Profiles of Ohio

2015

Fourth Edition

Profiles of Ohio

A Universal Reference Book

Grey House Publishing

PUBLISHER: Leslie Mackenzie
EDITORIAL DIRECTOR: Laura Mars
EDITOR: David Garoogian
MARKETING DIRECTOR: Jessica Moody

Grey House Publishing, Inc.
4919 Route 22
Amenia, NY 12501
518.789.8700
FAX 845.373.6390
www.greyhouse.com
e-mail: books @greyhouse.com

First edition published 2006
Printed in Canada

ISBN: 978-1-61925-569-2

Table of Contents

Introduction
- Introduction . . . vii

User's Guides
- Profiles . . . ix
- Education . . . xxv
- Ancestry and Ethnicity . . . xxix
- Climate . . . xxxvii

About Ohio
- Key Facts and State Emblems . . . 3
- Photo Gallery . . . 4
- A Brief History . . . 10
- Government
  - Overview . . . 12
  - Congressional Districts (113th Congress) . . . 15
  - Percent of Population Who Voted for Barack Obama in 2012 by County . . . 16
- Land and Natural Resources
  - State Summary . . . 17
  - State Energy Profile . . . 18
  - Populated Places, Transportation and Physical Features . . . 21
  - Federal Lands and Indian Reservations . . . 22
  - Satellite View . . . 23
  - Economic Losses from Hazard Events, 1960–2009 . . . 24
  - Hazard Losses, 1960–2009 . . . 25
- Demographic Maps
  - Population . . . 26
  - Percent White . . . 27
  - Percent Black . . . 28
  - Percent Asian . . . 29
  - Percent Hispanic . . . 30
  - Median Age . . . 31
  - Median Household Income . . . 32
  - Median Home Value . . . 33
  - High School Graduates . . . 34
  - College Graduates . . . 35

Profiles
- Alphabetical by County/Place . . . 39
- Alphabetical Place Index . . . 309

Comparative Statistics
- Comparative statistics of 100 largest communities . . . 317

Community Rankings
- Rankings of top/bottom 150 communities with population of 10,000 or more . . . 347

Education
- Public School Profile . . . 474
- School District Rankings . . . 475
- National Assessment of Educational Progress (NAEP) . . . 501
- Ohio Assessment of Student Performance and Progress (CAASPP) . . . 509

Ancestry and Ethnicity

State Profile 514
County Profiles 515
Place Profiles 543
Ancestry Group Rankings 558
Hispanic Origin Rankings 578
Racial Group Rankings 583

Climate

State Physical Features and Climate Narrative 601
State Reference Map 602
State Relief Map 603
Weather Stations Map 604
Weather Stations by County 605
Weather Stations by City 606
Weather Stations by Elevation 608
National Weather Service Stations 609
Cooperative Weather Stations 617
Weather Station Rankings 629
Significant Storm Events 640

Introduction

This is the fourth edition of *Profiles of Ohio—Facts, Figures & Statistics for 1,336 Populated Places in Ohio.* As with the other titles in our *State Profiles* series, it was built with content from Grey House Publishing's award-winning *Profiles of America*—a 4-volume compilation of data on more than 43,000 places in the United States. We have updated and included the Ohio chapter from *Profiles of America,* and added several new chapters of demographic information and ranking sections, so that *Profiles of Ohio* is the most comprehensive portrait of the state of Ohio ever published.

Profiles of Ohio provides data on all populated communities and counties in the state of Ohio for which the US Census provides individual statistics. This edition also includes profiles of 132 unincorporated places based on US Census data by zip code.

This premier reference work includes seven major sections that cover everything from **Education** to **Ethnic Backgrounds** to **Climate**. All sections include **Comparative Statistics** or **Rankings**. **About Ohio** at the front of the book, is comprised of detailed narrative and colorful photos and maps. Here is an overview of each section:

1. About Ohio
This 4-color section gives the researcher a real sense of the state and its history. It includes a Photo Gallery, and comprehensive sections on Ohio's Government, Land and Natural Resources, State Energy Profile, and Demographic Maps. With charts and maps, these 35 pages help to anchor the researcher to the state, both physically and politically.

2. Profiles
This section, organized by county, gives detailed profiles of 1,336 places plus 88 counties, based on Census 2010 and data from the American Community Survey. We have added current government statistics and original research, so that these profiles pull together statistical and descriptive information on every Census-recognized place in the state. Major fields of information include:

Geography	*Housing*	*Education*	*Religion*
Ancestry	*Transportation*	*Population*	*Climate*
Economy	*Industry*	*Health*	

NEW categories to this edition include public and private health insurance, language spoken at home, people with disabilities and veterans. In addition to place profiles, this section includes an **Alphabetical Place Index**.

3. Comparative Statistics
This section includes tables that compare Ohio's 100 largest communities by dozens of data points.

4. Community Rankings
This NEW section includes tables that rank the top 150 and bottom 150 communities with popultion over 10,000, in dozens of categories.

5. Education
This section begins with an **Educational State Profile,** summarizing number of schools, students, diplomas granted and educational dollars spent. Following the state profile are **School District Rankings** on 16 topics ranging from *Teacher/Student Ratios* to *High School Drop-Out Rates.* Following these rankings are statewide *National Assessment of Educational Progress (NAEP)* results and information about school and district performance from the Ohio Department of Education.

6. Ancestry and Ethnicity
This section provides a detailed look at the ancestral, Hispanic and racial makeup of Ohio's 200+ ethnic categories. Profiles are included for the state and for all counties and places with 50,000 or more residents. In the ranking section, data is displayed three ways: 1) by number, based on all places regardless of population;

2) by percent, based on all places regardless of population; 3) by percent, based on places with populations of 50,000 or more. You will discover, for example, that the city of Mentor has the greatest number of people reporting Croatian ancestry in the state (1,797), and that 100% of the population of Miamiville are of German ancestry.

7. Climate

This section includes a State Summary, three colorful maps and profiles of both National and Cooperative Weather Stations. In addition, you'll find Weather Station Rankings with hundreds of interesting details, such as Danville 2 W and Millersburg reporting the lowest annual extreme minimum temperatures (-35° F).

This section also includes Significant Storm Event data from January 2000 through December 2009. Here you will learn that a winter storm caused $750 million in property damage in Knox, Stark and Trumbull Counties in March 2008 and that a F4 tornado was responsible for two deaths and 17 injuries in Van Wert in November 2002.

Note: The extensive **User Guide** that follows this introduction is segmented into four sections and examines, in some detail, each data field in the individual profiles and comparative sections for all chapters. It provides sources for all data points and statistical definitions as necessary.

User Guide

Places Covered

All 88 counties.

937 incorporated municipalities. Comprised of 248 cities and 689 villages.

267 Census Designated Places (CDP). The U.S. Bureau of the Census defines a CDP as "a statistical entity, defined for each decennial census according to Census Bureau guidelines, comprising a densely settled concentration of population that is not within an incorporated place, but is locally identified by a name. CDPs are delineated cooperatively by state and local officials and the Census Bureau, following Census Bureau guidelines.

132 unincorporated communities. The communities included have statistics for their ZIP Code Tabulation Area (ZCTA) available from the Census Bureau. They are referred to as "postal areas." "Postal areas" can span multiple ZCTAs. A ZCTA is a statistical entity developed by the Census Bureau to approximate the delivery area for a US Postal Service 5-digit or 3-digit ZIP Code in the US and Puerto Rico. A ZCTA is an aggregation of census blocks that have the same predominant ZIP Code associated with the mailing addresses in the Census Bureau's Master Address File. Thus, the Postal Service's delivery areas have been adjusted to encompass whole census blocks so that the Census Bureau can tabulate census data for the ZCTAs. ZCTAs do not include all ZIP Codes used for mail delivery and therefore do not precisely depict the area within which mail deliveries associated with that ZIP Code occur. Additionally, some areas that are known by a unique name, although they are part of a larger incorporated place, are also included as "postal areas."

For a more in-depth discussion of geographic areas, please refer to the Census Bureau's Geographic Areas Reference Manual at http://www.census.gov/geo/www/garm.html.

IMPORTANT NOTES

- Since the last decennial census, the U.S. Census replaced the long-form sample with the American Community Survey (ACS), which uses a series of monthly samples to produce annually updated estimates for the same areas. ACS estimates are based on data from a sample of housing units (3.54 million in 2013) and people in the population, not the full population. ACS sampling error (uncertainty of data) is greater for those areas with smaller populations. In an effort to provide the most accurate data, *Profiles of Ohio* reports ACS data for counties and communities with populations of 2,500 or more. The profiles for these places (2,500 or more population) also include data from Census 2010, including: population; population growth; population density; race; Hispanic origin; average household size; median age; age under 18; age 65 and over; males per 100 females; homeownership rate; homeowner vacancy rate; and rental vacancy rate. Profiles for counties and communities with 2,500 or less population show data from the Census 2010 only.
- *Profiles of Ohio* uses the term "community" to refer to all places except counties. The term "county" is used to refer to counties and county-equivalents. All places are defined as of the 2010 Census.
- If a community spans multiple counties, the community will be shown in the county that contains its largest population.
- When a county and city are coextensive (occupying the same geographic area and sharing the same government), they are given a single entry.
- In each community profile, only school districts that have schools that are physically located within the community are shown. In addition, statistics for each school district cover the entire district, regardless of the physical location of the schools within the district.
- Special care should be taken when interpreting certain statistics for communities containing large colleges or universities. College students were counted as residents of the area in which they were living while attending college (as they have been since the 1950 census). One effect this may have is skewing the figures for population, income, housing, and educational attainment.
- Some information (e.g. income) is available for both counties and individual communities. Other information is available for just counties (e.g. election results), or just individual communities (e.g. local newspapers). Refer to the "Data Explanation and Sources" section for a complete listing.
- Some statistical information is available only for larger communities. In addition, the larger places are more apt to have services such as newspapers, airports, school districts, etc.
- For the most complete information on any community, users should also check the entry for the county in which the community is located. In addition, more information and services will be listed under the larger places in the county.

Data Explanation and Sources: County Profiles

PHYSICAL AND GEOGRAPHICAL CHARACTERISTICS

Physical Location: Describes the physical location of the county. *Source: Columbia University Press, The Columbia Gazetteer of North America and original research.*

Land and Water Area: Land and water area in square miles. *Source: U.S. Census Bureau, Census 2010*

Latitude and Longitude: Latitude and longitude in degrees. *Source: U.S. Census Bureau, Census 2010*

Time Zone: Lists the time zone. *Source: Original research*

Year Organized: Year the county government was organized. *Source: National Association of Counties*

County Seat: Lists the county seat. If a county has more than one seat, then both are listed. *Source: National Association of Counties*

Metropolitan Area: Indicates the metropolitan area the county is located in. Also lists all the component counties of that metropolitan area. The Office of Management and Budget (OMB) defines metropolitan and micropolitan statistical areas. The most current definitions are as of February 2013. *Source: U.S. Census Bureau*

Climate: Includes all weather stations located within the county. Indicates the station name and elevation as well as the monthly average high and low temperatures, average precipitation, and average snowfall. The period of record is generally 1980-2009, however, certain weather stations contain averages going back as far as 1900. *Source: Grey House Publishing, Weather America: A Thirty-Year Summary of Statistical Weather Data and Rankings, 2010*

POPULATION

Population: 2010 figures are a 100% count of population. *Source: U.S. Census Bureau, Census 2010*

Population Growth: The increase or decrease in population between 2000 and 2010. *Source: U.S. Census Bureau, Census 2000, Census 2010*

Population Density: Total 2010 population divided by the land area in square miles. *Source: U.S. Census Bureau, U.S. Census Bureau, Census 2010*

Race/Hispanic Origin: Figures include the U.S. Census Bureau categories of White alone; Black/African American alone; Asian alone; American Indian/Alaska Native alone; Native Hawaiian/Other Pacific Islander alone; two or more races; and Hispanic of any race. Alone refers to the fact that these figures are not in combination with any other race. *Source: U.S. Census Bureau, Census 2010*

The concept of race, as used by the Census Bureau, reflects self-identification by people according to the race or races with which they most closely identify. These categories are socio-political constructs and should not be interpreted as being scientific or anthropological in nature. Furthermore, the race categories include both racial and national-origin groups.

- **White.** A person having origins in any of the original peoples of Europe, the Middle East, or North Africa. It includes people who indicated their race(s) as "White" or reported entries such as Irish, German, Italian, Lebanese, Arab, Moroccan, or Caucasian.
- **Black/African American.** A person having origins in any of the Black racial groups of Africa. It includes people who indicated their race(s) as "Black, African Am., or Negro" or reported entries such as African American, Kenyan, Nigerian, or Haitian.
- **Asian.** A person having origins in any of the original peoples of the Far East, Southeast Asia, or the Indian subcontinent, including, for example, Cambodia, China, India, Japan, Korea, Malaysia, Pakistan, the Philippine Islands, Thailand, and Vietnam. It includes people who indicated their race(s) as "Asian" or reported entries such as "Asian Indian," "Chinese," "Filipino," "Korean," "Japanese," "Vietnamese," and "Other Asian" or provided other detailed Asian responses.
- **American Indian/Alaska Native.** A person having origins in any of the original peoples of North and South America (including Central America) and who maintains tribal affiliation or community attachment. This category includes people who indicated their race(s) as "American Indian or Alaska Native" or

reported their enrolled or principal tribe, such as Navajo, Blackfeet, Inupiat, Yup'ik, or Central American Indian groups or South American Indian groups.

- **Native Hawaiian/Other Pacific Islander.** A person having origins in any of the original peoples of Hawaii, Guam, Samoa, or other Pacific Islands. It includes people who indicated their race(s) as "Pacific Islander" or reported entries such as "Native Hawaiian," "Guamanian or Chamorro," "Samoan," and "Other Pacific Islander" or provided other detailed Pacific Islander responses..
- **Two or More Races.** People may choose to provide two or more races either by checking two or more race response check boxes, by providing multiple responses, or by some combination of check boxes and other responses. The race response categories shown on the questionnaire are collapsed into the five minimum race groups identified by OMB, and the Census Bureau's "Some Other Race" category.
- **Hispanic.** The data on the Hispanic or Latino population were derived from answers to a question that was asked of all people. The terms "Spanish," "Hispanic origin," and "Latino" are used interchangeably. Some respondents identify with all three terms while others may identify with only one of these three specific terms. Hispanics or Latinos who identify with the terms "Spanish," "Hispanic," or "Latino" are those who classify themselves in one of the specific Spanish, Hispanic, or Latino categories listed on the questionnaire ("Mexican," "Puerto Rican," or "Cuban") as well as those who indicate that they are "other Spanish/Hispanic/Latino." People who do not identify with one of the specific origins listed on the questionnaire but indicate that they are "other Spanish/Hispanic/Latino" are those whose origins are from Spain, the Spanish-speaking countries of Central or South America, the Dominican Republic, or people identifying themselves generally as Spanish, Spanish-American, Hispanic, Hispano, Latino, and so on. All write-in responses to the "other Spanish/Hispanic/Latino" category were coded. Origin can be viewed as the heritage, nationality group, lineage, or country of birth of the person or the person's parents or ancestors before their arrival in the United States. People who identify their origin as Spanish, Hispanic, or Latino may be of any race.

Average Household Size: Number of persons in the average household. *Source: U.S. Census Bureau, Census 2010*

Median Age: Median age of the population. *Source: U.S. Census Bureau, Census 2010*

Age Under 18: Percent of the total population under 18 years old. *Source: U.S. Census Bureau, Census 2010*

Age 65 and Over: Percent of the total population age 65 and over. *Source: U.S. Census Bureau, Census 2010*

Males per 100 Females: Number of males per 100 females. *Source: U.S. Census Bureau, Census 2010*

Marital Status: Percentage of population never married, now married, separated, widowed, or divorced. *Source: U.S. Census Bureau, American Community Survey, 2009-2013 Five-Year Estimates*

The marital status classification refers to the status at the time of enumeration. Data on marital status are tabulated only for the population 15 years old and over. Each person was asked whether they were "Now married," "Widowed," "Separated," "Divorced," or "Never married." Couples who live together (for example, people in common-law marriages) were able to report the marital status they considered to be the most appropriate.

- **Never married.** Never married includes all people who have never been married, including people whose only marriage(s) was annulled.
- **Now married.** All people whose current marriage has not ended by widowhood or divorce. This category includes people defined as "separated."
- **Separated.** Includes people legally separated or otherwise absent from their spouse because of marital discord. Those without a final divorce decree are classified as "separated." This category also includes people who have been deserted or who have parted because they no longer want to live together, but who have not obtained a divorce.
- **Widowed**. This category includes widows and widowers who have not remarried.
- **Divorced.** This category includes people who are legally divorced and who have not remarried.

Foreign Born: Percentage of population who were not U.S. citizens at birth. Foreign-born people are those who indicated they were either a U.S. citizen by naturalization or they were not a citizen of the United States. *Source: U.S. Census Bureau, American Community Survey, 2009-2013 Five-Year Estimates*

Speak English Only: Percent of population that reported speaking only English at home. *Source: U.S. Census Bureau, American Community Survey, 2009-2013 Five-Year Estimates*

With Disability: Percent of the civilian noninstitutionalized population that reported having a disability. Disability status is determined from from six types of difficulty: vision, hearing, cognitive, ambulatory, self-care, and independent living. For children under 5 years old, hearing and vision difficulty are used to determine disability status. For children between the ages of 5 and 14, disability status is determined from hearing, vision, cognitive, ambulatory, and self-care difficulties. For people aged 15 years and older, they are considered to have a disability if they have difficulty with any one of the six difficulty types. *Source: U.S. Census Bureau, American Community Survey, 2009-2013 Five-Year Estimates*

Veterans: Percent of the civilian population 18 years and over who have served (even for a short time), but are not currently serving, on active duty in the U.S. Army, Navy, Air Force, Marine Corps, or the Coast Guard, or who served in the U.S. Merchant Marine during World War II. People who served in the National Guard or Reserves are classified as veterans only if they were ever called or ordered to active duty, not counting the 4-6 months for initial training or yearly summer camps. All other civilians are classified as nonveterans. Note: While it is possible for 17 year olds to be veterans of the Armed Forces, ACS data products are restricted to the population 18 years and older. *Source: U.S. Census Bureau, American Community Survey, 2009-2013 Five-Year Estimates*

Ancestry: Largest ancestry groups reported (up to five). The data includes persons who report multiple ancestries. For example, if a person reported being Irish and Italian, they would be included in both categories. Thus, the sum of the percentages may be greater than 100%. *Source: U.S. Census Bureau, American Community Survey, 2009-2013 Five-Year Estimates*

The data represent self-classification by people according to the ancestry group or groups with which they most closely identify. Ancestry refers to a person's ethnic origin or descent, "roots," heritage, or the place of birth of the person, the person's parents, or their ancestors before their arrival in the United States. Some ethnic identities, such as Egyptian or Polish, can be traced to geographic areas outside the United States, while other ethnicities such as Pennsylvania German or Cajun evolved in the United States.

The ancestry question was intended to provide data for groups that were not included in the Hispanic origin and race questions. Therefore, although data on all groups are collected, the ancestry data shown in these tabulations are for non-Hispanic and non-race groups. *See* Race/Hispanic Origin for information on Hispanic and race groups.

RELIGION

Religion: Lists the largest religious groups (up to six) based on the number of adherents divided by the population of the county. Adherents are defined as "all members, including full members, their children and the estimated number of other regular participants who are not considered as communicant, confirmed or full members." *Source: American Religious Bodies, 2010 U.S. Religion Census: Religious Congregations & Membership Study*

ECONOMY

Unemployment Rate: Unemployment rate as of October 2014. Includes all civilians age 16 or over who were unemployed and looking for work. *Source: U.S. Department of Labor, Bureau of Labor Statistics, Local Area Unemployment Statistics*

Leading Industries: Lists the three largest industries (excluding government) based on the number of employees. *Source: U.S. Census Bureau, County Business Patterns 2012*

Farms: The total number of farms and the total acreage they occupy. *Source: U.S. Department of Agriculture, National Agricultural Statistics Service, 2012 Census of Agriculture*

Company Size: The numbers of companies at various employee headcounts. Includes private employers only. *Source: U.S. Census Bureau, County Business Patterns 2012*

- **Employ 1,000 or more persons.** The numbers of companies that employ 1,000 or more persons.
- **Employ 500-999 persons.** The numbers of companies that employ 500 to 999 persons.
- **Employ 100-499 persons.** The numbers of companies that employ 100 to 499 persons.
- **Employ 1-99 persons.** The numbers of companies that employ 1 to 99 persons.

Business Ownership: Number of businesses that are majority-owned by women or various minority groups. *Source: U.S. Census Bureau, 2007 Economic Census, Survey of Business Owners: Black-Owned Firms, 2007 (latest statistics available at time of publication)*

- **Women-Owned.** Number of businesses that are majority-owned by a woman. Majority ownership is defined as having 51 percent or more of the stock or equity in the business.
- **Black-Owned.** Number of businesses that are majority-owned by a Black or African-American person(s). Majority ownership is defined as having 51 percent or more of the stock or equity in the business. Black or African American is defined as a person having origins in any of the black racial groups of Africa, including those who consider themselves to be "Haitian."
- **Hispanic-Owned.** Number of businesses that are majority-owned by a person(s) of Hispanic or Latino origin. Majority ownership is defined as having 51 percent or more of the stock or equity in the business. Hispanic or Latino origin is defined as a person of Cuban, Mexican, Puerto Rican, South or Central American, or other Spanish culture or origin, regardless of race.
- **Asian-Owned.** Number of businesses that are majority-owned by an Asian person(s). Majority ownership is defined as having 51 percent or more of the stock or equity in the business.

EMPLOYMENT

Employment by Occupation: Percentage of the employed civilian population 16 years and over in management, professional, service, sales, farming, construction, and production occupations. *Source: U.S. Census Bureau, American Community Survey, 2009-2013 Five-Year Estimates*

- Management, business, and financial occupations include:
    - Management occupations
    - Business and financial operations occupations

- Computer, engineering, and science occupations include:
    - Computer and mathematical occupations
    - Architecture and engineering occupations
    - Life, physical, and social science occupations

- Education, legal, community service, arts, and media occupations include:
    - Community and social service occupations
    - Legal occupations
    - Education, training, and library occupations
    - Arts, design, entertainment, sports, and media occupations

- Healthcare practitioners and technical occupations include:
    - Health diagnosing and treating practitioners and other technical occupations
    - Health technologists and technicians

- Service occupations include:
    - Healthcare support occupations
    - Protective service occupations:
        - Fire fighting and prevention, and other protective service workers including supervisors
        - Law enforcement workers including supervisors
    - Food preparation and serving related occupations
    - Building and grounds cleaning and maintenance occupations
    - Personal care and service occupations

- Sales and office occupations include:
    - Sales and related occupations
    - Office and administrative support occupations

- Natural resources, construction, and maintenance occupations include:
    - Farming, fishing, and forestry occupations
    - Construction and extraction occupations
    - Installation, maintenance, and repair occupations

- Production, transportation, and material moving occupations include:
    - Production occupations
    - Transportation occupations
    - Material moving occupations

INCOME

Per Capita Income: Per capita income is the mean income computed for every man, woman, and child in a particular group. It is derived by dividing the total income of a particular group by the total population in that group. Per capita income is rounded to the nearest whole dollar. *Source: U.S. Census Bureau, American Community Survey, 2009-2013 Five-Year Estimates*

Median Household Income: Includes the income of the householder and all other individuals 15 years old and over in the household, whether they are related to the householder or not. The median divides the income distribution into two equal parts: one-half of the cases falling below the median income and one-half above the median. For households, the median income is based on the distribution of the total number of households including those with no income. Median income for households is computed on the basis of a standard distribution and is rounded to the nearest whole dollar. *Source: U.S. Census Bureau, American Community Survey, 2009-2013 Five-Year Estimates*

Average Household Income: Average household income is obtained by dividing total household income by the total number of households. *Source: U.S. Census Bureau, American Community Survey, 2009-2013 Five-Year Estimates*

Percent of Households with Income of $100,000 or more: Percent of households with income of $100,000 or more. *Source: U.S. Census Bureau, American Community Survey, 2009-2013 Five-Year Estimates*

Poverty Rate: Percentage of population with income below the poverty level. Based on individuals for whom poverty status is determined. Poverty status was determined for all people except institutionalized people, people in military group quarters, people in college dormitories, and unrelated individuals under 15 years old. *Source: U.S. Census Bureau, American Community Survey, 2009-2013 Five-Year Estimates*

EDUCATIONAL ATTAINMENT

Figures show the percent of population age 25 and over with the following levels of educational attainment. *Source: U.S. Census Bureau, American Community Survey, 2009-2013 Five-Year Estimates*

- **High school diploma or higher.** Includes people whose highest degree is a high school diploma or its equivalent (GED), people who attended college but did not receive a degree, and people who received a college, university, or professional degree.
- **Bachelor's degree or higher.** Includes people who received a bachelor's, master's, doctorate, or professional degree.
- **Graduate/professional degree or higher.** Includes people who received a master's, doctorate, or professional degree.

HOUSING

Homeownership Rate: Percentage of housing units that are owner-occupied. *Source: U.S. Census Bureau, Census 2010*

Median Home Value: Median value in dollars of all owner-occupied housing units as reported by the owner. *Source: U.S. Census Bureau, American Community Survey, 2009-2013 Five-Year Estimates*

Median Year Structure Built: Year structure built refers to when the building was first constructed, not when it was remodeled, added to, or converted. For mobile homes, houseboats, RVs, etc, the manufacturer's model year was assumed to be the year built. The data relate to the number of units built during the specified periods that were still in existence at the time of enumeration. *Source: U.S. Census Bureau, American Community Survey, 2009-2013 Five-Year Estimates*

Homeowner Vacancy Rate: Proportion of the homeowner inventory that is vacant "for sale." It is computed by dividing the number of vacant units "for sale only" by the sum of the owner-occupied units, vacant units that are "for sale only," and vacant units that have been sold but not yet occupied, and then multiplying by 100. This measure is rounded to the nearest tenth. *Source: U.S. Census Bureau, Census 2010*

Median Gross Rent: Median monthly gross rent in dollars on specified renter-occupied and specified vacant-for-rent units. Specified renter-occupied and specified vacant-for-rent units exclude 1-family houses on 10 acres or more. Gross rent is the contract rent plus the estimated average monthly cost of utilities (electricity, gas, and water and sewer) and fuels (oil, coal, kerosene, wood, etc.) if these are paid by the renter (or paid for the renter by someone else). Gross rent is intended to eliminate differentials that result from varying practices with respect to the inclusion of utilities and fuels as part of the rental payment. Contract rent is the monthly rent agreed to or contracted for, regardless of any furnishings, utilities, fees, meals, or services that may be included. For vacant units, it is the monthly rent asked for the rental unit at the time of enumeration. *Source: U.S. Census Bureau, American Community Survey, 2009-2013 Five-Year Estimates*

Rental Vacancy Rate: Proportion of the rental inventory that is vacant "for rent." It is computed by dividing the number of vacant units "for rent" by the sum of the renter-occupied units, vacant units that are "for rent," and vacant units that have been rented but not yet occupied, and then multiplying by 100. This measure is rounded to the nearest tenth. *Source: U.S. Census Bureau, Census 2010*

VITAL STATISTICS

Birth Rate: Estimated number of births per 10,000 population in 2013. *Source: U.S. Census Bureau, Annual Components of Population Change, July 1, 2010 - July 1, 2013*

Death Rate: Estimated number of deaths per 10,000 population in 2013. *Source: U.S. Census Bureau, Annual Components of Population Change, July 1, 2010 - July 1, 2013*

Age-adjusted Cancer Mortality Rate: Number of age-adjusted deaths from cancer per 100,000 population in 2011. Cancer is defined as International Classification of Disease (ICD) codes C00–D48.9 Neoplasms. *Source: Centers for Disease Control, CDC Wonder, 2011*

Age-adjusted death rates are weighted averages of the age-specific death rates, where the weights represent a fixed population by age. They are used because the rates of almost all causes of death vary by age. Age adjustment is a technique for "removing" the effects of age from crude rates, so as to allow meaningful comparisons across populations with different underlying age structures. For example, comparing the crude rate of heart disease in Virginia to that of California is misleading, because the relatively older population in Virginia will lead to a higher crude death rate, even if the age-specific rates of heart disease in Virginia and California are the same. For such a comparison, age-adjusted rates would be preferable. Age-adjusted rates should be viewed as relative indexes rather than as direct or actual measures of mortality risk.

Death rates based on counts of twenty or less (≤ 20) are flagged as "Unreliable". Death rates based on fewer than three years of data for counties with populations of less than 100,000 in the 2000 Census counts, are also flagged as "Unreliable" if the number of deaths is five or less (≤ 5).

HEALTH INSURANCE

Health insurance coverage in the ACS and other Census Bureau surveys define coverage to include plans and programs that provide comprehensive health coverage. Plans that provide insurance for specific conditions or situations such as cancer and long-term care policies are not considered coverage. Likewise, other types of insurance like dental, vision, life, and disability insurance are not considered health insurance coverage.

For reporting purposes, the Census Bureau broadly classifies health insurance coverage as private health insurance or public coverage. Private health insurance is a plan provided through an employer or union, a plan purchased by an individual from a private company, or TRICARE or other military health care. Public health coverage includes the federal programs Medicare, Medicaid, and VA Health Care (provided through the Department of Veterans Affairs); the Children's Health Insurance Program (CHIP); and individual state health plans. The types of health insurance are not mutually exclusive; people may be covered by more than one at the same time. People who had no reported health coverage, or those whose only health coverage was Indian Health Service, were considered uninsured. *Source: U.S. Census Bureau, American Community Survey, 2009-2013 Five-Year Estimates*

- **Have Insurance:** Percent of the civilian noninstitutionalized population with any type of comprehensive health insurance.
- **Have Private Insurance.** Percent of the civilian noninstitutionalized population with private health insurance. A person may report that they have both public and private health insurance, thus, the sum of the percentages may be greater than 100%.
- **Have Public Insurance.** Percent of the civilian noninstitutionalized population with public health insurance. A person may report that they have both public and private health insurance, thus, the sum of the percentages may be greater than 100%.
- **Do Not Have Insurance.** Percent of the civilian noninstitutionalized population with no health insurance.
- **Children Under 18 With No Insurance.** Percent of the civilian noninstitutionalized population under age 18 with no health insurance.

HEALTH CARE

Number of physicians, hospital beds and hospital admission per 10,000 population. *Source: Area Resource File (ARF) 2012-2013. U.S. Department of Health and Human Services, Health Resources and Services Administration, Bureau of Health Professions, Rockville, MD.*

- **Number of Physicians.** The number of active, non-federal physicians (MDs and DOs) per 10,000 population in 2011.
- **Number of Hospital Beds.** The number of hospital beds per 10,000 population in 2010.
- **Number of Hospital Admissions.** The number of hospital admissions per 10,000 population in 2010.

AIR QUALITY INDEX

The percentage of days in 2013 the AQI fell into the Good (0-50), Moderate (51-100), Unhealthy for Sensitive Groups (101-150), Unhealthy (151-200), Very Unhealthy (201-300), and Hazardous (300+) ranges. If a range does not appear, its value is zero. Data covers January 2013 through December 2013. *Source: AirData: Access to Air Pollution Data, U.S. Environmental Protection Agency, Office of Air and Radiation*

The AQI is an index for reporting daily air quality. It tells you how clean or polluted your air is, and what associated health concerns you should be aware of. The AQI focuses on health effects that can happen within a few hours or days after breathing polluted air. EPA uses the AQI for five major air pollutants regulated by the Clean Air Act: ground-level ozone, particulate matter, carbon monoxide, sulfur dioxide, and nitrogen dioxide. For each of these pollutants, EPA has established national air quality standards to protect against harmful health effects.

The AQI runs from 0 to 500. The higher the AQI value, the greater the level of air pollution and the greater the health danger. For example, an AQI value of 50 represents good air quality and little potential to affect public health, while an AQI value over 300 represents hazardous air quality. An AQI value of 100 generally corresponds to the national air quality standard for the pollutant, which is the level EPA has set to protect public health. So, AQI values below 100 are generally thought of as satisfactory. When AQI values are above 100, air quality is considered to be unhealthy—at first for certain sensitive groups of people, then for everyone as AQI values get higher. Each category corresponds to a different level of health concern. For example, when the AQI for a pollutant is between 51 and 100, the health concern is "Moderate." Here are the six levels of health concern and what they mean:

- "Good" The AQI value for your community is between 0 and 50. Air quality is considered satisfactory and air pollution poses little or no risk.
- "Moderate" The AQI for your community is between 51 and 100. Air quality is acceptable; however, for some pollutants there may be a moderate health concern for a very small number of individuals. For example, people who are unusually sensitive to ozone may experience respiratory symptoms.
- "Unhealthy for Sensitive Groups" Certain groups of people are particularly sensitive to the harmful effects of certain air pollutants. This means they are likely to be affected at lower levels than the general public. For example, children and adults who are active outdoors and people with respiratory disease are at greater risk from exposure to ozone, while people with heart disease are at greater risk from carbon monoxide. Some people may be sensitive to more than one pollutant. When AQI values are between 101 and 150, members of sensitive groups may experience health effects. The general public is not likely to be affected when the AQI is in this range.
- "Unhealthy" AQI values are between 151 and 200. Everyone may begin to experience health effects. Members of sensitive groups may experience more serious health effects.
- "Very Unhealthy" AQI values between 201 and 300 trigger a health alert, meaning everyone may experience more serious health effects.
- "Hazardous" AQI values over 300 trigger health warnings of emergency conditions. The entire population is more likely to be affected.

TRANSPORTATION

Commute to Work: Percentage of workers 16 years old and over that use the following means of transportation to commute to work: car; public transportation; walk; work from home. The means of transportation data for some areas may show workers using modes of public transportation that are not available in those areas (e.g. subway or elevated riders in a metropolitan area where there actually is no subway or elevated service). This result is largely due to people who worked during the reference week at a location that was different from their usual place of work (such as people away from home on business in an area where subway service was available) and people who used more than one means of transportation each day but whose principal means was unavailable where they lived (e.g. residents of non-metropolitan areas who drove to the fringe of a metropolitan area and took the commuter railroad most of the distance to work). *Source: U.S. Census Bureau, American Community Survey, 2009-2013 Five-Year Estimates*

Median Travel Time to Work: Median travel time to work for workers 16 years old and over. Travel time to work refers to the total number of minutes that it usually took the person to get from home to work each day during the reference week. The elapsed time includes time spent waiting for public transportation, picking up passengers in carpools, and time spent in other activities related to getting to work. *Source: U.S. Census Bureau, American Community Survey, 2009-2013 Five-Year Estimates*

PRESIDENTIAL ELECTION

2012 Presidential election results. *Source: Dave Leip's Atlas of U.S. Presidential Elections*

NATIONAL AND STATE PARKS

Lists National/State parks located in the area. *Source: U.S. Geological Survey, Geographic Names Information System*

ADDITIONAL INFORMATION CONTACTS

General telephone number and website address (if available) of local government.

Data Explanation and Sources: Community Profiles

PHYSICAL AND GEOGRAPHICAL CHARACTERISTICS

Place Type: Lists the type of place (city, town, village, borough, Census-Designated Place (CDP), township, charter township, plantation, gore, district, grant, location, purchase, municipality, reservation, unorganized territory, or unincorporated postal area). *Source: U.S. Census Bureau, Census 2010 and U.S. Postal Service, City State File*

ZCTA: *This only appears within unincorporated postal areas.* The statistics that follow cover the corresponding ZIP Code Tabulation Area (ZCTA). A ZCTA is a statistical entity developed by the Census Bureau to approximate the delivery area for a US Postal Service 5-digit or 3-digit ZIP Code in the US and Puerto Rico. A ZCTA is an aggregation of census blocks that have the same predominant ZIP Code associated with the mailing addresses in the Census Bureau's Master Address File. Thus, the Postal Service's delivery areas have been adjusted to encompass whole census blocks so that the Census Bureau can tabulate census data for the ZCTAs. ZCTAs do not include all ZIP Codes used for mail delivery and therefore do not precisely depict the area within which mail deliveries associated with that ZIP Code occur. Additionally, some areas that are known by a unique name, although they are part of a larger incorporated place, are also included as "postal areas."

Land and Water Area: Land and water area in square miles. *Source: U.S. Census Bureau, Census 2010*

Latitude and Longitude: Latitude and longitude in degrees. *Source: U.S. Census Bureau, Census 2010.*

Elevation: Elevation in feet. *Source: U.S. Geological Survey, Geographic Names Information System (GNIS)*

HISTORY

Historical information. *Source: Columbia University Press, The Columbia Gazetteer of North America; Original research*

POPULATION

Population: 2010 figures are a 100% count of population. *Source: U.S. Census Bureau, Census 2010*

Population Growth: The increase or decrease in population between 2000 and 2010. *Source: U.S. Census Bureau, Census 2000, Census 2010*

Population Density: Total 2010 population divided by the land area in square miles. *Source: U.S. Census Bureau, U.S. Census Bureau, Census 2010*

Race/Hispanic Origin: Figures include the U.S. Census Bureau categories of White alone; Black/African American alone; Asian alone; American Indian/Alaska Native alone; Native Hawaiian/Other Pacific Islander alone; two or more races; and Hispanic of any race. Alone refers to the fact that these figures are not in combination with any other race. *Source: U.S. Census Bureau, Census 2010*

The concept of race, as used by the Census Bureau, reflects self-identification by people according to the race or races with which they most closely identify. These categories are socio-political constructs and should not be interpreted as being scientific or anthropological in nature. Furthermore, the race categories include both racial and national-origin groups.

- **White.** A person having origins in any of the original peoples of Europe, the Middle East, or North Africa. It includes people who indicated their race(s) as "White" or reported entries such as Irish, German, Italian, Lebanese, Arab, Moroccan, or Caucasian.
- **Black/African American.** A person having origins in any of the Black racial groups of Africa. It includes people who indicated their race(s) as "Black, African Am., or Negro" or reported entries such as African American, Kenyan, Nigerian, or Haitian.
- **Asian.** A person having origins in any of the original peoples of the Far East, Southeast Asia, or the Indian subcontinent, including, for example, Cambodia, China, India, Japan, Korea, Malaysia, Pakistan, the Philippine Islands, Thailand, and Vietnam. It includes people who indicated their race(s) as "Asian" or reported entries such as "Asian Indian," "Chinese," "Filipino," "Korean," "Japanese," "Vietnamese," and "Other Asian" or provided other detailed Asian responses.
- **American Indian/Alaska Native.** A person having origins in any of the original peoples of North and South America (including Central America) and who maintains tribal affiliation or community attachment.

This category includes people who indicated their race(s) as "American Indian or Alaska Native" or reported their enrolled or principal tribe, such as Navajo, Blackfeet, Inupiat, Yup'ik, or Central American Indian groups or South American Indian groups.

- **Native Hawaiian/Other Pacific Islander.** A person having origins in any of the original peoples of Hawaii, Guam, Samoa, or other Pacific Islands. It includes people who indicated their race(s) as "Pacific Islander" or reported entries such as "Native Hawaiian," "Guamanian or Chamorro," "Samoan," and "Other Pacific Islander" or provided other detailed Pacific Islander responses..
- **Two or More Races.** People may choose to provide two or more races either by checking two or more race response check boxes, by providing multiple responses, or by some combination of check boxes and other responses. The race response categories shown on the questionnaire are collapsed into the five minimum race groups identified by OMB, and the Census Bureau's "Some Other Race" category.
- **Hispanic.** The data on the Hispanic or Latino population were derived from answers to a question that was asked of all people. The terms "Spanish," "Hispanic origin," and "Latino" are used interchangeably. Some respondents identify with all three terms while others may identify with only one of these three specific terms. Hispanics or Latinos who identify with the terms "Spanish," "Hispanic," or "Latino" are those who classify themselves in one of the specific Spanish, Hispanic, or Latino categories listed on the questionnaire ("Mexican," "Puerto Rican," or "Cuban") as well as those who indicate that they are "other Spanish/Hispanic/Latino." People who do not identify with one of the specific origins listed on the questionnaire but indicate that they are "other Spanish/Hispanic/Latino" are those whose origins are from Spain, the Spanish-speaking countries of Central or South America, the Dominican Republic, or people identifying themselves generally as Spanish, Spanish-American, Hispanic, Hispano, Latino, and so on. All write-in responses to the "other Spanish/Hispanic/Latino" category were coded. Origin can be viewed as the heritage, nationality group, lineage, or country of birth of the person or the person's parents or ancestors before their arrival in the United States. People who identify their origin as Spanish, Hispanic, or Latino may be of any race.

Average Household Size: Number of persons in the average household. *Source: U.S. Census Bureau, Census 2010*

Median Age: Median age of the population. *Source: U.S. Census Bureau, Census 2010*

Age Under 18: Percent of the total population under 18 years old. *Source: U.S. Census Bureau, Census 2010*

Age 65 and Over: Percent of the total population age 65 and over. *Source: U.S. Census Bureau, Census 2010*

Males per 100 Females: Number of males per 100 females. *Source: U.S. Census Bureau, Census 2010*

Marital Status: Percentage of population never married, now married, separated, widowed, or divorced. *Source: U.S. Census Bureau, American Community Survey, 2009-2013 Five-Year Estimates*

The marital status classification refers to the status at the time of enumeration. Data on marital status are tabulated only for the population 15 years old and over. Each person was asked whether they were "Now married," "Widowed," "Separated," "Divorced," or "Never married." Couples who live together (for example, people in common-law marriages) were able to report the marital status they considered to be the most appropriate.

- **Never married**. Never married includes all people who have never been married, including people whose only marriage(s) was annulled.
- **Now married.** All people whose current marriage has not ended by widowhood or divorce. This category includes people defined as "separated."
- **Separated.** Includes people legally separated or otherwise absent from their spouse because of marital discord. Those without a final divorce decree are classified as "separated." This category also includes people who have been deserted or who have parted because they no longer want to live together, but who have not obtained a divorce.
- **Widowed**. This category includes widows and widowers who have not remarried.
- **Divorced.** This category includes people who are legally divorced and who have not remarried.

Foreign Born: Percentage of population who were not U.S. citizens at birth. Foreign-born people are those who indicated they were either a U.S. citizen by naturalization or they were not a citizen of the United States. *Source: U.S. Census Bureau, American Community Survey, 2009-2013 Five-Year Estimates*

Speak English Only: Percent of population that reported speaking only English at home. *Source: U.S. Census Bureau, American Community Survey, 2009-2013 Five-Year Estimates*

With Disability: Percent of the civilian noninstitutionalized population that reported having a disability. Disability status is determined from from six types of difficulty: vision, hearing, cognitive, ambulatory, self-care, and independent living. For children under 5 years old, hearing and vision difficulty are used to determine disability status. For children between the ages of 5 and 14, disability status is determined from hearing, vision, cognitive, ambulatory, and self-care difficulties. For people aged 15 years and older, they are considered to have a disability if they have difficulty with any one of the six difficulty types. *Source: U.S. Census Bureau, American Community Survey, 2009-2013 Five-Year Estimates*

Veterans: Percent of the civilian population 18 years and over who have served (even for a short time), but are not currently serving, on active duty in the U.S. Army, Navy, Air Force, Marine Corps, or the Coast Guard, or who served in the U.S. Merchant Marine during World War II. People who served in the National Guard or Reserves are classified as veterans only if they were ever called or ordered to active duty, not counting the 4-6 months for initial training or yearly summer camps. All other civilians are classified as nonveterans. Note: While it is possible for 17 year olds to be veterans of the Armed Forces, ACS data products are restricted to the population 18 years and older. *Source: U.S. Census Bureau, American Community Survey, 2009-2013 Five-Year Estimates*

Ancestry: Largest ancestry groups reported (up to five). The data includes persons who report multiple ancestries. For example, if a person reported being Irish and Italian, they would be included in both categories. Thus, the sum of the percentages may be greater than 100%. *Source: U.S. Census Bureau, American Community Survey, 2009-2013 Five-Year Estimates*

The data represent self-classification by people according to the ancestry group or groups with which they most closely identify. Ancestry refers to a person's ethnic origin or descent, "roots," heritage, or the place of birth of the person, the person's parents, or their ancestors before their arrival in the United States. Some ethnic identities, such as Egyptian or Polish, can be traced to geographic areas outside the United States, while other ethnicities such as Pennsylvania German or Cajun evolved in the United States.

The ancestry question was intended to provide data for groups that were not included in the Hispanic origin and race questions. Therefore, although data on all groups are collected, the ancestry data shown in these tabulations are for non-Hispanic and non-race groups. *See* Race/Hispanic Origin for information on Hispanic and race groups.

EMPLOYMENT

Employment by Occupation: Percentage of the employed civilian population 16 years and over in management, professional, service, sales, farming, construction, and production occupations. *Source: U.S. Census Bureau, American Community Survey, 2009-2013 Five-Year Estimates*

- Management, business, and financial occupations include:
  - Management occupations
  - Business and financial operations occupations
- Computer, engineering, and science occupations include:
  - Computer and mathematical occupations
  - Architecture and engineering occupations
  - Life, physical, and social science occupations
- Education, legal, community service, arts, and media occupations include:
  - Community and social service occupations
  - Legal occupations
  - Education, training, and library occupations
  - Arts, design, entertainment, sports, and media occupations
- Healthcare practitioners and technical occupations include:
  - Health diagnosing and treating practitioners and other technical occupations
  - Health technologists and technicians
- Service occupations include:
  - Healthcare support occupations
  - Protective service occupations:
    - Fire fighting and prevention, and other protective service workers including supervisors
    - Law enforcement workers including supervisors
  - Food preparation and serving related occupations
  - Building and grounds cleaning and maintenance occupations
  - Personal care and service occupations

- Sales and office occupations include:
  Sales and related occupations
  Office and administrative support occupations

- Natural resources, construction, and maintenance occupations include:
  Farming, fishing, and forestry occupations
  Construction and extraction occupations
  Installation, maintenance, and repair occupations

- Production, transportation, and material moving occupations include:
  Production occupations
  Transportation occupations
  Material moving occupations

INCOME

Per Capita Income: Per capita income is the mean income computed for every man, woman, and child in a particular group. It is derived by dividing the total income of a particular group by the total population in that group. Per capita income is rounded to the nearest whole dollar. *Source: U.S. Census Bureau, American Community Survey, 2009-2013 Five-Year Estimates*

Median Household Income: Includes the income of the householder and all other individuals 15 years old and over in the household, whether they are related to the householder or not. The median divides the income distribution into two equal parts: one-half of the cases falling below the median income and one-half above the median. For households, the median income is based on the distribution of the total number of households including those with no income. Median income for households is computed on the basis of a standard distribution and is rounded to the nearest whole dollar. *Source: U.S. Census Bureau, American Community Survey, 2009-2013 Five-Year Estimates*

Average Household Income: Average household income is obtained by dividing total household income by the total number of households. *Source: U.S. Census Bureau, American Community Survey, 2009-2013 Five-Year Estimates*

Percent of Households with Income of $100,000 or more: Percent of households with income of $100,000 or more. *Source: U.S. Census Bureau, American Community Survey, 2009-2013 Five-Year Estimates*

Poverty Rate: Percentage of population with income below the poverty level. Based on individuals for whom poverty status is determined. Poverty status was determined for all people except institutionalized people, people in military group quarters, people in college dormitories, and unrelated individuals under 15 years old. *Source: U.S. Census Bureau, American Community Survey, 2009-2013 Five-Year Estimates*

EDUCATIONAL ATTAINMENT

Figures show the percent of population age 25 and over with the following levels of educational attainment. *Source: U.S. Census Bureau, American Community Survey, 2009-2013 Five-Year Estimates*

- **High school diploma or higher.** Includes people whose highest degree is a high school diploma or its equivalent (GED), people who attended college but did not receive a degree, and people who received a college, university, or professional degree.
- **Bachelor's degree or higher.** Includes people who received a bachelor's, master's, doctorate, or professional degree.
- **Graduate/professional degree or higher.** Includes people who received a master's, doctorate, or professional degree.

SCHOOL DISTRICTS

Lists the name of each school district, the grade range (PK=pre-kindergarten; KG=kindergarten), the student enrollment, and the district headquarters' phone number. In each community profile, only school districts that have schools that are physically located within the community are shown. In addition, statistics for each school district cover the entire district, regardless of the physical location of the schools within the district. *Source: U.S. Department of Education, National Center for Educational Statistics, Directory of Public Elementary and Secondary Education Agencies, 2012-13*

COLLEGES

Four-year Colleges: Lists the name of each four-year college, the type of institution (private or public; for-profit or non-profit; religious affiliation; historically black), the total estimated student enrollment in 2013, the general telephone number, and the annual tuition and fees for full-time, first-time undergraduate students (in-state and out-of-state). *Source: U.S. Department of Education, National Center for Educational Statistics, IPEDS College Data, 2013-14*

Two-year Colleges: Lists the name of each two-year college, the type of institution (private or public; for-profit or non-profit; religious affiliation; historically black), the total estimated student enrollment in 2013, the general telephone number, and the annual tuition and fees for full-time, first-time undergraduate students (in-state and out-of-state). *Source: U.S. Department of Education, National Center for Educational Statistics, IPEDS College Data, 2013-14*

Vocational/Technical Schools: Lists the name of each vocational/technical school, the type of institution (private or public; for-profit or non-profit; religious affiliation; historically black), the total estimated student enrollment in 2013, the general telephone number, and the annual tuition and fees for full-time students. *Source: U.S. Department of Education, National Center for Educational Statistics, IPEDS College Data, 2013-14*

HOUSING

Homeownership Rate: Percentage of housing units that are owner-occupied. *Source: U.S. Census Bureau, Census 2010*

Median Home Value: Median value in dollars of all owner-occupied housing units as reported by the owner. *Source: U.S. Census Bureau, American Community Survey, 2009-2013 Five-Year Estimates*

Median Year Structure Built: Year structure built refers to when the building was first constructed, not when it was remodeled, added to, or converted. For mobile homes, houseboats, RVs, etc, the manufacturer's model year was assumed to be the year built. The data relate to the number of units built during the specified periods that were still in existence at the time of enumeration. *Source: U.S. Census Bureau, American Community Survey, 2009-2013 Five-Year Estimates*

Homeowner Vacancy Rate: Proportion of the homeowner inventory that is vacant "for sale." It is computed by dividing the number of vacant units "for sale only" by the sum of the owner-occupied units, vacant units that are "for sale only," and vacant units that have been sold but not yet occupied, and then multiplying by 100. This measure is rounded to the nearest tenth. *Source: U.S. Census Bureau, Census 2010*

Median Gross Rent: Median monthly gross rent in dollars on specified renter-occupied and specified vacant-for-rent units. Specified renter-occupied and specified vacant-for-rent units exclude 1-family houses on 10 acres or more. Gross rent is the contract rent plus the estimated average monthly cost of utilities (electricity, gas, and water and sewer) and fuels (oil, coal, kerosene, wood, etc.) if these are paid by the renter (or paid for the renter by someone else). Gross rent is intended to eliminate differentials that result from varying practices with respect to the inclusion of utilities and fuels as part of the rental payment. Contract rent is the monthly rent agreed to or contracted for, regardless of any furnishings, utilities, fees, meals, or services that may be included. For vacant units, it is the monthly rent asked for the rental unit at the time of enumeration. *Source: U.S. Census Bureau, American Community Survey, 2009-2013 Five-Year Estimates*

Rental Vacancy Rate: Proportion of the rental inventory that is vacant "for rent." It is computed by dividing the number of vacant units "for rent" by the sum of the renter-occupied units, vacant units that are "for rent," and vacant units that have been rented but not yet occupied, and then multiplying by 100. This measure is rounded to the nearest tenth. *Source: U.S. Census Bureau, Census 2010*

HEALTH INSURANCE

Health insurance coverage in the ACS and other Census Bureau surveys define coverage to include plans and programs that provide comprehensive health coverage. Plans that provide insurance for specific conditions or situations such as cancer and long-term care policies are not considered coverage. Likewise, other types of insurance like dental, vision, life, and disability insurance are not considered health insurance coverage.

For reporting purposes, the Census Bureau broadly classifies health insurance coverage as private health insurance or public coverage. Private health insurance is a plan provided through an employer or union, a plan purchased by an individual from a private company, or TRICARE or other military health care. Public health coverage includes the federal programs Medicare, Medicaid, and VA Health Care (provided through the Department of Veterans Affairs); the Children's Health Insurance Program (CHIP); and individual state health plans. The types of health insurance are not mutually exclusive; people may be covered by more than one at the same time. People who had no reported health coverage, or those whose only health coverage was Indian Health Service, were considered uninsured. *Source: U.S. Census Bureau, American Community Survey, 2009-2013 Five-Year Estimates*

- **Have Insurance:** Percent of the civilian noninstitutionalized population with any type of comprehensive health insurance.
- **Have Private Insurance.** Percent of the civilian noninstitutionalized population with private health insurance. A person may report that they have both public and private health insurance, thus, the sum of the percentages may be greater than 100%.
- **Have Public Insurance.** Percent of the civilian noninstitutionalized population with public health insurance. A person may report that they have both public and private health insurance, thus, the sum of the percentages may be greater than 100%.
- **Do Not Have Insurance.** Percent of the civilian noninstitutionalized population with no health insurance.
- **Children Under 18 With No Insurance.** Percent of the civilian noninstitutionalized population under age 18 with no health insurance.

HOSPITALS

Lists the hospital name and the number of licensed beds. *Source: Grey House Publishing, The Comparative Guide to American Hospitals, 2014*

NEWSPAPERS

List of daily and weekly newspapers with circulation figures. *Source: Gebbie Press, 2015 All-In-One Media Directory*

SAFETY

Violent Crime Rate: Number of violent crimes reported per 10,000 population. Violent crimes include murder, forcible rape, robbery, and aggravated assault. *Source: Federal Bureau of Investigation, Uniform Crime Reports 2013*

Property Crime Rate: Number of property crimes reported per 10,000 population. Property crimes include burglary, larceny-theft, and motor vehicle theft. *Source: Federal Bureau of Investigation, Uniform Crime Reports 2013*

TRANSPORTATION

Commute to Work: Percentage of workers 16 years old and over that use the following means of transportation to commute to work: car; public transportation; walk; work from home. The means of transportation data for some areas may show workers using modes of public transportation that are not available in those areas (e.g. subway or elevated riders in a metropolitan area where there actually is no subway or elevated service). This result is largely due to people who worked during the reference week at a location that was different from their usual place of work (such as people away from home on business in an area where subway service was available) and people who used more than one means of transportation each day but whose principal means was unavailable where they lived (e.g. residents of non-metropolitan areas who drove to the fringe of a metropolitan area and took the commuter railroad most of the distance to work). *Source: U.S. Census Bureau, American Community Survey, 2009-2013 Five-Year Estimates*

Median Travel Time to Work: Median travel time to work for workers 16 years old and over. Travel time to work refers to the total number of minutes that it usually took the person to get from home to work each day during the reference week. The elapsed time includes time spent waiting for public transportation, picking up passengers in carpools, and time spent in other activities related to getting to work. *Source: U.S. Census Bureau, American Community Survey, 2009-2013 Five-Year Estimates*

Amtrak: Indicates if Amtrak rail or bus service is available. Please note that the cities being served continually change. *Source: National Railroad Passenger Corporation, Amtrak National Timetable, 2015*

AIRPORTS

Lists the local airport(s) along with type of service and hub size. *Source: U.S. Department of Transportation, Bureau of Transportation Statistics*

ADDITIONAL INFORMATION CONTACTS

General telephone number and website address (if available) of local government.

User Guide: Education Section

School District Rankings

Number of Schools: Total number of schools in the district. *Source: U.S. Department of Education, National Center for Education Statistics, Common Core of Data, Public Elementary/Secondary School Universe Survey: School Year 2011-2012.*

Number of Teachers: Teachers are defined as individuals who provide instruction to pre-kindergarten, kindergarten, grades 1 through 12, or ungraded classes, or individuals who teach in an environment other than a classroom setting, and who maintain daily student attendance records. Numbers reported are full-time equivalents (FTE). *Source: U.S. Department of Education, National Center for Education Statistics, Common Core of Data, Local Education Agency (School District) Universe Survey: School Year 2011-2012.*

Number of Students: A student is an individual for whom instruction is provided in an elementary or secondary education program that is not an adult education program and is under the jurisdiction of a school, school system, or other education institution. *Sources: U.S. Department of Education, National Center for Education Statistics, Common Core of Data, Local Education Agency (School District) Universe Survey: School Year 2011-2012 and Public Elementary/Secondary School Universe Survey: School Year 2011-2012*

Individual Education Program (IEP) Students: A written instructional plan for students with disabilities designated as special education students under IDEA-Part B. The written instructional plan includes a statement of present levels of educational performance of a child; statement of annual goals, including short-term instructional objectives; statement of specific educational services to be provided and the extent to which the child will be able to participate in regular educational programs; the projected date for initiation and anticipated duration of services; the appropriate objectives, criteria and evaluation procedures; and the schedules for determining, on at least an annual basis, whether instructional objectives are being achieved. *Source: U.S. Department of Education, National Center for Education Statistics, Common Core of Data, Local Education Agency (School District) Universe Survey: School Year 2011-2012*

English Language Learner (ELL) Students: Formerly referred to as Limited English Proficient (LEP). Students being served in appropriate programs of language assistance (e.g., English as a Second Language, High Intensity Language Training, bilingual education). Does not include pupils enrolled in a class to learn a language other than English. Also Limited-English-Proficient students are individuals who were not born in the United States or whose native language is a language other than English; or individuals who come from environments where a language other than English is dominant; or individuals who are American Indians and Alaskan Natives and who come from environments where a language other than English has had a significant impact on their level of English language proficiency; and who, by reason thereof, have sufficient difficulty speaking, reading, writing, or understanding the English language, to deny such individuals the opportunity to learn successfully in classrooms where the language of instruction is English or to participate fully in our society. *Source: U.S. Department of Education, National Center for Education Statistics, Common Core of Data, Local Education Agency (School District) Universe Survey: School Year 2011-2012*

Students Eligible for Free Lunch Program: The free lunch program is defined as a program under the National School Lunch Act that provides cash subsidies for free lunches to students based on family size and income criteria. *Source: U.S. Department of Education, National Center for Education Statistics, Common Core of Data, Public Elementary/Secondary School Universe Survey: School Year 2011-2012*

Students Eligible for Reduced-Price Lunch Program: A student who is eligible to participate in the Reduced-Price Lunch Program under the National School Lunch Act. *Source: U.S. Department of Education, National Center for Education Statistics, Common Core of Data, Public Elementary/Secondary School Universe Survey: School Year 2011-2012*

Student/Teacher Ratio: The number of students divided by the number of teachers (FTE). See Number of Students and Number of Teachers above for for information.

Student/Librarian Ratio: The number of students divided by the number of library and media support staff. Library and media support staff are defined as staff members who render other professional library and media services; also includes library aides and those involved in library/media support. Their duties include selecting, preparing, caring for, and making available to instructional staff, equipment, films, filmstrips, transparencies, tapes, TV programs, and similar materials maintained separately or as part of an instructional materials center. Also included are activities in the audio-visual center, TV studio, related-work-study areas, and services provided by audio-visual personnel.

Numbers are based on full-time equivalents. *Source: U.S. Department of Education, National Center for Education Statistics, Common Core of Data, Local Education Agency (School District) Universe Survey: School Year 2011-2012.*

Student/Counselor Ratio: The number of students divided by the number of guidance counselors. Guidance counselors are professional staff assigned specific duties and school time for any of the following activities in an elementary or secondary setting: counseling with students and parents; consulting with other staff members on learning problems; evaluating student abilities; assisting students in making educational and career choices; assisting students in personal and social development; providing referral assistance; and/or working with other staff members in planning and conducting guidance programs for students. The state applies its own standards in apportioning the aggregate of guidance counselors/directors into the elementary and secondary level components. Numbers reported are full-time equivalents. *Source: U.S. Department of Education, National Center for Education Statistics, Common Core of Data, Local Education Agency (School District) Universe Survey: School Year 2011-2012.*

Current Spending per Student: Expenditure for Instruction, Support Services, and Other Elementary/Secondary Programs. Includes salaries, employee benefits, purchased services, and supplies, as well as payments made by states on behalf of school districts. Also includes transfers made by school districts into their own retirement system. Excludes expenditure for Non-Elementary/Secondary Programs, debt service, capital outlay, and transfers to other governments or school districts. This item is formally called "Current Expenditures for Public Elementary/Secondary Education."

Instruction: Includes payments from all funds for salaries, employee benefits, supplies, materials, and contractual services for elementary/secondary instruction. It excludes capital outlay, debt service, and interfund transfers for elementary/secondary instruction. Instruction covers regular, special, and vocational programs offered in both the regular school year and summer school. It excludes instructional support activities as well as adult education and community services. Instruction salaries includes salaries for teachers and teacher aides and assistants.

Support Services: Relates to support services functions (series 2000) defined in Financial Accounting for Local and State School Systems (National Center for Education Statistics 2000). Includes payments from all funds for salaries, employee benefits, supplies, materials, and contractual services. It excludes capital outlay, debt service, and interfund transfers. It includes expenditure for the following functions:

- Business/Central/Other Support Services
- General Administration
- Instructional Staff Support
- Operation and Maintenance
- Pupil Support Services
- Pupil Transportation Services
- School Administration
- Nonspecified Support Services

Values shown are dollars per pupil per year. They were calculated by dividing the total dollar amounts by the fall membership. Fall membership is comprised of the total student enrollment on October 1 (or the closest school day to October 1) for all grade levels (including prekindergarten and kindergarten) and ungraded pupils. Membership includes students both present and absent on the measurement day. *Source: U.S. Department of Education, National Center for Education Statistics, Common Core of Data, School District Finance Survey (F-33), Fiscal Year 2011.*

Drop-out Rate: A dropout is a student who was enrolled in school at some time during the previous school year; was not enrolled at the beginning of the current school year; has not graduated from high school or completed a state or district approved educational program; and does not meet any of the following exclusionary conditions: has transferred to another public school district, private school, or state- or district-approved educational program; is temporarily absent due to suspension or school-approved illness; or has died. The values shown cover grades 9 through 12. *Note: Drop-out rates are no longer available to the general public disaggregated by grade, race/ethnicity, and gender at the school district level. Beginning with the 2005–06 school year the CCD is reporting dropout data aggregated from the local education agency (district) level to the state level. This allows data users to compare event dropout rates across states, regions, and other jurisdictions. Source: U.S. Department of Education, National Center for Education Statistics, Common Core of Data, Local Education Agency (School District) Universe Survey Dropout and Completion Data, 2008-2009; U.S. Department of Education, National Center for Education Statistics, Common Core of Data, State Dropout and Completion Data File, 2009-2010*

Average Freshman Graduation Rate (AFGR): The AFGR is the number of regular diploma recipients in a given year divided by the average of the membership in grades 8, 9, and 10, reported 5, 4, and 3 years earlier, respectively. For example, the denominator of the 2008–09 AFGR is the average of the 8th-grade membership in 2004–05, 9th-grade membership in 2005–06, and 10th-grade membership in 2006–07. Ungraded students are prorated into these grades. Averaging these three grades provides an estimate of the number of first-time freshmen in the class of 2005–06 freshmen in order to estimate the on-time graduation rate for 2008–09.

Caution in interpreting the AFGR. Although the AFGR was selected as the best of the available alternatives, several factors make it fall short of a true on-time graduation rate. First, the AFGR does not take into account any imbalances in the number of students moving in and out of the nation or individual states over the high school years. As a result, the averaged freshman class is at best an approximation of the actual number of freshmen, where differences in the rates of transfers, retention, and dropping out in the three grades affect the average. Second, by including all graduates in a specific year, the graduates may include students who repeated a grade in high school or completed high school early and thus are not on-time graduates in that year. *Source: U.S. Department of Education, National Center for Education Statistics, Common Core of Data, Local Education Agency (School District) Universe Survey Dropout and Completion Data, 2008-2009; U.S. Department of Education, National Center for Education Statistics, Common Core of Data, State Dropout and Completion Data File, 2009-2010*

Number of Diploma Recipients: A student who has received a diploma during the previous school year or subsequent summer school. This category includes regular diploma recipients and other diploma recipients. A High School Diploma is a formal document certifying the successful completion of a secondary school program prescribed by the state education agency or other appropriate body. *Note: Diploma counts are no longer available to the general public disaggregated by grade, race/ethnicity, and gender at the school district level. Source: U.S. Department of Education, National Center for Education Statistics, Common Core of Data, Local Education Agency (School District) Universe Survey Dropout and Completion Data, 2008-2009; U.S. Department of Education, National Center for Education Statistics, Common Core of Data, State Dropout and Completion Data File, 2009-2010*

Note: n/a indicates data not available.

State Educational Profile

Please refer to the District Rankings section in the front of this User Guide for an explanation of data for all items except for the following:

Average Salary: The average salary for classroom teachers in 2013-2014. *Source: National Education Association, Rankings & Estimates: Rankings of the States 2013 and Estimates of School Statistics 2014*

College Entrance Exam Scores:

Scholastic Aptitude Test (SAT). *Note: Data covers all students during the 2013 school year. The College Board strongly discourages the comparison or ranking of states on the basis of SAT scores alone. Source: The College Board*

American College Testing Program (ACT). *Note: Data covers all students during the 2013 school year. Source: ACT, 2013 ACT National and State Scores*

National Assessment of Educational Progress (NAEP)

The National Assessment of Educational Progress (NAEP), also known as “the Nation’s Report Card,” is the only nationally representative and continuing assessment of what America’s students know and can do in various subject areas. As a result of the “No Child Left Behind” legislation, all states are required to participate in NAEP.

For more information, visit the U.S. Department of Education, National Center for Education Statistics at http://nces.ed.gov/nationsreportcard.

User Guide: Ancestry and Ethnicity Section

Places Covered

The ancestry and ethnicity profile section of this book covers the state and all counties and places with populations of 50,000 or more. Places included fall into one of the following categories:

Incorporated Places. Depending on the state, places are incorporated as either cities, towns, villages, boroughs, municipalities, independent cities, or corporations. A few municipalities have a form of government combined with another entity (e.g. county) and are listed as special cities or consolidated, unified, or metropolitan governments.

Census Designated Places (CDP). The U.S. Census Bureau defines a CDP as "a statistical entity," defined for each decennial census according to Census Bureau guidelines, comprising a densely settled concentration of population that is not within an incorporated place, but is locally identified by a name. CDPs are delineated cooperatively by state and local officials and the Census Bureau, following Census Bureau guidelines.

Minor Civil Divisions (called charter townships, districts, gores, grants, locations, plantations, purchases, reservations, towns, townships, and unorganized territories) for the states where the Census Bureau has determined that they serve as general-purpose governments. Those states are Connecticut, Maine, Massachusetts, Michigan, Minnesota, New Hampshire, New Jersey, New York, Pennsylvania, Rhode Island, Vermont, and Wisconsin. In some states incorporated municipalities are part of minor civil divisions and in some states they are independent of them.

Note: Several states have incorporated municipalities and minor civil divisions in the same county with the same name. Those communities are given separate entries (e.g. Burlington, New Jersey, in Burlington County will be listed under both the city and township of Burlington). A few states have Census Designated Places and minor civil divisions in the same county with the same name. Those communities are given separate entries (e.g. Bridgewater, Massachusetts, in Plymouth County will be listed under both the CDP and town of Bridgewater).

Source of Data

The ethnicities shown in this book were compiled from two different sources. Data for Race and Hispanic Origin was taken from Census 2010 Summary File 1 (SF1) while Ancestry data was taken from the American Community Survey (ACS) 2006-2010 Five-Year Estimate. The distinction is important because SF1 contains 100-percent data, which is the information compiled from the questions asked of all people and about every housing unit. ACS estimates are compiled from a sampling of households. The 2006-2010 Five-Year Estimate is based on data collected from January 1, 2006 to December 31, 2010.

The American Community Survey (ACS) is a relatively new survey conducted by the U.S. Census Bureau. It uses a series of monthly samples to produce annually updated data for the same small areas (census tracts and block groups) formerly surveyed via the decennial census long-form sample. While some version of this survey has been in the field since 1999, it was not fully implemented in terms of coverage until 2006. In 2005 it was expanded to cover all counties in the country and the 1-in-40 households sampling rate was first applied. The full implementation of the (household) sampling strategy for ACS entails having the survey mailed to about 250,000 households nationwide every month of every year and was begun in January 2005. In January 2006 sampling of group quarters was added to complete the sample as planned. In any given year about 2.5% (1 in 40) of U.S. households will receive the survey. Over any 5-year period about 1 in 8 households should receive the survey (as compared to about 1 in 6 that received the census long form in the 2000 census). Since receiving the survey is not the same as responding to it, the Bureau has adopted a strategy of sampling for non-response, resulting in something closer to 1 in 11 households actually participating in the survey over any 5-year period. For more information about the American Community Survey visit http://www.census.gov/acs/www.

Ancestry

Ancestry refers to a person's ethnic origin, heritage, descent, or "roots," which may reflect their place of birth or that of previous generations of their family. Some ethnic identities, such as "Egyptian" or "Polish" can be traced to geographic areas outside the United States, while other ethnicities such as "Pennsylvania German" or "Cajun" evolved in the United States.

The intent of the ancestry question in the ACS was not to measure the degree of attachment the respondent had to a particular ethnicity, but simply to establish that the respondent had a connection to and self-identified with a particular ethnic group. For example, a response of "Irish" might reflect total involvement in an Irish community or only a memory of ancestors several generations removed from the respondent.

The Census Bureau coded the responses into a numeric representation of over 1,000 categories. Responses initially were processed through an automated coding system; then, those that were not automatically assigned a code were coded by individuals trained in coding ancestry responses. The code list reflects the results of the Census Bureau's own research and consultations with many ethnic experts. Many decisions were made to determine the classification of responses. These decisions affected the grouping of the tabulated data. For example, the "Indonesian" category includes the responses of "Indonesian," "Celebesian," "Moluccan," and a number of other responses.

Ancestries Covered

- Afghan
- African, Sub-Saharan
  - African
  - Cape Verdean
  - Ethiopian
  - Ghanaian
  - Kenyan
  - Liberian
  - Nigerian
  - Senegalese
  - Sierra Leonean
  - Somalian
  - South African
  - Sudanese
  - Ugandan
  - Zimbabwean
  - Other Sub-Saharan African
- Albanian
- Alsatian
- American
- Arab
  - Arab
  - Egyptian
  - Iraqi
  - Jordanian
  - Lebanese
  - Moroccan
  - Palestinian
  - Syrian
  - Other Arab
- Armenian
- Assyrian/Chaldean/Syriac
- Australian
- Austrian
- Basque
- Belgian
- Brazilian
- British
- Bulgarian
- Cajun
- Canadian
- Carpatho Rusyn
- Celtic
- Croatian
- Cypriot
- Czech
- Czechoslovakian
- Danish
- Dutch
- Eastern European
- English
- Estonian
- European
- Finnish
- French, ex. Basque
- French Canadian
- German
- German Russian
- Greek
- Guyanese
- Hungarian
- Icelander
- Iranian
- Irish
- Israeli
- Italian
- Latvian
- Lithuanian
- Luxemburger
- Macedonian
- Maltese
- New Zealander
- Northern European
- Norwegian
- Pennsylvania German
- Polish
- Portuguese
- Romanian
- Russian
- Scandinavian
- Scotch-Irish
- Scottish
- Serbian
- Slavic
- Slovak
- Slovene
- Soviet Union
- Swedish
- Swiss
- Turkish
- Ukrainian
- Welsh
- West Indian, ex. Hispanic
  - Bahamian
  - Barbadian
  - Belizean
  - Bermudan
  - British West Indian
  - Dutch West Indian
  - Haitian
  - Jamaican
  - Trinidadian/Tobagonian
  - U.S. Virgin Islander
  - West Indian
  - Other West Indian
- Yugoslavian

The ancestry question allowed respondents to report one or more ancestry groups. Generally, only the first two responses reported were coded. If a response was in terms of a dual ancestry, for example, "Irish English," the person was assigned two codes, in this case one for Irish and another for English. However, in certain cases, multiple responses such as "French Canadian," "Scotch-Irish," "Greek Cypriot," and "Black Dutch" were assigned a single code reflecting their status as unique groups. If a person reported one of these unique groups in addition to another group, for example, "Scotch-Irish English," resulting in three terms, that person received one code for the unique group (Scotch-Irish) and another one for the remaining group (English). If a person reported "English Irish French," only English and Irish were coded. If there were more than two ancestries listed and one of the ancestries was a part of another, such as "German Bavarian Hawaiian," the responses were coded using the more detailed groups (Bavarian and Hawaiian).

The Census Bureau accepted "American" as a unique ethnicity if it was given alone or with one other ancestry. There were some groups such as "American Indian," "Mexican American," and "African American" that were coded and identified separately.

The ancestry question is asked for every person in the American Community Survey, regardless of age, place of birth, Hispanic origin, or race.

Although some people consider religious affiliation a component of ethnic identity, the ancestry question was not designed to collect any information concerning religion. Thus, if a religion was given as an answer to the ancestry question, it was listed in the "Other groups" category which is not shown in this book.

Ancestry should not be confused with a person's place of birth, although a person's place of birth and ancestry may be the same.

Hispanic Origin

The data on the Hispanic or Latino population were derived from answers to a Census 2010 question that was asked of all people. The terms "Spanish," "Hispanic origin," and "Latino" are used interchangeably. Some respondents identify with all three terms while others may identify with only one of these three specific terms. Hispanics or Latinos who identify with the terms "Spanish," "Hispanic," or "Latino" are those who classify themselves in one of the specific Spanish, Hispanic, or Latino categories listed on the questionnaire ("Mexican," "Puerto Rican," or "Cuban") as well as those who indicate that they are "other Spanish/Hispanic/Latino." People who do not identify with one of the specific origins listed on the questionnaire but indicate that they are "other Spanish/Hispanic/Latino" are those whose origins are from Spain, the Spanish-speaking countries of Central or South America, the Dominican Republic, or people identifying themselves generally as Spanish, Spanish-American, Hispanic, Hispano, Latino, and so on. All write-in responses to the "other Spanish/Hispanic/Latino" category were coded.

Hispanic Origins Covered

Hispanic or Latino	Salvadoran	Argentinean	Uruguayan
Central American, ex. Mexican	Other Central American	Bolivian	Venezuelan
Costa Rican	Cuban	Chilean	Other South American
Guatemalan	Dominican Republic	Colombian	Other Hispanic or Latino
Honduran	Mexican	Ecuadorian	
Nicaraguan	Puerto Rican	Paraguayan	
Panamanian	South American	Peruvian	

Origin can be viewed as the heritage, nationality group, lineage, or country of birth of the person or the person's parents or ancestors before their arrival in the United States. People who identify their origin as Hispanic, Latino, or Spanish may be of any race.

Ethnicities Based on Race

The data on race were derived from answers to the Census 2010 question on race that was asked of individuals in the United States. The Census Bureau collects racial data in accordance with guidelines provided by the U.S. Office of Management and Budget (OMB), and these data are based on self-identification.

The racial categories included in the census questionnaire generally reflect a social definition of race recognized in this country and not an attempt to define race biologically, anthropologically, or genetically. In addition, it is recognized that the categories of the race item include racial and national origin or sociocultural groups. People may choose to report more than one race to indicate their racial mixture, such as "American Indian" and "White." People who identify their origin as Hispanic, Latino, or Spanish may be of any race.

Racial Groups Covered

African-American/Black	Crow	Spanish American Indian	Korean
Not Hispanic	Delaware	Tlingit-Haida *(Alaska Native)*	Laotian
Hispanic	Hopi	Tohono O'Odham	Malaysian
American Indian/Alaska Native	Houma	Tsimshian *(Alaska Native)*	Nepalese
Not Hispanic	Inupiat *(Alaska Native)*	Ute	Pakistani
Hispanic	Iroquois	Yakama	Sri Lankan
Alaska Athabascan *(Ala. Nat.)*	Kiowa	Yaqui	Taiwanese
Aleut *(Alaska Native)*	Lumbee	Yuman	Thai
Apache	Menominee	Yup'ik *(Alaska Native)*	Vietnamese
Arapaho	Mexican American Indian	**Asian**	**Hawaii Native/Pacific Islander**
Blackfeet	Navajo	*Not Hispanic*	*Not Hispanic*
Canadian/French Am. Indian	Osage	*Hispanic*	*Hispanic*
Central American Indian	Ottawa	Bangladeshi	Fijian
Cherokee	Paiute	Bhutanese	Guamanian/Chamorro
Cheyenne	Pima	Burmese	Marshallese
Chickasaw	Potawatomi	Cambodian	Native Hawaiian
Chippewa	Pueblo	Chinese, ex. Taiwanese	Samoan
Choctaw	Puget Sound Salish	Filipino	Tongan
Colville	Seminole	Hmong	**White**
Comanche	Shoshone	Indian	*Not Hispanic*
Cree	Sioux	Indonesian	*Hispanic*
Creek	South American Indian	Japanese	

African American or Black: A person having origins in any of the Black racial groups of Africa. It includes people who indicated their race(s) as "Black, African Am., or Negro" or reported entries such as African American, Kenyan, Nigerian, or Haitian.

American Indian or Alaska Native: A person having origins in any of the original peoples of North and South America (including Central America) and who maintains tribal affiliation or community attachment. This category includes people who indicated their race(s) as "American Indian or Alaska Native" or reported their enrolled or principal tribe, such as Navajo, Blackfeet, Inupiat, Yup'ik, or Central American Indian groups or South American Indian groups.

Asian: A person having origins in any of the original peoples of the Far East, Southeast Asia, or the Indian subcontinent, including, for example, Cambodia, China, India, Japan, Korea, Malaysia, Pakistan, the Philippine Islands, Thailand, and Vietnam. It includes people who indicated their race(s) as "Asian" or reported entries such as "Asian Indian," "Chinese," "Filipino," "Korean," "Japanese," "Vietnamese," and "Other Asian" or provided other detailed Asian responses.

Native Hawaiian or Other Pacific Islander: A person having origins in any of the original peoples of Hawaii, Guam, Samoa, or other Pacific Islands. It includes people who indicated their race(s) as "Pacific Islander" or reported entries such as "Native Hawaiian," "Guamanian or Chamorro," "Samoan," and "Other Pacific Islander" or provided other detailed Pacific Islander responses.

White: A person having origins in any of the original peoples of Europe, the Middle East, or North Africa. It includes people who indicated their race(s) as "White" or reported entries such as Irish, German, Italian, Lebanese, Arab, Moroccan, or Caucasian.

Profiles

Each profile shows the name of the place, the county (if a place spans more than one county, the county that holds the majority of the population is shown), and the 2010 population (based on 100-percent data from Census 2010 Summary File 1). The rest of each profile is comprised of all 218 ethnicities grouped into three sections: ancestry; Hispanic origin; and race.

Column one displays the ancestry/Hispanic origin/race name, column two displays the number of people reporting each ancestry/Hispanic origin/race, and column three is the percent of the total population reporting each ancestry/Hispanic origin/race. The population figure shown is used to calculate the value in the "%" column for ethnicities based on race and Hispanic origin. The 2006-2010 estimated population figure from the American Community Survey (not shown) is used to calculate the value in the "%" column for all other ancestries.

For ethnicities in the ancestries group, the value in the "Number" column includes multiple ancestries reported. For example, if a person reported a multiple ancestry such as "French Danish," that response was counted twice in the tabulations, once in the French category and again in the Danish category. Thus, the sum of the counts is not the total population but the total of all responses. Numbers in parentheses indicate the number of people reporting a single ancestry. People reporting a single ancestry includes all people who reported only one ethnic group such as "German." Also included in this category are people with only a multiple-term response such as "Scotch-Irish" who are assigned a single code because they represent one distinct group. For example, the count for German would be interpreted as "The number of people who reported that German was their only ancestry."

For ethnicities based on Hispanic origin, the value in the "Number" column represents the number of people who reported being Mexican, Puerto Rican, Cuban or other Spanish/Hispanic/ Latino (all written-in responses were coded). All ethnicities based on Hispanic origin can be of any race.

For ethnicities based on race data the value in the "Number" column represents the total number of people who reported each category alone or in combination with one or more other race categories. This number represents the maximum number of people reporting and therefore the individual race categories may add up to more than the total population because people may be included in more than one category. The figures in parentheses show the number of people that reported that particular ethnicity alone, not in combination with any other race. For example, in Alabama, the entry for Korean shows 8,320 in parentheses and 10,624 in the "Number" column. This means that 8,320 people reported being Korean alone and 10,624 people reported being Korean alone or in combination with one or more other races.

Rankings

In the rankings section, each ethnicity has three tables. The first table shows the top 10 places sorted by ethnic population (based on all places, regardless of total population), the second table shows the top 10 places sorted by percent of the total population (based on all places, regardless of total population), the third table shows the top 10 places sorted by percent of the total population (based on places with total population of 50,000 or more).

Within each table, column one displays the place name, the state, and the county (if a place spans more than one county, the county that holds the majority of the population is shown). Column one in the first table displays the state only. Column two displays the number of people reporting each ancestry (includes people reporting multiple ancestries), Hispanic origin, or race (alone or in combination with any other race). Column three is the percent of the total population reporting each ancestry, Hispanic origin or race. For tables representing ethnicities based on race or Hispanic origin, the 100-percent population figure from SF1 is used to calculate the value in the "%" column. For all other ancestries, the 2006-2010 five-year estimated population figure from the American Community Survey is used to calculate the value in the "%" column.

Alphabetical Ethnicity Cross-Reference Guide

Afghan *see* Ancestry–Afghan
African *see* Ancestry–African, Sub-Saharan: African
African-American *see* Race–African-American/Black
African-American: Hispanic *see* Race–African-American/Black: Hispanic
African-American: Not Hispanic *see* Race–African-American/Black: Not Hispanic
Alaska Athabascan *see* Race–Alaska Native: Alaska Athabascan
Alaska Native *see* Race–American Indian/Alaska Native
Alaska Native: Hispanic *see* Race–American Indian/Alaska Native: Hispanic
Alaska Native: Not Hispanic *see* Race–American Indian/Alaska Native: Not Hispanic
Albanian *see* Ancestry–Albanian
Aleut *see* Race–Alaska Native: Aleut
Alsatian *see* Ancestry–Alsatian
American *see* Ancestry–American
American Indian *see* Race–American Indian/Alaska Native
American Indian: Hispanic *see* Race–American Indian/Alaska Native: Hispanic
American Indian: Not Hispanic *see* Race–American Indian/Alaska Native: Not Hispanic
Apache *see* Race–American Indian: Apache
Arab *see* Ancestry–Arab: Arab
Arab: Other *see* Ancestry–Arab: Other
Arapaho *see* Race–American Indian: Arapaho
Argentinean *see* Hispanic Origin–South American: Argentinean
Armenian *see* Ancestry–Armenian
Asian *see* Race–Asian
Asian Indian *see* Race–Asian: Indian
Asian: Hispanic *see* Race–Asian: Hispanic
Asian: Not Hispanic *see* Race–Asian: Not Hispanic
Assyrian *see* Ancestry–Assyrian/Chaldean/Syriac
Australian *see* Ancestry–Australian
Austrian *see* Ancestry–Austrian
Bahamian *see* Ancestry–West Indian: Bahamian, except Hispanic
Bangladeshi *see* Race–Asian: Bangladeshi
Barbadian *see* Ancestry–West Indian: Barbadian, except Hispanic
Basque *see* Ancestry–Basque
Belgian *see* Ancestry–Belgian
Belizean *see* Ancestry–West Indian: Belizean, except Hispanic
Bermudan *see* Ancestry–West Indian: Bermudan, except Hispanic
Bhutanese *see* Race–Asian: Bhutanese
Black *see* Race–African-American/Black
Black: Hispanic *see* Race–African-American/Black: Hispanic
Black: Not Hispanic *see* Race–African-American/Black: Not Hispanic
Blackfeet *see* Race–American Indian: Blackfeet
Bolivian *see* Hispanic Origin–South American: Bolivian
Brazilian *see* Ancestry–Brazilian
British *see* Ancestry–British

British West Indian *see* Ancestry–West Indian: British West Indian, except Hispanic
Bulgarian *see* Ancestry–Bulgarian
Burmese *see* Race–Asian: Burmese
Cajun *see* Ancestry–Cajun
Cambodian *see* Race–Asian: Cambodian
Canadian *see* Ancestry–Canadian
Canadian/French American Indian *see* Race–American Indian: Canadian/French American Indian
Cape Verdean *see* Ancestry–African, Sub-Saharan: Cape Verdean
Carpatho Rusyn *see* Ancestry–Carpatho Rusyn
Celtic *see* Ancestry–Celtic
Central American *see* Hispanic Origin–Central American, except Mexican
Central American Indian *see* Race–American Indian: Central American Indian
Central American: Other *see* Hispanic Origin–Central American: Other Central American
Chaldean *see* Ancestry–Assyrian/Chaldean/Syriac
Chamorro *see* Race–Hawaii Native/Pacific Islander: Guamanian or Chamorro
Cherokee *see* Race–American Indian: Cherokee
Cheyenne *see* Race–American Indian: Cheyenne
Chickasaw *see* Race–American Indian: Chickasaw
Chilean *see* Hispanic Origin–South American: Chilean
Chinese (except Taiwanese) *see* Race–Asian: Chinese, except Taiwanese
Chippewa *see* Race–American Indian: Chippewa
Choctaw *see* Race–American Indian: Choctaw
Colombian *see* Hispanic Origin–South American: Colombian
Colville *see* Race–American Indian: Colville
Comanche *see* Race–American Indian: Comanche
Costa Rican *see* Hispanic Origin–Central American: Costa Rican
Cree *see* Race–American Indian: Cree
Creek *see* Race–American Indian: Creek
Croatian *see* Ancestry–Croatian
Crow *see* Race–American Indian: Crow
Cuban *see* Hispanic Origin–Cuban
Cypriot *see* Ancestry–Cypriot
Czech *see* Ancestry–Czech
Czechoslovakian *see* Ancestry–Czechoslovakian
Danish *see* Ancestry–Danish
Delaware *see* Race–American Indian: Delaware
Dominican Republic *see* Hispanic Origin–Dominican Republic
Dutch *see* Ancestry–Dutch
Dutch West Indian *see* Ancestry–West Indian: Dutch West Indian, except Hispanic
Eastern European *see* Ancestry–Eastern European
Ecuadorian *see* Hispanic Origin–South American: Ecuadorian
Egyptian *see* Ancestry–Arab: Egyptian
English *see* Ancestry–English
Eskimo *see* Race–Alaska Native: Inupiat
Estonian *see* Ancestry–Estonian
Ethiopian *see* Ancestry–African, Sub-Saharan: Ethiopian
European *see* Ancestry–European
Fijian *see* Race–Hawaii Native/Pacific Islander: Fijian
Filipino *see* Race–Asian: Filipino
Finnish *see* Ancestry–Finnish
French (except Basque) *see* Ancestry–French, except Basque
French Canadian *see* Ancestry–French Canadian
German *see* Ancestry–German
German Russian *see* Ancestry–German Russian
Ghanaian *see* Ancestry–African, Sub-Saharan: Ghanaian
Greek *see* Ancestry–Greek
Guamanian *see* Race–Hawaii Native/Pacific Islander: Guamanian or Chamorro
Guatemalan *see* Hispanic Origin–Central American: Guatemalan
Guyanese *see* Ancestry–Guyanese
Haitian *see* Ancestry–West Indian: Haitian, except Hispanic
Hawaii Native *see* Race–Hawaii Native/Pacific Islander
Hawaii Native: Hispanic *see* Race–Hawaii Native/Pacific Islander: Hispanic

Hawaii Native: Not Hispanic *see* Race–Hawaii Native/Pacific Islander: Not Hispanic
Hispanic or Latino: *see* Hispanic Origin–Hispanic or Latino (of any race)
Hispanic or Latino: Other *see* Hispanic Origin–Other Hispanic or Latino
Hmong *see* Race–Asian: Hmong
Honduran *see* Hispanic Origin–Central American: Honduran
Hopi *see* Race–American Indian: Hopi
Houma *see* Race–American Indian: Houma
Hungarian *see* Ancestry–Hungarian
Icelander *see* Ancestry–Icelander
Indonesian *see* Race–Asian: Indonesian
Inupiat *see* Race–Alaska Native: Inupiat
Iranian *see* Ancestry–Iranian
Iraqi *see* Ancestry–Arab: Iraqi
Irish *see* Ancestry–Irish
Iroquois *see* Race–American Indian: Iroquois
Israeli *see* Ancestry–Israeli
Italian *see* Ancestry–Italian
Jamaican *see* Ancestry–West Indian: Jamaican, except Hispanic
Japanese *see* Race–Asian: Japanese
Jordanian *see* Ancestry–Arab: Jordanian
Kenyan *see* Ancestry–African, Sub-Saharan: Kenyan
Kiowa *see* Race–American Indian: Kiowa
Korean *see* Race–Asian: Korean
Laotian *see* Race–Asian: Laotian
Latvian *see* Ancestry–Latvian
Lebanese *see* Ancestry–Arab: Lebanese
Liberian *see* Ancestry–African, Sub-Saharan: Liberian
Lithuanian *see* Ancestry–Lithuanian
Lumbee *see* Race–American Indian: Lumbee
Luxemburger *see* Ancestry–Luxemburger
Macedonian *see* Ancestry–Macedonian
Malaysian *see* Race–Asian: Malaysian
Maltese *see* Ancestry–Maltese
Marshallese *see* Race–Hawaii Native/Pacific Islander: Marshallese
Menominee *see* Race–American Indian: Menominee
Mexican *see* Hispanic Origin–Mexican
Mexican American Indian *see* Race–American Indian: Mexican American Indian
Moroccan *see* Ancestry–Arab: Moroccan
Native Hawaiian *see* Race–Hawaii Native/Pacific Islander: Native Hawaiian
Navajo *see* Race–American Indian: Navajo
Nepalese *see* Race–Asian: Nepalese
New Zealander *see* Ancestry–New Zealander
Nicaraguan *see* Hispanic Origin–Central American: Nicaraguan
Nigerian *see* Ancestry–African, Sub-Saharan: Nigerian
Northern European *see* Ancestry–Northern European
Norwegian *see* Ancestry–Norwegian
Osage *see* Race–American Indian: Osage
Ottawa *see* Race–American Indian: Ottawa
Pacific Islander *see* Race–Hawaii Native/Pacific Islander
Pacific Islander: Hispanic *see* Race–Hawaii Native/Pacific Islander: Hispanic
Pacific Islander: Not Hispanic *see* Race–Hawaii Native/Pacific Islander: Not Hispanic
Paiute *see* Race–American Indian: Paiute
Pakistani *see* Race–Asian: Pakistani
Palestinian *see* Ancestry–Arab: Palestinian
Panamanian *see* Hispanic Origin–Central American: Panamanian
Paraguayan *see* Hispanic Origin–South American: Paraguayan
Pennsylvania German *see* Ancestry–Pennsylvania German
Peruvian *see* Hispanic Origin–South American: Peruvian
Pima *see* Race–American Indian: Pima
Polish *see* Ancestry–Polish
Portuguese *see* Ancestry–Portuguese
Potawatomi *see* Race–American Indian: Potawatomi

Pueblo *see* Race–American Indian: Pueblo
Puerto Rican *see* Hispanic Origin–Puerto Rican
Puget Sound Salish *see* Race–American Indian: Puget Sound Salish
Romanian *see* Ancestry–Romanian
Russian *see* Ancestry–Russian
Salvadoran *see* Hispanic Origin–Central American: Salvadoran
Samoan *see* Race–Hawaii Native/Pacific Islander: Samoan
Scandinavian *see* Ancestry–Scandinavian
Scotch-Irish *see* Ancestry–Scotch-Irish
Scottish *see* Ancestry–Scottish
Seminole *see* Race–American Indian: Seminole
Senegalese *see* Ancestry–African, Sub-Saharan: Senegalese
Serbian *see* Ancestry–Serbian
Shoshone *see* Race–American Indian: Shoshone
Sierra Leonean *see* Ancestry–African, Sub-Saharan: Sierra Leonean
Sioux *see* Race–American Indian: Sioux
Slavic *see* Ancestry–Slavic
Slovak *see* Ancestry–Slovak
Slovene *see* Ancestry–Slovene
Somalian *see* Ancestry–African, Sub-Saharan: Somalian
South African *see* Ancestry–African, Sub-Saharan: South African
South American *see* Hispanic Origin–South American
South American Indian *see* Race–American Indian: South American Indian
South American: Other *see* Hispanic Origin–South American: Other South American
Soviet Union *see* Ancestry–Soviet Union
Spanish American Indian *see* Race–American Indian: Spanish American Indian
Sri Lankan *see* Race–Asian: Sri Lankan
Sub-Saharan African *see* Ancestry–African, Sub-Saharan
Sub-Saharan African: Other *see* Ancestry–African, Sub-Saharan: Other
Sudanese *see* Ancestry–African, Sub-Saharan: Sudanese
Swedish *see* Ancestry–Swedish
Swiss *see* Ancestry–Swiss
Syriac *see* Ancestry–Assyrian/Chaldean/Syriac
Syrian *see* Ancestry–Arab: Syrian
Taiwanese *see* Race–Asian: Taiwanese
Thai *see* Race–Asian: Thai
Tlingit-Haida *see* Race–Alaska Native: Tlingit-Haida
Tohono O'Odham *see* Race–American Indian: Tohono O'Odham
Tongan *see* Race–Hawaii Native/Pacific Islander: Tongan
Trinidadian and Tobagonian *see* Ancestry–West Indian: Trinidadian and Tobagonian, except Hispanic
Tsimshian *see* Race–Alaska Native: Tsimshian
Turkish *see* Ancestry–Turkish
U.S. Virgin Islander *see* Ancestry–West Indian: U.S. Virgin Islander, except Hispanic
Ugandan *see* Ancestry–African, Sub-Saharan: Ugandan
Ukrainian *see* Ancestry–Ukrainian
Uruguayan *see* Hispanic Origin–South American: Uruguayan
Ute *see* Race–American Indian: Ute
Venezuelan *see* Hispanic Origin–South American: Venezuelan
Vietnamese *see* Race–Asian: Vietnamese
Welsh *see* Ancestry–Welsh
West Indian *see* Ancestry–West Indian: West Indian, except Hispanic
West Indian (except Hispanic) *see* Ancestry–West Indian, except Hispanic
West Indian: Other *see* Ancestry–West Indian: Other, except Hispanic
White *see* Race–White
White: Hispanic *see* Race–White: Hispanic
White: Not Hispanic *see* Race–White: Not Hispanic
Yakama *see* Race–American Indian: Yakama
Yaqui *see* Race–American Indian: Yaqui
Yugoslavian *see* Ancestry–Yugoslavian
Yuman *see* Race–American Indian: Yuman
Yup'ik *see* Race–Alaska Native: Yup'ik
Zimbabwean *see* Ancestry–African, Sub-Saharan: Zimbabwean

User Guide: Climate Section

SOURCES OF THE DATA

The National Climactic Data Center (NCDC) has two main classes or types of weather stations; first-order stations which are staffed by professional meteorologists and cooperative stations which are staffed by volunteers. All National Weather Service (NWS) stations included in this book are first-order stations.

The data in the climate section is compiled from several sources. The majority comes from the original NCDC computer tapes (DSI-3220 Summary of Month Cooperative). This data was used to create the entire table for each cooperative station and part of each National Weather Service station. The remainder of the data for each NWS station comes from the International Station Meteorological Climate Summary, Version 4.0, September 1996, which is also available from the NCDC.

Storm events come from the NCDC Storm Events Database which is accessible over the Internet at http://www4.ncdc.noaa.gov/ cgi-win/wwcgi.dll?wwevent~storms.

WEATHER STATION TABLES

The weather station tables are grouped by type (National Weather Service and Cooperative) and then arranged alphabetically. The station name is almost always a place name, and is shown here just as it appears in NCDC data. The station name is followed by the county in which the station is located (or by county equivalent name), the elevation of the station (at the time beginning of the thirty year period) and the latitude and longitude.

The National Weather Service Station tables contain 32 data elements which were compiled from two different sources, the International Station Meteorological Climate Summary (ISMCS) and NCDC DSI-3220 data tapes. The following 13 elements are from the ISMCS: maximum precipitation, minimum precipitation, maximum snowfall, maximum 24-hour snowfall, thunderstorm days, foggy days, predominant sky cover, relative humidity (morning and afternoon), dewpoint, wind speed and direction, and maximum wind gust. The remaining 19 elements come from the DSI-3220 data tapes. The period of record (POR) for data from the DSI-3220 data tapes is 1980-2009. The POR for ISMCS data varies from station to station and appears in a note below each station.

The Cooperative Station tables contain 19 data elements which were all compiled from the DSI-3220 data tapes with a POR of 1980-2009.

WEATHER ELEMENTS (NWS AND COOPERATIVE STATIONS)

The following elements were compiled by the editor from the NCDC DSI-3220 data tapes using a period of record of 1980-2009.

The average temperatures (maximum, minimum, and mean) are the average (see Methodology below) of those temperatures for all available values for a given month. For example, for a given station the average maximum temperature for July is the arithmetic average of all available maximum July temperatures for that station. (Maximum means the highest recorded temperature, minimum means the lowest recorded temperature, and mean means an arithmetic average temperature.)

The extreme maximum temperature is the highest temperature recorded in each month over the period 1980-2009. The extreme minimum temperature is the lowest temperature recorded in each month over the same time period. The extreme maximum daily precipitation is the largest amount of precipitation recorded over a 24-hour period in each month from 1980-2009. The maximum snow depth is the maximum snow depth recorded in each month over the period 1980-2009.

The days for maximum temperature and minimum temperature are the average number of days those criteria were met for all available instances. The symbol ≥ means greater than or equal to, the symbol ≤ means less than or equal to. For example, for a given station, the number of days the maximum temperature was greater than or equal to 90°F in July, is just an arithmetic average of the number of days in all the available Julys for that station.

Heating and cooling degree days are based on the median temperature for a given day and its variance from 65°F. For example, for a given station if the day's high temperature was 50°F and the day's low temperature was 30°F, the median (midpoint) temperature was 40°F. 40°F is 25 degrees below 65°F, hence on this day there would be 25 heating degree days. This also applies for cooling degree days. For example, for a given station if the day's high temperature was 80°F and the day's low temperature was 70°F, the median (midpoint) temperature was 75°F. 75°F is 10 degrees above 65°F, hence on this day there would be 10 cooling degree days. All heating and/or cooling degree days in a month are summed for the month giving respective totals for each element for that month. These sums for a given month for a given station over the past thirty years are again summed and then arithmetically averaged. It should be noted that the heating and cooling degree days do not cancel each other out. It is possible to have both for a given station in the same month.

Precipitation data is computed the same as heating and cooling degree days. Mean precipitation and mean snowfall are arithmetic averages of cumulative totals for the month. All available values for the thirty year period for a given month for a given station are summed and then divided by the number of values. The same is true for days of greater than or equal to 0.1", 0.5",and 1.0" of precipitation, and days of greater than or equal to 1.0" of snow depth on the ground. The word trace appears for precipitation and snowfall amounts that are too small to measure.

Finally, remember that all values presented in the tables and the rankings are averages, maximums, or minimums of available data (see Methodology below) for that specific data element for the last thirty years (1980-2009).

WEATHER ELEMENTS (NWS STATIONS ONLY)

The following elements were taken directly from the International Station Meteorological Climate Summary. The periods of records vary per station and are noted at the bottom of each table.

Maximum precipitation, minimum precipitation, maximum snowfall, maximum snow depth, maximum 24-hour snowfall, thunderstorm days, foggy days, relative humidity (morning and afternoon), dewpoint, prevailing wind speed and direction, and maximum wind gust are all self-explanatory.

The word trace appears for precipitation and snowfall amounts that are too small to measure.

Predominant sky cover contains four possible entries: CLR (clear); SCT (scattered); BRK (broken); and OVR (overcast).

INCLUSION CRITERIA—HOW STATIONS WERE SELECTED

The basic criteria is that a station must have data for temperature, precipitation, heating and cooling degree days of sufficient quantity in order to create a meaningful average. More specifically, the definition of sufficiency here has two parts. First, there must be 22 values for a given data element, and second, ten of the nineteen elements included in the table must pass this sufficiency test. For example, in regard to mean maximum temperature (the first element on every data table), a given station needs to have a value for every month of at least 22 of the last thirty years in order to meet the criteria, and, in addition, every station included must have at least ten of the nineteen elements with at least this minimal level of completeness in order to fulfill the criteria. We then removed stations that were geographically close together, giving preference to stations with better data quality.

METHODOLOGY

The following discussion applies only to data compiled from the NCDC DSI-3220 data tapes and excludes weather elements that are extreme maximums or minimums.

The data is based on an arithmetic average of all available data for a specific data element at a given station. For example, the average maximum daily high temperature during July for any given station was abstracted from NCDC source tapes for the thirty Julys, starting in July, 1980 and ending in July, 2009. These thirty figures were then summed and divided by thirty to produce an arithmetic average. As might be expected, there were not thirty values for every data element on every table. For a variety of reasons, NCDC data is sometimes incomplete. Thus the following standards were established.

For those data elements where there were 26-30 values, the data was taken to be essentially complete and an average was computed. For data elements where there were 22-25 values, the data was taken as being partly complete but still valid enough to use to compute an average. Such averages are shown in ***bold italic*** type to indicate that there was less than 26 values. For the few data elements where there were not even 22 values, no average was computed and 'na' appears in the space. If any of the twelve months for a given data element reported a value of 'na', no annual average was computed and the annual average was reported as 'na' as well.

Thus the basic computational methodology used is designed to provide an arithmetic average. Because of this, such a pure arithmetic average is somewhat different from the special type of average (called a "normal") which NCDC procedures produces and appears in federal publications.

Perhaps the best outline of the contrasting normalization methodology is found in the following paragraph (which appears as part of an NCDC technical document titled, CLIM81 1961-1990 NORMALS TD-9641 prepared by Lewis France of NCDC in May, 1992):

Normals have been defined as the arithmetic mean of a climatological element computed over a long time period. International agreements eventually led to the decision that the appropriate time period would be three consecutive decades (Guttman, 1989). The data record should be consistent (have no changes in location, instruments, observation practices, etc.; these are identified here as "exposure changes") and have no missing values so a normal will reflect the actual average climatic conditions. If any significant exposure changes have occurred, the data record is said to be "inhomogeneous," and the normal may not reflect a true climatic average. Such data need to be adjusted to remove the nonclimatic inhomogeneities. The resulting (adjusted) record is then said to be "homogeneous." If no exposure changes have occurred at a station, the normal is calculated simply by averaging the appropriate 30 values from the 1961-1990 record.

In the main, there are two "inhomogeneities" that NCDC is correcting for with normalization: adjusting for variances in time of day of observation (at the so-called First Order stations data is based on midnight to midnight observation times and this practice is not necessarily followed at cooperative stations which are staffed by volunteers), and second, estimating data that is either missing or incongruent.

The editors had some concerns regarding the comparative results of the two methodologies. Would our methodology produce strikingly different results than NCDC's? To allay concerns, results of the two processes were compared for the time period normalized results are available (1971-2000). In short, what was found was that the answer to this question is no. Never the less, users should be aware that because of both the time period covered (1980-2009) and the methodology used, data is not compatible with data from other sources.

POTENTIAL CAUTIONS

First, as with any statistical reference work of this type, users need to be aware of the source of the data. The information here comes from NOAA, and it is the most comprehensive and reliable core data available. Although it is the best, it is not perfect. Most weather stations are staffed by volunteers, times of observation sometimes vary, stations occasionally are moved (especially over a thirty year period), equipment is changed or upgraded, and all of these factors affect the uniformity of the data. The editors do not attempt to correct for these factors, and this data is not intended for either climatologists or atmospheric scientists. Users with concerns about data collection and reporting protocols are both referred to NCDC technical documentation.

Second, users need to be aware of the methodology here which is described above. Although this methodology has produced fully satisfactory results, it is not directly compatible with other methodologies, hence variances in the results published here and those which appear in other publications will doubtlessly arise.

Third, is the trap of that informal logical fallacy known as "hasty generalization," and its corollaries. This may involve presuming the future will be like the past (specifically, next year will be an average year), or it may involve misunderstanding the limitations of an arithmetic average, but more interestingly, it may involve those mistakes made most innocently by generalizing informally on too broad a basis. As weather is highly localized, the data should be taken in that context. A weather station collects data about climatic conditions at that spot, and that spot may or may not be an effective paradigm for an entire town or area.

About Ohio

Governor . . . . John Richard Kasich (R)
Lt Governor . . . . Mary Taylor (R)

State Capital . . . . Columbus
Date of Statehood . . . . March 1, 1803 (17th state)
State Nickname. . . . . The Buckeye State
Largest City . . . . Columbus
Highest Point . . . . Campbell Hill (1,549 feet)
Lowest Point. . . . . Ohio River at Indiana border (455 feet)

State Amphibian. . . . . Spotted Salamander *(Ambystoma maculatum)*
State Artifact. . . . . The Adena Pipe
State Beverage . . . . Tomato Juice
State Bicentennial Bridge . . . . Blaine Hill bridge built in 1828 (Belmont county)
State Bird . . . . Northern Cardinal *(Cardinalis cardinalis)*
State Flower . . . . Red Carnation *(Dianthus caryophyllus)*
State Fossil . . . . Isotelus (Trilobite)
State Frog . . . . Bullfrog *(Rana catesbeiana)*
State Fruit . . . . Tomato
State Gemstone. . . . . Ohio Flint
State Insect . . . . Ladybug (no specific species)
State Mammal. . . . . White-tailed Deer *(Odocoileus virginianus)*
State Motto . . . . "With God All Things Are Possible"
State Native Fruit . . . . Pawpaw *(Asimina triloba)*
State Prehistoric Monument . . Newark Earthworks
State Reptile . . . . Black Racer Snake *(Coluber constrictor constrictor)*
State Rock Song . . . . "Hang on Sloopy"
State Song. . . . . "Beautiful Ohio"
State Tree . . . . Ohio Buckeye *(Aesculus glabra)*
State Wildflower. . . . . White Trillium *(Trillium grandiflorum)*

Columbus, pictured above, is the capitol of Ohio. It is the state's largest city and the 28th largest metropolitan statistical area in the United States. In Greek Revival style, the Ohio Statehouse is predominant at the bottom of the photograph. Columbus was founded in 1812, and named for explorer Christopher Columbus.

The Ohio State University, pictured top, is located in Columbus. It was founded in 1873 and is the third largest university campus in the United States. The bottom photo shows Victorian architecture in Dayton, Ohio, the sixth largest city in the state. Dayton is the birthplace of Orville Wright and home to the National Museum of the United States Air Force.

Toledo, pictured top, on the Maumee River, is the fourth most populous city in Ohio. It is nicknamed "The Glass City" for its glass industry. The skyline of Cincinnait, the third largest city in the state, is shown in the bottom photo. Located on the Ohio River, at the border between Ohio and Kentucky, it is home to major league baseball team the Cincinnati Reds, whose stadium can be seen in the center of the photograph.

The Amish horse and buggy, pictured top, is part of the Holmes County, Ohio, Amish community. The largest Amish community in the world, this part of the state is called "Amish Country" and visitors to the area make tourism an important sector of the local economy. The Miami Erie Canal, in the bottom photo, connects the Ohio River in Cincinnati with Lake Erie in Toledo. It took 20 years (1825–1845) to complete the 301.49 mile waterway.

Agriculture is an important piece of the Ohio economy. Corn, pictured top, and soybeans, pictured bottom, are two of the most vital crops not only in Ohio, but also in Indiana, Illinois and Iowa. Both crops had bumper yields in 2014, due mostly to favorable weather.

Pictured here is a towboat pushing coal-laden barges along the Ohio River at Cincinnati, Ohio. Not only the drinking water source for more than 3 million people, the Ohio River is a major transportation route and flows through or along the border of six states.

A Brief History of Ohio

Ohio's earliest occupants probably followed retreating glaciers into the area while hunting mastadon and giant beaver. The earliest inhabitants were followed by the more advanced Mound Builders who ranged over Ohio between 1000 BC and 800 AD. They were noted for their burial practices, evidence of which remains in some 6,000 burial and ceremonial mounds.

Probably the first European to set foot in the Ohio Country was either Robert Cavelier, Sieur de La Salle, or Louis Jolliet. Between 1669 and 1670, La Salle explored the Ohio River area and Jolliet journeyed along Lake Erie. Based on La Salle's exploration and resulting map, the French later laid claim to the entire Ohio Valley. Both French and English hotly contested their control of the Ohio territory before permanent American settlement.

Among the historic Indian groups in Ohio were the Erie, Huron (Wyandot), Ottawa, and Tuscarora in the north; the Mingo (or Iroquois League) in the east; the Delaware and Shawnee in the south; and the Miami in the west. Remnants of these tribes, led by the Shawnee chief Blue Jacket, were defeated at the Battle of Fallen Timbers in 1794. This U.S. Army victory led to the establishment of the Greenville Treaty Line in 1795, which separated the Indian land to the northwest from the settlers' land to the east and south.

The Ohio Country became part of the Northwest Territory in 1787. With the passage of the Ordinances of 1785 and 1787, providing for stable government as well as land survey and sales in the territory, settlement by Anglo-Americans accelerated. Connecticut and Virginia retained title to Ohio land, forming the Connecticut Western Reserve in the northeast and the Virginia Military District between the Little Miami and Scioto rivers in the southwest. The Ohio Company of Associates acquired 1,875 sq miles in southeastern Ohio and in 1788 founded Ohio's first town, Marietta, at the confluence of the Muskingum and Ohio rivers.

Ohio statehood was guaranteed when more than 5,000 adult white males were counted during the area's census of 1797. In 1803, Ohio entered the Union with Edward Tiffin as its first governor. Chillicothe was the state capital from 1803 to 1810, when it was replaced by Zanesville. Chillicothe again was capital from 1812 to 1816, when Columbus assumed the honor.

The state's early years were characterized by dramatic population increases and political and military turmoil. Political intrigue was fomented by the supposedly treasonous activities of Aaron Burr on an Ohio River island owned by Harman Blennerhassett. Military problems resulted from Indian agitation and the campaigns of the War of 1812. Two names forever to be connected with Ohio and its early struggles are Tecumseh and William Henry Harrison. The first was the great Shawnee chief who almost succeeded in rallying the Indians for a last stand against the white man. The latter was the victor in the fight to bring peace to the New West and was the first of several U.S. presidents with strong ties to Ohio.

Transportation opened Ohio to internal development. Favored by navigable waters north and south, overland transportation surged with completion of the National Road through the state in 1838, and of the Ohio-Erie and Miami-Erie canals in 1832 and 1847, respectively. Ohio's railroad network was begun in 1836 but didn't really take off until about 1850. Efficient transportation gave impetus to the coal industry and boosted farm income and land values in the western and northern agricultural areas. By the Civil War period, Ohio had achieved national status as an agricultural and industrial state.

Preceding the Civil War, Ohio was strongly identified with abolitionist causes. The Underground Railroad was active along the Ohio River and on Lake Erie. The abolitionist movement received wide support, and in 1848, Ohio repealed its Black Laws, which had been restrictive of Blacks' civil rights. The Civil War was carried into Ohio during a cavalry foray led by Gen. John Hunt Morgan. The "invasion" lasted from July 13 to July 26, 1863, ending with the surrender of Morgan and his men and their imprisonment as horse thieves rather than combatants.

After the Civil War, Ohio became a political power on the national level. Seven U.S. presidents were born in Ohio: Ulysses S. Grant, Rutherford B. Hayes, James A. Garfield, Benjamin Harrison, William McKinley, William Howard Taft, and Warren G. Harding.

As an industrial state, Ohio was in the forefront of the union- organizing movement. The American Federation of Labor was formed in Columbus in 1886, followed by the United Mine Workers in 1888. Violence connected with labor unrest became commonplace in the mining areas of southeastern Ohio. During a strike in 1884 several mine shafts in Perry County were set afire and have been burning ever since. Many millions of tons of coal have been consumed, and despite a system of barricades and packing mud into the tunnels, some smoke from the fire is still visible.

During the 20th century Ohio moved to the forefront of the industrial states under the business leadership of such men as Benjamin F. Goodrich, Charles Franklin Kettering, and John D. Rockefeller. Two world wars and conflicts in Korea and Vietnam triggered massive industrialization, rapid in-migration, and subsequent urbanization. Ohio's fortunes can, however, be rapidly reversed by economic relocation such as a shift from coal to natural gas or by recession. These trends have had devastating results in the central cities and the traditional coal mining districts in Appalachia, where unemployment and poverty are chronic ills. Beset by overcapitalization and outdated facilities, Ohio struggles to remain an industrial giant. Steel plants with excess capacity have shut down, as have outmoded automobile plants. New Japanese-owned factories have opened in Ohio, however, offsetting gloomy economic developments at least in part.

Text written by Hubert G. H. Wilhelm. Sources: Havighurst, Walter, Ohio: A Bicentennial History (1976); Maizlish, Stephen E., The Triumph of Sectionalism (1983); Roseboom, E. H., and Weisenburger, F. P., A History of Ohio, 2d ed. (1977); Smith, Thomas H., ed., An Ohio Reader, 2 vols. (1975).

Ohio State Government

Organization

Ohio's state government contains three branches elected by Ohio voters. The legislative branch makes laws, the executive branch administers laws and the judicial branch interprets and enforces laws.

The legislative branch consists of the House of Representatives and the Senate, collectively called the General Assembly.

The executive branch includes the Governor, Lieutenant Governor, Attorney General, Auditor of State, Secretary of State, Treasurer of State, State Board of Education, the governor's cabinet, and boards and commissions whose members are appointed by the governor.

Ohio's judicial branch of government is comprised of the Supreme Court of Ohio and lower courts that all perform judicial functions for the people of Ohio.

The following are brief descriptions of the elected offices in Ohio government. These descriptions are not intended to be complete lists of responsibilities, but to give a broad overview of their duties.

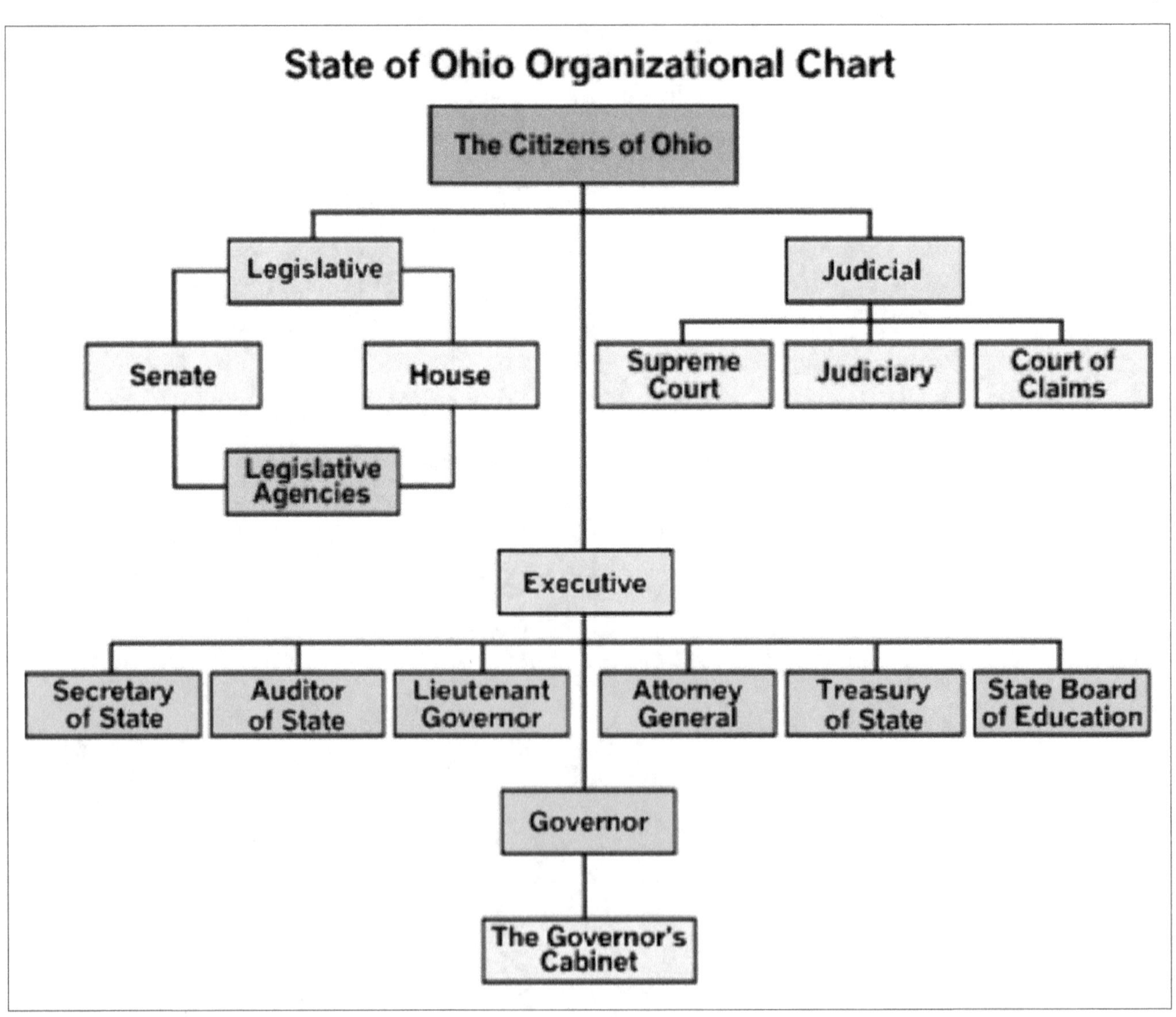

Legislative Branch

Ohio's House of Representatives has 99 members; the Senate has 33 (three House Districts within each Senate District). The General Assembly debates bills proposed for adoption as laws. Most bills require a majority vote in both the Senate and the House to pass. If a bill passes one chamber and is amended by the second chamber, the first chamber must concur with the changes. If there is no concurrence, the bill goes to a conference committee of members selected from both chambers. When both chambers approve a bill, it is then presented to the governor to be signed into law, vetoed or allowed to become law after 10 days without the governor's signature. The Legislature can override a governor's veto with a three-fifths vote of both chambers. When laws are finally adopted, they become part of Ohio Revised Code, and are known as "statutes."

Executive Branch

Governor
The governor is the chief executive officer of state government. The governor is responsible for proposing the state budget, appointing state department directors and members of boards and commissions (except for the state school board, whose members are elected) and signing into law or vetoing bills passed by the Ohio General Assembly. Term limit: two consecutive four-year terms.

Cabinet Offices

- Adjutant General
- Administrative Services
- Aging
- Agriculture
- Alcohol & Drug Addiction Services
- Board of Regents
- Budget & Management
- Commerce
- Development
- Environmental Protection Agency
- Health
- Insurance
- Job & Family Services
- Lottery
- Mental Health
- Mental Retardation & Developmental Disabilities
- Natural Resources
- Public Safety
- Rehabilitation & Correction
- Taxation
- Transportation
- Workers' Compensation
- Youth Services

Lieutenant Governor
The lieutenant governor, elected to a four-year term as a running mate to the governor, is also a member of the governor's cabinet and presides in the absence of the governor. The governor may appoint the lieutenant governor to be the director of one of the departments.

Attorney General
The attorney general is the lawyer for the state and all its departments. The attorney general has enforcement authority as empowered by the General Assembly. The attorney general also provides support to local law enforcement agencies. Term limit: two consecutive four-year terms.

Auditor of State
The auditor of state is the constitutional officer responsible for auditing all public offices in Ohio, including cities and villages, schools and universities, counties and townships, as well as the many departments, agencies and commissions of state government. The auditor's office also has the responsibility of making monthly distributions of state revenues to these entities. Term limit: two consecutive four-year terms.

Secretary of State
The Secretary of State is the chief election officer for the state, appointing members of the 88 county boards of elections and ensuring the integrity of the Ohio voting process. The Secretary is also charged with safely keeping the laws and resolutions passed by the Ohio General Assembly. The Secretary of state's office grants authority to companies to do business in Ohio and provides the public access to a wide variety of records and documents. Term limit: two consecutive four-year terms.

Treasurer of State
In general, the treasurer serves as the state's banker. The state treasurer manages the state's multi-billion dollar investment portfolios. Using sophisticated security measures and procedures, the treasurer maintains an accurate account of all state and custodial funds, including those of the state's five public pension systems. Term limit: two consecutive four-year terms.

State Board of Education
The Ohio State Board of Education regulates every school in the state, whether tax-supported or not, from preschool through high school. The board also sets standards for education and certifying Ohio teachers. The board provides leadership toward the continuous improvement of Ohio schools by making legislative and budgetary recommendations to the governor and the General Assembly. There are 19 board members, 11 elected and eight appointed by the governor. Term limit: two consecutive four-year terms.

Source: Ohio Secretary of State

nationalatlas.gov™
Where We Are
OHIO
CONGRESSIONAL DISTRICTS
113th Congress (January 2013–January 2015)
The Constitution prescribes Congressional apportionment based on decennial census population data. Each state has at least one Representative, no matter how small its population. Since 1941, distribution of Representatives has been based on total U.S. population, so that the average population per Representative has the least possible variation between one state and any other. Congress fixes the number of voting Representatives at each apportionment. States delineate the district boundaries. The first House of Representatives in 1789 had 65 members; currently there are 435. There are non-voting delegates from American Samoa, the District of Columbia, Guam, Puerto Rico, and the Virgin Islands.
1 2 3 4 5 6 7 8 9 10 11 12 13 14 15 16
MILES
0 10 20 30 40 50 60
Albers equal area projection
MICHIGAN
ONTARIO
CANADA
Lake Erie
NY
PENNSYLVANIA
INDIANA
KENTUCKY
WEST VIRGINIA
Ohio River
Toledo
Bowling Green
Defiance
Findlay
Fostoria
Fremont
Sandusky
Norwalk
Lorain
Elyria
Cleveland
Euclid
Parma
Akron
Youngstown
Alliance
Canton
Massillon
Wooster
Mansfield
Marion
Mt Vernon
New Philadelphia
Coshocton
East Liverpool
Steubenville
Cambridge
Zanesville
Westerville
Columbus
Lancaster
Marietta
Athens
Jackson
Gallipolis
Ironton
Portsmouth
Van Wert
Lima
Bellefontaine
Sidney
Greenville
Springfield
Dayton
Kettering
Beavercreek
Middletown
Hamilton
Fairfield
Cincinnati
U.S. Department of the Interior
U.S. Geological Survey
The National Atlas of the United States of America®

Percent of Population Who Voted for Barack Obama in 2012

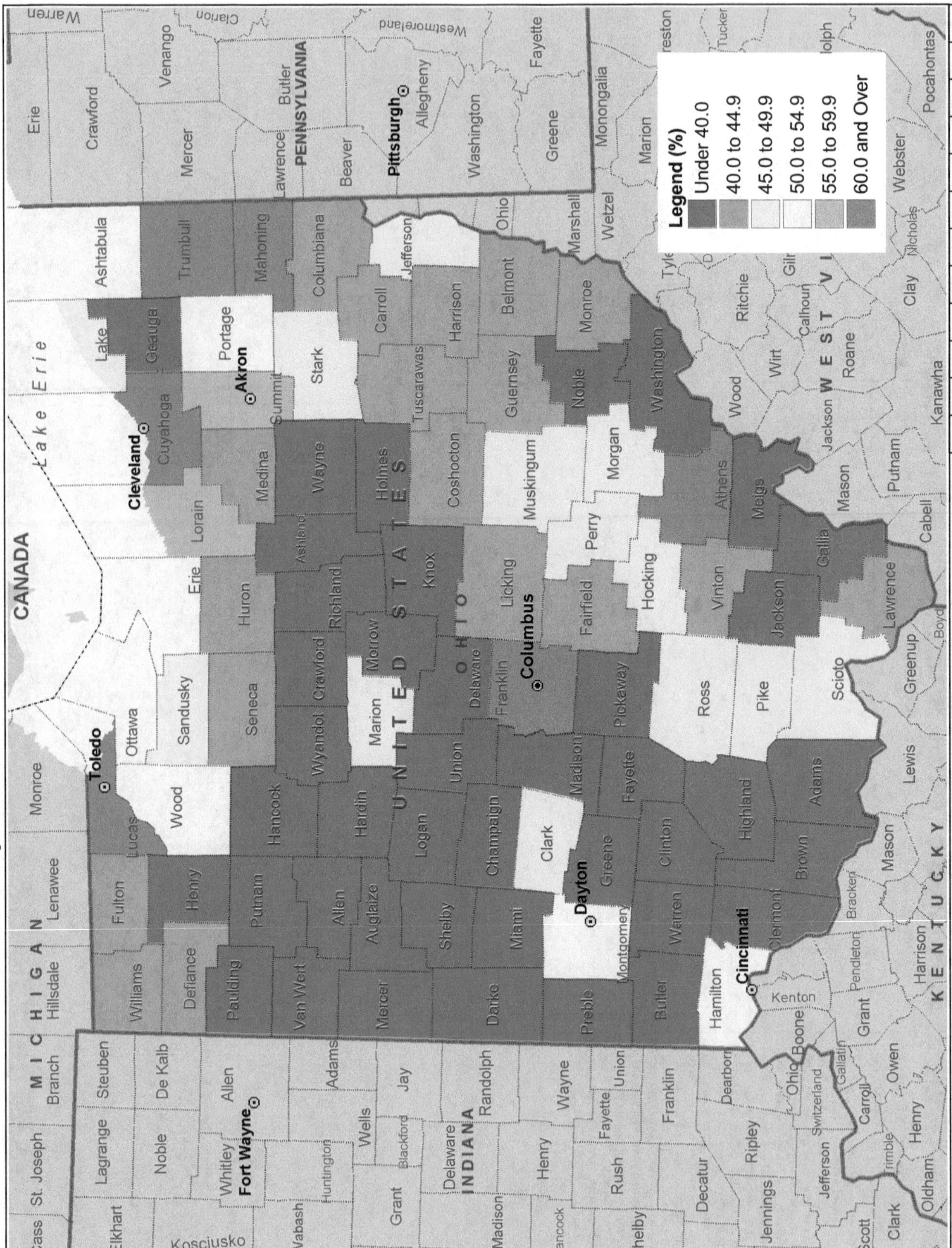

Legend (%)

- Under 40.0
- 40.0 to 44.9
- 45.0 to 49.9
- 50.0 to 54.9
- 55.0 to 59.9
- 60.0 and Over

0 mi 20 40 60 80 100 120

Ohio Land and Natural Resources

Topic	Value	Time Period
Total Surface Area (acres)	26,444,800	2010
Land	26,031,100	2010
Federal Land	373,300	2010
Non-Federal Land, Developed	4,166,300	2010
Non-Federal Land, Rural	21,491,500	2010
Cropland	11,108,900	2010
CRP Land	177,800	2010
Pastureland	2,190,700	2010
Rangeland	0	2010
Forest Land	7,079,300	2010
Other Rural Land	934,800	2010
Water	413,700	2010
National Heritage Areas	2	September 2014
National Natural Landmarks	23	September 2014
National Historic Landmarks	72	September 2014
National Register of Historic Places	3,901	September 2014
National Parks	8	September 2014
Visitors to National Parks	2,470,177	2014
Historic Places Documented by the National Park Service	895	September 2014
Archeological Sites in National Parks	257	September 2014
Threatened and Endangered Species in National Parks	1	2013
Economic Benefit from National Park Tourism	$149,000,000	2013
Natural Resources Conservation Programs (acres)		
Conservation Reserve Program (CRP)	21,709	2013
Conservation Stewardship Program (CSP)	51,952	2013
Conservation Technical Assistance (CTA)	386,069	2013
Environmental Quality Incentives Program (EQIP)	169,179	2013
Grassland Reserve Program (GRP)	78	2013
Emergency Watershed Protection Program (EWP)	0	2013
Wetlands Reserve Program (WRP)	1,290	2013
Wildlife Habitat Incentive Program (WHIP)	4,777	2013

Sources: *U.S. Department of the Interior, National Park Service, State Profiles; United States Department of Agriculture, Natural Resources Conservation Service, National Resources Inventory; U.S. Department of Agriculture, Farm Services Agency, Conservation Reserve Program*

Ohio State Energy Profile

Quick Facts

- Current interest in Ohio oil and natural gas exploration is focused on two Ohio shale plays-the Marcellus Shale and the Utica Shale.
- Ohio had the seventh largest crude oil refining capacity in the nation in 2014.
- In August 2003, a transmission failure in Ohio led to the largest blackout in North American history, affecting more than 50 million people.
- Coal fueled 67% of Ohio's net electricity generation in 2014, natural gas contributed 18%, and nuclear energy added another 12%.
- Ohio ranked sixth in the nation in 2012 in energy consumption by the industrial sector, and output from its factories accounted for 18% of the state's gross domestic product (GDP). Ohio contributed 3.4% to the total U.S. manufacturing GDP in 2013.

Analysis

Overview

Named after the river that forms its southern border, Ohio is a Great Lakes state, bordered on the north by Lake Erie. The Appalachian Plateau, part of the larger Appalachian Basin, crosses the eastern part of Ohio and contains considerable reserves of coal as well as many crude oil and natural gas fields. The state also has additional natural gas and crude oil resource potential from shales and coalbeds. Lake Erie influences Ohio's weather and provides an important offshore wind energy resource. Ohio's rolling plains have some of the most fertile farmland in the nation and mark the beginning of the Corn Belt, which extends westward across the Midwest. Corn produced in the state feeds Ohio's ethanol plants.

Ohio's primary economic activity is manufacturing. With its large population, heavily industrial economy, and highly variable climate, Ohio is among the top 10 states in total energy consumption. The industrial sector is the largest energy-consuming sector in the state. Most of Ohio's manufacturing is related to the transportation sector, but the state also has strong metals and chemical production industries. The transportation sector is the second-largest energy-consuming sector, followed closely by the residential sector. Despite Ohio's strong industrial base, per capita energy consumption in the state is only slightly above the national average.

Petroleum

Ohio's crude oil production and proved reserves are modest, although they are greater than each of the other Appalachian Basin states except Alabama. The Utica Shale formation has potential crude oil and natural gas liquids resources that could significantly add to Ohio's reserve base. Although Ohio's crude oil production was only about 5 million barrels annually over much of the past decade, increased drilling resulted in a 20-year high of almost 9 million barrels produced in 2013 and a 29-year high of more than 14 million barrels in 2014.

Ohio has the second-highest oil refining capacity among the north central states after Illinois. With a capacity of about 530,000 barrels of crude oil per calendar day, Ohio is consistently among the top 10 refining states in the nation. Ohio's four refineries include two in the Toledo area, one in Lima, and one in Canton. Collectively, those refineries process a wide suite of crude oils from light, sweet crudes to heavy, sour crudes. The crude oils come from Canada, the Midcontinent, North Dakota, and the U.S. Gulf Coast. Among the finished products from the Ohio refineries are transportation fuels, including motor gasoline, jet fuel, and ultra-low sulfur diesel, as well as a wide variety of other petroleum products. Ohio has several petroleum product pipelines that connect its refineries to markets in Ohio and adjacent states, and to petroleum product port facilities on Lake Erie.

Ohio is among the top 10 petroleum-consuming states in the nation. Total petroleum demand in Ohio far exceeds the state's production. Most of the petroleum consumed in Ohio is used as transportation fuels, either as motor gasoline or diesel fuel. Ohio gasoline stations can sell conventional motor gasoline throughout most of the state, but the U.S. Environmental Protection Agency requires gasoline to be formulated to reduce emissions that contribute to ozone formation in the summer months in the counties surrounding Cincinnati and Dayton. Ohio has substantial ethanol production capacity, and the additive is blended into the state's motor gasoline. Ohio is the seventh-largest ethanol producer in the nation, and the state's share of U.S. ethanol consumption is almost equal to its share of the nation's production capacity. Ohio's ethanol plants can produce more than 540 million gallons of ethanol per year.

Natural gas

Ohio's natural gas reserves and production more than doubled from 2012 to 2013 but are still less than 1% of the nation's total. Additional natural gas resource potential exists in the Utica and Marcellus Shales as well as from coalbed methane in the state's many coalfields. Ohio's marketed natural gas production typically meets no more than one-fifth of state demand. Natural gas enters the state from Indiana, West Virginia, Kentucky, and Pennsylvania via the many interstate pipelines that cross the state. The majority of the natural gas goes on to Michigan and West Virginia, but a substantial amount is used in state. To meet peak demand in the winter, Ohio uses natural gas from storage. The state has 24 natural gas storage fields in depleted oil and natural gas reservoirs. They have a combined total storage capacity of almost 580 billion cubic feet and a total working gas capacity of about 230 billion cubic feet.

Ohio is among the top 10 natural gas-consuming states. The industrial and residential sectors are the largest consumers. About two-thirds of Ohio households use natural gas for home heating. Natural gas use for electric power generation in Ohio has increased markedly in recent years as domestic natural gas production has increased. Much of the increase in production is from the Marcellus Shale region in or near eastern Ohio. The 2009 extension of the Rockies Express Pipeline to Clarington, Ohio, near the border with West Virginia, has led to the formation of new natural gas trading points.

Coal

Bituminous coal is Ohio's primary fossil fuel resource. The state is the 10th-largest coal-producer in the nation and the 6th-largest producer of bituminous coal. Although about two-thirds of Ohio's mining operations are surface mines, most of Ohio's coal comes from the state's underground mines. The state has 2% of the nation's recoverable coal at producing mines. However, almost twice as much coal is consumed in Ohio as is produced there.

Ohio is the fourth-largest coal-consuming state in the nation after Texas, Indiana, and Pennsylvania. To meet the state's needs, coal is brought in from several surrounding states by barge, rail, and truck. The largest share of coal from out of state typically comes from West Virginia. Substantial amounts also come from Illinois, Kentucky, Pennsylvania, and Wyoming. Almost 90% of the coal consumed in Ohio is used for electric power generation.

Two-fifths of the coal mined in Ohio is shipped out to other states by barge, truck, and rail. Coal also passes through Ohio from elsewhere and is shipped from the state's ports along Lake Erie. Cleveland, Ohio is a leading Great Lakes export point for coal. Coal is also transferred from rail to vessels at Toledo, Ohio and shipped from there throughout the Great Lakes region and overseas.

Electricity

The primary fuel for electricity generation in Ohio is coal. Eight of Ohio's 10 largest power plants by capacity are coal-fired. In recent years, the share of generation provided by coal has decreased overall, but coal still fuels about two-thirds of the state's electricity generation. Natural gas-fired generation has risen as prices of coal and natural gas have fluctuated. Even though the use of natural gas has increased dramatically since 2008, it accounts for less than one-fifth of the state's net generation. Electricity is also generated at Ohio's two nuclear power plants located along Lake Erie. Those plants supply almost one-eighth of Ohio's net generation. Renewable energy, particularly wind energy generation, is a small but rapidly growing source of net generation.

Ohio is among the top 10 electric power generators in the nation-eighth in 2014-and among the top 5 in retail sales. Because Ohio's net generation does not meet state demand, Ohio is a net recipient of electricity from outside the state. The residential sector accounts for the greatest share of retail sales of electricity in Ohio, followed by the industrial sector. Slightly more than one-fifth of Ohio households rely on electricity as their primary source of energy for home heating.

Ohio is part of an electric power grid that services 13 states between the Mississippi River and the Atlantic Ocean. In August 2003, a transmission failure in northeastern Ohio led to the largest blackout in North America, affecting an estimated 50 million people in the northeastern United States and Canada for up to two days. More than half a million Ohio homes and businesses lost power. It took only nine seconds for the grid to collapse.

Renewable energy

Wind is Ohio's primary renewable energy resource, and net electricity generation from wind has increased dramatically since 2010. Ohio's first utility-scale wind farm was constructed in Bowling Green in 2004. That wind farm's four turbines generate up to 7.2 megawatts of power. Since construction of the first wind farm, several larger wind generation facilities have been built, and by 2014 Ohio had 32 projects online-3 utility-scale and 29 smaller facilities. The 304-megawatt Blue Creek Wind Farm, located in northwestern Ohio, is the largest and has 152 2-megawatt turbines. Offshore wind-powered generation in Lake Erie is being explored, and a demonstration project called Icebreaker is in development in Lake Erie northwest of Cleveland.

Ohio's other renewable resources include biomass and solar energy. Biomass from wood and wood waste, as well as municipal solid waste and landfill gas, has contributed to Ohio's net electricity generation for some time. Researchers are investigating the use of native Ohio switchgrass for cellulosic ethanol production and the biofuel potential of giant miscanthus, a perennial grass native to Asia. Additionally, biodigesters could generate electricity using methane from the manure produced on Ohio's many farms. The solar power requirement in Ohio's renewable energy standard has encouraged solar projects. The state's two largest solar facilities are the 12-megawatt Wyandot Solar Farm and the 9.8-megawatt Napoleon Solar Project. Additional opportunities for solar generation exist on Ohio's residential and business rooftops.

Ohio has both an Alternative Energy Portfolio Standard (AEPS) and an Energy Portfolio Standard (EPS). The AEPS requires all of the state's retail electricity providers, except municipal utilities and electric cooperatives, to obtain 25% of their retail electricity sales from alternative energy resources by the end of 2026. Half of those resources must be renewables, but half of the requirement can be met by "any new, retrofitted, refueled, or repowered" generating facilities, including those using fossil fuels. The AEPS includes a carve-out for solar energy. The EPS requires utilities to put energy efficiency and peak demand reduction programs in place that achieve a cumulative energy savings of 22% by the end of 2026.

Source: U.S. Energy Information Administration, State Profile and Energy Estimates, March 19, 2015

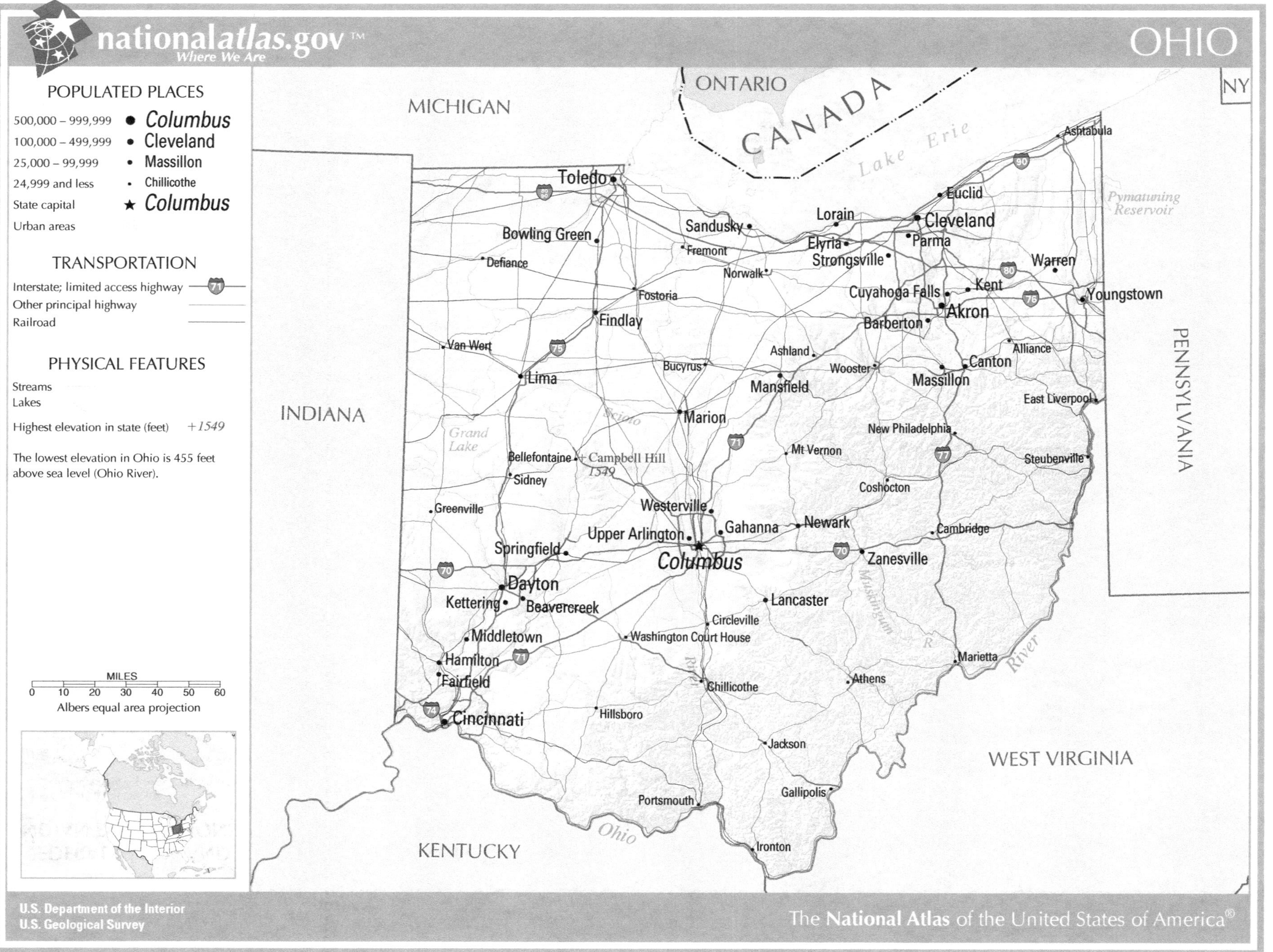
nationalatlas.gov™
Where We Are
OHIO
POPULATED PLACES
500,000 – 999,999 Columbus
100,000 – 499,999 Cleveland
25,000 – 99,999 Massillon
24,999 and less Chillicothe
State capital Columbus
Urban areas
TRANSPORTATION
Interstate; limited access highway
Other principal highway
Railroad
PHYSICAL FEATURES
Streams
Lakes
Highest elevation in state (feet) +1549
The lowest elevation in Ohio is 455 feet above sea level (Ohio River).
MILES
0 10 20 30 40 50 60
Albers equal area projection
U.S. Department of the Interior
U.S. Geological Survey
The National Atlas of the United States of America®
MICHIGAN
ONTARIO
CANADA
Lake Erie
NY
PENNSYLVANIA
WEST VIRGINIA
KENTUCKY
INDIANA
Pymatuning Reservoir
Ashtabula
Euclid
Cleveland
Parma
Lorain
Elyria
Strongsville
Warren
Youngstown
Kent
Cuyahoga Falls
Akron
Barberton
Alliance
Canton
Massillon
Wooster
Ashland
Mansfield
East Liverpool
New Philadelphia
Steubenville
Coshocton
Mt Vernon
Toledo
Bowling Green
Defiance
Sandusky
Fremont
Norwalk
Fostoria
Findlay
Van Wert
Lima
Bucyrus
Marion
Scioto
Grand Lake
Bellefontaine
Campbell Hill 1549
Sidney
Greenville
Westerville
Gahanna
Newark
Upper Arlington
Columbus
Springfield
Cambridge
Zanesville
Dayton
Kettering
Beavercreek
Lancaster
Muskingum R.
Circleville
Middletown
Washington Court House
Hamilton
Fairfield
Marietta
River
Athens
Chillicothe
Cincinnati
Hillsboro
Jackson
Gallipolis
Portsmouth
Ohio
Ironton

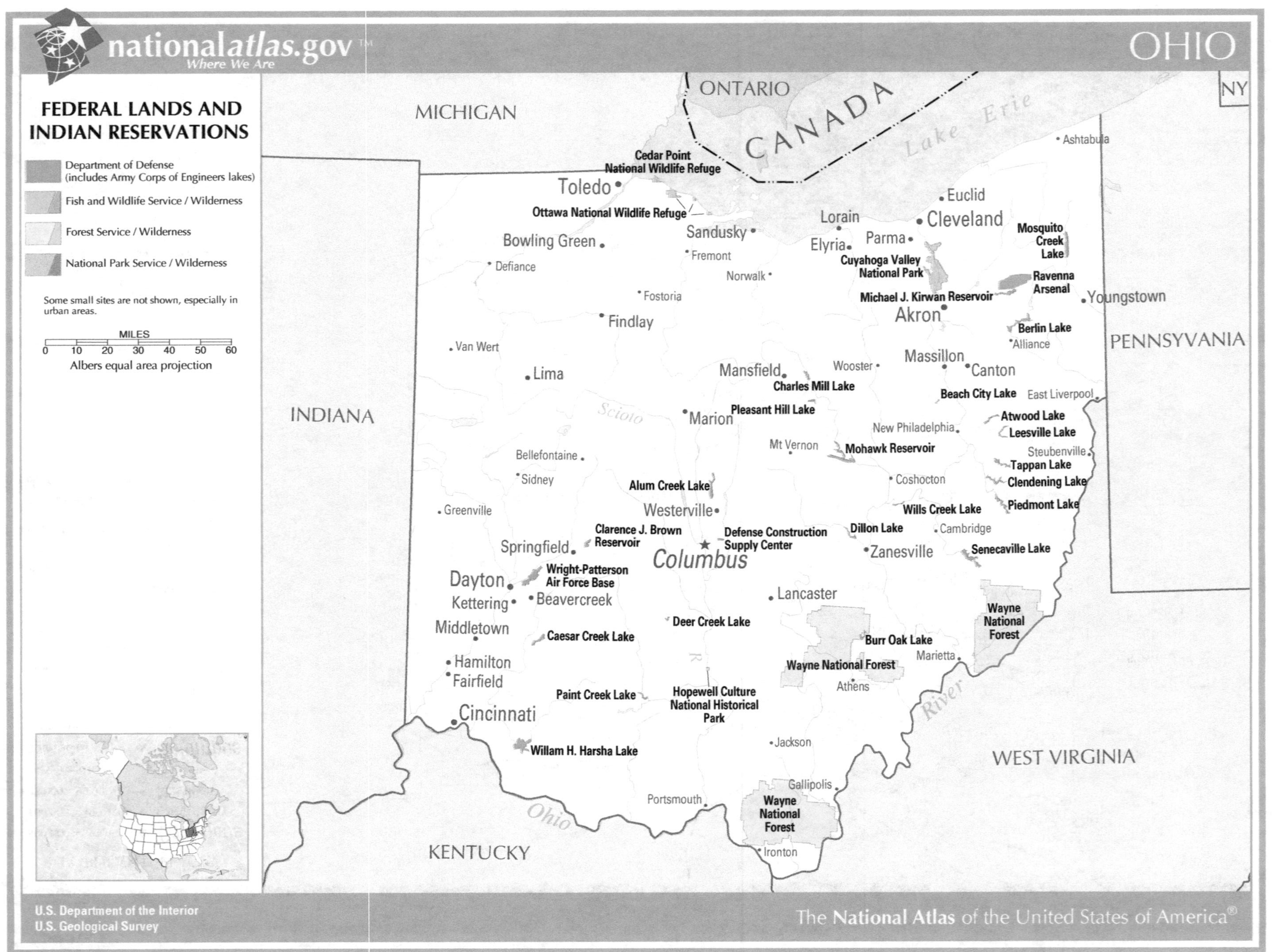
nationalatlas.gov™
Where We Are
OHIO
FEDERAL LANDS AND INDIAN RESERVATIONS
Department of Defense (includes Army Corps of Engineers lakes)
Fish and Wildlife Service / Wilderness
Forest Service / Wilderness
National Park Service / Wilderness
Some small sites are not shown, especially in urban areas.
MILES
0 10 20 30 40 50 60
Albers equal area projection
U.S. Department of the Interior
U.S. Geological Survey
The National Atlas of the United States of America®
MICHIGAN
ONTARIO
CANADA
Lake Erie
NY
PENNSYVANIA
WEST VIRGINIA
KENTUCKY
INDIANA
Ohio River
Scioto
Toledo
Cedar Point National Wildlife Refuge
Ottawa National Wildlife Refuge
Bowling Green
Defiance
Sandusky
Fremont
Fostoria
Findlay
Norwalk
Lorain
Elyria
Parma
Cleveland
Euclid
Cuyahoga Valley National Park
Michael J. Kirwan Reservoir
Akron
Mosquito Creek Lake
Ravenna Arsenal
Youngstown
Ashtabula
Berlin Lake
Alliance
Canton
Massillon
Wooster
Charles Mill Lake
Mansfield
Pleasant Hill Lake
Beach City Lake
East Liverpool
Atwood Lake
Leesville Lake
Steubenville
Tappan Lake
Clendening Lake
Piedmont Lake
Senecaville Lake
Wayne National Forest
New Philadelphia
Mohawk Reservoir
Coshocton
Cambridge
Wills Creek Lake
Dillon Lake
Zanesville
Mt Vernon
Marion
Lima
Van Wert
Bellefontaine
Sidney
Alum Creek Lake
Westerville
Defense Construction Supply Center
Columbus
Clarence J. Brown Reservoir
Springfield
Wright-Patterson Air Force Base
Beavercreek
Greenville
Dayton
Kettering
Middletown
Hamilton
Fairfield
Cincinnati
Caesar Creek Lake
Deer Creek Lake
Lancaster
Burr Oak Lake
Marietta
Athens
Hopewell Culture National Historical Park
Paint Creek Lake
Willam H. Harsha Lake
Portsmouth
Jackson
Gallipolis
Ironton

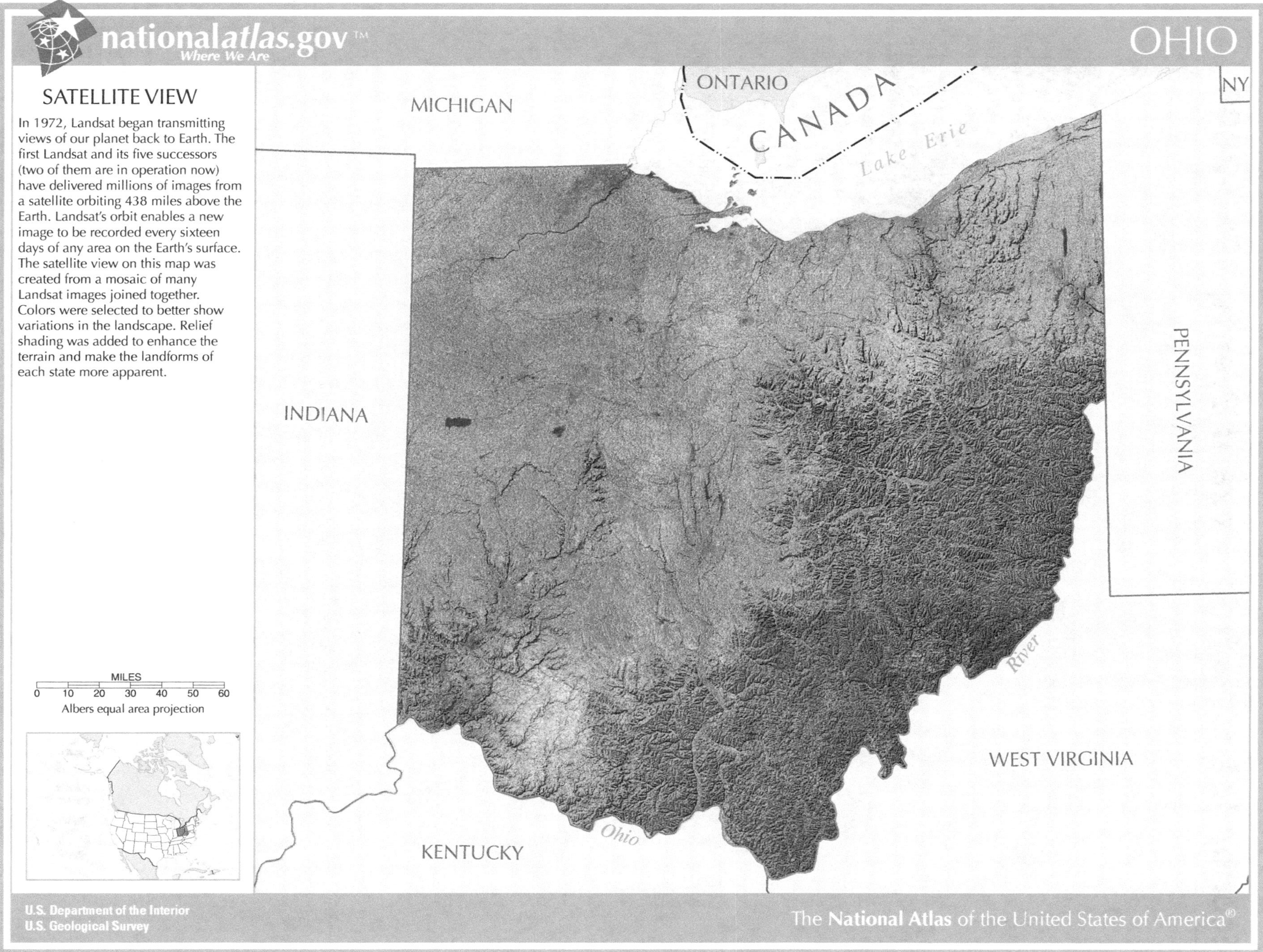
nationalatlas.gov™
Where We Are
OHIO
SATELLITE VIEW
In 1972, Landsat began transmitting views of our planet back to Earth. The first Landsat and its five successors (two of them are in operation now) have delivered millions of images from a satellite orbiting 438 miles above the Earth. Landsat's orbit enables a new image to be recorded every sixteen days of any area on the Earth's surface. The satellite view on this map was created from a mosaic of many Landsat images joined together. Colors were selected to better show variations in the landscape. Relief shading was added to enhance the terrain and make the landforms of each state more apparent.
MICHIGAN
ONTARIO
CANADA
Lake Erie
NY
INDIANA
PENNSYLVANIA
River
WEST VIRGINIA
Ohio
KENTUCKY
MILES
0 10 20 30 40 50 60
Albers equal area projection
U.S. Department of the Interior
U.S. Geological Survey
The National Atlas of the United States of America®

Economic Losses from Hazard Events, 1960-2009

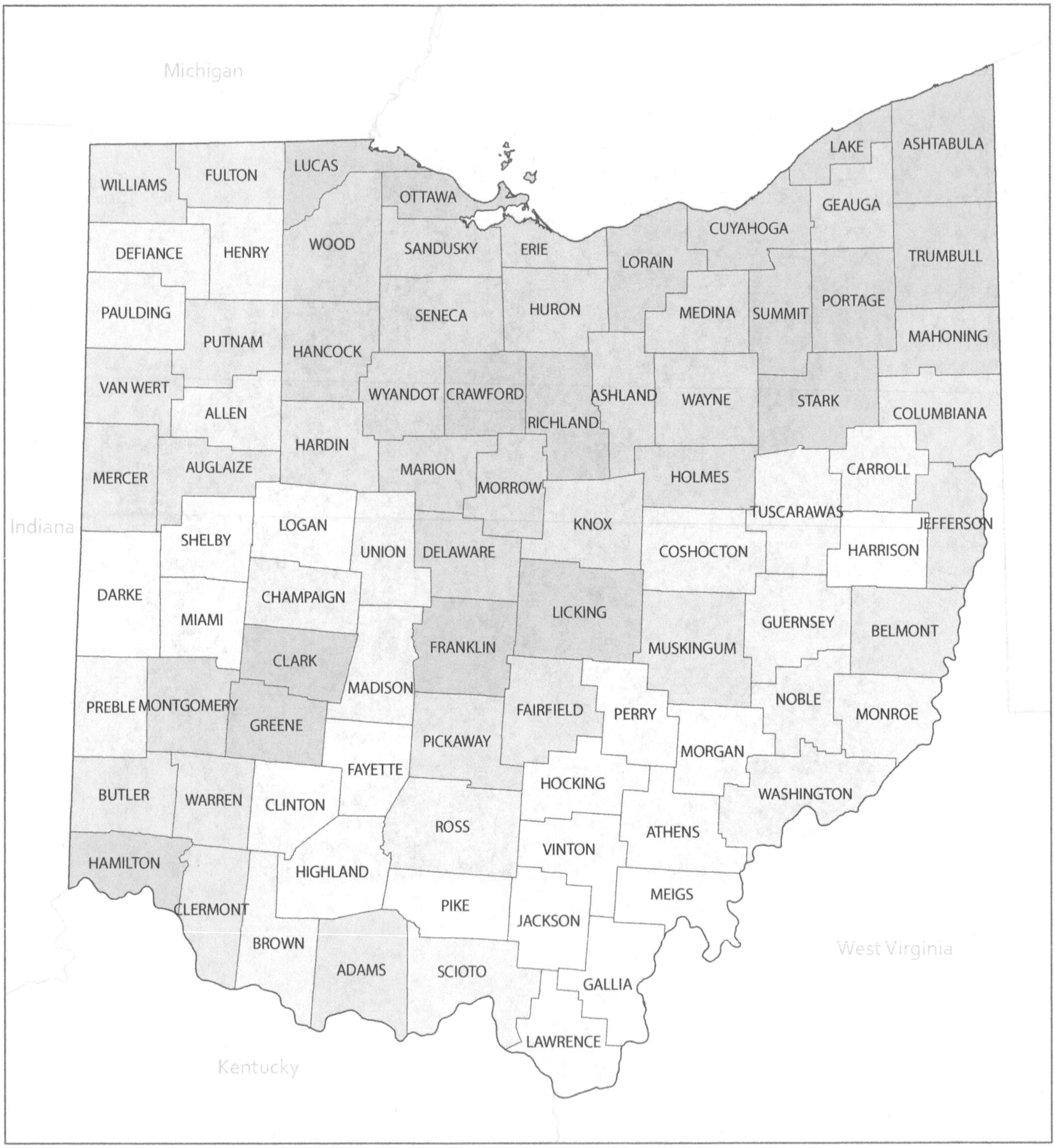

Michigan
Indiana
West Virginia
Kentucky

WILLIAMS
FULTON
LUCAS
OTTAWA
LAKE
ASHTABULA
GEAUGA
CUYAHOGA
DEFIANCE
HENRY
WOOD
SANDUSKY
ERIE
LORAIN
TRUMBULL
PAULDING
PUTNAM
HANCOCK
SENECA
HURON
MEDINA
SUMMIT
PORTAGE
MAHONING
VAN WERT
ALLEN
WYANDOT
CRAWFORD
ASHLAND
WAYNE
STARK
RICHLAND
COLUMBIANA
MERCER
AUGLAIZE
HARDIN
MARION
MORROW
HOLMES
CARROLL
TUSCARAWAS
JEFFERSON
SHELBY
LOGAN
UNION
DELAWARE
KNOX
COSHOCTON
HARRISON
DARKE
MIAMI
CHAMPAIGN
LICKING
GUERNSEY
BELMONT
CLARK
FRANKLIN
MUSKINGUM
MADISON
PREBLE
MONTGOMERY
GREENE
FAIRFIELD
PERRY
NOBLE
MONROE
PICKAWAY
MORGAN
FAYETTE
BUTLER
WARREN
CLINTON
HOCKING
WASHINGTON
ROSS
ATHENS
HAMILTON
VINTON
HIGHLAND
MEIGS
PIKE
CLERMONT
JACKSON
BROWN
ADAMS
SCIOTO
GALLIA
LAWRENCE

OHIO

Total Losses (Property and Crop)

44,626,565 - 60,451,644
60,451,645 - 73,029,169
73,029,170 - 108,792,439
108,792,440 - 155,398,218
155,398,219 - 467,844,281

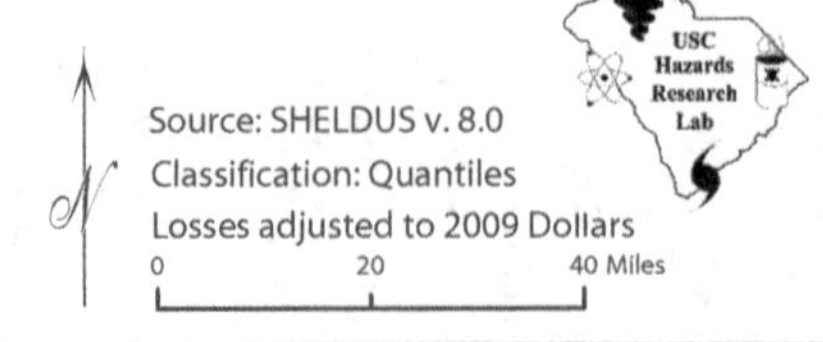

OHIO

Hazard Losses 1960-2009

Distribution of Losses by Hazard Type

(in 2009 USD million)

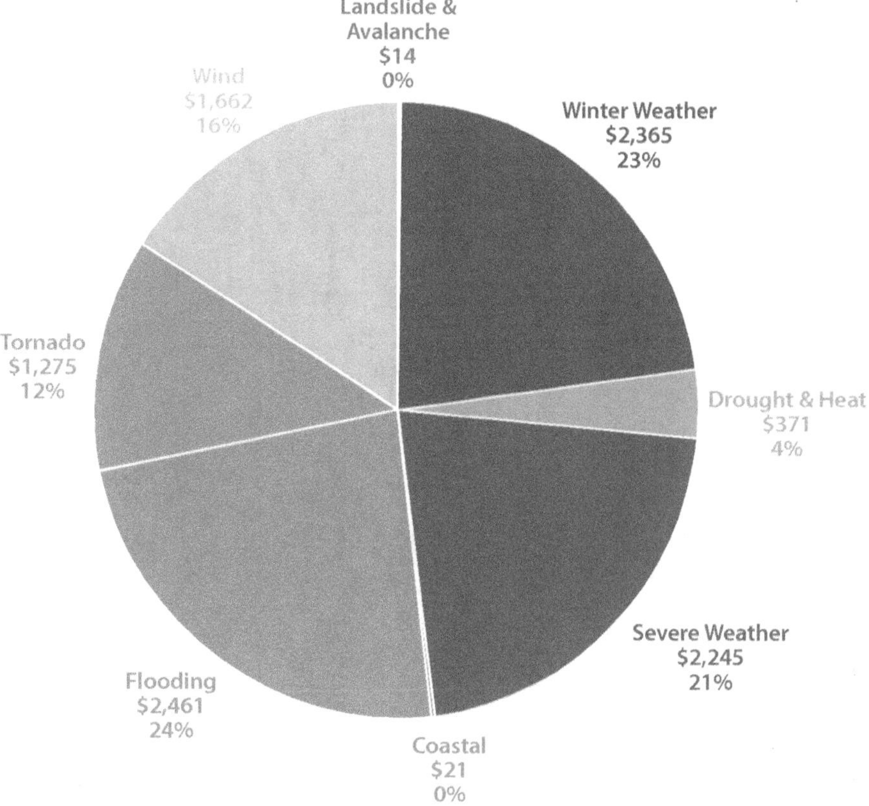

Distribution of Hazard Events

(number of events)

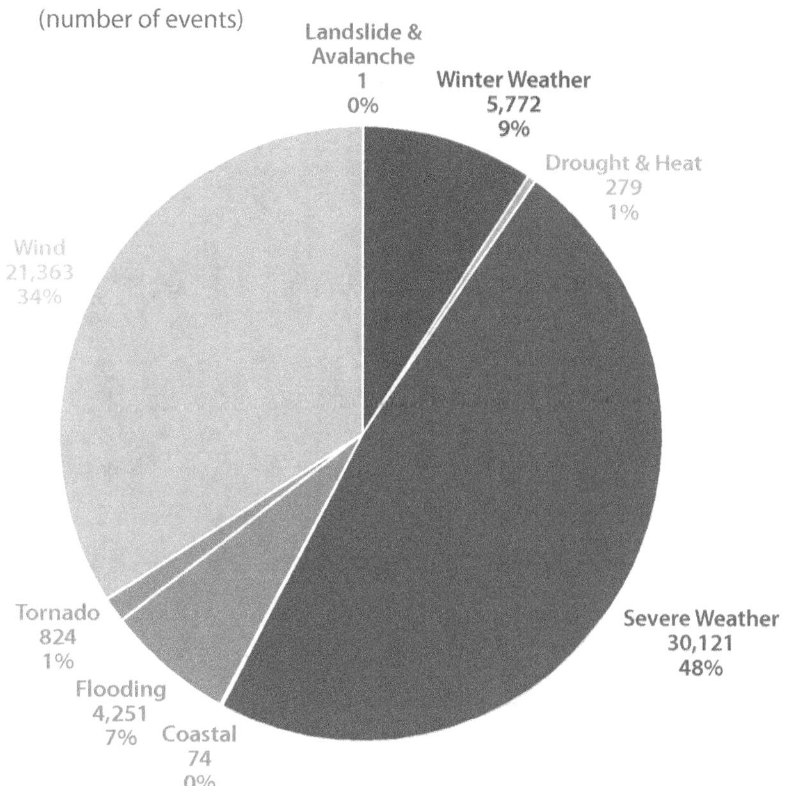

Demographic Maps

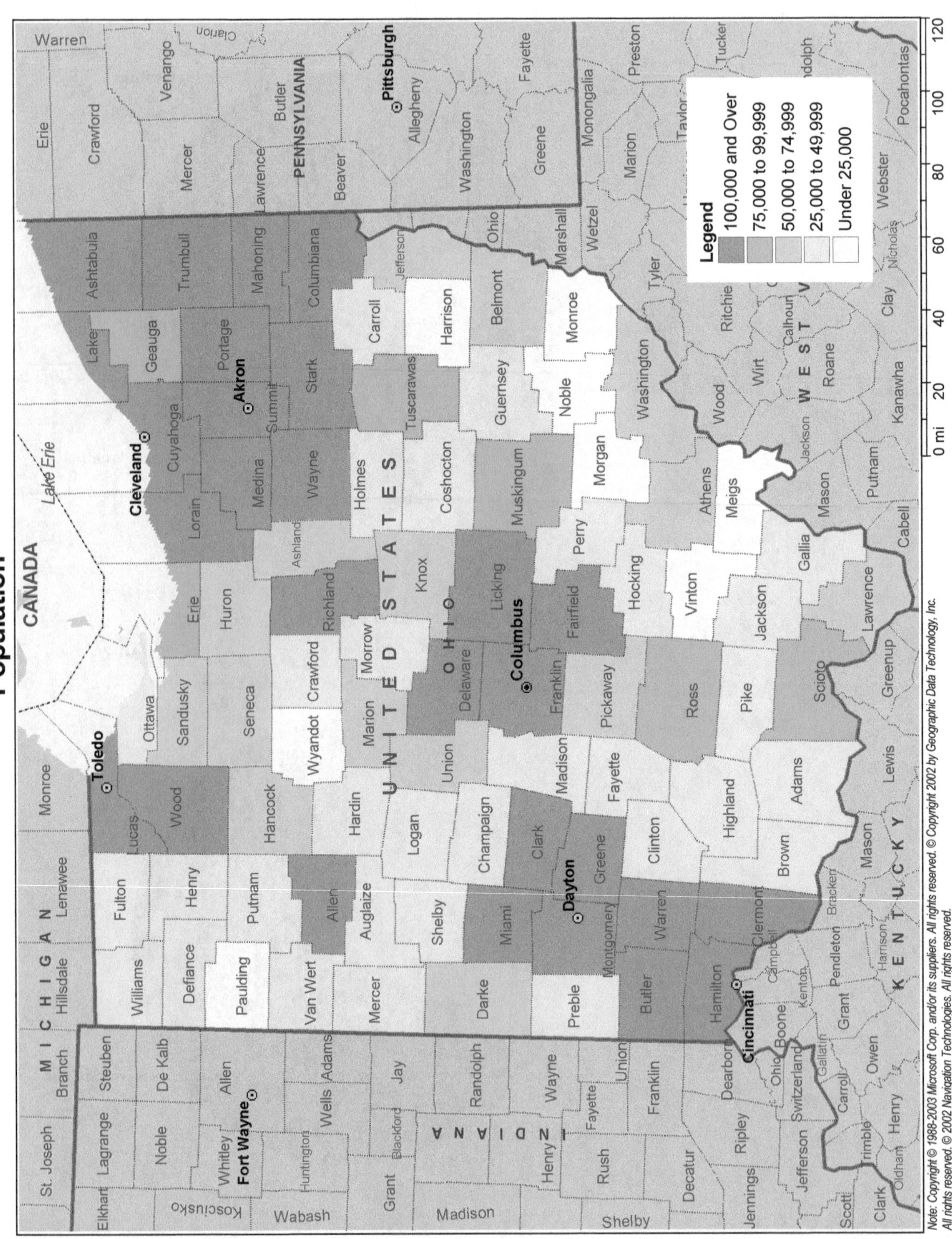

Percent White

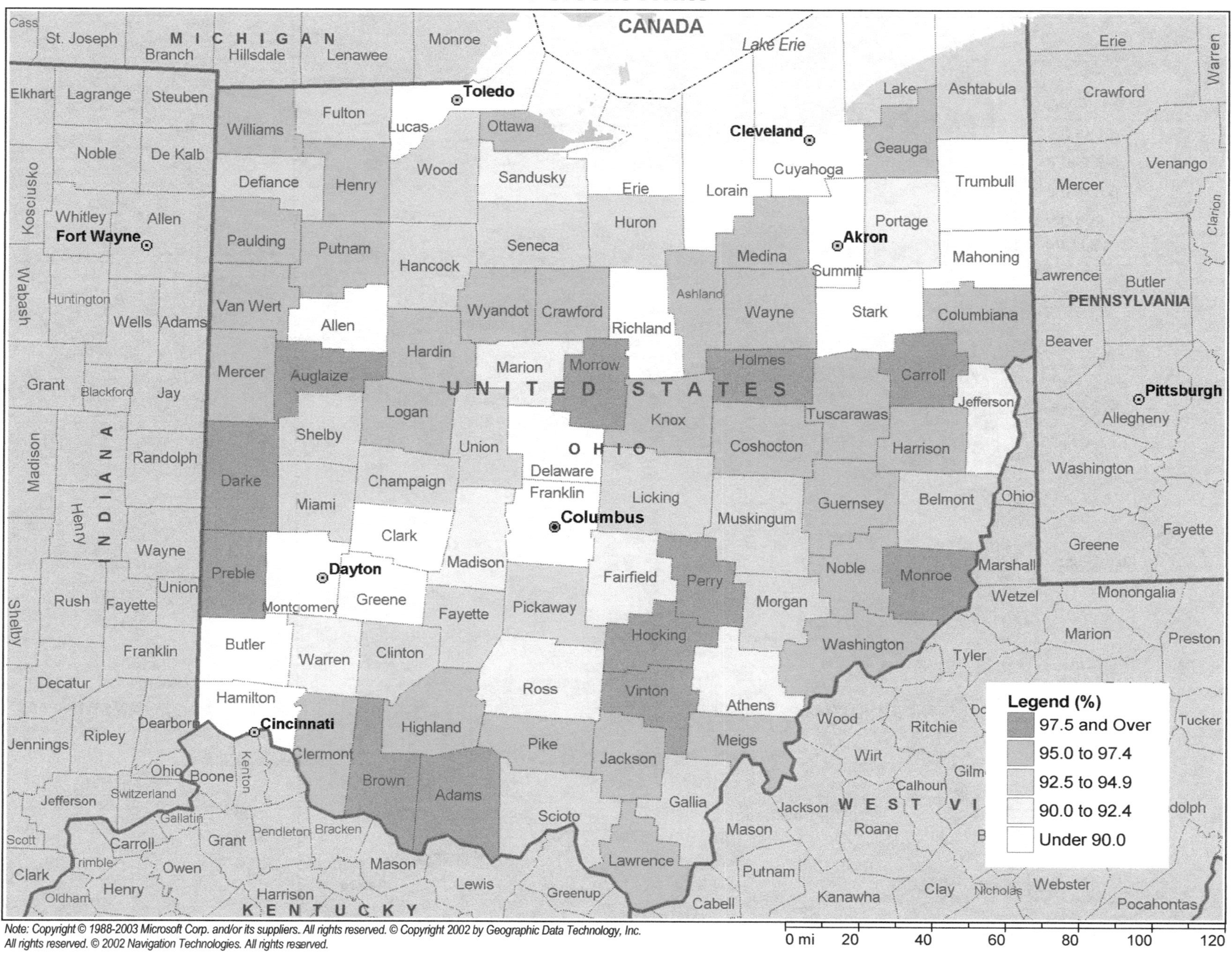

Percent Black

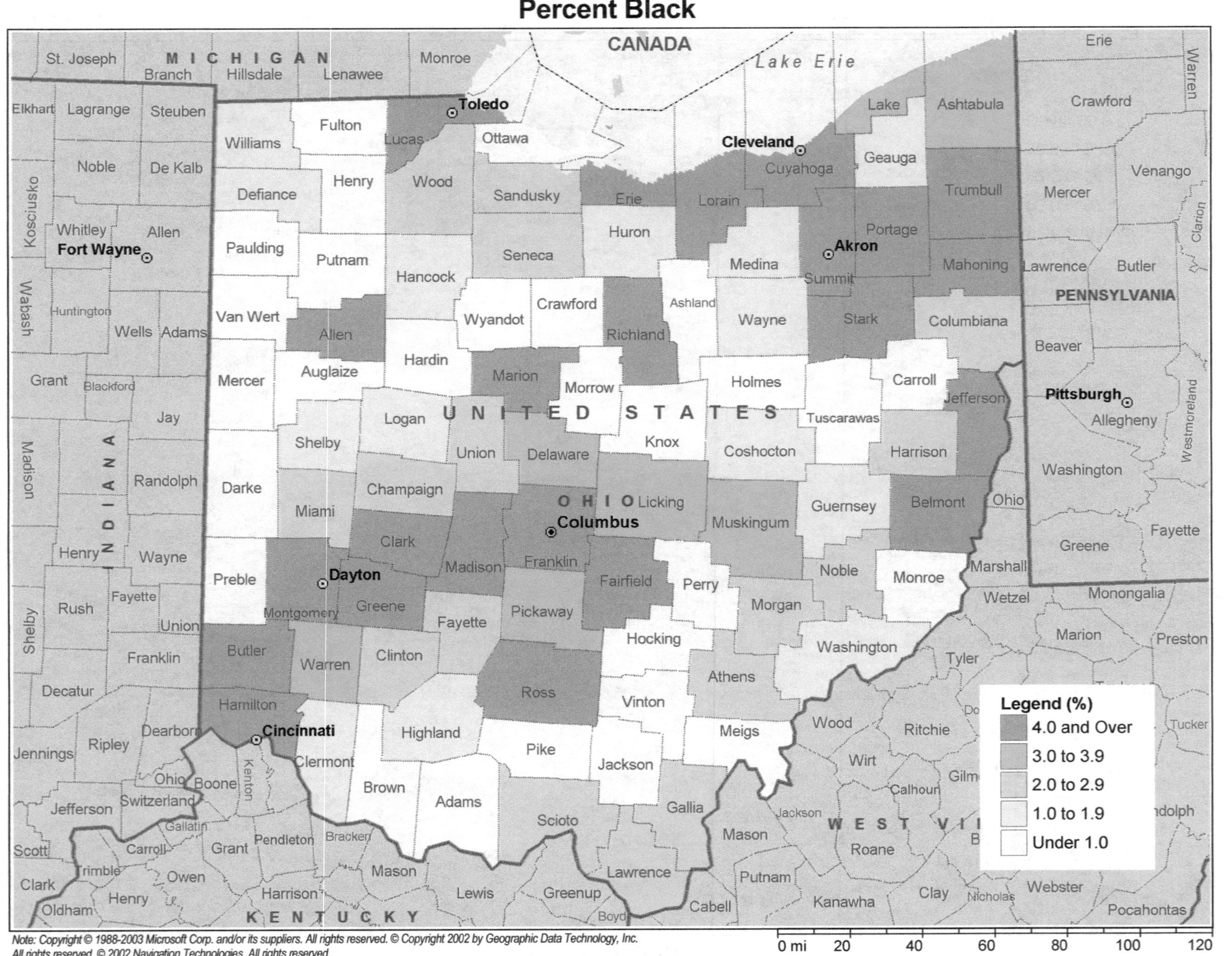

Percent Asian

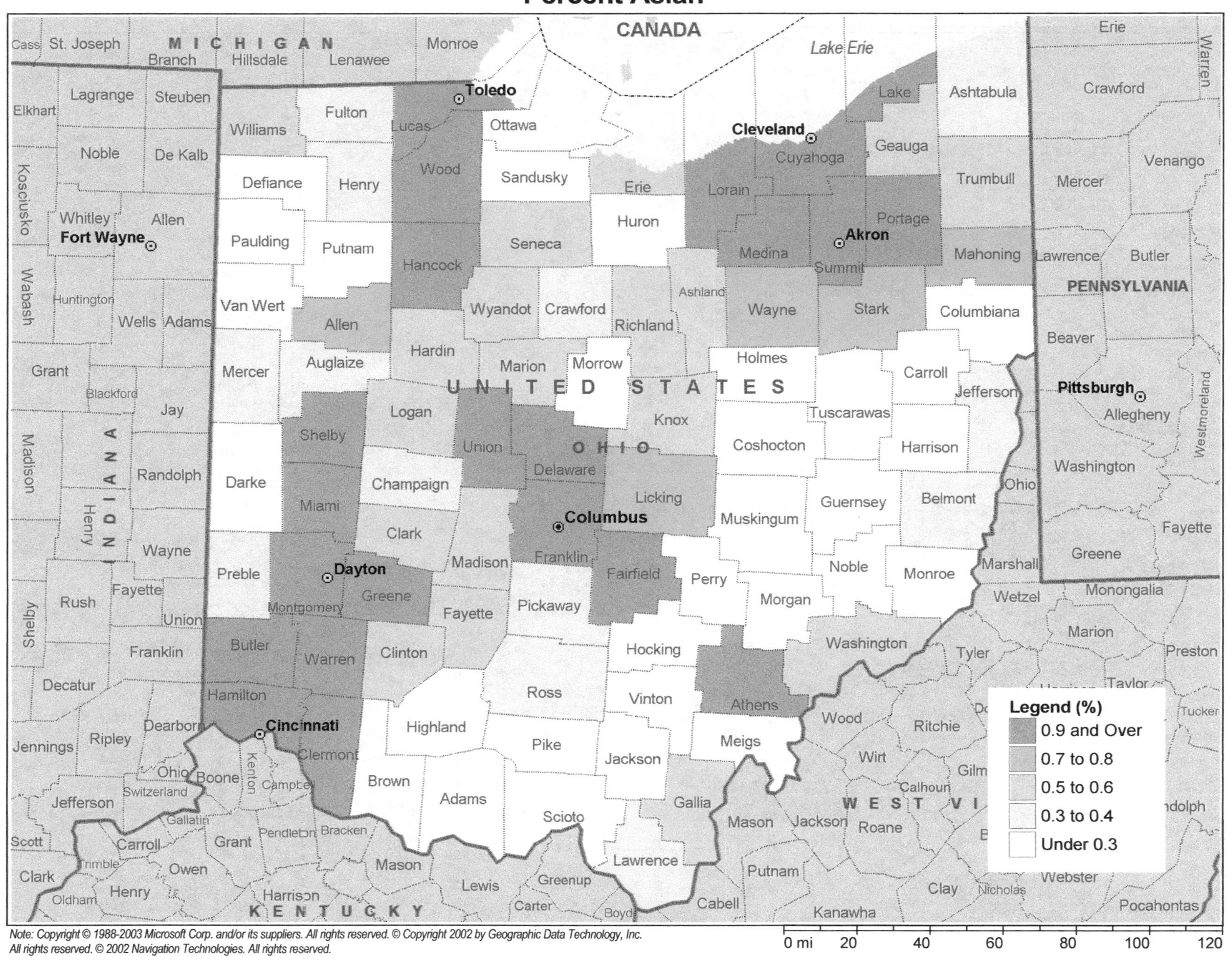

Percent Hispanic

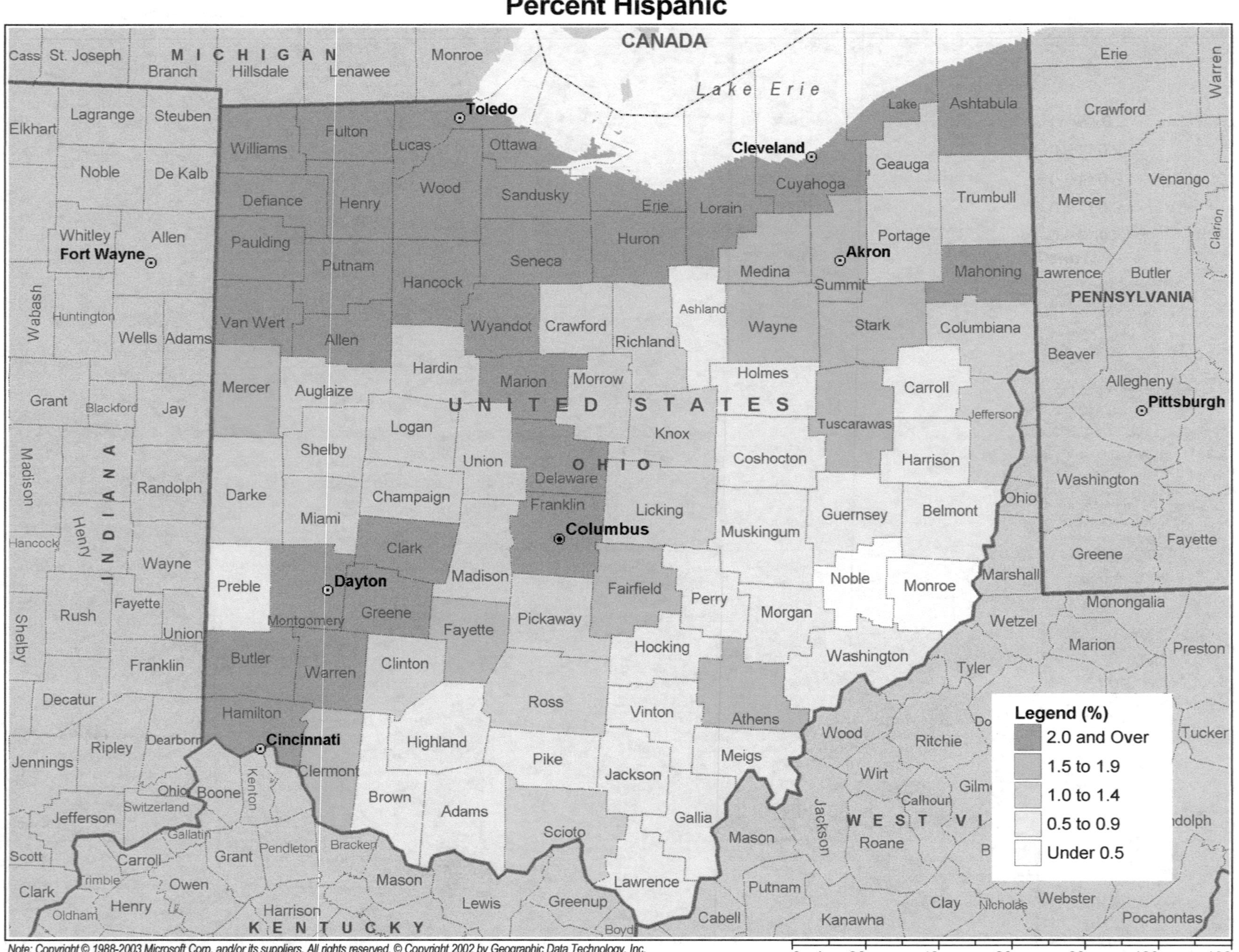

Median Age

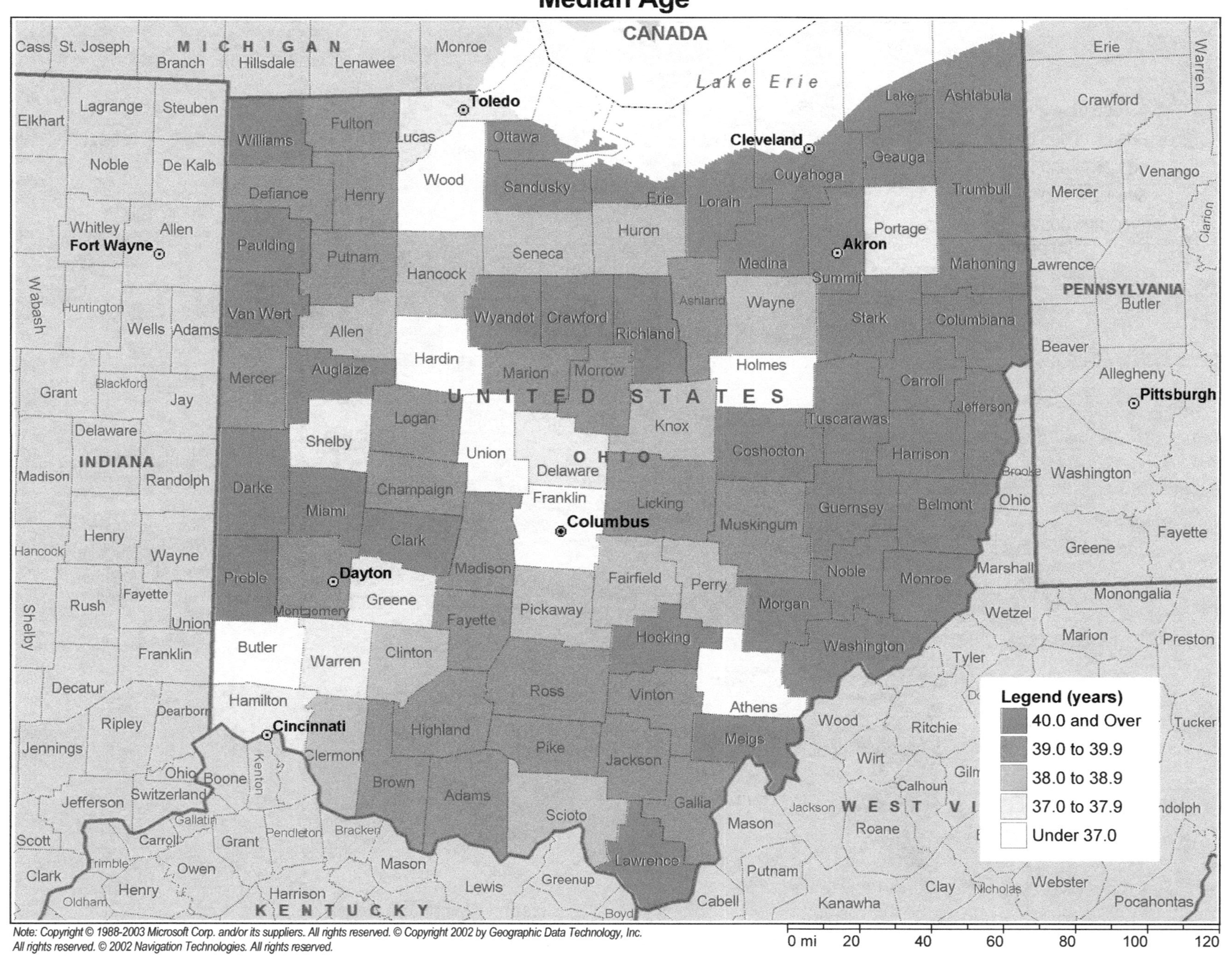
CANADA
Lake Erie
MICHIGAN
INDIANA
PENNSYLVANIA
WEST VIRGINIA
KENTUCKY
UNITED STATES
OHIO
Toledo
Cleveland
Akron
Columbus
Dayton
Cincinnati
Pittsburgh
Fort Wayne
Legend (years)
40.0 and Over
39.0 to 39.9
38.0 to 38.9
37.0 to 37.9
Under 37.0
0 mi 20 40 60 80 100 120

Median Household Income

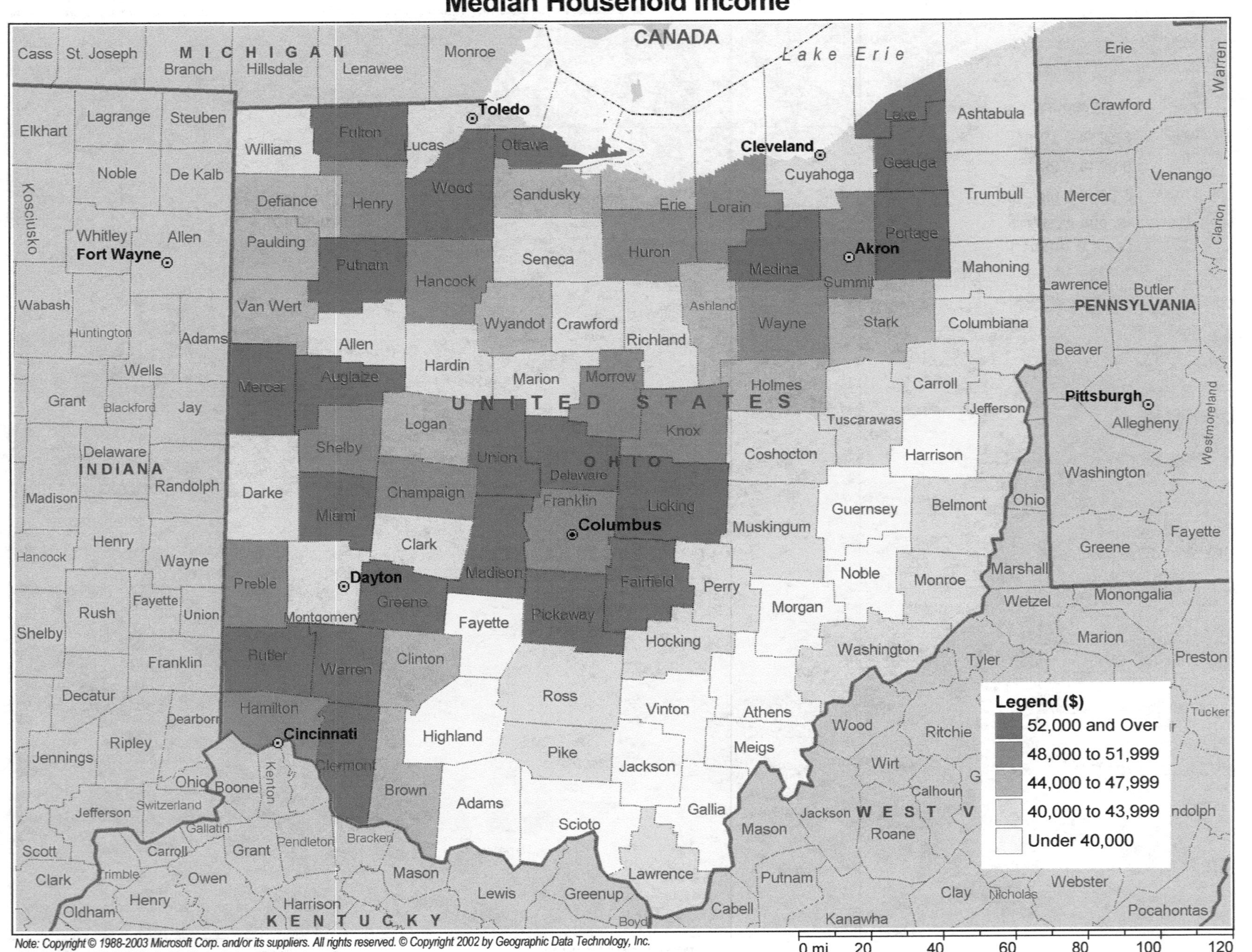

Legend ($)

- 140,000 and Over
- 120,000 to 139,999
- 100,000 to 119,999
- 80,000 to 99,999
- Under 80,000

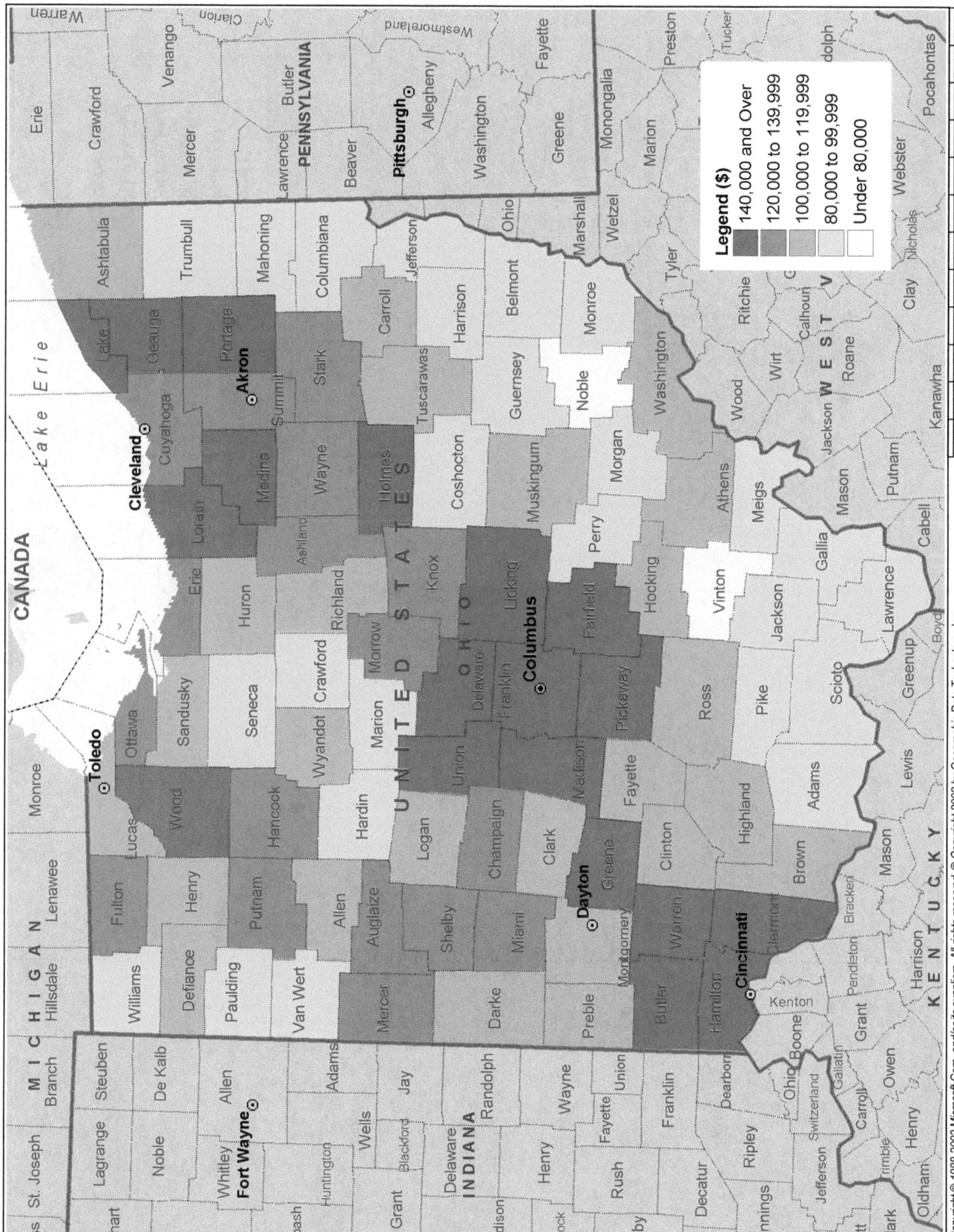

0 mi 20 40 60 80 100 120

High School Graduates*

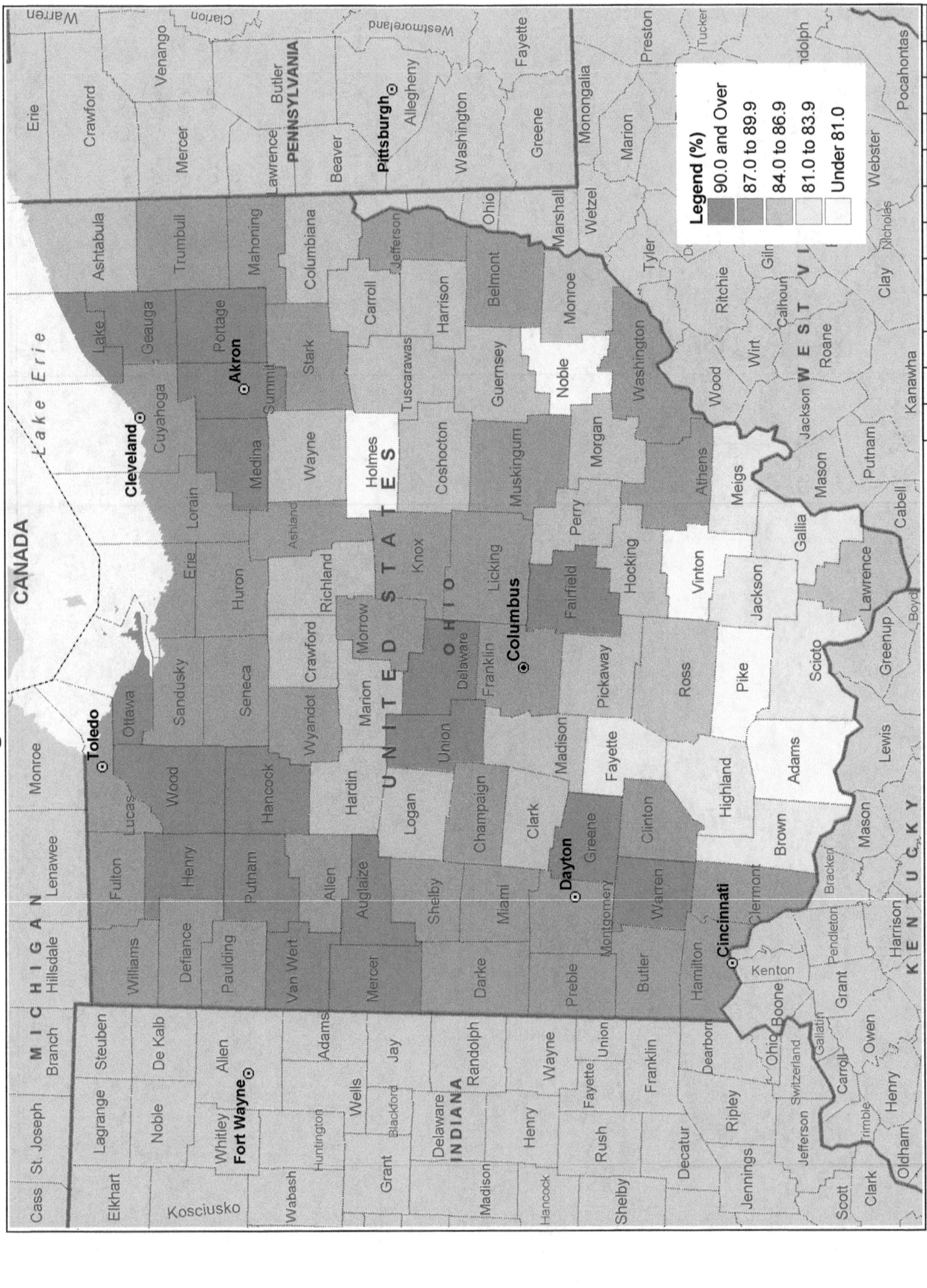

Legend (%)
- 90.0 and Over
- 87.0 to 89.9
- 84.0 to 86.9
- 81.0 to 83.9
- Under 81.0

0 mi 20 40 60 80 100 120

Note: *Percent of population age 25 and over with a high school diploma (including equivalency) or higher.

College Graduates*

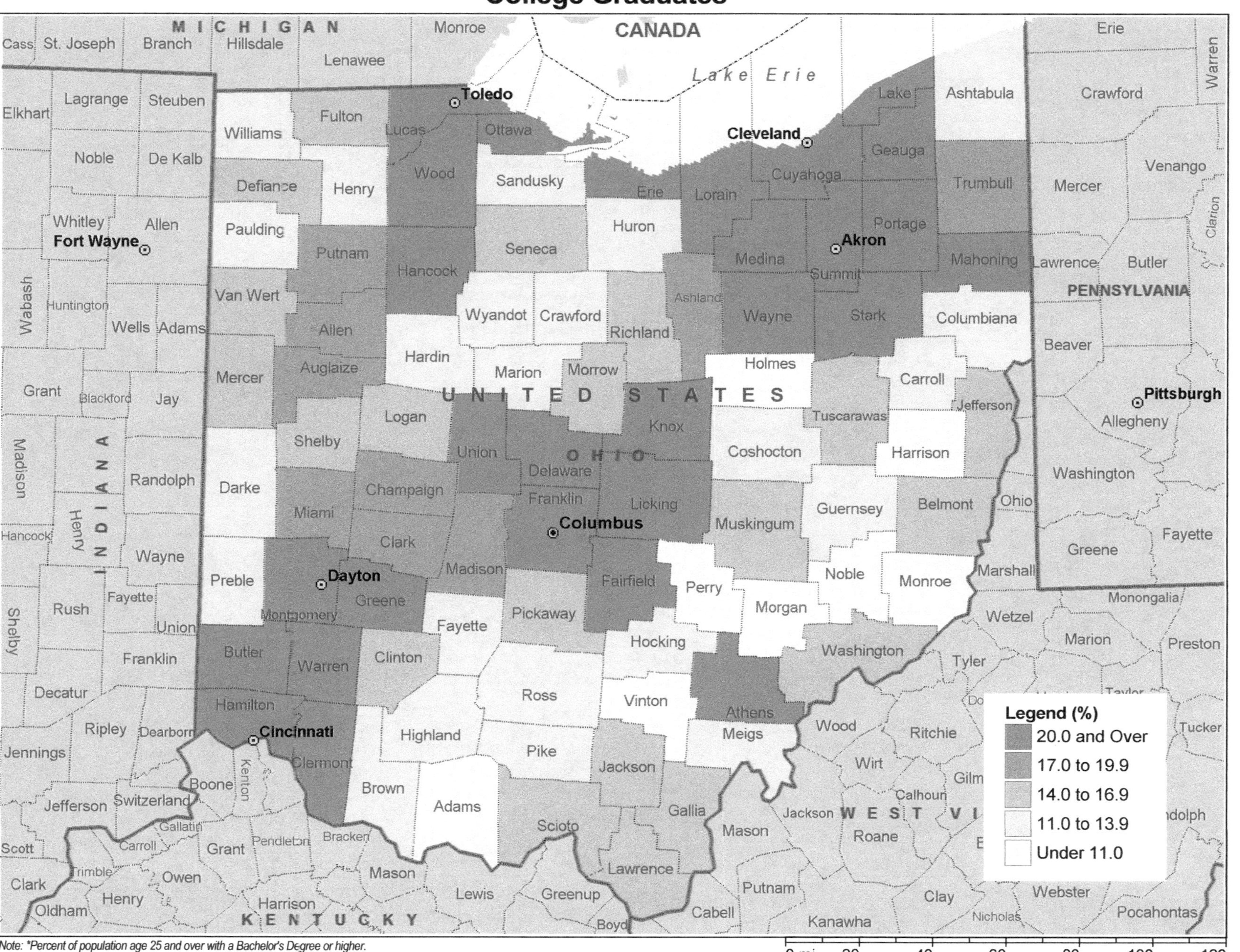

Note: *Percent of population age 25 and over with a Bachelor's Degree or higher.

Profiles

Adams County

Located in southern Ohio; bounded on the south by the Ohio River and the Kentucky border. Covers a land area of 583.867 square miles, a water area of 2.381 square miles, and is located in the Eastern Time Zone at 38.84° N. Lat., 83.47° W. Long. The county was founded in 1797. County seat is West Union.

Population: 28,550; Growth (since 2000): 4.5%; Density: 48.9 persons per square mile; Race: 97.7% White, 0.3% Black/African American, 0.1% Asian, 0.4% American Indian/Alaska Native, 0.0% Native Hawaiian/Other Pacific Islander, 1.3% two or more races, 0.9% Hispanic of any race; Average household size: 2.53; Median age: 39.6; Age under 18: 25.0%; Age 65 and over: 14.8%; Males per 100 females: 97.5; Marriage status: 21.8% never married, 58.1% now married, 2.2% separated, 7.2% widowed, 12.9% divorced; Foreign born: 0.2%; Speak English only: 96.8%; With disability: 20.4%; Veterans: 9.1%; Ancestry: 19.7% American, 17.3% German, 14.2% Irish, 9.5% English, 1.8% French

Religion: Six largest groups: 6.4% Baptist, 5.4% Non-denominational Protestant, 4.4% Methodist/Pietist, 1.8% Catholicism, 1.6% European Free-Church, 1.5% Presbyterian-Reformed

Economy: Unemployment rate: 5.9%; Leading industries: 20.7% retail trade; 13.2% health care and social assistance; 12.1% other services (except public administration); Farms: 1,351 totaling 172,408 acres; Company size: 0 employ 1,000 or more persons, 0 employ 500 to 999 persons, 6 employ 100 to 499 persons, 366 employ less than 100 persons; Business ownership: 652 women-owned, n/a Black-owned, n/a Hispanic-owned, n/a Asian-owned

Employment: 11.5% management, business, and financial, 1.8% computer, engineering, and science, 9.1% education, legal, community service, arts, and media, 5.6% healthcare practitioners, 19.8% service, 18.0% sales and office, 14.1% natural resources, construction, and maintenance, 20.1% production, transportation, and material moving

Income: Per capita: $18,235; Median household: $35,678; Average household: $45,859; Households with income of $100,000 or more: 10.2%; Poverty rate: 22.7%

Educational Attainment: High school diploma or higher: 76.7%; Bachelor's degree or higher: 10.6%; Graduate/professional degree or higher: 5.1%

Housing: Homeownership rate: 71.3%; Median home value: $92,900; Median year structure built: 1978; Homeowner vacancy rate: 2.3%; Median gross rent: $531 per month; Rental vacancy rate: 8.9%

Vital Statistics: Birth rate: 119.9 per 10,000 population; Death rate: 113.1 per 10,000 population; Age-adjusted cancer mortality rate: 207.9 deaths per 100,000 population

Health Insurance: 81.5% have insurance; 52.5% have private insurance; 40.7% have public insurance; 18.5% do not have insurance; 14.2% of children under 18 do not have insurance

Health Care: Physicians: 3.9 per 10,000 population; Hospital beds: 8.8 per 10,000 population; Hospital admissions: 335.6 per 10,000 population

Air Quality Index: 100.0% good, 0.0% moderate, 0.0% unhealthy for sensitive individuals, 0.0% unhealthy (percent of days)

Transportation: Commute: 91.2% car, 0.7% public transportation, 1.7% walk, 5.0% work from home; Median travel time to work: 32.3 minutes

Presidential Election: 35.8% Obama, 62.0% Romney (2012)

National and State Parks: Adams Lake State Park; Johnson Ridge State Nature Preserve; Ohio State Park; Serpent Mound State Memorial; Shawnee State Wilderness; Tranquility State Wildlife Area

Additional Information Contacts

Adams Government . . . . (937) 544-3286
http://www.adamscountyoh.com

Adams County Communities

BENTONVILLE (CDP). Covers a land area of 1.727 square miles and a water area of 0 square miles. Located at 38.75° N. Lat; 83.61° W. Long. Elevation is 915 feet.

Population: 287; Growth (since 2000): n/a; Density: 166.2 persons per square mile; Race: 99.7% White, 0.0% Black/African American, 0.0% Asian, 0.3% American Indian/Alaska Native, 0.0% Native Hawaiian/Other Pacific Islander, 0.0% Two or more races, 0.7% Hispanic of any race; Average household size: 2.41; Median age: 43.4; Age under 18: 20.6%; Age 65 and over: 21.6%; Males per 100 females: 78.3

Housing: Homeownership rate: 81.5%; Homeowner vacancy rate: 2.0%; Rental vacancy rate: 8.3%

BLUE CREEK (unincorporated postal area)

ZCTA: 45616

Covers a land area of 82.330 square miles and a water area of 0.121 square miles. Located at 38.76° N. Lat; 83.31° W. Long. Elevation is 673 feet.

Population: 1,559; Growth (since 2000): 12.8%; Density: 18.9 persons per square mile; Race: 96.7% White, 0.1% Black/African American, 0.2% Asian, 0.8% American Indian/Alaska Native, 0.0% Native Hawaiian/Other Pacific Islander, 2.1% Two or more races, 0.8% Hispanic of any race; Average household size: 2.48; Median age: 41.3; Age under 18: 22.7%; Age 65 and over: 13.1%; Males per 100 females: 98.6

Housing: Homeownership rate: 76.1%; Homeowner vacancy rate: 1.8%; Rental vacancy rate: 5.7%

CHERRY FORK (village). Covers a land area of 0.122 square miles and a water area of 0 square miles. Located at 38.89° N. Lat; 83.61° W. Long. Elevation is 902 feet.

Population: 155; Growth (since 2000): 22.0%; Density: 1,272.2 persons per square mile; Race: 96.8% White, 0.6% Black/African American, 0.0% Asian, 0.6% American Indian/Alaska Native, 0.0% Native Hawaiian/Other Pacific Islander, 1.9% Two or more races, 0.6% Hispanic of any race; Average household size: 2.42; Median age: 36.7; Age under 18: 29.0%; Age 65 and over: 10.3%; Males per 100 females: 118.3

Housing: Homeownership rate: 70.3%; Homeowner vacancy rate: 2.1%; Rental vacancy rate: 5.0%

LYNX (unincorporated postal area)

ZCTA: 45650

Covers a land area of 14.942 square miles and a water area of 0.060 square miles. Located at 38.74° N. Lat; 83.42° W. Long. Elevation is 820 feet.

Population: 435; Growth (since 2000): -8.2%; Density: 29.1 persons per square mile; Race: 98.2% White, 0.0% Black/African American, 0.0% Asian, 0.7% American Indian/Alaska Native, 0.0% Native Hawaiian/Other Pacific Islander, 1.1% Two or more races, 0.0% Hispanic of any race; Average household size: 2.23; Median age: 46.6; Age under 18: 17.7%; Age 65 and over: 16.1%; Males per 100 females: 109.1

Housing: Homeownership rate: 74.8%; Homeowner vacancy rate: 3.3%; Rental vacancy rate: 8.8%

MANCHESTER (village). Covers a land area of 1.283 square miles and a water area of 0.012 square miles. Located at 38.69° N. Lat; 83.60° W. Long. Elevation is 512 feet.

History: Manchester was founded in 1791 by General Nathaniel Massie. The town was an important steamboat landing in the mid-1800's, and in the later 1800's offered excursions on the river and showboats at the wharf.

Population: 2,023; Growth (since 2000): -1.0%; Density: 1,576.8 persons per square mile; Race: 96.2% White, 0.2% Black/African American, 0.1% Asian, 0.4% American Indian/Alaska Native, 0.0% Native Hawaiian/Other Pacific Islander, 2.4% Two or more races, 1.7% Hispanic of any race; Average household size: 2.47; Median age: 38.1; Age under 18: 26.7%; Age 65 and over: 15.6%; Males per 100 females: 93.2

School District(s)

Manchester Local (PK-12)
2012-13 Enrollment: 855. . . . . (937) 549-4777

Housing: Homeownership rate: 56.0%; Homeowner vacancy rate: 5.7%; Rental vacancy rate: 18.5%

Newspapers: Manchester Signal (weekly circulation 3500)

PEEBLES (village). Covers a land area of 1.182 square miles and a water area of 0 square miles. Located at 38.95° N. Lat; 83.41° W. Long. Elevation is 827 feet.

Population: 1,782; Growth (since 2000): 2.5%; Density: 1,507.8 persons per square mile; Race: 97.8% White, 0.3% Black/African American, 0.1% Asian, 0.4% American Indian/Alaska Native, 0.0% Native Hawaiian/Other Pacific Islander, 1.2% Two or more races, 1.5% Hispanic of any race; Average household size: 2.34; Median age: 36.5; Age under 18: 27.5%; Age 65 and over: 14.7%; Males per 100 females: 89.0

School District(s)

Adams County/ohio Valley Local (PK-12)
2012-13 Enrollment: 4,024 . . . . (937) 544-5586

Housing: Homeownership rate: 46.4%; Homeowner vacancy rate: 4.0%; Rental vacancy rate: 7.5%

ROME (village). Covers a land area of 0.230 square miles and a water area of 0.025 square miles. Located at 38.67° N. Lat; 83.38° W. Long. Elevation is 518 feet.
History: Also called Stout.
Population: 94; Growth (since 2000): -19.7%; Density: 408.3 persons per square mile; Race: 95.7% White, 0.0% Black/African American, 0.0% Asian, 2.1% American Indian/Alaska Native, 0.0% Native Hawaiian/Other Pacific Islander, 2.1% Two or more races, 1.1% Hispanic of any race; Average household size: 2.09; Median age: 49.3; Age under 18: 21.3%; Age 65 and over: 24.5%; Males per 100 females: 100.0
Housing: Homeownership rate: 64.4%; Homeowner vacancy rate: 6.5%; Rental vacancy rate: 11.1%

SEAMAN (village). Covers a land area of 1.067 square miles and a water area of 0 square miles. Located at 38.93° N. Lat; 83.57° W. Long. Elevation is 906 feet.
Population: 944; Growth (since 2000): -9.1%; Density: 884.4 persons per square mile; Race: 97.8% White, 0.1% Black/African American, 0.1% Asian, 0.3% American Indian/Alaska Native, 0.0% Native Hawaiian/Other Pacific Islander, 1.4% Two or more races, 1.3% Hispanic of any race; Average household size: 2.57; Median age: 35.5; Age under 18: 26.9%; Age 65 and over: 16.3%; Males per 100 females: 91.1

School District(s)

Adams County/ohio Valley Local (PK-12)
2012-13 Enrollment: 4,024 . . . . (937) 544-5586
Housing: Homeownership rate: 58.5%; Homeowner vacancy rate: 1.8%; Rental vacancy rate: 10.9%
Hospitals: Adams County Regional Medical Center

WEST UNION (village). County seat. Covers a land area of 2.831 square miles and a water area of 0 square miles. Located at 38.79° N. Lat; 83.54° W. Long. Elevation is 945 feet.
History: Laid out 1804.
Population: 3,241; Growth (since 2000): 11.6%; Density: 1,144.9 persons per square mile; Race: 97.4% White, 0.4% Black/African American, 0.2% Asian, 0.2% American Indian/Alaska Native, 0.0% Native Hawaiian/Other Pacific Islander, 1.5% Two or more races, 0.8% Hispanic of any race; Average household size: 2.29; Median age: 40.1; Age under 18: 23.4%; Age 65 and over: 20.2%; Males per 100 females: 83.4; Marriage status: 21.6% never married, 49.8% now married, 1.5% separated, 12.0% widowed, 16.6% divorced; Foreign born: 0.4%; Speak English only: 99.0%; With disability: 22.5%; Veterans: 9.2%; Ancestry: 17.1% American, 14.0% German, 10.6% Irish, 6.3% English, 1.8% Italian
Employment: 14.3% management, business, and financial, 3.0% computer, engineering, and science, 6.7% education, legal, community service, arts, and media, 7.4% healthcare practitioners, 14.4% service, 18.7% sales and office, 15.1% natural resources, construction, and maintenance, 20.3% production, transportation, and material moving
Income: Per capita: $16,533; Median household: $33,063; Average household: $39,974; Households with income of $100,000 or more: 4.8%; Poverty rate: 27.8%
Educational Attainment: High school diploma or higher: 72.4%; Bachelor's degree or higher: 5.6%; Graduate/professional degree or higher: 3.3%

School District(s)

Adams County/ohio Valley Local (PK-12)
2012-13 Enrollment: 4,024 . . . . (937) 544-5586
Housing: Homeownership rate: 50.3%; Median home value: $84,800; Median year structure built: 1971; Homeowner vacancy rate: 3.7%; Median gross rent: $482 per month; Rental vacancy rate: 8.7%
Health Insurance: 85.3% have insurance; 54.0% have private insurance; 47.1% have public insurance; 14.7% do not have insurance; 1.8% of children under 18 do not have insurance
Newspapers: The Peoples Defender (weekly circulation 7400)
Transportation: Commute: 89.1% car, 1.7% public transportation, 3.2% walk, 6.0% work from home; Median travel time to work: 23.2 minutes

WINCHESTER (village). Covers a land area of 2.612 square miles and a water area of 0.017 square miles. Located at 38.94° N. Lat; 83.65° W. Long. Elevation is 971 feet.
History: In agricultural area.
Population: 1,051; Growth (since 2000): 2.5%; Density: 402.3 persons per square mile; Race: 98.4% White, 0.2% Black/African American, 0.0% Asian, 0.5% American Indian/Alaska Native, 0.0% Native Hawaiian/Other Pacific Islander, 0.7% Two or more races, 1.0% Hispanic of any race; Average household size: 2.48; Median age: 35.9; Age under 18: 27.3%; Age 65 and over: 15.6%; Males per 100 females: 96.1
Housing: Homeownership rate: 59.3%; Homeowner vacancy rate: 4.5%; Rental vacancy rate: 3.9%

Allen County

Located in western Ohio; crossed by the Ottawa and Auglaize Rivers. Covers a land area of 402.496 square miles, a water area of 4.353 square miles, and is located in the Eastern Time Zone at 40.77° N. Lat., 84.11° W. Long. The county was founded in 1820. County seat is Lima.

Allen County is part of the Lima, OH Metropolitan Statistical Area. The entire metro area includes: Allen County, OH

Weather Station: Lima WWTP Elevation: 850 feet

	Jan	Feb	Mar	Apr	May	Jun	Jul	Aug	Sep	Oct	Nov	Dec
High	34	38	48	61	72	80	84	82	77	64	51	38
Low	20	22	30	40	51	60	64	63	55	44	35	24
Precip	2.4	2.2	2.7	3.4	4.2	3.9	4.3	3.5	3.2	2.7	3.3	2.8
Snow	na	na	na	tr	0.0	0.0	0.0	0.0	0.0	0.0	0.1	na

High and Low temperatures in degrees Fahrenheit; Precipitation and Snow in inches

Population: 106,331; Growth (since 2000): -2.0%; Density: 264.2 persons per square mile; Race: 83.8% White, 11.9% Black/African American, 0.7% Asian, 0.2% American Indian/Alaska Native, 0.0% Native Hawaiian/Other Pacific Islander, 2.6% two or more races, 2.4% Hispanic of any race; Average household size: 2.47; Median age: 38.3; Age under 18: 23.9%; Age 65 and over: 14.8%; Males per 100 females: 101.8; Marriage status: 30.8% never married, 49.3% now married, 1.6% separated, 6.8% widowed, 13.1% divorced; Foreign born: 1.6%; Speak English only: 97.0%; With disability: 14.5%; Veterans: 10.3%; Ancestry: 33.2% German, 12.1% Irish, 8.4% American, 7.6% English, 4.4% Italian
Religion: Six largest groups: 16.9% Catholicism, 8.3% Baptist, 7.4% Methodist/Pietist, 5.9% Holiness, 4.8% Non-denominational Protestant, 3.0% Lutheran
Economy: Unemployment rate: 4.5%; Leading industries: 16.7% retail trade; 12.8% other services (except public administration); 12.2% health care and social assistance; Farms: 904 totaling 183,186 acres; Company size: 2 employ 1,000 or more persons, 6 employ 500 to 999 persons, 56 employ 100 to 499 persons, 2,436 employ less than 100 persons; Business ownership: 2,003 women-owned, 365 Black-owned, n/a Hispanic-owned, n/a Asian-owned
Employment: 9.2% management, business, and financial, 2.9% computer, engineering, and science, 8.9% education, legal, community service, arts, and media, 5.9% healthcare practitioners, 21.1% service, 24.4% sales and office, 7.8% natural resources, construction, and maintenance, 19.9% production, transportation, and material moving
Income: Per capita: $22,295; Median household: $42,823; Average household: $56,189; Households with income of $100,000 or more: 13.3%; Poverty rate: 18.6%
Educational Attainment: High school diploma or higher: 88.4%; Bachelor's degree or higher: 17.2%; Graduate/professional degree or higher: 6.7%
Housing: Homeownership rate: 69.2%; Median home value: $105,000; Median year structure built: 1962; Homeowner vacancy rate: 2.2%; Median gross rent: $647 per month; Rental vacancy rate: 10.2%
Vital Statistics: Birth rate: 118.2 per 10,000 population; Death rate: 99.2 per 10,000 population; Age-adjusted cancer mortality rate: 194.6 deaths per 100,000 population
Health Insurance: 88.0% have insurance; 67.2% have private insurance; 35.3% have public insurance; 12.0% do not have insurance; 3.9% of children under 18 do not have insurance
Health Care: Physicians: 26.7 per 10,000 population; Hospital beds: 73.7 per 10,000 population; Hospital admissions: 2,820.7 per 10,000 population
Air Quality Index: 90.9% good, 9.1% moderate, 0.0% unhealthy for sensitive individuals, 0.0% unhealthy (percent of days)
Transportation: Commute: 94.7% car, 0.4% public transportation, 1.8% walk, 2.2% work from home; Median travel time to work: 19.3 minutes
Presidential Election: 36.3% Obama, 62.0% Romney (2012)
Additional Information Contacts
Allen Government . . . . (419) 228-3700
http://www.co.allen.oh.us

Allen County Communities

BEAVERDAM (village). Covers a land area of 0.612 square miles and a water area of <.001 square miles. Located at 40.83° N. Lat; 83.97° W. Long. Elevation is 856 feet.
Population: 382; Growth (since 2000): 7.3%; Density: 623.9 persons per square mile; Race: 96.9% White, 0.5% Black/African American, 0.3% Asian, 0.3% American Indian/Alaska Native, 0.0% Native Hawaiian/Other Pacific Islander, 2.1% Two or more races, 1.3% Hispanic of any race; Average household size: 2.65; Median age: 34.8; Age under 18: 24.9%; Age 65 and over: 12.6%; Males per 100 females: 106.5
Housing: Homeownership rate: 73.6%; Homeowner vacancy rate: 3.6%; Rental vacancy rate: 7.3%

BLUFFTON (village). Covers a land area of 3.547 square miles and a water area of 0.069 square miles. Located at 40.89° N. Lat; 83.89° W. Long. Elevation is 837 feet.
History: Bluffton was founded in 1833 and named for a Mennonite community in Indiana. Many of the early residents were Mennonites of Swiss descent. Limestone outcroppings in the vicinity created a crushed stone and lime industry here.
Population: 4,125; Growth (since 2000): 5.9%; Density: 1,163.0 persons per square mile; Race: 95.3% White, 1.6% Black/African American, 0.9% Asian, 0.2% American Indian/Alaska Native, 0.0% Native Hawaiian/Other Pacific Islander, 1.2% Two or more races, 1.5% Hispanic of any race; Average household size: 2.31; Median age: 34.0; Age under 18: 19.9%; Age 65 and over: 19.0%; Males per 100 females: 83.9; Marriage status: 30.8% never married, 53.9% now married, 1.2% separated, 8.3% widowed, 7.0% divorced; Foreign born: 2.6%; Speak English only: 97.7%; With disability: 10.6%; Veterans: 7.2%; Ancestry: 46.6% German, 10.9% Swiss, 7.1% American, 6.7% English, 6.7% Irish
Employment: 14.8% management, business, and financial, 2.9% computer, engineering, and science, 22.2% education, legal, community service, arts, and media, 5.8% healthcare practitioners, 18.7% service, 18.6% sales and office, 3.2% natural resources, construction, and maintenance, 13.7% production, transportation, and material moving
Income: Per capita: $26,808; Median household: $62,679; Average household: $69,916; Households with income of $100,000 or more: 20.0%; Poverty rate: 9.1%
Educational Attainment: High school diploma or higher: 95.3%; Bachelor's degree or higher: 45.8%; Graduate/professional degree or higher: 23.3%

School District(s)

Bluffton Exempted Village (PK-12)
2012-13 Enrollment: 1,116 . . . . (419) 358-5901

Four-year College(s)

Bluffton University (Private, Not-for-profit, Mennonite Church)
Fall 2013 Enrollment: 1,146 . . . . (419) 358-3000
2013-14 Tuition: In-state $28,504; Out-of-state $28,504
Housing: Homeownership rate: 67.0%; Median home value: $133,800; Median year structure built: 1963; Homeowner vacancy rate: 1.4%; Median gross rent: $620 per month; Rental vacancy rate: 5.6%
Health Insurance: 92.5% have insurance; 82.1% have private insurance; 24.3% have public insurance; 7.5% do not have insurance; 7.1% of children under 18 do not have insurance
Hospitals: Bluffton Hospital (25 beds)
Safety: Violent crime rate: 2.5 per 10,000 population; Property crime rate: 132.5 per 10,000 population
Newspapers: Bluffton News (weekly circulation 2900); North Baltimore News (weekly circulation 600)
Transportation: Commute: 80.5% car, 0.0% public transportation, 6.3% walk, 8.0% work from home; Median travel time to work: 18.4 minutes
Additional Information Contacts
Village of Bluffton . . . . (419) 358-2066
http://www.bluffton-ohio.com

CAIRO (village). Covers a land area of 0.225 square miles and a water area of 0 square miles. Located at 40.83° N. Lat; 84.08° W. Long. Elevation is 814 feet.
Population: 524; Growth (since 2000): 5.0%; Density: 2,329.2 persons per square mile; Race: 97.7% White, 0.6% Black/African American, 0.2% Asian, 0.2% American Indian/Alaska Native, 0.0% Native Hawaiian/Other Pacific Islander, 1.3% Two or more races, 1.5% Hispanic of any race; Average household size: 2.65; Median age: 37.2; Age under 18: 28.2%; Age 65 and over: 13.0%; Males per 100 females: 87.1
Housing: Homeownership rate: 81.3%; Homeowner vacancy rate: 3.0%; Rental vacancy rate: 5.1%

DELPHOS (city). Covers a land area of 3.435 square miles and a water area of 0.044 square miles. Located at 40.85° N. Lat; 84.34° W. Long. Elevation is 774 feet.
History: Delphos was platted in 1845 by Ferdinand Bredeick. Its location on the Miami & Erie Canal and the Pennsylvania Railroad brought it early growth. Large-scale honey production was one of the leading industries.
Population: 7,101; Growth (since 2000): 2.3%; Density: 2,067.0 persons per square mile; Race: 97.5% White, 0.4% Black/African American, 0.2% Asian, 0.2% American Indian/Alaska Native, 0.0% Native Hawaiian/Other Pacific Islander, 1.3% Two or more races, 1.8% Hispanic of any race; Average household size: 2.41; Median age: 38.6; Age under 18: 24.6%; Age 65 and over: 17.1%; Males per 100 females: 94.5; Marriage status: 26.3% never married, 56.3% now married, 0.9% separated, 7.4% widowed, 10.1% divorced; Foreign born: 0.3%; Speak English only: 97.0%; With disability: 15.9%; Veterans: 10.0%; Ancestry: 56.4% German, 8.4% Irish, 7.4% American, 4.9% English, 2.9% Lithuanian
Employment: 8.2% management, business, and financial, 1.9% computer, engineering, and science, 7.8% education, legal, community service, arts, and media, 4.3% healthcare practitioners, 15.3% service, 26.8% sales and office, 7.0% natural resources, construction, and maintenance, 28.7% production, transportation, and material moving
Income: Per capita: $21,329; Median household: $41,755; Average household: $50,486; Households with income of $100,000 or more: 9.0%; Poverty rate: 12.5%
Educational Attainment: High school diploma or higher: 89.4%; Bachelor's degree or higher: 14.4%; Graduate/professional degree or higher: 6.6%

School District(s)

Delphos City (PK-12)
2012-13 Enrollment: 1,104 . . . . (419) 692-2509
Housing: Homeownership rate: 73.3%; Median home value: $82,900; Median year structure built: 1955; Homeowner vacancy rate: 2.9%; Median gross rent: $631 per month; Rental vacancy rate: 9.3%
Health Insurance: 91.1% have insurance; 74.3% have private insurance; 31.6% have public insurance; 8.9% do not have insurance; 0.7% of children under 18 do not have insurance
Safety: Violent crime rate: 1.4 per 10,000 population; Property crime rate: 250.8 per 10,000 population
Newspapers: Delphos Daily Herald (daily circulation 3300)
Transportation: Commute: 94.2% car, 0.0% public transportation, 3.1% walk, 1.6% work from home; Median travel time to work: 19.2 minutes

ELIDA (village). Covers a land area of 1.220 square miles and a water area of <.001 square miles. Located at 40.79° N. Lat; 84.20° W. Long. Elevation is 797 feet.
Population: 1,905; Growth (since 2000): -0.6%; Density: 1,561.7 persons per square mile; Race: 94.3% White, 2.6% Black/African American, 0.8% Asian, 0.1% American Indian/Alaska Native, 0.0% Native Hawaiian/Other Pacific Islander, 1.6% Two or more races, 1.6% Hispanic of any race; Average household size: 2.69; Median age: 40.2; Age under 18: 26.4%; Age 65 and over: 12.1%; Males per 100 females: 95.0

School District(s)

Elida Local (PK-12)
2012-13 Enrollment: 2,445 . . . . (419) 331-4155
Housing: Homeownership rate: 87.8%; Homeowner vacancy rate: 2.3%; Rental vacancy rate: 2.3%

FORT SHAWNEE (CDP). Covers a land area of 7.208 square miles and a water area of 0.043 square miles. Located at 40.68° N. Lat; 84.13° W. Long. Elevation is 866 feet.
Population: 3,726; Growth (since 2000): -3.3%; Density: 516.9 persons per square mile; Race: 94.6% White, 2.5% Black/African American, 0.4% Asian, 0.2% American Indian/Alaska Native, 0.1% Native Hawaiian/Other Pacific Islander, 1.2% Two or more races, 1.9% Hispanic of any race; Average household size: 2.47; Median age: 42.0; Age under 18: 23.3%; Age 65 and over: 15.8%; Males per 100 females: 100.5; Marriage status: 21.6% never married, 60.0% now married, 1.3% separated, 6.1% widowed, 12.2% divorced; Foreign born: 2.7%; Speak English only: 94.9%; With disability: 11.3%; Veterans: 14.3%; Ancestry: 36.7% German, 12.7% Irish, 9.2% Italian, 8.8% American, 8.6% English

Employment: 9.6% management, business, and financial, 5.5% computer, engineering, and science, 11.7% education, legal, community service, arts, and media, 8.4% healthcare practitioners, 16.4% service, 26.2% sales and office, 7.6% natural resources, construction, and maintenance, 14.6% production, transportation, and material moving
Income: Per capita: $31,749; Median household: $54,330; Average household: $73,664; Households with income of $100,000 or more: 20.5%; Poverty rate: 8.0%
Educational Attainment: High school diploma or higher: 92.6%; Bachelor's degree or higher: 24.1%; Graduate/professional degree or higher: 8.3%
Housing: Homeownership rate: 86.7%; Median home value: $124,200; Median year structure built: 1966; Homeowner vacancy rate: 1.6%; Median gross rent: $822 per month; Rental vacancy rate: 15.1%
Health Insurance: 91.1% have insurance; 78.2% have private insurance; 30.6% have public insurance; 8.9% do not have insurance; 6.1% of children under 18 do not have insurance
Transportation: Commute: 97.4% car, 0.0% public transportation, 0.0% walk, 2.4% work from home; Median travel time to work: 19.4 minutes

GOMER (unincorporated postal area)

ZCTA: 45809

Covers a land area of 0.254 square miles and a water area of 0 square miles. Located at 40.85° N. Lat; 84.19° W. Long. Elevation is 778 feet.
Population: 157; Growth (since 2000): -24.5%; Density: 617.6 persons per square mile; Race: 98.7% White, 0.0% Black/African American, 0.6% Asian, 0.0% American Indian/Alaska Native, 0.0% Native Hawaiian/Other Pacific Islander, 0.6% Two or more races, 0.0% Hispanic of any race; Average household size: 2.42; Median age: 42.1; Age under 18: 23.6%; Age 65 and over: 10.8%; Males per 100 females: 101.3
Housing: Homeownership rate: 80.0%; Homeowner vacancy rate: 7.1%; Rental vacancy rate: 7.1%

HARROD (village). Covers a land area of 0.239 square miles and a water area of 0.001 square miles. Located at 40.71° N. Lat; 83.92° W. Long. Elevation is 981 feet.
Population: 417; Growth (since 2000): -15.1%; Density: 1,747.4 persons per square mile; Race: 99.3% White, 0.0% Black/African American, 0.0% Asian, 0.0% American Indian/Alaska Native, 0.0% Native Hawaiian/Other Pacific Islander, 0.7% Two or more races, 1.7% Hispanic of any race; Average household size: 2.92; Median age: 30.5; Age under 18: 29.7%; Age 65 and over: 9.6%; Males per 100 females: 97.6

School District(s)

Allen East Local (PK-12)
2012-13 Enrollment: 1,083 . . . . (419) 648-3333
Housing: Homeownership rate: 87.4%; Homeowner vacancy rate: 3.8%; Rental vacancy rate: 5.3%

LAFAYETTE (village). Covers a land area of 0.253 square miles and a water area of <.001 square miles. Located at 40.76° N. Lat; 83.95° W. Long. Elevation is 928 feet.
Population: 445; Growth (since 2000): 46.4%; Density: 1,762.0 persons per square mile; Race: 97.8% White, 0.0% Black/African American, 1.3% Asian, 0.2% American Indian/Alaska Native, 0.0% Native Hawaiian/Other Pacific Islander, 0.7% Two or more races, 1.1% Hispanic of any race; Average household size: 2.76; Median age: 33.4; Age under 18: 32.1%; Age 65 and over: 10.3%; Males per 100 females: 91.8
Housing: Homeownership rate: 74.5%; Homeowner vacancy rate: 0.8%; Rental vacancy rate: 4.7%

LIMA (city). County seat. Covers a land area of 13.565 square miles and a water area of 0.229 square miles. Located at 40.74° N. Lat; 84.11° W. Long. Elevation is 879 feet.
History: Lima was laid out on the Ottawa River in 1831 as the seat of Allen County. The name, the suggestion of minister and congressman Patrick Good, was drawn from a hat. Lima was incorporated in 1842. Oil was found here in 1885, bringing prosperity for a time until local industry turned to manufacturing railroad locomotives. It was in Lima that the Dillinger gang murdered Sheriff Jesse Sarber, starting a nation-wide hunt that ended in Dillinger's death and the end of his gang.
Population: 38,771; Growth (since 2000): -3.3%; Density: 2,858.2 persons per square mile; Race: 67.1% White, 26.4% Black/African American, 0.5% Asian, 0.3% American Indian/Alaska Native, 0.0% Native Hawaiian/Other Pacific Islander, 4.4% Two or more races, 3.7% Hispanic of any race; Average household size: 2.42; Median age: 32.9; Age under 18: 24.8%; Age 65 and over: 11.4%; Males per 100 females: 112.0; Marriage status: 41.3% never married, 35.2% now married, 3.2% separated, 6.3% widowed, 17.2% divorced; Foreign born: 1.4%; Speak English only: 97.1%; With disability: 17.7%; Veterans: 9.1%; Ancestry: 26.3% German, 13.0% Irish, 6.8% American, 5.7% English, 3.6% Italian
Employment: 7.4% management, business, and financial, 1.3% computer, engineering, and science, 8.1% education, legal, community service, arts, and media, 4.2% healthcare practitioners, 27.7% service, 23.9% sales and office, 6.0% natural resources, construction, and maintenance, 21.4% production, transportation, and material moving
Income: Per capita: $15,266; Median household: $28,050; Average household: $38,996; Households with income of $100,000 or more: 6.1%; Poverty rate: 33.9%
Educational Attainment: High school diploma or higher: 82.5%; Bachelor's degree or higher: 10.8%; Graduate/professional degree or higher: 4.5%

School District(s)

Apollo (07-12)
2012-13 Enrollment: n/a . . . . (419) 998-2908
Auglaize County Educational Academy (KG-12)
2012-13 Enrollment: 90. . . . . (419) 738-4572
Bath Local (PK-12)
2012-13 Enrollment: 1,787 . . . . (419) 221-0807
Heir Force Community School (KG-08)
2012-13 Enrollment: 301. . . . . (419) 228-9241
Lima City (PK-12)
2012-13 Enrollment: 3,863 . . . . (419) 996-3400
Perry Local (PK-12)
2012-13 Enrollment: 799. . . . . (419) 221-2770
Quest Academy Community (KG-05)
2012-13 Enrollment: 119. . . . . (419) 227-7730
Shawnee Local (PK-12)
2012-13 Enrollment: 2,458 . . . . (419) 998-8031
West Central Learning Academy II (07-12)
2012-13 Enrollment: 57. . . . . (419) 227-9252

Four-year College(s)

Ohio State University-Lima Campus (Public)
Fall 2013 Enrollment: 1,077 . . . . (419) 995-8600
2013-14 Tuition: In-state $7,140; Out-of-state $22,860
University of Northwestern Ohio (Private, Not-for-profit)
Fall 2013 Enrollment: 4,167 . . . . (419) 227-3141
2013-14 Tuition: In-state $9,565; Out-of-state $9,565

Two-year College(s)

James A Rhodes State College (Public)
Fall 2013 Enrollment: 3,599 . . . . (419) 221-1112
2013-14 Tuition: In-state $4,713; Out-of-state $9,412
Ohio State Beauty Academy (Private, For-profit)
Fall 2013 Enrollment: 171 . . . . (419) 229-7896

Vocational/Technical School(s)

Apollo Career Center (Public)
Fall 2013 Enrollment: 654 . . . . (419) 998-3000
2013-14 Tuition: $10,260
Institute of Therapeutic Massage (Private, For-profit)
Fall 2013 Enrollment: 66 . . . . (419) 523-9580
2013-14 Tuition: $15,983
Housing: Homeownership rate: 50.6%; Median home value: $70,500; Median year structure built: 1953; Homeowner vacancy rate: 3.4%; Median gross rent: $623 per month; Rental vacancy rate: 12.0%
Health Insurance: 82.6% have insurance; 50.3% have private insurance; 44.6% have public insurance; 17.4% do not have insurance; 3.6% of children under 18 do not have insurance
Hospitals: Institute For Orthopaedic Surgery; Lima Memorial Health System (308 beds); Saint Rita's Medical Center (424 beds)
Safety: Violent crime rate: 95.8 per 10,000 population; Property crime rate: 505.6 per 10,000 population
Newspapers: Lima News (daily circulation 32900)
Transportation: Commute: 93.9% car, 1.1% public transportation, 2.9% walk, 1.3% work from home; Median travel time to work: 17.7 minutes
Airports: Lima Allen County (general aviation)
Additional Information Contacts
City of Lima . . . . (419) 228-5462
http://www.cityhall.lima.oh.us

SPENCERVILLE (village). Covers a land area of 0.969 square miles and a water area of <.001 square miles. Located at 40.71° N. Lat; 84.35° W. Long. Elevation is 830 feet.
History: Laid out 1844-1845, incorporated 1866.
Population: 2,223; Growth (since 2000): -0.5%; Density: 2,293.1 persons per square mile; Race: 96.5% White, 0.4% Black/African American, 0.4% Asian, 0.2% American Indian/Alaska Native, 0.0% Native Hawaiian/Other Pacific Islander, 2.5% Two or more races, 0.7% Hispanic of any race; Average household size: 2.66; Median age: 33.4; Age under 18: 30.6%; Age 65 and over: 15.2%; Males per 100 females: 94.8

School District(s)

Spencerville Local (PK-12)
2012-13 Enrollment: 924. . . . . (419) 647-4111

Housing: Homeownership rate: 72.7%; Homeowner vacancy rate: 2.9%; Rental vacancy rate: 7.8%
Safety: Violent crime rate: 4.6 per 10,000 population; Property crime rate: 186.5 per 10,000 population
Newspapers: The Journal News (weekly circulation 2100)

Ashland County

Located in north central Ohio; drained by forks of the Mohican River. Covers a land area of 422.950 square miles, a water area of 3.849 square miles, and is located in the Eastern Time Zone at 40.84° N. Lat., 82.27° W. Long. The county was founded in 1846. County seat is Ashland.

Ashland County is part of the Ashland, OH Micropolitan Statistical Area. The entire metro area includes: Ashland County, OH

Population: 53,139; Growth (since 2000): 1.2%; Density: 125.6 persons per square mile; Race: 97.3% White, 0.7% Black/African American, 0.5% Asian, 0.2% American Indian/Alaska Native, 0.1% Native Hawaiian/Other Pacific Islander, 1.0% two or more races, 0.9% Hispanic of any race; Average household size: 2.53; Median age: 39.3; Age under 18: 23.9%; Age 65 and over: 15.8%; Males per 100 females: 95.6; Marriage status: 26.4% never married, 58.3% now married, 1.5% separated, 5.8% widowed, 9.5% divorced; Foreign born: 2.2%; Speak English only: 94.3%; With disability: 12.9%; Veterans: 10.1%; Ancestry: 33.1% German, 15.2% American, 11.0% Irish, 10.0% English, 4.6% Italian
Religion: Six largest groups: 12.9% Baptist, 7.4% Methodist/Pietist, 6.2% European Free-Church, 5.9% Non-denominational Protestant, 3.1% Lutheran, 2.8% Catholicism
Economy: Unemployment rate: 4.2%; Leading industries: 16.0% other services (except public administration); 15.3% retail trade; 11.1% health care and social assistance; Farms: 1,034 totaling 152,972 acres; Company size: 0 employ 1,000 or more persons, 2 employ 500 to 999 persons, 24 employ 100 to 499 persons, 984 employ less than 100 persons; Business ownership: 697 women-owned, n/a Black-owned, n/a Hispanic-owned, 35 Asian-owned
Employment: 11.7% management, business, and financial, 3.0% computer, engineering, and science, 8.6% education, legal, community service, arts, and media, 6.0% healthcare practitioners, 18.9% service, 22.4% sales and office, 10.1% natural resources, construction, and maintenance, 19.4% production, transportation, and material moving
Income: Per capita: $21,940; Median household: $46,548; Average household: $57,197; Households with income of $100,000 or more: 11.6%; Poverty rate: 16.3%
Educational Attainment: High school diploma or higher: 87.1%; Bachelor's degree or higher: 19.3%; Graduate/professional degree or higher: 7.7%
Housing: Homeownership rate: 75.1%; Median home value: $122,100; Median year structure built: 1971; Homeowner vacancy rate: 2.4%; Median gross rent: $674 per month; Rental vacancy rate: 9.0%
Vital Statistics: Birth rate: 106.1 per 10,000 population; Death rate: 102.4 per 10,000 population; Age-adjusted cancer mortality rate: 194.1 deaths per 100,000 population
Health Insurance: 85.1% have insurance; 70.2% have private insurance; 29.9% have public insurance; 14.9% do not have insurance; 16.8% of children under 18 do not have insurance
Health Care: Physicians: 10.0 per 10,000 population; Hospital beds: 9.2 per 10,000 population; Hospital admissions: 442.4 per 10,000 population
Transportation: Commute: 90.7% car, 0.2% public transportation, 3.8% walk, 4.1% work from home; Median travel time to work: 22.8 minutes
Presidential Election: 33.9% Obama, 63.9% Romney (2012)
National and State Parks: Mohican State Forest; Mohican State Park

Additional Information Contacts

Ashland Government. . . . . (419) 289-0000
http://www.ashlandcounty.org

Ashland County Communities

ASHLAND (city). County seat. Covers a land area of 11.169 square miles and a water area of 0.062 square miles. Located at 40.87° N. Lat; 82.32° W. Long. Elevation is 1,066 feet.
History: Ashland was platted in 1815 by William Montgomery, who called it Uniontown. In 1822 the town was renamed Ashland, for Henry Clay's estate at Lexington, Kentucky. A memorial to Johnny Appleseed, who often came through Ashland, was erected in 1915 through the donations of Ashland County children.
Population: 20,362; Growth (since 2000): -4.2%; Density: 1,823.1 persons per square mile; Race: 95.8% White, 1.4% Black/African American, 1.0% Asian, 0.1% American Indian/Alaska Native, 0.1% Native Hawaiian/Other Pacific Islander, 1.3% Two or more races, 1.2% Hispanic of any race; Average household size: 2.28; Median age: 36.1; Age under 18: 21.0%; Age 65 and over: 17.7%; Males per 100 females: 88.1; Marriage status: 33.0% never married, 47.5% now married, 1.2% separated, 7.5% widowed, 11.9% divorced; Foreign born: 3.9%; Speak English only: 95.1%; With disability: 13.3%; Veterans: 9.4%; Ancestry: 31.1% German, 12.5% Irish, 11.0% American, 10.3% English, 6.0% Italian
Employment: 12.3% management, business, and financial, 3.0% computer, engineering, and science, 12.5% education, legal, community service, arts, and media, 4.8% healthcare practitioners, 19.8% service, 25.9% sales and office, 6.1% natural resources, construction, and maintenance, 15.6% production, transportation, and material moving
Income: Per capita: $20,983; Median household: $40,219; Average household: $52,194; Households with income of $100,000 or more: 12.2%; Poverty rate: 16.3%
Educational Attainment: High school diploma or higher: 87.7%; Bachelor's degree or higher: 27.7%; Graduate/professional degree or higher: 12.8%

School District(s)

Ashland City (PK-12)
2012-13 Enrollment: 3,241 . . . . (419) 289-1117
Ashland County Community Academy (09-12)
2012-13 Enrollment: 108. . . . . (419) 903-0295
Ashland County-West Holmes (10-12)
2012-13 Enrollment: n/a . . . . (419) 289-3313
Crestview Local (PK-12)
2012-13 Enrollment: 1,172 . . . . (419) 895-1700
Mapleton Local (PK-12)
2012-13 Enrollment: 879. . . . . (419) 945-2188

Four-year College(s)

Ashland University (Private, Not-for-profit, Brethren Church)
Fall 2013 Enrollment: 5,979 . . . . (419) 289-4142
2013-14 Tuition: In-state $29,836; Out-of-state $29,836

Vocational/Technical School(s)

Ashland County-West Holmes Career Center (Public)
Fall 2013 Enrollment: 74 . . . . (419) 289-3313
2013-14 Tuition: $4,810

Housing: Homeownership rate: 61.9%; Median home value: $101,600; Median year structure built: 1962; Homeowner vacancy rate: 3.2%; Median gross rent: $688 per month; Rental vacancy rate: 10.1%
Health Insurance: 86.3% have insurance; 69.6% have private insurance; 31.2% have public insurance; 13.7% do not have insurance; 8.3% of children under 18 do not have insurance
Hospitals: Samaritan Regional Health System (110 beds)
Safety: Violent crime rate: 6.9 per 10,000 population; Property crime rate: 255.6 per 10,000 population
Newspapers: Ashland Times-Gazette (daily circulation 11900)
Transportation: Commute: 89.4% car, 0.0% public transportation, 6.4% walk, 3.4% work from home; Median travel time to work: 17.7 minutes

Additional Information Contacts

City of Ashland . . . . (419) 289-8622
http://www.ashland-ohio.com

BAILEY LAKES (village). Covers a land area of 0.388 square miles and a water area of 0.075 square miles. Located at 40.95° N. Lat; 82.36° W. Long. Elevation is 1,053 feet.
Population: 371; Growth (since 2000): -6.5%; Density: 955.9 persons per square mile; Race: 97.0% White, 1.6% Black/African American, 0.0%

Asian, 0.0% American Indian/Alaska Native, 0.0% Native Hawaiian/Other Pacific Islander, 1.3% Two or more races, 0.3% Hispanic of any race; Average household size: 2.39; Median age: 43.5; Age under 18: 22.4%; Age 65 and over: 17.5%; Males per 100 females: 94.2

Housing: Homeownership rate: 61.3%; Homeowner vacancy rate: 2.1%; Rental vacancy rate: 9.0%

CINNAMON LAKE (CDP). Covers a land area of 1.618 square miles and a water area of 0.225 square miles. Located at 40.98° N. Lat; 82.19° W. Long.

Population: 1,243; Growth (since 2000): n/a; Density: 768.2 persons per square mile; Race: 98.2% White, 0.6% Black/African American, 0.2% Asian, 0.2% American Indian/Alaska Native, 0.0% Native Hawaiian/Other Pacific Islander, 0.7% Two or more races, 0.6% Hispanic of any race; Average household size: 2.64; Median age: 41.0; Age under 18: 25.0%; Age 65 and over: 14.5%; Males per 100 females: 97.9

Housing: Homeownership rate: 90.6%; Homeowner vacancy rate: 5.3%; Rental vacancy rate: 4.3%

HAYESVILLE (village). Covers a land area of 0.738 square miles and a water area of 0.003 square miles. Located at 40.78° N. Lat; 82.26° W. Long. Elevation is 1,247 feet.

History: Hayesville was laid out in 1830 by Linus Hayes, a tavern owner, and Reverend John Cox. It was in Hayesville that William McKinley pleaded his first law case.

Population: 448; Growth (since 2000): 28.7%; Density: 607.1 persons per square mile; Race: 98.4% White, 0.0% Black/African American, 0.2% Asian, 0.0% American Indian/Alaska Native, 0.0% Native Hawaiian/Other Pacific Islander, 1.3% Two or more races, 0.4% Hispanic of any race; Average household size: 2.43; Median age: 42.8; Age under 18: 23.7%; Age 65 and over: 17.9%; Males per 100 females: 109.3

School District(s)

Hillsdale Local (PK-12)
2012-13 Enrollment: 959. . . . . (419) 368-8231

Housing: Homeownership rate: 84.2%; Homeowner vacancy rate: 0.6%; Rental vacancy rate: 3.3%

JEROMESVILLE (village). Covers a land area of 0.363 square miles and a water area of <.001 square miles. Located at 40.80° N. Lat; 82.20° W. Long. Elevation is 1,007 feet.

History: Jeromesville was named for a French trader, Jean Baptiste Jerome, who lived here. The town grew as a rural trading center.

Population: 562; Growth (since 2000): 17.6%; Density: 1,548.8 persons per square mile; Race: 99.1% White, 0.0% Black/African American, 0.0% Asian, 0.9% American Indian/Alaska Native, 0.0% Native Hawaiian/Other Pacific Islander, 0.0% Two or more races, 1.1% Hispanic of any race; Average household size: 2.70; Median age: 33.3; Age under 18: 32.4%; Age 65 and over: 10.7%; Males per 100 females: 98.6

School District(s)

Hillsdale Local (PK-12)
2012-13 Enrollment: 959. . . . . (419) 368-8231

Housing: Homeownership rate: 65.0%; Homeowner vacancy rate: 4.3%; Rental vacancy rate: 3.9%

LOUDONVILLE (village). Covers a land area of 2.599 square miles and a water area of 0.024 square miles. Located at 40.63° N. Lat; 82.23° W. Long. Elevation is 971 feet.

History: Loudonville was laid out in 1814 and named for a Revolutionary War soldier, James Louden Priest, who helped to survey the town. An early industry was the building of buses and ambulances.

Population: 2,641; Growth (since 2000): -9.1%; Density: 1,016.2 persons per square mile; Race: 97.8% White, 0.6% Black/African American, 0.4% Asian, 0.1% American Indian/Alaska Native, 0.0% Native Hawaiian/Other Pacific Islander, 0.5% Two or more races, 1.0% Hispanic of any race; Average household size: 2.35; Median age: 43.0; Age under 18: 22.2%; Age 65 and over: 20.0%; Males per 100 females: 87.6; Marriage status: 27.7% never married, 53.3% now married, 1.5% separated, 7.1% widowed, 11.8% divorced; Foreign born: 0.3%; Speak English only: 99.6%; With disability: 14.6%; Veterans: 11.3%; Ancestry: 35.2% German, 16.9% American, 11.9% Irish, 5.5% English, 3.2% European

Employment: 5.3% management, business, and financial, 4.4% computer, engineering, and science, 5.3% education, legal, community service, arts, and media, 6.3% healthcare practitioners, 16.4% service, 28.2% sales and office, 12.9% natural resources, construction, and maintenance, 21.3% production, transportation, and material moving

Income: Per capita: $18,680; Median household: $40,795; Average household: $48,543; Households with income of $100,000 or more: 6.8%; Poverty rate: 21.8%

Educational Attainment: High school diploma or higher: 86.1%; Bachelor's degree or higher: 13.0%; Graduate/professional degree or higher: 4.6%

School District(s)

Loudonville-Perrysville Exempted Village (PK-12)
2012-13 Enrollment: 1,122 . . . . (419) 994-3912

Housing: Homeownership rate: 66.2%; Median home value: $96,600; Median year structure built: 1954; Homeowner vacancy rate: 2.7%; Median gross rent: $622 per month; Rental vacancy rate: 11.9%

Health Insurance: 92.3% have insurance; 67.4% have private insurance; 41.0% have public insurance; 7.7% do not have insurance; 0.0% of children under 18 do not have insurance

Safety: Violent crime rate: 0.0 per 10,000 population; Property crime rate: 160.6 per 10,000 population

Newspapers: Loudonville Times (weekly circulation 2500)

Transportation: Commute: 90.5% car, 1.4% public transportation, 5.8% walk, 2.0% work from home; Median travel time to work: 19.3 minutes

MIFFLIN (village). Covers a land area of 0.183 square miles and a water area of 0 square miles. Located at 40.77° N. Lat; 82.36° W. Long. Elevation is 1,066 feet.

Population: 137; Growth (since 2000): -4.9%; Density: 749.7 persons per square mile; Race: 99.3% White, 0.0% Black/African American, 0.0% Asian, 0.0% American Indian/Alaska Native, 0.0% Native Hawaiian/Other Pacific Islander, 0.0% Two or more races, 0.7% Hispanic of any race; Average household size: 2.40; Median age: 39.3; Age under 18: 25.5%; Age 65 and over: 15.3%; Males per 100 females: 93.0

Housing: Homeownership rate: 66.7%; Homeowner vacancy rate: 0.0%; Rental vacancy rate: 13.6%

NOVA (unincorporated postal area)

ZCTA: 44859

Covers a land area of 30.319 square miles and a water area of 0.204 square miles. Located at 41.02° N. Lat; 82.33° W. Long. Elevation is 1,129 feet.

Population: 1,737; Growth (since 2000): -1.3%; Density: 57.3 persons per square mile; Race: 98.8% White, 0.1% Black/African American, 0.1% Asian, 0.2% American Indian/Alaska Native, 0.0% Native Hawaiian/Other Pacific Islander, 0.7% Two or more races, 0.6% Hispanic of any race; Average household size: 2.69; Median age: 41.7; Age under 18: 24.1%; Age 65 and over: 13.7%; Males per 100 females: 103.4

Housing: Homeownership rate: 91.8%; Homeowner vacancy rate: 1.5%; Rental vacancy rate: 1.9%

PERRYSVILLE (village). Covers a land area of 0.787 square miles and a water area of 0 square miles. Located at 40.66° N. Lat; 82.31° W. Long. Elevation is 988 feet.

Population: 735; Growth (since 2000): -9.9%; Density: 933.4 persons per square mile; Race: 97.3% White, 0.3% Black/African American, 0.4% Asian, 0.1% American Indian/Alaska Native, 0.0% Native Hawaiian/Other Pacific Islander, 1.2% Two or more races, 1.5% Hispanic of any race; Average household size: 2.25; Median age: 37.8; Age under 18: 24.6%; Age 65 and over: 14.3%; Males per 100 females: 95.5

School District(s)

Loudonville-Perrysville Exempted Village (PK-12)
2012-13 Enrollment: 1,122 . . . . (419) 994-3912

Housing: Homeownership rate: 62.6%; Homeowner vacancy rate: 5.1%; Rental vacancy rate: 14.7%

Safety: Violent crime rate: 0.0 per 10,000 population; Property crime rate: 292.1 per 10,000 population

POLK (village). Covers a land area of 1.012 square miles and a water area of 0.024 square miles. Located at 40.95° N. Lat; 82.21° W. Long. Elevation is 1,263 feet.

Population: 336; Growth (since 2000): -5.9%; Density: 332.0 persons per square mile; Race: 97.0% White, 0.3% Black/African American, 0.0% Asian, 0.0% American Indian/Alaska Native, 0.0% Native Hawaiian/Other Pacific Islander, 1.8% Two or more races, 2.4% Hispanic of any race; Average household size: 2.60; Median age: 39.3; Age under 18: 27.1%; Age 65 and over: 11.3%; Males per 100 females: 90.9

Housing: Homeownership rate: 80.6%; Homeowner vacancy rate: 1.9%; Rental vacancy rate: 0.0%

SAVANNAH (village). Covers a land area of 0.572 square miles and a water area of 0.009 square miles. Located at 40.97° N. Lat; 82.37° W. Long. Elevation is 1,102 feet.
Population: 413; Growth (since 2000): 11.0%; Density: 722.0 persons per square mile; Race: 97.3% White, 1.2% Black/African American, 0.0% Asian, 1.0% American Indian/Alaska Native, 0.0% Native Hawaiian/Other Pacific Islander, 0.5% Two or more races, 1.7% Hispanic of any race; Average household size: 2.97; Median age: 33.3; Age under 18: 29.8%; Age 65 and over: 9.4%; Males per 100 females: 97.6
Housing: Homeownership rate: 76.2%; Homeowner vacancy rate: 0.9%; Rental vacancy rate: 15.4%

SULLIVAN (unincorporated postal area)
ZCTA: 44880
Covers a land area of 30.787 square miles and a water area of 0.229 square miles. Located at 41.03° N. Lat; 82.22° W. Long. Elevation is 1,125 feet.
Population: 2,864; Growth (since 2000): 21.4%; Density: 93.0 persons per square mile; Race: 98.1% White, 0.6% Black/African American, 0.1% Asian, 0.2% American Indian/Alaska Native, 0.0% Native Hawaiian/Other Pacific Islander, 0.9% Two or more races, 1.3% Hispanic of any race; Average household size: 2.89; Median age: 39.2; Age under 18: 27.9%; Age 65 and over: 12.1%; Males per 100 females: 105.2; Marriage status: 29.5% never married, 57.8% now married, 2.1% separated, 6.5% widowed, 6.2% divorced; Foreign born: 1.8%; Speak English only: 95.1%; With disability: 11.6%; Veterans: 11.1%; Ancestry: 46.1% German, 15.0% Irish, 14.7% French, 10.0% American, 9.4% Polish
Employment: 4.2% management, business, and financial, 0.0% computer, engineering, and science, 3.9% education, legal, community service, arts, and media, 9.2% healthcare practitioners, 21.9% service, 17.0% sales and office, 14.0% natural resources, construction, and maintenance, 29.8% production, transportation, and material moving
Income: Per capita: $17,246; Median household: $43,368; Average household: $50,879; Households with income of $100,000 or more: 7.8%; Poverty rate: 11.2%
Educational Attainment: High school diploma or higher: 79.2%; Bachelor's degree or higher: 5.8%; Graduate/professional degree or higher: 3.6%

School District(s)

Black River Local (PK-12)
2012-13 Enrollment: 1,225 . . . . (419) 736-3300
Housing: Homeownership rate: 88.5%; Median home value: $143,000; Median year structure built: 1990; Homeowner vacancy rate: 2.0%; Median gross rent: $1,112 per month; Rental vacancy rate: 5.7%
Health Insurance: 85.8% have insurance; 71.6% have private insurance; 36.7% have public insurance; 14.2% do not have insurance; 2.3% of children under 18 do not have insurance
Transportation: Commute: 92.7% car, 0.0% public transportation, 2.8% walk, 3.1% work from home; Median travel time to work: 30.9 minutes

Ashtabula County

Located in northeastern Ohio; bounded on the north by Lake Erie; crossed by the Grand and Ashtabula Rivers. Covers a land area of 701.931 square miles, a water area of 665.971 square miles, and is located in the Eastern Time Zone at 41.91° N. Lat., 80.75° W. Long. The county was founded in 1807. County seat is Jefferson.

Ashtabula County is part of the Ashtabula, OH Micropolitan Statistical Area. The entire metro area includes: Ashtabula County, OH

Weather Station: Dorset Elevation: 979 feet

	Jan	Feb	Mar	Apr	May	Jun	Jul	Aug	Sep	Oct	Nov	Dec
High	33	35	45	58	68	77	81	80	74	61	49	37
Low	16	17	25	35	44	54	58	57	50	40	33	22
Precip	2.6	2.2	2.9	3.6	3.9	4.5	4.8	3.8	4.4	4.0	3.7	3.2
Snow	21.2	13.5	11.6	3.5	tr	0.0	0.0	0.0	0.0	0.5	8.3	20.4

High and Low temperatures in degrees Fahrenheit; Precipitation and Snow in inches

Population: 101,497; Growth (since 2000): -1.2%; Density: 144.6 persons per square mile; Race: 92.7% White, 3.5% Black/African American, 0.4% Asian, 0.2% American Indian/Alaska Native, 0.0% Native Hawaiian/Other Pacific Islander, 2.1% two or more races, 3.4% Hispanic of any race; Average household size: 2.50; Median age: 41.0; Age under 18: 23.7%; Age 65 and over: 15.6%; Males per 100 females: 99.8; Marriage status: 26.7% never married, 50.7% now married, 1.5% separated, 7.7% widowed, 15.0% divorced; Foreign born: 1.4%; Speak English only: 94.3%; With disability: 14.8%; Veterans: 12.0%; Ancestry: 23.3% German, 15.7% Irish, 12.7% English, 11.8% American, 10.6% Italian
Religion: Six largest groups: 13.9% Catholicism, 5.0% Methodist/Pietist, 3.7% Baptist, 2.7% Presbyterian-Reformed, 2.5% Lutheran, 2.2% European Free-Church
Economy: Unemployment rate: 5.2%; Leading industries: 16.9% retail trade; 12.1% other services (except public administration); 11.7% accommodation and food services; Farms: 1,099 totaling 165,967 acres; Company size: 0 employ 1,000 or more persons, 1 employs 500 to 999 persons, 48 employ 100 to 499 persons, 1,907 employ less than 100 persons; Business ownership: 2,035 women-owned, n/a Black-owned, n/a Hispanic-owned, 97 Asian-owned
Employment: 9.3% management, business, and financial, 2.1% computer, engineering, and science, 6.9% education, legal, community service, arts, and media, 5.9% healthcare practitioners, 19.1% service, 22.8% sales and office, 11.3% natural resources, construction, and maintenance, 22.7% production, transportation, and material moving
Income: Per capita: $20,011; Median household: $40,516; Average household: $50,023; Households with income of $100,000 or more: 10.5%; Poverty rate: 18.7%
Educational Attainment: High school diploma or higher: 85.1%; Bachelor's degree or higher: 12.6%; Graduate/professional degree or higher: 4.2%
Housing: Homeownership rate: 71.8%; Median home value: $110,800; Median year structure built: 1959; Homeowner vacancy rate: 2.9%; Median gross rent: $616 per month; Rental vacancy rate: 10.1%
Vital Statistics: Birth rate: 110.8 per 10,000 population; Death rate: 108.9 per 10,000 population; Age-adjusted cancer mortality rate: 224.7 deaths per 100,000 population
Health Insurance: 86.1% have insurance; 62.9% have private insurance; 36.7% have public insurance; 13.9% do not have insurance; 7.8% of children under 18 do not have insurance
Health Care: Physicians: 6.7 per 10,000 population; Hospital beds: 31.6 per 10,000 population; Hospital admissions: 1,007.7 per 10,000 population
Air Quality Index: 94.0% good, 6.0% moderate, 0.0% unhealthy for sensitive individuals, 0.0% unhealthy (percent of days)
Transportation: Commute: 92.9% car, 0.7% public transportation, 1.9% walk, 3.4% work from home; Median travel time to work: 25.0 minutes
Presidential Election: 55.0% Obama, 42.8% Romney (2012)
National and State Parks: Geneva-On-The-Lake State Park; Orwell State Wildlife Area; Pymatuning State Park
Additional Information Contacts
Ashtabula Government . . . . (440) 576-3750
http://www.co.ashtabula.oh.us

Ashtabula County Communities

ANDOVER (village). Covers a land area of 1.366 square miles and a water area of 0 square miles. Located at 41.61° N. Lat; 80.57° W. Long. Elevation is 1,093 feet.
Population: 1,145; Growth (since 2000): -9.8%; Density: 838.2 persons per square mile; Race: 95.5% White, 2.8% Black/African American, 0.1% Asian, 0.3% American Indian/Alaska Native, 0.0% Native Hawaiian/Other Pacific Islander, 1.4% Two or more races, 1.7% Hispanic of any race; Average household size: 2.44; Median age: 44.2; Age under 18: 22.9%; Age 65 and over: 21.4%; Males per 100 females: 83.2

School District(s)

Pymatuning Valley Local (PK-12)
2012-13 Enrollment: 1,300 . . . . (440) 293-6488
Housing: Homeownership rate: 59.1%; Homeowner vacancy rate: 4.3%; Rental vacancy rate: 7.2%
Newspapers: Pymatuning Area News (weekly circulation 2200)

ASHTABULA (city). Covers a land area of 7.735 square miles and a water area of 0.171 square miles. Located at 41.88° N. Lat; 80.80° W. Long. Elevation is 669 feet.
History: The surveying party of Moses Cleaveland stopped here in 1796, and two members of the group remained as settlers. The town that was incorporated in 1831 was named Ashtabula for the river that emptied into Lake Erie at the site. Ashtabula developed as a shipping center for coal and iron ore, and as a fishing and farm trading center. Strong abolitionist sentiment made it a key station on the Underground Railroad.

Population: 19,124; Growth (since 2000): -8.8%; Density: 2,472.5 persons per square mile; Race: 82.0% White, 8.9% Black/African American, 0.3% Asian, 0.4% American Indian/Alaska Native, 0.0% Native Hawaiian/Other Pacific Islander, 5.0% Two or more races, 9.3% Hispanic of any race; Average household size: 2.42; Median age: 37.0; Age under 18: 26.4%; Age 65 and over: 14.7%; Males per 100 females: 90.9; Marriage status: 31.6% never married, 43.4% now married, 1.7% separated, 7.9% widowed, 17.1% divorced; Foreign born: 1.1%; Speak English only: 93.3%; With disability: 17.0%; Veterans: 9.9%; Ancestry: 16.1% Italian, 16.0% German, 13.5% American, 11.8% Irish, 10.3% English
Employment: 6.7% management, business, and financial, 1.4% computer, engineering, and science, 6.6% education, legal, community service, arts, and media, 4.7% healthcare practitioners, 24.5% service, 24.3% sales and office, 7.7% natural resources, construction, and maintenance, 24.0% production, transportation, and material moving
Income: Per capita: $16,356; Median household: $27,876; Average household: $38,007; Households with income of $100,000 or more: 5.1%; Poverty rate: 32.9%
Educational Attainment: High school diploma or higher: 83.5%; Bachelor's degree or higher: 8.9%; Graduate/professional degree or higher: 4.5%

School District(s)

Ashtabula Area City (PK-12)
2012-13 Enrollment: 3,862 . . . . (440) 992-1200
Buckeye Local (PK-12)
2012-13 Enrollment: 1,763 . . . . (440) 998-4411

Four-year College(s)

Kent State University at Ashtabula (Public)
Fall 2013 Enrollment: 2,341 . . . . (440) 964-3322
2013-14 Tuition: In-state $5,554; Out-of-state $13,514

Housing: Homeownership rate: 52.2%; Median home value: $78,700; Median year structure built: 1950; Homeowner vacancy rate: 4.9%; Median gross rent: $621 per month; Rental vacancy rate: 11.6%
Health Insurance: 85.7% have insurance; 50.0% have private insurance; 48.4% have public insurance; 14.3% do not have insurance; 6.8% of children under 18 do not have insurance
Hospitals: Ashtabula County Medical Center (234 beds)
Newspapers: Star-Beacon (daily circulation 17600)
Transportation: Commute: 91.3% car, 0.8% public transportation, 3.0% walk, 2.4% work from home; Median travel time to work: 19.4 minutes
Additional Information Contacts
City of Ashtabula . . . . (440) 992-7103
http://ci.ashtabula.oh.us

AUSTINBURG (CDP). Covers a land area of 3.283 square miles and a water area of 0 square miles. Located at 41.77° N. Lat; 80.86° W. Long. Elevation is 810 feet.
Population: 516; Growth (since 2000): n/a; Density: 157.2 persons per square mile; Race: 97.5% White, 0.8% Black/African American, 0.4% Asian, 0.6% American Indian/Alaska Native, 0.0% Native Hawaiian/Other Pacific Islander, 0.8% Two or more races, 1.4% Hispanic of any race; Average household size: 2.28; Median age: 52.5; Age under 18: 15.7%; Age 65 and over: 31.2%; Males per 100 females: 76.1

School District(s)

Geneva Area City (PK-12)
2012-13 Enrollment: 2,570 . . . . (440) 466-4831

Housing: Homeownership rate: 59.6%; Homeowner vacancy rate: 0.0%; Rental vacancy rate: 2.8%

CONNEAUT (city). Covers a land area of 26.355 square miles and a water area of 0.066 square miles. Located at 41.93° N. Lat; 80.57° W. Long. Elevation is 650 feet.
History: Conneaut was settled in 1799 by Thomas Montgomery and Aaron Wright. The village grew around the natural harbor, which attracted shipping of coal and ores.
Population: 12,841; Growth (since 2000): 2.9%; Density: 487.2 persons per square mile; Race: 89.8% White, 7.5% Black/African American, 0.4% Asian, 0.2% American Indian/Alaska Native, 0.0% Native Hawaiian/Other Pacific Islander, 1.8% Two or more races, 1.8% Hispanic of any race; Average household size: 2.37; Median age: 39.6; Age under 18: 20.2%; Age 65 and over: 15.7%; Males per 100 females: 119.5; Marriage status: 32.5% never married, 45.6% now married, 1.5% separated, 7.1% widowed, 14.8% divorced; Foreign born: 1.0%; Speak English only: 96.8%; With disability: 14.1%; Veterans: 12.4%; Ancestry: 25.1% German, 17.5% Irish, 13.0% American, 10.4% Italian, 10.2% English
Employment: 7.5% management, business, and financial, 1.8% computer, engineering, and science, 8.0% education, legal, community service, arts, and media, 3.5% healthcare practitioners, 19.6% service, 26.0% sales and office, 9.6% natural resources, construction, and maintenance, 24.0% production, transportation, and material moving
Income: Per capita: $16,212; Median household: $33,065; Average household: $41,085; Households with income of $100,000 or more: 6.3%; Poverty rate: 22.8%
Educational Attainment: High school diploma or higher: 84.6%; Bachelor's degree or higher: 9.7%; Graduate/professional degree or higher: 3.5%

School District(s)

Conneaut Area City (PK-12)
2012-13 Enrollment: 1,786 . . . . (440) 593-7200

Housing: Homeownership rate: 66.2%; Median home value: $87,200; Median year structure built: 1944; Homeowner vacancy rate: 4.2%; Median gross rent: $582 per month; Rental vacancy rate: 11.1%
Health Insurance: 86.7% have insurance; 62.6% have private insurance; 41.0% have public insurance; 13.3% do not have insurance; 3.1% of children under 18 do not have insurance
Hospitals: University Hospitals Conneaut Medical Center (86 beds)
Safety: Violent crime rate: 7.8 per 10,000 population; Property crime rate: 220.2 per 10,000 population
Transportation: Commute: 91.8% car, 1.3% public transportation, 2.1% walk, 3.6% work from home; Median travel time to work: 22.4 minutes
Additional Information Contacts
City of Conneaut . . . . (440) 593-7401
http://www.conneaut.net

DORSET (unincorporated postal area)
ZCTA: 44032
Covers a land area of 40.250 square miles and a water area of 0.028 square miles. Located at 41.67° N. Lat; 80.67° W. Long. Elevation is 981 feet.
Population: 1,557; Growth (since 2000): 4.2%; Density: 38.7 persons per square mile; Race: 94.3% White, 1.3% Black/African American, 1.2% Asian, 0.9% American Indian/Alaska Native, 0.0% Native Hawaiian/Other Pacific Islander, 2.2% Two or more races, 0.6% Hispanic of any race; Average household size: 2.74; Median age: 42.4; Age under 18: 23.0%; Age 65 and over: 12.8%; Males per 100 females: 105.4
Housing: Homeownership rate: 86.1%; Homeowner vacancy rate: 1.6%; Rental vacancy rate: 3.7%

EDGEWOOD (CDP). Covers a land area of 6.831 square miles and a water area of 0.006 square miles. Located at 41.88° N. Lat; 80.75° W. Long. Elevation is 682 feet.
Population: 4,432; Growth (since 2000): -6.9%; Density: 648.8 persons per square mile; Race: 94.2% White, 1.9% Black/African American, 0.5% Asian, 0.1% American Indian/Alaska Native, 0.0% Native Hawaiian/Other Pacific Islander, 2.6% Two or more races, 3.2% Hispanic of any race; Average household size: 2.29; Median age: 44.0; Age under 18: 21.7%; Age 65 and over: 18.2%; Males per 100 females: 97.7; Marriage status: 26.2% never married, 52.7% now married, 0.7% separated, 8.7% widowed, 12.4% divorced; Foreign born: 1.0%; Speak English only: 98.7%; With disability: 19.5%; Veterans: 13.9%; Ancestry: 24.0% German, 20.2% Italian, 14.4% Irish, 12.5% American, 10.1% English
Employment: 8.9% management, business, and financial, 3.4% computer, engineering, and science, 7.0% education, legal, community service, arts, and media, 6.1% healthcare practitioners, 23.3% service, 24.5% sales and office, 8.1% natural resources, construction, and maintenance, 18.7% production, transportation, and material moving
Income: Per capita: $20,894; Median household: $35,026; Average household: $48,452; Households with income of $100,000 or more: 12.5%; Poverty rate: 20.2%
Educational Attainment: High school diploma or higher: 84.8%; Bachelor's degree or higher: 8.3%; Graduate/professional degree or higher: 2.9%
Housing: Homeownership rate: 74.4%; Median home value: $85,800; Median year structure built: 1958; Homeowner vacancy rate: 1.7%; Median gross rent: $588 per month; Rental vacancy rate: 10.1%
Health Insurance: 87.4% have insurance; 63.2% have private insurance; 42.9% have public insurance; 12.6% do not have insurance; 7.7% of children under 18 do not have insurance
Transportation: Commute: 92.9% car, 0.6% public transportation, 3.7% walk, 2.6% work from home; Median travel time to work: 19.3 minutes

GENEVA (city). Covers a land area of 4.136 square miles and a water area of 0 square miles. Located at 41.80° N. Lat; 80.95° W. Long. Elevation is 673 feet.
History: Geneva was founded in 1805. In Geneva's cemetery is a monument to Platt R. Spencer (1800-1864) who founded business schools in many cities and created the Spencerian penmanship system.
Population: 6,215; Growth (since 2000): -5.8%; Density: 1,502.7 persons per square mile; Race: 94.3% White, 1.7% Black/African American, 0.5% Asian, 0.1% American Indian/Alaska Native, 0.0% Native Hawaiian/Other Pacific Islander, 1.7% Two or more races, 5.5% Hispanic of any race; Average household size: 2.36; Median age: 40.9; Age under 18: 22.2%; Age 65 and over: 17.8%; Males per 100 females: 95.5; Marriage status: 27.2% never married, 46.6% now married, 1.4% separated, 10.5% widowed, 15.7% divorced; Foreign born: 2.8%; Speak English only: 90.4%; With disability: 16.6%; Veterans: 14.0%; Ancestry: 27.2% German, 14.9% Irish, 13.4% English, 7.7% Italian, 6.9% American
Employment: 6.9% management, business, and financial, 0.3% computer, engineering, and science, 4.5% education, legal, community service, arts, and media, 5.6% healthcare practitioners, 19.0% service, 28.4% sales and office, 12.1% natural resources, construction, and maintenance, 23.3% production, transportation, and material moving
Income: Per capita: $19,504; Median household: $41,305; Average household: $48,412; Households with income of $100,000 or more: 9.3%; Poverty rate: 15.5%
Educational Attainment: High school diploma or higher: 85.2%; Bachelor's degree or higher: 13.6%; Graduate/professional degree or higher: 4.1%

School District(s)

Geneva Area City (PK-12)
2012-13 Enrollment: 2,570 . . . . (440) 466-4831
Housing: Homeownership rate: 63.3%; Median home value: $103,700; Median year structure built: 1955; Homeowner vacancy rate: 4.4%; Median gross rent: $583 per month; Rental vacancy rate: 11.3%
Health Insurance: 88.7% have insurance; 63.2% have private insurance; 38.3% have public insurance; 11.3% do not have insurance; 5.2% of children under 18 do not have insurance
Hospitals: UHHS Memorial Hospital of Geneva (46 beds)
Transportation: Commute: 96.0% car, 1.2% public transportation, 0.2% walk, 1.4% work from home; Median travel time to work: 24.9 minutes

GENEVA-ON-THE-LAKE (village). Covers a land area of 2.257 square miles and a water area of 0.021 square miles. Located at 41.86° N. Lat; 80.95° W. Long. Elevation is 604 feet.
Population: 1,288; Growth (since 2000): -16.6%; Density: 570.6 persons per square mile; Race: 95.9% White, 0.2% Black/African American, 0.2% Asian, 0.2% American Indian/Alaska Native, 0.2% Native Hawaiian/Other Pacific Islander, 2.4% Two or more races, 3.2% Hispanic of any race; Average household size: 2.19; Median age: 42.7; Age under 18: 19.3%; Age 65 and over: 13.8%; Males per 100 females: 102.8
Housing: Homeownership rate: 56.2%; Homeowner vacancy rate: 5.1%; Rental vacancy rate: 14.0%

JEFFERSON (village). County seat. Covers a land area of 2.519 square miles and a water area of 0 square miles. Located at 41.74° N. Lat; 80.77° W. Long. Elevation is 961 feet.
History: Jefferson was named by Gideon Granger, Postmaster General in Jefferson's cabinet. The Republican Party's first national platform was written here at the law office of Joshua R. Giddings.
Population: 3,120; Growth (since 2000): -12.7%; Density: 1,238.5 persons per square mile; Race: 97.1% White, 1.1% Black/African American, 0.4% Asian, 0.1% American Indian/Alaska Native, 0.0% Native Hawaiian/Other Pacific Islander, 1.3% Two or more races, 1.0% Hispanic of any race; Average household size: 2.30; Median age: 43.0; Age under 18: 22.5%; Age 65 and over: 20.4%; Males per 100 females: 83.9; Marriage status: 27.6% never married, 38.2% now married, 1.0% separated, 14.7% widowed, 19.5% divorced; Foreign born: 0.4%; Speak English only: 95.9%; With disability: 17.0%; Veterans: 8.6%; Ancestry: 29.5% German, 18.0% Irish, 13.7% English, 9.9% American, 6.9% Italian
Employment: 5.3% management, business, and financial, 0.0% computer, engineering, and science, 15.2% education, legal, community service, arts, and media, 10.8% healthcare practitioners, 19.1% service, 20.5% sales and office, 8.7% natural resources, construction, and maintenance, 20.3% production, transportation, and material moving
Income: Per capita: $22,571; Median household: $42,604; Average household: $51,590; Households with income of $100,000 or more: 14.2%; Poverty rate: 10.9%
Educational Attainment: High school diploma or higher: 88.1%; Bachelor's degree or higher: 20.9%; Graduate/professional degree or higher: 10.3%

School District(s)

Ashtabula County Technical and Career Center (05-12)
2012-13 Enrollment: n/a . . . . (614) 995-1985
Jefferson Area Local (PK-12)
2012-13 Enrollment: 1,755 . . . . (440) 576-9180

Vocational/Technical School(s)

Ashtabula County Technical and Career Campus (Public)
Fall 2013 Enrollment: 159 . . . . (440) 576-6015
2013-14 Tuition: $9,275
Housing: Homeownership rate: 61.7%; Median home value: $99,000; Median year structure built: 1971; Homeowner vacancy rate: 3.3%; Median gross rent: $616 per month; Rental vacancy rate: 5.9%
Health Insurance: 89.2% have insurance; 65.8% have private insurance; 38.0% have public insurance; 10.8% do not have insurance; 0.0% of children under 18 do not have insurance
Newspapers: Gazette Newspapers (weekly circulation 13000); Gazette Newspapers (weekly circulation 31000)
Transportation: Commute: 89.2% car, 0.0% public transportation, 5.4% walk, 5.3% work from home; Median travel time to work: 21.8 minutes

KINGSVILLE (unincorporated postal area)

ZCTA: 44048

Covers a land area of 30.431 square miles and a water area of 0.042 square miles. Located at 41.85° N. Lat; 80.64° W. Long. Elevation is 791 feet.
Population: 2,565; Growth (since 2000): 0.5%; Density: 84.3 persons per square mile; Race: 97.0% White, 1.4% Black/African American, 0.2% Asian, 0.1% American Indian/Alaska Native, 0.0% Native Hawaiian/Other Pacific Islander, 1.0% Two or more races, 0.8% Hispanic of any race; Average household size: 2.66; Median age: 45.3; Age under 18: 22.6%; Age 65 and over: 19.5%; Males per 100 females: 100.5; Marriage status: 16.6% never married, 48.4% now married, 0.0% separated, 11.7% widowed, 23.4% divorced; Foreign born: 2.6%; Speak English only: 96.8%; With disability: 14.2%; Veterans: 20.3%; Ancestry: 21.8% German, 19.8% Irish, 13.2% American, 10.5% English, 9.9% Slovak
Employment: 16.1% management, business, and financial, 0.7% computer, engineering, and science, 11.4% education, legal, community service, arts, and media, 11.7% healthcare practitioners, 9.2% service, 18.8% sales and office, 9.3% natural resources, construction, and maintenance, 22.8% production, transportation, and material moving
Income: Per capita: $20,711; Median household: $45,559; Average household: $53,533; Households with income of $100,000 or more: 12.2%; Poverty rate: 14.3%
Educational Attainment: High school diploma or higher: 81.3%; Bachelor's degree or higher: 11.4%; Graduate/professional degree or higher: 4.5%

School District(s)

Buckeye Local (PK-12)
2012-13 Enrollment: 1,763 . . . . (440) 998-4411
Housing: Homeownership rate: 80.6%; Median home value: $117,800; Median year structure built: 1960; Homeowner vacancy rate: 0.8%; Median gross rent: $589 per month; Rental vacancy rate: 2.7%
Health Insurance: 93.3% have insurance; 74.0% have private insurance; 35.6% have public insurance; 6.7% do not have insurance; 2.3% of children under 18 do not have insurance
Transportation: Commute: 91.6% car, 0.0% public transportation, 2.0% walk, 6.4% work from home; Median travel time to work: 25.8 minutes

NORTH KINGSVILLE (village). Covers a land area of 8.887 square miles and a water area of 0.019 square miles. Located at 41.93° N. Lat; 80.68° W. Long. Elevation is 709 feet.
Population: 2,923; Growth (since 2000): 10.0%; Density: 328.9 persons per square mile; Race: 96.5% White, 0.7% Black/African American, 1.2% Asian, 0.1% American Indian/Alaska Native, 0.2% Native Hawaiian/Other Pacific Islander, 1.1% Two or more races, 1.5% Hispanic of any race; Average household size: 2.53; Median age: 44.8; Age under 18: 23.0%; Age 65 and over: 15.9%; Males per 100 females: 95.3; Marriage status: 23.2% never married, 59.6% now married, 0.7% separated, 5.3% widowed, 11.9% divorced; Foreign born: 0.8%; Speak English only: 98.3%;

With disability: 10.5%; Veterans: 11.0%; Ancestry: 24.1% German, 18.8% Irish, 15.9% Italian, 15.1% English, 9.0% American
Employment: 14.4% management, business, and financial, 2.4% computer, engineering, and science, 7.9% education, legal, community service, arts, and media, 9.5% healthcare practitioners, 15.0% service, 20.4% sales and office, 10.8% natural resources, construction, and maintenance, 19.7% production, transportation, and material moving
Income: Per capita: $27,459; Median household: $54,806; Average household: $64,043; Households with income of $100,000 or more: 16.6%; Poverty rate: 4.6%
Educational Attainment: High school diploma or higher: 95.3%; Bachelor's degree or higher: 18.5%; Graduate/professional degree or higher: 5.9%
Housing: Homeownership rate: 84.8%; Median home value: $124,500; Median year structure built: 1965; Homeowner vacancy rate: 1.9%; Median gross rent: $800 per month; Rental vacancy rate: 8.4%
Health Insurance: 90.5% have insurance; 80.6% have private insurance; 22.2% have public insurance; 9.5% do not have insurance; 0.8% of children under 18 do not have insurance
Transportation: Commute: 96.4% car, 0.3% public transportation, 1.0% walk, 2.0% work from home; Median travel time to work: 19.7 minutes

ORWELL (village). Covers a land area of 1.966 square miles and a water area of 0 square miles. Located at 41.54° N. Lat; 80.86° W. Long. Elevation is 889 feet.
Population: 1,660; Growth (since 2000): 9.3%; Density: 844.5 persons per square mile; Race: 94.7% White, 1.3% Black/African American, 0.2% Asian, 0.4% American Indian/Alaska Native, 0.0% Native Hawaiian/Other Pacific Islander, 3.1% Two or more races, 0.7% Hispanic of any race; Average household size: 2.52; Median age: 35.4; Age under 18: 26.2%; Age 65 and over: 13.9%; Males per 100 females: 93.7

School District(s)

Grand Valley Local (PK-12)
2012-13 Enrollment: 1,340 . . . . (440) 437-6260
Housing: Homeownership rate: 57.9%; Homeowner vacancy rate: 0.0%; Rental vacancy rate: 12.0%
Additional Information Contacts
Village of Orwell . . . . (440) 437-6459
http://www.orwellvillage.org

PIERPONT (unincorporated postal area)
ZCTA: 44082
Covers a land area of 33.880 square miles and a water area of 0.020 square miles. Located at 41.76° N. Lat; 80.57° W. Long. Elevation is 997 feet.
Population: 1,619; Growth (since 2000): 10.2%; Density: 47.8 persons per square mile; Race: 97.3% White, 1.4% Black/African American, 0.3% Asian, 0.2% American Indian/Alaska Native, 0.0% Native Hawaiian/Other Pacific Islander, 0.8% Two or more races, 1.4% Hispanic of any race; Average household size: 2.95; Median age: 38.4; Age under 18: 28.1%; Age 65 and over: 14.9%; Males per 100 females: 105.2
Housing: Homeownership rate: 83.0%; Homeowner vacancy rate: 1.7%; Rental vacancy rate: 6.0%

ROAMING SHORES (village). Covers a land area of 2.098 square miles and a water area of 0.719 square miles. Located at 41.64° N. Lat; 80.83° W. Long. Elevation is 869 feet.
Population: 1,508; Growth (since 2000): 21.7%; Density: 718.8 persons per square mile; Race: 98.6% White, 0.5% Black/African American, 0.3% Asian, 0.0% American Indian/Alaska Native, 0.0% Native Hawaiian/Other Pacific Islander, 0.6% Two or more races, 0.5% Hispanic of any race; Average household size: 2.59; Median age: 40.2; Age under 18: 24.9%; Age 65 and over: 13.5%; Males per 100 females: 102.4
Housing: Homeownership rate: 94.2%; Homeowner vacancy rate: 3.5%; Rental vacancy rate: 18.6%

ROCK CREEK (village). Covers a land area of 0.889 square miles and a water area of 0 square miles. Located at 41.66° N. Lat; 80.85° W. Long. Elevation is 804 feet.
Population: 529; Growth (since 2000): -9.4%; Density: 594.8 persons per square mile; Race: 97.5% White, 1.5% Black/African American, 0.2% Asian, 0.0% American Indian/Alaska Native, 0.0% Native Hawaiian/Other Pacific Islander, 0.8% Two or more races, 0.2% Hispanic of any race; Average household size: 2.70; Median age: 36.8; Age under 18: 27.2%; Age 65 and over: 11.3%; Males per 100 females: 101.9

School District(s)

Jefferson Area Local (PK-12)
2012-13 Enrollment: 1,755 . . . . (440) 576-9180
Housing: Homeownership rate: 68.9%; Homeowner vacancy rate: 2.1%; Rental vacancy rate: 3.1%
Hospitals: Glenbeigh (80 beds)

WILLIAMSFIELD (unincorporated postal area)
ZCTA: 44093
Covers a land area of 32.164 square miles and a water area of 0.110 square miles. Located at 41.53° N. Lat; 80.61° W. Long. Elevation is 1,135 feet.
Population: 1,467; Growth (since 2000): -3.8%; Density: 45.6 persons per square mile; Race: 97.5% White, 1.1% Black/African American, 0.1% Asian, 0.3% American Indian/Alaska Native, 0.0% Native Hawaiian/Other Pacific Islander, 1.0% Two or more races, 0.4% Hispanic of any race; Average household size: 2.65; Median age: 40.3; Age under 18: 27.4%; Age 65 and over: 14.7%; Males per 100 females: 104.6
Housing: Homeownership rate: 80.8%; Homeowner vacancy rate: 4.2%; Rental vacancy rate: 7.0%

WINDSOR (unincorporated postal area)
ZCTA: 44099
Covers a land area of 21.981 square miles and a water area of 0.085 square miles. Located at 41.55° N. Lat; 80.98° W. Long. Elevation is 827 feet.
Population: 2,314; Growth (since 2000): 40.5%; Density: 105.3 persons per square mile; Race: 98.1% White, 1.0% Black/African American, 0.3% Asian, 0.2% American Indian/Alaska Native, 0.0% Native Hawaiian/Other Pacific Islander, 0.4% Two or more races, 0.8% Hispanic of any race; Average household size: 3.37; Median age: 29.0; Age under 18: 36.8%; Age 65 and over: 7.5%; Males per 100 females: 98.3
Housing: Homeownership rate: 87.6%; Homeowner vacancy rate: 1.3%; Rental vacancy rate: 7.6%

Athens County

Located in southeastern Ohio; bounded on the southeast by the Ohio River and the West Virginia border. Covers a land area of 503.598 square miles, a water area of 4.843 square miles, and is located in the Eastern Time Zone at 39.33° N. Lat., 82.05° W. Long. The county was founded in 1805. County seat is Athens.

Athens County is part of the Athens, OH Micropolitan Statistical Area. The entire metro area includes: Athens County, OH

Population: 64,757; Growth (since 2000): 4.1%; Density: 128.6 persons per square mile; Race: 91.8% White, 2.7% Black/African American, 2.7% Asian, 0.3% American Indian/Alaska Native, 0.0% Native Hawaiian/Other Pacific Islander, 2.1% two or more races, 1.5% Hispanic of any race; Average household size: 2.35; Median age: 26.3; Age under 18: 15.8%; Age 65 and over: 10.1%; Males per 100 females: 100.3; Marriage status: 50.6% never married, 35.4% now married, 1.1% separated, 4.2% widowed, 9.8% divorced; Foreign born: 3.9%; Speak English only: 95.2%; With disability: 13.1%; Veterans: 6.6%; Ancestry: 20.1% German, 15.6% American, 12.7% Irish, 9.6% English, 4.4% Italian
Religion: Six largest groups: 4.7% Methodist/Pietist, 4.2% Baptist, 3.0% Catholicism, 2.8% Non-denominational Protestant, 2.0% Holiness, 0.7% Presbyterian-Reformed
Economy: Unemployment rate: 4.7%; Leading industries: 17.9% retail trade; 13.4% health care and social assistance; 13.3% accommodation and food services; Farms: 722 totaling 90,473 acres; Company size: 0 employ 1,000 or more persons, 0 employ 500 to 999 persons, 13 employ 100 to 499 persons, 1,066 employ less than 100 persons; Business ownership: 1,106 women-owned, n/a Black-owned, 66 Hispanic-owned, n/a Asian-owned
Employment: 8.5% management, business, and financial, 3.3% computer, engineering, and science, 18.4% education, legal, community service, arts, and media, 4.6% healthcare practitioners, 23.9% service, 23.7% sales and office, 8.4% natural resources, construction, and maintenance, 9.1% production, transportation, and material moving
Income: Per capita: $17,019; Median household: $33,823; Average household: $46,791; Households with income of $100,000 or more: 10.3%; Poverty rate: 31.7%

Educational Attainment: High school diploma or higher: 89.4%; Bachelor's degree or higher: 28.2%; Graduate/professional degree or higher: 15.6%
Housing: Homeownership rate: 56.9%; Median home value: $115,500; Median year structure built: 1975; Homeowner vacancy rate: 2.3%; Median gross rent: $689 per month; Rental vacancy rate: 7.4%
Vital Statistics: Birth rate: 79.9 per 10,000 population; Death rate: 70.5 per 10,000 population; Age-adjusted cancer mortality rate: 191.5 deaths per 100,000 population
Health Insurance: 89.3% have insurance; 71.9% have private insurance; 27.3% have public insurance; 10.7% do not have insurance; 4.9% of children under 18 do not have insurance
Health Care: Physicians: 23.1 per 10,000 population; Hospital beds: 58.6 per 10,000 population; Hospital admissions: 628.7 per 10,000 population
Air Quality Index: 86.0% good, 14.0% moderate, 0.0% unhealthy for sensitive individuals, 0.0% unhealthy (percent of days)
Transportation: Commute: 78.7% car, 0.9% public transportation, 14.5% walk, 4.3% work from home; Median travel time to work: 20.7 minutes
Presidential Election: 66.1% Obama, 31.1% Romney (2012)
National and State Parks: Gifford State Forest; Strouds Run State Park; Trimble State Wildlife Area; Waterloo State Forest
Additional Information Contacts
Athens Government .... (740) 592-3219
http://www.co.athensoh.org

Athens County Communities

ALBANY (village). Covers a land area of 1.248 square miles and a water area of 0.015 square miles. Located at 39.22° N. Lat; 82.20° W. Long. Elevation is 761 feet.
History: Albany was laid out in 1831 and named for Albany, New York.
Population: 828; Growth (since 2000): 2.5%; Density: 663.2 persons per square mile; Race: 98.3% White, 0.1% Black/African American, 0.7% Asian, 0.1% American Indian/Alaska Native, 0.0% Native Hawaiian/Other Pacific Islander, 0.4% Two or more races, 1.6% Hispanic of any race; Average household size: 2.32; Median age: 40.8; Age under 18: 21.3%; Age 65 and over: 18.6%; Males per 100 females: 84.8

School District(s)

Alexander Local (PK-12)
2012-13 Enrollment: 1,577 .... (740) 698-8831
Housing: Homeownership rate: 70.3%; Homeowner vacancy rate: 5.0%; Rental vacancy rate: 14.9%
Safety: Violent crime rate: 0.0 per 10,000 population; Property crime rate: 250.9 per 10,000 population

AMESVILLE (village). Covers a land area of 0.219 square miles and a water area of 0 square miles. Located at 39.40° N. Lat; 81.95° W. Long. Elevation is 633 feet.
Population: 154; Growth (since 2000): -16.3%; Density: 703.8 persons per square mile; Race: 88.3% White, 3.2% Black/African American, 4.5% Asian, 0.6% American Indian/Alaska Native, 0.0% Native Hawaiian/Other Pacific Islander, 3.2% Two or more races, 2.6% Hispanic of any race; Average household size: 2.44; Median age: 36.5; Age under 18: 25.3%; Age 65 and over: 14.3%; Males per 100 females: 94.9

School District(s)

Federal Hocking Local (PK-12)
2012-13 Enrollment: 987......................... (740) 662-6691
Housing: Homeownership rate: 76.2%; Homeowner vacancy rate: 3.9%; Rental vacancy rate: 6.3%

ATHENS (city). County seat. Covers a land area of 9.827 square miles and a water area of 0.219 square miles. Located at 39.33° N. Lat; 82.10° W. Long. Elevation is 718 feet.
History: Athens was selected by the territorial legislature as the site of a university, which was chartered in 1804 and became Ohio University. Athens was incorporated as a city in 1912.
Population: 23,832; Growth (since 2000): 11.7%; Density: 2,425.2 persons per square mile; Race: 86.4% White, 4.4% Black/African American, 6.1% Asian, 0.2% American Indian/Alaska Native, 0.0% Native Hawaiian/Other Pacific Islander, 2.3% Two or more races, 2.4% Hispanic of any race; Average household size: 2.28; Median age: 21.6; Age under 18: 5.8%; Age 65 and over: 4.3%; Males per 100 females: 100.0; Marriage status: 81.3% never married, 13.9% now married, 0.6% separated, 1.6% widowed, 3.2% divorced; Foreign born: 8.3%; Speak English only: 90.9%; With disability: 5.5%; Veterans: 2.3%; Ancestry: 24.5% German, 14.1% Irish, 7.3% English, 6.8% Italian, 5.8% American
Employment: 7.1% management, business, and financial, 5.1% computer, engineering, and science, 24.5% education, legal, community service, arts, and media, 3.3% healthcare practitioners, 28.8% service, 24.0% sales and office, 1.3% natural resources, construction, and maintenance, 5.9% production, transportation, and material moving
Income: Per capita: $11,929; Median household: $17,933; Average household: $39,622; Households with income of $100,000 or more: 11.0%; Poverty rate: 57.4%
Educational Attainment: High school diploma or higher: 94.3%; Bachelor's degree or higher: 63.7%; Graduate/professional degree or higher: 40.1%

School District(s)

Athens City (PK-12)
2012-13 Enrollment: 2,718 .... (740) 797-4544

Four-year College(s)

Ohio University-Main Campus (Public)
Fall 2013 Enrollment: 28,786 .... (740) 593-1000
2013-14 Tuition: In-state $10,446; Out-of-state $19,410
Housing: Homeownership rate: 27.5%; Median home value: $162,300; Median year structure built: 1970; Homeowner vacancy rate: 2.3%; Median gross rent: $762 per month; Rental vacancy rate: 4.7%
Health Insurance: 95.3% have insurance; 88.8% have private insurance; 11.3% have public insurance; 4.7% do not have insurance; 0.5% of children under 18 do not have insurance
Hospitals: O'Bleness Memorial Hospital (114 beds)
Safety: Violent crime rate: 7.2 per 10,000 population; Property crime rate: 171.2 per 10,000 population
Newspapers: Athens Messenger (daily circulation 11300); Athens News (weekly circulation 18000)
Transportation: Commute: 51.9% car, 2.0% public transportation, 36.9% walk, 6.4% work from home; Median travel time to work: 14.0 minutes
Airports: Ohio University Snyder Field (general aviation)
Additional Information Contacts
City of Athens .... (740) 592-3338
http://www.ci.athens.oh.us

BUCHTEL (village). Covers a land area of 0.486 square miles and a water area of 0.001 square miles. Located at 39.46° N. Lat; 82.18° W. Long. Elevation is 689 feet.
Population: 558; Growth (since 2000): -2.8%; Density: 1,147.6 persons per square mile; Race: 97.8% White, 1.1% Black/African American, 0.0% Asian, 0.0% American Indian/Alaska Native, 0.0% Native Hawaiian/Other Pacific Islander, 1.1% Two or more races, 1.1% Hispanic of any race; Average household size: 2.37; Median age: 38.0; Age under 18: 21.9%; Age 65 and over: 14.7%; Males per 100 females: 94.4
Housing: Homeownership rate: 73.6%; Homeowner vacancy rate: 3.3%; Rental vacancy rate: 13.9%

CHAUNCEY (village). Covers a land area of 0.664 square miles and a water area of 0.002 square miles. Located at 39.40° N. Lat; 82.13° W. Long. Elevation is 653 feet.
History: Chauncey was first a salt town, and later a coal town.
Population: 1,049; Growth (since 2000): -1.7%; Density: 1,578.7 persons per square mile; Race: 96.6% White, 0.9% Black/African American, 0.4% Asian, 0.3% American Indian/Alaska Native, 0.1% Native Hawaiian/Other Pacific Islander, 1.7% Two or more races, 0.6% Hispanic of any race; Average household size: 2.48; Median age: 37.4; Age under 18: 24.2%; Age 65 and over: 13.3%; Males per 100 females: 101.7

School District(s)

Athens City (PK-12)
2012-13 Enrollment: 2,718 .... (740) 797-4544
Housing: Homeownership rate: 59.4%; Homeowner vacancy rate: 4.2%; Rental vacancy rate: 11.2%

COOLVILLE (village). Covers a land area of 0.833 square miles and a water area of 0.024 square miles. Located at 39.22° N. Lat; 81.80° W. Long. Elevation is 699 feet.
Population: 496; Growth (since 2000): -6.1%; Density: 595.6 persons per square mile; Race: 98.0% White, 0.4% Black/African American, 0.0% Asian, 0.0% American Indian/Alaska Native, 0.0% Native Hawaiian/Other Pacific Islander, 1.6% Two or more races, 0.2% Hispanic of any race; Average household size: 2.64; Median age: 39.0; Age under 18: 25.0%; Age 65 and over: 12.7%; Males per 100 females: 92.2

School District(s)

Federal Hocking Local (PK-12)
2012-13 Enrollment: 987. . . . . (740) 662-6691

Housing: Homeownership rate: 77.7%; Homeowner vacancy rate: 2.0%; Rental vacancy rate: 12.5%

GLOUSTER (village). Covers a land area of 1.327 square miles and a water area of 0.012 square miles. Located at 39.50° N. Lat; 82.08° W. Long. Elevation is 673 feet.

Population: 1,791; Growth (since 2000): -9.2%; Density: 1,349.3 persons per square mile; Race: 96.1% White, 1.4% Black/African American, 0.2% Asian, 0.1% American Indian/Alaska Native, 0.0% Native Hawaiian/Other Pacific Islander, 2.1% Two or more races, 0.8% Hispanic of any race; Average household size: 2.49; Median age: 35.8; Age under 18: 27.7%; Age 65 and over: 11.9%; Males per 100 females: 91.6

School District(s)

Trimble Local (PK-12)
2012-13 Enrollment: 852. . . . . (740) 767-4444

Housing: Homeownership rate: 68.5%; Homeowner vacancy rate: 5.9%; Rental vacancy rate: 16.2%

GUYSVILLE (unincorporated postal area)

ZCTA: 45735

Covers a land area of 50.061 square miles and a water area of 0.177 square miles. Located at 39.26° N. Lat; 81.93° W. Long. Elevation is 643 feet.

Population: 1,730; Growth (since 2000): 2.2%; Density: 34.6 persons per square mile; Race: 96.6% White, 0.8% Black/African American, 0.4% Asian, 0.3% American Indian/Alaska Native, 0.0% Native Hawaiian/Other Pacific Islander, 1.8% Two or more races, 0.2% Hispanic of any race; Average household size: 2.47; Median age: 41.3; Age under 18: 23.1%; Age 65 and over: 13.1%; Males per 100 females: 103.8

Housing: Homeownership rate: 85.9%; Homeowner vacancy rate: 1.1%; Rental vacancy rate: 9.2%

HOCKINGPORT (CDP). Covers a land area of 0.426 square miles and a water area of 0.044 square miles. Located at 39.19° N. Lat; 81.74° W. Long. Elevation is 617 feet.

Population: 212; Growth (since 2000): n/a; Density: 497.5 persons per square mile; Race: 98.1% White, 1.4% Black/African American, 0.0% Asian, 0.0% American Indian/Alaska Native, 0.0% Native Hawaiian/Other Pacific Islander, 0.5% Two or more races, 0.0% Hispanic of any race; Average household size: 2.08; Median age: 46.2; Age under 18: 19.3%; Age 65 and over: 21.7%; Males per 100 females: 84.3

Housing: Homeownership rate: 75.5%; Homeowner vacancy rate: 3.8%; Rental vacancy rate: 19.4%

JACKSONVILLE (village). Covers a land area of 0.242 square miles and a water area of 0.002 square miles. Located at 39.48° N. Lat; 82.08° W. Long. Elevation is 679 feet.

Population: 481; Growth (since 2000): -11.6%; Density: 1,987.0 persons per square mile; Race: 96.9% White, 0.6% Black/African American, 0.0% Asian, 0.0% American Indian/Alaska Native, 0.0% Native Hawaiian/Other Pacific Islander, 2.5% Two or more races, 0.0% Hispanic of any race; Average household size: 2.36; Median age: 42.5; Age under 18: 19.5%; Age 65 and over: 18.3%; Males per 100 females: 91.6

Housing: Homeownership rate: 73.1%; Homeowner vacancy rate: 1.3%; Rental vacancy rate: 22.5%

MILLFIELD (CDP). Covers a land area of 0.567 square miles and a water area of 0.011 square miles. Located at 39.44° N. Lat; 82.10° W. Long. Elevation is 679 feet.

Population: 341; Growth (since 2000): n/a; Density: 601.1 persons per square mile; Race: 95.9% White, 2.1% Black/African American, 0.0% Asian, 0.0% American Indian/Alaska Native, 0.0% Native Hawaiian/Other Pacific Islander, 1.8% Two or more races, 2.3% Hispanic of any race; Average household size: 2.69; Median age: 33.3; Age under 18: 28.4%; Age 65 and over: 8.8%; Males per 100 females: 104.2

Housing: Homeownership rate: 68.5%; Homeowner vacancy rate: 2.2%; Rental vacancy rate: 13.0%

NELSONVILLE (city). Covers a land area of 4.892 square miles and a water area of 0.111 square miles. Located at 39.46° N. Lat; 82.22° W. Long. Elevation is 679 feet.

History: First called Englishtown, the name was changed in 1824 to Nelsonville, in honor of Daniel Nelson, an enterprising citizen. Nelsonville developed as a coal town.

Population: 5,392; Growth (since 2000): 3.1%; Density: 1,102.1 persons per square mile; Race: 94.2% White, 2.8% Black/African American, 0.3% Asian, 0.5% American Indian/Alaska Native, 0.1% Native Hawaiian/Other Pacific Islander, 1.7% Two or more races, 1.4% Hispanic of any race; Average household size: 2.24; Median age: 25.1; Age under 18: 17.4%; Age 65 and over: 9.0%; Males per 100 females: 121.2; Marriage status: 49.3% never married, 28.6% now married, 1.3% separated, 6.7% widowed, 15.4% divorced; Foreign born: 1.1%; Speak English only: 98.4%; With disability: 19.0%; Veterans: 7.1%; Ancestry: 22.2% American, 17.8% German, 14.0% Irish, 7.6% English, 6.6% Italian

Employment: 6.8% management, business, and financial, 1.7% computer, engineering, and science, 11.9% education, legal, community service, arts, and media, 4.3% healthcare practitioners, 18.9% service, 39.3% sales and office, 7.3% natural resources, construction, and maintenance, 9.8% production, transportation, and material moving

Income: Per capita: $12,251; Median household: $24,422; Average household: $33,367; Households with income of $100,000 or more: 3.9%; Poverty rate: 34.6%

Educational Attainment: High school diploma or higher: 83.8%; Bachelor's degree or higher: 9.4%; Graduate/professional degree or higher: 4.6%

School District(s)

Nelsonville-York City (PK-12)
2012-13 Enrollment: 1,285 . . . . (740) 753-4441
Tri-County Career Center (11-12)
2012-13 Enrollment: n/a . . . . (740) 753-3511

Two-year College(s)

Hocking College (Public)
Fall 2013 Enrollment: 4,094 . . . . (740) 753-3591
2013-14 Tuition: In-state $4,290; Out-of-state $8,580
Tri-County Adult Career Center (Public)
Fall 2013 Enrollment: 129. . . . . (740) 753-5464

Housing: Homeownership rate: 40.3%; Median home value: $71,200; Median year structure built: 1951; Homeowner vacancy rate: 4.3%; Median gross rent: $575 per month; Rental vacancy rate: 8.5%

Health Insurance: 85.6% have insurance; 54.5% have private insurance; 41.0% have public insurance; 14.4% do not have insurance; 0.8% of children under 18 do not have insurance

Hospitals: Doctors Hospital of Nelsonville (50 beds)

Safety: Violent crime rate: 24.4 per 10,000 population; Property crime rate: 376.8 per 10,000 population

Transportation: Commute: 90.6% car, 0.3% public transportation, 6.4% walk, 1.4% work from home; Median travel time to work: 19.9 minutes

NEW MARSHFIELD (CDP). Covers a land area of 0.392 square miles and a water area of 0.001 square miles. Located at 39.32° N. Lat; 82.22° W. Long. Elevation is 820 feet.

Population: 326; Growth (since 2000): n/a; Density: 831.8 persons per square mile; Race: 98.2% White, 0.0% Black/African American, 0.0% Asian, 0.6% American Indian/Alaska Native, 0.0% Native Hawaiian/Other Pacific Islander, 1.2% Two or more races, 0.3% Hispanic of any race; Average household size: 2.26; Median age: 44.3; Age under 18: 19.6%; Age 65 and over: 14.4%; Males per 100 females: 88.4

Housing: Homeownership rate: 72.9%; Homeowner vacancy rate: 0.0%; Rental vacancy rate: 9.3%

STEWART (CDP). Covers a land area of 0.296 square miles and a water area of 0 square miles. Located at 39.31° N. Lat; 81.90° W. Long. Elevation is 669 feet.

Population: 247; Growth (since 2000): n/a; Density: 835.2 persons per square mile; Race: 97.2% White, 0.8% Black/African American, 0.0% Asian, 0.8% American Indian/Alaska Native, 0.0% Native Hawaiian/Other Pacific Islander, 1.2% Two or more races, 0.0% Hispanic of any race; Average household size: 2.40; Median age: 41.3; Age under 18: 25.9%; Age 65 and over: 12.1%; Males per 100 females: 96.0

School District(s)

Federal Hocking Local (PK-12)
2012-13 Enrollment: 987. . . . . (740) 662-6691

Housing: Homeownership rate: 73.8%; Homeowner vacancy rate: 0.0%; Rental vacancy rate: 10.0%

THE PLAINS (CDP). Covers a land area of 2.277 square miles and a water area of 0.006 square miles. Located at 39.37° N. Lat; 82.13° W. Long. Elevation is 715 feet.

Population: 3,080; Growth (since 2000): 5.1%; Density: 1,352.6 persons per square mile; Race: 92.0% White, 3.1% Black/African American, 1.0% Asian, 0.4% American Indian/Alaska Native, 0.0% Native Hawaiian/Other Pacific Islander, 3.3% Two or more races, 1.8% Hispanic of any race; Average household size: 2.12; Median age: 40.8; Age under 18: 19.9%; Age 65 and over: 19.6%; Males per 100 females: 80.0; Marriage status: 21.4% never married, 46.4% now married, 2.3% separated, 14.0% widowed, 18.2% divorced; Foreign born: 2.3%; Speak English only: 96.4%; With disability: 22.0%; Veterans: 14.8%; Ancestry: 22.4% American, 14.0% German, 13.1% Irish, 12.6% English, 4.4% Scottish

Employment: 6.4% management, business, and financial, 4.9% computer, engineering, and science, 20.4% education, legal, community service, arts, and media, 3.5% healthcare practitioners, 18.9% service, 22.8% sales and office, 13.1% natural resources, construction, and maintenance, 10.0% production, transportation, and material moving

Income: Per capita: $17,909; Median household: $35,777; Average household: $38,866; Households with income of $100,000 or more: 3.7%; Poverty rate: 25.3%

Educational Attainment: High school diploma or higher: 90.0%; Bachelor's degree or higher: 25.7%; Graduate/professional degree or higher: 12.0%

School District(s)

Athens City (PK-12)
2012-13 Enrollment: 2,718 . . . . (740) 797-4544

Housing: Homeownership rate: 48.8%; Median home value: $148,100; Median year structure built: 1985; Homeowner vacancy rate: 2.4%; Median gross rent: $723 per month; Rental vacancy rate: 8.4%

Health Insurance: 91.1% have insurance; 64.5% have private insurance; 53.3% have public insurance; 8.9% do not have insurance; 4.7% of children under 18 do not have insurance

Transportation: Commute: 93.9% car, 0.0% public transportation, 5.4% walk, 0.0% work from home; Median travel time to work: 21.2 minutes

TRIMBLE (village). Covers a land area of 0.662 square miles and a water area of 0.010 square miles. Located at 39.49° N. Lat; 82.08° W. Long. Elevation is 679 feet.

Population: 390; Growth (since 2000): -16.3%; Density: 588.8 persons per square mile; Race: 97.4% White, 0.0% Black/African American, 0.0% Asian, 0.3% American Indian/Alaska Native, 0.0% Native Hawaiian/Other Pacific Islander, 2.3% Two or more races, 0.0% Hispanic of any race; Average household size: 2.69; Median age: 39.5; Age under 18: 22.8%; Age 65 and over: 15.9%; Males per 100 females: 109.7

Housing: Homeownership rate: 69.6%; Homeowner vacancy rate: 6.4%; Rental vacancy rate: 6.4%

Auglaize County

Located in western Ohio; drained by the Auglaize and Saint Marys Rivers; includes part of Grand Lake. Covers a land area of 401.386 square miles, a water area of 0.519 square miles, and is located in the Eastern Time Zone at 40.56° N. Lat., 84.22° W. Long. The county was founded in 1848. County seat is Wapakoneta.

Auglaize County is part of the Wapakoneta, OH Micropolitan Statistical Area. The entire metro area includes: Auglaize County, OH

Population: 45,949; Growth (since 2000): -1.4%; Density: 114.5 persons per square mile; Race: 97.8% White, 0.3% Black/African American, 0.4% Asian, 0.2% American Indian/Alaska Native, 0.0% Native Hawaiian/Other Pacific Islander, 0.9% two or more races, 1.2% Hispanic of any race; Average household size: 2.53; Median age: 40.0; Age under 18: 25.4%; Age 65 and over: 15.4%; Males per 100 females: 98.4; Marriage status: 22.0% never married, 60.6% now married, 1.2% separated, 7.8% widowed, 9.6% divorced; Foreign born: 1.0%; Speak English only: 97.5%; With disability: 11.2%; Veterans: 10.3%; Ancestry: 51.9% German, 12.1% Irish, 9.8% American, 6.9% English, 3.3% French

Religion: Six largest groups: 25.3% Catholicism, 8.1% Presbyterian-Reformed, 7.1% Methodist/Pietist, 6.5% Holiness, 5.4% Lutheran, 1.9% Baptist

Economy: Unemployment rate: 3.2%; Leading industries: 16.9% retail trade; 13.7% other services (except public administration); 10.2% health care and social assistance; Farms: 1,040 totaling 210,084 acres; Company size: 1 employs 1,000 or more persons, 1 employs 500 to 999 persons, 28 employ 100 to 499 persons, 946 employ less than 100 persons; Business ownership: 993 women-owned, n/a Black-owned, n/a Hispanic-owned, 33 Asian-owned

Employment: 10.7% management, business, and financial, 3.6% computer, engineering, and science, 9.6% education, legal, community service, arts, and media, 6.1% healthcare practitioners, 14.8% service, 20.1% sales and office, 10.5% natural resources, construction, and maintenance, 24.6% production, transportation, and material moving

Income: Per capita: $25,323; Median household: $52,239; Average household: $63,293; Households with income of $100,000 or more: 16.1%; Poverty rate: 8.8%

Educational Attainment: High school diploma or higher: 91.4%; Bachelor's degree or higher: 17.1%; Graduate/professional degree or higher: 7.0%

Housing: Homeownership rate: 76.5%; Median home value: $129,400; Median year structure built: 1968; Homeowner vacancy rate: 1.9%; Median gross rent: $657 per month; Rental vacancy rate: 10.0%

Vital Statistics: Birth rate: 114.8 per 10,000 population; Death rate: 103.9 per 10,000 population; Age-adjusted cancer mortality rate: 163.2 deaths per 100,000 population

Health Insurance: 92.3% have insurance; 78.6% have private insurance; 28.5% have public insurance; 7.7% do not have insurance; 3.8% of children under 18 do not have insurance

Health Care: Physicians: 8.1 per 10,000 population; Hospital beds: 12.4 per 10,000 population; Hospital admissions: 448.6 per 10,000 population

Transportation: Commute: 92.9% car, 0.3% public transportation, 2.6% walk, 2.5% work from home; Median travel time to work: 20.3 minutes

Presidential Election: 24.7% Obama, 73.6% Romney (2012)

National and State Parks: Fort Amanda State Park

Additional Information Contacts

Auglaize Government . . . . (419) 739-6710
http://www2.auglaizecounty.org

Auglaize County Communities

BUCKLAND (village). Covers a land area of 0.258 square miles and a water area of 0 square miles. Located at 40.62° N. Lat; 84.26° W. Long. Elevation is 850 feet.

Population: 233; Growth (since 2000): -8.6%; Density: 904.1 persons per square mile; Race: 98.7% White, 0.0% Black/African American, 0.4% Asian, 0.0% American Indian/Alaska Native, 0.0% Native Hawaiian/Other Pacific Islander, 0.9% Two or more races, 2.1% Hispanic of any race; Average household size: 2.43; Median age: 36.3; Age under 18: 28.3%; Age 65 and over: 14.2%; Males per 100 females: 102.6

Housing: Homeownership rate: 64.6%; Homeowner vacancy rate: 0.0%; Rental vacancy rate: 0.0%

CRIDERSVILLE (village). Covers a land area of 0.897 square miles and a water area of 0 square miles. Located at 40.65° N. Lat; 84.15° W. Long. Elevation is 883 feet.

Population: 1,852; Growth (since 2000): 1.9%; Density: 2,065.5 persons per square mile; Race: 98.3% White, 0.4% Black/African American, 0.0% Asian, 0.1% American Indian/Alaska Native, 0.0% Native Hawaiian/Other Pacific Islander, 1.2% Two or more races, 1.6% Hispanic of any race; Average household size: 2.32; Median age: 41.8; Age under 18: 24.4%; Age 65 and over: 20.8%; Males per 100 females: 87.3

School District(s)

Wapakoneta City (PK-12)
2012-13 Enrollment: 2,996 . . . . (419) 739-2900

Housing: Homeownership rate: 64.7%; Homeowner vacancy rate: 1.0%; Rental vacancy rate: 3.2%

MINSTER (village). Covers a land area of 1.932 square miles and a water area of 0 square miles. Located at 40.40° N. Lat; 84.38° W. Long. Elevation is 965 feet.

History: Incorporated 1833.

Population: 2,805; Growth (since 2000): 0.4%; Density: 1,452.1 persons per square mile; Race: 99.3% White, 0.0% Black/African American, 0.1% Asian, 0.0% American Indian/Alaska Native, 0.1% Native Hawaiian/Other Pacific Islander, 0.4% Two or more races, 0.7% Hispanic of any race; Average household size: 2.60; Median age: 39.9; Age under 18: 28.9%;

Age 65 and over: 16.9%; Males per 100 females: 98.7; Marriage status: 20.7% never married, 64.7% now married, 0.8% separated, 10.3% widowed, 4.3% divorced; Foreign born: 0.5%; Speak English only: 97.9%; With disability: 9.4%; Veterans: 8.8%; Ancestry: 69.9% German, 11.7% Irish, 6.6% French, 3.8% American, 3.0% Italian
Employment: 13.7% management, business, and financial, 4.9% computer, engineering, and science, 10.7% education, legal, community service, arts, and media, 8.3% healthcare practitioners, 11.3% service, 24.7% sales and office, 8.3% natural resources, construction, and maintenance, 18.1% production, transportation, and material moving
Income: Per capita: $30,607; Median household: $71,912; Average household: $81,095; Households with income of $100,000 or more: 28.4%; Poverty rate: 6.2%
Educational Attainment: High school diploma or higher: 94.6%; Bachelor's degree or higher: 28.0%; Graduate/professional degree or higher: 10.5%

School District(s)

Minster Local (PK-12)
2012-13 Enrollment: 849. . . . . (419) 628-3397
Housing: Homeownership rate: 83.9%; Median home value: $170,400; Median year structure built: 1969; Homeowner vacancy rate: 2.1%; Median gross rent: $740 per month; Rental vacancy rate: 18.2%
Health Insurance: 95.7% have insurance; 85.5% have private insurance; 22.0% have public insurance; 4.3% do not have insurance; 1.5% of children under 18 do not have insurance
Newspapers: Community Post (weekly circulation 6800)
Transportation: Commute: 84.9% car, 1.3% public transportation, 3.5% walk, 5.4% work from home; Median travel time to work: 15.7 minutes
Additional Information Contacts
Village of Minster. . . . . (419) 628-3497
http://www.minsteroh.com

NEW BREMEN (village). Covers a land area of 2.145 square miles and a water area of 0 square miles. Located at 40.43° N. Lat; 84.38° W. Long. Elevation is 945 feet.
History: Incorporated 1833.
Population: 2,978; Growth (since 2000): 2.4%; Density: 1,388.6 persons per square mile; Race: 97.8% White, 0.1% Black/African American, 0.5% Asian, 0.1% American Indian/Alaska Native, 0.0% Native Hawaiian/Other Pacific Islander, 1.0% Two or more races, 1.2% Hispanic of any race; Average household size: 2.60; Median age: 38.2; Age under 18: 27.8%; Age 65 and over: 12.0%; Males per 100 females: 99.3; Marriage status: 21.7% never married, 65.4% now married, 0.5% separated, 4.8% widowed, 8.1% divorced; Foreign born: 1.1%; Speak English only: 96.9%; With disability: 8.4%; Veterans: 8.6%; Ancestry: 63.9% German, 8.7% Irish, 8.3% English, 7.5% French, 6.2% American
Employment: 12.7% management, business, and financial, 6.7% computer, engineering, and science, 11.0% education, legal, community service, arts, and media, 5.9% healthcare practitioners, 11.0% service, 18.7% sales and office, 8.5% natural resources, construction, and maintenance, 25.6% production, transportation, and material moving
Income: Per capita: $27,508; Median household: $55,121; Average household: $68,377; Households with income of $100,000 or more: 21.5%; Poverty rate: 9.2%
Educational Attainment: High school diploma or higher: 94.8%; Bachelor's degree or higher: 26.1%; Graduate/professional degree or higher: 9.7%

School District(s)

New Bremen Local (PK-12)
2012-13 Enrollment: 836. . . . . (419) 629-8606
Housing: Homeownership rate: 77.8%; Median home value: $148,800; Median year structure built: 1971; Homeowner vacancy rate: 2.2%; Median gross rent: $582 per month; Rental vacancy rate: 13.8%
Health Insurance: 94.9% have insurance; 88.3% have private insurance; 19.7% have public insurance; 5.1% do not have insurance; 0.0% of children under 18 do not have insurance
Transportation: Commute: 91.4% car, 0.0% public transportation, 4.0% walk, 2.2% work from home; Median travel time to work: 18.6 minutes
Additional Information Contacts
Village of New Bremen . . . . (419) 629-2827
http://www.newbremen.com

NEW HAMPSHIRE (CDP). Covers a land area of 0.610 square miles and a water area of 0 square miles. Located at 40.55° N. Lat; 83.95° W. Long. Elevation is 1,037 feet.
Population: 174; Growth (since 2000): n/a; Density: 285.2 persons per square mile; Race: 100.0% White, 0.0% Black/African American, 0.0% Asian, 0.0% American Indian/Alaska Native, 0.0% Native Hawaiian/Other Pacific Islander, 0.0% Two or more races, 0.0% Hispanic of any race; Average household size: 3.00; Median age: 38.0; Age under 18: 28.7%; Age 65 and over: 14.4%; Males per 100 females: 95.5
Housing: Homeownership rate: 79.3%; Homeowner vacancy rate: 2.1%; Rental vacancy rate: 14.3%

NEW KNOXVILLE (village). Covers a land area of 0.885 square miles and a water area of 0 square miles. Located at 40.49° N. Lat; 84.32° W. Long. Elevation is 899 feet.
Population: 879; Growth (since 2000): -1.3%; Density: 993.3 persons per square mile; Race: 98.6% White, 0.0% Black/African American, 0.0% Asian, 0.3% American Indian/Alaska Native, 0.0% Native Hawaiian/Other Pacific Islander, 0.7% Two or more races, 1.3% Hispanic of any race; Average household size: 2.48; Median age: 39.4; Age under 18: 27.6%; Age 65 and over: 15.4%; Males per 100 females: 97.5

School District(s)

New Knoxville Local (PK-12)
2012-13 Enrollment: 438. . . . . (419) 753-2431
Housing: Homeownership rate: 68.4%; Homeowner vacancy rate: 2.8%; Rental vacancy rate: 11.1%
Additional Information Contacts
Village of New Knoxville . . . . (419) 753-2160
http://www.newknoxville.com

SAINT JOHNS (CDP). Covers a land area of 0.384 square miles and a water area of 0.007 square miles. Located at 40.56° N. Lat; 84.08° W. Long. Elevation is 1,007 feet.
Population: 185; Growth (since 2000): n/a; Density: 482.1 persons per square mile; Race: 95.1% White, 2.7% Black/African American, 0.0% Asian, 0.0% American Indian/Alaska Native, 0.0% Native Hawaiian/Other Pacific Islander, 2.2% Two or more races, 10.8% Hispanic of any race; Average household size: 2.61; Median age: 36.5; Age under 18: 29.2%; Age 65 and over: 8.1%; Males per 100 females: 105.6
Housing: Homeownership rate: 81.7%; Homeowner vacancy rate: 3.2%; Rental vacancy rate: 0.0%

SAINT MARYS (city). Covers a land area of 4.589 square miles and a water area of 0.030 square miles. Located at 40.55° N. Lat; 84.39° W. Long. Elevation is 869 feet.
History: St. Marys began as a trading post, and was organized as a town after 1818. It was called Girty's Town when it served as headquarters and supply depot for Generals Harmar, Wayne, and Harrison. Later, its location on the Miami & Erie Canal made it a shipping center for farm produce, which arrived in St. Marys by boat and was transferred to wagons for the overland haul to the Ohio River.
Population: 8,332; Growth (since 2000): -0.1%; Density: 1,815.8 persons per square mile; Race: 96.7% White, 0.4% Black/African American, 0.7% Asian, 0.1% American Indian/Alaska Native, 0.1% Native Hawaiian/Other Pacific Islander, 1.5% Two or more races, 1.3% Hispanic of any race; Average household size: 2.51; Median age: 37.5; Age under 18: 26.6%; Age 65 and over: 14.4%; Males per 100 females: 96.9; Marriage status: 23.7% never married, 55.5% now married, 2.3% separated, 10.5% widowed, 10.3% divorced; Foreign born: 1.3%; Speak English only: 97.5%; With disability: 12.7%; Veterans: 9.8%; Ancestry: 48.7% German, 11.6% Irish, 7.8% English, 6.9% Dutch, 5.7% American
Employment: 9.1% management, business, and financial, 1.9% computer, engineering, and science, 9.9% education, legal, community service, arts, and media, 6.8% healthcare practitioners, 20.0% service, 22.2% sales and office, 10.3% natural resources, construction, and maintenance, 20.0% production, transportation, and material moving
Income: Per capita: $21,738; Median household: $40,926; Average household: $52,099; Households with income of $100,000 or more: 12.6%; Poverty rate: 13.7%
Educational Attainment: High school diploma or higher: 87.4%; Bachelor's degree or higher: 14.2%; Graduate/professional degree or higher: 5.0%

School District(s)

Saint Marys City (PK-12)
2012-13 Enrollment: 2,201 . . . . (419) 394-4312

Housing: Homeownership rate: 68.3%; Median home value: $96,300; Median year structure built: 1959; Homeowner vacancy rate: 2.7%; Median gross rent: $631 per month; Rental vacancy rate: 13.8%
Health Insurance: 91.2% have insurance; 70.1% have private insurance; 34.7% have public insurance; 8.8% do not have insurance; 0.0% of children under 18 do not have insurance
Hospitals: Grand Lake Health System (130 beds)
Newspapers: The Evening Leader (daily circulation 4500)
Transportation: Commute: 93.7% car, 0.3% public transportation, 3.2% walk, 1.1% work from home; Median travel time to work: 17.7 minutes

UNIOPOLIS (village). Covers a land area of 0.156 square miles and a water area of 0 square miles. Located at 40.60° N. Lat; 84.09° W. Long. Elevation is 935 feet.
Population: 222; Growth (since 2000): -13.3%; Density: 1,425.6 persons per square mile; Race: 100.0% White, 0.0% Black/African American, 0.0% Asian, 0.0% American Indian/Alaska Native, 0.0% Native Hawaiian/Other Pacific Islander, 0.0% Two or more races, 0.0% Hispanic of any race; Average household size: 2.67; Median age: 41.5; Age under 18: 18.9%; Age 65 and over: 17.6%; Males per 100 females: 109.4
Housing: Homeownership rate: 83.1%; Homeowner vacancy rate: 2.7%; Rental vacancy rate: 12.5%

WAPAKONETA (city). County seat. Covers a land area of 6.206 square miles and a water area of 0.053 square miles. Located at 40.57° N. Lat; 84.19° W. Long. Elevation is 892 feet.
History: Wapakoneta was platted in 1833 and settled by people of German heritage. Woodworking industries provided the economic base in the late 1800's. The town's name was first Wapaghkonetta, a combination of two Indian names, Wapaugh and Konetta.
Population: 9,867; Growth (since 2000): 4.1%; Density: 1,590.0 persons per square mile; Race: 97.1% White, 0.4% Black/African American, 0.4% Asian, 0.3% American Indian/Alaska Native, 0.0% Native Hawaiian/Other Pacific Islander, 1.2% Two or more races, 1.6% Hispanic of any race; Average household size: 2.39; Median age: 37.0; Age under 18: 25.2%; Age 65 and over: 15.6%; Males per 100 females: 91.6; Marriage status: 25.6% never married, 52.6% now married, 2.0% separated, 9.8% widowed, 11.9% divorced; Foreign born: 1.1%; Speak English only: 97.2%; With disability: 13.5%; Veterans: 10.8%; Ancestry: 46.4% German, 16.3% Irish, 11.2% American, 5.3% English, 3.2% Italian
Employment: 5.9% management, business, and financial, 2.2% computer, engineering, and science, 9.0% education, legal, community service, arts, and media, 6.1% healthcare practitioners, 20.4% service, 19.9% sales and office, 9.3% natural resources, construction, and maintenance, 27.3% production, transportation, and material moving
Income: Per capita: $21,106; Median household: $46,180; Average household: $52,131; Households with income of $100,000 or more: 8.1%; Poverty rate: 10.7%
Educational Attainment: High school diploma or higher: 90.6%; Bachelor's degree or higher: 13.7%; Graduate/professional degree or higher: 5.4%

School District(s)

Wapakoneta City (PK-12)
2012-13 Enrollment: 2,996 . . . . (419) 739-2900
Housing: Homeownership rate: 68.4%; Median home value: $98,100; Median year structure built: 1965; Homeowner vacancy rate: 1.8%; Median gross rent: $612 per month; Rental vacancy rate: 8.5%
Health Insurance: 89.9% have insurance; 71.3% have private insurance; 36.1% have public insurance; 10.1% do not have insurance; 7.4% of children under 18 do not have insurance
Safety: Violent crime rate: 9.2 per 10,000 population; Property crime rate: 180.4 per 10,000 population
Newspapers: Wapakoneta Daily News (daily circulation 5000)
Transportation: Commute: 91.9% car, 0.3% public transportation, 3.3% walk, 1.5% work from home; Median travel time to work: 20.6 minutes
Airports: Neil Armstrong (general aviation)
Additional Information Contacts
City of Wapakoneta . . . . (419) 738-3011
http://www.wapakoneta.net

WAYNESFIELD (village). Covers a land area of 0.740 square miles and a water area of 0 square miles. Located at 40.60° N. Lat; 83.97° W. Long. Elevation is 1,063 feet.
Population: 847; Growth (since 2000): 5.5%; Density: 1,144.6 persons per square mile; Race: 97.8% White, 0.6% Black/African American, 0.1% Asian, 0.2% American Indian/Alaska Native, 0.0% Native Hawaiian/Other Pacific Islander, 0.6% Two or more races, 2.1% Hispanic of any race; Average household size: 2.74; Median age: 33.5; Age under 18: 31.4%; Age 65 and over: 10.7%; Males per 100 females: 92.1

School District(s)

Waynesfield-Goshen Local (PK-12)
2012-13 Enrollment: 560. . . . . (419) 568-9100
Housing: Homeownership rate: 72.5%; Homeowner vacancy rate: 3.8%; Rental vacancy rate: 13.0%

Belmont County

Located in eastern Ohio; bounded on the east by the Ohio River and the West Virginia border. Covers a land area of 532.129 square miles, a water area of 9.145 square miles, and is located in the Eastern Time Zone at 40.02° N. Lat., 80.97° W. Long. The county was founded in 1801. County seat is Saint Clairsville.

Belmont County is part of the Wheeling, WV-OH Metropolitan Statistical Area. The entire metro area includes: Belmont County, OH; Marshall County, WV; Ohio County, WV

Weather Station: Barnesville Elevation: 1,240 feet

	Jan	Feb	Mar	Apr	May	Jun	Jul	Aug	Sep	Oct	Nov	Dec
High	36	39	49	61	70	79	83	81	74	63	51	39
Low	20	21	28	39	48	57	62	60	52	41	33	24
Precip	3.0	2.6	3.5	3.9	4.5	4.6	4.4	3.7	3.2	3.1	4.0	3.0
Snow	10.1	7.7	4.9	1.2	tr	0.0	0.0	tr	0.0	0.1	1.8	5.8

High and Low temperatures in degrees Fahrenheit; Precipitation and Snow in inches

Population: 70,400; Growth (since 2000): 0.2%; Density: 132.3 persons per square mile; Race: 94.0% White, 4.0% Black/African American, 0.4% Asian, 0.1% American Indian/Alaska Native, 0.0% Native Hawaiian/Other Pacific Islander, 1.3% two or more races, 0.6% Hispanic of any race; Average household size: 2.32; Median age: 43.4; Age under 18: 19.7%; Age 65 and over: 17.6%; Males per 100 females: 101.7; Marriage status: 26.8% never married, 52.4% now married, 1.7% separated, 8.4% widowed, 12.4% divorced; Foreign born: 0.8%; Speak English only: 97.9%; With disability: 17.5%; Veterans: 11.0%; Ancestry: 25.5% German, 18.3% Irish, 11.0% English, 9.9% Italian, 9.1% Polish
Religion: Six largest groups: 11.6% Catholicism, 8.7% Methodist/Pietist, 6.4% Baptist, 3.5% Presbyterian-Reformed, 1.8% Non-denominational Protestant, 1.5% Lutheran
Economy: Unemployment rate: 4.7%; Leading industries: 20.3% retail trade; 14.1% health care and social assistance; 13.4% other services (except public administration); Farms: 700 totaling 113,233 acres; Company size: 0 employ 1,000 or more persons, 2 employ 500 to 999 persons, 26 employ 100 to 499 persons, 1,440 employ less than 100 persons; Business ownership: 1,215 women-owned, n/a Black-owned, n/a Hispanic-owned, n/a Asian-owned
Employment: 8.0% management, business, and financial, 1.5% computer, engineering, and science, 8.2% education, legal, community service, arts, and media, 8.4% healthcare practitioners, 20.5% service, 24.5% sales and office, 13.5% natural resources, construction, and maintenance, 15.4% production, transportation, and material moving
Income: Per capita: $22,380; Median household: $41,534; Average household: $53,195; Households with income of $100,000 or more: 11.6%; Poverty rate: 14.6%
Educational Attainment: High school diploma or higher: 87.7%; Bachelor's degree or higher: 14.4%; Graduate/professional degree or higher: 4.8%
Housing: Homeownership rate: 73.2%; Median home value: $88,500; Median year structure built: 1957; Homeowner vacancy rate: 1.8%; Median gross rent: $533 per month; Rental vacancy rate: 8.5%
Vital Statistics: Birth rate: 104.1 per 10,000 population; Death rate: 120.0 per 10,000 population; Age-adjusted cancer mortality rate: 194.6 deaths per 100,000 population
Health Insurance: 89.0% have insurance; 69.1% have private insurance; 36.3% have public insurance; 11.0% do not have insurance; 3.0% of children under 18 do not have insurance
Health Care: Physicians: 10.9 per 10,000 population; Hospital beds: 37.6 per 10,000 population; Hospital admissions: 933.7 per 10,000 population
Air Quality Index: 100.0% good, 0.0% moderate, 0.0% unhealthy for sensitive individuals, 0.0% unhealthy (percent of days)
Transportation: Commute: 94.5% car, 0.4% public transportation, 2.5% walk, 1.9% work from home; Median travel time to work: 23.7 minutes

Presidential Election: 44.8% Obama, 53.2% Romney (2012)
National and State Parks: Belmont Lake State Reserve
Additional Information Contacts
Belmont Government . . . . (740) 699-2155
http://www.belcc.com

Belmont County Communities

ALLEDONIA (unincorporated postal area)
ZCTA: 43902
Covers a land area of 17.276 square miles and a water area of 0.327 square miles. Located at 39.88° N. Lat; 80.95° W. Long. Elevation is 830 feet.
Population: 202; Growth (since 2000): -4.7%; Density: 11.7 persons per square mile; Race: 100.0% White, 0.0% Black/African American, 0.0% Asian, 0.0% American Indian/Alaska Native, 0.0% Native Hawaiian/Other Pacific Islander, 0.0% Two or more races, 1.0% Hispanic of any race; Average household size: 2.49; Median age: 43.8; Age under 18: 18.8%; Age 65 and over: 15.8%; Males per 100 females: 119.6
Housing: Homeownership rate: 81.5%; Homeowner vacancy rate: 0.0%; Rental vacancy rate: 0.0%

BANNOCK (CDP). Covers a land area of 0.296 square miles and a water area of <.001 square miles. Located at 40.10° N. Lat; 80.98° W. Long. Elevation is 1,004 feet.
Population: 211; Growth (since 2000): n/a; Density: 713.2 persons per square mile; Race: 100.0% White, 0.0% Black/African American, 0.0% Asian, 0.0% American Indian/Alaska Native, 0.0% Native Hawaiian/Other Pacific Islander, 0.0% Two or more races, 0.0% Hispanic of any race; Average household size: 2.57; Median age: 46.3; Age under 18: 15.6%; Age 65 and over: 13.7%; Males per 100 females: 111.0
Housing: Homeownership rate: 82.9%; Homeowner vacancy rate: 2.8%; Rental vacancy rate: 0.0%

BARNESVILLE (village). Covers a land area of 1.943 square miles and a water area of 0.012 square miles. Located at 39.99° N. Lat; 81.17° W. Long. Elevation is 1,273 feet.
Population: 4,193; Growth (since 2000): -0.8%; Density: 2,157.7 persons per square mile; Race: 97.0% White, 0.9% Black/African American, 0.3% Asian, 0.1% American Indian/Alaska Native, 0.0% Native Hawaiian/Other Pacific Islander, 1.6% Two or more races, 0.6% Hispanic of any race; Average household size: 2.28; Median age: 41.4; Age under 18: 21.4%; Age 65 and over: 20.5%; Males per 100 females: 85.9; Marriage status: 22.0% never married, 53.3% now married, 2.3% separated, 10.8% widowed, 13.8% divorced; Foreign born: 0.0%; Speak English only: 99.2%; With disability: 22.2%; Veterans: 10.2%; Ancestry: 30.6% German, 23.6% Irish, 9.0% American, 6.5% English, 4.1% Scotch-Irish
Employment: 6.4% management, business, and financial, 1.3% computer, engineering, and science, 3.7% education, legal, community service, arts, and media, 8.0% healthcare practitioners, 18.9% service, 27.5% sales and office, 20.6% natural resources, construction, and maintenance, 13.6% production, transportation, and material moving
Income: Per capita: $19,827; Median household: $40,994; Average household: $45,920; Households with income of $100,000 or more: 2.9%; Poverty rate: 12.9%
Educational Attainment: High school diploma or higher: 86.4%; Bachelor's degree or higher: 13.1%; Graduate/professional degree or higher: 3.3%

School District(s)

Barnesville Exempted Village (PK-12)
2012-13 Enrollment: 1,162 . . . . (740) 425-3615
Housing: Homeownership rate: 65.2%; Median home value: $82,700; Median year structure built: 1943; Homeowner vacancy rate: 3.5%; Median gross rent: $513 per month; Rental vacancy rate: 4.9%
Health Insurance: 89.8% have insurance; 68.1% have private insurance; 36.0% have public insurance; 10.2% do not have insurance; 1.7% of children under 18 do not have insurance
Hospitals: Barnesville Hospital Association (25 beds)
Newspapers: Barnesville Enterprise (weekly circulation 4500)
Transportation: Commute: 93.6% car, 0.0% public transportation, 5.8% walk, 0.0% work from home; Median travel time to work: 27.7 minutes

BARTON (unincorporated postal area)
ZCTA: 43905
Covers a land area of 0.387 square miles and a water area of 0.006 square miles. Located at 40.10° N. Lat; 80.84° W. Long. Elevation is 797 feet.
Population: 237; Growth (since 2000): 1.3%; Density: 612.9 persons per square mile; Race: 97.0% White, 0.0% Black/African American, 0.8% Asian, 0.0% American Indian/Alaska Native, 0.0% Native Hawaiian/Other Pacific Islander, 2.1% Two or more races, 0.0% Hispanic of any race; Average household size: 2.15; Median age: 43.2; Age under 18: 22.8%; Age 65 and over: 21.1%; Males per 100 females: 94.3
Housing: Homeownership rate: 85.4%; Homeowner vacancy rate: 2.1%; Rental vacancy rate: 5.9%

BELLAIRE (village). Covers a land area of 1.650 square miles and a water area of 0.026 square miles. Located at 40.02° N. Lat; 80.75° W. Long. Elevation is 666 feet.
History: Bellaire was named for the home of a Maryland settler who purchased part of the townsite in 1802. After 1900, coal mining and the manufacture of glass and enamel ware became the leading industries.
Population: 4,278; Growth (since 2000): -12.6%; Density: 2,592.6 persons per square mile; Race: 91.9% White, 5.5% Black/African American, 0.2% Asian, 0.3% American Indian/Alaska Native, 0.0% Native Hawaiian/Other Pacific Islander, 2.2% Two or more races, 0.8% Hispanic of any race; Average household size: 2.32; Median age: 38.9; Age under 18: 23.4%; Age 65 and over: 15.9%; Males per 100 females: 92.1; Marriage status: 29.1% never married, 43.8% now married, 4.2% separated, 9.0% widowed, 18.1% divorced; Foreign born: 0.4%; Speak English only: 96.9%; With disability: 22.5%; Veterans: 9.5%; Ancestry: 24.0% German, 18.4% Irish, 11.2% Italian, 9.5% Polish, 8.5% American
Employment: 6.7% management, business, and financial, 0.0% computer, engineering, and science, 7.1% education, legal, community service, arts, and media, 8.9% healthcare practitioners, 29.4% service, 21.7% sales and office, 10.2% natural resources, construction, and maintenance, 16.0% production, transportation, and material moving
Income: Per capita: $16,127; Median household: $26,833; Average household: $37,118; Households with income of $100,000 or more: 4.3%; Poverty rate: 29.1%
Educational Attainment: High school diploma or higher: 78.4%; Bachelor's degree or higher: 7.8%; Graduate/professional degree or higher: 2.5%

School District(s)

Bellaire Local (PK-12)
2012-13 Enrollment: 1,196 . . . . (740) 676-1826
Housing: Homeownership rate: 52.5%; Median home value: $53,400; Median year structure built: Before 1940; Homeowner vacancy rate: 2.6%; Median gross rent: $533 per month; Rental vacancy rate: 11.7%
Health Insurance: 79.5% have insurance; 46.8% have private insurance; 44.0% have public insurance; 20.5% do not have insurance; 5.3% of children under 18 do not have insurance
Hospitals: Belmont Community Hospital (99 beds)
Safety: Violent crime rate: 7.1 per 10,000 population; Property crime rate: 85.7 per 10,000 population
Transportation: Commute: 88.0% car, 0.4% public transportation, 8.9% walk, 2.7% work from home; Median travel time to work: 19.5 minutes

BELMONT (village). Covers a land area of 0.266 square miles and a water area of 0 square miles. Located at 40.03° N. Lat; 81.04° W. Long. Elevation is 1,191 feet.
Population: 453; Growth (since 2000): -14.8%; Density: 1,701.3 persons per square mile; Race: 97.4% White, 0.4% Black/African American, 0.0% Asian, 1.3% American Indian/Alaska Native, 0.0% Native Hawaiian/Other Pacific Islander, 0.9% Two or more races, 0.2% Hispanic of any race; Average household size: 2.26; Median age: 44.0; Age under 18: 20.8%; Age 65 and over: 15.9%; Males per 100 females: 85.7

School District(s)

Union Local (PK-12)
2012-13 Enrollment: 1,478 . . . . (740) 782-1978
Housing: Homeownership rate: 80.7%; Homeowner vacancy rate: 3.0%; Rental vacancy rate: 0.0%

BETHESDA (village). Covers a land area of 0.624 square miles and a water area of 0.020 square miles. Located at 40.02° N. Lat; 81.07° W. Long. Elevation is 1,227 feet.

Population: 1,256; Growth (since 2000): -11.1%; Density: 2,013.2 persons per square mile; Race: 96.6% White, 0.3% Black/African American, 0.2% Asian, 0.1% American Indian/Alaska Native, 0.2% Native Hawaiian/Other Pacific Islander, 2.7% Two or more races, 0.2% Hispanic of any race; Average household size: 2.29; Median age: 39.6; Age under 18: 24.0%; Age 65 and over: 13.6%; Males per 100 females: 87.2

Housing: Homeownership rate: 67.6%; Homeowner vacancy rate: 2.3%; Rental vacancy rate: 10.9%

BRIDGEPORT (village). Covers a land area of 1.366 square miles and a water area of 0.010 square miles. Located at 40.06° N. Lat; 80.75° W. Long. Elevation is 656 feet.

History: Bridgeport was platted by Ebenezer Zane in 1806, when it was called Canton. The present name was given in 1836. An early boatbuilding industry was replaced by glass-making in the late 1800's.

Population: 1,831; Growth (since 2000): -16.2%; Density: 1,340.0 persons per square mile; Race: 89.7% White, 6.9% Black/African American, 0.2% Asian, 0.0% American Indian/Alaska Native, 0.0% Native Hawaiian/Other Pacific Islander, 3.0% Two or more races, 0.2% Hispanic of any race; Average household size: 2.26; Median age: 43.3; Age under 18: 19.5%; Age 65 and over: 17.4%; Males per 100 females: 95.2

School District(s)

Bridgeport Exempted Village (PK-12)
2012-13 Enrollment: 791. . . . . (740) 635-1713

Housing: Homeownership rate: 66.3%; Homeowner vacancy rate: 2.0%; Rental vacancy rate: 6.5%

Safety: Violent crime rate: 0.0 per 10,000 population; Property crime rate: 83.3 per 10,000 population

BROOKSIDE (village). Covers a land area of 0.173 square miles and a water area of 0.003 square miles. Located at 40.07° N. Lat; 80.76° W. Long. Elevation is 650 feet.

History: Brookside was settled along Wheeling Creek, where grist mills, sawmills, and woolen mills were established. Later it became a coal mining town.

Population: 632; Growth (since 2000): -1.9%; Density: 3,649.7 persons per square mile; Race: 96.2% White, 1.9% Black/African American, 0.0% Asian, 0.5% American Indian/Alaska Native, 0.0% Native Hawaiian/Other Pacific Islander, 1.3% Two or more races, 0.3% Hispanic of any race; Average household size: 2.24; Median age: 44.5; Age under 18: 19.1%; Age 65 and over: 17.7%; Males per 100 females: 93.9

Housing: Homeownership rate: 78.1%; Homeowner vacancy rate: 1.8%; Rental vacancy rate: 12.5%

FAIRPOINT (unincorporated postal area)

ZCTA: 43927

Covers a land area of 0.410 square miles and a water area of 0.008 square miles. Located at 40.12° N. Lat; 80.94° W. Long. Elevation is 948 feet.

Population: 74; Growth (since 2000): 68.2%; Density: 180.5 persons per square mile; Race: 100.0% White, 0.0% Black/African American, 0.0% Asian, 0.0% American Indian/Alaska Native, 0.0% Native Hawaiian/Other Pacific Islander, 0.0% Two or more races, 0.0% Hispanic of any race; Average household size: 2.24; Median age: 39.3; Age under 18: 24.3%; Age 65 and over: 18.9%; Males per 100 females: 94.7

Housing: Homeownership rate: 81.8%; Homeowner vacancy rate: 0.0%; Rental vacancy rate: 0.0%

FLUSHING (village). Covers a land area of 0.614 square miles and a water area of 0 square miles. Located at 40.15° N. Lat; 81.06° W. Long. Elevation is 1,286 feet.

Population: 879; Growth (since 2000): -2.3%; Density: 1,432.7 persons per square mile; Race: 97.6% White, 1.4% Black/African American, 0.0% Asian, 0.2% American Indian/Alaska Native, 0.0% Native Hawaiian/Other Pacific Islander, 0.8% Two or more races, 0.7% Hispanic of any race; Average household size: 2.29; Median age: 40.7; Age under 18: 22.5%; Age 65 and over: 16.3%; Males per 100 females: 96.6

Housing: Homeownership rate: 71.4%; Homeowner vacancy rate: 2.1%; Rental vacancy rate: 5.2%

GLENCOE (CDP). Covers a land area of 1.223 square miles and a water area of 0.011 square miles. Located at 40.01° N. Lat; 80.88° W. Long. Elevation is 830 feet.

Population: 310; Growth (since 2000): n/a; Density: 253.6 persons per square mile; Race: 98.7% White, 0.0% Black/African American, 0.3% Asian, 0.0% American Indian/Alaska Native, 0.0% Native Hawaiian/Other Pacific Islander, 0.0% Two or more races, 1.3% Hispanic of any race; Average household size: 2.61; Median age: 39.8; Age under 18: 24.2%; Age 65 and over: 12.9%; Males per 100 females: 109.5

Housing: Homeownership rate: 89.1%; Homeowner vacancy rate: 2.7%; Rental vacancy rate: 7.1%

HOLLOWAY (village). Covers a land area of 0.949 square miles and a water area of 0.011 square miles. Located at 40.16° N. Lat; 81.13° W. Long. Elevation is 925 feet.

Population: 338; Growth (since 2000): -2.0%; Density: 356.1 persons per square mile; Race: 97.6% White, 0.0% Black/African American, 0.3% Asian, 0.6% American Indian/Alaska Native, 0.0% Native Hawaiian/Other Pacific Islander, 0.3% Two or more races, 1.5% Hispanic of any race; Average household size: 2.43; Median age: 39.0; Age under 18: 23.1%; Age 65 and over: 16.0%; Males per 100 females: 100.0

Housing: Homeownership rate: 81.3%; Homeowner vacancy rate: 0.0%; Rental vacancy rate: 3.6%

JACOBSBURG (unincorporated postal area)

ZCTA: 43933

Covers a land area of 47.582 square miles and a water area of 0.371 square miles. Located at 39.94° N. Lat; 80.90° W. Long. Elevation is 1,296 feet.

Population: 2,070; Growth (since 2000): 18.7%; Density: 43.5 persons per square mile; Race: 98.4% White, 0.1% Black/African American, 0.1% Asian, 0.0% American Indian/Alaska Native, 0.0% Native Hawaiian/Other Pacific Islander, 1.3% Two or more races, 0.3% Hispanic of any race; Average household size: 2.45; Median age: 45.0; Age under 18: 19.7%; Age 65 and over: 15.2%; Males per 100 females: 103.3

Housing: Homeownership rate: 86.1%; Homeowner vacancy rate: 0.8%; Rental vacancy rate: 9.8%

LAFFERTY (CDP). Covers a land area of 0.936 square miles and a water area of 0.014 square miles. Located at 40.12° N. Lat; 81.02° W. Long. Elevation is 1,060 feet.

Population: 304; Growth (since 2000): n/a; Density: 325.0 persons per square mile; Race: 97.0% White, 1.0% Black/African American, 0.3% Asian, 0.3% American Indian/Alaska Native, 0.0% Native Hawaiian/Other Pacific Islander, 1.3% Two or more races, 1.0% Hispanic of any race; Average household size: 2.27; Median age: 42.3; Age under 18: 21.1%; Age 65 and over: 17.1%; Males per 100 females: 97.4

Housing: Homeownership rate: 78.3%; Homeowner vacancy rate: 0.0%; Rental vacancy rate: 3.3%

LANSING (CDP). Covers a land area of 0.281 square miles and a water area of 0.003 square miles. Located at 40.08° N. Lat; 80.79° W. Long. Elevation is 705 feet.

Population: 634; Growth (since 2000): n/a; Density: 2,252.6 persons per square mile; Race: 96.8% White, 0.8% Black/African American, 0.3% Asian, 0.0% American Indian/Alaska Native, 0.0% Native Hawaiian/Other Pacific Islander, 2.1% Two or more races, 1.4% Hispanic of any race; Average household size: 2.34; Median age: 42.7; Age under 18: 20.2%; Age 65 and over: 18.9%; Males per 100 females: 93.3

Housing: Homeownership rate: 73.0%; Homeowner vacancy rate: 2.9%; Rental vacancy rate: 13.1%

MARTINS FERRY (city). Covers a land area of 2.329 square miles and a water area of 0.002 square miles. Located at 40.11° N. Lat; 80.73° W. Long. Elevation is 709 feet.

History: The settlement that formed here in the 1780's was known as Norristown. In 1795 Absalom Martin laid out a town that he called Jefferson, but he later voided his town plat when he failed to get the county seat. Settlers continued to come, and in 1835 Absalom's son, Ebenezer Martin, replatted the town and named it Martinsville. Because Martin owned the ferry, the town became known as Martins Ferry. Writer William Dean Howells was born here in 1837.

Population: 6,915; Growth (since 2000): -4.3%; Density: 2,969.5 persons per square mile; Race: 91.6% White, 5.6% Black/African American, 0.1% Asian, 0.3% American Indian/Alaska Native, 0.0% Native Hawaiian/Other

Pacific Islander, 2.2% Two or more races, 0.7% Hispanic of any race; Average household size: 2.26; Median age: 42.1; Age under 18: 21.3%; Age 65 and over: 17.2%; Males per 100 females: 88.1; Marriage status: 30.6% never married, 45.7% now married, 2.8% separated, 8.4% widowed, 15.3% divorced; Foreign born: 0.6%; Speak English only: 98.8%; With disability: 19.2%; Veterans: 9.5%; Ancestry: 27.9% German, 15.9% Irish, 13.5% Italian, 12.9% English, 8.1% Polish
Employment: 7.0% management, business, and financial, 2.1% computer, engineering, and science, 8.3% education, legal, community service, arts, and media, 5.7% healthcare practitioners, 23.0% service, 28.6% sales and office, 8.5% natural resources, construction, and maintenance, 16.7% production, transportation, and material moving
Income: Per capita: $20,038; Median household: $31,795; Average household: $45,360; Households with income of $100,000 or more: 10.0%; Poverty rate: 25.0%
Educational Attainment: High school diploma or higher: 85.9%; Bachelor's degree or higher: 12.7%; Graduate/professional degree or higher: 3.5%

School District(s)

Martins Ferry City (PK-12)
2012-13 Enrollment: 1,452 . . . . (740) 633-1732
Housing: Homeownership rate: 57.9%; Median home value: $73,400; Median year structure built: 1947; Homeowner vacancy rate: 2.6%; Median gross rent: $466 per month; Rental vacancy rate: 12.4%
Health Insurance: 87.4% have insurance; 59.6% have private insurance; 41.7% have public insurance; 12.6% do not have insurance; 1.7% of children under 18 do not have insurance
Hospitals: East Ohio Regional Hospital (250 beds)
Safety: Violent crime rate: 14.7 per 10,000 population; Property crime rate: 98.5 per 10,000 population
Newspapers: Times-Leader (daily circulation 16100)
Transportation: Commute: 89.3% car, 2.4% public transportation, 5.8% walk, 1.7% work from home; Median travel time to work: 19.3 minutes

MORRISTOWN (village). Covers a land area of 0.505 square miles and a water area of 0.002 square miles. Located at 40.06° N. Lat; 81.07° W. Long. Elevation is 1,260 feet.
History: Morristown was laid out in 1802 and served as a toll station on the National Road.
Population: 303; Growth (since 2000): 1.3%; Density: 600.5 persons per square mile; Race: 96.7% White, 1.7% Black/African American, 0.0% Asian, 0.3% American Indian/Alaska Native, 0.0% Native Hawaiian/Other Pacific Islander, 0.7% Two or more races, 1.0% Hispanic of any race; Average household size: 2.24; Median age: 43.8; Age under 18: 24.4%; Age 65 and over: 18.5%; Males per 100 females: 118.0
Housing: Homeownership rate: 76.6%; Homeowner vacancy rate: 2.0%; Rental vacancy rate: 0.0%

NEFFS (CDP). Covers a land area of 3.986 square miles and a water area of 0.038 square miles. Located at 40.04° N. Lat; 80.82° W. Long. Elevation is 735 feet.
Population: 993; Growth (since 2000): -12.7%; Density: 249.1 persons per square mile; Race: 98.9% White, 0.2% Black/African American, 0.1% Asian, 0.0% American Indian/Alaska Native, 0.0% Native Hawaiian/Other Pacific Islander, 0.3% Two or more races, 0.2% Hispanic of any race; Average household size: 2.42; Median age: 44.7; Age under 18: 19.0%; Age 65 and over: 16.6%; Males per 100 females: 98.2
Housing: Homeownership rate: 88.3%; Homeowner vacancy rate: 0.5%; Rental vacancy rate: 9.4%

PIEDMONT (unincorporated postal area)
ZCTA: 43983
Covers a land area of 20.556 square miles and a water area of 1.980 square miles. Located at 40.14° N. Lat; 81.20° W. Long..
Population: 440; Growth (since 2000): 1.6%; Density: 21.4 persons per square mile; Race: 97.7% White, 1.6% Black/African American, 0.0% Asian, 0.5% American Indian/Alaska Native, 0.0% Native Hawaiian/Other Pacific Islander, 0.2% Two or more races, 0.5% Hispanic of any race; Average household size: 2.24; Median age: 49.0; Age under 18: 19.1%; Age 65 and over: 22.5%; Males per 100 females: 116.7
Housing: Homeownership rate: 86.3%; Homeowner vacancy rate: 3.9%; Rental vacancy rate: 6.9%

POWHATAN POINT (village). Covers a land area of 1.470 square miles and a water area of 0.163 square miles. Located at 39.86° N. Lat; 80.81° W. Long. Elevation is 679 feet.
History: Powhatan Point was established in the 1820's along the Ohio River. A coal boom during the 1920's brought growth to the town.
Population: 1,592; Growth (since 2000): -8.7%; Density: 1,083.4 persons per square mile; Race: 98.7% White, 0.4% Black/African American, 0.1% Asian, 0.3% American Indian/Alaska Native, 0.0% Native Hawaiian/Other Pacific Islander, 0.6% Two or more races, 0.3% Hispanic of any race; Average household size: 2.24; Median age: 43.6; Age under 18: 21.4%; Age 65 and over: 17.5%; Males per 100 females: 91.6

School District(s)

Switzerland of Ohio Local (PK-12)
2012-13 Enrollment: 2,481 . . . . (740) 472-5801
Housing: Homeownership rate: 69.8%; Homeowner vacancy rate: 2.0%; Rental vacancy rate: 6.9%
Safety: Violent crime rate: 6.4 per 10,000 population; Property crime rate: 114.4 per 10,000 population

SAINT CLAIRSVILLE (city). County seat. Covers a land area of 2.418 square miles and a water area of 0.019 square miles. Located at 40.08° N. Lat; 80.90° W. Long. Elevation is 1,266 feet.
History: St. Clairsville was named for Arthur St. Clair, first governor of the Northwest Territory. It became the seat of Belmont County in 1804.
Population: 5,184; Growth (since 2000): 2.5%; Density: 2,143.8 persons per square mile; Race: 94.7% White, 2.8% Black/African American, 1.0% Asian, 0.1% American Indian/Alaska Native, 0.0% Native Hawaiian/Other Pacific Islander, 1.2% Two or more races, 0.7% Hispanic of any race; Average household size: 2.10; Median age: 49.7; Age under 18: 17.7%; Age 65 and over: 25.8%; Males per 100 females: 84.9; Marriage status: 15.5% never married, 58.3% now married, 0.8% separated, 13.6% widowed, 12.6% divorced; Foreign born: 2.2%; Speak English only: 98.6%; With disability: 15.4%; Veterans: 12.3%; Ancestry: 24.4% German, 19.1% Irish, 15.6% English, 11.8% Italian, 10.2% Polish
Employment: 7.2% management, business, and financial, 4.1% computer, engineering, and science, 11.1% education, legal, community service, arts, and media, 13.0% healthcare practitioners, 15.3% service, 20.2% sales and office, 11.5% natural resources, construction, and maintenance, 17.6% production, transportation, and material moving
Income: Per capita: $27,053; Median household: $50,625; Average household: $60,668; Households with income of $100,000 or more: 15.6%; Poverty rate: 4.6%
Educational Attainment: High school diploma or higher: 93.7%; Bachelor's degree or higher: 23.9%; Graduate/professional degree or higher: 9.0%

School District(s)

Belmont-Harrison (08-12)
2012-13 Enrollment: n/a . . . . (740) 695-9130
Saint Clairsville-Richland City (PK-12)
2012-13 Enrollment: 1,653 . . . . (740) 695-1624

Four-year College(s)

Ohio University-Eastern Campus (Public)
Fall 2013 Enrollment: 1,091 . . . . (740) 695-1720
2013-14 Tuition: In-state $4,778; Out-of-state $6,624

Two-year College(s)

Belmont College (Public)
Fall 2013 Enrollment: 1,259 . . . . (740) 695-9500
2013-14 Tuition: In-state $3,452; Out-of-state $5,876
Housing: Homeownership rate: 64.9%; Median home value: $139,200; Median year structure built: 1967; Homeowner vacancy rate: 2.4%; Median gross rent: $656 per month; Rental vacancy rate: 4.9%
Health Insurance: 95.2% have insurance; 82.6% have private insurance; 36.0% have public insurance; 4.8% do not have insurance; 3.4% of children under 18 do not have insurance
Transportation: Commute: 96.2% car, 0.1% public transportation, 1.8% walk, 0.9% work from home; Median travel time to work: 20.3 minutes
Additional Information Contacts
City of Saint Clairsville. . . . . (740) 695-1410
http://www.stclairsville.com

SHADYSIDE (village). Covers a land area of 1.011 square miles and a water area of 0.020 square miles. Located at 39.97° N. Lat; 80.75° W. Long. Elevation is 689 feet.
History: Shadyside was platted in 1901. It developed as a residential town, with casket making as a primary industry.

Population: 3,785; Growth (since 2000): 3.0%; Density: 3,745.3 persons per square mile; Race: 99.0% White, 0.2% Black/African American, 0.2% Asian, 0.1% American Indian/Alaska Native, 0.0% Native Hawaiian/Other Pacific Islander, 0.5% Two or more races, 0.5% Hispanic of any race; Average household size: 2.15; Median age: 47.9; Age under 18: 17.5%; Age 65 and over: 23.5%; Males per 100 females: 84.7; Marriage status: 26.3% never married, 51.1% now married, 0.8% separated, 11.7% widowed, 10.9% divorced; Foreign born: 0.3%; Speak English only: 98.3%; With disability: 18.7%; Veterans: 13.9%; Ancestry: 32.2% German, 13.3% Irish, 11.3% English, 10.9% Italian, 8.8% American
Employment: 10.7% management, business, and financial, 1.6% computer, engineering, and science, 11.8% education, legal, community service, arts, and media, 10.9% healthcare practitioners, 21.2% service, 23.7% sales and office, 9.9% natural resources, construction, and maintenance, 10.2% production, transportation, and material moving
Income: Per capita: $23,870; Median household: $43,453; Average household: $51,168; Households with income of $100,000 or more: 12.1%; Poverty rate: 10.0%
Educational Attainment: High school diploma or higher: 92.2%; Bachelor's degree or higher: 18.1%; Graduate/professional degree or higher: 6.5%

School District(s)

Shadyside Local (PK-12)
2012-13 Enrollment: 828. . . . . (740) 676-3121
Housing: Homeownership rate: 69.8%; Median home value: $88,900; Median year structure built: 1950; Homeowner vacancy rate: 1.3%; Median gross rent: $577 per month; Rental vacancy rate: 5.6%
Health Insurance: 87.3% have insurance; 72.2% have private insurance; 33.7% have public insurance; 12.7% do not have insurance; 5.4% of children under 18 do not have insurance
Transportation: Commute: 95.4% car, 0.0% public transportation, 2.3% walk, 0.7% work from home; Median travel time to work: 20.8 minutes

WOLFHURST (CDP). Covers a land area of 0.486 square miles and a water area of 0.017 square miles. Located at 40.07° N. Lat; 80.78° W. Long. Elevation is 676 feet.
Population: 1,239; Growth (since 2000): n/a; Density: 2,549.9 persons per square mile; Race: 94.2% White, 3.5% Black/African American, 0.4% Asian, 0.0% American Indian/Alaska Native, 0.0% Native Hawaiian/Other Pacific Islander, 1.9% Two or more races, 0.2% Hispanic of any race; Average household size: 1.96; Median age: 49.9; Age under 18: 15.8%; Age 65 and over: 26.1%; Males per 100 females: 85.5
Housing: Homeownership rate: 59.0%; Homeowner vacancy rate: 0.9%; Rental vacancy rate: 9.1%

Brown County

Located in southwestern Ohio; bounded on the south by the Ohio River and the Kentucky border. Covers a land area of 490.016 square miles, a water area of 3.436 square miles, and is located in the Eastern Time Zone at 38.93° N. Lat., 83.87° W. Long. The county was founded in 1817. County seat is Georgetown.

Brown County is part of the Cincinnati, OH-KY-IN Metropolitan Statistical Area. The entire metro area includes: Dearborn County, IN; Ohio County, IN; Union County, IN; Boone County, KY; Bracken County, KY; Campbell County, KY; Gallatin County, KY; Grant County, KY; Kenton County, KY; Pendleton County, KY; Brown County, OH; Butler County, OH; Clermont County, OH; Hamilton County, OH; Warren County, OH

Weather Station: Ripley Exp Farm Elevation: 879 feet

	Jan	Feb	Mar	Apr	May	Jun	Jul	Aug	Sep	Oct	Nov	Dec
High	39	44	52	64	74	82	86	85	78	67	54	43
Low	20	23	30	40	50	59	63	61	53	41	33	24
Precip	2.9	2.9	4.2	4.0	5.4	4.1	5.0	3.8	2.9	3.2	3.5	3.4
Snow	6.4	5.1	3.0	0.4	tr	0.0	0.0	0.0	0.0	0.1	0.5	3.2

High and Low temperatures in degrees Fahrenheit; Precipitation and Snow in inches

Population: 44,846; Growth (since 2000): 6.1%; Density: 91.5 persons per square mile; Race: 97.5% White, 0.9% Black/African American, 0.2% Asian, 0.2% American Indian/Alaska Native, 0.0% Native Hawaiian/Other Pacific Islander, 1.0% two or more races, 0.6% Hispanic of any race; Average household size: 2.60; Median age: 39.9; Age under 18: 24.6%; Age 65 and over: 14.4%; Males per 100 females: 98.5; Marriage status: 22.9% never married, 57.4% now married, 2.0% separated, 7.2% widowed, 12.4% divorced; Foreign born: 0.5%; Speak English only: 98.8%; With disability: 16.5%; Veterans: 10.9%; Ancestry: 24.6% German, 19.0% American, 12.5% Irish, 8.6% English, 2.2% Dutch
Religion: Six largest groups: 10.6% Baptist, 8.0% Non-denominational Protestant, 6.4% Catholicism, 3.4% Methodist/Pietist, 1.3% Presbyterian-Reformed, 1.0% Holiness
Economy: Unemployment rate: 5.2%; Leading industries: 18.9% retail trade; 12.5% other services (except public administration); 12.1% accommodation and food services; Farms: 1,379 totaling 206,446 acres; Company size: 0 employ 1,000 or more persons, 0 employ 500 to 999 persons, 8 employ 100 to 499 persons, 537 employ less than 100 persons; Business ownership: 1,073 women-owned, n/a Black-owned, n/a Hispanic-owned, n/a Asian-owned
Employment: 10.3% management, business, and financial, 2.3% computer, engineering, and science, 7.2% education, legal, community service, arts, and media, 5.6% healthcare practitioners, 19.9% service, 22.9% sales and office, 11.8% natural resources, construction, and maintenance, 20.0% production, transportation, and material moving
Income: Per capita: $21,206; Median household: $44,341; Average household: $55,432; Households with income of $100,000 or more: 11.9%; Poverty rate: 14.1%
Educational Attainment: High school diploma or higher: 81.5%; Bachelor's degree or higher: 11.0%; Graduate/professional degree or higher: 3.9%
Housing: Homeownership rate: 75.6%; Median home value: $116,300; Median year structure built: 1981; Homeowner vacancy rate: 2.2%; Median gross rent: $667 per month; Rental vacancy rate: 8.9%
Vital Statistics: Birth rate: 112.7 per 10,000 population; Death rate: 103.9 per 10,000 population; Age-adjusted cancer mortality rate: 217.4 deaths per 100,000 population
Health Insurance: 86.0% have insurance; 64.8% have private insurance; 33.8% have public insurance; 14.0% do not have insurance; 6.6% of children under 18 do not have insurance
Health Care: Physicians: 4.3 per 10,000 population; Hospital beds: 13.2 per 10,000 population; Hospital admissions: 118.1 per 10,000 population
Transportation: Commute: 94.1% car, 0.3% public transportation, 1.3% walk, 3.6% work from home; Median travel time to work: 35.6 minutes
Presidential Election: 36.5% Obama, 61.6% Romney (2012)
National and State Parks: Rankin House State Memorial
Additional Information Contacts
Brown Government . . . . (937) 378-3956
http://www.browncountyohio.gov

Brown County Communities

ABERDEEN (village). Covers a land area of 1.347 square miles and a water area of 0.284 square miles. Located at 38.67° N. Lat; 83.77° W. Long. Elevation is 515 feet.
History: Aberdeen was the Ohio River terminus of Zane's Trace, and a ferry point for people and goods going across the river to Kentucky.
Population: 1,638; Growth (since 2000): 2.2%; Density: 1,216.0 persons per square mile; Race: 96.2% White, 1.8% Black/African American, 0.2% Asian, 0.1% American Indian/Alaska Native, 0.0% Native Hawaiian/Other Pacific Islander, 1.5% Two or more races, 0.9% Hispanic of any race; Average household size: 2.16; Median age: 41.9; Age under 18: 21.1%; Age 65 and over: 16.6%; Males per 100 females: 87.2

School District(s)

Ripley-Union-Lewis-Huntington Local (PK-12)
2012-13 Enrollment: 1,024 . . . . (937) 392-4396
Housing: Homeownership rate: 52.9%; Homeowner vacancy rate: 3.6%; Rental vacancy rate: 14.3%

DECATUR (unincorporated postal area)
ZCTA: 45115
Covers a land area of 1.041 square miles and a water area of 0 square miles. Located at 38.82° N. Lat; 83.70° W. Long. Elevation is 922 feet.
Population: 78; Growth (since 2000): 178.6%; Density: 74.9 persons per square mile; Race: 96.2% White, 1.3% Black/African American, 0.0% Asian, 0.0% American Indian/Alaska Native, 0.0% Native Hawaiian/Other Pacific Islander, 2.6% Two or more races, 0.0% Hispanic of any race; Average household size: 2.23; Median age: 40.0; Age under 18: 20.5%; Age 65 and over: 20.5%; Males per 100 females: 100.0
Housing: Homeownership rate: 82.9%; Homeowner vacancy rate: 3.3%; Rental vacancy rate: 0.0%

FAYETTEVILLE (village). Covers a land area of 0.521 square miles and a water area of 0 square miles. Located at 39.18° N. Lat; 83.93° W. Long. Elevation is 948 feet.

History: Fayetteville was settled in 1811 and became a village in 1868. St. Aloysius Academy, a Catholic school for boys, was founded here in 1850.

Population: 330; Growth (since 2000): -11.3%; Density: 633.7 persons per square mile; Race: 99.4% White, 0.3% Black/African American, 0.0% Asian, 0.0% American Indian/Alaska Native, 0.0% Native Hawaiian/Other Pacific Islander, 0.0% Two or more races, 1.2% Hispanic of any race; Average household size: 2.58; Median age: 36.8; Age under 18: 26.4%; Age 65 and over: 13.9%; Males per 100 females: 96.4

School District(s)

Fayetteville-Perry Local (PK-12)
2012-13 Enrollment: 835. . . . . (513) 875-2423

Housing: Homeownership rate: 68.0%; Homeowner vacancy rate: 7.4%; Rental vacancy rate: 12.5%

GEORGETOWN (village). County seat. Covers a land area of 4.044 square miles and a water area of 0 square miles. Located at 38.87° N. Lat; 83.90° W. Long. Elevation is 922 feet.

History: Georgetown was surveyed in 1819 and named for Georgetown, Kentucky. In the second half of the 1800's, the town was a distribution point for tobacco grown in the area.

Population: 4,331; Growth (since 2000): 17.3%; Density: 1,070.9 persons per square mile; Race: 95.5% White, 1.9% Black/African American, 0.5% Asian, 0.3% American Indian/Alaska Native, 0.0% Native Hawaiian/Other Pacific Islander, 1.6% Two or more races, 0.6% Hispanic of any race; Average household size: 2.36; Median age: 38.6; Age under 18: 24.5%; Age 65 and over: 18.7%; Males per 100 females: 93.1; Marriage status: 26.7% never married, 45.8% now married, 4.3% separated, 8.5% widowed, 19.0% divorced; Foreign born: 0.9%; Speak English only: 99.1%; With disability: 14.7%; Veterans: 6.6%; Ancestry: 24.5% German, 17.9% American, 14.7% Irish, 8.7% English, 3.9% Scottish

Employment: 6.2% management, business, and financial, 1.9% computer, engineering, and science, 12.3% education, legal, community service, arts, and media, 7.2% healthcare practitioners, 32.6% service, 18.0% sales and office, 11.2% natural resources, construction, and maintenance, 10.7% production, transportation, and material moving

Income: Per capita: $17,075; Median household: $33,333; Average household: $39,004; Households with income of $100,000 or more: 6.3%; Poverty rate: 17.4%

Educational Attainment: High school diploma or higher: 83.5%; Bachelor's degree or higher: 9.4%; Graduate/professional degree or higher: 4.2%

School District(s)

Georgetown Exempted Village (PK-12)
2012-13 Enrollment: 952. . . . . (937) 378-3565
Southern Hills (09-12)
2012-13 Enrollment: n/a . . . . (937) 378-6131

Housing: Homeownership rate: 53.9%; Median home value: $107,300; Median year structure built: 1970; Homeowner vacancy rate: 4.9%; Median gross rent: $518 per month; Rental vacancy rate: 9.5%

Health Insurance: 83.8% have insurance; 56.0% have private insurance; 39.3% have public insurance; 16.2% do not have insurance; 2.1% of children under 18 do not have insurance

Hospitals: Southwest Regional Medical Center (127 beds)

Safety: Violent crime rate: 6.7 per 10,000 population; Property crime rate: 262.5 per 10,000 population

Newspapers: The News Democrat (weekly circulation 4000)

Transportation: Commute: 92.9% car, 0.1% public transportation, 2.8% walk, 4.3% work from home; Median travel time to work: 30.6 minutes

HAMERSVILLE (village). Covers a land area of 0.393 square miles and a water area of 0 square miles. Located at 38.92° N. Lat; 83.99° W. Long. Elevation is 965 feet.

Population: 546; Growth (since 2000): 6.0%; Density: 1,390.7 persons per square mile; Race: 98.2% White, 0.0% Black/African American, 0.2% Asian, 0.0% American Indian/Alaska Native, 0.0% Native Hawaiian/Other Pacific Islander, 1.1% Two or more races, 0.5% Hispanic of any race; Average household size: 2.90; Median age: 34.5; Age under 18: 29.3%; Age 65 and over: 9.9%; Males per 100 females: 100.0

School District(s)

Western Brown Local (PK-12)
2012-13 Enrollment: 3,100 . . . . (937) 444-2044

Housing: Homeownership rate: 65.4%; Homeowner vacancy rate: 3.9%; Rental vacancy rate: 8.5%

HIGGINSPORT (village). Covers a land area of 0.251 square miles and a water area of 0.043 square miles. Located at 38.79° N. Lat; 83.97° W. Long. Elevation is 512 feet.

Population: 251; Growth (since 2000): -13.7%; Density: 1,000.7 persons per square mile; Race: 96.8% White, 0.0% Black/African American, 0.0% Asian, 0.4% American Indian/Alaska Native, 0.0% Native Hawaiian/Other Pacific Islander, 2.0% Two or more races, 1.2% Hispanic of any race; Average household size: 2.41; Median age: 44.5; Age under 18: 19.5%; Age 65 and over: 18.7%; Males per 100 females: 96.1

Housing: Homeownership rate: 70.2%; Homeowner vacancy rate: 1.3%; Rental vacancy rate: 18.4%

LAKE LORELEI (CDP). Covers a land area of 2.201 square miles and a water area of 0.249 square miles. Located at 39.19° N. Lat; 83.97° W. Long.

Population: 1,170; Growth (since 2000): n/a; Density: 531.5 persons per square mile; Race: 96.2% White, 0.3% Black/African American, 0.8% Asian, 0.1% American Indian/Alaska Native, 0.1% Native Hawaiian/Other Pacific Islander, 2.1% Two or more races, 1.0% Hispanic of any race; Average household size: 2.61; Median age: 44.0; Age under 18: 23.7%; Age 65 and over: 14.9%; Males per 100 females: 99.3

Housing: Homeownership rate: 94.4%; Homeowner vacancy rate: 2.9%; Rental vacancy rate: 3.7%

LAKE WAYNOKA (CDP). Covers a land area of 4.281 square miles and a water area of 0.521 square miles. Located at 38.94° N. Lat; 83.78° W. Long.

Population: 1,173; Growth (since 2000): n/a; Density: 274.0 persons per square mile; Race: 98.6% White, 0.7% Black/African American, 0.0% Asian, 0.0% American Indian/Alaska Native, 0.0% Native Hawaiian/Other Pacific Islander, 0.7% Two or more races, 0.8% Hispanic of any race; Average household size: 2.53; Median age: 46.7; Age under 18: 20.6%; Age 65 and over: 22.5%; Males per 100 females: 99.8

Housing: Homeownership rate: 92.9%; Homeowner vacancy rate: 2.7%; Rental vacancy rate: 15.4%

MOUNT ORAB (village). Covers a land area of 8.887 square miles and a water area of 0 square miles. Located at 39.03° N. Lat; 83.92° W. Long. Elevation is 942 feet.

History: The name of Mount Orab was derived from the biblical Horeb.

Population: 3,664; Growth (since 2000): 58.8%; Density: 412.3 persons per square mile; Race: 97.7% White, 0.7% Black/African American, 0.6% Asian, 0.1% American Indian/Alaska Native, 0.0% Native Hawaiian/Other Pacific Islander, 0.7% Two or more races, 0.6% Hispanic of any race; Average household size: 2.64; Median age: 33.7; Age under 18: 29.7%; Age 65 and over: 11.6%; Males per 100 females: 91.0; Marriage status: 20.4% never married, 55.7% now married, 1.5% separated, 11.5% widowed, 12.4% divorced; Foreign born: 0.0%; Speak English only: 99.1%; With disability: 12.6%; Veterans: 5.3%; Ancestry: 27.5% American, 23.4% German, 14.1% Irish, 5.4% English, 5.0% Italian

Employment: 8.7% management, business, and financial, 1.2% computer, engineering, and science, 7.3% education, legal, community service, arts, and media, 4.8% healthcare practitioners, 26.7% service, 32.3% sales and office, 6.9% natural resources, construction, and maintenance, 12.3% production, transportation, and material moving

Income: Per capita: $16,611; Median household: $39,335; Average household: $47,423; Households with income of $100,000 or more: 8.3%; Poverty rate: 18.8%

Educational Attainment: High school diploma or higher: 78.2%; Bachelor's degree or higher: 9.6%; Graduate/professional degree or higher: 4.4%

School District(s)

Western Brown Local (PK-12)
2012-13 Enrollment: 3,100 . . . . (937) 444-2044

Housing: Homeownership rate: 61.5%; Median home value: $114,300; Median year structure built: 1990; Homeowner vacancy rate: 1.9%; Median gross rent: $697 per month; Rental vacancy rate: 6.1%

Health Insurance: 76.6% have insurance; 51.5% have private insurance; 34.4% have public insurance; 23.4% do not have insurance; 10.4% of children under 18 do not have insurance

Newspapers: Brown County Press (weekly circulation 16500)

Transportation: Commute: 96.6% car, 0.5% public transportation, 1.3% walk, 1.6% work from home; Median travel time to work: 34.0 minutes

RIPLEY (village). Covers a land area of 1.988 square miles and a water area of 0.305 square miles. Located at 38.73° N. Lat; 83.83° W. Long. Elevation is 505 feet.

History: Ripley was laid out in 1812 by Colonel James Poage of Virginia. It was an early center for steamboat building, and for piano manufacturing. The 1937 flooding of the Ohio River ruined Ripley's wharf area. The Rankin House in Ripley was a station on the Underground Railroad.

Population: 1,750; Growth (since 2000): 0.3%; Density: 880.5 persons per square mile; Race: 92.6% White, 4.9% Black/African American, 0.2% Asian, 0.2% American Indian/Alaska Native, 0.0% Native Hawaiian/Other Pacific Islander, 2.2% Two or more races, 0.5% Hispanic of any race; Average household size: 2.31; Median age: 42.2; Age under 18: 24.1%; Age 65 and over: 15.9%; Males per 100 females: 90.6

School District(s)

Ripley-Union-Lewis-Huntington Local (PK-12)
2012-13 Enrollment: 1,024 . . . . (937) 392-4396

Housing: Homeownership rate: 60.2%; Homeowner vacancy rate: 5.4%; Rental vacancy rate: 13.5%

Newspapers: Ripley Bee (weekly circulation 1300)

RUSSELLVILLE (village). Covers a land area of 0.729 square miles and a water area of 0 square miles. Located at 38.87° N. Lat; 83.79° W. Long. Elevation is 971 feet.

Population: 561; Growth (since 2000): 23.8%; Density: 769.1 persons per square mile; Race: 99.1% White, 0.5% Black/African American, 0.0% Asian, 0.0% American Indian/Alaska Native, 0.0% Native Hawaiian/Other Pacific Islander, 0.4% Two or more races, 0.5% Hispanic of any race; Average household size: 2.68; Median age: 33.7; Age under 18: 30.3%; Age 65 and over: 13.9%; Males per 100 females: 92.8

School District(s)

Eastern Local (PK-12)
2012-13 Enrollment: 1,289 . . . . (937) 378-3981

Housing: Homeownership rate: 69.9%; Homeowner vacancy rate: 2.0%; Rental vacancy rate: 11.1%

SAINT MARTIN (village). Covers a land area of 1.093 square miles and a water area of 0 square miles. Located at 39.21° N. Lat; 83.89° W. Long. Elevation is 978 feet.

Population: 129; Growth (since 2000): 41.8%; Density: 118.0 persons per square mile; Race: 99.2% White, 0.0% Black/African American, 0.0% Asian, 0.0% American Indian/Alaska Native, 0.0% Native Hawaiian/Other Pacific Islander, 0.8% Two or more races, 0.0% Hispanic of any race; Average household size: 2.66; Median age: 49.2; Age under 18: 19.4%; Age 65 and over: 15.5%; Males per 100 females: 95.5

Two-year College(s)

Chatfield College (Private, Not-for-profit, Roman Catholic)
Fall 2013 Enrollment: 427 . . . . (513) 875-3344
2013-14 Tuition: In-state $9,070; Out-of-state $9,070

Housing: Homeownership rate: 91.5%; Homeowner vacancy rate: 0.0%; Rental vacancy rate: 0.0%

SARDINIA (village). Covers a land area of 1.239 square miles and a water area of 0 square miles. Located at 39.01° N. Lat; 83.80° W. Long. Elevation is 958 feet.

Population: 980; Growth (since 2000): 13.7%; Density: 791.3 persons per square mile; Race: 99.2% White, 0.2% Black/African American, 0.0% Asian, 0.3% American Indian/Alaska Native, 0.0% Native Hawaiian/Other Pacific Islander, 0.2% Two or more races, 0.3% Hispanic of any race; Average household size: 2.67; Median age: 30.0; Age under 18: 33.1%; Age 65 and over: 9.9%; Males per 100 females: 86.3

School District(s)

Eastern Local (PK-12)
2012-13 Enrollment: 1,289 . . . . (937) 378-3981
Eastern Local (PK-12)
2012-13 Enrollment: 782. . . . . (740) 226-4851

Housing: Homeownership rate: 55.9%; Homeowner vacancy rate: 4.2%; Rental vacancy rate: 5.9%

Butler County

Located in southwestern Ohio; bounded on the west by Indiana; crossed by the Great Miami River. Covers a land area of 467.056 square miles, a water area of 3.077 square miles, and is located in the Eastern Time Zone at 39.44° N. Lat., 84.57° W. Long. The county was founded in 1803. County seat is Hamilton.

Butler County is part of the Cincinnati, OH-KY-IN Metropolitan Statistical Area. The entire metro area includes: Dearborn County, IN; Ohio County, IN; Union County, IN; Boone County, KY; Bracken County, KY; Campbell County, KY; Gallatin County, KY; Grant County, KY; Kenton County, KY; Pendleton County, KY; Brown County, OH; Butler County, OH; Clermont County, OH; Hamilton County, OH; Warren County, OH

Weather Station: Fairfield Elevation: 575 feet

	Jan	Feb	Mar	Apr	May	Jun	Jul	Aug	Sep	Oct	Nov	Dec
High	40	43	54	66	75	84	88	87	80	68	55	42
Low	22	24	31	41	51	61	65	63	55	43	34	26
Precip	3.2	2.9	3.8	4.5	5.0	4.1	4.2	3.2	3.1	3.2	3.0	3.7
Snow	3.1	2.1	0.8	0.0	0.0	0.0	0.0	0.0	0.0	0.2	0.1	1.5

High and Low temperatures in degrees Fahrenheit; Precipitation and Snow in inches

Population: 368,130; Growth (since 2000): 10.6%; Density: 788.2 persons per square mile; Race: 86.0% White, 7.3% Black/African American, 2.4% Asian, 0.2% American Indian/Alaska Native, 0.1% Native Hawaiian/Other Pacific Islander, 2.1% two or more races, 4.0% Hispanic of any race; Average household size: 2.63; Median age: 36.0; Age under 18: 25.2%; Age 65 and over: 11.5%; Males per 100 females: 95.8; Marriage status: 29.9% never married, 53.3% now married, 1.9% separated, 5.5% widowed, 11.3% divorced; Foreign born: 5.2%; Speak English only: 93.1%; With disability: 11.3%; Veterans: 9.2%; Ancestry: 27.3% German, 13.0% Irish, 11.0% American, 9.0% English, 4.5% Italian

Religion: Six largest groups: 12.1% Catholicism, 7.4% Baptist, 4.4% Non-denominational Protestant, 3.7% Pentecostal, 3.0% Methodist/Pietist, 2.2% Holiness

Economy: Unemployment rate: 4.1%; Leading industries: 14.5% retail trade; 10.5% health care and social assistance; 10.3% other services (except public administration); Farms: 865 totaling 146,054 acres; Company size: 6 employ 1,000 or more persons, 8 employ 500 to 999 persons, 188 employ 100 to 499 persons, 6,748 employ less than 100 persons; Business ownership: 7,357 women-owned, 861 Black-owned, 365 Hispanic-owned, 679 Asian-owned

Employment: 14.3% management, business, and financial, 5.9% computer, engineering, and science, 9.4% education, legal, community service, arts, and media, 6.0% healthcare practitioners, 17.2% service, 25.9% sales and office, 7.3% natural resources, construction, and maintenance, 14.0% production, transportation, and material moving

Income: Per capita: $26,813; Median household: $56,610; Average household: $71,993; Households with income of $100,000 or more: 23.3%; Poverty rate: 13.6%

Educational Attainment: High school diploma or higher: 88.9%; Bachelor's degree or higher: 27.4%; Graduate/professional degree or higher: 9.8%

Housing: Homeownership rate: 69.7%; Median home value: $157,400; Median year structure built: 1976; Homeowner vacancy rate: 2.1%; Median gross rent: $798 per month; Rental vacancy rate: 12.4%

Vital Statistics: Birth rate: 120.7 per 10,000 population; Death rate: 84.1 per 10,000 population; Age-adjusted cancer mortality rate: 192.3 deaths per 100,000 population

Health Insurance: 89.4% have insurance; 74.3% have private insurance; 25.3% have public insurance; 10.6% do not have insurance; 5.2% of children under 18 do not have insurance

Health Care: Physicians: 12.3 per 10,000 population; Hospital beds: 16.3 per 10,000 population; Hospital admissions: 888.6 per 10,000 population

Air Quality Index: 73.7% good, 26.0% moderate, 0.3% unhealthy for sensitive individuals, 0.0% unhealthy (percent of days)

Transportation: Commute: 92.1% car, 0.8% public transportation, 2.5% walk, 3.6% work from home; Median travel time to work: 23.5 minutes

Presidential Election: 36.1% Obama, 62.3% Romney (2012)

Additional Information Contacts

Butler Government . . . . (513) 887-3247
http://www.butlercountyohio.org

Butler County Communities

BECKETT RIDGE (CDP). Covers a land area of 4.802 square miles and a water area of 0 square miles. Located at 39.34° N. Lat; 84.44° W. Long. Elevation is 820 feet.

History: Beckett Ridge's planning began in 1976 with the purchase of 1,800 acres of farmland from the Beckett family who owned the land since 1810.

Population: 9,187; Growth (since 2000): 6.0%; Density: 1,913.0 persons per square mile; Race: 81.9% White, 8.7% Black/African American, 6.6% Asian, 0.2% American Indian/Alaska Native, 0.1% Native Hawaiian/Other Pacific Islander, 1.7% Two or more races, 3.0% Hispanic of any race; Average household size: 2.60; Median age: 39.0; Age under 18: 26.8%; Age 65 and over: 8.8%; Males per 100 females: 96.7; Marriage status: 23.7% never married, 61.0% now married, 0.1% separated, 5.4% widowed, 10.0% divorced; Foreign born: 9.3%; Speak English only: 91.3%; With disability: 7.2%; Veterans: 6.8%; Ancestry: 30.5% German, 13.6% Irish, 8.8% Italian, 8.5% English, 7.8% American

Employment: 24.5% management, business, and financial, 12.2% computer, engineering, and science, 9.4% education, legal, community service, arts, and media, 10.1% healthcare practitioners, 10.4% service, 22.8% sales and office, 2.1% natural resources, construction, and maintenance, 8.5% production, transportation, and material moving

Income: Per capita: $46,219; Median household: $87,382; Average household: $116,250; Households with income of $100,000 or more: 42.4%; Poverty rate: 3.3%

Educational Attainment: High school diploma or higher: 97.7%; Bachelor's degree or higher: 53.0%; Graduate/professional degree or higher: 19.5%

Housing: Homeownership rate: 77.0%; Median home value: $219,900; Median year structure built: 1991; Homeowner vacancy rate: 1.9%; Median gross rent: $1,212 per month; Rental vacancy rate: 5.1%

Health Insurance: 94.7% have insurance; 89.8% have private insurance; 14.8% have public insurance; 5.3% do not have insurance; 1.9% of children under 18 do not have insurance

Transportation: Commute: 90.7% car, 1.0% public transportation, 0.7% walk, 6.4% work from home; Median travel time to work: 24.6 minutes

DARRTOWN (CDP). Covers a land area of 2.356 square miles and a water area of 0 square miles. Located at 39.50° N. Lat; 84.67° W. Long. Elevation is 738 feet.

Population: 516; Growth (since 2000): n/a; Density: 219.0 persons per square mile; Race: 98.4% White, 0.4% Black/African American, 0.0% Asian, 0.4% American Indian/Alaska Native, 0.0% Native Hawaiian/Other Pacific Islander, 0.8% Two or more races, 0.4% Hispanic of any race; Average household size: 2.37; Median age: 44.2; Age under 18: 19.2%; Age 65 and over: 12.2%; Males per 100 females: 94.0

Housing: Homeownership rate: 84.8%; Homeowner vacancy rate: 1.6%; Rental vacancy rate: 2.9%

FAIRFIELD (city). Covers a land area of 20.939 square miles and a water area of 0.121 square miles. Located at 39.33° N. Lat; 84.54° W. Long. Elevation is 594 feet.

Population: 42,510; Growth (since 2000): 1.0%; Density: 2,030.2 persons per square mile; Race: 79.0% White, 12.8% Black/African American, 2.4% Asian, 0.3% American Indian/Alaska Native, 0.1% Native Hawaiian/Other Pacific Islander, 2.4% Two or more races, 5.5% Hispanic of any race; Average household size: 2.41; Median age: 38.3; Age under 18: 23.2%; Age 65 and over: 13.0%; Males per 100 females: 92.9; Marriage status: 28.0% never married, 52.8% now married, 1.9% separated, 5.8% widowed, 13.4% divorced; Foreign born: 7.0%; Speak English only: 91.6%; With disability: 9.0%; Veterans: 9.1%; Ancestry: 29.6% German, 13.7% Irish, 8.4% American, 8.1% English, 4.5% Italian

Employment: 13.3% management, business, and financial, 5.8% computer, engineering, and science, 8.8% education, legal, community service, arts, and media, 6.0% healthcare practitioners, 15.7% service, 28.1% sales and office, 6.7% natural resources, construction, and maintenance, 15.7% production, transportation, and material moving

Income: Per capita: $28,663; Median household: $56,318; Average household: $69,488; Households with income of $100,000 or more: 20.2%; Poverty rate: 8.1%

Educational Attainment: High school diploma or higher: 91.7%; Bachelor's degree or higher: 26.5%; Graduate/professional degree or higher: 8.5%

School District(s)

Fairfield City (PK-12)
2012-13 Enrollment: 9,703 . . . . (513) 829-6300

Two-year College(s)

Moler-Pickens Beauty Academy (Private, For-profit)
Fall 2013 Enrollment: 74 . . . . (513) 874-5116

Housing: Homeownership rate: 63.8%; Median home value: $147,100; Median year structure built: 1978; Homeowner vacancy rate: 1.7%; Median gross rent: $855 per month; Rental vacancy rate: 12.0%

Health Insurance: 88.0% have insurance; 76.5% have private insurance; 21.1% have public insurance; 12.0% do not have insurance; 3.5% of children under 18 do not have insurance

Hospitals: Mercy Hospital Fairfield (167 beds)

Safety: Violent crime rate: 28.1 per 10,000 population; Property crime rate: 257.8 per 10,000 population

Transportation: Commute: 96.6% car, 0.3% public transportation, 0.5% walk, 2.0% work from home; Median travel time to work: 23.0 minutes

Additional Information Contacts

City of Fairfield . . . . (513) 867-5300
http://www.fairfield-city.org

FOUR BRIDGES (CDP). Covers a land area of 2.194 square miles and a water area of 0.003 square miles. Located at 39.38° N. Lat; 84.36° W. Long.

Population: 2,919; Growth (since 2000): n/a; Density: 1,330.2 persons per square mile; Race: 88.4% White, 5.1% Black/African American, 4.5% Asian, 0.0% American Indian/Alaska Native, 0.0% Native Hawaiian/Other Pacific Islander, 1.5% Two or more races, 1.7% Hispanic of any race; Average household size: 2.62; Median age: 40.4; Age under 18: 27.1%; Age 65 and over: 13.9%; Males per 100 females: 92.8; Marriage status: 22.7% never married, 61.8% now married, 1.2% separated, 8.8% widowed, 6.8% divorced; Foreign born: 4.6%; Speak English only: 94.3%; With disability: 11.5%; Veterans: 6.9%; Ancestry: 30.9% German, 18.9% Irish, 12.2% English, 4.9% Polish, 4.6% American

Employment: 28.5% management, business, and financial, 16.1% computer, engineering, and science, 8.6% education, legal, community service, arts, and media, 5.8% healthcare practitioners, 5.0% service, 32.6% sales and office, 1.1% natural resources, construction, and maintenance, 2.3% production, transportation, and material moving

Income: Per capita: $44,187; Median household: $91,164; Average household: $114,903; Households with income of $100,000 or more: 44.6%; Poverty rate: 0.9%

Educational Attainment: High school diploma or higher: 96.2%; Bachelor's degree or higher: 57.7%; Graduate/professional degree or higher: 22.6%

Housing: Homeownership rate: 70.8%; Median home value: $377,900; Median year structure built: 2002; Homeowner vacancy rate: 2.2%; Median gross rent: $1,279 per month; Rental vacancy rate: 18.6%

Health Insurance: 95.8% have insurance; 88.2% have private insurance; 19.0% have public insurance; 4.2% do not have insurance; 5.7% of children under 18 do not have insurance

Transportation: Commute: 91.9% car, 0.0% public transportation, 0.0% walk, 8.1% work from home; Median travel time to work: 24.4 minutes

HAMILTON (city). County seat. Covers a land area of 21.596 square miles and a water area of 0.479 square miles. Located at 39.39° N. Lat; 84.57° W. Long. Elevation is 597 feet.

History: Settlement at Hamilton began in 1791 when General St. Clair built Fort Hamilton as a military and trading post. The town was platted in 1794 by Colonel Israel Ludlow, and named Fairfield, but the site was abandoned in 1796. When the plat was recorded in 1802, the town was named Hamilton for the fort, and became the seat of Butler County. In 1854 Rossville, settled in 1804 on the other side of the Great Miami River, became part of Hamilton. It was the Hamilton Hydraulic water-power plant completed in 1852 that changed Hamilton into an industrial center. A resident here at that time was William Dean Howells, who describes the city in "A Boy's Town."

Population: 62,477; Growth (since 2000): 2.9%; Density: 2,893.0 persons per square mile; Race: 84.0% White, 8.5% Black/African American, 0.6% Asian, 0.2% American Indian/Alaska Native, 0.1% Native Hawaiian/Other Pacific Islander, 2.9% Two or more races, 6.4% Hispanic of any race; Average household size: 2.47; Median age: 35.3; Age under 18: 24.9%; Age 65 and over: 13.2%; Males per 100 females: 95.4; Marriage status: 31.9% never married, 45.3% now married, 3.2% separated, 7.0% widowed, 15.8% divorced; Foreign born: 3.8%; Speak English only: 94.3%;

With disability: 15.2%; Veterans: 10.0%; Ancestry: 28.0% German, 16.0% American, 12.9% Irish, 7.8% English, 4.6% Italian
Employment: 8.0% management, business, and financial, 3.4% computer, engineering, and science, 8.4% education, legal, community service, arts, and media, 4.9% healthcare practitioners, 21.5% service, 26.3% sales and office, 9.5% natural resources, construction, and maintenance, 18.0% production, transportation, and material moving
Income: Per capita: $20,283; Median household: $40,426; Average household: $50,466; Households with income of $100,000 or more: 10.2%; Poverty rate: 22.9%
Educational Attainment: High school diploma or higher: 83.1%; Bachelor's degree or higher: 14.8%; Graduate/professional degree or higher: 4.6%

School District(s)

Butler Technology & Career Development Schools (07-12)
2012-13 Enrollment: n/a . . . . (513) 868-1911
Edgewood City (PK-12)
2012-13 Enrollment: 3,606 . . . . (513) 863-4692
Fairfield City (PK-12)
2012-13 Enrollment: 9,703 . . . . (513) 829-6300
Hamilton City (PK-12)
2012-13 Enrollment: 9,868 . . . . (513) 887-5000
New Miami Local (PK-12)
2012-13 Enrollment: 739. . . . . (513) 863-0833
Richard Allen Academy III (KG-06)
2012-13 Enrollment: 180. . . . . (513) 868-2900
Ross Local (PK-12)
2012-13 Enrollment: 2,764 . . . . (513) 863-1253

Four-year College(s)

Miami University-Hamilton (Public)
Fall 2013 Enrollment: 3,621 . . . . (513) 785-3000
2013-14 Tuition: In-state $5,072; Out-of-state $14,165

Vocational/Technical School(s)

Butler Tech-D Russel Lee Career Center (Public)
Fall 2013 Enrollment: 303 . . . . (513) 645-8205
2013-14 Tuition: $13,896

Housing: Homeownership rate: 55.9%; Median home value: $104,300; Median year structure built: 1954; Homeowner vacancy rate: 2.9%; Median gross rent: $707 per month; Rental vacancy rate: 11.9%
Health Insurance: 84.5% have insurance; 59.9% have private insurance; 36.2% have public insurance; 15.5% do not have insurance; 7.0% of children under 18 do not have insurance
Hospitals: Fort Hamilton Hughes Memorial Hospital (310 beds)
Safety: Violent crime rate: 60.7 per 10,000 population; Property crime rate: 630.3 per 10,000 population
Newspapers: Journal-News (daily circulation 20300)
Transportation: Commute: 94.1% car, 0.2% public transportation, 2.4% walk, 1.6% work from home; Median travel time to work: 24.2 minutes
Airports: Butler Co Regional-Hogan Field (general aviation)

Additional Information Contacts

City of Hamilton . . . . (513) 785-7000
http://www.hamilton-city.org

JACKSONBURG (village). Covers a land area of 0.020 square miles and a water area of 0 square miles. Located at 39.54° N. Lat; 84.50° W. Long. Elevation is 955 feet.
History: Sometimes spelled Jacksonburgh.
Population: 63; Growth (since 2000): -6.0%; Density: 3,159.6 persons per square mile; Race: 90.5% White, 0.0% Black/African American, 0.0% Asian, 4.8% American Indian/Alaska Native, 0.0% Native Hawaiian/Other Pacific Islander, 4.8% Two or more races, 0.0% Hispanic of any race; Average household size: 3.00; Median age: 29.8; Age under 18: 30.2%; Age 65 and over: 4.8%; Males per 100 females: 117.2
Housing: Homeownership rate: 76.2%; Homeowner vacancy rate: 0.0%; Rental vacancy rate: 16.7%

MIDDLETOWN (city). Covers a land area of 26.185 square miles and a water area of 0.235 square miles. Located at 39.50° N. Lat; 84.36° W. Long. Elevation is 656 feet.
History: Middletown was platted in 1802 by Stephen Vail and James Sutton, who named it for its position midway between Cincinnati and Dayton. It was in Middletown in 1825 that Governor DeWitt Clinton of New York took the first shovelful of dirt to signify the beginning of the Miami & Erie Canal.
Population: 48,694; Growth (since 2000): -5.6%; Density: 1,859.6 persons per square mile; Race: 83.3% White, 11.7% Black/African American, 0.5% Asian, 0.2% American Indian/Alaska Native, 0.0% Native Hawaiian/Other Pacific Islander, 2.7% Two or more races, 3.8% Hispanic of any race; Average household size: 2.38; Median age: 38.3; Age under 18: 24.3%; Age 65 and over: 14.9%; Males per 100 females: 90.6; Marriage status: 29.6% never married, 47.2% now married, 2.7% separated, 7.1% widowed, 16.1% divorced; Foreign born: 3.0%; Speak English only: 94.9%; With disability: 19.3%; Veterans: 9.9%; Ancestry: 18.7% German, 12.5% Irish, 9.5% American, 7.8% English, 3.6% Italian
Employment: 10.8% management, business, and financial, 3.4% computer, engineering, and science, 6.9% education, legal, community service, arts, and media, 5.3% healthcare practitioners, 21.4% service, 26.0% sales and office, 8.0% natural resources, construction, and maintenance, 18.2% production, transportation, and material moving
Income: Per capita: $20,199; Median household: $35,853; Average household: $48,185; Households with income of $100,000 or more: 8.7%; Poverty rate: 23.0%
Educational Attainment: High school diploma or higher: 82.4%; Bachelor's degree or higher: 15.5%; Graduate/professional degree or higher: 4.6%

School District(s)

Life Skills Center-Middletown (09-12)
2012-13 Enrollment: 201. . . . . (513) 423-1800
Madison Local (PK-12)
2012-13 Enrollment: 1,519 . . . . (513) 420-4750
Middletown City (PK-12)
2012-13 Enrollment: 6,315 . . . . (513) 423-0781
Middletown Fitness & Prep Acad (KG-08)
2012-13 Enrollment: 267. . . . . (513) 424-6110
Summit Academy Secondary School - Middletown (09-12)
2012-13 Enrollment: 52. . . . . (513) 420-9767
Summit Acdy Community Schl for Alternative Learner (01-08)
2012-13 Enrollment: 103. . . . . (513) 422-8540

Four-year College(s)

Miami University-Middletown (Public)
Fall 2013 Enrollment: 2,221 . . . . (513) 727-3200
2013-14 Tuition: In-state $5,072; Out-of-state $14,165

Two-year College(s)

Carousel Beauty College-Middletown (Private, For-profit)
Fall 2013 Enrollment: 25 . . . . (937) 223-3572

Housing: Homeownership rate: 53.8%; Median home value: $97,200; Median year structure built: 1958; Homeowner vacancy rate: 4.0%; Median gross rent: $732 per month; Rental vacancy rate: 14.1%
Health Insurance: 85.0% have insurance; 55.4% have private insurance; 43.3% have public insurance; 15.0% do not have insurance; 5.1% of children under 18 do not have insurance
Safety: Violent crime rate: 61.8 per 10,000 population; Property crime rate: 816.2 per 10,000 population
Newspapers: Middletown Journal (daily circulation 18300)
Transportation: Commute: 95.0% car, 0.9% public transportation, 1.0% walk, 2.0% work from home; Median travel time to work: 21.2 minutes
Airports: Middletown Regional/Hook Field (general aviation)

Additional Information Contacts

City of Middletown . . . . (513) 425-7730
http://www.ci.middletown.oh.us

MILLVILLE (village). Covers a land area of 0.583 square miles and a water area of 0 square miles. Located at 39.39° N. Lat; 84.65° W. Long. Elevation is 623 feet.
Population: 708; Growth (since 2000): -13.3%; Density: 1,213.7 persons per square mile; Race: 97.5% White, 0.1% Black/African American, 0.8% Asian, 0.1% American Indian/Alaska Native, 0.0% Native Hawaiian/Other Pacific Islander, 1.0% Two or more races, 0.3% Hispanic of any race; Average household size: 2.63; Median age: 38.9; Age under 18: 23.0%; Age 65 and over: 14.0%; Males per 100 females: 92.9
Housing: Homeownership rate: 81.8%; Homeowner vacancy rate: 3.0%; Rental vacancy rate: 7.4%

MONROE (city). Covers a land area of 15.873 square miles and a water area of 0.023 square miles. Located at 39.45° N. Lat; 84.37° W. Long. Elevation is 830 feet.
Population: 12,442; Growth (since 2000): 74.4%; Density: 783.9 persons per square mile; Race: 92.6% White, 3.7% Black/African American, 1.7% Asian, 0.2% American Indian/Alaska Native, 0.0% Native Hawaiian/Other

Pacific Islander, 1.3% Two or more races, 1.8% Hispanic of any race; Average household size: 2.63; Median age: 36.9; Age under 18: 27.0%; Age 65 and over: 14.3%; Males per 100 females: 95.1; Marriage status: 23.5% never married, 58.0% now married, 1.1% separated, 8.9% widowed, 9.6% divorced; Foreign born: 2.7%; Speak English only: 94.6%; With disability: 10.6%; Veterans: 13.2%; Ancestry: 32.3% German, 14.6% Irish, 11.0% English, 7.8% American, 3.9% Scottish
Employment: 14.9% management, business, and financial, 5.9% computer, engineering, and science, 7.9% education, legal, community service, arts, and media, 6.6% healthcare practitioners, 14.8% service, 30.0% sales and office, 6.1% natural resources, construction, and maintenance, 13.9% production, transportation, and material moving
Income: Per capita: $27,149; Median household: $67,046; Average household: $72,716; Households with income of $100,000 or more: 23.7%; Poverty rate: 8.0%
Educational Attainment: High school diploma or higher: 92.9%; Bachelor's degree or higher: 30.6%; Graduate/professional degree or higher: 6.7%

School District(s)

Butler Technology & Career Development Schools (07-12)
2012-13 Enrollment: n/a . . . . (513) 868-1911
Monroe Local SD (PK-12)
2012-13 Enrollment: 2,410 . . . . (513) 539-2536

Housing: Homeownership rate: 78.4%; Median home value: $158,100; Median year structure built: 1999; Homeowner vacancy rate: 1.6%; Median gross rent: $968 per month; Rental vacancy rate: 10.2%
Health Insurance: 92.7% have insurance; 81.0% have private insurance; 21.9% have public insurance; 7.3% do not have insurance; 3.8% of children under 18 do not have insurance
Safety: Violent crime rate: 39.9 per 10,000 population; Property crime rate: 410.2 per 10,000 population
Transportation: Commute: 94.6% car, 0.2% public transportation, 0.8% walk, 4.2% work from home; Median travel time to work: 27.0 minutes
Additional Information Contacts
City of Monroe. . . . . (513) 539-7374
http://www.monroeohio.org

NEW MIAMI (village). Covers a land area of 0.905 square miles and a water area of 0.036 square miles. Located at 39.43° N. Lat; 84.54° W. Long. Elevation is 594 feet.
Population: 2,249; Growth (since 2000): -8.9%; Density: 2,485.4 persons per square mile; Race: 92.0% White, 5.2% Black/African American, 0.1% Asian, 0.3% American Indian/Alaska Native, 0.1% Native Hawaiian/Other Pacific Islander, 2.2% Two or more races, 1.2% Hispanic of any race; Average household size: 2.84; Median age: 36.1; Age under 18: 26.1%; Age 65 and over: 11.1%; Males per 100 females: 101.5
Housing: Homeownership rate: 63.4%; Homeowner vacancy rate: 2.9%; Rental vacancy rate: 9.1%

OKEANA (unincorporated postal area)

ZCTA: 45053

Covers a land area of 27.128 square miles and a water area of <.001 square miles. Located at 39.35° N. Lat; 84.79° W. Long. Elevation is 640 feet.
Population: 3,420; Growth (since 2000): 12.2%; Density: 126.1 persons per square mile; Race: 98.6% White, 0.1% Black/African American, 0.1% Asian, 0.3% American Indian/Alaska Native, 0.0% Native Hawaiian/Other Pacific Islander, 0.7% Two or more races, 0.9% Hispanic of any race; Average household size: 2.81; Median age: 43.3; Age under 18: 24.1%; Age 65 and over: 12.5%; Males per 100 females: 104.7; Marriage status: 20.8% never married, 66.4% now married, 0.0% separated, 7.2% widowed, 5.7% divorced; Foreign born: 0.3%; Speak English only: 97.8%; With disability: 10.8%; Veterans: 9.3%; Ancestry: 49.0% German, 13.0% American, 10.0% English, 8.7% Irish, 3.3% Italian
Employment: 15.8% management, business, and financial, 3.6% computer, engineering, and science, 12.2% education, legal, community service, arts, and media, 9.8% healthcare practitioners, 15.1% service, 17.8% sales and office, 15.2% natural resources, construction, and maintenance, 10.5% production, transportation, and material moving
Income: Per capita: $31,705; Median household: $77,361; Average household: $79,920; Households with income of $100,000 or more: 38.7%; Poverty rate: 7.0%
Educational Attainment: High school diploma or higher: 94.5%; Bachelor's degree or higher: 29.7%; Graduate/professional degree or higher: 11.6%
Housing: Homeownership rate: 93.2%; Median home value: $237,100; Median year structure built: 1986; Homeowner vacancy rate: 0.7%; Median gross rent: n/a per month; Rental vacancy rate: 4.5%
Health Insurance: 93.8% have insurance; 88.3% have private insurance; 19.7% have public insurance; 6.2% do not have insurance; 5.1% of children under 18 do not have insurance
Transportation: Commute: 95.0% car, 1.6% public transportation, 0.0% walk, 3.5% work from home; Median travel time to work: 31.6 minutes

OLDE WEST CHESTER (CDP). Covers a land area of 0.357 square miles and a water area of 0 square miles. Located at 39.34° N. Lat; 84.40° W. Long. Elevation is 676 feet.
Population: 240; Growth (since 2000): 3.4%; Density: 671.9 persons per square mile; Race: 87.9% White, 3.8% Black/African American, 1.7% Asian, 0.0% American Indian/Alaska Native, 0.0% Native Hawaiian/Other Pacific Islander, 0.0% Two or more races, 7.5% Hispanic of any race; Average household size: 2.70; Median age: 42.1; Age under 18: 23.7%; Age 65 and over: 8.8%; Males per 100 females: 103.4
Housing: Homeownership rate: 67.4%; Homeowner vacancy rate: 6.3%; Rental vacancy rate: 0.0%

OXFORD (city). Covers a land area of 6.676 square miles and a water area of 0.002 square miles. Located at 39.51° N. Lat; 84.75° W. Long. Elevation is 922 feet.
History: Named for Oxford, the university town in Oxfordshire, England. Oxford was planned, even before the land had been surveyed and cleared, as the site of Miami University, authorized by the Ohio Legislature in 1809. The University actually opened in 1824, and the town grew around it. It was joined in 1848 by the Oxford College for Women, which flourished for 80 years before it was absorbed by Miami University. One of the instructors at the University was William Holmes McGuffey, whose name became synonymous with the "Eclectic Readers" that he compiled to help children learn to read.
Population: 21,371; Growth (since 2000): -2.6%; Density: 3,201.0 persons per square mile; Race: 87.6% White, 4.0% Black/African American, 5.4% Asian, 0.2% American Indian/Alaska Native, 0.0% Native Hawaiian/Other Pacific Islander, 2.2% Two or more races, 2.3% Hispanic of any race; Average household size: 2.40; Median age: 21.4; Age under 18: 6.8%; Age 65 and over: 5.6%; Males per 100 females: 90.7; Marriage status: 77.6% never married, 17.2% now married, 0.9% separated, 2.0% widowed, 3.2% divorced; Foreign born: 6.8%; Speak English only: 91.8%; With disability: 6.5%; Veterans: 2.8%; Ancestry: 22.8% German, 12.1% American, 11.0% Irish, 7.8% English, 5.6% Italian
Employment: 11.0% management, business, and financial, 3.7% computer, engineering, and science, 21.5% education, legal, community service, arts, and media, 2.3% healthcare practitioners, 29.9% service, 23.5% sales and office, 2.1% natural resources, construction, and maintenance, 6.0% production, transportation, and material moving
Income: Per capita: $14,950; Median household: $28,429; Average household: $51,136; Households with income of $100,000 or more: 14.9%; Poverty rate: 46.0%
Educational Attainment: High school diploma or higher: 92.3%; Bachelor's degree or higher: 59.8%; Graduate/professional degree or higher: 31.8%

School District(s)

Talawanda City (PK-12)
2012-13 Enrollment: 2,963 . . . . (513) 273-3333

Four-year College(s)

Miami University-Oxford (Public)
Fall 2013 Enrollment: 17,901 . . . . (513) 529-1809
2013-14 Tuition: In-state $13,800; Out-of-state $29,590

Housing: Homeownership rate: 30.5%; Median home value: $188,100; Median year structure built: 1979; Homeowner vacancy rate: 2.8%; Median gross rent: $768 per month; Rental vacancy rate: 13.8%
Health Insurance: 94.2% have insurance; 88.3% have private insurance; 11.7% have public insurance; 5.8% do not have insurance; 5.9% of children under 18 do not have insurance
Hospitals: McCullough - Hyde Memorial Hospital (60 beds)
Safety: Violent crime rate: 22.0 per 10,000 population; Property crime rate: 270.9 per 10,000 population
Newspapers: Oxford Press (weekly circulation 3700)
Transportation: Commute: 54.8% car, 5.7% public transportation, 26.9% walk, 11.0% work from home; Median travel time to work: 14.0 minutes
Airports: Miami University (general aviation)
Additional Information Contacts

City of Oxford . . . . (513) 524-5200
http://www.cityofoxford.org

ROSS (CDP). Covers a land area of 3.117 square miles and a water area of 0.027 square miles. Located at 39.31° N. Lat; 84.66° W. Long. Elevation is 554 feet.
Population: 3,417; Growth (since 2000): 73.4%; Density: 1,096.3 persons per square mile; Race: 98.3% White, 0.2% Black/African American, 0.0% Asian, 0.2% American Indian/Alaska Native, 0.1% Native Hawaiian/Other Pacific Islander, 0.9% Two or more races, 0.7% Hispanic of any race; Average household size: 2.76; Median age: 39.2; Age under 18: 26.1%; Age 65 and over: 11.6%; Males per 100 females: 99.1; Marriage status: 28.6% never married, 59.2% now married, 2.3% separated, 5.0% widowed, 7.2% divorced; Foreign born: 0.4%; Speak English only: 99.1%; With disability: 9.9%; Veterans: 14.9%; Ancestry: 41.0% German, 19.7% Irish, 10.2% English, 9.2% American, 2.4% French
Employment: 13.2% management, business, and financial, 5.2% computer, engineering, and science, 7.8% education, legal, community service, arts, and media, 7.9% healthcare practitioners, 13.8% service, 15.9% sales and office, 12.7% natural resources, construction, and maintenance, 23.3% production, transportation, and material moving
Income: Per capita: $27,327; Median household: $59,788; Average household: $71,378; Households with income of $100,000 or more: 22.8%; Poverty rate: 2.4%
Educational Attainment: High school diploma or higher: 86.9%; Bachelor's degree or higher: 21.3%; Graduate/professional degree or higher: 5.4%
Housing: Homeownership rate: 78.1%; Median home value: $165,000; Median year structure built: 1975; Homeowner vacancy rate: 1.4%; Median gross rent: $878 per month; Rental vacancy rate: 6.2%
Health Insurance: 90.3% have insurance; 81.8% have private insurance; 22.6% have public insurance; 9.7% do not have insurance; 5.9% of children under 18 do not have insurance
Transportation: Commute: 97.0% car, 1.5% public transportation, 0.0% walk, 1.5% work from home; Median travel time to work: 25.8 minutes

SEVEN MILE (village). Covers a land area of 0.723 square miles and a water area of 0 square miles. Located at 39.49° N. Lat; 84.55° W. Long. Elevation is 653 feet.
Population: 751; Growth (since 2000): 10.8%; Density: 1,038.6 persons per square mile; Race: 97.6% White, 0.1% Black/African American, 0.3% Asian, 0.1% American Indian/Alaska Native, 0.0% Native Hawaiian/Other Pacific Islander, 1.2% Two or more races, 1.3% Hispanic of any race; Average household size: 2.55; Median age: 40.3; Age under 18: 23.3%; Age 65 and over: 14.4%; Males per 100 females: 94.1

School District(s)

Edgewood City (PK-12)
2012-13 Enrollment: 3,606 . . . . (513) 863-4692
Housing: Homeownership rate: 71.8%; Homeowner vacancy rate: 1.9%; Rental vacancy rate: 8.8%

SOMERVILLE (village). Covers a land area of 0.252 square miles and a water area of 0 square miles. Located at 39.56° N. Lat; 84.64° W. Long. Elevation is 768 feet.
Population: 281; Growth (since 2000): -4.4%; Density: 1,113.1 persons per square mile; Race: 98.2% White, 0.0% Black/African American, 0.0% Asian, 0.0% American Indian/Alaska Native, 0.0% Native Hawaiian/Other Pacific Islander, 1.8% Two or more races, 0.0% Hispanic of any race; Average household size: 2.93; Median age: 37.8; Age under 18: 24.9%; Age 65 and over: 12.5%; Males per 100 females: 112.9
Housing: Homeownership rate: 69.8%; Homeowner vacancy rate: 4.2%; Rental vacancy rate: 6.5%

TRENTON (city). Covers a land area of 4.563 square miles and a water area of 0 square miles. Located at 39.48° N. Lat; 84.46° W. Long. Elevation is 650 feet.
Population: 11,869; Growth (since 2000): 35.7%; Density: 2,600.9 persons per square mile; Race: 96.2% White, 1.0% Black/African American, 0.5% Asian, 0.2% American Indian/Alaska Native, 0.0% Native Hawaiian/Other Pacific Islander, 1.9% Two or more races, 1.7% Hispanic of any race; Average household size: 2.85; Median age: 32.2; Age under 18: 31.0%; Age 65 and over: 9.4%; Males per 100 females: 94.6; Marriage status: 22.8% never married, 60.4% now married, 4.3% separated, 5.8% widowed, 11.1% divorced; Foreign born: 0.1%; Speak English only: 98.8%; With disability: 13.0%; Veterans: 9.9%; Ancestry: 27.3% German, 10.2% American, 10.2% Irish, 7.2% English, 3.7% Italian
Employment: 9.8% management, business, and financial, 4.7% computer, engineering, and science, 6.2% education, legal, community service, arts, and media, 3.4% healthcare practitioners, 15.5% service, 31.9% sales and office, 7.9% natural resources, construction, and maintenance, 20.5% production, transportation, and material moving
Income: Per capita: $22,474; Median household: $58,181; Average household: $62,718; Households with income of $100,000 or more: 16.8%; Poverty rate: 9.6%
Educational Attainment: High school diploma or higher: 89.6%; Bachelor's degree or higher: 11.0%; Graduate/professional degree or higher: 3.6%

School District(s)

Edgewood City (PK-12)
2012-13 Enrollment: 3,606 . . . . (513) 863-4692
Housing: Homeownership rate: 72.6%; Median home value: $125,100; Median year structure built: 1977; Homeowner vacancy rate: 2.4%; Median gross rent: $780 per month; Rental vacancy rate: 7.8%
Health Insurance: 89.4% have insurance; 75.6% have private insurance; 22.5% have public insurance; 10.6% do not have insurance; 8.2% of children under 18 do not have insurance
Transportation: Commute: 97.2% car, 0.3% public transportation, 1.3% walk, 1.2% work from home; Median travel time to work: 26.9 minutes
Additional Information Contacts
City of Trenton. . . . . (513) 988-6304
http://www.ci.trenton.oh.us

WEST CHESTER (unincorporated postal area)

ZCTA: 45069

Covers a land area of 28.438 square miles and a water area of 0.019 square miles. Located at 39.35° N. Lat; 84.41° W. Long..
Population: 49,060; Growth (since 2000): 14.6%; Density: 1,725.1 persons per square mile; Race: 82.7% White, 7.0% Black/African American, 6.8% Asian, 0.2% American Indian/Alaska Native, 0.1% Native Hawaiian/Other Pacific Islander, 2.0% Two or more races, 3.6% Hispanic of any race; Average household size: 2.75; Median age: 38.9; Age under 18: 27.2%; Age 65 and over: 10.6%; Males per 100 females: 96.9; Marriage status: 23.0% never married, 62.9% now married, 1.5% separated, 5.6% widowed, 8.4% divorced; Foreign born: 10.6%; Speak English only: 87.2%; With disability: 7.4%; Veterans: 9.0%; Ancestry: 28.8% German, 13.1% Irish, 10.2% English, 8.1% American, 5.8% Italian
Employment: 22.0% management, business, and financial, 11.4% computer, engineering, and science, 10.6% education, legal, community service, arts, and media, 6.8% healthcare practitioners, 12.5% service, 24.1% sales and office, 4.2% natural resources, construction, and maintenance, 8.4% production, transportation, and material moving
Income: Per capita: $37,794; Median household: $84,010; Average household: $104,419; Households with income of $100,000 or more: 41.0%; Poverty rate: 5.1%
Educational Attainment: High school diploma or higher: 95.2%; Bachelor's degree or higher: 46.1%; Graduate/professional degree or higher: 18.6%

School District(s)

Lakota Local (PK-12)
2012-13 Enrollment: 16,526 . . . . (513) 874-5505

Four-year College(s)

Aveda Fredric's Institute-Cincinnati (Private, For-profit)
Fall 2013 Enrollment: 212. . . . . (513) 533-0700

Two-year College(s)

Aveda Fredric's Institute-Cincinnati (Private, For-profit)
Fall 2013 Enrollment: 212. . . . . (513) 533-0700

Vocational/Technical School(s)

Aveda Fredric's Institute-Cincinnati (Private, For-profit)
Fall 2013 Enrollment: 212. . . . . (513) 533-0700
2013-14 Tuition: $17,150
Housing: Homeownership rate: 82.1%; Median home value: $203,900; Median year structure built: 1989; Homeowner vacancy rate: 1.9%; Median gross rent: $1,055 per month; Rental vacancy rate: 15.4%
Health Insurance: 92.9% have insurance; 86.1% have private insurance; 17.7% have public insurance; 7.1% do not have insurance; 4.1% of children under 18 do not have insurance
Hospitals: West Chester Hospital
Transportation: Commute: 91.3% car, 0.8% public transportation, 1.3% walk, 5.9% work from home; Median travel time to work: 22.8 minutes

WETHERINGTON (CDP). Covers a land area of 0.906 square miles and a water area of 0 square miles. Located at 39.36° N. Lat; 84.38° W. Long. Elevation is 860 feet.
Population: 1,302; Growth (since 2000): 28.9%; Density: 1,437.2 persons per square mile; Race: 90.6% White, 2.8% Black/African American, 5.8% Asian, 0.2% American Indian/Alaska Native, 0.0% Native Hawaiian/Other Pacific Islander, 0.6% Two or more races, 1.8% Hispanic of any race; Average household size: 2.44; Median age: 48.1; Age under 18: 20.3%; Age 65 and over: 14.7%; Males per 100 females: 95.5
Housing: Homeownership rate: 94.6%; Homeowner vacancy rate: 6.1%; Rental vacancy rate: 3.2%

WILLIAMSDALE (CDP). Covers a land area of 0.174 square miles and a water area of 0 square miles. Located at 39.44° N. Lat; 84.53° W. Long. Elevation is 600 feet.
Population: 581; Growth (since 2000): n/a; Density: 3,335.4 persons per square mile; Race: 97.2% White, 0.2% Black/African American, 0.0% Asian, 0.7% American Indian/Alaska Native, 0.0% Native Hawaiian/Other Pacific Islander, 1.9% Two or more races, 1.5% Hispanic of any race; Average household size: 2.65; Median age: 39.9; Age under 18: 24.8%; Age 65 and over: 14.5%; Males per 100 females: 106.8
Housing: Homeownership rate: 72.1%; Homeowner vacancy rate: 3.1%; Rental vacancy rate: 9.0%

Carroll County

Located in eastern Ohio; drained by Small Sandy, Conotton, and Yellow Creeks. Covers a land area of 394.609 square miles, a water area of 4.322 square miles, and is located in the Eastern Time Zone at 40.58° N. Lat., 81.09° W. Long. The county was founded in 1832. County seat is Carrollton.

Carroll County is part of the Canton-Massillon, OH Metropolitan Statistical Area. The entire metro area includes: Carroll County, OH; Stark County, OH

Population: 28,836; Growth (since 2000): 0.0%; Density: 73.1 persons per square mile; Race: 97.8% White, 0.5% Black/African American, 0.2% Asian, 0.3% American Indian/Alaska Native, 0.0% Native Hawaiian/Other Pacific Islander, 1.1% two or more races, 0.8% Hispanic of any race; Average household size: 2.50; Median age: 43.1; Age under 18: 23.0%; Age 65 and over: 16.7%; Males per 100 females: 99.7; Marriage status: 21.1% never married, 59.6% now married, 1.2% separated, 7.0% widowed, 12.3% divorced; Foreign born: 0.9%; Speak English only: 96.9%; With disability: 13.6%; Veterans: 10.8%; Ancestry: 26.9% German, 15.7% American, 14.7% Irish, 9.3% English, 5.8% Italian
Religion: Six largest groups: 9.0% Methodist/Pietist, 6.3% Catholicism, 4.0% Lutheran, 3.4% Baptist, 2.1% European Free-Church, 2.1% Non-denominational Protestant
Economy: Unemployment rate: 4.6%; Leading industries: 16.3% other services (except public administration); 14.6% retail trade; 9.8% construction; Farms: 733 totaling 106,256 acres; Company size: 0 employ 1,000 or more persons, 0 employ 500 to 999 persons, 7 employ 100 to 499 persons, 452 employ less than 100 persons; Business ownership: n/a women-owned, n/a Black-owned, n/a Hispanic-owned, n/a Asian-owned
Employment: 11.2% management, business, and financial, 2.0% computer, engineering, and science, 5.7% education, legal, community service, arts, and media, 6.5% healthcare practitioners, 16.2% service, 21.9% sales and office, 13.7% natural resources, construction, and maintenance, 22.7% production, transportation, and material moving
Income: Per capita: $21,783; Median household: $43,779; Average household: $54,849; Households with income of $100,000 or more: 11.6%; Poverty rate: 15.5%
Educational Attainment: High school diploma or higher: 85.1%; Bachelor's degree or higher: 11.0%; Graduate/professional degree or higher: 4.3%
Housing: Homeownership rate: 78.2%; Median home value: $110,400; Median year structure built: 1972; Homeowner vacancy rate: 1.7%; Median gross rent: $589 per month; Rental vacancy rate: 9.5%
Vital Statistics: Birth rate: 92.0 per 10,000 population; Death rate: 95.5 per 10,000 population; Age-adjusted cancer mortality rate: 238.4 deaths per 100,000 population
Health Insurance: 85.2% have insurance; 66.0% have private insurance; 33.3% have public insurance; 14.8% do not have insurance; 13.8% of children under 18 do not have insurance
Health Care: Physicians: 4.9 per 10,000 population; Hospital beds: 0.0 per 10,000 population; Hospital admissions: 0.0 per 10,000 population
Transportation: Commute: 92.7% car, 0.6% public transportation, 2.1% walk, 4.2% work from home; Median travel time to work: 31.0 minutes
Presidential Election: 41.6% Obama, 55.4% Romney (2012)
National and State Parks: Leesville State Wildlife Area
Additional Information Contacts
Carroll Government. . . . . (330) 627-4869
http://www.carrollcountyohio.us

Carroll County Communities

AUGUSTA (unincorporated postal area)
ZCTA: 44607
Covers a land area of 2.094 square miles and a water area of 0 square miles. Located at 40.69° N. Lat; 81.03° W. Long. Elevation is 1,230 feet.
Population: 234; Growth (since 2000): n/a; Density: 111.8 persons per square mile; Race: 97.0% White, 0.4% Black/African American, 0.4% Asian, 0.9% American Indian/Alaska Native, 0.0% Native Hawaiian/Other Pacific Islander, 1.3% Two or more races, 0.0% Hispanic of any race; Average household size: 2.96; Median age: 34.5; Age under 18: 32.5%; Age 65 and over: 12.4%; Males per 100 females: 105.3
Housing: Homeownership rate: 81.0%; Homeowner vacancy rate: 1.5%; Rental vacancy rate: 11.8%

CARROLLTON (village). County seat. Covers a land area of 2.447 square miles and a water area of 0 square miles. Located at 40.58° N. Lat; 81.09° W. Long. Elevation is 1,106 feet.
History: Laid out 1815.
Population: 3,241; Growth (since 2000): 1.6%; Density: 1,324.6 persons per square mile; Race: 98.2% White, 0.4% Black/African American, 0.4% Asian, 0.0% American Indian/Alaska Native, 0.0% Native Hawaiian/Other Pacific Islander, 0.9% Two or more races, 0.9% Hispanic of any race; Average household size: 2.26; Median age: 42.2; Age under 18: 22.3%; Age 65 and over: 22.2%; Males per 100 females: 79.2; Marriage status: 32.5% never married, 45.0% now married, 0.9% separated, 9.0% widowed, 13.6% divorced; Foreign born: 1.2%; Speak English only: 97.6%; With disability: 15.7%; Veterans: 9.8%; Ancestry: 25.5% German, 15.4% Irish, 11.6% American, 11.0% English, 6.3% Dutch
Employment: 12.4% management, business, and financial, 0.7% computer, engineering, and science, 5.2% education, legal, community service, arts, and media, 2.7% healthcare practitioners, 25.9% service, 24.7% sales and office, 12.9% natural resources, construction, and maintenance, 15.5% production, transportation, and material moving
Income: Per capita: $18,757; Median household: $38,513; Average household: $45,527; Households with income of $100,000 or more: 7.2%; Poverty rate: 18.9%
Educational Attainment: High school diploma or higher: 80.8%; Bachelor's degree or higher: 12.2%; Graduate/professional degree or higher: 6.1%

School District(s)

Carrollton Exempted Village (PK-12)
2012-13 Enrollment: 2,309 . . . . (330) 627-2181
Housing: Homeownership rate: 60.6%; Median home value: $108,100; Median year structure built: 1962; Homeowner vacancy rate: 2.3%; Median gross rent: $534 per month; Rental vacancy rate: 12.2%
Health Insurance: 88.4% have insurance; 65.8% have private insurance; 38.9% have public insurance; 11.6% do not have insurance; 5.0% of children under 18 do not have insurance
Newspapers: Free Press Standard (weekly circulation 8500)
Transportation: Commute: 86.8% car, 2.9% public transportation, 5.3% walk, 5.0% work from home; Median travel time to work: 24.6 minutes
Airports: Carroll County-Tolson (general aviation)

DELLROY (village). Covers a land area of 0.180 square miles and a water area of 0.032 square miles. Located at 40.56° N. Lat; 81.20° W. Long. Elevation is 958 feet.
Population: 356; Growth (since 2000): 21.1%; Density: 1,980.1 persons per square mile; Race: 97.2% White, 0.6% Black/African American, 0.0% Asian, 1.4% American Indian/Alaska Native, 0.0% Native Hawaiian/Other Pacific Islander, 0.8% Two or more races, 0.6% Hispanic of any race; Average household size: 2.66; Median age: 38.0; Age under 18: 25.6%; Age 65 and over: 17.1%; Males per 100 females: 94.5

School District(s)

Carrollton Exempted Village (PK-12)
2012-13 Enrollment: 2,309 . . . . (330) 627-2181

Housing: Homeownership rate: 70.1%; Homeowner vacancy rate: 2.1%; Rental vacancy rate: 4.8%

LAKE MOHAWK (CDP). Covers a land area of 3.670 square miles and a water area of 0.805 square miles. Located at 40.66° N. Lat; 81.19° W. Long. Elevation is 1,204 feet.

Population: 1,652; Growth (since 2000): n/a; Density: 450.2 persons per square mile; Race: 98.5% White, 0.4% Black/African American, 0.0% Asian, 0.0% American Indian/Alaska Native, 0.0% Native Hawaiian/Other Pacific Islander, 1.1% Two or more races, 0.5% Hispanic of any race; Average household size: 2.47; Median age: 49.5; Age under 18: 19.6%; Age 65 and over: 19.0%; Males per 100 females: 102.0

Housing: Homeownership rate: 97.6%; Homeowner vacancy rate: 1.4%; Rental vacancy rate: 0.0%

LEESVILLE (village). Covers a land area of 0.257 square miles and a water area of 0 square miles. Located at 40.45° N. Lat; 81.21° W. Long. Elevation is 994 feet.

Population: 158; Growth (since 2000): -14.1%; Density: 615.4 persons per square mile; Race: 97.5% White, 0.0% Black/African American, 0.0% Asian, 0.0% American Indian/Alaska Native, 0.0% Native Hawaiian/Other Pacific Islander, 2.5% Two or more races, 0.0% Hispanic of any race; Average household size: 2.39; Median age: 46.3; Age under 18: 19.6%; Age 65 and over: 25.9%; Males per 100 females: 92.7

Housing: Homeownership rate: 84.9%; Homeowner vacancy rate: 3.4%; Rental vacancy rate: 9.1%

MALVERN (village). Covers a land area of 0.668 square miles and a water area of 0 square miles. Located at 40.69° N. Lat; 81.18° W. Long. Elevation is 994 feet.

Population: 1,189; Growth (since 2000): -2.4%; Density: 1,780.2 persons per square mile; Race: 93.8% White, 3.8% Black/African American, 0.3% Asian, 0.3% American Indian/Alaska Native, 0.0% Native Hawaiian/Other Pacific Islander, 1.3% Two or more races, 2.2% Hispanic of any race; Average household size: 2.27; Median age: 42.4; Age under 18: 20.6%; Age 65 and over: 17.8%; Males per 100 females: 93.6

School District(s)

Brown Local (PK-12)
2012-13 Enrollment: 648. . . . . (330) 863-1170

Housing: Homeownership rate: 56.8%; Homeowner vacancy rate: 1.3%; Rental vacancy rate: 11.0%

MECHANICSTOWN (unincorporated postal area)

ZCTA: 44651

Covers a land area of 24.093 square miles and a water area of 0.009 square miles. Located at 40.63° N. Lat; 80.95° W. Long. Elevation is 1,253 feet.

Population: 861; Growth (since 2000): 3.4%; Density: 35.7 persons per square mile; Race: 97.6% White, 0.3% Black/African American, 0.0% Asian, 0.2% American Indian/Alaska Native, 0.0% Native Hawaiian/Other Pacific Islander, 1.7% Two or more races, 0.9% Hispanic of any race; Average household size: 2.80; Median age: 36.7; Age under 18: 30.4%; Age 65 and over: 10.6%; Males per 100 females: 108.0

Housing: Homeownership rate: 84.1%; Homeowner vacancy rate: 1.1%; Rental vacancy rate: 9.1%

SHERRODSVILLE (village). Covers a land area of 0.316 square miles and a water area of 0 square miles. Located at 40.49° N. Lat; 81.24° W. Long. Elevation is 909 feet.

Population: 304; Growth (since 2000): -3.8%; Density: 963.3 persons per square mile; Race: 98.4% White, 0.0% Black/African American, 0.0% Asian, 1.0% American Indian/Alaska Native, 0.0% Native Hawaiian/Other Pacific Islander, 0.3% Two or more races, 0.3% Hispanic of any race; Average household size: 2.69; Median age: 36.5; Age under 18: 26.6%; Age 65 and over: 10.9%; Males per 100 females: 108.2

School District(s)

Conotton Valley Union Local (PK-12)
2012-13 Enrollment: 428. . . . . (740) 269-2000

Housing: Homeownership rate: 76.1%; Homeowner vacancy rate: 3.3%; Rental vacancy rate: 6.9%

Champaign County

Located in west central Ohio; crossed by the Mad River, and Darby, Small Buck, and Little Darby Creeks. Covers a land area of 428.669 square miles, a water area of 1.164 square miles, and is located in the Eastern Time Zone at 40.13° N. Lat., 83.77° W. Long. The county was founded in 1805. County seat is Urbana.

Champaign County is part of the Urbana, OH Micropolitan Statistical Area. The entire metro area includes: Champaign County, OH

Weather Station: Urbana WWTP Elevation: 1,000 feet

	Jan	Feb	Mar	Apr	May	Jun	Jul	Aug	Sep	Oct	Nov	Dec
High	34	39	48	61	71	80	84	83	76	64	51	38
Low	19	22	29	39	49	59	62	60	52	41	33	23
Precip	2.6	2.1	2.8	3.8	4.8	4.5	5.5	3.4	3.1	2.9	3.2	3.0
Snow	na	na	na	0.1	0.0	0.0	0.0	0.0	0.0	0.0	tr	na

High and Low temperatures in degrees Fahrenheit; Precipitation and Snow in inches

Population: 40,097; Growth (since 2000): 3.1%; Density: 93.5 persons per square mile; Race: 94.7% White, 2.2% Black/African American, 0.4% Asian, 0.4% American Indian/Alaska Native, 0.0% Native Hawaiian/Other Pacific Islander, 1.9% two or more races, 1.1% Hispanic of any race; Average household size: 2.56; Median age: 39.7; Age under 18: 25.0%; Age 65 and over: 14.4%; Males per 100 females: 98.0; Marriage status: 23.1% never married, 57.7% now married, 2.0% separated, 5.9% widowed, 13.3% divorced; Foreign born: 1.0%; Speak English only: 97.9%; With disability: 13.5%; Veterans: 11.3%; Ancestry: 27.6% German, 15.1% Irish, 13.1% American, 10.1% English, 3.1% Dutch

Religion: Six largest groups: 8.3% Methodist/Pietist, 4.9% Non-denominational Protestant, 4.3% Baptist, 3.7% Catholicism, 2.8% Holiness, 1.7% Lutheran

Economy: Unemployment rate: 3.9%; Leading industries: 16.4% retail trade; 14.2% other services (except public administration); 9.8% construction; Farms: 873 totaling 190,060 acres; Company size: 0 employ 1,000 or more persons, 2 employ 500 to 999 persons, 16 employ 100 to 499 persons, 581 employs less than 100 persons; Business ownership: 841 women-owned, n/a Black-owned, n/a Hispanic-owned, n/a Asian-owned

Employment: 14.1% management, business, and financial, 3.1% computer, engineering, and science, 7.6% education, legal, community service, arts, and media, 5.1% healthcare practitioners, 15.6% service, 21.2% sales and office, 9.1% natural resources, construction, and maintenance, 24.3% production, transportation, and material moving

Income: Per capita: $23,358; Median household: $49,157; Average household: $60,528; Households with income of $100,000 or more: 15.7%; Poverty rate: 13.4%

Educational Attainment: High school diploma or higher: 87.4%; Bachelor's degree or higher: 17.0%; Graduate/professional degree or higher: 5.1%

Housing: Homeownership rate: 74.6%; Median home value: $124,600; Median year structure built: 1970; Homeowner vacancy rate: 2.3%; Median gross rent: $688 per month; Rental vacancy rate: 9.1%

Vital Statistics: Birth rate: 104.7 per 10,000 population; Death rate: 92.3 per 10,000 population; Age-adjusted cancer mortality rate: 191.4 deaths per 100,000 population

Health Insurance: 89.4% have insurance; 71.3% have private insurance; 31.7% have public insurance; 10.6% do not have insurance; 5.7% of children under 18 do not have insurance

Health Care: Physicians: 3.8 per 10,000 population; Hospital beds: 6.3 per 10,000 population; Hospital admissions: 270.8 per 10,000 population

Transportation: Commute: 94.0% car, 0.4% public transportation, 1.6% walk, 2.9% work from home; Median travel time to work: 26.4 minutes

Presidential Election: 37.9% Obama, 60.3% Romney (2012)

National and State Parks: Cedar Bog State Nature Preserve; Kiser Lake State Park; Siegenthaler-Kaestner Esker State Nature Preserve

Additional Information Contacts

Champaign Government . . . . (937) 484-1611
http://www.co.champaign.oh.us

Champaign County Communities

CABLE (unincorporated postal area)

ZCTA: 43009

Covers a land area of 34.470 square miles and a water area of 0.018 square miles. Located at 40.17° N. Lat; 83.64° W. Long. Elevation is 1,184 feet.

Population: 2,135; Growth (since 2000): 20.3%; Density: 61.9 persons per square mile; Race: 95.8% White, 1.6% Black/African American, 0.2% Asian, 0.3% American Indian/Alaska Native, 0.0% Native Hawaiian/Other Pacific Islander, 1.8% Two or more races, 0.6% Hispanic of any race; Average household size: 2.84; Median age: 39.2; Age under 18: 26.9%; Age 65 and over: 10.4%; Males per 100 females: 102.2

Housing: Homeownership rate: 89.1%; Homeowner vacancy rate: 1.0%; Rental vacancy rate: 6.8%

CHRISTIANSBURG (village). Covers a land area of 0.216 square miles and a water area of 0 square miles. Located at 40.06° N. Lat; 84.03° W. Long. Elevation is 1,115 feet.

Population: 526; Growth (since 2000): -4.9%; Density: 2,435.4 persons per square mile; Race: 96.0% White, 0.0% Black/African American, 0.2% Asian, 0.6% American Indian/Alaska Native, 0.0% Native Hawaiian/Other Pacific Islander, 2.1% Two or more races, 1.3% Hispanic of any race; Average household size: 2.42; Median age: 39.6; Age under 18: 25.1%; Age 65 and over: 16.9%; Males per 100 females: 97.0

Housing: Homeownership rate: 75.1%; Homeowner vacancy rate: 3.5%; Rental vacancy rate: 1.8%

CONOVER (unincorporated postal area)

ZCTA: 45317

Covers a land area of 24.688 square miles and a water area of 0.004 square miles. Located at 40.21° N. Lat; 83.99° W. Long..

Population: 1,180; Growth (since 2000): 9.5%; Density: 47.8 persons per square mile; Race: 98.9% White, 0.2% Black/African American, 0.2% Asian, 0.0% American Indian/Alaska Native, 0.0% Native Hawaiian/Other Pacific Islander, 0.6% Two or more races, 0.9% Hispanic of any race; Average household size: 2.74; Median age: 40.2; Age under 18: 25.2%; Age 65 and over: 13.9%; Males per 100 females: 108.1

Housing: Homeownership rate: 85.3%; Homeowner vacancy rate: 1.6%; Rental vacancy rate: 6.0%

MECHANICSBURG (village). Covers a land area of 1.010 square miles and a water area of 0.007 square miles. Located at 40.07° N. Lat; 83.56° W. Long. Elevation is 1,083 feet.

Population: 1,644; Growth (since 2000): -5.7%; Density: 1,628.5 persons per square mile; Race: 95.4% White, 1.6% Black/African American, 0.1% Asian, 0.5% American Indian/Alaska Native, 0.0% Native Hawaiian/Other Pacific Islander, 2.1% Two or more races, 1.0% Hispanic of any race; Average household size: 2.49; Median age: 35.5; Age under 18: 24.5%; Age 65 and over: 13.2%; Males per 100 females: 109.4

School District(s)

Mechanicsburg Exempted Village (PK-12)
2012-13 Enrollment: 890. . . . . (937) 834-2453

Housing: Homeownership rate: 63.4%; Homeowner vacancy rate: 3.0%; Rental vacancy rate: 8.7%

MUTUAL (village). Covers a land area of 0.133 square miles and a water area of 0 square miles. Located at 40.08° N. Lat; 83.64° W. Long. Elevation is 1,194 feet.

Population: 104; Growth (since 2000): -21.2%; Density: 781.0 persons per square mile; Race: 97.1% White, 2.9% Black/African American, 0.0% Asian, 0.0% American Indian/Alaska Native, 0.0% Native Hawaiian/Other Pacific Islander, 0.0% Two or more races, 0.0% Hispanic of any race; Average household size: 2.17; Median age: 45.5; Age under 18: 23.1%; Age 65 and over: 26.0%; Males per 100 females: 103.9

Housing: Homeownership rate: 75.0%; Homeowner vacancy rate: 5.0%; Rental vacancy rate: 0.0%

NORTH LEWISBURG (village). Covers a land area of 1.151 square miles and a water area of 0 square miles. Located at 40.22° N. Lat; 83.56° W. Long. Elevation is 1,089 feet.

Population: 1,490; Growth (since 2000): -6.2%; Density: 1,295.0 persons per square mile; Race: 95.6% White, 0.4% Black/African American, 0.5% Asian, 0.6% American Indian/Alaska Native, 0.0% Native Hawaiian/Other Pacific Islander, 2.9% Two or more races, 0.9% Hispanic of any race; Average household size: 2.51; Median age: 35.4; Age under 18: 27.0%; Age 65 and over: 11.0%; Males per 100 females: 101.9

School District(s)

Triad Local (PK-12)
2012-13 Enrollment: 953. . . . . (937) 826-4961

Housing: Homeownership rate: 67.8%; Homeowner vacancy rate: 3.7%; Rental vacancy rate: 11.5%

ROSEWOOD (CDP). Covers a land area of 1.354 square miles and a water area of 0 square miles. Located at 40.22° N. Lat; 83.96° W. Long. Elevation is 1,132 feet.

Population: 257; Growth (since 2000): n/a; Density: 189.8 persons per square mile; Race: 97.7% White, 0.0% Black/African American, 0.0% Asian, 0.0% American Indian/Alaska Native, 0.0% Native Hawaiian/Other Pacific Islander, 2.3% Two or more races, 2.3% Hispanic of any race; Average household size: 2.62; Median age: 38.1; Age under 18: 27.2%; Age 65 and over: 19.5%; Males per 100 females: 116.0

Housing: Homeownership rate: 78.6%; Homeowner vacancy rate: 0.0%; Rental vacancy rate: 0.0%

SAINT PARIS (village). Covers a land area of 1.677 square miles and a water area of 0 square miles. Located at 40.13° N. Lat; 83.96° W. Long. Elevation is 1,204 feet.

History: St. Paris was settled in 1813 by David Huffman, when it was called simply Paris.

Population: 2,089; Growth (since 2000): 4.6%; Density: 1,245.5 persons per square mile; Race: 97.8% White, 0.2% Black/African American, 0.0% Asian, 0.1% American Indian/Alaska Native, 0.2% Native Hawaiian/Other Pacific Islander, 1.4% Two or more races, 0.5% Hispanic of any race; Average household size: 2.63; Median age: 33.7; Age under 18: 31.2%; Age 65 and over: 12.3%; Males per 100 females: 91.7

School District(s)

A.b. Graham Academy (KG-12)
2012-13 Enrollment: 232. . . . . (937) 663-0370

Graham Local (PK-12)
2012-13 Enrollment: 2,055 . . . . (937) 663-4123

Housing: Homeownership rate: 66.7%; Homeowner vacancy rate: 2.7%; Rental vacancy rate: 7.4%

URBANA (city). County seat. Covers a land area of 7.753 square miles and a water area of 0.023 square miles. Located at 40.11° N. Lat; 83.75° W. Long. Elevation is 1,050 feet.

History: Urbana was laid out in 1805, and selected in 1812 by General Hull as the site of a training camp. After the war, many of the soldiers who had trained here remained as residents.

Population: 11,793; Growth (since 2000): 1.5%; Density: 1,521.0 persons per square mile; Race: 89.7% White, 5.4% Black/African American, 0.7% Asian, 0.4% American Indian/Alaska Native, 0.0% Native Hawaiian/Other Pacific Islander, 3.1% Two or more races, 2.0% Hispanic of any race; Average household size: 2.34; Median age: 38.2; Age under 18: 23.7%; Age 65 and over: 16.4%; Males per 100 females: 89.1; Marriage status: 27.6% never married, 48.7% now married, 3.4% separated, 7.0% widowed, 16.7% divorced; Foreign born: 1.1%; Speak English only: 97.7%; With disability: 17.5%; Veterans: 10.9%; Ancestry: 19.8% German, 17.1% Irish, 11.4% American, 7.8% English, 2.8% Italian

Employment: 11.0% management, business, and financial, 4.2% computer, engineering, and science, 7.6% education, legal, community service, arts, and media, 5.2% healthcare practitioners, 17.7% service, 19.9% sales and office, 7.0% natural resources, construction, and maintenance, 27.5% production, transportation, and material moving

Income: Per capita: $19,517; Median household: $37,010; Average household: $48,102; Households with income of $100,000 or more: 7.6%; Poverty rate: 19.3%

Educational Attainment: High school diploma or higher: 84.7%; Bachelor's degree or higher: 16.1%; Graduate/professional degree or higher: 4.3%

School District(s)

Urbana City (PK-12)
2012-13 Enrollment: 2,115 . . . . (937) 653-1402

Urbana Community School (06-12)
2012-13 Enrollment: 37. . . . . (937) 653-1477

Four-year College(s)

Urbana University (Private, Not-for-profit)
Fall 2013 Enrollment: 1,748 . . . . (937) 484-1301
2013-14 Tuition: In-state $21,566; Out-of-state $21,566

Housing: Homeownership rate: 57.2%; Median home value: $98,300; Median year structure built: 1958; Homeowner vacancy rate: 3.7%; Median gross rent: $659 per month; Rental vacancy rate: 11.1%

Health Insurance: 86.1% have insurance; 61.8% have private insurance; 39.8% have public insurance; 13.9% do not have insurance; 6.3% of children under 18 do not have insurance

Hospitals: Mercy Memorial Hospital (73 beds)

Safety: Violent crime rate: 17.2 per 10,000 population; Property crime rate: 329.3 per 10,000 population

Newspapers: Urbana Daily Citizen (daily circulation 5600)

Transportation: Commute: 94.7% car, 0.3% public transportation, 1.4% walk, 1.7% work from home; Median travel time to work: 20.8 minutes

Additional Information Contacts

City of Urbana . . . . (937) 652-4300
http://urbanaohio.com

WOODSTOCK (village). Covers a land area of 0.293 square miles and a water area of 0 square miles. Located at 40.17° N. Lat; 83.53° W. Long. Elevation is 1,043 feet.

Population: 305; Growth (since 2000): -3.8%; Density: 1,042.6 persons per square mile; Race: 98.4% White, 0.0% Black/African American, 0.0% Asian, 1.0% American Indian/Alaska Native, 0.0% Native Hawaiian/Other Pacific Islander, 0.3% Two or more races, 0.7% Hispanic of any race; Average household size: 2.96; Median age: 33.2; Age under 18: 33.4%; Age 65 and over: 7.9%; Males per 100 females: 111.8

Housing: Homeownership rate: 72.9%; Homeowner vacancy rate: 2.5%; Rental vacancy rate: 0.0%

Clark County

Located in west central Ohio; crossed by the Mad and Little Miami Rivers. Covers a land area of 397.473 square miles, a water area of 5.054 square miles, and is located in the Eastern Time Zone at 39.92° N. Lat., 83.78° W. Long. The county was founded in 1817. County seat is Springfield.

Clark County is part of the Springfield, OH Metropolitan Statistical Area. The entire metro area includes: Clark County, OH

Weather Station: Springfield New Water Works Elevation: 930 feet

	Jan	Feb	Mar	Apr	May	Jun	Jul	Aug	Sep	Oct	Nov	Dec
High	35	39	49	61	72	80	84	83	77	64	52	39
Low	19	21	29	38	49	59	62	60	52	41	32	23
Precip	2.4	1.8	2.4	3.4	4.7	4.4	4.6	3.3	3.1	2.8	2.9	2.7
Snow	na	2.7	na	tr	0.0	0.0	0.0	0.0	0.0	tr	tr	1.4

High and Low temperatures in degrees Fahrenheit; Precipitation and Snow in inches

Population: 138,333; Growth (since 2000): -4.4%; Density: 348.0 persons per square mile; Race: 86.3% White, 8.8% Black/African American, 0.6% Asian, 0.3% American Indian/Alaska Native, 0.0% Native Hawaiian/Other Pacific Islander, 2.5% two or more races, 2.8% Hispanic of any race; Average household size: 2.45; Median age: 40.5; Age under 18: 23.6%; Age 65 and over: 16.2%; Males per 100 females: 93.9; Marriage status: 27.8% never married, 50.9% now married, 2.1% separated, 7.5% widowed, 13.8% divorced; Foreign born: 2.2%; Speak English only: 96.1%; With disability: 16.5%; Veterans: 13.0%; Ancestry: 22.7% German, 14.2% Irish, 13.0% American, 9.5% English, 3.2% Italian

Religion: Six largest groups: 7.0% Baptist, 6.6% Catholicism, 4.3% Methodist/Pietist, 2.7% Non-denominational Protestant, 2.5% Lutheran, 2.4% Holiness

Economy: Unemployment rate: 4.2%; Leading industries: 17.2% retail trade; 14.0% other services (except public administration); 13.1% health care and social assistance; Farms: 785 totaling 174,337 acres; Company size: 5 employ 1,000 or more persons, 1 employs 500 to 999 persons, 55 employ 100 to 499 persons, 2,296 employ less than 100 persons; Business ownership: 2,516 women-owned, n/a Black-owned, n/a Hispanic-owned, 113 Asian-owned

Employment: 11.0% management, business, and financial, 3.0% computer, engineering, and science, 9.2% education, legal, community service, arts, and media, 5.8% healthcare practitioners, 18.6% service, 25.1% sales and office, 8.4% natural resources, construction, and maintenance, 18.9% production, transportation, and material moving

Income: Per capita: $22,780; Median household: $43,136; Average household: $56,049; Households with income of $100,000 or more: 13.5%; Poverty rate: 18.6%

Educational Attainment: High school diploma or higher: 86.1%; Bachelor's degree or higher: 17.6%; Graduate/professional degree or higher: 6.2%

Housing: Homeownership rate: 68.7%; Median home value: $106,400; Median year structure built: 1961; Homeowner vacancy rate: 2.8%; Median gross rent: $662 per month; Rental vacancy rate: 10.6%

Vital Statistics: Birth rate: 115.8 per 10,000 population; Death rate: 118.4 per 10,000 population; Age-adjusted cancer mortality rate: 207.2 deaths per 100,000 population

Health Insurance: 88.1% have insurance; 64.5% have private insurance; 38.4% have public insurance; 11.9% do not have insurance; 4.4% of children under 18 do not have insurance

Health Care: Physicians: 14.1 per 10,000 population; Hospital beds: 18.3 per 10,000 population; Hospital admissions: 1,044.5 per 10,000 population

Air Quality Index: 70.1% good, 29.9% moderate, 0.0% unhealthy for sensitive individuals, 0.0% unhealthy (percent of days)

Transportation: Commute: 93.5% car, 0.7% public transportation, 2.9% walk, 2.2% work from home; Median travel time to work: 22.1 minutes

Presidential Election: 48.3% Obama, 50.1% Romney (2012)

National and State Parks: Buck Creek State Park; Prairie Road Fen State Nature Preserve

Additional Information Contacts

Clark Government . . . . (937) 328-2405
http://www.clarkcountyohio.gov

Clark County Communities

CATAWBA (village). Covers a land area of 0.255 square miles and a water area of 0 square miles. Located at 40.00° N. Lat; 83.62° W. Long. Elevation is 1,234 feet.

Population: 272; Growth (since 2000): -12.8%; Density: 1,065.0 persons per square mile; Race: 98.9% White, 0.7% Black/African American, 0.4% Asian, 0.0% American Indian/Alaska Native, 0.0% Native Hawaiian/Other Pacific Islander, 0.0% Two or more races, 0.4% Hispanic of any race; Average household size: 2.86; Median age: 36.5; Age under 18: 30.5%; Age 65 and over: 11.4%; Males per 100 females: 107.6

Housing: Homeownership rate: 77.9%; Homeowner vacancy rate: 2.6%; Rental vacancy rate: 4.5%

CRYSTAL LAKES (CDP). Covers a land area of 0.474 square miles and a water area of 0.031 square miles. Located at 39.89° N. Lat; 84.02° W. Long. Elevation is 850 feet.

Population: 1,483; Growth (since 2000): 5.1%; Density: 3,129.1 persons per square mile; Race: 88.3% White, 0.4% Black/African American, 0.2% Asian, 0.4% American Indian/Alaska Native, 0.0% Native Hawaiian/Other Pacific Islander, 2.0% Two or more races, 13.7% Hispanic of any race; Average household size: 2.68; Median age: 37.0; Age under 18: 25.4%; Age 65 and over: 10.9%; Males per 100 females: 107.7

Housing: Homeownership rate: 73.8%; Homeowner vacancy rate: 3.3%; Rental vacancy rate: 4.6%

DONNELSVILLE (village). Covers a land area of 0.389 square miles and a water area of 0 square miles. Located at 39.92° N. Lat; 83.94° W. Long. Elevation is 928 feet.

Population: 304; Growth (since 2000): 3.8%; Density: 781.4 persons per square mile; Race: 98.7% White, 0.0% Black/African American, 0.3% Asian, 0.3% American Indian/Alaska Native, 0.0% Native Hawaiian/Other Pacific Islander, 0.3% Two or more races, 0.3% Hispanic of any race; Average household size: 2.67; Median age: 39.3; Age under 18: 28.9%; Age 65 and over: 8.6%; Males per 100 females: 102.7

School District(s)

Tecumseh Local (PK-12)
2012-13 Enrollment: 3,113 . . . . (937) 845-3576

Housing: Homeownership rate: 78.1%; Homeowner vacancy rate: 8.2%; Rental vacancy rate: 24.2%

ENON (village). Covers a land area of 1.276 square miles and a water area of 0 square miles. Located at 39.87° N. Lat; 83.93° W. Long. Elevation is 896 feet.

Population: 2,415; Growth (since 2000): -8.5%; Density: 1,892.1 persons per square mile; Race: 96.6% White, 0.4% Black/African American, 1.3% Asian, 0.3% American Indian/Alaska Native, 0.0% Native Hawaiian/Other

Pacific Islander, 0.9% Two or more races, 0.8% Hispanic of any race; Average household size: 2.26; Median age: 48.1; Age under 18: 19.1%; Age 65 and over: 20.8%; Males per 100 females: 94.9

School District(s)

Greenon Local (PK-12)
2012-13 Enrollment: 1,751 . . . . (937) 864-1202

Housing: Homeownership rate: 76.5%; Homeowner vacancy rate: 1.3%; Rental vacancy rate: 6.7%

GREEN MEADOWS (CDP). Covers a land area of 0.798 square miles and a water area of 0 square miles. Located at 39.87° N. Lat; 83.95° W. Long. Elevation is 892 feet.

Population: 2,327; Growth (since 2000): 0.4%; Density: 2,915.5 persons per square mile; Race: 95.7% White, 0.7% Black/African American, 1.3% Asian, 0.1% American Indian/Alaska Native, 0.0% Native Hawaiian/Other Pacific Islander, 1.9% Two or more races, 1.8% Hispanic of any race; Average household size: 2.41; Median age: 40.4; Age under 18: 23.8%; Age 65 and over: 17.4%; Males per 100 females: 96.2

Housing: Homeownership rate: 75.7%; Homeowner vacancy rate: 2.5%; Rental vacancy rate: 8.5%

HOLIDAY VALLEY (CDP). Covers a land area of 1.820 square miles and a water area of 0 square miles. Located at 39.85° N. Lat; 83.96° W. Long. Elevation is 866 feet.

Population: 1,510; Growth (since 2000): -11.8%; Density: 829.5 persons per square mile; Race: 95.0% White, 1.5% Black/African American, 1.0% Asian, 0.1% American Indian/Alaska Native, 0.0% Native Hawaiian/Other Pacific Islander, 1.4% Two or more races, 2.3% Hispanic of any race; Average household size: 2.60; Median age: 44.5; Age under 18: 20.1%; Age 65 and over: 21.5%; Males per 100 females: 90.2

Housing: Homeownership rate: 91.7%; Homeowner vacancy rate: 1.6%; Rental vacancy rate: 4.3%

MEDWAY (unincorporated postal area)

ZCTA: 45341

Covers a land area of 6.062 square miles and a water area of 0.364 square miles. Located at 39.88° N. Lat; 84.02° W. Long. Elevation is 846 feet.

Population: 3,883; Growth (since 2000): -5.5%; Density: 640.6 persons per square mile; Race: 91.2% White, 0.8% Black/African American, 0.3% Asian, 0.4% American Indian/Alaska Native, 0.0% Native Hawaiian/Other Pacific Islander, 1.8% Two or more races, 9.4% Hispanic of any race; Average household size: 2.40; Median age: 45.0; Age under 18: 21.2%; Age 65 and over: 19.3%; Males per 100 females: 103.0; Marriage status: 25.5% never married, 53.3% now married, 5.1% separated, 7.2% widowed, 14.0% divorced; Foreign born: 6.2%; Speak English only: 90.8%; With disability: 16.7%; Veterans: 15.1%; Ancestry: 25.7% German, 15.1% Irish, 11.3% American, 7.7% English, 6.4% French

Employment: 9.9% management, business, and financial, 2.5% computer, engineering, and science, 4.1% education, legal, community service, arts, and media, 5.8% healthcare practitioners, 13.9% service, 28.6% sales and office, 11.0% natural resources, construction, and maintenance, 24.2% production, transportation, and material moving

Income: Per capita: $20,184; Median household: $37,902; Average household: $46,712; Households with income of $100,000 or more: 8.4%; Poverty rate: 18.2%

Educational Attainment: High school diploma or higher: 80.9%; Bachelor's degree or higher: 13.9%; Graduate/professional degree or higher: 4.1%

School District(s)

Tecumseh Local (PK-12)
2012-13 Enrollment: 3,113 . . . . (937) 845-3576

Housing: Homeownership rate: 80.4%; Median home value: $71,500; Median year structure built: 1965; Homeowner vacancy rate: 4.8%; Median gross rent: $668 per month; Rental vacancy rate: 8.1%

Health Insurance: 85.4% have insurance; 60.7% have private insurance; 41.0% have public insurance; 14.6% do not have insurance; 4.2% of children under 18 do not have insurance

Transportation: Commute: 95.8% car, 0.0% public transportation, 1.3% walk, 2.3% work from home; Median travel time to work: 24.8 minutes

NEW CARLISLE (city). Covers a land area of 2.738 square miles and a water area of 0.016 square miles. Located at 39.95° N. Lat; 84.03° W. Long. Elevation is 899 feet.

History: Founded 1810.

Population: 5,785; Growth (since 2000): 0.9%; Density: 2,113.1 persons per square mile; Race: 90.1% White, 0.5% Black/African American, 0.4% Asian, 0.1% American Indian/Alaska Native, 0.0% Native Hawaiian/Other Pacific Islander, 1.3% Two or more races, 11.3% Hispanic of any race; Average household size: 2.58; Median age: 36.2; Age under 18: 26.0%; Age 65 and over: 14.7%; Males per 100 females: 91.2; Marriage status: 26.6% never married, 51.3% now married, 1.5% separated, 7.7% widowed, 14.4% divorced; Foreign born: 6.7%; Speak English only: 89.3%; With disability: 15.3%; Veterans: 12.6%; Ancestry: 25.7% German, 13.5% Irish, 9.9% American, 8.8% English, 3.5% Italian

Employment: 8.4% management, business, and financial, 3.4% computer, engineering, and science, 4.8% education, legal, community service, arts, and media, 3.7% healthcare practitioners, 17.9% service, 24.3% sales and office, 10.8% natural resources, construction, and maintenance, 26.7% production, transportation, and material moving

Income: Per capita: $17,577; Median household: $39,518; Average household: $44,993; Households with income of $100,000 or more: 4.2%; Poverty rate: 14.9%

Educational Attainment: High school diploma or higher: 82.3%; Bachelor's degree or higher: 9.3%; Graduate/professional degree or higher: 2.4%

School District(s)

Tecumseh Local (PK-12)
2012-13 Enrollment: 3,113 . . . . (937) 845-3576

Housing: Homeownership rate: 67.5%; Median home value: $91,700; Median year structure built: 1964; Homeowner vacancy rate: 2.8%; Median gross rent: $703 per month; Rental vacancy rate: 6.3%

Health Insurance: 81.3% have insurance; 58.5% have private insurance; 34.6% have public insurance; 18.7% do not have insurance; 13.4% of children under 18 do not have insurance

Transportation: Commute: 96.3% car, 0.6% public transportation, 2.5% walk, 0.5% work from home; Median travel time to work: 23.9 minutes

NORTH HAMPTON (village). Covers a land area of 0.432 square miles and a water area of 0 square miles. Located at 39.99° N. Lat; 83.94° W. Long. Elevation is 1,096 feet.

Population: 478; Growth (since 2000): 29.2%; Density: 1,107.3 persons per square mile; Race: 96.9% White, 0.0% Black/African American, 0.2% Asian, 0.2% American Indian/Alaska Native, 0.0% Native Hawaiian/Other Pacific Islander, 2.5% Two or more races, 1.0% Hispanic of any race; Average household size: 2.76; Median age: 37.4; Age under 18: 28.9%; Age 65 and over: 11.3%; Males per 100 females: 93.5

Housing: Homeownership rate: 74.0%; Homeowner vacancy rate: 0.8%; Rental vacancy rate: 4.3%

NORTHRIDGE (CDP). Covers a land area of 3.051 square miles and a water area of 0 square miles. Located at 40.00° N. Lat; 83.78° W. Long. Elevation is 1,079 feet.

Population: 7,572; Growth (since 2000): 10.5%; Density: 2,481.9 persons per square mile; Race: 96.0% White, 1.7% Black/African American, 0.6% Asian, 0.1% American Indian/Alaska Native, 0.0% Native Hawaiian/Other Pacific Islander, 1.2% Two or more races, 1.1% Hispanic of any race; Average household size: 2.40; Median age: 44.0; Age under 18: 22.3%; Age 65 and over: 21.5%; Males per 100 females: 89.4; Marriage status: 18.2% never married, 59.4% now married, 0.4% separated, 8.6% widowed, 13.8% divorced; Foreign born: 0.8%; Speak English only: 97.6%; With disability: 12.2%; Veterans: 14.8%; Ancestry: 27.1% German, 19.9% Irish, 9.3% American, 7.3% English, 4.7% Italian

Employment: 10.6% management, business, and financial, 2.4% computer, engineering, and science, 6.8% education, legal, community service, arts, and media, 10.1% healthcare practitioners, 14.3% service, 27.2% sales and office, 6.2% natural resources, construction, and maintenance, 22.3% production, transportation, and material moving

Income: Per capita: $28,289; Median household: $58,208; Average household: $67,232; Households with income of $100,000 or more: 19.2%; Poverty rate: 3.8%

Educational Attainment: High school diploma or higher: 89.7%; Bachelor's degree or higher: 19.4%; Graduate/professional degree or higher: 3.9%

Housing: Homeownership rate: 82.3%; Median home value: $116,000; Median year structure built: 1976; Homeowner vacancy rate: 1.6%; Median gross rent: $704 per month; Rental vacancy rate: 3.1%

Health Insurance: 94.7% have insurance; 83.3% have private insurance; 28.3% have public insurance; 5.3% do not have insurance; 2.7% of children under 18 do not have insurance

Transportation: Commute: 99.6% car, 0.0% public transportation, 0.0% walk, 0.2% work from home; Median travel time to work: 21.8 minutes

PARK LAYNE (CDP). Covers a land area of 1.465 square miles and a water area of 0 square miles. Located at 39.89° N. Lat; 84.04° W. Long. Elevation is 840 feet.

Population: 4,343; Growth (since 2000): -3.9%; Density: 2,965.4 persons per square mile; Race: 94.6% White, 0.7% Black/African American, 0.3% Asian, 0.3% American Indian/Alaska Native, 0.1% Native Hawaiian/Other Pacific Islander, 1.9% Two or more races, 4.1% Hispanic of any race; Average household size: 2.79; Median age: 34.4; Age under 18: 28.8%; Age 65 and over: 11.2%; Males per 100 females: 97.1; Marriage status: 34.5% never married, 48.7% now married, 3.0% separated, 4.9% widowed, 11.9% divorced; Foreign born: 2.2%; Speak English only: 97.1%; With disability: 12.0%; Veterans: 13.9%; Ancestry: 27.7% German, 24.6% Irish, 6.9% Italian, 6.7% English, 6.5% American

Employment: 2.6% management, business, and financial, 4.7% computer, engineering, and science, 1.6% education, legal, community service, arts, and media, 2.6% healthcare practitioners, 23.2% service, 32.7% sales and office, 13.9% natural resources, construction, and maintenance, 18.7% production, transportation, and material moving

Income: Per capita: $17,117; Median household: $48,139; Average household: $53,442; Households with income of $100,000 or more: 9.8%; Poverty rate: 15.8%

Educational Attainment: High school diploma or higher: 77.7%; Bachelor's degree or higher: 6.8%; Graduate/professional degree or higher: 1.4%

Housing: Homeownership rate: 73.8%; Median home value: $81,000; Median year structure built: 1965; Homeowner vacancy rate: 2.7%; Median gross rent: $757 per month; Rental vacancy rate: 5.8%

Health Insurance: 80.4% have insurance; 55.9% have private insurance; 34.2% have public insurance; 19.6% do not have insurance; 6.4% of children under 18 do not have insurance

Transportation: Commute: 95.4% car, 0.0% public transportation, 3.6% walk, 0.4% work from home; Median travel time to work: 23.3 minutes

SOUTH CHARLESTON (village). Covers a land area of 1.284 square miles and a water area of <.001 square miles. Located at 39.82° N. Lat; 83.64° W. Long. Elevation is 1,129 feet.

History: South Charleston developed as a rural distributing center.

Population: 1,693; Growth (since 2000): -8.5%; Density: 1,318.7 persons per square mile; Race: 97.6% White, 0.4% Black/African American, 0.1% Asian, 0.0% American Indian/Alaska Native, 0.0% Native Hawaiian/Other Pacific Islander, 1.5% Two or more races, 0.9% Hispanic of any race; Average household size: 2.35; Median age: 38.0; Age under 18: 25.0%; Age 65 and over: 16.2%; Males per 100 females: 90.7

School District(s)

Southeastern Local (PK-12)
2012-13 Enrollment: 697. . . . . (888) 627-6745

Housing: Homeownership rate: 58.6%; Homeowner vacancy rate: 1.8%; Rental vacancy rate: 10.8%

Safety: Violent crime rate: 0.0 per 10,000 population; Property crime rate: 167.2 per 10,000 population

SOUTH VIENNA (village). Covers a land area of 0.523 square miles and a water area of 0 square miles. Located at 39.93° N. Lat; 83.61° W. Long. Elevation is 1,191 feet.

Population: 384; Growth (since 2000): -18.1%; Density: 734.3 persons per square mile; Race: 90.4% White, 0.8% Black/African American, 0.5% Asian, 0.5% American Indian/Alaska Native, 0.0% Native Hawaiian/Other Pacific Islander, 2.1% Two or more races, 7.8% Hispanic of any race; Average household size: 2.59; Median age: 40.7; Age under 18: 26.8%; Age 65 and over: 9.6%; Males per 100 females: 93.9

School District(s)

Northeastern Local (PK-12)
2012-13 Enrollment: 3,527 . . . . (937) 325-7615

Housing: Homeownership rate: 70.3%; Homeowner vacancy rate: 3.7%; Rental vacancy rate: 4.3%

SPRINGFIELD (city). County seat. Covers a land area of 25.294 square miles and a water area of 0.205 square miles. Located at 39.93° N. Lat; 83.80° W. Long. Elevation is 974 feet.

History: Springfield's first settler was James Demint, who came in 1799. Surveyor John Daugherty platted a town in 1801. The settlement was called Springfield for the spring water coming down the cliffs that bordered the valley of Buck Creek. Simon Kenton from Kentucky set up a gristmill and sawmill on the site that was later the International Harvester plant. The National Road, completed in 1838, put Springfield on the route of the Ohio Stage Company and provided a means for the area's produce to get to a market. In the 1850's the Champion Binder Company was producing farm machinery here, its facility later purchased by the McCormick interests, which were subsequently acquired by International Harvester Company.

Population: 60,608; Growth (since 2000): -7.3%; Density: 2,396.1 persons per square mile; Race: 75.2% White, 18.1% Black/African American, 0.8% Asian, 0.3% American Indian/Alaska Native, 0.0% Native Hawaiian/Other Pacific Islander, 4.0% Two or more races, 3.0% Hispanic of any race; Average household size: 2.38; Median age: 36.0; Age under 18: 24.4%; Age 65 and over: 15.3%; Males per 100 females: 90.9; Marriage status: 35.3% never married, 40.3% now married, 3.1% separated, 8.2% widowed, 16.2% divorced; Foreign born: 2.6%; Speak English only: 95.1%; With disability: 18.3%; Veterans: 11.1%; Ancestry: 18.9% German, 12.9% Irish, 11.5% American, 7.8% English, 3.1% Italian

Employment: 9.7% management, business, and financial, 2.2% computer, engineering, and science, 10.2% education, legal, community service, arts, and media, 5.0% healthcare practitioners, 23.9% service, 24.1% sales and office, 5.6% natural resources, construction, and maintenance, 19.4% production, transportation, and material moving

Income: Per capita: $18,633; Median household: $31,635; Average household: $44,778; Households with income of $100,000 or more: 8.4%; Poverty rate: 30.4%

Educational Attainment: High school diploma or higher: 82.1%; Bachelor's degree or higher: 14.9%; Graduate/professional degree or higher: 5.6%

School District(s)

Clark-Shawnee Local (PK-12)
2012-13 Enrollment: 2,108 . . . . (937) 328-5378
Greenon Local (PK-12)
2012-13 Enrollment: 1,751 . . . . (937) 864-1202
Life Skills Center-Springfield (09-12)
2012-13 Enrollment: 143. . . . . (937) 322-2940
Northeastern Local (PK-12)
2012-13 Enrollment: 3,527 . . . . (937) 325-7615
Northwestern Local (PK-12)
2012-13 Enrollment: 1,719 . . . . (937) 964-1318
Springfield Academy of Excellence (KG-06)
2012-13 Enrollment: 244. . . . . (937) 325-0933
Springfield City (PK-12)
2012-13 Enrollment: 7,374 . . . . (937) 505-2800
Springfield Preparatory and Fitness Academy (KG-08)
2012-13 Enrollment: 190. . . . . (937) 323-6250
Springfield-Clark County (08-12)
2012-13 Enrollment: n/a . . . . (937) 325-7368

Four-year College(s)

Wittenberg University (Private, Not-for-profit, Lutheran Church in America)
Fall 2013 Enrollment: 1,979 . . . . (937) 327-6231
2013-14 Tuition: In-state $38,030; Out-of-state $38,030

Two-year College(s)

Carousel Beauty College-Springfield (Private, For-profit)
Fall 2013 Enrollment: 57 . . . . (937) 223-3572
Clark State Community College (Public)
Fall 2013 Enrollment: 5,653 . . . . (937) 325-0691
2013-14 Tuition: In-state $3,279; Out-of-state $6,111

Housing: Homeownership rate: 52.8%; Median home value: $82,100; Median year structure built: 1951; Homeowner vacancy rate: 3.7%; Median gross rent: $638 per month; Rental vacancy rate: 11.6%

Health Insurance: 85.6% have insurance; 53.2% have private insurance; 45.8% have public insurance; 14.4% do not have insurance; 4.9% of children under 18 do not have insurance

Hospitals: Ohio Valley Medical Center; Springfield Regional Medical Center (324 beds)

Safety: Violent crime rate: 71.2 per 10,000 population; Property crime rate: 743.7 per 10,000 population

Newspapers: Springfield News-Sun (daily circulation 25700)

Transportation: Commute: 90.2% car, 1.3% public transportation, 5.6% walk, 2.1% work from home; Median travel time to work: 19.4 minutes

Airports: Springfield-Beckley Municipal (general aviation)

Additional Information Contacts

City of Springfield . . . . (937) 324-7700
http://www.ci.springfield.oh.us

TREMONT CITY (village). Covers a land area of 0.256 square miles and a water area of 0 square miles. Located at 40.02° N. Lat; 83.84° W. Long. Elevation is 955 feet.
Population: 375; Growth (since 2000): 7.4%; Density: 1,463.3 persons per square mile; Race: 98.9% White, 0.3% Black/African American, 0.3% Asian, 0.0% American Indian/Alaska Native, 0.0% Native Hawaiian/Other Pacific Islander, 0.3% Two or more races, 1.6% Hispanic of any race; Average household size: 2.48; Median age: 39.4; Age under 18: 20.8%; Age 65 and over: 10.9%; Males per 100 females: 108.3
Housing: Homeownership rate: 66.3%; Homeowner vacancy rate: 1.9%; Rental vacancy rate: 10.5%

Clermont County

Located in southwestern Ohio; bounded on the southwest by the Ohio River and the Kentucky border, and on the northwest by the Little Miami River. Covers a land area of 452.100 square miles, a water area of 7.666 square miles, and is located in the Eastern Time Zone at 39.05° N. Lat., 84.15° W. Long. The county was founded in 1800. County seat is Batavia.

Clermont County is part of the Cincinnati, OH-KY-IN Metropolitan Statistical Area. The entire metro area includes: Dearborn County, IN; Ohio County, IN; Union County, IN; Boone County, KY; Bracken County, KY; Campbell County, KY; Gallatin County, KY; Grant County, KY; Kenton County, KY; Pendleton County, KY; Brown County, OH; Butler County, OH; Clermont County, OH; Hamilton County, OH; Warren County, OH

Weather Station: Chilo Meldahl L&D Elevation: 500 feet

	Jan	Feb	Mar	Apr	May	Jun	Jul	Aug	Sep	Oct	Nov	Dec
High	40	44	54	65	74	82	86	86	80	68	56	44
Low	23	24	32	42	51	60	65	64	56	45	36	27
Precip	2.9	2.8	4.3	3.4	4.6	3.6	3.9	3.2	2.8	3.1	2.9	3.0
Snow	0.6	na	0.7	0.0	0.0	0.0	0.0	0.0	0.0	0.0	tr	1.4

High and Low temperatures in degrees Fahrenheit; Precipitation and Snow in inches

Weather Station: Milford Elevation: 520 feet

	Jan	Feb	Mar	Apr	May	Jun	Jul	Aug	Sep	Oct	Nov	Dec
High	38	43	53	65	75	83	87	86	79	68	55	43
Low	20	23	30	40	50	59	63	62	53	41	33	25
Precip	3.1	2.6	3.7	4.1	5.6	4.4	4.3	4.1	3.0	3.0	3.6	3.3
Snow	na	4.5	1.3	0.3	tr	0.0	0.0	tr	0.0	0.2	0.1	2.6

High and Low temperatures in degrees Fahrenheit; Precipitation and Snow in inches

Population: 197,363; Growth (since 2000): 10.9%; Density: 436.5 persons per square mile; Race: 95.9% White, 1.2% Black/African American, 1.0% Asian, 0.2% American Indian/Alaska Native, 0.0% Native Hawaiian/Other Pacific Islander, 1.3% two or more races, 1.5% Hispanic of any race; Average household size: 2.61; Median age: 38.5; Age under 18: 25.6%; Age 65 and over: 11.8%; Males per 100 females: 97.3; Marriage status: 25.3% never married, 57.4% now married, 1.7% separated, 5.7% widowed, 11.6% divorced; Foreign born: 2.4%; Speak English only: 96.4%; With disability: 12.3%; Veterans: 9.9%; Ancestry: 28.1% German, 23.2% American, 14.7% Irish, 10.5% English, 3.6% Italian
Religion: Six largest groups: 15.9% Catholicism, 8.0% Baptist, 5.1% Methodist/Pietist, 3.3% Non-denominational Protestant, 1.7% Pentecostal, 0.9% Holiness
Economy: Unemployment rate: 4.0%; Leading industries: 15.0% retail trade; 12.1% construction; 10.9% other services (except public administration); Farms: 822 totaling 121,125 acres; Company size: 1 employs 1,000 or more persons, 5 employ 500 to 999 persons, 77 employ 100 to 499 persons, 3,464 employ less than 100 persons; Business ownership: 4,680 women-owned, 69 Black-owned, 162 Hispanic-owned, n/a Asian-owned
Employment: 15.2% management, business, and financial, 5.6% computer, engineering, and science, 8.9% education, legal, community service, arts, and media, 5.9% healthcare practitioners, 16.2% service, 25.5% sales and office, 8.8% natural resources, construction, and maintenance, 13.8% production, transportation, and material moving
Income: Per capita: $28,761; Median household: $60,365; Average household: $75,825; Households with income of $100,000 or more: 25.0%; Poverty rate: 10.2%
Educational Attainment: High school diploma or higher: 88.3%; Bachelor's degree or higher: 25.6%; Graduate/professional degree or higher: 8.7%
Housing: Homeownership rate: 74.5%; Median home value: $154,500; Median year structure built: 1982; Homeowner vacancy rate: 2.1%; Median gross rent: $754 per month; Rental vacancy rate: 10.4%
Vital Statistics: Birth rate: 114.8 per 10,000 population; Death rate: 76.1 per 10,000 population; Age-adjusted cancer mortality rate: 189.4 deaths per 100,000 population
Health Insurance: 89.3% have insurance; 75.1% have private insurance; 25.0% have public insurance; 10.7% do not have insurance; 4.7% of children under 18 do not have insurance
Health Care: Physicians: 19.4 per 10,000 population; Hospital beds: 6.0 per 10,000 population; Hospital admissions: 311.4 per 10,000 population
Air Quality Index: 92.1% good, 7.5% moderate, 0.5% unhealthy for sensitive individuals, 0.0% unhealthy (percent of days)
Transportation: Commute: 93.6% car, 0.7% public transportation, 0.9% walk, 4.5% work from home; Median travel time to work: 27.5 minutes
Presidential Election: 31.4% Obama, 67.0% Romney (2012)
National and State Parks: East Fork State Park; East Fork Tailwater State Wildlife Area; Stonelick Lake State Park
Additional Information Contacts
Clermont Government. . . . . (513) 732-7300
http://www.clermontcountyohio.gov

Clermont County Communities

AMELIA (village). Covers a land area of 1.791 square miles and a water area of 0 square miles. Located at 39.02° N. Lat; 84.22° W. Long. Elevation is 876 feet.
Population: 4,801; Growth (since 2000): 74.5%; Density: 2,680.6 persons per square mile; Race: 95.1% White, 1.6% Black/African American, 0.7% Asian, 0.3% American Indian/Alaska Native, 0.0% Native Hawaiian/Other Pacific Islander, 1.6% Two or more races, 1.9% Hispanic of any race; Average household size: 2.62; Median age: 30.5; Age under 18: 29.7%; Age 65 and over: 5.9%; Males per 100 females: 94.1; Marriage status: 29.1% never married, 52.0% now married, 1.9% separated, 2.7% widowed, 16.2% divorced; Foreign born: 1.6%; Speak English only: 95.7%; With disability: 11.8%; Veterans: 10.7%; Ancestry: 27.1% American, 25.9% German, 18.2% Irish, 12.9% English, 3.7% Italian
Employment: 12.1% management, business, and financial, 5.4% computer, engineering, and science, 9.1% education, legal, community service, arts, and media, 0.8% healthcare practitioners, 25.3% service, 23.7% sales and office, 17.8% natural resources, construction, and maintenance, 5.7% production, transportation, and material moving
Income: Per capita: $22,016; Median household: $57,037; Average household: $58,544; Households with income of $100,000 or more: 14.7%; Poverty rate: 6.7%
Educational Attainment: High school diploma or higher: 93.6%; Bachelor's degree or higher: 14.3%; Graduate/professional degree or higher: 2.1%

School District(s)

West Clermont Local (PK-12)
2012-13 Enrollment: 8,448 . . . . (513) 943-5000
Housing: Homeownership rate: 63.9%; Median home value: $131,700; Median year structure built: 1993; Homeowner vacancy rate: 2.8%; Median gross rent: $725 per month; Rental vacancy rate: 8.9%
Health Insurance: 86.4% have insurance; 72.3% have private insurance; 19.8% have public insurance; 13.6% do not have insurance; 5.5% of children under 18 do not have insurance
Safety: Violent crime rate: 2.1 per 10,000 population; Property crime rate: 65.7 per 10,000 population
Transportation: Commute: 97.4% car, 0.9% public transportation, 0.4% walk, 1.2% work from home; Median travel time to work: 32.7 minutes

BATAVIA (village). County seat. Covers a land area of 1.590 square miles and a water area of 0.030 square miles. Located at 39.08° N. Lat; 84.18° W. Long. Elevation is 594 feet.
History: Settled c.1797, laid out 1814, incorporated 1842.
Population: 1,509; Growth (since 2000): -6.7%; Density: 949.0 persons per square mile; Race: 93.6% White, 3.4% Black/African American, 0.6% Asian, 0.5% American Indian/Alaska Native, 0.0% Native Hawaiian/Other Pacific Islander, 1.8% Two or more races, 0.9% Hispanic of any race; Average household size: 2.37; Median age: 37.7; Age under 18: 24.5%; Age 65 and over: 13.5%; Males per 100 females: 89.1

School District(s)

Batavia Local (PK-12)
2012-13 Enrollment: 2,070 . . . . (513) 732-2343

Clermont Northeastern Local (PK-12)
2012-13 Enrollment: 1,570 . . . . (513) 625-5478
West Clermont Local (PK-12)
2012-13 Enrollment: 8,448 . . . . (513) 943-5000

Four-year College(s)

University of Cincinnati-Clermont College (Public)
Fall 2013 Enrollment: 3,461 . . . . (513) 732-5200
2013-14 Tuition: In-state $5,210; Out-of-state $12,302

Housing: Homeownership rate: 59.9%; Homeowner vacancy rate: 2.8%; Rental vacancy rate: 11.5%

Hospitals: Mercy Hospital Clermont (114 beds)

Safety: Violent crime rate: 12.2 per 10,000 population; Property crime rate: 398.0 per 10,000 population

Newspapers: Clermont Sun (weekly circulation 3000)

BETHEL (village). Covers a land area of 1.395 square miles and a water area of 0.005 square miles. Located at 38.96° N. Lat; 84.08° W. Long. Elevation is 889 feet.

History: Settled 1797.

Population: 2,711; Growth (since 2000): 2.8%; Density: 1,942.8 persons per square mile; Race: 97.3% White, 0.4% Black/African American, 0.1% Asian, 0.1% American Indian/Alaska Native, 0.4% Native Hawaiian/Other Pacific Islander, 1.6% Two or more races, 1.0% Hispanic of any race; Average household size: 2.56; Median age: 33.8; Age under 18: 29.0%; Age 65 and over: 12.9%; Males per 100 females: 86.8; Marriage status: 31.0% never married, 46.6% now married, 1.5% separated, 7.5% widowed, 15.0% divorced; Foreign born: 0.8%; Speak English only: 98.1%; With disability: 22.9%; Veterans: 9.0%; Ancestry: 33.1% American, 20.0% German, 12.0% Irish, 10.5% English, 2.4% Italian

Employment: 5.5% management, business, and financial, 4.5% computer, engineering, and science, 7.1% education, legal, community service, arts, and media, 4.7% healthcare practitioners, 26.6% service, 16.4% sales and office, 13.4% natural resources, construction, and maintenance, 22.0% production, transportation, and material moving

Income: Per capita: $18,164; Median household: $32,278; Average household: $45,955; Households with income of $100,000 or more: 8.4%; Poverty rate: 22.0%

Educational Attainment: High school diploma or higher: 79.0%; Bachelor's degree or higher: 12.5%; Graduate/professional degree or higher: 3.9%

School District(s)

Bethel-Tate Local (PK-12)
2012-13 Enrollment: 1,686 . . . . (513) 734-2271
U S Grant (11-12)
2012-13 Enrollment: n/a . . . . (513) 734-6222

Vocational/Technical School(s)

U S Grant Joint Vocational School (Public)
Fall 2013 Enrollment: 18 . . . . (513) 734-6222
2013-14 Tuition: In-state $5,645; Out-of-state $5,645

Housing: Homeownership rate: 47.9%; Median home value: $98,400; Median year structure built: 1960; Homeowner vacancy rate: 4.4%; Median gross rent: $547 per month; Rental vacancy rate: 8.5%

Health Insurance: 78.6% have insurance; 50.8% have private insurance; 39.2% have public insurance; 21.4% do not have insurance; 9.7% of children under 18 do not have insurance

Safety: Violent crime rate: 14.6 per 10,000 population; Property crime rate: 347.1 per 10,000 population

Transportation: Commute: 91.2% car, 0.7% public transportation, 5.0% walk, 2.2% work from home; Median travel time to work: 32.0 minutes

Additional Information Contacts

Village of Bethel . . . . (513) 734-2243
http://bethel-oh.gov

CHILO (village). Covers a land area of 0.202 square miles and a water area of 0.043 square miles. Located at 38.79° N. Lat; 84.14° W. Long. Elevation is 502 feet.

History: Chilo was a boat-building center and river port before the 1937 floods destroyed most of the town.

Population: 63; Growth (since 2000): -35.1%; Density: 311.2 persons per square mile; Race: 98.4% White, 0.0% Black/African American, 0.0% Asian, 1.6% American Indian/Alaska Native, 0.0% Native Hawaiian/Other Pacific Islander, 0.0% Two or more races, 0.0% Hispanic of any race; Average household size: 2.25; Median age: 50.8; Age under 18: 14.3%; Age 65 and over: 22.2%; Males per 100 females: 70.3

Housing: Homeownership rate: 71.4%; Homeowner vacancy rate: 16.7%; Rental vacancy rate: 11.1%

DAY HEIGHTS (CDP). Covers a land area of 1.178 square miles and a water area of 0 square miles. Located at 39.18° N. Lat; 84.23° W. Long. Elevation is 873 feet.

Population: 2,620; Growth (since 2000): -7.2%; Density: 2,223.8 persons per square mile; Race: 97.0% White, 1.3% Black/African American, 0.5% Asian, 0.2% American Indian/Alaska Native, 0.0% Native Hawaiian/Other Pacific Islander, 0.7% Two or more races, 1.6% Hispanic of any race; Average household size: 2.66; Median age: 42.6; Age under 18: 22.8%; Age 65 and over: 15.3%; Males per 100 females: 102.3; Marriage status: 18.5% never married, 61.0% now married, 0.9% separated, 7.4% widowed, 13.1% divorced; Foreign born: 1.6%; Speak English only: 97.7%; With disability: 11.8%; Veterans: 13.1%; Ancestry: 30.9% German, 23.2% English, 19.5% Irish, 13.8% American, 7.1% Scottish

Employment: 19.5% management, business, and financial, 7.1% computer, engineering, and science, 9.7% education, legal, community service, arts, and media, 6.3% healthcare practitioners, 19.0% service, 22.8% sales and office, 5.1% natural resources, construction, and maintenance, 10.6% production, transportation, and material moving

Income: Per capita: $27,852; Median household: $60,938; Average household: $68,862; Households with income of $100,000 or more: 20.0%; Poverty rate: 7.6%

Educational Attainment: High school diploma or higher: 89.1%; Bachelor's degree or higher: 26.4%; Graduate/professional degree or higher: 9.4%

Housing: Homeownership rate: 91.5%; Median home value: $145,100; Median year structure built: 1967; Homeowner vacancy rate: 2.0%; Median gross rent: $1,348 per month; Rental vacancy rate: 1.1%

Health Insurance: 91.6% have insurance; 79.4% have private insurance; 28.0% have public insurance; 8.4% do not have insurance; 8.1% of children under 18 do not have insurance

Transportation: Commute: 89.3% car, 0.0% public transportation, 2.0% walk, 8.7% work from home; Median travel time to work: 23.6 minutes

---

FELICITY (village). Covers a land area of 0.272 square miles and a water area of 0 square miles. Located at 38.84° N. Lat; 84.10° W. Long. Elevation is 919 feet.

Population: 818; Growth (since 2000): -11.3%; Density: 3,011.3 persons per square mile; Race: 98.7% White, 0.2% Black/African American, 0.1% Asian, 0.5% American Indian/Alaska Native, 0.0% Native Hawaiian/Other Pacific Islander, 0.4% Two or more races, 1.2% Hispanic of any race; Average household size: 2.44; Median age: 37.5; Age under 18: 27.8%; Age 65 and over: 12.2%; Males per 100 females: 87.2

School District(s)

Felicity-Franklin Local (PK-12)
2012-13 Enrollment: 937 . . . . (513) 876-2113

Housing: Homeownership rate: 36.4%; Homeowner vacancy rate: 4.6%; Rental vacancy rate: 9.0%

GOSHEN (unincorporated postal area)

ZCTA: 45122

Covers a land area of 44.174 square miles and a water area of 0.220 square miles. Located at 39.22° N. Lat; 84.12° W. Long. Elevation is 837 feet.

Population: 11,054; Growth (since 2000): -3.1%; Density: 250.2 persons per square mile; Race: 97.7% White, 0.6% Black/African American, 0.2% Asian, 0.2% American Indian/Alaska Native, 0.0% Native Hawaiian/Other Pacific Islander, 1.2% Two or more races, 0.9% Hispanic of any race; Average household size: 2.72; Median age: 40.3; Age under 18: 24.4%; Age 65 and over: 12.8%; Males per 100 females: 101.6; Marriage status: 23.8% never married, 59.8% now married, 1.1% separated, 5.8% widowed, 10.5% divorced; Foreign born: 1.1%; Speak English only: 97.8%; With disability: 13.7%; Veterans: 9.7%; Ancestry: 30.2% American, 22.4% German, 12.7% Irish, 8.3% English, 2.6% Italian

Employment: 11.7% management, business, and financial, 4.2% computer, engineering, and science, 6.1% education, legal, community service, arts, and media, 5.5% healthcare practitioners, 14.9% service, 23.1% sales and office, 13.1% natural resources, construction, and maintenance, 21.5% production, transportation, and material moving

Income: Per capita: $22,148; Median household: $52,507; Average household: $60,001; Households with income of $100,000 or more: 13.9%; Poverty rate: 11.4%

Educational Attainment: High school diploma or higher: 84.3%; Bachelor's degree or higher: 12.5%; Graduate/professional degree or higher: 2.7%

School District(s)

Goshen Local (PK-12)
2012-13 Enrollment: 2,595 . . . . (513) 722-2222

Housing: Homeownership rate: 83.2%; Median home value: $131,800; Median year structure built: 1979; Homeowner vacancy rate: 2.6%; Median gross rent: $839 per month; Rental vacancy rate: 8.8%

Health Insurance: 84.1% have insurance; 66.8% have private insurance; 32.8% have public insurance; 15.9% do not have insurance; 10.5% of children under 18 do not have insurance

Transportation: Commute: 94.7% car, 0.4% public transportation, 0.4% walk, 4.0% work from home; Median travel time to work: 29.0 minutes

MIAMIVILLE (CDP). Covers a land area of 0.338 square miles and a water area of 0.030 square miles. Located at 39.21° N. Lat; 84.30° W. Long. Elevation is 584 feet.

Population: 242; Growth (since 2000): n/a; Density: 715.7 persons per square mile; Race: 95.5% White, 0.0% Black/African American, 0.4% Asian, 0.8% American Indian/Alaska Native, 0.4% Native Hawaiian/Other Pacific Islander, 1.7% Two or more races, 0.8% Hispanic of any race; Average household size: 2.52; Median age: 42.5; Age under 18: 21.5%; Age 65 and over: 14.0%; Males per 100 females: 112.3

Housing: Homeownership rate: 69.8%; Homeowner vacancy rate: 6.7%; Rental vacancy rate: 3.3%

MILFORD (city). Covers a land area of 3.727 square miles and a water area of 0.124 square miles. Located at 39.17° N. Lat; 84.28° W. Long. Elevation is 551 feet.

History: Milford was settled in an area of glacial moraines, on the Little Miami River. A prehistoric civilization left mounds in this region.

Population: 6,709; Growth (since 2000): 6.8%; Density: 1,800.0 persons per square mile; Race: 94.6% White, 2.3% Black/African American, 0.8% Asian, 0.1% American Indian/Alaska Native, 0.0% Native Hawaiian/Other Pacific Islander, 1.6% Two or more races, 1.1% Hispanic of any race; Average household size: 2.12; Median age: 43.2; Age under 18: 21.4%; Age 65 and over: 21.9%; Males per 100 females: 82.6; Marriage status: 26.4% never married, 50.2% now married, 2.2% separated, 11.1% widowed, 12.3% divorced; Foreign born: 1.9%; Speak English only: 96.5%; With disability: 15.9%; Veterans: 11.4%; Ancestry: 27.1% German, 21.4% American, 16.4% Irish, 9.1% English, 4.8% Italian

Employment: 9.7% management, business, and financial, 4.3% computer, engineering, and science, 9.0% education, legal, community service, arts, and media, 5.4% healthcare practitioners, 21.9% service, 27.4% sales and office, 7.9% natural resources, construction, and maintenance, 14.4% production, transportation, and material moving

Income: Per capita: $25,710; Median household: $40,024; Average household: $60,297; Households with income of $100,000 or more: 20.8%; Poverty rate: 19.3%

Educational Attainment: High school diploma or higher: 91.6%; Bachelor's degree or higher: 27.4%; Graduate/professional degree or higher: 10.0%

School District(s)

Great Oaks Inst of Technology (05-12)
2012-13 Enrollment: n/a . . . . (513) 771-8840
Milford Exempted Village (PK-12)
2012-13 Enrollment: 6,452 . . . . (513) 831-1314

Housing: Homeownership rate: 52.3%; Median home value: $165,800; Median year structure built: 1967; Homeowner vacancy rate: 2.5%; Median gross rent: $671 per month; Rental vacancy rate: 8.3%

Health Insurance: 88.6% have insurance; 67.1% have private insurance; 34.8% have public insurance; 11.4% do not have insurance; 5.7% of children under 18 do not have insurance

Safety: Violent crime rate: 9.0 per 10,000 population; Property crime rate: 526.2 per 10,000 population

Transportation: Commute: 83.3% car, 1.5% public transportation, 3.1% walk, 12.1% work from home; Median travel time to work: 23.9 minutes

MOSCOW (village). Covers a land area of 0.367 square miles and a water area of 0.022 square miles. Located at 38.86° N. Lat; 84.23° W. Long. Elevation is 499 feet.

History: Moscow was one of the first stations on the Underground Railroad. During the Reconstruction Period, Moscow was a busy shipping point, and a producer of large quantities of brandy.

Population: 185; Growth (since 2000): -24.2%; Density: 504.3 persons per square mile; Race: 98.4% White, 1.1% Black/African American, 0.0% Asian, 0.0% American Indian/Alaska Native, 0.0% Native Hawaiian/Other Pacific Islander, 0.0% Two or more races, 1.6% Hispanic of any race; Average household size: 2.28; Median age: 47.7; Age under 18: 16.8%; Age 65 and over: 15.1%; Males per 100 females: 107.9

Housing: Homeownership rate: 69.1%; Homeowner vacancy rate: 6.7%; Rental vacancy rate: 13.8%

MOUNT CARMEL (CDP). Covers a land area of 1.834 square miles and a water area of 0.002 square miles. Located at 39.10° N. Lat; 84.30° W. Long. Elevation is 883 feet.

Population: 4,741; Growth (since 2000): 10.1%; Density: 2,585.0 persons per square mile; Race: 94.1% White, 1.3% Black/African American, 0.9% Asian, 0.2% American Indian/Alaska Native, 0.0% Native Hawaiian/Other Pacific Islander, 1.9% Two or more races, 3.1% Hispanic of any race; Average household size: 2.48; Median age: 36.3; Age under 18: 23.8%; Age 65 and over: 10.8%; Males per 100 females: 95.4; Marriage status: 25.8% never married, 55.5% now married, 0.8% separated, 4.8% widowed, 13.9% divorced; Foreign born: 1.2%; Speak English only: 95.7%; With disability: 14.8%; Veterans: 10.3%; Ancestry: 37.3% American, 24.6% German, 9.0% Irish, 5.5% English, 4.0% Italian

Employment: 14.2% management, business, and financial, 4.1% computer, engineering, and science, 9.4% education, legal, community service, arts, and media, 6.7% healthcare practitioners, 18.6% service, 24.3% sales and office, 10.2% natural resources, construction, and maintenance, 12.4% production, transportation, and material moving

Income: Per capita: $24,493; Median household: $47,199; Average household: $64,187; Households with income of $100,000 or more: 19.0%; Poverty rate: 15.6%

Educational Attainment: High school diploma or higher: 88.1%; Bachelor's degree or higher: 20.6%; Graduate/professional degree or higher: 6.5%

Housing: Homeownership rate: 61.5%; Median home value: $119,100; Median year structure built: 1968; Homeowner vacancy rate: 2.1%; Median gross rent: $720 per month; Rental vacancy rate: 12.5%

Health Insurance: 91.5% have insurance; 74.9% have private insurance; 27.0% have public insurance; 8.5% do not have insurance; 2.4% of children under 18 do not have insurance

Transportation: Commute: 95.7% car, 0.0% public transportation, 1.1% walk, 3.0% work from home; Median travel time to work: 23.5 minutes

MOUNT REPOSE (CDP). Covers a land area of 2.033 square miles and a water area of <.001 square miles. Located at 39.19° N. Lat; 84.22° W. Long. Elevation is 866 feet.

Population: 4,672; Growth (since 2000): 13.9%; Density: 2,297.6 persons per square mile; Race: 95.7% White, 0.9% Black/African American, 1.7% Asian, 0.2% American Indian/Alaska Native, 0.0% Native Hawaiian/Other Pacific Islander, 1.2% Two or more races, 1.7% Hispanic of any race; Average household size: 2.75; Median age: 37.2; Age under 18: 28.8%; Age 65 and over: 10.9%; Males per 100 females: 96.1; Marriage status: 21.9% never married, 59.0% now married, 1.1% separated, 9.9% widowed, 9.3% divorced; Foreign born: 2.1%; Speak English only: 96.2%; With disability: 11.7%; Veterans: 9.1%; Ancestry: 37.0% German, 21.0% American, 15.6% Irish, 6.0% English, 4.3% Italian

Employment: 14.2% management, business, and financial, 9.6% computer, engineering, and science, 9.6% education, legal, community service, arts, and media, 4.0% healthcare practitioners, 16.3% service, 27.0% sales and office, 7.0% natural resources, construction, and maintenance, 12.3% production, transportation, and material moving

Income: Per capita: $28,309; Median household: $72,574; Average household: $73,414; Households with income of $100,000 or more: 23.8%; Poverty rate: 3.0%

Educational Attainment: High school diploma or higher: 89.2%; Bachelor's degree or higher: 31.3%; Graduate/professional degree or higher: 8.8%

Housing: Homeownership rate: 85.0%; Median home value: $143,700; Median year structure built: 1981; Homeowner vacancy rate: 1.5%; Median gross rent: $709 per month; Rental vacancy rate: 7.2%

Health Insurance: 95.0% have insurance; 84.8% have private insurance; 23.2% have public insurance; 5.0% do not have insurance; 1.0% of children under 18 do not have insurance

Transportation: Commute: 94.1% car, 0.9% public transportation, 0.0% walk, 4.6% work from home; Median travel time to work: 27.6 minutes

MULBERRY (CDP). Covers a land area of 1.590 square miles and a water area of 0 square miles. Located at 39.20° N. Lat; 84.25° W. Long. Elevation is 843 feet.
Population: 3,323; Growth (since 2000): 5.9%; Density: 2,089.8 persons per square mile; Race: 95.0% White, 2.1% Black/African American, 1.0% Asian, 0.2% American Indian/Alaska Native, 0.1% Native Hawaiian/Other Pacific Islander, 1.1% Two or more races, 1.3% Hispanic of any race; Average household size: 2.11; Median age: 49.5; Age under 18: 17.0%; Age 65 and over: 24.5%; Males per 100 females: 80.6; Marriage status: 24.7% never married, 50.1% now married, 1.5% separated, 9.2% widowed, 16.1% divorced; Foreign born: 4.1%; Speak English only: 95.1%; With disability: 7.2%; Veterans: 16.7%; Ancestry: 30.2% German, 19.7% American, 16.0% Irish, 8.6% English, 8.3% Scottish
Employment: 18.2% management, business, and financial, 4.4% computer, engineering, and science, 13.3% education, legal, community service, arts, and media, 3.4% healthcare practitioners, 13.6% service, 34.7% sales and office, 1.2% natural resources, construction, and maintenance, 11.2% production, transportation, and material moving
Income: Per capita: $34,152; Median household: $59,881; Average household: $78,542; Households with income of $100,000 or more: 22.0%; Poverty rate: 3.5%
Educational Attainment: High school diploma or higher: 89.3%; Bachelor's degree or higher: 34.9%; Graduate/professional degree or higher: 15.5%
Housing: Homeownership rate: 76.2%; Median home value: $133,100; Median year structure built: 1986; Homeowner vacancy rate: 2.5%; Median gross rent: $773 per month; Rental vacancy rate: 27.2%
Health Insurance: 92.8% have insurance; 83.4% have private insurance; 26.3% have public insurance; 7.2% do not have insurance; 1.3% of children under 18 do not have insurance
Transportation: Commute: 95.1% car, 1.1% public transportation, 0.0% walk, 3.8% work from home; Median travel time to work: 22.6 minutes

NEVILLE (village). Covers a land area of 0.395 square miles and a water area of 0.064 square miles. Located at 38.81° N. Lat; 84.21° W. Long. Elevation is 499 feet.
History: Neville was founded in 1808 and named for a Virginia officer in the Revolutionary War who was given land here for his military service. More than half of the houses in Neville were destroyed by the 1937 flooding of the Ohio River.
Population: 100; Growth (since 2000): -21.3%; Density: 253.4 persons per square mile; Race: 99.0% White, 0.0% Black/African American, 1.0% Asian, 0.0% American Indian/Alaska Native, 0.0% Native Hawaiian/Other Pacific Islander, 0.0% Two or more races, 0.0% Hispanic of any race; Average household size: 2.56; Median age: 43.0; Age under 18: 20.0%; Age 65 and over: 11.0%; Males per 100 females: 100.0
Housing: Homeownership rate: 77.0%; Homeowner vacancy rate: 0.0%; Rental vacancy rate: 18.2%

NEW RICHMOND (village). Covers a land area of 3.413 square miles and a water area of 0.309 square miles. Located at 38.97° N. Lat; 84.28° W. Long. Elevation is 492 feet.
History: New Richmond was created when two villages were joined. One of them, Susanna, had been laid out in 1816 by Thomas Ashburn as a model town. The 1937 flooding of the Ohio River devastated New Richmond.
Population: 2,582; Growth (since 2000): 16.4%; Density: 756.5 persons per square mile; Race: 95.6% White, 1.6% Black/African American, 0.3% Asian, 0.2% American Indian/Alaska Native, 0.2% Native Hawaiian/Other Pacific Islander, 1.5% Two or more races, 1.5% Hispanic of any race; Average household size: 2.63; Median age: 36.7; Age under 18: 28.4%; Age 65 and over: 10.7%; Males per 100 females: 100.5; Marriage status: 26.7% never married, 51.8% now married, 2.7% separated, 6.8% widowed, 14.7% divorced; Foreign born: 0.0%; Speak English only: 98.3%; With disability: 15.7%; Veterans: 12.0%; Ancestry: 24.8% American, 18.1% German, 10.6% English, 10.3% Irish, 2.9% Italian
Employment: 9.6% management, business, and financial, 6.6% computer, engineering, and science, 7.8% education, legal, community service, arts, and media, 2.7% healthcare practitioners, 22.0% service, 26.4% sales and office, 13.1% natural resources, construction, and maintenance, 11.9% production, transportation, and material moving
Income: Per capita: $22,872; Median household: $50,893; Average household: $58,692; Households with income of $100,000 or more: 15.2%; Poverty rate: 14.2%
Educational Attainment: High school diploma or higher: 84.7%; Bachelor's degree or higher: 14.9%; Graduate/professional degree or higher: 5.2%

School District(s)

New Richmond Exempted Village (PK-12)
2012-13 Enrollment: 2,327 . . . . (513) 553-2616
Housing: Homeownership rate: 59.4%; Median home value: $153,800; Median year structure built: 1969; Homeowner vacancy rate: 4.9%; Median gross rent: $662 per month; Rental vacancy rate: 9.2%
Health Insurance: 84.5% have insurance; 68.4% have private insurance; 31.0% have public insurance; 15.5% do not have insurance; 6.0% of children under 18 do not have insurance
Transportation: Commute: 93.5% car, 0.0% public transportation, 1.2% walk, 5.3% work from home; Median travel time to work: 26.5 minutes

NEWTONSVILLE (village). Covers a land area of 0.254 square miles and a water area of 0 square miles. Located at 39.18° N. Lat; 84.09° W. Long. Elevation is 906 feet.
Population: 392; Growth (since 2000): -20.3%; Density: 1,544.9 persons per square mile; Race: 99.0% White, 0.0% Black/African American, 0.0% Asian, 0.3% American Indian/Alaska Native, 0.0% Native Hawaiian/Other Pacific Islander, 0.8% Two or more races, 1.0% Hispanic of any race; Average household size: 2.97; Median age: 32.6; Age under 18: 30.9%; Age 65 and over: 10.5%; Males per 100 females: 92.2
Housing: Homeownership rate: 69.7%; Homeowner vacancy rate: 4.2%; Rental vacancy rate: 9.1%

OWENSVILLE (village). Covers a land area of 0.430 square miles and a water area of 0 square miles. Located at 39.12° N. Lat; 84.14° W. Long. Elevation is 860 feet.
Population: 794; Growth (since 2000): -2.7%; Density: 1,845.6 persons per square mile; Race: 97.9% White, 0.1% Black/African American, 0.3% Asian, 0.0% American Indian/Alaska Native, 0.0% Native Hawaiian/Other Pacific Islander, 1.8% Two or more races, 0.8% Hispanic of any race; Average household size: 2.05; Median age: 44.3; Age under 18: 20.9%; Age 65 and over: 18.4%; Males per 100 females: 82.9
Housing: Homeownership rate: 36.0%; Homeowner vacancy rate: 2.8%; Rental vacancy rate: 8.5%

SUMMERSIDE (CDP). Covers a land area of 2.087 square miles and a water area of 0.007 square miles. Located at 39.12° N. Lat; 84.29° W. Long. Elevation is 873 feet.
Population: 5,083; Growth (since 2000): -8.0%; Density: 2,435.8 persons per square mile; Race: 94.6% White, 1.2% Black/African American, 1.4% Asian, 0.3% American Indian/Alaska Native, 0.0% Native Hawaiian/Other Pacific Islander, 1.7% Two or more races, 2.1% Hispanic of any race; Average household size: 2.45; Median age: 35.2; Age under 18: 24.8%; Age 65 and over: 11.0%; Males per 100 females: 87.4; Marriage status: 22.4% never married, 57.1% now married, 2.4% separated, 5.2% widowed, 15.4% divorced; Foreign born: 2.0%; Speak English only: 95.8%; With disability: 9.7%; Veterans: 10.4%; Ancestry: 27.9% German, 19.4% American, 17.6% English, 13.7% Irish, 3.9% French
Employment: 12.4% management, business, and financial, 6.8% computer, engineering, and science, 11.4% education, legal, community service, arts, and media, 5.2% healthcare practitioners, 16.2% service, 27.9% sales and office, 4.1% natural resources, construction, and maintenance, 17.1% production, transportation, and material moving
Income: Per capita: $26,944; Median household: $58,018; Average household: $66,022; Households with income of $100,000 or more: 20.6%; Poverty rate: 13.3%
Educational Attainment: High school diploma or higher: 89.5%; Bachelor's degree or higher: 24.8%; Graduate/professional degree or higher: 8.2%
Housing: Homeownership rate: 65.3%; Median home value: $127,100; Median year structure built: 1979; Homeowner vacancy rate: 2.2%; Median gross rent: $785 per month; Rental vacancy rate: 6.6%
Health Insurance: 93.8% have insurance; 80.8% have private insurance; 27.8% have public insurance; 6.2% do not have insurance; 5.1% of children under 18 do not have insurance
Transportation: Commute: 94.3% car, 1.4% public transportation, 0.0% walk, 3.5% work from home; Median travel time to work: 25.1 minutes

WILLIAMSBURG (village). Covers a land area of 1.947 square miles and a water area of 0.020 square miles. Located at 39.05° N. Lat; 84.05° W. Long. Elevation is 814 feet.
History: Incorporated 1800.
Population: 2,490; Growth (since 2000): 5.6%; Density: 1,279.2 persons per square mile; Race: 98.0% White, 0.5% Black/African American, 0.1% Asian, 0.2% American Indian/Alaska Native, 0.0% Native Hawaiian/Other Pacific Islander, 1.0% Two or more races, 0.5% Hispanic of any race; Average household size: 2.46; Median age: 36.6; Age under 18: 26.7%; Age 65 and over: 11.8%; Males per 100 females: 93.8

School District(s)

Williamsburg Local (PK-12)
2012-13 Enrollment: 981. . . . . (513) 724-3077
Housing: Homeownership rate: 51.8%; Homeowner vacancy rate: 5.5%; Rental vacancy rate: 7.5%
Safety: Violent crime rate: 19.9 per 10,000 population; Property crime rate: 326.2 per 10,000 population

WITHAMSVILLE (CDP). Covers a land area of 3.117 square miles and a water area of 0 square miles. Located at 39.06° N. Lat; 84.28° W. Long. Elevation is 879 feet.
Population: 7,021; Growth (since 2000): 123.2%; Density: 2,252.8 persons per square mile; Race: 94.9% White, 1.4% Black/African American, 1.5% Asian, 0.2% American Indian/Alaska Native, 0.0% Native Hawaiian/Other Pacific Islander, 1.5% Two or more races, 1.8% Hispanic of any race; Average household size: 2.30; Median age: 36.3; Age under 18: 22.0%; Age 65 and over: 12.3%; Males per 100 females: 95.9; Marriage status: 32.8% never married, 46.3% now married, 1.1% separated, 5.8% widowed, 15.1% divorced; Foreign born: 1.2%; Speak English only: 98.0%; With disability: 15.6%; Veterans: 13.5%; Ancestry: 31.7% American, 31.5% German, 14.6% Irish, 7.7% English, 3.5% Italian
Employment: 14.0% management, business, and financial, 3.3% computer, engineering, and science, 8.0% education, legal, community service, arts, and media, 8.3% healthcare practitioners, 17.6% service, 25.5% sales and office, 10.1% natural resources, construction, and maintenance, 13.2% production, transportation, and material moving
Income: Per capita: $28,721; Median household: $60,617; Average household: $63,141; Households with income of $100,000 or more: 14.9%; Poverty rate: 9.3%
Educational Attainment: High school diploma or higher: 93.5%; Bachelor's degree or higher: 20.2%; Graduate/professional degree or higher: 5.3%
Housing: Homeownership rate: 53.0%; Median home value: $142,000; Median year structure built: 1977; Homeowner vacancy rate: 2.3%; Median gross rent: $828 per month; Rental vacancy rate: 10.3%
Health Insurance: 92.0% have insurance; 79.4% have private insurance; 20.5% have public insurance; 8.0% do not have insurance; 0.0% of children under 18 do not have insurance
Transportation: Commute: 95.7% car, 1.5% public transportation, 0.0% walk, 2.9% work from home; Median travel time to work: 26.6 minutes

Clinton County

Located in southwestern Ohio; drained by forks of the Little Miami River and Caesar Creek. Covers a land area of 408.684 square miles, a water area of 3.610 square miles, and is located in the Eastern Time Zone at 39.41° N. Lat., 83.81° W. Long. The county was founded in 1810. County seat is Wilmington.

Clinton County is part of the Wilmington, OH Micropolitan Statistical Area. The entire metro area includes: Clinton County, OH

Weather Station: Wilmington 3 N Elevation: 1,029 feet

	Jan	Feb	Mar	Apr	May	Jun	Jul	Aug	Sep	Oct	Nov	Dec
High	36	39	50	62	72	80	84	83	77	65	52	39
Low	20	22	30	40	50	59	62	60	53	42	34	24
Precip	2.8	2.4	3.5	3.9	5.2	3.8	4.2	3.0	2.8	3.1	3.1	3.0
Snow	6.9	5.8	3.3	0.4	tr	0.0	0.0	0.0	0.0	0.2	0.9	3.5

High and Low temperatures in degrees Fahrenheit; Precipitation and Snow in inches

Population: 42,040; Growth (since 2000): 3.7%; Density: 102.9 persons per square mile; Race: 94.7% White, 2.2% Black/African American, 0.5% Asian, 0.2% American Indian/Alaska Native, 0.0% Native Hawaiian/Other Pacific Islander, 1.9% two or more races, 1.3% Hispanic of any race; Average household size: 2.52; Median age: 38.7; Age under 18: 24.4%; Age 65 and over: 13.5%; Males per 100 females: 96.2; Marriage status: 25.3% never married, 55.8% now married, 2.1% separated, 6.5% widowed, 12.4% divorced; Foreign born: 1.3%; Speak English only: 98.4%; With disability: 13.7%; Veterans: 12.3%; Ancestry: 23.2% German, 14.3% Irish, 13.6% American, 10.4% English, 2.6% Italian
Religion: Six largest groups: 11.5% Baptist, 5.8% Non-denominational Protestant, 5.2% Catholicism, 4.7% Methodist/Pietist, 2.0% Holiness, 1.8% European Free-Church
Economy: Unemployment rate: 5.7%; Leading industries: 18.0% retail trade; 12.8% health care and social assistance; 12.7% other services (except public administration); Farms: 759 totaling 208,142 acres; Company size: 0 employ 1,000 or more persons, 4 employ 500 to 999 persons, 16 employ 100 to 499 persons, 697 employ less than 100 persons; Business ownership: 726 women-owned, n/a Black-owned, n/a Hispanic-owned, n/a Asian-owned
Employment: 9.9% management, business, and financial, 4.4% computer, engineering, and science, 7.3% education, legal, community service, arts, and media, 5.2% healthcare practitioners, 17.9% service, 25.1% sales and office, 9.4% natural resources, construction, and maintenance, 20.7% production, transportation, and material moving
Income: Per capita: $22,026; Median household: $46,048; Average household: $56,558; Households with income of $100,000 or more: 13.2%; Poverty rate: 16.5%
Educational Attainment: High school diploma or higher: 87.7%; Bachelor's degree or higher: 14.5%; Graduate/professional degree or higher: 4.9%
Housing: Homeownership rate: 67.2%; Median home value: $118,600; Median year structure built: 1973; Homeowner vacancy rate: 2.9%; Median gross rent: $668 per month; Rental vacancy rate: 11.8%
Vital Statistics: Birth rate: 119.2 per 10,000 population; Death rate: 99.9 per 10,000 population; Age-adjusted cancer mortality rate: 249.1 deaths per 100,000 population
Health Insurance: 88.2% have insurance; 67.8% have private insurance; 33.5% have public insurance; 11.8% do not have insurance; 4.9% of children under 18 do not have insurance
Health Care: Physicians: 16.2 per 10,000 population; Hospital beds: 20.3 per 10,000 population; Hospital admissions: 1,070.8 per 10,000 population
Air Quality Index: 95.8% good, 3.7% moderate, 0.5% unhealthy for sensitive individuals, 0.0% unhealthy (percent of days)
Transportation: Commute: 91.1% car, 0.4% public transportation, 3.8% walk, 3.5% work from home; Median travel time to work: 26.2 minutes
Presidential Election: 31.4% Obama, 66.5% Romney (2012)
National and State Parks: Cowan State Park
Additional Information Contacts
Clinton Government . . . . (937) 382-2103
http://co.clinton.oh.us

Clinton County Communities

BLANCHESTER (village). Covers a land area of 4.148 square miles and a water area of 0.097 square miles. Located at 39.30° N. Lat; 83.97° W. Long. Elevation is 968 feet.
Population: 4,243; Growth (since 2000): 0.5%; Density: 1,022.8 persons per square mile; Race: 97.8% White, 0.4% Black/African American, 0.3% Asian, 0.3% American Indian/Alaska Native, 0.0% Native Hawaiian/Other Pacific Islander, 1.1% Two or more races, 0.4% Hispanic of any race; Average household size: 2.53; Median age: 37.3; Age under 18: 25.5%; Age 65 and over: 15.6%; Males per 100 females: 89.0; Marriage status: 28.8% never married, 50.8% now married, 2.9% separated, 6.5% widowed, 13.8% divorced; Foreign born: 0.0%; Speak English only: 98.8%; With disability: 17.4%; Veterans: 19.0%; Ancestry: 24.0% German, 18.2% Irish, 15.0% English, 12.9% American, 2.4% Italian
Employment: 3.3% management, business, and financial, 0.0% computer, engineering, and science, 7.7% education, legal, community service, arts, and media, 4.9% healthcare practitioners, 26.5% service, 21.4% sales and office, 10.7% natural resources, construction, and maintenance, 25.6% production, transportation, and material moving
Income: Per capita: $20,104; Median household: $43,182; Average household: $51,167; Households with income of $100,000 or more: 11.6%; Poverty rate: 20.8%
Educational Attainment: High school diploma or higher: 82.6%; Bachelor's degree or higher: 7.6%; Graduate/professional degree or higher: 3.4%

School District(s)
Blanchester Local (PK-12)
2012-13 Enrollment: 1,691 . . . . (937) 783-3523
Housing: Homeownership rate: 64.1%; Median home value: $94,800; Median year structure built: 1966; Homeowner vacancy rate: 3.3%; Median gross rent: $630 per month; Rental vacancy rate: 14.8%
Health Insurance: 83.9% have insurance; 62.5% have private insurance; 40.2% have public insurance; 16.1% do not have insurance; 12.1% of children under 18 do not have insurance
Safety: Violent crime rate: 2.4 per 10,000 population; Property crime rate: 137.1 per 10,000 population
Transportation: Commute: 85.4% car, 0.0% public transportation, 7.1% walk, 5.0% work from home; Median travel time to work: 24.0 minutes

CLARKSVILLE (village). Covers a land area of 0.463 square miles and a water area of 0.030 square miles. Located at 39.40° N. Lat; 83.99° W. Long. Elevation is 814 feet.
Population: 548; Growth (since 2000): 10.3%; Density: 1,184.8 persons per square mile; Race: 96.0% White, 0.0% Black/African American, 2.2% Asian, 0.2% American Indian/Alaska Native, 0.0% Native Hawaiian/Other Pacific Islander, 0.7% Two or more races, 0.9% Hispanic of any race; Average household size: 2.69; Median age: 31.5; Age under 18: 31.4%; Age 65 and over: 7.3%; Males per 100 females: 105.2

School District(s)
Clinton-Massie Local (PK-12)
2012-13 Enrollment: 1,894 . . . . (937) 289-2471
Housing: Homeownership rate: 51.4%; Homeowner vacancy rate: 0.0%; Rental vacancy rate: 11.6%

MARTINSVILLE (village). Covers a land area of 0.439 square miles and a water area of 0.002 square miles. Located at 39.32° N. Lat; 83.81° W. Long. Elevation is 1,089 feet.
Population: 463; Growth (since 2000): 5.2%; Density: 1,053.9 persons per square mile; Race: 96.1% White, 1.3% Black/African American, 0.2% Asian, 0.0% American Indian/Alaska Native, 0.0% Native Hawaiian/Other Pacific Islander, 0.0% Two or more races, 2.8% Hispanic of any race; Average household size: 3.11; Median age: 32.8; Age under 18: 32.4%; Age 65 and over: 12.1%; Males per 100 females: 98.7
Housing: Homeownership rate: 67.8%; Homeowner vacancy rate: 5.6%; Rental vacancy rate: 2.0%

MIDLAND (village). Covers a land area of 0.352 square miles and a water area of 0 square miles. Located at 39.31° N. Lat; 83.91° W. Long. Elevation is 988 feet.
History: Midland developed as a junction town for two branches of the Baltimore & Ohio Railroad.
Population: 315; Growth (since 2000): 18.9%; Density: 893.9 persons per square mile; Race: 96.2% White, 1.0% Black/African American, 0.0% Asian, 0.0% American Indian/Alaska Native, 0.0% Native Hawaiian/Other Pacific Islander, 2.9% Two or more races, 0.0% Hispanic of any race; Average household size: 2.89; Median age: 28.6; Age under 18: 29.8%; Age 65 and over: 5.4%; Males per 100 females: 92.1
Housing: Homeownership rate: 46.8%; Homeowner vacancy rate: 1.9%; Rental vacancy rate: 11.9%

NEW VIENNA (village). Covers a land area of 0.853 square miles and a water area of 0.019 square miles. Located at 39.33° N. Lat; 83.69° W. Long. Elevation is 1,122 feet.
Population: 1,224; Growth (since 2000): -5.4%; Density: 1,435.2 persons per square mile; Race: 96.7% White, 0.8% Black/African American, 0.3% Asian, 0.4% American Indian/Alaska Native, 0.0% Native Hawaiian/Other Pacific Islander, 1.2% Two or more races, 0.7% Hispanic of any race; Average household size: 2.56; Median age: 35.7; Age under 18: 26.5%; Age 65 and over: 10.8%; Males per 100 females: 91.8

School District(s)
East Clinton Local (PK-12)
2012-13 Enrollment: 1,427 . . . . (937) 584-2461
Housing: Homeownership rate: 55.9%; Homeowner vacancy rate: 2.9%; Rental vacancy rate: 8.2%

PORT WILLIAM (village). Covers a land area of 0.116 square miles and a water area of 0.003 square miles. Located at 39.55° N. Lat; 83.79° W. Long. Elevation is 1,020 feet.
Population: 254; Growth (since 2000): -1.6%; Density: 2,185.0 persons per square mile; Race: 95.7% White, 1.2% Black/African American, 0.8% Asian, 2.0% American Indian/Alaska Native, 0.0% Native Hawaiian/Other Pacific Islander, 0.4% Two or more races, 1.2% Hispanic of any race; Average household size: 2.62; Median age: 35.6; Age under 18: 29.5%; Age 65 and over: 7.9%; Males per 100 females: 96.9
Housing: Homeownership rate: 62.9%; Homeowner vacancy rate: 4.7%; Rental vacancy rate: 2.7%

REESVILLE (unincorporated postal area)
ZCTA: 45166
Covers a land area of 0.740 square miles and a water area of 0 square miles. Located at 39.48° N. Lat; 83.69° W. Long. Elevation is 1,083 feet.
Population: 98; Growth (since 2000): n/a; Density: 132.5 persons per square mile; Race: 94.9% White, 0.0% Black/African American, 1.0% Asian, 0.0% American Indian/Alaska Native, 0.0% Native Hawaiian/Other Pacific Islander, 1.0% Two or more races, 3.1% Hispanic of any race; Average household size: 2.58; Median age: 39.6; Age under 18: 26.5%; Age 65 and over: 13.3%; Males per 100 females: 127.9
Housing: Homeownership rate: 71.0%; Homeowner vacancy rate: 6.7%; Rental vacancy rate: 0.0%

SABINA (village). Covers a land area of 1.282 square miles and a water area of 0.008 square miles. Located at 39.49° N. Lat; 83.63° W. Long. Elevation is 1,050 feet.
Population: 2,564; Growth (since 2000): -7.8%; Density: 1,999.7 persons per square mile; Race: 97.0% White, 0.9% Black/African American, 0.3% Asian, 0.3% American Indian/Alaska Native, 0.0% Native Hawaiian/Other Pacific Islander, 1.4% Two or more races, 0.9% Hispanic of any race; Average household size: 2.45; Median age: 38.5; Age under 18: 24.2%; Age 65 and over: 15.4%; Males per 100 females: 94.8; Marriage status: 25.8% never married, 54.4% now married, 1.4% separated, 5.6% widowed, 14.2% divorced; Foreign born: 0.8%; Speak English only: 99.6%; With disability: 17.5%; Veterans: 10.8%; Ancestry: 25.1% German, 13.6% American, 12.6% Irish, 10.0% English, 5.8% Dutch
Employment: 5.4% management, business, and financial, 1.1% computer, engineering, and science, 5.5% education, legal, community service, arts, and media, 2.9% healthcare practitioners, 17.2% service, 31.9% sales and office, 15.3% natural resources, construction, and maintenance, 20.8% production, transportation, and material moving
Income: Per capita: $17,648; Median household: $38,661; Average household: $46,232; Households with income of $100,000 or more: 7.9%; Poverty rate: 22.1%
Educational Attainment: High school diploma or higher: 83.6%; Bachelor's degree or higher: 7.8%; Graduate/professional degree or higher: 0.9%

School District(s)
East Clinton Local (PK-12)
2012-13 Enrollment: 1,427 . . . . (937) 584-2461
Housing: Homeownership rate: 59.1%; Median home value: $77,100; Median year structure built: 1959; Homeowner vacancy rate: 2.7%; Median gross rent: $631 per month; Rental vacancy rate: 9.1%
Health Insurance: 87.0% have insurance; 58.5% have private insurance; 43.5% have public insurance; 13.0% do not have insurance; 2.1% of children under 18 do not have insurance
Safety: Violent crime rate: 7.9 per 10,000 population; Property crime rate: 306.4 per 10,000 population
Transportation: Commute: 93.9% car, 0.8% public transportation, 3.7% walk, 0.7% work from home; Median travel time to work: 23.2 minutes

WILMINGTON (city). County seat. Covers a land area of 10.889 square miles and a water area of 0.041 square miles. Located at 39.44° N. Lat; 83.82° W. Long. Elevation is 1,017 feet.
History: Seat of Wilmington College. Settled 1810, incorporated 1828.
Population: 12,520; Growth (since 2000): 5.0%; Density: 1,149.8 persons per square mile; Race: 88.3% White, 6.1% Black/African American, 0.8% Asian, 0.2% American Indian/Alaska Native, 0.1% Native Hawaiian/Other Pacific Islander, 3.5% Two or more races, 2.6% Hispanic of any race; Average household size: 2.27; Median age: 33.7; Age under 18: 23.5%; Age 65 and over: 14.5%; Males per 100 females: 87.7; Marriage status: 30.8% never married, 45.5% now married, 2.9% separated, 9.3% widowed, 14.5% divorced; Foreign born: 1.9%; Speak English only: 96.7%; With disability: 15.4%; Veterans: 10.0%; Ancestry: 19.5% German, 13.8% American, 10.7% Irish, 9.9% English, 2.7% Italian
Employment: 9.6% management, business, and financial, 3.3% computer, engineering, and science, 10.0% education, legal, community service, arts, and media, 3.3% healthcare practitioners, 19.9% service, 24.8% sales and

office, 6.4% natural resources, construction, and maintenance, 22.6% production, transportation, and material moving
Income: Per capita: $18,887; Median household: $29,828; Average household: $43,161; Households with income of $100,000 or more: 5.1%; Poverty rate: 24.8%
Educational Attainment: High school diploma or higher: 85.2%; Bachelor's degree or higher: 14.1%; Graduate/professional degree or higher: 5.1%

School District(s)

Great Oaks Inst of Technology (05-12)
2012-13 Enrollment: n/a . . . . (513) 771-8840
Wilmington City (PK-12)
2012-13 Enrollment: 3,104 . . . . (937) 382-1641

Four-year College(s)

Wilmington College (Private, Not-for-profit, Friends)
Fall 2013 Enrollment: 1,173 . . . . (800) 341-9318
2013-14 Tuition: In-state $28,190; Out-of-state $28,190
Housing: Homeownership rate: 47.7%; Median home value: $97,700; Median year structure built: 1968; Homeowner vacancy rate: 4.1%; Median gross rent: $670 per month; Rental vacancy rate: 14.1%
Health Insurance: 88.7% have insurance; 59.9% have private insurance; 44.0% have public insurance; 11.3% do not have insurance; 2.8% of children under 18 do not have insurance
Hospitals: Clinton Memorial Hospital (150 beds)
Newspapers: Wilmington News Journal (daily circulation 7400)
Transportation: Commute: 86.8% car, 0.3% public transportation, 7.5% walk, 3.4% work from home; Median travel time to work: 20.0 minutes
Airports: Wilmington Air Park (general aviation)
Additional Information Contacts
City of Wilmington . . . . (937) 382-5458
http://ci.wilmington.oh.us

Columbiana County

Located in eastern Ohio; bounded on the east by Pennsylvania, and on the southeast by the Ohio River; drained by the Little Beaver River. Covers a land area of 531.893 square miles, a water area of 2.795 square miles, and is located in the Eastern Time Zone at 40.77° N. Lat., 80.78° W. Long. The county was founded in 1803. County seat is Lisbon.

Columbiana County is part of the Salem, OH Micropolitan Statistical Area. The entire metro area includes: Columbiana County, OH

Weather Station: Millport 2 NW Elevation: 1,149 feet

	Jan	Feb	Mar	Apr	May	Jun	Jul	Aug	Sep	Oct	Nov	Dec
High	36	40	50	62	72	80	84	82	76	64	51	39
Low	18	20	27	37	46	55	59	57	50	39	31	22
Precip	2.5	2.2	2.8	3.3	4.0	3.8	4.0	3.3	3.3	2.6	3.1	2.8
Snow	8.0	6.6	5.1	1.5	tr	0.0	0.0	0.0	0.0	tr	1.6	6.0

High and Low temperatures in degrees Fahrenheit; Precipitation and Snow in inches

Population: 107,841; Growth (since 2000): -3.8%; Density: 202.7 persons per square mile; Race: 95.5% White, 2.2% Black/African American, 0.3% Asian, 0.2% American Indian/Alaska Native, 0.0% Native Hawaiian/Other Pacific Islander, 1.3% two or more races, 1.2% Hispanic of any race; Average household size: 2.43; Median age: 42.3; Age under 18: 21.9%; Age 65 and over: 16.5%; Males per 100 females: 101.0; Marriage status: 24.4% never married, 55.0% now married, 2.4% separated, 7.4% widowed, 13.2% divorced; Foreign born: 1.2%; Speak English only: 97.5%; With disability: 16.2%; Veterans: 12.0%; Ancestry: 27.8% German, 17.0% Irish, 13.3% American, 12.8% English, 9.3% Italian
Religion: Six largest groups: 9.0% Catholicism, 7.1% Methodist/Pietist, 6.2% Baptist, 4.5% Non-denominational Protestant, 3.8% Presbyterian-Reformed, 2.9% Lutheran
Economy: Unemployment rate: 4.9%; Leading industries: 16.3% retail trade; 14.1% other services (except public administration); 13.9% health care and social assistance; Farms: 1,045 totaling 127,846 acres; Company size: 0 employ 1,000 or more persons, 3 employ 500 to 999 persons, 28 employ 100 to 499 persons, 2,067 employ less than 100 persons; Business ownership: 2,220 women-owned, n/a Black-owned, 60 Hispanic-owned, n/a Asian-owned
Employment: 10.0% management, business, and financial, 2.0% computer, engineering, and science, 7.9% education, legal, community service, arts, and media, 5.4% healthcare practitioners, 19.9% service, 22.4% sales and office, 10.4% natural resources, construction, and maintenance, 22.0% production, transportation, and material moving
Income: Per capita: $21,575; Median household: $42,300; Average household: $53,654; Households with income of $100,000 or more: 10.9%; Poverty rate: 16.9%
Educational Attainment: High school diploma or higher: 86.5%; Bachelor's degree or higher: 12.6%; Graduate/professional degree or higher: 4.2%
Housing: Homeownership rate: 73.1%; Median home value: $96,000; Median year structure built: 1962; Homeowner vacancy rate: 2.4%; Median gross rent: $589 per month; Rental vacancy rate: 8.8%
Vital Statistics: Birth rate: 100.7 per 10,000 population; Death rate: 105.9 per 10,000 population; Age-adjusted cancer mortality rate: 198.5 deaths per 100,000 population
Health Insurance: 87.7% have insurance; 65.5% have private insurance; 36.7% have public insurance; 12.3% do not have insurance; 5.4% of children under 18 do not have insurance
Health Care: Physicians: 10.3 per 10,000 population; Hospital beds: 23.2 per 10,000 population; Hospital admissions: 930.5 per 10,000 population
Air Quality Index: 99.7% good, 0.3% moderate, 0.0% unhealthy for sensitive individuals, 0.0% unhealthy (percent of days)
Transportation: Commute: 94.0% car, 0.4% public transportation, 1.8% walk, 2.8% work from home; Median travel time to work: 24.6 minutes
Presidential Election: 42.9% Obama, 55.0% Romney (2012)
National and State Parks: Beaver Creek State Forest; Guilford Lake State Park
Additional Information Contacts
Columbiana Government . . . . (330) 424-9511
http://www.columbianacounty.org

Columbiana County Communities

CALCUTTA (CDP). Covers a land area of 11.865 square miles and a water area of 0.013 square miles. Located at 40.69° N. Lat; 80.55° W. Long. Elevation is 1,112 feet.
Population: 3,742; Growth (since 2000): 7.2%; Density: 315.4 persons per square mile; Race: 97.3% White, 0.4% Black/African American, 0.8% Asian, 0.2% American Indian/Alaska Native, 0.2% Native Hawaiian/Other Pacific Islander, 1.1% Two or more races, 0.7% Hispanic of any race; Average household size: 2.31; Median age: 47.5; Age under 18: 20.3%; Age 65 and over: 23.9%; Males per 100 females: 91.7; Marriage status: 18.7% never married, 60.6% now married, 1.8% separated, 13.5% widowed, 7.2% divorced; Foreign born: 1.8%; Speak English only: 98.2%; With disability: 14.2%; Veterans: 14.9%; Ancestry: 22.4% German, 19.4% American, 14.4% Irish, 13.6% English, 5.7% Italian
Employment: 17.4% management, business, and financial, 1.7% computer, engineering, and science, 13.2% education, legal, community service, arts, and media, 3.6% healthcare practitioners, 13.1% service, 22.0% sales and office, 10.1% natural resources, construction, and maintenance, 18.9% production, transportation, and material moving
Income: Per capita: $27,914; Median household: $52,356; Average household: $68,113; Households with income of $100,000 or more: 22.1%; Poverty rate: 7.4%
Educational Attainment: High school diploma or higher: 86.0%; Bachelor's degree or higher: 18.4%; Graduate/professional degree or higher: 10.4%
Housing: Homeownership rate: 76.5%; Median home value: $124,300; Median year structure built: 1976; Homeowner vacancy rate: 2.1%; Median gross rent: $589 per month; Rental vacancy rate: 3.9%
Health Insurance: 93.5% have insurance; 75.7% have private insurance; 36.5% have public insurance; 6.5% do not have insurance; 0.0% of children under 18 do not have insurance
Transportation: Commute: 93.7% car, 1.2% public transportation, 2.5% walk, 2.6% work from home; Median travel time to work: 23.0 minutes

COLUMBIANA (city). Covers a land area of 6.000 square miles and a water area of 0.143 square miles. Located at 40.89° N. Lat; 80.67° W. Long. Elevation is 1,148 feet.
History: Columbiana was laid out in 1805, when it was called Dixonville for its founder, Joshua Dixon. Harvey S. Firestone (1868-1938), who had the idea of making rubber tires for buggies, was born in Columbiana.
Population: 6,384; Growth (since 2000): 13.3%; Density: 1,064.0 persons per square mile; Race: 97.7% White, 0.6% Black/African American, 0.5% Asian, 0.0% American Indian/Alaska Native, 0.0% Native Hawaiian/Other Pacific Islander, 0.8% Two or more races, 1.0% Hispanic of any race; Average household size: 2.15; Median age: 49.4; Age under 18: 17.5%; Age 65 and over: 27.4%; Males per 100 females: 87.4; Marriage status:

24.1% never married, 53.6% now married, 0.9% separated, 10.9% widowed, 11.4% divorced; Foreign born: 0.5%; Speak English only: 98.9%; With disability: 16.6%; Veterans: 13.7%; Ancestry: 32.4% German, 18.2% Irish, 13.0% American, 11.1% English, 9.3% Italian
Employment: 9.0% management, business, and financial, 2.9% computer, engineering, and science, 8.4% education, legal, community service, arts, and media, 6.2% healthcare practitioners, 17.3% service, 27.5% sales and office, 5.4% natural resources, construction, and maintenance, 23.4% production, transportation, and material moving
Income: Per capita: $21,651; Median household: $40,598; Average household: $48,309; Households with income of $100,000 or more: 9.8%; Poverty rate: 12.0%
Educational Attainment: High school diploma or higher: 90.5%; Bachelor's degree or higher: 16.7%; Graduate/professional degree or higher: 7.7%

School District(s)

Columbiana Exempted Village (01-12)
2012-13 Enrollment: 1,043 . . . . (330) 482-5352
Crestview Local (PK-12)
2012-13 Enrollment: 1,235 . . . . (330) 482-5526

Housing: Homeownership rate: 66.3%; Median home value: $124,600; Median year structure built: 1970; Homeowner vacancy rate: 4.3%; Median gross rent: $588 per month; Rental vacancy rate: 9.5%
Health Insurance: 90.0% have insurance; 69.2% have private insurance; 44.8% have public insurance; 10.0% do not have insurance; 1.5% of children under 18 do not have insurance
Safety: Violent crime rate: 6.3 per 10,000 population; Property crime rate: 174.2 per 10,000 population
Transportation: Commute: 90.6% car, 0.0% public transportation, 5.6% walk, 2.3% work from home; Median travel time to work: 17.1 minutes

---

EAST LIVERPOOL (city). Covers a land area of 4.563 square miles and a water area of 0.196 square miles. Located at 40.63° N. Lat; 80.57° W. Long. Elevation is 768 feet.
History: East Liverpool was called St. Clair in 1798 by its founder, Thomas Fawcett of Ireland. Early residents called it Fawcett's Town, but in 1860 the name became Liverpool, because many of the residents had come from the English pottery city. James Bennett, a young potter from England, arrived here in 1838, and East Liverpool began the pottery production that shaped its character for many years.
Population: 11,195; Growth (since 2000): -14.5%; Density: 2,453.7 persons per square mile; Race: 91.7% White, 4.6% Black/African American, 0.2% Asian, 0.2% American Indian/Alaska Native, 0.0% Native Hawaiian/Other Pacific Islander, 3.0% Two or more races, 1.1% Hispanic of any race; Average household size: 2.39; Median age: 37.6; Age under 18: 25.4%; Age 65 and over: 14.6%; Males per 100 females: 90.7; Marriage status: 31.1% never married, 46.0% now married, 3.8% separated, 8.5% widowed, 14.4% divorced; Foreign born: 0.9%; Speak English only: 98.7%; With disability: 21.8%; Veterans: 11.9%; Ancestry: 22.6% German, 19.2% Irish, 16.4% English, 12.9% American, 8.9% Italian
Employment: 8.8% management, business, and financial, 1.0% computer, engineering, and science, 7.3% education, legal, community service, arts, and media, 6.8% healthcare practitioners, 22.1% service, 20.5% sales and office, 8.1% natural resources, construction, and maintenance, 25.4% production, transportation, and material moving
Income: Per capita: $16,584; Median household: $27,886; Average household: $38,568; Households with income of $100,000 or more: 6.1%; Poverty rate: 30.1%
Educational Attainment: High school diploma or higher: 81.2%; Bachelor's degree or higher: 6.6%; Graduate/professional degree or higher: 3.5%

School District(s)

Beaver Local (PK-12)
2012-13 Enrollment: 1,909 . . . . (330) 385-6831
Buckeye Online School for Success (KG-12)
2012-13 Enrollment: 1,240 . . . . (330) 385-1987
East Liverpool City (PK-12)
2012-13 Enrollment: 2,268 . . . . (330) 385-7132

Four-year College(s)

Kent State University at East Liverpool (Public)
Fall 2013 Enrollment: 1,672 . . . . (330) 385-3805
2013-14 Tuition: In-state $5,554; Out-of-state $13,514

Two-year College(s)

Ohio Valley College of Technology (Private, For-profit)
Fall 2013 Enrollment: 183 . . . . (330) 385-1070
2013-14 Tuition: In-state $11,698; Out-of-state $11,698

Housing: Homeownership rate: 54.7%; Median home value: $54,700; Median year structure built: 1943; Homeowner vacancy rate: 3.5%; Median gross rent: $557 per month; Rental vacancy rate: 11.8%
Health Insurance: 87.3% have insurance; 51.9% have private insurance; 48.8% have public insurance; 12.7% do not have insurance; 3.2% of children under 18 do not have insurance
Hospitals: East Liverpool City Hospital (199 beds)
Newspapers: The Review (daily circulation 9300)
Transportation: Commute: 95.3% car, 1.0% public transportation, 1.8% walk, 1.0% work from home; Median travel time to work: 24.4 minutes
Additional Information Contacts
City of East Liverpool . . . . (330) 385-3381
http://www.eastliverpool.com

EAST PALESTINE (village). Covers a land area of 3.152 square miles and a water area of 0 square miles. Located at 40.84° N. Lat; 80.55° W. Long. Elevation is 997 feet.
History: East Palestine was established in 1828 by Thomas McCalla and William Grate. It developed as a pottery town, first using deposits of local clay, but later employing finer materials.
Population: 4,721; Growth (since 2000): -4.0%; Density: 1,497.7 persons per square mile; Race: 98.2% White, 0.2% Black/African American, 0.3% Asian, 0.1% American Indian/Alaska Native, 0.0% Native Hawaiian/Other Pacific Islander, 0.7% Two or more races, 0.9% Hispanic of any race; Average household size: 2.46; Median age: 40.7; Age under 18: 23.1%; Age 65 and over: 16.5%; Males per 100 females: 96.2; Marriage status: 26.8% never married, 54.2% now married, 2.6% separated, 6.9% widowed, 12.2% divorced; Foreign born: 2.7%; Speak English only: 97.0%; With disability: 16.2%; Veterans: 9.1%; Ancestry: 37.9% German, 17.6% Irish, 14.2% English, 12.9% Italian, 8.0% American
Employment: 10.4% management, business, and financial, 3.0% computer, engineering, and science, 8.4% education, legal, community service, arts, and media, 4.0% healthcare practitioners, 18.1% service, 20.9% sales and office, 12.4% natural resources, construction, and maintenance, 22.9% production, transportation, and material moving
Income: Per capita: $19,459; Median household: $41,368; Average household: $50,253; Households with income of $100,000 or more: 9.1%; Poverty rate: 17.1%
Educational Attainment: High school diploma or higher: 86.1%; Bachelor's degree or higher: 10.1%; Graduate/professional degree or higher: 2.3%

School District(s)

East Palestine City (PK-12)
2012-13 Enrollment: 1,185 . . . . (330) 426-4191

Housing: Homeownership rate: 72.4%; Median home value: $83,300; Median year structure built: Before 1940; Homeowner vacancy rate: 3.3%; Median gross rent: $567 per month; Rental vacancy rate: 11.4%
Health Insurance: 89.6% have insurance; 68.4% have private insurance; 33.4% have public insurance; 10.4% do not have insurance; 0.0% of children under 18 do not have insurance
Safety: Violent crime rate: 13.0 per 10,000 population; Property crime rate: 252.6 per 10,000 population
Transportation: Commute: 95.3% car, 0.5% public transportation, 3.2% walk, 0.7% work from home; Median travel time to work: 26.8 minutes
Additional Information Contacts
City of East Palestine . . . . (330) 426-4367
http://www.eastpalestine-oh.gov

EAST ROCHESTER (CDP). Covers a land area of 0.426 square miles and a water area of 0 square miles. Located at 40.75° N. Lat; 81.04° W. Long. Elevation is 1,093 feet.
Population: 231; Growth (since 2000): n/a; Density: 542.2 persons per square mile; Race: 98.7% White, 1.3% Black/African American, 0.0% Asian, 0.0% American Indian/Alaska Native, 0.0% Native Hawaiian/Other Pacific Islander, 0.0% Two or more races, 0.4% Hispanic of any race; Average household size: 2.78; Median age: 35.1; Age under 18: 27.3%; Age 65 and over: 13.4%; Males per 100 females: 104.4
Housing: Homeownership rate: 80.7%; Homeowner vacancy rate: 4.2%; Rental vacancy rate: 11.1%

GLENMOOR (CDP). Covers a land area of 2.796 square miles and a water area of <.001 square miles. Located at 40.66° N. Lat; 80.61° W. Long. Elevation is 1,122 feet.
Population: 1,987; Growth (since 2000): -9.4%; Density: 710.7 persons per square mile; Race: 97.4% White, 1.2% Black/African American, 0.0% Asian, 0.3% American Indian/Alaska Native, 0.0% Native Hawaiian/Other Pacific Islander, 1.1% Two or more races, 0.4% Hispanic of any race; Average household size: 2.40; Median age: 45.1; Age under 18: 20.5%; Age 65 and over: 17.3%; Males per 100 females: 103.0
Housing: Homeownership rate: 78.1%; Homeowner vacancy rate: 2.4%; Rental vacancy rate: 4.7%

HANOVERTON (village). Covers a land area of 0.695 square miles and a water area of 0 square miles. Located at 40.75° N. Lat; 80.94° W. Long. Elevation is 1,132 feet.
Population: 408; Growth (since 2000): 5.4%; Density: 587.2 persons per square mile; Race: 100.0% White, 0.0% Black/African American, 0.0% Asian, 0.0% American Indian/Alaska Native, 0.0% Native Hawaiian/Other Pacific Islander, 0.0% Two or more races, 0.0% Hispanic of any race; Average household size: 2.52; Median age: 39.6; Age under 18: 23.8%; Age 65 and over: 15.4%; Males per 100 females: 91.5

School District(s)

United Local (PK-12)
2012-13 Enrollment: 1,300 . . . . (330) 223-1521
Housing: Homeownership rate: 83.3%; Homeowner vacancy rate: 2.2%; Rental vacancy rate: 3.6%

HOMEWORTH (CDP). Covers a land area of 1.239 square miles and a water area of 0.015 square miles. Located at 40.84° N. Lat; 81.07° W. Long. Elevation is 1,142 feet.
Population: 481; Growth (since 2000): n/a; Density: 388.3 persons per square mile; Race: 99.2% White, 0.2% Black/African American, 0.0% Asian, 0.0% American Indian/Alaska Native, 0.0% Native Hawaiian/Other Pacific Islander, 0.6% Two or more races, 0.0% Hispanic of any race; Average household size: 2.72; Median age: 35.6; Age under 18: 24.1%; Age 65 and over: 8.1%; Males per 100 females: 104.7
Housing: Homeownership rate: 70.6%; Homeowner vacancy rate: 2.3%; Rental vacancy rate: 7.1%

KENSINGTON (unincorporated postal area)

ZCTA: 44427

Covers a land area of 30.596 square miles and a water area of 0.043 square miles. Located at 40.71° N. Lat; 80.95° W. Long. Elevation is 1,115 feet.
Population: 1,612; Growth (since 2000): -6.7%; Density: 52.7 persons per square mile; Race: 98.6% White, 0.2% Black/African American, 0.1% Asian, 0.1% American Indian/Alaska Native, 0.0% Native Hawaiian/Other Pacific Islander, 0.9% Two or more races, 0.9% Hispanic of any race; Average household size: 2.77; Median age: 39.1; Age under 18: 27.7%; Age 65 and over: 13.0%; Males per 100 females: 99.5
Housing: Homeownership rate: 82.8%; Homeowner vacancy rate: 1.2%; Rental vacancy rate: 6.5%

LA CROFT (CDP). Covers a land area of 1.145 square miles and a water area of 0 square miles. Located at 40.65° N. Lat; 80.60° W. Long. Elevation is 1,168 feet.
Population: 1,144; Growth (since 2000): -12.5%; Density: 999.4 persons per square mile; Race: 97.2% White, 0.9% Black/African American, 0.0% Asian, 0.2% American Indian/Alaska Native, 0.0% Native Hawaiian/Other Pacific Islander, 1.6% Two or more races, 0.7% Hispanic of any race; Average household size: 2.36; Median age: 44.7; Age under 18: 19.8%; Age 65 and over: 16.6%; Males per 100 females: 89.7
Housing: Homeownership rate: 78.1%; Homeowner vacancy rate: 2.6%; Rental vacancy rate: 1.8%

LAKE TOMAHAWK (CDP). Covers a land area of 0.829 square miles and a water area of 0.197 square miles. Located at 40.76° N. Lat; 80.60° W. Long.
Population: 485; Growth (since 2000): n/a; Density: 585.2 persons per square mile; Race: 97.9% White, 0.2% Black/African American, 0.0% Asian, 0.4% American Indian/Alaska Native, 0.2% Native Hawaiian/Other Pacific Islander, 1.2% Two or more races, 0.8% Hispanic of any race; Average household size: 2.54; Median age: 45.1; Age under 18: 20.6%; Age 65 and over: 11.5%; Males per 100 females: 106.4
Housing: Homeownership rate: 96.9%; Homeowner vacancy rate: 3.6%; Rental vacancy rate: 0.0%

LEETONIA (village). Covers a land area of 2.263 square miles and a water area of 0.007 square miles. Located at 40.88° N. Lat; 80.76° W. Long. Elevation is 1,017 feet.
History: Laid out 1866.
Population: 1,959; Growth (since 2000): -4.1%; Density: 865.6 persons per square mile; Race: 97.8% White, 0.2% Black/African American, 0.3% Asian, 0.2% American Indian/Alaska Native, 0.1% Native Hawaiian/Other Pacific Islander, 1.5% Two or more races, 0.8% Hispanic of any race; Average household size: 2.62; Median age: 38.2; Age under 18: 26.1%; Age 65 and over: 13.3%; Males per 100 females: 96.1

School District(s)

Leetonia Exempted Village (PK-12)
2012-13 Enrollment: 749. . . . . (330) 427-6594
Housing: Homeownership rate: 76.7%; Homeowner vacancy rate: 5.2%; Rental vacancy rate: 10.7%

LISBON (village). County seat. Covers a land area of 1.687 square miles and a water area of 0 square miles. Located at 40.78° N. Lat; 80.76° W. Long. Elevation is 965 feet.
History: Lisbon was founded in 1802, and grew as a coal and pottery town. This was the birthplace of politicians Marcus A. Hanna (1837-1904) and Clement L. Vallandigham (1820-1871).
Population: 2,821; Growth (since 2000): 1.2%; Density: 1,671.8 persons per square mile; Race: 97.4% White, 1.1% Black/African American, 0.2% Asian, 0.2% American Indian/Alaska Native, 0.0% Native Hawaiian/Other Pacific Islander, 0.9% Two or more races, 1.2% Hispanic of any race; Average household size: 2.35; Median age: 39.6; Age under 18: 23.1%; Age 65 and over: 15.5%; Males per 100 females: 89.7; Marriage status: 29.8% never married, 52.5% now married, 4.0% separated, 5.9% widowed, 11.7% divorced; Foreign born: 0.7%; Speak English only: 97.3%; With disability: 20.8%; Veterans: 9.7%; Ancestry: 40.5% German, 20.7% American, 17.7% Irish, 7.6% English, 4.8% Italian
Employment: 9.8% management, business, and financial, 1.9% computer, engineering, and science, 7.3% education, legal, community service, arts, and media, 5.4% healthcare practitioners, 22.5% service, 24.6% sales and office, 13.4% natural resources, construction, and maintenance, 15.0% production, transportation, and material moving
Income: Per capita: $20,070; Median household: $40,071; Average household: $48,461; Households with income of $100,000 or more: 10.4%; Poverty rate: 21.3%
Educational Attainment: High school diploma or higher: 88.1%; Bachelor's degree or higher: 13.7%; Graduate/professional degree or higher: 4.3%

School District(s)

Beaver Local (PK-12)
2012-13 Enrollment: 1,909 . . . . (330) 385-6831
Columbiana County (09-12)
2012-13 Enrollment: n/a . . . . (330) 424-9561
Lisbon Exempted Village (PK-12)
2012-13 Enrollment: 949. . . . . (330) 424-7714

Vocational/Technical School(s)

Columbiana County Career and Technical Center (Public)
Fall 2013 Enrollment: 190 . . . . (330) 424-9561
2013-14 Tuition: In-state $5,645; Out-of-state $5,645
Housing: Homeownership rate: 58.1%; Median home value: $72,400; Median year structure built: 1942; Homeowner vacancy rate: 3.0%; Median gross rent: $566 per month; Rental vacancy rate: 9.7%
Health Insurance: 87.0% have insurance; 58.0% have private insurance; 38.5% have public insurance; 13.0% do not have insurance; 0.0% of children under 18 do not have insurance
Newspapers: Morning Journal (daily circulation 11800)
Transportation: Commute: 91.9% car, 0.0% public transportation, 4.3% walk, 3.8% work from home; Median travel time to work: 24.4 minutes

NEGLEY (CDP). Covers a land area of 0.891 square miles and a water area of 0 square miles. Located at 40.79° N. Lat; 80.54° W. Long. Elevation is 856 feet.
Population: 281; Growth (since 2000): n/a; Density: 315.2 persons per square mile; Race: 98.6% White, 0.0% Black/African American, 0.0% Asian, 0.0% American Indian/Alaska Native, 0.0% Native Hawaiian/Other Pacific Islander, 0.0% Two or more races, 1.1% Hispanic of any race;

Average household size: 2.25; Median age: 47.7; Age under 18: 15.3%; Age 65 and over: 22.8%; Males per 100 females: 102.2
Housing: Homeownership rate: 80.8%; Homeowner vacancy rate: 1.9%; Rental vacancy rate: 4.0%

NEW WATERFORD (village). Covers a land area of 0.887 square miles and a water area of 0 square miles. Located at 40.85° N. Lat; 80.62° W. Long. Elevation is 1,047 feet.
Population: 1,238; Growth (since 2000): -11.0%; Density: 1,395.0 persons per square mile; Race: 98.1% White, 0.2% Black/African American, 0.5% Asian, 0.2% American Indian/Alaska Native, 0.0% Native Hawaiian/Other Pacific Islander, 0.9% Two or more races, 0.6% Hispanic of any race; Average household size: 2.41; Median age: 40.1; Age under 18: 24.0%; Age 65 and over: 16.0%; Males per 100 females: 89.0
Housing: Homeownership rate: 70.6%; Homeowner vacancy rate: 1.9%; Rental vacancy rate: 12.6%

ROGERS (village). Covers a land area of 0.227 square miles and a water area of 0 square miles. Located at 40.79° N. Lat; 80.63° W. Long. Elevation is 1,027 feet.
Population: 237; Growth (since 2000): -10.9%; Density: 1,042.2 persons per square mile; Race: 98.3% White, 0.4% Black/African American, 0.0% Asian, 0.0% American Indian/Alaska Native, 0.0% Native Hawaiian/Other Pacific Islander, 1.3% Two or more races, 0.0% Hispanic of any race; Average household size: 2.79; Median age: 39.3; Age under 18: 21.1%; Age 65 and over: 11.4%; Males per 100 females: 91.1
Housing: Homeownership rate: 83.5%; Homeowner vacancy rate: 1.4%; Rental vacancy rate: 0.0%

SALEM (city). Covers a land area of 6.425 square miles and a water area of 0.003 square miles. Located at 40.90° N. Lat; 80.85° W. Long. Elevation is 1,227 feet.
History: The Quakers came to Salem in 1801 from Salem, New Jersey, and were joined by others from Pennsylvania and Virginia. The town was a station on the Underground Railroad.
Population: 12,303; Growth (since 2000): 0.9%; Density: 1,915.0 persons per square mile; Race: 95.9% White, 0.7% Black/African American, 0.4% Asian, 0.2% American Indian/Alaska Native, 0.0% Native Hawaiian/Other Pacific Islander, 1.2% Two or more races, 2.5% Hispanic of any race; Average household size: 2.25; Median age: 42.8; Age under 18: 21.2%; Age 65 and over: 19.1%; Males per 100 females: 91.8; Marriage status: 25.7% never married, 48.9% now married, 1.9% separated, 7.4% widowed, 18.0% divorced; Foreign born: 1.3%; Speak English only: 97.9%; With disability: 17.8%; Veterans: 12.6%; Ancestry: 29.3% German, 18.4% Irish, 12.5% American, 10.1% Italian, 8.8% English
Employment: 6.5% management, business, and financial, 1.4% computer, engineering, and science, 7.0% education, legal, community service, arts, and media, 5.6% healthcare practitioners, 21.8% service, 22.6% sales and office, 8.5% natural resources, construction, and maintenance, 26.6% production, transportation, and material moving
Income: Per capita: $19,997; Median household: $36,122; Average household: $45,689; Households with income of $100,000 or more: 7.4%; Poverty rate: 22.8%
Educational Attainment: High school diploma or higher: 86.2%; Bachelor's degree or higher: 12.3%; Graduate/professional degree or higher: 4.1%

School District(s)

Salem City (PK-12)
2012-13 Enrollment: 2,050 . . . . (330) 332-0316
West Branch Local (PK-12)
2012-13 Enrollment: 2,149 . . . . (330) 938-9324

Four-year College(s)

Allegheny Wesleyan College (Private, Not-for-profit, Other Protestant)
Fall 2013 Enrollment: 43 . . . . (330) 337-6403
2013-14 Tuition: In-state $4,800; Out-of-state $4,800
Kent State University at Salem (Public)
Fall 2013 Enrollment: 1,846 . . . . (330) 332-0361
2013-14 Tuition: In-state $5,554; Out-of-state $13,514

Vocational/Technical School(s)

Hannah E Mullins School of Practical Nursing (Public)
Fall 2013 Enrollment: 77 . . . . (330) 332-8940
2013-14 Tuition: $10,500
Housing: Homeownership rate: 61.3%; Median home value: $85,600; Median year structure built: 1953; Homeowner vacancy rate: 2.4%; Median gross rent: $586 per month; Rental vacancy rate: 6.1%
Health Insurance: 84.3% have insurance; 60.6% have private insurance; 39.4% have public insurance; 15.7% do not have insurance; 3.7% of children under 18 do not have insurance
Hospitals: Salem Regional Medical Center (183 beds)
Safety: Violent crime rate: 5.0 per 10,000 population; Property crime rate: 203.9 per 10,000 population
Newspapers: Salem News (daily circulation 6100)
Transportation: Commute: 96.2% car, 0.0% public transportation, 2.0% walk, 1.6% work from home; Median travel time to work: 20.3 minutes
Additional Information Contacts
City of Salem . . . . (330) 332-4241
http://www.cityofsalemohio.org

SALINEVILLE (village). Covers a land area of 2.208 square miles and a water area of 0 square miles. Located at 40.62° N. Lat; 80.83° W. Long. Elevation is 909 feet.
History: Salineville was named for the salt springs nearby. A salt well was sunk here in 1809, and by 1835 twenty wells were operating along Little Yellow Creek. The arrival of the railroad in 1852 led to the opening of drift coal mines, bringing prosperity to Salineville after the Civil War.
Population: 1,311; Growth (since 2000): -6.2%; Density: 593.9 persons per square mile; Race: 97.1% White, 1.4% Black/African American, 0.1% Asian, 0.2% American Indian/Alaska Native, 0.0% Native Hawaiian/Other Pacific Islander, 1.3% Two or more races, 0.4% Hispanic of any race; Average household size: 2.52; Median age: 36.5; Age under 18: 27.8%; Age 65 and over: 14.0%; Males per 100 females: 91.7

School District(s)

Southern Local (PK-12)
2012-13 Enrollment: 843 . . . . (330) 679-2343
Housing: Homeownership rate: 66.6%; Homeowner vacancy rate: 2.7%; Rental vacancy rate: 19.2%
Safety: Violent crime rate: 15.5 per 10,000 population; Property crime rate: 294.8 per 10,000 population

SUMMITVILLE (village). Covers a land area of 0.924 square miles and a water area of 0.027 square miles. Located at 40.67° N. Lat; 80.89° W. Long. Elevation is 1,106 feet.
Population: 135; Growth (since 2000): 25.0%; Density: 146.1 persons per square mile; Race: 95.6% White, 0.7% Black/African American, 0.0% Asian, 0.0% American Indian/Alaska Native, 0.0% Native Hawaiian/Other Pacific Islander, 3.7% Two or more races, 4.4% Hispanic of any race; Average household size: 2.65; Median age: 38.2; Age under 18: 25.9%; Age 65 and over: 19.3%; Males per 100 females: 101.5
Housing: Homeownership rate: 84.4%; Homeowner vacancy rate: 6.5%; Rental vacancy rate: 0.0%

WASHINGTONVILLE (village). Covers a land area of 0.668 square miles and a water area of <.001 square miles. Located at 40.90° N. Lat; 80.77° W. Long. Elevation is 1,056 feet.
Population: 801; Growth (since 2000): 1.5%; Density: 1,198.3 persons per square mile; Race: 98.0% White, 0.9% Black/African American, 0.0% Asian, 0.0% American Indian/Alaska Native, 0.0% Native Hawaiian/Other Pacific Islander, 1.0% Two or more races, 0.5% Hispanic of any race; Average household size: 2.48; Median age: 37.5; Age under 18: 24.7%; Age 65 and over: 13.7%; Males per 100 females: 94.9
Housing: Homeownership rate: 59.8%; Homeowner vacancy rate: 4.0%; Rental vacancy rate: 4.4%

WELLSVILLE (village). Covers a land area of 1.802 square miles and a water area of 0.109 square miles. Located at 40.60° N. Lat; 80.65° W. Long. Elevation is 696 feet.
History: Wellsville was founded in 1797 by William Wells, and grew as a stagecoach stop, a shipping center during the steamboat era, and the location of brickyards, potteries, and tile plants.
Population: 3,541; Growth (since 2000): -14.3%; Density: 1,965.0 persons per square mile; Race: 89.3% White, 6.8% Black/African American, 0.4% Asian, 0.1% American Indian/Alaska Native, 0.0% Native Hawaiian/Other Pacific Islander, 3.0% Two or more races, 1.2% Hispanic of any race; Average household size: 2.40; Median age: 37.6; Age under 18: 26.0%; Age 65 and over: 14.8%; Males per 100 females: 88.2; Marriage status: 26.3% never married, 47.4% now married, 6.4% separated, 10.4% widowed, 15.9% divorced; Foreign born: 0.0%; Speak English only: 96.6%; With disability: 18.9%; Veterans: 7.8%; Ancestry: 17.5% German, 17.3% American, 15.9% Irish, 11.8% Italian, 7.8% English

Employment: 5.1% management, business, and financial, 0.8% computer, engineering, and science, 6.1% education, legal, community service, arts, and media, 7.5% healthcare practitioners, 20.0% service, 31.0% sales and office, 4.7% natural resources, construction, and maintenance, 24.9% production, transportation, and material moving
Income: Per capita: $16,723; Median household: $32,754; Average household: $45,154; Households with income of $100,000 or more: 4.9%; Poverty rate: 33.9%
Educational Attainment: High school diploma or higher: 78.2%; Bachelor's degree or higher: 4.6%; Graduate/professional degree or higher: 0.7%

School District(s)

Wellsville Local (PK-12)
2012-13 Enrollment: 828. . . . . (330) 532-2643
Housing: Homeownership rate: 58.8%; Median home value: $58,000; Median year structure built: Before 1940; Homeowner vacancy rate: 4.3%; Median gross rent: $563 per month; Rental vacancy rate: 12.8%
Health Insurance: 89.0% have insurance; 50.1% have private insurance; 50.8% have public insurance; 11.0% do not have insurance; 0.0% of children under 18 do not have insurance
Transportation: Commute: 90.1% car, 0.6% public transportation, 4.1% walk, 1.4% work from home; Median travel time to work: 25.8 minutes

WINONA (unincorporated postal area)

ZCTA: 44493

Covers a land area of 0.251 square miles and a water area of 0 square miles. Located at 40.83° N. Lat; 80.89° W. Long. Elevation is 1,194 feet.
Population: 25; Growth (since 2000): n/a; Density: 99.8 persons per square mile; Race: 100.0% White, 0.0% Black/African American, 0.0% Asian, 0.0% American Indian/Alaska Native, 0.0% Native Hawaiian/Other Pacific Islander, 0.0% Two or more races, 0.0% Hispanic of any race; Average household size: 2.27; Median age: 38.3; Age under 18: 20.0%; Age 65 and over: 12.0%; Males per 100 females: 92.3
Housing: Homeownership rate: 36.4%; Homeowner vacancy rate: 0.0%; Rental vacancy rate: 12.5%

Coshocton County

Located in central Ohio; drained by the Muskingum, Tuscarawas, and Walhonding Rivers. Covers a land area of 563.913 square miles, a water area of 3.569 square miles, and is located in the Eastern Time Zone at 40.30° N. Lat., 81.93° W. Long. The county was founded in 1811. County seat is Coshocton.

Coshocton County is part of the Coshocton, OH Micropolitan Statistical Area. The entire metro area includes: Coshocton County, OH

Weather Station: Coshocton Agr Res Stn Elevation: 1,140 feet

	Jan	Feb	Mar	Apr	May	Jun	Jul	Aug	Sep	Oct	Nov	Dec
High	35	38	48	61	70	79	83	82	75	63	51	39
Low	19	22	29	41	51	59	63	62	55	43	34	24
Precip	2.5	2.1	3.0	3.4	4.1	4.0	4.4	3.8	3.0	2.6	3.0	2.8
Snow	na	na	na	tr	tr	0.0	0.0	0.0	0.0	tr	tr	na

High and Low temperatures in degrees Fahrenheit; Precipitation and Snow in inches

Weather Station: Coshocton Wpc Plant Elevation: 759 feet

	Jan	Feb	Mar	Apr	May	Jun	Jul	Aug	Sep	Oct	Nov	Dec
High	37	41	51	63	72	80	84	83	76	64	53	41
Low	20	22	30	39	49	58	62	61	53	41	33	24
Precip	2.9	2.4	3.4	3.9	4.6	4.0	4.5	4.0	3.1	2.9	3.4	3.1
Snow	7.8	5.4	3.0	0.8	tr	0.0	0.0	0.0	0.0	tr	0.8	3.5

High and Low temperatures in degrees Fahrenheit; Precipitation and Snow in inches

Population: 36,901; Growth (since 2000): 0.7%; Density: 65.4 persons per square mile; Race: 97.0% White, 1.1% Black/African American, 0.3% Asian, 0.2% American Indian/Alaska Native, 0.0% Native Hawaiian/Other Pacific Islander, 1.2% two or more races, 0.8% Hispanic of any race; Average household size: 2.49; Median age: 40.8; Age under 18: 24.1%; Age 65 and over: 16.2%; Males per 100 females: 97.6; Marriage status: 23.2% never married, 56.7% now married, 1.3% separated, 7.7% widowed, 12.4% divorced; Foreign born: 0.5%; Speak English only: 94.7%; With disability: 13.6%; Veterans: 11.9%; Ancestry: 26.6% German, 12.1% Irish, 10.1% English, 9.9% American, 2.9% Italian
Religion: Six largest groups: 13.6% Methodist/Pietist, 5.4% Baptist, 5.2% European Free-Church, 3.9% Holiness, 3.9% Non-denominational Protestant, 3.7% Catholicism
Economy: Unemployment rate: 5.3%; Leading industries: 16.5% retail trade; 15.1% other services (except public administration); 12.8% health care and social assistance; Farms: 1,122 totaling 169,762 acres; Company size: 0 employ 1,000 or more persons, 1 employs 500 to 999 persons, 11 employs 100 to 499 persons, 642 employ less than 100 persons; Business ownership: 728 women-owned, n/a Black-owned, n/a Hispanic-owned, n/a Asian-owned
Employment: 9.5% management, business, and financial, 2.2% computer, engineering, and science, 7.2% education, legal, community service, arts, and media, 5.0% healthcare practitioners, 18.8% service, 18.7% sales and office, 13.6% natural resources, construction, and maintenance, 25.0% production, transportation, and material moving
Income: Per capita: $20,526; Median household: $41,274; Average household: $51,136; Households with income of $100,000 or more: 10.6%; Poverty rate: 16.9%
Educational Attainment: High school diploma or higher: 84.9%; Bachelor's degree or higher: 12.3%; Graduate/professional degree or higher: 4.1%
Housing: Homeownership rate: 73.2%; Median home value: $93,300; Median year structure built: 1964; Homeowner vacancy rate: 1.8%; Median gross rent: $564 per month; Rental vacancy rate: 8.7%
Vital Statistics: Birth rate: 125.4 per 10,000 population; Death rate: 99.0 per 10,000 population; Age-adjusted cancer mortality rate: 199.6 deaths per 100,000 population
Health Insurance: 84.1% have insurance; 62.7% have private insurance; 35.5% have public insurance; 15.9% do not have insurance; 14.2% of children under 18 do not have insurance
Health Care: Physicians: 7.1 per 10,000 population; Hospital beds: 15.2 per 10,000 population; Hospital admissions: 690.6 per 10,000 population
Transportation: Commute: 91.3% car, 0.5% public transportation, 2.5% walk, 4.0% work from home; Median travel time to work: 23.9 minutes
Presidential Election: 44.0% Obama, 53.4% Romney (2012)
Additional Information Contacts
Coshocton Government . . . . (740) 622-1753
http://www.coshoctoncounty.net

Coshocton County Communities

BLISSFIELD (unincorporated postal area)

ZCTA: 43805

Covers a land area of 1.193 square miles and a water area of 0.014 square miles. Located at 40.39° N. Lat; 81.97° W. Long. Elevation is 823 feet.
Population: 71; Growth (since 2000): n/a; Density: 59.5 persons per square mile; Race: 100.0% White, 0.0% Black/African American, 0.0% Asian, 0.0% American Indian/Alaska Native, 0.0% Native Hawaiian/Other Pacific Islander, 0.0% Two or more races, 0.0% Hispanic of any race; Average household size: 2.22; Median age: 50.9; Age under 18: 15.5%; Age 65 and over: 23.9%; Males per 100 females: 129.0
Housing: Homeownership rate: 71.9%; Homeowner vacancy rate: 4.2%; Rental vacancy rate: 0.0%

CANAL LEWISVILLE (CDP). Covers a land area of 0.418 square miles and a water area of 0 square miles. Located at 40.30° N. Lat; 81.84° W. Long. Elevation is 761 feet.
Population: 320; Growth (since 2000): n/a; Density: 766.0 persons per square mile; Race: 96.3% White, 1.3% Black/African American, 0.0% Asian, 0.0% American Indian/Alaska Native, 0.0% Native Hawaiian/Other Pacific Islander, 2.5% Two or more races, 0.3% Hispanic of any race; Average household size: 2.34; Median age: 47.0; Age under 18: 17.2%; Age 65 and over: 21.9%; Males per 100 females: 78.8
Housing: Homeownership rate: 83.2%; Homeowner vacancy rate: 0.0%; Rental vacancy rate: 20.0%

CONESVILLE (village). Covers a land area of 0.160 square miles and a water area of 0 square miles. Located at 40.18° N. Lat; 81.89° W. Long. Elevation is 741 feet.
Population: 347; Growth (since 2000): -4.7%; Density: 2,169.4 persons per square mile; Race: 100.0% White, 0.0% Black/African American, 0.0% Asian, 0.0% American Indian/Alaska Native, 0.0% Native Hawaiian/Other Pacific Islander, 0.0% Two or more races, 0.0% Hispanic of any race; Average household size: 2.59; Median age: 37.5; Age under 18: 25.6%; Age 65 and over: 17.9%; Males per 100 females: 87.6

School District(s)

River View Local (PK-12)
2012-13 Enrollment: 2,066 . . . . (740) 824-3521

Housing: Homeownership rate: 77.6%; Homeowner vacancy rate: 1.9%; Rental vacancy rate: 3.2%

COSHOCTON (city). County seat. Covers a land area of 8.084 square miles and a water area of 0.124 square miles. Located at 40.26° N. Lat; 81.85° W. Long. Elevation is 774 feet.

History: Coshocton was established on a plateau southeast of the juncture of the Walhonding and Tuscarawas Rivers, and developed as an industrial city. The town's name is of Indian origin. An advertising novelty plant built in 1887 by J.F. Meek was a leading industry. Coshocton suffered repeated floodings from the rivers until Wills Creek Dam and Mohawk Dam were built on the Walhonding in the 1930's.

Population: 11,216; Growth (since 2000): -4.0%; Density: 1,387.5 persons per square mile; Race: 95.7% White, 1.8% Black/African American, 0.4% Asian, 0.2% American Indian/Alaska Native, 0.0% Native Hawaiian/Other Pacific Islander, 1.6% Two or more races, 1.1% Hispanic of any race; Average household size: 2.25; Median age: 42.9; Age under 18: 21.7%; Age 65 and over: 20.5%; Males per 100 females: 88.0; Marriage status: 24.5% never married, 51.9% now married, 1.7% separated, 10.7% widowed, 12.9% divorced; Foreign born: 0.6%; Speak English only: 98.8%; With disability: 15.2%; Veterans: 12.2%; Ancestry: 23.6% German, 12.7% Irish, 11.6% American, 11.5% English, 3.5% Italian

Employment: 9.2% management, business, and financial, 2.0% computer, engineering, and science, 9.3% education, legal, community service, arts, and media, 3.8% healthcare practitioners, 23.5% service, 17.9% sales and office, 8.8% natural resources, construction, and maintenance, 25.4% production, transportation, and material moving

Income: Per capita: $21,115; Median household: $34,663; Average household: $48,231; Households with income of $100,000 or more: 9.9%; Poverty rate: 19.5%

Educational Attainment: High school diploma or higher: 85.8%; Bachelor's degree or higher: 14.9%; Graduate/professional degree or higher: 5.3%

School District(s)

Coshocton City (PK-12)
2012-13 Enrollment: 1,607 . . . . (740) 622-1901
Coshocton County (08-12)
2012-13 Enrollment: n/a . . . . (740) 622-0211
Coshocton Opportunity School (10-12)
2012-13 Enrollment: 49. . . . . (740) 622-3600

Housing: Homeownership rate: 60.7%; Median home value: $87,000; Median year structure built: 1946; Homeowner vacancy rate: 3.2%; Median gross rent: $569 per month; Rental vacancy rate: 10.6%

Health Insurance: 88.3% have insurance; 61.6% have private insurance; 44.7% have public insurance; 11.7% do not have insurance; 1.7% of children under 18 do not have insurance

Hospitals: Coshocton County Memorial Hospital (61 beds)

Newspapers: Coshocton Tribune (daily circulation 6200)

Transportation: Commute: 90.9% car, 0.3% public transportation, 3.9% walk, 3.2% work from home; Median travel time to work: 14.6 minutes

Airports: Richard Downing (general aviation)

Additional Information Contacts

City of Coshocton . . . . (740) 622-1373

FRESNO (CDP). Covers a land area of 0.230 square miles and a water area of 0 square miles. Located at 40.33° N. Lat; 81.74° W. Long. Elevation is 794 feet.

Population: 140; Growth (since 2000): n/a; Density: 609.3 persons per square mile; Race: 95.7% White, 0.0% Black/African American, 0.0% Asian, 2.1% American Indian/Alaska Native, 0.0% Native Hawaiian/Other Pacific Islander, 2.1% Two or more races, 0.0% Hispanic of any race; Average household size: 2.64; Median age: 32.5; Age under 18: 30.0%; Age 65 and over: 8.6%; Males per 100 females: 97.2

Housing: Homeownership rate: 79.2%; Homeowner vacancy rate: 0.0%; Rental vacancy rate: 21.4%

NELLIE (village). Covers a land area of 0.714 square miles and a water area of 0 square miles. Located at 40.34° N. Lat; 82.07° W. Long. Elevation is 817 feet.

Population: 131; Growth (since 2000): -2.2%; Density: 183.4 persons per square mile; Race: 98.5% White, 0.0% Black/African American, 0.0% Asian, 0.0% American Indian/Alaska Native, 0.0% Native Hawaiian/Other Pacific Islander, 0.8% Two or more races, 0.0% Hispanic of any race; Average household size: 2.67; Median age: 37.5; Age under 18: 28.2%; Age 65 and over: 14.5%; Males per 100 females: 111.3

Housing: Homeownership rate: 77.5%; Homeowner vacancy rate: 4.8%; Rental vacancy rate: 8.3%

PLAINFIELD (village). Covers a land area of 0.410 square miles and a water area of 0 square miles. Located at 40.21° N. Lat; 81.72° W. Long. Elevation is 797 feet.

Population: 157; Growth (since 2000): -0.6%; Density: 383.2 persons per square mile; Race: 96.8% White, 0.6% Black/African American, 0.0% Asian, 0.0% American Indian/Alaska Native, 0.0% Native Hawaiian/Other Pacific Islander, 2.5% Two or more races, 0.0% Hispanic of any race; Average household size: 2.28; Median age: 50.5; Age under 18: 19.1%; Age 65 and over: 18.5%; Males per 100 females: 96.3

Housing: Homeownership rate: 88.4%; Homeowner vacancy rate: 0.0%; Rental vacancy rate: 0.0%

WALHONDING (unincorporated postal area)

ZCTA: 43843

Covers a land area of 42.303 square miles and a water area of 0.045 square miles. Located at 40.35° N. Lat; 82.18° W. Long. Elevation is 889 feet.

Population: 1,123; Growth (since 2000): 26.2%; Density: 26.5 persons per square mile; Race: 97.7% White, 0.3% Black/African American, 0.2% Asian, 0.1% American Indian/Alaska Native, 0.0% Native Hawaiian/Other Pacific Islander, 1.6% Two or more races, 1.2% Hispanic of any race; Average household size: 2.89; Median age: 35.6; Age under 18: 29.9%; Age 65 and over: 11.4%; Males per 100 females: 106.8

Housing: Homeownership rate: 84.4%; Homeowner vacancy rate: 1.5%; Rental vacancy rate: 7.4%

WARSAW (village). Covers a land area of 0.438 square miles and a water area of 0.016 square miles. Located at 40.34° N. Lat; 82.00° W. Long. Elevation is 801 feet.

Population: 682; Growth (since 2000): -12.7%; Density: 1,558.2 persons per square mile; Race: 98.8% White, 0.1% Black/African American, 0.3% Asian, 0.1% American Indian/Alaska Native, 0.0% Native Hawaiian/Other Pacific Islander, 0.6% Two or more races, 0.7% Hispanic of any race; Average household size: 2.46; Median age: 40.5; Age under 18: 23.8%; Age 65 and over: 16.7%; Males per 100 females: 99.4

School District(s)

River View Local (PK-12)
2012-13 Enrollment: 2,066 . . . . (740) 824-3521

Housing: Homeownership rate: 71.9%; Homeowner vacancy rate: 0.5%; Rental vacancy rate: 13.3%

WEST LAFAYETTE (village). Covers a land area of 0.885 square miles and a water area of 0 square miles. Located at 40.28° N. Lat; 81.75° W. Long. Elevation is 804 feet.

History: West Lafayette began when John Coles, an Englishman, opened a store here in 1850. The town prospered with the arrival of the Pennsylvania Railroad. Early industries were an enameling plant, a metal-products company, and a novelty factory.

Population: 2,321; Growth (since 2000): 0.3%; Density: 2,623.9 persons per square mile; Race: 99.0% White, 0.1% Black/African American, 0.1% Asian, 0.0% American Indian/Alaska Native, 0.0% Native Hawaiian/Other Pacific Islander, 0.6% Two or more races, 0.6% Hispanic of any race; Average household size: 2.38; Median age: 39.1; Age under 18: 23.3%; Age 65 and over: 17.4%; Males per 100 females: 86.7

School District(s)

Ridgewood Local (PK-12)
2012-13 Enrollment: 1,246 . . . . (740) 545-6354

Housing: Homeownership rate: 67.3%; Homeowner vacancy rate: 1.8%; Rental vacancy rate: 8.4%

Safety: Violent crime rate: 0.0 per 10,000 population; Property crime rate: 86.8 per 10,000 population

Crawford County

Located in north central Ohio; drained by the Sandusky and Olentangy Rivers. Covers a land area of 401.786 square miles, a water area of 0.911 square miles, and is located in the Eastern Time Zone at 40.85° N. Lat., 82.92° W. Long. The county was founded in 1820. County seat is Bucyrus.

Crawford County is part of the Bucyrus, OH Micropolitan Statistical Area. The entire metro area includes: Crawford County, OH

Weather Station: Bucyrus Elevation: 955 feet

	Jan	Feb	Mar	Apr	May	Jun	Jul	Aug	Sep	Oct	Nov	Dec
High	33	36	46	60	70	80	83	81	75	62	49	37
Low	18	20	27	37	47	57	61	60	52	41	32	23
Precip	2.5	2.0	2.7	3.4	4.3	4.2	4.4	3.8	3.2	2.6	3.1	2.9
Snow	7.4	4.6	3.4	0.9	0.1	0.0	0.0	0.0	0.0	0.1	0.9	5.1

High and Low temperatures in degrees Fahrenheit; Precipitation and Snow in inches

Population: 43,784; Growth (since 2000): -6.8%; Density: 109.0 persons per square mile; Race: 97.2% White, 0.9% Black/African American, 0.4% Asian, 0.1% American Indian/Alaska Native, 0.0% Native Hawaiian/Other Pacific Islander, 1.1% two or more races, 1.2% Hispanic of any race; Average household size: 2.39; Median age: 41.9; Age under 18: 23.1%; Age 65 and over: 17.8%; Males per 100 females: 94.4; Marriage status: 23.4% never married, 56.9% now married, 1.6% separated, 8.0% widowed, 11.6% divorced; Foreign born: 0.6%; Speak English only: 98.6%; With disability: 15.5%; Veterans: 10.6%; Ancestry: 40.9% German, 15.0% Irish, 11.5% American, 11.4% English, 3.7% Italian
Religion: Six largest groups: 13.3% Catholicism, 10.5% Lutheran, 8.1% Methodist/Pietist, 4.9% Non-denominational Protestant, 4.2% Presbyterian-Reformed, 4.2% Holiness
Economy: Unemployment rate: 5.7%; Leading industries: 16.1% retail trade; 14.0% other services (except public administration); 11.6% health care and social assistance; Farms: 634 totaling 240,022 acres; Company size: 0 employ 1,000 or more persons, 2 employ 500 to 999 persons, 19 employ 100 to 499 persons, 830 employ less than 100 persons; Business ownership: 664 women-owned, n/a Black-owned, n/a Hispanic-owned, n/a Asian-owned
Employment: 9.6% management, business, and financial, 2.2% computer, engineering, and science, 8.3% education, legal, community service, arts, and media, 5.2% healthcare practitioners, 18.7% service, 21.9% sales and office, 9.2% natural resources, construction, and maintenance, 24.8% production, transportation, and material moving
Income: Per capita: $21,478; Median household: $40,783; Average household: $51,782; Households with income of $100,000 or more: 8.6%; Poverty rate: 16.6%
Educational Attainment: High school diploma or higher: 86.8%; Bachelor's degree or higher: 11.8%; Graduate/professional degree or higher: 4.2%
Housing: Homeownership rate: 69.3%; Median home value: $87,300; Median year structure built: 1956; Homeowner vacancy rate: 2.5%; Median gross rent: $643 per month; Rental vacancy rate: 10.1%
Vital Statistics: Birth rate: 105.1 per 10,000 population; Death rate: 106.5 per 10,000 population; Age-adjusted cancer mortality rate: 182.9 deaths per 100,000 population
Health Insurance: 88.5% have insurance; 67.3% have private insurance; 38.4% have public insurance; 11.5% do not have insurance; 4.0% of children under 18 do not have insurance
Health Care: Physicians: 6.5 per 10,000 population; Hospital beds: 13.8 per 10,000 population; Hospital admissions: 512.1 per 10,000 population
Transportation: Commute: 93.8% car, 0.6% public transportation, 2.1% walk, 2.2% work from home; Median travel time to work: 21.8 minutes
Presidential Election: 37.6% Obama, 60.2% Romney (2012)
National and State Parks: Carmean Woods State Nature Preserve; Paul B Sears Woods State Nature Preserve
Additional Information Contacts
Crawford Government . . . . (419) 562-5876
http://www.crawford-co.org

Crawford County Communities

BUCYRUS (city). County seat. Covers a land area of 7.422 square miles and a water area of 0.014 square miles. Located at 40.81° N. Lat; 82.97° W. Long. Elevation is 994 feet.
History: The site of Bucyrus was purchased by Samuel Norton and Colonel James Kilbourne in 1819, and settled by a group from Pennsylvania. Kilbourne surveyed the village in 1822 and named it for Cyrus, an ancient Persian leader. He prefixed it with "bu" to suggest "beautiful."
Population: 12,362; Growth (since 2000): -6.5%; Density: 1,665.6 persons per square mile; Race: 96.3% White, 1.1% Black/African American, 0.7% Asian, 0.2% American Indian/Alaska Native, 0.0% Native Hawaiian/Other Pacific Islander, 1.3% Two or more races, 1.6% Hispanic of any race; Average household size: 2.26; Median age: 41.1; Age under 18: 22.0%; Age 65 and over: 18.2%; Males per 100 females: 91.4; Marriage status: 24.6% never married, 51.7% now married, 2.1% separated, 8.6% widowed, 15.1% divorced; Foreign born: 0.7%; Speak English only: 98.9%; With disability: 17.6%; Veterans: 11.6%; Ancestry: 40.7% German, 19.2% Irish, 11.9% English, 11.7% American, 3.8% Dutch
Employment: 9.3% management, business, and financial, 1.8% computer, engineering, and science, 7.0% education, legal, community service, arts, and media, 4.2% healthcare practitioners, 19.1% service, 24.0% sales and office, 7.9% natural resources, construction, and maintenance, 26.7% production, transportation, and material moving
Income: Per capita: $19,189; Median household: $35,280; Average household: $43,389; Households with income of $100,000 or more: 3.5%; Poverty rate: 21.4%
Educational Attainment: High school diploma or higher: 86.1%; Bachelor's degree or higher: 10.1%; Graduate/professional degree or higher: 3.0%

School District(s)

Bucyrus City (PK-12)
2012-13 Enrollment: 1,480 . . . . (419) 562-4045
Wynford Local (PK-12)
2012-13 Enrollment: 1,128 . . . . (419) 562-7828
Housing: Homeownership rate: 59.2%; Median home value: $80,700; Median year structure built: 1954; Homeowner vacancy rate: 3.3%; Median gross rent: $632 per month; Rental vacancy rate: 10.6%
Health Insurance: 87.9% have insurance; 63.3% have private insurance; 43.2% have public insurance; 12.1% do not have insurance; 2.4% of children under 18 do not have insurance
Hospitals: Bucyrus Community Hospital (25 beds)
Newspapers: Telegraph-Forum (daily circulation 6200)
Transportation: Commute: 93.7% car, 0.5% public transportation, 2.3% walk, 1.5% work from home; Median travel time to work: 22.2 minutes

CHATFIELD (village). Covers a land area of 0.300 square miles and a water area of 0 square miles. Located at 40.95° N. Lat; 82.94° W. Long. Elevation is 978 feet.
Population: 189; Growth (since 2000): -13.3%; Density: 629.5 persons per square mile; Race: 97.4% White, 0.0% Black/African American, 0.0% Asian, 0.5% American Indian/Alaska Native, 0.0% Native Hawaiian/Other Pacific Islander, 2.1% Two or more races, 1.6% Hispanic of any race; Average household size: 2.52; Median age: 42.1; Age under 18: 23.8%; Age 65 and over: 13.2%; Males per 100 females: 101.1
Housing: Homeownership rate: 85.4%; Homeowner vacancy rate: 0.0%; Rental vacancy rate: 0.0%

CRESTLINE (village). Covers a land area of 3.166 square miles and a water area of 0.005 square miles. Located at 40.78° N. Lat; 82.75° W. Long. Elevation is 1,145 feet.
History: Crestline (Crest Line) was established when the Pennsylvania Railroad became the second line in the area. It joined Livingston, founded two years earlier when the first railroad came through. When the two villages grew to the point where their borders touched, they joined as Crestline.
Population: 4,630; Growth (since 2000): -9.0%; Density: 1,462.4 persons per square mile; Race: 94.1% White, 2.7% Black/African American, 0.5% Asian, 0.2% American Indian/Alaska Native, 0.0% Native Hawaiian/Other Pacific Islander, 2.3% Two or more races, 1.1% Hispanic of any race; Average household size: 2.41; Median age: 37.8; Age under 18: 26.6%; Age 65 and over: 16.5%; Males per 100 females: 90.7; Marriage status: 28.5% never married, 49.7% now married, 1.4% separated, 8.9% widowed, 12.9% divorced; Foreign born: 0.5%; Speak English only: 99.4%; With disability: 15.3%; Veterans: 10.8%; Ancestry: 31.6% German, 11.2% Irish, 9.5% English, 7.8% American, 7.0% Italian
Employment: 4.6% management, business, and financial, 1.4% computer, engineering, and science, 7.8% education, legal, community service, arts, and media, 3.3% healthcare practitioners, 26.0% service, 25.2% sales and office, 6.7% natural resources, construction, and maintenance, 24.9% production, transportation, and material moving
Income: Per capita: $17,580; Median household: $35,313; Average household: $42,849; Households with income of $100,000 or more: 5.3%; Poverty rate: 25.5%
Educational Attainment: High school diploma or higher: 85.2%; Bachelor's degree or higher: 10.1%; Graduate/professional degree or higher: 1.2%

School District(s)

Colonel Crawford Local (PK-12)
2012-13 Enrollment: 872. . . . . (419) 562-4666
Crestline Exempted Village (PK-12)
2012-13 Enrollment: 716. . . . . (419) 683-3647

Housing: Homeownership rate: 64.1%; Median home value: $73,000; Median year structure built: 1956; Homeowner vacancy rate: 3.7%; Median gross rent: $612 per month; Rental vacancy rate: 10.8%
Health Insurance: 85.1% have insurance; 58.5% have private insurance; 43.6% have public insurance; 14.9% do not have insurance; 9.0% of children under 18 do not have insurance
Safety: Violent crime rate: 11.1 per 10,000 population; Property crime rate: 173.8 per 10,000 population
Newspapers: Crestline Advocate (weekly circulation 2300)
Transportation: Commute: 96.5% car, 1.1% public transportation, 1.2% walk, 0.4% work from home; Median travel time to work: 19.6 minutes

Additional Information Contacts

Village of Crestline . . . . (419) 683-3800
http://www.crestlineoh.com

GALION (city). Covers a land area of 7.607 square miles and a water area of 0.018 square miles. Located at 40.74° N. Lat; 82.78° W. Long. Elevation is 1,168 feet.
History: Galion was setttled by German Lutherans from Pennsylvania in 1831. In the 1890's C.H. North organized a company for the manufacture of telephone equipment, inventing improvements that made Galion a pioneering center for this industry.
Population: 10,512; Growth (since 2000): -7.3%; Density: 1,381.9 persons per square mile; Race: 97.6% White, 0.5% Black/African American, 0.2% Asian, 0.1% American Indian/Alaska Native, 0.0% Native Hawaiian/Other Pacific Islander, 1.1% Two or more races, 1.3% Hispanic of any race; Average household size: 2.32; Median age: 39.7; Age under 18: 24.3%; Age 65 and over: 17.3%; Males per 100 females: 88.9; Marriage status: 24.0% never married, 53.1% now married, 1.9% separated, 9.9% widowed, 13.0% divorced; Foreign born: 0.8%; Speak English only: 98.8%; With disability: 19.7%; Veterans: 8.9%; Ancestry: 38.3% German, 19.7% Irish, 12.1% English, 10.1% American, 4.8% Italian
Employment: 7.5% management, business, and financial, 2.1% computer, engineering, and science, 9.8% education, legal, community service, arts, and media, 4.1% healthcare practitioners, 22.0% service, 23.8% sales and office, 6.7% natural resources, construction, and maintenance, 24.1% production, transportation, and material moving
Income: Per capita: $16,690; Median household: $33,414; Average household: $40,847; Households with income of $100,000 or more: 5.1%; Poverty rate: 22.0%
Educational Attainment: High school diploma or higher: 83.3%; Bachelor's degree or higher: 9.9%; Graduate/professional degree or higher: 4.6%

School District(s)

Galion City (PK-12)
2012-13 Enrollment: 1,841 . . . . (419) 468-3432
Northmor Local (PK-12)
2012-13 Enrollment: 1,089 . . . . (419) 946-8861

Housing: Homeownership rate: 60.8%; Median home value: $71,100; Median year structure built: 1952; Homeowner vacancy rate: 3.1%; Median gross rent: $662 per month; Rental vacancy rate: 12.1%
Health Insurance: 88.1% have insurance; 55.2% have private insurance; 49.0% have public insurance; 11.9% do not have insurance; 2.9% of children under 18 do not have insurance
Hospitals: Galion Community Hospital (25 beds)
Safety: Violent crime rate: 21.6 per 10,000 population; Property crime rate: 577.3 per 10,000 population
Newspapers: Galion Inquirer (daily circulation 3900)
Transportation: Commute: 93.7% car, 0.3% public transportation, 3.5% walk, 1.9% work from home; Median travel time to work: 21.5 minutes

Additional Information Contacts

City of Galion. . . . . (419) 468-1857
http://www.ci.galion.oh.us

NEW WASHINGTON (village). Covers a land area of 1.373 square miles and a water area of 0 square miles. Located at 40.96° N. Lat; 82.85° W. Long. Elevation is 994 feet.
Population: 967; Growth (since 2000): -2.0%; Density: 704.1 persons per square mile; Race: 98.7% White, 0.2% Black/African American, 0.0% Asian, 0.0% American Indian/Alaska Native, 0.0% Native Hawaiian/Other Pacific Islander, 0.5% Two or more races, 1.0% Hispanic of any race; Average household size: 2.42; Median age: 38.5; Age under 18: 26.0%; Age 65 and over: 15.8%; Males per 100 females: 97.8

School District(s)

Buckeye Central Local (PK-12)
2012-13 Enrollment: 655. . . . . (419) 492-2864

Housing: Homeownership rate: 75.8%; Homeowner vacancy rate: 2.2%; Rental vacancy rate: 4.0%
Newspapers: New Washington Herald (weekly circulation 1600)

NORTH ROBINSON (village). Covers a land area of 0.097 square miles and a water area of 0 square miles. Located at 40.79° N. Lat; 82.86° W. Long. Elevation is 1,070 feet.
Population: 205; Growth (since 2000): -2.8%; Density: 2,105.7 persons per square mile; Race: 97.6% White, 0.0% Black/African American, 0.5% Asian, 0.0% American Indian/Alaska Native, 0.0% Native Hawaiian/Other Pacific Islander, 2.0% Two or more races, 2.9% Hispanic of any race; Average household size: 2.50; Median age: 41.8; Age under 18: 24.4%; Age 65 and over: 15.6%; Males per 100 females: 103.0

School District(s)

Colonel Crawford Local (PK-12)
2012-13 Enrollment: 872. . . . . (419) 562-4666

Housing: Homeownership rate: 81.7%; Homeowner vacancy rate: 1.5%; Rental vacancy rate: 11.8%

OCEOLA (CDP). Covers a land area of 0.501 square miles and a water area of 0 square miles. Located at 40.84° N. Lat; 83.09° W. Long. Elevation is 932 feet.
Population: 190; Growth (since 2000): n/a; Density: 379.0 persons per square mile; Race: 98.9% White, 0.0% Black/African American, 0.0% Asian, 0.5% American Indian/Alaska Native, 0.0% Native Hawaiian/Other Pacific Islander, 0.0% Two or more races, 2.1% Hispanic of any race; Average household size: 2.64; Median age: 39.0; Age under 18: 25.8%; Age 65 and over: 11.6%; Males per 100 females: 95.9
Housing: Homeownership rate: 63.9%; Homeowner vacancy rate: 0.0%; Rental vacancy rate: 3.7%

SULPHUR SPRINGS (CDP). Covers a land area of 0.241 square miles and a water area of 0 square miles. Located at 40.87° N. Lat; 82.88° W. Long. Elevation is 1,027 feet.
Population: 194; Growth (since 2000): n/a; Density: 806.3 persons per square mile; Race: 96.9% White, 0.5% Black/African American, 0.0% Asian, 0.5% American Indian/Alaska Native, 0.5% Native Hawaiian/Other Pacific Islander, 1.5% Two or more races, 0.5% Hispanic of any race; Average household size: 2.66; Median age: 37.7; Age under 18: 24.2%; Age 65 and over: 13.4%; Males per 100 females: 104.2
Housing: Homeownership rate: 83.6%; Homeowner vacancy rate: 1.6%; Rental vacancy rate: 0.0%

TIRO (village). Covers a land area of 0.411 square miles and a water area of 0 square miles. Located at 40.91° N. Lat; 82.77° W. Long. Elevation is 1,053 feet.
Population: 280; Growth (since 2000): -0.4%; Density: 680.6 persons per square mile; Race: 96.8% White, 0.7% Black/African American, 0.7% Asian, 0.0% American Indian/Alaska Native, 0.0% Native Hawaiian/Other Pacific Islander, 1.8% Two or more races, 3.9% Hispanic of any race; Average household size: 3.29; Median age: 35.6; Age under 18: 31.1%; Age 65 and over: 13.6%; Males per 100 females: 98.6
Housing: Homeownership rate: 76.4%; Homeowner vacancy rate: 5.8%; Rental vacancy rate: 9.1%

Cuyahoga County

Located in northern Ohio; bounded on the north by Lake Erie; drained by the Cuyahoga and Rocky Rivers. Covers a land area of 457.191 square miles, a water area of 788.396 square miles, and is located in the Eastern Time Zone at 41.76° N. Lat., 81.72° W. Long. The county was founded in 1808. County seat is Cleveland.

Cuyahoga County is part of the Cleveland-Elyria, OH Metropolitan Statistical Area. The entire metro area includes: Cuyahoga County, OH; Geauga County, OH; Lake County, OH; Lorain County, OH; Medina County, OH

Weather Station: Cleveland Hopkins Intl Arpt Elevation: 770 feet

	Jan	Feb	Mar	Apr	May	Jun	Jul	Aug	Sep	Oct	Nov	Dec
High	34	37	46	59	69	78	82	81	74	62	50	38
Low	20	22	29	39	49	58	63	62	55	44	36	25
Precip	2.7	2.3	3.0	3.5	3.6	3.4	3.5	3.5	3.8	3.1	3.5	3.1
Snow	18.4	14.5	12.6	3.4	tr	tr	tr	tr	tr	0.2	4.5	14.1

High and Low temperatures in degrees Fahrenheit; Precipitation and Snow in inches

Population: 1,280,122; Growth (since 2000): -8.2%; Density: 2,800.0 persons per square mile; Race: 63.6% White, 29.7% Black/African American, 2.6% Asian, 0.2% American Indian/Alaska Native, 0.0% Native Hawaiian/Other Pacific Islander, 2.1% two or more races, 4.8% Hispanic of any race; Average household size: 2.29; Median age: 40.2; Age under 18: 22.7%; Age 65 and over: 15.5%; Males per 100 females: 90.3; Marriage status: 37.1% never married, 42.9% now married, 2.0% separated, 7.6% widowed, 12.4% divorced; Foreign born: 7.0%; Speak English only: 88.7%; With disability: 14.3%; Veterans: 8.8%; Ancestry: 16.5% German, 12.7% Irish, 9.1% Italian, 8.1% Polish, 5.9% English
Religion: Six largest groups: 28.6% Catholicism, 5.3% Baptist, 3.3% Non-denominational Protestant, 2.5% Lutheran, 2.4% Methodist/Pietist, 2.4% Judaism
Economy: Unemployment rate: 5.6%; Leading industries: 13.0% retail trade; 12.1% professional, scientific, and technical services; 10.9% health care and social assistance; Farms: 114 totaling 2,608 acres; Company size: 47 employ 1,000 or more persons, 55 employ 500 to 999 persons, 935 employ 100 to 499 persons, 32,150 employ less than 100 persons; Business ownership: 29,969 women-owned, 14,527 Black-owned, 1,678 Hispanic-owned, 3,106 Asian-owned
Employment: 14.6% management, business, and financial, 5.4% computer, engineering, and science, 11.0% education, legal, community service, arts, and media, 7.3% healthcare practitioners, 18.7% service, 25.4% sales and office, 5.6% natural resources, construction, and maintenance, 12.1% production, transportation, and material moving
Income: Per capita: $27,423; Median household: $43,804; Average household: $63,539; Households with income of $100,000 or more: 17.5%; Poverty rate: 18.3%
Educational Attainment: High school diploma or higher: 87.5%; Bachelor's degree or higher: 29.7%; Graduate/professional degree or higher: 12.0%
Housing: Homeownership rate: 60.8%; Median home value: $125,700; Median year structure built: 1954; Homeowner vacancy rate: 2.8%; Median gross rent: $732 per month; Rental vacancy rate: 13.2%
Vital Statistics: Birth rate: 117.9 per 10,000 population; Death rate: 104.7 per 10,000 population; Age-adjusted cancer mortality rate: 193.4 deaths per 100,000 population
Health Insurance: 88.5% have insurance; 66.2% have private insurance; 34.4% have public insurance; 11.5% do not have insurance; 4.1% of children under 18 do not have insurance
Health Care: Physicians: 57.9 per 10,000 population; Hospital beds: 54.0 per 10,000 population; Hospital admissions: 2,211.1 per 10,000 population
Air Quality Index: 44.4% good, 53.7% moderate, 1.9% unhealthy for sensitive individuals, 0.0% unhealthy (percent of days)
Transportation: Commute: 87.7% car, 5.2% public transportation, 2.5% walk, 3.4% work from home; Median travel time to work: 24.1 minutes
Presidential Election: 68.8% Obama, 30.2% Romney (2012)
National and State Parks: Chagrin State Scenic River; Cleveland Lakefront State Park; Cuyahoga Valley National Recreation Area; Edgewater State Park
Additional Information Contacts
Cuyahoga Government . . . . (216) 443-7000
http://www.cuyahogacounty.us

Cuyahoga County Communities

BAY VILLAGE (city). Covers a land area of 4.566 square miles and a water area of 2.488 square miles. Located at 41.49° N. Lat; 81.93° W. Long. Elevation is 633 feet.
History: Named for its location on a bay of Lake Erie. Incorporated 1903.
Population: 15,651; Growth (since 2000): -2.7%; Density: 3,428.0 persons per square mile; Race: 97.0% White, 0.5% Black/African American, 0.9% Asian, 0.1% American Indian/Alaska Native, 0.0% Native Hawaiian/Other Pacific Islander, 1.1% Two or more races, 1.6% Hispanic of any race; Average household size: 2.50; Median age: 43.4; Age under 18: 25.4%; Age 65 and over: 15.5%; Males per 100 females: 90.4; Marriage status: 20.9% never married, 61.9% now married, 0.4% separated, 6.0% widowed, 11.2% divorced; Foreign born: 3.2%; Speak English only: 94.9%; With disability: 8.3%; Veterans: 9.9%; Ancestry: 33.2% German, 28.3% Irish, 14.5% English, 12.7% Italian, 8.6% Polish
Employment: 24.7% management, business, and financial, 4.2% computer, engineering, and science, 19.6% education, legal, community service, arts, and media, 7.8% healthcare practitioners, 10.3% service, 23.7% sales and office, 4.5% natural resources, construction, and maintenance, 5.0% production, transportation, and material moving
Income: Per capita: $43,498; Median household: $83,679; Average household: $110,102; Households with income of $100,000 or more: 39.1%; Poverty rate: 4.0%
Educational Attainment: High school diploma or higher: 98.1%; Bachelor's degree or higher: 56.2%; Graduate/professional degree or higher: 21.9%

School District(s)

Bay Village City (PK-12)
2012-13 Enrollment: 2,541 . . . . (440) 617-7300
Housing: Homeownership rate: 91.5%; Median home value: $197,800; Median year structure built: 1957; Homeowner vacancy rate: 1.1%; Median gross rent: $1,012 per month; Rental vacancy rate: 4.3%
Health Insurance: 96.3% have insurance; 89.1% have private insurance; 20.5% have public insurance; 3.7% do not have insurance; 1.9% of children under 18 do not have insurance
Newspapers: Gottschalk Publishing (weekly circulation 19000)
Transportation: Commute: 89.9% car, 2.0% public transportation, 0.8% walk, 6.1% work from home; Median travel time to work: 23.6 minutes
Additional Information Contacts
City of Bay Village . . . . (440) 899-3415
http://www.cityofbayvillage.com

BEACHWOOD (city). Covers a land area of 5.325 square miles and a water area of 0.014 square miles. Located at 41.48° N. Lat; 81.50° W. Long. Elevation is 1,184 feet.
History: On June 26, 1915, the trustees of Warrensville Township ordered the incorporation of Beachwood Village; in 1960, Beachwood attained "City" status.
Population: 11,953; Growth (since 2000): -1.9%; Density: 2,244.6 persons per square mile; Race: 77.3% White, 13.7% Black/African American, 7.4% Asian, 0.0% American Indian/Alaska Native, 0.0% Native Hawaiian/Other Pacific Islander, 1.2% Two or more races, 1.9% Hispanic of any race; Average household size: 2.16; Median age: 52.5; Age under 18: 19.6%; Age 65 and over: 32.3%; Males per 100 females: 79.6; Marriage status: 18.2% never married, 58.0% now married, 0.8% separated, 15.2% widowed, 8.6% divorced; Foreign born: 17.6%; Speak English only: 80.4%; With disability: 11.1%; Veterans: 9.0%; Ancestry: 11.6% Russian, 9.9% German, 9.8% Polish, 7.8% American, 6.4% Eastern European
Employment: 23.4% management, business, and financial, 8.6% computer, engineering, and science, 19.5% education, legal, community service, arts, and media, 11.2% healthcare practitioners, 7.2% service, 27.0% sales and office, 0.7% natural resources, construction, and maintenance, 2.3% production, transportation, and material moving
Income: Per capita: $54,099; Median household: $79,722; Average household: $126,291; Households with income of $100,000 or more: 42.4%; Poverty rate: 3.2%
Educational Attainment: High school diploma or higher: 94.3%; Bachelor's degree or higher: 57.9%; Graduate/professional degree or higher: 30.6%

School District(s)

Beachwood City (PK-12)
2012-13 Enrollment: 1,579 . . . . (216) 464-2600

Four-year College(s)

University of Phoenix-Cleveland Campus (Private, For-profit)
Fall 2013 Enrollment: 385 . . . . (866) 766-0766
2013-14 Tuition: In-state $12,400; Out-of-state $12,400
Housing: Homeownership rate: 62.3%; Median home value: $280,800; Median year structure built: 1969; Homeowner vacancy rate: 2.6%; Median gross rent: $1,580 per month; Rental vacancy rate: 5.9%
Health Insurance: 97.5% have insurance; 88.7% have private insurance; 27.2% have public insurance; 2.5% do not have insurance; 1.3% of children under 18 do not have insurance
Hospitals: University Hospitals Ahuja Medical Center
Transportation: Commute: 86.7% car, 2.5% public transportation, 2.2% walk, 8.0% work from home; Median travel time to work: 21.1 minutes
Additional Information Contacts

City of Beachwood . . . . (216) 464-1070
http://www.beachwoodohio.com

BEDFORD (city). Covers a land area of 5.351 square miles and a water area of 0.048 square miles. Located at 41.39° N. Lat; 81.54° W. Long. Elevation is 948 feet.

History: Named for Bedford in Bedfordshire, England. The first settlement at Bedford was made in 1786 by a group of Moravian missionaries, and was called Pilgerruh, meaning pilgrim's rest. In 1810 the town site was surveyed by the Connecticut Land Company, and in 1813 permanent settlers arrived. Benjamin Fitch, who began the manufacture of chairs in Bedford, was one of the first settlers.

Population: 13,074; Growth (since 2000): -8.0%; Density: 2,443.2 persons per square mile; Race: 53.9% White, 41.9% Black/African American, 0.9% Asian, 0.2% American Indian/Alaska Native, 0.0% Native Hawaiian/Other Pacific Islander, 2.5% Two or more races, 2.0% Hispanic of any race; Average household size: 2.08; Median age: 41.9; Age under 18: 21.2%; Age 65 and over: 17.0%; Males per 100 females: 84.4; Marriage status: 33.8% never married, 43.7% now married, 3.5% separated, 9.0% widowed, 13.6% divorced; Foreign born: 2.2%; Speak English only: 95.4%; With disability: 13.9%; Veterans: 12.2%; Ancestry: 9.1% Irish, 9.0% German, 9.0% Italian, 8.0% Polish, 7.1% English

Employment: 10.0% management, business, and financial, 3.3% computer, engineering, and science, 7.9% education, legal, community service, arts, and media, 3.2% healthcare practitioners, 18.3% service, 34.2% sales and office, 5.9% natural resources, construction, and maintenance, 17.4% production, transportation, and material moving

Income: Per capita: $23,216; Median household: $40,417; Average household: $48,925; Households with income of $100,000 or more: 8.3%; Poverty rate: 13.5%

Educational Attainment: High school diploma or higher: 87.7%; Bachelor's degree or higher: 19.2%; Graduate/professional degree or higher: 5.4%

School District(s)

Bedford City (PK-12)
2012-13 Enrollment: 3,549 . . . . (440) 439-1500

Housing: Homeownership rate: 56.3%; Median home value: $95,000; Median year structure built: 1957; Homeowner vacancy rate: 3.7%; Median gross rent: $769 per month; Rental vacancy rate: 10.8%

Health Insurance: 89.1% have insurance; 72.3% have private insurance; 32.2% have public insurance; 10.9% do not have insurance; 3.3% of children under 18 do not have insurance

Safety: Violent crime rate: 24.1 per 10,000 population; Property crime rate: 308.0 per 10,000 population

Transportation: Commute: 91.5% car, 3.8% public transportation, 1.7% walk, 0.8% work from home; Median travel time to work: 22.0 minutes

Additional Information Contacts

City of Bedford. . . . . (440) 232-1600
http://www.bedfordoh.gov

BEDFORD HEIGHTS (city). Covers a land area of 4.535 square miles and a water area of 0.012 square miles. Located at 41.40° N. Lat; 81.50° W. Long. Elevation is 1,040 feet.

History: Named for Bedford in Bedfordshire, England. Incorporated 1951.

Population: 10,751; Growth (since 2000): -5.5%; Density: 2,370.9 persons per square mile; Race: 18.7% White, 76.9% Black/African American, 1.2% Asian, 0.1% American Indian/Alaska Native, 0.0% Native Hawaiian/Other Pacific Islander, 2.1% Two or more races, 2.6% Hispanic of any race; Average household size: 2.09; Median age: 43.3; Age under 18: 19.9%; Age 65 and over: 16.8%; Males per 100 females: 84.9; Marriage status: 37.6% never married, 36.2% now married, 4.0% separated, 7.8% widowed, 18.4% divorced; Foreign born: 4.6%; Speak English only: 92.8%; With disability: 15.4%; Veterans: 12.2%; Ancestry: 3.6% Italian, 3.5% German, 3.4% Irish, 1.7% Polish, 1.7% African

Employment: 10.0% management, business, and financial, 2.4% computer, engineering, and science, 9.9% education, legal, community service, arts, and media, 3.2% healthcare practitioners, 21.0% service, 30.2% sales and office, 6.9% natural resources, construction, and maintenance, 16.4% production, transportation, and material moving

Income: Per capita: $21,649; Median household: $34,662; Average household: $45,553; Households with income of $100,000 or more: 8.2%; Poverty rate: 14.0%

Educational Attainment: High school diploma or higher: 88.6%; Bachelor's degree or higher: 16.6%; Graduate/professional degree or higher: 6.1%

Housing: Homeownership rate: 51.0%; Median home value: $111,500; Median year structure built: 1966; Homeowner vacancy rate: 3.0%; Median gross rent: $714 per month; Rental vacancy rate: 15.4%

Health Insurance: 84.6% have insurance; 62.8% have private insurance; 36.1% have public insurance; 15.4% do not have insurance; 8.2% of children under 18 do not have insurance

Transportation: Commute: 93.3% car, 2.3% public transportation, 2.0% walk, 0.4% work from home; Median travel time to work: 22.9 minutes

Additional Information Contacts

City of Bedford Heights . . . . (440) 786-3200
http://www.bedfordheights.gov

BENTLEYVILLE (village). Covers a land area of 2.557 square miles and a water area of 0.043 square miles. Located at 41.41° N. Lat; 81.41° W. Long. Elevation is 938 feet.

Population: 864; Growth (since 2000): -8.8%; Density: 337.9 persons per square mile; Race: 95.0% White, 0.7% Black/African American, 2.8% Asian, 0.0% American Indian/Alaska Native, 0.0% Native Hawaiian/Other Pacific Islander, 1.5% Two or more races, 0.6% Hispanic of any race; Average household size: 2.85; Median age: 46.2; Age under 18: 29.3%; Age 65 and over: 10.1%; Males per 100 females: 98.2

Housing: Homeownership rate: 96.7%; Homeowner vacancy rate: 1.3%; Rental vacancy rate: 0.0%

Additional Information Contacts

Village of Bentleyville . . . . (440) 247-5055
http://www.villageofbentleyville.com

BEREA (city). Covers a land area of 5.718 square miles and a water area of 0.109 square miles. Located at 41.37° N. Lat; 81.86° W. Long. Elevation is 755 feet.

History: Named for the city in ancient Syria, mentioned in the Bible. Berea was founded by John Baldwin in 1827, on land owned by Gideon Granger, Postmaster General under President Jefferson. Baldwin discovered the vein of abrasive sandstone that provided the early industry for the community.

Population: 19,093; Growth (since 2000): 0.6%; Density: 3,339.3 persons per square mile; Race: 88.8% White, 6.6% Black/African American, 1.5% Asian, 0.2% American Indian/Alaska Native, 0.0% Native Hawaiian/Other Pacific Islander, 2.3% Two or more races, 2.8% Hispanic of any race; Average household size: 2.26; Median age: 37.1; Age under 18: 18.3%; Age 65 and over: 13.9%; Males per 100 females: 91.3; Marriage status: 40.2% never married, 42.4% now married, 1.2% separated, 6.5% widowed, 11.0% divorced; Foreign born: 4.4%; Speak English only: 92.8%; With disability: 13.2%; Veterans: 8.0%; Ancestry: 31.3% German, 20.4% Irish, 10.9% English, 9.9% Italian, 8.1% Polish

Employment: 12.3% management, business, and financial, 5.9% computer, engineering, and science, 12.6% education, legal, community service, arts, and media, 5.6% healthcare practitioners, 17.0% service, 26.6% sales and office, 7.2% natural resources, construction, and maintenance, 12.7% production, transportation, and material moving

Income: Per capita: $25,732; Median household: $55,942; Average household: $65,886; Households with income of $100,000 or more: 18.4%; Poverty rate: 11.2%

Educational Attainment: High school diploma or higher: 91.8%; Bachelor's degree or higher: 30.7%; Graduate/professional degree or higher: 10.6%

School District(s)

Berea City (PK-12)
2012-13 Enrollment: 7,066 . . . . (216) 898-8300
Columbia Local (PK-12)
2012-13 Enrollment: 904. . . . . (440) 236-5008

Four-year College(s)

Baldwin Wallace University (Private, Not-for-profit, United Methodist)
Fall 2013 Enrollment: 4,053 . . . . (440) 826-2900
2013-14 Tuition: In-state $27,840; Out-of-state $27,840

Housing: Homeownership rate: 70.2%; Median home value: $128,100; Median year structure built: 1959; Homeowner vacancy rate: 2.1%; Median gross rent: $693 per month; Rental vacancy rate: 7.5%

Health Insurance: 92.0% have insurance; 78.3% have private insurance; 25.7% have public insurance; 8.0% do not have insurance; 1.9% of children under 18 do not have insurance

Safety: Violent crime rate: 9.5 per 10,000 population; Property crime rate: 130.9 per 10,000 population

Transportation: Commute: 85.1% car, 1.7% public transportation, 5.7% walk, 5.3% work from home; Median travel time to work: 21.4 minutes

Additional Information Contacts
City of Berea . . . . (440) 826-5800
http://www.bereaohio.com

BRATENAHL (village). Covers a land area of 1.023 square miles and a water area of 0.581 square miles. Located at 41.56° N. Lat; 81.61° W. Long. Elevation is 614 feet.
Population: 1,197; Growth (since 2000): -10.5%; Density: 1,170.6 persons per square mile; Race: 80.5% White, 15.5% Black/African American, 2.5% Asian, 0.3% American Indian/Alaska Native, 0.0% Native Hawaiian/Other Pacific Islander, 0.9% Two or more races, 0.9% Hispanic of any race; Average household size: 1.75; Median age: 57.8; Age under 18: 6.5%; Age 65 and over: 31.1%; Males per 100 females: 94.6
Housing: Homeownership rate: 81.7%; Homeowner vacancy rate: 7.5%; Rental vacancy rate: 17.4%

BRECKSVILLE (city). Covers a land area of 19.574 square miles and a water area of 0.113 square miles. Located at 41.31° N. Lat; 81.62° W. Long. Elevation is 889 feet.
History: Brecksville was settled about 1811 and named for John and Robert Breck, early residents.
Population: 13,656; Growth (since 2000): 2.0%; Density: 697.7 persons per square mile; Race: 93.3% White, 1.7% Black/African American, 3.4% Asian, 0.1% American Indian/Alaska Native, 0.0% Native Hawaiian/Other Pacific Islander, 1.1% Two or more races, 1.4% Hispanic of any race; Average household size: 2.50; Median age: 47.4; Age under 18: 22.8%; Age 65 and over: 17.8%; Males per 100 females: 99.5; Marriage status: 26.1% never married, 58.2% now married, 0.7% separated, 5.4% widowed, 10.3% divorced; Foreign born: 7.4%; Speak English only: 90.6%; With disability: 11.0%; Veterans: 10.5%; Ancestry: 25.7% German, 18.3% Polish, 16.1% Irish, 12.9% Italian, 12.2% English
Employment: 26.7% management, business, and financial, 6.7% computer, engineering, and science, 14.1% education, legal, community service, arts, and media, 10.8% healthcare practitioners, 9.3% service, 23.5% sales and office, 4.9% natural resources, construction, and maintenance, 3.9% production, transportation, and material moving
Income: Per capita: $49,686; Median household: $90,924; Average household: $125,171; Households with income of $100,000 or more: 46.2%; Poverty rate: 2.5%
Educational Attainment: High school diploma or higher: 94.4%; Bachelor's degree or higher: 51.3%; Graduate/professional degree or higher: 23.1%

School District(s)
Brecksville-Broadview Heights City (PK-12)
2012-13 Enrollment: 4,160 . . . . (440) 740-4000
Cuyahoga Valley Career Center (09-12)
2012-13 Enrollment: n/a . . . . (440) 526-5200

Two-year College(s)
Stautzenberger College-Brecksville (Private, For-profit)
Fall 2013 Enrollment: 317 . . . . (440) 838-1999
2013-14 Tuition: In-state $10,494; Out-of-state $10,494

Vocational/Technical School(s)
Cuyahoga Valley Career Center (Public)
Fall 2013 Enrollment: 106 . . . . (440) 746-8230
2013-14 Tuition: $12,400

Housing: Homeownership rate: 87.7%; Median home value: $243,800; Median year structure built: 1976; Homeowner vacancy rate: 1.5%; Median gross rent: $1,378 per month; Rental vacancy rate: 9.9%
Health Insurance: 94.8% have insurance; 87.4% have private insurance; 22.1% have public insurance; 5.2% do not have insurance; 4.7% of children under 18 do not have insurance
Safety: Violent crime rate: 0.7 per 10,000 population; Property crime rate: 47.4 per 10,000 population
Newspapers: Gazette Newspaper (weekly circulation 10000)
Transportation: Commute: 91.9% car, 1.1% public transportation, 1.2% walk, 5.2% work from home; Median travel time to work: 23.7 minutes
Additional Information Contacts
City of Brecksville . . . . (440) 526-4351
http://www.brecksville.oh.us

BROADVIEW HEIGHTS (city). Covers a land area of 13.048 square miles and a water area of 0.021 square miles. Located at 41.32° N. Lat; 81.68° W. Long. Elevation is 1,191 feet.
History: Named for the beautiful local views. Incorporated 1926.
Population: 19,400; Growth (since 2000): 21.5%; Density: 1,486.8 persons per square mile; Race: 91.0% White, 2.1% Black/African American, 5.2% Asian, 0.1% American Indian/Alaska Native, 0.0% Native Hawaiian/Other Pacific Islander, 1.3% Two or more races, 1.8% Hispanic of any race; Average household size: 2.50; Median age: 41.5; Age under 18: 24.6%; Age 65 and over: 14.8%; Males per 100 females: 92.7; Marriage status: 26.7% never married, 56.3% now married, 1.2% separated, 6.6% widowed, 10.4% divorced; Foreign born: 8.7%; Speak English only: 86.4%; With disability: 8.3%; Veterans: 8.1%; Ancestry: 22.3% German, 17.4% Polish, 16.1% Italian, 13.1% Irish, 7.7% Hungarian
Employment: 19.8% management, business, and financial, 8.8% computer, engineering, and science, 11.5% education, legal, community service, arts, and media, 8.9% healthcare practitioners, 9.6% service, 26.2% sales and office, 3.6% natural resources, construction, and maintenance, 11.6% production, transportation, and material moving
Income: Per capita: $37,115; Median household: $75,882; Average household: $92,040; Households with income of $100,000 or more: 34.7%; Poverty rate: 6.6%
Educational Attainment: High school diploma or higher: 94.5%; Bachelor's degree or higher: 44.1%; Graduate/professional degree or higher: 19.1%

School District(s)
Brecksville-Broadview Heights City (PK-12)
2012-13 Enrollment: 4,160 . . . . (440) 740-4000
North Royalton City (PK-12)
2012-13 Enrollment: 4,618 . . . . (440) 237-8800

Two-year College(s)
Vatterott College-Cleveland (Private, For-profit)
Fall 2013 Enrollment: 229 . . . . (440) 526-1660
2013-14 Tuition: In-state $12,736; Out-of-state $12,736

Housing: Homeownership rate: 82.2%; Median home value: $213,700; Median year structure built: 1980; Homeowner vacancy rate: 1.3%; Median gross rent: $858 per month; Rental vacancy rate: 17.7%
Health Insurance: 93.7% have insurance; 86.8% have private insurance; 20.2% have public insurance; 6.3% do not have insurance; 3.1% of children under 18 do not have insurance
Safety: Violent crime rate: 5.7 per 10,000 population; Property crime rate: 0.0 per 10,000 population
Transportation: Commute: 91.8% car, 1.5% public transportation, 1.4% walk, 5.0% work from home; Median travel time to work: 28.0 minutes
Additional Information Contacts
City of Broadview Heights . . . . (440) 526-4357
http://www.broadview-heights.org

BROOK PARK (city). Covers a land area of 7.530 square miles and a water area of 0.003 square miles. Located at 41.40° N. Lat; 81.82° W. Long. Elevation is 797 feet.
History: Named for its location near a branch of the Rocky River. Incorporated 1914.
Population: 19,212; Growth (since 2000): -9.5%; Density: 2,551.5 persons per square mile; Race: 92.2% White, 3.2% Black/African American, 1.6% Asian, 0.2% American Indian/Alaska Native, 0.0% Native Hawaiian/Other Pacific Islander, 1.9% Two or more races, 3.4% Hispanic of any race; Average household size: 2.45; Median age: 43.8; Age under 18: 21.0%; Age 65 and over: 19.8%; Males per 100 females: 92.4; Marriage status: 30.4% never married, 49.0% now married, 1.2% separated, 9.1% widowed, 11.6% divorced; Foreign born: 4.3%; Speak English only: 93.3%; With disability: 15.4%; Veterans: 11.6%; Ancestry: 25.1% German, 16.1% Irish, 14.7% Italian, 13.6% Polish, 8.8% English
Employment: 8.6% management, business, and financial, 3.0% computer, engineering, and science, 6.6% education, legal, community service, arts, and media, 4.4% healthcare practitioners, 22.9% service, 26.5% sales and office, 10.1% natural resources, construction, and maintenance, 17.8% production, transportation, and material moving
Income: Per capita: $23,893; Median household: $49,010; Average household: $57,740; Households with income of $100,000 or more: 12.2%; Poverty rate: 8.7%
Educational Attainment: High school diploma or higher: 85.3%; Bachelor's degree or higher: 11.3%; Graduate/professional degree or higher: 2.8%

School District(s)
Berea City (PK-12)
2012-13 Enrollment: 7,066 . . . . (216) 898-8300
Quest Community School (09-12)
2012-13 Enrollment: 41 . . . . (614) 995-1985

Housing: Homeownership rate: 81.0%; Median home value: $117,700; Median year structure built: 1961; Homeowner vacancy rate: 1.2%; Median gross rent: $831 per month; Rental vacancy rate: 9.3%
Health Insurance: 89.2% have insurance; 70.6% have private insurance; 33.0% have public insurance; 10.8% do not have insurance; 3.2% of children under 18 do not have insurance
Transportation: Commute: 93.3% car, 2.0% public transportation, 2.1% walk, 1.4% work from home; Median travel time to work: 21.2 minutes
Additional Information Contacts
City of Brook Park . . . . (216) 433-1300
http://www.cityofbrookpark.com

BROOKLYN (city). Covers a land area of 4.248 square miles and a water area of 0.036 square miles. Located at 41.43° N. Lat; 81.75° W. Long. Elevation is 764 feet.
History: Brooklyn is a city in Cuyahoga County, Ohio, and a suburb of Cleveland.
Population: 11,169; Growth (since 2000): -3.6%; Density: 2,628.9 persons per square mile; Race: 84.3% White, 5.2% Black/African American, 3.9% Asian, 0.2% American Indian/Alaska Native, 0.0% Native Hawaiian/Other Pacific Islander, 2.4% Two or more races, 10.4% Hispanic of any race; Average household size: 2.17; Median age: 42.9; Age under 18: 19.1%; Age 65 and over: 19.2%; Males per 100 females: 93.1; Marriage status: 31.2% never married, 46.3% now married, 1.3% separated, 8.1% widowed, 14.4% divorced; Foreign born: 10.9%; Speak English only: 82.3%; With disability: 14.1%; Veterans: 12.1%; Ancestry: 24.9% German, 17.0% Irish, 13.0% Italian, 8.6% Polish, 7.4% English
Employment: 9.0% management, business, and financial, 5.6% computer, engineering, and science, 7.0% education, legal, community service, arts, and media, 4.7% healthcare practitioners, 22.0% service, 24.1% sales and office, 10.0% natural resources, construction, and maintenance, 17.5% production, transportation, and material moving
Income: Per capita: $22,668; Median household: $41,637; Average household: $50,619; Households with income of $100,000 or more: 7.6%; Poverty rate: 15.4%
Educational Attainment: High school diploma or higher: 85.4%; Bachelor's degree or higher: 15.6%; Graduate/professional degree or higher: 4.9%

School District(s)

Brooklyn City (PK-12)
2012-13 Enrollment: 1,452 . . . . (216) 485-8100

Two-year College(s)

Kaplan Career Institute-Cleveland (Private, For-profit)
Fall 2013 Enrollment: 302 . . . . (216) 485-0900
Housing: Homeownership rate: 58.7%; Median home value: $115,100; Median year structure built: 1958; Homeowner vacancy rate: 1.8%; Median gross rent: $684 per month; Rental vacancy rate: 7.6%
Health Insurance: 87.6% have insurance; 66.8% have private insurance; 36.4% have public insurance; 12.4% do not have insurance; 7.4% of children under 18 do not have insurance
Safety: Violent crime rate: 18.2 per 10,000 population; Property crime rate: 645.4 per 10,000 population
Transportation: Commute: 94.1% car, 2.6% public transportation, 0.9% walk, 1.7% work from home; Median travel time to work: 21.2 minutes
Additional Information Contacts
City of Brooklyn . . . . (216) 351-2133
http://www.brooklynohio.gov

BROOKLYN HEIGHTS (village). Covers a land area of 1.744 square miles and a water area of 0.019 square miles. Located at 41.42° N. Lat; 81.67° W. Long. Elevation is 764 feet.
Population: 1,543; Growth (since 2000): -1.0%; Density: 885.0 persons per square mile; Race: 94.6% White, 1.2% Black/African American, 1.7% Asian, 0.6% American Indian/Alaska Native, 0.0% Native Hawaiian/Other Pacific Islander, 1.6% Two or more races, 2.5% Hispanic of any race; Average household size: 2.58; Median age: 43.6; Age under 18: 23.7%; Age 65 and over: 17.1%; Males per 100 females: 89.3
Housing: Homeownership rate: 88.7%; Homeowner vacancy rate: 1.3%; Rental vacancy rate: 4.2%

CHAGRIN FALLS (village). Covers a land area of 2.075 square miles and a water area of 0.058 square miles. Located at 41.43° N. Lat; 81.39° W. Long. Elevation is 1,001 feet.
History: Noah Graves from Massachusetts built a grist mill here in 1833, and the town of Chagrin Falls developed as a residential community. The town was named for the Chagrin River, said to have been named by surveyor Moses Cleaveland to express his embarrassment at mistaking it for the Cuyahoga River.
Population: 4,113; Growth (since 2000): 2.2%; Density: 1,982.0 persons per square mile; Race: 98.0% White, 0.4% Black/African American, 0.8% Asian, 0.0% American Indian/Alaska Native, 0.1% Native Hawaiian/Other Pacific Islander, 0.5% Two or more races, 0.9% Hispanic of any race; Average household size: 2.16; Median age: 46.1; Age under 18: 23.8%; Age 65 and over: 22.8%; Males per 100 females: 86.0; Marriage status: 18.9% never married, 52.6% now married, 3.1% separated, 13.5% widowed, 15.0% divorced; Foreign born: 4.2%; Speak English only: 93.8%; With disability: 10.5%; Veterans: 10.3%; Ancestry: 25.9% German, 21.9% English, 19.8% Irish, 13.2% Italian, 8.7% Polish
Employment: 22.8% management, business, and financial, 1.9% computer, engineering, and science, 12.2% education, legal, community service, arts, and media, 10.2% healthcare practitioners, 14.0% service, 24.8% sales and office, 7.6% natural resources, construction, and maintenance, 6.6% production, transportation, and material moving
Income: Per capita: $45,351; Median household: $57,434; Average household: $93,191; Households with income of $100,000 or more: 30.1%; Poverty rate: 5.5%
Educational Attainment: High school diploma or higher: 98.2%; Bachelor's degree or higher: 58.6%; Graduate/professional degree or higher: 27.4%

School District(s)

Chagrin Falls Exempted Village (PK-12)
2012-13 Enrollment: 2,011 . . . . (440) 247-5500
Kenston Local (PK-12)
2012-13 Enrollment: 3,028 . . . . (440) 543-9677
Housing: Homeownership rate: 70.3%; Median home value: $322,900; Median year structure built: 1957; Homeowner vacancy rate: 1.8%; Median gross rent: $1,213 per month; Rental vacancy rate: 8.5%
Health Insurance: 94.5% have insurance; 85.6% have private insurance; 23.4% have public insurance; 5.5% do not have insurance; 0.0% of children under 18 do not have insurance
Safety: Violent crime rate: 2.5 per 10,000 population; Property crime rate: 130.3 per 10,000 population
Newspapers: Chagrin Valley Publishing (weekly circulation 30000)
Transportation: Commute: 91.2% car, 0.7% public transportation, 1.0% walk, 6.6% work from home; Median travel time to work: 25.1 minutes
Additional Information Contacts
Village of Chagrin Falls . . . . (440) 247-5050
http://www.chagrin-falls.org

CLEVELAND (city). County seat. Covers a land area of 77.697 square miles and a water area of 4.769 square miles. Located at 41.48° N. Lat; 81.68° W. Long. Elevation is 653 feet.
History: Moses Cleaveland platted the city of Cleveland on the shores of Lake Erie in 1796 for the Connecticut Land Company, but stayed only a few months in the town that would bear his name. It was Lorenzo Carter who pulled the community together, and launched the first boat from Cleveland harbor in 1804, a prophesy of the many freighters and passenger steamers that would one day enter this harbor. The spelling of the town's name changed from Cleaveland to Cleveland about 1832, when a newspaper editor had to drop one letter from his masthead to make it fit the space, and decided to drop the "a" from Cleaveland. Cleveland expanded when the Ohio & Erie Canal was completed, becoming a commercial center. In 1836 it was incorporated as a city, and over the next half-century developed into an industrial giant. The Cuyahoga Steam Furnace Company began making locomotives, the Cleveland Iron Company and the Standard Oil Company were organized, along with many other industries.
Population: 396,815; Growth (since 2000): -17.1%; Density: 5,107.2 persons per square mile; Race: 37.3% White, 53.3% Black/African American, 1.8% Asian, 0.3% American Indian/Alaska Native, 0.0% Native Hawaiian/Other Pacific Islander, 2.8% Two or more races, 10.0% Hispanic of any race; Average household size: 2.29; Median age: 35.7; Age under 18: 24.6%; Age 65 and over: 12.0%; Males per 100 females: 92.1; Marriage status: 48.6% never married, 29.1% now married, 3.5% separated, 7.4% widowed, 14.9% divorced; Foreign born: 4.6%; Speak English only: 88.2%; With disability: 19.1%; Veterans: 8.3%; Ancestry: 9.9% German, 9.0% Irish, 4.4% Italian, 4.1% Polish, 3.2% English
Employment: 9.1% management, business, and financial, 3.0% computer, engineering, and science, 8.6% education, legal, community service, arts, and media, 5.4% healthcare practitioners, 27.3% service, 23.6% sales and

office, 6.2% natural resources, construction, and maintenance, 16.8% production, transportation, and material moving
Income: Per capita: $16,992; Median household: $26,217; Average household: $38,274; Households with income of $100,000 or more: 6.6%; Poverty rate: 35.4%
Educational Attainment: High school diploma or higher: 77.4%; Bachelor's degree or higher: 14.9%; Graduate/professional degree or higher: 5.6%

School District(s)

Apex Academy (KG-08)
2012-13 Enrollment: 574. . . . . (216) 451-1725
Arts and Science Preparatory Academy (KG-08)
2012-13 Enrollment: 166. . . . . (216) 344-2081
Bella Academy of Excellence (KG-07)
2012-13 Enrollment: 431. . . . . (216) 481-1500
Broadway Academy (KG-08)
2012-13 Enrollment: 365. . . . . (614) 995-1985
Citizens Academy (KG-05)
2012-13 Enrollment: 410. . . . . (216) 791-4195
Citizens Leadership Academy (06-06)
2012-13 Enrollment: 198. . . . . (614) 995-1985
Cleveland Academy for Scholarship Technology and L (09-12)
2012-13 Enrollment: 253. . . . . (216) 443-5400
Cleveland Arts and Social Sciences Academy (KG-08)
2012-13 Enrollment: 351. . . . . (216) 229-3182
Cleveland College Preparatory School (KG-08)
2012-13 Enrollment: 297. . . . . (216) 341-1347
Cleveland Community School (KG-04)
2012-13 Enrollment: 157. . . . . (216) 523-1133
Cleveland Entrepreneurship Preparatory School (06-08)
2012-13 Enrollment: 271. . . . . (216) 456-2080
Cleveland Municipal (PK-12)
2012-13 Enrollment: 39,813 . . . . (216) 574-8000
Constellation Schools: Collinwood Village Academy (KG-03)
2012-13 Enrollment: 83. . . . . (614) 995-1985
Constellation Schools: Eastside Arts Academy (KG-03)
2012-13 Enrollment: 87. . . . . (614) 995-1985
Constellation Schools: Madison Community Elementar (KG-08)
2012-13 Enrollment: 303. . . . . (216) 651-5212
Constellation Schools: Old Brooklyn Community Elem (KG-04)
2012-13 Enrollment: 332. . . . . (216) 661-7888
Constellation Schools: Old Brooklyn Community Midd (05-08)
2012-13 Enrollment: 194. . . . . (216) 351-0280
Constellation Schools: Outreach Academy for Studen (04-12)
2012-13 Enrollment: 43. . . . . (614) 995-1985
Constellation Schools: Puritas Community Elementar (KG-04)
2012-13 Enrollment: 198. . . . . (216) 688-0680
Constellation Schools: Puritas Community Middle (05-08)
2012-13 Enrollment: 140. . . . . (216) 251-1596
Constellation Schools: Stockyard Community Element (KG-06)
2012-13 Enrollment: 292. . . . . (216) 651-5143
Constellation Schools: Westpark Community Elementa (KG-04)
2012-13 Enrollment: 329. . . . . (216) 688-0271
Constellation Schools: Westpark Community Middle (05-08)
2012-13 Enrollment: 214. . . . . (216) 251-7200
Constellation Schools: Westside Community School o (KG-07)
2012-13 Enrollment: 349. . . . . (216) 688-1900
Dow Leadership Institute the (KG-06)
2012-13 Enrollment: 116. . . . . (614) 995-1985
Entrepreneurship Preparatory School - Woodland Hills Campus
2012-13 Enrollment: 75. . . . . (216) 298-1164
Frederick Douglass Reclamation Academy
2012-13 Enrollment: 81. . . . . (216) 941-9661
George V. Voinovich Reclamation Academy (09-12)
2012-13 Enrollment: 80. . . . . (216) 295-1493
Harvard Avenue Community School (KG-08)
2012-13 Enrollment: 627. . . . . (216) 283-5100
Hope Academy Chapelside Campus (KG-08)
2012-13 Enrollment: 478. . . . . (216) 283-6589
Hope Academy Cuyahoga Campus (KG-08)
2012-13 Enrollment: 449. . . . . (216) 251-5450
Hope Academy East Campus (KG-08)
2012-13 Enrollment: 393. . . . . (216) 383-1214
Hope Academy Lincoln Park (KG-08)
2012-13 Enrollment: 218. . . . . (216) 263-7008
Hope Academy Northcoast (KG-08)
2012-13 Enrollment: 293. . . . . (216) 429-0232
Hope Academy Northwest Campus (KG-08)
2012-13 Enrollment: 412. . . . . (216) 226-6800
Horizon Science Acad Cleveland (09-12)
2012-13 Enrollment: 490. . . . . (216) 432-3660
Horizon Science Academy Cleveland Elementary Schoo (KG-05)
2012-13 Enrollment: 161. . . . . (216) 432-9576
Horizon Science Academy Denison Elementary School (KG-05)
2012-13 Enrollment: 225. . . . . (216) 661-8840
Horizon Science Academy-Cleveland Middle School (06-08)
2012-13 Enrollment: 159. . . . . (216) 432-9940
Horizon Science Academy-Denison Middle School (KG-08)
2012-13 Enrollment: 304. . . . . (216) 739-9911
Imagine Cleveland Academy (KG-04)
2012-13 Enrollment: 237. . . . . (614) 995-1985
Intergenerational School the (KG-08)
2012-13 Enrollment: 224. . . . . (216) 721-0120
Invictus High School (09-12)
2012-13 Enrollment: 84. . . . . (216) 431-7571
Lake Erie International High School (09-12)
2012-13 Enrollment: 153. . . . . (216) 539-7229
Langston Hughes High School
2012-13 Enrollment: 114. . . . . (216) 721-0845
Life Skills of Northeast Ohio (09-12)
2012-13 Enrollment: 230. . . . . (216) 421-7587
Lion of Judah Academy (KG-08)
2012-13 Enrollment: 156. . . . . (216) 881-9200
Mayfield City (PK-12)
2012-13 Enrollment: 4,502 . . . . (440) 995-7201
Menlo Park Academy (KG-08)
2012-13 Enrollment: 334. . . . . (440) 925-6365
Near West Intergenerational School (KG-04)
2012-13 Enrollment: 109. . . . . (216) 461-4308
Northeast Ohio College Preparatory School (KG-09)
2012-13 Enrollment: 440. . . . . (216) 965-0580
O.n.e. Academy the
2012-13 Enrollment: n/a . . . . (614) 995-1985
Ohio Connections Academy Inc (KG-12)
2012-13 Enrollment: 3,052 . . . . (513) 234-4900
Pearl Academy (KG-08)
2012-13 Enrollment: 277. . . . . (216) 741-2991
Phoenix Village Academy Primary 2 (04-05)
2012-13 Enrollment: 65. . . . . (216) 812-0244
Phoenix Village Academy: Secondary I (KG-03)
2012-13 Enrollment: 98. . . . . (216) 426-8601
Promise Academy (09-12)
2012-13 Enrollment: 521. . . . . (216) 443-0500
South Euclid-Lyndhurst City (PK-12)
2012-13 Enrollment: 3,981 . . . . (216) 691-2000
Steve Sanders Academy the (KG-05)
2012-13 Enrollment: n/a . . . . (216) 361-1883
Thurgood Marshall High School (09-12)
2012-13 Enrollment: 111. . . . . (216) 961-9813
University of Cleveland Preparatory School (KG-08)
2012-13 Enrollment: 456. . . . . (614) 995-1985
Village Preparatory School (KG-02)
2012-13 Enrollment: 355. . . . . (216) 456-2070
Villaview Community School (05-08)
2012-13 Enrollment: 132. . . . . (216) 523-1133
Virtual Schoolhouse Inc. (KG-12)
2012-13 Enrollment: 358. . . . . (216) 541-2048
Woodland Academy (KG-08)
2012-13 Enrollment: 404. . . . . (216) 721-6909

Four-year College(s)

Bryant & Stratton College-Cleveland (Private, For-profit)
Fall 2013 Enrollment: 538 . . . . (216) 771-1700
2013-14 Tuition: In-state $16,565; Out-of-state $16,565
Case Western Reserve University (Private, Not-for-profit)
Fall 2013 Enrollment: 10,325 . . . . (216) 368-2000
2013-14 Tuition: In-state $41,800; Out-of-state $41,800
Cleveland Institute of Art (Private, Not-for-profit)
Fall 2013 Enrollment: 568 . . . . (216) 421-7000
2013-14 Tuition: In-state $36,509; Out-of-state $36,509

Cleveland Institute of Music (Private, Not-for-profit)
Fall 2013 Enrollment: 451 . . . . (216) 791-5000
2013-14 Tuition: In-state $44,039; Out-of-state $44,039
Cleveland State University (Public)
Fall 2013 Enrollment: 17,497 . . . . (216) 687-2000
2013-14 Tuition: In-state $9,499; Out-of-state $12,678
Notre Dame College (Private, Not-for-profit, Roman Catholic)
Fall 2013 Enrollment: 2,269 . . . . (216) 381-1680
2013-14 Tuition: In-state $26,344; Out-of-state $26,344
South University-Cleveland (Private, For-profit)
Fall 2013 Enrollment: 254 . . . . (855) 398-9280
2013-14 Tuition: In-state $16,360; Out-of-state $16,360

Two-year College(s)

Allstate Hairstyling & Barber College (Private, For-profit)
Fall 2013 Enrollment: 35 . . . . (216) 241-6684
Cuyahoga Community College District (Public)
Fall 2013 Enrollment: 27,910 . . . . (800) 954-8742
2013-14 Tuition: In-state $3,853; Out-of-state $7,368
Lincoln College of Technology-Cleveland (Private, For-profit)
Fall 2013 Enrollment: 79 . . . . (216) 706-6481
2013-14 Tuition: In-state $12,020; Out-of-state $12,020
Ohio Technical College (Private, For-profit)
Fall 2013 Enrollment: 1,119 . . . . (216) 881-1700
Remington College-Cleveland Campus (Private, Not-for-profit)
Fall 2013 Enrollment: 438 . . . . (216) 475-7520
2013-14 Tuition: In-state $15,995; Out-of-state $15,995

Vocational/Technical School(s)

Cleveland Institute of Dental-Medical Assistants-Cleveland (Private, For-profit)
Fall 2013 Enrollment: 113 . . . . (216) 241-2930
2013-14 Tuition: $9,050

Housing: Homeownership rate: 44.1%; Median home value: $76,700; Median year structure built: Before 1940; Homeowner vacancy rate: 3.9%; Median gross rent: $659 per month; Rental vacancy rate: 15.0%
Health Insurance: 83.1% have insurance; 45.3% have private insurance; 47.2% have public insurance; 16.9% do not have insurance; 3.9% of children under 18 do not have insurance
Hospitals: Cleveland - Wade Park VA Medical Center (688 beds); Cleveland Clinic (1113 beds); Fairview Hospital (511 beds); Lutheran Hospital (209 beds); Metrohealth System (728 beds); Saint Vincent Charity Medical Center (492 beds); University Hospitals Case Medical Center (1032 beds)
Safety: Violent crime rate: 147.8 per 10,000 population; Property crime rate: 595.3 per 10,000 population
Newspapers: Call & Post (weekly circulation 34000); Cleveland Scene (weekly circulation 90000); Plain Dealer (daily circulation 292000)
Transportation: Commute: 80.0% car, 10.9% public transportation, 4.6% walk, 2.8% work from home; Median travel time to work: 24.3 minutes; Amtrak: Train service available.
Airports: Burke Lakefront (general aviation); Cleveland-Hopkins International (primary service/medium hub); Cuyahoga County (general aviation)
Additional Information Contacts
City of Cleveland . . . . (216) 664-2000
http://www.city.cleveland.oh.us

CLEVELAND HEIGHTS (city). Covers a land area of 8.107 square miles and a water area of 0.018 square miles. Located at 41.51° N. Lat; 81.56° W. Long. Elevation is 942 feet.
History: Named for Moses Cleaveland (1754-1806), surveyor of the Western Reserve. Cleveland Heights was established in 1905, and became a city in 1921. It grew as a collection of neighborhoods serving as residential suburbs for Cleveland.
Population: 46,121; Growth (since 2000): -7.7%; Density: 5,689.3 persons per square mile; Race: 49.8% White, 42.5% Black/African American, 4.1% Asian, 0.2% American Indian/Alaska Native, 0.0% Native Hawaiian/Other Pacific Islander, 2.8% Two or more races, 2.0% Hispanic of any race; Average household size: 2.27; Median age: 35.8; Age under 18: 22.3%; Age 65 and over: 13.5%; Males per 100 females: 87.2; Marriage status: 41.8% never married, 40.7% now married, 1.7% separated, 5.7% widowed, 11.8% divorced; Foreign born: 8.5%; Speak English only: 89.7%; With disability: 11.1%; Veterans: 6.9%; Ancestry: 12.3% German, 9.4% Irish, 5.8% Italian, 5.7% English, 3.2% Hungarian
Employment: 14.6% management, business, and financial, 8.1% computer, engineering, and science, 19.9% education, legal, community service, arts, and media, 12.5% healthcare practitioners, 15.8% service, 19.8% sales and office, 2.5% natural resources, construction, and maintenance, 6.8% production, transportation, and material moving
Income: Per capita: $30,167; Median household: $50,109; Average household: $69,089; Households with income of $100,000 or more: 20.0%; Poverty rate: 20.0%
Educational Attainment: High school diploma or higher: 94.0%; Bachelor's degree or higher: 50.2%; Graduate/professional degree or higher: 26.4%

School District(s)

Cleveland Heights-University Heights City (PK-12)
2012-13 Enrollment: 5,845 . . . . (216) 371-7171

Vocational/Technical School(s)

Cut Beauty School (Private, For-profit)
Fall 2013 Enrollment: n/a . . . . (216) 320-1444
2013-14 Tuition: $14,300

Housing: Homeownership rate: 56.3%; Median home value: $132,600; Median year structure built: Before 1940; Homeowner vacancy rate: 3.9%; Median gross rent: $831 per month; Rental vacancy rate: 10.0%
Health Insurance: 89.7% have insurance; 70.7% have private insurance; 30.4% have public insurance; 10.3% do not have insurance; 5.2% of children under 18 do not have insurance
Safety: Violent crime rate: 31.1 per 10,000 population; Property crime rate: 336.0 per 10,000 population
Transportation: Commute: 82.7% car, 5.9% public transportation, 5.0% walk, 4.6% work from home; Median travel time to work: 22.3 minutes
Additional Information Contacts
City of Cleveland Heights . . . . (216) 291-4444
http://www.clevelandheights.com

CUYAHOGA HEIGHTS (village). Covers a land area of 3.072 square miles and a water area of 0.142 square miles. Located at 41.44° N. Lat; 81.65° W. Long. Elevation is 715 feet.
Population: 638; Growth (since 2000): 6.5%; Density: 207.7 persons per square mile; Race: 97.3% White, 0.6% Black/African American, 1.4% Asian, 0.2% American Indian/Alaska Native, 0.0% Native Hawaiian/Other Pacific Islander, 0.3% Two or more races, 0.9% Hispanic of any race; Average household size: 2.47; Median age: 40.5; Age under 18: 25.9%; Age 65 and over: 16.1%; Males per 100 females: 83.9

School District(s)

Cuyahoga Heights Local (PK-12)
2012-13 Enrollment: 883 . . . . (216) 429-5700

Housing: Homeownership rate: 67.5%; Homeowner vacancy rate: 1.1%; Rental vacancy rate: 3.3%

EAST CLEVELAND (city). Covers a land area of 3.086 square miles and a water area of 0.007 square miles. Located at 41.53° N. Lat; 81.58° W. Long. Elevation is 686 feet.
History: Named for its location east of Cleveland. The original East Cleveland was annexed by Cleveland in 1872, and the name disappeared from the map until 1892, when the neighboring Collamer became East Cleveland Hamlet. In 1911 the village became a city.
Population: 17,843; Growth (since 2000): -34.4%; Density: 5,782.4 persons per square mile; Race: 4.6% White, 93.2% Black/African American, 0.2% Asian, 0.2% American Indian/Alaska Native, 0.0% Native Hawaiian/Other Pacific Islander, 1.5% Two or more races, 1.0% Hispanic of any race; Average household size: 2.11; Median age: 42.6; Age under 18: 22.2%; Age 65 and over: 18.8%; Males per 100 females: 82.1; Marriage status: 46.4% never married, 26.0% now married, 3.8% separated, 10.4% widowed, 17.3% divorced; Foreign born: 3.5%; Speak English only: 95.0%; With disability: 21.8%; Veterans: 9.3%; Ancestry: 2.2% African, 1.4% German, 1.2% American, 0.9% English, 0.9% Jamaican
Employment: 4.1% management, business, and financial, 0.9% computer, engineering, and science, 7.2% education, legal, community service, arts, and media, 5.7% healthcare practitioners, 38.8% service, 21.5% sales and office, 3.5% natural resources, construction, and maintenance, 18.3% production, transportation, and material moving
Income: Per capita: $13,902; Median household: $20,577; Average household: $29,297; Households with income of $100,000 or more: 2.8%; Poverty rate: 42.6%
Educational Attainment: High school diploma or higher: 78.3%; Bachelor's degree or higher: 11.1%; Graduate/professional degree or higher: 4.5%

School District(s)

Cleveland Municipal (PK-12)
2012-13 Enrollment: 39,813 . . . . (216) 574-8000
East Cleveland City SD (PK-12)
2012-13 Enrollment: 2,780 . . . . (216) 268-6570

Housing: Homeownership rate: 33.5%; Median home value: $68,900; Median year structure built: Before 1940; Homeowner vacancy rate: 11.4%; Median gross rent: $608 per month; Rental vacancy rate: 22.1%

Health Insurance: 80.4% have insurance; 36.5% have private insurance; 56.9% have public insurance; 19.6% do not have insurance; 8.8% of children under 18 do not have insurance

Transportation: Commute: 69.2% car, 23.7% public transportation, 3.9% walk, 2.7% work from home; Median travel time to work: 26.2 minutes

Additional Information Contacts

City of East Cleveland . . . . (216) 681-2208
http://www.eastcleveland.org

EUCLID (city). Covers a land area of 10.630 square miles and a water area of 0.852 square miles. Located at 41.59° N. Lat; 81.52° W. Long. Elevation is 617 feet.

History: Euclid was settled in 1798 and named for the Greek mathematician by surveyors in the party of Moses Cleaveland. Euclid developed as a residential community near Cleveland.

Population: 48,920; Growth (since 2000): -7.2%; Density: 4,602.1 persons per square mile; Race: 43.8% White, 52.6% Black/African American, 0.7% Asian, 0.2% American Indian/Alaska Native, 0.0% Native Hawaiian/Other Pacific Islander, 2.3% Two or more races, 1.6% Hispanic of any race; Average household size: 2.13; Median age: 41.0; Age under 18: 22.9%; Age 65 and over: 15.9%; Males per 100 females: 81.1; Marriage status: 43.4% never married, 34.8% now married, 2.6% separated, 8.0% widowed, 13.9% divorced; Foreign born: 3.2%; Speak English only: 95.7%; With disability: 15.5%; Veterans: 9.4%; Ancestry: 9.9% German, 7.8% Irish, 6.4% Italian, 4.2% Slovene, 3.8% Polish

Employment: 11.3% management, business, and financial, 4.0% computer, engineering, and science, 7.3% education, legal, community service, arts, and media, 7.5% healthcare practitioners, 21.3% service, 27.1% sales and office, 5.6% natural resources, construction, and maintenance, 16.0% production, transportation, and material moving

Income: Per capita: $22,378; Median household: $36,272; Average household: $47,878; Households with income of $100,000 or more: 9.3%; Poverty rate: 19.9%

Educational Attainment: High school diploma or higher: 88.0%; Bachelor's degree or higher: 19.5%; Graduate/professional degree or higher: 6.6%

School District(s)

Euclid City (PK-12)
2012-13 Enrollment: 5,448 . . . . (216) 261-2900
New Day Academy Boarding & Day School (KG-12)
2012-13 Enrollment: 260. . . . . (216) 797-1602
Noble Academy-Cleveland (KG-08)
2012-13 Enrollment: 304. . . . . (216) 486-8866
Pinnacle Academy (KG-08)
2012-13 Enrollment: 682. . . . . (216) 731-0127

Two-year College(s)

Cleveland Clinic Health System-School of Diagnostic Imaging (Private, Not-for-profit)
Fall 2013 Enrollment: 44 . . . . (216) 692-8665

Housing: Homeownership rate: 54.0%; Median home value: $91,200; Median year structure built: 1956; Homeowner vacancy rate: 4.1%; Median gross rent: $733 per month; Rental vacancy rate: 14.6%

Health Insurance: 85.4% have insurance; 63.3% have private insurance; 34.3% have public insurance; 14.6% do not have insurance; 7.8% of children under 18 do not have insurance

Hospitals: Euclid Hospital (371 beds)

Transportation: Commute: 88.4% car, 7.0% public transportation, 1.4% walk, 2.6% work from home; Median travel time to work: 24.3 minutes

Additional Information Contacts

City of Euclid . . . . (216) 289-2751
http://www.ci.euclid.oh.us

FAIRVIEW PARK (city). Covers a land area of 4.678 square miles and a water area of 0 square miles. Located at 41.44° N. Lat; 81.85° W. Long. Elevation is 745 feet.

History: Named to promote the town as a good place to live. Incorporated 1950.

Population: 16,826; Growth (since 2000): -4.2%; Density: 3,596.6 persons per square mile; Race: 94.4% White, 1.8% Black/African American, 1.6% Asian, 0.1% American Indian/Alaska Native, 0.0% Native Hawaiian/Other Pacific Islander, 1.2% Two or more races, 3.3% Hispanic of any race; Average household size: 2.22; Median age: 42.3; Age under 18: 21.1%; Age 65 and over: 16.8%; Males per 100 females: 92.1; Marriage status: 31.8% never married, 50.0% now married, 0.6% separated, 6.5% widowed, 11.7% divorced; Foreign born: 7.9%; Speak English only: 88.2%; With disability: 10.4%; Veterans: 8.3%; Ancestry: 28.5% German, 27.4% Irish, 10.1% Italian, 8.8% English, 8.0% Polish

Employment: 15.2% management, business, and financial, 6.4% computer, engineering, and science, 11.0% education, legal, community service, arts, and media, 7.8% healthcare practitioners, 15.2% service, 27.6% sales and office, 7.8% natural resources, construction, and maintenance, 9.0% production, transportation, and material moving

Income: Per capita: $30,503; Median household: $52,844; Average household: $67,778; Households with income of $100,000 or more: 19.9%; Poverty rate: 8.2%

Educational Attainment: High school diploma or higher: 95.0%; Bachelor's degree or higher: 37.8%; Graduate/professional degree or higher: 13.5%

School District(s)

Fairview Park City (PK-12)
2012-13 Enrollment: 1,815 . . . . (440) 331-5500

Two-year College(s)

Fairview Beauty Academy (Private, For-profit)
Fall 2013 Enrollment: 105 . . . . (440) 734-5555

Housing: Homeownership rate: 73.4%; Median home value: $144,600; Median year structure built: 1956; Homeowner vacancy rate: 1.6%; Median gross rent: $704 per month; Rental vacancy rate: 12.3%

Health Insurance: 90.3% have insurance; 77.2% have private insurance; 27.2% have public insurance; 9.7% do not have insurance; 5.5% of children under 18 do not have insurance

Transportation: Commute: 91.5% car, 2.2% public transportation, 0.9% walk, 3.6% work from home; Median travel time to work: 25.0 minutes

Additional Information Contacts

City of Fairview Park . . . . (440) 356-4411
http://www.fairviewpark.org

GARFIELD HEIGHTS (city). Covers a land area of 7.230 square miles and a water area of 0.061 square miles. Located at 41.42° N. Lat; 81.60° W. Long. Elevation is 955 feet.

History: Founded 1904, incorporated 1932.

Population: 28,849; Growth (since 2000): -6.1%; Density: 3,990.3 persons per square mile; Race: 60.2% White, 35.7% Black/African American, 1.3% Asian, 0.2% American Indian/Alaska Native, 0.0% Native Hawaiian/Other Pacific Islander, 2.1% Two or more races, 2.3% Hispanic of any race; Average household size: 2.43; Median age: 38.5; Age under 18: 25.0%; Age 65 and over: 15.4%; Males per 100 females: 85.2; Marriage status: 38.6% never married, 40.3% now married, 1.6% separated, 9.4% widowed, 11.7% divorced; Foreign born: 3.5%; Speak English only: 94.2%; With disability: 14.5%; Veterans: 10.7%; Ancestry: 19.3% Polish, 12.9% German, 9.2% Irish, 8.5% Italian, 4.2% Slovak

Employment: 9.4% management, business, and financial, 3.0% computer, engineering, and science, 7.0% education, legal, community service, arts, and media, 4.6% healthcare practitioners, 18.7% service, 34.0% sales and office, 7.8% natural resources, construction, and maintenance, 15.5% production, transportation, and material moving

Income: Per capita: $20,993; Median household: $42,511; Average household: $49,619; Households with income of $100,000 or more: 8.6%; Poverty rate: 14.8%

Educational Attainment: High school diploma or higher: 86.2%; Bachelor's degree or higher: 13.7%; Graduate/professional degree or higher: 4.9%

School District(s)

Cleveland Municipal (PK-12)
2012-13 Enrollment: 39,813 . . . . (216) 574-8000
Garfield Heights City Schools (PK-12)
2012-13 Enrollment: 3,628 . . . . (216) 475-8100

Housing: Homeownership rate: 69.6%; Median home value: $85,900; Median year structure built: 1954; Homeowner vacancy rate: 4.2%; Median gross rent: $745 per month; Rental vacancy rate: 9.5%

Health Insurance: 89.5% have insurance; 66.8% have private insurance; 37.5% have public insurance; 10.5% do not have insurance; 4.1% of children under 18 do not have insurance

Hospitals: Marymount Hospital (322 beds)
Transportation: Commute: 91.2% car, 4.1% public transportation, 1.8% walk, 1.9% work from home; Median travel time to work: 22.4 minutes
Additional Information Contacts
City of Garfield Heights . . . . (216) 475-1100
http://www.garfieldhts.org

GATES MILLS (village). Covers a land area of 8.968 square miles and a water area of 0.129 square miles. Located at 41.53° N. Lat; 81.41° W. Long. Elevation is 718 feet.
Population: 2,270; Growth (since 2000): -8.9%; Density: 253.1 persons per square mile; Race: 93.0% White, 1.3% Black/African American, 4.0% Asian, 0.1% American Indian/Alaska Native, 0.0% Native Hawaiian/Other Pacific Islander, 1.2% Two or more races, 1.9% Hispanic of any race; Average household size: 2.45; Median age: 52.5; Age under 18: 18.2%; Age 65 and over: 23.4%; Males per 100 females: 103.0

School District(s)

Mayfield City (PK-12)
2012-13 Enrollment: 4,502 . . . . (440) 995-7201
Housing: Homeownership rate: 92.8%; Homeowner vacancy rate: 1.3%; Rental vacancy rate: 9.5%
Safety: Violent crime rate: 0.0 per 10,000 population; Property crime rate: 75.4 per 10,000 population

GLENWILLOW (village). Covers a land area of 2.720 square miles and a water area of 0.061 square miles. Located at 41.36° N. Lat; 81.47° W. Long. Elevation is 942 feet.
Population: 923; Growth (since 2000): 105.6%; Density: 339.3 persons per square mile; Race: 57.4% White, 28.7% Black/African American, 10.4% Asian, 0.2% American Indian/Alaska Native, 0.0% Native Hawaiian/Other Pacific Islander, 2.9% Two or more races, 1.1% Hispanic of any race; Average household size: 2.64; Median age: 41.2; Age under 18: 28.3%; Age 65 and over: 20.4%; Males per 100 females: 91.9
Housing: Homeownership rate: 82.9%; Homeowner vacancy rate: 4.3%; Rental vacancy rate: 36.5%

HIGHLAND HEIGHTS (city). Covers a land area of 5.152 square miles and a water area of 0 square miles. Located at 41.55° N. Lat; 81.47° W. Long. Elevation is 935 feet.
History: Originally part of Mayfield Township, the City of Highland Heights was founded in 1920 and incorporated in 1967. It was the first city in Cuyahoga County to require new residential neighborhoods to have underground wiring and ornamental lamp posts.
Population: 8,345; Growth (since 2000): 3.3%; Density: 1,619.7 persons per square mile; Race: 91.0% White, 1.9% Black/African American, 5.8% Asian, 0.1% American Indian/Alaska Native, 0.0% Native Hawaiian/Other Pacific Islander, 0.9% Two or more races, 1.4% Hispanic of any race; Average household size: 2.60; Median age: 48.2; Age under 18: 21.8%; Age 65 and over: 20.0%; Males per 100 females: 97.0; Marriage status: 27.4% never married, 62.7% now married, 0.2% separated, 4.6% widowed, 5.3% divorced; Foreign born: 12.6%; Speak English only: 83.0%; With disability: 8.5%; Veterans: 7.8%; Ancestry: 31.0% Italian, 16.0% German, 14.1% Irish, 8.2% Polish, 6.7% English
Employment: 25.5% management, business, and financial, 8.6% computer, engineering, and science, 11.1% education, legal, community service, arts, and media, 7.7% healthcare practitioners, 12.9% service, 25.4% sales and office, 3.8% natural resources, construction, and maintenance, 5.0% production, transportation, and material moving
Income: Per capita: $42,573; Median household: $100,469; Average household: $111,464; Households with income of $100,000 or more: 50.5%; Poverty rate: 2.6%
Educational Attainment: High school diploma or higher: 95.7%; Bachelor's degree or higher: 52.2%; Graduate/professional degree or higher: 22.0%

Two-year College(s)

ATS Institute of Technology (Private, For-profit)
Fall 2013 Enrollment: 504 . . . . (440) 449-1700
2013-14 Tuition: In-state $26,281; Out-of-state $26,281
Housing: Homeownership rate: 95.3%; Median home value: $267,300; Median year structure built: 1976; Homeowner vacancy rate: 1.9%; Median gross rent: $993 per month; Rental vacancy rate: 31.4%
Health Insurance: 95.9% have insurance; 89.7% have private insurance; 23.0% have public insurance; 4.1% do not have insurance; 0.4% of children under 18 do not have insurance
Safety: Violent crime rate: 7.2 per 10,000 population; Property crime rate: 120.8 per 10,000 population
Transportation: Commute: 93.4% car, 0.4% public transportation, 1.3% walk, 4.6% work from home; Median travel time to work: 20.7 minutes

HIGHLAND HILLS (village). Covers a land area of 1.959 square miles and a water area of 0.007 square miles. Located at 41.45° N. Lat; 81.52° W. Long. Elevation is 1,086 feet.
Population: 1,130; Growth (since 2000): -30.2%; Density: 576.9 persons per square mile; Race: 23.5% White, 74.4% Black/African American, 0.3% Asian, 0.1% American Indian/Alaska Native, 0.0% Native Hawaiian/Other Pacific Islander, 1.5% Two or more races, 2.7% Hispanic of any race; Average household size: 1.79; Median age: 33.0; Age under 18: 23.1%; Age 65 and over: 14.8%; Males per 100 females: 206.2

School District(s)

Buckeye United SD (08-12)
2012-13 Enrollment: 369. . . . . (614) 466-0720
Housing: Homeownership rate: 42.9%; Homeowner vacancy rate: 5.7%; Rental vacancy rate: 17.3%

HUNTING VALLEY (village). Covers a land area of 7.892 square miles and a water area of 0.121 square miles. Located at 41.48° N. Lat; 81.41° W. Long. Elevation is 761 feet.
Population: 705; Growth (since 2000): -4.1%; Density: 89.3 persons per square mile; Race: 97.0% White, 0.6% Black/African American, 1.1% Asian, 0.0% American Indian/Alaska Native, 0.0% Native Hawaiian/Other Pacific Islander, 1.0% Two or more races, 2.7% Hispanic of any race; Average household size: 2.55; Median age: 50.3; Age under 18: 23.1%; Age 65 and over: 26.4%; Males per 100 females: 96.9
Housing: Homeownership rate: 85.2%; Homeowner vacancy rate: 4.4%; Rental vacancy rate: 8.9%
Safety: Violent crime rate: 0.0 per 10,000 population; Property crime rate: 0.0 per 10,000 population

INDEPENDENCE (city). Covers a land area of 9.540 square miles and a water area of 0.103 square miles. Located at 41.38° N. Lat; 81.63° W. Long. Elevation is 860 feet.
Population: 7,133; Growth (since 2000): 0.3%; Density: 747.7 persons per square mile; Race: 96.6% White, 0.4% Black/African American, 1.9% Asian, 0.1% American Indian/Alaska Native, 0.0% Native Hawaiian/Other Pacific Islander, 0.8% Two or more races, 1.1% Hispanic of any race; Average household size: 2.57; Median age: 47.0; Age under 18: 22.9%; Age 65 and over: 19.5%; Males per 100 females: 94.2; Marriage status: 23.4% never married, 59.1% now married, 0.6% separated, 10.7% widowed, 6.8% divorced; Foreign born: 4.0%; Speak English only: 92.6%; With disability: 11.2%; Veterans: 8.3%; Ancestry: 31.8% Polish, 22.7% German, 16.9% Irish, 15.0% Italian, 7.8% English
Employment: 16.8% management, business, and financial, 5.3% computer, engineering, and science, 10.0% education, legal, community service, arts, and media, 9.2% healthcare practitioners, 14.2% service, 29.2% sales and office, 6.5% natural resources, construction, and maintenance, 8.7% production, transportation, and material moving
Income: Per capita: $33,613; Median household: $67,662; Average household: $85,376; Households with income of $100,000 or more: 29.6%; Poverty rate: 3.0%
Educational Attainment: High school diploma or higher: 93.3%; Bachelor's degree or higher: 34.6%; Graduate/professional degree or higher: 14.2%

School District(s)

Independence Local (PK-12)
2012-13 Enrollment: 1,097 . . . . (216) 642-5850

Two-year College(s)

Miami-Jacobs Career College-Independence (Private, For-profit)
Fall 2013 Enrollment: 243 . . . . (216) 861-3222
2013-14 Tuition: In-state $11,964; Out-of-state $11,964

Vocational/Technical School(s)

Central School of Practical Nursing (Private, Not-for-profit)
Fall 2013 Enrollment: 123 . . . . (216) 901-4400
2013-14 Tuition: $13,805
Housing: Homeownership rate: 91.8%; Median home value: $214,900; Median year structure built: 1961; Homeowner vacancy rate: 1.2%; Median gross rent: $922 per month; Rental vacancy rate: 3.4%
Health Insurance: 97.6% have insurance; 88.1% have private insurance; 25.4% have public insurance; 2.4% do not have insurance; 1.1% of children under 18 do not have insurance

Safety: Violent crime rate: 5.6 per 10,000 population; Property crime rate: 217.1 per 10,000 population
Transportation: Commute: 93.4% car, 1.4% public transportation, 0.1% walk, 5.1% work from home; Median travel time to work: 20.4 minutes
Additional Information Contacts
City of Independence . . . . (216) 524-4131
http://www.independenceohio.org

LAKEWOOD (city). Covers a land area of 5.534 square miles and a water area of 1.159 square miles. Located at 41.48° N. Lat; 81.80° W. Long. Elevation is 702 feet.
History: Named for its location on the wooded shores of Lake Erie. Lakewood was known as East Rockport until 1889, when its name was changed to Lakewood, refering to its location on the wooded shore of Lake Erie. Lakewood was incorporated as a city in 1911.
Population: 52,131; Growth (since 2000): -8.0%; Density: 9,419.3 persons per square mile; Race: 87.5% White, 6.4% Black/African American, 1.9% Asian, 0.3% American Indian/Alaska Native, 0.0% Native Hawaiian/Other Pacific Islander, 2.7% Two or more races, 4.1% Hispanic of any race; Average household size: 2.05; Median age: 35.4; Age under 18: 19.6%; Age 65 and over: 11.0%; Males per 100 females: 96.6; Marriage status: 43.5% never married, 37.9% now married, 1.6% separated, 5.4% widowed, 13.3% divorced; Foreign born: 8.0%; Speak English only: 89.1%; With disability: 12.0%; Veterans: 8.1%; Ancestry: 24.6% German, 24.1% Irish, 11.5% Italian, 10.2% English, 7.3% Polish
Employment: 16.5% management, business, and financial, 5.5% computer, engineering, and science, 14.2% education, legal, community service, arts, and media, 7.4% healthcare practitioners, 17.4% service, 25.1% sales and office, 5.2% natural resources, construction, and maintenance, 8.8% production, transportation, and material moving
Income: Per capita: $27,858; Median household: $43,218; Average household: $56,813; Households with income of $100,000 or more: 14.7%; Poverty rate: 16.4%
Educational Attainment: High school diploma or higher: 92.2%; Bachelor's degree or higher: 40.7%; Graduate/professional degree or higher: 14.0%

School District(s)

Lakewood City (PK-12)
2012-13 Enrollment: 5,818 . . . . (216) 529-4092
Lakewood City Academy (04-12)
2012-13 Enrollment: 156. . . . . (216) 529-4037

Two-year College(s)

Virginia Marti College of Art and Design (Private, For-profit)
Fall 2013 Enrollment: 173. . . . . (216) 221-8584
2013-14 Tuition: In-state $17,459; Out-of-state $17,459
Housing: Homeownership rate: 43.3%; Median home value: $129,400; Median year structure built: Before 1940; Homeowner vacancy rate: 2.7%; Median gross rent: $699 per month; Rental vacancy rate: 12.0%
Health Insurance: 85.7% have insurance; 66.8% have private insurance; 27.1% have public insurance; 14.3% do not have insurance; 5.3% of children under 18 do not have insurance
Hospitals: Lakewood Hospital (400 beds)
Transportation: Commute: 86.7% car, 6.3% public transportation, 2.3% walk, 3.1% work from home; Median travel time to work: 24.3 minutes
Additional Information Contacts
City of Lakewood. . . . . (216) 529-6600
http://www.ci.lakewood.oh.us

LINNDALE (village). Covers a land area of 0.081 square miles and a water area of 0 square miles. Located at 41.44° N. Lat; 81.77° W. Long. Elevation is 755 feet.
Population: 179; Growth (since 2000): 53.0%; Density: 2,223.0 persons per square mile; Race: 65.9% White, 27.9% Black/African American, 0.0% Asian, 0.0% American Indian/Alaska Native, 1.7% Native Hawaiian/Other Pacific Islander, 0.0% Two or more races, 17.3% Hispanic of any race; Average household size: 2.71; Median age: 35.1; Age under 18: 26.3%; Age 65 and over: 7.3%; Males per 100 females: 94.6
Housing: Homeownership rate: 34.9%; Homeowner vacancy rate: 0.0%; Rental vacancy rate: 12.0%

LYNDHURST (city). Covers a land area of 4.432 square miles and a water area of 0.006 square miles. Located at 41.52° N. Lat; 81.49° W. Long. Elevation is 1,033 feet.
History: Incorporated 1917.
Population: 14,001; Growth (since 2000): -8.4%; Density: 3,159.3 persons per square mile; Race: 90.3% White, 6.4% Black/African American, 1.6% Asian, 0.0% American Indian/Alaska Native, 0.0% Native Hawaiian/Other Pacific Islander, 1.2% Two or more races, 1.3% Hispanic of any race; Average household size: 2.15; Median age: 47.0; Age under 18: 17.4%; Age 65 and over: 24.3%; Males per 100 females: 85.3; Marriage status: 25.1% never married, 58.1% now married, 0.7% separated, 8.3% widowed, 8.4% divorced; Foreign born: 7.8%; Speak English only: 91.2%; With disability: 10.5%; Veterans: 8.6%; Ancestry: 20.5% Italian, 18.5% German, 15.4% Irish, 7.2% English, 6.4% Polish
Employment: 20.9% management, business, and financial, 6.2% computer, engineering, and science, 14.3% education, legal, community service, arts, and media, 9.0% healthcare practitioners, 14.8% service, 27.8% sales and office, 2.6% natural resources, construction, and maintenance, 4.3% production, transportation, and material moving
Income: Per capita: $36,432; Median household: $63,593; Average household: $81,818; Households with income of $100,000 or more: 28.3%; Poverty rate: 4.3%
Educational Attainment: High school diploma or higher: 93.9%; Bachelor's degree or higher: 45.2%; Graduate/professional degree or higher: 15.2%

School District(s)

South Euclid-Lyndhurst City (PK-12)
2012-13 Enrollment: 3,981 . . . . (216) 691-2000

Two-year College(s)

Inner State Beauty School (Private, For-profit)
Fall 2013 Enrollment: 139 . . . . (440) 442-4500

Vocational/Technical School(s)

Cleveland Institute of Dental-Medical Assistants-Lyndhurst (Private, For-profit)
Fall 2013 Enrollment: 64 . . . . (216) 241-2930
2013-14 Tuition: $9,050
Housing: Homeownership rate: 85.9%; Median home value: $143,900; Median year structure built: 1956; Homeowner vacancy rate: 2.7%; Median gross rent: $1,092 per month; Rental vacancy rate: 11.2%
Health Insurance: 95.6% have insurance; 87.0% have private insurance; 25.7% have public insurance; 4.4% do not have insurance; 1.2% of children under 18 do not have insurance
Safety: Violent crime rate: 3.6 per 10,000 population; Property crime rate: 0.0 per 10,000 population
Transportation: Commute: 90.6% car, 2.2% public transportation, 1.5% walk, 4.9% work from home; Median travel time to work: 22.3 minutes
Additional Information Contacts
City of Lyndhurst . . . . (440) 442-5777
http://www.lyndhurst-oh.com

MAPLE HEIGHTS (city). Covers a land area of 5.172 square miles and a water area of <.001 square miles. Located at 41.41° N. Lat; 81.56° W. Long. Elevation is 896 feet.
History: Named for its abundance of maple trees. Incorporated 1932.
Population: 23,138; Growth (since 2000): -11.5%; Density: 4,473.6 persons per square mile; Race: 28.0% White, 68.2% Black/African American, 1.0% Asian, 0.2% American Indian/Alaska Native, 0.0% Native Hawaiian/Other Pacific Islander, 2.1% Two or more races, 1.5% Hispanic of any race; Average household size: 2.41; Median age: 39.2; Age under 18: 25.1%; Age 65 and over: 13.2%; Males per 100 females: 86.1; Marriage status: 39.8% never married, 39.0% now married, 2.6% separated, 7.5% widowed, 13.7% divorced; Foreign born: 3.0%; Speak English only: 96.7%; With disability: 16.2%; Veterans: 10.3%; Ancestry: 6.8% German, 6.4% Polish, 4.9% Italian, 4.8% Irish, 2.5% Czech
Employment: 8.3% management, business, and financial, 3.4% computer, engineering, and science, 6.6% education, legal, community service, arts, and media, 4.3% healthcare practitioners, 20.1% service, 33.8% sales and office, 7.9% natural resources, construction, and maintenance, 15.7% production, transportation, and material moving
Income: Per capita: $19,471; Median household: $36,664; Average household: $44,755; Households with income of $100,000 or more: 7.2%; Poverty rate: 19.5%
Educational Attainment: High school diploma or higher: 88.2%; Bachelor's degree or higher: 14.0%; Graduate/professional degree or higher: 4.1%

School District(s)

Maple Heights City (PK-12)
2012-13 Enrollment: 3,807 . . . . (216) 587-6100

Housing: Homeownership rate: 73.7%; Median home value: $84,400; Median year structure built: 1956; Homeowner vacancy rate: 4.5%; Median gross rent: $777 per month; Rental vacancy rate: 13.7%
Health Insurance: 88.2% have insurance; 61.4% have private insurance; 39.4% have public insurance; 11.8% do not have insurance; 0.7% of children under 18 do not have insurance
Transportation: Commute: 90.2% car, 4.8% public transportation, 1.8% walk, 1.5% work from home; Median travel time to work: 22.7 minutes
Additional Information Contacts
City of Maple Heights .... (216) 662-6000
http://mapleheights.cuyahogacounty.us

MAYFIELD (village). Covers a land area of 3.950 square miles and a water area of 0.008 square miles. Located at 41.55° N. Lat; 81.43° W. Long. Elevation is 925 feet.
Population: 3,460; Growth (since 2000): 0.7%; Density: 875.9 persons per square mile; Race: 90.1% White, 2.8% Black/African American, 6.0% Asian, 0.0% American Indian/Alaska Native, 0.0% Native Hawaiian/Other Pacific Islander, 1.0% Two or more races, 1.2% Hispanic of any race; Average household size: 2.26; Median age: 48.3; Age under 18: 19.3%; Age 65 and over: 24.2%; Males per 100 females: 98.3; Marriage status: 29.5% never married, 52.4% now married, 1.4% separated, 8.4% widowed, 9.7% divorced; Foreign born: 18.0%; Speak English only: 77.1%; With disability: 10.4%; Veterans: 9.9%; Ancestry: 25.4% Italian, 15.2% Irish, 12.5% German, 7.7% Polish, 5.8% English
Employment: 23.6% management, business, and financial, 4.1% computer, engineering, and science, 17.1% education, legal, community service, arts, and media, 5.9% healthcare practitioners, 8.7% service, 30.1% sales and office, 5.9% natural resources, construction, and maintenance, 4.7% production, transportation, and material moving
Income: Per capita: $42,286; Median household: $75,375; Average household: $101,527; Households with income of $100,000 or more: 36.0%; Poverty rate: 3.3%
Educational Attainment: High school diploma or higher: 95.2%; Bachelor's degree or higher: 55.7%; Graduate/professional degree or higher: 20.7%

School District(s)

Mayfield City (PK-12)
2012-13 Enrollment: 4,502 .... (440) 995-7201
Housing: Homeownership rate: 70.9%; Median home value: $229,800; Median year structure built: 1964; Homeowner vacancy rate: 1.4%; Median gross rent: $1,012 per month; Rental vacancy rate: 7.0%
Health Insurance: 94.8% have insurance; 81.7% have private insurance; 28.2% have public insurance; 5.2% do not have insurance; 1.7% of children under 18 do not have insurance
Transportation: Commute: 91.1% car, 2.9% public transportation, 1.2% walk, 4.2% work from home; Median travel time to work: 24.9 minutes
Additional Information Contacts
Village of Mayfield .... (440) 461-2210
http://www.mayfieldvillage.com

MAYFIELD HEIGHTS (city). Covers a land area of 4.168 square miles and a water area of 0.009 square miles. Located at 41.52° N. Lat; 81.45° W. Long. Elevation is 1,086 feet.
History: Named either for Mayfield in Derby, England, or for the month of May. Incorporated 1925.
Population: 19,155; Growth (since 2000): -1.2%; Density: 4,595.4 persons per square mile; Race: 80.4% White, 10.3% Black/African American, 7.0% Asian, 0.1% American Indian/Alaska Native, 0.0% Native Hawaiian/Other Pacific Islander, 1.7% Two or more races, 2.0% Hispanic of any race; Average household size: 1.97; Median age: 42.9; Age under 18: 17.6%; Age 65 and over: 23.8%; Males per 100 females: 82.7; Marriage status: 32.5% never married, 45.4% now married, 0.9% separated, 11.5% widowed, 10.7% divorced; Foreign born: 17.3%; Speak English only: 79.1%; With disability: 13.0%; Veterans: 7.7%; Ancestry: 24.8% Italian, 16.7% German, 11.2% Irish, 7.0% Polish, 6.5% English
Employment: 14.8% management, business, and financial, 13.4% computer, engineering, and science, 12.1% education, legal, community service, arts, and media, 7.6% healthcare practitioners, 18.3% service, 22.7% sales and office, 4.1% natural resources, construction, and maintenance, 6.9% production, transportation, and material moving
Income: Per capita: $27,279; Median household: $43,615; Average household: $55,259; Households with income of $100,000 or more: 13.3%; Poverty rate: 7.6%
Educational Attainment: High school diploma or higher: 90.8%; Bachelor's degree or higher: 38.2%; Graduate/professional degree or higher: 15.5%
Housing: Homeownership rate: 50.8%; Median home value: $142,700; Median year structure built: 1964; Homeowner vacancy rate: 2.2%; Median gross rent: $821 per month; Rental vacancy rate: 10.2%
Health Insurance: 91.4% have insurance; 79.4% have private insurance; 27.3% have public insurance; 8.6% do not have insurance; 9.1% of children under 18 do not have insurance
Hospitals: Hillcrest Hospital (424 beds)
Transportation: Commute: 96.1% car, 1.1% public transportation, 1.2% walk, 1.5% work from home; Median travel time to work: 21.2 minutes
Additional Information Contacts
City of Mayfield Heights............................ (440) 442-2626
http://www.mayfieldheights.org

MIDDLEBURG HEIGHTS (city). Covers a land area of 8.065 square miles and a water area of 0.011 square miles. Located at 41.37° N. Lat; 81.81° W. Long. Elevation is 853 feet.
Population: 15,946; Growth (since 2000): 2.6%; Density: 1,977.2 persons per square mile; Race: 91.1% White, 1.6% Black/African American, 5.6% Asian, 0.2% American Indian/Alaska Native, 0.0% Native Hawaiian/Other Pacific Islander, 0.9% Two or more races, 2.2% Hispanic of any race; Average household size: 2.18; Median age: 46.6; Age under 18: 17.5%; Age 65 and over: 23.1%; Males per 100 females: 89.6; Marriage status: 25.5% never married, 50.9% now married, 0.8% separated, 9.3% widowed, 14.3% divorced; Foreign born: 14.3%; Speak English only: 81.5%; With disability: 12.4%; Veterans: 10.0%; Ancestry: 25.0% German, 15.3% Italian, 15.1% Irish, 14.5% Polish, 6.7% English
Employment: 18.0% management, business, and financial, 10.5% computer, engineering, and science, 7.5% education, legal, community service, arts, and media, 6.8% healthcare practitioners, 14.6% service, 25.9% sales and office, 5.7% natural resources, construction, and maintenance, 10.9% production, transportation, and material moving
Income: Per capita: $29,202; Median household: $56,002; Average household: $64,817; Households with income of $100,000 or more: 19.7%; Poverty rate: 7.8%
Educational Attainment: High school diploma or higher: 91.0%; Bachelor's degree or higher: 32.1%; Graduate/professional degree or higher: 13.8%

School District(s)

Berea City (PK-12)
2012-13 Enrollment: 7,066 .... (216) 898-8300
Polaris (09-12)
2012-13 Enrollment: n/a .... (440) 891-7600

Two-year College(s)

Sanford-Brown College-Middleburg Heights (Private, For-profit)
Fall 2013 Enrollment: 495........................ (440) 202-3232
2013-14 Tuition: In-state $15,262; Out-of-state $15,262

Vocational/Technical School(s)

Polaris Career Center (Public)
Fall 2013 Enrollment: 350........................ (440) 891-7600
2013-14 Tuition: $7,495
Housing: Homeownership rate: 72.8%; Median home value: $160,300; Median year structure built: 1971; Homeowner vacancy rate: 2.1%; Median gross rent: $788 per month; Rental vacancy rate: 10.4%
Health Insurance: 92.0% have insurance; 80.1% have private insurance; 28.2% have public insurance; 8.0% do not have insurance; 3.7% of children under 18 do not have insurance
Hospitals: Southwest General Health Center (336 beds)
Transportation: Commute: 93.4% car, 1.4% public transportation, 0.8% walk, 2.9% work from home; Median travel time to work: 21.7 minutes
Additional Information Contacts
City of Middleburg Heights .... (440) 234-8811
http://www.middleburgheights.com

MORELAND HILLS (village). Covers a land area of 7.149 square miles and a water area of 0.078 square miles. Located at 41.44° N. Lat; 81.44° W. Long. Elevation is 1,040 feet.
History: In 1815, settlement began near the point where State Route 87 crosses the Chagrin River. The village, which in 1831 was still part of Orange Township, was the birthplace of James A. Garfield, the 20th President of the United States.
Population: 3,320; Growth (since 2000): 0.7%; Density: 464.4 persons per square mile; Race: 89.6% White, 3.7% Black/African American, 4.6%

Asian, 0.1% American Indian/Alaska Native, 0.1% Native Hawaiian/Other Pacific Islander, 1.7% Two or more races, 1.1% Hispanic of any race; Average household size: 2.63; Median age: 49.1; Age under 18: 24.2%; Age 65 and over: 18.6%; Males per 100 females: 97.1; Marriage status: 16.7% never married, 65.8% now married, 0.3% separated, 6.0% widowed, 11.6% divorced; Foreign born: 11.9%; Speak English only: 87.0%; With disability: 9.1%; Veterans: 7.3%; Ancestry: 21.6% German, 14.2% Irish, 11.7% English, 9.0% Italian, 7.7% Polish

Employment: 30.0% management, business, and financial, 9.1% computer, engineering, and science, 9.9% education, legal, community service, arts, and media, 14.2% healthcare practitioners, 8.4% service, 21.1% sales and office, 2.9% natural resources, construction, and maintenance, 4.3% production, transportation, and material moving

Income: Per capita: $76,232; Median household: $119,194; Average household: $191,969; Households with income of $100,000 or more: 57.4%; Poverty rate: 3.4%

Educational Attainment: High school diploma or higher: 98.4%; Bachelor's degree or higher: 71.4%; Graduate/professional degree or higher: 30.7%

Housing: Homeownership rate: 94.0%; Median home value: $392,100; Median year structure built: 1961; Homeowner vacancy rate: 2.3%; Median gross rent: $1,307 per month; Rental vacancy rate: 5.0%

Health Insurance: 97.0% have insurance; 89.1% have private insurance; 20.1% have public insurance; 3.0% do not have insurance; 0.0% of children under 18 do not have insurance

Safety: Violent crime rate: 0.0 per 10,000 population; Property crime rate: 33.3 per 10,000 population

Transportation: Commute: 85.9% car, 4.5% public transportation, 0.9% walk, 6.3% work from home; Median travel time to work: 26.0 minutes

Additional Information Contacts

Village of Moreland Hills . . . . (440) 248-1188
http://www.morelandhills.com

NEWBURGH HEIGHTS (village). Covers a land area of 0.583 square miles and a water area of <.001 square miles. Located at 41.45° N. Lat; 81.66° W. Long. Elevation is 692 feet.

Population: 2,167; Growth (since 2000): -9.3%; Density: 3,719.4 persons per square mile; Race: 79.1% White, 14.9% Black/African American, 0.3% Asian, 0.1% American Indian/Alaska Native, 0.0% Native Hawaiian/Other Pacific Islander, 3.2% Two or more races, 5.4% Hispanic of any race; Average household size: 2.26; Median age: 37.2; Age under 18: 24.8%; Age 65 and over: 12.6%; Males per 100 females: 104.0

School District(s)

Cleveland Municipal (PK-12)
2012-13 Enrollment: 39,813 . . . . (216) 574-8000
Washington Park Community (KG-08)
2012-13 Enrollment: 233. . . . . (216) 271-6055

Housing: Homeownership rate: 53.2%; Homeowner vacancy rate: 4.2%; Rental vacancy rate: 14.2%

NORTH OLMSTED (city). Covers a land area of 11.674 square miles and a water area of 0 square miles. Located at 41.41° N. Lat; 81.92° W. Long. Elevation is 761 feet.

History: Named for Charles H. Olmsted. First U.S. municipal bus line began operations in North Olmstead in 1931. Incorporated as a city 1951.

Population: 32,718; Growth (since 2000): -4.1%; Density: 2,802.7 persons per square mile; Race: 92.6% White, 2.0% Black/African American, 2.7% Asian, 0.1% American Indian/Alaska Native, 0.0% Native Hawaiian/Other Pacific Islander, 1.7% Two or more races, 3.5% Hispanic of any race; Average household size: 2.37; Median age: 43.5; Age under 18: 20.7%; Age 65 and over: 17.8%; Males per 100 females: 93.4; Marriage status: 26.8% never married, 55.7% now married, 1.0% separated, 7.2% widowed, 10.3% divorced; Foreign born: 8.6%; Speak English only: 86.6%; With disability: 12.4%; Veterans: 9.3%; Ancestry: 28.4% German, 22.4% Irish, 11.7% Italian, 9.0% Polish, 8.7% English

Employment: 16.3% management, business, and financial, 6.1% computer, engineering, and science, 10.0% education, legal, community service, arts, and media, 7.1% healthcare practitioners, 13.9% service, 29.9% sales and office, 6.2% natural resources, construction, and maintenance, 10.4% production, transportation, and material moving

Income: Per capita: $30,152; Median household: $59,411; Average household: $70,525; Households with income of $100,000 or more: 21.7%; Poverty rate: 7.2%

Educational Attainment: High school diploma or higher: 92.7%; Bachelor's degree or higher: 30.5%; Graduate/professional degree or higher: 9.7%

School District(s)

North Olmsted City (PK-12)
2012-13 Enrollment: 4,086 . . . . (440) 779-3549

Two-year College(s)

Remington College-Cleveland West Campus (Private, Not-for-profit)
Fall 2013 Enrollment: 73 . . . . (440) 777-2560

Vocational/Technical School(s)

Regency Beauty Institute-North Olmsted (Private, For-profit)
Fall 2013 Enrollment: 96 . . . . (800) 787-6456
2013-14 Tuition: $16,200

Housing: Homeownership rate: 76.3%; Median home value: $147,400; Median year structure built: 1966; Homeowner vacancy rate: 1.6%; Median gross rent: $796 per month; Rental vacancy rate: 11.3%

Health Insurance: 92.2% have insurance; 78.5% have private insurance; 28.1% have public insurance; 7.8% do not have insurance; 2.5% of children under 18 do not have insurance

Transportation: Commute: 92.4% car, 2.5% public transportation, 1.2% walk, 3.2% work from home; Median travel time to work: 23.1 minutes

Additional Information Contacts

City of North Olmsted . . . . (440) 777-8000
http://www.north-olmsted.com

NORTH RANDALL (village). Covers a land area of 0.769 square miles and a water area of 0.001 square miles. Located at 41.43° N. Lat; 81.53° W. Long. Elevation is 1,043 feet.

Population: 1,027; Growth (since 2000): 13.4%; Density: 1,335.5 persons per square mile; Race: 10.2% White, 86.3% Black/African American, 1.3% Asian, 0.9% American Indian/Alaska Native, 0.0% Native Hawaiian/Other Pacific Islander, 1.2% Two or more races, 0.7% Hispanic of any race; Average household size: 1.84; Median age: 51.2; Age under 18: 15.2%; Age 65 and over: 27.4%; Males per 100 females: 75.0

Two-year College(s)

Ohio Technical College-PowerSport Institute (Private, For-profit)
Fall 2013 Enrollment: 267 . . . . (216) 587-5000

Housing: Homeownership rate: 25.1%; Homeowner vacancy rate: 4.8%; Rental vacancy rate: 21.7%

NORTH ROYALTON (city). Covers a land area of 21.310 square miles and a water area of 0.013 square miles. Located at 41.31° N. Lat; 81.75° W. Long. Elevation is 1,197 feet.

History: Dairy-processing and sawmilling center in the 19th century, North Royalton has since developed a variety of light industries. Settled 1811, incorporated as a village 1927, as a city 1960.

Population: 30,444; Growth (since 2000): 6.3%; Density: 1,428.6 persons per square mile; Race: 94.6% White, 1.1% Black/African American, 2.7% Asian, 0.1% American Indian/Alaska Native, 0.0% Native Hawaiian/Other Pacific Islander, 1.1% Two or more races, 1.6% Hispanic of any race; Average household size: 2.33; Median age: 43.5; Age under 18: 20.1%; Age 65 and over: 15.1%; Males per 100 females: 95.3; Marriage status: 28.9% never married, 54.0% now married, 0.8% separated, 6.8% widowed, 10.2% divorced; Foreign born: 9.2%; Speak English only: 86.7%; With disability: 11.2%; Veterans: 8.8%; Ancestry: 21.8% German, 17.2% Italian, 17.1% Polish, 14.3% Irish, 7.6% English

Employment: 20.0% management, business, and financial, 6.6% computer, engineering, and science, 8.6% education, legal, community service, arts, and media, 9.1% healthcare practitioners, 14.2% service, 24.7% sales and office, 6.6% natural resources, construction, and maintenance, 10.4% production, transportation, and material moving

Income: Per capita: $34,352; Median household: $66,683; Average household: $82,526; Households with income of $100,000 or more: 28.0%; Poverty rate: 4.3%

Educational Attainment: High school diploma or higher: 94.3%; Bachelor's degree or higher: 34.4%; Graduate/professional degree or higher: 13.5%

School District(s)

North Royalton City (PK-12)
2012-13 Enrollment: 4,618 . . . . (440) 237-8800

Housing: Homeownership rate: 71.6%; Median home value: $193,700; Median year structure built: 1982; Homeowner vacancy rate: 1.5%; Median gross rent: $764 per month; Rental vacancy rate: 9.3%

Health Insurance: 91.6% have insurance; 82.2% have private insurance; 22.3% have public insurance; 8.4% do not have insurance; 4.3% of children under 18 do not have insurance

Transportation: Commute: 92.6% car, 0.5% public transportation, 0.4% walk, 5.6% work from home; Median travel time to work: 27.5 minutes

Additional Information Contacts

City of North Royalton . . . . (440) 237-5686
http://www.northroyalton.org

OAKWOOD (village). Covers a land area of 3.436 square miles and a water area of 0.008 square miles. Located at 41.37° N. Lat; 81.50° W. Long. Elevation is 1,047 feet.

Population: 3,667; Growth (since 2000): 0.0%; Density: 1,067.1 persons per square mile; Race: 30.7% White, 64.7% Black/African American, 0.7% Asian, 0.2% American Indian/Alaska Native, 0.1% Native Hawaiian/Other Pacific Islander, 3.4% Two or more races, 2.3% Hispanic of any race; Average household size: 2.28; Median age: 46.7; Age under 18: 18.7%; Age 65 and over: 19.3%; Males per 100 females: 90.8; Marriage status: 28.5% never married, 50.4% now married, 0.9% separated, 8.9% widowed, 12.3% divorced; Foreign born: 8.1%; Speak English only: 89.8%; With disability: 15.7%; Veterans: 11.6%; Ancestry: 6.3% German, 4.7% Russian, 4.2% Irish, 3.3% Hungarian, 3.0% Polish

Employment: 10.2% management, business, and financial, 4.2% computer, engineering, and science, 12.6% education, legal, community service, arts, and media, 7.2% healthcare practitioners, 21.6% service, 18.2% sales and office, 2.6% natural resources, construction, and maintenance, 23.4% production, transportation, and material moving

Income: Per capita: $24,707; Median household: $54,274; Average household: $60,592; Households with income of $100,000 or more: 14.3%; Poverty rate: 14.1%

Educational Attainment: High school diploma or higher: 81.9%; Bachelor's degree or higher: 23.6%; Graduate/professional degree or higher: 11.5%

Housing: Homeownership rate: 73.2%; Median home value: $153,400; Median year structure built: 1968; Homeowner vacancy rate: 2.6%; Median gross rent: $660 per month; Rental vacancy rate: 3.7%

Health Insurance: 84.0% have insurance; 64.7% have private insurance; 31.9% have public insurance; 16.0% do not have insurance; 0.0% of children under 18 do not have insurance

Transportation: Commute: 99.0% car, 0.0% public transportation, 0.0% walk, 0.4% work from home; Median travel time to work: 22.4 minutes

OLMSTED FALLS (city). Covers a land area of 4.122 square miles and a water area of 0 square miles. Located at 41.37° N. Lat; 81.90° W. Long. Elevation is 774 feet.

Population: 9,024; Growth (since 2000): 13.3%; Density: 2,189.0 persons per square mile; Race: 94.9% White, 2.0% Black/African American, 1.2% Asian, 0.1% American Indian/Alaska Native, 0.0% Native Hawaiian/Other Pacific Islander, 1.3% Two or more races, 2.6% Hispanic of any race; Average household size: 2.42; Median age: 41.6; Age under 18: 24.5%; Age 65 and over: 13.7%; Males per 100 females: 87.6; Marriage status: 25.1% never married, 57.4% now married, 1.1% separated, 5.7% widowed, 11.8% divorced; Foreign born: 3.7%; Speak English only: 93.2%; With disability: 8.8%; Veterans: 8.9%; Ancestry: 29.7% German, 19.9% Irish, 18.1% Italian, 12.0% Polish, 9.8% English

Employment: 20.8% management, business, and financial, 6.0% computer, engineering, and science, 9.9% education, legal, community service, arts, and media, 6.6% healthcare practitioners, 11.8% service, 25.4% sales and office, 7.3% natural resources, construction, and maintenance, 12.1% production, transportation, and material moving

Income: Per capita: $31,225; Median household: $71,364; Average household: $80,018; Households with income of $100,000 or more: 30.2%; Poverty rate: 3.3%

Educational Attainment: High school diploma or higher: 93.8%; Bachelor's degree or higher: 38.0%; Graduate/professional degree or higher: 13.6%

School District(s)

Olmsted Falls City (PK-12)
2012-13 Enrollment: 3,766 . . . . (440) 427-6000

Housing: Homeownership rate: 80.7%; Median home value: $151,700; Median year structure built: 1978; Homeowner vacancy rate: 1.9%; Median gross rent: $771 per month; Rental vacancy rate: 7.0%

Health Insurance: 93.1% have insurance; 83.0% have private insurance; 21.3% have public insurance; 6.9% do not have insurance; 4.4% of children under 18 do not have insurance

Safety: Violent crime rate: 1.1 per 10,000 population; Property crime rate: 42.6 per 10,000 population

Transportation: Commute: 94.3% car, 1.8% public transportation, 1.1% walk, 1.9% work from home; Median travel time to work: 28.6 minutes

Additional Information Contacts

City of Olmsted Falls . . . . (440) 235-5550
http://www.olmstedfalls.org

ORANGE (village). Covers a land area of 3.803 square miles and a water area of 0.019 square miles. Located at 41.44° N. Lat; 81.47° W. Long. Elevation is 1,158 feet.

History: Orange Village, the southwest quadrant of the original Orange township, was incorporated as a village in 1929.

Population: 3,323; Growth (since 2000): 2.7%; Density: 873.8 persons per square mile; Race: 77.1% White, 14.4% Black/African American, 5.7% Asian, 0.1% American Indian/Alaska Native, 0.1% Native Hawaiian/Other Pacific Islander, 1.9% Two or more races, 1.6% Hispanic of any race; Average household size: 2.59; Median age: 46.8; Age under 18: 24.8%; Age 65 and over: 18.1%; Males per 100 females: 92.5; Marriage status: 18.1% never married, 65.8% now married, 0.5% separated, 5.3% widowed, 10.8% divorced; Foreign born: 14.3%; Speak English only: 83.4%; With disability: 10.4%; Veterans: 8.9%; Ancestry: 12.0% Russian, 8.7% Hungarian, 8.0% Polish, 7.2% German, 4.7% American

Employment: 24.7% management, business, and financial, 9.8% computer, engineering, and science, 18.0% education, legal, community service, arts, and media, 16.1% healthcare practitioners, 5.3% service, 22.1% sales and office, 1.8% natural resources, construction, and maintenance, 2.3% production, transportation, and material moving

Income: Per capita: $62,134; Median household: $114,833; Average household: $154,897; Households with income of $100,000 or more: 52.6%; Poverty rate: 4.3%

Educational Attainment: High school diploma or higher: 96.0%; Bachelor's degree or higher: 72.6%; Graduate/professional degree or higher: 36.7%

Housing: Homeownership rate: 92.5%; Median home value: $297,400; Median year structure built: 1980; Homeowner vacancy rate: 1.7%; Median gross rent: $1,941 per month; Rental vacancy rate: 8.7%

Health Insurance: 95.5% have insurance; 86.8% have private insurance; 26.1% have public insurance; 4.5% do not have insurance; 0.0% of children under 18 do not have insurance

Transportation: Commute: 95.7% car, 0.3% public transportation, 0.0% walk, 4.1% work from home; Median travel time to work: 19.9 minutes

Additional Information Contacts

Village of Orange . . . . (440) 498-4400
http://www.orangevillage.com

PARMA (city). Covers a land area of 20.024 square miles and a water area of 0.049 square miles. Located at 41.38° N. Lat; 81.73° W. Long. Elevation is 863 feet.

History: Named for the Italian city of Parma. Population declined between 1970 and 1990, reflecting the pattern in conjunction with the greater Northern Ohio area. Settled 1816. Incorporated 1924.

Population: 81,601; Growth (since 2000): -4.7%; Density: 4,075.1 persons per square mile; Race: 93.0% White, 2.3% Black/African American, 1.9% Asian, 0.2% American Indian/Alaska Native, 0.0% Native Hawaiian/Other Pacific Islander, 1.6% Two or more races, 3.6% Hispanic of any race; Average household size: 2.34; Median age: 41.5; Age under 18: 20.4%; Age 65 and over: 17.7%; Males per 100 females: 92.8; Marriage status: 31.5% never married, 48.6% now married, 1.2% separated, 8.2% widowed, 11.8% divorced; Foreign born: 9.8%; Speak English only: 85.9%; With disability: 14.2%; Veterans: 9.4%; Ancestry: 24.6% German, 17.2% Polish, 14.9% Irish, 14.4% Italian, 7.2% Slovak

Employment: 11.7% management, business, and financial, 4.1% computer, engineering, and science, 7.7% education, legal, community service, arts, and media, 5.9% healthcare practitioners, 19.0% service, 27.6% sales and office, 8.4% natural resources, construction, and maintenance, 15.5% production, transportation, and material moving

Income: Per capita: $24,713; Median household: $49,654; Average household: $58,530; Households with income of $100,000 or more: 14.0%; Poverty rate: 10.9%

Educational Attainment: High school diploma or higher: 89.1%; Bachelor's degree or higher: 19.6%; Graduate/professional degree or higher: 6.0%

School District(s)

Avon Local (PK-12)
2012-13 Enrollment: 4,096 . . . . (440) 937-4680
Constellation Schools: Parma Community (KG-12)
2012-13 Enrollment: 1,033 . . . . (440) 888-5490
Constellation Schools: Stockyard Community Middle (07-08)
2012-13 Enrollment: 85. . . . . (216) 961-5052
Global Village Academy (KG-05)
2012-13 Enrollment: 117. . . . . (216) 767-5956
Parma City (PK-12)
2012-13 Enrollment: 11,315 . . . . (440) 842-5300
Summit Academy Community School-Parma (KG-12)
2012-13 Enrollment: 219. . . . . (440) 888-5407

Four-year College(s)

Bryant & Stratton College-Parma (Private, For-profit)
Fall 2013 Enrollment: 662 . . . . (216) 265-3151
2013-14 Tuition: In-state $16,565; Out-of-state $16,565

Housing: Homeownership rate: 74.1%; Median home value: $115,700; Median year structure built: 1958; Homeowner vacancy rate: 1.7%; Median gross rent: $758 per month; Rental vacancy rate: 8.7%

Health Insurance: 89.1% have insurance; 71.4% have private insurance; 31.8% have public insurance; 10.9% do not have insurance; 5.0% of children under 18 do not have insurance

Hospitals: Parma Community General Hospital (348 beds)

Transportation: Commute: 94.0% car, 2.0% public transportation, 1.4% walk, 1.8% work from home; Median travel time to work: 24.3 minutes

Additional Information Contacts

City of Parma. . . . . (440) 885-8000
http://www.cityofparma-oh.gov

PARMA HEIGHTS (city).

Covers a land area of 4.186 square miles and a water area of <.001 square miles. Located at 41.38° N. Lat; 81.76° W. Long. Elevation is 856 feet.

History: Named for the city in Italy. Settled 1818; set off from Parma and incorporated 1912.

Population: 20,718; Growth (since 2000): -4.3%; Density: 4,949.9 persons per square mile; Race: 91.1% White, 2.8% Black/African American, 3.0% Asian, 0.2% American Indian/Alaska Native, 0.0% Native Hawaiian/Other Pacific Islander, 1.8% Two or more races, 3.8% Hispanic of any race; Average household size: 2.15; Median age: 43.2; Age under 18: 18.9%; Age 65 and over: 20.5%; Males per 100 females: 87.0; Marriage status: 29.2% never married, 48.4% now married, 0.8% separated, 9.7% widowed, 12.8% divorced; Foreign born: 13.0%; Speak English only: 83.4%; With disability: 16.1%; Veterans: 9.3%; Ancestry: 23.3% German, 15.3% Irish, 12.5% Polish, 12.3% Italian, 7.2% English

Employment: 10.7% management, business, and financial, 5.3% computer, engineering, and science, 6.7% education, legal, community service, arts, and media, 5.9% healthcare practitioners, 19.9% service, 27.4% sales and office, 8.0% natural resources, construction, and maintenance, 16.1% production, transportation, and material moving

Income: Per capita: $24,331; Median household: $43,502; Average household: $54,156; Households with income of $100,000 or more: 12.9%; Poverty rate: 12.1%

Educational Attainment: High school diploma or higher: 89.2%; Bachelor's degree or higher: 21.0%; Graduate/professional degree or higher: 5.8%

School District(s)

Parma City (PK-12)
2012-13 Enrollment: 11,315 . . . . (440) 842-5300

Housing: Homeownership rate: 59.4%; Median home value: $117,700; Median year structure built: 1960; Homeowner vacancy rate: 1.8%; Median gross rent: $736 per month; Rental vacancy rate: 10.5%

Health Insurance: 88.1% have insurance; 68.7% have private insurance; 34.1% have public insurance; 11.9% do not have insurance; 7.4% of children under 18 do not have insurance

Safety: Violent crime rate: 8.3 per 10,000 population; Property crime rate: 214.3 per 10,000 population

Transportation: Commute: 94.2% car, 2.2% public transportation, 1.1% walk, 1.7% work from home; Median travel time to work: 25.2 minutes

Additional Information Contacts

City of Parma Heights . . . . (440) 884-9600
http://www.parmaheightsoh.gov

PEPPER PIKE (city).

Covers a land area of 7.059 square miles and a water area of 0.033 square miles. Located at 41.48° N. Lat; 81.46° W. Long. Elevation is 1,056 feet.

History: In 1820, Orange Township was established, which included the present municipalities of Pepper Pike, Hunting Valley, Moreland Hills, Orange Village and Woodmere. The name "Pepper Pike" was selected after the Pepper family, who lived and worked along the primary transportation corridor (i.e., turnpike).

Population: 5,979; Growth (since 2000): -1.0%; Density: 847.0 persons per square mile; Race: 86.3% White, 6.5% Black/African American, 5.5% Asian, 0.2% American Indian/Alaska Native, 0.0% Native Hawaiian/Other Pacific Islander, 1.6% Two or more races, 1.4% Hispanic of any race; Average household size: 2.59; Median age: 49.2; Age under 18: 23.6%; Age 65 and over: 23.4%; Males per 100 females: 87.0; Marriage status: 21.4% never married, 71.1% now married, 1.4% separated, 4.9% widowed, 2.6% divorced; Foreign born: 11.9%; Speak English only: 85.8%; With disability: 7.9%; Veterans: 7.3%; Ancestry: 13.5% German, 11.3% English, 11.1% Irish, 10.6% Russian, 10.4% Polish

Employment: 31.4% management, business, and financial, 4.3% computer, engineering, and science, 16.3% education, legal, community service, arts, and media, 15.4% healthcare practitioners, 9.4% service, 20.2% sales and office, 1.4% natural resources, construction, and maintenance, 1.6% production, transportation, and material moving

Income: Per capita: $80,882; Median household: $141,845; Average household: $215,681; Households with income of $100,000 or more: 62.0%; Poverty rate: 5.0%

Educational Attainment: High school diploma or higher: 98.0%; Bachelor's degree or higher: 72.2%; Graduate/professional degree or higher: 41.1%

School District(s)

Orange City (PK-12)
2012-13 Enrollment: 2,199 . . . . (216) 831-8600

Four-year College(s)

Ursuline College (Private, Not-for-profit, Roman Catholic)
Fall 2013 Enrollment: 1,357 . . . . (440) 449-4200
2013-14 Tuition: In-state $26,720; Out-of-state $26,720

Housing: Homeownership rate: 94.9%; Median home value: $426,200; Median year structure built: 1967; Homeowner vacancy rate: 2.3%; Median gross rent: $1,182 per month; Rental vacancy rate: 1.7%

Health Insurance: 96.8% have insurance; 90.2% have private insurance; 25.6% have public insurance; 3.2% do not have insurance; 0.6% of children under 18 do not have insurance

Transportation: Commute: 90.6% car, 0.0% public transportation, 0.6% walk, 7.7% work from home; Median travel time to work: 22.7 minutes

Additional Information Contacts

City of Pepper Pike . . . . (216) 831-8500
http://www.pepperpike.org

RICHMOND HEIGHTS (city).

Covers a land area of 4.436 square miles and a water area of 0.008 square miles. Located at 41.56° N. Lat; 81.51° W. Long. Elevation is 869 feet.

Population: 10,546; Growth (since 2000): -3.6%; Density: 2,377.6 persons per square mile; Race: 48.5% White, 44.9% Black/African American, 4.3% Asian, 0.1% American Indian/Alaska Native, 0.0% Native Hawaiian/Other Pacific Islander, 1.8% Two or more races, 1.8% Hispanic of any race; Average household size: 2.17; Median age: 46.1; Age under 18: 18.4%; Age 65 and over: 20.5%; Males per 100 females: 81.5; Marriage status: 37.3% never married, 44.2% now married, 1.0% separated, 8.5% widowed, 10.0% divorced; Foreign born: 11.0%; Speak English only: 85.1%; With disability: 11.8%; Veterans: 9.9%; Ancestry: 10.8% German, 8.3% Italian, 7.4% Irish, 4.7% English, 3.2% African

Employment: 10.7% management, business, and financial, 7.1% computer, engineering, and science, 13.7% education, legal, community service, arts, and media, 6.1% healthcare practitioners, 14.9% service, 30.2% sales and office, 4.0% natural resources, construction, and maintenance, 13.3% production, transportation, and material moving

Income: Per capita: $29,925; Median household: $48,233; Average household: $63,887; Households with income of $100,000 or more: 17.9%; Poverty rate: 7.0%

Educational Attainment: High school diploma or higher: 92.2%; Bachelor's degree or higher: 40.3%; Graduate/professional degree or higher: 15.3%

School District(s)

Richmond Heights Local (PK-12)
2012-13 Enrollment: 837. . . . . (216) 692-8485

Housing: Homeownership rate: 64.1%; Median home value: $155,400; Median year structure built: 1967; Homeowner vacancy rate: 3.0%; Median gross rent: $710 per month; Rental vacancy rate: 19.0%
Health Insurance: 86.0% have insurance; 74.7% have private insurance; 25.9% have public insurance; 14.0% do not have insurance; 13.7% of children under 18 do not have insurance
Hospitals: UHHS Richmond Heights Hospital (250 beds)
Safety: Violent crime rate: 12.4 per 10,000 population; Property crime rate: 312.3 per 10,000 population
Transportation: Commute: 92.4% car, 1.8% public transportation, 0.8% walk, 4.5% work from home; Median travel time to work: 24.4 minutes
Additional Information Contacts
City of Richmond Heights .... (216) 383-6300
http://www.richmondheightsohio.org

ROCKY RIVER (city). Covers a land area of 4.738 square miles and a water area of 0.873 square miles. Located at 41.47° N. Lat; 81.85° W. Long. Elevation is 692 feet.
History: Named for its location at the mouth of the Rocky River, so named because of its rocky river bed. The town of Rocky River was established in 1815 on Lake Erie at the mouth of the Rocky River.
Population: 20,213; Growth (since 2000): -2.5%; Density: 4,266.2 persons per square mile; Race: 95.5% White, 1.0% Black/African American, 1.8% Asian, 0.1% American Indian/Alaska Native, 0.0% Native Hawaiian/Other Pacific Islander, 1.3% Two or more races, 1.8% Hispanic of any race; Average household size: 2.16; Median age: 45.6; Age under 18: 21.8%; Age 65 and over: 22.4%; Males per 100 females: 85.5; Marriage status: 26.8% never married, 54.7% now married, 0.8% separated, 9.7% widowed, 8.8% divorced; Foreign born: 11.2%; Speak English only: 86.6%; With disability: 9.5%; Veterans: 10.9%; Ancestry: 26.5% Irish, 25.8% German, 10.1% English, 9.3% Italian, 7.7% Polish
Employment: 26.7% management, business, and financial, 7.6% computer, engineering, and science, 14.4% education, legal, community service, arts, and media, 8.7% healthcare practitioners, 11.3% service, 23.6% sales and office, 3.2% natural resources, construction, and maintenance, 4.5% production, transportation, and material moving
Income: Per capita: $45,176; Median household: $67,926; Average household: $103,122; Households with income of $100,000 or more: 33.4%; Poverty rate: 5.0%
Educational Attainment: High school diploma or higher: 94.6%; Bachelor's degree or higher: 55.1%; Graduate/professional degree or higher: 20.8%

School District(s)

Rocky River City (PK-12)
2012-13 Enrollment: 2,627 .... (440) 333-6000

Two-year College(s)

Brown Aveda Institute-Rocky River (Private, For-profit)
Fall 2013 Enrollment: 151 .... (440) 255-9494

Vocational/Technical School(s)

Harmony Path School of Massage Therapy (Private, For-profit)
Fall 2013 Enrollment: 16 .... (440) 333-6633
Housing: Homeownership rate: 72.1%; Median home value: $199,100; Median year structure built: 1958; Homeowner vacancy rate: 2.4%; Median gross rent: $802 per month; Rental vacancy rate: 13.1%
Health Insurance: 94.0% have insurance; 83.1% have private insurance; 28.1% have public insurance; 6.0% do not have insurance; 1.9% of children under 18 do not have insurance
Transportation: Commute: 90.5% car, 2.5% public transportation, 0.9% walk, 5.4% work from home; Median travel time to work: 23.6 minutes
Additional Information Contacts
City of Rocky River .... (440) 331-0600
http://www.rrcity.com

SEVEN HILLS (city). Covers a land area of 4.907 square miles and a water area of 0.007 square miles. Located at 41.38° N. Lat; 81.68° W. Long. Elevation is 883 feet.
History: Named for the seven hills of Rome. Incorporated as a city 1961. Part of its city hall is an old schoolhouse, built in 1861.
Population: 11,804; Growth (since 2000): -2.3%; Density: 2,405.3 persons per square mile; Race: 95.6% White, 0.8% Black/African American, 2.5% Asian, 0.1% American Indian/Alaska Native, 0.0% Native Hawaiian/Other Pacific Islander, 0.7% Two or more races, 1.3% Hispanic of any race; Average household size: 2.36; Median age: 50.0; Age under 18: 16.3%; Age 65 and over: 26.3%; Males per 100 females: 95.0; Marriage status: 25.0% never married, 58.8% now married, 0.6% separated, 8.2% widowed, 8.0% divorced; Foreign born: 14.3%; Speak English only: 79.6%; With disability: 13.5%; Veterans: 10.9%; Ancestry: 23.5% Polish, 19.4% Italian, 18.1% German, 12.3% Irish, 7.0% Slovak
Employment: 18.1% management, business, and financial, 9.2% computer, engineering, and science, 11.7% education, legal, community service, arts, and media, 8.2% healthcare practitioners, 10.4% service, 25.5% sales and office, 7.5% natural resources, construction, and maintenance, 9.4% production, transportation, and material moving
Income: Per capita: $34,559; Median household: $66,794; Average household: $82,262; Households with income of $100,000 or more: 28.6%; Poverty rate: 4.1%
Educational Attainment: High school diploma or higher: 89.3%; Bachelor's degree or higher: 34.2%; Graduate/professional degree or higher: 10.8%

School District(s)

Parma City (PK-12)
2012-13 Enrollment: 11,315 .... (440) 842-5300
Housing: Homeownership rate: 94.7%; Median home value: $166,000; Median year structure built: 1966; Homeowner vacancy rate: 1.3%; Median gross rent: $1,110 per month; Rental vacancy rate: 2.6%
Health Insurance: 95.2% have insurance; 82.8% have private insurance; 30.6% have public insurance; 4.8% do not have insurance; 2.4% of children under 18 do not have insurance
Safety: Violent crime rate: 4.3 per 10,000 population; Property crime rate: 41.0 per 10,000 population
Transportation: Commute: 94.4% car, 1.3% public transportation, 0.4% walk, 3.0% work from home; Median travel time to work: 25.7 minutes
Additional Information Contacts
City of Seven Hills .... (216) 524-4421
http://www.sevenhillsohio.org

SHAKER HEIGHTS (city). Covers a land area of 6.282 square miles and a water area of 0.042 square miles. Located at 41.48° N. Lat; 81.55° W. Long. Elevation is 1,050 feet.
History: Named for a community of Shakers founded in the region in the early 1800s. The Shakers founded a religious community here in the early 1800's. The site was acquired in 1905 by O.P. and M.J. VanSweringen, railroad tycoons, who connected it with downtown Cleveland by a rapid transit line. Shaker Heights grew as a residential area.
Population: 28,448; Growth (since 2000): -3.3%; Density: 4,528.2 persons per square mile; Race: 55.0% White, 37.1% Black/African American, 4.6% Asian, 0.1% American Indian/Alaska Native, 0.0% Native Hawaiian/Other Pacific Islander, 2.7% Two or more races, 2.2% Hispanic of any race; Average household size: 2.39; Median age: 40.9; Age under 18: 26.7%; Age 65 and over: 15.5%; Males per 100 females: 82.5; Marriage status: 28.7% never married, 54.4% now married, 1.1% separated, 6.4% widowed, 10.5% divorced; Foreign born: 8.8%; Speak English only: 89.4%; With disability: 8.5%; Veterans: 6.7%; Ancestry: 11.4% German, 8.7% English, 8.3% Irish, 5.7% Italian, 4.0% Polish
Employment: 21.5% management, business, and financial, 7.4% computer, engineering, and science, 24.6% education, legal, community service, arts, and media, 12.5% healthcare practitioners, 10.0% service, 17.1% sales and office, 2.3% natural resources, construction, and maintenance, 4.5% production, transportation, and material moving
Income: Per capita: $48,868; Median household: $77,951; Average household: $122,111; Households with income of $100,000 or more: 39.7%; Poverty rate: 9.2%
Educational Attainment: High school diploma or higher: 95.9%; Bachelor's degree or higher: 65.3%; Graduate/professional degree or higher: 38.7%

School District(s)

Shaker Heights City (PK-12)
2012-13 Enrollment: 5,396 .... (216) 295-4000
Housing: Homeownership rate: 63.9%; Median home value: $223,800; Median year structure built: 1945; Homeowner vacancy rate: 4.0%; Median gross rent: $943 per month; Rental vacancy rate: 13.7%
Health Insurance: 93.7% have insurance; 83.3% have private insurance; 24.2% have public insurance; 6.3% do not have insurance; 2.1% of children under 18 do not have insurance
Safety: Violent crime rate: 14.7 per 10,000 population; Property crime rate: 230.7 per 10,000 population
Transportation: Commute: 83.7% car, 5.8% public transportation, 2.0% walk, 6.6% work from home; Median travel time to work: 23.0 minutes
Additional Information Contacts

City of Shaker Heights. . . . . (216) 491-1400
http://www.shakeronline.com

SOLON (city). Covers a land area of 20.361 square miles and a water area of 0.130 square miles. Located at 41.39° N. Lat; 81.44° W. Long. Elevation is 1,040 feet.

History: Named for Solon Bull, one of the town's early settlers. Founded 1820. Incorporated as a city 1960.

Population: 23,348; Growth (since 2000): 7.1%; Density: 1,146.7 persons per square mile; Race: 77.5% White, 10.6% Black/African American, 10.0% Asian, 0.1% American Indian/Alaska Native, 0.0% Native Hawaiian/Other Pacific Islander, 1.4% Two or more races, 1.5% Hispanic of any race; Average household size: 2.78; Median age: 43.1; Age under 18: 27.8%; Age 65 and over: 12.4%; Males per 100 females: 95.1; Marriage status: 20.9% never married, 66.4% now married, 0.7% separated, 5.1% widowed, 7.6% divorced; Foreign born: 13.8%; Speak English only: 82.5%; With disability: 7.5%; Veterans: 6.9%; Ancestry: 15.1% German, 11.1% Italian, 9.1% Irish, 8.6% Polish, 7.9% Russian

Employment: 23.8% management, business, and financial, 7.1% computer, engineering, and science, 14.3% education, legal, community service, arts, and media, 9.8% healthcare practitioners, 12.1% service, 24.5% sales and office, 3.5% natural resources, construction, and maintenance, 4.9% production, transportation, and material moving

Income: Per capita: $47,332; Median household: $97,181; Average household: $133,209; Households with income of $100,000 or more: 48.4%; Poverty rate: 3.8%

Educational Attainment: High school diploma or higher: 96.3%; Bachelor's degree or higher: 56.6%; Graduate/professional degree or higher: 27.4%

School District(s)

Solon City (PK-12)
2012-13 Enrollment: 4,965 . . . . (440) 248-1600

Housing: Homeownership rate: 86.9%; Median home value: $266,300; Median year structure built: 1982; Homeowner vacancy rate: 1.3%; Median gross rent: $1,047 per month; Rental vacancy rate: 7.9%

Health Insurance: 95.0% have insurance; 87.0% have private insurance; 18.7% have public insurance; 5.0% do not have insurance; 2.9% of children under 18 do not have insurance

Safety: Violent crime rate: 3.0 per 10,000 population; Property crime rate: 111.2 per 10,000 population

Transportation: Commute: 93.3% car, 0.2% public transportation, 0.6% walk, 5.4% work from home; Median travel time to work: 25.5 minutes

Additional Information Contacts

City of Solon . . . . (440) 248-1155
http://www.solonohio.org

SOUTH EUCLID (city). Covers a land area of 4.651 square miles and a water area of 0 square miles. Located at 41.52° N. Lat; 81.52° W. Long. Elevation is 958 feet.

History: Named for Euclid, the mathematician of Alexandria. Site of Notre Dame College, a Roman Catholic school for women. Incorporated as a city 1940.

Population: 22,295; Growth (since 2000): -5.3%; Density: 4,794.0 persons per square mile; Race: 54.1% White, 40.7% Black/African American, 2.0% Asian, 0.1% American Indian/Alaska Native, 0.0% Native Hawaiian/Other Pacific Islander, 2.5% Two or more races, 2.0% Hispanic of any race; Average household size: 2.43; Median age: 37.9; Age under 18: 24.0%; Age 65 and over: 12.9%; Males per 100 females: 83.9; Marriage status: 41.0% never married, 39.9% now married, 1.6% separated, 7.1% widowed, 12.1% divorced; Foreign born: 6.3%; Speak English only: 91.1%; With disability: 10.0%; Veterans: 6.2%; Ancestry: 12.9% German, 10.6% Irish, 10.3% Italian, 5.8% Polish, 4.5% Russian

Employment: 15.4% management, business, and financial, 6.8% computer, engineering, and science, 13.1% education, legal, community service, arts, and media, 8.1% healthcare practitioners, 16.6% service, 27.0% sales and office, 5.3% natural resources, construction, and maintenance, 7.8% production, transportation, and material moving

Income: Per capita: $27,704; Median household: $59,968; Average household: $68,039; Households with income of $100,000 or more: 20.7%; Poverty rate: 8.3%

Educational Attainment: High school diploma or higher: 93.7%; Bachelor's degree or higher: 38.8%; Graduate/professional degree or higher: 16.0%

School District(s)

South Euclid-Lyndhurst City (PK-12)
2012-13 Enrollment: 3,981 . . . . (216) 691-2000

Housing: Homeownership rate: 80.2%; Median home value: $114,100; Median year structure built: 1954; Homeowner vacancy rate: 3.3%; Median gross rent: $966 per month; Rental vacancy rate: 6.9%

Health Insurance: 90.3% have insurance; 74.1% have private insurance; 25.1% have public insurance; 9.7% do not have insurance; 4.9% of children under 18 do not have insurance

Safety: Violent crime rate: 14.1 per 10,000 population; Property crime rate: 215.2 per 10,000 population

Transportation: Commute: 89.9% car, 2.7% public transportation, 2.0% walk, 4.0% work from home; Median travel time to work: 24.2 minutes

Additional Information Contacts

City of South Euclid . . . . (216) 381-0400
http://www.cityofsoutheuclid.com

STRONGSVILLE (city). Covers a land area of 24.627 square miles and a water area of 0.007 square miles. Located at 41.31° N. Lat; 81.83° W. Long. Elevation is 932 feet.

History: Named for Caleb Strong (1745-1819), a Massachusetts statesman. The city's population doubled between 1970 and 1990. Settled 1816. Incorporated 1927.

Population: 44,750; Growth (since 2000): 2.0%; Density: 1,817.1 persons per square mile; Race: 92.0% White, 1.9% Black/African American, 4.1% Asian, 0.1% American Indian/Alaska Native, 0.0% Native Hawaiian/Other Pacific Islander, 1.4% Two or more races, 2.0% Hispanic of any race; Average household size: 2.52; Median age: 44.2; Age under 18: 23.3%; Age 65 and over: 16.1%; Males per 100 females: 94.7; Marriage status: 23.4% never married, 62.1% now married, 0.8% separated, 7.1% widowed, 7.5% divorced; Foreign born: 8.4%; Speak English only: 89.4%; With disability: 9.2%; Veterans: 8.4%; Ancestry: 28.5% German, 16.5% Irish, 13.0% Polish, 12.6% Italian, 10.1% English

Employment: 20.9% management, business, and financial, 8.5% computer, engineering, and science, 10.3% education, legal, community service, arts, and media, 7.7% healthcare practitioners, 11.0% service, 28.2% sales and office, 4.5% natural resources, construction, and maintenance, 8.8% production, transportation, and material moving

Income: Per capita: $37,401; Median household: $76,397; Average household: $94,668; Households with income of $100,000 or more: 37.9%; Poverty rate: 5.0%

Educational Attainment: High school diploma or higher: 94.5%; Bachelor's degree or higher: 43.0%; Graduate/professional degree or higher: 16.1%

School District(s)

Strongsville City (PK-12)
2012-13 Enrollment: 6,179 . . . . (440) 572-7000

Four-year College(s)

ITT Technical Institute-Strongsville (Private, For-profit)
Fall 2013 Enrollment: 391 . . . . (440) 234-9091
2013-14 Tuition: In-state $18,048; Out-of-state $18,048

Housing: Homeownership rate: 80.8%; Median home value: $193,700; Median year structure built: 1980; Homeowner vacancy rate: 1.4%; Median gross rent: $810 per month; Rental vacancy rate: 8.5%

Health Insurance: 94.6% have insurance; 85.4% have private insurance; 21.6% have public insurance; 5.4% do not have insurance; 3.1% of children under 18 do not have insurance

Safety: Violent crime rate: 6.1 per 10,000 population; Property crime rate: 167.3 per 10,000 population

Transportation: Commute: 91.8% car, 2.0% public transportation, 1.2% walk, 4.3% work from home; Median travel time to work: 27.3 minutes

Additional Information Contacts

City of Strongsville. . . . . (440) 580-3100
http://www.strongsville.org

UNIVERSITY HEIGHTS (city). Covers a land area of 1.820 square miles and a water area of 0 square miles. Located at 41.49° N. Lat; 81.53° W. Long. Elevation is 1,027 feet.

History: Named for it being home to John Carroll University. University Heights grew as a residential community. It took its name from John Carroll University, a liberal arts college founded here by the Jesuit Order in 1886.

Population: 13,539; Growth (since 2000): -4.3%; Density: 7,437.9 persons per square mile; Race: 71.8% White, 23.1% Black/African American, 2.4% Asian, 0.1% American Indian/Alaska Native, 0.0% Native Hawaiian/Other

Pacific Islander, 1.6% Two or more races, 2.8% Hispanic of any race; Average household size: 2.48; Median age: 30.7; Age under 18: 22.7%; Age 65 and over: 11.7%; Males per 100 females: 91.0; Marriage status: 41.6% never married, 47.8% now married, 0.8% separated, 4.2% widowed, 6.4% divorced; Foreign born: 7.9%; Speak English only: 88.8%; With disability: 8.5%; Veterans: 5.0%; Ancestry: 18.6% German, 16.5% Irish, 9.9% Italian, 6.2% Polish, 5.8% English
Employment: 21.9% management, business, and financial, 8.4% computer, engineering, and science, 19.4% education, legal, community service, arts, and media, 11.6% healthcare practitioners, 11.0% service, 22.2% sales and office, 2.0% natural resources, construction, and maintenance, 3.5% production, transportation, and material moving
Income: Per capita: $30,541; Median household: $67,826; Average household: $84,553; Households with income of $100,000 or more: 32.6%; Poverty rate: 8.9%
Educational Attainment: High school diploma or higher: 96.3%; Bachelor's degree or higher: 64.1%; Graduate/professional degree or higher: 33.9%

School District(s)

Cleveland Heights-University Heights City (PK-12)
2012-13 Enrollment: 5,845 . . . . (216) 371-7171

Four-year College(s)

John Carroll University (Private, Not-for-profit, Roman Catholic)
Fall 2013 Enrollment: 3,711 . . . . (216) 397-1886
2013-14 Tuition: In-state $34,480; Out-of-state $34,480
Housing: Homeownership rate: 69.8%; Median home value: $159,100; Median year structure built: 1948; Homeowner vacancy rate: 3.4%; Median gross rent: $1,011 per month; Rental vacancy rate: 9.5%
Health Insurance: 95.9% have insurance; 82.4% have private insurance; 23.8% have public insurance; 4.1% do not have insurance; 1.5% of children under 18 do not have insurance
Safety: Violent crime rate: 17.1 per 10,000 population; Property crime rate: 208.7 per 10,000 population
Transportation: Commute: 82.5% car, 2.6% public transportation, 7.2% walk, 7.1% work from home; Median travel time to work: 22.2 minutes
Additional Information Contacts
City of University Heights . . . . (216) 932-7800
http://www.universityheights.com

VALLEY VIEW (village). Covers a land area of 5.437 square miles and a water area of 0.134 square miles. Located at 41.38° N. Lat; 81.61° W. Long. Elevation is 643 feet.
Population: 2,034; Growth (since 2000): -6.7%; Density: 374.1 persons per square mile; Race: 96.9% White, 0.2% Black/African American, 0.9% Asian, 0.0% American Indian/Alaska Native, 0.1% Native Hawaiian/Other Pacific Islander, 1.4% Two or more races, 1.3% Hispanic of any race; Average household size: 2.68; Median age: 47.3; Age under 18: 21.2%; Age 65 and over: 16.3%; Males per 100 females: 102.6

Vocational/Technical School(s)

Ohio Center for Broadcasting-Valley View (Private, For-profit)
Fall 2013 Enrollment: 172 . . . . (216) 503-5900
2013-14 Tuition: $16,322
Housing: Homeownership rate: 91.1%; Homeowner vacancy rate: 0.3%; Rental vacancy rate: 5.6%
Newspapers: Sun Newspapers (weekly circulation 355000)
Additional Information Contacts
Village of Valley View . . . . (216) 524-6511
http://www.valleyview.net

WALTON HILLS (village). Covers a land area of 6.756 square miles and a water area of 0.046 square miles. Located at 41.37° N. Lat; 81.55° W. Long. Elevation is 988 feet.
Population: 2,281; Growth (since 2000): -5.0%; Density: 337.6 persons per square mile; Race: 90.7% White, 8.1% Black/African American, 0.3% Asian, 0.2% American Indian/Alaska Native, 0.0% Native Hawaiian/Other Pacific Islander, 0.7% Two or more races, 0.7% Hispanic of any race; Average household size: 2.27; Median age: 55.4; Age under 18: 11.2%; Age 65 and over: 30.8%; Males per 100 females: 91.7
Housing: Homeownership rate: 96.3%; Homeowner vacancy rate: 0.8%; Rental vacancy rate: 7.5%
Safety: Violent crime rate: 0.0 per 10,000 population; Property crime rate: 111.1 per 10,000 population

---

WARRENSVILLE HEIGHTS (city). Covers a land area of 4.132 square miles and a water area of 0.005 square miles. Located at 41.44° N. Lat; 81.52° W. Long. Elevation is 1,037 feet.
History: Named for the David Warren family. Incorporated 1927.
Population: 13,542; Growth (since 2000): -10.4%; Density: 3,277.7 persons per square mile; Race: 3.6% White, 93.5% Black/African American, 0.3% Asian, 0.2% American Indian/Alaska Native, 0.0% Native Hawaiian/Other Pacific Islander, 2.0% Two or more races, 1.4% Hispanic of any race; Average household size: 2.22; Median age: 39.2; Age under 18: 24.5%; Age 65 and over: 17.5%; Males per 100 females: 74.4; Marriage status: 40.7% never married, 34.9% now married, 3.7% separated, 8.0% widowed, 16.4% divorced; Foreign born: 2.3%; Speak English only: 95.8%; With disability: 12.8%; Veterans: 10.0%; Ancestry: 3.2% African, 1.5% American, 1.2% Irish, 1.2% Somalian, 1.1% Jamaican
Employment: 7.8% management, business, and financial, 2.5% computer, engineering, and science, 11.9% education, legal, community service, arts, and media, 3.1% healthcare practitioners, 21.7% service, 30.5% sales and office, 4.8% natural resources, construction, and maintenance, 17.6% production, transportation, and material moving
Income: Per capita: $19,831; Median household: $35,461; Average household: $43,183; Households with income of $100,000 or more: 5.0%; Poverty rate: 19.3%
Educational Attainment: High school diploma or higher: 87.2%; Bachelor's degree or higher: 16.3%; Graduate/professional degree or higher: 4.2%

School District(s)

Warrensville Heights City (PK-12)
2012-13 Enrollment: 1,744 . . . . (216) 295-7710

Four-year College(s)

ITT Technical Institute-Warrensville Heights (Private, For-profit)
Fall 2013 Enrollment: 458 . . . . (216) 896-6500
2013-14 Tuition: In-state $18,048; Out-of-state $18,048
Housing: Homeownership rate: 43.3%; Median home value: $93,600; Median year structure built: 1960; Homeowner vacancy rate: 2.9%; Median gross rent: $773 per month; Rental vacancy rate: 10.0%
Health Insurance: 87.6% have insurance; 58.9% have private insurance; 42.8% have public insurance; 12.4% do not have insurance; 2.8% of children under 18 do not have insurance
Hospitals: South Pointe Hospital (232 beds)
Transportation: Commute: 87.1% car, 9.4% public transportation, 1.9% walk, 1.3% work from home; Median travel time to work: 26.2 minutes
Additional Information Contacts
City of Warrensville Heights . . . . (216) 587-6500
http://www.cityofwarrensville.com

WESTLAKE (city). Covers a land area of 15.926 square miles and a water area of 0.004 square miles. Located at 41.45° N. Lat; 81.93° W. Long. Elevation is 709 feet.
History: Named for its location southwest of Lakewood. Incorporated as a city 1956.
Population: 32,729; Growth (since 2000): 3.2%; Density: 2,055.1 persons per square mile; Race: 91.2% White, 1.6% Black/African American, 4.9% Asian, 0.1% American Indian/Alaska Native, 0.1% Native Hawaiian/Other Pacific Islander, 1.6% Two or more races, 2.5% Hispanic of any race; Average household size: 2.30; Median age: 45.0; Age under 18: 21.5%; Age 65 and over: 19.0%; Males per 100 females: 90.2; Marriage status: 24.8% never married, 56.9% now married, 0.6% separated, 8.2% widowed, 10.1% divorced; Foreign born: 11.2%; Speak English only: 84.2%; With disability: 9.6%; Veterans: 8.8%; Ancestry: 27.0% German, 21.9% Irish, 11.4% English, 8.0% Italian, 6.6% Polish
Employment: 24.4% management, business, and financial, 8.5% computer, engineering, and science, 12.5% education, legal, community service, arts, and media, 11.2% healthcare practitioners, 11.2% service, 22.6% sales and office, 3.5% natural resources, construction, and maintenance, 6.0% production, transportation, and material moving
Income: Per capita: $46,684; Median household: $76,358; Average household: $110,717; Households with income of $100,000 or more: 37.7%; Poverty rate: 4.2%
Educational Attainment: High school diploma or higher: 95.1%; Bachelor's degree or higher: 52.4%; Graduate/professional degree or higher: 20.9%

School District(s)

Westlake City (PK-12)
2012-13 Enrollment: 3,929 . . . . (440) 871-7300

Housing: Homeownership rate: 72.5%; Median home value: $228,800; Median year structure built: 1981; Homeowner vacancy rate: 2.1%; Median gross rent: $997 per month; Rental vacancy rate: 9.1%
Health Insurance: 95.0% have insurance; 86.7% have private insurance; 21.8% have public insurance; 5.0% do not have insurance; 3.6% of children under 18 do not have insurance
Hospitals: Saint John Medical Center (200 beds)
Transportation: Commute: 92.0% car, 1.4% public transportation, 1.0% walk, 4.6% work from home; Median travel time to work: 24.3 minutes
Additional Information Contacts
City of Westlake . . . . (440) 871-3300
http://www.cityofwestlake.org

WOODMERE (village). Covers a land area of 0.334 square miles and a water area of 0 square miles. Located at 41.46° N. Lat; 81.48° W. Long. Elevation is 1,171 feet.
Population: 884; Growth (since 2000): 6.8%; Density: 2,650.3 persons per square mile; Race: 29.5% White, 61.9% Black/African American, 3.7% Asian, 0.0% American Indian/Alaska Native, 0.0% Native Hawaiian/Other Pacific Islander, 3.8% Two or more races, 3.7% Hispanic of any race; Average household size: 1.98; Median age: 37.9; Age under 18: 23.5%; Age 65 and over: 11.0%; Males per 100 females: 72.0
Housing: Homeownership rate: 30.7%; Homeowner vacancy rate: 2.1%; Rental vacancy rate: 3.1%
Safety: Violent crime rate: 45.9 per 10,000 population; Property crime rate: 401.8 per 10,000 population

Darke County

Located in western Ohio; bounded on the west by Indiana; drained by Greenville Creek and the Stillwater and Mississinewa Rivers. Covers a land area of 598.100 square miles, a water area of 1.657 square miles, and is located in the Eastern Time Zone at 40.13° N. Lat., 84.62° W. Long. The county was founded in 1809. County seat is Greenville.

Darke County is part of the Greenville, OH Micropolitan Statistical Area. The entire metro area includes: Darke County, OH

Weather Station: Greenville Water Plant Elevation: 1,023 feet

	Jan	Feb	Mar	Apr	May	Jun	Jul	Aug	Sep	Oct	Nov	Dec
High	33	37	48	61	71	80	83	82	77	64	51	38
Low	17	19	28	38	49	59	62	59	51	40	32	22
Precip	2.4	2.1	3.0	3.7	4.5	4.2	4.3	3.2	2.6	2.9	3.2	2.8
Snow	7.3	6.0	3.0	0.5	tr	0.0	0.0	0.0	0.0	0.2	0.7	4.3

High and Low temperatures in degrees Fahrenheit; Precipitation and Snow in inches

Population: 52,959; Growth (since 2000): -0.7%; Density: 88.5 persons per square mile; Race: 97.8% White, 0.4% Black/African American, 0.3% Asian, 0.2% American Indian/Alaska Native, 0.0% Native Hawaiian/Other Pacific Islander, 0.9% two or more races, 1.2% Hispanic of any race; Average household size: 2.50; Median age: 40.8; Age under 18: 24.9%; Age 65 and over: 16.9%; Males per 100 females: 96.6; Marriage status: 23.3% never married, 58.7% now married, 1.1% separated, 7.1% widowed, 11.0% divorced; Foreign born: 0.7%; Speak English only: 98.5%; With disability: 13.0%; Veterans: 9.5%; Ancestry: 40.2% German, 13.4% American, 11.5% Irish, 8.9% English, 6.0% French
Religion: Six largest groups: 13.4% Catholicism, 6.5% Methodist/Pietist, 4.3% European Free-Church, 4.0% Lutheran, 3.6% Baptist, 3.5% Non-denominational Protestant
Economy: Unemployment rate: 3.7%; Leading industries: 14.9% retail trade; 14.7% other services (except public administration); 14.5% construction; Farms: 1,693 totaling 339,981 acres; Company size: 0 employ 1,000 or more persons, 3 employ 500 to 999 persons, 15 employ 100 to 499 persons, 1,133 employ less than 100 persons; Business ownership: 1,108 women-owned, n/a Black-owned, n/a Hispanic-owned, n/a Asian-owned
Employment: 10.4% management, business, and financial, 2.4% computer, engineering, and science, 7.3% education, legal, community service, arts, and media, 4.7% healthcare practitioners, 16.4% service, 20.6% sales and office, 12.4% natural resources, construction, and maintenance, 25.8% production, transportation, and material moving
Income: Per capita: $22,511; Median household: $43,425; Average household: $56,065; Households with income of $100,000 or more: 11.9%; Poverty rate: 13.7%
Educational Attainment: High school diploma or higher: 87.0%; Bachelor's degree or higher: 11.9%; Graduate/professional degree or higher: 4.9%
Housing: Homeownership rate: 74.7%; Median home value: $110,600; Median year structure built: 1957; Homeowner vacancy rate: 2.0%; Median gross rent: $585 per month; Rental vacancy rate: 7.9%
Vital Statistics: Birth rate: 119.7 per 10,000 population; Death rate: 108.4 per 10,000 population; Age-adjusted cancer mortality rate: 171.0 deaths per 100,000 population
Health Insurance: 87.6% have insurance; 69.2% have private insurance; 33.3% have public insurance; 12.4% do not have insurance; 8.9% of children under 18 do not have insurance
Health Care: Physicians: 6.7 per 10,000 population; Hospital beds: 13.9 per 10,000 population; Hospital admissions: 429.9 per 10,000 population
Transportation: Commute: 92.5% car, 0.7% public transportation, 1.6% walk, 4.1% work from home; Median travel time to work: 22.5 minutes
Presidential Election: 26.6% Obama, 71.5% Romney (2012)
National and State Parks: Fort Jefferson State Memorial; Treaty of Greenville State Park
Additional Information Contacts
Darke Government . . . . (937) 547-7370
http://www.co.darke.oh.us

Darke County Communities

ANSONIA (village). Covers a land area of 0.785 square miles and a water area of 0.021 square miles. Located at 40.21° N. Lat; 84.63° W. Long. Elevation is 1,001 feet.
Population: 1,174; Growth (since 2000): 2.5%; Density: 1,495.3 persons per square mile; Race: 98.8% White, 0.0% Black/African American, 0.2% Asian, 0.3% American Indian/Alaska Native, 0.0% Native Hawaiian/Other Pacific Islander, 0.6% Two or more races, 1.6% Hispanic of any race; Average household size: 2.62; Median age: 35.4; Age under 18: 27.6%; Age 65 and over: 10.3%; Males per 100 females: 94.0

School District(s)

Ansonia Local (PK-12)
2012-13 Enrollment: 789. . . . . (937) 337-4000
Housing: Homeownership rate: 67.6%; Homeowner vacancy rate: 1.3%; Rental vacancy rate: 11.0%

ARCANUM (village). Covers a land area of 1.299 square miles and a water area of 0 square miles. Located at 39.99° N. Lat; 84.55° W. Long. Elevation is 1,047 feet.
Population: 2,129; Growth (since 2000): 2.6%; Density: 1,638.4 persons per square mile; Race: 98.8% White, 0.1% Black/African American, 0.2% Asian, 0.0% American Indian/Alaska Native, 0.0% Native Hawaiian/Other Pacific Islander, 0.7% Two or more races, 0.3% Hispanic of any race; Average household size: 2.40; Median age: 37.4; Age under 18: 26.5%; Age 65 and over: 17.1%; Males per 100 females: 89.9

School District(s)

Arcanum-Butler Local (PK-12)
2012-13 Enrollment: 1,038 . . . . (937) 692-5174
Franklin Monroe Local (PK-12)
2012-13 Enrollment: 718. . . . . (937) 947-1212
Housing: Homeownership rate: 70.4%; Homeowner vacancy rate: 3.8%; Rental vacancy rate: 10.1%
Safety: Violent crime rate: 0.0 per 10,000 population; Property crime rate: 157.3 per 10,000 population

CASTINE (village). Covers a land area of 0.076 square miles and a water area of 0 square miles. Located at 39.93° N. Lat; 84.62° W. Long. Elevation is 1,076 feet.
Population: 130; Growth (since 2000): 0.8%; Density: 1,714.9 persons per square mile; Race: 97.7% White, 0.0% Black/African American, 0.0% Asian, 0.8% American Indian/Alaska Native, 0.0% Native Hawaiian/Other Pacific Islander, 0.8% Two or more races, 0.0% Hispanic of any race; Average household size: 2.41; Median age: 35.5; Age under 18: 23.8%; Age 65 and over: 16.2%; Males per 100 females: 97.0
Housing: Homeownership rate: 61.1%; Homeowner vacancy rate: 0.0%; Rental vacancy rate: 4.3%

GETTYSBURG (village). Covers a land area of 0.436 square miles and a water area of <.001 square miles. Located at 40.12° N. Lat; 84.50° W. Long. Elevation is 994 feet.
Population: 513; Growth (since 2000): -8.1%; Density: 1,177.2 persons per square mile; Race: 97.5% White, 0.4% Black/African American, 0.2% Asian, 0.0% American Indian/Alaska Native, 0.0% Native Hawaiian/Other Pacific Islander, 1.8% Two or more races, 0.6% Hispanic of any race; Average household size: 3.02; Median age: 32.7; Age under 18: 32.4%; Age 65 and over: 9.6%; Males per 100 females: 96.6
Housing: Homeownership rate: 78.3%; Homeowner vacancy rate: 4.3%; Rental vacancy rate: 9.8%

GORDON (village). Covers a land area of 0.165 square miles and a water area of 0 square miles. Located at 39.93° N. Lat; 84.51° W. Long. Elevation is 1,047 feet.
Population: 212; Growth (since 2000): 11.6%; Density: 1,288.2 persons per square mile; Race: 97.6% White, 0.5% Black/African American, 0.0% Asian, 0.5% American Indian/Alaska Native, 0.0% Native Hawaiian/Other Pacific Islander, 0.9% Two or more races, 0.0% Hispanic of any race; Average household size: 2.86; Median age: 40.8; Age under 18: 25.0%; Age 65 and over: 13.7%; Males per 100 females: 114.1
Housing: Homeownership rate: 90.5%; Homeowner vacancy rate: 1.5%; Rental vacancy rate: 0.0%

GREENVILLE (city). County seat. Covers a land area of 6.604 square miles and a water area of 0.063 square miles. Located at 40.10° N. Lat; 84.62° W. Long. Elevation is 1,043 feet.
History: Fort Greenville, established here and named for General Nathanael Greene, was abandoned in 1795. A town was founded here in 1805 by the Swawnee chieftain, Tecumseh, and his brother, Tenakwatawa, known as The Prophet. After Prophet's Town was moved to Indiana, other settlers came and the town of Greenville was founded.
Population: 13,227; Growth (since 2000): -0.5%; Density: 2,002.9 persons per square mile; Race: 96.7% White, 0.9% Black/African American, 0.7% Asian, 0.2% American Indian/Alaska Native, 0.0% Native Hawaiian/Other Pacific Islander, 1.1% Two or more races, 1.4% Hispanic of any race; Average household size: 2.17; Median age: 43.4; Age under 18: 21.5%; Age 65 and over: 22.5%; Males per 100 females: 85.4; Marriage status: 26.8% never married, 46.6% now married, 1.6% separated, 11.4% widowed, 15.2% divorced; Foreign born: 0.9%; Speak English only: 98.2%; With disability: 19.2%; Veterans: 8.3%; Ancestry: 37.8% German, 14.9% Irish, 14.3% American, 7.8% English, 3.0% French
Employment: 9.2% management, business, and financial, 1.7% computer, engineering, and science, 7.1% education, legal, community service, arts, and media, 5.1% healthcare practitioners, 17.6% service, 24.7% sales and office, 6.5% natural resources, construction, and maintenance, 28.1% production, transportation, and material moving
Income: Per capita: $20,286; Median household: $31,758; Average household: $42,742; Households with income of $100,000 or more: 7.1%; Poverty rate: 18.4%
Educational Attainment: High school diploma or higher: 84.8%; Bachelor's degree or higher: 11.0%; Graduate/professional degree or higher: 4.6%

School District(s)

Greenville City (PK-12)
2012-13 Enrollment: 2,678 . . . . (937) 548-3185
Housing: Homeownership rate: 59.0%; Median home value: $87,000; Median year structure built: 1957; Homeowner vacancy rate: 2.5%; Median gross rent: $558 per month; Rental vacancy rate: 8.6%
Health Insurance: 85.8% have insurance; 59.5% have private insurance; 44.3% have public insurance; 14.2% do not have insurance; 7.3% of children under 18 do not have insurance
Hospitals: Wayne Hospital (92 beds)
Safety: Violent crime rate: 26.0 per 10,000 population; Property crime rate: 421.8 per 10,000 population
Newspapers: Daily Advocate (daily circulation 6500); The Early Bird (weekly circulation 22400)
Transportation: Commute: 91.2% car, 2.2% public transportation, 1.3% walk, 4.1% work from home; Median travel time to work: 18.3 minutes
Additional Information Contacts
City of Greenville. . . . . (937) 548-1819
http://www.cityofgreenville.org

HOLLANSBURG (village). Covers a land area of 0.121 square miles and a water area of 0 square miles. Located at 40.00° N. Lat; 84.79° W. Long. Elevation is 1,161 feet.
Population: 227; Growth (since 2000): 6.1%; Density: 1,877.3 persons per square mile; Race: 93.8% White, 0.4% Black/African American, 0.0% Asian, 0.0% American Indian/Alaska Native, 0.4% Native Hawaiian/Other Pacific Islander, 3.5% Two or more races, 1.3% Hispanic of any race; Average household size: 2.32; Median age: 40.3; Age under 18: 26.4%; Age 65 and over: 16.3%; Males per 100 females: 116.2
Housing: Homeownership rate: 76.5%; Homeowner vacancy rate: 0.0%; Rental vacancy rate: 14.8%

ITHACA (village). Covers a land area of 0.031 square miles and a water area of 0 square miles. Located at 39.94° N. Lat; 84.55° W. Long. Elevation is 1,033 feet.
Population: 136; Growth (since 2000): 33.3%; Density: 4,355.1 persons per square mile; Race: 99.3% White, 0.0% Black/African American, 0.7% Asian, 0.0% American Indian/Alaska Native, 0.0% Native Hawaiian/Other Pacific Islander, 0.0% Two or more races, 3.7% Hispanic of any race; Average household size: 3.09; Median age: 34.3; Age under 18: 27.9%; Age 65 and over: 12.5%; Males per 100 females: 86.3
Housing: Homeownership rate: 77.3%; Homeowner vacancy rate: 2.6%; Rental vacancy rate: 15.4%

NEW MADISON (village). Covers a land area of 0.410 square miles and a water area of 0 square miles. Located at 39.97° N. Lat; 84.71° W. Long. Elevation is 1,106 feet.
Population: 892; Growth (since 2000): 9.2%; Density: 2,174.8 persons per square mile; Race: 97.8% White, 0.7% Black/African American, 0.3% Asian, 0.1% American Indian/Alaska Native, 0.0% Native Hawaiian/Other Pacific Islander, 0.7% Two or more races, 0.9% Hispanic of any race; Average household size: 2.53; Median age: 36.0; Age under 18: 28.3%; Age 65 and over: 13.3%; Males per 100 females: 91.0

School District(s)

Tri-Village Local (PK-12)
2012-13 Enrollment: 730. . . . . (937) 996-6261
Housing: Homeownership rate: 71.6%; Homeowner vacancy rate: 2.7%; Rental vacancy rate: 10.7%

NEW WESTON (village). Covers a land area of 0.256 square miles and a water area of 0 square miles. Located at 40.34° N. Lat; 84.64° W. Long. Elevation is 1,010 feet.
Population: 136; Growth (since 2000): 0.7%; Density: 531.8 persons per square mile; Race: 97.8% White, 1.5% Black/African American, 0.0% Asian, 0.0% American Indian/Alaska Native, 0.0% Native Hawaiian/Other Pacific Islander, 0.7% Two or more races, 5.1% Hispanic of any race; Average household size: 3.02; Median age: 28.0; Age under 18: 38.2%; Age 65 and over: 7.4%; Males per 100 females: 106.1
Housing: Homeownership rate: 82.2%; Homeowner vacancy rate: 2.6%; Rental vacancy rate: 0.0%

NORTH STAR (village). Covers a land area of 0.525 square miles and a water area of 0 square miles. Located at 40.32° N. Lat; 84.57° W. Long. Elevation is 1,007 feet.
History: North Star was founded in 1844 by John Houston and Heronimus Star. This was the birthplace of Annie Oakley, born in 1860, who became an expert markswoman.
Population: 236; Growth (since 2000): 12.9%; Density: 449.7 persons per square mile; Race: 100.0% White, 0.0% Black/African American, 0.0% Asian, 0.0% American Indian/Alaska Native, 0.0% Native Hawaiian/Other Pacific Islander, 0.0% Two or more races, 0.0% Hispanic of any race; Average household size: 2.68; Median age: 37.0; Age under 18: 30.1%; Age 65 and over: 22.5%; Males per 100 females: 90.3
Housing: Homeownership rate: 84.1%; Homeowner vacancy rate: 0.0%; Rental vacancy rate: 6.7%

OSGOOD (village). Covers a land area of 0.341 square miles and a water area of 0 square miles. Located at 40.34° N. Lat; 84.50° W. Long. Elevation is 958 feet.
Population: 302; Growth (since 2000): 18.4%; Density: 885.4 persons per square mile; Race: 98.3% White, 0.0% Black/African American, 0.0% Asian, 1.7% American Indian/Alaska Native, 0.0% Native Hawaiian/Other Pacific Islander, 0.0% Two or more races, 1.3% Hispanic of any race; Average household size: 2.52; Median age: 38.4; Age under 18: 28.5%; Age 65 and over: 22.2%; Males per 100 females: 111.2

Housing: Homeownership rate: 88.4%; Homeowner vacancy rate: 0.0%; Rental vacancy rate: 0.0%

PALESTINE (village). Covers a land area of 0.146 square miles and a water area of 0 square miles. Located at 40.05° N. Lat; 84.74° W. Long. Elevation is 1,109 feet.
Population: 200; Growth (since 2000): 17.6%; Density: 1,369.2 persons per square mile; Race: 93.5% White, 5.0% Black/African American, 0.0% Asian, 0.0% American Indian/Alaska Native, 0.0% Native Hawaiian/Other Pacific Islander, 1.5% Two or more races, 0.0% Hispanic of any race; Average household size: 2.53; Median age: 33.5; Age under 18: 30.0%; Age 65 and over: 16.0%; Males per 100 females: 100.0
Housing: Homeownership rate: 64.5%; Homeowner vacancy rate: 3.8%; Rental vacancy rate: 15.2%

PITSBURG (village). Covers a land area of 0.189 square miles and a water area of 0 square miles. Located at 39.99° N. Lat; 84.49° W. Long. Elevation is 1,024 feet.
History: Also spelled Pittsburg.
Population: 388; Growth (since 2000): -1.0%; Density: 2,050.2 persons per square mile; Race: 98.7% White, 0.0% Black/African American, 1.0% Asian, 0.3% American Indian/Alaska Native, 0.0% Native Hawaiian/Other Pacific Islander, 0.0% Two or more races, 0.0% Hispanic of any race; Average household size: 2.62; Median age: 40.3; Age under 18: 27.1%; Age 65 and over: 13.9%; Males per 100 females: 92.1
Housing: Homeownership rate: 79.7%; Homeowner vacancy rate: 4.8%; Rental vacancy rate: 3.2%

ROSSBURG (village). Covers a land area of 0.140 square miles and a water area of 0 square miles. Located at 40.28° N. Lat; 84.64° W. Long. Elevation is 1,030 feet.
Population: 201; Growth (since 2000): -10.3%; Density: 1,433.6 persons per square mile; Race: 100.0% White, 0.0% Black/African American, 0.0% Asian, 0.0% American Indian/Alaska Native, 0.0% Native Hawaiian/Other Pacific Islander, 0.0% Two or more races, 0.5% Hispanic of any race; Average household size: 2.61; Median age: 39.8; Age under 18: 22.4%; Age 65 and over: 10.4%; Males per 100 females: 103.0
Housing: Homeownership rate: 81.8%; Homeowner vacancy rate: 1.5%; Rental vacancy rate: 6.7%

UNION CITY (village). Covers a land area of 0.919 square miles and a water area of 0.047 square miles. Located at 40.20° N. Lat; 84.79° W. Long. Elevation is 1,106 feet.
Population: 1,666; Growth (since 2000): -5.7%; Density: 1,812.1 persons per square mile; Race: 93.1% White, 0.9% Black/African American, 0.4% Asian, 0.2% American Indian/Alaska Native, 0.0% Native Hawaiian/Other Pacific Islander, 2.5% Two or more races, 6.1% Hispanic of any race; Average household size: 2.41; Median age: 38.3; Age under 18: 26.6%; Age 65 and over: 15.2%; Males per 100 females: 90.0

School District(s)

Mississinawa Valley Local (PK-12)
2012-13 Enrollment: 703. . . . . (937) 968-5656
Housing: Homeownership rate: 53.6%; Homeowner vacancy rate: 5.9%; Rental vacancy rate: 7.8%

VERSAILLES (village). Covers a land area of 1.867 square miles and a water area of 0.006 square miles. Located at 40.22° N. Lat; 84.48° W. Long. Elevation is 981 feet.
History: Settled 1819, incorporated 1855.
Population: 2,687; Growth (since 2000): 3.8%; Density: 1,439.4 persons per square mile; Race: 99.0% White, 0.2% Black/African American, 0.0% Asian, 0.1% American Indian/Alaska Native, 0.0% Native Hawaiian/Other Pacific Islander, 0.7% Two or more races, 0.6% Hispanic of any race; Average household size: 2.39; Median age: 39.8; Age under 18: 25.9%; Age 65 and over: 19.4%; Males per 100 females: 91.4; Marriage status: 21.3% never married, 62.1% now married, 0.5% separated, 8.2% widowed, 8.4% divorced; Foreign born: 0.3%; Speak English only: 99.7%; With disability: 10.0%; Veterans: 12.0%; Ancestry: 46.3% German, 28.1% French, 10.4% Irish, 8.5% American, 7.2% English
Employment: 14.7% management, business, and financial, 5.7% computer, engineering, and science, 7.7% education, legal, community service, arts, and media, 5.3% healthcare practitioners, 14.5% service, 20.1% sales and office, 7.2% natural resources, construction, and maintenance, 25.0% production, transportation, and material moving
Income: Per capita: $24,709; Median household: $47,480; Average household: $60,552; Households with income of $100,000 or more: 20.0%; Poverty rate: 5.8%
Educational Attainment: High school diploma or higher: 90.8%; Bachelor's degree or higher: 22.5%; Graduate/professional degree or higher: 7.8%

School District(s)

Versailles Exempted Village (PK-12)
2012-13 Enrollment: 1,386 . . . . (937) 526-4773
Housing: Homeownership rate: 71.5%; Median home value: $129,400; Median year structure built: 1951; Homeowner vacancy rate: 1.3%; Median gross rent: $564 per month; Rental vacancy rate: 8.5%
Health Insurance: 94.3% have insurance; 86.9% have private insurance; 19.8% have public insurance; 5.7% do not have insurance; 1.2% of children under 18 do not have insurance
Newspapers: Versailles Policy (weekly circulation 2400)
Transportation: Commute: 95.1% car, 0.6% public transportation, 2.3% walk, 1.4% work from home; Median travel time to work: 18.7 minutes
Additional Information Contacts
Village of Versailles. . . . . (937) 526-3294
http://www.versaillesohio.cc

WAYNE LAKES (village). Covers a land area of 0.530 square miles and a water area of 0.119 square miles. Located at 40.02° N. Lat; 84.66° W. Long. Elevation is 1,047 feet.
Population: 718; Growth (since 2000): 5.0%; Density: 1,353.6 persons per square mile; Race: 98.2% White, 0.7% Black/African American, 0.0% Asian, 0.1% American Indian/Alaska Native, 0.0% Native Hawaiian/Other Pacific Islander, 0.8% Two or more races, 0.4% Hispanic of any race; Average household size: 2.36; Median age: 43.6; Age under 18: 20.3%; Age 65 and over: 15.9%; Males per 100 females: 97.8
Housing: Homeownership rate: 79.0%; Homeowner vacancy rate: 2.4%; Rental vacancy rate: 1.5%

YORKSHIRE (village). Covers a land area of 0.283 square miles and a water area of 0 square miles. Located at 40.33° N. Lat; 84.50° W. Long. Elevation is 981 feet.
Population: 96; Growth (since 2000): -12.7%; Density: 339.7 persons per square mile; Race: 95.8% White, 0.0% Black/African American, 0.0% Asian, 0.0% American Indian/Alaska Native, 0.0% Native Hawaiian/Other Pacific Islander, 4.2% Two or more races, 0.0% Hispanic of any race; Average household size: 2.67; Median age: 31.3; Age under 18: 24.0%; Age 65 and over: 12.5%; Males per 100 females: 113.3
Housing: Homeownership rate: 83.4%; Homeowner vacancy rate: 3.2%; Rental vacancy rate: 25.0%

Defiance County

Located in northwestern Ohio; bounded on the west by Indiana; intersected by the Maumee, Auglize, and Tiffin Rivers. Covers a land area of 411.460 square miles, a water area of 2.730 square miles, and is located in the Eastern Time Zone at 41.32° N. Lat., 84.49° W. Long. The county was founded in 1845. County seat is Defiance.

Defiance County is part of the Defiance, OH Micropolitan Statistical Area. The entire metro area includes: Defiance County, OH

Weather Station: Defiance Elevation: 700 feet

	Jan	Feb	Mar	Apr	May	Jun	Jul	Aug	Sep	Oct	Nov	Dec
High	32	35	46	60	71	81	84	82	76	63	49	36
Low	17	19	27	38	48	58	62	61	53	42	32	22
Precip	2.0	2.1	2.5	3.4	3.9	3.6	4.1	3.2	3.3	3.0	3.0	2.7
Snow	6.7	5.6	2.5	0.5	tr	0.0	0.0	0.0	0.0	0.1	0.9	4.5

High and Low temperatures in degrees Fahrenheit; Precipitation and Snow in inches

Population: 39,037; Growth (since 2000): -1.2%; Density: 94.9 persons per square mile; Race: 92.8% White, 1.9% Black/African American, 0.3% Asian, 0.3% American Indian/Alaska Native, 0.0% Native Hawaiian/Other Pacific Islander, 2.0% two or more races, 8.7% Hispanic of any race; Average household size: 2.51; Median age: 39.4; Age under 18: 24.6%; Age 65 and over: 15.0%; Males per 100 females: 97.0; Marriage status: 26.8% never married, 56.5% now married, 1.6% separated, 5.8% widowed, 10.9% divorced; Foreign born: 1.8%; Speak English only: 94.4%; With disability: 13.2%; Veterans: 10.9%; Ancestry: 40.0% German, 12.0% Irish, 9.7% English, 7.6% American, 3.6% French

Religion: Six largest groups: 20.5% Catholicism, 15.7% Lutheran, 7.5% Methodist/Pietist, 5.5% Baptist, 4.7% Non-denominational Protestant, 2.6% Holiness
Economy: Unemployment rate: 4.1%; Leading industries: 18.4% retail trade; 14.7% other services (except public administration); 10.8% health care and social assistance; Farms: 1,030 totaling 225,250 acres; Company size: 1 employs 1,000 or more persons, 1 employs 500 to 999 persons, 22 employ 100 to 499 persons, 785 employ less than 100 persons; Business ownership: 863 women-owned, n/a Black-owned, n/a Hispanic-owned, n/a Asian-owned
Employment: 9.4% management, business, and financial, 2.5% computer, engineering, and science, 9.3% education, legal, community service, arts, and media, 5.4% healthcare practitioners, 16.6% service, 22.6% sales and office, 10.5% natural resources, construction, and maintenance, 23.8% production, transportation, and material moving
Income: Per capita: $22,739; Median household: $47,593; Average household: $57,654; Households with income of $100,000 or more: 13.1%; Poverty rate: 13.9%
Educational Attainment: High school diploma or higher: 88.4%; Bachelor's degree or higher: 16.5%; Graduate/professional degree or higher: 5.9%
Housing: Homeownership rate: 77.4%; Median home value: $106,100; Median year structure built: 1963; Homeowner vacancy rate: 2.3%; Median gross rent: $632 per month; Rental vacancy rate: 9.8%
Vital Statistics: Birth rate: 118.1 per 10,000 population; Death rate: 99.7 per 10,000 population; Age-adjusted cancer mortality rate: 225.0 deaths per 100,000 population
Health Insurance: 88.8% have insurance; 72.7% have private insurance; 31.7% have public insurance; 11.2% do not have insurance; 4.7% of children under 18 do not have insurance
Health Care: Physicians: 11.9 per 10,000 population; Hospital beds: 21.3 per 10,000 population; Hospital admissions: 1,315.7 per 10,000 population
Transportation: Commute: 95.1% car, 0.3% public transportation, 1.3% walk, 2.0% work from home; Median travel time to work: 19.8 minutes
Presidential Election: 41.9% Obama, 56.0% Romney (2012)
National and State Parks: Independence Dam State Park; Oxbow Lake State Wildlife Area
Additional Information Contacts
Defiance Government . . . . (419) 782-4761
http://www.defiance-county.com

Defiance County Communities

DEFIANCE (city). County seat. Covers a land area of 11.617 square miles and a water area of 0.509 square miles. Located at 41.28° N. Lat; 84.37° W. Long. Elevation is 676 feet.
History: General Anthony Wayne built a fort here in 1794 and called it Fort Defiance. It was replaced in 1812 by General William Henry Harrison, who built Fort Winchester near Wayne's old fort. The town that developed after the War of 1812 was spurred by the Wabash & Erie Canal and the Miami & Erie Canal, which joined near here.
Population: 16,494; Growth (since 2000): 0.2%; Density: 1,419.8 persons per square mile; Race: 88.1% White, 3.6% Black/African American, 0.4% Asian, 0.3% American Indian/Alaska Native, 0.0% Native Hawaiian/Other Pacific Islander, 2.8% Two or more races, 14.4% Hispanic of any race; Average household size: 2.38; Median age: 37.1; Age under 18: 24.1%; Age 65 and over: 15.3%; Males per 100 females: 93.4; Marriage status: 31.7% never married, 49.0% now married, 1.5% separated, 7.2% widowed, 12.2% divorced; Foreign born: 1.3%; Speak English only: 92.1%; With disability: 15.4%; Veterans: 10.3%; Ancestry: 35.2% German, 12.8% Irish, 9.9% English, 8.1% American, 3.2% Italian
Employment: 8.4% management, business, and financial, 1.5% computer, engineering, and science, 13.2% education, legal, community service, arts, and media, 4.1% healthcare practitioners, 19.2% service, 24.0% sales and office, 7.2% natural resources, construction, and maintenance, 22.3% production, transportation, and material moving
Income: Per capita: $21,962; Median household: $42,395; Average household: $52,910; Households with income of $100,000 or more: 10.4%; Poverty rate: 18.4%
Educational Attainment: High school diploma or higher: 87.1%; Bachelor's degree or higher: 19.5%; Graduate/professional degree or higher: 7.2%

School District(s)

Ayersville Local (PK-12)
2012-13 Enrollment: 759. . . . . (419) 395-1111
Defiance City (PK-12)
2012-13 Enrollment: 2,506 . . . . (419) 782-0070
Northeastern Local (PK-12)
2012-13 Enrollment: 1,114 . . . . (419) 497-3461

Four-year College(s)

Defiance College (Private, Not-for-profit, United Church of Christ)
Fall 2013 Enrollment: 989 . . . . (419) 784-4010
2013-14 Tuition: In-state $28,690; Out-of-state $28,690
Housing: Homeownership rate: 67.1%; Median home value: $98,400; Median year structure built: 1960; Homeowner vacancy rate: 3.3%; Median gross rent: $639 per month; Rental vacancy rate: 9.8%
Health Insurance: 88.0% have insurance; 68.4% have private insurance; 34.4% have public insurance; 12.0% do not have insurance; 1.4% of children under 18 do not have insurance
Hospitals: Defiance Regional Medical Center (61 beds); Mercy Hospital of Defiance
Safety: Violent crime rate: 18.5 per 10,000 population; Property crime rate: 281.7 per 10,000 population
Newspapers: Crescent-News (daily circulation 17300)
Transportation: Commute: 94.5% car, 0.4% public transportation, 1.6% walk, 1.7% work from home; Median travel time to work: 17.5 minutes
Additional Information Contacts
City of Defiance. . . . . (419) 784-2101
http://www.cityofdefiance.com

EVANSPORT (unincorporated postal area)
ZCTA: 43519
Covers a land area of 1.289 square miles and a water area of 0.003 square miles. Located at 41.42° N. Lat; 84.41° W. Long. Elevation is 696 feet.
Population: 184; Growth (since 2000): n/a; Density: 142.7 persons per square mile; Race: 97.3% White, 0.0% Black/African American, 0.0% Asian, 0.0% American Indian/Alaska Native, 0.0% Native Hawaiian/Other Pacific Islander, 1.6% Two or more races, 3.3% Hispanic of any race; Average household size: 2.75; Median age: 37.0; Age under 18: 25.5%; Age 65 and over: 10.9%; Males per 100 females: 100.0
Housing: Homeownership rate: 83.6%; Homeowner vacancy rate: 6.7%; Rental vacancy rate: 0.0%

HICKSVILLE (village). Covers a land area of 2.656 square miles and a water area of 0 square miles. Located at 41.29° N. Lat; 84.76° W. Long. Elevation is 761 feet.
History: Hicksville was founded in 1836 by Henry Hicks, Isaac Smith, and John Bryan as a trading post dealing in furs. The town's industry passed from lumber, to mills and tanneries, and to canning and wood products.
Population: 3,581; Growth (since 2000): -1.9%; Density: 1,348.1 persons per square mile; Race: 94.9% White, 0.3% Black/African American, 0.4% Asian, 0.3% American Indian/Alaska Native, 0.0% Native Hawaiian/Other Pacific Islander, 2.0% Two or more races, 5.1% Hispanic of any race; Average household size: 2.47; Median age: 36.9; Age under 18: 26.0%; Age 65 and over: 16.0%; Males per 100 females: 92.7; Marriage status: 31.0% never married, 45.1% now married, 3.1% separated, 8.5% widowed, 15.4% divorced; Foreign born: 3.0%; Speak English only: 95.5%; With disability: 14.1%; Veterans: 10.2%; Ancestry: 36.9% German, 11.8% American, 10.2% English, 5.1% Irish, 2.5% Dutch
Employment: 7.0% management, business, and financial, 2.5% computer, engineering, and science, 3.3% education, legal, community service, arts, and media, 4.3% healthcare practitioners, 12.3% service, 21.7% sales and office, 7.8% natural resources, construction, and maintenance, 41.1% production, transportation, and material moving
Income: Per capita: $17,089; Median household: $37,544; Average household: $41,746; Households with income of $100,000 or more: 4.2%; Poverty rate: 14.9%
Educational Attainment: High school diploma or higher: 80.8%; Bachelor's degree or higher: 9.7%; Graduate/professional degree or higher: 3.7%

School District(s)

Hicksville Exempted Village (PK-12)
2012-13 Enrollment: 903. . . . . (419) 542-7665
Housing: Homeownership rate: 70.4%; Median home value: $81,400; Median year structure built: 1956; Homeowner vacancy rate: 2.5%; Median gross rent: $565 per month; Rental vacancy rate: 8.2%
Health Insurance: 86.0% have insurance; 59.3% have private insurance; 38.4% have public insurance; 14.0% do not have insurance; 5.1% of children under 18 do not have insurance

Hospitals: Community Memorial Hospital
Newspapers: Hicksville News-Tribune (weekly circulation 2500)
Transportation: Commute: 96.5% car, 0.0% public transportation, 2.3% walk, 1.2% work from home; Median travel time to work: 21.3 minutes

MARK CENTER (unincorporated postal area)
ZCTA: 43536
Covers a land area of 15.402 square miles and a water area of 0 square miles. Located at 41.31° N. Lat; 84.63° W. Long. Elevation is 718 feet.
Population: 394; Growth (since 2000): -12.6%; Density: 25.6 persons per square mile; Race: 96.7% White, 1.0% Black/African American, 0.0% Asian, 0.0% American Indian/Alaska Native, 0.0% Native Hawaiian/Other Pacific Islander, 0.3% Two or more races, 5.3% Hispanic of any race; Average household size: 2.81; Median age: 37.2; Age under 18: 25.1%; Age 65 and over: 11.9%; Males per 100 females: 110.7
Housing: Homeownership rate: 87.8%; Homeowner vacancy rate: 2.3%; Rental vacancy rate: 10.5%

NEY (village). Covers a land area of 0.408 square miles and a water area of 0 square miles. Located at 41.38° N. Lat; 84.52° W. Long. Elevation is 712 feet.
Population: 354; Growth (since 2000): -2.7%; Density: 866.7 persons per square mile; Race: 96.3% White, 0.0% Black/African American, 0.0% Asian, 0.0% American Indian/Alaska Native, 0.0% Native Hawaiian/Other Pacific Islander, 1.1% Two or more races, 4.5% Hispanic of any race; Average household size: 2.72; Median age: 35.8; Age under 18: 31.4%; Age 65 and over: 11.9%; Males per 100 females: 104.6
Housing: Homeownership rate: 76.1%; Homeowner vacancy rate: 4.8%; Rental vacancy rate: 0.0%

SHERWOOD (village). Covers a land area of 1.467 square miles and a water area of 0.015 square miles. Located at 41.29° N. Lat; 84.55° W. Long. Elevation is 709 feet.
Population: 827; Growth (since 2000): 3.2%; Density: 563.9 persons per square mile; Race: 96.7% White, 0.4% Black/African American, 0.1% Asian, 0.2% American Indian/Alaska Native, 0.0% Native Hawaiian/Other Pacific Islander, 1.7% Two or more races, 4.8% Hispanic of any race; Average household size: 2.53; Median age: 36.0; Age under 18: 28.4%; Age 65 and over: 15.6%; Males per 100 females: 88.4

School District(s)

Central Local (PK-12)
2012-13 Enrollment: 1,088 . . . . (419) 658-2808
Housing: Homeownership rate: 75.5%; Homeowner vacancy rate: 2.4%; Rental vacancy rate: 17.5%

Delaware County

Located in central Ohio; crossed by the Olentangy and Scioto Rivers. Covers a land area of 443.098 square miles, a water area of 14.231 square miles, and is located in the Eastern Time Zone at 40.28° N. Lat., 83.01° W. Long. The county was founded in 1808. County seat is Delaware.

Delaware County is part of the Columbus, OH Metropolitan Statistical Area. The entire metro area includes: Delaware County, OH; Fairfield County, OH; Franklin County, OH; Hocking County, OH; Licking County, OH; Madison County, OH; Morrow County, OH; Perry County, OH; Pickaway County, OH; Union County, OH

Population: 174,214; Growth (since 2000): 58.4%; Density: 393.2 persons per square mile; Race: 89.7% White, 3.4% Black/African American, 4.3% Asian, 0.1% American Indian/Alaska Native, 0.0% Native Hawaiian/Other Pacific Islander, 1.8% two or more races, 2.1% Hispanic of any race; Average household size: 2.74; Median age: 37.4; Age under 18: 29.0%; Age 65 and over: 9.5%; Males per 100 females: 97.3; Marriage status: 22.3% never married, 65.3% now married, 1.1% separated, 3.6% widowed, 8.7% divorced; Foreign born: 6.1%; Speak English only: 91.9%; With disability: 7.1%; Veterans: 8.1%; Ancestry: 32.2% German, 16.1% Irish, 12.0% English, 8.0% Italian, 7.8% American
Religion: Six largest groups: 12.7% Catholicism, 4.5% Methodist/Pietist, 3.6% Hindu, 2.9% Presbyterian-Reformed, 2.5% Baptist, 1.7% Non-denominational Protestant
Economy: Unemployment rate: 3.4%; Leading industries: 14.3% retail trade; 13.1% professional, scientific, and technical services; 10.2% accommodation and food services; Farms: 755 totaling 140,902 acres; Company size: 3 employ 1,000 or more persons, 7 employ 500 to 999 persons, 99 employ 100 to 499 persons, 3,985 employ less than 100 persons; Business ownership: 4,661 women-owned, 345 Black-owned, n/a Hispanic-owned, 670 Asian-owned
Employment: 24.3% management, business, and financial, 8.4% computer, engineering, and science, 11.3% education, legal, community service, arts, and media, 7.4% healthcare practitioners, 12.2% service, 23.8% sales and office, 5.2% natural resources, construction, and maintenance, 7.3% production, transportation, and material moving
Income: Per capita: $40,189; Median household: $89,757; Average household: $110,852; Households with income of $100,000 or more: 44.0%; Poverty rate: 4.9%
Educational Attainment: High school diploma or higher: 96.0%; Bachelor's degree or higher: 50.5%; Graduate/professional degree or higher: 17.5%
Housing: Homeownership rate: 81.8%; Median home value: $246,300; Median year structure built: 1995; Homeowner vacancy rate: 2.0%; Median gross rent: $883 per month; Rental vacancy rate: 7.7%
Vital Statistics: Birth rate: 111.7 per 10,000 population; Death rate: 52.7 per 10,000 population; Age-adjusted cancer mortality rate: 148.1 deaths per 100,000 population
Health Insurance: 94.7% have insurance; 87.2% have private insurance; 16.3% have public insurance; 5.3% do not have insurance; 2.3% of children under 18 do not have insurance
Health Care: Physicians: 36.4 per 10,000 population; Hospital beds: 3.4 per 10,000 population; Hospital admissions: 146.9 per 10,000 population
Air Quality Index: 92.5% good, 7.5% moderate, 0.0% unhealthy for sensitive individuals, 0.0% unhealthy (percent of days)
Transportation: Commute: 91.0% car, 0.3% public transportation, 1.2% walk, 6.9% work from home; Median travel time to work: 25.3 minutes
Presidential Election: 37.5% Obama, 61.2% Romney (2012)
National and State Parks: Alum Creek State Park
Additional Information Contacts
Delaware Government . . . . (740) 833-2100
http://www.co.delaware.oh.us

Delaware County Communities

ASHLEY (village). Covers a land area of 0.659 square miles and a water area of 0 square miles. Located at 40.41° N. Lat; 82.95° W. Long. Elevation is 984 feet.
Population: 1,330; Growth (since 2000): 9.4%; Density: 2,018.8 persons per square mile; Race: 97.2% White, 0.5% Black/African American, 0.2% Asian, 0.1% American Indian/Alaska Native, 0.0% Native Hawaiian/Other Pacific Islander, 2.0% Two or more races, 1.5% Hispanic of any race; Average household size: 2.62; Median age: 36.3; Age under 18: 27.1%; Age 65 and over: 13.6%; Males per 100 females: 89.2

School District(s)

Buckeye Valley Local (PK-12)
2012-13 Enrollment: 2,205 . . . . (740) 369-8735
Housing: Homeownership rate: 65.4%; Homeowner vacancy rate: 1.2%; Rental vacancy rate: 6.5%

DELAWARE (city). County seat. Covers a land area of 18.952 square miles and a water area of 0.122 square miles. Located at 40.29° N. Lat; 83.07° W. Long. Elevation is 869 feet.
History: Named for Thomas West, Lord Delaware, first British governor of the colony of Virginia. Delaware was established around a sulphur spring, called Medicine Waters by the Mingo and Delaware tribes who lived here in the early 1800's. Joseph Barber settled on the present town site in 1807 and opened a tavern, and the town was platted in 1808. In 1833 a company, formed to exploit the local mineral springs, built a resort hotel. The resort was unsuccessful, but the hotel became the first building of Ohio Wesleyan University, chartered in 1842.
Population: 34,753; Growth (since 2000): 37.7%; Density: 1,833.7 persons per square mile; Race: 90.6% White, 4.5% Black/African American, 1.4% Asian, 0.2% American Indian/Alaska Native, 0.0% Native Hawaiian/Other Pacific Islander, 2.5% Two or more races, 2.5% Hispanic of any race; Average household size: 2.47; Median age: 33.2; Age under 18: 25.5%; Age 65 and over: 11.1%; Males per 100 females: 92.2; Marriage status: 31.8% never married, 50.8% now married, 1.5% separated, 4.8% widowed, 12.7% divorced; Foreign born: 3.4%; Speak English only: 96.0%; With disability: 10.5%; Veterans: 9.9%; Ancestry: 32.8% German, 15.6% Irish, 11.3% English, 8.2% American, 4.7% Italian

Employment: 16.4% management, business, and financial, 7.0% computer, engineering, and science, 11.8% education, legal, community service, arts, and media, 5.2% healthcare practitioners, 18.0% service, 25.1% sales and office, 5.3% natural resources, construction, and maintenance, 11.1% production, transportation, and material moving
Income: Per capita: $26,992; Median household: $56,963; Average household: $69,356; Households with income of $100,000 or more: 21.7%; Poverty rate: 9.6%
Educational Attainment: High school diploma or higher: 92.4%; Bachelor's degree or higher: 34.2%; Graduate/professional degree or higher: 12.3%

School District(s)

Buckeye United SD (08-12)
2012-13 Enrollment: 369. . . . . (614) 466-0720
Buckeye Valley Local (PK-12)
2012-13 Enrollment: 2,205 . . . . (740) 369-8735
Delaware Area Career Center (08-12)
2012-13 Enrollment: n/a . . . . (740) 548-0708
Delaware City (PK-12)
2012-13 Enrollment: 5,326 . . . . (740) 833-1100
Olentangy Local (PK-12)
2012-13 Enrollment: 17,383 . . . . (740) 657-4050

Four-year College(s)

Methodist Theological School in Ohio (Private, Not-for-profit, United Methodist)
Fall 2013 Enrollment: 193 . . . . (740) 363-1146
Ohio Wesleyan University (Private, Not-for-profit, United Methodist)
Fall 2013 Enrollment: 1,830 . . . . (740) 368-2000
2013-14 Tuition: In-state $40,510; Out-of-state $40,510

Vocational/Technical School(s)

Delaware Area Career Center (Public)
Fall 2013 Enrollment: 68 . . . . (740) 201-3206
2013-14 Tuition: $3,100

Housing: Homeownership rate: 60.9%; Median home value: $158,500; Median year structure built: 1988; Homeowner vacancy rate: 2.5%; Median gross rent: $807 per month; Rental vacancy rate: 8.4%
Health Insurance: 92.5% have insurance; 79.2% have private insurance; 23.3% have public insurance; 7.5% do not have insurance; 3.9% of children under 18 do not have insurance
Hospitals: Grady Memorial Hospital (135 beds)
Safety: Violent crime rate: 14.6 per 10,000 population; Property crime rate: 255.9 per 10,000 population
Newspapers: Delaware Gazette (daily circulation 8400)
Transportation: Commute: 90.0% car, 0.3% public transportation, 3.6% walk, 5.3% work from home; Median travel time to work: 26.4 minutes
Airports: Delaware Municipal - Jim Moore Field (general aviation)
Additional Information Contacts
City of Delaware . . . . (740) 203-1000
http://www.delawareohio.net

GALENA (village). Covers a land area of 1.598 square miles and a water area of 0.102 square miles. Located at 40.23° N. Lat; 82.88° W. Long. Elevation is 919 feet.
Population: 653; Growth (since 2000): 114.1%; Density: 408.7 persons per square mile; Race: 90.8% White, 2.6% Black/African American, 3.4% Asian, 0.5% American Indian/Alaska Native, 0.5% Native Hawaiian/Other Pacific Islander, 1.1% Two or more races, 2.3% Hispanic of any race; Average household size: 3.05; Median age: 35.2; Age under 18: 30.9%; Age 65 and over: 9.2%; Males per 100 females: 97.9

School District(s)

Big Walnut Local (PK-12)
2012-13 Enrollment: 3,045 . . . . (740) 965-3010
Olentangy Local (PK-12)
2012-13 Enrollment: 17,383 . . . . (740) 657-4050

Housing: Homeownership rate: 82.2%; Homeowner vacancy rate: 3.2%; Rental vacancy rate: 11.6%

KILBOURNE (CDP). Covers a land area of 0.449 square miles and a water area of 0 square miles. Located at 40.33° N. Lat; 82.96° W. Long. Elevation is 915 feet.
Population: 139; Growth (since 2000): n/a; Density: 309.5 persons per square mile; Race: 97.8% White, 0.0% Black/African American, 0.0% Asian, 0.7% American Indian/Alaska Native, 0.0% Native Hawaiian/Other Pacific Islander, 0.7% Two or more races, 0.0% Hispanic of any race; Average household size: 2.48; Median age: 46.8; Age under 18: 12.9%; Age 65 and over: 11.5%; Males per 100 females: 127.9
Housing: Homeownership rate: 76.8%; Homeowner vacancy rate: 2.1%; Rental vacancy rate: 18.8%

LEWIS CENTER (unincorporated postal area)
ZCTA: 43035
Covers a land area of 19.590 square miles and a water area of 3.102 square miles. Located at 40.19° N. Lat; 83.00° W. Long. Elevation is 938 feet.
Population: 24,721; Growth (since 2000): 119.5%; Density: 1,261.9 persons per square mile; Race: 81.7% White, 5.0% Black/African American, 9.7% Asian, 0.1% American Indian/Alaska Native, 0.0% Native Hawaiian/Other Pacific Islander, 2.2% Two or more races, 3.4% Hispanic of any race; Average household size: 2.93; Median age: 33.0; Age under 18: 34.6%; Age 65 and over: 4.4%; Males per 100 females: 99.4; Marriage status: 22.7% never married, 68.6% now married, 1.5% separated, 1.8% widowed, 6.9% divorced; Foreign born: 12.6%; Speak English only: 81.8%; With disability: 4.9%; Veterans: 6.1%; Ancestry: 28.3% German, 16.2% Irish, 9.6% English, 8.4% Italian, 5.5% American
Employment: 25.9% management, business, and financial, 11.1% computer, engineering, and science, 11.4% education, legal, community service, arts, and media, 8.0% healthcare practitioners, 12.1% service, 22.0% sales and office, 3.6% natural resources, construction, and maintenance, 6.0% production, transportation, and material moving
Income: Per capita: $37,674; Median household: $101,295; Average household: $113,106; Households with income of $100,000 or more: 50.7%; Poverty rate: 5.9%
Educational Attainment: High school diploma or higher: 96.4%; Bachelor's degree or higher: 59.3%; Graduate/professional degree or higher: 20.0%

School District(s)

Olentangy Local (PK-12)
2012-13 Enrollment: 17,383 . . . . (740) 657-4050

Housing: Homeownership rate: 82.0%; Median home value: $250,900; Median year structure built: 2000; Homeowner vacancy rate: 1.9%; Median gross rent: $867 per month; Rental vacancy rate: 6.7%
Health Insurance: 93.2% have insurance; 85.8% have private insurance; 11.4% have public insurance; 6.8% do not have insurance; 5.0% of children under 18 do not have insurance
Newspapers: Grove City Record (weekly circulation 3500); ThisWeek Newspapers (weekly circulation 307000)
Transportation: Commute: 93.9% car, 0.2% public transportation, 0.5% walk, 5.1% work from home; Median travel time to work: 22.7 minutes

---

OSTRANDER (village). Covers a land area of 0.842 square miles and a water area of 0 square miles. Located at 40.26° N. Lat; 83.22° W. Long. Elevation is 928 feet.
Population: 643; Growth (since 2000): 58.8%; Density: 763.6 persons per square mile; Race: 97.7% White, 0.5% Black/African American, 0.3% Asian, 0.0% American Indian/Alaska Native, 0.0% Native Hawaiian/Other Pacific Islander, 1.6% Two or more races, 1.7% Hispanic of any race; Average household size: 2.91; Median age: 35.0; Age under 18: 32.8%; Age 65 and over: 8.2%; Males per 100 females: 108.8

School District(s)

Buckeye Valley Local (PK-12)
2012-13 Enrollment: 2,205 . . . . (740) 369-8735

Housing: Homeownership rate: 83.2%; Homeowner vacancy rate: 1.1%; Rental vacancy rate: 5.1%

POWELL (city). Covers a land area of 4.932 square miles and a water area of 0.004 square miles. Located at 40.17° N. Lat; 83.08° W. Long. Elevation is 906 feet.
History: It was named "Middlebury" at the time, because the first settlers came from the Middlebury, Connecticut area. In 1857, Judge Thomas Powell established the first post office in the community, and the residents decided to adopt his name. Powell was finally incorporated as a municipality in 1947.
Population: 11,500; Growth (since 2000): 84.1%; Density: 2,331.9 persons per square mile; Race: 88.5% White, 1.9% Black/African American, 7.5% Asian, 0.1% American Indian/Alaska Native, 0.0% Native Hawaiian/Other Pacific Islander, 1.7% Two or more races, 1.4% Hispanic of any race; Average household size: 3.03; Median age: 37.4; Age under 18: 34.7%; Age 65 and over: 7.7%; Males per 100 females: 97.0; Marriage status: 19.0% never married, 71.4% now married, 0.6% separated, 2.5%

widowed, 7.1% divorced; Foreign born: 9.9%; Speak English only: 87.6%; With disability: 4.6%; Veterans: 5.2%; Ancestry: 24.8% German, 17.7% Irish, 12.8% Italian, 10.3% English, 7.3% American
Employment: 27.2% management, business, and financial, 12.2% computer, engineering, and science, 11.3% education, legal, community service, arts, and media, 12.4% healthcare practitioners, 5.2% service, 25.0% sales and office, 2.1% natural resources, construction, and maintenance, 4.7% production, transportation, and material moving
Income: Per capita: $48,246; Median household: $132,598; Average household: $142,845; Households with income of $100,000 or more: 67.4%; Poverty rate: 1.2%
Educational Attainment: High school diploma or higher: 98.8%; Bachelor's degree or higher: 70.6%; Graduate/professional degree or higher: 28.1%

School District(s)

Dublin City (PK-12)
2012-13 Enrollment: 14,627 . . . . (614) 764-5913
Olentangy Local (PK-12)
2012-13 Enrollment: 17,383 . . . . (740) 657-4050
Worthington City (PK-12)
2012-13 Enrollment: 9,423 . . . . (614) 450-6000

Housing: Homeownership rate: 94.1%; Median home value: $324,400; Median year structure built: 1999; Homeowner vacancy rate: 2.0%; Median gross rent: $1,897 per month; Rental vacancy rate: 10.5%
Health Insurance: 98.4% have insurance; 94.9% have private insurance; 12.1% have public insurance; 1.6% do not have insurance; 0.0% of children under 18 do not have insurance
Safety: Violent crime rate: 1.7 per 10,000 population; Property crime rate: 68.6 per 10,000 population
Transportation: Commute: 89.2% car, 0.8% public transportation, 1.0% walk, 9.0% work from home; Median travel time to work: 24.7 minutes
Additional Information Contacts
Village of Powell . . . . (614) 885-5380
http://www.cityofpowell.us

RADNOR (CDP). Covers a land area of 0.721 square miles and a water area of 0 square miles. Located at 40.39° N. Lat; 83.15° W. Long. Elevation is 935 feet.
Population: 201; Growth (since 2000): n/a; Density: 278.9 persons per square mile; Race: 94.5% White, 0.0% Black/African American, 0.5% Asian, 0.0% American Indian/Alaska Native, 0.0% Native Hawaiian/Other Pacific Islander, 5.0% Two or more races, 1.5% Hispanic of any race; Average household size: 2.79; Median age: 38.5; Age under 18: 25.9%; Age 65 and over: 14.9%; Males per 100 females: 105.1

School District(s)

Buckeye Valley Local (PK-12)
2012-13 Enrollment: 2,205 . . . . (740) 369-8735

Housing: Homeownership rate: 79.1%; Homeowner vacancy rate: 0.0%; Rental vacancy rate: 11.8%

SHAWNEE HILLS (village). Covers a land area of 0.442 square miles and a water area of 0 square miles. Located at 40.16° N. Lat; 83.14° W. Long. Elevation is 892 feet.
Population: 681; Growth (since 2000): 62.5%; Density: 1,540.5 persons per square mile; Race: 92.5% White, 2.5% Black/African American, 3.2% Asian, 0.1% American Indian/Alaska Native, 0.0% Native Hawaiian/Other Pacific Islander, 1.3% Two or more races, 1.9% Hispanic of any race; Average household size: 2.54; Median age: 40.6; Age under 18: 24.1%; Age 65 and over: 9.1%; Males per 100 females: 108.9
Housing: Homeownership rate: 88.4%; Homeowner vacancy rate: 5.9%; Rental vacancy rate: 0.0%
Additional Information Contacts
Village of Shawnee Hills . . . . (614) 889-2824
http://www.shawneehillsoh.com

SUNBURY (village). Covers a land area of 3.278 square miles and a water area of 0.018 square miles. Located at 40.25° N. Lat; 82.87° W. Long. Elevation is 968 feet.
Population: 4,389; Growth (since 2000): 66.9%; Density: 1,339.0 persons per square mile; Race: 95.2% White, 1.1% Black/African American, 1.1% Asian, 0.2% American Indian/Alaska Native, 0.1% Native Hawaiian/Other Pacific Islander, 1.5% Two or more races, 1.7% Hispanic of any race; Average household size: 2.62; Median age: 33.6; Age under 18: 29.8%; Age 65 and over: 11.4%; Males per 100 females: 90.1; Marriage status: 21.5% never married, 59.8% now married, 0.5% separated, 5.0% widowed, 13.6% divorced; Foreign born: 2.4%; Speak English only: 96.2%; With disability: 10.8%; Veterans: 5.5%; Ancestry: 36.9% German, 14.1% Irish, 10.7% English, 6.9% Italian, 4.2% Polish
Employment: 15.9% management, business, and financial, 4.5% computer, engineering, and science, 11.5% education, legal, community service, arts, and media, 8.3% healthcare practitioners, 13.3% service, 25.9% sales and office, 8.0% natural resources, construction, and maintenance, 12.8% production, transportation, and material moving
Income: Per capita: $26,756; Median household: $62,353; Average household: $65,843; Households with income of $100,000 or more: 20.6%; Poverty rate: 5.8%
Educational Attainment: High school diploma or higher: 94.1%; Bachelor's degree or higher: 37.1%; Graduate/professional degree or higher: 10.2%

School District(s)

Big Walnut Local (PK-12)
2012-13 Enrollment: 3,045 . . . . (740) 965-3010

Housing: Homeownership rate: 71.0%; Median home value: $158,800; Median year structure built: 1991; Homeowner vacancy rate: 2.2%; Median gross rent: <$100 per month; Rental vacancy rate: 6.7%
Health Insurance: 95.8% have insurance; 82.8% have private insurance; 28.1% have public insurance; 4.2% do not have insurance; 0.0% of children under 18 do not have insurance
Newspapers: Sunbury News (weekly circulation 3200)
Transportation: Commute: 93.0% car, 0.0% public transportation, 3.2% walk, 3.8% work from home; Median travel time to work: 27.1 minutes

Erie County

Located in northern Ohio; bounded on the north by Lake Erie; drained by the Huron and Vermilion Rivers; includes Kelleys Island. Covers a land area of 251.558 square miles, a water area of 374.429 square miles, and is located in the Eastern Time Zone at 41.55° N. Lat., 82.53° W. Long. The county was founded in 1838. County seat is Sandusky.

Erie County is part of the Sandusky, OH Micropolitan Statistical Area. The entire metro area includes: Erie County, OH

Weather Station: Sandusky Elevation: 583 feet

	Jan	Feb	Mar	Apr	May	Jun	Jul	Aug	Sep	Oct	Nov	Dec
High	33	36	44	57	67	78	82	80	74	62	50	37
Low	20	22	29	40	52	61	66	65	57	45	36	25
Precip	1.8	1.7	2.4	3.2	3.3	3.8	3.5	3.3	2.8	2.4	2.7	2.3
Snow	6.7	4.3	2.6	0.5	tr	0.0	0.0	0.0	0.0	0.0	0.2	2.9

High and Low temperatures in degrees Fahrenheit; Precipitation and Snow in inches

Population: 77,079; Growth (since 2000): -3.1%; Density: 306.4 persons per square mile; Race: 87.0% White, 8.6% Black/African American, 0.6% Asian, 0.3% American Indian/Alaska Native, 0.0% Native Hawaiian/Other Pacific Islander, 2.8% two or more races, 3.4% Hispanic of any race; Average household size: 2.37; Median age: 43.4; Age under 18: 22.2%; Age 65 and over: 17.3%; Males per 100 females: 96.1; Marriage status: 26.3% never married, 54.1% now married, 1.8% separated, 7.5% widowed, 12.0% divorced; Foreign born: 1.7%; Speak English only: 96.7%; With disability: 14.9%; Veterans: 11.5%; Ancestry: 36.8% German, 15.7% Irish, 9.1% English, 9.0% Italian, 4.8% American
Religion: Six largest groups: 25.6% Catholicism, 6.0% Non-denominational Protestant, 5.9% Lutheran, 5.2% Presbyterian-Reformed, 3.7% Methodist/Pietist, 3.5% Baptist
Economy: Unemployment rate: 4.5%; Leading industries: 16.5% retail trade; 14.2% accommodation and food services; 11.1% other services (except public administration); Farms: 345 totaling 83,330 acres; Company size: 2 employ 1,000 or more persons, 2 employ 500 to 999 persons, 38 employ 100 to 499 persons, 1,835 employ less than 100 persons; Business ownership: 1,733 women-owned, 181 Black-owned, n/a Hispanic-owned, n/a Asian-owned
Employment: 10.5% management, business, and financial, 2.5% computer, engineering, and science, 9.4% education, legal, community service, arts, and media, 7.1% healthcare practitioners, 21.0% service, 23.9% sales and office, 8.2% natural resources, construction, and maintenance, 17.3% production, transportation, and material moving
Income: Per capita: $26,135; Median household: $46,498; Average household: $61,916; Households with income of $100,000 or more: 16.1%; Poverty rate: 13.3%

Educational Attainment: High school diploma or higher: 89.3%; Bachelor's degree or higher: 21.0%; Graduate/professional degree or higher: 8.0%
Housing: Homeownership rate: 69.9%; Median home value: $135,200; Median year structure built: 1963; Homeowner vacancy rate: 2.6%; Median gross rent: $696 per month; Rental vacancy rate: 11.4%
Vital Statistics: Birth rate: 99.5 per 10,000 population; Death rate: 113.3 per 10,000 population; Age-adjusted cancer mortality rate: 201.7 deaths per 100,000 population
Health Insurance: 88.6% have insurance; 71.7% have private insurance; 33.6% have public insurance; 11.4% do not have insurance; 5.5% of children under 18 do not have insurance
Health Care: Physicians: 24.6 per 10,000 population; Hospital beds: 30.8 per 10,000 population; Hospital admissions: 1,085.4 per 10,000 population
Transportation: Commute: 92.9% car, 0.6% public transportation, 2.0% walk, 2.8% work from home; Median travel time to work: 20.1 minutes
Presidential Election: 54.8% Obama, 43.5% Romney (2012)
National and State Parks: Glacial Grooves State Memorial; Kelleys Island State Park
Additional Information Contacts
Erie Government . . . . (419) 627-7682
http://www.eriecounty.oh.gov

Erie County Communities

BAY VIEW (village). Covers a land area of 0.276 square miles and a water area of 0.002 square miles. Located at 41.47° N. Lat; 82.82° W. Long. Elevation is 577 feet.
History: Bay View developed as a resort community with swimming, boating, and camping facilities.
Population: 632; Growth (since 2000): -8.7%; Density: 2,289.0 persons per square mile; Race: 96.8% White, 0.3% Black/African American, 0.8% Asian, 0.9% American Indian/Alaska Native, 0.0% Native Hawaiian/Other Pacific Islander, 1.1% Two or more races, 0.5% Hispanic of any race; Average household size: 2.27; Median age: 47.7; Age under 18: 19.5%; Age 65 and over: 19.3%; Males per 100 females: 98.7
Housing: Homeownership rate: 80.6%; Homeowner vacancy rate: 1.3%; Rental vacancy rate: 0.0%

BERLIN HEIGHTS (village). Covers a land area of 1.603 square miles and a water area of 0.001 square miles. Located at 41.32° N. Lat; 82.49° W. Long. Elevation is 774 feet.
History: Berlin Heights developed as the center of an apple and peach district, begun in 1812 when John Hoak and John Fleming brought from Canada a number of young fruit trees.
Population: 714; Growth (since 2000): 4.2%; Density: 445.5 persons per square mile; Race: 96.8% White, 0.7% Black/African American, 0.1% Asian, 0.1% American Indian/Alaska Native, 0.0% Native Hawaiian/Other Pacific Islander, 2.2% Two or more races, 1.4% Hispanic of any race; Average household size: 2.65; Median age: 40.2; Age under 18: 25.8%; Age 65 and over: 15.4%; Males per 100 females: 89.9

School District(s)

Edison Local (Formerly Berlin-Milan) (PK-12)
2012-13 Enrollment: 1,574 . . . . (419) 499-4272
Housing: Homeownership rate: 79.9%; Homeowner vacancy rate: 2.7%; Rental vacancy rate: 1.8%

BEULAH BEACH (CDP). Covers a land area of 0.046 square miles and a water area of 0 square miles. Located at 41.39° N. Lat; 82.44° W. Long. Elevation is 600 feet.
Population: 53; Growth (since 2000): n/a; Density: 1,154.7 persons per square mile; Race: 96.2% White, 0.0% Black/African American, 1.9% Asian, 0.0% American Indian/Alaska Native, 0.0% Native Hawaiian/Other Pacific Islander, 1.9% Two or more races, 3.8% Hispanic of any race; Average household size: 1.83; Median age: 61.5; Age under 18: 7.5%; Age 65 and over: 47.2%; Males per 100 females: 82.8
Housing: Homeownership rate: 55.2%; Homeowner vacancy rate: 5.9%; Rental vacancy rate: 12.5%

BIRMINGHAM (unincorporated postal area)
ZCTA: 44816
Covers a land area of 0.026 square miles and a water area of 0 square miles. Located at 41.33° N. Lat; 82.35° W. Long. Elevation is 784 feet.
Population: 42; Growth (since 2000): -60.0%; Density: 1,628.8 persons per square mile; Race: 100.0% White, 0.0% Black/African American, 0.0% Asian, 0.0% American Indian/Alaska Native, 0.0% Native Hawaiian/Other Pacific Islander, 0.0% Two or more races, 0.0% Hispanic of any race; Average household size: 1.68; Median age: 55.5; Age under 18: 7.1%; Age 65 and over: 33.3%; Males per 100 females: 100.0
Housing: Homeownership rate: 64.0%; Homeowner vacancy rate: 5.9%; Rental vacancy rate: 0.0%

CASTALIA (village). Covers a land area of 1.044 square miles and a water area of 0.009 square miles. Located at 41.40° N. Lat; 82.80° W. Long. Elevation is 636 feet.
Population: 852; Growth (since 2000): -8.9%; Density: 816.1 persons per square mile; Race: 97.1% White, 0.1% Black/African American, 0.1% Asian, 0.4% American Indian/Alaska Native, 0.0% Native Hawaiian/Other Pacific Islander, 1.6% Two or more races, 3.3% Hispanic of any race; Average household size: 2.42; Median age: 40.5; Age under 18: 23.1%; Age 65 and over: 13.3%; Males per 100 females: 96.3

School District(s)

Margaretta Local (PK-12)
2012-13 Enrollment: 1,142 . . . . (419) 684-5322
Townsend North Community School (09-12)
2012-13 Enrollment: 272. . . . . (419) 684-5351
Housing: Homeownership rate: 72.1%; Homeowner vacancy rate: 2.3%; Rental vacancy rate: 3.9%

CRYSTAL ROCK (CDP). Covers a land area of 0.106 square miles and a water area of 0 square miles. Located at 41.45° N. Lat; 82.84° W. Long. Elevation is 581 feet.
Population: 176; Growth (since 2000): n/a; Density: 1,653.4 persons per square mile; Race: 94.3% White, 0.0% Black/African American, 0.0% Asian, 0.6% American Indian/Alaska Native, 0.0% Native Hawaiian/Other Pacific Islander, 2.3% Two or more races, 7.4% Hispanic of any race; Average household size: 2.23; Median age: 45.8; Age under 18: 18.2%; Age 65 and over: 20.5%; Males per 100 females: 100.0
Housing: Homeownership rate: 78.4%; Homeowner vacancy rate: 3.1%; Rental vacancy rate: 5.6%

HURON (city). Covers a land area of 4.837 square miles and a water area of 2.891 square miles. Located at 41.40° N. Lat; 82.56° W. Long. Elevation is 587 feet.
History: A French trading post was established here about 1749. In 1805, trader B.F. Flemond arrived, and the town of Huron soon grew up around the harbor at the mouth of the Huron River. Shipping and shipbuilding supported the town.
Population: 7,149; Growth (since 2000): -10.2%; Density: 1,478.1 persons per square mile; Race: 96.4% White, 0.9% Black/African American, 0.5% Asian, 0.3% American Indian/Alaska Native, 0.0% Native Hawaiian/Other Pacific Islander, 1.5% Two or more races, 2.3% Hispanic of any race; Average household size: 2.30; Median age: 43.9; Age under 18: 22.7%; Age 65 and over: 18.4%; Males per 100 females: 92.7; Marriage status: 24.1% never married, 57.1% now married, 3.0% separated, 8.7% widowed, 10.1% divorced; Foreign born: 1.3%; Speak English only: 97.9%; With disability: 11.5%; Veterans: 9.9%; Ancestry: 42.7% German, 17.0% Irish, 13.3% English, 11.3% Italian, 5.6% American
Employment: 12.7% management, business, and financial, 2.0% computer, engineering, and science, 9.1% education, legal, community service, arts, and media, 8.8% healthcare practitioners, 19.2% service, 30.3% sales and office, 6.1% natural resources, construction, and maintenance, 11.8% production, transportation, and material moving
Income: Per capita: $30,160; Median household: $52,321; Average household: $71,112; Households with income of $100,000 or more: 19.5%; Poverty rate: 11.1%
Educational Attainment: High school diploma or higher: 94.5%; Bachelor's degree or higher: 35.0%; Graduate/professional degree or higher: 9.7%

School District(s)

Huron City Schools (PK-12)
2012-13 Enrollment: 1,482 . . . . (419) 433-1234

Two-year College(s)

Bowling Green State University-Firelands (Public)
Fall 2013 Enrollment: 2,441 . . . . (419) 433-5560
2013-14 Tuition: In-state $4,946; Out-of-state $12,254

Housing: Homeownership rate: 73.2%; Median home value: $145,300; Median year structure built: 1966; Homeowner vacancy rate: 2.4%; Median gross rent: $715 per month; Rental vacancy rate: 9.1%
Health Insurance: 89.9% have insurance; 76.5% have private insurance; 29.6% have public insurance; 10.1% do not have insurance; 4.4% of children under 18 do not have insurance
Transportation: Commute: 92.3% car, 0.0% public transportation, 4.2% walk, 3.1% work from home; Median travel time to work: 20.9 minutes
Additional Information Contacts
City of Huron . . . . (419) 433-5000
http://www.cityofhuron.org

KELLEYS ISLAND (village). Covers a land area of 4.348 square miles and a water area of 0.058 square miles. Located at 41.60° N. Lat; 82.71° W. Long. Elevation is 594 feet.
History: In 1833 Irad and Datus Kelley acquired the island in Lake Erie, and settled here. They first harvested the forests of red cedar. In 1846 they planted an acre of grapes, and the island was soon known for its wine, as well as its peaches and grapes. Later, quarrying of the limestone became an important industry.
Population: 312; Growth (since 2000): -15.0%; Density: 71.8 persons per square mile; Race: 98.1% White, 0.3% Black/African American, 0.6% Asian, 0.0% American Indian/Alaska Native, 0.0% Native Hawaiian/Other Pacific Islander, 0.3% Two or more races, 1.3% Hispanic of any race; Average household size: 1.78; Median age: 58.8; Age under 18: 9.6%; Age 65 and over: 34.3%; Males per 100 females: 110.8

School District(s)

Kelleys Island Local (03-12)
2012-13 Enrollment: 1. . . . . (419) 746-2730
Housing: Homeownership rate: 82.3%; Homeowner vacancy rate: 3.3%; Rental vacancy rate: 56.2%
Airports: Kelleys Island Land Field (general aviation)

MILAN (village). Covers a land area of 1.185 square miles and a water area of 0.019 square miles. Located at 41.29° N. Lat; 82.60° W. Long. Elevation is 663 feet.
History: Several villages occupied this site on the Huron River before the permanent settlement of Milan was laid out in 1816 by Ebenezer Merry. The town became a shipping port in 1839, when residents completed a canal to the Huron River, three miles away. Wheat was the principal cargo of the ships that left Milan. Milan prospered until the river became unnavigable for lake boats and the canal ceased to be used in the 1880 's.
Population: 1,367; Growth (since 2000): -5.4%; Density: 1,153.8 persons per square mile; Race: 97.5% White, 0.7% Black/African American, 0.6% Asian, 0.1% American Indian/Alaska Native, 0.0% Native Hawaiian/Other Pacific Islander, 0.9% Two or more races, 1.8% Hispanic of any race; Average household size: 2.52; Median age: 44.5; Age under 18: 23.6%; Age 65 and over: 16.8%; Males per 100 females: 98.1

School District(s)

Edison Local (Formerly Berlin-Milan) (PK-12)
2012-13 Enrollment: 1,574 . . . . (419) 499-4272
Ehove Career Center (09-12)
2012-13 Enrollment: n/a . . . . (866) 256-9707

Two-year College(s)

EHOVE Career Center (Public)
Fall 2013 Enrollment: 302 . . . . (419) 499-4663
Housing: Homeownership rate: 77.4%; Homeowner vacancy rate: 0.5%; Rental vacancy rate: 7.8%

SANDUSKY (city). County seat. Covers a land area of 9.726 square miles and a water area of 12.175 square miles. Located at 41.46° N. Lat; 82.71° W. Long. Elevation is 594 feet.
History: Sandusky was platted in 1818, replacing a smaller tract laid out in 1816 and called Portland. Its location on the southeastern corner of Sandusky Bay (named Lac Sandouske by French explorers, after the Wyandotte San-doos-tee) made the town a tourist and vacation destination, as well as an industrial community. The town was a port of entry and a shipping center, a stopping place for all vessels that sailed the Great Lakes. Sandusky became the seat of Erie County in 1838, but the 1840's brought epidemics of cholera that killed hundreds of people. In the 1850's Sandusky was an important station on the Underground Railroad.
Population: 25,793; Growth (since 2000): -7.4%; Density: 2,652.1 persons per square mile; Race: 70.4% White, 22.0% Black/African American, 0.6% Asian, 0.4% American Indian/Alaska Native, 0.0% Native Hawaiian/Other Pacific Islander, 5.5% Two or more races, 4.9% Hispanic of any race; Average household size: 2.28; Median age: 38.5; Age under 18: 23.9%; Age 65 and over: 15.0%; Males per 100 females: 91.0; Marriage status: 36.2% never married, 41.9% now married, 2.9% separated, 7.5% widowed, 14.4% divorced; Foreign born: 1.8%; Speak English only: 96.0%; With disability: 18.0%; Veterans: 10.7%; Ancestry: 31.1% German, 13.8% Irish, 7.6% Italian, 6.4% English, 3.8% Polish
Employment: 9.4% management, business, and financial, 1.8% computer, engineering, and science, 9.2% education, legal, community service, arts, and media, 4.4% healthcare practitioners, 25.5% service, 22.7% sales and office, 6.9% natural resources, construction, and maintenance, 20.0% production, transportation, and material moving
Income: Per capita: $20,883; Median household: $35,776; Average household: $46,922; Households with income of $100,000 or more: 9.3%; Poverty rate: 23.1%
Educational Attainment: High school diploma or higher: 83.1%; Bachelor's degree or higher: 14.6%; Graduate/professional degree or higher: 5.2%

School District(s)

Perkins Local (PK-12)
2012-13 Enrollment: 2,328 . . . . (419) 625-0484
Sandusky City (PK-12)
2012-13 Enrollment: 3,228 . . . . (419) 626-6940

Two-year College(s)

Firelands Regional Medical Center School of Nursing (Private, Not-for-profit)
Fall 2013 Enrollment: 99 . . . . (419) 557-7110
Ohio Business College-Sandusky (Private, For-profit)
Fall 2013 Enrollment: 387 . . . . (419) 627-8345
2013-14 Tuition: In-state $8,500; Out-of-state $8,500

Vocational/Technical School(s)

Sandusky Career Center (Public)
Fall 2013 Enrollment: 95 . . . . (419) 984-1100
2013-14 Tuition: $9,905
Housing: Homeownership rate: 53.4%; Median home value: $85,000; Median year structure built: 1952; Homeowner vacancy rate: 4.2%; Median gross rent: $622 per month; Rental vacancy rate: 13.3%
Health Insurance: 83.6% have insurance; 55.7% have private insurance; 42.6% have public insurance; 16.4% do not have insurance; 7.1% of children under 18 do not have insurance
Hospitals: Firelands Regional Medical Center (325 beds)
Safety: Violent crime rate: 30.7 per 10,000 population; Property crime rate: 450.0 per 10,000 population
Newspapers: Sandusky Register (daily circulation 22200)
Transportation: Commute: 90.8% car, 1.3% public transportation, 2.7% walk, 2.7% work from home; Median travel time to work: 16.6 minutes; Amtrak: Train service available.
Airports: Griffing Sandusky (general aviation)
Additional Information Contacts
City of Sandusky . . . . (419) 627-5844
http://www.ci.sandusky.oh.us

WHITES LANDING (CDP). Covers a land area of 0.293 square miles and a water area of <.001 square miles. Located at 41.43° N. Lat; 82.89° W. Long. Elevation is 577 feet.
Population: 375; Growth (since 2000): n/a; Density: 1,280.1 persons per square mile; Race: 93.9% White, 0.8% Black/African American, 0.3% Asian, 2.1% American Indian/Alaska Native, 0.3% Native Hawaiian/Other Pacific Islander, 2.7% Two or more races, 2.4% Hispanic of any race; Average household size: 2.55; Median age: 43.5; Age under 18: 21.9%; Age 65 and over: 11.2%; Males per 100 females: 115.5
Housing: Homeownership rate: 80.3%; Homeowner vacancy rate: 2.5%; Rental vacancy rate: 12.1%

Fairfield County

Located in central Ohio; drained by the Hocking River; includes part of Buckeye Lake. Covers a land area of 504.411 square miles, a water area of 4.150 square miles, and is located in the Eastern Time Zone at 39.75° N. Lat., 82.63° W. Long. The county was founded in 1800. County seat is Lancaster.

Fairfield County is part of the Columbus, OH Metropolitan Statistical Area. The entire metro area includes: Delaware County, OH; Fairfield County, OH; Franklin County, OH; Hocking County, OH; Licking County, OH;

Madison County, OH; Morrow County, OH; Perry County, OH; Pickaway County, OH; Union County, OH

Population: 146,156; Growth (since 2000): 19.1%; Density: 289.8 persons per square mile; Race: 90.2% White, 6.0% Black/African American, 1.1% Asian, 0.2% American Indian/Alaska Native, 0.0% Native Hawaiian/Other Pacific Islander, 1.9% two or more races, 1.7% Hispanic of any race; Average household size: 2.64; Median age: 38.2; Age under 18: 26.3%; Age 65 and over: 12.4%; Males per 100 females: 98.3; Marriage status: 25.9% never married, 56.8% now married, 1.6% separated, 5.4% widowed, 11.9% divorced; Foreign born: 2.6%; Speak English only: 96.1%; With disability: 12.5%; Veterans: 10.9%; Ancestry: 29.9% German, 15.8% Irish, 10.7% English, 9.3% American, 4.4% Italian
Religion: Six largest groups: 12.0% Catholicism, 6.8% Methodist/Pietist, 6.4% Baptist, 3.9% Lutheran, 3.8% Non-denominational Protestant, 2.0% Pentecostal
Economy: Unemployment rate: 4.0%; Leading industries: 16.0% retail trade; 11.9% health care and social assistance; 11.2% other services (except public administration); Farms: 1,184 totaling 206,699 acres; Company size: 3 employ 1,000 or more persons, 0 employ 500 to 999 persons, 47 employ 100 to 499 persons, 2,507 employ less than 100 persons; Business ownership: 3,611 women-owned, n/a Black-owned, 156 Hispanic-owned, n/a Asian-owned
Employment: 15.8% management, business, and financial, 4.1% computer, engineering, and science, 9.5% education, legal, community service, arts, and media, 6.3% healthcare practitioners, 17.9% service, 25.3% sales and office, 8.8% natural resources, construction, and maintenance, 12.3% production, transportation, and material moving
Income: Per capita: $27,031; Median household: $58,786; Average household: $71,763; Households with income of $100,000 or more: 23.0%; Poverty rate: 11.9%
Educational Attainment: High school diploma or higher: 91.5%; Bachelor's degree or higher: 26.0%; Graduate/professional degree or higher: 8.7%
Housing: Homeownership rate: 74.0%; Median home value: $163,700; Median year structure built: 1979; Homeowner vacancy rate: 2.2%; Median gross rent: $774 per month; Rental vacancy rate: 8.5%
Vital Statistics: Birth rate: 110.6 per 10,000 population; Death rate: 80.1 per 10,000 population; Age-adjusted cancer mortality rate: 169.9 deaths per 100,000 population
Health Insurance: 90.9% have insurance; 73.8% have private insurance; 29.1% have public insurance; 9.1% do not have insurance; 3.5% of children under 18 do not have insurance
Health Care: Physicians: 15.5 per 10,000 population; Hospital beds: 15.1 per 10,000 population; Hospital admissions: 707.9 per 10,000 population
Transportation: Commute: 93.3% car, 0.2% public transportation, 1.6% walk, 3.9% work from home; Median travel time to work: 26.4 minutes
Presidential Election: 41.1% Obama, 57.3% Romney (2012)
National and State Parks: Rock Mill Dam State Wildlife Area; Shallenberger State Nature Reserve; Sherman House State Memorial; Tarlton State Park
Additional Information Contacts
Fairfield Government. . . . . (740) 687-7190
http://www.co.fairfield.oh.us

Fairfield County Communities

AMANDA (village). Covers a land area of 0.300 square miles and a water area of 0 square miles. Located at 39.65° N. Lat; 82.74° W. Long. Elevation is 922 feet.
Population: 737; Growth (since 2000): 4.2%; Density: 2,453.8 persons per square mile; Race: 96.6% White, 0.9% Black/African American, 0.0% Asian, 0.0% American Indian/Alaska Native, 0.1% Native Hawaiian/Other Pacific Islander, 1.8% Two or more races, 1.4% Hispanic of any race; Average household size: 2.73; Median age: 37.0; Age under 18: 30.0%; Age 65 and over: 12.6%; Males per 100 females: 106.4

School District(s)

Amanda-Clearcreek Local (PK-12)
2012-13 Enrollment: 1,633 . . . . (740) 969-7250
Housing: Homeownership rate: 72.2%; Homeowner vacancy rate: 3.4%; Rental vacancy rate: 6.2%

BALTIMORE (village). Covers a land area of 2.090 square miles and a water area of 0 square miles. Located at 39.85° N. Lat; 82.61° W. Long. Elevation is 866 feet.
Population: 2,966; Growth (since 2000): 3.0%; Density: 1,419.2 persons per square mile; Race: 97.5% White, 0.3% Black/African American, 0.5% Asian, 0.0% American Indian/Alaska Native, 0.0% Native Hawaiian/Other Pacific Islander, 1.5% Two or more races, 0.5% Hispanic of any race; Average household size: 2.44; Median age: 37.0; Age under 18: 26.8%; Age 65 and over: 13.0%; Males per 100 females: 90.1; Marriage status: 26.6% never married, 53.6% now married, 2.9% separated, 5.9% widowed, 14.0% divorced; Foreign born: 0.8%; Speak English only: 96.7%; With disability: 15.0%; Veterans: 14.5%; Ancestry: 37.7% German, 17.4% Irish, 8.8% English, 5.7% American, 5.6% Polish
Employment: 6.7% management, business, and financial, 3.5% computer, engineering, and science, 9.3% education, legal, community service, arts, and media, 4.9% healthcare practitioners, 18.3% service, 30.2% sales and office, 14.1% natural resources, construction, and maintenance, 13.0% production, transportation, and material moving
Income: Per capita: $18,977; Median household: $44,738; Average household: $52,849; Households with income of $100,000 or more: 16.3%; Poverty rate: 24.7%
Educational Attainment: High school diploma or higher: 87.5%; Bachelor's degree or higher: 14.9%; Graduate/professional degree or higher: 4.7%

School District(s)

Liberty Union-Thurston Local (PK-12)
2012-13 Enrollment: 1,389 . . . . (740) 862-4171
Housing: Homeownership rate: 58.8%; Median home value: $125,700; Median year structure built: 1958; Homeowner vacancy rate: 1.2%; Median gross rent: $758 per month; Rental vacancy rate: 7.9%
Health Insurance: 94.4% have insurance; 68.1% have private insurance; 42.2% have public insurance; 5.6% do not have insurance; 0.3% of children under 18 do not have insurance
Newspapers: Towne Crier (weekly circulation 30000)
Transportation: Commute: 96.1% car, 0.0% public transportation, 0.0% walk, 3.9% work from home; Median travel time to work: 26.7 minutes
Additional Information Contacts
Village of Baltimore . . . . (740) 862-4491
http://www.baltimoreohio.org

BREMEN (village). Covers a land area of 0.861 square miles and a water area of 0.002 square miles. Located at 39.71° N. Lat; 82.43° W. Long. Elevation is 794 feet.
Population: 1,425; Growth (since 2000): 12.6%; Density: 1,654.1 persons per square mile; Race: 98.2% White, 0.3% Black/African American, 0.0% Asian, 0.3% American Indian/Alaska Native, 0.1% Native Hawaiian/Other Pacific Islander, 1.2% Two or more races, 0.4% Hispanic of any race; Average household size: 2.79; Median age: 34.5; Age under 18: 31.1%; Age 65 and over: 13.2%; Males per 100 females: 99.0

School District(s)

Fairfield Union Local (PK-12)
2012-13 Enrollment: 1,963 . . . . (740) 536-7384
Housing: Homeownership rate: 72.0%; Homeowner vacancy rate: 2.1%; Rental vacancy rate: 10.1%

CARROLL (village). Covers a land area of 0.315 square miles and a water area of 0 square miles. Located at 39.80° N. Lat; 82.70° W. Long. Elevation is 833 feet.
Population: 524; Growth (since 2000): 7.4%; Density: 1,661.2 persons per square mile; Race: 96.2% White, 0.6% Black/African American, 0.2% Asian, 0.4% American Indian/Alaska Native, 0.0% Native Hawaiian/Other Pacific Islander, 2.7% Two or more races, 0.0% Hispanic of any race; Average household size: 2.52; Median age: 38.0; Age under 18: 25.4%; Age 65 and over: 13.7%; Males per 100 females: 103.9

School District(s)

Bloom-Carroll Local (PK-12)
2012-13 Enrollment: 1,776 . . . . (614) 837-6560
Eastland-Fairfield Career/tech (09-12)
2012-13 Enrollment: n/a . . . . (614) 836-4530
Housing: Homeownership rate: 59.1%; Homeowner vacancy rate: 1.6%; Rental vacancy rate: 4.4%

FAIRFIELD BEACH (CDP). Covers a land area of 0.653 square miles and a water area of 0.315 square miles. Located at 39.92° N. Lat; 82.48° W. Long. Elevation is 925 feet.

Population: 1,292; Growth (since 2000): 11.1%; Density: 1,977.8 persons per square mile; Race: 96.7% White, 0.4% Black/African American, 0.0% Asian, 0.2% American Indian/Alaska Native, 0.0% Native Hawaiian/Other Pacific Islander, 2.2% Two or more races, 1.1% Hispanic of any race; Average household size: 2.52; Median age: 41.0; Age under 18: 22.4%; Age 65 and over: 13.7%; Males per 100 females: 111.1

Housing: Homeownership rate: 79.5%; Homeowner vacancy rate: 6.6%; Rental vacancy rate: 10.3%

LANCASTER (city). County seat. Covers a land area of 18.841 square miles and a water area of 0.064 square miles. Located at 39.72° N. Lat; 82.61° W. Long. Elevation is 886 feet.

History: Lancaster was established on one of the three sections of land given to Ebenezer Zane for his work in laying out Zane's Trace. In 1800 the settlement on the banks of the Hocking River was named New Lancaster, because settlers had come from Lancaster, Pennsylvania. The first newspaper was printed in German, which was the language used in the early schools.

Population: 38,780; Growth (since 2000): 9.7%; Density: 2,058.3 persons per square mile; Race: 95.9% White, 1.0% Black/African American, 0.5% Asian, 0.3% American Indian/Alaska Native, 0.0% Native Hawaiian/Other Pacific Islander, 1.7% Two or more races, 1.6% Hispanic of any race; Average household size: 2.36; Median age: 37.5; Age under 18: 24.0%; Age 65 and over: 15.7%; Males per 100 females: 92.2; Marriage status: 28.5% never married, 46.2% now married, 2.7% separated, 7.8% widowed, 17.4% divorced; Foreign born: 1.2%; Speak English only: 98.4%; With disability: 18.8%; Veterans: 11.6%; Ancestry: 28.7% German, 15.8% Irish, 11.7% American, 10.3% English, 3.4% Italian

Employment: 9.8% management, business, and financial, 2.8% computer, engineering, and science, 7.7% education, legal, community service, arts, and media, 6.6% healthcare practitioners, 22.2% service, 27.7% sales and office, 6.8% natural resources, construction, and maintenance, 16.4% production, transportation, and material moving

Income: Per capita: $21,397; Median household: $37,087; Average household: $49,988; Households with income of $100,000 or more: 10.4%; Poverty rate: 21.1%

Educational Attainment: High school diploma or higher: 86.4%; Bachelor's degree or higher: 16.5%; Graduate/professional degree or higher: 5.6%

School District(s)

Fairfield Union Local (PK-12)
2012-13 Enrollment: 1,963 .... (740) 536-7384
Lancaster City (PK-12)
2012-13 Enrollment: 5,996 .... (740) 687-7300
Lancaster Digital Academy (03-12)
2012-13 Enrollment: 103.......................... (740) 277-7450
Lancaster Fairfield Community School (09-12)
2012-13 Enrollment: 48.......................... (740) 652-7200

Four-year College(s)

Ohio University-Lancaster Campus (Public)
Fall 2013 Enrollment: 2,596 .... (740) 654-6711
2013-14 Tuition: In-state $4,974; Out-of-state $9,510

Two-year College(s)

Daymar College-Lancaster (Private, For-profit)
Fall 2013 Enrollment: 69.......................... (740) 687-6126
2013-14 Tuition: In-state $18,000; Out-of-state $18,000

Housing: Homeownership rate: 57.7%; Median home value: $115,900; Median year structure built: 1962; Homeowner vacancy rate: 2.7%; Median gross rent: $712 per month; Rental vacancy rate: 8.7%

Health Insurance: 87.6% have insurance; 59.4% have private insurance; 43.5% have public insurance; 12.4% do not have insurance; 4.3% of children under 18 do not have insurance

Hospitals: Fairfield Medical Center (229 beds)

Newspapers: Eagle-Gazette (daily circulation 13200)

Transportation: Commute: 93.6% car, 0.1% public transportation, 3.3% walk, 1.4% work from home; Median travel time to work: 23.9 minutes

Airports: Fairfield County (general aviation)

Additional Information Contacts

City of Lancaster .... (740) 687-6600
http://www.ci.lancaster.oh.us

LITHOPOLIS (village). Covers a land area of 2.024 square miles and a water area of 0.004 square miles. Located at 39.82° N. Lat; 82.82° W. Long. Elevation is 942 feet.

History: The name of Lithopolis means "stone city" in the Greek, an appropriate name for a town that grew around sandstone quarries.

Population: 1,106; Growth (since 2000): 84.3%; Density: 546.4 persons per square mile; Race: 94.3% White, 3.4% Black/African American, 0.7% Asian, 0.0% American Indian/Alaska Native, 0.0% Native Hawaiian/Other Pacific Islander, 1.5% Two or more races, 2.3% Hispanic of any race; Average household size: 2.50; Median age: 38.2; Age under 18: 25.6%; Age 65 and over: 12.6%; Males per 100 females: 93.4

School District(s)

Bloom-Carroll Local (PK-12)
2012-13 Enrollment: 1,776 .... (614) 837-6560

Housing: Homeownership rate: 75.4%; Homeowner vacancy rate: 7.9%; Rental vacancy rate: 11.4%

Safety: Violent crime rate: 0.0 per 10,000 population; Property crime rate: 49.9 per 10,000 population

MILLERSPORT (village). Covers a land area of 0.873 square miles and a water area of 0.031 square miles. Located at 39.90° N. Lat; 82.54° W. Long. Elevation is 899 feet.

Population: 1,044; Growth (since 2000): 8.4%; Density: 1,196.1 persons per square mile; Race: 98.1% White, 0.4% Black/African American, 0.0% Asian, 0.4% American Indian/Alaska Native, 0.1% Native Hawaiian/Other Pacific Islander, 1.0% Two or more races, 1.1% Hispanic of any race; Average household size: 2.37; Median age: 39.1; Age under 18: 23.5%; Age 65 and over: 14.1%; Males per 100 females: 89.5

School District(s)

Walnut Township Local (PK-12)
2012-13 Enrollment: 577.......................... (740) 467-2802

Housing: Homeownership rate: 67.9%; Homeowner vacancy rate: 1.6%; Rental vacancy rate: 13.5%

PICKERINGTON (city). Covers a land area of 9.745 square miles and a water area of 0.001 square miles. Located at 39.89° N. Lat; 82.77° W. Long. Elevation is 840 feet.

Population: 18,291; Growth (since 2000): 86.8%; Density: 1,877.0 persons per square mile; Race: 80.1% White, 13.0% Black/African American, 2.9% Asian, 0.2% American Indian/Alaska Native, 0.0% Native Hawaiian/Other Pacific Islander, 3.1% Two or more races, 2.5% Hispanic of any race; Average household size: 2.92; Median age: 32.9; Age under 18: 33.3%; Age 65 and over: 6.8%; Males per 100 females: 94.7; Marriage status: 24.5% never married, 62.9% now married, 1.9% separated, 3.2% widowed, 9.4% divorced; Foreign born: 4.8%; Speak English only: 94.4%; With disability: 5.5%; Veterans: 10.2%; Ancestry: 29.3% German, 18.1% Irish, 11.6% English, 7.0% American, 5.2% Italian

Employment: 21.1% management, business, and financial, 4.8% computer, engineering, and science, 10.6% education, legal, community service, arts, and media, 7.6% healthcare practitioners, 16.4% service, 24.7% sales and office, 6.5% natural resources, construction, and maintenance, 8.2% production, transportation, and material moving

Income: Per capita: $31,347; Median household: $81,540; Average household: $87,917; Households with income of $100,000 or more: 35.2%; Poverty rate: 4.4%

Educational Attainment: High school diploma or higher: 96.8%; Bachelor's degree or higher: 38.8%; Graduate/professional degree or higher: 13.6%

School District(s)

Pickerington Community School (09-12)
2012-13 Enrollment: 66.......................... (614) 995-1985
Pickerington Local (PK-12)
2012-13 Enrollment: 10,061 .... (614) 833-2110

Housing: Homeownership rate: 77.4%; Median home value: $183,200; Median year structure built: 1999; Homeowner vacancy rate: 3.4%; Median gross rent: $949 per month; Rental vacancy rate: 11.7%

Health Insurance: 94.1% have insurance; 88.6% have private insurance; 13.4% have public insurance; 5.9% do not have insurance; 2.6% of children under 18 do not have insurance

Transportation: Commute: 92.5% car, 0.0% public transportation, 0.3% walk, 5.3% work from home; Median travel time to work: 26.7 minutes

Additional Information Contacts

City of Pickerington .... (614) 837-3974
http://www.ci.pickerington.oh.us

PLEASANTVILLE (village). Covers a land area of 0.266 square miles and a water area of 0 square miles. Located at 39.81° N. Lat; 82.52° W. Long. Elevation is 915 feet.
Population: 960; Growth (since 2000): 9.5%; Density: 3,613.7 persons per square mile; Race: 95.4% White, 0.1% Black/African American, 0.3% Asian, 0.5% American Indian/Alaska Native, 0.5% Native Hawaiian/Other Pacific Islander, 2.3% Two or more races, 0.8% Hispanic of any race; Average household size: 2.62; Median age: 32.4; Age under 18: 29.9%; Age 65 and over: 10.2%; Males per 100 females: 100.0

School District(s)

Fairfield Union Local (PK-12)
2012-13 Enrollment: 1,963 . . . . (740) 536-7384
Housing: Homeownership rate: 54.1%; Homeowner vacancy rate: 4.9%; Rental vacancy rate: 7.8%

RUSHVILLE (village). Covers a land area of 0.240 square miles and a water area of 0 square miles. Located at 39.76° N. Lat; 82.43° W. Long. Elevation is 1,053 feet.
History: Rushville was the birthplace of Benjamin Russell Hanby (1833-1867), who wrote the song "Darling Nellie Gray." Though it was published and became popular across the country, Hanby never received royalties for his work.
Population: 302; Growth (since 2000): 12.7%; Density: 1,260.4 persons per square mile; Race: 96.0% White, 0.0% Black/African American, 0.7% Asian, 0.0% American Indian/Alaska Native, 0.0% Native Hawaiian/Other Pacific Islander, 3.3% Two or more races, 0.0% Hispanic of any race; Average household size: 2.82; Median age: 32.3; Age under 18: 30.5%; Age 65 and over: 5.3%; Males per 100 females: 89.9
Housing: Homeownership rate: 72.0%; Homeowner vacancy rate: 2.5%; Rental vacancy rate: 0.0%

STOUTSVILLE (village). Covers a land area of 1.156 square miles and a water area of 0 square miles. Located at 39.60° N. Lat; 82.82° W. Long. Elevation is 968 feet.
Population: 560; Growth (since 2000): -3.6%; Density: 484.5 persons per square mile; Race: 99.8% White, 0.0% Black/African American, 0.0% Asian, 0.0% American Indian/Alaska Native, 0.0% Native Hawaiian/Other Pacific Islander, 0.2% Two or more races, 0.5% Hispanic of any race; Average household size: 2.65; Median age: 38.4; Age under 18: 28.2%; Age 65 and over: 10.9%; Males per 100 females: 102.2
Housing: Homeownership rate: 76.8%; Homeowner vacancy rate: 0.6%; Rental vacancy rate: 9.1%

SUGAR GROVE (village). Covers a land area of 0.289 square miles and a water area of 0.012 square miles. Located at 39.63° N. Lat; 82.55° W. Long. Elevation is 778 feet.
Population: 426; Growth (since 2000): -4.9%; Density: 1,473.3 persons per square mile; Race: 98.1% White, 0.0% Black/African American, 0.0% Asian, 1.4% American Indian/Alaska Native, 0.0% Native Hawaiian/Other Pacific Islander, 0.5% Two or more races, 0.5% Hispanic of any race; Average household size: 2.75; Median age: 34.8; Age under 18: 30.8%; Age 65 and over: 6.6%; Males per 100 females: 100.9

School District(s)

Berne Union Local (PK-12)
2012-13 Enrollment: 891 . . . . (740) 746-8341
Housing: Homeownership rate: 60.7%; Homeowner vacancy rate: 5.1%; Rental vacancy rate: 7.4%

THURSTON (village). Covers a land area of 0.260 square miles and a water area of 0 square miles. Located at 39.84° N. Lat; 82.54° W. Long. Elevation is 886 feet.
Population: 604; Growth (since 2000): 8.8%; Density: 2,323.2 persons per square mile; Race: 95.4% White, 0.0% Black/African American, 0.2% Asian, 0.3% American Indian/Alaska Native, 0.0% Native Hawaiian/Other Pacific Islander, 3.8% Two or more races, 1.3% Hispanic of any race; Average household size: 2.76; Median age: 34.6; Age under 18: 29.1%; Age 65 and over: 11.8%; Males per 100 females: 92.4
Housing: Homeownership rate: 68.9%; Homeowner vacancy rate: 2.6%; Rental vacancy rate: 12.8%

Additional Information Contacts

Village of Thurston . . . . (740) 862-6003
http://www.thurstonohio.com

WEST RUSHVILLE (village). Covers a land area of 0.065 square miles and a water area of <.001 square miles. Located at 39.76° N. Lat; 82.45° W. Long. Elevation is 1,020 feet.
Population: 134; Growth (since 2000): 1.5%; Density: 2,066.7 persons per square mile; Race: 97.0% White, 0.0% Black/African American, 0.0% Asian, 0.0% American Indian/Alaska Native, 0.0% Native Hawaiian/Other Pacific Islander, 3.0% Two or more races, 0.7% Hispanic of any race; Average household size: 2.63; Median age: 36.0; Age under 18: 29.1%; Age 65 and over: 9.0%; Males per 100 females: 103.0
Housing: Homeownership rate: 68.6%; Homeowner vacancy rate: 5.4%; Rental vacancy rate: 5.9%

Fayette County

Located in south central Ohio; drained by Paint, Sugar, and Rattlesnakes Creeks. Covers a land area of 406.357 square miles, a water area of 0.658 square miles, and is located in the Eastern Time Zone at 39.55° N. Lat., 83.46° W. Long. The county was founded in 1810. County seat is Washington Court House.

Fayette County is part of the Washington Court House, OH Micropolitan Statistical Area. The entire metro area includes: Fayette County, OH

Population: 29,030; Growth (since 2000): 2.1%; Density: 71.4 persons per square mile; Race: 94.6% White, 2.0% Black/African American, 0.5% Asian, 0.2% American Indian/Alaska Native, 0.0% Native Hawaiian/Other Pacific Islander, 1.7% two or more races, 1.8% Hispanic of any race; Average household size: 2.49; Median age: 39.4; Age under 18: 24.7%; Age 65 and over: 15.0%; Males per 100 females: 96.7; Marriage status: 25.2% never married, 52.9% now married, 3.0% separated, 6.7% widowed, 15.2% divorced; Foreign born: 1.3%; Speak English only: 97.3%; With disability: 17.4%; Veterans: 10.0%; Ancestry: 19.0% German, 13.7% American, 10.0% Irish, 10.0% English, 2.4% Scottish
Religion: Six largest groups: 7.0% Methodist/Pietist, 6.2% Baptist, 5.9% Non-denominational Protestant, 2.2% Catholicism, 1.5% Presbyterian-Reformed, 0.8% Episcopalianism/Anglicanism
Economy: Unemployment rate: 4.0%; Leading industries: 32.1% retail trade; 10.7% other services (except public administration); 10.4% accommodation and food services; Farms: 504 totaling 196,529 acres; Company size: 0 employ 1,000 or more persons, 1 employs 500 to 999 persons, 13 employ 100 to 499 persons, 556 employ less than 100 persons; Business ownership: 377 women-owned, n/a Black-owned, n/a Hispanic-owned, n/a Asian-owned
Employment: 11.5% management, business, and financial, 2.0% computer, engineering, and science, 6.8% education, legal, community service, arts, and media, 4.0% healthcare practitioners, 19.7% service, 26.8% sales and office, 7.9% natural resources, construction, and maintenance, 21.3% production, transportation, and material moving
Income: Per capita: $20,603; Median household: $37,619; Average household: $50,683; Households with income of $100,000 or more: 9.2%; Poverty rate: 20.1%
Educational Attainment: High school diploma or higher: 83.4%; Bachelor's degree or higher: 13.7%; Graduate/professional degree or higher: 4.6%
Housing: Homeownership rate: 63.2%; Median home value: $107,000; Median year structure built: 1969; Homeowner vacancy rate: 3.4%; Median gross rent: $696 per month; Rental vacancy rate: 8.4%
Vital Statistics: Birth rate: 126.0 per 10,000 population; Death rate: 102.8 per 10,000 population; Age-adjusted cancer mortality rate: 182.5 deaths per 100,000 population
Health Insurance: 84.8% have insurance; 59.5% have private insurance; 37.8% have public insurance; 15.2% do not have insurance; 4.2% of children under 18 do not have insurance
Health Care: Physicians: 5.2 per 10,000 population; Hospital beds: 8.6 per 10,000 population; Hospital admissions: 348.3 per 10,000 population
Air Quality Index: 97.5% good, 2.5% moderate, 0.0% unhealthy for sensitive individuals, 0.0% unhealthy (percent of days)
Transportation: Commute: 93.2% car, 0.5% public transportation, 2.9% walk, 2.6% work from home; Median travel time to work: 22.2 minutes
Presidential Election: 38.2% Obama, 60.5% Romney (2012)

Additional Information Contacts

Fayette Government . . . . (740) 335-0720
http://www.fayette-co-oh.com

Fayette County Communities

BLOOMINGBURG (village). Covers a land area of 0.701 square miles and a water area of 0 square miles. Located at 39.61° N. Lat; 83.40° W. Long. Elevation is 994 feet.

Population: 938; Growth (since 2000): 7.3%; Density: 1,337.7 persons per square mile; Race: 88.6% White, 3.1% Black/African American, 0.0% Asian, 0.6% American Indian/Alaska Native, 0.0% Native Hawaiian/Other Pacific Islander, 1.5% Two or more races, 6.9% Hispanic of any race; Average household size: 2.92; Median age: 30.8; Age under 18: 32.1%; Age 65 and over: 9.7%; Males per 100 females: 107.1

Housing: Homeownership rate: 69.8%; Homeowner vacancy rate: 3.4%; Rental vacancy rate: 17.1%

GOOD HOPE (CDP). Covers a land area of 0.753 square miles and a water area of 0 square miles. Located at 39.45° N. Lat; 83.36° W. Long. Elevation is 922 feet.

Population: 234; Growth (since 2000): n/a; Density: 310.9 persons per square mile; Race: 98.3% White, 0.9% Black/African American, 0.0% Asian, 0.0% American Indian/Alaska Native, 0.0% Native Hawaiian/Other Pacific Islander, 0.4% Two or more races, 0.4% Hispanic of any race; Average household size: 2.60; Median age: 38.8; Age under 18: 24.4%; Age 65 and over: 12.8%; Males per 100 females: 91.8

Housing: Homeownership rate: 80.0%; Homeowner vacancy rate: 2.6%; Rental vacancy rate: 9.5%

JEFFERSONVILLE (village). Covers a land area of 1.700 square miles and a water area of 0.035 square miles. Located at 39.65° N. Lat; 83.56° W. Long. Elevation is 1,050 feet.

Population: 1,203; Growth (since 2000): -6.6%; Density: 707.8 persons per square mile; Race: 92.3% White, 4.2% Black/African American, 0.2% Asian, 0.2% American Indian/Alaska Native, 0.0% Native Hawaiian/Other Pacific Islander, 2.8% Two or more races, 1.9% Hispanic of any race; Average household size: 2.40; Median age: 33.9; Age under 18: 27.8%; Age 65 and over: 12.2%; Males per 100 females: 95.0

Housing: Homeownership rate: 51.2%; Homeowner vacancy rate: 7.9%; Rental vacancy rate: 10.9%

MILLEDGEVILLE (village). Covers a land area of 0.101 square miles and a water area of 0 square miles. Located at 39.59° N. Lat; 83.59° W. Long. Elevation is 1,050 feet.

Population: 112; Growth (since 2000): -8.2%; Density: 1,106.3 persons per square mile; Race: 95.5% White, 1.8% Black/African American, 0.9% Asian, 0.0% American Indian/Alaska Native, 0.0% Native Hawaiian/Other Pacific Islander, 0.9% Two or more races, 0.0% Hispanic of any race; Average household size: 2.24; Median age: 45.7; Age under 18: 22.3%; Age 65 and over: 17.0%; Males per 100 females: 133.3

Housing: Homeownership rate: 78.0%; Homeowner vacancy rate: 4.9%; Rental vacancy rate: 0.0%

OCTA (village). Covers a land area of 0.278 square miles and a water area of 0 square miles. Located at 39.61° N. Lat; 83.61° W. Long. Elevation is 1,040 feet.

Population: 59; Growth (since 2000): -28.9%; Density: 212.6 persons per square mile; Race: 84.7% White, 15.3% Black/African American, 0.0% Asian, 0.0% American Indian/Alaska Native, 0.0% Native Hawaiian/Other Pacific Islander, 0.0% Two or more races, 1.7% Hispanic of any race; Average household size: 1.97; Median age: 45.8; Age under 18: 20.3%; Age 65 and over: 23.7%; Males per 100 females: 96.7

Housing: Homeownership rate: 46.7%; Homeowner vacancy rate: 12.5%; Rental vacancy rate: 0.0%

PANCOASTBURG (CDP). Covers a land area of 0.341 square miles and a water area of 0.006 square miles. Located at 39.62° N. Lat; 83.27° W. Long. Elevation is 866 feet.

Population: 87; Growth (since 2000): n/a; Density: 255.4 persons per square mile; Race: 98.9% White, 0.0% Black/African American, 1.1% Asian, 0.0% American Indian/Alaska Native, 0.0% Native Hawaiian/Other Pacific Islander, 0.0% Two or more races, 0.0% Hispanic of any race; Average household size: 2.07; Median age: 44.8; Age under 18: 11.5%; Age 65 and over: 11.5%; Males per 100 females: 107.1

Housing: Homeownership rate: 61.9%; Homeowner vacancy rate: 0.0%; Rental vacancy rate: 11.1%

WASHINGTON COURT HOUSE (city). County seat. Covers a land area of 8.739 square miles and a water area of 0.060 square miles. Located at 39.54° N. Lat; 83.43° W. Long. Elevation is 978 feet.

Population: 14,192; Growth (since 2000): n/a; Density: 1,624.1 persons per square mile; Race: 93.5% White, 2.7% Black/African American, 0.8% Asian, 0.3% American Indian/Alaska Native, 0.0% Native Hawaiian/Other Pacific Islander, 2.1% Two or more races, 1.8% Hispanic of any race; Average household size: 2.37; Median age: 38.4; Age under 18: 25.0%; Age 65 and over: 15.9%; Males per 100 females: 91.1; Marriage status: 25.2% never married, 48.6% now married, 4.2% separated, 7.9% widowed, 18.3% divorced; Foreign born: 1.9%; Speak English only: 96.4%; With disability: 20.0%; Veterans: 10.2%; Ancestry: 17.0% German, 14.5% American, 11.0% Irish, 9.3% English, 3.0% Dutch

Employment: 11.1% management, business, and financial, 1.6% computer, engineering, and science, 7.1% education, legal, community service, arts, and media, 3.8% healthcare practitioners, 23.1% service, 24.5% sales and office, 7.3% natural resources, construction, and maintenance, 21.5% production, transportation, and material moving

Income: Per capita: $19,696; Median household: $32,186; Average household: $45,521; Households with income of $100,000 or more: 6.2%; Poverty rate: 23.1%

Educational Attainment: High school diploma or higher: 81.0%; Bachelor's degree or higher: 15.0%; Graduate/professional degree or higher: 4.8%

School District(s)

Miami Trace Local (PK-12)
2012-13 Enrollment: 2,433 . . . . (740) 335-3010
Washington Court House City (PK-12)
2012-13 Enrollment: 2,240 . . . . (740) 335-6620

Housing: Homeownership rate: 52.3%; Median home value: $98,500; Median year structure built: 1966; Homeowner vacancy rate: 4.6%; Median gross rent: $692 per month; Rental vacancy rate: 8.0%

Health Insurance: 83.8% have insurance; 55.5% have private insurance; 41.5% have public insurance; 16.2% do not have insurance; 4.0% of children under 18 do not have insurance

Hospitals: Fayette County Memorial Hospital (70 beds)

Safety: Violent crime rate: 17.0 per 10,000 population; Property crime rate: 484.3 per 10,000 population

Newspapers: Record-Herald (daily circulation 5200)

Transportation: Commute: 93.9% car, 0.5% public transportation, 3.1% walk, 1.4% work from home; Median travel time to work: 20.1 minutes

Airports: Fayette County (general aviation)

Additional Information Contacts

City of Washington Court House . . . . (740) 636-2340
http://www.ci.washington-court-house.oh.us

Franklin County

Located in central Ohio; crossed by the Scioto and Olentangy Rivers. Covers a land area of 532.188 square miles, a water area of 11.320 square miles, and is located in the Eastern Time Zone at 39.97° N. Lat., 83.01° W. Long. The county was founded in 1803. County seat is Columbus.

Franklin County is part of the Columbus, OH Metropolitan Statistical Area. The entire metro area includes: Delaware County, OH; Fairfield County, OH; Franklin County, OH; Hocking County, OH; Licking County, OH; Madison County, OH; Morrow County, OH; Perry County, OH; Pickaway County, OH; Union County, OH

Weather Station: Columbus Valley Crossing Elevation: 734 feet

	Jan	Feb	Mar	Apr	May	Jun	Jul	Aug	Sep	Oct	Nov	Dec
High	37	41	52	64	73	82	85	84	78	66	54	41
Low	21	23	31	41	51	60	64	62	54	43	34	25
Precip	2.9	2.1	3.3	3.7	4.5	4.0	4.5	3.3	3.0	2.9	3.2	3.0
Snow	5.7	4.0	1.6	0.5	tr	0.0	0.0	0.0	0.0	tr	0.4	2.7

High and Low temperatures in degrees Fahrenheit; Precipitation and Snow in inches

Weather Station: Columbus-Port Columbus Intl Elevation: 810 feet

	Jan	Feb	Mar	Apr	May	Jun	Jul	Aug	Sep	Oct	Nov	Dec
High	37	41	51	63	73	81	85	84	77	65	52	40
Low	22	24	32	42	51	61	65	63	56	44	35	26
Precip	2.7	2.2	3.1	3.4	4.2	4.0	4.7	3.5	2.9	2.6	3.1	3.0
Snow	9.3	6.3	4.4	1.1	tr	tr	tr	tr	tr	0.2	1.2	5.4

High and Low temperatures in degrees Fahrenheit; Precipitation and Snow in inches

Weather Station: Westerville Elevation: 810 feet

	Jan	Feb	Mar	Apr	May	Jun	Jul	Aug	Sep	Oct	Nov	Dec
High	37	41	52	65	74	82	85	84	78	66	53	41
Low	21	23	31	41	50	59	63	62	54	43	35	26
Precip	2.7	2.2	2.9	3.5	4.4	4.5	4.3	3.2	2.8	2.8	3.1	2.9
Snow	6.9	4.6	2.5	0.5	tr	0.0	0.0	0.0	0.0	tr	0.3	3.7

High and Low temperatures in degrees Fahrenheit; Precipitation and Snow in inches

Population: 1,163,414; Growth (since 2000): 8.8%; Density: 2,186.1 persons per square mile; Race: 69.2% White, 21.2% Black/African American, 3.9% Asian, 0.2% American Indian/Alaska Native, 0.1% Native Hawaiian/Other Pacific Islander, 3.0% two or more races, 4.8% Hispanic of any race; Average household size: 2.38; Median age: 33.4; Age under 18: 23.9%; Age 65 and over: 9.9%; Males per 100 females: 94.9; Marriage status: 38.1% never married, 44.9% now married, 2.2% separated, 5.0% widowed, 12.0% divorced; Foreign born: 9.4%; Speak English only: 87.9%; With disability: 11.5%; Veterans: 7.7%; Ancestry: 23.2% German, 13.8% Irish, 8.5% English, 5.7% American, 5.6% Italian
Religion: Six largest groups: 13.2% Catholicism, 5.3% Baptist, 4.4% Non-denominational Protestant, 4.0% Methodist/Pietist, 2.6% Lutheran, 2.2% Pentecostal
Economy: Unemployment rate: 3.9%; Leading industries: 13.5% retail trade; 12.8% professional, scientific, and technical services; 12.4% health care and social assistance; Farms: 388 totaling 62,017 acres; Company size: 42 employ 1,000 or more persons, 68 employ 500 to 999 persons, 913 employ 100 to 499 persons, 25,848 employ less than 100 persons; Business ownership: 31,093 women-owned, 11,470 Black-owned, 1,714 Hispanic-owned, 3,708 Asian-owned
Employment: 16.8% management, business, and financial, 6.5% computer, engineering, and science, 11.6% education, legal, community service, arts, and media, 5.7% healthcare practitioners, 16.9% service, 26.3% sales and office, 5.4% natural resources, construction, and maintenance, 10.7% production, transportation, and material moving
Income: Per capita: $28,283; Median household: $50,877; Average household: $69,197; Households with income of $100,000 or more: 20.6%; Poverty rate: 18.1%
Educational Attainment: High school diploma or higher: 89.7%; Bachelor's degree or higher: 36.4%; Graduate/professional degree or higher: 13.0%
Housing: Homeownership rate: 55.4%; Median home value: $150,800; Median year structure built: 1974; Homeowner vacancy rate: 2.9%; Median gross rent: $819 per month; Rental vacancy rate: 9.8%
Vital Statistics: Birth rate: 150.0 per 10,000 population; Death rate: 74.2 per 10,000 population; Age-adjusted cancer mortality rate: 182.2 deaths per 100,000 population
Health Insurance: 86.7% have insurance; 68.6% have private insurance; 26.8% have public insurance; 13.3% do not have insurance; 6.2% of children under 18 do not have insurance
Health Care: Physicians: 40.3 per 10,000 population; Hospital beds: 40.2 per 10,000 population; Hospital admissions: 1,955.8 per 10,000 population
Air Quality Index: 67.7% good, 31.8% moderate, 0.5% unhealthy for sensitive individuals, 0.0% unhealthy (percent of days)
Transportation: Commute: 89.7% car, 2.4% public transportation, 2.4% walk, 3.9% work from home; Median travel time to work: 21.5 minutes
Presidential Election: 60.1% Obama, 38.4% Romney (2012)
National and State Parks: Olentangy River State Wildlife Access Area; Sawmill State Wildlife Education Area
Additional Information Contacts
Franklin Government. . . . . (614) 462-3322
http://www.co.franklin.oh.us

Franklin County Communities

AMLIN (unincorporated postal area)

ZCTA: 43002

Covers a land area of 0.994 square miles and a water area of 0.002 square miles. Located at 40.06° N. Lat; 83.17° W. Long. Elevation is 945 feet.
Population: 2,262; Growth (since 2000): 73.5%; Density: 2,275.2 persons per square mile; Race: 84.4% White, 5.1% Black/African American, 6.5% Asian, 0.0% American Indian/Alaska Native, 0.0% Native Hawaiian/Other Pacific Islander, 1.9% Two or more races, 4.1% Hispanic of any race; Average household size: 2.00; Median age: 30.7; Age under 18: 12.3%; Age 65 and over: 4.8%; Males per 100 females: 91.5
Housing: Homeownership rate: 92.2%; Homeowner vacancy rate: 7.5%; Rental vacancy rate: 8.9%

BEXLEY (city). Covers a land area of 2.431 square miles and a water area of 0.020 square miles. Located at 39.97° N. Lat; 82.93° W. Long. Elevation is 794 feet.
History: Named for Bexley, England. Bexley developed as a residential suburb of Columbus, and as the location of Capital University, founded in 1830 as a Lutheran divinity school.
Population: 13,057; Growth (since 2000): -1.1%; Density: 5,370.9 persons per square mile; Race: 89.6% White, 5.9% Black/African American, 1.5% Asian, 0.1% American Indian/Alaska Native, 0.0% Native Hawaiian/Other Pacific Islander, 2.5% Two or more races, 1.8% Hispanic of any race; Average household size: 2.59; Median age: 35.5; Age under 18: 25.7%; Age 65 and over: 10.1%; Males per 100 females: 88.4; Marriage status: 36.0% never married, 52.6% now married, 0.9% separated, 3.1% widowed, 8.3% divorced; Foreign born: 6.4%; Speak English only: 92.5%; With disability: 7.2%; Veterans: 4.7%; Ancestry: 31.7% German, 13.5% Irish, 11.7% English, 8.1% Italian, 6.2% American
Employment: 24.3% management, business, and financial, 6.8% computer, engineering, and science, 23.7% education, legal, community service, arts, and media, 5.8% healthcare practitioners, 13.6% service, 20.4% sales and office, 2.8% natural resources, construction, and maintenance, 2.5% production, transportation, and material moving
Income: Per capita: $46,147; Median household: $93,478; Average household: $132,664; Households with income of $100,000 or more: 46.5%; Poverty rate: 8.8%
Educational Attainment: High school diploma or higher: 98.4%; Bachelor's degree or higher: 69.2%; Graduate/professional degree or higher: 30.7%

School District(s)

Bexley City (PK-12)
2012-13 Enrollment: 2,130 . . . . (614) 231-7611
Housing: Homeownership rate: 75.6%; Median home value: $274,600; Median year structure built: 1943; Homeowner vacancy rate: 1.5%; Median gross rent: $895 per month; Rental vacancy rate: 16.3%
Health Insurance: 94.2% have insurance; 88.0% have private insurance; 15.0% have public insurance; 5.8% do not have insurance; 2.0% of children under 18 do not have insurance
Safety: Violent crime rate: 15.0 per 10,000 population; Property crime rate: 271.9 per 10,000 population
Transportation: Commute: 84.9% car, 0.9% public transportation, 7.1% walk, 4.8% work from home; Median travel time to work: 16.7 minutes
Additional Information Contacts
City of Bexley . . . . (614) 559-4200
http://www.bexley.org

BLACKLICK ESTATES (CDP). Covers a land area of 1.891 square miles and a water area of 0.024 square miles. Located at 39.90° N. Lat; 82.87° W. Long. Elevation is 758 feet.
Population: 8,682; Growth (since 2000): -8.8%; Density: 4,592.4 persons per square mile; Race: 73.5% White, 19.6% Black/African American, 1.3% Asian, 0.2% American Indian/Alaska Native, 0.1% Native Hawaiian/Other Pacific Islander, 3.8% Two or more races, 3.2% Hispanic of any race; Average household size: 2.81; Median age: 34.5; Age under 18: 28.0%; Age 65 and over: 10.5%; Males per 100 females: 95.0; Marriage status: 34.6% never married, 43.8% now married, 3.1% separated, 5.9% widowed, 15.7% divorced; Foreign born: 2.2%; Speak English only: 97.5%; With disability: 15.4%; Veterans: 9.3%; Ancestry: 15.6% German, 14.3% English, 10.6% Irish, 9.6% American, 5.0% Italian
Employment: 8.6% management, business, and financial, 2.3% computer, engineering, and science, 5.3% education, legal, community service, arts, and media, 0.7% healthcare practitioners, 19.1% service, 35.8% sales and office, 9.5% natural resources, construction, and maintenance, 18.5% production, transportation, and material moving
Income: Per capita: $19,143; Median household: $49,816; Average household: $53,411; Households with income of $100,000 or more: 7.0%; Poverty rate: 16.4%
Educational Attainment: High school diploma or higher: 85.0%; Bachelor's degree or higher: 8.8%; Graduate/professional degree or higher: 3.1%

School District(s)

Gahanna-Jefferson City (PK-12)
2012-13 Enrollment: 7,041 . . . . (614) 471-7065

Licking Heights Local (PK-12)
2012-13 Enrollment: 3,616 . . . . (740) 927-6926
Housing: Homeownership rate: 73.7%; Median home value: $95,400; Median year structure built: 1969; Homeowner vacancy rate: 2.5%; Median gross rent: $970 per month; Rental vacancy rate: 17.8%
Health Insurance: 78.9% have insurance; 52.4% have private insurance; 37.3% have public insurance; 21.1% do not have insurance; 15.4% of children under 18 do not have insurance
Transportation: Commute: 96.3% car, 1.2% public transportation, 1.2% walk, 0.4% work from home; Median travel time to work: 24.5 minutes

BRICE (village). Covers a land area of 0.098 square miles and a water area of <.001 square miles. Located at 39.92° N. Lat; 82.83° W. Long. Elevation is 781 feet.
Population: 114; Growth (since 2000): 62.9%; Density: 1,163.4 persons per square mile; Race: 78.1% White, 10.5% Black/African American, 1.8% Asian, 0.0% American Indian/Alaska Native, 0.9% Native Hawaiian/Other Pacific Islander, 7.9% Two or more races, 0.0% Hispanic of any race; Average household size: 2.78; Median age: 40.0; Age under 18: 26.3%; Age 65 and over: 12.3%; Males per 100 females: 93.2
Housing: Homeownership rate: 78.1%; Homeowner vacancy rate: 0.0%; Rental vacancy rate: 0.0%

CANAL WINCHESTER (city). Covers a land area of 7.465 square miles and a water area of 0.136 square miles. Located at 39.84° N. Lat; 82.82° W. Long. Elevation is 761 feet.
History: The town of Canal Winchester developed as a produce center on the Ohio & Erie Canal.
Population: 7,101; Growth (since 2000): 58.6%; Density: 951.2 persons per square mile; Race: 91.6% White, 5.1% Black/African American, 1.2% Asian, 0.1% American Indian/Alaska Native, 0.0% Native Hawaiian/Other Pacific Islander, 1.6% Two or more races, 1.2% Hispanic of any race; Average household size: 2.62; Median age: 39.7; Age under 18: 26.7%; Age 65 and over: 14.8%; Males per 100 females: 89.3; Marriage status: 20.9% never married, 61.9% now married, 0.3% separated, 7.0% widowed, 10.2% divorced; Foreign born: 3.8%; Speak English only: 95.5%; With disability: 11.2%; Veterans: 14.1%; Ancestry: 28.4% German, 15.3% English, 13.7% Irish, 10.6% American, 5.3% Italian
Employment: 20.9% management, business, and financial, 5.1% computer, engineering, and science, 12.9% education, legal, community service, arts, and media, 7.7% healthcare practitioners, 12.2% service, 31.1% sales and office, 4.1% natural resources, construction, and maintenance, 6.1% production, transportation, and material moving
Income: Per capita: $33,559; Median household: $76,500; Average household: $88,004; Households with income of $100,000 or more: 35.3%; Poverty rate: 2.0%
Educational Attainment: High school diploma or higher: 97.1%; Bachelor's degree or higher: 35.8%; Graduate/professional degree or higher: 17.0%

School District(s)

Canal Winchester Local (PK-12)
2012-13 Enrollment: 3,589 . . . . (614) 837-4533

Two-year College(s)

Ohio State School of Cosmetology-Canal Winchester (Private, For-profit)
Fall 2013 Enrollment: 89 . . . . (614) 252-5252
Housing: Homeownership rate: 84.0%; Median home value: $186,300; Median year structure built: 1998; Homeowner vacancy rate: 5.9%; Median gross rent: $561 per month; Rental vacancy rate: 8.8%
Health Insurance: 94.5% have insurance; 86.9% have private insurance; 20.3% have public insurance; 5.5% do not have insurance; 0.6% of children under 18 do not have insurance
Hospitals: Diley Ridge Medical Center
Transportation: Commute: 93.5% car, 0.0% public transportation, 0.5% walk, 5.3% work from home; Median travel time to work: 25.1 minutes
Additional Information Contacts
Village of Canal Winchester . . . . (614) 837-7493
http://www.canalwinchesterohio.gov

COLUMBUS (city). State capital. County seat. Covers a land area of 217.169 square miles and a water area of 5.936 square miles. Located at 39.98° N. Lat; 82.99° W. Long. Elevation is 781 feet.
History: The site of Columbus was selected for the capital of Ohio in 1812, and the town was laid out. Columbus' early problems of cholera and lack of transportation were solved by draining the nearby swamps, and by the the Ohio & Erie Canal connected to Columbus by a feeder canal. The National Road reached Columbus in 1833, with stagecoaches arriving daily from the east. By 1872 transportation was being provided by five rail lines, and in 1873 Ohio State University was founded in Columbus.
Population: 787,033; Growth (since 2000): 10.6%; Density: 3,624.1 persons per square mile; Race: 61.5% White, 28.0% Black/African American, 4.1% Asian, 0.3% American Indian/Alaska Native, 0.1% Native Hawaiian/Other Pacific Islander, 3.3% Two or more races, 5.6% Hispanic of any race; Average household size: 2.31; Median age: 31.2; Age under 18: 23.2%; Age 65 and over: 8.6%; Males per 100 females: 95.4; Marriage status: 43.3% never married, 39.4% now married, 2.5% separated, 4.7% widowed, 12.6% divorced; Foreign born: 10.9%; Speak English only: 86.0%; With disability: 11.8%; Veterans: 7.2%; Ancestry: 20.5% German, 12.4% Irish, 6.8% English, 5.2% Italian, 4.9% American
Employment: 15.2% management, business, and financial, 6.2% computer, engineering, and science, 11.3% education, legal, community service, arts, and media, 5.3% healthcare practitioners, 18.3% service, 26.8% sales and office, 5.5% natural resources, construction, and maintenance, 11.4% production, transportation, and material moving
Income: Per capita: $24,351; Median household: $44,072; Average household: $57,570; Households with income of $100,000 or more: 14.7%; Poverty rate: 22.4%
Educational Attainment: High school diploma or higher: 88.3%; Bachelor's degree or higher: 33.1%; Graduate/professional degree or higher: 11.1%

School District(s)

A+ Arts Academy (KG-08)
2012-13 Enrollment: 310. . . . . (614) 338-0767
Academy of Columbus (KG-08)
2012-13 Enrollment: 363. . . . . (614) 433-7510
Academy of New Media Middle (06-08)
2012-13 Enrollment: 82. . . . . (614) 252-4441
Arts & College Preparatory Academy (09-12)
2012-13 Enrollment: 269. . . . . (614) 986-9974
C.m. Grant Leadership Academy (KG-08)
2012-13 Enrollment: 154. . . . . (614) 252-2087
Capital High School (09-12)
2012-13 Enrollment: 170. . . . . (614) 299-9802
Cesar Chavez College Preparatory School (KG-05)
2012-13 Enrollment: 42. . . . . (614) 351-1774
Charles School At Ohio Dominican University (09-12)
2012-13 Enrollment: 381. . . . . (614) 258-8588
Columbus Arts & Technology Academy (KG-08)
2012-13 Enrollment: 497. . . . . (614) 577-0900
Columbus Bilingual Academy (KG-08)
2012-13 Enrollment: 96. . . . . (614) 324-1492
Columbus Bilingual Academy-North (KG-04)
2012-13 Enrollment: 159. . . . . (614) 324-1492
Columbus City SD (PK-12)
2012-13 Enrollment: 50,384 . . . . (614) 365-5000
Columbus Collegiate Academy (06-08)
2012-13 Enrollment: 190. . . . . (614) 299-5284
Columbus Humanities Arts and Technology Academy (KG-08)
2012-13 Enrollment: 330. . . . . (614) 261-1200
Columbus Performance Academy (KG-06)
2012-13 Enrollment: 166. . . . . (614) 318-0720
Columbus Preparatory Academy (KG-08)
2012-13 Enrollment: 621. . . . . (614) 275-3600
Columbus Preparatory and Fitness Academy (KG-08)
2012-13 Enrollment: 200. . . . . (614) 318-0606
Crittenton Community School (06-09)
2012-13 Enrollment: 49. . . . . (614) 372-2401
Cruiser Academy (09-12)
2012-13 Enrollment: 158. . . . . (614) 237-8756
Dublin City (PK-12)
2012-13 Enrollment: 14,627 . . . . (614) 764-5913
Early College Academy (09-12)
2012-13 Enrollment: 189. . . . . (614) 298-4742
Educational Academy At Linden (KG-05)
2012-13 Enrollment: 86. . . . . (614) 291-0235
Educational Academy for Boys & Girls (KG-05)
2012-13 Enrollment: 92. . . . . (614) 261-7480
Electronic Classroom of Tomorrow (KG-12)
2012-13 Enrollment: 12,202 . . . . (614) 492-8884
Fci Academy (KG-12)
2012-13 Enrollment: 445. . . . . (614) 471-4527

Focus Learning Academy of Northern Columbus (KG-08)
2012-13 Enrollment: 168 (614) 547-0927
Focus Learning Academy of Southeastern Columbus (09-12)
2012-13 Enrollment: 194 (614) 269-0150
Focus Learning Academy of Southwest Columbus (09-12)
2012-13 Enrollment: 241 (614) 545-2000
Focus North High School (09-12)
2012-13 Enrollment: 161 (614) 310-0430
Graham Expeditionary Middle School (06-08)
2012-13 Enrollment: 162 (614) 262-1111
Graham School the (09-12)
2012-13 Enrollment: 260 (614) 262-1111
Grandview Heights City (PK-12)
2012-13 Enrollment: 1,080 (614) 481-3600
Great Western Academy (KG-08)
2012-13 Enrollment: 852 (614) 276-1028
Groveport Madison Local (PK-12)
2012-13 Enrollment: 5,535 (614) 492-2520
Hamilton Local (PK-12)
2012-13 Enrollment: 3,093 (614) 491-8044
Hamilton Local Digital Academy (01-12)
2012-13 Enrollment: 60 (614) 491-8044
Harrisburg Pike Community School (KG-05)
2012-13 Enrollment: 441 (614) 223-1510
Hilliard City (PK-12)
2012-13 Enrollment: 15,435 (614) 921-7000
Horizon Science Academy Columbus (09-12)
2012-13 Enrollment: 428 (614) 846-7616
Horizon Science Academy Columbus Middle School (06-08)
2012-13 Enrollment: 433 (614) 428-6564
Horizon Science Academy Elementary School (KG-05)
2012-13 Enrollment: 497 (614) 475-4585
Imagine Integrity Academy (KG-04)
2012-13 Enrollment: 131 (614) 995-1985
International Acad of Columbus (KG-08)
2012-13 Enrollment: 213 (614) 844-5539
Kipp: Journey Academy (05-08)
2012-13 Enrollment: 335 (614) 263-6137
Life Skills Center of Columbus North (09-12)
2012-13 Enrollment: 154 (614) 891-9041
Life Skills Center of Columbus Southeast (09-12)
2012-13 Enrollment: 176 (614) 863-9175
Midnimo Cross Cultural Community School (06-09)
2012-13 Enrollment: 75 (614) 261-7480
Millennium Community School (KG-08)
2012-13 Enrollment: 723 (614) 255-5585
New Beginnings Academy (09-12)
2012-13 Enrollment: 85 (614) 237-9540
Noble Academy-Columbus (KG-08)
2012-13 Enrollment: 257 (614) 326-0687
Northland Preparatory and Fitness Academy (KG-08)
2012-13 Enrollment: 248 (614) 318-0600
Notten School for Science Technology Engineering a (KG-06)
2012-13 Enrollment: n/a (614) 622-7839
Oakstone Community School (01-12)
2012-13 Enrollment: 247 (614) 458-1085
Ohio School for the Deaf (PK-12)
2012-13 Enrollment: 148 (614) 728-4030
Ohio State School for the Blin (KG-12)
2012-13 Enrollment: 114 (614) 752-1152
Patriot Preparatory Academy (KG-12)
2012-13 Enrollment: 585 (614) 864-5332
Performance Academy Eastland (KG-08)
2012-13 Enrollment: 254 (614) 759-9113
Premier Academy of Ohio (06-12)
2012-13 Enrollment: 118 (614) 501-3820
Pschtecin Public Schools (09-12)
2012-13 Enrollment: 66 (614) 985-3428
Renaissance Academy (KG-08)
2012-13 Enrollment: 162 (614) 866-7277
Road To Success Academy (09-12)
2012-13 Enrollment: 113 (614) 421-5838
Scholarts Preparatory and Career Center for Childr (01-12)
2012-13 Enrollment: 116 (614) 443-1480
South Scioto Academy (KG-06)
2012-13 Enrollment: 171 (614) 445-7684
South-Western City (PK-12)
2012-13 Enrollment: 20,906 (614) 801-3000
Sullivant Avenue Community School (KG-06)
2012-13 Enrollment: 455 (614) 308-5991
Summit Academy Columbus (KG-05)
2012-13 Enrollment: 57 (614) 237-5497
Summit Academy Middle School - Columbus (06-08)
2012-13 Enrollment: 51 (614) 237-5497
Summit Academy Transition High School-Columbus (09-12)
2012-13 Enrollment: 70 (614) 880-0714
The Academy for Urban Solutions (09-12)
2012-13 Enrollment: 226 (614) 545-9890
The Arch Academy (09-12)
2012-13 Enrollment: 70 (614) 299-9802
Ubah Math & Reading Academy
2012-13 Enrollment: 67 (614) 272-5722
Virtual Community School of Ohio (KG-12)
2012-13 Enrollment: 1,066 (614) 501-9473
Westerville City (PK-12)
2012-13 Enrollment: 14,629 (614) 797-5700
Westside Academy (KG-04)
2012-13 Enrollment: 158 (614) 272-9392
Whitehall Preparatory and Fitness Academy (KG-08)
2012-13 Enrollment: 287 (614) 324-4585
World Collegiate Preparatory School (KG-05)
2012-13 Enrollment: 116 (614) 299-1007
Worthington City (PK-12)
2012-13 Enrollment: 9,423 (614) 450-6000
Youthbuild Columbus Community (10-12)
2012-13 Enrollment: 252 (614) 291-0805
Zenith Academy (KG-10)
2012-13 Enrollment: 324 (614) 419-6753
Zenith Academy East (KG-08)
2012-13 Enrollment: 207 (614) 577-0999

Four-year College(s)

Bexley Hall Episcopal Seminary (Private, Not-for-profit, Protestant Episcopal)
Fall 2013 Enrollment: 15 (614) 231-3095
Capital University (Private, Not-for-profit, Evangelical Lutheran Church)
Fall 2013 Enrollment: 3,628 (614) 236-6011
2013-14 Tuition: In-state $31,990; Out-of-state $31,990
Chamberlain College of Nursing-Ohio (Private, For-profit)
Fall 2013 Enrollment: 667 (614) 252-8890
2013-14 Tuition: In-state $17,280; Out-of-state $17,280
Columbus College of Art and Design (Private, Not-for-profit)
Fall 2013 Enrollment: 1,379 (614) 224-9101
2013-14 Tuition: In-state $30,390; Out-of-state $30,390
DeVry University-Ohio (Private, For-profit)
Fall 2013 Enrollment: 3,578 (614) 253-7291
2013-14 Tuition: In-state $16,010; Out-of-state $16,010
Franklin University (Private, Not-for-profit)
Fall 2013 Enrollment: 6,274 (614) 797-4700
2013-14 Tuition: In-state $10,681; Out-of-state $10,681
ITT Technical Institute-Columbus (Private, For-profit)
Fall 2013 Enrollment: 345 (614) 868-2000
2013-14 Tuition: In-state $18,048; Out-of-state $18,048
Mount Carmel College of Nursing (Private, Not-for-profit, Roman Catholic)
Fall 2013 Enrollment: 1,121 (614) 234-5800
2013-14 Tuition: In-state $11,675; Out-of-state $11,675
Ohio Dominican University (Private, Not-for-profit, Roman Catholic)
Fall 2013 Enrollment: 2,573 (614) 253-2741
2013-14 Tuition: In-state $28,932; Out-of-state $28,932
Ohio State University-Main Campus (Public)
Fall 2013 Enrollment: 57,466 (614) 292-6446
2013-14 Tuition: In-state $10,037; Out-of-state $25,757
Pontifical College Josephinum (Private, Not-for-profit, Roman Catholic)
Fall 2013 Enrollment: 213 (614) 885-5585
2013-14 Tuition: In-state $20,614; Out-of-state $20,614
Trinity Lutheran Seminary (Private, Not-for-profit, Evangelical Lutheran Church)
Fall 2013 Enrollment: 116 (614) 235-4136

Two-year College(s)

American Institute of Alternative Medicine (Private, For-profit)
Fall 2013 Enrollment: 263 (614) 825-6255
2013-14 Tuition: In-state $13,895; Out-of-state $13,895

Bradford School (Private, For-profit)
Fall 2013 Enrollment: 449 . . . . (614) 416-6200
2013-14 Tuition: In-state $13,980; Out-of-state $13,980
Columbus State Community College (Public)
Fall 2013 Enrollment: 25,249 . . . . (614) 287-5353
2013-14 Tuition: In-state $3,790; Out-of-state $8,186
Miami-Jacobs Career College-Columbus (Private, For-profit)
Fall 2013 Enrollment: 304 . . . . (614) 221-7770
2013-14 Tuition: In-state $11,964; Out-of-state $11,964
National College-Columbus (Private, For-profit)
Fall 2013 Enrollment: 99 . . . . (614) 212-2800
2013-14 Tuition: In-state $11,550; Out-of-state $11,550
Nationwide Beauty Academy (Private, For-profit)
Fall 2013 Enrollment: 57 . . . . (614) 252-5252
Ohio Business College-Hilliard (Private, For-profit)
Fall 2013 Enrollment: 165 . . . . (614) 891-5030
2013-14 Tuition: In-state $8,500; Out-of-state $8,500
Ohio State College of Barber Styling (Private, For-profit)
Fall 2013 Enrollment: 142 . . . . (614) 868-1015
Sanford-Brown College-Columbus (Private, For-profit)
Fall 2013 Enrollment: 31 . . . . (847) 781-3600
The Spa School (Private, For-profit)
Fall 2013 Enrollment: 61 . . . . (614) 252-5252

Vocational/Technical School(s)

Adult and Community Education-Hudson (Public)
Fall 2013 Enrollment: 140 . . . . (614) 365-6000
2013-14 Tuition: $13,500
American School of Technology (Private, For-profit)
Fall 2013 Enrollment: 250 . . . . (614) 436-4820
2013-14 Tuition: $15,600
Aveda Institute-Columbus (Private, For-profit)
Fall 2013 Enrollment: 271 . . . . (614) 291-2421
2013-14 Tuition: $19,750
Dental Assistant Pro LLC-Columbus (Private, For-profit)
Fall 2013 Enrollment: 16 . . . . (614) 891-7075
Heritage College-Columbus (Private, For-profit)
Fall 2013 Enrollment: 520 . . . . (614) 328-4700
2013-14 Tuition: $17,264
MyComputerCareer.Com-TechSkills (Private, For-profit)
Fall 2013 Enrollment: 292 . . . . (614) 891-3200
2013-14 Tuition: $16,036
National Personal Training Institute of Columbus (Private, For-profit)
Fall 2013 Enrollment: 75 . . . . (614) 336-2664
Ohio Center for Broadcasting-Columbus (Private, For-profit)
Fall 2013 Enrollment: 102 . . . . (614) 655-5250
2013-14 Tuition: In-state $15,557; Out-of-state $15,557
Regency Beauty Institute-Columbus (Private, For-profit)
Fall 2013 Enrollment: 92 . . . . (800) 787-6456
2013-14 Tuition: $16,200
The Ohio Academy Paul Mitchell Partner School-Columbus (Private, For-profit)
Fall 2013 Enrollment: 216 . . . . (614) 478-0922
2013-14 Tuition: $14,850

Housing: Homeownership rate: 47.0%; Median home value: $130,700; Median year structure built: 1974; Homeowner vacancy rate: 3.3%; Median gross rent: $809 per month; Rental vacancy rate: 9.6%

Health Insurance: 84.7% have insurance; 63.7% have private insurance; 28.6% have public insurance; 15.3% do not have insurance; 7.0% of children under 18 do not have insurance

Hospitals: Doctors Hospital (478 beds); Grant Medical Center (337 beds); James Cancer Hospital & Solove Research Institute; Mount Carmel West (523 beds); Ohio State University Hospitals (156 beds); Riverside Methodist Hospital (1049 beds)

Newspapers: Columbus Alive (weekly circulation 46000); Columbus Dispatch (daily circulation 217000); Columbus Messenger Company (weekly circulation 100000); Suburban News Publications (weekly circulation 293000)

Transportation: Commute: 89.1% car, 3.0% public transportation, 2.8% walk, 3.4% work from home; Median travel time to work: 21.3 minutes; Amtrak: Bus service available.

Airports: Bolton Field (general aviation); Ohio State University (general aviation); Port Columbus International (primary service/medium hub); Rickenbacker International (primary service/non-hub)

Additional Information Contacts

City of Columbus . . . . (614) 645-8100
http://www.ci.columbus.oh.us

DARBYDALE (CDP). Covers a land area of 0.987 square miles and a water area of 0.002 square miles. Located at 39.86° N. Lat; 83.17° W. Long. Elevation is 873 feet.

Population: 793; Growth (since 2000): n/a; Density: 803.6 persons per square mile; Race: 97.2% White, 0.4% Black/African American, 0.0% Asian, 0.4% American Indian/Alaska Native, 0.0% Native Hawaiian/Other Pacific Islander, 1.5% Two or more races, 0.9% Hispanic of any race; Average household size: 2.64; Median age: 40.8; Age under 18: 22.3%; Age 65 and over: 13.9%; Males per 100 females: 99.2

Housing: Homeownership rate: 85.7%; Homeowner vacancy rate: 2.2%; Rental vacancy rate: 6.4%

DUBLIN (city). Covers a land area of 24.437 square miles and a water area of 0.361 square miles. Located at 40.11° N. Lat; 83.14° W. Long. Elevation is 830 feet.

History: Named for Dublin, Ireland. Dublin was laid out in 1818 by John Sells, whose descendants organized the Sells Brothers' Circus. At one time, Dublin was selected to be the state capital by a commission appointed for that purpose, but "political horse trading" changed the selection.

Population: 41,751; Growth (since 2000): 33.0%; Density: 1,708.5 persons per square mile; Race: 80.5% White, 1.8% Black/African American, 15.3% Asian, 0.1% American Indian/Alaska Native, 0.0% Native Hawaiian/Other Pacific Islander, 1.8% Two or more races, 1.8% Hispanic of any race; Average household size: 2.78; Median age: 38.3; Age under 18: 30.4%; Age 65 and over: 7.8%; Males per 100 females: 97.6; Marriage status: 22.7% never married, 67.4% now married, 0.5% separated, 3.4% widowed, 6.6% divorced; Foreign born: 15.0%; Speak English only: 83.1%; With disability: 5.3%; Veterans: 6.8%; Ancestry: 30.1% German, 16.3% Irish, 11.1% English, 7.8% Italian, 6.1% American

Employment: 30.1% management, business, and financial, 14.4% computer, engineering, and science, 11.8% education, legal, community service, arts, and media, 8.6% healthcare practitioners, 8.7% service, 22.6% sales and office, 1.3% natural resources, construction, and maintenance, 2.5% production, transportation, and material moving

Income: Per capita: $52,906; Median household: $113,182; Average household: $146,145; Households with income of $100,000 or more: 59.1%; Poverty rate: 3.0%

Educational Attainment: High school diploma or higher: 98.5%; Bachelor's degree or higher: 73.4%; Graduate/professional degree or higher: 28.5%

School District(s)

Dublin City (PK-12)
2012-13 Enrollment: 14,627 . . . . (614) 764-5913
Hilliard City (PK-12)
2012-13 Enrollment: 15,435 . . . . (614) 921-7000

Housing: Homeownership rate: 79.1%; Median home value: $330,900; Median year structure built: 1993; Homeowner vacancy rate: 2.2%; Median gross rent: $1,161 per month; Rental vacancy rate: 7.0%

Health Insurance: 96.9% have insurance; 93.4% have private insurance; 10.2% have public insurance; 3.1% do not have insurance; 1.4% of children under 18 do not have insurance

Hospitals: Dublin Methodist Hospital

Safety: Violent crime rate: 2.3 per 10,000 population; Property crime rate: 129.1 per 10,000 population

Transportation: Commute: 90.5% car, 0.3% public transportation, 0.5% walk, 7.7% work from home; Median travel time to work: 22.4 minutes

Additional Information Contacts

City of Dublin . . . . (614) 410-4400
http://www.dublin.oh.us

GAHANNA (city). Covers a land area of 12.427 square miles and a water area of 0.171 square miles. Located at 40.04° N. Lat; 82.88° W. Long. Elevation is 797 feet.

History: Named for an Algonquian Indian translation of "stream". Incorporated 1881.

Population: 33,248; Growth (since 2000): 1.9%; Density: 2,675.4 persons per square mile; Race: 82.1% White, 11.2% Black/African American, 3.1% Asian, 0.2% American Indian/Alaska Native, 0.0% Native Hawaiian/Other Pacific Islander, 2.4% Two or more races, 2.6% Hispanic of any race; Average household size: 2.54; Median age: 39.4; Age under 18: 25.3%; Age 65 and over: 11.7%; Males per 100 females: 91.9; Marriage status:

28.8% never married, 55.2% now married, 1.8% separated, 4.9% widowed, 11.1% divorced; Foreign born: 5.6%; Speak English only: 94.1%; With disability: 10.5%; Veterans: 8.4%; Ancestry: 29.9% German, 16.6% Irish, 12.9% English, 6.2% Italian, 5.6% American
Employment: 22.8% management, business, and financial, 7.9% computer, engineering, and science, 13.2% education, legal, community service, arts, and media, 5.5% healthcare practitioners, 15.7% service, 24.1% sales and office, 3.6% natural resources, construction, and maintenance, 7.3% production, transportation, and material moving
Income: Per capita: $35,037; Median household: $71,201; Average household: $89,591; Households with income of $100,000 or more: 34.5%; Poverty rate: 5.5%
Educational Attainment: High school diploma or higher: 95.1%; Bachelor's degree or higher: 47.0%; Graduate/professional degree or higher: 16.1%

School District(s)

Gahanna Community School (09-12)
2012-13 Enrollment: 102. . . . . (614) 478-5500
Gahanna-Jefferson City (PK-12)
2012-13 Enrollment: 7,041 . . . . (614) 471-7065

Vocational/Technical School(s)

Everest Institute-Gahanna (Private, For-profit)
Fall 2013 Enrollment: 462. . . . . (614) 322-3414
2013-14 Tuition: $18,750
Housing: Homeownership rate: 75.0%; Median home value: $186,300; Median year structure built: 1984; Homeowner vacancy rate: 1.2%; Median gross rent: $955 per month; Rental vacancy rate: 6.5%
Health Insurance: 94.4% have insurance; 85.7% have private insurance; 18.9% have public insurance; 5.6% do not have insurance; 2.1% of children under 18 do not have insurance
Safety: Violent crime rate: 6.8 per 10,000 population; Property crime rate: 209.9 per 10,000 population
Transportation: Commute: 91.3% car, 0.3% public transportation, 0.7% walk, 7.1% work from home; Median travel time to work: 21.0 minutes
Additional Information Contacts
City of Gahanna . . . . (614) 342-4000
http://www.gahanna.gov

GALLOWAY (unincorporated postal area)
ZCTA: 43119
Covers a land area of 31.791 square miles and a water area of 0.317 square miles. Located at 39.94° N. Lat; 83.21° W. Long. Elevation is 899 feet.
Population: 27,698; Growth (since 2000): 27.7%; Density: 871.3 persons per square mile; Race: 82.6% White, 7.5% Black/African American, 2.4% Asian, 0.2% American Indian/Alaska Native, 0.0% Native Hawaiian/Other Pacific Islander, 3.0% Two or more races, 7.4% Hispanic of any race; Average household size: 2.78; Median age: 32.2; Age under 18: 29.0%; Age 65 and over: 5.8%; Males per 100 females: 95.2; Marriage status: 25.9% never married, 60.7% now married, 2.2% separated, 2.5% widowed, 10.9% divorced; Foreign born: 9.5%; Speak English only: 84.1%; With disability: 9.1%; Veterans: 6.5%; Ancestry: 27.7% German, 14.9% Irish, 9.2% English, 8.7% American, 7.3% Italian
Employment: 14.9% management, business, and financial, 5.1% computer, engineering, and science, 6.3% education, legal, community service, arts, and media, 5.3% healthcare practitioners, 18.3% service, 27.2% sales and office, 7.2% natural resources, construction, and maintenance, 15.7% production, transportation, and material moving
Income: Per capita: $24,629; Median household: $56,506; Average household: $68,605; Households with income of $100,000 or more: 19.8%; Poverty rate: 10.2%
Educational Attainment: High school diploma or higher: 89.9%; Bachelor's degree or higher: 26.5%; Graduate/professional degree or higher: 6.3%

School District(s)

South-Western City (PK-12)
2012-13 Enrollment: 20,906 . . . . (614) 801-3000
Housing: Homeownership rate: 73.1%; Median home value: $139,600; Median year structure built: 1993; Homeowner vacancy rate: 1.8%; Median gross rent: $770 per month; Rental vacancy rate: 9.4%
Health Insurance: 86.5% have insurance; 69.7% have private insurance; 23.8% have public insurance; 13.5% do not have insurance; 7.8% of children under 18 do not have insurance
Transportation: Commute: 95.7% car, 0.1% public transportation, 0.2% walk, 2.9% work from home; Median travel time to work: 23.3 minutes

GRANDVIEW HEIGHTS (city). Covers a land area of 1.332 square miles and a water area of 0.004 square miles. Located at 39.98° N. Lat; 83.04° W. Long. Elevation is 771 feet.
Population: 6,536; Growth (since 2000): -2.4%; Density: 4,908.2 persons per square mile; Race: 94.6% White, 1.4% Black/African American, 1.2% Asian, 0.2% American Indian/Alaska Native, 0.0% Native Hawaiian/Other Pacific Islander, 1.9% Two or more races, 2.4% Hispanic of any race; Average household size: 2.23; Median age: 35.7; Age under 18: 21.5%; Age 65 and over: 9.5%; Males per 100 females: 94.3; Marriage status: 34.2% never married, 50.8% now married, 1.0% separated, 3.7% widowed, 11.4% divorced; Foreign born: 2.8%; Speak English only: 94.7%; With disability: 5.2%; Veterans: 4.8%; Ancestry: 38.0% German, 19.0% Irish, 11.6% Italian, 11.6% English, 4.7% American
Employment: 23.5% management, business, and financial, 7.2% computer, engineering, and science, 21.8% education, legal, community service, arts, and media, 9.2% healthcare practitioners, 11.1% service, 19.7% sales and office, 3.8% natural resources, construction, and maintenance, 3.7% production, transportation, and material moving
Income: Per capita: $42,537; Median household: $85,089; Average household: $104,745; Households with income of $100,000 or more: 42.6%; Poverty rate: 6.9%
Educational Attainment: High school diploma or higher: 97.5%; Bachelor's degree or higher: 62.4%; Graduate/professional degree or higher: 29.4%
Housing: Homeownership rate: 63.7%; Median home value: $257,400; Median year structure built: Before 1940; Homeowner vacancy rate: 2.6%; Median gross rent: $902 per month; Rental vacancy rate: 2.6%
Health Insurance: 93.4% have insurance; 82.7% have private insurance; 16.7% have public insurance; 6.6% do not have insurance; 0.7% of children under 18 do not have insurance
Safety: Violent crime rate: 11.3 per 10,000 population; Property crime rate: 191.4 per 10,000 population
Transportation: Commute: 91.8% car, 1.1% public transportation, 2.0% walk, 3.9% work from home; Median travel time to work: 17.8 minutes
Additional Information Contacts
City of Grandview Heights. . . . . (614) 481-6211
http://www.grandviewheights.org

GROVE CITY (city). Covers a land area of 16.196 square miles and a water area of 0.157 square miles. Located at 39.87° N. Lat; 83.07° W. Long. Elevation is 846 feet.
History: Named for its many tree groves, by William F. Brock. Grove City developed around an agricultural and truck gardening region. Many of its early residents were of German ancestry.
Population: 35,575; Growth (since 2000): 31.4%; Density: 2,196.5 persons per square mile; Race: 92.6% White, 2.8% Black/African American, 1.3% Asian, 0.2% American Indian/Alaska Native, 0.0% Native Hawaiian/Other Pacific Islander, 2.1% Two or more races, 2.6% Hispanic of any race; Average household size: 2.53; Median age: 37.8; Age under 18: 25.4%; Age 65 and over: 12.2%; Males per 100 females: 93.5; Marriage status: 26.1% never married, 56.5% now married, 1.9% separated, 5.6% widowed, 11.8% divorced; Foreign born: 2.4%; Speak English only: 95.6%; With disability: 12.8%; Veterans: 9.5%; Ancestry: 31.0% German, 18.5% Irish, 10.3% English, 9.3% American, 5.1% Italian
Employment: 15.6% management, business, and financial, 5.1% computer, engineering, and science, 7.1% education, legal, community service, arts, and media, 8.1% healthcare practitioners, 16.6% service, 26.9% sales and office, 7.7% natural resources, construction, and maintenance, 13.0% production, transportation, and material moving
Income: Per capita: $30,638; Median household: $66,299; Average household: $77,809; Households with income of $100,000 or more: 26.9%; Poverty rate: 8.7%
Educational Attainment: High school diploma or higher: 94.1%; Bachelor's degree or higher: 27.3%; Graduate/professional degree or higher: 8.6%

School District(s)

South-Western City (PK-12)
2012-13 Enrollment: 20,906 . . . . (614) 801-3000

Four-year College(s)

Harrison College-Grove City (Private, For-profit)
Fall 2013 Enrollment: 244 . . . . (888) 544-4422
2013-14 Tuition: In-state $16,740; Out-of-state $16,740
Housing: Homeownership rate: 69.7%; Median home value: $160,100; Median year structure built: 1988; Homeowner vacancy rate: 1.9%; Median gross rent: $847 per month; Rental vacancy rate: 6.9%

Health Insurance: 90.2% have insurance; 78.9% have private insurance; 23.3% have public insurance; 9.8% do not have insurance; 5.3% of children under 18 do not have insurance
Safety: Violent crime rate: 10.8 per 10,000 population; Property crime rate: 341.3 per 10,000 population
Transportation: Commute: 93.5% car, 0.7% public transportation, 0.3% walk, 3.8% work from home; Median travel time to work: 21.9 minutes
Additional Information Contacts
City of Grove City . . . . (614) 277-3000
http://www.grovecityohio.gov

GROVEPORT (city). Covers a land area of 8.560 square miles and a water area of 0.227 square miles. Located at 39.86° N. Lat; 82.89° W. Long. Elevation is 741 feet.
Population: 5,363; Growth (since 2000): 38.8%; Density: 626.5 persons per square mile; Race: 82.1% White, 12.5% Black/African American, 1.9% Asian, 0.3% American Indian/Alaska Native, 0.0% Native Hawaiian/Other Pacific Islander, 2.3% Two or more races, 2.2% Hispanic of any race; Average household size: 2.56; Median age: 39.9; Age under 18: 23.7%; Age 65 and over: 12.5%; Males per 100 females: 92.8; Marriage status: 23.4% never married, 58.4% now married, 1.4% separated, 6.8% widowed, 11.4% divorced; Foreign born: 2.8%; Speak English only: 96.6%; With disability: 13.2%; Veterans: 12.8%; Ancestry: 26.5% German, 13.7% Irish, 10.0% English, 7.9% American, 4.4% Italian
Employment: 11.3% management, business, and financial, 4.5% computer, engineering, and science, 11.5% education, legal, community service, arts, and media, 5.0% healthcare practitioners, 15.5% service, 25.8% sales and office, 7.3% natural resources, construction, and maintenance, 19.1% production, transportation, and material moving
Income: Per capita: $28,796; Median household: $58,065; Average household: $73,097; Households with income of $100,000 or more: 22.7%; Poverty rate: 10.5%
Educational Attainment: High school diploma or higher: 92.4%; Bachelor's degree or higher: 24.4%; Graduate/professional degree or higher: 8.4%

School District(s)

Eastland-Fairfield Career/tech (09-12)
2012-13 Enrollment: n/a . . . . (614) 836-4530
Groveport Community School (KG-08)
2012-13 Enrollment: 995. . . . . (614) 574-0037
Groveport Madison Local (PK-12)
2012-13 Enrollment: 5,535 . . . . (614) 492-2520

Vocational/Technical School(s)

Eastland-Fairfield Career and Technical Schools (Public)
Fall 2013 Enrollment: 188. . . . . (614) 836-4541
2013-14 Tuition: $4,850
Housing: Homeownership rate: 74.4%; Median home value: $144,100; Median year structure built: 1977; Homeowner vacancy rate: 3.6%; Median gross rent: $641 per month; Rental vacancy rate: 13.2%
Health Insurance: 88.2% have insurance; 73.0% have private insurance; 26.7% have public insurance; 11.8% do not have insurance; 14.9% of children under 18 do not have insurance
Safety: Violent crime rate: 5.4 per 10,000 population; Property crime rate: 294.7 per 10,000 population
Transportation: Commute: 96.2% car, 0.8% public transportation, 0.3% walk, 2.1% work from home; Median travel time to work: 19.7 minutes
Additional Information Contacts
Village of Groveport. . . . . (614) 836-5301
http://www.groveport.org

HARRISBURG (village). Covers a land area of 0.154 square miles and a water area of 0 square miles. Located at 39.81° N. Lat; 83.17° W. Long. Elevation is 794 feet.
Population: 320; Growth (since 2000): -3.6%; Density: 2,077.0 persons per square mile; Race: 96.9% White, 0.6% Black/African American, 0.6% Asian, 0.9% American Indian/Alaska Native, 0.0% Native Hawaiian/Other Pacific Islander, 0.9% Two or more races, 0.3% Hispanic of any race; Average household size: 2.32; Median age: 44.7; Age under 18: 19.1%; Age 65 and over: 14.4%; Males per 100 females: 103.8
Housing: Homeownership rate: 68.8%; Homeowner vacancy rate: 3.1%; Rental vacancy rate: 4.4%

HILLIARD (city). Covers a land area of 13.167 square miles and a water area of 0.168 square miles. Located at 40.04° N. Lat; 83.15° W. Long. Elevation is 932 feet.
Population: 28,435; Growth (since 2000): 17.4%; Density: 2,159.6 persons per square mile; Race: 88.5% White, 3.0% Black/African American, 5.6% Asian, 0.2% American Indian/Alaska Native, 0.0% Native Hawaiian/Other Pacific Islander, 1.9% Two or more races, 2.3% Hispanic of any race; Average household size: 2.77; Median age: 35.9; Age under 18: 30.1%; Age 65 and over: 8.6%; Males per 100 females: 95.5; Marriage status: 22.4% never married, 62.8% now married, 0.8% separated, 5.3% widowed, 9.5% divorced; Foreign born: 5.7%; Speak English only: 91.7%; With disability: 7.2%; Veterans: 7.7%; Ancestry: 31.8% German, 15.3% Irish, 13.2% English, 8.6% American, 7.4% Italian
Employment: 22.1% management, business, and financial, 9.3% computer, engineering, and science, 13.0% education, legal, community service, arts, and media, 6.9% healthcare practitioners, 12.5% service, 24.5% sales and office, 3.4% natural resources, construction, and maintenance, 8.3% production, transportation, and material moving
Income: Per capita: $35,604; Median household: $85,052; Average household: $98,726; Households with income of $100,000 or more: 42.0%; Poverty rate: 4.7%
Educational Attainment: High school diploma or higher: 95.7%; Bachelor's degree or higher: 46.0%; Graduate/professional degree or higher: 16.5%

School District(s)

Hilliard City (PK-12)
2012-13 Enrollment: 15,435 . . . . (614) 921-7000

Four-year College(s)

ITT Technical Institute-Hilliard (Private, For-profit)
Fall 2013 Enrollment: 322 . . . . (614) 771-4888
2013-14 Tuition: In-state $18,048; Out-of-state $18,048
Housing: Homeownership rate: 79.2%; Median home value: $205,000; Median year structure built: 1992; Homeowner vacancy rate: 1.7%; Median gross rent: $968 per month; Rental vacancy rate: 7.3%
Health Insurance: 92.6% have insurance; 83.3% have private insurance; 17.8% have public insurance; 7.4% do not have insurance; 2.9% of children under 18 do not have insurance
Safety: Violent crime rate: 8.3 per 10,000 population; Property crime rate: 229.3 per 10,000 population
Transportation: Commute: 92.9% car, 0.1% public transportation, 0.9% walk, 4.8% work from home; Median travel time to work: 22.1 minutes
Additional Information Contacts
City of Hilliard . . . . (614) 876-7361
http://hilliardohio.gov

HUBER RIDGE (CDP). Covers a land area of 1.041 square miles and a water area of 0.010 square miles. Located at 40.09° N. Lat; 82.92° W. Long. Elevation is 830 feet.
Population: 4,604; Growth (since 2000): -5.7%; Density: 4,421.4 persons per square mile; Race: 82.9% White, 11.0% Black/African American, 1.3% Asian, 0.1% American Indian/Alaska Native, 0.1% Native Hawaiian/Other Pacific Islander, 3.2% Two or more races, 3.4% Hispanic of any race; Average household size: 2.79; Median age: 32.0; Age under 18: 29.5%; Age 65 and over: 8.9%; Males per 100 females: 93.5; Marriage status: 30.2% never married, 51.4% now married, 1.3% separated, 6.6% widowed, 11.7% divorced; Foreign born: 5.7%; Speak English only: 88.3%; With disability: 6.7%; Veterans: 10.1%; Ancestry: 27.3% German, 16.9% Irish, 7.8% English, 6.6% American, 4.1% Italian
Employment: 14.2% management, business, and financial, 9.4% computer, engineering, and science, 6.8% education, legal, community service, arts, and media, 4.2% healthcare practitioners, 22.8% service, 25.0% sales and office, 4.7% natural resources, construction, and maintenance, 12.8% production, transportation, and material moving
Income: Per capita: $24,226; Median household: $62,000; Average household: $66,681; Households with income of $100,000 or more: 16.4%; Poverty rate: 9.1%
Educational Attainment: High school diploma or higher: 91.2%; Bachelor's degree or higher: 25.7%; Graduate/professional degree or higher: 7.2%
Housing: Homeownership rate: 71.9%; Median home value: $118,500; Median year structure built: 1969; Homeowner vacancy rate: 1.7%; Median gross rent: <$100 per month; Rental vacancy rate: 12.0%
Health Insurance: 89.0% have insurance; 72.5% have private insurance; 28.1% have public insurance; 11.0% do not have insurance; 4.3% of children under 18 do not have insurance

Transportation: Commute: 98.0% car, 0.0% public transportation, 0.0% walk, 1.7% work from home; Median travel time to work: 23.6 minutes

LAKE DARBY (CDP). Covers a land area of 3.463 square miles and a water area of 0.040 square miles. Located at 39.96° N. Lat; 83.22° W. Long. Elevation is 925 feet.

Population: 4,592; Growth (since 2000): 23.2%; Density: 1,326.0 persons per square mile; Race: 92.4% White, 2.6% Black/African American, 1.5% Asian, 0.3% American Indian/Alaska Native, 0.0% Native Hawaiian/Other Pacific Islander, 1.8% Two or more races, 3.1% Hispanic of any race; Average household size: 3.06; Median age: 32.5; Age under 18: 32.5%; Age 65 and over: 3.7%; Males per 100 females: 100.6; Marriage status: 15.9% never married, 73.7% now married, 1.7% separated, 0.7% widowed, 9.7% divorced; Foreign born: 5.6%; Speak English only: 91.2%; With disability: 9.1%; Veterans: 6.4%; Ancestry: 39.6% German, 16.2% Irish, 10.2% American, 10.2% English, 4.9% Ukrainian

Employment: 12.6% management, business, and financial, 12.0% computer, engineering, and science, 9.0% education, legal, community service, arts, and media, 5.6% healthcare practitioners, 13.3% service, 27.4% sales and office, 10.2% natural resources, construction, and maintenance, 9.9% production, transportation, and material moving

Income: Per capita: $29,129; Median household: $77,607; Average household: $86,597; Households with income of $100,000 or more: 30.3%; Poverty rate: 5.4%

Educational Attainment: High school diploma or higher: 95.1%; Bachelor's degree or higher: 33.5%; Graduate/professional degree or higher: 11.4%

Housing: Homeownership rate: 93.4%; Median home value: $142,300; Median year structure built: 1991; Homeowner vacancy rate: 1.1%; Median gross rent: $1,177 per month; Rental vacancy rate: 7.5%

Health Insurance: 91.9% have insurance; 78.8% have private insurance; 17.6% have public insurance; 8.1% do not have insurance; 10.3% of children under 18 do not have insurance

Transportation: Commute: 94.6% car, 0.9% public transportation, 0.3% walk, 2.7% work from home; Median travel time to work: 27.5 minutes

LINCOLN VILLAGE (CDP). Covers a land area of 1.836 square miles and a water area of <.001 square miles. Located at 39.95° N. Lat; 83.13° W. Long. Elevation is 909 feet.

Population: 9,032; Growth (since 2000): -4.7%; Density: 4,919.8 persons per square mile; Race: 82.1% White, 6.3% Black/African American, 0.9% Asian, 0.4% American Indian/Alaska Native, 0.0% Native Hawaiian/Other Pacific Islander, 3.0% Two or more races, 10.7% Hispanic of any race; Average household size: 2.42; Median age: 38.2; Age under 18: 23.6%; Age 65 and over: 14.5%; Males per 100 females: 96.8; Marriage status: 33.2% never married, 42.9% now married, 3.5% separated, 8.6% widowed, 15.4% divorced; Foreign born: 11.5%; Speak English only: 83.3%; With disability: 19.9%; Veterans: 10.5%; Ancestry: 20.4% German, 17.0% Irish, 9.5% English, 7.3% American, 3.1% Italian

Employment: 9.3% management, business, and financial, 1.9% computer, engineering, and science, 4.9% education, legal, community service, arts, and media, 3.2% healthcare practitioners, 16.7% service, 29.8% sales and office, 16.1% natural resources, construction, and maintenance, 18.1% production, transportation, and material moving

Income: Per capita: $20,830; Median household: $38,831; Average household: $51,048; Households with income of $100,000 or more: 7.1%; Poverty rate: 16.7%

Educational Attainment: High school diploma or higher: 76.2%; Bachelor's degree or higher: 10.0%; Graduate/professional degree or higher: 2.2%

Housing: Homeownership rate: 61.2%; Median home value: $101,400; Median year structure built: 1962; Homeowner vacancy rate: 2.8%; Median gross rent: $721 per month; Rental vacancy rate: 16.8%

Health Insurance: 79.2% have insurance; 54.6% have private insurance; 35.1% have public insurance; 20.8% do not have insurance; 5.8% of children under 18 do not have insurance

Transportation: Commute: 89.6% car, 2.3% public transportation, 2.8% walk, 2.8% work from home; Median travel time to work: 22.6 minutes

LOCKBOURNE (village). Covers a land area of 0.750 square miles and a water area of 0.046 square miles. Located at 39.81° N. Lat; 82.99° W. Long. Elevation is 712 feet.

Population: 237; Growth (since 2000): -15.4%; Density: 315.9 persons per square mile; Race: 97.9% White, 0.0% Black/African American, 0.0% Asian, 0.0% American Indian/Alaska Native, 0.0% Native Hawaiian/Other Pacific Islander, 1.7% Two or more races, 2.5% Hispanic of any race; Average household size: 2.49; Median age: 38.9; Age under 18: 24.5%; Age 65 and over: 20.7%; Males per 100 females: 91.1

Housing: Homeownership rate: 64.2%; Homeowner vacancy rate: 1.6%; Rental vacancy rate: 8.1%

MARBLE CLIFF (village). Covers a land area of 0.266 square miles and a water area of 0 square miles. Located at 39.99° N. Lat; 83.06° W. Long. Elevation is 794 feet.

History: Limestone quarry gave its name.

Population: 573; Growth (since 2000): -11.3%; Density: 2,155.2 persons per square mile; Race: 97.9% White, 0.5% Black/African American, 1.0% Asian, 0.0% American Indian/Alaska Native, 0.0% Native Hawaiian/Other Pacific Islander, 0.3% Two or more races, 1.6% Hispanic of any race; Average household size: 1.96; Median age: 48.6; Age under 18: 17.8%; Age 65 and over: 20.6%; Males per 100 females: 97.6

Housing: Homeownership rate: 63.3%; Homeowner vacancy rate: 6.9%; Rental vacancy rate: 3.6%

MINERVA PARK (village). Covers a land area of 0.506 square miles and a water area of 0.011 square miles. Located at 40.08° N. Lat; 82.95° W. Long. Elevation is 846 feet.

Population: 1,272; Growth (since 2000): -1.2%; Density: 2,512.2 persons per square mile; Race: 88.5% White, 6.1% Black/African American, 1.7% Asian, 0.3% American Indian/Alaska Native, 0.1% Native Hawaiian/Other Pacific Islander, 3.0% Two or more races, 3.2% Hispanic of any race; Average household size: 2.36; Median age: 45.2; Age under 18: 19.9%; Age 65 and over: 19.0%; Males per 100 females: 92.1

Housing: Homeownership rate: 93.3%; Homeowner vacancy rate: 2.7%; Rental vacancy rate: 7.7%

Safety: Violent crime rate: 7.7 per 10,000 population; Property crime rate: 223.6 per 10,000 population

NEW ALBANY (city). Covers a land area of 11.557 square miles and a water area of 0.144 square miles. Located at 40.08° N. Lat; 82.80° W. Long. Elevation is 1,024 feet.

History: Founded in 1837, it is now a growing suburb in the Columbus area. The Village of New Albany is a master planned community built upon the best traditions of small town America.

Population: 7,724; Growth (since 2000): 108.1%; Density: 668.3 persons per square mile; Race: 87.7% White, 3.1% Black/African American, 6.5% Asian, 0.1% American Indian/Alaska Native, 0.1% Native Hawaiian/Other Pacific Islander, 2.1% Two or more races, 2.0% Hispanic of any race; Average household size: 3.21; Median age: 37.9; Age under 18: 36.6%; Age 65 and over: 6.5%; Males per 100 females: 98.3; Marriage status: 16.9% never married, 73.6% now married, 0.5% separated, 3.2% widowed, 6.3% divorced; Foreign born: 6.8%; Speak English only: 90.1%; With disability: 4.1%; Veterans: 8.9%; Ancestry: 28.8% German, 14.1% Irish, 11.2% Italian, 10.2% American, 8.9% English

Employment: 44.3% management, business, and financial, 4.8% computer, engineering, and science, 15.3% education, legal, community service, arts, and media, 8.6% healthcare practitioners, 6.7% service, 15.3% sales and office, 0.2% natural resources, construction, and maintenance, 4.8% production, transportation, and material moving

Income: Per capita: $79,333; Median household: $185,076; Average household: $250,888; Households with income of $100,000 or more: 72.6%; Poverty rate: 1.2%

Educational Attainment: High school diploma or higher: 99.2%; Bachelor's degree or higher: 79.0%; Graduate/professional degree or higher: 41.2%

School District(s)

New Albany-Plain Local (PK-12)
2012-13 Enrollment: 4,623 . . . . (614) 855-2040

Housing: Homeownership rate: 93.0%; Median home value: $485,200; Median year structure built: 2001; Homeowner vacancy rate: 5.6%; Median gross rent: $1,803 per month; Rental vacancy rate: 5.1%

Health Insurance: 98.9% have insurance; 97.3% have private insurance; 9.3% have public insurance; 1.1% do not have insurance; 0.4% of children under 18 do not have insurance

Hospitals: Mount Carmel New Albany Surgical Hospital

Safety: Violent crime rate: 2.3 per 10,000 population; Property crime rate: 112.9 per 10,000 population

Transportation: Commute: 90.3% car, 0.0% public transportation, 0.5% walk, 8.0% work from home; Median travel time to work: 21.7 minutes

Additional Information Contacts

Village of New Albany . . . . (614) 855-3913
http://www.villageofnewalbany.org

OBETZ (village). Covers a land area of 5.784 square miles and a water area of 0.144 square miles. Located at 39.86° N. Lat; 82.94° W. Long. Elevation is 748 feet.
Population: 4,532; Growth (since 2000): 14.0%; Density: 783.6 persons per square mile; Race: 85.8% White, 7.7% Black/African American, 2.1% Asian, 0.5% American Indian/Alaska Native, 0.0% Native Hawaiian/Other Pacific Islander, 2.4% Two or more races, 2.8% Hispanic of any race; Average household size: 2.72; Median age: 35.9; Age under 18: 27.6%; Age 65 and over: 10.0%; Males per 100 females: 96.0; Marriage status: 36.4% never married, 42.6% now married, 2.2% separated, 6.1% widowed, 14.9% divorced; Foreign born: 2.8%; Speak English only: 94.3%; With disability: 16.1%; Veterans: 8.1%; Ancestry: 32.6% German, 16.0% Irish, 10.7% American, 9.7% Italian, 9.6% English
Employment: 13.0% management, business, and financial, 1.3% computer, engineering, and science, 2.9% education, legal, community service, arts, and media, 8.9% healthcare practitioners, 13.4% service, 26.0% sales and office, 12.0% natural resources, construction, and maintenance, 22.5% production, transportation, and material moving
Income: Per capita: $20,930; Median household: $49,779; Average household: $57,528; Households with income of $100,000 or more: 11.1%; Poverty rate: 12.2%
Educational Attainment: High school diploma or higher: 78.8%; Bachelor's degree or higher: 12.3%; Graduate/professional degree or higher: 4.8%
Housing: Homeownership rate: 77.7%; Median home value: $101,200; Median year structure built: 1976; Homeowner vacancy rate: 4.6%; Median gross rent: $824 per month; Rental vacancy rate: 7.5%
Health Insurance: 85.9% have insurance; 67.0% have private insurance; 26.1% have public insurance; 14.1% do not have insurance; 9.0% of children under 18 do not have insurance
Safety: Violent crime rate: 8.6 per 10,000 population; Property crime rate: 330.7 per 10,000 population
Transportation: Commute: 99.2% car, 0.0% public transportation, 0.3% walk, 0.4% work from home; Median travel time to work: 22.7 minutes
Additional Information Contacts
Village of Obetz . . . . (614) 491-1080
http://www.obetz.oh.us

REYNOLDSBURG (city). Covers a land area of 11.157 square miles and a water area of 0.083 square miles. Located at 39.96° N. Lat; 82.80° W. Long. Elevation is 879 feet.
Population: 35,893; Growth (since 2000): 11.9%; Density: 3,217.0 persons per square mile; Race: 69.7% White, 23.3% Black/African American, 1.8% Asian, 0.2% American Indian/Alaska Native, 0.1% Native Hawaiian/Other Pacific Islander, 3.5% Two or more races, 3.4% Hispanic of any race; Average household size: 2.49; Median age: 37.3; Age under 18: 26.3%; Age 65 and over: 11.6%; Males per 100 females: 90.0; Marriage status: 32.1% never married, 48.2% now married, 1.9% separated, 5.3% widowed, 14.3% divorced; Foreign born: 5.9%; Speak English only: 92.1%; With disability: 11.2%; Veterans: 10.0%; Ancestry: 21.4% German, 16.6% Irish, 7.7% English, 6.0% American, 5.5% Italian
Employment: 16.4% management, business, and financial, 6.5% computer, engineering, and science, 9.5% education, legal, community service, arts, and media, 5.0% healthcare practitioners, 16.6% service, 29.7% sales and office, 6.4% natural resources, construction, and maintenance, 10.0% production, transportation, and material moving
Income: Per capita: $28,959; Median household: $58,257; Average household: $71,357; Households with income of $100,000 or more: 23.1%; Poverty rate: 12.8%
Educational Attainment: High school diploma or higher: 92.1%; Bachelor's degree or higher: 29.9%; Graduate/professional degree or higher: 8.4%

School District(s)

Everest High School (10-12)
2012-13 Enrollment: 107. . . . . (614) 367-1980
Pickerington Local (PK-12)
2012-13 Enrollment: 10,061 . . . . (614) 833-2110
Reynoldsburg City (PK-12)
2012-13 Enrollment: 6,125 . . . . (614) 501-1020

Housing: Homeownership rate: 63.5%; Median home value: $145,200; Median year structure built: 1982; Homeowner vacancy rate: 2.7%; Median gross rent: $827 per month; Rental vacancy rate: 11.6%
Health Insurance: 90.3% have insurance; 74.7% have private insurance; 27.1% have public insurance; 9.7% do not have insurance; 3.8% of children under 18 do not have insurance
Transportation: Commute: 91.4% car, 1.8% public transportation, 1.8% walk, 4.1% work from home; Median travel time to work: 23.5 minutes
Additional Information Contacts
City of Reynoldsburg . . . . (614) 322-6800
http://www.ci.reynoldsburg.oh.us

RIVERLEA (village). Covers a land area of 0.153 square miles and a water area of 0 square miles. Located at 40.08° N. Lat; 83.02° W. Long. Elevation is 787 feet.
Population: 545; Growth (since 2000): 9.2%; Density: 3,572.2 persons per square mile; Race: 97.1% White, 0.4% Black/African American, 1.5% Asian, 0.2% American Indian/Alaska Native, 0.0% Native Hawaiian/Other Pacific Islander, 0.9% Two or more races, 0.6% Hispanic of any race; Average household size: 2.47; Median age: 44.5; Age under 18: 27.0%; Age 65 and over: 15.8%; Males per 100 females: 81.7
Housing: Homeownership rate: 89.6%; Homeowner vacancy rate: 1.5%; Rental vacancy rate: 14.8%

UPPER ARLINGTON (city). Covers a land area of 9.839 square miles and a water area of 0.030 square miles. Located at 40.03° N. Lat; 83.07° W. Long. Elevation is 814 feet.
History: Named for the Upper Arlington Company, a development organization. Incorporated 1918.
Population: 33,771; Growth (since 2000): 0.3%; Density: 3,432.5 persons per square mile; Race: 92.1% White, 0.8% Black/African American, 4.9% Asian, 0.1% American Indian/Alaska Native, 0.0% Native Hawaiian/Other Pacific Islander, 1.6% Two or more races, 1.6% Hispanic of any race; Average household size: 2.44; Median age: 42.8; Age under 18: 25.1%; Age 65 and over: 16.7%; Males per 100 females: 91.7; Marriage status: 24.0% never married, 63.3% now married, 1.0% separated, 5.3% widowed, 7.4% divorced; Foreign born: 7.6%; Speak English only: 89.5%; With disability: 8.0%; Veterans: 7.4%; Ancestry: 33.5% German, 20.3% Irish, 16.6% English, 9.0% Italian, 5.9% American
Employment: 23.6% management, business, and financial, 10.8% computer, engineering, and science, 19.6% education, legal, community service, arts, and media, 10.6% healthcare practitioners, 8.7% service, 21.4% sales and office, 2.4% natural resources, construction, and maintenance, 3.1% production, transportation, and material moving
Income: Per capita: $51,932; Median household: $97,829; Average household: $130,971; Households with income of $100,000 or more: 48.8%; Poverty rate: 4.6%
Educational Attainment: High school diploma or higher: 98.4%; Bachelor's degree or higher: 72.9%; Graduate/professional degree or higher: 33.7%

School District(s)

Upper Arlington City (PK-12)
2012-13 Enrollment: 5,802 . . . . (614) 487-5000

Housing: Homeownership rate: 80.8%; Median home value: $306,800; Median year structure built: 1958; Homeowner vacancy rate: 2.3%; Median gross rent: $989 per month; Rental vacancy rate: 7.0%
Health Insurance: 95.2% have insurance; 88.4% have private insurance; 19.0% have public insurance; 4.8% do not have insurance; 3.7% of children under 18 do not have insurance
Safety: Violent crime rate: 2.9 per 10,000 population; Property crime rate: 129.5 per 10,000 population
Transportation: Commute: 88.8% car, 1.4% public transportation, 1.5% walk, 6.8% work from home; Median travel time to work: 19.1 minutes
Additional Information Contacts
City of Upper Arlington . . . . (614) 583-5000
http://www.ua-ohio.net

URBANCREST (village). Covers a land area of 0.598 square miles and a water area of <.001 square miles. Located at 39.90° N. Lat; 83.09° W. Long. Elevation is 840 feet.
Population: 960; Growth (since 2000): 10.6%; Density: 1,606.1 persons per square mile; Race: 26.4% White, 55.1% Black/African American, 2.9% Asian, 0.1% American Indian/Alaska Native, 8.8% Native Hawaiian/Other Pacific Islander, 5.8% Two or more races, 3.8% Hispanic of any race; Average household size: 2.85; Median age: 25.3; Age under 18: 38.1%; Age 65 and over: 7.4%; Males per 100 females: 81.8
Housing: Homeownership rate: 38.0%; Homeowner vacancy rate: 6.5%; Rental vacancy rate: 2.8%

VALLEYVIEW (village). Covers a land area of 0.149 square miles and a water area of 0.003 square miles. Located at 39.96° N. Lat; 83.07° W. Long. Elevation is 778 feet.
Population: 620; Growth (since 2000): 3.2%; Density: 4,167.9 persons per square mile; Race: 90.0% White, 5.0% Black/African American, 0.8% Asian, 0.3% American Indian/Alaska Native, 1.0% Native Hawaiian/Other Pacific Islander, 1.0% Two or more races, 4.4% Hispanic of any race; Average household size: 2.52; Median age: 39.4; Age under 18: 23.1%; Age 65 and over: 12.6%; Males per 100 females: 98.7
Housing: Homeownership rate: 68.3%; Homeowner vacancy rate: 1.8%; Rental vacancy rate: 2.5%

WESTERVILLE (city). Covers a land area of 12.473 square miles and a water area of 0.138 square miles. Located at 40.12° N. Lat; 82.91° W. Long. Elevation is 869 feet.
History: Named for the Westervelt family, prominent farmers in the area. Westerville was settled in 1813 by Virginia Cavalier families and Quakers from Pennsylvania, and became the headquarters of the Anti-Saloon League in 1909.
Population: 36,120; Growth (since 2000): 2.3%; Density: 2,895.9 persons per square mile; Race: 88.6% White, 6.4% Black/African American, 2.3% Asian, 0.2% American Indian/Alaska Native, 0.0% Native Hawaiian/Other Pacific Islander, 2.1% Two or more races, 1.9% Hispanic of any race; Average household size: 2.48; Median age: 41.2; Age under 18: 22.4%; Age 65 and over: 14.3%; Males per 100 females: 88.5; Marriage status: 27.3% never married, 58.0% now married, 0.6% separated, 5.9% widowed, 8.8% divorced; Foreign born: 6.4%; Speak English only: 92.3%; With disability: 9.5%; Veterans: 9.0%; Ancestry: 30.9% German, 17.2% Irish, 13.2% English, 6.0% Italian, 5.4% American
Employment: 22.7% management, business, and financial, 6.6% computer, engineering, and science, 14.6% education, legal, community service, arts, and media, 5.6% healthcare practitioners, 13.3% service, 28.3% sales and office, 3.9% natural resources, construction, and maintenance, 5.2% production, transportation, and material moving
Income: Per capita: $37,431; Median household: $82,146; Average household: $99,206; Households with income of $100,000 or more: 40.0%; Poverty rate: 6.6%
Educational Attainment: High school diploma or higher: 95.9%; Bachelor's degree or higher: 51.8%; Graduate/professional degree or higher: 18.0%

School District(s)

Cornerstone Academy Community (KG-08)
2012-13 Enrollment: 504 . . . . (614) 775-0615
Westerville City (PK-12)
2012-13 Enrollment: 14,629 . . . . (614) 797-5700
Worthington City (PK-12)
2012-13 Enrollment: 9,423 . . . . (614) 450-6000

Four-year College(s)

Hondros College (Private, For-profit)
Fall 2013 Enrollment: 1,656 . . . . (855) 906-8773
2013-14 Tuition: In-state $18,105; Out-of-state $18,105
Otterbein University (Private, Not-for-profit, United Methodist)
Fall 2013 Enrollment: 2,919 . . . . (614) 890-3000
2013-14 Tuition: In-state $31,424; Out-of-state $31,424

Two-year College(s)

Fortis College-Columbus (Private, For-profit)
Fall 2013 Enrollment: 628 . . . . (614) 882-2551
2013-14 Tuition: In-state $13,489; Out-of-state $13,489
Ohio State School of Cosmetology-Westerville (Private, For-profit)
Fall 2013 Enrollment: 79 . . . . (614) 252-5252

Housing: Homeownership rate: 77.0%; Median home value: $204,900; Median year structure built: 1980; Homeowner vacancy rate: 1.4%; Median gross rent: $904 per month; Rental vacancy rate: 6.8%
Health Insurance: 94.6% have insurance; 85.9% have private insurance; 19.6% have public insurance; 5.4% do not have insurance; 1.7% of children under 18 do not have insurance
Hospitals: Mount Carmel Saint Ann's (180 beds)
Safety: Violent crime rate: 3.5 per 10,000 population; Property crime rate: 226.4 per 10,000 population
Transportation: Commute: 90.5% car, 0.4% public transportation, 3.1% walk, 5.4% work from home; Median travel time to work: 20.7 minutes
Additional Information Contacts
City of Westerville . . . . (614) 901-6400
http://www.westerville.org

WHITEHALL (city). Covers a land area of 5.257 square miles and a water area of 0.028 square miles. Located at 39.97° N. Lat; 82.88° W. Long. Elevation is 791 feet.
History: Named for Whitehall, site of government offices in London, England. Incorporated 1948.
Population: 18,062; Growth (since 2000): -5.9%; Density: 3,435.8 persons per square mile; Race: 58.8% White, 29.3% Black/African American, 1.5% Asian, 0.5% American Indian/Alaska Native, 0.0% Native Hawaiian/Other Pacific Islander, 4.4% Two or more races, 9.9% Hispanic of any race; Average household size: 2.40; Median age: 35.0; Age under 18: 25.8%; Age 65 and over: 11.2%; Males per 100 females: 94.6; Marriage status: 37.3% never married, 37.3% now married, 3.3% separated, 6.2% widowed, 19.3% divorced; Foreign born: 11.7%; Speak English only: 82.8%; With disability: 16.9%; Veterans: 8.2%; Ancestry: 15.3% German, 10.4% Irish, 6.6% American, 4.7% English, 3.8% Italian
Employment: 8.5% management, business, and financial, 2.3% computer, engineering, and science, 5.1% education, legal, community service, arts, and media, 1.8% healthcare practitioners, 23.2% service, 26.5% sales and office, 7.9% natural resources, construction, and maintenance, 24.7% production, transportation, and material moving
Income: Per capita: $18,259; Median household: $33,311; Average household: $42,594; Households with income of $100,000 or more: 5.0%; Poverty rate: 24.3%
Educational Attainment: High school diploma or higher: 79.2%; Bachelor's degree or higher: 9.8%; Graduate/professional degree or higher: 2.5%

School District(s)

Whitehall City (PK-12)
2012-13 Enrollment: 3,087 . . . . (614) 801-3000

Housing: Homeownership rate: 41.6%; Median home value: $90,900; Median year structure built: 1960; Homeowner vacancy rate: 2.6%; Median gross rent: $744 per month; Rental vacancy rate: 17.7%
Health Insurance: 77.4% have insurance; 47.7% have private insurance; 38.4% have public insurance; 22.6% do not have insurance; 9.6% of children under 18 do not have insurance
Safety: Violent crime rate: 68.7 per 10,000 population; Property crime rate: 725.6 per 10,000 population
Transportation: Commute: 89.6% car, 6.0% public transportation, 1.8% walk, 1.3% work from home; Median travel time to work: 21.1 minutes
Additional Information Contacts
City of Whitehall . . . . (614) 338-3106
http://whitehall-oh.us

WORTHINGTON (city). Covers a land area of 5.545 square miles and a water area of 0.076 square miles. Located at 40.10° N. Lat; 83.02° W. Long. Elevation is 863 feet.
History: Worthington was settled in 1803 by a group led by Colonel James Kilbourne, who named the place after a parish in Connecticut. A series of educational institutions opened and closed in Worthington over the next century.
Population: 13,575; Growth (since 2000): -3.9%; Density: 2,448.2 persons per square mile; Race: 93.0% White, 2.2% Black/African American, 2.3% Asian, 0.0% American Indian/Alaska Native, 0.0% Native Hawaiian/Other Pacific Islander, 2.0% Two or more races, 1.7% Hispanic of any race; Average household size: 2.35; Median age: 44.9; Age under 18: 23.2%; Age 65 and over: 19.1%; Males per 100 females: 89.3; Marriage status: 20.3% never married, 63.1% now married, 1.2% separated, 6.3% widowed, 10.2% divorced; Foreign born: 4.6%; Speak English only: 94.7%; With disability: 7.4%; Veterans: 8.0%; Ancestry: 34.8% German, 21.1% Irish, 16.2% English, 7.0% Italian, 4.1% Polish
Employment: 24.1% management, business, and financial, 7.3% computer, engineering, and science, 23.4% education, legal, community service, arts, and media, 7.2% healthcare practitioners, 7.5% service, 22.9% sales and office, 3.1% natural resources, construction, and maintenance, 4.4% production, transportation, and material moving
Income: Per capita: $45,272; Median household: $86,855; Average household: $110,528; Households with income of $100,000 or more: 43.7%; Poverty rate: 3.5%
Educational Attainment: High school diploma or higher: 98.2%; Bachelor's degree or higher: 66.5%; Graduate/professional degree or higher: 29.7%

School District(s)

Worthington City (PK-12)
2012-13 Enrollment: 9,423 . . . . (614) 450-6000

Housing: Homeownership rate: 82.3%; Median home value: $239,100; Median year structure built: 1963; Homeowner vacancy rate: 1.5%; Median gross rent: $836 per month; Rental vacancy rate: 5.9%
Health Insurance: 95.0% have insurance; 88.6% have private insurance; 20.6% have public insurance; 5.0% do not have insurance; 1.3% of children under 18 do not have insurance
Safety: Violent crime rate: 3.6 per 10,000 population; Property crime rate: 277.9 per 10,000 population
Transportation: Commute: 90.3% car, 0.9% public transportation, 0.7% walk, 7.1% work from home; Median travel time to work: 21.0 minutes
Additional Information Contacts
City of Worthington . . . . (614) 436-3100
http://www.worthington.org

Fulton County

Located in northwestern Ohio; bounded on the north by Michigan; drained by the Tiffin River. Covers a land area of 405.443 square miles, a water area of 1.784 square miles, and is located in the Eastern Time Zone at 41.60° N. Lat., 84.12° W. Long. The county was founded in 1850. County seat is Wauseon.

Fulton County is part of the Toledo, OH Metropolitan Statistical Area. The entire metro area includes: Fulton County, OH; Lucas County, OH; Wood County, OH

Weather Station: Wauseon Water Plant Elevation: 750 feet

	Jan	Feb	Mar	Apr	May	Jun	Jul	Aug	Sep	Oct	Nov	Dec
High	32	36	46	60	71	81	84	82	76	63	49	36
Low	17	19	27	38	48	58	61	60	52	41	32	22
Precip	1.9	1.6	2.3	3.1	3.7	3.4	3.7	3.7	3.2	2.9	2.9	2.5
Snow	8.2	6.1	4.1	0.6	tr	0.0	0.0	0.0	0.0	0.1	1.2	5.3

High and Low temperatures in degrees Fahrenheit; Precipitation and Snow in inches

Population: 42,698; Growth (since 2000): 1.5%; Density: 105.3 persons per square mile; Race: 94.9% White, 0.4% Black/African American, 0.4% Asian, 0.3% American Indian/Alaska Native, 0.0% Native Hawaiian/Other Pacific Islander, 1.5% two or more races, 7.8% Hispanic of any race; Average household size: 2.61; Median age: 39.9; Age under 18: 25.8%; Age 65 and over: 14.1%; Males per 100 females: 96.6; Marriage status: 22.8% never married, 61.8% now married, 1.0% separated, 5.8% widowed, 9.7% divorced; Foreign born: 1.8%; Speak English only: 95.8%; With disability: 10.7%; Veterans: 8.7%; Ancestry: 43.5% German, 11.3% English, 11.0% Irish, 6.0% American, 5.5% Polish
Religion: Six largest groups: 17.8% Catholicism, 9.2% European Free-Church, 8.5% Lutheran, 6.1% Baptist, 4.9% Holiness, 4.6% Methodist/Pietist
Economy: Unemployment rate: 4.2%; Leading industries: 16.7% retail trade; 12.5% other services (except public administration); 12.1% construction; Farms: 825 totaling 195,356 acres; Company size: 1 employs 1,000 or more persons, 2 employ 500 to 999 persons, 18 employ 100 to 499 persons, 913 employ less than 100 persons; Business ownership: 827 women-owned, n/a Black-owned, n/a Hispanic-owned, n/a Asian-owned
Employment: 11.5% management, business, and financial, 2.5% computer, engineering, and science, 8.5% education, legal, community service, arts, and media, 6.2% healthcare practitioners, 15.3% service, 21.9% sales and office, 11.9% natural resources, construction, and maintenance, 22.3% production, transportation, and material moving
Income: Per capita: $24,771; Median household: $52,856; Average household: $64,226; Households with income of $100,000 or more: 15.5%; Poverty rate: 11.4%
Educational Attainment: High school diploma or higher: 88.6%; Bachelor's degree or higher: 16.3%; Graduate/professional degree or higher: 5.7%
Housing: Homeownership rate: 79.0%; Median home value: $128,900; Median year structure built: 1968; Homeowner vacancy rate: 1.8%; Median gross rent: $668 per month; Rental vacancy rate: 9.2%
Vital Statistics: Birth rate: 111.6 per 10,000 population; Death rate: 92.5 per 10,000 population; Age-adjusted cancer mortality rate: 190.0 deaths per 100,000 population
Health Insurance: 92.1% have insurance; 77.7% have private insurance; 26.7% have public insurance; 7.9% do not have insurance; 3.3% of children under 18 do not have insurance
Health Care: Physicians: 8.7 per 10,000 population; Hospital beds: 24.9 per 10,000 population; Hospital admissions: 478.7 per 10,000 population
Transportation: Commute: 93.2% car, 0.1% public transportation, 1.7% walk, 3.5% work from home; Median travel time to work: 23.3 minutes
Presidential Election: 42.3% Obama, 55.5% Romney (2012)
National and State Parks: Harrison Lake State Reservation
Additional Information Contacts
Fulton Government . . . . (419) 337-9255
http://www.fultoncountyoh.com

Fulton County Communities

ARCHBOLD (village). Covers a land area of 4.932 square miles and a water area of 0.139 square miles. Located at 41.52° N. Lat; 84.30° W. Long. Elevation is 732 feet.
Population: 4,346; Growth (since 2000): 1.3%; Density: 881.2 persons per square mile; Race: 90.5% White, 0.5% Black/African American, 0.9% Asian, 0.5% American Indian/Alaska Native, 0.0% Native Hawaiian/Other Pacific Islander, 2.0% Two or more races, 16.8% Hispanic of any race; Average household size: 2.41; Median age: 41.0; Age under 18: 25.7%; Age 65 and over: 19.9%; Males per 100 females: 88.5; Marriage status: 23.0% never married, 63.7% now married, 1.6% separated, 5.3% widowed, 8.0% divorced; Foreign born: 3.8%; Speak English only: 91.5%; With disability: 9.7%; Veterans: 5.0%; Ancestry: 40.9% German, 9.8% English, 4.8% French, 4.4% American, 4.1% Irish
Employment: 10.8% management, business, and financial, 0.0% computer, engineering, and science, 15.5% education, legal, community service, arts, and media, 4.3% healthcare practitioners, 14.2% service, 23.2% sales and office, 7.2% natural resources, construction, and maintenance, 24.8% production, transportation, and material moving
Income: Per capita: $24,841; Median household: $48,216; Average household: $62,612; Households with income of $100,000 or more: 18.0%; Poverty rate: 14.1%
Educational Attainment: High school diploma or higher: 84.3%; Bachelor's degree or higher: 25.9%; Graduate/professional degree or higher: 11.6%

School District(s)
Archbold-Area Local (PK-12)
2012-13 Enrollment: 1,199 . . . . (419) 446-2728
Four County Career Center (07-12)
2012-13 Enrollment: n/a . . . . (419) 267-3331

Two-year College(s)
Northwest State Community College (Public)
Fall 2013 Enrollment: 4,603 . . . . (419) 267-5511
2013-14 Tuition: In-state $3,574; Out-of-state $6,934

Vocational/Technical School(s)
Four County Career Center (Public)
Fall 2013 Enrollment: 142 . . . . (419) 267-3331

Housing: Homeownership rate: 71.8%; Median home value: $124,900; Median year structure built: 1975; Homeowner vacancy rate: 2.6%; Median gross rent: $615 per month; Rental vacancy rate: 5.3%
Health Insurance: 91.5% have insurance; 75.2% have private insurance; 30.2% have public insurance; 8.5% do not have insurance; 6.5% of children under 18 do not have insurance
Newspapers: Archbold Buckeye (weekly circulation 3200); Farmland News (weekly circulation 3500)
Transportation: Commute: 95.2% car, 0.0% public transportation, 0.8% walk, 2.2% work from home; Median travel time to work: 17.1 minutes
Additional Information Contacts
Village of Archbold . . . . (419) 445-4726
http://www.archbold.com

DELTA (village). Covers a land area of 2.670 square miles and a water area of 0.001 square miles. Located at 41.58° N. Lat; 84.00° W. Long. Elevation is 722 feet.
Population: 3,103; Growth (since 2000): 5.9%; Density: 1,162.2 persons per square mile; Race: 96.1% White, 0.4% Black/African American, 0.5% Asian, 0.5% American Indian/Alaska Native, 0.0% Native Hawaiian/Other Pacific Islander, 1.6% Two or more races, 5.3% Hispanic of any race; Average household size: 2.58; Median age: 35.5; Age under 18: 27.7%; Age 65 and over: 12.2%; Males per 100 females: 93.9; Marriage status: 26.4% never married, 52.2% now married, 1.2% separated, 5.2% widowed, 16.2% divorced; Foreign born: 0.6%; Speak English only: 96.0%; With disability: 9.8%; Veterans: 11.5%; Ancestry: 40.1% German, 18.2% Irish, 7.4% English, 5.4% Italian, 5.3% American
Employment: 8.4% management, business, and financial, 7.2% computer, engineering, and science, 3.7% education, legal, community service, arts,

and media, 6.4% healthcare practitioners, 20.3% service, 19.3% sales and office, 11.0% natural resources, construction, and maintenance, 23.8% production, transportation, and material moving
Income: Per capita: $20,847; Median household: $44,412; Average household: $52,777; Households with income of $100,000 or more: 9.1%; Poverty rate: 13.1%
Educational Attainment: High school diploma or higher: 91.7%; Bachelor's degree or higher: 15.3%; Graduate/professional degree or higher: 5.2%

School District(s)

Pike-Delta-York Local (PK-12)
2012-13 Enrollment: 1,237 . . . . (419) 822-3391
Housing: Homeownership rate: 75.1%; Median home value: $106,500; Median year structure built: 1956; Homeowner vacancy rate: 2.6%; Median gross rent: $582 per month; Rental vacancy rate: 7.4%
Health Insurance: 92.1% have insurance; 74.5% have private insurance; 32.8% have public insurance; 7.9% do not have insurance; 3.1% of children under 18 do not have insurance
Safety: Violent crime rate: 3.2 per 10,000 population; Property crime rate: 107.2 per 10,000 population
Newspapers: Delta Atlas (weekly circulation 2000)
Transportation: Commute: 91.8% car, 0.0% public transportation, 2.0% walk, 1.9% work from home; Median travel time to work: 26.9 minutes

---

FAYETTE (village). Covers a land area of 0.984 square miles and a water area of 0 square miles. Located at 41.67° N. Lat; 84.33° W. Long. Elevation is 791 feet.
History: Fayette developed as a grain and livestock shipping center.
Population: 1,283; Growth (since 2000): -4.3%; Density: 1,303.6 persons per square mile; Race: 94.0% White, 1.0% Black/African American, 0.1% Asian, 0.4% American Indian/Alaska Native, 0.0% Native Hawaiian/Other Pacific Islander, 2.2% Two or more races, 14.3% Hispanic of any race; Average household size: 2.54; Median age: 35.3; Age under 18: 28.4%; Age 65 and over: 12.8%; Males per 100 females: 90.1

School District(s)

Fayette Local (PK-12)
2012-13 Enrollment: 435. . . . . (419) 237-2573
Housing: Homeownership rate: 64.1%; Homeowner vacancy rate: 1.5%; Rental vacancy rate: 24.3%

LYONS (village). Covers a land area of 0.708 square miles and a water area of <.001 square miles. Located at 41.70° N. Lat; 84.07° W. Long. Elevation is 768 feet.
Population: 562; Growth (since 2000): 0.5%; Density: 794.3 persons per square mile; Race: 97.9% White, 0.2% Black/African American, 0.4% Asian, 0.0% American Indian/Alaska Native, 0.0% Native Hawaiian/Other Pacific Islander, 1.2% Two or more races, 3.0% Hispanic of any race; Average household size: 2.48; Median age: 39.5; Age under 18: 24.9%; Age 65 and over: 12.5%; Males per 100 females: 95.1
Housing: Homeownership rate: 72.2%; Homeowner vacancy rate: 4.7%; Rental vacancy rate: 10.0%

METAMORA (village). Covers a land area of 0.825 square miles and a water area of 0.014 square miles. Located at 41.71° N. Lat; 83.91° W. Long. Elevation is 718 feet.
Population: 627; Growth (since 2000): 11.4%; Density: 760.2 persons per square mile; Race: 99.2% White, 0.0% Black/African American, 0.0% Asian, 0.2% American Indian/Alaska Native, 0.0% Native Hawaiian/Other Pacific Islander, 0.6% Two or more races, 2.2% Hispanic of any race; Average household size: 2.84; Median age: 36.9; Age under 18: 29.8%; Age 65 and over: 10.8%; Males per 100 females: 97.2

School District(s)

Evergreen Local (PK-12)
2012-13 Enrollment: 1,188 . . . . (419) 644-3521
Housing: Homeownership rate: 77.3%; Homeowner vacancy rate: 1.1%; Rental vacancy rate: 13.6%

PETTISVILLE (CDP). Covers a land area of 0.952 square miles and a water area of <.001 square miles. Located at 41.53° N. Lat; 84.22° W. Long. Elevation is 758 feet.
Population: 498; Growth (since 2000): n/a; Density: 523.4 persons per square mile; Race: 95.6% White, 0.0% Black/African American, 1.0% Asian, 0.2% American Indian/Alaska Native, 0.0% Native Hawaiian/Other Pacific Islander, 1.0% Two or more races, 9.8% Hispanic of any race; Average household size: 2.68; Median age: 41.8; Age under 18: 26.7%; Age 65 and over: 17.5%; Males per 100 females: 93.8

School District(s)

Pettisville Local (PK-12)
2012-13 Enrollment: 494. . . . . (419) 446-2705
Housing: Homeownership rate: 82.3%; Homeowner vacancy rate: 1.9%; Rental vacancy rate: 8.3%

SWANTON (village). Covers a land area of 3.094 square miles and a water area of 0.037 square miles. Located at 41.58° N. Lat; 83.89° W. Long. Elevation is 682 feet.
Population: 3,690; Growth (since 2000): 11.6%; Density: 1,192.6 persons per square mile; Race: 97.1% White, 0.9% Black/African American, 0.1% Asian, 0.2% American Indian/Alaska Native, 0.0% Native Hawaiian/Other Pacific Islander, 1.3% Two or more races, 3.5% Hispanic of any race; Average household size: 2.56; Median age: 38.0; Age under 18: 26.0%; Age 65 and over: 13.9%; Males per 100 females: 95.1; Marriage status: 24.8% never married, 58.9% now married, 2.3% separated, 7.9% widowed, 8.4% divorced; Foreign born: 0.0%; Speak English only: 99.2%; With disability: 12.7%; Veterans: 9.9%; Ancestry: 38.9% German, 14.3% Irish, 12.9% English, 10.2% Polish, 5.4% American
Employment: 11.0% management, business, and financial, 2.8% computer, engineering, and science, 8.0% education, legal, community service, arts, and media, 8.1% healthcare practitioners, 16.6% service, 24.6% sales and office, 10.1% natural resources, construction, and maintenance, 18.7% production, transportation, and material moving
Income: Per capita: $23,756; Median household: $52,824; Average household: $57,753; Households with income of $100,000 or more: 11.9%; Poverty rate: 9.3%
Educational Attainment: High school diploma or higher: 89.0%; Bachelor's degree or higher: 14.1%; Graduate/professional degree or higher: 3.7%

School District(s)

Swanton Local (PK-12)
2012-13 Enrollment: 1,255 . . . . (419) 826-7085
Housing: Homeownership rate: 72.6%; Median home value: $129,500; Median year structure built: 1959; Homeowner vacancy rate: 2.4%; Median gross rent: $804 per month; Rental vacancy rate: 5.4%
Health Insurance: 92.8% have insurance; 82.2% have private insurance; 22.5% have public insurance; 7.2% do not have insurance; 1.1% of children under 18 do not have insurance
Newspapers: Swanton Enterprise (weekly circulation 1900)
Transportation: Commute: 95.2% car, 0.0% public transportation, 0.9% walk, 3.9% work from home; Median travel time to work: 24.5 minutes
Additional Information Contacts
Village of Swanton. . . . . (419) 826-9515
http://www.villageofswantonohio.us

TEDROW (CDP). Covers a land area of 0.321 square miles and a water area of 0 square miles. Located at 41.60° N. Lat; 84.20° W. Long. Elevation is 768 feet.
Population: 173; Growth (since 2000): n/a; Density: 539.5 persons per square mile; Race: 92.5% White, 0.0% Black/African American, 0.0% Asian, 0.0% American Indian/Alaska Native, 0.0% Native Hawaiian/Other Pacific Islander, 0.0% Two or more races, 30.6% Hispanic of any race; Average household size: 2.51; Median age: 44.4; Age under 18: 22.0%; Age 65 and over: 19.7%; Males per 100 females: 111.0
Housing: Homeownership rate: 76.8%; Homeowner vacancy rate: 1.9%; Rental vacancy rate: 5.9%

WAUSEON (city). County seat. Covers a land area of 5.168 square miles and a water area of 0.023 square miles. Located at 41.55° N. Lat; 84.14° W. Long. Elevation is 768 feet.
History: Settled 1835, incorporated 1852.
Population: 7,332; Growth (since 2000): 3.4%; Density: 1,418.6 persons per square mile; Race: 90.3% White, 0.9% Black/African American, 1.0% Asian, 0.3% American Indian/Alaska Native, 0.0% Native Hawaiian/Other Pacific Islander, 2.3% Two or more races, 14.2% Hispanic of any race; Average household size: 2.58; Median age: 35.4; Age under 18: 28.6%; Age 65 and over: 13.1%; Males per 100 females: 92.1; Marriage status: 22.8% never married, 57.4% now married, 0.7% separated, 6.5% widowed, 13.3% divorced; Foreign born: 3.5%; Speak English only: 90.8%; With disability: 11.5%; Veterans: 8.9%; Ancestry: 37.3% German, 12.3% Irish, 9.3% English, 7.0% Polish, 5.2% French

Employment: 6.9% management, business, and financial, 1.1% computer, engineering, and science, 6.5% education, legal, community service, arts, and media, 7.3% healthcare practitioners, 15.2% service, 25.1% sales and office, 8.6% natural resources, construction, and maintenance, 29.3% production, transportation, and material moving
Income: Per capita: $20,208; Median household: $44,954; Average household: $51,409; Households with income of $100,000 or more: 10.1%; Poverty rate: 18.9%
Educational Attainment: High school diploma or higher: 83.2%; Bachelor's degree or higher: 17.2%; Graduate/professional degree or higher: 6.4%

School District(s)

Wauseon Exempted Village (PK-12)
2012-13 Enrollment: 1,843 . . . . (419) 335-6616
Housing: Homeownership rate: 67.4%; Median home value: $111,000; Median year structure built: 1963; Homeowner vacancy rate: 2.3%; Median gross rent: $623 per month; Rental vacancy rate: 9.3%
Health Insurance: 91.5% have insurance; 67.5% have private insurance; 35.2% have public insurance; 8.5% do not have insurance; 2.0% of children under 18 do not have insurance
Hospitals: Fulton County Health Center (119 beds)
Safety: Violent crime rate: 11.0 per 10,000 population; Property crime rate: 282.2 per 10,000 population
Newspapers: Fulton County Expositor (weekly circulation 13000)
Transportation: Commute: 93.3% car, 0.2% public transportation, 1.9% walk, 3.5% work from home; Median travel time to work: 17.9 minutes

Gallia County

Located in southern Ohio; bounded on the east by the Ohio River and the West Virginia border; crossed by Raccoon Creek. Covers a land area of 466.530 square miles, a water area of 4.666 square miles, and is located in the Eastern Time Zone at 38.82° N. Lat., 82.30° W. Long. The county was founded in 1803. County seat is Gallipolis.

Gallia County is part of the Point Pleasant, WV-OH Micropolitan Statistical Area. The entire metro area includes: Gallia County, OH; Mason County, WV

Weather Station: Gallipolis Elevation: 568 feet

	Jan	Feb	Mar	Apr	May	Jun	Jul	Aug	Sep	Oct	Nov	Dec
High	43	47	57	68	76	84	87	87	80	69	58	46
Low	23	25	32	41	51	60	65	63	56	44	35	27
Precip	2.8	3.0	3.8	3.5	4.4	3.7	4.1	3.4	3.0	2.8	3.1	3.2
Snow	4.2	2.9	1.2	tr	0.0	0.0	0.0	0.0	0.0	0.0	tr	1.0

High and Low temperatures in degrees Fahrenheit; Precipitation and Snow in inches

Population: 30,934; Growth (since 2000): -0.4%; Density: 66.3 persons per square mile; Race: 94.7% White, 2.6% Black/African American, 0.5% Asian, 0.4% American Indian/Alaska Native, 0.0% Native Hawaiian/Other Pacific Islander, 1.6% two or more races, 0.9% Hispanic of any race; Average household size: 2.49; Median age: 39.9; Age under 18: 23.8%; Age 65 and over: 16.0%; Males per 100 females: 97.1; Marriage status: 23.0% never married, 55.4% now married, 1.7% separated, 7.3% widowed, 14.4% divorced; Foreign born: 1.0%; Speak English only: 97.4%; With disability: 18.1%; Veterans: 9.9%; Ancestry: 17.7% German, 13.8% Irish, 12.7% American, 9.7% English, 2.8% French
Religion: Six largest groups: 9.7% Baptist, 4.6% Methodist/Pietist, 3.3% Non-denominational Protestant, 2.4% European Free-Church, 2.0% Holiness, 1.6% Catholicism
Economy: Unemployment rate: 5.7%; Leading industries: 21.8% retail trade; 12.5% health care and social assistance; 12.3% other services (except public administration); Farms: 957 totaling 115,838 acres; Company size: 1 employs 1,000 or more persons, 1 employs 500 to 999 persons, 11 employs 100 to 499 persons, 547 employ less than 100 persons; Business ownership: 533 women-owned, n/a Black-owned, n/a Hispanic-owned, n/a Asian-owned
Employment: 9.8% management, business, and financial, 1.8% computer, engineering, and science, 9.4% education, legal, community service, arts, and media, 9.2% healthcare practitioners, 19.9% service, 20.1% sales and office, 11.9% natural resources, construction, and maintenance, 18.0% production, transportation, and material moving
Income: Per capita: $21,168; Median household: $39,226; Average household: $54,833; Households with income of $100,000 or more: 13.8%; Poverty rate: 17.7%
Educational Attainment: High school diploma or higher: 81.3%; Bachelor's degree or higher: 15.2%; Graduate/professional degree or higher: 6.2%
Housing: Homeownership rate: 72.5%; Median home value: $95,500; Median year structure built: 1980; Homeowner vacancy rate: 2.4%; Median gross rent: $580 per month; Rental vacancy rate: 9.9%
Vital Statistics: Birth rate: 116.6 per 10,000 population; Death rate: 109.7 per 10,000 population; Age-adjusted cancer mortality rate: 202.1 deaths per 100,000 population
Health Insurance: 85.3% have insurance; 60.0% have private insurance; 40.3% have public insurance; 14.7% do not have insurance; 8.0% of children under 18 do not have insurance
Health Care: Physicians: 26.6 per 10,000 population; Hospital beds: 58.5 per 10,000 population; Hospital admissions: 2,206.1 per 10,000 population
Transportation: Commute: 93.6% car, 0.1% public transportation, 3.2% walk, 2.4% work from home; Median travel time to work: 26.1 minutes
Presidential Election: 36.0% Obama, 61.7% Romney (2012)
National and State Parks: Tycoon Lake State Wildlife Area
Additional Information Contacts
Gallia Government . . . . (740) 446-8510
http://www.gallianet.net

Gallia County Communities

BIDWELL (unincorporated postal area)

ZCTA: 45614

Covers a land area of 73.163 square miles and a water area of 0.725 square miles. Located at 38.93° N. Lat; 82.28° W. Long. Elevation is 686 feet.
Population: 5,080; Growth (since 2000): 14.8%; Density: 69.4 persons per square mile; Race: 91.8% White, 5.2% Black/African American, 0.3% Asian, 0.4% American Indian/Alaska Native, 0.0% Native Hawaiian/Other Pacific Islander, 2.1% Two or more races, 0.7% Hispanic of any race; Average household size: 2.63; Median age: 39.6; Age under 18: 25.5%; Age 65 and over: 16.8%; Males per 100 females: 91.5; Marriage status: 20.6% never married, 58.7% now married, 1.4% separated, 9.7% widowed, 11.0% divorced; Foreign born: 0.7%; Speak English only: 98.0%; With disability: 15.5%; Veterans: 11.8%; Ancestry: 20.1% Irish, 19.9% German, 14.7% American, 9.4% English, 4.9% Dutch
Employment: 3.3% management, business, and financial, 2.1% computer, engineering, and science, 12.8% education, legal, community service, arts, and media, 5.7% healthcare practitioners, 6.4% service, 31.5% sales and office, 19.5% natural resources, construction, and maintenance, 18.7% production, transportation, and material moving
Income: Per capita: $21,421; Median household: $41,417; Average household: $57,181; Households with income of $100,000 or more: 13.6%; Poverty rate: 20.5%
Educational Attainment: High school diploma or higher: 84.5%; Bachelor's degree or higher: 14.5%; Graduate/professional degree or higher: 4.4%

School District(s)

Gallia County Local (PK-12)
2012-13 Enrollment: 2,211 . . . . (740) 446-7917
Housing: Homeownership rate: 73.3%; Median home value: $89,400; Median year structure built: 1983; Homeowner vacancy rate: 1.4%; Median gross rent: $636 per month; Rental vacancy rate: 12.5%
Health Insurance: 89.3% have insurance; 62.6% have private insurance; 45.1% have public insurance; 10.7% do not have insurance; 5.7% of children under 18 do not have insurance
Transportation: Commute: 95.0% car, 0.1% public transportation, 3.3% walk, 1.7% work from home; Median travel time to work: 29.5 minutes

CENTERVILLE (village). Covers a land area of 0.100 square miles and a water area of 0 square miles. Located at 38.90° N. Lat; 82.45° W. Long. Elevation is 679 feet.
Population: 103; Growth (since 2000): -23.1%; Density: 1,027.4 persons per square mile; Race: 98.1% White, 1.0% Black/African American, 0.0% Asian, 0.0% American Indian/Alaska Native, 0.0% Native Hawaiian/Other Pacific Islander, 1.0% Two or more races, 0.0% Hispanic of any race; Average household size: 2.40; Median age: 44.3; Age under 18: 12.6%; Age 65 and over: 22.3%; Males per 100 females: 110.2
Housing: Homeownership rate: 79.1%; Homeowner vacancy rate: 5.6%; Rental vacancy rate: 18.2%

CHESHIRE (village). Covers a land area of 0.770 square miles and a water area of 0.012 square miles. Located at 38.95° N. Lat; 82.11° W. Long. Elevation is 571 feet.
Population: 132; Growth (since 2000): -40.3%; Density: 171.4 persons per square mile; Race: 96.2% White, 0.8% Black/African American, 0.0% Asian, 0.0% American Indian/Alaska Native, 0.0% Native Hawaiian/Other Pacific Islander, 0.8% Two or more races, 1.5% Hispanic of any race; Average household size: 1.97; Median age: 52.0; Age under 18: 15.2%; Age 65 and over: 24.2%; Males per 100 females: 112.9
Housing: Homeownership rate: 73.2%; Homeowner vacancy rate: 0.0%; Rental vacancy rate: 10.0%

CROWN CITY (village). Covers a land area of 1.161 square miles and a water area of 0.036 square miles. Located at 38.59° N. Lat; 82.30° W. Long. Elevation is 568 feet.
Population: 413; Growth (since 2000): 0.5%; Density: 355.8 persons per square mile; Race: 98.8% White, 0.0% Black/African American, 1.0% Asian, 0.0% American Indian/Alaska Native, 0.0% Native Hawaiian/Other Pacific Islander, 0.2% Two or more races, 0.5% Hispanic of any race; Average household size: 2.35; Median age: 42.6; Age under 18: 19.9%; Age 65 and over: 18.9%; Males per 100 females: 90.3

School District(s)

Gallia County Local (PK-12)
2012-13 Enrollment: 2,211 . . . . (740) 446-7917
Housing: Homeownership rate: 67.6%; Homeowner vacancy rate: 4.7%; Rental vacancy rate: 6.6%

GALLIPOLIS (village). County seat. Covers a land area of 3.597 square miles and a water area of 0.228 square miles. Located at 38.82° N. Lat; 82.19° W. Long. Elevation is 571 feet.
History: Gallipolis was settled in 1790 by French immigrants who had been induced to leave France and purchase land in Ohio. After their long journey, they found that the deeds they had purchased were worthless, and those who stayed in Gallipolis had to buy their land all over again.
Population: 3,641; Growth (since 2000): -12.9%; Density: 1,012.1 persons per square mile; Race: 89.7% White, 5.1% Black/African American, 1.1% Asian, 0.6% American Indian/Alaska Native, 0.0% Native Hawaiian/Other Pacific Islander, 3.0% Two or more races, 1.2% Hispanic of any race; Average household size: 2.14; Median age: 44.6; Age under 18: 18.9%; Age 65 and over: 20.8%; Males per 100 females: 93.3; Marriage status: 29.9% never married, 44.9% now married, 1.6% separated, 6.9% widowed, 18.3% divorced; Foreign born: 0.8%; Speak English only: 98.5%; With disability: 26.8%; Veterans: 10.7%; Ancestry: 13.3% American, 13.3% German, 12.8% Irish, 8.3% English, 7.3% French
Employment: 12.4% management, business, and financial, 0.6% computer, engineering, and science, 12.3% education, legal, community service, arts, and media, 11.3% healthcare practitioners, 20.6% service, 28.1% sales and office, 9.1% natural resources, construction, and maintenance, 5.7% production, transportation, and material moving
Income: Per capita: $22,835; Median household: $32,193; Average household: $50,755; Households with income of $100,000 or more: 12.0%; Poverty rate: 22.9%
Educational Attainment: High school diploma or higher: 79.8%; Bachelor's degree or higher: 20.1%; Graduate/professional degree or higher: 7.5%

School District(s)

Gallia County Local (PK-12)
2012-13 Enrollment: 2,211 . . . . (740) 446-7917
Gallipolis City (PK-12)
2012-13 Enrollment: 2,163 . . . . (740) 446-3211

Two-year College(s)

Gallipolis Career College (Private, For-profit)
Fall 2013 Enrollment: 105 . . . . (740) 446-4367
2013-14 Tuition: In-state $11,570; Out-of-state $11,570
Housing: Homeownership rate: 48.9%; Median home value: $119,700; Median year structure built: 1951; Homeowner vacancy rate: 5.7%; Median gross rent: $592 per month; Rental vacancy rate: 8.9%
Health Insurance: 88.0% have insurance; 57.6% have private insurance; 47.2% have public insurance; 12.0% do not have insurance; 0.0% of children under 18 do not have insurance
Hospitals: Holzer Medical Center (269 beds)
Safety: Violent crime rate: 11.0 per 10,000 population; Property crime rate: 938.4 per 10,000 population
Newspapers: Gallipolis Daily Tribune (daily circulation 4500)
Transportation: Commute: 90.6% car, 1.3% public transportation, 4.3% walk, 3.8% work from home; Median travel time to work: 17.1 minutes
Airports: Gallia-Meigs Regional (general aviation)
Additional Information Contacts
City of Gallipolis. . . . . (740) 446-1789
http://www.gallianet.net/Gallipolis/index.htm

KANAUGA (CDP). Covers a land area of 0.289 square miles and a water area of 0.031 square miles. Located at 38.84° N. Lat; 82.15° W. Long. Elevation is 571 feet.
Population: 175; Growth (since 2000): n/a; Density: 604.6 persons per square mile; Race: 95.4% White, 4.6% Black/African American, 0.0% Asian, 0.0% American Indian/Alaska Native, 0.0% Native Hawaiian/Other Pacific Islander, 0.0% Two or more races, 0.0% Hispanic of any race; Average household size: 2.27; Median age: 43.2; Age under 18: 18.3%; Age 65 and over: 20.6%; Males per 100 females: 110.8
Housing: Homeownership rate: 52.0%; Homeowner vacancy rate: 4.8%; Rental vacancy rate: 11.9%

PATRIOT (unincorporated postal area)

ZCTA: 45658

Covers a land area of 97.157 square miles and a water area of 0.391 square miles. Located at 38.76° N. Lat; 82.41° W. Long. Elevation is 718 feet.
Population: 2,787; Growth (since 2000): 20.4%; Density: 28.7 persons per square mile; Race: 96.7% White, 1.1% Black/African American, 0.2% Asian, 0.7% American Indian/Alaska Native, 0.0% Native Hawaiian/Other Pacific Islander, 0.8% Two or more races, 1.2% Hispanic of any race; Average household size: 2.95; Median age: 34.5; Age under 18: 30.9%; Age 65 and over: 12.3%; Males per 100 females: 108.1; Marriage status: 18.2% never married, 61.7% now married, 3.6% separated, 4.8% widowed, 15.3% divorced; Foreign born: 6.0%; Speak English only: 91.8%; With disability: 20.1%; Veterans: 8.4%; Ancestry: 23.3% German, 12.4% American, 9.3% English, 7.7% Irish, 6.7% Welsh
Employment: 11.6% management, business, and financial, 2.3% computer, engineering, and science, 15.4% education, legal, community service, arts, and media, 2.6% healthcare practitioners, 18.0% service, 16.6% sales and office, 8.2% natural resources, construction, and maintenance, 25.4% production, transportation, and material moving
Income: Per capita: $17,768; Median household: $32,361; Average household: $44,310; Households with income of $100,000 or more: 10.0%; Poverty rate: 19.9%
Educational Attainment: High school diploma or higher: 75.8%; Bachelor's degree or higher: 13.5%; Graduate/professional degree or higher: 7.5%

School District(s)

Gallia County Local (PK-12)
2012-13 Enrollment: 2,211 . . . . (740) 446-7917
Housing: Homeownership rate: 82.2%; Median home value: $73,500; Median year structure built: 1986; Homeowner vacancy rate: 2.3%; Median gross rent: $556 per month; Rental vacancy rate: 4.5%
Health Insurance: 72.0% have insurance; 49.6% have private insurance; 37.1% have public insurance; 28.0% do not have insurance; 24.2% of children under 18 do not have insurance
Transportation: Commute: 92.8% car, 0.0% public transportation, 5.1% walk, 2.1% work from home; Median travel time to work: 33.2 minutes

RIO GRANDE (village). Covers a land area of 1.357 square miles and a water area of 0.011 square miles. Located at 38.88° N. Lat; 82.38° W. Long. Elevation is 656 feet.
History: Rio Grande was settled by Nehemiah Atwood, who served under General William Henry Harrison in the War of 1812 and, in 1818, opened a tavern at this site. Atwood provided the endowment for Rio Grande College, established in 1876 under the supervision of the Baptist church.
Population: 830; Growth (since 2000): -9.3%; Density: 611.8 persons per square mile; Race: 87.2% White, 8.8% Black/African American, 0.6% Asian, 0.2% American Indian/Alaska Native, 0.0% Native Hawaiian/Other Pacific Islander, 2.4% Two or more races, 1.3% Hispanic of any race; Average household size: 2.35; Median age: 21.9; Age under 18: 16.0%; Age 65 and over: 7.3%; Males per 100 females: 101.5

School District(s)

Gallia-Jackson-Vinton (07-12)
2012-13 Enrollment: n/a . . . . (740) 245-5334
Gallipolis City (PK-12)
2012-13 Enrollment: 2,163 . . . . (740) 446-3211

Four-year College(s)

University of Rio Grande (Private, Not-for-profit)
Fall 2013 Enrollment: 2,314 . . . . (740) 245-7206
2013-14 Tuition: In-state $20,780; Out-of-state $20,780

Vocational/Technical School(s)

Buckeye Hills Career Center (Public)
Fall 2013 Enrollment: 108 . . . . (740) 245-5334
2013-14 Tuition: $7,800

Housing: Homeownership rate: 40.4%; Homeowner vacancy rate: 9.6%; Rental vacancy rate: 7.6%

Safety: Violent crime rate: 13.2 per 10,000 population; Property crime rate: 79.2 per 10,000 population

THURMAN (unincorporated postal area)

ZCTA: 45685

Covers a land area of 30.275 square miles and a water area of 0.019 square miles. Located at 38.93° N. Lat; 82.46° W. Long. Elevation is 682 feet.

Population: 1,251; Growth (since 2000): 36.3%; Density: 41.3 persons per square mile; Race: 94.9% White, 2.8% Black/African American, 0.0% Asian, 0.1% American Indian/Alaska Native, 0.0% Native Hawaiian/Other Pacific Islander, 1.8% Two or more races, 1.2% Hispanic of any race; Average household size: 2.63; Median age: 35.9; Age under 18: 24.7%; Age 65 and over: 13.2%; Males per 100 females: 92.2

Housing: Homeownership rate: 65.7%; Homeowner vacancy rate: 2.8%; Rental vacancy rate: 9.4%

VINTON (village). Covers a land area of 1.177 square miles and a water area of 0.033 square miles. Located at 38.98° N. Lat; 82.33° W. Long. Elevation is 610 feet.

Population: 222; Growth (since 2000): -31.5%; Density: 188.5 persons per square mile; Race: 99.1% White, 0.9% Black/African American, 0.0% Asian, 0.0% American Indian/Alaska Native, 0.0% Native Hawaiian/Other Pacific Islander, 0.0% Two or more races, 0.5% Hispanic of any race; Average household size: 2.34; Median age: 46.7; Age under 18: 20.3%; Age 65 and over: 16.7%; Males per 100 females: 89.7

School District(s)

Gallia County Local (PK-12)
2012-13 Enrollment: 2,211 . . . . (740) 446-7917

Housing: Homeownership rate: 77.9%; Homeowner vacancy rate: 5.1%; Rental vacancy rate: 25.0%

Geauga County

Located in northeastern Ohio; drained by the Cuyahoga, Chagrin, and Grand Rivers; includes several lakes. Covers a land area of 400.164 square miles, a water area of 8.129 square miles, and is located in the Eastern Time Zone at 41.50° N. Lat., 81.17° W. Long. The county was founded in 1805. County seat is Chardon.

Geauga County is part of the Cleveland-Elyria, OH Metropolitan Statistical Area. The entire metro area includes: Cuyahoga County, OH; Geauga County, OH; Lake County, OH; Lorain County, OH; Medina County, OH

Weather Station: Chardon Elevation: 1,129 feet

	Jan	Feb	Mar	Apr	May	Jun	Jul	Aug	Sep	Oct	Nov	Dec
High	32	35	44	57	68	77	80	79	72	60	49	37
Low	16	17	24	35	45	54	58	57	50	40	32	22
Precip	3.6	2.8	3.3	4.0	4.4	4.5	4.4	4.2	4.3	4.1	4.3	4.4
Snow	28.6	19.2	14.4	4.5	tr	0.0	0.0	0.0	0.0	0.9	9.5	25.7

High and Low temperatures in degrees Fahrenheit; Precipitation and Snow in inches

Population: 93,389; Growth (since 2000): 2.7%; Density: 233.4 persons per square mile; Race: 96.9% White, 1.3% Black/African American, 0.6% Asian, 0.1% American Indian/Alaska Native, 0.0% Native Hawaiian/Other Pacific Islander, 0.8% two or more races, 1.1% Hispanic of any race; Average household size: 2.70; Median age: 43.3; Age under 18: 26.0%; Age 65 and over: 15.5%; Males per 100 females: 96.7; Marriage status: 24.3% never married, 61.2% now married, 1.0% separated, 5.6% widowed, 8.9% divorced; Foreign born: 3.0%; Speak English only: 88.1%; With disability: 9.6%; Veterans: 9.1%; Ancestry: 26.1% German, 15.5% Irish, 14.1% Italian, 12.3% English, 8.0% Polish

Religion: Six largest groups: 33.1% Catholicism, 9.6% European Free-Church, 3.6% Methodist/Pietist, 3.1% Presbyterian-Reformed, 2.3% Lutheran, 1.9% Baptist

Economy: Unemployment rate: 4.3%; Leading industries: 14.2% construction; 12.8% professional, scientific, and technical services; 10.3% retail trade; Farms: 959 totaling 66,809 acres; Company size: 1 employs 1,000 or more persons, 2 employ 500 to 999 persons, 33 employ 100 to 499 persons, 2,712 employ less than 100 persons; Business ownership: 2,771 women-owned, n/a Black-owned, 48 Hispanic-owned, 44 Asian-owned

Employment: 17.4% management, business, and financial, 5.5% computer, engineering, and science, 9.4% education, legal, community service, arts, and media, 6.6% healthcare practitioners, 14.5% service, 24.9% sales and office, 11.2% natural resources, construction, and maintenance, 10.6% production, transportation, and material moving

Income: Per capita: $34,455; Median household: $67,663; Average household: $92,481; Households with income of $100,000 or more: 31.9%; Poverty rate: 8.1%

Educational Attainment: High school diploma or higher: 90.9%; Bachelor's degree or higher: 35.9%; Graduate/professional degree or higher: 13.3%

Housing: Homeownership rate: 85.7%; Median home value: $224,700; Median year structure built: 1974; Homeowner vacancy rate: 2.1%; Median gross rent: $802 per month; Rental vacancy rate: 8.2%

Vital Statistics: Birth rate: 97.3 per 10,000 population; Death rate: 78.1 per 10,000 population; Age-adjusted cancer mortality rate: 162.8 deaths per 100,000 population

Health Insurance: 87.9% have insurance; 78.1% have private insurance; 22.8% have public insurance; 12.1% do not have insurance; 14.4% of children under 18 do not have insurance

Health Care: Physicians: 22.9 per 10,000 population; Hospital beds: 36.4 per 10,000 population; Hospital admissions: 1,107.7 per 10,000 population

Air Quality Index: 93.5% good, 6.5% moderate, 0.0% unhealthy for sensitive individuals, 0.0% unhealthy (percent of days)

Transportation: Commute: 90.0% car, 0.4% public transportation, 1.6% walk, 6.4% work from home; Median travel time to work: 27.6 minutes

Presidential Election: 38.5% Obama, 60.1% Romney (2012)

National and State Parks: Auburn State Wildlife Area; Punderson State Park

Additional Information Contacts

Geauga Government. . . . . (440) 285-2222
http://www.co.geauga.oh.us

Geauga County Communities

AQUILLA (village). Covers a land area of 0.147 square miles and a water area of 0 square miles. Located at 41.55° N. Lat; 81.17° W. Long. Elevation is 1,266 feet.

Population: 340; Growth (since 2000): -8.6%; Density: 2,305.6 persons per square mile; Race: 97.9% White, 0.0% Black/African American, 0.3% Asian, 0.0% American Indian/Alaska Native, 0.0% Native Hawaiian/Other Pacific Islander, 1.8% Two or more races, 0.0% Hispanic of any race; Average household size: 2.66; Median age: 39.3; Age under 18: 28.5%; Age 65 and over: 9.7%; Males per 100 females: 97.7

Housing: Homeownership rate: 84.4%; Homeowner vacancy rate: 3.5%; Rental vacancy rate: 20.0%

BAINBRIDGE (CDP). Covers a land area of 3.392 square miles and a water area of 0.072 square miles. Located at 41.40° N. Lat; 81.34° W. Long. Elevation is 1,168 feet.

History: In 1817, Bainbridge Township was established and named for a well-known naval hero of the War of 1812, Commodore William Bainbridge.

Population: 3,267; Growth (since 2000): -4.4%; Density: 963.3 persons per square mile; Race: 96.3% White, 1.5% Black/African American, 0.6% Asian, 0.1% American Indian/Alaska Native, 0.1% Native Hawaiian/Other Pacific Islander, 1.0% Two or more races, 0.9% Hispanic of any race; Average household size: 2.59; Median age: 44.9; Age under 18: 27.0%; Age 65 and over: 17.0%; Males per 100 females: 91.5; Marriage status: 22.0% never married, 59.7% now married, 0.5% separated, 8.0% widowed, 10.3% divorced; Foreign born: 7.8%; Speak English only: 90.6%; With disability: 7.8%; Veterans: 7.3%; Ancestry: 32.3% German, 21.1% Irish, 13.3% English, 10.5% Italian, 9.3% Polish

Employment: 18.0% management, business, and financial, 5.2% computer, engineering, and science, 18.2% education, legal, community service, arts, and media, 8.6% healthcare practitioners, 9.6% service, 29.4% sales and office, 6.9% natural resources, construction, and maintenance, 4.1% production, transportation, and material moving

Income: Per capita: $53,450; Median household: $85,604; Average household: $122,119; Households with income of $100,000 or more: 41.6%; Poverty rate: 1.6%
Educational Attainment: High school diploma or higher: 97.7%; Bachelor's degree or higher: 65.6%; Graduate/professional degree or higher: 27.1%
Housing: Homeownership rate: 93.1%; Median home value: $256,700; Median year structure built: 1972; Homeowner vacancy rate: 2.5%; Median gross rent: $1,433 per month; Rental vacancy rate: 0.0%
Health Insurance: 92.7% have insurance; 86.4% have private insurance; 17.1% have public insurance; 7.3% do not have insurance; 0.0% of children under 18 do not have insurance
Transportation: Commute: 91.5% car, 0.0% public transportation, 1.5% walk, 7.1% work from home; Median travel time to work: 26.5 minutes

BURTON (village). Covers a land area of 1.047 square miles and a water area of 0.002 square miles. Located at 41.47° N. Lat; 81.15° W. Long. Elevation is 1,312 feet.
Population: 1,455; Growth (since 2000): 0.3%; Density: 1,389.2 persons per square mile; Race: 97.2% White, 1.2% Black/African American, 0.8% Asian, 0.1% American Indian/Alaska Native, 0.0% Native Hawaiian/Other Pacific Islander, 0.4% Two or more races, 1.3% Hispanic of any race; Average household size: 2.32; Median age: 42.8; Age under 18: 21.9%; Age 65 and over: 21.1%; Males per 100 females: 93.7

School District(s)

Berkshire Local (PK-12)
2012-13 Enrollment: 976. . . . . (440) 834-3380

Four-year College(s)

Kent State University at Geauga (Public)
Fall 2013 Enrollment: 2,653 . . . . (440) 834-4187
2013-14 Tuition: In-state $5,554; Out-of-state $13,514
Housing: Homeownership rate: 58.0%; Homeowner vacancy rate: 0.9%; Rental vacancy rate: 14.4%
Safety: Violent crime rate: 0.0 per 10,000 population; Property crime rate: 6.9 per 10,000 population

CHARDON (city). County seat. Covers a land area of 4.580 square miles and a water area of 0.035 square miles. Located at 41.58° N. Lat; 81.21° W. Long. Elevation is 1,309 feet.
History: Chardon was named for Peter Chardon Brooks, first owner of the site. The town developed as the maple syrup and sugar center of Ohio, from its location on the crest of a hill, surrounded by maple groves.
Population: 5,148; Growth (since 2000): -0.2%; Density: 1,124.1 persons per square mile; Race: 96.9% White, 0.8% Black/African American, 0.6% Asian, 0.2% American Indian/Alaska Native, 0.0% Native Hawaiian/Other Pacific Islander, 1.3% Two or more races, 1.5% Hispanic of any race; Average household size: 2.21; Median age: 41.1; Age under 18: 23.5%; Age 65 and over: 17.7%; Males per 100 females: 82.2; Marriage status: 30.4% never married, 47.1% now married, 2.5% separated, 6.3% widowed, 16.1% divorced; Foreign born: 3.7%; Speak English only: 93.1%; With disability: 14.3%; Veterans: 12.8%; Ancestry: 22.7% Italian, 20.1% German, 17.8% Irish, 12.1% English, 9.2% Polish
Employment: 9.3% management, business, and financial, 2.2% computer, engineering, and science, 11.0% education, legal, community service, arts, and media, 7.6% healthcare practitioners, 13.2% service, 35.9% sales and office, 5.7% natural resources, construction, and maintenance, 15.1% production, transportation, and material moving
Income: Per capita: $24,791; Median household: $52,318; Average household: $58,415; Households with income of $100,000 or more: 13.1%; Poverty rate: 8.2%
Educational Attainment: High school diploma or higher: 94.1%; Bachelor's degree or higher: 29.4%; Graduate/professional degree or higher: 13.9%

School District(s)

Chardon Local (PK-12)
2012-13 Enrollment: 3,024 . . . . (440) 285-4052
Gcesc Community School
2012-13 Enrollment: n/a . . . . (614) 995-1985
Housing: Homeownership rate: 59.2%; Median home value: $179,900; Median year structure built: 1967; Homeowner vacancy rate: 2.3%; Median gross rent: $699 per month; Rental vacancy rate: 6.5%
Health Insurance: 92.9% have insurance; 82.6% have private insurance; 24.3% have public insurance; 7.1% do not have insurance; 7.0% of children under 18 do not have insurance
Hospitals: UH Geauga Medical Center
Safety: Violent crime rate: 11.6 per 10,000 population; Property crime rate: 199.1 per 10,000 population
Newspapers: Geauga County Maple Leaf (weekly circulation 3000)
Transportation: Commute: 88.5% car, 0.0% public transportation, 5.9% walk, 2.3% work from home; Median travel time to work: 23.1 minutes
Additional Information Contacts
Village of Chardon. . . . . (440) 286-2600
http://www.chardon.cc

CHESTERLAND (CDP). Covers a land area of 4.377 square miles and a water area of 0.014 square miles. Located at 41.52° N. Lat; 81.34° W. Long. Elevation is 1,211 feet.
Population: 2,521; Growth (since 2000): -4.7%; Density: 575.9 persons per square mile; Race: 97.6% White, 0.9% Black/African American, 0.4% Asian, 0.0% American Indian/Alaska Native, 0.0% Native Hawaiian/Other Pacific Islander, 1.0% Two or more races, 2.4% Hispanic of any race; Average household size: 2.50; Median age: 46.7; Age under 18: 20.5%; Age 65 and over: 19.8%; Males per 100 females: 93.5; Marriage status: 21.1% never married, 59.2% now married, 1.2% separated, 8.5% widowed, 11.2% divorced; Foreign born: 6.1%; Speak English only: 90.2%; With disability: 11.5%; Veterans: 9.6%; Ancestry: 22.3% Italian, 15.3% Irish, 14.4% German, 11.7% English, 9.5% Polish
Employment: 13.2% management, business, and financial, 4.4% computer, engineering, and science, 9.8% education, legal, community service, arts, and media, 3.6% healthcare practitioners, 22.2% service, 28.5% sales and office, 9.7% natural resources, construction, and maintenance, 8.5% production, transportation, and material moving
Income: Per capita: $36,248; Median household: $62,545; Average household: $76,068; Households with income of $100,000 or more: 25.6%; Poverty rate: 4.6%
Educational Attainment: High school diploma or higher: 93.8%; Bachelor's degree or higher: 32.8%; Graduate/professional degree or higher: 12.3%

School District(s)

West Geauga Local (PK-12)
2012-13 Enrollment: 2,204 . . . . (440) 729-5900

Vocational/Technical School(s)

International Culinary Arts and Sciences Institute (Private, For-profit)
Fall 2013 Enrollment: 40. . . . . (440) 729-7340
2013-14 Tuition: $21,905
Housing: Homeownership rate: 90.2%; Median home value: $183,000; Median year structure built: 1958; Homeowner vacancy rate: 1.3%; Median gross rent: n/a per month; Rental vacancy rate: 8.5%
Health Insurance: 94.5% have insurance; 86.8% have private insurance; 27.3% have public insurance; 5.5% do not have insurance; 0.0% of children under 18 do not have insurance
Newspapers: Chesterland News (weekly circulation 6400)
Transportation: Commute: 94.1% car, 0.0% public transportation, 4.3% walk, 1.6% work from home; Median travel time to work: 24.6 minutes

HUNTSBURG (unincorporated postal area)

ZCTA: 44046

Covers a land area of 15.412 square miles and a water area of 0.731 square miles. Located at 41.54° N. Lat; 81.07° W. Long. Elevation is 1,253 feet.
Population: 2,222; Growth (since 2000): 9.8%; Density: 144.2 persons per square mile; Race: 97.9% White, 1.3% Black/African American, 0.0% Asian, 0.1% American Indian/Alaska Native, 0.0% Native Hawaiian/Other Pacific Islander, 0.8% Two or more races, 0.3% Hispanic of any race; Average household size: 2.97; Median age: 39.8; Age under 18: 28.7%; Age 65 and over: 16.2%; Males per 100 females: 90.4
Housing: Homeownership rate: 84.2%; Homeowner vacancy rate: 1.5%; Rental vacancy rate: 15.3%

MIDDLEFIELD (village). Covers a land area of 3.021 square miles and a water area of 0.022 square miles. Located at 41.46° N. Lat; 81.07° W. Long. Elevation is 1,125 feet.
Population: 2,694; Growth (since 2000): 20.6%; Density: 891.7 persons per square mile; Race: 96.9% White, 0.8% Black/African American, 0.6% Asian, 0.0% American Indian/Alaska Native, 0.0% Native Hawaiian/Other Pacific Islander, 1.6% Two or more races, 0.8% Hispanic of any race; Average household size: 2.20; Median age: 43.8; Age under 18: 21.9%; Age 65 and over: 22.5%; Males per 100 females: 82.9; Marriage status: 23.1% never married, 48.0% now married, 1.4% separated, 13.8% widowed, 15.1% divorced; Foreign born: 2.2%; Speak English only: 92.3%;

With disability: 14.9%; Veterans: 8.2%; Ancestry: 28.8% German, 14.4% Irish, 10.3% English, 9.7% Italian, 5.9% American
Employment: 7.8% management, business, and financial, 2.4% computer, engineering, and science, 11.1% education, legal, community service, arts, and media, 4.2% healthcare practitioners, 27.5% service, 21.1% sales and office, 9.6% natural resources, construction, and maintenance, 16.3% production, transportation, and material moving
Income: Per capita: $22,936; Median household: $41,632; Average household: $52,774; Households with income of $100,000 or more: 13.5%; Poverty rate: 9.0%
Educational Attainment: High school diploma or higher: 85.0%; Bachelor's degree or higher: 18.8%; Graduate/professional degree or higher: 5.9%

School District(s)

Cardinal Local (PK-12)
2012-13 Enrollment: 1,224 . . . . (440) 632-0261
Housing: Homeownership rate: 56.0%; Median home value: $151,600; Median year structure built: 1981; Homeowner vacancy rate: 3.2%; Median gross rent: $701 per month; Rental vacancy rate: 7.4%
Health Insurance: 92.8% have insurance; 78.3% have private insurance; 29.7% have public insurance; 7.2% do not have insurance; 5.2% of children under 18 do not have insurance
Safety: Violent crime rate: 14.8 per 10,000 population; Property crime rate: 173.6 per 10,000 population
Transportation: Commute: 90.9% car, 0.0% public transportation, 3.8% walk, 4.0% work from home; Median travel time to work: 26.2 minutes
Airports: Geauga County (general aviation)
Additional Information Contacts
Village of Middlefield . . . . (440) 632-5248
http://www.middlefieldohio.com

MONTVILLE (unincorporated postal area)

ZCTA: 44064

Covers a land area of 22.510 square miles and a water area of 0.324 square miles. Located at 41.60° N. Lat; 81.03° W. Long. Elevation is 1,204 feet.
Population: 1,657; Growth (since 2000): -0.1%; Density: 73.6 persons per square mile; Race: 97.1% White, 1.0% Black/African American, 0.2% Asian, 0.1% American Indian/Alaska Native, 0.0% Native Hawaiian/Other Pacific Islander, 1.5% Two or more races, 0.6% Hispanic of any race; Average household size: 2.65; Median age: 43.8; Age under 18: 22.8%; Age 65 and over: 13.5%; Males per 100 females: 110.3
Housing: Homeownership rate: 89.5%; Homeowner vacancy rate: 1.2%; Rental vacancy rate: 10.8%

NEWBURY (unincorporated postal area)

ZCTA: 44065

Covers a land area of 21.752 square miles and a water area of 0.633 square miles. Located at 41.48° N. Lat; 81.22° W. Long..
Population: 4,433; Growth (since 2000): 7.2%; Density: 203.8 persons per square mile; Race: 96.1% White, 1.5% Black/African American, 0.6% Asian, 0.1% American Indian/Alaska Native, 0.0% Native Hawaiian/Other Pacific Islander, 1.2% Two or more races, 0.9% Hispanic of any race; Average household size: 2.52; Median age: 46.6; Age under 18: 21.1%; Age 65 and over: 18.0%; Males per 100 females: 95.3; Marriage status: 33.7% never married, 52.8% now married, 1.9% separated, 4.3% widowed, 9.2% divorced; Foreign born: 1.1%; Speak English only: 96.7%; With disability: 10.0%; Veterans: 6.6%; Ancestry: 33.0% German, 22.3% Irish, 14.7% English, 13.6% Polish, 13.3% Italian
Employment: 20.9% management, business, and financial, 3.8% computer, engineering, and science, 10.4% education, legal, community service, arts, and media, 4.5% healthcare practitioners, 16.8% service, 20.0% sales and office, 6.7% natural resources, construction, and maintenance, 16.8% production, transportation, and material moving
Income: Per capita: $32,006; Median household: $56,005; Average household: $82,800; Households with income of $100,000 or more: 27.5%; Poverty rate: 8.7%
Educational Attainment: High school diploma or higher: 93.4%; Bachelor's degree or higher: 25.5%; Graduate/professional degree or higher: 10.6%

School District(s)

Newbury Local (PK-12)
2012-13 Enrollment: 544. . . . . (440) 564-5501
Housing: Homeownership rate: 80.9%; Median home value: $209,400; Median year structure built: 1962; Homeowner vacancy rate: 1.7%; Median gross rent: $850 per month; Rental vacancy rate: 6.0%
Health Insurance: 93.2% have insurance; 77.2% have private insurance; 27.9% have public insurance; 6.8% do not have insurance; 0.0% of children under 18 do not have insurance
Transportation: Commute: 90.4% car, 0.0% public transportation, 0.5% walk, 9.1% work from home; Median travel time to work: 24.3 minutes

NOVELTY (unincorporated postal area)

ZCTA: 44072

Covers a land area of 18.750 square miles and a water area of 0.188 square miles. Located at 41.47° N. Lat; 81.32° W. Long. Elevation is 1,063 feet.
Population: 4,383; Growth (since 2000): 7.4%; Density: 233.8 persons per square mile; Race: 97.2% White, 1.2% Black/African American, 1.0% Asian, 0.0% American Indian/Alaska Native, 0.0% Native Hawaiian/Other Pacific Islander, 0.3% Two or more races, 1.1% Hispanic of any race; Average household size: 2.51; Median age: 49.9; Age under 18: 19.9%; Age 65 and over: 20.0%; Males per 100 females: 98.8; Marriage status: 19.3% never married, 69.0% now married, 2.2% separated, 6.4% widowed, 5.3% divorced; Foreign born: 8.1%; Speak English only: 92.1%; With disability: 5.2%; Veterans: 9.5%; Ancestry: 23.5% German, 20.6% Italian, 15.0% English, 11.5% Polish, 10.7% Irish
Employment: 23.8% management, business, and financial, 7.2% computer, engineering, and science, 5.6% education, legal, community service, arts, and media, 16.4% healthcare practitioners, 7.5% service, 31.0% sales and office, 6.7% natural resources, construction, and maintenance, 1.7% production, transportation, and material moving
Income: Per capita: $49,214; Median household: $64,115; Average household: $114,632; Households with income of $100,000 or more: 37.7%; Poverty rate: 8.6%
Educational Attainment: High school diploma or higher: 95.8%; Bachelor's degree or higher: 47.2%; Graduate/professional degree or higher: 21.8%

School District(s)

The Gatehouse School
2012-13 Enrollment: n/a . . . . (614) 995-1985
West Geauga Local (PK-12)
2012-13 Enrollment: 2,204 . . . . (440) 729-5900
Housing: Homeownership rate: 91.7%; Median home value: $301,100; Median year structure built: 1972; Homeowner vacancy rate: 1.6%; Median gross rent: $824 per month; Rental vacancy rate: 5.8%
Health Insurance: 94.7% have insurance; 86.4% have private insurance; 26.1% have public insurance; 5.3% do not have insurance; 0.0% of children under 18 do not have insurance
Transportation: Commute: 92.4% car, 0.9% public transportation, 0.0% walk, 6.6% work from home; Median travel time to work: 27.8 minutes

PARKMAN (unincorporated postal area)

ZCTA: 44080

Covers a land area of 0.997 square miles and a water area of 0.015 square miles. Located at 41.37° N. Lat; 81.06° W. Long. Elevation is 1,096 feet.
Population: 226; Growth (since 2000): 109.3%; Density: 226.8 persons per square mile; Race: 97.8% White, 0.4% Black/African American, 0.0% Asian, 0.0% American Indian/Alaska Native, 0.0% Native Hawaiian/Other Pacific Islander, 1.8% Two or more races, 0.0% Hispanic of any race; Average household size: 2.35; Median age: 43.4; Age under 18: 22.1%; Age 65 and over: 11.9%; Males per 100 females: 119.4
Housing: Homeownership rate: 63.6%; Homeowner vacancy rate: 4.7%; Rental vacancy rate: 5.4%

SOUTH RUSSELL (village). Covers a land area of 3.754 square miles and a water area of 0.079 square miles. Located at 41.43° N. Lat; 81.33° W. Long. Elevation is 1,122 feet.
History: The southern part of the township had incorporated early in 1923 as South Russell Village and had asked for annexation to Chagrin Falls School District and had been accepted. South Russell students began attending Chagrin Falls Schools in 1926. Thus South Russell was born in controversy over educational issues, proving that still, as over one hundred years before, people in the Western Reserve considered a good education paramount. After World War II, rapid growth in South Russell led to the opening in 1966 of Gurney Elementary School on Bell Road.

Population: 3,810; Growth (since 2000): -5.3%; Density: 1,014.9 persons per square mile; Race: 97.5% White, 0.4% Black/African American, 1.2% Asian, 0.1% American Indian/Alaska Native, 0.1% Native Hawaiian/Other Pacific Islander, 0.7% Two or more races, 0.8% Hispanic of any race; Average household size: 2.77; Median age: 44.9; Age under 18: 29.1%; Age 65 and over: 14.1%; Males per 100 females: 99.0; Marriage status: 14.2% never married, 72.5% now married, 0.2% separated, 6.8% widowed, 6.5% divorced; Foreign born: 1.1%; Speak English only: 97.6%; With disability: 4.7%; Veterans: 7.5%; Ancestry: 25.2% German, 23.0% Irish, 21.3% English, 13.4% Italian, 6.2% Polish
Employment: 33.9% management, business, and financial, 6.8% computer, engineering, and science, 22.3% education, legal, community service, arts, and media, 5.2% healthcare practitioners, 4.7% service, 23.5% sales and office, 1.2% natural resources, construction, and maintenance, 2.6% production, transportation, and material moving
Income: Per capita: $55,382; Median household: $112,431; Average household: $150,515; Households with income of $100,000 or more: 52.5%; Poverty rate: 0.9%
Educational Attainment: High school diploma or higher: 97.6%; Bachelor's degree or higher: 74.7%; Graduate/professional degree or higher: 27.6%
Housing: Homeownership rate: 95.9%; Median home value: $311,800; Median year structure built: 1973; Homeowner vacancy rate: 1.8%; Median gross rent: $729 per month; Rental vacancy rate: 11.3%
Health Insurance: 96.8% have insurance; 92.9% have private insurance; 15.7% have public insurance; 3.2% do not have insurance; 0.0% of children under 18 do not have insurance
Safety: Violent crime rate: 0.0 per 10,000 population; Property crime rate: 34.0 per 10,000 population
Transportation: Commute: 85.4% car, 0.0% public transportation, 0.0% walk, 14.6% work from home; Median travel time to work: 30.4 minutes
Additional Information Contacts
Village of South Russell . . . . (440) 338-6700
http://www.southrussell.com

THOMPSON (unincorporated postal area)

ZCTA: 44086

Covers a land area of 27.571 square miles and a water area of 0.213 square miles. Located at 41.68° N. Lat; 81.06° W. Long. Elevation is 1,270 feet.
Population: 2,391; Growth (since 2000): 3.5%; Density: 86.7 persons per square mile; Race: 98.4% White, 0.2% Black/African American, 0.3% Asian, 0.2% American Indian/Alaska Native, 0.0% Native Hawaiian/Other Pacific Islander, 1.0% Two or more races, 0.2% Hispanic of any race; Average household size: 2.64; Median age: 43.2; Age under 18: 22.5%; Age 65 and over: 12.7%; Males per 100 females: 102.1

School District(s)

Ledgemont Local (PK-12)
2012-13 Enrollment: 526. . . . . (440) 298-3341
Housing: Homeownership rate: 89.7%; Homeowner vacancy rate: 1.4%; Rental vacancy rate: 9.4%

Greene County

Located in southwest central Ohio; crossed by the Little Miami and Mad Rivers. Covers a land area of 413.729 square miles, a water area of 2.526 square miles, and is located in the Eastern Time Zone at 39.69° N. Lat., 83.89° W. Long. The county was founded in 1803. County seat is Xenia.

Greene County is part of the Dayton, OH Metropolitan Statistical Area. The entire metro area includes: Greene County, OH; Miami County, OH; Montgomery County, OH

Weather Station: Xenia 6 SSE Elevation: 967 feet

	Jan	Feb	Mar	Apr	May	Jun	Jul	Aug	Sep	Oct	Nov	Dec
High	37	41	52	64	73	80	83	82	77	65	53	41
Low	21	24	32	42	51	60	63	61	54	44	35	25
Precip	2.9	2.4	3.4	3.9	4.9	4.2	4.4	3.1	2.6	3.1	3.2	3.1
Snow	7.0	5.4	2.6	0.4	tr	0.0	0.0	0.0	0.0	0.2	0.6	4.1

High and Low temperatures in degrees Fahrenheit; Precipitation and Snow in inches

Population: 161,573; Growth (since 2000): 9.3%; Density: 390.5 persons per square mile; Race: 86.4% White, 7.2% Black/African American, 2.9% Asian, 0.3% American Indian/Alaska Native, 0.1% Native Hawaiian/Other Pacific Islander, 2.6% two or more races, 2.1% Hispanic of any race; Average household size: 2.43; Median age: 37.2; Age under 18: 21.7%; Age 65 and over: 13.6%; Males per 100 females: 95.9; Marriage status: 31.5% never married, 52.7% now married, 1.6% separated, 5.8% widowed, 10.0% divorced; Foreign born: 4.5%; Speak English only: 93.8%; With disability: 11.8%; Veterans: 14.3%; Ancestry: 23.2% German, 16.8% American, 12.8% Irish, 10.6% English, 3.7% Italian
Religion: Six largest groups: 8.7% Catholicism, 7.2% Baptist, 3.9% Non-denominational Protestant, 3.6% Methodist/Pietist, 3.0% Presbyterian-Reformed, 2.5% Hindu
Economy: Unemployment rate: 4.4%; Leading industries: 17.0% retail trade; 14.4% professional, scientific, and technical services; 11.6% other services (except public administration); Farms: 800 totaling 145,790 acres; Company size: 1 employs 1,000 or more persons, 6 employ 500 to 999 persons, 71 employs 100 to 499 persons, 2,933 employ less than 100 persons; Business ownership: 3,632 women-owned, n/a Black-owned, 171 Hispanic-owned, 287 Asian-owned
Employment: 16.2% management, business, and financial, 8.5% computer, engineering, and science, 11.5% education, legal, community service, arts, and media, 7.3% healthcare practitioners, 16.4% service, 23.1% sales and office, 6.3% natural resources, construction, and maintenance, 10.7% production, transportation, and material moving
Income: Per capita: $30,040; Median household: $58,080; Average household: $75,764; Households with income of $100,000 or more: 25.1%; Poverty rate: 13.9%
Educational Attainment: High school diploma or higher: 92.4%; Bachelor's degree or higher: 36.0%; Graduate/professional degree or higher: 17.4%
Housing: Homeownership rate: 67.8%; Median home value: $158,000; Median year structure built: 1973; Homeowner vacancy rate: 2.1%; Median gross rent: $834 per month; Rental vacancy rate: 10.4%
Vital Statistics: Birth rate: 108.9 per 10,000 population; Death rate: 81.4 per 10,000 population; Age-adjusted cancer mortality rate: 152.0 deaths per 100,000 population
Health Insurance: 91.6% have insurance; 77.5% have private insurance; 27.5% have public insurance; 8.4% do not have insurance; 3.7% of children under 18 do not have insurance
Health Care: Physicians: 28.7 per 10,000 population; Hospital beds: 8.6 per 10,000 population; Hospital admissions: 507.8 per 10,000 population
Air Quality Index: 71.3% good, 28.4% moderate, 0.3% unhealthy for sensitive individuals, 0.0% unhealthy (percent of days)
Transportation: Commute: 91.2% car, 0.3% public transportation, 3.3% walk, 4.3% work from home; Median travel time to work: 20.2 minutes
Presidential Election: 38.3% Obama, 60.0% Romney (2012)
National and State Parks: Beaver Creek State Wildlife Area; Charles Young Buffalo Soldiers National Monument; Clifton Gorge State Nature Preserve; Dayton Aviation Heritage National Historical Park; Glen Thompson State Reserve; Huffman Prairie National Historic Landmark; John Bryan State Park; Little Miami State Forest Preserve; The Narrows State Scenic River Reserve; Williamson Mound State Memorial
Additional Information Contacts
Greene Government . . . . (937) 562-5006
http://www.co.greene.oh.us

Greene County Communities

ALPHA (unincorporated postal area)

ZCTA: 45301

Covers a land area of 0.092 square miles and a water area of 0 square miles. Located at 39.71° N. Lat; 84.02° W. Long. Elevation is 801 feet.
Population: 130; Growth (since 2000): -5.1%; Density: 1,407.5 persons per square mile; Race: 94.6% White, 0.8% Black/African American, 0.8% Asian, 0.8% American Indian/Alaska Native, 0.0% Native Hawaiian/Other Pacific Islander, 1.5% Two or more races, 3.1% Hispanic of any race; Average household size: 2.55; Median age: 34.0; Age under 18: 25.4%; Age 65 and over: 16.2%; Males per 100 females: 94.0
Housing: Homeownership rate: 86.2%; Homeowner vacancy rate: 4.3%; Rental vacancy rate: 22.2%

BEAVERCREEK (city). Covers a land area of 26.399 square miles and a water area of 0.037 square miles. Located at 39.73° N. Lat; 84.06° W. Long. Elevation is 876 feet.
Population: 45,193; Growth (since 2000): 19.0%; Density: 1,711.9 persons per square mile; Race: 88.5% White, 2.5% Black/African American, 5.9% Asian, 0.2% American Indian/Alaska Native, 0.0% Native Hawaiian/Other Pacific Islander, 2.3% Two or more races, 2.6% Hispanic of any race; Average household size: 2.47; Median age: 40.4; Age under

18: 22.6%; Age 65 and over: 14.3%; Males per 100 females: 99.7; Marriage status: 26.3% never married, 59.6% now married, 1.3% separated, 6.2% widowed, 7.9% divorced; Foreign born: 7.2%; Speak English only: 90.6%; With disability: 9.8%; Veterans: 19.1%; Ancestry: 26.1% German, 14.6% American, 13.3% Irish, 10.9% English, 4.7% Italian
Employment: 23.6% management, business, and financial, 12.8% computer, engineering, and science, 11.5% education, legal, community service, arts, and media, 9.0% healthcare practitioners, 12.6% service, 19.0% sales and office, 3.3% natural resources, construction, and maintenance, 8.2% production, transportation, and material moving
Income: Per capita: $39,212; Median household: $76,162; Average household: $95,686; Households with income of $100,000 or more: 35.3%; Poverty rate: 5.5%
Educational Attainment: High school diploma or higher: 96.4%; Bachelor's degree or higher: 49.5%; Graduate/professional degree or higher: 26.0%

School District(s)

Beavercreek City (PK-12)
2012-13 Enrollment: 7,502 . . . . (937) 426-1522
Housing: Homeownership rate: 74.0%; Median home value: $174,100; Median year structure built: 1979; Homeowner vacancy rate: 1.7%; Median gross rent: $1,080 per month; Rental vacancy rate: 10.3%
Health Insurance: 94.2% have insurance; 86.3% have private insurance; 22.4% have public insurance; 5.8% do not have insurance; 3.6% of children under 18 do not have insurance
Hospitals: Indu & Raj Soin Medical Center
Safety: Violent crime rate: 2.6 per 10,000 population; Property crime rate: 248.4 per 10,000 population
Transportation: Commute: 92.4% car, 0.2% public transportation, 1.6% walk, 5.0% work from home; Median travel time to work: 18.7 minutes
Additional Information Contacts
City of Beavercreek. . . . . (937) 427-5510
http://www.ci.beavercreek.oh.us

BELLBROOK (city). Covers a land area of 3.125 square miles and a water area of 0.001 square miles. Located at 39.64° N. Lat; 84.09° W. Long. Elevation is 778 feet.
Population: 6,943; Growth (since 2000): -0.9%; Density: 2,221.5 persons per square mile; Race: 96.0% White, 1.3% Black/African American, 0.7% Asian, 0.3% American Indian/Alaska Native, 0.0% Native Hawaiian/Other Pacific Islander, 1.3% Two or more races, 2.1% Hispanic of any race; Average household size: 2.51; Median age: 42.5; Age under 18: 23.9%; Age 65 and over: 12.9%; Males per 100 females: 97.7; Marriage status: 23.5% never married, 61.5% now married, 2.2% separated, 3.9% widowed, 11.1% divorced; Foreign born: 3.8%; Speak English only: 96.6%; With disability: 6.8%; Veterans: 15.6%; Ancestry: 30.3% German, 16.1% Irish, 14.0% English, 11.2% American, 6.5% Italian
Employment: 16.9% management, business, and financial, 9.5% computer, engineering, and science, 15.4% education, legal, community service, arts, and media, 5.6% healthcare practitioners, 11.4% service, 22.9% sales and office, 10.2% natural resources, construction, and maintenance, 8.1% production, transportation, and material moving
Income: Per capita: $33,053; Median household: $71,935; Average household: $82,519; Households with income of $100,000 or more: 29.4%; Poverty rate: 6.8%
Educational Attainment: High school diploma or higher: 95.7%; Bachelor's degree or higher: 38.4%; Graduate/professional degree or higher: 18.1%

School District(s)

Bellbrook-Sugarcreek Local SD (PK-12)
2012-13 Enrollment: 2,605 . . . . (937) 848-5001
Housing: Homeownership rate: 81.7%; Median home value: $156,200; Median year structure built: 1968; Homeowner vacancy rate: 1.6%; Median gross rent: $964 per month; Rental vacancy rate: 10.1%
Health Insurance: 96.1% have insurance; 84.1% have private insurance; 22.3% have public insurance; 3.9% do not have insurance; 0.0% of children under 18 do not have insurance
Safety: Violent crime rate: 2.8 per 10,000 population; Property crime rate: 131.7 per 10,000 population
Transportation: Commute: 89.6% car, 0.0% public transportation, 0.9% walk, 8.3% work from home; Median travel time to work: 20.1 minutes
Additional Information Contacts
City of Bellbrook . . . . (937) 848-4666
http://www.cityofbellbrook.org

BOWERSVILLE (village). Covers a land area of 0.150 square miles and a water area of 0 square miles. Located at 39.58° N. Lat; 83.72° W. Long. Elevation is 1,089 feet.
Population: 312; Growth (since 2000): 7.6%; Density: 2,082.7 persons per square mile; Race: 97.1% White, 0.6% Black/African American, 0.0% Asian, 0.0% American Indian/Alaska Native, 0.0% Native Hawaiian/Other Pacific Islander, 1.9% Two or more races, 2.2% Hispanic of any race; Average household size: 2.62; Median age: 36.0; Age under 18: 26.0%; Age 65 and over: 13.1%; Males per 100 females: 96.2
Housing: Homeownership rate: 73.9%; Homeowner vacancy rate: 2.2%; Rental vacancy rate: 6.1%

CEDARVILLE (village). Covers a land area of 1.282 square miles and a water area of 0.043 square miles. Located at 39.75° N. Lat; 83.81° W. Long. Elevation is 1,050 feet.
History: Cedarville was settled in 1805 and developed around Cedarville College, chartered in 1887 and opened in 1894 under the Reformed Presbyterian Church.
Population: 4,019; Growth (since 2000): 5.0%; Density: 3,134.8 persons per square mile; Race: 94.4% White, 2.3% Black/African American, 1.1% Asian, 0.1% American Indian/Alaska Native, 0.0% Native Hawaiian/Other Pacific Islander, 1.7% Two or more races, 2.2% Hispanic of any race; Average household size: 2.45; Median age: 21.0; Age under 18: 9.2%; Age 65 and over: 6.0%; Males per 100 females: 87.0; Marriage status: 74.9% never married, 18.6% now married, 0.1% separated, 3.2% widowed, 3.3% divorced; Foreign born: 2.6%; Speak English only: 96.8%; With disability: 8.7%; Veterans: 3.9%; Ancestry: 23.4% German, 15.8% American, 11.6% Irish, 11.4% English, 3.7% Dutch
Employment: 4.3% management, business, and financial, 1.9% computer, engineering, and science, 16.3% education, legal, community service, arts, and media, 2.9% healthcare practitioners, 39.2% service, 22.1% sales and office, 5.0% natural resources, construction, and maintenance, 8.3% production, transportation, and material moving
Income: Per capita: $11,855; Median household: $30,511; Average household: $46,920; Households with income of $100,000 or more: 10.3%; Poverty rate: 32.1%
Educational Attainment: High school diploma or higher: 96.0%; Bachelor's degree or higher: 36.2%; Graduate/professional degree or higher: 18.1%

School District(s)

Cedar Cliff Local (PK-12)
2012-13 Enrollment: 551. . . . . (937) 766-6000

Four-year College(s)

Cedarville University (Private, Not-for-profit, Baptist)
Fall 2013 Enrollment: 3,462 . . . . (937) 766-2211
2013-14 Tuition: In-state $26,420; Out-of-state $26,420
Housing: Homeownership rate: 50.4%; Median home value: $137,200; Median year structure built: 1964; Homeowner vacancy rate: 4.1%; Median gross rent: $589 per month; Rental vacancy rate: 9.1%
Health Insurance: 92.4% have insurance; 81.9% have private insurance; 17.6% have public insurance; 7.6% do not have insurance; 9.7% of children under 18 do not have insurance
Transportation: Commute: 53.9% car, 0.0% public transportation, 31.2% walk, 14.0% work from home; Median travel time to work: 14.9 minutes

CLIFTON (village). Covers a land area of 0.179 square miles and a water area of 0.007 square miles. Located at 39.80° N. Lat; 83.83° W. Long. Elevation is 1,004 feet.
History: Clifton was settled on the Little Miami River where water-power was plentiful. Isaac Kaufman Funk, who formed a partnership with college classmate Adam Willis Wagnalls, was born in Clifton in 1839. Funk was the editor of "A Standard Dictionary of the English Language."
Population: 152; Growth (since 2000): -15.1%; Density: 849.6 persons per square mile; Race: 92.1% White, 2.6% Black/African American, 1.3% Asian, 0.0% American Indian/Alaska Native, 0.0% Native Hawaiian/Other Pacific Islander, 3.9% Two or more races, 3.9% Hispanic of any race; Average household size: 2.38; Median age: 45.5; Age under 18: 22.4%; Age 65 and over: 13.8%; Males per 100 females: 85.4
Housing: Homeownership rate: 76.5%; Homeowner vacancy rate: 7.5%; Rental vacancy rate: 31.8%

FAIRBORN (city). Covers a land area of 13.160 square miles and a water area of 0.009 square miles. Located at 39.80° N. Lat; 84.01° W. Long. Elevation is 837 feet.
History: Air Force Museum nearby. Settled 1799, incorporated 1950 with the merging of Osborn and Fairborn.
Population: 32,352; Growth (since 2000): 0.9%; Density: 2,458.4 persons per square mile; Race: 84.8% White, 7.7% Black/African American, 3.1% Asian, 0.3% American Indian/Alaska Native, 0.1% Native Hawaiian/Other Pacific Islander, 3.1% Two or more races, 2.4% Hispanic of any race; Average household size: 2.24; Median age: 32.4; Age under 18: 20.4%; Age 65 and over: 13.2%; Males per 100 females: 95.8; Marriage status: 38.3% never married, 42.3% now married, 1.8% separated, 5.7% widowed, 13.7% divorced; Foreign born: 5.0%; Speak English only: 93.1%; With disability: 15.4%; Veterans: 14.2%; Ancestry: 20.1% German, 20.0% American, 11.0% Irish, 9.3% English, 2.4% Italian
Employment: 10.4% management, business, and financial, 7.6% computer, engineering, and science, 8.7% education, legal, community service, arts, and media, 5.6% healthcare practitioners, 20.5% service, 28.1% sales and office, 6.2% natural resources, construction, and maintenance, 12.9% production, transportation, and material moving
Income: Per capita: $22,959; Median household: $41,720; Average household: $52,770; Households with income of $100,000 or more: 12.4%; Poverty rate: 24.3%
Educational Attainment: High school diploma or higher: 86.7%; Bachelor's degree or higher: 25.2%; Graduate/professional degree or higher: 10.9%

School District(s)

Fairborn City (PK-12)
2012-13 Enrollment: 4,273 . . . . (937) 878-3961
Fairborn Digital Academy (09-12)
2012-13 Enrollment: 136. . . . . (937) 879-0511
Housing: Homeownership rate: 50.7%; Median home value: $109,100; Median year structure built: 1969; Homeowner vacancy rate: 2.6%; Median gross rent: $760 per month; Rental vacancy rate: 12.2%
Health Insurance: 88.8% have insurance; 67.4% have private insurance; 35.6% have public insurance; 11.2% do not have insurance; 3.2% of children under 18 do not have insurance
Safety: Violent crime rate: 18.9 per 10,000 population; Property crime rate: 281.8 per 10,000 population
Transportation: Commute: 94.8% car, 0.3% public transportation, 2.2% walk, 1.8% work from home; Median travel time to work: 19.5 minutes
Additional Information Contacts
City of Fairborn . . . . (937) 754-3030
http://www.ci.fairborn.oh.us

JAMESTOWN (village). Covers a land area of 1.207 square miles and a water area of 0.004 square miles. Located at 39.66° N. Lat; 83.74° W. Long. Elevation is 1,060 feet.
History: Jamestown was settled near the old route of Chiuxso's Trail, a wagon road through the forest connecting Ripley on the Ohio River with the Mad River Valley. The town was rebuilt after a cyclone destroyed the buildings in 1844.
Population: 1,993; Growth (since 2000): 4.0%; Density: 1,650.9 persons per square mile; Race: 95.1% White, 2.4% Black/African American, 0.2% Asian, 0.1% American Indian/Alaska Native, 0.0% Native Hawaiian/Other Pacific Islander, 1.7% Two or more races, 0.7% Hispanic of any race; Average household size: 2.56; Median age: 36.7; Age under 18: 25.7%; Age 65 and over: 16.0%; Males per 100 females: 82.8

School District(s)

Greeneview Local (PK-12)
2012-13 Enrollment: 1,371 . . . . (937) 675-2728
Housing: Homeownership rate: 62.5%; Homeowner vacancy rate: 2.5%; Rental vacancy rate: 8.9%

SHAWNEE HILLS (CDP). Covers a land area of 2.670 square miles and a water area of 0.284 square miles. Located at 39.65° N. Lat; 83.79° W. Long. Elevation is 1,047 feet.
Population: 2,171; Growth (since 2000): -7.8%; Density: 813.2 persons per square mile; Race: 97.0% White, 0.7% Black/African American, 0.5% Asian, 0.4% American Indian/Alaska Native, 0.0% Native Hawaiian/Other Pacific Islander, 1.2% Two or more races, 0.9% Hispanic of any race; Average household size: 2.63; Median age: 40.6; Age under 18: 23.7%; Age 65 and over: 11.2%; Males per 100 females: 100.8
Housing: Homeownership rate: 92.3%; Homeowner vacancy rate: 1.9%; Rental vacancy rate: 1.5%

SPRING VALLEY (village). Covers a land area of 0.266 square miles and a water area of 0.002 square miles. Located at 39.61° N. Lat; 84.01° W. Long. Elevation is 764 feet.
History: Spring Valley was named for the nearby springs, whose water was bottled and shipped from the town. Spring Valley developed as a farming community, with tobacco grown here as early as 1825.
Population: 479; Growth (since 2000): -6.1%; Density: 1,803.7 persons per square mile; Race: 97.3% White, 0.2% Black/African American, 0.0% Asian, 0.2% American Indian/Alaska Native, 0.0% Native Hawaiian/Other Pacific Islander, 2.1% Two or more races, 0.8% Hispanic of any race; Average household size: 2.42; Median age: 43.8; Age under 18: 19.4%; Age 65 and over: 14.4%; Males per 100 females: 101.3
Housing: Homeownership rate: 77.8%; Homeowner vacancy rate: 3.7%; Rental vacancy rate: 8.3%

WILBERFORCE (CDP). Covers a land area of 3.081 square miles and a water area of 0.024 square miles. Located at 39.71° N. Lat; 83.88° W. Long. Elevation is 1,007 feet.
History: Wilberforce was named for William Wilberforce, an English reformer. The town grew around Wilberforce University, opened in 1856 by the Methodist Episcopal Church and purchased in 1863 by the African M.E. Church.
Population: 2,271; Growth (since 2000): 43.8%; Density: 737.1 persons per square mile; Race: 12.9% White, 82.3% Black/African American, 0.1% Asian, 0.2% American Indian/Alaska Native, 0.0% Native Hawaiian/Other Pacific Islander, 4.3% Two or more races, 1.8% Hispanic of any race; Average household size: 2.50; Median age: 20.5; Age under 18: 6.5%; Age 65 and over: 4.4%; Males per 100 females: 94.4

Four-year College(s)

Central State University (Public, Historically black)
Fall 2013 Enrollment: 2,068 . . . . (937) 376-6011
2013-14 Tuition: In-state $6,058; Out-of-state $13,510
Payne Theological Seminary (Private, Not-for-profit, African Methodist Episcopal)
Fall 2013 Enrollment: 135 . . . . (937) 376-2946
Wilberforce University (Private, Not-for-profit, Historically black, African Methodist Episcopal)
Fall 2013 Enrollment: 479 . . . . (937) 376-2911
2013-14 Tuition: In-state $15,140; Out-of-state $15,140
Housing: Homeownership rate: 66.5%; Homeowner vacancy rate: 4.7%; Rental vacancy rate: 14.7%

WRIGHT-PATTERSON AFB (CDP). Covers a land area of 9.929 square miles and a water area of 0.080 square miles. Located at 39.82° N. Lat; 84.05° W. Long.
Population: 1,821; Growth (since 2000): -72.6%; Density: 183.4 persons per square mile; Race: 79.7% White, 10.7% Black/African American, 3.2% Asian, 0.1% American Indian/Alaska Native, 0.2% Native Hawaiian/Other Pacific Islander, 4.4% Two or more races, 7.5% Hispanic of any race; Average household size: 2.92; Median age: 24.0; Age under 18: 24.2%; Age 65 and over: 0.5%; Males per 100 females: 128.2

Four-year College(s)

Air Force Institute of Technology-Graduate School of Engineering & Manageme (Public)
Fall 2013 Enrollment: 853 . . . . (937) 255-3636
Housing: Homeownership rate: 0.7%; Homeowner vacancy rate: 0.0%; Rental vacancy rate: 6.7%

XENIA (city). County seat. Covers a land area of 13.281 square miles and a water area of 0.014 square miles. Located at 39.68° N. Lat; 83.94° W. Long. Elevation is 935 feet.
History: Xenia developed around an agricultural area. An early industry was the production of rope and twine.
Population: 25,719; Growth (since 2000): 6.4%; Density: 1,936.5 persons per square mile; Race: 82.0% White, 13.4% Black/African American, 0.5% Asian, 0.4% American Indian/Alaska Native, 0.0% Native Hawaiian/Other Pacific Islander, 3.2% Two or more races, 1.7% Hispanic of any race; Average household size: 2.39; Median age: 37.1; Age under 18: 24.8%; Age 65 and over: 15.7%; Males per 100 females: 89.3; Marriage status: 27.7% never married, 49.7% now married, 2.4% separated, 8.7% widowed, 13.9% divorced; Foreign born: 1.6%; Speak English only: 97.2%; With disability: 16.2%; Veterans: 11.1%; Ancestry: 19.1% American, 18.3% German, 13.3% Irish, 9.0% English, 3.5% Italian
Employment: 10.4% management, business, and financial, 2.6% computer, engineering, and science, 10.3% education, legal, community

service, arts, and media, 5.1% healthcare practitioners, 19.6% service, 26.6% sales and office, 12.2% natural resources, construction, and maintenance, 13.2% production, transportation, and material moving
Income: Per capita: $20,514; Median household: $39,756; Average household: $49,228; Households with income of $100,000 or more: 10.0%; Poverty rate: 24.5%
Educational Attainment: High school diploma or higher: 88.1%; Bachelor's degree or higher: 18.3%; Graduate/professional degree or higher: 6.8%

School District(s)

Greene County Jt Voc SD (07-12)
2012-13 Enrollment: n/a . . . . (937) 372-6941
Summit Academy-Xenia (KG-08)
2012-13 Enrollment: 143. . . . . (937) 372-5210
Xenia Community City (PK-12)
2012-13 Enrollment: 4,338 . . . . (937) 376-2961

Vocational/Technical School(s)

Greene County Vocational School District (Public)
Fall 2013 Enrollment: 171 . . . . (937) 426-6636
2013-14 Tuition: $3,698

Housing: Homeownership rate: 61.6%; Median home value: $98,400; Median year structure built: 1969; Homeowner vacancy rate: 2.9%; Median gross rent: $651 per month; Rental vacancy rate: 9.2%
Health Insurance: 88.3% have insurance; 63.1% have private insurance; 39.5% have public insurance; 11.7% do not have insurance; 2.4% of children under 18 do not have insurance
Hospitals: Greene Memorial Hospital (231 beds)
Safety: Violent crime rate: 21.1 per 10,000 population; Property crime rate: 402.9 per 10,000 population
Newspapers: Fairborn Daily Herald (daily circulation 4000); Xenia Daily Gazette (daily circulation 5900)
Transportation: Commute: 93.5% car, 1.1% public transportation, 2.5% walk, 2.0% work from home; Median travel time to work: 22.1 minutes
Airports: Greene County-Lewis A. Jackson Regional (general aviation)
Additional Information Contacts
City of Xenia . . . . (937) 376-7232
http://www.ci.xenia.oh.us

YELLOW SPRINGS (village). Covers a land area of 2.016 square miles and a water area of <.001 square miles. Located at 39.80° N. Lat; 83.89° W. Long. Elevation is 961 feet.
History: Yellow Springs was founded in 1804 and named for the yellowed water of the nearby iron springs. Antioch College was founded here in 1853 with Horace Mann as its first president.
Population: 3,487; Growth (since 2000): -7.3%; Density: 1,729.6 persons per square mile; Race: 78.1% White, 12.0% Black/African American, 1.5% Asian, 0.6% American Indian/Alaska Native, 0.0% Native Hawaiian/Other Pacific Islander, 7.3% Two or more races, 2.0% Hispanic of any race; Average household size: 2.04; Median age: 48.5; Age under 18: 19.7%; Age 65 and over: 21.6%; Males per 100 females: 85.1; Marriage status: 32.6% never married, 44.2% now married, 0.8% separated, 7.0% widowed, 16.2% divorced; Foreign born: 4.1%; Speak English only: 90.4%; With disability: 13.0%; Veterans: 9.0%; Ancestry: 27.3% German, 16.4% Irish, 14.8% English, 4.2% Scottish, 4.2% American
Employment: 13.3% management, business, and financial, 11.1% computer, engineering, and science, 24.4% education, legal, community service, arts, and media, 10.3% healthcare practitioners, 13.6% service, 16.0% sales and office, 5.2% natural resources, construction, and maintenance, 6.1% production, transportation, and material moving
Income: Per capita: $37,107; Median household: $60,707; Average household: $78,974; Households with income of $100,000 or more: 28.3%; Poverty rate: 14.9%
Educational Attainment: High school diploma or higher: 98.2%; Bachelor's degree or higher: 63.5%; Graduate/professional degree or higher: 34.3%

School District(s)

Yellow Springs Exempted Village (PK-12)
2012-13 Enrollment: 699. . . . . (937) 767-7381

Four-year College(s)

Antioch College (Private, Not-for-profit)
Fall 2013 Enrollment: 186 . . . . (937) 319-6082
2013-14 Tuition: In-state $27,505; Out-of-state $27,505
Antioch University-Midwest (Private, Not-for-profit)
Fall 2013 Enrollment: 310 . . . . (937) 769-1800
Antioch University-PhD Program in Leadership and Change (Private, Not-for-profit)
Fall 2013 Enrollment: 152 . . . . (937) 769-1360

Housing: Homeownership rate: 64.3%; Median home value: $203,700; Median year structure built: 1956; Homeowner vacancy rate: 2.1%; Median gross rent: $731 per month; Rental vacancy rate: 7.9%
Health Insurance: 86.0% have insurance; 73.5% have private insurance; 32.9% have public insurance; 14.0% do not have insurance; 7.7% of children under 18 do not have insurance
Safety: Violent crime rate: 8.5 per 10,000 population; Property crime rate: 70.6 per 10,000 population
Newspapers: Yellow Springs News (weekly circulation 1800)
Transportation: Commute: 79.0% car, 0.0% public transportation, 7.0% walk, 10.3% work from home; Median travel time to work: 22.9 minutes
Additional Information Contacts
Village of Yellow Springs. . . . . (937) 767-7202
http://www.yso.com

Guernsey County

Located in eastern Ohio; drained by Wills Creek; includes Salt Fork Lake. Covers a land area of 522.254 square miles, a water area of 6.049 square miles, and is located in the Eastern Time Zone at 40.06° N. Lat., 81.50° W. Long. The county was founded in 1810. County seat is Cambridge.

Guernsey County is part of the Cambridge, OH Micropolitan Statistical Area. The entire metro area includes: Guernsey County, OH

Weather Station: Cambridge Elevation: 799 feet

	Jan	Feb	Mar	Apr	May	Jun	Jul	Aug	Sep	Oct	Nov	Dec
High	38	43	53	66	74	82	85	84	78	66	54	42
Low	22	24	31	41	50	58	63	62	54	43	34	26
Precip	3.0	2.2	3.1	3.5	4.2	3.9	4.3	3.6	3.3	2.8	3.3	2.8
Snow	6.3	4.5	2.8	0.7	tr	0.0	0.0	0.0	0.0	tr	0.7	3.2

High and Low temperatures in degrees Fahrenheit; Precipitation and Snow in inches

Population: 40,087; Growth (since 2000): -1.7%; Density: 76.8 persons per square mile; Race: 96.0% White, 1.5% Black/African American, 0.3% Asian, 0.2% American Indian/Alaska Native, 0.0% Native Hawaiian/Other Pacific Islander, 1.8% two or more races, 0.9% Hispanic of any race; Average household size: 2.44; Median age: 40.9; Age under 18: 24.0%; Age 65 and over: 16.0%; Males per 100 females: 96.1; Marriage status: 23.7% never married, 54.7% now married, 2.5% separated, 7.7% widowed, 13.9% divorced; Foreign born: 0.6%; Speak English only: 96.9%; With disability: 16.7%; Veterans: 11.0%; Ancestry: 21.5% German, 16.5% Irish, 11.2% English, 9.5% American, 3.0% Dutch
Religion: Six largest groups: 10.4% Methodist/Pietist, 7.8% Baptist, 5.3% Catholicism, 2.1% Presbyterian-Reformed, 2.0% European Free-Church, 1.8% Pentecostal
Economy: Unemployment rate: 4.9%; Leading industries: 16.9% retail trade; 14.3% health care and social assistance; 12.4% other services (except public administration); Farms: 1,228 totaling 143,763 acres; Company size: 0 employ 1,000 or more persons, 2 employ 500 to 999 persons, 16 employ 100 to 499 persons, 836 employ less than 100 persons; Business ownership: 450 women-owned, n/a Black-owned, n/a Hispanic-owned, 28 Asian-owned
Employment: 7.4% management, business, and financial, 1.8% computer, engineering, and science, 9.6% education, legal, community service, arts, and media, 7.2% healthcare practitioners, 18.7% service, 22.6% sales and office, 10.5% natural resources, construction, and maintenance, 22.1% production, transportation, and material moving
Income: Per capita: $20,537; Median household: $38,841; Average household: $50,388; Households with income of $100,000 or more: 11.4%; Poverty rate: 20.3%
Educational Attainment: High school diploma or higher: 84.9%; Bachelor's degree or higher: 12.9%; Graduate/professional degree or higher: 4.5%
Housing: Homeownership rate: 71.7%; Median home value: $94,000; Median year structure built: 1968; Homeowner vacancy rate: 1.9%; Median gross rent: $570 per month; Rental vacancy rate: 8.5%
Vital Statistics: Birth rate: 113.5 per 10,000 population; Death rate: 108.2 per 10,000 population; Age-adjusted cancer mortality rate: 221.7 deaths per 100,000 population
Health Insurance: 85.8% have insurance; 59.7% have private insurance; 39.4% have public insurance; 14.2% do not have insurance; 9.7% of children under 18 do not have insurance

Health Care: Physicians: 13.3 per 10,000 population; Hospital beds: 23.8 per 10,000 population; Hospital admissions: 1,121.2 per 10,000 population
Transportation: Commute: 93.4% car, 0.4% public transportation, 1.4% walk, 4.0% work from home; Median travel time to work: 23.3 minutes
Presidential Election: 44.1% Obama, 53.7% Romney (2012)
National and State Parks: Salt Fork State Park and Wildlife Area
Additional Information Contacts
Guernsey Government . . . . (740) 432-9200
http://www.guernseycounty.org

Guernsey County Communities

BUFFALO (CDP). Covers a land area of 0.490 square miles and a water area of 0 square miles. Located at 39.92° N. Lat; 81.52° W. Long. Elevation is 856 feet.
Population: 401; Growth (since 2000): n/a; Density: 818.2 persons per square mile; Race: 99.0% White, 0.0% Black/African American, 0.0% Asian, 0.2% American Indian/Alaska Native, 0.0% Native Hawaiian/Other Pacific Islander, 0.7% Two or more races, 0.7% Hispanic of any race; Average household size: 2.19; Median age: 44.4; Age under 18: 21.4%; Age 65 and over: 15.2%; Males per 100 females: 100.5
Housing: Homeownership rate: 77.0%; Homeowner vacancy rate: 0.7%; Rental vacancy rate: 6.5%

BYESVILLE (village). Covers a land area of 1.187 square miles and a water area of 0 square miles. Located at 39.97° N. Lat; 81.55° W. Long. Elevation is 810 feet.
History: Byesville was named for Jonathan Bye, who built a flour mill here in the early 1800's. Later, the town's economy depended on coal mining.
Population: 2,438; Growth (since 2000): -5.3%; Density: 2,054.1 persons per square mile; Race: 98.2% White, 0.1% Black/African American, 0.2% Asian, 0.2% American Indian/Alaska Native, 0.0% Native Hawaiian/Other Pacific Islander, 1.2% Two or more races, 0.2% Hispanic of any race; Average household size: 2.37; Median age: 39.2; Age under 18: 25.4%; Age 65 and over: 16.2%; Males per 100 females: 87.1

School District(s)

Rolling Hills Local (PK-12)
2012-13 Enrollment: 1,675 . . . . (740) 432-5370
Housing: Homeownership rate: 60.3%; Homeowner vacancy rate: 1.1%; Rental vacancy rate: 6.8%

CAMBRIDGE (city). County seat. Covers a land area of 6.352 square miles and a water area of 0.004 square miles. Located at 40.02° N. Lat; 81.59° W. Long. Elevation is 814 feet.
History: Cambridge was laid out in 1806 by Jacob Gomber and Zacheus Beatty, and named for Cambridge, Maryland, the former home of many of the first settlers. Oil and gas discovered in the area in the 1880's led to industrial development, including a glass factory founded in 1901.
Population: 10,635; Growth (since 2000): -7.7%; Density: 1,674.2 persons per square mile; Race: 92.7% White, 3.4% Black/African American, 0.3% Asian, 0.3% American Indian/Alaska Native, 0.0% Native Hawaiian/Other Pacific Islander, 3.0% Two or more races, 1.2% Hispanic of any race; Average household size: 2.23; Median age: 38.8; Age under 18: 24.6%; Age 65 and over: 17.3%; Males per 100 females: 87.4; Marriage status: 28.3% never married, 44.7% now married, 3.5% separated, 10.2% widowed, 16.8% divorced; Foreign born: 1.0%; Speak English only: 97.8%; With disability: 20.7%; Veterans: 12.8%; Ancestry: 20.0% German, 14.8% Irish, 11.3% American, 8.9% English, 2.7% French
Employment: 8.7% management, business, and financial, 1.7% computer, engineering, and science, 9.0% education, legal, community service, arts, and media, 9.1% healthcare practitioners, 24.2% service, 20.8% sales and office, 6.4% natural resources, construction, and maintenance, 20.0% production, transportation, and material moving
Income: Per capita: $18,550; Median household: $26,987; Average household: $39,690; Households with income of $100,000 or more: 7.2%; Poverty rate: 28.6%
Educational Attainment: High school diploma or higher: 84.6%; Bachelor's degree or higher: 13.3%; Graduate/professional degree or higher: 5.2%

School District(s)

Cambridge City (PK-12)
2012-13 Enrollment: 2,159 . . . . (740) 439-5021
East Muskingum Local (PK-12)
2012-13 Enrollment: 2,105 . . . . (740) 826-7655

Two-year College(s)

Valley Beauty School (Private, For-profit)
Fall 2013 Enrollment: 29 . . . . (740) 373-3617
Housing: Homeownership rate: 49.5%; Median home value: $84,300; Median year structure built: 1947; Homeowner vacancy rate: 3.6%; Median gross rent: $554 per month; Rental vacancy rate: 8.9%
Health Insurance: 87.4% have insurance; 53.6% have private insurance; 48.7% have public insurance; 12.6% do not have insurance; 0.9% of children under 18 do not have insurance
Hospitals: Southeastern Ohio Regional Medical Center (209 beds)
Safety: Violent crime rate: 35.1 per 10,000 population; Property crime rate: 520.2 per 10,000 population
Newspapers: Daily Jeffersonian (daily circulation 12700); New Concord Leader (weekly circulation 1200); Village Reporter (weekly circulation 1000)
Transportation: Commute: 89.6% car, 1.4% public transportation, 2.9% walk, 5.8% work from home; Median travel time to work: 17.9 minutes
Additional Information Contacts
City of Cambridge . . . . (740) 439-1050
http://www.cambridgeoh.org

CUMBERLAND (village). Covers a land area of 0.486 square miles and a water area of 0 square miles. Located at 39.85° N. Lat; 81.66° W. Long. Elevation is 856 feet.
Population: 367; Growth (since 2000): -8.7%; Density: 755.7 persons per square mile; Race: 94.3% White, 2.2% Black/African American, 0.3% Asian, 0.0% American Indian/Alaska Native, 0.0% Native Hawaiian/Other Pacific Islander, 2.2% Two or more races, 1.6% Hispanic of any race; Average household size: 2.78; Median age: 37.6; Age under 18: 25.3%; Age 65 and over: 14.4%; Males per 100 females: 96.3
Housing: Homeownership rate: 75.0%; Homeowner vacancy rate: 2.9%; Rental vacancy rate: 19.5%

DERWENT (unincorporated postal area)

ZCTA: 43733

Covers a land area of 0.923 square miles and a water area of 0 square miles. Located at 39.93° N. Lat; 81.54° W. Long. Elevation is 814 feet.
Population: 95; Growth (since 2000): n/a; Density: 103.0 persons per square mile; Race: 100.0% White, 0.0% Black/African American, 0.0% Asian, 0.0% American Indian/Alaska Native, 0.0% Native Hawaiian/Other Pacific Islander, 0.0% Two or more races, 0.0% Hispanic of any race; Average household size: 2.50; Median age: 38.8; Age under 18: 20.0%; Age 65 and over: 18.9%; Males per 100 females: 102.1
Housing: Homeownership rate: 84.2%; Homeowner vacancy rate: 0.0%; Rental vacancy rate: 0.0%

FAIRVIEW (village). Covers a land area of 0.401 square miles and a water area of 0 square miles. Located at 40.06° N. Lat; 81.23° W. Long. Elevation is 1,217 feet.
History: Fairview was once the leading U.S. producer of pennyroyal, an herb used in early medicines.
Population: 83; Growth (since 2000): 2.5%; Density: 206.8 persons per square mile; Race: 97.6% White, 1.2% Black/African American, 0.0% Asian, 0.0% American Indian/Alaska Native, 0.0% Native Hawaiian/Other Pacific Islander, 1.2% Two or more races, 1.2% Hispanic of any race; Average household size: 2.59; Median age: 43.3; Age under 18: 20.5%; Age 65 and over: 16.9%; Males per 100 females: 130.6
Housing: Homeownership rate: 84.4%; Homeowner vacancy rate: 6.7%; Rental vacancy rate: 16.7%

KIMBOLTON (CDP). Covers a land area of 0.498 square miles and a water area of 0 square miles. Located at 40.15° N. Lat; 81.58° W. Long. Elevation is 801 feet.
Population: 144; Growth (since 2000): -24.2%; Density: 289.4 persons per square mile; Race: 97.9% White, 0.0% Black/African American, 0.0% Asian, 0.0% American Indian/Alaska Native, 0.0% Native Hawaiian/Other Pacific Islander, 2.1% Two or more races, 0.0% Hispanic of any race; Average household size: 2.62; Median age: 36.0; Age under 18: 28.5%; Age 65 and over: 7.6%; Males per 100 females: 105.7
Housing: Homeownership rate: 83.6%; Homeowner vacancy rate: 4.2%; Rental vacancy rate: 10.0%

KIPLING (unincorporated postal area)

ZCTA: 43750

Covers a land area of 1.079 square miles and a water area of 0.003 square miles. Located at 40.00° N. Lat; 81.51° W. Long. Elevation is 820 feet.

Population: 164; Growth (since 2000): n/a; Density: 152.0 persons per square mile; Race: 98.2% White, 0.0% Black/African American, 0.0% Asian, 0.0% American Indian/Alaska Native, 0.0% Native Hawaiian/Other Pacific Islander, 1.8% Two or more races, 1.2% Hispanic of any race; Average household size: 2.48; Median age: 39.0; Age under 18: 23.2%; Age 65 and over: 10.4%; Males per 100 females: 90.7

Housing: Homeownership rate: 93.9%; Homeowner vacancy rate: 3.1%; Rental vacancy rate: 0.0%

LORE CITY (village). Covers a land area of 0.328 square miles and a water area of 0 square miles. Located at 39.98° N. Lat; 81.46° W. Long. Elevation is 817 feet.

History: Lore City grew around the coal mines. Morgan's Confederate raiders burned buildings here on their flight across Ohio.

Population: 325; Growth (since 2000): 6.6%; Density: 991.1 persons per square mile; Race: 95.7% White, 0.6% Black/African American, 0.0% Asian, 0.3% American Indian/Alaska Native, 0.0% Native Hawaiian/Other Pacific Islander, 2.5% Two or more races, 2.5% Hispanic of any race; Average household size: 2.75; Median age: 32.8; Age under 18: 31.4%; Age 65 and over: 16.6%; Males per 100 females: 91.2

School District(s)

East Guernsey Local (PK-12)
2012-13 Enrollment: 1,001 . . . . (740) 489-5190

Housing: Homeownership rate: 82.2%; Homeowner vacancy rate: 2.0%; Rental vacancy rate: 4.5%

OLD WASHINGTON (village). Covers a land area of 0.672 square miles and a water area of 0 square miles. Located at 40.04° N. Lat; 81.44° W. Long. Elevation is 1,017 feet.

History: Old Washington was a stagecoach stop on the National Road, with several inns providing rooms and meals for travelers.

Population: 279; Growth (since 2000): 5.3%; Density: 415.3 persons per square mile; Race: 98.9% White, 0.0% Black/African American, 0.0% Asian, 0.4% American Indian/Alaska Native, 0.0% Native Hawaiian/Other Pacific Islander, 0.7% Two or more races, 1.4% Hispanic of any race; Average household size: 2.51; Median age: 40.1; Age under 18: 21.9%; Age 65 and over: 19.7%; Males per 100 females: 109.8

Housing: Homeownership rate: 79.2%; Homeowner vacancy rate: 1.1%; Rental vacancy rate: 0.0%

PLEASANT CITY (village). Covers a land area of 0.176 square miles and a water area of 0 square miles. Located at 39.90° N. Lat; 81.54° W. Long. Elevation is 823 feet.

History: Pleasant City, first called Point Pleasant, developed around the coal mines in the 1890's.

Population: 447; Growth (since 2000): 1.8%; Density: 2,534.1 persons per square mile; Race: 98.0% White, 0.0% Black/African American, 0.2% Asian, 0.0% American Indian/Alaska Native, 0.0% Native Hawaiian/Other Pacific Islander, 1.8% Two or more races, 1.1% Hispanic of any race; Average household size: 2.69; Median age: 32.5; Age under 18: 28.0%; Age 65 and over: 10.3%; Males per 100 females: 93.5

Housing: Homeownership rate: 69.3%; Homeowner vacancy rate: 3.3%; Rental vacancy rate: 7.0%

QUAKER CITY (village). Covers a land area of 0.526 square miles and a water area of 0 square miles. Located at 39.97° N. Lat; 81.30° W. Long. Elevation is 863 feet.

Population: 502; Growth (since 2000): -10.8%; Density: 955.3 persons per square mile; Race: 99.0% White, 0.0% Black/African American, 0.4% Asian, 0.0% American Indian/Alaska Native, 0.0% Native Hawaiian/Other Pacific Islander, 0.2% Two or more races, 0.8% Hispanic of any race; Average household size: 2.49; Median age: 37.8; Age under 18: 25.5%; Age 65 and over: 15.5%; Males per 100 females: 94.6

Housing: Homeownership rate: 68.9%; Homeowner vacancy rate: 2.8%; Rental vacancy rate: 6.0%

SALESVILLE (village). Covers a land area of 0.096 square miles and a water area of 0 square miles. Located at 39.97° N. Lat; 81.34° W. Long. Elevation is 866 feet.

History: Salesville was established near Leatherwood Creek, and was the setting for William Dean Howells' novel "The Leatherwood God."

Population: 129; Growth (since 2000): -16.2%; Density: 1,348.5 persons per square mile; Race: 96.9% White, 1.6% Black/African American, 0.0% Asian, 0.0% American Indian/Alaska Native, 0.0% Native Hawaiian/Other Pacific Islander, 1.6% Two or more races, 0.0% Hispanic of any race; Average household size: 2.58; Median age: 37.5; Age under 18: 26.4%; Age 65 and over: 11.6%; Males per 100 females: 98.5

Housing: Homeownership rate: 86.0%; Homeowner vacancy rate: 0.0%; Rental vacancy rate: 0.0%

SENECAVILLE (village). Covers a land area of 0.475 square miles and a water area of 0 square miles. Located at 39.93° N. Lat; 81.46° W. Long. Elevation is 896 feet.

Population: 457; Growth (since 2000): 0.9%; Density: 962.1 persons per square mile; Race: 98.9% White, 0.0% Black/African American, 0.0% Asian, 0.4% American Indian/Alaska Native, 0.0% Native Hawaiian/Other Pacific Islander, 0.7% Two or more races, 0.0% Hispanic of any race; Average household size: 2.51; Median age: 39.7; Age under 18: 26.9%; Age 65 and over: 15.3%; Males per 100 females: 104.9

School District(s)

Mid-East Career and Technology Centers (09-12)
2012-13 Enrollment: n/a . . . . (740) 454-0105
Rolling Hills Local (PK-12)
2012-13 Enrollment: 1,675 . . . . (740) 432-5370

Housing: Homeownership rate: 70.9%; Homeowner vacancy rate: 1.5%; Rental vacancy rate: 0.0%

Hamilton County

Located in southwestern Ohio; bounded on the west by Indiana, and on the south by the Ohio River and the Kentucky border; drained by Great Miami, Little Miami, and Whitewater Rivers. Covers a land area of 405.910 square miles, a water area of 6.721 square miles, and is located in the Eastern Time Zone at 39.20° N. Lat., 84.54° W. Long. The county was founded in 1790. County seat is Cincinnati.

Hamilton County is part of the Cincinnati, OH-KY-IN Metropolitan Statistical Area. The entire metro area includes: Dearborn County, IN; Ohio County, IN; Union County, IN; Boone County, KY; Bracken County, KY; Campbell County, KY; Gallatin County, KY; Grant County, KY; Kenton County, KY; Pendleton County, KY; Brown County, OH; Butler County, OH; Clermont County, OH; Hamilton County, OH; Warren County, OH

Weather Station: Cincinnati Fernbank — Elevation: 500 feet

	Jan	Feb	Mar	Apr	May	Jun	Jul	Aug	Sep	Oct	Nov	Dec
High	40	44	54	65	74	82	86	85	79	67	56	43
Low	22	24	32	41	51	61	65	64	56	44	36	27
Precip	3.3	3.0	4.4	4.4	5.8	4.3	4.5	3.7	3.0	3.6	3.5	3.8
Snow	4.4	4.5	2.3	tr	tr	0.0	0.0	0.0	0.0	tr	0.2	2.9

High and Low temperatures in degrees Fahrenheit; Precipitation and Snow in inches

Population: 802,374; Growth (since 2000): -5.1%; Density: 1,976.7 persons per square mile; Race: 68.8% White, 25.7% Black/African American, 2.0% Asian, 0.2% American Indian/Alaska Native, 0.1% Native Hawaiian/Other Pacific Islander, 2.1% two or more races, 2.6% Hispanic of any race; Average household size: 2.34; Median age: 37.1; Age under 18: 23.6%; Age 65 and over: 13.3%; Males per 100 females: 92.3; Marriage status: 37.2% never married, 45.3% now married, 2.3% separated, 6.3% widowed, 11.1% divorced; Foreign born: 4.9%; Speak English only: 93.1%; With disability: 12.3%; Veterans: 8.5%; Ancestry: 29.8% German, 14.0% Irish, 7.1% English, 6.3% American, 4.5% Italian

Religion: Six largest groups: 25.6% Catholicism, 6.3% Baptist, 4.9% Non-denominational Protestant, 4.5% Methodist/Pietist, 2.6% Pentecostal, 2.4% Presbyterian-Reformed

Economy: Unemployment rate: 4.4%; Leading industries: 13.5% retail trade; 12.1% professional, scientific, and technical services; 11.4% health care and social assistance; Farms: 295 totaling 21,618 acres; Company size: 31 employs 1,000 or more persons, 55 employ 500 to 999 persons, 695 employ 100 to 499 persons, 20,145 employ less than 100 persons; Business ownership: 19,988 women-owned, 7,603 Black-owned, 568 Hispanic-owned, 1,592 Asian-owned

Employment: 15.7% management, business, and financial, 5.9% computer, engineering, and science, 11.0% education, legal, community service, arts, and media, 6.8% healthcare practitioners, 18.5% service, 25.4% sales and office, 5.6% natural resources, construction, and maintenance, 11.1% production, transportation, and material moving
Income: Per capita: $29,681; Median household: $48,593; Average household: $70,632; Households with income of $100,000 or more: 20.9%; Poverty rate: 18.0%
Educational Attainment: High school diploma or higher: 88.6%; Bachelor's degree or higher: 33.7%; Graduate/professional degree or higher: 12.9%
Housing: Homeownership rate: 59.6%; Median home value: $144,400; Median year structure built: 1959; Homeowner vacancy rate: 3.0%; Median gross rent: $698 per month; Rental vacancy rate: 12.9%
Vital Statistics: Birth rate: 136.9 per 10,000 population; Death rate: 94.9 per 10,000 population; Age-adjusted cancer mortality rate: 202.4 deaths per 100,000 population
Health Insurance: 88.7% have insurance; 68.9% have private insurance; 30.0% have public insurance; 11.3% do not have insurance; 4.7% of children under 18 do not have insurance
Health Care: Physicians: 49.8 per 10,000 population; Hospital beds: 50.4 per 10,000 population; Hospital admissions: 2,127.1 per 10,000 population
Air Quality Index: 50.7% good, 47.9% moderate, 1.4% unhealthy for sensitive individuals, 0.0% unhealthy (percent of days)
Transportation: Commute: 88.6% car, 3.8% public transportation, 3.0% walk, 3.8% work from home; Median travel time to work: 22.7 minutes
Presidential Election: 51.8% Obama, 46.9% Romney (2012)
National and State Parks: Harrison State Park; Kroger Hills State Reserve; LIttle Miami State Scenic River; Little Miami Scenic State Park; National Steamboat Monument; National Underground Railroad Freedom Center; William Howard Taft National Historic Site
Additional Information Contacts
Hamilton Government . . . . (513) 946-4400
http://www.hamilton-co.org

Hamilton County Communities

ADDYSTON (village). Covers a land area of 0.852 square miles and a water area of 0.056 square miles. Located at 39.14° N. Lat; 84.71° W. Long. Elevation is 482 feet.
History: Addyston became a town in 1871 when Matthew Addy of Cincinnati established a pipe foundry.
Population: 938; Growth (since 2000): -7.1%; Density: 1,101.1 persons per square mile; Race: 89.7% White, 5.7% Black/African American, 0.2% Asian, 0.2% American Indian/Alaska Native, 0.0% Native Hawaiian/Other Pacific Islander, 4.2% Two or more races, 1.9% Hispanic of any race; Average household size: 2.52; Median age: 34.2; Age under 18: 25.3%; Age 65 and over: 10.2%; Males per 100 females: 102.2
Housing: Homeownership rate: 46.3%; Homeowner vacancy rate: 6.3%; Rental vacancy rate: 10.3%

AMBERLEY (village). Covers a land area of 3.499 square miles and a water area of 0 square miles. Located at 39.20° N. Lat; 84.43° W. Long. Elevation is 801 feet.
History: Amberley Village was incorporated as a village on April 5, 1940. It was designated a Tree City USA by the National Arbor Day Foundation.
Population: 3,585; Growth (since 2000): 4.7%; Density: 1,024.7 persons per square mile; Race: 85.7% White, 9.5% Black/African American, 3.0% Asian, 0.1% American Indian/Alaska Native, 0.0% Native Hawaiian/Other Pacific Islander, 1.4% Two or more races, 1.3% Hispanic of any race; Average household size: 2.59; Median age: 49.1; Age under 18: 24.0%; Age 65 and over: 21.4%; Males per 100 females: 92.0; Marriage status: 14.3% never married, 77.3% now married, 1.1% separated, 4.8% widowed, 3.6% divorced; Foreign born: 8.5%; Speak English only: 92.4%; With disability: 9.6%; Veterans: 10.5%; Ancestry: 23.6% German, 14.0% Russian, 11.7% Irish, 9.3% Polish, 7.2% American
Employment: 30.5% management, business, and financial, 3.7% computer, engineering, and science, 18.8% education, legal, community service, arts, and media, 17.8% healthcare practitioners, 8.3% service, 18.5% sales and office, 0.3% natural resources, construction, and maintenance, 2.2% production, transportation, and material moving
Income: Per capita: $60,976; Median household: $112,202; Average household: $164,013; Households with income of $100,000 or more: 57.1%; Poverty rate: 6.1%
Educational Attainment: High school diploma or higher: 97.9%; Bachelor's degree or higher: 73.0%; Graduate/professional degree or higher: 34.2%
Housing: Homeownership rate: 95.0%; Median home value: $317,700; Median year structure built: 1958; Homeowner vacancy rate: 2.0%; Median gross rent: $1,875 per month; Rental vacancy rate: 1.4%
Health Insurance: 96.1% have insurance; 80.4% have private insurance; 29.8% have public insurance; 3.9% do not have insurance; 0.0% of children under 18 do not have insurance
Safety: Violent crime rate: 2.8 per 10,000 population; Property crime rate: 167.4 per 10,000 population
Transportation: Commute: 95.0% car, 0.2% public transportation, 0.4% walk, 3.8% work from home; Median travel time to work: 20.5 minutes

ARLINGTON HEIGHTS (village). Covers a land area of 0.268 square miles and a water area of 0 square miles. Located at 39.22° N. Lat; 84.46° W. Long. Elevation is 554 feet.
Population: 745; Growth (since 2000): -17.1%; Density: 2,782.1 persons per square mile; Race: 80.7% White, 14.8% Black/African American, 0.4% Asian, 0.0% American Indian/Alaska Native, 0.1% Native Hawaiian/Other Pacific Islander, 3.6% Two or more races, 0.9% Hispanic of any race; Average household size: 2.26; Median age: 36.3; Age under 18: 23.1%; Age 65 and over: 10.9%; Males per 100 females: 99.2
Housing: Homeownership rate: 48.4%; Homeowner vacancy rate: 3.0%; Rental vacancy rate: 12.3%

BLUE ASH (city). Covers a land area of 7.580 square miles and a water area of 0.014 square miles. Located at 39.25° N. Lat; 84.39° W. Long. Elevation is 846 feet.
History: The Carpenter's Run Baptist Church (1797-1828) served the earliest settlers of Blue Ash. Built of logs from the blue ash tree, the church gave the community its name.
Population: 12,114; Growth (since 2000): -3.2%; Density: 1,598.2 persons per square mile; Race: 79.9% White, 6.5% Black/African American, 10.6% Asian, 0.2% American Indian/Alaska Native, 0.0% Native Hawaiian/Other Pacific Islander, 2.1% Two or more races, 2.5% Hispanic of any race; Average household size: 2.40; Median age: 41.6; Age under 18: 22.7%; Age 65 and over: 15.4%; Males per 100 females: 96.0; Marriage status: 25.1% never married, 58.7% now married, 1.0% separated, 6.0% widowed, 10.2% divorced; Foreign born: 15.5%; Speak English only: 83.0%; With disability: 8.6%; Veterans: 9.9%; Ancestry: 26.7% German, 17.2% Irish, 11.3% English, 6.2% American, 4.2% Italian
Employment: 19.6% management, business, and financial, 7.9% computer, engineering, and science, 16.7% education, legal, community service, arts, and media, 10.7% healthcare practitioners, 13.9% service, 17.3% sales and office, 4.6% natural resources, construction, and maintenance, 9.3% production, transportation, and material moving
Income: Per capita: $44,114; Median household: $70,787; Average household: $103,933; Households with income of $100,000 or more: 35.3%; Poverty rate: 5.6%
Educational Attainment: High school diploma or higher: 92.4%; Bachelor's degree or higher: 54.5%; Graduate/professional degree or higher: 27.5%

Four-year College(s)

University of Cincinnati-Blue Ash College (Public)
Fall 2013 Enrollment: 4,816 . . . . (513) 745-5600
2013-14 Tuition: In-state $5,890; Out-of-state $14,516
Housing: Homeownership rate: 71.1%; Median home value: $214,500; Median year structure built: 1978; Homeowner vacancy rate: 2.1%; Median gross rent: $1,034 per month; Rental vacancy rate: 6.6%
Health Insurance: 94.1% have insurance; 85.0% have private insurance; 21.6% have public insurance; 5.9% do not have insurance; 2.1% of children under 18 do not have insurance
Safety: Violent crime rate: 5.8 per 10,000 population; Property crime rate: 321.4 per 10,000 population
Transportation: Commute: 93.6% car, 1.0% public transportation, 0.9% walk, 3.8% work from home; Median travel time to work: 20.2 minutes
Additional Information Contacts
City of Blue Ash. . . . . (513) 745-8500
http://www.blueash.com

BLUE JAY (CDP). Covers a land area of 4.373 square miles and a water area of 0.035 square miles. Located at 39.24° N. Lat; 84.74° W. Long. Elevation is 781 feet.
Population: 959; Growth (since 2000): n/a; Density: 219.3 persons per square mile; Race: 98.3% White, 0.1% Black/African American, 0.2% Asian, 0.1% American Indian/Alaska Native, 0.0% Native Hawaiian/Other Pacific Islander, 0.5% Two or more races, 1.3% Hispanic of any race; Average household size: 2.63; Median age: 46.3; Age under 18: 18.7%; Age 65 and over: 18.7%; Males per 100 females: 103.6
Housing: Homeownership rate: 87.9%; Homeowner vacancy rate: 0.6%; Rental vacancy rate: 2.2%

BRECON (CDP). Covers a land area of 0.560 square miles and a water area of <.001 square miles. Located at 39.28° N. Lat; 84.35° W. Long. Elevation is 869 feet.
Population: 244; Growth (since 2000): n/a; Density: 436.0 persons per square mile; Race: 84.8% White, 2.0% Black/African American, 0.0% Asian, 0.0% American Indian/Alaska Native, 2.0% Native Hawaiian/Other Pacific Islander, 3.3% Two or more races, 28.3% Hispanic of any race; Average household size: 2.49; Median age: 36.0; Age under 18: 24.2%; Age 65 and over: 19.3%; Males per 100 females: 101.7
Housing: Homeownership rate: 85.7%; Homeowner vacancy rate: 5.6%; Rental vacancy rate: 12.5%

BRIDGETOWN (CDP). Covers a land area of 4.323 square miles and a water area of 0 square miles. Located at 39.16° N. Lat; 84.64° W. Long. Elevation is 899 feet.
Population: 14,407; Growth (since 2000): n/a; Density: 3,333.0 persons per square mile; Race: 96.9% White, 0.9% Black/African American, 0.8% Asian, 0.1% American Indian/Alaska Native, 0.1% Native Hawaiian/Other Pacific Islander, 1.1% Two or more races, 0.8% Hispanic of any race; Average household size: 2.46; Median age: 40.2; Age under 18: 23.7%; Age 65 and over: 18.8%; Males per 100 females: 90.0; Marriage status: 27.9% never married, 52.0% now married, 0.6% separated, 10.8% widowed, 9.2% divorced; Foreign born: 1.2%; Speak English only: 96.7%; With disability: 12.1%; Veterans: 10.2%; Ancestry: 52.9% German, 17.1% Irish, 8.1% English, 6.9% American, 6.9% Italian
Employment: 14.2% management, business, and financial, 3.9% computer, engineering, and science, 8.0% education, legal, community service, arts, and media, 9.1% healthcare practitioners, 17.0% service, 29.6% sales and office, 9.2% natural resources, construction, and maintenance, 9.0% production, transportation, and material moving
Income: Per capita: $28,450; Median household: $57,424; Average household: $68,912; Households with income of $100,000 or more: 20.4%; Poverty rate: 6.4%
Educational Attainment: High school diploma or higher: 92.5%; Bachelor's degree or higher: 25.1%; Graduate/professional degree or higher: 7.7%
Housing: Homeownership rate: 85.3%; Median home value: $128,300; Median year structure built: 1960; Homeowner vacancy rate: 2.0%; Median gross rent: $871 per month; Rental vacancy rate: 9.7%
Health Insurance: 93.2% have insurance; 80.2% have private insurance; 29.1% have public insurance; 6.8% do not have insurance; 4.2% of children under 18 do not have insurance
Transportation: Commute: 96.3% car, 0.5% public transportation, 0.8% walk, 2.0% work from home; Median travel time to work: 24.5 minutes

CAMP DENNISON (CDP). Covers a land area of 0.401 square miles and a water area of 0 square miles. Located at 39.20° N. Lat; 84.29° W. Long. Elevation is 574 feet.
Population: 375; Growth (since 2000): n/a; Density: 935.7 persons per square mile; Race: 75.2% White, 19.5% Black/African American, 0.0% Asian, 0.0% American Indian/Alaska Native, 0.0% Native Hawaiian/Other Pacific Islander, 4.0% Two or more races, 2.4% Hispanic of any race; Average household size: 2.33; Median age: 46.6; Age under 18: 20.8%; Age 65 and over: 12.8%; Males per 100 females: 107.2
Housing: Homeownership rate: 77.1%; Homeowner vacancy rate: 0.8%; Rental vacancy rate: 5.1%

CHERRY GROVE (CDP). Covers a land area of 1.132 square miles and a water area of 0 square miles. Located at 39.08° N. Lat; 84.32° W. Long. Elevation is 876 feet.
Population: 4,378; Growth (since 2000): -3.9%; Density: 3,865.8 persons per square mile; Race: 94.9% White, 1.2% Black/African American, 2.0% Asian, 0.2% American Indian/Alaska Native, 0.0% Native Hawaiian/Other Pacific Islander, 1.4% Two or more races, 1.9% Hispanic of any race; Average household size: 2.89; Median age: 38.8; Age under 18: 29.1%; Age 65 and over: 13.6%; Males per 100 females: 91.8; Marriage status: 26.0% never married, 65.9% now married, 1.3% separated, 3.5% widowed, 4.6% divorced; Foreign born: 3.4%; Speak English only: 97.3%; With disability: 6.1%; Veterans: 8.4%; Ancestry: 40.6% German, 17.1% Irish, 13.8% American, 11.4% English, 4.8% Italian
Employment: 14.8% management, business, and financial, 8.0% computer, engineering, and science, 17.9% education, legal, community service, arts, and media, 6.7% healthcare practitioners, 16.3% service, 21.4% sales and office, 6.5% natural resources, construction, and maintenance, 8.3% production, transportation, and material moving
Income: Per capita: $30,094; Median household: $80,872; Average household: $90,198; Households with income of $100,000 or more: 40.8%; Poverty rate: 7.2%
Educational Attainment: High school diploma or higher: 97.1%; Bachelor's degree or higher: 38.9%; Graduate/professional degree or higher: 9.8%
Housing: Homeownership rate: 93.6%; Median home value: $170,200; Median year structure built: 1971; Homeowner vacancy rate: 0.6%; Median gross rent: $1,274 per month; Rental vacancy rate: 3.0%
Health Insurance: 95.7% have insurance; 84.3% have private insurance; 27.1% have public insurance; 4.3% do not have insurance; 0.9% of children under 18 do not have insurance
Transportation: Commute: 91.5% car, 0.0% public transportation, 0.7% walk, 7.0% work from home; Median travel time to work: 23.5 minutes

CHEVIOT (city). Covers a land area of 1.168 square miles and a water area of <.001 square miles. Located at 39.16° N. Lat; 84.61° W. Long. Elevation is 909 feet.
History: Settled early 1800s; incorporated 1904.
Population: 8,375; Growth (since 2000): -7.1%; Density: 7,172.0 persons per square mile; Race: 89.0% White, 7.3% Black/African American, 0.5% Asian, 0.2% American Indian/Alaska Native, 0.0% Native Hawaiian/Other Pacific Islander, 2.1% Two or more races, 2.0% Hispanic of any race; Average household size: 2.18; Median age: 34.6; Age under 18: 21.8%; Age 65 and over: 13.3%; Males per 100 females: 92.9; Marriage status: 35.9% never married, 40.2% now married, 2.5% separated, 6.9% widowed, 17.0% divorced; Foreign born: 3.2%; Speak English only: 93.5%; With disability: 19.3%; Veterans: 9.0%; Ancestry: 49.0% German, 21.6% Irish, 8.6% Italian, 5.3% English, 3.4% American
Employment: 11.8% management, business, and financial, 6.5% computer, engineering, and science, 10.1% education, legal, community service, arts, and media, 6.2% healthcare practitioners, 17.2% service, 29.6% sales and office, 7.2% natural resources, construction, and maintenance, 11.3% production, transportation, and material moving
Income: Per capita: $22,948; Median household: $37,302; Average household: $47,262; Households with income of $100,000 or more: 10.5%; Poverty rate: 15.6%
Educational Attainment: High school diploma or higher: 87.0%; Bachelor's degree or higher: 22.4%; Graduate/professional degree or higher: 6.7%
Housing: Homeownership rate: 58.8%; Median home value: $95,400; Median year structure built: 1946; Homeowner vacancy rate: 3.1%; Median gross rent: $662 per month; Rental vacancy rate: 13.5%
Health Insurance: 90.1% have insurance; 69.1% have private insurance; 32.5% have public insurance; 9.9% do not have insurance; 1.3% of children under 18 do not have insurance
Transportation: Commute: 87.9% car, 4.6% public transportation, 3.8% walk, 3.0% work from home; Median travel time to work: 23.2 minutes
Additional Information Contacts
City of Cheviot. . . . . (513) 661-2700
http://www.cheviot.org

CINCINNATI (city). County seat. Covers a land area of 77.942 square miles and a water area of 1.604 square miles. Located at 39.14° N. Lat; 84.51° W. Long. Elevation is 627 feet.
History: Cincinnati was settled at an Ohio River crossroads in 1788 when developers platted a village that they named Losantiville. In 1790 the name was changed to Cincinnati by General Arthur St. Clair, Governor of the Northwest Territory, in honor of the Revolutionary Officers' Society. The Ohio River was the avenue down which settlers came to find space to establish farms, and Cincinnati became the center of commerce. Immigrants from Germany and Ireland joined other Europeans who came straight to Cincinnati. Steamboat travel on the Ohio River and the opening

of the Miami & Erie Canal spurred trading. When Charles Dickens visited Cincinnati in 1842, he described it as "a place that commends itself... favorably and pleasantly to a stranger." The Civil War tore Cincinnati apart. Its sympathies were with the North, but its trade was with the South, and there was great rejoicing when the war ended.

Population: 296,943; Growth (since 2000): -10.4%; Density: 3,809.8 persons per square mile; Race: 49.3% White, 44.8% Black/African American, 1.8% Asian, 0.3% American Indian/Alaska Native, 0.1% Native Hawaiian/Other Pacific Islander, 2.5% Two or more races, 2.8% Hispanic of any race; Average household size: 2.12; Median age: 32.5; Age under 18: 22.1%; Age 65 and over: 10.8%; Males per 100 females: 92.5; Marriage status: 50.9% never married, 31.0% now married, 3.1% separated, 5.9% widowed, 12.2% divorced; Foreign born: 5.2%; Speak English only: 92.4%; With disability: 14.0%; Veterans: 7.0%; Ancestry: 19.1% German, 10.4% Irish, 5.4% American, 5.2% English, 3.6% Italian

Employment: 14.3% management, business, and financial, 6.3% computer, engineering, and science, 12.2% education, legal, community service, arts, and media, 5.7% healthcare practitioners, 22.0% service, 24.0% sales and office, 4.6% natural resources, construction, and maintenance, 10.9% production, transportation, and material moving

Income: Per capita: $24,779; Median household: $34,116; Average household: $54,204; Households with income of $100,000 or more: 13.4%; Poverty rate: 30.4%

Educational Attainment: High school diploma or higher: 84.3%; Bachelor's degree or higher: 31.5%; Graduate/professional degree or higher: 12.9%

School District(s)

Accelerated Achievement Academy of East Cincinnati (09-12)
2012-13 Enrollment: 166 . . . . (614) 995-1985
Accelerated Achievement Academy of North Cincinnat
2012-13 Enrollment: 95 . . . . (513) 246-4260
Alliance Academy of Cincinnati (KG-08)
2012-13 Enrollment: 320 . . . . (513) 751-5555
Cincinnati City (PK-12)
2012-13 Enrollment: 31,615 . . . . (513) 363-0000
Cincinnati College Preparatory Academy (KG-12)
2012-13 Enrollment: 909 . . . . (513) 684-0777
Cincinnati College Preparatory Academy East (KG-06)
2012-13 Enrollment: 358 . . . . (614) 995-1985
Cincinnati Leadership Academy (KG-08)
2012-13 Enrollment: 250 . . . . (513) 351-5737
Cincinnati Speech & Reading Intervention Center (KG-08)
2012-13 Enrollment: 270 . . . . (513) 651-9624
College Hill Leadership Academy (KG-08)
2012-13 Enrollment: 94 . . . . (513) 541-3274
Deer Park Community City (PK-12)
2012-13 Enrollment: 1,250 . . . . (513) 891-0222
Dohn Community (09-12)
2012-13 Enrollment: 169 . . . . (513) 281-6100
East End Community Heritage School (KG-12)
2012-13 Enrollment: 72 . . . . (513) 281-3900
Finneytown Local (PK-12)
2012-13 Enrollment: 1,421 . . . . (513) 728-3700
Forest Hills Local (PK-12)
2012-13 Enrollment: 7,508 . . . . (513) 231-3600
Great Oaks Inst of Technology (05-12)
2012-13 Enrollment: n/a . . . . (513) 771-8840
Hamilton Cnty Math & Science (KG-08)
2012-13 Enrollment: 501 . . . . (513) 728-8620
Horizon Science Academy-Cincinnati (KG-12)
2012-13 Enrollment: 454 . . . . (513) 242-0099
Impact Academy Cincinnati (KG-02)
2012-13 Enrollment: 105 . . . . (937) 654-6697
Indian Hill Exempted Village (PK-12)
2012-13 Enrollment: 1,930 . . . . (513) 272-4500
King Academy Community School (KG-08)
2012-13 Enrollment: 108 . . . . (513) 421-7519
Lakota Local (PK-12)
2012-13 Enrollment: 16,526 . . . . (513) 874-5505
Leadership Academy of Mathematics & Science Focus
2012-13 Enrollment: n/a . . . . (614) 995-1985
Leadership Academy of Mathematics & Science of Cin (09-12)
2012-13 Enrollment: n/a . . . . (740) 971-8749
Life Skills Center of Hamilton County (09-12)
2012-13 Enrollment: 105 . . . . (513) 821-6695
Life Skills Ctr of Cincinnati (09-12)
2012-13 Enrollment: 121 . . . . (513) 475-0222
Lighthouse Community Sch Inc (07-12)
2012-13 Enrollment: 53 . . . . (513) 561-7888
Lockland Local (PK-12)
2012-13 Enrollment: 580 . . . . (513) 563-5000
Madeira City (PK-12)
2012-13 Enrollment: 1,446 . . . . (513) 985-6070
Mariemont City (PK-12)
2012-13 Enrollment: 1,668 . . . . (513) 272-7500
Mount Auburn International Academy (KG-12)
2012-13 Enrollment: 525 . . . . (513) 241-5500
Mt Healthy City (PK-12)
2012-13 Enrollment: 3,203 . . . . (513) 729-0077
Mt. Healthy Preparatory and Fitness Academy (KG-08)
2012-13 Enrollment: 260 . . . . (513) 587-6280
New Richmond Exempted Village (PK-12)
2012-13 Enrollment: 2,327 . . . . (513) 553-2616
North College Hill City (PK-12)
2012-13 Enrollment: 1,611 . . . . (513) 931-8181
Northwest Local (PK-12)
2012-13 Enrollment: 9,197 . . . . (513) 923-1000
Oak Hills Local (PK-12)
2012-13 Enrollment: 7,976 . . . . (513) 574-3200
Orion Academy (KG-08)
2012-13 Enrollment: 672 . . . . (513) 251-6000
P.a.c.e. High School (09-12)
2012-13 Enrollment: 116 . . . . (513) 751-7223
Phoenix Community Learning Ctr (KG-08)
2012-13 Enrollment: 359 . . . . (513) 351-5801
Princeton City (PK-12)
2012-13 Enrollment: 5,379 . . . . (513) 864-1000
Riverside Academy (KG-08)
2012-13 Enrollment: 291 . . . . (513) 921-7777
Saint Bernard-Elmwood Place City (PK-12)
2012-13 Enrollment: 1,034 . . . . (513) 482-7121
Summit Academy Cincinnati (KG-07)
2012-13 Enrollment: 137 . . . . (513) 321-0561
Summit Academy Transition High School-Cincinnati (08-12)
2012-13 Enrollment: 80 . . . . (513) 541-4000
Sycamore Community City (PK-12)
2012-13 Enrollment: 5,298 . . . . (513) 686-1700
T.c.p. World Academy (KG-06)
2012-13 Enrollment: 455 . . . . (513) 531-9500
Theodore Roosevelt Public Community School (KG-12)
2012-13 Enrollment: 232 . . . . (513) 244-6960
Three Rivers Local (PK-12)
2012-13 Enrollment: 1,924 . . . . (513) 941-6400
V L T Academy (KG-12)
2012-13 Enrollment: 869 . . . . (513) 421-1129
West Clermont Local (PK-12)
2012-13 Enrollment: 8,448 . . . . (513) 943-5000
Winton Woods City (PK-12)
2012-13 Enrollment: 3,447 . . . . (513) 619-2300

Four-year College(s)

Art Academy of Cincinnati (Private, Not-for-profit)
Fall 2013 Enrollment: 215 . . . . (513) 562-6262
2013-14 Tuition: In-state $24,330; Out-of-state $24,330
Athenaeum of Ohio (Private, Not-for-profit, Roman Catholic)
Fall 2013 Enrollment: 208 . . . . (513) 231-2223
Brown Mackie College-Cincinnati (Private, For-profit)
Fall 2013 Enrollment: 1,045 . . . . (513) 771-2424
2013-14 Tuition: In-state $12,474; Out-of-state $12,474
Cincinnati Christian University (Private, Not-for-profit, Christian Churches and Churches of Christ)
Fall 2013 Enrollment: 918 . . . . (513) 244-8100
2013-14 Tuition: In-state $15,266; Out-of-state $15,266
Cincinnati College of Mortuary Science (Private, Not-for-profit)
Fall 2013 Enrollment: 81 . . . . (513) 761-2020
College of Mount St Joseph (Private, Not-for-profit, Roman Catholic)
Fall 2013 Enrollment: 2,326 . . . . (513) 244-4200
2013-14 Tuition: In-state $25,800; Out-of-state $25,800
Gods Bible School and College (Private, Not-for-profit, Other Protestant)
Fall 2013 Enrollment: 305 . . . . (513) 721-7944
2013-14 Tuition: In-state $7,000; Out-of-state $7,000

Good Samaritan College of Nursing and Health Science (Private, Not-for-profit, Roman Catholic)
Fall 2013 Enrollment: 355 . . . . (513) 862-2631
2013-14 Tuition: In-state $18,825; Out-of-state $18,825
Ohio Mid-Western College (Private, Not-for-profit, Baptist)
Fall 2013 Enrollment: 140 . . . . (513) 772-9888
2013-14 Tuition: In-state $10,944; Out-of-state $10,944
The Art Institute of Cincinnati (Private, For-profit)
Fall 2013 Enrollment: 38 . . . . (513) 751-1206
2013-14 Tuition: In-state $23,341; Out-of-state $23,341
The Art Institute of Ohio-Cincinnati (Private, For-profit)
Fall 2013 Enrollment: 834 . . . . (513) 833-2400
2013-14 Tuition: In-state $17,391; Out-of-state $17,391
The Christ College of Nursing and Health Sciences (Private, Not-for-profit)
Fall 2013 Enrollment: 535 . . . . (513) 585-0032
2013-14 Tuition: In-state $18,883; Out-of-state $18,883
Union Institute & University (Private, Not-for-profit)
Fall 2013 Enrollment: 1,660 . . . . (800) 861-6400
2013-14 Tuition: In-state $11,904; Out-of-state $11,904
University of Cincinnati-Main Campus (Public)
Fall 2013 Enrollment: 34,379 . . . . (513) 556-6000
2013-14 Tuition: In-state $10,784; Out-of-state $25,816
Xavier University (Private, Not-for-profit, Roman Catholic)
Fall 2013 Enrollment: 6,633 . . . . (513) 745-3000
2013-14 Tuition: In-state $33,000; Out-of-state $33,000

Two-year College(s)

Antonelli College-Cincinnati (Private, For-profit)
Fall 2013 Enrollment: 180 . . . . (513) 241-4338
2013-14 Tuition: In-state $15,980; Out-of-state $15,980
Cincinnati State Technical and Community College (Public)
Fall 2013 Enrollment: 11,167 . . . . (513) 569-1500
2013-14 Tuition: In-state $3,745; Out-of-state $7,232
Eastern Hills Academy of Hair Design (Private, For-profit)
Fall 2013 Enrollment: 71 . . . . (513) 231-8621
Fortis College-Cincinnati (Private, For-profit)
Fall 2013 Enrollment: 501 . . . . (513) 771-2795
2013-14 Tuition: In-state $21,661; Out-of-state $21,661
Galen College of Nursing-Cincinnati (Private, For-profit)
Fall 2013 Enrollment: 505 . . . . (513) 475-3600
Great Oaks Institute of Technology and Career Development (Public)
Fall 2013 Enrollment: 289 . . . . (513) 771-8925
Lincoln College of Technology-Tri-County (Private, For-profit)
Fall 2013 Enrollment: 123 . . . . (513) 874-0432
2013-14 Tuition: In-state $12,020; Out-of-state $12,020
Moler Hollywood Beauty Academy (Private, For-profit)
Fall 2013 Enrollment: 80 . . . . (513) 621-5262
National College-Cincinnati (Private, For-profit)
Fall 2013 Enrollment: 137 . . . . (513) 761-1291
2013-14 Tuition: In-state $11,550; Out-of-state $11,550
Western Hills School of Beauty and Hair Design (Private, For-profit)
Fall 2013 Enrollment: 259 . . . . (513) 574-3818

Vocational/Technical School(s)

Empire Beauty School-Cincinnati (Private, For-profit)
Fall 2013 Enrollment: 186 . . . . (800) 920-4593
2013-14 Tuition: $16,320
Ohio Center for Broadcasting-Cincinnati (Private, For-profit)
Fall 2013 Enrollment: 19 . . . . (513) 271-6060
2013-14 Tuition: $15,188
Paul Mitchell The School-Cincinnati (Private, For-profit)
Fall 2013 Enrollment: 244 . . . . (513) 769-7699
2013-14 Tuition: $15,113
Regency Beauty Institute-Eastgate (Private, For-profit)
Fall 2013 Enrollment: 84 . . . . (800) 787-6456
2013-14 Tuition: $16,200
Ross Medical Education Center-Cincinnati (Private, For-profit)
Fall 2013 Enrollment: 126 . . . . (513) 851-8500
2013-14 Tuition: $15,680
The Salon Professional Academy-Cincinnati (Private, For-profit)
Fall 2013 Enrollment: 58 . . . . (513) 481-2222
2013-14 Tuition: $16,840

Housing: Homeownership rate: 38.9%; Median home value: $123,600; Median year structure built: 1947; Homeowner vacancy rate: 5.1%; Median gross rent: $640 per month; Rental vacancy rate: 14.7%

Health Insurance: 84.9% have insurance; 57.6% have private insurance; 35.3% have public insurance; 15.1% do not have insurance; 5.5% of children under 18 do not have insurance

Hospitals: Bethesda North (314 beds); Christ Hospital; Cincinnati VA Medical Center (378 beds); Good Samaritan Hospital (700 beds); Jewish Hospital; Mercy Health - West Hospital (269 beds); Mercy Hospital Anderson (186 beds); Trihealth Evendale Hospital; University of Cincinnati Medical Center

Safety: Violent crime rate: 95.3 per 10,000 population; Property crime rate: 581.2 per 10,000 population

Newspapers: CIN Weekly (weekly circulation 65000); Cincinnati Enquirer (daily circulation 198000); City Beat (weekly circulation 53000); Community Press (weekly circulation 72000); Pulse (weekly circulation 18000); Valley Courier (weekly circulation 2200)

Transportation: Commute: 81.3% car, 7.9% public transportation, 5.6% walk, 4.0% work from home; Median travel time to work: 22.4 minutes; Amtrak: Train service available.

Airports: Cincinnati Municipal Airport Lunken Field (general aviation); Cincinnati/Northern Kentucky International (primary service/medium hub)

Additional Information Contacts

City of Cincinnati . . . . (513) 591-6000
http://www.cincinnati-oh.gov

CLEVES (village). Covers a land area of 1.583 square miles and a water area of 0.003 square miles. Located at 39.16° N. Lat; 84.74° W. Long. Elevation is 499 feet.

History: Cleves was platted in 1818 and named for John Cleves Symmes, a pioneer who had founded North Bend.

Population: 3,234; Growth (since 2000): 15.9%; Density: 2,042.5 persons per square mile; Race: 96.9% White, 0.6% Black/African American, 0.4% Asian, 0.4% American Indian/Alaska Native, 0.0% Native Hawaiian/Other Pacific Islander, 1.6% Two or more races, 1.2% Hispanic of any race; Average household size: 3.00; Median age: 33.2; Age under 18: 32.5%; Age 65 and over: 7.7%; Males per 100 females: 101.2; Marriage status: 29.0% never married, 53.4% now married, 1.9% separated, 5.9% widowed, 11.7% divorced; Foreign born: 0.5%; Speak English only: 98.2%; With disability: 13.0%; Veterans: 10.0%; Ancestry: 43.4% German, 19.3% Irish, 6.2% American, 6.2% English, 4.9% Italian

Employment: 13.0% management, business, and financial, 2.9% computer, engineering, and science, 10.9% education, legal, community service, arts, and media, 4.0% healthcare practitioners, 16.7% service, 29.6% sales and office, 12.8% natural resources, construction, and maintenance, 10.2% production, transportation, and material moving

Income: Per capita: $24,429; Median household: $54,961; Average household: $69,571; Households with income of $100,000 or more: 24.8%; Poverty rate: 13.2%

Educational Attainment: High school diploma or higher: 90.4%; Bachelor's degree or higher: 17.7%; Graduate/professional degree or higher: 4.7%

School District(s)

Three Rivers Local (PK-12)
2012-13 Enrollment: 1,924 . . . . (513) 941-6400

Housing: Homeownership rate: 75.3%; Median home value: $118,700; Median year structure built: 1964; Homeowner vacancy rate: 1.3%; Median gross rent: $690 per month; Rental vacancy rate: 15.7%

Health Insurance: 87.5% have insurance; 74.3% have private insurance; 20.0% have public insurance; 12.5% do not have insurance; 8.0% of children under 18 do not have insurance

Transportation: Commute: 94.1% car, 0.5% public transportation, 1.5% walk, 1.9% work from home; Median travel time to work: 26.8 minutes

Additional Information Contacts

Village of Cleves . . . . (513) 941-5127
http://www.cleves.org

COLDSTREAM (CDP). Covers a land area of 2.766 square miles and a water area of 0.084 square miles. Located at 39.04° N. Lat; 84.34° W. Long.

Population: 1,173; Growth (since 2000): n/a; Density: 424.1 persons per square mile; Race: 96.2% White, 0.9% Black/African American, 1.8% Asian, 0.1% American Indian/Alaska Native, 0.0% Native Hawaiian/Other Pacific Islander, 0.7% Two or more races, 2.5% Hispanic of any race; Average household size: 2.77; Median age: 48.4; Age under 18: 24.8%; Age 65 and over: 13.1%; Males per 100 females: 99.8

Housing: Homeownership rate: 97.4%; Homeowner vacancy rate: 1.4%; Rental vacancy rate: 8.3%

CONCORDE HILLS (CDP). Covers a land area of 0.383 square miles and a water area of 0 square miles. Located at 39.21° N. Lat; 84.36° W. Long.
Population: 663; Growth (since 2000): n/a; Density: 1,729.4 persons per square mile; Race: 92.8% White, 1.5% Black/African American, 3.9% Asian, 0.0% American Indian/Alaska Native, 0.0% Native Hawaiian/Other Pacific Islander, 1.5% Two or more races, 3.5% Hispanic of any race; Average household size: 2.50; Median age: 49.0; Age under 18: 25.8%; Age 65 and over: 23.8%; Males per 100 females: 83.7
Housing: Homeownership rate: 76.6%; Homeowner vacancy rate: 2.8%; Rental vacancy rate: 10.0%

COVEDALE (CDP). Covers a land area of 2.800 square miles and a water area of 0 square miles. Located at 39.13° N. Lat; 84.64° W. Long. Elevation is 886 feet.
Population: 6,447; Growth (since 2000): 1.4%; Density: 2,302.4 persons per square mile; Race: 93.7% White, 3.4% Black/African American, 1.1% Asian, 0.0% American Indian/Alaska Native, 0.0% Native Hawaiian/Other Pacific Islander, 1.4% Two or more races, 1.0% Hispanic of any race; Average household size: 2.53; Median age: 43.6; Age under 18: 22.9%; Age 65 and over: 18.3%; Males per 100 females: 89.0; Marriage status: 25.9% never married, 55.7% now married, 1.9% separated, 7.7% widowed, 10.7% divorced; Foreign born: 1.5%; Speak English only: 97.3%; With disability: 12.7%; Veterans: 7.6%; Ancestry: 51.8% German, 25.7% Irish, 7.2% Italian, 6.1% English, 4.9% Lebanese
Employment: 14.1% management, business, and financial, 10.0% computer, engineering, and science, 11.3% education, legal, community service, arts, and media, 6.4% healthcare practitioners, 17.2% service, 22.8% sales and office, 10.2% natural resources, construction, and maintenance, 8.1% production, transportation, and material moving
Income: Per capita: $31,974; Median household: $70,718; Average household: $81,491; Households with income of $100,000 or more: 31.6%; Poverty rate: 9.5%
Educational Attainment: High school diploma or higher: 93.7%; Bachelor's degree or higher: 32.1%; Graduate/professional degree or higher: 12.3%
Housing: Homeownership rate: 89.2%; Median home value: $150,400; Median year structure built: 1957; Homeowner vacancy rate: 1.9%; Median gross rent: $956 per month; Rental vacancy rate: 6.5%
Health Insurance: 91.1% have insurance; 78.8% have private insurance; 24.2% have public insurance; 8.9% do not have insurance; 0.0% of children under 18 do not have insurance
Transportation: Commute: 92.0% car, 1.2% public transportation, 1.4% walk, 3.8% work from home; Median travel time to work: 27.7 minutes

DEER PARK (city). Covers a land area of 0.874 square miles and a water area of 0 square miles. Located at 39.20° N. Lat; 84.40° W. Long. Elevation is 873 feet.
Population: 5,736; Growth (since 2000): -4.1%; Density: 6,564.2 persons per square mile; Race: 91.9% White, 4.6% Black/African American, 1.3% Asian, 0.1% American Indian/Alaska Native, 0.0% Native Hawaiian/Other Pacific Islander, 1.5% Two or more races, 1.7% Hispanic of any race; Average household size: 2.12; Median age: 38.5; Age under 18: 18.8%; Age 65 and over: 15.8%; Males per 100 females: 90.1; Marriage status: 32.7% never married, 43.0% now married, 1.6% separated, 11.1% widowed, 13.1% divorced; Foreign born: 1.9%; Speak English only: 96.7%; With disability: 15.1%; Veterans: 5.8%; Ancestry: 39.0% German, 19.2% Irish, 10.5% English, 6.9% American, 3.3% Italian
Employment: 16.4% management, business, and financial, 5.1% computer, engineering, and science, 10.1% education, legal, community service, arts, and media, 5.6% healthcare practitioners, 17.1% service, 29.4% sales and office, 7.6% natural resources, construction, and maintenance, 8.7% production, transportation, and material moving
Income: Per capita: $27,203; Median household: $45,618; Average household: $58,361; Households with income of $100,000 or more: 11.4%; Poverty rate: 8.6%
Educational Attainment: High school diploma or higher: 88.3%; Bachelor's degree or higher: 29.0%; Graduate/professional degree or higher: 7.4%
Housing: Homeownership rate: 68.1%; Median home value: $124,700; Median year structure built: 1949; Homeowner vacancy rate: 2.4%; Median gross rent: $703 per month; Rental vacancy rate: 5.9%
Health Insurance: 90.7% have insurance; 73.8% have private insurance; 26.4% have public insurance; 9.3% do not have insurance; 1.8% of children under 18 do not have insurance
Safety: Violent crime rate: 14.0 per 10,000 population; Property crime rate: 156.3 per 10,000 population
Transportation: Commute: 94.8% car, 0.6% public transportation, 2.2% walk, 1.9% work from home; Median travel time to work: 18.8 minutes

DELHI HILLS (CDP). Covers a land area of 1.488 square miles and a water area of 0 square miles. Located at 39.09° N. Lat; 84.62° W. Long. Elevation is 873 feet.
Population: 5,259; Growth (since 2000): n/a; Density: 3,535.3 persons per square mile; Race: 96.7% White, 1.0% Black/African American, 0.9% Asian, 0.0% American Indian/Alaska Native, 0.0% Native Hawaiian/Other Pacific Islander, 1.1% Two or more races, 0.5% Hispanic of any race; Average household size: 2.94; Median age: 37.5; Age under 18: 25.9%; Age 65 and over: 10.5%; Males per 100 females: 97.3; Marriage status: 27.9% never married, 61.7% now married, 0.6% separated, 5.4% widowed, 5.1% divorced; Foreign born: 2.4%; Speak English only: 97.2%; With disability: 10.1%; Veterans: 8.6%; Ancestry: 54.9% German, 28.7% Irish, 8.9% English, 6.7% Italian, 6.4% American
Employment: 18.6% management, business, and financial, 3.6% computer, engineering, and science, 6.3% education, legal, community service, arts, and media, 5.6% healthcare practitioners, 9.8% service, 33.7% sales and office, 9.8% natural resources, construction, and maintenance, 12.6% production, transportation, and material moving
Income: Per capita: $30,619; Median household: $85,326; Average household: $87,617; Households with income of $100,000 or more: 35.6%; Poverty rate: 7.6%
Educational Attainment: High school diploma or higher: 93.2%; Bachelor's degree or higher: 24.0%; Graduate/professional degree or higher: 6.4%
Housing: Homeownership rate: 93.5%; Median home value: $138,000; Median year structure built: 1969; Homeowner vacancy rate: 1.2%; Median gross rent: $1,172 per month; Rental vacancy rate: 0.0%
Health Insurance: 93.8% have insurance; 82.2% have private insurance; 21.6% have public insurance; 6.2% do not have insurance; 4.5% of children under 18 do not have insurance
Transportation: Commute: 93.9% car, 1.5% public transportation, 1.5% walk, 3.2% work from home; Median travel time to work: 25.9 minutes

DELSHIRE (CDP). Covers a land area of 0.699 square miles and a water area of 0 square miles. Located at 39.09° N. Lat; 84.59° W. Long.
Population: 3,180; Growth (since 2000): n/a; Density: 4,549.9 persons per square mile; Race: 93.0% White, 2.9% Black/African American, 1.7% Asian, 0.2% American Indian/Alaska Native, 0.1% Native Hawaiian/Other Pacific Islander, 1.8% Two or more races, 0.9% Hispanic of any race; Average household size: 2.98; Median age: 33.5; Age under 18: 29.4%; Age 65 and over: 10.0%; Males per 100 females: 97.6; Marriage status: 30.4% never married, 51.9% now married, 0.3% separated, 4.6% widowed, 13.2% divorced; Foreign born: 1.6%; Speak English only: 94.6%; With disability: 11.0%; Veterans: 11.2%; Ancestry: 49.3% German, 16.2% Irish, 9.6% Italian, 7.8% American, 5.4% English
Employment: 8.3% management, business, and financial, 7.3% computer, engineering, and science, 9.8% education, legal, community service, arts, and media, 2.0% healthcare practitioners, 18.7% service, 30.2% sales and office, 11.0% natural resources, construction, and maintenance, 12.6% production, transportation, and material moving
Income: Per capita: $23,447; Median household: $65,980; Average household: $71,352; Households with income of $100,000 or more: 19.7%; Poverty rate: 4.8%
Educational Attainment: High school diploma or higher: 88.7%; Bachelor's degree or higher: 20.1%; Graduate/professional degree or higher: 5.7%
Housing: Homeownership rate: 75.5%; Median home value: $123,800; Median year structure built: 1968; Homeowner vacancy rate: 1.7%; Median gross rent: $714 per month; Rental vacancy rate: 17.4%
Health Insurance: 84.3% have insurance; 69.8% have private insurance; 21.7% have public insurance; 15.7% do not have insurance; 19.6% of children under 18 do not have insurance
Transportation: Commute: 91.0% car, 5.5% public transportation, 1.5% walk, 2.0% work from home; Median travel time to work: 27.0 minutes

DENT (CDP). Covers a land area of 5.930 square miles and a water area of 0 square miles. Located at 39.19° N. Lat; 84.66° W. Long. Elevation is 840 feet.
Population: 10,497; Growth (since 2000): 37.9%; Density: 1,770.2 persons per square mile; Race: 95.7% White, 1.3% Black/African

American, 1.6% Asian, 0.1% American Indian/Alaska Native, 0.0% Native Hawaiian/Other Pacific Islander, 1.0% Two or more races, 1.1% Hispanic of any race; Average household size: 2.39; Median age: 40.2; Age under 18: 23.0%; Age 65 and over: 15.7%; Males per 100 females: 91.9; Marriage status: 26.2% never married, 57.0% now married, 1.5% separated, 6.2% widowed, 10.6% divorced; Foreign born: 2.5%; Speak English only: 96.5%; With disability: 10.3%; Veterans: 8.9%; Ancestry: 53.8% German, 19.4% Irish, 11.8% Italian, 6.6% English, 6.3% American
Employment: 19.4% management, business, and financial, 5.8% computer, engineering, and science, 7.5% education, legal, community service, arts, and media, 6.8% healthcare practitioners, 13.0% service, 36.5% sales and office, 6.4% natural resources, construction, and maintenance, 4.6% production, transportation, and material moving
Income: Per capita: $33,694; Median household: $64,878; Average household: $78,409; Households with income of $100,000 or more: 28.6%; Poverty rate: 4.8%
Educational Attainment: High school diploma or higher: 92.9%; Bachelor's degree or higher: 35.0%; Graduate/professional degree or higher: 9.5%
Housing: Homeownership rate: 77.6%; Median home value: $188,000; Median year structure built: 1989; Homeowner vacancy rate: 3.6%; Median gross rent: $826 per month; Rental vacancy rate: 7.6%
Health Insurance: 96.6% have insurance; 88.4% have private insurance; 20.4% have public insurance; 3.4% do not have insurance; 1.1% of children under 18 do not have insurance
Transportation: Commute: 94.9% car, 1.1% public transportation, 1.3% walk, 2.7% work from home; Median travel time to work: 24.0 minutes

DILLONVALE (CDP). Covers a land area of 0.891 square miles and a water area of 0 square miles. Located at 39.22° N. Lat; 84.40° W. Long. Elevation is 784 feet.
Population: 3,474; Growth (since 2000): -6.5%; Density: 3,900.5 persons per square mile; Race: 94.0% White, 3.3% Black/African American, 0.8% Asian, 0.4% American Indian/Alaska Native, 0.0% Native Hawaiian/Other Pacific Islander, 1.2% Two or more races, 1.3% Hispanic of any race; Average household size: 2.21; Median age: 43.9; Age under 18: 19.2%; Age 65 and over: 18.9%; Males per 100 females: 92.3; Marriage status: 28.4% never married, 50.0% now married, 2.9% separated, 7.5% widowed, 14.2% divorced; Foreign born: 1.1%; Speak English only: 93.0%; With disability: 13.4%; Veterans: 7.6%; Ancestry: 37.9% German, 15.3% English, 15.1% Irish, 10.3% American, 7.1% Italian
Employment: 20.2% management, business, and financial, 3.7% computer, engineering, and science, 10.6% education, legal, community service, arts, and media, 2.1% healthcare practitioners, 18.1% service, 29.0% sales and office, 3.5% natural resources, construction, and maintenance, 12.9% production, transportation, and material moving
Income: Per capita: $28,374; Median household: $57,402; Average household: $68,935; Households with income of $100,000 or more: 18.4%; Poverty rate: 11.3%
Educational Attainment: High school diploma or higher: 94.6%; Bachelor's degree or higher: 23.9%; Graduate/professional degree or higher: 5.8%
Housing: Homeownership rate: 84.4%; Median home value: $135,400; Median year structure built: n/a; Homeowner vacancy rate: 1.7%; Median gross rent: $749 per month; Rental vacancy rate: 2.7%
Health Insurance: 85.8% have insurance; 76.7% have private insurance; 23.8% have public insurance; 14.2% do not have insurance; 9.3% of children under 18 do not have insurance
Transportation: Commute: 96.8% car, 1.3% public transportation, 0.0% walk, 0.8% work from home; Median travel time to work: 19.1 minutes

DRY RIDGE (CDP). Covers a land area of 4.141 square miles and a water area of 0 square miles. Located at 39.26° N. Lat; 84.63° W. Long. Elevation is 919 feet.
Population: 2,782; Growth (since 2000): n/a; Density: 671.9 persons per square mile; Race: 93.1% White, 4.2% Black/African American, 1.6% Asian, 0.0% American Indian/Alaska Native, 0.0% Native Hawaiian/Other Pacific Islander, 0.9% Two or more races, 1.8% Hispanic of any race; Average household size: 2.31; Median age: 47.1; Age under 18: 17.5%; Age 65 and over: 20.0%; Males per 100 females: 90.0; Marriage status: 19.5% never married, 65.9% now married, 0.6% separated, 8.9% widowed, 5.7% divorced; Foreign born: 4.0%; Speak English only: 90.4%; With disability: 12.1%; Veterans: 9.9%; Ancestry: 44.7% German, 9.6% Irish, 7.4% Italian, 6.3% English, 5.7% American
Employment: 18.7% management, business, and financial, 6.7% computer, engineering, and science, 11.7% education, legal, community service, arts, and media, 6.2% healthcare practitioners, 7.9% service, 32.4% sales and office, 7.5% natural resources, construction, and maintenance, 9.1% production, transportation, and material moving
Income: Per capita: $41,659; Median household: $70,213; Average household: $98,419; Households with income of $100,000 or more: 32.0%; Poverty rate: 1.2%
Educational Attainment: High school diploma or higher: 92.7%; Bachelor's degree or higher: 35.0%; Graduate/professional degree or higher: 16.8%
Housing: Homeownership rate: 93.0%; Median home value: $197,500; Median year structure built: 1991; Homeowner vacancy rate: 1.6%; Median gross rent: n/a per month; Rental vacancy rate: 1.2%
Health Insurance: 92.0% have insurance; 83.8% have private insurance; 24.0% have public insurance; 8.0% do not have insurance; 18.5% of children under 18 do not have insurance
Transportation: Commute: 97.1% car, 0.5% public transportation, 0.0% walk, 2.4% work from home; Median travel time to work: 23.6 minutes

DRY RUN (CDP). Covers a land area of 4.671 square miles and a water area of 0.009 square miles. Located at 39.10° N. Lat; 84.33° W. Long. Elevation is 860 feet.
History: Dry Run is a part of the village of Newtown, which was founded in 1792. The original fort, Fort Mercer, was settled near the current Jones Fish Hatchery on Church Street. It was originally called Mercersburg, named after early settler Captain Aaron Mercer.
Population: 7,281; Growth (since 2000): 11.1%; Density: 1,558.6 persons per square mile; Race: 93.8% White, 0.9% Black/African American, 3.2% Asian, 0.1% American Indian/Alaska Native, 0.0% Native Hawaiian/Other Pacific Islander, 1.7% Two or more races, 1.8% Hispanic of any race; Average household size: 3.13; Median age: 40.4; Age under 18: 32.1%; Age 65 and over: 8.7%; Males per 100 females: 99.5; Marriage status: 21.1% never married, 71.8% now married, 0.5% separated, 3.1% widowed, 3.9% divorced; Foreign born: 5.7%; Speak English only: 93.4%; With disability: 5.4%; Veterans: 6.5%; Ancestry: 39.3% German, 20.4% Irish, 13.5% English, 8.3% American, 7.4% Italian
Employment: 39.9% management, business, and financial, 5.1% computer, engineering, and science, 11.9% education, legal, community service, arts, and media, 9.0% healthcare practitioners, 9.2% service, 19.2% sales and office, 2.2% natural resources, construction, and maintenance, 3.5% production, transportation, and material moving
Income: Per capita: $50,672; Median household: $130,577; Average household: $160,690; Households with income of $100,000 or more: 66.2%; Poverty rate: 0.8%
Educational Attainment: High school diploma or higher: 98.4%; Bachelor's degree or higher: 72.5%; Graduate/professional degree or higher: 28.6%
Housing: Homeownership rate: 97.4%; Median home value: $296,300; Median year structure built: 1981; Homeowner vacancy rate: 1.5%; Median gross rent: $1,174 per month; Rental vacancy rate: 6.0%
Health Insurance: 95.6% have insurance; 92.0% have private insurance; 10.2% have public insurance; 4.4% do not have insurance; 2.8% of children under 18 do not have insurance
Transportation: Commute: 88.4% car, 2.6% public transportation, 0.4% walk, 8.6% work from home; Median travel time to work: 26.1 minutes

DUNLAP (CDP). Covers a land area of 6.533 square miles and a water area of 0.160 square miles. Located at 39.29° N. Lat; 84.64° W. Long. Elevation is 856 feet.
Population: 1,719; Growth (since 2000): n/a; Density: 263.1 persons per square mile; Race: 98.1% White, 0.7% Black/African American, 0.3% Asian, 0.0% American Indian/Alaska Native, 0.1% Native Hawaiian/Other Pacific Islander, 0.5% Two or more races, 0.6% Hispanic of any race; Average household size: 2.62; Median age: 48.8; Age under 18: 19.4%; Age 65 and over: 13.3%; Males per 100 females: 102.7
Housing: Homeownership rate: 95.4%; Homeowner vacancy rate: 0.6%; Rental vacancy rate: 9.1%

ELIZABETHTOWN (CDP). Covers a land area of 0.890 square miles and a water area of 0.014 square miles. Located at 39.16° N. Lat; 84.80° W. Long. Elevation is 492 feet.
Population: 350; Growth (since 2000): n/a; Density: 393.3 persons per square mile; Race: 98.6% White, 0.0% Black/African American, 0.0% Asian, 0.0% American Indian/Alaska Native, 0.0% Native Hawaiian/Other

Pacific Islander, 0.6% Two or more races, 2.6% Hispanic of any race; Average household size: 2.73; Median age: 32.1; Age under 18: 28.0%; Age 65 and over: 10.0%; Males per 100 females: 112.1
Housing: Homeownership rate: 60.9%; Homeowner vacancy rate: 0.0%; Rental vacancy rate: 18.0%

ELMWOOD PLACE (village). Covers a land area of 0.319 square miles and a water area of 0 square miles. Located at 39.19° N. Lat; 84.49° W. Long. Elevation is 525 feet.
History: Settled 1875, incorporated 1890.
Population: 2,188; Growth (since 2000): -18.4%; Density: 6,853.0 persons per square mile; Race: 79.1% White, 14.9% Black/African American, 0.7% Asian, 0.3% American Indian/Alaska Native, 0.5% Native Hawaiian/Other Pacific Islander, 3.6% Two or more races, 3.6% Hispanic of any race; Average household size: 2.51; Median age: 35.2; Age under 18: 26.6%; Age 65 and over: 9.6%; Males per 100 females: 103.0
Housing: Homeownership rate: 40.2%; Homeowner vacancy rate: 10.8%; Rental vacancy rate: 10.3%

EVENDALE (village). Covers a land area of 4.742 square miles and a water area of 0 square miles. Located at 39.25° N. Lat; 84.43° W. Long. Elevation is 594 feet.
Population: 2,767; Growth (since 2000): -10.5%; Density: 583.5 persons per square mile; Race: 88.0% White, 6.5% Black/African American, 4.3% Asian, 0.3% American Indian/Alaska Native, 0.0% Native Hawaiian/Other Pacific Islander, 0.6% Two or more races, 0.4% Hispanic of any race; Average household size: 2.60; Median age: 50.3; Age under 18: 20.6%; Age 65 and over: 19.6%; Males per 100 females: 97.5; Marriage status: 21.6% never married, 69.1% now married, 0.6% separated, 4.3% widowed, 5.0% divorced; Foreign born: 7.5%; Speak English only: 91.5%; With disability: 9.8%; Veterans: 9.6%; Ancestry: 31.2% German, 15.6% Irish, 11.5% English, 6.6% Italian, 5.2% American
Employment: 27.7% management, business, and financial, 6.2% computer, engineering, and science, 11.3% education, legal, community service, arts, and media, 6.7% healthcare practitioners, 13.7% service, 25.0% sales and office, 2.2% natural resources, construction, and maintenance, 7.2% production, transportation, and material moving
Income: Per capita: $51,563; Median household: $109,853; Average household: $136,066; Households with income of $100,000 or more: 54.0%; Poverty rate: 3.7%
Educational Attainment: High school diploma or higher: 94.3%; Bachelor's degree or higher: 57.6%; Graduate/professional degree or higher: 27.3%
Housing: Homeownership rate: 94.7%; Median home value: $260,900; Median year structure built: 1977; Homeowner vacancy rate: 0.9%; Median gross rent: $1,347 per month; Rental vacancy rate: 1.8%
Health Insurance: 98.4% have insurance; 91.8% have private insurance; 23.0% have public insurance; 1.6% do not have insurance; 0.0% of children under 18 do not have insurance
Safety: Violent crime rate: 29.0 per 10,000 population; Property crime rate: 1,317.9 per 10,000 population
Transportation: Commute: 92.7% car, 0.4% public transportation, 0.7% walk, 5.9% work from home; Median travel time to work: 20.1 minutes

FAIRFAX (village). Covers a land area of 0.763 square miles and a water area of 0 square miles. Located at 39.14° N. Lat; 84.40° W. Long. Elevation is 568 feet.
Population: 1,699; Growth (since 2000): -12.3%; Density: 2,228.0 persons per square mile; Race: 94.8% White, 2.4% Black/African American, 0.8% Asian, 0.3% American Indian/Alaska Native, 0.0% Native Hawaiian/Other Pacific Islander, 1.6% Two or more races, 1.3% Hispanic of any race; Average household size: 2.40; Median age: 37.7; Age under 18: 24.4%; Age 65 and over: 11.4%; Males per 100 females: 86.9
Housing: Homeownership rate: 77.2%; Homeowner vacancy rate: 3.3%; Rental vacancy rate: 6.9%
Safety: Violent crime rate: 5.9 per 10,000 population; Property crime rate: 1,412.5 per 10,000 population
Additional Information Contacts
Village of Fairfax . . . . (513) 527-6503
http://www.fairfaxohio.org

FINNEYTOWN (CDP). Covers a land area of 4.057 square miles and a water area of 0 square miles. Located at 39.22° N. Lat; 84.51° W. Long. Elevation is 889 feet.
Population: 12,741; Growth (since 2000): -5.6%; Density: 3,140.2 persons per square mile; Race: 61.7% White, 33.7% Black/African American, 1.4% Asian, 0.1% American Indian/Alaska Native, 0.1% Native Hawaiian/Other Pacific Islander, 2.3% Two or more races, 1.9% Hispanic of any race; Average household size: 2.53; Median age: 39.5; Age under 18: 25.8%; Age 65 and over: 16.2%; Males per 100 females: 87.1; Marriage status: 30.2% never married, 52.9% now married, 2.4% separated, 7.2% widowed, 9.7% divorced; Foreign born: 4.9%; Speak English only: 95.1%; With disability: 10.3%; Veterans: 11.0%; Ancestry: 29.6% German, 10.8% Irish, 8.4% English, 5.0% American, 3.7% Italian
Employment: 11.6% management, business, and financial, 6.4% computer, engineering, and science, 10.6% education, legal, community service, arts, and media, 6.2% healthcare practitioners, 19.0% service, 29.4% sales and office, 3.4% natural resources, construction, and maintenance, 13.5% production, transportation, and material moving
Income: Per capita: $26,299; Median household: $53,165; Average household: $64,486; Households with income of $100,000 or more: 19.9%; Poverty rate: 12.1%
Educational Attainment: High school diploma or higher: 92.3%; Bachelor's degree or higher: 31.6%; Graduate/professional degree or higher: 10.0%
Housing: Homeownership rate: 79.4%; Median home value: $128,300; Median year structure built: 1958; Homeowner vacancy rate: 2.3%; Median gross rent: $848 per month; Rental vacancy rate: 6.3%
Health Insurance: 91.8% have insurance; 67.8% have private insurance; 36.3% have public insurance; 8.2% do not have insurance; 4.9% of children under 18 do not have insurance
Transportation: Commute: 92.2% car, 1.9% public transportation, 2.3% walk, 2.6% work from home; Median travel time to work: 22.3 minutes

FOREST PARK (city). Covers a land area of 6.480 square miles and a water area of 0 square miles. Located at 39.29° N. Lat; 84.53° W. Long. Elevation is 833 feet.
Population: 18,720; Growth (since 2000): -3.8%; Density: 2,888.9 persons per square mile; Race: 24.9% White, 65.0% Black/African American, 2.2% Asian, 0.2% American Indian/Alaska Native, 0.2% Native Hawaiian/Other Pacific Islander, 3.6% Two or more races, 6.4% Hispanic of any race; Average household size: 2.59; Median age: 35.8; Age under 18: 26.9%; Age 65 and over: 11.7%; Males per 100 females: 86.6; Marriage status: 34.1% never married, 48.4% now married, 3.8% separated, 4.9% widowed, 12.5% divorced; Foreign born: 9.8%; Speak English only: 88.2%; With disability: 12.7%; Veterans: 10.0%; Ancestry: 8.6% German, 5.2% Irish, 3.9% Other Subsaharan African, 2.5% English, 1.7% American
Employment: 8.9% management, business, and financial, 3.6% computer, engineering, and science, 8.8% education, legal, community service, arts, and media, 5.4% healthcare practitioners, 20.9% service, 26.7% sales and office, 5.8% natural resources, construction, and maintenance, 19.9% production, transportation, and material moving
Income: Per capita: $22,367; Median household: $46,949; Average household: $56,240; Households with income of $100,000 or more: 12.5%; Poverty rate: 17.2%
Educational Attainment: High school diploma or higher: 87.7%; Bachelor's degree or higher: 24.4%; Graduate/professional degree or higher: 8.0%
Housing: Homeownership rate: 59.3%; Median home value: $110,800; Median year structure built: 1971; Homeowner vacancy rate: 2.9%; Median gross rent: $900 per month; Rental vacancy rate: 11.1%
Health Insurance: 81.8% have insurance; 63.0% have private insurance; 29.7% have public insurance; 18.2% do not have insurance; 9.2% of children under 18 do not have insurance
Safety: Violent crime rate: 16.1 per 10,000 population; Property crime rate: 250.6 per 10,000 population
Transportation: Commute: 93.3% car, 2.6% public transportation, 0.6% walk, 3.0% work from home; Median travel time to work: 24.4 minutes
Additional Information Contacts
City of Forest Park. . . . . (513) 595-5200
http://www.forestpark.org

FORESTVILLE (CDP). Covers a land area of 3.724 square miles and a water area of <.001 square miles. Located at 39.07° N. Lat; 84.34° W. Long. Elevation is 820 feet.
Population: 10,532; Growth (since 2000): -4.1%; Density: 2,827.8 persons per square mile; Race: 93.4% White, 1.4% Black/African American, 2.5% Asian, 0.1% American Indian/Alaska Native, 0.1% Native Hawaiian/Other Pacific Islander, 2.0% Two or more races, 1.5% Hispanic of any race; Average household size: 2.43; Median age: 42.0; Age under 18: 25.1%; Age 65 and over: 17.5%; Males per 100 females: 86.1; Marriage status: 20.5% never married, 58.8% now married, 1.1% separated, 10.2% widowed, 10.5% divorced; Foreign born: 4.9%; Speak English only: 93.0%; With disability: 13.3%; Veterans: 10.9%; Ancestry: 34.7% German, 20.7% Irish, 17.0% American, 11.8% English, 5.5% Italian
Employment: 21.0% management, business, and financial, 5.0% computer, engineering, and science, 19.2% education, legal, community service, arts, and media, 5.6% healthcare practitioners, 14.1% service, 25.6% sales and office, 4.2% natural resources, construction, and maintenance, 5.2% production, transportation, and material moving
Income: Per capita: $33,853; Median household: $64,250; Average household: $79,987; Households with income of $100,000 or more: 31.5%; Poverty rate: 7.5%
Educational Attainment: High school diploma or higher: 94.8%; Bachelor's degree or higher: 49.5%; Graduate/professional degree or higher: 19.8%
Housing: Homeownership rate: 72.8%; Median home value: $207,600; Median year structure built: 1979; Homeowner vacancy rate: 2.0%; Median gross rent: $907 per month; Rental vacancy rate: 9.0%
Health Insurance: 95.3% have insurance; 83.7% have private insurance; 27.8% have public insurance; 4.7% do not have insurance; 1.9% of children under 18 do not have insurance
Transportation: Commute: 90.0% car, 3.2% public transportation, 2.6% walk, 4.1% work from home; Median travel time to work: 25.0 minutes

FRUIT HILL (CDP). Covers a land area of 1.275 square miles and a water area of 0 square miles. Located at 39.07° N. Lat; 84.37° W. Long. Elevation is 732 feet.
Population: 3,755; Growth (since 2000): -4.8%; Density: 2,944.3 persons per square mile; Race: 96.1% White, 1.5% Black/African American, 1.0% Asian, 0.1% American Indian/Alaska Native, 0.1% Native Hawaiian/Other Pacific Islander, 1.0% Two or more races, 1.2% Hispanic of any race; Average household size: 2.65; Median age: 41.0; Age under 18: 25.9%; Age 65 and over: 15.7%; Males per 100 females: 91.4; Marriage status: 20.1% never married, 60.4% now married, 0.6% separated, 7.0% widowed, 12.5% divorced; Foreign born: 6.1%; Speak English only: 94.1%; With disability: 12.0%; Veterans: 16.4%; Ancestry: 39.4% German, 23.9% Irish, 18.3% American, 12.1% English, 7.4% Italian
Employment: 23.8% management, business, and financial, 3.1% computer, engineering, and science, 17.5% education, legal, community service, arts, and media, 5.5% healthcare practitioners, 20.0% service, 21.1% sales and office, 2.0% natural resources, construction, and maintenance, 7.2% production, transportation, and material moving
Income: Per capita: $38,309; Median household: $75,469; Average household: $97,262; Households with income of $100,000 or more: 33.1%; Poverty rate: 10.2%
Educational Attainment: High school diploma or higher: 96.6%; Bachelor's degree or higher: 40.4%; Graduate/professional degree or higher: 13.3%
Housing: Homeownership rate: 87.6%; Median home value: $164,300; Median year structure built: 1967; Homeowner vacancy rate: 1.6%; Median gross rent: $985 per month; Rental vacancy rate: 1.2%
Health Insurance: 96.0% have insurance; 82.8% have private insurance; 27.1% have public insurance; 4.0% do not have insurance; 2.5% of children under 18 do not have insurance
Transportation: Commute: 88.4% car, 0.0% public transportation, 4.9% walk, 6.1% work from home; Median travel time to work: 20.4 minutes

GLENDALE (village). Covers a land area of 1.686 square miles and a water area of 0 square miles. Located at 39.27° N. Lat; 84.46° W. Long. Elevation is 633 feet.
History: Incorporated 1855.
Population: 2,155; Growth (since 2000): -1.5%; Density: 1,278.2 persons per square mile; Race: 81.4% White, 15.4% Black/African American, 1.5% Asian, 0.0% American Indian/Alaska Native, 0.0% Native Hawaiian/Other Pacific Islander, 1.3% Two or more races, 1.3% Hispanic of any race; Average household size: 2.20; Median age: 49.6; Age under 18: 19.6%; Age 65 and over: 20.1%; Males per 100 females: 94.0
Housing: Homeownership rate: 84.4%; Homeowner vacancy rate: 4.0%; Rental vacancy rate: 11.5%
Additional Information Contacts
Village of Glendale . . . . (513) 771-7200
http://www.glendaleohio.org

GOLF MANOR (village). Covers a land area of 0.575 square miles and a water area of 0 square miles. Located at 39.19° N. Lat; 84.45° W. Long. Elevation is 663 feet.
History: Incorporated 1947.
Population: 3,611; Growth (since 2000): -9.7%; Density: 6,275.5 persons per square mile; Race: 24.3% White, 72.6% Black/African American, 0.2% Asian, 0.1% American Indian/Alaska Native, 0.0% Native Hawaiian/Other Pacific Islander, 2.3% Two or more races, 1.2% Hispanic of any race; Average household size: 2.24; Median age: 38.1; Age under 18: 26.1%; Age 65 and over: 12.7%; Males per 100 females: 80.5; Marriage status: 36.6% never married, 32.8% now married, 2.5% separated, 7.3% widowed, 23.2% divorced; Foreign born: 4.4%; Speak English only: 95.4%; With disability: 12.2%; Veterans: 7.7%; Ancestry: 6.3% German, 5.6% Italian, 5.4% Armenian, 2.4% Russian, 2.4% English
Employment: 10.4% management, business, and financial, 1.8% computer, engineering, and science, 9.9% education, legal, community service, arts, and media, 5.1% healthcare practitioners, 26.9% service, 27.7% sales and office, 2.2% natural resources, construction, and maintenance, 15.9% production, transportation, and material moving
Income: Per capita: $19,203; Median household: $35,191; Average household: $41,404; Households with income of $100,000 or more: 2.1%; Poverty rate: 21.6%
Educational Attainment: High school diploma or higher: 89.2%; Bachelor's degree or higher: 25.0%; Graduate/professional degree or higher: 4.9%
Housing: Homeownership rate: 54.3%; Median home value: $93,800; Median year structure built: 1953; Homeowner vacancy rate: 4.2%; Median gross rent: $689 per month; Rental vacancy rate: 14.5%
Health Insurance: 91.5% have insurance; 60.5% have private insurance; 38.7% have public insurance; 8.5% do not have insurance; 1.1% of children under 18 do not have insurance
Transportation: Commute: 92.6% car, 3.3% public transportation, 2.4% walk, 0.7% work from home; Median travel time to work: 19.7 minutes
Additional Information Contacts
Village of Golf Manor. . . . . (513) 531-7418
http://www.golfmanor.org

GRANDVIEW (CDP). Covers a land area of 4.349 square miles and a water area of 0.309 square miles. Located at 39.20° N. Lat; 84.72° W. Long. Elevation is 646 feet.
Population: 1,466; Growth (since 2000): 5.4%; Density: 337.1 persons per square mile; Race: 98.0% White, 0.5% Black/African American, 0.2% Asian, 0.1% American Indian/Alaska Native, 0.1% Native Hawaiian/Other Pacific Islander, 0.9% Two or more races, 0.1% Hispanic of any race; Average household size: 2.85; Median age: 37.7; Age under 18: 25.7%; Age 65 and over: 10.1%; Males per 100 females: 105.0
Housing: Homeownership rate: 79.4%; Homeowner vacancy rate: 2.2%; Rental vacancy rate: 7.8%

GREENHILLS (village). Covers a land area of 1.246 square miles and a water area of 0 square miles. Located at 39.27° N. Lat; 84.52° W. Long. Elevation is 804 feet.
History: Greenhills was completed in 1937 as a Resettlement Administration project to provide housing.
Population: 3,615; Growth (since 2000): -11.9%; Density: 2,901.9 persons per square mile; Race: 88.0% White, 6.7% Black/African American, 0.8% Asian, 0.1% American Indian/Alaska Native, 0.1% Native Hawaiian/Other Pacific Islander, 3.6% Two or more races, 2.4% Hispanic of any race; Average household size: 2.37; Median age: 39.0; Age under 18: 23.8%; Age 65 and over: 16.0%; Males per 100 females: 89.4; Marriage status: 26.1% never married, 58.2% now married, 0.4% separated, 5.4% widowed, 10.3% divorced; Foreign born: 2.0%; Speak English only: 94.8%; With disability: 8.7%; Veterans: 7.9%; Ancestry: 33.3% German, 24.9% Irish, 8.1% English, 4.1% American, 3.1% French
Employment: 15.9% management, business, and financial, 5.4% computer, engineering, and science, 18.5% education, legal, community service, arts, and media, 3.6% healthcare practitioners, 15.4% service,

24.3% sales and office, 10.8% natural resources, construction, and maintenance, 6.2% production, transportation, and material moving
Income: Per capita: $26,930; Median household: $54,214; Average household: $67,016; Households with income of $100,000 or more: 14.3%; Poverty rate: 9.9%
Educational Attainment: High school diploma or higher: 91.9%; Bachelor's degree or higher: 36.7%; Graduate/professional degree or higher: 13.7%
Housing: Homeownership rate: 71.7%; Median home value: $121,700; Median year structure built: 1956; Homeowner vacancy rate: 3.1%; Median gross rent: $741 per month; Rental vacancy rate: 12.3%
Health Insurance: 86.6% have insurance; 71.0% have private insurance; 26.3% have public insurance; 13.4% do not have insurance; 1.6% of children under 18 do not have insurance
Safety: Violent crime rate: 2.8 per 10,000 population; Property crime rate: 100.3 per 10,000 population
Transportation: Commute: 92.4% car, 3.0% public transportation, 0.5% walk, 4.1% work from home; Median travel time to work: 21.2 minutes
Additional Information Contacts
Village of Greenhills . . . . (513) 825-2100
http://www.greenhillsohio.org

GROESBECK (CDP). Covers a land area of 2.945 square miles and a water area of 0 square miles. Located at 39.23° N. Lat; 84.60° W. Long. Elevation is 863 feet.
Population: 6,788; Growth (since 2000): -5.7%; Density: 2,305.1 persons per square mile; Race: 84.5% White, 11.7% Black/African American, 0.7% Asian, 0.1% American Indian/Alaska Native, 0.0% Native Hawaiian/Other Pacific Islander, 2.5% Two or more races, 1.4% Hispanic of any race; Average household size: 2.50; Median age: 38.9; Age under 18: 24.4%; Age 65 and over: 14.6%; Males per 100 females: 96.0; Marriage status: 27.5% never married, 54.8% now married, 1.7% separated, 7.2% widowed, 10.5% divorced; Foreign born: 3.6%; Speak English only: 96.4%; With disability: 12.8%; Veterans: 9.7%; Ancestry: 39.7% German, 13.8% Irish, 7.9% English, 6.0% American, 5.1% Italian
Employment: 15.6% management, business, and financial, 4.2% computer, engineering, and science, 6.5% education, legal, community service, arts, and media, 3.6% healthcare practitioners, 16.4% service, 31.6% sales and office, 8.4% natural resources, construction, and maintenance, 13.8% production, transportation, and material moving
Income: Per capita: $23,396; Median household: $48,233; Average household: $60,533; Households with income of $100,000 or more: 17.2%; Poverty rate: 11.6%
Educational Attainment: High school diploma or higher: 83.8%; Bachelor's degree or higher: 17.9%; Graduate/professional degree or higher: 4.8%
Housing: Homeownership rate: 81.0%; Median home value: $119,000; Median year structure built: 1966; Homeowner vacancy rate: 2.4%; Median gross rent: $792 per month; Rental vacancy rate: 11.8%
Health Insurance: 87.0% have insurance; 66.6% have private insurance; 31.0% have public insurance; 13.0% do not have insurance; 3.5% of children under 18 do not have insurance
Transportation: Commute: 91.3% car, 1.1% public transportation, 2.3% walk, 3.8% work from home; Median travel time to work: 23.0 minutes

HARRISON (city). Covers a land area of 4.921 square miles and a water area of 0.038 square miles. Located at 39.26° N. Lat; 84.79° W. Long. Elevation is 522 feet.
History: Harrison was settled before 1800, and the town was laid out in 1813 on the Ohio-Indiana border. It was named for William Henry Harrison.
Population: 9,897; Growth (since 2000): 32.2%; Density: 2,011.1 persons per square mile; Race: 97.6% White, 0.3% Black/African American, 0.6% Asian, 0.2% American Indian/Alaska Native, 0.0% Native Hawaiian/Other Pacific Islander, 0.8% Two or more races, 1.1% Hispanic of any race; Average household size: 2.63; Median age: 34.7; Age under 18: 26.2%; Age 65 and over: 11.3%; Males per 100 females: 94.9; Marriage status: 29.1% never married, 55.5% now married, 1.5% separated, 3.8% widowed, 11.5% divorced; Foreign born: 0.4%; Speak English only: 97.8%; With disability: 8.4%; Veterans: 13.1%; Ancestry: 57.3% German, 21.8% Irish, 9.4% English, 7.9% American, 4.8% French
Employment: 13.4% management, business, and financial, 3.1% computer, engineering, and science, 7.3% education, legal, community service, arts, and media, 7.2% healthcare practitioners, 17.8% service, 30.1% sales and office, 8.5% natural resources, construction, and maintenance, 12.6% production, transportation, and material moving
Income: Per capita: $25,557; Median household: $62,569; Average household: $71,433; Households with income of $100,000 or more: 27.1%; Poverty rate: 5.9%
Educational Attainment: High school diploma or higher: 91.9%; Bachelor's degree or higher: 22.5%; Graduate/professional degree or higher: 6.4%

School District(s)

Southwest Local (PK-12)
2012-13 Enrollment: 3,441 . . . . (513) 367-4139
Housing: Homeownership rate: 70.7%; Median home value: $147,500; Median year structure built: 1985; Homeowner vacancy rate: 2.2%; Median gross rent: $830 per month; Rental vacancy rate: 12.0%
Health Insurance: 93.9% have insurance; 80.3% have private insurance; 22.4% have public insurance; 6.1% do not have insurance; 3.2% of children under 18 do not have insurance
Safety: Violent crime rate: 3.0 per 10,000 population; Property crime rate: 241.2 per 10,000 population
Newspapers: Harrison Press (weekly circulation 5400)
Transportation: Commute: 94.5% car, 1.4% public transportation, 1.1% walk, 2.6% work from home; Median travel time to work: 25.6 minutes
Additional Information Contacts
City of Harrison . . . . (513) 367-2111
http://www.harrisonoh.org

HIGHPOINT (CDP). Covers a land area of 0.344 square miles and a water area of 0 square miles. Located at 39.29° N. Lat; 84.35° W. Long. Elevation is 873 feet.
Population: 1,503; Growth (since 2000): n/a; Density: 4,366.2 persons per square mile; Race: 85.8% White, 4.7% Black/African American, 2.9% Asian, 0.2% American Indian/Alaska Native, 1.1% Native Hawaiian/Other Pacific Islander, 2.9% Two or more races, 4.3% Hispanic of any race; Average household size: 2.60; Median age: 35.9; Age under 18: 24.7%; Age 65 and over: 8.8%; Males per 100 females: 96.5
Housing: Homeownership rate: 84.1%; Homeowner vacancy rate: 2.0%; Rental vacancy rate: 6.1%

HOOVEN (CDP). Covers a land area of 2.566 square miles and a water area of 0.078 square miles. Located at 39.18° N. Lat; 84.77° W. Long. Elevation is 502 feet.
Population: 534; Growth (since 2000): n/a; Density: 208.1 persons per square mile; Race: 92.7% White, 1.1% Black/African American, 0.0% Asian, 1.9% American Indian/Alaska Native, 0.0% Native Hawaiian/Other Pacific Islander, 2.4% Two or more races, 5.2% Hispanic of any race; Average household size: 2.77; Median age: 38.8; Age under 18: 25.8%; Age 65 and over: 14.4%; Males per 100 females: 117.1
Housing: Homeownership rate: 69.4%; Homeowner vacancy rate: 1.5%; Rental vacancy rate: 10.3%

KENWOOD (CDP). Covers a land area of 2.304 square miles and a water area of <.001 square miles. Located at 39.21° N. Lat; 84.38° W. Long. Elevation is 801 feet.
History: Sycamore Township remained virtually unnoticed until after World War II when developers moved in to build subdivisions known as Kenwood and Dillionvale and the township's population grew from only a few thousand to well over 20,000 in just a few short years. Kenwood stands as the commercial district, the "downtown" of Sycamore township.
Population: 6,981; Growth (since 2000): -6.0%; Density: 3,030.6 persons per square mile; Race: 84.1% White, 6.9% Black/African American, 6.6% Asian, 0.1% American Indian/Alaska Native, 0.1% Native Hawaiian/Other Pacific Islander, 1.9% Two or more races, 2.8% Hispanic of any race; Average household size: 2.16; Median age: 46.3; Age under 18: 21.8%; Age 65 and over: 24.2%; Males per 100 females: 84.1; Marriage status: 18.0% never married, 58.4% now married, 1.5% separated, 13.1% widowed, 10.5% divorced; Foreign born: 11.8%; Speak English only: 85.0%; With disability: 13.3%; Veterans: 8.4%; Ancestry: 35.3% German, 17.6% Irish, 8.7% English, 7.2% American, 4.4% Italian
Employment: 20.2% management, business, and financial, 5.0% computer, engineering, and science, 17.5% education, legal, community service, arts, and media, 16.1% healthcare practitioners, 7.5% service, 28.2% sales and office, 2.5% natural resources, construction, and maintenance, 3.1% production, transportation, and material moving

Income: Per capita: $43,658; Median household: $69,231; Average household: $96,663; Households with income of $100,000 or more: 34.3%; Poverty rate: 5.4%
Educational Attainment: High school diploma or higher: 95.6%; Bachelor's degree or higher: 59.4%; Graduate/professional degree or higher: 31.5%
Housing: Homeownership rate: 59.1%; Median home value: $247,300; Median year structure built: 1967; Homeowner vacancy rate: 2.1%; Median gross rent: $1,299 per month; Rental vacancy rate: 14.6%
Health Insurance: 96.2% have insurance; 82.6% have private insurance; 30.9% have public insurance; 3.8% do not have insurance; 0.7% of children under 18 do not have insurance
Transportation: Commute: 88.0% car, 2.3% public transportation, 1.3% walk, 7.0% work from home; Median travel time to work: 19.9 minutes

LINCOLN HEIGHTS (village). Covers a land area of 0.757 square miles and a water area of 0 square miles. Located at 39.24° N. Lat; 84.46° W. Long. Elevation is 597 feet.
History: Incorporated 1946.
Population: 3,286; Growth (since 2000): -20.1%; Density: 4,343.5 persons per square mile; Race: 1.7% White, 95.5% Black/African American, 0.0% Asian, 0.3% American Indian/Alaska Native, 0.2% Native Hawaiian/Other Pacific Islander, 2.0% Two or more races, 0.5% Hispanic of any race; Average household size: 2.55; Median age: 31.9; Age under 18: 30.6%; Age 65 and over: 12.2%; Males per 100 females: 76.3; Marriage status: 49.4% never married, 28.5% now married, 4.0% separated, 8.5% widowed, 13.6% divorced; Foreign born: 0.8%; Speak English only: 97.2%; With disability: 14.2%; Veterans: 4.8%; Ancestry: 1.6% German, 1.2% American, 0.4% African, 0.2% English
Employment: 2.9% management, business, and financial, 0.0% computer, engineering, and science, 1.6% education, legal, community service, arts, and media, 0.4% healthcare practitioners, 38.3% service, 29.7% sales and office, 4.0% natural resources, construction, and maintenance, 23.1% production, transportation, and material moving
Income: Per capita: $15,634; Median household: $25,568; Average household: $36,753; Households with income of $100,000 or more: 7.2%; Poverty rate: 32.8%
Educational Attainment: High school diploma or higher: 75.9%; Bachelor's degree or higher: 4.8%; Graduate/professional degree or higher: 2.1%
Housing: Homeownership rate: 35.6%; Median home value: $82,600; Median year structure built: 1962; Homeowner vacancy rate: 1.9%; Median gross rent: $627 per month; Rental vacancy rate: 8.3%
Health Insurance: 74.1% have insurance; 37.8% have private insurance; 42.5% have public insurance; 25.9% do not have insurance; 16.4% of children under 18 do not have insurance
Transportation: Commute: 88.7% car, 1.5% public transportation, 1.2% walk, 7.0% work from home; Median travel time to work: 17.2 minutes

LOCKLAND (village). Covers a land area of 1.231 square miles and a water area of 0 square miles. Located at 39.23° N. Lat; 84.46° W. Long. Elevation is 581 feet.
History: Plotted 1828, incorporated 1865.
Population: 3,449; Growth (since 2000): -7.0%; Density: 2,801.5 persons per square mile; Race: 64.5% White, 29.9% Black/African American, 0.2% Asian, 0.2% American Indian/Alaska Native, 0.1% Native Hawaiian/Other Pacific Islander, 3.4% Two or more races, 4.2% Hispanic of any race; Average household size: 2.36; Median age: 35.7; Age under 18: 23.8%; Age 65 and over: 10.4%; Males per 100 females: 105.5; Marriage status: 42.4% never married, 37.6% now married, 3.4% separated, 6.3% widowed, 13.7% divorced; Foreign born: 18.9%; Speak English only: 77.4%; With disability: 9.8%; Veterans: 7.1%; Ancestry: 16.0% German, 8.5% Irish, 6.9% American, 5.2% English, 4.4% Nigerian
Employment: 8.1% management, business, and financial, 0.7% computer, engineering, and science, 0.9% education, legal, community service, arts, and media, 3.0% healthcare practitioners, 26.1% service, 22.7% sales and office, 9.5% natural resources, construction, and maintenance, 29.0% production, transportation, and material moving
Income: Per capita: $15,782; Median household: $33,163; Average household: $39,855; Households with income of $100,000 or more: 5.0%; Poverty rate: 33.6%
Educational Attainment: High school diploma or higher: 69.4%; Bachelor's degree or higher: 7.5%; Graduate/professional degree or higher: 2.2%

School District(s)

Lockland Local (PK-12)
2012-13 Enrollment: 580 . . . . (513) 563-5000
Housing: Homeownership rate: 43.7%; Median home value: $88,500; Median year structure built: 1946; Homeowner vacancy rate: 4.0%; Median gross rent: $594 per month; Rental vacancy rate: 16.4%
Health Insurance: 71.0% have insurance; 46.8% have private insurance; 31.9% have public insurance; 29.0% do not have insurance; 7.3% of children under 18 do not have insurance
Safety: Violent crime rate: 61.3 per 10,000 population; Property crime rate: 467.0 per 10,000 population
Transportation: Commute: 85.8% car, 3.1% public transportation, 5.8% walk, 3.2% work from home; Median travel time to work: 23.4 minutes
Additional Information Contacts
Village of Lockland . . . . (513) 761-1124
http://www.lockland.com

LOVELAND (city). Covers a land area of 4.927 square miles and a water area of 0.074 square miles. Located at 39.27° N. Lat; 84.27° W. Long. Elevation is 600 feet.
Population: 12,081; Growth (since 2000): 3.5%; Density: 2,452.0 persons per square mile; Race: 93.5% White, 2.1% Black/African American, 1.7% Asian, 0.1% American Indian/Alaska Native, 0.1% Native Hawaiian/Other Pacific Islander, 1.9% Two or more races, 2.4% Hispanic of any race; Average household size: 2.55; Median age: 38.0; Age under 18: 27.9%; Age 65 and over: 12.8%; Males per 100 females: 91.8; Marriage status: 26.1% never married, 50.8% now married, 0.6% separated, 8.9% widowed, 14.2% divorced; Foreign born: 4.8%; Speak English only: 92.2%; With disability: 8.6%; Veterans: 8.4%; Ancestry: 37.3% German, 13.8% Irish, 13.7% English, 11.7% American, 4.6% Italian
Employment: 18.3% management, business, and financial, 8.3% computer, engineering, and science, 12.9% education, legal, community service, arts, and media, 6.3% healthcare practitioners, 11.9% service, 27.4% sales and office, 5.8% natural resources, construction, and maintenance, 9.1% production, transportation, and material moving
Income: Per capita: $34,896; Median household: $74,020; Average household: $90,053; Households with income of $100,000 or more: 37.4%; Poverty rate: 8.0%
Educational Attainment: High school diploma or higher: 94.0%; Bachelor's degree or higher: 43.3%; Graduate/professional degree or higher: 15.7%

School District(s)

Loveland City (PK-12)
2012-13 Enrollment: 4,687 . . . . (513) 683-5600
Milford Exempted Village (PK-12)
2012-13 Enrollment: 6,452 . . . . (513) 831-1314
Sycamore Community City (PK-12)
2012-13 Enrollment: 5,298 . . . . (513) 686-1700
Housing: Homeownership rate: 73.3%; Median home value: $167,300; Median year structure built: 1977; Homeowner vacancy rate: 1.8%; Median gross rent: $862 per month; Rental vacancy rate: 7.0%
Health Insurance: 94.0% have insurance; 80.9% have private insurance; 23.7% have public insurance; 6.0% do not have insurance; 2.2% of children under 18 do not have insurance
Safety: Violent crime rate: 5.7 per 10,000 population; Property crime rate: 103.0 per 10,000 population
Newspapers: Community Press (weekly circulation 113000)
Transportation: Commute: 92.4% car, 0.0% public transportation, 1.5% walk, 5.1% work from home; Median travel time to work: 23.4 minutes
Additional Information Contacts
City of Loveland. . . . . (513) 683-0150
http://www.lovelandoh.com

MACK (CDP). Covers a land area of 9.273 square miles and a water area of 0 square miles. Located at 39.15° N. Lat; 84.68° W. Long. Elevation is 906 feet.
Population: 11,585; Growth (since 2000): n/a; Density: 1,249.4 persons per square mile; Race: 98.2% White, 0.4% Black/African American, 0.4% Asian, 0.1% American Indian/Alaska Native, 0.0% Native Hawaiian/Other Pacific Islander, 0.7% Two or more races, 0.6% Hispanic of any race; Average household size: 2.87; Median age: 44.4; Age under 18: 24.6%; Age 65 and over: 13.8%; Males per 100 females: 100.1; Marriage status: 23.9% never married, 65.6% now married, 0.1% separated, 5.0% widowed, 5.5% divorced; Foreign born: 1.9%; Speak English only: 97.3%;

With disability: 11.1%; Veterans: 8.3%; Ancestry: 54.1% German, 24.1% Irish, 9.2% English, 8.2% American, 7.6% Italian
Employment: 21.8% management, business, and financial, 6.6% computer, engineering, and science, 8.1% education, legal, community service, arts, and media, 9.1% healthcare practitioners, 13.2% service, 26.1% sales and office, 5.6% natural resources, construction, and maintenance, 9.7% production, transportation, and material moving
Income: Per capita: $37,896; Median household: $83,861; Average household: $106,386; Households with income of $100,000 or more: 43.8%; Poverty rate: 3.9%
Educational Attainment: High school diploma or higher: 94.0%; Bachelor's degree or higher: 35.0%; Graduate/professional degree or higher: 10.6%
Housing: Homeownership rate: 96.4%; Median home value: $209,800; Median year structure built: 1976; Homeowner vacancy rate: 0.9%; Median gross rent: $1,348 per month; Rental vacancy rate: 2.6%
Health Insurance: 95.9% have insurance; 86.9% have private insurance; 21.3% have public insurance; 4.1% do not have insurance; 1.9% of children under 18 do not have insurance
Transportation: Commute: 91.7% car, 0.6% public transportation, 0.4% walk, 6.6% work from home; Median travel time to work: 28.2 minutes

MADEIRA (city). Covers a land area of 3.377 square miles and a water area of 0.003 square miles. Located at 39.19° N. Lat; 84.37° W. Long. Elevation is 764 feet.
Population: 8,726; Growth (since 2000): -2.2%; Density: 2,584.0 persons per square mile; Race: 93.0% White, 2.5% Black/African American, 2.8% Asian, 0.1% American Indian/Alaska Native, 0.0% Native Hawaiian/Other Pacific Islander, 1.2% Two or more races, 2.3% Hispanic of any race; Average household size: 2.58; Median age: 42.9; Age under 18: 25.6%; Age 65 and over: 16.0%; Males per 100 females: 92.8; Marriage status: 19.7% never married, 64.2% now married, 0.7% separated, 6.8% widowed, 9.3% divorced; Foreign born: 6.9%; Speak English only: 92.4%; With disability: 5.3%; Veterans: 8.1%; Ancestry: 42.7% German, 17.7% Irish, 10.0% English, 9.7% Italian, 5.9% American
Employment: 26.1% management, business, and financial, 7.3% computer, engineering, and science, 15.2% education, legal, community service, arts, and media, 6.7% healthcare practitioners, 10.3% service, 23.0% sales and office, 5.4% natural resources, construction, and maintenance, 6.1% production, transportation, and material moving
Income: Per capita: $38,941; Median household: $87,750; Average household: $102,721; Households with income of $100,000 or more: 42.2%; Poverty rate: 3.6%
Educational Attainment: High school diploma or higher: 95.6%; Bachelor's degree or higher: 56.6%; Graduate/professional degree or higher: 23.4%

School District(s)

Madeira City (PK-12)
2012-13 Enrollment: 1,446 . . . . (513) 985-6070
Housing: Homeownership rate: 89.5%; Median home value: $223,300; Median year structure built: 1956; Homeowner vacancy rate: 2.9%; Median gross rent: $794 per month; Rental vacancy rate: 9.9%
Health Insurance: 93.8% have insurance; 86.2% have private insurance; 18.3% have public insurance; 6.2% do not have insurance; 2.4% of children under 18 do not have insurance
Safety: Violent crime rate: 0.0 per 10,000 population; Property crime rate: 36.2 per 10,000 population
Transportation: Commute: 89.9% car, 2.0% public transportation, 1.6% walk, 6.2% work from home; Median travel time to work: 20.1 minutes
Additional Information Contacts
City of Madeira . . . . (513) 561-7228
http://www.madeiracity.com

MARIEMONT (village). Covers a land area of 0.864 square miles and a water area of 0.029 square miles. Located at 39.14° N. Lat; 84.38° W. Long. Elevation is 584 feet.
History: Mariemont was laid out in 1922 along the Little Miami River on land owned by Marie Emery of Cincinnati. A large stone tower on a knoll above the town housed the Bells of Mariemont, 23 bells weighing from 100 pounds to two tons.
Population: 3,403; Growth (since 2000): -0.1%; Density: 3,939.0 persons per square mile; Race: 94.7% White, 1.6% Black/African American, 1.3% Asian, 0.2% American Indian/Alaska Native, 0.1% Native Hawaiian/Other Pacific Islander, 1.7% Two or more races, 1.6% Hispanic of any race; Average household size: 2.34; Median age: 36.6; Age under 18: 28.2%; Age 65 and over: 12.9%; Males per 100 females: 82.5; Marriage status: 23.7% never married, 60.0% now married, 1.3% separated, 7.3% widowed, 9.1% divorced; Foreign born: 1.7%; Speak English only: 98.6%; With disability: 7.2%; Veterans: 5.9%; Ancestry: 31.4% German, 19.1% English, 18.2% Irish, 7.0% American, 5.3% European
Employment: 22.7% management, business, and financial, 9.0% computer, engineering, and science, 18.8% education, legal, community service, arts, and media, 7.5% healthcare practitioners, 10.0% service, 25.6% sales and office, 1.3% natural resources, construction, and maintenance, 5.1% production, transportation, and material moving
Income: Per capita: $47,308; Median household: $84,740; Average household: $121,525; Households with income of $100,000 or more: 39.1%; Poverty rate: 3.8%
Educational Attainment: High school diploma or higher: 95.1%; Bachelor's degree or higher: 69.8%; Graduate/professional degree or higher: 30.6%
Housing: Homeownership rate: 61.0%; Median home value: $301,000; Median year structure built: 1945; Homeowner vacancy rate: 3.3%; Median gross rent: $861 per month; Rental vacancy rate: 10.6%
Health Insurance: 96.0% have insurance; 86.2% have private insurance; 20.3% have public insurance; 4.0% do not have insurance; 2.3% of children under 18 do not have insurance
Safety: Violent crime rate: 0.0 per 10,000 population; Property crime rate: 153.9 per 10,000 population
Transportation: Commute: 93.5% car, 0.6% public transportation, 2.0% walk, 2.4% work from home; Median travel time to work: 23.4 minutes

MIAMI HEIGHTS (CDP). Covers a land area of 3.513 square miles and a water area of 0 square miles. Located at 39.17° N. Lat; 84.72° W. Long. Elevation is 823 feet.
Population: 4,731; Growth (since 2000): n/a; Density: 1,346.9 persons per square mile; Race: 97.9% White, 0.6% Black/African American, 0.7% Asian, 0.1% American Indian/Alaska Native, 0.0% Native Hawaiian/Other Pacific Islander, 0.7% Two or more races, 0.5% Hispanic of any race; Average household size: 2.84; Median age: 40.1; Age under 18: 28.0%; Age 65 and over: 14.1%; Males per 100 females: 95.4; Marriage status: 23.1% never married, 63.7% now married, 0.7% separated, 5.7% widowed, 7.5% divorced; Foreign born: 1.2%; Speak English only: 95.2%; With disability: 7.0%; Veterans: 8.1%; Ancestry: 60.8% German, 26.8% Irish, 7.3% English, 6.1% Italian, 3.2% American
Employment: 18.0% management, business, and financial, 4.4% computer, engineering, and science, 10.6% education, legal, community service, arts, and media, 6.0% healthcare practitioners, 13.1% service, 30.5% sales and office, 7.9% natural resources, construction, and maintenance, 9.4% production, transportation, and material moving
Income: Per capita: $30,954; Median household: $72,650; Average household: $86,487; Households with income of $100,000 or more: 35.5%; Poverty rate: 4.9%
Educational Attainment: High school diploma or higher: 92.9%; Bachelor's degree or higher: 36.0%; Graduate/professional degree or higher: 8.4%
Housing: Homeownership rate: 94.6%; Median home value: $214,700; Median year structure built: 1997; Homeowner vacancy rate: 1.5%; Median gross rent: $842 per month; Rental vacancy rate: 2.2%
Health Insurance: 98.6% have insurance; 91.8% have private insurance; 18.3% have public insurance; 1.4% do not have insurance; 0.6% of children under 18 do not have insurance
Transportation: Commute: 96.8% car, 0.4% public transportation, 2.3% walk, 0.5% work from home; Median travel time to work: 26.5 minutes

MIAMITOWN (CDP). Covers a land area of 1.343 square miles and a water area of 0.024 square miles. Located at 39.21° N. Lat; 84.71° W. Long. Elevation is 522 feet.
Population: 1,259; Growth (since 2000): n/a; Density: 937.3 persons per square mile; Race: 96.3% White, 0.5% Black/African American, 0.0% Asian, 0.2% American Indian/Alaska Native, 0.0% Native Hawaiian/Other Pacific Islander, 1.7% Two or more races, 3.3% Hispanic of any race; Average household size: 2.20; Median age: 31.2; Age under 18: 24.9%; Age 65 and over: 8.2%; Males per 100 females: 101.1

School District(s)

Southwest Local (PK-12)
2012-13 Enrollment: 3,441 . . . . (513) 367-4139
Housing: Homeownership rate: 15.9%; Homeowner vacancy rate: 3.2%; Rental vacancy rate: 16.0%

MONFORT HEIGHTS (CDP). Covers a land area of 5.913 square miles and a water area of <.001 square miles. Located at 39.18° N. Lat; 84.61° W. Long. Elevation is 899 feet.

Population: 11,948; Growth (since 2000): n/a; Density: 2,020.6 persons per square mile; Race: 90.1% White, 6.6% Black/African American, 1.3% Asian, 0.1% American Indian/Alaska Native, 0.0% Native Hawaiian/Other Pacific Islander, 1.5% Two or more races, 0.9% Hispanic of any race; Average household size: 2.48; Median age: 41.6; Age under 18: 23.5%; Age 65 and over: 16.9%; Males per 100 females: 92.7; Marriage status: 26.0% never married, 60.6% now married, 1.1% separated, 7.0% widowed, 6.4% divorced; Foreign born: 2.2%; Speak English only: 96.3%; With disability: 11.1%; Veterans: 9.3%; Ancestry: 54.2% German, 24.2% Irish, 7.2% American, 6.1% English, 5.3% Italian

Employment: 18.2% management, business, and financial, 3.2% computer, engineering, and science, 8.4% education, legal, community service, arts, and media, 11.1% healthcare practitioners, 15.2% service, 26.7% sales and office, 6.7% natural resources, construction, and maintenance, 10.5% production, transportation, and material moving

Income: Per capita: $36,227; Median household: $69,000; Average household: $89,339; Households with income of $100,000 or more: 29.3%; Poverty rate: 3.9%

Educational Attainment: High school diploma or higher: 95.0%; Bachelor's degree or higher: 38.2%; Graduate/professional degree or higher: 13.3%

Housing: Homeownership rate: 85.1%; Median home value: $165,200; Median year structure built: 1974; Homeowner vacancy rate: 1.8%; Median gross rent: $879 per month; Rental vacancy rate: 15.8%

Health Insurance: 96.4% have insurance; 83.6% have private insurance; 27.7% have public insurance; 3.6% do not have insurance; 0.0% of children under 18 do not have insurance

Transportation: Commute: 92.6% car, 0.8% public transportation, 1.5% walk, 4.5% work from home; Median travel time to work: 20.9 minutes

MONTGOMERY (city). Covers a land area of 5.286 square miles and a water area of 0.013 square miles. Located at 39.25° N. Lat; 84.35° W. Long. Elevation is 801 feet.

History: Montgomery was named after the town of Montgomery, New York, where the original settlers came from. Montgomery, New York was named in honor of Richard Montgomery, Brigadier General of the Continental Army during the American Revolution.

Population: 10,251; Growth (since 2000): 0.9%; Density: 1,939.1 persons per square mile; Race: 89.9% White, 2.7% Black/African American, 5.6% Asian, 0.1% American Indian/Alaska Native, 0.0% Native Hawaiian/Other Pacific Islander, 1.4% Two or more races, 1.8% Hispanic of any race; Average household size: 2.60; Median age: 46.9; Age under 18: 25.3%; Age 65 and over: 19.9%; Males per 100 females: 92.7; Marriage status: 18.3% never married, 68.7% now married, 0.7% separated, 7.9% widowed, 5.2% divorced; Foreign born: 7.7%; Speak English only: 93.1%; With disability: 8.6%; Veterans: 7.9%; Ancestry: 28.2% German, 17.3% Irish, 9.5% American, 9.2% English, 7.9% Italian

Employment: 27.9% management, business, and financial, 10.6% computer, engineering, and science, 19.6% education, legal, community service, arts, and media, 8.1% healthcare practitioners, 10.3% service, 18.3% sales and office, 2.5% natural resources, construction, and maintenance, 2.8% production, transportation, and material moving

Income: Per capita: $53,322; Median household: $107,620; Average household: $143,390; Households with income of $100,000 or more: 52.6%; Poverty rate: 3.0%

Educational Attainment: High school diploma or higher: 97.7%; Bachelor's degree or higher: 70.4%; Graduate/professional degree or higher: 31.1%

Housing: Homeownership rate: 86.5%; Median home value: $309,200; Median year structure built: 1975; Homeowner vacancy rate: 1.8%; Median gross rent: $1,221 per month; Rental vacancy rate: 7.5%

Health Insurance: 96.7% have insurance; 90.7% have private insurance; 19.3% have public insurance; 3.3% do not have insurance; 3.9% of children under 18 do not have insurance

Safety: Violent crime rate: 2.9 per 10,000 population; Property crime rate: 159.1 per 10,000 population

Transportation: Commute: 92.8% car, 1.3% public transportation, 0.6% walk, 4.6% work from home; Median travel time to work: 23.9 minutes

Additional Information Contacts

City of Montgomery . . . . (513) 891-2424
http://www.ci.montgomery.oh.us

MOUNT HEALTHY (city). Covers a land area of 1.406 square miles and a water area of 0 square miles. Located at 39.23° N. Lat; 84.55° W. Long. Elevation is 837 feet.

History: Mount Healthy was founded in 1817 by John Laboyteaux and Samuel Hill. It was first called Mount Pleasant, but the name was later changed to reflect the village's escape from the cholera epidemic of the 1850's.

Population: 6,098; Growth (since 2000): -14.7%; Density: 4,336.5 persons per square mile; Race: 62.4% White, 33.0% Black/African American, 0.7% Asian, 0.2% American Indian/Alaska Native, 0.1% Native Hawaiian/Other Pacific Islander, 2.6% Two or more races, 1.9% Hispanic of any race; Average household size: 2.17; Median age: 40.0; Age under 18: 22.9%; Age 65 and over: 18.2%; Males per 100 females: 81.4; Marriage status: 34.2% never married, 41.5% now married, 0.9% separated, 9.7% widowed, 14.6% divorced; Foreign born: 2.7%; Speak English only: 95.1%; With disability: 15.7%; Veterans: 10.1%; Ancestry: 33.3% German, 13.4% Irish, 5.7% English, 4.1% Scottish, 3.6% American

Employment: 8.5% management, business, and financial, 4.5% computer, engineering, and science, 10.8% education, legal, community service, arts, and media, 2.5% healthcare practitioners, 21.0% service, 29.7% sales and office, 6.8% natural resources, construction, and maintenance, 16.3% production, transportation, and material moving

Income: Per capita: $21,316; Median household: $34,167; Average household: $44,162; Households with income of $100,000 or more: 8.6%; Poverty rate: 24.1%

Educational Attainment: High school diploma or higher: 89.7%; Bachelor's degree or higher: 21.2%; Graduate/professional degree or higher: 6.5%

Housing: Homeownership rate: 48.7%; Median home value: $94,400; Median year structure built: 1960; Homeowner vacancy rate: 2.6%; Median gross rent: $630 per month; Rental vacancy rate: 10.5%

Health Insurance: 88.8% have insurance; 64.4% have private insurance; 35.7% have public insurance; 11.2% do not have insurance; 2.5% of children under 18 do not have insurance

Transportation: Commute: 90.5% car, 6.2% public transportation, 2.1% walk, 0.4% work from home; Median travel time to work: 26.2 minutes

Additional Information Contacts

City of Mount Healthy . . . . (513) 931-8840
http://www.mthealthy.org

MOUNT HEALTHY HEIGHTS (CDP). Covers a land area of 0.777 square miles and a water area of 0 square miles. Located at 39.27° N. Lat; 84.57° W. Long. Elevation is 846 feet.

Population: 3,264; Growth (since 2000): -5.4%; Density: 4,199.1 persons per square mile; Race: 57.5% White, 37.5% Black/African American, 0.6% Asian, 0.0% American Indian/Alaska Native, 0.2% Native Hawaiian/Other Pacific Islander, 3.2% Two or more races, 2.0% Hispanic of any race; Average household size: 2.63; Median age: 31.9; Age under 18: 29.6%; Age 65 and over: 8.7%; Males per 100 females: 83.2; Marriage status: 40.4% never married, 38.6% now married, 3.5% separated, 6.0% widowed, 15.0% divorced; Foreign born: 0.3%; Speak English only: 99.3%; With disability: 7.7%; Veterans: 5.2%; Ancestry: 20.5% German, 11.4% Irish, 4.3% English, 3.3% Polish, 3.2% American

Employment: 10.3% management, business, and financial, 1.9% computer, engineering, and science, 0.0% education, legal, community service, arts, and media, 10.8% healthcare practitioners, 23.3% service, 23.0% sales and office, 12.4% natural resources, construction, and maintenance, 18.4% production, transportation, and material moving

Income: Per capita: $14,872; Median household: $37,500; Average household: $41,316; Households with income of $100,000 or more: 2.3%; Poverty rate: 29.8%

Educational Attainment: High school diploma or higher: 83.8%; Bachelor's degree or higher: 6.7%; Graduate/professional degree or higher: 0.8%

Housing: Homeownership rate: 63.4%; Median home value: $94,300; Median year structure built: 1967; Homeowner vacancy rate: 2.5%; Median gross rent: $872 per month; Rental vacancy rate: 6.6%

Health Insurance: 88.0% have insurance; 57.3% have private insurance; 36.5% have public insurance; 12.0% do not have insurance; 6.8% of children under 18 do not have insurance

Transportation: Commute: 96.9% car, 0.8% public transportation, 0.0% walk, 2.3% work from home; Median travel time to work: 22.6 minutes

MOUNT SAINT JOSEPH (unincorporated postal area)

ZCTA: 45051

Covers a land area of 0.086 square miles and a water area of 0 square miles. Located at 39.10° N. Lat; 84.65° W. Long. Elevation is 817 feet.
Population: 177; Growth (since 2000): n/a; Density: 2,047.9 persons per square mile; Race: 96.6% White, 0.0% Black/African American, 3.4% Asian, 0.0% American Indian/Alaska Native, 0.0% Native Hawaiian/Other Pacific Islander, 0.0% Two or more races, 0.6% Hispanic of any race; Average household size: 0.00; Median age: 84.6; Age under 18: 0.0%; Age 65 and over: 98.3%; Males per 100 females: 0.0
Housing: Homeownership rate: n/a; Homeowner vacancy rate: 0.0%; Rental vacancy rate: 0.0%

NEW BALTIMORE (CDP). Covers a land area of 1.371 square miles and a water area of 0.017 square miles. Located at 39.28° N. Lat; 84.67° W. Long. Elevation is 564 feet.
Population: 661; Growth (since 2000): n/a; Density: 482.1 persons per square mile; Race: 96.4% White, 0.5% Black/African American, 0.2% Asian, 0.0% American Indian/Alaska Native, 0.0% Native Hawaiian/Other Pacific Islander, 3.0% Two or more races, 0.6% Hispanic of any race; Average household size: 2.61; Median age: 35.2; Age under 18: 27.4%; Age 65 and over: 9.8%; Males per 100 females: 94.4
Housing: Homeownership rate: 90.1%; Homeowner vacancy rate: 6.1%; Rental vacancy rate: 19.4%

NEW BURLINGTON (CDP). Covers a land area of 3.068 square miles and a water area of 0 square miles. Located at 39.26° N. Lat; 84.55° W. Long. Elevation is 823 feet.
Population: 5,069; Growth (since 2000): n/a; Density: 1,652.1 persons per square mile; Race: 52.3% White, 42.8% Black/African American, 1.2% Asian, 0.2% American Indian/Alaska Native, 0.1% Native Hawaiian/Other Pacific Islander, 2.3% Two or more races, 2.4% Hispanic of any race; Average household size: 2.67; Median age: 41.9; Age under 18: 25.6%; Age 65 and over: 17.6%; Males per 100 females: 85.9; Marriage status: 33.9% never married, 52.8% now married, 2.0% separated, 4.5% widowed, 8.9% divorced; Foreign born: 4.0%; Speak English only: 93.6%; With disability: 13.9%; Veterans: 11.0%; Ancestry: 32.2% German, 10.0% Irish, 5.4% English, 4.1% American, 2.8% Italian
Employment: 13.2% management, business, and financial, 2.4% computer, engineering, and science, 8.8% education, legal, community service, arts, and media, 2.7% healthcare practitioners, 23.7% service, 23.7% sales and office, 4.5% natural resources, construction, and maintenance, 21.1% production, transportation, and material moving
Income: Per capita: $24,107; Median household: $52,641; Average household: $64,007; Households with income of $100,000 or more: 20.8%; Poverty rate: 20.1%
Educational Attainment: High school diploma or higher: 87.0%; Bachelor's degree or higher: 14.5%; Graduate/professional degree or higher: 3.8%
Housing: Homeownership rate: 73.5%; Median home value: $142,500; Median year structure built: 1973; Homeowner vacancy rate: 3.0%; Median gross rent: $1,018 per month; Rental vacancy rate: 9.2%
Health Insurance: 88.8% have insurance; 57.6% have private insurance; 43.4% have public insurance; 11.2% do not have insurance; 0.0% of children under 18 do not have insurance
Transportation: Commute: 93.6% car, 1.1% public transportation, 1.7% walk, 3.2% work from home; Median travel time to work: 24.3 minutes

NEW HAVEN (CDP). Covers a land area of 1.294 square miles and a water area of 0.005 square miles. Located at 39.28° N. Lat; 84.75° W. Long. Elevation is 561 feet.
Population: 583; Growth (since 2000): n/a; Density: 450.4 persons per square mile; Race: 97.3% White, 0.7% Black/African American, 0.0% Asian, 0.5% American Indian/Alaska Native, 0.0% Native Hawaiian/Other Pacific Islander, 0.7% Two or more races, 1.4% Hispanic of any race; Average household size: 2.43; Median age: 42.8; Age under 18: 23.5%; Age 65 and over: 13.4%; Males per 100 females: 105.3
Housing: Homeownership rate: 86.7%; Homeowner vacancy rate: 1.4%; Rental vacancy rate: 17.9%

NEWTOWN (village). Covers a land area of 2.172 square miles and a water area of 0.199 square miles. Located at 39.12° N. Lat; 84.35° W. Long. Elevation is 499 feet.
History: Laid out 1801.
Population: 2,672; Growth (since 2000): 10.4%; Density: 1,230.3 persons per square mile; Race: 94.6% White, 1.4% Black/African American, 1.6% Asian, 0.2% American Indian/Alaska Native, 0.0% Native Hawaiian/Other Pacific Islander, 1.4% Two or more races, 2.1% Hispanic of any race; Average household size: 2.38; Median age: 39.0; Age under 18: 24.5%; Age 65 and over: 12.5%; Males per 100 females: 93.1; Marriage status: 25.1% never married, 57.9% now married, 1.2% separated, 5.3% widowed, 11.6% divorced; Foreign born: 3.0%; Speak English only: 94.4%; With disability: 11.6%; Veterans: 7.7%; Ancestry: 24.9% German, 17.2% American, 14.6% Irish, 11.3% English, 4.7% Italian
Employment: 24.7% management, business, and financial, 6.3% computer, engineering, and science, 11.0% education, legal, community service, arts, and media, 5.8% healthcare practitioners, 14.3% service, 22.7% sales and office, 5.1% natural resources, construction, and maintenance, 10.0% production, transportation, and material moving
Income: Per capita: $38,989; Median household: $69,122; Average household: $96,875; Households with income of $100,000 or more: 31.5%; Poverty rate: 5.8%
Educational Attainment: High school diploma or higher: 87.0%; Bachelor's degree or higher: 43.9%; Graduate/professional degree or higher: 14.7%
Housing: Homeownership rate: 69.6%; Median home value: $148,900; Median year structure built: 1989; Homeowner vacancy rate: 2.0%; Median gross rent: $1,042 per month; Rental vacancy rate: 9.8%
Health Insurance: 92.5% have insurance; 83.0% have private insurance; 22.2% have public insurance; 7.5% do not have insurance; 3.7% of children under 18 do not have insurance
Safety: Violent crime rate: 7.5 per 10,000 population; Property crime rate: 123.9 per 10,000 population
Transportation: Commute: 96.5% car, 0.0% public transportation, 0.0% walk, 2.0% work from home; Median travel time to work: 25.1 minutes

NORTH BEND (village). Covers a land area of 1.070 square miles and a water area of 0.075 square miles. Located at 39.15° N. Lat; 84.74° W. Long. Elevation is 574 feet.
History: North Bend was founded in 1789 by John Cleves Symmes. William Henry Harrison lived here until he became the 9th President of the U.S. in 1841. This was the birthplace of his grandson, William Henry Harrison (1833-1901), the 23rd U.S. President.
Population: 857; Growth (since 2000): 42.1%; Density: 800.6 persons per square mile; Race: 97.3% White, 0.6% Black/African American, 0.5% Asian, 0.1% American Indian/Alaska Native, 0.0% Native Hawaiian/Other Pacific Islander, 0.7% Two or more races, 1.2% Hispanic of any race; Average household size: 2.32; Median age: 52.7; Age under 18: 15.9%; Age 65 and over: 23.7%; Males per 100 females: 100.2

School District(s)

Three Rivers Local (PK-12)
2012-13 Enrollment: 1,924 . . . . (513) 941-6400
Housing: Homeownership rate: 76.8%; Homeowner vacancy rate: 1.4%; Rental vacancy rate: 18.7%

NORTH COLLEGE HILL (city). Covers a land area of 1.826 square miles and a water area of 0.001 square miles. Located at 39.22° N. Lat; 84.55° W. Long. Elevation is 823 feet.
History: Named for its location north of Cincinnati. Revolutionary War cemetery is in the city. Incorporated as a city 1940.
Population: 9,397; Growth (since 2000): -6.8%; Density: 5,145.3 persons per square mile; Race: 49.0% White, 46.6% Black/African American, 0.6% Asian, 0.1% American Indian/Alaska Native, 0.1% Native Hawaiian/Other Pacific Islander, 3.2% Two or more races, 1.3% Hispanic of any race; Average household size: 2.39; Median age: 36.2; Age under 18: 25.3%; Age 65 and over: 12.1%; Males per 100 females: 89.8; Marriage status: 37.0% never married, 43.9% now married, 4.1% separated, 5.2% widowed, 13.9% divorced; Foreign born: 2.0%; Speak English only: 97.5%; With disability: 14.6%; Veterans: 8.8%; Ancestry: 20.2% German, 7.3% Irish, 3.8% American, 3.2% English, 2.8% Italian
Employment: 11.5% management, business, and financial, 1.6% computer, engineering, and science, 9.0% education, legal, community service, arts, and media, 6.9% healthcare practitioners, 19.6% service, 26.6% sales and office, 9.8% natural resources, construction, and maintenance, 15.0% production, transportation, and material moving
Income: Per capita: $22,358; Median household: $42,367; Average household: $50,563; Households with income of $100,000 or more: 8.5%; Poverty rate: 15.5%

Educational Attainment: High school diploma or higher: 90.4%; Bachelor's degree or higher: 14.9%; Graduate/professional degree or higher: 6.3%

School District(s)

North College Hill City (PK-12)
2012-13 Enrollment: 1,611 . . . . (513) 931-8181

Housing: Homeownership rate: 62.1%; Median home value: $88,400; Median year structure built: 1953; Homeowner vacancy rate: 3.9%; Median gross rent: $765 per month; Rental vacancy rate: 8.6%

Health Insurance: 85.1% have insurance; 61.9% have private insurance; 32.6% have public insurance; 14.9% do not have insurance; 5.8% of children under 18 do not have insurance

Safety: Violent crime rate: 25.7 per 10,000 population; Property crime rate: 446.5 per 10,000 population

Transportation: Commute: 90.5% car, 2.8% public transportation, 4.2% walk, 2.4% work from home; Median travel time to work: 23.0 minutes

Additional Information Contacts

City of North College Hill . . . . (513) 521-7413
http://www.northcollegehill.org

NORTHBROOK (CDP). Covers a land area of 1.949 square miles and a water area of 0 square miles. Located at 39.25° N. Lat; 84.58° W. Long. Elevation is 833 feet.

Population: 10,668; Growth (since 2000): -3.7%; Density: 5,474.5 persons per square mile; Race: 65.6% White, 27.9% Black/African American, 1.2% Asian, 0.4% American Indian/Alaska Native, 0.1% Native Hawaiian/Other Pacific Islander, 3.6% Two or more races, 3.5% Hispanic of any race; Average household size: 2.65; Median age: 33.6; Age under 18: 28.2%; Age 65 and over: 11.4%; Males per 100 females: 88.4; Marriage status: 32.8% never married, 45.1% now married, 3.7% separated, 6.1% widowed, 16.0% divorced; Foreign born: 2.7%; Speak English only: 96.8%; With disability: 13.3%; Veterans: 12.4%; Ancestry: 28.8% German, 12.0% Irish, 7.2% American, 5.8% English, 5.0% Italian

Employment: 6.2% management, business, and financial, 1.6% computer, engineering, and science, 6.9% education, legal, community service, arts, and media, 4.1% healthcare practitioners, 22.8% service, 35.3% sales and office, 8.3% natural resources, construction, and maintenance, 14.8% production, transportation, and material moving

Income: Per capita: $18,117; Median household: $38,807; Average household: $46,844; Households with income of $100,000 or more: 5.5%; Poverty rate: 15.2%

Educational Attainment: High school diploma or higher: 83.4%; Bachelor's degree or higher: 10.4%; Graduate/professional degree or higher: 2.1%

Housing: Homeownership rate: 69.8%; Median home value: $86,600; Median year structure built: 1966; Homeowner vacancy rate: 2.7%; Median gross rent: $945 per month; Rental vacancy rate: 4.0%

Health Insurance: 85.6% have insurance; 61.0% have private insurance; 34.4% have public insurance; 14.4% do not have insurance; 10.5% of children under 18 do not have insurance

Transportation: Commute: 94.0% car, 1.4% public transportation, 1.3% walk, 2.9% work from home; Median travel time to work: 21.6 minutes

---

NORTHGATE (CDP). Covers a land area of 2.530 square miles and a water area of 0.021 square miles. Located at 39.25° N. Lat; 84.59° W. Long. Elevation is 879 feet.

Population: 7,377; Growth (since 2000): -8.0%; Density: 2,915.8 persons per square mile; Race: 78.8% White, 16.7% Black/African American, 1.4% Asian, 0.1% American Indian/Alaska Native, 0.3% Native Hawaiian/Other Pacific Islander, 2.1% Two or more races, 1.3% Hispanic of any race; Average household size: 2.71; Median age: 38.7; Age under 18: 25.6%; Age 65 and over: 13.5%; Males per 100 females: 94.2; Marriage status: 31.6% never married, 52.4% now married, 0.9% separated, 6.5% widowed, 9.5% divorced; Foreign born: 1.7%; Speak English only: 96.3%; With disability: 12.1%; Veterans: 10.8%; Ancestry: 34.9% German, 13.9% Irish, 5.9% American, 5.8% English, 2.9% French

Employment: 9.2% management, business, and financial, 4.2% computer, engineering, and science, 5.0% education, legal, community service, arts, and media, 4.7% healthcare practitioners, 18.0% service, 28.0% sales and office, 12.8% natural resources, construction, and maintenance, 18.2% production, transportation, and material moving

Income: Per capita: $25,645; Median household: $59,066; Average household: $67,999; Households with income of $100,000 or more: 19.4%; Poverty rate: 4.4%

Educational Attainment: High school diploma or higher: 89.7%; Bachelor's degree or higher: 16.9%; Graduate/professional degree or higher: 3.4%

Housing: Homeownership rate: 81.4%; Median home value: $119,700; Median year structure built: 1969; Homeowner vacancy rate: 1.7%; Median gross rent: $926 per month; Rental vacancy rate: 6.8%

Health Insurance: 89.3% have insurance; 79.4% have private insurance; 24.4% have public insurance; 10.7% do not have insurance; 0.8% of children under 18 do not have insurance

Transportation: Commute: 96.3% car, 0.9% public transportation, 0.8% walk, 0.8% work from home; Median travel time to work: 22.1 minutes

---

NORWOOD (city). Covers a land area of 3.147 square miles and a water area of 0 square miles. Located at 39.16° N. Lat; 84.45° W. Long. Elevation is 653 feet.

History: Named for the shortened form of north woods. Norwood began in the early 1800's, and until 1888 was called Sharpsburg, for early settler John Sharp. The U.S. Playing Card Company was established here, and maintained a Playing Card Museum.

Population: 19,207; Growth (since 2000): -11.4%; Density: 6,102.8 persons per square mile; Race: 86.6% White, 7.6% Black/African American, 0.8% Asian, 0.4% American Indian/Alaska Native, 0.1% Native Hawaiian/Other Pacific Islander, 2.5% Two or more races, 5.1% Hispanic of any race; Average household size: 2.28; Median age: 33.4; Age under 18: 20.2%; Age 65 and over: 11.1%; Males per 100 females: 99.5; Marriage status: 44.1% never married, 38.1% now married, 2.8% separated, 6.0% widowed, 11.8% divorced; Foreign born: 2.6%; Speak English only: 94.9%; With disability: 16.0%; Veterans: 8.7%; Ancestry: 27.9% German, 17.5% American, 17.1% Irish, 8.7% English, 4.0% Italian

Employment: 13.1% management, business, and financial, 5.1% computer, engineering, and science, 10.1% education, legal, community service, arts, and media, 3.4% healthcare practitioners, 17.9% service, 29.3% sales and office, 7.7% natural resources, construction, and maintenance, 13.4% production, transportation, and material moving

Income: Per capita: $22,503; Median household: $37,303; Average household: $49,369; Households with income of $100,000 or more: 10.9%; Poverty rate: 20.7%

Educational Attainment: High school diploma or higher: 80.9%; Bachelor's degree or higher: 24.2%; Graduate/professional degree or higher: 7.1%

School District(s)

Norwood City (PK-12)
2012-13 Enrollment: 2,073 . . . . (513) 924-2500

Four-year College(s)

ITT Technical Institute-Norwood (Private, For-profit)
Fall 2013 Enrollment: 419 . . . . (513) 531-8300
2013-14 Tuition: In-state $18,048; Out-of-state $18,048

Two-year College(s)

ITT Technical Institute-West Chester (Private, For-profit)
Fall 2013 Enrollment: 61 . . . . (513) 531-8300
2013-14 Tuition: In-state $18,048; Out-of-state $18,048

Housing: Homeownership rate: 49.0%; Median home value: $121,900; Median year structure built: Before 1940; Homeowner vacancy rate: 3.5%; Median gross rent: $636 per month; Rental vacancy rate: 10.9%

Health Insurance: 82.7% have insurance; 62.0% have private insurance; 30.0% have public insurance; 17.3% do not have insurance; 10.2% of children under 18 do not have insurance

Safety: Violent crime rate: 32.5 per 10,000 population; Property crime rate: 661.9 per 10,000 population

Transportation: Commute: 90.7% car, 2.1% public transportation, 2.6% walk, 2.9% work from home; Median travel time to work: 19.1 minutes

Additional Information Contacts

City of Norwood. . . . . (513) 458-4500
http://www.norwood-ohio.com

PLAINVILLE (CDP). Covers a land area of 0.093 square miles and a water area of 0 square miles. Located at 39.14° N. Lat; 84.36° W. Long. Elevation is 499 feet.

Population: 87; Growth (since 2000): n/a; Density: 934.1 persons per square mile; Race: 100.0% White, 0.0% Black/African American, 0.0% Asian, 0.0% American Indian/Alaska Native, 0.0% Native Hawaiian/Other Pacific Islander, 0.0% Two or more races, 0.0% Hispanic of any race; Average household size: 1.71; Median age: 54.8; Age under 18: 10.3%; Age 65 and over: 35.6%; Males per 100 females: 74.0

Housing: Homeownership rate: 94.2%; Homeowner vacancy rate: 7.5%; Rental vacancy rate: 25.0%

PLEASANT HILLS (CDP). Covers a land area of 0.330 square miles and a water area of 0 square miles. Located at 39.24° N. Lat; 84.52° W. Long. Elevation is 787 feet.
Population: 606; Growth (since 2000): n/a; Density: 1,838.5 persons per square mile; Race: 43.6% White, 53.0% Black/African American, 0.8% Asian, 0.0% American Indian/Alaska Native, 0.0% Native Hawaiian/Other Pacific Islander, 1.8% Two or more races, 0.3% Hispanic of any race; Average household size: 2.25; Median age: 46.7; Age under 18: 19.6%; Age 65 and over: 21.1%; Males per 100 females: 90.0
Housing: Homeownership rate: 86.2%; Homeowner vacancy rate: 7.1%; Rental vacancy rate: 0.0%

PLEASANT RUN (CDP). Covers a land area of 2.069 square miles and a water area of 0 square miles. Located at 39.29° N. Lat; 84.58° W. Long. Elevation is 748 feet.
Population: 4,953; Growth (since 2000): -6.0%; Density: 2,393.8 persons per square mile; Race: 79.8% White, 14.5% Black/African American, 1.8% Asian, 0.5% American Indian/Alaska Native, 0.0% Native Hawaiian/Other Pacific Islander, 2.5% Two or more races, 2.2% Hispanic of any race; Average household size: 2.78; Median age: 38.5; Age under 18: 24.8%; Age 65 and over: 13.6%; Males per 100 females: 94.3; Marriage status: 35.9% never married, 46.8% now married, 0.8% separated, 8.7% widowed, 8.6% divorced; Foreign born: 2.4%; Speak English only: 97.1%; With disability: 10.6%; Veterans: 11.8%; Ancestry: 34.6% German, 11.0% Irish, 7.5% English, 5.6% American, 4.3% Italian
Employment: 12.9% management, business, and financial, 6.7% computer, engineering, and science, 6.6% education, legal, community service, arts, and media, 4.0% healthcare practitioners, 17.9% service, 31.6% sales and office, 7.2% natural resources, construction, and maintenance, 13.1% production, transportation, and material moving
Income: Per capita: $24,409; Median household: $60,849; Average household: $65,289; Households with income of $100,000 or more: 12.6%; Poverty rate: 6.1%
Educational Attainment: High school diploma or higher: 92.3%; Bachelor's degree or higher: 15.2%; Graduate/professional degree or higher: 3.3%
Housing: Homeownership rate: 89.5%; Median home value: $113,700; Median year structure built: 1971; Homeowner vacancy rate: 2.0%; Median gross rent: $1,057 per month; Rental vacancy rate: 18.9%
Health Insurance: 87.3% have insurance; 74.5% have private insurance; 19.6% have public insurance; 12.7% do not have insurance; 7.2% of children under 18 do not have insurance
Transportation: Commute: 93.9% car, 0.1% public transportation, 0.4% walk, 5.6% work from home; Median travel time to work: 23.8 minutes

PLEASANT RUN FARM (CDP). Covers a land area of 1.058 square miles and a water area of 0 square miles. Located at 39.30° N. Lat; 84.55° W. Long. Elevation is 764 feet.
Population: 4,654; Growth (since 2000): -1.6%; Density: 4,397.0 persons per square mile; Race: 54.0% White, 40.2% Black/African American, 0.5% Asian, 0.2% American Indian/Alaska Native, 0.1% Native Hawaiian/Other Pacific Islander, 3.7% Two or more races, 2.1% Hispanic of any race; Average household size: 2.79; Median age: 35.0; Age under 18: 29.2%; Age 65 and over: 9.0%; Males per 100 females: 91.1; Marriage status: 25.7% never married, 54.0% now married, 1.6% separated, 7.7% widowed, 12.6% divorced; Foreign born: 1.6%; Speak English only: 96.3%; With disability: 11.3%; Veterans: 12.5%; Ancestry: 23.8% German, 10.1% Irish, 9.8% English, 3.0% Ethiopian, 2.8% American
Employment: 13.4% management, business, and financial, 6.1% computer, engineering, and science, 9.3% education, legal, community service, arts, and media, 8.1% healthcare practitioners, 20.3% service, 27.3% sales and office, 4.0% natural resources, construction, and maintenance, 11.4% production, transportation, and material moving
Income: Per capita: $25,256; Median household: $59,200; Average household: $68,828; Households with income of $100,000 or more: 23.0%; Poverty rate: 8.2%
Educational Attainment: High school diploma or higher: 91.2%; Bachelor's degree or higher: 30.8%; Graduate/professional degree or higher: 10.5%
Housing: Homeownership rate: 84.1%; Median home value: $133,700; Median year structure built: 1976; Homeowner vacancy rate: 2.4%; Median gross rent: $966 per month; Rental vacancy rate: 16.9%
Health Insurance: 89.7% have insurance; 70.0% have private insurance; 31.5% have public insurance; 10.3% do not have insurance; 4.7% of children under 18 do not have insurance
Transportation: Commute: 92.7% car, 0.5% public transportation, 0.5% walk, 6.3% work from home; Median travel time to work: 23.2 minutes

READING (city). Covers a land area of 2.892 square miles and a water area of 0 square miles. Located at 39.22° N. Lat; 84.43° W. Long. Elevation is 561 feet.
History: Reading was platted in 1798 by Adam Vorhees, and named Vorheestown. The name was changed to honor Redingbo, William Penn 's son-in-law.
Population: 10,385; Growth (since 2000): -8.0%; Density: 3,591.6 persons per square mile; Race: 89.1% White, 7.3% Black/African American, 1.0% Asian, 0.1% American Indian/Alaska Native, 0.0% Native Hawaiian/Other Pacific Islander, 1.9% Two or more races, 1.7% Hispanic of any race; Average household size: 2.26; Median age: 39.5; Age under 18: 21.6%; Age 65 and over: 14.9%; Males per 100 females: 96.4; Marriage status: 35.5% never married, 45.0% now married, 1.7% separated, 7.9% widowed, 11.7% divorced; Foreign born: 4.1%; Speak English only: 94.8%; With disability: 15.8%; Veterans: 10.3%; Ancestry: 31.6% German, 17.4% Irish, 9.2% English, 8.0% American, 3.3% Italian
Employment: 11.8% management, business, and financial, 5.0% computer, engineering, and science, 8.5% education, legal, community service, arts, and media, 4.1% healthcare practitioners, 22.9% service, 24.5% sales and office, 7.6% natural resources, construction, and maintenance, 15.6% production, transportation, and material moving
Income: Per capita: $24,810; Median household: $39,662; Average household: $54,701; Households with income of $100,000 or more: 15.7%; Poverty rate: 20.6%
Educational Attainment: High school diploma or higher: 84.9%; Bachelor's degree or higher: 15.6%; Graduate/professional degree or higher: 6.8%

School District(s)

Reading Community City (PK-12)
2012-13 Enrollment: 1,609 . . . . (513) 554-1800
Housing: Homeownership rate: 57.4%; Median home value: $127,400; Median year structure built: 1957; Homeowner vacancy rate: 1.9%; Median gross rent: $623 per month; Rental vacancy rate: 11.5%
Health Insurance: 86.6% have insurance; 59.9% have private insurance; 36.9% have public insurance; 13.4% do not have insurance; 3.8% of children under 18 do not have insurance
Transportation: Commute: 92.0% car, 1.5% public transportation, 4.7% walk, 1.4% work from home; Median travel time to work: 19.5 minutes
Additional Information Contacts
City of Reading . . . . (513) 733-3725
http://www.readingohio.org

REMINGTON (CDP). Covers a land area of 0.211 square miles and a water area of 0.003 square miles. Located at 39.23° N. Lat; 84.32° W. Long. Elevation is 577 feet.
Population: 328; Growth (since 2000): n/a; Density: 1,551.3 persons per square mile; Race: 86.0% White, 0.9% Black/African American, 11.0% Asian, 0.3% American Indian/Alaska Native, 0.0% Native Hawaiian/Other Pacific Islander, 1.5% Two or more races, 0.6% Hispanic of any race; Average household size: 2.56; Median age: 45.1; Age under 18: 24.7%; Age 65 and over: 15.5%; Males per 100 females: 108.9
Housing: Homeownership rate: 89.9%; Homeowner vacancy rate: 2.5%; Rental vacancy rate: 13.3%

ROSSMOYNE (CDP). Covers a land area of 0.591 square miles and a water area of 0 square miles. Located at 39.21° N. Lat; 84.39° W. Long. Elevation is 833 feet.
Population: 2,230; Growth (since 2000): n/a; Density: 3,775.7 persons per square mile; Race: 86.1% White, 8.8% Black/African American, 1.9% Asian, 0.4% American Indian/Alaska Native, 0.2% Native Hawaiian/Other Pacific Islander, 2.1% Two or more races, 1.7% Hispanic of any race; Average household size: 2.42; Median age: 37.2; Age under 18: 22.2%; Age 65 and over: 13.4%; Males per 100 females: 94.3
Housing: Homeownership rate: 72.9%; Homeowner vacancy rate: 2.2%; Rental vacancy rate: 6.0%

SAINT BERNARD (city). Covers a land area of 1.546 square miles and a water area of 0.012 square miles. Located at 39.17° N. Lat; 84.49° W. Long. Elevation is 568 feet.
Population: 4,368; Growth (since 2000): -11.3%; Density: 2,825.4 persons per square mile; Race: 80.0% White, 15.7% Black/African American, 0.7% Asian, 0.3% American Indian/Alaska Native, 0.1% Native Hawaiian/Other Pacific Islander, 2.3% Two or more races, 1.9% Hispanic of any race; Average household size: 2.33; Median age: 38.2; Age under 18: 23.6%; Age 65 and over: 13.0%; Males per 100 females: 89.4; Marriage status: 31.3% never married, 47.0% now married, 3.8% separated, 3.9% widowed, 17.8% divorced; Foreign born: 1.1%; Speak English only: 98.6%; With disability: 16.4%; Veterans: 8.2%; Ancestry: 38.6% German, 15.2% Irish, 5.3% English, 4.3% American, 4.2% Italian
Employment: 9.7% management, business, and financial, 2.9% computer, engineering, and science, 5.1% education, legal, community service, arts, and media, 8.0% healthcare practitioners, 25.2% service, 28.8% sales and office, 3.9% natural resources, construction, and maintenance, 16.5% production, transportation, and material moving
Income: Per capita: $23,245; Median household: $46,737; Average household: $56,667; Households with income of $100,000 or more: 16.5%; Poverty rate: 13.6%
Educational Attainment: High school diploma or higher: 91.1%; Bachelor's degree or higher: 14.0%; Graduate/professional degree or higher: 3.4%

School District(s)

Saint Bernard-Elmwood Place City (PK-12)
2012-13 Enrollment: 1,034 . . . . (513) 482-7121
Housing: Homeownership rate: 60.0%; Median home value: $95,800; Median year structure built: Before 1940; Homeowner vacancy rate: 4.8%; Median gross rent: $659 per month; Rental vacancy rate: 11.8%
Health Insurance: 91.7% have insurance; 68.0% have private insurance; 33.9% have public insurance; 8.3% do not have insurance; 2.2% of children under 18 do not have insurance
Transportation: Commute: 83.8% car, 3.4% public transportation, 9.0% walk, 2.1% work from home; Median travel time to work: 21.6 minutes

SALEM HEIGHTS (CDP). Covers a land area of 1.645 square miles and a water area of 0 square miles. Located at 39.07° N. Lat; 84.38° W. Long. Elevation is 745 feet.
Population: 3,839; Growth (since 2000): n/a; Density: 2,333.8 persons per square mile; Race: 95.5% White, 1.3% Black/African American, 1.3% Asian, 0.4% American Indian/Alaska Native, 0.0% Native Hawaiian/Other Pacific Islander, 1.4% Two or more races, 1.4% Hispanic of any race; Average household size: 2.65; Median age: 39.3; Age under 18: 26.9%; Age 65 and over: 13.4%; Males per 100 females: 96.3; Marriage status: 24.1% never married, 59.9% now married, 3.0% separated, 6.9% widowed, 9.0% divorced; Foreign born: 0.2%; Speak English only: 96.3%; With disability: 9.8%; Veterans: 8.2%; Ancestry: 42.8% German, 24.5% Irish, 16.5% American, 15.3% English, 9.7% Italian
Employment: 16.3% management, business, and financial, 2.2% computer, engineering, and science, 10.5% education, legal, community service, arts, and media, 11.8% healthcare practitioners, 16.5% service, 23.3% sales and office, 6.2% natural resources, construction, and maintenance, 13.2% production, transportation, and material moving
Income: Per capita: $42,658; Median household: $75,897; Average household: $112,481; Households with income of $100,000 or more: 28.4%; Poverty rate: 2.5%
Educational Attainment: High school diploma or higher: 92.9%; Bachelor's degree or higher: 35.8%; Graduate/professional degree or higher: 15.3%
Housing: Homeownership rate: 90.0%; Median home value: $156,600; Median year structure built: 1962; Homeowner vacancy rate: 1.7%; Median gross rent: $1,038 per month; Rental vacancy rate: 4.8%
Health Insurance: 93.4% have insurance; 85.4% have private insurance; 25.1% have public insurance; 6.6% do not have insurance; 6.2% of children under 18 do not have insurance
Transportation: Commute: 91.4% car, 0.7% public transportation, 0.0% walk, 5.3% work from home; Median travel time to work: 20.1 minutes

SHARONVILLE (city). Covers a land area of 9.832 square miles and a water area of 0.058 square miles. Located at 39.28° N. Lat; 84.41° W. Long. Elevation is 587 feet.
History: Named for Sharon, Pennsylvania, which was named for the region in Palestine mentioned in the Bible. Sharonville was surveyed in 1796 by Simon Hegerman, and became a transportation center when the New York Central Lines built their freight yards and shops here.
Population: 13,560; Growth (since 2000): -1.8%; Density: 1,379.2 persons per square mile; Race: 79.7% White, 8.7% Black/African American, 4.0% Asian, 0.2% American Indian/Alaska Native, 0.3% Native Hawaiian/Other Pacific Islander, 3.0% Two or more races, 7.0% Hispanic of any race; Average household size: 2.17; Median age: 40.8; Age under 18: 20.0%; Age 65 and over: 17.6%; Males per 100 females: 91.5; Marriage status: 31.5% never married, 46.1% now married, 1.4% separated, 8.3% widowed, 14.1% divorced; Foreign born: 10.4%; Speak English only: 86.7%; With disability: 13.4%; Veterans: 11.5%; Ancestry: 26.9% German, 11.6% Irish, 8.4% English, 5.7% American, 2.1% Italian
Employment: 17.6% management, business, and financial, 8.8% computer, engineering, and science, 6.0% education, legal, community service, arts, and media, 6.2% healthcare practitioners, 15.7% service, 22.4% sales and office, 4.3% natural resources, construction, and maintenance, 19.0% production, transportation, and material moving
Income: Per capita: $29,712; Median household: $51,892; Average household: $64,422; Households with income of $100,000 or more: 17.6%; Poverty rate: 11.2%
Educational Attainment: High school diploma or higher: 89.9%; Bachelor's degree or higher: 30.7%; Graduate/professional degree or higher: 12.7%

Two-year College(s)

Miami-Jacobs Career College-Sharonville (Private, For-profit)
Fall 2013 Enrollment: 156 . . . . (513) 693-4400
2013-14 Tuition: In-state $12,024; Out-of-state $12,024
Housing: Homeownership rate: 61.0%; Median home value: $143,300; Median year structure built: 1978; Homeowner vacancy rate: 1.4%; Median gross rent: $824 per month; Rental vacancy rate: 10.6%
Health Insurance: 87.2% have insurance; 69.9% have private insurance; 28.9% have public insurance; 12.8% do not have insurance; 8.6% of children under 18 do not have insurance
Transportation: Commute: 93.5% car, 0.0% public transportation, 2.7% walk, 2.4% work from home; Median travel time to work: 18.8 minutes
Additional Information Contacts
City of Sharonville . . . . (513) 563-1144
http://www.sharonville.org

SHAWNEE (CDP). Covers a land area of 6.418 square miles and a water area of 0.530 square miles. Located at 39.14° N. Lat; 84.78° W. Long.
Population: 724; Growth (since 2000): n/a; Density: 112.8 persons per square mile; Race: 96.8% White, 0.4% Black/African American, 0.0% Asian, 0.7% American Indian/Alaska Native, 0.0% Native Hawaiian/Other Pacific Islander, 1.9% Two or more races, 0.6% Hispanic of any race; Average household size: 2.57; Median age: 46.4; Age under 18: 20.7%; Age 65 and over: 17.5%; Males per 100 females: 101.1
Housing: Homeownership rate: 84.4%; Homeowner vacancy rate: 3.2%; Rental vacancy rate: 4.3%

SHERWOOD (CDP). Covers a land area of 1.069 square miles and a water area of 0 square miles. Located at 39.09° N. Lat; 84.36° W. Long. Elevation is 725 feet.
History: During the Civil War, Morgan's Raid (a Confederate cavalry assault) passed through this part of Hamilton County in 1863.
Population: 3,719; Growth (since 2000): n/a; Density: 3,478.1 persons per square mile; Race: 95.4% White, 1.1% Black/African American, 1.9% Asian, 0.2% American Indian/Alaska Native, 0.0% Native Hawaiian/Other Pacific Islander, 1.0% Two or more races, 1.5% Hispanic of any race; Average household size: 2.76; Median age: 39.3; Age under 18: 29.1%; Age 65 and over: 12.8%; Males per 100 females: 93.9; Marriage status: 20.6% never married, 64.2% now married, 2.4% separated, 3.3% widowed, 11.8% divorced; Foreign born: 3.8%; Speak English only: 91.5%; With disability: 7.5%; Veterans: 8.0%; Ancestry: 38.6% German, 15.8% Irish, 15.3% American, 11.9% English, 6.7% Italian
Employment: 26.9% management, business, and financial, 5.5% computer, engineering, and science, 11.6% education, legal, community service, arts, and media, 10.7% healthcare practitioners, 12.7% service, 20.9% sales and office, 4.6% natural resources, construction, and maintenance, 7.0% production, transportation, and material moving
Income: Per capita: $43,636; Median household: $84,150; Average household: $110,965; Households with income of $100,000 or more: 40.2%; Poverty rate: 5.6%

Educational Attainment: High school diploma or higher: 94.1%; Bachelor's degree or higher: 52.0%; Graduate/professional degree or higher: 20.4%
Housing: Homeownership rate: 94.9%; Median home value: $165,600; Median year structure built: 1965; Homeowner vacancy rate: 0.8%; Median gross rent: n/a per month; Rental vacancy rate: 5.6%
Health Insurance: 92.7% have insurance; 85.3% have private insurance; 17.7% have public insurance; 7.3% do not have insurance; 1.6% of children under 18 do not have insurance
Transportation: Commute: 92.4% car, 1.5% public transportation, 0.8% walk, 5.3% work from home; Median travel time to work: 23.0 minutes

SILVERTON (village). Covers a land area of 1.112 square miles and a water area of 0 square miles. Located at 39.19° N. Lat; 84.40° W. Long. Elevation is 853 feet.
History: Silverton developed as a residential community on the outskirts of Cincinnati.
Population: 4,788; Growth (since 2000): -7.5%; Density: 4,307.2 persons per square mile; Race: 44.0% White, 51.4% Black/African American, 0.8% Asian, 0.3% American Indian/Alaska Native, 0.0% Native Hawaiian/Other Pacific Islander, 2.7% Two or more races, 2.5% Hispanic of any race; Average household size: 1.95; Median age: 43.3; Age under 18: 15.9%; Age 65 and over: 16.8%; Males per 100 females: 85.7; Marriage status: 38.7% never married, 39.2% now married, 3.7% separated, 4.8% widowed, 17.3% divorced; Foreign born: 2.2%; Speak English only: 98.0%; With disability: 10.2%; Veterans: 5.9%; Ancestry: 23.5% German, 6.6% Irish, 5.4% American, 3.8% African, 3.2% Italian
Employment: 9.9% management, business, and financial, 6.6% computer, engineering, and science, 9.3% education, legal, community service, arts, and media, 6.9% healthcare practitioners, 21.9% service, 20.1% sales and office, 6.2% natural resources, construction, and maintenance, 19.1% production, transportation, and material moving
Income: Per capita: $25,129; Median household: $37,351; Average household: $48,184; Households with income of $100,000 or more: 10.5%; Poverty rate: 15.2%
Educational Attainment: High school diploma or higher: 89.8%; Bachelor's degree or higher: 34.1%; Graduate/professional degree or higher: 9.3%
Housing: Homeownership rate: 54.3%; Median home value: $124,700; Median year structure built: 1952; Homeowner vacancy rate: 2.0%; Median gross rent: $583 per month; Rental vacancy rate: 9.9%
Health Insurance: 82.6% have insurance; 68.1% have private insurance; 27.5% have public insurance; 17.4% do not have insurance; 5.2% of children under 18 do not have insurance
Safety: Violent crime rate: 35.6 per 10,000 population; Property crime rate: 280.9 per 10,000 population
Transportation: Commute: 90.4% car, 1.7% public transportation, 1.8% walk, 6.1% work from home; Median travel time to work: 19.6 minutes
Additional Information Contacts
City of Silverton . . . . (513) 936-6240
http://silvertonohio.us

SIXTEEN MILE STAND (CDP). Covers a land area of 1.116 square miles and a water area of 0.003 square miles. Located at 39.28° N. Lat; 84.33° W. Long. Elevation is 807 feet.
Population: 2,928; Growth (since 2000): n/a; Density: 2,624.4 persons per square mile; Race: 76.9% White, 6.1% Black/African American, 13.3% Asian, 0.0% American Indian/Alaska Native, 0.1% Native Hawaiian/Other Pacific Islander, 2.3% Two or more races, 3.9% Hispanic of any race; Average household size: 2.37; Median age: 39.4; Age under 18: 23.5%; Age 65 and over: 8.6%; Males per 100 females: 102.3; Marriage status: 29.5% never married, 51.6% now married, 1.1% separated, 4.4% widowed, 14.5% divorced; Foreign born: 18.9%; Speak English only: 78.1%; With disability: 6.1%; Veterans: 7.0%; Ancestry: 22.9% German, 17.7% Irish, 9.8% Italian, 8.4% English, 4.3% American
Employment: 23.5% management, business, and financial, 11.7% computer, engineering, and science, 10.7% education, legal, community service, arts, and media, 8.4% healthcare practitioners, 8.4% service, 28.9% sales and office, 0.9% natural resources, construction, and maintenance, 7.5% production, transportation, and material moving
Income: Per capita: $52,968; Median household: $74,745; Average household: $130,591; Households with income of $100,000 or more: 41.3%; Poverty rate: 7.6%

Educational Attainment: High school diploma or higher: 99.4%; Bachelor's degree or higher: 58.0%; Graduate/professional degree or higher: 22.9%
Housing: Homeownership rate: 50.7%; Median home value: $384,600; Median year structure built: 1986; Homeowner vacancy rate: 0.9%; Median gross rent: $1,238 per month; Rental vacancy rate: 11.5%
Health Insurance: 92.7% have insurance; 86.7% have private insurance; 12.9% have public insurance; 7.3% do not have insurance; 0.0% of children under 18 do not have insurance
Transportation: Commute: 89.9% car, 0.5% public transportation, 1.7% walk, 7.3% work from home; Median travel time to work: 22.4 minutes

SKYLINE ACRES (CDP). Covers a land area of 0.657 square miles and a water area of 0 square miles. Located at 39.23° N. Lat; 84.57° W. Long. Elevation is 827 feet.
Population: 1,717; Growth (since 2000): n/a; Density: 2,611.9 persons per square mile; Race: 15.2% White, 81.5% Black/African American, 0.3% Asian, 0.2% American Indian/Alaska Native, 0.1% Native Hawaiian/Other Pacific Islander, 2.7% Two or more races, 0.4% Hispanic of any race; Average household size: 2.76; Median age: 36.4; Age under 18: 30.5%; Age 65 and over: 16.6%; Males per 100 females: 87.4
Housing: Homeownership rate: 70.0%; Homeowner vacancy rate: 1.6%; Rental vacancy rate: 7.0%

SPRINGDALE (city). Covers a land area of 4.963 square miles and a water area of 0.011 square miles. Located at 39.29° N. Lat; 84.48° W. Long. Elevation is 738 feet.
History: Springdale was the site in 1801-1802 of a meeting of the religious sect called the New Lights, who evidenced pronounced physical manifestations of jerking, rolling, whirling, falling, and barking.
Population: 11,223; Growth (since 2000): 6.2%; Density: 2,261.4 persons per square mile; Race: 55.0% White, 29.9% Black/African American, 2.8% Asian, 0.3% American Indian/Alaska Native, 0.4% Native Hawaiian/Other Pacific Islander, 2.9% Two or more races, 17.5% Hispanic of any race; Average household size: 2.38; Median age: 38.7; Age under 18: 22.6%; Age 65 and over: 20.0%; Males per 100 females: 86.8; Marriage status: 33.2% never married, 44.9% now married, 1.5% separated, 10.0% widowed, 11.8% divorced; Foreign born: 14.2%; Speak English only: 78.3%; With disability: 12.4%; Veterans: 10.4%; Ancestry: 18.4% German, 9.1% Irish, 8.3% English, 4.9% American, 1.7% Scotch-Irish
Employment: 9.0% management, business, and financial, 9.1% computer, engineering, and science, 10.8% education, legal, community service, arts, and media, 6.6% healthcare practitioners, 19.7% service, 21.9% sales and office, 7.8% natural resources, construction, and maintenance, 15.0% production, transportation, and material moving
Income: Per capita: $22,381; Median household: $49,222; Average household: $59,147; Households with income of $100,000 or more: 17.3%; Poverty rate: 23.5%
Educational Attainment: High school diploma or higher: 84.2%; Bachelor's degree or higher: 28.4%; Graduate/professional degree or higher: 8.8%

Two-year College(s)

Beckfield College-Tri-County (Private, For-profit)
Fall 2013 Enrollment: 554 . . . . (513) 671-1920
2013-14 Tuition: In-state $12,546; Out-of-state $12,546

Vocational/Technical School(s)

Regency Beauty Institute-Tri-County (Private, For-profit)
Fall 2013 Enrollment: 46 . . . . (800) 787-6456
2013-14 Tuition: $16,200

Housing: Homeownership rate: 54.5%; Median home value: $127,600; Median year structure built: 1972; Homeowner vacancy rate: 2.5%; Median gross rent: $868 per month; Rental vacancy rate: 6.4%
Health Insurance: 83.0% have insurance; 60.5% have private insurance; 34.3% have public insurance; 17.0% do not have insurance; 5.8% of children under 18 do not have insurance
Safety: Violent crime rate: 36.6 per 10,000 population; Property crime rate: 691.6 per 10,000 population
Transportation: Commute: 96.1% car, 0.6% public transportation, 1.4% walk, 1.5% work from home; Median travel time to work: 21.3 minutes
Additional Information Contacts
City of Springdale . . . . (513) 346-5700
http://www.springdale.org

TAYLOR CREEK (CDP). Covers a land area of 8.435 square miles and a water area of 0 square miles. Located at 39.24° N. Lat; 84.68° W. Long.

Population: 3,062; Growth (since 2000): n/a; Density: 363.0 persons per square mile; Race: 95.7% White, 2.2% Black/African American, 1.0% Asian, 0.1% American Indian/Alaska Native, 0.0% Native Hawaiian/Other Pacific Islander, 0.8% Two or more races, 1.1% Hispanic of any race; Average household size: 2.42; Median age: 44.3; Age under 18: 21.4%; Age 65 and over: 15.1%; Males per 100 females: 98.4; Marriage status: 31.7% never married, 56.9% now married, 1.0% separated, 3.5% widowed, 7.9% divorced; Foreign born: 0.9%; Speak English only: 94.2%; With disability: 9.0%; Veterans: 13.9%; Ancestry: 50.3% German, 17.3% Irish, 7.8% Italian, 6.7% Czechoslovakian, 6.6% English

Employment: 10.0% management, business, and financial, 6.6% computer, engineering, and science, 12.0% education, legal, community service, arts, and media, 12.5% healthcare practitioners, 16.2% service, 23.4% sales and office, 13.0% natural resources, construction, and maintenance, 6.4% production, transportation, and material moving

Income: Per capita: $33,991; Median household: $68,750; Average household: $91,040; Households with income of $100,000 or more: 35.5%; Poverty rate: 6.6%

Educational Attainment: High school diploma or higher: 91.5%; Bachelor's degree or higher: 25.4%; Graduate/professional degree or higher: 4.4%

Housing: Homeownership rate: 84.0%; Median home value: $209,300; Median year structure built: 1986; Homeowner vacancy rate: 2.9%; Median gross rent: $1,092 per month; Rental vacancy rate: 8.6%

Health Insurance: 93.5% have insurance; 82.3% have private insurance; 21.5% have public insurance; 6.5% do not have insurance; 0.6% of children under 18 do not have insurance

Transportation: Commute: 96.6% car, 1.2% public transportation, 0.5% walk, 1.6% work from home; Median travel time to work: 22.4 minutes

TERRACE PARK (village). Covers a land area of 1.174 square miles and a water area of 0.054 square miles. Located at 39.16° N. Lat; 84.31° W. Long. Elevation is 568 feet.

History: Terrace Park developed as a suburban community near Cincinnati.

Population: 2,251; Growth (since 2000): -1.0%; Density: 1,918.0 persons per square mile; Race: 98.6% White, 0.1% Black/African American, 0.4% Asian, 0.0% American Indian/Alaska Native, 0.0% Native Hawaiian/Other Pacific Islander, 0.7% Two or more races, 0.8% Hispanic of any race; Average household size: 2.97; Median age: 41.4; Age under 18: 35.0%; Age 65 and over: 10.5%; Males per 100 females: 101.0

School District(s)

Mariemont City (PK-12)
2012-13 Enrollment: 1,668 . . . . (513) 272-7500

Housing: Homeownership rate: 94.0%; Homeowner vacancy rate: 2.4%; Rental vacancy rate: 10.0%

THE VILLAGE OF INDIAN HILL (city). Covers a land area of 18.554 square miles and a water area of 0.095 square miles. Located at 39.19° N. Lat; 84.34° W. Long. Elevation is 564 feet.

History: Indian Hill began as a farming community, which from about 1904 began to attract Cincinnatians, who bought up its farmhouses as rural weekend designations. The rolling country appealed to a group of four Cincinnati businessmen who had built homes there in the early 1920s and envisioned a more ambitious rural settlement, persuading friends to join them in 1924 in forming the Camargo Realty Co.

Population: 5,785; Growth (since 2000): -2.1%; Density: 311.8 persons per square mile; Race: 92.2% White, 0.7% Black/African American, 5.7% Asian, 0.1% American Indian/Alaska Native, 0.0% Native Hawaiian/Other Pacific Islander, 1.1% Two or more races, 1.6% Hispanic of any race; Average household size: 2.81; Median age: 48.4; Age under 18: 27.0%; Age 65 and over: 17.5%; Males per 100 females: 93.9; Marriage status: 17.6% never married, 77.1% now married, 0.3% separated, 2.8% widowed, 2.4% divorced; Foreign born: 10.5%; Speak English only: 89.8%; With disability: 4.7%; Veterans: 7.2%; Ancestry: 35.3% German, 19.0% Irish, 13.6% English, 7.1% Italian, 5.5% European

Employment: 35.4% management, business, and financial, 4.9% computer, engineering, and science, 12.1% education, legal, community service, arts, and media, 26.0% healthcare practitioners, 6.8% service, 11.3% sales and office, 0.6% natural resources, construction, and maintenance, 3.0% production, transportation, and material moving

Income: Per capita: $113,863; Median household: $207,069; Average household: $324,959; Households with income of $100,000 or more: 71.9%; Poverty rate: 2.1%

Educational Attainment: High school diploma or higher: 98.9%; Bachelor's degree or higher: 85.4%; Graduate/professional degree or higher: 40.9%

Housing: Homeownership rate: 94.8%; Median home value: $934,500; Median year structure built: 1973; Homeowner vacancy rate: 2.7%; Median gross rent: $1,165 per month; Rental vacancy rate: 7.7%

Health Insurance: 99.4% have insurance; 91.2% have private insurance; 22.6% have public insurance; 0.6% do not have insurance; 0.0% of children under 18 do not have insurance

Transportation: Commute: 88.8% car, 0.0% public transportation, 2.7% walk, 8.5% work from home; Median travel time to work: 20.0 minutes

TURPIN HILLS (CDP). Covers a land area of 2.978 square miles and a water area of 0.003 square miles. Located at 39.11° N. Lat; 84.38° W. Long. Elevation is 650 feet.

History: The development of Turpin Hills (TH) began in the spring of 1956. A sign appeared on the site announcing lots "for sale" and the current name.

Population: 5,099; Growth (since 2000): 2.8%; Density: 1,712.5 persons per square mile; Race: 96.7% White, 0.7% Black/African American, 1.2% Asian, 0.0% American Indian/Alaska Native, 0.1% Native Hawaiian/Other Pacific Islander, 0.9% Two or more races, 1.5% Hispanic of any race; Average household size: 2.73; Median age: 42.4; Age under 18: 28.5%; Age 65 and over: 12.6%; Males per 100 females: 96.7; Marriage status: 19.8% never married, 69.3% now married, 1.1% separated, 3.8% widowed, 7.0% divorced; Foreign born: 0.9%; Speak English only: 96.9%; With disability: 8.0%; Veterans: 10.9%; Ancestry: 33.9% German, 22.3% Irish, 13.0% American, 12.5% English, 12.0% Italian

Employment: 31.1% management, business, and financial, 4.3% computer, engineering, and science, 17.8% education, legal, community service, arts, and media, 8.2% healthcare practitioners, 7.5% service, 24.3% sales and office, 1.4% natural resources, construction, and maintenance, 5.4% production, transportation, and material moving

Income: Per capita: $49,622; Median household: $122,200; Average household: $142,105; Households with income of $100,000 or more: 59.0%; Poverty rate: 2.8%

Educational Attainment: High school diploma or higher: 99.5%; Bachelor's degree or higher: 68.3%; Graduate/professional degree or higher: 25.4%

Housing: Homeownership rate: 82.8%; Median home value: $284,900; Median year structure built: 1974; Homeowner vacancy rate: 1.0%; Median gross rent: $691 per month; Rental vacancy rate: 15.1%

Health Insurance: 97.6% have insurance; 91.0% have private insurance; 13.6% have public insurance; 2.4% do not have insurance; 0.0% of children under 18 do not have insurance

Transportation: Commute: 87.3% car, 3.1% public transportation, 0.0% walk, 9.6% work from home; Median travel time to work: 24.5 minutes

WHITE OAK (CDP). Covers a land area of 6.167 square miles and a water area of 0 square miles. Located at 39.21° N. Lat; 84.61° W. Long. Elevation is 915 feet.

Population: 19,167; Growth (since 2000): 44.4%; Density: 3,108.2 persons per square mile; Race: 87.8% White, 8.5% Black/African American, 1.1% Asian, 0.2% American Indian/Alaska Native, 0.0% Native Hawaiian/Other Pacific Islander, 1.8% Two or more races, 1.4% Hispanic of any race; Average household size: 2.43; Median age: 40.2; Age under 18: 23.2%; Age 65 and over: 15.5%; Males per 100 females: 93.0; Marriage status: 27.2% never married, 55.3% now married, 1.7% separated, 6.2% widowed, 11.3% divorced; Foreign born: 3.0%; Speak English only: 96.2%; With disability: 11.5%; Veterans: 10.0%; Ancestry: 48.4% German, 19.5% Irish, 6.3% English, 5.5% Italian, 4.6% American

Employment: 14.8% management, business, and financial, 4.5% computer, engineering, and science, 8.4% education, legal, community service, arts, and media, 11.5% healthcare practitioners, 16.7% service, 26.8% sales and office, 5.8% natural resources, construction, and maintenance, 11.5% production, transportation, and material moving

Income: Per capita: $29,989; Median household: $56,066; Average household: $71,824; Households with income of $100,000 or more: 24.2%; Poverty rate: 12.6%

Educational Attainment: High school diploma or higher: 91.1%; Bachelor's degree or higher: 27.7%; Graduate/professional degree or higher: 9.1%

Housing: Homeownership rate: 72.7%; Median home value: $132,500; Median year structure built: 1967; Homeowner vacancy rate: 2.0%; Median gross rent: $682 per month; Rental vacancy rate: 9.0%
Health Insurance: 90.5% have insurance; 73.8% have private insurance; 28.3% have public insurance; 9.5% do not have insurance; 6.5% of children under 18 do not have insurance
Transportation: Commute: 96.4% car, 0.9% public transportation, 1.1% walk, 1.2% work from home; Median travel time to work: 22.4 minutes

WOODLAWN (village). Covers a land area of 2.570 square miles and a water area of 0 square miles. Located at 39.26° N. Lat; 84.47° W. Long. Elevation is 587 feet.
Population: 3,294; Growth (since 2000): 17.0%; Density: 1,281.5 persons per square mile; Race: 26.1% White, 67.2% Black/African American, 2.9% Asian, 0.2% American Indian/Alaska Native, 0.1% Native Hawaiian/Other Pacific Islander, 2.5% Two or more races, 2.3% Hispanic of any race; Average household size: 2.10; Median age: 39.6; Age under 18: 18.9%; Age 65 and over: 15.8%; Males per 100 females: 81.8; Marriage status: 43.6% never married, 35.3% now married, 3.2% separated, 8.0% widowed, 13.1% divorced; Foreign born: 6.8%; Speak English only: 93.9%; With disability: 10.4%; Veterans: 8.2%; Ancestry: 10.2% German, 9.5% American, 3.8% Irish, 3.3% English, 3.2% African
Employment: 14.6% management, business, and financial, 8.4% computer, engineering, and science, 9.7% education, legal, community service, arts, and media, 5.0% healthcare practitioners, 16.6% service, 24.0% sales and office, 7.3% natural resources, construction, and maintenance, 14.5% production, transportation, and material moving
Income: Per capita: $24,958; Median household: $50,814; Average household: $54,325; Households with income of $100,000 or more: 7.2%; Poverty rate: 14.9%
Educational Attainment: High school diploma or higher: 88.6%; Bachelor's degree or higher: 32.7%; Graduate/professional degree or higher: 8.7%
Housing: Homeownership rate: 39.6%; Median home value: $96,800; Median year structure built: 1971; Homeowner vacancy rate: 2.8%; Median gross rent: $978 per month; Rental vacancy rate: 8.7%
Health Insurance: 91.2% have insurance; 71.6% have private insurance; 31.6% have public insurance; 8.8% do not have insurance; 4.1% of children under 18 do not have insurance
Safety: Violent crime rate: 36.6 per 10,000 population; Property crime rate: 350.3 per 10,000 population
Transportation: Commute: 93.9% car, 2.5% public transportation, 1.2% walk, 1.9% work from home; Median travel time to work: 19.3 minutes

WYOMING (city). Covers a land area of 2.868 square miles and a water area of 0 square miles. Located at 39.23° N. Lat; 84.48° W. Long. Elevation is 577 feet.
History: Settled 1865, incorporated 1874.
Population: 8,428; Growth (since 2000): 2.0%; Density: 2,938.8 persons per square mile; Race: 83.6% White, 11.3% Black/African American, 2.1% Asian, 0.1% American Indian/Alaska Native, 0.0% Native Hawaiian/Other Pacific Islander, 2.2% Two or more races, 1.8% Hispanic of any race; Average household size: 2.68; Median age: 42.4; Age under 18: 29.7%; Age 65 and over: 14.2%; Males per 100 females: 90.4; Marriage status: 28.5% never married, 59.4% now married, 1.4% separated, 5.6% widowed, 6.5% divorced; Foreign born: 5.5%; Speak English only: 91.7%; With disability: 8.1%; Veterans: 5.9%; Ancestry: 37.6% German, 12.8% English, 11.4% Irish, 6.7% Russian, 5.1% Polish
Employment: 27.3% management, business, and financial, 7.9% computer, engineering, and science, 21.3% education, legal, community service, arts, and media, 7.8% healthcare practitioners, 10.3% service, 20.9% sales and office, 1.7% natural resources, construction, and maintenance, 2.7% production, transportation, and material moving
Income: Per capita: $47,247; Median household: $106,912; Average household: $129,626; Households with income of $100,000 or more: 52.7%; Poverty rate: 4.7%
Educational Attainment: High school diploma or higher: 97.3%; Bachelor's degree or higher: 70.8%; Graduate/professional degree or higher: 33.6%

School District(s)

Wyoming City (PK-12)
2012-13 Enrollment: 1,879 . . . . (513) 206-7000
Housing: Homeownership rate: 85.5%; Median home value: $288,700; Median year structure built: 1954; Homeowner vacancy rate: 1.7%; Median gross rent: $1,073 per month; Rental vacancy rate: 9.5%
Health Insurance: 94.6% have insurance; 88.6% have private insurance; 17.3% have public insurance; 5.4% do not have insurance; 2.6% of children under 18 do not have insurance
Safety: Violent crime rate: 2.4 per 10,000 population; Property crime rate: 203.9 per 10,000 population
Transportation: Commute: 90.7% car, 1.4% public transportation, 0.7% walk, 6.3% work from home; Median travel time to work: 21.2 minutes
Additional Information Contacts
City of Wyoming . . . . (513) 821-7600
http://www.wyoming.oh.us

Hancock County

Located in northwestern Ohio; crossed by the Blanchard River. Covers a land area of 531.358 square miles, a water area of 2.301 square miles, and is located in the Eastern Time Zone at 41.00° N. Lat., 83.67° W. Long. The county was founded in 1820. County seat is Findlay.

Hancock County is part of the Findlay, OH Micropolitan Statistical Area. The entire metro area includes: Hancock County, OH

Weather Station: Findlay Airport — Elevation: 799 feet

	Jan	Feb	Mar	Apr	May	Jun	Jul	Aug	Sep	Oct	Nov	Dec
High	33	36	47	60	70	79	83	81	75	63	50	37
Low	19	22	29	39	50	59	63	61	54	43	34	24
Precip	1.9	1.7	2.4	3.2	3.8	3.9	3.7	3.4	2.5	2.4	2.8	2.4
Snow	na	na	na	na	na	na	na	na	na	na	na	na

High and Low temperatures in degrees Fahrenheit; Precipitation and Snow in inches

Weather Station: Findlay Wpcc — Elevation: 768 feet

	Jan	Feb	Mar	Apr	May	Jun	Jul	Aug	Sep	Oct	Nov	Dec
High	33	37	47	60	71	80	84	82	76	63	50	37
Low	19	22	29	40	50	60	64	63	55	44	34	24
Precip	2.3	2.1	2.6	3.4	4.1	4.2	4.0	3.8	2.7	2.7	2.9	2.8
Snow	8.4	5.5	4.4	1.1	0.1	0.0	0.0	0.0	0.0	0.2	1.3	5.9

High and Low temperatures in degrees Fahrenheit; Precipitation and Snow in inches

Population: 74,782; Growth (since 2000): 4.9%; Density: 140.7 persons per square mile; Race: 93.4% White, 1.5% Black/African American, 1.7% Asian, 0.2% American Indian/Alaska Native, 0.0% Native Hawaiian/Other Pacific Islander, 1.8% two or more races, 4.5% Hispanic of any race; Average household size: 2.42; Median age: 38.5; Age under 18: 23.6%; Age 65 and over: 14.3%; Males per 100 females: 94.2; Marriage status: 27.9% never married, 54.1% now married, 1.8% separated, 6.9% widowed, 11.0% divorced; Foreign born: 2.3%; Speak English only: 95.7%; With disability: 11.1%; Veterans: 9.4%; Ancestry: 40.0% German, 11.6% American, 10.4% Irish, 9.4% English, 4.0% Italian
Religion: Six largest groups: 12.6% Catholicism, 11.3% Methodist/Pietist, 7.4% Lutheran, 4.0% Presbyterian-Reformed, 2.6% Non-denominational Protestant, 2.3% Baptist
Economy: Unemployment rate: 3.4%; Leading industries: 15.3% retail trade; 12.5% other services (except public administration); 10.7% health care and social assistance; Farms: 831 totaling 230,261 acres; Company size: 5 employ 1,000 or more persons, 3 employ 500 to 999 persons, 63 employ 100 to 499 persons, 1,641 employs less than 100 persons; Business ownership: 1,631 women-owned, n/a Black-owned, n/a Hispanic-owned, n/a Asian-owned
Employment: 16.5% management, business, and financial, 4.5% computer, engineering, and science, 7.9% education, legal, community service, arts, and media, 5.5% healthcare practitioners, 16.8% service, 20.1% sales and office, 8.1% natural resources, construction, and maintenance, 20.6% production, transportation, and material moving
Income: Per capita: $26,139; Median household: $49,589; Average household: $63,169; Households with income of $100,000 or more: 17.7%; Poverty rate: 14.0%
Educational Attainment: High school diploma or higher: 91.7%; Bachelor's degree or higher: 25.7%; Graduate/professional degree or higher: 8.9%
Housing: Homeownership rate: 70.3%; Median home value: $127,800; Median year structure built: 1968; Homeowner vacancy rate: 2.4%; Median gross rent: $652 per month; Rental vacancy rate: 11.7%
Vital Statistics: Birth rate: 115.3 per 10,000 population; Death rate: 85.9 per 10,000 population; Age-adjusted cancer mortality rate: 201.9 deaths per 100,000 population

Health Insurance: 89.3% have insurance; 75.4% have private insurance; 27.8% have public insurance; 10.7% do not have insurance; 5.7% of children under 18 do not have insurance
Health Care: Physicians: 17.0 per 10,000 population; Hospital beds: 24.1 per 10,000 population; Hospital admissions: 1,019.4 per 10,000 population
Transportation: Commute: 92.5% car, 0.2% public transportation, 2.4% walk, 3.7% work from home; Median travel time to work: 16.9 minutes
Presidential Election: 34.9% Obama, 63.2% Romney (2012)
National and State Parks: Van Buren Lake State Park
Additional Information Contacts
Hancock Government . . . . (419) 424-7044
http://www.co.hancock.oh.us

Hancock County Communities

ARCADIA (village). Covers a land area of 0.577 square miles and a water area of 0 square miles. Located at 41.11° N. Lat; 83.51° W. Long. Elevation is 807 feet.
Population: 590; Growth (since 2000): 9.9%; Density: 1,023.2 persons per square mile; Race: 96.1% White, 1.4% Black/African American, 0.2% Asian, 0.2% American Indian/Alaska Native, 0.0% Native Hawaiian/Other Pacific Islander, 1.5% Two or more races, 3.1% Hispanic of any race; Average household size: 2.72; Median age: 35.0; Age under 18: 29.5%; Age 65 and over: 11.4%; Males per 100 females: 100.0

School District(s)

Arcadia Local (PK-12)
2012-13 Enrollment: 588. . . . . (419) 894-6431
Housing: Homeownership rate: 79.2%; Homeowner vacancy rate: 3.8%; Rental vacancy rate: 6.3%

ARLINGTON (village). Covers a land area of 0.804 square miles and a water area of 0 square miles. Located at 40.89° N. Lat; 83.65° W. Long. Elevation is 863 feet.
Population: 1,455; Growth (since 2000): 7.7%; Density: 1,808.6 persons per square mile; Race: 98.9% White, 0.3% Black/African American, 0.1% Asian, 0.1% American Indian/Alaska Native, 0.0% Native Hawaiian/Other Pacific Islander, 0.5% Two or more races, 0.8% Hispanic of any race; Average household size: 2.53; Median age: 38.0; Age under 18: 27.1%; Age 65 and over: 17.0%; Males per 100 females: 87.7

School District(s)

Arlington Local (PK-12)
2012-13 Enrollment: 591. . . . . (419) 365-5121
Housing: Homeownership rate: 72.4%; Homeowner vacancy rate: 3.6%; Rental vacancy rate: 9.5%

BENTON RIDGE (village). Covers a land area of 0.343 square miles and a water area of 0 square miles. Located at 41.00° N. Lat; 83.79° W. Long. Elevation is 791 feet.
Population: 299; Growth (since 2000): -5.1%; Density: 872.0 persons per square mile; Race: 95.7% White, 0.0% Black/African American, 0.0% Asian, 0.7% American Indian/Alaska Native, 0.0% Native Hawaiian/Other Pacific Islander, 2.0% Two or more races, 2.0% Hispanic of any race; Average household size: 2.58; Median age: 37.4; Age under 18: 24.4%; Age 65 and over: 13.7%; Males per 100 females: 103.4
Housing: Homeownership rate: 89.7%; Homeowner vacancy rate: 0.0%; Rental vacancy rate: 7.7%

FINDLAY (city). County seat. Covers a land area of 19.134 square miles and a water area of 0.120 square miles. Located at 41.05° N. Lat; 83.64° W. Long. Elevation is 774 feet.
History: Findlay was laid out in 1821 by Joseph Vance and Elnathan Cory, and named for Fort Findlay, an outpost built under the direction of General Hull during the War of 1812. After the Civil War, the Findlay Natural Gas Company began to make commercial use of the gas and oil beneath the city. It was in the Findlay "Jeffersonian" in 1860 that Petroleum V. Nasby (pen name of David Ross Locke, the editor) wrote satirical letters attacking the institution of slavery.
Population: 41,202; Growth (since 2000): 5.7%; Density: 2,153.3 persons per square mile; Race: 91.2% White, 2.2% Black/African American, 2.5% Asian, 0.3% American Indian/Alaska Native, 0.0% Native Hawaiian/Other Pacific Islander, 2.1% Two or more races, 5.7% Hispanic of any race; Average household size: 2.29; Median age: 35.9; Age under 18: 22.2%; Age 65 and over: 14.5%; Males per 100 females: 90.7; Marriage status: 32.1% never married, 47.7% now married, 1.8% separated, 7.7% widowed, 12.4% divorced; Foreign born: 3.4%; Speak English only: 94.6%; With disability: 13.0%; Veterans: 9.8%; Ancestry: 36.0% German, 12.4% American, 11.1% Irish, 8.6% English, 4.1% Italian
Employment: 15.7% management, business, and financial, 5.1% computer, engineering, and science, 9.0% education, legal, community service, arts, and media, 5.8% healthcare practitioners, 19.2% service, 19.7% sales and office, 6.9% natural resources, construction, and maintenance, 18.5% production, transportation, and material moving
Income: Per capita: $24,783; Median household: $42,901; Average household: $57,491; Households with income of $100,000 or more: 14.1%; Poverty rate: 20.2%
Educational Attainment: High school diploma or higher: 90.2%; Bachelor's degree or higher: 27.1%; Graduate/professional degree or higher: 10.1%

School District(s)

Findlay City (PK-12)
2012-13 Enrollment: 5,720 . . . . (419) 425-8212
Findlay Digital Academy (09-12)
2012-13 Enrollment: 131. . . . . (419) 425-3598
Liberty-Benton Local (PK-12)
2012-13 Enrollment: 1,321 . . . . (419) 422-8526

Four-year College(s)

Brown Mackie College-Findlay (Private, For-profit)
Fall 2013 Enrollment: 448 . . . . (419) 423-2211
2013-14 Tuition: In-state $12,114; Out-of-state $12,114
The University of Findlay (Private, Not-for-profit, Church of God)
Fall 2013 Enrollment: 4,880 . . . . (419) 422-8313
2013-14 Tuition: In-state $29,798; Out-of-state $29,798
Winebrenner Theological Seminary (Private, Not-for-profit, Other Protestant)
Fall 2013 Enrollment: 60 . . . . (419) 434-4200

Two-year College(s)

The Artisan College of Cosmetology (Private, For-profit)
Fall 2013 Enrollment: 30 . . . . (419) 425-1485
Housing: Homeownership rate: 60.4%; Median home value: $123,300; Median year structure built: 1966; Homeowner vacancy rate: 2.7%; Median gross rent: $642 per month; Rental vacancy rate: 12.0%
Health Insurance: 87.8% have insurance; 70.0% have private insurance; 31.6% have public insurance; 12.2% do not have insurance; 5.9% of children under 18 do not have insurance
Hospitals: Blanchard Valley Hospital (150 beds)
Safety: Violent crime rate: 18.0 per 10,000 population; Property crime rate: 348.5 per 10,000 population
Newspapers: The Courier (daily circulation 21200)
Transportation: Commute: 91.5% car, 0.1% public transportation, 3.0% walk, 3.8% work from home; Median travel time to work: 14.5 minutes
Airports: Findlay (general aviation)
Additional Information Contacts
City of Findlay . . . . (419) 424-7137
http://www.ci.findlay.oh.us

JENERA (village). Covers a land area of 0.270 square miles and a water area of 0 square miles. Located at 40.90° N. Lat; 83.73° W. Long. Elevation is 850 feet.
Population: 221; Growth (since 2000): -6.0%; Density: 819.0 persons per square mile; Race: 99.1% White, 0.0% Black/African American, 0.0% Asian, 0.0% American Indian/Alaska Native, 0.0% Native Hawaiian/Other Pacific Islander, 0.9% Two or more races, 0.9% Hispanic of any race; Average household size: 2.80; Median age: 32.5; Age under 18: 28.1%; Age 65 and over: 9.5%; Males per 100 females: 102.8
Housing: Homeownership rate: 78.5%; Homeowner vacancy rate: 7.5%; Rental vacancy rate: 5.3%

MCCOMB (village). Covers a land area of 0.887 square miles and a water area of 0.036 square miles. Located at 41.11° N. Lat; 83.79° W. Long. Elevation is 771 feet.
Population: 1,648; Growth (since 2000): -1.7%; Density: 1,858.8 persons per square mile; Race: 93.9% White, 0.4% Black/African American, 0.7% Asian, 0.4% American Indian/Alaska Native, 0.0% Native Hawaiian/Other Pacific Islander, 2.4% Two or more races, 8.9% Hispanic of any race; Average household size: 2.80; Median age: 34.8; Age under 18: 30.6%; Age 65 and over: 10.4%; Males per 100 females: 95.3

School District(s)

Mccomb Local (PK-12)
2012-13 Enrollment: 761. . . . . (419) 293-3979

Housing: Homeownership rate: 75.0%; Homeowner vacancy rate: 2.6%; Rental vacancy rate: 12.0%

MOUNT BLANCHARD (village). Covers a land area of 0.538 square miles and a water area of 0 square miles. Located at 40.90° N. Lat; 83.56° W. Long. Elevation is 846 feet.
Population: 492; Growth (since 2000): 1.7%; Density: 915.0 persons per square mile; Race: 96.5% White, 0.4% Black/African American, 0.0% Asian, 0.0% American Indian/Alaska Native, 0.4% Native Hawaiian/Other Pacific Islander, 1.6% Two or more races, 2.6% Hispanic of any race; Average household size: 2.69; Median age: 34.3; Age under 18: 30.7%; Age 65 and over: 13.8%; Males per 100 females: 97.6

School District(s)

Riverdale Local (PK-12)
2012-13 Enrollment: 990. . . . . (419) 694-4994
Housing: Homeownership rate: 73.2%; Homeowner vacancy rate: 4.3%; Rental vacancy rate: 21.0%

MOUNT CORY (village). Covers a land area of 0.384 square miles and a water area of 0 square miles. Located at 40.93° N. Lat; 83.82° W. Long. Elevation is 814 feet.
Population: 204; Growth (since 2000): 0.5%; Density: 531.1 persons per square mile; Race: 96.1% White, 0.0% Black/African American, 1.5% Asian, 0.5% American Indian/Alaska Native, 0.0% Native Hawaiian/Other Pacific Islander, 2.0% Two or more races, 0.0% Hispanic of any race; Average household size: 2.65; Median age: 39.7; Age under 18: 28.4%; Age 65 and over: 14.2%; Males per 100 females: 102.0
Housing: Homeownership rate: 89.6%; Homeowner vacancy rate: 4.1%; Rental vacancy rate: 0.0%

RAWSON (village). Covers a land area of 0.396 square miles and a water area of 0 square miles. Located at 40.96° N. Lat; 83.78° W. Long. Elevation is 810 feet.
Population: 570; Growth (since 2000): 22.6%; Density: 1,441.2 persons per square mile; Race: 95.6% White, 1.9% Black/African American, 0.9% Asian, 0.0% American Indian/Alaska Native, 0.0% Native Hawaiian/Other Pacific Islander, 1.4% Two or more races, 1.9% Hispanic of any race; Average household size: 2.98; Median age: 30.8; Age under 18: 33.5%; Age 65 and over: 8.1%; Males per 100 females: 96.6

School District(s)

Cory-Rawson Local (PK-12)
2012-13 Enrollment: 613. . . . . (419) 963-3415
Housing: Homeownership rate: 68.0%; Homeowner vacancy rate: 1.5%; Rental vacancy rate: 12.9%

VAN BUREN (village). Covers a land area of 0.258 square miles and a water area of 0 square miles. Located at 41.14° N. Lat; 83.65° W. Long. Elevation is 768 feet.
History: Van Buren was named for President Martin Van Buren. For a time, Van Buren was an oil center.
Population: 328; Growth (since 2000): 4.8%; Density: 1,270.6 persons per square mile; Race: 97.3% White, 0.0% Black/African American, 0.0% Asian, 0.0% American Indian/Alaska Native, 0.0% Native Hawaiian/Other Pacific Islander, 0.9% Two or more races, 4.3% Hispanic of any race; Average household size: 2.76; Median age: 34.5; Age under 18: 30.5%; Age 65 and over: 12.8%; Males per 100 females: 98.8

School District(s)

Van Buren Local (PK-12)
2012-13 Enrollment: 1,044 . . . . (419) 299-3578
Housing: Homeownership rate: 95.0%; Homeowner vacancy rate: 4.2%; Rental vacancy rate: 0.0%

VANLUE (village). Covers a land area of 0.349 square miles and a water area of 0.007 square miles. Located at 40.97° N. Lat; 83.48° W. Long. Elevation is 820 feet.
Population: 359; Growth (since 2000): -3.2%; Density: 1,028.8 persons per square mile; Race: 98.3% White, 0.3% Black/African American, 0.0% Asian, 0.0% American Indian/Alaska Native, 0.0% Native Hawaiian/Other Pacific Islander, 0.8% Two or more races, 5.3% Hispanic of any race; Average household size: 2.55; Median age: 35.8; Age under 18: 26.5%; Age 65 and over: 14.2%; Males per 100 females: 88.9

School District(s)

Vanlue Local (PK-12)
2012-13 Enrollment: 238. . . . . (419) 387-7724
Housing: Homeownership rate: 80.2%; Homeowner vacancy rate: 0.0%; Rental vacancy rate: 24.3%

WILLIAMSTOWN (unincorporated postal area)

ZCTA: 45897

Covers a land area of 1.376 square miles and a water area of 0.007 square miles. Located at 40.83° N. Lat; 83.66° W. Long. Elevation is 932 feet.
Population: 101; Growth (since 2000): 48.5%; Density: 73.4 persons per square mile; Race: 99.0% White, 0.0% Black/African American, 0.0% Asian, 0.0% American Indian/Alaska Native, 0.0% Native Hawaiian/Other Pacific Islander, 1.0% Two or more races, 2.0% Hispanic of any race; Average household size: 2.24; Median age: 46.5; Age under 18: 20.8%; Age 65 and over: 17.8%; Males per 100 females: 83.6
Housing: Homeownership rate: 82.2%; Homeowner vacancy rate: 0.0%; Rental vacancy rate: 20.0%

Hardin County

Located in west central Ohio; crossed by the Sciota, Blanchard, and Ottawa Rivers. Covers a land area of 470.405 square miles, a water area of 0.243 square miles, and is located in the Eastern Time Zone at 40.66° N. Lat., 83.66° W. Long. The county was founded in 1820. County seat is Kenton.

Weather Station: Kenton Elevation: 995 feet

	Jan	Feb	Mar	Apr	May	Jun	Jul	Aug	Sep	Oct	Nov	Dec
High	33	37	47	60	71	81	85	83	76	63	50	37
Low	18	20	28	39	50	59	63	61	53	42	33	23
Precip	2.3	2.1	2.6	3.3	4.1	3.6	3.9	3.1	2.7	2.4	2.9	2.7
Snow	8.3	6.6	3.9	0.4	0.0	0.0	0.0	0.0	0.0	tr	1.0	5.0

High and Low temperatures in degrees Fahrenheit; Precipitation and Snow in inches

Population: 32,058; Growth (since 2000): 0.4%; Density: 68.1 persons per square mile; Race: 96.7% White, 0.8% Black/African American, 0.6% Asian, 0.2% American Indian/Alaska Native, 0.0% Native Hawaiian/Other Pacific Islander, 1.3% two or more races, 1.3% Hispanic of any race; Average household size: 2.53; Median age: 34.7; Age under 18: 23.6%; Age 65 and over: 13.4%; Males per 100 females: 98.5; Marriage status: 32.0% never married, 48.6% now married, 1.2% separated, 7.0% widowed, 12.4% divorced; Foreign born: 1.5%; Speak English only: 95.1%; With disability: 14.4%; Veterans: 9.4%; Ancestry: 29.5% German, 15.2% American, 13.1% Irish, 8.8% English, 2.2% Italian
Religion: Six largest groups: 10.7% Methodist/Pietist, 5.6% Catholicism, 5.2% Presbyterian-Reformed, 4.3% Baptist, 2.9% European Free-Church, 2.8% Pentecostal
Economy: Unemployment rate: 4.0%; Leading industries: 19.5% retail trade; 13.9% other services (except public administration); 10.6% accommodation and food services; Farms: 793 totaling 247,839 acres; Company size: 1 employs 1,000 or more persons, 0 employ 500 to 999 persons, 9 employ 100 to 499 persons, 452 employ less than 100 persons; Business ownership: 475 women-owned, n/a Black-owned, n/a Hispanic-owned, n/a Asian-owned
Employment: 8.9% management, business, and financial, 2.4% computer, engineering, and science, 9.3% education, legal, community service, arts, and media, 3.8% healthcare practitioners, 20.2% service, 21.9% sales and office, 6.5% natural resources, construction, and maintenance, 26.9% production, transportation, and material moving
Income: Per capita: $19,626; Median household: $40,415; Average household: $51,886; Households with income of $100,000 or more: 10.3%; Poverty rate: 18.1%
Educational Attainment: High school diploma or higher: 86.8%; Bachelor's degree or higher: 13.4%; Graduate/professional degree or higher: 6.1%
Housing: Homeownership rate: 70.8%; Median home value: $95,600; Median year structure built: 1960; Homeowner vacancy rate: 2.5%; Median gross rent: $645 per month; Rental vacancy rate: 10.4%
Vital Statistics: Birth rate: 109.4 per 10,000 population; Death rate: 99.2 per 10,000 population; Age-adjusted cancer mortality rate: 164.7 deaths per 100,000 population
Health Insurance: 85.4% have insurance; 67.1% have private insurance; 30.7% have public insurance; 14.6% do not have insurance; 11.7% of children under 18 do not have insurance
Health Care: Physicians: 4.4 per 10,000 population; Hospital beds: 7.8 per 10,000 population; Hospital admissions: 316.4 per 10,000 population

Transportation: Commute: 89.2% car, 0.3% public transportation, 3.6% walk, 5.0% work from home; Median travel time to work: 22.9 minutes
Presidential Election: 36.9% Obama, 60.4% Romney (2012)
Additional Information Contacts
Hardin Government . . . . (419) 674-2205
http://www.hardincountyoh.com

Hardin County Communities

ADA (village). Covers a land area of 2.078 square miles and a water area of 0 square miles. Located at 40.77° N. Lat; 83.82° W. Long. Elevation is 961 feet.
History: Ada grew up around Ohio Northern University, founded in 1871 as the Northwestern Ohio Normal School by Henry Solomon Lehr.
Population: 5,952; Growth (since 2000): 6.6%; Density: 2,864.1 persons per square mile; Race: 93.5% White, 1.9% Black/African American, 1.9% Asian, 0.1% American Indian/Alaska Native, 0.0% Native Hawaiian/Other Pacific Islander, 1.9% Two or more races, 1.6% Hispanic of any race; Average household size: 2.26; Median age: 22.2; Age under 18: 13.6%; Age 65 and over: 6.3%; Males per 100 females: 103.4; Marriage status: 59.5% never married, 26.6% now married, 0.2% separated, 4.1% widowed, 9.8% divorced; Foreign born: 2.5%; Speak English only: 96.0%; With disability: 9.5%; Veterans: 3.6%; Ancestry: 38.0% German, 18.2% Irish, 9.8% English, 9.4% American, 6.0% Italian
Employment: 4.8% management, business, and financial, 4.9% computer, engineering, and science, 13.4% education, legal, community service, arts, and media, 5.4% healthcare practitioners, 23.6% service, 27.8% sales and office, 3.2% natural resources, construction, and maintenance, 16.8% production, transportation, and material moving
Income: Per capita: $13,227; Median household: $28,981; Average household: $43,496; Households with income of $100,000 or more: 7.9%; Poverty rate: 22.6%
Educational Attainment: High school diploma or higher: 85.4%; Bachelor's degree or higher: 26.1%; Graduate/professional degree or higher: 15.5%

School District(s)
Ada Exempted Village (PK-12)
2012-13 Enrollment: 869. . . . . (419) 634-6421

Four-year College(s)
Ohio Northern University (Private, Not-for-profit, United Methodist)
Fall 2013 Enrollment: 3,619 . . . . (419) 772-2000
2013-14 Tuition: In-state $36,720; Out-of-state $36,720

Housing: Homeownership rate: 47.1%; Median home value: $97,900; Median year structure built: 1965; Homeowner vacancy rate: 3.5%; Median gross rent: $679 per month; Rental vacancy rate: 8.2%
Health Insurance: 92.4% have insurance; 81.3% have private insurance; 22.8% have public insurance; 7.6% do not have insurance; 0.0% of children under 18 do not have insurance
Safety: Violent crime rate: 12.2 per 10,000 population; Property crime rate: 132.1 per 10,000 population
Newspapers: Ada Herald (weekly circulation 2800)
Transportation: Commute: 73.5% car, 0.1% public transportation, 7.4% walk, 16.7% work from home; Median travel time to work: 21.1 minutes

ALGER (village). Covers a land area of 0.285 square miles and a water area of 0 square miles. Located at 40.71° N. Lat; 83.84° W. Long. Elevation is 974 feet.
Population: 860; Growth (since 2000): -3.2%; Density: 3,019.9 persons per square mile; Race: 97.2% White, 0.2% Black/African American, 0.1% Asian, 0.5% American Indian/Alaska Native, 0.0% Native Hawaiian/Other Pacific Islander, 1.9% Two or more races, 1.2% Hispanic of any race; Average household size: 2.48; Median age: 37.1; Age under 18: 26.7%; Age 65 and over: 14.8%; Males per 100 females: 85.7
Housing: Homeownership rate: 67.2%; Homeowner vacancy rate: 3.6%; Rental vacancy rate: 14.2%

DOLA (CDP). Covers a land area of 0.832 square miles and a water area of 0 square miles. Located at 40.78° N. Lat; 83.70° W. Long. Elevation is 948 feet.
Population: 140; Growth (since 2000): n/a; Density: 168.4 persons per square mile; Race: 95.0% White, 1.4% Black/African American, 0.0% Asian, 0.7% American Indian/Alaska Native, 0.0% Native Hawaiian/Other Pacific Islander, 2.9% Two or more races, 0.0% Hispanic of any race; Average household size: 2.46; Median age: 44.0; Age under 18: 26.4%; Age 65 and over: 18.6%; Males per 100 females: 94.4

School District(s)
Hardin Northern Local (PK-12)
2012-13 Enrollment: 466. . . . . (419) 759-2331

Housing: Homeownership rate: 79.0%; Homeowner vacancy rate: 2.1%; Rental vacancy rate: 7.7%

DUNKIRK (village). Covers a land area of 0.664 square miles and a water area of 0.059 square miles. Located at 40.79° N. Lat; 83.64° W. Long. Elevation is 945 feet.
Population: 875; Growth (since 2000): -8.1%; Density: 1,318.4 persons per square mile; Race: 97.4% White, 0.3% Black/African American, 0.5% Asian, 0.3% American Indian/Alaska Native, 0.0% Native Hawaiian/Other Pacific Islander, 1.5% Two or more races, 0.5% Hispanic of any race; Average household size: 2.64; Median age: 35.5; Age under 18: 28.1%; Age 65 and over: 12.1%; Males per 100 females: 100.7
Housing: Homeownership rate: 79.5%; Homeowner vacancy rate: 1.8%; Rental vacancy rate: 8.1%

FOREST (village). Covers a land area of 1.605 square miles and a water area of 0 square miles. Located at 40.81° N. Lat; 83.51° W. Long. Elevation is 928 feet.
Population: 1,461; Growth (since 2000): -1.8%; Density: 910.5 persons per square mile; Race: 98.0% White, 0.4% Black/African American, 0.0% Asian, 0.1% American Indian/Alaska Native, 0.0% Native Hawaiian/Other Pacific Islander, 1.4% Two or more races, 1.0% Hispanic of any race; Average household size: 2.66; Median age: 34.2; Age under 18: 29.4%; Age 65 and over: 11.9%; Males per 100 females: 102.1
Housing: Homeownership rate: 72.8%; Homeowner vacancy rate: 2.2%; Rental vacancy rate: 13.2%

KENTON (city). County seat. Covers a land area of 5.038 square miles and a water area of 0.094 square miles. Located at 40.64° N. Lat; 83.61° W. Long. Elevation is 991 feet.
History: Kenton was platted in 1833 on the Scioto River, and named for pioneer Simon Kenton. The town's economic base moved from agriculture to ornamental iron fences and then back to agriculture.
Population: 8,262; Growth (since 2000): -0.9%; Density: 1,639.8 persons per square mile; Race: 96.2% White, 0.9% Black/African American, 0.3% Asian, 0.2% American Indian/Alaska Native, 0.1% Native Hawaiian/Other Pacific Islander, 1.4% Two or more races, 2.2% Hispanic of any race; Average household size: 2.40; Median age: 37.2; Age under 18: 25.5%; Age 65 and over: 15.5%; Males per 100 females: 88.9; Marriage status: 32.3% never married, 38.4% now married, 3.0% separated, 10.8% widowed, 18.5% divorced; Foreign born: 1.4%; Speak English only: 96.6%; With disability: 21.2%; Veterans: 10.3%; Ancestry: 20.9% German, 18.5% American, 11.6% Irish, 7.6% English, 2.4% Scottish
Employment: 7.3% management, business, and financial, 0.5% computer, engineering, and science, 11.1% education, legal, community service, arts, and media, 1.8% healthcare practitioners, 22.7% service, 24.8% sales and office, 4.7% natural resources, construction, and maintenance, 27.1% production, transportation, and material moving
Income: Per capita: $16,838; Median household: $31,700; Average household: $38,485; Households with income of $100,000 or more: 3.5%; Poverty rate: 22.6%
Educational Attainment: High school diploma or higher: 84.6%; Bachelor's degree or higher: 6.3%; Graduate/professional degree or higher: 2.5%

School District(s)
Hardin Community School (07-12)
2012-13 Enrollment: 34. . . . . (419) 674-2288
Kenton City (PK-12)
2012-13 Enrollment: 1,928 . . . . (419) 673-0775

Housing: Homeownership rate: 58.6%; Median home value: $73,600; Median year structure built: 1956; Homeowner vacancy rate: 3.4%; Median gross rent: $551 per month; Rental vacancy rate: 12.1%
Health Insurance: 77.8% have insurance; 49.6% have private insurance; 38.5% have public insurance; 22.2% do not have insurance; 4.1% of children under 18 do not have insurance
Hospitals: Hardin Memorial Hospital (103 beds)
Safety: Violent crime rate: 15.9 per 10,000 population; Property crime rate: 425.9 per 10,000 population
Newspapers: Kenton Times (daily circulation 7200)
Transportation: Commute: 92.9% car, 0.2% public transportation, 2.1% walk, 0.8% work from home; Median travel time to work: 19.3 minutes

MCGUFFEY (village). Covers a land area of 0.364 square miles and a water area of 0 square miles. Located at 40.69° N. Lat; 83.79° W. Long. Elevation is 971 feet.
History: McGuffey was settled in a marshy region, and took to the growing of onions. Those who tended the onion fields were sometimes called "marsh rats."
Population: 501; Growth (since 2000): -4.0%; Density: 1,374.5 persons per square mile; Race: 96.6% White, 0.6% Black/African American, 0.4% Asian, 0.4% American Indian/Alaska Native, 0.0% Native Hawaiian/Other Pacific Islander, 2.0% Two or more races, 0.2% Hispanic of any race; Average household size: 2.61; Median age: 35.6; Age under 18: 26.7%; Age 65 and over: 14.0%; Males per 100 females: 85.6

School District(s)

Upper Scioto Valley Local (PK-12)
2012-13 Enrollment: 579. . . . . (419) 757-3231
Housing: Homeownership rate: 70.8%; Homeowner vacancy rate: 2.2%; Rental vacancy rate: 9.7%

MOUNT VICTORY (village). Covers a land area of 0.766 square miles and a water area of 0 square miles. Located at 40.53° N. Lat; 83.52° W. Long. Elevation is 1,040 feet.
Population: 627; Growth (since 2000): 4.5%; Density: 819.0 persons per square mile; Race: 98.1% White, 0.6% Black/African American, 0.5% Asian, 0.0% American Indian/Alaska Native, 0.0% Native Hawaiian/Other Pacific Islander, 0.3% Two or more races, 1.1% Hispanic of any race; Average household size: 2.52; Median age: 37.3; Age under 18: 25.4%; Age 65 and over: 16.3%; Males per 100 females: 97.2

School District(s)

Ridgemont Local (PK-12)
2012-13 Enrollment: 478. . . . . (937) 354-2441
Housing: Homeownership rate: 73.9%; Homeowner vacancy rate: 3.2%; Rental vacancy rate: 9.7%

PATTERSON (village). Covers a land area of 0.107 square miles and a water area of 0 square miles. Located at 40.78° N. Lat; 83.53° W. Long. Elevation is 925 feet.
Population: 139; Growth (since 2000): 0.7%; Density: 1,304.5 persons per square mile; Race: 99.3% White, 0.0% Black/African American, 0.0% Asian, 0.0% American Indian/Alaska Native, 0.0% Native Hawaiian/Other Pacific Islander, 0.7% Two or more races, 2.2% Hispanic of any race; Average household size: 2.62; Median age: 42.3; Age under 18: 22.3%; Age 65 and over: 13.7%; Males per 100 females: 80.5
Housing: Homeownership rate: 75.4%; Homeowner vacancy rate: 2.4%; Rental vacancy rate: 7.1%

RIDGEWAY (village). Covers a land area of 0.592 square miles and a water area of 0 square miles. Located at 40.51° N. Lat; 83.57° W. Long. Elevation is 1,060 feet.
Population: 338; Growth (since 2000): -4.5%; Density: 570.6 persons per square mile; Race: 97.0% White, 1.5% Black/African American, 0.3% Asian, 0.0% American Indian/Alaska Native, 0.0% Native Hawaiian/Other Pacific Islander, 1.2% Two or more races, 0.9% Hispanic of any race; Average household size: 2.70; Median age: 34.4; Age under 18: 29.3%; Age 65 and over: 9.2%; Males per 100 females: 88.8

School District(s)

Ridgemont Local (PK-12)
2012-13 Enrollment: 478. . . . . (937) 354-2441
Housing: Homeownership rate: 85.6%; Homeowner vacancy rate: 3.6%; Rental vacancy rate: 0.0%

Harrison County

Located in eastern Ohio; drained by Stillwater and Conotton Creeks; includes Tappan and Clendening Lakes. Covers a land area of 402.339 square miles, a water area of 8.428 square miles, and is located in the Eastern Time Zone at 40.29° N. Lat., 81.09° W. Long. The county was founded in 1813. County seat is Cadiz.

Weather Station: Cadiz Elevation: 1,259 feet

	Jan	Feb	Mar	Apr	May	Jun	Jul	Aug	Sep	Oct	Nov	Dec
High	35	39	48	61	70	79	82	81	75	63	51	39
Low	19	22	29	40	49	58	63	61	54	43	34	24
Precip	3.0	2.4	3.2	3.5	4.4	4.3	4.3	3.8	3.4	2.8	3.4	2.9
Snow	8.8	6.1	4.9	1.3	0.0	0.0	0.0	0.0	0.0	0.1	1.5	5.6

High and Low temperatures in degrees Fahrenheit; Precipitation and Snow in inches

Population: 15,864; Growth (since 2000): 0.1%; Density: 39.4 persons per square mile; Race: 95.9% White, 2.1% Black/African American, 0.1% Asian, 0.1% American Indian/Alaska Native, 0.0% Native Hawaiian/Other Pacific Islander, 1.6% two or more races, 0.5% Hispanic of any race; Average household size: 2.40; Median age: 44.4; Age under 18: 21.9%; Age 65 and over: 18.2%; Males per 100 females: 98.4; Marriage status: 21.7% never married, 58.5% now married, 1.2% separated, 8.1% widowed, 11.8% divorced; Foreign born: 0.4%; Speak English only: 97.7%; With disability: 15.6%; Veterans: 12.8%; Ancestry: 20.5% German, 15.1% Irish, 9.7% English, 7.8% Polish, 7.0% American
Religion: Six largest groups: 12.9% Methodist/Pietist, 3.7% Presbyterian-Reformed, 3.6% Baptist, 3.4% Catholicism, 2.4% European Free-Church, 0.9% Holiness
Economy: Unemployment rate: 4.5%; Leading industries: 16.3% other services (except public administration); 13.2% retail trade; 11.2% construction; Farms: 444 totaling 95,387 acres; Company size: 0 employ 1,000 or more persons, 0 employ 500 to 999 persons, 4 employ 100 to 499 persons, 254 employ less than 100 persons; Business ownership: 309 women-owned, n/a Black-owned, n/a Hispanic-owned, n/a Asian-owned
Employment: 8.2% management, business, and financial, 1.1% computer, engineering, and science, 7.3% education, legal, community service, arts, and media, 4.9% healthcare practitioners, 18.6% service, 22.5% sales and office, 17.0% natural resources, construction, and maintenance, 20.3% production, transportation, and material moving
Income: Per capita: $21,029; Median household: $39,002; Average household: $50,896; Households with income of $100,000 or more: 9.9%; Poverty rate: 18.4%
Educational Attainment: High school diploma or higher: 85.7%; Bachelor's degree or higher: 9.2%; Graduate/professional degree or higher: 2.9%
Housing: Homeownership rate: 75.6%; Median home value: $83,500; Median year structure built: 1961; Homeowner vacancy rate: 2.0%; Median gross rent: $577 per month; Rental vacancy rate: 7.3%
Vital Statistics: Birth rate: 92.8 per 10,000 population; Death rate: 128.7 per 10,000 population; Age-adjusted cancer mortality rate: 184.1 deaths per 100,000 population
Health Insurance: 88.5% have insurance; 65.4% have private insurance; 38.4% have public insurance; 11.5% do not have insurance; 5.4% of children under 18 do not have insurance
Health Care: Physicians: 6.4 per 10,000 population; Hospital beds: 15.8 per 10,000 population; Hospital admissions: 292.5 per 10,000 population
Transportation: Commute: 95.3% car, 0.3% public transportation, 1.5% walk, 2.4% work from home; Median travel time to work: 29.1 minutes
Presidential Election: 41.4% Obama, 56.2% Romney (2012)
National and State Parks: Harrison County State Forest
Additional Information Contacts
Harrison Government . . . . (740) 942-4623
http://www.harrisoncountyohio.org

Harrison County Communities

BOWERSTON (village). Covers a land area of 0.506 square miles and a water area of 0 square miles. Located at 40.43° N. Lat; 81.19° W. Long. Elevation is 955 feet.
Population: 398; Growth (since 2000): -3.9%; Density: 786.0 persons per square mile; Race: 98.7% White, 0.8% Black/African American, 0.0% Asian, 0.3% American Indian/Alaska Native, 0.0% Native Hawaiian/Other Pacific Islander, 0.3% Two or more races, 0.0% Hispanic of any race; Average household size: 2.26; Median age: 41.1; Age under 18: 22.6%; Age 65 and over: 20.9%; Males per 100 females: 81.7

School District(s)

Conotton Valley Union Local (PK-12)
2012-13 Enrollment: 428. . . . . (740) 269-2000
Housing: Homeownership rate: 62.1%; Homeowner vacancy rate: 3.8%; Rental vacancy rate: 10.4%

CADIZ (village). County seat. Covers a land area of 8.777 square miles and a water area of 0.163 square miles. Located at 40.26° N. Lat; 80.99° W. Long. Elevation is 1,266 feet.
History: The town of Cadiz, settled at the junction of the Mingo and Moravian trails, was surveyed in 1803, and in 1830 became the seat of Harrison County.
Population: 3,353; Growth (since 2000): 1.4%; Density: 382.0 persons per square mile; Race: 87.4% White, 8.4% Black/African American, 0.3% Asian, 0.0% American Indian/Alaska Native, 0.0% Native Hawaiian/Other

Pacific Islander, 3.5% Two or more races, 0.8% Hispanic of any race; Average household size: 2.32; Median age: 42.3; Age under 18: 22.5%; Age 65 and over: 18.3%; Males per 100 females: 89.3; Marriage status: 27.8% never married, 52.2% now married, 2.9% separated, 8.3% widowed, 11.7% divorced; Foreign born: 0.0%; Speak English only: 98.9%; With disability: 15.9%; Veterans: 12.2%; Ancestry: 15.4% Irish, 13.4% German, 9.4% Polish, 8.1% English, 6.4% Italian

Employment: 8.5% management, business, and financial, 1.3% computer, engineering, and science, 9.9% education, legal, community service, arts, and media, 6.1% healthcare practitioners, 13.3% service, 26.7% sales and office, 24.7% natural resources, construction, and maintenance, 9.5% production, transportation, and material moving

Income: Per capita: $20,895; Median household: $36,578; Average household: $49,526; Households with income of $100,000 or more: 11.2%; Poverty rate: 15.2%

Educational Attainment: High school diploma or higher: 86.3%; Bachelor's degree or higher: 14.1%; Graduate/professional degree or higher: 5.3%

School District(s)

Belmont-Harrison (08-12)
2012-13 Enrollment: n/a . . . . (740) 695-9130
Harrison Hills City (PK-12)
2012-13 Enrollment: 1,559 . . . . (740) 942-7800

Housing: Homeownership rate: 61.0%; Median home value: $86,000; Median year structure built: 1954; Homeowner vacancy rate: 2.3%; Median gross rent: $546 per month; Rental vacancy rate: 9.9%

Health Insurance: 91.8% have insurance; 68.1% have private insurance; 39.1% have public insurance; 8.2% do not have insurance; 0.0% of children under 18 do not have insurance

Hospitals: Harrison Community Hospital (48 beds)

Newspapers: Harrison News-Herald (weekly circulation 6500)

Transportation: Commute: 94.8% car, 0.0% public transportation, 2.3% walk, 1.9% work from home; Median travel time to work: 18.5 minutes

DEERSVILLE (village). Covers a land area of 0.345 square miles and a water area of 0 square miles. Located at 40.31° N. Lat; 81.19° W. Long. Elevation is 1,230 feet.

Population: 79; Growth (since 2000): -3.7%; Density: 229.3 persons per square mile; Race: 94.9% White, 0.0% Black/African American, 2.5% Asian, 0.0% American Indian/Alaska Native, 0.0% Native Hawaiian/Other Pacific Islander, 2.5% Two or more races, 0.0% Hispanic of any race; Average household size: 2.39; Median age: 45.5; Age under 18: 16.5%; Age 65 and over: 17.7%; Males per 100 females: 107.9

Housing: Homeownership rate: 87.9%; Homeowner vacancy rate: 14.7%; Rental vacancy rate: 20.0%

FREEPORT (village). Covers a land area of 0.599 square miles and a water area of 0 square miles. Located at 40.21° N. Lat; 81.27° W. Long. Elevation is 997 feet.

Population: 369; Growth (since 2000): -7.3%; Density: 616.1 persons per square mile; Race: 97.6% White, 0.0% Black/African American, 0.0% Asian, 0.0% American Indian/Alaska Native, 0.0% Native Hawaiian/Other Pacific Islander, 2.4% Two or more races, 0.0% Hispanic of any race; Average household size: 2.29; Median age: 41.2; Age under 18: 23.3%; Age 65 and over: 17.9%; Males per 100 females: 99.5

Housing: Homeownership rate: 70.2%; Homeowner vacancy rate: 2.6%; Rental vacancy rate: 4.0%

HARRISVILLE (village). Covers a land area of 0.152 square miles and a water area of <.001 square miles. Located at 40.18° N. Lat; 80.89° W. Long. Elevation is 1,250 feet.

Population: 235; Growth (since 2000): -9.3%; Density: 1,544.7 persons per square mile; Race: 99.6% White, 0.0% Black/African American, 0.0% Asian, 0.0% American Indian/Alaska Native, 0.0% Native Hawaiian/Other Pacific Islander, 0.4% Two or more races, 0.9% Hispanic of any race; Average household size: 2.37; Median age: 41.2; Age under 18: 18.7%; Age 65 and over: 14.5%; Males per 100 females: 106.1

Housing: Homeownership rate: 77.8%; Homeowner vacancy rate: 8.3%; Rental vacancy rate: 12.0%

HOPEDALE (village). Covers a land area of 1.117 square miles and a water area of <.001 square miles. Located at 40.33° N. Lat; 80.90° W. Long. Elevation is 1,158 feet.

History: Hopedale was the home of motion picture actor Clark Gable, who spent part of his boyhood here. The town developed around the coal mines.

Population: 950; Growth (since 2000): -3.5%; Density: 850.8 persons per square mile; Race: 97.1% White, 0.8% Black/African American, 0.3% Asian, 0.3% American Indian/Alaska Native, 0.0% Native Hawaiian/Other Pacific Islander, 1.5% Two or more races, 0.5% Hispanic of any race; Average household size: 2.35; Median age: 48.0; Age under 18: 21.6%; Age 65 and over: 25.3%; Males per 100 females: 95.9

School District(s)

Harrison Hills City (PK-12)
2012-13 Enrollment: 1,559 . . . . (740) 942-7800

Housing: Homeownership rate: 72.4%; Homeowner vacancy rate: 2.2%; Rental vacancy rate: 6.4%

JEWETT (village). Covers a land area of 0.509 square miles and a water area of 0 square miles. Located at 40.37° N. Lat; 81.00° W. Long. Elevation is 1,007 feet.

History: Laid out 1851, incorporated 1886.

Population: 692; Growth (since 2000): -11.7%; Density: 1,359.6 persons per square mile; Race: 96.7% White, 0.3% Black/African American, 0.0% Asian, 0.0% American Indian/Alaska Native, 0.0% Native Hawaiian/Other Pacific Islander, 2.9% Two or more races, 0.1% Hispanic of any race; Average household size: 2.53; Median age: 36.9; Age under 18: 25.6%; Age 65 and over: 14.9%; Males per 100 females: 102.3

Housing: Homeownership rate: 71.4%; Homeowner vacancy rate: 3.9%; Rental vacancy rate: 8.2%

NEW ATHENS (village). Covers a land area of 0.279 square miles and a water area of <.001 square miles. Located at 40.18° N. Lat; 80.99° W. Long. Elevation is 1,184 feet.

Population: 320; Growth (since 2000): -6.4%; Density: 1,145.4 persons per square mile; Race: 99.4% White, 0.3% Black/African American, 0.0% Asian, 0.0% American Indian/Alaska Native, 0.0% Native Hawaiian/Other Pacific Islander, 0.3% Two or more races, 0.0% Hispanic of any race; Average household size: 2.29; Median age: 44.9; Age under 18: 19.1%; Age 65 and over: 18.8%; Males per 100 females: 93.9

Housing: Homeownership rate: 82.2%; Homeowner vacancy rate: 1.7%; Rental vacancy rate: 0.0%

SCIO (village). Covers a land area of 0.557 square miles and a water area of 0 square miles. Located at 40.40° N. Lat; 81.09° W. Long. Elevation is 997 feet.

Population: 763; Growth (since 2000): -4.5%; Density: 1,370.4 persons per square mile; Race: 98.3% White, 0.0% Black/African American, 0.0% Asian, 0.0% American Indian/Alaska Native, 0.0% Native Hawaiian/Other Pacific Islander, 1.7% Two or more races, 0.1% Hispanic of any race; Average household size: 2.35; Median age: 38.5; Age under 18: 26.1%; Age 65 and over: 15.3%; Males per 100 females: 90.3

School District(s)

Harrison Hills City (PK-12)
2012-13 Enrollment: 1,559 . . . . (740) 942-7800

Housing: Homeownership rate: 60.5%; Homeowner vacancy rate: 4.7%; Rental vacancy rate: 6.5%

TIPPECANOE (CDP). Covers a land area of 0.537 square miles and a water area of 0 square miles. Located at 40.27° N. Lat; 81.28° W. Long. Elevation is 902 feet.

Population: 121; Growth (since 2000): n/a; Density: 225.3 persons per square mile; Race: 100.0% White, 0.0% Black/African American, 0.0% Asian, 0.0% American Indian/Alaska Native, 0.0% Native Hawaiian/Other Pacific Islander, 0.0% Two or more races, 0.0% Hispanic of any race; Average household size: 2.75; Median age: 37.8; Age under 18: 31.4%; Age 65 and over: 17.4%; Males per 100 females: 105.1

Housing: Homeownership rate: 84.1%; Homeowner vacancy rate: 0.0%; Rental vacancy rate: 12.5%

Henry County

Located in northwestern Ohio; crossed by the Maumee River. Covers a land area of 416.010 square miles, a water area of 3.740 square miles, and is located in the Eastern Time Zone at 41.34° N. Lat., 84.07° W. Long. The county was founded in 1820. County seat is Napoleon.

Weather Station: Napoleon Elevation: 682 feet

	Jan	Feb	Mar	Apr	May	Jun	Jul	Aug	Sep	Oct	Nov	Dec
High	32	35	47	60	71	81	85	83	76	63	50	36
Low	16	17	27	37	47	58	62	60	52	41	33	22
Precip	2.1	2.0	2.5	3.5	3.8	3.5	3.8	3.4	3.2	2.8	2.9	2.7
Snow	8.1	5.8	2.9	0.5	0.0	0.0	0.0	0.0	0.0	0.1	0.7	5.5

High and Low temperatures in degrees Fahrenheit; Precipitation and Snow in inches

Population: 28,215; Growth (since 2000): -3.4%; Density: 67.8 persons per square mile; Race: 95.2% White, 0.4% Black/African American, 0.4% Asian, 0.3% American Indian/Alaska Native, 0.0% Native Hawaiian/Other Pacific Islander, 1.3% two or more races, 6.6% Hispanic of any race; Average household size: 2.55; Median age: 39.8; Age under 18: 25.1%; Age 65 and over: 15.4%; Males per 100 females: 98.1; Marriage status: 24.3% never married, 57.3% now married, 1.1% separated, 7.3% widowed, 11.1% divorced; Foreign born: 1.6%; Speak English only: 96.4%; With disability: 12.8%; Veterans: 11.4%; Ancestry: 51.0% German, 10.2% Irish, 8.7% American, 8.1% English, 3.6% French
Religion: Six largest groups: 34.1% Lutheran, 12.2% Catholicism, 9.8% Methodist/Pietist, 4.1% Baptist, 2.8% Presbyterian-Reformed, 2.4% Holiness
Economy: Unemployment rate: 3.9%; Leading industries: 13.9% other services (except public administration); 13.8% retail trade; 11.5% construction; Farms: 848 totaling 235,919 acres; Company size: 1 employs 1,000 or more persons, 0 employ 500 to 999 persons, 9 employ 100 to 499 persons, 557 employ less than 100 persons; Business ownership: 561 women-owned, n/a Black-owned, n/a Hispanic-owned, n/a Asian-owned
Employment: 10.9% management, business, and financial, 1.7% computer, engineering, and science, 7.8% education, legal, community service, arts, and media, 6.6% healthcare practitioners, 17.5% service, 18.8% sales and office, 10.4% natural resources, construction, and maintenance, 26.2% production, transportation, and material moving
Income: Per capita: $23,347; Median household: $49,439; Average household: $58,759; Households with income of $100,000 or more: 14.7%; Poverty rate: 13.5%
Educational Attainment: High school diploma or higher: 90.4%; Bachelor's degree or higher: 13.8%; Graduate/professional degree or higher: 4.7%
Housing: Homeownership rate: 80.0%; Median home value: $114,000; Median year structure built: 1958; Homeowner vacancy rate: 2.4%; Median gross rent: $673 per month; Rental vacancy rate: 9.2%
Vital Statistics: Birth rate: 120.3 per 10,000 population; Death rate: 83.3 per 10,000 population; Age-adjusted cancer mortality rate: 208.9 deaths per 100,000 population
Health Insurance: 90.2% have insurance; 74.1% have private insurance; 30.5% have public insurance; 9.8% do not have insurance; 4.9% of children under 18 do not have insurance
Health Care: Physicians: 5.3 per 10,000 population; Hospital beds: 8.9 per 10,000 population; Hospital admissions: 303.7 per 10,000 population
Transportation: Commute: 94.2% car, 0.5% public transportation, 1.0% walk, 3.0% work from home; Median travel time to work: 20.8 minutes
Presidential Election: 39.6% Obama, 58.2% Romney (2012)
National and State Parks: Maumee State Forest; North Turkeyfoot State Park
Additional Information Contacts
Henry Government . . . . (419) 592-4876
http://www.henrycountyohio.com

Henry County Communities

DESHLER (village). Covers a land area of 2.255 square miles and a water area of 0.035 square miles. Located at 41.21° N. Lat; 83.91° W. Long. Elevation is 709 feet.
Population: 1,799; Growth (since 2000): -1.7%; Density: 797.6 persons per square mile; Race: 91.9% White, 0.1% Black/African American, 0.4% Asian, 0.3% American Indian/Alaska Native, 0.0% Native Hawaiian/Other Pacific Islander, 2.8% Two or more races, 9.9% Hispanic of any race; Average household size: 2.60; Median age: 36.5; Age under 18: 28.8%; Age 65 and over: 14.9%; Males per 100 females: 97.9

School District(s)

Patrick Henry Local (PK-12)
2012-13 Enrollment: 921. . . . . (419) 274-5451
Housing: Homeownership rate: 75.9%; Homeowner vacancy rate: 3.9%; Rental vacancy rate: 13.6%
Newspapers: Deshler Flag (weekly circulation 1500)

FLORIDA (village). Covers a land area of 0.225 square miles and a water area of 0 square miles. Located at 41.32° N. Lat; 84.20° W. Long. Elevation is 669 feet.
Population: 232; Growth (since 2000): -5.7%; Density: 1,031.6 persons per square mile; Race: 96.6% White, 0.0% Black/African American, 0.4% Asian, 0.0% American Indian/Alaska Native, 0.0% Native Hawaiian/Other Pacific Islander, 1.3% Two or more races, 6.0% Hispanic of any race; Average household size: 2.47; Median age: 42.7; Age under 18: 22.8%; Age 65 and over: 19.4%; Males per 100 females: 85.6
Housing: Homeownership rate: 70.2%; Homeowner vacancy rate: 1.4%; Rental vacancy rate: 6.7%

HAMLER (village). Covers a land area of 0.797 square miles and a water area of 0.005 square miles. Located at 41.23° N. Lat; 84.04° W. Long. Elevation is 709 feet.
Population: 576; Growth (since 2000): -11.4%; Density: 722.4 persons per square mile; Race: 90.8% White, 0.3% Black/African American, 0.0% Asian, 1.0% American Indian/Alaska Native, 0.0% Native Hawaiian/Other Pacific Islander, 1.4% Two or more races, 21.5% Hispanic of any race; Average household size: 2.50; Median age: 35.6; Age under 18: 27.4%; Age 65 and over: 16.7%; Males per 100 females: 100.0

School District(s)

Patrick Henry Local (PK-12)
2012-13 Enrollment: 921. . . . . (419) 274-5451
Housing: Homeownership rate: 80.0%; Homeowner vacancy rate: 4.1%; Rental vacancy rate: 9.6%

HOLGATE (village). Covers a land area of 1.154 square miles and a water area of 0 square miles. Located at 41.25° N. Lat; 84.13° W. Long. Elevation is 709 feet.
Population: 1,109; Growth (since 2000): -7.1%; Density: 961.0 persons per square mile; Race: 90.2% White, 0.6% Black/African American, 0.2% Asian, 0.3% American Indian/Alaska Native, 0.0% Native Hawaiian/Other Pacific Islander, 1.7% Two or more races, 19.0% Hispanic of any race; Average household size: 2.61; Median age: 38.0; Age under 18: 27.1%; Age 65 and over: 15.6%; Males per 100 females: 94.9

School District(s)

Holgate Local (PK-12)
2012-13 Enrollment: 458. . . . . (419) 264-5141
Housing: Homeownership rate: 79.9%; Homeowner vacancy rate: 4.7%; Rental vacancy rate: 7.9%

LIBERTY CENTER (village). Covers a land area of 1.037 square miles and a water area of 0 square miles. Located at 41.44° N. Lat; 84.01° W. Long. Elevation is 679 feet.
Population: 1,180; Growth (since 2000): 6.4%; Density: 1,138.2 persons per square mile; Race: 98.2% White, 0.1% Black/African American, 0.2% Asian, 0.1% American Indian/Alaska Native, 0.0% Native Hawaiian/Other Pacific Islander, 1.2% Two or more races, 3.3% Hispanic of any race; Average household size: 2.65; Median age: 33.9; Age under 18: 30.7%; Age 65 and over: 10.7%; Males per 100 females: 97.3

School District(s)

Liberty Center Local (PK-12)
2012-13 Enrollment: 1,086 . . . . (419) 533-5011
Housing: Homeownership rate: 75.6%; Homeowner vacancy rate: 2.6%; Rental vacancy rate: 8.3%
Newspapers: The Liberty Press (weekly circulation 1200)

MALINTA (village). Covers a land area of 0.770 square miles and a water area of 0 square miles. Located at 41.32° N. Lat; 84.04° W. Long. Elevation is 682 feet.
Population: 265; Growth (since 2000): -7.0%; Density: 344.3 persons per square mile; Race: 93.2% White, 0.4% Black/African American, 0.4% Asian, 0.0% American Indian/Alaska Native, 0.0% Native Hawaiian/Other Pacific Islander, 2.6% Two or more races, 14.0% Hispanic of any race; Average household size: 2.60; Median age: 36.2; Age under 18: 28.7%; Age 65 and over: 14.7%; Males per 100 females: 92.0

School District(s)

Patrick Henry Local (PK-12)
2012-13 Enrollment: 921. . . . . (419) 274-5451

Housing: Homeownership rate: 80.4%; Homeowner vacancy rate: 1.2%; Rental vacancy rate: 20.0%

MCCLURE (village). Covers a land area of 0.498 square miles and a water area of 0 square miles. Located at 41.37° N. Lat; 83.94° W. Long. Elevation is 676 feet.
Population: 725; Growth (since 2000): -4.7%; Density: 1,455.6 persons per square mile; Race: 96.1% White, 0.1% Black/African American, 0.4% Asian, 0.1% American Indian/Alaska Native, 0.0% Native Hawaiian/Other Pacific Islander, 1.0% Two or more races, 7.3% Hispanic of any race; Average household size: 2.52; Median age: 37.4; Age under 18: 26.5%; Age 65 and over: 10.9%; Males per 100 females: 100.3
Housing: Homeownership rate: 78.1%; Homeowner vacancy rate: 3.0%; Rental vacancy rate: 3.1%

NAPOLEON (city). County seat. Covers a land area of 6.186 square miles and a water area of 0.400 square miles. Located at 41.40° N. Lat; 84.13° W. Long. Elevation is 679 feet.
History: Napoleon was named by a group of Frenchmen who settled here in the midst of a predominantly German population. Napoleon developed as the seat of Henry County, and as the market center for a rural area.
Population: 8,749; Growth (since 2000): -6.1%; Density: 1,414.3 persons per square mile; Race: 93.7% White, 0.9% Black/African American, 0.4% Asian, 0.4% American Indian/Alaska Native, 0.0% Native Hawaiian/Other Pacific Islander, 1.7% Two or more races, 8.0% Hispanic of any race; Average household size: 2.36; Median age: 39.2; Age under 18: 23.7%; Age 65 and over: 17.7%; Males per 100 females: 89.9; Marriage status: 28.0% never married, 46.9% now married, 1.3% separated, 9.5% widowed, 15.6% divorced; Foreign born: 2.8%; Speak English only: 96.4%; With disability: 17.2%; Veterans: 11.8%; Ancestry: 41.7% German, 10.8% Irish, 10.5% American, 7.9% English, 5.2% Dutch
Employment: 12.2% management, business, and financial, 2.2% computer, engineering, and science, 5.1% education, legal, community service, arts, and media, 5.6% healthcare practitioners, 22.6% service, 15.9% sales and office, 7.2% natural resources, construction, and maintenance, 29.2% production, transportation, and material moving
Income: Per capita: $23,070; Median household: $42,578; Average household: $53,098; Households with income of $100,000 or more: 12.1%; Poverty rate: 20.6%
Educational Attainment: High school diploma or higher: 88.7%; Bachelor's degree or higher: 12.8%; Graduate/professional degree or higher: 4.8%

School District(s)

Napoleon Area City (PK-12)
2012-13 Enrollment: 1,990 . . . . (419) 599-7015
Housing: Homeownership rate: 67.5%; Median home value: $102,400; Median year structure built: 1965; Homeowner vacancy rate: 3.7%; Median gross rent: $636 per month; Rental vacancy rate: 10.2%
Health Insurance: 85.8% have insurance; 66.6% have private insurance; 34.6% have public insurance; 14.2% do not have insurance; 10.7% of children under 18 do not have insurance
Hospitals: Henry County Hospital (52 beds)
Safety: Violent crime rate: 5.8 per 10,000 population; Property crime rate: 357.8 per 10,000 population
Newspapers: Northwest Signal (daily circulation 5700)
Transportation: Commute: 92.9% car, 1.5% public transportation, 1.7% walk, 1.4% work from home; Median travel time to work: 15.4 minutes
Additional Information Contacts
City of Napoleon . . . . (419) 592-4010
http://www.napoleonohio.com

NEW BAVARIA (village). Covers a land area of 0.070 square miles and a water area of 0 square miles. Located at 41.20° N. Lat; 84.17° W. Long. Elevation is 735 feet.
Population: 99; Growth (since 2000): 26.9%; Density: 1,415.3 persons per square mile; Race: 98.0% White, 0.0% Black/African American, 0.0% Asian, 0.0% American Indian/Alaska Native, 0.0% Native Hawaiian/Other Pacific Islander, 0.0% Two or more races, 5.1% Hispanic of any race; Average household size: 2.48; Median age: 35.8; Age under 18: 30.3%; Age 65 and over: 11.1%; Males per 100 females: 115.2
Housing: Homeownership rate: 90.0%; Homeowner vacancy rate: 2.7%; Rental vacancy rate: 0.0%

RIDGEVILLE CORNERS (CDP). Covers a land area of 0.914 square miles and a water area of 0 square miles. Located at 41.44° N. Lat; 84.26° W. Long. Elevation is 735 feet.
Population: 435; Growth (since 2000): n/a; Density: 475.7 persons per square mile; Race: 94.9% White, 0.0% Black/African American, 0.0% Asian, 0.0% American Indian/Alaska Native, 0.0% Native Hawaiian/Other Pacific Islander, 2.5% Two or more races, 3.7% Hispanic of any race; Average household size: 2.42; Median age: 39.2; Age under 18: 23.4%; Age 65 and over: 17.5%; Males per 100 females: 106.2
Housing: Homeownership rate: 79.4%; Homeowner vacancy rate: 0.0%; Rental vacancy rate: 11.9%

Highland County

Located in southwestern Ohio; drained by the East Fork of Little Miami River, and by several creeks. Covers a land area of 553.084 square miles, a water area of 4.709 square miles, and is located in the Eastern Time Zone at 39.18° N. Lat., 83.60° W. Long. The county was founded in 1805. County seat is Hillsboro.

Weather Station: Hillsboro Elevation: 1,100 feet

	Jan	Feb	Mar	Apr	May	Jun	Jul	Aug	Sep	Oct	Nov	Dec
High	37	41	51	62	71	79	83	82	76	65	53	40
Low	21	23	31	41	51	60	64	62	55	44	35	25
Precip	3.1	2.9	3.7	4.1	5.1	3.9	3.8	3.5	3.1	3.1	3.1	3.0
Snow	6.0	4.8	2.8	0.5	tr	0.0	0.0	0.0	0.0	0.2	0.4	2.6

High and Low temperatures in degrees Fahrenheit; Precipitation and Snow in inches

Population: 43,589; Growth (since 2000): 6.6%; Density: 78.8 persons per square mile; Race: 96.5% White, 1.4% Black/African American, 0.2% Asian, 0.3% American Indian/Alaska Native, 0.0% Native Hawaiian/Other Pacific Islander, 1.5% two or more races, 0.7% Hispanic of any race; Average household size: 2.58; Median age: 39.2; Age under 18: 25.4%; Age 65 and over: 15.2%; Males per 100 females: 96.0; Marriage status: 22.2% never married, 54.8% now married, 2.5% separated, 8.7% widowed, 14.3% divorced; Foreign born: 0.6%; Speak English only: 97.9%; With disability: 17.6%; Veterans: 11.0%; Ancestry: 23.4% German, 17.8% American, 14.2% Irish, 9.2% English, 2.1% Dutch
Religion: Six largest groups: 11.3% Baptist, 6.5% Methodist/Pietist, 6.3% Non-denominational Protestant, 2.1% European Free-Church, 1.8% Pentecostal, 1.8% Catholicism
Economy: Unemployment rate: 5.6%; Leading industries: 20.9% retail trade; 14.6% health care and social assistance; 12.5% other services (except public administration); Farms: 1,412 totaling 264,521 acres; Company size: 0 employ 1,000 or more persons, 0 employ 500 to 999 persons, 15 employ 100 to 499 persons, 655 employ less than 100 persons; Business ownership: n/a women-owned, n/a Black-owned, n/a Hispanic-owned, n/a Asian-owned
Employment: 10.7% management, business, and financial, 1.9% computer, engineering, and science, 6.5% education, legal, community service, arts, and media, 5.9% healthcare practitioners, 15.6% service, 19.7% sales and office, 13.9% natural resources, construction, and maintenance, 25.9% production, transportation, and material moving
Income: Per capita: $19,348; Median household: $39,091; Average household: $48,468; Households with income of $100,000 or more: 8.5%; Poverty rate: 19.5%
Educational Attainment: High school diploma or higher: 82.2%; Bachelor's degree or higher: 11.4%; Graduate/professional degree or higher: 4.2%
Housing: Homeownership rate: 72.0%; Median home value: $101,800; Median year structure built: 1977; Homeowner vacancy rate: 2.8%; Median gross rent: $631 per month; Rental vacancy rate: 10.7%
Vital Statistics: Birth rate: 119.2 per 10,000 population; Death rate: 105.8 per 10,000 population; Age-adjusted cancer mortality rate: 248.7 deaths per 100,000 population
Health Insurance: 83.7% have insurance; 56.0% have private insurance; 40.6% have public insurance; 16.3% do not have insurance; 12.1% of children under 18 do not have insurance
Health Care: Physicians: 5.8 per 10,000 population; Hospital beds: 11.5 per 10,000 population; Hospital admissions: 628.4 per 10,000 population
Transportation: Commute: 93.0% car, 0.4% public transportation, 1.7% walk, 3.7% work from home; Median travel time to work: 29.9 minutes
Presidential Election: 33.6% Obama, 64.3% Romney (2012)
National and State Parks: Fallsville State Wildlife Area; Fort Hill State Memorial; Oldaker State Wildlife Area; Rocky Fork State Park

Additional Information Contacts
Highland Government . . . . (937) 393-1911
http://www.co.highland.oh.us

Highland County Communities

BUFORD (CDP). Covers a land area of 1.483 square miles and a water area of 0 square miles. Located at 39.07° N. Lat; 83.84° W. Long. Elevation is 948 feet.
Population: 352; Growth (since 2000): n/a; Density: 237.3 persons per square mile; Race: 98.9% White, 0.3% Black/African American, 0.3% Asian, 0.0% American Indian/Alaska Native, 0.0% Native Hawaiian/Other Pacific Islander, 0.6% Two or more races, 0.3% Hispanic of any race; Average household size: 2.96; Median age: 32.6; Age under 18: 31.0%; Age 65 and over: 11.1%; Males per 100 females: 93.4
Housing: Homeownership rate: 81.5%; Homeowner vacancy rate: 1.0%; Rental vacancy rate: 4.3%

GREENFIELD (village). Covers a land area of 2.061 square miles and a water area of 0 square miles. Located at 39.35° N. Lat; 83.39° W. Long. Elevation is 909 feet.
History: Platted 1798, incorporated 1841.
Population: 4,639; Growth (since 2000): -5.4%; Density: 2,250.7 persons per square mile; Race: 95.9% White, 1.7% Black/African American, 0.2% Asian, 0.1% American Indian/Alaska Native, 0.0% Native Hawaiian/Other Pacific Islander, 1.7% Two or more races, 0.8% Hispanic of any race; Average household size: 2.47; Median age: 37.1; Age under 18: 25.9%; Age 65 and over: 15.8%; Males per 100 females: 90.4; Marriage status: 23.5% never married, 43.0% now married, 2.7% separated, 13.7% widowed, 19.8% divorced; Foreign born: 0.3%; Speak English only: 98.0%; With disability: 21.1%; Veterans: 12.1%; Ancestry: 28.0% German, 17.3% Irish, 13.3% American, 8.6% English, 3.8% Scottish
Employment: 8.1% management, business, and financial, 1.3% computer, engineering, and science, 6.3% education, legal, community service, arts, and media, 3.7% healthcare practitioners, 21.2% service, 19.1% sales and office, 5.6% natural resources, construction, and maintenance, 34.7% production, transportation, and material moving
Income: Per capita: $13,826; Median household: $27,945; Average household: $32,052; Households with income of $100,000 or more: 1.7%; Poverty rate: 30.3%
Educational Attainment: High school diploma or higher: 72.6%; Bachelor's degree or higher: 6.0%; Graduate/professional degree or higher: 2.5%

School District(s)

Greenfield Exempted Village (PK-12)
2012-13 Enrollment: 2,080 . . . . (937) 981-2152
Housing: Homeownership rate: 52.9%; Median home value: $71,800; Median year structure built: 1959; Homeowner vacancy rate: 3.7%; Median gross rent: $517 per month; Rental vacancy rate: 13.0%
Health Insurance: 85.8% have insurance; 48.2% have private insurance; 51.4% have public insurance; 14.2% do not have insurance; 6.4% of children under 18 do not have insurance
Hospitals: Greenfield Area Medical Center (46 beds)
Safety: Violent crime rate: 8.8 per 10,000 population; Property crime rate: 449.5 per 10,000 population
Transportation: Commute: 90.6% car, 1.4% public transportation, 5.1% walk, 2.9% work from home; Median travel time to work: 23.1 minutes

HIGHLAND (village). Covers a land area of 0.170 square miles and a water area of 0 square miles. Located at 39.34° N. Lat; 83.60° W. Long. Elevation is 1,066 feet.
Population: 254; Growth (since 2000): -10.2%; Density: 1,494.9 persons per square mile; Race: 96.5% White, 0.8% Black/African American, 0.0% Asian, 1.2% American Indian/Alaska Native, 0.0% Native Hawaiian/Other Pacific Islander, 1.6% Two or more races, 2.8% Hispanic of any race; Average household size: 2.73; Median age: 33.0; Age under 18: 30.3%; Age 65 and over: 13.0%; Males per 100 females: 88.1
Housing: Homeownership rate: 63.5%; Homeowner vacancy rate: 6.2%; Rental vacancy rate: 5.4%

HIGHLAND HOLIDAY (CDP). Covers a land area of 0.604 square miles and a water area of 0.493 square miles. Located at 39.19° N. Lat; 83.47° W. Long. Elevation is 938 feet.
Population: 550; Growth (since 2000): n/a; Density: 910.3 persons per square mile; Race: 98.2% White, 0.4% Black/African American, 0.7% Asian, 0.2% American Indian/Alaska Native, 0.0% Native Hawaiian/Other Pacific Islander, 0.5% Two or more races, 0.0% Hispanic of any race; Average household size: 2.67; Median age: 34.8; Age under 18: 27.5%; Age 65 and over: 14.0%; Males per 100 females: 103.0
Housing: Homeownership rate: 71.4%; Homeowner vacancy rate: 9.2%; Rental vacancy rate: 13.2%

HILLSBORO (city). County seat. Covers a land area of 5.429 square miles and a water area of 0 square miles. Located at 39.21° N. Lat; 83.61° W. Long. Elevation is 1,132 feet.
History: Hillsboro was platted in 1807, and developed around brickyards, tanneries, and grist and woolen mills. In 1873, The Women 's Temperance Crusade was organized and managed to close all of the saloons in the town when the women marched into each in turn and held a prayer meeting.
Population: 6,605; Growth (since 2000): 3.7%; Density: 1,216.6 persons per square mile; Race: 90.0% White, 5.8% Black/African American, 0.8% Asian, 0.3% American Indian/Alaska Native, 0.0% Native Hawaiian/Other Pacific Islander, 2.9% Two or more races, 1.3% Hispanic of any race; Average household size: 2.28; Median age: 38.7; Age under 18: 24.3%; Age 65 and over: 20.1%; Males per 100 females: 81.6; Marriage status: 21.6% never married, 50.2% now married, 3.4% separated, 12.1% widowed, 16.2% divorced; Foreign born: 1.6%; Speak English only: 96.7%; With disability: 20.6%; Veterans: 10.0%; Ancestry: 20.4% German, 15.3% Irish, 11.4% American, 9.9% English, 2.4% Dutch
Employment: 10.4% management, business, and financial, 1.6% computer, engineering, and science, 5.8% education, legal, community service, arts, and media, 8.4% healthcare practitioners, 17.6% service, 29.2% sales and office, 8.6% natural resources, construction, and maintenance, 18.5% production, transportation, and material moving
Income: Per capita: $18,101; Median household: $33,682; Average household: $41,053; Households with income of $100,000 or more: 8.0%; Poverty rate: 27.3%
Educational Attainment: High school diploma or higher: 81.8%; Bachelor's degree or higher: 15.0%; Graduate/professional degree or higher: 3.8%

School District(s)

Bright Local (PK-12)
2012-13 Enrollment: 720. . . . . (937) 442-3114
Hillsboro City (PK-12)
2012-13 Enrollment: 2,646 . . . . (937) 393-3475

Two-year College(s)

Southern State Community College (Public)
Fall 2013 Enrollment: 2,431 . . . . (937) 393-3431
2013-14 Tuition: In-state $4,132; Out-of-state $7,752
Housing: Homeownership rate: 51.1%; Median home value: $96,400; Median year structure built: 1963; Homeowner vacancy rate: 5.1%; Median gross rent: $595 per month; Rental vacancy rate: 9.6%
Health Insurance: 85.4% have insurance; 50.7% have private insurance; 48.7% have public insurance; 14.6% do not have insurance; 7.6% of children under 18 do not have insurance
Hospitals: Highland District Hospital (65 beds)
Safety: Violent crime rate: 13.9 per 10,000 population; Property crime rate: 477.3 per 10,000 population
Newspapers: Times Gazette (daily circulation 5000)
Transportation: Commute: 94.1% car, 0.0% public transportation, 3.0% walk, 2.5% work from home; Median travel time to work: 24.1 minutes

LEESBURG (village). Covers a land area of 1.168 square miles and a water area of 0 square miles. Located at 39.34° N. Lat; 83.55° W. Long. Elevation is 1,014 feet.
History: Shortly after Leesburg was founded in 1802, Quakers from Pennsylvania settled here. Prior to 1900, Leesburg hosted the annual meeting of the Society of Friends, attended by members from all parts of the United States.
Population: 1,314; Growth (since 2000): 4.9%; Density: 1,124.7 persons per square mile; Race: 97.6% White, 0.2% Black/African American, 0.1% Asian, 0.5% American Indian/Alaska Native, 0.0% Native Hawaiian/Other Pacific Islander, 1.6% Two or more races, 0.7% Hispanic of any race; Average household size: 2.56; Median age: 33.8; Age under 18: 28.4%; Age 65 and over: 12.9%; Males per 100 females: 90.2

School District(s)

Fairfield Local (PK-12)
2012-13 Enrollment: 939. . . . . (937) 780-2221

Housing: Homeownership rate: 56.1%; Homeowner vacancy rate: 3.3%; Rental vacancy rate: 8.5%
Safety: Violent crime rate: 0.0 per 10,000 population; Property crime rate: 263.6 per 10,000 population

LYNCHBURG (village). Covers a land area of 0.940 square miles and a water area of 0.007 square miles. Located at 39.24° N. Lat; 83.79° W. Long. Elevation is 1,007 feet.
Population: 1,499; Growth (since 2000): 11.0%; Density: 1,595.4 persons per square mile; Race: 98.8% White, 0.0% Black/African American, 0.0% Asian, 0.0% American Indian/Alaska Native, 0.0% Native Hawaiian/Other Pacific Islander, 0.9% Two or more races, 0.8% Hispanic of any race; Average household size: 2.61; Median age: 35.5; Age under 18: 27.4%; Age 65 and over: 14.0%; Males per 100 females: 90.0

School District(s)

Lynchburg-Clay Local (PK-12)
2012-13 Enrollment: 1,187 . . . . (937) 364-2338
Housing: Homeownership rate: 68.0%; Homeowner vacancy rate: 2.9%; Rental vacancy rate: 12.3%

MOWRYSTOWN (village). Covers a land area of 0.482 square miles and a water area of 0.007 square miles. Located at 39.04° N. Lat; 83.75° W. Long. Elevation is 997 feet.
Population: 360; Growth (since 2000): -3.5%; Density: 746.6 persons per square mile; Race: 99.7% White, 0.0% Black/African American, 0.0% Asian, 0.0% American Indian/Alaska Native, 0.0% Native Hawaiian/Other Pacific Islander, 0.3% Two or more races, 0.0% Hispanic of any race; Average household size: 2.79; Median age: 34.8; Age under 18: 28.1%; Age 65 and over: 15.0%; Males per 100 females: 102.2

School District(s)

Bright Local (PK-12)
2012-13 Enrollment: 720. . . . . (937) 442-3114
Housing: Homeownership rate: 71.3%; Homeowner vacancy rate: 6.1%; Rental vacancy rate: 2.6%

ROCKY FORK POINT (CDP). Covers a land area of 0.712 square miles and a water area of 0.512 square miles. Located at 39.19° N. Lat; 83.49° W. Long. Elevation is 974 feet.
Population: 639; Growth (since 2000): n/a; Density: 897.1 persons per square mile; Race: 98.9% White, 0.3% Black/African American, 0.5% Asian, 0.0% American Indian/Alaska Native, 0.0% Native Hawaiian/Other Pacific Islander, 0.3% Two or more races, 1.6% Hispanic of any race; Average household size: 2.31; Median age: 46.5; Age under 18: 21.3%; Age 65 and over: 20.8%; Males per 100 females: 99.1
Housing: Homeownership rate: 74.7%; Homeowner vacancy rate: 6.2%; Rental vacancy rate: 18.6%

SINKING SPRING (village). Covers a land area of 0.467 square miles and a water area of 0 square miles. Located at 39.07° N. Lat; 83.39° W. Long. Elevation is 866 feet.
History: Nearby are Fort Hill and Serpent Mound, prehistoric earthworks.
Population: 133; Growth (since 2000): -15.8%; Density: 284.8 persons per square mile; Race: 100.0% White, 0.0% Black/African American, 0.0% Asian, 0.0% American Indian/Alaska Native, 0.0% Native Hawaiian/Other Pacific Islander, 0.0% Two or more races, 0.0% Hispanic of any race; Average household size: 2.51; Median age: 45.2; Age under 18: 23.3%; Age 65 and over: 23.3%; Males per 100 females: 98.5
Housing: Homeownership rate: 77.4%; Homeowner vacancy rate: 2.3%; Rental vacancy rate: 7.7%

Hocking County

Located in south central Ohio; crossed by the Hocking River. Covers a land area of 421.323 square miles, a water area of 2.305 square miles, and is located in the Eastern Time Zone at 39.49° N. Lat., 82.48° W. Long. The county was founded in 1818. County seat is Logan.

Hocking County is part of the Columbus, OH Metropolitan Statistical Area. The entire metro area includes: Delaware County, OH; Fairfield County, OH; Franklin County, OH; Hocking County, OH; Licking County, OH; Madison County, OH; Morrow County, OH; Perry County, OH; Pickaway County, OH; Union County, OH

Population: 29,380; Growth (since 2000): 4.0%; Density: 69.7 persons per square mile; Race: 97.5% White, 0.7% Black/African American, 0.2% Asian, 0.3% American Indian/Alaska Native, 0.0% Native Hawaiian/Other Pacific Islander, 1.1% two or more races, 0.7% Hispanic of any race; Average household size: 2.52; Median age: 40.9; Age under 18: 23.8%; Age 65 and over: 15.3%; Males per 100 females: 99.9; Marriage status: 22.2% never married, 57.3% now married, 1.8% separated, 7.6% widowed, 12.9% divorced; Foreign born: 0.9%; Speak English only: 98.6%; With disability: 16.2%; Veterans: 12.9%; Ancestry: 25.6% German, 14.5% American, 13.4% Irish, 9.8% English, 2.8% Dutch
Religion: Six largest groups: 8.1% Methodist/Pietist, 4.2% Baptist, 3.4% Catholicism, 2.7% Holiness, 2.4% Lutheran, 2.0% Non-denominational Protestant
Economy: Unemployment rate: 4.7%; Leading industries: 14.8% retail trade; 12.4% accommodation and food services; 12.4% other services (except public administration); Farms: 367 totaling 38,085 acres; Company size: 0 employ 1,000 or more persons, 0 employ 500 to 999 persons, 8 employ 100 to 499 persons, 458 employ less than 100 persons; Business ownership: 461 women-owned, n/a Black-owned, n/a Hispanic-owned, n/a Asian-owned
Employment: 9.6% management, business, and financial, 2.1% computer, engineering, and science, 10.0% education, legal, community service, arts, and media, 6.8% healthcare practitioners, 19.1% service, 20.8% sales and office, 12.2% natural resources, construction, and maintenance, 19.4% production, transportation, and material moving
Income: Per capita: $21,037; Median household: $42,089; Average household: $53,061; Households with income of $100,000 or more: 12.6%; Poverty rate: 15.9%
Educational Attainment: High school diploma or higher: 86.7%; Bachelor's degree or higher: 12.7%; Graduate/professional degree or higher: 4.8%
Housing: Homeownership rate: 73.4%; Median home value: $109,800; Median year structure built: 1977; Homeowner vacancy rate: 3.7%; Median gross rent: $584 per month; Rental vacancy rate: 6.8%
Vital Statistics: Birth rate: 104.0 per 10,000 population; Death rate: 102.6 per 10,000 population; Age-adjusted cancer mortality rate: 215.1 deaths per 100,000 population
Health Insurance: 87.3% have insurance; 64.8% have private insurance; 37.2% have public insurance; 12.7% do not have insurance; 6.8% of children under 18 do not have insurance
Health Care: Physicians: 6.8 per 10,000 population; Hospital beds: 18.0 per 10,000 population; Hospital admissions: 478.7 per 10,000 population
Transportation: Commute: 94.2% car, 0.2% public transportation, 1.7% walk, 3.1% work from home; Median travel time to work: 31.1 minutes
Presidential Election: 48.3% Obama, 49.4% Romney (2012)
National and State Parks: Conkles Hollow State Nature Preserve; Hocking Hills State Park; Hocking State Forest; Lake Logan State Park; Sunday Creek State Wildlife Area; Wayne National Forest
Additional Information Contacts
Hocking Government. . . . . (740) 385-5195
http://www.co.hocking.oh.us

Hocking County Communities

CARBON HILL (CDP). Covers a land area of 0.405 square miles and a water area of 0.002 square miles. Located at 39.50° N. Lat; 82.24° W. Long. Elevation is 705 feet.
Population: 233; Growth (since 2000): n/a; Density: 576.0 persons per square mile; Race: 94.8% White, 0.0% Black/African American, 1.3% Asian, 1.7% American Indian/Alaska Native, 0.0% Native Hawaiian/Other Pacific Islander, 1.7% Two or more races, 0.4% Hispanic of any race; Average household size: 2.48; Median age: 41.3; Age under 18: 23.2%; Age 65 and over: 9.9%; Males per 100 females: 102.6
Housing: Homeownership rate: 79.8%; Homeowner vacancy rate: 1.3%; Rental vacancy rate: 0.0%

HAYDENVILLE (CDP). Covers a land area of 0.856 square miles and a water area of 0.025 square miles. Located at 39.48° N. Lat; 82.32° W. Long. Elevation is 705 feet.
Population: 381; Growth (since 2000): n/a; Density: 445.2 persons per square mile; Race: 95.0% White, 0.0% Black/African American, 0.3% Asian, 0.3% American Indian/Alaska Native, 0.0% Native Hawaiian/Other Pacific Islander, 4.5% Two or more races, 2.6% Hispanic of any race; Average household size: 2.70; Median age: 35.5; Age under 18: 28.3%; Age 65 and over: 10.5%; Males per 100 females: 97.4
Housing: Homeownership rate: 67.4%; Homeowner vacancy rate: 3.0%; Rental vacancy rate: 8.0%

HIDE-A-WAY HILLS (CDP). Covers a land area of 2.606 square miles and a water area of 0.218 square miles. Located at 39.65° N. Lat; 82.47° W. Long. Elevation is 948 feet.
Population: 794; Growth (since 2000): n/a; Density: 304.7 persons per square mile; Race: 98.5% White, 0.5% Black/African American, 0.3% Asian, 0.3% American Indian/Alaska Native, 0.0% Native Hawaiian/Other Pacific Islander, 0.5% Two or more races, 0.4% Hispanic of any race; Average household size: 2.20; Median age: 53.4; Age under 18: 16.0%; Age 65 and over: 23.6%; Males per 100 females: 105.2
Housing: Homeownership rate: 94.7%; Homeowner vacancy rate: 3.1%; Rental vacancy rate: 9.5%

LAURELVILLE (village). Covers a land area of 0.209 square miles and a water area of 0.002 square miles. Located at 39.47° N. Lat; 82.74° W. Long. Elevation is 738 feet.
Population: 527; Growth (since 2000): -1.1%; Density: 2,527.1 persons per square mile; Race: 97.3% White, 0.0% Black/African American, 0.6% Asian, 0.4% American Indian/Alaska Native, 0.0% Native Hawaiian/Other Pacific Islander, 0.9% Two or more races, 0.4% Hispanic of any race; Average household size: 2.09; Median age: 39.5; Age under 18: 25.0%; Age 65 and over: 20.9%; Males per 100 females: 80.5

School District(s)

Logan Elm Local (PK-12)
2012-13 Enrollment: 1,988 . . . . (740) 474-7501
Housing: Homeownership rate: 48.0%; Homeowner vacancy rate: 4.7%; Rental vacancy rate: 9.5%

LOGAN (city). County seat. Covers a land area of 4.791 square miles and a water area of 0.139 square miles. Located at 39.54° N. Lat; 82.41° W. Long. Elevation is 741 feet.
History: Logan was founded in 1816 by Governor Thomas Worthington, who purchased a tract near the Hocking Falls and set up mills. Logan flourished with the opening of the Hocking Canal in 1840, and the completion of the Hocking Valley Railroad in 1869.
Population: 7,152; Growth (since 2000): 6.7%; Density: 1,492.8 persons per square mile; Race: 97.5% White, 0.8% Black/African American, 0.2% Asian, 0.3% American Indian/Alaska Native, 0.0% Native Hawaiian/Other Pacific Islander, 0.9% Two or more races, 0.8% Hispanic of any race; Average household size: 2.34; Median age: 38.0; Age under 18: 24.3%; Age 65 and over: 17.5%; Males per 100 females: 86.7; Marriage status: 24.1% never married, 50.0% now married, 3.3% separated, 11.2% widowed, 14.7% divorced; Foreign born: 1.4%; Speak English only: 98.0%; With disability: 19.3%; Veterans: 11.0%; Ancestry: 27.0% German, 15.5% Irish, 13.4% American, 10.6% English, 4.0% Italian
Employment: 8.0% management, business, and financial, 2.2% computer, engineering, and science, 13.1% education, legal, community service, arts, and media, 5.9% healthcare practitioners, 20.0% service, 25.5% sales and office, 11.0% natural resources, construction, and maintenance, 14.3% production, transportation, and material moving
Income: Per capita: $19,768; Median household: $36,136; Average household: $45,779; Households with income of $100,000 or more: 8.7%; Poverty rate: 26.1%
Educational Attainment: High school diploma or higher: 87.3%; Bachelor's degree or higher: 15.6%; Graduate/professional degree or higher: 6.3%

School District(s)

Logan-Hocking Local (PK-12)
2012-13 Enrollment: 3,987 . . . . (740) 385-8517
Housing: Homeownership rate: 55.8%; Median home value: $100,700; Median year structure built: 1956; Homeowner vacancy rate: 9.7%; Median gross rent: $534 per month; Rental vacancy rate: 5.8%
Health Insurance: 83.8% have insurance; 59.3% have private insurance; 40.7% have public insurance; 16.2% do not have insurance; 11.8% of children under 18 do not have insurance
Hospitals: Hocking Valley Community Hospital (93 beds)
Safety: Violent crime rate: 9.8 per 10,000 population; Property crime rate: 471.1 per 10,000 population
Newspapers: Logan Daily News (daily circulation 4200)
Transportation: Commute: 92.5% car, 0.0% public transportation, 2.5% walk, 3.0% work from home; Median travel time to work: 22.9 minutes

MURRAY CITY (village). Covers a land area of 0.317 square miles and a water area of <.001 square miles. Located at 39.51° N. Lat; 82.17° W. Long. Elevation is 712 feet.
Population: 449; Growth (since 2000): -0.7%; Density: 1,414.3 persons per square mile; Race: 99.1% White, 0.2% Black/African American, 0.0% Asian, 0.0% American Indian/Alaska Native, 0.0% Native Hawaiian/Other Pacific Islander, 0.7% Two or more races, 1.3% Hispanic of any race; Average household size: 2.57; Median age: 37.4; Age under 18: 23.6%; Age 65 and over: 12.9%; Males per 100 females: 99.6
Housing: Homeownership rate: 66.8%; Homeowner vacancy rate: 5.6%; Rental vacancy rate: 18.1%

ROCKBRIDGE (CDP). Covers a land area of 0.378 square miles and a water area of 0 square miles. Located at 39.59° N. Lat; 82.53° W. Long. Elevation is 751 feet.
Population: 182; Growth (since 2000): n/a; Density: 481.8 persons per square mile; Race: 97.8% White, 0.0% Black/African American, 0.0% Asian, 0.0% American Indian/Alaska Native, 0.0% Native Hawaiian/Other Pacific Islander, 2.2% Two or more races, 0.0% Hispanic of any race; Average household size: 2.36; Median age: 37.0; Age under 18: 23.6%; Age 65 and over: 12.1%; Males per 100 females: 102.2
Housing: Homeownership rate: 68.9%; Homeowner vacancy rate: 1.9%; Rental vacancy rate: 0.0%

SOUTH BLOOMINGVILLE (unincorporated postal area)
ZCTA: 43152
Covers a land area of 43.495 square miles and a water area of 0.169 square miles. Located at 39.40° N. Lat; 82.62° W. Long. Elevation is 702 feet.
Population: 921; Growth (since 2000): -16.1%; Density: 21.2 persons per square mile; Race: 98.8% White, 0.1% Black/African American, 0.1% Asian, 0.5% American Indian/Alaska Native, 0.0% Native Hawaiian/Other Pacific Islander, 0.4% Two or more races, 0.2% Hispanic of any race; Average household size: 2.44; Median age: 42.3; Age under 18: 23.5%; Age 65 and over: 14.2%; Males per 100 females: 101.5
Housing: Homeownership rate: 76.9%; Homeowner vacancy rate: 3.3%; Rental vacancy rate: 16.2%

UNION FURNACE (unincorporated postal area)
ZCTA: 43158
Covers a land area of 2.039 square miles and a water area of 0.009 square miles. Located at 39.45° N. Lat; 82.36° W. Long. Elevation is 748 feet.
Population: 268; Growth (since 2000): 119.7%; Density: 131.4 persons per square mile; Race: 95.9% White, 0.4% Black/African American, 0.0% Asian, 1.9% American Indian/Alaska Native, 0.0% Native Hawaiian/Other Pacific Islander, 0.7% Two or more races, 0.0% Hispanic of any race; Average household size: 2.55; Median age: 42.5; Age under 18: 20.5%; Age 65 and over: 13.4%; Males per 100 females: 103.0

School District(s)

Logan-Hocking Local (PK-12)
2012-13 Enrollment: 3,987 . . . . (740) 385-8517
Housing: Homeownership rate: 77.1%; Homeowner vacancy rate: 2.4%; Rental vacancy rate: 0.0%

Holmes County

Located in central Ohio; crossed by Killbuck Creek and Walhonding River. Covers a land area of 422.533 square miles, a water area of 1.446 square miles, and is located in the Eastern Time Zone at 40.57° N. Lat., 81.93° W. Long. The county was founded in 1824. County seat is Millersburg.

Weather Station: Millersburg — Elevation: 818 feet

	Jan	Feb	Mar	Apr	May	Jun	Jul	Aug	Sep	Oct	Nov	Dec
High	36	39	49	62	71	80	84	83	76	64	52	39
Low	18	19	27	36	45	56	60	58	50	38	31	22
Precip	2.9	1.8	2.9	3.5	4.6	4.8	4.3	3.5	3.1	2.9	2.8	2.7
Snow	6.3	3.9	2.5	0.3	tr	0.0	0.0	0.0	0.0	tr	0.7	3.9

High and Low temperatures in degrees Fahrenheit; Precipitation and Snow in inches

Population: 42,366; Growth (since 2000): 8.8%; Density: 100.3 persons per square mile; Race: 98.7% White, 0.3% Black/African American, 0.1% Asian, 0.1% American Indian/Alaska Native, 0.0% Native Hawaiian/Other Pacific Islander, 0.5% two or more races, 0.8% Hispanic of any race; Average household size: 3.31; Median age: 29.7; Age under 18: 34.3%;

Age 65 and over: 11.3%; Males per 100 females: 99.5; Marriage status: 28.1% never married, 61.0% now married, 0.6% separated, 5.0% widowed, 5.9% divorced; Foreign born: 0.8%; Speak English only: 50.9%; With disability: 7.9%; Veterans: 5.5%; Ancestry: 32.2% German, 10.0% American, 9.9% Swiss, 8.6% Pennsylvania German, 6.0% Irish
Religion: Six largest groups: 51.5% European Free-Church, 4.8% Baptist, 3.7% Methodist/Pietist, 2.8% Non-denominational Protestant, 1.7% Presbyterian-Reformed, 1.5% Catholicism
Economy: Unemployment rate: 2.9%; Leading industries: 22.7% manufacturing; 18.6% construction; 13.7% retail trade; Farms: 1,969 totaling 220,948 acres; Company size: 0 employ 1,000 or more persons, 2 employ 500 to 999 persons, 25 employ 100 to 499 persons, 1,101 employs less than 100 persons; Business ownership: 787 women-owned, n/a Black-owned, n/a Hispanic-owned, n/a Asian-owned
Employment: 11.6% management, business, and financial, 1.7% computer, engineering, and science, 4.3% education, legal, community service, arts, and media, 3.0% healthcare practitioners, 14.2% service, 19.6% sales and office, 15.3% natural resources, construction, and maintenance, 30.2% production, transportation, and material moving
Income: Per capita: $17,177; Median household: $45,477; Average household: $56,607; Households with income of $100,000 or more: 11.9%; Poverty rate: 15.8%
Educational Attainment: High school diploma or higher: 55.2%; Bachelor's degree or higher: 8.5%; Graduate/professional degree or higher: 3.3%
Housing: Homeownership rate: 76.3%; Median home value: $151,400; Median year structure built: 1978; Homeowner vacancy rate: 1.0%; Median gross rent: $564 per month; Rental vacancy rate: 7.6%
Vital Statistics: Birth rate: 184.4 per 10,000 population; Death rate: 71.6 per 10,000 population; Age-adjusted cancer mortality rate: 132.5 deaths per 100,000 population
Health Insurance: 54.3% have insurance; 42.5% have private insurance; 18.7% have public insurance; 45.7% do not have insurance; 53.5% of children under 18 do not have insurance
Health Care: Physicians: 5.3 per 10,000 population; Hospital beds: 9.4 per 10,000 population; Hospital admissions: 395.8 per 10,000 population
Transportation: Commute: 74.4% car, 0.3% public transportation, 6.4% walk, 8.8% work from home; Median travel time to work: 22.7 minutes
Presidential Election: 22.6% Obama, 75.4% Romney (2012)
Additional Information Contacts
Holmes Government . . . . (330) 674-0286
http://www.co.holmes.oh.us

Holmes County Communities

BERLIN (CDP). Covers a land area of 1.411 square miles and a water area of <.001 square miles. Located at 40.57° N. Lat; 81.81° W. Long. Elevation is 1,293 feet.
Population: 898; Growth (since 2000): n/a; Density: 636.3 persons per square mile; Race: 98.0% White, 0.4% Black/African American, 0.7% Asian, 0.1% American Indian/Alaska Native, 0.0% Native Hawaiian/Other Pacific Islander, 0.7% Two or more races, 0.9% Hispanic of any race; Average household size: 2.47; Median age: 38.0; Age under 18: 23.7%; Age 65 and over: 17.0%; Males per 100 females: 97.8

School District(s)

East Holmes Local (PK-12)
2012-13 Enrollment: 1,843 . . . . (330) 893-2610
Housing: Homeownership rate: 73.3%; Homeowner vacancy rate: 1.5%; Rental vacancy rate: 8.4%

BIG PRAIRIE (unincorporated postal area)
ZCTA: 44611
Covers a land area of 29.071 square miles and a water area of 0.048 square miles. Located at 40.61° N. Lat; 82.07° W. Long. Elevation is 951 feet.
Population: 2,025; Growth (since 2000): -0.1%; Density: 69.7 persons per square mile; Race: 97.9% White, 0.3% Black/African American, 0.2% Asian, 0.0% American Indian/Alaska Native, 0.1% Native Hawaiian/Other Pacific Islander, 0.6% Two or more races, 0.5% Hispanic of any race; Average household size: 2.77; Median age: 38.5; Age under 18: 27.9%; Age 65 and over: 14.2%; Males per 100 females: 100.3
Housing: Homeownership rate: 83.1%; Homeowner vacancy rate: 2.3%; Rental vacancy rate: 6.1%

BRINKHAVEN (unincorporated postal area)
ZCTA: 43006
Covers a land area of 23.906 square miles and a water area of 0.060 square miles. Located at 40.46° N. Lat; 82.15° W. Long..
Population: 822; Growth (since 2000): 37.7%; Density: 34.4 persons per square mile; Race: 97.6% White, 0.2% Black/African American, 0.1% Asian, 0.1% American Indian/Alaska Native, 0.0% Native Hawaiian/Other Pacific Islander, 1.9% Two or more races, 0.7% Hispanic of any race; Average household size: 3.08; Median age: 33.4; Age under 18: 36.4%; Age 65 and over: 11.6%; Males per 100 females: 102.5
Housing: Homeownership rate: 76.8%; Homeowner vacancy rate: 1.4%; Rental vacancy rate: 16.2%

GLENMONT (village). Covers a land area of 0.268 square miles and a water area of 0 square miles. Located at 40.52° N. Lat; 82.09° W. Long. Elevation is 886 feet.
History: Glenmont grew up around the sandstone quarries that furnished the material for some of New York's brownstone houses.
Population: 272; Growth (since 2000): -3.9%; Density: 1,013.1 persons per square mile; Race: 98.2% White, 0.0% Black/African American, 0.7% Asian, 0.4% American Indian/Alaska Native, 0.0% Native Hawaiian/Other Pacific Islander, 0.4% Two or more races, 0.4% Hispanic of any race; Average household size: 2.34; Median age: 37.8; Age under 18: 25.7%; Age 65 and over: 16.5%; Males per 100 females: 101.5
Housing: Homeownership rate: 72.4%; Homeowner vacancy rate: 1.2%; Rental vacancy rate: 0.0%

HOLMESVILLE (village). Covers a land area of 0.226 square miles and a water area of 0.007 square miles. Located at 40.63° N. Lat; 81.92° W. Long. Elevation is 863 feet.
Population: 372; Growth (since 2000): -3.6%; Density: 1,646.8 persons per square mile; Race: 98.7% White, 0.0% Black/African American, 0.3% Asian, 0.0% American Indian/Alaska Native, 0.0% Native Hawaiian/Other Pacific Islander, 1.1% Two or more races, 0.3% Hispanic of any race; Average household size: 2.55; Median age: 36.0; Age under 18: 23.4%; Age 65 and over: 12.6%; Males per 100 females: 98.9

School District(s)

Southeast Local (PK-12)
2012-13 Enrollment: 1,486 . . . . (330) 698-3001
Housing: Homeownership rate: 70.6%; Homeowner vacancy rate: 1.9%; Rental vacancy rate: 0.0%

KILLBUCK (village). Covers a land area of 0.357 square miles and a water area of 0 square miles. Located at 40.50° N. Lat; 81.98° W. Long. Elevation is 810 feet.
History: Killbuck was settled in 1811, and named for the creek on which it was established.
Population: 817; Growth (since 2000): -2.6%; Density: 2,287.1 persons per square mile; Race: 99.1% White, 0.0% Black/African American, 0.1% Asian, 0.0% American Indian/Alaska Native, 0.0% Native Hawaiian/Other Pacific Islander, 0.6% Two or more races, 0.5% Hispanic of any race; Average household size: 2.45; Median age: 38.0; Age under 18: 27.5%; Age 65 and over: 14.9%; Males per 100 females: 80.8

School District(s)

West Holmes Local (PK-12)
2012-13 Enrollment: 2,410 . . . . (330) 674-3556
Housing: Homeownership rate: 62.5%; Homeowner vacancy rate: 3.2%; Rental vacancy rate: 11.3%

LAKE BUCKHORN (CDP). Covers a land area of 1.757 square miles and a water area of 0.255 square miles. Located at 40.47° N. Lat; 81.91° W. Long.
Population: 601; Growth (since 2000): n/a; Density: 342.1 persons per square mile; Race: 99.2% White, 0.2% Black/African American, 0.0% Asian, 0.2% American Indian/Alaska Native, 0.0% Native Hawaiian/Other Pacific Islander, 0.3% Two or more races, 0.0% Hispanic of any race; Average household size: 2.58; Median age: 45.1; Age under 18: 24.5%; Age 65 and over: 18.1%; Males per 100 females: 97.7
Housing: Homeownership rate: 97.8%; Homeowner vacancy rate: 1.3%; Rental vacancy rate: 0.0%

LAKEVILLE (unincorporated postal area)

ZCTA: 44638

Covers a land area of 28.111 square miles and a water area of 0.420 square miles. Located at 40.65° N. Lat; 82.14° W. Long. Elevation is 961 feet.

Population: 1,497; Growth (since 2000): -2.3%; Density: 53.3 persons per square mile; Race: 98.7% White, 0.0% Black/African American, 0.3% Asian, 0.3% American Indian/Alaska Native, 0.0% Native Hawaiian/Other Pacific Islander, 0.3% Two or more races, 1.8% Hispanic of any race; Average household size: 2.69; Median age: 38.1; Age under 18: 26.9%; Age 65 and over: 12.0%; Males per 100 females: 102.0

School District(s)

West Holmes Local (PK-12)
2012-13 Enrollment: 2,410 . . . . (330) 674-3556

Housing: Homeownership rate: 75.7%; Homeowner vacancy rate: 1.6%; Rental vacancy rate: 14.6%

MILLERSBURG (village).

County seat. Covers a land area of 2.217 square miles and a water area of 0.009 square miles. Located at 40.55° N. Lat; 81.91° W. Long. Elevation is 892 feet.

History: Settlement in Millersburg began in 1816, when many "Pennsylvania Dutch" came here. The town has been the seat of Holmes County since 1824.

Population: 3,025; Growth (since 2000): -9.0%; Density: 1,364.4 persons per square mile; Race: 96.3% White, 0.6% Black/African American, 0.3% Asian, 0.2% American Indian/Alaska Native, 0.1% Native Hawaiian/Other Pacific Islander, 1.3% Two or more races, 2.6% Hispanic of any race; Average household size: 2.38; Median age: 37.7; Age under 18: 24.0%; Age 65 and over: 15.1%; Males per 100 females: 86.2; Marriage status: 31.9% never married, 39.4% now married, 1.5% separated, 8.6% widowed, 20.2% divorced; Foreign born: 1.2%; Speak English only: 90.7%; With disability: 13.6%; Veterans: 6.7%; Ancestry: 32.8% German, 13.0% Irish, 7.8% American, 7.4% English, 6.7% Polish

Employment: 6.0% management, business, and financial, 5.3% computer, engineering, and science, 6.8% education, legal, community service, arts, and media, 2.5% healthcare practitioners, 18.6% service, 18.8% sales and office, 12.1% natural resources, construction, and maintenance, 30.0% production, transportation, and material moving

Income: Per capita: $19,175; Median household: $32,419; Average household: $42,669; Households with income of $100,000 or more: 4.9%; Poverty rate: 20.8%

Educational Attainment: High school diploma or higher: 78.7%; Bachelor's degree or higher: 14.0%; Graduate/professional degree or higher: 5.3%

School District(s)

East Holmes Local (PK-12)
2012-13 Enrollment: 1,843 . . . . (330) 893-2610
West Holmes Local (PK-12)
2012-13 Enrollment: 2,410 . . . . (330) 674-3556

Housing: Homeownership rate: 55.7%; Median home value: $94,000; Median year structure built: 1955; Homeowner vacancy rate: 3.0%; Median gross rent: $518 per month; Rental vacancy rate: 10.8%

Health Insurance: 86.5% have insurance; 66.5% have private insurance; 31.2% have public insurance; 13.5% do not have insurance; 5.9% of children under 18 do not have insurance

Hospitals: Pomerene Hospital (55 beds)

Safety: Violent crime rate: 9.7 per 10,000 population; Property crime rate: 421.5 per 10,000 population

Newspapers: Holmes County Hub (weekly circulation 4400)

Transportation: Commute: 95.5% car, 0.0% public transportation, 2.4% walk, 1.3% work from home; Median travel time to work: 19.1 minutes

Additional Information Contacts

Village of Millersburg . . . . (330) 674-1886
http://www.millersburgohio.com

NASHVILLE (village).

Covers a land area of 0.075 square miles and a water area of 0 square miles. Located at 40.60° N. Lat; 82.11° W. Long. Elevation is 1,234 feet.

Population: 197; Growth (since 2000): 14.5%; Density: 2,642.1 persons per square mile; Race: 99.5% White, 0.0% Black/African American, 0.0% Asian, 0.0% American Indian/Alaska Native, 0.0% Native Hawaiian/Other Pacific Islander, 0.5% Two or more races, 0.5% Hispanic of any race; Average household size: 2.59; Median age: 28.9; Age under 18: 34.0%; Age 65 and over: 11.2%; Males per 100 females: 105.2

School District(s)

West Holmes Local (PK-12)
2012-13 Enrollment: 2,410 . . . . (330) 674-3556

Housing: Homeownership rate: 76.3%; Homeowner vacancy rate: 7.8%; Rental vacancy rate: 14.3%

WALNUT CREEK (CDP).

Covers a land area of 2.223 square miles and a water area of 0.002 square miles. Located at 40.55° N. Lat; 81.73° W. Long. Elevation is 1,188 feet.

Population: 878; Growth (since 2000): n/a; Density: 394.9 persons per square mile; Race: 99.2% White, 0.1% Black/African American, 0.1% Asian, 0.0% American Indian/Alaska Native, 0.0% Native Hawaiian/Other Pacific Islander, 0.5% Two or more races, 0.2% Hispanic of any race; Average household size: 2.83; Median age: 52.2; Age under 18: 21.1%; Age 65 and over: 39.3%; Males per 100 females: 74.6

School District(s)

East Holmes Local (PK-12)
2012-13 Enrollment: 1,843 . . . . (330) 893-2610

Housing: Homeownership rate: 64.9%; Homeowner vacancy rate: 1.3%; Rental vacancy rate: 11.7%

WINESBURG (CDP).

Covers a land area of 0.627 square miles and a water area of 0.003 square miles. Located at 40.62° N. Lat; 81.69° W. Long. Elevation is 1,306 feet.

Population: 352; Growth (since 2000): n/a; Density: 561.2 persons per square mile; Race: 100.0% White, 0.0% Black/African American, 0.0% Asian, 0.0% American Indian/Alaska Native, 0.0% Native Hawaiian/Other Pacific Islander, 0.0% Two or more races, 0.0% Hispanic of any race; Average household size: 2.67; Median age: 32.8; Age under 18: 23.6%; Age 65 and over: 13.1%; Males per 100 females: 91.3

School District(s)

East Holmes Local (PK-12)
2012-13 Enrollment: 1,843 . . . . (330) 893-2610

Housing: Homeownership rate: 68.2%; Homeowner vacancy rate: 2.2%; Rental vacancy rate: 8.7%

Huron County

Located in northern Ohio; drained by the Huron and Vermilion Rivers. Covers a land area of 491.495 square miles, a water area of 3.327 square miles, and is located in the Eastern Time Zone at 41.15° N. Lat., 82.59° W. Long. The county was founded in 1815. County seat is Norwalk.

Huron County is part of the Norwalk, OH Micropolitan Statistical Area. The entire metro area includes: Huron County, OH

Weather Station: Norwalk Wwtp Elevation: 669 feet

	Jan	Feb	Mar	Apr	May	Jun	Jul	Aug	Sep	Oct	Nov	Dec
High	33	36	45	58	69	78	82	81	74	62	50	37
Low	18	20	28	38	49	58	62	61	53	42	34	24
Precip	2.3	2.0	2.7	3.5	3.8	4.2	3.9	3.7	3.3	2.7	3.0	2.8
Snow	8.9	6.0	5.4	1.3	tr	0.0	0.0	tr	0.0	tr	1.4	6.3

High and Low temperatures in degrees Fahrenheit; Precipitation and Snow in inches

Population: 59,626; Growth (since 2000): 0.2%; Density: 121.3 persons per square mile; Race: 94.9% White, 1.0% Black/African American, 0.3% Asian, 0.2% American Indian/Alaska Native, 0.0% Native Hawaiian/Other Pacific Islander, 1.6% two or more races, 5.6% Hispanic of any race; Average household size: 2.59; Median age: 38.4; Age under 18: 26.3%; Age 65 and over: 13.6%; Males per 100 females: 97.1; Marriage status: 25.6% never married, 56.0% now married, 1.8% separated, 5.8% widowed, 12.6% divorced; Foreign born: 2.8%; Speak English only: 94.2%; With disability: 13.5%; Veterans: 10.5%; Ancestry: 36.9% German, 13.7% Irish, 10.6% English, 9.0% American, 4.5% Italian

Religion: Six largest groups: 23.4% Catholicism, 5.4% Methodist/Pietist, 3.8% Lutheran, 3.6% Holiness, 3.0% Baptist, 2.5% Non-denominational Protestant

Economy: Unemployment rate: 5.8%; Leading industries: 15.0% retail trade; 14.2% other services (except public administration); 11.7% construction; Farms: 865 totaling 238,291 acres; Company size: 0 employ 1,000 or more persons, 4 employ 500 to 999 persons, 20 employ 100 to 499 persons, 1,138 employ less than 100 persons; Business ownership: 1,253 women-owned, n/a Black-owned, n/a Hispanic-owned, n/a Asian-owned

Employment: 9.1% management, business, and financial, 2.7% computer, engineering, and science, 7.4% education, legal, community service, arts,

and media, 5.1% healthcare practitioners, 16.2% service, 22.3% sales and office, 11.7% natural resources, construction, and maintenance, 25.5% production, transportation, and material moving

Income: Per capita: $22,257; Median household: $49,404; Average household: $57,894; Households with income of $100,000 or more: 13.2%; Poverty rate: 13.5%

Educational Attainment: High school diploma or higher: 87.7%; Bachelor's degree or higher: 13.1%; Graduate/professional degree or higher: 4.8%

Housing: Homeownership rate: 70.9%; Median home value: $118,800; Median year structure built: 1967; Homeowner vacancy rate: 2.4%; Median gross rent: $619 per month; Rental vacancy rate: 11.0%

Vital Statistics: Birth rate: 117.3 per 10,000 population; Death rate: 90.8 per 10,000 population; Age-adjusted cancer mortality rate: 213.5 deaths per 100,000 population

Health Insurance: 88.6% have insurance; 69.9% have private insurance; 33.1% have public insurance; 11.4% do not have insurance; 6.6% of children under 18 do not have insurance

Health Care: Physicians: 9.3 per 10,000 population; Hospital beds: 37.4 per 10,000 population; Hospital admissions: 1,194.7 per 10,000 population

Transportation: Commute: 92.5% car, 0.7% public transportation, 3.3% walk, 2.1% work from home; Median travel time to work: 21.5 minutes

Presidential Election: 44.3% Obama, 53.2% Romney (2012)

Additional Information Contacts

Huron Government . . . . (419) 668-3092
http://www.hccommissioners.com

Huron County Communities

CELERYVILLE (CDP). Covers a land area of 0.516 square miles and a water area of 0 square miles. Located at 41.03° N. Lat; 82.73° W. Long. Elevation is 942 feet.

Population: 210; Growth (since 2000): n/a; Density: 406.7 persons per square mile; Race: 96.7% White, 0.0% Black/African American, 0.0% Asian, 0.0% American Indian/Alaska Native, 0.0% Native Hawaiian/Other Pacific Islander, 1.4% Two or more races, 5.7% Hispanic of any race; Average household size: 2.41; Median age: 48.0; Age under 18: 19.5%; Age 65 and over: 21.9%; Males per 100 females: 114.3

Housing: Homeownership rate: 87.4%; Homeowner vacancy rate: 0.0%; Rental vacancy rate: 0.0%

COLLINS (CDP). Covers a land area of 4.618 square miles and a water area of 0.005 square miles. Located at 41.25° N. Lat; 82.48° W. Long. Elevation is 876 feet.

Population: 631; Growth (since 2000): n/a; Density: 136.6 persons per square mile; Race: 97.8% White, 0.0% Black/African American, 0.2% Asian, 0.5% American Indian/Alaska Native, 0.0% Native Hawaiian/Other Pacific Islander, 1.3% Two or more races, 1.4% Hispanic of any race; Average household size: 2.73; Median age: 39.8; Age under 18: 26.3%; Age 65 and over: 10.6%; Males per 100 females: 99.1

School District(s)

Western Reserve Local (PK-12)
2012-13 Enrollment: 1,193 . . . . (419) 660-8508

Housing: Homeownership rate: 87.4%; Homeowner vacancy rate: 2.4%; Rental vacancy rate: 14.7%

GREENWICH (village). Covers a land area of 1.353 square miles and a water area of 0.016 square miles. Located at 41.03° N. Lat; 82.52° W. Long. Elevation is 1,027 feet.

History: Greenwich was incorporated in 1879 and named for the town in Connecticut.

Population: 1,476; Growth (since 2000): -3.2%; Density: 1,091.2 persons per square mile; Race: 99.1% White, 0.2% Black/African American, 0.4% Asian, 0.0% American Indian/Alaska Native, 0.0% Native Hawaiian/Other Pacific Islander, 0.3% Two or more races, 1.1% Hispanic of any race; Average household size: 2.57; Median age: 36.1; Age under 18: 27.6%; Age 65 and over: 13.0%; Males per 100 females: 101.1

School District(s)

South Central Local (PK-12)
2012-13 Enrollment: 820. . . . . (419) 752-3815

Housing: Homeownership rate: 70.4%; Homeowner vacancy rate: 0.7%; Rental vacancy rate: 3.4%

Newspapers: Enterprise Review (weekly circulation 14000)

HOLIDAY LAKES (CDP). Covers a land area of 1.733 square miles and a water area of 0.350 square miles. Located at 41.10° N. Lat; 82.73° W. Long.

Population: 749; Growth (since 2000): n/a; Density: 432.1 persons per square mile; Race: 97.3% White, 0.7% Black/African American, 0.0% Asian, 0.0% American Indian/Alaska Native, 0.0% Native Hawaiian/Other Pacific Islander, 0.9% Two or more races, 2.8% Hispanic of any race; Average household size: 2.51; Median age: 48.6; Age under 18: 19.0%; Age 65 and over: 14.0%; Males per 100 females: 101.9

Housing: Homeownership rate: 94.3%; Homeowner vacancy rate: 4.4%; Rental vacancy rate: 0.0%

MONROEVILLE (village). Covers a land area of 1.400 square miles and a water area of 0.030 square miles. Located at 41.24° N. Lat; 82.70° W. Long. Elevation is 709 feet.

Population: 1,400; Growth (since 2000): -2.3%; Density: 1,000.3 persons per square mile; Race: 97.0% White, 0.1% Black/African American, 0.0% Asian, 0.1% American Indian/Alaska Native, 0.0% Native Hawaiian/Other Pacific Islander, 2.2% Two or more races, 2.0% Hispanic of any race; Average household size: 2.65; Median age: 34.5; Age under 18: 28.6%; Age 65 and over: 10.1%; Males per 100 females: 99.4

School District(s)

Monroeville Local (PK-12)
2012-13 Enrollment: 652. . . . . (419) 465-2610

Housing: Homeownership rate: 61.4%; Homeowner vacancy rate: 1.8%; Rental vacancy rate: 10.1%

Safety: Violent crime rate: 0.0 per 10,000 population; Property crime rate: 186.8 per 10,000 population

Additional Information Contacts

Village of Monroeville . . . . (419) 465-4443
http://www.monroevilleohio.com

NEW HAVEN (CDP). Covers a land area of 1.236 square miles and a water area of 0.003 square miles. Located at 41.03° N. Lat; 82.69° W. Long. Elevation is 932 feet.

Population: 399; Growth (since 2000): n/a; Density: 322.8 persons per square mile; Race: 93.2% White, 0.5% Black/African American, 0.3% Asian, 0.0% American Indian/Alaska Native, 0.0% Native Hawaiian/Other Pacific Islander, 1.8% Two or more races, 5.8% Hispanic of any race; Average household size: 2.42; Median age: 47.7; Age under 18: 18.8%; Age 65 and over: 21.6%; Males per 100 females: 106.7

School District(s)

Willard City (PK-12)
2012-13 Enrollment: 1,733 . . . . (419) 935-1541

Housing: Homeownership rate: 87.2%; Homeowner vacancy rate: 0.0%; Rental vacancy rate: 8.7%

NEW LONDON (village). Covers a land area of 2.205 square miles and a water area of 0.331 square miles. Located at 41.08° N. Lat; 82.41° W. Long. Elevation is 981 feet.

History: New London was settled in 1816 and developed as a rural trading and shipping center. The C.E. Ward Company was established here to produce band uniforms, graduation caps and gowns, church vestments, and other regalia for a worldwide market.

Population: 2,461; Growth (since 2000): -8.7%; Density: 1,116.0 persons per square mile; Race: 95.8% White, 1.8% Black/African American, 0.1% Asian, 0.0% American Indian/Alaska Native, 0.1% Native Hawaiian/Other Pacific Islander, 2.0% Two or more races, 1.1% Hispanic of any race; Average household size: 2.51; Median age: 37.4; Age under 18: 26.8%; Age 65 and over: 14.7%; Males per 100 females: 93.3

School District(s)

New London Local (PK-12)
2012-13 Enrollment: 991. . . . . (419) 929-8433

Housing: Homeownership rate: 63.9%; Homeowner vacancy rate: 4.3%; Rental vacancy rate: 13.7%

Safety: Violent crime rate: 0.0 per 10,000 population; Property crime rate: 86.6 per 10,000 population

Newspapers: New London Record (weekly circulation 2400)

Additional Information Contacts

Village of New London . . . . (419) 929-1809
http://www.newlondonohio.com

NORTH FAIRFIELD (village). Covers a land area of 0.462 square miles and a water area of 0.002 square miles. Located at 41.10° N. Lat; 82.61° W. Long. Elevation is 928 feet.
Population: 560; Growth (since 2000): -2.3%; Density: 1,212.5 persons per square mile; Race: 96.8% White, 0.0% Black/African American, 1.1% Asian, 0.2% American Indian/Alaska Native, 0.0% Native Hawaiian/Other Pacific Islander, 1.8% Two or more races, 0.9% Hispanic of any race; Average household size: 3.08; Median age: 32.9; Age under 18: 31.1%; Age 65 and over: 9.1%; Males per 100 females: 102.2
Housing: Homeownership rate: 81.9%; Homeowner vacancy rate: 5.7%; Rental vacancy rate: 19.5%

NORWALK (city). County seat. Covers a land area of 8.870 square miles and a water area of 0.282 square miles. Located at 41.24° N. Lat; 82.61° W. Long. Elevation is 728 feet.
History: Norwalk was founded in 1816 by Platt Benedict, and named for the Connecticut town which had been the home of many of its first settlers.
Population: 17,012; Growth (since 2000): 4.8%; Density: 1,917.9 persons per square mile; Race: 92.2% White, 1.9% Black/African American, 0.5% Asian, 0.2% American Indian/Alaska Native, 0.0% Native Hawaiian/Other Pacific Islander, 2.1% Two or more races, 7.2% Hispanic of any race; Average household size: 2.46; Median age: 37.0; Age under 18: 26.2%; Age 65 and over: 14.6%; Males per 100 females: 91.7; Marriage status: 27.1% never married, 50.4% now married, 1.4% separated, 6.8% widowed, 15.7% divorced; Foreign born: 3.4%; Speak English only: 94.3%; With disability: 14.9%; Veterans: 12.1%; Ancestry: 38.9% German, 14.1% Irish, 12.2% English, 9.7% American, 4.3% Italian
Employment: 9.2% management, business, and financial, 4.1% computer, engineering, and science, 8.9% education, legal, community service, arts, and media, 3.6% healthcare practitioners, 17.4% service, 23.6% sales and office, 9.9% natural resources, construction, and maintenance, 23.2% production, transportation, and material moving
Income: Per capita: $21,911; Median household: $42,142; Average household: $53,647; Households with income of $100,000 or more: 11.6%; Poverty rate: 16.2%
Educational Attainment: High school diploma or higher: 87.6%; Bachelor's degree or higher: 14.4%; Graduate/professional degree or higher: 6.1%

School District(s)

Norwalk City (PK-12)
2012-13 Enrollment: 2,898 . . . . (419) 668-2779

Two-year College(s)

Elite School of Cosmetology (Private, For-profit)
Fall 2013 Enrollment: 34 . . . . (419) 668-2333
Housing: Homeownership rate: 60.1%; Median home value: $118,100; Median year structure built: 1966; Homeowner vacancy rate: 2.8%; Median gross rent: $598 per month; Rental vacancy rate: 9.3%
Health Insurance: 89.4% have insurance; 67.3% have private insurance; 38.1% have public insurance; 10.6% do not have insurance; 3.5% of children under 18 do not have insurance
Hospitals: Fisher - Titus Hospital (112 beds)
Safety: Violent crime rate: 11.2 per 10,000 population; Property crime rate: 320.6 per 10,000 population
Newspapers: Norwalk Reflector (daily circulation 8800)
Transportation: Commute: 94.5% car, 0.3% public transportation, 2.8% walk, 1.2% work from home; Median travel time to work: 18.7 minutes
Additional Information Contacts
City of Norwalk . . . . (419) 663-6700
http://www.norwalkoh.com

WAKEMAN (village). Covers a land area of 0.825 square miles and a water area of 0.023 square miles. Located at 41.25° N. Lat; 82.40° W. Long. Elevation is 846 feet.
History: Wakeman was the home of the C.S. Clark Seed Company, founded in 1878 and specializing in varieties of seed corn.
Population: 1,047; Growth (since 2000): 10.1%; Density: 1,269.7 persons per square mile; Race: 99.0% White, 0.2% Black/African American, 0.0% Asian, 0.1% American Indian/Alaska Native, 0.0% Native Hawaiian/Other Pacific Islander, 0.6% Two or more races, 1.2% Hispanic of any race; Average household size: 2.60; Median age: 36.7; Age under 18: 28.7%; Age 65 and over: 11.3%; Males per 100 females: 92.5
Housing: Homeownership rate: 72.1%; Homeowner vacancy rate: 3.3%; Rental vacancy rate: 12.5%

WILLARD (city). Covers a land area of 3.549 square miles and a water area of 0.018 square miles. Located at 41.05° N. Lat; 82.72° W. Long. Elevation is 919 feet.
Population: 6,236; Growth (since 2000): -8.4%; Density: 1,756.9 persons per square mile; Race: 90.0% White, 1.8% Black/African American, 0.2% Asian, 0.2% American Indian/Alaska Native, 0.0% Native Hawaiian/Other Pacific Islander, 2.1% Two or more races, 18.9% Hispanic of any race; Average household size: 2.60; Median age: 34.6; Age under 18: 28.7%; Age 65 and over: 13.8%; Males per 100 females: 92.9; Marriage status: 30.5% never married, 52.7% now married, 2.5% separated, 4.2% widowed, 12.5% divorced; Foreign born: 6.5%; Speak English only: 86.4%; With disability: 16.6%; Veterans: 10.2%; Ancestry: 22.0% German, 14.5% Irish, 6.8% American, 6.2% English, 3.8% Italian
Employment: 9.2% management, business, and financial, 3.3% computer, engineering, and science, 6.9% education, legal, community service, arts, and media, 6.8% healthcare practitioners, 16.9% service, 20.4% sales and office, 7.0% natural resources, construction, and maintenance, 29.4% production, transportation, and material moving
Income: Per capita: $17,420; Median household: $42,244; Average household: $47,338; Households with income of $100,000 or more: 8.1%; Poverty rate: 25.9%
Educational Attainment: High school diploma or higher: 83.2%; Bachelor's degree or higher: 9.0%; Graduate/professional degree or higher: 2.5%

School District(s)

Willard City (PK-12)
2012-13 Enrollment: 1,733 . . . . (419) 935-1541
Housing: Homeownership rate: 52.5%; Median home value: $85,500; Median year structure built: 1957; Homeowner vacancy rate: 3.5%; Median gross rent: $584 per month; Rental vacancy rate: 13.7%
Health Insurance: 84.9% have insurance; 54.6% have private insurance; 45.3% have public insurance; 15.1% do not have insurance; 11.9% of children under 18 do not have insurance
Hospitals: Mercy Willard Hospital (25 beds)
Newspapers: The Times-Junction (weekly circulation 3800)
Transportation: Commute: 94.1% car, 0.2% public transportation, 1.4% walk, 1.1% work from home; Median travel time to work: 19.3 minutes
Additional Information Contacts
City of Willard . . . . (419) 933-2581
http://www.willardohio.com

Jackson County

Located in southern Ohio; drained by the Little Scioto River. Covers a land area of 420.304 square miles, a water area of 1.230 square miles, and is located in the Eastern Time Zone at 39.01° N. Lat., 82.61° W. Long. The county was founded in 1816. County seat is Jackson.

Jackson County is part of the Jackson, OH Micropolitan Statistical Area. The entire metro area includes: Jackson County, OH

Weather Station: Jackson 3 NW Elevation: 799 feet

	Jan	Feb	Mar	Apr	May	Jun	Jul	Aug	Sep	Oct	Nov	Dec
High	39	43	53	66	74	81	84	84	77	65	54	42
Low	21	23	30	40	49	58	62	61	54	42	33	25
Precip	2.9	2.9	3.9	3.5	4.5	3.9	4.4	3.3	2.9	3.0	3.3	3.2
Snow	na	4.8	2.0	0.7	0.0	0.0	0.0	0.0	0.0	0.0	0.5	2.7

High and Low temperatures in degrees Fahrenheit; Precipitation and Snow in inches

Population: 33,225; Growth (since 2000): 1.8%; Density: 79.0 persons per square mile; Race: 97.1% White, 0.6% Black/African American, 0.3% Asian, 0.4% American Indian/Alaska Native, 0.0% Native Hawaiian/Other Pacific Islander, 1.4% two or more races, 0.8% Hispanic of any race; Average household size: 2.53; Median age: 39.0; Age under 18: 24.5%; Age 65 and over: 14.1%; Males per 100 females: 95.6; Marriage status: 25.1% never married, 52.2% now married, 3.0% separated, 8.8% widowed, 13.9% divorced; Foreign born: 0.5%; Speak English only: 95.7%; With disability: 19.4%; Veterans: 11.8%; Ancestry: 18.3% German, 12.9% American, 12.6% Irish, 9.7% English, 5.8% Welsh
Religion: Six largest groups: 7.9% Methodist/Pietist, 6.2% Baptist, 5.1% Non-denominational Protestant, 2.5% Holiness, 1.9% Latter-day Saints, 1.3% Presbyterian-Reformed
Economy: Unemployment rate: 7.1%; Leading industries: 19.7% retail trade; 12.4% health care and social assistance; 11.7% other services (except public administration); Farms: 526 totaling 71,681 acres; Company

size: 2 employ 1,000 or more persons, 0 employ 500 to 999 persons, 12 employ 100 to 499 persons, 584 employ less than 100 persons; Business ownership: 543 women-owned, n/a Black-owned, n/a Hispanic-owned, n/a Asian-owned
Employment: 8.9% management, business, and financial, 2.9% computer, engineering, and science, 11.2% education, legal, community service, arts, and media, 6.9% healthcare practitioners, 16.7% service, 19.2% sales and office, 13.6% natural resources, construction, and maintenance, 20.7% production, transportation, and material moving
Income: Per capita: $19,405; Median household: $36,356; Average household: $47,537; Households with income of $100,000 or more: 9.0%; Poverty rate: 24.6%
Educational Attainment: High school diploma or higher: 81.4%; Bachelor's degree or higher: 15.2%; Graduate/professional degree or higher: 5.4%
Housing: Homeownership rate: 70.6%; Median home value: $89,600; Median year structure built: 1975; Homeowner vacancy rate: 2.6%; Median gross rent: $609 per month; Rental vacancy rate: 8.7%
Vital Statistics: Birth rate: 120.2 per 10,000 population; Death rate: 107.4 per 10,000 population; Age-adjusted cancer mortality rate: 217.5 deaths per 100,000 population
Health Insurance: 85.8% have insurance; 57.6% have private insurance; 40.6% have public insurance; 14.2% do not have insurance; 8.9% of children under 18 do not have insurance
Health Care: Physicians: 5.8 per 10,000 population; Hospital beds: 7.2 per 10,000 population; Hospital admissions: 409.9 per 10,000 population
Transportation: Commute: 94.8% car, 0.3% public transportation, 2.4% walk, 1.8% work from home; Median travel time to work: 27.2 minutes
Presidential Election: 38.4% Obama, 59.2% Romney (2012)
National and State Parks: Buckeye Furnace State Memorial; Jackson Lake State Reserve; Lake Katharine State Nature Preserve; Leo Petroglyph State Memorial; Richland Furnace State Forest
Additional Information Contacts
Jackson Government .... (740) 286-3301
http://www.jacksoncountygovernment.org

Jackson County Communities

COALTON (village). Covers a land area of 0.550 square miles and a water area of 0 square miles. Located at 39.11° N. Lat; 82.61° W. Long. Elevation is 696 feet.
History: During the 1880's, Coalton was a busy coal town.
Population: 479; Growth (since 2000): -12.1%; Density: 871.3 persons per square mile; Race: 97.5% White, 0.2% Black/African American, 0.0% Asian, 0.4% American Indian/Alaska Native, 0.0% Native Hawaiian/Other Pacific Islander, 1.9% Two or more races, 0.8% Hispanic of any race; Average household size: 2.34; Median age: 40.4; Age under 18: 21.7%; Age 65 and over: 14.8%; Males per 100 females: 97.9
Housing: Homeownership rate: 58.5%; Homeowner vacancy rate: 4.6%; Rental vacancy rate: 14.1%
Safety: Violent crime rate: 42.6 per 10,000 population; Property crime rate: 980.8 per 10,000 population

JACKSON (city). County seat. Covers a land area of 8.232 square miles and a water area of 0.261 square miles. Located at 39.05° N. Lat; 82.65° W. Long. Elevation is 686 feet.
History: Jackson was platted in 1817, and grew around the railroad that arrived in 1853. Many of Jackson's early settlers were Welsh who came to farm and later worked in the iron furnaces and coal mines.
Population: 6,397; Growth (since 2000): 3.4%; Density: 777.1 persons per square mile; Race: 96.4% White, 0.7% Black/African American, 0.4% Asian, 0.3% American Indian/Alaska Native, 0.0% Native Hawaiian/Other Pacific Islander, 1.7% Two or more races, 1.5% Hispanic of any race; Average household size: 2.32; Median age: 38.1; Age under 18: 23.8%; Age 65 and over: 14.7%; Males per 100 females: 87.0; Marriage status: 22.9% never married, 51.1% now married, 3.3% separated, 9.7% widowed, 16.3% divorced; Foreign born: 0.7%; Speak English only: 95.7%; With disability: 20.3%; Veterans: 13.6%; Ancestry: 21.4% German, 10.8% Irish, 10.5% English, 10.2% American, 5.8% Welsh
Employment: 4.8% management, business, and financial, 3.5% computer, engineering, and science, 18.9% education, legal, community service, arts, and media, 4.5% healthcare practitioners, 13.4% service, 25.7% sales and office, 7.9% natural resources, construction, and maintenance, 21.4% production, transportation, and material moving
Income: Per capita: $19,983; Median household: $36,545; Average household: $43,698; Households with income of $100,000 or more: 7.7%; Poverty rate: 20.6%
Educational Attainment: High school diploma or higher: 87.4%; Bachelor's degree or higher: 19.8%; Graduate/professional degree or higher: 8.3%

School District(s)

Center for Student Achievement (09-12)
2012-13 Enrollment: 57.......................... (740) 286-7839
Jackson City (PK-12)
2012-13 Enrollment: 2,417 .... (740) 286-6442

Two-year College(s)

Daymar College-Jackson (Private, For-profit)
Fall 2013 Enrollment: 77......................... (740) 286-1554
2013-14 Tuition: In-state $18,000; Out-of-state $18,000
Housing: Homeownership rate: 54.2%; Median home value: $93,200; Median year structure built: 1954; Homeowner vacancy rate: 3.6%; Median gross rent: $595 per month; Rental vacancy rate: 7.0%
Health Insurance: 88.1% have insurance; 59.2% have private insurance; 42.8% have public insurance; 11.9% do not have insurance; 0.0% of children under 18 do not have insurance
Hospitals: Holzer Medical Center Jackson
Safety: Violent crime rate: 11.1 per 10,000 population; Property crime rate: 386.4 per 10,000 population
Newspapers: Jackson Co. Times-Journal (weekly circulation 5800); Telegram (weekly circulation 6000)
Transportation: Commute: 93.6% car, 1.3% public transportation, 3.8% walk, 1.4% work from home; Median travel time to work: 23.5 minutes
Airports: James A Rhodes (general aviation)

OAK HILL (village). Covers a land area of 1.142 square miles and a water area of 0 square miles. Located at 38.90° N. Lat; 82.57° W. Long. Elevation is 702 feet.
Population: 1,551; Growth (since 2000): -8.0%; Density: 1,358.5 persons per square mile; Race: 97.5% White, 0.5% Black/African American, 0.3% Asian, 0.2% American Indian/Alaska Native, 0.0% Native Hawaiian/Other Pacific Islander, 1.6% Two or more races, 0.3% Hispanic of any race; Average household size: 2.49; Median age: 36.3; Age under 18: 25.2%; Age 65 and over: 15.0%; Males per 100 females: 90.8

School District(s)

Oak Hill Union Local (PK-12)
2012-13 Enrollment: 1,299 .... (740) 682-7595
Housing: Homeownership rate: 59.2%; Homeowner vacancy rate: 3.4%; Rental vacancy rate: 8.6%
Safety: Violent crime rate: 0.0 per 10,000 population; Property crime rate: 236.8 per 10,000 population

WELLSTON (city). Covers a land area of 6.970 square miles and a water area of 0.084 square miles. Located at 39.12° N. Lat; 82.54° W. Long. Elevation is 738 feet.
History: Wellston was named for Harvey Wells, who constructed a blast furnace in 1874 and platted a town around it.
Population: 5,663; Growth (since 2000): -6.8%; Density: 812.4 persons per square mile; Race: 97.7% White, 0.2% Black/African American, 0.2% Asian, 0.4% American Indian/Alaska Native, 0.0% Native Hawaiian/Other Pacific Islander, 1.3% Two or more races, 0.7% Hispanic of any race; Average household size: 2.47; Median age: 36.5; Age under 18: 25.6%; Age 65 and over: 14.8%; Males per 100 females: 88.0; Marriage status: 29.7% never married, 44.8% now married, 4.8% separated, 11.1% widowed, 14.4% divorced; Foreign born: 0.2%; Speak English only: 95.4%; With disability: 17.1%; Veterans: 11.1%; Ancestry: 18.0% Irish, 17.2% German, 12.9% English, 9.7% American, 5.8% Welsh
Employment: 11.3% management, business, and financial, 2.0% computer, engineering, and science, 11.0% education, legal, community service, arts, and media, 5.2% healthcare practitioners, 22.0% service, 15.9% sales and office, 11.4% natural resources, construction, and maintenance, 21.1% production, transportation, and material moving
Income: Per capita: $17,152; Median household: $33,643; Average household: $40,951; Households with income of $100,000 or more: 5.5%; Poverty rate: 33.9%
Educational Attainment: High school diploma or higher: 83.2%; Bachelor's degree or higher: 15.1%; Graduate/professional degree or higher: 3.1%

School District(s)

Wellston City (PK-12)
2012-13 Enrollment: 1,490 . . . . (740) 384-2152

Housing: Homeownership rate: 63.2%; Median home value: $77,100; Median year structure built: 1970; Homeowner vacancy rate: 4.5%; Median gross rent: $526 per month; Rental vacancy rate: 8.6%

Health Insurance: 90.5% have insurance; 52.3% have private insurance; 50.8% have public insurance; 9.5% do not have insurance; 0.0% of children under 18 do not have insurance

Safety: Violent crime rate: 21.5 per 10,000 population; Property crime rate: 468.0 per 10,000 population

Transportation: Commute: 96.0% car, 0.0% public transportation, 3.3% walk, 0.6% work from home; Median travel time to work: 32.2 minutes

Jefferson County

Located in eastern Ohio; bounded on the east by the Ohio River and the West Virginia border; drained by Yellow and Cross Creeks. Covers a land area of 408.329 square miles, a water area of 2.624 square miles, and is located in the Eastern Time Zone at 40.40° N. Lat., 80.76° W. Long. The county was founded in 1797. County seat is Steubenville.

Jefferson County is part of the Weirton-Steubenville, WV-OH Metropolitan Statistical Area. The entire metro area includes: Jefferson County, OH; Brooke County, WV; Hancock County, WV

Weather Station: Steubenville — Elevation: 992 feet

	Jan	Feb	Mar	Apr	May	Jun	Jul	Aug	Sep	Oct	Nov	Dec
High	37	41	50	63	72	80	83	82	76	64	52	41
Low	22	23	30	40	50	59	64	63	55	43	35	25
Precip	3.0	2.3	3.3	3.4	4.4	4.2	4.4	4.0	3.4	2.8	3.5	3.0
Snow	na	na	0.4	tr	0.0	0.0	0.0	0.0	0.0	0.2	0.2	na

High and Low temperatures in degrees Fahrenheit; Precipitation and Snow in inches

Population: 69,709; Growth (since 2000): -5.7%; Density: 170.7 persons per square mile; Race: 91.9% White, 5.6% Black/African American, 0.4% Asian, 0.1% American Indian/Alaska Native, 0.0% Native Hawaiian/Other Pacific Islander, 1.7% two or more races, 1.1% Hispanic of any race; Average household size: 2.32; Median age: 43.9; Age under 18: 20.2%; Age 65 and over: 18.3%; Males per 100 females: 92.3; Marriage status: 28.5% never married, 51.9% now married, 1.7% separated, 8.0% widowed, 11.6% divorced; Foreign born: 1.1%; Speak English only: 97.4%; With disability: 16.6%; Veterans: 12.2%; Ancestry: 19.0% German, 16.0% Irish, 14.2% Italian, 8.8% English, 7.3% Polish

Religion: Six largest groups: 19.9% Catholicism, 11.2% Methodist/Pietist, 3.8% Baptist, 3.2% Presbyterian-Reformed, 2.0% Holiness, 1.9% Non-denominational Protestant

Economy: Unemployment rate: 6.0%; Leading industries: 16.8% retail trade; 15.4% other services (except public administration); 11.7% health care and social assistance; Farms: 493 totaling 68,341 acres; Company size: 2 employ 1,000 or more persons, 2 employ 500 to 999 persons, 22 employ 100 to 499 persons, 1,277 employ less than 100 persons; Business ownership: 1,178 women-owned, n/a Black-owned, n/a Hispanic-owned, 63 Asian-owned

Employment: 9.7% management, business, and financial, 2.3% computer, engineering, and science, 7.7% education, legal, community service, arts, and media, 7.8% healthcare practitioners, 20.8% service, 24.1% sales and office, 11.3% natural resources, construction, and maintenance, 16.2% production, transportation, and material moving

Income: Per capita: $22,324; Median household: $40,577; Average household: $52,864; Households with income of $100,000 or more: 11.2%; Poverty rate: 16.6%

Educational Attainment: High school diploma or higher: 89.0%; Bachelor's degree or higher: 14.7%; Graduate/professional degree or higher: 5.3%

Housing: Homeownership rate: 72.1%; Median home value: $86,400; Median year structure built: 1957; Homeowner vacancy rate: 2.2%; Median gross rent: $575 per month; Rental vacancy rate: 9.1%

Vital Statistics: Birth rate: 92.7 per 10,000 population; Death rate: 138.5 per 10,000 population; Age-adjusted cancer mortality rate: 200.2 deaths per 100,000 population

Health Insurance: 88.9% have insurance; 68.7% have private insurance; 36.5% have public insurance; 11.1% do not have insurance; 4.4% of children under 18 do not have insurance

Health Care: Physicians: 11.8 per 10,000 population; Hospital beds: 57.4 per 10,000 population; Hospital admissions: 1,786.6 per 10,000 population

Air Quality Index: 60.0% good, 38.9% moderate, 1.1% unhealthy for sensitive individuals, 0.0% unhealthy (percent of days)

Transportation: Commute: 91.6% car, 0.6% public transportation, 3.9% walk, 3.2% work from home; Median travel time to work: 24.8 minutes

Presidential Election: 46.3% Obama, 51.7% Romney (2012)

National and State Parks: Fernwood State Forest; Jefferson Lake State Park

Additional Information Contacts

Jefferson Government. . . . . (740) 283-8500
http://www.jeffersoncountyoh.com

Jefferson County Communities

ADENA (village). Covers a land area of 0.537 square miles and a water area of 0 square miles. Located at 40.22° N. Lat; 80.88° W. Long. Elevation is 856 feet.

Population: 759; Growth (since 2000): -6.9%; Density: 1,413.0 persons per square mile; Race: 97.9% White, 0.3% Black/African American, 0.0% Asian, 0.0% American Indian/Alaska Native, 0.1% Native Hawaiian/Other Pacific Islander, 1.7% Two or more races, 0.4% Hispanic of any race; Average household size: 2.38; Median age: 43.9; Age under 18: 21.6%; Age 65 and over: 19.8%; Males per 100 females: 91.7

School District(s)

Buckeye Local (PK-12)
2012-13 Enrollment: 1,922 . . . . (740) 769-7395

Housing: Homeownership rate: 79.9%; Homeowner vacancy rate: 1.1%; Rental vacancy rate: 4.5%

AMSTERDAM (village). Covers a land area of 0.319 square miles and a water area of 0 square miles. Located at 40.47° N. Lat; 80.92° W. Long. Elevation is 928 feet.

History: Settled 1830, incorporated 1904.

Population: 511; Growth (since 2000): -10.0%; Density: 1,600.9 persons per square mile; Race: 99.0% White, 0.0% Black/African American, 0.2% Asian, 0.2% American Indian/Alaska Native, 0.0% Native Hawaiian/Other Pacific Islander, 0.6% Two or more races, 1.0% Hispanic of any race; Average household size: 2.50; Median age: 39.6; Age under 18: 25.0%; Age 65 and over: 16.2%; Males per 100 females: 86.5

Housing: Homeownership rate: 70.1%; Homeowner vacancy rate: 1.4%; Rental vacancy rate: 12.9%

BERGHOLZ (village). Covers a land area of 0.563 square miles and a water area of 0 square miles. Located at 40.52° N. Lat; 80.89° W. Long. Elevation is 925 feet.

History: Settled 1885, incorporated 1906.

Population: 664; Growth (since 2000): -13.7%; Density: 1,178.5 persons per square mile; Race: 98.2% White, 0.8% Black/African American, 0.2% Asian, 0.3% American Indian/Alaska Native, 0.0% Native Hawaiian/Other Pacific Islander, 0.6% Two or more races, 0.2% Hispanic of any race; Average household size: 2.50; Median age: 38.3; Age under 18: 24.2%; Age 65 and over: 14.0%; Males per 100 females: 91.4

School District(s)

Edison Local (PK-12)
2012-13 Enrollment: 1,858 . . . . (330) 532-3199

Housing: Homeownership rate: 74.1%; Homeowner vacancy rate: 4.4%; Rental vacancy rate: 15.9%

BLOOMINGDALE (village). Covers a land area of 0.088 square miles and a water area of 0 square miles. Located at 40.34° N. Lat; 80.82° W. Long. Elevation is 1,263 feet.

History: Laid out 1816. Also called Bloomfield.

Population: 202; Growth (since 2000): -8.6%; Density: 2,286.0 persons per square mile; Race: 98.0% White, 0.5% Black/African American, 0.0% Asian, 0.5% American Indian/Alaska Native, 0.0% Native Hawaiian/Other Pacific Islander, 1.0% Two or more races, 0.0% Hispanic of any race; Average household size: 2.53; Median age: 41.5; Age under 18: 18.8%; Age 65 and over: 14.4%; Males per 100 females: 112.6

School District(s)

Indian Creek Local (PK-12)
2012-13 Enrollment: 2,194 . . . . (740) 264-3502

Jefferson County (11-12)
2012-13 Enrollment: n/a . . . . (740) 264-5545

Housing: Homeownership rate: 83.8%; Homeowner vacancy rate: 0.0%; Rental vacancy rate: 12.5%

BRILLIANT (CDP). Covers a land area of 1.754 square miles and a water area of 0.014 square miles. Located at 40.27° N. Lat; 80.64° W. Long. Elevation is 689 feet.

Population: 1,482; Growth (since 2000): n/a; Density: 845.0 persons per square mile; Race: 98.8% White, 0.3% Black/African American, 0.0% Asian, 0.1% American Indian/Alaska Native, 0.0% Native Hawaiian/Other Pacific Islander, 0.8% Two or more races, 0.3% Hispanic of any race; Average household size: 2.27; Median age: 44.6; Age under 18: 20.4%; Age 65 and over: 18.6%; Males per 100 females: 90.5

School District(s)

Buckeye Local (PK-12)
2012-13 Enrollment: 1,922 . . . . (740) 769-7395

Housing: Homeownership rate: 67.6%; Homeowner vacancy rate: 2.6%; Rental vacancy rate: 10.5%

DILLONVALE (village). Covers a land area of 0.386 square miles and a water area of 0.008 square miles. Located at 40.20° N. Lat; 80.78° W. Long. Elevation is 735 feet.

History: Dillonvale grew in the center of a large coal-mining region.

Population: 665; Growth (since 2000): -14.9%; Density: 1,722.4 persons per square mile; Race: 98.0% White, 0.9% Black/African American, 0.0% Asian, 0.2% American Indian/Alaska Native, 0.0% Native Hawaiian/Other Pacific Islander, 0.8% Two or more races, 0.2% Hispanic of any race; Average household size: 2.23; Median age: 43.4; Age under 18: 20.2%; Age 65 and over: 20.5%; Males per 100 females: 89.5

Housing: Homeownership rate: 83.0%; Homeowner vacancy rate: 0.4%; Rental vacancy rate: 9.1%

EAST SPRINGFIELD (unincorporated postal area)

ZCTA: 43925

Covers a land area of 0.120 square miles and a water area of 0 square miles. Located at 40.45° N. Lat; 80.86° W. Long. Elevation is 1,266 feet.

Population: 82; Growth (since 2000): -3.5%; Density: 685.0 persons per square mile; Race: 100.0% White, 0.0% Black/African American, 0.0% Asian, 0.0% American Indian/Alaska Native, 0.0% Native Hawaiian/Other Pacific Islander, 0.0% Two or more races, 0.0% Hispanic of any race; Average household size: 2.56; Median age: 38.0; Age under 18: 25.6%; Age 65 and over: 11.0%; Males per 100 females: 100.0

Housing: Homeownership rate: 71.9%; Homeowner vacancy rate: 0.0%; Rental vacancy rate: 0.0%

EMPIRE (village). Covers a land area of 0.300 square miles and a water area of 0 square miles. Located at 40.51° N. Lat; 80.63° W. Long. Elevation is 682 feet.

Population: 299; Growth (since 2000): -0.3%; Density: 995.7 persons per square mile; Race: 94.6% White, 2.7% Black/African American, 0.0% Asian, 2.0% American Indian/Alaska Native, 0.0% Native Hawaiian/Other Pacific Islander, 0.7% Two or more races, 0.0% Hispanic of any race; Average household size: 2.51; Median age: 36.7; Age under 18: 25.1%; Age 65 and over: 9.4%; Males per 100 females: 88.1

Housing: Homeownership rate: 63.8%; Homeowner vacancy rate: 1.3%; Rental vacancy rate: 10.0%

HAMMONDSVILLE (unincorporated postal area)

ZCTA: 43930

Covers a land area of 37.618 square miles and a water area of 0.121 square miles. Located at 40.56° N. Lat; 80.76° W. Long. Elevation is 689 feet.

Population: 882; Growth (since 2000): 18.7%; Density: 23.4 persons per square mile; Race: 97.7% White, 0.1% Black/African American, 0.0% Asian, 0.1% American Indian/Alaska Native, 0.0% Native Hawaiian/Other Pacific Islander, 1.8% Two or more races, 0.0% Hispanic of any race; Average household size: 2.40; Median age: 44.7; Age under 18: 19.5%; Age 65 and over: 14.7%; Males per 100 females: 101.4

School District(s)

Edison Local (PK-12)
2012-13 Enrollment: 1,858 . . . . (330) 532-3199

Housing: Homeownership rate: 80.2%; Homeowner vacancy rate: 1.7%; Rental vacancy rate: 1.4%

IRONDALE (village). Covers a land area of 1.449 square miles and a water area of 0.027 square miles. Located at 40.57° N. Lat; 80.73° W. Long. Elevation is 712 feet.

Population: 387; Growth (since 2000): -7.4%; Density: 267.0 persons per square mile; Race: 99.7% White, 0.3% Black/African American, 0.0% Asian, 0.0% American Indian/Alaska Native, 0.0% Native Hawaiian/Other Pacific Islander, 0.0% Two or more races, 0.0% Hispanic of any race; Average household size: 2.73; Median age: 36.1; Age under 18: 28.4%; Age 65 and over: 11.6%; Males per 100 females: 112.6

Housing: Homeownership rate: 80.2%; Homeowner vacancy rate: 1.7%; Rental vacancy rate: 3.4%

MINGO JUNCTION (village). Covers a land area of 2.690 square miles and a water area of 0.171 square miles. Located at 40.33° N. Lat; 80.62° W. Long. Elevation is 794 feet.

History: Mingo Junction developed near Steubenville as a steel town.

Population: 3,454; Growth (since 2000): -4.9%; Density: 1,284.2 persons per square mile; Race: 94.5% White, 3.6% Black/African American, 0.1% Asian, 0.3% American Indian/Alaska Native, 0.0% Native Hawaiian/Other Pacific Islander, 1.4% Two or more races, 0.8% Hispanic of any race; Average household size: 2.32; Median age: 44.2; Age under 18: 21.1%; Age 65 and over: 19.9%; Males per 100 females: 90.6; Marriage status: 29.9% never married, 47.7% now married, 1.3% separated, 8.1% widowed, 14.4% divorced; Foreign born: 0.0%; Speak English only: 98.8%; With disability: 17.2%; Veterans: 15.3%; Ancestry: 22.4% German, 19.0% Italian, 18.0% Irish, 10.0% English, 6.9% Slovak

Employment: 6.7% management, business, and financial, 1.1% computer, engineering, and science, 8.8% education, legal, community service, arts, and media, 2.4% healthcare practitioners, 24.6% service, 24.8% sales and office, 6.8% natural resources, construction, and maintenance, 24.8% production, transportation, and material moving

Income: Per capita: $21,276; Median household: $40,720; Average household: $48,262; Households with income of $100,000 or more: 9.4%; Poverty rate: 14.6%

Educational Attainment: High school diploma or higher: 91.6%; Bachelor's degree or higher: 11.1%; Graduate/professional degree or higher: 5.5%

School District(s)

Indian Creek Local (PK-12)
2012-13 Enrollment: 2,194 . . . . (740) 264-3502

Housing: Homeownership rate: 70.6%; Median home value: $77,800; Median year structure built: 1955; Homeowner vacancy rate: 2.4%; Median gross rent: $512 per month; Rental vacancy rate: 8.9%

Health Insurance: 84.0% have insurance; 61.7% have private insurance; 43.4% have public insurance; 16.0% do not have insurance; 8.2% of children under 18 do not have insurance

Transportation: Commute: 97.2% car, 0.0% public transportation, 0.7% walk, 2.1% work from home; Median travel time to work: 26.3 minutes

MOUNT PLEASANT (village). Covers a land area of 0.255 square miles and a water area of 0 square miles. Located at 40.18° N. Lat; 80.80° W. Long. Elevation is 1,247 feet.

History: Mount Pleasant began in the early 1800's as a Quaker community. The town was an abolitionist stronghold, and a refuge for fugitive slaves from the south long before the Civil War. The first abolitionist newspaper, the "Philanthopist," was published here in 1817 by Charles Osborn.

Population: 478; Growth (since 2000): -10.7%; Density: 1,874.7 persons per square mile; Race: 97.7% White, 0.8% Black/African American, 0.6% Asian, 0.4% American Indian/Alaska Native, 0.0% Native Hawaiian/Other Pacific Islander, 0.4% Two or more races, 0.2% Hispanic of any race; Average household size: 2.49; Median age: 44.5; Age under 18: 20.9%; Age 65 and over: 16.9%; Males per 100 females: 93.5

Housing: Homeownership rate: 86.5%; Homeowner vacancy rate: 2.9%; Rental vacancy rate: 3.7%

NEW ALEXANDRIA (village). Covers a land area of 0.367 square miles and a water area of 0 square miles. Located at 40.29° N. Lat; 80.68° W. Long. Elevation is 1,224 feet.

Population: 272; Growth (since 2000): 22.5%; Density: 741.4 persons per square mile; Race: 97.1% White, 1.5% Black/African American, 0.0% Asian, 0.0% American Indian/Alaska Native, 0.0% Native Hawaiian/Other Pacific Islander, 1.5% Two or more races, 0.0% Hispanic of any race; Average household size: 2.54; Median age: 45.7; Age under 18: 21.0%; Age 65 and over: 18.8%; Males per 100 females: 114.2

Housing: Homeownership rate: 80.4%; Homeowner vacancy rate: 3.4%; Rental vacancy rate: 4.2%

POTTERY ADDITION (CDP). Covers a land area of 0.908 square miles and a water area of 0.185 square miles. Located at 40.40° N. Lat; 80.62° W. Long. Elevation is 686 feet.
Population: 293; Growth (since 2000): n/a; Density: 322.7 persons per square mile; Race: 99.3% White, 0.7% Black/African American, 0.0% Asian, 0.0% American Indian/Alaska Native, 0.0% Native Hawaiian/Other Pacific Islander, 0.0% Two or more races, 0.3% Hispanic of any race; Average household size: 2.33; Median age: 40.9; Age under 18: 21.8%; Age 65 and over: 17.1%; Males per 100 females: 102.1
Housing: Homeownership rate: 73.8%; Homeowner vacancy rate: 1.0%; Rental vacancy rate: 5.7%

RAYLAND (village). Covers a land area of 0.472 square miles and a water area of 0.027 square miles. Located at 40.18° N. Lat; 80.69° W. Long. Elevation is 679 feet.
Population: 417; Growth (since 2000): -3.9%; Density: 882.7 persons per square mile; Race: 97.8% White, 1.0% Black/African American, 0.0% Asian, 0.2% American Indian/Alaska Native, 0.0% Native Hawaiian/Other Pacific Islander, 0.5% Two or more races, 0.0% Hispanic of any race; Average household size: 2.41; Median age: 43.7; Age under 18: 22.8%; Age 65 and over: 18.0%; Males per 100 females: 95.8

School District(s)

Buckeye Local (PK-12)
2012-13 Enrollment: 1,922 . . . . (740) 769-7395
Housing: Homeownership rate: 78.6%; Homeowner vacancy rate: 2.8%; Rental vacancy rate: 5.1%

RICHMOND (village). Covers a land area of 0.553 square miles and a water area of 0 square miles. Located at 40.43° N. Lat; 80.77° W. Long. Elevation is 1,240 feet.
Population: 481; Growth (since 2000): 2.1%; Density: 869.7 persons per square mile; Race: 98.8% White, 0.6% Black/African American, 0.4% Asian, 0.0% American Indian/Alaska Native, 0.0% Native Hawaiian/Other Pacific Islander, 0.2% Two or more races, 0.8% Hispanic of any race; Average household size: 2.26; Median age: 43.8; Age under 18: 18.7%; Age 65 and over: 16.0%; Males per 100 females: 87.9

School District(s)

Edison Local (PK-12)
2012-13 Enrollment: 1,858 . . . . (330) 532-3199
Housing: Homeownership rate: 68.6%; Homeowner vacancy rate: 3.9%; Rental vacancy rate: 6.9%

SMITHFIELD (village). Covers a land area of 0.945 square miles and a water area of 0 square miles. Located at 40.27° N. Lat; 80.78° W. Long. Elevation is 1,247 feet.
Population: 869; Growth (since 2000): 0.2%; Density: 919.2 persons per square mile; Race: 86.7% White, 11.3% Black/African American, 0.0% Asian, 0.0% American Indian/Alaska Native, 0.1% Native Hawaiian/Other Pacific Islander, 1.6% Two or more races, 1.2% Hispanic of any race; Average household size: 2.35; Median age: 42.9; Age under 18: 22.4%; Age 65 and over: 17.3%; Males per 100 females: 90.6
Housing: Homeownership rate: 75.5%; Homeowner vacancy rate: 4.2%; Rental vacancy rate: 10.0%

STEUBENVILLE (city). County seat. Covers a land area of 10.545 square miles and a water area of 0.082 square miles. Located at 40.37° N. Lat; 80.66° W. Long. Elevation is 1,050 feet.
History: Jacob Walker came to the Ohio River in 1765. He was followed in 1786 by government scouts who selected this site for a fort, called Fort Steuben for Baron Frederick William von Steuben, a Prussian drillmaster who aided the colonies in the Revolutionary War. A community called La Belle sprang up around the fort, and when the fort was destroyed in 1790, the settlement remained. Bezaleel Wells and James Ross laid out the town in 1797. It was named Steubenville, and became the seat of Jefferson County. Industries began in the early 1800's with a pottery, a drift coal mine, nail factory and foundry. As river traffic increased, Steubenville became an important port. The Frazier, Kilgore and Company rolling mill, using the labels of Wheeling Steel and Weirton Steel, was erected in 1856.
Population: 18,659; Growth (since 2000): -1.9%; Density: 1,769.5 persons per square mile; Race: 79.0% White, 15.9% Black/African American, 0.8% Asian, 0.2% American Indian/Alaska Native, 0.0% Native Hawaiian/Other Pacific Islander, 3.5% Two or more races, 2.4% Hispanic of any race; Average household size: 2.22; Median age: 38.8; Age under 18: 20.3%; Age 65 and over: 17.5%; Males per 100 females: 85.7; Marriage status: 38.7% never married, 41.0% now married, 2.5% separated, 8.2% widowed, 12.1% divorced; Foreign born: 1.7%; Speak English only: 95.3%; With disability: 16.6%; Veterans: 10.1%; Ancestry: 17.7% German, 17.2% Italian, 16.5% Irish, 6.1% Polish, 5.9% English
Employment: 11.4% management, business, and financial, 3.6% computer, engineering, and science, 10.3% education, legal, community service, arts, and media, 8.4% healthcare practitioners, 20.8% service, 27.7% sales and office, 5.4% natural resources, construction, and maintenance, 12.4% production, transportation, and material moving
Income: Per capita: $20,359; Median household: $32,092; Average household: $48,830; Households with income of $100,000 or more: 12.7%; Poverty rate: 28.6%
Educational Attainment: High school diploma or higher: 87.6%; Bachelor's degree or higher: 20.6%; Graduate/professional degree or higher: 7.7%

School District(s)

Edison Local (PK-12)
2012-13 Enrollment: 1,858 . . . . (330) 532-3199
Steubenville City (PK-12)
2012-13 Enrollment: 2,415 . . . . (740) 283-3767

Four-year College(s)

Franciscan University of Steubenville (Private, Not-for-profit, Roman Catholic)
Fall 2013 Enrollment: 2,733 . . . . (740) 283-3771
2013-14 Tuition: In-state $23,160; Out-of-state $23,160

Two-year College(s)

Eastern Gateway Community College (Public)
Fall 2013 Enrollment: 2,929 . . . . (740) 264-5591
2013-14 Tuition: In-state $3,420; Out-of-state $4,260
Trinity Health System School of Nursing (Private, Not-for-profit, Roman Catholic)
Fall 2013 Enrollment: 87 . . . . (740) 283-7467
2013-14 Tuition: In-state $7,120; Out-of-state $7,120
Housing: Homeownership rate: 56.0%; Median home value: $93,300; Median year structure built: 1954; Homeowner vacancy rate: 4.0%; Median gross rent: $561 per month; Rental vacancy rate: 10.5%
Health Insurance: 89.3% have insurance; 63.8% have private insurance; 41.0% have public insurance; 10.7% do not have insurance; 3.9% of children under 18 do not have insurance
Hospitals: Trinity Medical Center East & Trinity Medical Center West (401 beds)
Newspapers: Herald-Star (daily circulation 13200)
Transportation: Commute: 81.8% car, 2.1% public transportation, 9.5% walk, 5.9% work from home; Median travel time to work: 17.1 minutes
Airports: Jefferson County Airpark (general aviation)
Additional Information Contacts
City of Steubenville . . . . (740) 283-6000
http://www.ci.steubenville.oh.us

STRATTON (village). Covers a land area of 0.537 square miles and a water area of 0 square miles. Located at 40.53° N. Lat; 80.63° W. Long. Elevation is 650 feet.
Population: 294; Growth (since 2000): 6.1%; Density: 547.0 persons per square mile; Race: 99.0% White, 0.0% Black/African American, 0.0% Asian, 0.0% American Indian/Alaska Native, 0.0% Native Hawaiian/Other Pacific Islander, 1.0% Two or more races, 1.4% Hispanic of any race; Average household size: 2.03; Median age: 49.5; Age under 18: 20.1%; Age 65 and over: 25.9%; Males per 100 females: 88.5
Housing: Homeownership rate: 68.9%; Homeowner vacancy rate: 1.0%; Rental vacancy rate: 4.3%

TILTONSVILLE (village). Covers a land area of 0.525 square miles and a water area of 0.031 square miles. Located at 40.17° N. Lat; 80.70° W. Long. Elevation is 673 feet.
Population: 1,372; Growth (since 2000): 3.2%; Density: 2,613.8 persons per square mile; Race: 97.6% White, 0.6% Black/African American, 0.1% Asian, 0.1% American Indian/Alaska Native, 0.1% Native Hawaiian/Other Pacific Islander, 1.4% Two or more races, 0.7% Hispanic of any race; Average household size: 2.27; Median age: 44.3; Age under 18: 18.4%; Age 65 and over: 19.1%; Males per 100 females: 85.9

School District(s)

Buckeye Local (PK-12)
2012-13 Enrollment: 1,922 . . . . (740) 769-7395

Housing: Homeownership rate: 62.8%; Homeowner vacancy rate: 0.3%; Rental vacancy rate: 11.8%

TORONTO (city). Covers a land area of 1.858 square miles and a water area of 0.276 square miles. Located at 40.46° N. Lat; 80.61° W. Long. Elevation is 696 feet.

History: Toronto was laid out in 1818 by John Depuy when it was called Newburg, and later Sloan's Station. In 1881 it was renamed Toronto for a prominent citizen who had come from Toronto, Canada.

Population: 5,091; Growth (since 2000): -10.3%; Density: 2,739.7 persons per square mile; Race: 97.1% White, 1.1% Black/African American, 0.2% Asian, 0.2% American Indian/Alaska Native, 0.0% Native Hawaiian/Other Pacific Islander, 1.3% Two or more races, 0.8% Hispanic of any race; Average household size: 2.23; Median age: 44.0; Age under 18: 20.7%; Age 65 and over: 18.1%; Males per 100 females: 88.2; Marriage status: 29.9% never married, 48.6% now married, 0.9% separated, 7.7% widowed, 13.7% divorced; Foreign born: 0.4%; Speak English only: 99.1%; With disability: 19.1%; Veterans: 9.9%; Ancestry: 20.5% Irish, 17.0% German, 8.7% Italian, 8.0% American, 7.8% Polish

Employment: 4.7% management, business, and financial, 2.6% computer, engineering, and science, 7.1% education, legal, community service, arts, and media, 8.6% healthcare practitioners, 25.1% service, 24.4% sales and office, 9.7% natural resources, construction, and maintenance, 17.7% production, transportation, and material moving

Income: Per capita: $22,154; Median household: $39,483; Average household: $49,556; Households with income of $100,000 or more: 8.9%; Poverty rate: 20.8%

Educational Attainment: High school diploma or higher: 94.1%; Bachelor's degree or higher: 12.6%; Graduate/professional degree or higher: 5.5%

School District(s)

Toronto City (PK-12)
2012-13 Enrollment: 844. . . . . (740) 537-2456

Housing: Homeownership rate: 66.7%; Median home value: $79,100; Median year structure built: 1949; Homeowner vacancy rate: 2.4%; Median gross rent: $578 per month; Rental vacancy rate: 10.0%

Health Insurance: 89.0% have insurance; 65.5% have private insurance; 39.2% have public insurance; 11.0% do not have insurance; 1.2% of children under 18 do not have insurance

Safety: Violent crime rate: 18.2 per 10,000 population; Property crime rate: 16.2 per 10,000 population

Transportation: Commute: 92.0% car, 0.0% public transportation, 5.3% walk, 2.3% work from home; Median travel time to work: 23.4 minutes

WINTERSVILLE (village). Covers a land area of 3.119 square miles and a water area of <.001 square miles. Located at 40.38° N. Lat; 80.71° W. Long. Elevation is 1,260 feet.

History: Land office here for first land sales in Northwest Territory. Incorporated 1947.

Population: 3,924; Growth (since 2000): -3.5%; Density: 1,257.9 persons per square mile; Race: 91.4% White, 6.4% Black/African American, 0.8% Asian, 0.1% American Indian/Alaska Native, 0.0% Native Hawaiian/Other Pacific Islander, 1.1% Two or more races, 0.9% Hispanic of any race; Average household size: 2.20; Median age: 48.8; Age under 18: 17.8%; Age 65 and over: 24.9%; Males per 100 females: 87.9; Marriage status: 23.2% never married, 58.1% now married, 2.3% separated, 8.4% widowed, 10.3% divorced; Foreign born: 4.0%; Speak English only: 96.7%; With disability: 12.7%; Veterans: 10.5%; Ancestry: 22.0% German, 19.0% Italian, 11.5% Irish, 8.8% English, 4.4% American

Employment: 15.1% management, business, and financial, 2.2% computer, engineering, and science, 8.8% education, legal, community service, arts, and media, 13.6% healthcare practitioners, 17.2% service, 22.6% sales and office, 9.1% natural resources, construction, and maintenance, 11.3% production, transportation, and material moving

Income: Per capita: $29,472; Median household: $40,321; Average household: $62,472; Households with income of $100,000 or more: 14.7%; Poverty rate: 7.5%

Educational Attainment: High school diploma or higher: 93.6%; Bachelor's degree or higher: 21.3%; Graduate/professional degree or higher: 6.2%

School District(s)

Indian Creek Local (PK-12)
2012-13 Enrollment: 2,194 . . . . (740) 264-3502

Housing: Homeownership rate: 66.1%; Median home value: $112,100; Median year structure built: 1968; Homeowner vacancy rate: 1.4%; Median gross rent: $632 per month; Rental vacancy rate: 6.3%

Health Insurance: 93.9% have insurance; 77.3% have private insurance; 32.2% have public insurance; 6.1% do not have insurance; 3.4% of children under 18 do not have insurance

Safety: Violent crime rate: 7.9 per 10,000 population; Property crime rate: 164.9 per 10,000 population

Transportation: Commute: 97.1% car, 0.5% public transportation, 0.9% walk, 1.5% work from home; Median travel time to work: 22.6 minutes

YORKVILLE (village). Covers a land area of 0.595 square miles and a water area of 0.002 square miles. Located at 40.15° N. Lat; 80.71° W. Long. Elevation is 659 feet.

History: Yorkville grew around the Wheeling Steel Corporation's mill. It was named for York, Pennsylvania, the former home of many of the early settlers.

Population: 1,079; Growth (since 2000): -12.3%; Density: 1,813.4 persons per square mile; Race: 98.1% White, 1.4% Black/African American, 0.0% Asian, 0.1% American Indian/Alaska Native, 0.0% Native Hawaiian/Other Pacific Islander, 0.4% Two or more races, 0.1% Hispanic of any race; Average household size: 2.11; Median age: 46.4; Age under 18: 17.0%; Age 65 and over: 22.1%; Males per 100 females: 90.3

Housing: Homeownership rate: 58.8%; Homeowner vacancy rate: 1.3%; Rental vacancy rate: 12.7%

Knox County

Located in central Ohio; drained by the Kokosing and Mohican Rivers and the North Fork of the Licking River. Covers a land area of 525.494 square miles, a water area of 4.139 square miles, and is located in the Eastern Time Zone at 40.40° N. Lat., 82.42° W. Long. The county was founded in 1808. County seat is Mount Vernon.

Knox County is part of the Mount Vernon, OH Micropolitan Statistical Area. The entire metro area includes: Knox County, OH

Weather Station: Centerburg 2 SE — Elevation: 1,205 feet

	Jan	Feb	Mar	Apr	May	Jun	Jul	Aug	Sep	Oct	Nov	Dec
High	34	37	48	61	71	79	83	81	75	63	50	37
Low	17	20	28	39	49	58	62	60	52	41	32	22
Precip	2.9	2.4	3.1	3.8	4.5	4.6	4.4	3.7	3.2	2.9	3.5	3.1
Snow	4.6	2.1	2.1	0.2	tr	0.0	0.0	0.0	0.0	0.1	0.8	2.5

High and Low temperatures in degrees Fahrenheit; Precipitation and Snow in inches

Weather Station: Danville 2 W — Elevation: 970 feet

	Jan	Feb	Mar	Apr	May	Jun	Jul	Aug	Sep	Oct	Nov	Dec
High	35	39	49	61	71	80	83	82	76	64	51	39
Low	17	19	26	35	45	55	59	57	49	37	30	22
Precip	2.8	2.4	3.2	3.6	4.7	4.6	4.6	3.7	3.1	2.8	3.2	3.2
Snow	12.2	8.5	6.2	1.8	tr	0.0	0.0	0.0	0.0	tr	2.2	8.2

High and Low temperatures in degrees Fahrenheit; Precipitation and Snow in inches

Weather Station: Fredericktown 4 S — Elevation: 1,049 feet

	Jan	Feb	Mar	Apr	May	Jun	Jul	Aug	Sep	Oct	Nov	Dec
High	33	37	47	60	70	79	82	81	75	63	51	39
Low	15	18	26	36	46	55	59	56	49	37	30	22
Precip	2.4	1.9	3.0	3.4	4.3	4.1	4.3	3.4	3.1	2.7	3.0	2.7
Snow	8.7	5.6	3.5	0.7	tr	0.0	0.0	0.0	0.0	0.0	1.1	5.4

High and Low temperatures in degrees Fahrenheit; Precipitation and Snow in inches

Population: 60,921; Growth (since 2000): 11.8%; Density: 115.9 persons per square mile; Race: 96.7% White, 0.8% Black/African American, 0.6% Asian, 0.2% American Indian/Alaska Native, 0.0% Native Hawaiian/Other Pacific Islander, 1.2% two or more races, 1.2% Hispanic of any race; Average household size: 2.54; Median age: 38.3; Age under 18: 24.1%; Age 65 and over: 14.8%; Males per 100 females: 95.4; Marriage status: 26.6% never married, 56.4% now married, 1.6% separated, 7.2% widowed, 9.8% divorced; Foreign born: 1.6%; Speak English only: 94.3%; With disability: 13.9%; Veterans: 9.7%; Ancestry: 27.4% German, 13.4% Irish, 12.6% English, 10.4% American, 4.4% Italian

Religion: Six largest groups: 7.3% Baptist, 6.1% Methodist/Pietist, 5.3% Catholicism, 4.7% Holiness, 4.2% European Free-Church, 2.6% Pentecostal

Economy: Unemployment rate: 4.0%; Leading industries: 16.8% retail trade; 13.7% other services (except public administration); 12.5% health

care and social assistance; Farms: 1,374 totaling 186,047 acres; Company size: 4 employ 1,000 or more persons, 2 employ 500 to 999 persons, 17 employ 100 to 499 persons, 1,022 employ less than 100 persons; Business ownership: 1,208 women-owned, n/a Black-owned, n/a Hispanic-owned, n/a Asian-owned
Employment: 12.9% management, business, and financial, 2.9% computer, engineering, and science, 10.9% education, legal, community service, arts, and media, 4.4% healthcare practitioners, 17.1% service, 22.8% sales and office, 10.9% natural resources, construction, and maintenance, 18.2% production, transportation, and material moving
Income: Per capita: $23,878; Median household: $49,750; Average household: $62,500; Households with income of $100,000 or more: 14.7%; Poverty rate: 14.2%
Educational Attainment: High school diploma or higher: 88.1%; Bachelor's degree or higher: 21.2%; Graduate/professional degree or higher: 7.3%
Housing: Homeownership rate: 72.5%; Median home value: $133,500; Median year structure built: 1973; Homeowner vacancy rate: 2.0%; Median gross rent: $681 per month; Rental vacancy rate: 7.9%
Vital Statistics: Birth rate: 107.9 per 10,000 population; Death rate: 96.2 per 10,000 population; Age-adjusted cancer mortality rate: 178.7 deaths per 100,000 population
Health Insurance: 85.1% have insurance; 68.6% have private insurance; 29.9% have public insurance; 14.9% do not have insurance; 15.6% of children under 18 do not have insurance
Health Care: Physicians: 8.4 per 10,000 population; Hospital beds: 14.2 per 10,000 population; Hospital admissions: 553.0 per 10,000 population
Air Quality Index: 93.0% good, 7.0% moderate, 0.0% unhealthy for sensitive individuals, 0.0% unhealthy (percent of days)
Transportation: Commute: 87.4% car, 0.3% public transportation, 5.4% walk, 5.9% work from home; Median travel time to work: 26.4 minutes
Presidential Election: 36.8% Obama, 61.1% Romney (2012)
National and State Parks: Knox Lake State Wildlife Area; Knox Woods State Nature Preserve
Additional Information Contacts
Knox Government . . . . (740) 393-6703
http://www.co.knox.oh.us

Knox County Communities

APPLE VALLEY (CDP). Covers a land area of 6.013 square miles and a water area of 0.795 square miles. Located at 40.44° N. Lat; 82.35° W. Long. Elevation is 1,125 feet.
Population: 5,058; Growth (since 2000): n/a; Density: 841.1 persons per square mile; Race: 96.9% White, 1.1% Black/African American, 0.6% Asian, 0.3% American Indian/Alaska Native, 0.0% Native Hawaiian/Other Pacific Islander, 0.8% Two or more races, 1.4% Hispanic of any race; Average household size: 2.60; Median age: 42.3; Age under 18: 24.2%; Age 65 and over: 17.8%; Males per 100 females: 101.4; Marriage status: 11.6% never married, 76.3% now married, 0.0% separated, 4.5% widowed, 7.7% divorced; Foreign born: 4.2%; Speak English only: 97.1%; With disability: 10.5%; Veterans: 14.5%; Ancestry: 34.5% German, 16.0% English, 13.5% Irish, 9.1% American, 3.4% Scottish
Employment: 14.0% management, business, and financial, 4.7% computer, engineering, and science, 17.5% education, legal, community service, arts, and media, 6.5% healthcare practitioners, 8.6% service, 31.2% sales and office, 5.7% natural resources, construction, and maintenance, 11.8% production, transportation, and material moving
Income: Per capita: $31,955; Median household: $65,424; Average household: $80,175; Households with income of $100,000 or more: 21.3%; Poverty rate: 5.8%
Educational Attainment: High school diploma or higher: 93.8%; Bachelor's degree or higher: 30.7%; Graduate/professional degree or higher: 8.3%
Housing: Homeownership rate: 89.8%; Median home value: $156,300; Median year structure built: 1996; Homeowner vacancy rate: 3.1%; Median gross rent: <$100 per month; Rental vacancy rate: 4.3%
Health Insurance: 96.7% have insurance; 86.9% have private insurance; 32.1% have public insurance; 3.3% do not have insurance; 2.6% of children under 18 do not have insurance
Transportation: Commute: 91.6% car, 0.0% public transportation, 0.0% walk, 7.7% work from home; Median travel time to work: 32.7 minutes

BLADENSBURG (CDP). Covers a land area of 0.330 square miles and a water area of 0.002 square miles. Located at 40.29° N. Lat; 82.28° W. Long. Elevation is 961 feet.
Population: 191; Growth (since 2000): n/a; Density: 578.5 persons per square mile; Race: 99.5% White, 0.0% Black/African American, 0.0% Asian, 0.0% American Indian/Alaska Native, 0.0% Native Hawaiian/Other Pacific Islander, 0.5% Two or more races, 1.0% Hispanic of any race; Average household size: 2.73; Median age: 32.3; Age under 18: 30.9%; Age 65 and over: 12.6%; Males per 100 females: 83.7
School District(s)
East Knox Local (PK-12)
2012-13 Enrollment: 1,054 . . . . (740) 599-7493
Housing: Homeownership rate: 58.6%; Homeowner vacancy rate: 2.4%; Rental vacancy rate: 6.5%

CENTERBURG (village). Covers a land area of 0.895 square miles and a water area of 0.003 square miles. Located at 40.30° N. Lat; 82.70° W. Long. Elevation is 1,227 feet.
History: Centerburg was settled in 1806 and named for its position near the geographical center of the state.
Population: 1,773; Growth (since 2000): 23.8%; Density: 1,981.3 persons per square mile; Race: 96.9% White, 1.2% Black/African American, 0.3% Asian, 0.1% American Indian/Alaska Native, 0.0% Native Hawaiian/Other Pacific Islander, 1.4% Two or more races, 0.2% Hispanic of any race; Average household size: 2.63; Median age: 36.2; Age under 18: 28.5%; Age 65 and over: 14.3%; Males per 100 females: 89.8
School District(s)
Centerburg Local (PK-12)
2012-13 Enrollment: 1,074 . . . . (740) 625-6346
Housing: Homeownership rate: 56.4%; Homeowner vacancy rate: 3.5%; Rental vacancy rate: 5.9%

DANVILLE (village). Covers a land area of 0.553 square miles and a water area of 0.005 square miles. Located at 40.45° N. Lat; 82.26° W. Long. Elevation is 988 feet.
Population: 1,044; Growth (since 2000): -5.4%; Density: 1,886.2 persons per square mile; Race: 97.9% White, 0.6% Black/African American, 0.1% Asian, 0.4% American Indian/Alaska Native, 0.0% Native Hawaiian/Other Pacific Islander, 0.9% Two or more races, 1.2% Hispanic of any race; Average household size: 2.46; Median age: 33.8; Age under 18: 28.3%; Age 65 and over: 12.8%; Males per 100 females: 97.0
School District(s)
Danville Local (PK-12)
2012-13 Enrollment: 646. . . . . (740) 599-6116
Housing: Homeownership rate: 58.1%; Homeowner vacancy rate: 5.3%; Rental vacancy rate: 10.9%
Safety: Violent crime rate: 0.0 per 10,000 population; Property crime rate: 313.4 per 10,000 population

FREDERICKTOWN (village). Covers a land area of 1.974 square miles and a water area of 0.102 square miles. Located at 40.48° N. Lat; 82.55° W. Long. Elevation is 1,096 feet.
Population: 2,493; Growth (since 2000): 2.7%; Density: 1,262.6 persons per square mile; Race: 98.0% White, 0.4% Black/African American, 0.0% Asian, 0.2% American Indian/Alaska Native, 0.0% Native Hawaiian/Other Pacific Islander, 1.0% Two or more races, 0.9% Hispanic of any race; Average household size: 2.37; Median age: 37.6; Age under 18: 25.8%; Age 65 and over: 15.4%; Males per 100 females: 94.9
School District(s)
Fredericktown Local (PK-12)
2012-13 Enrollment: 1,132 . . . . (740) 694-2956
Housing: Homeownership rate: 66.7%; Homeowner vacancy rate: 2.1%; Rental vacancy rate: 7.7%
Safety: Violent crime rate: 0.0 per 10,000 population; Property crime rate: 206.6 per 10,000 population
Newspapers: Knox County Citizen (weekly circulation 1400)

GAMBIER (village). Covers a land area of 0.935 square miles and a water area of <.001 square miles. Located at 40.38° N. Lat; 82.39° W. Long. Elevation is 1,076 feet.
History: Gambier was the site of the founding of Kenyon College, established in 1824 by Philander Chase, first Episcopal bishop of Ohio, as a Theological Seminary. The college was located on land donated by Lord Gambier, for whom the town was named.

Population: 2,391; Growth (since 2000): 27.8%; Density: 2,557.2 persons per square mile; Race: 90.5% White, 2.8% Black/African American, 2.0% Asian, 0.2% American Indian/Alaska Native, 0.0% Native Hawaiian/Other Pacific Islander, 3.7% Two or more races, 2.8% Hispanic of any race; Average household size: 2.39; Median age: 21.2; Age under 18: 4.0%; Age 65 and over: 4.5%; Males per 100 females: 89.9

School District(s)

Mount Vernon City (PK-12)
2012-13 Enrollment: 3,864 . . . . (740) 397-7422

Four-year College(s)

Kenyon College (Private, Not-for-profit)
Fall 2013 Enrollment: 1,705 . . . . (740) 427-5000
2013-14 Tuition: In-state $45,640; Out-of-state $45,640

Housing: Homeownership rate: 42.3%; Homeowner vacancy rate: 2.0%; Rental vacancy rate: 5.7%

GANN (village). Covers a land area of 0.187 square miles and a water area of 0.012 square miles. Located at 40.47° N. Lat; 82.19° W. Long. Elevation is 902 feet.

Population: 125; Growth (since 2000): -12.6%; Density: 669.2 persons per square mile; Race: 100.0% White, 0.0% Black/African American, 0.0% Asian, 0.0% American Indian/Alaska Native, 0.0% Native Hawaiian/Other Pacific Islander, 0.0% Two or more races, 2.4% Hispanic of any race; Average household size: 2.31; Median age: 42.2; Age under 18: 24.8%; Age 65 and over: 12.8%; Males per 100 females: 104.9

Housing: Homeownership rate: 64.8%; Homeowner vacancy rate: 5.4%; Rental vacancy rate: 9.5%

HOWARD (CDP). Covers a land area of 0.224 square miles and a water area of 0 square miles. Located at 40.41° N. Lat; 82.33° W. Long. Elevation is 902 feet.

Population: 242; Growth (since 2000): n/a; Density: 1,081.3 persons per square mile; Race: 98.3% White, 0.0% Black/African American, 0.0% Asian, 0.4% American Indian/Alaska Native, 0.0% Native Hawaiian/Other Pacific Islander, 1.2% Two or more races, 0.0% Hispanic of any race; Average household size: 2.57; Median age: 40.0; Age under 18: 20.7%; Age 65 and over: 20.2%; Males per 100 females: 112.3

School District(s)

East Knox Local (PK-12)
2012-13 Enrollment: 1,054 . . . . (740) 599-7493

Housing: Homeownership rate: 70.2%; Homeowner vacancy rate: 8.2%; Rental vacancy rate: 15.2%

MARTINSBURG (village). Covers a land area of 0.177 square miles and a water area of <.001 square miles. Located at 40.27° N. Lat; 82.35° W. Long. Elevation is 1,175 feet.

Population: 237; Growth (since 2000): 28.1%; Density: 1,341.8 persons per square mile; Race: 93.7% White, 1.7% Black/African American, 0.4% Asian, 1.3% American Indian/Alaska Native, 0.0% Native Hawaiian/Other Pacific Islander, 2.5% Two or more races, 0.0% Hispanic of any race; Average household size: 2.44; Median age: 37.6; Age under 18: 27.8%; Age 65 and over: 15.2%; Males per 100 females: 107.9

Housing: Homeownership rate: 56.7%; Homeowner vacancy rate: 0.0%; Rental vacancy rate: 4.5%

MOUNT VERNON (city). County seat. Covers a land area of 9.408 square miles and a water area of 0.185 square miles. Located at 40.39° N. Lat; 82.47° W. Long. Elevation is 1,004 feet.

History: Mount Vernon was laid out in 1805 by Benjamin Butler, Thomas Patterson, and Joseph Walker, all of whom became prominent citizens here. The town developed as a rural commercial center, and later as a manufacturer of steam, diesel, and gas engines. John Chapman, known as Johnny Appleseed, owned lots in Mount Vernon. This was the birthplace of Daniel Decatur Emmett (1815-1904) who wrote the song "Dixie."

Population: 16,990; Growth (since 2000): 18.2%; Density: 1,805.9 persons per square mile; Race: 95.3% White, 1.1% Black/African American, 1.1% Asian, 0.2% American Indian/Alaska Native, 0.0% Native Hawaiian/Other Pacific Islander, 1.5% Two or more races, 1.8% Hispanic of any race; Average household size: 2.19; Median age: 37.2; Age under 18: 21.8%; Age 65 and over: 17.3%; Males per 100 females: 86.9; Marriage status: 32.3% never married, 45.1% now married, 3.5% separated, 9.1% widowed, 13.5% divorced; Foreign born: 1.2%; Speak English only: 98.4%; With disability: 18.6%; Veterans: 9.7%; Ancestry: 22.0% German, 13.7% Irish, 11.3% English, 10.6% American, 6.3% Italian

Employment: 11.1% management, business, and financial, 2.9% computer, engineering, and science, 11.3% education, legal, community service, arts, and media, 3.8% healthcare practitioners, 22.4% service, 24.3% sales and office, 6.3% natural resources, construction, and maintenance, 17.9% production, transportation, and material moving

Income: Per capita: $19,843; Median household: $35,162; Average household: $47,309; Households with income of $100,000 or more: 7.9%; Poverty rate: 20.2%

Educational Attainment: High school diploma or higher: 88.1%; Bachelor's degree or higher: 20.3%; Graduate/professional degree or higher: 8.6%

School District(s)

Knox County Jvsd (08-12)
2012-13 Enrollment: n/a . . . . (740) 397-5820
Mount Vernon City (PK-12)
2012-13 Enrollment: 3,864 . . . . (740) 397-7422

Four-year College(s)

Mount Vernon Nazarene University (Private, Not-for-profit, Church of the Nazarene)
Fall 2013 Enrollment: 2,229 . . . . (740) 392-6868
2013-14 Tuition: In-state $23,690; Out-of-state $23,690

Vocational/Technical School(s)

Knox County Career Center (Public)
Fall 2013 Enrollment: 252 . . . . (740) 393-2933
2013-14 Tuition: $13,035

Housing: Homeownership rate: 53.3%; Median home value: $102,600; Median year structure built: 1958; Homeowner vacancy rate: 2.5%; Median gross rent: $658 per month; Rental vacancy rate: 9.0%

Health Insurance: 86.8% have insurance; 61.4% have private insurance; 40.5% have public insurance; 13.2% do not have insurance; 5.0% of children under 18 do not have insurance

Hospitals: Knox Community Hospital (115 beds)

Safety: Violent crime rate: 8.4 per 10,000 population; Property crime rate: 534.4 per 10,000 population

Newspapers: Mount Vernon News (daily circulation 9200)

Transportation: Commute: 87.8% car, 0.0% public transportation, 9.5% walk, 1.9% work from home; Median travel time to work: 19.1 minutes

Airports: Knox County (general aviation)

Additional Information Contacts

City of Mount Vernon. . . . . (740) 393-9517
http://www.mountvernonohio.org

Lake County

Located in northeastern Ohio; bounded on the north by Lake Erie; drained by the Grand and Chagrin Rivers. Covers a land area of 227.493 square miles, a water area of 751.705 square miles, and is located in the Eastern Time Zone at 41.92° N. Lat., 81.39° W. Long. The county was founded in 1840. County seat is Painesville.

Lake County is part of the Cleveland-Elyria, OH Metropolitan Statistical Area. The entire metro area includes: Cuyahoga County, OH; Geauga County, OH; Lake County, OH; Lorain County, OH; Medina County, OH

Weather Station: Painesville 4 NW Elevation: 600 feet

	Jan	Feb	Mar	Apr	May	Jun	Jul	Aug	Sep	Oct	Nov	Dec
High	35	37	45	57	67	77	81	80	74	63	52	40
Low	22	23	29	40	50	60	65	64	57	47	38	28
Precip	2.4	2.0	2.8	3.3	3.3	3.7	3.8	3.4	4.0	3.5	3.5	3.0
Snow	11.5	8.1	6.5	1.2	tr	0.0	0.0	0.0	0.0	tr	2.2	9.7

High and Low temperatures in degrees Fahrenheit; Precipitation and Snow in inches

Population: 230,041; Growth (since 2000): 1.1%; Density: 1,011.2 persons per square mile; Race: 92.5% White, 3.2% Black/African American, 1.1% Asian, 0.1% American Indian/Alaska Native, 0.0% Native Hawaiian/Other Pacific Islander, 1.5% two or more races, 3.4% Hispanic of any race; Average household size: 2.41; Median age: 42.3; Age under 18: 22.2%; Age 65 and over: 16.1%; Males per 100 females: 95.1; Marriage status: 27.3% never married, 53.4% now married, 1.2% separated, 7.3% widowed, 12.0% divorced; Foreign born: 5.3%; Speak English only: 92.8%; With disability: 11.5%; Veterans: 10.3%; Ancestry: 25.1% German, 18.5% Irish, 16.5% Italian, 10.8% English, 7.2% Polish

Religion: Six largest groups: 35.2% Catholicism, 3.9% Methodist/Pietist, 2.4% Lutheran, 2.0% Non-denominational Protestant, 1.6% Pentecostal, 1.4% Baptist

Economy: Unemployment rate: 4.6%; Leading industries: 13.0% retail trade; 10.1% manufacturing; 10.0% health care and social assistance; Farms: 214 totaling 17,125 acres; Company size: 3 employ 1,000 or more persons, 5 employ 500 to 999 persons, 135 employ 100 to 499 persons, 5,972 employ less than 100 persons; Business ownership: 5,226 women-owned, 215 Black-owned, n/a Hispanic-owned, 334 Asian-owned
Employment: 14.0% management, business, and financial, 5.3% computer, engineering, and science, 8.5% education, legal, community service, arts, and media, 6.7% healthcare practitioners, 16.3% service, 26.3% sales and office, 7.5% natural resources, construction, and maintenance, 15.4% production, transportation, and material moving
Income: Per capita: $29,132; Median household: $56,018; Average household: $70,236; Households with income of $100,000 or more: 21.0%; Poverty rate: 9.2%
Educational Attainment: High school diploma or higher: 91.2%; Bachelor's degree or higher: 24.9%; Graduate/professional degree or higher: 8.3%
Housing: Homeownership rate: 75.7%; Median home value: $151,300; Median year structure built: 1969; Homeowner vacancy rate: 2.0%; Median gross rent: $806 per month; Rental vacancy rate: 9.8%
Vital Statistics: Birth rate: 98.2 per 10,000 population; Death rate: 101.1 per 10,000 population; Age-adjusted cancer mortality rate: 180.0 deaths per 100,000 population
Health Insurance: 90.3% have insurance; 76.8% have private insurance; 26.8% have public insurance; 9.7% do not have insurance; 6.1% of children under 18 do not have insurance
Health Care: Physicians: 14.3 per 10,000 population; Hospital beds: 22.1 per 10,000 population; Hospital admissions: 994.9 per 10,000 population
Air Quality Index: 83.6% good, 14.2% moderate, 2.2% unhealthy for sensitive individuals, 0.0% unhealthy (percent of days)
Transportation: Commute: 94.5% car, 0.9% public transportation, 1.2% walk, 2.7% work from home; Median travel time to work: 23.3 minutes
Presidential Election: 48.3% Obama, 50.0% Romney (2012)
National and State Parks: Chaplin State Forest; Hach-Otis Sanctuary State Nature Preserve; Headlands Beach State Park; Headlands Dunes State Nature Preserve; James A Garfield National Historic Site; Mentor Marsh State Nature Preserve
Additional Information Contacts
Lake Government . . . . (440) 350-2500
http://www.lakecountyohio.gov

Lake County Communities

EASTLAKE (city). Covers a land area of 6.395 square miles and a water area of 0.130 square miles. Located at 41.66° N. Lat; 81.43° W. Long. Elevation is 617 feet.
Population: 18,577; Growth (since 2000): -8.3%; Density: 2,904.9 persons per square mile; Race: 95.9% White, 1.4% Black/African American, 1.0% Asian, 0.1% American Indian/Alaska Native, 0.0% Native Hawaiian/Other Pacific Islander, 1.2% Two or more races, 1.4% Hispanic of any race; Average household size: 2.37; Median age: 42.7; Age under 18: 20.6%; Age 65 and over: 15.4%; Males per 100 females: 97.2; Marriage status: 30.7% never married, 49.8% now married, 0.7% separated, 7.4% widowed, 12.1% divorced; Foreign born: 6.2%; Speak English only: 92.1%; With disability: 12.4%; Veterans: 10.5%; Ancestry: 27.1% German, 17.4% Irish, 17.3% Italian, 9.0% English, 8.2% Polish
Employment: 12.9% management, business, and financial, 5.1% computer, engineering, and science, 6.2% education, legal, community service, arts, and media, 6.3% healthcare practitioners, 17.6% service, 24.9% sales and office, 9.3% natural resources, construction, and maintenance, 17.7% production, transportation, and material moving
Income: Per capita: $25,624; Median household: $52,441; Average household: $59,474; Households with income of $100,000 or more: 14.5%; Poverty rate: 7.3%
Educational Attainment: High school diploma or higher: 88.8%; Bachelor's degree or higher: 16.5%; Graduate/professional degree or higher: 5.8%

School District(s)
Willoughby-Eastlake City (PK-12)
2012-13 Enrollment: 8,418 . . . . (440) 946-5000

Four-year College(s)
Bryant & Stratton College-Eastlake (Private, For-profit)
Fall 2013 Enrollment: 614 . . . . (440) 510-1112
2013-14 Tuition: In-state $16,565; Out-of-state $16,565

Vocational/Technical School(s)
Willoughby-Eastlake School of Practical Nursing (Public)
Fall 2013 Enrollment: 67 . . . . (440) 602-5094
2013-14 Tuition: In-state $11,125; Out-of-state $11,125
Housing: Homeownership rate: 74.6%; Median home value: $128,000; Median year structure built: 1965; Homeowner vacancy rate: 1.6%; Median gross rent: $768 per month; Rental vacancy rate: 6.1%
Health Insurance: 88.0% have insurance; 73.0% have private insurance; 27.7% have public insurance; 12.0% do not have insurance; 10.2% of children under 18 do not have insurance
Safety: Violent crime rate: 8.7 per 10,000 population; Property crime rate: 234.5 per 10,000 population
Transportation: Commute: 94.9% car, 1.0% public transportation, 1.7% walk, 2.0% work from home; Median travel time to work: 23.4 minutes
Additional Information Contacts
City of Eastlake . . . . (330) 426-4367
http://www.eastlakeohio.com

FAIRPORT HARBOR (village). Covers a land area of 1.027 square miles and a water area of 0.081 square miles. Located at 41.75° N. Lat; 81.27° W. Long. Elevation is 610 feet.
History: Fairport Harbor grew around fishing, salt-making, and the shipping of iron ore. Many of the early residents were Hungarians and Finns.
Population: 3,109; Growth (since 2000): -2.2%; Density: 3,027.0 persons per square mile; Race: 94.7% White, 2.1% Black/African American, 0.3% Asian, 0.2% American Indian/Alaska Native, 0.0% Native Hawaiian/Other Pacific Islander, 2.1% Two or more races, 2.2% Hispanic of any race; Average household size: 2.17; Median age: 41.0; Age under 18: 20.7%; Age 65 and over: 14.8%; Males per 100 females: 94.7; Marriage status: 30.5% never married, 45.5% now married, 0.8% separated, 6.9% widowed, 17.0% divorced; Foreign born: 2.0%; Speak English only: 90.2%; With disability: 14.9%; Veterans: 14.2%; Ancestry: 18.9% English, 16.3% German, 15.6% Irish, 14.7% Hungarian, 12.5% Finnish
Employment: 11.2% management, business, and financial, 0.6% computer, engineering, and science, 12.3% education, legal, community service, arts, and media, 1.8% healthcare practitioners, 13.8% service, 32.3% sales and office, 9.7% natural resources, construction, and maintenance, 18.3% production, transportation, and material moving
Income: Per capita: $23,065; Median household: $40,523; Average household: $50,086; Households with income of $100,000 or more: 11.9%; Poverty rate: 21.6%
Educational Attainment: High school diploma or higher: 88.5%; Bachelor's degree or higher: 21.3%; Graduate/professional degree or higher: 6.6%

School District(s)
Fairport Harbor Exempted Village (PK-12)
2012-13 Enrollment: 556. . . . . (440) 354-5400
Housing: Homeownership rate: 58.5%; Median home value: $98,200; Median year structure built: 1942; Homeowner vacancy rate: 4.2%; Median gross rent: $859 per month; Rental vacancy rate: 13.6%
Health Insurance: 76.9% have insurance; 54.6% have private insurance; 33.9% have public insurance; 23.1% do not have insurance; 15.7% of children under 18 do not have insurance
Safety: Violent crime rate: 32.3 per 10,000 population; Property crime rate: 426.2 per 10,000 population
Transportation: Commute: 96.0% car, 0.0% public transportation, 0.8% walk, 1.8% work from home; Median travel time to work: 20.1 minutes

GRAND RIVER (village). Covers a land area of 0.541 square miles and a water area of 0.094 square miles. Located at 41.74° N. Lat; 81.29° W. Long. Elevation is 610 feet.
History: Formerly Richmond.
Population: 399; Growth (since 2000): 15.7%; Density: 736.9 persons per square mile; Race: 96.7% White, 1.5% Black/African American, 0.0% Asian, 0.0% American Indian/Alaska Native, 0.0% Native Hawaiian/Other Pacific Islander, 0.5% Two or more races, 4.5% Hispanic of any race; Average household size: 2.51; Median age: 43.8; Age under 18: 21.1%; Age 65 and over: 13.8%; Males per 100 females: 106.7
Housing: Homeownership rate: 69.8%; Homeowner vacancy rate: 2.6%; Rental vacancy rate: 5.9%

KIRTLAND (city). Covers a land area of 16.671 square miles and a water area of 0.130 square miles. Located at 41.60° N. Lat; 81.34° W. Long. Elevation is 666 feet.
History: Kirtland was the location in 1831 where Joseph Smith led a group of his followers. The town flourished as a Mormon stronghold until 1838, when Smith moved on. The Kirtland Temple built by the group remained a dominant factor in the town.
Population: 6,866; Growth (since 2000): 2.9%; Density: 411.8 persons per square mile; Race: 97.7% White, 0.4% Black/African American, 0.7% Asian, 0.1% American Indian/Alaska Native, 0.0% Native Hawaiian/Other Pacific Islander, 0.9% Two or more races, 1.1% Hispanic of any race; Average household size: 2.63; Median age: 46.9; Age under 18: 23.0%; Age 65 and over: 19.1%; Males per 100 females: 97.1; Marriage status: 25.7% never married, 57.0% now married, 1.4% separated, 7.1% widowed, 10.2% divorced; Foreign born: 5.7%; Speak English only: 92.4%; With disability: 7.7%; Veterans: 9.3%; Ancestry: 23.7% German, 20.1% Irish, 14.5% Italian, 12.9% English, 8.9% Slovene
Employment: 22.4% management, business, and financial, 4.6% computer, engineering, and science, 11.7% education, legal, community service, arts, and media, 9.1% healthcare practitioners, 12.5% service, 22.6% sales and office, 6.1% natural resources, construction, and maintenance, 11.0% production, transportation, and material moving
Income: Per capita: $39,594; Median household: $83,281; Average household: $105,857; Households with income of $100,000 or more: 43.9%; Poverty rate: 4.1%
Educational Attainment: High school diploma or higher: 95.1%; Bachelor's degree or higher: 36.3%; Graduate/professional degree or higher: 15.0%

School District(s)

Kirtland Local (PK-12)
2012-13 Enrollment: 1,188 . . . . (440) 256-3360

Two-year College(s)

Lakeland Community College (Public)
Fall 2013 Enrollment: 8,839 . . . . (440) 525-7000
2013-14 Tuition: In-state $4,066; Out-of-state $8,906

Housing: Homeownership rate: 86.5%; Median home value: $261,700; Median year structure built: 1969; Homeowner vacancy rate: 1.5%; Median gross rent: $737 per month; Rental vacancy rate: 10.2%
Health Insurance: 96.8% have insurance; 89.7% have private insurance; 21.3% have public insurance; 3.2% do not have insurance; 1.0% of children under 18 do not have insurance
Safety: Violent crime rate: 0.0 per 10,000 population; Property crime rate: 52.5 per 10,000 population
Transportation: Commute: 96.1% car, 0.2% public transportation, 0.6% walk, 3.1% work from home; Median travel time to work: 24.9 minutes
Additional Information Contacts
City of Kirtland . . . . (440) 256-3332
http://kirtlandohio.com

KIRTLAND HILLS (village). Covers a land area of 5.567 square miles and a water area of 0.076 square miles. Located at 41.64° N. Lat; 81.33° W. Long. Elevation is 843 feet.
History: The first Mormon temple was built here (1833-1836) by Joseph Smith and his followers. Settled 1808, incorporated 1926.
Population: 646; Growth (since 2000): 8.2%; Density: 116.0 persons per square mile; Race: 96.7% White, 0.0% Black/African American, 1.7% Asian, 0.0% American Indian/Alaska Native, 0.0% Native Hawaiian/Other Pacific Islander, 1.5% Two or more races, 2.8% Hispanic of any race; Average household size: 2.64; Median age: 48.0; Age under 18: 22.4%; Age 65 and over: 19.2%; Males per 100 females: 94.6
Housing: Homeownership rate: 88.2%; Homeowner vacancy rate: 1.8%; Rental vacancy rate: 0.0%
Safety: Violent crime rate: 0.0 per 10,000 population; Property crime rate: 31.1 per 10,000 population

LAKELINE (village). Covers a land area of 0.088 square miles and a water area of 0 square miles. Located at 41.66° N. Lat; 81.45° W. Long. Elevation is 617 feet.
Population: 226; Growth (since 2000): 37.0%; Density: 2,578.2 persons per square mile; Race: 97.8% White, 0.9% Black/African American, 0.0% Asian, 0.0% American Indian/Alaska Native, 0.0% Native Hawaiian/Other Pacific Islander, 1.3% Two or more races, 0.9% Hispanic of any race; Average household size: 2.38; Median age: 45.1; Age under 18: 19.5%; Age 65 and over: 16.8%; Males per 100 females: 105.5
Housing: Homeownership rate: 90.5%; Homeowner vacancy rate: 3.4%; Rental vacancy rate: 9.1%

MADISON (village). Covers a land area of 5.087 square miles and a water area of 0 square miles. Located at 41.77° N. Lat; 81.05° W. Long. Elevation is 728 feet.
History: Madison grew around its orchards, nurseries, and potato fields. It was known for Madison Willowcraft, the product of its basket-making industry.
Population: 3,184; Growth (since 2000): 9.0%; Density: 625.9 persons per square mile; Race: 96.3% White, 0.6% Black/African American, 0.5% Asian, 0.1% American Indian/Alaska Native, 0.0% Native Hawaiian/Other Pacific Islander, 1.6% Two or more races, 1.5% Hispanic of any race; Average household size: 2.55; Median age: 41.1; Age under 18: 25.2%; Age 65 and over: 14.7%; Males per 100 females: 90.3; Marriage status: 21.1% never married, 56.0% now married, 0.4% separated, 7.6% widowed, 15.4% divorced; Foreign born: 2.5%; Speak English only: 96.0%; With disability: 13.2%; Veterans: 10.8%; Ancestry: 28.2% German, 21.2% English, 18.1% Irish, 14.2% Italian, 6.0% Polish
Employment: 15.4% management, business, and financial, 5.8% computer, engineering, and science, 9.8% education, legal, community service, arts, and media, 4.6% healthcare practitioners, 16.4% service, 25.2% sales and office, 11.6% natural resources, construction, and maintenance, 11.2% production, transportation, and material moving
Income: Per capita: $25,319; Median household: $53,011; Average household: $62,599; Households with income of $100,000 or more: 17.2%; Poverty rate: 15.1%
Educational Attainment: High school diploma or higher: 88.7%; Bachelor's degree or higher: 24.5%; Graduate/professional degree or higher: 6.0%

School District(s)

Madison Local (PK-12)
2012-13 Enrollment: 3,290 . . . . (440) 428-2166

Housing: Homeownership rate: 79.1%; Median home value: $142,100; Median year structure built: 1975; Homeowner vacancy rate: 1.4%; Median gross rent: $734 per month; Rental vacancy rate: 7.1%
Health Insurance: 88.8% have insurance; 73.4% have private insurance; 29.5% have public insurance; 11.2% do not have insurance; 7.0% of children under 18 do not have insurance
Transportation: Commute: 95.4% car, 0.8% public transportation, 0.5% walk, 0.6% work from home; Median travel time to work: 27.6 minutes
Additional Information Contacts
Village of Madison . . . . (440) 428-7526
http://www.madisonvillage.org

MENTOR (city). Covers a land area of 26.645 square miles and a water area of 1.353 square miles. Located at 41.69° N. Lat; 81.34° W. Long. Elevation is 692 feet.
History: Named, possibly, for Hiram Mentor, an early settler. Mentor was founded in 1799. James A. Garfield lived in Mentor prior to his time as president of the U.S.
Population: 47,159; Growth (since 2000): -6.2%; Density: 1,769.9 persons per square mile; Race: 96.3% White, 1.0% Black/African American, 1.4% Asian, 0.1% American Indian/Alaska Native, 0.0% Native Hawaiian/Other Pacific Islander, 1.0% Two or more races, 1.3% Hispanic of any race; Average household size: 2.44; Median age: 44.8; Age under 18: 21.2%; Age 65 and over: 16.5%; Males per 100 females: 93.7; Marriage status: 24.6% never married, 58.5% now married, 0.7% separated, 6.8% widowed, 10.1% divorced; Foreign born: 3.5%; Speak English only: 94.9%; With disability: 11.3%; Veterans: 10.4%; Ancestry: 28.1% German, 19.0% Irish, 18.4% Italian, 12.7% English, 8.5% Polish
Employment: 16.6% management, business, and financial, 6.4% computer, engineering, and science, 8.3% education, legal, community service, arts, and media, 7.2% healthcare practitioners, 14.5% service, 27.8% sales and office, 5.8% natural resources, construction, and maintenance, 13.6% production, transportation, and material moving
Income: Per capita: $32,485; Median household: $65,888; Average household: $79,468; Households with income of $100,000 or more: 27.3%; Poverty rate: 6.8%
Educational Attainment: High school diploma or higher: 94.5%; Bachelor's degree or higher: 28.9%; Graduate/professional degree or higher: 9.6%

School District(s)

Mentor Exempted Village (PK-12)
2012-13 Enrollment: 8,071 . . . . (440) 255-4444

Two-year College(s)
Brown Aveda Institute-Mentor (Private, For-profit)
Fall 2013 Enrollment: 149 . . . . (440) 255-9494

Vocational/Technical School(s)
Cleveland Institute of Dental-Medical Assistants-Mentor (Private, For-profit)
Fall 2013 Enrollment: 135 . . . . (216) 241-2930
2013-14 Tuition: $9,050

Housing: Homeownership rate: 85.5%; Median home value: $169,000; Median year structure built: 1972; Homeowner vacancy rate: 1.6%; Median gross rent: $885 per month; Rental vacancy rate: 11.2%
Health Insurance: 94.0% have insurance; 83.7% have private insurance; 24.7% have public insurance; 6.0% do not have insurance; 3.3% of children under 18 do not have insurance
Safety: Violent crime rate: 9.2 per 10,000 population; Property crime rate: 225.4 per 10,000 population
Transportation: Commute: 94.4% car, 1.0% public transportation, 1.1% walk, 3.0% work from home; Median travel time to work: 24.1 minutes
Additional Information Contacts
City of Mentor . . . . (440) 255-1100
http://www.cityofmentor.com

MENTOR-ON-THE-LAKE (city). Covers a land area of 1.613 square miles and a water area of 0.040 square miles. Located at 41.71° N. Lat; 81.37° W. Long. Elevation is 627 feet.
History: Mentor-on-the-Lake is a city in Lake County, Ohio. Established October 22, 1924, it was incorporated city on February 12, 1971. A vast majority of its land was originally deeded as the Dickey-Moore tract and property known as Mooreland, once owned by the Moore family, is situated on land that now houses Lakeland Community College.
Population: 7,443; Growth (since 2000): -8.4%; Density: 4,614.0 persons per square mile; Race: 95.6% White, 1.8% Black/African American, 1.0% Asian, 0.1% American Indian/Alaska Native, 0.0% Native Hawaiian/Other Pacific Islander, 1.3% Two or more races, 1.4% Hispanic of any race; Average household size: 2.33; Median age: 40.3; Age under 18: 21.7%; Age 65 and over: 14.1%; Males per 100 females: 96.0; Marriage status: 28.2% never married, 47.6% now married, 1.8% separated, 6.6% widowed, 17.6% divorced; Foreign born: 1.8%; Speak English only: 96.7%; With disability: 11.9%; Veterans: 11.6%; Ancestry: 23.5% Irish, 21.7% German, 17.7% Italian, 10.3% English, 8.4% Hungarian
Employment: 8.0% management, business, and financial, 3.0% computer, engineering, and science, 5.4% education, legal, community service, arts, and media, 7.1% healthcare practitioners, 19.6% service, 31.5% sales and office, 7.9% natural resources, construction, and maintenance, 17.6% production, transportation, and material moving
Income: Per capita: $27,000; Median household: $46,721; Average household: $59,189; Households with income of $100,000 or more: 13.5%; Poverty rate: 8.5%
Educational Attainment: High school diploma or higher: 90.0%; Bachelor's degree or higher: 13.3%; Graduate/professional degree or higher: 2.7%

School District(s)
Mentor Exempted Village (PK-12)
2012-13 Enrollment: 8,071 . . . . (440) 255-4444

Housing: Homeownership rate: 67.5%; Median home value: $133,700; Median year structure built: 1971; Homeowner vacancy rate: 1.5%; Median gross rent: $871 per month; Rental vacancy rate: 11.6%
Health Insurance: 90.1% have insurance; 75.1% have private insurance; 29.6% have public insurance; 9.9% do not have insurance; 0.4% of children under 18 do not have insurance
Transportation: Commute: 96.5% car, 0.6% public transportation, 1.2% walk, 1.1% work from home; Median travel time to work: 22.9 minutes

NORTH MADISON (CDP). Covers a land area of 3.907 square miles and a water area of 0 square miles. Located at 41.83° N. Lat; 81.05° W. Long. Elevation is 673 feet.
Population: 8,547; Growth (since 2000): 1.1%; Density: 2,187.4 persons per square mile; Race: 97.3% White, 0.5% Black/African American, 0.4% Asian, 0.2% American Indian/Alaska Native, 0.0% Native Hawaiian/Other Pacific Islander, 1.2% Two or more races, 1.8% Hispanic of any race; Average household size: 2.57; Median age: 38.5; Age under 18: 25.8%; Age 65 and over: 11.9%; Males per 100 females: 97.1; Marriage status: 28.7% never married, 48.9% now married, 1.7% separated, 5.8% widowed, 16.6% divorced; Foreign born: 1.2%; Speak English only: 98.7%; With disability: 12.3%; Veterans: 13.8%; Ancestry: 24.1% Irish, 23.3% German, 22.8% Italian, 13.3% English, 7.8% Polish
Employment: 7.9% management, business, and financial, 3.3% computer, engineering, and science, 5.2% education, legal, community service, arts, and media, 5.4% healthcare practitioners, 14.2% service, 26.3% sales and office, 13.7% natural resources, construction, and maintenance, 24.0% production, transportation, and material moving
Income: Per capita: $23,358; Median household: $54,422; Average household: $63,996; Households with income of $100,000 or more: 15.6%; Poverty rate: 12.6%
Educational Attainment: High school diploma or higher: 86.5%; Bachelor's degree or higher: 14.9%; Graduate/professional degree or higher: 5.8%
Housing: Homeownership rate: 76.3%; Median home value: $118,500; Median year structure built: 1967; Homeowner vacancy rate: 3.1%; Median gross rent: $880 per month; Rental vacancy rate: 5.6%
Health Insurance: 87.4% have insurance; 68.3% have private insurance; 29.3% have public insurance; 12.6% do not have insurance; 7.1% of children under 18 do not have insurance
Transportation: Commute: 97.0% car, 0.4% public transportation, 0.6% walk, 1.2% work from home; Median travel time to work: 32.5 minutes

NORTH PERRY (village). Covers a land area of 3.867 square miles and a water area of 0 square miles. Located at 41.80° N. Lat; 81.12° W. Long. Elevation is 679 feet.
Population: 893; Growth (since 2000): 6.6%; Density: 230.9 persons per square mile; Race: 99.3% White, 0.0% Black/African American, 0.2% Asian, 0.0% American Indian/Alaska Native, 0.1% Native Hawaiian/Other Pacific Islander, 0.3% Two or more races, 0.6% Hispanic of any race; Average household size: 2.66; Median age: 44.9; Age under 18: 24.7%; Age 65 and over: 13.9%; Males per 100 females: 106.7
Housing: Homeownership rate: 83.6%; Homeowner vacancy rate: 1.1%; Rental vacancy rate: 1.8%
Additional Information Contacts
Village of North Perry . . . . (440) 259-4994
http://www.northperry.org

PAINESVILLE (city). County seat. Covers a land area of 6.285 square miles and a water area of 0.726 square miles. Located at 41.72° N. Lat; 81.25° W. Long. Elevation is 676 feet.
History: Named for Edward Paine, first settler, who had been a general in the American Revolution. Painesville was settled in the early 1800's by pioneers from Connecticut. Architect-builder Jonathan Goldsmith lived in Painesville from 1811 until his death in 1847, and the town had several examples of Goldsmith's work.
Population: 19,563; Growth (since 2000): 11.8%; Density: 3,112.7 persons per square mile; Race: 68.2% White, 13.1% Black/African American, 0.8% Asian, 0.3% American Indian/Alaska Native, 0.0% Native Hawaiian/Other Pacific Islander, 4.5% Two or more races, 22.0% Hispanic of any race; Average household size: 2.64; Median age: 30.2; Age under 18: 28.3%; Age 65 and over: 8.7%; Males per 100 females: 101.2; Marriage status: 41.1% never married, 41.0% now married, 2.7% separated, 4.5% widowed, 13.4% divorced; Foreign born: 13.0%; Speak English only: 80.5%; With disability: 14.0%; Veterans: 7.2%; Ancestry: 21.2% German, 15.4% Irish, 9.4% Italian, 7.0% English, 4.1% Polish
Employment: 7.6% management, business, and financial, 2.7% computer, engineering, and science, 8.2% education, legal, community service, arts, and media, 3.4% healthcare practitioners, 25.7% service, 22.4% sales and office, 8.4% natural resources, construction, and maintenance, 21.5% production, transportation, and material moving
Income: Per capita: $18,797; Median household: $35,536; Average household: $50,756; Households with income of $100,000 or more: 9.4%; Poverty rate: 25.6%
Educational Attainment: High school diploma or higher: 79.0%; Bachelor's degree or higher: 14.9%; Graduate/professional degree or higher: 4.5%

School District(s)
Auburn (10-12)
2012-13 Enrollment: n/a . . . . (440) 357-7542
Painesville City Local (PK-12)
2012-13 Enrollment: 3,126 . . . . (440) 392-5060
Riverside Local (PK-12)
2012-13 Enrollment: 4,655 . . . . (440) 352-0668
Summit Academy Community School - Painesville (KG-09)
2012-13 Enrollment: 93. . . . . (440) 358-0877

Four-year College(s)

Lake Erie College (Private, Not-for-profit)
Fall 2013 Enrollment: 1,086 . . . . (440) 375-7000
2013-14 Tuition: In-state $27,368; Out-of-state $27,368

Vocational/Technical School(s)

Auburn Career Center (Public)
Fall 2013 Enrollment: 203 . . . . (440) 357-7542
2013-14 Tuition: $12,950

Housing: Homeownership rate: 50.2%; Median home value: $110,500; Median year structure built: 1960; Homeowner vacancy rate: 3.8%; Median gross rent: $726 per month; Rental vacancy rate: 8.8%
Health Insurance: 80.8% have insurance; 55.2% have private insurance; 34.1% have public insurance; 19.2% do not have insurance; 12.6% of children under 18 do not have insurance
Hospitals: TriPoint Medical center
Safety: Violent crime rate: 22.9 per 10,000 population; Property crime rate: 259.0 per 10,000 population
Transportation: Commute: 90.9% car, 1.7% public transportation, 4.0% walk, 1.6% work from home; Median travel time to work: 19.2 minutes
Additional Information Contacts
City of Painesville . . . . (440) 352-9301
http://www.painesville.com

PERRY (village). Covers a land area of 2.181 square miles and a water area of 0 square miles. Located at 41.76° N. Lat; 81.14° W. Long. Elevation is 699 feet.
Population: 1,663; Growth (since 2000): 39.2%; Density: 762.6 persons per square mile; Race: 96.1% White, 0.8% Black/African American, 1.4% Asian, 0.0% American Indian/Alaska Native, 0.0% Native Hawaiian/Other Pacific Islander, 1.1% Two or more races, 2.6% Hispanic of any race; Average household size: 2.78; Median age: 39.9; Age under 18: 28.8%; Age 65 and over: 10.6%; Males per 100 females: 98.4

School District(s)

Perry Local (PK-12)
2012-13 Enrollment: 1,776 . . . . (440) 259-3881
Housing: Homeownership rate: 84.7%; Homeowner vacancy rate: 2.5%; Rental vacancy rate: 3.2%

TIMBERLAKE (village). Covers a land area of 0.211 square miles and a water area of 0 square miles. Located at 41.67° N. Lat; 81.44° W. Long. Elevation is 617 feet.
Population: 675; Growth (since 2000): -12.9%; Density: 3,199.1 persons per square mile; Race: 96.3% White, 0.6% Black/African American, 0.6% Asian, 0.6% American Indian/Alaska Native, 0.0% Native Hawaiian/Other Pacific Islander, 0.7% Two or more races, 2.4% Hispanic of any race; Average household size: 2.29; Median age: 49.6; Age under 18: 18.2%; Age 65 and over: 22.4%; Males per 100 females: 96.8
Housing: Homeownership rate: 92.2%; Homeowner vacancy rate: 1.4%; Rental vacancy rate: 11.5%

WAITE HILL (village). Covers a land area of 4.182 square miles and a water area of 0.066 square miles. Located at 41.61° N. Lat; 81.39° W. Long. Elevation is 768 feet.
Population: 471; Growth (since 2000): 5.6%; Density: 112.6 persons per square mile; Race: 96.8% White, 0.4% Black/African American, 1.3% Asian, 0.0% American Indian/Alaska Native, 0.0% Native Hawaiian/Other Pacific Islander, 0.4% Two or more races, 0.2% Hispanic of any race; Average household size: 2.44; Median age: 52.6; Age under 18: 20.6%; Age 65 and over: 29.3%; Males per 100 females: 102.1
Housing: Homeownership rate: 89.7%; Homeowner vacancy rate: 2.8%; Rental vacancy rate: 0.0%
Safety: Violent crime rate: 0.0 per 10,000 population; Property crime rate: 42.6 per 10,000 population

WICKLIFFE (city). Covers a land area of 4.639 square miles and a water area of 0.021 square miles. Located at 41.61° N. Lat; 81.47° W. Long. Elevation is 764 feet.
History: Named for Charles A. Wickliffe, a Kentucky lawyer. Borromeo College of Ohio and the Rabbinical College of Telshe are here. Incorporated 1916.
Population: 12,750; Growth (since 2000): -5.4%; Density: 2,748.7 persons per square mile; Race: 92.8% White, 4.5% Black/African American, 0.8% Asian, 0.1% American Indian/Alaska Native, 0.0% Native Hawaiian/Other Pacific Islander, 1.6% Two or more races, 1.2% Hispanic of any race; Average household size: 2.29; Median age: 44.0; Age under 18: 20.4%; Age 65 and over: 21.7%; Males per 100 females: 93.7; Marriage status: 27.2% never married, 49.4% now married, 1.2% separated, 11.0% widowed, 12.4% divorced; Foreign born: 4.0%; Speak English only: 93.6%; With disability: 14.3%; Veterans: 12.7%; Ancestry: 22.3% Italian, 19.7% Irish, 19.5% German, 9.0% Slovene, 9.0% Polish
Employment: 10.1% management, business, and financial, 5.5% computer, engineering, and science, 9.6% education, legal, community service, arts, and media, 7.1% healthcare practitioners, 18.4% service, 26.6% sales and office, 7.7% natural resources, construction, and maintenance, 14.9% production, transportation, and material moving
Income: Per capita: $25,418; Median household: $47,155; Average household: $57,741; Households with income of $100,000 or more: 15.3%; Poverty rate: 8.8%
Educational Attainment: High school diploma or higher: 91.7%; Bachelor's degree or higher: 20.9%; Graduate/professional degree or higher: 6.5%

School District(s)

Wickliffe City (PK-12)
2012-13 Enrollment: 1,518 . . . . (440) 943-6900

Four-year College(s)

Rabbinical College Telshe (Private, Not-for-profit, Jewish)
Fall 2013 Enrollment: 96 . . . . (440) 943-5300
2013-14 Tuition: In-state $9,600; Out-of-state $9,600
Housing: Homeownership rate: 79.4%; Median home value: $126,200; Median year structure built: 1957; Homeowner vacancy rate: 1.6%; Median gross rent: $778 per month; Rental vacancy rate: 7.0%
Health Insurance: 91.9% have insurance; 76.2% have private insurance; 31.8% have public insurance; 8.1% do not have insurance; 3.5% of children under 18 do not have insurance
Transportation: Commute: 95.8% car, 1.0% public transportation, 0.5% walk, 2.3% work from home; Median travel time to work: 19.9 minutes
Additional Information Contacts
City of Wickliffe . . . . (440) 943-7100
http://www.cityofwickliffe.com

WILLOUGHBY (city). Covers a land area of 10.249 square miles and a water area of 0.090 square miles. Located at 41.65° N. Lat; 81.41° W. Long. Elevation is 659 feet.
History: Willoughby was first called Chagrin, but was renamed for an instructor in the Willoughby Medical College, established in 1834. The college had a good reputation until 1843, when a local resident discovered her newly-buried husband was missing from his grave. The medical school's method of acquiring cadavers for research soon brought about its own demise.
Population: 22,268; Growth (since 2000): -1.6%; Density: 2,172.7 persons per square mile; Race: 93.6% White, 3.1% Black/African American, 1.5% Asian, 0.1% American Indian/Alaska Native, 0.0% Native Hawaiian/Other Pacific Islander, 1.5% Two or more races, 1.3% Hispanic of any race; Average household size: 2.12; Median age: 43.6; Age under 18: 19.1%; Age 65 and over: 19.1%; Males per 100 females: 88.1; Marriage status: 29.7% never married, 47.8% now married, 0.8% separated, 8.7% widowed, 13.8% divorced; Foreign born: 6.3%; Speak English only: 92.4%; With disability: 11.7%; Veterans: 9.4%; Ancestry: 25.9% German, 20.1% Irish, 17.4% Italian, 10.4% English, 7.5% Polish
Employment: 11.7% management, business, and financial, 5.6% computer, engineering, and science, 9.9% education, legal, community service, arts, and media, 7.5% healthcare practitioners, 16.4% service, 27.3% sales and office, 7.6% natural resources, construction, and maintenance, 14.0% production, transportation, and material moving
Income: Per capita: $29,383; Median household: $51,245; Average household: $63,031; Households with income of $100,000 or more: 15.5%; Poverty rate: 7.8%
Educational Attainment: High school diploma or higher: 93.1%; Bachelor's degree or higher: 27.6%; Graduate/professional degree or higher: 9.1%

School District(s)

Willoughby-Eastlake City (PK-12)
2012-13 Enrollment: 8,418 . . . . (440) 946-5000

Vocational/Technical School(s)

Regency Beauty Institute-Cleveland (Private, For-profit)
Fall 2013 Enrollment: 86 . . . . (800) 787-6456
2013-14 Tuition: $16,200
Housing: Homeownership rate: 61.1%; Median home value: $147,400; Median year structure built: 1971; Homeowner vacancy rate: 3.4%; Median gross rent: $826 per month; Rental vacancy rate: 11.1%

Health Insurance: 89.5% have insurance; 77.1% have private insurance; 26.1% have public insurance; 10.5% do not have insurance; 8.5% of children under 18 do not have insurance
Safety: Violent crime rate: 6.3 per 10,000 population; Property crime rate: 219.9 per 10,000 population
Newspapers: News-Herald (daily circulation 40600)
Transportation: Commute: 95.1% car, 1.1% public transportation, 1.3% walk, 2.1% work from home; Median travel time to work: 21.4 minutes
Airports: Willoughby Lost Nation Municipal (general aviation)
Additional Information Contacts
City of Willoughby . . . . (440) 951-2800
http://www.willoughbyohio.com

WILLOUGHBY HILLS (city). Covers a land area of 10.729 square miles and a water area of 0.085 square miles. Located at 41.58° N. Lat; 81.43° W. Long. Elevation is 804 feet.
History: Willoughby Hills, incorporated as a village in Lake County, Ohio, in 1954, became a city in 1970.
Population: 9,485; Growth (since 2000): 10.4%; Density: 884.0 persons per square mile; Race: 77.6% White, 16.1% Black/African American, 4.3% Asian, 0.0% American Indian/Alaska Native, 0.0% Native Hawaiian/Other Pacific Islander, 1.6% Two or more races, 1.3% Hispanic of any race; Average household size: 2.16; Median age: 44.4; Age under 18: 18.6%; Age 65 and over: 18.1%; Males per 100 females: 92.9; Marriage status: 29.6% never married, 52.0% now married, 2.9% separated, 5.7% widowed, 12.7% divorced; Foreign born: 11.8%; Speak English only: 86.7%; With disability: 7.2%; Veterans: 11.7%; Ancestry: 15.1% Italian, 14.7% German, 10.1% Irish, 9.7% Slovene, 9.4% English
Employment: 13.2% management, business, and financial, 10.6% computer, engineering, and science, 7.7% education, legal, community service, arts, and media, 9.0% healthcare practitioners, 11.2% service, 29.5% sales and office, 4.8% natural resources, construction, and maintenance, 14.0% production, transportation, and material moving
Income: Per capita: $33,826; Median household: $56,593; Average household: $73,145; Households with income of $100,000 or more: 22.3%; Poverty rate: 3.8%
Educational Attainment: High school diploma or higher: 94.6%; Bachelor's degree or higher: 34.7%; Graduate/professional degree or higher: 10.2%

Two-year College(s)

National College-Willoughby Hills (Private, For-profit)
Fall 2013 Enrollment: 66 . . . . (440) 944-0825
2013-14 Tuition: In-state $11,442; Out-of-state $11,442
Housing: Homeownership rate: 50.5%; Median home value: $230,400; Median year structure built: 1971; Homeowner vacancy rate: 2.0%; Median gross rent: $810 per month; Rental vacancy rate: 15.0%
Health Insurance: 92.7% have insurance; 82.0% have private insurance; 25.3% have public insurance; 7.3% do not have insurance; 1.5% of children under 18 do not have insurance
Transportation: Commute: 95.5% car, 1.2% public transportation, 0.0% walk, 1.5% work from home; Median travel time to work: 22.3 minutes

WILLOWICK (city). Covers a land area of 2.536 square miles and a water area of 0 square miles. Located at 41.63° N. Lat; 81.47° W. Long. Elevation is 623 feet.
History: Named for the Willoughby and Wickliff families. Incorporated 1924.
Population: 14,171; Growth (since 2000): -1.3%; Density: 5,587.0 persons per square mile; Race: 95.0% White, 2.5% Black/African American, 0.8% Asian, 0.1% American Indian/Alaska Native, 0.0% Native Hawaiian/Other Pacific Islander, 1.3% Two or more races, 1.3% Hispanic of any race; Average household size: 2.32; Median age: 41.5; Age under 18: 20.9%; Age 65 and over: 19.1%; Males per 100 females: 93.8; Marriage status: 30.1% never married, 49.4% now married, 1.6% separated, 10.3% widowed, 10.1% divorced; Foreign born: 5.1%; Speak English only: 93.4%; With disability: 12.7%; Veterans: 9.8%; Ancestry: 23.5% German, 19.0% Irish, 18.6% Italian, 9.0% English, 8.6% Polish
Employment: 12.4% management, business, and financial, 3.9% computer, engineering, and science, 8.3% education, legal, community service, arts, and media, 5.0% healthcare practitioners, 17.9% service, 25.5% sales and office, 9.1% natural resources, construction, and maintenance, 17.9% production, transportation, and material moving
Income: Per capita: $27,873; Median household: $47,071; Average household: $62,468; Households with income of $100,000 or more: 11.7%; Poverty rate: 8.4%
Educational Attainment: High school diploma or higher: 90.0%; Bachelor's degree or higher: 19.0%; Graduate/professional degree or higher: 5.3%

School District(s)

Willoughby-Eastlake City (PK-12)
2012-13 Enrollment: 8,418 . . . . (440) 946-5000
Housing: Homeownership rate: 80.1%; Median home value: $121,000; Median year structure built: 1957; Homeowner vacancy rate: 1.7%; Median gross rent: $734 per month; Rental vacancy rate: 7.8%
Health Insurance: 91.7% have insurance; 76.4% have private insurance; 30.1% have public insurance; 8.3% do not have insurance; 2.4% of children under 18 do not have insurance
Transportation: Commute: 94.1% car, 1.1% public transportation, 1.0% walk, 3.1% work from home; Median travel time to work: 20.1 minutes
Additional Information Contacts
City of Willowick . . . . (440) 585-3700
http://www.cityofwillowick.com

Lawrence County

Located in southern Ohio; bounded on the south by the Ohio River and the Kentucky and West Virginia borders. Covers a land area of 453.371 square miles, a water area of 3.904 square miles, and is located in the Eastern Time Zone at 38.60° N. Lat., 82.52° W. Long. The county was founded in 1815. County seat is Ironton.

Lawrence County is part of the Huntington-Ashland, WV-KY-OH Metropolitan Statistical Area. The entire metro area includes: Boyd County, KY; Greenup County, KY; Lawrence County, OH; Cabell County, WV; Lincoln County, WV; Putnam County, WV; Wayne County, WV

Population: 62,450; Growth (since 2000): 0.2%; Density: 137.7 persons per square mile; Race: 95.9% White, 2.0% Black/African American, 0.4% Asian, 0.2% American Indian/Alaska Native, 0.0% Native Hawaiian/Other Pacific Islander, 1.4% two or more races, 0.7% Hispanic of any race; Average household size: 2.47; Median age: 40.1; Age under 18: 23.5%; Age 65 and over: 15.6%; Males per 100 females: 94.6; Marriage status: 24.7% never married, 52.1% now married, 2.5% separated, 8.8% widowed, 14.4% divorced; Foreign born: 0.4%; Speak English only: 98.7%; With disability: 21.1%; Veterans: 11.7%; Ancestry: 15.6% German, 12.9% American, 11.7% Irish, 10.5% English, 1.9% Scottish
Religion: Six largest groups: 11.4% Baptist, 3.1% Catholicism, 2.9% Methodist/Pietist, 2.4% Non-denominational Protestant, 1.6% Holiness, 0.7% Pentecostal
Economy: Unemployment rate: 5.1%; Leading industries: 18.7% retail trade; 15.0% health care and social assistance; 13.6% other services (except public administration); Farms: 592 totaling 64,575 acres; Company size: 0 employ 1,000 or more persons, 0 employ 500 to 999 persons, 17 employ 100 to 499 persons, 801 employs less than 100 persons; Business ownership: n/a women-owned, n/a Black-owned, n/a Hispanic-owned, n/a Asian-owned
Employment: 10.4% management, business, and financial, 1.9% computer, engineering, and science, 9.6% education, legal, community service, arts, and media, 7.9% healthcare practitioners, 18.2% service, 24.0% sales and office, 11.4% natural resources, construction, and maintenance, 16.7% production, transportation, and material moving
Income: Per capita: $21,365; Median household: $41,552; Average household: $53,143; Households with income of $100,000 or more: 11.4%; Poverty rate: 18.3%
Educational Attainment: High school diploma or higher: 85.0%; Bachelor's degree or higher: 14.9%; Graduate/professional degree or higher: 4.8%
Housing: Homeownership rate: 72.4%; Median home value: $97,200; Median year structure built: 1973; Homeowner vacancy rate: 1.7%; Median gross rent: $618 per month; Rental vacancy rate: 7.1%
Vital Statistics: Birth rate: 110.8 per 10,000 population; Death rate: 108.0 per 10,000 population; Age-adjusted cancer mortality rate: 206.1 deaths per 100,000 population
Health Insurance: 87.2% have insurance; 62.2% have private insurance; 39.6% have public insurance; 12.8% do not have insurance; 3.5% of children under 18 do not have insurance
Health Care: Physicians: 9.8 per 10,000 population; Hospital beds: 1.3 per 10,000 population; Hospital admissions: 40.1 per 10,000 population
Air Quality Index: 87.4% good, 12.1% moderate, 0.5% unhealthy for sensitive individuals, 0.0% unhealthy (percent of days)

Transportation: Commute: 95.5% car, 1.1% public transportation, 0.7% walk, 1.9% work from home; Median travel time to work: 24.2 minutes
Presidential Election: 41.4% Obama, 56.9% Romney (2012)
National and State Parks: Dean State Forest; Wayne National Forest; Wayne National Forest - Ironton Ranger District
Additional Information Contacts
Lawrence Government . . . . (740) 533-4300
http://www.lawrencecountyohio.org

Lawrence County Communities

ATHALIA (village). Covers a land area of 0.686 square miles and a water area of <.001 square miles. Located at 38.51° N. Lat; 82.31° W. Long. Elevation is 558 feet.
Population: 373; Growth (since 2000): 13.7%; Density: 544.0 persons per square mile; Race: 97.9% White, 0.8% Black/African American, 0.3% Asian, 0.8% American Indian/Alaska Native, 0.0% Native Hawaiian/Other Pacific Islander, 0.3% Two or more races, 2.1% Hispanic of any race; Average household size: 2.45; Median age: 39.7; Age under 18: 21.4%; Age 65 and over: 12.6%; Males per 100 females: 91.3
Housing: Homeownership rate: 69.1%; Homeowner vacancy rate: 0.0%; Rental vacancy rate: 2.1%

BURLINGTON (CDP). Covers a land area of 1.393 square miles and a water area of 0.025 square miles. Located at 38.41° N. Lat; 82.53° W. Long. Elevation is 558 feet.
History: Burlington was founded by Reverend Plymale, a Baptist minister in Virginia who had been a slave-holder. He purchased the land in Ohio and presented each of his former slaves with an equal portion of it. In 1817 Burlington became the first seat of Lawrence County.
Population: 2,676; Growth (since 2000): -4.2%; Density: 1,921.1 persons per square mile; Race: 88.6% White, 8.4% Black/African American, 0.1% Asian, 0.5% American Indian/Alaska Native, 0.0% Native Hawaiian/Other Pacific Islander, 1.9% Two or more races, 1.3% Hispanic of any race; Average household size: 2.31; Median age: 45.3; Age under 18: 19.6%; Age 65 and over: 23.4%; Males per 100 females: 85.8; Marriage status: 24.2% never married, 38.4% now married, 1.9% separated, 18.8% widowed, 18.6% divorced; Foreign born: 1.0%; Speak English only: 99.2%; With disability: 27.1%; Veterans: 12.9%; Ancestry: 14.2% Irish, 13.8% English, 12.6% German, 9.1% American, 4.1% Scottish
Employment: 9.0% management, business, and financial, 2.4% computer, engineering, and science, 4.1% education, legal, community service, arts, and media, 2.6% healthcare practitioners, 23.3% service, 30.7% sales and office, 6.5% natural resources, construction, and maintenance, 21.4% production, transportation, and material moving
Income: Per capita: $23,129; Median household: $34,940; Average household: $46,790; Households with income of $100,000 or more: 7.3%; Poverty rate: 14.4%
Educational Attainment: High school diploma or higher: 79.9%; Bachelor's degree or higher: 14.1%; Graduate/professional degree or higher: 2.7%
Housing: Homeownership rate: 65.6%; Median home value: $77,200; Median year structure built: 1978; Homeowner vacancy rate: 1.0%; Median gross rent: $597 per month; Rental vacancy rate: 7.7%
Health Insurance: 77.2% have insurance; 53.8% have private insurance; 41.9% have public insurance; 22.8% do not have insurance; 0.0% of children under 18 do not have insurance
Transportation: Commute: 97.7% car, 0.0% public transportation, 2.3% walk, 0.0% work from home; Median travel time to work: 16.4 minutes

CHESAPEAKE (village). Covers a land area of 0.472 square miles and a water area of 0.086 square miles. Located at 38.43° N. Lat; 82.46° W. Long. Elevation is 558 feet.
History: Chesapeake developed as a residential community, with many of its citizens commuting to Huntington, across the Ohio River in West Virginia.
Population: 745; Growth (since 2000): -11.5%; Density: 1,576.8 persons per square mile; Race: 96.8% White, 0.5% Black/African American, 0.4% Asian, 0.7% American Indian/Alaska Native, 0.0% Native Hawaiian/Other Pacific Islander, 1.2% Two or more races, 0.9% Hispanic of any race; Average household size: 2.16; Median age: 44.4; Age under 18: 20.8%; Age 65 and over: 21.5%; Males per 100 females: 90.1

School District(s)

Chesapeake Union Exempted Village (PK-12)
2012-13 Enrollment: 1,389 . . . . (740) 867-3135
Lawrence County (06-12)
2012-13 Enrollment: n/a . . . . (740) 867-6641

Two-year College(s)

O C Collins Career Center (Public)
Fall 2013 Enrollment: 407 . . . . (740) 867-6641
Housing: Homeownership rate: 60.9%; Homeowner vacancy rate: 0.9%; Rental vacancy rate: 11.8%
Airports: Lawrence County Airpark (general aviation)

COAL GROVE (village). Covers a land area of 1.902 square miles and a water area of 0.144 square miles. Located at 38.49° N. Lat; 82.64° W. Long. Elevation is 571 feet.
Population: 2,165; Growth (since 2000): 6.8%; Density: 1,138.5 persons per square mile; Race: 97.7% White, 0.6% Black/African American, 0.0% Asian, 0.4% American Indian/Alaska Native, 0.0% Native Hawaiian/Other Pacific Islander, 1.1% Two or more races, 0.3% Hispanic of any race; Average household size: 2.55; Median age: 38.5; Age under 18: 24.4%; Age 65 and over: 16.3%; Males per 100 females: 88.9

School District(s)

Dawson-Bryant Local (PK-12)
2012-13 Enrollment: 1,183 . . . . (740) 532-6451
Housing: Homeownership rate: 64.7%; Homeowner vacancy rate: 1.8%; Rental vacancy rate: 3.3%

HANGING ROCK (village). Covers a land area of 0.556 square miles and a water area of 0.086 square miles. Located at 38.56° N. Lat; 82.73° W. Long. Elevation is 538 feet.
History: Hanging Rock was named for the sandstone cliff, 400 feet high, which has an overhang at the top. Hanging Rock was founded in 1820 and developed around an iron furnace.
Population: 221; Growth (since 2000): -20.8%; Density: 397.2 persons per square mile; Race: 98.6% White, 0.0% Black/African American, 0.0% Asian, 0.0% American Indian/Alaska Native, 0.0% Native Hawaiian/Other Pacific Islander, 1.4% Two or more races, 1.4% Hispanic of any race; Average household size: 2.33; Median age: 47.4; Age under 18: 14.9%; Age 65 and over: 19.9%; Males per 100 females: 90.5
Housing: Homeownership rate: 80.0%; Homeowner vacancy rate: 0.0%; Rental vacancy rate: 17.4%

IRONTON (city). County seat. Covers a land area of 4.161 square miles and a water area of 0.296 square miles. Located at 38.53° N. Lat; 82.68° W. Long. Elevation is 551 feet.
History: Ironton was founded in 1848 by John Campbell, one of the first ironmasters of the region. The ore deposits in the Ironton district were discovered about 1826, and a charcoal furnace was set up to make pigiron. The iron industry supported Ironton for a century.
Population: 11,129; Growth (since 2000): -0.7%; Density: 2,674.5 persons per square mile; Race: 92.6% White, 4.7% Black/African American, 0.3% Asian, 0.2% American Indian/Alaska Native, 0.0% Native Hawaiian/Other Pacific Islander, 2.1% Two or more races, 0.5% Hispanic of any race; Average household size: 2.23; Median age: 42.1; Age under 18: 21.1%; Age 65 and over: 19.2%; Males per 100 females: 89.1; Marriage status: 29.4% never married, 43.3% now married, 2.3% separated, 10.4% widowed, 17.0% divorced; Foreign born: 0.3%; Speak English only: 98.7%; With disability: 25.0%; Veterans: 9.9%; Ancestry: 16.1% German, 12.7% American, 11.1% Irish, 10.0% English, 2.7% French
Employment: 9.6% management, business, and financial, 1.7% computer, engineering, and science, 11.6% education, legal, community service, arts, and media, 6.6% healthcare practitioners, 20.8% service, 27.1% sales and office, 7.8% natural resources, construction, and maintenance, 14.7% production, transportation, and material moving
Income: Per capita: $19,902; Median household: $34,448; Average household: $45,886; Households with income of $100,000 or more: 10.3%; Poverty rate: 18.1%
Educational Attainment: High school diploma or higher: 87.8%; Bachelor's degree or higher: 16.8%; Graduate/professional degree or higher: 6.5%

School District(s)

Dawson-Bryant Local (PK-12)
2012-13 Enrollment: 1,183 . . . . (740) 532-6451
Ironton City (PK-12)
2012-13 Enrollment: 1,529 . . . . (740) 532-4133
Rock Hill Local (PK-12)
2012-13 Enrollment: 1,462 . . . . (740) 532-7030

Four-year College(s)

Ohio University-Southern Campus (Public)
Fall 2013 Enrollment: 2,012 . . . . (740) 533-4600
2013-14 Tuition: In-state $4,778; Out-of-state $6,624

Housing: Homeownership rate: 59.4%; Median home value: $87,300; Median year structure built: 1951; Homeowner vacancy rate: 2.5%; Median gross rent: $537 per month; Rental vacancy rate: 7.0%

Health Insurance: 85.9% have insurance; 62.2% have private insurance; 37.9% have public insurance; 14.1% do not have insurance; 4.2% of children under 18 do not have insurance

Newspapers: Ironton Tribune (daily circulation 5200)

Transportation: Commute: 93.7% car, 0.1% public transportation, 1.5% walk, 2.2% work from home; Median travel time to work: 16.7 minutes

Additional Information Contacts

City of Ironton . . . . (740) 532-3833
http://ironton-ohio.com

KITTS HILL (unincorporated postal area)

ZCTA: 45645

Covers a land area of 46.737 square miles and a water area of 0.134 square miles. Located at 38.57° N. Lat; 82.53° W. Long. Elevation is 955 feet.

Population: 3,036; Growth (since 2000): 4.3%; Density: 65.0 persons per square mile; Race: 98.9% White, 0.1% Black/African American, 0.1% Asian, 0.1% American Indian/Alaska Native, 0.0% Native Hawaiian/Other Pacific Islander, 0.6% Two or more races, 0.2% Hispanic of any race; Average household size: 2.68; Median age: 39.0; Age under 18: 25.0%; Age 65 and over: 12.2%; Males per 100 females: 99.6; Marriage status: 18.1% never married, 66.3% now married, 3.7% separated, 8.1% widowed, 7.5% divorced; Foreign born: 0.6%; Speak English only: 97.6%; With disability: 21.9%; Veterans: 14.5%; Ancestry: 25.6% German, 18.0% English, 11.6% Irish, 10.2% American, 2.7% Russian

Employment: 22.3% management, business, and financial, 2.5% computer, engineering, and science, 7.4% education, legal, community service, arts, and media, 12.6% healthcare practitioners, 8.9% service, 27.1% sales and office, 7.7% natural resources, construction, and maintenance, 11.4% production, transportation, and material moving

Income: Per capita: $26,743; Median household: $53,125; Average household: $66,827; Households with income of $100,000 or more: 22.3%; Poverty rate: 9.8%

Educational Attainment: High school diploma or higher: 88.2%; Bachelor's degree or higher: 15.8%; Graduate/professional degree or higher: 8.3%

Housing: Homeownership rate: 82.8%; Median home value: $91,300; Median year structure built: 1980; Homeowner vacancy rate: 0.8%; Median gross rent: $594 per month; Rental vacancy rate: 10.5%

Health Insurance: 91.0% have insurance; 67.5% have private insurance; 36.2% have public insurance; 9.0% do not have insurance; 0.0% of children under 18 do not have insurance

Transportation: Commute: 100.0% car, 0.0% public transportation, 0.0% walk, 0.0% work from home; Median travel time to work: 29.4 minutes

PEDRO (unincorporated postal area)

ZCTA: 45659

Covers a land area of 98.267 square miles and a water area of 0.608 square miles. Located at 38.66° N. Lat; 82.64° W. Long. Elevation is 610 feet.

Population: 2,973; Growth (since 2000): -5.7%; Density: 30.3 persons per square mile; Race: 97.5% White, 0.5% Black/African American, 0.0% Asian, 0.2% American Indian/Alaska Native, 0.0% Native Hawaiian/Other Pacific Islander, 1.4% Two or more races, 0.9% Hispanic of any race; Average household size: 2.71; Median age: 36.7; Age under 18: 26.9%; Age 65 and over: 11.3%; Males per 100 females: 100.9; Marriage status: 22.6% never married, 50.7% now married, 3.7% separated, 8.6% widowed, 18.1% divorced; Foreign born: 0.0%; Speak English only: 100.0%; With disability: 22.8%; Veterans: 11.5%; Ancestry: 18.9% American, 15.7% German, 7.5% English, 5.1% Irish, 1.9% Scotch-Irish

Employment: 8.3% management, business, and financial, 0.0% computer, engineering, and science, 11.8% education, legal, community service, arts, and media, 10.8% healthcare practitioners, 24.8% service, 9.3% sales and office, 17.5% natural resources, construction, and maintenance, 17.5% production, transportation, and material moving

Income: Per capita: $18,910; Median household: $36,635; Average household: $44,111; Households with income of $100,000 or more: 7.7%; Poverty rate: 22.6%

Educational Attainment: High school diploma or higher: 77.6%; Bachelor's degree or higher: 14.8%; Graduate/professional degree or higher: 6.7%

Housing: Homeownership rate: 80.5%; Median home value: $80,800; Median year structure built: 1981; Homeowner vacancy rate: 1.1%; Median gross rent: $632 per month; Rental vacancy rate: 4.1%

Health Insurance: 84.1% have insurance; 58.6% have private insurance; 37.9% have public insurance; 15.9% do not have insurance; 0.0% of children under 18 do not have insurance

Transportation: Commute: 98.6% car, 0.0% public transportation, 0.9% walk, 0.5% work from home; Median travel time to work: 36.0 minutes

PROCTORVILLE (village). Covers a land area of 0.238 square miles and a water area of 0.034 square miles. Located at 38.44° N. Lat; 82.38° W. Long. Elevation is 551 feet.

Population: 574; Growth (since 2000): -7.4%; Density: 2,413.8 persons per square mile; Race: 97.9% White, 0.3% Black/African American, 0.0% Asian, 0.2% American Indian/Alaska Native, 0.0% Native Hawaiian/Other Pacific Islander, 1.4% Two or more races, 1.0% Hispanic of any race; Average household size: 2.29; Median age: 40.2; Age under 18: 21.4%; Age 65 and over: 18.1%; Males per 100 females: 93.3

School District(s)

Fairland Local (PK-12)
2012-13 Enrollment: 1,671 . . . . (740) 886-3100

Housing: Homeownership rate: 58.2%; Homeowner vacancy rate: 3.3%; Rental vacancy rate: 7.8%

Hospitals: Three Gables Surgery Center

SCOTTOWN (unincorporated postal area)

ZCTA: 45678

Covers a land area of 40.737 square miles and a water area of 0.239 square miles. Located at 38.61° N. Lat; 82.38° W. Long. Elevation is 594 feet.

Population: 1,101; Growth (since 2000): 2.1%; Density: 27.0 persons per square mile; Race: 99.3% White, 0.0% Black/African American, 0.0% Asian, 0.3% American Indian/Alaska Native, 0.0% Native Hawaiian/Other Pacific Islander, 0.4% Two or more races, 1.1% Hispanic of any race; Average household size: 2.51; Median age: 42.6; Age under 18: 21.9%; Age 65 and over: 15.3%; Males per 100 females: 108.9

Housing: Homeownership rate: 86.8%; Homeowner vacancy rate: 1.8%; Rental vacancy rate: 9.4%

SOUTH POINT (village). Covers a land area of 2.939 square miles and a water area of 0.289 square miles. Located at 38.42° N. Lat; 82.58° W. Long. Elevation is 561 feet.

History: South Point was named for its location at the southern tip of Ohio. The residents of South Point enjoyed a view of three states: Kentucky, West Virginia, and Ohio.

Population: 3,958; Growth (since 2000): 5.8%; Density: 1,346.7 persons per square mile; Race: 94.2% White, 3.2% Black/African American, 0.5% Asian, 0.1% American Indian/Alaska Native, 0.0% Native Hawaiian/Other Pacific Islander, 1.8% Two or more races, 0.4% Hispanic of any race; Average household size: 2.47; Median age: 40.3; Age under 18: 23.3%; Age 65 and over: 17.3%; Males per 100 females: 88.1; Marriage status: 28.3% never married, 51.8% now married, 1.2% separated, 7.4% widowed, 12.5% divorced; Foreign born: 0.0%; Speak English only: 99.6%; With disability: 18.3%; Veterans: 15.1%; Ancestry: 19.4% German, 18.3% Irish, 11.9% American, 11.5% English, 3.0% French

Employment: 11.6% management, business, and financial, 3.7% computer, engineering, and science, 12.1% education, legal, community service, arts, and media, 5.8% healthcare practitioners, 18.5% service, 26.3% sales and office, 6.5% natural resources, construction, and maintenance, 15.4% production, transportation, and material moving

Income: Per capita: $25,908; Median household: $46,875; Average household: $58,192; Households with income of $100,000 or more: 13.8%; Poverty rate: 13.9%

Educational Attainment: High school diploma or higher: 92.1%; Bachelor's degree or higher: 18.5%; Graduate/professional degree or higher: 7.4%

School District(s)

South Point Local (PK-12)
2012-13 Enrollment: 1,748 . . . . (740) 377-4315

Four-year College(s)

Tri-State Bible College (Private, Not-for-profit, Undenominational)
Fall 2013 Enrollment: 59 . . . . (740) 377-2520
2013-14 Tuition: In-state $7,700; Out-of-state $7,700

Housing: Homeownership rate: 70.8%; Median home value: $128,900; Median year structure built: 1977; Homeowner vacancy rate: 2.1%; Median gross rent: $673 per month; Rental vacancy rate: 4.1%

Health Insurance: 92.5% have insurance; 69.6% have private insurance; 43.0% have public insurance; 7.5% do not have insurance; 2.6% of children under 18 do not have insurance

Safety: Violent crime rate: 20.2 per 10,000 population; Property crime rate: 131.3 per 10,000 population

Transportation: Commute: 93.6% car, 3.4% public transportation, 0.3% walk, 2.8% work from home; Median travel time to work: 22.8 minutes

Additional Information Contacts

Village of South Point . . . . (740) 377-4838
http://www.villageofsouthpoint.com

WATERLOO (unincorporated postal area)

ZCTA: 45688

Covers a land area of 36.711 square miles and a water area of 0.124 square miles. Located at 38.73° N. Lat; 82.54° W. Long. Elevation is 636 feet.

Population: 475; Growth (since 2000): 8.0%; Density: 12.9 persons per square mile; Race: 99.4% White, 0.2% Black/African American, 0.0% Asian, 0.0% American Indian/Alaska Native, 0.0% Native Hawaiian/Other Pacific Islander, 0.4% Two or more races, 0.0% Hispanic of any race; Average household size: 2.51; Median age: 40.7; Age under 18: 24.0%; Age 65 and over: 11.2%; Males per 100 females: 96.3

Housing: Homeownership rate: 77.3%; Homeowner vacancy rate: 2.6%; Rental vacancy rate: 6.4%

WILLOW WOOD (unincorporated postal area)

ZCTA: 45696

Covers a land area of 36.009 square miles and a water area of 0.168 square miles. Located at 38.60° N. Lat; 82.45° W. Long. Elevation is 620 feet.

Population: 1,438; Growth (since 2000): 5.3%; Density: 39.9 persons per square mile; Race: 99.2% White, 0.1% Black/African American, 0.1% Asian, 0.0% American Indian/Alaska Native, 0.0% Native Hawaiian/Other Pacific Islander, 0.6% Two or more races, 0.8% Hispanic of any race; Average household size: 2.65; Median age: 40.1; Age under 18: 25.2%; Age 65 and over: 12.9%; Males per 100 females: 101.4

School District(s)

Symmes Valley Local (PK-12)
2012-13 Enrollment: 784 . . . . (740) 643-2451

Housing: Homeownership rate: 81.2%; Homeowner vacancy rate: 1.6%; Rental vacancy rate: 5.6%

Licking County

Located in central Ohio; drained by the Licking River and Raccoon Creek; includes part of Buckeye Lake. Covers a land area of 682.500 square miles, a water area of 4.991 square miles, and is located in the Eastern Time Zone at 40.09° N. Lat., 82.48° W. Long. The county was founded in 1808. County seat is Newark.

Licking County is part of the Columbus, OH Metropolitan Statistical Area. The entire metro area includes: Delaware County, OH; Fairfield County, OH; Franklin County, OH; Hocking County, OH; Licking County, OH; Madison County, OH; Morrow County, OH; Perry County, OH; Pickaway County, OH; Union County, OH

Weather Station: Newark Water Works Elevation: 834 feet

	Jan	Feb	Mar	Apr	May	Jun	Jul	Aug	Sep	Oct	Nov	Dec
High	36	40	50	63	72	81	84	83	76	64	52	40
Low	20	22	29	39	48	58	62	60	53	41	33	24
Precip	3.0	2.5	3.2	3.7	4.4	4.5	4.4	3.7	2.9	3.0	3.2	3.2
Snow	6.8	4.7	2.2	0.7	tr	0.0	0.0	0.0	0.0	tr	0.4	2.6

High and Low temperatures in degrees Fahrenheit; Precipitation and Snow in inches

Population: 166,492; Growth (since 2000): 14.4%; Density: 243.9 persons per square mile; Race: 93.2% White, 3.4% Black/African American, 0.7% Asian, 0.3% American Indian/Alaska Native, 0.0% Native Hawaiian/Other Pacific Islander, 1.9% two or more races, 1.4% Hispanic of any race; Average household size: 2.55; Median age: 39.1; Age under 18: 24.7%; Age 65 and over: 13.3%; Males per 100 females: 95.9; Marriage status: 25.6% never married, 56.6% now married, 1.9% separated, 5.8% widowed, 12.1% divorced; Foreign born: 1.7%; Speak English only: 96.9%; With disability: 13.2%; Veterans: 11.6%; Ancestry: 29.2% German, 16.7% Irish, 11.3% English, 10.4% American, 6.0% Italian

Religion: Six largest groups: 9.6% Catholicism, 8.9% Baptist, 5.4% Methodist/Pietist, 2.3% Presbyterian-Reformed, 2.2% Non-denominational Protestant, 1.7% Pentecostal

Economy: Unemployment rate: 4.1%; Leading industries: 15.4% retail trade; 11.1% other services (except public administration); 10.9% construction; Farms: 1,484 totaling 224,015 acres; Company size: 3 employ 1,000 or more persons, 5 employ 500 to 999 persons, 65 employ 100 to 499 persons, 2,819 employ less than 100 persons; Business ownership: 4,024 women-owned, n/a Black-owned, n/a Hispanic-owned, n/a Asian-owned

Employment: 14.7% management, business, and financial, 4.4% computer, engineering, and science, 9.0% education, legal, community service, arts, and media, 5.2% healthcare practitioners, 17.0% service, 27.1% sales and office, 9.0% natural resources, construction, and maintenance, 13.7% production, transportation, and material moving

Income: Per capita: $26,716; Median household: $55,114; Average household: $68,701; Households with income of $100,000 or more: 20.1%; Poverty rate: 12.0%

Educational Attainment: High school diploma or higher: 89.2%; Bachelor's degree or higher: 21.9%; Graduate/professional degree or higher: 7.1%

Housing: Homeownership rate: 73.3%; Median home value: $149,500; Median year structure built: 1975; Homeowner vacancy rate: 2.1%; Median gross rent: $732 per month; Rental vacancy rate: 8.7%

Vital Statistics: Birth rate: 113.3 per 10,000 population; Death rate: 87.4 per 10,000 population; Age-adjusted cancer mortality rate: 186.2 deaths per 100,000 population

Health Insurance: 89.1% have insurance; 72.5% have private insurance; 29.1% have public insurance; 10.9% do not have insurance; 4.5% of children under 18 do not have insurance

Health Care: Physicians: 10.4 per 10,000 population; Hospital beds: 13.1 per 10,000 population; Hospital admissions: 444.1 per 10,000 population

Air Quality Index: 94.4% good, 5.6% moderate, 0.0% unhealthy for sensitive individuals, 0.0% unhealthy (percent of days)

Transportation: Commute: 91.7% car, 0.4% public transportation, 2.5% walk, 4.6% work from home; Median travel time to work: 25.1 minutes

Presidential Election: 41.7% Obama, 56.3% Romney (2012)

National and State Parks: Black Hand State Nature Preserve; Cranberry Bog State Nature Preserve; Morris Woods State Nature Preserve; Moundbuilders State Memorial; Octagon State Memorial

Additional Information Contacts

Licking Government . . . . (740) 349-6066
http://www.lcounty.com

Licking County Communities

ALEXANDRIA (village). Covers a land area of 0.245 square miles and a water area of <.001 square miles. Located at 40.09° N. Lat; 82.61° W. Long. Elevation is 974 feet.

Population: 517; Growth (since 2000): 508.2%; Density: 2,109.7 persons per square mile; Race: 98.5% White, 0.0% Black/African American, 0.0% Asian, 0.6% American Indian/Alaska Native, 0.0% Native Hawaiian/Other Pacific Islander, 1.0% Two or more races, 1.2% Hispanic of any race; Average household size: 2.84; Median age: 34.9; Age under 18: 30.2%; Age 65 and over: 11.4%; Males per 100 females: 98.1

School District(s)

Northridge Local (PK-12)
2012-13 Enrollment: 1,255 . . . . (740) 967-6631

Housing: Homeownership rate: 75.8%; Homeowner vacancy rate: 2.1%; Rental vacancy rate: 10.2%

BEECHWOOD TRAILS (CDP). Covers a land area of 3.910 square miles and a water area of 0.013 square miles. Located at 40.03° N. Lat; 82.66° W. Long. Elevation is 1,207 feet.

Population: 3,020; Growth (since 2000): 33.7%; Density: 772.4 persons per square mile; Race: 95.7% White, 2.0% Black/African American, 0.6% Asian, 0.3% American Indian/Alaska Native, 0.0% Native Hawaiian/Other Pacific Islander, 1.1% Two or more races, 1.2% Hispanic of any race; Average household size: 2.77; Median age: 43.6; Age under 18: 23.1%; Age 65 and over: 9.9%; Males per 100 females: 95.1; Marriage status:

17.7% never married, 76.4% now married, 0.5% separated, 3.3% widowed, 2.5% divorced; Foreign born: 1.1%; Speak English only: 95.4%; With disability: 6.3%; Veterans: 11.4%; Ancestry: 33.6% German, 15.2% Irish, 11.3% English, 10.0% American, 6.3% Scottish
Employment: 23.4% management, business, and financial, 9.2% computer, engineering, and science, 16.5% education, legal, community service, arts, and media, 4.8% healthcare practitioners, 12.9% service, 21.8% sales and office, 5.0% natural resources, construction, and maintenance, 6.5% production, transportation, and material moving
Income: Per capita: $34,411; Median household: $91,797; Average household: $96,493; Households with income of $100,000 or more: 42.3%; Poverty rate: n/a
Educational Attainment: High school diploma or higher: 94.0%; Bachelor's degree or higher: 41.2%; Graduate/professional degree or higher: 14.1%
Housing: Homeownership rate: 97.7%; Median home value: $185,000; Median year structure built: 1991; Homeowner vacancy rate: 1.1%; Median gross rent: n/a per month; Rental vacancy rate: 7.1%
Health Insurance: 96.0% have insurance; 89.6% have private insurance; 15.7% have public insurance; 4.0% do not have insurance; 0.0% of children under 18 do not have insurance
Transportation: Commute: 88.9% car, 5.0% public transportation, 0.0% walk, 6.1% work from home; Median travel time to work: 32.2 minutes

BROWNSVILLE (CDP). Covers a land area of 0.892 square miles and a water area of <.001 square miles. Located at 39.94° N. Lat; 82.25° W. Long. Elevation is 948 feet.
Population: 220; Growth (since 2000): n/a; Density: 246.7 persons per square mile; Race: 96.8% White, 0.9% Black/African American, 0.0% Asian, 0.0% American Indian/Alaska Native, 0.0% Native Hawaiian/Other Pacific Islander, 1.8% Two or more races, 0.0% Hispanic of any race; Average household size: 2.39; Median age: 45.8; Age under 18: 20.9%; Age 65 and over: 19.1%; Males per 100 females: 105.6
Housing: Homeownership rate: 88.0%; Homeowner vacancy rate: 0.0%; Rental vacancy rate: 21.4%

BUCKEYE LAKE (village). Covers a land area of 2.000 square miles and a water area of 0.020 square miles. Located at 39.94° N. Lat; 82.49° W. Long. Elevation is 899 feet.
History: Beside lake created for Ohio Canal c.1827.
Population: 2,746; Growth (since 2000): -9.9%; Density: 1,373.1 persons per square mile; Race: 96.6% White, 0.8% Black/African American, 0.3% Asian, 0.3% American Indian/Alaska Native, 0.0% Native Hawaiian/Other Pacific Islander, 1.9% Two or more races, 0.9% Hispanic of any race; Average household size: 2.31; Median age: 41.4; Age under 18: 22.7%; Age 65 and over: 13.4%; Males per 100 females: 94.6; Marriage status: 34.6% never married, 34.6% now married, 2.8% separated, 6.8% widowed, 24.0% divorced; Foreign born: 0.0%; Speak English only: 99.0%; With disability: 19.2%; Veterans: 13.6%; Ancestry: 36.3% German, 29.7% Irish, 6.4% Dutch, 6.3% English, 6.1% American
Employment: 8.2% management, business, and financial, 0.0% computer, engineering, and science, 3.1% education, legal, community service, arts, and media, 3.1% healthcare practitioners, 21.6% service, 24.9% sales and office, 22.9% natural resources, construction, and maintenance, 16.3% production, transportation, and material moving
Income: Per capita: $16,708; Median household: $27,764; Average household: $35,628; Households with income of $100,000 or more: 4.1%; Poverty rate: 30.8%
Educational Attainment: High school diploma or higher: 70.3%; Bachelor's degree or higher: 9.8%; Graduate/professional degree or higher: 4.4%
Housing: Homeownership rate: 60.3%; Median home value: $74,500; Median year structure built: 1972; Homeowner vacancy rate: 7.3%; Median gross rent: $597 per month; Rental vacancy rate: 7.1%
Health Insurance: 82.3% have insurance; 35.1% have private insurance; 56.5% have public insurance; 17.7% do not have insurance; 0.0% of children under 18 do not have insurance
Newspapers: Buckeye Lake Beacon (weekly circulation 14800)
Transportation: Commute: 96.0% car, 0.0% public transportation, 0.0% walk, 1.8% work from home; Median travel time to work: 24.1 minutes

CROTON (unincorporated postal area)
ZCTA: 43013
Covers a land area of 19.222 square miles and a water area of 0.043 square miles. Located at 40.23° N. Lat; 82.69° W. Long. Elevation is 1,168 feet.
Population: 1,201; Growth (since 2000): 22.7%; Density: 62.5 persons per square mile; Race: 97.5% White, 0.3% Black/African American, 0.2% Asian, 0.2% American Indian/Alaska Native, 0.0% Native Hawaiian/Other Pacific Islander, 0.6% Two or more races, 2.0% Hispanic of any race; Average household size: 2.69; Median age: 40.3; Age under 18: 24.5%; Age 65 and over: 12.2%; Males per 100 females: 100.5
Housing: Homeownership rate: 85.9%; Homeowner vacancy rate: 1.8%; Rental vacancy rate: 6.0%

ETNA (CDP). Covers a land area of 0.630 square miles and a water area of 0.004 square miles. Located at 39.96° N. Lat; 82.69° W. Long. Elevation is 1,060 feet.
Population: 1,215; Growth (since 2000): n/a; Density: 1,928.2 persons per square mile; Race: 91.7% White, 3.6% Black/African American, 1.9% Asian, 0.0% American Indian/Alaska Native, 0.0% Native Hawaiian/Other Pacific Islander, 2.4% Two or more races, 1.5% Hispanic of any race; Average household size: 2.96; Median age: 32.1; Age under 18: 30.5%; Age 65 and over: 4.9%; Males per 100 females: 109.5
Housing: Homeownership rate: 87.8%; Homeowner vacancy rate: 1.4%; Rental vacancy rate: 0.0%

GRANVILLE (village). Covers a land area of 4.675 square miles and a water area of 0.029 square miles. Located at 40.06° N. Lat; 82.50° W. Long. Elevation is 958 feet.
History: Granville was laid out in 1806 and named for the Massachusetts home of its early settlers. In 1831 the Granville Literary and Theological Institute was established, becoming Denison University in 1856.
Population: 5,646; Growth (since 2000): 78.3%; Density: 1,207.7 persons per square mile; Race: 91.9% White, 2.1% Black/African American, 3.6% Asian, 0.1% American Indian/Alaska Native, 0.0% Native Hawaiian/Other Pacific Islander, 1.7% Two or more races, 2.7% Hispanic of any race; Average household size: 2.52; Median age: 22.0; Age under 18: 18.1%; Age 65 and over: 9.6%; Males per 100 females: 86.1; Marriage status: 52.0% never married, 39.8% now married, 0.5% separated, 2.9% widowed, 5.3% divorced; Foreign born: 5.5%; Speak English only: 93.0%; With disability: 6.3%; Veterans: 5.6%; Ancestry: 30.6% German, 22.5% Irish, 12.2% English, 8.5% Italian, 4.9% Swedish
Employment: 18.7% management, business, and financial, 3.9% computer, engineering, and science, 24.7% education, legal, community service, arts, and media, 5.7% healthcare practitioners, 17.9% service, 23.1% sales and office, 1.5% natural resources, construction, and maintenance, 4.5% production, transportation, and material moving
Income: Per capita: $32,287; Median household: $103,333; Average household: $125,896; Households with income of $100,000 or more: 53.3%; Poverty rate: 6.6%
Educational Attainment: High school diploma or higher: 99.5%; Bachelor's degree or higher: 65.4%; Graduate/professional degree or higher: 36.3%

School District(s)

Granville Exempted Village (PK-12)
2012-13 Enrollment: 2,490 . . . . (740) 587-8101

Four-year College(s)

Denison University (Private, Not-for-profit)
Fall 2013 Enrollment: 2,274 . . . . (740) 587-0810
2013-14 Tuition: In-state $43,910; Out-of-state $43,910

Housing: Homeownership rate: 78.2%; Median home value: $310,300; Median year structure built: 1965; Homeowner vacancy rate: 2.7%; Median gross rent: $848 per month; Rental vacancy rate: 6.8%
Health Insurance: 96.8% have insurance; 92.5% have private insurance; 12.1% have public insurance; 3.2% do not have insurance; 0.0% of children under 18 do not have insurance
Newspapers: Granville Sentinel (weekly circulation 2400)
Transportation: Commute: 52.9% car, 0.0% public transportation, 31.1% walk, 15.0% work from home; Median travel time to work: 18.3 minutes
Additional Information Contacts
Village of Granville . . . . (740) 587-0707
http://www.granville.oh.us

GRANVILLE SOUTH (CDP). Covers a land area of 6.096 square miles and a water area of 0.055 square miles. Located at 40.05° N. Lat; 82.55° W. Long.

Population: 1,410; Growth (since 2000): 18.1%; Density: 231.3 persons per square mile; Race: 96.9% White, 0.9% Black/African American, 1.4% Asian, 0.1% American Indian/Alaska Native, 0.0% Native Hawaiian/Other Pacific Islander, 0.6% Two or more races, 0.9% Hispanic of any race; Average household size: 2.53; Median age: 48.0; Age under 18: 25.2%; Age 65 and over: 23.0%; Males per 100 females: 93.2

Housing: Homeownership rate: 80.1%; Homeowner vacancy rate: 0.4%; Rental vacancy rate: 8.4%

GRATIOT (village). Covers a land area of 0.131 square miles and a water area of 0 square miles. Located at 39.95° N. Lat; 82.22° W. Long. Elevation is 984 feet.

Population: 221; Growth (since 2000): 18.2%; Density: 1,688.5 persons per square mile; Race: 98.6% White, 0.5% Black/African American, 0.0% Asian, 0.0% American Indian/Alaska Native, 0.0% Native Hawaiian/Other Pacific Islander, 0.9% Two or more races, 0.0% Hispanic of any race; Average household size: 2.43; Median age: 44.4; Age under 18: 19.5%; Age 65 and over: 15.4%; Males per 100 females: 90.5

Housing: Homeownership rate: 86.8%; Homeowner vacancy rate: 0.0%; Rental vacancy rate: 0.0%

HANOVER (village). Covers a land area of 1.663 square miles and a water area of 0.018 square miles. Located at 40.08° N. Lat; 82.27° W. Long. Elevation is 823 feet.

Population: 921; Growth (since 2000): 4.1%; Density: 553.9 persons per square mile; Race: 97.5% White, 1.0% Black/African American, 0.2% Asian, 0.3% American Indian/Alaska Native, 0.0% Native Hawaiian/Other Pacific Islander, 0.5% Two or more races, 0.7% Hispanic of any race; Average household size: 2.85; Median age: 37.5; Age under 18: 29.3%; Age 65 and over: 13.8%; Males per 100 females: 107.4

Housing: Homeownership rate: 86.1%; Homeowner vacancy rate: 1.8%; Rental vacancy rate: 4.2%

HARBOR HILLS (CDP). Covers a land area of 2.764 square miles and a water area of 0.729 square miles. Located at 39.94° N. Lat; 82.43° W. Long. Elevation is 928 feet.

Population: 1,509; Growth (since 2000): 15.8%; Density: 545.9 persons per square mile; Race: 98.6% White, 0.3% Black/African American, 0.1% Asian, 0.1% American Indian/Alaska Native, 0.0% Native Hawaiian/Other Pacific Islander, 0.9% Two or more races, 0.7% Hispanic of any race; Average household size: 2.25; Median age: 49.9; Age under 18: 17.2%; Age 65 and over: 22.3%; Males per 100 females: 101.7

Housing: Homeownership rate: 86.0%; Homeowner vacancy rate: 3.3%; Rental vacancy rate: 7.6%

HARTFORD (village). Covers a land area of 0.549 square miles and a water area of 0.004 square miles. Located at 40.24° N. Lat; 82.69° W. Long. Elevation is 1,168 feet.

Population: 397; Growth (since 2000): -3.6%; Density: 722.9 persons per square mile; Race: 99.0% White, 0.3% Black/African American, 0.5% Asian, 0.0% American Indian/Alaska Native, 0.0% Native Hawaiian/Other Pacific Islander, 0.0% Two or more races, 1.3% Hispanic of any race; Average household size: 2.63; Median age: 37.4; Age under 18: 26.2%; Age 65 and over: 15.6%; Males per 100 females: 91.8

Housing: Homeownership rate: 77.5%; Homeowner vacancy rate: 0.8%; Rental vacancy rate: 8.1%

HEATH (city). Covers a land area of 10.922 square miles and a water area of 0.078 square miles. Located at 40.02° N. Lat; 82.44° W. Long. Elevation is 860 feet.

History: Former Newark Air Force Base nearby that specialized in guidance of navigation systems; closed base scheduled for privatization.

Population: 10,310; Growth (since 2000): 20.9%; Density: 943.9 persons per square mile; Race: 93.7% White, 2.6% Black/African American, 0.7% Asian, 0.2% American Indian/Alaska Native, 0.0% Native Hawaiian/Other Pacific Islander, 2.2% Two or more races, 1.5% Hispanic of any race; Average household size: 2.45; Median age: 40.1; Age under 18: 24.3%; Age 65 and over: 16.9%; Males per 100 females: 91.9; Marriage status: 24.7% never married, 53.5% now married, 2.1% separated, 8.1% widowed, 13.7% divorced; Foreign born: 2.0%; Speak English only: 96.9%; With disability: 16.8%; Veterans: 12.6%; Ancestry: 28.2% German, 17.7% Irish, 13.2% American, 9.4% English, 5.2% Italian

Employment: 13.1% management, business, and financial, 2.3% computer, engineering, and science, 10.0% education, legal, community service, arts, and media, 6.3% healthcare practitioners, 17.0% service, 27.2% sales and office, 7.4% natural resources, construction, and maintenance, 16.6% production, transportation, and material moving

Income: Per capita: $24,598; Median household: $43,657; Average household: $57,172; Households with income of $100,000 or more: 14.5%; Poverty rate: 12.8%

Educational Attainment: High school diploma or higher: 87.7%; Bachelor's degree or higher: 17.9%; Graduate/professional degree or higher: 5.3%

School District(s)

Heath City (PK-12)
2012-13 Enrollment: 1,642 . . . . (740) 522-2816

Housing: Homeownership rate: 65.8%; Median home value: $129,600; Median year structure built: 1978; Homeowner vacancy rate: 2.8%; Median gross rent: $794 per month; Rental vacancy rate: 7.4%

Health Insurance: 89.5% have insurance; 70.4% have private insurance; 34.1% have public insurance; 10.5% do not have insurance; 4.5% of children under 18 do not have insurance

Safety: Violent crime rate: 19.2 per 10,000 population; Property crime rate: 575.4 per 10,000 population

Newspapers: Heath News (weekly circulation 4500)

Transportation: Commute: 93.4% car, 0.7% public transportation, 1.4% walk, 2.7% work from home; Median travel time to work: 21.5 minutes

HEBRON (village). Covers a land area of 3.065 square miles and a water area of 0.004 square miles. Located at 39.97° N. Lat; 82.49° W. Long. Elevation is 889 feet.

History: Hebron developed as a commercial center on the Ohio & Erie Canal and the old National Road.

Population: 2,336; Growth (since 2000): 14.8%; Density: 762.2 persons per square mile; Race: 96.4% White, 0.4% Black/African American, 0.5% Asian, 0.3% American Indian/Alaska Native, 0.2% Native Hawaiian/Other Pacific Islander, 2.0% Two or more races, 1.7% Hispanic of any race; Average household size: 2.39; Median age: 36.9; Age under 18: 25.4%; Age 65 and over: 13.7%; Males per 100 females: 88.1

School District(s)

Lakewood Digital Academy (01-12)
2012-13 Enrollment: 51. . . . . (740) 928-5878

Lakewood Local (PK-12)
2012-13 Enrollment: 1,965 . . . . (740) 928-5878

Housing: Homeownership rate: 60.0%; Homeowner vacancy rate: 2.2%; Rental vacancy rate: 6.8%

Safety: Violent crime rate: 4.2 per 10,000 population; Property crime rate: 140.2 per 10,000 population

Additional Information Contacts

Village of Hebron. . . . . (740) 928-2261
http://www.hebronvillage.com

JACKSONTOWN (unincorporated postal area)

ZCTA: 43030

Covers a land area of 0.092 square miles and a water area of 0 square miles. Located at 39.96° N. Lat; 82.42° W. Long. Elevation is 991 feet.

Population: 114; Growth (since 2000): n/a; Density: 1,236.1 persons per square mile; Race: 100.0% White, 0.0% Black/African American, 0.0% Asian, 0.0% American Indian/Alaska Native, 0.0% Native Hawaiian/Other Pacific Islander, 0.0% Two or more races, 0.0% Hispanic of any race; Average household size: 2.71; Median age: 40.3; Age under 18: 22.8%; Age 65 and over: 17.5%; Males per 100 females: 93.2

Housing: Homeownership rate: 66.6%; Homeowner vacancy rate: 0.0%; Rental vacancy rate: 12.5%

JOHNSTOWN (village). Covers a land area of 2.904 square miles and a water area of 0.009 square miles. Located at 40.15° N. Lat; 82.69° W. Long. Elevation is 1,158 feet.

History: Johnstown was the site of the discovery in 1926 of the skeleton of a mastodon. A farmer digging in his garden uncovered the bones of an animal that had been 8 feet tall and 15 feet long. The skeleton was purchased by the Cleveland Museum of Natural History.

Population: 4,632; Growth (since 2000): 34.7%; Density: 1,595.0 persons per square mile; Race: 97.1% White, 0.6% Black/African American, 0.5% Asian, 0.5% American Indian/Alaska Native, 0.0% Native Hawaiian/Other Pacific Islander, 0.9% Two or more races, 1.8% Hispanic of any race; Average household size: 2.42; Median age: 35.6; Age under 18: 26.7%;

Age 65 and over: 13.5%; Males per 100 females: 90.3; Marriage status: 31.3% never married, 57.9% now married, 3.9% separated, 3.9% widowed, 6.9% divorced; Foreign born: 4.7%; Speak English only: 92.6%; With disability: 11.7%; Veterans: 8.1%; Ancestry: 35.3% German, 28.1% Irish, 9.0% Italian, 8.6% English, 7.2% American
Employment: 17.0% management, business, and financial, 2.0% computer, engineering, and science, 8.3% education, legal, community service, arts, and media, 4.2% healthcare practitioners, 24.1% service, 22.4% sales and office, 9.9% natural resources, construction, and maintenance, 12.1% production, transportation, and material moving
Income: Per capita: $24,008; Median household: $60,714; Average household: $67,478; Households with income of $100,000 or more: 20.3%; Poverty rate: 8.7%
Educational Attainment: High school diploma or higher: 88.2%; Bachelor's degree or higher: 21.3%; Graduate/professional degree or higher: 9.4%

School District(s)

Johnstown-Monroe Local (PK-12)
2012-13 Enrollment: 1,578 . . . . (740) 967-6846
Northridge Local (PK-12)
2012-13 Enrollment: 1,255 . . . . (740) 967-6631

Housing: Homeownership rate: 59.4%; Median home value: $152,400; Median year structure built: 1969; Homeowner vacancy rate: 2.2%; Median gross rent: $677 per month; Rental vacancy rate: 5.0%
Health Insurance: 87.7% have insurance; 72.5% have private insurance; 24.4% have public insurance; 12.3% do not have insurance; 9.7% of children under 18 do not have insurance
Safety: Violent crime rate: 6.2 per 10,000 population; Property crime rate: 183.1 per 10,000 population
Newspapers: Johnstown Independent (weekly circulation 2400)
Transportation: Commute: 90.1% car, 0.7% public transportation, 2.7% walk, 6.5% work from home; Median travel time to work: 31.9 minutes

Additional Information Contacts

Village of Johnstown . . . . (740) 967-3177
http://www.villageofjohnstown.org

KIRKERSVILLE (village). Covers a land area of 2.237 square miles and a water area of <.001 square miles. Located at 39.95° N. Lat; 82.60° W. Long. Elevation is 935 feet.
Population: 525; Growth (since 2000): 1.0%; Density: 234.6 persons per square mile; Race: 94.5% White, 2.9% Black/African American, 1.1% Asian, 0.2% American Indian/Alaska Native, 0.0% Native Hawaiian/Other Pacific Islander, 1.0% Two or more races, 0.6% Hispanic of any race; Average household size: 2.58; Median age: 39.4; Age under 18: 22.7%; Age 65 and over: 9.9%; Males per 100 females: 106.7

School District(s)

Southwest Licking Local (PK-12)
2012-13 Enrollment: 3,751 . . . . (740) 927-3941

Housing: Homeownership rate: 73.7%; Homeowner vacancy rate: 0.7%; Rental vacancy rate: 17.7%

MARNE (CDP). Covers a land area of 0.884 square miles and a water area of 0.001 square miles. Located at 40.07° N. Lat; 82.30° W. Long. Elevation is 801 feet.
Population: 783; Growth (since 2000): n/a; Density: 885.6 persons per square mile; Race: 96.4% White, 0.6% Black/African American, 0.1% Asian, 0.1% American Indian/Alaska Native, 0.0% Native Hawaiian/Other Pacific Islander, 2.7% Two or more races, 2.2% Hispanic of any race; Average household size: 2.71; Median age: 39.4; Age under 18: 24.6%; Age 65 and over: 13.5%; Males per 100 females: 99.2
Housing: Homeownership rate: 83.0%; Homeowner vacancy rate: 0.8%; Rental vacancy rate: 9.3%

NEWARK (city). County seat. Covers a land area of 20.884 square miles and a water area of 0.486 square miles. Located at 40.07° N. Lat; 82.42° W. Long. Elevation is 833 feet.
History: In 1802, near the ancient mounds of a vanished people, General William Schenck platted a settlement and named it for his hometown in New Jersey. When Newark became the seat of Licking County in 1808, its citizens hammered together a one-room log cabin, with slab benches on a sawdust floor, as the courthouse. The canal came to Newark in 1832, and the population tripled, only to be cut again by a cholera epidemic in 1849. Natural gas discovered here in 1887 attracted iron and glass industries with its cheap fuel, and Newark again grew.
Population: 47,573; Growth (since 2000): 2.8%; Density: 2,278.0 persons per square mile; Race: 92.8% White, 3.3% Black/African American, 0.6% Asian, 0.3% American Indian/Alaska Native, 0.0% Native Hawaiian/Other Pacific Islander, 2.6% Two or more races, 1.2% Hispanic of any race; Average household size: 2.35; Median age: 37.3; Age under 18: 24.0%; Age 65 and over: 14.5%; Males per 100 females: 91.5; Marriage status: 29.0% never married, 47.9% now married, 2.3% separated, 7.7% widowed, 15.4% divorced; Foreign born: 1.1%; Speak English only: 97.7%; With disability: 17.5%; Veterans: 11.0%; Ancestry: 27.9% German, 16.1% Irish, 10.7% English, 10.1% American, 5.8% Italian
Employment: 10.0% management, business, and financial, 3.9% computer, engineering, and science, 9.1% education, legal, community service, arts, and media, 5.5% healthcare practitioners, 21.2% service, 26.8% sales and office, 7.7% natural resources, construction, and maintenance, 15.9% production, transportation, and material moving
Income: Per capita: $21,654; Median household: $38,295; Average household: $51,331; Households with income of $100,000 or more: 10.6%; Poverty rate: 21.0%
Educational Attainment: High school diploma or higher: 86.1%; Bachelor's degree or higher: 15.4%; Graduate/professional degree or higher: 4.1%

School District(s)

Career and Technology Educational Centers (09-12)
2012-13 Enrollment: n/a . . . . (740) 366-3351
Licking Valley Local (PK-12)
2012-13 Enrollment: 2,013 . . . . (740) 763-3525
Newark City (PK-12)
2012-13 Enrollment: 6,218 . . . . (740) 670-7000
Newark Digital Academy (KG-12)
2012-13 Enrollment: 269. . . . . (740) 328-2022
North Fork Local (PK-12)
2012-13 Enrollment: 1,614 . . . . (740) 892-3666
Par Excellence Academy (KG-05)
2012-13 Enrollment: 137. . . . . (740) 344-7279

Four-year College(s)

Ohio State University-Newark Campus (Public)
Fall 2013 Enrollment: 2,315 . . . . (740) 366-9333
2013-14 Tuition: In-state $7,140; Out-of-state $22,860

Two-year College(s)

Career and Technology Education Centers of Licking County (Public)
Fall 2013 Enrollment: 348 . . . . (740) 364-2333
Central Ohio Technical College (Public)
Fall 2013 Enrollment: 3,648 . . . . (740) 366-1351
2013-14 Tuition: In-state $4,296; Out-of-state $7,056

Housing: Homeownership rate: 56.4%; Median home value: $113,900; Median year structure built: 1961; Homeowner vacancy rate: 2.8%; Median gross rent: $667 per month; Rental vacancy rate: 10.3%
Health Insurance: 86.0% have insurance; 60.2% have private insurance; 38.1% have public insurance; 14.0% do not have insurance; 4.2% of children under 18 do not have insurance
Hospitals: Licking Memorial Hospital (195 beds)
Safety: Violent crime rate: 14.0 per 10,000 population; Property crime rate: 496.8 per 10,000 population
Newspapers: The Advocate (daily circulation 19400)
Transportation: Commute: 93.4% car, 0.2% public transportation, 2.2% walk, 2.6% work from home; Median travel time to work: 21.1 minutes
Airports: Newark-Heath (general aviation)

Additional Information Contacts

City of Newark . . . . (740) 670-7500
http://www.ci.newark.oh.us

PATASKALA (city). Covers a land area of 28.617 square miles and a water area of 0.096 square miles. Located at 40.01° N. Lat; 82.71° W. Long. Elevation is 1,001 feet.
Population: 14,962; Growth (since 2000): 46.0%; Density: 522.8 persons per square mile; Race: 90.0% White, 6.0% Black/African American, 0.7% Asian, 0.3% American Indian/Alaska Native, 0.0% Native Hawaiian/Other Pacific Islander, 2.5% Two or more races, 2.0% Hispanic of any race; Average household size: 2.66; Median age: 35.8; Age under 18: 27.6%; Age 65 and over: 10.6%; Males per 100 females: 96.5; Marriage status: 26.6% never married, 55.3% now married, 2.0% separated, 5.9% widowed, 12.3% divorced; Foreign born: 1.5%; Speak English only: 96.7%; With disability: 12.4%; Veterans: 12.0%; Ancestry: 31.6% German, 14.9% Irish, 11.9% American, 10.9% English, 8.6% Italian

Employment: 15.9% management, business, and financial, 3.4% computer, engineering, and science, 7.9% education, legal, community service, arts, and media, 5.8% healthcare practitioners, 17.0% service, 29.2% sales and office, 8.7% natural resources, construction, and maintenance, 12.2% production, transportation, and material moving
Income: Per capita: $27,586; Median household: $65,593; Average household: $73,250; Households with income of $100,000 or more: 19.2%; Poverty rate: 9.4%
Educational Attainment: High school diploma or higher: 91.3%; Bachelor's degree or higher: 28.1%; Graduate/professional degree or higher: 8.9%

School District(s)

Licking Heights Local (PK-12)
2012-13 Enrollment: 3,616 . . . . (740) 927-6926
Southwest Licking Digital Acad (01-12)
2012-13 Enrollment: 28. . . . . (740) 927-3941
Southwest Licking Local (PK-12)
2012-13 Enrollment: 3,751 . . . . (740) 927-3941

Housing: Homeownership rate: 77.2%; Median home value: $161,200; Median year structure built: 1992; Homeowner vacancy rate: 2.1%; Median gross rent: $887 per month; Rental vacancy rate: 7.7%
Health Insurance: 89.2% have insurance; 75.7% have private insurance; 25.6% have public insurance; 10.8% do not have insurance; 1.2% of children under 18 do not have insurance
Newspapers: Pataskala Post (weekly circulation 11100); Pataskala Standard (weekly circulation 5200)
Transportation: Commute: 94.2% car, 0.0% public transportation, 0.8% walk, 4.5% work from home; Median travel time to work: 25.3 minutes
Additional Information Contacts
City of Pataskala . . . . (740) 927-2021
http://www.ci.pataskala.oh.us

SAINT LOUISVILLE (village). Covers a land area of 0.249 square miles and a water area of 0 square miles. Located at 40.17° N. Lat; 82.42° W. Long. Elevation is 902 feet.
Population: 373; Growth (since 2000): 7.8%; Density: 1,498.3 persons per square mile; Race: 97.3% White, 0.3% Black/African American, 0.0% Asian, 1.1% American Indian/Alaska Native, 0.0% Native Hawaiian/Other Pacific Islander, 0.5% Two or more races, 0.8% Hispanic of any race; Average household size: 2.61; Median age: 36.1; Age under 18: 29.0%; Age 65 and over: 16.1%; Males per 100 females: 91.3
Housing: Homeownership rate: 79.7%; Homeowner vacancy rate: 0.9%; Rental vacancy rate: 0.0%

UTICA (village). Covers a land area of 1.691 square miles and a water area of 0.016 square miles. Located at 40.24° N. Lat; 82.44° W. Long. Elevation is 958 feet.
Population: 2,132; Growth (since 2000): 0.1%; Density: 1,261.0 persons per square mile; Race: 97.7% White, 0.5% Black/African American, 0.2% Asian, 0.1% American Indian/Alaska Native, 0.1% Native Hawaiian/Other Pacific Islander, 1.2% Two or more races, 0.9% Hispanic of any race; Average household size: 2.50; Median age: 37.4; Age under 18: 27.1%; Age 65 and over: 15.8%; Males per 100 females: 87.3

School District(s)

North Fork Local (PK-12)
2012-13 Enrollment: 1,614 . . . . (740) 892-3666

Housing: Homeownership rate: 62.4%; Homeowner vacancy rate: 1.1%; Rental vacancy rate: 13.9%
Safety: Violent crime rate: 14.1 per 10,000 population; Property crime rate: 333.5 per 10,000 population
Newspapers: Utica Herald (weekly circulation 2300)

Logan County

Located in west central Ohio; drained by the Great Miami and Mad Rivers; includes Campbell Hill, the highest point in the state (1,550 ft). Covers a land area of 458.429 square miles, a water area of 8.343 square miles, and is located in the Eastern Time Zone at 40.39° N. Lat., 83.77° W. Long. The county was founded in 1817. County seat is Bellefontaine.

Logan County is part of the Bellefontaine, OH Micropolitan Statistical Area. The entire metro area includes: Logan County, OH

Weather Station: Bellefontaine Elevation: 1,185 feet

	Jan	Feb	Mar	Apr	May	Jun	Jul	Aug	Sep	Oct	Nov	Dec
High	33	37	48	61	71	80	83	82	76	63	50	38
Low	18	20	28	39	50	59	63	61	54	42	33	23
Precip	2.6	2.1	2.9	3.6	4.1	4.4	4.2	3.6	2.8	2.6	3.2	3.0
Snow	na	3.2	1.2	0.2	0.0	0.0	0.0	0.0	0.0	0.2	0.4	2.5

High and Low temperatures in degrees Fahrenheit; Precipitation and Snow in inches

Population: 45,858; Growth (since 2000): -0.3%; Density: 100.0 persons per square mile; Race: 95.3% White, 1.6% Black/African American, 0.5% Asian, 0.3% American Indian/Alaska Native, 0.0% Native Hawaiian/Other Pacific Islander, 1.9% two or more races, 1.2% Hispanic of any race; Average household size: 2.51; Median age: 39.9; Age under 18: 25.3%; Age 65 and over: 14.7%; Males per 100 females: 97.2; Marriage status: 23.0% never married, 56.4% now married, 2.7% separated, 6.9% widowed, 13.7% divorced; Foreign born: 1.2%; Speak English only: 96.2%; With disability: 15.1%; Veterans: 10.1%; Ancestry: 29.7% German, 14.1% American, 14.1% Irish, 9.6% English, 3.5% Italian
Religion: Six largest groups: 7.2% Methodist/Pietist, 4.9% Catholicism, 4.8% Baptist, 3.4% European Free-Church, 2.8% Presbyterian-Reformed, 2.7% Holiness
Economy: Unemployment rate: 3.7%; Leading industries: 17.0% retail trade; 12.9% other services (except public administration); 11.3% accommodation and food services; Farms: 868 totaling 212,937 acres; Company size: 2 employ 1,000 or more persons, 2 employ 500 to 999 persons, 20 employ 100 to 499 persons, 847 employ less than 100 persons; Business ownership: 1,015 women-owned, n/a Black-owned, n/a Hispanic-owned, n/a Asian-owned
Employment: 11.4% management, business, and financial, 2.9% computer, engineering, and science, 8.4% education, legal, community service, arts, and media, 4.3% healthcare practitioners, 15.5% service, 20.9% sales and office, 11.5% natural resources, construction, and maintenance, 25.1% production, transportation, and material moving
Income: Per capita: $22,878; Median household: $47,542; Average household: $57,199; Households with income of $100,000 or more: 13.6%; Poverty rate: 15.9%
Educational Attainment: High school diploma or higher: 86.1%; Bachelor's degree or higher: 14.8%; Graduate/professional degree or higher: 5.5%
Housing: Homeownership rate: 73.4%; Median home value: $118,600; Median year structure built: 1969; Homeowner vacancy rate: 3.0%; Median gross rent: $700 per month; Rental vacancy rate: 10.0%
Vital Statistics: Birth rate: 114.8 per 10,000 population; Death rate: 106.9 per 10,000 population; Age-adjusted cancer mortality rate: 196.5 deaths per 100,000 population
Health Insurance: 85.7% have insurance; 66.8% have private insurance; 32.0% have public insurance; 14.3% do not have insurance; 9.3% of children under 18 do not have insurance
Health Care: Physicians: 10.8 per 10,000 population; Hospital beds: 21.9 per 10,000 population; Hospital admissions: 403.0 per 10,000 population
Transportation: Commute: 92.2% car, 0.3% public transportation, 2.3% walk, 3.8% work from home; Median travel time to work: 23.3 minutes
Presidential Election: 33.1% Obama, 64.9% Romney (2012)
National and State Parks: Fox Island State Park; Indian Lake State Park; Indian Lake State Wildlife Area
Additional Information Contacts
Logan Government . . . . (937) 599-7283
http://www.co.logan.oh.us

Logan County Communities

BELLE CENTER (village). Covers a land area of 0.695 square miles and a water area of 0.013 square miles. Located at 40.51° N. Lat; 83.75° W. Long. Elevation is 1,043 feet.
History: Belle Center developed as a rural trading village. A large butter and cheese plant was established here.
Population: 813; Growth (since 2000): 0.7%; Density: 1,170.0 persons per square mile; Race: 98.2% White, 0.1% Black/African American, 0.2% Asian, 0.1% American Indian/Alaska Native, 0.0% Native Hawaiian/Other Pacific Islander, 1.1% Two or more races, 0.6% Hispanic of any race; Average household size: 2.50; Median age: 37.2; Age under 18: 26.6%; Age 65 and over: 15.5%; Males per 100 females: 92.7
Housing: Homeownership rate: 81.6%; Homeowner vacancy rate: 2.9%; Rental vacancy rate: 1.6%

BELLEFONTAINE (city). County seat. Covers a land area of 10.036 square miles and a water area of 0 square miles. Located at 40.36° N. Lat; 83.76° W. Long. Elevation is 1,243 feet.
History: Bellefontaine was settled in 1806, and became the seat of Logan County in 1820. The name means "beautiful fountain," referring to the natural springs at the site.
Population: 13,370; Growth (since 2000): 2.3%; Density: 1,332.2 persons per square mile; Race: 90.1% White, 4.3% Black/African American, 1.2% Asian, 0.2% American Indian/Alaska Native, 0.0% Native Hawaiian/Other Pacific Islander, 3.7% Two or more races, 1.9% Hispanic of any race; Average household size: 2.44; Median age: 34.8; Age under 18: 27.1%; Age 65 and over: 12.8%; Males per 100 females: 93.9; Marriage status: 27.4% never married, 48.3% now married, 5.3% separated, 8.3% widowed, 16.0% divorced; Foreign born: 2.0%; Speak English only: 96.1%; With disability: 19.5%; Veterans: 7.4%; Ancestry: 27.9% German, 15.1% American, 14.6% Irish, 9.1% English, 6.3% Italian
Employment: 8.2% management, business, and financial, 3.7% computer, engineering, and science, 11.6% education, legal, community service, arts, and media, 6.3% healthcare practitioners, 16.2% service, 18.4% sales and office, 9.2% natural resources, construction, and maintenance, 26.4% production, transportation, and material moving
Income: Per capita: $20,669; Median household: $39,821; Average household: $51,085; Households with income of $100,000 or more: 10.8%; Poverty rate: 24.3%
Educational Attainment: High school diploma or higher: 83.2%; Bachelor's degree or higher: 16.0%; Graduate/professional degree or higher: 7.0%

School District(s)

Bellefontaine City (KG-12)
2012-13 Enrollment: 2,534 . . . . (937) 593-9060
Benjamin Logan Local (KG-12)
2012-13 Enrollment: 1,729 . . . . (937) 593-9211
Ohio Hi-Point Career Center (07-12)
2012-13 Enrollment: n/a . . . . (937) 599-3010

Vocational/Technical School(s)

Ohio Hi Point Joint Vocational School District (Public)
Fall 2013 Enrollment: 32 . . . . (937) 599-3010
2013-14 Tuition: $11,170

Housing: Homeownership rate: 56.0%; Median home value: $100,500; Median year structure built: 1962; Homeowner vacancy rate: 3.3%; Median gross rent: $711 per month; Rental vacancy rate: 10.8%
Health Insurance: 86.5% have insurance; 57.7% have private insurance; 42.1% have public insurance; 13.5% do not have insurance; 1.0% of children under 18 do not have insurance
Hospitals: Mary Rutan Hospital (105 beds)
Safety: Violent crime rate: 34.2 per 10,000 population; Property crime rate: 442.7 per 10,000 population
Newspapers: Bellefontaine Examiner (daily circulation 8900)
Transportation: Commute: 94.3% car, 0.5% public transportation, 1.8% walk, 2.7% work from home; Median travel time to work: 20.2 minutes
Airports: Bellefontaine Regional (general aviation)
Additional Information Contacts
City of Bellefontaine . . . . (937) 592-4376
http://www.ci.bellefontaine.oh.us

CHIPPEWA PARK (CDP). Covers a land area of 0.440 square miles and a water area of 0.053 square miles. Located at 40.52° N. Lat; 83.89° W. Long. Elevation is 1,014 feet.
Population: 891; Growth (since 2000): n/a; Density: 2,024.0 persons per square mile; Race: 98.0% White, 0.2% Black/African American, 0.2% Asian, 0.2% American Indian/Alaska Native, 0.0% Native Hawaiian/Other Pacific Islander, 1.2% Two or more races, 1.3% Hispanic of any race; Average household size: 2.03; Median age: 50.6; Age under 18: 15.7%; Age 65 and over: 23.0%; Males per 100 females: 106.3
Housing: Homeownership rate: 73.6%; Homeowner vacancy rate: 3.0%; Rental vacancy rate: 12.3%

DE GRAFF (village). Covers a land area of 1.010 square miles and a water area of 0 square miles. Located at 40.31° N. Lat; 83.92° W. Long. Elevation is 1,001 feet.
History: Sometimes spelled Degraff.
Population: 1,285; Growth (since 2000): 6.0%; Density: 1,272.0 persons per square mile; Race: 97.5% White, 0.9% Black/African American, 0.2% Asian, 0.3% American Indian/Alaska Native, 0.2% Native Hawaiian/Other Pacific Islander, 0.7% Two or more races, 0.2% Hispanic of any race; Average household size: 2.70; Median age: 34.8; Age under 18: 30.7%; Age 65 and over: 12.9%; Males per 100 females: 95.6

School District(s)

Riverside Local (PK-12)
2012-13 Enrollment: 685. . . . . (937) 585-5981

Housing: Homeownership rate: 75.2%; Homeowner vacancy rate: 3.5%; Rental vacancy rate: 10.6%

EAST LIBERTY (CDP). Covers a land area of 1.577 square miles and a water area of 0 square miles. Located at 40.33° N. Lat; 83.59° W. Long. Elevation is 1,135 feet.
Population: 366; Growth (since 2000): n/a; Density: 232.0 persons per square mile; Race: 98.6% White, 0.0% Black/African American, 0.0% Asian, 0.5% American Indian/Alaska Native, 0.0% Native Hawaiian/Other Pacific Islander, 0.0% Two or more races, 1.6% Hispanic of any race; Average household size: 2.58; Median age: 41.4; Age under 18: 22.7%; Age 65 and over: 15.3%; Males per 100 females: 95.7
Housing: Homeownership rate: 81.0%; Homeowner vacancy rate: 0.0%; Rental vacancy rate: 18.2%

HUNTSVILLE (village). Covers a land area of 0.302 square miles and a water area of 0 square miles. Located at 40.44° N. Lat; 83.80° W. Long. Elevation is 1,076 feet.
Population: 431; Growth (since 2000): -5.1%; Density: 1,425.4 persons per square mile; Race: 98.4% White, 0.5% Black/African American, 0.0% Asian, 0.0% American Indian/Alaska Native, 0.0% Native Hawaiian/Other Pacific Islander, 0.7% Two or more races, 0.9% Hispanic of any race; Average household size: 2.71; Median age: 35.6; Age under 18: 30.9%; Age 65 and over: 13.9%; Males per 100 females: 93.3
Housing: Homeownership rate: 69.1%; Homeowner vacancy rate: 3.5%; Rental vacancy rate: 19.7%
Additional Information Contacts
Village of Huntsville . . . . (937) 686-7275
http://huntsvilleohio.com

LAKEVIEW (village). Covers a land area of 0.707 square miles and a water area of 0.005 square miles. Located at 40.49° N. Lat; 83.93° W. Long. Elevation is 991 feet.
History: Lakeview developed as a resort on Indian Lake.
Population: 1,072; Growth (since 2000): -0.2%; Density: 1,515.3 persons per square mile; Race: 97.2% White, 0.7% Black/African American, 0.1% Asian, 0.3% American Indian/Alaska Native, 0.1% Native Hawaiian/Other Pacific Islander, 1.2% Two or more races, 1.0% Hispanic of any race; Average household size: 2.39; Median age: 39.8; Age under 18: 23.2%; Age 65 and over: 14.7%; Males per 100 females: 92.5
Housing: Homeownership rate: 74.4%; Homeowner vacancy rate: 7.3%; Rental vacancy rate: 11.5%

LEWISTOWN (CDP). Covers a land area of 0.768 square miles and a water area of 0 square miles. Located at 40.42° N. Lat; 83.88° W. Long. Elevation is 1,014 feet.
Population: 222; Growth (since 2000): n/a; Density: 289.2 persons per square mile; Race: 99.1% White, 0.0% Black/African American, 0.0% Asian, 0.0% American Indian/Alaska Native, 0.0% Native Hawaiian/Other Pacific Islander, 0.9% Two or more races, 0.0% Hispanic of any race; Average household size: 2.96; Median age: 35.3; Age under 18: 30.6%; Age 65 and over: 7.2%; Males per 100 females: 93.0

School District(s)

Indian Lake Local (KG-12)
2012-13 Enrollment: 1,676 . . . . (937) 686-8601

Housing: Homeownership rate: 86.6%; Homeowner vacancy rate: 2.9%; Rental vacancy rate: 0.0%

QUINCY (village). Covers a land area of 1.132 square miles and a water area of 0 square miles. Located at 40.30° N. Lat; 83.97° W. Long. Elevation is 1,056 feet.
Population: 706; Growth (since 2000): -3.8%; Density: 623.5 persons per square mile; Race: 96.5% White, 0.3% Black/African American, 0.1% Asian, 0.4% American Indian/Alaska Native, 0.0% Native Hawaiian/Other Pacific Islander, 2.4% Two or more races, 0.6% Hispanic of any race; Average household size: 2.94; Median age: 33.2; Age under 18: 31.3%; Age 65 and over: 8.4%; Males per 100 females: 99.4
Housing: Homeownership rate: 67.5%; Homeowner vacancy rate: 5.2%; Rental vacancy rate: 9.2%

RUSHSYLVANIA (village). Covers a land area of 0.784 square miles and a water area of 0 square miles. Located at 40.46° N. Lat; 83.67° W. Long. Elevation is 1,243 feet.
Population: 516; Growth (since 2000): -5.0%; Density: 658.3 persons per square mile; Race: 96.5% White, 0.0% Black/African American, 0.6% Asian, 0.8% American Indian/Alaska Native, 0.0% Native Hawaiian/Other Pacific Islander, 1.6% Two or more races, 0.6% Hispanic of any race; Average household size: 2.66; Median age: 37.3; Age under 18: 27.9%; Age 65 and over: 12.0%; Males per 100 females: 94.0
Housing: Homeownership rate: 77.9%; Homeowner vacancy rate: 6.2%; Rental vacancy rate: 2.3%

RUSSELLS POINT (village). Covers a land area of 0.932 square miles and a water area of 0.079 square miles. Located at 40.47° N. Lat; 83.89° W. Long. Elevation is 1,004 feet.
History: Russells Point developed as a resort and vacation center on Indian Lake.
Population: 1,391; Growth (since 2000): -14.1%; Density: 1,492.4 persons per square mile; Race: 97.3% White, 0.6% Black/African American, 0.1% Asian, 0.2% American Indian/Alaska Native, 0.0% Native Hawaiian/Other Pacific Islander, 1.3% Two or more races, 1.1% Hispanic of any race; Average household size: 2.25; Median age: 38.0; Age under 18: 25.7%; Age 65 and over: 16.9%; Males per 100 females: 94.5
Housing: Homeownership rate: 52.4%; Homeowner vacancy rate: 10.2%; Rental vacancy rate: 13.2%

VALLEY HI (village). Covers a land area of 0.617 square miles and a water area of 0 square miles. Located at 40.32° N. Lat; 83.68° W. Long. Elevation is 1,270 feet.
Population: 212; Growth (since 2000): -13.1%; Density: 343.9 persons per square mile; Race: 95.8% White, 1.4% Black/African American, 0.0% Asian, 0.9% American Indian/Alaska Native, 0.0% Native Hawaiian/Other Pacific Islander, 1.4% Two or more races, 3.3% Hispanic of any race; Average household size: 2.44; Median age: 32.0; Age under 18: 25.9%; Age 65 and over: 6.6%; Males per 100 females: 107.8
Housing: Homeownership rate: 33.3%; Homeowner vacancy rate: 14.7%; Rental vacancy rate: 23.7%

WEST LIBERTY (village). Covers a land area of 1.120 square miles and a water area of 0 square miles. Located at 40.26° N. Lat; 83.76° W. Long. Elevation is 1,086 feet.
History: West Liberty developed as a rural trading center around a milk plant, a flour mill, and grain elevators.
Population: 1,805; Growth (since 2000): -0.4%; Density: 1,611.1 persons per square mile; Race: 96.1% White, 1.3% Black/African American, 0.6% Asian, 0.1% American Indian/Alaska Native, 0.1% Native Hawaiian/Other Pacific Islander, 1.7% Two or more races, 0.8% Hispanic of any race; Average household size: 2.26; Median age: 41.0; Age under 18: 25.2%; Age 65 and over: 23.2%; Males per 100 females: 80.5

School District(s)

West Liberty-Salem Local (PK-12)
2012-13 Enrollment: 1,231 . . . . (937) 465-1075
Housing: Homeownership rate: 61.4%; Homeowner vacancy rate: 1.3%; Rental vacancy rate: 7.7%
Safety: Violent crime rate: 11.2 per 10,000 population; Property crime rate: 56.1 per 10,000 population

WEST MANSFIELD (village). Covers a land area of 0.834 square miles and a water area of 0.025 square miles. Located at 40.40° N. Lat; 83.54° W. Long. Elevation is 1,089 feet.
Population: 682; Growth (since 2000): -2.6%; Density: 817.3 persons per square mile; Race: 96.6% White, 0.9% Black/African American, 0.1% Asian, 0.1% American Indian/Alaska Native, 0.0% Native Hawaiian/Other Pacific Islander, 2.2% Two or more races, 0.1% Hispanic of any race; Average household size: 2.52; Median age: 36.0; Age under 18: 26.2%; Age 65 and over: 14.5%; Males per 100 females: 100.0
Housing: Homeownership rate: 78.9%; Homeowner vacancy rate: 5.7%; Rental vacancy rate: 7.9%

ZANESFIELD (village). Covers a land area of 0.106 square miles and a water area of 0 square miles. Located at 40.34° N. Lat; 83.68° W. Long. Elevation is 1,171 feet.
History: Zanesfield was settled in 1819 on the site of a blockhouse built by the English during the French and Indian War. The land once belonged to Isaac Zane, who was adopted by the Wyandot tribe when he was nine years old, and married the daughter of Chief Tarhe. He was known as White Eagle.
Population: 197; Growth (since 2000): -10.5%; Density: 1,855.8 persons per square mile; Race: 96.4% White, 2.0% Black/African American, 0.0% Asian, 0.0% American Indian/Alaska Native, 1.0% Native Hawaiian/Other Pacific Islander, 0.5% Two or more races, 0.0% Hispanic of any race; Average household size: 2.24; Median age: 42.4; Age under 18: 22.8%; Age 65 and over: 14.2%; Males per 100 females: 77.5
Housing: Homeownership rate: 71.6%; Homeowner vacancy rate: 1.5%; Rental vacancy rate: 7.1%

Lorain County

Located in northern Ohio; bounded on the north by Lake Erie; drained by the Black and Vermilion Rivers. Covers a land area of 491.101 square miles, a water area of 432.230 square miles, and is located in the Eastern Time Zone at 41.44° N. Lat., 82.18° W. Long. The county was founded in 1822. County seat is Elyria.

Lorain County is part of the Cleveland-Elyria, OH Metropolitan Statistical Area. The entire metro area includes: Cuyahoga County, OH; Geauga County, OH; Lake County, OH; Lorain County, OH; Medina County, OH

Weather Station: Elyria 3 E — Elevation: 729 feet

	Jan	Feb	Mar	Apr	May	Jun	Jul	Aug	Sep	Oct	Nov	Dec
High	35	39	48	61	72	81	85	83	76	64	52	39
Low	21	22	29	39	49	59	63	62	55	44	36	25
Precip	2.6	2.3	2.8	3.4	3.7	3.8	3.8	3.8	3.7	3.1	3.3	3.2
Snow	11.6	9.0	7.2	2.2	tr	tr	0.0	0.0	0.0	tr	2.4	8.6

High and Low temperatures in degrees Fahrenheit; Precipitation and Snow in inches

Weather Station: Oberlin — Elevation: 815 feet

	Jan	Feb	Mar	Apr	May	Jun	Jul	Aug	Sep	Oct	Nov	Dec
High	34	37	46	59	70	79	83	81	75	63	50	38
Low	18	19	27	37	47	57	61	59	52	41	33	23
Precip	2.5	2.1	2.7	3.4	3.9	3.7	3.9	3.4	3.3	2.9	3.1	2.8
Snow	13.3	10.0	8.6	2.2	tr	0.0	0.0	0.0	0.0	tr	2.1	9.6

High and Low temperatures in degrees Fahrenheit; Precipitation and Snow in inches

Population: 301,356; Growth (since 2000): 5.9%; Density: 613.6 persons per square mile; Race: 84.8% White, 8.6% Black/African American, 0.9% Asian, 0.3% American Indian/Alaska Native, 0.0% Native Hawaiian/Other Pacific Islander, 3.0% two or more races, 8.4% Hispanic of any race; Average household size: 2.51; Median age: 40.0; Age under 18: 23.9%; Age 65 and over: 14.3%; Males per 100 females: 96.7; Marriage status: 29.5% never married, 52.6% now married, 1.8% separated, 6.4% widowed, 11.5% divorced; Foreign born: 2.9%; Speak English only: 92.3%; With disability: 13.7%; Veterans: 10.3%; Ancestry: 25.8% German, 16.5% Irish, 10.4% English, 8.7% Italian, 8.3% Polish
Religion: Six largest groups: 24.4% Catholicism, 4.9% Non-denominational Protestant, 4.2% Baptist, 2.9% Methodist/Pietist, 2.6% Presbyterian-Reformed, 1.8% Lutheran
Economy: Unemployment rate: 6.3%; Leading industries: 14.7% retail trade; 11.6% other services (except public administration); 11.1% health care and social assistance; Farms: 768 totaling 122,692 acres; Company size: 5 employ 1,000 or more persons, 5 employ 500 to 999 persons, 122 employ 100 to 499 persons, 5,441 employs less than 100 persons; Business ownership: 5,608 women-owned, n/a Black-owned, 391 Hispanic-owned, 385 Asian-owned
Employment: 13.1% management, business, and financial, 4.2% computer, engineering, and science, 9.6% education, legal, community service, arts, and media, 6.1% healthcare practitioners, 18.5% service, 24.3% sales and office, 7.9% natural resources, construction, and maintenance, 16.2% production, transportation, and material moving
Income: Per capita: $26,030; Median household: $51,816; Average household: $65,972; Households with income of $100,000 or more: 19.2%; Poverty rate: 14.6%
Educational Attainment: High school diploma or higher: 88.8%; Bachelor's degree or higher: 22.2%; Graduate/professional degree or higher: 8.2%
Housing: Homeownership rate: 72.9%; Median home value: $140,700; Median year structure built: 1969; Homeowner vacancy rate: 2.4%; Median gross rent: $733 per month; Rental vacancy rate: 11.6%
Vital Statistics: Birth rate: 112.5 per 10,000 population; Death rate: 90.1 per 10,000 population; Age-adjusted cancer mortality rate: 181.0 deaths per 100,000 population

Health Insurance: 90.3% have insurance; 72.1% have private insurance; 31.9% have public insurance; 9.7% do not have insurance; 3.4% of children under 18 do not have insurance
Health Care: Physicians: 16.6 per 10,000 population; Hospital beds: 19.2 per 10,000 population; Hospital admissions: 985.3 per 10,000 population
Air Quality Index: 84.8% good, 15.2% moderate, 0.0% unhealthy for sensitive individuals, 0.0% unhealthy (percent of days)
Transportation: Commute: 92.8% car, 0.8% public transportation, 2.2% walk, 3.0% work from home; Median travel time to work: 24.3 minutes
Presidential Election: 56.4% Obama, 41.9% Romney (2012)
National and State Parks: Black River State Reservation; Findley State Park; French Creek State Reservation
Additional Information Contacts
Lorain Government . . . . (440) 329-5000
http://www.loraincounty.us

Lorain County Communities

AMHERST (city). Covers a land area of 7.062 square miles and a water area of 0.059 square miles. Located at 41.41° N. Lat; 82.23° W. Long. Elevation is 689 feet.
History: Named for Baron Jeffrey Amherst (1717-1797), British general in the French and Indian Wars. Amherst grew around an extensive sandstone quarry.
Population: 12,021; Growth (since 2000): 1.9%; Density: 1,702.2 persons per square mile; Race: 95.7% White, 0.7% Black/African American, 0.7% Asian, 0.2% American Indian/Alaska Native, 0.0% Native Hawaiian/Other Pacific Islander, 1.7% Two or more races, 5.3% Hispanic of any race; Average household size: 2.50; Median age: 45.0; Age under 18: 22.1%; Age 65 and over: 17.8%; Males per 100 females: 93.4; Marriage status: 25.1% never married, 56.7% now married, 0.6% separated, 7.0% widowed, 11.2% divorced; Foreign born: 2.5%; Speak English only: 96.3%; With disability: 11.4%; Veterans: 11.2%; Ancestry: 38.6% German, 15.6% Irish, 11.9% Polish, 10.9% English, 7.5% Italian
Employment: 12.8% management, business, and financial, 5.6% computer, engineering, and science, 9.9% education, legal, community service, arts, and media, 6.6% healthcare practitioners, 15.7% service, 30.2% sales and office, 7.5% natural resources, construction, and maintenance, 11.6% production, transportation, and material moving
Income: Per capita: $28,708; Median household: $63,895; Average household: $75,310; Households with income of $100,000 or more: 30.0%; Poverty rate: 7.9%
Educational Attainment: High school diploma or higher: 92.6%; Bachelor's degree or higher: 26.0%; Graduate/professional degree or higher: 11.0%

School District(s)

Amherst Exempted Village (PK-12)
2012-13 Enrollment: 3,921 . . . . (440) 988-4406
Housing: Homeownership rate: 84.5%; Median home value: $153,700; Median year structure built: 1969; Homeowner vacancy rate: 1.9%; Median gross rent: $746 per month; Rental vacancy rate: 9.3%
Health Insurance: 93.9% have insurance; 80.9% have private insurance; 29.4% have public insurance; 6.1% do not have insurance; 3.4% of children under 18 do not have insurance
Safety: Violent crime rate: 7.5 per 10,000 population; Property crime rate: 181.9 per 10,000 population
Newspapers: Amherst News Times (weekly circulation 2500)
Transportation: Commute: 94.6% car, 0.1% public transportation, 0.4% walk, 4.1% work from home; Median travel time to work: 20.6 minutes
Additional Information Contacts
City of Amherst . . . . (440) 988-4380
http://www.amherstohio.org

AVON (city). Covers a land area of 20.808 square miles and a water area of 0.057 square miles. Located at 41.45° N. Lat; 82.01° W. Long. Elevation is 669 feet.
History: Named for Avon, New York. Settled c.1814. Incorporated 1918.
Population: 21,193; Growth (since 2000): 85.2%; Density: 1,018.5 persons per square mile; Race: 92.4% White, 2.3% Black/African American, 3.1% Asian, 0.1% American Indian/Alaska Native, 0.0% Native Hawaiian/Other Pacific Islander, 1.4% Two or more races, 3.4% Hispanic of any race; Average household size: 2.76; Median age: 38.4; Age under 18: 30.5%; Age 65 and over: 12.6%; Males per 100 females: 93.8; Marriage status: 19.5% never married, 64.4% now married, 0.7% separated, 6.2% widowed, 9.9% divorced; Foreign born: 5.5%; Speak English only: 90.7%; With disability: 8.1%; Veterans: 9.1%; Ancestry: 31.9% German, 22.7% Irish, 13.6% English, 11.0% Italian, 9.5% Polish
Employment: 24.0% management, business, and financial, 7.7% computer, engineering, and science, 13.2% education, legal, community service, arts, and media, 8.3% healthcare practitioners, 13.7% service, 23.5% sales and office, 2.9% natural resources, construction, and maintenance, 6.6% production, transportation, and material moving
Income: Per capita: $41,876; Median household: $82,603; Average household: $113,883; Households with income of $100,000 or more: 42.0%; Poverty rate: 4.5%
Educational Attainment: High school diploma or higher: 96.0%; Bachelor's degree or higher: 51.3%; Graduate/professional degree or higher: 21.0%

School District(s)

Avon Local (PK-12)
2012-13 Enrollment: 4,096 . . . . (440) 937-4680

Vocational/Technical School(s)

Reflexology Certification Institute (Private, For-profit)
Fall 2013 Enrollment: n/a . . . . (614) 565-1047
Housing: Homeownership rate: 84.2%; Median home value: $249,100; Median year structure built: 1998; Homeowner vacancy rate: 1.6%; Median gross rent: $1,145 per month; Rental vacancy rate: 8.9%
Health Insurance: 96.0% have insurance; 90.4% have private insurance; 18.7% have public insurance; 4.0% do not have insurance; 0.7% of children under 18 do not have insurance
Transportation: Commute: 91.7% car, 1.3% public transportation, 0.7% walk, 5.6% work from home; Median travel time to work: 25.9 minutes
Additional Information Contacts
City of Avon. . . . . (440) 937-7800
http://www.cityofavon.com

AVON LAKE (city). Covers a land area of 11.129 square miles and a water area of 0 square miles. Located at 41.49° N. Lat; 82.02° W. Long. Elevation is 610 feet.
History: Named for Avon New York, which was named for the river in England. Avon Lake developed as a vacation area, with beaches for water sports.
Population: 22,581; Growth (since 2000): 24.4%; Density: 2,029.0 persons per square mile; Race: 95.7% White, 1.1% Black/African American, 1.3% Asian, 0.1% American Indian/Alaska Native, 0.0% Native Hawaiian/Other Pacific Islander, 1.4% Two or more races, 2.4% Hispanic of any race; Average household size: 2.53; Median age: 41.9; Age under 18: 26.2%; Age 65 and over: 14.5%; Males per 100 females: 93.3; Marriage status: 22.1% never married, 61.4% now married, 0.5% separated, 6.9% widowed, 9.6% divorced; Foreign born: 4.2%; Speak English only: 93.7%; With disability: 10.1%; Veterans: 10.2%; Ancestry: 28.9% German, 24.1% Irish, 13.6% English, 12.2% Italian, 8.0% Polish
Employment: 24.2% management, business, and financial, 3.5% computer, engineering, and science, 13.8% education, legal, community service, arts, and media, 7.4% healthcare practitioners, 12.2% service, 28.2% sales and office, 4.5% natural resources, construction, and maintenance, 6.2% production, transportation, and material moving
Income: Per capita: $40,049; Median household: $80,271; Average household: $100,905; Households with income of $100,000 or more: 38.3%; Poverty rate: 4.6%
Educational Attainment: High school diploma or higher: 96.7%; Bachelor's degree or higher: 50.1%; Graduate/professional degree or higher: 18.8%

School District(s)

Avon Lake City (PK-12)
2012-13 Enrollment: 3,766 . . . . (440) 933-6210
Housing: Homeownership rate: 82.2%; Median home value: $213,300; Median year structure built: 1986; Homeowner vacancy rate: 2.6%; Median gross rent: $1,052 per month; Rental vacancy rate: 6.6%
Health Insurance: 95.8% have insurance; 89.8% have private insurance; 19.5% have public insurance; 4.2% do not have insurance; 1.1% of children under 18 do not have insurance
Newspapers: North Ridgeville Press (weekly circulation 3500); The Press (weekly circulation 9000); West Life (weekly circulation 7500)
Transportation: Commute: 92.1% car, 1.1% public transportation, 2.0% walk, 3.6% work from home; Median travel time to work: 26.3 minutes
Additional Information Contacts
City of Avon Lake . . . . (440) 933-6141
http://www.avonlake.org

COLUMBIA STATION (unincorporated postal area)

ZCTA: 44028

Covers a land area of 33.199 square miles and a water area of 0.220 square miles. Located at 41.30° N. Lat; 81.94° W. Long. Elevation is 804 feet.

Population: 8,467; Growth (since 2000): -17.0%; Density: 255.0 persons per square mile; Race: 97.7% White, 0.4% Black/African American, 0.5% Asian, 0.3% American Indian/Alaska Native, 0.0% Native Hawaiian/Other Pacific Islander, 0.8% Two or more races, 1.7% Hispanic of any race; Average household size: 2.70; Median age: 45.5; Age under 18: 21.1%; Age 65 and over: 14.6%; Males per 100 females: 105.1; Marriage status: 23.9% never married, 60.5% now married, 1.6% separated, 5.3% widowed, 10.3% divorced; Foreign born: 1.9%; Speak English only: 96.9%; With disability: 9.6%; Veterans: 10.1%; Ancestry: 35.5% German, 21.5% Irish, 14.3% English, 10.3% American, 9.3% Polish

Employment: 17.4% management, business, and financial, 3.6% computer, engineering, and science, 5.6% education, legal, community service, arts, and media, 4.4% healthcare practitioners, 16.0% service, 24.2% sales and office, 12.0% natural resources, construction, and maintenance, 16.8% production, transportation, and material moving

Income: Per capita: $30,338; Median household: $69,007; Average household: $81,571; Households with income of $100,000 or more: 26.0%; Poverty rate: 6.0%

Educational Attainment: High school diploma or higher: 90.9%; Bachelor's degree or higher: 19.3%; Graduate/professional degree or higher: 5.6%

School District(s)

Columbia Local (PK-12)
2012-13 Enrollment: 904. . . . . (440) 236-5008

Housing: Homeownership rate: 90.2%; Median home value: $180,800; Median year structure built: 1969; Homeowner vacancy rate: 1.1%; Median gross rent: $994 per month; Rental vacancy rate: 6.7%

Health Insurance: 92.4% have insurance; 82.5% have private insurance; 22.3% have public insurance; 7.6% do not have insurance; 3.1% of children under 18 do not have insurance

Newspapers: The Rural-Urban Record (weekly circulation 10000)

Transportation: Commute: 88.9% car, 0.5% public transportation, 1.7% walk, 8.0% work from home; Median travel time to work: 26.8 minutes

EATON ESTATES (CDP). Covers a land area of 0.869 square miles and a water area of 0.003 square miles. Located at 41.30° N. Lat; 82.01° W. Long. Elevation is 801 feet.

Population: 1,222; Growth (since 2000): -13.3%; Density: 1,405.4 persons per square mile; Race: 96.6% White, 0.7% Black/African American, 0.2% Asian, 0.5% American Indian/Alaska Native, 0.0% Native Hawaiian/Other Pacific Islander, 1.6% Two or more races, 2.0% Hispanic of any race; Average household size: 2.81; Median age: 38.2; Age under 18: 24.7%; Age 65 and over: 10.8%; Males per 100 females: 103.0

Housing: Homeownership rate: 83.2%; Homeowner vacancy rate: 3.9%; Rental vacancy rate: 3.9%

ELYRIA (city). County seat. Covers a land area of 20.571 square miles and a water area of 0.274 square miles. Located at 41.37° N. Lat; 82.11° W. Long. Elevation is 738 feet.

History: Named for Herman Ely (1775-1852), merchant and founder of the town. Settlement at Elyria began in 1817 when Heman Ely, a New Englander, acquired land around the falls of the Black River and built a dam, grist mill, sawmill, and house. Novelist Sherwood Anderson managed a paint factory in Elyria before he became a writer.

Population: 54,533; Growth (since 2000): -2.5%; Density: 2,650.9 persons per square mile; Race: 78.1% White, 15.5% Black/African American, 0.8% Asian, 0.3% American Indian/Alaska Native, 0.0% Native Hawaiian/Other Pacific Islander, 4.1% Two or more races, 4.9% Hispanic of any race; Average household size: 2.39; Median age: 38.1; Age under 18: 24.2%; Age 65 and over: 14.3%; Males per 100 females: 91.6; Marriage status: 34.4% never married, 47.3% now married, 2.6% separated, 6.2% widowed, 12.1% divorced; Foreign born: 1.6%; Speak English only: 96.3%; With disability: 15.8%; Veterans: 10.7%; Ancestry: 25.4% German, 14.2% Irish, 9.6% English, 8.1% American, 7.9% Polish

Employment: 9.6% management, business, and financial, 3.9% computer, engineering, and science, 8.2% education, legal, community service, arts, and media, 5.6% healthcare practitioners, 21.7% service, 23.9% sales and office, 7.6% natural resources, construction, and maintenance, 19.5% production, transportation, and material moving

Income: Per capita: $21,276; Median household: $41,600; Average household: $49,873; Households with income of $100,000 or more: 9.7%; Poverty rate: 18.8%

Educational Attainment: High school diploma or higher: 87.9%; Bachelor's degree or higher: 15.0%; Graduate/professional degree or higher: 5.4%

School District(s)

Constellation Schools: Elyria Community Elementary (KG-07)
2012-13 Enrollment: 461. . . . . (440) 366-5225
Elyria City Schools (PK-12)
2012-13 Enrollment: 6,547 . . . . (440) 284-8201
Life Skills Center of Elyria (09-12)
2012-13 Enrollment: 145. . . . . (440) 324-1755

Two-year College(s)

Lorain County Community College (Public)
Fall 2013 Enrollment: 12,274 . . . . (440) 366-5222
2013-14 Tuition: In-state $3,558; Out-of-state $7,059

Housing: Homeownership rate: 60.9%; Median home value: $100,400; Median year structure built: 1965; Homeowner vacancy rate: 3.0%; Median gross rent: $718 per month; Rental vacancy rate: 13.3%

Health Insurance: 87.8% have insurance; 63.9% have private insurance; 38.2% have public insurance; 12.2% do not have insurance; 3.0% of children under 18 do not have insurance

Hospitals: University Hospitals - Elyria Medical Center (348 beds)

Newspapers: Chronicle-Telegram (daily circulation 24400)

Transportation: Commute: 94.6% car, 0.7% public transportation, 1.0% walk, 2.1% work from home; Median travel time to work: 21.9 minutes; Amtrak: Train service available.

Additional Information Contacts

City of Elyria . . . . (440) 326-1500
http://www.cityofelyria.org

GRAFTON (village). Covers a land area of 4.712 square miles and a water area of 0.029 square miles. Located at 41.28° N. Lat; 82.03° W. Long. Elevation is 801 feet.

Population: 6,636; Growth (since 2000): 188.3%; Density: 1,408.2 persons per square mile; Race: 65.0% White, 32.7% Black/African American, 0.3% Asian, 0.2% American Indian/Alaska Native, 0.0% Native Hawaiian/Other Pacific Islander, 0.7% Two or more races, 2.3% Hispanic of any race; Average household size: 2.68; Median age: 36.2; Age under 18: 10.4%; Age 65 and over: 5.6%; Males per 100 females: 392.3; Marriage status: 43.0% never married, 38.3% now married, 2.2% separated, 3.9% widowed, 14.8% divorced; Foreign born: 1.2%; Speak English only: 94.9%; With disability: 10.0%; Veterans: 9.3%; Ancestry: 22.8% German, 19.5% Irish, 7.7% English, 7.3% Italian, 5.4% Polish

Employment: 8.6% management, business, and financial, 6.6% computer, engineering, and science, 8.7% education, legal, community service, arts, and media, 5.1% healthcare practitioners, 9.7% service, 32.0% sales and office, 7.4% natural resources, construction, and maintenance, 21.8% production, transportation, and material moving

Income: Per capita: $16,129; Median household: $51,932; Average household: $61,691; Households with income of $100,000 or more: 16.3%; Poverty rate: 5.5%

Educational Attainment: High school diploma or higher: 77.8%; Bachelor's degree or higher: 7.6%; Graduate/professional degree or higher: 2.9%

School District(s)

Midview Local (PK-12)
2012-13 Enrollment: 3,091 . . . . (440) 926-3737

Housing: Homeownership rate: 79.5%; Median home value: $138,100; Median year structure built: 1971; Homeowner vacancy rate: 0.8%; Median gross rent: $695 per month; Rental vacancy rate: 7.5%

Health Insurance: 88.5% have insurance; 75.6% have private insurance; 24.3% have public insurance; 11.5% do not have insurance; 10.6% of children under 18 do not have insurance

Safety: Violent crime rate: 7.0 per 10,000 population; Property crime rate: 29.7 per 10,000 population

Transportation: Commute: 93.1% car, 0.9% public transportation, 3.4% walk, 2.1% work from home; Median travel time to work: 25.0 minutes

KIPTON (village). Covers a land area of 0.440 square miles and a water area of 0.005 square miles. Located at 41.27° N. Lat; 82.30° W. Long. Elevation is 850 feet.

Population: 243; Growth (since 2000): -8.3%; Density: 551.7 persons per square mile; Race: 97.1% White, 0.0% Black/African American, 0.0%

Asian, 0.0% American Indian/Alaska Native, 0.0% Native Hawaiian/Other Pacific Islander, 2.1% Two or more races, 2.5% Hispanic of any race; Average household size: 2.38; Median age: 42.8; Age under 18: 19.3%; Age 65 and over: 15.2%; Males per 100 females: 120.9
Housing: Homeownership rate: 81.4%; Homeowner vacancy rate: 1.2%; Rental vacancy rate: 13.6%

LAGRANGE (village). Covers a land area of 2.010 square miles and a water area of 0.004 square miles. Located at 41.24° N. Lat; 82.12° W. Long. Elevation is 823 feet.
Population: 2,103; Growth (since 2000): 15.9%; Density: 1,046.5 persons per square mile; Race: 96.6% White, 0.4% Black/African American, 0.2% Asian, 0.7% American Indian/Alaska Native, 0.0% Native Hawaiian/Other Pacific Islander, 1.7% Two or more races, 1.9% Hispanic of any race; Average household size: 2.73; Median age: 41.4; Age under 18: 25.7%; Age 65 and over: 14.4%; Males per 100 females: 94.0

School District(s)

Keystone Local (PK-12)
2012-13 Enrollment: 1,601 . . . . (440) 355-5131
Housing: Homeownership rate: 74.9%; Homeowner vacancy rate: 2.3%; Rental vacancy rate: 9.8%

LORAIN (city). Covers a land area of 23.673 square miles and a water area of 0.474 square miles. Located at 41.44° N. Lat; 82.18° W. Long. Elevation is 610 feet.
History: Named for the province of Lorraine in France. Lorain had its beginnings in 1807 when Nathan Perry and the Azariah Beebes established a trading post on the south shore of Lake Erie, at the mouth of the Black River. In 1810 others arrived, including John Reid, whose home became the post office, justice's office, and tavern. By 1819 shipbuilding began in Lorain. The town had first been known as Mouth of Black River, but in 1836 it was incorporated as Charleston. When the Cleveland, Lorain & Wheeling Railroad arrived in 1872, a new charter was granted under the name of Lorain. The first steel company came to Lorain in 1894, and was later acquired by the United States Steel Corporation, bringing immigrants from many countries to work here.
Population: 64,097; Growth (since 2000): -6.6%; Density: 2,707.6 persons per square mile; Race: 67.9% White, 17.6% Black/African American, 0.4% Asian, 0.5% American Indian/Alaska Native, 0.0% Native Hawaiian/Other Pacific Islander, 5.4% Two or more races, 25.2% Hispanic of any race; Average household size: 2.48; Median age: 36.8; Age under 18: 26.7%; Age 65 and over: 13.9%; Males per 100 females: 90.5; Marriage status: 35.6% never married, 43.2% now married, 2.9% separated, 7.8% widowed, 13.4% divorced; Foreign born: 3.2%; Speak English only: 81.8%; With disability: 18.6%; Veterans: 9.4%; Ancestry: 14.3% German, 11.8% Irish, 8.5% Italian, 6.2% English, 6.2% Polish
Employment: 8.9% management, business, and financial, 2.5% computer, engineering, and science, 7.5% education, legal, community service, arts, and media, 4.6% healthcare practitioners, 23.9% service, 23.9% sales and office, 7.4% natural resources, construction, and maintenance, 21.2% production, transportation, and material moving
Income: Per capita: $18,698; Median household: $33,610; Average household: $45,347; Households with income of $100,000 or more: 9.1%; Poverty rate: 30.4%
Educational Attainment: High school diploma or higher: 81.1%; Bachelor's degree or higher: 11.8%; Graduate/professional degree or higher: 4.0%

School District(s)

Academy of Arts and Sciences (KG-03)
2012-13 Enrollment: 236. . . . . (440) 244-0156
Clearview Local (PK-12)
2012-13 Enrollment: 1,708 . . . . (440) 233-5412
Constellation Schools: Lorain Community Elementary (KG-04)
2012-13 Enrollment: 209. . . . . (440) 204-2130
Constellation Schools: Lorain Community Middle (05-08)
2012-13 Enrollment: 122. . . . . (440) 242-2023
Horizon Science Academy Lorain (KG-07)
2012-13 Enrollment: 423. . . . . (440) 282-4277
Lorain City (PK-12)
2012-13 Enrollment: 6,858 . . . . (440) 233-2271
Lorain High School Digital (03-12)
2012-13 Enrollment: 119. . . . . (440) 282-4087
Mansfield Preparatory Academy of Excellence (03-08)
2012-13 Enrollment: 130. . . . . (440) 282-3127
Summit Academy Middle School - Lorain (06-08)
2012-13 Enrollment: 88. . . . . (440) 288-0448
Summit Academy Secondary - Lorain (09-12)
2012-13 Enrollment: 78. . . . . (440) 288-0448
Summit Academy-Lorain (KG-05)
2012-13 Enrollment: 138. . . . . (440) 277-4110

Vocational/Technical School(s)

Northern Institute of Cosmetology (Private, For-profit)
Fall 2013 Enrollment: 33 . . . . (440) 244-4282
2013-14 Tuition: $7,181
Housing: Homeownership rate: 57.8%; Median home value: $93,400; Median year structure built: 1958; Homeowner vacancy rate: 3.6%; Median gross rent: $630 per month; Rental vacancy rate: 13.2%
Health Insurance: 86.8% have insurance; 53.1% have private insurance; 46.0% have public insurance; 13.2% do not have insurance; 3.6% of children under 18 do not have insurance
Hospitals: Mercy Regional Medical Center
Safety: Violent crime rate: 47.8 per 10,000 population; Property crime rate: 439.0 per 10,000 population
Newspapers: Morning Journal (daily circulation 26700)
Transportation: Commute: 95.2% car, 0.9% public transportation, 1.4% walk, 1.7% work from home; Median travel time to work: 22.9 minutes
Airports: Lorain County Regional (general aviation)
Additional Information Contacts
City of Lorain . . . . (440) 204-2002
http://www.cityoflorain.org

NORTH RIDGEVILLE (city). Covers a land area of 23.438 square miles and a water area of 0.140 square miles. Located at 41.39° N. Lat; 82.02° W. Long. Elevation is 728 feet.
Population: 29,465; Growth (since 2000): 31.9%; Density: 1,257.1 persons per square mile; Race: 95.0% White, 1.5% Black/African American, 1.2% Asian, 0.2% American Indian/Alaska Native, 0.0% Native Hawaiian/Other Pacific Islander, 1.6% Two or more races, 3.3% Hispanic of any race; Average household size: 2.54; Median age: 40.7; Age under 18: 23.1%; Age 65 and over: 15.0%; Males per 100 females: 96.3; Marriage status: 21.9% never married, 62.1% now married, 2.0% separated, 5.5% widowed, 10.5% divorced; Foreign born: 4.7%; Speak English only: 94.4%; With disability: 9.6%; Veterans: 9.6%; Ancestry: 27.6% German, 19.6% Irish, 13.2% Polish, 11.0% Italian, 9.8% English
Employment: 17.0% management, business, and financial, 5.5% computer, engineering, and science, 9.6% education, legal, community service, arts, and media, 6.6% healthcare practitioners, 14.5% service, 24.8% sales and office, 7.8% natural resources, construction, and maintenance, 14.2% production, transportation, and material moving
Income: Per capita: $30,468; Median household: $67,156; Average household: $76,027; Households with income of $100,000 or more: 26.4%; Poverty rate: 6.6%
Educational Attainment: High school diploma or higher: 93.0%; Bachelor's degree or higher: 27.3%; Graduate/professional degree or higher: 8.7%

School District(s)

North Ridgeville City (PK-12)
2012-13 Enrollment: 4,116 . . . . (440) 327-4444
Housing: Homeownership rate: 90.0%; Median home value: $161,900; Median year structure built: 1979; Homeowner vacancy rate: 2.0%; Median gross rent: $829 per month; Rental vacancy rate: 9.3%
Health Insurance: 92.6% have insurance; 82.8% have private insurance; 23.5% have public insurance; 7.4% do not have insurance; 1.6% of children under 18 do not have insurance
Safety: Violent crime rate: 4.5 per 10,000 population; Property crime rate: 86.1 per 10,000 population
Transportation: Commute: 94.4% car, 1.4% public transportation, 0.4% walk, 3.4% work from home; Median travel time to work: 27.1 minutes
Additional Information Contacts
City of North Ridgeville . . . . (440) 353-0819
http://www.nridgeville.org

OBERLIN (city). Covers a land area of 4.919 square miles and a water area of 0.038 square miles. Located at 41.29° N. Lat; 82.22° W. Long. Elevation is 810 feet.
History: Oberlin College was founded in 1833 by John L. Shipherd, a Presbyterian minister from Elyria, and Philo P. Steward, a missionary. In 1837 four women applied for the regular college course. When they were accepted, Oberlin became the first coeducational college in the country.

Population: 8,286; Growth (since 2000): 1.1%; Density: 1,684.6 persons per square mile; Race: 73.0% White, 14.8% Black/African American, 4.0% Asian, 0.2% American Indian/Alaska Native, 0.0% Native Hawaiian/Other Pacific Islander, 6.5% Two or more races, 5.1% Hispanic of any race; Average household size: 2.19; Median age: 23.3; Age under 18: 14.8%; Age 65 and over: 14.7%; Males per 100 females: 85.1; Marriage status: 56.4% never married, 28.9% now married, 1.0% separated, 6.7% widowed, 7.9% divorced; Foreign born: 6.4%; Speak English only: 90.3%; With disability: 11.2%; Veterans: 6.0%; Ancestry: 19.8% German, 16.3% English, 13.3% Irish, 6.7% American, 4.6% Italian
Employment: 9.0% management, business, and financial, 3.7% computer, engineering, and science, 26.3% education, legal, community service, arts, and media, 2.3% healthcare practitioners, 26.9% service, 19.9% sales and office, 3.6% natural resources, construction, and maintenance, 8.3% production, transportation, and material moving
Income: Per capita: $21,572; Median household: $51,013; Average household: $65,311; Households with income of $100,000 or more: 22.6%; Poverty rate: 19.8%
Educational Attainment: High school diploma or higher: 93.4%; Bachelor's degree or higher: 40.3%; Graduate/professional degree or higher: 24.7%

School District(s)

Firelands Local (PK-12)
2012-13 Enrollment: 1,728 . . . . (440) 965-5821
Lorain County Jvs (08-12)
2012-13 Enrollment: n/a . . . . (440) 774-1051
Oberlin City Schools (PK-12)
2012-13 Enrollment: 1,023 . . . . (440) 774-1458

Four-year College(s)

Oberlin College (Private, Not-for-profit)
Fall 2013 Enrollment: 2,911 . . . . (440) 775-8411
2013-14 Tuition: In-state $46,870; Out-of-state $46,870

Two-year College(s)

Lorain County Joint Vocational School District (Public)
Fall 2013 Enrollment: 106 . . . . (440) 774-1051
Housing: Homeownership rate: 49.4%; Median home value: $139,700; Median year structure built: 1957; Homeowner vacancy rate: 2.5%; Median gross rent: $715 per month; Rental vacancy rate: 8.3%
Health Insurance: 90.3% have insurance; 78.6% have private insurance; 23.7% have public insurance; 9.7% do not have insurance; 2.6% of children under 18 do not have insurance
Hospitals: Mercy Allen Hospital (25 beds)
Safety: Violent crime rate: 14.4 per 10,000 population; Property crime rate: 231.2 per 10,000 population
Newspapers: Oberlin News Tribune (weekly circulation 3500)
Transportation: Commute: 54.6% car, 0.5% public transportation, 31.3% walk, 6.0% work from home; Median travel time to work: 14.4 minutes

PHEASANT RUN (CDP). Covers a land area of 0.934 square miles and a water area of 0.036 square miles. Located at 41.21° N. Lat; 82.15° W. Long. Elevation is 833 feet.
Population: 1,397; Growth (since 2000): n/a; Density: 1,496.3 persons per square mile; Race: 96.4% White, 0.8% Black/African American, 0.1% Asian, 0.1% American Indian/Alaska Native, 0.3% Native Hawaiian/Other Pacific Islander, 2.1% Two or more races, 3.1% Hispanic of any race; Average household size: 2.76; Median age: 36.7; Age under 18: 27.0%; Age 65 and over: 9.4%; Males per 100 females: 101.0
Housing: Homeownership rate: 85.4%; Homeowner vacancy rate: 3.5%; Rental vacancy rate: 1.3%

ROCHESTER (village). Covers a land area of 1.118 square miles and a water area of 0.007 square miles. Located at 41.12° N. Lat; 82.31° W. Long. Elevation is 928 feet.
Population: 182; Growth (since 2000): -4.2%; Density: 162.8 persons per square mile; Race: 98.4% White, 0.0% Black/African American, 0.0% Asian, 0.5% American Indian/Alaska Native, 0.0% Native Hawaiian/Other Pacific Islander, 1.1% Two or more races, 2.2% Hispanic of any race; Average household size: 2.56; Median age: 41.3; Age under 18: 24.7%; Age 65 and over: 15.9%; Males per 100 females: 95.7
Housing: Homeownership rate: 84.5%; Homeowner vacancy rate: 1.6%; Rental vacancy rate: 0.0%

SHEFFIELD (village). Covers a land area of 10.743 square miles and a water area of 0.098 square miles. Located at 41.46° N. Lat; 82.09° W. Long. Elevation is 669 feet.
History: Incorporated 1933.
Population: 3,982; Growth (since 2000): 35.0%; Density: 370.7 persons per square mile; Race: 89.3% White, 4.0% Black/African American, 2.7% Asian, 0.3% American Indian/Alaska Native, 0.0% Native Hawaiian/Other Pacific Islander, 2.2% Two or more races, 6.1% Hispanic of any race; Average household size: 2.51; Median age: 45.2; Age under 18: 20.2%; Age 65 and over: 16.2%; Males per 100 females: 97.4; Marriage status: 20.0% never married, 62.5% now married, 0.7% separated, 7.3% widowed, 10.2% divorced; Foreign born: 6.8%; Speak English only: 88.6%; With disability: 11.5%; Veterans: 13.3%; Ancestry: 24.9% German, 19.1% Irish, 8.2% English, 7.6% Italian, 6.9% American
Employment: 17.3% management, business, and financial, 4.8% computer, engineering, and science, 6.6% education, legal, community service, arts, and media, 3.2% healthcare practitioners, 21.3% service, 25.9% sales and office, 6.7% natural resources, construction, and maintenance, 14.2% production, transportation, and material moving
Income: Per capita: $29,079; Median household: $63,144; Average household: $75,011; Households with income of $100,000 or more: 25.7%; Poverty rate: 6.7%
Educational Attainment: High school diploma or higher: 90.9%; Bachelor's degree or higher: 25.4%; Graduate/professional degree or higher: 9.0%

School District(s)

Sheffield-Sheffield Lake City (PK-12)
2012-13 Enrollment: 1,777 . . . . (440) 949-6181

Two-year College(s)

Ohio Business College-Sheffield (Private, For-profit)
Fall 2013 Enrollment: 415 . . . . (440) 934-3101
2013-14 Tuition: In-state $8,500; Out-of-state $8,500
Vanity School of Cosmetology (Private, For-profit)
Fall 2013 Enrollment: 53 . . . . (888) 809-4247
Housing: Homeownership rate: 76.7%; Median home value: $185,100; Median year structure built: 1994; Homeowner vacancy rate: 1.1%; Median gross rent: $1,140 per month; Rental vacancy rate: 8.4%
Health Insurance: 93.2% have insurance; 79.3% have private insurance; 33.5% have public insurance; 6.8% do not have insurance; 2.3% of children under 18 do not have insurance
Transportation: Commute: 94.3% car, 0.0% public transportation, 0.7% walk, 3.5% work from home; Median travel time to work: 25.7 minutes

SHEFFIELD LAKE (city). Covers a land area of 2.477 square miles and a water area of 0 square miles. Located at 41.49° N. Lat; 82.10° W. Long. Elevation is 600 feet.
History: Incorporated 1920.
Population: 9,137; Growth (since 2000): -2.5%; Density: 3,689.3 persons per square mile; Race: 94.5% White, 1.7% Black/African American, 0.5% Asian, 0.3% American Indian/Alaska Native, 0.0% Native Hawaiian/Other Pacific Islander, 2.2% Two or more races, 4.9% Hispanic of any race; Average household size: 2.46; Median age: 39.4; Age under 18: 22.5%; Age 65 and over: 12.0%; Males per 100 females: 97.9; Marriage status: 30.7% never married, 49.4% now married, 0.9% separated, 6.7% widowed, 13.2% divorced; Foreign born: 1.9%; Speak English only: 94.2%; With disability: 13.9%; Veterans: 11.2%; Ancestry: 27.7% German, 14.9% Irish, 12.0% Italian, 11.6% English, 10.9% Polish
Employment: 5.8% management, business, and financial, 2.8% computer, engineering, and science, 10.0% education, legal, community service, arts, and media, 8.6% healthcare practitioners, 21.0% service, 23.0% sales and office, 11.5% natural resources, construction, and maintenance, 17.2% production, transportation, and material moving
Income: Per capita: $23,433; Median household: $47,707; Average household: $54,647; Households with income of $100,000 or more: 9.8%; Poverty rate: 13.9%
Educational Attainment: High school diploma or higher: 90.3%; Bachelor's degree or higher: 18.0%; Graduate/professional degree or higher: 5.1%

School District(s)

Sheffield-Sheffield Lake City (PK-12)
2012-13 Enrollment: 1,777 . . . . (440) 949-6181
Housing: Homeownership rate: 72.9%; Median home value: $113,100; Median year structure built: 1967; Homeowner vacancy rate: 2.3%; Median gross rent: $863 per month; Rental vacancy rate: 13.9%

Health Insurance: 84.8% have insurance; 69.5% have private insurance; 28.5% have public insurance; 15.2% do not have insurance; 17.2% of children under 18 do not have insurance
Safety: Violent crime rate: 5.5 per 10,000 population; Property crime rate: 127.1 per 10,000 population
Transportation: Commute: 94.8% car, 1.1% public transportation, 1.1% walk, 1.1% work from home; Median travel time to work: 26.6 minutes

SOUTH AMHERST (village). Covers a land area of 2.472 square miles and a water area of 0.020 square miles. Located at 41.35° N. Lat; 82.24° W. Long. Elevation is 791 feet.
History: South Amherst was at one time called Podunk. The town developed as a quarrying center.
Population: 1,688; Growth (since 2000): -9.4%; Density: 682.9 persons per square mile; Race: 96.2% White, 0.4% Black/African American, 0.1% Asian, 0.7% American Indian/Alaska Native, 0.0% Native Hawaiian/Other Pacific Islander, 2.1% Two or more races, 2.7% Hispanic of any race; Average household size: 2.51; Median age: 46.1; Age under 18: 20.2%; Age 65 and over: 17.8%; Males per 100 females: 95.6

School District(s)

Firelands Local (PK-12)
2012-13 Enrollment: 1,728 . . . . (440) 965-5821
Housing: Homeownership rate: 84.5%; Homeowner vacancy rate: 1.6%; Rental vacancy rate: 2.8%

VERMILION (city). Covers a land area of 10.655 square miles and a water area of 0.166 square miles. Located at 41.41° N. Lat; 82.32° W. Long.
History: Vermilion was settled in 1808 along the Vermilion River, named for the red clay found along the river bottom. Vermilion developed as a fishing center and a tourist resort.
Population: 10,594; Growth (since 2000): -3.0%; Density: 994.3 persons per square mile; Race: 96.8% White, 0.3% Black/African American, 0.3% Asian, 0.2% American Indian/Alaska Native, 0.0% Native Hawaiian/Other Pacific Islander, 1.8% Two or more races, 2.8% Hispanic of any race; Average household size: 2.50; Median age: 43.5; Age under 18: 22.6%; Age 65 and over: 16.8%; Males per 100 females: 94.5; Marriage status: 23.4% never married, 55.5% now married, 1.2% separated, 8.0% widowed, 13.1% divorced; Foreign born: 1.0%; Speak English only: 98.2%; With disability: 12.6%; Veterans: 12.6%; Ancestry: 28.0% German, 18.0% Irish, 12.8% English, 9.2% American, 9.0% Polish
Employment: 8.3% management, business, and financial, 3.4% computer, engineering, and science, 8.8% education, legal, community service, arts, and media, 9.4% healthcare practitioners, 20.8% service, 23.0% sales and office, 10.4% natural resources, construction, and maintenance, 15.8% production, transportation, and material moving
Income: Per capita: $26,856; Median household: $51,899; Average household: $64,033; Households with income of $100,000 or more: 19.0%; Poverty rate: 12.5%
Educational Attainment: High school diploma or higher: 89.0%; Bachelor's degree or higher: 18.4%; Graduate/professional degree or higher: 8.1%

School District(s)

Vermilion Local (PK-12)
2012-13 Enrollment: 2,027 . . . . (440) 204-1716
Housing: Homeownership rate: 78.1%; Median home value: $130,300; Median year structure built: 1966; Homeowner vacancy rate: 2.7%; Median gross rent: $771 per month; Rental vacancy rate: 11.3%
Health Insurance: 88.6% have insurance; 73.5% have private insurance; 33.0% have public insurance; 11.4% do not have insurance; 5.3% of children under 18 do not have insurance
Safety: Violent crime rate: 10.5 per 10,000 population; Property crime rate: 131.7 per 10,000 population
Newspapers: Vermilion Photojournal (weekly circulation 3000)
Transportation: Commute: 92.0% car, 0.0% public transportation, 5.1% walk, 2.2% work from home; Median travel time to work: 27.7 minutes

WELLINGTON (village). Covers a land area of 3.595 square miles and a water area of 0.291 square miles. Located at 41.15° N. Lat; 82.23° W. Long. Elevation is 850 feet.
History: Wellington developed in the dairy and grain area of Lorain County. It was an abolitionist center, and in 1858, when a Federal marshal stopped in Wellington with a runaway slave, the residents rescued the slave. Many of them were then arrested and charged with aiding a fugitive slave.
Population: 4,802; Growth (since 2000): 6.5%; Density: 1,335.6 persons per square mile; Race: 95.8% White, 1.2% Black/African American, 0.4% Asian, 0.3% American Indian/Alaska Native, 0.0% Native Hawaiian/Other Pacific Islander, 1.8% Two or more races, 2.0% Hispanic of any race; Average household size: 2.39; Median age: 39.5; Age under 18: 24.9%; Age 65 and over: 17.0%; Males per 100 females: 92.1; Marriage status: 25.9% never married, 55.0% now married, 1.1% separated, 9.3% widowed, 9.8% divorced; Foreign born: 0.4%; Speak English only: 98.9%; With disability: 14.9%; Veterans: 8.2%; Ancestry: 30.7% German, 16.6% Irish, 10.0% Italian, 8.5% American, 7.8% English
Employment: 4.5% management, business, and financial, 3.8% computer, engineering, and science, 10.7% education, legal, community service, arts, and media, 5.6% healthcare practitioners, 11.4% service, 25.3% sales and office, 12.3% natural resources, construction, and maintenance, 26.4% production, transportation, and material moving
Income: Per capita: $23,357; Median household: $55,690; Average household: $63,401; Households with income of $100,000 or more: 14.6%; Poverty rate: 10.1%
Educational Attainment: High school diploma or higher: 89.6%; Bachelor's degree or higher: 13.2%; Graduate/professional degree or higher: 7.4%

School District(s)

Wellington Exempted Village (PK-12)
2012-13 Enrollment: 1,242 . . . . (440) 647-4286
Housing: Homeownership rate: 62.3%; Median home value: $132,300; Median year structure built: 1968; Homeowner vacancy rate: 2.7%; Median gross rent: $718 per month; Rental vacancy rate: 6.5%
Health Insurance: 90.2% have insurance; 71.1% have private insurance; 31.6% have public insurance; 9.8% do not have insurance; 1.0% of children under 18 do not have insurance
Newspapers: Wellington Enterprise (weekly circulation 3000)
Transportation: Commute: 93.4% car, 0.0% public transportation, 1.5% walk, 4.6% work from home; Median travel time to work: 32.3 minutes

Lucas County

Located in northwestern Ohio; bounded on the north by Michigan, on the southeast by the Maumee River, and on the northeast by the west end of Lake Erie. Covers a land area of 340.855 square miles, a water area of 255.022 square miles, and is located in the Eastern Time Zone at 41.68° N. Lat., 83.47° W. Long. The county was founded in 1835. County seat is Toledo.

Lucas County is part of the Toledo, OH Metropolitan Statistical Area. The entire metro area includes: Fulton County, OH; Lucas County, OH; Wood County, OH

Weather Station: Toledo Express Arpt Elevation: 668 feet

	Jan	Feb	Mar	Apr	May	Jun	Jul	Aug	Sep	Oct	Nov	Dec
High	32	36	46	60	71	80	84	82	75	62	49	36
Low	18	20	28	38	48	58	62	61	53	41	33	23
Precip	2.1	2.0	2.5	3.1	3.5	3.5	3.2	3.3	2.8	2.6	2.8	2.7
Snow	11.3	8.6	5.9	1.4	na	na	na	na	na	na	1.9	7.4

High and Low temperatures in degrees Fahrenheit; Precipitation and Snow in inches

Population: 441,815; Growth (since 2000): -2.0%; Density: 1,296.2 persons per square mile; Race: 74.0% White, 19.0% Black/African American, 1.5% Asian, 0.3% American Indian/Alaska Native, 0.0% Native Hawaiian/Other Pacific Islander, 3.1% two or more races, 6.1% Hispanic of any race; Average household size: 2.39; Median age: 37.0; Age under 18: 24.0%; Age 65 and over: 13.1%; Males per 100 females: 93.9; Marriage status: 35.6% never married, 44.5% now married, 2.0% separated, 6.5% widowed, 13.4% divorced; Foreign born: 3.4%; Speak English only: 94.0%; With disability: 15.1%; Veterans: 8.7%; Ancestry: 28.0% German, 12.5% Irish, 9.8% Polish, 7.3% English, 4.6% French
Religion: Six largest groups: 20.9% Catholicism, 5.5% Lutheran, 4.4% Baptist, 3.0% Non-denominational Protestant, 2.8% Methodist/Pietist, 2.2% Pentecostal
Economy: Unemployment rate: 4.9%; Leading industries: 15.0% retail trade; 13.2% health care and social assistance; 10.7% other services (except public administration); Farms: 330 totaling 63,022 acres; Company size: 11 employs 1,000 or more persons, 15 employ 500 to 999 persons, 264 employ 100 to 499 persons, 9,377 employ less than 100 persons; Business ownership: 8,011 women-owned, 2,193 Black-owned, 639 Hispanic-owned, 587 Asian-owned

Employment: 11.4% management, business, and financial, 3.5% computer, engineering, and science, 10.1% education, legal, community service, arts, and media, 6.9% healthcare practitioners, 20.1% service, 24.6% sales and office, 7.1% natural resources, construction, and maintenance, 16.3% production, transportation, and material moving
Income: Per capita: $23,885; Median household: $41,556; Average household: $57,207; Households with income of $100,000 or more: 14.7%; Poverty rate: 20.8%
Educational Attainment: High school diploma or higher: 87.8%; Bachelor's degree or higher: 23.4%; Graduate/professional degree or higher: 8.8%
Housing: Homeownership rate: 63.0%; Median home value: $108,700; Median year structure built: 1958; Homeowner vacancy rate: 2.7%; Median gross rent: $649 per month; Rental vacancy rate: 11.3%
Vital Statistics: Birth rate: 123.1 per 10,000 population; Death rate: 98.9 per 10,000 population; Age-adjusted cancer mortality rate: 192.9 deaths per 100,000 population
Health Insurance: 87.4% have insurance; 65.6% have private insurance; 34.3% have public insurance; 12.6% do not have insurance; 4.7% of children under 18 do not have insurance
Health Care: Physicians: 38.4 per 10,000 population; Hospital beds: 51.3 per 10,000 population; Hospital admissions: 2,330.5 per 10,000 population
Air Quality Index: 83.4% good, 16.6% moderate, 0.0% unhealthy for sensitive individuals, 0.0% unhealthy (percent of days)
Transportation: Commute: 92.8% car, 1.6% public transportation, 2.2% walk, 2.6% work from home; Median travel time to work: 19.9 minutes
Presidential Election: 64.3% Obama, 33.9% Romney (2012)
National and State Parks: Cedar Point National Wildlife Refuge; Fallen Timbers State Memorial; Fort Miamis State Memorial; Irwin Prairie State Nature Preserve; Mallard Club Marsh State Wildlife Area; Maumee Bay State Park; Missionary Island State Wildlife Area; West Sister Island National Wildlife Refuge

Additional Information Contacts
Lucas Government . . . . (419) 213-4000
http://www.co.lucas.oh.us

Lucas County Communities

BERKEY (village). Covers a land area of 4.176 square miles and a water area of 0 square miles. Located at 41.71° N. Lat; 83.84° W. Long. Elevation is 702 feet.
Population: 237; Growth (since 2000): -10.6%; Density: 56.8 persons per square mile; Race: 99.2% White, 0.0% Black/African American, 0.8% Asian, 0.0% American Indian/Alaska Native, 0.0% Native Hawaiian/Other Pacific Islander, 0.0% Two or more races, 1.3% Hispanic of any race; Average household size: 2.39; Median age: 48.2; Age under 18: 21.1%; Age 65 and over: 18.1%; Males per 100 females: 104.3
Housing: Homeownership rate: 81.8%; Homeowner vacancy rate: 6.9%; Rental vacancy rate: 5.3%

HARBOR VIEW (village). Covers a land area of 0.029 square miles and a water area of 0 square miles. Located at 41.69° N. Lat; 83.44° W. Long. Elevation is 581 feet.
Population: 123; Growth (since 2000): 24.2%; Density: 4,233.4 persons per square mile; Race: 96.7% White, 0.0% Black/African American, 2.4% Asian, 0.0% American Indian/Alaska Native, 0.0% Native Hawaiian/Other Pacific Islander, 0.8% Two or more races, 1.6% Hispanic of any race; Average household size: 2.56; Median age: 39.3; Age under 18: 23.6%; Age 65 and over: 12.2%; Males per 100 females: 89.2
Housing: Homeownership rate: 72.9%; Homeowner vacancy rate: 2.8%; Rental vacancy rate: 0.0%

HOLLAND (village). Covers a land area of 0.990 square miles and a water area of 0 square miles. Located at 41.62° N. Lat; 83.71° W. Long. Elevation is 636 feet.
Population: 1,764; Growth (since 2000): 35.1%; Density: 1,782.4 persons per square mile; Race: 84.1% White, 10.4% Black/African American, 2.9% Asian, 0.3% American Indian/Alaska Native, 0.0% Native Hawaiian/Other Pacific Islander, 1.2% Two or more races, 4.0% Hispanic of any race; Average household size: 2.23; Median age: 45.2; Age under 18: 21.0%; Age 65 and over: 23.0%; Males per 100 females: 84.7

School District(s)
Springfield Local (PK-12)
2012-13 Enrollment: 3,942 . . . . (419) 867-5600

Vocational/Technical School(s)
Regency Beauty Institute-Toledo (Private, For-profit)
Fall 2013 Enrollment: 83 . . . . (800) 787-6456
2013-14 Tuition: $16,200
Housing: Homeownership rate: 56.6%; Homeowner vacancy rate: 0.9%; Rental vacancy rate: 3.3%
Safety: Violent crime rate: 45.5 per 10,000 population; Property crime rate: 1,461.9 per 10,000 population

MAUMEE (city). Covers a land area of 9.886 square miles and a water area of 0.716 square miles. Located at 41.57° N. Lat; 83.67° W. Long. Elevation is 633 feet.
History: A French-Canadian trading post was here from 1680 to 1693. In 1764 the British built Fort Miami. When a store opened in 1817, the town began to grow around it. Earlier names of Waynesville and South Toledo gave way to the name of Maumee, a corruption of the Indian name Miami.
Population: 14,286; Growth (since 2000): -6.2%; Density: 1,445.1 persons per square mile; Race: 94.7% White, 1.8% Black/African American, 0.9% Asian, 0.2% American Indian/Alaska Native, 0.0% Native Hawaiian/Other Pacific Islander, 1.7% Two or more races, 3.4% Hispanic of any race; Average household size: 2.37; Median age: 39.7; Age under 18: 22.6%; Age 65 and over: 13.7%; Males per 100 females: 95.9; Marriage status: 25.8% never married, 55.1% now married, 1.4% separated, 6.4% widowed, 12.6% divorced; Foreign born: 2.3%; Speak English only: 96.4%; With disability: 10.6%; Veterans: 9.1%; Ancestry: 42.1% German, 18.6% Irish, 11.5% English, 10.8% Polish, 6.4% American
Employment: 11.8% management, business, and financial, 3.7% computer, engineering, and science, 10.4% education, legal, community service, arts, and media, 9.0% healthcare practitioners, 16.3% service, 26.1% sales and office, 8.5% natural resources, construction, and maintenance, 14.3% production, transportation, and material moving
Income: Per capita: $28,792; Median household: $54,128; Average household: $67,291; Households with income of $100,000 or more: 17.6%; Poverty rate: 8.2%
Educational Attainment: High school diploma or higher: 94.8%; Bachelor's degree or higher: 32.3%; Graduate/professional degree or higher: 11.9%

School District(s)
Maumee City (PK-12)
2012-13 Enrollment: 2,479 . . . . (419) 893-3200
Ohio Virtual Academy (KG-12)
2012-13 Enrollment: 12,944 . . . . (419) 482-0948
Wildwood Environmental Academy (KG-12)
2012-13 Enrollment: 286. . . . . (419) 868-9885

Four-year College(s)
ITT Technical Institute-Maumee (Private, For-profit)
Fall 2013 Enrollment: 219 . . . . (419) 861-6500
2013-14 Tuition: In-state $18,048; Out-of-state $18,048

Two-year College(s)
Professional Skills Institute (Private, For-profit)
Fall 2013 Enrollment: 311 . . . . (419) 720-6670
2013-14 Tuition: In-state $15,318; Out-of-state $15,318
Stautzenberger College-Maumee (Private, For-profit)
Fall 2013 Enrollment: 790 . . . . (419) 866-0261
2013-14 Tuition: In-state $10,476; Out-of-state $10,476
Housing: Homeownership rate: 72.8%; Median home value: $127,000; Median year structure built: 1961; Homeowner vacancy rate: 1.7%; Median gross rent: $735 per month; Rental vacancy rate: 9.7%
Health Insurance: 92.4% have insurance; 83.3% have private insurance; 23.2% have public insurance; 7.6% do not have insurance; 3.0% of children under 18 do not have insurance
Hospitals: Saint Luke's Hospital (314 beds)
Safety: Violent crime rate: 7.8 per 10,000 population; Property crime rate: 372.1 per 10,000 population
Transportation: Commute: 95.4% car, 0.6% public transportation, 0.8% walk, 2.6% work from home; Median travel time to work: 19.1 minutes

Additional Information Contacts
City of Maumee . . . . (419) 897-7100
http://www.maumee.org

MONCLOVA (unincorporated postal area)
ZCTA: 43542
Covers a land area of 14.535 square miles and a water area of 0 square miles. Located at 41.57° N. Lat; 83.77° W. Long. Elevation is 633 feet.

Population: 3,591; Growth (since 2000): 50.3%; Density: 247.1 persons per square mile; Race: 94.7% White, 1.2% Black/African American, 2.0% Asian, 0.1% American Indian/Alaska Native, 0.0% Native Hawaiian/Other Pacific Islander, 1.1% Two or more races, 3.3% Hispanic of any race; Average household size: 2.94; Median age: 39.7; Age under 18: 28.3%; Age 65 and over: 9.7%; Males per 100 females: 107.1; Marriage status: 23.1% never married, 64.5% now married, 0.0% separated, 6.6% widowed, 5.7% divorced; Foreign born: 0.9%; Speak English only: 98.1%; With disability: 6.9%; Veterans: 5.6%; Ancestry: 43.8% German, 20.0% Irish, 14.8% Italian, 12.0% Polish, 9.2% Hungarian
Employment: 19.2% management, business, and financial, 4.0% computer, engineering, and science, 9.3% education, legal, community service, arts, and media, 10.2% healthcare practitioners, 14.5% service, 27.9% sales and office, 8.7% natural resources, construction, and maintenance, 6.3% production, transportation, and material moving
Income: Per capita: $39,406; Median household: $112,653; Average household: $124,445; Households with income of $100,000 or more: 55.6%; Poverty rate: 0.9%
Educational Attainment: High school diploma or higher: 96.0%; Bachelor's degree or higher: 32.6%; Graduate/professional degree or higher: 16.8%

School District(s)

Anthony Wayne Local (PK-12)
2012-13 Enrollment: 4,298 . . . . (419) 877-5377
Housing: Homeownership rate: 91.4%; Median home value: $207,800; Median year structure built: 1984; Homeowner vacancy rate: 1.5%; Median gross rent: n/a per month; Rental vacancy rate: 5.4%
Health Insurance: 96.7% have insurance; 90.0% have private insurance; 16.1% have public insurance; 3.3% do not have insurance; 0.0% of children under 18 do not have insurance
Transportation: Commute: 94.9% car, 0.0% public transportation, 0.6% walk, 4.6% work from home; Median travel time to work: 23.6 minutes

---

NEAPOLIS (CDP). Covers a land area of 0.710 square miles and a water area of 0 square miles. Located at 41.49° N. Lat; 83.87° W. Long. Elevation is 669 feet.
Population: 423; Growth (since 2000): n/a; Density: 596.0 persons per square mile; Race: 95.3% White, 0.0% Black/African American, 0.0% Asian, 0.0% American Indian/Alaska Native, 0.0% Native Hawaiian/Other Pacific Islander, 1.2% Two or more races, 5.4% Hispanic of any race; Average household size: 2.68; Median age: 39.7; Age under 18: 24.8%; Age 65 and over: 11.8%; Males per 100 females: 104.3
Housing: Homeownership rate: 83.6%; Homeowner vacancy rate: 1.5%; Rental vacancy rate: 29.7%

OREGON (city). Covers a land area of 29.976 square miles and a water area of 8.055 square miles. Located at 41.67° N. Lat; 83.42° W. Long. Elevation is 604 feet.
History: Incorporated 1958.
Population: 20,291; Growth (since 2000): 4.8%; Density: 676.9 persons per square mile; Race: 93.5% White, 1.4% Black/African American, 0.8% Asian, 0.2% American Indian/Alaska Native, 0.0% Native Hawaiian/Other Pacific Islander, 1.9% Two or more races, 7.5% Hispanic of any race; Average household size: 2.44; Median age: 42.3; Age under 18: 22.6%; Age 65 and over: 17.6%; Males per 100 females: 92.7; Marriage status: 25.2% never married, 55.3% now married, 1.7% separated, 7.7% widowed, 11.8% divorced; Foreign born: 2.5%; Speak English only: 95.1%; With disability: 14.4%; Veterans: 9.5%; Ancestry: 37.2% German, 11.8% Irish, 9.3% Hungarian, 9.0% Polish, 8.3% English
Employment: 8.4% management, business, and financial, 3.8% computer, engineering, and science, 8.8% education, legal, community service, arts, and media, 7.6% healthcare practitioners, 16.7% service, 27.0% sales and office, 9.3% natural resources, construction, and maintenance, 18.3% production, transportation, and material moving
Income: Per capita: $28,062; Median household: $54,191; Average household: $66,236; Households with income of $100,000 or more: 19.9%; Poverty rate: 9.4%
Educational Attainment: High school diploma or higher: 88.4%; Bachelor's degree or higher: 18.7%; Graduate/professional degree or higher: 7.1%

School District(s)

Eagle Learning Center (09-12)
2012-13 Enrollment: 62. . . . . (419) 720-2003
Oregon City (PK-12)
2012-13 Enrollment: 3,778 . . . . (419) 693-0661

Two-year College(s)

Toledo Academy of Beauty Culture-East (Private, For-profit)
Fall 2013 Enrollment: 111 . . . . (419) 693-7257
Housing: Homeownership rate: 71.5%; Median home value: $133,100; Median year structure built: 1969; Homeowner vacancy rate: 2.1%; Median gross rent: $617 per month; Rental vacancy rate: 7.6%
Health Insurance: 90.6% have insurance; 78.5% have private insurance; 28.4% have public insurance; 9.4% do not have insurance; 4.0% of children under 18 do not have insurance
Hospitals: Bay Park Community Hospital (70 beds); Mercy Saint Charles Hospital (390 beds)
Safety: Violent crime rate: 12.9 per 10,000 population; Property crime rate: 389.3 per 10,000 population
Transportation: Commute: 96.6% car, 0.1% public transportation, 0.5% walk, 2.4% work from home; Median travel time to work: 19.5 minutes
Additional Information Contacts
City of Oregon . . . . (419) 698-7095
http://www.ci.oregon.oh.us

OTTAWA HILLS (village). Covers a land area of 1.846 square miles and a water area of 0.016 square miles. Located at 41.67° N. Lat; 83.64° W. Long. Elevation is 604 feet.
History: Settled 1916, incorporated 1924.
Population: 4,517; Growth (since 2000): -1.0%; Density: 2,446.4 persons per square mile; Race: 87.8% White, 3.7% Black/African American, 6.0% Asian, 0.2% American Indian/Alaska Native, 0.0% Native Hawaiian/Other Pacific Islander, 1.8% Two or more races, 2.0% Hispanic of any race; Average household size: 2.60; Median age: 43.6; Age under 18: 28.6%; Age 65 and over: 16.2%; Males per 100 females: 89.8; Marriage status: 22.6% never married, 64.2% now married, 0.3% separated, 6.1% widowed, 7.1% divorced; Foreign born: 6.8%; Speak English only: 90.0%; With disability: 8.9%; Veterans: 7.6%; Ancestry: 26.8% German, 17.8% Irish, 13.3% English, 7.5% Polish, 6.5% French
Employment: 27.6% management, business, and financial, 4.6% computer, engineering, and science, 19.6% education, legal, community service, arts, and media, 13.8% healthcare practitioners, 10.0% service, 17.3% sales and office, 1.8% natural resources, construction, and maintenance, 5.2% production, transportation, and material moving
Income: Per capita: $58,731; Median household: $111,364; Average household: $158,249; Households with income of $100,000 or more: 54.5%; Poverty rate: 3.1%
Educational Attainment: High school diploma or higher: 97.2%; Bachelor's degree or higher: 77.0%; Graduate/professional degree or higher: 37.8%
Housing: Homeownership rate: 83.5%; Median home value: $254,800; Median year structure built: 1953; Homeowner vacancy rate: 2.2%; Median gross rent: $1,054 per month; Rental vacancy rate: 7.4%
Health Insurance: 97.9% have insurance; 93.7% have private insurance; 13.3% have public insurance; 2.1% do not have insurance; 0.6% of children under 18 do not have insurance
Safety: Violent crime rate: 11.2 per 10,000 population; Property crime rate: 71.4 per 10,000 population
Transportation: Commute: 90.4% car, 0.0% public transportation, 1.0% walk, 6.7% work from home; Median travel time to work: 18.1 minutes
Additional Information Contacts
Village of Ottawa Hills . . . . (419) 536-1111
http://www.ottawahills.org

SYLVANIA (city). Covers a land area of 6.478 square miles and a water area of 0.045 square miles. Located at 41.71° N. Lat; 83.71° W. Long. Elevation is 666 feet.
History: Incorporated 1867.
Population: 18,965; Growth (since 2000): 1.6%; Density: 2,927.8 persons per square mile; Race: 92.4% White, 2.7% Black/African American, 2.3% Asian, 0.1% American Indian/Alaska Native, 0.1% Native Hawaiian/Other Pacific Islander, 1.7% Two or more races, 2.9% Hispanic of any race; Average household size: 2.43; Median age: 42.7; Age under 18: 23.6%; Age 65 and over: 17.2%; Males per 100 females: 89.7; Marriage status: 27.7% never married, 57.3% now married, 0.9% separated, 6.1% widowed, 9.0% divorced; Foreign born: 6.1%; Speak English only: 93.0%; With disability: 10.1%; Veterans: 8.9%; Ancestry: 34.8% German, 13.8% Polish, 13.4% Irish, 12.8% English, 6.5% Italian
Employment: 16.1% management, business, and financial, 6.1% computer, engineering, and science, 16.0% education, legal, community service, arts, and media, 8.3% healthcare practitioners, 16.6% service,

22.3% sales and office, 2.9% natural resources, construction, and maintenance, 11.7% production, transportation, and material moving
Income: Per capita: $34,478; Median household: $67,817; Average household: $85,088; Households with income of $100,000 or more: 33.3%; Poverty rate: 7.1%
Educational Attainment: High school diploma or higher: 94.6%; Bachelor's degree or higher: 40.4%; Graduate/professional degree or higher: 16.0%

School District(s)

Sylvania City (PK-12)
2012-13 Enrollment: 7,497 . . . . (419) 824-8501

Four-year College(s)

Lourdes University (Private, Not-for-profit, Roman Catholic)
Fall 2013 Enrollment: 2,187 . . . . (419) 885-3211
2013-14 Tuition: In-state $17,655; Out-of-state $17,655

Two-year College(s)

Ross College-Sylvania (Private, For-profit)
Fall 2013 Enrollment: 423 . . . . (419) 882-3203

Housing: Homeownership rate: 71.5%; Median home value: $171,800; Median year structure built: 1975; Homeowner vacancy rate: 2.1%; Median gross rent: $781 per month; Rental vacancy rate: 9.1%
Health Insurance: 93.5% have insurance; 84.0% have private insurance; 24.6% have public insurance; 6.5% do not have insurance; 2.6% of children under 18 do not have insurance
Hospitals: Flower Hospital (279 beds)
Transportation: Commute: 94.6% car, 1.1% public transportation, 0.5% walk, 3.4% work from home; Median travel time to work: 20.0 minutes
Additional Information Contacts
City of Sylvania . . . . (419) 885-8925
http://www.cityofsylvania.com

TOLEDO (city). County seat. Covers a land area of 80.692 square miles and a water area of 3.432 square miles. Located at 41.66° N. Lat; 83.58° W. Long. Elevation is 610 feet.
History: Toledo was established along the Maumee River on the westernmost tip of Lake Erie. A stockade called Fort Industry was built here around 1800, but was short-lived. In 1833 two small settlements voted to consolidate, and the residents chose the name of Toledo for the new town. The early years were difficult for the town, with cholera, a drought, business failures, and the Toledo War of 1835, a protracted boundary dispute between Ohio and Michigan which ended with Michigan being given the Upper Peninsula in exchange for Ohio keeping the disputed territory. In the 1840's things improved, with Toledo the logical choice as terminus of the Wabash & Erie Canal, followed by the Miami & Erie Canal. When the 1850's came, Toledo was a station on the Underground Railroad for escaping slaves. Among the industries that developed after the Civil War was the Libby Glass Company, which revolutionized the glass industry, and the Owens Bottle Machine Company.
Population: 287,208; Growth (since 2000): -8.4%; Density: 3,559.3 persons per square mile; Race: 64.8% White, 27.2% Black/African American, 1.1% Asian, 0.4% American Indian/Alaska Native, 0.0% Native Hawaiian/Other Pacific Islander, 3.9% Two or more races, 7.4% Hispanic of any race; Average household size: 2.33; Median age: 34.2; Age under 18: 24.0%; Age 65 and over: 12.1%; Males per 100 females: 93.8; Marriage status: 41.0% never married, 37.7% now married, 2.4% separated, 6.5% widowed, 14.8% divorced; Foreign born: 3.2%; Speak English only: 93.9%; With disability: 17.3%; Veterans: 8.4%; Ancestry: 24.0% German, 11.6% Irish, 9.0% Polish, 5.8% English, 4.0% French
Employment: 8.9% management, business, and financial, 2.8% computer, engineering, and science, 9.3% education, legal, community service, arts, and media, 5.6% healthcare practitioners, 23.3% service, 24.4% sales and office, 7.3% natural resources, construction, and maintenance, 18.6% production, transportation, and material moving
Income: Per capita: $18,760; Median household: $33,317; Average household: $43,543; Households with income of $100,000 or more: 7.4%; Poverty rate: 27.2%
Educational Attainment: High school diploma or higher: 84.8%; Bachelor's degree or higher: 17.2%; Graduate/professional degree or higher: 5.9%

School District(s)

Achieve Career Preparatory Academy (09-12)
2012-13 Enrollment: 201 . . . . (419) 243-8559
Alternative Education Academy (KG-12)
2012-13 Enrollment: 2,051 . . . . (330) 253-8680
Aurora Academy (KG-08)
2012-13 Enrollment: 139 . . . . (419) 693-6841
Autism Model School (01-12)
2012-13 Enrollment: 103 . . . . (419) 897-4400
Bennett Venture Academy (KG-08)
2012-13 Enrollment: 664 . . . . (419) 269-2247
Bridge Academy of Ohio (KG-03)
2012-13 Enrollment: n/a . . . . (419) 475-6620
Central Academy of Ohio (KG-08)
2012-13 Enrollment: 165 . . . . (419) 475-6740
Clay Avenue Community School (KG-07)
2012-13 Enrollment: 524 . . . . (419) 727-9900
Eagle Academy (KG-09)
2012-13 Enrollment: 535 . . . . (419) 697-2760
Glass City Academy (11-12)
2012-13 Enrollment: 235 . . . . (419) 720-6311
Great Expectations Elementary School (KG-04)
2012-13 Enrollment: 182 . . . . (419) 490-6252
Horizon Science Academy Toledo (09-12)
2012-13 Enrollment: 514 . . . . (419) 474-3350
Horizon Science Academy Toledo Downtown (KG-08)
2012-13 Enrollment: 313 . . . . (419) 244-3333
Horizon Science Academy-Springfield (KG-08)
2012-13 Enrollment: 441 . . . . (419) 535-0524
Imani Learning Academy (KG-08)
2012-13 Enrollment: 129 . . . . (419) 535-7078
Knight Academy (05-08)
2012-13 Enrollment: 167 . . . . (419) 720-4444
L. Hollingworth School for Talented and Gifted (KG-07)
2012-13 Enrollment: 207 . . . . (419) 705-3411
Lake Erie Academy (KG-09)
2012-13 Enrollment: 269 . . . . (419) 475-3786
Life Skills Center of Toledo (09-12)
2012-13 Enrollment: 114 . . . . (419) 241-5504
Madison Avenue School of Arts (KG-05)
2012-13 Enrollment: 591 . . . . (419) 259-4000
Maritime Academy of Toledo the (05-12)
2012-13 Enrollment: 218 . . . . (419) 244-9999
Northpointe Academy (KG-07)
2012-13 Enrollment: 294 . . . . (419) 537-0911
Ottawa Hills Local (PK-12)
2012-13 Enrollment: 988 . . . . (419) 536-6371
Phoenix Academy Community School (07-12)
2012-13 Enrollment: 542 . . . . (419) 720-4500
Polly Fox Academy Community School (07-12)
2012-13 Enrollment: 112 . . . . (419) 720-4503
Springfield Local (PK-12)
2012-13 Enrollment: 3,942 . . . . (419) 867-5600
Star Academy of Toledo (KG-08)
2012-13 Enrollment: 196 . . . . (419) 720-6330
Summit Academy Community School-Toledo (KG-08)
2012-13 Enrollment: 135 . . . . (419) 476-0784
Summit Academy Toledo Learning Center (KG-12)
2012-13 Enrollment: 168 . . . . (419) 476-7859
Sylvania City (PK-12)
2012-13 Enrollment: 7,497 . . . . (419) 824-8501
The Autism Academy of Learning (KG-12)
2012-13 Enrollment: 52 . . . . (419) 865-7487
Toledo City (PK-12)
2012-13 Enrollment: 22,107 . . . . (419) 671-8200
Toledo Preparatory and Fitness Academy (KG-08)
2012-13 Enrollment: 148 . . . . (419) 535-3700
Toledo School for the Arts (06-12)
2012-13 Enrollment: 579 . . . . (419) 246-8732
Washington Local (PK-12)
2012-13 Enrollment: 6,820 . . . . (419) 473-8220
Winterfield Venture Academy (KG-08)
2012-13 Enrollment: 524 . . . . (419) 531-3285

Four-year College(s)

Herzing University-Toledo (Private, For-profit)
Fall 2013 Enrollment: 205 . . . . (419) 776-0300
2013-14 Tuition: In-state $10,800; Out-of-state $10,800
Mercy College of Ohio (Private, Not-for-profit, Roman Catholic)
Fall 2013 Enrollment: 1,195 . . . . (419) 251-1313
2013-14 Tuition: In-state $11,430; Out-of-state $11,430

University of Toledo (Public)
Fall 2013 Enrollment: 20,743 . . . . (419) 530-4636
2013-14 Tuition: In-state $9,275; Out-of-state $18,395

Two-year College(s)

Davis College (Private, For-profit)
Fall 2013 Enrollment: 218 . . . . (419) 473-2700
2013-14 Tuition: In-state $14,130; Out-of-state $14,130
Lincoln College of Technology-Toledo (Private, For-profit)
Fall 2013 Enrollment: 60 . . . . (419) 389-4725
2013-14 Tuition: In-state $12,020; Out-of-state $12,020
Toledo Public Schools Adult and Continuing Education (Public)
Fall 2013 Enrollment: 145 . . . . (419) 671-8700
Toni & Guy Hairdressing Academy-Toledo (Private, For-profit)
Fall 2013 Enrollment: 116 . . . . (419) 866-4489

Vocational/Technical School(s)

Athena Career Academy (Private, For-profit)
Fall 2013 Enrollment: 188 . . . . (419) 472-1150
2013-14 Tuition: $20,415
Toledo Restaurant Training Center (Private, Not-for-profit)
Fall 2013 Enrollment: 40 . . . . (419) 241-5100
2013-14 Tuition: $5,650

Housing: Homeownership rate: 55.5%; Median home value: $83,600; Median year structure built: 1953; Homeowner vacancy rate: 3.2%; Median gross rent: $629 per month; Rental vacancy rate: 12.0%
Health Insurance: 84.7% have insurance; 56.9% have private insurance; 39.4% have public insurance; 15.3% do not have insurance; 5.4% of children under 18 do not have insurance
Hospitals: Mercy Saint Anne Hospital (88 beds); Mercy Saint Vincent Medical Center (588 beds); The Toledo Hospital (794 beds); University of Toledo Medical Center (319 beds)
Safety: Violent crime rate: 102.5 per 10,000 population; Property crime rate: n/a per 10,000 population
Newspapers: Herald Newspapers (weekly circulation 10000); The Blade (daily circulation 123000); Toledo Free Press (weekly circulation 115000)
Transportation: Commute: 91.5% car, 2.3% public transportation, 3.0% walk, 2.1% work from home; Median travel time to work: 19.0 minutes; Amtrak: Train service available.
Airports: Toledo Express (primary service/non-hub)
Additional Information Contacts
City of Toledo . . . . (419) 245-1001
http://www.ci.toledo.oh.us

WATERVILLE (city). Covers a land area of 4.689 square miles and a water area of 0.188 square miles. Located at 41.50° N. Lat; 83.74° W. Long. Elevation is 614 feet.
History: Waterville was platted in 1818 by John Pray. It grew as the center of a garden nursery region.
Population: 5,523; Growth (since 2000): 14.4%; Density: 1,177.9 persons per square mile; Race: 96.7% White, 0.5% Black/African American, 1.0% Asian, 0.1% American Indian/Alaska Native, 0.0% Native Hawaiian/Other Pacific Islander, 1.2% Two or more races, 2.7% Hispanic of any race; Average household size: 2.62; Median age: 41.6; Age under 18: 25.9%; Age 65 and over: 13.9%; Males per 100 females: 92.8; Marriage status: 16.6% never married, 61.3% now married, 2.3% separated, 7.9% widowed, 14.1% divorced; Foreign born: 3.0%; Speak English only: 96.5%; With disability: 8.1%; Veterans: 7.8%; Ancestry: 33.1% German, 14.5% Irish, 13.8% Polish, 10.7% English, 5.5% French
Employment: 17.9% management, business, and financial, 3.5% computer, engineering, and science, 8.1% education, legal, community service, arts, and media, 10.8% healthcare practitioners, 12.6% service, 28.1% sales and office, 9.4% natural resources, construction, and maintenance, 9.7% production, transportation, and material moving
Income: Per capita: $30,556; Median household: $70,475; Average household: $78,133; Households with income of $100,000 or more: 27.3%; Poverty rate: 4.8%
Educational Attainment: High school diploma or higher: 94.1%; Bachelor's degree or higher: 31.8%; Graduate/professional degree or higher: 12.2%

School District(s)

Anthony Wayne Local (PK-12)
2012-13 Enrollment: 4,298 . . . . (419) 877-5377
Housing: Homeownership rate: 85.6%; Median home value: $170,200; Median year structure built: 1976; Homeowner vacancy rate: 0.8%; Median gross rent: $861 per month; Rental vacancy rate: 14.4%
Health Insurance: 94.2% have insurance; 87.3% have private insurance; 17.5% have public insurance; 5.8% do not have insurance; 2.7% of children under 18 do not have insurance
Safety: Violent crime rate: 9.1 per 10,000 population; Property crime rate: 101.9 per 10,000 population
Transportation: Commute: 94.4% car, 0.9% public transportation, 0.3% walk, 4.3% work from home; Median travel time to work: 23.1 minutes
Additional Information Contacts
Village of Waterville . . . . (419) 878-8100
http://www.waterville.org

WHITEHOUSE (village). Covers a land area of 4.292 square miles and a water area of 0 square miles. Located at 41.52° N. Lat; 83.80° W. Long. Elevation is 653 feet.
Population: 4,149; Growth (since 2000): 51.8%; Density: 966.7 persons per square mile; Race: 96.4% White, 0.9% Black/African American, 0.6% Asian, 0.2% American Indian/Alaska Native, 0.0% Native Hawaiian/Other Pacific Islander, 1.2% Two or more races, 2.3% Hispanic of any race; Average household size: 2.67; Median age: 39.0; Age under 18: 27.9%; Age 65 and over: 12.0%; Males per 100 females: 94.5; Marriage status: 25.3% never married, 60.3% now married, 0.4% separated, 5.2% widowed, 9.3% divorced; Foreign born: 1.0%; Speak English only: 98.4%; With disability: 8.4%; Veterans: 8.0%; Ancestry: 47.9% German, 20.5% Irish, 10.3% English, 7.9% Polish, 5.1% American
Employment: 14.2% management, business, and financial, 6.2% computer, engineering, and science, 11.8% education, legal, community service, arts, and media, 11.2% healthcare practitioners, 12.3% service, 25.6% sales and office, 6.2% natural resources, construction, and maintenance, 12.7% production, transportation, and material moving
Income: Per capita: $27,908; Median household: $70,394; Average household: $77,824; Households with income of $100,000 or more: 27.5%; Poverty rate: 7.6%
Educational Attainment: High school diploma or higher: 96.0%; Bachelor's degree or higher: 25.9%; Graduate/professional degree or higher: 13.1%

School District(s)

Anthony Wayne Local (PK-12)
2012-13 Enrollment: 4,298 . . . . (419) 877-5377
Housing: Homeownership rate: 79.1%; Median home value: $168,700; Median year structure built: 1987; Homeowner vacancy rate: 1.4%; Median gross rent: $595 per month; Rental vacancy rate: 7.6%
Health Insurance: 96.8% have insurance; 83.0% have private insurance; 28.1% have public insurance; 3.2% do not have insurance; 0.7% of children under 18 do not have insurance
Safety: Violent crime rate: 6.9 per 10,000 population; Property crime rate: 50.9 per 10,000 population
Transportation: Commute: 96.4% car, 0.0% public transportation, 0.9% walk, 2.8% work from home; Median travel time to work: 22.9 minutes
Additional Information Contacts
Village of Whitehouse . . . . (419) 877-5383
http://whitehouseoh.gov

Madison County

Located in central Ohio; drained by Deer, Paint, and Darby Creeks. Covers a land area of 465.875 square miles, a water area of 0.755 square miles, and is located in the Eastern Time Zone at 39.90° N. Lat., 83.40° W. Long. The county was founded in 1810. County seat is London.

Madison County is part of the Columbus, OH Metropolitan Statistical Area. The entire metro area includes: Delaware County, OH; Fairfield County, OH; Franklin County, OH; Hocking County, OH; Licking County, OH; Madison County, OH; Morrow County, OH; Perry County, OH; Pickaway County, OH; Union County, OH

Population: 43,435; Growth (since 2000): 8.0%; Density: 93.2 persons per square mile; Race: 90.6% White, 6.6% Black/African American, 0.5% Asian, 0.2% American Indian/Alaska Native, 0.0% Native Hawaiian/Other Pacific Islander, 1.5% two or more races, 1.4% Hispanic of any race; Average household size: 2.59; Median age: 39.1; Age under 18: 22.6%; Age 65 and over: 12.4%; Males per 100 females: 120.4; Marriage status: 29.5% never married, 51.4% now married, 1.5% separated, 5.9% widowed, 13.2% divorced; Foreign born: 1.7%; Speak English only: 96.8%; With disability: 13.6%; Veterans: 10.2%; Ancestry: 30.1% German, 15.1% American, 15.0% Irish, 11.5% English, 3.9% Italian

Religion: Six largest groups: 5.8% Catholicism, 5.6% Methodist/Pietist, 4.0% Baptist, 4.0% Hindu, 2.7% European Free-Church, 2.4% Presbyterian-Reformed
Economy: Unemployment rate: 4.0%; Leading industries: 15.4% retail trade; 13.5% construction; 12.1% other services (except public administration); Farms: 699 totaling 263,275 acres; Company size: 0 employ 1,000 or more persons, 3 employ 500 to 999 persons, 19 employ 100 to 499 persons, 646 employ less than 100 persons; Business ownership: 661 women-owned, n/a Black-owned, n/a Hispanic-owned, n/a Asian-owned
Employment: 11.9% management, business, and financial, 4.0% computer, engineering, and science, 7.6% education, legal, community service, arts, and media, 4.6% healthcare practitioners, 17.6% service, 25.1% sales and office, 10.7% natural resources, construction, and maintenance, 18.4% production, transportation, and material moving
Income: Per capita: $24,014; Median household: $54,956; Average household: $69,267; Households with income of $100,000 or more: 21.3%; Poverty rate: 11.0%
Educational Attainment: High school diploma or higher: 85.7%; Bachelor's degree or higher: 17.6%; Graduate/professional degree or higher: 4.9%
Housing: Homeownership rate: 72.2%; Median home value: $144,100; Median year structure built: 1973; Homeowner vacancy rate: 2.2%; Median gross rent: $741 per month; Rental vacancy rate: 8.3%
Vital Statistics: Birth rate: 94.3 per 10,000 population; Death rate: 83.6 per 10,000 population; Age-adjusted cancer mortality rate: 220.6 deaths per 100,000 population
Health Insurance: 87.9% have insurance; 73.1% have private insurance; 27.5% have public insurance; 12.1% do not have insurance; 5.3% of children under 18 do not have insurance
Health Care: Physicians: 10.9 per 10,000 population; Hospital beds: 12.8 per 10,000 population; Hospital admissions: 318.7 per 10,000 population
Air Quality Index: 93.5% good, 6.5% moderate, 0.0% unhealthy for sensitive individuals, 0.0% unhealthy (percent of days)
Transportation: Commute: 93.7% car, 0.2% public transportation, 3.1% walk, 2.3% work from home; Median travel time to work: 23.4 minutes
Presidential Election: 38.9% Obama, 59.3% Romney (2012)
National and State Parks: Bigelow Cemetery State Nature Preserve; Madison Lake State Park; Madison Lake State Reserve
Additional Information Contacts
Madison Government . . . . (740) 852-2972
http://www.co.madison.oh.us

Madison County Communities

CHOCTAW LAKE (CDP). Covers a land area of 0.824 square miles and a water area of 0.386 square miles. Located at 39.96° N. Lat; 83.49° W. Long. Elevation is 1,053 feet.
Population: 1,546; Growth (since 2000): -1.0%; Density: 1,877.2 persons per square mile; Race: 97.9% White, 0.8% Black/African American, 0.4% Asian, 0.1% American Indian/Alaska Native, 0.0% Native Hawaiian/Other Pacific Islander, 0.8% Two or more races, 1.0% Hispanic of any race; Average household size: 2.63; Median age: 44.8; Age under 18: 22.2%; Age 65 and over: 10.9%; Males per 100 females: 98.0
Housing: Homeownership rate: 94.7%; Homeowner vacancy rate: 2.6%; Rental vacancy rate: 3.1%

IRWIN (unincorporated postal area)

ZCTA: 43029

Covers a land area of 23.619 square miles and a water area of 0.013 square miles. Located at 40.10° N. Lat; 83.44° W. Long..
Population: 664; Growth (since 2000): 6.9%; Density: 28.1 persons per square mile; Race: 95.6% White, 0.3% Black/African American, 1.2% Asian, 1.1% American Indian/Alaska Native, 0.0% Native Hawaiian/Other Pacific Islander, 1.7% Two or more races, 0.5% Hispanic of any race; Average household size: 3.06; Median age: 31.8; Age under 18: 28.0%; Age 65 and over: 10.4%; Males per 100 females: 90.8

Four-year College(s)
Rosedale Bible College (Private, Not-for-profit, Mennonite Church)
Fall 2013 Enrollment: 45 . . . . (740) 857-1311
2013-14 Tuition: In-state $8,426; Out-of-state $8,426

Two-year College(s)
Rosedale Bible College (Private, Not-for-profit, Mennonite Church)
Fall 2013 Enrollment: 45 . . . . (740) 857-1311
2013-14 Tuition: In-state $8,426; Out-of-state $8,426

Vocational/Technical School(s)
Rosedale Bible College (Private, Not-for-profit, Mennonite Church)
Fall 2013 Enrollment: 45 . . . . (740) 857-1311
2013-14 Tuition: In-state $8,426; Out-of-state $8,426
Housing: Homeownership rate: 72.0%; Homeowner vacancy rate: 0.0%; Rental vacancy rate: 5.3%

LAFAYETTE (CDP). Covers a land area of 1.048 square miles and a water area of 0 square miles. Located at 39.94° N. Lat; 83.41° W. Long. Elevation is 1,010 feet.
Population: 202; Growth (since 2000): n/a; Density: 192.8 persons per square mile; Race: 97.0% White, 1.5% Black/African American, 0.0% Asian, 0.0% American Indian/Alaska Native, 0.0% Native Hawaiian/Other Pacific Islander, 1.5% Two or more races, 0.0% Hispanic of any race; Average household size: 2.27; Median age: 45.0; Age under 18: 21.8%; Age 65 and over: 20.3%; Males per 100 females: 102.0
Housing: Homeownership rate: 56.2%; Homeowner vacancy rate: 0.0%; Rental vacancy rate: 7.1%

LONDON (city). County seat. Covers a land area of 8.448 square miles and a water area of 0 square miles. Located at 39.89° N. Lat; 83.44° W. Long. Elevation is 1,053 feet.
History: London was established on a site that had formerly been a swamp, known for malaria and ague. When the swamp was drained, the land was good for farming and livestock raising. The town was incorporated in 1831 and soon became a stockyard and trading center.
Population: 9,904; Growth (since 2000): 12.9%; Density: 1,172.4 persons per square mile; Race: 89.2% White, 6.0% Black/African American, 1.0% Asian, 0.3% American Indian/Alaska Native, 0.0% Native Hawaiian/Other Pacific Islander, 2.9% Two or more races, 1.7% Hispanic of any race; Average household size: 2.43; Median age: 37.1; Age under 18: 25.6%; Age 65 and over: 14.6%; Males per 100 females: 88.3; Marriage status: 26.4% never married, 49.1% now married, 1.7% separated, 8.7% widowed, 15.8% divorced; Foreign born: 2.8%; Speak English only: 95.5%; With disability: 17.6%; Veterans: 8.9%; Ancestry: 28.6% German, 19.6% American, 11.7% Irish, 11.1% English, 3.3% Italian
Employment: 12.0% management, business, and financial, 2.8% computer, engineering, and science, 6.0% education, legal, community service, arts, and media, 4.5% healthcare practitioners, 24.2% service, 26.4% sales and office, 8.1% natural resources, construction, and maintenance, 16.1% production, transportation, and material moving
Income: Per capita: $21,632; Median household: $44,558; Average household: $51,857; Households with income of $100,000 or more: 11.7%; Poverty rate: 13.6%
Educational Attainment: High school diploma or higher: 87.3%; Bachelor's degree or higher: 18.0%; Graduate/professional degree or higher: 4.3%

School District(s)
Jonathan Alder Local (PK-12)
2012-13 Enrollment: 2,190 . . . . (614) 873-5621
London Academy (09-12)
2012-13 Enrollment: 266. . . . . (740) 852-5703
London City (PK-12)
2012-13 Enrollment: 1,965 . . . . (740) 852-5700
Madison-Plains Local (KG-12)
2012-13 Enrollment: 1,234 . . . . (740) 852-0290
Housing: Homeownership rate: 55.9%; Median home value: $118,000; Median year structure built: 1972; Homeowner vacancy rate: 3.5%; Median gross rent: $760 per month; Rental vacancy rate: 8.3%
Health Insurance: 83.4% have insurance; 67.1% have private insurance; 31.1% have public insurance; 16.6% do not have insurance; 9.5% of children under 18 do not have insurance
Hospitals: Madison County Hospital (102 beds)
Safety: Violent crime rate: 16.2 per 10,000 population; Property crime rate: 255.4 per 10,000 population
Newspapers: Madison Press (daily circulation 5500); Madison Press (weekly circulation 20000)
Transportation: Commute: 94.3% car, 0.4% public transportation, 3.7% walk, 0.4% work from home; Median travel time to work: 19.8 minutes
Additional Information Contacts
City of London . . . . (740) 852-3243
http://ci.london.oh.us

MIDWAY (village). Covers a land area of 0.291 square miles and a water area of 0 square miles. Located at 39.73° N. Lat; 83.48° W. Long. Elevation is 1,066 feet.
History: Also called Sedalia.
Population: 322; Growth (since 2000): 17.5%; Density: 1,107.5 persons per square mile; Race: 97.2% White, 0.9% Black/African American, 0.0% Asian, 0.6% American Indian/Alaska Native, 0.0% Native Hawaiian/Other Pacific Islander, 1.2% Two or more races, 3.1% Hispanic of any race; Average household size: 2.78; Median age: 34.7; Age under 18: 30.7%; Age 65 and over: 11.8%; Males per 100 females: 95.2
Housing: Homeownership rate: 72.4%; Homeowner vacancy rate: 1.2%; Rental vacancy rate: 5.9%

MOUNT STERLING (village). Covers a land area of 1.725 square miles and a water area of 0 square miles. Located at 39.72° N. Lat; 83.26° W. Long. Elevation is 902 feet.
History: Mount Sterling was founded in 1828 by John J. Smith, who named the town after his former home in Kentucky. An early industry was the Ohio Willow Wood Company, manufacturers of artificial limbs, polo balls and mallets.
Population: 1,782; Growth (since 2000): -4.5%; Density: 1,032.8 persons per square mile; Race: 97.5% White, 0.3% Black/African American, 0.7% Asian, 0.4% American Indian/Alaska Native, 0.0% Native Hawaiian/Other Pacific Islander, 0.7% Two or more races, 2.0% Hispanic of any race; Average household size: 2.40; Median age: 36.3; Age under 18: 24.1%; Age 65 and over: 13.1%; Males per 100 females: 90.4
Housing: Homeownership rate: 53.8%; Homeowner vacancy rate: 3.3%; Rental vacancy rate: 12.8%

PLAIN CITY (village). Covers a land area of 2.379 square miles and a water area of 0.016 square miles. Located at 40.11° N. Lat; 83.27° W. Long. Elevation is 935 feet.
History: Plain City was laid out in 1818 by Isaac Bigelow. It was first called Westminster, then Pleasant Valley, and finally named Plain City in 1851 because of its location on Big Darby Plain.
Population: 4,225; Growth (since 2000): 49.2%; Density: 1,776.1 persons per square mile; Race: 96.0% White, 0.6% Black/African American, 0.7% Asian, 0.7% American Indian/Alaska Native, 0.0% Native Hawaiian/Other Pacific Islander, 1.9% Two or more races, 1.5% Hispanic of any race; Average household size: 2.63; Median age: 37.2; Age under 18: 29.3%; Age 65 and over: 14.8%; Males per 100 females: 88.9; Marriage status: 21.4% never married, 58.2% now married, 1.4% separated, 6.9% widowed, 13.5% divorced; Foreign born: 0.5%; Speak English only: 98.1%; With disability: 10.6%; Veterans: 9.5%; Ancestry: 37.1% German, 16.4% American, 14.4% Irish, 8.8% English, 6.1% Belgian
Employment: 12.0% management, business, and financial, 8.9% computer, engineering, and science, 9.0% education, legal, community service, arts, and media, 4.4% healthcare practitioners, 10.4% service, 27.2% sales and office, 11.8% natural resources, construction, and maintenance, 16.2% production, transportation, and material moving
Income: Per capita: $27,393; Median household: $51,890; Average household: $71,854; Households with income of $100,000 or more: 27.5%; Poverty rate: 17.4%
Educational Attainment: High school diploma or higher: 91.5%; Bachelor's degree or higher: 32.1%; Graduate/professional degree or highor: 7.5%

School District(s)

Jonathan Alder Local (PK-12)
2012-13 Enrollment: 2,190 . . . . (614) 873-5621
Tolles Career & Technical Center (09-12)
2012-13 Enrollment: n/a . . . . (614) 873-4666

Vocational/Technical School(s)

Tolles Career and Technical Center (Public)
Fall 2013 Enrollment: n/a . . . . (614) 873-4666
2013-14 Tuition: $2,340

Housing: Homeownership rate: 69.6%; Median home value: $179,100; Median year structure built: 1973; Homeowner vacancy rate: 1.4%; Median gross rent: $589 per month; Rental vacancy rate: 3.7%
Health Insurance: 94.1% have insurance; 75.0% have private insurance; 30.5% have public insurance; 5.9% do not have insurance; 0.4% of children under 18 do not have insurance
Transportation: Commute: 94.8% car, 0.0% public transportation, 2.2% walk, 3.0% work from home; Median travel time to work: 21.3 minutes

PLUMWOOD (CDP). Covers a land area of 0.622 square miles and a water area of 0 square miles. Located at 40.01° N. Lat; 83.41° W. Long. Elevation is 1,007 feet.
Population: 319; Growth (since 2000): n/a; Density: 513.1 persons per square mile; Race: 96.9% White, 0.0% Black/African American, 0.3% Asian, 0.0% American Indian/Alaska Native, 0.0% Native Hawaiian/Other Pacific Islander, 2.8% Two or more races, 1.3% Hispanic of any race; Average household size: 2.95; Median age: 36.7; Age under 18: 29.5%; Age 65 and over: 10.3%; Males per 100 females: 118.5
Housing: Homeownership rate: 72.2%; Homeowner vacancy rate: 0.0%; Rental vacancy rate: 6.3%

SEDALIA (unincorporated postal area)
ZCTA: 43151
Covers a land area of 0.291 square miles and a water area of 0 square miles. Located at 39.73° N. Lat; 83.48° W. Long..
Population: 322; Growth (since 2000): 17.5%; Density: 1,107.5 persons per square mile; Race: 97.2% White, 0.9% Black/African American, 0.0% Asian, 0.6% American Indian/Alaska Native, 0.0% Native Hawaiian/Other Pacific Islander, 1.2% Two or more races, 3.1% Hispanic of any race; Average household size: 2.78; Median age: 34.7; Age under 18: 30.7%; Age 65 and over: 11.8%; Males per 100 females: 95.2
Housing: Homeownership rate: 72.4%; Homeowner vacancy rate: 1.2%; Rental vacancy rate: 5.9%

SOUTH SOLON (village). Covers a land area of 0.251 square miles and a water area of 0 square miles. Located at 39.74° N. Lat; 83.61° W. Long. Elevation is 1,112 feet.
Population: 355; Growth (since 2000): -12.3%; Density: 1,416.4 persons per square mile; Race: 96.9% White, 0.3% Black/African American, 0.0% Asian, 0.3% American Indian/Alaska Native, 0.0% Native Hawaiian/Other Pacific Islander, 2.5% Two or more races, 2.5% Hispanic of any race; Average household size: 2.89; Median age: 37.5; Age under 18: 24.5%; Age 65 and over: 11.3%; Males per 100 females: 102.9
Housing: Homeownership rate: 74.8%; Homeowner vacancy rate: 3.2%; Rental vacancy rate: 6.1%

WEST JEFFERSON (village). Covers a land area of 4.850 square miles and a water area of 0.021 square miles. Located at 39.95° N. Lat; 83.31° W. Long. Elevation is 912 feet.
Population: 4,222; Growth (since 2000): -2.5%; Density: 870.5 persons per square mile; Race: 97.6% White, 0.5% Black/African American, 0.3% Asian, 0.0% American Indian/Alaska Native, 0.0% Native Hawaiian/Other Pacific Islander, 1.4% Two or more races, 0.9% Hispanic of any race; Average household size: 2.55; Median age: 38.5; Age under 18: 25.5%; Age 65 and over: 15.6%; Males per 100 females: 95.6; Marriage status: 25.4% never married, 54.7% now married, 0.4% separated, 7.0% widowed, 12.8% divorced; Foreign born: 1.0%; Speak English only: 98.2%; With disability: 16.0%; Veterans: 11.0%; Ancestry: 28.9% German, 22.4% Irish, 18.3% American, 11.1% English, 4.2% Scottish
Employment: 7.3% management, business, and financial, 1.4% computer, engineering, and science, 5.6% education, legal, community service, arts, and media, 4.8% healthcare practitioners, 25.7% service, 28.5% sales and office, 9.2% natural resources, construction, and maintenance, 17.6% production, transportation, and material moving
Income: Per capita: $24,008; Median household: $48,459; Average household: $62,121; Households with income of $100,000 or more: 11.5%; Poverty rate: 10.5%
Educational Attainment: High school diploma or higher: 85.8%; Bachelor's degree or higher: 9.3%; Graduate/professional degree or higher: 3.6%

School District(s)

Jefferson Local (PK-12)
2012-13 Enrollment: 1,207 . . . . (614) 879-7654

Housing: Homeownership rate: 68.7%; Median home value: $122,000; Median year structure built: 1967; Homeowner vacancy rate: 1.4%; Median gross rent: $828 per month; Rental vacancy rate: 5.4%
Health Insurance: 87.5% have insurance; 67.6% have private insurance; 31.0% have public insurance; 12.5% do not have insurance; 7.3% of children under 18 do not have insurance
Safety: Violent crime rate: 4.8 per 10,000 population; Property crime rate: 245.7 per 10,000 population
Transportation: Commute: 96.5% car, 0.0% public transportation, 1.7% walk, 1.1% work from home; Median travel time to work: 25.0 minutes

Additional Information Contacts
Village of West Jefferson . . . . (614) 879-7674
http://www.villageofwestjefferson.com

Mahoning County

Located in eastern Ohio; bounded on the east by Pennsylvania; crossed by the Mahoning and Little Beaver Rivers. Covers a land area of 411.623 square miles, a water area of 13.663 square miles, and is located in the Eastern Time Zone at 41.01° N. Lat., 80.77° W. Long. The county was founded in 1846. County seat is Youngstown.

Mahoning County is part of the Youngstown-Warren-Boardman, OH-PA Metropolitan Statistical Area. The entire metro area includes: Mahoning County, OH; Trumbull County, OH; Mercer County, PA

Population: 238,823; Growth (since 2000): -7.3%; Density: 580.2 persons per square mile; Race: 79.9% White, 15.7% Black/African American, 0.7% Asian, 0.2% American Indian/Alaska Native, 0.0% Native Hawaiian/Other Pacific Islander, 2.1% two or more races, 4.7% Hispanic of any race; Average household size: 2.34; Median age: 42.9; Age under 18: 21.5%; Age 65 and over: 17.9%; Males per 100 females: 93.7; Marriage status: 30.7% never married, 47.5% now married, 1.9% separated, 9.2% widowed, 12.6% divorced; Foreign born: 3.2%; Speak English only: 93.3%; With disability: 15.8%; Veterans: 10.6%; Ancestry: 20.9% German, 18.4% Italian, 17.1% Irish, 7.7% English, 7.1% Slovak
Religion: Six largest groups: 29.8% Catholicism, 7.6% Baptist, 3.9% Pentecostal, 3.6% Methodist/Pietist, 3.5% Lutheran, 2.8% Presbyterian-Reformed
Economy: Unemployment rate: 4.9%; Leading industries: 15.9% retail trade; 13.6% health care and social assistance; 11.2% other services (except public administration); Farms: 578 totaling 74,966 acres; Company size: 3 employ 1,000 or more persons, 8 employ 500 to 999 persons, 133 employ 100 to 499 persons, 5,503 employ less than 100 persons; Business ownership: 5,652 women-owned, n/a Black-owned, n/a Hispanic-owned, 296 Asian-owned
Employment: 11.1% management, business, and financial, 2.8% computer, engineering, and science, 9.2% education, legal, community service, arts, and media, 7.5% healthcare practitioners, 19.9% service, 25.8% sales and office, 7.6% natural resources, construction, and maintenance, 16.1% production, transportation, and material moving
Income: Per capita: $23,975; Median household: $41,058; Average household: $56,335; Households with income of $100,000 or more: 13.2%; Poverty rate: 17.6%
Educational Attainment: High school diploma or higher: 88.6%; Bachelor's degree or higher: 20.8%; Graduate/professional degree or higher: 7.3%
Housing: Homeownership rate: 70.6%; Median home value: $95,800; Median year structure built: 1959; Homeowner vacancy rate: 2.4%; Median gross rent: $616 per month; Rental vacancy rate: 10.9%
Vital Statistics: Birth rate: 98.1 per 10,000 population; Death rate: 126.6 per 10,000 population; Age-adjusted cancer mortality rate: 200.4 deaths per 100,000 population
Health Insurance: 89.0% have insurance; 64.2% have private insurance; 38.1% have public insurance; 11.0% do not have insurance; 4.5% of children under 18 do not have insurance
Health Care: Physicians: 30.5 per 10,000 population; Hospital beds: 46.5 per 10,000 population; Hospital admissions: 2,177.9 per 10,000 population
Air Quality Index: 86.8% good, 12.9% moderate, 0.3% unhealthy for sensitive individuals, 0.0% unhealthy (percent of days)
Transportation: Commute: 93.6% car, 1.1% public transportation, 1.3% walk, 2.7% work from home; Median travel time to work: 21.5 minutes
Presidential Election: 63.2% Obama, 35.5% Romney (2012)
Additional Information Contacts
Mahoning Government . . . . (330) 740-2130
http://www.mahoningcountyoh.gov

Mahoning County Communities

AUSTINTOWN (CDP). Covers a land area of 11.630 square miles and a water area of 0.034 square miles. Located at 41.09° N. Lat; 80.74° W. Long. Elevation is 1,129 feet.
Population: 29,677; Growth (since 2000): -6.2%; Density: 2,551.8 persons per square mile; Race: 89.9% White, 6.9% Black/African American, 0.6% Asian, 0.2% American Indian/Alaska Native, 0.0% Native Hawaiian/Other Pacific Islander, 1.8% Two or more races, 2.7% Hispanic of any race; Average household size: 2.22; Median age: 42.8; Age under 18: 20.0%; Age 65 and over: 18.8%; Males per 100 females: 90.6; Marriage status: 28.5% never married, 48.5% now married, 1.1% separated, 10.1% widowed, 13.0% divorced; Foreign born: 1.8%; Speak English only: 97.1%; With disability: 15.2%; Veterans: 13.2%; Ancestry: 27.4% German, 22.4% Irish, 19.1% Italian, 9.2% English, 7.5% Slovak
Employment: 9.4% management, business, and financial, 2.7% computer, engineering, and science, 9.5% education, legal, community service, arts, and media, 7.5% healthcare practitioners, 18.6% service, 26.2% sales and office, 7.5% natural resources, construction, and maintenance, 18.6% production, transportation, and material moving
Income: Per capita: $22,861; Median household: $41,713; Average household: $50,576; Households with income of $100,000 or more: 10.2%; Poverty rate: 12.2%
Educational Attainment: High school diploma or higher: 91.1%; Bachelor's degree or higher: 18.3%; Graduate/professional degree or higher: 6.2%

Two-year College(s)

Casal Aveda Institute (Private, For-profit)
Fall 2013 Enrollment: 156 . . . . (330) 792-6504
Housing: Homeownership rate: 65.9%; Median home value: $91,400; Median year structure built: 1966; Homeowner vacancy rate: 2.0%; Median gross rent: $591 per month; Rental vacancy rate: 12.3%
Health Insurance: 88.7% have insurance; 68.2% have private insurance; 35.4% have public insurance; 11.3% do not have insurance; 6.4% of children under 18 do not have insurance
Safety: Violent crime rate: 14.6 per 10,000 population; Property crime rate: 262.8 per 10,000 population
Transportation: Commute: 96.9% car, 0.3% public transportation, 0.1% walk, 2.0% work from home; Median travel time to work: 19.5 minutes

BELOIT (village). Covers a land area of 0.975 square miles and a water area of 0.008 square miles. Located at 40.92° N. Lat; 81.00° W. Long. Elevation is 1,125 feet.
Population: 978; Growth (since 2000): -4.5%; Density: 1,002.9 persons per square mile; Race: 97.3% White, 0.3% Black/African American, 0.4% Asian, 0.1% American Indian/Alaska Native, 0.0% Native Hawaiian/Other Pacific Islander, 1.8% Two or more races, 0.3% Hispanic of any race; Average household size: 2.30; Median age: 43.4; Age under 18: 23.8%; Age 65 and over: 22.1%; Males per 100 females: 91.0

School District(s)

West Branch Local (PK-12)
2012-13 Enrollment: 2,149 . . . . (330) 938-9324
Housing: Homeownership rate: 70.4%; Homeowner vacancy rate: 3.2%; Rental vacancy rate: 9.3%

BERLIN CENTER (unincorporated postal area)
ZCTA: 44401
Covers a land area of 32.162 square miles and a water area of 1.922 square miles. Located at 41.02° N. Lat; 80.94° W. Long. Elevation is 1,073 feet.
Population: 2,892; Growth (since 2000): -8.9%; Density: 89.9 persons per square mile; Race: 98.8% White, 0.2% Black/African American, 0.0% Asian, 0.2% American Indian/Alaska Native, 0.0% Native Hawaiian/Other Pacific Islander, 0.8% Two or more races, 0.7% Hispanic of any race; Average household size: 2.52; Median age: 47.2; Age under 18: 19.6%; Age 65 and over: 16.6%; Males per 100 females: 106.7; Marriage status: 22.0% never married, 61.8% now married, 1.9% separated, 8.0% widowed, 8.2% divorced; Foreign born: 3.0%; Speak English only: 92.9%; With disability: 15.3%; Veterans: 11.4%; Ancestry: 35.8% German, 26.1% Irish, 9.5% Italian, 7.7% English, 7.4% American
Employment: 7.2% management, business, and financial, 4.0% computer, engineering, and science, 3.2% education, legal, community service, arts, and media, 6.4% healthcare practitioners, 21.1% service, 12.5% sales and office, 15.1% natural resources, construction, and maintenance, 30.6% production, transportation, and material moving
Income: Per capita: $27,498; Median household: $61,654; Average household: $67,837; Households with income of $100,000 or more: 16.7%; Poverty rate: 5.5%
Educational Attainment: High school diploma or higher: 87.4%; Bachelor's degree or higher: 11.1%; Graduate/professional degree or higher: 4.8%

School District(s)

Western Reserve Local (01-12)
2012-13 Enrollment: 683 . . . . (330) 547-4100

Housing: Homeownership rate: 90.4%; Median home value: $157,400; Median year structure built: 1976; Homeowner vacancy rate: 1.2%; Median gross rent: $792 per month; Rental vacancy rate: 11.3%

Health Insurance: 88.3% have insurance; 73.2% have private insurance; 31.5% have public insurance; 11.7% do not have insurance; 4.0% of children under 18 do not have insurance

Transportation: Commute: 95.6% car, 0.0% public transportation, 0.0% walk, 3.6% work from home; Median travel time to work: 28.9 minutes

---

BOARDMAN (CDP). Covers a land area of 15.121 square miles and a water area of 0.172 square miles. Located at 41.03° N. Lat; 80.67° W. Long. Elevation is 1,112 feet.

Population: 35,376; Growth (since 2000): -4.9%; Density: 2,339.5 persons per square mile; Race: 89.6% White, 6.4% Black/African American, 1.2% Asian, 0.1% American Indian/Alaska Native, 0.0% Native Hawaiian/Other Pacific Islander, 1.7% Two or more races, 3.3% Hispanic of any race; Average household size: 2.23; Median age: 43.8; Age under 18: 20.0%; Age 65 and over: 18.4%; Males per 100 females: 90.7; Marriage status: 28.7% never married, 49.5% now married, 1.8% separated, 8.9% widowed, 13.0% divorced; Foreign born: 2.9%; Speak English only: 93.7%; With disability: 13.0%; Veterans: 10.6%; Ancestry: 26.7% Italian, 21.7% German, 18.9% Irish, 8.9% Slovak, 6.9% English

Employment: 14.2% management, business, and financial, 3.3% computer, engineering, and science, 10.8% education, legal, community service, arts, and media, 7.3% healthcare practitioners, 16.6% service, 30.2% sales and office, 6.4% natural resources, construction, and maintenance, 11.3% production, transportation, and material moving

Income: Per capita: $28,039; Median household: $47,381; Average household: $61,583; Households with income of $100,000 or more: 15.4%; Poverty rate: 10.3%

Educational Attainment: High school diploma or higher: 92.7%; Bachelor's degree or higher: 27.1%; Graduate/professional degree or higher: 9.1%

Two-year College(s)

Raphael's School of Beauty Culture Inc-Boardman (Private, For-profit)
Fall 2013 Enrollment: 124 . . . . (330) 782-3395

Housing: Homeownership rate: 68.5%; Median home value: $111,500; Median year structure built: 1964; Homeowner vacancy rate: 2.6%; Median gross rent: $612 per month; Rental vacancy rate: 10.9%

Health Insurance: 89.9% have insurance; 72.3% have private insurance; 31.0% have public insurance; 10.1% do not have insurance; 5.9% of children under 18 do not have insurance

Hospitals: Saint Elizabeth Boardman Health Center

Newspapers: Town Crier Newspapers (weekly circulation 20000)

Transportation: Commute: 95.5% car, 0.7% public transportation, 1.0% walk, 2.0% work from home; Median travel time to work: 20.4 minutes

---

CAMPBELL (city). Covers a land area of 3.712 square miles and a water area of 0.032 square miles. Located at 41.08° N. Lat; 80.59° W. Long. Elevation is 1,033 feet.

History: Until 1926, called East Youngstown.

Population: 8,235; Growth (since 2000): -12.9%; Density: 2,218.4 persons per square mile; Race: 69.1% White, 21.2% Black/African American, 0.4% Asian, 0.3% American Indian/Alaska Native, 0.0% Native Hawaiian/Other Pacific Islander, 3.8% Two or more races, 15.8% Hispanic of any race; Average household size: 2.43; Median age: 41.5; Age under 18: 23.2%; Age 65 and over: 19.6%; Males per 100 females: 90.0; Marriage status: 31.4% never married, 49.7% now married, 3.2% separated, 9.2% widowed, 9.6% divorced; Foreign born: 5.1%; Speak English only: 81.5%; With disability: 20.7%; Veterans: 13.0%; Ancestry: 13.0% Italian, 12.0% Greek, 10.3% German, 10.2% Irish, 6.3% Polish

Employment: 7.0% management, business, and financial, 0.7% computer, engineering, and science, 7.1% education, legal, community service, arts, and media, 6.7% healthcare practitioners, 22.3% service, 26.0% sales and office, 7.3% natural resources, construction, and maintenance, 23.0% production, transportation, and material moving

Income: Per capita: $17,802; Median household: $32,724; Average household: $41,948; Households with income of $100,000 or more: 4.7%; Poverty rate: 21.7%

Educational Attainment: High school diploma or higher: 84.3%; Bachelor's degree or higher: 9.5%; Graduate/professional degree or higher: 3.3%

School District(s)

Campbell City (PK-12)
2012-13 Enrollment: 1,201 . . . . (330) 799-8777

Housing: Homeownership rate: 69.8%; Median home value: $71,600; Median year structure built: 1955; Homeowner vacancy rate: 2.9%; Median gross rent: $681 per month; Rental vacancy rate: 10.8%

Health Insurance: 90.7% have insurance; 54.9% have private insurance; 48.1% have public insurance; 9.3% do not have insurance; 0.7% of children under 18 do not have insurance

Transportation: Commute: 95.8% car, 0.8% public transportation, 0.7% walk, 1.1% work from home; Median travel time to work: 22.2 minutes

Additional Information Contacts

City of Campbell . . . . (330) 755-1451
http://cityofcampbellohio.org

CANFIELD (city). Covers a land area of 4.579 square miles and a water area of 0.027 square miles. Located at 41.03° N. Lat; 80.77° W. Long. Elevation is 1,148 feet.

History: Canfield was surveyed in 1798. After a brief oil boom, the town turned to lumber, clay, coal, and farm products for its revenue source.

Population: 7,515; Growth (since 2000): 1.9%; Density: 1,641.1 persons per square mile; Race: 96.4% White, 0.4% Black/African American, 1.8% Asian, 0.1% American Indian/Alaska Native, 0.0% Native Hawaiian/Other Pacific Islander, 0.7% Two or more races, 1.5% Hispanic of any race; Average household size: 2.44; Median age: 45.8; Age under 18: 23.6%; Age 65 and over: 19.0%; Males per 100 females: 92.4; Marriage status: 18.2% never married, 64.9% now married, 0.3% separated, 7.6% widowed, 9.3% divorced; Foreign born: 4.8%; Speak English only: 94.5%; With disability: 8.7%; Veterans: 10.3%; Ancestry: 26.2% German, 23.3% Italian, 21.6% Irish, 12.3% English, 8.8% Slovak

Employment: 16.0% management, business, and financial, 4.4% computer, engineering, and science, 12.4% education, legal, community service, arts, and media, 11.9% healthcare practitioners, 11.8% service, 31.0% sales and office, 5.4% natural resources, construction, and maintenance, 7.1% production, transportation, and material moving

Income: Per capita: $40,947; Median household: $71,133; Average household: $97,425; Households with income of $100,000 or more: 35.2%; Poverty rate: 8.7%

Educational Attainment: High school diploma or higher: 96.4%; Bachelor's degree or higher: 40.2%; Graduate/professional degree or higher: 15.3%

School District(s)

Canfield Local (PK-12)
2012-13 Enrollment: 2,826 . . . . (330) 533-3303
Mahoning County Career & Tech Ctr (07-12)
2012-13 Enrollment: n/a . . . . (330) 729-4000
South Range Local (PK-12)
2012-13 Enrollment: 1,165 . . . . (330) 549-5226

Vocational/Technical School(s)

Mahoning County Career and Technical Center (Public)
Fall 2013 Enrollment: 96 . . . . (330) 729-4100
2013-14 Tuition: $8,329

Housing: Homeownership rate: 84.1%; Median home value: $159,200; Median year structure built: 1975; Homeowner vacancy rate: 2.7%; Median gross rent: $638 per month; Rental vacancy rate: 12.7%

Health Insurance: 93.9% have insurance; 86.0% have private insurance; 22.6% have public insurance; 6.1% do not have insurance; 4.0% of children under 18 do not have insurance

Safety: Violent crime rate: 2.7 per 10,000 population; Property crime rate: 99.9 per 10,000 population

Transportation: Commute: 94.5% car, 0.0% public transportation, 1.2% walk, 4.0% work from home; Median travel time to work: 24.6 minutes

Additional Information Contacts

City of Canfield . . . . (330) 533-1101
http://www.ci.canfield.oh.us

CRAIG BEACH (village). Covers a land area of 0.784 square miles and a water area of 0.785 square miles. Located at 41.12° N. Lat; 80.98° W. Long. Elevation is 951 feet.

Population: 1,180; Growth (since 2000): -5.9%; Density: 1,504.4 persons per square mile; Race: 95.6% White, 0.2% Black/African American, 0.4% Asian, 0.5% American Indian/Alaska Native, 0.0% Native Hawaiian/Other Pacific Islander, 2.8% Two or more races, 2.1% Hispanic of any race; Average household size: 2.44; Median age: 40.4; Age under 18: 22.5%; Age 65 and over: 14.1%; Males per 100 females: 94.1

Housing: Homeownership rate: 70.2%; Homeowner vacancy rate: 3.1%; Rental vacancy rate: 5.8%

DAMASCUS (CDP). Covers a land area of 0.799 square miles and a water area of 0.007 square miles. Located at 40.91° N. Lat; 80.95° W. Long. Elevation is 1,211 feet.
Population: 443; Growth (since 2000): n/a; Density: 554.4 persons per square mile; Race: 99.3% White, 0.0% Black/African American, 0.2% Asian, 0.0% American Indian/Alaska Native, 0.0% Native Hawaiian/Other Pacific Islander, 0.2% Two or more races, 0.5% Hispanic of any race; Average household size: 2.53; Median age: 38.4; Age under 18: 24.4%; Age 65 and over: 11.3%; Males per 100 females: 98.7
Housing: Homeownership rate: 65.7%; Homeowner vacancy rate: 4.1%; Rental vacancy rate: 7.7%

LAKE MILTON (unincorporated postal area)
ZCTA: 44429
Covers a land area of 6.496 square miles and a water area of 2.607 square miles. Located at 41.10° N. Lat; 80.98° W. Long. Elevation is 988 feet.
Population: 2,576; Growth (since 2000): -10.7%; Density: 396.6 persons per square mile; Race: 97.3% White, 0.1% Black/African American, 0.3% Asian, 0.3% American Indian/Alaska Native, 0.0% Native Hawaiian/Other Pacific Islander, 1.7% Two or more races, 1.5% Hispanic of any race; Average household size: 2.34; Median age: 45.7; Age under 18: 19.3%; Age 65 and over: 15.7%; Males per 100 females: 99.8; Marriage status: 21.7% never married, 59.0% now married, 1.3% separated, 6.4% widowed, 13.0% divorced; Foreign born: 1.1%; Speak English only: 98.2%; With disability: 15.7%; Veterans: 12.9%; Ancestry: 28.7% German, 26.6% Irish, 12.3% Italian, 10.4% English, 9.3% Slovak
Employment: 8.4% management, business, and financial, 3.6% computer, engineering, and science, 10.0% education, legal, community service, arts, and media, 9.7% healthcare practitioners, 15.5% service, 24.0% sales and office, 13.4% natural resources, construction, and maintenance, 15.3% production, transportation, and material moving
Income: Per capita: $27,572; Median household: $49,432; Average household: $61,617; Households with income of $100,000 or more: 14.1%; Poverty rate: 14.9%
Educational Attainment: High school diploma or higher: 89.5%; Bachelor's degree or higher: 18.9%; Graduate/professional degree or higher: 5.8%

Four-year College(s)
TDDS Technical Institute (Private, For-profit)
Fall 2013 Enrollment: 374 . . . . (330) 538-2216

Two-year College(s)
TDDS Technical Institute (Private, For-profit)
Fall 2013 Enrollment: 374 . . . . (330) 538-2216

Vocational/Technical School(s)
TDDS Technical Institute (Private, For-profit)
Fall 2013 Enrollment: 374 . . . . (330) 538-2216
2013-14 Tuition: $6,245

Housing: Homeownership rate: 75.6%; Median home value: $124,200; Median year structure built: 1964; Homeowner vacancy rate: 3.6%; Median gross rent: $717 per month; Rental vacancy rate: 5.3%
Health Insurance: 87.8% have insurance; 65.9% have private insurance; 37.6% have public insurance; 12.2% do not have insurance; 5.2% of children under 18 do not have insurance
Transportation: Commute: 95.1% car, 0.0% public transportation, 3.0% walk, 1.9% work from home; Median travel time to work: 29.3 minutes

LOWELLVILLE (village). Covers a land area of 1.361 square miles and a water area of 0.082 square miles. Located at 41.04° N. Lat; 80.54° W. Long. Elevation is 823 feet.
History: Lowellville was settled in 1800 and incorporated in 1836. First a coal town, after 1845 the economy depended more on iron and steel.
Population: 1,155; Growth (since 2000): -9.8%; Density: 848.7 persons per square mile; Race: 98.9% White, 0.3% Black/African American, 0.2% Asian, 0.1% American Indian/Alaska Native, 0.0% Native Hawaiian/Other Pacific Islander, 0.6% Two or more races, 1.2% Hispanic of any race; Average household size: 2.45; Median age: 41.6; Age under 18: 23.2%; Age 65 and over: 16.9%; Males per 100 females: 84.2

School District(s)
Lowellville Local (PK-12)
2012-13 Enrollment: 594 . . . . (330) 536-6318

Housing: Homeownership rate: 71.4%; Homeowner vacancy rate: 2.3%; Rental vacancy rate: 9.4%
Safety: Violent crime rate: 0.0 per 10,000 population; Property crime rate: 124.0 per 10,000 population

MAPLE RIDGE (CDP). Covers a land area of 1.840 square miles and a water area of 0.057 square miles. Located at 40.91° N. Lat; 81.05° W. Long. Elevation is 1,102 feet.
Population: 761; Growth (since 2000): -16.4%; Density: 413.6 persons per square mile; Race: 97.2% White, 0.5% Black/African American, 0.1% Asian, 0.1% American Indian/Alaska Native, 0.0% Native Hawaiian/Other Pacific Islander, 1.8% Two or more races, 0.4% Hispanic of any race; Average household size: 2.50; Median age: 42.8; Age under 18: 23.3%; Age 65 and over: 14.8%; Males per 100 females: 96.1
Housing: Homeownership rate: 84.2%; Homeowner vacancy rate: 1.2%; Rental vacancy rate: 7.7%

NEW MIDDLETOWN (village). Covers a land area of 0.873 square miles and a water area of 0.002 square miles. Located at 40.97° N. Lat; 80.56° W. Long. Elevation is 1,253 feet.
Population: 1,621; Growth (since 2000): -3.6%; Density: 1,856.5 persons per square mile; Race: 98.8% White, 0.1% Black/African American, 0.1% Asian, 0.0% American Indian/Alaska Native, 0.0% Native Hawaiian/Other Pacific Islander, 0.6% Two or more races, 1.7% Hispanic of any race; Average household size: 2.29; Median age: 47.0; Age under 18: 19.6%; Age 65 and over: 21.3%; Males per 100 females: 81.7

School District(s)
Springfield Local (PK-12)
2012-13 Enrollment: 1,113 . . . . (330) 542-2929

Housing: Homeownership rate: 75.7%; Homeowner vacancy rate: 2.2%; Rental vacancy rate: 5.5%

NEW SPRINGFIELD (unincorporated postal area)
ZCTA: 44443
Covers a land area of 12.843 square miles and a water area of 0.222 square miles. Located at 40.93° N. Lat; 80.60° W. Long. Elevation is 1,211 feet.
Population: 1,704; Growth (since 2000): -17.1%; Density: 132.7 persons per square mile; Race: 99.2% White, 0.0% Black/African American, 0.0% Asian, 0.1% American Indian/Alaska Native, 0.1% Native Hawaiian/Other Pacific Islander, 0.7% Two or more races, 0.5% Hispanic of any race; Average household size: 2.44; Median age: 44.9; Age under 18: 20.5%; Age 65 and over: 18.0%; Males per 100 females: 96.5
Housing: Homeownership rate: 85.6%; Homeowner vacancy rate: 2.3%; Rental vacancy rate: 17.7%

NORTH JACKSON (unincorporated postal area)
ZCTA: 44451
Covers a land area of 37.483 square miles and a water area of 0.601 square miles. Located at 41.08° N. Lat; 80.87° W. Long. Elevation is 1,020 feet.
Population: 3,032; Growth (since 2000): -2.2%; Density: 80.9 persons per square mile; Race: 98.0% White, 0.4% Black/African American, 0.1% Asian, 0.3% American Indian/Alaska Native, 0.0% Native Hawaiian/Other Pacific Islander, 0.8% Two or more races, 0.8% Hispanic of any race; Average household size: 2.49; Median age: 45.9; Age under 18: 18.9%; Age 65 and over: 15.8%; Males per 100 females: 107.0; Marriage status: 24.0% never married, 60.2% now married, 1.1% separated, 4.5% widowed, 11.3% divorced; Foreign born: 2.7%; Speak English only: 95.5%; With disability: 15.4%; Veterans: 12.0%; Ancestry: 38.1% German, 20.6% Irish, 11.9% Italian, 8.1% Slovak, 7.5% American
Employment: 10.4% management, business, and financial, 0.5% computer, engineering, and science, 8.1% education, legal, community service, arts, and media, 8.9% healthcare practitioners, 15.1% service, 20.3% sales and office, 12.1% natural resources, construction, and maintenance, 24.7% production, transportation, and material moving
Income: Per capita: $27,487; Median household: $61,236; Average household: $67,711; Households with income of $100,000 or more: 17.6%; Poverty rate: 6.5%
Educational Attainment: High school diploma or higher: 93.9%; Bachelor's degree or higher: 18.7%; Graduate/professional degree or higher: 5.2%

School District(s)
Jackson-Milton Local (PK-12)
2012-13 Enrollment: 799 . . . . (330) 538-3232

Housing: Homeownership rate: 82.5%; Median home value: $159,600; Median year structure built: 1973; Homeowner vacancy rate: 1.1%; Median gross rent: $843 per month; Rental vacancy rate: 13.8%
Health Insurance: 93.2% have insurance; 79.6% have private insurance; 26.5% have public insurance; 6.8% do not have insurance; 3.2% of children under 18 do not have insurance
Transportation: Commute: 92.8% car, 0.0% public transportation, 1.9% walk, 4.0% work from home; Median travel time to work: 21.7 minutes

NORTH LIMA (unincorporated postal area)

ZCTA: 44452

Covers a land area of 13.354 square miles and a water area of 0.849 square miles. Located at 40.95° N. Lat; 80.66° W. Long. Elevation is 1,102 feet.
Population: 3,167; Growth (since 2000): 16.3%; Density: 237.2 persons per square mile; Race: 97.8% White, 0.8% Black/African American, 0.5% Asian, 0.1% American Indian/Alaska Native, 0.0% Native Hawaiian/Other Pacific Islander, 0.8% Two or more races, 0.4% Hispanic of any race; Average household size: 2.48; Median age: 48.1; Age under 18: 21.3%; Age 65 and over: 25.1%; Males per 100 females: 88.7; Marriage status: 23.9% never married, 48.4% now married, 0.4% separated, 13.0% widowed, 14.6% divorced; Foreign born: 2.6%; Speak English only: 95.3%; With disability: 17.4%; Veterans: 9.6%; Ancestry: 29.4% German, 19.6% Irish, 15.8% Italian, 11.4% English, 10.8% Polish
Employment: 6.9% management, business, and financial, 7.9% computer, engineering, and science, 6.0% education, legal, community service, arts, and media, 2.2% healthcare practitioners, 25.9% service, 28.7% sales and office, 7.9% natural resources, construction, and maintenance, 14.6% production, transportation, and material moving
Income: Per capita: $20,653; Median household: $37,238; Average household: $49,435; Households with income of $100,000 or more: 7.9%; Poverty rate: 14.7%
Educational Attainment: High school diploma or higher: 89.0%; Bachelor's degree or higher: 15.4%; Graduate/professional degree or higher: 5.4%
Housing: Homeownership rate: 75.8%; Median home value: $144,000; Median year structure built: 1968; Homeowner vacancy rate: 2.5%; Median gross rent: $631 per month; Rental vacancy rate: 12.3%
Health Insurance: 89.5% have insurance; 70.2% have private insurance; 37.0% have public insurance; 10.5% do not have insurance; 5.4% of children under 18 do not have insurance
Transportation: Commute: 96.0% car, 0.0% public transportation, 0.0% walk, 2.5% work from home; Median travel time to work: 27.0 minutes

PETERSBURG (unincorporated postal area)

ZCTA: 44454

Covers a land area of 8.286 square miles and a water area of 0.147 square miles. Located at 40.92° N. Lat; 80.55° W. Long. Elevation is 1,129 feet.
Population: 1,153; Growth (since 2000): -9.7%; Density: 139.1 persons per square mile; Race: 97.6% White, 0.3% Black/African American, 0.1% Asian, 0.3% American Indian/Alaska Native, 0.0% Native Hawaiian/Other Pacific Islander, 1.3% Two or more races, 2.0% Hispanic of any race; Average household size: 2.71; Median age: 43.7; Age under 18: 22.4%; Age 65 and over: 14.2%; Males per 100 females: 100.2
Housing: Homeownership rate: 85.4%; Homeowner vacancy rate: 1.9%; Rental vacancy rate: 6.1%

POLAND (village). Covers a land area of 1.634 square miles and a water area of 0.022 square miles. Located at 41.02° N. Lat; 80.62° W. Long. Elevation is 1,043 feet.

History: Poland was settled in 1799 by Jonathan Fowler, and originally named for him. Fowler operated the Stone Tavern, a stop on the Pittsburgh to Cleveland stage route. The town became a residential suburb of Youngstown.
Population: 2,555; Growth (since 2000): -10.9%; Density: 1,563.3 persons per square mile; Race: 98.5% White, 0.2% Black/African American, 0.4% Asian, 0.0% American Indian/Alaska Native, 0.0% Native Hawaiian/Other Pacific Islander, 0.9% Two or more races, 1.1% Hispanic of any race; Average household size: 2.40; Median age: 46.3; Age under 18: 21.4%; Age 65 and over: 21.3%; Males per 100 females: 93.1; Marriage status: 24.8% never married, 58.4% now married, 2.1% separated, 8.1% widowed, 8.7% divorced; Foreign born: 4.0%; Speak English only: 96.1%; With disability: 11.7%; Veterans: 7.4%; Ancestry: 27.8% German, 22.4% Italian, 20.0% Irish, 16.0% English, 7.5% Slovak
Employment: 11.9% management, business, and financial, 2.6% computer, engineering, and science, 14.7% education, legal, community service, arts, and media, 11.1% healthcare practitioners, 12.2% service, 23.9% sales and office, 6.5% natural resources, construction, and maintenance, 17.1% production, transportation, and material moving
Income: Per capita: $31,154; Median household: $57,159; Average household: $77,789; Households with income of $100,000 or more: 25.7%; Poverty rate: 6.6%
Educational Attainment: High school diploma or higher: 94.1%; Bachelor's degree or higher: 41.3%; Graduate/professional degree or higher: 16.4%

School District(s)

Poland Local (PK-12)
2012-13 Enrollment: 2,164 . . . . (330) 757-7000
Housing: Homeownership rate: 87.6%; Median home value: $130,400; Median year structure built: 1951; Homeowner vacancy rate: 1.6%; Median gross rent: $880 per month; Rental vacancy rate: 5.7%
Health Insurance: 95.4% have insurance; 82.5% have private insurance; 27.6% have public insurance; 4.6% do not have insurance; 1.8% of children under 18 do not have insurance
Safety: Violent crime rate: 0.0 per 10,000 population; Property crime rate: 67.7 per 10,000 population
Transportation: Commute: 92.2% car, 2.8% public transportation, 1.0% walk, 2.7% work from home; Median travel time to work: 27.8 minutes

SEBRING (village). Covers a land area of 2.496 square miles and a water area of 0.016 square miles. Located at 40.92° N. Lat; 81.03° W. Long. Elevation is 1,102 feet.

Population: 4,420; Growth (since 2000): -10.0%; Density: 1,771.1 persons per square mile; Race: 97.8% White, 0.2% Black/African American, 0.2% Asian, 0.1% American Indian/Alaska Native, 0.0% Native Hawaiian/Other Pacific Islander, 1.2% Two or more races, 0.7% Hispanic of any race; Average household size: 2.23; Median age: 45.3; Age under 18: 20.4%; Age 65 and over: 26.9%; Males per 100 females: 84.2; Marriage status: 23.9% never married, 42.9% now married, 0.8% separated, 18.9% widowed, 14.3% divorced; Foreign born: 4.5%; Speak English only: 94.1%; With disability: 21.6%; Veterans: 9.3%; Ancestry: 27.6% German, 12.8% English, 12.5% American, 12.3% Irish, 4.8% Italian
Employment: 5.2% management, business, and financial, 0.4% computer, engineering, and science, 1.1% education, legal, community service, arts, and media, 5.0% healthcare practitioners, 24.7% service, 21.2% sales and office, 16.8% natural resources, construction, and maintenance, 25.5% production, transportation, and material moving
Income: Per capita: $22,001; Median household: $35,403; Average household: $46,383; Households with income of $100,000 or more: 4.0%; Poverty rate: 14.8%
Educational Attainment: High school diploma or higher: 83.7%; Bachelor's degree or higher: 16.0%; Graduate/professional degree or higher: 3.5%

School District(s)

Sebring Local (PK-12)
2012-13 Enrollment: 557. . . . . (330) 938-6165
Housing: Homeownership rate: 54.7%; Median home value: $70,300; Median year structure built: 1958; Homeowner vacancy rate: 2.7%; Median gross rent: $743 per month; Rental vacancy rate: 17.3%
Health Insurance: 85.7% have insurance; 60.7% have private insurance; 45.8% have public insurance; 14.3% do not have insurance; 2.1% of children under 18 do not have insurance
Safety: Violent crime rate: 20.8 per 10,000 population; Property crime rate: 246.7 per 10,000 population
Transportation: Commute: 94.8% car, 0.0% public transportation, 1.2% walk, 2.1% work from home; Median travel time to work: 20.9 minutes
Additional Information Contacts
Village of Sebring . . . . (330) 938-9340
http://www.sebringohio.net

STRUTHERS (city). Covers a land area of 3.642 square miles and a water area of 0.096 square miles. Located at 41.05° N. Lat; 80.59° W. Long. Elevation is 1,007 feet.

History: Principal steel industry has declined. Founded 1800, incorporated 1922.
Population: 10,713; Growth (since 2000): -8.9%; Density: 2,941.4 persons per square mile; Race: 94.3% White, 2.9% Black/African American, 0.2% Asian, 0.2% American Indian/Alaska Native, 0.0% Native Hawaiian/Other Pacific Islander, 1.9% Two or more races, 3.1% Hispanic of any race;

Average household size: 2.43; Median age: 41.4; Age under 18: 22.2%; Age 65 and over: 18.0%; Males per 100 females: 90.9; Marriage status: 30.8% never married, 42.9% now married, 2.7% separated, 10.5% widowed, 15.8% divorced; Foreign born: 0.8%; Speak English only: 93.5%; With disability: 18.6%; Veterans: 8.5%; Ancestry: 27.2% Italian, 21.6% German, 19.4% Irish, 11.9% Slovak, 6.4% Polish

Employment: 8.3% management, business, and financial, 0.9% computer, engineering, and science, 6.8% education, legal, community service, arts, and media, 3.8% healthcare practitioners, 23.3% service, 30.1% sales and office, 10.2% natural resources, construction, and maintenance, 16.6% production, transportation, and material moving

Income: Per capita: $18,643; Median household: $36,628; Average household: $44,790; Households with income of $100,000 or more: 5.1%; Poverty rate: 19.8%

Educational Attainment: High school diploma or higher: 90.0%; Bachelor's degree or higher: 12.8%; Graduate/professional degree or higher: 3.9%

School District(s)

Struthers City (PK-12)
2012-13 Enrollment: 1,940 . . . . (330) 750-1061

Housing: Homeownership rate: 73.0%; Median home value: $71,100; Median year structure built: 1954; Homeowner vacancy rate: 2.4%; Median gross rent: $623 per month; Rental vacancy rate: 6.5%

Health Insurance: 86.2% have insurance; 56.5% have private insurance; 41.1% have public insurance; 13.8% do not have insurance; 2.4% of children under 18 do not have insurance

Safety: Violent crime rate: 10.5 per 10,000 population; Property crime rate: 158.7 per 10,000 population

Newspapers: Hometown Journal (weekly circulation 6000)

Transportation: Commute: 95.8% car, 0.5% public transportation, 0.9% walk, 0.7% work from home; Median travel time to work: 19.2 minutes

Additional Information Contacts

City of Struthers. . . . . (330) 755-2181
http://www.cityofstruthers.com

YOUNGSTOWN (city). County seat. Covers a land area of 33.955 square miles and a water area of 0.635 square miles. Located at 41.10° N. Lat; 80.65° W. Long. Elevation is 856 feet.

History: Youngstown, established along the Mahoning River, was shaped by the steel industry. In 1797 John Young of New York led a party of settlers to this site. By 1802 James and Daniel Heaton had set up a crude smelter on Yellow Creek, utilizing native bog ores and limestones. The first coal mine in the Mahoning Valley opened in 1826, and Mahoning coal was soon used in the reduction of iron ore. In 1892 the Union Iron & Steel Company built a plant in Youngstown, and the banks of the river were soon lined with Bessemer converters, open-hearth furnaces, strip and rolling mills, pipe plants, and manufactories of steel accessories and products.

Population: 66,982; Growth (since 2000): -18.3%; Density: 1,972.7 persons per square mile; Race: 47.0% White, 45.2% Black/African American, 0.4% Asian, 0.4% American Indian/Alaska Native, 0.0% Native Hawaiian/Other Pacific Islander, 3.7% Two or more races, 9.3% Hispanic of any race; Average household size: 2.28; Median age: 38.0; Age under 18: 22.8%; Age 65 and over: 15.8%; Males per 100 females: 96.9; Marriage status: 43.8% never married, 31.6% now married, 3.3% separated, 9.2% widowed, 15.4% divorced; Foreign born: 4.3%; Speak English only: 90.3%; With disability: 20.9%; Veterans: 9.8%; Ancestry: 11.0% Italian, 10.4% German, 10.2% Irish, 6.1% American, 6.1% African

Employment: 7.0% management, business, and financial, 1.8% computer, engineering, and science, 7.7% education, legal, community service, arts, and media, 5.5% healthcare practitioners, 29.3% service, 23.9% sales and office, 7.1% natural resources, construction, and maintenance, 17.7% production, transportation, and material moving

Income: Per capita: $14,876; Median household: $24,454; Average household: $34,894; Households with income of $100,000 or more: 4.2%; Poverty rate: 36.4%

Educational Attainment: High school diploma or higher: 80.4%; Bachelor's degree or higher: 11.0%; Graduate/professional degree or higher: 4.0%

School District(s)

Austintown Local (PK-12)
2012-13 Enrollment: 5,216 . . . . (330) 797-3900

Boardman Local (PK-12)
2012-13 Enrollment: 4,421 . . . . (330) 726-3404

Horizon Science Academy Youngstown (KG-08)
2012-13 Enrollment: 388. . . . . (330) 782-3003

Liberty Local (PK-12)
2012-13 Enrollment: 1,282 . . . . (330) 759-0807

Life Skills Ctr of Youngstown (09-12)
2012-13 Enrollment: 217. . . . . (330) 743-6698

Mahoning County High School (09-12)
2012-13 Enrollment: 100. . . . . (330) 965-2860

Mahoning Unlimited Classroom (04-12)
2012-13 Enrollment: 120. . . . . (330) 965-7828

Mahoning Valley Opportunity Center (09-12)
2012-13 Enrollment: 103. . . . . (330) 744-7656

Mollie Kessler (01-08)
2012-13 Enrollment: 65. . . . . (330) 746-3095

Southside Academy (KG-08)
2012-13 Enrollment: 305. . . . . (330) 742-9090

Stambaugh Charter Academy (KG-08)
2012-13 Enrollment: 467. . . . . (330) 792-4806

Steam Academy of Youngstown (KG-05)
2012-13 Enrollment: n/a . . . . (330) 480-0844

Summit Academy Secondary - Youngstown (08-12)
2012-13 Enrollment: 196. . . . . (330) 747-0950

Summit Academy-Youngstown (KG-08)
2012-13 Enrollment: 169. . . . . (330) 259-0421

Youngstown Academy of Excellence (KG-08)
2012-13 Enrollment: 214. . . . . (330) 746-3970

Youngstown City Schools (PK-12)
2012-13 Enrollment: 5,555 . . . . (330) 744-6915

Youngstown Community School (KG-06)
2012-13 Enrollment: 321. . . . . (330) 746-2240

Four-year College(s)

ITT Technical Institute-Youngstown (Private, For-profit)
Fall 2013 Enrollment: 472 . . . . (330) 270-1600
2013-14 Tuition: In-state $18,048; Out-of-state $18,048

Youngstown State University (Public)
Fall 2013 Enrollment: 13,352 . . . . (877) 468-6978
2013-14 Tuition: In-state $8,129; Out-of-state $8,358

Two-year College(s)

National College-Youngstown (Private, For-profit)
Fall 2013 Enrollment: 130 . . . . (330) 759-0205
2013-14 Tuition: In-state $11,550; Out-of-state $11,550

Vocational/Technical School(s)

Choffin Career and Technical Center (Public)
Fall 2013 Enrollment: 154 . . . . (330) 744-8700
2013-14 Tuition: In-state $8,000; Out-of-state $8,000

Housing: Homeownership rate: 58.2%; Median home value: $46,600; Median year structure built: 1948; Homeowner vacancy rate: 3.2%; Median gross rent: $585 per month; Rental vacancy rate: 11.1%

Health Insurance: 84.9% have insurance; 42.0% have private insurance; 54.4% have public insurance; 15.1% do not have insurance; 3.3% of children under 18 do not have insurance

Hospitals: Northside Medical Center (830 beds); Saint Elizabeth Health Center (350 beds); Surgical Hospital at Southwoods

Safety: Violent crime rate: 81.0 per 10,000 population; Property crime rate: 549.8 per 10,000 population

Newspapers: Boardman News (weekly circulation 9000); The Vindicator (daily circulation 58300)

Transportation: Commute: 88.4% car, 3.2% public transportation, 2.9% walk, 2.7% work from home; Median travel time to work: 20.3 minutes

Airports: Youngstown-Warren Regional (primary service/non-hub)

Additional Information Contacts

City of Youngstown . . . . (330) 742-8701
http://www.cityofyoungstownoh.org

Marion County

Located in central Ohio; crossed by the Scioto River; drained by the Olentangy and Little Scioto Rivers. Covers a land area of 403.757 square miles, a water area of 0.351 square miles, and is located in the Eastern Time Zone at 40.59° N. Lat., 83.17° W. Long. The county was founded in 1820. County seat is Marion.

Marion County is part of the Marion, OH Micropolitan Statistical Area. The entire metro area includes: Marion County, OH

Weather Station: Marion 2 N Elevation: 964 feet

	Jan	Feb	Mar	Apr	May	Jun	Jul	Aug	Sep	Oct	Nov	Dec
High	33	37	47	60	71	80	83	82	76	63	50	38
Low	18	20	28	38	49	59	62	60	52	41	33	23
Precip	2.5	1.9	2.3	3.6	4.5	4.4	4.3	3.8	3.2	2.9	3.0	2.8
Snow	7.6	5.2	3.5	0.6	0.0	0.0	0.0	0.0	0.0	tr	0.8	5.3

High and Low temperatures in degrees Fahrenheit; Precipitation and Snow in inches

Population: 66,501; Growth (since 2000): 0.4%; Density: 164.7 persons per square mile; Race: 91.1% White, 5.7% Black/African American, 0.5% Asian, 0.2% American Indian/Alaska Native, 0.1% Native Hawaiian/Other Pacific Islander, 1.7% two or more races, 2.3% Hispanic of any race; Average household size: 2.47; Median age: 39.9; Age under 18: 22.1%; Age 65 and over: 14.2%; Males per 100 females: 110.3; Marriage status: 26.8% never married, 52.1% now married, 2.3% separated, 7.1% widowed, 13.9% divorced; Foreign born: 1.2%; Speak English only: 96.5%; With disability: 17.4%; Veterans: 10.6%; Ancestry: 28.1% German, 14.8% Irish, 12.1% American, 9.8% English, 4.6% Italian
Religion: Six largest groups: 5.5% Methodist/Pietist, 5.3% Baptist, 4.4% Lutheran, 3.8% Catholicism, 3.7% Holiness, 2.3% Non-denominational Protestant
Economy: Unemployment rate: 4.9%; Leading industries: 15.8% retail trade; 13.6% health care and social assistance; 13.6% other services (except public administration); Farms: 578 totaling 189,210 acres; Company size: 2 employ 1,000 or more persons, 1 employs 500 to 999 persons, 25 employ 100 to 499 persons, 1,123 employ less than 100 persons; Business ownership: 1,018 women-owned, 76 Black-owned, n/a Hispanic-owned, n/a Asian-owned
Employment: 9.5% management, business, and financial, 2.4% computer, engineering, and science, 8.3% education, legal, community service, arts, and media, 6.3% healthcare practitioners, 18.3% service, 20.6% sales and office, 8.9% natural resources, construction, and maintenance, 25.7% production, transportation, and material moving
Income: Per capita: $20,624; Median household: $42,572; Average household: $54,751; Households with income of $100,000 or more: 12.1%; Poverty rate: 18.5%
Educational Attainment: High school diploma or higher: 85.5%; Bachelor's degree or higher: 12.4%; Graduate/professional degree or higher: 5.4%
Housing: Homeownership rate: 68.6%; Median home value: $98,600; Median year structure built: 1960; Homeowner vacancy rate: 2.5%; Median gross rent: $702 per month; Rental vacancy rate: 12.1%
Vital Statistics: Birth rate: 114.1 per 10,000 population; Death rate: 103.3 per 10,000 population; Age-adjusted cancer mortality rate: 194.3 deaths per 100,000 population
Health Insurance: 86.6% have insurance; 63.5% have private insurance; 37.2% have public insurance; 13.4% do not have insurance; 6.0% of children under 18 do not have insurance
Health Care: Physicians: 15.0 per 10,000 population; Hospital beds: 25.5 per 10,000 population; Hospital admissions: 1,228.1 per 10,000 population
Transportation: Commute: 95.3% car, 0.6% public transportation, 1.2% walk, 2.1% work from home; Median travel time to work: 22.1 minutes
Presidential Election: 45.1% Obama, 52.7% Romney (2012)

Additional Information Contacts

Marion Government. . . . . (740) 223-4001
http://www.co.marion.oh.us

Marion County Communities

CALEDONIA (village). Covers a land area of 0.230 square miles and a water area of 0 square miles. Located at 40.64° N. Lat; 82.97° W. Long. Elevation is 997 feet.
History: Caledonia was the boyhood home of Warren G. Harding, 29th President of the United States.
Population: 577; Growth (since 2000): -0.2%; Density: 2,505.3 persons per square mile; Race: 97.4% White, 1.6% Black/African American, 0.2% Asian, 0.0% American Indian/Alaska Native, 0.0% Native Hawaiian/Other Pacific Islander, 0.2% Two or more races, 0.5% Hispanic of any race; Average household size: 2.49; Median age: 40.2; Age under 18: 24.1%; Age 65 and over: 16.3%; Males per 100 females: 90.4

School District(s)

River Valley Academy (04-12)
2012-13 Enrollment: n/a . . . . (740) 725-5451
River Valley Local (PK-12)
2012-13 Enrollment: 1,953 . . . . (740) 725-5401

Housing: Homeownership rate: 77.5%; Homeowner vacancy rate: 4.2%; Rental vacancy rate: 5.5%

GREEN CAMP (village). Covers a land area of 0.338 square miles and a water area of 0 square miles. Located at 40.53° N. Lat; 83.21° W. Long. Elevation is 912 feet.
Population: 374; Growth (since 2000): 9.4%; Density: 1,106.8 persons per square mile; Race: 96.5% White, 0.0% Black/African American, 0.0% Asian, 0.0% American Indian/Alaska Native, 0.0% Native Hawaiian/Other Pacific Islander, 3.5% Two or more races, 0.5% Hispanic of any race; Average household size: 2.63; Median age: 40.0; Age under 18: 25.7%; Age 65 and over: 13.9%; Males per 100 females: 118.7

School District(s)

Elgin Local (PK-12)
2012-13 Enrollment: 1,105 . . . . (740) 382-1101

Housing: Homeownership rate: 73.9%; Homeowner vacancy rate: 2.7%; Rental vacancy rate: 9.8%

LA RUE (village). Covers a land area of 0.478 square miles and a water area of 0 square miles. Located at 40.58° N. Lat; 83.38° W. Long. Elevation is 928 feet.
History: La Rue was the home of the Oorang Dog Kennels, which used Olympic athlete Jim Thorpe and other Indian athletes to play exhibition football games advertising their highly trained dogs.
Population: 747; Growth (since 2000): -3.6%; Density: 1,562.6 persons per square mile; Race: 94.9% White, 0.3% Black/African American, 0.0% Asian, 0.1% American Indian/Alaska Native, 0.0% Native Hawaiian/Other Pacific Islander, 2.1% Two or more races, 3.7% Hispanic of any race; Average household size: 2.57; Median age: 39.8; Age under 18: 25.4%; Age 65 and over: 17.5%; Males per 100 females: 95.5

School District(s)

Elgin Local (PK-12)
2012-13 Enrollment: 1,105 . . . . (740) 382-1101

Housing: Homeownership rate: 66.3%; Homeowner vacancy rate: 2.5%; Rental vacancy rate: 7.5%

MARION (city). County seat. Covers a land area of 11.736 square miles and a water area of 0.078 square miles. Located at 40.59° N. Lat; 83.12° W. Long. Elevation is 981 feet.
History: The site of Marion was selected as the seat of Marion County in 1824 because of the abundance of well water, discovered when some thirsty travelers stuck a wooden spade in the ground and named the spot Jacob's Well. The Marion Steam Shovel Company was organized in 1884, sending the name of Marion all over the world on its digging equipment.
Population: 36,837; Growth (since 2000): 4.3%; Density: 3,138.8 persons per square mile; Race: 86.7% White, 9.6% Black/African American, 0.4% Asian, 0.2% American Indian/Alaska Native, 0.0% Native Hawaiian/Other Pacific Islander, 2.1% Two or more races, 3.0% Hispanic of any race; Average household size: 2.45; Median age: 37.3; Age under 18: 22.2%; Age 65 and over: 12.6%; Males per 100 females: 121.6; Marriage status: 32.6% never married, 43.6% now married, 3.4% separated, 7.1% widowed, 16.7% divorced; Foreign born: 1.2%; Speak English only: 95.4%; With disability: 19.5%; Veterans: 10.7%; Ancestry: 25.1% German, 15.8% Irish, 10.8% American, 9.3% English, 5.2% Italian
Employment: 5.6% management, business, and financial, 2.5% computer, engineering, and science, 7.4% education, legal, community service, arts, and media, 3.6% healthcare practitioners, 22.2% service, 22.2% sales and office, 8.4% natural resources, construction, and maintenance, 28.1% production, transportation, and material moving
Income: Per capita: $15,815; Median household: $33,586; Average household: $44,647; Households with income of $100,000 or more: 7.3%; Poverty rate: 27.9%
Educational Attainment: High school diploma or higher: 81.8%; Bachelor's degree or higher: 9.9%; Graduate/professional degree or higher: 3.9%

School District(s)

Elgin Local (PK-12)
2012-13 Enrollment: 1,105 . . . . (740) 382-1101
Marion City (PK-12)
2012-13 Enrollment: 4,197 . . . . (740) 387-3300
Marion City Digital Academy (KG-12)
2012-13 Enrollment: 85. . . . . (740) 223-4417
Pleasant Community Digital (KG-01)
2012-13 Enrollment: 93. . . . . (740) 389-4476

Pleasant Education Academy (09-12)
2012-13 Enrollment: 52. . . . . (740) 389-4476
Pleasant Local (01-12)
2012-13 Enrollment: 1,177 . . . . (740) 389-4476
River Valley Local (PK-12)
2012-13 Enrollment: 1,953 . . . . (740) 725-5401
Rushmore Academy (08-12)
2012-13 Enrollment: 162. . . . . (740) 387-3300
Treca Digital Academy (KG-12)
2012-13 Enrollment: 1,805 . . . . (740) 389-4798
Tri-Rivers (09-12)
2012-13 Enrollment: n/a . . . . (740) 389-4681

Four-year College(s)

Ohio State University-Marion Campus (Public)
Fall 2013 Enrollment: 1,259 . . . . (740) 725-6111
2013-14 Tuition: In-state $7,140; Out-of-state $22,860

Two-year College(s)

Marion Technical College (Public)
Fall 2013 Enrollment: 2,698 . . . . (740) 389-4636
2013-14 Tuition: In-state $4,422; Out-of-state $6,532

Vocational/Technical School(s)

Tri-Rivers Career Center (Public)
Fall 2013 Enrollment: 158. . . . . (740) 389-4682
2013-14 Tuition: $11,753

Housing: Homeownership rate: 57.4%; Median home value: $77,500; Median year structure built: 1950; Homeowner vacancy rate: 3.4%; Median gross rent: $670 per month; Rental vacancy rate: 12.9%

Health Insurance: 84.2% have insurance; 53.1% have private insurance; 44.2% have public insurance; 15.8% do not have insurance; 5.0% of children under 18 do not have insurance

Hospitals: Marion General Hospital

Newspapers: Marion Star (daily circulation 12400)

Transportation: Commute: 94.9% car, 0.8% public transportation, 1.5% walk, 1.8% work from home; Median travel time to work: 19.5 minutes

Airports: Marion Municipal (general aviation)

Additional Information Contacts

City of Marion . . . . (740) 387-3591
http://www.marionohio.us

MORRAL (village). Covers a land area of 2.701 square miles and a water area of 0 square miles. Located at 40.69° N. Lat; 83.21° W. Long. Elevation is 909 feet.

Population: 399; Growth (since 2000): 2.8%; Density: 147.7 persons per square mile; Race: 96.5% White, 0.8% Black/African American, 0.3% Asian, 0.8% American Indian/Alaska Native, 0.0% Native Hawaiian/Other Pacific Islander, 1.3% Two or more races, 1.5% Hispanic of any race; Average household size: 2.56; Median age: 39.3; Age under 18: 24.8%; Age 65 and over: 11.3%; Males per 100 females: 98.5

School District(s)

Ridgedale Community School (03-12)
2012-13 Enrollment: 36. . . . . (740) 382-6065
Ridgedale Local (PK-12)
2012-13 Enrollment: 721. . . . . (740) 382-6065

Housing: Homeownership rate: 86.5%; Homeowner vacancy rate: 1.4%; Rental vacancy rate: 8.7%

NEW BLOOMINGTON (village). Covers a land area of 0.440 square miles and a water area of 0 square miles. Located at 40.58° N. Lat; 83.31° W. Long. Elevation is 942 feet.

Population: 515; Growth (since 2000): -6.0%; Density: 1,169.6 persons per square mile; Race: 93.6% White, 0.4% Black/African American, 0.2% Asian, 0.2% American Indian/Alaska Native, 0.0% Native Hawaiian/Other Pacific Islander, 3.1% Two or more races, 14.4% Hispanic of any race; Average household size: 2.70; Median age: 35.2; Age under 18: 25.2%; Age 65 and over: 9.9%; Males per 100 females: 122.9

Housing: Homeownership rate: 79.1%; Homeowner vacancy rate: 0.6%; Rental vacancy rate: 23.1%

PROSPECT (village). Covers a land area of 0.724 square miles and a water area of 0 square miles. Located at 40.45° N. Lat; 83.18° W. Long. Elevation is 909 feet.

History: Settled 1832, incorporated as village 1876.

Population: 1,112; Growth (since 2000): -6.6%; Density: 1,536.7 persons per square mile; Race: 98.1% White, 0.3% Black/African American, 0.2% Asian, 0.0% American Indian/Alaska Native, 0.0% Native Hawaiian/Other Pacific Islander, 1.1% Two or more races, 1.3% Hispanic of any race; Average household size: 2.45; Median age: 37.5; Age under 18: 25.5%; Age 65 and over: 12.1%; Males per 100 females: 100.0

School District(s)

Elgin Local (PK-12)
2012-13 Enrollment: 1,105 . . . . (740) 382-1101

Housing: Homeownership rate: 70.4%; Homeowner vacancy rate: 3.0%; Rental vacancy rate: 10.0%

WALDO (village). Covers a land area of 0.648 square miles and a water area of 0 square miles. Located at 40.46° N. Lat; 83.08° W. Long. Elevation is 938 feet.

Population: 338; Growth (since 2000): 1.8%; Density: 521.5 persons per square mile; Race: 96.4% White, 0.3% Black/African American, 0.9% Asian, 0.0% American Indian/Alaska Native, 0.0% Native Hawaiian/Other Pacific Islander, 2.4% Two or more races, 1.2% Hispanic of any race; Average household size: 2.45; Median age: 41.5; Age under 18: 21.6%; Age 65 and over: 16.0%; Males per 100 females: 94.3

Housing: Homeownership rate: 71.7%; Homeowner vacancy rate: 3.9%; Rental vacancy rate: 22.0%

Medina County

Located in northern Ohio; drained by the Rocky and Black Rivers; includes Chippewa Lake. Covers a land area of 421.357 square miles, a water area of 1.658 square miles, and is located in the Eastern Time Zone at 41.12° N. Lat., 81.90° W. Long. The county was founded in 1812. County seat is Medina.

Medina County is part of the Cleveland-Elyria, OH Metropolitan Statistical Area. The entire metro area includes: Cuyahoga County, OH; Geauga County, OH; Lake County, OH; Lorain County, OH; Medina County, OH

Weather Station: Chippewa Lake Elevation: 1,180 feet

	Jan	Feb	Mar	Apr	May	Jun	Jul	Aug	Sep	Oct	Nov	Dec
High	33	37	46	59	70	79	83	81	74	62	50	37
Low	18	19	27	37	47	56	60	59	52	41	33	23
Precip	2.5	2.1	2.9	3.5	4.0	3.9	4.2	3.7	3.4	2.8	3.3	3.0
Snow	9.4	7.1	6.7	1.9	tr	0.0	0.0	0.0	0.0	0.1	2.6	8.1

High and Low temperatures in degrees Fahrenheit; Precipitation and Snow in inches

Population: 172,332; Growth (since 2000): 14.1%; Density: 409.0 persons per square mile; Race: 96.1% White, 1.2% Black/African American, 1.0% Asian, 0.1% American Indian/Alaska Native, 0.0% Native Hawaiian/Other Pacific Islander, 1.2% two or more races, 1.6% Hispanic of any race; Average household size: 2.63; Median age: 40.4; Age under 18: 25.4%; Age 65 and over: 13.1%; Males per 100 females: 97.2; Marriage status: 23.7% never married, 60.8% now married, 0.9% separated, 5.6% widowed, 9.9% divorced; Foreign born: 2.8%; Speak English only: 94.8%; With disability: 9.5%; Veterans: 10.0%; Ancestry: 29.9% German, 16.9% Irish, 11.3% Italian, 10.4% Polish, 10.3% English

Religion: Six largest groups: 28.2% Catholicism, 4.3% Methodist/Pietist, 4.1% Lutheran, 3.9% Non-denominational Protestant, 3.6% Baptist, 2.4% Presbyterian-Reformed

Economy: Unemployment rate: 4.4%; Leading industries: 12.4% retail trade; 12.2% construction; 10.3% professional, scientific, and technical services; Farms: 920 totaling 94,978 acres; Company size: 1 employs 1,000 or more persons, 3 employ 500 to 999 persons, 77 employ 100 to 499 persons, 3,853 employ less than 100 persons; Business ownership: 3,872 women-owned, 80 Black-owned, n/a Hispanic-owned, n/a Asian-owned

Employment: 16.2% management, business, and financial, 5.3% computer, engineering, and science, 8.9% education, legal, community service, arts, and media, 6.7% healthcare practitioners, 15.3% service, 25.9% sales and office, 8.7% natural resources, construction, and maintenance, 13.1% production, transportation, and material moving

Income: Per capita: $30,707; Median household: $65,951; Average household: $80,696; Households with income of $100,000 or more: 27.0%; Poverty rate: 7.4%

Educational Attainment: High school diploma or higher: 93.2%; Bachelor's degree or higher: 29.6%; Graduate/professional degree or higher: 9.7%

Housing: Homeownership rate: 80.6%; Median home value: $181,000; Median year structure built: 1979; Homeowner vacancy rate: 1.6%; Median gross rent: $821 per month; Rental vacancy rate: 10.0%

Vital Statistics: Birth rate: 99.4 per 10,000 population; Death rate: 75.1 per 10,000 population; Age-adjusted cancer mortality rate: 190.3 deaths per 100,000 population
Health Insurance: 91.8% have insurance; 81.1% have private insurance; 22.8% have public insurance; 8.2% do not have insurance; 4.4% of children under 18 do not have insurance
Health Care: Physicians: 16.0 per 10,000 population; Hospital beds: 11.4 per 10,000 population; Hospital admissions: 541.2 per 10,000 population
Air Quality Index: 86.4% good, 13.6% moderate, 0.0% unhealthy for sensitive individuals, 0.0% unhealthy (percent of days)
Transportation: Commute: 93.1% car, 0.6% public transportation, 1.1% walk, 4.4% work from home; Median travel time to work: 28.0 minutes
Presidential Election: 42.6% Obama, 55.7% Romney (2012)
National and State Parks: Spencer Lake State Wildlife Area
Additional Information Contacts
Medina Government . . . . (330) 722-9208
http://www.co.medina.oh.us

Medina County Communities

BRUNSWICK (city). Covers a land area of 12.916 square miles and a water area of 0.037 square miles. Located at 41.25° N. Lat; 81.82° W. Long. Elevation is 1,168 feet.
History: Named for its pleasing sound to early residents. Small farm community for many years; population burgeoned with the housing boom after World War II. Settled 1815 as part of the Conn. Western Reserve. Incorporated 1960.
Population: 34,255; Growth (since 2000): 2.6%; Density: 2,652.2 persons per square mile; Race: 95.5% White, 1.2% Black/African American, 1.2% Asian, 0.1% American Indian/Alaska Native, 0.0% Native Hawaiian/Other Pacific Islander, 1.3% Two or more races, 2.3% Hispanic of any race; Average household size: 2.63; Median age: 39.1; Age under 18: 25.2%; Age 65 and over: 11.9%; Males per 100 females: 96.6; Marriage status: 28.7% never married, 56.1% now married, 0.8% separated, 5.6% widowed, 9.7% divorced; Foreign born: 3.1%; Speak English only: 94.1%; With disability: 9.2%; Veterans: 9.5%; Ancestry: 28.5% German, 18.8% Irish, 14.1% Italian, 13.7% Polish, 8.0% English
Employment: 13.0% management, business, and financial, 4.5% computer, engineering, and science, 7.3% education, legal, community service, arts, and media, 7.1% healthcare practitioners, 16.6% service, 27.1% sales and office, 8.5% natural resources, construction, and maintenance, 15.8% production, transportation, and material moving
Income: Per capita: $28,225; Median household: $63,924; Average household: $72,755; Households with income of $100,000 or more: 19.5%; Poverty rate: 6.7%
Educational Attainment: High school diploma or higher: 92.1%; Bachelor's degree or higher: 20.8%; Graduate/professional degree or higher: 5.8%

School District(s)

Brunswick City (PK-12)
2012-13 Enrollment: 7,334 . . . . (330) 225-7731

Two-year College(s)

Raphael's School of Beauty Culture Inc-Brunswick (Private, For-profit)
Fall 2013 Enrollment: 53 . . . . (330) 225-0195
Housing: Homeownership rate: 78.5%; Median home value: $157,400; Median year structure built: 1977; Homeowner vacancy rate: 1.3%; Median gross rent: $810 per month; Rental vacancy rate: 10.4%
Health Insurance: 91.1% have insurance; 79.9% have private insurance; 23.1% have public insurance; 8.9% do not have insurance; 3.9% of children under 18 do not have insurance
Safety: Violent crime rate: 4.7 per 10,000 population; Property crime rate: 83.7 per 10,000 population
Transportation: Commute: 94.0% car, 1.1% public transportation, 1.6% walk, 2.7% work from home; Median travel time to work: 28.9 minutes
Additional Information Contacts
City of Brunswick. . . . . (330) 225-9144
http://www.brunswick.oh.us

CHIPPEWA LAKE (village). Covers a land area of 0.247 square miles and a water area of <.001 square miles. Located at 41.07° N. Lat; 81.90° W. Long. Elevation is 1,024 feet.
Population: 711; Growth (since 2000): n/a; Density: 2,881.8 persons per square mile; Race: 97.2% White, 0.6% Black/African American, 0.0% Asian, 0.3% American Indian/Alaska Native, 0.0% Native Hawaiian/Other Pacific Islander, 1.1% Two or more races, 1.4% Hispanic of any race; Average household size: 2.29; Median age: 42.6; Age under 18: 19.7%; Age 65 and over: 12.7%; Males per 100 females: 104.9
Housing: Homeownership rate: 76.2%; Homeowner vacancy rate: 5.6%; Rental vacancy rate: 14.9%

GLORIA GLENS PARK (village). Covers a land area of 0.107 square miles and a water area of 0.005 square miles. Located at 41.06° N. Lat; 81.90° W. Long. Elevation is 1,020 feet.
Population: 425; Growth (since 2000): -21.0%; Density: 3,965.2 persons per square mile; Race: 98.6% White, 0.2% Black/African American, 0.5% Asian, 0.2% American Indian/Alaska Native, 0.0% Native Hawaiian/Other Pacific Islander, 0.5% Two or more races, 1.4% Hispanic of any race; Average household size: 2.37; Median age: 39.5; Age under 18: 22.4%; Age 65 and over: 11.3%; Males per 100 females: 107.3
Housing: Homeownership rate: 75.4%; Homeowner vacancy rate: 3.6%; Rental vacancy rate: 4.3%

HINCKLEY (unincorporated postal area)
ZCTA: 44233
Covers a land area of 26.704 square miles and a water area of 0.139 square miles. Located at 41.25° N. Lat; 81.74° W. Long. Elevation is 1,096 feet.
Population: 7,646; Growth (since 2000): 12.8%; Density: 286.3 persons per square mile; Race: 97.5% White, 0.4% Black/African American, 1.2% Asian, 0.1% American Indian/Alaska Native, 0.0% Native Hawaiian/Other Pacific Islander, 0.6% Two or more races, 1.2% Hispanic of any race; Average household size: 2.77; Median age: 45.3; Age under 18: 24.0%; Age 65 and over: 14.4%; Males per 100 females: 101.5; Marriage status: 19.2% never married, 65.8% now married, 1.2% separated, 4.6% widowed, 10.3% divorced; Foreign born: 6.5%; Speak English only: 89.8%; With disability: 6.6%; Veterans: 6.2%; Ancestry: 27.0% German, 14.4% Italian, 13.9% Polish, 11.4% Irish, 7.9% Hungarian
Employment: 17.7% management, business, and financial, 5.7% computer, engineering, and science, 5.0% education, legal, community service, arts, and media, 8.9% healthcare practitioners, 12.5% service, 26.9% sales and office, 9.6% natural resources, construction, and maintenance, 13.8% production, transportation, and material moving
Income: Per capita: $37,644; Median household: $78,507; Average household: $102,577; Households with income of $100,000 or more: 41.3%; Poverty rate: 2.5%
Educational Attainment: High school diploma or higher: 97.0%; Bachelor's degree or higher: 38.1%; Graduate/professional degree or higher: 14.4%

School District(s)

Highland Local (PK-12)
2012-13 Enrollment: 3,193 . . . . (330) 239-1901
Housing: Homeownership rate: 94.6%; Median home value: $265,500; Median year structure built: 1979; Homeowner vacancy rate: 1.2%; Median gross rent: n/a per month; Rental vacancy rate: 8.6%
Health Insurance: 94.7% have insurance; 88.5% have private insurance; 18.3% have public insurance; 5.3% do not have insurance; 2.2% of children under 18 do not have insurance
Transportation: Commute: 94.5% car, 0.4% public transportation, 0.4% walk, 4.0% work from home; Median travel time to work: 26.6 minutes

HOMERVILLE (unincorporated postal area)
ZCTA: 44235
Covers a land area of 25.034 square miles and a water area of 0.033 square miles. Located at 41.03° N. Lat; 82.12° W. Long. Elevation is 1,073 feet.
Population: 1,825; Growth (since 2000): -2.6%; Density: 72.9 persons per square mile; Race: 98.4% White, 0.5% Black/African American, 0.2% Asian, 0.0% American Indian/Alaska Native, 0.0% Native Hawaiian/Other Pacific Islander, 0.7% Two or more races, 0.4% Hispanic of any race; Average household size: 3.20; Median age: 34.1; Age under 18: 32.5%; Age 65 and over: 10.3%; Males per 100 females: 102.8
Housing: Homeownership rate: 86.9%; Homeowner vacancy rate: 1.8%; Rental vacancy rate: 0.0%

LITCHFIELD (unincorporated postal area)
ZCTA: 44253
Covers a land area of 24.631 square miles and a water area of 0.018 square miles. Located at 41.17° N. Lat; 82.03° W. Long. Elevation is 1,004 feet.

Population: 3,218; Growth (since 2000): -2.8%; Density: 130.6 persons per square mile; Race: 97.9% White, 0.7% Black/African American, 0.1% Asian, 0.1% American Indian/Alaska Native, 0.0% Native Hawaiian/Other Pacific Islander, 1.1% Two or more races, 1.6% Hispanic of any race; Average household size: 2.74; Median age: 44.8; Age under 18: 22.0%; Age 65 and over: 12.7%; Males per 100 females: 106.3; Marriage status: 20.3% never married, 66.0% now married, 0.0% separated, 4.7% widowed, 9.0% divorced; Foreign born: 1.0%; Speak English only: 96.4%; With disability: 10.0%; Veterans: 6.4%; Ancestry: 28.7% German, 16.9% Irish, 12.7% Italian, 11.6% Polish, 8.4% English
Employment: 17.6% management, business, and financial, 4.0% computer, engineering, and science, 6.7% education, legal, community service, arts, and media, 8.0% healthcare practitioners, 10.6% service, 22.0% sales and office, 15.8% natural resources, construction, and maintenance, 15.3% production, transportation, and material moving
Income: Per capita: $29,826; Median household: $74,662; Average household: $79,076; Households with income of $100,000 or more: 30.3%; Poverty rate: 12.9%
Educational Attainment: High school diploma or higher: 91.9%; Bachelor's degree or higher: 22.3%; Graduate/professional degree or higher: 8.3%
Housing: Homeownership rate: 92.5%; Median home value: $193,400; Median year structure built: 1979; Homeowner vacancy rate: 1.2%; Median gross rent: $1,026 per month; Rental vacancy rate: 5.4%
Health Insurance: 88.7% have insurance; 76.4% have private insurance; 24.9% have public insurance; 11.3% do not have insurance; 8.6% of children under 18 do not have insurance
Transportation: Commute: 95.1% car, 0.0% public transportation, 1.3% walk, 3.6% work from home; Median travel time to work: 30.2 minutes

---

LODI (village). Covers a land area of 2.246 square miles and a water area of 0.008 square miles. Located at 41.04° N. Lat; 82.01° W. Long. Elevation is 925 feet.
History: Lodi was founded in 1824 by Judge Joseph Harris, who built his house on an ancient Indian mound. The town developed as a distribution center for dairy products and fertilizers.
Population: 2,746; Growth (since 2000): -10.3%; Density: 1,222.6 persons per square mile; Race: 98.1% White, 0.4% Black/African American, 0.2% Asian, 0.1% American Indian/Alaska Native, 0.0% Native Hawaiian/Other Pacific Islander, 1.0% Two or more races, 1.1% Hispanic of any race; Average household size: 2.31; Median age: 41.6; Age under 18: 22.0%; Age 65 and over: 17.0%; Males per 100 females: 92.4; Marriage status: 30.7% never married, 46.7% now married, 2.5% separated, 5.8% widowed, 16.8% divorced; Foreign born: 1.4%; Speak English only: 95.7%; With disability: 17.9%; Veterans: 12.7%; Ancestry: 33.7% German, 16.1% Irish, 12.7% American, 7.4% Italian, 7.1% Polish
Employment: 3.9% management, business, and financial, 1.1% computer, engineering, and science, 3.0% education, legal, community service, arts, and media, 4.8% healthcare practitioners, 21.6% service, 23.5% sales and office, 9.5% natural resources, construction, and maintenance, 32.5% production, transportation, and material moving
Income: Per capita: $19,986; Median household: $36,897; Average household: $43,818; Households with income of $100,000 or more: 4.5%; Poverty rate: 20.1%
Educational Attainment: High school diploma or higher: 87.0%; Bachelor's degree or higher: 8.2%; Graduate/professional degree or higher: 1.3%

School District(s)

Cloverleaf Local (PK-12)
2012-13 Enrollment: 2,632 . . . . (330) 948-2500
Housing: Homeownership rate: 64.8%; Median home value: $84,100; Median year structure built: 1963; Homeowner vacancy rate: 2.9%; Median gross rent: $668 per month; Rental vacancy rate: 20.2%
Health Insurance: 86.3% have insurance; 60.7% have private insurance; 41.1% have public insurance; 13.7% do not have insurance; 2.0% of children under 18 do not have insurance
Hospitals: Lodi Community Hospital (25 beds)
Safety: Violent crime rate: 3.6 per 10,000 population; Property crime rate: 190.8 per 10,000 population
Transportation: Commute: 96.3% car, 0.3% public transportation, 0.0% walk, 2.2% work from home; Median travel time to work: 23.1 minutes

---

MEDINA (city). County seat. Covers a land area of 11.572 square miles and a water area of 0.210 square miles. Located at 41.13° N. Lat; 81.87° W. Long. Elevation is 1,089 feet.
History: Named for the city of Hejaz, Saudi Arabia, to which Mohammed made his flight from Mecca in 622. Medina was platted in 1818 by a Captain Badger, who built a log cabin on the site. The town, first called Mecca, became known for its bee culture and honey products, calling itself the "sweetest town on earth."
Population: 26,678; Growth (since 2000): 6.1%; Density: 2,305.4 persons per square mile; Race: 93.3% White, 3.1% Black/African American, 0.9% Asian, 0.1% American Indian/Alaska Native, 0.0% Native Hawaiian/Other Pacific Islander, 2.1% Two or more races, 1.8% Hispanic of any race; Average household size: 2.53; Median age: 36.4; Age under 18: 28.3%; Age 65 and over: 11.6%; Males per 100 females: 92.5; Marriage status: 27.6% never married, 53.4% now married, 1.3% separated, 6.1% widowed, 12.9% divorced; Foreign born: 2.6%; Speak English only: 95.4%; With disability: 10.9%; Veterans: 10.7%; Ancestry: 30.4% German, 18.3% Irish, 13.9% Italian, 11.7% English, 9.9% Polish
Employment: 14.0% management, business, and financial, 4.8% computer, engineering, and science, 8.7% education, legal, community service, arts, and media, 5.7% healthcare practitioners, 17.0% service, 29.8% sales and office, 8.2% natural resources, construction, and maintenance, 11.8% production, transportation, and material moving
Income: Per capita: $26,352; Median household: $53,586; Average household: $68,887; Households with income of $100,000 or more: 21.3%; Poverty rate: 13.3%
Educational Attainment: High school diploma or higher: 93.6%; Bachelor's degree or higher: 31.7%; Graduate/professional degree or higher: 9.3%

School District(s)

Buckeye Local (PK-12)
2012-13 Enrollment: 2,206 . . . . (330) 722-8257
Highland Local (PK-12)
2012-13 Enrollment: 3,193 . . . . (330) 239-1901
Medina City SD (PK-12)
2012-13 Enrollment: 7,168 . . . . (330) 636-3031
Medina County Joint Vocational SD (09-12)
2012-13 Enrollment: n/a . . . . (330) 725-8461
New Directions Academy
2012-13 Enrollment: n/a . . . . (614) 995-1985

Vocational/Technical School(s)

Hamrick School (Private, For-profit)
Fall 2013 Enrollment: 187 . . . . (330) 239-2229
2013-14 Tuition: $9,727
Medina County Career Center (Public)
Fall 2013 Enrollment: 105 . . . . (330) 725-8461
2013-14 Tuition: $3,900
Housing: Homeownership rate: 66.3%; Median home value: $161,700; Median year structure built: 1979; Homeowner vacancy rate: 1.9%; Median gross rent: $802 per month; Rental vacancy rate: 10.3%
Health Insurance: 90.8% have insurance; 76.7% have private insurance; 24.8% have public insurance; 9.2% do not have insurance; 5.0% of children under 18 do not have insurance
Hospitals: Medina Hospital (118 beds)
Safety: Violent crime rate: 7.2 per 10,000 population; Property crime rate: 164.6 per 10,000 population
Newspapers: Medina County Gazette (daily circulation 14400)
Transportation: Commute: 93.7% car, 0.6% public transportation, 1.2% walk, 3.2% work from home; Median travel time to work: 26.1 minutes
Airports: Medina Municipal (general aviation)
Additional Information Contacts
City of Medina . . . . (330) 725-8861
http://www.medinaoh.org

SEVILLE (village). Covers a land area of 2.603 square miles and a water area of 0 square miles. Located at 41.02° N. Lat; 81.87° W. Long. Elevation is 988 feet.
Population: 2,296; Growth (since 2000): 6.3%; Density: 882.2 persons per square mile; Race: 96.9% White, 0.7% Black/African American, 0.5% Asian, 0.2% American Indian/Alaska Native, 0.0% Native Hawaiian/Other Pacific Islander, 1.3% Two or more races, 1.5% Hispanic of any race; Average household size: 2.40; Median age: 41.8; Age under 18: 20.9%; Age 65 and over: 16.1%; Males per 100 females: 92.0

School District(s)

Cloverleaf Local (PK-12)
2012-13 Enrollment: 2,632 . . . . (330) 948-2500

Housing: Homeownership rate: 78.3%; Homeowner vacancy rate: 1.8%; Rental vacancy rate: 6.9%

Additional Information Contacts

Village of Seville . . . . (330) 769-4146
http://www.villageofseville.com

SHARON CENTER (unincorporated postal area)

ZCTA: 44274

Covers a land area of 0.432 square miles and a water area of 0 square miles. Located at 41.10° N. Lat; 81.73° W. Long. Elevation is 1,129 feet.

Population: 225; Growth (since 2000): n/a; Density: 521.2 persons per square mile; Race: 97.3% White, 1.3% Black/African American, 0.0% Asian, 0.9% American Indian/Alaska Native, 0.0% Native Hawaiian/Other Pacific Islander, 0.4% Two or more races, 1.8% Hispanic of any race; Average household size: 2.53; Median age: 38.1; Age under 18: 25.3%; Age 65 and over: 16.0%; Males per 100 females: 106.4

School District(s)

Highland Local (PK-12)
2012-13 Enrollment: 3,193 . . . . (330) 239-1901

Housing: Homeownership rate: 77.0%; Homeowner vacancy rate: 0.0%; Rental vacancy rate: 0.0%

SPENCER (village). Covers a land area of 0.986 square miles and a water area of 0.007 square miles. Located at 41.10° N. Lat; 82.12° W. Long. Elevation is 915 feet.

Population: 753; Growth (since 2000): 0.8%; Density: 763.5 persons per square mile; Race: 97.5% White, 0.1% Black/African American, 0.3% Asian, 0.1% American Indian/Alaska Native, 0.0% Native Hawaiian/Other Pacific Islander, 1.5% Two or more races, 3.1% Hispanic of any race; Average household size: 2.66; Median age: 37.3; Age under 18: 27.5%; Age 65 and over: 13.9%; Males per 100 females: 97.6

Housing: Homeownership rate: 66.5%; Homeowner vacancy rate: 2.6%; Rental vacancy rate: 7.8%

VALLEY CITY (unincorporated postal area)

ZCTA: 44280

Covers a land area of 24.503 square miles and a water area of 0.004 square miles. Located at 41.25° N. Lat; 81.93° W. Long. Elevation is 814 feet.

Population: 4,557; Growth (since 2000): 9.8%; Density: 186.0 persons per square mile; Race: 97.7% White, 0.4% Black/African American, 0.8% Asian, 0.2% American Indian/Alaska Native, 0.0% Native Hawaiian/Other Pacific Islander, 0.7% Two or more races, 1.6% Hispanic of any race; Average household size: 2.67; Median age: 46.9; Age under 18: 20.8%; Age 65 and over: 15.0%; Males per 100 females: 101.2; Marriage status: 23.3% never married, 60.8% now married, 0.5% separated, 6.0% widowed, 9.8% divorced; Foreign born: 1.8%; Speak English only: 96.9%; With disability: 13.2%; Veterans: 9.1%; Ancestry: 38.5% German, 15.4% Irish, 14.1% Polish, 11.3% Italian, 8.3% English

Employment: 18.7% management, business, and financial, 5.9% computer, engineering, and science, 10.0% education, legal, community service, arts, and media, 7.9% healthcare practitioners, 13.5% service, 24.3% sales and office, 10.5% natural resources, construction, and maintenance, 9.2% production, transportation, and material moving

Income: Per capita: $34,967; Median household: $71,929; Average household: $90,368; Households with income of $100,000 or more: 32.9%; Poverty rate: 5.6%

Educational Attainment: High school diploma or higher: 89.5%; Bachelor's degree or higher: 26.4%; Graduate/professional degree or higher: 11.3%

Housing: Homeownership rate: 92.1%; Median home value: $226,700; Median year structure built: 1978; Homeowner vacancy rate: 1.0%; Median gross rent: $588 per month; Rental vacancy rate: 6.3%

Health Insurance: 95.6% have insurance; 88.7% have private insurance; 22.0% have public insurance; 4.4% do not have insurance; 0.0% of children under 18 do not have insurance

Transportation: Commute: 89.6% car, 1.0% public transportation, 2.4% walk, 3.8% work from home; Median travel time to work: 27.2 minutes

WADSWORTH (city). Covers a land area of 10.621 square miles and a water area of 0 square miles. Located at 41.03° N. Lat; 81.73° W. Long. Elevation is 1,171 feet.

History: Named for Colonel E. Wadsworth. Wadsworth developed as an industrial town, manufacturing matches, valves, locomotive appliances, and lubricators.

Population: 21,567; Growth (since 2000): 17.0%; Density: 2,030.5 persons per square mile; Race: 96.9% White, 0.8% Black/African American, 0.7% Asian, 0.2% American Indian/Alaska Native, 0.0% Native Hawaiian/Other Pacific Islander, 1.1% Two or more races, 1.2% Hispanic of any race; Average household size: 2.48; Median age: 38.7; Age under 18: 25.6%; Age 65 and over: 15.8%; Males per 100 females: 92.5; Marriage status: 21.3% never married, 55.7% now married, 0.6% separated, 8.7% widowed, 14.3% divorced; Foreign born: 2.0%; Speak English only: 96.0%; With disability: 9.4%; Veterans: 11.0%; Ancestry: 24.3% German, 14.6% Irish, 13.1% English, 8.7% American, 8.3% Italian

Employment: 17.3% management, business, and financial, 5.6% computer, engineering, and science, 10.4% education, legal, community service, arts, and media, 5.5% healthcare practitioners, 17.7% service, 26.1% sales and office, 5.0% natural resources, construction, and maintenance, 12.2% production, transportation, and material moving

Income: Per capita: $26,999; Median household: $57,539; Average household: $68,991; Households with income of $100,000 or more: 22.0%; Poverty rate: 7.3%

Educational Attainment: High school diploma or higher: 92.4%; Bachelor's degree or higher: 32.0%; Graduate/professional degree or higher: 10.4%

School District(s)

Wadsworth City (PK-12)
2012-13 Enrollment: 4,871 . . . . (330) 336-3571

Housing: Homeownership rate: 72.4%; Median home value: $159,200; Median year structure built: 1973; Homeowner vacancy rate: 2.2%; Median gross rent: $787 per month; Rental vacancy rate: 10.8%

Health Insurance: 90.7% have insurance; 77.2% have private insurance; 26.4% have public insurance; 9.3% do not have insurance; 5.4% of children under 18 do not have insurance

Hospitals: Summa Wadsworth - Rittman Hospital (113 beds)

Safety: Violent crime rate: 8.3 per 10,000 population; Property crime rate: 212.8 per 10,000 population

Transportation: Commute: 93.4% car, 0.0% public transportation, 1.3% walk, 4.3% work from home; Median travel time to work: 22.6 minutes

Additional Information Contacts

City of Wadsworth . . . . (330) 335-1521
http://www.wadsworthcity.com

WESTFIELD CENTER (village). Covers a land area of 2.108 square miles and a water area of 0 square miles. Located at 41.03° N. Lat; 81.93° W. Long. Elevation is 1,099 feet.

Population: 1,115; Growth (since 2000): 5.8%; Density: 529.0 persons per square mile; Race: 97.5% White, 0.1% Black/African American, 0.9% Asian, 0.0% American Indian/Alaska Native, 0.0% Native Hawaiian/Other Pacific Islander, 1.3% Two or more races, 1.3% Hispanic of any race; Average household size: 2.48; Median age: 48.4; Age under 18: 20.5%; Age 65 and over: 22.5%; Males per 100 females: 102.4

Housing: Homeownership rate: 91.3%; Homeowner vacancy rate: 2.1%; Rental vacancy rate: 0.0%

Meigs County

Located in southeastern Ohio; bounded on the southeast by the Ohio River and the West Virginia border; drained by the Shade River and Leading Creek. Covers a land area of 430.098 square miles, a water area of 2.903 square miles, and is located in the Eastern Time Zone at 39.09° N. Lat., 82.03° W. Long. The county was founded in 1819. County seat is Pomeroy.

Weather Station: Carpenter 2 S Elevation: 821 feet

	Jan	Feb	Mar	Apr	May	Jun	Jul	Aug	Sep	Oct	Nov	Dec
High	39	43	53	65	73	81	85	84	77	66	55	43
Low	21	23	31	40	49	58	62	60	52	41	33	25
Precip	2.9	2.8	3.7	3.6	4.4	3.8	4.5	3.3	3.2	2.9	3.2	2.8
Snow	6.9	4.4	2.7	0.9	tr	0.0	0.0	0.0	0.0	tr	0.6	3.1

High and Low temperatures in degrees Fahrenheit; Precipitation and Snow in inches

Population: 23,770; Growth (since 2000): 3.0%; Density: 55.3 persons per square mile; Race: 97.4% White, 0.9% Black/African American, 0.2% Asian, 0.2% American Indian/Alaska Native, 0.0% Native Hawaiian/Other Pacific Islander, 1.2% two or more races, 0.5% Hispanic of any race; Average household size: 2.46; Median age: 41.2; Age under 18: 22.8%; Age 65 and over: 15.7%; Males per 100 females: 96.3; Marriage status: 23.5% never married, 55.3% now married, 1.9% separated, 7.7% widowed, 13.5% divorced; Foreign born: 0.3%; Speak English only: 99.3%; With disability: 20.2%; Veterans: 11.0%; Ancestry: 25.7% German, 13.4% Irish, 12.2% American, 9.2% English, 3.7% Dutch
Religion: Six largest groups: 7.4% Baptist, 7.2% Methodist/Pietist, 4.5% Non-denominational Protestant, 3.0% Holiness, 1.2% Catholicism, 1.1% Pentecostal
Economy: Unemployment rate: 7.0%; Leading industries: 20.5% retail trade; 16.2% other services (except public administration); 13.6% health care and social assistance; Farms: 588 totaling 75,801 acres; Company size: 0 employ 1,000 or more persons, 0 employ 500 to 999 persons, 3 employ 100 to 499 persons, 299 employ less than 100 persons; Business ownership: n/a women-owned, n/a Black-owned, n/a Hispanic-owned, n/a Asian-owned
Employment: 8.0% management, business, and financial, 1.8% computer, engineering, and science, 10.1% education, legal, community service, arts, and media, 5.4% healthcare practitioners, 17.9% service, 22.4% sales and office, 16.1% natural resources, construction, and maintenance, 18.2% production, transportation, and material moving
Income: Per capita: $18,816; Median household: $35,469; Average household: $45,737; Households with income of $100,000 or more: 9.5%; Poverty rate: 21.9%
Educational Attainment: High school diploma or higher: 83.4%; Bachelor's degree or higher: 12.2%; Graduate/professional degree or higher: 4.3%
Housing: Homeownership rate: 77.1%; Median home value: $82,600; Median year structure built: 1977; Homeowner vacancy rate: 2.0%; Median gross rent: $566 per month; Rental vacancy rate: 10.5%
Vital Statistics: Birth rate: 112.4 per 10,000 population; Death rate: 106.0 per 10,000 population; Age-adjusted cancer mortality rate: 230.8 deaths per 100,000 population
Health Insurance: 84.5% have insurance; 57.0% have private insurance; 42.4% have public insurance; 15.5% do not have insurance; 5.9% of children under 18 do not have insurance
Health Care: Physicians: 2.1 per 10,000 population; Hospital beds: 0.0 per 10,000 population; Hospital admissions: 0.0 per 10,000 population
Air Quality Index: 99.2% good, 0.8% moderate, 0.0% unhealthy for sensitive individuals, 0.0% unhealthy (percent of days)
Transportation: Commute: 94.0% car, 0.1% public transportation, 2.3% walk, 2.5% work from home; Median travel time to work: 28.3 minutes
Presidential Election: 39.2% Obama, 57.9% Romney (2012)
National and State Parks: Buffington Island State Memorial; Forked Run State Park
Additional Information Contacts
Meigs Government . . . . (740) 992-2895
http://www.meigscountyohio.com

Meigs County Communities

LANGSVILLE (unincorporated postal area)

ZCTA: 45741

Covers a land area of 42.678 square miles and a water area of 0.007 square miles. Located at 39.08° N. Lat; 82.25° W. Long. Elevation is 571 feet.
Population: 918; Growth (since 2000): 0.0%; Density: 21.5 persons per square mile; Race: 97.9% White, 0.7% Black/African American, 0.0% Asian, 0.1% American Indian/Alaska Native, 0.0% Native Hawaiian/Other Pacific Islander, 1.2% Two or more races, 0.4% Hispanic of any race; Average household size: 2.47; Median age: 40.8; Age under 18: 22.9%; Age 65 and over: 13.7%; Males per 100 females: 97.8
Housing: Homeownership rate: 78.2%; Homeowner vacancy rate: 3.6%; Rental vacancy rate: 2.4%

LONG BOTTOM (unincorporated postal area)

ZCTA: 45743

Covers a land area of 36.714 square miles and a water area of 0.275 square miles. Located at 39.08° N. Lat; 81.85° W. Long. Elevation is 604 feet.
Population: 1,449; Growth (since 2000): -9.0%; Density: 39.5 persons per square mile; Race: 98.5% White, 0.6% Black/African American, 0.1% Asian, 0.1% American Indian/Alaska Native, 0.0% Native Hawaiian/Other Pacific Islander, 0.4% Two or more races, 1.0% Hispanic of any race; Average household size: 2.52; Median age: 41.5; Age under 18: 21.7%; Age 65 and over: 14.9%; Males per 100 females: 103.5
Housing: Homeownership rate: 86.2%; Homeowner vacancy rate: 1.0%; Rental vacancy rate: 4.8%

MIDDLEPORT (village). Covers a land area of 1.798 square miles and a water area of 0.098 square miles. Located at 38.99° N. Lat; 82.07° W. Long. Elevation is 571 feet.
History: Middleport was an active river town along the Ohio River during the last half of the 1800's. The disastrous flooding of the river in 1937 destroyed Middleport's waterfront.
Population: 2,530; Growth (since 2000): 0.2%; Density: 1,406.9 persons per square mile; Race: 94.5% White, 3.0% Black/African American, 0.2% Asian, 0.4% American Indian/Alaska Native, 0.0% Native Hawaiian/Other Pacific Islander, 1.6% Two or more races, 0.6% Hispanic of any race; Average household size: 2.23; Median age: 42.5; Age under 18: 21.3%; Age 65 and over: 20.4%; Males per 100 females: 85.6; Marriage status: 29.7% never married, 47.0% now married, 3.5% separated, 10.8% widowed, 12.6% divorced; Foreign born: 0.2%; Speak English only: 99.0%; With disability: 26.6%; Veterans: 8.9%; Ancestry: 25.4% German, 16.8% Irish, 14.2% American, 8.1% English, 4.2% Dutch
Employment: 6.2% management, business, and financial, 0.0% computer, engineering, and science, 6.6% education, legal, community service, arts, and media, 0.7% healthcare practitioners, 28.4% service, 35.2% sales and office, 9.4% natural resources, construction, and maintenance, 13.4% production, transportation, and material moving
Income: Per capita: $15,193; Median household: $24,311; Average household: $33,971; Households with income of $100,000 or more: 2.7%; Poverty rate: 34.4%
Educational Attainment: High school diploma or higher: 78.9%; Bachelor's degree or higher: 9.9%; Graduate/professional degree or higher: 5.0%

School District(s)

Meigs Local (PK-12)
2012-13 Enrollment: 1,786 . . . . (740) 992-2153
Housing: Homeownership rate: 56.9%; Median home value: $55,300; Median year structure built: 1950; Homeowner vacancy rate: 5.3%; Median gross rent: $513 per month; Rental vacancy rate: 13.8%
Health Insurance: 77.1% have insurance; 40.2% have private insurance; 52.6% have public insurance; 22.9% do not have insurance; 13.7% of children under 18 do not have insurance
Safety: Violent crime rate: 12.0 per 10,000 population; Property crime rate: 95.8 per 10,000 population
Transportation: Commute: 92.4% car, 0.6% public transportation, 1.9% walk, 5.1% work from home; Median travel time to work: 23.4 minutes

POMEROY (village). County seat. Covers a land area of 3.246 square miles and a water area of 0.063 square miles. Located at 39.03° N. Lat; 82.03° W. Long. Elevation is 574 feet.
History: Pomeroy began in 1804 when Samuel Pomeroy, a Boston merchant, purchased land here. Coal mining began in Pomeroy in the early 1800's, making the town the primary shipper of coal in Ohio prior to 1850. Salt making was also a leading early industry.
Population: 1,852; Growth (since 2000): -5.8%; Density: 570.5 persons per square mile; Race: 94.3% White, 2.7% Black/African American, 0.1% Asian, 0.5% American Indian/Alaska Native, 0.0% Native Hawaiian/Other Pacific Islander, 2.3% Two or more races, 0.5% Hispanic of any race; Average household size: 2.44; Median age: 35.2; Age under 18: 27.0%; Age 65 and over: 13.4%; Males per 100 females: 84.6

School District(s)

Meigs Local (PK-12)
2012-13 Enrollment: 1,786 . . . . (740) 992-2153
Housing: Homeownership rate: 56.8%; Homeowner vacancy rate: 7.1%; Rental vacancy rate: 10.8%
Newspapers: The Daily Sentinel (daily circulation 3500)

PORTLAND (unincorporated postal area)

ZCTA: 45770

Covers a land area of 20.453 square miles and a water area of 0.557 square miles. Located at 38.98° N. Lat; 81.80° W. Long. Elevation is 614 feet.

Population: 620; Growth (since 2000): 14.4%; Density: 30.3 persons per square mile; Race: 98.4% White, 0.5% Black/African American, 0.0% Asian, 0.3% American Indian/Alaska Native, 0.0% Native Hawaiian/Other Pacific Islander, 0.5% Two or more races, 0.3% Hispanic of any race; Average household size: 2.44; Median age: 42.7; Age under 18: 20.0%; Age 65 and over: 14.4%; Males per 100 females: 104.6
Housing: Homeownership rate: 81.2%; Homeowner vacancy rate: 0.5%; Rental vacancy rate: 24.6%

RACINE (village). Covers a land area of 0.437 square miles and a water area of 0 square miles. Located at 38.97° N. Lat; 81.91° W. Long. Elevation is 577 feet.
Population: 675; Growth (since 2000): -9.5%; Density: 1,543.4 persons per square mile; Race: 98.1% White, 0.3% Black/African American, 0.0% Asian, 0.0% American Indian/Alaska Native, 0.0% Native Hawaiian/Other Pacific Islander, 1.5% Two or more races, 0.3% Hispanic of any race; Average household size: 2.34; Median age: 40.1; Age under 18: 21.6%; Age 65 and over: 18.7%; Males per 100 females: 87.5

School District(s)

Southern Local (PK-12)
2012-13 Enrollment: 757. . . . . (740) 949-2669
Housing: Homeownership rate: 69.5%; Homeowner vacancy rate: 1.0%; Rental vacancy rate: 14.8%

REEDSVILLE (unincorporated postal area)
ZCTA: 45772
Covers a land area of 43.164 square miles and a water area of 0.462 square miles. Located at 39.15° N. Lat; 81.82° W. Long. Elevation is 643 feet.
Population: 2,149; Growth (since 2000): 3.2%; Density: 49.8 persons per square mile; Race: 97.7% White, 0.2% Black/African American, 0.3% Asian, 0.2% American Indian/Alaska Native, 0.0% Native Hawaiian/Other Pacific Islander, 1.4% Two or more races, 0.5% Hispanic of any race; Average household size: 2.47; Median age: 41.4; Age under 18: 22.8%; Age 65 and over: 17.1%; Males per 100 females: 95.9

School District(s)

Eastern Local (PK-12)
2012-13 Enrollment: 831. . . . . (740) 667-6079
Housing: Homeownership rate: 84.6%; Homeowner vacancy rate: 1.5%; Rental vacancy rate: 7.6%

RUTLAND (village). Covers a land area of 0.827 square miles and a water area of 0 square miles. Located at 39.04° N. Lat; 82.13° W. Long. Elevation is 577 feet.
Population: 393; Growth (since 2000): -2.0%; Density: 475.2 persons per square mile; Race: 98.7% White, 0.0% Black/African American, 0.0% Asian, 0.0% American Indian/Alaska Native, 0.0% Native Hawaiian/Other Pacific Islander, 1.0% Two or more races, 1.0% Hispanic of any race; Average household size: 2.44; Median age: 39.3; Age under 18: 23.4%; Age 65 and over: 17.0%; Males per 100 females: 95.5
Housing: Homeownership rate: 77.0%; Homeowner vacancy rate: 1.6%; Rental vacancy rate: 7.5%

SHADE (unincorporated postal area)
ZCTA: 45776
Covers a land area of 19.676 square miles and a water area of 0.022 square miles. Located at 39.18° N. Lat; 82.02° W. Long..
Population: 765; Growth (since 2000): -4.1%; Density: 38.9 persons per square mile; Race: 96.3% White, 0.7% Black/African American, 0.8% Asian, 0.0% American Indian/Alaska Native, 0.0% Native Hawaiian/Other Pacific Islander, 1.6% Two or more races, 0.5% Hispanic of any race; Average household size: 2.43; Median age: 40.8; Age under 18: 22.5%; Age 65 and over: 14.0%; Males per 100 females: 105.1
Housing: Homeownership rate: 75.6%; Homeowner vacancy rate: 0.8%; Rental vacancy rate: 10.5%

SYRACUSE (village). Covers a land area of 0.927 square miles and a water area of 0.026 square miles. Located at 39.00° N. Lat; 81.97° W. Long. Elevation is 587 feet.
Population: 826; Growth (since 2000): -6.0%; Density: 890.7 persons per square mile; Race: 97.2% White, 0.8% Black/African American, 0.1% Asian, 0.4% American Indian/Alaska Native, 0.0% Native Hawaiian/Other Pacific Islander, 1.5% Two or more races, 0.1% Hispanic of any race; Average household size: 2.29; Median age: 45.8; Age under 18: 20.3%; Age 65 and over: 21.8%; Males per 100 females: 90.8
Housing: Homeownership rate: 73.6%; Homeowner vacancy rate: 4.0%; Rental vacancy rate: 12.7%

TUPPERS PLAINS (CDP). Covers a land area of 1.816 square miles and a water area of 0 square miles. Located at 39.17° N. Lat; 81.85° W. Long. Elevation is 735 feet.
Population: 465; Growth (since 2000): n/a; Density: 256.1 persons per square mile; Race: 97.2% White, 0.4% Black/African American, 0.2% Asian, 0.4% American Indian/Alaska Native, 0.2% Native Hawaiian/Other Pacific Islander, 1.5% Two or more races, 0.0% Hispanic of any race; Average household size: 2.53; Median age: 41.1; Age under 18: 22.8%; Age 65 and over: 15.7%; Males per 100 females: 82.4
Housing: Homeownership rate: 85.8%; Homeowner vacancy rate: 2.4%; Rental vacancy rate: 7.1%

Mercer County

Located in western Ohio; bounded on the west by Indiana; drained by the Wabash and Saint Marys Rivers; includes part of Grand Lake. Covers a land area of 462.449 square miles, a water area of 10.976 square miles, and is located in the Eastern Time Zone at 40.54° N. Lat., 84.63° W. Long. The county was founded in 1820. County seat is Celina.

Mercer County is part of the Celina, OH Micropolitan Statistical Area. The entire metro area includes: Mercer County, OH

Weather Station: Celina 3 NE Elevation: 859 feet

	Jan	Feb	Mar	Apr	May	Jun	Jul	Aug	Sep	Oct	Nov	Dec
High	34	38	49	62	72	81	84	82	77	64	50	37
Low	20	22	30	41	51	60	64	62	55	44	35	24
Precip	2.3	2.1	2.6	3.6	4.0	4.0	4.8	3.6	2.6	2.7	3.0	2.6
Snow	10.0	6.8	4.1	0.9	0.0	0.0	0.0	0.0	0.0	0.2	1.3	6.3

High and Low temperatures in degrees Fahrenheit; Precipitation and Snow in inches

Population: 40,814; Growth (since 2000): -0.3%; Density: 88.3 persons per square mile; Race: 97.4% White, 0.2% Black/African American, 0.4% Asian, 0.2% American Indian/Alaska Native, 0.2% Native Hawaiian/Other Pacific Islander, 0.9% two or more races, 1.5% Hispanic of any race; Average household size: 2.60; Median age: 39.4; Age under 18: 26.4%; Age 65 and over: 15.4%; Males per 100 females: 100.1; Marriage status: 23.2% never married, 61.0% now married, 0.9% separated, 7.6% widowed, 8.1% divorced; Foreign born: 0.9%; Speak English only: 97.6%; With disability: 10.7%; Veterans: 10.3%; Ancestry: 56.8% German, 9.7% American, 7.6% Irish, 5.7% English, 3.9% French
Religion: Six largest groups: 58.1% Catholicism, 7.3% Methodist/Pietist, 5.9% Lutheran, 3.1% Presbyterian-Reformed, 2.5% Non-denominational Protestant, 1.7% Holiness
Economy: Unemployment rate: 2.7%; Leading industries: 17.8% retail trade; 13.1% other services (except public administration); 10.4% construction; Farms: 1,208 totaling 273,152 acres; Company size: 0 employ 1,000 or more persons, 1 employs 500 to 999 persons, 21 employs 100 to 499 persons, 926 employ less than 100 persons; Business ownership: 850 women-owned, n/a Black-owned, n/a Hispanic-owned, n/a Asian-owned
Employment: 11.3% management, business, and financial, 2.8% computer, engineering, and science, 7.1% education, legal, community service, arts, and media, 4.1% healthcare practitioners, 15.1% service, 21.5% sales and office, 10.5% natural resources, construction, and maintenance, 27.7% production, transportation, and material moving
Income: Per capita: $24,157; Median household: $52,535; Average household: $62,288; Households with income of $100,000 or more: 15.0%; Poverty rate: 9.4%
Educational Attainment: High school diploma or higher: 90.7%; Bachelor's degree or higher: 16.2%; Graduate/professional degree or higher: 6.5%
Housing: Homeownership rate: 79.5%; Median home value: $124,200; Median year structure built: 1970; Homeowner vacancy rate: 1.7%; Median gross rent: $644 per month; Rental vacancy rate: 11.3%
Vital Statistics: Birth rate: 131.2 per 10,000 population; Death rate: 89.5 per 10,000 population; Age-adjusted cancer mortality rate: 176.4 deaths per 100,000 population
Health Insurance: 92.1% have insurance; 80.0% have private insurance; 26.7% have public insurance; 7.9% do not have insurance; 5.0% of children under 18 do not have insurance
Health Care: Physicians: 8.6 per 10,000 population; Hospital beds: 14.7 per 10,000 population; Hospital admissions: 473.7 per 10,000 population

Transportation: Commute: 94.1% car, 0.2% public transportation, 1.4% walk, 3.2% work from home; Median travel time to work: 18.4 minutes
Presidential Election: 21.8% Obama, 76.6% Romney (2012)
National and State Parks: Grand Lake State Park; Harbor Point State Park
Additional Information Contacts
Mercer Government . . . . (419) 586-3178
http://www.mercercountyohio.org

Mercer County Communities

BURKETTSVILLE (village). Covers a land area of 0.175 square miles and a water area of 0.002 square miles. Located at 40.35° N. Lat; 84.64° W. Long. Elevation is 974 feet.
Population: 244; Growth (since 2000): -3.9%; Density: 1,390.6 persons per square mile; Race: 99.2% White, 0.8% Black/African American, 0.0% Asian, 0.0% American Indian/Alaska Native, 0.0% Native Hawaiian/Other Pacific Islander, 0.0% Two or more races, 0.8% Hispanic of any race; Average household size: 2.54; Median age: 35.7; Age under 18: 24.6%; Age 65 and over: 16.8%; Males per 100 females: 112.2
Housing: Homeownership rate: 89.6%; Homeowner vacancy rate: 5.5%; Rental vacancy rate: 16.7%

CELINA (city). County seat. Covers a land area of 4.981 square miles and a water area of 0.289 square miles. Located at 40.56° N. Lat; 84.56° W. Long. Elevation is 873 feet.
History: Celina was settled in 1834 in a densely forested area. Lumber mills soon attracted woodworkers and cabinet makers, and furniture manufacture became the leading industry.
Population: 10,400; Growth (since 2000): 0.9%; Density: 2,088.0 persons per square mile; Race: 94.9% White, 0.5% Black/African American, 1.1% Asian, 0.4% American Indian/Alaska Native, 0.4% Native Hawaiian/Other Pacific Islander, 1.6% Two or more races, 2.8% Hispanic of any race; Average household size: 2.37; Median age: 38.3; Age under 18: 25.6%; Age 65 and over: 16.2%; Males per 100 females: 93.3; Marriage status: 23.7% never married, 52.6% now married, 1.6% separated, 9.6% widowed, 14.0% divorced; Foreign born: 1.4%; Speak English only: 96.9%; With disability: 14.9%; Veterans: 11.4%; Ancestry: 42.6% German, 10.2% American, 9.0% Irish, 7.1% English, 5.3% French
Employment: 10.8% management, business, and financial, 2.7% computer, engineering, and science, 8.4% education, legal, community service, arts, and media, 3.1% healthcare practitioners, 23.0% service, 18.8% sales and office, 8.5% natural resources, construction, and maintenance, 24.7% production, transportation, and material moving
Income: Per capita: $21,899; Median household: $40,665; Average household: $49,922; Households with income of $100,000 or more: 8.4%; Poverty rate: 14.8%
Educational Attainment: High school diploma or higher: 88.5%; Bachelor's degree or higher: 16.8%; Graduate/professional degree or higher: 8.7%

School District(s)

Celina City (PK-12)
2012-13 Enrollment: 2,706 . . . . (419) 586-8300

Four-year College(s)

Wright State University-Lake Campus (Public)
Fall 2013 Enrollment: 1,133 . . . . (419) 586-0300
2013-14 Tuition: In-state $5,740; Out-of-state $13,744
Housing: Homeownership rate: 66.2%; Median home value: $103,000; Median year structure built: 1969; Homeowner vacancy rate: 2.8%; Median gross rent: $669 per month; Rental vacancy rate: 13.4%
Health Insurance: 90.4% have insurance; 72.6% have private insurance; 31.6% have public insurance; 9.6% do not have insurance; 0.9% of children under 18 do not have insurance
Safety: Violent crime rate: 10.6 per 10,000 population; Property crime rate: 358.9 per 10,000 population
Newspapers: Daily Standard (daily circulation 11000)
Transportation: Commute: 93.4% car, 0.2% public transportation, 1.4% walk, 2.3% work from home; Median travel time to work: 16.8 minutes
Airports: Lakefield (general aviation)
Additional Information Contacts
City of Celina . . . . (419) 586-6464
http://www.ci.celina.oh.us

CHICKASAW (village). Covers a land area of 0.234 square miles and a water area of 0.001 square miles. Located at 40.44° N. Lat; 84.49° W. Long. Elevation is 942 feet.
Population: 290; Growth (since 2000): -20.3%; Density: 1,236.9 persons per square mile; Race: 99.7% White, 0.0% Black/African American, 0.0% Asian, 0.0% American Indian/Alaska Native, 0.0% Native Hawaiian/Other Pacific Islander, 0.0% Two or more races, 0.3% Hispanic of any race; Average household size: 2.38; Median age: 42.3; Age under 18: 22.8%; Age 65 and over: 19.7%; Males per 100 females: 98.6
Housing: Homeownership rate: 85.3%; Homeowner vacancy rate: 0.0%; Rental vacancy rate: 25.0%

COLDWATER (village). Covers a land area of 1.923 square miles and a water area of 0.052 square miles. Located at 40.48° N. Lat; 84.63° W. Long. Elevation is 909 feet.
Population: 4,427; Growth (since 2000): -1.2%; Density: 2,301.6 persons per square mile; Race: 99.0% White, 0.1% Black/African American, 0.1% Asian, 0.0% American Indian/Alaska Native, 0.3% Native Hawaiian/Other Pacific Islander, 0.3% Two or more races, 0.7% Hispanic of any race; Average household size: 2.49; Median age: 39.2; Age under 18: 26.2%; Age 65 and over: 17.1%; Males per 100 females: 92.0; Marriage status: 23.9% never married, 60.9% now married, 0.2% separated, 11.4% widowed, 3.8% divorced; Foreign born: 2.4%; Speak English only: 97.6%; With disability: 10.2%; Veterans: 9.4%; Ancestry: 63.0% German, 9.3% American, 8.2% Irish, 4.7% English, 2.4% French
Employment: 12.7% management, business, and financial, 1.3% computer, engineering, and science, 6.6% education, legal, community service, arts, and media, 3.5% healthcare practitioners, 16.7% service, 23.7% sales and office, 14.2% natural resources, construction, and maintenance, 21.5% production, transportation, and material moving
Income: Per capita: $23,757; Median household: $54,825; Average household: $62,075; Households with income of $100,000 or more: 15.6%; Poverty rate: 4.8%
Educational Attainment: High school diploma or higher: 90.9%; Bachelor's degree or higher: 16.1%; Graduate/professional degree or higher: 5.3%

School District(s)

Coldwater Exempted Village (PK-12)
2012-13 Enrollment: 1,452 . . . . (419) 678-2611
Housing: Homeownership rate: 76.8%; Median home value: $119,300; Median year structure built: 1970; Homeowner vacancy rate: 1.4%; Median gross rent: $518 per month; Rental vacancy rate: 10.9%
Health Insurance: 93.2% have insurance; 85.8% have private insurance; 23.7% have public insurance; 6.8% do not have insurance; 4.9% of children under 18 do not have insurance
Hospitals: Mercer County Joint Township Community Hospital (76 beds)
Newspapers: Mercer County Chronicle (weekly circulation 3000)
Transportation: Commute: 98.1% car, 0.0% public transportation, 1.4% walk, 0.5% work from home; Median travel time to work: 16.1 minutes

FORT RECOVERY (village). Covers a land area of 1.053 square miles and a water area of 0.021 square miles. Located at 40.41° N. Lat; 84.78° W. Long. Elevation is 938 feet.
History: The original Fort Recovery was built by General Anthony Wayne in 1793.
Population: 1,430; Growth (since 2000): 12.3%; Density: 1,358.6 persons per square mile; Race: 97.7% White, 0.1% Black/African American, 0.1% Asian, 0.1% American Indian/Alaska Native, 0.0% Native Hawaiian/Other Pacific Islander, 1.3% Two or more races, 1.1% Hispanic of any race; Average household size: 2.58; Median age: 34.8; Age under 18: 28.2%; Age 65 and over: 14.7%; Males per 100 females: 104.3

School District(s)

Fort Recovery Local (PK-12)
2012-13 Enrollment: 1,056 . . . . (419) 375-4139
Housing: Homeownership rate: 78.5%; Homeowner vacancy rate: 2.0%; Rental vacancy rate: 7.0%
Safety: Violent crime rate: 0.0 per 10,000 population; Property crime rate: 77.4 per 10,000 population

MARIA STEIN (unincorporated postal area)

ZCTA: 45860

Covers a land area of 34.984 square miles and a water area of 0.028 square miles. Located at 40.40° N. Lat; 84.52° W. Long. Elevation is 968 feet.

Population: 2,274; Growth (since 2000): 0.2%; Density: 65.0 persons per square mile; Race: 99.4% White, 0.0% Black/African American, 0.1% Asian, 0.0% American Indian/Alaska Native, 0.0% Native Hawaiian/Other Pacific Islander, 0.2% Two or more races, 0.6% Hispanic of any race; Average household size: 3.14; Median age: 34.5; Age under 18: 33.3%; Age 65 and over: 11.5%; Males per 100 females: 105.6

School District(s)

Marion Local (PK-12)
2012-13 Enrollment: 869. . . . . (419) 925-4294

Housing: Homeownership rate: 88.4%; Homeowner vacancy rate: 0.3%; Rental vacancy rate: 6.7%

MENDON (village). Covers a land area of 0.555 square miles and a water area of 0.010 square miles. Located at 40.67° N. Lat; 84.52° W. Long. Elevation is 820 feet.

Population: 662; Growth (since 2000): -5.0%; Density: 1,192.9 persons per square mile; Race: 97.1% White, 0.3% Black/African American, 0.0% Asian, 0.9% American Indian/Alaska Native, 0.3% Native Hawaiian/Other Pacific Islander, 1.4% Two or more races, 1.7% Hispanic of any race; Average household size: 2.60; Median age: 38.3; Age under 18: 25.2%; Age 65 and over: 12.5%; Males per 100 females: 100.0

Housing: Homeownership rate: 77.6%; Homeowner vacancy rate: 2.9%; Rental vacancy rate: 19.7%

MONTEZUMA (village). Covers a land area of 0.116 square miles and a water area of 0.007 square miles. Located at 40.49° N. Lat; 84.55° W. Long. Elevation is 883 feet.

Population: 165; Growth (since 2000): -13.6%; Density: 1,420.0 persons per square mile; Race: 99.4% White, 0.0% Black/African American, 0.0% Asian, 0.0% American Indian/Alaska Native, 0.0% Native Hawaiian/Other Pacific Islander, 0.6% Two or more races, 1.2% Hispanic of any race; Average household size: 2.23; Median age: 44.3; Age under 18: 13.9%; Age 65 and over: 12.1%; Males per 100 females: 111.5

Housing: Homeownership rate: 74.3%; Homeowner vacancy rate: 3.4%; Rental vacancy rate: 5.0%

ROCKFORD (village). Covers a land area of 0.819 square miles and a water area of 0.020 square miles. Located at 40.69° N. Lat; 84.65° W. Long. Elevation is 814 feet.

History: Rockford was settled after the Treaty of 1818 on the site of a trading post operated by Anthony Shane. The town was first called Shane's Crossing.

Population: 1,120; Growth (since 2000): -0.5%; Density: 1,366.9 persons per square mile; Race: 96.3% White, 0.5% Black/African American, 0.3% Asian, 0.2% American Indian/Alaska Native, 0.0% Native Hawaiian/Other Pacific Islander, 1.7% Two or more races, 2.5% Hispanic of any race; Average household size: 2.41; Median age: 41.5; Age under 18: 24.3%; Age 65 and over: 18.8%; Males per 100 females: 88.6

School District(s)

Parkway Local (PK-12)
2012-13 Enrollment: 1,075 . . . . (419) 363-3045

Housing: Homeownership rate: 73.1%; Homeowner vacancy rate: 3.7%; Rental vacancy rate: 8.8%

SAINT HENRY (village). Covers a land area of 1.604 square miles and a water area of 0.047 square miles. Located at 40.42° N. Lat; 84.63° W. Long. Elevation is 971 feet.

Population: 2,427; Growth (since 2000): 6.9%; Density: 1,513.3 persons per square mile; Race: 99.1% White, 0.1% Black/African American, 0.0% Asian, 0.0% American Indian/Alaska Native, 0.0% Native Hawaiian/Other Pacific Islander, 0.2% Two or more races, 1.4% Hispanic of any race; Average household size: 2.79; Median age: 35.2; Age under 18: 29.5%; Age 65 and over: 15.7%; Males per 100 females: 100.1

School District(s)

Saint Henry Consolidated Local (PK-12)
2012-13 Enrollment: 986. . . . . (419) 678-4834

Housing: Homeownership rate: 80.5%; Homeowner vacancy rate: 0.9%; Rental vacancy rate: 6.1%

Miami County

Located in western Ohio; crossed by the Great Miami and Stillwater Rivers. Covers a land area of 406.580 square miles, a water area of 3.076 square miles, and is located in the Eastern Time Zone at 40.05° N. Lat., 84.23° W. Long. The county was founded in 1807. County seat is Troy.

Miami County is part of the Dayton, OH Metropolitan Statistical Area. The entire metro area includes: Greene County, OH; Miami County, OH; Montgomery County, OH

Population: 102,506; Growth (since 2000): 3.7%; Density: 252.1 persons per square mile; Race: 94.4% White, 2.0% Black/African American, 1.2% Asian, 0.2% American Indian/Alaska Native, 0.0% Native Hawaiian/Other Pacific Islander, 1.8% two or more races, 1.3% Hispanic of any race; Average household size: 2.48; Median age: 40.6; Age under 18: 24.2%; Age 65 and over: 15.3%; Males per 100 females: 96.7; Marriage status: 24.0% never married, 56.5% now married, 1.4% separated, 6.7% widowed, 12.8% divorced; Foreign born: 1.7%; Speak English only: 97.3%; With disability: 12.1%; Veterans: 10.9%; Ancestry: 34.1% German, 13.0% Irish, 10.7% American, 9.4% English, 3.4% French

Religion: Six largest groups: 10.6% Catholicism, 8.8% Methodist/Pietist, 4.3% Baptist, 3.8% Non-denominational Protestant, 2.7% Presbyterian-Reformed, 2.2% Holiness

Economy: Unemployment rate: 4.2%; Leading industries: 14.7% retail trade; 12.8% other services (except public administration); 10.3% manufacturing; Farms: 1,068 totaling 184,233 acres; Company size: 1 employs 1,000 or more persons, 7 employ 500 to 999 persons, 55 employ 100 to 499 persons, 2,044 employ less than 100 persons; Business ownership: 2,757 women-owned, n/a Black-owned, 69 Hispanic-owned, 160 Asian-owned

Employment: 12.1% management, business, and financial, 4.6% computer, engineering, and science, 8.4% education, legal, community service, arts, and media, 5.4% healthcare practitioners, 15.2% service, 23.4% sales and office, 9.2% natural resources, construction, and maintenance, 21.7% production, transportation, and material moving

Income: Per capita: $25,369; Median household: $52,040; Average household: $62,385; Households with income of $100,000 or more: 16.0%; Poverty rate: 13.0%

Educational Attainment: High school diploma or higher: 88.4%; Bachelor's degree or higher: 19.7%; Graduate/professional degree or higher: 6.9%

Housing: Homeownership rate: 71.5%; Median home value: $133,700; Median year structure built: 1965; Homeowner vacancy rate: 2.3%; Median gross rent: $711 per month; Rental vacancy rate: 10.2%

Vital Statistics: Birth rate: 109.5 per 10,000 population; Death rate: 90.7 per 10,000 population; Age-adjusted cancer mortality rate: 179.1 deaths per 100,000 population

Health Insurance: 89.3% have insurance; 73.2% have private insurance; 29.2% have public insurance; 10.7% do not have insurance; 6.1% of children under 18 do not have insurance

Health Care: Physicians: 12.0 per 10,000 population; Hospital beds: 16.3 per 10,000 population; Hospital admissions: 791.9 per 10,000 population

Air Quality Index: 92.5% good, 7.5% moderate, 0.0% unhealthy for sensitive individuals, 0.0% unhealthy (percent of days)

Transportation: Commute: 94.8% car, 0.5% public transportation, 1.6% walk, 2.6% work from home; Median travel time to work: 20.6 minutes

Presidential Election: 31.3% Obama, 66.9% Romney (2012)

National and State Parks: Greenville Falls State Nature Preserve

Additional Information Contacts

Miami Government . . . . (937) 332-7000
http://www.co.miami.oh.us

Miami County Communities

BRADFORD (village). Covers a land area of 0.858 square miles and a water area of 0.021 square miles. Located at 40.13° N. Lat; 84.43° W. Long. Elevation is 988 feet.

Population: 1,842; Growth (since 2000): -0.9%; Density: 2,145.7 persons per square mile; Race: 98.9% White, 0.2% Black/African American, 0.2% Asian, 0.1% American Indian/Alaska Native, 0.1% Native Hawaiian/Other Pacific Islander, 0.3% Two or more races, 0.9% Hispanic of any race; Average household size: 2.72; Median age: 35.6; Age under 18: 28.5%; Age 65 and over: 13.7%; Males per 100 females: 91.5

School District(s)

Bradford Exempted Village (PK-12)
2012-13 Enrollment: 514. . . . . (937) 448-2770

Housing: Homeownership rate: 73.2%; Homeowner vacancy rate: 2.5%; Rental vacancy rate: 8.1%

CASSTOWN (village). Covers a land area of 0.097 square miles and a water area of 0 square miles. Located at 40.05° N. Lat; 84.13° W. Long. Elevation is 935 feet.
Population: 267; Growth (since 2000): -17.1%; Density: 2,750.1 persons per square mile; Race: 100.0% White, 0.0% Black/African American, 0.0% Asian, 0.0% American Indian/Alaska Native, 0.0% Native Hawaiian/Other Pacific Islander, 0.0% Two or more races, 0.0% Hispanic of any race; Average household size: 2.36; Median age: 36.8; Age under 18: 24.0%; Age 65 and over: 13.5%; Males per 100 females: 88.0

School District(s)

Miami East Local (PK-12)
2012-13 Enrollment: 1,198 . . . . (937) 335-7505
Housing: Homeownership rate: 71.7%; Homeowner vacancy rate: 3.5%; Rental vacancy rate: 5.9%

COVINGTON (village). Covers a land area of 1.324 square miles and a water area of 0.026 square miles. Located at 40.12° N. Lat; 84.35° W. Long. Elevation is 928 feet.
History: Covington was settled in 1807 on the site of an outpost built by General Anthony Wayne.
Population: 2,584; Growth (since 2000): 1.0%; Density: 1,951.4 persons per square mile; Race: 98.1% White, 0.3% Black/African American, 0.0% Asian, 0.1% American Indian/Alaska Native, 0.0% Native Hawaiian/Other Pacific Islander, 1.3% Two or more races, 0.6% Hispanic of any race; Average household size: 2.42; Median age: 38.7; Age under 18: 24.9%; Age 65 and over: 18.9%; Males per 100 females: 93.6; Marriage status: 20.6% never married, 56.9% now married, 0.4% separated, 8.1% widowed, 14.4% divorced; Foreign born: 0.8%; Speak English only: 99.0%; With disability: 9.3%; Veterans: 10.1%; Ancestry: 32.0% German, 10.4% American, 9.5% Irish, 8.8% English, 3.2% Italian
Employment: 6.6% management, business, and financial, 4.4% computer, engineering, and science, 3.8% education, legal, community service, arts, and media, 7.1% healthcare practitioners, 13.4% service, 24.6% sales and office, 10.3% natural resources, construction, and maintenance, 29.8% production, transportation, and material moving
Income: Per capita: $20,479; Median household: $41,806; Average household: $54,636; Households with income of $100,000 or more: 11.8%; Poverty rate: 16.5%
Educational Attainment: High school diploma or higher: 88.9%; Bachelor's degree or higher: 10.8%; Graduate/professional degree or higher: 3.2%

School District(s)

Covington Exempted Village (PK-12)
2012-13 Enrollment: 852. . . . . (937) 473-9816
Housing: Homeownership rate: 69.7%; Median home value: $105,700; Median year structure built: 1949; Homeowner vacancy rate: 3.8%; Median gross rent: $643 per month; Rental vacancy rate: 10.5%
Health Insurance: 89.6% have insurance; 73.6% have private insurance; 31.1% have public insurance; 10.4% do not have insurance; 2.8% of children under 18 do not have insurance
Safety: Violent crime rate: 3.9 per 10,000 population; Property crime rate: 131.0 per 10,000 population
Newspapers: Stillwater Advertiser (weekly circulation 11000)
Transportation: Commute: 95.8% car, 0.0% public transportation, 2.1% walk, 2.1% work from home; Median travel time to work: 18.6 minutes

FLETCHER (village). Covers a land area of 0.311 square miles and a water area of 0 square miles. Located at 40.14° N. Lat; 84.11° W. Long. Elevation is 1,050 feet.
Population: 473; Growth (since 2000): -7.3%; Density: 1,522.0 persons per square mile; Race: 97.0% White, 0.0% Black/African American, 0.0% Asian, 0.2% American Indian/Alaska Native, 0.0% Native Hawaiian/Other Pacific Islander, 2.1% Two or more races, 0.8% Hispanic of any race; Average household size: 2.70; Median age: 36.0; Age under 18: 27.7%; Age 65 and over: 12.9%; Males per 100 females: 106.6
Housing: Homeownership rate: 81.7%; Homeowner vacancy rate: 4.0%; Rental vacancy rate: 11.1%

LAURA (village). Covers a land area of 0.271 square miles and a water area of 0 square miles. Located at 40.00° N. Lat; 84.41° W. Long. Elevation is 991 feet.
Population: 474; Growth (since 2000): -2.7%; Density: 1,750.3 persons per square mile; Race: 96.6% White, 1.7% Black/African American, 0.2% Asian, 0.4% American Indian/Alaska Native, 0.0% Native Hawaiian/Other Pacific Islander, 0.4% Two or more races, 1.5% Hispanic of any race; Average household size: 2.72; Median age: 38.0; Age under 18: 23.4%; Age 65 and over: 12.9%; Males per 100 females: 99.2
Housing: Homeownership rate: 76.4%; Homeowner vacancy rate: 2.9%; Rental vacancy rate: 6.8%

LUDLOW FALLS (village). Covers a land area of 0.179 square miles and a water area of 0 square miles. Located at 40.00° N. Lat; 84.34° W. Long. Elevation is 902 feet.
Population: 208; Growth (since 2000): -1.0%; Density: 1,165.2 persons per square mile; Race: 100.0% White, 0.0% Black/African American, 0.0% Asian, 0.0% American Indian/Alaska Native, 0.0% Native Hawaiian/Other Pacific Islander, 0.0% Two or more races, 0.5% Hispanic of any race; Average household size: 2.57; Median age: 34.0; Age under 18: 28.8%; Age 65 and over: 7.2%; Males per 100 females: 110.1
Housing: Homeownership rate: 70.4%; Homeowner vacancy rate: 0.0%; Rental vacancy rate: 4.0%

PIQUA (city). Covers a land area of 11.620 square miles and a water area of 0.267 square miles. Located at 40.15° N. Lat; 84.24° W. Long. Elevation is 876 feet.
History: Piqua was settled in 1797 and called Washington until 1816, when the legislature renamed it for a tribe of the Shawnee, who previously had villages near the site. The earlier fur trading was replaced by a flatboat business, as cargoes of lumber and farm products were sent to New Orleans. In 1815 Piqua became a producer of linseed oil. The Miami & Erie Canal and the railroads stimulated Piqua's growth in the later 1800's.
Population: 20,522; Growth (since 2000): -1.0%; Density: 1,766.2 persons per square mile; Race: 92.4% White, 3.3% Black/African American, 0.7% Asian, 0.2% American Indian/Alaska Native, 0.0% Native Hawaiian/Other Pacific Islander, 2.9% Two or more races, 1.4% Hispanic of any race; Average household size: 2.44; Median age: 38.1; Age under 18: 24.8%; Age 65 and over: 14.7%; Males per 100 females: 92.2; Marriage status: 28.1% never married, 48.4% now married, 1.9% separated, 8.6% widowed, 14.9% divorced; Foreign born: 1.0%; Speak English only: 97.4%; With disability: 16.0%; Veterans: 10.5%; Ancestry: 32.9% German, 14.7% Irish, 9.5% American, 8.5% English, 3.8% Italian
Employment: 7.5% management, business, and financial, 3.2% computer, engineering, and science, 6.9% education, legal, community service, arts, and media, 3.4% healthcare practitioners, 16.5% service, 25.0% sales and office, 8.8% natural resources, construction, and maintenance, 28.8% production, transportation, and material moving
Income: Per capita: $19,419; Median household: $36,260; Average household: $45,503; Households with income of $100,000 or more: 7.2%; Poverty rate: 23.4%
Educational Attainment: High school diploma or higher: 82.4%; Bachelor's degree or higher: 10.4%; Graduate/professional degree or higher: 3.8%

School District(s)

Piqua City (PK-12)
2012-13 Enrollment: 3,485 . . . . (937) 773-4321
Upper Valley (07-12)
2012-13 Enrollment: n/a . . . . (937) 778-1980

Two-year College(s)

Edison State Community College (Public)
Fall 2013 Enrollment: 2,993 . . . . (937) 778-8600
2013-14 Tuition: In-state $4,149; Out-of-state $7,659

Vocational/Technical School(s)

Upper Valley Career Center (Public)
Fall 2013 Enrollment: 405. . . . . (937) 778-1980
2013-14 Tuition: $14,065
Housing: Homeownership rate: 61.1%; Median home value: $87,400; Median year structure built: 1954; Homeowner vacancy rate: 4.2%; Median gross rent: $652 per month; Rental vacancy rate: 12.7%
Health Insurance: 85.5% have insurance; 61.8% have private insurance; 37.8% have public insurance; 14.5% do not have insurance; 7.3% of children under 18 do not have insurance
Safety: Violent crime rate: 16.0 per 10,000 population; Property crime rate: 504.0 per 10,000 population
Newspapers: Piqua Daily Call (daily circulation 6100)
Transportation: Commute: 95.2% car, 0.4% public transportation, 2.1% walk, 1.2% work from home; Median travel time to work: 17.9 minutes
Additional Information Contacts
City of Piqua . . . . (937) 778-2051
http://www.piquaoh.org

PLEASANT HILL (village). Covers a land area of 0.608 square miles and a water area of 0 square miles. Located at 40.05° N. Lat; 84.35° W. Long. Elevation is 932 feet.
Population: 1,200; Growth (since 2000): 5.8%; Density: 1,974.6 persons per square mile; Race: 98.7% White, 0.3% Black/African American, 0.3% Asian, 0.1% American Indian/Alaska Native, 0.0% Native Hawaiian/Other Pacific Islander, 0.6% Two or more races, 1.9% Hispanic of any race; Average household size: 2.62; Median age: 35.7; Age under 18: 27.7%; Age 65 and over: 14.1%; Males per 100 females: 93.9

School District(s)

Newton Local (PK-12)
2012-13 Enrollment: 574. . . . . (937) 676-2002
Housing: Homeownership rate: 76.0%; Homeowner vacancy rate: 3.0%; Rental vacancy rate: 4.3%

POTSDAM (village). Covers a land area of 0.445 square miles and a water area of 0 square miles. Located at 39.96° N. Lat; 84.41° W. Long. Elevation is 1,007 feet.
Population: 288; Growth (since 2000): 41.9%; Density: 646.7 persons per square mile; Race: 96.2% White, 0.0% Black/African American, 0.0% Asian, 1.4% American Indian/Alaska Native, 0.0% Native Hawaiian/Other Pacific Islander, 2.4% Two or more races, 0.0% Hispanic of any race; Average household size: 2.82; Median age: 37.5; Age under 18: 25.7%; Age 65 and over: 12.2%; Males per 100 females: 108.7
Housing: Homeownership rate: 81.3%; Homeowner vacancy rate: 0.0%; Rental vacancy rate: 0.0%

TIPP CITY (city). Covers a land area of 7.529 square miles and a water area of 0.114 square miles. Located at 39.97° N. Lat; 84.19° W. Long. Elevation is 827 feet.
History: Formerly called Tippecanoe City.
Population: 9,689; Growth (since 2000): 5.1%; Density: 1,286.8 persons per square mile; Race: 95.9% White, 0.6% Black/African American, 1.5% Asian, 0.2% American Indian/Alaska Native, 0.0% Native Hawaiian/Other Pacific Islander, 1.2% Two or more races, 1.6% Hispanic of any race; Average household size: 2.48; Median age: 40.3; Age under 18: 25.9%; Age 65 and over: 15.0%; Males per 100 females: 93.2; Marriage status: 23.3% never married, 56.1% now married, 1.7% separated, 5.2% widowed, 15.4% divorced; Foreign born: 1.5%; Speak English only: 98.2%; With disability: 10.0%; Veterans: 8.6%; Ancestry: 33.8% German, 11.6% English, 10.0% American, 9.0% Irish, 3.5% European
Employment: 13.7% management, business, and financial, 9.1% computer, engineering, and science, 9.5% education, legal, community service, arts, and media, 9.3% healthcare practitioners, 13.8% service, 21.0% sales and office, 11.3% natural resources, construction, and maintenance, 12.3% production, transportation, and material moving
Income: Per capita: $29,188; Median household: $58,984; Average household: $73,130; Households with income of $100,000 or more: 21.2%; Poverty rate: 6.7%
Educational Attainment: High school diploma or higher: 93.4%; Bachelor's degree or higher: 29.6%; Graduate/professional degree or higher: 11.7%

School District(s)

Bethel Local (PK-12)
2012-13 Enrollment: 905. . . . . (937) 845-9414
Tipp City Exempted Village (PK-12)
2012-13 Enrollment: 2,518 . . . . (937) 667-8444
Housing: Homeownership rate: 69.2%; Median home value: $155,800; Median year structure built: 1976; Homeowner vacancy rate: 2.0%; Median gross rent: $723 per month; Rental vacancy rate: 13.4%
Health Insurance: 91.5% have insurance; 83.2% have private insurance; 19.9% have public insurance; 8.5% do not have insurance; 4.7% of children under 18 do not have insurance
Safety: Violent crime rate: 9.2 per 10,000 population; Property crime rate: 192.9 per 10,000 population
Newspapers: Vandalia Drummer News (weekly circulation 5000)
Transportation: Commute: 96.9% car, 0.0% public transportation, 1.3% walk, 1.8% work from home; Median travel time to work: 18.9 minutes
Additional Information Contacts
City of Tipp City. . . . . (937) 669-8477
http://www.tippcityohio.gov

TROY (city). County seat. Covers a land area of 11.722 square miles and a water area of 0.219 square miles. Located at 40.04° N. Lat; 84.22° W. Long. Elevation is 837 feet.
History: Troy was settled in 1798 by Michael Garver, who built a cabin here and encouraged other settlers to follow him. The coming of the canal in 1837 and the railroad in 1850 brought industrial growth to Troy.
Population: 25,058; Growth (since 2000): 13.9%; Density: 2,137.8 persons per square mile; Race: 90.1% White, 4.2% Black/African American, 2.4% Asian, 0.2% American Indian/Alaska Native, 0.0% Native Hawaiian/Other Pacific Islander, 2.4% Two or more races, 1.8% Hispanic of any race; Average household size: 2.38; Median age: 36.9; Age under 18: 25.2%; Age 65 and over: 13.1%; Males per 100 females: 94.9; Marriage status: 27.8% never married, 50.6% now married, 1.4% separated, 6.5% widowed, 15.2% divorced; Foreign born: 2.9%; Speak English only: 95.4%; With disability: 12.8%; Veterans: 10.8%; Ancestry: 27.6% German, 12.7% Irish, 11.1% American, 8.8% English, 3.5% French
Employment: 12.9% management, business, and financial, 5.3% computer, engineering, and science, 9.4% education, legal, community service, arts, and media, 4.4% healthcare practitioners, 14.9% service, 23.9% sales and office, 6.1% natural resources, construction, and maintenance, 23.0% production, transportation, and material moving
Income: Per capita: $23,779; Median household: $48,570; Average household: $56,728; Households with income of $100,000 or more: 13.1%; Poverty rate: 16.2%
Educational Attainment: High school diploma or higher: 88.5%; Bachelor's degree or higher: 22.5%; Graduate/professional degree or higher: 7.2%

School District(s)

Troy City (PK-12)
2012-13 Enrollment: 4,357 . . . . (937) 332-6700

Two-year College(s)

Miami-Jacobs Career College-Troy (Private, For-profit)
Fall 2013 Enrollment: 277. . . . . (937) 332-8580
2013-14 Tuition: In-state $12,024; Out-of-state $12,024

Vocational/Technical School(s)

Hobart Institute of Welding Technology (Private, Not-for-profit)
Fall 2013 Enrollment: 285. . . . . (937) 332-9500
2013-14 Tuition: $14,870
Housing: Homeownership rate: 59.2%; Median home value: $123,800; Median year structure built: 1969; Homeowner vacancy rate: 2.3%; Median gross rent: $704 per month; Rental vacancy rate: 9.0%
Health Insurance: 88.8% have insurance; 71.7% have private insurance; 29.3% have public insurance; 11.2% do not have insurance; 8.0% of children under 18 do not have insurance
Hospitals: Upper Valley Medical Center (128 beds)
Safety: Violent crime rate: 7.5 per 10,000 population; Property crime rate: 311.1 per 10,000 population
Newspapers: Record Herald (weekly circulation 5500); Troy Daily News (daily circulation 9300)
Transportation: Commute: 94.4% car, 0.8% public transportation, 2.1% walk, 2.3% work from home; Median travel time to work: 18.1 minutes
Additional Information Contacts
City of Troy . . . . (937) 339-1221
http://www.troyohio.gov

WEST MILTON (village). Covers a land area of 3.244 square miles and a water area of 0.098 square miles. Located at 39.96° N. Lat; 84.33° W. Long. Elevation is 902 feet.
History: Settled 1807, incorporated 1835.
Population: 4,630; Growth (since 2000): -0.3%; Density: 1,427.2 persons per square mile; Race: 97.4% White, 0.5% Black/African American, 0.3% Asian, 0.1% American Indian/Alaska Native, 0.0% Native Hawaiian/Other Pacific Islander, 1.5% Two or more races, 0.8% Hispanic of any race; Average household size: 2.35; Median age: 39.3; Age under 18: 25.2%; Age 65 and over: 16.5%; Males per 100 females: 90.5; Marriage status: 22.0% never married, 52.2% now married, 0.8% separated, 5.4% widowed, 20.5% divorced; Foreign born: 1.9%; Speak English only: 97.0%; With disability: 9.4%; Veterans: 9.8%; Ancestry: 41.4% German, 13.1% Irish, 6.6% English, 6.3% American, 3.6% French
Employment: 7.6% management, business, and financial, 3.4% computer, engineering, and science, 6.6% education, legal, community service, arts, and media, 5.4% healthcare practitioners, 16.5% service, 25.9% sales and office, 7.9% natural resources, construction, and maintenance, 26.8% production, transportation, and material moving

Income: Per capita: $23,593; Median household: $50,833; Average household: $54,975; Households with income of $100,000 or more: 8.5%; Poverty rate: 8.0%
Educational Attainment: High school diploma or higher: 89.6%; Bachelor's degree or higher: 16.9%; Graduate/professional degree or higher: 4.1%

School District(s)

Milton-Union Exempted Village (PK-12)
2012-13 Enrollment: 1,431 . . . . (937) 884-7910
Housing: Homeownership rate: 64.3%; Median home value: $104,600; Median year structure built: 1963; Homeowner vacancy rate: 1.5%; Median gross rent: $787 per month; Rental vacancy rate: 8.5%
Health Insurance: 91.6% have insurance; 78.3% have private insurance; 26.2% have public insurance; 8.4% do not have insurance; 2.5% of children under 18 do not have insurance
Transportation: Commute: 94.7% car, 0.0% public transportation, 4.6% walk, 0.0% work from home; Median travel time to work: 21.9 minutes

Monroe County

Located in eastern Ohio; bounded on the southeast by the Ohio River and the West Virginia border; drained by Little Muskingum River and Sunfish Creek. Covers a land area of 455.721 square miles, a water area of 1.737 square miles, and is located in the Eastern Time Zone at 39.73° N. Lat., 81.09° W. Long. The county was founded in 1813. County seat is Woodsfield.

Weather Station: Hannibal Lock & Dam — Elevation: 620 feet

	Jan	Feb	Mar	Apr	May	Jun	Jul	Aug	Sep	Oct	Nov	Dec
High	38	42	51	64	72	81	84	83	77	65	54	42
Low	21	23	29	38	48	57	62	62	55	43	34	26
Precip	3.1	2.8	3.7	3.4	4.3	4.0	4.4	3.5	3.2	2.6	3.4	3.1
Snow	na	na	1.9	tr	0.0	0.0	0.0	0.0	0.0	0.0	tr	0.5

High and Low temperatures in degrees Fahrenheit; Precipitation and Snow in inches

Population: 14,642; Growth (since 2000): -3.5%; Density: 32.1 persons per square mile; Race: 98.1% White, 0.4% Black/African American, 0.1% Asian, 0.1% American Indian/Alaska Native, 0.0% Native Hawaiian/Other Pacific Islander, 1.2% two or more races, 0.4% Hispanic of any race; Average household size: 2.39; Median age: 44.7; Age under 18: 21.5%; Age 65 and over: 19.4%; Males per 100 females: 99.1; Marriage status: 19.4% never married, 60.6% now married, 1.0% separated, 8.4% widowed, 11.5% divorced; Foreign born: 0.2%; Speak English only: 96.8%; With disability: 16.7%; Veterans: 12.5%; Ancestry: 34.5% German, 15.0% Irish, 9.9% English, 9.0% American, 3.7% Italian
Religion: Six largest groups: 22.2% Baptist, 10.8% Methodist/Pietist, 6.9% Presbyterian-Reformed, 5.2% Catholicism, 4.2% European Free-Church, 1.1% Holiness
Economy: Unemployment rate: 9.5%; Leading industries: 18.5% retail trade; 17.3% other services (except public administration); 13.8% construction; Farms: 823 totaling 111,161 acres; Company size: 1 employs 1,000 or more persons, 1 employs 500 to 999 persons, 1 employs 100 to 499 persons, 251 employs less than 100 persons; Business ownership: n/a women-owned, n/a Black-owned, n/a Hispanic-owned, n/a Asian-owned
Employment: 8.5% management, business, and financial, 2.3% computer, engineering, and science, 7.8% education, legal, community service, arts, and media, 5.8% healthcare practitioners, 13.9% service, 22.3% sales and office, 21.8% natural resources, construction, and maintenance, 17.6% production, transportation, and material moving
Income: Per capita: $21,487; Median household: $40,573; Average household: $50,706; Households with income of $100,000 or more: 8.8%; Poverty rate: 19.0%
Educational Attainment: High school diploma or higher: 86.4%; Bachelor's degree or higher: 10.4%; Graduate/professional degree or higher: 4.0%
Housing: Homeownership rate: 78.5%; Median home value: $89,100; Median year structure built: 1963; Homeowner vacancy rate: 1.4%; Median gross rent: $506 per month; Rental vacancy rate: 9.2%
Vital Statistics: Birth rate: 100.1 per 10,000 population; Death rate: 138.5 per 10,000 population; Age-adjusted cancer mortality rate: 171.7 deaths per 100,000 population
Health Insurance: 88.1% have insurance; 68.6% have private insurance; 37.3% have public insurance; 11.9% do not have insurance; 11.7% of children under 18 do not have insurance
Health Care: Physicians: 2.1 per 10,000 population; Hospital beds: 0.0 per 10,000 population; Hospital admissions: 0.0 per 10,000 population
Transportation: Commute: 92.2% car, 0.8% public transportation, 3.2% walk, 3.4% work from home; Median travel time to work: 32.1 minutes
Presidential Election: 44.6% Obama, 52.5% Romney (2012)
National and State Parks: Monroe Lake State Wildlife Area; Sunfish Creek State Forest; Wayne National Forest
Additional Information Contacts
Monroe Government . . . . (740) 472-1341
http://www.monroecountyohio.com

Monroe County Communities

ANTIOCH (village). Covers a land area of 0.106 square miles and a water area of 0 square miles. Located at 39.66° N. Lat; 81.07° W. Long. Elevation is 1,066 feet.
Population: 86; Growth (since 2000): -3.4%; Density: 813.8 persons per square mile; Race: 97.7% White, 1.2% Black/African American, 0.0% Asian, 0.0% American Indian/Alaska Native, 0.0% Native Hawaiian/Other Pacific Islander, 1.2% Two or more races, 0.0% Hispanic of any race; Average household size: 2.61; Median age: 42.5; Age under 18: 25.6%; Age 65 and over: 11.6%; Males per 100 females: 109.8
Housing: Homeownership rate: 81.9%; Homeowner vacancy rate: 3.6%; Rental vacancy rate: 0.0%

BEALLSVILLE (village). Covers a land area of 0.363 square miles and a water area of 0 square miles. Located at 39.85° N. Lat; 81.04° W. Long. Elevation is 1,257 feet.
Population: 409; Growth (since 2000): -3.3%; Density: 1,127.3 persons per square mile; Race: 97.8% White, 0.0% Black/African American, 0.0% Asian, 0.0% American Indian/Alaska Native, 0.0% Native Hawaiian/Other Pacific Islander, 2.2% Two or more races, 0.0% Hispanic of any race; Average household size: 2.35; Median age: 39.8; Age under 18: 22.5%; Age 65 and over: 13.4%; Males per 100 females: 95.7

School District(s)

Switzerland of Ohio Local (PK-12)
2012-13 Enrollment: 2,481 . . . . (740) 472-5801
Housing: Homeownership rate: 60.9%; Homeowner vacancy rate: 0.9%; Rental vacancy rate: 11.3%

CAMERON (unincorporated postal area)
ZCTA: 43914
Covers a land area of 0.580 square miles and a water area of 0 square miles. Located at 39.78° N. Lat; 80.95° W. Long. Elevation is 696 feet.
Population: 94; Growth (since 2000): 27.0%; Density: 162.1 persons per square mile; Race: 98.9% White, 0.0% Black/African American, 0.0% Asian, 0.0% American Indian/Alaska Native, 0.0% Native Hawaiian/Other Pacific Islander, 1.1% Two or more races, 0.0% Hispanic of any race; Average household size: 2.76; Median age: 39.8; Age under 18: 17.0%; Age 65 and over: 11.7%; Males per 100 females: 104.3
Housing: Homeownership rate: 76.4%; Homeowner vacancy rate: 0.0%; Rental vacancy rate: 0.0%

CLARINGTON (village). Covers a land area of 1.139 square miles and a water area of 0.099 square miles. Located at 39.78° N. Lat; 80.87° W. Long. Elevation is 633 feet.
History: Clarington was originally settled by Swiss immigrants, who engaged in clock-making. Many of the later residents were of Slavic and Italian descent.
Population: 384; Growth (since 2000): -13.5%; Density: 337.0 persons per square mile; Race: 96.9% White, 1.0% Black/African American, 0.0% Asian, 0.0% American Indian/Alaska Native, 0.0% Native Hawaiian/Other Pacific Islander, 2.1% Two or more races, 0.3% Hispanic of any race; Average household size: 2.33; Median age: 40.3; Age under 18: 23.4%; Age 65 and over: 15.4%; Males per 100 females: 80.3
Housing: Homeownership rate: 70.3%; Homeowner vacancy rate: 5.7%; Rental vacancy rate: 2.0%

GRAYSVILLE (village). Covers a land area of 1.007 square miles and a water area of 0 square miles. Located at 39.66° N. Lat; 81.17° W. Long. Elevation is 1,096 feet.
Population: 76; Growth (since 2000): -32.7%; Density: 75.5 persons per square mile; Race: 89.5% White, 0.0% Black/African American, 0.0% Asian, 0.0% American Indian/Alaska Native, 0.0% Native Hawaiian/Other

Pacific Islander, 10.5% Two or more races, 0.0% Hispanic of any race; Average household size: 2.24; Median age: 48.0; Age under 18: 18.4%; Age 65 and over: 15.8%; Males per 100 females: 100.0

School District(s)

Switzerland of Ohio Local (PK-12)
2012-13 Enrollment: 2,481 . . . . (740) 472-5801

Housing: Homeownership rate: 85.3%; Homeowner vacancy rate: 0.0%; Rental vacancy rate: 14.3%

HANNIBAL (CDP). Covers a land area of 1.115 square miles and a water area of 0 square miles. Located at 39.67° N. Lat; 80.87° W. Long. Elevation is 653 feet.

Population: 411; Growth (since 2000): n/a; Density: 368.6 persons per square mile; Race: 97.8% White, 0.0% Black/African American, 0.0% Asian, 0.7% American Indian/Alaska Native, 0.0% Native Hawaiian/Other Pacific Islander, 1.5% Two or more races, 1.0% Hispanic of any race; Average household size: 2.23; Median age: 51.6; Age under 18: 19.0%; Age 65 and over: 26.3%; Males per 100 females: 94.8

School District(s)

Switzerland of Ohio Local (PK-12)
2012-13 Enrollment: 2,481 . . . . (740) 472-5801

Housing: Homeownership rate: 85.3%; Homeowner vacancy rate: 0.0%; Rental vacancy rate: 10.0%

JERUSALEM (village). Covers a land area of 0.242 square miles and a water area of 0 square miles. Located at 39.85° N. Lat; 81.10° W. Long. Elevation is 1,263 feet.

Population: 161; Growth (since 2000): 5.9%; Density: 666.5 persons per square mile; Race: 100.0% White, 0.0% Black/African American, 0.0% Asian, 0.0% American Indian/Alaska Native, 0.0% Native Hawaiian/Other Pacific Islander, 0.0% Two or more races, 1.2% Hispanic of any race; Average household size: 2.30; Median age: 43.8; Age under 18: 21.7%; Age 65 and over: 23.0%; Males per 100 females: 106.4

Housing: Homeownership rate: 71.4%; Homeowner vacancy rate: 0.0%; Rental vacancy rate: 4.8%

LEWISVILLE (village). Covers a land area of 0.368 square miles and a water area of 0 square miles. Located at 39.77° N. Lat; 81.22° W. Long. Elevation is 1,201 feet.

Population: 176; Growth (since 2000): -24.5%; Density: 478.8 persons per square mile; Race: 98.3% White, 0.0% Black/African American, 0.6% Asian, 0.0% American Indian/Alaska Native, 0.0% Native Hawaiian/Other Pacific Islander, 1.1% Two or more races, 0.6% Hispanic of any race; Average household size: 2.11; Median age: 48.5; Age under 18: 17.0%; Age 65 and over: 20.5%; Males per 100 females: 87.2

Housing: Homeownership rate: 80.3%; Homeowner vacancy rate: 1.6%; Rental vacancy rate: 11.8%

MILTONSBURG (village). Covers a land area of 0.073 square miles and a water area of 0 square miles. Located at 39.83° N. Lat; 81.16° W. Long. Elevation is 1,293 feet.

Population: 43; Growth (since 2000): 48.3%; Density: 591.4 persons per square mile; Race: 100.0% White, 0.0% Black/African American, 0.0% Asian, 0.0% American Indian/Alaska Native, 0.0% Native Hawaiian/Other Pacific Islander, 0.0% Two or more races, 0.0% Hispanic of any race; Average household size: 2.26; Median age: 42.8; Age under 18: 20.9%; Age 65 and over: 11.6%; Males per 100 females: 126.3

Housing: Homeownership rate: 79.0%; Homeowner vacancy rate: 11.1%; Rental vacancy rate: 20.0%

NEW MATAMORAS (unincorporated postal area)

ZCTA: 45767

Covers a land area of 113.815 square miles and a water area of 0.672 square miles. Located at 39.54° N. Lat; 81.13° W. Long..

Population: 2,800; Growth (since 2000): -1.4%; Density: 24.6 persons per square mile; Race: 98.2% White, 0.4% Black/African American, 0.1% Asian, 0.1% American Indian/Alaska Native, 0.0% Native Hawaiian/Other Pacific Islander, 1.2% Two or more races, 0.6% Hispanic of any race; Average household size: 2.32; Median age: 45.0; Age under 18: 20.5%; Age 65 and over: 19.6%; Males per 100 females: 102.3; Marriage status: 20.1% never married, 63.2% now married, 0.7% separated, 7.8% widowed, 8.9% divorced; Foreign born: 0.0%; Speak English only: 98.7%; With disability: 24.8%; Veterans: 5.8%; Ancestry: 26.5% German, 16.7% Irish, 14.5% English, 4.6% American, 2.7% Dutch

Employment: 4.3% management, business, and financial, 0.8% computer, engineering, and science, 5.5% education, legal, community service, arts, and media, 2.1% healthcare practitioners, 13.1% service, 36.1% sales and office, 16.6% natural resources, construction, and maintenance, 21.6% production, transportation, and material moving

Income: Per capita: $18,986; Median household: $36,064; Average household: $42,914; Households with income of $100,000 or more: 7.9%; Poverty rate: 22.5%

Educational Attainment: High school diploma or higher: 80.2%; Bachelor's degree or higher: 5.7%; Graduate/professional degree or higher: 0.9%

School District(s)

Frontier Local (PK-12)
2012-13 Enrollment: 673. . . . . (740) 865-3473

Housing: Homeownership rate: 75.4%; Median home value: $87,000; Median year structure built: 1960; Homeowner vacancy rate: 1.2%; Median gross rent: $473 per month; Rental vacancy rate: 3.2%

Health Insurance: 91.2% have insurance; 62.4% have private insurance; 45.6% have public insurance; 8.8% do not have insurance; 5.1% of children under 18 do not have insurance

Transportation: Commute: 98.6% car, 0.4% public transportation, 0.6% walk, 0.5% work from home; Median travel time to work: 33.2 minutes

SARDIS (CDP). Covers a land area of 1.232 square miles and a water area of 0 square miles. Located at 39.63° N. Lat; 80.91° W. Long. Elevation is 666 feet.

Population: 559; Growth (since 2000): n/a; Density: 453.7 persons per square mile; Race: 97.9% White, 0.4% Black/African American, 0.0% Asian, 0.4% American Indian/Alaska Native, 0.0% Native Hawaiian/Other Pacific Islander, 1.4% Two or more races, 0.0% Hispanic of any race; Average household size: 2.16; Median age: 45.9; Age under 18: 19.0%; Age 65 and over: 22.0%; Males per 100 females: 92.8

School District(s)

Switzerland of Ohio Local (PK-12)
2012-13 Enrollment: 2,481 . . . . (740) 472-5801

Housing: Homeownership rate: 70.3%; Homeowner vacancy rate: 0.5%; Rental vacancy rate: 7.1%

STAFFORD (village). Covers a land area of 0.340 square miles and a water area of 0 square miles. Located at 39.71° N. Lat; 81.28° W. Long. Elevation is 1,079 feet.

Population: 81; Growth (since 2000): -5.8%; Density: 238.5 persons per square mile; Race: 93.8% White, 4.9% Black/African American, 0.0% Asian, 1.2% American Indian/Alaska Native, 0.0% Native Hawaiian/Other Pacific Islander, 0.0% Two or more races, 0.0% Hispanic of any race; Average household size: 2.32; Median age: 47.2; Age under 18: 18.5%; Age 65 and over: 19.8%; Males per 100 females: 92.9

Housing: Homeownership rate: 67.6%; Homeowner vacancy rate: 4.2%; Rental vacancy rate: 0.0%

WILSON (village). Covers a land area of 0.413 square miles and a water area of 0.058 square miles. Located at 39.86° N. Lat; 81.07° W. Long. Elevation is 1,250 feet.

Population: 125; Growth (since 2000): 5.9%; Density: 302.9 persons per square mile; Race: 96.0% White, 0.0% Black/African American, 0.0% Asian, 0.0% American Indian/Alaska Native, 0.0% Native Hawaiian/Other Pacific Islander, 4.0% Two or more races, 2.4% Hispanic of any race; Average household size: 2.23; Median age: 49.8; Age under 18: 20.0%; Age 65 and over: 25.6%; Males per 100 females: 111.9

Housing: Homeownership rate: 85.7%; Homeowner vacancy rate: 0.0%; Rental vacancy rate: 11.1%

WOODSFIELD (village). County seat. Covers a land area of 2.015 square miles and a water area of 0 square miles. Located at 39.76° N. Lat; 81.12° W. Long. Elevation is 1,207 feet.

History: Settled 1815, incorporated 1834.

Population: 2,384; Growth (since 2000): -8.2%; Density: 1,182.9 persons per square mile; Race: 97.3% White, 0.7% Black/African American, 0.2% Asian, 0.0% American Indian/Alaska Native, 0.0% Native Hawaiian/Other Pacific Islander, 1.4% Two or more races, 1.0% Hispanic of any race; Average household size: 2.17; Median age: 45.9; Age under 18: 21.4%; Age 65 and over: 26.6%; Males per 100 females: 83.5

School District(s)

Switzerland of Ohio Local (PK-12)
2012-13 Enrollment: 2,481 . . . . (740) 472-5801

Housing: Homeownership rate: 62.3%; Homeowner vacancy rate: 2.4%; Rental vacancy rate: 15.9%
Newspapers: Monroe County Beacon (weekly circulation 5000)

Montgomery County

Located in western Ohio; crossed by the Great Miami, Stillwater, and Mad Rivers. Covers a land area of 461.553 square miles, a water area of 2.782 square miles, and is located in the Eastern Time Zone at 39.76° N. Lat., 84.29° W. Long. The county was founded in 1803. County seat is Dayton.

Montgomery County is part of the Dayton, OH Metropolitan Statistical Area. The entire metro area includes: Greene County, OH; Miami County, OH; Montgomery County, OH

Weather Station: Dayton Intl Arpt Elevation: 1,000 feet

	Jan	Feb	Mar	Apr	May	Jun	Jul	Aug	Sep	Oct	Nov	Dec
High	35	39	50	62	72	81	84	83	76	64	51	39
Low	20	23	31	41	51	61	64	63	55	44	35	24
Precip	2.8	2.3	3.4	4.1	4.6	4.3	4.1	3.1	3.1	3.0	3.3	3.1
Snow	8.0	6.3	4.1	0.6	tr	0.0	tr	tr	tr	0.4	0.8	5.1

High and Low temperatures in degrees Fahrenheit; Precipitation and Snow in inches

Weather Station: Dayton Mcd Elevation: 745 feet

	Jan	Feb	Mar	Apr	May	Jun	Jul	Aug	Sep	Oct	Nov	Dec
High	36	41	51	64	74	84	87	86	79	66	53	40
Low	22	25	32	43	53	63	67	65	57	45	36	26
Precip	2.9	2.3	3.3	4.0	4.9	4.1	4.4	3.0	2.7	2.9	3.2	3.0
Snow	4.8	2.7	1.6	0.1	0.0	0.0	0.0	0.0	0.0	tr	0.3	2.9

High and Low temperatures in degrees Fahrenheit; Precipitation and Snow in inches

Population: 535,153; Growth (since 2000): -4.3%; Density: 1,159.5 persons per square mile; Race: 73.9% White, 20.9% Black/African American, 1.7% Asian, 0.2% American Indian/Alaska Native, 0.0% Native Hawaiian/Other Pacific Islander, 2.4% two or more races, 2.3% Hispanic of any race; Average household size: 2.33; Median age: 39.2; Age under 18: 23.0%; Age 65 and over: 15.1%; Males per 100 females: 92.4; Marriage status: 32.5% never married, 46.2% now married, 2.3% separated, 7.3% widowed, 14.1% divorced; Foreign born: 3.7%; Speak English only: 94.5%; With disability: 15.1%; Veterans: 10.9%; Ancestry: 24.0% German, 13.0% Irish, 8.5% English, 8.0% American, 3.8% Italian
Religion: Six largest groups: 14.7% Catholicism, 11.5% Baptist, 4.6% Non-denominational Protestant, 4.0% Methodist/Pietist, 3.0% Holiness, 2.2% Lutheran
Economy: Unemployment rate: 4.8%; Leading industries: 14.6% retail trade; 12.8% health care and social assistance; 11.0% other services (except public administration); Farms: 770 totaling 124,105 acres; Company size: 12 employ 1,000 or more persons, 16 employ 500 to 999 persons, 298 employ 100 to 499 persons, 11,139 employ less than 100 persons; Business ownership: 11,216 women-owned, 4,040 Black-owned, 342 Hispanic-owned, 974 Asian-owned
Employment: 13.1% management, business, and financial, 5.2% computer, engineering, and science, 10.1% education, legal, community service, arts, and media, 6.5% healthcare practitioners, 19.3% service, 25.5% sales and office, 6.7% natural resources, construction, and maintenance, 13.5% production, transportation, and material moving
Income: Per capita: $24,997; Median household: $43,401; Average household: $58,719; Households with income of $100,000 or more: 15.4%; Poverty rate: 17.7%
Educational Attainment: High school diploma or higher: 88.2%; Bachelor's degree or higher: 24.6%; Graduate/professional degree or higher: 10.0%
Housing: Homeownership rate: 63.0%; Median home value: $112,800; Median year structure built: 1964; Homeowner vacancy rate: 2.9%; Median gross rent: $723 per month; Rental vacancy rate: 12.9%
Vital Statistics: Birth rate: 121.2 per 10,000 population; Death rate: 103.5 per 10,000 population; Age-adjusted cancer mortality rate: 190.6 deaths per 100,000 population
Health Insurance: 87.7% have insurance; 66.2% have private insurance; 34.1% have public insurance; 12.3% do not have insurance; 5.2% of children under 18 do not have insurance
Health Care: Physicians: 34.6 per 10,000 population; Hospital beds: 53.5 per 10,000 population; Hospital admissions: 2,053.8 per 10,000 population
Air Quality Index: 65.2% good, 34.8% moderate, 0.0% unhealthy for sensitive individuals, 0.0% unhealthy (percent of days)
Transportation: Commute: 90.7% car, 2.2% public transportation, 2.7% walk, 3.2% work from home; Median travel time to work: 21.3 minutes
Presidential Election: 50.7% Obama, 47.7% Romney (2012)
National and State Parks: Miamisburg Mound State Memorial; Sycamore State Park
Additional Information Contacts
Montgomery Government . . . . (937) 225-4690
http://www.co.montgomery.oh.us

Montgomery County Communities

BROOKVILLE (city). Covers a land area of 3.822 square miles and a water area of 0 square miles. Located at 39.84° N. Lat; 84.42° W. Long. Elevation is 1,030 feet.
Population: 5,884; Growth (since 2000): 11.2%; Density: 1,539.4 persons per square mile; Race: 97.6% White, 0.4% Black/African American, 0.9% Asian, 0.1% American Indian/Alaska Native, 0.0% Native Hawaiian/Other Pacific Islander, 0.7% Two or more races, 0.7% Hispanic of any race; Average household size: 2.29; Median age: 42.3; Age under 18: 23.3%; Age 65 and over: 22.2%; Males per 100 females: 85.7; Marriage status: 16.6% never married, 54.3% now married, 1.4% separated, 13.4% widowed, 15.7% divorced; Foreign born: 0.9%; Speak English only: 98.9%; With disability: 15.2%; Veterans: 10.3%; Ancestry: 36.3% German, 12.9% American, 12.3% Irish, 7.5% English, 4.3% Italian
Employment: 7.8% management, business, and financial, 4.9% computer, engineering, and science, 9.0% education, legal, community service, arts, and media, 8.5% healthcare practitioners, 15.2% service, 24.4% sales and office, 5.5% natural resources, construction, and maintenance, 24.7% production, transportation, and material moving
Income: Per capita: $23,908; Median household: $41,784; Average household: $53,568; Households with income of $100,000 or more: 10.0%; Poverty rate: 9.3%
Educational Attainment: High school diploma or higher: 89.8%; Bachelor's degree or higher: 14.7%; Graduate/professional degree or higher: 4.1%

School District(s)

Brookville Local (PK-12)
2012-13 Enrollment: 1,447 . . . . (937) 833-2181
Housing: Homeownership rate: 64.4%; Median home value: $109,300; Median year structure built: 1968; Homeowner vacancy rate: 2.7%; Median gross rent: $616 per month; Rental vacancy rate: 7.3%
Health Insurance: 90.8% have insurance; 74.8% have private insurance; 34.1% have public insurance; 9.2% do not have insurance; 4.6% of children under 18 do not have insurance
Safety: Violent crime rate: 3.4 per 10,000 population; Property crime rate: 172.1 per 10,000 population
Newspapers: Brookville Star (weekly circulation 6500)
Transportation: Commute: 95.3% car, 0.0% public transportation, 1.5% walk, 1.1% work from home; Median travel time to work: 21.9 minutes
Additional Information Contacts
Village of Brookville. . . . . (937) 833-2135
http://www.brookvilleohio.com

CENTERVILLE (city). Covers a land area of 10.780 square miles and a water area of 0.065 square miles. Located at 39.63° N. Lat; 84.15° W. Long. Elevation is 1,020 feet.
History: Incorporated 1879.
Population: 23,999; Growth (since 2000): 4.2%; Density: 2,226.2 persons per square mile; Race: 90.2% White, 4.0% Black/African American, 3.2% Asian, 0.2% American Indian/Alaska Native, 0.0% Native Hawaiian/Other Pacific Islander, 1.9% Two or more races, 1.8% Hispanic of any race; Average household size: 2.19; Median age: 46.9; Age under 18: 20.1%; Age 65 and over: 24.4%; Males per 100 females: 86.0; Marriage status: 22.3% never married, 56.8% now married, 1.1% separated, 9.8% widowed, 11.1% divorced; Foreign born: 5.3%; Speak English only: 93.1%; With disability: 14.2%; Veterans: 12.4%; Ancestry: 31.6% German, 17.1% Irish, 13.2% English, 8.8% American, 4.6% Italian
Employment: 18.7% management, business, and financial, 7.2% computer, engineering, and science, 14.7% education, legal, community service, arts, and media, 9.0% healthcare practitioners, 15.0% service, 24.7% sales and office, 3.2% natural resources, construction, and maintenance, 7.5% production, transportation, and material moving
Income: Per capita: $35,825; Median household: $60,162; Average household: $77,576; Households with income of $100,000 or more: 25.7%; Poverty rate: 7.5%

Educational Attainment: High school diploma or higher: 94.7%; Bachelor's degree or higher: 45.2%; Graduate/professional degree or higher: 19.4%

School District(s)

Centerville City (PK-12)
2012-13 Enrollment: 8,357 . . . . (937) 433-8841
Springboro Community City (PK-12)
2012-13 Enrollment: 5,734 . . . . (937) 748-3960

Four-year College(s)

Fortis College-Centerville (Private, For-profit)
Fall 2013 Enrollment: 2,802 . . . . (937) 433-3410
2013-14 Tuition: In-state $11,586; Out-of-state $11,586

Vocational/Technical School(s)

David-Curtis School of Floral Design (Private, For-profit)
Fall 2013 Enrollment: 2 . . . . (937) 433-0566
2013-14 Tuition: $2,450

Housing: Homeownership rate: 72.1%; Median home value: $169,500; Median year structure built: 1976; Homeowner vacancy rate: 1.9%; Median gross rent: $841 per month; Rental vacancy rate: 10.9%

Health Insurance: 93.4% have insurance; 81.0% have private insurance; 31.7% have public insurance; 6.6% do not have insurance; 3.8% of children under 18 do not have insurance

Safety: Violent crime rate: 7.9 per 10,000 population; Property crime rate: 181.6 per 10,000 population

Transportation: Commute: 93.1% car, 1.8% public transportation, 0.1% walk, 4.7% work from home; Median travel time to work: 21.8 minutes

Additional Information Contacts

City of Centerville . . . . (937) 433-7151
http://www.ci.centerville.oh.us

CLAYTON (city). Covers a land area of 18.506 square miles and a water area of 0.089 square miles. Located at 39.87° N. Lat; 84.33° W. Long. Elevation is 1,001 feet.

Population: 13,209; Growth (since 2000): -1.0%; Density: 713.8 persons per square mile; Race: 76.5% White, 18.8% Black/African American, 1.4% Asian, 0.2% American Indian/Alaska Native, 0.0% Native Hawaiian/Other Pacific Islander, 2.5% Two or more races, 1.4% Hispanic of any race; Average household size: 2.56; Median age: 42.6; Age under 18: 23.4%; Age 65 and over: 14.0%; Males per 100 females: 95.9; Marriage status: 25.3% never married, 57.4% now married, 1.2% separated, 5.4% widowed, 11.8% divorced; Foreign born: 2.0%; Speak English only: 95.7%; With disability: 12.2%; Veterans: 12.2%; Ancestry: 28.8% German, 11.9% Irish, 9.6% English, 5.1% American, 4.2% Italian

Employment: 16.1% management, business, and financial, 4.3% computer, engineering, and science, 11.0% education, legal, community service, arts, and media, 7.3% healthcare practitioners, 14.9% service, 29.5% sales and office, 5.9% natural resources, construction, and maintenance, 11.0% production, transportation, and material moving

Income: Per capita: $30,471; Median household: $65,187; Average household: $76,941; Households with income of $100,000 or more: 25.6%; Poverty rate: 7.6%

Educational Attainment: High school diploma or higher: 93.8%; Bachelor's degree or higher: 33.3%; Graduate/professional degree or higher: 14.3%

School District(s)

Miami Valley Career Tech (07-12)
2012-13 Enrollment: n/a . . . . (937) 837-7781
Northmont City (PK-12)
2012-13 Enrollment: 5,251 . . . . (937) 832-5000

Vocational/Technical School(s)

Miami Valley Career Technology Center (Public)
Fall 2013 Enrollment: 407 . . . . (800) 716-7161
2013-14 Tuition: $12,660

Housing: Homeownership rate: 82.8%; Median home value: $135,800; Median year structure built: 1971; Homeowner vacancy rate: 2.4%; Median gross rent: $873 per month; Rental vacancy rate: 8.6%

Health Insurance: 93.4% have insurance; 79.2% have private insurance; 25.4% have public insurance; 6.6% do not have insurance; 1.5% of children under 18 do not have insurance

Safety: Violent crime rate: 3.8 per 10,000 population; Property crime rate: 159.0 per 10,000 population

Transportation: Commute: 96.4% car, 0.6% public transportation, 0.6% walk, 1.8% work from home; Median travel time to work: 24.1 minutes

Additional Information Contacts

City of Clayton . . . . (937) 836-3500
http://www.clayton.oh.us

DAYTON (city). County seat. Covers a land area of 55.652 square miles and a water area of 0.853 square miles. Located at 39.78° N. Lat; 84.20° W. Long. Elevation is 738 feet.

History: Settlers began coming in 1795 to the site where the Great Miami River was joined by the Stillwater and Mad Rivers and Wolf Creek. When Ohio became a state in 1803, Dayton became the Montgomery County seat, and two years later the town was incorporated. The opening of the canal system in the 1830's increased Dayton's river traffic, augmented by the railroad traffic that began in 1851. Industries such as the railroad car works and the National Cash Register Company were founded between 1850 and 1890, and by the early 1900's locally-made Stoddard-Dayton, Speedwell, and Big Four automobiles were wheeling around Dayton. Wilbur and Orville Wright used the Dayton Public Library to learn about aerodynamics, and soon established an experimental airplane factory here. Charles F. Kettering came to Dayton to work at the cash register plant, invented a quick-starting electric motor, and started the Dayton Engineering Laboratories Company (Delco). Dayton suffered recurring floods until a system of levees and dams to restrain the rivers was completed in 1921.

Population: 141,527; Growth (since 2000): -14.8%; Density: 2,543.1 persons per square mile; Race: 51.7% White, 42.9% Black/African American, 0.9% Asian, 0.3% American Indian/Alaska Native, 0.0% Native Hawaiian/Other Pacific Islander, 2.9% Two or more races, 3.0% Hispanic of any race; Average household size: 2.26; Median age: 34.4; Age under 18: 22.9%; Age 65 and over: 11.8%; Males per 100 females: 95.0; Marriage status: 48.7% never married, 29.0% now married, 3.0% separated, 6.5% widowed, 15.7% divorced; Foreign born: 3.8%; Speak English only: 94.3%; With disability: 19.0%; Veterans: 9.0%; Ancestry: 16.8% German, 10.9% Irish, 6.4% American, 5.1% English, 3.7% Italian

Employment: 9.1% management, business, and financial, 3.8% computer, engineering, and science, 10.6% education, legal, community service, arts, and media, 4.3% healthcare practitioners, 25.5% service, 24.4% sales and office, 7.3% natural resources, construction, and maintenance, 15.0% production, transportation, and material moving

Income: Per capita: $16,494; Median household: $28,456; Average household: $39,105; Households with income of $100,000 or more: 5.9%; Poverty rate: 34.7%

Educational Attainment: High school diploma or higher: 80.8%; Bachelor's degree or higher: 16.4%; Graduate/professional degree or higher: 6.5%

School District(s)

Centerville City (PK-12)
2012-13 Enrollment: 8,357 . . . . (937) 433-8841
City Day Community School (KG-08)
2012-13 Enrollment: 132. . . . . (937) 223-8130
Dayton City (PK-12)
2012-13 Enrollment: 14,357 . . . . (937) 542-3000
Dayton Early College Academy Inc (07-12)
2012-13 Enrollment: 459. . . . . (937) 229-5780
Dayton Leadership Academies-Dayton Liberty Campus (KG-08)
2012-13 Enrollment: 316. . . . . (937) 262-4080
Dayton Leadership Academies-Dayton View Campus (KG-08)
2012-13 Enrollment: 415. . . . . (937) 567-9426
Dayton Technology Design High School (09-12)
2012-13 Enrollment: 149. . . . . (937) 225-3989
Emerson Academy (KG-08)
2012-13 Enrollment: 700. . . . . (937) 223-2889
General Chappie James Leadership Academy (09-12)
2012-13 Enrollment: 104. . . . . (937) 835-3580
Horizon Science Academy Dayton Downtown (KG-07)
2012-13 Enrollment: 220. . . . . (937) 554-2437
Horizon Science Academy Dayton High School (07-12)
2012-13 Enrollment: 373. . . . . (937) 281-1480
Horizon Science Academy-Dayton (KG-06)
2012-13 Enrollment: 149. . . . . (937) 277-1177
Imagine Woodbury Academy (KG-04)
2012-13 Enrollment: 158. . . . . (614) 995-1985
Jefferson Township Local (PK-12)
2012-13 Enrollment: 421. . . . . (937) 835-5682
Klepinger Community School (KG-08)
2012-13 Enrollment: 425. . . . . (937) 610-1710

Life Skills Center of Dayton (09-12)
2012-13 Enrollment: 323. . . . . (937) 274-2841
Mad River Local (PK-12)
2012-13 Enrollment: 3,772 . . . . (937) 259-6606
Miami Valley Academies (KG-12)
2012-13 Enrollment: 180. . . . . (937) 294-4522
Miami Valley Career Tech (07-12)
2012-13 Enrollment: n/a . . . . (937) 837-7781
Miamisburg City (PK-12)
2012-13 Enrollment: 5,542 . . . . (937) 866-3381
Mound Street Health Careers Acadmy (09-12)
2012-13 Enrollment: 121. . . . . (937) 223-3041
Mound Street It Careers Academy (09-11)
2012-13 Enrollment: 71. . . . . (937) 223-3041
Mound Street Military Careers Academy (09-12)
2012-13 Enrollment: 71. . . . . (937) 223-3041
North Dayton School of Science & Discovery (KG-08)
2012-13 Enrollment: 523. . . . . (937) 278-6671
Northmont City (PK-12)
2012-13 Enrollment: 5,251 . . . . (937) 832-5000
Northridge Local (PK-12)
2012-13 Enrollment: 1,734 . . . . (937) 278-5885
Oakwood City (KG-12)
2012-13 Enrollment: 2,102 . . . . (937) 297-5332
Pathway School of Discovery (KG-08)
2012-13 Enrollment: 762. . . . . (937) 235-5498
Richard Allen Academy (07-09)
2012-13 Enrollment: 102. . . . . (937) 586-9815
Richard Allen Academy II (02-06)
2012-13 Enrollment: 466. . . . . (937) 586-9756
Richard Allen Preparatory (KG-01)
2012-13 Enrollment: 225. . . . . (937) 278-4201
Summit Academy Dayton (KG-08)
2012-13 Enrollment: 111. . . . . (937) 278-4298
Summit Academy Transition High School Dayton (09-12)
2012-13 Enrollment: 85. . . . . (937) 223-3154
The Isus Institute of Health Care (09-11)
2012-13 Enrollment: n/a . . . . (937) 223-2323
Vandalia-Butler City (PK-12)
2012-13 Enrollment: 3,235 . . . . (937) 415-6400
West Carrollton City (PK-12)
2012-13 Enrollment: 3,726 . . . . (937) 859-5121

Four-year College(s)

ITT Technical Institute-Dayton (Private, For-profit)
Fall 2013 Enrollment: 304. . . . . (937) 264-7700
2013-14 Tuition: In-state $18,048; Out-of-state $18,048
United Theological Seminary (Private, Not-for-profit, United Methodist)
Fall 2013 Enrollment: 640. . . . . (937) 529-2201
University of Dayton (Private, Not-for-profit, Roman Catholic)
Fall 2013 Enrollment: 10,835 . . . . (937) 229-1000
2013-14 Tuition: In-state $35,800; Out-of-state $35,800
Wright State University-Main Campus (Public)
Fall 2013 Enrollment: 16,656 . . . . (937) 775-3333
2013-14 Tuition: In-state $8,542; Out-of-state $16,546

Two-year College(s)

Carousel Beauty College-Dayton (Private, For-profit)
Fall 2013 Enrollment: 31. . . . . (937) 223-3572
Creative Images Institute of Cosmetology-North Dayton (Private, For-profit)
Fall 2013 Enrollment: 181. . . . . (937) 454-1200
Creative Images Institute of Cosmetology-South Dayton (Private, For-profit)
Fall 2013 Enrollment: 99. . . . . (937) 433-1944
International College of Broadcasting (Private, For-profit)
Fall 2013 Enrollment: 74. . . . . (937) 258-8251
2013-14 Tuition: In-state $14,660; Out-of-state $14,660
Kaplan College-Dayton (Private, For-profit)
Fall 2013 Enrollment: 404. . . . . (937) 294-6155
Lincoln College of Technology-Dayton (Private, For-profit)
Fall 2013 Enrollment: 58. . . . . (937) 224-0061
2013-14 Tuition: In-state $12,020; Out-of-state $12,020
Miami-Jacobs Career College-Dayton (Private, For-profit)
Fall 2013 Enrollment: 258. . . . . (937) 668-0203
2013-14 Tuition: In-state $12,024; Out-of-state $12,024
Ohio Medical Career Center (Private, For-profit)
Fall 2013 Enrollment: n/a . . . . (937) 567-8880
Sinclair Community College (Public)
Fall 2013 Enrollment: 19,176 . . . . (937) 512-3000
2013-14 Tuition: In-state $3,432; Out-of-state $6,600

Vocational/Technical School(s)

Dayton School of Medical Massage (Private, For-profit)
Fall 2013 Enrollment: 505. . . . . (937) 294-6994
2013-14 Tuition: In-state $15,400; Out-of-state $15,400
Ohio Business College-Dayton (Private, For-profit)
Fall 2013 Enrollment: 54. . . . . (937) 443-0223
2013-14 Tuition: In-state $8,500; Out-of-state $8,500
Regency Beauty Institute-Dayton (Private, For-profit)
Fall 2013 Enrollment: 87. . . . . (800) 787-6456
2013-14 Tuition: $16,200
Ross Medical Education Center-Dayton (Private, For-profit)
Fall 2013 Enrollment: 94. . . . . (937) 235-0510
2013-14 Tuition: $15,680

Housing: Homeownership rate: 49.9%; Median home value: $69,600; Median year structure built: 1950; Homeowner vacancy rate: 4.6%; Median gross rent: $637 per month; Rental vacancy rate: 15.7%

Health Insurance: 83.1% have insurance; 51.1% have private insurance; 42.0% have public insurance; 16.9% do not have insurance; 5.2% of children under 18 do not have insurance

Hospitals: Dayton VA Medical Center (539 beds); Good Samaritan Hospital (560 beds); Grandview Hospital & Medical Center (452 beds); Medical Center at Elizabeth Place (26 beds); Miami Valley Hospital (848 beds)

Safety: Violent crime rate: 87.1 per 10,000 population; Property crime rate: 542.3 per 10,000 population

Newspapers: Dayton City Paper (weekly circulation 23000); Dayton Daily News (daily circulation 123000); Dayton Weekly News (weekly circulation 30000); Oakwood Register (weekly circulation 10000); Times Community Papers (weekly circulation 78000)

Transportation: Commute: 82.5% car, 5.3% public transportation, 8.1% walk, 2.2% work from home; Median travel time to work: 20.2 minutes

Airports: Dayton-Wright Brothers (general aviation); James M Cox Dayton International (primary service/small hub); Wright-Patterson AFB (general aviation)

Additional Information Contacts

City of Dayton . . . . (937) 333-3333
http://www.cityofdayton.org

DREXEL (CDP). Covers a land area of 2.184 square miles and a water area of 0 square miles. Located at 39.74° N. Lat; 84.29° W. Long. Elevation is 951 feet.

Population: 2,076; Growth (since 2000): 0.9%; Density: 950.4 persons per square mile; Race: 50.5% White, 45.3% Black/African American, 0.0% Asian, 0.4% American Indian/Alaska Native, 0.0% Native Hawaiian/Other Pacific Islander, 3.3% Two or more races, 3.5% Hispanic of any race; Average household size: 2.68; Median age: 30.7; Age under 18: 33.8%; Age 65 and over: 10.3%; Males per 100 females: 89.8

Housing: Homeownership rate: 47.6%; Homeowner vacancy rate: 1.6%; Rental vacancy rate: 5.4%

ENGLEWOOD (city). Covers a land area of 6.551 square miles and a water area of 0.041 square miles. Located at 39.87° N. Lat; 84.31° W. Long. Elevation is 919 feet.

History: Englewood was established as a Mennonite community by descendants of a group that had been invited to Pennsylvania by William Penn.

Population: 13,465; Growth (since 2000): 10.1%; Density: 2,055.4 persons per square mile; Race: 82.3% White, 12.9% Black/African American, 1.6% Asian, 0.2% American Indian/Alaska Native, 0.1% Native Hawaiian/Other Pacific Islander, 2.3% Two or more races, 1.1% Hispanic of any race; Average household size: 2.37; Median age: 42.1; Age under 18: 23.0%; Age 65 and over: 19.2%; Males per 100 females: 87.2; Marriage status: 24.1% never married, 55.4% now married, 3.4% separated, 7.8% widowed, 12.6% divorced; Foreign born: 4.4%; Speak English only: 94.8%; With disability: 13.8%; Veterans: 13.3%; Ancestry: 33.1% German, 10.5% English, 9.8% Irish, 8.4% American, 4.0% Italian

Employment: 11.8% management, business, and financial, 5.5% computer, engineering, and science, 10.7% education, legal, community service, arts, and media, 8.4% healthcare practitioners, 19.7% service, 27.7% sales and office, 5.0% natural resources, construction, and maintenance, 11.1% production, transportation, and material moving

Income: Per capita: $25,377; Median household: $51,042; Average household: $60,989; Households with income of $100,000 or more: 16.2%; Poverty rate: 9.3%
Educational Attainment: High school diploma or higher: 94.4%; Bachelor's degree or higher: 27.7%; Graduate/professional degree or higher: 10.1%

School District(s)

Northmont City (PK-12)
2012-13 Enrollment: 5,251 . . . . (937) 832-5000
Housing: Homeownership rate: 73.8%; Median home value: $120,200; Median year structure built: 1974; Homeowner vacancy rate: 2.3%; Median gross rent: $690 per month; Rental vacancy rate: 8.9%
Health Insurance: 92.0% have insurance; 74.2% have private insurance; 33.7% have public insurance; 8.0% do not have insurance; 3.7% of children under 18 do not have insurance
Safety: Violent crime rate: 11.1 per 10,000 population; Property crime rate: 328.5 per 10,000 population
Newspapers: Englewood Independent (weekly circulation 4000)
Transportation: Commute: 94.9% car, 0.4% public transportation, 1.1% walk, 2.9% work from home; Median travel time to work: 21.8 minutes
Additional Information Contacts
City of Englewood . . . . (937) 836-5106
http://www.ci.englewood.oh.us

FARMERSVILLE (village). Covers a land area of 0.715 square miles and a water area of 0 square miles. Located at 39.68° N. Lat; 84.43° W. Long. Elevation is 879 feet.
Population: 1,009; Growth (since 2000): 3.0%; Density: 1,411.7 persons per square mile; Race: 97.6% White, 0.0% Black/African American, 0.2% Asian, 0.0% American Indian/Alaska Native, 0.0% Native Hawaiian/Other Pacific Islander, 2.0% Two or more races, 0.6% Hispanic of any race; Average household size: 2.72; Median age: 36.8; Age under 18: 28.5%; Age 65 and over: 11.1%; Males per 100 females: 88.6

School District(s)

Valley View Local (PK-12)
2012-13 Enrollment: 1,914 . . . . (937) 855-6581
Housing: Homeownership rate: 75.7%; Homeowner vacancy rate: 2.1%; Rental vacancy rate: 6.2%

GERMANTOWN (city). Covers a land area of 4.262 square miles and a water area of 0 square miles. Located at 39.63° N. Lat; 84.36° W. Long. Elevation is 718 feet.
History: Laid out 1814.
Population: 5,547; Growth (since 2000): 13.6%; Density: 1,301.4 persons per square mile; Race: 97.5% White, 0.8% Black/African American, 0.5% Asian, 0.2% American Indian/Alaska Native, 0.0% Native Hawaiian/Other Pacific Islander, 0.8% Two or more races, 1.2% Hispanic of any race; Average household size: 2.57; Median age: 37.5; Age under 18: 27.3%; Age 65 and over: 13.1%; Males per 100 females: 92.5; Marriage status: 19.4% never married, 61.7% now married, 0.7% separated, 5.1% widowed, 13.7% divorced; Foreign born: 2.1%; Speak English only: 97.7%; With disability: 10.0%; Veterans: 12.2%; Ancestry: 34.3% German, 22.3% Irish, 8.5% English, 8.3% American, 3.8% Welsh
Employment: 12.0% management, business, and financial, 3.9% computer, engineering, and science, 6.7% education, legal, community service, arts, and media, 0.4% healthcare practitioners, 20.6% service, 25.2% sales and office, 4.8% natural resources, construction, and maintenance, 17.5% production, transportation, and material moving
Income: Per capita: $29,214; Median household: $52,418; Average household: $73,717; Households with income of $100,000 or more: 18.4%; Poverty rate: 8.1%
Educational Attainment: High school diploma or higher: 90.9%; Bachelor's degree or higher: 19.9%; Graduate/professional degree or higher: 7.9%

School District(s)

Valley View Local (PK-12)
2012-13 Enrollment: 1,914 . . . . (937) 855-6581
Housing: Homeownership rate: 74.1%; Median home value: $125,200; Median year structure built: 1961; Homeowner vacancy rate: 1.8%; Median gross rent: $635 per month; Rental vacancy rate: 13.2%
Health Insurance: 88.8% have insurance; 74.0% have private insurance; 28.0% have public insurance; 11.2% do not have insurance; 2.2% of children under 18 do not have insurance
Safety: Violent crime rate: 1.8 per 10,000 population; Property crime rate: 76.1 per 10,000 population
Transportation: Commute: 93.4% car, 0.0% public transportation, 0.9% walk, 4.0% work from home; Median travel time to work: 25.6 minutes
Additional Information Contacts
Village of Germantown . . . . (937) 855-7255
http://germantown.oh.us

HUBER HEIGHTS (city). Covers a land area of 22.272 square miles and a water area of 0.095 square miles. Located at 39.86° N. Lat; 84.11° W. Long. Elevation is 932 feet.
Population: 38,101; Growth (since 2000): -0.3%; Density: 1,710.7 persons per square mile; Race: 79.6% White, 13.0% Black/African American, 2.5% Asian, 0.3% American Indian/Alaska Native, 0.1% Native Hawaiian/Other Pacific Islander, 3.5% Two or more races, 3.1% Hispanic of any race; Average household size: 2.58; Median age: 37.4; Age under 18: 25.4%; Age 65 and over: 12.9%; Males per 100 females: 93.4; Marriage status: 26.9% never married, 55.5% now married, 3.0% separated, 5.0% widowed, 12.6% divorced; Foreign born: 4.9%; Speak English only: 92.7%; With disability: 14.5%; Veterans: 15.5%; Ancestry: 23.3% German, 13.8% Irish, 9.0% English, 8.6% American, 3.7% Italian
Employment: 11.8% management, business, and financial, 6.4% computer, engineering, and science, 8.3% education, legal, community service, arts, and media, 5.8% healthcare practitioners, 19.0% service, 26.1% sales and office, 7.1% natural resources, construction, and maintenance, 15.5% production, transportation, and material moving
Income: Per capita: $25,013; Median household: $52,261; Average household: $63,383; Households with income of $100,000 or more: 16.0%; Poverty rate: 11.0%
Educational Attainment: High school diploma or higher: 91.6%; Bachelor's degree or higher: 22.1%; Graduate/professional degree or higher: 8.6%

School District(s)

Huber Heights City (PK-12)
2012-13 Enrollment: 6,143 . . . . (937) 237-6300

Two-year College(s)

Carousel of Miami Valley Beauty College (Private, For-profit)
Fall 2013 Enrollment: 34 . . . . (937) 223-3572
Housing: Homeownership rate: 72.0%; Median home value: $108,000; Median year structure built: 1973; Homeowner vacancy rate: 2.2%; Median gross rent: $852 per month; Rental vacancy rate: 11.5%
Health Insurance: 87.8% have insurance; 70.8% have private insurance; 30.9% have public insurance; 12.2% do not have insurance; 8.2% of children under 18 do not have insurance
Safety: Violent crime rate: 16.0 per 10,000 population; Property crime rate: 361.0 per 10,000 population
Newspapers: Huber Heights Courier (weekly circulation 9000)
Transportation: Commute: 93.8% car, 1.6% public transportation, 1.1% walk, 1.6% work from home; Median travel time to work: 22.3 minutes
Additional Information Contacts
City of Huber Heights . . . . (937) 233-1423
http://www.hhoh.org

KETTERING (city). Covers a land area of 18.677 square miles and a water area of 0.039 square miles. Located at 39.70° N. Lat; 84.15° W. Long. Elevation is 1,004 feet.
History: Settled c.1812, incorporated 1952.
Population: 56,163; Growth (since 2000): -2.3%; Density: 3,007.0 persons per square mile; Race: 92.6% White, 3.3% Black/African American, 1.3% Asian, 0.2% American Indian/Alaska Native, 0.0% Native Hawaiian/Other Pacific Islander, 2.1% Two or more races, 2.1% Hispanic of any race; Average household size: 2.19; Median age: 40.9; Age under 18: 21.0%; Age 65 and over: 18.0%; Males per 100 females: 91.2; Marriage status: 28.5% never married, 49.7% now married, 1.5% separated, 7.3% widowed, 14.6% divorced; Foreign born: 3.0%; Speak English only: 94.8%; With disability: 12.7%; Veterans: 10.6%; Ancestry: 33.3% German, 16.1% Irish, 11.1% English, 9.5% American, 4.4% Italian
Employment: 13.1% management, business, and financial, 7.2% computer, engineering, and science, 11.2% education, legal, community service, arts, and media, 7.0% healthcare practitioners, 17.1% service, 27.2% sales and office, 5.6% natural resources, construction, and maintenance, 11.7% production, transportation, and material moving
Income: Per capita: $29,489; Median household: $49,522; Average household: $64,557; Households with income of $100,000 or more: 17.0%; Poverty rate: 11.1%

Educational Attainment: High school diploma or higher: 93.9%; Bachelor's degree or higher: 31.1%; Graduate/professional degree or higher: 12.6%

School District(s)

Dayton Regional Stem School (07-11)
2012-13 Enrollment: 429. . . . . (937) 256-3777
Kettering City (PK-12)
2012-13 Enrollment: 7,724 . . . . (937) 499-1400

Four-year College(s)

Kettering College (Private, Not-for-profit, Seventh Day Adventists)
Fall 2013 Enrollment: 880. . . . . (937) 395-8601
2013-14 Tuition: In-state $10,032; Out-of-state $10,032

Two-year College(s)

Advertising Art Educational Services DBA School of Advertising Art (Private, For-profit)
Fall 2013 Enrollment: 140. . . . . (937) 294-0592
2013-14 Tuition: In-state $23,628; Out-of-state $23,628
Carousel Beauty College-Kettering (Private, For-profit)
Fall 2013 Enrollment: 61. . . . . (937) 223-3572
National College-Dayton (Private, For-profit)
Fall 2013 Enrollment: 167. . . . . (937) 299-9450
2013-14 Tuition: In-state $11,550; Out-of-state $11,550

Housing: Homeownership rate: 64.8%; Median home value: $130,100; Median year structure built: 1960; Homeowner vacancy rate: 2.4%; Median gross rent: $741 per month; Rental vacancy rate: 10.2%
Health Insurance: 90.4% have insurance; 75.5% have private insurance; 28.9% have public insurance; 9.6% do not have insurance; 5.3% of children under 18 do not have insurance
Hospitals: Kettering Medical Center (522 beds)
Safety: Violent crime rate: 9.5 per 10,000 population; Property crime rate: 230.2 per 10,000 population
Transportation: Commute: 91.7% car, 1.2% public transportation, 1.7% walk, 4.0% work from home; Median travel time to work: 20.2 minutes
Additional Information Contacts
City of Kettering. . . . . (937) 296-2400
http://www.ketteringoh.org

MIAMISBURG (city). Covers a land area of 12.184 square miles and a water area of 0.185 square miles. Located at 39.63° N. Lat; 84.27° W. Long. Elevation is 705 feet.
History: Miamisburg was laid out in 1818 on the site of a blockhouse called Hole's Station, which had been built by Zachariah Hole about 1800. The Hoover and Gamble Company, manufacturer of reapers, was founded here in 1840. Tobacco warehouses were situated in Miamisburg in the late 1800's.
Population: 20,181; Growth (since 2000): 3.6%; Density: 1,656.3 persons per square mile; Race: 93.8% White, 3.0% Black/African American, 1.0% Asian, 0.2% American Indian/Alaska Native, 0.0% Native Hawaiian/Other Pacific Islander, 1.5% Two or more races, 1.6% Hispanic of any race; Average household size: 2.50; Median age: 40.2; Age under 18: 25.1%; Age 65 and over: 16.2%; Males per 100 females: 90.7; Marriage status: 21.4% never married, 54.5% now married, 1.3% separated, 10.5% widowed, 13.6% divorced; Foreign born: 1.3%; Speak English only: 98.3%; With disability: 14.1%; Veterans: 11.7%; Ancestry: 31.1% German, 18.2% Irish, 11.6% American, 11.4% English, 3.4% Scottish
Employment: 15.7% management, business, and financial, 5.8% computer, engineering, and science, 9.9% education, legal, community service, arts, and media, 5.7% healthcare practitioners, 15.3% service, 27.7% sales and office, 6.0% natural resources, construction, and maintenance, 13.9% production, transportation, and material moving
Income: Per capita: $27,730; Median household: $52,007; Average household: $65,598; Households with income of $100,000 or more: 22.9%; Poverty rate: 11.6%
Educational Attainment: High school diploma or higher: 90.0%; Bachelor's degree or higher: 22.5%; Graduate/professional degree or higher: 8.8%

School District(s)

Miamisburg City (PK-12)
2012-13 Enrollment: 5,542 . . . . (937) 866-3381
Miamisburg Secondary Academy (07-12)
2012-13 Enrollment: 108. . . . . (937) 866-3381

Two-year College(s)

Dayton Barber College (Private, For-profit)
Fall 2013 Enrollment: 57. . . . . (937) 222-9101

Housing: Homeownership rate: 71.5%; Median home value: $136,800; Median year structure built: 1971; Homeowner vacancy rate: 2.3%; Median gross rent: $680 per month; Rental vacancy rate: 12.6%
Health Insurance: 91.0% have insurance; 72.1% have private insurance; 34.4% have public insurance; 9.0% do not have insurance; 1.7% of children under 18 do not have insurance
Hospitals: Sycamore Medical Center (181 beds)
Safety: Violent crime rate: 9.4 per 10,000 population; Property crime rate: 333.5 per 10,000 population
Newspapers: Franklin Chronicle (weekly circulation 8000); Germantown Press (weekly circulation 2700); Miamisburg News (weekly circulation 6500); Springboro Star Press (weekly circulation 12000)
Transportation: Commute: 93.3% car, 0.8% public transportation, 1.3% walk, 4.1% work from home; Median travel time to work: 20.9 minutes
Additional Information Contacts
City of Miamisburg. . . . . (937) 866-3303
http://www.ci.miamisburg.oh.us

MORAINE (city). Covers a land area of 9.251 square miles and a water area of 0.266 square miles. Located at 39.70° N. Lat; 84.24° W. Long. Elevation is 738 feet.
Population: 6,307; Growth (since 2000): -8.6%; Density: 681.8 persons per square mile; Race: 81.1% White, 12.4% Black/African American, 1.3% Asian, 0.3% American Indian/Alaska Native, 0.1% Native Hawaiian/Other Pacific Islander, 2.5% Two or more races, 3.6% Hispanic of any race; Average household size: 2.37; Median age: 37.0; Age under 18: 23.7%; Age 65 and over: 12.7%; Males per 100 females: 95.7; Marriage status: 31.0% never married, 49.6% now married, 3.1% separated, 6.1% widowed, 13.3% divorced; Foreign born: 1.6%; Speak English only: 96.7%; With disability: 15.1%; Veterans: 6.3%; Ancestry: 17.1% German, 15.3% Irish, 9.2% American, 3.6% English, 2.7% Italian
Employment: 10.3% management, business, and financial, 2.3% computer, engineering, and science, 4.2% education, legal, community service, arts, and media, 9.7% healthcare practitioners, 22.1% service, 23.1% sales and office, 9.5% natural resources, construction, and maintenance, 18.8% production, transportation, and material moving
Income: Per capita: $17,811; Median household: $40,080; Average household: $44,934; Households with income of $100,000 or more: 8.5%; Poverty rate: 25.9%
Educational Attainment: High school diploma or higher: 84.1%; Bachelor's degree or higher: 10.8%; Graduate/professional degree or higher: 3.4%
Housing: Homeownership rate: 55.3%; Median home value: $92,400; Median year structure built: 1973; Homeowner vacancy rate: 3.3%; Median gross rent: $733 per month; Rental vacancy rate: 11.5%
Health Insurance: 83.6% have insurance; 55.2% have private insurance; 37.0% have public insurance; 16.4% do not have insurance; 9.8% of children under 18 do not have insurance
Safety: Violent crime rate: 47.5 per 10,000 population; Property crime rate: 1,139.8 per 10,000 population
Transportation: Commute: 92.7% car, 1.3% public transportation, 2.1% walk, 3.3% work from home; Median travel time to work: 19.1 minutes
Additional Information Contacts
City of Moraine . . . . (937) 535-1000
http://www.ci.moraine.oh.us

NEW LEBANON (village). Covers a land area of 2.045 square miles and a water area of 0 square miles. Located at 39.74° N. Lat; 84.39° W. Long. Elevation is 909 feet.
History: New Lebanon was established as a community of Dunkards. A murder and the burning of the town in 1876 were attributed to a conflict between warring gangs.
Population: 3,995; Growth (since 2000): -5.6%; Density: 1,953.7 persons per square mile; Race: 96.2% White, 1.2% Black/African American, 0.4% Asian, 0.1% American Indian/Alaska Native, 0.0% Native Hawaiian/Other Pacific Islander, 2.0% Two or more races, 0.7% Hispanic of any race; Average household size: 2.55; Median age: 36.9; Age under 18: 26.3%; Age 65 and over: 15.2%; Males per 100 females: 93.3; Marriage status: 31.0% never married, 46.8% now married, 3.4% separated, 6.5% widowed, 15.7% divorced; Foreign born: 0.4%; Speak English only: 98.7%; With disability: 20.5%; Veterans: 9.0%; Ancestry: 30.4% German, 22.2% Irish, 16.9% American, 9.3% English, 3.3% Italian
Employment: 3.3% management, business, and financial, 3.1% computer, engineering, and science, 1.4% education, legal, community service, arts, and media, 9.2% healthcare practitioners, 21.6% service, 28.3% sales and

office, 22.0% natural resources, construction, and maintenance, 11.0% production, transportation, and material moving
Income: Per capita: $18,221; Median household: $37,232; Average household: $46,620; Households with income of $100,000 or more: 7.9%; Poverty rate: 13.9%
Educational Attainment: High school diploma or higher: 89.7%; Bachelor's degree or higher: 7.2%; Graduate/professional degree or higher: 1.5%

School District(s)

New Lebanon Local (PK-12)
2012-13 Enrollment: 1,135 . . . . (937) 687-1301
Housing: Homeownership rate: 67.7%; Median home value: $84,800; Median year structure built: 1965; Homeowner vacancy rate: 2.4%; Median gross rent: $693 per month; Rental vacancy rate: 10.1%
Health Insurance: 90.6% have insurance; 71.1% have private insurance; 32.9% have public insurance; 9.4% do not have insurance; 1.2% of children under 18 do not have insurance
Safety: Violent crime rate: 2.5 per 10,000 population; Property crime rate: 373.2 per 10,000 population
Transportation: Commute: 95.4% car, 0.0% public transportation, 2.0% walk, 0.9% work from home; Median travel time to work: 23.5 minutes
Additional Information Contacts
Village of New Lebanon . . . . (937) 687-1341
http://www.newlebanonoh.com

OAKWOOD (city). Covers a land area of 2.195 square miles and a water area of 0 square miles. Located at 39.72° N. Lat; 84.17° W. Long. Elevation is 988 feet.
History: Incorporated as village in 1907; became city after 1930.
Population: 9,202; Growth (since 2000): -0.1%; Density: 4,192.3 persons per square mile; Race: 95.3% White, 0.9% Black/African American, 1.4% Asian, 0.2% American Indian/Alaska Native, 0.0% Native Hawaiian/Other Pacific Islander, 1.6% Two or more races, 1.8% Hispanic of any race; Average household size: 2.58; Median age: 40.5; Age under 18: 30.6%; Age 65 and over: 11.9%; Males per 100 females: 90.2; Marriage status: 23.3% never married, 61.4% now married, 0.3% separated, 5.4% widowed, 9.9% divorced; Foreign born: 2.3%; Speak English only: 95.1%; With disability: 5.3%; Veterans: 9.8%; Ancestry: 32.9% German, 18.4% Irish, 14.9% English, 6.9% Italian, 5.3% Polish
Employment: 25.7% management, business, and financial, 6.0% computer, engineering, and science, 19.1% education, legal, community service, arts, and media, 15.5% healthcare practitioners, 6.4% service, 22.5% sales and office, 1.9% natural resources, construction, and maintenance, 2.9% production, transportation, and material moving
Income: Per capita: $51,989; Median household: $99,975; Average household: $135,123; Households with income of $100,000 or more: 50.1%; Poverty rate: 2.5%
Educational Attainment: High school diploma or higher: 99.2%; Bachelor's degree or higher: 70.7%; Graduate/professional degree or higher: 35.9%
Housing: Homeownership rate: 81.7%; Median home value: $235,900; Median year structure built: Before 1940; Homeowner vacancy rate: 1.8%; Median gross rent: $950 per month; Rental vacancy rate: 9.7%
Health Insurance: 94.8% have insurance; 90.9% have private insurance; 14.1% have public insurance; 5.2% do not have insurance; 2.5% of children under 18 do not have insurance
Transportation: Commute: 94.3% car, 0.1% public transportation, 1.2% walk, 3.5% work from home; Median travel time to work: 18.8 minutes

PHILLIPSBURG (village). Covers a land area of 0.266 square miles and a water area of 0 square miles. Located at 39.90° N. Lat; 84.40° W. Long. Elevation is 1,033 feet.
Population: 557; Growth (since 2000): -11.3%; Density: 2,090.3 persons per square mile; Race: 97.7% White, 1.4% Black/African American, 0.4% Asian, 0.0% American Indian/Alaska Native, 0.0% Native Hawaiian/Other Pacific Islander, 0.2% Two or more races, 3.2% Hispanic of any race; Average household size: 2.37; Median age: 40.4; Age under 18: 21.5%; Age 65 and over: 18.5%; Males per 100 females: 105.5
Housing: Homeownership rate: 75.7%; Homeowner vacancy rate: 3.2%; Rental vacancy rate: 8.1%

RIVERSIDE (city). Covers a land area of 9.720 square miles and a water area of 0.042 square miles. Located at 39.78° N. Lat; 84.12° W. Long. Elevation is 778 feet.
Population: 25,201; Growth (since 2000): 7.0%; Density: 2,592.8 persons per square mile; Race: 87.2% White, 6.6% Black/African American, 1.9% Asian, 0.3% American Indian/Alaska Native, 0.0% Native Hawaiian/Other Pacific Islander, 2.8% Two or more races, 3.3% Hispanic of any race; Average household size: 2.45; Median age: 34.8; Age under 18: 24.7%; Age 65 and over: 13.8%; Males per 100 females: 94.2; Marriage status: 27.5% never married, 50.6% now married, 2.2% separated, 7.7% widowed, 14.2% divorced; Foreign born: 3.0%; Speak English only: 95.0%; With disability: 16.3%; Veterans: 15.9%; Ancestry: 22.7% German, 15.4% Irish, 13.3% American, 8.0% English, 3.3% French
Employment: 11.5% management, business, and financial, 6.6% computer, engineering, and science, 5.2% education, legal, community service, arts, and media, 5.9% healthcare practitioners, 20.0% service, 23.4% sales and office, 9.3% natural resources, construction, and maintenance, 18.3% production, transportation, and material moving
Income: Per capita: $21,247; Median household: $41,104; Average household: $50,984; Households with income of $100,000 or more: 11.5%; Poverty rate: 17.6%
Educational Attainment: High school diploma or higher: 85.7%; Bachelor's degree or higher: 15.2%; Graduate/professional degree or higher: 5.8%
Housing: Homeownership rate: 57.1%; Median home value: $92,800; Median year structure built: 1963; Homeowner vacancy rate: 2.0%; Median gross rent: $742 per month; Rental vacancy rate: 10.7%
Health Insurance: 86.3% have insurance; 62.8% have private insurance; 36.1% have public insurance; 13.7% do not have insurance; 5.8% of children under 18 do not have insurance
Safety: Violent crime rate: 17.5 per 10,000 population; Property crime rate: 246.5 per 10,000 population
Transportation: Commute: 96.3% car, 0.6% public transportation, 1.2% walk, 1.3% work from home; Median travel time to work: 17.6 minutes
Additional Information Contacts
City of Riverside . . . . (937) 233-1801
http://www.riverside.oh.us

TROTWOOD (city). Covers a land area of 30.494 square miles and a water area of 0.014 square miles. Located at 39.79° N. Lat; 84.32° W. Long. Elevation is 837 feet.
Population: 24,431; Growth (since 2000): -10.9%; Density: 801.2 persons per square mile; Race: 28.1% White, 68.2% Black/African American, 0.3% Asian, 0.2% American Indian/Alaska Native, 0.0% Native Hawaiian/Other Pacific Islander, 2.6% Two or more races, 0.9% Hispanic of any race; Average household size: 2.29; Median age: 41.8; Age under 18: 23.6%; Age 65 and over: 17.8%; Males per 100 females: 79.9; Marriage status: 38.1% never married, 37.0% now married, 2.6% separated, 9.2% widowed, 15.7% divorced; Foreign born: 1.8%; Speak English only: 97.0%; With disability: 19.0%; Veterans: 11.6%; Ancestry: 8.0% German, 4.3% Irish, 3.7% American, 2.7% English, 2.2% African
Employment: 10.9% management, business, and financial, 3.4% computer, engineering, and science, 7.7% education, legal, community service, arts, and media, 5.8% healthcare practitioners, 20.9% service, 28.3% sales and office, 5.9% natural resources, construction, and maintenance, 17.1% production, transportation, and material moving
Income: Per capita: $20,396; Median household: $36,277; Average household: $46,623; Households with income of $100,000 or more: 10.4%; Poverty rate: 21.2%
Educational Attainment: High school diploma or higher: 83.5%; Bachelor's degree or higher: 14.4%; Graduate/professional degree or higher: 5.6%

School District(s)

Trotwood Fitness & Prep Acad (KG-08)
2012-13 Enrollment: 325. . . . . (937) 854-4100
Trotwood-Madison City (PK-12)
2012-13 Enrollment: 2,542 . . . . (937) 854-3050
Housing: Homeownership rate: 57.5%; Median home value: $81,300; Median year structure built: 1965; Homeowner vacancy rate: 3.6%; Median gross rent: $708 per month; Rental vacancy rate: 14.2%
Health Insurance: 84.3% have insurance; 57.1% have private insurance; 40.2% have public insurance; 15.7% do not have insurance; 6.8% of children under 18 do not have insurance
Safety: Violent crime rate: 45.3 per 10,000 population; Property crime rate: 511.5 per 10,000 population

Transportation: Commute: 92.6% car, 4.1% public transportation, 1.4% walk, 1.1% work from home; Median travel time to work: 24.3 minutes
Additional Information Contacts
City of Trotwood . . . . (937) 837-7771
http://www.trotwood.org

UNION (city). Covers a land area of 7.050 square miles and a water area of 0.076 square miles. Located at 39.92° N. Lat; 84.29° W. Long. Elevation is 922 feet.
Population: 6,419; Growth (since 2000): 15.2%; Density: 910.5 persons per square mile; Race: 93.5% White, 3.6% Black/African American, 0.7% Asian, 0.2% American Indian/Alaska Native, 0.0% Native Hawaiian/Other Pacific Islander, 1.8% Two or more races, 1.6% Hispanic of any race; Average household size: 2.51; Median age: 38.6; Age under 18: 25.5%; Age 65 and over: 12.8%; Males per 100 females: 92.6; Marriage status: 16.5% never married, 64.7% now married, 1.9% separated, 5.5% widowed, 13.3% divorced; Foreign born: 0.5%; Speak English only: 97.6%; With disability: 11.4%; Veterans: 11.6%; Ancestry: 41.6% German, 20.5% Irish, 7.7% American, 6.3% English, 2.7% Polish
Employment: 11.5% management, business, and financial, 1.3% computer, engineering, and science, 8.9% education, legal, community service, arts, and media, 4.5% healthcare practitioners, 25.0% service, 22.7% sales and office, 10.4% natural resources, construction, and maintenance, 15.7% production, transportation, and material moving
Income: Per capita: $25,852; Median household: $52,132; Average household: $66,000; Households with income of $100,000 or more: 14.0%; Poverty rate: 3.2%
Educational Attainment: High school diploma or higher: 92.9%; Bachelor's degree or higher: 14.2%; Graduate/professional degree or higher: 7.8%

School District(s)

Northmont City (PK-12)
2012-13 Enrollment: 5,251 . . . . (937) 832-5000
Housing: Homeownership rate: 82.0%; Median home value: $98,700; Median year structure built: 1974; Homeowner vacancy rate: 2.6%; Median gross rent: $900 per month; Rental vacancy rate: 8.0%
Health Insurance: 91.3% have insurance; 81.1% have private insurance; 23.2% have public insurance; 8.7% do not have insurance; 1.0% of children under 18 do not have insurance
Safety: Violent crime rate: 10.9 per 10,000 population; Property crime rate: 245.6 per 10,000 population
Transportation: Commute: 96.2% car, 0.5% public transportation, 0.0% walk, 1.8% work from home; Median travel time to work: 28.7 minutes
Additional Information Contacts
City of Union . . . . (937) 836-8624
http://www.ci.union.oh.us

VANDALIA (city). Covers a land area of 12.344 square miles and a water area of 0.068 square miles. Located at 39.88° N. Lat; 84.19° W. Long. Elevation is 991 feet.
History: Vandalia was settled in 1838 and named for Vandalia, Illinois. Vandalia was known as the site of the largest shotgun tournament in the world, held by the Amateur Trapshooters' Association.
Population: 15,246; Growth (since 2000): 4.4%; Density: 1,235.1 persons per square mile; Race: 91.5% White, 4.1% Black/African American, 1.4% Asian, 0.1% American Indian/Alaska Native, 0.0% Native Hawaiian/Other Pacific Islander, 2.1% Two or more races, 1.6% Hispanic of any race; Average household size: 2.30; Median age: 40.6; Age under 18: 23.1%; Age 65 and over: 15.7%; Males per 100 females: 93.9; Marriage status: 26.9% never married, 54.8% now married, 2.2% separated, 6.5% widowed, 11.8% divorced; Foreign born: 2.2%; Speak English only: 96.9%; With disability: 12.1%; Veterans: 10.9%; Ancestry: 28.6% German, 17.5% Irish, 10.7% English, 5.5% American, 4.6% Italian
Employment: 14.5% management, business, and financial, 4.0% computer, engineering, and science, 8.1% education, legal, community service, arts, and media, 7.0% healthcare practitioners, 20.8% service, 25.4% sales and office, 5.9% natural resources, construction, and maintenance, 14.2% production, transportation, and material moving
Income: Per capita: $26,774; Median household: $52,164; Average household: $63,367; Households with income of $100,000 or more: 18.9%; Poverty rate: 10.9%
Educational Attainment: High school diploma or higher: 90.9%; Bachelor's degree or higher: 21.3%; Graduate/professional degree or higher: 9.0%

School District(s)

Vandalia-Butler City (PK-12)
2012-13 Enrollment: 3,235 . . . . (937) 415-6400
Housing: Homeownership rate: 64.3%; Median home value: $137,700; Median year structure built: 1972; Homeowner vacancy rate: 1.7%; Median gross rent: $662 per month; Rental vacancy rate: 10.3%
Health Insurance: 89.8% have insurance; 72.7% have private insurance; 28.3% have public insurance; 10.2% do not have insurance; 2.8% of children under 18 do not have insurance
Safety: Violent crime rate: 14.5 per 10,000 population; Property crime rate: 223.3 per 10,000 population
Transportation: Commute: 94.6% car, 0.5% public transportation, 0.3% walk, 2.6% work from home; Median travel time to work: 20.8 minutes
Additional Information Contacts
City of Vandalia . . . . (937) 415-2254
http://www.ci.vandalia.oh.us

WEST CARROLLTON (city). Covers a land area of 6.439 square miles and a water area of 0.218 square miles. Located at 39.67° N. Lat; 84.26° W. Long. Elevation is 715 feet.
Population: 13,143; Growth (since 2000): n/a; Density: 2,041.3 persons per square mile; Race: 86.8% White, 8.9% Black/African American, 1.1% Asian, 0.3% American Indian/Alaska Native, 0.0% Native Hawaiian/Other Pacific Islander, 2.0% Two or more races, 2.6% Hispanic of any race; Average household size: 2.18; Median age: 37.5; Age under 18: 21.1%; Age 65 and over: 14.5%; Males per 100 females: 93.0; Marriage status: 28.9% never married, 46.2% now married, 1.9% separated, 8.3% widowed, 16.6% divorced; Foreign born: 4.4%; Speak English only: 94.8%; With disability: 15.4%; Veterans: 9.3%; Ancestry: 23.2% German, 14.1% Irish, 9.2% English, 7.9% American, 2.6% French
Employment: 11.1% management, business, and financial, 4.9% computer, engineering, and science, 6.2% education, legal, community service, arts, and media, 6.3% healthcare practitioners, 19.0% service, 26.0% sales and office, 10.5% natural resources, construction, and maintenance, 15.9% production, transportation, and material moving
Income: Per capita: $22,534; Median household: $38,255; Average household: $47,763; Households with income of $100,000 or more: 9.5%; Poverty rate: 16.2%
Educational Attainment: High school diploma or higher: 87.8%; Bachelor's degree or higher: 15.5%; Graduate/professional degree or higher: 3.6%

School District(s)

West Carrollton City (PK-12)
2012-13 Enrollment: 3,726 . . . . (937) 859-5121
Housing: Homeownership rate: 56.8%; Median home value: $102,200; Median year structure built: 1971; Homeowner vacancy rate: 3.1%; Median gross rent: $738 per month; Rental vacancy rate: 10.4%
Health Insurance: 85.1% have insurance; 67.1% have private insurance; 29.8% have public insurance; 14.9% do not have insurance; 8.9% of children under 18 do not have insurance
Safety: Violent crime rate: 22.2 per 10,000 population; Property crime rate: 300.5 per 10,000 population
Transportation: Commute: 91.3% car, 2.3% public transportation, 0.9% walk, 3.1% work from home; Median travel time to work: 20.7 minutes
Additional Information Contacts
City of West Carrollton . . . . (937) 859-5183
http://www.westcarrollton.org

Morgan County

Located in east central Ohio; crossed by the Muskingum River, and Meigs and Wolf Creeks. Covers a land area of 416.423 square miles, a water area of 5.360 square miles, and is located in the Eastern Time Zone at 39.62° N. Lat., 81.86° W. Long. The county was founded in 1817. County seat is McConnelsville.

Weather Station: Mc Connelsville Lock 7 Elevation: 759 feet

	Jan	Feb	Mar	Apr	May	Jun	Jul	Aug	Sep	Oct	Nov	Dec
High	38	42	52	64	73	81	84	83	77	65	54	42
Low	20	21	28	38	47	57	61	60	52	40	32	24
Precip	3.1	2.5	3.7	3.8	4.7	4.1	4.6	3.6	3.2	2.9	3.5	3.2
Snow	6.6	5.4	2.4	0.7	0.0	0.0	0.0	0.0	0.0	tr	0.4	3.3

High and Low temperatures in degrees Fahrenheit; Precipitation and Snow in inches

Population: 15,054; Growth (since 2000): 1.1%; Density: 36.2 persons per square mile; Race: 93.2% White, 2.9% Black/African American, 0.1% Asian, 0.3% American Indian/Alaska Native, 0.0% Native Hawaiian/Other Pacific Islander, 3.3% two or more races, 0.6% Hispanic of any race; Average household size: 2.46; Median age: 42.4; Age under 18: 23.4%; Age 65 and over: 17.3%; Males per 100 females: 99.3; Marriage status: 20.8% never married, 60.9% now married, 1.6% separated, 7.5% widowed, 10.8% divorced; Foreign born: 0.4%; Speak English only: 98.2%; With disability: 16.8%; Veterans: 11.4%; Ancestry: 20.3% German, 13.8% Irish, 12.7% English, 9.2% American, 2.2% Scottish
Religion: Six largest groups: 9.9% Methodist/Pietist, 9.2% Baptist, 1.7% European Free-Church, 1.4% Non-denominational Protestant, 0.9% Catholicism, 0.8% Presbyterian-Reformed
Economy: Unemployment rate: 6.0%; Leading industries: 16.7% other services (except public administration); 15.4% retail trade; 10.3% health care and social assistance; Farms: 510 totaling 95,174 acres; Company size: 0 employ 1,000 or more persons, 0 employ 500 to 999 persons, 3 employ 100 to 499 persons, 153 employ less than 100 persons; Business ownership: n/a women-owned, n/a Black-owned, n/a Hispanic-owned, n/a Asian-owned
Employment: 9.8% management, business, and financial, 1.6% computer, engineering, and science, 7.0% education, legal, community service, arts, and media, 7.5% healthcare practitioners, 19.2% service, 18.9% sales and office, 17.2% natural resources, construction, and maintenance, 18.7% production, transportation, and material moving
Income: Per capita: $21,027; Median household: $37,865; Average household: $51,300; Households with income of $100,000 or more: 9.4%; Poverty rate: 20.2%
Educational Attainment: High school diploma or higher: 85.6%; Bachelor's degree or higher: 10.5%; Graduate/professional degree or higher: 3.6%
Housing: Homeownership rate: 76.9%; Median home value: $89,000; Median year structure built: 1973; Homeowner vacancy rate: 1.5%; Median gross rent: $550 per month; Rental vacancy rate: 7.9%
Vital Statistics: Birth rate: 90.6 per 10,000 population; Death rate: 93.9 per 10,000 population; Age-adjusted cancer mortality rate: 191.3 deaths per 100,000 population
Health Insurance: 86.4% have insurance; 61.7% have private insurance; 39.9% have public insurance; 13.6% do not have insurance; 6.1% of children under 18 do not have insurance
Health Care: Physicians: 0.7 per 10,000 population; Hospital beds: 0.0 per 10,000 population; Hospital admissions: 0.0 per 10,000 population
Air Quality Index: 85.6% good, 9.4% moderate, 4.7% unhealthy for sensitive individuals, 0.3% unhealthy (percent of days)
Transportation: Commute: 91.3% car, 0.6% public transportation, 2.8% walk, 4.4% work from home; Median travel time to work: 32.2 minutes
Presidential Election: 45.9% Obama, 51.9% Romney (2012)
National and State Parks: Big Bottom State Memorial Park; Burr Oak State Park; Muskingum River Parkway State Park
Additional Information Contacts
Morgan Government . . . . (740) 962-3183
http://www.morgancounty-oh.gov

Morgan County Communities

CHESTERHILL (village). Covers a land area of 0.539 square miles and a water area of 0.003 square miles. Located at 39.49° N. Lat; 81.87° W. Long. Elevation is 974 feet.
Population: 289; Growth (since 2000): -5.2%; Density: 535.7 persons per square mile; Race: 73.7% White, 9.7% Black/African American, 0.3% Asian, 0.3% American Indian/Alaska Native, 0.0% Native Hawaiian/Other Pacific Islander, 15.6% Two or more races, 0.3% Hispanic of any race; Average household size: 2.39; Median age: 41.4; Age under 18: 25.3%; Age 65 and over: 18.7%; Males per 100 females: 90.1
Housing: Homeownership rate: 71.9%; Homeowner vacancy rate: 4.4%; Rental vacancy rate: 15.0%

MALTA (village). Covers a land area of 0.343 square miles and a water area of 0.043 square miles. Located at 39.65° N. Lat; 81.86° W. Long. Elevation is 676 feet.
History: Malta was founded in 1816 by Simeon Pool and John Bell, who owned the land. The town was named for the island of Malta in the Mediterranean where Pool had visited.
Population: 671; Growth (since 2000): -3.6%; Density: 1,953.8 persons per square mile; Race: 91.1% White, 4.0% Black/African American, 0.0% Asian, 0.0% American Indian/Alaska Native, 0.0% Native Hawaiian/Other Pacific Islander, 4.8% Two or more races, 0.3% Hispanic of any race; Average household size: 2.41; Median age: 36.0; Age under 18: 27.3%; Age 65 and over: 14.8%; Males per 100 females: 96.2

School District(s)

Morgan Local (PK-12)
2012-13 Enrollment: 2,043 . . . . (740) 962-2782
Housing: Homeownership rate: 65.1%; Homeowner vacancy rate: 1.6%; Rental vacancy rate: 6.7%

MCCONNELSVILLE (village). County seat. Covers a land area of 1.785 square miles and a water area of 0.112 square miles. Located at 39.66° N. Lat; 81.84° W. Long. Elevation is 696 feet.
History: McConnelsville was platted in 1817 by General Robert McConnell, and became a Muskingum River shipping port for salt bound for Pittsburgh by keelboat.
Population: 1,784; Growth (since 2000): 6.4%; Density: 999.6 persons per square mile; Race: 93.3% White, 2.4% Black/African American, 0.4% Asian, 0.7% American Indian/Alaska Native, 0.0% Native Hawaiian/Other Pacific Islander, 2.6% Two or more races, 1.3% Hispanic of any race; Average household size: 2.17; Median age: 47.1; Age under 18: 20.1%; Age 65 and over: 25.4%; Males per 100 females: 82.0

School District(s)

Morgan Local (PK-12)
2012-13 Enrollment: 2,043 . . . . (740) 962-2782
Housing: Homeownership rate: 52.2%; Homeowner vacancy rate: 3.4%; Rental vacancy rate: 10.5%
Safety: Violent crime rate: 5.5 per 10,000 population; Property crime rate: 110.5 per 10,000 population
Newspapers: Morgan County Herald (weekly circulation 5000)

STOCKPORT (village). Covers a land area of 0.329 square miles and a water area of 0 square miles. Located at 39.55° N. Lat; 81.79° W. Long. Elevation is 692 feet.
Population: 503; Growth (since 2000): -6.9%; Density: 1,530.8 persons per square mile; Race: 91.7% White, 3.0% Black/African American, 0.0% Asian, 0.0% American Indian/Alaska Native, 0.0% Native Hawaiian/Other Pacific Islander, 5.2% Two or more races, 0.6% Hispanic of any race; Average household size: 2.58; Median age: 35.1; Age under 18: 26.6%; Age 65 and over: 13.3%; Males per 100 females: 87.7

School District(s)

Morgan Local (PK-12)
2012-13 Enrollment: 2,043 . . . . (740) 962-2782
Housing: Homeownership rate: 65.7%; Homeowner vacancy rate: 1.5%; Rental vacancy rate: 20.9%

Morrow County

Located in central Ohio; drained by the Kokosing River and Whetstone and Big Walnut Creeks. Covers a land area of 406.079 square miles, a water area of 1.143 square miles, and is located in the Eastern Time Zone at 40.53° N. Lat., 82.80° W. Long. The county was founded in 1848. County seat is Mount Gilead.

Morrow County is part of the Columbus, OH Metropolitan Statistical Area. The entire metro area includes: Delaware County, OH; Fairfield County, OH; Franklin County, OH; Hocking County, OH; Licking County, OH; Madison County, OH; Morrow County, OH; Perry County, OH; Pickaway County, OH; Union County, OH

Population: 34,827; Growth (since 2000): 10.1%; Density: 85.8 persons per square mile; Race: 97.7% White, 0.3% Black/African American, 0.3% Asian, 0.1% American Indian/Alaska Native, 0.0% Native Hawaiian/Other Pacific Islander, 1.3% two or more races, 1.1% Hispanic of any race; Average household size: 2.68; Median age: 39.5; Age under 18: 25.8%; Age 65 and over: 13.4%; Males per 100 females: 100.5; Marriage status: 22.0% never married, 60.8% now married, 1.2% separated, 6.5% widowed, 10.7% divorced; Foreign born: 0.7%; Speak English only: 96.0%; With disability: 13.7%; Veterans: 11.1%; Ancestry: 28.1% German, 15.1% Irish, 14.0% English, 13.4% American, 4.1% Italian
Religion: Six largest groups: 8.2% Methodist/Pietist, 4.5% Baptist, 3.4% Holiness, 3.1% European Free-Church, 1.9% Non-denominational Protestant, 1.2% Catholicism
Economy: Unemployment rate: 4.2%; Leading industries: 14.1% construction; 13.3% retail trade; 12.5% health care and social assistance;

Farms: 824 totaling 167,736 acres; Company size: 0 employ 1,000 or more persons, 1 employs 500 to 999 persons, 4 employ 100 to 499 persons, 378 employ less than 100 persons; Business ownership: 592 women-owned, n/a Black-owned, n/a Hispanic-owned, n/a Asian-owned
Employment: 9.4% management, business, and financial, 3.7% computer, engineering, and science, 6.5% education, legal, community service, arts, and media, 6.2% healthcare practitioners, 14.1% service, 22.5% sales and office, 15.0% natural resources, construction, and maintenance, 22.6% production, transportation, and material moving
Income: Per capita: $22,228; Median household: $51,484; Average household: $60,066; Households with income of $100,000 or more: 14.6%; Poverty rate: 13.6%
Educational Attainment: High school diploma or higher: 87.8%; Bachelor's degree or higher: 14.1%; Graduate/professional degree or higher: 5.0%
Housing: Homeownership rate: 79.6%; Median home value: $127,400; Median year structure built: 1979; Homeowner vacancy rate: 2.2%; Median gross rent: $652 per month; Rental vacancy rate: 9.7%
Vital Statistics: Birth rate: 116.5 per 10,000 population; Death rate: 84.2 per 10,000 population; Age-adjusted cancer mortality rate: 202.5 deaths per 100,000 population
Health Insurance: 87.8% have insurance; 69.3% have private insurance; 32.4% have public insurance; 12.2% do not have insurance; 9.0% of children under 18 do not have insurance
Health Care: Physicians: 2.9 per 10,000 population; Hospital beds: 15.2 per 10,000 population; Hospital admissions: 269.3 per 10,000 population
Transportation: Commute: 93.8% car, 0.3% public transportation, 1.2% walk, 4.0% work from home; Median travel time to work: 30.3 minutes
Presidential Election: 36.6% Obama, 61.1% Romney (2012)
National and State Parks: Mount Gilead State Park
Additional Information Contacts
Morrow Government . . . . (419) 947-4085
http://www.morrowcounty.info

Morrow County Communities

CANDLEWOOD LAKE (CDP). Covers a land area of 2.254 square miles and a water area of 0.309 square miles. Located at 40.62° N. Lat; 82.77° W. Long.
Population: 1,147; Growth (since 2000): n/a; Density: 508.8 persons per square mile; Race: 97.8% White, 0.3% Black/African American, 0.4% Asian, 0.4% American Indian/Alaska Native, 0.0% Native Hawaiian/Other Pacific Islander, 0.8% Two or more races, 0.7% Hispanic of any race; Average household size: 2.58; Median age: 45.7; Age under 18: 24.2%; Age 65 and over: 16.0%; Males per 100 females: 98.8
Housing: Homeownership rate: 94.1%; Homeowner vacancy rate: 3.2%; Rental vacancy rate: 18.8%

CARDINGTON (village). Covers a land area of 2.006 square miles and a water area of 0 square miles. Located at 40.50° N. Lat; 82.89° W. Long. Elevation is 1,007 feet.
History: Cardington was founded in 1822 and named for an old carding mill here. After the Civil War, Cardington became a lumber town.
Population: 2,047; Growth (since 2000): 10.7%; Density: 1,020.3 persons per square mile; Race: 97.9% White, 0.1% Black/African American, 0.2% Asian, 0.0% American Indian/Alaska Native, 0.0% Native Hawaiian/Other Pacific Islander, 1.3% Two or more races, 0.8% Hispanic of any race; Average household size: 2.57; Median age: 33.5; Age under 18: 30.6%; Age 65 and over: 10.0%; Males per 100 females: 93.1

School District(s)

Cardington Lincoln Local Digital Academy (03-12)
2012-13 Enrollment: 30. . . . . (419) 864-4566
Cardington-Lincoln Local (PK-12)
2012-13 Enrollment: 1,062 . . . . (419) 864-3691
Housing: Homeownership rate: 58.9%; Homeowner vacancy rate: 3.3%; Rental vacancy rate: 17.3%
Safety: Violent crime rate: 4.9 per 10,000 population; Property crime rate: 381.2 per 10,000 population

CHESTERVILLE (village). Covers a land area of 0.205 square miles and a water area of 0.007 square miles. Located at 40.47° N. Lat; 82.68° W. Long. Elevation is 1,145 feet.
Population: 228; Growth (since 2000): 18.1%; Density: 1,114.6 persons per square mile; Race: 97.8% White, 0.0% Black/African American, 0.0% Asian, 0.0% American Indian/Alaska Native, 0.0% Native Hawaiian/Other Pacific Islander, 2.2% Two or more races, 0.4% Hispanic of any race; Average household size: 2.56; Median age: 40.5; Age under 18: 25.4%; Age 65 and over: 20.2%; Males per 100 females: 83.9
Housing: Homeownership rate: 72.2%; Homeowner vacancy rate: 3.4%; Rental vacancy rate: 4.3%

EDISON (village). Covers a land area of 0.287 square miles and a water area of 0 square miles. Located at 40.56° N. Lat; 82.86° W. Long. Elevation is 1,063 feet.
Population: 437; Growth (since 2000): 0.0%; Density: 1,520.4 persons per square mile; Race: 98.9% White, 0.2% Black/African American, 0.2% Asian, 0.0% American Indian/Alaska Native, 0.0% Native Hawaiian/Other Pacific Islander, 0.7% Two or more races, 1.8% Hispanic of any race; Average household size: 2.63; Median age: 36.9; Age under 18: 25.4%; Age 65 and over: 15.6%; Males per 100 females: 92.5

School District(s)

Tomorrow Center (01-12)
2012-13 Enrollment: 87. . . . . (419) 946-1900
Housing: Homeownership rate: 69.9%; Homeowner vacancy rate: 7.9%; Rental vacancy rate: 7.1%

FULTON (village). Covers a land area of 0.153 square miles and a water area of 0 square miles. Located at 40.46° N. Lat; 82.83° W. Long. Elevation is 1,106 feet.
Population: 258; Growth (since 2000): -2.3%; Density: 1,686.1 persons per square mile; Race: 96.9% White, 0.0% Black/African American, 0.0% Asian, 0.0% American Indian/Alaska Native, 0.0% Native Hawaiian/Other Pacific Islander, 1.9% Two or more races, 1.9% Hispanic of any race; Average household size: 2.46; Median age: 35.7; Age under 18: 27.5%; Age 65 and over: 13.6%; Males per 100 females: 88.3
Housing: Homeownership rate: 66.6%; Homeowner vacancy rate: 6.7%; Rental vacancy rate: 7.9%

IBERIA (CDP). Covers a land area of 3.854 square miles and a water area of 0.013 square miles. Located at 40.68° N. Lat; 82.83° W. Long. Elevation is 1,079 feet.
Population: 452; Growth (since 2000): n/a; Density: 117.3 persons per square mile; Race: 97.6% White, 1.8% Black/African American, 0.0% Asian, 0.2% American Indian/Alaska Native, 0.0% Native Hawaiian/Other Pacific Islander, 0.4% Two or more races, 0.4% Hispanic of any race; Average household size: 2.76; Median age: 41.5; Age under 18: 26.5%; Age 65 and over: 17.5%; Males per 100 females: 96.5
Housing: Homeownership rate: 84.8%; Homeowner vacancy rate: 0.7%; Rental vacancy rate: 0.0%

MARENGO (village). Covers a land area of 0.168 square miles and a water area of 0 square miles. Located at 40.40° N. Lat; 82.81° W. Long. Elevation is 1,158 feet.
Population: 342; Growth (since 2000): 15.2%; Density: 2,031.3 persons per square mile; Race: 95.3% White, 0.0% Black/African American, 0.0% Asian, 0.0% American Indian/Alaska Native, 0.0% Native Hawaiian/Other Pacific Islander, 3.5% Two or more races, 1.5% Hispanic of any race; Average household size: 2.57; Median age: 31.8; Age under 18: 31.0%; Age 65 and over: 10.5%; Males per 100 females: 92.1

School District(s)

Highland Local (PK-12)
2012-13 Enrollment: 1,828 . . . . (419) 768-2206
Housing: Homeownership rate: 44.4%; Homeowner vacancy rate: 4.8%; Rental vacancy rate: 6.3%

MOUNT GILEAD (village). County seat. Covers a land area of 3.387 square miles and a water area of 0.011 square miles. Located at 40.55° N. Lat; 82.83° W. Long. Elevation is 1,135 feet.
History: Mount Gilead was settled in 1817 by Lewis and Ralph Hardenbrook, whose farm was in a tulip-tree forest. Until 1824 the settlement was called Whetstone, and later Youngstown. In 1832 the Ohio legislature changed the name again to honor Mount Gilead, Virginia.
Population: 3,660; Growth (since 2000): 11.2%; Density: 1,080.6 persons per square mile; Race: 97.1% White, 0.3% Black/African American, 0.2% Asian, 0.1% American Indian/Alaska Native, 0.0% Native Hawaiian/Other Pacific Islander, 2.0% Two or more races, 1.9% Hispanic of any race; Average household size: 2.34; Median age: 36.9; Age under 18: 24.5%; Age 65 and over: 17.3%; Males per 100 females: 89.9; Marriage status: 29.2% never married, 49.4% now married, 2.0% separated, 11.0% widowed, 10.3% divorced; Foreign born: 2.8%; Speak English only: 97.9%;

With disability: 18.9%; Veterans: 12.9%; Ancestry: 35.3% German, 16.1% English, 14.7% Irish, 7.7% American, 5.4% Scotch-Irish
Employment: 6.8% management, business, and financial, 6.8% computer, engineering, and science, 7.3% education, legal, community service, arts, and media, 5.2% healthcare practitioners, 13.4% service, 20.5% sales and office, 13.7% natural resources, construction, and maintenance, 26.2% production, transportation, and material moving
Income: Per capita: $21,739; Median household: $38,299; Average household: $54,669; Households with income of $100,000 or more: 16.0%; Poverty rate: 20.9%
Educational Attainment: High school diploma or higher: 87.6%; Bachelor's degree or higher: 17.2%; Graduate/professional degree or higher: 3.2%

School District(s)

Mount Gilead Exempted Village (PK-12)
2012-13 Enrollment: 1,277 . . . . (419) 946-1646
Housing: Homeownership rate: 50.4%; Median home value: $99,100; Median year structure built: 1961; Homeowner vacancy rate: 4.3%; Median gross rent: $545 per month; Rental vacancy rate: 8.4%
Health Insurance: 85.5% have insurance; 53.4% have private insurance; 46.8% have public insurance; 14.5% do not have insurance; 6.8% of children under 18 do not have insurance
Hospitals: Morrow County Hospital (79 beds)
Newspapers: Morrow Co. Independent (weekly circulation 1000); Morrow County Sentinel (weekly circulation 4800)
Transportation: Commute: 94.9% car, 0.0% public transportation, 2.2% walk, 0.8% work from home; Median travel time to work: 27.5 minutes
Additional Information Contacts
Village of Mount Gilead . . . . (419) 946-3926
http://www.mountgilead.net

SPARTA (village). Covers a land area of 0.087 square miles and a water area of 0 square miles. Located at 40.39° N. Lat; 82.70° W. Long. Elevation is 1,358 feet.
Population: 161; Growth (since 2000): -15.7%; Density: 1,854.2 persons per square mile; Race: 95.7% White, 1.9% Black/African American, 0.0% Asian, 0.0% American Indian/Alaska Native, 0.0% Native Hawaiian/Other Pacific Islander, 1.9% Two or more races, 0.6% Hispanic of any race; Average household size: 2.48; Median age: 40.6; Age under 18: 25.5%; Age 65 and over: 14.3%; Males per 100 females: 78.9

School District(s)

Highland Local (PK-12)
2012-13 Enrollment: 1,828 . . . . (419) 768-2206
Housing: Homeownership rate: 61.6%; Homeowner vacancy rate: 0.0%; Rental vacancy rate: 10.7%

Muskingum County

Located in central Ohio; crossed by the Muskingum and Licking Rivers, and Salt and Jonathan Creeks. Covers a land area of 664.579 square miles, a water area of 8.004 square miles, and is located in the Eastern Time Zone at 39.97° N. Lat., 81.94° W. Long. The county was founded in 1804. County seat is Zanesville.

Muskingum County is part of the Zanesville, OH Micropolitan Statistical Area. The entire metro area includes: Muskingum County, OH

Weather Station: Philo 3 SW — Elevation: 1,020 feet

	Jan	Feb	Mar	Apr	May	Jun	Jul	Aug	Sep	Oct	Nov	Dec
High	36	40	50	62	70	77	81	81	74	63	51	39
Low	20	23	30	40	49	57	61	60	53	42	34	24
Precip	2.5	2.0	3.0	3.4	4.3	4.1	4.2	3.4	3.2	2.7	3.0	2.6
Snow	8.6	6.3	3.8	0.9	tr	0.0	0.0	0.0	0.0	tr	1.0	4.2

High and Low temperatures in degrees Fahrenheit; Precipitation and Snow in inches

Weather Station: Zanesville Municipal Arpt — Elevation: 879 feet

	Jan	Feb	Mar	Apr	May	Jun	Jul	Aug	Sep	Oct	Nov	Dec
High	37	41	51	63	72	80	84	83	76	64	53	41
Low	22	24	31	40	50	59	63	61	54	42	34	25
Precip	2.7	2.2	3.1	3.5	4.2	4.0	3.9	3.5	3.0	2.6	3.1	2.6
Snow	na	na	na	na	na	na	na	na	na	na	na	na

High and Low temperatures in degrees Fahrenheit; Precipitation and Snow in inches

Population: 86,074; Growth (since 2000): 1.8%; Density: 129.5 persons per square mile; Race: 93.0% White, 3.8% Black/African American, 0.3% Asian, 0.2% American Indian/Alaska Native, 0.0% Native Hawaiian/Other Pacific Islander, 2.5% two or more races, 0.8% Hispanic of any race; Average household size: 2.46; Median age: 39.5; Age under 18: 24.0%; Age 65 and over: 15.3%; Males per 100 females: 93.7; Marriage status: 27.1% never married, 52.3% now married, 1.9% separated, 7.2% widowed, 13.3% divorced; Foreign born: 1.0%; Speak English only: 97.7%; With disability: 15.4%; Veterans: 10.0%; Ancestry: 21.7% German, 14.7% Irish, 11.0% American, 9.8% English, 2.9% Italian
Religion: Six largest groups: 10.6% Methodist/Pietist, 6.6% Baptist, 6.0% Catholicism, 2.8% Non-denominational Protestant, 2.4% Presbyterian-Reformed, 2.4% Lutheran
Economy: Unemployment rate: 5.6%; Leading industries: 19.5% retail trade; 13.9% other services (except public administration); 11.1% health care and social assistance; Farms: 1,259 totaling 173,269 acres; Company size: 2 employ 1,000 or more persons, 1 employs 500 to 999 persons, 42 employ 100 to 499 persons, 1,705 employ less than 100 persons; Business ownership: 1,545 women-owned, 143 Black-owned, n/a Hispanic-owned, n/a Asian-owned
Employment: 8.7% management, business, and financial, 2.2% computer, engineering, and science, 8.4% education, legal, community service, arts, and media, 6.4% healthcare practitioners, 19.7% service, 26.0% sales and office, 9.9% natural resources, construction, and maintenance, 18.7% production, transportation, and material moving
Income: Per capita: $20,775; Median household: $40,524; Average household: $51,460; Households with income of $100,000 or more: 11.5%; Poverty rate: 18.1%
Educational Attainment: High school diploma or higher: 87.1%; Bachelor's degree or higher: 14.2%; Graduate/professional degree or higher: 5.3%
Housing: Homeownership rate: 69.2%; Median home value: $108,500; Median year structure built: 1967; Homeowner vacancy rate: 2.5%; Median gross rent: $624 per month; Rental vacancy rate: 8.7%
Vital Statistics: Birth rate: 122.5 per 10,000 population; Death rate: 106.2 per 10,000 population; Age-adjusted cancer mortality rate: 213.4 deaths per 100,000 population
Health Insurance: 88.0% have insurance; 63.0% have private insurance; 38.9% have public insurance; 12.0% do not have insurance; 4.7% of children under 18 do not have insurance
Health Care: Physicians: 18.3 per 10,000 population; Hospital beds: 45.6 per 10,000 population; Hospital admissions: 2,027.0 per 10,000 population
Transportation: Commute: 94.4% car, 0.3% public transportation, 2.0% walk, 3.0% work from home; Median travel time to work: 24.4 minutes
Presidential Election: 45.4% Obama, 52.4% Romney (2012)
National and State Parks: Blue Rock State Forest; Blue Rock State Park; Dillon State Park; Dillon State Wildlife Area; Monroe Basin State Wildlife Area; Muskingum River Parkway State Park; Powelson State Wildlife Area
Additional Information Contacts
Muskingum Government . . . . (740) 455-7100
http://www.muskingumcounty.org

Muskingum County Communities

ADAMSVILLE (village). Covers a land area of 0.053 square miles and a water area of 0 square miles. Located at 40.07° N. Lat; 81.88° W. Long. Elevation is 1,020 feet.
Population: 114; Growth (since 2000): -10.2%; Density: 2,144.4 persons per square mile; Race: 99.1% White, 0.0% Black/African American, 0.0% Asian, 0.0% American Indian/Alaska Native, 0.0% Native Hawaiian/Other Pacific Islander, 0.9% Two or more races, 0.0% Hispanic of any race; Average household size: 2.53; Median age: 39.6; Age under 18: 27.2%; Age 65 and over: 14.0%; Males per 100 females: 103.6

School District(s)

Tri-Valley Local (PK-12)
2012-13 Enrollment: 3,019 . . . . (740) 754-1442
Housing: Homeownership rate: 68.9%; Homeowner vacancy rate: 0.0%; Rental vacancy rate: 0.0%

BLUE ROCK (unincorporated postal area)
ZCTA: 43720
Covers a land area of 45.399 square miles and a water area of 0.550 square miles. Located at 39.80° N. Lat; 81.88° W. Long. Elevation is 715 feet.
Population: 1,300; Growth (since 2000): 7.8%; Density: 28.6 persons per square mile; Race: 97.8% White, 0.6% Black/African American, 0.2% Asian, 0.3% American Indian/Alaska Native, 0.0% Native Hawaiian/Other Pacific Islander, 1.2% Two or more races, 0.1% Hispanic of any race;

Average household size: 2.51; Median age: 43.6; Age under 18: 22.4%; Age 65 and over: 12.3%; Males per 100 females: 99.1

Housing: Homeownership rate: 82.5%; Homeowner vacancy rate: 2.3%; Rental vacancy rate: 2.2%

CHANDLERSVILLE (unincorporated postal area)

ZCTA: 43727

Covers a land area of 75.218 square miles and a water area of 0.558 square miles. Located at 39.86° N. Lat; 81.79° W. Long. Elevation is 735 feet.

Population: 1,473; Growth (since 2000): 13.3%; Density: 19.6 persons per square mile; Race: 97.8% White, 0.9% Black/African American, 0.1% Asian, 0.1% American Indian/Alaska Native, 0.0% Native Hawaiian/Other Pacific Islander, 1.0% Two or more races, 0.2% Hispanic of any race; Average household size: 2.60; Median age: 41.1; Age under 18: 23.6%; Age 65 and over: 13.4%; Males per 100 females: 107.2

Housing: Homeownership rate: 87.3%; Homeowner vacancy rate: 0.4%; Rental vacancy rate: 6.5%

DRESDEN (village). Covers a land area of 1.141 square miles and a water area of 0.035 square miles. Located at 40.12° N. Lat; 82.01° W. Long. Elevation is 741 feet.

Population: 1,529; Growth (since 2000): 7.4%; Density: 1,339.5 persons per square mile; Race: 97.4% White, 0.3% Black/African American, 0.5% Asian, 0.1% American Indian/Alaska Native, 0.0% Native Hawaiian/Other Pacific Islander, 1.8% Two or more races, 0.3% Hispanic of any race; Average household size: 2.35; Median age: 39.0; Age under 18: 25.1%; Age 65 and over: 16.7%; Males per 100 females: 87.1

School District(s)

Tri-Valley Local (PK-12)
2012-13 Enrollment: 3,019 . . . . (740) 754-1442

Housing: Homeownership rate: 62.5%; Homeowner vacancy rate: 2.1%; Rental vacancy rate: 10.6%

Newspapers: Dresden Transcript (weekly circulation 5500)

DUNCAN FALLS (CDP). Covers a land area of 1.240 square miles and a water area of 0.077 square miles. Located at 39.88° N. Lat; 81.91° W. Long. Elevation is 709 feet.

Population: 880; Growth (since 2000): n/a; Density: 709.5 persons per square mile; Race: 98.6% White, 0.5% Black/African American, 0.1% Asian, 0.0% American Indian/Alaska Native, 0.0% Native Hawaiian/Other Pacific Islander, 0.6% Two or more races, 0.1% Hispanic of any race; Average household size: 2.49; Median age: 39.0; Age under 18: 26.1%; Age 65 and over: 18.9%; Males per 100 females: 88.8

School District(s)

Franklin Local (PK-12)
2012-13 Enrollment: 2,046 . . . . (740) 674-5203

Housing: Homeownership rate: 78.8%; Homeowner vacancy rate: 1.0%; Rental vacancy rate: 9.6%

EAST FULTONHAM (CDP). Covers a land area of 0.466 square miles and a water area of 0.124 square miles. Located at 39.84° N. Lat; 82.12° W. Long. Elevation is 768 feet.

Population: 335; Growth (since 2000): n/a; Density: 719.2 persons per square mile; Race: 97.0% White, 0.9% Black/African American, 0.3% Asian, 0.0% American Indian/Alaska Native, 0.0% Native Hawaiian/Other Pacific Islander, 1.5% Two or more races, 0.9% Hispanic of any race; Average household size: 2.77; Median age: 37.9; Age under 18: 30.7%; Age 65 and over: 13.4%; Males per 100 females: 93.6

Housing: Homeownership rate: 76.8%; Homeowner vacancy rate: 4.1%; Rental vacancy rate: 12.5%

FRAZEYSBURG (village). Covers a land area of 0.924 square miles and a water area of 0 square miles. Located at 40.12° N. Lat; 82.12° W. Long. Elevation is 751 feet.

Population: 1,326; Growth (since 2000): 10.4%; Density: 1,435.0 persons per square mile; Race: 97.6% White, 0.1% Black/African American, 0.3% Asian, 0.2% American Indian/Alaska Native, 0.0% Native Hawaiian/Other Pacific Islander, 1.7% Two or more races, 0.5% Hispanic of any race; Average household size: 2.53; Median age: 35.4; Age under 18: 27.5%; Age 65 and over: 13.7%; Males per 100 females: 91.3

School District(s)

Tri-Valley Local (PK-12)
2012-13 Enrollment: 3,019 . . . . (740) 754-1442

Housing: Homeownership rate: 59.4%; Homeowner vacancy rate: 2.4%; Rental vacancy rate: 14.1%

FULTONHAM (village). Covers a land area of 0.156 square miles and a water area of 0 square miles. Located at 39.86° N. Lat; 82.14° W. Long. Elevation is 994 feet.

History: Fultonham developed around the Columbia Cement Company plant, which used the local desposits of limestone.

Population: 176; Growth (since 2000): 16.6%; Density: 1,127.7 persons per square mile; Race: 100.0% White, 0.0% Black/African American, 0.0% Asian, 0.0% American Indian/Alaska Native, 0.0% Native Hawaiian/Other Pacific Islander, 0.0% Two or more races, 0.0% Hispanic of any race; Average household size: 2.89; Median age: 33.7; Age under 18: 27.8%; Age 65 and over: 11.4%; Males per 100 females: 97.8

Housing: Homeownership rate: 70.5%; Homeowner vacancy rate: 2.3%; Rental vacancy rate: 10.0%

HOPEWELL (unincorporated postal area)

ZCTA: 43746

Covers a land area of 21.020 square miles and a water area of 0.017 square miles. Located at 39.97° N. Lat; 82.18° W. Long. Elevation is 1,089 feet.

Population: 1,425; Growth (since 2000): 5.9%; Density: 67.8 persons per square mile; Race: 97.7% White, 1.0% Black/African American, 0.0% Asian, 0.1% American Indian/Alaska Native, 0.0% Native Hawaiian/Other Pacific Islander, 0.9% Two or more races, 0.4% Hispanic of any race; Average household size: 2.63; Median age: 39.5; Age under 18: 24.8%; Age 65 and over: 12.5%; Males per 100 females: 103.0

School District(s)

West Muskingum Local (PK-12)
2012-13 Enrollment: 1,499 . . . . (740) 455-4052

Housing: Homeownership rate: 84.2%; Homeowner vacancy rate: 1.1%; Rental vacancy rate: 8.4%

NASHPORT (unincorporated postal area)

ZCTA: 43830

Covers a land area of 50.922 square miles and a water area of 1.241 square miles. Located at 40.06° N. Lat; 82.14° W. Long. Elevation is 823 feet.

Population: 6,158; Growth (since 2000): 12.3%; Density: 120.9 persons per square mile; Race: 96.2% White, 1.6% Black/African American, 0.3% Asian, 0.1% American Indian/Alaska Native, 0.0% Native Hawaiian/Other Pacific Islander, 1.7% Two or more races, 0.6% Hispanic of any race; Average household size: 2.70; Median age: 37.9; Age under 18: 27.4%; Age 65 and over: 10.9%; Males per 100 females: 100.9; Marriage status: 23.0% never married, 63.8% now married, 0.7% separated, 4.5% widowed, 8.7% divorced; Foreign born: 1.5%; Speak English only: 97.4%; With disability: 8.4%; Veterans: 11.8%; Ancestry: 26.4% German, 17.2% Irish, 8.9% English, 8.4% American, 2.9% Dutch

Employment: 12.5% management, business, and financial, 2.5% computer, engineering, and science, 7.9% education, legal, community service, arts, and media, 8.1% healthcare practitioners, 14.3% service, 27.1% sales and office, 7.7% natural resources, construction, and maintenance, 19.9% production, transportation, and material moving

Income: Per capita: $23,722; Median household: $51,648; Average household: $64,815; Households with income of $100,000 or more: 22.8%; Poverty rate: 7.0%

Educational Attainment: High school diploma or higher: 92.2%; Bachelor's degree or higher: 21.8%; Graduate/professional degree or higher: 6.3%

School District(s)

Tri-Valley Local (PK-12)
2012-13 Enrollment: 3,019 . . . . (740) 754-1442

Housing: Homeownership rate: 78.1%; Median home value: $147,800; Median year structure built: 1983; Homeowner vacancy rate: 1.4%; Median gross rent: $592 per month; Rental vacancy rate: 9.2%

Health Insurance: 88.0% have insurance; 78.1% have private insurance; 23.4% have public insurance; 12.0% do not have insurance; 5.3% of children under 18 do not have insurance

Transportation: Commute: 99.6% car, 0.0% public transportation, 0.0% walk, 0.4% work from home; Median travel time to work: 28.6 minutes

NEW CONCORD (village). Covers a land area of 1.626 square miles and a water area of 0 square miles. Located at 39.99° N. Lat; 81.74° W. Long. Elevation is 869 feet.
History: New Concord began in 1807 when the National Road was opened. Muskingum College was founded here in 1836.
Population: 2,491; Growth (since 2000): -6.0%; Density: 1,532.4 persons per square mile; Race: 96.1% White, 1.2% Black/African American, 1.0% Asian, 0.1% American Indian/Alaska Native, 0.0% Native Hawaiian/Other Pacific Islander, 1.1% Two or more races, 1.0% Hispanic of any race; Average household size: 2.27; Median age: 22.5; Age under 18: 12.0%; Age 65 and over: 13.0%; Males per 100 females: 82.4

School District(s)

East Muskingum Local (PK-12)
2012-13 Enrollment: 2,105 . . . . (740) 826-7655

Four-year College(s)

Muskingum University (Private, Not-for-profit, Presbyterian Church (USA))
Fall 2013 Enrollment: 2,154 . . . . (740) 826-8211
2013-14 Tuition: In-state $23,662; Out-of-state $23,662
Housing: Homeownership rate: 50.0%; Homeowner vacancy rate: 3.5%; Rental vacancy rate: 7.9%
Safety: Violent crime rate: 4.0 per 10,000 population; Property crime rate: 16.1 per 10,000 population

NORTH ZANESVILLE (CDP). Covers a land area of 3.552 square miles and a water area of 0.003 square miles. Located at 39.99° N. Lat; 81.99° W. Long. Elevation is 902 feet.
Population: 2,816; Growth (since 2000): -6.5%; Density: 792.7 persons per square mile; Race: 95.6% White, 1.3% Black/African American, 1.1% Asian, 0.3% American Indian/Alaska Native, 0.0% Native Hawaiian/Other Pacific Islander, 1.5% Two or more races, 0.7% Hispanic of any race; Average household size: 2.21; Median age: 50.5; Age under 18: 17.2%; Age 65 and over: 24.8%; Males per 100 females: 90.5; Marriage status: 18.8% never married, 63.1% now married, 2.0% separated, 8.3% widowed, 9.8% divorced; Foreign born: 0.8%; Speak English only: 96.7%; With disability: 10.1%; Veterans: 16.5%; Ancestry: 27.2% German, 23.6% Irish, 14.4% American, 11.8% English, 7.2% Italian
Employment: 9.7% management, business, and financial, 2.7% computer, engineering, and science, 20.8% education, legal, community service, arts, and media, 9.8% healthcare practitioners, 9.4% service, 32.1% sales and office, 1.0% natural resources, construction, and maintenance, 14.4% production, transportation, and material moving
Income: Per capita: $29,829; Median household: $68,750; Average household: $72,320; Households with income of $100,000 or more: 21.1%; Poverty rate: 4.0%
Educational Attainment: High school diploma or higher: 92.6%; Bachelor's degree or higher: 36.8%; Graduate/professional degree or higher: 22.4%
Housing: Homeownership rate: 84.9%; Median home value: $158,700; Median year structure built: 1963; Homeowner vacancy rate: 2.6%; Median gross rent: $830 per month; Rental vacancy rate: 11.4%
Health Insurance: 96.3% have insurance; 86.2% have private insurance; 26.2% have public insurance; 3.7% do not have insurance; 0.0% of children under 18 do not have insurance
Transportation: Commute: 96.8% car, 0.0% public transportation, 0.7% walk, 2.5% work from home; Median travel time to work: 20.1 minutes

NORWICH (village). Covers a land area of 0.100 square miles and a water area of 0 square miles. Located at 39.98° N. Lat; 81.79° W. Long. Elevation is 968 feet.
History: The village of Norwich was reported in the 1800's to be the home of a headless creature which roamed Stumpy Hollow at night, frightening the residents and leaving them speechless.
Population: 102; Growth (since 2000): -9.7%; Density: 1,021.0 persons per square mile; Race: 100.0% White, 0.0% Black/African American, 0.0% Asian, 0.0% American Indian/Alaska Native, 0.0% Native Hawaiian/Other Pacific Islander, 0.0% Two or more races, 0.0% Hispanic of any race; Average household size: 2.08; Median age: 49.0; Age under 18: 11.8%; Age 65 and over: 16.7%; Males per 100 females: 104.0
Housing: Homeownership rate: 85.7%; Homeowner vacancy rate: 0.0%; Rental vacancy rate: 12.5%

PHILO (village). Covers a land area of 0.422 square miles and a water area of 0 square miles. Located at 39.86° N. Lat; 81.91° W. Long. Elevation is 732 feet.
Population: 733; Growth (since 2000): -4.7%; Density: 1,738.8 persons per square mile; Race: 97.8% White, 0.8% Black/African American, 0.1% Asian, 0.0% American Indian/Alaska Native, 0.0% Native Hawaiian/Other Pacific Islander, 1.1% Two or more races, 0.7% Hispanic of any race; Average household size: 2.64; Median age: 33.8; Age under 18: 29.7%; Age 65 and over: 12.3%; Males per 100 females: 93.4

School District(s)

Franklin Local (PK-12)
2012-13 Enrollment: 2,046 . . . . (740) 674-5203
Housing: Homeownership rate: 77.7%; Homeowner vacancy rate: 4.1%; Rental vacancy rate: 4.4%

PLEASANT GROVE (CDP). Covers a land area of 3.211 square miles and a water area of 0.007 square miles. Located at 39.95° N. Lat; 81.96° W. Long. Elevation is 932 feet.
Population: 1,742; Growth (since 2000): -13.6%; Density: 542.5 persons per square mile; Race: 93.9% White, 2.8% Black/African American, 0.3% Asian, 0.1% American Indian/Alaska Native, 0.0% Native Hawaiian/Other Pacific Islander, 2.8% Two or more races, 0.6% Hispanic of any race; Average household size: 2.24; Median age: 45.1; Age under 18: 20.1%; Age 65 and over: 19.7%; Males per 100 females: 94.4
Housing: Homeownership rate: 68.3%; Homeowner vacancy rate: 2.7%; Rental vacancy rate: 9.1%

SOUTH ZANESVILLE (village). Covers a land area of 0.828 square miles and a water area of 0 square miles. Located at 39.90° N. Lat; 82.02° W. Long. Elevation is 722 feet.
Population: 1,989; Growth (since 2000): 2.7%; Density: 2,400.7 persons per square mile; Race: 94.1% White, 3.0% Black/African American, 0.1% Asian, 0.3% American Indian/Alaska Native, 0.1% Native Hawaiian/Other Pacific Islander, 2.4% Two or more races, 0.3% Hispanic of any race; Average household size: 2.40; Median age: 37.1; Age under 18: 25.9%; Age 65 and over: 13.4%; Males per 100 females: 93.5
Housing: Homeownership rate: 70.0%; Homeowner vacancy rate: 3.5%; Rental vacancy rate: 7.4%

TRINWAY (CDP). Covers a land area of 0.378 square miles and a water area of 0 square miles. Located at 40.14° N. Lat; 82.01° W. Long. Elevation is 738 feet.
Population: 365; Growth (since 2000): n/a; Density: 965.4 persons per square mile; Race: 97.0% White, 0.3% Black/African American, 0.0% Asian, 0.0% American Indian/Alaska Native, 0.0% Native Hawaiian/Other Pacific Islander, 2.7% Two or more races, 0.3% Hispanic of any race; Average household size: 2.64; Median age: 35.1; Age under 18: 30.1%; Age 65 and over: 12.6%; Males per 100 females: 117.3
Housing: Homeownership rate: 81.2%; Homeowner vacancy rate: 0.8%; Rental vacancy rate: 0.0%

ZANESVILLE (city). County seat. Covers a land area of 11.768 square miles and a water area of 0.373 square miles. Located at 39.96° N. Lat; 82.01° W. Long. Elevation is 676 feet.
History: Zanesville, situated at the confluence of the Licking and Muskingum Rivers, was established in the late 1790's. Clay suitable for pottery-making was discovered in the vicinity, and by 1808 dishes, stoneware, and bricks were bearing the Zanesville imprint. Local sands were used in the glass plant started in Zanesville in 1815, making goblets and water pitchers that became prized collectors items. Zanesville was named for Ebenezer Zane, who surveyed Zane's Trace, an overland route through Ohio, in 1797. A descendant of Zane was western writer Zane Grey, who was born in Zanesville in 1875.
Population: 25,487; Growth (since 2000): -0.4%; Density: 2,165.8 persons per square mile; Race: 84.4% White, 9.7% Black/African American, 0.4% Asian, 0.4% American Indian/Alaska Native, 0.0% Native Hawaiian/Other Pacific Islander, 4.7% Two or more races, 1.2% Hispanic of any race; Average household size: 2.29; Median age: 36.3; Age under 18: 25.1%; Age 65 and over: 15.2%; Males per 100 females: 87.3; Marriage status: 33.6% never married, 39.8% now married, 3.3% separated, 8.9% widowed, 17.7% divorced; Foreign born: 1.3%; Speak English only: 97.3%; With disability: 22.0%; Veterans: 8.8%; Ancestry: 16.5% German, 12.8% Irish, 9.5% American, 8.2% English, 3.2% Italian
Employment: 7.5% management, business, and financial, 3.2% computer, engineering, and science, 8.4% education, legal, community service, arts,

and media, 5.1% healthcare practitioners, 25.3% service, 24.5% sales and office, 7.8% natural resources, construction, and maintenance, 18.3% production, transportation, and material moving
Income: Per capita: $16,876; Median household: $26,986; Average household: $38,989; Households with income of $100,000 or more: 5.3%; Poverty rate: 29.7%
Educational Attainment: High school diploma or higher: 79.7%; Bachelor's degree or higher: 11.1%; Graduate/professional degree or higher: 4.1%

School District(s)

East Muskingum Local (PK-12)
2012-13 Enrollment: 2,105 . . . . (740) 826-7655
Foxfire High School (09-12)
2012-13 Enrollment: 209. . . . . (740) 453-4509
Foxfire Intermediate School (05-08)
2012-13 Enrollment: 61. . . . . (740) 453-4509
Maysville Local (PK-12)
2012-13 Enrollment: 2,356 . . . . (740) 453-0754
Mid-East Career and Technology Centers (09-12)
2012-13 Enrollment: n/a . . . . (740) 454-0105
Muskingum Valley Stemm Academy
2012-13 Enrollment: n/a . . . . (614) 995-1985
West Muskingum Local (PK-12)
2012-13 Enrollment: 1,499 . . . . (740) 455-4052
Zanesville City (PK-12)
2012-13 Enrollment: 3,443 . . . . (740) 454-9751
Zanesville Community School (09-12)
2012-13 Enrollment: 95. . . . . (740) 454-9751

Four-year College(s)

Ohio University-Zanesville Campus (Public)
Fall 2013 Enrollment: 2,042 . . . . (740) 453-0762
2013-14 Tuition: In-state $4,982; Out-of-state $9,510

Two-year College(s)

Valley Beauty School (Private, For-profit)
Fall 2013 Enrollment: 19. . . . . (740) 373-3617
Zane State College (Public)
Fall 2013 Enrollment: 3,652 . . . . (740) 454-2501
2013-14 Tuition: In-state $4,556; Out-of-state $9,026

Vocational/Technical School(s)

Mid-EastCTC-Adult Education (Public)
Fall 2013 Enrollment: 385. . . . . (740) 455-3111
2013-14 Tuition: $7,803

Housing: Homeownership rate: 47.0%; Median home value: $76,200; Median year structure built: 1948; Homeowner vacancy rate: 5.3%; Median gross rent: $605 per month; Rental vacancy rate: 8.9%
Health Insurance: 85.6% have insurance; 43.3% have private insurance; 55.9% have public insurance; 14.4% do not have insurance; 5.3% of children under 18 do not have insurance
Hospitals: Genesis Healthcare System (352 beds)
Safety: Violent crime rate: 40.6 per 10,000 population; Property crime rate: 630.9 per 10,000 population
Newspapers: Times Recorder (daily circulation 18000)
Transportation: Commute: 92.2% car, 0.5% public transportation, 2.6% walk, 4.4% work from home; Median travel time to work: 21.0 minutes
Airports: Zanesville Municipal (general aviation)
Additional Information Contacts
City of Zanesville. . . . . (740) 455-0603
http://www.coz.org

Noble County

Located in eastern Ohio; drained by Wills, Duck, and Seneca Creeks. Covers a land area of 398.012 square miles, a water area of 6.558 square miles, and is located in the Eastern Time Zone at 39.77° N. Lat., 81.45° W. Long. The county was founded in 1851. County seat is Caldwell.
Population: 14,645; Growth (since 2000): 4.2%; Density: 36.8 persons per square mile; Race: 96.1% White, 2.5% Black/African American, 0.1% Asian, 0.3% American Indian/Alaska Native, 0.0% Native Hawaiian/Other Pacific Islander, 0.8% two or more races, 0.4% Hispanic of any race; Average household size: 2.47; Median age: 48.6; Age under 18: 19.1%; Age 65 and over: 20.8%; Males per 100 females: 137.2; Marriage status: 29.4% never married, 51.2% now married, 2.3% separated, 8.1% widowed, 11.4% divorced; Foreign born: 0.6%; Speak English only: 97.4%; With disability: 17.1%; Veterans: 13.8%; Ancestry: 20.7% German, 12.2% Irish, 8.7% American, 7.2% English, 2.8% Polish
Religion: Six largest groups: 10.5% Catholicism, 7.7% Baptist, 6.5% Methodist/Pietist, 2.2% Holiness, 0.5% Presbyterian-Reformed, 0.0% Other Groups
Economy: Unemployment rate: 5.6%; Leading industries: 15.9% retail trade; 15.9% other services (except public administration); 10.7% construction; Farms: 595 totaling 86,117 acres; Company size: 0 employ 1,000 or more persons, 0 employ 500 to 999 persons, 2 employ 100 to 499 persons, 212 employ less than 100 persons; Business ownership: 320 women-owned, n/a Black-owned, n/a Hispanic-owned, n/a Asian-owned
Employment: 10.8% management, business, and financial, 0.3% computer, engineering, and science, 6.4% education, legal, community service, arts, and media, 6.1% healthcare practitioners, 14.1% service, 23.1% sales and office, 8.4% natural resources, construction, and maintenance, 30.7% production, transportation, and material moving
Income: Per capita: $18,853; Median household: $38,290; Average household: $46,315; Households with income of $100,000 or more: 7.3%; Poverty rate: 15.2%
Educational Attainment: High school diploma or higher: 80.1%; Bachelor's degree or higher: 9.7%; Graduate/professional degree or higher: 3.3%
Housing: Homeownership rate: 77.9%; Median home value: $77,300; Median year structure built: 1973; Homeowner vacancy rate: 1.5%; Median gross rent: $581 per month; Rental vacancy rate: 6.9%
Vital Statistics: Birth rate: 112.1 per 10,000 population; Death rate: 83.4 per 10,000 population; Age-adjusted cancer mortality rate: 119.1 deaths per 100,000 population
Health Insurance: 87.1% have insurance; 61.8% have private insurance; 40.5% have public insurance; 12.9% do not have insurance; 14.8% of children under 18 do not have insurance
Health Care: Physicians: 2.1 per 10,000 population; Hospital beds: 0.0 per 10,000 population; Hospital admissions: 0.0 per 10,000 population
Air Quality Index: 96.3% good, 3.7% moderate, 0.0% unhealthy for sensitive individuals, 0.0% unhealthy (percent of days)
Transportation: Commute: 95.9% car, 0.1% public transportation, 1.9% walk, 1.8% work from home; Median travel time to work: 28.7 minutes
Presidential Election: 36.2% Obama, 60.8% Romney (2012)
National and State Parks: Wolf Run State Park
Additional Information Contacts
Noble Government . . . . (740) 732-2969
http://www.noblecountyohio.com

Noble County Communities

AVA (unincorporated postal area)

ZCTA: 43711

Covers a land area of 0.213 square miles and a water area of <.001 square miles. Located at 39.84° N. Lat; 81.58° W. Long. Elevation is 774 feet.
Population: 91; Growth (since 2000): n/a; Density: 427.7 persons per square mile; Race: 96.7% White, 0.0% Black/African American, 0.0% Asian, 0.0% American Indian/Alaska Native, 0.0% Native Hawaiian/Other Pacific Islander, 3.3% Two or more races, 0.0% Hispanic of any race; Average household size: 2.76; Median age: 29.5; Age under 18: 40.7%; Age 65 and over: 9.9%; Males per 100 females: 111.6
Housing: Homeownership rate: 63.6%; Homeowner vacancy rate: 0.0%; Rental vacancy rate: 7.7%

BATESVILLE (village). Covers a land area of 0.136 square miles and a water area of 0 square miles. Located at 39.91° N. Lat; 81.28° W. Long. Elevation is 912 feet.
Population: 71; Growth (since 2000): -29.0%; Density: 520.8 persons per square mile; Race: 95.8% White, 1.4% Black/African American, 0.0% Asian, 0.0% American Indian/Alaska Native, 0.0% Native Hawaiian/Other Pacific Islander, 2.8% Two or more races, 0.0% Hispanic of any race; Average household size: 2.54; Median age: 41.3; Age under 18: 23.9%; Age 65 and over: 16.9%; Males per 100 females: 91.9
Housing: Homeownership rate: 75.0%; Homeowner vacancy rate: 0.0%; Rental vacancy rate: 0.0%

BELLE VALLEY (village). Covers a land area of 0.407 square miles and a water area of 0 square miles. Located at 39.79° N. Lat; 81.56° W. Long. Elevation is 748 feet.
History: Belle Valley developed around a large coal mine. In the early 1900's the mine attracted many Eastern European immigrants who found work here.

Population: 223; Growth (since 2000): -15.2%; Density: 548.4 persons per square mile; Race: 97.3% White, 0.0% Black/African American, 0.0% Asian, 0.0% American Indian/Alaska Native, 0.0% Native Hawaiian/Other Pacific Islander, 1.8% Two or more races, 0.4% Hispanic of any race; Average household size: 2.40; Median age: 40.6; Age under 18: 23.3%; Age 65 and over: 18.8%; Males per 100 females: 102.7
Housing: Homeownership rate: 67.8%; Homeowner vacancy rate: 4.5%; Rental vacancy rate: 9.1%

CALDWELL (village). County seat. Covers a land area of 0.889 square miles and a water area of 0.013 square miles. Located at 39.75° N. Lat; 81.51° W. Long. Elevation is 745 feet.
History: Caldwell was founded in 1857 as the seat of Noble County, and named for the owners of the town site. Coal mining was Caldwell's primary industry.
Population: 1,748; Growth (since 2000): -10.6%; Density: 1,966.4 persons per square mile; Race: 97.7% White, 0.2% Black/African American, 0.5% Asian, 0.3% American Indian/Alaska Native, 0.0% Native Hawaiian/Other Pacific Islander, 1.1% Two or more races, 0.1% Hispanic of any race; Average household size: 2.01; Median age: 45.6; Age under 18: 18.9%; Age 65 and over: 23.6%; Males per 100 females: 83.6

School District(s)

Caldwell Exempted Village (PK-12)
2012-13 Enrollment: 759. . . . . (740) 732-5637
Housing: Homeownership rate: 56.7%; Homeowner vacancy rate: 1.8%; Rental vacancy rate: 6.5%
Newspapers: Journal & Noble Co. Leader (weekly circulation 4500)

DEXTER CITY (village). Covers a land area of 0.167 square miles and a water area of 0.006 square miles. Located at 39.66° N. Lat; 81.47° W. Long. Elevation is 709 feet.
Population: 129; Growth (since 2000): -22.3%; Density: 774.0 persons per square mile; Race: 95.3% White, 0.8% Black/African American, 0.0% Asian, 0.0% American Indian/Alaska Native, 0.0% Native Hawaiian/Other Pacific Islander, 3.9% Two or more races, 0.0% Hispanic of any race; Average household size: 2.53; Median age: 38.5; Age under 18: 27.1%; Age 65 and over: 10.9%; Males per 100 females: 98.5
Housing: Homeownership rate: 70.6%; Homeowner vacancy rate: 0.0%; Rental vacancy rate: 6.3%

SARAHSVILLE (village). Covers a land area of 0.154 square miles and a water area of <.001 square miles. Located at 39.81° N. Lat; 81.47° W. Long. Elevation is 978 feet.
Population: 166; Growth (since 2000): -16.2%; Density: 1,074.7 persons per square mile; Race: 98.8% White, 1.2% Black/African American, 0.0% Asian, 0.0% American Indian/Alaska Native, 0.0% Native Hawaiian/Other Pacific Islander, 0.0% Two or more races, 0.0% Hispanic of any race; Average household size: 2.96; Median age: 32.5; Age under 18: 27.7%; Age 65 and over: 5.4%; Males per 100 females: 100.0

School District(s)

Noble Local (PK-12)
2012-13 Enrollment: 920. . . . . (740) 732-2084
Housing: Homeownership rate: 84.0%; Homeowner vacancy rate: 4.1%; Rental vacancy rate: 0.0%

SUMMERFIELD (village). Covers a land area of 0.371 square miles and a water area of <.001 square miles. Located at 39.80° N. Lat; 81.34° W. Long. Elevation is 1,204 feet.
Population: 254; Growth (since 2000): -14.2%; Density: 683.7 persons per square mile; Race: 98.4% White, 0.0% Black/African American, 0.4% Asian, 0.0% American Indian/Alaska Native, 0.0% Native Hawaiian/Other Pacific Islander, 0.0% Two or more races, 1.2% Hispanic of any race; Average household size: 2.37; Median age: 39.0; Age under 18: 24.0%; Age 65 and over: 13.0%; Males per 100 females: 96.9
Housing: Homeownership rate: 72.0%; Homeowner vacancy rate: 3.8%; Rental vacancy rate: 0.0%

Ottawa County

Located in northern Ohio; bounded on the northeast by Lake Erie; drained by Portage River; includes the Bass Islands. Covers a land area of 254.917 square miles, a water area of 330.146 square miles, and is located in the Eastern Time Zone at 41.54° N. Lat., 83.01° W. Long. The county was founded in 1840. County seat is Port Clinton.

Ottawa County is part of the Port Clinton, OH Micropolitan Statistical Area. The entire metro area includes: Ottawa County, OH

Population: 41,428; Growth (since 2000): 1.1%; Density: 162.5 persons per square mile; Race: 96.5% White, 0.8% Black/African American, 0.3% Asian, 0.2% American Indian/Alaska Native, 0.0% Native Hawaiian/Other Pacific Islander, 1.3% two or more races, 4.2% Hispanic of any race; Average household size: 2.34; Median age: 46.3; Age under 18: 20.7%; Age 65 and over: 19.0%; Males per 100 females: 97.4; Marriage status: 20.6% never married, 60.4% now married, 1.3% separated, 8.3% widowed, 10.7% divorced; Foreign born: 1.3%; Speak English only: 96.2%; With disability: 14.6%; Veterans: 10.9%; Ancestry: 41.7% German, 12.8% Irish, 9.4% English, 6.4% American, 6.3% Polish
Religion: Six largest groups: 17.5% Catholicism, 16.7% Lutheran, 6.3% Presbyterian-Reformed, 5.3% Methodist/Pietist, 1.7% Baptist, 1.3% Holiness
Economy: Unemployment rate: 5.3%; Leading industries: 16.4% accommodation and food services; 14.1% retail trade; 12.4% other services (except public administration); Farms: 620 totaling 112,677 acres; Company size: 0 employ 1,000 or more persons, 4 employ 500 to 999 persons, 8 employ 100 to 499 persons, 992 employ less than 100 persons; Business ownership: n/a women-owned, n/a Black-owned, n/a Hispanic-owned, n/a Asian-owned
Employment: 12.3% management, business, and financial, 2.6% computer, engineering, and science, 7.5% education, legal, community service, arts, and media, 6.3% healthcare practitioners, 17.8% service, 23.0% sales and office, 12.4% natural resources, construction, and maintenance, 18.2% production, transportation, and material moving
Income: Per capita: $27,979; Median household: $53,202; Average household: $65,723; Households with income of $100,000 or more: 19.4%; Poverty rate: 11.0%
Educational Attainment: High school diploma or higher: 91.5%; Bachelor's degree or higher: 20.3%; Graduate/professional degree or higher: 6.6%
Housing: Homeownership rate: 79.7%; Median home value: $136,000; Median year structure built: 1971; Homeowner vacancy rate: 3.1%; Median gross rent: $716 per month; Rental vacancy rate: 13.5%
Vital Statistics: Birth rate: 83.3 per 10,000 population; Death rate: 114.7 per 10,000 population; Age-adjusted cancer mortality rate: 173.1 deaths per 100,000 population
Health Insurance: 89.3% have insurance; 74.9% have private insurance; 31.8% have public insurance; 10.7% do not have insurance; 5.1% of children under 18 do not have insurance
Health Care: Physicians: 9.9 per 10,000 population; Hospital beds: 6.0 per 10,000 population; Hospital admissions: 244.9 per 10,000 population
Transportation: Commute: 92.2% car, 1.0% public transportation, 1.2% walk, 4.4% work from home; Median travel time to work: 23.4 minutes
Presidential Election: 51.1% Obama, 47.1% Romney (2012)
National and State Parks: Catawba Island State Park; Crane Creek State Park; East Harbor State Park; Lakeside Daisy State Nature Preserve; Ottawa National Wildlife Refuge; South Bass Island State Park

Additional Information Contacts

Ottawa Government . . . . (419) 734-6710
http://www.co.ottawa.oh.us

Ottawa County Communities

CLAY CENTER (village). Covers a land area of 1.037 square miles and a water area of 0 square miles. Located at 41.57° N. Lat; 83.36° W. Long. Elevation is 610 feet.
Population: 276; Growth (since 2000): -6.1%; Density: 266.3 persons per square mile; Race: 98.2% White, 0.0% Black/African American, 0.0% Asian, 0.0% American Indian/Alaska Native, 0.0% Native Hawaiian/Other Pacific Islander, 0.7% Two or more races, 5.8% Hispanic of any race; Average household size: 2.68; Median age: 32.8; Age under 18: 26.4%; Age 65 and over: 14.5%; Males per 100 females: 85.2
Housing: Homeownership rate: 86.4%; Homeowner vacancy rate: 3.3%; Rental vacancy rate: 12.5%

CURTICE (CDP). Covers a land area of 3.636 square miles and a water area of 0 square miles. Located at 41.62° N. Lat; 83.37° W. Long. Elevation is 594 feet.
Population: 1,526; Growth (since 2000): n/a; Density: 419.7 persons per square mile; Race: 97.1% White, 0.2% Black/African American, 0.9% Asian, 0.2% American Indian/Alaska Native, 0.0% Native Hawaiian/Other

Pacific Islander, 1.3% Two or more races, 2.5% Hispanic of any race; Average household size: 2.73; Median age: 44.1; Age under 18: 22.3%; Age 65 and over: 13.5%; Males per 100 females: 105.1

School District(s)

Oregon City (PK-12)
2012-13 Enrollment: 3,778 . . . . (419) 693-0661

Housing: Homeownership rate: 92.0%; Homeowner vacancy rate: 0.8%; Rental vacancy rate: 17.9%

ELMORE (village). Covers a land area of 0.814 square miles and a water area of 0 square miles. Located at 41.47° N. Lat; 83.29° W. Long. Elevation is 604 feet.

Population: 1,410; Growth (since 2000): -1.1%; Density: 1,732.8 persons per square mile; Race: 96.4% White, 0.5% Black/African American, 0.1% Asian, 0.2% American Indian/Alaska Native, 0.0% Native Hawaiian/Other Pacific Islander, 2.1% Two or more races, 5.7% Hispanic of any race; Average household size: 2.53; Median age: 38.6; Age under 18: 27.2%; Age 65 and over: 17.0%; Males per 100 females: 94.8

School District(s)

Woodmore Local (PK-12)
2012-13 Enrollment: 1,127 . . . . (419) 862-1060

Housing: Homeownership rate: 73.1%; Homeowner vacancy rate: 3.3%; Rental vacancy rate: 2.6%

GENOA (village). Covers a land area of 1.551 square miles and a water area of 0 square miles. Located at 41.52° N. Lat; 83.36° W. Long. Elevation is 623 feet.

History: Settled 1835 as Stony Ridge Station.

Population: 2,336; Growth (since 2000): 4.8%; Density: 1,506.5 persons per square mile; Race: 96.2% White, 0.4% Black/African American, 0.1% Asian, 0.1% American Indian/Alaska Native, 0.0% Native Hawaiian/Other Pacific Islander, 1.3% Two or more races, 7.4% Hispanic of any race; Average household size: 2.38; Median age: 40.6; Age under 18: 22.9%; Age 65 and over: 19.3%; Males per 100 females: 95.8

School District(s)

Genoa Area Local (PK-12)
2012-13 Enrollment: 1,323 . . . . (419) 855-7741

Housing: Homeownership rate: 72.3%; Homeowner vacancy rate: 2.3%; Rental vacancy rate: 7.4%

Additional Information Contacts

Village of Genoa . . . . (419) 855-7791
http://www.genoaohio.org

GRAYTOWN (unincorporated postal area)

ZCTA: 43432

Covers a land area of 22.769 square miles and a water area of 0.017 square miles. Located at 41.56° N. Lat; 83.25° W. Long. Elevation is 594 feet.

Population: 1,366; Growth (since 2000): 0.7%; Density: 60.0 persons per square mile; Race: 98.9% White, 0.1% Black/African American, 0.0% Asian, 0.1% American Indian/Alaska Native, 0.0% Native Hawaiian/Other Pacific Islander, 0.7% Two or more races, 2.9% Hispanic of any race; Average household size: 2.74; Median age: 41.8; Age under 18: 23.9%; Age 65 and over: 12.2%; Males per 100 females: 100.9

School District(s)

Benton Carroll Salem Local (PK-12)
2012-13 Enrollment: 1,645 . . . . (419) 898-6210

Housing: Homeownership rate: 89.8%; Homeowner vacancy rate: 1.3%; Rental vacancy rate: 10.5%

GYPSUM (unincorporated postal area)

ZCTA: 43433

Covers a land area of 0.501 square miles and a water area of 0 square miles. Located at 41.50° N. Lat; 82.88° W. Long. Elevation is 581 feet.

Population: 95; Growth (since 2000): n/a; Density: 189.8 persons per square mile; Race: 98.9% White, 0.0% Black/African American, 0.0% Asian, 0.0% American Indian/Alaska Native, 0.0% Native Hawaiian/Other Pacific Islander, 0.0% Two or more races, 5.3% Hispanic of any race; Average household size: 2.57; Median age: 39.3; Age under 18: 23.2%; Age 65 and over: 9.5%; Males per 100 females: 93.9

Housing: Homeownership rate: 83.8%; Homeowner vacancy rate: 13.9%; Rental vacancy rate: 0.0%

LACARNE (unincorporated postal area)

ZCTA: 43439

Covers a land area of 0.055 square miles and a water area of 0 square miles. Located at 41.52° N. Lat; 83.04° W. Long. Elevation is 577 feet.

Population: 113; Growth (since 2000): 52.7%; Density: 2,043.0 persons per square mile; Race: 97.3% White, 0.0% Black/African American, 0.0% Asian, 0.0% American Indian/Alaska Native, 0.0% Native Hawaiian/Other Pacific Islander, 2.7% Two or more races, 5.3% Hispanic of any race; Average household size: 2.76; Median age: 40.1; Age under 18: 23.0%; Age 65 and over: 11.5%; Males per 100 females: 79.4

Housing: Homeownership rate: 78.1%; Homeowner vacancy rate: 0.0%; Rental vacancy rate: 18.2%

LAKESIDE (CDP). Covers a land area of 0.688 square miles and a water area of 0 square miles. Located at 41.54° N. Lat; 82.75° W. Long. Elevation is 607 feet.

Population: 694; Growth (since 2000): n/a; Density: 1,008.6 persons per square mile; Race: 98.0% White, 1.0% Black/African American, 0.3% Asian, 0.1% American Indian/Alaska Native, 0.0% Native Hawaiian/Other Pacific Islander, 0.4% Two or more races, 1.9% Hispanic of any race; Average household size: 1.77; Median age: 60.1; Age under 18: 11.0%; Age 65 and over: 39.2%; Males per 100 females: 76.6

School District(s)

Danbury Local (PK-12)
2012-13 Enrollment: 556. . . . . (419) 798-5185

Housing: Homeownership rate: 66.2%; Homeowner vacancy rate: 6.4%; Rental vacancy rate: 39.2%

LAKESIDE MARBLEHEAD (unincorporated postal area)

ZCTA: 43440

Covers a land area of 16.096 square miles and a water area of 2.544 square miles. Located at 41.53° N. Lat; 82.78° W. Long..

Population: 4,875; Growth (since 2000): 12.9%; Density: 302.9 persons per square mile; Race: 97.8% White, 0.6% Black/African American, 0.2% Asian, 0.3% American Indian/Alaska Native, 0.0% Native Hawaiian/Other Pacific Islander, 0.8% Two or more races, 1.9% Hispanic of any race; Average household size: 2.05; Median age: 54.9; Age under 18: 14.4%; Age 65 and over: 27.4%; Males per 100 females: 95.8; Marriage status: 14.5% never married, 62.6% now married, 0.6% separated, 12.5% widowed, 10.4% divorced; Foreign born: 2.4%; Speak English only: 96.6%; With disability: 18.4%; Veterans: 15.4%; Ancestry: 33.3% German, 15.7% Irish, 12.9% English, 8.0% Polish, 6.8% Italian

Employment: 12.3% management, business, and financial, 1.3% computer, engineering, and science, 3.9% education, legal, community service, arts, and media, 8.2% healthcare practitioners, 18.3% service, 33.0% sales and office, 10.7% natural resources, construction, and maintenance, 12.3% production, transportation, and material moving

Income: Per capita: $36,255; Median household: $53,490; Average household: $71,662; Households with income of $100,000 or more: 19.3%; Poverty rate: 7.6%

Educational Attainment: High school diploma or higher: 95.0%; Bachelor's degree or higher: 24.1%; Graduate/professional degree or higher: 6.8%

School District(s)

Danbury Local (PK-12)
2012-13 Enrollment: 556. . . . . (419) 798-5185

Housing: Homeownership rate: 83.6%; Median home value: $165,700; Median year structure built: 1979; Homeowner vacancy rate: 4.5%; Median gross rent: $747 per month; Rental vacancy rate: 29.9%

Health Insurance: 87.4% have insurance; 74.2% have private insurance; 42.0% have public insurance; 12.6% do not have insurance; 14.1% of children under 18 do not have insurance

Transportation: Commute: 88.8% car, 0.1% public transportation, 1.2% walk, 7.0% work from home; Median travel time to work: 24.3 minutes

MARBLEHEAD (village). Covers a land area of 3.305 square miles and a water area of 0.997 square miles. Located at 41.53° N. Lat; 82.72° W. Long. Elevation is 623 feet.

History: The Benajah Wolcott family settled here in 1809 and found three orchards which the French had planted earlier. Quarrying began in 1834 when John Clemens, a relative of Mark Twain, established himself here. Marblehead may have been called Marble Headland by an early visitor, who thought the white limestone cliffs were marble.

Population: 903; Growth (since 2000): 18.5%; Density: 273.3 persons per square mile; Race: 98.7% White, 0.2% Black/African American, 0.3% Asian, 0.1% American Indian/Alaska Native, 0.0% Native Hawaiian/Other Pacific Islander, 0.6% Two or more races, 1.7% Hispanic of any race; Average household size: 2.17; Median age: 55.7; Age under 18: 15.9%; Age 65 and over: 28.8%; Males per 100 females: 98.9
Housing: Homeownership rate: 87.0%; Homeowner vacancy rate: 7.8%; Rental vacancy rate: 21.7%
Newspapers: Peninsula News (weekly circulation 1800)

MARTIN (unincorporated postal area)

ZCTA: 43445

Covers a land area of 18.882 square miles and a water area of 0.103 square miles. Located at 41.58° N. Lat; 83.30° W. Long. Elevation is 604 feet.
Population: 1,161; Growth (since 2000): -0.8%; Density: 61.5 persons per square mile; Race: 97.1% White, 0.3% Black/African American, 0.3% Asian, 0.0% American Indian/Alaska Native, 0.0% Native Hawaiian/Other Pacific Islander, 0.6% Two or more races, 6.4% Hispanic of any race; Average household size: 2.71; Median age: 43.1; Age under 18: 24.1%; Age 65 and over: 12.3%; Males per 100 females: 110.7
Housing: Homeownership rate: 89.8%; Homeowner vacancy rate: 1.0%; Rental vacancy rate: 4.3%

MIDDLE BASS (unincorporated postal area)

ZCTA: 43446

Covers a land area of 1.258 square miles and a water area of 0.023 square miles. Located at 41.68° N. Lat; 82.81° W. Long. Elevation is 581 feet.
Population: 25; Growth (since 2000): n/a; Density: 19.9 persons per square mile; Race: 96.0% White, 0.0% Black/African American, 4.0% Asian, 0.0% American Indian/Alaska Native, 0.0% Native Hawaiian/Other Pacific Islander, 0.0% Two or more races, 0.0% Hispanic of any race; Average household size: 2.08; Median age: 60.5; Age under 18: 16.0%; Age 65 and over: 36.0%; Males per 100 females: 66.7
Housing: Homeownership rate: 100.0%; Homeowner vacancy rate: 7.7%; Rental vacancy rate: 0.0%
Airports: Middle Bass Island (general aviation)

OAK HARBOR (village). Covers a land area of 1.550 square miles and a water area of 0.153 square miles. Located at 41.51° N. Lat; 83.13° W. Long. Elevation is 584 feet.

History: Sometimes spelled Oakharbor.
Population: 2,759; Growth (since 2000): -2.9%; Density: 1,779.7 persons per square mile; Race: 97.5% White, 0.3% Black/African American, 0.1% Asian, 0.1% American Indian/Alaska Native, 0.0% Native Hawaiian/Other Pacific Islander, 1.4% Two or more races, 2.9% Hispanic of any race; Average household size: 2.39; Median age: 39.2; Age under 18: 26.4%; Age 65 and over: 16.7%; Males per 100 females: 86.8; Marriage status: 23.8% never married, 55.1% now married, 1.2% separated, 10.2% widowed, 10.9% divorced; Foreign born: 0.1%; Speak English only: 96.2%; With disability: 16.1%; Veterans: 6.8%; Ancestry: 47.9% German, 11.1% Irish, 7.8% French, 5.8% Polish, 5.6% English
Employment: 14.2% management, business, and financial, 4.7% computer, engineering, and science, 7.1% education, legal, community service, arts, and media, 2.7% healthcare practitioners, 16.5% service, 23.6% sales and office, 11.1% natural resources, construction, and maintenance, 20.1% production, transportation, and material moving
Income: Per capita: $24,656; Median household: $47,219; Average household: $56,330; Households with income of $100,000 or more: 11.3%; Poverty rate: 4.5%
Educational Attainment: High school diploma or higher: 95.9%; Bachelor's degree or higher: 17.6%; Graduate/professional degree or higher: 5.7%

School District(s)

Benton Carroll Salem Local (PK-12)
2012-13 Enrollment: 1,645 . . . . (419) 898-6210
Housing: Homeownership rate: 69.5%; Median home value: $115,000; Median year structure built: 1952; Homeowner vacancy rate: 3.8%; Median gross rent: $777 per month; Rental vacancy rate: 5.9%
Health Insurance: 87.6% have insurance; 80.4% have private insurance; 24.5% have public insurance; 12.4% do not have insurance; 3.3% of children under 18 do not have insurance
Safety: Violent crime rate: 10.9 per 10,000 population; Property crime rate: 181.8 per 10,000 population
Newspapers: The Exponent (weekly circulation 2000)
Transportation: Commute: 98.2% car, 0.0% public transportation, 1.0% walk, 0.5% work from home; Median travel time to work: 21.5 minutes
Additional Information Contacts
Village of Oak Harbor . . . . (419) 898-5561
http://www.oakharbor.oh.us

PORT CLINTON (city). County seat. Covers a land area of 2.078 square miles and a water area of 0.201 square miles. Located at 41.51° N. Lat; 82.94° W. Long. Elevation is 577 feet.

History: Port Clinton was platted in 1828 and settled by some Scotch immigrants, bound for Chicago, who were shipwrecked at this point and settled here. The town was named for DeWitt Clinton.
Population: 6,056; Growth (since 2000): -5.2%; Density: 2,913.9 persons per square mile; Race: 93.3% White, 2.3% Black/African American, 0.2% Asian, 0.1% American Indian/Alaska Native, 0.0% Native Hawaiian/Other Pacific Islander, 2.1% Two or more races, 7.8% Hispanic of any race; Average household size: 2.24; Median age: 41.5; Age under 18: 22.1%; Age 65 and over: 17.6%; Males per 100 females: 91.5; Marriage status: 24.3% never married, 53.4% now married, 1.8% separated, 7.4% widowed, 14.9% divorced; Foreign born: 0.8%; Speak English only: 93.2%; With disability: 12.9%; Veterans: 9.0%; Ancestry: 35.3% German, 9.9% Irish, 8.0% Italian, 6.1% English, 5.9% American
Employment: 9.6% management, business, and financial, 3.1% computer, engineering, and science, 7.7% education, legal, community service, arts, and media, 6.3% healthcare practitioners, 20.0% service, 25.8% sales and office, 12.2% natural resources, construction, and maintenance, 15.1% production, transportation, and material moving
Income: Per capita: $24,034; Median household: $45,505; Average household: $55,127; Households with income of $100,000 or more: 13.8%; Poverty rate: 16.9%
Educational Attainment: High school diploma or higher: 90.4%; Bachelor's degree or higher: 18.0%; Graduate/professional degree or higher: 5.7%

School District(s)

Port Clinton City (PK-12)
2012-13 Enrollment: 1,726 . . . . (419) 732-2102
Housing: Homeownership rate: 63.3%; Median home value: $107,200; Median year structure built: 1957; Homeowner vacancy rate: 3.7%; Median gross rent: $623 per month; Rental vacancy rate: 11.8%
Health Insurance: 85.3% have insurance; 69.5% have private insurance; 29.6% have public insurance; 14.7% do not have insurance; 10.5% of children under 18 do not have insurance
Hospitals: H B Magruder Memorial Hospital (98 beds)
Safety: Violent crime rate: 26.5 per 10,000 population; Property crime rate: 253.1 per 10,000 population
Newspapers: News-Herald (daily circulation 5200); The Beacon (weekly circulation 17000)
Transportation: Commute: 91.3% car, 1.1% public transportation, 0.8% walk, 5.2% work from home; Median travel time to work: 21.8 minutes
Airports: Carl R Keller Field (general aviation)
Additional Information Contacts
City of Port Clinton . . . . (419) 734-5522

PUT-IN-BAY (village). Covers a land area of 0.453 square miles and a water area of 0.178 square miles. Located at 41.65° N. Lat; 82.82° W. Long. Elevation is 568 feet.

History: Perry's Victory and International Peace Memorial national monument (est. 1936) is near here. A granite column 352 feet high commemorates battle of Lake Erie (1813), in which Admiral Perry's U.S. fleet defeated the British, and symbolizes century of peace between U.S. and Canada.
Population: 138; Growth (since 2000): 7.8%; Density: 304.8 persons per square mile; Race: 100.0% White, 0.0% Black/African American, 0.0% Asian, 0.0% American Indian/Alaska Native, 0.0% Native Hawaiian/Other Pacific Islander, 0.0% Two or more races, 0.0% Hispanic of any race; Average household size: 1.94; Median age: 54.7; Age under 18: 15.2%; Age 65 and over: 29.0%; Males per 100 females: 112.3

School District(s)

Put-In-Bay Local (PK-12)
2012-13 Enrollment: 73. . . . . (419) 285-3614
Housing: Homeownership rate: 72.9%; Homeowner vacancy rate: 1.9%; Rental vacancy rate: 20.8%
Airports: Put-in-Bay (general aviation)

ROCKY RIDGE (village). Covers a land area of 1.011 square miles and a water area of 0.015 square miles. Located at 41.53° N. Lat; 83.21° W. Long. Elevation is 604 feet.
Population: 417; Growth (since 2000): 7.2%; Density: 412.6 persons per square mile; Race: 95.7% White, 0.0% Black/African American, 0.0% Asian, 0.5% American Indian/Alaska Native, 0.0% Native Hawaiian/Other Pacific Islander, 2.6% Two or more races, 5.0% Hispanic of any race; Average household size: 2.62; Median age: 38.9; Age under 18: 27.6%; Age 65 and over: 11.3%; Males per 100 females: 106.4
Housing: Homeownership rate: 81.8%; Homeowner vacancy rate: 1.5%; Rental vacancy rate: 12.1%
Safety: Violent crime rate: 0.0 per 10,000 population; Property crime rate: 0.0 per 10,000 population

WILLISTON (CDP). Covers a land area of 0.611 square miles and a water area of 0 square miles. Located at 41.60° N. Lat; 83.34° W. Long. Elevation is 594 feet.
Population: 487; Growth (since 2000): n/a; Density: 796.6 persons per square mile; Race: 95.9% White, 1.6% Black/African American, 0.0% Asian, 0.2% American Indian/Alaska Native, 0.0% Native Hawaiian/Other Pacific Islander, 1.6% Two or more races, 3.7% Hispanic of any race; Average household size: 2.45; Median age: 49.4; Age under 18: 19.3%; Age 65 and over: 23.6%; Males per 100 females: 94.8
Housing: Homeownership rate: 85.2%; Homeowner vacancy rate: 2.3%; Rental vacancy rate: 18.5%

Paulding County

Located in northwestern Ohio; bounded on the west by Indiana; drained by the Auglaize and Maumee Rivers. Covers a land area of 416.438 square miles, a water area of 2.410 square miles, and is located in the Eastern Time Zone at 41.12° N. Lat., 84.58° W. Long. The county was founded in 1820. County seat is Paulding.

Weather Station: Paulding Elevation: 725 feet

	Jan	Feb	Mar	Apr	May	Jun	Jul	Aug	Sep	Oct	Nov	Dec
High	32	35	46	60	71	80	84	82	76	63	49	36
Low	16	18	27	37	48	58	61	59	51	40	31	21
Precip	2.1	2.0	2.5	3.2	4.1	3.4	3.9	3.2	3.0	2.7	2.8	2.6
Snow	5.9	5.8	3.6	0.3	0.0	0.0	0.0	0.0	0.0	0.1	0.6	4.2

High and Low temperatures in degrees Fahrenheit; Precipitation and Snow in inches

Population: 19,614; Growth (since 2000): -3.3%; Density: 47.1 persons per square mile; Race: 95.7% White, 0.9% Black/African American, 0.2% Asian, 0.3% American Indian/Alaska Native, 0.0% Native Hawaiian/Other Pacific Islander, 1.6% two or more races, 4.3% Hispanic of any race; Average household size: 2.51; Median age: 40.0; Age under 18: 25.2%; Age 65 and over: 14.8%; Males per 100 females: 97.9; Marriage status: 21.9% never married, 59.8% now married, 1.0% separated, 8.3% widowed, 10.0% divorced; Foreign born: 1.1%; Speak English only: 96.2%; With disability: 15.5%; Veterans: 10.4%; Ancestry: 36.3% German, 11.9% Irish, 11.0% American, 8.4% English, 3.2% French
Religion: Six largest groups: 23.1% Catholicism, 9.4% Methodist/Pietist, 4.5% Baptist, 4.4% Lutheran, 4.4% Holiness, 2.7% European Free-Church
Economy: Unemployment rate: 3.9%; Leading industries: 16.6% retail trade; 12.8% manufacturing; 12.5% other services (except public administration); Farms: 676 totaling 220,878 acres; Company size: 0 employ 1,000 or more persons, 0 employ 500 to 999 persons, 5 employ 100 to 499 persons, 291 employs less than 100 persons; Business ownership: 192 women-owned, n/a Black-owned, n/a Hispanic-owned, n/a Asian-owned
Employment: 10.1% management, business, and financial, 1.5% computer, engineering, and science, 5.4% education, legal, community service, arts, and media, 6.2% healthcare practitioners, 14.7% service, 20.6% sales and office, 10.2% natural resources, construction, and maintenance, 31.4% production, transportation, and material moving
Income: Per capita: $22,714; Median household: $44,861; Average household: $57,147; Households with income of $100,000 or more: 12.0%; Poverty rate: 13.7%
Educational Attainment: High school diploma or higher: 88.6%; Bachelor's degree or higher: 12.1%; Graduate/professional degree or higher: 4.7%
Housing: Homeownership rate: 79.1%; Median home value: $92,300; Median year structure built: 1969; Homeowner vacancy rate: 2.2%; Median gross rent: $582 per month; Rental vacancy rate: 11.1%
Vital Statistics: Birth rate: 120.0 per 10,000 population; Death rate: 90.9 per 10,000 population; Age-adjusted cancer mortality rate: 246.7 deaths per 100,000 population
Health Insurance: 91.7% have insurance; 71.7% have private insurance; 35.8% have public insurance; 8.3% do not have insurance; 2.9% of children under 18 do not have insurance
Health Care: Physicians: 4.1 per 10,000 population; Hospital beds: 12.9 per 10,000 population; Hospital admissions: 270.1 per 10,000 population
Transportation: Commute: 93.7% car, 0.5% public transportation, 1.5% walk, 4.1% work from home; Median travel time to work: 23.1 minutes
Presidential Election: 38.5% Obama, 58.9% Romney (2012)
Additional Information Contacts
Paulding Government . . . . (419) 399-8215

Paulding County Communities

ANTWERP (village). Covers a land area of 1.334 square miles and a water area of <.001 square miles. Located at 41.18° N. Lat; 84.74° W. Long. Elevation is 728 feet.
Population: 1,736; Growth (since 2000): -0.2%; Density: 1,301.7 persons per square mile; Race: 96.6% White, 0.7% Black/African American, 0.1% Asian, 0.1% American Indian/Alaska Native, 0.0% Native Hawaiian/Other Pacific Islander, 1.4% Two or more races, 4.8% Hispanic of any race; Average household size: 2.31; Median age: 37.9; Age under 18: 26.3%; Age 65 and over: 15.7%; Males per 100 females: 92.9

School District(s)

Antwerp Local (PK-12)
2012-13 Enrollment: 635. . . . . (419) 258-5421
Housing: Homeownership rate: 64.2%; Homeowner vacancy rate: 2.2%; Rental vacancy rate: 12.9%
Newspapers: Antwerp Bee-Argus (weekly circulation 1000)

BROUGHTON (village). Covers a land area of 0.217 square miles and a water area of 0 square miles. Located at 41.09° N. Lat; 84.53° W. Long. Elevation is 725 feet.
Population: 120; Growth (since 2000): -27.7%; Density: 552.3 persons per square mile; Race: 97.5% White, 0.0% Black/African American, 0.0% Asian, 1.7% American Indian/Alaska Native, 0.0% Native Hawaiian/Other Pacific Islander, 0.0% Two or more races, 0.8% Hispanic of any race; Average household size: 2.45; Median age: 50.2; Age under 18: 15.0%; Age 65 and over: 20.0%; Males per 100 females: 100.0
Housing: Homeownership rate: 89.8%; Homeowner vacancy rate: 0.0%; Rental vacancy rate: 0.0%

CECIL (village). Covers a land area of 1.462 square miles and a water area of <.001 square miles. Located at 41.22° N. Lat; 84.60° W. Long. Elevation is 722 feet.
Population: 188; Growth (since 2000): -13.0%; Density: 128.6 persons per square mile; Race: 94.7% White, 2.7% Black/African American, 0.0% Asian, 0.5% American Indian/Alaska Native, 0.0% Native Hawaiian/Other Pacific Islander, 2.1% Two or more races, 4.8% Hispanic of any race; Average household size: 2.65; Median age: 37.5; Age under 18: 27.7%; Age 65 and over: 9.6%; Males per 100 females: 121.2
Housing: Homeownership rate: 70.4%; Homeowner vacancy rate: 5.6%; Rental vacancy rate: 8.3%

GROVER HILL (village). Covers a land area of 0.275 square miles and a water area of 0 square miles. Located at 41.02° N. Lat; 84.48° W. Long. Elevation is 725 feet.
Population: 402; Growth (since 2000): -2.4%; Density: 1,461.3 persons per square mile; Race: 98.5% White, 0.2% Black/African American, 0.0% Asian, 0.0% American Indian/Alaska Native, 0.0% Native Hawaiian/Other Pacific Islander, 1.2% Two or more races, 1.0% Hispanic of any race; Average household size: 2.53; Median age: 37.1; Age under 18: 28.6%; Age 65 and over: 14.9%; Males per 100 females: 104.1

School District(s)

Wayne Trace Local (PK-12)
2012-13 Enrollment: 902. . . . . (419) 263-2415
Housing: Homeownership rate: 79.2%; Homeowner vacancy rate: 2.3%; Rental vacancy rate: 5.7%

HAVILAND (village). Covers a land area of 0.393 square miles and a water area of 0 square miles. Located at 41.02° N. Lat; 84.59° W. Long. Elevation is 735 feet.
Population: 215; Growth (since 2000): 19.4%; Density: 546.8 persons per square mile; Race: 96.3% White, 0.5% Black/African American, 0.0% Asian, 0.0% American Indian/Alaska Native, 0.0% Native Hawaiian/Other Pacific Islander, 0.9% Two or more races, 5.6% Hispanic of any race; Average household size: 2.72; Median age: 34.9; Age under 18: 26.5%; Age 65 and over: 13.0%; Males per 100 females: 92.0

School District(s)

Wayne Trace Local (PK-12)
2012-13 Enrollment: 902. . . . . (419) 263-2415
Housing: Homeownership rate: 76.0%; Homeowner vacancy rate: 0.0%; Rental vacancy rate: 0.0%

LATTY (village). Covers a land area of 0.269 square miles and a water area of 0 square miles. Located at 41.09° N. Lat; 84.58° W. Long. Elevation is 728 feet.
Population: 193; Growth (since 2000): -3.5%; Density: 718.2 persons per square mile; Race: 88.6% White, 5.2% Black/African American, 0.0% Asian, 3.1% American Indian/Alaska Native, 0.0% Native Hawaiian/Other Pacific Islander, 3.1% Two or more races, 3.6% Hispanic of any race; Average household size: 2.76; Median age: 37.3; Age under 18: 28.5%; Age 65 and over: 9.8%; Males per 100 females: 101.0
Housing: Homeownership rate: 90.0%; Homeowner vacancy rate: 4.5%; Rental vacancy rate: 0.0%

MELROSE (village). Covers a land area of 0.856 square miles and a water area of 0 square miles. Located at 41.09° N. Lat; 84.42° W. Long. Elevation is 709 feet.
Population: 275; Growth (since 2000): -14.6%; Density: 321.2 persons per square mile; Race: 99.3% White, 0.0% Black/African American, 0.4% Asian, 0.0% American Indian/Alaska Native, 0.0% Native Hawaiian/Other Pacific Islander, 0.4% Two or more races, 2.5% Hispanic of any race; Average household size: 2.70; Median age: 33.8; Age under 18: 30.5%; Age 65 and over: 12.0%; Males per 100 females: 93.7
Housing: Homeownership rate: 70.6%; Homeowner vacancy rate: 0.0%; Rental vacancy rate: 9.1%

OAKWOOD (village). Covers a land area of 0.588 square miles and a water area of 0 square miles. Located at 41.09° N. Lat; 84.38° W. Long. Elevation is 709 feet.
Population: 608; Growth (since 2000): 0.2%; Density: 1,033.9 persons per square mile; Race: 96.9% White, 0.0% Black/African American, 0.0% Asian, 0.2% American Indian/Alaska Native, 0.0% Native Hawaiian/Other Pacific Islander, 2.1% Two or more races, 4.3% Hispanic of any race; Average household size: 2.67; Median age: 33.4; Age under 18: 28.1%; Age 65 and over: 14.5%; Males per 100 females: 101.3

School District(s)

Paulding Exempted Village (PK-12)
2012-13 Enrollment: 1,492 . . . . (419) 399-4656
Housing: Homeownership rate: 69.3%; Homeowner vacancy rate: 1.8%; Rental vacancy rate: 4.1%

PAULDING (village). County seat. Covers a land area of 2.364 square miles and a water area of 0.098 square miles. Located at 41.14° N. Lat; 84.58° W. Long. Elevation is 722 feet.
Population: 3,605; Growth (since 2000): 0.3%; Density: 1,525.1 persons per square mile; Race: 91.6% White, 2.4% Black/African American, 0.3% Asian, 0.3% American Indian/Alaska Native, 0.0% Native Hawaiian/Other Pacific Islander, 2.6% Two or more races, 8.5% Hispanic of any race; Average household size: 2.35; Median age: 38.4; Age under 18: 25.2%; Age 65 and over: 16.0%; Males per 100 females: 87.2; Marriage status: 28.0% never married, 54.8% now married, 0.0% separated, 9.6% widowed, 7.6% divorced; Foreign born: 3.3%; Speak English only: 91.8%; With disability: 17.4%; Veterans: 7.6%; Ancestry: 30.6% German, 11.4% American, 9.4% Irish, 5.3% English, 3.4% Italian
Employment: 7.7% management, business, and financial, 0.6% computer, engineering, and science, 5.2% education, legal, community service, arts, and media, 5.0% healthcare practitioners, 13.8% service, 24.5% sales and office, 9.2% natural resources, construction, and maintenance, 34.1% production, transportation, and material moving
Income: Per capita: $19,830; Median household: $36,610; Average household: $47,882; Households with income of $100,000 or more: 8.1%; Poverty rate: 18.4%
Educational Attainment: High school diploma or higher: 87.0%; Bachelor's degree or higher: 13.1%; Graduate/professional degree or higher: 6.9%

School District(s)

Paulding Exempted Village (PK-12)
2012-13 Enrollment: 1,492 . . . . (419) 399-4656
Housing: Homeownership rate: 64.2%; Median home value: $83,900; Median year structure built: 1969; Homeowner vacancy rate: 4.4%; Median gross rent: $555 per month; Rental vacancy rate: 13.6%
Health Insurance: 89.3% have insurance; 67.8% have private insurance; 37.6% have public insurance; 10.7% do not have insurance; 6.8% of children under 18 do not have insurance
Hospitals: Paulding County Hospital (25 beds)
Safety: Violent crime rate: 0.0 per 10,000 population; Property crime rate: 45.4 per 10,000 population
Newspapers: Paulding Progress (weekly circulation 4200)
Transportation: Commute: 92.6% car, 1.5% public transportation, 3.3% walk, 2.6% work from home; Median travel time to work: 18.7 minutes

PAYNE (village). Covers a land area of 0.677 square miles and a water area of 0 square miles. Located at 41.08° N. Lat; 84.73° W. Long. Elevation is 748 feet.
Population: 1,194; Growth (since 2000): 2.4%; Density: 1,763.2 persons per square mile; Race: 95.5% White, 0.4% Black/African American, 0.1% Asian, 0.1% American Indian/Alaska Native, 0.1% Native Hawaiian/Other Pacific Islander, 1.8% Two or more races, 4.0% Hispanic of any race; Average household size: 2.36; Median age: 39.4; Age under 18: 25.3%; Age 65 and over: 19.4%; Males per 100 females: 89.5

School District(s)

Wayne Trace Local (PK-12)
2012-13 Enrollment: 902. . . . . (419) 263-2415
Housing: Homeownership rate: 72.1%; Homeowner vacancy rate: 3.0%; Rental vacancy rate: 15.2%

Perry County

Located in central Ohio; drained by Rush, Sunday, Jonathan, and Moxahala Creeks; includes part of Buckeye Lake. Covers a land area of 407.971 square miles, a water area of 4.515 square miles, and is located in the Eastern Time Zone at 39.74° N. Lat., 82.24° W. Long. The county was founded in 1817. County seat is New Lexington.

Perry County is part of the Columbus, OH Metropolitan Statistical Area. The entire metro area includes: Delaware County, OH; Fairfield County, OH; Franklin County, OH; Hocking County, OH; Licking County, OH; Madison County, OH; Morrow County, OH; Perry County, OH; Pickaway County, OH; Union County, OH

Weather Station: New Lexington 2 NW Elevation: 890 feet

	Jan	Feb	Mar	Apr	May	Jun	Jul	Aug	Sep	Oct	Nov	Dec
High	37	41	51	64	73	81	84	83	77	65	53	41
Low	18	20	27	37	47	56	61	59	51	39	31	23
Precip	3.0	2.5	3.6	3.9	4.6	4.0	4.7	3.2	3.0	3.0	3.4	3.0
Snow	7.9	5.2	2.8	0.3	tr	0.0	0.0	0.0	0.0	tr	0.5	3.0

High and Low temperatures in degrees Fahrenheit; Precipitation and Snow in inches

Population: 36,058; Growth (since 2000): 5.8%; Density: 88.4 persons per square mile; Race: 97.9% White, 0.3% Black/African American, 0.1% Asian, 0.2% American Indian/Alaska Native, 0.0% Native Hawaiian/Other Pacific Islander, 1.4% two or more races, 0.5% Hispanic of any race; Average household size: 2.63; Median age: 38.6; Age under 18: 26.2%; Age 65 and over: 12.9%; Males per 100 females: 99.4; Marriage status: 24.6% never married, 57.9% now married, 2.4% separated, 6.6% widowed, 11.0% divorced; Foreign born: 0.4%; Speak English only: 98.8%; With disability: 16.3%; Veterans: 10.3%; Ancestry: 24.0% German, 12.5% Irish, 10.7% American, 8.4% English, 3.6% Italian
Religion: Six largest groups: 8.3% Catholicism, 7.1% Methodist/Pietist, 3.4% Baptist, 2.6% Non-denominational Protestant, 1.8% Lutheran, 1.4% Presbyterian-Reformed
Economy: Unemployment rate: 5.3%; Leading industries: 16.6% retail trade; 14.3% health care and social assistance; 11.9% other services (except public administration); Farms: 699 totaling 107,224 acres; Company size: 0 employ 1,000 or more persons, 0 employ 500 to 999 persons, 6 employ 100 to 499 persons, 421 employs less than 100 persons; Business ownership: 1,009 women-owned, n/a Black-owned, n/a Hispanic-owned, n/a Asian-owned

Employment: 9.6% management, business, and financial, 2.1% computer, engineering, and science, 7.6% education, legal, community service, arts, and media, 5.5% healthcare practitioners, 21.0% service, 19.7% sales and office, 13.4% natural resources, construction, and maintenance, 21.1% production, transportation, and material moving
Income: Per capita: $19,372; Median household: $41,446; Average household: $50,003; Households with income of $100,000 or more: 10.0%; Poverty rate: 19.6%
Educational Attainment: High school diploma or higher: 84.2%; Bachelor's degree or higher: 10.2%; Graduate/professional degree or higher: 3.6%
Housing: Homeownership rate: 75.3%; Median home value: $93,100; Median year structure built: 1973; Homeowner vacancy rate: 1.9%; Median gross rent: $583 per month; Rental vacancy rate: 7.4%
Vital Statistics: Birth rate: 118.3 per 10,000 population; Death rate: 98.1 per 10,000 population; Age-adjusted cancer mortality rate: 265.8 deaths per 100,000 population
Health Insurance: 86.2% have insurance; 62.8% have private insurance; 36.0% have public insurance; 13.8% do not have insurance; 5.2% of children under 18 do not have insurance
Health Care: Physicians: 3.1 per 10,000 population; Hospital beds: 0.0 per 10,000 population; Hospital admissions: 0.0 per 10,000 population
Transportation: Commute: 94.2% car, 0.3% public transportation, 2.1% walk, 2.7% work from home; Median travel time to work: 34.7 minutes
Presidential Election: 46.7% Obama, 51.1% Romney (2012)
National and State Parks: Avondale State Wildlife Area; Perry State Forest
Additional Information Contacts
Perry Government . . . . (740) 342-2045
http://www.perrycountyohiocofc.com/govnment.htm

Perry County Communities

CORNING (village). Covers a land area of 0.431 square miles and a water area of 0 square miles. Located at 39.60° N. Lat; 82.09° W. Long. Elevation is 732 feet.
Population: 583; Growth (since 2000): -1.7%; Density: 1,351.1 persons per square mile; Race: 97.3% White, 0.5% Black/African American, 0.0% Asian, 0.3% American Indian/Alaska Native, 0.0% Native Hawaiian/Other Pacific Islander, 1.9% Two or more races, 0.3% Hispanic of any race; Average household size: 2.58; Median age: 30.9; Age under 18: 30.0%; Age 65 and over: 13.7%; Males per 100 females: 95.6

School District(s)

Southern Local (PK-12)
2012-13 Enrollment: 664 . . . . (740) 394-2402
Housing: Homeownership rate: 69.9%; Homeowner vacancy rate: 3.6%; Rental vacancy rate: 6.8%

CROOKSVILLE (village). Covers a land area of 1.624 square miles and a water area of 0.021 square miles. Located at 39.77° N. Lat; 82.10° W. Long. Elevation is 791 feet.
Population: 2,534; Growth (since 2000): 2.1%; Density: 1,560.4 persons per square mile; Race: 98.5% White, 0.1% Black/African American, 0.1% Asian, 0.1% American Indian/Alaska Native, 0.0% Native Hawaiian/Other Pacific Islander, 0.9% Two or more races, 0.7% Hispanic of any race; Average household size: 2.59; Median age: 34.4; Age under 18: 29.7%; Age 65 and over: 12.8%; Males per 100 females: 92.8; Marriage status: 24.2% never married, 54.4% now married, 2.8% separated, 6.7% widowed, 14.8% divorced; Foreign born: 0.6%; Speak English only: 98.2%; With disability: 19.1%; Veterans: 10.1%; Ancestry: 23.0% German, 15.5% Irish, 13.8% American, 10.6% English, 3.2% French
Employment: 6.1% management, business, and financial, 3.8% computer, engineering, and science, 3.9% education, legal, community service, arts, and media, 4.7% healthcare practitioners, 23.0% service, 23.2% sales and office, 9.1% natural resources, construction, and maintenance, 26.1% production, transportation, and material moving
Income: Per capita: $15,226; Median household: $31,447; Average household: $35,567; Households with income of $100,000 or more: 2.1%; Poverty rate: 20.6%
Educational Attainment: High school diploma or higher: 82.5%; Bachelor's degree or higher: 8.0%; Graduate/professional degree or higher: 1.9%

School District(s)

Crooksville Exempted Village (PK-12)
2012-13 Enrollment: 1,090 . . . . (740) 982-7040
Housing: Homeownership rate: 61.1%; Median home value: $68,700; Median year structure built: 1942; Homeowner vacancy rate: 3.4%; Median gross rent: $471 per month; Rental vacancy rate: 11.0%
Health Insurance: 83.4% have insurance; 57.9% have private insurance; 44.7% have public insurance; 16.6% do not have insurance; 9.0% of children under 18 do not have insurance
Transportation: Commute: 83.1% car, 0.0% public transportation, 13.5% walk, 0.7% work from home; Median travel time to work: 30.1 minutes
Additional Information Contacts
Village of Crooksville . . . . (740) 982-2656
http://www.crooksville.com

GLENFORD (village). Covers a land area of 0.113 square miles and a water area of 0.002 square miles. Located at 39.89° N. Lat; 82.32° W. Long. Elevation is 846 feet.
History: Glenford was established near a prehistoric fortification known as Glenford Fort. A stone wall 7-10 feet high and 6,600 feet long enclosed an area with a central mound.
Population: 173; Growth (since 2000): -12.6%; Density: 1,534.0 persons per square mile; Race: 98.3% White, 0.6% Black/African American, 0.6% Asian, 0.0% American Indian/Alaska Native, 0.0% Native Hawaiian/Other Pacific Islander, 0.6% Two or more races, 0.0% Hispanic of any race; Average household size: 2.84; Median age: 32.1; Age under 18: 30.1%; Age 65 and over: 6.9%; Males per 100 females: 103.5

School District(s)

Northern Local (PK-12)
2012-13 Enrollment: 2,122 . . . . (740) 743-1303
Housing: Homeownership rate: 73.8%; Homeowner vacancy rate: 0.0%; Rental vacancy rate: 11.1%

HEMLOCK (village). Covers a land area of 0.372 square miles and a water area of 0.002 square miles. Located at 39.59° N. Lat; 82.15° W. Long. Elevation is 764 feet.
Population: 155; Growth (since 2000): 9.2%; Density: 416.4 persons per square mile; Race: 100.0% White, 0.0% Black/African American, 0.0% Asian, 0.0% American Indian/Alaska Native, 0.0% Native Hawaiian/Other Pacific Islander, 0.0% Two or more races, 0.0% Hispanic of any race; Average household size: 2.77; Median age: 39.4; Age under 18: 25.2%; Age 65 and over: 11.6%; Males per 100 females: 98.7
Housing: Homeownership rate: 75.0%; Homeowner vacancy rate: 2.1%; Rental vacancy rate: 17.6%

JUNCTION CITY (village). Covers a land area of 0.633 square miles and a water area of 0.005 square miles. Located at 39.72° N. Lat; 82.30° W. Long. Elevation is 840 feet.
Population: 819; Growth (since 2000): 0.1%; Density: 1,293.7 persons per square mile; Race: 97.3% White, 0.2% Black/African American, 0.1% Asian, 0.1% American Indian/Alaska Native, 0.0% Native Hawaiian/Other Pacific Islander, 1.8% Two or more races, 1.0% Hispanic of any race; Average household size: 2.60; Median age: 35.5; Age under 18: 26.6%; Age 65 and over: 11.4%; Males per 100 females: 101.7

School District(s)

New Lexington City (PK-12)
2012-13 Enrollment: 1,893 . . . . (740) 342-4133
Housing: Homeownership rate: 57.5%; Homeowner vacancy rate: 3.2%; Rental vacancy rate: 3.6%

MOUNT PERRY (unincorporated postal area)
ZCTA: 43760
Covers a land area of 34.670 square miles and a water area of 0.059 square miles. Located at 39.89° N. Lat; 82.19° W. Long. Elevation is 846 feet.
Population: 1,831; Growth (since 2000): 4.7%; Density: 52.8 persons per square mile; Race: 96.7% White, 0.4% Black/African American, 0.3% Asian, 0.4% American Indian/Alaska Native, 0.0% Native Hawaiian/Other Pacific Islander, 2.2% Two or more races, 0.3% Hispanic of any race; Average household size: 2.83; Median age: 38.6; Age under 18: 27.6%; Age 65 and over: 11.9%; Males per 100 females: 107.4
Housing: Homeownership rate: 84.9%; Homeowner vacancy rate: 0.5%; Rental vacancy rate: 10.0%

MOXAHALA (unincorporated postal area)

ZCTA: 43761

Covers a land area of 0.621 square miles and a water area of 0.007 square miles. Located at 39.67° N. Lat; 82.15° W. Long. Elevation is 817 feet.

Population: 111; Growth (since 2000): n/a; Density: 178.7 persons per square mile; Race: 100.0% White, 0.0% Black/African American, 0.0% Asian, 0.0% American Indian/Alaska Native, 0.0% Native Hawaiian/Other Pacific Islander, 0.0% Two or more races, 0.0% Hispanic of any race; Average household size: 2.52; Median age: 37.8; Age under 18: 20.7%; Age 65 and over: 12.6%; Males per 100 females: 101.8

Housing: Homeownership rate: 77.3%; Homeowner vacancy rate: 0.0%; Rental vacancy rate: 0.0%

NEW LEXINGTON (village). County seat. Covers a land area of 1.947 square miles and a water area of 0.002 square miles. Located at 39.72° N. Lat; 82.21° W. Long. Elevation is 958 feet.

History: New Lexington developed around the tile and pottery works, which used the excellent clays found in the vicinity.

Population: 4,731; Growth (since 2000): 0.9%; Density: 2,429.5 persons per square mile; Race: 97.9% White, 0.5% Black/African American, 0.1% Asian, 0.2% American Indian/Alaska Native, 0.1% Native Hawaiian/Other Pacific Islander, 1.1% Two or more races, 0.6% Hispanic of any race; Average household size: 2.53; Median age: 33.8; Age under 18: 28.2%; Age 65 and over: 13.3%; Males per 100 females: 89.6; Marriage status: 33.2% never married, 45.8% now married, 2.3% separated, 7.5% widowed, 13.4% divorced; Foreign born: 0.0%; Speak English only: 98.1%; With disability: 18.3%; Veterans: 7.7%; Ancestry: 17.2% German, 15.4% American, 8.3% Irish, 5.5% English, 2.2% Welsh

Employment: 8.9% management, business, and financial, 1.4% computer, engineering, and science, 6.9% education, legal, community service, arts, and media, 8.6% healthcare practitioners, 23.5% service, 19.7% sales and office, 8.0% natural resources, construction, and maintenance, 23.2% production, transportation, and material moving

Income: Per capita: $15,351; Median household: $32,277; Average household: $40,786; Households with income of $100,000 or more: 3.1%; Poverty rate: 28.3%

Educational Attainment: High school diploma or higher: 84.3%; Bachelor's degree or higher: 6.6%; Graduate/professional degree or higher: 3.4%

School District(s)

New Lexington City (PK-12)
2012-13 Enrollment: 1,893 . . . . (740) 342-4133

Housing: Homeownership rate: 55.6%; Median home value: $82,600; Median year structure built: 1953; Homeowner vacancy rate: 1.3%; Median gross rent: $613 per month; Rental vacancy rate: 7.1%

Health Insurance: 80.7% have insurance; 54.8% have private insurance; 38.5% have public insurance; 19.3% do not have insurance; 8.2% of children under 18 do not have insurance

Safety: Violent crime rate: 27.4 per 10,000 population; Property crime rate: 385.3 per 10,000 population

Newspapers: Perry Co Tribune (weekly circulation 3800)

Transportation: Commute: 95.2% car, 0.2% public transportation, 3.9% walk, 0.8% work from home; Median travel time to work: 33.5 minutes

Additional Information Contacts

City of New Lexington . . . . (740) 342-2177
http://www.newlexington.org

NEW STRAITSVILLE (village). Covers a land area of 1.300 square miles and a water area of 0.001 square miles. Located at 39.58° N. Lat; 82.23° W. Long. Elevation is 794 feet.

History: New Straitsville was laid out in 1870 by a mining company. An undergound coal fire began to burn here in 1884, when some desperate miners set fire to loaded coal cars and pushed them down five mine shafts.

Population: 722; Growth (since 2000): -6.7%; Density: 555.6 persons per square mile; Race: 95.7% White, 0.4% Black/African American, 0.0% Asian, 0.0% American Indian/Alaska Native, 0.0% Native Hawaiian/Other Pacific Islander, 3.9% Two or more races, 0.7% Hispanic of any race; Average household size: 2.46; Median age: 37.4; Age under 18: 25.6%; Age 65 and over: 11.8%; Males per 100 females: 84.2

Housing: Homeownership rate: 65.6%; Homeowner vacancy rate: 2.4%; Rental vacancy rate: 20.3%

RENDVILLE (village). Covers a land area of 0.312 square miles and a water area of 0.001 square miles. Located at 39.62° N. Lat; 82.09° W. Long. Elevation is 748 feet.

Population: 36; Growth (since 2000): -21.7%; Density: 115.5 persons per square mile; Race: 80.6% White, 8.3% Black/African American, 0.0% Asian, 0.0% American Indian/Alaska Native, 0.0% Native Hawaiian/Other Pacific Islander, 11.1% Two or more races, 0.0% Hispanic of any race; Average household size: 2.00; Median age: 54.5; Age under 18: 11.1%; Age 65 and over: 27.8%; Males per 100 females: 80.0

Housing: Homeownership rate: 88.9%; Homeowner vacancy rate: 0.0%; Rental vacancy rate: 0.0%

ROSEVILLE (village). Covers a land area of 0.700 square miles and a water area of 0.005 square miles. Located at 39.81° N. Lat; 82.08° W. Long.

Population: 1,852; Growth (since 2000): -4.3%; Density: 2,644.9 persons per square mile; Race: 97.5% White, 0.5% Black/African American, 0.2% Asian, 0.2% American Indian/Alaska Native, 0.0% Native Hawaiian/Other Pacific Islander, 1.5% Two or more races, 0.6% Hispanic of any race; Average household size: 2.65; Median age: 33.7; Age under 18: 29.2%; Age 65 and over: 11.7%; Males per 100 females: 94.3

School District(s)

Franklin Local (PK-12)
2012-13 Enrollment: 2,046 . . . . (740) 674-5203
Franklin Local Community School (07-12)
2012-13 Enrollment: 87. . . . . (740) 697-7317

Housing: Homeownership rate: 64.1%; Homeowner vacancy rate: 6.1%; Rental vacancy rate: 7.7%

Safety: Violent crime rate: 10.8 per 10,000 population; Property crime rate: 140.2 per 10,000 population

SHAWNEE (village). Covers a land area of 2.247 square miles and a water area of 0.014 square miles. Located at 39.61° N. Lat; 82.20° W. Long. Elevation is 850 feet.

Population: 655; Growth (since 2000): 7.7%; Density: 291.5 persons per square mile; Race: 98.0% White, 0.2% Black/African American, 0.0% Asian, 0.0% American Indian/Alaska Native, 0.0% Native Hawaiian/Other Pacific Islander, 1.8% Two or more races, 0.3% Hispanic of any race; Average household size: 2.79; Median age: 34.9; Age under 18: 27.8%; Age 65 and over: 11.3%; Males per 100 females: 110.6

Housing: Homeownership rate: 79.6%; Homeowner vacancy rate: 2.1%; Rental vacancy rate: 21.3%

SOMERSET (village). Covers a land area of 1.163 square miles and a water area of 0.003 square miles. Located at 39.81° N. Lat; 82.30° W. Long. Elevation is 1,083 feet.

History: Somerset was laid out in 1810 by John Fink and Jacob Miller, and served as the seat of Perry County from 1829 to 1857. Civil War general Philip Henry Sheridan spent his boyhood in Somerset.

Population: 1,481; Growth (since 2000): -4.4%; Density: 1,273.2 persons per square mile; Race: 98.3% White, 0.3% Black/African American, 0.1% Asian, 0.0% American Indian/Alaska Native, 0.1% Native Hawaiian/Other Pacific Islander, 1.1% Two or more races, 0.6% Hispanic of any race; Average household size: 2.31; Median age: 41.1; Age under 18: 25.3%; Age 65 and over: 17.0%; Males per 100 females: 92.3

School District(s)

Northern Local (PK-12)
2012-13 Enrollment: 2,122 . . . . (740) 743-1303

Housing: Homeownership rate: 57.2%; Homeowner vacancy rate: 3.3%; Rental vacancy rate: 4.0%

THORNPORT (CDP). Covers a land area of 1.221 square miles and a water area of 0.467 square miles. Located at 39.92° N. Lat; 82.43° W. Long. Elevation is 899 feet.

Population: 1,004; Growth (since 2000): n/a; Density: 822.0 persons per square mile; Race: 97.9% White, 0.2% Black/African American, 0.5% Asian, 0.3% American Indian/Alaska Native, 0.0% Native Hawaiian/Other Pacific Islander, 0.6% Two or more races, 0.2% Hispanic of any race; Average household size: 2.25; Median age: 50.4; Age under 18: 16.8%; Age 65 and over: 21.1%; Males per 100 females: 99.6

Housing: Homeownership rate: 78.5%; Homeowner vacancy rate: 6.9%; Rental vacancy rate: 4.0%

THORNVILLE (village). Covers a land area of 1.104 square miles and a water area of 0.004 square miles. Located at 39.89° N. Lat; 82.41° W. Long. Elevation is 1,030 feet.
Population: 991; Growth (since 2000): 35.6%; Density: 897.9 persons per square mile; Race: 98.8% White, 0.1% Black/African American, 0.1% Asian, 0.1% American Indian/Alaska Native, 0.0% Native Hawaiian/Other Pacific Islander, 0.9% Two or more races, 0.0% Hispanic of any race; Average household size: 2.38; Median age: 39.7; Age under 18: 25.1%; Age 65 and over: 16.0%; Males per 100 females: 91.7

School District(s)

Northern Local (PK-12)
2012-13 Enrollment: 2,122 . . . . (740) 743-1303
Housing: Homeownership rate: 63.3%; Homeowner vacancy rate: 1.5%; Rental vacancy rate: 8.2%

Pickaway County

Located in south central Ohio; crossed by the Scioto River. Covers a land area of 501.320 square miles, a water area of 5.232 square miles, and is located in the Eastern Time Zone at 39.65° N. Lat., 83.05° W. Long. The county was founded in 1810. County seat is Circleville.

Pickaway County is part of the Columbus, OH Metropolitan Statistical Area. The entire metro area includes: Delaware County, OH; Fairfield County, OH; Franklin County, OH; Hocking County, OH; Licking County, OH; Madison County, OH; Morrow County, OH; Perry County, OH; Pickaway County, OH; Union County, OH

Weather Station: Circleville Elevation: 672 feet

	Jan	Feb	Mar	Apr	May	Jun	Jul	Aug	Sep	Oct	Nov	Dec
High	38	41	51	64	73	82	85	84	78	66	54	41
Low	22	23	31	41	51	60	63	62	54	43	34	26
Precip	2.6	2.2	3.0	3.5	4.8	3.7	4.0	3.4	2.9	3.0	3.0	2.8
Snow	5.5	3.9	1.7	0.4	0.0	0.0	0.0	0.0	0.0	0.0	0.3	2.1

High and Low temperatures in degrees Fahrenheit; Precipitation and Snow in inches

Population: 55,698; Growth (since 2000): 5.6%; Density: 111.1 persons per square mile; Race: 94.5% White, 3.4% Black/African American, 0.4% Asian, 0.2% American Indian/Alaska Native, 0.0% Native Hawaiian/Other Pacific Islander, 1.2% two or more races, 1.1% Hispanic of any race; Average household size: 2.61; Median age: 38.5; Age under 18: 23.6%; Age 65 and over: 12.8%; Males per 100 females: 110.4; Marriage status: 26.7% never married, 55.2% now married, 2.2% separated, 5.8% widowed, 12.3% divorced; Foreign born: 0.6%; Speak English only: 98.4%; With disability: 15.1%; Veterans: 10.1%; Ancestry: 29.1% German, 16.8% American, 15.4% Irish, 11.4% English, 4.0% Dutch
Religion: Six largest groups: 6.9% Methodist/Pietist, 3.4% Baptist, 3.1% Catholicism, 2.1% Lutheran, 1.8% Holiness, 1.4% Non-denominational Protestant
Economy: Unemployment rate: 4.9%; Leading industries: 15.6% retail trade; 11.7% construction; 10.6% health care and social assistance; Farms: 803 totaling 293,684 acres; Company size: 0 employ 1,000 or more persons, 2 employ 500 to 999 persons, 19 employ 100 to 499 persons, 782 employ less than 100 persons; Business ownership: 941 women-owned, n/a Black-owned, n/a Hispanic-owned, n/a Asian-owned
Employment: 13.4% management, business, and financial, 3.4% computer, engineering, and science, 9.2% education, legal, community service, arts, and media, 5.2% healthcare practitioners, 18.3% service, 23.5% sales and office, 10.4% natural resources, construction, and maintenance, 16.7% production, transportation, and material moving
Income: Per capita: $23,851; Median household: $54,003; Average household: $67,287; Households with income of $100,000 or more: 19.6%; Poverty rate: 13.3%
Educational Attainment: High school diploma or higher: 84.9%; Bachelor's degree or higher: 16.1%; Graduate/professional degree or higher: 5.3%
Housing: Homeownership rate: 74.2%; Median home value: $149,200; Median year structure built: 1976; Homeowner vacancy rate: 2.2%; Median gross rent: $732 per month; Rental vacancy rate: 10.7%
Vital Statistics: Birth rate: 97.7 per 10,000 population; Death rate: 92.2 per 10,000 population; Age-adjusted cancer mortality rate: 179.2 deaths per 100,000 population
Health Insurance: 90.3% have insurance; 71.2% have private insurance; 31.1% have public insurance; 9.7% do not have insurance; 4.2% of children under 18 do not have insurance
Health Care: Physicians: 7.5 per 10,000 population; Hospital beds: 14.1 per 10,000 population; Hospital admissions: 483.7 per 10,000 population
Transportation: Commute: 94.0% car, 0.4% public transportation, 1.4% walk, 3.7% work from home; Median travel time to work: 27.3 minutes
Presidential Election: 39.8% Obama, 58.5% Romney (2012)
National and State Parks: A W Marion State Park; Logan Elm State Memorial; Stages Pond State Nature Preserve
Additional Information Contacts
Pickaway Government . . . . (740) 474-6093
http://www.pickaway.org

Pickaway County Communities

ASHVILLE (village). Covers a land area of 2.507 square miles and a water area of 0 square miles. Located at 39.72° N. Lat; 82.95° W. Long. Elevation is 712 feet.
Population: 4,097; Growth (since 2000): 29.1%; Density: 1,634.4 persons per square mile; Race: 96.7% White, 1.0% Black/African American, 0.3% Asian, 0.4% American Indian/Alaska Native, 0.0% Native Hawaiian/Other Pacific Islander, 1.4% Two or more races, 1.4% Hispanic of any race; Average household size: 2.56; Median age: 32.8; Age under 18: 29.3%; Age 65 and over: 9.5%; Males per 100 females: 94.1; Marriage status: 22.4% never married, 64.0% now married, 3.2% separated, 3.7% widowed, 9.9% divorced; Foreign born: 1.0%; Speak English only: 96.0%; With disability: 11.8%; Veterans: 8.1%; Ancestry: 22.1% American, 21.4% German, 16.0% Irish, 8.1% English, 4.7% Scottish
Employment: 10.5% management, business, and financial, 5.2% computer, engineering, and science, 9.7% education, legal, community service, arts, and media, 3.2% healthcare practitioners, 21.3% service, 25.8% sales and office, 8.2% natural resources, construction, and maintenance, 16.2% production, transportation, and material moving
Income: Per capita: $21,289; Median household: $51,923; Average household: $61,267; Households with income of $100,000 or more: 17.8%; Poverty rate: 19.9%
Educational Attainment: High school diploma or higher: 83.4%; Bachelor's degree or higher: 16.9%; Graduate/professional degree or higher: 6.9%

School District(s)

Teays Valley Local (PK-12)
2012-13 Enrollment: 3,697 . . . . (740) 983-5000
Housing: Homeownership rate: 54.7%; Median home value: $149,100; Median year structure built: 1983; Homeowner vacancy rate: 3.3%; Median gross rent: $660 per month; Rental vacancy rate: 8.1%
Health Insurance: 90.5% have insurance; 69.0% have private insurance; 27.8% have public insurance; 9.5% do not have insurance; 4.9% of children under 18 do not have insurance
Safety: Violent crime rate: 2.4 per 10,000 population; Property crime rate: 97.1 per 10,000 population
Transportation: Commute: 90.5% car, 0.0% public transportation, 1.0% walk, 7.8% work from home; Median travel time to work: 28.4 minutes
Additional Information Contacts
Village of Ashville . . . . (740) 983-6367
http://ashvilleohio.gov

CIRCLEVILLE (city). County seat. Covers a land area of 6.644 square miles and a water area of 0.121 square miles. Located at 39.60° N. Lat; 82.93° W. Long. Elevation is 696 feet.
History: Named for local circular earthworks made by prehistoric mound builders. Circleville was settled in 1810 on the site of two ancient forts erected by the mound builders, one of them a round enclosure from which Circleville took its name.
Population: 13,314; Growth (since 2000): -1.3%; Density: 2,003.9 persons per square mile; Race: 95.4% White, 1.9% Black/African American, 0.4% Asian, 0.2% American Indian/Alaska Native, 0.0% Native Hawaiian/Other Pacific Islander, 1.7% Two or more races, 1.1% Hispanic of any race; Average household size: 2.36; Median age: 39.3; Age under 18: 23.3%; Age 65 and over: 17.7%; Males per 100 females: 92.0; Marriage status: 27.2% never married, 48.4% now married, 2.1% separated, 9.5% widowed, 14.9% divorced; Foreign born: 0.1%; Speak English only: 98.4%; With disability: 20.4%; Veterans: 11.4%; Ancestry: 31.0% German, 15.0% Irish, 14.5% American, 11.7% English, 3.8% Dutch
Employment: 11.4% management, business, and financial, 1.9% computer, engineering, and science, 9.6% education, legal, community service, arts, and media, 3.7% healthcare practitioners, 23.2% service,

24.5% sales and office, 4.2% natural resources, construction, and maintenance, 21.5% production, transportation, and material moving
Income: Per capita: $20,453; Median household: $38,480; Average household: $49,944; Households with income of $100,000 or more: 10.8%; Poverty rate: 19.8%
Educational Attainment: High school diploma or higher: 83.6%; Bachelor's degree or higher: 13.4%; Graduate/professional degree or higher: 5.0%

School District(s)

Buckeye United SD (08-12)
2012-13 Enrollment: 369. . . . . (614) 466-0720
Circleville City (PK-12)
2012-13 Enrollment: 2,148 . . . . (740) 474-4340
Logan Elm Local (PK-12)
2012-13 Enrollment: 1,988 . . . . (740) 474-7501

Four-year College(s)

Ohio Christian University (Private, Not-for-profit, Other Protestant)
Fall 2013 Enrollment: 3,711 . . . . (740) 474-8896
2013-14 Tuition: In-state $17,720; Out-of-state $17,720
Housing: Homeownership rate: 58.0%; Median home value: $119,100; Median year structure built: 1963; Homeowner vacancy rate: 2.8%; Median gross rent: $731 per month; Rental vacancy rate: 11.9%
Health Insurance: 86.9% have insurance; 59.7% have private insurance; 41.4% have public insurance; 13.1% do not have insurance; 4.8% of children under 18 do not have insurance
Hospitals: Berger Hospital (91 beds)
Safety: Violent crime rate: 17.0 per 10,000 population; Property crime rate: 613.7 per 10,000 population
Newspapers: Circleville Herald (daily circulation 5000)
Transportation: Commute: 93.4% car, 0.5% public transportation, 1.9% walk, 3.5% work from home; Median travel time to work: 24.0 minutes
Additional Information Contacts
City of Circleville . . . . (740) 477-2551
http://www.ci.circleville.oh.us

COMMERCIAL POINT (village). Covers a land area of 1.126 square miles and a water area of 0 square miles. Located at 39.77° N. Lat; 83.06° W. Long. Elevation is 791 feet.
Population: 1,582; Growth (since 2000): 103.9%; Density: 1,405.5 persons per square mile; Race: 94.4% White, 1.3% Black/African American, 1.3% Asian, 0.3% American Indian/Alaska Native, 0.0% Native Hawaiian/Other Pacific Islander, 1.8% Two or more races, 2.0% Hispanic of any race; Average household size: 3.12; Median age: 32.1; Age under 18: 34.8%; Age 65 and over: 6.4%; Males per 100 females: 92.5

School District(s)

Teays Valley Local (PK-12)
2012-13 Enrollment: 3,697 . . . . (740) 983-5000
Housing: Homeownership rate: 89.5%; Homeowner vacancy rate: 3.2%; Rental vacancy rate: 13.1%
Safety: Violent crime rate: 0.0 per 10,000 population; Property crime rate: 113.4 per 10,000 population

DARBYVILLE (village). Covers a land area of 0.465 square miles and a water area of 0.016 square miles. Located at 39.70° N. Lat; 83.11° W. Long. Elevation is 745 feet.
Population: 222; Growth (since 2000): -24.2%; Density: 477.5 persons per square mile; Race: 98.2% White, 0.5% Black/African American, 0.0% Asian, 0.0% American Indian/Alaska Native, 0.0% Native Hawaiian/Other Pacific Islander, 1.4% Two or more races, 0.0% Hispanic of any race; Average household size: 2.81; Median age: 38.4; Age under 18: 26.6%; Age 65 and over: 14.9%; Males per 100 females: 91.4
Housing: Homeownership rate: 65.8%; Homeowner vacancy rate: 7.0%; Rental vacancy rate: 3.6%

DERBY (CDP). Covers a land area of 1.333 square miles and a water area of 0 square miles. Located at 39.76° N. Lat; 83.21° W. Long. Elevation is 915 feet.
Population: 408; Growth (since 2000): n/a; Density: 306.2 persons per square mile; Race: 97.3% White, 0.5% Black/African American, 0.2% Asian, 0.0% American Indian/Alaska Native, 0.0% Native Hawaiian/Other Pacific Islander, 1.7% Two or more races, 0.5% Hispanic of any race; Average household size: 2.76; Median age: 38.3; Age under 18: 26.0%; Age 65 and over: 12.5%; Males per 100 females: 101.0
Housing: Homeownership rate: 71.7%; Homeowner vacancy rate: 0.9%; Rental vacancy rate: 2.3%

LOGAN ELM VILLAGE (CDP). Covers a land area of 0.525 square miles and a water area of <.001 square miles. Located at 39.57° N. Lat; 82.95° W. Long. Elevation is 705 feet.
Population: 1,118; Growth (since 2000): 5.3%; Density: 2,129.6 persons per square mile; Race: 98.4% White, 0.4% Black/African American, 0.5% Asian, 0.2% American Indian/Alaska Native, 0.0% Native Hawaiian/Other Pacific Islander, 0.2% Two or more races, 0.5% Hispanic of any race; Average household size: 2.40; Median age: 45.0; Age under 18: 22.1%; Age 65 and over: 24.4%; Males per 100 females: 85.4
Housing: Homeownership rate: 72.9%; Homeowner vacancy rate: 1.9%; Rental vacancy rate: 3.4%

NEW HOLLAND (village). Covers a land area of 1.880 square miles and a water area of 0 square miles. Located at 39.55° N. Lat; 83.26° W. Long. Elevation is 856 feet.
History: New Holland was founded in 1818, and grew as a center for poultry and hog raising.
Population: 801; Growth (since 2000): 2.0%; Density: 426.0 persons per square mile; Race: 97.6% White, 0.2% Black/African American, 0.2% Asian, 0.4% American Indian/Alaska Native, 0.0% Native Hawaiian/Other Pacific Islander, 0.5% Two or more races, 1.0% Hispanic of any race; Average household size: 2.60; Median age: 41.2; Age under 18: 22.7%; Age 65 and over: 14.5%; Males per 100 females: 101.8
Housing: Homeownership rate: 69.5%; Homeowner vacancy rate: 5.3%; Rental vacancy rate: 11.1%

ORIENT (village). Covers a land area of 0.119 square miles and a water area of 0 square miles. Located at 39.81° N. Lat; 83.15° W. Long. Elevation is 837 feet.
Population: 270; Growth (since 2000): 0.4%; Density: 2,269.6 persons per square mile; Race: 96.3% White, 0.7% Black/African American, 0.0% Asian, 2.2% American Indian/Alaska Native, 0.0% Native Hawaiian/Other Pacific Islander, 0.7% Two or more races, 0.4% Hispanic of any race; Average household size: 2.81; Median age: 38.5; Age under 18: 23.3%; Age 65 and over: 11.5%; Males per 100 females: 106.1
Housing: Homeownership rate: 75.0%; Homeowner vacancy rate: 0.0%; Rental vacancy rate: 0.0%

SOUTH BLOOMFIELD (village). Covers a land area of 4.278 square miles and a water area of 0 square miles. Located at 39.72° N. Lat; 82.99° W. Long. Elevation is 696 feet.
Population: 1,744; Growth (since 2000): 47.9%; Density: 407.7 persons per square mile; Race: 97.1% White, 0.9% Black/African American, 0.2% Asian, 0.3% American Indian/Alaska Native, 0.0% Native Hawaiian/Other Pacific Islander, 1.4% Two or more races, 1.1% Hispanic of any race; Average household size: 2.67; Median age: 34.3; Age under 18: 28.1%; Age 65 and over: 10.1%; Males per 100 females: 95.5

School District(s)

Teays Valley Local (PK-12)
2012-13 Enrollment: 3,697 . . . . (740) 983-5000
Housing: Homeownership rate: 84.7%; Homeowner vacancy rate: 1.9%; Rental vacancy rate: 7.4%
Safety: Violent crime rate: 0.0 per 10,000 population; Property crime rate: 213.7 per 10,000 population

TARLTON (village). Covers a land area of 0.418 square miles and a water area of 0 square miles. Located at 39.55° N. Lat; 82.78° W. Long. Elevation is 902 feet.
History: Tarlton Cross Mound nearby.
Population: 282; Growth (since 2000): -5.4%; Density: 674.8 persons per square mile; Race: 98.9% White, 0.7% Black/African American, 0.0% Asian, 0.0% American Indian/Alaska Native, 0.0% Native Hawaiian/Other Pacific Islander, 0.4% Two or more races, 2.8% Hispanic of any race; Average household size: 2.82; Median age: 39.2; Age under 18: 27.0%; Age 65 and over: 10.3%; Males per 100 females: 90.5
Housing: Homeownership rate: 73.0%; Homeowner vacancy rate: 2.6%; Rental vacancy rate: 10.0%

WILLIAMSPORT (village). Covers a land area of 1.812 square miles and a water area of 0.030 square miles. Located at 39.58° N. Lat; 83.12° W. Long. Elevation is 768 feet.
Population: 1,023; Growth (since 2000): 2.1%; Density: 564.5 persons per square mile; Race: 97.7% White, 0.3% Black/African American, 0.0% Asian, 0.2% American Indian/Alaska Native, 0.0% Native Hawaiian/Other Pacific Islander, 1.7% Two or more races, 0.3% Hispanic of any race;

Average household size: 2.99; Median age: 30.5; Age under 18: 34.0%; Age 65 and over: 8.8%; Males per 100 females: 93.0

School District(s)

Westfall Local (PK-12)
2012-13 Enrollment: 1,571 . . . . (740) 986-3671

Housing: Homeownership rate: 64.0%; Homeowner vacancy rate: 3.9%; Rental vacancy rate: 6.1%

Pike County

Located in southern Ohio; crossed by the Scioto River. Covers a land area of 440.282 square miles, a water area of 3.694 square miles, and is located in the Eastern Time Zone at 39.07° N. Lat., 83.05° W. Long. The county was founded in 1815. County seat is Waverly.

Weather Station: Waverly Elevation: 560 feet

	Jan	Feb	Mar	Apr	May	Jun	Jul	Aug	Sep	Oct	Nov	Dec
High	40	44	54	66	75	83	86	85	79	68	56	43
Low	20	22	30	39	49	59	63	61	52	40	32	24
Precip	2.8	2.5	3.7	3.6	4.5	3.5	4.2	3.8	2.6	3.0	3.1	2.9
Snow	4.6	3.3	1.7	tr	0.0	0.0	0.0	0.0	0.0	0.0	0.1	2.2

High and Low temperatures in degrees Fahrenheit; Precipitation and Snow in inches

Population: 28,709; Growth (since 2000): 3.7%; Density: 65.2 persons per square mile; Race: 96.6% White, 0.9% Black/African American, 0.2% Asian, 0.5% American Indian/Alaska Native, 0.0% Native Hawaiian/Other Pacific Islander, 1.6% two or more races, 0.7% Hispanic of any race; Average household size: 2.56; Median age: 39.2; Age under 18: 24.8%; Age 65 and over: 14.7%; Males per 100 females: 98.6; Marriage status: 23.2% never married, 52.2% now married, 2.5% separated, 7.4% widowed, 17.3% divorced; Foreign born: 0.6%; Speak English only: 97.2%; With disability: 20.7%; Veterans: 10.4%; Ancestry: 17.7% German, 14.3% Irish, 13.3% American, 10.8% English, 1.8% Dutch
Religion: Six largest groups: 11.3% Baptist, 3.4% Methodist/Pietist, 2.9% Non-denominational Protestant, 1.0% Catholicism, 0.5% Presbyterian-Reformed, 0.3% European Free-Church
Economy: Unemployment rate: 6.9%; Leading industries: 19.5% retail trade; 15.1% health care and social assistance; 10.4% other services (except public administration); Farms: 490 totaling 97,446 acres; Company size: 1 employs 1,000 or more persons, 1 employs 500 to 999 persons, 13 employ 100 to 499 persons, 390 employ less than 100 persons; Business ownership: 278 women-owned, n/a Black-owned, n/a Hispanic-owned, n/a Asian-owned
Employment: 12.5% management, business, and financial, 3.1% computer, engineering, and science, 8.4% education, legal, community service, arts, and media, 6.9% healthcare practitioners, 19.1% service, 17.8% sales and office, 12.9% natural resources, construction, and maintenance, 19.3% production, transportation, and material moving
Income: Per capita: $20,071; Median household: $42,165; Average household: $51,535; Households with income of $100,000 or more: 11.7%; Poverty rate: 23.5%
Educational Attainment: High school diploma or higher: 77.6%; Bachelor's degree or higher: 12.2%; Graduate/professional degree or higher: 5.1%
Housing: Homeownership rate: 68.4%; Median home value: $96,200; Median year structure built: 1981; Homeowner vacancy rate: 1.5%; Median gross rent: $676 per month; Rental vacancy rate: 11.2%
Vital Statistics: Birth rate: 118.4 per 10,000 population; Death rate: 121.3 per 10,000 population; Age-adjusted cancer mortality rate: 215.1 deaths per 100,000 population
Health Insurance: 85.6% have insurance; 53.7% have private insurance; 45.2% have public insurance; 14.4% do not have insurance; 4.5% of children under 18 do not have insurance
Health Care: Physicians: 4.2 per 10,000 population; Hospital beds: 8.7 per 10,000 population; Hospital admissions: 249.9 per 10,000 population
Transportation: Commute: 94.3% car, 0.3% public transportation, 0.5% walk, 3.9% work from home; Median travel time to work: 27.8 minutes
Presidential Election: 48.9% Obama, 49.3% Romney (2012)
National and State Parks: Lake White State Park
Additional Information Contacts
Pike Government. . . . . (740) 947-4817
http://www.pike-co.org

Pike County Communities

BEAVER (village). Covers a land area of 0.390 square miles and a water area of <.001 square miles. Located at 39.03° N. Lat; 82.83° W. Long. Elevation is 689 feet.
Population: 449; Growth (since 2000): -3.2%; Density: 1,150.6 persons per square mile; Race: 94.7% White, 0.0% Black/African American, 0.0% Asian, 0.0% American Indian/Alaska Native, 0.0% Native Hawaiian/Other Pacific Islander, 4.9% Two or more races, 2.2% Hispanic of any race; Average household size: 2.47; Median age: 31.8; Age under 18: 27.4%; Age 65 and over: 13.6%; Males per 100 females: 84.8

School District(s)

Eastern Local (PK-12)
2012-13 Enrollment: 782. . . . . (740) 226-4851

Housing: Homeownership rate: 45.0%; Homeowner vacancy rate: 2.3%; Rental vacancy rate: 14.4%

CYNTHIANA (CDP). Covers a land area of 0.035 square miles and a water area of 0 square miles. Located at 39.17° N. Lat; 83.35° W. Long. Elevation is 971 feet.
Population: 68; Growth (since 2000): n/a; Density: 1,961.5 persons per square mile; Race: 98.5% White, 0.0% Black/African American, 0.0% Asian, 0.0% American Indian/Alaska Native, 0.0% Native Hawaiian/Other Pacific Islander, 1.5% Two or more races, 0.0% Hispanic of any race; Average household size: 2.06; Median age: 53.0; Age under 18: 11.8%; Age 65 and over: 26.5%; Males per 100 females: 100.0
Housing: Homeownership rate: 69.7%; Homeowner vacancy rate: 4.2%; Rental vacancy rate: 9.1%

LATHAM (unincorporated postal area)
ZCTA: 45646
Covers a land area of 15.673 square miles and a water area of 0.072 square miles. Located at 39.08° N. Lat; 83.32° W. Long. Elevation is 636 feet.
Population: 370; Growth (since 2000): 25.4%; Density: 23.6 persons per square mile; Race: 98.6% White, 0.0% Black/African American, 0.0% Asian, 0.5% American Indian/Alaska Native, 0.0% Native Hawaiian/Other Pacific Islander, 0.5% Two or more races, 0.0% Hispanic of any race; Average household size: 2.57; Median age: 43.5; Age under 18: 21.6%; Age 65 and over: 17.0%; Males per 100 females: 93.7

School District(s)

Western Local (PK-12)
2012-13 Enrollment: 746. . . . . (740) 493-3113

Housing: Homeownership rate: 76.4%; Homeowner vacancy rate: 1.8%; Rental vacancy rate: 5.6%

PIKETON (village). Covers a land area of 2.503 square miles and a water area of 0.054 square miles. Located at 39.06° N. Lat; 82.99° W. Long. Elevation is 577 feet.
History: Piketon was settled in 1814, when it was called Jefferson. Piketon served as the seat of Pike County until 1861.
Population: 2,181; Growth (since 2000): 14.4%; Density: 871.3 persons per square mile; Race: 97.3% White, 0.9% Black/African American, 0.2% Asian, 0.1% American Indian/Alaska Native, 0.0% Native Hawaiian/Other Pacific Islander, 1.5% Two or more races, 0.3% Hispanic of any race; Average household size: 2.41; Median age: 38.2; Age under 18: 25.5%; Age 65 and over: 18.6%; Males per 100 females: 87.7

School District(s)

Pike County Area (09-12)
2012-13 Enrollment: n/a . . . . (740) 289-2721
Scioto Valley Local (PK-12)
2012-13 Enrollment: 1,380 . . . . (740) 289-4456

Vocational/Technical School(s)

Pike County Joint Vocational School District (Public)
Fall 2013 Enrollment: 83. . . . . (740) 289-2282
2013-14 Tuition: $7,980

Housing: Homeownership rate: 50.3%; Homeowner vacancy rate: 2.1%; Rental vacancy rate: 7.9%

STOCKDALE (CDP). Covers a land area of 0.534 square miles and a water area of <.001 square miles. Located at 38.96° N. Lat; 82.86° W. Long. Elevation is 718 feet.
Population: 135; Growth (since 2000): n/a; Density: 252.8 persons per square mile; Race: 99.3% White, 0.0% Black/African American, 0.0%

Asian, 0.7% American Indian/Alaska Native, 0.0% Native Hawaiian/Other Pacific Islander, 0.0% Two or more races, 0.0% Hispanic of any race; Average household size: 2.65; Median age: 34.5; Age under 18: 26.7%; Age 65 and over: 11.1%; Males per 100 females: 84.9
Housing: Homeownership rate: 68.6%; Homeowner vacancy rate: 0.0%; Rental vacancy rate: 5.9%

WAVERLY (village). Aka Waverly City. County seat.
Note: Statistics that would complete this profile are not available because the village was incorporated after the 2010 Census was released.

Portage County

Located in northeastern Ohio; crossed by the Cuyahoga River and tributaries of the Mahoning; includes many small lakes. Covers a land area of 487.381 square miles, a water area of 16.683 square miles, and is located in the Eastern Time Zone at 41.17° N. Lat., 81.20° W. Long. The county was founded in 1807. County seat is Ravenna.

Portage County is part of the Akron, OH Metropolitan Statistical Area. The entire metro area includes: Portage County, OH; Summit County, OH

Weather Station: Hiram | Elevation: 1,229 feet

	Jan	Feb	Mar	Apr	May	Jun	Jul	Aug	Sep	Oct	Nov	Dec
High	32	36	45	58	68	77	81	80	73	60	49	36
Low	17	19	26	37	47	56	61	60	52	41	33	22
Precip	3.0	2.4	3.3	3.8	4.1	4.0	4.1	3.7	3.8	3.4	3.6	3.5
Snow	18.2	12.7	10.4	1.9	tr	0.0	0.0	0.0	0.0	0.4	5.3	14.3

High and Low temperatures in degrees Fahrenheit; Precipitation and Snow in inches

Population: 161,419; Growth (since 2000): 6.2%; Density: 331.2 persons per square mile; Race: 92.3% White, 4.1% Black/African American, 1.4% Asian, 0.2% American Indian/Alaska Native, 0.0% Native Hawaiian/Other Pacific Islander, 1.7% two or more races, 1.3% Hispanic of any race; Average household size: 2.47; Median age: 37.4; Age under 18: 20.9%; Age 65 and over: 12.9%; Males per 100 females: 95.5; Marriage status: 35.9% never married, 48.5% now married, 1.6% separated, 4.8% widowed, 10.8% divorced; Foreign born: 3.1%; Speak English only: 95.7%; With disability: 11.5%; Veterans: 9.4%; Ancestry: 30.0% German, 16.9% Irish, 11.5% Italian, 11.3% English, 6.4% Polish
Religion: Six largest groups: 12.3% Catholicism, 4.0% Methodist/Pietist, 2.9% Non-denominational Protestant, 2.2% Baptist, 1.5% Presbyterian-Reformed, 1.2% Lutheran
Economy: Unemployment rate: 4.1%; Leading industries: 14.8% retail trade; 10.8% other services (except public administration); 10.2% construction; Farms: 847 totaling 83,321 acres; Company size: 1 employs 1,000 or more persons, 2 employ 500 to 999 persons, 72 employ 100 to 499 persons, 2,906 employ less than 100 persons; Business ownership: 2,849 women-owned, 137 Black-owned, n/a Hispanic-owned, 172 Asian-owned
Employment: 12.6% management, business, and financial, 3.9% computer, engineering, and science, 9.3% education, legal, community service, arts, and media, 4.3% healthcare practitioners, 19.8% service, 24.8% sales and office, 8.3% natural resources, construction, and maintenance, 17.0% production, transportation, and material moving
Income: Per capita: $25,332; Median household: $52,697; Average household: $65,457; Households with income of $100,000 or more: 18.4%; Poverty rate: 16.1%
Educational Attainment: High school diploma or higher: 91.0%; Bachelor's degree or higher: 25.1%; Graduate/professional degree or higher: 9.2%
Housing: Homeownership rate: 69.9%; Median home value: $150,300; Median year structure built: 1974; Homeowner vacancy rate: 1.9%; Median gross rent: $802 per month; Rental vacancy rate: 9.2%
Vital Statistics: Birth rate: 87.8 per 10,000 population; Death rate: 78.9 per 10,000 population; Age-adjusted cancer mortality rate: 194.1 deaths per 100,000 population
Health Insurance: 89.7% have insurance; 74.4% have private insurance; 26.9% have public insurance; 10.3% do not have insurance; 4.0% of children under 18 do not have insurance
Health Care: Physicians: 12.6 per 10,000 population; Hospital beds: 8.6 per 10,000 population; Hospital admissions: 616.4 per 10,000 population
Air Quality Index: 90.8% good, 9.2% moderate, 0.0% unhealthy for sensitive individuals, 0.0% unhealthy (percent of days)
Transportation: Commute: 91.6% car, 0.7% public transportation, 3.2% walk, 3.7% work from home; Median travel time to work: 24.5 minutes
Presidential Election: 51.4% Obama, 46.6% Romney (2012)
National and State Parks: Charles Tummonds State Nature Preserve; Eagle Creek State Nature Preserve; Marsh Wetlands State Nature Preserve; Nelson-Kennedy Ledges State Park; Tinkers Creek State Park; Tom S Cooperrider-Kent Bog State Nature Preserve; Triangle Lake Bog State Nature Preserve; West Branch State Park
Additional Information Contacts
Portage Government . . . . (330) 297-3600
http://www.co.portage.oh.us

Portage County Communities

ATWATER (CDP). Covers a land area of 0.842 square miles and a water area of 0.011 square miles. Located at 41.03° N. Lat; 81.16° W. Long. Elevation is 1,129 feet.
Population: 758; Growth (since 2000): n/a; Density: 900.1 persons per square mile; Race: 97.8% White, 1.1% Black/African American, 0.1% Asian, 0.0% American Indian/Alaska Native, 0.0% Native Hawaiian/Other Pacific Islander, 1.1% Two or more races, 1.2% Hispanic of any race; Average household size: 2.76; Median age: 34.4; Age under 18: 30.2%; Age 65 and over: 8.6%; Males per 100 females: 87.6

School District(s)

Waterloo Local (PK-12)
2012-13 Enrollment: 1,139 . . . . (330) 947-2664
Housing: Homeownership rate: 76.0%; Homeowner vacancy rate: 2.3%; Rental vacancy rate: 1.5%

AURORA (city). Covers a land area of 22.918 square miles and a water area of 1.147 square miles. Located at 41.30° N. Lat; 81.33° W. Long. Elevation is 1,129 feet.
History: Founded in 1799, Aurora was designated a Tree City USA by the National Arbor Day Foundation.
Population: 15,548; Growth (since 2000): 14.7%; Density: 678.4 persons per square mile; Race: 93.9% White, 3.0% Black/African American, 1.9% Asian, 0.1% American Indian/Alaska Native, 0.0% Native Hawaiian/Other Pacific Islander, 1.0% Two or more races, 1.3% Hispanic of any race; Average household size: 2.54; Median age: 45.4; Age under 18: 24.6%; Age 65 and over: 19.1%; Males per 100 females: 92.0; Marriage status: 21.8% never married, 61.8% now married, 1.9% separated, 7.9% widowed, 8.5% divorced; Foreign born: 6.6%; Speak English only: 90.7%; With disability: 10.0%; Veterans: 10.9%; Ancestry: 22.8% German, 14.8% Italian, 14.4% Irish, 10.9% Polish, 8.9% English
Employment: 26.8% management, business, and financial, 5.3% computer, engineering, and science, 10.7% education, legal, community service, arts, and media, 7.3% healthcare practitioners, 14.9% service, 22.7% sales and office, 3.4% natural resources, construction, and maintenance, 8.9% production, transportation, and material moving
Income: Per capita: $42,549; Median household: $80,400; Average household: $107,375; Households with income of $100,000 or more: 39.4%; Poverty rate: 5.0%
Educational Attainment: High school diploma or higher: 95.7%; Bachelor's degree or higher: 47.9%; Graduate/professional degree or higher: 18.5%

School District(s)

Aurora City (PK-12)
2012-13 Enrollment: 2,936 . . . . (330) 562-6106
Housing: Homeownership rate: 80.3%; Median home value: $247,600; Median year structure built: 1986; Homeowner vacancy rate: 2.1%; Median gross rent: $1,442 per month; Rental vacancy rate: 6.3%
Health Insurance: 93.8% have insurance; 86.2% have private insurance; 21.7% have public insurance; 6.2% do not have insurance; 4.0% of children under 18 do not have insurance
Safety: Violent crime rate: 5.8 per 10,000 population; Property crime rate: 102.2 per 10,000 population
Transportation: Commute: 91.2% car, 0.5% public transportation, 0.9% walk, 6.4% work from home; Median travel time to work: 26.3 minutes
Additional Information Contacts
City of Aurora . . . . (330) 562-6131
http://www.auroraoh.com

BRADY LAKE (village). Covers a land area of 0.314 square miles and a water area of 0.098 square miles. Located at 41.16° N. Lat; 81.31° W. Long. Elevation is 1,079 feet.
Population: 464; Growth (since 2000): -9.6%; Density: 1,475.8 persons per square mile; Race: 94.4% White, 0.2% Black/African American, 1.1%

Asian, 1.3% American Indian/Alaska Native, 0.0% Native Hawaiian/Other Pacific Islander, 3.0% Two or more races, 0.9% Hispanic of any race; Average household size: 2.31; Median age: 47.4; Age under 18: 14.9%; Age 65 and over: 12.9%; Males per 100 females: 108.1
Housing: Homeownership rate: 73.1%; Homeowner vacancy rate: 2.0%; Rental vacancy rate: 11.1%

BRIMFIELD (CDP). Covers a land area of 3.970 square miles and a water area of 0.037 square miles. Located at 41.10° N. Lat; 81.35° W. Long. Elevation is 1,102 feet.
Population: 3,343; Growth (since 2000): 2.9%; Density: 842.0 persons per square mile; Race: 95.3% White, 2.4% Black/African American, 0.7% Asian, 0.2% American Indian/Alaska Native, 0.0% Native Hawaiian/Other Pacific Islander, 1.3% Two or more races, 0.8% Hispanic of any race; Average household size: 2.64; Median age: 38.2; Age under 18: 23.8%; Age 65 and over: 12.8%; Males per 100 females: 97.6; Marriage status: 34.4% never married, 56.0% now married, 1.7% separated, 3.5% widowed, 6.1% divorced; Foreign born: 1.1%; Speak English only: 95.3%; With disability: 14.1%; Veterans: 11.1%; Ancestry: 35.1% German, 15.9% Irish, 9.7% Italian, 8.6% English, 6.2% Polish
Employment: 8.4% management, business, and financial, 4.3% computer, engineering, and science, 8.5% education, legal, community service, arts, and media, 2.5% healthcare practitioners, 11.8% service, 29.7% sales and office, 17.6% natural resources, construction, and maintenance, 17.1% production, transportation, and material moving
Income: Per capita: $25,812; Median household: $67,308; Average household: $75,345; Households with income of $100,000 or more: 26.5%; Poverty rate: 13.2%
Educational Attainment: High school diploma or higher: 92.6%; Bachelor's degree or higher: 19.1%; Graduate/professional degree or higher: 7.9%
Housing: Homeownership rate: 81.9%; Median home value: $130,300; Median year structure built: 1967; Homeowner vacancy rate: 1.9%; Median gross rent: $988 per month; Rental vacancy rate: 7.6%
Health Insurance: 93.7% have insurance; 85.4% have private insurance; 20.0% have public insurance; 6.3% do not have insurance; 1.2% of children under 18 do not have insurance
Transportation: Commute: 94.9% car, 0.0% public transportation, 0.0% walk, 2.8% work from home; Median travel time to work: 20.4 minutes

DEERFIELD (unincorporated postal area)
ZCTA: 44411
Covers a land area of 17.838 square miles and a water area of 1.917 square miles. Located at 41.04° N. Lat; 81.04° W. Long. Elevation is 1,070 feet.
Population: 2,181; Growth (since 2000): -19.4%; Density: 122.3 persons per square mile; Race: 97.7% White, 0.4% Black/African American, 0.2% Asian, 0.2% American Indian/Alaska Native, 0.0% Native Hawaiian/Other Pacific Islander, 1.5% Two or more races, 0.7% Hispanic of any race; Average household size: 2.57; Median age: 40.9; Age under 18: 24.2%; Age 65 and over: 13.0%; Males per 100 females: 101.4
Housing: Homeownership rate: 85.5%; Homeowner vacancy rate: 3.1%; Rental vacancy rate: 10.1%

DIAMOND (unincorporated postal area)
ZCTA: 44412
Covers a land area of 22.844 square miles and a water area of 0.209 square miles. Located at 41.09° N. Lat; 81.03° W. Long. Elevation is 991 feet.
Population: 2,644; Growth (since 2000): -2.1%; Density: 115.7 persons per square mile; Race: 97.5% White, 0.7% Black/African American, 0.1% Asian, 0.5% American Indian/Alaska Native, 0.0% Native Hawaiian/Other Pacific Islander, 1.1% Two or more races, 0.9% Hispanic of any race; Average household size: 2.75; Median age: 42.6; Age under 18: 24.8%; Age 65 and over: 13.0%; Males per 100 females: 103.5; Marriage status: 26.0% never married, 58.0% now married, 2.8% separated, 4.4% widowed, 11.6% divorced; Foreign born: 0.5%; Speak English only: 98.2%; With disability: 10.0%; Veterans: 8.7%; Ancestry: 39.4% German, 21.6% Irish, 9.8% Italian, 9.6% English, 6.3% American
Employment: 6.6% management, business, and financial, 1.2% computer, engineering, and science, 2.9% education, legal, community service, arts, and media, 3.3% healthcare practitioners, 20.3% service, 25.8% sales and office, 12.7% natural resources, construction, and maintenance, 27.1% production, transportation, and material moving
Income: Per capita: $29,145; Median household: $58,929; Average household: $72,413; Households with income of $100,000 or more: 14.2%; Poverty rate: 8.8%
Educational Attainment: High school diploma or higher: 93.2%; Bachelor's degree or higher: 9.0%; Graduate/professional degree or higher: 2.9%

School District(s)

Southeast Local (PK-12)
2012-13 Enrollment: 1,749 . . . . (330) 654-5841
Housing: Homeownership rate: 83.7%; Median home value: $151,600; Median year structure built: 1972; Homeowner vacancy rate: 1.2%; Median gross rent: $869 per month; Rental vacancy rate: 13.7%
Health Insurance: 91.0% have insurance; 76.9% have private insurance; 28.1% have public insurance; 9.0% do not have insurance; 6.0% of children under 18 do not have insurance
Transportation: Commute: 95.9% car, 0.0% public transportation, 0.8% walk, 2.6% work from home; Median travel time to work: 28.4 minutes

GARRETTSVILLE (village). Covers a land area of 2.513 square miles and a water area of 0.016 square miles. Located at 41.28° N. Lat; 81.09° W. Long. Elevation is 1,001 feet.
Population: 2,325; Growth (since 2000): 2.8%; Density: 925.1 persons per square mile; Race: 97.8% White, 0.5% Black/African American, 0.3% Asian, 0.0% American Indian/Alaska Native, 0.0% Native Hawaiian/Other Pacific Islander, 1.0% Two or more races, 0.9% Hispanic of any race; Average household size: 2.41; Median age: 41.0; Age under 18: 23.9%; Age 65 and over: 13.8%; Males per 100 females: 93.3

School District(s)

James A Garfield Local (PK-12)
2012-13 Enrollment: 1,457 . . . . (330) 527-4336
Housing: Homeownership rate: 65.1%; Homeowner vacancy rate: 2.9%; Rental vacancy rate: 12.0%
Newspapers: Weekly Villager (weekly circulation 13000)
Additional Information Contacts
Village of Garrettsville . . . . (330) 527-2682
http://www.garrettsville.org

HIRAM (village). Covers a land area of 0.927 square miles and a water area of 0 square miles. Located at 41.31° N. Lat; 81.14° W. Long. Elevation is 1,250 feet.
History: Hiram grew up around Hiram College, founded in 1850 by the Disciples of Christ as the Western Reserve Eclectic Institute. President James A. Garfield was valedictorian of his class when he graduated from the Institute in 1853.
Population: 1,406; Growth (since 2000): 13.2%; Density: 1,516.1 persons per square mile; Race: 85.3% White, 8.2% Black/African American, 3.3% Asian, 0.4% American Indian/Alaska Native, 0.0% Native Hawaiian/Other Pacific Islander, 2.1% Two or more races, 2.1% Hispanic of any race; Average household size: 2.35; Median age: 21.0; Age under 18: 8.1%; Age 65 and over: 4.8%; Males per 100 females: 95.0

Four-year College(s)

Hiram College (Private, Not-for-profit)
Fall 2013 Enrollment: 1,311 . . . . (330) 569-3211
2013-14 Tuition: In-state $30,290; Out-of-state $30,290
Housing: Homeownership rate: 43.9%; Homeowner vacancy rate: 2.9%; Rental vacancy rate: 6.6%

KENT (city). Covers a land area of 9.174 square miles and a water area of 0.109 square miles. Located at 41.15° N. Lat; 81.36° W. Long. Elevation is 1,063 feet.
History: Kent developed around Kent State University, founded in 1910 as a state normal school and accredited as a university in 1935.
Population: 28,904; Growth (since 2000): 3.6%; Density: 3,150.5 persons per square mile; Race: 83.1% White, 9.6% Black/African American, 3.7% Asian, 0.2% American Indian/Alaska Native, 0.1% Native Hawaiian/Other Pacific Islander, 2.9% Two or more races, 2.2% Hispanic of any race; Average household size: 2.22; Median age: 22.7; Age under 18: 14.1%; Age 65 and over: 7.4%; Males per 100 females: 86.2; Marriage status: 61.1% never married, 28.5% now married, 1.1% separated, 2.9% widowed, 7.4% divorced; Foreign born: 6.2%; Speak English only: 92.4%; With disability: 9.3%; Veterans: 4.8%; Ancestry: 31.4% German, 18.1% Irish, 14.1% Italian, 9.2% English, 4.9% Polish
Employment: 9.1% management, business, and financial, 4.9% computer, engineering, and science, 16.1% education, legal, community service, arts, and media, 4.1% healthcare practitioners, 27.9% service, 24.3% sales and

office, 3.7% natural resources, construction, and maintenance, 9.9% production, transportation, and material moving
Income: Per capita: $19,143; Median household: $31,035; Average household: $51,507; Households with income of $100,000 or more: 12.3%; Poverty rate: 35.3%
Educational Attainment: High school diploma or higher: 91.7%; Bachelor's degree or higher: 42.0%; Graduate/professional degree or higher: 17.8%

School District(s)

Field Local (PK-12)
2012-13 Enrollment: 2,055 . . . . (330) 673-2659
Kent City (PK-12)
2012-13 Enrollment: 3,524 . . . . (330) 673-6515

Four-year College(s)

Kent State University at Kent (Public)
Fall 2013 Enrollment: 28,998 . . . . (330) 672-3000
2013-14 Tuition: In-state $9,816; Out-of-state $17,776

Vocational/Technical School(s)

Northcoast Medical Training Academy (Private, For-profit)
Fall 2013 Enrollment: 202 . . . . (330) 678-6600
2013-14 Tuition: $20,040
Housing: Homeownership rate: 37.0%; Median home value: $138,600; Median year structure built: 1970; Homeowner vacancy rate: 2.3%; Median gross rent: $716 per month; Rental vacancy rate: 8.0%
Health Insurance: 87.8% have insurance; 72.6% have private insurance; 23.5% have public insurance; 12.2% do not have insurance; 4.0% of children under 18 do not have insurance
Safety: Violent crime rate: 18.6 per 10,000 population; Property crime rate: 219.4 per 10,000 population
Transportation: Commute: 81.5% car, 2.4% public transportation, 10.6% walk, 4.2% work from home; Median travel time to work: 21.3 minutes
Additional Information Contacts
City of Kent . . . . (330) 676-7500
http://www.kentohio.org

MANTUA (village). Covers a land area of 1.403 square miles and a water area of 0.015 square miles. Located at 41.28° N. Lat; 81.22° W. Long. Elevation is 1,148 feet.
Population: 1,043; Growth (since 2000): -0.3%; Density: 743.3 persons per square mile; Race: 98.2% White, 0.3% Black/African American, 0.1% Asian, 0.1% American Indian/Alaska Native, 0.1% Native Hawaiian/Other Pacific Islander, 1.2% Two or more races, 0.5% Hispanic of any race; Average household size: 2.31; Median age: 41.5; Age under 18: 22.8%; Age 65 and over: 13.3%; Males per 100 females: 92.8

School District(s)

Crestwood Local (PK-12)
2012-13 Enrollment: 1,977 . . . . (330) 274-8511
Housing: Homeownership rate: 57.6%; Homeowner vacancy rate: 1.5%; Rental vacancy rate: 6.8%

NORTH BENTON (unincorporated postal area)
ZCTA: 44449
Covers a land area of 11.841 square miles and a water area of 0.470 square miles. Located at 40.98° N. Lat; 81.04° W. Long..
Population: 1,323; Growth (since 2000): 1.4%; Density: 111.7 persons per square mile; Race: 99.2% White, 0.1% Black/African American, 0.2% Asian, 0.0% American Indian/Alaska Native, 0.0% Native Hawaiian/Other Pacific Islander, 0.4% Two or more races, 0.4% Hispanic of any race; Average household size: 2.47; Median age: 46.3; Age under 18: 19.4%; Age 65 and over: 15.8%; Males per 100 females: 105.1
Housing: Homeownership rate: 86.4%; Homeowner vacancy rate: 2.9%; Rental vacancy rate: 3.9%

RAVENNA (city). County seat. Covers a land area of 5.630 square miles and a water area of 0.047 square miles. Located at 41.16° N. Lat; 81.24° W. Long. Elevation is 1,135 feet.
History: Ravenna was settled in 1799 by Benjamin Tappan, Jr., a New Englander and later U.S. senator from Ohio. The town was named for the Italian city.
Population: 11,724; Growth (since 2000): -0.4%; Density: 2,082.4 persons per square mile; Race: 91.1% White, 5.6% Black/African American, 0.4% Asian, 0.2% American Indian/Alaska Native, 0.0% Native Hawaiian/Other Pacific Islander, 2.3% Two or more races, 1.4% Hispanic of any race; Average household size: 2.28; Median age: 37.9; Age under 18: 22.5%; Age 65 and over: 14.9%; Males per 100 females: 92.8; Marriage status: 35.5% never married, 41.4% now married, 1.6% separated, 6.2% widowed, 16.9% divorced; Foreign born: 1.0%; Speak English only: 98.2%; With disability: 19.3%; Veterans: 8.4%; Ancestry: 31.2% German, 17.9% Irish, 11.9% Italian, 10.9% English, 4.7% Polish
Employment: 8.7% management, business, and financial, 2.6% computer, engineering, and science, 5.6% education, legal, community service, arts, and media, 4.0% healthcare practitioners, 27.5% service, 23.3% sales and office, 7.6% natural resources, construction, and maintenance, 20.7% production, transportation, and material moving
Income: Per capita: $20,084; Median household: $35,756; Average household: $45,623; Households with income of $100,000 or more: 7.1%; Poverty rate: 25.1%
Educational Attainment: High school diploma or higher: 84.0%; Bachelor's degree or higher: 13.2%; Graduate/professional degree or higher: 6.1%

School District(s)

Maplewood Career Center (11-12)
2012-13 Enrollment: n/a . . . . (330) 296-2892
Ravenna City (PK-12)
2012-13 Enrollment: 2,769 . . . . (330) 296-9679
Southeast Local (PK-12)
2012-13 Enrollment: 1,749 . . . . (330) 654-5841

Two-year College(s)

Fortis College-Ravenna (Private, For-profit)
Fall 2013 Enrollment: 356 . . . . (330) 297-7319
2013-14 Tuition: In-state $13,174; Out-of-state $13,174

Vocational/Technical School(s)

Community Technology Learning Center of Portage (Private, Not-for-profit)
Fall 2013 Enrollment: n/a . . . . (330) 296-8720
Housing: Homeownership rate: 54.2%; Median home value: $106,100; Median year structure built: 1954; Homeowner vacancy rate: 2.5%; Median gross rent: $626 per month; Rental vacancy rate: 10.0%
Health Insurance: 88.8% have insurance; 56.7% have private insurance; 43.7% have public insurance; 11.2% do not have insurance; 3.0% of children under 18 do not have insurance
Hospitals: Robinson Memorial Hospital (285 beds)
Newspapers: Record-Courier (daily circulation 17900)
Transportation: Commute: 94.6% car, 0.8% public transportation, 2.4% walk, 2.0% work from home; Median travel time to work: 21.2 minutes
Additional Information Contacts
City of Ravenna. . . . . (330) 296-3864
http://www.ci.ravenna.oh.us

ROOTSTOWN (unincorporated postal area)
ZCTA: 44272
Covers a land area of 22.423 square miles and a water area of 0.169 square miles. Located at 41.09° N. Lat; 81.18° W. Long. Elevation is 1,125 feet.
Population: 5,208; Growth (since 2000): 28.7%; Density: 232.3 persons per square mile; Race: 96.3% White, 0.9% Black/African American, 1.2% Asian, 0.1% American Indian/Alaska Native, 0.1% Native Hawaiian/Other Pacific Islander, 1.2% Two or more races, 1.0% Hispanic of any race; Average household size: 2.68; Median age: 39.8; Age under 18: 23.9%; Age 65 and over: 13.2%; Males per 100 females: 96.9; Marriage status: 25.7% never married, 59.6% now married, 0.5% separated, 3.8% widowed, 10.9% divorced; Foreign born: 0.3%; Speak English only: 98.6%; With disability: 9.5%; Veterans: 9.5%; Ancestry: 37.6% German, 14.1% English, 13.6% Irish, 8.1% American, 7.9% Italian
Employment: 7.7% management, business, and financial, 2.8% computer, engineering, and science, 6.7% education, legal, community service, arts, and media, 3.6% healthcare practitioners, 16.9% service, 26.3% sales and office, 15.3% natural resources, construction, and maintenance, 20.7% production, transportation, and material moving
Income: Per capita: $24,053; Median household: $62,083; Average household: $65,504; Households with income of $100,000 or more: 16.4%; Poverty rate: 4.7%
Educational Attainment: High school diploma or higher: 92.9%; Bachelor's degree or higher: 13.4%; Graduate/professional degree or higher: 4.8%

School District(s)

Rootstown Local (PK-12)
2012-13 Enrollment: 1,198 . . . . (330) 325-9911

Four-year College(s)

Northeast Ohio Medical University (Public)
Fall 2013 Enrollment: 832 . . . . (800) 686-2511

Two-year College(s)

Northeast Ohio Medical University (Public)
Fall 2013 Enrollment: 832 . . . . (800) 686-2511

Vocational/Technical School(s)

Northeast Ohio Medical University (Public)
Fall 2013 Enrollment: 832 . . . . (800) 686-2511

Housing: Homeownership rate: 80.7%; Median home value: $157,800; Median year structure built: 1975; Homeowner vacancy rate: 1.1%; Median gross rent: $893 per month; Rental vacancy rate: 4.3%

Health Insurance: 91.3% have insurance; 80.7% have private insurance; 25.3% have public insurance; 8.7% do not have insurance; 2.0% of children under 18 do not have insurance

Transportation: Commute: 95.0% car, 0.0% public transportation, 1.2% walk, 3.2% work from home; Median travel time to work: 30.1 minutes

STREETSBORO (city). Covers a land area of 23.459 square miles and a water area of 0.902 square miles. Located at 41.24° N. Lat; 81.35° W. Long. Elevation is 1,129 feet.

History: Streetsboro was settled in 1822 and named for Titus Street, original owner of the land.

Population: 16,028; Growth (since 2000): 30.2%; Density: 683.2 persons per square mile; Race: 87.7% White, 7.9% Black/African American, 2.2% Asian, 0.2% American Indian/Alaska Native, 0.0% Native Hawaiian/Other Pacific Islander, 1.8% Two or more races, 1.7% Hispanic of any race; Average household size: 2.43; Median age: 37.9; Age under 18: 22.3%; Age 65 and over: 11.7%; Males per 100 females: 94.2; Marriage status: 31.9% never married, 50.1% now married, 1.0% separated, 5.9% widowed, 12.1% divorced; Foreign born: 3.5%; Speak English only: 96.1%; With disability: 9.6%; Veterans: 9.8%; Ancestry: 25.3% German, 16.5% Irish, 13.4% Italian, 12.0% English, 7.5% Polish

Employment: 17.0% management, business, and financial, 2.9% computer, engineering, and science, 7.1% education, legal, community service, arts, and media, 3.0% healthcare practitioners, 18.9% service, 29.4% sales and office, 5.9% natural resources, construction, and maintenance, 15.8% production, transportation, and material moving

Income: Per capita: $27,533; Median household: $61,940; Average household: $67,570; Households with income of $100,000 or more: 20.0%; Poverty rate: 7.5%

Educational Attainment: High school diploma or higher: 92.5%; Bachelor's degree or higher: 24.3%; Graduate/professional degree or higher: 7.5%

School District(s)

Streetsboro City (PK-12)
2012-13 Enrollment: 2,104 . . . . (330) 626-4900

Housing: Homeownership rate: 70.1%; Median home value: $149,500; Median year structure built: 1989; Homeowner vacancy rate: 2.3%; Median gross rent: $918 per month; Rental vacancy rate: 11.3%

Health Insurance: 89.5% have insurance; 77.0% have private insurance; 23.1% have public insurance; 10.5% do not have insurance; 5.3% of children under 18 do not have insurance

Safety: Violent crime rate: 6.2 per 10,000 population; Property crime rate: 43.4 per 10,000 population

Transportation: Commute: 95.5% car, 0.5% public transportation, 0.9% walk, 2.6% work from home; Median travel time to work: 23.8 minutes

Additional Information Contacts

City of Streetsboro. . . . . (330) 626-4942
http://cityofstreetsboro.com

SUGAR BUSH KNOLLS (village). Covers a land area of 0.214 square miles and a water area of 0.017 square miles. Located at 41.20° N. Lat; 81.35° W. Long. Elevation is 1,099 feet.

Population: 177; Growth (since 2000): -22.0%; Density: 827.0 persons per square mile; Race: 91.5% White, 1.1% Black/African American, 2.3% Asian, 0.6% American Indian/Alaska Native, 0.0% Native Hawaiian/Other Pacific Islander, 3.4% Two or more races, 2.3% Hispanic of any race; Average household size: 2.57; Median age: 51.6; Age under 18: 17.5%; Age 65 and over: 19.8%; Males per 100 females: 92.4

Housing: Homeownership rate: 98.5%; Homeowner vacancy rate: 2.9%; Rental vacancy rate: 0.0%

WAYLAND (unincorporated postal area)

ZCTA: 44285

Covers a land area of 0.138 square miles and a water area of 0 square miles. Located at 41.16° N. Lat; 81.07° W. Long. Elevation is 942 feet.

Population: 85; Growth (since 2000): n/a; Density: 614.0 persons per square mile; Race: 96.5% White, 0.0% Black/African American, 0.0% Asian, 0.0% American Indian/Alaska Native, 0.0% Native Hawaiian/Other Pacific Islander, 3.5% Two or more races, 3.5% Hispanic of any race; Average household size: 2.74; Median age: 40.1; Age under 18: 27.1%; Age 65 and over: 11.8%; Males per 100 females: 123.7

Housing: Homeownership rate: 71.0%; Homeowner vacancy rate: 0.0%; Rental vacancy rate: 18.2%

WINDHAM (village). Covers a land area of 2.057 square miles and a water area of 0.002 square miles. Located at 41.24° N. Lat; 81.04° W. Long. Elevation is 971 feet.

Population: 2,209; Growth (since 2000): -21.3%; Density: 1,074.0 persons per square mile; Race: 91.2% White, 4.5% Black/African American, 0.2% Asian, 0.2% American Indian/Alaska Native, 0.0% Native Hawaiian/Other Pacific Islander, 3.5% Two or more races, 1.3% Hispanic of any race; Average household size: 2.80; Median age: 31.6; Age under 18: 31.1%; Age 65 and over: 9.6%; Males per 100 females: 87.8

School District(s)

Windham Exempted Village (PK-12)
2012-13 Enrollment: 647. . . . . (330) 326-2711

Housing: Homeownership rate: 50.4%; Homeowner vacancy rate: 11.4%; Rental vacancy rate: 18.0%

Preble County

Located in western Ohio; bounded on the west by Indiana; drained by the East Fork of the Whitewater River. Covers a land area of 424.120 square miles, a water area of 2.342 square miles, and is located in the Eastern Time Zone at 39.74° N. Lat., 84.65° W. Long. The county was founded in 1808. County seat is Eaton.

Weather Station: Eaton Elevation: 1,001 feet

	Jan	Feb	Mar	Apr	May	Jun	Jul	Aug	Sep	Oct	Nov	Dec
High	35	39	49	62	72	81	84	84	77	65	52	39
Low	18	20	28	38	49	58	62	60	52	41	32	22
Precip	2.7	2.2	3.3	4.0	5.2	4.1	4.3	3.0	2.8	3.1	3.3	3.2
Snow	na	na	1.3	0.2	0.0	0.0	0.0	0.0	0.0	0.0	0.1	2.1

High and Low temperatures in degrees Fahrenheit; Precipitation and Snow in inches

Population: 42,270; Growth (since 2000): -0.2%; Density: 99.7 persons per square mile; Race: 97.6% White, 0.4% Black/African American, 0.4% Asian, 0.2% American Indian/Alaska Native, 0.0% Native Hawaiian/Other Pacific Islander, 1.2% two or more races, 0.6% Hispanic of any race; Average household size: 2.56; Median age: 40.9; Age under 18: 24.2%; Age 65 and over: 15.2%; Males per 100 females: 98.4; Marriage status: 22.2% never married, 58.1% now married, 1.4% separated, 7.0% widowed, 12.7% divorced; Foreign born: 1.1%; Speak English only: 97.8%; With disability: 15.6%; Veterans: 11.8%; Ancestry: 30.5% German, 14.4% Irish, 12.3% American, 10.7% English, 2.4% French

Religion: Six largest groups: 8.4% Baptist, 4.2% Methodist/Pietist, 4.0% Presbyterian-Reformed, 3.5% Lutheran, 2.9% European Free-Church, 2.7% Non-denominational Protestant

Economy: Unemployment rate: 4.6%; Leading industries: 16.4% retail trade; 13.4% other services (except public administration); 11.3% construction; Farms: 1,088 totaling 224,243 acres; Company size: 0 employ 1,000 or more persons, 1 employs 500 to 999 persons, 13 employ 100 to 499 persons, 634 employ less than 100 persons; Business ownership: n/a women-owned, n/a Black-owned, n/a Hispanic-owned, n/a Asian-owned

Employment: 9.6% management, business, and financial, 2.3% computer, engineering, and science, 7.4% education, legal, community service, arts, and media, 5.6% healthcare practitioners, 19.3% service, 20.9% sales and office, 11.8% natural resources, construction, and maintenance, 23.2% production, transportation, and material moving

Income: Per capita: $23,374; Median household: $48,405; Average household: $59,273; Households with income of $100,000 or more: 13.8%; Poverty rate: 12.2%

Educational Attainment: High school diploma or higher: 87.8%; Bachelor's degree or higher: 11.3%; Graduate/professional degree or higher: 3.7%

Housing: Homeownership rate: 76.9%; Median home value: $116,700; Median year structure built: 1966; Homeowner vacancy rate: 2.2%; Median gross rent: $717 per month; Rental vacancy rate: 8.3%

Vital Statistics: Birth rate: 102.1 per 10,000 population; Death rate: 98.5 per 10,000 population; Age-adjusted cancer mortality rate: 208.2 deaths per 100,000 population
Health Insurance: 88.1% have insurance; 68.7% have private insurance; 33.2% have public insurance; 11.9% do not have insurance; 5.6% of children under 18 do not have insurance
Health Care: Physicians: 2.6 per 10,000 population; Hospital beds: 0.0 per 10,000 population; Hospital admissions: 0.0 per 10,000 population
Air Quality Index: 66.5% good, 33.2% moderate, 0.3% unhealthy for sensitive individuals, 0.0% unhealthy (percent of days)
Transportation: Commute: 93.8% car, 0.5% public transportation, 2.1% walk, 2.8% work from home; Median travel time to work: 25.7 minutes
Presidential Election: 30.6% Obama, 67.3% Romney (2012)
National and State Parks: Fort Saint Clair State Park; Hueston Woods State Nature Preserve; Hueston Woods State Park
Additional Information Contacts
Preble Government . . . . (937) 456-8143
http://www.prebco.org

Preble County Communities

CAMDEN (village). Covers a land area of 1.241 square miles and a water area of 0.007 square miles. Located at 39.64° N. Lat; 84.64° W. Long. Elevation is 837 feet.
Population: 2,046; Growth (since 2000): -11.1%; Density: 1,648.7 persons per square mile; Race: 98.8% White, 0.1% Black/African American, 0.0% Asian, 0.2% American Indian/Alaska Native, 0.0% Native Hawaiian/Other Pacific Islander, 0.6% Two or more races, 1.1% Hispanic of any race; Average household size: 2.45; Median age: 35.2; Age under 18: 28.0%; Age 65 and over: 13.1%; Males per 100 females: 89.6

School District(s)

Preble Shawnee Local (PK-12)
2012-13 Enrollment: 1,352 . . . . (937) 452-1283
Housing: Homeownership rate: 63.5%; Homeowner vacancy rate: 2.7%; Rental vacancy rate: 11.5%

COLLEGE CORNER (village). Covers a land area of 0.250 square miles and a water area of 0.013 square miles. Located at 39.57° N. Lat; 84.81° W. Long. Elevation is 981 feet.
Population: 407; Growth (since 2000): -4.0%; Density: 1,627.3 persons per square mile; Race: 97.1% White, 1.0% Black/African American, 0.2% Asian, 0.5% American Indian/Alaska Native, 0.0% Native Hawaiian/Other Pacific Islander, 1.2% Two or more races, 0.2% Hispanic of any race; Average household size: 2.37; Median age: 38.1; Age under 18: 23.6%; Age 65 and over: 11.8%; Males per 100 females: 101.5

School District(s)

College Corner Local (PK-12)
2012-13 Enrollment: 92. . . . . (765) 732-3183
Union Co/clg Corner Joint SD (KG-12)
2012-13 Enrollment: 1,494 . . . . (765) 458-7471
Housing: Homeownership rate: 57.6%; Homeowner vacancy rate: 3.8%; Rental vacancy rate: 23.7%

EATON (city). County seat. Covers a land area of 6.194 square miles and a water area of 0.007 square miles. Located at 39.75° N. Lat; 84.63° W. Long. Elevation is 1,040 feet.
History: Eaton was founded in 1806 and named for General William Eaton, who served in the Tripolitan War of 1805.
Population: 8,407; Growth (since 2000): 3.4%; Density: 1,357.2 persons per square mile; Race: 96.3% White, 0.6% Black/African American, 1.0% Asian, 0.2% American Indian/Alaska Native, 0.0% Native Hawaiian/Other Pacific Islander, 1.5% Two or more races, 0.8% Hispanic of any race; Average household size: 2.33; Median age: 40.4; Age under 18: 23.3%; Age 65 and over: 19.1%; Males per 100 females: 89.5; Marriage status: 26.9% never married, 49.0% now married, 1.1% separated, 10.2% widowed, 13.9% divorced; Foreign born: 1.5%; Speak English only: 96.7%; With disability: 14.9%; Veterans: 13.3%; Ancestry: 30.3% German, 17.9% Irish, 11.7% English, 11.6% American, 3.3% French
Employment: 5.1% management, business, and financial, 4.0% computer, engineering, and science, 7.0% education, legal, community service, arts, and media, 5.4% healthcare practitioners, 23.3% service, 19.7% sales and office, 9.3% natural resources, construction, and maintenance, 26.1% production, transportation, and material moving
Income: Per capita: $19,663; Median household: $34,677; Average household: $47,480; Households with income of $100,000 or more: 7.1%; Poverty rate: 21.6%
Educational Attainment: High school diploma or higher: 88.7%; Bachelor's degree or higher: 10.8%; Graduate/professional degree or higher: 2.7%

School District(s)

Eaton Community City (PK-12)
2012-13 Enrollment: 2,140 . . . . (937) 456-1107
Housing: Homeownership rate: 63.7%; Median home value: $93,700; Median year structure built: 1964; Homeowner vacancy rate: 3.3%; Median gross rent: $648 per month; Rental vacancy rate: 11.3%
Health Insurance: 88.3% have insurance; 55.7% have private insurance; 45.3% have public insurance; 11.7% do not have insurance; 0.7% of children under 18 do not have insurance
Safety: Violent crime rate: 14.4 per 10,000 population; Property crime rate: 444.2 per 10,000 population
Newspapers: The Register-Herald (weekly circulation 7200)
Transportation: Commute: 93.1% car, 0.1% public transportation, 2.4% walk, 3.7% work from home; Median travel time to work: 21.6 minutes

ELDORADO (village). Covers a land area of 0.229 square miles and a water area of 0 square miles. Located at 39.90° N. Lat; 84.68° W. Long. Elevation is 1,132 feet.
Population: 509; Growth (since 2000): -6.3%; Density: 2,226.5 persons per square mile; Race: 99.0% White, 0.0% Black/African American, 0.6% Asian, 0.0% American Indian/Alaska Native, 0.0% Native Hawaiian/Other Pacific Islander, 0.2% Two or more races, 0.2% Hispanic of any race; Average household size: 2.60; Median age: 39.2; Age under 18: 27.1%; Age 65 and over: 12.0%; Males per 100 females: 98.1
Housing: Homeownership rate: 73.5%; Homeowner vacancy rate: 6.5%; Rental vacancy rate: 1.9%

GRATIS (village). Covers a land area of 0.965 square miles and a water area of <.001 square miles. Located at 39.65° N. Lat; 84.53° W. Long. Elevation is 876 feet.
Population: 881; Growth (since 2000): -5.7%; Density: 913.3 persons per square mile; Race: 97.7% White, 0.5% Black/African American, 0.0% Asian, 0.6% American Indian/Alaska Native, 0.0% Native Hawaiian/Other Pacific Islander, 1.2% Two or more races, 0.3% Hispanic of any race; Average household size: 2.57; Median age: 38.1; Age under 18: 23.3%; Age 65 and over: 12.4%; Males per 100 females: 98.9
Housing: Homeownership rate: 79.3%; Homeowner vacancy rate: 1.5%; Rental vacancy rate: 4.1%

LAKE LAKENGREN (CDP). Covers a land area of 2.860 square miles and a water area of 0.327 square miles. Located at 39.69° N. Lat; 84.69° W. Long. Elevation is 1,089 feet.
Population: 3,383; Growth (since 2000): n/a; Density: 1,183.0 persons per square mile; Race: 97.1% White, 0.8% Black/African American, 0.4% Asian, 0.1% American Indian/Alaska Native, 0.0% Native Hawaiian/Other Pacific Islander, 1.2% Two or more races, 0.9% Hispanic of any race; Average household size: 2.79; Median age: 38.4; Age under 18: 25.8%; Age 65 and over: 12.5%; Males per 100 females: 100.8; Marriage status: 17.8% never married, 63.3% now married, 1.3% separated, 4.0% widowed, 14.3% divorced; Foreign born: 2.5%; Speak English only: 95.9%; With disability: 7.9%; Veterans: 10.2%; Ancestry: 22.1% German, 15.7% American, 12.5% English, 7.8% Irish, 2.3% European
Employment: 13.2% management, business, and financial, 2.7% computer, engineering, and science, 8.6% education, legal, community service, arts, and media, 4.5% healthcare practitioners, 19.1% service, 22.9% sales and office, 7.6% natural resources, construction, and maintenance, 21.4% production, transportation, and material moving
Income: Per capita: $24,072; Median household: $61,456; Average household: $67,811; Households with income of $100,000 or more: 19.1%; Poverty rate: 4.2%
Educational Attainment: High school diploma or higher: 90.8%; Bachelor's degree or higher: 14.4%; Graduate/professional degree or higher: 5.1%
Housing: Homeownership rate: 92.8%; Median home value: $126,200; Median year structure built: 1993; Homeowner vacancy rate: 3.5%; Median gross rent: $921 per month; Rental vacancy rate: 4.2%
Health Insurance: 95.3% have insurance; 84.5% have private insurance; 22.7% have public insurance; 4.7% do not have insurance; 1.2% of children under 18 do not have insurance

Transportation: Commute: 96.1% car, 1.0% public transportation, 0.0% walk, 2.9% work from home; Median travel time to work: 29.7 minutes

LEWISBURG (village). Covers a land area of 1.074 square miles and a water area of 0 square miles. Located at 39.85° N. Lat; 84.54° W. Long. Elevation is 997 feet.

History: Lewisburg developed as a rural trade center. Tobacco was once a leading crop here.

Population: 1,820; Growth (since 2000): 1.2%; Density: 1,694.3 persons per square mile; Race: 97.1% White, 0.2% Black/African American, 0.5% Asian, 0.3% American Indian/Alaska Native, 0.0% Native Hawaiian/Other Pacific Islander, 1.9% Two or more races, 0.8% Hispanic of any race; Average household size: 2.56; Median age: 36.2; Age under 18: 27.3%; Age 65 and over: 15.4%; Males per 100 females: 97.8

School District(s)

Tri-County North Local (PK-12)
2012-13 Enrollment: 950. . . . . (937) 962-2671

Housing: Homeownership rate: 71.6%; Homeowner vacancy rate: 2.8%; Rental vacancy rate: 8.2%

NEW PARIS (village). Covers a land area of 0.735 square miles and a water area of 0.023 square miles. Located at 39.86° N. Lat; 84.79° W. Long. Elevation is 1,033 feet.

Population: 1,629; Growth (since 2000): 0.4%; Density: 2,215.4 persons per square mile; Race: 97.7% White, 0.1% Black/African American, 0.1% Asian, 0.6% American Indian/Alaska Native, 0.1% Native Hawaiian/Other Pacific Islander, 1.3% Two or more races, 0.4% Hispanic of any race; Average household size: 2.28; Median age: 36.7; Age under 18: 25.6%; Age 65 and over: 14.7%; Males per 100 females: 87.9

School District(s)

National Trail Local (PK-12)
2012-13 Enrollment: 1,063 . . . . (937) 437-3333

Housing: Homeownership rate: 59.7%; Homeowner vacancy rate: 2.1%; Rental vacancy rate: 6.9%

VERONA (village). Covers a land area of 0.456 square miles and a water area of 0.007 square miles. Located at 39.90° N. Lat; 84.51° W. Long. Elevation is 1,024 feet.

Population: 494; Growth (since 2000): 14.9%; Density: 1,083.3 persons per square mile; Race: 98.6% White, 0.0% Black/African American, 0.0% Asian, 0.0% American Indian/Alaska Native, 0.0% Native Hawaiian/Other Pacific Islander, 1.4% Two or more races, 0.0% Hispanic of any race; Average household size: 2.74; Median age: 37.3; Age under 18: 25.5%; Age 65 and over: 12.3%; Males per 100 females: 101.6

Housing: Homeownership rate: 76.6%; Homeowner vacancy rate: 2.8%; Rental vacancy rate: 0.0%

WEST ALEXANDRIA (village). Covers a land area of 0.674 square miles and a water area of 0 square miles. Located at 39.74° N. Lat; 84.53° W. Long. Elevation is 892 feet.

Population: 1,340; Growth (since 2000): -3.9%; Density: 1,989.1 persons per square mile; Race: 96.4% White, 1.0% Black/African American, 0.6% Asian, 0.1% American Indian/Alaska Native, 0.0% Native Hawaiian/Other Pacific Islander, 1.8% Two or more races, 1.4% Hispanic of any race; Average household size: 2.43; Median age: 37.8; Age under 18: 25.4%; Age 65 and over: 14.8%; Males per 100 females: 91.2

School District(s)

Twin Valley Community Local (PK-12)
2012-13 Enrollment: 898. . . . . (937) 839-4688

Housing: Homeownership rate: 63.2%; Homeowner vacancy rate: 3.9%; Rental vacancy rate: 8.4%

Safety: Violent crime rate: 0.0 per 10,000 population; Property crime rate: 140.2 per 10,000 population

Newspapers: Twin Valley Publications (weekly circulation 8000)

WEST ELKTON (village). Covers a land area of 0.583 square miles and a water area of 0 square miles. Located at 39.59° N. Lat; 84.56° W. Long. Elevation is 1,030 feet.

Population: 197; Growth (since 2000): 1.5%; Density: 337.7 persons per square mile; Race: 97.0% White, 0.5% Black/African American, 1.5% Asian, 0.0% American Indian/Alaska Native, 0.0% Native Hawaiian/Other Pacific Islander, 0.5% Two or more races, 0.5% Hispanic of any race; Average household size: 2.59; Median age: 39.3; Age under 18: 24.4%; Age 65 and over: 14.2%; Males per 100 females: 121.3

School District(s)

Preble Shawnee Local (PK-12)
2012-13 Enrollment: 1,352 . . . . (937) 452-1283

Housing: Homeownership rate: 73.7%; Homeowner vacancy rate: 1.8%; Rental vacancy rate: 4.8%

WEST MANCHESTER (village). Covers a land area of 0.272 square miles and a water area of 0 square miles. Located at 39.90° N. Lat; 84.63° W. Long. Elevation is 1,093 feet.

Population: 474; Growth (since 2000): 9.5%; Density: 1,743.2 persons per square mile; Race: 95.4% White, 1.9% Black/African American, 0.0% Asian, 0.4% American Indian/Alaska Native, 0.0% Native Hawaiian/Other Pacific Islander, 2.1% Two or more races, 1.1% Hispanic of any race; Average household size: 2.84; Median age: 33.3; Age under 18: 27.6%; Age 65 and over: 10.3%; Males per 100 females: 95.1

Housing: Homeownership rate: 73.1%; Homeowner vacancy rate: 2.4%; Rental vacancy rate: 0.0%

Putnam County

Located in northwestern Ohio; crossed by the Auglize and Blanchard Rivers. Covers a land area of 482.522 square miles, a water area of 1.778 square miles, and is located in the Eastern Time Zone at 41.02° N. Lat., 84.13° W. Long. The county was founded in 1820. County seat is Ottawa.

Weather Station: Pandora Elevation: 770 feet

	Jan	Feb	Mar	Apr	May	Jun	Jul	Aug	Sep	Oct	Nov	Dec
High	33	37	47	61	71	80	84	82	76	63	50	37
Low	18	21	28	39	49	59	63	60	53	42	33	23
Precip	2.3	2.0	2.7	3.5	3.9	4.1	4.0	3.4	3.0	2.7	3.1	2.7
Snow	9.4	6.9	4.4	1.2	tr	0.0	0.0	0.0	tr	0.1	1.9	6.6

High and Low temperatures in degrees Fahrenheit; Precipitation and Snow in inches

Population: 34,499; Growth (since 2000): -0.7%; Density: 71.5 persons per square mile; Race: 95.7% White, 0.3% Black/African American, 0.2% Asian, 0.2% American Indian/Alaska Native, 0.0% Native Hawaiian/Other Pacific Islander, 0.9% two or more races, 5.5% Hispanic of any race; Average household size: 2.66; Median age: 39.0; Age under 18: 26.7%; Age 65 and over: 14.3%; Males per 100 females: 99.9; Marriage status: 22.7% never married, 63.3% now married, 0.5% separated, 7.0% widowed, 6.9% divorced; Foreign born: 1.0%; Speak English only: 96.6%; With disability: 9.4%; Veterans: 7.9%; Ancestry: 60.0% German, 9.8% American, 6.9% Irish, 5.0% English, 2.4% French

Religion: Six largest groups: 60.3% Catholicism, 5.0% Methodist/Pietist, 4.4% European Free-Church, 2.4% Non-denominational Protestant, 2.2% Holiness, 1.6% Baptist

Economy: Unemployment rate: 3.5%; Leading industries: 17.7% construction; 14.3% retail trade; 11.6% other services (except public administration); Farms: 1,272 totaling 305,567 acres; Company size: 0 employ 1,000 or more persons, 0 employ 500 to 999 persons, 15 employ 100 to 499 persons, 720 employ less than 100 persons; Business ownership: 643 women-owned, n/a Black-owned, n/a Hispanic-owned, n/a Asian-owned

Employment: 11.1% management, business, and financial, 3.8% computer, engineering, and science, 8.8% education, legal, community service, arts, and media, 7.9% healthcare practitioners, 13.1% service, 19.2% sales and office, 13.9% natural resources, construction, and maintenance, 22.4% production, transportation, and material moving

Income: Per capita: $25,481; Median household: $61,192; Average household: $67,868; Households with income of $100,000 or more: 20.4%; Poverty rate: 6.9%

Educational Attainment: High school diploma or higher: 91.9%; Bachelor's degree or higher: 19.9%; Graduate/professional degree or higher: 7.0%

Housing: Homeownership rate: 83.1%; Median home value: $133,500; Median year structure built: 1970; Homeowner vacancy rate: 1.4%; Median gross rent: $650 per month; Rental vacancy rate: 8.4%

Vital Statistics: Birth rate: 124.1 per 10,000 population; Death rate: 92.7 per 10,000 population; Age-adjusted cancer mortality rate: 152.6 deaths per 100,000 population

Health Insurance: 95.1% have insurance; 86.1% have private insurance; 23.4% have public insurance; 4.9% do not have insurance; 2.2% of children under 18 do not have insurance

Health Care: Physicians: 5.8 per 10,000 population; Hospital beds: 0.0 per 10,000 population; Hospital admissions: 0.0 per 10,000 population

Transportation: Commute: 94.4% car, 0.4% public transportation, 1.2% walk, 3.4% work from home; Median travel time to work: 22.9 minutes
Presidential Election: 23.4% Obama, 74.8% Romney (2012)
Additional Information Contacts
Putnam Government . . . . (419) 523-3656
http://www.putnamcountyohio.gov

Putnam County Communities

BELMORE (village). Covers a land area of 0.434 square miles and a water area of 0 square miles. Located at 41.15° N. Lat; 83.94° W. Long. Elevation is 735 feet.
Population: 143; Growth (since 2000): -16.4%; Density: 329.6 persons per square mile; Race: 71.3% White, 0.0% Black/African American, 0.0% Asian, 0.7% American Indian/Alaska Native, 0.0% Native Hawaiian/Other Pacific Islander, 2.8% Two or more races, 29.4% Hispanic of any race; Average household size: 3.58; Median age: 27.5; Age under 18: 39.2%; Age 65 and over: 11.2%; Males per 100 females: 101.4
Housing: Homeownership rate: 85.0%; Homeowner vacancy rate: 2.5%; Rental vacancy rate: 0.0%

CLOVERDALE (village). Covers a land area of 0.564 square miles and a water area of 0.006 square miles. Located at 41.02° N. Lat; 84.30° W. Long. Elevation is 722 feet.
Population: 168; Growth (since 2000): -16.4%; Density: 297.9 persons per square mile; Race: 95.8% White, 0.6% Black/African American, 0.0% Asian, 0.0% American Indian/Alaska Native, 0.0% Native Hawaiian/Other Pacific Islander, 3.0% Two or more races, 3.0% Hispanic of any race; Average household size: 2.43; Median age: 35.3; Age under 18: 29.8%; Age 65 and over: 8.3%; Males per 100 females: 97.6
Housing: Homeownership rate: 84.1%; Homeowner vacancy rate: 0.0%; Rental vacancy rate: 0.0%

COLUMBUS GROVE (village). Covers a land area of 1.081 square miles and a water area of 0.004 square miles. Located at 40.92° N. Lat; 84.06° W. Long. Elevation is 774 feet.
Population: 2,137; Growth (since 2000): -2.9%; Density: 1,976.0 persons per square mile; Race: 94.2% White, 0.8% Black/African American, 0.2% Asian, 0.6% American Indian/Alaska Native, 0.0% Native Hawaiian/Other Pacific Islander, 2.3% Two or more races, 4.8% Hispanic of any race; Average household size: 2.49; Median age: 37.1; Age under 18: 27.7%; Age 65 and over: 15.8%; Males per 100 females: 94.4

School District(s)

Columbus Grove Local (PK-12)
2012-13 Enrollment: 865. . . . . (419) 659-2639
Housing: Homeownership rate: 77.0%; Homeowner vacancy rate: 2.4%; Rental vacancy rate: 4.8%

CONTINENTAL (village). Covers a land area of 0.890 square miles and a water area of 0.021 square miles. Located at 41.10° N. Lat; 84.27° W. Long. Elevation is 722 feet.
Population: 1,153; Growth (since 2000): -2.9%; Density: 1,295.5 persons per square mile; Race: 98.4% White, 0.1% Black/African American, 0.1% Asian, 0.1% American Indian/Alaska Native, 0.2% Native Hawaiian/Other Pacific Islander, 0.3% Two or more races, 3.1% Hispanic of any race; Average household size: 2.37; Median age: 42.2; Age under 18: 22.8%; Age 65 and over: 16.0%; Males per 100 females: 99.5

School District(s)

Continental Local (PK-12)
2012-13 Enrollment: 447. . . . . (419) 596-3671
Housing: Homeownership rate: 74.0%; Homeowner vacancy rate: 4.2%; Rental vacancy rate: 6.0%
Newspapers: Continental News Review (weekly circulation 1000)

DUPONT (village). Covers a land area of 0.928 square miles and a water area of 0.003 square miles. Located at 41.05° N. Lat; 84.30° W. Long. Elevation is 725 feet.
Population: 318; Growth (since 2000): 18.7%; Density: 342.5 persons per square mile; Race: 99.4% White, 0.0% Black/African American, 0.0% Asian, 0.6% American Indian/Alaska Native, 0.0% Native Hawaiian/Other Pacific Islander, 0.0% Two or more races, 0.9% Hispanic of any race; Average household size: 2.37; Median age: 39.6; Age under 18: 18.6%; Age 65 and over: 9.7%; Males per 100 females: 107.8
Housing: Homeownership rate: 85.1%; Homeowner vacancy rate: 0.0%; Rental vacancy rate: 0.0%

FORT JENNINGS (village). Covers a land area of 0.522 square miles and a water area of 0.009 square miles. Located at 40.91° N. Lat; 84.30° W. Long. Elevation is 748 feet.
Population: 485; Growth (since 2000): 12.3%; Density: 928.6 persons per square mile; Race: 99.2% White, 0.0% Black/African American, 0.8% Asian, 0.0% American Indian/Alaska Native, 0.0% Native Hawaiian/Other Pacific Islander, 0.0% Two or more races, 0.0% Hispanic of any race; Average household size: 2.50; Median age: 39.1; Age under 18: 27.0%; Age 65 and over: 16.9%; Males per 100 females: 91.7

School District(s)

Jennings Local (PK-12)
2012-13 Enrollment: 382. . . . . (419) 286-2238
Housing: Homeownership rate: 85.1%; Homeowner vacancy rate: 2.4%; Rental vacancy rate: 14.7%

GILBOA (village). Covers a land area of 0.149 square miles and a water area of 0 square miles. Located at 41.02° N. Lat; 83.92° W. Long. Elevation is 748 feet.
Population: 184; Growth (since 2000): 8.2%; Density: 1,232.4 persons per square mile; Race: 94.6% White, 0.0% Black/African American, 0.5% Asian, 0.0% American Indian/Alaska Native, 0.0% Native Hawaiian/Other Pacific Islander, 1.1% Two or more races, 9.2% Hispanic of any race; Average household size: 2.59; Median age: 34.0; Age under 18: 25.5%; Age 65 and over: 19.0%; Males per 100 females: 97.8
Housing: Homeownership rate: 88.7%; Homeowner vacancy rate: 0.0%; Rental vacancy rate: 0.0%

GLANDORF (village). Covers a land area of 1.615 square miles and a water area of <.001 square miles. Located at 41.03° N. Lat; 84.08° W. Long. Elevation is 732 feet.
Population: 1,001; Growth (since 2000): 8.9%; Density: 619.7 persons per square mile; Race: 98.3% White, 0.0% Black/African American, 0.8% Asian, 0.0% American Indian/Alaska Native, 0.0% Native Hawaiian/Other Pacific Islander, 0.8% Two or more races, 1.6% Hispanic of any race; Average household size: 2.81; Median age: 38.8; Age under 18: 28.6%; Age 65 and over: 15.9%; Males per 100 females: 89.6

School District(s)

Ottawa-Glandorf Local (PK-12)
2012-13 Enrollment: 1,531 . . . . (419) 523-5261
Housing: Homeownership rate: 91.8%; Homeowner vacancy rate: 1.3%; Rental vacancy rate: 6.5%

KALIDA (village). Covers a land area of 1.440 square miles and a water area of 0.031 square miles. Located at 40.99° N. Lat; 84.19° W. Long. Elevation is 725 feet.
Population: 1,542; Growth (since 2000): 49.6%; Density: 1,070.6 persons per square mile; Race: 98.7% White, 0.2% Black/African American, 0.0% Asian, 0.0% American Indian/Alaska Native, 0.1% Native Hawaiian/Other Pacific Islander, 0.4% Two or more races, 1.1% Hispanic of any race; Average household size: 2.53; Median age: 39.6; Age under 18: 26.5%; Age 65 and over: 17.7%; Males per 100 females: 95.4

School District(s)

Kalida Local (PK-12)
2012-13 Enrollment: 600. . . . . (419) 532-3534
Housing: Homeownership rate: 73.2%; Homeowner vacancy rate: 1.6%; Rental vacancy rate: 6.0%

LEIPSIC (village). Covers a land area of 3.651 square miles and a water area of 0.011 square miles. Located at 41.11° N. Lat; 83.97° W. Long. Elevation is 764 feet.
Population: 2,093; Growth (since 2000): -6.4%; Density: 573.2 persons per square mile; Race: 77.8% White, 0.2% Black/African American, 0.4% Asian, 0.6% American Indian/Alaska Native, 0.0% Native Hawaiian/Other Pacific Islander, 2.9% Two or more races, 31.3% Hispanic of any race; Average household size: 2.58; Median age: 37.0; Age under 18: 27.9%; Age 65 and over: 16.1%; Males per 100 females: 90.8

School District(s)

Leipsic Local (PK-12)
2012-13 Enrollment: 635. . . . . (419) 943-2165
Housing: Homeownership rate: 68.8%; Homeowner vacancy rate: 1.9%; Rental vacancy rate: 11.6%
Newspapers: Leipsic Messenger (weekly circulation 1400)

MILLER CITY (village). Covers a land area of 0.301 square miles and a water area of 0 square miles. Located at 41.10° N. Lat; 84.13° W. Long. Elevation is 732 feet.

Population: 137; Growth (since 2000): 0.7%; Density: 454.8 persons per square mile; Race: 100.0% White, 0.0% Black/African American, 0.0% Asian, 0.0% American Indian/Alaska Native, 0.0% Native Hawaiian/Other Pacific Islander, 0.0% Two or more races, 0.0% Hispanic of any race; Average household size: 2.25; Median age: 40.8; Age under 18: 19.7%; Age 65 and over: 21.9%; Males per 100 females: 101.5

School District(s)

Miller City-New Cleveland Local (PK-12)
2012-13 Enrollment: 461. . . . . (419) 876-3172

Housing: Homeownership rate: 90.2%; Homeowner vacancy rate: 1.8%; Rental vacancy rate: 0.0%

OTTAWA (village). County seat. Covers a land area of 4.696 square miles and a water area of 0.068 square miles. Located at 41.02° N. Lat; 84.03° W. Long. Elevation is 725 feet.

History: Ottawa was established in 1833, and named for the Ottawa Indians. The Ohio Sugar Company, a beet-sugar refinery, was built here.

Population: 4,460; Growth (since 2000): 2.1%; Density: 949.8 persons per square mile; Race: 92.5% White, 0.8% Black/African American, 0.3% Asian, 0.4% American Indian/Alaska Native, 0.0% Native Hawaiian/Other Pacific Islander, 1.2% Two or more races, 10.3% Hispanic of any race; Average household size: 2.41; Median age: 38.8; Age under 18: 26.1%; Age 65 and over: 15.4%; Males per 100 females: 94.1; Marriage status: 21.0% never married, 59.7% now married, 0.9% separated, 11.0% widowed, 8.2% divorced; Foreign born: 2.4%; Speak English only: 95.1%; With disability: 9.2%; Veterans: 7.4%; Ancestry: 48.0% German, 10.4% Irish, 8.9% American, 6.6% English, 4.3% Italian

Employment: 11.3% management, business, and financial, 9.0% computer, engineering, and science, 13.2% education, legal, community service, arts, and media, 3.3% healthcare practitioners, 12.0% service, 20.8% sales and office, 7.8% natural resources, construction, and maintenance, 22.6% production, transportation, and material moving

Income: Per capita: $26,202; Median household: $53,697; Average household: $61,664; Households with income of $100,000 or more: 19.4%; Poverty rate: 8.5%

Educational Attainment: High school diploma or higher: 91.2%; Bachelor's degree or higher: 28.3%; Graduate/professional degree or higher: 8.1%

School District(s)

Ottawa-Glandorf Local (PK-12)
2012-13 Enrollment: 1,531 . . . . (419) 523-5261

Housing: Homeownership rate: 68.6%; Median home value: $137,500; Median year structure built: 1973; Homeowner vacancy rate: 1.9%; Median gross rent: $597 per month; Rental vacancy rate: 12.7%

Health Insurance: 92.1% have insurance; 76.9% have private insurance; 32.5% have public insurance; 7.9% do not have insurance; 2.3% of children under 18 do not have insurance

Newspapers: Putnam County Sentinel (weekly circulation 6000); Putnam County Vidette (weekly circulation 1100)

Transportation: Commute: 94.1% car, 0.0% public transportation, 3.8% walk, 1.1% work from home; Median travel time to work: 21.2 minutes

Additional Information Contacts

Village of Ottawa. . . . . (419) 523-5020
http://ottawaohio.us

OTTOVILLE (village). Covers a land area of 0.800 square miles and a water area of 0.005 square miles. Located at 40.93° N. Lat; 84.34° W. Long. Elevation is 741 feet.

Population: 976; Growth (since 2000): 11.8%; Density: 1,220.4 persons per square mile; Race: 97.5% White, 0.6% Black/African American, 0.6% Asian, 0.0% American Indian/Alaska Native, 0.0% Native Hawaiian/Other Pacific Islander, 0.3% Two or more races, 1.7% Hispanic of any race; Average household size: 2.49; Median age: 38.7; Age under 18: 25.3%; Age 65 and over: 16.2%; Males per 100 females: 93.7

School District(s)

Ottoville Local (PK-12)
2012-13 Enrollment: 441. . . . . (419) 453-3356

Housing: Homeownership rate: 79.3%; Homeowner vacancy rate: 1.9%; Rental vacancy rate: 7.9%

Additional Information Contacts

Village of Ottoville . . . . (419) 453-2426
http://www.villageofottoville.org

PANDORA (village). Covers a land area of 0.903 square miles and a water area of 0.024 square miles. Located at 40.95° N. Lat; 83.96° W. Long. Elevation is 774 feet.

Population: 1,153; Growth (since 2000): -2.9%; Density: 1,276.2 persons per square mile; Race: 97.2% White, 0.3% Black/African American, 0.0% Asian, 0.3% American Indian/Alaska Native, 0.0% Native Hawaiian/Other Pacific Islander, 0.6% Two or more races, 3.4% Hispanic of any race; Average household size: 2.43; Median age: 40.0; Age under 18: 24.4%; Age 65 and over: 18.6%; Males per 100 females: 96.4

School District(s)

Pandora-Gilboa Local (PK-12)
2012-13 Enrollment: 561. . . . . (419) 384-3227

Housing: Homeownership rate: 80.3%; Homeowner vacancy rate: 2.7%; Rental vacancy rate: 8.2%

VAUGHNSVILLE (CDP). Covers a land area of 0.171 square miles and a water area of 0.002 square miles. Located at 40.88° N. Lat; 84.15° W. Long. Elevation is 761 feet.

Population: 262; Growth (since 2000): n/a; Density: 1,531.9 persons per square mile; Race: 96.6% White, 0.0% Black/African American, 1.1% Asian, 0.0% American Indian/Alaska Native, 0.0% Native Hawaiian/Other Pacific Islander, 0.4% Two or more races, 1.9% Hispanic of any race; Average household size: 2.52; Median age: 36.0; Age under 18: 23.7%; Age 65 and over: 17.6%; Males per 100 females: 97.0

Housing: Homeownership rate: 81.7%; Homeowner vacancy rate: 6.6%; Rental vacancy rate: 5.0%

WEST LEIPSIC (village). Covers a land area of 0.238 square miles and a water area of 0 square miles. Located at 41.11° N. Lat; 84.00° W. Long. Elevation is 771 feet.

Population: 206; Growth (since 2000): -24.0%; Density: 865.4 persons per square mile; Race: 83.0% White, 0.5% Black/African American, 1.5% Asian, 0.0% American Indian/Alaska Native, 0.0% Native Hawaiian/Other Pacific Islander, 1.5% Two or more races, 29.6% Hispanic of any race; Average household size: 2.51; Median age: 40.4; Age under 18: 24.3%; Age 65 and over: 19.4%; Males per 100 females: 92.5

Housing: Homeownership rate: 80.5%; Homeowner vacancy rate: 1.5%; Rental vacancy rate: 0.0%

Richland County

Located in north central Ohio; drained by forks of the Mohican River. Covers a land area of 495.269 square miles, a water area of 4.809 square miles, and is located in the Eastern Time Zone at 40.77° N. Lat., 82.54° W. Long. The county was founded in 1813. County seat is Mansfield.

Richland County is part of the Mansfield, OH Metropolitan Statistical Area. The entire metro area includes: Richland County, OH

Weather Station: Mansfield 5 W — Elevation: 1,350 feet

	Jan	Feb	Mar	Apr	May	Jun	Jul	Aug	Sep	Oct	Nov	Dec
High	32	36	46	59	70	78	82	80	74	61	49	37
Low	17	19	27	37	47	56	60	59	52	40	32	22
Precip	2.2	1.8	2.8	3.6	4.6	4.4	4.0	3.8	3.2	2.8	3.1	2.9
Snow	na	na	na	0.4	0.0	0.0	0.0	0.0	0.0	tr	0.4	na

High and Low temperatures in degrees Fahrenheit; Precipitation and Snow in inches

Weather Station: Mansfield Lahm Municipal Arpt — Elevation: 1,294 feet

	Jan	Feb	Mar	Apr	May	Jun	Jul	Aug	Sep	Oct	Nov	Dec
High	33	36	46	59	69	78	82	80	73	62	49	37
Low	19	21	28	39	48	58	62	61	53	42	34	24
Precip	2.9	2.3	3.5	4.2	4.5	4.7	4.5	4.4	3.3	2.9	3.7	3.3
Snow	13.1	10.3	8.0	2.7	tr	tr	0.0	0.0	0.0	0.6	2.5	10.5

High and Low temperatures in degrees Fahrenheit; Precipitation and Snow in inches

Population: 124,475; Growth (since 2000): -3.4%; Density: 251.3 persons per square mile; Race: 87.5% White, 9.4% Black/African American, 0.6% Asian, 0.2% American Indian/Alaska Native, 0.0% Native Hawaiian/Other Pacific Islander, 1.9% two or more races, 1.4% Hispanic of any race; Average household size: 2.40; Median age: 40.9; Age under 18: 22.5%; Age 65 and over: 16.3%; Males per 100 females: 102.2; Marriage status: 28.0% never married, 51.2% now married, 2.8% separated, 7.9% widowed, 12.9% divorced; Foreign born: 1.5%; Speak English only: 96.6%; With disability: 13.9%; Veterans: 11.1%; Ancestry: 30.4% German, 13.4% Irish, 12.4% English, 9.3% American, 4.2% Italian

Religion: Six largest groups: 10.4% Non-denominational Protestant, 7.8% Catholicism, 6.1% Baptist, 4.4% Methodist/Pietist, 3.2% Lutheran, 3.1% Pentecostal
Economy: Unemployment rate: 5.0%; Leading industries: 16.7% retail trade; 13.4% other services (except public administration); 11.9% health care and social assistance; Farms: 1,010 totaling 160,623 acres; Company size: 2 employ 1,000 or more persons, 3 employ 500 to 999 persons, 69 employ 100 to 499 persons, 2,562 employ less than 100 persons; Business ownership: 2,424 women-owned, 215 Black-owned, n/a Hispanic-owned, 212 Asian-owned
Employment: 10.3% management, business, and financial, 2.7% computer, engineering, and science, 8.3% education, legal, community service, arts, and media, 6.0% healthcare practitioners, 19.2% service, 24.1% sales and office, 7.2% natural resources, construction, and maintenance, 22.2% production, transportation, and material moving
Income: Per capita: $21,932; Median household: $41,835; Average household: $54,211; Households with income of $100,000 or more: 11.7%; Poverty rate: 15.7%
Educational Attainment: High school diploma or higher: 86.2%; Bachelor's degree or higher: 14.9%; Graduate/professional degree or higher: 5.2%
Housing: Homeownership rate: 69.1%; Median home value: $103,500; Median year structure built: 1963; Homeowner vacancy rate: 2.4%; Median gross rent: $608 per month; Rental vacancy rate: 13.1%
Vital Statistics: Birth rate: 111.8 per 10,000 population; Death rate: 105.9 per 10,000 population; Age-adjusted cancer mortality rate: 184.2 deaths per 100,000 population
Health Insurance: 87.8% have insurance; 66.5% have private insurance; 37.3% have public insurance; 12.2% do not have insurance; 7.6% of children under 18 do not have insurance
Health Care: Physicians: 15.6 per 10,000 population; Hospital beds: 26.5 per 10,000 population; Hospital admissions: 1,200.0 per 10,000 population
Transportation: Commute: 94.0% car, 0.7% public transportation, 2.0% walk, 2.7% work from home; Median travel time to work: 21.2 minutes
Presidential Election: 38.9% Obama, 59.1% Romney (2012)
National and State Parks: Fowler Woods State Nature Preserve; Malabar Farm State Park
Additional Information Contacts
Richland Government . . . . (419) 774-5599
http://www.richlandcountyoh.us

Richland County Communities

BELLVILLE (village). Covers a land area of 2.735 square miles and a water area of 0.013 square miles. Located at 40.62° N. Lat; 82.51° W. Long. Elevation is 1,138 feet.
History: Bellville grew as a farm community surrounded by apple and peach orchards. Twice, the town's hopes for fortune were dashed. In 1853 Dr. James C. Lee, a former California miner, found gold here, but the amount turned out to be very small. In the 1890's it was thought that a spring might be of therapeutic value and a sanitarium was built, but failed to become a popular health spa.
Population: 1,918; Growth (since 2000): 8.2%; Density: 701.2 persons per square mile; Race: 97.7% White, 0.5% Black/African American, 0.1% Asian, 0.2% American Indian/Alaska Native, 0.0% Native Hawaiian/Other Pacific Islander, 1.5% Two or more races, 0.5% Hispanic of any race; Average household size: 2.32; Median age: 42.8; Age under 18: 23.4%; Age 65 and over: 20.5%; Males per 100 females: 92.8

School District(s)

Clear Fork Valley Local (PK-12)
2012-13 Enrollment: 1,832 . . . . (419) 886-3855
Housing: Homeownership rate: 68.0%; Homeowner vacancy rate: 1.6%; Rental vacancy rate: 6.7%
Newspapers: Star & Tri-Forks Press (weekly circulation 2100)
Additional Information Contacts
Village of Bellville . . . . (419) 886-2245
http://www.bellvilleohio.net/villageadmin.htm

BUTLER (village). Covers a land area of 1.140 square miles and a water area of 0.007 square miles. Located at 40.59° N. Lat; 82.42° W. Long. Elevation is 1,073 feet.
Population: 933; Growth (since 2000): 1.3%; Density: 818.5 persons per square mile; Race: 98.3% White, 0.4% Black/African American, 0.1% Asian, 0.1% American Indian/Alaska Native, 0.0% Native Hawaiian/Other Pacific Islander, 0.8% Two or more races, 1.5% Hispanic of any race; Average household size: 2.57; Median age: 37.2; Age under 18: 26.8%; Age 65 and over: 15.0%; Males per 100 females: 93.6

School District(s)

Clear Fork Valley Local (PK-12)
2012-13 Enrollment: 1,832 . . . . (419) 886-3855
Housing: Homeownership rate: 76.5%; Homeowner vacancy rate: 1.1%; Rental vacancy rate: 18.3%

LEXINGTON (village). Covers a land area of 3.812 square miles and a water area of 0.004 square miles. Located at 40.68° N. Lat; 82.58° W. Long. Elevation is 1,214 feet.
Population: 4,822; Growth (since 2000): 15.8%; Density: 1,264.8 persons per square mile; Race: 96.3% White, 1.2% Black/African American, 1.0% Asian, 0.2% American Indian/Alaska Native, 0.0% Native Hawaiian/Other Pacific Islander, 1.2% Two or more races, 1.2% Hispanic of any race; Average household size: 2.41; Median age: 39.9; Age under 18: 25.0%; Age 65 and over: 14.9%; Males per 100 females: 90.9; Marriage status: 22.0% never married, 61.4% now married, 3.6% separated, 6.1% widowed, 10.6% divorced; Foreign born: 1.9%; Speak English only: 97.8%; With disability: 8.9%; Veterans: 6.2%; Ancestry: 39.8% German, 15.8% Irish, 14.5% English, 10.5% American, 5.6% Italian
Employment: 18.5% management, business, and financial, 1.9% computer, engineering, and science, 15.5% education, legal, community service, arts, and media, 10.0% healthcare practitioners, 16.1% service, 26.2% sales and office, 4.8% natural resources, construction, and maintenance, 6.9% production, transportation, and material moving
Income: Per capita: $24,901; Median household: $54,350; Average household: $64,107; Households with income of $100,000 or more: 19.5%; Poverty rate: 10.1%
Educational Attainment: High school diploma or higher: 94.5%; Bachelor's degree or higher: 29.0%; Graduate/professional degree or higher: 9.5%

School District(s)

Lexington Local (PK-12)
2012-13 Enrollment: 2,397 . . . . (419) 884-2132
Housing: Homeownership rate: 68.4%; Median home value: $128,500; Median year structure built: 1972; Homeowner vacancy rate: 1.2%; Median gross rent: $578 per month; Rental vacancy rate: 7.9%
Health Insurance: 89.5% have insurance; 77.9% have private insurance; 24.1% have public insurance; 10.5% do not have insurance; 6.1% of children under 18 do not have insurance
Transportation: Commute: 95.8% car, 0.0% public transportation, 0.5% walk, 3.7% work from home; Median travel time to work: 24.2 minutes
Additional Information Contacts
Village of Lexington . . . . (419) 884-0765
http://www.lexingtonohio.us

LUCAS (village). Covers a land area of 0.688 square miles and a water area of <.001 square miles. Located at 40.70° N. Lat; 82.42° W. Long. Elevation is 1,086 feet.
Population: 615; Growth (since 2000): -0.8%; Density: 893.4 persons per square mile; Race: 98.0% White, 0.3% Black/African American, 0.0% Asian, 0.0% American Indian/Alaska Native, 0.0% Native Hawaiian/Other Pacific Islander, 1.6% Two or more races, 0.0% Hispanic of any race; Average household size: 2.59; Median age: 34.9; Age under 18: 20.1%; Age 65 and over: 11.7%; Males per 100 females: 96.5

School District(s)

Lucas Local (PK-12)
2012-13 Enrollment: 550. . . . . (419) 892-2338
Housing: Homeownership rate: 64.9%; Homeowner vacancy rate: 2.5%; Rental vacancy rate: 17.0%

MANSFIELD (city). County seat. Covers a land area of 30.872 square miles and a water area of 0.053 square miles. Located at 40.77° N. Lat; 82.53° W. Long. Elevation is 1,240 feet.
History: Mansfield was named for Jared Mansfield, U.S. Surveyor General, who directed the townsite to be laid out in 1808. Mansfield grew as the surrounding lands were cleared of timber and put under cultivation. During the War of 1812, Mansfield was threatened by British allies, but John Chapman (better known as Johnny Appleseed) made the 30-mile trip to bring troops from Mount Vernon, and Mansfield was saved. Mansfield's growth was slow, spurred only by the arrival of the railroad in 1846, until after the Civil War. By 1900 it was the home of the Ohio Brass Company, the Empire Sheet and Tin Plate Company, Tappan Stove Company, and a plant of the Westinghouse Electric and Manufacturing Company.

Population: 47,821; Growth (since 2000): -3.1%; Density: 1,549.0 persons per square mile; Race: 73.3% White, 22.1% Black/African American, 0.7% Asian, 0.2% American Indian/Alaska Native, 0.1% Native Hawaiian/Other Pacific Islander, 3.0% Two or more races, 1.9% Hispanic of any race; Average household size: 2.21; Median age: 38.5; Age under 18: 20.2%; Age 65 and over: 15.7%; Males per 100 females: 112.6; Marriage status: 35.8% never married, 39.7% now married, 3.7% separated, 8.5% widowed, 16.0% divorced; Foreign born: 1.7%; Speak English only: 96.7%; With disability: 18.1%; Veterans: 11.4%; Ancestry: 25.2% German, 12.2% Irish, 10.1% English, 7.0% American, 4.4% Italian
Employment: 8.3% management, business, and financial, 2.8% computer, engineering, and science, 7.5% education, legal, community service, arts, and media, 5.5% healthcare practitioners, 22.1% service, 25.7% sales and office, 4.5% natural resources, construction, and maintenance, 23.6% production, transportation, and material moving
Income: Per capita: $18,279; Median household: $32,722; Average household: $44,420; Households with income of $100,000 or more: 7.7%; Poverty rate: 24.4%
Educational Attainment: High school diploma or higher: 82.0%; Bachelor's degree or higher: 12.4%; Graduate/professional degree or higher: 4.6%

School District(s)

Constellation Schools: Mansfield Community Element (KG-03)
2012-13 Enrollment: 134. . . . . (419) 522-4578
Constellation Schools: Mansfield Community Middle (04-08)
2012-13 Enrollment: 131. . . . . (419) 522-2705
Foundation Academy (KG-08)
2012-13 Enrollment: 388. . . . . (419) 526-9540
Goal Digital Academy (01-12)
2012-13 Enrollment: 329. . . . . (419) 521-9008
Interactive Media & Construction (Imac) (09-12)
2012-13 Enrollment: 29. . . . . (419) 525-0105
Madison Local (PK-12)
2012-13 Enrollment: 3,112 . . . . (419) 589-2600
Mansfield City (PK-12)
2012-13 Enrollment: 3,663 . . . . (419) 525-6400
Mansfield Elective Academy (02-09)
2012-13 Enrollment: 29. . . . . (567) 247-4475
Mansfield Enhancement Academy (09-12)
2012-13 Enrollment: 49. . . . . (419) 525-0105
Ontario Local (PK-12)
2012-13 Enrollment: 1,814 . . . . (419) 747-4311
Richland Academy School of Excellence (04-08)
2012-13 Enrollment: 159. . . . . (419) 522-8224

Four-year College(s)

Ohio State University-Mansfield Campus (Public)
Fall 2013 Enrollment: 1,204 . . . . (419) 755-4011
2013-14 Tuition: In-state $7,140; Out-of-state $22,860

Two-year College(s)

Madison Adult Career Center (Public)
Fall 2013 Enrollment: 145. . . . . (419) 589-6363
North Central State College (Public)
Fall 2013 Enrollment: 2,958 . . . . (419) 755-4800
2013-14 Tuition: In-state $3,511; Out-of-state $7,023

Housing: Homeownership rate: 54.0%; Median home value: $79,900; Median year structure built: 1956; Homeowner vacancy rate: 3.4%; Median gross rent: $573 per month; Rental vacancy rate: 15.8%
Health Insurance: 86.7% have insurance; 54.7% have private insurance; 47.6% have public insurance; 13.3% do not have insurance; 4.1% of children under 18 do not have insurance
Hospitals: Medcentral Health System Mansfield Hospital (398 beds)
Safety: Violent crime rate: 36.1 per 10,000 population; Property crime rate: 676.2 per 10,000 population
Newspapers: News Journal (daily circulation 29100)
Transportation: Commute: 93.1% car, 1.6% public transportation, 2.6% walk, 1.7% work from home; Median travel time to work: 18.7 minutes
Airports: Mansfield Lahm Regional (general aviation)
Additional Information Contacts
City of Mansfield . . . . (419) 755-9626
http://www.ci.mansfield.oh.us

ONTARIO (city). Covers a land area of 11.084 square miles and a water area of 0.023 square miles. Located at 40.77° N. Lat; 82.62° W. Long. Elevation is 1,355 feet.
Population: 6,225; Growth (since 2000): 17.4%; Density: 561.6 persons per square mile; Race: 90.8% White, 4.0% Black/African American, 2.6% Asian, 0.3% American Indian/Alaska Native, 0.0% Native Hawaiian/Other Pacific Islander, 1.8% Two or more races, 1.6% Hispanic of any race; Average household size: 2.35; Median age: 43.1; Age under 18: 22.8%; Age 65 and over: 20.2%; Males per 100 females: 88.9; Marriage status: 24.0% never married, 53.8% now married, 0.8% separated, 10.1% widowed, 12.1% divorced; Foreign born: 5.3%; Speak English only: 92.1%; With disability: 12.2%; Veterans: 8.4%; Ancestry: 21.3% German, 15.7% English, 12.8% American, 11.8% Irish, 4.4% French
Employment: 11.1% management, business, and financial, 3.7% computer, engineering, and science, 7.9% education, legal, community service, arts, and media, 5.6% healthcare practitioners, 25.7% service, 23.9% sales and office, 5.2% natural resources, construction, and maintenance, 17.0% production, transportation, and material moving
Income: Per capita: $25,132; Median household: $47,698; Average household: $58,649; Households with income of $100,000 or more: 16.0%; Poverty rate: 5.8%
Educational Attainment: High school diploma or higher: 91.9%; Bachelor's degree or higher: 22.3%; Graduate/professional degree or higher: 6.3%

Vocational/Technical School(s)

Ross Medical Education Center-Ontario (Private, For-profit)
Fall 2013 Enrollment: 136 . . . . (419) 747-2206
2013-14 Tuition: $15,680

Housing: Homeownership rate: 68.7%; Median home value: $123,400; Median year structure built: 1979; Homeowner vacancy rate: 3.1%; Median gross rent: $692 per month; Rental vacancy rate: 8.5%
Health Insurance: 92.7% have insurance; 80.3% have private insurance; 33.7% have public insurance; 7.3% do not have insurance; 1.0% of children under 18 do not have insurance
Safety: Violent crime rate: 11.4 per 10,000 population; Property crime rate: 1,078.7 per 10,000 population
Newspapers: Tribune-Courier (weekly circulation 2400)
Transportation: Commute: 98.2% car, 0.6% public transportation, 0.0% walk, 1.2% work from home; Median travel time to work: 15.8 minutes
Additional Information Contacts
City of Ontario . . . . (419) 529-3818
http://www.ontarioohio.org

PLYMOUTH (village). Covers a land area of 2.465 square miles and a water area of 0.032 square miles. Located at 41.00° N. Lat; 82.67° W. Long. Elevation is 1,017 feet.
Population: 1,857; Growth (since 2000): 0.3%; Density: 753.3 persons per square mile; Race: 97.6% White, 0.3% Black/African American, 0.2% Asian, 0.2% American Indian/Alaska Native, 0.0% Native Hawaiian/Other Pacific Islander, 0.7% Two or more races, 2.5% Hispanic of any race; Average household size: 2.67; Median age: 34.1; Age under 18: 29.5%; Age 65 and over: 13.3%; Males per 100 females: 92.8

School District(s)

Plymouth-Shiloh Local (PK-12)
2012-13 Enrollment: 774. . . . . (419) 687-4733

Housing: Homeownership rate: 63.2%; Homeowner vacancy rate: 3.7%; Rental vacancy rate: 15.8%

SHELBY (city). Covers a land area of 6.348 square miles and a water area of 0.142 square miles. Located at 40.88° N. Lat; 82.66° W. Long. Elevation is 1,099 feet.
Population: 9,317; Growth (since 2000): -5.1%; Density: 1,467.8 persons per square mile; Race: 98.2% White, 0.2% Black/African American, 0.3% Asian, 0.2% American Indian/Alaska Native, 0.0% Native Hawaiian/Other Pacific Islander, 1.0% Two or more races, 1.2% Hispanic of any race; Average household size: 2.34; Median age: 40.1; Age under 18: 24.5%; Age 65 and over: 17.6%; Males per 100 females: 88.6; Marriage status: 23.3% never married, 50.8% now married, 2.9% separated, 9.2% widowed, 16.7% divorced; Foreign born: 0.4%; Speak English only: 99.5%; With disability: 12.2%; Veterans: 9.2%; Ancestry: 35.9% German, 18.2% Irish, 13.7% English, 10.8% American, 5.2% Italian
Employment: 9.2% management, business, and financial, 1.7% computer, engineering, and science, 8.5% education, legal, community service, arts, and media, 6.1% healthcare practitioners, 17.9% service, 22.4% sales and

office, 7.8% natural resources, construction, and maintenance, 26.3% production, transportation, and material moving
Income: Per capita: $22,668; Median household: $41,650; Average household: $52,057; Households with income of $100,000 or more: 9.3%; Poverty rate: 12.1%
Educational Attainment: High school diploma or higher: 87.8%; Bachelor's degree or higher: 12.0%; Graduate/professional degree or higher: 4.9%

School District(s)

Pioneer Career & Technology (07-12)
2012-13 Enrollment: n/a . . . . (419) 347-7926
Shelby City (PK-12)
2012-13 Enrollment: 1,880 . . . . (419) 342-3520

Vocational/Technical School(s)

Pioneer Career and Technology Center (Public)
Fall 2013 Enrollment: 35 . . . . (419) 347-7744
2013-14 Tuition: $4,240

Housing: Homeownership rate: 63.8%; Median home value: $87,700; Median year structure built: 1958; Homeowner vacancy rate: 2.9%; Median gross rent: $550 per month; Rental vacancy rate: 12.5%
Health Insurance: 89.1% have insurance; 70.2% have private insurance; 33.9% have public insurance; 10.9% do not have insurance; 1.1% of children under 18 do not have insurance
Hospitals: Medcentral Health System Shelby Hospital (68 beds)
Safety: Violent crime rate: 12.0 per 10,000 population; Property crime rate: 399.7 per 10,000 population
Newspapers: Daily Globe (daily circulation 4000)
Transportation: Commute: 93.6% car, 0.0% public transportation, 3.7% walk, 2.3% work from home; Median travel time to work: 18.4 minutes

SHILOH (village). Covers a land area of 0.905 square miles and a water area of 0.004 square miles. Located at 40.97° N. Lat; 82.60° W. Long. Elevation is 1,079 feet.
Population: 649; Growth (since 2000): -10.0%; Density: 717.0 persons per square mile; Race: 97.8% White, 0.6% Black/African American, 0.3% Asian, 0.8% American Indian/Alaska Native, 0.0% Native Hawaiian/Other Pacific Islander, 0.5% Two or more races, 0.5% Hispanic of any race; Average household size: 2.76; Median age: 38.4; Age under 18: 25.0%; Age 65 and over: 11.9%; Males per 100 females: 99.7
Housing: Homeownership rate: 78.3%; Homeowner vacancy rate: 3.6%; Rental vacancy rate: 8.9%

Ross County

Located in southern Ohio; crossed by the Scioto River and several creeks. Covers a land area of 689.188 square miles, a water area of 3.837 square miles, and is located in the Eastern Time Zone at 39.32° N. Lat., 83.06° W. Long. The county was founded in 1798. County seat is Chillicothe.

Ross County is part of the Chillicothe, OH Micropolitan Statistical Area. The entire metro area includes: Ross County, OH

Weather Station: Chillicothe Mound City Elevation: 649 feet

	Jan	Feb	Mar	Apr	May	Jun	Jul	Aug	Sep	Oct	Nov	Dec
High	38	43	52	65	73	82	86	85	78	67	54	42
Low	20	23	30	40	50	59	63	61	53	41	34	25
Precip	2.6	2.5	3.5	3.6	4.6	3.3	4.0	3.1	2.7	2.6	2.9	2.8
Snow	5.2	4.0	2.4	0.4	tr	0.0	0.0	0.0	0.0	0.1	0.4	2.3

High and Low temperatures in degrees Fahrenheit; Precipitation and Snow in inches

Population: 78,064; Growth (since 2000): 6.4%; Density: 113.3 persons per square mile; Race: 90.7% White, 6.2% Black/African American, 0.4% Asian, 0.3% American Indian/Alaska Native, 0.0% Native Hawaiian/Other Pacific Islander, 2.1% two or more races, 1.0% Hispanic of any race; Average household size: 2.48; Median age: 39.8; Age under 18: 22.5%; Age 65 and over: 13.5%; Males per 100 females: 111.6; Marriage status: 27.8% never married, 51.5% now married, 2.4% separated, 6.4% widowed, 14.3% divorced; Foreign born: 0.7%; Speak English only: 96.9%; With disability: 17.5%; Veterans: 11.9%; Ancestry: 26.1% German, 15.1% Irish, 12.1% American, 10.0% English, 1.9% French
Religion: Six largest groups: 5.9% Baptist, 5.5% Methodist/Pietist, 4.2% Non-denominational Protestant, 3.5% Catholicism, 1.9% Holiness, 1.3% Pentecostal
Economy: Unemployment rate: 4.9%; Leading industries: 19.0% retail trade; 12.9% health care and social assistance; 12.0% other services (except public administration); Farms: 980 totaling 221,723 acres; Company size: 4 employ 1,000 or more persons, 1 employs 500 to 999 persons, 27 employ 100 to 499 persons, 1,205 employ less than 100 persons; Business ownership: 1,576 women-owned, n/a Black-owned, n/a Hispanic-owned, n/a Asian-owned
Employment: 9.6% management, business, and financial, 3.4% computer, engineering, and science, 7.2% education, legal, community service, arts, and media, 6.8% healthcare practitioners, 19.9% service, 21.4% sales and office, 9.9% natural resources, construction, and maintenance, 21.9% production, transportation, and material moving
Income: Per capita: $21,310; Median household: $43,264; Average household: $56,902; Households with income of $100,000 or more: 14.4%; Poverty rate: 19.7%
Educational Attainment: High school diploma or higher: 84.1%; Bachelor's degree or higher: 13.7%; Graduate/professional degree or higher: 5.4%
Housing: Homeownership rate: 70.5%; Median home value: $111,100; Median year structure built: 1972; Homeowner vacancy rate: 2.6%; Median gross rent: $641 per month; Rental vacancy rate: 8.8%
Vital Statistics: Birth rate: 108.2 per 10,000 population; Death rate: 98.4 per 10,000 population; Age-adjusted cancer mortality rate: 205.8 deaths per 100,000 population
Health Insurance: 87.0% have insurance; 62.1% have private insurance; 37.5% have public insurance; 13.0% do not have insurance; 6.0% of children under 18 do not have insurance
Health Care: Physicians: 17.8 per 10,000 population; Hospital beds: 71.0 per 10,000 population; Hospital admissions: 2,350.7 per 10,000 population
Transportation: Commute: 94.0% car, 0.7% public transportation, 1.5% walk, 2.5% work from home; Median travel time to work: 25.9 minutes
Presidential Election: 48.0% Obama, 50.4% Romney (2012)
National and State Parks: Adena State Memorial; Great Seal State Park; Hopewell Culture National Historical Park; Paint Creek State Park; Ross County Lake State Wildlife Area; Scioto River Canal Lands Access State Wildlife Area; Scioto Trail State Forest; Scioto Trail State Park; Seip Mound State Memorial; Story Mound State Memorial; Tar Hollow State Forest

Additional Information Contacts

Ross Government . . . . (740) 702-3085
http://www.co.ross.oh.us

Ross County Communities

ADELPHI (village). Covers a land area of 0.274 square miles and a water area of <.001 square miles. Located at 39.46° N. Lat; 82.75° W. Long. Elevation is 837 feet.
Population: 380; Growth (since 2000): 2.4%; Density: 1,386.3 persons per square mile; Race: 95.0% White, 1.6% Black/African American, 0.3% Asian, 0.0% American Indian/Alaska Native, 0.0% Native Hawaiian/Other Pacific Islander, 3.2% Two or more races, 0.0% Hispanic of any race; Average household size: 2.47; Median age: 39.0; Age under 18: 26.8%; Age 65 and over: 15.3%; Males per 100 females: 104.3
Housing: Homeownership rate: 75.4%; Homeowner vacancy rate: 4.1%; Rental vacancy rate: 9.5%

ANDERSONVILLE (CDP). Covers a land area of 2.274 square miles and a water area of 0 square miles. Located at 39.43° N. Lat, 83.02° W. Long. Elevation is 653 feet.
Population: 779; Growth (since 2000): n/a; Density: 342.6 persons per square mile; Race: 96.3% White, 1.9% Black/African American, 0.4% Asian, 0.0% American Indian/Alaska Native, 0.0% Native Hawaiian/Other Pacific Islander, 1.2% Two or more races, 1.7% Hispanic of any race; Average household size: 2.59; Median age: 42.9; Age under 18: 25.5%; Age 65 and over: 11.8%; Males per 100 females: 93.3
Housing: Homeownership rate: 86.7%; Homeowner vacancy rate: 1.9%; Rental vacancy rate: 11.1%

BAINBRIDGE (village). Covers a land area of 0.512 square miles and a water area of 0 square miles. Located at 39.23° N. Lat; 83.27° W. Long. Elevation is 735 feet.
History: Bainbridge was founded in 1805 by Nathaniel Massie, a landowner and surveyor. In 1826 Dr. John Harris established a school for teaching dentistry here, where Chapin A. Harris was trained. Harris later founded the dental college at Baltimore and the "American Journal of Dental Science."
Population: 860; Growth (since 2000): -15.0%; Density: 1,679.2 persons per square mile; Race: 96.4% White, 0.8% Black/African American, 0.0%

Asian, 0.2% American Indian/Alaska Native, 0.0% Native Hawaiian/Other Pacific Islander, 2.6% Two or more races, 0.6% Hispanic of any race; Average household size: 2.36; Median age: 43.2; Age under 18: 22.6%; Age 65 and over: 20.9%; Males per 100 females: 84.9

School District(s)

Paint Valley Local (PK-12)
2012-13 Enrollment: 981 . . . . (740) 634-2826

Housing: Homeownership rate: 65.0%; Homeowner vacancy rate: 2.9%; Rental vacancy rate: 6.0%

BOURNEVILLE (CDP). Covers a land area of 0.503 square miles and a water area of 0 square miles. Located at 39.28° N. Lat; 83.16° W. Long. Elevation is 679 feet.

Population: 199; Growth (since 2000): n/a; Density: 396.0 persons per square mile; Race: 98.5% White, 0.0% Black/African American, 0.0% Asian, 0.5% American Indian/Alaska Native, 0.0% Native Hawaiian/Other Pacific Islander, 1.0% Two or more races, 0.5% Hispanic of any race; Average household size: 2.49; Median age: 39.8; Age under 18: 22.1%; Age 65 and over: 20.1%; Males per 100 females: 80.9

Housing: Homeownership rate: 65.0%; Homeowner vacancy rate: 8.8%; Rental vacancy rate: 6.5%

CHILLICOTHE (city). County seat. Covers a land area of 10.428 square miles and a water area of 0.167 square miles. Located at 39.34° N. Lat; 82.99° W. Long. Elevation is 633 feet.

History: In 1796 Nathaniel Massie established a community of settlers on the Scioto River at the mouth of Paint Creek. When Edward Tiffin and other young men came from Virginia in 1798, the town of Chillicothe was founded and became the capitol of the Northwest Territory. Ohio became a state in 1803, and Chillicothe continued as the capitol until 1810. Then industrial growth replaced the business of state, and the first paper mill was founded in 1812. By 1815 a flour mill was turning out 50 barrels daily, and by 1835, when the canal made agriculture profitable, cereal mills constructed along its banks shipped their products east and south. By 1890 the town had factories manufacturing a variety of items, including the Champion bed lounge, Mosher ratchet jack, Neely razor blade, Scioto grain elevator, and Crown baking powder and spices.

Population: 21,901; Growth (since 2000): 0.5%; Density: 2,100.2 persons per square mile; Race: 88.1% White, 7.2% Black/African American, 0.5% Asian, 0.3% American Indian/Alaska Native, 0.0% Native Hawaiian/Other Pacific Islander, 3.4% Two or more races, 1.3% Hispanic of any race; Average household size: 2.25; Median age: 41.5; Age under 18: 21.8%; Age 65 and over: 17.9%; Males per 100 females: 90.8; Marriage status: 30.7% never married, 45.3% now married, 3.1% separated, 9.0% widowed, 15.0% divorced; Foreign born: 0.9%; Speak English only: 96.6%; With disability: 21.6%; Veterans: 12.3%; Ancestry: 27.6% German, 14.4% Irish, 11.5% American, 10.5% English, 2.7% French

Employment: 9.4% management, business, and financial, 3.8% computer, engineering, and science, 6.1% education, legal, community service, arts, and media, 6.2% healthcare practitioners, 24.9% service, 24.9% sales and office, 8.5% natural resources, construction, and maintenance, 16.0% production, transportation, and material moving

Income: Per capita: $21,776; Median household: $36,927; Average household: $49,767; Households with income of $100,000 or more: 10.1%; Poverty rate: 23.6%

Educational Attainment: High school diploma or higher: 83.2%; Bachelor's degree or higher: 18.4%; Graduate/professional degree or higher: 7.2%

School District(s)

Chillicothe City (PK-12)
2012-13 Enrollment: 2,894 . . . . (740) 775-4250
Huntington Local (PK-12)
2012-13 Enrollment: 1,219 . . . . (740) 663-5892
Pickaway-Ross County Jvsd (07-12)
2012-13 Enrollment: n/a . . . . (740) 642-1200
Southeastern Local (PK-12)
2012-13 Enrollment: 1,188 . . . . (740) 774-2003
Union-Scioto Local (PK-12)
2012-13 Enrollment: 2,177 . . . . (740) 773-4102
Zane Trace Local (PK-12)
2012-13 Enrollment: 1,508 . . . . (740) 775-1355

Four-year College(s)

Ohio University-Chillicothe Campus (Public)
Fall 2013 Enrollment: 2,330 . . . . (740) 774-7200
2013-14 Tuition: In-state $4,974; Out-of-state $9,510

Two-year College(s)

Daymar College-Chillicothe (Private, For-profit)
Fall 2013 Enrollment: 76 . . . . (740) 774-6300
2013-14 Tuition: In-state $18,000; Out-of-state $18,000

Vocational/Technical School(s)

Pickaway Ross Joint Vocational School District (Public)
Fall 2013 Enrollment: 374 . . . . (740) 642-1200
2013-14 Tuition: $539

Housing: Homeownership rate: 59.1%; Median home value: $97,800; Median year structure built: 1953; Homeowner vacancy rate: 4.2%; Median gross rent: $640 per month; Rental vacancy rate: 9.9%

Health Insurance: 85.3% have insurance; 56.8% have private insurance; 44.3% have public insurance; 14.7% do not have insurance; 5.8% of children under 18 do not have insurance

Hospitals: Adena Regional Medical Center (238 beds); Chillicothe VA Medical Center (297 beds)

Safety: Violent crime rate: 33.7 per 10,000 population; Property crime rate: 896.3 per 10,000 population

Newspapers: Chillicothe Gazette (daily circulation 14500)

Transportation: Commute: 94.2% car, 0.7% public transportation, 1.8% walk, 2.7% work from home; Median travel time to work: 21.5 minutes

Airports: Ross County (general aviation)

Additional Information Contacts

City of Chillicothe. . . . . (740) 774-1185
http://ci.chillicothe.oh.us

CLARKSBURG (village). Covers a land area of 0.173 square miles and a water area of 0 square miles. Located at 39.51° N. Lat; 83.15° W. Long. Elevation is 771 feet.

Population: 455; Growth (since 2000): -11.8%; Density: 2,637.3 persons per square mile; Race: 98.5% White, 0.2% Black/African American, 0.0% Asian, 0.0% American Indian/Alaska Native, 0.0% Native Hawaiian/Other Pacific Islander, 0.9% Two or more races, 1.8% Hispanic of any race; Average household size: 2.74; Median age: 34.8; Age under 18: 29.0%; Age 65 and over: 14.3%; Males per 100 females: 89.6

Housing: Homeownership rate: 69.3%; Homeowner vacancy rate: 0.9%; Rental vacancy rate: 8.9%

FRANKFORT (village). Covers a land area of 0.564 square miles and a water area of 0 square miles. Located at 39.40° N. Lat; 83.18° W. Long. Elevation is 738 feet.

History: Frankfort was established on the site of a Shawnee village that was burned and plundered by Simon Kenton in 1787.

Population: 1,064; Growth (since 2000): 5.2%; Density: 1,887.8 persons per square mile; Race: 92.6% White, 3.9% Black/African American, 0.4% Asian, 0.7% American Indian/Alaska Native, 0.0% Native Hawaiian/Other Pacific Islander, 2.4% Two or more races, 0.2% Hispanic of any race; Average household size: 2.35; Median age: 41.2; Age under 18: 24.1%; Age 65 and over: 18.8%; Males per 100 females: 88.7

School District(s)

Adena Local (PK-12)
2012-13 Enrollment: 1,230 . . . . (740) 998-4633

Housing: Homeownership rate: 65.6%; Homeowner vacancy rate: 4.2%; Rental vacancy rate: 13.4%

KINGSTON (village). Covers a land area of 0.369 square miles and a water area of 0 square miles. Located at 39.47° N. Lat; 82.91° W. Long. Elevation is 791 feet.

Population: 1,032; Growth (since 2000): 0.0%; Density: 2,798.0 persons per square mile; Race: 98.8% White, 0.6% Black/African American, 0.0% Asian, 0.0% American Indian/Alaska Native, 0.0% Native Hawaiian/Other Pacific Islander, 0.4% Two or more races, 1.5% Hispanic of any race; Average household size: 2.25; Median age: 40.2; Age under 18: 22.3%; Age 65 and over: 17.4%; Males per 100 females: 93.6

School District(s)

Logan Elm Local (PK-12)
2012-13 Enrollment: 1,988 . . . . (740) 474-7501

Housing: Homeownership rate: 69.4%; Homeowner vacancy rate: 2.1%; Rental vacancy rate: 7.9%

LONDONDERRY (unincorporated postal area)

ZCTA: 45647

Covers a land area of 66.486 square miles and a water area of 0.144 square miles. Located at 39.29° N. Lat; 82.73° W. Long. Elevation is 686 feet.

Population: 2,484; Growth (since 2000): 31.5%; Density: 37.4 persons per square mile; Race: 98.1% White, 0.4% Black/African American, 0.3% Asian, 0.5% American Indian/Alaska Native, 0.1% Native Hawaiian/Other Pacific Islander, 0.6% Two or more races, 0.3% Hispanic of any race; Average household size: 2.55; Median age: 42.0; Age under 18: 23.4%; Age 65 and over: 15.2%; Males per 100 females: 104.6
Housing: Homeownership rate: 81.9%; Homeowner vacancy rate: 1.6%; Rental vacancy rate: 12.7%

RICHMOND DALE (CDP). Covers a land area of 0.496 square miles and a water area of 0 square miles. Located at 39.20° N. Lat; 82.81° W. Long. Elevation is 594 feet.
Population: 377; Growth (since 2000): n/a; Density: 759.6 persons per square mile; Race: 93.9% White, 0.8% Black/African American, 0.0% Asian, 0.3% American Indian/Alaska Native, 0.0% Native Hawaiian/Other Pacific Islander, 5.0% Two or more races, 0.3% Hispanic of any race; Average household size: 2.37; Median age: 38.9; Age under 18: 25.7%; Age 65 and over: 18.6%; Males per 100 females: 98.4
Housing: Homeownership rate: 65.4%; Homeowner vacancy rate: 0.0%; Rental vacancy rate: 6.8%

SOUTH SALEM (village). Covers a land area of 0.206 square miles and a water area of 0 square miles. Located at 39.34° N. Lat; 83.31° W. Long. Elevation is 928 feet.
Population: 204; Growth (since 2000): -4.2%; Density: 990.2 persons per square mile; Race: 98.5% White, 1.0% Black/African American, 0.0% Asian, 0.0% American Indian/Alaska Native, 0.0% Native Hawaiian/Other Pacific Islander, 0.5% Two or more races, 0.0% Hispanic of any race; Average household size: 2.55; Median age: 42.0; Age under 18: 23.0%; Age 65 and over: 12.3%; Males per 100 females: 96.2

School District(s)

Greenfield Exempted Village (PK-12)
2012-13 Enrollment: 2,080 . . . . (937) 981-2152
Housing: Homeownership rate: 77.5%; Homeowner vacancy rate: 1.6%; Rental vacancy rate: 0.0%

Sandusky County

Located in northern Ohio; bounded on the northeast by Sandusky Bay of Lake Erie; crossed by the Sandusky and Portage Rivers. Covers a land area of 408.453 square miles, a water area of 9.254 square miles, and is located in the Eastern Time Zone at 41.36° N. Lat., 83.14° W. Long. The county was founded in 1820. County seat is Fremont.

Sandusky County is part of the Fremont, OH Micropolitan Statistical Area. The entire metro area includes: Sandusky County, OH

Weather Station: Fremont Elevation: 600 feet

	Jan	Feb	Mar	Apr	May	Jun	Jul	Aug	Sep	Oct	Nov	Dec
High	32	36	46	59	70	80	84	82	75	63	50	37
Low	17	20	28	38	49	59	63	61	53	41	33	23
Precip	2.3	2.2	2.6	3.4	4.0	4.1	3.6	3.2	3.1	2.9	2.9	2.9
Snow	8.0	6.3	4.1	0.5	tr	0.0	0.0	0.0	0.0	tr	0.6	5.0

High and Low temperatures in degrees Fahrenheit; Precipitation and Snow in inches

Population: 60,944; Growth (since 2000): -1.4%; Density: 149.2 persons per square mile; Race: 91.2% White, 2.8% Black/African American, 0.3% Asian, 0.2% American Indian/Alaska Native, 0.0% Native Hawaiian/Other Pacific Islander, 2.6% two or more races, 8.9% Hispanic of any race; Average household size: 2.48; Median age: 40.4; Age under 18: 24.4%; Age 65 and over: 15.3%; Males per 100 females: 96.9; Marriage status: 26.1% never married, 55.0% now married, 1.8% separated, 7.0% widowed, 11.9% divorced; Foreign born: 1.8%; Speak English only: 94.8%; With disability: 13.6%; Veterans: 10.2%; Ancestry: 39.8% German, 11.5% Irish, 8.9% English, 8.2% American, 4.1% Polish
Religion: Six largest groups: 20.3% Catholicism, 10.1% Lutheran, 6.2% Methodist/Pietist, 4.1% Non-denominational Protestant, 1.6% Pentecostal, 1.6% Presbyterian-Reformed
Economy: Unemployment rate: 4.1%; Leading industries: 15.2% retail trade; 12.3% health care and social assistance; 12.0% other services (except public administration); Farms: 737 totaling 181,440 acres; Company size: 1 employs 1,000 or more persons, 1 employs 500 to 999 persons, 30 employ 100 to 499 persons, 1,288 employ less than 100 persons; Business ownership: 1,111 women-owned, 28 Black-owned, 118 Hispanic-owned, n/a Asian-owned
Employment: 8.9% management, business, and financial, 3.1% computer, engineering, and science, 7.4% education, legal, community service, arts, and media, 5.7% healthcare practitioners, 16.9% service, 20.2% sales and office, 11.1% natural resources, construction, and maintenance, 26.7% production, transportation, and material moving
Income: Per capita: $22,799; Median household: $46,140; Average household: $56,439; Households with income of $100,000 or more: 13.5%; Poverty rate: 14.3%
Educational Attainment: High school diploma or higher: 88.6%; Bachelor's degree or higher: 13.7%; Graduate/professional degree or higher: 4.8%
Housing: Homeownership rate: 73.8%; Median home value: $110,400; Median year structure built: 1958; Homeowner vacancy rate: 2.1%; Median gross rent: $613 per month; Rental vacancy rate: 8.6%
Vital Statistics: Birth rate: 114.3 per 10,000 population; Death rate: 97.2 per 10,000 population; Age-adjusted cancer mortality rate: 190.7 deaths per 100,000 population
Health Insurance: 88.9% have insurance; 71.7% have private insurance; 31.6% have public insurance; 11.1% do not have insurance; 4.6% of children under 18 do not have insurance
Health Care: Physicians: 12.4 per 10,000 population; Hospital beds: 42.4 per 10,000 population; Hospital admissions: 817.7 per 10,000 population
Transportation: Commute: 92.7% car, 1.0% public transportation, 2.6% walk, 2.4% work from home; Median travel time to work: 19.7 minutes
Presidential Election: 49.8% Obama, 47.9% Romney (2012)
National and State Parks: Green Springs State Nursery; Pfizer State Park; Sandusky Scenic River State Access Area; Spiegel Grove State Park
Additional Information Contacts
Sandusky Government . . . . (419) 334-6100
http://www.sandusky-county.org

Sandusky County Communities

BALLVILLE (CDP). Covers a land area of 2.703 square miles and a water area of 0.205 square miles. Located at 41.33° N. Lat; 83.13° W. Long. Elevation is 623 feet.
Population: 2,976; Growth (since 2000): -8.6%; Density: 1,101.1 persons per square mile; Race: 95.1% White, 1.4% Black/African American, 0.5% Asian, 0.1% American Indian/Alaska Native, 0.0% Native Hawaiian/Other Pacific Islander, 1.4% Two or more races, 3.9% Hispanic of any race; Average household size: 2.27; Median age: 50.3; Age under 18: 18.3%; Age 65 and over: 22.4%; Males per 100 females: 95.5; Marriage status: 17.4% never married, 63.5% now married, 0.0% separated, 7.9% widowed, 11.2% divorced; Foreign born: 3.5%; Speak English only: 95.8%; With disability: 11.2%; Veterans: 11.2%; Ancestry: 48.8% German, 12.3% Irish, 10.8% English, 7.1% American, 6.5% Polish
Employment: 13.9% management, business, and financial, 3.6% computer, engineering, and science, 13.5% education, legal, community service, arts, and media, 11.1% healthcare practitioners, 15.1% service, 19.4% sales and office, 4.4% natural resources, construction, and maintenance, 19.0% production, transportation, and material moving
Income: Per capita: $30,332; Median household: $56,458; Average household: $67,469; Households with income of $100,000 or more: 15.2%; Poverty rate: 3.3%
Educational Attainment: High school diploma or higher: 92.5%; Bachelor's degree or higher: 26.5%; Graduate/professional degree or higher: 11.7%
Housing: Homeownership rate: 87.0%; Median home value: $143,000; Median year structure built: 1967; Homeowner vacancy rate: 2.8%; Median gross rent: $711 per month; Rental vacancy rate: 6.6%
Health Insurance: 91.2% have insurance; 85.4% have private insurance; 28.1% have public insurance; 8.8% do not have insurance; 4.5% of children under 18 do not have insurance
Transportation: Commute: 95.2% car, 0.0% public transportation, 2.7% walk, 1.3% work from home; Median travel time to work: 17.3 minutes

BELLEVUE (city). Covers a land area of 6.136 square miles and a water area of 0.118 square miles. Located at 41.27° N. Lat; 82.84° W. Long. Elevation is 751 feet.
History: Bellevue was established as a railroad town in 1839 and named by James Bell, a railroad employee.
Population: 8,202; Growth (since 2000): 0.1%; Density: 1,336.7 persons per square mile; Race: 96.3% White, 0.6% Black/African American, 0.2% Asian, 0.2% American Indian/Alaska Native, 0.0% Native Hawaiian/Other Pacific Islander, 2.0% Two or more races, 3.2% Hispanic of any race;

Average household size: 2.45; Median age: 36.5; Age under 18: 26.0%; Age 65 and over: 14.5%; Males per 100 females: 91.8; Marriage status: 26.8% never married, 51.3% now married, 4.9% separated, 7.4% widowed, 14.5% divorced; Foreign born: 0.3%; Speak English only: 97.8%; With disability: 14.3%; Veterans: 8.5%; Ancestry: 42.1% German, 15.6% Irish, 10.0% Italian, 9.0% English, 7.9% American
Employment: 8.0% management, business, and financial, 2.7% computer, engineering, and science, 6.2% education, legal, community service, arts, and media, 7.7% healthcare practitioners, 19.8% service, 19.5% sales and office, 9.4% natural resources, construction, and maintenance, 26.7% production, transportation, and material moving
Income: Per capita: $22,399; Median household: $46,509; Average household: $57,058; Households with income of $100,000 or more: 12.8%; Poverty rate: 11.7%
Educational Attainment: High school diploma or higher: 90.5%; Bachelor's degree or higher: 12.4%; Graduate/professional degree or higher: 3.5%

School District(s)

Bellevue City (PK-12)
2012-13 Enrollment: 2,042 . . . . (419) 484-5000
Housing: Homeownership rate: 65.3%; Median home value: $96,000; Median year structure built: 1954; Homeowner vacancy rate: 2.7%; Median gross rent: $701 per month; Rental vacancy rate: 12.7%
Health Insurance: 90.3% have insurance; 70.9% have private insurance; 32.7% have public insurance; 9.7% do not have insurance; 1.2% of children under 18 do not have insurance
Hospitals: Bellevue Hospital (64 beds)
Newspapers: Bellevue Gazette (daily circulation 2800)
Transportation: Commute: 91.4% car, 0.2% public transportation, 2.8% walk, 3.8% work from home; Median travel time to work: 18.0 minutes
Additional Information Contacts
City of Bellevue . . . . (419) 484-8400
http://www.cityofbellevue.com

BURGOON (village). Covers a land area of 0.121 square miles and a water area of 0 square miles. Located at 41.27° N. Lat; 83.25° W. Long. Elevation is 705 feet.
Population: 172; Growth (since 2000): -13.6%; Density: 1,416.3 persons per square mile; Race: 95.9% White, 0.0% Black/African American, 0.6% Asian, 0.6% American Indian/Alaska Native, 0.0% Native Hawaiian/Other Pacific Islander, 0.0% Two or more races, 7.0% Hispanic of any race; Average household size: 2.57; Median age: 39.8; Age under 18: 25.6%; Age 65 and over: 15.7%; Males per 100 females: 95.5
Housing: Homeownership rate: 86.5%; Homeowner vacancy rate: 3.3%; Rental vacancy rate: 10.0%

CLYDE (city). Covers a land area of 5.043 square miles and a water area of 0.052 square miles. Located at 41.31° N. Lat; 82.98° W. Long. Elevation is 696 feet.
History: The story of Clyde's beginnings tells of an officer during the War of 1812 who drove a stake into the ground here and said: "At this spot I shall build my future home, which shall be the nucleus of a thriving town." It was 1820 when the soldier returned, recovered his chosen land, and the city of Clyde came into being. Writer Sherwood Anderson spent his boyhood in Clyde, and portrayed the town in the novel "Winesburg, Ohio."
Population: 6,325; Growth (since 2000): 4.3%; Density: 1,254.2 persons per square mile; Race: 94.4% White, 0.6% Black/African American, 0.4% Asian, 0.3% American Indian/Alaska Native, 0.0% Native Hawaiian/Other Pacific Islander, 2.7% Two or more races, 5.9% Hispanic of any race; Average household size: 2.50; Median age: 37.4; Age under 18: 26.3%; Age 65 and over: 13.8%; Males per 100 females: 95.1; Marriage status: 26.8% never married, 54.9% now married, 1.8% separated, 6.8% widowed, 11.4% divorced; Foreign born: 0.9%; Speak English only: 97.8%; With disability: 12.1%; Veterans: 12.2%; Ancestry: 33.6% German, 16.7% Irish, 10.3% English, 9.5% American, 3.3% Scottish
Employment: 6.9% management, business, and financial, 1.9% computer, engineering, and science, 10.4% education, legal, community service, arts, and media, 6.2% healthcare practitioners, 16.6% service, 18.4% sales and office, 8.7% natural resources, construction, and maintenance, 30.9% production, transportation, and material moving
Income: Per capita: $23,764; Median household: $44,071; Average household: $57,624; Households with income of $100,000 or more: 12.4%; Poverty rate: 15.2%
Educational Attainment: High school diploma or higher: 93.0%; Bachelor's degree or higher: 17.4%; Graduate/professional degree or higher: 5.5%

School District(s)

Bellevue City (PK-12)
2012-13 Enrollment: 2,042 . . . . (419) 484-5000
Clyde-Green Springs Exempted Village (PK-12)
2012-13 Enrollment: 2,273 . . . . (419) 547-0588
Housing: Homeownership rate: 68.4%; Median home value: $96,200; Median year structure built: 1963; Homeowner vacancy rate: 2.5%; Median gross rent: $625 per month; Rental vacancy rate: 8.6%
Health Insurance: 91.0% have insurance; 71.8% have private insurance; 29.0% have public insurance; 9.0% do not have insurance; 1.9% of children under 18 do not have insurance
Newspapers: Clyde Enterprise (weekly circulation 1700)
Transportation: Commute: 96.2% car, 0.4% public transportation, 2.1% walk, 0.8% work from home; Median travel time to work: 19.5 minutes
Additional Information Contacts
City of Clyde . . . . (419) 547-6898
http://www.clydeohio.org

FREMONT (city). County seat. Covers a land area of 8.346 square miles and a water area of 0.219 square miles. Located at 41.35° N. Lat; 83.12° W. Long. Elevation is 627 feet.
History: Settlement began here after the War of 1812, when the two small towns of Croghansville and Lower Sandusky were established on the Sandusky River. In 1829 the two united, and in 1849 the name was changed to Fremont, for explorer John C. Fremont. Fremont grew as a sugar-beet and cannery center.
Population: 16,734; Growth (since 2000): -3.7%; Density: 2,005.1 persons per square mile; Race: 80.7% White, 8.3% Black/African American, 0.3% Asian, 0.2% American Indian/Alaska Native, 0.0% Native Hawaiian/Other Pacific Islander, 5.1% Two or more races, 16.1% Hispanic of any race; Average household size: 2.42; Median age: 35.3; Age under 18: 27.2%; Age 65 and over: 13.9%; Males per 100 females: 91.7; Marriage status: 33.3% never married, 45.6% now married, 2.3% separated, 7.0% widowed, 14.1% divorced; Foreign born: 2.8%; Speak English only: 90.1%; With disability: 15.2%; Veterans: 9.0%; Ancestry: 29.3% German, 8.2% Irish, 7.6% American, 6.6% English, 5.8% Polish
Employment: 5.5% management, business, and financial, 3.8% computer, engineering, and science, 6.1% education, legal, community service, arts, and media, 4.0% healthcare practitioners, 18.3% service, 21.8% sales and office, 8.0% natural resources, construction, and maintenance, 32.6% production, transportation, and material moving
Income: Per capita: $18,230; Median household: $37,948; Average household: $45,080; Households with income of $100,000 or more: 8.4%; Poverty rate: 22.8%
Educational Attainment: High school diploma or higher: 84.7%; Bachelor's degree or higher: 12.0%; Graduate/professional degree or higher: 4.2%

School District(s)

Fremont City (PK-12)
2012-13 Enrollment: 4,121 . . . . (419) 332-6454
North Central Academy-Fremont (06-12)
2012-13 Enrollment: 117. . . . . (419) 448-5786
Vanguard-Sentinel Career & Technology Centers (06-12)
2012-13 Enrollment: n/a . . . . (419) 332-2626

Two-year College(s)

Terra State Community College (Public)
Fall 2013 Enrollment: 2,923 . . . . (419) 334-8400
2013-14 Tuition: In-state $4,344; Out-of-state $6,824

Vocational/Technical School(s)

Vanguard-Sentinel Adult Career and Technology Center (Public)
Fall 2013 Enrollment: 54 . . . . (567) 201-2942
2013-14 Tuition: $6,044
Housing: Homeownership rate: 58.1%; Median home value: $85,800; Median year structure built: 1946; Homeowner vacancy rate: 2.5%; Median gross rent: $600 per month; Rental vacancy rate: 10.5%
Health Insurance: 83.8% have insurance; 60.3% have private insurance; 37.0% have public insurance; 16.2% do not have insurance; 7.5% of children under 18 do not have insurance
Hospitals: Memorial Hospital (186 beds)
Safety: Violent crime rate: 25.4 per 10,000 population; Property crime rate: 580.7 per 10,000 population
Newspapers: News-Messenger (daily circulation 12000)

Transportation: Commute: 92.8% car, 0.4% public transportation, 2.5% walk, 2.5% work from home; Median travel time to work: 16.6 minutes
Additional Information Contacts
City of Fremont . . . . (419) 334-5900
http://www.fremontohio.org

GIBSONBURG (village). Covers a land area of 2.395 square miles and a water area of 0.478 square miles. Located at 41.39° N. Lat; 83.32° W. Long. Elevation is 682 feet.
History: Founded 1871.
Population: 2,581; Growth (since 2000): 3.0%; Density: 1,077.5 persons per square mile; Race: 94.2% White, 0.6% Black/African American, 0.0% Asian, 0.2% American Indian/Alaska Native, 0.0% Native Hawaiian/Other Pacific Islander, 1.5% Two or more races, 8.6% Hispanic of any race; Average household size: 2.55; Median age: 36.9; Age under 18: 26.2%; Age 65 and over: 14.5%; Males per 100 females: 93.3; Marriage status: 29.3% never married, 51.0% now married, 2.0% separated, 5.9% widowed, 13.8% divorced; Foreign born: 0.4%; Speak English only: 95.5%; With disability: 12.4%; Veterans: 9.1%; Ancestry: 50.4% German, 12.7% Irish, 9.6% American, 5.1% Polish, 4.8% English
Employment: 10.7% management, business, and financial, 5.0% computer, engineering, and science, 6.8% education, legal, community service, arts, and media, 2.7% healthcare practitioners, 19.0% service, 18.8% sales and office, 11.8% natural resources, construction, and maintenance, 25.2% production, transportation, and material moving
Income: Per capita: $18,608; Median household: $42,857; Average household: $50,694; Households with income of $100,000 or more: 8.2%; Poverty rate: 13.1%
Educational Attainment: High school diploma or higher: 90.0%; Bachelor's degree or higher: 9.4%; Graduate/professional degree or higher: 3.5%

School District(s)

Gibsonburg Exempted Village (PK-12)
2012-13 Enrollment: 1,081 . . . . (419) 637-2479
Housing: Homeownership rate: 69.3%; Median home value: $106,700; Median year structure built: 1948; Homeowner vacancy rate: 3.1%; Median gross rent: $571 per month; Rental vacancy rate: 6.8%
Health Insurance: 87.6% have insurance; 71.0% have private insurance; 30.3% have public insurance; 12.4% do not have insurance; 7.2% of children under 18 do not have insurance
Transportation: Commute: 91.9% car, 0.0% public transportation, 3.2% walk, 3.5% work from home; Median travel time to work: 22.2 minutes

GREEN SPRINGS (village). Covers a land area of 1.207 square miles and a water area of 0.003 square miles. Located at 41.26° N. Lat; 83.05° W. Long. Elevation is 709 feet.
Population: 1,368; Growth (since 2000): 9.7%; Density: 1,133.2 persons per square mile; Race: 96.4% White, 0.6% Black/African American, 0.1% Asian, 0.7% American Indian/Alaska Native, 0.0% Native Hawaiian/Other Pacific Islander, 1.4% Two or more races, 8.4% Hispanic of any race; Average household size: 2.51; Median age: 40.4; Age under 18: 24.9%; Age 65 and over: 18.6%; Males per 100 females: 93.5

School District(s)

Clyde-Green Springs Exempted Village (PK-12)
2012-13 Enrollment: 2,273 . . . . (419) 547-0588
Housing: Homeownership rate: 74.2%; Homeowner vacancy rate: 1.1%; Rental vacancy rate: 8.8%

HELENA (village). Covers a land area of 0.295 square miles and a water area of 0 square miles. Located at 41.34° N. Lat; 83.29° W. Long. Elevation is 696 feet.
Population: 224; Growth (since 2000): -5.1%; Density: 759.1 persons per square mile; Race: 99.6% White, 0.0% Black/African American, 0.0% Asian, 0.0% American Indian/Alaska Native, 0.0% Native Hawaiian/Other Pacific Islander, 0.0% Two or more races, 3.6% Hispanic of any race; Average household size: 2.31; Median age: 41.8; Age under 18: 20.5%; Age 65 and over: 13.8%; Males per 100 females: 121.8
Housing: Homeownership rate: 82.5%; Homeowner vacancy rate: 2.4%; Rental vacancy rate: 10.0%

HESSVILLE (CDP). Covers a land area of 0.699 square miles and a water area of 0 square miles. Located at 41.40° N. Lat; 83.24° W. Long. Elevation is 630 feet.
Population: 214; Growth (since 2000): n/a; Density: 306.2 persons per square mile; Race: 89.3% White, 0.0% Black/African American, 0.0% Asian, 0.0% American Indian/Alaska Native, 0.0% Native Hawaiian/Other Pacific Islander, 4.2% Two or more races, 25.7% Hispanic of any race; Average household size: 2.71; Median age: 35.3; Age under 18: 32.2%; Age 65 and over: 15.4%; Males per 100 females: 107.8
Housing: Homeownership rate: 70.9%; Homeowner vacancy rate: 3.4%; Rental vacancy rate: 0.0%

LINDSEY (village). Covers a land area of 1.562 square miles and a water area of 0 square miles. Located at 41.42° N. Lat; 83.22° W. Long. Elevation is 620 feet.
Population: 446; Growth (since 2000): -11.5%; Density: 285.6 persons per square mile; Race: 94.2% White, 0.4% Black/African American, 0.4% Asian, 0.0% American Indian/Alaska Native, 0.0% Native Hawaiian/Other Pacific Islander, 2.9% Two or more races, 11.4% Hispanic of any race; Average household size: 2.39; Median age: 41.0; Age under 18: 23.8%; Age 65 and over: 15.2%; Males per 100 females: 92.2

School District(s)

Fremont City (PK-12)
2012-13 Enrollment: 4,121 . . . . (419) 332-6454
Housing: Homeownership rate: 85.6%; Homeowner vacancy rate: 3.6%; Rental vacancy rate: 0.0%

STONY PRAIRIE (CDP). Covers a land area of 1.699 square miles and a water area of 0 square miles. Located at 41.35° N. Lat; 83.14° W. Long. Elevation is 633 feet.
Population: 1,284; Growth (since 2000): 53.6%; Density: 755.8 persons per square mile; Race: 84.8% White, 3.9% Black/African American, 0.5% Asian, 0.2% American Indian/Alaska Native, 0.0% Native Hawaiian/Other Pacific Islander, 3.3% Two or more races, 18.5% Hispanic of any race; Average household size: 2.49; Median age: 41.9; Age under 18: 23.8%; Age 65 and over: 18.1%; Males per 100 females: 99.1
Housing: Homeownership rate: 73.3%; Homeowner vacancy rate: 2.3%; Rental vacancy rate: 2.8%

VICKERY (CDP). Covers a land area of 0.423 square miles and a water area of 0 square miles. Located at 41.38° N. Lat; 82.94° W. Long. Elevation is 600 feet.
Population: 121; Growth (since 2000): n/a; Density: 286.3 persons per square mile; Race: 99.2% White, 0.0% Black/African American, 0.0% Asian, 0.0% American Indian/Alaska Native, 0.0% Native Hawaiian/Other Pacific Islander, 0.8% Two or more races, 0.8% Hispanic of any race; Average household size: 2.81; Median age: 40.3; Age under 18: 20.7%; Age 65 and over: 10.7%; Males per 100 females: 101.7
Housing: Homeownership rate: 86.1%; Homeowner vacancy rate: 5.1%; Rental vacancy rate: 14.3%

WIGHTMANS GROVE (CDP). Covers a land area of 0.141 square miles and a water area of 0.014 square miles. Located at 41.42° N. Lat; 83.05° W. Long. Elevation is 574 feet.
Population: 72; Growth (since 2000): n/a; Density: 508.9 persons per square mile; Race: 100.0% White, 0.0% Black/African American, 0.0% Asian, 0.0% American Indian/Alaska Native, 0.0% Native Hawaiian/Other Pacific Islander, 0.0% Two or more races, 2.8% Hispanic of any race; Average household size: 2.18; Median age: 45.5; Age under 18: 19.4%; Age 65 and over: 9.7%; Males per 100 females: 125.0
Housing: Homeownership rate: 78.8%; Homeowner vacancy rate: 7.1%; Rental vacancy rate: 22.2%

WOODVILLE (village). Covers a land area of 1.325 square miles and a water area of 0 square miles. Located at 41.45° N. Lat; 83.36° W. Long. Elevation is 636 feet.
History: Woodville developed in the center of an extensive limestone area. The lime produced here was noted for its whiteness, plasticity, and sand-carrying qualities.
Population: 2,135; Growth (since 2000): 8.0%; Density: 1,611.8 persons per square mile; Race: 96.3% White, 0.3% Black/African American, 0.8% Asian, 0.1% American Indian/Alaska Native, 0.0% Native Hawaiian/Other Pacific Islander, 0.8% Two or more races, 6.0% Hispanic of any race; Average household size: 2.51; Median age: 39.1; Age under 18: 25.5%; Age 65 and over: 15.4%; Males per 100 females: 95.0

School District(s)

Woodmore Local (PK-12)
2012-13 Enrollment: 1,127 . . . . (419) 862-1060
Housing: Homeownership rate: 75.6%; Homeowner vacancy rate: 2.7%; Rental vacancy rate: 5.9%

Scioto County

Located in southern Ohio; bounded on the south by the Ohio River and the Kentucky border; crossed by the Scioto and Little Scioto Rivers. Covers a land area of 610.213 square miles, a water area of 5.935 square miles, and is located in the Eastern Time Zone at 38.82° N. Lat., 83.00° W. Long. The county was founded in 1803. County seat is Portsmouth.

Scioto County is part of the Portsmouth, OH Micropolitan Statistical Area. The entire metro area includes: Scioto County, OH

Weather Station: Portsmouth Sciotoville Elevation: 540 feet

	Jan	Feb	Mar	Apr	May	Jun	Jul	Aug	Sep	Oct	Nov	Dec
High	41	45	55	67	75	83	87	86	80	68	56	44
Low	23	25	33	42	51	60	64	62	54	42	34	26
Precip	3.1	2.8	3.8	3.6	4.7	3.4	4.4	3.8	2.6	2.6	3.1	3.2
Snow	3.4	2.1	1.2	0.2	tr	0.0	0.0	0.0	0.0	0.0	0.1	1.0

High and Low temperatures in degrees Fahrenheit; Precipitation and Snow in inches

Population: 79,499; Growth (since 2000): 0.4%; Density: 130.3 persons per square mile; Race: 94.4% White, 2.7% Black/African American, 0.3% Asian, 0.5% American Indian/Alaska Native, 0.0% Native Hawaiian/Other Pacific Islander, 1.7% two or more races, 1.1% Hispanic of any race; Average household size: 2.46; Median age: 38.8; Age under 18: 22.8%; Age 65 and over: 15.5%; Males per 100 females: 97.6; Marriage status: 28.0% never married, 51.5% now married, 2.5% separated, 7.7% widowed, 12.8% divorced; Foreign born: 1.0%; Speak English only: 97.8%; With disability: 21.2%; Veterans: 10.5%; Ancestry: 22.3% German, 13.4% American, 13.3% Irish, 11.1% English, 2.4% French
Religion: Six largest groups: 5.6% Baptist, 4.8% Non-denominational Protestant, 4.1% Catholicism, 3.9% Methodist/Pietist, 2.1% Holiness, 1.1% Pentecostal
Economy: Unemployment rate: 6.6%; Leading industries: 19.8% retail trade; 16.6% health care and social assistance; 12.9% other services (except public administration); Farms: 689 totaling 94,342 acres; Company size: 1 employs 1,000 or more persons, 0 employ 500 to 999 persons, 29 employ 100 to 499 persons, 1,259 employ less than 100 persons; Business ownership: 1,639 women-owned, n/a Black-owned, n/a Hispanic-owned, n/a Asian-owned
Employment: 10.2% management, business, and financial, 2.4% computer, engineering, and science, 10.7% education, legal, community service, arts, and media, 9.9% healthcare practitioners, 21.0% service, 22.1% sales and office, 9.7% natural resources, construction, and maintenance, 14.0% production, transportation, and material moving
Income: Per capita: $19,437; Median household: $35,379; Average household: $49,798; Households with income of $100,000 or more: 11.0%; Poverty rate: 23.3%
Educational Attainment: High school diploma or higher: 81.3%; Bachelor's degree or higher: 14.2%; Graduate/professional degree or higher: 5.2%
Housing: Homeownership rate: 68.4%; Median home value: $88,200; Median year structure built: 1964; Homeowner vacancy rate: 1.7%; Median gross rent: $553 per month; Rental vacancy rate: 7.8%
Vital Statistics: Birth rate: 114.9 per 10,000 population; Death rate: 112.5 per 10,000 population; Age-adjusted cancer mortality rate: 195.0 deaths per 100,000 population
Health Insurance: 85.2% have insurance; 55.9% have private insurance; 42.1% have public insurance; 14.8% do not have insurance; 4.8% of children under 18 do not have insurance
Health Care: Physicians: 18.7 per 10,000 population; Hospital beds: 29.0 per 10,000 population; Hospital admissions: 1,491.2 per 10,000 population
Air Quality Index: 93.7% good, 6.3% moderate, 0.0% unhealthy for sensitive individuals, 0.0% unhealthy (percent of days)
Transportation: Commute: 93.1% car, 0.1% public transportation, 3.3% walk, 2.6% work from home; Median travel time to work: 24.6 minutes
Presidential Election: 48.1% Obama, 50.0% Romney (2012)
National and State Parks: Brush Creek State Forest; Shawnee State Forest; Shawnee State Park
Additional Information Contacts
Scioto Government . . . . (740) 355-8313
http://www.sciotocountyohio.com

Scioto County Communities

CLARKTOWN (CDP). Covers a land area of 2.044 square miles and a water area of 0.002 square miles. Located at 38.85° N. Lat; 82.91° W. Long. Elevation is 689 feet.
Population: 958; Growth (since 2000): n/a; Density: 468.7 persons per square mile; Race: 97.1% White, 0.3% Black/African American, 0.3% Asian, 0.6% American Indian/Alaska Native, 0.0% Native Hawaiian/Other Pacific Islander, 1.7% Two or more races, 0.3% Hispanic of any race; Average household size: 2.43; Median age: 40.5; Age under 18: 21.5%; Age 65 and over: 17.6%; Males per 100 females: 98.3
Housing: Homeownership rate: 80.2%; Homeowner vacancy rate: 1.9%; Rental vacancy rate: 2.4%

FRANKLIN FURNACE (CDP). Covers a land area of 2.355 square miles and a water area of 0.395 square miles. Located at 38.61° N. Lat; 82.85° W. Long. Elevation is 574 feet.
Population: 1,660; Growth (since 2000): 8.0%; Density: 704.8 persons per square mile; Race: 87.8% White, 9.8% Black/African American, 0.1% Asian, 0.6% American Indian/Alaska Native, 0.0% Native Hawaiian/Other Pacific Islander, 1.0% Two or more races, 1.3% Hispanic of any race; Average household size: 2.47; Median age: 33.8; Age under 18: 23.4%; Age 65 and over: 13.7%; Males per 100 females: 126.5

School District(s)

Green Local (PK-12)
2012-13 Enrollment: 582. . . . . (740) 354-9221
Housing: Homeownership rate: 74.7%; Homeowner vacancy rate: 1.5%; Rental vacancy rate: 20.9%

FRIENDSHIP (CDP). Covers a land area of 1.168 square miles and a water area of 0.013 square miles. Located at 38.70° N. Lat; 83.10° W. Long. Elevation is 548 feet.
Population: 351; Growth (since 2000): n/a; Density: 300.4 persons per square mile; Race: 96.3% White, 0.9% Black/African American, 0.6% Asian, 0.0% American Indian/Alaska Native, 0.0% Native Hawaiian/Other Pacific Islander, 2.3% Two or more races, 0.0% Hispanic of any race; Average household size: 2.28; Median age: 45.1; Age under 18: 21.9%; Age 65 and over: 18.8%; Males per 100 females: 87.7
Housing: Homeownership rate: 77.7%; Homeowner vacancy rate: 0.9%; Rental vacancy rate: 11.1%

HAVERHILL (unincorporated postal area)
ZCTA: 45636
Covers a land area of 0.648 square miles and a water area of 0.046 square miles. Located at 38.59° N. Lat; 82.83° W. Long. Elevation is 548 feet.
Population: 148; Growth (since 2000): n/a; Density: 228.3 persons per square mile; Race: 100.0% White, 0.0% Black/African American, 0.0% Asian, 0.0% American Indian/Alaska Native, 0.0% Native Hawaiian/Other Pacific Islander, 0.0% Two or more races, 0.7% Hispanic of any race; Average household size: 2.51; Median age: 43.0; Age under 18: 22.3%; Age 65 and over: 16.9%; Males per 100 females: 108.5
Housing: Homeownership rate: 66.1%; Homeowner vacancy rate: 0.0%; Rental vacancy rate: 44.4%

LUCASVILLE (CDP). Covers a land area of 2.513 square miles and a water area of 0.040 square miles. Located at 38.87° N. Lat; 82.99° W. Long. Elevation is 554 feet.
History: Lucasville was founded in 1819 by John Lucas on land received by his father, William Lucas, for Revolutionary War service. The founder's son, Robert Lucas, was governor of Ohio (1832-1836) and territorial governor of Iowa (1838-1841).
Population: 2,757; Growth (since 2000): 73.6%; Density: 1,096.9 persons per square mile; Race: 70.3% White, 28.7% Black/African American, 0.1% Asian, 0.1% American Indian/Alaska Native, 0.0% Native Hawaiian/Other Pacific Islander, 0.7% Two or more races, 0.8% Hispanic of any race; Average household size: 2.54; Median age: 33.2; Age under 18: 11.7%; Age 65 and over: 7.8%; Males per 100 females: 303.1; Marriage status: 43.9% never married, 46.0% now married, 4.5% separated, 1.8% widowed, 8.4% divorced; Foreign born: 0.0%; Speak English only: 97.8%; With disability: 19.9%; Veterans: 11.1%; Ancestry: 21.2% German, 15.9% English, 9.1% Irish, 6.0% American, 4.3% Scotch-Irish
Employment: 11.6% management, business, and financial, 2.2% computer, engineering, and science, 9.5% education, legal, community

service, arts, and media, 8.5% healthcare practitioners, 21.1% service, 31.5% sales and office, 11.3% natural resources, construction, and maintenance, 4.2% production, transportation, and material moving

Income: Per capita: $15,185; Median household: $35,969; Average household: $54,009; Households with income of $100,000 or more: 4.9%; Poverty rate: 32.9%

Educational Attainment: High school diploma or higher: 75.1%; Bachelor's degree or higher: 15.9%; Graduate/professional degree or higher: 4.8%

School District(s)

Scioto County Career Technical Center (09-12)
2012-13 Enrollment: n/a . . . . (740) 259-5522
Valley Local (PK-12)
2012-13 Enrollment: 1,042 . . . . (740) 259-3115

Vocational/Technical School(s)

Scioto County Career Technical Center (Public)
Fall 2013 Enrollment: 321 . . . . (740) 259-5526
2013-14 Tuition: $9,135

Housing: Homeownership rate: 72.6%; Median home value: $130,900; Median year structure built: 1971; Homeowner vacancy rate: 1.8%; Median gross rent: $521 per month; Rental vacancy rate: 8.0%

Health Insurance: 79.4% have insurance; 51.1% have private insurance; 42.9% have public insurance; 20.6% do not have insurance; 4.0% of children under 18 do not have insurance

Transportation: Commute: 98.4% car, 0.0% public transportation, 0.0% walk, 1.6% work from home; Median travel time to work: 24.9 minutes

MCDERMOTT (CDP). Covers a land area of 0.579 square miles and a water area of <.001 square miles. Located at 38.83° N. Lat; 83.06° W. Long. Elevation is 584 feet.

Population: 434; Growth (since 2000): n/a; Density: 749.5 persons per square mile; Race: 98.6% White, 0.0% Black/African American, 0.0% Asian, 0.0% American Indian/Alaska Native, 0.0% Native Hawaiian/Other Pacific Islander, 1.4% Two or more races, 0.2% Hispanic of any race; Average household size: 2.66; Median age: 38.9; Age under 18: 25.6%; Age 65 and over: 17.1%; Males per 100 females: 96.4

School District(s)

Northwest Local (PK-12)
2012-13 Enrollment: 1,612 . . . . (614) 995-1985

Housing: Homeownership rate: 80.1%; Homeowner vacancy rate: 2.3%; Rental vacancy rate: 6.1%

MINFORD (CDP). Covers a land area of 1.743 square miles and a water area of 0.005 square miles. Located at 38.86° N. Lat; 82.85° W. Long. Elevation is 656 feet.

Population: 693; Growth (since 2000): n/a; Density: 397.5 persons per square mile; Race: 97.3% White, 0.0% Black/African American, 0.1% Asian, 0.4% American Indian/Alaska Native, 0.0% Native Hawaiian/Other Pacific Islander, 1.9% Two or more races, 0.9% Hispanic of any race; Average household size: 2.30; Median age: 46.4; Age under 18: 20.9%; Age 65 and over: 27.0%; Males per 100 females: 80.5

School District(s)

Minford Local (PK-12)
2012-13 Enrollment: 1,519 . . . . (740) 820-3896

Housing: Homeownership rate: 68.8%; Homeowner vacancy rate: 0.5%; Rental vacancy rate: 8.6%

NEW BOSTON (village). Covers a land area of 1.111 square miles and a water area of 0.030 square miles. Located at 38.75° N. Lat; 82.93° W. Long. Elevation is 535 feet.

History: New Boston was founded in 1891 and named for Boston, whose capitalists financed a sawmill here. New Boston later became a river steel town.

Population: 2,272; Growth (since 2000): -2.9%; Density: 2,044.5 persons per square mile; Race: 96.0% White, 1.1% Black/African American, 0.3% Asian, 0.3% American Indian/Alaska Native, 0.0% Native Hawaiian/Other Pacific Islander, 2.1% Two or more races, 0.9% Hispanic of any race; Average household size: 2.08; Median age: 40.3; Age under 18: 22.7%; Age 65 and over: 19.5%; Males per 100 females: 84.4

School District(s)

New Boston Local (PK-12)
2012-13 Enrollment: 511. . . . . (740) 456-4626

Two-year College(s)

Daymar College-New Boston (Private, For-profit)
Fall 2013 Enrollment: 87 . . . . (740) 456-4124
2013-14 Tuition: In-state $18,000; Out-of-state $18,000

Housing: Homeownership rate: 34.0%; Homeowner vacancy rate: 3.9%; Rental vacancy rate: 7.8%

Safety: Violent crime rate: 4.5 per 10,000 population; Property crime rate: 709.5 per 10,000 population

OTWAY (village). Covers a land area of 0.204 square miles and a water area of 0.004 square miles. Located at 38.86° N. Lat; 83.19° W. Long. Elevation is 600 feet.

Population: 87; Growth (since 2000): 1.2%; Density: 426.4 persons per square mile; Race: 94.3% White, 0.0% Black/African American, 0.0% Asian, 3.4% American Indian/Alaska Native, 0.0% Native Hawaiian/Other Pacific Islander, 2.3% Two or more races, 0.0% Hispanic of any race; Average household size: 2.23; Median age: 40.5; Age under 18: 18.4%; Age 65 and over: 19.5%; Males per 100 females: 67.3

Housing: Homeownership rate: 66.7%; Homeowner vacancy rate: 6.9%; Rental vacancy rate: 23.5%

PORTSMOUTH (city). County seat. Covers a land area of 10.734 square miles and a water area of 0.338 square miles. Located at 38.75° N. Lat; 82.95° W. Long. Elevation is 535 feet.

History: Portsmouth was founded in 1803 by Major Henry Massie, a Virginia land speculator. By 1815 Portsmouth was an incorporated town. Industry moved from lumbering and fur trading, to canal-boat center, to iron works and brickyards. In 1927, a suspension bridge was built across the Ohio River to connect the town with South Portsmouth in Kentucky.

Population: 20,226; Growth (since 2000): -3.3%; Density: 1,884.2 persons per square mile; Race: 90.1% White, 5.1% Black/African American, 0.6% Asian, 0.4% American Indian/Alaska Native, 0.0% Native Hawaiian/Other Pacific Islander, 3.0% Two or more races, 2.2% Hispanic of any race; Average household size: 2.28; Median age: 36.1; Age under 18: 21.6%; Age 65 and over: 16.4%; Males per 100 females: 86.6; Marriage status: 33.9% never married, 40.4% now married, 2.3% separated, 9.1% widowed, 16.6% divorced; Foreign born: 2.3%; Speak English only: 96.1%; With disability: 23.9%; Veterans: 10.0%; Ancestry: 22.1% German, 16.5% Irish, 10.8% American, 10.4% English, 2.7% Italian

Employment: 10.5% management, business, and financial, 1.4% computer, engineering, and science, 12.6% education, legal, community service, arts, and media, 10.0% healthcare practitioners, 24.4% service, 23.8% sales and office, 6.0% natural resources, construction, and maintenance, 11.3% production, transportation, and material moving

Income: Per capita: $17,818; Median household: $27,976; Average household: $42,528; Households with income of $100,000 or more: 8.9%; Poverty rate: 30.6%

Educational Attainment: High school diploma or higher: 77.8%; Bachelor's degree or higher: 17.4%; Graduate/professional degree or higher: 6.6%

School District(s)

Clay Local (PK-12)
2012-13 Enrollment: 625. . . . . (740) 354-6645
Portsmouth City (PK-12)
2012-13 Enrollment: 1,863 . . . . (740) 354-4727
Sciotoville (05-12)
2012-13 Enrollment: 300. . . . . (740) 776-6777
Sciotoville Elementary Academy (KG-04)
2012-13 Enrollment: 140. . . . . (740) 776-2920

Four-year College(s)

Shawnee State University (Public)
Fall 2013 Enrollment: 4,341 . . . . (740) 354-3205
2013-14 Tuition: In-state $7,177; Out-of-state $12,291

Two-year College(s)

Paramount Beauty Academy (Private, For-profit)
Fall 2013 Enrollment: 101 . . . . (740) 353-2436

Housing: Homeownership rate: 50.1%; Median home value: $74,200; Median year structure built: Before 1940; Homeowner vacancy rate: 2.9%; Median gross rent: $536 per month; Rental vacancy rate: 8.0%

Health Insurance: 82.4% have insurance; 50.1% have private insurance; 45.4% have public insurance; 17.6% do not have insurance; 4.9% of children under 18 do not have insurance

Hospitals: Kings Daughters Medical Center Ohio; Southern Ohio Medical Center (488 beds)

Safety: Violent crime rate: 43.8 per 10,000 population; Property crime rate: 776.5 per 10,000 population
Newspapers: Community Common (weekly circulation 39000); Portsmouth Daily Times (daily circulation 12400)
Transportation: Commute: 89.4% car, 0.1% public transportation, 7.5% walk, 1.8% work from home; Median travel time to work: 18.7 minutes
Airports: Greater Portsmouth Regional (general aviation)
Additional Information Contacts
City of Portsmouth. . . . . (740) 354-8807
http://www.ci.portsmouth.oh.us

RARDEN (village). Covers a land area of 0.212 square miles and a water area of <.001 square miles. Located at 38.92° N. Lat; 83.24° W. Long. Elevation is 617 feet.
Population: 159; Growth (since 2000): -9.7%; Density: 751.5 persons per square mile; Race: 99.4% White, 0.0% Black/African American, 0.6% Asian, 0.0% American Indian/Alaska Native, 0.0% Native Hawaiian/Other Pacific Islander, 0.0% Two or more races, 0.0% Hispanic of any race; Average household size: 2.37; Median age: 42.5; Age under 18: 23.9%; Age 65 and over: 17.0%; Males per 100 females: 87.1
Housing: Homeownership rate: 70.2%; Homeowner vacancy rate: 4.1%; Rental vacancy rate: 23.1%

ROSEMOUNT (CDP). Covers a land area of 5.748 square miles and a water area of 0.003 square miles. Located at 38.77° N. Lat; 82.97° W. Long. Elevation is 617 feet.
Population: 2,112; Growth (since 2000): 3.4%; Density: 367.4 persons per square mile; Race: 97.5% White, 0.7% Black/African American, 0.5% Asian, 0.1% American Indian/Alaska Native, 0.0% Native Hawaiian/Other Pacific Islander, 0.9% Two or more races, 0.6% Hispanic of any race; Average household size: 2.46; Median age: 43.8; Age under 18: 21.2%; Age 65 and over: 20.9%; Males per 100 females: 85.1
Housing: Homeownership rate: 78.5%; Homeowner vacancy rate: 2.0%; Rental vacancy rate: 2.7%

SCIOTODALE (CDP). Covers a land area of 1.949 square miles and a water area of 0.005 square miles. Located at 38.75° N. Lat; 82.85° W. Long. Elevation is 597 feet.
Population: 1,081; Growth (since 2000): 10.1%; Density: 554.7 persons per square mile; Race: 96.7% White, 0.8% Black/African American, 0.4% Asian, 0.7% American Indian/Alaska Native, 0.0% Native Hawaiian/Other Pacific Islander, 1.3% Two or more races, 1.4% Hispanic of any race; Average household size: 2.57; Median age: 41.0; Age under 18: 24.0%; Age 65 and over: 16.4%; Males per 100 females: 95.8
Housing: Homeownership rate: 79.8%; Homeowner vacancy rate: 2.0%; Rental vacancy rate: 4.5%

SOUTH WEBSTER (village). Covers a land area of 1.311 square miles and a water area of 0.014 square miles. Located at 38.82° N. Lat; 82.73° W. Long. Elevation is 705 feet.
Population: 866; Growth (since 2000): 13.4%; Density: 660.8 persons per square mile; Race: 98.2% White, 0.1% Black/African American, 0.3% Asian, 0.1% American Indian/Alaska Native, 0.0% Native Hawaiian/Other Pacific Islander, 1.3% Two or more races, 0.3% Hispanic of any race; Average household size: 2.34; Median age: 43.9; Age under 18: 22.7%; Age 65 and over: 19.7%; Males per 100 females: 91.2

School District(s)

Bloom-Vernon Local (PK-12)
2012-13 Enrollment: 909. . . . . (740) 778-2281
Housing: Homeownership rate: 76.7%; Homeowner vacancy rate: 2.4%; Rental vacancy rate: 5.5%

STOUT (unincorporated postal area)

ZCTA: 45684

Covers a land area of 79.263 square miles and a water area of 1.169 square miles. Located at 38.65° N. Lat; 83.19° W. Long..
Population: 1,804; Growth (since 2000): -1.3%; Density: 22.8 persons per square mile; Race: 96.7% White, 0.2% Black/African American, 0.3% Asian, 0.6% American Indian/Alaska Native, 0.0% Native Hawaiian/Other Pacific Islander, 2.1% Two or more races, 0.9% Hispanic of any race; Average household size: 2.41; Median age: 43.8; Age under 18: 21.1%; Age 65 and over: 16.2%; Males per 100 females: 98.2
Housing: Homeownership rate: 81.8%; Homeowner vacancy rate: 3.4%; Rental vacancy rate: 8.5%

WEST PORTSMOUTH (CDP). Covers a land area of 4.705 square miles and a water area of 0.003 square miles. Located at 38.77° N. Lat; 83.04° W. Long. Elevation is 617 feet.
Population: 3,149; Growth (since 2000): -8.9%; Density: 669.3 persons per square mile; Race: 96.6% White, 0.3% Black/African American, 0.1% Asian, 0.6% American Indian/Alaska Native, 0.0% Native Hawaiian/Other Pacific Islander, 2.0% Two or more races, 1.4% Hispanic of any race; Average household size: 2.55; Median age: 39.1; Age under 18: 23.3%; Age 65 and over: 14.5%; Males per 100 females: 93.3; Marriage status: 20.9% never married, 59.4% now married, 4.2% separated, 7.6% widowed, 12.2% divorced; Foreign born: 0.0%; Speak English only: 99.8%; With disability: 20.3%; Veterans: 10.4%; Ancestry: 21.3% German, 16.8% American, 7.4% French, 7.3% Irish, 5.8% English
Employment: 1.9% management, business, and financial, 0.0% computer, engineering, and science, 5.6% education, legal, community service, arts, and media, 5.2% healthcare practitioners, 27.6% service, 31.1% sales and office, 9.9% natural resources, construction, and maintenance, 18.7% production, transportation, and material moving
Income: Per capita: $16,668; Median household: $35,979; Average household: $43,838; Households with income of $100,000 or more: 5.0%; Poverty rate: 14.0%
Educational Attainment: High school diploma or higher: 81.4%; Bachelor's degree or higher: 4.0%; Graduate/professional degree or higher: 1.4%

School District(s)

Washington-Nile Local (PK-12)
2012-13 Enrollment: 1,536 . . . . (740) 858-1111
Housing: Homeownership rate: 72.5%; Median home value: $60,800; Median year structure built: 1959; Homeowner vacancy rate: 1.8%; Median gross rent: $609 per month; Rental vacancy rate: 10.2%
Health Insurance: 89.0% have insurance; 58.3% have private insurance; 43.1% have public insurance; 11.0% do not have insurance; 0.6% of children under 18 do not have insurance
Transportation: Commute: 95.7% car, 0.0% public transportation, 0.9% walk, 2.1% work from home; Median travel time to work: 25.4 minutes

WHEELERSBURG (CDP). Covers a land area of 5.804 square miles and a water area of 0.094 square miles. Located at 38.74° N. Lat; 82.85° W. Long. Elevation is 554 feet.
Population: 6,437; Growth (since 2000): -0.5%; Density: 1,109.1 persons per square mile; Race: 97.3% White, 0.3% Black/African American, 0.5% Asian, 0.4% American Indian/Alaska Native, 0.0% Native Hawaiian/Other Pacific Islander, 1.2% Two or more races, 0.9% Hispanic of any race; Average household size: 2.35; Median age: 41.1; Age under 18: 22.6%; Age 65 and over: 19.3%; Males per 100 females: 89.4; Marriage status: 26.5% never married, 54.3% now married, 2.0% separated, 7.6% widowed, 11.6% divorced; Foreign born: 1.0%; Speak English only: 99.4%; With disability: 19.1%; Veterans: 10.3%; Ancestry: 33.7% German, 14.8% Irish, 13.4% English, 11.4% American, 3.1% Scottish
Employment: 18.2% management, business, and financial, 3.0% computer, engineering, and science, 9.2% education, legal, community service, arts, and media, 10.5% healthcare practitioners, 13.8% service, 23.3% sales and office, 12.0% natural resources, construction, and maintenance, 10.0% production, transportation, and material moving
Income: Per capita: $24,242; Median household: $45,761; Average household: $58,213; Households with income of $100,000 or more: 14.6%; Poverty rate: 15.5%
Educational Attainment: High school diploma or higher: 85.5%; Bachelor's degree or higher: 19.8%; Graduate/professional degree or higher: 5.9%

School District(s)

Wheelersburg Local (PK-12)
2012-13 Enrollment: 1,540 . . . . (740) 574-8484
Housing: Homeownership rate: 67.5%; Median home value: $128,600; Median year structure built: 1972; Homeowner vacancy rate: 1.3%; Median gross rent: $578 per month; Rental vacancy rate: 8.2%
Health Insurance: 83.0% have insurance; 59.4% have private insurance; 34.3% have public insurance; 17.0% do not have insurance; 9.8% of children under 18 do not have insurance
Newspapers: The Scioto Voice (weekly circulation 3600)
Transportation: Commute: 94.2% car, 0.0% public transportation, 0.0% walk, 5.2% work from home; Median travel time to work: 23.4 minutes

Seneca County

Located in northern Ohio; drained by the Sandusky River and its tributaries. Covers a land area of 551.017 square miles, a water area of 1.776 square miles, and is located in the Eastern Time Zone at 41.12° N. Lat., 83.13° W. Long. The county was founded in 1820. County seat is Tiffin.

Seneca County is part of the Tiffin, OH Micropolitan Statistical Area. The entire metro area includes: Seneca County, OH

Weather Station: Tiffin | Elevation: 740 feet

	Jan	Feb	Mar	Apr	May	Jun	Jul	Aug	Sep	Oct	Nov	Dec
High	33	36	47	60	71	80	84	83	76	63	50	37
Low	18	21	29	39	49	59	63	61	53	42	34	23
Precip	2.3	2.0	2.5	3.3	3.9	4.1	3.6	3.7	3.4	2.6	3.0	2.9
Snow	9.3	6.0	4.4	1.3	tr	0.0	0.0	0.0	0.0	tr	1.0	7.0

High and Low temperatures in degrees Fahrenheit; Precipitation and Snow in inches

Population: 56,745; Growth (since 2000): -3.3%; Density: 103.0 persons per square mile; Race: 93.7% White, 2.3% Black/African American, 0.6% Asian, 0.2% American Indian/Alaska Native, 0.0% Native Hawaiian/Other Pacific Islander, 1.9% two or more races, 4.4% Hispanic of any race; Average household size: 2.49; Median age: 38.8; Age under 18: 23.6%; Age 65 and over: 14.8%; Males per 100 females: 99.8; Marriage status: 29.0% never married, 53.4% now married, 1.5% separated, 6.4% widowed, 11.2% divorced; Foreign born: 1.2%; Speak English only: 97.3%; With disability: 13.9%; Veterans: 10.9%; Ancestry: 45.7% German, 9.8% Irish, 8.2% American, 7.0% English, 5.1% Italian
Religion: Six largest groups: 33.1% Catholicism, 6.5% Methodist/Pietist, 5.7% Presbyterian-Reformed, 3.0% Lutheran, 2.4% Baptist, 1.8% Pentecostal
Economy: Unemployment rate: 4.1%; Leading industries: 13.6% other services (except public administration); 13.5% retail trade; 12.6% health care and social assistance; Farms: 1,113 totaling 290,511 acres; Company size: 0 employ 1,000 or more persons, 2 employ 500 to 999 persons, 31 employs 100 to 499 persons, 1,141 employs less than 100 persons; Business ownership: 1,111 women-owned, n/a Black-owned, n/a Hispanic-owned, n/a Asian-owned
Employment: 8.7% management, business, and financial, 2.2% computer, engineering, and science, 8.3% education, legal, community service, arts, and media, 5.7% healthcare practitioners, 19.2% service, 18.9% sales and office, 9.5% natural resources, construction, and maintenance, 27.6% production, transportation, and material moving
Income: Per capita: $22,075; Median household: $43,764; Average household: $56,020; Households with income of $100,000 or more: 12.0%; Poverty rate: 15.5%
Educational Attainment: High school diploma or higher: 89.4%; Bachelor's degree or higher: 15.3%; Graduate/professional degree or higher: 5.8%
Housing: Homeownership rate: 73.7%; Median home value: $97,900; Median year structure built: 1956; Homeowner vacancy rate: 2.6%; Median gross rent: $619 per month; Rental vacancy rate: 12.3%
Vital Statistics: Birth rate: 105.5 per 10,000 population; Death rate: 94.6 per 10,000 population; Age-adjusted cancer mortality rate: 179.8 deaths per 100,000 population
Health Insurance: 89.0% have insurance; 70.7% have private insurance; 32.8% have public insurance; 11.0% do not have insurance; 3.3% of children under 18 do not have insurance
Health Care: Physicians: 8.4 per 10,000 population; Hospital beds: 13.5 per 10,000 population; Hospital admissions: 608.7 per 10,000 population
Transportation: Commute: 92.4% car, 0.3% public transportation, 3.5% walk, 2.1% work from home; Median travel time to work: 20.0 minutes
Presidential Election: 44.5% Obama, 52.9% Romney (2012)
National and State Parks: Sandusky Scenic River State Access Area; Springville Marsh State Natural Area
Additional Information Contacts
Seneca Government . . . . (419) 447-4550
http://www.seneca-county.com

Seneca County Communities

ALVADA (unincorporated postal area)
ZCTA: 44802
Covers a land area of 28.449 square miles and a water area of 0 square miles. Located at 41.05° N. Lat; 83.42° W. Long. Elevation is 846 feet.
Population: 1,032; Growth (since 2000): 1.9%; Density: 36.3 persons per square mile; Race: 97.3% White, 0.0% Black/African American, 0.8% Asian, 0.0% American Indian/Alaska Native, 0.0% Native Hawaiian/Other Pacific Islander, 0.8% Two or more races, 2.6% Hispanic of any race; Average household size: 2.75; Median age: 39.4; Age under 18: 26.6%; Age 65 and over: 11.2%; Males per 100 females: 108.1
Housing: Homeownership rate: 86.9%; Homeowner vacancy rate: 1.2%; Rental vacancy rate: 3.9%

ATTICA (village). Covers a land area of 0.663 square miles and a water area of 0.009 square miles. Located at 41.06° N. Lat; 82.89° W. Long. Elevation is 948 feet.
Population: 899; Growth (since 2000): -5.9%; Density: 1,355.5 persons per square mile; Race: 96.3% White, 0.8% Black/African American, 0.0% Asian, 0.0% American Indian/Alaska Native, 0.0% Native Hawaiian/Other Pacific Islander, 2.7% Two or more races, 1.3% Hispanic of any race; Average household size: 2.47; Median age: 39.8; Age under 18: 25.6%; Age 65 and over: 17.5%; Males per 100 females: 95.4
School District(s)
Seneca East Local (PK-12)
2012-13 Enrollment: 969. . . . . (419) 426-7041
Housing: Homeownership rate: 73.9%; Homeowner vacancy rate: 2.9%; Rental vacancy rate: 26.4%
Newspapers: Attica Hub (weekly circulation 4400)

BASCOM (CDP). Covers a land area of 1.514 square miles and a water area of 0 square miles. Located at 41.13° N. Lat; 83.29° W. Long. Elevation is 774 feet.
Population: 390; Growth (since 2000): n/a; Density: 257.6 persons per square mile; Race: 99.5% White, 0.0% Black/African American, 0.0% Asian, 0.0% American Indian/Alaska Native, 0.0% Native Hawaiian/Other Pacific Islander, 0.5% Two or more races, 1.8% Hispanic of any race; Average household size: 2.60; Median age: 39.3; Age under 18: 23.8%; Age 65 and over: 14.1%; Males per 100 females: 109.7
School District(s)
Hopewell-Loudon Local (PK-12)
2012-13 Enrollment: 894. . . . . (419) 937-2216
Housing: Homeownership rate: 80.7%; Homeowner vacancy rate: 1.6%; Rental vacancy rate: 9.1%

BETTSVILLE (village). Covers a land area of 0.521 square miles and a water area of 0 square miles. Located at 41.24° N. Lat; 83.23° W. Long. Elevation is 702 feet.
Population: 661; Growth (since 2000): -15.7%; Density: 1,268.9 persons per square mile; Race: 97.3% White, 0.0% Black/African American, 1.2% Asian, 0.2% American Indian/Alaska Native, 0.0% Native Hawaiian/Other Pacific Islander, 0.3% Two or more races, 8.3% Hispanic of any race; Average household size: 2.35; Median age: 40.3; Age under 18: 23.4%; Age 65 and over: 15.6%; Males per 100 females: 102.8
School District(s)
Bettsville Local (PK-12)
2012-13 Enrollment: 165. . . . . (419) 986-5166
Housing: Homeownership rate: 78.7%; Homeowner vacancy rate: 4.3%; Rental vacancy rate: 12.9%

BLOOMVILLE (village). Covers a land area of 0.603 square miles and a water area of 0 square miles. Located at 41.05° N. Lat; 83.01° W. Long. Elevation is 928 feet.
Population: 956; Growth (since 2000): -8.5%; Density: 1,584.3 persons per square mile; Race: 97.4% White, 0.2% Black/African American, 0.0% Asian, 0.1% American Indian/Alaska Native, 0.0% Native Hawaiian/Other Pacific Islander, 1.6% Two or more races, 2.1% Hispanic of any race; Average household size: 2.66; Median age: 34.3; Age under 18: 29.7%; Age 65 and over: 14.2%; Males per 100 females: 102.1
Housing: Homeownership rate: 68.5%; Homeowner vacancy rate: 1.6%; Rental vacancy rate: 12.0%

FLAT ROCK (CDP). Covers a land area of 0.209 square miles and a water area of 0 square miles. Located at 41.24° N. Lat; 82.86° W. Long. Elevation is 797 feet.
Population: 233; Growth (since 2000): n/a; Density: 1,114.0 persons per square mile; Race: 97.9% White, 1.3% Black/African American, 0.0% Asian, 0.4% American Indian/Alaska Native, 0.0% Native Hawaiian/Other Pacific Islander, 0.4% Two or more races, 2.1% Hispanic of any race;

Average household size: 2.68; Median age: 28.8; Age under 18: 29.2%; Age 65 and over: 15.0%; Males per 100 females: 111.8
Housing: Homeownership rate: 74.0%; Homeowner vacancy rate: 5.3%; Rental vacancy rate: 9.5%

FORT SENECA (CDP). Covers a land area of 0.625 square miles and a water area of 0 square miles. Located at 41.20° N. Lat; 83.17° W. Long. Elevation is 699 feet.
Population: 254; Growth (since 2000): n/a; Density: 406.1 persons per square mile; Race: 98.4% White, 0.0% Black/African American, 0.0% Asian, 0.0% American Indian/Alaska Native, 0.0% Native Hawaiian/Other Pacific Islander, 1.2% Two or more races, 2.0% Hispanic of any race; Average household size: 2.44; Median age: 46.0; Age under 18: 20.5%; Age 65 and over: 18.5%; Males per 100 females: 92.4
Housing: Homeownership rate: 83.7%; Homeowner vacancy rate: 0.0%; Rental vacancy rate: 5.6%

FOSTORIA (city). Covers a land area of 7.545 square miles and a water area of 0.218 square miles. Located at 41.16° N. Lat; 83.41° W. Long. Elevation is 781 feet.
History: Fostoria grew from the union in 1854 of two rival settlements, Rome and Risdon, which had been established in 1832. The town was named for C.W. Foster, a local real estate developer whose son, Charles, served as governor of Ohio (1880-1884).
Population: 13,441; Growth (since 2000): -3.5%; Density: 1,781.5 persons per square mile; Race: 84.1% White, 6.4% Black/African American, 0.4% Asian, 0.1% American Indian/Alaska Native, 0.0% Native Hawaiian/Other Pacific Islander, 4.7% Two or more races, 11.5% Hispanic of any race; Average household size: 2.42; Median age: 37.9; Age under 18: 26.0%; Age 65 and over: 16.0%; Males per 100 females: 89.7; Marriage status: 28.6% never married, 44.7% now married, 3.7% separated, 10.5% widowed, 16.2% divorced; Foreign born: 0.7%; Speak English only: 96.7%; With disability: 17.0%; Veterans: 12.8%; Ancestry: 36.7% German, 9.7% Irish, 7.7% American, 5.7% English, 5.3% Italian
Employment: 5.6% management, business, and financial, 1.3% computer, engineering, and science, 5.8% education, legal, community service, arts, and media, 4.5% healthcare practitioners, 24.8% service, 18.3% sales and office, 5.7% natural resources, construction, and maintenance, 33.9% production, transportation, and material moving
Income: Per capita: $18,004; Median household: $35,090; Average household: $42,326; Households with income of $100,000 or more: 5.4%; Poverty rate: 24.7%
Educational Attainment: High school diploma or higher: 86.7%; Bachelor's degree or higher: 9.4%; Graduate/professional degree or higher: 3.0%

School District(s)

Fostoria City (PK-12)
2012-13 Enrollment: 1,836 . . . . (419) 435-8163
Housing: Homeownership rate: 63.8%; Median home value: $68,100; Median year structure built: 1952; Homeowner vacancy rate: 4.5%; Median gross rent: $579 per month; Rental vacancy rate: 11.3%
Health Insurance: 84.2% have insurance; 59.4% have private insurance; 42.7% have public insurance; 15.8% do not have insurance; 3.1% of children under 18 do not have insurance
Hospitals: Fostoria Community Hospital (66 beds)
Newspapers: Review Times (daily circulation 4100); The Focus (weekly circulation 12000)
Transportation: Commute: 94.7% car, 0.3% public transportation, 3.2% walk, 1.2% work from home; Median travel time to work: 20.2 minutes
Additional Information Contacts
City of Fostoria . . . . (419) 435-8282
http://www.ci.fostoria.oh.us

KANSAS (CDP). Covers a land area of 0.439 square miles and a water area of 0 square miles. Located at 41.25° N. Lat; 83.28° W. Long. Elevation is 728 feet.
Population: 179; Growth (since 2000): n/a; Density: 407.6 persons per square mile; Race: 97.8% White, 0.0% Black/African American, 0.0% Asian, 0.0% American Indian/Alaska Native, 0.0% Native Hawaiian/Other Pacific Islander, 0.0% Two or more races, 4.5% Hispanic of any race; Average household size: 2.67; Median age: 40.7; Age under 18: 24.0%; Age 65 and over: 14.5%; Males per 100 females: 82.7

School District(s)

Lakota Local (PK-12)
2012-13 Enrollment: 995. . . . . (419) 986-6650
Housing: Homeownership rate: 95.6%; Homeowner vacancy rate: 0.0%; Rental vacancy rate: 0.0%

MELMORE (CDP). Covers a land area of 0.593 square miles and a water area of 0 square miles. Located at 41.03° N. Lat; 83.10° W. Long. Elevation is 863 feet.
Population: 153; Growth (since 2000): n/a; Density: 258.0 persons per square mile; Race: 96.7% White, 0.0% Black/African American, 1.3% Asian, 0.0% American Indian/Alaska Native, 0.0% Native Hawaiian/Other Pacific Islander, 1.3% Two or more races, 1.3% Hispanic of any race; Average household size: 2.22; Median age: 43.3; Age under 18: 19.0%; Age 65 and over: 15.7%; Males per 100 females: 104.0
Housing: Homeownership rate: 78.2%; Homeowner vacancy rate: 0.0%; Rental vacancy rate: 0.0%

NEW RIEGEL (village). Covers a land area of 0.200 square miles and a water area of 0 square miles. Located at 41.05° N. Lat; 83.32° W. Long. Elevation is 833 feet.
Population: 249; Growth (since 2000): 10.2%; Density: 1,243.2 persons per square mile; Race: 98.8% White, 0.8% Black/African American, 0.0% Asian, 0.0% American Indian/Alaska Native, 0.4% Native Hawaiian/Other Pacific Islander, 0.0% Two or more races, 2.0% Hispanic of any race; Average household size: 2.25; Median age: 41.9; Age under 18: 22.1%; Age 65 and over: 19.7%; Males per 100 females: 97.6

School District(s)

New Riegel Local (PK-12)
2012-13 Enrollment: 374. . . . . (419) 595-2265
Housing: Homeownership rate: 70.0%; Homeowner vacancy rate: 0.0%; Rental vacancy rate: 15.4%

OLD FORT (CDP). Covers a land area of 0.577 square miles and a water area of 0 square miles. Located at 41.24° N. Lat; 83.15° W. Long. Elevation is 686 feet.
Population: 186; Growth (since 2000): n/a; Density: 322.1 persons per square mile; Race: 94.6% White, 1.6% Black/African American, 0.0% Asian, 0.0% American Indian/Alaska Native, 0.0% Native Hawaiian/Other Pacific Islander, 3.2% Two or more races, 5.4% Hispanic of any race; Average household size: 2.62; Median age: 34.0; Age under 18: 30.1%; Age 65 and over: 17.7%; Males per 100 females: 93.8

School District(s)

Old Fort Local (PK-12)
2012-13 Enrollment: 458. . . . . (419) 992-4291
Housing: Homeownership rate: 81.7%; Homeowner vacancy rate: 4.9%; Rental vacancy rate: 0.0%

REPUBLIC (village). Covers a land area of 0.863 square miles and a water area of 0 square miles. Located at 41.13° N. Lat; 83.02° W. Long. Elevation is 886 feet.
Population: 549; Growth (since 2000): -10.6%; Density: 636.5 persons per square mile; Race: 98.2% White, 0.4% Black/African American, 0.2% Asian, 0.5% American Indian/Alaska Native, 0.0% Native Hawaiian/Other Pacific Islander, 0.7% Two or more races, 1.8% Hispanic of any race; Average household size: 2.50; Median age: 35.5; Age under 18: 25.9%; Age 65 and over: 11.3%; Males per 100 females: 100.4
Housing: Homeownership rate: 75.0%; Homeowner vacancy rate: 1.2%; Rental vacancy rate: 17.9%

TIFFIN (city). County seat. Covers a land area of 6.764 square miles and a water area of 0.136 square miles. Located at 41.12° N. Lat; 83.18° W. Long. Elevation is 745 feet.
History: In 1817, Erastus Bowe built the Pan Yan Tavern on the north side of the Sandusky River, and a town called Oakley grew up around it. In 1820 Josiah Hedges established a settlement on the south side of the river opposite Oakley, calling it Tiffin after Edward Tiffin, the first governor of Ohio. The two villages were united as Tiffin in 1850.
Population: 17,963; Growth (since 2000): -0.9%; Density: 2,655.8 persons per square mile; Race: 93.9% White, 2.6% Black/African American, 1.0% Asian, 0.2% American Indian/Alaska Native, 0.0% Native Hawaiian/Other Pacific Islander, 1.6% Two or more races, 3.1% Hispanic of any race; Average household size: 2.29; Median age: 35.2; Age under 18: 20.7%; Age 65 and over: 15.8%; Males per 100 females: 95.8; Marriage status: 37.7% never married, 44.7% now married, 1.2% separated, 6.4% widowed, 11.2% divorced; Foreign born: 2.9%; Speak English only: 96.2%; With disability: 15.1%; Veterans: 10.2%; Ancestry: 46.3% German, 12.6% Irish, 7.8% American, 6.3% Italian, 5.6% English

Employment: 7.1% management, business, and financial, 1.8% computer, engineering, and science, 11.3% education, legal, community service, arts, and media, 4.5% healthcare practitioners, 21.6% service, 22.6% sales and office, 6.6% natural resources, construction, and maintenance, 24.4% production, transportation, and material moving
Income: Per capita: $18,801; Median household: $35,179; Average household: $47,517; Households with income of $100,000 or more: 6.5%; Poverty rate: 17.2%
Educational Attainment: High school diploma or higher: 87.9%; Bachelor's degree or higher: 17.3%; Graduate/professional degree or higher: 6.2%

School District(s)

Bridges Community Academy (KG-12)
2012-13 Enrollment: 128. . . . . (419) 455-9295
Lakeland Academy Community School (08-12)
2012-13 Enrollment: 26. . . . . (740) 658-1042
Tiffin City (PK-12)
2012-13 Enrollment: 2,768 . . . . (419) 447-2515
Vanguard-Sentinel Career & Technology Centers (06-12)
2012-13 Enrollment: n/a . . . . (419) 332-2626

Four-year College(s)

Heidelberg University (Private, Not-for-profit, United Church of Christ)
Fall 2013 Enrollment: 1,241 . . . . (419) 448-2000
2013-14 Tuition: In-state $26,180; Out-of-state $26,180
Tiffin University (Private, Not-for-profit)
Fall 2013 Enrollment: 4,954 . . . . (800) 968-6446
2013-14 Tuition: In-state $20,700; Out-of-state $20,700

Two-year College(s)

Tiffin Academy of Hair Design (Private, For-profit)
Fall 2013 Enrollment: 42. . . . . (419) 447-3117
Housing: Homeownership rate: 62.6%; Median home value: $91,400; Median year structure built: 1951; Homeowner vacancy rate: 3.8%; Median gross rent: $622 per month; Rental vacancy rate: 13.9%
Health Insurance: 87.6% have insurance; 66.6% have private insurance; 34.9% have public insurance; 12.4% do not have insurance; 3.5% of children under 18 do not have insurance
Hospitals: Mercy Tiffin Hospital (105 beds)
Newspapers: Advertiser-Tribune (daily circulation 9800)
Transportation: Commute: 87.7% car, 0.4% public transportation, 6.9% walk, 1.4% work from home; Median travel time to work: 16.3 minutes
Additional Information Contacts
City of Tiffin . . . . (419) 448-5401
http://www.tiffinohio.com

Shelby County

Located in western Ohio; crossed by the Great Miami River; includes Lake Loramie. Covers a land area of 407.675 square miles, a water area of 3.017 square miles, and is located in the Eastern Time Zone at 40.34° N. Lat., 84.20° W. Long. The county was founded in 1819. County seat is Sidney.

Shelby County is part of the Sidney, OH Micropolitan Statistical Area. The entire metro area includes: Shelby County, OH

Weather Station: Sidney 1 S Elevation: 939 feet

	Jan	Feb	Mar	Apr	May	Jun	Jul	Aug	Sep	Oct	Nov	Dec
High	34	38	48	61	71	81	84	83	77	64	51	38
Low	17	20	28	38	48	58	62	60	52	41	32	22
Precip	2.6	2.2	2.8	3.6	4.1	4.5	4.2	3.8	2.7	2.8	3.3	2.9
Snow	na	na	na	tr	0.0	0.0	0.0	0.0	0.0	0.0	tr	na

High and Low temperatures in degrees Fahrenheit; Precipitation and Snow in inches

Population: 49,423; Growth (since 2000): 3.2%; Density: 121.2 persons per square mile; Race: 94.7% White, 1.9% Black/African American, 0.9% Asian, 0.2% American Indian/Alaska Native, 0.1% Native Hawaiian/Other Pacific Islander, 1.9% two or more races, 1.3% Hispanic of any race; Average household size: 2.64; Median age: 37.9; Age under 18: 27.3%; Age 65 and over: 12.9%; Males per 100 females: 99.5; Marriage status: 24.0% never married, 57.9% now married, 1.3% separated, 6.3% widowed, 11.8% divorced; Foreign born: 1.6%; Speak English only: 97.5%; With disability: 11.5%; Veterans: 9.6%; Ancestry: 37.1% German, 11.2% American, 9.5% Irish, 8.0% English, 5.1% French
Religion: Six largest groups: 27.0% Catholicism, 7.3% Lutheran, 6.0% Non-denominational Protestant, 5.9% Methodist/Pietist, 3.0% Baptist, 2.9% Presbyterian-Reformed
Economy: Unemployment rate: 3.7%; Leading industries: 14.4% retail trade; 12.2% manufacturing; 11.0% other services (except public administration); Farms: 986 totaling 206,283 acres; Company size: 1 employs 1,000 or more persons, 3 employ 500 to 999 persons, 41 employs 100 to 499 persons, 947 employ less than 100 persons; Business ownership: n/a women-owned, n/a Black-owned, 34 Hispanic-owned, n/a Asian-owned
Employment: 13.0% management, business, and financial, 3.1% computer, engineering, and science, 5.9% education, legal, community service, arts, and media, 5.1% healthcare practitioners, 16.7% service, 18.2% sales and office, 8.8% natural resources, construction, and maintenance, 29.3% production, transportation, and material moving
Income: Per capita: $24,028; Median household: $50,427; Average household: $63,549; Households with income of $100,000 or more: 14.8%; Poverty rate: 11.4%
Educational Attainment: High school diploma or higher: 88.2%; Bachelor's degree or higher: 14.5%; Graduate/professional degree or higher: 5.7%
Housing: Homeownership rate: 72.3%; Median home value: $123,400; Median year structure built: 1970; Homeowner vacancy rate: 2.2%; Median gross rent: $689 per month; Rental vacancy rate: 8.6%
Vital Statistics: Birth rate: 126.4 per 10,000 population; Death rate: 81.5 per 10,000 population; Age-adjusted cancer mortality rate: 178.7 deaths per 100,000 population
Health Insurance: 89.5% have insurance; 74.0% have private insurance; 27.6% have public insurance; 10.5% do not have insurance; 4.7% of children under 18 do not have insurance
Health Care: Physicians: 7.9 per 10,000 population; Hospital beds: 14.4 per 10,000 population; Hospital admissions: 542.5 per 10,000 population
Transportation: Commute: 94.8% car, 0.1% public transportation, 1.5% walk, 2.8% work from home; Median travel time to work: 18.7 minutes
Presidential Election: 26.2% Obama, 72.2% Romney (2012)
National and State Parks: Lake Loramie State Park
Additional Information Contacts
Shelby Government. . . . . (937) 498-7226
http://www.co.shelby.oh.us

Shelby County Communities

ANNA (village). Covers a land area of 1.029 square miles and a water area of <.001 square miles. Located at 40.40° N. Lat; 84.18° W. Long. Elevation is 1,027 feet.
Population: 1,567; Growth (since 2000): 18.8%; Density: 1,522.7 persons per square mile; Race: 97.4% White, 0.4% Black/African American, 0.2% Asian, 0.4% American Indian/Alaska Native, 0.0% Native Hawaiian/Other Pacific Islander, 1.5% Two or more races, 0.6% Hispanic of any race; Average household size: 2.84; Median age: 31.1; Age under 18: 33.4%; Age 65 and over: 7.1%; Males per 100 females: 93.7

School District(s)

Anna Local (KG-12)
2012-13 Enrollment: 1,248 . . . . (937) 394-2011
Housing: Homeownership rate: 74.3%; Homeowner vacancy rate: 2.2%; Rental vacancy rate: 10.1%

BOTKINS (village). Covers a land area of 1.241 square miles and a water area of 0.013 square miles. Located at 40.45° N. Lat; 84.18° W. Long. Elevation is 997 feet.
Population: 1,155; Growth (since 2000): -4.1%; Density: 930.9 persons per square mile; Race: 97.7% White, 0.4% Black/African American, 0.6% Asian, 0.1% American Indian/Alaska Native, 0.1% Native Hawaiian/Other Pacific Islander, 1.0% Two or more races, 0.7% Hispanic of any race; Average household size: 2.41; Median age: 37.8; Age under 18: 25.4%; Age 65 and over: 13.2%; Males per 100 females: 98.5

School District(s)

Botkins Local (KG-12)
2012-13 Enrollment: 588. . . . . (937) 693-3756
Housing: Homeownership rate: 75.0%; Homeowner vacancy rate: 0.8%; Rental vacancy rate: 10.2%

FORT LORAMIE (village). Covers a land area of 0.957 square miles and a water area of <.001 square miles. Located at 40.35° N. Lat; 84.37° W. Long. Elevation is 951 feet.
History: Fort Loramie built here (1794) by Anthony Wayne.
Population: 1,478; Growth (since 2000): 10.0%; Density: 1,544.3 persons per square mile; Race: 99.7% White, 0.1% Black/African American, 0.1%

Asian, 0.0% American Indian/Alaska Native, 0.0% Native Hawaiian/Other Pacific Islander, 0.1% Two or more races, 0.4% Hispanic of any race; Average household size: 2.79; Median age: 35.0; Age under 18: 31.1%; Age 65 and over: 14.6%; Males per 100 females: 96.0

School District(s)

Fort Loramie Local (KG-12)
2012-13 Enrollment: 818. . . . . (937) 295-3931

Housing: Homeownership rate: 82.8%; Homeowner vacancy rate: 0.7%; Rental vacancy rate: 14.0%

HOUSTON (unincorporated postal area)

ZCTA: 45333

Covers a land area of 22.162 square miles and a water area of 0.244 square miles. Located at 40.25° N. Lat; 84.33° W. Long. Elevation is 961 feet.

Population: 1,345; Growth (since 2000): -9.7%; Density: 60.7 persons per square mile; Race: 97.8% White, 0.9% Black/African American, 0.3% Asian, 0.0% American Indian/Alaska Native, 0.0% Native Hawaiian/Other Pacific Islander, 1.0% Two or more races, 0.1% Hispanic of any race; Average household size: 2.80; Median age: 38.7; Age under 18: 27.1%; Age 65 and over: 11.2%; Males per 100 females: 107.6

School District(s)

Hardin-Houston Local (KG-12)
2012-13 Enrollment: 851. . . . . (937) 295-3010

Housing: Homeownership rate: 84.6%; Homeowner vacancy rate: 0.5%; Rental vacancy rate: 9.5%

JACKSON CENTER (village). Covers a land area of 1.676 square miles and a water area of 0.008 square miles. Located at 40.44° N. Lat; 84.04° W. Long. Elevation is 1,027 feet.

Population: 1,462; Growth (since 2000): 6.8%; Density: 872.3 persons per square mile; Race: 98.1% White, 0.0% Black/African American, 0.1% Asian, 0.0% American Indian/Alaska Native, 0.0% Native Hawaiian/Other Pacific Islander, 1.2% Two or more races, 1.7% Hispanic of any race; Average household size: 2.54; Median age: 35.7; Age under 18: 29.7%; Age 65 and over: 13.6%; Males per 100 females: 99.7

School District(s)

Jackson Center Local (PK-12)
2012-13 Enrollment: 537. . . . . (937) 596-6053

Housing: Homeownership rate: 70.0%; Homeowner vacancy rate: 2.2%; Rental vacancy rate: 16.4%

Safety: Violent crime rate: 0.0 per 10,000 population; Property crime rate: 158.6 per 10,000 population

KETTLERSVILLE (village). Covers a land area of 1.021 square miles and a water area of 0.004 square miles. Located at 40.44° N. Lat; 84.26° W. Long. Elevation is 978 feet.

History: Also spelled Kettlerville.

Population: 179; Growth (since 2000): 2.3%; Density: 175.3 persons per square mile; Race: 98.9% White, 0.0% Black/African American, 0.0% Asian, 0.0% American Indian/Alaska Native, 1.1% Native Hawaiian/Other Pacific Islander, 0.0% Two or more races, 2.2% Hispanic of any race; Average household size: 2.63; Median age: 30.8; Age under 18: 30.2%; Age 65 and over: 12.8%; Males per 100 females: 115.7

Housing: Homeownership rate: 82.3%; Homeowner vacancy rate: 3.4%; Rental vacancy rate: 0.0%

LOCKINGTON (village). Covers a land area of 0.082 square miles and a water area of 0 square miles. Located at 40.21° N. Lat; 84.24° W. Long. Elevation is 948 feet.

Population: 141; Growth (since 2000): -32.2%; Density: 1,718.1 persons per square mile; Race: 97.9% White, 0.0% Black/African American, 0.7% Asian, 0.0% American Indian/Alaska Native, 0.0% Native Hawaiian/Other Pacific Islander, 1.4% Two or more races, 0.7% Hispanic of any race; Average household size: 2.52; Median age: 44.8; Age under 18: 22.0%; Age 65 and over: 11.3%; Males per 100 females: 116.9

Housing: Homeownership rate: 75.0%; Homeowner vacancy rate: 6.7%; Rental vacancy rate: 22.2%

MAPLEWOOD (unincorporated postal area)

ZCTA: 45340

Covers a land area of 23.095 square miles and a water area of 0.052 square miles. Located at 40.37° N. Lat; 84.05° W. Long. Elevation is 1,033 feet.

Population: 830; Growth (since 2000): 12.3%; Density: 35.9 persons per square mile; Race: 98.4% White, 0.7% Black/African American, 0.1% Asian, 0.1% American Indian/Alaska Native, 0.0% Native Hawaiian/Other Pacific Islander, 0.5% Two or more races, 0.5% Hispanic of any race; Average household size: 2.83; Median age: 42.6; Age under 18: 24.7%; Age 65 and over: 13.3%; Males per 100 females: 97.1

Housing: Homeownership rate: 92.9%; Homeowner vacancy rate: 0.4%; Rental vacancy rate: 0.0%

NEWPORT (CDP). Covers a land area of 0.360 square miles and a water area of 0.033 square miles. Located at 40.30° N. Lat; 84.37° W. Long. Elevation is 971 feet.

Population: 198; Growth (since 2000): n/a; Density: 550.7 persons per square mile; Race: 100.0% White, 0.0% Black/African American, 0.0% Asian, 0.0% American Indian/Alaska Native, 0.0% Native Hawaiian/Other Pacific Islander, 0.0% Two or more races, 0.5% Hispanic of any race; Average household size: 2.33; Median age: 36.3; Age under 18: 23.7%; Age 65 and over: 15.7%; Males per 100 females: 127.6

Housing: Homeownership rate: 73.0%; Homeowner vacancy rate: 0.0%; Rental vacancy rate: 0.0%

PEMBERTON (unincorporated postal area)

ZCTA: 45353

Covers a land area of 2.812 square miles and a water area of 0 square miles. Located at 40.29° N. Lat; 84.04° W. Long. Elevation is 1,056 feet.

Population: 196; Growth (since 2000): 75.0%; Density: 69.7 persons per square mile; Race: 95.4% White, 1.0% Black/African American, 1.0% Asian, 0.5% American Indian/Alaska Native, 0.0% Native Hawaiian/Other Pacific Islander, 1.5% Two or more races, 0.0% Hispanic of any race; Average household size: 2.88; Median age: 35.0; Age under 18: 27.6%; Age 65 and over: 12.2%; Males per 100 females: 104.2

Housing: Homeownership rate: 77.9%; Homeowner vacancy rate: 0.0%; Rental vacancy rate: 11.8%

PORT JEFFERSON (village). Covers a land area of 0.166 square miles and a water area of 0.022 square miles. Located at 40.33° N. Lat; 84.09° W. Long. Elevation is 971 feet.

Population: 371; Growth (since 2000): 15.6%; Density: 2,229.5 persons per square mile; Race: 100.0% White, 0.0% Black/African American, 0.0% Asian, 0.0% American Indian/Alaska Native, 0.0% Native Hawaiian/Other Pacific Islander, 0.0% Two or more races, 0.0% Hispanic of any race; Average household size: 2.61; Median age: 36.6; Age under 18: 25.3%; Age 65 and over: 10.5%; Males per 100 females: 105.0

Housing: Homeownership rate: 76.8%; Homeowner vacancy rate: 1.8%; Rental vacancy rate: 5.7%

RUSSIA (village). Covers a land area of 0.779 square miles and a water area of 0.008 square miles. Located at 40.23° N. Lat; 84.41° W. Long. Elevation is 968 feet.

Population: 640; Growth (since 2000): 16.2%; Density: 821.2 persons per square mile; Race: 99.2% White, 0.0% Black/African American, 0.0% Asian, 0.0% American Indian/Alaska Native, 0.0% Native Hawaiian/Other Pacific Islander, 0.8% Two or more races, 0.2% Hispanic of any race; Average household size: 2.86; Median age: 31.6; Age under 18: 35.0%; Age 65 and over: 13.1%; Males per 100 females: 93.9

School District(s)

Russia Local (KG-12)
2012-13 Enrollment: 454. . . . . (937) 526-3156

Housing: Homeownership rate: 79.9%; Homeowner vacancy rate: 1.6%; Rental vacancy rate: 16.7%

SIDNEY (city). County seat. Covers a land area of 12.023 square miles and a water area of 0.132 square miles. Located at 40.29° N. Lat; 84.17° W. Long. Elevation is 955 feet.

History: Sidney was platted in 1820 and named for Sir Philip Sidney, the English poet. The town developed around sawmills and woodworking mills. In 1879, Benjamin Slusser built a factory to produce the sheet-steel road scraper that he had invented.

Population: 21,229; Growth (since 2000): 5.0%; Density: 1,765.8 persons per square mile; Race: 90.3% White, 3.7% Black/African American, 1.6% Asian, 0.2% American Indian/Alaska Native, 0.2% Native Hawaiian/Other Pacific Islander, 3.3% Two or more races, 2.2% Hispanic of any race; Average household size: 2.51; Median age: 36.1; Age under 18: 27.2%; Age 65 and over: 12.4%; Males per 100 females: 96.4; Marriage status: 27.8% never married, 49.5% now married, 2.1% separated, 7.0%

widowed, 15.8% divorced; Foreign born: 2.5%; Speak English only: 96.3%; With disability: 15.0%; Veterans: 9.6%; Ancestry: 27.1% German, 12.3% American, 9.5% Irish, 8.3% English, 3.6% French
Employment: 11.7% management, business, and financial, 2.2% computer, engineering, and science, 4.6% education, legal, community service, arts, and media, 3.8% healthcare practitioners, 21.2% service, 16.6% sales and office, 5.8% natural resources, construction, and maintenance, 34.3% production, transportation, and material moving
Income: Per capita: $21,494; Median household: $43,347; Average household: $54,121; Households with income of $100,000 or more: 8.2%; Poverty rate: 16.4%
Educational Attainment: High school diploma or higher: 83.9%; Bachelor's degree or higher: 11.6%; Graduate/professional degree or higher: 5.4%

School District(s)

Fairlawn Local (PK-12)
2012-13 Enrollment: 653 . . . . (937) 492-1974
Sidney City (KG-12)
2012-13 Enrollment: 3,445 . . . . (937) 497-2200

Housing: Homeownership rate: 59.3%; Median home value: $105,200; Median year structure built: 1968; Homeowner vacancy rate: 3.5%; Median gross rent: $673 per month; Rental vacancy rate: 8.6%
Health Insurance: 86.6% have insurance; 64.0% have private insurance; 35.3% have public insurance; 13.4% do not have insurance; 5.1% of children under 18 do not have insurance
Hospitals: Wilson Memorial Hospital (112 beds)
Safety: Violent crime rate: 16.2 per 10,000 population; Property crime rate: 588.7 per 10,000 population
Newspapers: Sidney Daily News (daily circulation 13000)
Transportation: Commute: 95.9% car, 0.1% public transportation, 1.0% walk, 2.1% work from home; Median travel time to work: 16.6 minutes
Additional Information Contacts
City of Sidney . . . . (937) 498-2335
http://www.sidneyoh.com

Stark County

Located in east central Ohio; crossed by the Tuscarawas River. Covers a land area of 575.271 square miles, a water area of 5.262 square miles, and is located in the Eastern Time Zone at 40.81° N. Lat., 81.37° W. Long. The county was founded in 1808. County seat is Canton.

Stark County is part of the Canton-Massillon, OH Metropolitan Statistical Area. The entire metro area includes: Carroll County, OH; Stark County, OH

Population: 375,586; Growth (since 2000): -0.7%; Density: 652.9 persons per square mile; Race: 88.7% White, 7.6% Black/African American, 0.7% Asian, 0.3% American Indian/Alaska Native, 0.0% Native Hawaiian/Other Pacific Islander, 2.2% two or more races, 1.6% Hispanic of any race; Average household size: 2.42; Median age: 41.1; Age under 18: 22.9%; Age 65 and over: 16.2%; Males per 100 females: 93.8; Marriage status: 28.5% never married, 52.0% now married, 1.7% separated, 7.1% widowed, 12.5% divorced; Foreign born: 1.9%; Speak English only: 96.4%; With disability: 13.4%; Veterans: 10.8%; Ancestry: 32.5% German, 15.3% Irish, 10.2% Italian, 9.1% English, 8.3% American
Religion: Six largest groups: 14.9% Catholicism, 7.5% Non-denominational Protestant, 5.8% Baptist, 5.4% Methodist/Pietist, 2.9% Lutheran, 2.9% Presbyterian-Reformed
Economy: Unemployment rate: 4.5%; Leading industries: 15.2% retail trade; 12.4% other services (except public administration); 11.9% health care and social assistance; Farms: 1,168 totaling 135,749 acres; Company size: 7 employ 1,000 or more persons, 11 employs 500 to 999 persons, 189 employ 100 to 499 persons, 8,137 employ less than 100 persons; Business ownership: 8,080 women-owned, 1,045 Black-owned, 140 Hispanic-owned, 362 Asian-owned
Employment: 12.0% management, business, and financial, 3.5% computer, engineering, and science, 9.3% education, legal, community service, arts, and media, 6.5% healthcare practitioners, 19.9% service, 24.5% sales and office, 8.1% natural resources, construction, and maintenance, 16.2% production, transportation, and material moving
Income: Per capita: $24,453; Median household: $45,641; Average household: $59,807; Households with income of $100,000 or more: 15.4%; Poverty rate: 15.0%
Educational Attainment: High school diploma or higher: 89.1%; Bachelor's degree or higher: 21.1%; Graduate/professional degree or higher: 7.0%
Housing: Homeownership rate: 70.4%; Median home value: $122,400; Median year structure built: 1963; Homeowner vacancy rate: 2.2%; Median gross rent: $666 per month; Rental vacancy rate: 10.0%
Vital Statistics: Birth rate: 108.9 per 10,000 population; Death rate: 102.5 per 10,000 population; Age-adjusted cancer mortality rate: 179.4 deaths per 100,000 population
Health Insurance: 88.8% have insurance; 69.7% have private insurance; 33.3% have public insurance; 11.2% do not have insurance; 5.3% of children under 18 do not have insurance
Health Care: Physicians: 24.9 per 10,000 population; Hospital beds: 38.6 per 10,000 population; Hospital admissions: 1,381.6 per 10,000 population
Air Quality Index: 74.5% good, 25.5% moderate, 0.0% unhealthy for sensitive individuals, 0.0% unhealthy (percent of days)
Transportation: Commute: 94.1% car, 1.0% public transportation, 1.5% walk, 2.9% work from home; Median travel time to work: 21.4 minutes
Presidential Election: 48.9% Obama, 49.2% Romney (2012)
National and State Parks: First Ladies National Historic Site; Jackson Bog State Nature Preserve; Quail Hollow State Park
Additional Information Contacts
Stark Government . . . . (330) 451-7371
http://www.co.stark.oh.us

Stark County Communities

ALLIANCE (city). Covers a land area of 8.924 square miles and a water area of 0.044 square miles. Located at 40.91° N. Lat; 81.12° W. Long. Elevation is 1,158 feet.
History: Between 1805 and 1835, four small towns were established along the Mahoning River. In 1854 the four communities were united under the name of Alliance. Alliance was incorporated in 1889, and became known for its production of cranes and heavy mill machinery.
Population: 22,322; Growth (since 2000): -4.0%; Density: 2,501.3 persons per square mile; Race: 84.6% White, 10.5% Black/African American, 0.8% Asian, 0.2% American Indian/Alaska Native, 0.0% Native Hawaiian/Other Pacific Islander, 3.4% Two or more races, 1.9% Hispanic of any race; Average household size: 2.38; Median age: 35.3; Age under 18: 22.0%; Age 65 and over: 15.7%; Males per 100 females: 91.9; Marriage status: 38.4% never married, 38.9% now married, 2.3% separated, 7.7% widowed, 15.0% divorced; Foreign born: 1.7%; Speak English only: 97.2%; With disability: 16.3%; Veterans: 9.5%; Ancestry: 25.7% German, 14.1% Irish, 9.0% Italian, 8.2% American, 7.5% English
Employment: 7.7% management, business, and financial, 2.3% computer, engineering, and science, 6.9% education, legal, community service, arts, and media, 3.7% healthcare practitioners, 23.1% service, 24.9% sales and office, 6.9% natural resources, construction, and maintenance, 24.5% production, transportation, and material moving
Income: Per capita: $17,205; Median household: $31,152; Average household: $41,900; Households with income of $100,000 or more: 7.4%; Poverty rate: 26.9%
Educational Attainment: High school diploma or higher: 83.7%; Bachelor's degree or higher: 13.5%; Graduate/professional degree or higher: 4.0%

School District(s)

Alliance City (PK-12)
2012-13 Enrollment: 3,039 . . . . (330) 821-2100
Marlington Local (PK-12)
2012-13 Enrollment: 2,393 . . . . (330) 823-7458
West Branch Local (PK-12)
2012-13 Enrollment: 2,149 . . . . (330) 938-9324

Four-year College(s)

University of Mount Union (Private, Not-for-profit, United Methodist)
Fall 2013 Enrollment: 2,187 . . . . (800) 992-6682
2013-14 Tuition: In-state $27,380; Out-of-state $27,380

Two-year College(s)

Raphael's School of Beauty Culture Inc-Alliance (Private, For-profit)
Fall 2013 Enrollment: 87 . . . . (330) 823-3884

Vocational/Technical School(s)

Community Services Division-Alliance City (Public)
Fall 2013 Enrollment: 106 . . . . (330) 821-2102
2013-14 Tuition: $6,616

Housing: Homeownership rate: 54.9%; Median home value: $81,200; Median year structure built: 1951; Homeowner vacancy rate: 3.1%; Median gross rent: $611 per month; Rental vacancy rate: 12.8%
Health Insurance: 85.5% have insurance; 56.4% have private insurance; 41.8% have public insurance; 14.5% do not have insurance; 7.4% of children under 18 do not have insurance
Hospitals: Alliance Community Hospital (184 beds)
Safety: Violent crime rate: 37.5 per 10,000 population; Property crime rate: 441.7 per 10,000 population
Newspapers: The Review (daily circulation 11800)
Transportation: Commute: 92.5% car, 0.2% public transportation, 3.5% walk, 2.7% work from home; Median travel time to work: 17.8 minutes; Amtrak: Train service available.
Additional Information Contacts
City of Alliance. . . . . (330) 821-3110
http://www.cityofalliance.com

BEACH CITY (village). Covers a land area of 0.458 square miles and a water area of 0 square miles. Located at 40.65° N. Lat; 81.58° W. Long. Elevation is 1,004 feet.
History: Flood control dam completed in 1937 nearby.
Population: 1,033; Growth (since 2000): -9.1%; Density: 2,257.7 persons per square mile; Race: 97.6% White, 0.4% Black/African American, 0.0% Asian, 0.2% American Indian/Alaska Native, 0.0% Native Hawaiian/Other Pacific Islander, 1.6% Two or more races, 0.8% Hispanic of any race; Average household size: 2.47; Median age: 39.5; Age under 18: 23.8%; Age 65 and over: 16.2%; Males per 100 females: 92.0
Housing: Homeownership rate: 69.9%; Homeowner vacancy rate: 2.3%; Rental vacancy rate: 3.8%

BREWSTER (village). Covers a land area of 2.232 square miles and a water area of 0.008 square miles. Located at 40.71° N. Lat; 81.60° W. Long. Elevation is 991 feet.
Population: 2,112; Growth (since 2000): -9.1%; Density: 946.0 persons per square mile; Race: 98.5% White, 0.1% Black/African American, 0.3% Asian, 0.0% American Indian/Alaska Native, 0.0% Native Hawaiian/Other Pacific Islander, 0.5% Two or more races, 0.9% Hispanic of any race; Average household size: 2.48; Median age: 42.9; Age under 18: 21.4%; Age 65 and over: 20.1%; Males per 100 females: 95.9
Housing: Homeownership rate: 76.8%; Homeowner vacancy rate: 0.9%; Rental vacancy rate: 8.5%
Safety: Violent crime rate: 0.0 per 10,000 population; Property crime rate: 60.1 per 10,000 population

CANAL FULTON (city). Covers a land area of 3.258 square miles and a water area of 0.057 square miles. Located at 40.89° N. Lat; 81.59° W. Long. Elevation is 951 feet.
History: Canal Fulton was first called Milan, but the name was changed during the construction of the Ohio & Erie Canal to honor Robert Fulton, inventor of the steamboat.
Population: 5,479; Growth (since 2000): 8.3%; Density: 1,681.9 persons per square mile; Race: 97.0% White, 0.6% Black/African American, 0.4% Asian, 0.1% American Indian/Alaska Native, 0.0% Native Hawaiian/Other Pacific Islander, 1.7% Two or more races, 1.5% Hispanic of any race; Average household size: 2.43; Median age: 40.3; Age under 18: 23.1%; Age 65 and over: 17.6%; Males per 100 females: 89.4; Marriage status: 24.7% never married, 51.8% now married, 1.2% separated, 9.8% widowed, 13.7% divorced; Foreign born: 1.1%; Speak English only: 98.5%; With disability: 11.2%; Veterans: 15.3%; Ancestry: 39.5% German, 23.4% Irish, 10.8% American, 9.1% English, 8.5% Italian
Employment: 8.4% management, business, and financial, 3.5% computer, engineering, and science, 6.8% education, legal, community service, arts, and media, 12.2% healthcare practitioners, 16.8% service, 30.2% sales and office, 8.4% natural resources, construction, and maintenance, 13.7% production, transportation, and material moving
Income: Per capita: $21,941; Median household: $50,332; Average household: $53,340; Households with income of $100,000 or more: 9.3%; Poverty rate: 11.5%
Educational Attainment: High school diploma or higher: 91.1%; Bachelor's degree or higher: 20.5%; Graduate/professional degree or higher: 3.6%

School District(s)

Northwest Local (PK-12)
2012-13 Enrollment: 1,940 . . . . (330) 854-2291

Housing: Homeownership rate: 64.3%; Median home value: $133,900; Median year structure built: 1979; Homeowner vacancy rate: 3.5%; Median gross rent: $687 per month; Rental vacancy rate: 9.3%
Health Insurance: 84.8% have insurance; 73.5% have private insurance; 25.5% have public insurance; 15.2% do not have insurance; 12.2% of children under 18 do not have insurance
Safety: Violent crime rate: 1.8 per 10,000 population; Property crime rate: 145.8 per 10,000 population
Transportation: Commute: 94.9% car, 0.7% public transportation, 1.2% walk, 3.2% work from home; Median travel time to work: 26.5 minutes

CANTON (city). County seat. Covers a land area of 25.462 square miles and a water area of 0.016 square miles. Located at 40.81° N. Lat; 81.37° W. Long. Elevation is 1,056 feet.
History: Pioneer settlers from New England built homes along Nimishillen Creek in 1805. The town was platted in 1806 by Bezaleel Wells, the "Father of Canton," and incorporated in 1822. Canton's first major industry began in 1827 when Joshua Gibbs developed an improved metal plow. This was the start of Canton's future as a processor of steel, manufacturing reapers, roller bearings, and other products. German and Swiss artisans came to Canton to work in the Dueber-Hampden Watch Company. President William McKinley was a resident of Canton, and conducted his campaign for the presidency from his home here. After his assassination in Buffalo in 1901, his remains were brought back to Canton for burial.
Population: 73,007; Growth (since 2000): -9.7%; Density: 2,867.3 persons per square mile; Race: 69.1% White, 24.2% Black/African American, 0.3% Asian, 0.5% American Indian/Alaska Native, 0.0% Native Hawaiian/Other Pacific Islander, 4.8% Two or more races, 2.6% Hispanic of any race; Average household size: 2.35; Median age: 35.6; Age under 18: 25.1%; Age 65 and over: 12.8%; Males per 100 females: 90.0; Marriage status: 37.9% never married, 39.3% now married, 3.1% separated, 6.9% widowed, 16.0% divorced; Foreign born: 2.2%; Speak English only: 95.3%; With disability: 16.8%; Veterans: 10.4%; Ancestry: 22.6% German, 13.1% Irish, 8.9% Italian, 7.2% American, 5.7% English
Employment: 7.9% management, business, and financial, 2.5% computer, engineering, and science, 8.1% education, legal, community service, arts, and media, 5.6% healthcare practitioners, 28.7% service, 22.8% sales and office, 6.6% natural resources, construction, and maintenance, 17.9% production, transportation, and material moving
Income: Per capita: $16,669; Median household: $30,209; Average household: $39,787; Households with income of $100,000 or more: 5.9%; Poverty rate: 31.7%
Educational Attainment: High school diploma or higher: 82.7%; Bachelor's degree or higher: 13.8%; Graduate/professional degree or higher: 4.1%

School District(s)

Canton City (PK-12)
2012-13 Enrollment: 9,612 . . . . (330) 438-2500
Canton Local (PK-12)
2012-13 Enrollment: 2,174 . . . . (330) 484-8010
Canton Local Digital Academy
2012-13 Enrollment: n/a . . . . (330) 484-8010
Five R's Academy (09-11)
2012-13 Enrollment: n/a . . . . (330) 484-8010
Garfield Academy (KG-08)
2012-13 Enrollment: 243. . . . . (330) 454-3128
Imagine On Superior (KG-03)
2012-13 Enrollment: 219. . . . . (330) 451-2050
Jackson Local (PK-12)
2012-13 Enrollment: 5,854 . . . . (330) 830-8000
Life Skills Center of Canton (09-12)
2012-13 Enrollment: 123. . . . . (330) 456-4490
Perry Local (PK-12)
2012-13 Enrollment: 4,848 . . . . (330) 477-8121
Plain Local (PK-12)
2012-13 Enrollment: 6,024 . . . . (330) 492-3500
Project Rebuild Community School (10-12)
2012-13 Enrollment: 75. . . . . (330) 452-8414
Summit Academy Secondary - Canton (09-12)
2012-13 Enrollment: 71. . . . . (330) 453-8547
Summit Academy-Canton (KG-08)
2012-13 Enrollment: 98. . . . . (330) 458-0393

Four-year College(s)

Aultman College of Nursing and Health Sciences (Private, Not-for-profit)
Fall 2013 Enrollment: 306 . . . . (330) 363-6347
2013-14 Tuition: In-state $17,336; Out-of-state $17,336
Brown Mackie College-North Canton (Private, For-profit)
Fall 2013 Enrollment: 563 . . . . (330) 494-1214
2013-14 Tuition: In-state $12,114; Out-of-state $12,114
Kent State University at Stark (Public)
Fall 2013 Enrollment: 4,886 . . . . (330) 499-9600
2013-14 Tuition: In-state $5,554; Out-of-state $13,514
Malone University (Private, Not-for-profit, Friends)
Fall 2013 Enrollment: 2,074 . . . . (330) 471-8100
2013-14 Tuition: In-state $25,678; Out-of-state $25,678

Two-year College(s)

National College-Canton (Private, For-profit)
Fall 2013 Enrollment: 89 . . . . (330) 492-5300
2013-14 Tuition: In-state $11,550; Out-of-state $11,550

Vocational/Technical School(s)

Canton City Schools Adult Career and Technical Education (Public)
Fall 2013 Enrollment: 91 . . . . (330) 453-3271
2013-14 Tuition: $11,200
National Beauty College (Private, For-profit)
Fall 2013 Enrollment: 78 . . . . (330) 499-5596
2013-14 Tuition: $15,750
Regency Beauty Institute-Canton (Private, For-profit)
Fall 2013 Enrollment: 138 . . . . (800) 787-6456
2013-14 Tuition: $16,200

Housing: Homeownership rate: 53.3%; Median home value: $77,200; Median year structure built: 1946; Homeowner vacancy rate: 4.3%; Median gross rent: $582 per month; Rental vacancy rate: 10.4%

Health Insurance: 83.4% have insurance; 49.6% have private insurance; 45.2% have public insurance; 16.6% do not have insurance; 7.1% of children under 18 do not have insurance

Hospitals: Aultman Hospital (808 beds); Mercy Medical Center (476 beds)

Safety: Violent crime rate: 92.7 per 10,000 population; Property crime rate: 585.8 per 10,000 population

Newspapers: The Repository (daily circulation 64100)

Transportation: Commute: 91.3% car, 3.0% public transportation, 2.9% walk, 2.0% work from home; Median travel time to work: 19.4 minutes

Additional Information Contacts

City of Canton . . . . (330) 489-3283
http://www.ci.canton.oh.us

EAST CANTON (village). Covers a land area of 1.317 square miles and a water area of 0 square miles. Located at 40.79° N. Lat; 81.28° W. Long. Elevation is 1,165 feet.

History: East Canton was founded in 1805 as Osnaburg. The name was changed in 1821. The town developed as a residential suburb for Canton, and as a center for glazed brick making.

Population: 1,591; Growth (since 2000): -2.3%; Density: 1,208.4 persons per square mile; Race: 94.0% White, 3.3% Black/African American, 0.1% Asian, 0.1% American Indian/Alaska Native, 0.0% Native Hawaiian/Other Pacific Islander, 1.8% Two or more races, 1.7% Hispanic of any race; Average household size: 2.40; Median age: 39.8; Age under 18: 23.1%; Age 65 and over: 15.0%; Males per 100 females: 96.7

School District(s)

Osnaburg Local (PK-12)
2012-13 Enrollment: 865 . . . . (330) 488-1609

Housing: Homeownership rate: 66.2%; Homeowner vacancy rate: 1.1%; Rental vacancy rate: 5.9%

EAST SPARTA (village). Covers a land area of 1.681 square miles and a water area of 0 square miles. Located at 40.66° N. Lat; 81.36° W. Long. Elevation is 971 feet.

Population: 819; Growth (since 2000): 1.6%; Density: 487.1 persons per square mile; Race: 99.3% White, 0.2% Black/African American, 0.0% Asian, 0.0% American Indian/Alaska Native, 0.0% Native Hawaiian/Other Pacific Islander, 0.5% Two or more races, 0.9% Hispanic of any race; Average household size: 2.50; Median age: 42.3; Age under 18: 24.3%; Age 65 and over: 17.6%; Males per 100 females: 98.8

Housing: Homeownership rate: 76.8%; Homeowner vacancy rate: 1.6%; Rental vacancy rate: 6.2%

GREENTOWN (CDP). Covers a land area of 2.741 square miles and a water area of 0 square miles. Located at 40.93° N. Lat; 81.40° W. Long. Elevation is 1,197 feet.

Population: 3,804; Growth (since 2000): 20.6%; Density: 1,388.0 persons per square mile; Race: 94.5% White, 1.6% Black/African American, 1.8% Asian, 0.2% American Indian/Alaska Native, 0.0% Native Hawaiian/Other Pacific Islander, 1.4% Two or more races, 1.6% Hispanic of any race; Average household size: 2.81; Median age: 39.1; Age under 18: 27.1%; Age 65 and over: 9.4%; Males per 100 females: 98.7; Marriage status: 22.8% never married, 66.3% now married, 0.7% separated, 4.1% widowed, 6.8% divorced; Foreign born: 2.6%; Speak English only: 98.7%; With disability: 5.4%; Veterans: 13.5%; Ancestry: 36.0% German, 19.3% Italian, 15.9% English, 15.5% Irish, 7.2% American

Employment: 14.4% management, business, and financial, 13.6% computer, engineering, and science, 9.8% education, legal, community service, arts, and media, 5.4% healthcare practitioners, 14.9% service, 30.3% sales and office, 5.3% natural resources, construction, and maintenance, 6.2% production, transportation, and material moving

Income: Per capita: $30,960; Median household: $80,564; Average household: $86,988; Households with income of $100,000 or more: 38.2%; Poverty rate: 2.4%

Educational Attainment: High school diploma or higher: 94.7%; Bachelor's degree or higher: 36.0%; Graduate/professional degree or higher: 9.6%

Housing: Homeownership rate: 84.3%; Median home value: $195,000; Median year structure built: 1991; Homeowner vacancy rate: 0.8%; Median gross rent: $750 per month; Rental vacancy rate: 4.4%

Health Insurance: 92.1% have insurance; 84.5% have private insurance; 17.7% have public insurance; 7.9% do not have insurance; 0.0% of children under 18 do not have insurance

Transportation: Commute: 97.2% car, 0.0% public transportation, 0.0% walk, 2.8% work from home; Median travel time to work: 19.9 minutes

---

HARTVILLE (village). Covers a land area of 2.576 square miles and a water area of 0.001 square miles. Located at 40.96° N. Lat; 81.33° W. Long. Elevation is 1,168 feet.

Population: 2,944; Growth (since 2000): 35.4%; Density: 1,142.8 persons per square mile; Race: 96.1% White, 0.8% Black/African American, 0.7% Asian, 0.1% American Indian/Alaska Native, 0.0% Native Hawaiian/Other Pacific Islander, 1.9% Two or more races, 1.0% Hispanic of any race; Average household size: 2.52; Median age: 38.0; Age under 18: 26.8%; Age 65 and over: 14.5%; Males per 100 females: 89.6; Marriage status: 26.8% never married, 55.6% now married, 0.9% separated, 6.5% widowed, 11.1% divorced; Foreign born: 1.0%; Speak English only: 97.4%; With disability: 7.4%; Veterans: 7.0%; Ancestry: 36.5% German, 13.0% Irish, 10.7% English, 9.8% American, 8.2% Italian

Employment: 15.7% management, business, and financial, 4.2% computer, engineering, and science, 5.8% education, legal, community service, arts, and media, 4.2% healthcare practitioners, 18.2% service, 31.0% sales and office, 7.2% natural resources, construction, and maintenance, 13.7% production, transportation, and material moving

Income: Per capita: $27,206; Median household: $58,044; Average household: $73,045; Households with income of $100,000 or more: 20.1%; Poverty rate: 11.3%

Educational Attainment: High school diploma or higher: 88.7%; Bachelor's degree or higher: 27.8%; Graduate/professional degree or higher: 9.9%

School District(s)

Lake Local (PK-12)
2012-13 Enrollment: 3,532 . . . . (330) 877-9383

Housing: Homeownership rate: 59.1%; Median home value: $149,400; Median year structure built: 1976; Homeowner vacancy rate: 3.7%; Median gross rent: $703 per month; Rental vacancy rate: 12.4%

Health Insurance: 90.7% have insurance; 79.4% have private insurance; 27.6% have public insurance; 9.3% do not have insurance; 4.3% of children under 18 do not have insurance

Safety: Violent crime rate: 0.0 per 10,000 population; Property crime rate: 173.2 per 10,000 population

Newspapers: Hartville News (weekly circulation 2900)

Transportation: Commute: 94.0% car, 0.0% public transportation, 0.3% walk, 4.9% work from home; Median travel time to work: 25.2 minutes

HILLS AND DALES (village). Covers a land area of 0.323 square miles and a water area of 0 square miles. Located at 40.83° N. Lat; 81.44° W. Long. Elevation is 1,122 feet.
Population: 221; Growth (since 2000): -15.0%; Density: 684.9 persons per square mile; Race: 92.8% White, 0.0% Black/African American, 6.3% Asian, 0.0% American Indian/Alaska Native, 0.0% Native Hawaiian/Other Pacific Islander, 0.9% Two or more races, 2.7% Hispanic of any race; Average household size: 2.28; Median age: 56.4; Age under 18: 16.7%; Age 65 and over: 30.8%; Males per 100 females: 108.5
Housing: Homeownership rate: 97.9%; Homeowner vacancy rate: 4.0%; Rental vacancy rate: 0.0%

LIMAVILLE (village). Covers a land area of 0.273 square miles and a water area of 0.007 square miles. Located at 40.99° N. Lat; 81.15° W. Long. Elevation is 1,053 feet.
Population: 151; Growth (since 2000): -21.8%; Density: 554.1 persons per square mile; Race: 98.0% White, 2.0% Black/African American, 0.0% Asian, 0.0% American Indian/Alaska Native, 0.0% Native Hawaiian/Other Pacific Islander, 0.0% Two or more races, 0.7% Hispanic of any race; Average household size: 2.52; Median age: 42.2; Age under 18: 25.8%; Age 65 and over: 20.5%; Males per 100 females: 109.7
Housing: Homeownership rate: 91.7%; Homeowner vacancy rate: 0.0%; Rental vacancy rate: 0.0%

LOUISVILLE (city). Covers a land area of 5.492 square miles and a water area of 0 square miles. Located at 40.84° N. Lat; 81.26° W. Long. Elevation is 1,138 feet.
Population: 9,186; Growth (since 2000): 3.2%; Density: 1,672.5 persons per square mile; Race: 98.3% White, 0.2% Black/African American, 0.3% Asian, 0.2% American Indian/Alaska Native, 0.0% Native Hawaiian/Other Pacific Islander, 0.9% Two or more races, 1.3% Hispanic of any race; Average household size: 2.44; Median age: 39.4; Age under 18: 25.4%; Age 65 and over: 18.0%; Males per 100 females: 86.8; Marriage status: 22.8% never married, 53.0% now married, 1.8% separated, 9.4% widowed, 14.9% divorced; Foreign born: 0.9%; Speak English only: 97.9%; With disability: 11.2%; Veterans: 11.5%; Ancestry: 34.0% German, 14.6% Irish, 14.0% Italian, 11.1% English, 8.5% French
Employment: 10.6% management, business, and financial, 4.4% computer, engineering, and science, 9.7% education, legal, community service, arts, and media, 7.0% healthcare practitioners, 17.9% service, 26.5% sales and office, 7.3% natural resources, construction, and maintenance, 16.5% production, transportation, and material moving
Income: Per capita: $24,951; Median household: $48,401; Average household: $59,516; Households with income of $100,000 or more: 13.5%; Poverty rate: 7.3%
Educational Attainment: High school diploma or higher: 92.5%; Bachelor's degree or higher: 22.7%; Graduate/professional degree or higher: 7.7%

School District(s)

Louisville City (PK-12)
2012-13 Enrollment: 3,039 . . . . (330) 875-9687
Marlington Local (PK-12)
2012-13 Enrollment: 2,393 . . . . (330) 823-7458

Housing: Homeownership rate: 64.5%; Median home value: $134,600; Median year structure built: 1969; Homeowner vacancy rate: 2.1%; Median gross rent: $701 per month; Rental vacancy rate: 8.1%
Health Insurance: 92.9% have insurance; 80.2% have private insurance; 27.2% have public insurance; 7.1% do not have insurance; 0.9% of children under 18 do not have insurance
Safety: Violent crime rate: 6.6 per 10,000 population; Property crime rate: 201.2 per 10,000 population
Newspapers: Louisville Herald (weekly circulation 3000)
Transportation: Commute: 95.5% car, 0.4% public transportation, 2.5% walk, 1.5% work from home; Median travel time to work: 22.5 minutes

Additional Information Contacts

City of Louisville . . . . (330) 875-3321
http://www.louisvilleohio.com

MAGNOLIA (village). Covers a land area of 0.868 square miles and a water area of 0 square miles. Located at 40.65° N. Lat; 81.29° W. Long. Elevation is 948 feet.
Population: 978; Growth (since 2000): 5.0%; Density: 1,126.9 persons per square mile; Race: 97.8% White, 0.2% Black/African American, 0.3% Asian, 0.3% American Indian/Alaska Native, 0.0% Native Hawaiian/Other Pacific Islander, 1.3% Two or more races, 1.2% Hispanic of any race; Average household size: 2.55; Median age: 38.9; Age under 18: 26.0%; Age 65 and over: 14.9%; Males per 100 females: 102.1

School District(s)

Sandy Valley Local (PK-12)
2012-13 Enrollment: 1,499 . . . . (330) 866-3339

Housing: Homeownership rate: 75.8%; Homeowner vacancy rate: 0.7%; Rental vacancy rate: 11.4%

MASSILLON (city). Covers a land area of 18.578 square miles and a water area of 0.181 square miles. Located at 40.78° N. Lat; 81.53° W. Long. Elevation is 948 feet.
History: Massillon came into existence in 1826 when the Ohio & Erie Canal was planned. The town was laid out on both sides of the Tuscarawas River by James Duncan and Ferdinand Hurxthal, and named for Jean Baptiste Massillon, a French divine and Mrs. Duncan's favorite writer. Two years later the canal was completed, and Massillon became a marketing and industrial town.
Population: 32,149; Growth (since 2000): 2.6%; Density: 1,730.4 persons per square mile; Race: 87.4% White, 8.8% Black/African American, 0.4% Asian, 0.3% American Indian/Alaska Native, 0.0% Native Hawaiian/Other Pacific Islander, 2.6% Two or more races, 2.0% Hispanic of any race; Average household size: 2.37; Median age: 40.1; Age under 18: 22.9%; Age 65 and over: 16.7%; Males per 100 females: 94.0; Marriage status: 31.3% never married, 46.1% now married, 1.8% separated, 7.4% widowed, 15.3% divorced; Foreign born: 1.1%; Speak English only: 97.0%; With disability: 16.5%; Veterans: 11.6%; Ancestry: 37.2% German, 17.2% Irish, 10.6% American, 8.7% Italian, 6.9% English
Employment: 8.3% management, business, and financial, 2.1% computer, engineering, and science, 6.7% education, legal, community service, arts, and media, 4.9% healthcare practitioners, 22.0% service, 26.5% sales and office, 8.3% natural resources, construction, and maintenance, 21.1% production, transportation, and material moving
Income: Per capita: $20,701; Median household: $38,142; Average household: $48,390; Households with income of $100,000 or more: 8.8%; Poverty rate: 19.0%
Educational Attainment: High school diploma or higher: 86.6%; Bachelor's degree or higher: 14.3%; Graduate/professional degree or higher: 4.7%

School District(s)

Buckeye United SD (08-12)
2012-13 Enrollment: 369. . . . . (614) 466-0720
Jackson Local (PK-12)
2012-13 Enrollment: 5,854 . . . . (330) 830-8000
Massillon City (PK-12)
2012-13 Enrollment: 4,001 . . . . (330) 830-3900
Massillon Digital Academy Inc (06-12)
2012-13 Enrollment: 101. . . . . (330) 830-3900
Perry Local (PK-12)
2012-13 Enrollment: 4,848 . . . . (330) 477-8121
Stark County Area (08-12)
2012-13 Enrollment: n/a . . . . (330) 832-1591
Tuslaw Local (PK-12)
2012-13 Enrollment: 1,345 . . . . (330) 837-7813

Housing: Homeownership rate: 66.6%; Median home value: $98,100; Median year structure built: 1955; Homeowner vacancy rate: 3.0%; Median gross rent: $638 per month; Rental vacancy rate: 10.4%
Health Insurance: 88.5% have insurance; 64.6% have private insurance; 41.6% have public insurance; 11.5% do not have insurance; 5.0% of children under 18 do not have insurance
Hospitals: Affinity Medical Center (451 beds)
Safety: Violent crime rate: 21.5 per 10,000 population; Property crime rate: 303.2 per 10,000 population
Newspapers: The Independent (daily circulation 12200)
Transportation: Commute: 94.8% car, 1.0% public transportation, 2.2% walk, 1.5% work from home; Median travel time to work: 20.6 minutes

Additional Information Contacts

City of Massillon . . . . (330) 830-1700
http://www.massillonohio.com

MEYERS LAKE (village). Covers a land area of 0.224 square miles and a water area of 0.210 square miles. Located at 40.81° N. Lat; 81.42° W. Long. Elevation is 1,112 feet.
History: Former site of amusement park at streetcar line terminus.
Population: 569; Growth (since 2000): 0.7%; Density: 2,537.7 persons per square mile; Race: 95.6% White, 2.6% Black/African American, 0.7%

Asian, 0.0% American Indian/Alaska Native, 0.0% Native Hawaiian/Other Pacific Islander, 1.1% Two or more races, 0.9% Hispanic of any race; Average household size: 1.69; Median age: 59.3; Age under 18: 6.5%; Age 65 and over: 34.6%; Males per 100 females: 84.1
Housing: Homeownership rate: 82.3%; Homeowner vacancy rate: 5.5%; Rental vacancy rate: 6.3%

MINERVA (village). Covers a land area of 2.230 square miles and a water area of 0 square miles. Located at 40.73° N. Lat; 81.10° W. Long. Elevation is 1,056 feet.
History: Minerva was established as a town in 1835, when the Sandy & Beaver Canal was under construction. The town was named for the niece of John Whitacre, the founder.
Population: 3,720; Growth (since 2000): -5.4%; Density: 1,668.0 persons per square mile; Race: 97.7% White, 0.3% Black/African American, 0.3% Asian, 0.1% American Indian/Alaska Native, 0.0% Native Hawaiian/Other Pacific Islander, 1.3% Two or more races, 0.7% Hispanic of any race; Average household size: 2.34; Median age: 41.2; Age under 18: 23.6%; Age 65 and over: 19.9%; Males per 100 females: 90.1; Marriage status: 28.2% never married, 50.8% now married, 2.4% separated, 9.0% widowed, 12.0% divorced; Foreign born: 0.0%; Speak English only: 99.3%; With disability: 13.0%; Veterans: 9.5%; Ancestry: 30.3% German, 16.2% Irish, 11.2% English, 10.4% American, 5.3% Italian
Employment: 8.6% management, business, and financial, 1.4% computer, engineering, and science, 7.8% education, legal, community service, arts, and media, 5.9% healthcare practitioners, 15.4% service, 29.0% sales and office, 6.3% natural resources, construction, and maintenance, 25.6% production, transportation, and material moving
Income: Per capita: $19,493; Median household: $39,817; Average household: $48,563; Households with income of $100,000 or more: 8.5%; Poverty rate: 13.7%
Educational Attainment: High school diploma or higher: 86.8%; Bachelor's degree or higher: 13.0%; Graduate/professional degree or higher: 5.3%

School District(s)

Minerva Local (PK-12)
2012-13 Enrollment: 1,824 . . . . (330) 868-4332
Housing: Homeownership rate: 63.2%; Median home value: $85,200; Median year structure built: 1952; Homeowner vacancy rate: 2.4%; Median gross rent: $603 per month; Rental vacancy rate: 12.3%
Health Insurance: 90.0% have insurance; 71.8% have private insurance; 34.4% have public insurance; 10.0% do not have insurance; 4.2% of children under 18 do not have insurance
Newspapers: Press-News (weekly circulation 2200); The News Leader (weekly circulation 3900)
Transportation: Commute: 94.8% car, 0.7% public transportation, 4.4% walk, 0.0% work from home; Median travel time to work: 29.4 minutes

NAVARRE (village). Covers a land area of 2.054 square miles and a water area of 0.004 square miles. Located at 40.73° N. Lat; 81.51° W. Long. Elevation is 961 feet.
History: Navarre was founded by James Duncan and named by his wife for a prince of Navarre. A lock of the Ohio & Erie Canal was located in Navarre, which became a shipping center for farm produce.
Population: 1,957; Growth (since 2000): 35.9%; Density: 952.5 persons per square mile; Race: 98.2% White, 0.7% Black/African American, 0.2% Asian, 0.1% American Indian/Alaska Native, 0.1% Native Hawaiian/Other Pacific Islander, 0.8% Two or more races, 0.7% Hispanic of any race; Average household size: 2.10; Median age: 48.9; Age under 18: 17.7%; Age 65 and over: 26.2%; Males per 100 females: 89.3

School District(s)

Fairless Local (PK-12)
2012-13 Enrollment: 1,520 . . . . (330) 767-3577
Perry Local (PK-12)
2012-13 Enrollment: 4,848 . . . . (330) 477-8121
Housing: Homeownership rate: 66.9%; Homeowner vacancy rate: 2.5%; Rental vacancy rate: 4.5%
Safety: Violent crime rate: 0.0 per 10,000 population; Property crime rate: 180.7 per 10,000 population
Additional Information Contacts
Village of Navarre . . . . (330) 879-5508
http://www.navarreohio.net

NORTH CANTON (city). Covers a land area of 6.400 square miles and a water area of 0 square miles. Located at 40.87° N. Lat; 81.40° W. Long. Elevation is 1,158 feet.
History: Settled c.1815, incorporated as a city 1961.
Population: 17,488; Growth (since 2000): 6.8%; Density: 2,732.5 persons per square mile; Race: 94.8% White, 2.0% Black/African American, 1.1% Asian, 0.2% American Indian/Alaska Native, 0.0% Native Hawaiian/Other Pacific Islander, 1.5% Two or more races, 1.5% Hispanic of any race; Average household size: 2.15; Median age: 42.5; Age under 18: 18.6%; Age 65 and over: 21.5%; Males per 100 females: 86.1; Marriage status: 29.6% never married, 47.7% now married, 1.2% separated, 9.1% widowed, 13.6% divorced; Foreign born: 2.7%; Speak English only: 96.5%; With disability: 12.0%; Veterans: 11.2%; Ancestry: 37.5% German, 17.4% Irish, 15.1% Italian, 12.9% English, 4.7% French
Employment: 14.6% management, business, and financial, 5.2% computer, engineering, and science, 14.7% education, legal, community service, arts, and media, 5.7% healthcare practitioners, 18.6% service, 27.6% sales and office, 4.7% natural resources, construction, and maintenance, 9.0% production, transportation, and material moving
Income: Per capita: $28,256; Median household: $50,728; Average household: $64,572; Households with income of $100,000 or more: 16.9%; Poverty rate: 6.8%
Educational Attainment: High school diploma or higher: 93.8%; Bachelor's degree or higher: 32.7%; Graduate/professional degree or higher: 11.5%

School District(s)

North Canton City (PK-12)
2012-13 Enrollment: 4,634 . . . . (330) 497-5600

Four-year College(s)

Walsh University (Private, Not-for-profit, Roman Catholic)
Fall 2013 Enrollment: 2,963 . . . . (330) 499-7090
2013-14 Tuition: In-state $25,840; Out-of-state $25,840

Two-year College(s)

Stark State College (Public)
Fall 2013 Enrollment: 15,450 . . . . (330) 494-6170
2013-14 Tuition: In-state $3,607; Out-of-state $5,791
Housing: Homeownership rate: 67.7%; Median home value: $137,300; Median year structure built: 1968; Homeowner vacancy rate: 1.7%; Median gross rent: $757 per month; Rental vacancy rate: 8.5%
Health Insurance: 92.1% have insurance; 80.3% have private insurance; 29.0% have public insurance; 7.9% do not have insurance; 1.7% of children under 18 do not have insurance
Safety: Violent crime rate: 6.9 per 10,000 population; Property crime rate: 201.4 per 10,000 population
Transportation: Commute: 90.3% car, 0.8% public transportation, 2.5% walk, 6.0% work from home; Median travel time to work: 18.3 minutes
Additional Information Contacts
City of North Canton . . . . (330) 499-5081
http://www.northcantonohio.com

NORTH LAWRENCE (CDP). Covers a land area of 0.339 square miles and a water area of 0.011 square miles. Located at 40.84° N. Lat; 81.64° W. Long. Elevation is 1,033 feet.
Population: 268; Growth (since 2000): n/a; Density: 791.5 persons per square mile; Race: 90.9% White, 0.0% Black/African American, 0.0% Asian, 0.0% American Indian/Alaska Native, 0.0% Native Hawaiian/Other Pacific Islander, 0.7% Two or more races, 0.0% Hispanic of any race; Average household size: 2.88; Median age: 38.6; Age under 18: 27.2%; Age 65 and over: 10.1%; Males per 100 females: 106.2
Housing: Homeownership rate: 90.4%; Homeowner vacancy rate: 5.6%; Rental vacancy rate: 10.0%

PARIS (unincorporated postal area)

ZCTA: 44669

Covers a land area of 17.383 square miles and a water area of 0.032 square miles. Located at 40.79° N. Lat; 81.16° W. Long. Elevation is 1,263 feet.
Population: 1,382; Growth (since 2000): -11.6%; Density: 79.5 persons per square mile; Race: 97.4% White, 0.3% Black/African American, 0.2% Asian, 0.0% American Indian/Alaska Native, 0.0% Native Hawaiian/Other Pacific Islander, 1.7% Two or more races, 0.3% Hispanic of any race; Average household size: 2.55; Median age: 43.7; Age under 18: 23.1%; Age 65 and over: 16.5%; Males per 100 females: 103.5

Housing: Homeownership rate: 86.9%; Homeowner vacancy rate: 1.0%; Rental vacancy rate: 7.6%

PERRY HEIGHTS (CDP). Covers a land area of 2.863 square miles and a water area of 0.041 square miles. Located at 40.80° N. Lat; 81.47° W. Long. Elevation is 1,099 feet.
Population: 8,441; Growth (since 2000): -5.2%; Density: 2,948.7 persons per square mile; Race: 93.6% White, 2.9% Black/African American, 0.5% Asian, 0.1% American Indian/Alaska Native, 0.0% Native Hawaiian/Other Pacific Islander, 1.8% Two or more races, 2.2% Hispanic of any race; Average household size: 2.38; Median age: 41.4; Age under 18: 22.9%; Age 65 and over: 17.4%; Males per 100 females: 92.0; Marriage status: 27.2% never married, 49.0% now married, 2.1% separated, 8.7% widowed, 15.1% divorced; Foreign born: 1.9%; Speak English only: 96.4%; With disability: 11.4%; Veterans: 11.2%; Ancestry: 34.7% German, 12.4% Irish, 10.8% Italian, 9.0% American, 7.8% English
Employment: 9.9% management, business, and financial, 3.7% computer, engineering, and science, 7.7% education, legal, community service, arts, and media, 6.3% healthcare practitioners, 24.0% service, 25.0% sales and office, 8.2% natural resources, construction, and maintenance, 15.2% production, transportation, and material moving
Income: Per capita: $21,305; Median household: $40,455; Average household: $47,989; Households with income of $100,000 or more: 6.8%; Poverty rate: 16.7%
Educational Attainment: High school diploma or higher: 88.2%; Bachelor's degree or higher: 12.5%; Graduate/professional degree or higher: 3.1%
Housing: Homeownership rate: 71.3%; Median home value: $101,800; Median year structure built: 1966; Homeowner vacancy rate: 1.8%; Median gross rent: $675 per month; Rental vacancy rate: 9.8%
Health Insurance: 85.4% have insurance; 68.4% have private insurance; 29.3% have public insurance; 14.6% do not have insurance; 7.8% of children under 18 do not have insurance
Transportation: Commute: 95.9% car, 1.0% public transportation, 1.9% walk, 0.7% work from home; Median travel time to work: 21.8 minutes

RICHVILLE (CDP). Covers a land area of 3.128 square miles and a water area of 0.011 square miles. Located at 40.75° N. Lat; 81.47° W. Long. Elevation is 1,060 feet.
Population: 3,324; Growth (since 2000): n/a; Density: 1,062.5 persons per square mile; Race: 94.4% White, 3.5% Black/African American, 0.3% Asian, 0.1% American Indian/Alaska Native, 0.0% Native Hawaiian/Other Pacific Islander, 1.6% Two or more races, 0.9% Hispanic of any race; Average household size: 2.51; Median age: 43.5; Age under 18: 21.3%; Age 65 and over: 17.3%; Males per 100 females: 100.8; Marriage status: 26.7% never married, 54.9% now married, 0.0% separated, 4.8% widowed, 13.6% divorced; Foreign born: 1.1%; Speak English only: 94.6%; With disability: 14.4%; Veterans: 9.3%; Ancestry: 45.1% German, 13.8% English, 13.5% Irish, 11.4% Italian, 6.7% American
Employment: 12.3% management, business, and financial, 4.0% computer, engineering, and science, 8.5% education, legal, community service, arts, and media, 6.5% healthcare practitioners, 16.8% service, 24.0% sales and office, 7.6% natural resources, construction, and maintenance, 20.2% production, transportation, and material moving
Income: Per capita: $21,431; Median household: $54,005; Average household: $56,960; Households with income of $100,000 or more: 12.3%; Poverty rate: 10.6%
Educational Attainment: High school diploma or higher: 90.5%; Bachelor's degree or higher: 10.0%; Graduate/professional degree or higher: 2.8%
Housing: Homeownership rate: 81.6%; Median home value: $119,100; Median year structure built: 1967; Homeowner vacancy rate: 1.2%; Median gross rent: $756 per month; Rental vacancy rate: 5.4%
Health Insurance: 88.3% have insurance; 73.5% have private insurance; 30.8% have public insurance; 11.7% do not have insurance; 2.5% of children under 18 do not have insurance
Transportation: Commute: 97.9% car, 0.1% public transportation, 0.7% walk, 1.3% work from home; Median travel time to work: 21.3 minutes

ROBERTSVILLE (CDP). Covers a land area of 0.309 square miles and a water area of 0 square miles. Located at 40.76° N. Lat; 81.19° W. Long. Elevation is 1,086 feet.
Population: 331; Growth (since 2000): n/a; Density: 1,069.5 persons per square mile; Race: 95.5% White, 1.2% Black/African American, 0.0% Asian, 0.0% American Indian/Alaska Native, 0.0% Native Hawaiian/Other Pacific Islander, 3.0% Two or more races, 1.8% Hispanic of any race; Average household size: 2.57; Median age: 39.5; Age under 18: 25.4%; Age 65 and over: 19.3%; Males per 100 females: 93.6
Housing: Homeownership rate: 82.2%; Homeowner vacancy rate: 3.6%; Rental vacancy rate: 17.9%

UNIONTOWN (CDP). Covers a land area of 2.492 square miles and a water area of 0.025 square miles. Located at 40.97° N. Lat; 81.40° W. Long. Elevation is 1,119 feet.
Population: 3,309; Growth (since 2000): 18.1%; Density: 1,327.7 persons per square mile; Race: 97.4% White, 0.7% Black/African American, 0.3% Asian, 0.2% American Indian/Alaska Native, 0.0% Native Hawaiian/Other Pacific Islander, 1.2% Two or more races, 0.8% Hispanic of any race; Average household size: 2.59; Median age: 41.8; Age under 18: 25.0%; Age 65 and over: 17.6%; Males per 100 females: 96.0; Marriage status: 14.2% never married, 67.9% now married, 0.7% separated, 5.9% widowed, 12.0% divorced; Foreign born: 0.4%; Speak English only: 98.1%; With disability: 17.0%; Veterans: 13.6%; Ancestry: 33.8% German, 16.5% Irish, 10.3% English, 6.9% American, 5.2% Polish
Employment: 25.4% management, business, and financial, 6.9% computer, engineering, and science, 6.2% education, legal, community service, arts, and media, 6.1% healthcare practitioners, 7.8% service, 25.0% sales and office, 4.7% natural resources, construction, and maintenance, 17.9% production, transportation, and material moving
Income: Per capita: $25,139; Median household: $60,300; Average household: $67,564; Households with income of $100,000 or more: 17.4%; Poverty rate: 6.2%
Educational Attainment: High school diploma or higher: 96.8%; Bachelor's degree or higher: 31.2%; Graduate/professional degree or higher: 9.2%

School District(s)

Green Local (PK-12)
2012-13 Enrollment: 4,147 . . . . (330) 896-7500
Lake Local (PK-12)
2012-13 Enrollment: 3,532 . . . . (330) 877-9383
Portage Lakes (09-12)
2012-13 Enrollment: n/a . . . . (330) 896-8200

Vocational/Technical School(s)

Portage Lakes Career Center (Public)
Fall 2013 Enrollment: 55 . . . . (330) 896-8200
2013-14 Tuition: $11,300
W Howard Nicol School of Practical Nursing (Public)
Fall 2013 Enrollment: n/a . . . . (330) 896-8105
2013-14 Tuition: $9,300

Housing: Homeownership rate: 83.2%; Median home value: $147,500; Median year structure built: 1971; Homeowner vacancy rate: 1.7%; Median gross rent: $731 per month; Rental vacancy rate: 5.2%
Health Insurance: 94.4% have insurance; 80.6% have private insurance; 29.4% have public insurance; 5.6% do not have insurance; 0.4% of children under 18 do not have insurance
Safety: Violent crime rate: 0.0 per 10,000 population; Property crime rate: 241.3 per 10,000 population
Transportation: Commute: 97.2% car, 0.0% public transportation, 0.0% walk, 2.8% work from home; Median travel time to work: 26.7 minutes

WAYNESBURG (village). Covers a land area of 0.517 square miles and a water area of 0 square miles. Located at 40.67° N. Lat; 81.26° W. Long. Elevation is 997 feet.
Population: 923; Growth (since 2000): -8.0%; Density: 1,786.8 persons per square mile; Race: 97.6% White, 1.0% Black/African American, 0.1% Asian, 0.1% American Indian/Alaska Native, 0.0% Native Hawaiian/Other Pacific Islander, 1.2% Two or more races, 0.7% Hispanic of any race; Average household size: 2.56; Median age: 39.0; Age under 18: 25.7%; Age 65 and over: 13.5%; Males per 100 females: 100.7
Housing: Homeownership rate: 69.9%; Homeowner vacancy rate: 3.4%; Rental vacancy rate: 17.3%

WILMOT (village). Covers a land area of 0.139 square miles and a water area of 0 square miles. Located at 40.66° N. Lat; 81.63° W. Long. Elevation is 1,027 feet.
History: Wilmot was platted in 1836, and developed as a trading center in the midst of the Amish country.
Population: 304; Growth (since 2000): -9.3%; Density: 2,180.4 persons per square mile; Race: 98.0% White, 0.3% Black/African American, 0.3% Asian, 0.0% American Indian/Alaska Native, 0.0% Native Hawaiian/Other

Pacific Islander, 1.3% Two or more races, 0.3% Hispanic of any race; Average household size: 2.58; Median age: 31.7; Age under 18: 27.3%; Age 65 and over: 9.2%; Males per 100 females: 111.1
Housing: Homeownership rate: 61.9%; Homeowner vacancy rate: 2.6%; Rental vacancy rate: 7.8%

Summit County

Located in northeastern Ohio; drained by the Cuyahoga and Tuscarawas Rivers; includes Portage Lakes. Covers a land area of 412.748 square miles, a water area of 7.307 square miles, and is located in the Eastern Time Zone at 41.12° N. Lat., 81.53° W. Long. The county was founded in 1840. County seat is Akron.

Summit County is part of the Akron, OH Metropolitan Statistical Area. The entire metro area includes: Portage County, OH; Summit County, OH

Weather Station: Akron Akron-Canton Reg Arpt Elevation: 1,208 feet

	Jan	Feb	Mar	Apr	May	Jun	Jul	Aug	Sep	Oct	Nov	Dec
High	34	37	47	60	70	78	82	81	73	61	50	38
Low	19	21	28	39	49	58	62	61	53	42	34	24
Precip	2.6	2.3	3.0	3.6	4.3	3.8	4.1	3.7	3.4	2.8	3.2	2.8
Snow	12.2	9.6	8.4	2.8	0.1	tr	0.0	tr	tr	0.5	2.9	9.9

High and Low temperatures in degrees Fahrenheit; Precipitation and Snow in inches

Population: 541,781; Growth (since 2000): -0.2%; Density: 1,312.6 persons per square mile; Race: 80.6% White, 14.4% Black/African American, 2.2% Asian, 0.2% American Indian/Alaska Native, 0.0% Native Hawaiian/Other Pacific Islander, 2.1% two or more races, 1.6% Hispanic of any race; Average household size: 2.39; Median age: 40.0; Age under 18: 22.8%; Age 65 and over: 14.6%; Males per 100 females: 93.7; Marriage status: 31.7% never married, 49.5% now married, 1.6% separated, 6.9% widowed, 11.9% divorced; Foreign born: 4.5%; Speak English only: 94.1%; With disability: 12.5%; Veterans: 9.8%; Ancestry: 22.6% German, 14.2% Irish, 9.2% Italian, 9.2% English, 6.0% American
Religion: Six largest groups: 21.6% Catholicism, 8.0% Non-denominational Protestant, 3.9% Methodist/Pietist, 3.1% Baptist, 2.4% Presbyterian-Reformed, 1.9% Lutheran
Economy: Unemployment rate: 4.4%; Leading industries: 13.1% retail trade; 11.2% health care and social assistance; 11.1% professional, scientific, and technical services; Farms: 304 totaling 16,545 acres; Company size: 7 employ 1,000 or more persons, 27 employ 500 to 999 persons, 379 employ 100 to 499 persons, 13,194 employ less than 100 persons; Business ownership: 11,785 women-owned, 2,968 Black-owned, 275 Hispanic-owned, 932 Asian-owned
Employment: 14.5% management, business, and financial, 5.5% computer, engineering, and science, 10.4% education, legal, community service, arts, and media, 6.4% healthcare practitioners, 17.1% service, 26.0% sales and office, 7.0% natural resources, construction, and maintenance, 13.1% production, transportation, and material moving
Income: Per capita: $27,818; Median household: $49,669; Average household: $66,568; Households with income of $100,000 or more: 18.9%; Poverty rate: 15.4%
Educational Attainment: High school diploma or higher: 90.3%; Bachelor's degree or higher: 29.6%; Graduate/professional degree or higher: 10.4%
Housing: Homeownership rate: 67.8%; Median home value: $135,600; Median year structure built: 1963; Homeowner vacancy rate: 2.5%; Median gross rent: $741 per month; Rental vacancy rate: 9.8%
Vital Statistics: Birth rate: 112.7 per 10,000 population; Death rate: 101.3 per 10,000 population; Age-adjusted cancer mortality rate: 189.8 deaths per 100,000 population
Health Insurance: 88.9% have insurance; 71.1% have private insurance; 30.2% have public insurance; 11.1% do not have insurance; 5.4% of children under 18 do not have insurance
Health Care: Physicians: 34.3 per 10,000 population; Hospital beds: 36.6 per 10,000 population; Hospital admissions: 1,548.6 per 10,000 population
Air Quality Index: 81.9% good, 17.3% moderate, 0.8% unhealthy for sensitive individuals, 0.0% unhealthy (percent of days)
Transportation: Commute: 93.4% car, 1.6% public transportation, 1.4% walk, 3.0% work from home; Median travel time to work: 22.6 minutes
Presidential Election: 56.7% Obama, 41.9% Romney (2012)
National and State Parks: Cuyahoga Valley National Park; Portage Lakes State Park; Portage Lakes Wetland State Nature Preserve
Additional Information Contacts

Summit Government . . . . (330) 643-2510
http://www.co.summit.oh.us

Summit County Communities

AKRON (city). County seat. Covers a land area of 62.033 square miles and a water area of 0.340 square miles. Located at 41.08° N. Lat; 81.52° W. Long. Elevation is 961 feet.
History: The first settler in the Akron area was Captain Joseph Hart, who established Middlebury, now East Akron, in 1807. The city of Akron was laid out in 1825 by General Simon Perkins, commissioner of the Ohio Canal Fund, who saw a great future for a town on the summit of the course of the Ohio & Erie Canal. When the canal opened to traffic in 1827, the town grew rapidly. In 1840 trade was improved further with the opening of the Ohio & Pennsylvania Canal. In 1859, former resident John Brown was executed here for his raid at Harper's Ferry. Dr. Benjamin Franklin Goodrich came to Akron in 1870 and founded a plant for manufacturing fire hose and other articles from rubber. Around 1900 Akron was the national center for the manufacture of farm machinery, and the American Cereal Company (Quaker Oats) emerged as a leading cereal producer. But it was the rubber industry that by 1915 made Akron a boom town.
Population: 199,110; Growth (since 2000): -8.3%; Density: 3,209.8 persons per square mile; Race: 62.2% White, 31.5% Black/African American, 2.1% Asian, 0.2% American Indian/Alaska Native, 0.0% Native Hawaiian/Other Pacific Islander, 3.2% Two or more races, 2.1% Hispanic of any race; Average household size: 2.31; Median age: 35.7; Age under 18: 22.9%; Age 65 and over: 12.6%; Males per 100 females: 93.6; Marriage status: 41.5% never married, 37.6% now married, 2.5% separated, 6.6% widowed, 14.3% divorced; Foreign born: 4.5%; Speak English only: 93.6%; With disability: 15.1%; Veterans: 9.6%; Ancestry: 17.6% German, 12.4% Irish, 6.6% English, 6.2% Italian, 5.2% American
Employment: 10.1% management, business, and financial, 3.5% computer, engineering, and science, 9.6% education, legal, community service, arts, and media, 5.2% healthcare practitioners, 22.0% service, 27.1% sales and office, 6.6% natural resources, construction, and maintenance, 15.8% production, transportation, and material moving
Income: Per capita: $19,968; Median household: $33,909; Average household: $45,847; Households with income of $100,000 or more: 8.7%; Poverty rate: 27.5%
Educational Attainment: High school diploma or higher: 85.4%; Bachelor's degree or higher: 20.2%; Graduate/professional degree or higher: 6.6%

School District(s)

Akron City (PK-12)
2012-13 Enrollment: 22,394 . . . . (330) 761-1661
Akron Digital Academy (KG-12)
2012-13 Enrollment: 496. . . . . (330) 237-2232
Akros Middle School (06-08)
2012-13 Enrollment: 133. . . . . (330) 374-6704
Coventry Local (PK-12)
2012-13 Enrollment: 2,242 . . . . (330) 644-8489
Edge Academy the (KG-05)
2012-13 Enrollment: 273. . . . . (330) 535-4581
Gain Productive Skills Academy
2012-13 Enrollment: n/a . . . . (614) 995-1985
Greater Summit County Early Learning Center (KG-02)
2012-13 Enrollment: 99. . . . . (330) 945-5600
Hope Academy Brown Saint Campus (KG-08)
2012-13 Enrollment: 287. . . . . (330) 785-0180
Hope Academy University (KG-08)
2012-13 Enrollment: 380. . . . . (330) 535-7728
Imagine Akron Academy (KG-KG)
2012-13 Enrollment: 104. . . . . (330) 379-1034
Life Skills Center of North Akron (09-12)
2012-13 Enrollment: 109. . . . . (330) 633-5990
Life Skills Center of Summit County (09-12)
2012-13 Enrollment: 117. . . . . (330) 745-3678
Manchester Local (PK-12)
2012-13 Enrollment: 1,358 . . . . (330) 882-6926
Phoenix Village Academy Primary 1 (KG-04)
2012-13 Enrollment: n/a . . . . (330) 773-6800
Revere Local (PK-12)
2012-13 Enrollment: 2,630 . . . . (330) 666-4155
Romig Road Community School (01-06)
2012-13 Enrollment: 452. . . . . (330) 848-1100

Springfield Local (PK-12)
2012-13 Enrollment: 2,358 . . . . (330) 798-1111
Summit Academy Community School for Alt Learners o (KG-05)
2012-13 Enrollment: 111 . . . . (330) 253-7441
Summit Academy Middle School-Akron (06-08)
2012-13 Enrollment: 63 . . . . (330) 252-1510
Summit Academy Secondary - Akron (09-12)
2012-13 Enrollment: 72 . . . . (330) 434-2343
Towpath Trail High School (09-12)
2012-13 Enrollment: 159 . . . . (234) 542-0102
Youth Experiencing Success
2012-13 Enrollment: n/a . . . . (614) 995-1985

Four-year College(s)

Akron Institute of Herzing University (Private, For-profit)
Fall 2013 Enrollment: 302 . . . . (330) 724-1600
2013-14 Tuition: In-state $10,800; Out-of-state $10,800
Brown Mackie College-Akron (Private, For-profit)
Fall 2013 Enrollment: 694 . . . . (330) 869-3600
2013-14 Tuition: In-state $12,114; Out-of-state $12,114
Bryant & Stratton College-Akron (Private, For-profit)
Fall 2013 Enrollment: 313 . . . . (330) 598-2500
2013-14 Tuition: In-state $16,565; Out-of-state $16,565
ITT Technical Institute-Akron (Private, For-profit)
Fall 2013 Enrollment: 249 . . . . (330) 865-8600
2013-14 Tuition: In-state $18,048; Out-of-state $18,048
University of Akron Main Campus (Public)
Fall 2013 Enrollment: 24,932 . . . . (330) 972-7111
2013-14 Tuition: In-state $10,054; Out-of-state $18,418

Two-year College(s)

National Institute of Massotherapy (Private, For-profit)
Fall 2013 Enrollment: 56 . . . . (330) 867-1996
Ohio College of Massotherapy Inc (Private, Not-for-profit)
Fall 2013 Enrollment: 103 . . . . (330) 665-1084
2013-14 Tuition: In-state $8,475; Out-of-state $8,475

Vocational/Technical School(s)

Akron School of Practical Nursing (Public)
Fall 2013 Enrollment: 34 . . . . (330) 873-3355
2013-14 Tuition: $11,035
Fortis College-Akron (Private, For-profit)
Fall 2013 Enrollment: 144 . . . . (330) 923-9959
2013-14 Tuition: $12,579
Gerbers Akron Beauty School (Private, For-profit)
Fall 2013 Enrollment: 67 . . . . (330) 867-6200
2013-14 Tuition: $8,780
Regency Beauty Institute-Akron (Private, For-profit)
Fall 2013 Enrollment: 123 . . . . (800) 787-6456
2013-14 Tuition: $16,200

Housing: Homeownership rate: 54.5%; Median home value: $83,900; Median year structure built: 1953; Homeowner vacancy rate: 3.7%; Median gross rent: $680 per month; Rental vacancy rate: 10.5%

Health Insurance: 84.0% have insurance; 56.0% have private insurance; 39.2% have public insurance; 16.0% do not have insurance; 7.3% of children under 18 do not have insurance

Hospitals: Akron General Medical Center (532 beds); Crystal Clinic Orthopaedic Center; Summa Health Systems Hospitals (658 beds)

Safety: Violent crime rate: 79.1 per 10,000 population; Property crime rate: 486.3 per 10,000 population

Newspapers: Akron Beacon Journal (daily circulation 119000); Akron Suburbanite (weekly circulation 33000); Jackson Suburbanite (weekly circulation 12500); South Side News Leader (weekly circulation 23000); West Side Leader (weekly circulation 43000)

Transportation: Commute: 91.2% car, 3.8% public transportation, 2.2% walk, 2.1% work from home; Median travel time to work: 20.5 minutes

Airports: Akron Fulton International (general aviation); Akron-Canton Regional (primary service/small hub)

Additional Information Contacts

City of Akron . . . . (330) 375-2345
http://www.ci.akron.oh.us

BARBERTON (city). Covers a land area of 9.038 square miles and a water area of 0.219 square miles. Located at 41.01° N. Lat; 81.60° W. Long. Elevation is 971 feet.

History: Barberton was laid out in 1891 by Ohio Columbus Barber, the owner of the Diamond Match Company. Barber dominated the town until his death in 1920, spending millions of dollars on the Anna Dean Experimental Farm, known as Barber's Folly, where cows and horses lived in luxury.

Population: 26,550; Growth (since 2000): -4.8%; Density: 2,937.5 persons per square mile; Race: 90.8% White, 5.9% Black/African American, 0.3% Asian, 0.3% American Indian/Alaska Native, 0.0% Native Hawaiian/Other Pacific Islander, 2.2% Two or more races, 1.4% Hispanic of any race; Average household size: 2.37; Median age: 39.8; Age under 18: 23.5%; Age 65 and over: 16.5%; Males per 100 females: 92.0; Marriage status: 33.4% never married, 41.3% now married, 2.2% separated, 10.2% widowed, 15.1% divorced; Foreign born: 3.1%; Speak English only: 95.6%; With disability: 16.0%; Veterans: 9.6%; Ancestry: 21.3% German, 14.3% Irish, 8.1% English, 7.5% American, 5.0% Italian

Employment: 7.2% management, business, and financial, 3.9% computer, engineering, and science, 5.0% education, legal, community service, arts, and media, 4.8% healthcare practitioners, 23.0% service, 26.5% sales and office, 9.8% natural resources, construction, and maintenance, 19.8% production, transportation, and material moving

Income: Per capita: $20,506; Median household: $37,819; Average household: $48,233; Households with income of $100,000 or more: 7.6%; Poverty rate: 20.5%

Educational Attainment: High school diploma or higher: 85.2%; Bachelor's degree or higher: 11.4%; Graduate/professional degree or higher: 2.4%

School District(s)

Barberton City (PK-12)
2012-13 Enrollment: 4,148 . . . . (330) 753-1025

Housing: Homeownership rate: 62.4%; Median home value: $86,800; Median year structure built: 1953; Homeowner vacancy rate: 3.3%; Median gross rent: $683 per month; Rental vacancy rate: 7.4%

Health Insurance: 85.8% have insurance; 59.6% have private insurance; 38.5% have public insurance; 14.2% do not have insurance; 7.3% of children under 18 do not have insurance

Hospitals: Summa Health System Barberton Hospital (311 beds)

Safety: Violent crime rate: 33.1 per 10,000 population; Property crime rate: 368.1 per 10,000 population

Newspapers: Barberton Herald (weekly circulation 7900)

Transportation: Commute: 94.5% car, 1.0% public transportation, 1.9% walk, 1.3% work from home; Median travel time to work: 21.3 minutes

Additional Information Contacts

City of Barberton . . . . (330) 848-6719
http://www.cityofbarberton.com

BOSTON HEIGHTS (village). Covers a land area of 6.895 square miles and a water area of <.001 square miles. Located at 41.25° N. Lat; 81.51° W. Long. Elevation is 1,070 feet.

Population: 1,300; Growth (since 2000): 9.6%; Density: 188.5 persons per square mile; Race: 95.9% White, 2.1% Black/African American, 0.7% Asian, 0.1% American Indian/Alaska Native, 0.0% Native Hawaiian/Other Pacific Islander, 1.2% Two or more races, 0.8% Hispanic of any race; Average household size: 2.81; Median age: 44.4; Age under 18: 26.1%; Age 65 and over: 12.1%; Males per 100 females: 95.5

Housing: Homeownership rate: 89.5%; Homeowner vacancy rate: 2.6%; Rental vacancy rate: 2.0%

CLINTON (village). Covers a land area of 3.549 square miles and a water area of 0.090 square miles. Located at 40.93° N. Lat; 81.63° W. Long. Elevation is 945 feet.

Population: 1,214; Growth (since 2000): -9.2%; Density: 342.1 persons per square mile; Race: 97.5% White, 0.3% Black/African American, 0.3% Asian, 0.2% American Indian/Alaska Native, 0.0% Native Hawaiian/Other Pacific Islander, 1.3% Two or more races, 0.7% Hispanic of any race; Average household size: 2.58; Median age: 43.1; Age under 18: 21.4%; Age 65 and over: 13.3%; Males per 100 females: 106.5

School District(s)

Norton City (PK-12)
2012-13 Enrollment: 2,583 . . . . (330) 825-0863

Housing: Homeownership rate: 88.3%; Homeowner vacancy rate: 1.6%; Rental vacancy rate: 15.2%

CUYAHOGA FALLS (city). Covers a land area of 25.648 square miles and a water area of 0.099 square miles. Located at 41.18° N. Lat; 81.55° W. Long. Elevation is 1,027 feet.

History: The city greatly expanded its area by annexing Northampton township in the 1980s. Incorporated 1836.

Population: 49,652; Growth (since 2000): 0.6%; Density: 1,935.9 persons per square mile; Race: 93.4% White, 3.3% Black/African American, 1.2% Asian, 0.2% American Indian/Alaska Native, 0.0% Native Hawaiian/Other Pacific Islander, 1.6% Two or more races, 1.4% Hispanic of any race; Average household size: 2.21; Median age: 39.4; Age under 18: 20.9%; Age 65 and over: 15.3%; Males per 100 females: 89.7; Marriage status: 30.2% never married, 49.2% now married, 1.3% separated, 6.7% widowed, 13.9% divorced; Foreign born: 3.0%; Speak English only: 95.9%; With disability: 12.9%; Veterans: 9.9%; Ancestry: 27.6% German, 15.9% Irish, 11.5% English, 11.1% Italian, 6.9% American
Employment: 14.0% management, business, and financial, 6.2% computer, engineering, and science, 11.0% education, legal, community service, arts, and media, 6.6% healthcare practitioners, 14.5% service, 27.6% sales and office, 7.5% natural resources, construction, and maintenance, 12.5% production, transportation, and material moving
Income: Per capita: $26,402; Median household: $49,438; Average household: $58,490; Households with income of $100,000 or more: 14.4%; Poverty rate: 12.0%
Educational Attainment: High school diploma or higher: 93.4%; Bachelor's degree or higher: 30.4%; Graduate/professional degree or higher: 9.6%

School District(s)

Cuyahoga Falls City (PK-12)
2012-13 Enrollment: 4,951 . . . . (330) 926-3800
Schnee Learning Center (09-12)
2012-13 Enrollment: 104. . . . . (330) 922-1966
Woodridge Local (PK-12)
2012-13 Enrollment: 2,067 . . . . (330) 928-9074

Two-year College(s)

Fortis College-Cuyahoga Falls (Private, For-profit)
Fall 2013 Enrollment: 471 . . . . (330) 923-9959
2013-14 Tuition: In-state $12,299; Out-of-state $12,299

Housing: Homeownership rate: 63.7%; Median home value: $120,400; Median year structure built: 1958; Homeowner vacancy rate: 1.7%; Median gross rent: $761 per month; Rental vacancy rate: 8.3%
Health Insurance: 89.8% have insurance; 75.9% have private insurance; 26.3% have public insurance; 10.2% do not have insurance; 5.3% of children under 18 do not have insurance
Hospitals: Edwin Shaw Rehab Institute; Summa Western Reserve Hospital (257 beds)
Safety: Violent crime rate: 14.0 per 10,000 population; Property crime rate: 261.9 per 10,000 population
Transportation: Commute: 94.7% car, 0.8% public transportation, 1.0% walk, 2.9% work from home; Median travel time to work: 22.6 minutes
Additional Information Contacts
City of Cuyahoga Falls . . . . (330) 971-8000
http://cfo.cityofcf.com/web

FAIRLAWN (city). Covers a land area of 4.476 square miles and a water area of 0.011 square miles. Located at 41.13° N. Lat; 81.62° W. Long. Elevation is 1,007 feet.
Population: 7,437; Growth (since 2000): 1.8%; Density: 1,661.6 persons per square mile; Race: 82.1% White, 11.0% Black/African American, 4.3% Asian, 0.0% American Indian/Alaska Native, 0.0% Native Hawaiian/Other Pacific Islander, 2.0% Two or more races, 2.3% Hispanic of any race; Average household size: 2.20; Median age: 46.8; Age under 18: 19.4%; Age 65 and over: 23.4%; Males per 100 females: 88.9; Marriage status: 28.9% never married, 48.3% now married, 1.3% separated, 11.4% widowed, 11.4% divorced; Foreign born: 9.7%; Speak English only: 86.0%; With disability: 8.9%; Veterans: 9.1%; Ancestry: 17.6% German, 13.9% Irish, 13.8% English, 11.3% Italian, 5.1% Hungarian
Employment: 22.3% management, business, and financial, 7.7% computer, engineering, and science, 14.7% education, legal, community service, arts, and media, 10.7% healthcare practitioners, 8.3% service, 25.1% sales and office, 2.6% natural resources, construction, and maintenance, 8.6% production, transportation, and material moving
Income: Per capita: $41,786; Median household: $62,662; Average household: $85,805; Households with income of $100,000 or more: 29.9%; Poverty rate: 2.9%
Educational Attainment: High school diploma or higher: 96.1%; Bachelor's degree or higher: 50.4%; Graduate/professional degree or higher: 18.2%

School District(s)

Copley-Fairlawn City (PK-12)
2012-13 Enrollment: 3,196 . . . . (330) 664-4800

Housing: Homeownership rate: 66.1%; Median home value: $171,700; Median year structure built: 1971; Homeowner vacancy rate: 2.2%; Median gross rent: $909 per month; Rental vacancy rate: 6.5%
Health Insurance: 92.6% have insurance; 84.9% have private insurance; 26.4% have public insurance; 7.4% do not have insurance; 4.4% of children under 18 do not have insurance
Transportation: Commute: 92.1% car, 1.4% public transportation, 0.0% walk, 6.2% work from home; Median travel time to work: 20.8 minutes
Additional Information Contacts
City of Fairlawn . . . . (330) 668-9500
http://www.cityoffairlawn.com

GREEN (city). Covers a land area of 32.055 square miles and a water area of 1.479 square miles. Located at 40.95° N. Lat; 81.47° W. Long. Elevation is 1,142 feet.
Population: 25,699; Growth (since 2000): 12.6%; Density: 801.7 persons per square mile; Race: 95.0% White, 1.8% Black/African American, 1.5% Asian, 0.2% American Indian/Alaska Native, 0.0% Native Hawaiian/Other Pacific Islander, 1.2% Two or more races, 1.2% Hispanic of any race; Average household size: 2.54; Median age: 41.8; Age under 18: 24.1%; Age 65 and over: 14.5%; Males per 100 females: 95.1; Marriage status: 23.5% never married, 60.4% now married, 0.5% separated, 7.5% widowed, 8.6% divorced; Foreign born: 3.2%; Speak English only: 93.7%; With disability: 10.7%; Veterans: 9.6%; Ancestry: 29.2% German, 14.6% Irish, 13.0% Italian, 10.3% English, 6.6% American
Employment: 17.1% management, business, and financial, 4.7% computer, engineering, and science, 11.7% education, legal, community service, arts, and media, 6.5% healthcare practitioners, 14.2% service, 26.3% sales and office, 7.3% natural resources, construction, and maintenance, 12.2% production, transportation, and material moving
Income: Per capita: $31,909; Median household: $61,150; Average household: $78,756; Households with income of $100,000 or more: 25.3%; Poverty rate: 8.3%
Educational Attainment: High school diploma or higher: 92.3%; Bachelor's degree or higher: 33.5%; Graduate/professional degree or higher: 11.5%

School District(s)

Green Local (PK-12)
2012-13 Enrollment: 4,147 . . . . (330) 896-7500

Housing: Homeownership rate: 78.6%; Median home value: $174,300; Median year structure built: 1980; Homeowner vacancy rate: 2.2%; Median gross rent: $811 per month; Rental vacancy rate: 13.4%
Health Insurance: 90.6% have insurance; 78.1% have private insurance; 24.4% have public insurance; 9.4% do not have insurance; 5.3% of children under 18 do not have insurance
Transportation: Commute: 95.8% car, 0.0% public transportation, 0.3% walk, 3.6% work from home; Median travel time to work: 22.5 minutes
Additional Information Contacts
City of Green . . . . (330) 896-5510
http://www.cityofgreen.org

HUDSON (city). Covers a land area of 25.596 square miles and a water area of 0.265 square miles. Located at 41.24° N. Lat; 81.44° W. Long. Elevation is 1,066 feet.
History: The city is named after its founder, David Hudson. Hudson moved here from Goshen, Connecticut in 1799. The Underground Railroad passed through Hudson, and Hudson was the childhood home of John Brown after his family moved there in 1805.
Population: 22,262; Growth (since 2000): -0.8%; Density: 869.7 persons per square mile; Race: 92.7% White, 1.3% Black/African American, 4.3% Asian, 0.1% American Indian/Alaska Native, 0.0% Native Hawaiian/Other Pacific Islander, 1.3% Two or more races, 1.7% Hispanic of any race; Average household size: 2.87; Median age: 42.5; Age under 18: 30.1%; Age 65 and over: 11.8%; Males per 100 females: 96.4; Marriage status: 20.4% never married, 68.7% now married, 0.5% separated, 4.9% widowed, 6.0% divorced; Foreign born: 8.1%; Speak English only: 91.7%; With disability: 6.3%; Veterans: 7.5%; Ancestry: 25.6% German, 15.4% Irish, 14.0% English, 10.1% Italian, 6.8% Polish
Employment: 29.0% management, business, and financial, 8.8% computer, engineering, and science, 15.4% education, legal, community service, arts, and media, 7.7% healthcare practitioners, 7.9% service, 24.5% sales and office, 2.0% natural resources, construction, and maintenance, 4.8% production, transportation, and material moving

Income: Per capita: $49,903; Median household: $119,212; Average household: $144,323; Households with income of $100,000 or more: 57.6%; Poverty rate: 3.6%
Educational Attainment: High school diploma or higher: 98.5%; Bachelor's degree or higher: 68.4%; Graduate/professional degree or higher: 28.3%

School District(s)

Hudson City (PK-12)
2012-13 Enrollment: 4,626 . . . . (330) 653-1200
Housing: Homeownership rate: 89.7%; Median home value: $289,900; Median year structure built: 1980; Homeowner vacancy rate: 1.6%; Median gross rent: $1,972 per month; Rental vacancy rate: 10.0%
Health Insurance: 96.2% have insurance; 92.5% have private insurance; 15.7% have public insurance; 3.8% do not have insurance; 2.8% of children under 18 do not have insurance
Safety: Violent crime rate: 1.3 per 10,000 population; Property crime rate: 59.1 per 10,000 population
Transportation: Commute: 88.2% car, 0.8% public transportation, 1.5% walk, 8.1% work from home; Median travel time to work: 28.3 minutes
Additional Information Contacts
City of Hudson. . . . . (330) 650-1799
http://www.hudson.oh.us

LAKEMORE (village). Covers a land area of 1.476 square miles and a water area of 0.191 square miles. Located at 41.02° N. Lat; 81.42° W. Long. Elevation is 1,083 feet.
History: Incorporated 1920.
Population: 3,068; Growth (since 2000): 19.8%; Density: 2,078.5 persons per square mile; Race: 95.4% White, 2.0% Black/African American, 0.7% Asian, 0.2% American Indian/Alaska Native, 0.0% Native Hawaiian/Other Pacific Islander, 1.4% Two or more races, 1.1% Hispanic of any race; Average household size: 2.47; Median age: 40.3; Age under 18: 21.3%; Age 65 and over: 14.2%; Males per 100 females: 89.3; Marriage status: 29.4% never married, 52.5% now married, 1.9% separated, 7.7% widowed, 10.4% divorced; Foreign born: 4.1%; Speak English only: 96.1%; With disability: 16.7%; Veterans: 11.2%; Ancestry: 26.0% German, 19.5% Irish, 12.1% English, 7.9% American, 6.9% Italian
Employment: 8.7% management, business, and financial, 4.8% computer, engineering, and science, 9.7% education, legal, community service, arts, and media, 8.0% healthcare practitioners, 17.4% service, 19.1% sales and office, 6.8% natural resources, construction, and maintenance, 25.5% production, transportation, and material moving
Income: Per capita: $21,904; Median household: $40,982; Average household: $50,206; Households with income of $100,000 or more: 9.3%; Poverty rate: 11.6%
Educational Attainment: High school diploma or higher: 85.3%; Bachelor's degree or higher: 15.1%; Graduate/professional degree or higher: 4.0%
Housing: Homeownership rate: 73.9%; Median home value: $112,400; Median year structure built: 1956; Homeowner vacancy rate: 3.0%; Median gross rent: $805 per month; Rental vacancy rate: 6.9%
Health Insurance: 91.4% have insurance; 68.4% have private insurance; 37.2% have public insurance; 8.6% do not have insurance; 0.0% of children under 18 do not have insurance
Transportation: Commute: 96.3% car, 0.0% public transportation, 0.5% walk, 3.3% work from home; Median travel time to work: 26.7 minutes

MACEDONIA (city). Covers a land area of 9.706 square miles and a water area of 0.038 square miles. Located at 41.31° N. Lat; 81.50° W. Long. Elevation is 988 feet.
Population: 11,188; Growth (since 2000): 21.3%; Density: 1,152.7 persons per square mile; Race: 83.6% White, 10.4% Black/African American, 3.9% Asian, 0.1% American Indian/Alaska Native, 0.0% Native Hawaiian/Other Pacific Islander, 1.6% Two or more races, 1.3% Hispanic of any race; Average household size: 2.58; Median age: 43.4; Age under 18: 22.3%; Age 65 and over: 14.7%; Males per 100 females: 94.1; Marriage status: 23.1% never married, 61.3% now married, 1.1% separated, 7.2% widowed, 8.4% divorced; Foreign born: 6.5%; Speak English only: 92.4%; With disability: 9.8%; Veterans: 10.9%; Ancestry: 25.3% German, 12.8% Irish, 12.5% Polish, 11.9% English, 11.9% Italian
Employment: 18.9% management, business, and financial, 7.7% computer, engineering, and science, 10.4% education, legal, community service, arts, and media, 7.7% healthcare practitioners, 13.6% service, 22.7% sales and office, 6.9% natural resources, construction, and maintenance, 12.0% production, transportation, and material moving
Income: Per capita: $39,132; Median household: $80,930; Average household: $100,586; Households with income of $100,000 or more: 35.4%; Poverty rate: 1.0%
Educational Attainment: High school diploma or higher: 96.0%; Bachelor's degree or higher: 39.5%; Graduate/professional degree or higher: 15.2%

School District(s)

Nordonia Hills City (PK-12)
2012-13 Enrollment: 3,773 . . . . (330) 467-0580
Housing: Homeownership rate: 92.2%; Median home value: $187,900; Median year structure built: 1985; Homeowner vacancy rate: 1.9%; Median gross rent: $1,165 per month; Rental vacancy rate: 8.2%
Health Insurance: 96.2% have insurance; 89.1% have private insurance; 19.3% have public insurance; 3.8% do not have insurance; 0.5% of children under 18 do not have insurance
Transportation: Commute: 95.7% car, 0.4% public transportation, 0.8% walk, 3.1% work from home; Median travel time to work: 23.4 minutes
Additional Information Contacts
City of Macedonia . . . . (330) 468-8300
http://www.macedonia.oh.us

MOGADORE (village). Covers a land area of 2.094 square miles and a water area of 0.020 square miles. Located at 41.05° N. Lat; 81.41° W. Long. Elevation is 1,145 feet.
Population: 3,853; Growth (since 2000): -1.0%; Density: 1,839.8 persons per square mile; Race: 97.6% White, 0.3% Black/African American, 0.3% Asian, 0.2% American Indian/Alaska Native, 0.0% Native Hawaiian/Other Pacific Islander, 1.5% Two or more races, 0.9% Hispanic of any race; Average household size: 2.60; Median age: 41.0; Age under 18: 23.0%; Age 65 and over: 16.9%; Males per 100 females: 94.2; Marriage status: 34.0% never married, 50.4% now married, 0.5% separated, 7.0% widowed, 8.5% divorced; Foreign born: 1.2%; Speak English only: 97.9%; With disability: 7.4%; Veterans: 10.4%; Ancestry: 34.1% German, 16.7% Irish, 12.0% Italian, 7.4% American, 7.2% English
Employment: 8.7% management, business, and financial, 2.9% computer, engineering, and science, 9.9% education, legal, community service, arts, and media, 4.8% healthcare practitioners, 12.8% service, 34.0% sales and office, 11.9% natural resources, construction, and maintenance, 15.0% production, transportation, and material moving
Income: Per capita: $22,581; Median household: $55,212; Average household: $63,281; Households with income of $100,000 or more: 12.1%; Poverty rate: 15.6%
Educational Attainment: High school diploma or higher: 91.9%; Bachelor's degree or higher: 13.5%; Graduate/professional degree or higher: 4.7%

School District(s)

Falcon Academy of Creative Arts (03-06)
2012-13 Enrollment: 172. . . . . (330) 673-2659
Field Local (PK-12)
2012-13 Enrollment: 2,055 . . . . (330) 673-2659
Mogadore Local (PK-12)
2012-13 Enrollment: 887. . . . . (330) 628-9945
Housing: Homeownership rate: 82.2%; Median home value: $118,900; Median year structure built: 1958; Homeowner vacancy rate: 1.8%; Median gross rent: $781 per month; Rental vacancy rate: 5.0%
Health Insurance: 94.3% have insurance; 82.9% have private insurance; 30.4% have public insurance; 5.7% do not have insurance; 0.6% of children under 18 do not have insurance
Transportation: Commute: 97.7% car, 0.0% public transportation, 0.0% walk, 1.6% work from home; Median travel time to work: 20.6 minutes

MONTROSE-GHENT (CDP). Covers a land area of 9.423 square miles and a water area of 0.091 square miles. Located at 41.16° N. Lat; 81.64° W. Long. Elevation is 915 feet.
History: Montrose-Ghent is composed of the unincorporated communities of Montrose and Ghent. Despite sharing a commercial district with Fairlawn, the regions are administratively separate.
Population: 5,177; Growth (since 2000): -1.6%; Density: 549.4 persons per square mile; Race: 94.4% White, 1.6% Black/African American, 2.7% Asian, 0.1% American Indian/Alaska Native, 0.0% Native Hawaiian/Other Pacific Islander, 1.0% Two or more races, 0.9% Hispanic of any race; Average household size: 2.49; Median age: 50.0; Age under 18: 20.7%; Age 65 and over: 21.0%; Males per 100 females: 98.5; Marriage status: 17.4% never married, 68.3% now married, 0.3% separated, 4.2% widowed, 10.1% divorced; Foreign born: 6.4%; Speak English only: 93.6%;

With disability: 8.2%; Veterans: 10.5%; Ancestry: 24.3% German, 15.2% Irish, 13.7% Italian, 9.5% English, 7.0% American
Employment: 23.2% management, business, and financial, 5.8% computer, engineering, and science, 13.2% education, legal, community service, arts, and media, 19.4% healthcare practitioners, 12.3% service, 22.2% sales and office, 2.3% natural resources, construction, and maintenance, 1.5% production, transportation, and material moving
Income: Per capita: $61,348; Median household: $104,638; Average household: $150,003; Households with income of $100,000 or more: 51.7%; Poverty rate: 4.6%
Educational Attainment: High school diploma or higher: 98.0%; Bachelor's degree or higher: 67.9%; Graduate/professional degree or higher: 32.8%
Housing: Homeownership rate: 92.2%; Median home value: $318,300; Median year structure built: 1977; Homeowner vacancy rate: 2.1%; Median gross rent: $1,166 per month; Rental vacancy rate: 12.4%
Health Insurance: 94.3% have insurance; 87.9% have private insurance; 24.4% have public insurance; 5.7% do not have insurance; 3.4% of children under 18 do not have insurance
Transportation: Commute: 93.7% car, 0.5% public transportation, 0.6% walk, 5.2% work from home; Median travel time to work: 22.4 minutes

MUNROE FALLS (city). Covers a land area of 2.718 square miles and a water area of 0.092 square miles. Located at 41.14° N. Lat; 81.44° W. Long. Elevation is 1,030 feet.
Population: 5,012; Growth (since 2000): -5.7%; Density: 1,843.8 persons per square mile; Race: 95.6% White, 1.5% Black/African American, 1.4% Asian, 0.1% American Indian/Alaska Native, 0.0% Native Hawaiian/Other Pacific Islander, 1.2% Two or more races, 1.2% Hispanic of any race; Average household size: 2.40; Median age: 45.1; Age under 18: 20.2%; Age 65 and over: 16.3%; Males per 100 females: 94.9; Marriage status: 20.0% never married, 64.3% now married, 1.1% separated, 6.0% widowed, 9.7% divorced; Foreign born: 3.6%; Speak English only: 93.6%; With disability: 8.2%; Veterans: 9.6%; Ancestry: 26.3% German, 18.6% Irish, 13.4% Italian, 10.6% English, 4.9% American
Employment: 16.7% management, business, and financial, 7.1% computer, engineering, and science, 17.5% education, legal, community service, arts, and media, 6.6% healthcare practitioners, 13.5% service, 27.6% sales and office, 3.3% natural resources, construction, and maintenance, 7.7% production, transportation, and material moving
Income: Per capita: $35,021; Median household: $64,654; Average household: $82,063; Households with income of $100,000 or more: 24.9%; Poverty rate: 2.0%
Educational Attainment: High school diploma or higher: 92.3%; Bachelor's degree or higher: 42.8%; Graduate/professional degree or higher: 18.6%

School District(s)

Stow-Munroe Falls City SD (PK-12)
2012-13 Enrollment: 5,321 . . . . (330) 689-5445
Housing: Homeownership rate: 81.3%; Median home value: $162,800; Median year structure built: 1975; Homeowner vacancy rate: 1.6%; Median gross rent: $625 per month; Rental vacancy rate: 9.9%
Health Insurance: 95.1% have insurance; 85.1% have private insurance; 24.4% have public insurance; 4.9% do not have insurance; 0.0% of children under 18 do not have insurance
Transportation: Commute: 95.0% car, 0.0% public transportation, 2.3% walk, 2.7% work from home; Median travel time to work: 22.4 minutes
Additional Information Contacts
City of Munroe Falls . . . . (330) 688-7491
http://www.munroefalls.com

NEW FRANKLIN (city). Covers a land area of 25.036 square miles and a water area of 1.642 square miles. Located at 40.95° N. Lat; 81.58° W. Long. Elevation is 1,089 feet.
History: In 1997 the village of New Franklin was incorporated from a section of Franklin Township to thwart annexation attempts from neighboring cities. New Franklin expanded significantly in November 2003 when the residents of Franklin Township and New Franklin voted to merge the two entities. The merger took effect January 1, 2005. The village officially became a city on March 6, 2006.
Population: 14,227; Growth (since 2000): 549.3%; Density: 568.3 persons per square mile; Race: 97.7% White, 0.6% Black/African American, 0.4% Asian, 0.1% American Indian/Alaska Native, 0.0% Native Hawaiian/Other Pacific Islander, 1.0% Two or more races, 0.8% Hispanic of any race; Average household size: 2.51; Median age: 45.5; Age under 18: 21.2%; Age 65 and over: 17.7%; Males per 100 females: 98.0; Marriage status: 21.5% never married, 64.0% now married, 0.8% separated, 5.4% widowed, 9.0% divorced; Foreign born: 2.4%; Speak English only: 97.0%; With disability: 12.0%; Veterans: 12.1%; Ancestry: 29.6% German, 20.0% Irish, 12.6% English, 9.8% American, 9.8% Italian
Employment: 11.7% management, business, and financial, 5.6% computer, engineering, and science, 7.4% education, legal, community service, arts, and media, 6.8% healthcare practitioners, 18.0% service, 22.0% sales and office, 14.0% natural resources, construction, and maintenance, 14.4% production, transportation, and material moving
Income: Per capita: $29,808; Median household: $65,892; Average household: $76,535; Households with income of $100,000 or more: 20.5%; Poverty rate: 6.6%
Educational Attainment: High school diploma or higher: 92.4%; Bachelor's degree or higher: 21.8%; Graduate/professional degree or higher: 5.7%
Housing: Homeownership rate: 87.2%; Median home value: $139,200; Median year structure built: 1964; Homeowner vacancy rate: 1.4%; Median gross rent: $838 per month; Rental vacancy rate: 8.1%
Health Insurance: 92.4% have insurance; 80.3% have private insurance; 28.1% have public insurance; 7.6% do not have insurance; 1.6% of children under 18 do not have insurance
Safety: Violent crime rate: 3.5 per 10,000 population; Property crime rate: 49.2 per 10,000 population
Transportation: Commute: 96.6% car, 0.3% public transportation, 0.2% walk, 2.4% work from home; Median travel time to work: 24.2 minutes
Additional Information Contacts
City of New Franklin . . . . (330) 882-4324
http://www.newfranklin.org

NORTHFIELD (village). Covers a land area of 1.083 square miles and a water area of 0 square miles. Located at 41.34° N. Lat; 81.53° W. Long. Elevation is 1,050 feet.
Population: 3,677; Growth (since 2000): -3.9%; Density: 3,396.4 persons per square mile; Race: 85.6% White, 5.8% Black/African American, 5.3% Asian, 0.2% American Indian/Alaska Native, 0.0% Native Hawaiian/Other Pacific Islander, 2.3% Two or more races, 1.7% Hispanic of any race; Average household size: 2.38; Median age: 40.5; Age under 18: 21.7%; Age 65 and over: 13.2%; Males per 100 females: 97.8; Marriage status: 35.6% never married, 41.9% now married, 0.7% separated, 7.9% widowed, 14.6% divorced; Foreign born: 6.8%; Speak English only: 90.3%; With disability: 14.4%; Veterans: 9.7%; Ancestry: 18.9% Polish, 13.1% German, 9.9% Irish, 9.8% Italian, 7.0% American
Employment: 11.1% management, business, and financial, 3.1% computer, engineering, and science, 5.2% education, legal, community service, arts, and media, 5.7% healthcare practitioners, 21.5% service, 25.9% sales and office, 7.8% natural resources, construction, and maintenance, 19.8% production, transportation, and material moving
Income: Per capita: $24,047; Median household: $55,401; Average household: $60,447; Households with income of $100,000 or more: 13.5%; Poverty rate: 5.9%
Educational Attainment: High school diploma or higher: 87.9%; Bachelor's degree or higher: 14.5%; Graduate/professional degree or higher: 4.5%

School District(s)

Nordonia Hills City (PK-12)
2012-13 Enrollment: 3,773 . . . . (330) 467-0580
Housing: Homeownership rate: 68.4%; Median home value: $127,600; Median year structure built: 1963; Homeowner vacancy rate: 1.7%; Median gross rent: $699 per month; Rental vacancy rate: 5.5%
Health Insurance: 89.7% have insurance; 76.2% have private insurance; 25.0% have public insurance; 10.3% do not have insurance; 2.0% of children under 18 do not have insurance
Transportation: Commute: 96.3% car, 0.9% public transportation, 2.0% walk, 0.8% work from home; Median travel time to work: 27.4 minutes

NORTON (city). Covers a land area of 20.162 square miles and a water area of 0.327 square miles. Located at 41.03° N. Lat; 81.65° W. Long. Elevation is 1,060 feet.
Population: 12,085; Growth (since 2000): 4.9%; Density: 599.4 persons per square mile; Race: 96.2% White, 1.7% Black/African American, 0.8% Asian, 0.2% American Indian/Alaska Native, 0.1% Native Hawaiian/Other Pacific Islander, 1.0% Two or more races, 0.9% Hispanic of any race; Average household size: 2.53; Median age: 43.7; Age under 18: 21.8%; Age 65 and over: 16.1%; Males per 100 females: 97.2; Marriage status:

20.5% never married, 62.7% now married, 1.3% separated, 7.1% widowed, 9.7% divorced; Foreign born: 2.0%; Speak English only: 96.8%; With disability: 12.6%; Veterans: 10.3%; Ancestry: 23.2% German, 11.8% Irish, 10.2% American, 10.1% English, 6.1% Italian
Employment: 13.2% management, business, and financial, 5.7% computer, engineering, and science, 11.1% education, legal, community service, arts, and media, 6.9% healthcare practitioners, 15.7% service, 22.9% sales and office, 10.7% natural resources, construction, and maintenance, 13.6% production, transportation, and material moving
Income: Per capita: $26,648; Median household: $59,261; Average household: $66,921; Households with income of $100,000 or more: 21.3%; Poverty rate: 6.2%
Educational Attainment: High school diploma or higher: 91.4%; Bachelor's degree or higher: 21.3%; Graduate/professional degree or higher: 6.7%

School District(s)

L.e.a.d. Academy (07-08)
2012-13 Enrollment: n/a . . . . (330) 207-5890
L.e.a.r.n. Academy (KG-03)
2012-13 Enrollment: n/a . . . . (330) 207-5890
Norton City (PK-12)
2012-13 Enrollment: 2,583 . . . . (330) 825-0863

Housing: Homeownership rate: 84.9%; Median home value: $137,800; Median year structure built: 1963; Homeowner vacancy rate: 1.4%; Median gross rent: $920 per month; Rental vacancy rate: 5.8%
Health Insurance: 92.0% have insurance; 79.3% have private insurance; 26.6% have public insurance; 8.0% do not have insurance; 1.4% of children under 18 do not have insurance
Safety: Violent crime rate: 5.8 per 10,000 population; Property crime rate: 188.1 per 10,000 population
Transportation: Commute: 95.4% car, 0.0% public transportation, 1.3% walk, 2.4% work from home; Median travel time to work: 21.9 minutes

Additional Information Contacts

City of Norton . . . . (330) 825-7815
http://www.cityofnorton.org

PENINSULA (village). Covers a land area of 4.671 square miles and a water area of 0.010 square miles. Located at 41.23° N. Lat; 81.55° W. Long. Elevation is 755 feet.
Population: 565; Growth (since 2000): -6.1%; Density: 120.9 persons per square mile; Race: 98.4% White, 0.4% Black/African American, 0.4% Asian, 0.0% American Indian/Alaska Native, 0.0% Native Hawaiian/Other Pacific Islander, 0.9% Two or more races, 0.4% Hispanic of any race; Average household size: 2.38; Median age: 47.3; Age under 18: 20.5%; Age 65 and over: 13.5%; Males per 100 females: 97.6

School District(s)

Woodridge Local (PK-12)
2012-13 Enrollment: 2,067 . . . . (330) 928-9074

Housing: Homeownership rate: 78.1%; Homeowner vacancy rate: 0.0%; Rental vacancy rate: 7.1%

PIGEON CREEK (CDP). Covers a land area of 0.895 square miles and a water area of 0 square miles. Located at 41.11° N. Lat; 81.67° W. Long. Elevation is 1,040 feet.
Population: 882; Growth (since 2000): -6.7%; Density: 985.8 persons per square mile; Race: 96.1% White, 1.9% Black/African American, 1.2% Asian, 0.0% American Indian/Alaska Native, 0.0% Native Hawaiian/Other Pacific Islander, 0.7% Two or more races, 0.9% Hispanic of any race; Average household size: 2.73; Median age: 47.5; Age under 18: 22.4%; Age 65 and over: 17.1%; Males per 100 females: 100.5
Housing: Homeownership rate: 99.1%; Homeowner vacancy rate: 1.8%; Rental vacancy rate: 0.0%

PORTAGE LAKES (CDP). Covers a land area of 3.945 square miles and a water area of 0.994 square miles. Located at 41.00° N. Lat; 81.54° W. Long. Elevation is 1,053 feet.
Population: 6,968; Growth (since 2000): -29.4%; Density: 1,766.2 persons per square mile; Race: 95.9% White, 1.7% Black/African American, 0.6% Asian, 0.3% American Indian/Alaska Native, 0.0% Native Hawaiian/Other Pacific Islander, 1.4% Two or more races, 0.7% Hispanic of any race; Average household size: 2.14; Median age: 43.1; Age under 18: 17.1%; Age 65 and over: 15.1%; Males per 100 females: 102.1; Marriage status: 37.0% never married, 43.4% now married, 3.4% separated, 4.0% widowed, 15.7% divorced; Foreign born: 1.5%; Speak English only: 96.7%; With disability: 16.7%; Veterans: 12.6%; Ancestry: 30.9% German, 19.4% Irish, 9.9% English, 9.7% American, 7.8% Italian
Employment: 11.8% management, business, and financial, 4.9% computer, engineering, and science, 3.6% education, legal, community service, arts, and media, 5.1% healthcare practitioners, 18.9% service, 27.4% sales and office, 16.9% natural resources, construction, and maintenance, 11.4% production, transportation, and material moving
Income: Per capita: $27,136; Median household: $49,113; Average household: $57,486; Households with income of $100,000 or more: 13.4%; Poverty rate: 10.1%
Educational Attainment: High school diploma or higher: 93.3%; Bachelor's degree or higher: 20.2%; Graduate/professional degree or higher: 4.3%
Housing: Homeownership rate: 63.4%; Median home value: $132,000; Median year structure built: 1958; Homeowner vacancy rate: 2.9%; Median gross rent: $746 per month; Rental vacancy rate: 7.2%
Health Insurance: 86.7% have insurance; 74.4% have private insurance; 25.2% have public insurance; 13.3% do not have insurance; 4.9% of children under 18 do not have insurance
Transportation: Commute: 97.0% car, 0.0% public transportation, 0.4% walk, 1.7% work from home; Median travel time to work: 20.8 minutes

REMINDERVILLE (village). Covers a land area of 2.180 square miles and a water area of 0.030 square miles. Located at 41.33° N. Lat; 81.40° W. Long. Elevation is 1,014 feet.
Population: 3,404; Growth (since 2000): 45.0%; Density: 1,561.2 persons per square mile; Race: 82.3% White, 9.0% Black/African American, 5.3% Asian, 0.1% American Indian/Alaska Native, 0.0% Native Hawaiian/Other Pacific Islander, 2.8% Two or more races, 1.1% Hispanic of any race; Average household size: 2.43; Median age: 38.3; Age under 18: 24.5%; Age 65 and over: 11.7%; Males per 100 females: 95.6; Marriage status: 23.2% never married, 58.7% now married, 0.3% separated, 3.4% widowed, 14.7% divorced; Foreign born: 3.0%; Speak English only: 95.4%; With disability: 9.4%; Veterans: 8.3%; Ancestry: 28.4% German, 23.9% Italian, 13.5% Polish, 12.6% Irish, 10.9% English
Employment: 17.2% management, business, and financial, 9.6% computer, engineering, and science, 16.9% education, legal, community service, arts, and media, 6.7% healthcare practitioners, 14.7% service, 24.3% sales and office, 5.4% natural resources, construction, and maintenance, 5.2% production, transportation, and material moving
Income: Per capita: $31,568; Median household: $73,611; Average household: $83,196; Households with income of $100,000 or more: 28.7%; Poverty rate: 0.8%
Educational Attainment: High school diploma or higher: 95.7%; Bachelor's degree or higher: 36.5%; Graduate/professional degree or higher: 17.5%
Housing: Homeownership rate: 84.5%; Median home value: $178,600; Median year structure built: 1981; Homeowner vacancy rate: 2.3%; Median gross rent: $1,026 per month; Rental vacancy rate: 5.6%
Health Insurance: 95.6% have insurance; 87.1% have private insurance; 19.4% have public insurance; 4.4% do not have insurance; 0.2% of children under 18 do not have insurance
Safety: Violent crime rate: 5.4 per 10,000 population; Property crime rate: 67.8 per 10,000 population
Transportation: Commute: 96.2% car, 0.0% public transportation, 0.5% walk, 1.9% work from home; Median travel time to work: 26.2 minutes

Additional Information Contacts

Village of Reminderville. . . . . (330) 562-1234
http://www.reminderville.com

RICHFIELD (village). Covers a land area of 9.319 square miles and a water area of 0.003 square miles. Located at 41.23° N. Lat; 81.64° W. Long. Elevation is 1,152 feet.
History: Richfield was the home of John Brown (1800-1859) during the 1840's, when he was a sheep raiser and wool broker. Brown became a symbol of the Northern sympathies in the Civil War after his raid on the arsenal at Harpers Ferry in 1859, for which he was convicted of treason and hung.
Population: 3,648; Growth (since 2000): 11.0%; Density: 391.4 persons per square mile; Race: 96.8% White, 0.7% Black/African American, 1.4% Asian, 0.1% American Indian/Alaska Native, 0.0% Native Hawaiian/Other Pacific Islander, 1.0% Two or more races, 0.6% Hispanic of any race; Average household size: 2.57; Median age: 46.4; Age under 18: 23.4%; Age 65 and over: 17.8%; Males per 100 females: 101.5; Marriage status: 22.6% never married, 59.5% now married, 0.4% separated, 7.8%

widowed, 10.1% divorced; Foreign born: 4.7%; Speak English only: 93.6%; With disability: 11.5%; Veterans: 11.0%; Ancestry: 29.5% German, 14.4% Italian, 13.8% Polish, 11.9% Irish, 11.5% English
Employment: 27.5% management, business, and financial, 7.5% computer, engineering, and science, 10.1% education, legal, community service, arts, and media, 5.0% healthcare practitioners, 10.1% service, 29.5% sales and office, 5.2% natural resources, construction, and maintenance, 5.2% production, transportation, and material moving
Income: Per capita: $41,633; Median household: $77,540; Average household: $109,474; Households with income of $100,000 or more: 38.8%; Poverty rate: 2.8%
Educational Attainment: High school diploma or higher: 95.8%; Bachelor's degree or higher: 45.6%; Graduate/professional degree or higher: 13.6%

School District(s)

Revere Local (PK-12)
2012-13 Enrollment: 2,630 . . . . (330) 666-4155
Housing: Homeownership rate: 89.1%; Median home value: $238,700; Median year structure built: 1970; Homeowner vacancy rate: 2.0%; Median gross rent: $839 per month; Rental vacancy rate: 3.8%
Health Insurance: 93.0% have insurance; 85.8% have private insurance; 19.5% have public insurance; 7.0% do not have insurance; 2.4% of children under 18 do not have insurance
Safety: Violent crime rate: 0.0 per 10,000 population; Property crime rate: 87.6 per 10,000 population
Transportation: Commute: 87.5% car, 0.6% public transportation, 0.1% walk, 11.5% work from home; Median travel time to work: 26.2 minutes
Additional Information Contacts
Village of Richfield. . . . . (330) 659-9201
http://www.richfieldvillageohio.org

SAWYERWOOD (CDP). Covers a land area of 0.744 square miles and a water area of 0.277 square miles. Located at 41.03° N. Lat; 81.45° W. Long. Elevation is 1,096 feet.
Population: 1,540; Growth (since 2000): n/a; Density: 2,070.6 persons per square mile; Race: 96.0% White, 1.2% Black/African American, 0.2% Asian, 0.1% American Indian/Alaska Native, 0.0% Native Hawaiian/Other Pacific Islander, 2.0% Two or more races, 1.2% Hispanic of any race; Average household size: 2.34; Median age: 44.1; Age under 18: 19.7%; Age 65 and over: 14.4%; Males per 100 females: 106.2
Housing: Homeownership rate: 72.8%; Homeowner vacancy rate: 3.2%; Rental vacancy rate: 12.2%

SILVER LAKE (village). Covers a land area of 1.417 square miles and a water area of 0.181 square miles. Located at 41.15° N. Lat; 81.46° W. Long. Elevation is 1,053 feet.
History: Beginning in 1874, the lake and the land surrounding it was a popular amusement park in the Akron area. It was sold in 1917 and subdivided for residential development, leading to the incorporation of the village in 1918.
Population: 2,519; Growth (since 2000): -16.6%; Density: 1,777.2 persons per square mile; Race: 96.9% White, 0.6% Black/African American, 1.5% Asian, 0.1% American Indian/Alaska Native, 0.1% Native Hawaiian/Other Pacific Islander, 0.6% Two or more races, 1.3% Hispanic of any race; Average household size: 2.50; Median age: 49.9; Age under 18: 20.5%; Age 65 and over: 19.7%; Males per 100 females: 99.1; Marriage status: 19.9% never married, 64.0% now married, 0.4% separated, 6.6% widowed, 9.5% divorced; Foreign born: 1.2%; Speak English only: 97.9%; With disability: 7.3%; Veterans: 11.6%; Ancestry: 21.3% German, 15.8% Irish, 15.2% Italian, 10.6% English, 4.8% European
Employment: 26.6% management, business, and financial, 9.0% computer, engineering, and science, 17.5% education, legal, community service, arts, and media, 9.5% healthcare practitioners, 6.8% service, 25.1% sales and office, 1.8% natural resources, construction, and maintenance, 3.6% production, transportation, and material moving
Income: Per capita: $51,386; Median household: $96,833; Average household: $120,695; Households with income of $100,000 or more: 47.5%; Poverty rate: 3.1%
Educational Attainment: High school diploma or higher: 97.2%; Bachelor's degree or higher: 59.9%; Graduate/professional degree or higher: 23.3%

School District(s)

Cuyahoga Falls City (PK-12)
2012-13 Enrollment: 4,951 . . . . (330) 926-3800
Housing: Homeownership rate: 94.8%; Median home value: $204,200; Median year structure built: 1958; Homeowner vacancy rate: 2.0%; Median gross rent: $1,514 per month; Rental vacancy rate: 13.1%
Health Insurance: 97.1% have insurance; 89.9% have private insurance; 24.4% have public insurance; 2.9% do not have insurance; 1.5% of children under 18 do not have insurance
Transportation: Commute: 89.5% car, 0.9% public transportation, 1.9% walk, 6.1% work from home; Median travel time to work: 19.9 minutes

STOW (city). Covers a land area of 17.088 square miles and a water area of 0.233 square miles. Located at 41.18° N. Lat; 81.44° W. Long. Elevation is 1,089 feet.
History: Settled 1802, incorporated as a city 1960.
Population: 34,837; Growth (since 2000): 8.4%; Density: 2,038.7 persons per square mile; Race: 93.0% White, 2.7% Black/African American, 2.4% Asian, 0.1% American Indian/Alaska Native, 0.0% Native Hawaiian/Other Pacific Islander, 1.4% Two or more races, 1.5% Hispanic of any race; Average household size: 2.42; Median age: 39.7; Age under 18: 22.7%; Age 65 and over: 13.8%; Males per 100 females: 93.0; Marriage status: 26.5% never married, 55.7% now married, 1.3% separated, 6.7% widowed, 11.1% divorced; Foreign born: 4.4%; Speak English only: 95.6%; With disability: 9.4%; Veterans: 9.6%; Ancestry: 26.9% German, 15.1% Irish, 12.0% English, 9.6% Italian, 6.1% Polish
Employment: 17.2% management, business, and financial, 7.5% computer, engineering, and science, 11.3% education, legal, community service, arts, and media, 7.0% healthcare practitioners, 14.4% service, 27.0% sales and office, 5.6% natural resources, construction, and maintenance, 10.0% production, transportation, and material moving
Income: Per capita: $31,365; Median household: $63,085; Average household: $77,534; Households with income of $100,000 or more: 27.3%; Poverty rate: 7.6%
Educational Attainment: High school diploma or higher: 94.1%; Bachelor's degree or higher: 40.0%; Graduate/professional degree or higher: 13.4%

School District(s)

Stow-Munroe Falls City SD (PK-12)
2012-13 Enrollment: 5,321 . . . . (330) 689-5445

Two-year College(s)

National College-Stow (Private, For-profit)
Fall 2013 Enrollment: 82. . . . . (330) 676-1351
2013-14 Tuition: In-state $11,442; Out-of-state $11,442
Housing: Homeownership rate: 69.6%; Median home value: $165,900; Median year structure built: 1979; Homeowner vacancy rate: 1.6%; Median gross rent: $843 per month; Rental vacancy rate: 9.3%
Health Insurance: 93.0% have insurance; 84.4% have private insurance; 20.3% have public insurance; 7.0% do not have insurance; 5.9% of children under 18 do not have insurance
Safety: Violent crime rate: 6.6 per 10,000 population; Property crime rate: 205.1 per 10,000 population
Newspapers: Record Publishing (weekly circulation 25000)
Transportation: Commute: 94.1% car, 1.0% public transportation, 1.3% walk, 3.4% work from home; Median travel time to work: 24.3 minutes
Airports: Kent State University (general aviation)
Additional Information Contacts
City of Stow. . . . . (330) 689 2700
http://www.stow.oh.us

TALLMADGE (city). Covers a land area of 13.996 square miles and a water area of 0.024 square miles. Located at 41.11° N. Lat; 81.43° W. Long. Elevation is 1,112 feet.
History: Settled 1807, incorporated 1950. Its historic architecture includes a 19th-century Congregational church near the city's center.
Population: 17,537; Growth (since 2000): 7.0%; Density: 1,253.0 persons per square mile; Race: 93.6% White, 3.3% Black/African American, 1.0% Asian, 0.3% American Indian/Alaska Native, 0.1% Native Hawaiian/Other Pacific Islander, 1.5% Two or more races, 1.0% Hispanic of any race; Average household size: 2.45; Median age: 45.1; Age under 18: 21.6%; Age 65 and over: 19.5%; Males per 100 females: 91.5; Marriage status: 25.8% never married, 56.4% now married, 0.8% separated, 7.5% widowed, 10.2% divorced; Foreign born: 2.7%; Speak English only: 96.2%; With disability: 12.1%; Veterans: 11.4%; Ancestry: 29.2% German, 19.1% Irish, 13.4% English, 11.2% Italian, 7.6% American
Employment: 13.7% management, business, and financial, 4.8% computer, engineering, and science, 11.9% education, legal, community service, arts, and media, 7.0% healthcare practitioners, 16.1% service,

24.0% sales and office, 9.7% natural resources, construction, and maintenance, 13.0% production, transportation, and material moving
Income: Per capita: $28,072; Median household: $54,225; Average household: $70,158; Households with income of $100,000 or more: 21.2%; Poverty rate: 10.1%
Educational Attainment: High school diploma or higher: 92.5%; Bachelor's degree or higher: 28.5%; Graduate/professional degree or higher: 9.6%

School District(s)

Tallmadge City (PK-12)
2012-13 Enrollment: 2,475 . . . . (330) 633-3291
Housing: Homeownership rate: 78.0%; Median home value: $155,200; Median year structure built: 1968; Homeowner vacancy rate: 1.7%; Median gross rent: $674 per month; Rental vacancy rate: 7.8%
Health Insurance: 94.3% have insurance; 80.5% have private insurance; 30.8% have public insurance; 5.7% do not have insurance; 1.0% of children under 18 do not have insurance
Safety: Violent crime rate: 12.0 per 10,000 population; Property crime rate: 202.8 per 10,000 population
Transportation: Commute: 96.7% car, 0.4% public transportation, 0.8% walk, 1.6% work from home; Median travel time to work: 20.9 minutes
Additional Information Contacts
City of Tallmadge . . . . (330) 633-0857
http://www.tallmadge-ohio.org

TWINSBURG (city). Covers a land area of 13.769 square miles and a water area of 0.032 square miles. Located at 41.32° N. Lat; 81.44° W. Long. Elevation is 1,004 feet.
History: Twinsburg was named for Moses and Aaron Wilcox, twins who built adjacent houses here in 1818.
Population: 18,795; Growth (since 2000): 10.5%; Density: 1,365.0 persons per square mile; Race: 78.5% White, 13.4% Black/African American, 5.7% Asian, 0.1% American Indian/Alaska Native, 0.0% Native Hawaiian/Other Pacific Islander, 1.9% Two or more races, 1.2% Hispanic of any race; Average household size: 2.49; Median age: 41.4; Age under 18: 25.4%; Age 65 and over: 14.5%; Males per 100 females: 88.0; Marriage status: 24.8% never married, 60.4% now married, 0.6% separated, 7.9% widowed, 6.9% divorced; Foreign born: 7.7%; Speak English only: 90.9%; With disability: 8.6%; Veterans: 7.1%; Ancestry: 19.3% German, 16.7% Italian, 13.8% Irish, 8.7% Polish, 8.3% English
Employment: 23.1% management, business, and financial, 9.6% computer, engineering, and science, 11.9% education, legal, community service, arts, and media, 6.0% healthcare practitioners, 12.0% service, 22.2% sales and office, 3.5% natural resources, construction, and maintenance, 11.7% production, transportation, and material moving
Income: Per capita: $37,484; Median household: $70,958; Average household: $93,154; Households with income of $100,000 or more: 32.7%; Poverty rate: 3.7%
Educational Attainment: High school diploma or higher: 93.3%; Bachelor's degree or higher: 44.3%; Graduate/professional degree or higher: 15.3%

School District(s)

Twinsburg City (PK-12)
2012-13 Enrollment: 4,327 . . . . (330) 486-2000

Vocational/Technical School(s)

The Ohio Academy Paul Mitchell Partner School-Cleveland (Private, For-profit)
Fall 2013 Enrollment: 181 . . . . (330) 963-0119
2013-14 Tuition: $14,850
Housing: Homeownership rate: 76.7%; Median home value: $206,700; Median year structure built: 1991; Homeowner vacancy rate: 1.2%; Median gross rent: $954 per month; Rental vacancy rate: 9.1%
Health Insurance: 96.4% have insurance; 88.0% have private insurance; 20.1% have public insurance; 3.6% do not have insurance; 1.3% of children under 18 do not have insurance
Safety: Violent crime rate: 4.8 per 10,000 population; Property crime rate: 70.4 per 10,000 population
Transportation: Commute: 94.4% car, 0.2% public transportation, 0.7% walk, 4.1% work from home; Median travel time to work: 26.3 minutes
Additional Information Contacts
City of Twinsburg. . . . . (330) 425-7161
http://www.mytwinsburg.com

TWINSBURG HEIGHTS (CDP). Covers a land area of 0.288 square miles and a water area of 0 square miles. Located at 41.31° N. Lat; 81.46° W. Long. Elevation is 1,135 feet.
Population: 925; Growth (since 2000): n/a; Density: 3,210.7 persons per square mile; Race: 10.4% White, 82.1% Black/African American, 0.3% Asian, 0.2% American Indian/Alaska Native, 0.0% Native Hawaiian/Other Pacific Islander, 6.3% Two or more races, 1.6% Hispanic of any race; Average household size: 2.93; Median age: 23.6; Age under 18: 40.3%; Age 65 and over: 5.0%; Males per 100 females: 76.5
Housing: Homeownership rate: 51.0%; Homeowner vacancy rate: 6.9%; Rental vacancy rate: 4.9%

Trumbull County

Located in northeastern Ohio; bounded on the east by Pennsylvania; drained by the Mahoning and Grand Rivers. Covers a land area of 618.296 square miles, a water area of 18.271 square miles, and is located in the Eastern Time Zone at 41.31° N. Lat., 80.77° W. Long. The county was founded in 1800. County seat is Warren.

Trumbull County is part of the Youngstown-Warren-Boardman, OH-PA Metropolitan Statistical Area. The entire metro area includes: Mahoning County, OH; Trumbull County, OH; Mercer County, PA

Weather Station: Warren 3 S Elevation: 899 feet

	Jan	Feb	Mar	Apr	May	Jun	Jul	Aug	Sep	Oct	Nov	Dec
High	35	38	47	61	71	79	83	82	74	63	51	39
Low	17	18	25	35	44	54	58	57	50	39	31	22
Precip	2.6	1.8	3.1	3.5	4.0	4.0	4.8	3.5	3.8	2.9	3.1	2.8
Snow	11.5	6.9	5.2	0.4	0.0	0.0	0.0	0.0	0.0	tr	0.8	7.1

High and Low temperatures in degrees Fahrenheit; Precipitation and Snow in inches

Weather Station: Youngstown Municipal Arpt Elevation: 1,180 feet

	Jan	Feb	Mar	Apr	May	Jun	Jul	Aug	Sep	Oct	Nov	Dec
High	33	37	46	59	70	78	82	80	73	61	49	37
Low	19	21	27	38	46	55	60	58	51	41	34	24
Precip	2.5	2.1	3.0	3.4	3.7	3.9	4.4	3.4	3.8	2.7	3.1	2.9
Snow	15.9	11.9	10.8	3.0	tr	tr	tr	tr	tr	0.8	4.0	13.3

High and Low temperatures in degrees Fahrenheit; Precipitation and Snow in inches

Population: 210,312; Growth (since 2000): -6.6%; Density: 340.1 persons per square mile; Race: 89.0% White, 8.3% Black/African American, 0.5% Asian, 0.2% American Indian/Alaska Native, 0.0% Native Hawaiian/Other Pacific Islander, 1.8% two or more races, 1.3% Hispanic of any race; Average household size: 2.40; Median age: 42.8; Age under 18: 22.2%; Age 65 and over: 17.4%; Males per 100 females: 94.4; Marriage status: 27.8% never married, 50.6% now married, 1.9% separated, 8.3% widowed, 13.2% divorced; Foreign born: 1.6%; Speak English only: 95.0%; With disability: 14.7%; Veterans: 11.6%; Ancestry: 19.4% German, 19.1% American, 13.5% Irish, 13.2% Italian, 8.9% English
Religion: Six largest groups: 18.9% Catholicism, 5.4% Methodist/Pietist, 4.9% Baptist, 4.1% Non-denominational Protestant, 2.8% Pentecostal, 2.0% Holiness
Economy: Unemployment rate: 4.9%; Leading industries: 16.4% retail trade; 13.7% health care and social assistance; 12.0% other services (except public administration); Farms: 888 totaling 113,896 acres; Company size: 8 employ 1,000 or more persons, 4 employ 500 to 999 persons, 90 employ 100 to 499 persons, 4,102 employ less than 100 persons; Business ownership: 3,754 women-owned, 531 Black-owned, n/a Hispanic-owned, 194 Asian-owned
Employment: 10.0% management, business, and financial, 2.7% computer, engineering, and science, 8.0% education, legal, community service, arts, and media, 6.4% healthcare practitioners, 19.6% service, 24.0% sales and office, 9.3% natural resources, construction, and maintenance, 19.9% production, transportation, and material moving
Income: Per capita: $22,568; Median household: $42,880; Average household: $53,566; Households with income of $100,000 or more: 11.8%; Poverty rate: 17.4%
Educational Attainment: High school diploma or higher: 87.7%; Bachelor's degree or higher: 17.0%; Graduate/professional degree or higher: 5.2%
Housing: Homeownership rate: 72.5%; Median home value: $97,400; Median year structure built: 1962; Homeowner vacancy rate: 2.6%; Median gross rent: $625 per month; Rental vacancy rate: 12.3%

Vital Statistics: Birth rate: 99.6 per 10,000 population; Death rate: 115.9 per 10,000 population; Age-adjusted cancer mortality rate: 204.4 deaths per 100,000 population
Health Insurance: 87.1% have insurance; 64.9% have private insurance; 36.7% have public insurance; 12.9% do not have insurance; 6.3% of children under 18 do not have insurance
Health Care: Physicians: 13.9 per 10,000 population; Hospital beds: 23.7 per 10,000 population; Hospital admissions: 1,109.9 per 10,000 population
Air Quality Index: 81.0% good, 18.6% moderate, 0.4% unhealthy for sensitive individuals, 0.0% unhealthy (percent of days)
Transportation: Commute: 94.5% car, 0.5% public transportation, 1.2% walk, 2.7% work from home; Median travel time to work: 22.3 minutes
Presidential Election: 60.2% Obama, 38.0% Romney (2012)
National and State Parks: Grand River State Wildlife Area; Mosquito Creek State Park; Mosquito Creek State Wildlife Area
Additional Information Contacts
Trumbull Government . . . . (330) 675-2451
http://www.co.trumbull.oh.us

Trumbull County Communities

BOLINDALE (CDP). Covers a land area of 0.994 square miles and a water area of 0 square miles. Located at 41.21° N. Lat; 80.78° W. Long. Elevation is 948 feet.
Population: 2,089; Growth (since 2000): -16.1%; Density: 2,102.6 persons per square mile; Race: 92.5% White, 5.3% Black/African American, 0.4% Asian, 0.1% American Indian/Alaska Native, 0.0% Native Hawaiian/Other Pacific Islander, 1.4% Two or more races, 2.2% Hispanic of any race; Average household size: 2.37; Median age: 44.2; Age under 18: 20.7%; Age 65 and over: 18.2%; Males per 100 females: 95.1
Housing: Homeownership rate: 73.7%; Homeowner vacancy rate: 2.9%; Rental vacancy rate: 12.4%

BRISTOLVILLE (unincorporated postal area)
ZCTA: 44402
Covers a land area of 36.198 square miles and a water area of 0.583 square miles. Located at 41.38° N. Lat; 80.85° W. Long. Elevation is 899 feet.
Population: 3,352; Growth (since 2000): 0.8%; Density: 92.6 persons per square mile; Race: 98.1% White, 0.3% Black/African American, 0.1% Asian, 0.1% American Indian/Alaska Native, 0.0% Native Hawaiian/Other Pacific Islander, 1.3% Two or more races, 0.6% Hispanic of any race; Average household size: 2.68; Median age: 43.0; Age under 18: 23.4%; Age 65 and over: 15.2%; Males per 100 females: 102.8; Marriage status: 23.7% never married, 62.1% now married, 1.4% separated, 2.8% widowed, 11.3% divorced; Foreign born: 0.5%; Speak English only: 99.5%; With disability: 7.8%; Veterans: 12.9%; Ancestry: 28.1% American, 17.6% German, 10.8% English, 8.9% Irish, 6.8% Polish
Employment: 12.1% management, business, and financial, 2.1% computer, engineering, and science, 5.6% education, legal, community service, arts, and media, 6.2% healthcare practitioners, 13.0% service, 18.4% sales and office, 8.7% natural resources, construction, and maintenance, 33.8% production, transportation, and material moving
Income: Per capita: $22,466; Median household: $56,074; Average household: $62,882; Households with income of $100,000 or more: 12.8%; Poverty rate: 4.3%
Educational Attainment: High school diploma or higher: 91.5%; Bachelor's degree or higher: 12.9%; Graduate/professional degree or higher: 2.7%

School District(s)

Bristol Local (PK-12)
2012-13 Enrollment: 664. . . . . (330) 889-3882
Housing: Homeownership rate: 84.2%; Median home value: $131,400; Median year structure built: 1973; Homeowner vacancy rate: 1.8%; Median gross rent: $652 per month; Rental vacancy rate: 6.6%
Health Insurance: 92.1% have insurance; 80.3% have private insurance; 27.4% have public insurance; 7.9% do not have insurance; 6.5% of children under 18 do not have insurance
Transportation: Commute: 90.2% car, 0.0% public transportation, 2.5% walk, 6.2% work from home; Median travel time to work: 27.6 minutes

BROOKFIELD CENTER (CDP). Covers a land area of 2.800 square miles and a water area of 0 square miles. Located at 41.24° N. Lat; 80.56° W. Long. Elevation is 1,063 feet.
Population: 1,207; Growth (since 2000): -6.3%; Density: 431.1 persons per square mile; Race: 97.0% White, 1.3% Black/African American, 0.4% Asian, 0.1% American Indian/Alaska Native, 0.0% Native Hawaiian/Other Pacific Islander, 1.2% Two or more races, 0.5% Hispanic of any race; Average household size: 2.24; Median age: 50.0; Age under 18: 15.5%; Age 65 and over: 22.9%; Males per 100 females: 97.5

School District(s)

Brookfield Local (PK-12)
2012-13 Enrollment: 1,122 . . . . (330) 448-4930
Housing: Homeownership rate: 78.5%; Homeowner vacancy rate: 2.5%; Rental vacancy rate: 2.5%

BURGHILL (unincorporated postal area)
ZCTA: 44404
Covers a land area of 17.040 square miles and a water area of 0.588 square miles. Located at 41.32° N. Lat; 80.56° W. Long. Elevation is 1,030 feet.
Population: 1,624; Growth (since 2000): -4.6%; Density: 95.3 persons per square mile; Race: 98.3% White, 0.1% Black/African American, 0.1% Asian, 0.1% American Indian/Alaska Native, 0.0% Native Hawaiian/Other Pacific Islander, 1.0% Two or more races, 0.7% Hispanic of any race; Average household size: 2.57; Median age: 46.3; Age under 18: 20.4%; Age 65 and over: 17.5%; Males per 100 females: 100.0
Housing: Homeownership rate: 84.5%; Homeowner vacancy rate: 1.5%; Rental vacancy rate: 4.9%

CHAMPION HEIGHTS (CDP). Covers a land area of 8.367 square miles and a water area of 0 square miles. Located at 41.30° N. Lat; 80.85° W. Long. Elevation is 932 feet.
Population: 6,498; Growth (since 2000): 37.5%; Density: 776.7 persons per square mile; Race: 97.8% White, 0.9% Black/African American, 0.3% Asian, 0.1% American Indian/Alaska Native, 0.0% Native Hawaiian/Other Pacific Islander, 0.8% Two or more races, 0.9% Hispanic of any race; Average household size: 2.46; Median age: 44.1; Age under 18: 22.5%; Age 65 and over: 20.6%; Males per 100 females: 91.5; Marriage status: 25.3% never married, 53.1% now married, 1.0% separated, 9.3% widowed, 12.2% divorced; Foreign born: 0.9%; Speak English only: 97.7%; With disability: 13.5%; Veterans: 11.2%; Ancestry: 22.6% American, 22.0% German, 12.9% English, 10.4% Irish, 8.2% Italian
Employment: 11.5% management, business, and financial, 2.2% computer, engineering, and science, 6.0% education, legal, community service, arts, and media, 7.7% healthcare practitioners, 13.8% service, 27.6% sales and office, 7.8% natural resources, construction, and maintenance, 23.4% production, transportation, and material moving
Income: Per capita: $25,552; Median household: $50,964; Average household: $62,557; Households with income of $100,000 or more: 13.7%; Poverty rate: 10.4%
Educational Attainment: High school diploma or higher: 91.7%; Bachelor's degree or higher: 16.6%; Graduate/professional degree or higher: 4.1%
Housing: Homeownership rate: 82.6%; Median home value: $110,000; Median year structure built: 1965; Homeowner vacancy rate: 2.3%; Median gross rent: $680 per month; Rental vacancy rate: 7.1%
Health Insurance: 92.5% have insurance; 75.3% have private insurance; 32.1% have public insurance; 7.5% do not have insurance; 0.0% of children under 18 do not have insurance
Transportation: Commute: 94.0% car, 0.5% public transportation, 1.1% walk, 4.5% work from home; Median travel time to work: 22.8 minutes

CHURCHILL (CDP). Covers a land area of 2.560 square miles and a water area of 0 square miles. Located at 41.17° N. Lat; 80.67° W. Long. Elevation is 1,063 feet.
Population: 2,149; Growth (since 2000): -17.4%; Density: 839.3 persons per square mile; Race: 86.2% White, 11.2% Black/African American, 0.4% Asian, 0.3% American Indian/Alaska Native, 0.0% Native Hawaiian/Other Pacific Islander, 1.9% Two or more races, 2.5% Hispanic of any race; Average household size: 2.37; Median age: 44.9; Age under 18: 20.4%; Age 65 and over: 18.8%; Males per 100 females: 94.3
Housing: Homeownership rate: 77.7%; Homeowner vacancy rate: 2.2%; Rental vacancy rate: 10.2%

CORTLAND (city). Covers a land area of 4.248 square miles and a water area of 0 square miles. Located at 41.33° N. Lat; 80.72° W. Long. Elevation is 1,024 feet.

Population: 7,104; Growth (since 2000): 4.0%; Density: 1,672.2 persons per square mile; Race: 97.0% White, 1.2% Black/African American, 0.5% Asian, 0.2% American Indian/Alaska Native, 0.0% Native Hawaiian/Other Pacific Islander, 0.9% Two or more races, 0.9% Hispanic of any race; Average household size: 2.33; Median age: 44.4; Age under 18: 22.0%; Age 65 and over: 18.6%; Males per 100 females: 88.8; Marriage status: 20.1% never married, 61.1% now married, 1.5% separated, 8.9% widowed, 10.0% divorced; Foreign born: 1.3%; Speak English only: 96.4%; With disability: 11.7%; Veterans: 12.2%; Ancestry: 26.3% German, 18.7% Irish, 16.8% American, 14.3% Italian, 11.8% English

Employment: 17.2% management, business, and financial, 7.2% computer, engineering, and science, 9.7% education, legal, community service, arts, and media, 5.8% healthcare practitioners, 15.9% service, 24.8% sales and office, 4.5% natural resources, construction, and maintenance, 14.9% production, transportation, and material moving

Income: Per capita: $30,618; Median household: $59,656; Average household: $67,300; Households with income of $100,000 or more: 20.0%; Poverty rate: 6.0%

Educational Attainment: High school diploma or higher: 95.7%; Bachelor's degree or higher: 29.5%; Graduate/professional degree or higher: 6.7%

School District(s)

Lakeview Local (PK-12)
2012-13 Enrollment: 1,795 . . . . (330) 637-8741
Maplewood Local (PK-12)
2012-13 Enrollment: 807. . . . . (330) 637-7506
Mathews Local (PK-12)
2012-13 Enrollment: 790. . . . . (330) 394-1800

Housing: Homeownership rate: 72.1%; Median home value: $140,000; Median year structure built: 1980; Homeowner vacancy rate: 2.5%; Median gross rent: $622 per month; Rental vacancy rate: 9.3%

Health Insurance: 91.6% have insurance; 81.5% have private insurance; 27.6% have public insurance; 8.4% do not have insurance; 3.1% of children under 18 do not have insurance

Safety: Violent crime rate: 5.7 per 10,000 population; Property crime rate: 113.9 per 10,000 population

Transportation: Commute: 97.2% car, 0.0% public transportation, 0.0% walk, 1.7% work from home; Median travel time to work: 24.8 minutes

Additional Information Contacts

City of Cortland . . . . (330) 637-4003
http://www.cityofcortland.org

FARMDALE (unincorporated postal area)

ZCTA: 44417

Covers a land area of 33.322 square miles and a water area of 0 square miles. Located at 41.44° N. Lat; 80.66° W. Long. Elevation is 935 feet.

Population: 1,659; Growth (since 2000): -6.2%; Density: 49.8 persons per square mile; Race: 98.3% White, 0.6% Black/African American, 0.2% Asian, 0.1% American Indian/Alaska Native, 0.1% Native Hawaiian/Other Pacific Islander, 0.7% Two or more races, 0.6% Hispanic of any race; Average household size: 2.58; Median age: 45.6; Age under 18: 20.7%; Age 65 and over: 16.5%; Males per 100 females: 98.0

Housing: Homeownership rate: 86.6%; Homeowner vacancy rate: 1.1%; Rental vacancy rate: 6.5%

FOWLER (unincorporated postal area)

ZCTA: 44418

Covers a land area of 17.426 square miles and a water area of 0 square miles. Located at 41.31° N. Lat; 80.60° W. Long. Elevation is 1,142 feet.

Population: 1,357; Growth (since 2000): 9.7%; Density: 77.9 persons per square mile; Race: 99.0% White, 0.5% Black/African American, 0.1% Asian, 0.1% American Indian/Alaska Native, 0.0% Native Hawaiian/Other Pacific Islander, 0.3% Two or more races, 0.4% Hispanic of any race; Average household size: 2.51; Median age: 46.2; Age under 18: 20.4%; Age 65 and over: 18.2%; Males per 100 females: 98.4

Housing: Homeownership rate: 87.1%; Homeowner vacancy rate: 2.8%; Rental vacancy rate: 4.2%

GIRARD (city). Covers a land area of 5.875 square miles and a water area of 0.486 square miles. Located at 41.17° N. Lat; 80.70° W. Long. Elevation is 906 feet.

History: Girard was settled about 1800, but growth was slow until the Ohio & Erie Canal was completed. The town was probably named for Stephen Girard, philanthropist and founder of Girard College in Philadelphia, Pennsylvania.

Population: 9,958; Growth (since 2000): -8.7%; Density: 1,694.8 persons per square mile; Race: 93.2% White, 4.0% Black/African American, 0.3% Asian, 0.1% American Indian/Alaska Native, 0.0% Native Hawaiian/Other Pacific Islander, 2.2% Two or more races, 2.1% Hispanic of any race; Average household size: 2.31; Median age: 41.8; Age under 18: 21.9%; Age 65 and over: 17.1%; Males per 100 females: 87.7; Marriage status: 33.7% never married, 43.4% now married, 1.6% separated, 8.0% widowed, 14.9% divorced; Foreign born: 2.0%; Speak English only: 96.2%; With disability: 16.1%; Veterans: 11.4%; Ancestry: 24.4% Italian, 20.0% American, 14.7% Irish, 14.6% German, 6.4% English

Employment: 9.7% management, business, and financial, 1.7% computer, engineering, and science, 11.4% education, legal, community service, arts, and media, 4.2% healthcare practitioners, 22.7% service, 23.4% sales and office, 8.6% natural resources, construction, and maintenance, 18.2% production, transportation, and material moving

Income: Per capita: $21,044; Median household: $40,298; Average household: $48,712; Households with income of $100,000 or more: 8.4%; Poverty rate: 21.5%

Educational Attainment: High school diploma or higher: 89.8%; Bachelor's degree or higher: 20.8%; Graduate/professional degree or higher: 7.2%

School District(s)

Girard City SD (PK-12)
2012-13 Enrollment: 1,691 . . . . (330) 545-2596

Housing: Homeownership rate: 63.8%; Median home value: $82,700; Median year structure built: 1956; Homeowner vacancy rate: 2.8%; Median gross rent: $604 per month; Rental vacancy rate: 8.9%

Health Insurance: 89.0% have insurance; 62.0% have private insurance; 40.0% have public insurance; 11.0% do not have insurance; 2.1% of children under 18 do not have insurance

Safety: Violent crime rate: 35.8 per 10,000 population; Property crime rate: 277.4 per 10,000 population

Transportation: Commute: 95.9% car, 0.0% public transportation, 1.7% walk, 2.2% work from home; Median travel time to work: 22.0 minutes

Additional Information Contacts

City of Girard . . . . (330) 545-3879
http://www.cityofgirard.com

HILLTOP (CDP). Covers a land area of 0.571 square miles and a water area of 0 square miles. Located at 41.16° N. Lat; 80.74° W. Long. Elevation is 974 feet.

Population: 532; Growth (since 2000): -0.4%; Density: 932.2 persons per square mile; Race: 97.4% White, 1.7% Black/African American, 0.2% Asian, 0.0% American Indian/Alaska Native, 0.2% Native Hawaiian/Other Pacific Islander, 0.6% Two or more races, 1.7% Hispanic of any race; Average household size: 2.56; Median age: 42.8; Age under 18: 23.1%; Age 65 and over: 15.8%; Males per 100 females: 108.6

Housing: Homeownership rate: 84.6%; Homeowner vacancy rate: 2.2%; Rental vacancy rate: 3.0%

HOWLAND CENTER (CDP). Covers a land area of 4.036 square miles and a water area of 0 square miles. Located at 41.25° N. Lat; 80.74° W. Long. Elevation is 892 feet.

Population: 6,351; Growth (since 2000): -2.0%; Density: 1,573.8 persons per square mile; Race: 93.5% White, 3.4% Black/African American, 1.4% Asian, 0.3% American Indian/Alaska Native, 0.0% Native Hawaiian/Other Pacific Islander, 1.1% Two or more races, 1.4% Hispanic of any race; Average household size: 2.37; Median age: 45.4; Age under 18: 21.1%; Age 65 and over: 20.8%; Males per 100 females: 89.6; Marriage status: 20.1% never married, 60.8% now married, 1.3% separated, 7.8% widowed, 11.3% divorced; Foreign born: 1.9%; Speak English only: 96.2%; With disability: 11.0%; Veterans: 10.5%; Ancestry: 21.7% German, 19.0% Italian, 13.3% English, 13.1% American, 9.7% Irish

Employment: 13.8% management, business, and financial, 5.4% computer, engineering, and science, 12.1% education, legal, community service, arts, and media, 5.1% healthcare practitioners, 17.0% service, 23.1% sales and office, 12.0% natural resources, construction, and maintenance, 11.6% production, transportation, and material moving

Income: Per capita: $28,550; Median household: $60,447; Average household: $70,954; Households with income of $100,000 or more: 22.0%; Poverty rate: 8.2%
Educational Attainment: High school diploma or higher: 92.6%; Bachelor's degree or higher: 30.8%; Graduate/professional degree or higher: 12.7%
Housing: Homeownership rate: 81.5%; Median home value: $127,000; Median year structure built: 1972; Homeowner vacancy rate: 3.0%; Median gross rent: $882 per month; Rental vacancy rate: 17.8%
Health Insurance: 89.4% have insurance; 76.6% have private insurance; 25.3% have public insurance; 10.6% do not have insurance; 6.7% of children under 18 do not have insurance
Transportation: Commute: 95.8% car, 0.0% public transportation, 0.9% walk, 3.3% work from home; Median travel time to work: 22.4 minutes

HUBBARD (city). Covers a land area of 3.902 square miles and a water area of 0.006 square miles. Located at 41.16° N. Lat; 80.57° W. Long. Elevation is 981 feet.
History: Hubbard was named for Nehemiah Hubbard, who purchased the land on which the town was founded in 1801. Until 1880, coal mining was the principal industry.
Population: 7,874; Growth (since 2000): -4.9%; Density: 2,018.1 persons per square mile; Race: 96.5% White, 1.5% Black/African American, 0.3% Asian, 0.1% American Indian/Alaska Native, 0.1% Native Hawaiian/Other Pacific Islander, 1.2% Two or more races, 1.3% Hispanic of any race; Average household size: 2.29; Median age: 43.9; Age under 18: 20.3%; Age 65 and over: 19.1%; Males per 100 females: 90.8; Marriage status: 23.5% never married, 50.2% now married, 1.7% separated, 11.6% widowed, 14.7% divorced; Foreign born: 1.0%; Speak English only: 95.5%; With disability: 16.8%; Veterans: 12.8%; Ancestry: 25.8% Italian, 22.9% German, 18.1% Irish, 14.3% American, 9.4% English
Employment: 12.6% management, business, and financial, 4.7% computer, engineering, and science, 9.6% education, legal, community service, arts, and media, 5.7% healthcare practitioners, 20.0% service, 28.7% sales and office, 7.0% natural resources, construction, and maintenance, 11.7% production, transportation, and material moving
Income: Per capita: $23,347; Median household: $41,101; Average household: $49,919; Households with income of $100,000 or more: 8.7%; Poverty rate: 13.2%
Educational Attainment: High school diploma or higher: 90.9%; Bachelor's degree or higher: 20.3%; Graduate/professional degree or higher: 4.5%

School District(s)

Hubbard Exempted Village (PK-12)
2012-13 Enrollment: 1,985 . . . . (330) 534-1921
Housing: Homeownership rate: 71.1%; Median home value: $91,100; Median year structure built: 1958; Homeowner vacancy rate: 1.4%; Median gross rent: $627 per month; Rental vacancy rate: 10.2%
Health Insurance: 90.6% have insurance; 69.8% have private insurance; 36.1% have public insurance; 9.4% do not have insurance; 2.0% of children under 18 do not have insurance
Safety: Violent crime rate: 6.4 per 10,000 population; Property crime rate: 175.3 per 10,000 population
Transportation: Commute: 93.7% car, 0.2% public transportation, 1.0% walk, 3.8% work from home; Median travel time to work: 20.2 minutes
Additional Information Contacts
City of Hubbard . . . . (330) 534-3090
http://www.cityofhubbard.com

KINSMAN (unincorporated postal area)
ZCTA: 44428
Covers a land area of 54.467 square miles and a water area of 2.826 square miles. Located at 41.44° N. Lat; 80.57° W. Long. Elevation is 935 feet.
Population: 3,290; Growth (since 2000): -5.6%; Density: 60.4 persons per square mile; Race: 97.7% White, 0.3% Black/African American, 0.3% Asian, 0.6% American Indian/Alaska Native, 0.0% Native Hawaiian/Other Pacific Islander, 0.9% Two or more races, 0.9% Hispanic of any race; Average household size: 2.55; Median age: 44.6; Age under 18: 22.6%; Age 65 and over: 17.1%; Males per 100 females: 98.0; Marriage status: 23.3% never married, 60.2% now married, 1.2% separated, 6.3% widowed, 10.1% divorced; Foreign born: 0.9%; Speak English only: 98.3%; With disability: 17.0%; Veterans: 11.5%; Ancestry: 39.5% American, 12.9% German, 9.5% English, 8.9% Irish, 5.9% Italian
Employment: 3.8% management, business, and financial, 0.7% computer, engineering, and science, 1.3% education, legal, community service, arts, and media, 1.2% healthcare practitioners, 16.6% service, 31.3% sales and office, 12.1% natural resources, construction, and maintenance, 33.0% production, transportation, and material moving
Income: Per capita: $22,167; Median household: $44,082; Average household: $53,547; Households with income of $100,000 or more: 8.4%; Poverty rate: 15.1%
Educational Attainment: High school diploma or higher: 83.2%; Bachelor's degree or higher: 6.9%; Graduate/professional degree or higher: 1.2%

School District(s)

Joseph Badger Local (PK-12)
2012-13 Enrollment: 868. . . . . (330) 876-2800
Housing: Homeownership rate: 81.8%; Median home value: $109,900; Median year structure built: 1966; Homeowner vacancy rate: 2.4%; Median gross rent: $534 per month; Rental vacancy rate: 16.3%
Health Insurance: 82.3% have insurance; 64.4% have private insurance; 37.6% have public insurance; 17.7% do not have insurance; 0.0% of children under 18 do not have insurance
Transportation: Commute: 94.2% car, 0.9% public transportation, 3.1% walk, 1.1% work from home; Median travel time to work: 31.4 minutes

KINSMAN CENTER (CDP). Covers a land area of 2.186 square miles and a water area of 0.008 square miles. Located at 41.45° N. Lat; 80.58° W. Long.
Population: 616; Growth (since 2000): n/a; Density: 281.8 persons per square mile; Race: 99.2% White, 0.2% Black/African American, 0.0% Asian, 0.3% American Indian/Alaska Native, 0.0% Native Hawaiian/Other Pacific Islander, 0.3% Two or more races, 0.3% Hispanic of any race; Average household size: 2.44; Median age: 42.1; Age under 18: 23.5%; Age 65 and over: 19.3%; Males per 100 females: 93.7
Housing: Homeownership rate: 70.7%; Homeowner vacancy rate: 4.7%; Rental vacancy rate: 18.7%

LEAVITTSBURG (CDP). Covers a land area of 1.735 square miles and a water area of 0.062 square miles. Located at 41.25° N. Lat; 80.88° W. Long. Elevation is 912 feet.
Population: 1,973; Growth (since 2000): -10.3%; Density: 1,137.2 persons per square mile; Race: 95.3% White, 1.6% Black/African American, 0.2% Asian, 0.4% American Indian/Alaska Native, 0.1% Native Hawaiian/Other Pacific Islander, 2.5% Two or more races, 0.9% Hispanic of any race; Average household size: 2.69; Median age: 39.6; Age under 18: 25.0%; Age 65 and over: 13.7%; Males per 100 females: 102.2

School District(s)

Labrae Local (PK-12)
2012-13 Enrollment: 1,399 . . . . (330) 898-0800
Housing: Homeownership rate: 78.0%; Homeowner vacancy rate: 2.2%; Rental vacancy rate: 1.8%

LORDSTOWN (village). Covers a land area of 23.137 square miles and a water area of 0.001 square miles. Located at 41.17° N. Lat; 80.87° W. Long. Elevation is 955 feet.
Population: 3,417; Growth (since 2000): -5.9%; Density: 147.7 persons per square mile; Race: 95.1% White, 3.2% Black/African American, 0.4% Asian, 0.1% American Indian/Alaska Native, 0.0% Native Hawaiian/Other Pacific Islander, 1.1% Two or more races, 0.9% Hispanic of any race; Average household size: 2.46; Median age: 45.0; Age under 18: 21.1%; Age 65 and over: 17.2%; Males per 100 females: 94.5; Marriage status: 20.5% never married, 59.3% now married, 0.0% separated, 7.7% widowed, 12.5% divorced; Foreign born: 1.7%; Speak English only: 97.4%; With disability: 14.6%; Veterans: 8.9%; Ancestry: 24.6% American, 23.4% German, 13.1% Irish, 11.6% Italian, 11.4% English
Employment: 9.6% management, business, and financial, 2.0% computer, engineering, and science, 4.3% education, legal, community service, arts, and media, 10.0% healthcare practitioners, 13.1% service, 24.5% sales and office, 10.0% natural resources, construction, and maintenance, 26.4% production, transportation, and material moving
Income: Per capita: $25,555; Median household: $48,795; Average household: $55,672; Households with income of $100,000 or more: 12.6%; Poverty rate: 10.5%
Educational Attainment: High school diploma or higher: 89.3%; Bachelor's degree or higher: 11.7%; Graduate/professional degree or higher: 5.1%

Housing: Homeownership rate: 85.3%; Median home value: $128,100; Median year structure built: 1976; Homeowner vacancy rate: 1.2%; Median gross rent: $563 per month; Rental vacancy rate: 14.2%
Health Insurance: 89.4% have insurance; 71.4% have private insurance; 37.0% have public insurance; 10.6% do not have insurance; 3.0% of children under 18 do not have insurance
Transportation: Commute: 97.0% car, 0.6% public transportation, 0.0% walk, 0.6% work from home; Median travel time to work: 22.1 minutes

MAPLEWOOD PARK (CDP). Covers a land area of 0.788 square miles and a water area of 0 square miles. Located at 41.14° N. Lat; 80.58° W. Long. Elevation is 1,093 feet.
Population: 280; Growth (since 2000): -12.8%; Density: 355.3 persons per square mile; Race: 46.4% White, 47.9% Black/African American, 0.0% Asian, 0.0% American Indian/Alaska Native, 0.0% Native Hawaiian/Other Pacific Islander, 5.7% Two or more races, 1.8% Hispanic of any race; Average household size: 2.35; Median age: 45.8; Age under 18: 18.2%; Age 65 and over: 20.0%; Males per 100 females: 81.8
Housing: Homeownership rate: 77.3%; Homeowner vacancy rate: 2.1%; Rental vacancy rate: 0.0%

MASURY (CDP). Covers a land area of 3.422 square miles and a water area of 0.040 square miles. Located at 41.21° N. Lat; 80.54° W. Long. Elevation is 922 feet.
Population: 2,064; Growth (since 2000): -21.2%; Density: 603.1 persons per square mile; Race: 96.5% White, 2.0% Black/African American, 0.0% Asian, 0.0% American Indian/Alaska Native, 0.0% Native Hawaiian/Other Pacific Islander, 1.0% Two or more races, 1.4% Hispanic of any race; Average household size: 2.30; Median age: 44.0; Age under 18: 20.2%; Age 65 and over: 17.2%; Males per 100 females: 96.8
Housing: Homeownership rate: 72.9%; Homeowner vacancy rate: 2.1%; Rental vacancy rate: 8.3%

MCDONALD (village). Covers a land area of 1.688 square miles and a water area of 0 square miles. Located at 41.16° N. Lat; 80.72° W. Long. Elevation is 961 feet.
Population: 3,263; Growth (since 2000): -6.3%; Density: 1,933.6 persons per square mile; Race: 97.3% White, 1.1% Black/African American, 0.2% Asian, 0.2% American Indian/Alaska Native, 0.0% Native Hawaiian/Other Pacific Islander, 1.1% Two or more races, 1.5% Hispanic of any race; Average household size: 2.57; Median age: 41.3; Age under 18: 24.2%; Age 65 and over: 14.9%; Males per 100 females: 93.9; Marriage status: 24.6% never married, 58.7% now married, 1.4% separated, 5.3% widowed, 11.5% divorced; Foreign born: 2.3%; Speak English only: 96.2%; With disability: 10.7%; Veterans: 12.0%; Ancestry: 26.2% American, 17.9% German, 17.8% Italian, 14.1% Irish, 8.0% Slovak
Employment: 16.0% management, business, and financial, 0.6% computer, engineering, and science, 9.4% education, legal, community service, arts, and media, 6.3% healthcare practitioners, 20.8% service, 24.6% sales and office, 4.0% natural resources, construction, and maintenance, 18.4% production, transportation, and material moving
Income: Per capita: $24,630; Median household: $49,139; Average household: $61,966; Households with income of $100,000 or more: 13.3%; Poverty rate: 20.6%
Educational Attainment: High school diploma or higher: 87.7%; Bachelor's degree or higher: 20.8%; Graduate/professional degree or higher: 5.8%

School District(s)

Mcdonald Local (PK-12)
2012-13 Enrollment: 859. . . . . (330) 530-8051
Housing: Homeownership rate: 84.9%; Median home value: $101,200; Median year structure built: 1957; Homeowner vacancy rate: 2.5%; Median gross rent: $729 per month; Rental vacancy rate: 11.7%
Health Insurance: 90.0% have insurance; 72.4% have private insurance; 34.1% have public insurance; 10.0% do not have insurance; 8.6% of children under 18 do not have insurance
Transportation: Commute: 98.7% car, 0.5% public transportation, 0.0% walk, 0.8% work from home; Median travel time to work: 21.3 minutes

MCKINLEY HEIGHTS (CDP). Covers a land area of 0.871 square miles and a water area of <.001 square miles. Located at 41.19° N. Lat; 80.72° W. Long. Elevation is 991 feet.
Population: 1,060; Growth (since 2000): n/a; Density: 1,216.5 persons per square mile; Race: 97.4% White, 1.2% Black/African American, 0.7% Asian, 0.3% American Indian/Alaska Native, 0.0% Native Hawaiian/Other Pacific Islander, 0.5% Two or more races, 0.3% Hispanic of any race; Average household size: 2.44; Median age: 42.4; Age under 18: 23.2%; Age 65 and over: 15.3%; Males per 100 females: 101.1
Housing: Homeownership rate: 79.3%; Homeowner vacancy rate: 2.0%; Rental vacancy rate: 51.3%

MESOPOTAMIA (unincorporated postal area)
ZCTA: 44439
Covers a land area of 0.174 square miles and a water area of 0 square miles. Located at 41.46° N. Lat; 80.96° W. Long. Elevation is 856 feet.
Population: 115; Growth (since 2000): n/a; Density: 659.1 persons per square mile; Race: 97.4% White, 0.0% Black/African American, 0.0% Asian, 2.6% American Indian/Alaska Native, 0.0% Native Hawaiian/Other Pacific Islander, 0.0% Two or more races, 0.0% Hispanic of any race; Average household size: 3.11; Median age: 31.3; Age under 18: 30.4%; Age 65 and over: 10.4%; Males per 100 females: 101.8
Housing: Homeownership rate: 64.8%; Homeowner vacancy rate: 0.0%; Rental vacancy rate: 0.0%

MINERAL RIDGE (CDP). Covers a land area of 3.263 square miles and a water area of 0.017 square miles. Located at 41.14° N. Lat; 80.77° W. Long. Elevation is 1,004 feet.
Population: 3,892; Growth (since 2000): -0.2%; Density: 1,192.9 persons per square mile; Race: 95.3% White, 2.5% Black/African American, 0.1% Asian, 0.1% American Indian/Alaska Native, 0.0% Native Hawaiian/Other Pacific Islander, 1.5% Two or more races, 2.3% Hispanic of any race; Average household size: 2.44; Median age: 43.0; Age under 18: 20.9%; Age 65 and over: 16.5%; Males per 100 females: 95.4; Marriage status: 32.3% never married, 47.6% now married, 0.6% separated, 5.6% widowed, 14.5% divorced; Foreign born: 0.8%; Speak English only: 96.1%; With disability: 16.7%; Veterans: 13.7%; Ancestry: 23.7% American, 18.5% Irish, 18.1% Italian, 17.5% German, 8.5% English
Employment: 8.0% management, business, and financial, 4.2% computer, engineering, and science, 9.8% education, legal, community service, arts, and media, 10.6% healthcare practitioners, 13.5% service, 28.0% sales and office, 9.9% natural resources, construction, and maintenance, 16.0% production, transportation, and material moving
Income: Per capita: $25,347; Median household: $53,997; Average household: $64,304; Households with income of $100,000 or more: 19.6%; Poverty rate: 13.1%
Educational Attainment: High school diploma or higher: 85.0%; Bachelor's degree or higher: 21.2%; Graduate/professional degree or higher: 5.4%

School District(s)

Weathersfield Local (PK-12)
2012-13 Enrollment: 914. . . . . (330) 652-0287
Housing: Homeownership rate: 74.0%; Median home value: $111,000; Median year structure built: 1972; Homeowner vacancy rate: 1.3%; Median gross rent: $503 per month; Rental vacancy rate: 8.3%
Health Insurance: 93.6% have insurance; 74.1% have private insurance; 30.4% have public insurance; 6.4% do not have insurance; 10.1% of children under 18 do not have insurance
Transportation: Commute: 92.9% car, 6.1% public transportation, 0.5% walk, 0.5% work from home; Median travel time to work: 22.3 minutes

MORGANDALE (CDP). Covers a land area of 2.658 square miles and a water area of 0 square miles. Located at 41.27° N. Lat; 80.80° W. Long. Elevation is 925 feet.
Population: 1,224; Growth (since 2000): n/a; Density: 460.6 persons per square mile; Race: 94.1% White, 2.5% Black/African American, 0.5% Asian, 0.2% American Indian/Alaska Native, 0.0% Native Hawaiian/Other Pacific Islander, 1.7% Two or more races, 1.7% Hispanic of any race; Average household size: 2.24; Median age: 42.8; Age under 18: 20.7%; Age 65 and over: 15.8%; Males per 100 females: 102.3
Housing: Homeownership rate: 70.0%; Homeowner vacancy rate: 3.0%; Rental vacancy rate: 13.7%

NEWTON FALLS (village). Covers a land area of 2.307 square miles and a water area of 0.082 square miles. Located at 41.19° N. Lat; 80.97° W. Long. Elevation is 928 feet.
Population: 4,795; Growth (since 2000): -4.1%; Density: 2,078.4 persons per square mile; Race: 97.6% White, 0.8% Black/African American, 0.1% Asian, 0.1% American Indian/Alaska Native, 0.0% Native Hawaiian/Other Pacific Islander, 1.2% Two or more races, 1.1% Hispanic of any race; Average household size: 2.30; Median age: 40.0; Age under 18: 23.4%;

Age 65 and over: 17.1%; Males per 100 females: 90.4; Marriage status: 28.7% never married, 49.6% now married, 2.7% separated, 9.2% widowed, 12.5% divorced; Foreign born: 2.1%; Speak English only: 97.9%; With disability: 12.7%; Veterans: 12.5%; Ancestry: 21.9% American, 21.9% German, 13.2% English, 11.7% Irish, 8.4% Polish
Employment: 5.2% management, business, and financial, 0.0% computer, engineering, and science, 6.9% education, legal, community service, arts, and media, 6.1% healthcare practitioners, 12.3% service, 27.0% sales and office, 9.5% natural resources, construction, and maintenance, 33.1% production, transportation, and material moving
Income: Per capita: $20,584; Median household: $35,434; Average household: $45,243; Households with income of $100,000 or more: 8.0%; Poverty rate: 22.4%
Educational Attainment: High school diploma or higher: 85.6%; Bachelor's degree or higher: 8.8%; Graduate/professional degree or higher: 5.2%

School District(s)

Newton Falls Exempted Village (PK-12)
2012-13 Enrollment: 1,270 . . . . (330) 872-5445
Housing: Homeownership rate: 54.3%; Median home value: $86,000; Median year structure built: 1955; Homeowner vacancy rate: 3.0%; Median gross rent: $670 per month; Rental vacancy rate: 15.5%
Health Insurance: 87.5% have insurance; 67.7% have private insurance; 35.6% have public insurance; 12.5% do not have insurance; 0.0% of children under 18 do not have insurance
Transportation: Commute: 97.0% car, 1.0% public transportation, 0.7% walk, 1.3% work from home; Median travel time to work: 26.2 minutes

---

NILES (city). Covers a land area of 8.611 square miles and a water area of 0.019 square miles. Located at 41.19° N. Lat; 80.75° W. Long. Elevation is 883 feet.
History: Niles was settled in 1806 by James Heaton, who built a gristmill and blast furnace in the area. It was known as Heaton's Furnace until 1834, when the name was changed to Nilestown for a Baltimore newspaper editor whom Heaton admired. The post office later shortened the name. William McKinley, the 25th president of the United States, was born in Niles in 1843.
Population: 19,266; Growth (since 2000): -8.0%; Density: 2,237.3 persons per square mile; Race: 93.1% White, 3.5% Black/African American, 0.7% Asian, 0.2% American Indian/Alaska Native, 0.0% Native Hawaiian/Other Pacific Islander, 2.2% Two or more races, 1.3% Hispanic of any race; Average household size: 2.24; Median age: 42.0; Age under 18: 20.7%; Age 65 and over: 17.8%; Males per 100 females: 90.9; Marriage status: 30.0% never married, 43.7% now married, 2.3% separated, 10.1% widowed, 16.3% divorced; Foreign born: 1.4%; Speak English only: 96.3%; With disability: 17.9%; Veterans: 10.6%; Ancestry: 20.8% Italian, 20.0% German, 19.6% American, 15.4% Irish, 8.2% English
Employment: 7.0% management, business, and financial, 1.5% computer, engineering, and science, 5.6% education, legal, community service, arts, and media, 8.7% healthcare practitioners, 23.2% service, 25.2% sales and office, 9.6% natural resources, construction, and maintenance, 19.2% production, transportation, and material moving
Income: Per capita: $20,507; Median household: $37,169; Average household: $46,184; Households with income of $100,000 or more: 8.0%; Poverty rate: 19.4%
Educational Attainment: High school diploma or higher: 85.9%; Bachelor's degree or higher: 15.8%; Graduate/professional degree or higher: 4.6%

School District(s)

Niles City (PK-12)
2012-13 Enrollment: 2,485 . . . . (330) 652-2509

Two-year College(s)

ETI Technical College (Private, For-profit)
Fall 2013 Enrollment: 161 . . . . (330) 652-9919
2013-14 Tuition: In-state $9,352; Out-of-state $9,352
Raphael's School of Beauty Culture Inc-Niles (Private, For-profit)
Fall 2013 Enrollment: 145 . . . . (330) 652-1559

Vocational/Technical School(s)

Ross Medical Education Center-Niles (Private, For-profit)
Fall 2013 Enrollment: 151 . . . . (330) 505-1436
2013-14 Tuition: $15,680
Housing: Homeownership rate: 60.0%; Median home value: $81,600; Median year structure built: 1956; Homeowner vacancy rate: 3.1%; Median gross rent: $608 per month; Rental vacancy rate: 10.5%
Health Insurance: 83.5% have insurance; 60.6% have private insurance; 38.2% have public insurance; 16.5% do not have insurance; 12.6% of children under 18 do not have insurance
Safety: Violent crime rate: 26.9 per 10,000 population; Property crime rate: 493.9 per 10,000 population
Newspapers: The Review Newspapers (weekly circulation 3000)
Transportation: Commute: 96.6% car, 0.6% public transportation, 1.0% walk, 1.1% work from home; Median travel time to work: 17.1 minutes
Additional Information Contacts
City of Niles . . . . (330) 544-9000
http://www.thecityofniles.com

NORTH BLOOMFIELD (unincorporated postal area)
ZCTA: 44450
Covers a land area of 45.710 square miles and a water area of 1.533 square miles. Located at 41.45° N. Lat; 80.83° W. Long. Elevation is 896 feet.
Population: 2,042; Growth (since 2000): -3.5%; Density: 44.7 persons per square mile; Race: 95.2% White, 3.4% Black/African American, 0.1% Asian, 0.2% American Indian/Alaska Native, 0.0% Native Hawaiian/Other Pacific Islander, 0.9% Two or more races, 0.9% Hispanic of any race; Average household size: 2.79; Median age: 38.1; Age under 18: 27.6%; Age 65 and over: 12.9%; Males per 100 females: 104.8

School District(s)

Bloomfield-Mespo Local (PK-12)
2012-13 Enrollment: 286. . . . . (440) 685-4752
Maplewood Local (PK-12)
2012-13 Enrollment: 807. . . . . (330) 637-7506
Housing: Homeownership rate: 74.8%; Homeowner vacancy rate: 0.9%; Rental vacancy rate: 4.6%

ORANGEVILLE (village). Covers a land area of 0.836 square miles and a water area of 0.322 square miles. Located at 41.35° N. Lat; 80.53° W. Long. Elevation is 919 feet.
Population: 197; Growth (since 2000): 4.2%; Density: 235.6 persons per square mile; Race: 95.4% White, 1.0% Black/African American, 0.5% Asian, 0.0% American Indian/Alaska Native, 0.0% Native Hawaiian/Other Pacific Islander, 1.0% Two or more races, 1.0% Hispanic of any race; Average household size: 2.63; Median age: 38.4; Age under 18: 26.9%; Age 65 and over: 15.2%; Males per 100 females: 111.8
Housing: Homeownership rate: 80.0%; Homeowner vacancy rate: 3.1%; Rental vacancy rate: 11.8%

SOUTH CANAL (CDP). Covers a land area of 1.705 square miles and a water area of 0.036 square miles. Located at 41.18° N. Lat; 80.99° W. Long. Elevation is 935 feet.
Population: 1,100; Growth (since 2000): -18.3%; Density: 645.2 persons per square mile; Race: 97.6% White, 0.4% Black/African American, 0.1% Asian, 0.0% American Indian/Alaska Native, 0.1% Native Hawaiian/Other Pacific Islander, 1.5% Two or more races, 0.6% Hispanic of any race; Average household size: 2.45; Median age: 47.3; Age under 18: 18.8%; Age 65 and over: 21.2%; Males per 100 females: 101.5
Housing: Homeownership rate: 90.0%; Homeowner vacancy rate: 1.2%; Rental vacancy rate: 5.8%

SOUTHINGTON (unincorporated postal area)
ZCTA: 44470
Covers a land area of 26.769 square miles and a water area of 0.030 square miles. Located at 41.30° N. Lat; 80.97° W. Long. Elevation is 892 feet.
Population: 3,790; Growth (since 2000): 6.6%; Density: 141.6 persons per square mile; Race: 98.1% White, 0.8% Black/African American, 0.2% Asian, 0.1% American Indian/Alaska Native, 0.0% Native Hawaiian/Other Pacific Islander, 0.6% Two or more races, 0.7% Hispanic of any race; Average household size: 2.63; Median age: 43.4; Age under 18: 22.8%; Age 65 and over: 16.0%; Males per 100 females: 101.6; Marriage status: 22.6% never married, 62.3% now married, 0.4% separated, 8.1% widowed, 7.0% divorced; Foreign born: 0.5%; Speak English only: 96.2%; With disability: 14.9%; Veterans: 14.1%; Ancestry: 20.0% German, 18.2% American, 15.2% English, 11.0% Irish, 6.5% Polish
Employment: 5.1% management, business, and financial, 2.8% computer, engineering, and science, 6.0% education, legal, community service, arts, and media, 8.8% healthcare practitioners, 8.9% service, 26.8% sales and office, 17.2% natural resources, construction, and maintenance, 24.4% production, transportation, and material moving

Income: Per capita: $23,795; Median household: $51,815; Average household: $58,334; Households with income of $100,000 or more: 11.5%; Poverty rate: 7.8%
Educational Attainment: High school diploma or higher: 89.8%; Bachelor's degree or higher: 13.1%; Graduate/professional degree or higher: 1.6%

School District(s)

Southington Local (PK-12)
2012-13 Enrollment: 554. . . . . (330) 898-7480
Housing: Homeownership rate: 89.9%; Median home value: $142,500; Median year structure built: 1970; Homeowner vacancy rate: 3.4%; Median gross rent: $912 per month; Rental vacancy rate: 10.4%
Health Insurance: 88.2% have insurance; 77.8% have private insurance; 27.0% have public insurance; 11.8% do not have insurance; 1.0% of children under 18 do not have insurance
Transportation: Commute: 93.5% car, 1.8% public transportation, 0.8% walk, 2.8% work from home; Median travel time to work: 27.2 minutes

VIENNA CENTER (CDP). Covers a land area of 0.957 square miles and a water area of 0 square miles. Located at 41.23° N. Lat; 80.65° W. Long. Elevation is 1,148 feet.
Population: 650; Growth (since 2000): -34.6%; Density: 679.4 persons per square mile; Race: 97.7% White, 0.8% Black/African American, 0.0% Asian, 0.0% American Indian/Alaska Native, 0.0% Native Hawaiian/Other Pacific Islander, 1.5% Two or more races, 0.5% Hispanic of any race; Average household size: 2.36; Median age: 48.4; Age under 18: 17.2%; Age 65 and over: 20.5%; Males per 100 females: 98.8

School District(s)

Mathews Local (PK-12)
2012-13 Enrollment: 790. . . . . (330) 394-1800
Housing: Homeownership rate: 82.2%; Homeowner vacancy rate: 0.9%; Rental vacancy rate: 0.0%

WARREN (city). County seat. Covers a land area of 16.127 square miles and a water area of 0.028 square miles. Located at 41.24° N. Lat; 80.82° W. Long. Elevation is 886 feet.
History: Warren was settled in 1798 when Ephraim Quinby and Richard Storr of the Connecticut Land Company came from Pennsylvania. In 1800 the settlement was made the seat of the newly formed Trumbull County. Warren, named for a surveyor, grew slowly, and was incorporated as a village in 1834. The opening of the canal brought a shipping industry, and manufacturing developed. In 1899 J. Ward Packard made the first Packard automobiles in Warren, as well as founding the forerunner of the Peerless Electric Company and other lamp manufacturing companies.
Population: 41,557; Growth (since 2000): -11.3%; Density: 2,576.8 persons per square mile; Race: 67.7% White, 27.7% Black/African American, 0.4% Asian, 0.2% American Indian/Alaska Native, 0.0% Native Hawaiian/Other Pacific Islander, 3.3% Two or more races, 1.9% Hispanic of any race; Average household size: 2.30; Median age: 38.3; Age under 18: 23.7%; Age 65 and over: 16.0%; Males per 100 females: 92.6; Marriage status: 37.1% never married, 38.3% now married, 3.0% separated, 9.2% widowed, 15.4% divorced; Foreign born: 1.7%; Speak English only: 95.7%; With disability: 16.7%; Veterans: 10.4%; Ancestry: 17.0% American, 12.9% German, 10.3% Irish, 8.0% Italian, 5.6% English
Employment: 8.0% management, business, and financial, 1.9% computer, engineering, and science, 7.1% education, legal, community service, arts, and media, 6.1% healthcare practitioners, 25.9% service, 24.9% sales and office, 7.6% natural resources, construction, and maintenance, 18.7% production, transportation, and material moving
Income: Per capita: $16,939; Median household: $29,317; Average household: $39,453; Households with income of $100,000 or more: 6.4%; Poverty rate: 32.3%
Educational Attainment: High school diploma or higher: 83.2%; Bachelor's degree or higher: 12.1%; Graduate/professional degree or higher: 3.5%

School District(s)

Champion Local (PK-12)
2012-13 Enrollment: 1,482 . . . . (330) 847-2330
Howland Local (PK-12)
2012-13 Enrollment: 2,971 . . . . (330) 856-8200
Lakeview Local (PK-12)
2012-13 Enrollment: 1,795 . . . . (330) 637-8741
Life Skills of Trumbull County (09-12)
2012-13 Enrollment: 220. . . . . (330) 392-0231
Lordstown Local (PK-12)
2012-13 Enrollment: 490. . . . . (330) 824-2534
Steam Academy of Warren (KG-06)
2012-13 Enrollment: 149. . . . . (330) 394-3200
Summit Academy Community School-Warren (KG-06)
2012-13 Enrollment: 101. . . . . (330) 369-4233
Summit Academy Warren Middle & Secondary (07-12)
2012-13 Enrollment: 96. . . . . (330) 399-1692
Trumbull Career & Tech Ctr (08-12)
2012-13 Enrollment: n/a . . . . (330) 847-0503
Warren City (PK-12)
2012-13 Enrollment: 5,169 . . . . (330) 841-2321

Four-year College(s)

Kent State University at Trumbull (Public)
Fall 2013 Enrollment: 3,087 . . . . (330) 847-0571
2013-14 Tuition: In-state $5,554; Out-of-state $13,514

Two-year College(s)

Trumbull Business College (Private, For-profit)
Fall 2013 Enrollment: 240. . . . . (330) 369-3200
2013-14 Tuition: In-state $12,389; Out-of-state $12,389

Vocational/Technical School(s)

Trumbull Career & Technical Center (Public)
Fall 2013 Enrollment: 230. . . . . (330) 847-0503
2013-14 Tuition: $10,356
Housing: Homeownership rate: 56.6%; Median home value: $65,600; Median year structure built: 1955; Homeowner vacancy rate: 4.0%; Median gross rent: $596 per month; Rental vacancy rate: 13.3%
Health Insurance: 86.9% have insurance; 50.0% have private insurance; 49.4% have public insurance; 13.1% do not have insurance; 2.3% of children under 18 do not have insurance
Hospitals: Saint Joseph Health Center (165 beds); Trumbull Memorial Hospital (350 beds)
Safety: Violent crime rate: 65.0 per 10,000 population; Property crime rate: 472.2 per 10,000 population
Newspapers: Tribune Chronicle (daily circulation 30600)
Transportation: Commute: 93.7% car, 0.9% public transportation, 1.2% walk, 2.8% work from home; Median travel time to work: 19.5 minutes
Additional Information Contacts
City of Warren . . . . (330) 841-2601
http://www.warren.org

WEST FARMINGTON (village). Covers a land area of 0.878 square miles and a water area of 0 square miles. Located at 41.39° N. Lat; 80.97° W. Long. Elevation is 869 feet.
Population: 499; Growth (since 2000): -3.9%; Density: 568.1 persons per square mile; Race: 98.8% White, 0.0% Black/African American, 0.0% Asian, 0.4% American Indian/Alaska Native, 0.0% Native Hawaiian/Other Pacific Islander, 0.8% Two or more races, 0.2% Hispanic of any race; Average household size: 2.92; Median age: 32.3; Age under 18: 29.9%; Age 65 and over: 9.6%; Males per 100 females: 107.1
Housing: Homeownership rate: 69.0%; Homeowner vacancy rate: 5.5%; Rental vacancy rate: 8.5%

WEST HILL (CDP). Covers a land area of 1.577 square miles and a water area of 0 square miles. Located at 41.23° N. Lat; 80.53° W. Long. Elevation is 1,043 feet.
Population: 2,273; Growth (since 2000): -9.9%; Density: 1,441.5 persons per square mile; Race: 86.1% White, 9.4% Black/African American, 0.1% Asian, 0.0% American Indian/Alaska Native, 0.0% Native Hawaiian/Other Pacific Islander, 4.1% Two or more races, 1.2% Hispanic of any race; Average household size: 2.30; Median age: 42.7; Age under 18: 22.6%; Age 65 and over: 19.0%; Males per 100 females: 95.3
Housing: Homeownership rate: 57.9%; Homeowner vacancy rate: 3.0%; Rental vacancy rate: 14.7%

YANKEE LAKE (village). Covers a land area of 0.508 square miles and a water area of 0 square miles. Located at 41.27° N. Lat; 80.57° W. Long. Elevation is 1,007 feet.
Population: 79; Growth (since 2000): -20.2%; Density: 155.6 persons per square mile; Race: 98.7% White, 0.0% Black/African American, 0.0% Asian, 0.0% American Indian/Alaska Native, 0.0% Native Hawaiian/Other Pacific Islander, 0.0% Two or more races, 1.3% Hispanic of any race; Average household size: 2.55; Median age: 50.3; Age under 18: 15.2%; Age 65 and over: 17.7%; Males per 100 females: 88.1

Housing: Homeownership rate: 83.8%; Homeowner vacancy rate: 0.0%; Rental vacancy rate: 16.7%

Tuscarawas County

Located in eastern Ohio; crossed by the Tuscarawas River. Covers a land area of 567.636 square miles, a water area of 3.815 square miles, and is located in the Eastern Time Zone at 40.45° N. Lat., 81.47° W. Long. The county was founded in 1808. County seat is New Philadelphia.

Tuscarawas County is part of the New Philadelphia-Dover, OH Micropolitan Statistical Area. The entire metro area includes: Tuscarawas County, OH

Population: 92,582; Growth (since 2000): 1.8%; Density: 163.1 persons per square mile; Race: 96.6% White, 0.8% Black/African American, 0.3% Asian, 0.3% American Indian/Alaska Native, 0.2% Native Hawaiian/Other Pacific Islander, 1.2% two or more races, 1.9% Hispanic of any race; Average household size: 2.47; Median age: 40.9; Age under 18: 23.7%; Age 65 and over: 16.4%; Males per 100 females: 96.6; Marriage status: 22.9% never married, 57.5% now married, 1.6% separated, 7.4% widowed, 12.1% divorced; Foreign born: 1.3%; Speak English only: 94.4%; With disability: 12.9%; Veterans: 10.9%; Ancestry: 34.2% German, 14.5% Irish, 9.8% English, 9.1% American, 8.0% Italian
Religion: Six largest groups: 10.8% Methodist/Pietist, 9.5% Catholicism, 6.7% Holiness, 5.5% Presbyterian-Reformed, 3.8% Lutheran, 3.5% European Free-Church
Economy: Unemployment rate: 4.0%; Leading industries: 16.8% retail trade; 14.6% other services (except public administration); 9.8% manufacturing; Farms: 1,014 totaling 138,083 acres; Company size: 0 employ 1,000 or more persons, 2 employ 500 to 999 persons, 45 employ 100 to 499 persons, 2,106 employ less than 100 persons; Business ownership: 1,526 women-owned, n/a Black-owned, n/a Hispanic-owned, n/a Asian-owned
Employment: 9.7% management, business, and financial, 3.0% computer, engineering, and science, 7.9% education, legal, community service, arts, and media, 6.2% healthcare practitioners, 18.4% service, 22.3% sales and office, 9.6% natural resources, construction, and maintenance, 23.0% production, transportation, and material moving
Income: Per capita: $21,966; Median household: $43,739; Average household: $54,561; Households with income of $100,000 or more: 11.6%; Poverty rate: 14.6%
Educational Attainment: High school diploma or higher: 86.7%; Bachelor's degree or higher: 15.2%; Graduate/professional degree or higher: 5.3%
Housing: Homeownership rate: 72.2%; Median home value: $108,700; Median year structure built: 1965; Homeowner vacancy rate: 1.8%; Median gross rent: $622 per month; Rental vacancy rate: 8.7%
Vital Statistics: Birth rate: 114.6 per 10,000 population; Death rate: 102.9 per 10,000 population; Age-adjusted cancer mortality rate: 164.6 deaths per 100,000 population
Health Insurance: 87.3% have insurance; 68.7% have private insurance; 32.7% have public insurance; 12.7% do not have insurance; 7.6% of children under 18 do not have insurance
Health Care: Physicians: 10.9 per 10,000 population; Hospital beds: 21.1 per 10,000 population; Hospital admissions: 722.3 per 10,000 population
Transportation: Commute: 92.7% car, 0.2% public transportation, 1.8% walk, 3.4% work from home; Median travel time to work: 20.7 minutes
Presidential Election: 43.9% Obama, 53.7% Romney (2012)
National and State Parks: Fort Laurens State Memorial
Additional Information Contacts
Tuscarawas Government . . . . (330) 364-8811
http://www.co.tuscarawas.oh.us

Tuscarawas County Communities

BALTIC (village). Covers a land area of 0.803 square miles and a water area of 0 square miles. Located at 40.44° N. Lat; 81.70° W. Long. Elevation is 1,060 feet.
Population: 795; Growth (since 2000): 7.0%; Density: 990.3 persons per square mile; Race: 98.5% White, 0.6% Black/African American, 0.1% Asian, 0.0% American Indian/Alaska Native, 0.0% Native Hawaiian/Other Pacific Islander, 0.8% Two or more races, 0.3% Hispanic of any race; Average household size: 2.53; Median age: 40.9; Age under 18: 25.2%; Age 65 and over: 21.4%; Males per 100 females: 100.3

School District(s)
Garaway Local (PK-12)
2012-13 Enrollment: 1,196 . . . . (330) 852-2421
Housing: Homeownership rate: 74.4%; Homeowner vacancy rate: 1.9%; Rental vacancy rate: 13.1%

BARNHILL (village). Covers a land area of 0.362 square miles and a water area of 0 square miles. Located at 40.45° N. Lat; 81.37° W. Long. Elevation is 879 feet.
Population: 396; Growth (since 2000): 8.8%; Density: 1,093.6 persons per square mile; Race: 98.2% White, 0.8% Black/African American, 0.0% Asian, 0.5% American Indian/Alaska Native, 0.0% Native Hawaiian/Other Pacific Islander, 0.5% Two or more races, 1.5% Hispanic of any race; Average household size: 2.71; Median age: 36.8; Age under 18: 27.5%; Age 65 and over: 12.1%; Males per 100 females: 101.0
Housing: Homeownership rate: 80.8%; Homeowner vacancy rate: 0.8%; Rental vacancy rate: 6.7%

BOLIVAR (village). Covers a land area of 0.694 square miles and a water area of 0.006 square miles. Located at 40.65° N. Lat; 81.46° W. Long. Elevation is 928 feet.
History: Bolivar was an important grain market during the boom days of the Ohio & Erie and the Sandy & Beaver Canals. Near Bolivar was the site of the cabin built in 1761 by Christian Frederick Post, a Moravian missionary.
Population: 994; Growth (since 2000): 11.2%; Density: 1,431.8 persons per square mile; Race: 98.8% White, 0.1% Black/African American, 0.2% Asian, 0.4% American Indian/Alaska Native, 0.0% Native Hawaiian/Other Pacific Islander, 0.5% Two or more races, 0.7% Hispanic of any race; Average household size: 2.37; Median age: 45.9; Age under 18: 21.0%; Age 65 and over: 21.4%; Males per 100 females: 88.3

School District(s)
Tuscarawas Valley Local (PK-12)
2012-13 Enrollment: 1,449 . . . . (330) 859-2213
Housing: Homeownership rate: 83.4%; Homeowner vacancy rate: 0.9%; Rental vacancy rate: 6.0%

DENNISON (village). Covers a land area of 1.349 square miles and a water area of 0 square miles. Located at 40.40° N. Lat; 81.33° W. Long. Elevation is 863 feet.
History: The site of Dennison was selected in 1864 by the Pittsburgh, Columbus & St. Louis Railroad for its division shops. The town was named for William Dennison, a Civil War governor of Ohio.
Population: 2,655; Growth (since 2000): -11.3%; Density: 1,968.2 persons per square mile; Race: 96.8% White, 1.0% Black/African American, 0.2% Asian, 0.4% American Indian/Alaska Native, 0.0% Native Hawaiian/Other Pacific Islander, 1.4% Two or more races, 1.0% Hispanic of any race; Average household size: 2.54; Median age: 35.5; Age under 18: 26.6%; Age 65 and over: 12.2%; Males per 100 females: 95.2; Marriage status: 31.1% never married, 43.8% now married, 2.4% separated, 9.3% widowed, 15.8% divorced; Foreign born: 2.0%; Speak English only: 97.6%; With disability: 15.4%; Veterans: 8.8%; Ancestry: 30.6% German, 24.6% Irish, 7.3% American, 6.1% Italian, 5.8% English
Employment: 6.6% management, business, and financial, 3.7% computer, engineering, and science, 7.3% education, legal, community service, arts, and media, 5.1% healthcare practitioners, 28.8% service, 19.5% sales and office, 5.4% natural resources, construction, and maintenance, 23.7% production, transportation, and material moving
Income: Per capita: $16,164; Median household: $32,604; Average household: $40,842; Households with income of $100,000 or more: 4.7%; Poverty rate: 24.6%
Educational Attainment: High school diploma or higher: 84.9%; Bachelor's degree or higher: 9.8%; Graduate/professional degree or higher: 1.7%

School District(s)
Claymont City (PK-12)
2012-13 Enrollment: 2,113 . . . . (740) 922-5478
Housing: Homeownership rate: 61.6%; Median home value: $66,400; Median year structure built: Before 1940; Homeowner vacancy rate: 2.0%; Median gross rent: $610 per month; Rental vacancy rate: 12.7%
Health Insurance: 88.4% have insurance; 54.9% have private insurance; 46.5% have public insurance; 11.6% do not have insurance; 0.0% of children under 18 do not have insurance
Hospitals: Trinity Hospital Twin City (25 beds)

Transportation: Commute: 93.9% car, 1.1% public transportation, 1.0% walk, 2.2% work from home; Median travel time to work: 21.2 minutes

DOVER (city). Covers a land area of 5.685 square miles and a water area of 0.103 square miles. Located at 40.53° N. Lat; 81.48° W. Long. Elevation is 892 feet.

History: Dover was laid out in 1807 on land owned by Jesse Slingluff and Christian Deardorff, and settled by German immigrants from Pennsylvania. For a time it was known as Canal Dover, and was the collector's port for the Ohio & Erie Canal in Tuscarawas County.

Population: 12,826; Growth (since 2000): 5.0%; Density: 2,256.2 persons per square mile; Race: 94.1% White, 1.1% Black/African American, 0.5% Asian, 0.6% American Indian/Alaska Native, 0.7% Native Hawaiian/Other Pacific Islander, 1.4% Two or more races, 4.1% Hispanic of any race; Average household size: 2.37; Median age: 42.9; Age under 18: 22.3%; Age 65 and over: 22.0%; Males per 100 females: 90.3; Marriage status: 20.6% never married, 54.8% now married, 1.8% separated, 9.1% widowed, 15.5% divorced; Foreign born: 3.1%; Speak English only: 94.4%; With disability: 13.1%; Veterans: 13.1%; Ancestry: 36.8% German, 14.2% Irish, 9.8% Italian, 8.5% American, 8.1% English

Employment: 10.9% management, business, and financial, 3.1% computer, engineering, and science, 10.5% education, legal, community service, arts, and media, 8.5% healthcare practitioners, 16.4% service, 25.8% sales and office, 6.6% natural resources, construction, and maintenance, 18.2% production, transportation, and material moving

Income: Per capita: $23,055; Median household: $41,732; Average household: $55,034; Households with income of $100,000 or more: 11.8%; Poverty rate: 13.9%

Educational Attainment: High school diploma or higher: 91.0%; Bachelor's degree or higher: 23.4%; Graduate/professional degree or higher: 8.0%

School District(s)

Dover City (PK-12)
2012-13 Enrollment: 2,735 . . . . (330) 364-1906

Housing: Homeownership rate: 69.4%; Median home value: $111,700; Median year structure built: 1956; Homeowner vacancy rate: 1.9%; Median gross rent: $629 per month; Rental vacancy rate: 10.5%

Health Insurance: 85.9% have insurance; 71.7% have private insurance; 30.7% have public insurance; 14.1% do not have insurance; 2.8% of children under 18 do not have insurance

Hospitals: Union Hospital (105 beds)

Safety: Violent crime rate: 10.9 per 10,000 population; Property crime rate: 45.4 per 10,000 population

Transportation: Commute: 93.3% car, 0.0% public transportation, 1.9% walk, 4.1% work from home; Median travel time to work: 19.6 minutes

Additional Information Contacts

City of Dover . . . . (330) 343-6726
http://www.doverohio.com

DUNDEE (CDP). Covers a land area of 0.779 square miles and a water area of 0 square miles. Located at 40.59° N. Lat; 81.61° W. Long. Elevation is 1,030 feet.

Population: 297; Growth (since 2000): n/a; Density: 381.3 persons per square mile; Race: 99.3% White, 0.0% Black/African American, 0.0% Asian, 0.3% American Indian/Alaska Native, 0.0% Native Hawaiian/Other Pacific Islander, 0.3% Two or more races, 0.3% Hispanic of any race; Average household size: 2.56; Median age: 38.9; Age under 18: 22.9%; Age 65 and over: 8.8%; Males per 100 females: 98.0

School District(s)

Beacon Hill Academy (07-10)
2012-13 Enrollment: 68. . . . . (614) 995-1985

Garaway Local (PK-12)
2012-13 Enrollment: 1,196 . . . . (330) 852-2421

Housing: Homeownership rate: 69.8%; Homeowner vacancy rate: 0.0%; Rental vacancy rate: 2.8%

GNADENHUTTEN (village). Covers a land area of 0.966 square miles and a water area of <.001 square miles. Located at 40.36° N. Lat; 81.43° W. Long. Elevation is 850 feet.

History: The name of Gnadenhutten is of German origin, meaning "tents of grace." A community was established here in 1772 by Joshua, a Mohican elder of a group of Indians from the Moravian mission founded by David Zeisberger at Schoenbrunn. The group was massacred by militiamen from Pennsylvania in 1782.

Population: 1,288; Growth (since 2000): 0.6%; Density: 1,333.6 persons per square mile; Race: 99.1% White, 0.0% Black/African American, 0.0% Asian, 0.0% American Indian/Alaska Native, 0.0% Native Hawaiian/Other Pacific Islander, 0.7% Two or more races, 0.5% Hispanic of any race; Average household size: 2.52; Median age: 39.3; Age under 18: 25.6%; Age 65 and over: 17.4%; Males per 100 females: 98.2

School District(s)

Indian Valley Local Schools (PK-12)
2012-13 Enrollment: 1,774 . . . . (740) 254-4334

Housing: Homeownership rate: 80.3%; Homeowner vacancy rate: 1.4%; Rental vacancy rate: 10.7%

MIDVALE (village). Covers a land area of 0.759 square miles and a water area of 0 square miles. Located at 40.44° N. Lat; 81.37° W. Long. Elevation is 856 feet.

Population: 754; Growth (since 2000): 37.8%; Density: 993.1 persons per square mile; Race: 98.0% White, 0.8% Black/African American, 0.0% Asian, 0.0% American Indian/Alaska Native, 0.0% Native Hawaiian/Other Pacific Islander, 0.8% Two or more races, 1.2% Hispanic of any race; Average household size: 2.70; Median age: 33.7; Age under 18: 29.0%; Age 65 and over: 10.7%; Males per 100 females: 98.9

School District(s)

Indian Valley Local Schools (PK-12)
2012-13 Enrollment: 1,774 . . . . (740) 254-4334

Housing: Homeownership rate: 71.7%; Homeowner vacancy rate: 1.0%; Rental vacancy rate: 5.9%

MINERAL CITY (village). Covers a land area of 0.818 square miles and a water area of 0 square miles. Located at 40.60° N. Lat; 81.36° W. Long. Elevation is 951 feet.

Population: 727; Growth (since 2000): -13.6%; Density: 888.6 persons per square mile; Race: 95.5% White, 1.8% Black/African American, 1.0% Asian, 0.1% American Indian/Alaska Native, 0.1% Native Hawaiian/Other Pacific Islander, 1.5% Two or more races, 0.7% Hispanic of any race; Average household size: 2.62; Median age: 36.3; Age under 18: 27.2%; Age 65 and over: 8.9%; Males per 100 females: 92.3

School District(s)

Tuscarawas Valley Local (PK-12)
2012-13 Enrollment: 1,449 . . . . (330) 859-2213

Housing: Homeownership rate: 72.3%; Homeowner vacancy rate: 3.4%; Rental vacancy rate: 11.5%

NEW PHILADELPHIA (city). County seat. Covers a land area of 8.216 square miles and a water area of 0.170 square miles. Located at 40.49° N. Lat; 81.44° W. Long. Elevation is 902 feet.

History: New Philadelphia was founded in 1804 by John Knisely, and settled by many Swiss-German immigrants from Pennsylvania.

Population: 17,288; Growth (since 2000): 1.4%; Density: 2,104.2 persons per square mile; Race: 94.0% White, 1.2% Black/African American, 0.6% Asian, 0.4% American Indian/Alaska Native, 0.4% Native Hawaiian/Other Pacific Islander, 1.8% Two or more races, 4.2% Hispanic of any race; Average household size: 2.32; Median age: 40.4; Age under 18: 21.9%; Age 65 and over: 16.8%; Males per 100 females: 94.1; Marriage status: 27.9% never married, 52.4% now married, 2.1% separated, 6.1% widowed, 13.6% divorced; Foreign born: 1.2%; Speak English only: 96.3%; With disability: 13.3%; Veterans: 12.2%; Ancestry: 32.9% German, 15.3% Irish, 11.7% Italian, 9.7% English, 6.3% American

Employment: 11.5% management, business, and financial, 2.8% computer, engineering, and science, 8.4% education, legal, community service, arts, and media, 5.3% healthcare practitioners, 23.6% service, 23.2% sales and office, 5.4% natural resources, construction, and maintenance, 19.8% production, transportation, and material moving

Income: Per capita: $21,616; Median household: $39,905; Average household: $51,643; Households with income of $100,000 or more: 10.2%; Poverty rate: 18.3%

Educational Attainment: High school diploma or higher: 87.8%; Bachelor's degree or higher: 17.4%; Graduate/professional degree or higher: 6.8%

School District(s)

Buckeye (07-12)
2012-13 Enrollment: n/a . . . . (330) 339-2288

New Philadelphia City (PK-12)
2012-13 Enrollment: 2,954 . . . . (330) 364-0600

Quaker Digital Academy (KG-12)
2012-13 Enrollment: 576. . . . . (330) 364-0618

Four-year College(s)

Kent State University at Tuscarawas (Public)
Fall 2013 Enrollment: 2,408 . . . . (330) 339-3391
2013-14 Tuition: In-state $5,554; Out-of-state $13,514

Vocational/Technical School(s)

Buckeye Joint Vocational School (Public)
Fall 2013 Enrollment: 89 . . . . (330) 308-5720
2013-14 Tuition: $5,670

Housing: Homeownership rate: 63.5%; Median home value: $102,800; Median year structure built: 1962; Homeowner vacancy rate: 1.9%; Median gross rent: $634 per month; Rental vacancy rate: 11.0%

Health Insurance: 89.0% have insurance; 63.9% have private insurance; 37.6% have public insurance; 11.0% do not have insurance; 4.0% of children under 18 do not have insurance

Safety: Violent crime rate: 4.6 per 10,000 population; Property crime rate: 165.4 per 10,000 population

Newspapers: Times Reporter (daily circulation 19100)

Transportation: Commute: 92.9% car, 0.2% public transportation, 2.5% walk, 1.5% work from home; Median travel time to work: 17.4 minutes

Additional Information Contacts

City of New Philadelphia . . . . (330) 364-4491
http://www.newphilaoh.com

NEWCOMERSTOWN (village). Covers a land area of 2.843 square miles and a water area of 0.097 square miles. Located at 40.28° N. Lat; 81.60° W. Long. Elevation is 801 feet.

History: First called Neighbor Town when it was settled in 1815 by the Neighbor brothers from New Jersey, the town became Newcomerstown in remembrance of Chief Eagle Feather who was called "the newcomer."

Population: 3,822; Growth (since 2000): -4.6%; Density: 1,344.5 persons per square mile; Race: 95.6% White, 1.6% Black/African American, 0.3% Asian, 0.2% American Indian/Alaska Native, 0.0% Native Hawaiian/Other Pacific Islander, 1.8% Two or more races, 1.2% Hispanic of any race; Average household size: 2.35; Median age: 40.3; Age under 18: 24.1%; Age 65 and over: 17.6%; Males per 100 females: 90.1; Marriage status: 23.8% never married, 48.5% now married, 3.5% separated, 10.4% widowed, 17.3% divorced; Foreign born: 1.5%; Speak English only: 98.3%; With disability: 18.9%; Veterans: 8.1%; Ancestry: 23.0% German, 13.8% Irish, 12.8% American, 10.7% English, 6.2% Italian

Employment: 7.4% management, business, and financial, 0.0% computer, engineering, and science, 3.1% education, legal, community service, arts, and media, 6.0% healthcare practitioners, 14.1% service, 17.5% sales and office, 12.3% natural resources, construction, and maintenance, 39.5% production, transportation, and material moving

Income: Per capita: $15,224; Median household: $29,269; Average household: $37,276; Households with income of $100,000 or more: 1.9%; Poverty rate: 32.4%

Educational Attainment: High school diploma or higher: 82.4%; Bachelor's degree or higher: 5.7%; Graduate/professional degree or higher: 1.7%

School District(s)

Newcomerstown Exempted Village (PK-12)
2012-13 Enrollment: 1,050 . . . . (740) 498-8373

Housing: Homeownership rate: 61.2%; Median home value: $67,200; Median year structure built: 1944; Homeowner vacancy rate: 3.7%; Median gross rent: $601 per month; Rental vacancy rate: 5.5%

Health Insurance: 85.6% have insurance; 51.8% have private insurance; 51.8% have public insurance; 14.4% do not have insurance; 4.4% of children under 18 do not have insurance

Safety: Violent crime rate: 50.1 per 10,000 population; Property crime rate: 271.8 per 10,000 population

Newspapers: Newcomerstown News (weekly circulation 3500)

Transportation: Commute: 98.6% car, 0.0% public transportation, 0.0% walk, 0.0% work from home; Median travel time to work: 27.5 minutes

PARRAL (village). Covers a land area of 0.180 square miles and a water area of 0 square miles. Located at 40.56° N. Lat; 81.49° W. Long. Elevation is 906 feet.

Population: 218; Growth (since 2000): -9.5%; Density: 1,210.6 persons per square mile; Race: 95.0% White, 0.5% Black/African American, 0.0% Asian, 0.0% American Indian/Alaska Native, 0.0% Native Hawaiian/Other Pacific Islander, 2.8% Two or more races, 2.3% Hispanic of any race; Average household size: 2.18; Median age: 49.0; Age under 18: 17.4%; Age 65 and over: 19.7%; Males per 100 females: 107.6

Housing: Homeownership rate: 77.0%; Homeowner vacancy rate: 0.0%; Rental vacancy rate: 4.2%

PORT WASHINGTON (village). Covers a land area of 0.514 square miles and a water area of 0 square miles. Located at 40.33° N. Lat; 81.52° W. Long. Elevation is 814 feet.

History: Port Washington was once a shipping center on the Ohio & Erie Canal. Nearby was the settlement of Salem, established in 1780 for members of the Lichtenau community.

Population: 569; Growth (since 2000): 3.1%; Density: 1,106.8 persons per square mile; Race: 97.7% White, 0.0% Black/African American, 0.2% Asian, 0.0% American Indian/Alaska Native, 0.0% Native Hawaiian/Other Pacific Islander, 0.4% Two or more races, 1.8% Hispanic of any race; Average household size: 2.72; Median age: 39.1; Age under 18: 26.4%; Age 65 and over: 16.0%; Males per 100 females: 94.9

School District(s)

Indian Valley Local Schools (PK-12)
2012-13 Enrollment: 1,774 . . . . (740) 254-4334

Housing: Homeownership rate: 72.7%; Homeowner vacancy rate: 3.7%; Rental vacancy rate: 1.7%

ROSWELL (village). Covers a land area of 0.262 square miles and a water area of 0 square miles. Located at 40.48° N. Lat; 81.35° W. Long. Elevation is 948 feet.

Population: 219; Growth (since 2000): -20.7%; Density: 835.9 persons per square mile; Race: 98.6% White, 0.5% Black/African American, 0.0% Asian, 0.0% American Indian/Alaska Native, 0.0% Native Hawaiian/Other Pacific Islander, 0.5% Two or more races, 0.5% Hispanic of any race; Average household size: 2.58; Median age: 34.1; Age under 18: 28.3%; Age 65 and over: 9.1%; Males per 100 females: 90.4

Housing: Homeownership rate: 68.2%; Homeowner vacancy rate: 4.7%; Rental vacancy rate: 6.9%

SANDYVILLE (CDP). Covers a land area of 0.628 square miles and a water area of 0 square miles. Located at 40.65° N. Lat; 81.37° W. Long. Elevation is 965 feet.

Population: 368; Growth (since 2000): n/a; Density: 586.1 persons per square mile; Race: 97.3% White, 0.0% Black/African American, 0.0% Asian, 0.3% American Indian/Alaska Native, 0.0% Native Hawaiian/Other Pacific Islander, 0.5% Two or more races, 1.9% Hispanic of any race; Average household size: 2.36; Median age: 46.0; Age under 18: 18.5%; Age 65 and over: 18.8%; Males per 100 females: 95.7

Housing: Homeownership rate: 75.0%; Homeowner vacancy rate: 0.0%; Rental vacancy rate: 2.4%

SOMERDALE (unincorporated postal area)

ZCTA: 44678

Covers a land area of 0.931 square miles and a water area of 0 square miles. Located at 40.57° N. Lat; 81.35° W. Long. Elevation is 915 feet.

Population: 152; Growth (since 2000): -28.6%; Density: 163.2 persons per square mile; Race: 99.3% White, 0.0% Black/African American, 0.0% Asian, 0.0% American Indian/Alaska Native, 0.0% Native Hawaiian/Other Pacific Islander, 0.7% Two or more races, 0.0% Hispanic of any race; Average household size: 2.24; Median age: 45.0; Age under 18: 16.4%; Age 65 and over: 15.8%; Males per 100 females: 94.9

Housing: Homeownership rate: 86.8%; Homeowner vacancy rate: 3.3%; Rental vacancy rate: 10.0%

STONE CREEK (village). Covers a land area of 0.429 square miles and a water area of <.001 square miles. Located at 40.40° N. Lat; 81.56° W. Long. Elevation is 938 feet.

History: Stone Creek was laid out in 1854 by Phillip Leonard, and first called Phillipsburg. Settlers had come here as early as 1837 from Pennsylvania. The town grew around the iron ore mined in the area, and the clay used in brick plants. Early Swiss settlers also started a Swiss cheese industry.

Population: 177; Growth (since 2000): -3.8%; Density: 412.7 persons per square mile; Race: 97.7% White, 0.6% Black/African American, 0.0% Asian, 0.0% American Indian/Alaska Native, 0.0% Native Hawaiian/Other Pacific Islander, 1.1% Two or more races, 0.6% Hispanic of any race; Average household size: 2.72; Median age: 35.5; Age under 18: 24.3%; Age 65 and over: 13.0%; Males per 100 females: 113.3

Housing: Homeownership rate: 75.4%; Homeowner vacancy rate: 0.0%; Rental vacancy rate: 5.6%

STRASBURG (village). Covers a land area of 1.388 square miles and a water area of 0 square miles. Located at 40.60° N. Lat; 81.53° W. Long. Elevation is 912 feet.
History: Strasburg was notable as the location of the Garver Brothers Store, founded in 1866 by Phillip A. Garver. When his sons, Rudolph and Albert, took over the store in the 1880's, they made it the focal point of the community by keeping a card index record of every man, woman, and child living within 18 miles of Strasburg, and anticipating their needs.
Population: 2,608; Growth (since 2000): 12.9%; Density: 1,879.0 persons per square mile; Race: 97.5% White, 0.2% Black/African American, 0.4% Asian, 0.1% American Indian/Alaska Native, 0.6% Native Hawaiian/Other Pacific Islander, 0.3% Two or more races, 1.6% Hispanic of any race; Average household size: 2.33; Median age: 44.1; Age under 18: 20.3%; Age 65 and over: 19.7%; Males per 100 females: 94.8; Marriage status: 21.8% never married, 58.2% now married, 0.8% separated, 7.2% widowed, 12.8% divorced; Foreign born: 3.4%; Speak English only: 94.9%; With disability: 17.8%; Veterans: 11.7%; Ancestry: 36.3% German, 12.8% English, 12.0% Irish, 7.3% Italian, 5.5% Swiss
Employment: 7.3% management, business, and financial, 0.7% computer, engineering, and science, 10.4% education, legal, community service, arts, and media, 6.0% healthcare practitioners, 21.1% service, 25.0% sales and office, 7.4% natural resources, construction, and maintenance, 22.0% production, transportation, and material moving
Income: Per capita: $25,508; Median household: $50,038; Average household: $59,824; Households with income of $100,000 or more: 14.4%; Poverty rate: 10.9%
Educational Attainment: High school diploma or higher: 89.7%; Bachelor's degree or higher: 18.3%; Graduate/professional degree or higher: 6.2%

School District(s)

Strasburg-Franklin Local (PK-12)
2012-13 Enrollment: 603. . . . . (330) 878-5571
Housing: Homeownership rate: 61.6%; Median home value: $121,500; Median year structure built: 1969; Homeowner vacancy rate: 1.7%; Median gross rent: $728 per month; Rental vacancy rate: 5.0%
Health Insurance: 90.8% have insurance; 75.4% have private insurance; 35.7% have public insurance; 9.2% do not have insurance; 0.0% of children under 18 do not have insurance
Safety: Violent crime rate: 3.8 per 10,000 population; Property crime rate: 137.5 per 10,000 population
Transportation: Commute: 94.1% car, 0.0% public transportation, 1.3% walk, 3.1% work from home; Median travel time to work: 21.1 minutes

SUGARCREEK (village). Covers a land area of 3.790 square miles and a water area of 0 square miles. Located at 40.51° N. Lat; 81.64° W. Long. Elevation is 1,001 feet.
Population: 2,220; Growth (since 2000): 2.1%; Density: 585.7 persons per square mile; Race: 97.8% White, 0.1% Black/African American, 0.1% Asian, 0.1% American Indian/Alaska Native, 0.0% Native Hawaiian/Other Pacific Islander, 1.2% Two or more races, 1.5% Hispanic of any race; Average household size: 2.46; Median age: 40.0; Age under 18: 22.3%; Age 65 and over: 17.9%; Males per 100 females: 98.4

School District(s)

Garaway Local (PK-12)
2012-13 Enrollment: 1,196 . . . . (330) 852-2421
Housing: Homeownership rate: 71.9%; Homeowner vacancy rate: 1.4%; Rental vacancy rate: 6.9%
Newspapers: The Budget (weekly circulation 19500)

TUSCARAWAS (village). Covers a land area of 0.711 square miles and a water area of 0.025 square miles. Located at 40.39° N. Lat; 81.40° W. Long. Elevation is 846 feet.
Population: 1,056; Growth (since 2000): 13.1%; Density: 1,484.6 persons per square mile; Race: 99.0% White, 0.1% Black/African American, 0.5% Asian, 0.0% American Indian/Alaska Native, 0.0% Native Hawaiian/Other Pacific Islander, 0.5% Two or more races, 0.4% Hispanic of any race; Average household size: 2.41; Median age: 39.9; Age under 18: 24.1%; Age 65 and over: 17.0%; Males per 100 females: 99.2

School District(s)

Indian Valley Local Schools (PK-12)
2012-13 Enrollment: 1,774 . . . . (740) 254-4334
Housing: Homeownership rate: 78.1%; Homeowner vacancy rate: 2.0%; Rental vacancy rate: 12.6%

UHRICHSVILLE (city). Covers a land area of 2.811 square miles and a water area of 0.003 square miles. Located at 40.40° N. Lat; 81.35° W. Long. Elevation is 869 feet.
History: Uhrichsville was settled in 1804 by Michael Uhrich of Pennsylvania, who purchased land in the area and built a flour mill. The town was platted in 1833 and became a center for the manufacture of vitrified clay products.
Population: 5,413; Growth (since 2000): -4.4%; Density: 1,925.9 persons per square mile; Race: 96.3% White, 1.4% Black/African American, 0.3% Asian, 0.1% American Indian/Alaska Native, 0.0% Native Hawaiian/Other Pacific Islander, 1.6% Two or more races, 0.8% Hispanic of any race; Average household size: 2.44; Median age: 36.5; Age under 18: 26.7%; Age 65 and over: 15.3%; Males per 100 females: 89.8; Marriage status: 24.2% never married, 45.7% now married, 2.1% separated, 15.3% widowed, 14.8% divorced; Foreign born: 0.4%; Speak English only: 98.9%; With disability: 14.5%; Veterans: 10.6%; Ancestry: 25.7% German, 14.7% Irish, 11.3% American, 9.4% Italian, 7.5% English
Employment: 6.7% management, business, and financial, 1.4% computer, engineering, and science, 9.6% education, legal, community service, arts, and media, 2.9% healthcare practitioners, 22.6% service, 23.5% sales and office, 10.9% natural resources, construction, and maintenance, 22.5% production, transportation, and material moving
Income: Per capita: $15,014; Median household: $30,343; Average household: $36,716; Households with income of $100,000 or more: 3.9%; Poverty rate: 27.7%
Educational Attainment: High school diploma or higher: 81.9%; Bachelor's degree or higher: 6.1%; Graduate/professional degree or higher: 2.0%

School District(s)

Claymont City (PK-12)
2012-13 Enrollment: 2,113 . . . . (740) 922-5478
Housing: Homeownership rate: 58.9%; Median home value: $65,200; Median year structure built: 1943; Homeowner vacancy rate: 3.6%; Median gross rent: $516 per month; Rental vacancy rate: 8.1%
Health Insurance: 81.9% have insurance; 53.3% have private insurance; 40.4% have public insurance; 18.1% do not have insurance; 9.7% of children under 18 do not have insurance
Safety: Violent crime rate: 1.9 per 10,000 population; Property crime rate: 215.3 per 10,000 population
Transportation: Commute: 90.0% car, 0.1% public transportation, 2.1% walk, 6.2% work from home; Median travel time to work: 16.7 minutes

ZOAR (village). Covers a land area of 0.583 square miles and a water area of 0.090 square miles. Located at 40.61° N. Lat; 81.42° W. Long. Elevation is 906 feet.
History: Named for the biblical city to which Lot fled after leaving Sodom, Zoar was settled in 1817 by a group of Separatists from southern Germany who came seeking religious freedom. They established a communal corporation, chartered in 1832 as the Separatist Society of Zoar, which prospered for 80 years.
Population: 169; Growth (since 2000): -12.4%; Density: 290.0 persons per square mile; Race: 98.2% White, 0.0% Black/African American, 0.6% Asian, 0.0% American Indian/Alaska Native, 0.0% Native Hawaiian/Other Pacific Islander, 1.2% Two or more races, 0.6% Hispanic of any race; Average household size: 2.19; Median age: 52.6; Age under 18: 10.1%; Age 65 and over: 26.0%; Males per 100 females: 108.6

School District(s)

Tuscarawas Valley Local (PK-12)
2012-13 Enrollment: 1,449 . . . . (330) 859-2213
Housing: Homeownership rate: 87.0%; Homeowner vacancy rate: 1.4%; Rental vacancy rate: 0.0%

Union County

Located in central Ohio; drained by Darby Creek. Covers a land area of 431.730 square miles, a water area of 5.142 square miles, and is located in the Eastern Time Zone at 40.30° N. Lat., 83.37° W. Long. The county was founded in 1820. County seat is Marysville.

Union County is part of the Columbus, OH Metropolitan Statistical Area. The entire metro area includes: Delaware County, OH; Fairfield County, OH; Franklin County, OH; Hocking County, OH; Licking County, OH; Madison County, OH; Morrow County, OH; Perry County, OH; Pickaway County, OH; Union County, OH

Weather Station: Marysville Elevation: 1,000 feet

	Jan	Feb	Mar	Apr	May	Jun	Jul	Aug	Sep	Oct	Nov	Dec
High	34	39	49	62	72	81	84	83	76	64	51	38
Low	20	22	30	40	50	59	64	62	54	43	34	24
Precip	2.4	2.0	2.7	3.3	4.4	4.3	4.3	3.3	2.9	2.6	3.0	2.8
Snow	6.2	4.6	3.8	0.4	0.0	0.0	0.0	0.0	0.0	0.1	0.9	4.5

High and Low temperatures in degrees Fahrenheit; Precipitation and Snow in inches

Population: 52,300; Growth (since 2000): 27.8%; Density: 121.1 persons per square mile; Race: 92.9% White, 2.4% Black/African American, 2.7% Asian, 0.2% American Indian/Alaska Native, 0.0% Native Hawaiian/Other Pacific Islander, 1.4% two or more races, 1.3% Hispanic of any race; Average household size: 2.73; Median age: 36.4; Age under 18: 27.2%; Age 65 and over: 9.5%; Males per 100 females: 89.5; Marriage status: 25.1% never married, 58.7% now married, 1.9% separated, 4.2% widowed, 11.9% divorced; Foreign born: 2.8%; Speak English only: 95.8%; With disability: 10.6%; Veterans: 9.2%; Ancestry: 31.8% German, 15.3% Irish, 14.4% American, 11.8% English, 4.2% Italian
Religion: Six largest groups: 9.7% Methodist/Pietist, 6.3% Lutheran, 4.8% Catholicism, 4.4% Baptist, 1.6% Pentecostal, 1.3% Presbyterian-Reformed
Economy: Unemployment rate: 3.7%; Leading industries: 12.3% retail trade; 11.5% other services (except public administration); 10.2% construction; Farms: 995 totaling 241,935 acres; Company size: 6 employ 1,000 or more persons, 1 employs 500 to 999 persons, 22 employ 100 to 499 persons, 961 employs less than 100 persons; Business ownership: 1,208 women-owned, n/a Black-owned, n/a Hispanic-owned, n/a Asian-owned
Employment: 15.7% management, business, and financial, 8.0% computer, engineering, and science, 7.5% education, legal, community service, arts, and media, 5.4% healthcare practitioners, 15.4% service, 22.1% sales and office, 7.1% natural resources, construction, and maintenance, 18.9% production, transportation, and material moving
Income: Per capita: $28,852; Median household: $65,086; Average household: $81,415; Households with income of $100,000 or more: 28.4%; Poverty rate: 7.8%
Educational Attainment: High school diploma or higher: 92.2%; Bachelor's degree or higher: 27.0%; Graduate/professional degree or higher: 8.9%
Housing: Homeownership rate: 77.4%; Median home value: $171,800; Median year structure built: 1986; Homeowner vacancy rate: 2.4%; Median gross rent: $810 per month; Rental vacancy rate: 7.8%
Vital Statistics: Birth rate: 105.8 per 10,000 population; Death rate: 58.7 per 10,000 population; Age-adjusted cancer mortality rate: 157.9 deaths per 100,000 population
Health Insurance: 91.3% have insurance; 78.6% have private insurance; 22.5% have public insurance; 8.7% do not have insurance; 3.6% of children under 18 do not have insurance
Health Care: Physicians: 8.7 per 10,000 population; Hospital beds: 10.5 per 10,000 population; Hospital admissions: 318.9 per 10,000 population
Transportation: Commute: 93.0% car, 0.2% public transportation, 1.3% walk, 4.9% work from home; Median travel time to work: 23.5 minutes
Presidential Election: 34.3% Obama, 63.9% Romney (2012)
National and State Parks: Milford Center Prairie State Nature Preserve
Additional Information Contacts
Union Government . . . . (937) 645-3012
http://www.co.union.oh.us

Union County Communities

MAGNETIC SPRINGS (village). Covers a land area of 0.231 square miles and a water area of 0.005 square miles. Located at 40.35° N. Lat; 83.26° W. Long. Elevation is 932 feet.
Population: 268; Growth (since 2000): -17.0%; Density: 1,158.6 persons per square mile; Race: 97.4% White, 0.4% Black/African American, 0.0% Asian, 0.7% American Indian/Alaska Native, 0.0% Native Hawaiian/Other Pacific Islander, 1.5% Two or more races, 0.0% Hispanic of any race; Average household size: 2.44; Median age: 39.8; Age under 18: 25.4%; Age 65 and over: 7.5%; Males per 100 females: 107.8
Housing: Homeownership rate: 56.3%; Homeowner vacancy rate: 4.6%; Rental vacancy rate: 12.5%

MARYSVILLE (city). County seat. Covers a land area of 16.271 square miles and a water area of 0.291 square miles. Located at 40.23° N. Lat; 83.36° W. Long. Elevation is 994 feet.
History: Marysville was settled in 1816 by Jonathan Summers, and platted in 1820 by Samuel Culbertson, who named the town for his daughter. The log cabin that became a symbol of William Henry Harrison's presidential campaign of 1840 came from Marysville.
Population: 22,094; Growth (since 2000): 38.6%; Density: 1,357.8 persons per square mile; Race: 90.4% White, 4.5% Black/African American, 2.3% Asian, 0.3% American Indian/Alaska Native, 0.1% Native Hawaiian/Other Pacific Islander, 1.8% Two or more races, 1.8% Hispanic of any race; Average household size: 2.62; Median age: 33.1; Age under 18: 26.6%; Age 65 and over: 8.1%; Males per 100 females: 74.9; Marriage status: 29.6% never married, 49.6% now married, 2.9% separated, 4.3% widowed, 16.5% divorced; Foreign born: 3.1%; Speak English only: 95.6%; With disability: 11.7%; Veterans: 8.8%; Ancestry: 29.2% German, 16.1% Irish, 13.0% American, 10.3% English, 4.6% Italian
Employment: 13.1% management, business, and financial, 9.5% computer, engineering, and science, 6.9% education, legal, community service, arts, and media, 5.0% healthcare practitioners, 15.0% service, 24.5% sales and office, 6.7% natural resources, construction, and maintenance, 19.4% production, transportation, and material moving
Income: Per capita: $22,888; Median household: $53,880; Average household: $65,960; Households with income of $100,000 or more: 21.6%; Poverty rate: 9.4%
Educational Attainment: High school diploma or higher: 90.0%; Bachelor's degree or higher: 25.0%; Graduate/professional degree or higher: 6.3%

School District(s)

Marysville Exempted Village (PK-12)
2012-13 Enrollment: 5,251 . . . . (937) 644-8105
Housing: Homeownership rate: 65.1%; Median home value: $159,500; Median year structure built: 1992; Homeowner vacancy rate: 3.3%; Median gross rent: $833 per month; Rental vacancy rate: 9.0%
Health Insurance: 90.9% have insurance; 77.2% have private insurance; 21.6% have public insurance; 9.1% do not have insurance; 4.1% of children under 18 do not have insurance
Hospitals: Memorial Hospital of Union County (82 beds)
Safety: Violent crime rate: 5.4 per 10,000 population; Property crime rate: 193.4 per 10,000 population
Newspapers: Marysville Journal-Tribune (daily circulation 6000)
Transportation: Commute: 93.5% car, 0.4% public transportation, 1.4% walk, 4.2% work from home; Median travel time to work: 21.7 minutes
Airports: Union County (general aviation)
Additional Information Contacts
City of Marysville . . . . (937) 642-6015
http://www.marysvilleohio.org

MILFORD CENTER (village). Covers a land area of 0.409 square miles and a water area of 0.014 square miles. Located at 40.18° N. Lat; 83.44° W. Long. Elevation is 997 feet.
Population: 792; Growth (since 2000): 26.5%; Density: 1,937.4 persons per square mile; Race: 96.8% White, 0.5% Black/African American, 0.3% Asian, 0.4% American Indian/Alaska Native, 0.0% Native Hawaiian/Other Pacific Islander, 2.0% Two or more races, 0.6% Hispanic of any race; Average household size: 2.65; Median age: 34.9; Age under 18: 28.0%; Age 65 and over: 10.6%; Males per 100 females: 88.6

School District(s)

Fairbanks Local (PK-12)
2012-13 Enrollment: 995. . . . . (937) 349-3731
Housing: Homeownership rate: 78.3%; Homeowner vacancy rate: 2.5%; Rental vacancy rate: 5.7%

NEW CALIFORNIA (CDP). Covers a land area of 2.065 square miles and a water area of 0.032 square miles. Located at 40.15° N. Lat; 83.24° W. Long. Elevation is 997 feet.
Population: 1,411; Growth (since 2000): n/a; Density: 683.3 persons per square mile; Race: 96.0% White, 1.1% Black/African American, 1.6% Asian, 0.0% American Indian/Alaska Native, 0.0% Native Hawaiian/Other Pacific Islander, 1.1% Two or more races, 0.7% Hispanic of any race; Average household size: 3.01; Median age: 35.5; Age under 18: 31.5%; Age 65 and over: 6.2%; Males per 100 females: 103.6
Housing: Homeownership rate: 97.0%; Homeowner vacancy rate: 1.3%; Rental vacancy rate: 30.0%

RAYMOND (CDP). Covers a land area of 1.269 square miles and a water area of 0.027 square miles. Located at 40.34° N. Lat; 83.47° W. Long. Elevation is 1,070 feet.

Population: 257; Growth (since 2000): n/a; Density: 202.5 persons per square mile; Race: 98.8% White, 1.2% Black/African American, 0.0% Asian, 0.0% American Indian/Alaska Native, 0.0% Native Hawaiian/Other Pacific Islander, 0.0% Two or more races, 0.0% Hispanic of any race; Average household size: 2.68; Median age: 38.4; Age under 18: 29.2%; Age 65 and over: 8.9%; Males per 100 females: 87.6

School District(s)

Marysville Exempted Village (PK-12)
2012-13 Enrollment: 5,251 . . . . (937) 644-8105

Housing: Homeownership rate: 79.2%; Homeowner vacancy rate: 1.3%; Rental vacancy rate: 0.0%

RICHWOOD (village). Covers a land area of 1.255 square miles and a water area of 0.026 square miles. Located at 40.43° N. Lat; 83.29° W. Long. Elevation is 948 feet.

Population: 2,229; Growth (since 2000): 3.4%; Density: 1,776.8 persons per square mile; Race: 98.3% White, 0.4% Black/African American, 0.0% Asian, 0.2% American Indian/Alaska Native, 0.0% Native Hawaiian/Other Pacific Islander, 0.9% Two or more races, 0.7% Hispanic of any race; Average household size: 2.54; Median age: 34.2; Age under 18: 29.6%; Age 65 and over: 12.7%; Males per 100 females: 90.2

School District(s)

North Union Local (PK-12)
2012-13 Enrollment: 1,476 . . . . (740) 943-2509

Housing: Homeownership rate: 61.8%; Homeowner vacancy rate: 2.0%; Rental vacancy rate: 10.8%

Safety: Violent crime rate: 13.4 per 10,000 population; Property crime rate: 285.7 per 10,000 population

Newspapers: Richwood Gazette (weekly circulation 2500)

UNIONVILLE CENTER (village). Covers a land area of 0.159 square miles and a water area of 0.005 square miles. Located at 40.14° N. Lat; 83.34° W. Long. Elevation is 971 feet.

Population: 233; Growth (since 2000): -22.1%; Density: 1,466.4 persons per square mile; Race: 96.1% White, 0.0% Black/African American, 2.6% Asian, 0.4% American Indian/Alaska Native, 0.0% Native Hawaiian/Other Pacific Islander, 0.9% Two or more races, 0.9% Hispanic of any race; Average household size: 2.99; Median age: 39.8; Age under 18: 29.6%; Age 65 and over: 12.0%; Males per 100 females: 106.2

Housing: Homeownership rate: 78.2%; Homeowner vacancy rate: 0.0%; Rental vacancy rate: 5.6%

Van Wert County

Located in western Ohio; bounded on the west by Indiana; drained by the Little Auglaize River. Covers a land area of 409.158 square miles, a water area of 1.267 square miles, and is located in the Eastern Time Zone at 40.86° N. Lat., 84.59° W. Long. The county was founded in 1820. County seat is Van Wert.

Van Wert County is part of the Van Wert, OH Micropolitan Statistical Area. The entire metro area includes: Van Wert County, OH

Weather Station: Van Wert 1 S Elevation: 790 feet

	Jan	Feb	Mar	Apr	May	Jun	Jul	Aug	Sep	Oct	Nov	Dec
High	33	36	47	60	72	81	85	83	77	63	50	37
Low	18	20	28	39	50	60	64	62	53	42	33	23
Precip	2.2	1.9	2.3	3.4	4.1	4.2	4.3	3.7	2.9	3.0	3.0	2.6
Snow	5.3	4.6	2.2	0.6	0.0	0.0	0.0	0.0	0.0	0.1	1.0	5.6

High and Low temperatures in degrees Fahrenheit; Precipitation and Snow in inches

Population: 28,744; Growth (since 2000): -3.1%; Density: 70.3 persons per square mile; Race: 96.6% White, 0.9% Black/African American, 0.2% Asian, 0.1% American Indian/Alaska Native, 0.0% Native Hawaiian/Other Pacific Islander, 1.4% two or more races, 2.6% Hispanic of any race; Average household size: 2.48; Median age: 40.3; Age under 18: 24.9%; Age 65 and over: 16.3%; Males per 100 females: 95.0; Marriage status: 22.4% never married, 59.4% now married, 1.3% separated, 6.5% widowed, 11.6% divorced; Foreign born: 0.8%; Speak English only: 97.9%; With disability: 14.8%; Veterans: 9.9%; Ancestry: 42.7% German, 12.0% Irish, 9.9% American, 9.6% English, 2.3% French

Religion: Six largest groups: 10.9% Methodist/Pietist, 8.9% Lutheran, 8.4% Catholicism, 6.3% Presbyterian-Reformed, 4.5% Non-denominational Protestant, 1.2% Pentecostal

Economy: Unemployment rate: 3.9%; Leading industries: 15.8% retail trade; 15.1% other services (except public administration); 11.3% health care and social assistance; Farms: 655 totaling 227,277 acres; Company size: 0 employ 1,000 or more persons, 3 employ 500 to 999 persons, 10 employ 100 to 499 persons, 537 employ less than 100 persons; Business ownership: 663 women-owned, n/a Black-owned, n/a Hispanic-owned, n/a Asian-owned

Employment: 9.2% management, business, and financial, 2.5% computer, engineering, and science, 8.1% education, legal, community service, arts, and media, 6.0% healthcare practitioners, 16.0% service, 19.7% sales and office, 8.5% natural resources, construction, and maintenance, 29.9% production, transportation, and material moving

Income: Per capita: $22,790; Median household: $45,355; Average household: $55,992; Households with income of $100,000 or more: 12.1%; Poverty rate: 12.5%

Educational Attainment: High school diploma or higher: 90.8%; Bachelor's degree or higher: 15.4%; Graduate/professional degree or higher: 6.1%

Housing: Homeownership rate: 78.6%; Median home value: $88,600; Median year structure built: 1956; Homeowner vacancy rate: 2.7%; Median gross rent: $618 per month; Rental vacancy rate: 10.0%

Vital Statistics: Birth rate: 106.1 per 10,000 population; Death rate: 102.6 per 10,000 population; Age-adjusted cancer mortality rate: 173.4 deaths per 100,000 population

Health Insurance: 90.7% have insurance; 73.8% have private insurance; 31.7% have public insurance; 9.3% do not have insurance; 5.1% of children under 18 do not have insurance

Health Care: Physicians: 8.0 per 10,000 population; Hospital beds: 27.5 per 10,000 population; Hospital admissions: 480.4 per 10,000 population

Transportation: Commute: 93.5% car, 0.2% public transportation, 2.4% walk, 2.4% work from home; Median travel time to work: 18.7 minutes

Presidential Election: 31.6% Obama, 66.8% Romney (2012)

Additional Information Contacts

Van Wert Government . . . . (419) 238-6159
http://www.vanwertcounty.org

Van Wert County Communities

CONVOY (village). Covers a land area of 0.561 square miles and a water area of <.001 square miles. Located at 40.92° N. Lat; 84.71° W. Long. Elevation is 781 feet.

Population: 1,085; Growth (since 2000): -2.3%; Density: 1,933.7 persons per square mile; Race: 97.2% White, 0.4% Black/African American, 0.1% Asian, 0.2% American Indian/Alaska Native, 0.0% Native Hawaiian/Other Pacific Islander, 1.3% Two or more races, 2.6% Hispanic of any race; Average household size: 2.55; Median age: 35.2; Age under 18: 30.0%; Age 65 and over: 15.4%; Males per 100 females: 85.5

School District(s)

Crestview Local (PK-12)
2012-13 Enrollment: 861 . . . . (419) 749-2893

Housing: Homeownership rate: 73.5%; Homeowner vacancy rate: 3.5%; Rental vacancy rate: 11.3%

ELGIN (village). Covers a land area of 0.225 square miles and a water area of 0 square miles. Located at 40.74° N. Lat; 84.48° W. Long. Elevation is 814 feet.

Population: 57; Growth (since 2000): 14.0%; Density: 253.8 persons per square mile; Race: 98.2% White, 0.0% Black/African American, 0.0% Asian, 0.0% American Indian/Alaska Native, 0.0% Native Hawaiian/Other Pacific Islander, 1.8% Two or more races, 0.0% Hispanic of any race; Average household size: 2.59; Median age: 37.3; Age under 18: 22.8%; Age 65 and over: 7.0%; Males per 100 females: 128.0

Housing: Homeownership rate: 86.4%; Homeowner vacancy rate: 0.0%; Rental vacancy rate: 0.0%

MIDDLE POINT (village). Covers a land area of 0.560 square miles and a water area of 0.008 square miles. Located at 40.86° N. Lat; 84.45° W. Long. Elevation is 778 feet.

Population: 576; Growth (since 2000): -2.9%; Density: 1,028.0 persons per square mile; Race: 99.3% White, 0.0% Black/African American, 0.0% Asian, 0.0% American Indian/Alaska Native, 0.0% Native Hawaiian/Other Pacific Islander, 0.5% Two or more races, 0.7% Hispanic of any race;

Average household size: 2.54; Median age: 39.0; Age under 18: 27.1%; Age 65 and over: 14.2%; Males per 100 females: 99.3
Housing: Homeownership rate: 82.0%; Homeowner vacancy rate: 3.6%; Rental vacancy rate: 4.7%

OHIO CITY (village). Covers a land area of 0.531 square miles and a water area of 0 square miles. Located at 40.77° N. Lat; 84.62° W. Long. Elevation is 820 feet.
Population: 705; Growth (since 2000): -10.1%; Density: 1,327.4 persons per square mile; Race: 97.4% White, 0.0% Black/African American, 0.1% Asian, 0.3% American Indian/Alaska Native, 0.0% Native Hawaiian/Other Pacific Islander, 0.9% Two or more races, 3.8% Hispanic of any race; Average household size: 2.46; Median age: 40.1; Age under 18: 24.4%; Age 65 and over: 13.6%; Males per 100 females: 95.8
Housing: Homeownership rate: 84.0%; Homeowner vacancy rate: 7.3%; Rental vacancy rate: 12.7%

SCOTT (village). Covers a land area of 0.811 square miles and a water area of <.001 square miles. Located at 40.99° N. Lat; 84.58° W. Long. Elevation is 738 feet.
Population: 286; Growth (since 2000): -11.2%; Density: 352.6 persons per square mile; Race: 98.6% White, 0.0% Black/African American, 0.0% Asian, 0.0% American Indian/Alaska Native, 0.0% Native Hawaiian/Other Pacific Islander, 0.7% Two or more races, 0.7% Hispanic of any race; Average household size: 2.58; Median age: 34.7; Age under 18: 28.3%; Age 65 and over: 12.9%; Males per 100 females: 90.7
Housing: Homeownership rate: 82.9%; Homeowner vacancy rate: 2.1%; Rental vacancy rate: 9.5%

VAN WERT (city). County seat. Covers a land area of 7.325 square miles and a water area of 0.281 square miles. Located at 40.87° N. Lat; 84.59° W. Long. Elevation is 778 feet.
History: The site of Van Wert was chosen in 1835 by Captain James Watson Riley, who correctly foresaw that the location would make it a thoroughfare. The town developed into the peony center of Ohio, raising many flowers.
Population: 10,846; Growth (since 2000): 1.5%; Density: 1,480.7 persons per square mile; Race: 94.6% White, 1.7% Black/African American, 0.4% Asian, 0.1% American Indian/Alaska Native, 0.0% Native Hawaiian/Other Pacific Islander, 2.0% Two or more races, 4.0% Hispanic of any race; Average household size: 2.33; Median age: 39.6; Age under 18: 24.4%; Age 65 and over: 18.1%; Males per 100 females: 88.0; Marriage status: 24.8% never married, 51.6% now married, 1.9% separated, 8.4% widowed, 15.1% divorced; Foreign born: 1.2%; Speak English only: 97.7%; With disability: 16.4%; Veterans: 10.7%; Ancestry: 36.8% German, 14.1% Irish, 9.6% American, 9.4% English, 2.4% Italian
Employment: 6.1% management, business, and financial, 3.4% computer, engineering, and science, 8.9% education, legal, community service, arts, and media, 6.1% healthcare practitioners, 20.1% service, 20.3% sales and office, 6.2% natural resources, construction, and maintenance, 28.8% production, transportation, and material moving
Income: Per capita: $20,433; Median household: $37,205; Average household: $49,599; Households with income of $100,000 or more: 8.8%; Poverty rate: 19.8%
Educational Attainment: High school diploma or higher: 88.1%; Bachelor's degree or higher: 15.2%; Graduate/professional degree or higher: 6.2%

School District(s)

Lifelinks Community School (06-12)
2012-13 Enrollment: 56. . . . . (419) 238-0648
Lincolnview Local (PK-12)
2012-13 Enrollment: 875. . . . . (419) 968-2226
Van Wert City (PK-12)
2012-13 Enrollment: 2,034 . . . . (419) 238-0648
Vantage Career Center (07-12)
2012-13 Enrollment: n/a . . . . (419) 238-5411

Vocational/Technical School(s)

Vantage Career Center (Public)
Fall 2013 Enrollment: 62. . . . . (419) 238-5411
2013-14 Tuition: $620

Housing: Homeownership rate: 66.0%; Median home value: $82,100; Median year structure built: 1955; Homeowner vacancy rate: 3.4%; Median gross rent: $615 per month; Rental vacancy rate: 11.0%
Health Insurance: 88.4% have insurance; 63.5% have private insurance; 39.6% have public insurance; 11.6% do not have insurance; 6.1% of children under 18 do not have insurance
Hospitals: Van Wert County Hospital (100 beds)
Safety: Violent crime rate: 19.4 per 10,000 population; Property crime rate: 361.2 per 10,000 population
Newspapers: Times-Bulletin (daily circulation 6400)
Transportation: Commute: 91.3% car, 0.3% public transportation, 3.6% walk, 1.4% work from home; Median travel time to work: 14.5 minutes

Additional Information Contacts

City of Van Wert . . . . (419) 238-0308
http://vanwert.org

VENEDOCIA (village). Covers a land area of 0.134 square miles and a water area of 0 square miles. Located at 40.79° N. Lat; 84.46° W. Long. Elevation is 804 feet.
Population: 124; Growth (since 2000): -22.5%; Density: 923.2 persons per square mile; Race: 97.6% White, 0.8% Black/African American, 0.0% Asian, 0.0% American Indian/Alaska Native, 0.0% Native Hawaiian/Other Pacific Islander, 1.6% Two or more races, 0.0% Hispanic of any race; Average household size: 2.34; Median age: 42.0; Age under 18: 20.2%; Age 65 and over: 14.5%; Males per 100 females: 117.5
Housing: Homeownership rate: 83.0%; Homeowner vacancy rate: 0.0%; Rental vacancy rate: 0.0%

WILLSHIRE (village). Covers a land area of 0.371 square miles and a water area of 0.002 square miles. Located at 40.75° N. Lat; 84.79° W. Long. Elevation is 794 feet.
Population: 397; Growth (since 2000): -14.3%; Density: 1,068.9 persons per square mile; Race: 97.7% White, 1.0% Black/African American, 0.0% Asian, 0.5% American Indian/Alaska Native, 0.3% Native Hawaiian/Other Pacific Islander, 0.5% Two or more races, 0.8% Hispanic of any race; Average household size: 2.45; Median age: 41.1; Age under 18: 25.2%; Age 65 and over: 18.1%; Males per 100 females: 98.5
Housing: Homeownership rate: 80.8%; Homeowner vacancy rate: 7.6%; Rental vacancy rate: 18.4%
Newspapers: Photo Star (weekly circulation 11000)

WREN (village). Covers a land area of 0.310 square miles and a water area of <.001 square miles. Located at 40.80° N. Lat; 84.77° W. Long. Elevation is 807 feet.
Population: 194; Growth (since 2000): -2.5%; Density: 626.8 persons per square mile; Race: 95.4% White, 1.0% Black/African American, 0.0% Asian, 0.0% American Indian/Alaska Native, 0.0% Native Hawaiian/Other Pacific Islander, 3.6% Two or more races, 2.1% Hispanic of any race; Average household size: 2.49; Median age: 39.5; Age under 18: 23.2%; Age 65 and over: 14.4%; Males per 100 females: 102.1
Housing: Homeownership rate: 84.6%; Homeowner vacancy rate: 5.7%; Rental vacancy rate: 7.7%

Vinton County

Located in southern Ohio; drained by Raccoon Creek. Covers a land area of 412.360 square miles, a water area of 2.618 square miles, and is located in the Eastern Time Zone at 39.26° N. Lat., 82.49° W. Long. The county was founded in 1850. County seat is McArthur.
Population: 13,435; Growth (since 2000): 4.9%; Density: 32.6 persons per square mile; Race: 97.9% White, 0.3% Black/African American, 0.2% Asian, 0.4% American Indian/Alaska Native, 0.0% Native Hawaiian/Other Pacific Islander, 1.1% two or more races, 0.5% Hispanic of any race; Average household size: 2.54; Median age: 39.6; Age under 18: 24.8%; Age 65 and over: 14.0%; Males per 100 females: 99.1; Marriage status: 22.7% never married, 55.8% now married, 0.8% separated, 7.3% widowed, 14.3% divorced; Foreign born: 0.2%; Speak English only: 98.2%; With disability: 18.2%; Veterans: 8.6%; Ancestry: 16.3% German, 15.6% Irish, 14.2% American, 8.0% English, 2.4% Scottish
Religion: Six largest groups: 7.4% Baptist, 4.3% Methodist/Pietist, 2.0% Non-denominational Protestant, 1.7% Pentecostal, 1.5% Catholicism, 1.0% Holiness
Economy: Unemployment rate: 6.3%; Leading industries: 20.1% retail trade; 14.8% health care and social assistance; 10.1% manufacturing; Farms: 226 totaling 33,400 acres; Company size: 0 employ 1,000 or more persons, 0 employ 500 to 999 persons, 2 employ 100 to 499 persons, 147 employ less than 100 persons; Business ownership: 201 women-owned, n/a Black-owned, n/a Hispanic-owned, n/a Asian-owned

Employment: 10.3% management, business, and financial, 1.4% computer, engineering, and science, 8.0% education, legal, community service, arts, and media, 5.8% healthcare practitioners, 18.0% service, 18.1% sales and office, 12.3% natural resources, construction, and maintenance, 26.1% production, transportation, and material moving
Income: Per capita: $18,101; Median household: $36,705; Average household: $46,110; Households with income of $100,000 or more: 8.8%; Poverty rate: 20.6%
Educational Attainment: High school diploma or higher: 80.4%; Bachelor's degree or higher: 8.5%; Graduate/professional degree or higher: 2.9%
Housing: Homeownership rate: 75.6%; Median home value: $75,700; Median year structure built: 1983; Homeowner vacancy rate: 2.1%; Median gross rent: $617 per month; Rental vacancy rate: 5.8%
Vital Statistics: Birth rate: 91.9 per 10,000 population; Death rate: 114.5 per 10,000 population; Age-adjusted cancer mortality rate: 205.6 deaths per 100,000 population
Health Insurance: 86.4% have insurance; 53.4% have private insurance; 45.8% have public insurance; 13.6% do not have insurance; 8.0% of children under 18 do not have insurance
Health Care: Physicians: 1.5 per 10,000 population; Hospital beds: 0.0 per 10,000 population; Hospital admissions: 0.0 per 10,000 population
Transportation: Commute: 94.2% car, 0.1% public transportation, 2.2% walk, 3.3% work from home; Median travel time to work: 29.3 minutes
Presidential Election: 44.5% Obama, 52.3% Romney (2012)
National and State Parks: Lake Alma State Park; Lake Hope State Park; Wellston Reservoir State Wildlife Park; Zaleski State Forest
Additional Information Contacts
Vinton Government . . . . (740) 596-4571
http://www.vintoncounty.com/index.html

Vinton County Communities

CREOLA (unincorporated postal area)

ZCTA: 45622

Covers a land area of 14.474 square miles and a water area of 0.021 square miles. Located at 39.38° N. Lat; 82.49° W. Long. Elevation is 764 feet.
Population: 321; Growth (since 2000): -26.2%; Density: 22.2 persons per square mile; Race: 96.3% White, 0.0% Black/African American, 0.0% Asian, 0.0% American Indian/Alaska Native, 0.0% Native Hawaiian/Other Pacific Islander, 3.4% Two or more races, 1.6% Hispanic of any race; Average household size: 2.51; Median age: 45.2; Age under 18: 21.2%; Age 65 and over: 11.5%; Males per 100 females: 99.4
Housing: Homeownership rate: 88.3%; Homeowner vacancy rate: 1.7%; Rental vacancy rate: 11.8%

HAMDEN (village). Covers a land area of 0.569 square miles and a water area of <.001 square miles. Located at 39.16° N. Lat; 82.52° W. Long. Elevation is 722 feet.
Population: 879; Growth (since 2000): 0.9%; Density: 1,544.4 persons per square mile; Race: 99.3% White, 0.5% Black/African American, 0.1% Asian, 0.1% American Indian/Alaska Native, 0.0% Native Hawaiian/Other Pacific Islander, 0.0% Two or more races, 0.7% Hispanic of any race; Average household size: 2.60; Median age: 35.5; Age under 18: 26.4%; Age 65 and over: 14.3%; Males per 100 females: 96.6

School District(s)

Vinton County Local (PK-12)
2012-13 Enrollment: 2,270 . . . . (740) 596-5218
Housing: Homeownership rate: 70.1%; Homeowner vacancy rate: 1.6%; Rental vacancy rate: 4.7%

MCARTHUR (village). County seat. Covers a land area of 1.328 square miles and a water area of 0.006 square miles. Located at 39.25° N. Lat; 82.48° W. Long. Elevation is 764 feet.
History: McArthur was platted in 1815 and named McArthurstown for Duncan McArthur, later governor of Ohio. It was sited at the junction of two wilderness roads. Local clays were used in brickmaking, the town's early industry.
Population: 1,701; Growth (since 2000): -9.9%; Density: 1,281.1 persons per square mile; Race: 98.1% White, 0.1% Black/African American, 0.0% Asian, 0.8% American Indian/Alaska Native, 0.0% Native Hawaiian/Other Pacific Islander, 0.8% Two or more races, 0.8% Hispanic of any race; Average household size: 2.43; Median age: 35.3; Age under 18: 27.5%; Age 65 and over: 15.3%; Males per 100 females: 84.3

School District(s)

Vinton County Local (PK-12)
2012-13 Enrollment: 2,270 . . . . (740) 596-5218
Housing: Homeownership rate: 58.7%; Homeowner vacancy rate: 2.8%; Rental vacancy rate: 6.8%
Safety: Violent crime rate: 0.0 per 10,000 population; Property crime rate: 167.1 per 10,000 population
Newspapers: Vinton Co Courier (weekly circulation 2100)

NEW PLYMOUTH (unincorporated postal area)

ZCTA: 45654

Covers a land area of 56.066 square miles and a water area of 0.166 square miles. Located at 39.37° N. Lat; 82.38° W. Long. Elevation is 768 feet.
Population: 917; Growth (since 2000): -10.6%; Density: 16.4 persons per square mile; Race: 99.0% White, 0.2% Black/African American, 0.1% Asian, 0.2% American Indian/Alaska Native, 0.0% Native Hawaiian/Other Pacific Islander, 0.3% Two or more races, 0.5% Hispanic of any race; Average household size: 2.61; Median age: 41.2; Age under 18: 25.4%; Age 65 and over: 14.5%; Males per 100 females: 111.3
Housing: Homeownership rate: 82.9%; Homeowner vacancy rate: 0.7%; Rental vacancy rate: 6.2%

RAY (unincorporated postal area)

ZCTA: 45672

Covers a land area of 53.459 square miles and a water area of 0.153 square miles. Located at 39.19° N. Lat; 82.69° W. Long. Elevation is 614 feet.
Population: 1,749; Growth (since 2000): -1.9%; Density: 32.7 persons per square mile; Race: 96.7% White, 1.8% Black/African American, 0.1% Asian, 0.1% American Indian/Alaska Native, 0.0% Native Hawaiian/Other Pacific Islander, 1.3% Two or more races, 0.6% Hispanic of any race; Average household size: 2.55; Median age: 40.4; Age under 18: 23.5%; Age 65 and over: 12.3%; Males per 100 females: 106.7
Housing: Homeownership rate: 81.2%; Homeowner vacancy rate: 1.7%; Rental vacancy rate: 8.5%

WILKESVILLE (village). Covers a land area of 0.292 square miles and a water area of <.001 square miles. Located at 39.08° N. Lat; 82.33° W. Long. Elevation is 705 feet.
Population: 149; Growth (since 2000): -1.3%; Density: 510.0 persons per square mile; Race: 99.3% White, 0.7% Black/African American, 0.0% Asian, 0.0% American Indian/Alaska Native, 0.0% Native Hawaiian/Other Pacific Islander, 0.0% Two or more races, 2.7% Hispanic of any race; Average household size: 2.16; Median age: 42.8; Age under 18: 20.8%; Age 65 and over: 17.4%; Males per 100 females: 122.4
Housing: Homeownership rate: 76.8%; Homeowner vacancy rate: 7.0%; Rental vacancy rate: 11.1%

ZALESKI (village). Covers a land area of 0.440 square miles and a water area of 0.007 square miles. Located at 39.28° N. Lat; 82.39° W. Long. Elevation is 751 feet.
History: Zaleski was settled in a forested area, the site of the Zaleski Resettlement Project that sought to rehabilitate timberlands.
Population: 278; Growth (since 2000): -25.9%; Density: 631.7 persons per square mile; Race: 98.2% White, 0.0% Black/African American, 0.0% Asian, 0.0% American Indian/Alaska Native, 0.0% Native Hawaiian/Other Pacific Islander, 1.4% Two or more races, 0.0% Hispanic of any race; Average household size: 2.26; Median age: 43.0; Age under 18: 19.4%; Age 65 and over: 15.5%; Males per 100 females: 100.0
Housing: Homeownership rate: 73.2%; Homeowner vacancy rate: 2.2%; Rental vacancy rate: 8.3%

Warren County

Located in southwestern Ohio; crossed by the Little Miami River. Covers a land area of 401.314 square miles, a water area of 5.999 square miles, and is located in the Eastern Time Zone at 39.43° N. Lat., 84.17° W. Long. The county was founded in 1803. County seat is Lebanon.

Warren County is part of the Cincinnati, OH-KY-IN Metropolitan Statistical Area. The entire metro area includes: Dearborn County, IN; Ohio County, IN; Union County, IN; Boone County, KY; Bracken County, KY; Campbell County, KY; Gallatin County, KY; Grant County, KY; Kenton County, KY;

Pendleton County, KY; Brown County, OH; Butler County, OH; Clermont County, OH; Hamilton County, OH; Warren County, OH

Weather Station: Franklin Elevation: 669 feet

	Jan	Feb	Mar	Apr	May	Jun	Jul	Aug	Sep	Oct	Nov	Dec
High	37	41	52	63	73	82	85	85	78	66	53	41
Low	20	22	30	39	50	59	63	61	53	40	33	24
Precip	2.5	2.4	3.3	3.7	4.7	3.8	4.1	2.9	2.5	3.1	3.2	3.1
Snow	0.9	1.4	0.4	tr	0.0	0.0	0.0	0.0	0.0	0.0	0.2	na

High and Low temperatures in degrees Fahrenheit; Precipitation and Snow in inches

Population: 212,693; Growth (since 2000): 34.3%; Density: 530.0 persons per square mile; Race: 90.5% White, 3.3% Black/African American, 3.9% Asian, 0.2% American Indian/Alaska Native, 0.0% Native Hawaiian/Other Pacific Islander, 1.5% two or more races, 2.2% Hispanic of any race; Average household size: 2.70; Median age: 37.8; Age under 18: 27.5%; Age 65 and over: 10.8%; Males per 100 females: 101.0; Marriage status: 23.0% never married, 62.4% now married, 1.3% separated, 4.5% widowed, 10.1% divorced; Foreign born: 5.6%; Speak English only: 92.5%; With disability: 9.4%; Veterans: 9.6%; Ancestry: 27.8% German, 14.6% Irish, 11.8% American, 10.9% English, 4.5% Italian
Religion: Six largest groups: 9.2% Catholicism, 8.3% Baptist, 3.4% Methodist/Pietist, 2.9% Non-denominational Protestant, 1.7% Presbyterian-Reformed, 1.5% Pentecostal
Economy: Unemployment rate: 3.9%; Leading industries: 13.5% retail trade; 12.2% professional, scientific, and technical services; 11.0% health care and social assistance; Farms: 942 totaling 106,624 acres; Company size: 4 employ 1,000 or more persons, 10 employ 500 to 999 persons, 116 employ 100 to 499 persons, 3,783 employ less than 100 persons; Business ownership: 4,850 women-owned, 255 Black-owned, 302 Hispanic-owned, n/a Asian-owned
Employment: 19.4% management, business, and financial, 8.2% computer, engineering, and science, 9.0% education, legal, community service, arts, and media, 6.9% healthcare practitioners, 14.5% service, 25.6% sales and office, 5.3% natural resources, construction, and maintenance, 11.1% production, transportation, and material moving
Income: Per capita: $33,172; Median household: $72,487; Average household: $92,522; Households with income of $100,000 or more: 34.0%; Poverty rate: 6.3%
Educational Attainment: High school diploma or higher: 92.0%; Bachelor's degree or higher: 37.9%; Graduate/professional degree or higher: 13.9%
Housing: Homeownership rate: 78.7%; Median home value: $188,500; Median year structure built: 1991; Homeowner vacancy rate: 1.8%; Median gross rent: $919 per month; Rental vacancy rate: 7.8%
Vital Statistics: Birth rate: 112.8 per 10,000 population; Death rate: 71.8 per 10,000 population; Age-adjusted cancer mortality rate: 165.7 deaths per 100,000 population
Health Insurance: 93.0% have insurance; 83.4% have private insurance; 19.5% have public insurance; 7.0% do not have insurance; 3.2% of children under 18 do not have insurance
Health Care: Physicians: 24.3 per 10,000 population; Hospital beds: 17.5 per 10,000 population; Hospital admissions: 635.6 per 10,000 population
Air Quality Index: 95.3% good, 4.7% moderate, 0.0% unhealthy for sensitive individuals, 0.0% unhealthy (percent of days)
Transportation: Commute: 93.7% car, 0.7% public transportation, 0.9% walk, 4.3% work from home; Median travel time to work: 24.4 minutes
Presidential Election: 29.5% Obama, 69.1% Romney (2012)
National and State Parks: Caesar Creek Gorge State Natural Area; Caesar Creek State Park; Fort Ancient State Memorial
Additional Information Contacts
Warren Government . . . . (513) 695-1250
http://www.co.warren.oh.us

Warren County Communities

BUTLERVILLE (village). Covers a land area of 0.109 square miles and a water area of 0 square miles. Located at 39.30° N. Lat; 84.09° W. Long. Elevation is 866 feet.
Population: 163; Growth (since 2000): -29.4%; Density: 1,493.2 persons per square mile; Race: 99.4% White, 0.6% Black/African American, 0.0% Asian, 0.0% American Indian/Alaska Native, 0.0% Native Hawaiian/Other Pacific Islander, 0.0% Two or more races, 0.6% Hispanic of any race; Average household size: 2.91; Median age: 33.3; Age under 18: 29.4%; Age 65 and over: 7.4%; Males per 100 females: 103.8
Housing: Homeownership rate: 73.2%; Homeowner vacancy rate: 2.4%; Rental vacancy rate: 6.3%

CARLISLE (village). Covers a land area of 3.534 square miles and a water area of 0.198 square miles. Located at 39.58° N. Lat; 84.32° W. Long. Elevation is 689 feet.
Population: 4,915; Growth (since 2000): -4.0%; Density: 1,390.6 persons per square mile; Race: 98.3% White, 0.4% Black/African American, 0.1% Asian, 0.1% American Indian/Alaska Native, 0.0% Native Hawaiian/Other Pacific Islander, 0.8% Two or more races, 1.0% Hispanic of any race; Average household size: 2.60; Median age: 40.5; Age under 18: 24.3%; Age 65 and over: 15.1%; Males per 100 females: 94.2; Marriage status: 24.1% never married, 60.2% now married, 0.2% separated, 7.9% widowed, 7.8% divorced; Foreign born: 0.8%; Speak English only: 97.9%; With disability: 15.8%; Veterans: 8.2%; Ancestry: 21.6% German, 15.8% Irish, 12.6% American, 10.8% English, 3.9% Polish
Employment: 4.0% management, business, and financial, 4.5% computer, engineering, and science, 4.9% education, legal, community service, arts, and media, 7.4% healthcare practitioners, 15.8% service, 32.8% sales and office, 9.6% natural resources, construction, and maintenance, 21.0% production, transportation, and material moving
Income: Per capita: $23,054; Median household: $52,296; Average household: $60,871; Households with income of $100,000 or more: 15.2%; Poverty rate: 7.7%
Educational Attainment: High school diploma or higher: 84.9%; Bachelor's degree or higher: 7.3%; Graduate/professional degree or higher: 3.2%

School District(s)

Carlisle Local (PK-12)
2012-13 Enrollment: 1,661 . . . . (937) 746-0710
Housing: Homeownership rate: 79.5%; Median home value: $131,500; Median year structure built: 1973; Homeowner vacancy rate: 2.5%; Median gross rent: $698 per month; Rental vacancy rate: 21.2%
Health Insurance: 88.4% have insurance; 70.8% have private insurance; 29.8% have public insurance; 11.6% do not have insurance; 4.8% of children under 18 do not have insurance
Transportation: Commute: 97.9% car, 0.0% public transportation, 0.3% walk, 1.3% work from home; Median travel time to work: 26.6 minutes
Additional Information Contacts
Village of Carlisle . . . . (937) 746-0555
http://www.carlisleoh.org

CORWIN (village). Covers a land area of 0.345 square miles and a water area of 0 square miles. Located at 39.52° N. Lat; 84.07° W. Long. Elevation is 735 feet.
Population: 421; Growth (since 2000): 64.5%; Density: 1,221.0 persons per square mile; Race: 98.8% White, 0.0% Black/African American, 0.0% Asian, 0.0% American Indian/Alaska Native, 0.0% Native Hawaiian/Other Pacific Islander, 0.0% Two or more races, 1.9% Hispanic of any race; Average household size: 2.38; Median age: 42.6; Age under 18: 21.1%; Age 65 and over: 17.8%; Males per 100 females: 117.0
Housing: Homeownership rate: 87.0%; Homeowner vacancy rate: 1.9%; Rental vacancy rate: 4.2%

FIVE POINTS (CDP). Covers a land area of 2.059 square miles and a water area of 0 square miles. Located at 39.56° N. Lat; 84.19° W. Long. Elevation is 988 feet.
History: Five Points takes its name from the near-five way intersection on the western edge of the area.
Population: 1,824; Growth (since 2000): -16.8%; Density: 886.0 persons per square mile; Race: 96.1% White, 0.5% Black/African American, 1.8% Asian, 0.2% American Indian/Alaska Native, 0.0% Native Hawaiian/Other Pacific Islander, 1.3% Two or more races, 0.8% Hispanic of any race; Average household size: 2.85; Median age: 43.6; Age under 18: 27.7%; Age 65 and over: 10.4%; Males per 100 females: 101.5
Housing: Homeownership rate: 97.2%; Homeowner vacancy rate: 1.3%; Rental vacancy rate: 5.3%

FRANKLIN (city). Covers a land area of 9.173 square miles and a water area of 0.170 square miles. Located at 39.55° N. Lat; 84.30° W. Long. Elevation is 682 feet.
History: Named for Benjamin Franklin, American statesman and inventor. Franklin was founded in 1796 by William Schenck, an officer in Harrison 's Army in the War of 1812. The town was a port on the Great Miami River

after the Miami & Erie Canal was built. Later, paper mills were established here.

Population: 11,771; Growth (since 2000): 3.3%; Density: 1,283.2 persons per square mile; Race: 96.2% White, 0.9% Black/African American, 0.5% Asian, 0.2% American Indian/Alaska Native, 0.0% Native Hawaiian/Other Pacific Islander, 1.7% Two or more races, 1.6% Hispanic of any race; Average household size: 2.49; Median age: 36.7; Age under 18: 25.5%; Age 65 and over: 12.5%; Males per 100 females: 93.1; Marriage status: 22.7% never married, 54.7% now married, 3.7% separated, 5.3% widowed, 17.2% divorced; Foreign born: 0.7%; Speak English only: 98.8%; With disability: 18.3%; Veterans: 12.6%; Ancestry: 15.4% American, 15.2% German, 14.7% Irish, 7.9% English, 2.1% Scottish

Employment: 13.5% management, business, and financial, 4.4% computer, engineering, and science, 4.3% education, legal, community service, arts, and media, 5.5% healthcare practitioners, 13.9% service, 23.6% sales and office, 8.6% natural resources, construction, and maintenance, 26.2% production, transportation, and material moving

Income: Per capita: $21,081; Median household: $43,220; Average household: $51,242; Households with income of $100,000 or more: 10.9%; Poverty rate: 15.8%

Educational Attainment: High school diploma or higher: 83.2%; Bachelor's degree or higher: 11.4%; Graduate/professional degree or higher: 2.7%

School District(s)

Franklin City (PK-12)
2012-13 Enrollment: 2,907 . . . . (937) 746-1699

Housing: Homeownership rate: 57.6%; Median home value: $109,400; Median year structure built: 1967; Homeowner vacancy rate: 2.3%; Median gross rent: $760 per month; Rental vacancy rate: 6.8%

Health Insurance: 89.5% have insurance; 65.9% have private insurance; 37.1% have public insurance; 10.5% do not have insurance; 4.2% of children under 18 do not have insurance

Hospitals: Atrium Medical Center (250 beds)

Transportation: Commute: 97.7% car, 0.3% public transportation, 0.5% walk, 1.5% work from home; Median travel time to work: 22.1 minutes

Additional Information Contacts

City of Franklin . . . . (937) 746-9921
http://www.franklinohio.org

HARVEYSBURG (village). Covers a land area of 0.992 square miles and a water area of 0.024 square miles. Located at 39.50° N. Lat; 83.99° W. Long. Elevation is 925 feet.

Population: 546; Growth (since 2000): -3.0%; Density: 550.4 persons per square mile; Race: 95.1% White, 1.5% Black/African American, 0.4% Asian, 0.0% American Indian/Alaska Native, 0.0% Native Hawaiian/Other Pacific Islander, 2.9% Two or more races, 0.2% Hispanic of any race; Average household size: 2.68; Median age: 37.3; Age under 18: 26.4%; Age 65 and over: 9.3%; Males per 100 females: 104.5

Housing: Homeownership rate: 73.6%; Homeowner vacancy rate: 1.9%; Rental vacancy rate: 10.0%

HUNTER (CDP). Covers a land area of 1.626 square miles and a water area of 0 square miles. Located at 39.49° N. Lat; 84.29° W. Long. Elevation is 883 feet.

Population: 2,100; Growth (since 2000): 20.9%; Density: 1,291.2 persons per square mile; Race: 97.8% White, 0.4% Black/African American, 0.6% Asian, 0.1% American Indian/Alaska Native, 0.0% Native Hawaiian/Other Pacific Islander, 1.0% Two or more races, 0.6% Hispanic of any race; Average household size: 2.50; Median age: 45.6; Age under 18: 20.2%; Age 65 and over: 19.8%; Males per 100 females: 97.2

Housing: Homeownership rate: 89.1%; Homeowner vacancy rate: 1.4%; Rental vacancy rate: 3.2%

KINGS MILLS (CDP). Covers a land area of 1.344 square miles and a water area of 0.049 square miles. Located at 39.36° N. Lat; 84.24° W. Long. Elevation is 758 feet.

Population: 1,319; Growth (since 2000): n/a; Density: 981.4 persons per square mile; Race: 95.7% White, 1.4% Black/African American, 1.1% Asian, 0.0% American Indian/Alaska Native, 0.0% Native Hawaiian/Other Pacific Islander, 1.5% Two or more races, 2.1% Hispanic of any race; Average household size: 2.78; Median age: 40.3; Age under 18: 28.9%; Age 65 and over: 9.6%; Males per 100 females: 106.1

School District(s)

Kings Local (PK-12)
2012-13 Enrollment: 3,976 . . . . (513) 398-8050

Housing: Homeownership rate: 84.8%; Homeowner vacancy rate: 1.7%; Rental vacancy rate: 6.5%

LANDEN (CDP). Covers a land area of 2.028 square miles and a water area of 0.091 square miles. Located at 39.32° N. Lat; 84.28° W. Long. Elevation is 814 feet.

Population: 6,782; Growth (since 2000): -46.9%; Density: 3,343.8 persons per square mile; Race: 94.2% White, 1.8% Black/African American, 1.7% Asian, 0.1% American Indian/Alaska Native, 0.1% Native Hawaiian/Other Pacific Islander, 1.8% Two or more races, 2.6% Hispanic of any race; Average household size: 2.53; Median age: 38.0; Age under 18: 26.1%; Age 65 and over: 8.4%; Males per 100 females: 93.2; Marriage status: 24.7% never married, 59.1% now married, 0.4% separated, 3.2% widowed, 13.1% divorced; Foreign born: 5.5%; Speak English only: 94.2%; With disability: 6.8%; Veterans: 6.3%; Ancestry: 40.2% German, 18.8% Irish, 13.2% English, 6.2% Italian, 5.9% American

Employment: 23.3% management, business, and financial, 8.3% computer, engineering, and science, 10.0% education, legal, community service, arts, and media, 6.7% healthcare practitioners, 11.5% service, 31.2% sales and office, 4.9% natural resources, construction, and maintenance, 4.0% production, transportation, and material moving

Income: Per capita: $38,700; Median household: $87,951; Average household: $103,037; Households with income of $100,000 or more: 43.0%; Poverty rate: 1.9%

Educational Attainment: High school diploma or higher: 98.3%; Bachelor's degree or higher: 53.5%; Graduate/professional degree or higher: 18.6%

Housing: Homeownership rate: 80.6%; Median home value: $183,200; Median year structure built: 1983; Homeowner vacancy rate: 0.8%; Median gross rent: $1,050 per month; Rental vacancy rate: 9.4%

Health Insurance: 92.6% have insurance; 87.0% have private insurance; 14.7% have public insurance; 7.4% do not have insurance; 3.8% of children under 18 do not have insurance

Transportation: Commute: 93.6% car, 1.3% public transportation, 0.2% walk, 3.8% work from home; Median travel time to work: 22.4 minutes

LEBANON (city). County seat. Covers a land area of 12.963 square miles and a water area of 0.009 square miles. Located at 39.42° N. Lat; 84.22° W. Long. Elevation is 771 feet.

History: Named for the Semitic translation of "to be white". Lebanon was founded in 1803 and grew as the commercial center for the region between the two Miami Rivers. This was the home of Thomas Corwin (1794-1865) who was governor of Ohio, a U.S. senator, Secretary of the Treasury, and Minister to Mexico under Abraham Lincoln.

Population: 20,033; Growth (since 2000): 18.1%; Density: 1,545.3 persons per square mile; Race: 92.7% White, 2.6% Black/African American, 0.8% Asian, 0.2% American Indian/Alaska Native, 0.0% Native Hawaiian/Other Pacific Islander, 2.0% Two or more races, 3.5% Hispanic of any race; Average household size: 2.62; Median age: 34.7; Age under 18: 29.2%; Age 65 and over: 10.1%; Males per 100 females: 96.2; Marriage status: 28.6% never married, 52.7% now married, 2.2% separated, 5.6% widowed, 13.1% divorced; Foreign born: 3.5%; Speak English only: 94.8%; With disability: 9.9%; Veterans: 9.4%; Ancestry: 29.1% German, 20.8% Irish, 12.7% American, 10.2% English, 5.1% Italian

Employment: 14.1% management, business, and financial, 5.0% computer, engineering, and science, 9.2% education, legal, community service, arts, and media, 5.2% healthcare practitioners, 19.5% service, 32.4% sales and office, 3.4% natural resources, construction, and maintenance, 11.3% production, transportation, and material moving

Income: Per capita: $25,563; Median household: $58,649; Average household: $70,979; Households with income of $100,000 or more: 24.1%; Poverty rate: 13.7%

Educational Attainment: High school diploma or higher: 91.5%; Bachelor's degree or higher: 30.0%; Graduate/professional degree or higher: 9.9%

School District(s)

Greater Ohio Virtual School (09-12)
2012-13 Enrollment: 324. . . . . (513) 695-2924
Lebanon City (PK-12)
2012-13 Enrollment: 5,466 . . . . (513) 934-5770
Warren County Vocational School (07-12)
2012-13 Enrollment: n/a . . . . (513) 932-5677

Two-year College(s)

Warren County Career Center (Public)
Fall 2013 Enrollment: 392. . . . . (513) 932-8145

Vocational/Technical School(s)

Dental Assistant Pro-Lebanon (Private, For-profit)
Fall 2013 Enrollment: 18 . . . . (513) 932-4806

Housing: Homeownership rate: 61.8%; Median home value: $159,200; Median year structure built: 1989; Homeowner vacancy rate: 2.3%; Median gross rent: $794 per month; Rental vacancy rate: 7.0%

Health Insurance: 90.4% have insurance; 71.6% have private insurance; 26.8% have public insurance; 9.6% do not have insurance; 4.5% of children under 18 do not have insurance

Safety: Violent crime rate: 9.8 per 10,000 population; Property crime rate: 198.7 per 10,000 population

Newspapers: Western Star (weekly circulation 23000)

Transportation: Commute: 91.7% car, 1.4% public transportation, 2.5% walk, 3.9% work from home; Median travel time to work: 25.0 minutes

Airports: Warren County/John Lane Field (general aviation)

Additional Information Contacts

City of Lebanon . . . . (513) 932-3060
http://www.ci.lebanon.oh.us

LOVELAND PARK (CDP). Covers a land area of 1.145 square miles and a water area of 0.052 square miles. Located at 39.29° N. Lat; 84.26° W. Long. Elevation is 732 feet.

Population: 1,523; Growth (since 2000): -15.3%; Density: 1,329.6 persons per square mile; Race: 96.4% White, 0.7% Black/African American, 1.1% Asian, 0.1% American Indian/Alaska Native, 0.0% Native Hawaiian/Other Pacific Islander, 0.9% Two or more races, 2.6% Hispanic of any race; Average household size: 2.59; Median age: 42.2; Age under 18: 25.2%; Age 65 and over: 13.3%; Males per 100 females: 108.1

Housing: Homeownership rate: 83.0%; Homeowner vacancy rate: 1.4%; Rental vacancy rate: 1.9%

MAINEVILLE (village). Covers a land area of 1.369 square miles and a water area of 0 square miles. Located at 39.31° N. Lat; 84.21° W. Long. Elevation is 807 feet.

Population: 975; Growth (since 2000): 10.2%; Density: 712.4 persons per square mile; Race: 97.6% White, 0.5% Black/African American, 0.4% Asian, 0.1% American Indian/Alaska Native, 0.0% Native Hawaiian/Other Pacific Islander, 1.1% Two or more races, 0.8% Hispanic of any race; Average household size: 2.43; Median age: 38.4; Age under 18: 24.9%; Age 65 and over: 13.1%; Males per 100 females: 101.9

School District(s)

Kings Local (PK-12)
2012-13 Enrollment: 3,976 . . . . (513) 398-8050

Little Miami Local (PK-12)
2012-13 Enrollment: 3,814 . . . . (513) 899-2264

Housing: Homeownership rate: 73.8%; Homeowner vacancy rate: 1.3%; Rental vacancy rate: 4.5%

MASON (city). Covers a land area of 18.629 square miles and a water area of 0.036 square miles. Located at 39.35° N. Lat; 84.30° W. Long. Elevation is 807 feet.

Population: 30,712; Growth (since 2000): 39.5%; Density: 1,648.6 persons per square mile; Race: 85.1% White, 3.3% Black/African American, 9.0% Asian, 0.2% American Indian/Alaska Native, 0.1% Native Hawaiian/Other Pacific Islander, 1.5% Two or more races, 3.2% Hispanic of any race; Average household size: 2.77; Median age: 38.4; Age under 18: 30.8%; Age 65 and over: 9.9%; Males per 100 females: 94.1; Marriage status: 23.3% never married, 62.6% now married, 1.3% separated, 4.5% widowed, 9.7% divorced; Foreign born: 10.9%; Speak English only: 85.0%; With disability: 7.2%; Veterans: 7.8%; Ancestry: 30.2% German, 12.9% Irish, 11.1% English, 7.5% Italian, 6.8% American

Employment: 23.3% management, business, and financial, 9.3% computer, engineering, and science, 10.1% education, legal, community service, arts, and media, 7.0% healthcare practitioners, 13.9% service, 26.2% sales and office, 3.4% natural resources, construction, and maintenance, 6.8% production, transportation, and material moving

Income: Per capita: $37,849; Median household: $85,697; Average household: $105,916; Households with income of $100,000 or more: 42.9%; Poverty rate: 3.9%

Educational Attainment: High school diploma or higher: 96.1%; Bachelor's degree or higher: 54.0%; Graduate/professional degree or higher: 23.3%

School District(s)

Mason City SD (PK-12)
2012-13 Enrollment: 10,836 . . . . (513) 398-0474

Four-year College(s)

Strayer University-Ohio (Private, For-profit)
Fall 2013 Enrollment: 950 . . . . (513) 234-6450
2013-14 Tuition: In-state $15,495; Out-of-state $15,495

Housing: Homeownership rate: 83.5%; Median home value: $221,500; Median year structure built: 1994; Homeowner vacancy rate: 1.5%; Median gross rent: <$100 per month; Rental vacancy rate: 7.3%

Health Insurance: 94.7% have insurance; 89.9% have private insurance; 13.8% have public insurance; 5.3% do not have insurance; 1.9% of children under 18 do not have insurance

Safety: Violent crime rate: 3.5 per 10,000 population; Property crime rate: 134.9 per 10,000 population

Transportation: Commute: 94.0% car, 0.7% public transportation, 0.5% walk, 4.6% work from home; Median travel time to work: 23.2 minutes

Additional Information Contacts

City of Mason . . . . (513) 229-8500
http://www.imaginemason.org

MORROW (village). Covers a land area of 1.925 square miles and a water area of 0.037 square miles. Located at 39.35° N. Lat; 84.12° W. Long. Elevation is 643 feet.

History: Morrow was settled in 1844 and named for Jeremiah Morrow, Governor of Ohio from 1822 to 1826.

Population: 1,188; Growth (since 2000): -7.6%; Density: 617.3 persons per square mile; Race: 96.5% White, 0.4% Black/African American, 0.3% Asian, 0.2% American Indian/Alaska Native, 0.0% Native Hawaiian/Other Pacific Islander, 2.0% Two or more races, 2.0% Hispanic of any race; Average household size: 2.53; Median age: 39.0; Age under 18: 24.8%; Age 65 and over: 15.8%; Males per 100 females: 93.2

School District(s)

Little Miami Local (PK-12)
2012-13 Enrollment: 3,814 . . . . (513) 899-2264

Housing: Homeownership rate: 57.4%; Homeowner vacancy rate: 4.6%; Rental vacancy rate: 13.7%

OREGONIA (unincorporated postal area)

ZCTA: 45054

Covers a land area of 30.857 square miles and a water area of 0.022 square miles. Located at 39.44° N. Lat; 84.08° W. Long. Elevation is 696 feet.

Population: 2,471; Growth (since 2000): 46.3%; Density: 80.1 persons per square mile; Race: 97.2% White, 0.6% Black/African American, 0.2% Asian, 0.2% American Indian/Alaska Native, 0.0% Native Hawaiian/Other Pacific Islander, 0.9% Two or more races, 2.0% Hispanic of any race; Average household size: 2.75; Median age: 42.2; Age under 18: 23.8%; Age 65 and over: 10.2%; Males per 100 females: 106.8

Housing: Homeownership rate: 87.1%; Homeowner vacancy rate: 0.8%; Rental vacancy rate: 10.0%

PLEASANT PLAIN (village). Covers a land area of 0.162 square miles and a water area of 0 square miles. Located at 39.28° N. Lat; 84.11° W. Long. Elevation is 886 feet.

Population: 154; Growth (since 2000): -1.3%; Density: 950.8 persons per square mile; Race: 97.4% White, 1.9% Black/African American, 0.0% Asian, 0.0% American Indian/Alaska Native, 0.0% Native Hawaiian/Other Pacific Islander, 0.6% Two or more races, 0.0% Hispanic of any race; Average household size: 2.66; Median age: 32.0; Age under 18: 24.0%; Age 65 and over: 11.7%; Males per 100 females: 108.1

Housing: Homeownership rate: 69.0%; Homeowner vacancy rate: 0.0%; Rental vacancy rate: 0.0%

SOUTH LEBANON (village). Covers a land area of 2.647 square miles and a water area of 0.034 square miles. Located at 39.37° N. Lat; 84.22° W. Long. Elevation is 630 feet.

Population: 4,115; Growth (since 2000): 62.1%; Density: 1,554.8 persons per square mile; Race: 96.2% White, 1.4% Black/African American, 0.7% Asian, 0.1% American Indian/Alaska Native, 0.0% Native Hawaiian/Other Pacific Islander, 1.1% Two or more races, 2.3% Hispanic of any race; Average household size: 2.67; Median age: 35.3; Age under 18: 28.9%; Age 65 and over: 9.0%; Males per 100 females: 93.3; Marriage status: 28.0% never married, 57.8% now married, 0.7% separated, 3.3% widowed, 10.8% divorced; Foreign born: 4.0%; Speak English only: 92.9%; With disability: 14.2%; Veterans: 7.4%; Ancestry: 34.7% American, 25.4% German, 6.0% English, 5.5% Scottish, 5.4% Irish

Employment: 14.6% management, business, and financial, 15.3% computer, engineering, and science, 9.3% education, legal, community service, arts, and media, 4.6% healthcare practitioners, 17.3% service, 18.5% sales and office, 4.9% natural resources, construction, and maintenance, 15.6% production, transportation, and material moving
Income: Per capita: $26,569; Median household: $49,712; Average household: $72,831; Households with income of $100,000 or more: 24.9%; Poverty rate: 16.3%
Educational Attainment: High school diploma or higher: 86.6%; Bachelor's degree or higher: 34.5%; Graduate/professional degree or higher: 8.2%
Housing: Homeownership rate: 70.1%; Median home value: $193,700; Median year structure built: 2000; Homeowner vacancy rate: 2.6%; Median gross rent: $873 per month; Rental vacancy rate: 7.8%
Health Insurance: 82.5% have insurance; 69.5% have private insurance; 20.9% have public insurance; 17.5% do not have insurance; 5.7% of children under 18 do not have insurance
Transportation: Commute: 91.1% car, 0.7% public transportation, 0.4% walk, 7.8% work from home; Median travel time to work: 27.1 minutes
Additional Information Contacts
Village of South Lebanon .... (513) 494-2296
http://www.southlebanonohio.org

SPRINGBORO (city). Covers a land area of 9.355 square miles and a water area of <.001 square miles. Located at 39.56° N. Lat; 84.23° W. Long. Elevation is 781 feet.
History: Settled as early as 1796, Springboro was founded in 1815 by Jonathan Wright, a relative of the Wright Brothers, as "Springborough." Jonathan Wright's father, Joel Wright, was a surveyor who plotted Columbus, Ohio. Springboro was predominantly Quaker during its earlier years.
Population: 17,409; Growth (since 2000): 40.6%; Density: 1,860.9 persons per square mile; Race: 92.1% White, 2.3% Black/African American, 3.4% Asian, 0.1% American Indian/Alaska Native, 0.0% Native Hawaiian/Other Pacific Islander, 1.7% Two or more races, 1.8% Hispanic of any race; Average household size: 2.89; Median age: 36.4; Age under 18: 32.2%; Age 65 and over: 9.3%; Males per 100 females: 95.6; Marriage status: 18.4% never married, 69.3% now married, 0.8% separated, 2.8% widowed, 9.4% divorced; Foreign born: 5.9%; Speak English only: 92.8%; With disability: 6.6%; Veterans: 11.9%; Ancestry: 27.8% German, 14.9% Irish, 13.5% English, 8.7% American, 5.7% Italian
Employment: 25.4% management, business, and financial, 10.2% computer, engineering, and science, 11.0% education, legal, community service, arts, and media, 8.9% healthcare practitioners, 9.6% service, 23.4% sales and office, 4.1% natural resources, construction, and maintenance, 7.5% production, transportation, and material moving
Income: Per capita: $36,157; Median household: $96,094; Average household: $107,678; Households with income of $100,000 or more: 47.8%; Poverty rate: 3.9%
Educational Attainment: High school diploma or higher: 98.2%; Bachelor's degree or higher: 50.3%; Graduate/professional degree or higher: 19.6%

School District(s)

Springboro Community City (PK-12)
2012-13 Enrollment: 5,734 .... (937) 748-3960

Two-year College(s)

Miami-Jacobs Career College-Springboro (Private, For-profit)
Fall 2013 Enrollment: 222........................ (937) 746-1830
2013-14 Tuition: In-state $12,024; Out-of-state $12,024
Housing: Homeownership rate: 85.8%; Median home value: $201,900; Median year structure built: 1994; Homeowner vacancy rate: 1.6%; Median gross rent: $1,077 per month; Rental vacancy rate: 7.7%
Health Insurance: 95.8% have insurance; 88.6% have private insurance; 15.9% have public insurance; 4.2% do not have insurance; 1.3% of children under 18 do not have insurance
Safety: Violent crime rate: 6.2 per 10,000 population; Property crime rate: 111.8 per 10,000 population
Transportation: Commute: 95.1% car, 0.2% public transportation, 0.0% walk, 4.4% work from home; Median travel time to work: 22.4 minutes
Additional Information Contacts
City of Springboro .... (937) 748-4343
http://www.ci.springboro.oh.us

WAYNESVILLE (village). Covers a land area of 2.377 square miles and a water area of 0.006 square miles. Located at 39.53° N. Lat; 84.09° W. Long. Elevation is 751 feet.
History: Waynesville was laid out in 1796 by Samuel Highway and Dr. Evan Banes, and was named for General Anthony Wayne. Many of the early residents were Quakers from Carolina and Pennsylvania.
Population: 2,834; Growth (since 2000): 10.8%; Density: 1,192.4 persons per square mile; Race: 96.8% White, 0.4% Black/African American, 0.4% Asian, 0.1% American Indian/Alaska Native, 0.1% Native Hawaiian/Other Pacific Islander, 2.1% Two or more races, 1.2% Hispanic of any race; Average household size: 2.42; Median age: 41.6; Age under 18: 23.9%; Age 65 and over: 17.9%; Males per 100 females: 88.4; Marriage status: 22.1% never married, 54.3% now married, 0.7% separated, 8.3% widowed, 15.3% divorced; Foreign born: 1.2%; Speak English only: 97.4%; With disability: 11.2%; Veterans: 8.8%; Ancestry: 30.0% German, 11.7% Irish, 9.8% English, 7.9% American, 3.6% Dutch
Employment: 11.3% management, business, and financial, 2.3% computer, engineering, and science, 8.7% education, legal, community service, arts, and media, 7.6% healthcare practitioners, 21.7% service, 27.3% sales and office, 6.4% natural resources, construction, and maintenance, 14.7% production, transportation, and material moving
Income: Per capita: $23,142; Median household: $57,872; Average household: $62,946; Households with income of $100,000 or more: 17.4%; Poverty rate: 11.1%
Educational Attainment: High school diploma or higher: 90.5%; Bachelor's degree or higher: 23.2%; Graduate/professional degree or higher: 6.9%

School District(s)

Wayne Local (PK-12)
2012-13 Enrollment: 1,484 .... (513) 897-6971
Housing: Homeownership rate: 62.9%; Median home value: $160,300; Median year structure built: 1985; Homeowner vacancy rate: 1.2%; Median gross rent: $911 per month; Rental vacancy rate: 6.6%
Health Insurance: 90.3% have insurance; 76.1% have private insurance; 31.5% have public insurance; 9.7% do not have insurance; 6.1% of children under 18 do not have insurance
Transportation: Commute: 93.3% car, 0.0% public transportation, 4.2% walk, 2.5% work from home; Median travel time to work: 22.9 minutes

Washington County

Located in southeastern Ohio; bounded on the southeast by the Ohio River and the West Virginia border; crossed by the Muskingum and Little Muskingum Rivers. Covers a land area of 631.972 square miles, a water area of 8.025 square miles, and is located in the Eastern Time Zone at 39.45° N. Lat., 81.49° W. Long. The county was founded in 1788. County seat is Marietta.

Washington County is part of the Marietta, OH Micropolitan Statistical Area. The entire metro area includes: Washington County, OH

Weather Station: Marietta Wwtp Elevation: 580 feet

	Jan	Feb	Mar	Apr	May	Jun	Jul	Aug	Sep	Oct	Nov	Dec
High	40	44	53	66	74	82	85	85	78	67	55	43
Low	23	25	31	41	50	60	64	63	55	43	34	26
Precip	3.1	2.8	3.8	3.4	4.3	4.6	4.5	3.7	3.2	2.9	3.2	3.3
Snow	7.0	4.6	3.0	0.6	0.0	0.0	0.0	0.0	0.0	tr	0.6	3.0

High and Low temperatures in degrees Fahrenheit; Precipitation and Snow in inches

Population: 61,778; Growth (since 2000): -2.3%; Density: 97.8 persons per square mile; Race: 96.5% White, 1.1% Black/African American, 0.6% Asian, 0.2% American Indian/Alaska Native, 0.0% Native Hawaiian/Other Pacific Islander, 1.5% two or more races, 0.7% Hispanic of any race; Average household size: 2.34; Median age: 43.0; Age under 18: 20.9%; Age 65 and over: 17.5%; Males per 100 females: 95.4; Marriage status: 24.0% never married, 55.8% now married, 1.5% separated, 7.7% widowed, 12.5% divorced; Foreign born: 1.2%; Speak English only: 98.0%; With disability: 18.3%; Veterans: 11.0%; Ancestry: 26.1% German, 14.5% Irish, 12.1% American, 11.2% English, 2.6% Italian
Religion: Six largest groups: 11.5% Baptist, 8.8% Catholicism, 7.2% Methodist/Pietist, 3.4% Non-denominational Protestant, 2.4% Presbyterian-Reformed, 1.5% Holiness
Economy: Unemployment rate: 4.1%; Leading industries: 15.9% retail trade; 11.8% other services (except public administration); 11.3% construction; Farms: 1,122 totaling 138,940 acres; Company size: 1

employs 1,000 or more persons, 2 employ 500 to 999 persons, 31 employs 100 to 499 persons, 1,398 employ less than 100 persons; Business ownership: n/a women-owned, n/a Black-owned, n/a Hispanic-owned, n/a Asian-owned
Employment: 10.9% management, business, and financial, 3.4% computer, engineering, and science, 8.6% education, legal, community service, arts, and media, 6.3% healthcare practitioners, 17.7% service, 25.4% sales and office, 10.6% natural resources, construction, and maintenance, 17.1% production, transportation, and material moving
Income: Per capita: $23,496; Median household: $42,834; Average household: $56,439; Households with income of $100,000 or more: 14.0%; Poverty rate: 15.3%
Educational Attainment: High school diploma or higher: 88.8%; Bachelor's degree or higher: 16.0%; Graduate/professional degree or higher: 4.9%
Housing: Homeownership rate: 73.8%; Median home value: $108,600; Median year structure built: 1970; Homeowner vacancy rate: 1.7%; Median gross rent: $591 per month; Rental vacancy rate: 8.7%
Vital Statistics: Birth rate: 96.9 per 10,000 population; Death rate: 112.4 per 10,000 population; Age-adjusted cancer mortality rate: 206.0 deaths per 100,000 population
Health Insurance: 88.4% have insurance; 67.0% have private insurance; 36.4% have public insurance; 11.6% do not have insurance; 5.6% of children under 18 do not have insurance
Health Care: Physicians: 20.2 per 10,000 population; Hospital beds: 28.7 per 10,000 population; Hospital admissions: 1,441.2 per 10,000 population
Air Quality Index: 96.3% good, 3.7% moderate, 0.0% unhealthy for sensitive individuals, 0.0% unhealthy (percent of days)
Transportation: Commute: 93.3% car, 0.2% public transportation, 2.7% walk, 3.1% work from home; Median travel time to work: 22.7 minutes
Presidential Election: 36.7% Obama, 61.3% Romney (2012)
National and State Parks: Howes State Park; Marietta State Forest Nursery
Additional Information Contacts
Washington Government . . . . (740) 373-6623
http://www.washingtongov.org

Washington County Communities

BELPRE (city). Covers a land area of 3.485 square miles and a water area of 0.083 square miles. Located at 39.28° N. Lat; 81.59° W. Long. Elevation is 614 feet.
History: Belpre was established in 1789 by Captain Jonathan Stone who led a group of Revolutionary War veterans here from Marietta.
Population: 6,441; Growth (since 2000): -3.3%; Density: 1,848.3 persons per square mile; Race: 94.7% White, 2.1% Black/African American, 0.4% Asian, 0.2% American Indian/Alaska Native, 0.1% Native Hawaiian/Other Pacific Islander, 2.3% Two or more races, 0.8% Hispanic of any race; Average household size: 2.11; Median age: 44.7; Age under 18: 18.8%; Age 65 and over: 20.7%; Males per 100 females: 87.5; Marriage status: 23.1% never married, 47.5% now married, 0.7% separated, 9.8% widowed, 19.6% divorced; Foreign born: 0.5%; Speak English only: 97.7%; With disability: 26.8%; Veterans: 11.7%; Ancestry: 19.3% German, 15.7% Irish, 15.1% American, 11.8% English, 3.9% Dutch
Employment: 13.6% management, business, and financial, 2.2% computer, engineering, and science, 6.7% education, legal, community service, arts, and media, 7.8% healthcare practitioners, 21.6% service, 30.7% sales and office, 4.7% natural resources, construction, and maintenance, 12.6% production, transportation, and material moving
Income: Per capita: $22,479; Median household: $34,819; Average household: $45,514; Households with income of $100,000 or more: 11.6%; Poverty rate: 21.0%
Educational Attainment: High school diploma or higher: 87.2%; Bachelor's degree or higher: 10.7%; Graduate/professional degree or higher: 1.6%

School District(s)

Belpre City (PK-12)
2012-13 Enrollment: 972. . . . . (740) 423-9511
Housing: Homeownership rate: 63.5%; Median home value: $99,400; Median year structure built: 1966; Homeowner vacancy rate: 2.4%; Median gross rent: $623 per month; Rental vacancy rate: 9.6%
Health Insurance: 86.3% have insurance; 60.8% have private insurance; 46.4% have public insurance; 13.7% do not have insurance; 2.2% of children under 18 do not have insurance
Safety: Violent crime rate: 7.8 per 10,000 population; Property crime rate: 122.9 per 10,000 population
Transportation: Commute: 94.7% car, 0.4% public transportation, 3.1% walk, 1.5% work from home; Median travel time to work: 17.7 minutes

BEVERLY (village). Covers a land area of 0.682 square miles and a water area of 0.111 square miles. Located at 39.55° N. Lat; 81.64° W. Long. Elevation is 656 feet.
History: Beverly was settled in 1789 by a group of adventurers from Marietta. Fort Frye was erected, but it was abandoned in 1794 and a new community was established on the Muskingum River at the mouth of Olive Green Creek.
Population: 1,313; Growth (since 2000): 2.4%; Density: 1,924.1 persons per square mile; Race: 97.2% White, 0.3% Black/African American, 0.2% Asian, 0.0% American Indian/Alaska Native, 0.0% Native Hawaiian/Other Pacific Islander, 2.4% Two or more races, 0.5% Hispanic of any race; Average household size: 2.32; Median age: 41.2; Age under 18: 23.7%; Age 65 and over: 19.9%; Males per 100 females: 85.7

School District(s)

Fort Frye Local (PK-12)
2012-13 Enrollment: 954. . . . . (740) 984-2497
Housing: Homeownership rate: 65.7%; Homeowner vacancy rate: 1.4%; Rental vacancy rate: 8.7%
Safety: Violent crime rate: 7.7 per 10,000 population; Property crime rate: 192.0 per 10,000 population

COAL RUN (unincorporated postal area)

ZCTA: 45721

Covers a land area of 0.051 square miles and a water area of 0 square miles. Located at 39.57° N. Lat; 81.58° W. Long. Elevation is 646 feet.
Population: 29; Growth (since 2000): n/a; Density: 566.1 persons per square mile; Race: 96.6% White, 0.0% Black/African American, 0.0% Asian, 3.4% American Indian/Alaska Native, 0.0% Native Hawaiian/Other Pacific Islander, 0.0% Two or more races, 0.0% Hispanic of any race; Average household size: 2.42; Median age: 49.2; Age under 18: 17.2%; Age 65 and over: 13.8%; Males per 100 females: 222.2
Housing: Homeownership rate: 58.4%; Homeowner vacancy rate: 0.0%; Rental vacancy rate: 0.0%

CUTLER (unincorporated postal area)

ZCTA: 45724

Covers a land area of 53.286 square miles and a water area of 0.092 square miles. Located at 39.38° N. Lat; 81.80° W. Long. Elevation is 794 feet.
Population: 1,744; Growth (since 2000): 12.7%; Density: 32.7 persons per square mile; Race: 87.6% White, 6.7% Black/African American, 0.2% Asian, 0.5% American Indian/Alaska Native, 0.1% Native Hawaiian/Other Pacific Islander, 5.0% Two or more races, 0.5% Hispanic of any race; Average household size: 2.52; Median age: 42.1; Age under 18: 22.5%; Age 65 and over: 12.9%; Males per 100 females: 104.5
Housing: Homeownership rate: 88.6%; Homeowner vacancy rate: 1.7%; Rental vacancy rate: 4.7%

DEVOLA (CDP). Covers a land area of 5.135 square miles and a water area of 0.233 square miles. Located at 39.47° N. Lat; 81.47° W. Long. Elevation is 686 feet.
History: Also spelled De Vola.
Population: 2,652; Growth (since 2000): -4.3%; Density: 516.5 persons per square mile; Race: 97.9% White, 0.7% Black/African American, 0.5% Asian, 0.1% American Indian/Alaska Native, 0.0% Native Hawaiian/Other Pacific Islander, 0.6% Two or more races, 0.8% Hispanic of any race; Average household size: 2.33; Median age: 49.9; Age under 18: 19.5%; Age 65 and over: 24.4%; Males per 100 females: 89.7; Marriage status: 25.5% never married, 61.3% now married, 0.5% separated, 6.4% widowed, 6.9% divorced; Foreign born: 3.0%; Speak English only: 95.0%; With disability: 9.7%; Veterans: 9.6%; Ancestry: 33.4% German, 14.7% Irish, 12.0% English, 9.0% American, 3.7% Swiss
Employment: 19.4% management, business, and financial, 4.3% computer, engineering, and science, 6.0% education, legal, community service, arts, and media, 5.2% healthcare practitioners, 12.2% service, 31.5% sales and office, 10.5% natural resources, construction, and maintenance, 11.0% production, transportation, and material moving
Income: Per capita: $27,794; Median household: $62,798; Average household: $71,413; Households with income of $100,000 or more: 20.5%; Poverty rate: 7.5%

Educational Attainment: High school diploma or higher: 93.5%; Bachelor's degree or higher: 27.9%; Graduate/professional degree or higher: 10.4%
Housing: Homeownership rate: 86.7%; Median home value: $155,500; Median year structure built: 1967; Homeowner vacancy rate: 1.5%; Median gross rent: $1,090 per month; Rental vacancy rate: 5.7%
Health Insurance: 90.0% have insurance; 79.5% have private insurance; 24.8% have public insurance; 10.0% do not have insurance; 9.1% of children under 18 do not have insurance
Transportation: Commute: 90.7% car, 0.9% public transportation, 1.5% walk, 6.2% work from home; Median travel time to work: 18.9 minutes

FLEMING (unincorporated postal area)

ZCTA: 45729

Covers a land area of 25.572 square miles and a water area of 0.040 square miles. Located at 39.42° N. Lat; 81.60° W. Long. Elevation is 791 feet.
Population: 1,289; Growth (since 2000): -8.6%; Density: 50.4 persons per square mile; Race: 98.1% White, 0.9% Black/African American, 0.1% Asian, 0.4% American Indian/Alaska Native, 0.0% Native Hawaiian/Other Pacific Islander, 0.5% Two or more races, 0.2% Hispanic of any race; Average household size: 2.53; Median age: 44.4; Age under 18: 21.8%; Age 65 and over: 14.7%; Males per 100 females: 105.3
Housing: Homeownership rate: 88.6%; Homeowner vacancy rate: 0.4%; Rental vacancy rate: 7.9%

LITTLE HOCKING (CDP). Covers a land area of 0.415 square miles and a water area of 0.012 square miles. Located at 39.26° N. Lat; 81.70° W. Long. Elevation is 640 feet.
Population: 263; Growth (since 2000): n/a; Density: 633.8 persons per square mile; Race: 97.0% White, 0.8% Black/African American, 0.0% Asian, 0.0% American Indian/Alaska Native, 0.0% Native Hawaiian/Other Pacific Islander, 2.3% Two or more races, 0.0% Hispanic of any race; Average household size: 2.35; Median age: 44.1; Age under 18: 20.2%; Age 65 and over: 17.5%; Males per 100 females: 96.3

School District(s)

Warren Local (PK-12)
2012-13 Enrollment: 2,193 . . . . (740) 678-2366
Housing: Homeownership rate: 75.9%; Homeowner vacancy rate: 3.3%; Rental vacancy rate: 6.9%

LOWELL (village). Covers a land area of 0.228 square miles and a water area of 0.009 square miles. Located at 39.53° N. Lat; 81.51° W. Long. Elevation is 627 feet.
History: Lowell was founded in 1822 and grew around woolen mills. It was named for the textile town in Massachusetts.
Population: 549; Growth (since 2000): -12.6%; Density: 2,409.5 persons per square mile; Race: 98.7% White, 0.4% Black/African American, 0.0% Asian, 0.0% American Indian/Alaska Native, 0.0% Native Hawaiian/Other Pacific Islander, 0.7% Two or more races, 0.4% Hispanic of any race; Average household size: 2.21; Median age: 45.2; Age under 18: 22.6%; Age 65 and over: 22.8%; Males per 100 females: 84.8

School District(s)

Fort Frye Local (PK-12)
2012-13 Enrollment: 954 . . . . (740) 984-2497
Housing: Homeownership rate: 77.4%; Homeowner vacancy rate: 4.0%; Rental vacancy rate: 5.1%

LOWER SALEM (village). Covers a land area of 0.059 square miles and a water area of 0.003 square miles. Located at 39.56° N. Lat; 81.39° W. Long. Elevation is 653 feet.
History: Lower Salem was platted in 1850 by James Stanley.
Population: 86; Growth (since 2000): -21.1%; Density: 1,464.9 persons per square mile; Race: 93.0% White, 7.0% Black/African American, 0.0% Asian, 0.0% American Indian/Alaska Native, 0.0% Native Hawaiian/Other Pacific Islander, 0.0% Two or more races, 1.2% Hispanic of any race; Average household size: 2.77; Median age: 41.0; Age under 18: 23.3%; Age 65 and over: 14.0%; Males per 100 females: 79.2

School District(s)

Fort Frye Local (PK-12)
2012-13 Enrollment: 954 . . . . (740) 984-2497
Housing: Homeownership rate: 80.7%; Homeowner vacancy rate: 0.0%; Rental vacancy rate: 0.0%

MACKSBURG (village). Covers a land area of 0.216 square miles and a water area of 0.007 square miles. Located at 39.63° N. Lat; 81.46° W. Long. Elevation is 702 feet.
Population: 186; Growth (since 2000): -7.9%; Density: 861.3 persons per square mile; Race: 100.0% White, 0.0% Black/African American, 0.0% Asian, 0.0% American Indian/Alaska Native, 0.0% Native Hawaiian/Other Pacific Islander, 0.0% Two or more races, 0.0% Hispanic of any race; Average household size: 2.42; Median age: 40.0; Age under 18: 20.4%; Age 65 and over: 14.0%; Males per 100 females: 118.8
Housing: Homeownership rate: 83.1%; Homeowner vacancy rate: 0.0%; Rental vacancy rate: 0.0%

MARIETTA (city). County seat. Covers a land area of 8.433 square miles and a water area of 0.319 square miles. Located at 39.43° N. Lat; 81.45° W. Long. Elevation is 614 feet.
History: Marietta was settled at the confluence of the Muskingum and Ohio Rivers in 1788 by the Ohio Company of Associates, a group of New Englanders looking for land to the west. At first they called the settlement Muskingum, but soon the name was officially declared to be Marietta, a tribute to Queen Marie Antoinette of France for her help in the American Revolution.
Population: 14,085; Growth (since 2000): -3.0%; Density: 1,670.2 persons per square mile; Race: 94.9% White, 1.3% Black/African American, 1.4% Asian, 0.3% American Indian/Alaska Native, 0.0% Native Hawaiian/Other Pacific Islander, 1.5% Two or more races, 1.1% Hispanic of any race; Average household size: 2.14; Median age: 39.0; Age under 18: 18.9%; Age 65 and over: 18.4%; Males per 100 females: 88.4; Marriage status: 33.0% never married, 42.8% now married, 2.6% separated, 9.5% widowed, 14.6% divorced; Foreign born: 2.8%; Speak English only: 96.8%; With disability: 19.9%; Veterans: 11.5%; Ancestry: 25.5% German, 16.5% Irish, 11.3% American, 10.2% English, 3.5% Italian
Employment: 9.5% management, business, and financial, 4.3% computer, engineering, and science, 11.0% education, legal, community service, arts, and media, 7.2% healthcare practitioners, 24.7% service, 25.4% sales and office, 7.3% natural resources, construction, and maintenance, 10.5% production, transportation, and material moving
Income: Per capita: $24,101; Median household: $31,739; Average household: $52,985; Households with income of $100,000 or more: 12.1%; Poverty rate: 22.8%
Educational Attainment: High school diploma or higher: 87.5%; Bachelor's degree or higher: 23.3%; Graduate/professional degree or higher: 7.8%

School District(s)

Frontier Local (PK-12)
2012-13 Enrollment: 673 . . . . (740) 865-3473
Marietta City (PK-12)
2012-13 Enrollment: 2,728 . . . . (740) 374-6500
Warren Local (PK-12)
2012-13 Enrollment: 2,193 . . . . (740) 678-2366
Washington County (10-12)
2012-13 Enrollment: n/a . . . . (740) 373-2766

Four-year College(s)

Marietta College (Private, Not-for-profit)
Fall 2013 Enrollment: 1,542 . . . . (740) 376-4643
2013-14 Tuition: In-state $31,940; Out-of-state $31,940

Two-year College(s)

Washington County Career Center-Adult Technical Training (Public)
Fall 2013 Enrollment: 261 . . . . (740) 373-6283
Washington State Community College (Public)
Fall 2013 Enrollment: 1,759 . . . . (740) 374-8716
2013-14 Tuition: In-state $4,235; Out-of-state $8,315
Housing: Homeownership rate: 54.7%; Median home value: $100,000; Median year structure built: 1951; Homeowner vacancy rate: 2.8%; Median gross rent: $568 per month; Rental vacancy rate: 10.9%
Health Insurance: 86.9% have insurance; 63.2% have private insurance; 38.6% have public insurance; 13.1% do not have insurance; 11.6% of children under 18 do not have insurance
Hospitals: Marietta Memorial Hospital (204 beds); Selby General Hospital (80 beds)
Safety: Violent crime rate: 13.6 per 10,000 population; Property crime rate: 132.7 per 10,000 population
Newspapers: Marietta Times (daily circulation 10700)
Transportation: Commute: 88.2% car, 0.2% public transportation, 7.6% walk, 3.3% work from home; Median travel time to work: 15.1 minutes
Additional Information Contacts

City of Marietta . . . . (740) 373-1387
http://www.mariettaoh.net

MATAMORAS (village). Covers a land area of 0.348 square miles and a water area of 0.038 square miles. Located at 39.52° N. Lat; 81.07° W. Long. Elevation is 646 feet.
History: Matamoras, known as New Matamoras, was the center of a gas and oil boom during the latter decades of the 19th century.
Population: 896; Growth (since 2000): -6.4%; Density: 2,577.4 persons per square mile; Race: 97.2% White, 0.4% Black/African American, 0.2% Asian, 0.1% American Indian/Alaska Native, 0.0% Native Hawaiian/Other Pacific Islander, 2.0% Two or more races, 1.0% Hispanic of any race; Average household size: 2.23; Median age: 41.7; Age under 18: 23.4%; Age 65 and over: 20.2%; Males per 100 females: 88.6

School District(s)

Frontier Local (PK-12)
2012-13 Enrollment: 673. . . . . (740) 865-3473
Housing: Homeownership rate: 54.7%; Homeowner vacancy rate: 1.3%; Rental vacancy rate: 3.2%
Safety: Violent crime rate: 0.0 per 10,000 population; Property crime rate: 304.4 per 10,000 population

NEWPORT (CDP). Covers a land area of 1.619 square miles and a water area of 0.102 square miles. Located at 39.40° N. Lat; 81.22° W. Long. Elevation is 640 feet.
Population: 1,003; Growth (since 2000): n/a; Density: 619.7 persons per square mile; Race: 98.8% White, 0.0% Black/African American, 0.6% Asian, 0.1% American Indian/Alaska Native, 0.0% Native Hawaiian/Other Pacific Islander, 0.5% Two or more races, 0.4% Hispanic of any race; Average household size: 2.51; Median age: 42.2; Age under 18: 22.2%; Age 65 and over: 17.2%; Males per 100 females: 94.4

School District(s)

Frontier Local (PK-12)
2012-13 Enrollment: 673. . . . . (740) 865-3473
Housing: Homeownership rate: 85.5%; Homeowner vacancy rate: 1.4%; Rental vacancy rate: 16.7%

RENO (CDP). Covers a land area of 0.768 square miles and a water area of 0.017 square miles. Located at 39.37° N. Lat; 81.39° W. Long. Elevation is 646 feet.
Population: 1,293; Growth (since 2000): n/a; Density: 1,683.6 persons per square mile; Race: 97.5% White, 0.3% Black/African American, 0.6% Asian, 0.2% American Indian/Alaska Native, 0.0% Native Hawaiian/Other Pacific Islander, 1.3% Two or more races, 0.5% Hispanic of any race; Average household size: 2.07; Median age: 48.1; Age under 18: 18.3%; Age 65 and over: 24.7%; Males per 100 females: 89.6
Housing: Homeownership rate: 61.9%; Homeowner vacancy rate: 0.5%; Rental vacancy rate: 3.3%

VINCENT (CDP). Covers a land area of 0.383 square miles and a water area of 0.001 square miles. Located at 39.38° N. Lat; 81.67° W. Long. Elevation is 771 feet.
Population: 339; Growth (since 2000): n/a; Density: 885.5 persons per square mile; Race: 95.9% White, 2.9% Black/African American, 0.0% Asian, 0.6% American Indian/Alaska Native, 0.0% Native Hawaiian/Other Pacific Islander, 0.6% Two or more races, 2.1% Hispanic of any race; Average household size: 2.47; Median age: 40.2; Age under 18: 23.3%; Age 65 and over: 13.3%; Males per 100 females: 92.6

School District(s)

Warren Local (PK-12)
2012-13 Enrollment: 2,193 . . . . (740) 678-2366
Housing: Homeownership rate: 75.2%; Homeowner vacancy rate: 1.0%; Rental vacancy rate: 12.8%

WATERFORD (CDP). Covers a land area of 0.471 square miles and a water area of 0.051 square miles. Located at 39.54° N. Lat; 81.64° W. Long. Elevation is 653 feet.
Population: 450; Growth (since 2000): n/a; Density: 955.9 persons per square mile; Race: 98.7% White, 0.0% Black/African American, 0.0% Asian, 0.2% American Indian/Alaska Native, 0.0% Native Hawaiian/Other Pacific Islander, 1.1% Two or more races, 0.4% Hispanic of any race; Average household size: 2.47; Median age: 34.9; Age under 18: 27.3%; Age 65 and over: 17.3%; Males per 100 females: 94.8

School District(s)

Wolf Creek Local (PK-12)
2012-13 Enrollment: 587. . . . . (740) 984-2373
Housing: Homeownership rate: 67.0%; Homeowner vacancy rate: 2.3%; Rental vacancy rate: 6.3%

WHIPPLE (unincorporated postal area)
ZCTA: 45788
Covers a land area of 34.525 square miles and a water area of 0.165 square miles. Located at 39.51° N. Lat; 81.37° W. Long. Elevation is 646 feet.
Population: 1,129; Growth (since 2000): 12.8%; Density: 32.7 persons per square mile; Race: 98.2% White, 0.0% Black/African American, 0.4% Asian, 0.0% American Indian/Alaska Native, 0.0% Native Hawaiian/Other Pacific Islander, 1.4% Two or more races, 0.0% Hispanic of any race; Average household size: 2.59; Median age: 41.2; Age under 18: 22.9%; Age 65 and over: 13.6%; Males per 100 females: 101.2
Housing: Homeownership rate: 84.1%; Homeowner vacancy rate: 1.3%; Rental vacancy rate: 0.0%

WINGETT RUN (unincorporated postal area)
ZCTA: 45789
Covers a land area of 11.422 square miles and a water area of 0.065 square miles. Located at 39.55° N. Lat; 81.26° W. Long. Elevation is 656 feet.
Population: 177; Growth (since 2000): -42.5%; Density: 15.5 persons per square mile; Race: 94.9% White, 5.1% Black/African American, 0.0% Asian, 0.0% American Indian/Alaska Native, 0.0% Native Hawaiian/Other Pacific Islander, 0.0% Two or more races, 0.0% Hispanic of any race; Average household size: 2.57; Median age: 40.6; Age under 18: 23.2%; Age 65 and over: 10.7%; Males per 100 females: 126.9
Housing: Homeownership rate: 88.4%; Homeowner vacancy rate: 1.6%; Rental vacancy rate: 11.1%

Wayne County

Located in north central Ohio; crossed by the Lake Fork of the Mohican River. Covers a land area of 554.929 square miles, a water area of 1.888 square miles, and is located in the Eastern Time Zone at 40.83° N. Lat., 81.89° W. Long. The county was founded in 1786. County seat is Wooster.

Wayne County is part of the Wooster, OH Micropolitan Statistical Area. The entire metro area includes: Wayne County, OH

Weather Station: Wooster Exp Stn Elevation: 1,020 feet

	Jan	Feb	Mar	Apr	May	Jun	Jul	Aug	Sep	Oct	Nov	Dec
High	33	37	47	60	70	78	82	80	73	61	50	37
Low	19	21	28	38	48	57	61	59	52	41	33	24
Precip	2.3	2.0	2.8	3.7	4.4	4.3	4.2	4.1	3.4	3.0	3.1	2.7
Snow	8.4	6.4	5.6	1.1	tr	0.0	0.0	tr	0.0	0.1	1.5	6.2

High and Low temperatures in degrees Fahrenheit; Precipitation and Snow in inches

Population: 114,520; Growth (since 2000): 2.6%; Density: 206.4 persons per square mile; Race: 95.7% White, 1.5% Black/African American, 0.8% Asian, 0.2% American Indian/Alaska Native, 0.0% Native Hawaiian/Other Pacific Islander, 1.4% two or more races, 1.6% Hispanic of any race; Average household size: 2.61; Median age: 38.3; Age under 18: 25.4%; Age 65 and over: 14.6%; Males per 100 females: 97.7; Marriage status: 26.8% never married, 57.3% now married, 1.3% separated, 5.8% widowed, 10.0% divorced; Foreign born: 1.8%; Speak English only: 89.7%; With disability: 11.5%; Veterans: 9.4%; Ancestry: 31.6% German, 12.0% American, 12.0% Irish, 8.6% English, 5.9% Swiss
Religion: Six largest groups: 13.9% European Free-Church, 7.9% Catholicism, 6.3% Baptist, 5.8% Presbyterian-Reformed, 5.6% Non-denominational Protestant, 5.5% Methodist/Pietist
Economy: Unemployment rate: 3.7%; Leading industries: 14.9% retail trade; 13.0% construction; 12.4% other services (except public administration); Farms: 1,928 totaling 271,657 acres; Company size: 0 employ 1,000 or more persons, 5 employ 500 to 999 persons, 58 employ 100 to 499 persons, 2,387 employ less than 100 persons; Business ownership: 2,146 women-owned, 85 Black-owned, n/a Hispanic-owned, 121 Asian-owned
Employment: 10.3% management, business, and financial, 4.5% computer, engineering, and science, 9.8% education, legal, community service, arts, and media, 4.4% healthcare practitioners, 17.3% service,

22.3% sales and office, 10.4% natural resources, construction, and maintenance, 21.0% production, transportation, and material moving
Income: Per capita: $23,061; Median household: $49,135; Average household: $61,230; Households with income of $100,000 or more: 15.0%; Poverty rate: 12.4%
Educational Attainment: High school diploma or higher: 85.9%; Bachelor's degree or higher: 20.0%; Graduate/professional degree or higher: 7.3%
Housing: Homeownership rate: 73.0%; Median home value: $135,300; Median year structure built: 1972; Homeowner vacancy rate: 1.8%; Median gross rent: $665 per month; Rental vacancy rate: 9.6%
Vital Statistics: Birth rate: 132.1 per 10,000 population; Death rate: 90.0 per 10,000 population; Age-adjusted cancer mortality rate: 165.1 deaths per 100,000 population
Health Insurance: 84.9% have insurance; 69.2% have private insurance; 28.6% have public insurance; 15.1% do not have insurance; 16.1% of children under 18 do not have insurance
Health Care: Physicians: 12.9 per 10,000 population; Hospital beds: 15.3 per 10,000 population; Hospital admissions: 568.2 per 10,000 population
Transportation: Commute: 88.1% car, 0.2% public transportation, 5.3% walk, 4.8% work from home; Median travel time to work: 20.3 minutes
Presidential Election: 38.4% Obama, 59.7% Romney (2012)
National and State Parks: Johnson Woods State Nature Preserve; Killbuck Marsh State Wildlife Area
Additional Information Contacts
Wayne Government .... (330) 287-5400
http://www.wayneohio.org

Wayne County Communities

APPLE CREEK (village). Covers a land area of 0.581 square miles and a water area of 0.004 square miles. Located at 40.75° N. Lat; 81.83° W. Long. Elevation is 1,050 feet.
Population: 1,173; Growth (since 2000): 17.4%; Density: 2,019.7 persons per square mile; Race: 97.7% White, 0.3% Black/African American, 0.7% Asian, 0.3% American Indian/Alaska Native, 0.0% Native Hawaiian/Other Pacific Islander, 0.3% Two or more races, 3.7% Hispanic of any race; Average household size: 2.61; Median age: 37.9; Age under 18: 27.3%; Age 65 and over: 13.7%; Males per 100 females: 97.8

School District(s)

Southeast Local (PK-12)
2012-13 Enrollment: 1,486 .... (330) 698-3001
Housing: Homeownership rate: 74.8%; Homeowner vacancy rate: 2.9%; Rental vacancy rate: 10.2%

BURBANK (village). Covers a land area of 0.347 square miles and a water area of 0 square miles. Located at 40.99° N. Lat; 81.99° W. Long. Elevation is 955 feet.
Population: 207; Growth (since 2000): -25.8%; Density: 596.2 persons per square mile; Race: 97.6% White, 1.0% Black/African American, 0.0% Asian, 0.5% American Indian/Alaska Native, 0.0% Native Hawaiian/Other Pacific Islander, 1.0% Two or more races, 0.5% Hispanic of any race; Average household size: 2.56; Median age: 41.1; Age under 18: 23.7%; Age 65 and over: 15.5%; Males per 100 females: 107.0
Housing: Homeownership rate: 72.8%; Homeowner vacancy rate: 4.8%; Rental vacancy rate: 26.7%

CONGRESS (village). Covers a land area of 0.158 square miles and a water area of 0 square miles. Located at 40.93° N. Lat; 82.06° W. Long. Elevation is 1,161 feet.
History: Congress was established in 1827.
Population: 185; Growth (since 2000): -3.6%; Density: 1,168.6 persons per square mile; Race: 97.3% White, 0.5% Black/African American, 0.5% Asian, 0.0% American Indian/Alaska Native, 0.0% Native Hawaiian/Other Pacific Islander, 1.6% Two or more races, 2.7% Hispanic of any race; Average household size: 2.85; Median age: 35.7; Age under 18: 29.7%; Age 65 and over: 10.3%; Males per 100 females: 83.2
Housing: Homeownership rate: 70.8%; Homeowner vacancy rate: 2.1%; Rental vacancy rate: 9.5%

CRESTON (village). Covers a land area of 2.255 square miles and a water area of 0 square miles. Located at 40.98° N. Lat; 81.90° W. Long. Elevation is 991 feet.
Population: 2,171; Growth (since 2000): 0.5%; Density: 962.9 persons per square mile; Race: 96.9% White, 0.4% Black/African American, 0.7% Asian, 0.1% American Indian/Alaska Native, 0.0% Native Hawaiian/Other Pacific Islander, 1.8% Two or more races, 1.0% Hispanic of any race; Average household size: 2.51; Median age: 40.2; Age under 18: 24.5%; Age 65 and over: 17.0%; Males per 100 females: 92.5

School District(s)

Norwayne Local (PK-12)
2012-13 Enrollment: 1,434 .... (330) 435-6382
Housing: Homeownership rate: 76.6%; Homeowner vacancy rate: 1.8%; Rental vacancy rate: 9.8%

DALTON (village). Covers a land area of 1.505 square miles and a water area of 0 square miles. Located at 40.80° N. Lat; 81.70° W. Long. Elevation is 1,099 feet.
Population: 1,830; Growth (since 2000): 14.0%; Density: 1,215.8 persons per square mile; Race: 96.7% White, 0.3% Black/African American, 0.9% Asian, 0.1% American Indian/Alaska Native, 0.1% Native Hawaiian/Other Pacific Islander, 2.0% Two or more races, 1.5% Hispanic of any race; Average household size: 2.40; Median age: 43.4; Age under 18: 23.9%; Age 65 and over: 19.1%; Males per 100 females: 89.6

School District(s)

Dalton Local (PK-12)
2012-13 Enrollment: 890 .... (330) 828-2267
Housing: Homeownership rate: 73.0%; Homeowner vacancy rate: 2.0%; Rental vacancy rate: 11.2%
Newspapers: Dalton Gazette (weekly circulation 1400)

DOYLESTOWN (village). Covers a land area of 1.875 square miles and a water area of 0.002 square miles. Located at 40.97° N. Lat; 81.70° W. Long. Elevation is 1,247 feet.
Population: 3,051; Growth (since 2000): 9.0%; Density: 1,627.4 persons per square mile; Race: 97.9% White, 0.6% Black/African American, 0.2% Asian, 0.1% American Indian/Alaska Native, 0.0% Native Hawaiian/Other Pacific Islander, 0.9% Two or more races, 1.4% Hispanic of any race; Average household size: 2.45; Median age: 41.6; Age under 18: 24.8%; Age 65 and over: 18.8%; Males per 100 females: 86.2; Marriage status: 20.8% never married, 58.2% now married, 0.7% separated, 8.8% widowed, 12.3% divorced; Foreign born: 1.1%; Speak English only: 98.5%; With disability: 11.3%; Veterans: 10.8%; Ancestry: 31.9% German, 16.2% American, 12.1% English, 11.5% Irish, 4.3% Hungarian
Employment: 3.9% management, business, and financial, 10.5% computer, engineering, and science, 5.9% education, legal, community service, arts, and media, 6.9% healthcare practitioners, 24.3% service, 23.7% sales and office, 7.2% natural resources, construction, and maintenance, 17.5% production, transportation, and material moving
Income: Per capita: $25,766; Median household: $49,375; Average household: $58,414; Households with income of $100,000 or more: 13.3%; Poverty rate: 9.2%
Educational Attainment: High school diploma or higher: 93.4%; Bachelor's degree or higher: 23.1%; Graduate/professional degree or higher: 6.0%

School District(s)

Chippewa Local (PK-12)
2012-13 Enrollment: 1,426 .... (330) 658-6368
Housing: Homeownership rate: 70.1%; Median home value: $144,100; Median year structure built: 1970; Homeowner vacancy rate: 2.2%; Median gross rent: $675 per month; Rental vacancy rate: 8.1%
Health Insurance: 91.4% have insurance; 76.7% have private insurance; 29.3% have public insurance; 8.6% do not have insurance; 0.0% of children under 18 do not have insurance
Transportation: Commute: 90.5% car, 0.0% public transportation, 2.9% walk, 5.5% work from home; Median travel time to work: 19.8 minutes

FREDERICKSBURG (village). Covers a land area of 0.338 square miles and a water area of 0 square miles. Located at 40.68° N. Lat; 81.87° W. Long. Elevation is 974 feet.
Population: 423; Growth (since 2000): -13.1%; Density: 1,251.5 persons per square mile; Race: 99.3% White, 0.0% Black/African American, 0.5% Asian, 0.0% American Indian/Alaska Native, 0.0% Native Hawaiian/Other Pacific Islander, 0.2% Two or more races, 1.2% Hispanic of any race; Average household size: 2.37; Median age: 33.8; Age under 18: 24.1%; Age 65 and over: 15.1%; Males per 100 females: 97.7

School District(s)

Southeast Local (PK-12)
2012-13 Enrollment: 1,486 .... (330) 698-3001

Housing: Homeownership rate: 67.8%; Homeowner vacancy rate: 0.8%; Rental vacancy rate: 9.5%

KIDRON (CDP). Covers a land area of 2.927 square miles and a water area of <.001 square miles. Located at 40.75° N. Lat; 81.75° W. Long. Elevation is 1,102 feet.

Population: 944; Growth (since 2000): n/a; Density: 322.6 persons per square mile; Race: 97.6% White, 0.6% Black/African American, 0.8% Asian, 0.1% American Indian/Alaska Native, 0.0% Native Hawaiian/Other Pacific Islander, 0.7% Two or more races, 0.5% Hispanic of any race; Average household size: 2.97; Median age: 36.8; Age under 18: 29.9%; Age 65 and over: 18.9%; Males per 100 females: 99.2

Housing: Homeownership rate: 79.0%; Homeowner vacancy rate: 1.6%; Rental vacancy rate: 2.9%

MARSHALLVILLE (village). Covers a land area of 0.572 square miles and a water area of 0 square miles. Located at 40.90° N. Lat; 81.73° W. Long. Elevation is 1,119 feet.

Population: 756; Growth (since 2000): -8.5%; Density: 1,321.3 persons per square mile; Race: 98.4% White, 0.3% Black/African American, 0.0% Asian, 0.8% American Indian/Alaska Native, 0.0% Native Hawaiian/Other Pacific Islander, 0.5% Two or more races, 0.5% Hispanic of any race; Average household size: 2.60; Median age: 39.3; Age under 18: 24.1%; Age 65 and over: 13.6%; Males per 100 females: 98.4

School District(s)

Green Local (PK-12)
2012-13 Enrollment: 1,137 . . . . (330) 669-3921

Housing: Homeownership rate: 74.9%; Homeowner vacancy rate: 2.7%; Rental vacancy rate: 9.9%

MOUNT EATON (village). Covers a land area of 0.178 square miles and a water area of 0 square miles. Located at 40.70° N. Lat; 81.70° W. Long. Elevation is 1,250 feet.

Population: 241; Growth (since 2000): -2.0%; Density: 1,356.4 persons per square mile; Race: 98.8% White, 0.0% Black/African American, 0.0% Asian, 0.0% American Indian/Alaska Native, 0.0% Native Hawaiian/Other Pacific Islander, 0.8% Two or more races, 0.4% Hispanic of any race; Average household size: 2.59; Median age: 36.5; Age under 18: 24.9%; Age 65 and over: 12.4%; Males per 100 females: 92.8

School District(s)

Southeast Local (PK-12)
2012-13 Enrollment: 1,486 . . . . (330) 698-3001

Housing: Homeownership rate: 66.7%; Homeowner vacancy rate: 4.6%; Rental vacancy rate: 5.9%

NEW PITTSBURG (CDP). Covers a land area of 1.364 square miles and a water area of 0.008 square miles. Located at 40.85° N. Lat; 82.10° W. Long. Elevation is 1,135 feet.

Population: 388; Growth (since 2000): n/a; Density: 284.5 persons per square mile; Race: 99.0% White, 1.0% Black/African American, 0.0% Asian, 0.0% American Indian/Alaska Native, 0.0% Native Hawaiian/Other Pacific Islander, 0.0% Two or more races, 0.0% Hispanic of any race; Average household size: 2.90; Median age: 41.4; Age under 18: 21.6%; Age 65 and over: 20.4%; Males per 100 females: 89.3

Housing: Homeownership rate: 83.5%; Homeowner vacancy rate: 1.0%; Rental vacancy rate: 13.6%

ORRVILLE (city). Covers a land area of 5.740 square miles and a water area of 0.013 square miles. Located at 40.85° N. Lat; 81.78° W. Long. Elevation is 1,060 feet.

History: Settled c.1850, incorporated 1864.

Population: 8,380; Growth (since 2000): -2.0%; Density: 1,459.8 persons per square mile; Race: 89.7% White, 4.9% Black/African American, 1.3% Asian, 0.1% American Indian/Alaska Native, 0.0% Native Hawaiian/Other Pacific Islander, 2.6% Two or more races, 3.5% Hispanic of any race; Average household size: 2.48; Median age: 39.0; Age under 18: 24.3%; Age 65 and over: 16.1%; Males per 100 females: 95.1; Marriage status: 22.6% never married, 57.3% now married, 2.6% separated, 8.7% widowed, 11.3% divorced; Foreign born: 1.3%; Speak English only: 97.4%; With disability: 15.2%; Veterans: 10.3%; Ancestry: 34.4% German, 16.4% Irish, 9.0% American, 7.0% English, 6.8% Italian

Employment: 8.2% management, business, and financial, 1.5% computer, engineering, and science, 12.1% education, legal, community service, arts, and media, 4.3% healthcare practitioners, 17.1% service, 27.9% sales and office, 5.2% natural resources, construction, and maintenance, 23.7% production, transportation, and material moving

Income: Per capita: $20,424; Median household: $38,365; Average household: $49,521; Households with income of $100,000 or more: 13.1%; Poverty rate: 20.7%

Educational Attainment: High school diploma or higher: 90.7%; Bachelor's degree or higher: 18.0%; Graduate/professional degree or higher: 7.0%

School District(s)

Orrville City (PK-12)
2012-13 Enrollment: 1,552 . . . . (330) 682-4651

Two-year College(s)

University of Akron Wayne College (Public)
Fall 2013 Enrollment: 2,020 . . . . (800) 221-8308
2013-14 Tuition: In-state $6,116; Out-of-state $12,964

Housing: Homeownership rate: 63.2%; Median home value: $126,100; Median year structure built: 1965; Homeowner vacancy rate: 2.4%; Median gross rent: $717 per month; Rental vacancy rate: 14.6%

Health Insurance: 90.3% have insurance; 67.3% have private insurance; 38.8% have public insurance; 9.7% do not have insurance; 2.8% of children under 18 do not have insurance

Hospitals: Aultman Orrville Hospital (51 beds)

Safety: Violent crime rate: 8.3 per 10,000 population; Property crime rate: 145.2 per 10,000 population

Transportation: Commute: 95.6% car, 0.0% public transportation, 1.7% walk, 2.2% work from home; Median travel time to work: 17.9 minutes

Additional Information Contacts

City of Orrville . . . . (330) 684-5000
http://www.orrville.com

RITTMAN (city). Covers a land area of 6.431 square miles and a water area of 0.064 square miles. Located at 40.97° N. Lat; 81.78° W. Long. Elevation is 981 feet.

Population: 6,491; Growth (since 2000): 2.8%; Density: 1,009.4 persons per square mile; Race: 97.2% White, 0.4% Black/African American, 0.4% Asian, 0.2% American Indian/Alaska Native, 0.0% Native Hawaiian/Other Pacific Islander, 1.6% Two or more races, 1.2% Hispanic of any race; Average household size: 2.52; Median age: 38.5; Age under 18: 23.9%; Age 65 and over: 14.7%; Males per 100 females: 95.7; Marriage status: 20.1% never married, 62.3% now married, 1.1% separated, 6.6% widowed, 11.0% divorced; Foreign born: 1.7%; Speak English only: 97.2%; With disability: 14.4%; Veterans: 10.2%; Ancestry: 29.4% German, 19.3% Irish, 12.2% American, 9.6% English, 9.1% Italian

Employment: 8.6% management, business, and financial, 5.6% computer, engineering, and science, 4.7% education, legal, community service, arts, and media, 8.7% healthcare practitioners, 18.4% service, 20.0% sales and office, 9.1% natural resources, construction, and maintenance, 24.9% production, transportation, and material moving

Income: Per capita: $22,881; Median household: $45,913; Average household: $57,354; Households with income of $100,000 or more: 14.2%; Poverty rate: 13.3%

Educational Attainment: High school diploma or higher: 88.1%; Bachelor's degree or higher: 13.5%; Graduate/professional degree or higher: 3.4%

School District(s)

Rittman Academy (06-12)
2012-13 Enrollment: 36. . . . . (330) 927-7401
Rittman Exempted Village (PK-12)
2012-13 Enrollment: 1,017 . . . . (330) 927-7400

Housing: Homeownership rate: 66.4%; Median home value: $103,900; Median year structure built: 1959; Homeowner vacancy rate: 3.6%; Median gross rent: $632 per month; Rental vacancy rate: 8.1%

Health Insurance: 88.8% have insurance; 68.7% have private insurance; 32.8% have public insurance; 11.2% do not have insurance; 6.0% of children under 18 do not have insurance

Safety: Violent crime rate: 10.8 per 10,000 population; Property crime rate: 210.6 per 10,000 population

Transportation: Commute: 93.7% car, 0.3% public transportation, 1.3% walk, 3.2% work from home; Median travel time to work: 27.0 minutes

Additional Information Contacts

City of Rittman. . . . . (330) 925-2045
http://www.rittman.com

SHREVE (village). Covers a land area of 0.849 square miles and a water area of 0 square miles. Located at 40.68° N. Lat; 82.02° W. Long. Elevation is 896 feet.

Population: 1,514; Growth (since 2000): -4.3%; Density: 1,782.4 persons per square mile; Race: 97.7% White, 0.2% Black/African American, 0.3% Asian, 0.1% American Indian/Alaska Native, 0.1% Native Hawaiian/Other Pacific Islander, 0.9% Two or more races, 1.1% Hispanic of any race; Average household size: 2.49; Median age: 35.5; Age under 18: 27.9%; Age 65 and over: 12.6%; Males per 100 females: 92.6

School District(s)

Triway Local (PK-12)
2012-13 Enrollment: 1,704 . . . . (330) 264-9491

Housing: Homeownership rate: 65.6%; Homeowner vacancy rate: 3.6%; Rental vacancy rate: 18.4%

SMITHVILLE (village). Covers a land area of 1.238 square miles and a water area of 0.006 square miles. Located at 40.86° N. Lat; 81.86° W. Long. Elevation is 1,060 feet.

Population: 1,252; Growth (since 2000): -6.1%; Density: 1,011.6 persons per square mile; Race: 97.8% White, 0.9% Black/African American, 0.6% Asian, 0.4% American Indian/Alaska Native, 0.0% Native Hawaiian/Other Pacific Islander, 0.3% Two or more races, 1.3% Hispanic of any race; Average household size: 2.31; Median age: 44.2; Age under 18: 21.8%; Age 65 and over: 16.6%; Males per 100 females: 89.1

School District(s)

Green Local (PK-12)
2012-13 Enrollment: 1,137 . . . . (330) 669-3921
Wayne County Jvsd (09-12)
2012-13 Enrollment: n/a . . . . (330) 669-7000

Vocational/Technical School(s)

Wayne County Schools Career Center (Public)
Fall 2013 Enrollment: 360 . . . . (330) 669-7070
2013-14 Tuition: $12,450

Housing: Homeownership rate: 64.9%; Homeowner vacancy rate: 2.0%; Rental vacancy rate: 5.9%

STERLING (CDP). Covers a land area of 0.976 square miles and a water area of 0 square miles. Located at 40.97° N. Lat; 81.84° W. Long. Elevation is 968 feet.

Population: 457; Growth (since 2000): n/a; Density: 468.1 persons per square mile; Race: 97.8% White, 0.4% Black/African American, 0.0% Asian, 0.0% American Indian/Alaska Native, 0.2% Native Hawaiian/Other Pacific Islander, 1.3% Two or more races, 0.2% Hispanic of any race; Average household size: 2.69; Median age: 33.7; Age under 18: 23.2%; Age 65 and over: 9.4%; Males per 100 females: 100.4

Housing: Homeownership rate: 73.0%; Homeowner vacancy rate: 1.6%; Rental vacancy rate: 23.3%

WEST SALEM (village). Covers a land area of 1.088 square miles and a water area of 0.003 square miles. Located at 40.97° N. Lat; 82.11° W. Long. Elevation is 1,112 feet.

History: West Salem was laid out in 1834 by the Rickel brothers, who came from Wooster.

Population: 1,464; Growth (since 2000): -2.5%; Density: 1,345.5 persons per square mile; Race: 97.8% White, 0.1% Black/African American, 0.0% Asian, 0.1% American Indian/Alaska Native, 0.0% Native Hawaiian/Other Pacific Islander, 1.0% Two or more races, 2.1% Hispanic of any race; Average household size: 2.62; Median age: 37.1; Age under 18: 27.1%; Age 65 and over: 10.9%; Males per 100 females: 102.5

School District(s)

Northwestern Local (PK-12)
2012-13 Enrollment: 1,351 . . . . (419) 846-3151

Housing: Homeownership rate: 77.1%; Homeowner vacancy rate: 3.4%; Rental vacancy rate: 14.1%

WOOSTER (city). County seat. Covers a land area of 16.310 square miles and a water area of 0.051 square miles. Located at 40.82° N. Lat; 81.93° W. Long. Elevation is 994 feet.

History: Wooster was settled in 1807 by the Larwill family. The town that grew after the War of 1812 was named for Revolutionary War general David Wooster. Wooster claims to have had America's first Christmas tree in 1847, when a young German immigrant, August Imgard, cut and decorated a small spruce tree.

Population: 26,119; Growth (since 2000): 5.3%; Density: 1,601.4 persons per square mile; Race: 91.2% White, 3.6% Black/African American, 1.9% Asian, 0.3% American Indian/Alaska Native, 0.0% Native Hawaiian/Other Pacific Islander, 2.4% Two or more races, 2.2% Hispanic of any race; Average household size: 2.21; Median age: 37.3; Age under 18: 20.4%; Age 65 and over: 16.6%; Males per 100 females: 91.0; Marriage status: 36.3% never married, 46.1% now married, 1.1% separated, 6.0% widowed, 11.7% divorced; Foreign born: 3.9%; Speak English only: 93.4%; With disability: 12.3%; Veterans: 8.9%; Ancestry: 29.8% German, 11.6% American, 10.7% Irish, 10.0% English, 5.8% Italian

Employment: 8.7% management, business, and financial, 6.8% computer, engineering, and science, 15.1% education, legal, community service, arts, and media, 4.2% healthcare practitioners, 21.2% service, 22.5% sales and office, 5.7% natural resources, construction, and maintenance, 15.8% production, transportation, and material moving

Income: Per capita: $24,221; Median household: $40,633; Average household: $58,530; Households with income of $100,000 or more: 12.7%; Poverty rate: 17.4%

Educational Attainment: High school diploma or higher: 90.7%; Bachelor's degree or higher: 28.9%; Graduate/professional degree or higher: 11.6%

School District(s)

Triway Local (PK-12)
2012-13 Enrollment: 1,704 . . . . (330) 264-9491
Wooster City (PK-12)
2012-13 Enrollment: 3,602 . . . . (330) 264-0869

Four-year College(s)

The College of Wooster (Private, Not-for-profit)
Fall 2013 Enrollment: 2,116 . . . . (330) 263-2000
2013-14 Tuition: In-state $41,680; Out-of-state $41,680

Two-year College(s)

Ohio State University Agricultural Technical Institute (Public)
Fall 2013 Enrollment: 643 . . . . (330) 287-1330
2013-14 Tuition: In-state $7,104; Out-of-state $22,824

Housing: Homeownership rate: 58.9%; Median home value: $123,100; Median year structure built: 1972; Homeowner vacancy rate: 2.6%; Median gross rent: $656 per month; Rental vacancy rate: 10.2%

Health Insurance: 91.1% have insurance; 72.1% have private insurance; 34.9% have public insurance; 8.9% do not have insurance; 3.7% of children under 18 do not have insurance

Hospitals: Wooster Community Hospital (130 beds)

Safety: Violent crime rate: 15.9 per 10,000 population; Property crime rate: 370.6 per 10,000 population

Newspapers: Daily Record (daily circulation 21600)

Transportation: Commute: 83.8% car, 0.4% public transportation, 10.7% walk, 3.1% work from home; Median travel time to work: 16.4 minutes

Airports: Wayne County (general aviation)

Additional Information Contacts

City of Wooster . . . . (330) 263-5200
http://www.woosteroh.com

Williams County

Located in northwestern Ohio; bounded on the north by Michigan, and on the west by Indiana; crossed by the Saint Joseph and Tiffin Rivers. Covers a land area of 420.965 square miles, a water area of 2.126 square miles, and is located in the Eastern Time Zone at 41.56° N. Lat., 84.58° W. Long. The county was founded in 1820. County seat is Bryan.

Weather Station: Montpelier Elevation: 859 feet

	Jan	Feb	Mar	Apr	May	Jun	Jul	Aug	Sep	Oct	Nov	Dec
High	32	35	46	59	71	80	84	82	75	62	49	36
Low	15	17	25	36	46	56	60	59	50	39	31	21
Precip	2.2	2.0	2.7	3.4	4.0	3.5	3.7	4.0	3.3	3.0	3.1	2.7
Snow	9.1	8.4	4.7	0.9	tr	0.0	0.0	0.0	0.0	0.2	1.4	9.0

High and Low temperatures in degrees Fahrenheit; Precipitation and Snow in inches

Population: 37,642; Growth (since 2000): -3.9%; Density: 89.4 persons per square mile; Race: 95.9% White, 1.0% Black/African American, 0.6% Asian, 0.2% American Indian/Alaska Native, 0.0% Native Hawaiian/Other Pacific Islander, 1.2% two or more races, 3.7% Hispanic of any race; Average household size: 2.43; Median age: 40.7; Age under 18: 23.7%; Age 65 and over: 16.0%; Males per 100 females: 98.5; Marriage status: 22.5% never married, 57.0% now married, 1.7% separated, 6.6% widowed, 13.9% divorced; Foreign born: 1.6%; Speak English only: 96.9%;

With disability: 13.3%; Veterans: 10.9%; Ancestry: 40.9% German, 11.9% Irish, 10.6% English, 7.3% American, 3.8% French
Religion: Six largest groups: 10.3% Catholicism, 8.7% Methodist/Pietist, 5.2% Lutheran, 4.8% Baptist, 3.7% Non-denominational Protestant, 2.7% European Free-Church
Economy: Unemployment rate: 4.2%; Leading industries: 15.5% retail trade; 14.8% other services (except public administration); 13.9% manufacturing; Farms: 984 totaling 208,012 acres; Company size: 0 employ 1,000 or more persons, 2 employ 500 to 999 persons, 25 employ 100 to 499 persons, 786 employ less than 100 persons; Business ownership: n/a women-owned, n/a Black-owned, 33 Hispanic-owned, 49 Asian-owned
Employment: 8.8% management, business, and financial, 2.4% computer, engineering, and science, 6.8% education, legal, community service, arts, and media, 5.2% healthcare practitioners, 14.2% service, 21.7% sales and office, 9.8% natural resources, construction, and maintenance, 31.2% production, transportation, and material moving
Income: Per capita: $21,350; Median household: $43,089; Average household: $52,988; Households with income of $100,000 or more: 11.5%; Poverty rate: 13.7%
Educational Attainment: High school diploma or higher: 89.3%; Bachelor's degree or higher: 12.8%; Graduate/professional degree or higher: 3.8%
Housing: Homeownership rate: 74.9%; Median home value: $98,600; Median year structure built: 1965; Homeowner vacancy rate: 2.5%; Median gross rent: $625 per month; Rental vacancy rate: 10.0%
Vital Statistics: Birth rate: 115.5 per 10,000 population; Death rate: 98.7 per 10,000 population; Age-adjusted cancer mortality rate: 168.6 deaths per 100,000 population
Health Insurance: 88.8% have insurance; 70.0% have private insurance; 34.6% have public insurance; 11.2% do not have insurance; 4.5% of children under 18 do not have insurance
Health Care: Physicians: 10.1 per 10,000 population; Hospital beds: 39.4 per 10,000 population; Hospital admissions: 1,267.1 per 10,000 population
Transportation: Commute: 93.6% car, 0.2% public transportation, 2.5% walk, 1.6% work from home; Median travel time to work: 19.2 minutes
Presidential Election: 40.8% Obama, 57.1% Romney (2012)
Additional Information Contacts
Williams Government . . . . (419) 636-2059
http://www.co.williams.oh.us

Williams County Communities

ALVORDTON (CDP). Covers a land area of 0.252 square miles and a water area of <.001 square miles. Located at 41.66° N. Lat; 84.43° W. Long. Elevation is 856 feet.
Population: 217; Growth (since 2000): -28.9%; Density: 861.0 persons per square mile; Race: 95.9% White, 2.8% Black/African American, 0.0% Asian, 0.0% American Indian/Alaska Native, 0.0% Native Hawaiian/Other Pacific Islander, 0.5% Two or more races, 1.8% Hispanic of any race; Average household size: 2.27; Median age: 44.8; Age under 18: 19.4%; Age 65 and over: 17.1%; Males per 100 females: 128.4
Housing: Homeownership rate: 76.1%; Homeowner vacancy rate: 4.3%; Rental vacancy rate: 19.2%

BLAKESLEE (village). Covers a land area of 0.108 square miles and a water area of 0 square miles. Located at 41.52° N. Lat; 84.73° W. Long. Elevation is 860 feet.
Population: 96; Growth (since 2000): -26.2%; Density: 892.3 persons per square mile; Race: 100.0% White, 0.0% Black/African American, 0.0% Asian, 0.0% American Indian/Alaska Native, 0.0% Native Hawaiian/Other Pacific Islander, 0.0% Two or more races, 0.0% Hispanic of any race; Average household size: 2.13; Median age: 38.0; Age under 18: 22.9%; Age 65 and over: 22.9%; Males per 100 females: 95.9
Housing: Homeownership rate: 68.9%; Homeowner vacancy rate: 0.0%; Rental vacancy rate: 0.0%

BRYAN (city). County seat. Covers a land area of 5.528 square miles and a water area of 0.032 square miles. Located at 41.47° N. Lat; 84.55° W. Long. Elevation is 768 feet.
History: Bryan's early growth was attributed to its artesian wells, their supposed medicinal value creating a temporary business for the town, which became a trading and industrial center and the seat of Williams County.
Population: 8,545; Growth (since 2000): 2.5%; Density: 1,545.6 persons per square mile; Race: 94.3% White, 0.6% Black/African American, 0.9% Asian, 0.2% American Indian/Alaska Native, 0.1% Native Hawaiian/Other Pacific Islander, 2.0% Two or more races, 5.1% Hispanic of any race; Average household size: 2.24; Median age: 39.7; Age under 18: 23.6%; Age 65 and over: 16.8%; Males per 100 females: 90.6; Marriage status: 21.8% never married, 54.3% now married, 2.7% separated, 7.5% widowed, 16.5% divorced; Foreign born: 2.2%; Speak English only: 95.1%; With disability: 16.4%; Veterans: 10.7%; Ancestry: 41.5% German, 13.2% Irish, 12.1% English, 5.6% American, 5.1% Dutch
Employment: 8.3% management, business, and financial, 4.2% computer, engineering, and science, 8.3% education, legal, community service, arts, and media, 6.6% healthcare practitioners, 12.0% service, 21.9% sales and office, 5.1% natural resources, construction, and maintenance, 33.6% production, transportation, and material moving
Income: Per capita: $19,590; Median household: $37,374; Average household: $47,016; Households with income of $100,000 or more: 8.0%; Poverty rate: 17.6%
Educational Attainment: High school diploma or higher: 89.2%; Bachelor's degree or higher: 14.5%; Graduate/professional degree or higher: 4.2%
School District(s)
Bryan City (PK-12)
2012-13 Enrollment: 1,926 . . . . (419) 636-6973
Housing: Homeownership rate: 60.5%; Median home value: $102,300; Median year structure built: 1963; Homeowner vacancy rate: 2.7%; Median gross rent: $627 per month; Rental vacancy rate: 9.9%
Health Insurance: 92.1% have insurance; 70.4% have private insurance; 35.4% have public insurance; 7.9% do not have insurance; 2.1% of children under 18 do not have insurance
Hospitals: Community Hospitals & Wellness Centers (131 beds)
Safety: Violent crime rate: 1.2 per 10,000 population; Property crime rate: 27.0 per 10,000 population
Newspapers: Bryan Times (daily circulation 10200); The Countyline (weekly circulation 21000)
Transportation: Commute: 85.8% car, 0.7% public transportation, 4.5% walk, 2.6% work from home; Median travel time to work: 15.7 minutes; Amtrak: Train service available.

EDGERTON (village). Covers a land area of 1.867 square miles and a water area of 0.011 square miles. Located at 41.45° N. Lat; 84.75° W. Long. Elevation is 840 feet.
Population: 2,012; Growth (since 2000): -5.0%; Density: 1,077.7 persons per square mile; Race: 97.7% White, 0.2% Black/African American, 0.4% Asian, 0.1% American Indian/Alaska Native, 0.0% Native Hawaiian/Other Pacific Islander, 0.8% Two or more races, 2.5% Hispanic of any race; Average household size: 2.44; Median age: 41.3; Age under 18: 24.6%; Age 65 and over: 17.8%; Males per 100 females: 89.8
School District(s)
Edgerton Local (PK-12)
2012-13 Enrollment: 615. . . . . (419) 298-2112
Housing: Homeownership rate: 73.9%; Homeowner vacancy rate: 2.5%; Rental vacancy rate: 12.0%
Newspapers: Edgerton Earth (weekly circulation 1200)

EDON (village). Covers a land area of 1.122 square miles and a water area of 0 square miles. Located at 41.56° N. Lat; 84.77° W. Long. Elevation is 899 feet.
Population: 834; Growth (since 2000): -7.1%; Density: 743.3 persons per square mile; Race: 98.0% White, 0.1% Black/African American, 0.2% Asian, 0.2% American Indian/Alaska Native, 0.0% Native Hawaiian/Other Pacific Islander, 1.4% Two or more races, 0.8% Hispanic of any race; Average household size: 2.46; Median age: 37.8; Age under 18: 25.5%; Age 65 and over: 17.7%; Males per 100 females: 92.6
School District(s)
Edon-Northwest Local (PK-12)
2012-13 Enrollment: 571. . . . . (419) 272-3213
Housing: Homeownership rate: 79.9%; Homeowner vacancy rate: 3.6%; Rental vacancy rate: 4.1%

HOLIDAY CITY (village). Covers a land area of 2.666 square miles and a water area of 0.021 square miles. Located at 41.62° N. Lat; 84.54° W. Long. Elevation is 902 feet.
Population: 52; Growth (since 2000): 6.1%; Density: 19.5 persons per square mile; Race: 100.0% White, 0.0% Black/African American, 0.0%

Asian, 0.0% American Indian/Alaska Native, 0.0% Native Hawaiian/Other Pacific Islander, 0.0% Two or more races, 0.0% Hispanic of any race; Average household size: 2.89; Median age: 34.0; Age under 18: 26.9%; Age 65 and over: 15.4%; Males per 100 females: 116.7
Housing: Homeownership rate: 61.1%; Homeowner vacancy rate: 8.3%; Rental vacancy rate: 0.0%

KUNKLE (CDP). Covers a land area of 0.280 square miles and a water area of 0 square miles. Located at 41.64° N. Lat; 84.49° W. Long. Elevation is 879 feet.
Population: 246; Growth (since 2000): n/a; Density: 877.7 persons per square mile; Race: 93.1% White, 0.4% Black/African American, 0.0% Asian, 0.4% American Indian/Alaska Native, 0.0% Native Hawaiian/Other Pacific Islander, 1.2% Two or more races, 4.1% Hispanic of any race; Average household size: 2.96; Median age: 31.6; Age under 18: 30.1%; Age 65 and over: 10.2%; Males per 100 females: 112.1
Housing: Homeownership rate: 71.1%; Homeowner vacancy rate: 3.3%; Rental vacancy rate: 11.1%

LAKE SENECA (CDP). Covers a land area of 1.728 square miles and a water area of 0.060 square miles. Located at 41.67° N. Lat; 84.64° W. Long. Elevation is 932 feet.
Population: 465; Growth (since 2000): n/a; Density: 269.1 persons per square mile; Race: 99.4% White, 0.0% Black/African American, 0.0% Asian, 0.0% American Indian/Alaska Native, 0.0% Native Hawaiian/Other Pacific Islander, 0.2% Two or more races, 1.7% Hispanic of any race; Average household size: 2.41; Median age: 47.9; Age under 18: 17.4%; Age 65 and over: 17.6%; Males per 100 females: 108.5
Housing: Homeownership rate: 93.3%; Homeowner vacancy rate: 4.7%; Rental vacancy rate: 13.3%

MONTPELIER (village). Covers a land area of 2.909 square miles and a water area of 0.017 square miles. Located at 41.58° N. Lat; 84.59° W. Long. Elevation is 853 feet.
History: Settled 1855, incorporated 1875.
Population: 4,072; Growth (since 2000): -5.7%; Density: 1,399.7 persons per square mile; Race: 96.2% White, 0.1% Black/African American, 1.4% Asian, 0.5% American Indian/Alaska Native, 0.0% Native Hawaiian/Other Pacific Islander, 1.3% Two or more races, 3.4% Hispanic of any race; Average household size: 2.43; Median age: 36.1; Age under 18: 26.9%; Age 65 and over: 14.5%; Males per 100 females: 90.6; Marriage status: 31.2% never married, 45.6% now married, 0.8% separated, 5.1% widowed, 18.1% divorced; Foreign born: 1.0%; Speak English only: 98.1%; With disability: 12.9%; Veterans: 13.0%; Ancestry: 37.1% German, 12.1% Irish, 9.0% American, 8.2% English, 5.6% Dutch
Employment: 4.2% management, business, and financial, 1.4% computer, engineering, and science, 5.0% education, legal, community service, arts, and media, 2.1% healthcare practitioners, 17.3% service, 20.7% sales and office, 9.6% natural resources, construction, and maintenance, 39.7% production, transportation, and material moving
Income: Per capita: $16,174; Median household: $35,777; Average household: $39,991; Households with income of $100,000 or more: 4.4%; Poverty rate: 19.9%
Educational Attainment: High school diploma or higher: 86.4%; Bachelor's degree or higher: 11.5%; Graduate/professional degree or higher: 3.8%

School District(s)

Montpelier Exempted Village (PK-12)
2012-13 Enrollment: 983. . . . . (419) 485-3676
Housing: Homeownership rate: 63.2%; Median home value: $71,200; Median year structure built: 1945; Homeowner vacancy rate: 3.5%; Median gross rent: $523 per month; Rental vacancy rate: 8.4%
Health Insurance: 86.9% have insurance; 54.8% have private insurance; 45.4% have public insurance; 13.1% do not have insurance; 2.3% of children under 18 do not have insurance
Hospitals: Community Hospitals & Wellness Centers
Safety: Violent crime rate: 54.3 per 10,000 population; Property crime rate: 563.0 per 10,000 population
Newspapers: Montpelier Leader (weekly circulation 1800); Village Reporter (weekly circulation 1900)
Transportation: Commute: 94.9% car, 0.0% public transportation, 4.3% walk, 0.8% work from home; Median travel time to work: 19.1 minutes
Additional Information Contacts
Village of Montpelier . . . . (419) 485-5543
http://www.montpelieroh.net

PIONEER (village). Covers a land area of 2.016 square miles and a water area of 0.071 square miles. Located at 41.68° N. Lat; 84.55° W. Long. Elevation is 879 feet.
Population: 1,380; Growth (since 2000): -5.5%; Density: 684.7 persons per square mile; Race: 96.3% White, 0.8% Black/African American, 0.1% Asian, 0.4% American Indian/Alaska Native, 0.0% Native Hawaiian/Other Pacific Islander, 1.7% Two or more races, 4.6% Hispanic of any race; Average household size: 2.37; Median age: 36.6; Age under 18: 25.0%; Age 65 and over: 13.7%; Males per 100 females: 94.9

School District(s)

North Central Local (PK-12)
2012-13 Enrollment: 585. . . . . (419) 737-2392
Housing: Homeownership rate: 66.5%; Homeowner vacancy rate: 2.8%; Rental vacancy rate: 15.9%
Safety: Violent crime rate: 7.3 per 10,000 population; Property crime rate: 174.8 per 10,000 population

PULASKI (CDP). Covers a land area of 0.157 square miles and a water area of 0 square miles. Located at 41.51° N. Lat; 84.51° W. Long. Elevation is 761 feet.
Population: 132; Growth (since 2000): n/a; Density: 843.3 persons per square mile; Race: 97.0% White, 0.8% Black/African American, 0.0% Asian, 0.0% American Indian/Alaska Native, 0.0% Native Hawaiian/Other Pacific Islander, 0.8% Two or more races, 6.1% Hispanic of any race; Average household size: 2.20; Median age: 48.7; Age under 18: 18.2%; Age 65 and over: 14.4%; Males per 100 females: 106.3
Housing: Homeownership rate: 91.6%; Homeowner vacancy rate: 1.8%; Rental vacancy rate: 28.6%

STRYKER (village). Covers a land area of 0.868 square miles and a water area of 0.005 square miles. Located at 41.50° N. Lat; 84.42° W. Long. Elevation is 715 feet.
Population: 1,335; Growth (since 2000): -5.0%; Density: 1,538.5 persons per square mile; Race: 95.0% White, 0.4% Black/African American, 0.2% Asian, 0.4% American Indian/Alaska Native, 0.0% Native Hawaiian/Other Pacific Islander, 2.1% Two or more races, 8.4% Hispanic of any race; Average household size: 2.55; Median age: 34.7; Age under 18: 27.2%; Age 65 and over: 12.7%; Males per 100 females: 98.1

School District(s)

Stryker Local (KG-12)
2012-13 Enrollment: 396. . . . . (419) 682-6961
Housing: Homeownership rate: 75.1%; Homeowner vacancy rate: 2.7%; Rental vacancy rate: 18.2%

WEST UNITY (village). Covers a land area of 1.174 square miles and a water area of 0 square miles. Located at 41.59° N. Lat; 84.43° W. Long. Elevation is 787 feet.
Population: 1,671; Growth (since 2000): -6.6%; Density: 1,423.2 persons per square mile; Race: 95.9% White, 0.5% Black/African American, 0.6% Asian, 0.2% American Indian/Alaska Native, 0.0% Native Hawaiian/Other Pacific Islander, 1.4% Two or more races, 3.7% Hispanic of any race; Average household size: 2.37; Median age: 36.3; Age under 18: 27.0%; Age 65 and over: 13.0%; Males per 100 females: 93.2

School District(s)

Millcreek-West Unity Local (PK-12)
2012-13 Enrollment: 614. . . . . (419) 924-2366
Housing: Homeownership rate: 69.4%; Homeowner vacancy rate: 4.7%; Rental vacancy rate: 13.2%
Newspapers: Village Reporter (weekly circulation 3300)

Wood County

Located in northwestern Ohio; bounded on the northwest by the Maumee River; crossed by the Portage River. Covers a land area of 617.205 square miles, a water area of 3.286 square miles, and is located in the Eastern Time Zone at 41.36° N. Lat., 83.62° W. Long. The county was founded in 1820. County seat is Bowling Green.

Wood County is part of the Toledo, OH Metropolitan Statistical Area. The entire metro area includes: Fulton County, OH; Lucas County, OH; Wood County, OH

Weather Station: Bowling Green WWTP Elevation: 674 feet

	Jan	Feb	Mar	Apr	May	Jun	Jul	Aug	Sep	Oct	Nov	Dec
High	32	36	46	59	71	81	84	82	76	63	50	37
Low	18	20	27	38	48	59	62	60	52	41	33	23
Precip	1.9	1.8	2.2	3.1	3.8	3.4	3.7	3.6	2.6	2.8	2.6	2.4
Snow	7.1	5.4	3.2	0.6	tr	0.0	0.0	0.0	0.0	0.0	0.6	4.7

High and Low temperatures in degrees Fahrenheit; Precipitation and Snow in inches

Weather Station: Hoytville 2 NE Elevation: 700 feet

	Jan	Feb	Mar	Apr	May	Jun	Jul	Aug	Sep	Oct	Nov	Dec
High	33	36	46	60	71	81	84	82	76	63	50	37
Low	16	18	26	36	47	57	61	59	51	40	31	21
Precip	2.0	1.9	2.4	3.2	3.6	3.5	3.9	3.6	2.6	2.7	2.8	2.5
Snow	7.2	4.9	3.6	0.9	tr	0.0	0.0	0.0	0.0	tr	1.1	5.0

High and Low temperatures in degrees Fahrenheit; Precipitation and Snow in inches

Population: 125,488; Growth (since 2000): 3.7%; Density: 203.3 persons per square mile; Race: 92.8% White, 2.4% Black/African American, 1.5% Asian, 0.2% American Indian/Alaska Native, 0.0% Native Hawaiian/Other Pacific Islander, 1.7% two or more races, 4.5% Hispanic of any race; Average household size: 2.43; Median age: 35.3; Age under 18: 21.7%; Age 65 and over: 12.3%; Males per 100 females: 95.6; Marriage status: 34.5% never married, 50.8% now married, 1.5% separated, 5.2% widowed, 9.5% divorced; Foreign born: 3.3%; Speak English only: 94.8%; With disability: 9.6%; Veterans: 8.6%; Ancestry: 39.9% German, 15.0% Irish, 9.2% English, 6.9% Polish, 5.6% American

Religion: Six largest groups: 17.2% Catholicism, 9.9% Non-denominational Protestant, 8.5% Lutheran, 6.7% Methodist/Pietist, 2.7% Pentecostal, 2.4% Baptist

Economy: Unemployment rate: 4.1%; Leading industries: 13.9% retail trade; 11.9% accommodation and food services; 11.5% other services (except public administration); Farms: 1,091 totaling 267,957 acres; Company size: 2 employ 1,000 or more persons, 6 employ 500 to 999 persons, 78 employ 100 to 499 persons, 2,663 employ less than 100 persons; Business ownership: 2,178 women-owned, n/a Black-owned, 183 Hispanic-owned, 118 Asian-owned

Employment: 12.9% management, business, and financial, 4.0% computer, engineering, and science, 12.9% education, legal, community service, arts, and media, 5.9% healthcare practitioners, 17.3% service, 23.6% sales and office, 8.3% natural resources, construction, and maintenance, 15.0% production, transportation, and material moving

Income: Per capita: $26,326; Median household: $52,069; Average household: $66,861; Households with income of $100,000 or more: 20.8%; Poverty rate: 14.7%

Educational Attainment: High school diploma or higher: 93.1%; Bachelor's degree or higher: 29.5%; Graduate/professional degree or higher: 12.1%

Housing: Homeownership rate: 67.8%; Median home value: $149,500; Median year structure built: 1975; Homeowner vacancy rate: 2.2%; Median gross rent: $718 per month; Rental vacancy rate: 11.2%

Vital Statistics: Birth rate: 104.7 per 10,000 population; Death rate: 76.5 per 10,000 population; Age-adjusted cancer mortality rate: 174.2 deaths per 100,000 population

Health Insurance: 91.8% have insurance; 80.5% have private insurance; 23.1% have public insurance; 8.2% do not have insurance; 3.0% of children under 18 do not have insurance

Health Care: Physicians: 22.2 per 10,000 population; Hospital beds: 8.0 per 10,000 population; Hospital admissions: 287.1 per 10,000 population

Air Quality Index: 94.4% good, 5.6% moderate, 0.0% unhealthy for sensitive individuals, 0.0% unhealthy (percent of days)

Transportation: Commute: 90.6% car, 0.3% public transportation, 4.3% walk, 3.3% work from home; Median travel time to work: 19.9 minutes

Presidential Election: 51.0% Obama, 46.8% Romney (2012)

National and State Parks: Fort Meigs State Memorial; Thurston State Park

Additional Information Contacts

Wood Government . . . . (419) 354-9100
http://www.co.wood.oh.us

Wood County Communities

BAIRDSTOWN (village). Covers a land area of 0.270 square miles and a water area of 0 square miles. Located at 41.17° N. Lat; 83.61° W. Long. Elevation is 738 feet.

Population: 130; Growth (since 2000): 0.0%; Density: 480.6 persons per square mile; Race: 93.8% White, 0.0% Black/African American, 0.0% Asian, 0.0% American Indian/Alaska Native, 0.0% Native Hawaiian/Other Pacific Islander, 6.2% Two or more races, 3.8% Hispanic of any race; Average household size: 2.65; Median age: 42.0; Age under 18: 23.8%; Age 65 and over: 13.1%; Males per 100 females: 113.1

Housing: Homeownership rate: 83.6%; Homeowner vacancy rate: 0.0%; Rental vacancy rate: 0.0%

BLOOMDALE (village). Covers a land area of 0.665 square miles and a water area of 0.004 square miles. Located at 41.17° N. Lat; 83.55° W. Long. Elevation is 745 feet.

Population: 678; Growth (since 2000): -6.4%; Density: 1,019.7 persons per square mile; Race: 98.1% White, 0.0% Black/African American, 0.3% Asian, 0.0% American Indian/Alaska Native, 0.0% Native Hawaiian/Other Pacific Islander, 1.3% Two or more races, 2.7% Hispanic of any race; Average household size: 2.78; Median age: 36.4; Age under 18: 28.2%; Age 65 and over: 11.7%; Males per 100 females: 107.3

School District(s)

Elmwood Local (PK-12)
2012-13 Enrollment: 1,256 . . . . (419) 655-2583

Housing: Homeownership rate: 84.4%; Homeowner vacancy rate: 4.2%; Rental vacancy rate: 15.6%

BOWLING GREEN (city). County seat. Covers a land area of 12.557 square miles and a water area of 0.047 square miles. Located at 41.38° N. Lat; 83.65° W. Long. Elevation is 692 feet.

History: Bowling Green was laid out in 1835 and named by Joseph Gordon for his home town in Kentucky. Oil was found here in 1886, bringing an industrial boom. In 1914 the H.J. Heinz Company established a tomato-products plant in Bowling Green, and the same year Bowling Green State University opened as a normal school.

Population: 30,028; Growth (since 2000): 1.3%; Density: 2,391.3 persons per square mile; Race: 87.6% White, 6.4% Black/African American, 2.1% Asian, 0.2% American Indian/Alaska Native, 0.0% Native Hawaiian/Other Pacific Islander, 2.2% Two or more races, 4.8% Hispanic of any race; Average household size: 2.16; Median age: 23.2; Age under 18: 12.8%; Age 65 and over: 8.9%; Males per 100 females: 92.1; Marriage status: 60.6% never married, 29.6% now married, 1.4% separated, 2.8% widowed, 7.0% divorced; Foreign born: 5.2%; Speak English only: 92.9%; With disability: 6.8%; Veterans: 4.9%; Ancestry: 38.4% German, 16.8% Irish, 9.7% English, 6.7% Italian, 4.3% Polish

Employment: 9.4% management, business, and financial, 2.8% computer, engineering, and science, 20.3% education, legal, community service, arts, and media, 3.4% healthcare practitioners, 25.2% service, 22.5% sales and office, 7.2% natural resources, construction, and maintenance, 9.3% production, transportation, and material moving

Income: Per capita: $19,266; Median household: $34,550; Average household: $51,072; Households with income of $100,000 or more: 15.1%; Poverty rate: 32.5%

Educational Attainment: High school diploma or higher: 93.7%; Bachelor's degree or higher: 42.0%; Graduate/professional degree or higher: 21.5%

School District(s)

Bowling Green City SD (PK-12)
2012-13 Enrollment: 3,001 . . . . (419) 352-3576

Four-year College(s)

Bowling Green State University-Main Campus (Public)
Fall 2013 Enrollment: 16,958 . . . . (419) 372-2531
2013-14 Tuition: In-state $10,726; Out-of-state $18,034

Housing: Homeownership rate: 39.9%; Median home value: $159,900; Median year structure built: 1977; Homeowner vacancy rate: 2.6%; Median gross rent: $642 per month; Rental vacancy rate: 8.5%

Health Insurance: 91.8% have insurance; 82.9% have private insurance; 18.1% have public insurance; 8.2% do not have insurance; 2.5% of children under 18 do not have insurance

Hospitals: Wood County Hospital (162 beds)

Safety: Violent crime rate: 15.4 per 10,000 population; Property crime rate: 245.3 per 10,000 population

Newspapers: Sentinel-Tribune (daily circulation 11300)

Transportation: Commute: 78.4% car, 0.2% public transportation, 15.0% walk, 3.2% work from home; Median travel time to work: 15.5 minutes

Airports: Wood County (general aviation)

Additional Information Contacts

City of Bowling Green . . . . (419) 354-6204
http://www.bgohio.org

BRADNER (village). Covers a land area of 0.616 square miles and a water area of 0.002 square miles. Located at 41.32° N. Lat; 83.44° W. Long. Elevation is 692 feet.
Population: 985; Growth (since 2000): -15.9%; Density: 1,598.0 persons per square mile; Race: 97.2% White, 0.4% Black/African American, 0.3% Asian, 0.1% American Indian/Alaska Native, 0.0% Native Hawaiian/Other Pacific Islander, 1.5% Two or more races, 5.1% Hispanic of any race; Average household size: 2.54; Median age: 35.3; Age under 18: 25.4%; Age 65 and over: 11.6%; Males per 100 females: 102.7
Housing: Homeownership rate: 71.4%; Homeowner vacancy rate: 3.4%; Rental vacancy rate: 11.2%

CUSTAR (village). Covers a land area of 0.251 square miles and a water area of 0 square miles. Located at 41.28° N. Lat; 83.84° W. Long. Elevation is 692 feet.
Population: 179; Growth (since 2000): -13.9%; Density: 714.2 persons per square mile; Race: 94.4% White, 0.0% Black/African American, 0.0% Asian, 0.6% American Indian/Alaska Native, 0.0% Native Hawaiian/Other Pacific Islander, 2.8% Two or more races, 6.1% Hispanic of any race; Average household size: 2.45; Median age: 32.2; Age under 18: 25.7%; Age 65 and over: 10.6%; Males per 100 females: 108.1
Housing: Homeownership rate: 74.0%; Homeowner vacancy rate: 1.7%; Rental vacancy rate: 9.5%

CYGNET (village). Covers a land area of 0.331 square miles and a water area of 0.001 square miles. Located at 41.24° N. Lat; 83.64° W. Long. Elevation is 705 feet.
Population: 597; Growth (since 2000): 5.9%; Density: 1,803.0 persons per square mile; Race: 93.6% White, 1.2% Black/African American, 0.7% Asian, 0.7% American Indian/Alaska Native, 0.0% Native Hawaiian/Other Pacific Islander, 2.5% Two or more races, 5.7% Hispanic of any race; Average household size: 2.87; Median age: 33.4; Age under 18: 30.3%; Age 65 and over: 9.0%; Males per 100 females: 92.0
Housing: Homeownership rate: 81.3%; Homeowner vacancy rate: 2.8%; Rental vacancy rate: 23.5%

GRAND RAPIDS (village). Covers a land area of 0.879 square miles and a water area of 0.088 square miles. Located at 41.40° N. Lat; 83.87° W. Long. Elevation is 659 feet.
History: Grand Rapids developed as a rural trading center. It was the location of locks on the Miami & Erie Canal.
Population: 965; Growth (since 2000): -3.7%; Density: 1,097.6 persons per square mile; Race: 96.5% White, 0.5% Black/African American, 0.1% Asian, 0.2% American Indian/Alaska Native, 0.0% Native Hawaiian/Other Pacific Islander, 1.9% Two or more races, 3.9% Hispanic of any race; Average household size: 2.42; Median age: 38.9; Age under 18: 25.3%; Age 65 and over: 15.6%; Males per 100 females: 91.8

School District(s)

Otsego Local (PK-12)
2012-13 Enrollment: 1,530 . . . . (419) 823-4381
Housing: Homeownership rate: 73.5%; Homeowner vacancy rate: 2.1%; Rental vacancy rate: 10.5%
Additional Information Contacts
Village of Grand Rapids . . . . (419) 832-5305
http://www.grandrapidsohio.com

HASKINS (village). Covers a land area of 1.645 square miles and a water area of 0 square miles. Located at 41.46° N. Lat; 83.70° W. Long. Elevation is 659 feet.
Population: 1,188; Growth (since 2000): 86.2%; Density: 722.2 persons per square mile; Race: 97.4% White, 0.4% Black/African American, 0.3% Asian, 0.0% American Indian/Alaska Native, 0.0% Native Hawaiian/Other Pacific Islander, 0.9% Two or more races, 4.1% Hispanic of any race; Average household size: 2.90; Median age: 32.3; Age under 18: 33.8%; Age 65 and over: 5.5%; Males per 100 females: 100.3

School District(s)

Otsego Local (PK-12)
2012-13 Enrollment: 1,530 . . . . (419) 823-4381
Housing: Homeownership rate: 88.7%; Homeowner vacancy rate: 2.4%; Rental vacancy rate: 7.8%

HOYTVILLE (village). Covers a land area of 0.741 square miles and a water area of 0.012 square miles. Located at 41.19° N. Lat; 83.78° W. Long. Elevation is 709 feet.
Population: 303; Growth (since 2000): 2.4%; Density: 408.7 persons per square mile; Race: 89.8% White, 1.3% Black/African American, 0.7% Asian, 1.7% American Indian/Alaska Native, 0.0% Native Hawaiian/Other Pacific Islander, 1.3% Two or more races, 15.8% Hispanic of any race; Average household size: 3.16; Median age: 33.8; Age under 18: 33.3%; Age 65 and over: 8.9%; Males per 100 females: 100.7

School District(s)

Mccomb Local (PK-12)
2012-13 Enrollment: 761. . . . . (419) 293-3979
Housing: Homeownership rate: 74.0%; Homeowner vacancy rate: 1.4%; Rental vacancy rate: 3.8%

JERRY CITY (village). Covers a land area of 1.006 square miles and a water area of 0 square miles. Located at 41.25° N. Lat; 83.60° W. Long. Elevation is 692 feet.
Population: 427; Growth (since 2000): -5.7%; Density: 424.3 persons per square mile; Race: 99.3% White, 0.0% Black/African American, 0.0% Asian, 0.5% American Indian/Alaska Native, 0.0% Native Hawaiian/Other Pacific Islander, 0.0% Two or more races, 5.2% Hispanic of any race; Average household size: 2.64; Median age: 37.9; Age under 18: 26.5%; Age 65 and over: 11.2%; Males per 100 females: 100.5
Housing: Homeownership rate: 84.0%; Homeowner vacancy rate: 0.7%; Rental vacancy rate: 3.7%

LUCKEY (village). Covers a land area of 0.690 square miles and a water area of 0.001 square miles. Located at 41.45° N. Lat; 83.48° W. Long. Elevation is 669 feet.
Population: 1,012; Growth (since 2000): 1.4%; Density: 1,467.0 persons per square mile; Race: 97.6% White, 0.2% Black/African American, 0.8% Asian, 0.0% American Indian/Alaska Native, 0.0% Native Hawaiian/Other Pacific Islander, 1.3% Two or more races, 3.4% Hispanic of any race; Average household size: 2.64; Median age: 36.7; Age under 18: 26.1%; Age 65 and over: 13.1%; Males per 100 females: 97.3

School District(s)

Eastwood Local (PK-12)
2012-13 Enrollment: 1,488 . . . . (419) 833-6411
Housing: Homeownership rate: 81.8%; Homeowner vacancy rate: 1.2%; Rental vacancy rate: 9.1%

MILLBURY (village). Covers a land area of 0.996 square miles and a water area of 0 square miles. Located at 41.56° N. Lat; 83.43° W. Long. Elevation is 614 feet.
Population: 1,200; Growth (since 2000): 3.4%; Density: 1,204.7 persons per square mile; Race: 96.7% White, 0.7% Black/African American, 0.7% Asian, 0.0% American Indian/Alaska Native, 0.0% Native Hawaiian/Other Pacific Islander, 0.9% Two or more races, 4.8% Hispanic of any race; Average household size: 2.56; Median age: 40.7; Age under 18: 25.1%; Age 65 and over: 12.3%; Males per 100 females: 93.2

School District(s)

Lake Local (PK-12)
2012-13 Enrollment: 1,606 . . . . (419) 661-6690
Housing: Homeownership rate: 80.9%; Homeowner vacancy rate: 1.6%; Rental vacancy rate: 2.2%
Newspapers: Press Newspapers (weekly circulation 34000)

MILTON CENTER (village). Covers a land area of 0.398 square miles and a water area of 0 square miles. Located at 41.30° N. Lat; 83.83° W. Long. Elevation is 686 feet.
Population: 144; Growth (since 2000): -26.2%; Density: 361.8 persons per square mile; Race: 91.7% White, 0.0% Black/African American, 0.0% Asian, 0.7% American Indian/Alaska Native, 0.0% Native Hawaiian/Other Pacific Islander, 2.1% Two or more races, 22.9% Hispanic of any race; Average household size: 2.72; Median age: 36.5; Age under 18: 31.2%; Age 65 and over: 16.7%; Males per 100 females: 87.0
Housing: Homeownership rate: 83.0%; Homeowner vacancy rate: 8.2%; Rental vacancy rate: 18.2%

NORTH BALTIMORE (village). Covers a land area of 2.471 square miles and a water area of 0.028 square miles. Located at 41.18° N. Lat; 83.67° W. Long. Elevation is 732 feet.
History: Settled 1834.

Population: 3,432; Growth (since 2000): 2.1%; Density: 1,389.2 persons per square mile; Race: 96.3% White, 0.6% Black/African American, 0.4% Asian, 0.2% American Indian/Alaska Native, 0.0% Native Hawaiian/Other Pacific Islander, 1.3% Two or more races, 4.8% Hispanic of any race; Average household size: 2.56; Median age: 36.4; Age under 18: 26.9%; Age 65 and over: 13.9%; Males per 100 females: 95.2; Marriage status: 30.9% never married, 49.0% now married, 1.5% separated, 9.4% widowed, 10.7% divorced; Foreign born: 1.1%; Speak English only: 97.4%; With disability: 10.9%; Veterans: 10.2%; Ancestry: 31.4% German, 9.5% Irish, 8.1% American, 6.7% English, 6.0% Dutch

Employment: 9.6% management, business, and financial, 1.4% computer, engineering, and science, 4.5% education, legal, community service, arts, and media, 7.7% healthcare practitioners, 15.3% service, 20.7% sales and office, 8.3% natural resources, construction, and maintenance, 32.5% production, transportation, and material moving

Income: Per capita: $21,220; Median household: $43,393; Average household: $51,851; Households with income of $100,000 or more: 9.7%; Poverty rate: 10.3%

Educational Attainment: High school diploma or higher: 91.3%; Bachelor's degree or higher: 13.0%; Graduate/professional degree or higher: 1.9%

School District(s)

North Baltimore Local (PK-12)
2012-13 Enrollment: 653 . . . . (419) 257-3531

Housing: Homeownership rate: 69.4%; Median home value: $83,700; Median year structure built: 1955; Homeowner vacancy rate: 2.6%; Median gross rent: $586 per month; Rental vacancy rate: 12.7%

Health Insurance: 87.0% have insurance; 71.5% have private insurance; 26.5% have public insurance; 13.0% do not have insurance; 5.6% of children under 18 do not have insurance

Transportation: Commute: 97.6% car, 0.0% public transportation, 0.5% walk, 0.9% work from home; Median travel time to work: 19.2 minutes

NORTHWOOD (city).

Covers a land area of 8.523 square miles and a water area of 0.013 square miles. Located at 41.61° N. Lat; 83.48° W. Long. Elevation is 610 feet.

Population: 5,265; Growth (since 2000): -3.8%; Density: 617.8 persons per square mile; Race: 94.3% White, 0.7% Black/African American, 1.1% Asian, 0.6% American Indian/Alaska Native, 0.0% Native Hawaiian/Other Pacific Islander, 2.1% Two or more races, 5.8% Hispanic of any race; Average household size: 2.60; Median age: 39.0; Age under 18: 24.1%; Age 65 and over: 11.5%; Males per 100 females: 96.2; Marriage status: 23.5% never married, 59.0% now married, 2.3% separated, 5.4% widowed, 12.2% divorced; Foreign born: 0.5%; Speak English only: 97.8%; With disability: 14.2%; Veterans: 11.2%; Ancestry: 36.3% German, 15.6% Irish, 12.0% French, 9.4% English, 7.2% Polish

Employment: 7.3% management, business, and financial, 1.1% computer, engineering, and science, 6.7% education, legal, community service, arts, and media, 5.8% healthcare practitioners, 13.0% service, 36.8% sales and office, 5.1% natural resources, construction, and maintenance, 24.2% production, transportation, and material moving

Income: Per capita: $24,513; Median household: $46,767; Average household: $58,732; Households with income of $100,000 or more: 12.7%; Poverty rate: 9.7%

Educational Attainment: High school diploma or higher: 88.8%; Bachelor's degree or higher: 12.2%; Graduate/professional degree or higher: 1.4%

School District(s)

Northwood Local Schools (PK-12)
2012-13 Enrollment: 902 . . . . (419) 691-3888

Housing: Homeownership rate: 84.5%; Median home value: $108,500; Median year structure built: 1963; Homeowner vacancy rate: 1.8%; Median gross rent: $777 per month; Rental vacancy rate: 8.1%

Health Insurance: 89.0% have insurance; 78.0% have private insurance; 23.8% have public insurance; 11.0% do not have insurance; 6.7% of children under 18 do not have insurance

Safety: Violent crime rate: 16.8 per 10,000 population; Property crime rate: 398.5 per 10,000 population

Transportation: Commute: 94.9% car, 0.2% public transportation, 1.8% walk, 3.2% work from home; Median travel time to work: 18.3 minutes

Additional Information Contacts

City of Northwood . . . . (419) 693-9320
http://www.ci.northwood.oh.us

PEMBERVILLE (village).

Covers a land area of 1.160 square miles and a water area of 0 square miles. Located at 41.41° N. Lat; 83.46° W. Long. Elevation is 653 feet.

History: Settled 1834, incorporated 1876.

Population: 1,371; Growth (since 2000): 0.4%; Density: 1,181.8 persons per square mile; Race: 94.4% White, 0.1% Black/African American, 0.2% Asian, 0.1% American Indian/Alaska Native, 0.0% Native Hawaiian/Other Pacific Islander, 1.2% Two or more races, 6.6% Hispanic of any race; Average household size: 2.58; Median age: 39.6; Age under 18: 27.1%; Age 65 and over: 15.8%; Males per 100 females: 92.0

School District(s)

Eastwood Local (PK-12)
2012-13 Enrollment: 1,488 . . . . (419) 833-6411

Housing: Homeownership rate: 74.8%; Homeowner vacancy rate: 2.4%; Rental vacancy rate: 10.6%

Additional Information Contacts

Village of Pemberville . . . . (419) 287-3832
http://www.pemberville.org

PERRYSBURG (city).

Covers a land area of 11.514 square miles and a water area of 0 square miles. Located at 41.54° N. Lat; 83.64° W. Long. Elevation is 633 feet.

History: Perrysburg was settled in 1816 and named for Oliver Hazard Perry. Its site on the Maumee River made it a shipping and shipbuilding center. From 1822 to 1866, Perrysburg served as the seat of Wood County.

Population: 20,623; Growth (since 2000): 21.7%; Density: 1,791.1 persons per square mile; Race: 92.9% White, 1.4% Black/African American, 3.1% Asian, 0.1% American Indian/Alaska Native, 0.0% Native Hawaiian/Other Pacific Islander, 1.6% Two or more races, 3.2% Hispanic of any race; Average household size: 2.48; Median age: 38.4; Age under 18: 26.5%; Age 65 and over: 12.3%; Males per 100 females: 94.0; Marriage status: 23.4% never married, 59.9% now married, 1.5% separated, 7.2% widowed, 9.5% divorced; Foreign born: 5.2%; Speak English only: 93.1%; With disability: 8.3%; Veterans: 7.9%; Ancestry: 39.0% German, 16.9% Irish, 10.7% English, 9.4% Polish, 7.2% French

Employment: 23.2% management, business, and financial, 6.9% computer, engineering, and science, 13.5% education, legal, community service, arts, and media, 9.2% healthcare practitioners, 11.2% service, 23.4% sales and office, 4.9% natural resources, construction, and maintenance, 7.7% production, transportation, and material moving

Income: Per capita: $36,192; Median household: $71,220; Average household: $88,418; Households with income of $100,000 or more: 33.4%; Poverty rate: 5.3%

Educational Attainment: High school diploma or higher: 96.4%; Bachelor's degree or higher: 46.0%; Graduate/professional degree or higher: 17.6%

School District(s)

Penta Career Center (07-12)
2012-13 Enrollment: n/a . . . . (419) 666-1120
Perrysburg Exempted Village (PK-12)
2012-13 Enrollment: 4,618 . . . . (419) 874-9131
Rossford Exempted Village (PK-12)
2012-13 Enrollment: 1,747 . . . . (419) 666-2010

Two-year College(s)

Owens Community College (Public)
Fall 2013 Enrollment: 14,691 . . . . (567) 661-7000
2013-14 Tuition: In-state $3,826; Out-of-state $7,040
The Salon Professional Academy-Perrysburg (Private, For-profit)
Fall 2013 Enrollment: 76 . . . . (419) 873-9999

Vocational/Technical School(s)

Healing Arts Institute (Private, For-profit)
Fall 2013 Enrollment: 48 . . . . (419) 874-4496
Penta County Joint Vocational School (Public)
Fall 2013 Enrollment: 55 . . . . (419) 661-6555
2013-14 Tuition: $4,358

Housing: Homeownership rate: 70.5%; Median home value: $189,300; Median year structure built: 1981; Homeowner vacancy rate: 2.2%; Median gross rent: $845 per month; Rental vacancy rate: 11.1%

Health Insurance: 94.2% have insurance; 87.6% have private insurance; 17.1% have public insurance; 5.8% do not have insurance; 3.8% of children under 18 do not have insurance

Safety: Violent crime rate: 2.4 per 10,000 population; Property crime rate: 148.0 per 10,000 population

Newspapers: Welch Publishing (weekly circulation 33000)

Transportation: Commute: 93.2% car, 0.2% public transportation, 1.3% walk, 4.9% work from home; Median travel time to work: 20.1 minutes
Additional Information Contacts
City of Perrysburg . . . . (419) 872-8010
http://www.ci.perrysburg.oh.us

PORTAGE (village). Covers a land area of 1.488 square miles and a water area of 0 square miles. Located at 41.32° N. Lat; 83.65° W. Long. Elevation is 686 feet.
History: Portage began as a trading post in 1824 and grew during the oil and gas boom of the 1880's and 1890's.
Population: 438; Growth (since 2000): 2.3%; Density: 294.4 persons per square mile; Race: 94.1% White, 1.4% Black/African American, 0.0% Asian, 0.5% American Indian/Alaska Native, 0.5% Native Hawaiian/Other Pacific Islander, 0.7% Two or more races, 7.8% Hispanic of any race; Average household size: 2.50; Median age: 38.0; Age under 18: 20.5%; Age 65 and over: 8.9%; Males per 100 females: 99.1
Housing: Homeownership rate: 64.0%; Homeowner vacancy rate: 2.8%; Rental vacancy rate: 4.8%

RISINGSUN (village). Covers a land area of 0.570 square miles and a water area of 0 square miles. Located at 41.27° N. Lat; 83.43° W. Long. Elevation is 715 feet.
Population: 606; Growth (since 2000): -2.3%; Density: 1,063.2 persons per square mile; Race: 96.0% White, 0.0% Black/African American, 0.2% Asian, 0.7% American Indian/Alaska Native, 0.0% Native Hawaiian/Other Pacific Islander, 2.8% Two or more races, 4.5% Hispanic of any race; Average household size: 2.73; Median age: 36.0; Age under 18: 27.9%; Age 65 and over: 12.4%; Males per 100 females: 111.9
Housing: Homeownership rate: 68.5%; Homeowner vacancy rate: 3.1%; Rental vacancy rate: 10.1%

ROSSFORD (city). Covers a land area of 5.019 square miles and a water area of 0.306 square miles. Located at 41.60° N. Lat; 83.56° W. Long. Elevation is 617 feet.
History: Rossford began in 1896 when Edward Ford established a glass company that later merged with the Libbey-Owens corporation.
Population: 6,293; Growth (since 2000): -1.8%; Density: 1,253.9 persons per square mile; Race: 94.8% White, 1.7% Black/African American, 0.9% Asian, 0.4% American Indian/Alaska Native, 0.0% Native Hawaiian/Other Pacific Islander, 1.4% Two or more races, 3.5% Hispanic of any race; Average household size: 2.45; Median age: 39.1; Age under 18: 23.6%; Age 65 and over: 13.3%; Males per 100 females: 97.2; Marriage status: 30.0% never married, 53.7% now married, 0.9% separated, 4.2% widowed, 12.1% divorced; Foreign born: 1.6%; Speak English only: 96.3%; With disability: 9.9%; Veterans: 11.3%; Ancestry: 30.1% German, 18.1% Polish, 14.7% Irish, 6.2% American, 5.9% Italian
Employment: 10.5% management, business, and financial, 1.4% computer, engineering, and science, 11.2% education, legal, community service, arts, and media, 8.4% healthcare practitioners, 14.5% service, 27.3% sales and office, 8.1% natural resources, construction, and maintenance, 18.6% production, transportation, and material moving
Income: Per capita: $26,969; Median household: $50,513; Average household: $63,720; Households with income of $100,000 or more: 17.4%; Poverty rate: 7.9%
Educational Attainment: High school diploma or higher: 93.3%; Bachelor's degree or higher: 22.8%; Graduate/professional degree or higher: 10.4%

School District(s)

Rossford Exempted Village (PK-12)
2012-13 Enrollment: 1,747 . . . . (419) 666-2010
Housing: Homeownership rate: 70.6%; Median home value: $136,300; Median year structure built: 1959; Homeowner vacancy rate: 2.1%; Median gross rent: $669 per month; Rental vacancy rate: 13.7%
Health Insurance: 91.7% have insurance; 81.0% have private insurance; 24.7% have public insurance; 8.3% do not have insurance; 1.3% of children under 18 do not have insurance
Safety: Violent crime rate: 4.7 per 10,000 population; Property crime rate: 200.7 per 10,000 population
Transportation: Commute: 96.2% car, 0.7% public transportation, 0.5% walk, 1.7% work from home; Median travel time to work: 18.0 minutes
Additional Information Contacts
City of Rossford. . . . . (419) 666-0210
http://www.rossfordohio.com

RUDOLPH (CDP). Covers a land area of 0.819 square miles and a water area of 0 square miles. Located at 41.30° N. Lat; 83.66° W. Long. Elevation is 682 feet.
Population: 458; Growth (since 2000): n/a; Density: 559.0 persons per square mile; Race: 90.0% White, 0.0% Black/African American, 0.0% Asian, 0.2% American Indian/Alaska Native, 0.0% Native Hawaiian/Other Pacific Islander, 6.1% Two or more races, 9.0% Hispanic of any race; Average household size: 2.69; Median age: 33.7; Age under 18: 30.3%; Age 65 and over: 8.5%; Males per 100 females: 109.1
Housing: Homeownership rate: 78.2%; Homeowner vacancy rate: 2.9%; Rental vacancy rate: 5.1%

STONY RIDGE (CDP). Covers a land area of 1.704 square miles and a water area of 0 square miles. Located at 41.51° N. Lat; 83.51° W. Long. Elevation is 643 feet.
Population: 411; Growth (since 2000): n/a; Density: 241.2 persons per square mile; Race: 94.4% White, 2.9% Black/African American, 0.2% Asian, 0.0% American Indian/Alaska Native, 0.0% Native Hawaiian/Other Pacific Islander, 0.7% Two or more races, 3.4% Hispanic of any race; Average household size: 2.46; Median age: 44.1; Age under 18: 20.7%; Age 65 and over: 17.3%; Males per 100 females: 101.5
Housing: Homeownership rate: 80.8%; Homeowner vacancy rate: 2.2%; Rental vacancy rate: 22.0%

TONTOGANY (village). Covers a land area of 0.305 square miles and a water area of 0 square miles. Located at 41.42° N. Lat; 83.74° W. Long. Elevation is 666 feet.
Population: 367; Growth (since 2000): 0.8%; Density: 1,203.9 persons per square mile; Race: 97.8% White, 0.0% Black/African American, 0.0% Asian, 0.3% American Indian/Alaska Native, 0.0% Native Hawaiian/Other Pacific Islander, 0.8% Two or more races, 8.7% Hispanic of any race; Average household size: 2.51; Median age: 37.5; Age under 18: 28.1%; Age 65 and over: 13.4%; Males per 100 females: 105.0

School District(s)

Otsego Local (PK-12)
2012-13 Enrollment: 1,530 . . . . (419) 823-4381
Housing: Homeownership rate: 74.0%; Homeowner vacancy rate: 3.6%; Rental vacancy rate: 9.5%

WALBRIDGE (village). Covers a land area of 2.186 square miles and a water area of 0.015 square miles. Located at 41.59° N. Lat; 83.49° W. Long. Elevation is 617 feet.
Population: 3,019; Growth (since 2000): 18.6%; Density: 1,380.8 persons per square mile; Race: 95.9% White, 0.7% Black/African American, 0.3% Asian, 0.3% American Indian/Alaska Native, 0.0% Native Hawaiian/Other Pacific Islander, 1.8% Two or more races, 5.6% Hispanic of any race; Average household size: 2.07; Median age: 47.4; Age under 18: 17.7%; Age 65 and over: 23.8%; Males per 100 females: 85.4; Marriage status: 25.3% never married, 53.5% now married, 5.6% separated, 10.2% widowed, 11.0% divorced; Foreign born: 0.7%; Speak English only: 96.4%; With disability: 12.9%; Veterans: 10.3%; Ancestry: 42.3% German, 9.2% Irish, 9.1% Polish, 8.2% French, 7.7% Hungarian
Employment: 6.0% management, business, and financial, 0.0% computer, engineering, and science, 6.9% education, legal, community service, arts, and media, 3.0% healthcare practitioners, 28.0% service, 25.6% sales and office, 8.3% natural resources, construction, and maintenance, 22.1% production, transportation, and material moving
Income: Per capita: $22,224; Median household: $39,538; Average household: $46,999; Households with income of $100,000 or more: 9.8%; Poverty rate: 11.9%
Educational Attainment: High school diploma or higher: 90.8%; Bachelor's degree or higher: 7.6%; Graduate/professional degree or higher: 2.6%

School District(s)

Lake Local (PK-12)
2012-13 Enrollment: 1,606 . . . . (419) 661-6690
Housing: Homeownership rate: 75.2%; Median home value: $85,000; Median year structure built: 1967; Homeowner vacancy rate: 4.3%; Median gross rent: $632 per month; Rental vacancy rate: 14.2%
Health Insurance: 88.8% have insurance; 67.2% have private insurance; 41.3% have public insurance; 11.2% do not have insurance; 0.0% of children under 18 do not have insurance
Safety: Violent crime rate: 6.5 per 10,000 population; Property crime rate: 48.9 per 10,000 population

Transportation: Commute: 95.7% car, 0.0% public transportation, 0.8% walk, 0.9% work from home; Median travel time to work: 19.6 minutes
Airports: Toledo Executive (general aviation)

WAYNE (village). Covers a land area of 0.322 square miles and a water area of 0 square miles. Located at 41.30° N. Lat; 83.47° W. Long. Elevation is 699 feet.
History: Wayne was known as strongly abolitionist in sentiment prior to the Civil War. In the winter of 1858, Wayne was a transfer point for several hundred rifles headed for John Brown's hide-out in Maryland.
Population: 887; Growth (since 2000): 5.3%; Density: 2,753.3 persons per square mile; Race: 94.5% White, 0.2% Black/African American, 0.0% Asian, 0.2% American Indian/Alaska Native, 0.0% Native Hawaiian/Other Pacific Islander, 2.6% Two or more races, 6.0% Hispanic of any race; Average household size: 2.74; Median age: 32.3; Age under 18: 29.5%; Age 65 and over: 10.0%; Males per 100 females: 92.8
Housing: Homeownership rate: 71.0%; Homeowner vacancy rate: 3.7%; Rental vacancy rate: 6.0%

WEST MILLGROVE (village). Covers a land area of 0.260 square miles and a water area of 0 square miles. Located at 41.24° N. Lat; 83.49° W. Long. Elevation is 712 feet.
Population: 174; Growth (since 2000): 123.1%; Density: 669.3 persons per square mile; Race: 96.0% White, 0.0% Black/African American, 0.0% Asian, 0.0% American Indian/Alaska Native, 0.0% Native Hawaiian/Other Pacific Islander, 3.4% Two or more races, 1.7% Hispanic of any race; Average household size: 2.72; Median age: 32.0; Age under 18: 31.0%; Age 65 and over: 9.8%; Males per 100 females: 77.6
Housing: Homeownership rate: 82.8%; Homeowner vacancy rate: 0.0%; Rental vacancy rate: 0.0%

WESTON (village). Covers a land area of 1.130 square miles and a water area of 0.003 square miles. Located at 41.35° N. Lat; 83.79° W. Long. Elevation is 679 feet.
Population: 1,590; Growth (since 2000): -4.2%; Density: 1,406.9 persons per square mile; Race: 91.6% White, 0.1% Black/African American, 0.1% Asian, 1.0% American Indian/Alaska Native, 0.0% Native Hawaiian/Other Pacific Islander, 2.4% Two or more races, 11.8% Hispanic of any race; Average household size: 2.60; Median age: 35.8; Age under 18: 29.2%; Age 65 and over: 10.9%; Males per 100 females: 97.5
Housing: Homeownership rate: 73.6%; Homeowner vacancy rate: 3.8%; Rental vacancy rate: 11.0%

Wyandot County

Located in north central Ohio; drained by the Sandusky River. Covers a land area of 406.865 square miles, a water area of 0.689 square miles, and is located in the Eastern Time Zone at 40.84° N. Lat., 83.31° W. Long. The county was founded in 1845. County seat is Upper Sandusky.

Weather Station: Upper Sandusky Elevation: 854 feet

	Jan	Feb	Mar	Apr	May	Jun	Jul	Aug	Sep	Oct	Nov	Dec
High	33	37	47	61	71	80	84	83	77	64	50	37
Low	18	20	28	38	48	59	62	61	53	41	33	23
Precip	2.0	1.9	2.5	3.5	4.5	3.9	4.5	3.5	3.1	2.4	3.2	2.6
Snow	6.4	3.8	2.2	1.1	tr	0.0	0.0	0.0	0.0	tr	0.8	5.1

High and Low temperatures in degrees Fahrenheit; Precipitation and Snow in inches

Population: 22,615; Growth (since 2000): -1.3%; Density: 55.6 persons per square mile; Race: 96.9% White, 0.2% Black/African American, 0.6% Asian, 0.2% American Indian/Alaska Native, 0.0% Native Hawaiian/Other Pacific Islander, 1.0% two or more races, 2.2% Hispanic of any race; Average household size: 2.46; Median age: 40.5; Age under 18: 24.3%; Age 65 and over: 16.3%; Males per 100 females: 97.9; Marriage status: 22.6% never married, 58.2% now married, 2.3% separated, 8.1% widowed, 11.1% divorced; Foreign born: 0.9%; Speak English only: 96.5%; With disability: 14.2%; Veterans: 9.4%; Ancestry: 43.9% German, 12.3% American, 11.3% Irish, 8.1% English, 2.8% Italian
Religion: Six largest groups: 20.9% Catholicism, 12.1% Methodist/Pietist, 9.7% Lutheran, 6.5% Presbyterian-Reformed, 1.5% Holiness, 1.4% Pentecostal
Economy: Unemployment rate: 3.7%; Leading industries: 17.5% other services (except public administration); 13.4% retail trade; 10.2% construction; Farms: 593 totaling 220,841 acres; Company size: 0 employ 1,000 or more persons, 1 employs 500 to 999 persons, 10 employ 100 to 499 persons, 480 employ less than 100 persons; Business ownership: n/a women-owned, n/a Black-owned, n/a Hispanic-owned, n/a Asian-owned
Employment: 11.0% management, business, and financial, 2.0% computer, engineering, and science, 5.7% education, legal, community service, arts, and media, 5.5% healthcare practitioners, 17.8% service, 17.8% sales and office, 12.5% natural resources, construction, and maintenance, 27.7% production, transportation, and material moving
Income: Per capita: $22,382; Median household: $44,448; Average household: $54,131; Households with income of $100,000 or more: 9.6%; Poverty rate: 11.1%
Educational Attainment: High school diploma or higher: 89.6%; Bachelor's degree or higher: 12.0%; Graduate/professional degree or higher: 3.7%
Housing: Homeownership rate: 73.5%; Median home value: $103,500; Median year structure built: 1958; Homeowner vacancy rate: 1.6%; Median gross rent: $598 per month; Rental vacancy rate: 8.3%
Vital Statistics: Birth rate: 105.1 per 10,000 population; Death rate: 106.9 per 10,000 population; Age-adjusted cancer mortality rate: 184.4 deaths per 100,000 population
Health Insurance: 89.9% have insurance; 75.6% have private insurance; 28.4% have public insurance; 10.1% do not have insurance; 4.6% of children under 18 do not have insurance
Health Care: Physicians: 4.4 per 10,000 population; Hospital beds: 11.0 per 10,000 population; Hospital admissions: 318.4 per 10,000 population
Transportation: Commute: 94.3% car, 0.6% public transportation, 1.8% walk, 2.4% work from home; Median travel time to work: 22.5 minutes
Presidential Election: 38.6% Obama, 59.0% Romney (2012)
Additional Information Contacts
Wyandot Government . . . . (419) 294-3836
http://www.co.wyandot.oh.us

Wyandot County Communities

CAREY (village). Covers a land area of 1.976 square miles and a water area of 0.007 square miles. Located at 40.95° N. Lat; 83.38° W. Long. Elevation is 820 feet.
History: Carey was platted in 1843, and grew as a trading and shipping center for onions and celery. The Shrine of Our Lady of Consolation was established here in 1875 by Father Joseph P. Gloden.
Population: 3,674; Growth (since 2000): -5.8%; Density: 1,859.7 persons per square mile; Race: 96.2% White, 0.2% Black/African American, 1.6% Asian, 0.2% American Indian/Alaska Native, 0.0% Native Hawaiian/Other Pacific Islander, 1.0% Two or more races, 2.0% Hispanic of any race; Average household size: 2.41; Median age: 37.1; Age under 18: 26.4%; Age 65 and over: 13.0%; Males per 100 females: 97.1; Marriage status: 24.3% never married, 53.4% now married, 3.3% separated, 8.3% widowed, 13.9% divorced; Foreign born: 0.8%; Speak English only: 96.6%; With disability: 18.9%; Veterans: 11.9%; Ancestry: 49.4% German, 10.3% Irish, 9.5% American, 5.8% English, 2.5% Scottish
Employment: 9.3% management, business, and financial, 0.9% computer, engineering, and science, 4.5% education, legal, community service, arts, and media, 8.1% healthcare practitioners, 15.0% service, 12.2% sales and office, 7.9% natural resources, construction, and maintenance, 42.0% production, transportation, and material moving
Income: Per capita: $19,671; Median household: $37,519; Average household: $45,498; Households with income of $100,000 or more: 5.3%; Poverty rate: 9.0%
Educational Attainment: High school diploma or higher: 89.6%; Bachelor's degree or higher: 8.1%; Graduate/professional degree or higher: 1.6%

School District(s)

Carey Exempted Village (PK-12)
2012-13 Enrollment: 842. . . . . (419) 396-7922
Housing: Homeownership rate: 68.5%; Median home value: $88,800; Median year structure built: 1955; Homeowner vacancy rate: 3.1%; Median gross rent: $575 per month; Rental vacancy rate: 7.7%
Health Insurance: 87.3% have insurance; 69.9% have private insurance; 33.2% have public insurance; 12.7% do not have insurance; 0.0% of children under 18 do not have insurance
Newspapers: Progressor-Times Inc (weekly circulation 4000)
Transportation: Commute: 94.6% car, 0.0% public transportation, 3.9% walk, 1.1% work from home; Median travel time to work: 21.0 minutes

HARPSTER (village). Covers a land area of 1.971 square miles and a water area of 0 square miles. Located at 40.74° N. Lat; 83.25° W. Long. Elevation is 902 feet.
Population: 204; Growth (since 2000): 0.5%; Density: 103.5 persons per square mile; Race: 97.5% White, 1.0% Black/African American, 0.0% Asian, 0.0% American Indian/Alaska Native, 0.0% Native Hawaiian/Other Pacific Islander, 1.0% Two or more races, 0.5% Hispanic of any race; Average household size: 2.46; Median age: 44.0; Age under 18: 21.1%; Age 65 and over: 24.5%; Males per 100 females: 92.5
Housing: Homeownership rate: 79.5%; Homeowner vacancy rate: 1.5%; Rental vacancy rate: 5.3%

KIRBY (village). Covers a land area of 0.108 square miles and a water area of 0 square miles. Located at 40.81° N. Lat; 83.42° W. Long. Elevation is 873 feet.
Population: 118; Growth (since 2000): -10.6%; Density: 1,095.0 persons per square mile; Race: 99.2% White, 0.0% Black/African American, 0.0% Asian, 0.0% American Indian/Alaska Native, 0.0% Native Hawaiian/Other Pacific Islander, 0.8% Two or more races, 0.0% Hispanic of any race; Average household size: 2.36; Median age: 32.5; Age under 18: 20.3%; Age 65 and over: 11.0%; Males per 100 females: 151.1
Housing: Homeownership rate: 68.0%; Homeowner vacancy rate: 2.8%; Rental vacancy rate: 5.6%

MARSEILLES (village). Covers a land area of 0.098 square miles and a water area of 0 square miles. Located at 40.70° N. Lat; 83.39° W. Long. Elevation is 876 feet.
Population: 112; Growth (since 2000): -9.7%; Density: 1,147.3 persons per square mile; Race: 99.1% White, 0.0% Black/African American, 0.0% Asian, 0.9% American Indian/Alaska Native, 0.0% Native Hawaiian/Other Pacific Islander, 0.0% Two or more races, 0.0% Hispanic of any race; Average household size: 2.49; Median age: 40.0; Age under 18: 29.5%; Age 65 and over: 14.3%; Males per 100 females: 103.6
Housing: Homeownership rate: 88.9%; Homeowner vacancy rate: 0.0%; Rental vacancy rate: 0.0%

MCCUTCHENVILLE (CDP). Covers a land area of 2.780 square miles and a water area of 0.015 square miles. Located at 40.99° N. Lat; 83.25° W. Long. Elevation is 794 feet.
Population: 400; Growth (since 2000): n/a; Density: 143.9 persons per square mile; Race: 98.0% White, 0.0% Black/African American, 0.0% Asian, 0.0% American Indian/Alaska Native, 0.0% Native Hawaiian/Other Pacific Islander, 0.0% Two or more races, 3.5% Hispanic of any race; Average household size: 2.61; Median age: 39.8; Age under 18: 23.5%; Age 65 and over: 13.3%; Males per 100 females: 105.1
Housing: Homeownership rate: 81.1%; Homeowner vacancy rate: 1.6%; Rental vacancy rate: 6.5%

NEVADA (village). Covers a land area of 1.026 square miles and a water area of 0 square miles. Located at 40.82° N. Lat; 83.13° W. Long. Elevation is 932 feet.
Population: 760; Growth (since 2000): -6.6%; Density: 740.9 persons per square mile; Race: 97.1% White, 0.0% Black/African American, 0.0% Asian, 0.1% American Indian/Alaska Native, 0.0% Native Hawaiian/Other Pacific Islander, 2.1% Two or more races, 0.7% Hispanic of any race; Average household size: 2.58; Median age: 36.9; Age under 18: 26.4%; Age 65 and over: 12.8%; Males per 100 females: 99.0
Housing: Homeownership rate: 73.9%; Homeowner vacancy rate: 3.5%; Rental vacancy rate: 12.1%

SYCAMORE (village). Covers a land area of 0.637 square miles and a water area of 0 square miles. Located at 40.95° N. Lat; 83.17° W. Long. Elevation is 850 feet.
Population: 861; Growth (since 2000): -5.8%; Density: 1,352.4 persons per square mile; Race: 99.1% White, 0.1% Black/African American, 0.2% Asian, 0.0% American Indian/Alaska Native, 0.0% Native Hawaiian/Other Pacific Islander, 0.3% Two or more races, 1.5% Hispanic of any race; Average household size: 2.41; Median age: 40.2; Age under 18: 25.1%; Age 65 and over: 17.1%; Males per 100 females: 96.6

School District(s)

Mohawk Local (PK-12)
2012-13 Enrollment: 974. . . . . (419) 927-2414
Housing: Homeownership rate: 74.3%; Homeowner vacancy rate: 1.4%; Rental vacancy rate: 12.4%

UPPER SANDUSKY (city). County seat. Covers a land area of 7.011 square miles and a water area of 0.183 square miles. Located at 40.83° N. Lat; 83.27° W. Long. Elevation is 853 feet.
History: Upper Sandusky was laid out in 1843 on land that had belonged to the Wyandot tribe. The town of Upper Sandusky was preceded by Fort Ferree, built during the War of 1812 by General William Henry Harrison.
Population: 6,596; Growth (since 2000): 1.0%; Density: 940.8 persons per square mile; Race: 95.0% White, 0.3% Black/African American, 0.8% Asian, 0.2% American Indian/Alaska Native, 0.0% Native Hawaiian/Other Pacific Islander, 1.2% Two or more races, 4.3% Hispanic of any race; Average household size: 2.24; Median age: 41.0; Age under 18: 22.7%; Age 65 and over: 20.3%; Males per 100 females: 88.2; Marriage status: 21.0% never married, 56.4% now married, 3.0% separated, 11.6% widowed, 11.0% divorced; Foreign born: 2.4%; Speak English only: 94.2%; With disability: 14.9%; Veterans: 9.6%; Ancestry: 39.5% German, 12.4% Irish, 10.4% American, 9.0% English, 4.5% Italian
Employment: 13.5% management, business, and financial, 1.5% computer, engineering, and science, 7.6% education, legal, community service, arts, and media, 3.9% healthcare practitioners, 21.3% service, 17.8% sales and office, 10.3% natural resources, construction, and maintenance, 24.0% production, transportation, and material moving
Income: Per capita: $21,526; Median household: $36,227; Average household: $46,654; Households with income of $100,000 or more: 6.9%; Poverty rate: 19.0%
Educational Attainment: High school diploma or higher: 87.2%; Bachelor's degree or higher: 15.0%; Graduate/professional degree or higher: 5.3%

School District(s)

Upper Sandusky Exempted Village (PK-12)
2012-13 Enrollment: 1,661 . . . . (419) 294-2307
Housing: Homeownership rate: 58.0%; Median home value: $92,300; Median year structure built: 1960; Homeowner vacancy rate: 2.0%; Median gross rent: $591 per month; Rental vacancy rate: 9.8%
Health Insurance: 89.7% have insurance; 69.0% have private insurance; 36.0% have public insurance; 10.3% do not have insurance; 4.7% of children under 18 do not have insurance
Hospitals: Wyandot Memorial Hospital (45 beds)
Safety: Violent crime rate: 6.0 per 10,000 population; Property crime rate: 204.8 per 10,000 population
Newspapers: Daily Chief-Union (daily circulation 3800)
Transportation: Commute: 91.8% car, 1.8% public transportation, 2.9% walk, 1.9% work from home; Median travel time to work: 18.7 minutes

WHARTON (village). Covers a land area of 1.257 square miles and a water area of 0 square miles. Located at 40.86° N. Lat; 83.46° W. Long. Elevation is 883 feet.
Population: 358; Growth (since 2000): -12.5%; Density: 284.9 persons per square mile; Race: 99.2% White, 0.0% Black/African American, 0.0% Asian, 0.0% American Indian/Alaska Native, 0.0% Native Hawaiian/Other Pacific Islander, 0.8% Two or more races, 0.8% Hispanic of any race; Average household size: 2.69; Median age: 36.4; Age under 18: 26.0%; Age 65 and over: 12.3%; Males per 100 females: 105.7
Housing: Homeownership rate: 71.5%; Homeowner vacancy rate: 3.0%; Rental vacancy rate: 9.3%

Aberdeen (village) Brown County, 57
Ada (village) Hardin County, 156
Adams County, 39
Adamsville (village) Muskingum County, 227
Addyston (village) Hamilton County, 135
Adelphi (village) Ross County, 251
Adena (village) Jefferson County, 169
Akron (city) Summit County, 269
Albany (village) Athens County, 49
Alexandria (village) Licking County, 182
Alger (village) Hardin County, 156
Alledonia (unincorporated) Belmont County, 54
Allen County, 40
Alliance (city) Stark County, 263
Alpha (unincorporated) Greene County, 129
Alvada (unincorporated) Seneca County, 259
Alvordton (CDP) Williams County, 301
Amanda (village) Fairfield County, 109
Amberley (village) Hamilton County, 135
Amelia (village) Clermont County, 70
Amesville (village) Athens County, 49
Amherst (city) Lorain County, 189
Amlin (unincorporated) Franklin County, 113
Amsterdam (village) Jefferson County, 169
Andersonville (CDP) Ross County, 251
Andover (village) Ashtabula County, 45
Anna (village) Shelby County, 261
Ansonia (village) Darke County, 100
Antioch (village) Monroe County, 216
Antwerp (village) Paulding County, 234
Apple Creek (village) Wayne County, 298
Apple Valley (CDP) Knox County, 173
Aquilla (village) Geauga County, 126
Arcadia (village) Hancock County, 154
Arcanum (village) Darke County, 100
Archbold (village) Fulton County, 122
Arlington (village) Hancock County, 154
Arlington Heights (village) Hamilton County, 135
Ashland (city) Ashland County, 43
Ashland County, 43
Ashley (village) Delaware County, 104
Ashtabula (city) Ashtabula County, 45
Ashtabula County, 45
Ashville (village) Pickaway County, 238
Athalia (village) Lawrence County, 180
Athens (city) Athens County, 49
Athens County, 48
Attica (village) Seneca County, 259
Atwater (CDP) Portage County, 241
Auglaize County, 51
Augusta (unincorporated) Carroll County, 64
Aurora (city) Portage County, 241
Austinburg (CDP) Ashtabula County, 46
Austintown (CDP) Mahoning County, 200
Ava (unincorporated) Noble County, 230
Avon (city) Lorain County, 189
Avon Lake (city) Lorain County, 189
Bailey Lakes (village) Ashland County, 43
Bainbridge (CDP) Geauga County, 126
Bainbridge (village) Ross County, 251
Bairdstown (village) Wood County, 303
Ballville (CDP) Sandusky County, 253
Baltic (village) Tuscarawas County, 283
Baltimore (village) Fairfield County, 109
Bannock (CDP) Belmont County, 54
Barberton (city) Summit County, 270
Barnesville (village) Belmont County, 54
Barnhill (village) Tuscarawas County, 283
Barton (unincorporated) Belmont County, 54
Bascom (CDP) Seneca County, 259
Batavia (village) Clermont County, 70
Batesville (village) Noble County, 230
Bay View (village) Erie County, 107
Bay Village (city) Cuyahoga County, 84
Beach City (village) Stark County, 264
Beachwood (city) Cuyahoga County, 84
Beallsville (village) Monroe County, 216
Beaver (village) Pike County, 240
Beavercreek (city) Greene County, 129
Beaverdam (village) Allen County, 41
Beckett Ridge (CDP) Butler County, 60
Bedford (city) Cuyahoga County, 85
Bedford Heights (city) Cuyahoga County, 85
Beechwood Trails (CDP) Licking County, 182
Bellaire (village) Belmont County, 54
Bellbrook (city) Greene County, 130
Belle Center (village) Logan County, 186
Belle Valley (village) Noble County, 230
Bellefontaine (city) Logan County, 187
Bellevue (city) Sandusky County, 253
Bellville (village) Richland County, 249
Belmont (village) Belmont County, 54
Belmont County, 53
Belmore (village) Putnam County, 247
Beloit (village) Mahoning County, 200
Belpre (city) Washington County, 295
Bentleyville (village) Cuyahoga County, 85
Benton Ridge (village) Hancock County, 154
Bentonville (CDP) Adams County, 39
Berea (city) Cuyahoga County, 85
Bergholz (village) Jefferson County, 169
Berkey (village) Lucas County, 194
Berlin (CDP) Holmes County, 164
Berlin Center (unincorporated) Mahoning County, 200
Berlin Heights (village) Erie County, 107
Bethel (village) Clermont County, 71
Bethesda (village) Belmont County, 55
Bettsville (village) Seneca County, 259
Beulah Beach (CDP) Erie County, 107
Beverly (village) Washington County, 295
Bexley (city) Franklin County, 113
Bidwell (unincorporated) Gallia County, 124
Big Prairie (unincorporated) Holmes County, 164
Birmingham (unincorporated) Erie County, 107
Blacklick Estates (CDP) Franklin County, 113
Bladensburg (CDP) Knox County, 173
Blakeslee (village) Williams County, 301
Blanchester (village) Clinton County, 74
Blissfield (unincorporated) Coshocton County, 80
Bloomdale (village) Wood County, 303
Bloomingburg (village) Fayette County, 112
Bloomingdale (village) Jefferson County, 169
Bloomville (village) Seneca County, 259
Blue Ash (city) Hamilton County, 135
Blue Creek (unincorporated) Adams County, 39
Blue Jay (CDP) Hamilton County, 136
Blue Rock (unincorporated) Muskingum County, 227
Bluffton (village) Allen County, 41
Boardman (CDP) Mahoning County, 201
Bolindale (CDP) Trumbull County, 277
Bolivar (village) Tuscarawas County, 283
Boston Heights (village) Summit County, 270
Botkins (village) Shelby County, 261
Bourneville (CDP) Ross County, 252
Bowerston (village) Harrison County, 157
Bowersville (village) Greene County, 130
Bowling Green (city) Wood County, 303
Bradford (village) Miami County, 213
Bradner (village) Wood County, 304
Brady Lake (village) Portage County, 241
Bratenahl (village) Cuyahoga County, 86
Brecksville (city) Cuyahoga County, 86
Brecon (CDP) Hamilton County, 136
Bremen (village) Fairfield County, 109
Brewster (village) Stark County, 264
Brice (village) Franklin County, 114
Bridgeport (village) Belmont County, 55
Bridgetown (CDP) Hamilton County, 136
Brilliant (CDP) Jefferson County, 170
Brimfield (CDP) Portage County, 242
Brinkhaven (unincorporated) Holmes County, 164
Bristolville (unincorporated) Trumbull County, 277
Broadview Heights (city) Cuyahoga County, 86
Brook Park (city) Cuyahoga County, 86
Brookfield Center (CDP) Trumbull County, 277
Brooklyn (city) Cuyahoga County, 87
Brooklyn Heights (village) Cuyahoga County, 87
Brookside (village) Belmont County, 55
Brookville (city) Montgomery County, 218
Broughton (village) Paulding County, 234
Brown County, 57
Brownsville (CDP) Licking County, 183
Brunswick (city) Medina County, 207
Bryan (city) Williams County, 301
Buchtel (village) Athens County, 49
Buckeye Lake (village) Licking County, 183
Buckland (village) Auglaize County, 51
Bucyrus (city) Crawford County, 82
Buffalo (CDP) Guernsey County, 133
Buford (CDP) Highland County, 161
Burbank (village) Wayne County, 298
Burghill (unincorporated) Trumbull County, 277
Burgoon (village) Sandusky County, 254
Burkettsville (village) Mercer County, 212
Burlington (CDP) Lawrence County, 180
Burton (village) Geauga County, 127
Butler (village) Richland County, 249
Butler County, 59
Butlerville (village) Warren County, 291
Byesville (village) Guernsey County, 133
Cable (unincorporated) Champaign County, 66
Cadiz (village) Harrison County, 157
Cairo (village) Allen County, 41
Calcutta (CDP) Columbiana County, 76
Caldwell (village) Noble County, 231
Caledonia (village) Marion County, 205
Cambridge (city) Guernsey County, 133
Camden (village) Preble County, 245
Cameron (unincorporated) Monroe County, 216
Camp Dennison (CDP) Hamilton County, 136
Campbell (city) Mahoning County, 201
Canal Fulton (city) Stark County, 264
Canal Lewisville (CDP) Coshocton County, 80
Canal Winchester (city) Franklin County, 114
Candlewood Lake (CDP) Morrow County, 226
Canfield (city) Mahoning County, 201
Canton (city) Stark County, 264
Carbon Hill (CDP) Hocking County, 162
Cardington (village) Morrow County, 226
Carey (village) Wyandot County, 307
Carlisle (village) Warren County, 291
Carroll (village) Fairfield County, 109
Carroll County, 64
Carrollton (village) Carroll County, 64
Casstown (village) Miami County, 214
Castalia (village) Erie County, 107
Castine (village) Darke County, 100
Catawba (village) Clark County, 67
Cecil (village) Paulding County, 234
Cedarville (village) Greene County, 130
Celeryville (CDP) Huron County, 166
Celina (city) Mercer County, 212
Centerburg (village) Knox County, 173
Centerville (village) Gallia County, 124
Centerville (city) Montgomery County, 218
Chagrin Falls (village) Cuyahoga County, 87
Champaign County, 65

Champion Heights (CDP) Trumbull County, 277
Chandlersville (unincorporated) Muskingum County, 228
Chardon (city) Geauga County, 127
Chatfield (village) Crawford County, 82
Chauncey (village) Athens County, 49
Cherry Fork (village) Adams County, 39
Cherry Grove (CDP) Hamilton County, 136
Chesapeake (village) Lawrence County, 180
Cheshire (village) Gallia County, 125
Chesterhill (village) Morgan County, 225
Chesterland (CDP) Geauga County, 127
Chesterville (village) Morrow County, 226
Cheviot (city) Hamilton County, 136
Chickasaw (village) Mercer County, 212
Chillicothe (city) Ross County, 252
Chilo (village) Clermont County, 71
Chippewa Lake (village) Medina County, 207
Chippewa Park (CDP) Logan County, 187
Choctaw Lake (CDP) Madison County, 198
Christiansburg (village) Champaign County, 66
Churchill (CDP) Trumbull County, 277
Cincinnati (city) Hamilton County, 136
Cinnamon Lake (CDP) Ashland County, 44
Circleville (city) Pickaway County, 238
Clarington (village) Monroe County, 216
Clark County, 67
Clarksburg (village) Ross County, 252
Clarksville (village) Clinton County, 75
Clarktown (CDP) Scioto County, 256
Clay Center (village) Ottawa County, 231
Clayton (city) Montgomery County, 219
Clermont County, 70
Cleveland (city) Cuyahoga County, 87
Cleveland Heights (city) Cuyahoga County, 89
Cleves (village) Hamilton County, 138
Clifton (village) Greene County, 130
Clinton (village) Summit County, 270
Clinton County, 74
Cloverdale (village) Putnam County, 247
Clyde (city) Sandusky County, 254
Coal Grove (village) Lawrence County, 180
Coal Run (unincorporated) Washington County, 295
Coalton (village) Jackson County, 168
Coldstream (CDP) Hamilton County, 138
Coldwater (village) Mercer County, 212
College Corner (village) Preble County, 245
Collins (CDP) Huron County, 166
Columbia Station (unincorporated) Lorain County, 190
Columbiana (city) Columbiana County, 76
Columbiana County, 76
Columbus (city) Franklin County, 114
Columbus Grove (village) Putnam County, 247
Commercial Point (village) Pickaway County, 239
Concorde Hills (CDP) Hamilton County, 139
Conesville (village) Coshocton County, 80
Congress (village) Wayne County, 298
Conneaut (city) Ashtabula County, 46
Conover (unincorporated) Champaign County, 66
Continental (village) Putnam County, 247
Convoy (village) Van Wert County, 288
Coolville (village) Athens County, 49
Corning (village) Perry County, 236
Cortland (city) Trumbull County, 278
Corwin (village) Warren County, 291
Coshocton (city) Coshocton County, 81
Coshocton County, 80
Covedale (CDP) Hamilton County, 139
Covington (village) Miami County, 214
Craig Beach (village) Mahoning County, 201
Crawford County, 81
Creola (unincorporated) Vinton County, 290
Crestline (village) Crawford County, 82
Creston (village) Wayne County, 298
Cridersville (village) Auglaize County, 51
Crooksville (village) Perry County, 236
Croton (unincorporated) Licking County, 183
Crown City (village) Gallia County, 125
Crystal Lakes (CDP) Clark County, 67
Crystal Rock (CDP) Erie County, 107
Cumberland (village) Guernsey County, 133
Curtice (CDP) Ottawa County, 231
Custar (village) Wood County, 304
Cutler (unincorporated) Washington County, 295
Cuyahoga County, 83
Cuyahoga Falls (city) Summit County, 270
Cuyahoga Heights (village) Cuyahoga County, 89
Cygnet (village) Wood County, 304
Cynthiana (CDP) Pike County, 240
Dalton (village) Wayne County, 298
Damascus (CDP) Mahoning County, 202
Danville (village) Knox County, 173
Darbydale (CDP) Franklin County, 116
Darbyville (village) Pickaway County, 239
Darke County, 100
Darrtown (CDP) Butler County, 60
Day Heights (CDP) Clermont County, 71
Dayton (city) Montgomery County, 219
De Graff (village) Logan County, 187
Decatur (unincorporated) Brown County, 57
Deer Park (city) Hamilton County, 139
Deerfield (unincorporated) Portage County, 242
Deersville (village) Harrison County, 158
Defiance (city) Defiance County, 103
Defiance County, 102
Delaware (city) Delaware County, 104
Delaware County, 104
Delhi Hills (CDP) Hamilton County, 139
Dellroy (village) Carroll County, 64
Delphos (city) Allen County, 41
Delshire (CDP) Hamilton County, 139
Delta (village) Fulton County, 122
Dennison (village) Tuscarawas County, 283
Dent (CDP) Hamilton County, 139
Derby (CDP) Pickaway County, 239
Derwent (unincorporated) Guernsey County, 133
Deshler (village) Henry County, 159
Devola (CDP) Washington County, 295
Dexter City (village) Noble County, 231
Diamond (unincorporated) Portage County, 242
Dillonvale (CDP) Hamilton County, 140
Dillonvale (village) Jefferson County, 170
Dola (CDP) Hardin County, 156
Donnelsville (village) Clark County, 67
Dorset (unincorporated) Ashtabula County, 46
Dover (city) Tuscarawas County, 284
Doylestown (village) Wayne County, 298
Dresden (village) Muskingum County, 228
Drexel (CDP) Montgomery County, 220
Dry Ridge (CDP) Hamilton County, 140
Dry Run (CDP) Hamilton County, 140
Dublin (city) Franklin County, 116
Duncan Falls (CDP) Muskingum County, 228
Dundee (CDP) Tuscarawas County, 284
Dunkirk (village) Hardin County, 156
Dunlap (CDP) Hamilton County, 140
Dupont (village) Putnam County, 247
East Canton (village) Stark County, 265
East Cleveland (city) Cuyahoga County, 89
East Fultonham (CDP) Muskingum County, 228
East Liberty (CDP) Logan County, 187
East Liverpool (city) Columbiana County, 77
East Palestine (village) Columbiana County, 77
East Rochester (CDP) Columbiana County, 77
East Sparta (village) Stark County, 265
East Springfield (unincorporated) Jefferson County, 170
Eastlake (city) Lake County, 175
Eaton (city) Preble County, 245
Eaton Estates (CDP) Lorain County, 190
Edgerton (village) Williams County, 301
Edgewood (CDP) Ashtabula County, 46
Edison (village) Morrow County, 226
Edon (village) Williams County, 301
Eldorado (village) Preble County, 245
Elgin (village) Van Wert County, 288
Elida (village) Allen County, 41
Elizabethtown (CDP) Hamilton County, 140
Elmore (village) Ottawa County, 232
Elmwood Place (village) Hamilton County, 141
Elyria (city) Lorain County, 190
Empire (village) Jefferson County, 170
Englewood (city) Montgomery County, 220
Enon (village) Clark County, 67
Erie County, 106
Etna (CDP) Licking County, 183
Euclid (city) Cuyahoga County, 90
Evansport (unincorporated) Defiance County, 103
Evendale (village) Hamilton County, 141
Fairborn (city) Greene County, 131
Fairfax (village) Hamilton County, 141
Fairfield (city) Butler County, 60
Fairfield Beach (CDP) Fairfield County, 110
Fairfield County, 108
Fairlawn (city) Summit County, 271
Fairpoint (unincorporated) Belmont County, 55
Fairport Harbor (village) Lake County, 175
Fairview (village) Guernsey County, 133
Fairview Park (city) Cuyahoga County, 90
Farmdale (unincorporated) Trumbull County, 278
Farmersville (village) Montgomery County, 221
Fayette (village) Fulton County, 123
Fayette County, 111
Fayetteville (village) Brown County, 58
Felicity (village) Clermont County, 71
Findlay (city) Hancock County, 154
Finneytown (CDP) Hamilton County, 141
Five Points (CDP) Warren County, 291
Flat Rock (CDP) Seneca County, 259
Fleming (unincorporated) Washington County, 296
Fletcher (village) Miami County, 214
Florida (village) Henry County, 159
Flushing (village) Belmont County, 55
Forest (village) Hardin County, 156
Forest Park (city) Hamilton County, 141
Forestville (CDP) Hamilton County, 142
Fort Jennings (village) Putnam County, 247
Fort Loramie (village) Shelby County, 261
Fort Recovery (village) Mercer County, 212
Fort Seneca (CDP) Seneca County, 260
Fort Shawnee (CDP) Allen County, 41
Fostoria (city) Seneca County, 260
Four Bridges (CDP) Butler County, 60
Fowler (unincorporated) Trumbull County, 278
Frankfort (village) Ross County, 252
Franklin (city) Warren County, 291
Franklin County, 112
Franklin Furnace (CDP) Scioto County, 256
Frazeysburg (village) Muskingum County, 228
Fredericksburg (village) Wayne County, 298
Fredericktown (village) Knox County, 173
Freeport (village) Harrison County, 158
Fremont (city) Sandusky County, 254
Fresno (CDP) Coshocton County, 81
Friendship (CDP) Scioto County, 256
Fruit Hill (CDP) Hamilton County, 142

CDP = Census Designated Place

Fulton (village) Morrow County, 226
Fulton County, 122
Fultonham (village) Muskingum County, 228
Gahanna (city) Franklin County, 116
Galena (village) Delaware County, 105
Galion (city) Crawford County, 83
Gallia County, 124
Gallipolis (village) Gallia County, 125
Galloway (unincorporated) Franklin County, 117
Gambier (village) Knox County, 173
Gann (village) Knox County, 174
Garfield Heights (city) Cuyahoga County, 90
Garrettsville (village) Portage County, 242
Gates Mills (village) Cuyahoga County, 91
Geauga County, 126
Geneva (city) Ashtabula County, 47
Geneva-on-the-Lake (village) Ashtabula County, 47
Genoa (village) Ottawa County, 232
Georgetown (village) Brown County, 58
Germantown (city) Montgomery County, 221
Gettysburg (village) Darke County, 101
Gibsonburg (village) Sandusky County, 255
Gilboa (village) Putnam County, 247
Girard (city) Trumbull County, 278
Glandorf (village) Putnam County, 247
Glencoe (CDP) Belmont County, 55
Glendale (village) Hamilton County, 142
Glenford (village) Perry County, 236
Glenmont (village) Holmes County, 164
Glenmoor (CDP) Columbiana County, 78
Glenwillow (village) Cuyahoga County, 91
Gloria Glens Park (village) Medina County, 207
Glouster (village) Athens County, 50
Gnadenhutten (village) Tuscarawas County, 284
Golf Manor (village) Hamilton County, 142
Gomer (unincorporated) Allen County, 42
Good Hope (CDP) Fayette County, 112
Gordon (village) Darke County, 101
Goshen (unincorporated) Clermont County, 71
Grafton (village) Lorain County, 190
Grand Rapids (village) Wood County, 304
Grand River (village) Lake County, 175
Grandview (CDP) Hamilton County, 142
Grandview Heights (city) Franklin County, 117
Granville (village) Licking County, 183
Granville South (CDP) Licking County, 184
Gratiot (village) Licking County, 184
Gratis (village) Preble County, 245
Graysville (village) Monroe County, 216
Graytown (unincorporated) Ottawa County, 232
Green (city) Summit County, 271
Green Camp (village) Marion County, 205
Green Meadows (CDP) Clark County, 68
Green Springs (village) Sandusky County, 255
Greene County, 129
Greenfield (village) Highland County, 161
Greenhills (village) Hamilton County, 142
Greentown (CDP) Stark County, 265
Greenville (city) Darke County, 101
Greenwich (village) Huron County, 166
Groesbeck (CDP) Hamilton County, 143
Grove City (city) Franklin County, 117
Groveport (city) Franklin County, 118
Grover Hill (village) Paulding County, 234
Guernsey County, 132
Guysville (unincorporated) Athens County, 50
Gypsum (unincorporated) Ottawa County, 232
Hamden (village) Vinton County, 290
Hamersville (village) Brown County, 58
Hamilton (city) Butler County, 60
Hamilton County, 134
Hamler (village) Henry County, 159
Hammondsville (unincorporated) Jefferson County, 170
Hancock County, 153
Hanging Rock (village) Lawrence County, 180
Hannibal (CDP) Monroe County, 217
Hanover (village) Licking County, 184
Hanoverton (village) Columbiana County, 78
Harbor Hills (CDP) Licking County, 184
Harbor View (village) Lucas County, 194
Hardin County, 155
Harpster (village) Wyandot County, 308
Harrisburg (village) Franklin County, 118
Harrison (city) Hamilton County, 143
Harrison County, 157
Harrisville (village) Harrison County, 158
Harrod (village) Allen County, 42
Hartford (village) Licking County, 184
Hartville (village) Stark County, 265
Harveysburg (village) Warren County, 292
Haskins (village) Wood County, 304
Haverhill (unincorporated) Scioto County, 256
Haviland (village) Paulding County, 235
Haydenville (CDP) Hocking County, 162
Hayesville (village) Ashland County, 44
Heath (city) Licking County, 184
Hebron (village) Licking County, 184
Helena (village) Sandusky County, 255
Hemlock (village) Perry County, 236
Henry County, 158
Hessville (CDP) Sandusky County, 255
Hicksville (village) Defiance County, 103
Hide-A-Way Hills (CDP) Hocking County, 163
Higginsport (village) Brown County, 58
Highland (village) Highland County, 161
Highland County, 160
Highland Heights (city) Cuyahoga County, 91
Highland Hills (village) Cuyahoga County, 91
Highland Holiday (CDP) Highland County, 161
Highpoint (CDP) Hamilton County, 143
Hilliard (city) Franklin County, 118
Hills and Dales (village) Stark County, 266
Hillsboro (city) Highland County, 161
Hilltop (CDP) Trumbull County, 278
Hinckley (unincorporated) Medina County, 207
Hiram (village) Portage County, 242
Hocking County, 162
Hockingport (CDP) Athens County, 50
Holgate (village) Henry County, 159
Holiday City (village) Williams County, 301
Holiday Lakes (CDP) Huron County, 166
Holiday Valley (CDP) Clark County, 68
Holland (village) Lucas County, 194
Hollansburg (village) Darke County, 101
Holloway (village) Belmont County, 55
Holmes County, 163
Holmesville (village) Holmes County, 164
Homerville (unincorporated) Medina County, 207
Homeworth (CDP) Columbiana County, 78
Hooven (CDP) Hamilton County, 143
Hopedale (village) Harrison County, 158
Hopewell (unincorporated) Muskingum County, 228
Houston (unincorporated) Shelby County, 262
Howard (CDP) Knox County, 174
Howland Center (CDP) Trumbull County, 278
Hoytville (village) Wood County, 304
Hubbard (city) Trumbull County, 279
Huber Heights (city) Montgomery County, 221
Huber Ridge (CDP) Franklin County, 118
Hudson (city) Summit County, 271
Hunter (CDP) Warren County, 292
Hunting Valley (village) Cuyahoga County, 91
Huntsburg (unincorporated) Geauga County, 127
Huntsville (village) Logan County, 187
Huron (city) Erie County, 107
Huron County, 165
Iberia (CDP) Morrow County, 226
Independence (city) Cuyahoga County, 91
Irondale (village) Jefferson County, 170
Ironton (city) Lawrence County, 180
Irwin (unincorporated) Madison County, 198
Ithaca (village) Darke County, 101
Jackson (city) Jackson County, 168
Jackson Center (village) Shelby County, 262
Jackson County, 167
Jacksonburg (village) Butler County, 61
Jacksontown (unincorporated) Licking County, 184
Jacksonville (village) Athens County, 50
Jacobsburg (unincorporated) Belmont County, 55
Jamestown (village) Greene County, 131
Jefferson (village) Ashtabula County, 47
Jefferson County, 169
Jeffersonville (village) Fayette County, 112
Jenera (village) Hancock County, 154
Jeromesville (village) Ashland County, 44
Jerry City (village) Wood County, 304
Jerusalem (village) Monroe County, 217
Jewett (village) Harrison County, 158
Johnstown (village) Licking County, 184
Junction City (village) Perry County, 236
Kalida (village) Putnam County, 247
Kanauga (CDP) Gallia County, 125
Kansas (CDP) Seneca County, 260
Kelleys Island (village) Erie County, 108
Kensington (unincorporated) Columbiana County, 78
Kent (city) Portage County, 242
Kenton (city) Hardin County, 156
Kenwood (CDP) Hamilton County, 143
Kettering (city) Montgomery County, 221
Kettlersville (village) Shelby County, 262
Kidron (CDP) Wayne County, 299
Kilbourne (CDP) Delaware County, 105
Killbuck (village) Holmes County, 164
Kimbolton (CDP) Guernsey County, 133
Kings Mills (CDP) Warren County, 292
Kingston (village) Ross County, 252
Kingsville (unincorporated) Ashtabula County, 47
Kinsman (unincorporated) Trumbull County, 279
Kinsman Center (CDP) Trumbull County, 279
Kipling (unincorporated) Guernsey County, 134
Kipton (village) Lorain County, 190
Kirby (village) Wyandot County, 308
Kirkersville (village) Licking County, 185
Kirtland (city) Lake County, 176
Kirtland Hills (village) Lake County, 176
Kitts Hill (unincorporated) Lawrence County, 181
Knox County, 172
Kunkle (CDP) Williams County, 302
La Croft (CDP) Columbiana County, 78
La Rue (village) Marion County, 205
Lacarne (unincorporated) Ottawa County, 232
Lafayette (village) Allen County, 42
Lafayette (CDP) Madison County, 198
Lafferty (CDP) Belmont County, 55
LaGrange (village) Lorain County, 191
Lake Buckhorn (CDP) Holmes County, 164
Lake County, 174
Lake Darby (CDP) Franklin County, 119
Lake Lakengren (CDP) Preble County, 245
Lake Lorelei (CDP) Brown County, 58
Lake Milton (unincorporated) Mahoning County, 202
Lake Mohawk (CDP) Carroll County, 65
Lake Seneca (CDP) Williams County, 302

CDP = Census Designated Place

Lake Tomahawk (CDP) Columbiana County, 78
Lake Waynoka (CDP) Brown County, 58
Lakeline (village) Lake County, 176
Lakemore (village) Summit County, 272
Lakeside (CDP) Ottawa County, 232
Lakeside Marblehead (unincorporated) Ottawa County, 232
Lakeview (village) Logan County, 187
Lakeville (unincorporated) Holmes County, 165
Lakewood (city) Cuyahoga County, 92
Lancaster (city) Fairfield County, 110
Landen (CDP) Warren County, 292
Langsville (unincorporated) Meigs County, 210
Lansing (CDP) Belmont County, 55
Latham (unincorporated) Pike County, 240
Latty (village) Paulding County, 235
Laura (village) Miami County, 214
Laurelville (village) Hocking County, 163
Lawrence County, 179
Leavittsburg (CDP) Trumbull County, 279
Lebanon (city) Warren County, 292
Leesburg (village) Highland County, 161
Leesville (village) Carroll County, 65
Leetonia (village) Columbiana County, 78
Leipsic (village) Putnam County, 247
Lewis Center (unincorporated) Delaware County, 105
Lewisburg (village) Preble County, 246
Lewistown (CDP) Logan County, 187
Lewisville (village) Monroe County, 217
Lexington (village) Richland County, 249
Liberty Center (village) Henry County, 159
Licking County, 182
Lima (city) Allen County, 42
Limaville (village) Stark County, 266
Lincoln Heights (village) Hamilton County, 144
Lincoln Village (CDP) Franklin County, 119
Lindsey (village) Sandusky County, 255
Linndale (village) Cuyahoga County, 92
Lisbon (village) Columbiana County, 78
Litchfield (unincorporated) Medina County, 207
Lithopolis (village) Fairfield County, 110
Little Hocking (CDP) Washington County, 296
Lockbourne (village) Franklin County, 119
Lockington (village) Shelby County, 262
Lockland (village) Hamilton County, 144
Lodi (village) Medina County, 208
Logan (city) Hocking County, 163
Logan County, 186
Logan Elm Village (CDP) Pickaway County, 239
London (city) Madison County, 198
Londonderry (unincorporated) Ross County, 252
Long Bottom (unincorporated) Meigs County, 210
Lorain (city) Lorain County, 191
Lorain County, 188
Lordstown (village) Trumbull County, 279
Lore City (village) Guernsey County, 134
Loudonville (village) Ashland County, 44
Louisville (city) Stark County, 266
Loveland (city) Hamilton County, 144
Loveland Park (CDP) Warren County, 293
Lowell (village) Washington County, 296
Lowellville (village) Mahoning County, 202
Lower Salem (village) Washington County, 296
Lucas (village) Richland County, 249
Lucas County, 193
Lucasville (CDP) Scioto County, 256
Luckey (village) Wood County, 304
Ludlow Falls (village) Miami County, 214
Lynchburg (village) Highland County, 162
Lyndhurst (city) Cuyahoga County, 92
Lynx (unincorporated) Adams County, 39
Lyons (village) Fulton County, 123
Macedonia (city) Summit County, 272
Mack (CDP) Hamilton County, 144
Macksburg (village) Washington County, 296
Madeira (city) Hamilton County, 145
Madison (village) Lake County, 176
Madison County, 197
Magnetic Springs (village) Union County, 287
Magnolia (village) Stark County, 266
Mahoning County, 200
Maineville (village) Warren County, 293
Malinta (village) Henry County, 159
Malta (village) Morgan County, 225
Malvern (village) Carroll County, 65
Manchester (village) Adams County, 39
Mansfield (city) Richland County, 249
Mantua (village) Portage County, 243
Maple Heights (city) Cuyahoga County, 92
Maple Ridge (CDP) Mahoning County, 202
Maplewood (unincorporated) Shelby County, 262
Maplewood Park (CDP) Trumbull County, 280
Marble Cliff (village) Franklin County, 119
Marblehead (village) Ottawa County, 232
Marengo (village) Morrow County, 226
Maria Stein (unincorporated) Mercer County, 212
Mariemont (village) Hamilton County, 145
Marietta (city) Washington County, 296
Marion (city) Marion County, 205
Marion County, 204
Mark Center (unincorporated) Defiance County, 104
Marne (CDP) Licking County, 185
Marseilles (village) Wyandot County, 308
Marshallville (village) Wayne County, 299
Martin (unincorporated) Ottawa County, 233
Martins Ferry (city) Belmont County, 55
Martinsburg (village) Knox County, 174
Martinsville (village) Clinton County, 75
Marysville (city) Union County, 287
Mason (city) Warren County, 293
Massillon (city) Stark County, 266
Masury (CDP) Trumbull County, 280
Matamoras (village) Washington County, 297
Maumee (city) Lucas County, 194
Mayfield (village) Cuyahoga County, 93
Mayfield Heights (city) Cuyahoga County, 93
McArthur (village) Vinton County, 290
McClure (village) Henry County, 160
McComb (village) Hancock County, 154
McConnelsville (village) Morgan County, 225
McCutchenville (CDP) Wyandot County, 308
McDermott (CDP) Scioto County, 257
McDonald (village) Trumbull County, 280
McGuffey (village) Hardin County, 157
McKinley Heights (CDP) Trumbull County, 280
Mechanicsburg (village) Champaign County, 66
Mechanicstown (unincorporated) Carroll County, 65
Medina (city) Medina County, 208
Medina County, 206
Medway (unincorporated) Clark County, 68
Meigs County, 209
Melmore (CDP) Seneca County, 260
Melrose (village) Paulding County, 235
Mendon (village) Mercer County, 213
Mentor (city) Lake County, 176
Mentor-on-the-Lake (city) Lake County, 177
Mercer County, 211
Mesopotamia (unincorporated) Trumbull County, 280
Metamora (village) Fulton County, 123
Meyers Lake (village) Stark County, 266
Miami County, 213
Miami Heights (CDP) Hamilton County, 145
Miamisburg (city) Montgomery County, 222
Miamitown (CDP) Hamilton County, 145
Miamiville (CDP) Clermont County, 72
Middle Bass (unincorporated) Ottawa County, 233
Middle Point (village) Van Wert County, 288
Middleburg Heights (city) Cuyahoga County, 93
Middlefield (village) Geauga County, 127
Middleport (village) Meigs County, 210
Middletown (city) Butler County, 61
Midland (village) Clinton County, 75
Midvale (village) Tuscarawas County, 284
Midway (village) Madison County, 199
Mifflin (village) Ashland County, 44
Milan (village) Erie County, 108
Milford (city) Clermont County, 72
Milford Center (village) Union County, 287
Millbury (village) Wood County, 304
Milledgeville (village) Fayette County, 112
Miller City (village) Putnam County, 248
Millersburg (village) Holmes County, 165
Millersport (village) Fairfield County, 110
Millfield (CDP) Athens County, 50
Millville (village) Butler County, 61
Milton Center (village) Wood County, 304
Miltonsburg (village) Monroe County, 217
Mineral City (village) Tuscarawas County, 284
Mineral Ridge (CDP) Trumbull County, 280
Minerva (village) Stark County, 267
Minerva Park (village) Franklin County, 119
Minford (CDP) Scioto County, 257
Mingo Junction (village) Jefferson County, 170
Minster (village) Auglaize County, 51
Mogadore (village) Summit County, 272
Monclova (unincorporated) Lucas County, 194
Monfort Heights (CDP) Hamilton County, 146
Monroe (city) Butler County, 61
Monroe County, 216
Monroeville (village) Huron County, 166
Montezuma (village) Mercer County, 213
Montgomery (city) Hamilton County, 146
Montgomery County, 218
Montpelier (village) Williams County, 302
Montrose-Ghent (CDP) Summit County, 272
Montville (unincorporated) Geauga County, 128
Moraine (city) Montgomery County, 222
Moreland Hills (village) Cuyahoga County, 93
Morgan County, 224
Morgandale (CDP) Trumbull County, 280
Morral (village) Marion County, 206
Morristown (village) Belmont County, 56
Morrow (village) Warren County, 293
Morrow County, 225
Moscow (village) Clermont County, 72
Mount Blanchard (village) Hancock County, 155
Mount Carmel (CDP) Clermont County, 72
Mount Cory (village) Hancock County, 155
Mount Eaton (village) Wayne County, 299
Mount Gilead (village) Morrow County, 226
Mount Healthy (city) Hamilton County, 146
Mount Healthy Heights (CDP) Hamilton County, 146
Mount Orab (village) Brown County, 58
Mount Perry (unincorporated) Perry County, 236
Mount Pleasant (village) Jefferson County, 170
Mount Repose (CDP) Clermont County, 72
Mount Saint Joseph (unincorporated) Hamilton County, 147
Mount Sterling (village) Madison County, 199
Mount Vernon (city) Knox County, 174
Mount Victory (village) Hardin County, 157
Mowrystown (village) Highland County, 162
Moxahala (unincorporated) Perry County, 237
Mulberry (CDP) Clermont County, 73

CDP = Census Designated Place

Munroe Falls (city) Summit County, 273
Murray City (village) Hocking County, 163
Muskingum County, 227
Mutual (village) Champaign County, 66
Napoleon (city) Henry County, 160
Nashport (unincorporated) Muskingum County, 228
Nashville (village) Holmes County, 165
Navarre (village) Stark County, 267
Neapolis (CDP) Lucas County, 195
Neffs (CDP) Belmont County, 56
Negley (CDP) Columbiana County, 78
Nellie (village) Coshocton County, 81
Nelsonville (city) Athens County, 50
Nevada (village) Wyandot County, 308
Neville (village) Clermont County, 73
New Albany (city) Franklin County, 119
New Alexandria (village) Jefferson County, 170
New Athens (village) Harrison County, 158
New Baltimore (CDP) Hamilton County, 147
New Bavaria (village) Henry County, 160
New Bloomington (village) Marion County, 206
New Boston (village) Scioto County, 257
New Bremen (village) Auglaize County, 52
New Burlington (CDP) Hamilton County, 147
New California (CDP) Union County, 287
New Carlisle (city) Clark County, 68
New Concord (village) Muskingum County, 229
New Franklin (city) Summit County, 273
New Hampshire (CDP) Auglaize County, 52
New Haven (CDP) Hamilton County, 147
New Haven (CDP) Huron County, 166
New Holland (village) Pickaway County, 239
New Knoxville (village) Auglaize County, 52
New Lebanon (village) Montgomery County, 222
New Lexington (village) Perry County, 237
New London (village) Huron County, 166
New Madison (village) Darke County, 101
New Marshfield (CDP) Athens County, 50
New Matamoras (unincorporated) Monroe County, 217
New Miami (village) Butler County, 62
New Middletown (village) Mahoning County, 202
New Paris (village) Preble County, 246
New Philadelphia (city) Tuscarawas County, 284
New Pittsburg (CDP) Wayne County, 299
New Plymouth (unincorporated) Vinton County, 290
New Richmond (village) Clermont County, 73
New Riegel (village) Seneca County, 260
New Springfield (unincorporated) Mahoning County, 202
New Straitsville (village) Perry County, 237
New Vienna (village) Clinton County, 75
New Washington (village) Crawford County, 83
New Waterford (village) Columbiana County, 79
New Weston (village) Darke County, 101
Newark (city) Licking County, 185
Newburgh Heights (village) Cuyahoga County, 94
Newbury (unincorporated) Geauga County, 128
Newcomerstown (village) Tuscarawas County, 285
Newport (CDP) Shelby County, 262
Newport (CDP) Washington County, 297
Newton Falls (village) Trumbull County, 280
Newtonsville (village) Clermont County, 73
Newtown (village) Hamilton County, 147
Ney (village) Defiance County, 104
Niles (city) Trumbull County, 281
Noble County, 230
North Baltimore (village) Wood County, 304
North Bend (village) Hamilton County, 147
North Benton (unincorporated) Portage County, 243
North Bloomfield (unincorporated) Trumbull County, 281
North Canton (city) Stark County, 267
North College Hill (city) Hamilton County, 147
North Fairfield (village) Huron County, 167
North Hampton (village) Clark County, 68
North Jackson (unincorporated) Mahoning County, 202
North Kingsville (village) Ashtabula County, 47
North Lawrence (CDP) Stark County, 267
North Lewisburg (village) Champaign County, 66
North Lima (unincorporated) Mahoning County, 203
North Madison (CDP) Lake County, 177
North Olmsted (city) Cuyahoga County, 94
North Perry (village) Lake County, 177
North Randall (village) Cuyahoga County, 94
North Ridgeville (city) Lorain County, 191
North Robinson (village) Crawford County, 83
North Royalton (city) Cuyahoga County, 94
North Star (village) Darke County, 101
North Zanesville (CDP) Muskingum County, 229
Northbrook (CDP) Hamilton County, 148
Northfield (village) Summit County, 273
Northgate (CDP) Hamilton County, 148
Northridge (CDP) Clark County, 68
Northwood (city) Wood County, 305
Norton (city) Summit County, 273
Norwalk (city) Huron County, 167
Norwich (village) Muskingum County, 229
Norwood (city) Hamilton County, 148
Nova (unincorporated) Ashland County, 44
Novelty (unincorporated) Geauga County, 128
Oak Harbor (village) Ottawa County, 233
Oak Hill (village) Jackson County, 168
Oakwood (village) Cuyahoga County, 95
Oakwood (city) Montgomery County, 223
Oakwood (village) Paulding County, 235
Oberlin (city) Lorain County, 191
Obetz (village) Franklin County, 120
Oceola (CDP) Crawford County, 83
Octa (village) Fayette County, 112
Ohio City (village) Van Wert County, 289
Okeana (unincorporated) Butler County, 62
Old Fort (CDP) Seneca County, 260
Old Washington (village) Guernsey County, 134
Olde West Chester (CDP) Butler County, 62
Olmsted Falls (city) Cuyahoga County, 95
Ontario (city) Richland County, 250
Orange (village) Cuyahoga County, 95
Orangeville (village) Trumbull County, 281
Oregon (city) Lucas County, 195
Oregonia (unincorporated) Warren County, 293
Orient (village) Pickaway County, 239
Orrville (city) Wayne County, 299
Orwell (village) Ashtabula County, 48
Osgood (village) Darke County, 101
Ostrander (village) Delaware County, 105
Ottawa (village) Putnam County, 248
Ottawa County, 231
Ottawa Hills (village) Lucas County, 195
Ottoville (village) Putnam County, 248
Otway (village) Scioto County, 257
Owensville (village) Clermont County, 73
Oxford (city) Butler County, 62
Painesville (city) Lake County, 177
Palestine (village) Darke County, 102
Pancoastburg (CDP) Fayette County, 112
Pandora (village) Putnam County, 248
Paris (unincorporated) Stark County, 267
Park Layne (CDP) Clark County, 69
Parkman (unincorporated) Geauga County, 128
Parma (city) Cuyahoga County, 95
Parma Heights (city) Cuyahoga County, 96
Parral (village) Tuscarawas County, 285
Pataskala (city) Licking County, 185
Patriot (unincorporated) Gallia County, 125
Patterson (village) Hardin County, 157
Paulding (village) Paulding County, 235
Paulding County, 234
Payne (village) Paulding County, 235
Pedro (unincorporated) Lawrence County, 181
Peebles (village) Adams County, 39
Pemberton (unincorporated) Shelby County, 262
Pemberville (village) Wood County, 305
Peninsula (village) Summit County, 274
Pepper Pike (city) Cuyahoga County, 96
Perry (village) Lake County, 178
Perry County, 235
Perry Heights (CDP) Stark County, 268
Perrysburg (city) Wood County, 305
Perrysville (village) Ashland County, 44
Petersburg (unincorporated) Mahoning County, 203
Pettisville (CDP) Fulton County, 123
Pheasant Run (CDP) Lorain County, 192
Phillipsburg (village) Montgomery County, 223
Philo (village) Muskingum County, 229
Pickaway County, 238
Pickerington (city) Fairfield County, 110
Piedmont (unincorporated) Belmont County, 56
Pierpont (unincorporated) Ashtabula County, 48
Pigeon Creek (CDP) Summit County, 274
Pike County, 240
Piketon (village) Pike County, 240
Pioneer (village) Williams County, 302
Piqua (city) Miami County, 214
Pitsburg (village) Darke County, 102
Plain City (village) Madison County, 199
Plainfield (village) Coshocton County, 81
Plainville (CDP) Hamilton County, 148
Pleasant City (village) Guernsey County, 134
Pleasant Grove (CDP) Muskingum County, 229
Pleasant Hill (village) Miami County, 215
Pleasant Hills (CDP) Hamilton County, 149
Pleasant Plain (village) Warren County, 293
Pleasant Run (CDP) Hamilton County, 149
Pleasant Run Farm (CDP) Hamilton County, 149
Pleasantville (village) Fairfield County, 111
Plumwood (CDP) Madison County, 199
Plymouth (village) Richland County, 250
Poland (village) Mahoning County, 203
Polk (village) Ashland County, 44
Pomeroy (village) Meigs County, 210
Port Clinton (city) Ottawa County, 233
Port Jefferson (village) Shelby County, 262
Port Washington (village) Tuscarawas County, 285
Port William (village) Clinton County, 75
Portage (village) Wood County, 306
Portage County, 241
Portage Lakes (CDP) Summit County, 274
Portland (unincorporated) Meigs County, 210
Portsmouth (city) Scioto County, 257
Potsdam (village) Miami County, 215
Pottery Addition (CDP) Jefferson County, 171
Powell (city) Delaware County, 105
Powhatan Point (village) Belmont County, 56
Preble County, 244
Proctorville (village) Lawrence County, 181
Prospect (village) Marion County, 206
Pulaski (CDP) Williams County, 302
Put-in-Bay (village) Ottawa County, 233
Putnam County, 246

CDP = Census Designated Place

Quaker City (village) Guernsey County, 134
Quincy (village) Logan County, 187
Racine (village) Meigs County, 211
Radnor (CDP) Delaware County, 106
Rarden (village) Scioto County, 258
Ravenna (city) Portage County, 243
Rawson (village) Hancock County, 155
Ray (unincorporated) Vinton County, 290
Rayland (village) Jefferson County, 171
Raymond (CDP) Union County, 288
Reading (city) Hamilton County, 149
Reedsville (unincorporated) Meigs County, 211
Reesville (unincorporated) Clinton County, 75
Reminderville (village) Summit County, 274
Remington (CDP) Hamilton County, 149
Rendville (village) Perry County, 237
Reno (CDP) Washington County, 297
Republic (village) Seneca County, 260
Reynoldsburg (city) Franklin County, 120
Richfield (village) Summit County, 274
Richland County, 248
Richmond (village) Jefferson County, 171
Richmond Dale (CDP) Ross County, 253
Richmond Heights (city) Cuyahoga County, 96
Richville (CDP) Stark County, 268
Richwood (village) Union County, 288
Ridgeville Corners (CDP) Henry County, 160
Ridgeway (village) Hardin County, 157
Rio Grande (village) Gallia County, 125
Ripley (village) Brown County, 59
Risingsun (village) Wood County, 306
Rittman (city) Wayne County, 299
Riverlea (village) Franklin County, 120
Riverside (city) Montgomery County, 223
Roaming Shores (village) Ashtabula County, 48
Robertsville (CDP) Stark County, 268
Rochester (village) Lorain County, 192
Rock Creek (village) Ashtabula County, 48
Rockbridge (CDP) Hocking County, 163
Rockford (village) Mercer County, 213
Rocky Fork Point (CDP) Highland County, 162
Rocky Ridge (village) Ottawa County, 234
Rocky River (city) Cuyahoga County, 97
Rogers (village) Columbiana County, 79
Rome (village) Adams County, 40
Rootstown (unincorporated) Portage County, 243
Rosemount (CDP) Scioto County, 258
Roseville (village) Perry County, 237
Rosewood (CDP) Champaign County, 66
Ross (CDP) Butler County, 63
Ross County, 251
Rossburg (village) Darke County, 102
Rossford (city) Wood County, 306
Rossmoyne (CDP) Hamilton County, 149
Roswell (village) Tuscarawas County, 285
Rudolph (CDP) Wood County, 306
Rushsylvania (village) Logan County, 188
Rushville (village) Fairfield County, 111
Russells Point (village) Logan County, 188
Russellville (village) Brown County, 59
Russia (village) Shelby County, 262
Rutland (village) Meigs County, 211
Sabina (village) Clinton County, 75
Saint Bernard (city) Hamilton County, 150
Saint Clairsville (city) Belmont County, 56
Saint Henry (village) Mercer County, 213
Saint Johns (CDP) Auglaize County, 52
Saint Louisville (village) Licking County, 186
Saint Martin (village) Brown County, 59
Saint Marys (city) Auglaize County, 52
Saint Paris (village) Champaign County, 66
Salem (city) Columbiana County, 79
Salem Heights (CDP) Hamilton County, 150
Salesville (village) Guernsey County, 134
Salineville (village) Columbiana County, 79
Sandusky (city) Erie County, 108
Sandusky County, 253
Sandyville (CDP) Tuscarawas County, 285
Sarahsville (village) Noble County, 231
Sardinia (village) Brown County, 59
Sardis (CDP) Monroe County, 217
Savannah (village) Ashland County, 45
Sawyerwood (CDP) Summit County, 275
Scio (village) Harrison County, 158
Scioto County, 256
Sciotodale (CDP) Scioto County, 258
Scott (village) Van Wert County, 289
Scottown (unincorporated) Lawrence County, 181
Seaman (village) Adams County, 40
Sebring (village) Mahoning County, 203
Sedalia (unincorporated) Madison County, 199
Seneca County, 259
Senecaville (village) Guernsey County, 134
Seven Hills (city) Cuyahoga County, 97
Seven Mile (village) Butler County, 63
Seville (village) Medina County, 208
Shade (unincorporated) Meigs County, 211
Shadyside (village) Belmont County, 56
Shaker Heights (city) Cuyahoga County, 97
Sharon Center (unincorporated) Medina County, 209
Sharonville (city) Hamilton County, 150
Shawnee (CDP) Hamilton County, 150
Shawnee (village) Perry County, 237
Shawnee Hills (village) Delaware County, 106
Shawnee Hills (CDP) Greene County, 131
Sheffield (village) Lorain County, 192
Sheffield Lake (city) Lorain County, 192
Shelby (city) Richland County, 250
Shelby County, 261
Sherrodsville (village) Carroll County, 65
Sherwood (village) Defiance County, 104
Sherwood (CDP) Hamilton County, 150
Shiloh (village) Richland County, 251
Shreve (village) Wayne County, 300
Sidney (city) Shelby County, 262
Silver Lake (village) Summit County, 275
Silverton (village) Hamilton County, 151
Sinking Spring (village) Highland County, 162
Sixteen Mile Stand (CDP) Hamilton County, 151
Skyline Acres (CDP) Hamilton County, 151
Smithfield (village) Jefferson County, 171
Smithville (village) Wayne County, 300
Solon (city) Cuyahoga County, 98
Somerdale (unincorporated) Tuscarawas County, 285
Somerset (village) Perry County, 237
Somerville (village) Butler County, 63
South Amherst (village) Lorain County, 193
South Bloomfield (village) Pickaway County, 239
South Bloomingville (unincorporated) Hocking County, 163
South Canal (CDP) Trumbull County, 281
South Charleston (village) Clark County, 69
South Euclid (city) Cuyahoga County, 98
South Lebanon (village) Warren County, 293
South Point (village) Lawrence County, 181
South Russell (village) Geauga County, 128
South Salem (village) Ross County, 253
South Solon (village) Madison County, 199
South Vienna (village) Clark County, 69
South Webster (village) Scioto County, 258
South Zanesville (village) Muskingum County, 229
Southington (unincorporated) Trumbull County, 281
Sparta (village) Morrow County, 227
Spencer (village) Medina County, 209
Spencerville (village) Allen County, 43
Spring Valley (village) Greene County, 131
Springboro (city) Warren County, 294
Springdale (city) Hamilton County, 151
Springfield (city) Clark County, 69
Stafford (village) Monroe County, 217
Stark County, 263
Sterling (CDP) Wayne County, 300
Steubenville (city) Jefferson County, 171
Stewart (CDP) Athens County, 50
Stockdale (CDP) Pike County, 240
Stockport (village) Morgan County, 225
Stone Creek (village) Tuscarawas County, 285
Stony Prairie (CDP) Sandusky County, 255
Stony Ridge (CDP) Wood County, 306
Stout (unincorporated) Scioto County, 258
Stoutsville (village) Fairfield County, 111
Stow (city) Summit County, 275
Strasburg (village) Tuscarawas County, 286
Stratton (village) Jefferson County, 171
Streetsboro (city) Portage County, 244
Strongsville (city) Cuyahoga County, 98
Struthers (city) Mahoning County, 203
Stryker (village) Williams County, 302
Sugar Bush Knolls (village) Portage County, 244
Sugar Grove (village) Fairfield County, 111
Sugarcreek (village) Tuscarawas County, 286
Sullivan (unincorporated) Ashland County, 45
Sulphur Springs (CDP) Crawford County, 83
Summerfield (village) Noble County, 231
Summerside (CDP) Clermont County, 73
Summit County, 269
Summitville (village) Columbiana County, 79
Sunbury (village) Delaware County, 106
Swanton (village) Fulton County, 123
Sycamore (village) Wyandot County, 308
Sylvania (city) Lucas County, 195
Syracuse (village) Meigs County, 211
Tallmadge (city) Summit County, 275
Tarlton (village) Pickaway County, 239
Taylor Creek (CDP) Hamilton County, 152
Tedrow (CDP) Fulton County, 123
Terrace Park (village) Hamilton County, 152
The Plains (CDP) Athens County, 51
The Village of Indian Hill (city) Hamilton County, 152
Thompson (unincorporated) Geauga County, 129
Thornport (CDP) Perry County, 237
Thornville (village) Perry County, 238
Thurman (unincorporated) Gallia County, 126
Thurston (village) Fairfield County, 111
Tiffin (city) Seneca County, 260
Tiltonsville (village) Jefferson County, 171
Timberlake (village) Lake County, 178
Tipp City (city) Miami County, 215
Tippecanoe (CDP) Harrison County, 158
Tiro (village) Crawford County, 83
Toledo (city) Lucas County, 196
Tontogany (village) Wood County, 306
Toronto (city) Jefferson County, 172
Tremont City (village) Clark County, 70
Trenton (city) Butler County, 63
Trimble (village) Athens County, 51
Trinway (CDP) Muskingum County, 229
Trotwood (city) Montgomery County, 223
Troy (city) Miami County, 215
Trumbull County, 276
Tuppers Plains (CDP) Meigs County, 211
Turpin Hills (CDP) Hamilton County, 152
Tuscarawas (village) Tuscarawas County, 286
Tuscarawas County, 283

CDP = Census Designated Place

Twinsburg (city) Summit County, 276
Twinsburg Heights (CDP) Summit County, 276
Uhrichsville (city) Tuscarawas County, 286
Union (city) Montgomery County, 224
Union City (village) Darke County, 102
Union County, 286
Union Furnace (unincorporated) Hocking County, 163
Uniontown (CDP) Stark County, 268
Unionville Center (village) Union County, 288
Uniopolis (village) Auglaize County, 53
University Heights (city) Cuyahoga County, 98
Upper Arlington (city) Franklin County, 120
Upper Sandusky (city) Wyandot County, 308
Urbana (city) Champaign County, 66
Urbancrest (village) Franklin County, 120
Utica (village) Licking County, 186
Valley City (unincorporated) Medina County, 209
Valley Hi (village) Logan County, 188
Valley View (village) Cuyahoga County, 99
Valleyview (village) Franklin County, 121
Van Buren (village) Hancock County, 155
Van Wert (city) Van Wert County, 289
Van Wert County, 288
Vandalia (city) Montgomery County, 224
Vanlue (village) Hancock County, 155
Vaughnsville (CDP) Putnam County, 248
Venedocia (village) Van Wert County, 289
Vermilion (city) Lorain County, 193
Verona (village) Preble County, 246
Versailles (village) Darke County, 102
Vickery (CDP) Sandusky County, 255
Vienna Center (CDP) Trumbull County, 282
Vincent (CDP) Washington County, 297
Vinton (village) Gallia County, 126
Vinton County, 289
Wadsworth (city) Medina County, 209
Waite Hill (village) Lake County, 178
Wakeman (village) Huron County, 167
Walbridge (village) Wood County, 306
Waldo (village) Marion County, 206
Walhonding (unincorporated) Coshocton County, 81
Walnut Creek (CDP) Holmes County, 165
Walton Hills (village) Cuyahoga County, 99
Wapakoneta (city) Auglaize County, 53
Warren (city) Trumbull County, 282
Warren County, 290
Warrensville Heights (city) Cuyahoga County, 99
Warsaw (village) Coshocton County, 81
Washington County, 294
Washington Court House (city) Fayette County, 112
Washingtonville (village) Columbiana County, 79
Waterford (CDP) Washington County, 297
Waterloo (unincorporated) Lawrence County, 182
Waterville (city) Lucas County, 197
Wauseon (city) Fulton County, 123
Waverly (village) Pike County, 241
Wayland (unincorporated) Portage County, 244
Wayne (village) Wood County, 307
Wayne County, 297
Wayne Lakes (village) Darke County, 102
Waynesburg (village) Stark County, 268
Waynesfield (village) Auglaize County, 53
Waynesville (village) Warren County, 294
Wellington (village) Lorain County, 193
Wellston (city) Jackson County, 168
Wellsville (village) Columbiana County, 79
West Alexandria (village) Preble County, 246
West Carrollton (city) Montgomery County, 224
West Chester (unincorporated) Butler County, 63
West Elkton (village) Preble County, 246
West Farmington (village) Trumbull County, 282
West Hill (CDP) Trumbull County, 282
West Jefferson (village) Madison County, 199
West Lafayette (village) Coshocton County, 81
West Leipsic (village) Putnam County, 248
West Liberty (village) Logan County, 188
West Manchester (village) Preble County, 246
West Mansfield (village) Logan County, 188
West Millgrove (village) Wood County, 307
West Milton (village) Miami County, 215
West Portsmouth (CDP) Scioto County, 258
West Rushville (village) Fairfield County, 111
West Salem (village) Wayne County, 300
West Union (village) Adams County, 40
West Unity (village) Williams County, 302
Westerville (city) Franklin County, 121
Westfield Center (village) Medina County, 209
Westlake (city) Cuyahoga County, 99
Weston (village) Wood County, 307
Wetherington (CDP) Butler County, 64
Wharton (village) Wyandot County, 308
Wheelersburg (CDP) Scioto County, 258
Whipple (unincorporated) Washington County, 297
White Oak (CDP) Hamilton County, 152
Whitehall (city) Franklin County, 121
Whitehouse (village) Lucas County, 197
Whites Landing (CDP) Erie County, 108
Wickliffe (city) Lake County, 178
Wightmans Grove (CDP) Sandusky County, 255
Wilberforce (CDP) Greene County, 131
Wilkesville (village) Vinton County, 290
Willard (city) Huron County, 167
Williams County, 300
Williamsburg (village) Clermont County, 74
Williamsdale (CDP) Butler County, 64
Williamsfield (unincorporated) Ashtabula County, 48
Williamsport (village) Pickaway County, 239
Williamstown (unincorporated) Hancock County, 155
Williston (CDP) Ottawa County, 234
Willoughby (city) Lake County, 178
Willoughby Hills (city) Lake County, 179
Willow Wood (unincorporated) Lawrence County, 182
Willowick (city) Lake County, 179
Willshire (village) Van Wert County, 289
Wilmington (city) Clinton County, 75
Wilmot (village) Stark County, 268
Wilson (village) Monroe County, 217
Winchester (village) Adams County, 40
Windham (village) Portage County, 244
Windsor (unincorporated) Ashtabula County, 48
Winesburg (CDP) Holmes County, 165
Wingett Run (unincorporated) Washington County, 297
Winona (unincorporated) Columbiana County, 80
Wintersville (village) Jefferson County, 172
Withamsville (CDP) Clermont County, 74
Wolfhurst (CDP) Belmont County, 57
Wood County, 302
Woodlawn (village) Hamilton County, 153
Woodmere (village) Cuyahoga County, 100
Woodsfield (village) Monroe County, 217
Woodstock (village) Champaign County, 67
Woodville (village) Sandusky County, 255
Wooster (city) Wayne County, 300
Worthington (city) Franklin County, 121
Wren (village) Van Wert County, 289
Wright-Patterson AFB (CDP) Greene County, 131
Wyandot County, 307
Wyoming (city) Hamilton County, 153
Xenia (city) Greene County, 131
Yankee Lake (village) Trumbull County, 282
Yellow Springs (village) Greene County, 132
Yorkshire (village) Darke County, 102
Yorkville (village) Jefferson County, 172
Youngstown (city) Mahoning County, 204
Zaleski (village) Vinton County, 290
Zanesfield (village) Logan County, 188
Zanesville (city) Muskingum County, 229
Zoar (village) Tuscarawas County, 286

Comparative Statistics

This section compares the 100 largest cities by population in the state, by the following data points:

Population 318

Physical Characteristics 320

Population by Race/Hispanic Origin 322

Average Household Size, Age, and Male/Female Ratio 324

Foreign Born, Language Spoken, Disabled Persons, and Veterans 326

Five Largest Ancestry Groups 328

Marriage Status 330

Employment by Occupation 332

Educational Attainment 334

Health Insurance 336

Income and Poverty 338

Housing 340

Commute to Work 342

Crime 344

Population

Place	2000 Census	2010 Census	Growth 2000–2010 (%)
Akron	217,074	199,110	-8.2
Alliance	23,253	22,322	-4.0
Ashland	21,249	20,362	-4.1
Ashtabula	20,962	19,124	-8.7
Athens	21,342	23,832	11.6
Austintown	31,627	29,677	-6.1
Avon	11,446	21,193	85.1
Avon Lake	18,145	22,581	24.4
Barberton	27,899	26,550	-4.8
Beavercreek	37,984	45,193	18.9
Berea	18,970	19,093	0.6
Boardman	37,215	35,376	-4.9
Bowling Green	29,636	30,028	1.3
Broadview Heights	15,967	19,400	21.5
Brook Park	21,218	19,212	-9.4
Brunswick	33,388	34,255	2.6
Canton	80,806	73,007	-9.6
Centerville	23,024	23,999	4.2
Chillicothe	21,796	21,901	0.4
Cincinnati	331,285	296,943	-10.3
Cleveland	478,403	396,815	-17.0
Cleveland Heights	49,958	46,121	-7.6
Columbus	711,470	787,033	10.6
Cuyahoga Falls	49,374	49,652	0.5
Dayton	166,179	141,527	-14.8
Delaware	25,243	34,753	37.6
Dublin	31,392	41,751	33.0
Elyria	55,953	54,533	-2.5
Euclid	52,717	48,920	-7.2
Fairborn	32,052	32,352	0.9
Fairfield	42,097	42,510	0.9
Findlay	38,967	41,202	5.7
Forest Park	19,463	18,720	-3.8
Gahanna	32,636	33,248	1.8
Garfield Heights	30,734	28,849	-6.1
Green	22,817	25,699	12.6
Grove City	27,075	35,575	31.3
Hamilton	60,690	62,477	2.9
Hilliard	24,230	28,435	17.3
Huber Heights	38,212	38,101	-0.2
Hudson	22,439	22,262	-0.7
Kent	27,906	28,904	3.5
Kettering	57,502	56,163	-2.3
Lakewood	56,646	52,131	-7.9
Lancaster	35,335	38,780	9.7
Lebanon	16,962	20,033	18.1
Lima	40,081	38,771	-3.2
Lorain	68,652	64,097	-6.6
Mansfield	49,346	47,821	-3.0
Maple Heights	26,156	23,138	-11.5

Place	2000 Census	2010 Census	Growth 2000–2010 (%)
Marion	35,318	36,837	4.3
Marysville	15,942	22,094	38.5
Mason	22,016	30,712	39.5
Massillon	31,325	32,149	2.6
Mayfield Heights	19,386	19,155	-1.1
Medina	25,139	26,678	6.1
Mentor	50,278	47,159	-6.2
Miamisburg	19,489	20,181	3.5
Middletown	51,605	48,694	-5.6
Newark	46,279	47,573	2.8
Niles	20,932	19,266	-7.9
North Olmsted	34,113	32,718	-4.0
North Ridgeville	22,338	29,465	31.9
North Royalton	28,648	30,444	6.2
Norwood	21,675	19,207	-11.3
Oregon	19,355	20,291	4.8
Oxford	21,943	21,371	-2.6
Painesville	17,503	19,563	11.7
Parma	85,655	81,601	-4.7
Parma Heights	21,659	20,718	-4.3
Perrysburg	16,945	20,623	21.7
Piqua	20,738	20,522	-1.0
Portsmouth	20,909	20,226	-3.2
Reynoldsburg	32,069	35,893	11.9
Riverside	23,545	25,201	7.0
Rocky River	20,735	20,213	-2.5
Sandusky	27,844	25,793	-7.3
Shaker Heights	29,405	28,448	-3.2
Sidney	20,211	21,229	5.0
Solon	21,802	23,348	7.0
South Euclid	23,537	22,295	-5.2
Springfield	65,358	60,608	-7.2
Stow	32,139	34,837	8.3
Strongsville	43,858	44,750	2.0
Sylvania	18,670	18,965	1.5
Toledo	313,619	287,208	-8.4
Trotwood	27,420	24,431	-10.9
Troy	21,999	25,058	13.9
Twinsburg	17,006	18,795	10.5
Upper Arlington	33,686	33,771	0.2
Wadsworth	18,437	21,567	16.9
Warren	46,832	41,557	-11.2
Westerville	35,318	36,120	2.2
Westlake	31,719	32,729	3.1
White Oak	13,277	19,167	44.3
Willoughby	22,621	22,268	-1.5
Wooster	24,811	26,119	5.2
Xenia	24,164	25,719	6.4
Youngstown	82,026	66,982	-18.3
Zanesville	25,586	25,487	-0.3

SOURCE: U.S. Census Bureau, Census 2010, Census 2000

Physical Characteristics

Place	Density (persons per square mile)	Land Area (square miles)	Water Area (square miles)	Elevation (feet)
Akron	3,209.8	62.03	0.34	961
Alliance	2,501.3	8.92	0.04	1,158
Ashland	1,823.1	11.17	0.06	1,066
Ashtabula	2,472.5	7.73	0.17	669
Athens	2,425.2	9.83	0.22	718
Austintown	2,551.8	11.63	0.03	1,129
Avon	1,018.5	20.81	0.06	669
Avon Lake	2,029.0	11.13	0.00	610
Barberton	2,937.5	9.04	0.22	971
Beavercreek	1,711.9	26.40	0.04	876
Berea	3,339.3	5.72	0.11	755
Boardman	2,339.5	15.12	0.17	1,112
Bowling Green	2,391.3	12.56	0.05	692
Broadview Heights	1,486.8	13.05	0.02	1,191
Brook Park	2,551.5	7.53	0.00	797
Brunswick	2,652.2	12.92	0.04	1,168
Canton	2,867.3	25.46	0.02	1,056
Centerville	2,226.2	10.78	0.07	1,020
Chillicothe	2,100.2	10.43	0.17	633
Cincinnati	3,809.8	77.94	1.60	627
Cleveland	5,107.2	77.70	4.77	653
Cleveland Heights	5,689.3	8.11	0.02	942
Columbus	3,624.1	217.17	5.94	781
Cuyahoga Falls	1,935.9	25.65	0.10	1,027
Dayton	2,543.1	55.65	0.85	738
Delaware	1,833.7	18.95	0.12	869
Dublin	1,708.5	24.44	0.36	830
Elyria	2,650.9	20.57	0.27	738
Euclid	4,602.1	10.63	0.85	617
Fairborn	2,458.4	13.16	0.01	837
Fairfield	2,030.2	20.94	0.12	594
Findlay	2,153.3	19.13	0.12	774
Forest Park	2,888.9	6.48	0.00	833
Gahanna	2,675.4	12.43	0.17	797
Garfield Heights	3,990.3	7.23	0.06	955
Green	801.7	32.06	1.48	1,142
Grove City	2,196.5	16.20	0.16	846
Hamilton	2,893.0	21.60	0.48	597
Hilliard	2,159.6	13.17	0.17	932
Huber Heights	1,710.7	22.27	0.09	932
Hudson	869.7	25.60	0.27	1,066
Kent	3,150.5	9.17	0.11	1,063
Kettering	3,007.0	18.68	0.04	1,004
Lakewood	9,419.3	5.53	1.16	702
Lancaster	2,058.3	18.84	0.06	886
Lebanon	1,545.3	12.96	0.01	771
Lima	2,858.2	13.56	0.23	879
Lorain	2,707.6	23.67	0.47	610
Mansfield	1,549.0	30.87	0.05	1,240
Maple Heights	4,473.6	5.17	0.00	896

Place	Density (persons per square mile)	Land Area (square miles)	Water Area (square miles)	Elevation (feet)
Marion	3,138.8	11.74	0.08	981
Marysville	1,357.8	16.27	0.29	994
Mason	1,648.6	18.63	0.04	807
Massillon	1,730.4	18.58	0.18	948
Mayfield Heights	4,595.4	4.17	0.01	1,086
Medina	2,305.4	11.57	0.21	1,089
Mentor	1,769.9	26.64	1.35	692
Miamisburg	1,656.3	12.18	0.19	705
Middletown	1,859.6	26.18	0.23	656
Newark	2,278.0	20.88	0.49	833
Niles	2,237.3	8.61	0.02	883
North Olmsted	2,802.7	11.67	0.00	761
North Ridgeville	1,257.1	23.44	0.14	728
North Royalton	1,428.6	21.31	0.01	1,197
Norwood	6,102.8	3.15	0.00	653
Oregon	676.9	29.98	8.05	604
Oxford	3,201.0	6.68	0.00	922
Painesville	3,112.7	6.28	0.73	676
Parma	4,075.1	20.02	0.05	863
Parma Heights	4,949.9	4.19	0.00	856
Perrysburg	1,791.1	11.51	0.00	633
Piqua	1,766.2	11.62	0.27	876
Portsmouth	1,884.2	10.73	0.34	535
Reynoldsburg	3,217.0	11.16	0.08	879
Riverside	2,592.8	9.72	0.04	778
Rocky River	4,266.2	4.74	0.87	692
Sandusky	2,652.1	9.73	12.17	594
Shaker Heights	4,528.2	6.28	0.04	1,050
Sidney	1,765.8	12.02	0.13	955
Solon	1,146.7	20.36	0.13	1,040
South Euclid	4,794.0	4.65	0.00	958
Springfield	2,396.1	25.29	0.21	974
Stow	2,038.7	17.09	0.23	1,089
Strongsville	1,817.1	24.63	0.01	932
Sylvania	2,927.8	6.48	0.04	666
Toledo	3,559.3	80.69	3.43	610
Trotwood	801.2	30.49	0.01	837
Troy	2,137.8	11.72	0.22	837
Twinsburg	1,365.0	13.77	0.03	1,004
Upper Arlington	3,432.5	9.84	0.03	814
Wadsworth	2,030.5	10.62	0.00	1,171
Warren	2,576.8	16.13	0.03	886
Westerville	2,895.9	12.47	0.14	869
Westlake	2,055.1	15.93	0.00	709
White Oak	3,108.2	6.17	0.00	915
Willoughby	2,172.7	10.25	0.09	659
Wooster	1,601.4	16.31	0.05	994
Xenia	1,936.5	13.28	0.01	935
Youngstown	1,972.7	33.96	0.64	856
Zanesville	2,165.8	11.77	0.37	676

SOURCE: U.S. Census Bureau, Census 2010

Population by Race/Hispanic Origin

Place	White[1] (%)	Black[1] (%)	Asian[1] (%)	AIAN[1,2] (%)	NHOPI[1,3] (%)	Two or More Races (%)	Hispanic[4] (%)
Akron	62.2	31.5	2.1	0.2	0.0	3.2	2.1
Alliance	84.6	10.5	0.8	0.2	0.0	3.4	1.9
Ashland	95.8	1.4	1.0	0.1	0.1	1.3	1.2
Ashtabula	82.0	8.9	0.3	0.4	0.0	5.0	9.3
Athens	86.4	4.4	6.1	0.2	0.0	2.3	2.4
Austintown	89.9	6.9	0.6	0.2	0.0	1.8	2.7
Avon	92.4	2.3	3.1	0.1	0.0	1.4	3.4
Avon Lake	95.7	1.1	1.3	0.1	0.0	1.4	2.4
Barberton	90.8	5.9	0.3	0.3	0.0	2.2	1.4
Beavercreek	88.5	2.5	5.9	0.2	0.0	2.3	2.6
Berea	88.8	6.6	1.5	0.2	0.0	2.3	2.8
Boardman	89.6	6.4	1.2	0.1	0.0	1.7	3.3
Bowling Green	87.6	6.4	2.1	0.2	0.0	2.2	4.8
Broadview Heights	91.0	2.1	5.2	0.1	0.0	1.3	1.8
Brook Park	92.2	3.2	1.6	0.2	0.0	1.9	3.4
Brunswick	95.5	1.2	1.2	0.1	0.0	1.3	2.3
Canton	69.1	24.2	0.3	0.5	0.0	4.8	2.6
Centerville	90.2	4.0	3.2	0.2	0.0	1.9	1.8
Chillicothe	88.1	7.2	0.5	0.3	0.0	3.4	1.3
Cincinnati	49.3	44.8	1.8	0.3	0.1	2.5	2.8
Cleveland	37.3	53.3	1.8	0.3	0.0	2.8	10.0
Cleveland Heights	49.8	42.5	4.1	0.2	0.0	2.8	2.0
Columbus	61.5	28.0	4.1	0.3	0.1	3.3	5.6
Cuyahoga Falls	93.4	3.3	1.2	0.2	0.0	1.6	1.4
Dayton	51.7	42.9	0.9	0.3	0.0	2.9	3.0
Delaware	90.6	4.5	1.4	0.2	0.0	2.5	2.5
Dublin	80.5	1.8	15.3	0.1	0.0	1.8	1.8
Elyria	78.1	15.5	0.8	0.3	0.0	4.1	4.9
Euclid	43.8	52.6	0.7	0.2	0.0	2.3	1.6
Fairborn	84.8	7.7	3.1	0.3	0.1	3.1	2.4
Fairfield	79.0	12.8	2.4	0.3	0.1	2.4	5.5
Findlay	91.2	2.2	2.5	0.3	0.0	2.1	5.7
Forest Park	24.9	65.0	2.2	0.2	0.2	3.6	6.4
Gahanna	82.1	11.2	3.1	0.2	0.0	2.4	2.6
Garfield Heights	60.2	35.7	1.3	0.2	0.0	2.1	2.3
Green	95.0	1.8	1.5	0.2	0.0	1.2	1.2
Grove City	92.6	2.8	1.3	0.2	0.0	2.1	2.6
Hamilton	84.0	8.5	0.6	0.2	0.1	2.9	6.4
Hilliard	88.5	3.0	5.6	0.2	0.0	1.9	2.3
Huber Heights	79.6	13.0	2.5	0.3	0.1	3.5	3.1
Hudson	92.7	1.3	4.3	0.1	0.0	1.3	1.7
Kent	83.1	9.6	3.7	0.2	0.1	2.9	2.2
Kettering	92.6	3.3	1.3	0.2	0.0	2.1	2.1
Lakewood	87.5	6.4	1.9	0.3	0.0	2.7	4.1
Lancaster	95.9	1.0	0.5	0.3	0.0	1.7	1.6
Lebanon	92.7	2.6	0.8	0.2	0.0	2.0	3.5
Lima	67.1	26.4	0.5	0.3	0.0	4.4	3.7
Lorain	67.9	17.6	0.4	0.5	0.0	5.4	25.2
Mansfield	73.3	22.1	0.7	0.2	0.1	3.0	1.9
Maple Heights	28.0	68.2	1.0	0.2	0.0	2.1	1.5

Place	White[1] (%)	Black[1] (%)	Asian[1] (%)	AIAN[1,2] (%)	NHOPI[1,3] (%)	Two or More Races (%)	Hispanic[4] (%)
Marion	86.7	9.6	0.4	0.2	0.0	2.1	3.0
Marysville	90.4	4.5	2.3	0.3	0.1	1.8	1.8
Mason	85.1	3.3	9.0	0.2	0.1	1.5	3.2
Massillon	87.4	8.8	0.4	0.3	0.0	2.6	2.0
Mayfield Heights	80.4	10.3	7.0	0.1	0.0	1.7	2.0
Medina	93.3	3.1	0.9	0.1	0.0	2.1	1.8
Mentor	96.3	1.0	1.4	0.1	0.0	1.0	1.3
Miamisburg	93.8	3.0	1.0	0.2	0.0	1.5	1.6
Middletown	83.3	11.7	0.5	0.2	0.0	2.7	3.8
Newark	92.8	3.3	0.6	0.3	0.0	2.6	1.2
Niles	93.1	3.5	0.7	0.2	0.0	2.2	1.3
North Olmsted	92.6	2.0	2.7	0.1	0.0	1.7	3.5
North Ridgeville	95.0	1.5	1.2	0.2	0.0	1.6	3.3
North Royalton	94.6	1.1	2.7	0.1	0.0	1.1	1.6
Norwood	86.6	7.6	0.8	0.4	0.1	2.5	5.1
Oregon	93.5	1.4	0.8	0.2	0.0	1.9	7.5
Oxford	87.6	4.0	5.4	0.2	0.0	2.2	2.3
Painesville	68.2	13.1	0.8	0.3	0.0	4.5	22.0
Parma	93.0	2.3	1.9	0.2	0.0	1.6	3.6
Parma Heights	91.1	2.8	3.0	0.2	0.0	1.8	3.8
Perrysburg	92.9	1.4	3.1	0.1	0.0	1.6	3.2
Piqua	92.4	3.3	0.7	0.2	0.0	2.9	1.4
Portsmouth	90.1	5.1	0.6	0.4	0.0	3.0	2.2
Reynoldsburg	69.7	23.3	1.8	0.2	0.1	3.5	3.4
Riverside	87.2	6.6	1.9	0.3	0.0	2.8	3.3
Rocky River	95.5	1.0	1.8	0.1	0.0	1.3	1.8
Sandusky	70.4	22.0	0.6	0.4	0.0	5.5	4.9
Shaker Heights	55.0	37.1	4.6	0.1	0.0	2.7	2.2
Sidney	90.3	3.7	1.6	0.2	0.2	3.3	2.2
Solon	77.5	10.6	10.0	0.1	0.0	1.4	1.5
South Euclid	54.1	40.7	2.0	0.1	0.0	2.5	2.0
Springfield	75.2	18.1	0.8	0.3	0.0	4.0	3.0
Stow	93.0	2.7	2.4	0.1	0.0	1.4	1.5
Strongsville	92.0	1.9	4.1	0.1	0.0	1.4	2.0
Sylvania	92.4	2.7	2.3	0.1	0.1	1.7	2.9
Toledo	64.8	27.2	1.1	0.4	0.0	3.9	7.4
Trotwood	28.1	68.2	0.3	0.2	0.0	2.6	0.9
Troy	90.1	4.2	2.4	0.2	0.0	2.4	1.8
Twinsburg	78.5	13.4	5.7	0.1	0.0	1.9	1.2
Upper Arlington	92.1	0.8	4.9	0.1	0.0	1.6	1.6
Wadsworth	96.9	0.8	0.7	0.2	0.0	1.1	1.2
Warren	67.7	27.7	0.4	0.2	0.0	3.3	1.9
Westerville	88.6	6.4	2.3	0.2	0.0	2.1	1.9
Westlake	91.2	1.6	4.9	0.1	0.1	1.6	2.5
White Oak	87.8	8.5	1.1	0.2	0.0	1.8	1.4
Willoughby	93.6	3.1	1.5	0.1	0.0	1.5	1.3
Wooster	91.2	3.6	1.9	0.3	0.0	2.4	2.2
Xenia	82.0	13.4	0.5	0.4	0.0	3.2	1.7
Youngstown	47.0	45.2	0.4	0.4	0.0	3.7	9.3
Zanesville	84.4	9.7	0.4	0.4	0.0	4.7	1.2

NOTE: (1) Exclude multiple race combinations; (2) American Indian/Alaska Native; (3) Native Hawaiian/Other Pacific Islander; (4) May be of any race
SOURCE: U.S. Census Bureau, Census 2010

Average Household Size, Age, and Male/Female Ratio

Place	Average Household Size (persons)	Median Age (years)	Age Under 18 (%)	Age 65 and Over (%)	Males per 100 Females
Akron	2.31	35.7	22.9	12.6	93.6
Alliance	2.38	35.3	22.0	15.7	91.9
Ashland	2.28	36.1	21.0	17.7	88.1
Ashtabula	2.42	37.0	26.4	14.7	90.9
Athens	2.28	21.6	5.8	4.3	100.0
Austintown	2.22	42.8	20.0	18.8	90.6
Avon	2.76	38.4	30.5	12.6	93.8
Avon Lake	2.53	41.9	26.2	14.5	93.3
Barberton	2.37	39.8	23.5	16.5	92.0
Beavercreek	2.47	40.4	22.6	14.3	99.7
Berea	2.26	37.1	18.3	13.9	91.3
Boardman	2.23	43.8	20.0	18.4	90.7
Bowling Green	2.16	23.2	12.8	8.9	92.1
Broadview Heights	2.50	41.5	24.6	14.8	92.7
Brook Park	2.45	43.8	21.0	19.8	92.4
Brunswick	2.63	39.1	25.2	11.9	96.6
Canton	2.35	35.6	25.1	12.8	90.0
Centerville	2.19	46.9	20.1	24.4	86.0
Chillicothe	2.25	41.5	21.8	17.9	90.8
Cincinnati	2.12	32.5	22.1	10.8	92.5
Cleveland	2.29	35.7	24.6	12.0	92.1
Cleveland Heights	2.27	35.8	22.3	13.5	87.2
Columbus	2.31	31.2	23.2	8.6	95.4
Cuyahoga Falls	2.21	39.4	20.9	15.3	89.7
Dayton	2.26	34.4	22.9	11.8	95.0
Delaware	2.47	33.2	25.5	11.1	92.2
Dublin	2.78	38.3	30.4	7.8	97.6
Elyria	2.39	38.1	24.2	14.3	91.6
Euclid	2.13	41.0	22.9	15.9	81.1
Fairborn	2.24	32.4	20.4	13.2	95.8
Fairfield	2.41	38.3	23.2	13.0	92.9
Findlay	2.29	35.9	22.2	14.5	90.7
Forest Park	2.59	35.8	26.9	11.7	86.6
Gahanna	2.54	39.4	25.3	11.7	91.9
Garfield Heights	2.43	38.5	25.0	15.4	85.2
Green	2.54	41.8	24.1	14.5	95.1
Grove City	2.53	37.8	25.4	12.2	93.5
Hamilton	2.47	35.3	24.9	13.2	95.4
Hilliard	2.77	35.9	30.1	8.6	95.5
Huber Heights	2.58	37.4	25.4	12.9	93.4
Hudson	2.87	42.5	30.1	11.8	96.4
Kent	2.22	22.7	14.1	7.4	86.2
Kettering	2.19	40.9	21.0	18.0	91.2
Lakewood	2.05	35.4	19.6	11.0	96.6
Lancaster	2.36	37.5	24.0	15.7	92.2
Lebanon	2.62	34.7	29.2	10.1	96.2
Lima	2.42	32.9	24.8	11.4	112.0
Lorain	2.48	36.8	26.7	13.9	90.5
Mansfield	2.21	38.5	20.2	15.7	112.6
Maple Heights	2.41	39.2	25.1	13.2	86.1

Place	Average Household Size (persons)	Median Age (years)	Age Under 18 (%)	Age 65 and Over (%)	Males per 100 Females
Marion	2.45	37.3	22.2	12.6	121.6
Marysville	2.62	33.1	26.6	8.1	74.9
Mason	2.77	38.4	30.8	9.9	94.1
Massillon	2.37	40.1	22.9	16.7	94.0
Mayfield Heights	1.97	42.9	17.6	23.8	82.7
Medina	2.53	36.4	28.3	11.6	92.5
Mentor	2.44	44.8	21.2	16.5	93.7
Miamisburg	2.50	40.2	25.1	16.2	90.7
Middletown	2.38	38.3	24.3	14.9	90.6
Newark	2.35	37.3	24.0	14.5	91.5
Niles	2.24	42.0	20.7	17.8	90.9
North Olmsted	2.37	43.5	20.7	17.8	93.4
North Ridgeville	2.54	40.7	23.1	15.0	96.3
North Royalton	2.33	43.5	20.1	15.1	95.3
Norwood	2.28	33.4	20.2	11.1	99.5
Oregon	2.44	42.3	22.6	17.6	92.7
Oxford	2.40	21.4	6.8	5.6	90.7
Painesville	2.64	30.2	28.3	8.7	101.2
Parma	2.34	41.5	20.4	17.7	92.8
Parma Heights	2.15	43.2	18.9	20.5	87.0
Perrysburg	2.48	38.4	26.5	12.3	94.0
Piqua	2.44	38.1	24.8	14.7	92.2
Portsmouth	2.28	36.1	21.6	16.4	86.6
Reynoldsburg	2.49	37.3	26.3	11.6	90.0
Riverside	2.45	34.8	24.7	13.8	94.2
Rocky River	2.16	45.6	21.8	22.4	85.5
Sandusky	2.28	38.5	23.9	15.0	91.0
Shaker Heights	2.39	40.9	26.7	15.5	82.5
Sidney	2.51	36.1	27.2	12.4	96.4
Solon	2.78	43.1	27.8	12.4	95.1
South Euclid	2.43	37.9	24.0	12.9	83.9
Springfield	2.38	36.0	24.4	15.3	90.9
Stow	2.42	39.7	22.7	13.8	93.0
Strongsville	2.52	44.2	23.3	16.1	94.7
Sylvania	2.43	42.7	23.6	17.2	89.7
Toledo	2.33	34.2	24.0	12.1	93.8
Trotwood	2.29	41.8	23.6	17.8	79.9
Troy	2.38	36.9	25.2	13.1	94.9
Twinsburg	2.49	41.4	25.4	14.5	88.0
Upper Arlington	2.44	42.8	25.1	16.7	91.7
Wadsworth	2.48	38.7	25.6	15.8	92.5
Warren	2.30	38.3	23.7	16.0	92.6
Westerville	2.48	41.2	22.4	14.3	88.5
Westlake	2.30	45.0	21.5	19.0	90.2
White Oak	2.43	40.2	23.2	15.5	93.0
Willoughby	2.12	43.6	19.1	19.1	88.1
Wooster	2.21	37.3	20.4	16.6	91.0
Xenia	2.39	37.1	24.8	15.7	89.3
Youngstown	2.28	38.0	22.8	15.8	96.9
Zanesville	2.29	36.3	25.1	15.2	87.3

SOURCE: U.S. Census Bureau, Census 2010

Foreign Born, Language Spoken, Disabled Persons, and Veterans

Place	Foreign Born (%)	Speak English Only at Home (%)	With a Disability (%)	Veterans (%)
Akron	4.50	93.6	15.1	9.6
Alliance	1.70	97.2	16.3	9.5
Ashland	3.90	95.1	13.3	9.4
Ashtabula	1.10	93.3	17.0	9.9
Athens	8.30	90.9	5.5	2.3
Austintown	1.80	97.1	15.2	13.2
Avon	5.50	90.7	8.1	9.1
Avon Lake	4.20	93.7	10.1	10.2
Barberton	3.10	95.6	16.0	9.6
Beavercreek	7.20	90.6	9.8	19.1
Berea	4.40	92.8	13.2	8.0
Boardman	2.90	93.7	13.0	10.6
Bowling Green	5.20	92.9	6.8	4.9
Broadview Heights	8.70	86.4	8.3	8.1
Brook Park	4.30	93.3	15.4	11.6
Brunswick	3.10	94.1	9.2	9.5
Canton	2.20	95.3	16.8	10.4
Centerville	5.30	93.1	14.2	12.4
Chillicothe	0.90	96.6	21.6	12.3
Cincinnati	5.20	92.4	14.0	7.0
Cleveland	4.60	88.2	19.1	8.3
Cleveland Heights	8.50	89.7	11.1	6.9
Columbus	10.90	86.0	11.8	7.2
Cuyahoga Falls	3.00	95.9	12.9	9.9
Dayton	3.80	94.3	19.0	9.0
Delaware	3.40	96.0	10.5	9.9
Dublin	15.00	83.1	5.3	6.8
Elyria	1.60	96.3	15.8	10.7
Euclid	3.20	95.7	15.5	9.4
Fairborn	5.00	93.1	15.4	14.2
Fairfield	7.00	91.6	9.0	9.1
Findlay	3.40	94.6	13.0	9.8
Forest Park	9.80	88.2	12.7	10.0
Gahanna	5.60	94.1	10.5	8.4
Garfield Heights	3.50	94.2	14.5	10.7
Green	3.20	93.7	10.7	9.6
Grove City	2.40	95.6	12.8	9.5
Hamilton	3.80	94.3	15.2	10.0
Hilliard	5.70	91.7	7.2	7.7
Huber Heights	4.90	92.7	14.5	15.5
Hudson	8.10	91.7	6.3	7.5
Kent	6.20	92.4	9.3	4.8
Kettering	3.00	94.8	12.7	10.6
Lakewood	8.00	89.1	12.0	8.1
Lancaster	1.20	98.4	18.8	11.6
Lebanon	3.50	94.8	9.9	9.4
Lima	1.40	97.1	17.7	9.1
Lorain	3.20	81.8	18.6	9.4
Mansfield	1.70	96.7	18.1	11.4
Maple Heights	3.00	96.7	16.2	10.3

Place	Foreign Born (%)	Speak English Only at Home (%)	With a Disability (%)	Veterans (%)
Marion	1.20	95.4	19.5	10.7
Marysville	3.10	95.6	11.7	8.8
Mason	10.90	85.0	7.2	7.8
Massillon	1.10	97.0	16.5	11.6
Mayfield Heights	17.30	79.1	13.0	7.7
Medina	2.60	95.4	10.9	10.7
Mentor	3.50	94.9	11.3	10.4
Miamisburg	1.30	98.3	14.1	11.7
Middletown	3.00	94.9	19.3	9.9
Newark	1.10	97.7	17.5	11.0
Niles	1.40	96.3	17.9	10.6
North Olmsted	8.60	86.6	12.4	9.3
North Ridgeville	4.70	94.4	9.6	9.6
North Royalton	9.20	86.7	11.2	8.8
Norwood	2.60	94.9	16.0	8.7
Oregon	2.50	95.1	14.4	9.5
Oxford	6.80	91.8	6.5	2.8
Painesville	13.00	80.5	14.0	7.2
Parma	9.80	85.9	14.2	9.4
Parma Heights	13.00	83.4	16.1	9.3
Perrysburg	5.20	93.1	8.3	7.9
Piqua	1.00	97.4	16.0	10.5
Portsmouth	2.30	96.1	23.9	10.0
Reynoldsburg	5.90	92.1	11.2	10.0
Riverside	3.00	95.0	16.3	15.9
Rocky River	11.20	86.6	9.5	10.9
Sandusky	1.80	96.0	18.0	10.7
Shaker Heights	8.80	89.4	8.5	6.7
Sidney	2.50	96.3	15.0	9.6
Solon	13.80	82.5	7.5	6.9
South Euclid	6.30	91.1	10.0	6.2
Springfield	2.60	95.1	18.3	11.1
Stow	4.40	95.6	9.4	9.6
Strongsville	8.40	89.4	9.2	8.4
Sylvania	6.10	93.0	10.1	8.9
Toledo	3.20	93.9	17.3	8.4
Trotwood	1.80	97.0	19.0	11.6
Troy	2.90	95.4	12.8	10.8
Twinsburg	7.70	90.9	8.6	7.1
Upper Arlington	7.60	89.5	8.0	7.4
Wadsworth	2.00	96.0	9.4	11.0
Warren	1.70	95.7	16.7	10.4
Westerville	6.40	92.3	9.5	9.0
Westlake	11.20	84.2	9.6	8.8
White Oak	3.00	96.2	11.5	10.0
Willoughby	6.30	92.4	11.7	9.4
Wooster	3.90	93.4	12.3	8.9
Xenia	1.60	97.2	16.2	11.1
Youngstown	4.30	90.3	20.9	9.8
Zanesville	1.30	97.3	22.0	8.8

SOURCE: U.S. Census Bureau, American Community Survey, 2009-2013 Five-Year Estimates

Five Largest Ancestry Groups

Place	Group 1	Group 2	Group 3	Group 4	Group 5
Akron	German (17.6%)	Irish (12.4%)	English (6.6%)	Italian (6.2%)	American (5.2%)
Alliance	German (25.7%)	Irish (14.1%)	Italian (9.0%)	American (8.2%)	English (7.5%)
Ashland	German (31.1%)	Irish (12.5%)	American (11.0%)	English (10.3%)	Italian (6.0%)
Ashtabula	Italian (16.1%)	German (16.0%)	American (13.5%)	Irish (11.8%)	English (10.3%)
Athens	German (24.5%)	Irish (14.1%)	English (7.3%)	Italian (6.8%)	American (5.8%)
Austintown	German (27.4%)	Irish (22.4%)	Italian (19.1%)	English (9.2%)	Slovak (7.5%)
Avon	German (31.9%)	Irish (22.7%)	English (13.6%)	Italian (11.0%)	Polish (9.5%)
Avon Lake	German (28.9%)	Irish (24.1%)	English (13.6%)	Italian (12.2%)	Polish (8.0%)
Barberton	German (21.3%)	Irish (14.3%)	English (8.1%)	American (7.5%)	Italian (5.0%)
Beavercreek	German (26.1%)	American (14.6%)	Irish (13.3%)	English (10.9%)	Italian (4.7%)
Berea	German (31.3%)	Irish (20.4%)	English (10.9%)	Italian (9.9%)	Polish (8.1%)
Boardman	Italian (26.7%)	German (21.7%)	Irish (18.9%)	Slovak (8.9%)	English (6.9%)
Bowling Green	German (38.4%)	Irish (16.8%)	English (9.7%)	Italian (6.7%)	Polish (4.3%)
Broadview Heights	German (22.3%)	Polish (17.4%)	Italian (16.1%)	Irish (13.1%)	Hungarian (7.7%)
Brook Park	German (25.1%)	Irish (16.1%)	Italian (14.7%)	Polish (13.6%)	English (8.8%)
Brunswick	German (28.5%)	Irish (18.8%)	Italian (14.1%)	Polish (13.7%)	English (8.0%)
Canton	German (22.6%)	Irish (13.1%)	Italian (8.9%)	American (7.2%)	English (5.7%)
Centerville	German (31.6%)	Irish (17.1%)	English (13.2%)	American (8.8%)	Italian (4.6%)
Chillicothe	German (27.6%)	Irish (14.4%)	American (11.5%)	English (10.5%)	French (2.7%)
Cincinnati	German (19.1%)	Irish (10.4%)	American (5.4%)	English (5.2%)	Italian (3.6%)
Cleveland	German (9.9%)	Irish (9.0%)	Italian (4.4%)	Polish (4.1%)	English (3.2%)
Cleveland Heights	German (12.3%)	Irish (9.4%)	Italian (5.8%)	English (5.7%)	Hungarian (3.2%)
Columbus	German (20.5%)	Irish (12.4%)	English (6.8%)	Italian (5.2%)	American (4.9%)
Cuyahoga Falls	German (27.6%)	Irish (15.9%)	English (11.5%)	Italian (11.1%)	American (6.9%)
Dayton	German (16.8%)	Irish (10.9%)	American (6.4%)	English (5.1%)	Italian (3.7%)
Delaware	German (32.8%)	Irish (15.6%)	English (11.3%)	American (8.2%)	Italian (4.7%)
Dublin	German (30.1%)	Irish (16.3%)	English (11.1%)	Italian (7.8%)	American (6.1%)
Elyria	German (25.4%)	Irish (14.2%)	English (9.6%)	American (8.1%)	Polish (7.9%)
Euclid	German (9.9%)	Irish (7.8%)	Italian (6.4%)	Slovene (4.2%)	Polish (3.8%)
Fairborn	German (20.1%)	American (20.0%)	Irish (11.0%)	English (9.3%)	Italian (2.4%)
Fairfield	German (29.6%)	Irish (13.7%)	American (8.4%)	English (8.1%)	Italian (4.5%)
Findlay	German (36.0%)	American (12.4%)	Irish (11.1%)	English (8.6%)	Italian (4.1%)
Forest Park	German (8.6%)	Irish (5.2%)	(*) (3.9%)	English (2.5%)	American (1.7%)
Gahanna	German (29.9%)	Irish (16.6%)	English (12.9%)	Italian (6.2%)	American (5.6%)
Garfield Heights	Polish (19.3%)	German (12.9%)	Irish (9.2%)	Italian (8.5%)	Slovak (4.2%)
Green	German (29.2%)	Irish (14.6%)	Italian (13.0%)	English (10.3%)	American (6.6%)
Grove City	German (31.0%)	Irish (18.5%)	English (10.3%)	American (9.3%)	Italian (5.1%)
Hamilton	German (28.0%)	American (16.0%)	Irish (12.9%)	English (7.8%)	Italian (4.6%)
Hilliard	German (31.8%)	Irish (15.3%)	English (13.2%)	American (8.6%)	Italian (7.4%)
Huber Heights	German (23.3%)	Irish (13.8%)	English (9.0%)	American (8.6%)	Italian (3.7%)
Hudson	German (25.6%)	Irish (15.4%)	English (14.0%)	Italian (10.1%)	Polish (6.8%)
Kent	German (31.4%)	Irish (18.1%)	Italian (14.1%)	English (9.2%)	Polish (4.9%)
Kettering	German (33.3%)	Irish (16.1%)	English (11.1%)	American (9.5%)	Italian (4.4%)
Lakewood	German (24.6%)	Irish (24.1%)	Italian (11.5%)	English (10.2%)	Polish (7.3%)
Lancaster	German (28.7%)	Irish (15.8%)	American (11.7%)	English (10.3%)	Italian (3.4%)
Lebanon	German (29.1%)	Irish (20.8%)	American (12.7%)	English (10.2%)	Italian (5.1%)
Lima	German (26.3%)	Irish (13.0%)	American (6.8%)	English (5.7%)	Italian (3.6%)
Lorain	German (14.3%)	Irish (11.8%)	Italian (8.5%)	English (6.2%)	Polish (6.2%)
Mansfield	German (25.2%)	Irish (12.2%)	English (10.1%)	American (7.0%)	Italian (4.4%)
Maple Heights	German (6.8%)	Polish (6.4%)	Italian (4.9%)	Irish (4.8%)	Czech (2.5%)

Place	Group 1	Group 2	Group 3	Group 4	Group 5
Marion	German (25.1%)	Irish (15.8%)	American (10.8%)	English (9.3%)	Italian (5.2%)
Marysville	German (29.2%)	Irish (16.1%)	American (13.0%)	English (10.3%)	Italian (4.6%)
Mason	German (30.2%)	Irish (12.9%)	English (11.1%)	Italian (7.5%)	American (6.8%)
Massillon	German (37.2%)	Irish (17.2%)	American (10.6%)	Italian (8.7%)	English (6.9%)
Mayfield Heights	Italian (24.8%)	German (16.7%)	Irish (11.2%)	Polish (7.0%)	English (6.5%)
Medina	German (30.4%)	Irish (18.3%)	Italian (13.9%)	English (11.7%)	Polish (9.9%)
Mentor	German (28.1%)	Irish (19.0%)	Italian (18.4%)	English (12.7%)	Polish (8.5%)
Miamisburg	German (31.1%)	Irish (18.2%)	American (11.6%)	English (11.4%)	Scottish (3.4%)
Middletown	German (18.7%)	Irish (12.5%)	American (9.5%)	English (7.8%)	Italian (3.6%)
Newark	German (27.9%)	Irish (16.1%)	English (10.7%)	American (10.1%)	Italian (5.8%)
Niles	Italian (20.8%)	German (20.0%)	American (19.6%)	Irish (15.4%)	English (8.2%)
North Olmsted	German (28.4%)	Irish (22.4%)	Italian (11.7%)	Polish (9.0%)	English (8.7%)
North Ridgeville	German (27.6%)	Irish (19.6%)	Polish (13.2%)	Italian (11.0%)	English (9.8%)
North Royalton	German (21.8%)	Italian (17.2%)	Polish (17.1%)	Irish (14.3%)	English (7.6%)
Norwood	German (27.9%)	American (17.5%)	Irish (17.1%)	English (8.7%)	Italian (4.0%)
Oregon	German (37.2%)	Irish (11.8%)	Hungarian (9.3%)	Polish (9.0%)	English (8.3%)
Oxford	German (22.8%)	American (12.1%)	Irish (11.0%)	English (7.8%)	Italian (5.6%)
Painesville	German (21.2%)	Irish (15.4%)	Italian (9.4%)	English (7.0%)	Polish (4.1%)
Parma	German (24.6%)	Polish (17.2%)	Irish (14.9%)	Italian (14.4%)	Slovak (7.2%)
Parma Heights	German (23.3%)	Irish (15.3%)	Polish (12.5%)	Italian (12.3%)	English (7.2%)
Perrysburg	German (39.0%)	Irish (16.9%)	English (10.7%)	Polish (9.4%)	French (7.2%)
Piqua	German (32.9%)	Irish (14.7%)	American (9.5%)	English (8.5%)	Italian (3.8%)
Portsmouth	German (22.1%)	Irish (16.5%)	American (10.8%)	English (10.4%)	Italian (2.7%)
Reynoldsburg	German (21.4%)	Irish (16.6%)	English (7.7%)	American (6.0%)	Italian (5.5%)
Riverside	German (22.7%)	Irish (15.4%)	American (13.3%)	English (8.0%)	French (3.3%)
Rocky River	Irish (26.5%)	German (25.8%)	English (10.1%)	Italian (9.3%)	Polish (7.7%)
Sandusky	German (31.1%)	Irish (13.8%)	Italian (7.6%)	English (6.4%)	Polish (3.8%)
Shaker Heights	German (11.4%)	English (8.7%)	Irish (8.3%)	Italian (5.7%)	Polish (4.0%)
Sidney	German (27.1%)	American (12.3%)	Irish (9.5%)	English (8.3%)	French (3.6%)
Solon	German (15.1%)	Italian (11.1%)	Irish (9.1%)	Polish (8.6%)	Russian (7.9%)
South Euclid	German (12.9%)	Irish (10.6%)	Italian (10.3%)	Polish (5.8%)	Russian (4.5%)
Springfield	German (18.9%)	Irish (12.9%)	American (11.5%)	English (7.8%)	Italian (3.1%)
Stow	German (26.9%)	Irish (15.1%)	English (12.0%)	Italian (9.6%)	Polish (6.1%)
Strongsville	German (28.5%)	Irish (16.5%)	Polish (13.0%)	Italian (12.6%)	English (10.1%)
Sylvania	German (34.8%)	Polish (13.8%)	Irish (13.4%)	English (12.8%)	Italian (6.5%)
Toledo	German (24.0%)	Irish (11.6%)	Polish (9.0%)	English (5.8%)	French (4.0%)
Trotwood	German (8.0%)	Irish (4.3%)	American (3.7%)	English (2.7%)	African (2.2%)
Troy	German (27.6%)	Irish (12.7%)	American (11.1%)	English (8.8%)	French (3.5%)
Twinsburg	German (19.3%)	Italian (16.7%)	Irish (13.8%)	Polish (8.7%)	English (8.3%)
Upper Arlington	German (33.5%)	Irish (20.3%)	English (16.6%)	Italian (9.0%)	American (5.9%)
Wadsworth	German (24.3%)	Irish (14.6%)	English (13.1%)	American (8.7%)	Italian (8.3%)
Warren	American (17.0%)	German (12.0%)	Irish (10.3%)	Italian (8.0%)	English (5.6%)
Westerville	German (30.9%)	Irish (17.2%)	English (13.2%)	Italian (6.0%)	American (5.4%)
Westlake	German (27.0%)	Irish (21.9%)	English (11.4%)	Italian (8.0%)	Polish (6.6%)
White Oak	German (48.4%)	Irish (19.5%)	English (6.3%)	Italian (5.5%)	American (4.6%)
Willoughby	German (25.9%)	Irish (20.1%)	Italian (17.4%)	English (10.4%)	Polish (7.5%)
Wooster	German (29.8%)	American (11.6%)	Irish (10.7%)	English (10.0%)	Italian (5.8%)
Xenia	American (19.1%)	German (18.3%)	Irish (13.3%)	English (9.0%)	Italian (3.5%)
Youngstown	Italian (11.0%)	German (10.4%)	Irish (10.2%)	American (6.1%)	African (6.1%)
Zanesville	German (16.5%)	Irish (12.8%)	American (9.5%)	English (8.2%)	Italian (3.2%)

NOTE: (*) Other Subsaharan African; "French" excludes Basque; Please refer to the User Guide for more information.
SOURCE: U.S. Census Bureau, American Community Survey, 2009-2013 Five-Year Estimates

Marriage Status

Place	Never Married (%)	Now Married[1] (%)	Separated (%)	Widowed (%)	Divorced (%)
Akron	41.5	37.6	2.5	6.6	14.3
Alliance	38.4	38.9	2.3	7.7	15.0
Ashland	33.0	47.5	1.2	7.5	11.9
Ashtabula	31.6	43.4	1.7	7.9	17.1
Athens	81.3	13.9	0.6	1.6	3.2
Austintown	28.5	48.5	1.1	10.1	13.0
Avon	19.5	64.4	0.7	6.2	9.9
Avon Lake	22.1	61.4	0.5	6.9	9.6
Barberton	33.4	41.3	2.2	10.2	15.1
Beavercreek	26.3	59.6	1.3	6.2	7.9
Berea	40.2	42.4	1.2	6.5	11.0
Boardman	28.7	49.5	1.8	8.9	13.0
Bowling Green	60.6	29.6	1.4	2.8	7.0
Broadview Heights	26.7	56.3	1.2	6.6	10.4
Brook Park	30.4	49.0	1.2	9.1	11.6
Brunswick	28.7	56.1	0.8	5.6	9.7
Canton	37.9	39.3	3.1	6.9	16.0
Centerville	22.3	56.8	1.1	9.8	11.1
Chillicothe	30.7	45.3	3.1	9.0	15.0
Cincinnati	50.9	31.0	3.1	5.9	12.2
Cleveland	48.6	29.1	3.5	7.4	14.9
Cleveland Heights	41.8	40.7	1.7	5.7	11.8
Columbus	43.3	39.4	2.5	4.7	12.6
Cuyahoga Falls	30.2	49.2	1.3	6.7	13.9
Dayton	48.7	29.0	3.0	6.5	15.7
Delaware	31.8	50.8	1.5	4.8	12.7
Dublin	22.7	67.4	0.5	3.4	6.6
Elyria	34.4	47.3	2.6	6.2	12.1
Euclid	43.4	34.8	2.6	8.0	13.9
Fairborn	38.3	42.3	1.8	5.7	13.7
Fairfield	28.0	52.8	1.9	5.8	13.4
Findlay	32.1	47.7	1.8	7.7	12.4
Forest Park	34.1	48.4	3.8	4.9	12.5
Gahanna	28.8	55.2	1.8	4.9	11.1
Garfield Heights	38.6	40.3	1.6	9.4	11.7
Green	23.5	60.4	0.5	7.5	8.6
Grove City	26.1	56.5	1.9	5.6	11.8
Hamilton	31.9	45.3	3.2	7.0	15.8
Hilliard	22.4	62.8	0.8	5.3	9.5
Huber Heights	26.9	55.5	3.0	5.0	12.6
Hudson	20.4	68.7	0.5	4.9	6.0
Kent	61.1	28.5	1.1	2.9	7.4
Kettering	28.5	49.7	1.5	7.3	14.6
Lakewood	43.5	37.9	1.6	5.4	13.3
Lancaster	28.5	46.2	2.7	7.8	17.4
Lebanon	28.6	52.7	2.2	5.6	13.1
Lima	41.3	35.2	3.2	6.3	17.2
Lorain	35.6	43.2	2.9	7.8	13.4
Mansfield	35.8	39.7	3.7	8.5	16.0
Maple Heights	39.8	39.0	2.6	7.5	13.7

Place	Never Married (%)	Now Married[1] (%)	Separated (%)	Widowed (%)	Divorced (%)
Marion	32.6	43.6	3.4	7.1	16.7
Marysville	29.6	49.6	2.9	4.3	16.5
Mason	23.3	62.6	1.3	4.5	9.7
Massillon	31.3	46.1	1.8	7.4	15.3
Mayfield Heights	32.5	45.4	0.9	11.5	10.7
Medina	27.6	53.4	1.3	6.1	12.9
Mentor	24.6	58.5	0.7	6.8	10.1
Miamisburg	21.4	54.5	1.3	10.5	13.6
Middletown	29.6	47.2	2.7	7.1	16.1
Newark	29.0	47.9	2.3	7.7	15.4
Niles	30.0	43.7	2.3	10.1	16.3
North Olmsted	26.8	55.7	1.0	7.2	10.3
North Ridgeville	21.9	62.1	2.0	5.5	10.5
North Royalton	28.9	54.0	0.8	6.8	10.2
Norwood	44.1	38.1	2.8	6.0	11.8
Oregon	25.2	55.3	1.7	7.7	11.8
Oxford	77.6	17.2	0.9	2.0	3.2
Painesville	41.1	41.0	2.7	4.5	13.4
Parma	31.5	48.6	1.2	8.2	11.8
Parma Heights	29.2	48.4	0.8	9.7	12.8
Perrysburg	23.4	59.9	1.5	7.2	9.5
Piqua	28.1	48.4	1.9	8.6	14.9
Portsmouth	33.9	40.4	2.3	9.1	16.6
Reynoldsburg	32.1	48.2	1.9	5.3	14.3
Riverside	27.5	50.6	2.2	7.7	14.2
Rocky River	26.8	54.7	0.8	9.7	8.8
Sandusky	36.2	41.9	2.9	7.5	14.4
Shaker Heights	28.7	54.4	1.1	6.4	10.5
Sidney	27.8	49.5	2.1	7.0	15.8
Solon	20.9	66.4	0.7	5.1	7.6
South Euclid	41.0	39.9	1.6	7.1	12.1
Springfield	35.3	40.3	3.1	8.2	16.2
Stow	26.5	55.7	1.3	6.7	11.1
Strongsville	23.4	62.1	0.8	7.1	7.5
Sylvania	27.7	57.3	0.9	6.1	9.0
Toledo	41.0	37.7	2.4	6.5	14.8
Trotwood	38.1	37.0	2.6	9.2	15.7
Troy	27.8	50.6	1.4	6.5	15.2
Twinsburg	24.8	60.4	0.6	7.9	6.9
Upper Arlington	24.0	63.3	1.0	5.3	7.4
Wadsworth	21.3	55.7	0.6	8.7	14.3
Warren	37.1	38.3	3.0	9.2	15.4
Westerville	27.3	58.0	0.6	5.9	8.8
Westlake	24.8	56.9	0.6	8.2	10.1
White Oak	27.2	55.3	1.7	6.2	11.3
Willoughby	29.7	47.8	0.8	8.7	13.8
Wooster	36.3	46.1	1.1	6.0	11.7
Xenia	27.7	49.7	2.4	8.7	13.9
Youngstown	43.8	31.6	3.3	9.2	15.4
Zanesville	33.6	39.8	3.3	8.9	17.7

NOTE: (1) Includes separated.
zzz

SOURCE: U.S. Census Bureau, American Community Survey, 2009-2013 Five-Year Estimates

Employment by Occupation

Place	MBF[1] (%)	CES[2] (%)	ELCAM[3] (%)	HPT[4] (%)	S[5] (%)	SO[6] (%)	NRCM[7] (%)	PTMM[8] (%)
Akron	10.1	3.5	9.6	5.2	22.0	27.1	6.6	15.8
Alliance	7.7	2.3	6.9	3.7	23.1	24.9	6.9	24.5
Ashland	12.3	3.0	12.5	4.8	19.8	25.9	6.1	15.6
Ashtabula	6.7	1.4	6.6	4.7	24.5	24.3	7.7	24.0
Athens	7.1	5.1	24.5	3.3	28.8	24.0	1.3	5.9
Austintown	9.4	2.7	9.5	7.5	18.6	26.2	7.5	18.6
Avon	24.0	7.7	13.2	8.3	13.7	23.5	2.9	6.6
Avon Lake	24.2	3.5	13.8	7.4	12.2	28.2	4.5	6.2
Barberton	7.2	3.9	5.0	4.8	23.0	26.5	9.8	19.8
Beavercreek	23.6	12.8	11.5	9.0	12.6	19.0	3.3	8.2
Berea	12.3	5.9	12.6	5.6	17.0	26.6	7.2	12.7
Boardman	14.2	3.3	10.8	7.3	16.6	30.2	6.4	11.3
Bowling Green	9.4	2.8	20.3	3.4	25.2	22.5	7.2	9.3
Broadview Heights	19.8	8.8	11.5	8.9	9.6	26.2	3.6	11.6
Brook Park	8.6	3.0	6.6	4.4	22.9	26.5	10.1	17.8
Brunswick	13.0	4.5	7.3	7.1	16.6	27.1	8.5	15.8
Canton	7.9	2.5	8.1	5.6	28.7	22.8	6.6	17.9
Centerville	18.7	7.2	14.7	9.0	15.0	24.7	3.2	7.5
Chillicothe	9.4	3.8	6.1	6.2	24.9	24.9	8.5	16.0
Cincinnati	14.3	6.3	12.2	5.7	22.0	24.0	4.6	10.9
Cleveland	9.1	3.0	8.6	5.4	27.3	23.6	6.2	16.8
Cleveland Heights	14.6	8.1	19.9	12.5	15.8	19.8	2.5	6.8
Columbus	15.2	6.2	11.3	5.3	18.3	26.8	5.5	11.4
Cuyahoga Falls	14.0	6.2	11.0	6.6	14.5	27.6	7.5	12.5
Dayton	9.1	3.8	10.6	4.3	25.5	24.4	7.3	15.0
Delaware	16.4	7.0	11.8	5.2	18.0	25.1	5.3	11.1
Dublin	30.1	14.4	11.8	8.6	8.7	22.6	1.3	2.5
Elyria	9.6	3.9	8.2	5.6	21.7	23.9	7.6	19.5
Euclid	11.3	4.0	7.3	7.5	21.3	27.1	5.6	16.0
Fairborn	10.4	7.6	8.7	5.6	20.5	28.1	6.2	12.9
Fairfield	13.3	5.8	8.8	6.0	15.7	28.1	6.7	15.7
Findlay	15.7	5.1	9.0	5.8	19.2	19.7	6.9	18.5
Forest Park	8.9	3.6	8.8	5.4	20.9	26.7	5.8	19.9
Gahanna	22.8	7.9	13.2	5.5	15.7	24.1	3.6	7.3
Garfield Heights	9.4	3.0	7.0	4.6	18.7	34.0	7.8	15.5
Green	17.1	4.7	11.7	6.5	14.2	26.3	7.3	12.2
Grove City	15.6	5.1	7.1	8.1	16.6	26.9	7.7	13.0
Hamilton	8.0	3.4	8.4	4.9	21.5	26.3	9.5	18.0
Hilliard	22.1	9.3	13.0	6.9	12.5	24.5	3.4	8.3
Huber Heights	11.8	6.4	8.3	5.8	19.0	26.1	7.1	15.5
Hudson	29.0	8.8	15.4	7.7	7.9	24.5	2.0	4.8
Kent	9.1	4.9	16.1	4.1	27.9	24.3	3.7	9.9
Kettering	13.1	7.2	11.2	7.0	17.1	27.2	5.6	11.7
Lakewood	16.5	5.5	14.2	7.4	17.4	25.1	5.2	8.8
Lancaster	9.8	2.8	7.7	6.6	22.2	27.7	6.8	16.4
Lebanon	14.1	5.0	9.2	5.2	19.5	32.4	3.4	11.3
Lima	7.4	1.3	8.1	4.2	27.7	23.9	6.0	21.4
Lorain	8.9	2.5	7.5	4.6	23.9	23.9	7.4	21.2
Mansfield	8.3	2.8	7.5	5.5	22.1	25.7	4.5	23.6
Maple Heights	8.3	3.4	6.6	4.3	20.1	33.8	7.9	15.7

Place	MBF[1] (%)	CES[2] (%)	ELCAM[3] (%)	HPT[4] (%)	S[5] (%)	SO[6] (%)	NRCM[7] (%)	PTMM[8] (%)
Marion	5.6	2.5	7.4	3.6	22.2	22.2	8.4	28.1
Marysville	13.1	9.5	6.9	5.0	15.0	24.5	6.7	19.4
Mason	23.3	9.3	10.1	7.0	13.9	26.2	3.4	6.8
Massillon	8.3	2.1	6.7	4.9	22.0	26.5	8.3	21.1
Mayfield Heights	14.8	13.4	12.1	7.6	18.3	22.7	4.1	6.9
Medina	14.0	4.8	8.7	5.7	17.0	29.8	8.2	11.8
Mentor	16.6	6.4	8.3	7.2	14.5	27.8	5.8	13.6
Miamisburg	15.7	5.8	9.9	5.7	15.3	27.7	6.0	13.9
Middletown	10.8	3.4	6.9	5.3	21.4	26.0	8.0	18.2
Newark	10.0	3.9	9.1	5.5	21.2	26.8	7.7	15.9
Niles	7.0	1.5	5.6	8.7	23.2	25.2	9.6	19.2
North Olmsted	16.3	6.1	10.0	7.1	13.9	29.9	6.2	10.4
North Ridgeville	17.0	5.5	9.6	6.6	14.5	24.8	7.8	14.2
North Royalton	20.0	6.6	8.6	9.1	14.2	24.7	6.6	10.4
Norwood	13.1	5.1	10.1	3.4	17.9	29.3	7.7	13.4
Oregon	8.4	3.8	8.8	7.6	16.7	27.0	9.3	18.3
Oxford	11.0	3.7	21.5	2.3	29.9	23.5	2.1	6.0
Painesville	7.6	2.7	8.2	3.4	25.7	22.4	8.4	21.5
Parma	11.7	4.1	7.7	5.9	19.0	27.6	8.4	15.5
Parma Heights	10.7	5.3	6.7	5.9	19.9	27.4	8.0	16.1
Perrysburg	23.2	6.9	13.5	9.2	11.2	23.4	4.9	7.7
Piqua	7.5	3.2	6.9	3.4	16.5	25.0	8.8	28.8
Portsmouth	10.5	1.4	12.6	10.0	24.4	23.8	6.0	11.3
Reynoldsburg	16.4	6.5	9.5	5.0	16.6	29.7	6.4	10.0
Riverside	11.5	6.6	5.2	5.9	20.0	23.4	9.3	18.3
Rocky River	26.7	7.6	14.4	8.7	11.3	23.6	3.2	4.5
Sandusky	9.4	1.8	9.2	4.4	25.5	22.7	6.9	20.0
Shaker Heights	21.5	7.4	24.6	12.5	10.0	17.1	2.3	4.5
Sidney	11.7	2.2	4.6	3.8	21.2	16.6	5.8	34.3
Solon	23.8	7.1	14.3	9.8	12.1	24.5	3.5	4.9
South Euclid	15.4	6.8	13.1	8.1	16.6	27.0	5.3	7.8
Springfield	9.7	2.2	10.2	5.0	23.9	24.1	5.6	19.4
Stow	17.2	7.5	11.3	7.0	14.4	27.0	5.6	10.0
Strongsville	20.9	8.5	10.3	7.7	11.0	28.2	4.5	8.8
Sylvania	16.1	6.1	16.0	8.3	16.6	22.3	2.9	11.7
Toledo	8.9	2.8	9.3	5.6	23.3	24.4	7.3	18.6
Trotwood	10.9	3.4	7.7	5.8	20.9	28.3	5.9	17.1
Troy	12.9	5.3	9.4	4.4	14.9	23.9	6.1	23.0
Twinsburg	23.1	9.6	11.9	6.0	12.0	22.2	3.5	11.7
Upper Arlington	23.6	10.8	19.6	10.6	8.7	21.4	2.4	3.1
Wadsworth	17.3	5.6	10.4	5.5	17.7	26.1	5.0	12.2
Warren	8.0	1.9	7.1	6.1	25.9	24.9	7.6	18.7
Westerville	22.7	6.6	14.6	5.6	13.3	28.3	3.9	5.2
Westlake	24.4	8.5	12.5	11.2	11.2	22.6	3.5	6.0
White Oak	14.8	4.5	8.4	11.5	16.7	26.8	5.8	11.5
Willoughby	11.7	5.6	9.9	7.5	16.4	27.3	7.6	14.0
Wooster	8.7	6.8	15.1	4.2	21.2	22.5	5.7	15.8
Xenia	10.4	2.6	10.3	5.1	19.6	26.6	12.2	13.2
Youngstown	7.0	1.8	7.7	5.5	29.3	23.9	7.1	17.7
Zanesville	7.5	3.2	8.4	5.1	25.3	24.5	7.8	18.3

NOTES: (1) Management, business, and financial occupations; (2) Computer, engineering, and science occupations; (3) Education, legal, community service, arts, and media occupations; (4) Healthcare practitioners and technical occupations; (5) Service occupations; (6) Sales and office occupations; (7) Natural resources, construction, and maintenance occupations; (8) Production, transportation, and material moving occupations

SOURCE: U.S. Census Bureau, American Community Survey, 2009-2013 Five-Year Estimates

Educational Attainment

Place	Percent of Population 25 Years and Over with: High School Diploma or Higher[1]	Bachelor's Degree or Higher	Graduate/Professional Degree or Higher
Akron	85.4	20.2	6.6
Alliance	83.7	13.5	4.0
Ashland	87.7	27.7	12.8
Ashtabula	83.5	8.9	4.5
Athens	94.3	63.7	40.1
Austintown	91.1	18.3	6.2
Avon	96.0	51.3	21.0
Avon Lake	96.7	50.1	18.8
Barberton	85.2	11.4	2.4
Beavercreek	96.4	49.5	26.0
Berea	91.8	30.7	10.6
Boardman	92.7	27.1	9.1
Bowling Green	93.7	42.0	21.5
Broadview Heights	94.5	44.1	19.1
Brook Park	85.3	11.3	2.8
Brunswick	92.1	20.8	5.8
Canton	82.7	13.8	4.1
Centerville	94.7	45.2	19.4
Chillicothe	83.2	18.4	7.2
Cincinnati	84.3	31.5	12.9
Cleveland	77.4	14.9	5.6
Cleveland Heights	94.0	50.2	26.4
Columbus	88.3	33.1	11.1
Cuyahoga Falls	93.4	30.4	9.6
Dayton	80.8	16.4	6.5
Delaware	92.4	34.2	12.3
Dublin	98.5	73.4	28.5
Elyria	87.9	15.0	5.4
Euclid	88.0	19.5	6.6
Fairborn	86.7	25.2	10.9
Fairfield	91.7	26.5	8.5
Findlay	90.2	27.1	10.1
Forest Park	87.7	24.4	8.0
Gahanna	95.1	47.0	16.1
Garfield Heights	86.2	13.7	4.9
Green	92.3	33.5	11.5
Grove City	94.1	27.3	8.6
Hamilton	83.1	14.8	4.6
Hilliard	95.7	46.0	16.5
Huber Heights	91.6	22.1	8.6
Hudson	98.5	68.4	28.3
Kent	91.7	42.0	17.8
Kettering	93.9	31.1	12.6
Lakewood	92.2	40.7	14.0
Lancaster	86.4	16.5	5.6
Lebanon	91.5	30.0	9.9
Lima	82.5	10.8	4.5
Lorain	81.1	11.8	4.0
Mansfield	82.0	12.4	4.6
Maple Heights	88.2	14.0	4.1

Place	Percent of Population 25 Years and Over with:		
	High School Diploma or Higher[1]	Bachelor's Degree or Higher	Graduate/Professional Degree or Higher
Marion	81.8	9.9	3.9
Marysville	90.0	25.0	6.3
Mason	96.1	54.0	23.3
Massillon	86.6	14.3	4.7
Mayfield Heights	90.8	38.2	15.5
Medina	93.6	31.7	9.3
Mentor	94.5	28.9	9.6
Miamisburg	90.0	22.5	8.8
Middletown	82.4	15.5	4.6
Newark	86.1	15.4	4.1
Niles	85.9	15.8	4.6
North Olmsted	92.7	30.5	9.7
North Ridgeville	93.0	27.3	8.7
North Royalton	94.3	34.4	13.5
Norwood	80.9	24.2	7.1
Oregon	88.4	18.7	7.1
Oxford	92.3	59.8	31.8
Painesville	79.0	14.9	4.5
Parma	89.1	19.6	6.0
Parma Heights	89.2	21.0	5.8
Perrysburg	96.4	46.0	17.6
Piqua	82.4	10.4	3.8
Portsmouth	77.8	17.4	6.6
Reynoldsburg	92.1	29.9	8.4
Riverside	85.7	15.2	5.8
Rocky River	94.6	55.1	20.8
Sandusky	83.1	14.6	5.2
Shaker Heights	95.9	65.3	38.7
Sidney	83.9	11.6	5.4
Solon	96.3	56.6	27.4
South Euclid	93.7	38.8	16.0
Springfield	82.1	14.9	5.6
Stow	94.1	40.0	13.4
Strongsville	94.5	43.0	16.1
Sylvania	94.6	40.4	16.0
Toledo	84.8	17.2	5.9
Trotwood	83.5	14.4	5.6
Troy	88.5	22.5	7.2
Twinsburg	93.3	44.3	15.3
Upper Arlington	98.4	72.9	33.7
Wadsworth	92.4	32.0	10.4
Warren	83.2	12.1	3.5
Westerville	95.9	51.8	18.0
Westlake	95.1	52.4	20.9
White Oak	91.1	27.7	9.1
Willoughby	93.1	27.6	9.1
Wooster	90.7	28.9	11.6
Xenia	88.1	18.3	6.8
Youngstown	80.4	11.0	4.0
Zanesville	79.7	11.1	4.1

NOTE: (1) Includes General Equivalency Diploma (GED)
SOURCE: U.S. Census Bureau, American Community Survey, 2009-2013 Five-Year Estimates

Health Insurance

Place	Percent of Total Population with: Any Insurance	Private Insurance	Public Insurance	No Insurance	Percent of Population[1] Under Age 18 without Health Insurance
Akron	84.0	56.0	39.2	16.0	7.3
Alliance	85.5	56.4	41.8	14.5	7.4
Ashland	86.3	69.6	31.2	13.7	8.3
Ashtabula	85.7	50.0	48.4	14.3	6.8
Athens	95.3	88.8	11.3	4.7	0.5
Austintown	88.7	68.2	35.4	11.3	6.4
Avon	96.0	90.4	18.7	4.0	0.7
Avon Lake	95.8	89.8	19.5	4.2	1.1
Barberton	85.8	59.6	38.5	14.2	7.3
Beavercreek	94.2	86.3	22.4	5.8	3.6
Berea	92.0	78.3	25.7	8.0	1.9
Boardman	89.9	72.3	31.0	10.1	5.9
Bowling Green	91.8	82.9	18.1	8.2	2.5
Broadview Heights	93.7	86.8	20.2	6.3	3.1
Brook Park	89.2	70.6	33.0	10.8	3.2
Brunswick	91.1	79.9	23.1	8.9	3.9
Canton	83.4	49.6	45.2	16.6	7.1
Centerville	93.4	81.0	31.7	6.6	3.8
Chillicothe	85.3	56.8	44.3	14.7	5.8
Cincinnati	84.9	57.6	35.3	15.1	5.5
Cleveland	83.1	45.3	47.2	16.9	3.9
Cleveland Heights	89.7	70.7	30.4	10.3	5.2
Columbus	84.7	63.7	28.6	15.3	7.0
Cuyahoga Falls	89.8	75.9	26.3	10.2	5.3
Dayton	83.1	51.1	42.0	16.9	5.2
Delaware	92.5	79.2	23.3	7.5	3.9
Dublin	96.9	93.4	10.2	3.1	1.4
Elyria	87.8	63.9	38.2	12.2	3.0
Euclid	85.4	63.3	34.3	14.6	7.8
Fairborn	88.8	67.4	35.6	11.2	3.2
Fairfield	88.0	76.5	21.1	12.0	3.5
Findlay	87.8	70.0	31.6	12.2	5.9
Forest Park	81.8	63.0	29.7	18.2	9.2
Gahanna	94.4	85.7	18.9	5.6	2.1
Garfield Heights	89.5	66.8	37.5	10.5	4.1
Green	90.6	78.1	24.4	9.4	5.3
Grove City	90.2	78.9	23.3	9.8	5.3
Hamilton	84.5	59.9	36.2	15.5	7.0
Hilliard	92.6	83.3	17.8	7.4	2.9
Huber Heights	87.8	70.8	30.9	12.2	8.2
Hudson	96.2	92.5	15.7	3.8	2.8
Kent	87.8	72.6	23.5	12.2	4.0
Kettering	90.4	75.5	28.9	9.6	5.3
Lakewood	85.7	66.8	27.1	14.3	5.3
Lancaster	87.6	59.4	43.5	12.4	4.3
Lebanon	90.4	71.6	26.8	9.6	4.5
Lima	82.6	50.3	44.6	17.4	3.6
Lorain	86.8	53.1	46.0	13.2	3.6
Mansfield	86.7	54.7	47.6	13.3	4.1
Maple Heights	88.2	61.4	39.4	11.8	0.7

Place	Percent of Total Population with: Any Insurance	Private Insurance	Public Insurance	No Insurance	Percent of Population[1] Under Age 18 without Health Insurance
Marion	84.2	53.1	44.2	15.8	5.0
Marysville	90.9	77.2	21.6	9.1	4.1
Mason	94.7	89.9	13.8	5.3	1.9
Massillon	88.5	64.6	41.6	11.5	5.0
Mayfield Heights	91.4	79.4	27.3	8.6	9.1
Medina	90.8	76.7	24.8	9.2	5.0
Mentor	94.0	83.7	24.7	6.0	3.3
Miamisburg	91.0	72.1	34.4	9.0	1.7
Middletown	85.0	55.4	43.3	15.0	5.1
Newark	86.0	60.2	38.1	14.0	4.2
Niles	83.5	60.6	38.2	16.5	12.6
North Olmsted	92.2	78.5	28.1	7.8	2.5
North Ridgeville	92.6	82.8	23.5	7.4	1.6
North Royalton	91.6	82.2	22.3	8.4	4.3
Norwood	82.7	62.0	30.0	17.3	10.2
Oregon	90.6	78.5	28.4	9.4	4.0
Oxford	94.2	88.3	11.7	5.8	5.9
Painesville	80.8	55.2	34.1	19.2	12.6
Parma	89.1	71.4	31.8	10.9	5.0
Parma Heights	88.1	68.7	34.1	11.9	7.4
Perrysburg	94.2	87.6	17.1	5.8	3.8
Piqua	85.5	61.8	37.8	14.5	7.3
Portsmouth	82.4	50.1	45.4	17.6	4.9
Reynoldsburg	90.3	74.7	27.1	9.7	3.8
Riverside	86.3	62.8	36.1	13.7	5.8
Rocky River	94.0	83.1	28.1	6.0	1.9
Sandusky	83.6	55.7	42.6	16.4	7.1
Shaker Heights	93.7	83.3	24.2	6.3	2.1
Sidney	86.6	64.0	35.3	13.4	5.1
Solon	95.0	87.0	18.7	5.0	2.9
South Euclid	90.3	74.1	25.1	9.7	4.9
Springfield	85.6	53.2	45.8	14.4	4.9
Stow	93.0	84.4	20.3	7.0	5.9
Strongsville	94.6	85.4	21.6	5.4	3.1
Sylvania	93.5	84.0	24.6	6.5	2.6
Toledo	84.7	56.9	39.4	15.3	5.4
Trotwood	84.3	57.1	40.2	15.7	6.8
Troy	88.8	71.7	29.3	11.2	8.0
Twinsburg	96.4	88.0	20.1	3.6	1.3
Upper Arlington	95.2	88.4	19.0	4.8	3.7
Wadsworth	90.7	77.2	26.4	9.3	5.4
Warren	86.9	50.0	49.4	13.1	2.3
Westerville	94.6	85.9	19.6	5.4	1.7
Westlake	95.0	86.7	21.8	5.0	3.6
White Oak	90.5	73.8	28.3	9.5	6.5
Willoughby	89.5	77.1	26.1	10.5	8.5
Wooster	91.1	72.1	34.9	8.9	3.7
Xenia	88.3	63.1	39.5	11.7	2.4
Youngstown	84.9	42.0	54.4	15.1	3.3
Zanesville	85.6	43.3	55.9	14.4	5.3

NOTE: (1) Civilian noninstitutionalized population.
SOURCE: U.S. Census Bureau, American Community Survey, 2009-2013 Five-Year Estimates

Income and Poverty

Place	Average Household Income ($)	Median Household Income ($)	Per Capita Income ($)	Households w/$100,000+ Income (%)	Poverty Rate (%)
Akron	45,847	33,909	19,968	8.7	27.5
Alliance	41,900	31,152	17,205	7.4	26.9
Ashland	52,194	40,219	20,983	12.2	16.3
Ashtabula	38,007	27,876	16,356	5.1	32.9
Athens	39,622	17,933	11,929	11.0	57.4
Austintown	50,576	41,713	22,861	10.2	12.2
Avon	113,883	82,603	41,876	42.0	4.5
Avon Lake	100,905	80,271	40,049	38.3	4.6
Barberton	48,233	37,819	20,506	7.6	20.5
Beavercreek	95,686	76,162	39,212	35.3	5.5
Berea	65,886	55,942	25,732	18.4	11.2
Boardman	61,583	47,381	28,039	15.4	10.3
Bowling Green	51,072	34,550	19,266	15.1	32.5
Broadview Heights	92,040	75,882	37,115	34.7	6.6
Brook Park	57,740	49,010	23,893	12.2	8.7
Brunswick	72,755	63,924	28,225	19.5	6.7
Canton	39,787	30,209	16,669	5.9	31.7
Centerville	77,576	60,162	35,825	25.7	7.5
Chillicothe	49,767	36,927	21,776	10.1	23.6
Cincinnati	54,204	34,116	24,779	13.4	30.4
Cleveland	38,274	26,217	16,992	6.6	35.4
Cleveland Heights	69,089	50,109	30,167	20.0	20.0
Columbus	57,570	44,072	24,351	14.7	22.4
Cuyahoga Falls	58,490	49,438	26,402	14.4	12.0
Dayton	39,105	28,456	16,494	5.9	34.7
Delaware	69,356	56,963	26,992	21.7	9.6
Dublin	146,145	113,182	52,906	59.1	3.0
Elyria	49,873	41,600	21,276	9.7	18.8
Euclid	47,878	36,272	22,378	9.3	19.9
Fairborn	52,770	41,720	22,959	12.4	24.3
Fairfield	69,488	56,318	28,663	20.2	8.1
Findlay	57,491	42,901	24,783	14.1	20.2
Forest Park	56,240	46,949	22,367	12.5	17.2
Gahanna	89,591	71,201	35,037	34.5	5.5
Garfield Heights	49,619	42,511	20,993	8.6	14.8
Green	78,756	61,150	31,909	25.3	8.3
Grove City	77,809	66,299	30,638	26.9	8.7
Hamilton	50,466	40,426	20,283	10.2	22.9
Hilliard	98,726	85,052	35,604	42.0	4.7
Huber Heights	63,383	52,261	25,013	16.0	11.0
Hudson	144,323	119,212	49,903	57.6	3.6
Kent	51,507	31,035	19,143	12.3	35.3
Kettering	64,557	49,522	29,489	17.0	11.1
Lakewood	56,813	43,218	27,858	14.7	16.4
Lancaster	49,988	37,087	21,397	10.4	21.1
Lebanon	70,979	58,649	25,563	24.1	13.7
Lima	38,996	28,050	15,266	6.1	33.9
Lorain	45,347	33,610	18,698	9.1	30.4
Mansfield	44,420	32,722	18,279	7.7	24.4
Maple Heights	44,755	36,664	19,471	7.2	19.5

Place	Average Household Income ($)	Median Household Income ($)	Per Capita Income ($)	Households w/$100,000+ Income (%)	Poverty Rate (%)
Marion	44,647	33,586	15,815	7.3	27.9
Marysville	65,960	53,880	22,888	21.6	9.4
Mason	105,916	85,697	37,849	42.9	3.9
Massillon	48,390	38,142	20,701	8.8	19.0
Mayfield Heights	55,259	43,615	27,279	13.3	7.6
Medina	68,887	53,586	26,352	21.3	13.3
Mentor	79,468	65,888	32,485	27.3	6.8
Miamisburg	65,598	52,007	27,730	22.9	11.6
Middletown	48,185	35,853	20,199	8.7	23.0
Newark	51,331	38,295	21,654	10.6	21.0
Niles	46,184	37,169	20,507	8.0	19.4
North Olmsted	70,525	59,411	30,152	21.7	7.2
North Ridgeville	76,027	67,156	30,468	26.4	6.6
North Royalton	82,526	66,683	34,352	28.0	4.3
Norwood	49,369	37,303	22,503	10.9	20.7
Oregon	66,236	54,191	28,062	19.9	9.4
Oxford	51,136	28,429	14,950	14.9	46.0
Painesville	50,756	35,536	18,797	9.4	25.6
Parma	58,530	49,654	24,713	14.0	10.9
Parma Heights	54,156	43,502	24,331	12.9	12.1
Perrysburg	88,418	71,220	36,192	33.4	5.3
Piqua	45,503	36,260	19,419	7.2	23.4
Portsmouth	42,528	27,976	17,818	8.9	30.6
Reynoldsburg	71,357	58,257	28,959	23.1	12.8
Riverside	50,984	41,104	21,247	11.5	17.6
Rocky River	103,122	67,926	45,176	33.4	5.0
Sandusky	46,922	35,776	20,883	9.3	23.1
Shaker Heights	122,111	77,951	48,868	39.7	9.2
Sidney	54,121	43,347	21,494	8.2	16.4
Solon	133,209	97,181	47,332	48.4	3.8
South Euclid	68,039	59,968	27,704	20.7	8.3
Springfield	44,778	31,635	18,633	8.4	30.4
Stow	77,534	63,085	31,365	27.3	7.6
Strongsville	94,668	76,397	37,401	37.9	5.0
Sylvania	85,088	67,817	34,478	33.3	7.1
Toledo	43,543	33,317	18,760	7.4	27.2
Trotwood	46,623	36,277	20,396	10.4	21.2
Troy	56,728	48,570	23,779	13.1	16.2
Twinsburg	93,154	70,958	37,484	32.7	3.7
Upper Arlington	130,971	97,829	51,932	48.8	4.6
Wadsworth	68,991	57,539	26,999	22.0	7.3
Warren	39,453	29,317	16,939	6.4	32.3
Westerville	99,206	82,146	37,431	40.0	6.6
Westlake	110,717	76,358	46,684	37.7	4.2
White Oak	71,824	56,066	29,989	24.2	12.6
Willoughby	63,031	51,245	29,383	15.5	7.8
Wooster	58,530	40,633	24,221	12.7	17.4
Xenia	49,228	39,756	20,514	10.0	24.5
Youngstown	34,894	24,454	14,876	4.2	36.4
Zanesville	38,989	26,986	16,876	5.3	29.7

SOURCE: U.S. Census Bureau, American Community Survey, 2009-2013 Five-Year Estimates

Housing

Place	Homeownership Rate (%)	Median Home Value ($)	Median Year Structure Built	Homeowner Vacancy Rate (%)	Median Gross Rent ($/month)	Rental Vacancy Rate (%)
Akron	54.5	$83,900	1953	3.7	$680	10.5
Alliance	54.9	$81,200	1951	3.1	$611	12.8
Ashland	61.9	$101,600	1962	3.2	$688	10.1
Ashtabula	52.2	$78,700	1950	4.9	$621	11.6
Athens	27.5	$162,300	1970	2.3	$762	4.7
Austintown	65.9	$91,400	1966	2.0	$591	12.3
Avon	84.2	$249,100	1998	1.6	$1,145	8.9
Avon Lake	82.2	$213,300	1986	2.6	$1,052	6.6
Barberton	62.4	$86,800	1953	3.3	$683	7.4
Beavercreek	74.0	$174,100	1979	1.7	$1,080	10.3
Berea	70.2	$128,100	1959	2.1	$693	7.5
Boardman	68.5	$111,500	1964	2.6	$612	10.9
Bowling Green	39.9	$159,900	1977	2.6	$642	8.5
Broadview Heights	82.2	$213,700	1980	1.3	$858	17.7
Brook Park	81.0	$117,700	1961	1.2	$831	9.3
Brunswick	78.5	$157,400	1977	1.3	$810	10.4
Canton	53.3	$77,200	1946	4.3	$582	10.4
Centerville	72.1	$169,500	1976	1.9	$841	10.9
Chillicothe	59.1	$97,800	1953	4.2	$640	9.9
Cincinnati	38.9	$123,600	1947	5.1	$640	14.7
Cleveland	44.1	$76,700	Before 1940	3.9	$659	15.0
Cleveland Heights	56.3	$132,600	Before 1940	3.9	$831	10.0
Columbus	47.0	$130,700	1974	3.3	$809	9.6
Cuyahoga Falls	63.7	$120,400	1958	1.7	$761	8.3
Dayton	49.9	$69,600	1950	4.6	$637	15.7
Delaware	60.9	$158,500	1988	2.5	$807	8.4
Dublin	79.1	$330,900	1993	2.2	$1,161	7.0
Elyria	60.9	$100,400	1965	3.0	$718	13.3
Euclid	54.0	$91,200	1956	4.1	$733	14.6
Fairborn	50.7	$109,100	1969	2.6	$760	12.2
Fairfield	63.8	$147,100	1978	1.7	$855	12.0
Findlay	60.4	$123,300	1966	2.7	$642	12.0
Forest Park	59.3	$110,800	1971	2.9	$900	11.1
Gahanna	75.0	$186,300	1984	1.2	$955	6.5
Garfield Heights	69.6	$85,900	1954	4.2	$745	9.5
Green	78.6	$174,300	1980	2.2	$811	13.4
Grove City	69.7	$160,100	1988	1.9	$847	6.9
Hamilton	55.9	$104,300	1954	2.9	$707	11.9
Hilliard	79.2	$205,000	1992	1.7	$968	7.3
Huber Heights	72.0	$108,000	1973	2.2	$852	11.5
Hudson	89.7	$289,900	1980	1.6	$1,972	10.0
Kent	37.0	$138,600	1970	2.3	$716	8.0
Kettering	64.8	$130,100	1960	2.4	$741	10.2
Lakewood	43.3	$129,400	Before 1940	2.7	$699	12.0
Lancaster	57.7	$115,900	1962	2.7	$712	8.7
Lebanon	61.8	$159,200	1989	2.3	$794	7.0
Lima	50.6	$70,500	1953	3.4	$623	12.0
Lorain	57.8	$93,400	1958	3.6	$630	13.2
Mansfield	54.0	$79,900	1956	3.4	$573	15.8
Maple Heights	73.7	$84,400	1956	4.5	$777	13.7

Place	Homeownership Rate (%)	Median Home Value ($)	Median Year Structure Built	Homeowner Vacancy Rate (%)	Median Gross Rent ($/month)	Rental Vacancy Rate (%)
Marion	57.4	$77,500	1950	3.4	$670	12.9
Marysville	65.1	$159,500	1992	3.3	$833	9.0
Mason	83.5	$221,500	1994	1.5	<$101	7.3
Massillon	66.6	$98,100	1955	3.0	$638	10.4
Mayfield Heights	50.8	$142,700	1964	2.2	$821	10.2
Medina	66.3	$161,700	1979	1.9	$802	10.3
Mentor	85.5	$169,000	1972	1.6	$885	11.2
Miamisburg	71.5	$136,800	1971	2.3	$680	12.6
Middletown	53.8	$97,200	1958	4.0	$732	14.1
Newark	56.4	$113,900	1961	2.8	$667	10.3
Niles	60.0	$81,600	1956	3.1	$608	10.5
North Olmsted	76.3	$147,400	1966	1.6	$796	11.3
North Ridgeville	90.0	$161,900	1979	2.0	$829	9.3
North Royalton	71.6	$193,700	1982	1.5	$764	9.3
Norwood	49.0	$121,900	Before 1940	3.5	$636	10.9
Oregon	71.5	$133,100	1969	2.1	$617	7.6
Oxford	30.5	$188,100	1979	2.8	$768	13.8
Painesville	50.2	$110,500	1960	3.8	$726	8.8
Parma	74.1	$115,700	1958	1.7	$758	8.7
Parma Heights	59.4	$117,700	1960	1.8	$736	10.5
Perrysburg	70.5	$189,300	1981	2.2	$845	11.1
Piqua	61.1	$87,400	1954	4.2	$652	12.7
Portsmouth	50.1	$74,200	Before 1940	2.9	$536	8.0
Reynoldsburg	63.5	$145,200	1982	2.7	$827	11.6
Riverside	57.1	$92,800	1963	2.0	$742	10.7
Rocky River	72.1	$199,100	1958	2.4	$802	13.1
Sandusky	53.4	$85,000	1952	4.2	$622	13.3
Shaker Heights	63.9	$223,800	1945	4.0	$943	13.7
Sidney	59.3	$105,200	1968	3.5	$673	8.6
Solon	86.9	$266,300	1982	1.3	$1,047	7.9
South Euclid	80.2	$114,100	1954	3.3	$966	6.9
Springfield	52.8	$82,100	1951	3.7	$638	11.6
Stow	69.6	$165,900	1979	1.6	$843	9.3
Strongsville	80.8	$193,700	1980	1.4	$810	8.5
Sylvania	71.5	$171,800	1975	2.1	$781	9.1
Toledo	55.5	$83,600	1953	3.2	$629	12.0
Trotwood	57.5	$81,300	1965	3.6	$708	14.2
Troy	59.2	$123,800	1969	2.3	$704	9.0
Twinsburg	76.7	$206,700	1991	1.2	$954	9.1
Upper Arlington	80.8	$306,800	1958	2.3	$989	7.0
Wadsworth	72.4	$159,200	1973	2.2	$787	10.8
Warren	56.6	$65,600	1955	4.0	$596	13.3
Westerville	77.0	$204,900	1980	1.4	$904	6.8
Westlake	72.5	$228,800	1981	2.1	$997	9.1
White Oak	72.7	$132,500	1967	2.0	$682	9.0
Willoughby	61.1	$147,400	1971	3.4	$826	11.1
Wooster	58.9	$123,100	1972	2.6	$656	10.2
Xenia	61.6	$98,400	1969	2.9	$651	9.2
Youngstown	58.2	$46,600	1948	3.2	$585	11.1
Zanesville	47.0	$76,200	1948	5.3	$605	8.9

SOURCE: U.S. Census Bureau, Census 2010; U.S. Census Bureau, American Community Survey, 2009-2013 Five-Year Estimates

Commute to Work

Place	Automobile (%)	Public Transportation (%)	Walk (%)	Work from Home (%)	Median Travel Time to Work (minutes)
Akron	91.2	3.8	2.2	2.1	20.5
Alliance	92.5	0.2	3.5	2.7	17.8
Ashland	89.4	0.0	6.4	3.4	17.7
Ashtabula	91.3	0.8	3.0	2.4	19.4
Athens	51.9	2.0	36.9	6.4	14.0
Austintown	96.9	0.3	0.1	2.0	19.5
Avon	91.7	1.3	0.7	5.6	25.9
Avon Lake	92.1	1.1	2.0	3.6	26.3
Barberton	94.5	1.0	1.9	1.3	21.3
Beavercreek	92.4	0.2	1.6	5.0	18.7
Berea	85.1	1.7	5.7	5.3	21.4
Boardman	95.5	0.7	1.0	2.0	20.4
Bowling Green	78.4	0.2	15.0	3.2	15.5
Broadview Heights	91.8	1.5	1.4	5.0	28.0
Brook Park	93.3	2.0	2.1	1.4	21.2
Brunswick	94.0	1.1	1.6	2.7	28.9
Canton	91.3	3.0	2.9	2.0	19.4
Centerville	93.1	1.8	0.1	4.7	21.8
Chillicothe	94.2	0.7	1.8	2.7	21.5
Cincinnati	81.3	7.9	5.6	4.0	22.4
Cleveland	80.0	10.9	4.6	2.8	24.3
Cleveland Heights	82.7	5.9	5.0	4.6	22.3
Columbus	89.1	3.0	2.8	3.4	21.3
Cuyahoga Falls	94.7	0.8	1.0	2.9	22.6
Dayton	82.5	5.3	8.1	2.2	20.2
Delaware	90.0	0.3	3.6	5.3	26.4
Dublin	90.5	0.3	0.5	7.7	22.4
Elyria	94.6	0.7	1.0	2.1	21.9
Euclid	88.4	7.0	1.4	2.6	24.3
Fairborn	94.8	0.3	2.2	1.8	19.5
Fairfield	96.6	0.3	0.5	2.0	23.0
Findlay	91.5	0.1	3.0	3.8	14.5
Forest Park	93.3	2.6	0.6	3.0	24.4
Gahanna	91.3	0.3	0.7	7.1	21.0
Garfield Heights	91.2	4.1	1.8	1.9	22.4
Green	95.8	0.0	0.3	3.6	22.5
Grove City	93.5	0.7	0.3	3.8	21.9
Hamilton	94.1	0.2	2.4	1.6	24.2
Hilliard	92.9	0.1	0.9	4.8	22.1
Huber Heights	93.8	1.6	1.1	1.6	22.3
Hudson	88.2	0.8	1.5	8.1	28.3
Kent	81.5	2.4	10.6	4.2	21.3
Kettering	91.7	1.2	1.7	4.0	20.2
Lakewood	86.7	6.3	2.3	3.1	24.3
Lancaster	93.6	0.1	3.3	1.4	23.9
Lebanon	91.7	1.4	2.5	3.9	25.0
Lima	93.9	1.1	2.9	1.3	17.7
Lorain	95.2	0.9	1.4	1.7	22.9
Mansfield	93.1	1.6	2.6	1.7	18.7
Maple Heights	90.2	4.8	1.8	1.5	22.7

Place	Automobile (%)	Public Transportation (%)	Walk (%)	Work from Home (%)	Median Travel Time to Work (minutes)
Marion	94.9	0.8	1.5	1.8	19.5
Marysville	93.5	0.4	1.4	4.2	21.7
Mason	94.0	0.7	0.5	4.6	23.2
Massillon	94.8	1.0	2.2	1.5	20.6
Mayfield Heights	96.1	1.1	1.2	1.5	21.2
Medina	93.7	0.6	1.2	3.2	26.1
Mentor	94.4	1.0	1.1	3.0	24.1
Miamisburg	93.3	0.8	1.3	4.1	20.9
Middletown	95.0	0.9	1.0	2.0	21.2
Newark	93.4	0.2	2.2	2.6	21.1
Niles	96.6	0.6	1.0	1.1	17.1
North Olmsted	92.4	2.5	1.2	3.2	23.1
North Ridgeville	94.4	1.4	0.4	3.4	27.1
North Royalton	92.6	0.5	0.4	5.6	27.5
Norwood	90.7	2.1	2.6	2.9	19.1
Oregon	96.6	0.1	0.5	2.4	19.5
Oxford	54.8	5.7	26.9	11.0	14.0
Painesville	90.9	1.7	4.0	1.6	19.2
Parma	94.0	2.0	1.4	1.8	24.3
Parma Heights	94.2	2.2	1.1	1.7	25.2
Perrysburg	93.2	0.2	1.3	4.9	20.1
Piqua	95.2	0.4	2.1	1.2	17.9
Portsmouth	89.4	0.1	7.5	1.8	18.7
Reynoldsburg	91.4	1.8	1.8	4.1	23.5
Riverside	96.3	0.6	1.2	1.3	17.6
Rocky River	90.5	2.5	0.9	5.4	23.6
Sandusky	90.8	1.3	2.7	2.7	16.6
Shaker Heights	83.7	5.8	2.0	6.6	23.0
Sidney	95.9	0.1	1.0	2.1	16.6
Solon	93.3	0.2	0.6	5.4	25.5
South Euclid	89.9	2.7	2.0	4.0	24.2
Springfield	90.2	1.3	5.6	2.1	19.4
Stow	94.1	1.0	1.3	3.4	24.3
Strongsville	91.8	2.0	1.2	4.3	27.3
Sylvania	94.6	1.1	0.5	3.4	20.0
Toledo	91.5	2.3	3.0	2.1	19.0
Trotwood	92.6	4.1	1.4	1.1	24.3
Troy	94.4	0.8	2.1	2.3	18.1
Twinsburg	94.4	0.2	0.7	4.1	26.3
Upper Arlington	88.8	1.4	1.5	6.8	19.1
Wadsworth	93.4	0.0	1.3	4.3	22.6
Warren	93.7	0.9	1.2	2.8	19.5
Westerville	90.5	0.4	3.1	5.4	20.7
Westlake	92.0	1.4	1.0	4.6	24.3
White Oak	96.4	0.9	1.1	1.2	22.4
Willoughby	95.1	1.1	1.3	2.1	21.4
Wooster	83.8	0.4	10.7	3.1	16.4
Xenia	93.5	1.1	2.5	2.0	22.1
Youngstown	88.4	3.2	2.9	2.7	20.3
Zanesville	92.2	0.5	2.6	4.4	21.0

SOURCE: U.S. Census Bureau, American Community Survey, 2009-2013 Five-Year Estimates

Crime

Place	Violent Crime Rate (crimes per 10,000 population)	Property Crime Rate (crimes per 10,000 population)
Akron	79.1	486.3
Alliance	37.5	441.7
Ashland	6.9	255.6
Ashtabula	n/a	n/a
Athens	7.2	171.2
Austintown	14.6	262.8
Avon	n/a	n/a
Avon Lake	n/a	n/a
Barberton	33.1	368.1
Beavercreek	2.6	248.4
Berea	9.5	130.9
Boardman	n/a	n/a
Bowling Green	15.4	245.3
Broadview Heights	5.7	0.0
Brook Park	n/a	n/a
Brunswick	4.7	83.7
Canton	92.7	585.8
Centerville	7.9	181.6
Chillicothe	33.7	896.3
Cincinnati	95.3	581.2
Cleveland	147.8	595.3
Cleveland Heights	31.1	336.0
Columbus	n/a	n/a
Cuyahoga Falls	14.0	261.9
Dayton	87.1	542.3
Delaware	14.6	255.9
Dublin	2.3	129.1
Elyria	n/a	n/a
Euclid	n/a	n/a
Fairborn	18.9	281.8
Fairfield	28.1	257.8
Findlay	18.0	348.5
Forest Park	16.1	250.6
Gahanna	6.8	209.9
Garfield Heights	n/a	n/a
Green	n/a	n/a
Grove City	10.8	341.3
Hamilton	60.7	630.3
Hilliard	8.3	229.3
Huber Heights	16.0	361.0
Hudson	1.3	59.1
Kent	18.6	219.4
Kettering	9.5	230.2
Lakewood	n/a	n/a
Lancaster	n/a	n/a
Lebanon	9.8	198.7
Lima	95.8	505.6
Lorain	47.8	439.0
Mansfield	36.1	676.2
Maple Heights	n/a	n/a

Place	Violent Crime Rate (crimes per 10,000 population)	Property Crime Rate (crimes per 10,000 population)
Marion	n/a	n/a
Marysville	5.4	193.4
Mason	3.5	134.9
Massillon	21.5	303.2
Mayfield Heights	n/a	n/a
Medina	7.2	164.6
Mentor	9.2	225.4
Miamisburg	9.4	333.5
Middletown	61.8	816.2
Newark	14.0	496.8
Niles	26.9	493.9
North Olmsted	n/a	n/a
North Ridgeville	4.5	86.1
North Royalton	n/a	n/a
Norwood	32.5	661.9
Oregon	12.9	389.3
Oxford	22.0	270.9
Painesville	22.9	259.0
Parma	n/a	n/a
Parma Heights	8.3	214.3
Perrysburg	2.4	148.0
Piqua	16.0	504.0
Portsmouth	43.8	776.5
Reynoldsburg	n/a	n/a
Riverside	17.5	246.5
Rocky River	n/a	n/a
Sandusky	30.7	450.0
Shaker Heights	14.7	230.7
Sidney	16.2	588.7
Solon	3.0	111.2
South Euclid	14.1	215.2
Springfield	71.2	743.7
Stow	6.6	205.1
Strongsville	6.1	167.3
Sylvania	n/a	n/a
Toledo	102.5	n/a
Trotwood	45.3	511.5
Troy	7.5	311.1
Twinsburg	4.8	70.4
Upper Arlington	2.9	129.5
Wadsworth	8.3	212.8
Warren	65.0	472.2
Westerville	3.5	226.4
Westlake	n/a	n/a
White Oak	n/a	n/a
Willoughby	6.3	219.9
Wooster	15.9	370.6
Xenia	21.1	402.9
Youngstown	81.0	549.8
Zanesville	40.6	630.9

NOTE: n/a not available.
SOURCE: Federal Bureau of Investigation, Uniform Crime Reports, 2013

Community Rankings

This section ranks incorporated places and CDPs (Census Designated Places) with populations of 10,000 or more. Unincorporated postal areas were not considered. For each topic below, you will find two tables, one in Descending Order—highest to lowest, and one in Ascending Order—lowest to highest. Four topics are exceptions to this rule, and only include Descending Order—Water Area, Ancestry (five tables), Native Hawaiian/Other Pacific Islander, and Commute to Work: Public Transportation. This is because there are an extraordinarily large number of places that place at the bottom of these topics with zero numbers.

Land Area 349
Water Area 351
Elevation 352
Population 354
Population Growth 356
Population Density 358
White Population 360
Black/African American Population 362
Asian Population 364
American Indian/Alaska Native Population 366
Native Hawaiian/Other Pacific Islander Population 368
Two or More Races 369
Hispanic Population 371
Average Household Size 373
Median Age 375
Population Under Age 18 377
Population Age 65 and Over 379
Males per 100 Females 381
Marriage Status: Never Married 383
Marriage Status: Now Married 385
Marriage Status: Separated 387
Marriage Status: Widowed 389
Marriage Status: Divorced 391
Foreign Born 393
Speak English Only at Home 395
Population with a Disability 397
Veterans 399
Ancestry: German 401
Ancestry: English 402
Ancestry: American 403
Ancestry: Irish 404
Ancestry: Italian 405
Employment: Management, Business, and Financial Occupations 406
Employment: Computer, Engineering, and Science Occupations 408
Employment: Education, Legal, Community Service, Arts, and Media Occupations 410
Employment: Healthcare Practitioners 412
Employment: Service Occupations 414
Employment: Sales and Office Occupations 416
Employment: Natural Resources, Construction, and Maintenance Occupations 418

Employment: Production, Transportation, and Material Moving Occupations 420
Per Capita Income 422
Median Household Income 424
Average Household Income. 426
Households with Income of $100,000 or More 428
Poverty Rate 430
Educational Attainment: High School Diploma or Higher 432
Educational Attainment: Bachelor's Degree or Higher 434
Educational Attainment: Graduate/Professional Degree or Higher 436
Homeownership Rate 438
Median Home Value. 440
Median Year Structure Built 442
Homeowner Vacancy Rate 444
Median Gross Rent 446
Rental Vacancy Rate 448
Population with Health Insurance 450
Population with Private Health Insurance 452
Population with Public Health Insurance 454
Population with No Health Insurance 456
Population Under 18 Years Old with No Health Insurance 458
Commute to Work: Car 460
Commute to Work: Public Transportation 462
Commute to Work: Walk 463
Commute to Work: Work from Home 465
Median Travel Time to Work 467
Violent Crime Rate per 10,000 Population 469
Property Crime Rate per 10,000 Population. 471

Land Area

Top 150 Places Ranked in *Descending* Order

State Rank	Nat'l Rank	Sq. Miles	Place
1	33	217.169	**Columbus** (city) Franklin County
2	156	80.692	**Toledo** (city) Lucas County
3	160	77.942	**Cincinnati** (city) Hamilton County
4	161	77.697	**Cleveland** (city) Cuyahoga County
5	229	62.033	**Akron** (city) Summit County
6	300	55.652	**Dayton** (city) Montgomery County
7	788	33.955	**Youngstown** (city) Mahoning County
8	886	32.055	**Green** (city) Summit County
9	938	30.872	**Mansfield** (city) Richland County
10	958	30.494	**Trotwood** (city) Montgomery County
11	977	29.976	**Oregon** (city) Lucas County
12	1045	28.617	**Pataskala** (city) Licking County
13	1168	26.645	**Mentor** (city) Lake County
14	1178	26.399	**Beavercreek** (city) Greene County
15	1181	26.355	**Conneaut** (city) Ashtabula County
16	1196	26.185	**Middletown** (city) Butler County
17	1213	25.648	**Cuyahoga Falls** (city) Summit County
18	1216	25.596	**Hudson** (city) Summit County
19	1224	25.462	**Canton** (city) Stark County
20	1231	25.294	**Springfield** (city) Clark County
21	1249	25.036	**New Franklin** (city) Summit County
22	1270	24.627	**Strongsville** (city) Cuyahoga County
23	1281	24.437	**Dublin** (city) Franklin County
24	1331	23.673	**Lorain** (city) Lorain County
25	1341	23.459	**Streetsboro** (city) Portage County
26	1343	23.438	**North Ridgeville** (city) Lorain County
27	1388	22.918	**Aurora** (city) Portage County
28	1436	22.272	**Huber Heights** (city) Montgomery County
29	1489	21.596	**Hamilton** (city) Butler County
30	1505	21.310	**North Royalton** (city) Cuyahoga County
31	1521	20.939	**Fairfield** (city) Butler County
32	1531	20.884	**Newark** (city) Licking County
33	1539	20.808	**Avon** (city) Lorain County
34	1558	20.571	**Elyria** (city) Lorain County
35	1579	20.361	**Solon** (city) Cuyahoga County
36	1590	20.162	**Norton** (city) Summit County
37	1599	20.024	**Parma** (city) Cuyahoga County
38	1640	19.574	**Brecksville** (city) Cuyahoga County
39	1674	19.134	**Findlay** (city) Hancock County
40	1688	18.952	**Delaware** (city) Delaware County
41	1696	18.841	**Lancaster** (city) Fairfield County
42	1715	18.677	**Kettering** (city) Montgomery County
43	1719	18.629	**Mason** (city) Warren County
44	1722	18.578	**Massillon** (city) Stark County
45	1725	18.506	**Clayton** (city) Montgomery County
46	1849	17.088	**Stow** (city) Summit County
47	1920	16.310	**Wooster** (city) Wayne County
48	1925	16.271	**Marysville** (city) Union County
49	1940	16.196	**Grove City** (city) Franklin County
50	1946	16.127	**Warren** (city) Trumbull County
51	1975	15.926	**Westlake** (city) Cuyahoga County
52	1978	15.873	**Monroe** (city) Butler County
53	2064	15.121	**Boardman** (CDP) Mahoning County
54	2202	13.996	**Tallmadge** (city) Summit County
55	2234	13.769	**Twinsburg** (city) Summit County
56	2258	13.565	**Lima** (city) Allen County
57	2297	13.281	**Xenia** (city) Greene County
58	2309	13.167	**Hilliard** (city) Franklin County
59	2310	13.160	**Fairborn** (city) Greene County
60	2323	13.048	**Broadview Heights** (city) Cuyahoga County
61	2336	12.963	**Lebanon** (city) Warren County
62	2348	12.916	**Brunswick** (city) Medina County
63	2390	12.557	**Bowling Green** (city) Wood County
64	2395	12.473	**Westerville** (city) Franklin County
65	2398	12.427	**Gahanna** (city) Franklin County
66	2410	12.344	**Vandalia** (city) Montgomery County
67	2436	12.184	**Miamisburg** (city) Montgomery County
68	2458	12.023	**Sidney** (city) Shelby County
69	2496	11.768	**Zanesville** (city) Muskingum County
70	2500	11.736	**Marion** (city) Marion County
71	2503	11.722	**Troy** (city) Miami County
72	2509	11.674	**North Olmsted** (city) Cuyahoga County
73	2518	11.630	**Austintown** (CDP) Mahoning County
74	2521	11.620	**Piqua** (city) Miami County
75	2524	11.617	**Defiance** (city) Defiance County
76	2532	11.572	**Medina** (city) Medina County
77	2544	11.514	**Perrysburg** (city) Wood County
78	2590	11.169	**Ashland** (city) Ashland County
79	2592	11.157	**Reynoldsburg** (city) Franklin County
80	2598	11.129	**Avon Lake** (city) Lorain County
81	2623	10.922	**Heath** (city) Licking County
82	2628	10.889	**Wilmington** (city) Clinton County
83	2645	10.780	**Centerville** (city) Montgomery County
84	2655	10.734	**Portsmouth** (city) Scioto County
85	2666	10.655	**Vermilion** (city) Lorain County
86	2669	10.630	**Euclid** (city) Cuyahoga County
87	2671	10.621	**Wadsworth** (city) Medina County
88	2679	10.545	**Steubenville** (city) Jefferson County
89	2694	10.428	**Chillicothe** (city) Ross County
90	2730	10.249	**Willoughby** (city) Lake County
91	2776	10.036	**Bellefontaine** (city) Logan County
92	2814	9.886	**Maumee** (city) Lucas County
93	2832	9.839	**Upper Arlington** (city) Franklin County
94	2835	9.832	**Sharonville** (city) Hamilton County
95	2838	9.827	**Athens** (city) Athens County
96	2859	9.745	**Pickerington** (city) Fairfield County
97	2863	9.726	**Sandusky** (city) Erie County
98	2865	9.720	**Riverside** (city) Montgomery County
99	2868	9.706	**Macedonia** (city) Summit County
100	2905	9.408	**Mount Vernon** (city) Knox County
101	2910	9.355	**Springboro** (city) Warren County
102	2926	9.273	**Mack** (CDP) Hamilton County
103	2943	9.174	**Kent** (city) Portage County
104	2944	9.173	**Franklin** (city) Warren County
105	2972	9.038	**Barberton** (city) Summit County
106	2994	8.924	**Alliance** (city) Stark County
107	3009	8.870	**Norwalk** (city) Huron County
108	3033	8.739	**Washington Court House** (city) Fayette County
109	3060	8.611	**Niles** (city) Trumbull County
110	3089	8.433	**Marietta** (city) Washington County
111	3106	8.346	**Fremont** (city) Sandusky County
112	3133	8.216	**New Philadelphia** (city) Tuscarawas County
113	3152	8.107	**Cleveland Heights** (city) Cuyahoga County
114	3159	8.084	**Coshocton** (city) Coshocton County
115	3162	8.065	**Middleburg Heights** (city) Cuyahoga County
116	3231	7.753	**Urbana** (city) Champaign County
117	3239	7.735	**Ashtabula** (city) Ashtabula County
118	3261	7.607	**Galion** (city) Crawford County
119	3267	7.580	**Blue Ash** (city) Hamilton County
120	3275	7.545	**Fostoria** (city) Seneca County
121	3278	7.530	**Brook Park** (city) Cuyahoga County
122	3300	7.422	**Bucyrus** (city) Crawford County
123	3317	7.325	**Van Wert** (city) Van Wert County
124	3342	7.230	**Garfield Heights** (city) Cuyahoga County
125	3378	7.062	**Amherst** (city) Lorain County
126	3454	6.764	**Tiffin** (city) Seneca County
127	3471	6.676	**Oxford** (city) Butler County
128	3485	6.644	**Circleville** (city) Pickaway County
129	3495	6.604	**Greenville** (city) Darke County
130	3508	6.551	**Englewood** (city) Montgomery County
131	3523	6.480	**Forest Park** (city) Hamilton County
132	3524	6.478	**Sylvania** (city) Lucas County
133	3531	6.439	**West Carrollton** (city) Montgomery County
134	3532	6.425	**Salem** (city) Columbiana County
135	3538	6.400	**North Canton** (city) Stark County
136	3539	6.395	**Eastlake** (city) Lake County
137	3546	6.352	**Cambridge** (city) Guernsey County
138	3564	6.285	**Painesville** (city) Lake County
139	3565	6.282	**Shaker Heights** (city) Cuyahoga County
140	3588	6.167	**White Oak** (CDP) Hamilton County
141	3638	5.930	**Dent** (CDP) Hamilton County
142	3642	5.913	**Monfort Heights** (CDP) Hamilton County
143	3702	5.718	**Berea** (city) Cuyahoga County
144	3712	5.685	**Dover** (city) Tuscarawas County
145	3722	5.630	**Ravenna** (city) Portage County
146	3740	5.545	**Worthington** (city) Franklin County
147	3742	5.534	**Lakewood** (city) Cuyahoga County
148	3784	5.351	**Bedford** (city) Cuyahoga County
149	3789	5.325	**Beachwood** (city) Cuyahoga County
150	3803	5.286	**Montgomery** (city) Hamilton County

Note: *The state column ranks the top/bottom 150 places from all places in the state with population of 10,000 or more. The national column ranks the top/bottom 150 places from all places in the country with population of 10,000 or more. Places that are unincorporated were not considered in the rankings. Please refer to the User Guide for additional information.*

Land Area

Top 150 Places Ranked in *Ascending* Order

State Rank	Nat'l Rank	Sq. Miles	Place
1	77	1.820	**University Heights** (city) Cuyahoga County
2	97	1.949	**Northbrook** (CDP) Hamilton County
3	181	2.431	**Bexley** (city) Franklin County
4	199	2.536	**Willowick** (city) Lake County
5	296	2.892	**Reading** (city) Hamilton County
6	339	3.086	**East Cleveland** (city) Cuyahoga County
7	346	3.147	**Norwood** (city) Hamilton County
8	441	3.642	**Struthers** (city) Mahoning County
9	464	3.724	**Forestville** (CDP) Hamilton County
10	550	4.057	**Finneytown** (CDP) Hamilton County
11	565	4.132	**Warrensville Heights** (city) Cuyahoga County
12	571	4.161	**Ironton** (city) Lawrence County
13	577	4.168	**Mayfield Heights** (city) Cuyahoga County
14	582	4.186	**Parma Heights** (city) Cuyahoga County
15	596	4.248	**Brooklyn** (city) Cuyahoga County
16	616	4.323	**Bridgetown** (CDP) Hamilton County
17	648	4.432	**Lyndhurst** (city) Cuyahoga County
18	649	4.436	**Richmond Heights** (city) Cuyahoga County
19	667	4.535	**Bedford Heights** (city) Cuyahoga County
20	675	4.563	**East Liverpool** (city) Columbiana County
21	676	4.563	**Trenton** (city) Butler County
22	678	4.566	**Bay Village** (city) Cuyahoga County
23	701	4.639	**Wickliffe** (city) Lake County
24	704	4.651	**South Euclid** (city) Cuyahoga County
25	712	4.678	**Fairview Park** (city) Cuyahoga County
26	724	4.738	**Rocky River** (city) Cuyahoga County
27	768	4.907	**Seven Hills** (city) Cuyahoga County
28	775	4.927	**Loveland** (city) Hamilton County
29	776	4.932	**Powell** (city) Delaware County
30	783	4.963	**Springdale** (city) Hamilton County
31	787	4.981	**Celina** (city) Mercer County
32	834	5.172	**Maple Heights** (city) Cuyahoga County
33	848	5.257	**Whitehall** (city) Franklin County
34	853	5.286	**Montgomery** (city) Hamilton County
35	867	5.325	**Beachwood** (city) Cuyahoga County
36	872	5.351	**Bedford** (city) Cuyahoga County
37	914	5.534	**Lakewood** (city) Cuyahoga County
38	916	5.545	**Worthington** (city) Franklin County
39	934	5.630	**Ravenna** (city) Portage County
40	944	5.685	**Dover** (city) Tuscarawas County
41	954	5.718	**Berea** (city) Cuyahoga County
42	1014	5.913	**Monfort Heights** (CDP) Hamilton County
43	1018	5.930	**Dent** (CDP) Hamilton County
44	1068	6.167	**White Oak** (CDP) Hamilton County
45	1091	6.282	**Shaker Heights** (city) Cuyahoga County
46	1092	6.285	**Painesville** (city) Lake County
47	1110	6.352	**Cambridge** (city) Guernsey County
48	1117	6.395	**Eastlake** (city) Lake County
49	1118	6.400	**North Canton** (city) Stark County
50	1124	6.425	**Salem** (city) Columbiana County
51	1125	6.439	**West Carrollton** (city) Montgomery County
52	1132	6.478	**Sylvania** (city) Lucas County
53	1133	6.480	**Forest Park** (city) Hamilton County
54	1148	6.551	**Englewood** (city) Montgomery County
55	1161	6.604	**Greenville** (city) Darke County
56	1171	6.644	**Circleville** (city) Pickaway County
57	1185	6.676	**Oxford** (city) Butler County
58	1202	6.764	**Tiffin** (city) Seneca County
59	1278	7.062	**Amherst** (city) Lorain County
60	1314	7.230	**Garfield Heights** (city) Cuyahoga County
61	1339	7.325	**Van Wert** (city) Van Wert County
62	1356	7.422	**Bucyrus** (city) Crawford County
63	1378	7.530	**Brook Park** (city) Cuyahoga County
64	1381	7.545	**Fostoria** (city) Seneca County
65	1389	7.580	**Blue Ash** (city) Hamilton County
66	1395	7.607	**Galion** (city) Crawford County
67	1417	7.735	**Ashtabula** (city) Ashtabula County
68	1425	7.753	**Urbana** (city) Champaign County
69	1494	8.065	**Middleburg Heights** (city) Cuyahoga County
70	1497	8.084	**Coshocton** (city) Coshocton County
71	1504	8.107	**Cleveland Heights** (city) Cuyahoga County
72	1523	8.216	**New Philadelphia** (city) Tuscarawas County
73	1550	8.346	**Fremont** (city) Sandusky County
74	1567	8.433	**Marietta** (city) Washington County
75	1596	8.611	**Niles** (city) Trumbull County
76	1623	8.739	**Washington Court House** (city) Fayette County
77	1647	8.870	**Norwalk** (city) Huron County
78	1662	8.924	**Alliance** (city) Stark County
79	1684	9.038	**Barberton** (city) Summit County
80	1712	9.173	**Franklin** (city) Warren County
81	1713	9.174	**Kent** (city) Portage County
82	1730	9.273	**Mack** (CDP) Hamilton County
83	1746	9.355	**Springboro** (city) Warren County
84	1751	9.408	**Mount Vernon** (city) Knox County
85	1788	9.706	**Macedonia** (city) Summit County
86	1791	9.720	**Riverside** (city) Montgomery County
87	1793	9.726	**Sandusky** (city) Erie County
88	1797	9.745	**Pickerington** (city) Fairfield County
89	1818	9.827	**Athens** (city) Athens County
90	1821	9.832	**Sharonville** (city) Hamilton County
91	1824	9.839	**Upper Arlington** (city) Franklin County
92	1842	9.886	**Maumee** (city) Lucas County
93	1880	10.036	**Bellefontaine** (city) Logan County
94	1926	10.249	**Willoughby** (city) Lake County
95	1962	10.428	**Chillicothe** (city) Ross County
96	1977	10.545	**Steubenville** (city) Jefferson County
97	1985	10.621	**Wadsworth** (city) Medina County
98	1987	10.630	**Euclid** (city) Cuyahoga County
99	1990	10.655	**Vermilion** (city) Lorain County
100	2001	10.734	**Portsmouth** (city) Scioto County
101	2011	10.780	**Centerville** (city) Montgomery County
102	2028	10.889	**Wilmington** (city) Clinton County
103	2033	10.922	**Heath** (city) Licking County
104	2058	11.129	**Avon Lake** (city) Lorain County
105	2064	11.157	**Reynoldsburg** (city) Franklin County
106	2066	11.169	**Ashland** (city) Ashland County
107	2112	11.514	**Perrysburg** (city) Wood County
108	2124	11.572	**Medina** (city) Medina County
109	2132	11.617	**Defiance** (city) Defiance County
110	2135	11.620	**Piqua** (city) Miami County
111	2138	11.630	**Austintown** (CDP) Mahoning County
112	2147	11.674	**North Olmsted** (city) Cuyahoga County
113	2153	11.722	**Troy** (city) Miami County
114	2156	11.736	**Marion** (city) Marion County
115	2160	11.768	**Zanesville** (city) Muskingum County
116	2198	12.023	**Sidney** (city) Shelby County
117	2220	12.184	**Miamisburg** (city) Montgomery County
118	2246	12.344	**Vandalia** (city) Montgomery County
119	2258	12.427	**Gahanna** (city) Franklin County
120	2261	12.473	**Westerville** (city) Franklin County
121	2266	12.557	**Bowling Green** (city) Wood County
122	2308	12.916	**Brunswick** (city) Medina County
123	2320	12.963	**Lebanon** (city) Warren County
124	2333	13.048	**Broadview Heights** (city) Cuyahoga County
125	2346	13.160	**Fairborn** (city) Greene County
126	2347	13.167	**Hilliard** (city) Franklin County
127	2359	13.281	**Xenia** (city) Greene County
128	2398	13.565	**Lima** (city) Allen County
129	2422	13.769	**Twinsburg** (city) Summit County
130	2454	13.996	**Tallmadge** (city) Summit County
131	2592	15.121	**Boardman** (CDP) Mahoning County
132	2678	15.873	**Monroe** (city) Butler County
133	2681	15.926	**Westlake** (city) Cuyahoga County
134	2710	16.127	**Warren** (city) Trumbull County
135	2716	16.196	**Grove City** (city) Franklin County
136	2731	16.271	**Marysville** (city) Union County
137	2736	16.310	**Wooster** (city) Wayne County
138	2807	17.088	**Stow** (city) Summit County
139	2931	18.506	**Clayton** (city) Montgomery County
140	2934	18.578	**Massillon** (city) Stark County
141	2937	18.629	**Mason** (city) Warren County
142	2941	18.677	**Kettering** (city) Montgomery County
143	2960	18.841	**Lancaster** (city) Fairfield County
144	2968	18.952	**Delaware** (city) Delaware County
145	2982	19.134	**Findlay** (city) Hancock County
146	3016	19.574	**Brecksville** (city) Cuyahoga County
147	3057	20.024	**Parma** (city) Cuyahoga County
148	3066	20.162	**Norton** (city) Summit County
149	3077	20.361	**Solon** (city) Cuyahoga County
150	3098	20.571	**Elyria** (city) Lorain County

Note: *The state column ranks the top/bottom 150 places from all places in the state with population of 10,000 or more. The national column ranks the top/bottom 150 places from all places in the country with population of 10,000 or more. Places that are unincorporated were not considered in the rankings. Please refer to the User Guide for additional information.*

Water Area

Top 150 Places Ranked in *Descending* Order

State Rank	Nat'l Rank	Sq. Miles	Place
1	129	12.175	**Sandusky** (city) Erie County
2	184	8.055	**Oregon** (city) Lucas County
3	245	5.936	**Columbus** (city) Franklin County
4	282	4.769	**Cleveland** (city) Cuyahoga County
5	373	3.432	**Toledo** (city) Lucas County
6	482	2.488	**Bay Village** (city) Cuyahoga County
7	672	1.642	**New Franklin** (city) Summit County
8	684	1.604	**Cincinnati** (city) Hamilton County
9	721	1.479	**Green** (city) Summit County
10	782	1.353	**Mentor** (city) Lake County
11	880	1.159	**Lakewood** (city) Cuyahoga County
12	883	1.147	**Aurora** (city) Portage County
13	1026	0.902	**Streetsboro** (city) Portage County
14	1050	0.873	**Rocky River** (city) Cuyahoga County
15	1070	0.853	**Dayton** (city) Montgomery County
16	1071	0.852	**Euclid** (city) Cuyahoga County
17	1176	0.726	**Painesville** (city) Lake County
18	1185	0.716	**Maumee** (city) Lucas County
19	1262	0.635	**Youngstown** (city) Mahoning County
20	1412	0.509	**Defiance** (city) Defiance County
21	1443	0.486	**Newark** (city) Licking County
22	1456	0.479	**Hamilton** (city) Butler County
23	1464	0.474	**Lorain** (city) Lorain County
24	1622	0.373	**Zanesville** (city) Muskingum County
25	1641	0.361	**Dublin** (city) Franklin County
26	1693	0.340	**Akron** (city) Summit County
27	1700	0.338	**Portsmouth** (city) Scioto County
28	1729	0.327	**Norton** (city) Summit County
29	1754	0.319	**Marietta** (city) Washington County
30	1810	0.296	**Ironton** (city) Lawrence County
31	1829	0.291	**Marysville** (city) Union County
32	1837	0.289	**Celina** (city) Mercer County
33	1855	0.282	**Norwalk** (city) Huron County
34	1858	0.281	**Van Wert** (city) Van Wert County
35	1876	0.274	**Elyria** (city) Lorain County
36	1890	0.267	**Piqua** (city) Miami County
37	1893	0.265	**Hudson** (city) Summit County
38	2008	0.235	**Middletown** (city) Butler County
39	2015	0.233	**Stow** (city) Summit County
40	2023	0.229	**Lima** (city) Allen County
41	2055	0.219	**Fremont** (city) Sandusky County
42	2057	0.219	**Troy** (city) Miami County
43	2058	0.219	**Athens** (city) Athens County
44	2059	0.219	**Barberton** (city) Summit County
45	2065	0.218	**West Carrollton** (city) Montgomery County
46	2066	0.218	**Fostoria** (city) Seneca County
47	2087	0.210	**Medina** (city) Medina County
48	2114	0.205	**Springfield** (city) Clark County
49	2157	0.196	**East Liverpool** (city) Columbiana County
50	2191	0.185	**Miamisburg** (city) Montgomery County
51	2193	0.185	**Mount Vernon** (city) Knox County
52	2202	0.181	**Massillon** (city) Stark County
53	2245	0.172	**Boardman** (CDP) Mahoning County
54	2252	0.171	**Ashtabula** (city) Ashtabula County
55	2254	0.171	**Gahanna** (city) Franklin County
56	2264	0.170	**New Philadelphia** (city) Tuscarawas County
57	2266	0.170	**Franklin** (city) Warren County
58	2268	0.168	**Hilliard** (city) Franklin County
59	2279	0.167	**Chillicothe** (city) Ross County
60	2286	0.166	**Vermilion** (city) Lorain County
61	2332	0.157	**Grove City** (city) Franklin County
62	2405	0.140	**North Ridgeville** (city) Lorain County
63	2426	0.138	**Westerville** (city) Franklin County
64	2438	0.136	**Tiffin** (city) Seneca County
65	2469	0.132	**Sidney** (city) Shelby County
66	2487	0.130	**Eastlake** (city) Lake County
67	2488	0.130	**Solon** (city) Cuyahoga County
68	2520	0.124	**Coshocton** (city) Coshocton County
69	2533	0.122	**Delaware** (city) Delaware County
70	2537	0.121	**Circleville** (city) Pickaway County
71	2542	0.121	**Fairfield** (city) Butler County
72	2545	0.120	**Findlay** (city) Hancock County
73	2597	0.113	**Brecksville** (city) Cuyahoga County
74	2638	0.109	**Kent** (city) Portage County
75	2639	0.109	**Berea** (city) Cuyahoga County
76	2680	0.103	**Dover** (city) Tuscarawas County
77	2697	0.099	**Cuyahoga Falls** (city) Summit County
78	2716	0.096	**Pataskala** (city) Licking County
79	2726	0.096	**Struthers** (city) Mahoning County
80	2732	0.095	**Huber Heights** (city) Montgomery County
81	2763	0.090	**Willoughby** (city) Lake County
82	2771	0.089	**Clayton** (city) Montgomery County
83	2830	0.083	**Reynoldsburg** (city) Franklin County
84	2838	0.082	**Steubenville** (city) Jefferson County
85	2867	0.078	**Marion** (city) Marion County
86	2871	0.078	**Heath** (city) Licking County
87	2887	0.076	**Worthington** (city) Franklin County
88	2914	0.074	**Loveland** (city) Hamilton County
89	2964	0.068	**Vandalia** (city) Montgomery County
90	2979	0.066	**Conneaut** (city) Ashtabula County
91	2990	0.065	**Centerville** (city) Montgomery County
92	3003	0.064	**Lancaster** (city) Fairfield County
93	3013	0.063	**Greenville** (city) Darke County
94	3023	0.062	**Ashland** (city) Ashland County
95	3040	0.061	**Garfield Heights** (city) Cuyahoga County
96	3047	0.060	**Washington Court House** (city) Fayette County
97	3057	0.059	**Amherst** (city) Lorain County
98	3070	0.058	**Sharonville** (city) Hamilton County
99	3078	0.057	**Avon** (city) Lorain County
100	3108	0.053	**Mansfield** (city) Richland County
101	3135	0.051	**Wooster** (city) Wayne County
102	3160	0.049	**Parma** (city) Cuyahoga County
103	3175	0.048	**Bedford** (city) Cuyahoga County
104	3184	0.047	**Ravenna** (city) Portage County
105	3191	0.047	**Bowling Green** (city) Wood County
106	3210	0.045	**Sylvania** (city) Lucas County
107	3219	0.044	**Alliance** (city) Stark County
108	3248	0.042	**Shaker Heights** (city) Cuyahoga County
109	3259	0.042	**Riverside** (city) Montgomery County
110	3264	0.041	**Wilmington** (city) Clinton County
111	3271	0.041	**Englewood** (city) Montgomery County
112	3290	0.039	**Kettering** (city) Montgomery County
113	3310	0.038	**Macedonia** (city) Summit County
114	3317	0.037	**Brunswick** (city) Medina County
115	3332	0.037	**Beavercreek** (city) Greene County
116	3334	0.036	**Brooklyn** (city) Cuyahoga County
117	3340	0.036	**Mason** (city) Warren County
118	3369	0.034	**Austintown** (CDP) Mahoning County
119	3384	0.032	**Twinsburg** (city) Summit County
120	3424	0.030	**Upper Arlington** (city) Franklin County
121	3444	0.028	**Warren** (city) Trumbull County
122	3449	0.028	**Whitehall** (city) Franklin County
123	3500	0.024	**Tallmadge** (city) Summit County
124	3528	0.023	**Monroe** (city) Butler County
125	3536	0.023	**Urbana** (city) Champaign County
126	3556	0.021	**Wickliffe** (city) Lake County
127	3570	0.021	**Broadview Heights** (city) Cuyahoga County
128	3598	0.020	**Bexley** (city) Franklin County
129	3614	0.019	**Niles** (city) Trumbull County
130	3623	0.018	**Cleveland Heights** (city) Cuyahoga County
131	3624	0.018	**Galion** (city) Crawford County
132	3674	0.016	**Canton** (city) Stark County
133	3710	0.014	**Bucyrus** (city) Crawford County
134	3713	0.014	**Trotwood** (city) Montgomery County
135	3714	0.014	**Beachwood** (city) Cuyahoga County
136	3716	0.014	**Xenia** (city) Greene County
137	3722	0.014	**Blue Ash** (city) Hamilton County
138	3729	0.013	**Montgomery** (city) Hamilton County
139	3747	0.013	**North Royalton** (city) Cuyahoga County
140	3764	0.012	**Bedford Heights** (city) Cuyahoga County
141	3781	0.011	**Middleburg Heights** (city) Cuyahoga County
142	3782	0.011	**Springdale** (city) Hamilton County
143	3829	0.009	**Fairborn** (city) Greene County
144	3832	0.009	**Mayfield Heights** (city) Cuyahoga County
145	3842	0.009	**Lebanon** (city) Warren County
146	3873	0.008	**Richmond Heights** (city) Cuyahoga County
147	3876	0.007	**East Cleveland** (city) Cuyahoga County
148	3890	0.007	**Strongsville** (city) Cuyahoga County
149	3894	0.007	**Seven Hills** (city) Cuyahoga County
150	3920	0.006	**Lyndhurst** (city) Cuyahoga County

Note: *The state column ranks the top/bottom 150 places from all places in the state with population of 10,000 or more. The national column ranks the top/bottom 150 places from all places in the country with population of 10,000 or more. Places that are unincorporated were not considered in the rankings. Please refer to the User Guide for additional information.*

Elevation

Top 150 Places Ranked in *Descending* Order

State Rank	Nat'l Rank	Feet	Place
1	426	1,243	**Bellefontaine** (city) Logan County
2	427	1,240	**Mansfield** (city) Richland County
3	438	1,227	**Salem** (city) Columbiana County
4	461	1,197	**North Royalton** (city) Cuyahoga County
5	466	1,191	**Broadview Heights** (city) Cuyahoga County
6	468	1,184	**Beachwood** (city) Cuyahoga County
7	481	1,171	**Wadsworth** (city) Medina County
8	484	1,168	**Brunswick** (city) Medina County
8	484	1,168	**Galion** (city) Crawford County
10	492	1,158	**Alliance** (city) Stark County
10	492	1,158	**North Canton** (city) Stark County
12	505	1,142	**Green** (city) Summit County
13	515	1,135	**Ravenna** (city) Portage County
14	520	1,129	**Aurora** (city) Portage County
14	520	1,129	**Austintown** (CDP) Mahoning County
14	520	1,129	**Streetsboro** (city) Portage County
17	533	1,112	**Boardman** (CDP) Mahoning County
17	533	1,112	**Tallmadge** (city) Summit County
19	556	1,089	**Medina** (city) Medina County
19	556	1,089	**New Franklin** (city) Summit County
19	556	1,089	**Stow** (city) Summit County
22	563	1,086	**Mayfield Heights** (city) Cuyahoga County
23	580	1,066	**Ashland** (city) Ashland County
23	580	1,066	**Hudson** (city) Summit County
25	587	1,063	**Kent** (city) Portage County
26	591	1,060	**Norton** (city) Summit County
27	600	1,056	**Canton** (city) Stark County
28	608	1,050	**Shaker Heights** (city) Cuyahoga County
28	608	1,050	**Steubenville** (city) Jefferson County
28	608	1,050	**Urbana** (city) Champaign County
31	617	1,043	**Greenville** (city) Darke County
32	624	1,040	**Bedford Heights** (city) Cuyahoga County
32	624	1,040	**Solon** (city) Cuyahoga County
34	628	1,037	**Warrensville Heights** (city) Cuyahoga County
35	635	1,033	**Lyndhurst** (city) Cuyahoga County
36	649	1,027	**Cuyahoga Falls** (city) Summit County
36	649	1,027	**University Heights** (city) Cuyahoga County
38	660	1,020	**Centerville** (city) Montgomery County
39	664	1,017	**Wilmington** (city) Clinton County
40	677	1,007	**Struthers** (city) Mahoning County
41	680	1,004	**Kettering** (city) Montgomery County
41	680	1,004	**Mount Vernon** (city) Knox County
41	680	1,004	**Twinsburg** (city) Summit County
44	691	1,001	**Clayton** (city) Montgomery County
44	691	1,001	**Pataskala** (city) Licking County
46	697	994	**Bucyrus** (city) Crawford County
46	697	994	**Marysville** (city) Union County
46	697	994	**Wooster** (city) Wayne County
49	706	991	**Vandalia** (city) Montgomery County
50	710	988	**Macedonia** (city) Summit County
51	719	981	**Marion** (city) Marion County
52	724	978	**Washington Court House** (city) Fayette County
53	732	974	**Springfield** (city) Clark County
54	739	971	**Barberton** (city) Summit County
55	762	961	**Akron** (city) Summit County
56	764	958	**South Euclid** (city) Cuyahoga County
57	770	955	**Garfield Heights** (city) Cuyahoga County
57	770	955	**Sidney** (city) Shelby County
59	780	948	**Bedford** (city) Cuyahoga County
59	780	948	**Massillon** (city) Stark County
61	793	942	**Cleveland Heights** (city) Cuyahoga County
62	812	935	**Xenia** (city) Greene County
63	816	932	**Hilliard** (city) Franklin County
63	816	932	**Huber Heights** (city) Montgomery County
63	816	932	**Strongsville** (city) Cuyahoga County
66	838	922	**Oxford** (city) Butler County
67	844	919	**Englewood** (city) Montgomery County
68	846	915	**White Oak** (CDP) Hamilton County
69	869	906	**Mack** (CDP) Hamilton County
69	869	906	**Powell** (city) Delaware County
71	880	902	**New Philadelphia** (city) Tuscarawas County
72	889	899	**Bridgetown** (CDP) Hamilton County
72	889	899	**Monfort Heights** (CDP) Hamilton County
74	900	896	**Maple Heights** (city) Cuyahoga County
75	910	892	**Dover** (city) Tuscarawas County
76	913	889	**Brecksville** (city) Cuyahoga County
76	913	889	**Finneytown** (CDP) Hamilton County
78	924	886	**Lancaster** (city) Fairfield County
78	924	886	**Warren** (city) Trumbull County
80	932	883	**Niles** (city) Trumbull County
80	932	883	**Seven Hills** (city) Cuyahoga County
82	940	879	**Lima** (city) Allen County
82	940	879	**Reynoldsburg** (city) Franklin County
84	955	876	**Beavercreek** (city) Greene County
84	955	876	**Piqua** (city) Miami County
86	961	873	**Celina** (city) Mercer County
87	973	869	**Delaware** (city) Delaware County
87	973	869	**Richmond Heights** (city) Cuyahoga County
87	973	869	**Westerville** (city) Franklin County
90	990	863	**Parma** (city) Cuyahoga County
90	990	863	**Worthington** (city) Franklin County
92	999	860	**Heath** (city) Licking County
93	1007	856	**Parma Heights** (city) Cuyahoga County
93	1007	856	**Youngstown** (city) Mahoning County
95	1013	853	**Middleburg Heights** (city) Cuyahoga County
96	1029	846	**Blue Ash** (city) Hamilton County
96	1029	846	**Grove City** (city) Franklin County
98	1037	840	**Dent** (CDP) Hamilton County
98	1037	840	**Pickerington** (city) Fairfield County
100	1050	837	**Fairborn** (city) Greene County
100	1050	837	**Trotwood** (city) Montgomery County
100	1050	837	**Troy** (city) Miami County
103	1055	833	**Forest Park** (city) Hamilton County
103	1055	833	**Newark** (city) Licking County
103	1055	833	**Northbrook** (CDP) Hamilton County
106	1062	830	**Dublin** (city) Franklin County
106	1062	830	**Monroe** (city) Butler County
108	1088	820	**Forestville** (CDP) Hamilton County
109	1100	814	**Cambridge** (city) Guernsey County
109	1100	814	**Upper Arlington** (city) Franklin County
111	1114	807	**Mason** (city) Warren County
112	1131	801	**Montgomery** (city) Hamilton County
113	1140	797	**Brook Park** (city) Cuyahoga County
113	1140	797	**Gahanna** (city) Franklin County
115	1150	794	**Bexley** (city) Franklin County
116	1160	791	**Whitehall** (city) Franklin County
117	1183	781	**Columbus** (city) Franklin County
117	1183	781	**Fostoria** (city) Seneca County
117	1183	781	**Springboro** (city) Warren County
120	1188	778	**Riverside** (city) Montgomery County
120	1188	778	**Van Wert** (city) Van Wert County
122	1195	774	**Coshocton** (city) Coshocton County
122	1195	774	**Findlay** (city) Hancock County
124	1202	771	**Lebanon** (city) Warren County
125	1211	768	**East Liverpool** (city) Columbiana County
126	1223	764	**Brooklyn** (city) Cuyahoga County
126	1223	764	**Wickliffe** (city) Lake County
128	1234	761	**North Olmsted** (city) Cuyahoga County
129	1251	755	**Berea** (city) Cuyahoga County
130	1284	745	**Fairview Park** (city) Cuyahoga County
130	1284	745	**Tiffin** (city) Seneca County
132	1302	738	**Dayton** (city) Montgomery County
132	1302	738	**Elyria** (city) Lorain County
132	1302	738	**Springdale** (city) Hamilton County
135	1330	728	**North Ridgeville** (city) Lorain County
135	1330	728	**Norwalk** (city) Huron County
137	1363	718	**Athens** (city) Athens County
138	1375	715	**West Carrollton** (city) Montgomery County
139	1391	709	**Westlake** (city) Cuyahoga County
140	1403	705	**Miamisburg** (city) Montgomery County
141	1411	702	**Lakewood** (city) Cuyahoga County
142	1435	696	**Circleville** (city) Pickaway County
143	1443	692	**Bowling Green** (city) Wood County
143	1443	692	**Mentor** (city) Lake County
143	1443	692	**Rocky River** (city) Cuyahoga County
146	1453	689	**Amherst** (city) Lorain County
147	1458	686	**East Cleveland** (city) Cuyahoga County
148	1466	682	**Franklin** (city) Warren County
149	1491	676	**Defiance** (city) Defiance County
149	1491	676	**Painesville** (city) Lake County

Note: *The state column ranks the top/bottom 150 places from all places in the state with population of 10,000 or more. The national column ranks the top/bottom 150 places from all places in the country with population of 10,000 or more. Places that are unincorporated were not considered in the rankings. Please refer to the User Guide for additional information.*

Elevation

Top 150 Places Ranked in *Ascending* Order

State Rank	Nat'l Rank	Feet	Place
1	2371	535	**Portsmouth** (city) Scioto County
2	2403	551	**Ironton** (city) Lawrence County
3	2422	561	**Reading** (city) Hamilton County
4	2484	587	**Sharonville** (city) Hamilton County
5	2503	594	**Fairfield** (city) Butler County
5	2503	594	**Sandusky** (city) Erie County
7	2517	597	**Hamilton** (city) Butler County
8	2535	600	**Loveland** (city) Hamilton County
9	2556	604	**Oregon** (city) Lucas County
10	2598	610	**Avon Lake** (city) Lorain County
10	2598	610	**Lorain** (city) Lorain County
10	2598	610	**Toledo** (city) Lucas County
13	2619	614	**Marietta** (city) Washington County
14	2639	617	**Eastlake** (city) Lake County
14	2639	617	**Euclid** (city) Cuyahoga County
16	2665	623	**Willowick** (city) Lake County
17	2682	627	**Cincinnati** (city) Hamilton County
17	2682	627	**Fremont** (city) Sandusky County
19	2714	633	**Bay Village** (city) Cuyahoga County
19	2714	633	**Chillicothe** (city) Ross County
19	2714	633	**Maumee** (city) Lucas County
19	2714	633	**Perrysburg** (city) Wood County
23	2775	650	**Conneaut** (city) Ashtabula County
23	2775	650	**Trenton** (city) Butler County
25	2788	653	**Cleveland** (city) Cuyahoga County
25	2788	653	**Norwood** (city) Hamilton County
27	2802	656	**Middletown** (city) Butler County
28	2808	659	**Willoughby** (city) Lake County
29	2830	666	**Sylvania** (city) Lucas County
30	2844	669	**Ashtabula** (city) Ashtabula County
30	2844	669	**Avon** (city) Lorain County
32	2865	676	**Defiance** (city) Defiance County
32	2865	676	**Painesville** (city) Lake County
32	2865	676	**Zanesville** (city) Muskingum County
35	2889	682	**Franklin** (city) Warren County
36	2902	686	**East Cleveland** (city) Cuyahoga County
37	2910	689	**Amherst** (city) Lorain County
38	2915	692	**Bowling Green** (city) Wood County
38	2915	692	**Mentor** (city) Lake County
38	2915	692	**Rocky River** (city) Cuyahoga County
41	2925	696	**Circleville** (city) Pickaway County
42	2944	702	**Lakewood** (city) Cuyahoga County
43	2957	705	**Miamisburg** (city) Montgomery County
44	2965	709	**Westlake** (city) Cuyahoga County
45	2986	715	**West Carrollton** (city) Montgomery County
46	2993	718	**Athens** (city) Athens County
47	3025	728	**North Ridgeville** (city) Lorain County
47	3025	728	**Norwalk** (city) Huron County
49	3053	738	**Dayton** (city) Montgomery County
49	3053	738	**Elyria** (city) Lorain County
49	3053	738	**Springdale** (city) Hamilton County
52	3078	745	**Fairview Park** (city) Cuyahoga County
52	3078	745	**Tiffin** (city) Seneca County
54	3104	755	**Berea** (city) Cuyahoga County
55	3125	761	**North Olmsted** (city) Cuyahoga County
56	3134	764	**Brooklyn** (city) Cuyahoga County
56	3134	764	**Wickliffe** (city) Lake County
58	3145	768	**East Liverpool** (city) Columbiana County
59	3157	771	**Lebanon** (city) Warren County
60	3166	774	**Coshocton** (city) Coshocton County
60	3166	774	**Findlay** (city) Hancock County
62	3173	778	**Riverside** (city) Montgomery County
62	3173	778	**Van Wert** (city) Van Wert County
64	3180	781	**Columbus** (city) Franklin County
64	3180	781	**Fostoria** (city) Seneca County
64	3180	781	**Springboro** (city) Warren County
67	3205	791	**Whitehall** (city) Franklin County
68	3208	794	**Bexley** (city) Franklin County
69	3218	797	**Brook Park** (city) Cuyahoga County
69	3218	797	**Gahanna** (city) Franklin County
71	3228	801	**Montgomery** (city) Hamilton County
72	3246	807	**Mason** (city) Warren County
73	3259	814	**Cambridge** (city) Guernsey County
73	3259	814	**Upper Arlington** (city) Franklin County
75	3273	820	**Forestville** (CDP) Hamilton County
76	3295	830	**Dublin** (city) Franklin County
76	3295	830	**Monroe** (city) Butler County
78	3306	833	**Forest Park** (city) Hamilton County
78	3306	833	**Newark** (city) Licking County
78	3306	833	**Northbrook** (CDP) Hamilton County
81	3313	837	**Fairborn** (city) Greene County
81	3313	837	**Trotwood** (city) Montgomery County
81	3313	837	**Troy** (city) Miami County
84	3318	840	**Dent** (CDP) Hamilton County
84	3318	840	**Pickerington** (city) Fairfield County
86	3333	846	**Blue Ash** (city) Hamilton County
86	3333	846	**Grove City** (city) Franklin County
88	3347	853	**Middleburg Heights** (city) Cuyahoga County
89	3355	856	**Parma Heights** (city) Cuyahoga County
89	3355	856	**Youngstown** (city) Mahoning County
91	3361	860	**Heath** (city) Licking County
92	3369	863	**Parma** (city) Cuyahoga County
92	3369	863	**Worthington** (city) Franklin County
94	3387	869	**Delaware** (city) Delaware County
94	3387	869	**Richmond Heights** (city) Cuyahoga County
94	3387	869	**Westerville** (city) Franklin County
97	3395	873	**Celina** (city) Mercer County
98	3407	876	**Beavercreek** (city) Greene County
98	3407	876	**Piqua** (city) Miami County
100	3413	879	**Lima** (city) Allen County
100	3413	879	**Reynoldsburg** (city) Franklin County
102	3428	883	**Niles** (city) Trumbull County
102	3428	883	**Seven Hills** (city) Cuyahoga County
104	3436	886	**Lancaster** (city) Fairfield County
104	3436	886	**Warren** (city) Trumbull County
106	3444	889	**Brecksville** (city) Cuyahoga County
106	3444	889	**Finneytown** (CDP) Hamilton County
108	3455	892	**Dover** (city) Tuscarawas County
109	3458	896	**Maple Heights** (city) Cuyahoga County
110	3468	899	**Bridgetown** (CDP) Hamilton County
110	3468	899	**Monfort Heights** (CDP) Hamilton County
112	3479	902	**New Philadelphia** (city) Tuscarawas County
113	3488	906	**Mack** (CDP) Hamilton County
113	3488	906	**Powell** (city) Delaware County
115	3516	915	**White Oak** (CDP) Hamilton County
116	3522	919	**Englewood** (city) Montgomery County
117	3524	922	**Oxford** (city) Butler County
118	3544	932	**Hilliard** (city) Franklin County
118	3544	932	**Huber Heights** (city) Montgomery County
118	3544	932	**Strongsville** (city) Cuyahoga County
121	3552	935	**Xenia** (city) Greene County
122	3562	942	**Cleveland Heights** (city) Cuyahoga County
123	3579	948	**Bedford** (city) Cuyahoga County
123	3579	948	**Massillon** (city) Stark County
125	3590	955	**Garfield Heights** (city) Cuyahoga County
125	3590	955	**Sidney** (city) Shelby County
127	3598	958	**South Euclid** (city) Cuyahoga County
128	3604	961	**Akron** (city) Summit County
129	3620	971	**Barberton** (city) Summit County
130	3629	974	**Springfield** (city) Clark County
131	3636	978	**Washington Court House** (city) Fayette County
132	3644	981	**Marion** (city) Marion County
133	3654	988	**Macedonia** (city) Summit County
134	3658	991	**Vandalia** (city) Montgomery County
135	3662	994	**Bucyrus** (city) Crawford County
135	3662	994	**Marysville** (city) Union County
135	3662	994	**Wooster** (city) Wayne County
138	3673	1,001	**Clayton** (city) Montgomery County
138	3673	1,001	**Pataskala** (city) Licking County
140	3677	1,004	**Kettering** (city) Montgomery County
140	3677	1,004	**Mount Vernon** (city) Knox County
140	3677	1,004	**Twinsburg** (city) Summit County
143	3688	1,007	**Struthers** (city) Mahoning County
144	3698	1,017	**Wilmington** (city) Clinton County
145	3704	1,020	**Centerville** (city) Montgomery County
146	3713	1,027	**Cuyahoga Falls** (city) Summit County
146	3713	1,027	**University Heights** (city) Cuyahoga County
148	3726	1,033	**Lyndhurst** (city) Cuyahoga County
149	3733	1,037	**Warrensville Heights** (city) Cuyahoga County
150	3740	1,040	**Bedford Heights** (city) Cuyahoga County

Note: *The state column ranks the top/bottom 150 places from all places in the state with population of 10,000 or more. The national column ranks the top/bottom 150 places from all places in the country with population of 10,000 or more. Places that are unincorporated were not considered in the rankings. Please refer to the User Guide for additional information.*

Population

Top 150 Places Ranked in *Descending* Order

State Rank	Nat'l Rank	Number	Place
1	19	787,033	**Columbus** (city) Franklin County
2	52	396,815	**Cleveland** (city) Cuyahoga County
3	70	296,943	**Cincinnati** (city) Hamilton County
4	75	287,208	**Toledo** (city) Lucas County
5	123	199,110	**Akron** (city) Summit County
6	189	141,527	**Dayton** (city) Montgomery County
7	418	81,601	**Parma** (city) Cuyahoga County
8	497	73,007	**Canton** (city) Stark County
9	547	66,982	**Youngstown** (city) Mahoning County
10	590	64,097	**Lorain** (city) Lorain County
11	607	62,477	**Hamilton** (city) Butler County
12	637	60,608	**Springfield** (city) Clark County
13	719	56,163	**Kettering** (city) Montgomery County
14	748	54,533	**Elyria** (city) Lorain County
15	793	52,131	**Lakewood** (city) Cuyahoga County
16	840	49,652	**Cuyahoga Falls** (city) Summit County
17	857	48,920	**Euclid** (city) Cuyahoga County
18	865	48,694	**Middletown** (city) Butler County
19	889	47,821	**Mansfield** (city) Richland County
20	899	47,573	**Newark** (city) Licking County
21	910	47,159	**Mentor** (city) Lake County
22	929	46,121	**Cleveland Heights** (city) Cuyahoga County
23	947	45,193	**Beavercreek** (city) Greene County
24	957	44,750	**Strongsville** (city) Cuyahoga County
25	1017	42,510	**Fairfield** (city) Butler County
26	1031	41,751	**Dublin** (city) Franklin County
27	1039	41,557	**Warren** (city) Trumbull County
28	1053	41,202	**Findlay** (city) Hancock County
29	1125	38,780	**Lancaster** (city) Fairfield County
30	1126	38,771	**Lima** (city) Allen County
31	1148	38,101	**Huber Heights** (city) Montgomery County
32	1192	36,837	**Marion** (city) Marion County
33	1224	36,120	**Westerville** (city) Franklin County
34	1233	35,893	**Reynoldsburg** (city) Franklin County
35	1255	35,575	**Grove City** (city) Franklin County
36	1263	35,376	**Boardman** (CDP) Mahoning County
37	1285	34,837	**Stow** (city) Summit County
38	1287	34,753	**Delaware** (city) Delaware County
39	1311	34,255	**Brunswick** (city) Medina County
40	1331	33,771	**Upper Arlington** (city) Franklin County
41	1361	33,248	**Gahanna** (city) Franklin County
42	1390	32,729	**Westlake** (city) Cuyahoga County
43	1391	32,718	**North Olmsted** (city) Cuyahoga County
44	1409	32,352	**Fairborn** (city) Greene County
45	1414	32,149	**Massillon** (city) Stark County
46	1480	30,712	**Mason** (city) Warren County
47	1501	30,444	**North Royalton** (city) Cuyahoga County
48	1525	30,028	**Bowling Green** (city) Wood County
49	1549	29,677	**Austintown** (CDP) Mahoning County
50	1565	29,465	**North Ridgeville** (city) Lorain County
51	1611	28,904	**Kent** (city) Portage County
52	1615	28,849	**Garfield Heights** (city) Cuyahoga County
53	1637	28,448	**Shaker Heights** (city) Cuyahoga County
54	1639	28,435	**Hilliard** (city) Franklin County
55	1768	26,678	**Medina** (city) Medina County
56	1780	26,550	**Barberton** (city) Summit County
57	1814	26,119	**Wooster** (city) Wayne County
58	1838	25,793	**Sandusky** (city) Erie County
59	1842	25,719	**Xenia** (city) Greene County
60	1845	25,699	**Green** (city) Summit County
61	1866	25,487	**Zanesville** (city) Muskingum County
62	1887	25,201	**Riverside** (city) Montgomery County
63	1900	25,058	**Troy** (city) Miami County
64	1948	24,431	**Trotwood** (city) Montgomery County
65	1994	23,999	**Centerville** (city) Montgomery County
66	2011	23,832	**Athens** (city) Athens County
67	2064	23,348	**Solon** (city) Cuyahoga County
68	2076	23,138	**Maple Heights** (city) Cuyahoga County
69	2147	22,581	**Avon Lake** (city) Lorain County
70	2165	22,322	**Alliance** (city) Stark County
71	2167	22,295	**South Euclid** (city) Cuyahoga County
72	2168	22,268	**Willoughby** (city) Lake County
73	2169	22,262	**Hudson** (city) Summit County
74	2182	22,094	**Marysville** (city) Union County
75	2206	21,901	**Chillicothe** (city) Ross County
76	2237	21,567	**Wadsworth** (city) Medina County
77	2261	21,371	**Oxford** (city) Butler County
78	2278	21,229	**Sidney** (city) Shelby County
79	2284	21,193	**Avon** (city) Lorain County
80	2330	20,718	**Parma Heights** (city) Cuyahoga County
81	2341	20,623	**Perrysburg** (city) Wood County
82	2353	20,522	**Piqua** (city) Miami County
83	2370	20,362	**Ashland** (city) Ashland County
84	2384	20,291	**Oregon** (city) Lucas County
85	2395	20,226	**Portsmouth** (city) Scioto County
86	2399	20,213	**Rocky River** (city) Cuyahoga County
87	2400	20,181	**Miamisburg** (city) Montgomery County
88	2416	20,033	**Lebanon** (city) Warren County
89	2473	19,563	**Painesville** (city) Lake County
90	2498	19,400	**Broadview Heights** (city) Cuyahoga County
91	2516	19,266	**Niles** (city) Trumbull County
92	2525	19,212	**Brook Park** (city) Cuyahoga County
93	2526	19,207	**Norwood** (city) Hamilton County
94	2534	19,167	**White Oak** (CDP) Hamilton County
95	2536	19,155	**Mayfield Heights** (city) Cuyahoga County
96	2542	19,124	**Ashtabula** (city) Ashtabula County
97	2549	19,093	**Berea** (city) Cuyahoga County
98	2565	18,965	**Sylvania** (city) Lucas County
99	2593	18,795	**Twinsburg** (city) Summit County
100	2600	18,720	**Forest Park** (city) Hamilton County
101	2611	18,659	**Steubenville** (city) Jefferson County
102	2623	18,577	**Eastlake** (city) Lake County
103	2669	18,291	**Pickerington** (city) Fairfield County
104	2713	18,062	**Whitehall** (city) Franklin County
105	2729	17,963	**Tiffin** (city) Seneca County
106	2743	17,843	**East Cleveland** (city) Cuyahoga County
107	2790	17,537	**Tallmadge** (city) Summit County
108	2801	17,488	**North Canton** (city) Stark County
109	2814	17,409	**Springboro** (city) Warren County
110	2835	17,288	**New Philadelphia** (city) Tuscarawas County
111	2872	17,012	**Norwalk** (city) Huron County
112	2876	16,990	**Mount Vernon** (city) Knox County
113	2894	16,826	**Fairview Park** (city) Cuyahoga County
114	2912	16,734	**Fremont** (city) Sandusky County
115	2947	16,494	**Defiance** (city) Defiance County
116	3031	16,028	**Streetsboro** (city) Portage County
117	3049	15,946	**Middleburg Heights** (city) Cuyahoga County
118	3113	15,651	**Bay Village** (city) Cuyahoga County
119	3133	15,548	**Aurora** (city) Portage County
120	3196	15,246	**Vandalia** (city) Montgomery County
121	3259	14,962	**Pataskala** (city) Licking County
122	3385	14,407	**Bridgetown** (CDP) Hamilton County
123	3410	14,286	**Maumee** (city) Lucas County
124	3423	14,227	**New Franklin** (city) Summit County
125	3433	14,192	**Washington Court House** (city) Fayette County
126	3438	14,171	**Willowick** (city) Lake County
127	3458	14,085	**Marietta** (city) Washington County
128	3478	14,001	**Lyndhurst** (city) Cuyahoga County
129	3562	13,656	**Brecksville** (city) Cuyahoga County
130	3585	13,575	**Worthington** (city) Franklin County
131	3591	13,560	**Sharonville** (city) Hamilton County
132	3597	13,542	**Warrensville Heights** (city) Cuyahoga County
133	3599	13,539	**University Heights** (city) Cuyahoga County
134	3618	13,465	**Englewood** (city) Montgomery County
135	3624	13,441	**Fostoria** (city) Seneca County
136	3643	13,370	**Bellefontaine** (city) Logan County
137	3657	13,314	**Circleville** (city) Pickaway County
138	3677	13,227	**Greenville** (city) Darke County
139	3680	13,209	**Clayton** (city) Montgomery County
140	3700	13,143	**West Carrollton** (city) Montgomery County
141	3715	13,074	**Bedford** (city) Cuyahoga County
142	3724	13,057	**Bexley** (city) Franklin County
143	3770	12,841	**Conneaut** (city) Ashtabula County
144	3773	12,826	**Dover** (city) Tuscarawas County
145	3788	12,750	**Wickliffe** (city) Lake County
146	3792	12,741	**Finneytown** (CDP) Hamilton County
147	3847	12,520	**Wilmington** (city) Clinton County
148	3861	12,442	**Monroe** (city) Butler County
149	3880	12,362	**Bucyrus** (city) Crawford County
150	3908	12,303	**Salem** (city) Columbiana County

***Note:** The state column ranks the top/bottom 150 places from all places in the state with population of 10,000 or more. The national column ranks the top/bottom 150 places from all places in the country with population of 10,000 or more. Places that are unincorporated were not considered in the rankings. Please refer to the User Guide for additional information.*

Population

Top 150 Places Ranked in *Ascending* Order

State Rank	Nat'l Rank	Number	Place
1	93	10,251	**Montgomery** (city) Hamilton County
2	110	10,310	**Heath** (city) Licking County
3	139	10,385	**Reading** (city) Hamilton County
4	144	10,400	**Celina** (city) Mercer County
5	176	10,497	**Dent** (CDP) Hamilton County
6	184	10,512	**Galion** (city) Crawford County
7	193	10,532	**Forestville** (CDP) Hamilton County
8	198	10,546	**Richmond Heights** (city) Cuyahoga County
9	215	10,594	**Vermilion** (city) Lorain County
10	231	10,635	**Cambridge** (city) Guernsey County
11	248	10,668	**Northbrook** (CDP) Hamilton County
12	263	10,713	**Struthers** (city) Mahoning County
13	273	10,751	**Bedford Heights** (city) Cuyahoga County
14	308	10,846	**Van Wert** (city) Van Wert County
15	397	11,129	**Ironton** (city) Lawrence County
16	407	11,169	**Brooklyn** (city) Cuyahoga County
17	413	11,188	**Macedonia** (city) Summit County
18	415	11,195	**East Liverpool** (city) Columbiana County
19	424	11,216	**Coshocton** (city) Coshocton County
20	429	11,223	**Springdale** (city) Hamilton County
21	531	11,500	**Powell** (city) Delaware County
22	565	11,585	**Mack** (CDP) Hamilton County
23	598	11,724	**Ravenna** (city) Portage County
24	606	11,771	**Franklin** (city) Warren County
25	612	11,793	**Urbana** (city) Champaign County
26	617	11,804	**Seven Hills** (city) Cuyahoga County
27	636	11,869	**Trenton** (city) Butler County
28	654	11,948	**Monfort Heights** (CDP) Hamilton County
29	658	11,953	**Beachwood** (city) Cuyahoga County
30	676	12,021	**Amherst** (city) Lorain County
31	695	12,081	**Loveland** (city) Hamilton County
32	697	12,085	**Norton** (city) Summit County
33	705	12,114	**Blue Ash** (city) Hamilton County
34	748	12,303	**Salem** (city) Columbiana County
35	776	12,362	**Bucyrus** (city) Crawford County
36	793	12,442	**Monroe** (city) Butler County
37	809	12,520	**Wilmington** (city) Clinton County
38	864	12,741	**Finneytown** (CDP) Hamilton County
39	868	12,750	**Wickliffe** (city) Lake County
40	883	12,826	**Dover** (city) Tuscarawas County
41	886	12,841	**Conneaut** (city) Ashtabula County
42	932	13,057	**Bexley** (city) Franklin County
43	941	13,074	**Bedford** (city) Cuyahoga County
44	956	13,143	**West Carrollton** (city) Montgomery County
45	976	13,209	**Clayton** (city) Montgomery County
46	979	13,227	**Greenville** (city) Darke County
47	999	13,314	**Circleville** (city) Pickaway County
48	1013	13,370	**Bellefontaine** (city) Logan County
49	1032	13,441	**Fostoria** (city) Seneca County
50	1038	13,465	**Englewood** (city) Montgomery County
51	1057	13,539	**University Heights** (city) Cuyahoga County
52	1058	13,542	**Warrensville Heights** (city) Cuyahoga County
53	1065	13,560	**Sharonville** (city) Hamilton County
54	1071	13,575	**Worthington** (city) Franklin County
55	1092	13,656	**Brecksville** (city) Cuyahoga County
56	1178	14,001	**Lyndhurst** (city) Cuyahoga County
57	1198	14,085	**Marietta** (city) Washington County
58	1217	14,171	**Willowick** (city) Lake County
59	1222	14,192	**Washington Court House** (city) Fayette County
60	1233	14,227	**New Franklin** (city) Summit County
61	1246	14,286	**Maumee** (city) Lucas County
62	1270	14,407	**Bridgetown** (CDP) Hamilton County
63	1397	14,962	**Pataskala** (city) Licking County
64	1460	15,246	**Vandalia** (city) Montgomery County
65	1523	15,548	**Aurora** (city) Portage County
66	1542	15,651	**Bay Village** (city) Cuyahoga County
67	1606	15,946	**Middleburg Heights** (city) Cuyahoga County
68	1625	16,028	**Streetsboro** (city) Portage County
69	1709	16,494	**Defiance** (city) Defiance County
70	1744	16,734	**Fremont** (city) Sandusky County
71	1762	16,826	**Fairview Park** (city) Cuyahoga County
72	1780	16,990	**Mount Vernon** (city) Knox County
73	1784	17,012	**Norwalk** (city) Huron County
74	1820	17,288	**New Philadelphia** (city) Tuscarawas County
75	1842	17,409	**Springboro** (city) Warren County
76	1855	17,488	**North Canton** (city) Stark County
77	1866	17,537	**Tallmadge** (city) Summit County
78	1913	17,843	**East Cleveland** (city) Cuyahoga County
79	1927	17,963	**Tiffin** (city) Seneca County
80	1942	18,062	**Whitehall** (city) Franklin County
81	1987	18,291	**Pickerington** (city) Fairfield County
82	2033	18,577	**Eastlake** (city) Lake County
83	2045	18,659	**Steubenville** (city) Jefferson County
84	2055	18,720	**Forest Park** (city) Hamilton County
85	2063	18,795	**Twinsburg** (city) Summit County
86	2091	18,965	**Sylvania** (city) Lucas County
87	2107	19,093	**Berea** (city) Cuyahoga County
88	2114	19,124	**Ashtabula** (city) Ashtabula County
89	2120	19,155	**Mayfield Heights** (city) Cuyahoga County
90	2122	19,167	**White Oak** (CDP) Hamilton County
91	2130	19,207	**Norwood** (city) Hamilton County
92	2131	19,212	**Brook Park** (city) Cuyahoga County
93	2140	19,266	**Niles** (city) Trumbull County
94	2158	19,400	**Broadview Heights** (city) Cuyahoga County
95	2183	19,563	**Painesville** (city) Lake County
96	2240	20,033	**Lebanon** (city) Warren County
97	2256	20,181	**Miamisburg** (city) Montgomery County
98	2257	20,213	**Rocky River** (city) Cuyahoga County
99	2260	20,226	**Portsmouth** (city) Scioto County
100	2271	20,291	**Oregon** (city) Lucas County
101	2286	20,362	**Ashland** (city) Ashland County
102	2303	20,522	**Piqua** (city) Miami County
103	2315	20,623	**Perrysburg** (city) Wood County
104	2326	20,718	**Parma Heights** (city) Cuyahoga County
105	2372	21,193	**Avon** (city) Lorain County
106	2378	21,229	**Sidney** (city) Shelby County
107	2395	21,371	**Oxford** (city) Butler County
108	2419	21,567	**Wadsworth** (city) Medina County
109	2450	21,901	**Chillicothe** (city) Ross County
110	2474	22,094	**Marysville** (city) Union County
111	2487	22,262	**Hudson** (city) Summit County
112	2488	22,268	**Willoughby** (city) Lake County
113	2489	22,295	**South Euclid** (city) Cuyahoga County
114	2491	22,322	**Alliance** (city) Stark County
115	2509	22,581	**Avon Lake** (city) Lorain County
116	2580	23,138	**Maple Heights** (city) Cuyahoga County
117	2592	23,348	**Solon** (city) Cuyahoga County
118	2645	23,832	**Athens** (city) Athens County
119	2662	23,999	**Centerville** (city) Montgomery County
120	2708	24,431	**Trotwood** (city) Montgomery County
121	2756	25,058	**Troy** (city) Miami County
122	2769	25,201	**Riverside** (city) Montgomery County
123	2790	25,487	**Zanesville** (city) Muskingum County
124	2811	25,699	**Green** (city) Summit County
125	2814	25,719	**Xenia** (city) Greene County
126	2818	25,793	**Sandusky** (city) Erie County
127	2842	26,119	**Wooster** (city) Wayne County
128	2876	26,550	**Barberton** (city) Summit County
129	2888	26,678	**Medina** (city) Medina County
130	3017	28,435	**Hilliard** (city) Franklin County
131	3019	28,448	**Shaker Heights** (city) Cuyahoga County
132	3041	28,849	**Garfield Heights** (city) Cuyahoga County
133	3045	28,904	**Kent** (city) Portage County
134	3091	29,465	**North Ridgeville** (city) Lorain County
135	3107	29,677	**Austintown** (CDP) Mahoning County
136	3131	30,028	**Bowling Green** (city) Wood County
137	3155	30,444	**North Royalton** (city) Cuyahoga County
138	3176	30,712	**Mason** (city) Warren County
139	3242	32,149	**Massillon** (city) Stark County
140	3247	32,352	**Fairborn** (city) Greene County
141	3265	32,718	**North Olmsted** (city) Cuyahoga County
142	3266	32,729	**Westlake** (city) Cuyahoga County
143	3295	33,248	**Gahanna** (city) Franklin County
144	3325	33,771	**Upper Arlington** (city) Franklin County
145	3345	34,255	**Brunswick** (city) Medina County
146	3369	34,753	**Delaware** (city) Delaware County
147	3371	34,837	**Stow** (city) Summit County
148	3393	35,376	**Boardman** (CDP) Mahoning County
149	3401	35,575	**Grove City** (city) Franklin County
150	3423	35,893	**Reynoldsburg** (city) Franklin County

Note: *The state column ranks the top/bottom 150 places from all places in the state with population of 10,000 or more. The national column ranks the top/bottom 150 places from all places in the country with population of 10,000 or more. Places that are unincorporated were not considered in the rankings. Please refer to the User Guide for additional information.*

Population Growth

Top 150 Places Ranked in *Descending* Order

State Rank	Nat'l Rank	Percent	Place
1	19	549.3	**New Franklin** (city) Summit County
2	195	86.8	**Pickerington** (city) Fairfield County
3	202	85.2	**Avon** (city) Lorain County
4	206	84.1	**Powell** (city) Delaware County
5	241	74.4	**Monroe** (city) Butler County
6	451	46.0	**Pataskala** (city) Licking County
7	466	44.4	**White Oak** (CDP) Hamilton County
8	521	40.6	**Springboro** (city) Warren County
9	546	39.5	**Mason** (city) Warren County
10	566	38.6	**Marysville** (city) Union County
11	581	37.9	**Dent** (CDP) Hamilton County
12	586	37.7	**Delaware** (city) Delaware County
13	623	35.7	**Trenton** (city) Butler County
14	678	33.0	**Dublin** (city) Franklin County
15	704	31.9	**North Ridgeville** (city) Lorain County
16	716	31.4	**Grove City** (city) Franklin County
17	736	30.2	**Streetsboro** (city) Portage County
18	904	24.4	**Avon Lake** (city) Lorain County
19	1014	21.7	**Perrysburg** (city) Wood County
20	1023	21.5	**Broadview Heights** (city) Cuyahoga County
21	1033	21.3	**Macedonia** (city) Summit County
22	1052	20.9	**Heath** (city) Licking County
23	1134	19.0	**Beavercreek** (city) Greene County
24	1161	18.2	**Mount Vernon** (city) Knox County
25	1167	18.1	**Lebanon** (city) Warren County
26	1202	17.4	**Hilliard** (city) Franklin County
27	1225	17.0	**Wadsworth** (city) Medina County
28	1373	14.7	**Aurora** (city) Portage County
29	1423	13.9	**Troy** (city) Miami County
30	1536	12.6	**Green** (city) Summit County
31	1585	11.9	**Reynoldsburg** (city) Franklin County
32	1595	11.8	**Painesville** (city) Lake County
33	1602	11.7	**Athens** (city) Athens County
34	1681	10.6	**Columbus** (city) Franklin County
35	1689	10.5	**Twinsburg** (city) Summit County
36	1733	10.1	**Englewood** (city) Montgomery County
37	1770	9.7	**Lancaster** (city) Fairfield County
38	1922	8.4	**Stow** (city) Summit County
39	2078	7.1	**Solon** (city) Cuyahoga County
40	2093	7.0	**Riverside** (city) Montgomery County
40	2093	7.0	**Tallmadge** (city) Summit County
42	2127	6.8	**North Canton** (city) Stark County
43	2174	6.4	**Xenia** (city) Greene County
44	2187	6.3	**North Royalton** (city) Cuyahoga County
45	2204	6.2	**Springdale** (city) Hamilton County
46	2218	6.1	**Medina** (city) Medina County
47	2264	5.7	**Findlay** (city) Hancock County
48	2324	5.3	**Wooster** (city) Wayne County
49	2392	5.0	**Dover** (city) Tuscarawas County
49	2392	5.0	**Sidney** (city) Shelby County
49	2392	5.0	**Wilmington** (city) Clinton County
52	2407	4.9	**Norton** (city) Summit County
53	2429	4.8	**Norwalk** (city) Huron County
53	2429	4.8	**Oregon** (city) Lucas County
55	2481	4.4	**Vandalia** (city) Montgomery County
56	2501	4.3	**Marion** (city) Marion County
57	2515	4.2	**Centerville** (city) Montgomery County
58	2638	3.6	**Kent** (city) Portage County
58	2638	3.6	**Miamisburg** (city) Montgomery County
60	2669	3.5	**Loveland** (city) Hamilton County
61	2705	3.3	**Franklin** (city) Warren County
62	2723	3.2	**Westlake** (city) Cuyahoga County
63	2791	2.9	**Conneaut** (city) Ashtabula County
63	2791	2.9	**Hamilton** (city) Butler County
65	2812	2.8	**Newark** (city) Licking County
66	2846	2.6	**Brunswick** (city) Medina County
66	2846	2.6	**Massillon** (city) Stark County
66	2846	2.6	**Middleburg Heights** (city) Cuyahoga County
69	2923	2.3	**Bellefontaine** (city) Logan County
69	2923	2.3	**Westerville** (city) Franklin County
71	2993	2.0	**Brecksville** (city) Cuyahoga County
71	2993	2.0	**Strongsville** (city) Cuyahoga County
73	3013	1.9	**Amherst** (city) Lorain County
73	3013	1.9	**Gahanna** (city) Franklin County
75	3071	1.6	**Sylvania** (city) Lucas County
76	3092	1.5	**Urbana** (city) Champaign County
76	3092	1.5	**Van Wert** (city) Van Wert County
78	3112	1.4	**New Philadelphia** (city) Tuscarawas County
79	3133	1.3	**Bowling Green** (city) Wood County
80	3190	1.0	**Fairfield** (city) Butler County
81	3211	0.9	**Celina** (city) Mercer County
81	3211	0.9	**Fairborn** (city) Greene County
81	3211	0.9	**Montgomery** (city) Hamilton County
81	3211	0.9	**Salem** (city) Columbiana County
85	3281	0.6	**Berea** (city) Cuyahoga County
85	3281	0.6	**Cuyahoga Falls** (city) Summit County
87	3296	0.5	**Chillicothe** (city) Ross County
88	3342	0.3	**Upper Arlington** (city) Franklin County
89	3367	0.2	**Defiance** (city) Defiance County
90	3468	-0.3	**Huber Heights** (city) Montgomery County
91	3487	-0.4	**Ravenna** (city) Portage County
91	3487	-0.4	**Zanesville** (city) Muskingum County
93	3507	-0.5	**Greenville** (city) Darke County
94	3550	-0.7	**Ironton** (city) Lawrence County
95	3569	-0.8	**Hudson** (city) Summit County
96	3588	-0.9	**Tiffin** (city) Seneca County
97	3607	-1.0	**Bridgetown** (CDP) Hamilton County
97	3607	-1.0	**Clayton** (city) Montgomery County
97	3607	-1.0	**Mack** (CDP) Hamilton County
97	3607	-1.0	**Monfort Heights** (CDP) Hamilton County
97	3607	-1.0	**Piqua** (city) Miami County
97	3607	-1.0	**Washington Court House** (city) Fayette County
97	3607	-1.0	**West Carrollton** (city) Montgomery County
104	3794	-1.1	**Bexley** (city) Franklin County
105	3806	-1.2	**Mayfield Heights** (city) Cuyahoga County
106	3820	-1.3	**Circleville** (city) Pickaway County
106	3820	-1.3	**Willowick** (city) Lake County
108	3866	-1.6	**Willoughby** (city) Lake County
109	3897	-1.8	**Sharonville** (city) Hamilton County
110	3913	-1.9	**Beachwood** (city) Cuyahoga County
110	3913	-1.9	**Steubenville** (city) Jefferson County
112	3977	-2.3	**Kettering** (city) Montgomery County
112	3977	-2.3	**Seven Hills** (city) Cuyahoga County
114	4004	-2.5	**Elyria** (city) Lorain County
114	4004	-2.5	**Rocky River** (city) Cuyahoga County
116	4015	-2.6	**Oxford** (city) Butler County
117	4028	-2.7	**Bay Village** (city) Cuyahoga County
118	4064	-3.0	**Marietta** (city) Washington County
118	4064	-3.0	**Vermilion** (city) Lorain County
120	4079	-3.1	**Mansfield** (city) Richland County
121	4092	-3.2	**Blue Ash** (city) Hamilton County
122	4099	-3.3	**Lima** (city) Allen County
122	4099	-3.3	**Portsmouth** (city) Scioto County
122	4099	-3.3	**Shaker Heights** (city) Cuyahoga County
125	4128	-3.5	**Fostoria** (city) Seneca County
126	4136	-3.6	**Brooklyn** (city) Cuyahoga County
126	4136	-3.6	**Richmond Heights** (city) Cuyahoga County
128	4149	-3.7	**Fremont** (city) Sandusky County
128	4149	-3.7	**Northbrook** (CDP) Hamilton County
130	4164	-3.8	**Forest Park** (city) Hamilton County
131	4172	-3.9	**Worthington** (city) Franklin County
132	4180	-4.0	**Alliance** (city) Stark County
132	4180	-4.0	**Coshocton** (city) Coshocton County
134	4191	-4.1	**Forestville** (CDP) Hamilton County
134	4191	-4.1	**North Olmsted** (city) Cuyahoga County
136	4202	-4.2	**Ashland** (city) Ashland County
136	4202	-4.2	**Fairview Park** (city) Cuyahoga County
138	4215	-4.3	**Parma Heights** (city) Cuyahoga County
138	4215	-4.3	**University Heights** (city) Cuyahoga County
140	4264	-4.7	**Parma** (city) Cuyahoga County
141	4275	-4.8	**Barberton** (city) Summit County
142	4287	-4.9	**Boardman** (CDP) Mahoning County
143	4321	-5.3	**South Euclid** (city) Cuyahoga County
144	4326	-5.4	**Wickliffe** (city) Lake County
145	4333	-5.5	**Bedford Heights** (city) Cuyahoga County
146	4341	-5.6	**Finneytown** (CDP) Hamilton County
146	4341	-5.6	**Middletown** (city) Butler County
148	4363	-5.9	**Whitehall** (city) Franklin County
149	4373	-6.1	**Garfield Heights** (city) Cuyahoga County
150	4382	-6.2	**Austintown** (CDP) Mahoning County

***Note:** The state column ranks the top/bottom 150 places from all places in the state with population of 10,000 or more. The national column ranks the top/bottom 150 places from all places in the country with population of 10,000 or more. Places that are unincorporated were not considered in the rankings. Please refer to the User Guide for additional information.*

Population Growth

Top 150 Places Ranked in *Ascending* Order

State Rank	Nat'l Rank	Percent	Place
1	10	-34.4	**East Cleveland** (city) Cuyahoga County
2	37	-18.3	**Youngstown** (city) Mahoning County
3	46	-17.1	**Cleveland** (city) Cuyahoga County
4	57	-14.8	**Dayton** (city) Montgomery County
5	61	-14.5	**East Liverpool** (city) Columbiana County
6	89	-11.5	**Maple Heights** (city) Cuyahoga County
7	92	-11.4	**Norwood** (city) Hamilton County
8	94	-11.3	**Warren** (city) Trumbull County
9	98	-10.9	**Trotwood** (city) Montgomery County
10	106	-10.4	**Cincinnati** (city) Hamilton County
10	106	-10.4	**Warrensville Heights** (city) Cuyahoga County
12	124	-9.7	**Canton** (city) Stark County
13	133	-9.5	**Brook Park** (city) Cuyahoga County
14	147	-8.9	**Struthers** (city) Mahoning County
15	149	-8.8	**Ashtabula** (city) Ashtabula County
16	156	-8.4	**Lyndhurst** (city) Cuyahoga County
16	156	-8.4	**Toledo** (city) Lucas County
18	163	-8.3	**Akron** (city) Summit County
18	163	-8.3	**Eastlake** (city) Lake County
20	176	-8.0	**Bedford** (city) Cuyahoga County
20	176	-8.0	**Lakewood** (city) Cuyahoga County
20	176	-8.0	**Niles** (city) Trumbull County
20	176	-8.0	**Reading** (city) Hamilton County
24	190	-7.7	**Cambridge** (city) Guernsey County
24	190	-7.7	**Cleveland Heights** (city) Cuyahoga County
26	207	-7.4	**Sandusky** (city) Erie County
27	209	-7.3	**Galion** (city) Crawford County
27	209	-7.3	**Springfield** (city) Clark County
29	214	-7.2	**Euclid** (city) Cuyahoga County
30	243	-6.6	**Lorain** (city) Lorain County
31	250	-6.5	**Bucyrus** (city) Crawford County
32	265	-6.2	**Austintown** (CDP) Mahoning County
32	265	-6.2	**Maumee** (city) Lucas County
32	265	-6.2	**Mentor** (city) Lake County
35	275	-6.1	**Garfield Heights** (city) Cuyahoga County
36	286	-5.9	**Whitehall** (city) Franklin County
37	305	-5.6	**Finneytown** (CDP) Hamilton County
37	305	-5.6	**Middletown** (city) Butler County
39	316	-5.5	**Bedford Heights** (city) Cuyahoga County
40	324	-5.4	**Wickliffe** (city) Lake County
41	331	-5.3	**South Euclid** (city) Cuyahoga County
42	354	-4.9	**Boardman** (CDP) Mahoning County
43	370	-4.8	**Barberton** (city) Summit County
44	382	-4.7	**Parma** (city) Cuyahoga County
45	431	-4.3	**Parma Heights** (city) Cuyahoga County
45	431	-4.3	**University Heights** (city) Cuyahoga County
47	442	-4.2	**Ashland** (city) Ashland County
47	442	-4.2	**Fairview Park** (city) Cuyahoga County
49	455	-4.1	**Forestville** (CDP) Hamilton County
49	455	-4.1	**North Olmsted** (city) Cuyahoga County
51	466	-4.0	**Alliance** (city) Stark County
51	466	-4.0	**Coshocton** (city) Coshocton County
53	477	-3.9	**Worthington** (city) Franklin County
54	485	-3.8	**Forest Park** (city) Hamilton County
55	493	-3.7	**Fremont** (city) Sandusky County
55	493	-3.7	**Northbrook** (CDP) Hamilton County
57	508	-3.6	**Brooklyn** (city) Cuyahoga County
57	508	-3.6	**Richmond Heights** (city) Cuyahoga County
59	521	-3.5	**Fostoria** (city) Seneca County
60	546	-3.3	**Lima** (city) Allen County
60	546	-3.3	**Portsmouth** (city) Scioto County
60	546	-3.3	**Shaker Heights** (city) Cuyahoga County
63	558	-3.2	**Blue Ash** (city) Hamilton County
64	565	-3.1	**Mansfield** (city) Richland County
65	578	-3.0	**Marietta** (city) Washington County
65	578	-3.0	**Vermilion** (city) Lorain County
67	616	-2.7	**Bay Village** (city) Cuyahoga County
68	629	-2.6	**Oxford** (city) Butler County
69	642	-2.5	**Elyria** (city) Lorain County
69	642	-2.5	**Rocky River** (city) Cuyahoga County
71	665	-2.3	**Kettering** (city) Montgomery County
71	665	-2.3	**Seven Hills** (city) Cuyahoga County
73	724	-1.9	**Beachwood** (city) Cuyahoga County
73	724	-1.9	**Steubenville** (city) Jefferson County
75	744	-1.8	**Sharonville** (city) Hamilton County
76	773	-1.6	**Willoughby** (city) Lake County
77	821	-1.3	**Circleville** (city) Pickaway County
77	821	-1.3	**Willowick** (city) Lake County
79	837	-1.2	**Mayfield Heights** (city) Cuyahoga County
80	851	-1.1	**Bexley** (city) Franklin County
81	863	-1.0	**Clayton** (city) Montgomery County
81	863	-1.0	**Piqua** (city) Miami County
83	886	-0.9	**Tiffin** (city) Seneca County
84	905	-0.8	**Hudson** (city) Summit County
85	924	-0.7	**Ironton** (city) Lawrence County
86	962	-0.5	**Greenville** (city) Darke County
87	986	-0.4	**Ravenna** (city) Portage County
87	986	-0.4	**Zanesville** (city) Muskingum County
89	1006	-0.3	**Huber Heights** (city) Montgomery County
90	1104	0.2	**Defiance** (city) Defiance County
91	1126	0.3	**Upper Arlington** (city) Franklin County
92	1175	0.5	**Chillicothe** (city) Ross County
93	1197	0.6	**Berea** (city) Cuyahoga County
93	1197	0.6	**Cuyahoga Falls** (city) Summit County
95	1256	0.9	**Celina** (city) Mercer County
95	1256	0.9	**Fairborn** (city) Greene County
95	1256	0.9	**Montgomery** (city) Hamilton County
95	1256	0.9	**Salem** (city) Columbiana County
99	1282	1.0	**Fairfield** (city) Butler County
100	1337	1.3	**Bowling Green** (city) Wood County
101	1360	1.4	**New Philadelphia** (city) Tuscarawas County
102	1381	1.5	**Urbana** (city) Champaign County
102	1381	1.5	**Van Wert** (city) Van Wert County
104	1401	1.6	**Sylvania** (city) Lucas County
105	1463	1.9	**Amherst** (city) Lorain County
105	1463	1.9	**Gahanna** (city) Franklin County
107	1480	2.0	**Brecksville** (city) Cuyahoga County
107	1480	2.0	**Strongsville** (city) Cuyahoga County
109	1545	2.3	**Bellefontaine** (city) Logan County
109	1545	2.3	**Westerville** (city) Franklin County
111	1624	2.6	**Brunswick** (city) Medina County
111	1624	2.6	**Massillon** (city) Stark County
111	1624	2.6	**Middleburg Heights** (city) Cuyahoga County
114	1663	2.8	**Newark** (city) Licking County
115	1681	2.9	**Conneaut** (city) Ashtabula County
115	1681	2.9	**Hamilton** (city) Butler County
117	1746	3.2	**Westlake** (city) Cuyahoga County
118	1770	3.3	**Franklin** (city) Warren County
119	1806	3.5	**Loveland** (city) Hamilton County
120	1824	3.6	**Kent** (city) Portage County
120	1824	3.6	**Miamisburg** (city) Montgomery County
122	1964	4.2	**Centerville** (city) Montgomery County
123	1978	4.3	**Marion** (city) Marion County
124	1992	4.4	**Vandalia** (city) Montgomery County
125	2049	4.8	**Norwalk** (city) Huron County
125	2049	4.8	**Oregon** (city) Lucas County
127	2064	4.9	**Norton** (city) Summit County
128	2086	5.0	**Dover** (city) Tuscarawas County
128	2086	5.0	**Sidney** (city) Shelby County
128	2086	5.0	**Wilmington** (city) Clinton County
131	2152	5.3	**Wooster** (city) Wayne County
132	2213	5.7	**Findlay** (city) Hancock County
133	2264	6.1	**Medina** (city) Medina County
134	2275	6.2	**Springdale** (city) Hamilton County
135	2289	6.3	**North Royalton** (city) Cuyahoga County
136	2306	6.4	**Xenia** (city) Greene County
137	2352	6.8	**North Canton** (city) Stark County
138	2381	7.0	**Riverside** (city) Montgomery County
138	2381	7.0	**Tallmadge** (city) Summit County
140	2400	7.1	**Solon** (city) Cuyahoga County
141	2559	8.4	**Stow** (city) Summit County
142	2711	9.7	**Lancaster** (city) Fairfield County
143	2752	10.1	**Englewood** (city) Montgomery County
144	2797	10.5	**Twinsburg** (city) Summit County
145	2804	10.6	**Columbus** (city) Franklin County
146	2883	11.7	**Athens** (city) Athens County
147	2891	11.8	**Painesville** (city) Lake County
148	2898	11.9	**Reynoldsburg** (city) Franklin County
149	2949	12.6	**Green** (city) Summit County
150	3063	13.9	**Troy** (city) Miami County

Note: *The state column ranks the top/bottom 150 places from all places in the state with population of 10,000 or more. The national column ranks the top/bottom 150 places from all places in the country with population of 10,000 or more. Places that are unincorporated were not considered in the rankings. Please refer to the User Guide for additional information.*

Population Density

Top 150 Places Ranked in *Descending* Order

State Rank	Nat'l Rank	Pop./ Sq. Mi.	Place
1	152	9,419.3	**Lakewood** (city) Cuyahoga County
2	258	7,437.9	**University Heights** (city) Cuyahoga County
3	404	6,102.8	**Norwood** (city) Hamilton County
4	462	5,782.4	**East Cleveland** (city) Cuyahoga County
5	477	5,689.3	**Cleveland Heights** (city) Cuyahoga County
6	491	5,587.0	**Willowick** (city) Lake County
7	511	5,474.5	**Northbrook** (CDP) Hamilton County
8	526	5,370.9	**Bexley** (city) Franklin County
9	577	5,107.2	**Cleveland** (city) Cuyahoga County
10	615	4,949.9	**Parma Heights** (city) Cuyahoga County
11	661	4,794.0	**South Euclid** (city) Cuyahoga County
12	718	4,602.1	**Euclid** (city) Cuyahoga County
13	720	4,595.4	**Mayfield Heights** (city) Cuyahoga County
14	747	4,528.2	**Shaker Heights** (city) Cuyahoga County
15	771	4,473.6	**Maple Heights** (city) Cuyahoga County
16	822	4,266.2	**Rocky River** (city) Cuyahoga County
17	885	4,075.1	**Parma** (city) Cuyahoga County
18	918	3,990.3	**Garfield Heights** (city) Cuyahoga County
19	1002	3,809.8	**Cincinnati** (city) Hamilton County
20	1089	3,624.1	**Columbus** (city) Franklin County
21	1100	3,596.6	**Fairview Park** (city) Cuyahoga County
22	1102	3,591.6	**Reading** (city) Hamilton County
23	1126	3,559.3	**Toledo** (city) Lucas County
24	1192	3,435.8	**Whitehall** (city) Franklin County
25	1197	3,432.5	**Upper Arlington** (city) Franklin County
26	1202	3,428.0	**Bay Village** (city) Cuyahoga County
27	1258	3,339.3	**Berea** (city) Cuyahoga County
28	1265	3,333.0	**Bridgetown** (CDP) Hamilton County
29	1301	3,277.7	**Warrensville Heights** (city) Cuyahoga County
30	1335	3,217.0	**Reynoldsburg** (city) Franklin County
31	1342	3,209.8	**Akron** (city) Summit County
32	1348	3,201.0	**Oxford** (city) Butler County
33	1378	3,159.3	**Lyndhurst** (city) Cuyahoga County
34	1384	3,150.5	**Kent** (city) Portage County
35	1390	3,140.2	**Finneytown** (CDP) Hamilton County
36	1392	3,138.8	**Marion** (city) Marion County
37	1401	3,112.7	**Painesville** (city) Lake County
38	1403	3,108.2	**White Oak** (CDP) Hamilton County
39	1472	3,007.0	**Kettering** (city) Montgomery County
40	1518	2,941.4	**Struthers** (city) Mahoning County
41	1521	2,937.5	**Barberton** (city) Summit County
42	1524	2,927.8	**Sylvania** (city) Lucas County
43	1550	2,904.9	**Eastlake** (city) Lake County
44	1557	2,895.9	**Westerville** (city) Franklin County
45	1558	2,893.0	**Hamilton** (city) Butler County
46	1559	2,888.9	**Forest Park** (city) Hamilton County
47	1568	2,867.3	**Canton** (city) Stark County
48	1575	2,858.2	**Lima** (city) Allen County
49	1597	2,827.8	**Forestville** (CDP) Hamilton County
50	1620	2,802.7	**North Olmsted** (city) Cuyahoga County
51	1650	2,748.7	**Wickliffe** (city) Lake County
52	1663	2,732.5	**North Canton** (city) Stark County
53	1682	2,707.6	**Lorain** (city) Lorain County
54	1709	2,675.4	**Gahanna** (city) Franklin County
55	1712	2,674.5	**Ironton** (city) Lawrence County
56	1723	2,655.8	**Tiffin** (city) Seneca County
57	1730	2,652.2	**Brunswick** (city) Medina County
58	1731	2,652.1	**Sandusky** (city) Erie County
59	1732	2,650.9	**Elyria** (city) Lorain County
60	1744	2,628.9	**Brooklyn** (city) Cuyahoga County
61	1774	2,600.9	**Trenton** (city) Butler County
62	1784	2,592.8	**Riverside** (city) Montgomery County
63	1803	2,576.8	**Warren** (city) Trumbull County
64	1818	2,551.8	**Austintown** (CDP) Mahoning County
65	1819	2,551.5	**Brook Park** (city) Cuyahoga County
66	1824	2,543.1	**Dayton** (city) Montgomery County
67	1854	2,501.3	**Alliance** (city) Stark County
68	1874	2,472.5	**Ashtabula** (city) Ashtabula County
69	1882	2,458.4	**Fairborn** (city) Greene County
70	1887	2,453.7	**East Liverpool** (city) Columbiana County
71	1888	2,452.0	**Loveland** (city) Hamilton County
72	1896	2,448.2	**Worthington** (city) Franklin County
73	1901	2,443.2	**Bedford** (city) Cuyahoga County
74	1924	2,425.2	**Athens** (city) Athens County
75	1942	2,405.3	**Seven Hills** (city) Cuyahoga County
76	1948	2,396.1	**Springfield** (city) Clark County
77	1953	2,391.3	**Bowling Green** (city) Wood County
78	1966	2,377.6	**Richmond Heights** (city) Cuyahoga County
79	1973	2,370.9	**Bedford Heights** (city) Cuyahoga County
80	2003	2,339.5	**Boardman** (CDP) Mahoning County
81	2019	2,331.9	**Powell** (city) Delaware County
82	2046	2,305.4	**Medina** (city) Medina County
83	2078	2,278.0	**Newark** (city) Licking County
84	2098	2,261.4	**Springdale** (city) Hamilton County
85	2102	2,256.2	**Dover** (city) Tuscarawas County
86	2115	2,244.6	**Beachwood** (city) Cuyahoga County
87	2124	2,237.3	**Niles** (city) Trumbull County
88	2133	2,226.2	**Centerville** (city) Montgomery County
89	2150	2,196.5	**Grove City** (city) Franklin County
90	2172	2,172.7	**Willoughby** (city) Lake County
91	2182	2,165.8	**Zanesville** (city) Muskingum County
92	2188	2,159.6	**Hilliard** (city) Franklin County
93	2195	2,153.3	**Findlay** (city) Hancock County
94	2212	2,137.8	**Troy** (city) Miami County
95	2250	2,104.2	**New Philadelphia** (city) Tuscarawas County
96	2257	2,100.2	**Chillicothe** (city) Ross County
97	2270	2,088.0	**Celina** (city) Mercer County
98	2279	2,082.4	**Ravenna** (city) Portage County
99	2299	2,058.3	**Lancaster** (city) Fairfield County
100	2305	2,055.4	**Englewood** (city) Montgomery County
101	2306	2,055.1	**Westlake** (city) Cuyahoga County
102	2318	2,041.3	**West Carrollton** (city) Montgomery County
103	2319	2,038.7	**Stow** (city) Summit County
104	2325	2,030.5	**Wadsworth** (city) Medina County
105	2326	2,030.2	**Fairfield** (city) Butler County
106	2328	2,029.0	**Avon Lake** (city) Lorain County
107	2338	2,020.6	**Monfort Heights** (CDP) Hamilton County
108	2351	2,005.1	**Fremont** (city) Sandusky County
109	2352	2,003.9	**Circleville** (city) Pickaway County
110	2355	2,002.9	**Greenville** (city) Darke County
111	2378	1,977.2	**Middleburg Heights** (city) Cuyahoga County
112	2380	1,972.7	**Youngstown** (city) Mahoning County
113	2421	1,939.1	**Montgomery** (city) Hamilton County
114	2425	1,936.5	**Xenia** (city) Greene County
115	2427	1,935.9	**Cuyahoga Falls** (city) Summit County
116	2446	1,917.9	**Norwalk** (city) Huron County
117	2450	1,915.0	**Salem** (city) Columbiana County
118	2486	1,884.2	**Portsmouth** (city) Scioto County
119	2490	1,877.0	**Pickerington** (city) Fairfield County
120	2509	1,860.9	**Springboro** (city) Warren County
121	2512	1,859.6	**Middletown** (city) Butler County
122	2543	1,833.7	**Delaware** (city) Delaware County
123	2556	1,823.1	**Ashland** (city) Ashland County
124	2565	1,817.1	**Strongsville** (city) Cuyahoga County
125	2578	1,805.9	**Mount Vernon** (city) Knox County
126	2597	1,791.1	**Perrysburg** (city) Wood County
127	2613	1,781.5	**Fostoria** (city) Seneca County
128	2624	1,770.2	**Dent** (CDP) Hamilton County
129	2625	1,769.9	**Mentor** (city) Lake County
130	2627	1,769.5	**Steubenville** (city) Jefferson County
131	2633	1,766.2	**Piqua** (city) Miami County
132	2634	1,765.8	**Sidney** (city) Shelby County
133	2683	1,730.4	**Massillon** (city) Stark County
134	2704	1,711.9	**Beavercreek** (city) Greene County
135	2707	1,710.7	**Huber Heights** (city) Montgomery County
136	2710	1,708.5	**Dublin** (city) Franklin County
137	2716	1,702.2	**Amherst** (city) Lorain County
138	2754	1,674.2	**Cambridge** (city) Guernsey County
139	2760	1,670.2	**Marietta** (city) Washington County
140	2773	1,665.6	**Bucyrus** (city) Crawford County
141	2784	1,656.3	**Miamisburg** (city) Montgomery County
142	2794	1,648.6	**Mason** (city) Warren County
143	2824	1,624.1	**Washington Court House** (city) Fayette County
144	2849	1,601.4	**Wooster** (city) Wayne County
145	2853	1,598.2	**Blue Ash** (city) Hamilton County
146	2909	1,549.0	**Mansfield** (city) Richland County
147	2916	1,545.3	**Lebanon** (city) Warren County
148	2943	1,521.0	**Urbana** (city) Champaign County
149	2993	1,486.8	**Broadview Heights** (city) Cuyahoga County
150	2999	1,480.7	**Van Wert** (city) Van Wert County

Note: *The state column ranks the top/bottom 150 places from all places in the state with population of 10,000 or more. The national column ranks the top/bottom 150 places from all places in the country with population of 10,000 or more. Places that are unincorporated were not considered in the rankings. Please refer to the User Guide for additional information.*

Population Density

Top 150 Places Ranked in *Ascending* Order

State Rank	Nat'l Rank	Pop./ Sq. Mi.	Place
1	326	487.2	**Conneaut** (city) Ashtabula County
2	378	522.8	**Pataskala** (city) Licking County
3	433	568.3	**New Franklin** (city) Summit County
4	468	599.4	**Norton** (city) Summit County
5	561	676.9	**Oregon** (city) Lucas County
6	567	678.4	**Aurora** (city) Portage County
7	572	683.2	**Streetsboro** (city) Portage County
8	595	697.7	**Brecksville** (city) Cuyahoga County
9	612	713.8	**Clayton** (city) Montgomery County
10	703	783.9	**Monroe** (city) Butler County
11	722	801.2	**Trotwood** (city) Montgomery County
12	724	801.7	**Green** (city) Summit County
13	807	869.7	**Hudson** (city) Summit County
14	902	943.9	**Heath** (city) Licking County
15	970	994.3	**Vermilion** (city) Lorain County
16	1006	1,018.5	**Avon** (city) Lorain County
17	1177	1,146.7	**Solon** (city) Cuyahoga County
18	1184	1,149.8	**Wilmington** (city) Clinton County
19	1187	1,152.7	**Macedonia** (city) Summit County
20	1317	1,235.1	**Vandalia** (city) Montgomery County
21	1333	1,249.4	**Mack** (CDP) Hamilton County
22	1338	1,253.0	**Tallmadge** (city) Summit County
23	1343	1,257.1	**North Ridgeville** (city) Lorain County
24	1380	1,283.2	**Franklin** (city) Warren County
25	1447	1,332.2	**Bellefontaine** (city) Logan County
26	1474	1,357.8	**Marysville** (city) Union County
27	1488	1,365.0	**Twinsburg** (city) Summit County
28	1506	1,379.2	**Sharonville** (city) Hamilton County
29	1511	1,381.9	**Galion** (city) Crawford County
30	1519	1,387.5	**Coshocton** (city) Coshocton County
31	1564	1,419.8	**Defiance** (city) Defiance County
32	1580	1,428.6	**North Royalton** (city) Cuyahoga County
33	1610	1,445.1	**Maumee** (city) Lucas County
34	1657	1,480.7	**Van Wert** (city) Van Wert County
35	1663	1,486.8	**Broadview Heights** (city) Cuyahoga County
36	1713	1,521.0	**Urbana** (city) Champaign County
37	1740	1,545.3	**Lebanon** (city) Warren County
38	1747	1,549.0	**Mansfield** (city) Richland County
39	1803	1,598.2	**Blue Ash** (city) Hamilton County
40	1807	1,601.4	**Wooster** (city) Wayne County
41	1832	1,624.1	**Washington Court House** (city) Fayette County
42	1861	1,648.6	**Mason** (city) Warren County
43	1872	1,656.3	**Miamisburg** (city) Montgomery County
44	1883	1,665.6	**Bucyrus** (city) Crawford County
45	1896	1,670.2	**Marietta** (city) Washington County
46	1902	1,674.2	**Cambridge** (city) Guernsey County
47	1940	1,702.2	**Amherst** (city) Lorain County
48	1946	1,708.5	**Dublin** (city) Franklin County
49	1949	1,710.7	**Huber Heights** (city) Montgomery County
50	1952	1,711.9	**Beavercreek** (city) Greene County
51	1973	1,730.4	**Massillon** (city) Stark County
52	2022	1,765.8	**Sidney** (city) Shelby County
53	2023	1,766.2	**Piqua** (city) Miami County
54	2028	1,769.5	**Steubenville** (city) Jefferson County
55	2031	1,769.9	**Mentor** (city) Lake County
56	2032	1,770.2	**Dent** (CDP) Hamilton County
57	2043	1,781.5	**Fostoria** (city) Seneca County
58	2059	1,791.1	**Perrysburg** (city) Wood County
59	2078	1,805.9	**Mount Vernon** (city) Knox County
60	2091	1,817.1	**Strongsville** (city) Cuyahoga County
61	2099	1,823.1	**Ashland** (city) Ashland County
62	2113	1,833.7	**Delaware** (city) Delaware County
63	2144	1,859.6	**Middletown** (city) Butler County
64	2147	1,860.9	**Springboro** (city) Warren County
65	2166	1,877.0	**Pickerington** (city) Fairfield County
66	2170	1,884.2	**Portsmouth** (city) Scioto County
67	2206	1,915.0	**Salem** (city) Columbiana County
68	2210	1,917.9	**Norwalk** (city) Huron County
69	2229	1,935.9	**Cuyahoga Falls** (city) Summit County
70	2231	1,936.5	**Xenia** (city) Greene County
71	2235	1,939.1	**Montgomery** (city) Hamilton County
72	2276	1,972.7	**Youngstown** (city) Mahoning County
73	2278	1,977.2	**Middleburg Heights** (city) Cuyahoga County
74	2301	2,002.9	**Greenville** (city) Darke County
75	2304	2,003.9	**Circleville** (city) Pickaway County
76	2305	2,005.1	**Fremont** (city) Sandusky County
77	2318	2,020.6	**Monfort Heights** (CDP) Hamilton County
78	2328	2,029.0	**Avon Lake** (city) Lorain County
79	2330	2,030.2	**Fairfield** (city) Butler County
80	2331	2,030.5	**Wadsworth** (city) Medina County
81	2336	2,038.7	**Stow** (city) Summit County
82	2338	2,041.3	**West Carrollton** (city) Montgomery County
83	2350	2,055.1	**Westlake** (city) Cuyahoga County
84	2351	2,055.4	**Englewood** (city) Montgomery County
85	2357	2,058.3	**Lancaster** (city) Fairfield County
86	2377	2,082.4	**Ravenna** (city) Portage County
87	2386	2,088.0	**Celina** (city) Mercer County
88	2399	2,100.2	**Chillicothe** (city) Ross County
89	2405	2,104.2	**New Philadelphia** (city) Tuscarawas County
90	2444	2,137.8	**Troy** (city) Miami County
91	2461	2,153.3	**Findlay** (city) Hancock County
92	2468	2,159.6	**Hilliard** (city) Franklin County
93	2474	2,165.8	**Zanesville** (city) Muskingum County
94	2484	2,172.7	**Willoughby** (city) Lake County
95	2506	2,196.5	**Grove City** (city) Franklin County
96	2523	2,226.2	**Centerville** (city) Montgomery County
97	2532	2,237.3	**Niles** (city) Trumbull County
98	2541	2,244.6	**Beachwood** (city) Cuyahoga County
99	2554	2,256.2	**Dover** (city) Tuscarawas County
100	2558	2,261.4	**Springdale** (city) Hamilton County
101	2578	2,278.0	**Newark** (city) Licking County
102	2610	2,305.4	**Medina** (city) Medina County
103	2636	2,331.9	**Powell** (city) Delaware County
104	2653	2,339.5	**Boardman** (CDP) Mahoning County
105	2683	2,370.9	**Bedford Heights** (city) Cuyahoga County
106	2690	2,377.6	**Richmond Heights** (city) Cuyahoga County
107	2703	2,391.3	**Bowling Green** (city) Wood County
108	2708	2,396.1	**Springfield** (city) Clark County
109	2714	2,405.3	**Seven Hills** (city) Cuyahoga County
110	2732	2,425.2	**Athens** (city) Athens County
111	2755	2,443.2	**Bedford** (city) Cuyahoga County
112	2760	2,448.2	**Worthington** (city) Franklin County
113	2768	2,452.0	**Loveland** (city) Hamilton County
114	2769	2,453.7	**East Liverpool** (city) Columbiana County
115	2774	2,458.4	**Fairborn** (city) Greene County
116	2782	2,472.5	**Ashtabula** (city) Ashtabula County
117	2802	2,501.3	**Alliance** (city) Stark County
118	2832	2,543.1	**Dayton** (city) Montgomery County
119	2837	2,551.5	**Brook Park** (city) Cuyahoga County
120	2838	2,551.8	**Austintown** (CDP) Mahoning County
121	2853	2,576.8	**Warren** (city) Trumbull County
122	2872	2,592.8	**Riverside** (city) Montgomery County
123	2882	2,600.9	**Trenton** (city) Butler County
124	2912	2,628.9	**Brooklyn** (city) Cuyahoga County
125	2924	2,650.9	**Elyria** (city) Lorain County
126	2925	2,652.1	**Sandusky** (city) Erie County
127	2926	2,652.2	**Brunswick** (city) Medina County
128	2933	2,655.8	**Tiffin** (city) Seneca County
129	2944	2,674.5	**Ironton** (city) Lawrence County
130	2947	2,675.4	**Gahanna** (city) Franklin County
131	2974	2,707.6	**Lorain** (city) Lorain County
132	2993	2,732.5	**North Canton** (city) Stark County
133	3006	2,748.7	**Wickliffe** (city) Lake County
134	3036	2,802.7	**North Olmsted** (city) Cuyahoga County
135	3059	2,827.8	**Forestville** (CDP) Hamilton County
136	3081	2,858.2	**Lima** (city) Allen County
137	3088	2,867.3	**Canton** (city) Stark County
138	3097	2,888.9	**Forest Park** (city) Hamilton County
139	3098	2,893.0	**Hamilton** (city) Butler County
140	3099	2,895.9	**Westerville** (city) Franklin County
141	3106	2,904.9	**Eastlake** (city) Lake County
142	3132	2,927.8	**Sylvania** (city) Lucas County
143	3135	2,937.5	**Barberton** (city) Summit County
144	3138	2,941.4	**Struthers** (city) Mahoning County
145	3184	3,007.0	**Kettering** (city) Montgomery County
146	3253	3,108.2	**White Oak** (CDP) Hamilton County
147	3255	3,112.7	**Painesville** (city) Lake County
148	3264	3,138.8	**Marion** (city) Marion County
149	3266	3,140.2	**Finneytown** (CDP) Hamilton County
150	3272	3,150.5	**Kent** (city) Portage County

***Note:** The state column ranks the top/bottom 150 places from all places in the state with population of 10,000 or more. The national column ranks the top/bottom 150 places from all places in the country with population of 10,000 or more. Places that are unincorporated were not considered in the rankings. Please refer to the User Guide for additional information.*

White Population

Top 150 Places Ranked in *Descending* Order

State Rank	Nat'l Rank	Percent	Place
1	7	98.2	**Mack** (CDP) Hamilton County
2	17	97.7	**New Franklin** (city) Summit County
3	19	97.6	**Galion** (city) Crawford County
4	49	97.0	**Bay Village** (city) Cuyahoga County
5	57	96.9	**Bridgetown** (CDP) Hamilton County
5	57	96.9	**Wadsworth** (city) Medina County
7	68	96.8	**Vermilion** (city) Lorain County
8	77	96.7	**Greenville** (city) Darke County
9	124	96.3	**Bucyrus** (city) Crawford County
9	124	96.3	**Mentor** (city) Lake County
11	137	96.2	**Franklin** (city) Warren County
11	137	96.2	**Norton** (city) Summit County
11	137	96.2	**Trenton** (city) Butler County
14	189	95.9	**Eastlake** (city) Lake County
14	189	95.9	**Lancaster** (city) Fairfield County
14	189	95.9	**Salem** (city) Columbiana County
17	210	95.8	**Ashland** (city) Ashland County
18	224	95.7	**Amherst** (city) Lorain County
18	224	95.7	**Avon Lake** (city) Lorain County
18	224	95.7	**Coshocton** (city) Coshocton County
18	224	95.7	**Dent** (CDP) Hamilton County
22	244	95.6	**Seven Hills** (city) Cuyahoga County
23	258	95.5	**Brunswick** (city) Medina County
23	258	95.5	**Rocky River** (city) Cuyahoga County
25	276	95.4	**Circleville** (city) Pickaway County
26	291	95.3	**Mount Vernon** (city) Knox County
27	347	95.0	**Green** (city) Summit County
27	347	95.0	**North Ridgeville** (city) Lorain County
27	347	95.0	**Willowick** (city) Lake County
30	362	94.9	**Celina** (city) Mercer County
30	362	94.9	**Marietta** (city) Washington County
32	380	94.8	**North Canton** (city) Stark County
33	402	94.7	**Maumee** (city) Lucas County
34	427	94.6	**North Royalton** (city) Cuyahoga County
34	427	94.6	**Van Wert** (city) Van Wert County
36	461	94.4	**Fairview Park** (city) Cuyahoga County
37	477	94.3	**Struthers** (city) Mahoning County
38	500	94.1	**Dover** (city) Tuscarawas County
39	516	94.0	**New Philadelphia** (city) Tuscarawas County
40	536	93.9	**Aurora** (city) Portage County
40	536	93.9	**Tiffin** (city) Seneca County
42	559	93.8	**Miamisburg** (city) Montgomery County
43	577	93.7	**Heath** (city) Licking County
44	590	93.6	**Tallmadge** (city) Summit County
44	590	93.6	**Willoughby** (city) Lake County
46	610	93.5	**Loveland** (city) Hamilton County
46	610	93.5	**Oregon** (city) Lucas County
46	610	93.5	**Washington Court House** (city) Fayette County
49	632	93.4	**Cuyahoga Falls** (city) Summit County
49	632	93.4	**Forestville** (CDP) Hamilton County
51	655	93.3	**Brecksville** (city) Cuyahoga County
51	655	93.3	**Medina** (city) Medina County
53	693	93.1	**Niles** (city) Trumbull County
54	715	93.0	**Parma** (city) Cuyahoga County
54	715	93.0	**Stow** (city) Summit County
54	715	93.0	**Worthington** (city) Franklin County
57	732	92.9	**Perrysburg** (city) Wood County
58	749	92.8	**Newark** (city) Licking County
58	749	92.8	**Wickliffe** (city) Lake County
60	770	92.7	**Cambridge** (city) Guernsey County
60	770	92.7	**Hudson** (city) Summit County
60	770	92.7	**Lebanon** (city) Warren County
63	785	92.6	**Grove City** (city) Franklin County
63	785	92.6	**Ironton** (city) Lawrence County
63	785	92.6	**Kettering** (city) Montgomery County
63	785	92.6	**Monroe** (city) Butler County
63	785	92.6	**North Olmsted** (city) Cuyahoga County
68	817	92.4	**Avon** (city) Lorain County
68	817	92.4	**Piqua** (city) Miami County
68	817	92.4	**Sylvania** (city) Lucas County
71	854	92.2	**Brook Park** (city) Cuyahoga County
71	854	92.2	**Norwalk** (city) Huron County
73	870	92.1	**Springboro** (city) Warren County
73	870	92.1	**Upper Arlington** (city) Franklin County
75	896	92.0	**Strongsville** (city) Cuyahoga County
76	962	91.7	**East Liverpool** (city) Columbiana County
77	994	91.5	**Vandalia** (city) Montgomery County
78	1036	91.2	**Findlay** (city) Hancock County
78	1036	91.2	**Westlake** (city) Cuyahoga County
78	1036	91.2	**Wooster** (city) Wayne County
81	1053	91.1	**Middleburg Heights** (city) Cuyahoga County
81	1053	91.1	**Parma Heights** (city) Cuyahoga County
81	1053	91.1	**Ravenna** (city) Portage County
84	1070	91.0	**Broadview Heights** (city) Cuyahoga County
85	1106	90.8	**Barberton** (city) Summit County
86	1142	90.6	**Delaware** (city) Delaware County
87	1173	90.4	**Marysville** (city) Union County
88	1188	90.3	**Lyndhurst** (city) Cuyahoga County
88	1188	90.3	**Sidney** (city) Shelby County
90	1206	90.2	**Centerville** (city) Montgomery County
91	1218	90.1	**Bellefontaine** (city) Logan County
91	1218	90.1	**Monfort Heights** (CDP) Hamilton County
91	1218	90.1	**Portsmouth** (city) Scioto County
91	1218	90.1	**Troy** (city) Miami County
95	1235	90.0	**Pataskala** (city) Licking County
96	1250	89.9	**Austintown** (CDP) Mahoning County
96	1250	89.9	**Montgomery** (city) Hamilton County
98	1265	89.8	**Conneaut** (city) Ashtabula County
99	1280	89.7	**Urbana** (city) Champaign County
100	1294	89.6	**Bexley** (city) Franklin County
100	1294	89.6	**Boardman** (CDP) Mahoning County
102	1371	89.1	**Reading** (city) Hamilton County
103	1415	88.8	**Berea** (city) Cuyahoga County
104	1451	88.6	**Westerville** (city) Franklin County
105	1469	88.5	**Beavercreek** (city) Greene County
105	1469	88.5	**Hilliard** (city) Franklin County
105	1469	88.5	**Powell** (city) Delaware County
108	1494	88.3	**Wilmington** (city) Clinton County
109	1520	88.1	**Chillicothe** (city) Ross County
109	1520	88.1	**Defiance** (city) Defiance County
111	1569	87.8	**White Oak** (CDP) Hamilton County
112	1581	87.7	**Streetsboro** (city) Portage County
113	1594	87.6	**Bowling Green** (city) Wood County
113	1594	87.6	**Oxford** (city) Butler County
115	1608	87.5	**Lakewood** (city) Cuyahoga County
116	1626	87.4	**Massillon** (city) Stark County
117	1648	87.2	**Riverside** (city) Montgomery County
118	1707	86.8	**West Carrollton** (city) Montgomery County
119	1729	86.7	**Marion** (city) Marion County
120	1746	86.6	**Norwood** (city) Hamilton County
121	1768	86.4	**Athens** (city) Athens County
122	1932	85.1	**Mason** (city) Warren County
123	1971	84.8	**Fairborn** (city) Greene County
124	1990	84.6	**Alliance** (city) Stark County
125	2012	84.4	**Zanesville** (city) Muskingum County
126	2023	84.3	**Brooklyn** (city) Cuyahoga County
127	2053	84.1	**Fostoria** (city) Seneca County
128	2064	84.0	**Hamilton** (city) Butler County
129	2107	83.6	**Macedonia** (city) Summit County
130	2140	83.3	**Middletown** (city) Butler County
131	2165	83.1	**Kent** (city) Portage County
132	2251	82.3	**Englewood** (city) Montgomery County
133	2275	82.1	**Gahanna** (city) Franklin County
134	2280	82.0	**Ashtabula** (city) Ashtabula County
134	2280	82.0	**Xenia** (city) Greene County
136	2408	80.7	**Fremont** (city) Sandusky County
137	2430	80.5	**Dublin** (city) Franklin County
138	2436	80.4	**Mayfield Heights** (city) Cuyahoga County
139	2466	80.1	**Pickerington** (city) Fairfield County
140	2488	79.9	**Blue Ash** (city) Hamilton County
141	2506	79.7	**Sharonville** (city) Hamilton County
142	2517	79.6	**Huber Heights** (city) Montgomery County
143	2568	79.0	**Fairfield** (city) Butler County
143	2568	79.0	**Steubenville** (city) Jefferson County
145	2616	78.5	**Twinsburg** (city) Summit County
146	2648	78.1	**Elyria** (city) Lorain County
147	2694	77.5	**Solon** (city) Cuyahoga County
148	2716	77.3	**Beachwood** (city) Cuyahoga County
149	2777	76.5	**Clayton** (city) Montgomery County
150	2885	75.2	**Springfield** (city) Clark County

***Note:** The state column ranks the top/bottom 150 places from all places in the state with population of 10,000 or more. The national column ranks the top/bottom 150 places from all places in the country with population of 10,000 or more. Places that are unincorporated were not considered in the rankings. Please refer to the User Guide for additional information.*

White Population

Top 150 Places Ranked in *Ascending* Order

State Rank	Nat'l Rank	Percent	Place
1	11	3.6	**Warrensville Heights** (city) Cuyahoga County
2	16	4.6	**East Cleveland** (city) Cuyahoga County
3	91	18.7	**Bedford Heights** (city) Cuyahoga County
4	143	24.9	**Forest Park** (city) Hamilton County
5	168	28.0	**Maple Heights** (city) Cuyahoga County
6	170	28.1	**Trotwood** (city) Montgomery County
7	274	37.3	**Cleveland** (city) Cuyahoga County
8	392	43.8	**Euclid** (city) Cuyahoga County
9	466	47.0	**Youngstown** (city) Mahoning County
10	509	48.5	**Richmond Heights** (city) Cuyahoga County
11	532	49.3	**Cincinnati** (city) Hamilton County
12	542	49.8	**Cleveland Heights** (city) Cuyahoga County
13	598	51.7	**Dayton** (city) Montgomery County
14	666	53.9	**Bedford** (city) Cuyahoga County
15	677	54.1	**South Euclid** (city) Cuyahoga County
16	703	55.0	**Shaker Heights** (city) Cuyahoga County
16	703	55.0	**Springdale** (city) Hamilton County
18	828	58.8	**Whitehall** (city) Franklin County
19	887	60.2	**Garfield Heights** (city) Cuyahoga County
20	944	61.5	**Columbus** (city) Franklin County
21	954	61.7	**Finneytown** (CDP) Hamilton County
22	982	62.2	**Akron** (city) Summit County
23	1108	64.8	**Toledo** (city) Lucas County
24	1146	65.6	**Northbrook** (CDP) Hamilton County
25	1230	67.1	**Lima** (city) Allen County
26	1263	67.7	**Warren** (city) Trumbull County
27	1278	67.9	**Lorain** (city) Lorain County
28	1300	68.2	**Painesville** (city) Lake County
29	1352	69.1	**Canton** (city) Stark County
30	1387	69.7	**Reynoldsburg** (city) Franklin County
31	1437	70.4	**Sandusky** (city) Erie County
32	1540	71.8	**University Heights** (city) Cuyahoga County
33	1631	73.3	**Mansfield** (city) Richland County
34	1765	75.2	**Springfield** (city) Clark County
35	1871	76.5	**Clayton** (city) Montgomery County
36	1932	77.3	**Beachwood** (city) Cuyahoga County
37	1954	77.5	**Solon** (city) Cuyahoga County
38	2004	78.1	**Elyria** (city) Lorain County
39	2035	78.5	**Twinsburg** (city) Summit County
40	2081	79.0	**Fairfield** (city) Butler County
40	2081	79.0	**Steubenville** (city) Jefferson County
42	2134	79.6	**Huber Heights** (city) Montgomery County
43	2140	79.7	**Sharonville** (city) Hamilton County
44	2160	79.9	**Blue Ash** (city) Hamilton County
45	2182	80.1	**Pickerington** (city) Fairfield County
46	2204	80.4	**Mayfield Heights** (city) Cuyahoga County
47	2221	80.5	**Dublin** (city) Franklin County
48	2239	80.7	**Fremont** (city) Sandusky County
49	2363	82.0	**Ashtabula** (city) Ashtabula County
49	2363	82.0	**Xenia** (city) Greene County
51	2377	82.1	**Gahanna** (city) Franklin County
52	2393	82.3	**Englewood** (city) Montgomery County
53	2480	83.1	**Kent** (city) Portage County
54	2505	83.3	**Middletown** (city) Butler County
55	2539	83.6	**Macedonia** (city) Summit County
56	2580	84.0	**Hamilton** (city) Butler County
57	2593	84.1	**Fostoria** (city) Seneca County
58	2620	84.3	**Brooklyn** (city) Cuyahoga County
59	2634	84.4	**Zanesville** (city) Muskingum County
60	2661	84.6	**Alliance** (city) Stark County
61	2675	84.8	**Fairborn** (city) Greene County
62	2704	85.1	**Mason** (city) Warren County
63	2874	86.4	**Athens** (city) Athens County
64	2900	86.6	**Norwood** (city) Hamilton County
65	2911	86.7	**Marion** (city) Marion County
66	2928	86.8	**West Carrollton** (city) Montgomery County
67	2994	87.2	**Riverside** (city) Montgomery County
68	3021	87.4	**Massillon** (city) Stark County
69	3031	87.5	**Lakewood** (city) Cuyahoga County
70	3049	87.6	**Bowling Green** (city) Wood County
70	3049	87.6	**Oxford** (city) Butler County
72	3063	87.7	**Streetsboro** (city) Portage County
73	3076	87.8	**White Oak** (CDP) Hamilton County
74	3116	88.1	**Chillicothe** (city) Ross County
74	3116	88.1	**Defiance** (city) Defiance County
76	3150	88.3	**Wilmington** (city) Clinton County
77	3175	88.5	**Beavercreek** (city) Greene County
77	3175	88.5	**Hilliard** (city) Franklin County
77	3175	88.5	**Powell** (city) Delaware County
80	3188	88.6	**Westerville** (city) Franklin County
81	3222	88.8	**Berea** (city) Cuyahoga County
82	3272	89.1	**Reading** (city) Hamilton County
83	3348	89.6	**Bexley** (city) Franklin County
83	3348	89.6	**Boardman** (CDP) Mahoning County
85	3363	89.7	**Urbana** (city) Champaign County
86	3377	89.8	**Conneaut** (city) Ashtabula County
87	3392	89.9	**Austintown** (CDP) Mahoning County
87	3392	89.9	**Montgomery** (city) Hamilton County
89	3407	90.0	**Pataskala** (city) Licking County
90	3422	90.1	**Bellefontaine** (city) Logan County
90	3422	90.1	**Monfort Heights** (CDP) Hamilton County
90	3422	90.1	**Portsmouth** (city) Scioto County
90	3422	90.1	**Troy** (city) Miami County
94	3439	90.2	**Centerville** (city) Montgomery County
95	3451	90.3	**Lyndhurst** (city) Cuyahoga County
95	3451	90.3	**Sidney** (city) Shelby County
97	3469	90.4	**Marysville** (city) Union County
98	3496	90.6	**Delaware** (city) Delaware County
99	3530	90.8	**Barberton** (city) Summit County
100	3570	91.0	**Broadview Heights** (city) Cuyahoga County
101	3587	91.1	**Middleburg Heights** (city) Cuyahoga County
101	3587	91.1	**Parma Heights** (city) Cuyahoga County
101	3587	91.1	**Ravenna** (city) Portage County
104	3604	91.2	**Findlay** (city) Hancock County
104	3604	91.2	**Westlake** (city) Cuyahoga County
104	3604	91.2	**Wooster** (city) Wayne County
107	3646	91.5	**Vandalia** (city) Montgomery County
108	3680	91.7	**East Liverpool** (city) Columbiana County
109	3738	92.0	**Strongsville** (city) Cuyahoga County
110	3761	92.1	**Springboro** (city) Warren County
110	3761	92.1	**Upper Arlington** (city) Franklin County
112	3787	92.2	**Brook Park** (city) Cuyahoga County
112	3787	92.2	**Norwalk** (city) Huron County
114	3821	92.4	**Avon** (city) Lorain County
114	3821	92.4	**Piqua** (city) Miami County
114	3821	92.4	**Sylvania** (city) Lucas County
117	3850	92.6	**Grove City** (city) Franklin County
117	3850	92.6	**Ironton** (city) Lawrence County
117	3850	92.6	**Kettering** (city) Montgomery County
117	3850	92.6	**Monroe** (city) Butler County
117	3850	92.6	**North Olmsted** (city) Cuyahoga County
122	3872	92.7	**Cambridge** (city) Guernsey County
122	3872	92.7	**Hudson** (city) Summit County
122	3872	92.7	**Lebanon** (city) Warren County
125	3887	92.8	**Newark** (city) Licking County
125	3887	92.8	**Wickliffe** (city) Lake County
127	3908	92.9	**Perrysburg** (city) Wood County
128	3925	93.0	**Parma** (city) Cuyahoga County
128	3925	93.0	**Stow** (city) Summit County
128	3925	93.0	**Worthington** (city) Franklin County
131	3942	93.1	**Niles** (city) Trumbull County
132	3982	93.3	**Brecksville** (city) Cuyahoga County
132	3982	93.3	**Medina** (city) Medina County
134	4002	93.4	**Cuyahoga Falls** (city) Summit County
134	4002	93.4	**Forestville** (CDP) Hamilton County
136	4025	93.5	**Loveland** (city) Hamilton County
136	4025	93.5	**Oregon** (city) Lucas County
136	4025	93.5	**Washington Court House** (city) Fayette County
139	4047	93.6	**Tallmadge** (city) Summit County
139	4047	93.6	**Willoughby** (city) Lake County
141	4067	93.7	**Heath** (city) Licking County
142	4080	93.8	**Miamisburg** (city) Montgomery County
143	4098	93.9	**Aurora** (city) Portage County
143	4098	93.9	**Tiffin** (city) Seneca County
145	4121	94.0	**New Philadelphia** (city) Tuscarawas County
146	4141	94.1	**Dover** (city) Tuscarawas County
147	4173	94.3	**Struthers** (city) Mahoning County
148	4180	94.4	**Fairview Park** (city) Cuyahoga County
149	4217	94.6	**North Royalton** (city) Cuyahoga County
149	4217	94.6	**Van Wert** (city) Van Wert County

Note: *The state column ranks the top/bottom 150 places from all places in the state with population of 10,000 or more. The national column ranks the top/bottom 150 places from all places in the country with population of 10,000 or more. Places that are unincorporated were not considered in the rankings. Please refer to the User Guide for additional information.*

Black/African American Population

Top 150 Places Ranked in *Descending* Order

State Rank	Nat'l Rank	Percent	Place
1	6	93.5	**Warrensville Heights** (city) Cuyahoga County
2	8	93.2	**East Cleveland** (city) Cuyahoga County
3	56	76.9	**Bedford Heights** (city) Cuyahoga County
4	95	68.2	**Maple Heights** (city) Cuyahoga County
4	95	68.2	**Trotwood** (city) Montgomery County
6	113	65.0	**Forest Park** (city) Hamilton County
7	181	53.3	**Cleveland** (city) Cuyahoga County
8	185	52.6	**Euclid** (city) Cuyahoga County
9	259	45.2	**Youngstown** (city) Mahoning County
10	261	44.9	**Richmond Heights** (city) Cuyahoga County
11	262	44.8	**Cincinnati** (city) Hamilton County
12	276	42.9	**Dayton** (city) Montgomery County
13	280	42.5	**Cleveland Heights** (city) Cuyahoga County
14	289	41.9	**Bedford** (city) Cuyahoga County
15	309	40.7	**South Euclid** (city) Cuyahoga County
16	340	37.1	**Shaker Heights** (city) Cuyahoga County
17	359	35.7	**Garfield Heights** (city) Cuyahoga County
18	392	33.7	**Finneytown** (CDP) Hamilton County
19	437	31.5	**Akron** (city) Summit County
20	474	29.9	**Springdale** (city) Hamilton County
21	487	29.3	**Whitehall** (city) Franklin County
22	513	28.0	**Columbus** (city) Franklin County
23	521	27.9	**Northbrook** (CDP) Hamilton County
24	526	27.7	**Warren** (city) Trumbull County
25	541	27.2	**Toledo** (city) Lucas County
26	561	26.4	**Lima** (city) Allen County
27	613	24.2	**Canton** (city) Stark County
28	635	23.3	**Reynoldsburg** (city) Franklin County
29	641	23.1	**University Heights** (city) Cuyahoga County
30	677	22.1	**Mansfield** (city) Richland County
31	681	22.0	**Sandusky** (city) Erie County
32	786	18.8	**Clayton** (city) Montgomery County
33	827	18.1	**Springfield** (city) Clark County
34	849	17.6	**Lorain** (city) Lorain County
35	940	15.9	**Steubenville** (city) Jefferson County
36	963	15.5	**Elyria** (city) Lorain County
37	1078	13.7	**Beachwood** (city) Cuyahoga County
38	1097	13.4	**Twinsburg** (city) Summit County
38	1097	13.4	**Xenia** (city) Greene County
40	1117	13.1	**Painesville** (city) Lake County
41	1121	13.0	**Huber Heights** (city) Montgomery County
41	1121	13.0	**Pickerington** (city) Fairfield County
43	1128	12.9	**Englewood** (city) Montgomery County
44	1133	12.8	**Fairfield** (city) Butler County
45	1221	11.7	**Middletown** (city) Butler County
46	1263	11.2	**Gahanna** (city) Franklin County
47	1325	10.6	**Solon** (city) Cuyahoga County
48	1333	10.5	**Alliance** (city) Stark County
49	1343	10.4	**Macedonia** (city) Summit County
50	1352	10.3	**Mayfield Heights** (city) Cuyahoga County
51	1422	9.7	**Zanesville** (city) Muskingum County
52	1436	9.6	**Kent** (city) Portage County
52	1436	9.6	**Marion** (city) Marion County
54	1500	8.9	**Ashtabula** (city) Ashtabula County
54	1500	8.9	**West Carrollton** (city) Montgomery County
56	1510	8.8	**Massillon** (city) Stark County
57	1517	8.7	**Sharonville** (city) Hamilton County
58	1545	8.5	**Hamilton** (city) Butler County
58	1545	8.5	**White Oak** (CDP) Hamilton County
60	1563	8.3	**Fremont** (city) Sandusky County
61	1613	7.9	**Streetsboro** (city) Portage County
62	1640	7.7	**Fairborn** (city) Greene County
63	1653	7.6	**Norwood** (city) Hamilton County
64	1669	7.5	**Conneaut** (city) Ashtabula County
65	1696	7.3	**Reading** (city) Hamilton County
66	1712	7.2	**Chillicothe** (city) Ross County
67	1764	6.9	**Austintown** (CDP) Mahoning County
68	1808	6.6	**Berea** (city) Cuyahoga County
68	1808	6.6	**Monfort Heights** (CDP) Hamilton County
68	1808	6.6	**Riverside** (city) Montgomery County
71	1828	6.5	**Blue Ash** (city) Hamilton County
72	1840	6.4	**Boardman** (CDP) Mahoning County
72	1840	6.4	**Bowling Green** (city) Wood County
72	1840	6.4	**Fostoria** (city) Seneca County
72	1840	6.4	**Lakewood** (city) Cuyahoga County
72	1840	6.4	**Lyndhurst** (city) Cuyahoga County
72	1840	6.4	**Westerville** (city) Franklin County
78	1911	6.1	**Wilmington** (city) Clinton County
79	1926	6.0	**Pataskala** (city) Licking County
80	1947	5.9	**Barberton** (city) Summit County
80	1947	5.9	**Bexley** (city) Franklin County
82	2001	5.6	**Ravenna** (city) Portage County
83	2050	5.4	**Urbana** (city) Champaign County
84	2090	5.2	**Brooklyn** (city) Cuyahoga County
85	2116	5.1	**Portsmouth** (city) Scioto County
86	2206	4.7	**Ironton** (city) Lawrence County
87	2231	4.6	**East Liverpool** (city) Columbiana County
88	2253	4.5	**Delaware** (city) Delaware County
88	2253	4.5	**Marysville** (city) Union County
88	2253	4.5	**Wickliffe** (city) Lake County
91	2278	4.4	**Athens** (city) Athens County
92	2302	4.3	**Bellefontaine** (city) Logan County
93	2338	4.2	**Troy** (city) Miami County
94	2364	4.1	**Vandalia** (city) Montgomery County
95	2390	4.0	**Centerville** (city) Montgomery County
95	2390	4.0	**Oxford** (city) Butler County
97	2480	3.7	**Monroe** (city) Butler County
97	2480	3.7	**Sidney** (city) Shelby County
99	2510	3.6	**Defiance** (city) Defiance County
99	2510	3.6	**Wooster** (city) Wayne County
101	2534	3.5	**Niles** (city) Trumbull County
102	2568	3.4	**Cambridge** (city) Guernsey County
103	2602	3.3	**Cuyahoga Falls** (city) Summit County
103	2602	3.3	**Kettering** (city) Montgomery County
103	2602	3.3	**Mason** (city) Warren County
103	2602	3.3	**Newark** (city) Licking County
103	2602	3.3	**Piqua** (city) Miami County
103	2602	3.3	**Tallmadge** (city) Summit County
109	2654	3.2	**Brook Park** (city) Cuyahoga County
110	2693	3.1	**Medina** (city) Medina County
110	2693	3.1	**Willoughby** (city) Lake County
112	2726	3.0	**Aurora** (city) Portage County
112	2726	3.0	**Hilliard** (city) Franklin County
112	2726	3.0	**Miamisburg** (city) Montgomery County
115	2768	2.9	**Struthers** (city) Mahoning County
116	2800	2.8	**Grove City** (city) Franklin County
116	2800	2.8	**Parma Heights** (city) Cuyahoga County
118	2839	2.7	**Montgomery** (city) Hamilton County
118	2839	2.7	**Stow** (city) Summit County
118	2839	2.7	**Sylvania** (city) Lucas County
118	2839	2.7	**Washington Court House** (city) Fayette County
122	2884	2.6	**Heath** (city) Licking County
122	2884	2.6	**Lebanon** (city) Warren County
122	2884	2.6	**Tiffin** (city) Seneca County
125	2925	2.5	**Beavercreek** (city) Greene County
125	2925	2.5	**Willowick** (city) Lake County
127	3019	2.3	**Avon** (city) Lorain County
127	3019	2.3	**Parma** (city) Cuyahoga County
127	3019	2.3	**Springboro** (city) Warren County
130	3070	2.2	**Findlay** (city) Hancock County
130	3070	2.2	**Worthington** (city) Franklin County
132	3124	2.1	**Broadview Heights** (city) Cuyahoga County
132	3124	2.1	**Loveland** (city) Hamilton County
134	3175	2.0	**North Canton** (city) Stark County
134	3175	2.0	**North Olmsted** (city) Cuyahoga County
136	3239	1.9	**Circleville** (city) Pickaway County
136	3239	1.9	**Norwalk** (city) Huron County
136	3239	1.9	**Powell** (city) Delaware County
136	3239	1.9	**Strongsville** (city) Cuyahoga County
140	3304	1.8	**Coshocton** (city) Coshocton County
140	3304	1.8	**Dublin** (city) Franklin County
140	3304	1.8	**Fairview Park** (city) Cuyahoga County
140	3304	1.8	**Green** (city) Summit County
140	3304	1.8	**Maumee** (city) Lucas County
145	3359	1.7	**Brecksville** (city) Cuyahoga County
145	3359	1.7	**Norton** (city) Summit County
145	3359	1.7	**Van Wert** (city) Van Wert County
148	3428	1.6	**Middleburg Heights** (city) Cuyahoga County
148	3428	1.6	**Westlake** (city) Cuyahoga County
150	3502	1.5	**North Ridgeville** (city) Lorain County

Note: *The state column ranks the top/bottom 150 places from all places in the state with population of 10,000 or more. The national column ranks the top/bottom 150 places from all places in the country with population of 10,000 or more. Places that are unincorporated were not considered in the rankings. Please refer to the User Guide for additional information.*

Black/African American Population

Top 150 Places Ranked in *Ascending* Order

State Rank	Nat'l Rank	Percent	Place
1	15	0.3	**Vermilion** (city) Lorain County
2	56	0.4	**Mack** (CDP) Hamilton County
3	131	0.5	**Bay Village** (city) Cuyahoga County
3	131	0.5	**Celina** (city) Mercer County
3	131	0.5	**Galion** (city) Crawford County
6	234	0.6	**New Franklin** (city) Summit County
7	327	0.7	**Amherst** (city) Lorain County
7	327	0.7	**Salem** (city) Columbiana County
9	424	0.8	**Seven Hills** (city) Cuyahoga County
9	424	0.8	**Upper Arlington** (city) Franklin County
9	424	0.8	**Wadsworth** (city) Medina County
12	548	0.9	**Bridgetown** (CDP) Hamilton County
12	548	0.9	**Franklin** (city) Warren County
12	548	0.9	**Greenville** (city) Darke County
15	640	1.0	**Lancaster** (city) Fairfield County
15	640	1.0	**Mentor** (city) Lake County
15	640	1.0	**Rocky River** (city) Cuyahoga County
15	640	1.0	**Trenton** (city) Butler County
19	745	1.1	**Avon Lake** (city) Lorain County
19	745	1.1	**Bucyrus** (city) Crawford County
19	745	1.1	**Dover** (city) Tuscarawas County
19	745	1.1	**Mount Vernon** (city) Knox County
19	745	1.1	**North Royalton** (city) Cuyahoga County
24	830	1.2	**Brunswick** (city) Medina County
24	830	1.2	**New Philadelphia** (city) Tuscarawas County
26	919	1.3	**Dent** (CDP) Hamilton County
26	919	1.3	**Hudson** (city) Summit County
26	919	1.3	**Marietta** (city) Washington County
29	994	1.4	**Ashland** (city) Ashland County
29	994	1.4	**Eastlake** (city) Lake County
29	994	1.4	**Forestville** (CDP) Hamilton County
29	994	1.4	**Oregon** (city) Lucas County
29	994	1.4	**Perrysburg** (city) Wood County
34	1071	1.5	**North Ridgeville** (city) Lorain County
35	1155	1.6	**Middleburg Heights** (city) Cuyahoga County
35	1155	1.6	**Westlake** (city) Cuyahoga County
37	1229	1.7	**Brecksville** (city) Cuyahoga County
37	1229	1.7	**Norton** (city) Summit County
37	1229	1.7	**Van Wert** (city) Van Wert County
40	1298	1.8	**Coshocton** (city) Coshocton County
40	1298	1.8	**Dublin** (city) Franklin County
40	1298	1.8	**Fairview Park** (city) Cuyahoga County
40	1298	1.8	**Green** (city) Summit County
40	1298	1.8	**Maumee** (city) Lucas County
45	1353	1.9	**Circleville** (city) Pickaway County
45	1353	1.9	**Norwalk** (city) Huron County
45	1353	1.9	**Powell** (city) Delaware County
45	1353	1.9	**Strongsville** (city) Cuyahoga County
49	1418	2.0	**North Canton** (city) Stark County
49	1418	2.0	**North Olmsted** (city) Cuyahoga County
51	1482	2.1	**Broadview Heights** (city) Cuyahoga County
51	1482	2.1	**Loveland** (city) Hamilton County
53	1533	2.2	**Findlay** (city) Hancock County
53	1533	2.2	**Worthington** (city) Franklin County
55	1587	2.3	**Avon** (city) Lorain County
55	1587	2.3	**Parma** (city) Cuyahoga County
55	1587	2.3	**Springboro** (city) Warren County
58	1684	2.5	**Beavercreek** (city) Greene County
58	1684	2.5	**Willowick** (city) Lake County
60	1732	2.6	**Heath** (city) Licking County
60	1732	2.6	**Lebanon** (city) Warren County
60	1732	2.6	**Tiffin** (city) Seneca County
63	1773	2.7	**Montgomery** (city) Hamilton County
63	1773	2.7	**Stow** (city) Summit County
63	1773	2.7	**Sylvania** (city) Lucas County
63	1773	2.7	**Washington Court House** (city) Fayette County
67	1818	2.8	**Grove City** (city) Franklin County
67	1818	2.8	**Parma Heights** (city) Cuyahoga County
69	1857	2.9	**Struthers** (city) Mahoning County
70	1889	3.0	**Aurora** (city) Portage County
70	1889	3.0	**Hilliard** (city) Franklin County
70	1889	3.0	**Miamisburg** (city) Montgomery County
73	1931	3.1	**Medina** (city) Medina County
73	1931	3.1	**Willoughby** (city) Lake County
75	1964	3.2	**Brook Park** (city) Cuyahoga County
76	2003	3.3	**Cuyahoga Falls** (city) Summit County
76	2003	3.3	**Kettering** (city) Montgomery County
76	2003	3.3	**Mason** (city) Warren County
76	2003	3.3	**Newark** (city) Licking County
76	2003	3.3	**Piqua** (city) Miami County
76	2003	3.3	**Tallmadge** (city) Summit County
82	2055	3.4	**Cambridge** (city) Guernsey County
83	2089	3.5	**Niles** (city) Trumbull County
84	2123	3.6	**Defiance** (city) Defiance County
84	2123	3.6	**Wooster** (city) Wayne County
86	2147	3.7	**Monroe** (city) Butler County
86	2147	3.7	**Sidney** (city) Shelby County
88	2242	4.0	**Centerville** (city) Montgomery County
88	2242	4.0	**Oxford** (city) Butler County
90	2267	4.1	**Vandalia** (city) Montgomery County
91	2293	4.2	**Troy** (city) Miami County
92	2319	4.3	**Bellefontaine** (city) Logan County
93	2355	4.4	**Athens** (city) Athens County
94	2379	4.5	**Delaware** (city) Delaware County
94	2379	4.5	**Marysville** (city) Union County
94	2379	4.5	**Wickliffe** (city) Lake County
97	2404	4.6	**East Liverpool** (city) Columbiana County
98	2426	4.7	**Ironton** (city) Lawrence County
99	2518	5.1	**Portsmouth** (city) Scioto County
100	2541	5.2	**Brooklyn** (city) Cuyahoga County
101	2591	5.4	**Urbana** (city) Champaign County
102	2631	5.6	**Ravenna** (city) Portage County
103	2686	5.9	**Barberton** (city) Summit County
103	2686	5.9	**Bexley** (city) Franklin County
105	2710	6.0	**Pataskala** (city) Licking County
106	2731	6.1	**Wilmington** (city) Clinton County
107	2784	6.4	**Boardman** (CDP) Mahoning County
107	2784	6.4	**Bowling Green** (city) Wood County
107	2784	6.4	**Fostoria** (city) Seneca County
107	2784	6.4	**Lakewood** (city) Cuyahoga County
107	2784	6.4	**Lyndhurst** (city) Cuyahoga County
107	2784	6.4	**Westerville** (city) Franklin County
113	2817	6.5	**Blue Ash** (city) Hamilton County
114	2829	6.6	**Berea** (city) Cuyahoga County
114	2829	6.6	**Monfort Heights** (CDP) Hamilton County
114	2829	6.6	**Riverside** (city) Montgomery County
117	2877	6.9	**Austintown** (CDP) Mahoning County
118	2928	7.2	**Chillicothe** (city) Ross County
119	2945	7.3	**Reading** (city) Hamilton County
120	2973	7.5	**Conneaut** (city) Ashtabula County
121	2988	7.6	**Norwood** (city) Hamilton County
122	3004	7.7	**Fairborn** (city) Greene County
123	3032	7.9	**Streetsboro** (city) Portage County
124	3084	8.3	**Fremont** (city) Sandusky County
125	3101	8.5	**Hamilton** (city) Butler County
125	3101	8.5	**White Oak** (CDP) Hamilton County
127	3128	8.7	**Sharonville** (city) Hamilton County
128	3140	8.8	**Massillon** (city) Stark County
129	3147	8.9	**Ashtabula** (city) Ashtabula County
129	3147	8.9	**West Carrollton** (city) Montgomery County
131	3208	9.6	**Kent** (city) Portage County
131	3208	9.6	**Marion** (city) Marion County
133	3221	9.7	**Zanesville** (city) Muskingum County
134	3294	10.3	**Mayfield Heights** (city) Cuyahoga County
135	3305	10.4	**Macedonia** (city) Summit County
136	3314	10.5	**Alliance** (city) Stark County
137	3324	10.6	**Solon** (city) Cuyahoga County
138	3384	11.2	**Gahanna** (city) Franklin County
139	3428	11.7	**Middletown** (city) Butler County
140	3514	12.8	**Fairfield** (city) Butler County
141	3524	12.9	**Englewood** (city) Montgomery County
142	3529	13.0	**Huber Heights** (city) Montgomery County
142	3529	13.0	**Pickerington** (city) Fairfield County
144	3536	13.1	**Painesville** (city) Lake County
145	3550	13.4	**Twinsburg** (city) Summit County
145	3550	13.4	**Xenia** (city) Greene County
147	3572	13.7	**Beachwood** (city) Cuyahoga County
148	3687	15.5	**Elyria** (city) Lorain County
149	3711	15.9	**Steubenville** (city) Jefferson County
150	3806	17.6	**Lorain** (city) Lorain County

Note: *The state column ranks the top/bottom 150 places from all places in the state with population of 10,000 or more. The national column ranks the top/bottom 150 places from all places in the country with population of 10,000 or more. Places that are unincorporated were not considered in the rankings. Please refer to the User Guide for additional information.*

Asian Population

Top 150 Places Ranked in *Descending* Order

State Rank	Nat'l Rank	Percent	Place
1	281	15.3	**Dublin** (city) Franklin County
2	505	10.6	**Blue Ash** (city) Hamilton County
3	554	10.0	**Solon** (city) Cuyahoga County
4	621	9.0	**Mason** (city) Warren County
5	778	7.5	**Powell** (city) Delaware County
6	787	7.4	**Beachwood** (city) Cuyahoga County
7	845	7.0	**Mayfield Heights** (city) Cuyahoga County
8	958	6.1	**Athens** (city) Athens County
9	1001	5.9	**Beavercreek** (city) Greene County
10	1036	5.7	**Twinsburg** (city) Summit County
11	1058	5.6	**Hilliard** (city) Franklin County
11	1058	5.6	**Middleburg Heights** (city) Cuyahoga County
11	1058	5.6	**Montgomery** (city) Hamilton County
14	1103	5.4	**Oxford** (city) Butler County
15	1135	5.2	**Broadview Heights** (city) Cuyahoga County
16	1206	4.9	**Upper Arlington** (city) Franklin County
16	1206	4.9	**Westlake** (city) Cuyahoga County
18	1266	4.6	**Shaker Heights** (city) Cuyahoga County
19	1361	4.3	**Hudson** (city) Summit County
19	1361	4.3	**Richmond Heights** (city) Cuyahoga County
21	1423	4.1	**Cleveland Heights** (city) Cuyahoga County
21	1423	4.1	**Columbus** (city) Franklin County
21	1423	4.1	**Strongsville** (city) Cuyahoga County
24	1457	4.0	**Sharonville** (city) Hamilton County
25	1491	3.9	**Brooklyn** (city) Cuyahoga County
25	1491	3.9	**Macedonia** (city) Summit County
27	1569	3.7	**Kent** (city) Portage County
28	1700	3.4	**Brecksville** (city) Cuyahoga County
28	1700	3.4	**Springboro** (city) Warren County
30	1787	3.2	**Centerville** (city) Montgomery County
31	1850	3.1	**Avon** (city) Lorain County
31	1850	3.1	**Fairborn** (city) Greene County
31	1850	3.1	**Gahanna** (city) Franklin County
31	1850	3.1	**Perrysburg** (city) Wood County
35	1902	3.0	**Parma Heights** (city) Cuyahoga County
36	1953	2.9	**Pickerington** (city) Fairfield County
37	2010	2.8	**Springdale** (city) Hamilton County
38	2064	2.7	**North Olmsted** (city) Cuyahoga County
38	2064	2.7	**North Royalton** (city) Cuyahoga County
40	2173	2.5	**Findlay** (city) Hancock County
40	2173	2.5	**Forestville** (CDP) Hamilton County
40	2173	2.5	**Huber Heights** (city) Montgomery County
40	2173	2.5	**Seven Hills** (city) Cuyahoga County
44	2237	2.4	**Fairfield** (city) Butler County
44	2237	2.4	**Stow** (city) Summit County
44	2237	2.4	**Troy** (city) Miami County
44	2237	2.4	**University Heights** (city) Cuyahoga County
48	2314	2.3	**Marysville** (city) Union County
48	2314	2.3	**Sylvania** (city) Lucas County
48	2314	2.3	**Westerville** (city) Franklin County
48	2314	2.3	**Worthington** (city) Franklin County
52	2384	2.2	**Forest Park** (city) Hamilton County
52	2384	2.2	**Streetsboro** (city) Portage County
54	2465	2.1	**Akron** (city) Summit County
54	2465	2.1	**Bowling Green** (city) Wood County
56	2527	2.0	**South Euclid** (city) Cuyahoga County
57	2598	1.9	**Aurora** (city) Portage County
57	2598	1.9	**Lakewood** (city) Cuyahoga County
57	2598	1.9	**Parma** (city) Cuyahoga County
57	2598	1.9	**Riverside** (city) Montgomery County
57	2598	1.9	**Wooster** (city) Wayne County
62	2688	1.8	**Cincinnati** (city) Hamilton County
62	2688	1.8	**Cleveland** (city) Cuyahoga County
62	2688	1.8	**Reynoldsburg** (city) Franklin County
62	2688	1.8	**Rocky River** (city) Cuyahoga County
66	2801	1.7	**Loveland** (city) Hamilton County
66	2801	1.7	**Monroe** (city) Butler County
68	2898	1.6	**Brook Park** (city) Cuyahoga County
68	2898	1.6	**Dent** (CDP) Hamilton County
68	2898	1.6	**Englewood** (city) Montgomery County
68	2898	1.6	**Fairview Park** (city) Cuyahoga County
68	2898	1.6	**Lyndhurst** (city) Cuyahoga County
68	2898	1.6	**Sidney** (city) Shelby County
74	3009	1.5	**Berea** (city) Cuyahoga County
74	3009	1.5	**Bexley** (city) Franklin County
74	3009	1.5	**Green** (city) Summit County
74	3009	1.5	**Whitehall** (city) Franklin County
74	3009	1.5	**Willoughby** (city) Lake County
79	3111	1.4	**Clayton** (city) Montgomery County
79	3111	1.4	**Delaware** (city) Delaware County
79	3111	1.4	**Finneytown** (CDP) Hamilton County
79	3111	1.4	**Marietta** (city) Washington County
79	3111	1.4	**Mentor** (city) Lake County
79	3111	1.4	**Vandalia** (city) Montgomery County
85	3229	1.3	**Avon Lake** (city) Lorain County
85	3229	1.3	**Garfield Heights** (city) Cuyahoga County
85	3229	1.3	**Grove City** (city) Franklin County
85	3229	1.3	**Kettering** (city) Montgomery County
85	3229	1.3	**Monfort Heights** (CDP) Hamilton County
90	3327	1.2	**Bedford Heights** (city) Cuyahoga County
90	3327	1.2	**Bellefontaine** (city) Logan County
90	3327	1.2	**Boardman** (CDP) Mahoning County
90	3327	1.2	**Brunswick** (city) Medina County
90	3327	1.2	**Cuyahoga Falls** (city) Summit County
90	3327	1.2	**North Ridgeville** (city) Lorain County
90	3327	1.2	**Northbrook** (CDP) Hamilton County
97	3443	1.1	**Celina** (city) Mercer County
97	3443	1.1	**Mount Vernon** (city) Knox County
97	3443	1.1	**North Canton** (city) Stark County
97	3443	1.1	**Toledo** (city) Lucas County
97	3443	1.1	**West Carrollton** (city) Montgomery County
97	3443	1.1	**White Oak** (CDP) Hamilton County
103	3560	1.0	**Ashland** (city) Ashland County
103	3560	1.0	**Eastlake** (city) Lake County
103	3560	1.0	**Maple Heights** (city) Cuyahoga County
103	3560	1.0	**Miamisburg** (city) Montgomery County
103	3560	1.0	**Reading** (city) Hamilton County
103	3560	1.0	**Tallmadge** (city) Summit County
103	3560	1.0	**Tiffin** (city) Seneca County
110	3694	0.9	**Bay Village** (city) Cuyahoga County
110	3694	0.9	**Bedford** (city) Cuyahoga County
110	3694	0.9	**Dayton** (city) Montgomery County
110	3694	0.9	**Maumee** (city) Lucas County
110	3694	0.9	**Medina** (city) Medina County
115	3856	0.8	**Alliance** (city) Stark County
115	3856	0.8	**Bridgetown** (CDP) Hamilton County
115	3856	0.8	**Elyria** (city) Lorain County
115	3856	0.8	**Lebanon** (city) Warren County
115	3856	0.8	**Norton** (city) Summit County
115	3856	0.8	**Norwood** (city) Hamilton County
115	3856	0.8	**Oregon** (city) Lucas County
115	3856	0.8	**Painesville** (city) Lake County
115	3856	0.8	**Springfield** (city) Clark County
115	3856	0.8	**Steubenville** (city) Jefferson County
115	3856	0.8	**Washington Court House** (city) Fayette County
115	3856	0.8	**Wickliffe** (city) Lake County
115	3856	0.8	**Willowick** (city) Lake County
115	3856	0.8	**Wilmington** (city) Clinton County
129	4028	0.7	**Amherst** (city) Lorain County
129	4028	0.7	**Bucyrus** (city) Crawford County
129	4028	0.7	**Euclid** (city) Cuyahoga County
129	4028	0.7	**Greenville** (city) Darke County
129	4028	0.7	**Heath** (city) Licking County
129	4028	0.7	**Mansfield** (city) Richland County
129	4028	0.7	**Niles** (city) Trumbull County
129	4028	0.7	**Pataskala** (city) Licking County
129	4028	0.7	**Piqua** (city) Miami County
129	4028	0.7	**Urbana** (city) Champaign County
129	4028	0.7	**Wadsworth** (city) Medina County
140	4205	0.6	**Austintown** (CDP) Mahoning County
140	4205	0.6	**Hamilton** (city) Butler County
140	4205	0.6	**New Philadelphia** (city) Tuscarawas County
140	4205	0.6	**Newark** (city) Licking County
140	4205	0.6	**Portsmouth** (city) Scioto County
140	4205	0.6	**Sandusky** (city) Erie County
146	4336	0.5	**Chillicothe** (city) Ross County
146	4336	0.5	**Dover** (city) Tuscarawas County
146	4336	0.5	**Franklin** (city) Warren County
146	4336	0.5	**Lancaster** (city) Fairfield County
146	4336	0.5	**Lima** (city) Allen County

Note: *The state column ranks the top/bottom 150 places from all places in the state with population of 10,000 or more. The national column ranks the top/bottom 150 places from all places in the country with population of 10,000 or more. Places that are unincorporated were not considered in the rankings. Please refer to the User Guide for additional information.*

Asian Population

Top 150 Places Ranked in *Ascending* Order

State Rank	Nat'l Rank	Percent	Place
1	20	0.2	**East Cleveland** (city) Cuyahoga County
1	20	0.2	**East Liverpool** (city) Columbiana County
1	20	0.2	**Galion** (city) Crawford County
1	20	0.2	**Struthers** (city) Mahoning County
5	61	0.3	**Ashtabula** (city) Ashtabula County
5	61	0.3	**Barberton** (city) Summit County
5	61	0.3	**Cambridge** (city) Guernsey County
5	61	0.3	**Canton** (city) Stark County
5	61	0.3	**Fremont** (city) Sandusky County
5	61	0.3	**Ironton** (city) Lawrence County
5	61	0.3	**Trotwood** (city) Montgomery County
5	61	0.3	**Vermilion** (city) Lorain County
5	61	0.3	**Warrensville Heights** (city) Cuyahoga County
14	108	0.4	**Circleville** (city) Pickaway County
14	108	0.4	**Conneaut** (city) Ashtabula County
14	108	0.4	**Coshocton** (city) Coshocton County
14	108	0.4	**Defiance** (city) Defiance County
14	108	0.4	**Fostoria** (city) Seneca County
14	108	0.4	**Lorain** (city) Lorain County
14	108	0.4	**Mack** (CDP) Hamilton County
14	108	0.4	**Marion** (city) Marion County
14	108	0.4	**Massillon** (city) Stark County
14	108	0.4	**New Franklin** (city) Summit County
14	108	0.4	**Ravenna** (city) Portage County
14	108	0.4	**Salem** (city) Columbiana County
14	108	0.4	**Van Wert** (city) Van Wert County
14	108	0.4	**Warren** (city) Trumbull County
14	108	0.4	**Youngstown** (city) Mahoning County
14	108	0.4	**Zanesville** (city) Muskingum County
30	198	0.5	**Chillicothe** (city) Ross County
30	198	0.5	**Dover** (city) Tuscarawas County
30	198	0.5	**Franklin** (city) Warren County
30	198	0.5	**Lancaster** (city) Fairfield County
30	198	0.5	**Lima** (city) Allen County
30	198	0.5	**Middletown** (city) Butler County
30	198	0.5	**Norwalk** (city) Huron County
30	198	0.5	**Trenton** (city) Butler County
30	198	0.5	**Xenia** (city) Greene County
39	321	0.6	**Austintown** (CDP) Mahoning County
39	321	0.6	**Hamilton** (city) Butler County
39	321	0.6	**New Philadelphia** (city) Tuscarawas County
39	321	0.6	**Newark** (city) Licking County
39	321	0.6	**Portsmouth** (city) Scioto County
39	321	0.6	**Sandusky** (city) Erie County
45	452	0.7	**Amherst** (city) Lorain County
45	452	0.7	**Bucyrus** (city) Crawford County
45	452	0.7	**Euclid** (city) Cuyahoga County
45	452	0.7	**Greenville** (city) Darke County
45	452	0.7	**Heath** (city) Licking County
45	452	0.7	**Mansfield** (city) Richland County
45	452	0.7	**Niles** (city) Trumbull County
45	452	0.7	**Pataskala** (city) Licking County
45	452	0.7	**Piqua** (city) Miami County
45	452	0.7	**Urbana** (city) Champaign County
45	452	0.7	**Wadsworth** (city) Medina County
56	629	0.8	**Alliance** (city) Stark County
56	629	0.8	**Bridgetown** (CDP) Hamilton County
56	629	0.8	**Elyria** (city) Lorain County
56	629	0.8	**Lebanon** (city) Warren County
56	629	0.8	**Norton** (city) Summit County
56	629	0.8	**Norwood** (city) Hamilton County
56	629	0.8	**Oregon** (city) Lucas County
56	629	0.8	**Painesville** (city) Lake County
56	629	0.8	**Springfield** (city) Clark County
56	629	0.8	**Steubenville** (city) Jefferson County
56	629	0.8	**Washington Court House** (city) Fayette County
56	629	0.8	**Wickliffe** (city) Lake County
56	629	0.8	**Willowick** (city) Lake County
56	629	0.8	**Wilmington** (city) Clinton County
70	801	0.9	**Bay Village** (city) Cuyahoga County
70	801	0.9	**Bedford** (city) Cuyahoga County
70	801	0.9	**Dayton** (city) Montgomery County
70	801	0.9	**Maumee** (city) Lucas County
70	801	0.9	**Medina** (city) Medina County
75	963	1.0	**Ashland** (city) Ashland County
75	963	1.0	**Eastlake** (city) Lake County
75	963	1.0	**Maple Heights** (city) Cuyahoga County
75	963	1.0	**Miamisburg** (city) Montgomery County
75	963	1.0	**Reading** (city) Hamilton County
75	963	1.0	**Tallmadge** (city) Summit County
75	963	1.0	**Tiffin** (city) Seneca County
82	1097	1.1	**Celina** (city) Mercer County
82	1097	1.1	**Mount Vernon** (city) Knox County
82	1097	1.1	**North Canton** (city) Stark County
82	1097	1.1	**Toledo** (city) Lucas County
82	1097	1.1	**West Carrollton** (city) Montgomery County
82	1097	1.1	**White Oak** (CDP) Hamilton County
88	1214	1.2	**Bedford Heights** (city) Cuyahoga County
88	1214	1.2	**Bellefontaine** (city) Logan County
88	1214	1.2	**Boardman** (CDP) Mahoning County
88	1214	1.2	**Brunswick** (city) Medina County
88	1214	1.2	**Cuyahoga Falls** (city) Summit County
88	1214	1.2	**North Ridgeville** (city) Lorain County
88	1214	1.2	**Northbrook** (CDP) Hamilton County
95	1330	1.3	**Avon Lake** (city) Lorain County
95	1330	1.3	**Garfield Heights** (city) Cuyahoga County
95	1330	1.3	**Grove City** (city) Franklin County
95	1330	1.3	**Kettering** (city) Montgomery County
95	1330	1.3	**Monfort Heights** (CDP) Hamilton County
100	1428	1.4	**Clayton** (city) Montgomery County
100	1428	1.4	**Delaware** (city) Delaware County
100	1428	1.4	**Finneytown** (CDP) Hamilton County
100	1428	1.4	**Marietta** (city) Washington County
100	1428	1.4	**Mentor** (city) Lake County
100	1428	1.4	**Vandalia** (city) Montgomery County
106	1546	1.5	**Berea** (city) Cuyahoga County
106	1546	1.5	**Bexley** (city) Franklin County
106	1546	1.5	**Green** (city) Summit County
106	1546	1.5	**Whitehall** (city) Franklin County
106	1546	1.5	**Willoughby** (city) Lake County
111	1648	1.6	**Brook Park** (city) Cuyahoga County
111	1648	1.6	**Dent** (CDP) Hamilton County
111	1648	1.6	**Englewood** (city) Montgomery County
111	1648	1.6	**Fairview Park** (city) Cuyahoga County
111	1648	1.6	**Lyndhurst** (city) Cuyahoga County
111	1648	1.6	**Sidney** (city) Shelby County
117	1759	1.7	**Loveland** (city) Hamilton County
117	1759	1.7	**Monroe** (city) Butler County
119	1856	1.8	**Cincinnati** (city) Hamilton County
119	1856	1.8	**Cleveland** (city) Cuyahoga County
119	1856	1.8	**Reynoldsburg** (city) Franklin County
119	1856	1.8	**Rocky River** (city) Cuyahoga County
123	1969	1.9	**Aurora** (city) Portage County
123	1969	1.9	**Lakewood** (city) Cuyahoga County
123	1969	1.9	**Parma** (city) Cuyahoga County
123	1969	1.9	**Riverside** (city) Montgomery County
123	1969	1.9	**Wooster** (city) Wayne County
128	2059	2.0	**South Euclid** (city) Cuyahoga County
129	2130	2.1	**Akron** (city) Summit County
129	2130	2.1	**Bowling Green** (city) Wood County
131	2192	2.2	**Forest Park** (city) Hamilton County
131	2192	2.2	**Streetsboro** (city) Portage County
133	2273	2.3	**Marysville** (city) Union County
133	2273	2.3	**Sylvania** (city) Lucas County
133	2273	2.3	**Westerville** (city) Franklin County
133	2273	2.3	**Worthington** (city) Franklin County
137	2343	2.4	**Fairfield** (city) Butler County
137	2343	2.4	**Stow** (city) Summit County
137	2343	2.4	**Troy** (city) Miami County
137	2343	2.4	**University Heights** (city) Cuyahoga County
141	2420	2.5	**Findlay** (city) Hancock County
141	2420	2.5	**Forestville** (CDP) Hamilton County
141	2420	2.5	**Huber Heights** (city) Montgomery County
141	2420	2.5	**Seven Hills** (city) Cuyahoga County
145	2543	2.7	**North Olmsted** (city) Cuyahoga County
145	2543	2.7	**North Royalton** (city) Cuyahoga County
147	2593	2.8	**Springdale** (city) Hamilton County
148	2647	2.9	**Pickerington** (city) Fairfield County
149	2704	3.0	**Parma Heights** (city) Cuyahoga County
150	2755	3.1	**Avon** (city) Lorain County

Note: *The state column ranks the top/bottom 150 places from all places in the state with population of 10,000 or more. The national column ranks the top/bottom 150 places from all places in the country with population of 10,000 or more. Places that are unincorporated were not considered in the rankings. Please refer to the User Guide for additional information.*

American Indian/Alaska Native Population

Top 150 Places Ranked in *Descending* Order

State Rank	Nat'l Rank	Percent	Place
1	1134	0.6	**Dover** (city) Tuscarawas County
2	1413	0.5	**Canton** (city) Stark County
2	1413	0.5	**Lorain** (city) Lorain County
2	1413	0.5	**Whitehall** (city) Franklin County
5	1783	0.4	**Ashtabula** (city) Ashtabula County
5	1783	0.4	**Celina** (city) Mercer County
5	1783	0.4	**New Philadelphia** (city) Tuscarawas County
5	1783	0.4	**Northbrook** (CDP) Hamilton County
5	1783	0.4	**Norwood** (city) Hamilton County
5	1783	0.4	**Portsmouth** (city) Scioto County
5	1783	0.4	**Sandusky** (city) Erie County
5	1783	0.4	**Toledo** (city) Lucas County
5	1783	0.4	**Urbana** (city) Champaign County
5	1783	0.4	**Xenia** (city) Greene County
5	1783	0.4	**Youngstown** (city) Mahoning County
5	1783	0.4	**Zanesville** (city) Muskingum County
17	2288	0.3	**Barberton** (city) Summit County
17	2288	0.3	**Cambridge** (city) Guernsey County
17	2288	0.3	**Chillicothe** (city) Ross County
17	2288	0.3	**Cincinnati** (city) Hamilton County
17	2288	0.3	**Cleveland** (city) Cuyahoga County
17	2288	0.3	**Columbus** (city) Franklin County
17	2288	0.3	**Dayton** (city) Montgomery County
17	2288	0.3	**Defiance** (city) Defiance County
17	2288	0.3	**Elyria** (city) Lorain County
17	2288	0.3	**Fairborn** (city) Greene County
17	2288	0.3	**Fairfield** (city) Butler County
17	2288	0.3	**Findlay** (city) Hancock County
17	2288	0.3	**Huber Heights** (city) Montgomery County
17	2288	0.3	**Lakewood** (city) Cuyahoga County
17	2288	0.3	**Lancaster** (city) Fairfield County
17	2288	0.3	**Lima** (city) Allen County
17	2288	0.3	**Marietta** (city) Washington County
17	2288	0.3	**Marysville** (city) Union County
17	2288	0.3	**Massillon** (city) Stark County
17	2288	0.3	**Newark** (city) Licking County
17	2288	0.3	**Painesville** (city) Lake County
17	2288	0.3	**Pataskala** (city) Licking County
17	2288	0.3	**Riverside** (city) Montgomery County
17	2288	0.3	**Springdale** (city) Hamilton County
17	2288	0.3	**Springfield** (city) Clark County
17	2288	0.3	**Tallmadge** (city) Summit County
17	2288	0.3	**Washington Court House** (city) Fayette County
17	2288	0.3	**West Carrollton** (city) Montgomery County
17	2288	0.3	**Wooster** (city) Wayne County
46	3031	0.2	**Akron** (city) Summit County
46	3031	0.2	**Alliance** (city) Stark County
46	3031	0.2	**Amherst** (city) Lorain County
46	3031	0.2	**Athens** (city) Athens County
46	3031	0.2	**Austintown** (CDP) Mahoning County
46	3031	0.2	**Beavercreek** (city) Greene County
46	3031	0.2	**Bedford** (city) Cuyahoga County
46	3031	0.2	**Bellefontaine** (city) Logan County
46	3031	0.2	**Berea** (city) Cuyahoga County
46	3031	0.2	**Blue Ash** (city) Hamilton County
46	3031	0.2	**Bowling Green** (city) Wood County
46	3031	0.2	**Brook Park** (city) Cuyahoga County
46	3031	0.2	**Brooklyn** (city) Cuyahoga County
46	3031	0.2	**Bucyrus** (city) Crawford County
46	3031	0.2	**Centerville** (city) Montgomery County
46	3031	0.2	**Circleville** (city) Pickaway County
46	3031	0.2	**Clayton** (city) Montgomery County
46	3031	0.2	**Cleveland Heights** (city) Cuyahoga County
46	3031	0.2	**Conneaut** (city) Ashtabula County
46	3031	0.2	**Coshocton** (city) Coshocton County
46	3031	0.2	**Cuyahoga Falls** (city) Summit County
46	3031	0.2	**Delaware** (city) Delaware County
46	3031	0.2	**East Cleveland** (city) Cuyahoga County
46	3031	0.2	**East Liverpool** (city) Columbiana County
46	3031	0.2	**Englewood** (city) Montgomery County
46	3031	0.2	**Euclid** (city) Cuyahoga County
46	3031	0.2	**Forest Park** (city) Hamilton County
46	3031	0.2	**Franklin** (city) Warren County
46	3031	0.2	**Fremont** (city) Sandusky County
46	3031	0.2	**Gahanna** (city) Franklin County
46	3031	0.2	**Garfield Heights** (city) Cuyahoga County
46	3031	0.2	**Green** (city) Summit County
46	3031	0.2	**Greenville** (city) Darke County
46	3031	0.2	**Grove City** (city) Franklin County
46	3031	0.2	**Hamilton** (city) Butler County
46	3031	0.2	**Heath** (city) Licking County
46	3031	0.2	**Hilliard** (city) Franklin County
46	3031	0.2	**Ironton** (city) Lawrence County
46	3031	0.2	**Kent** (city) Portage County
46	3031	0.2	**Kettering** (city) Montgomery County
46	3031	0.2	**Lebanon** (city) Warren County
46	3031	0.2	**Mansfield** (city) Richland County
46	3031	0.2	**Maple Heights** (city) Cuyahoga County
46	3031	0.2	**Marion** (city) Marion County
46	3031	0.2	**Mason** (city) Warren County
46	3031	0.2	**Maumee** (city) Lucas County
46	3031	0.2	**Miamisburg** (city) Montgomery County
46	3031	0.2	**Middleburg Heights** (city) Cuyahoga County
46	3031	0.2	**Middletown** (city) Butler County
46	3031	0.2	**Monroe** (city) Butler County
46	3031	0.2	**Mount Vernon** (city) Knox County
46	3031	0.2	**Niles** (city) Trumbull County
46	3031	0.2	**North Canton** (city) Stark County
46	3031	0.2	**North Ridgeville** (city) Lorain County
46	3031	0.2	**Norton** (city) Summit County
46	3031	0.2	**Norwalk** (city) Huron County
46	3031	0.2	**Oregon** (city) Lucas County
46	3031	0.2	**Oxford** (city) Butler County
46	3031	0.2	**Parma** (city) Cuyahoga County
46	3031	0.2	**Parma Heights** (city) Cuyahoga County
46	3031	0.2	**Pickerington** (city) Fairfield County
46	3031	0.2	**Piqua** (city) Miami County
46	3031	0.2	**Ravenna** (city) Portage County
46	3031	0.2	**Reynoldsburg** (city) Franklin County
46	3031	0.2	**Salem** (city) Columbiana County
46	3031	0.2	**Sharonville** (city) Hamilton County
46	3031	0.2	**Sidney** (city) Shelby County
46	3031	0.2	**Steubenville** (city) Jefferson County
46	3031	0.2	**Streetsboro** (city) Portage County
46	3031	0.2	**Struthers** (city) Mahoning County
46	3031	0.2	**Tiffin** (city) Seneca County
46	3031	0.2	**Trenton** (city) Butler County
46	3031	0.2	**Trotwood** (city) Montgomery County
46	3031	0.2	**Troy** (city) Miami County
46	3031	0.2	**Vermilion** (city) Lorain County
46	3031	0.2	**Wadsworth** (city) Medina County
46	3031	0.2	**Warren** (city) Trumbull County
46	3031	0.2	**Warrensville Heights** (city) Cuyahoga County
46	3031	0.2	**Westerville** (city) Franklin County
46	3031	0.2	**White Oak** (CDP) Hamilton County
46	3031	0.2	**Wilmington** (city) Clinton County
127	3935	0.1	**Ashland** (city) Ashland County
127	3935	0.1	**Aurora** (city) Portage County
127	3935	0.1	**Avon** (city) Lorain County
127	3935	0.1	**Avon Lake** (city) Lorain County
127	3935	0.1	**Bay Village** (city) Cuyahoga County
127	3935	0.1	**Bedford Heights** (city) Cuyahoga County
127	3935	0.1	**Bexley** (city) Franklin County
127	3935	0.1	**Boardman** (CDP) Mahoning County
127	3935	0.1	**Brecksville** (city) Cuyahoga County
127	3935	0.1	**Bridgetown** (CDP) Hamilton County
127	3935	0.1	**Broadview Heights** (city) Cuyahoga County
127	3935	0.1	**Brunswick** (city) Medina County
127	3935	0.1	**Dent** (CDP) Hamilton County
127	3935	0.1	**Dublin** (city) Franklin County
127	3935	0.1	**Eastlake** (city) Lake County
127	3935	0.1	**Fairview Park** (city) Cuyahoga County
127	3935	0.1	**Finneytown** (CDP) Hamilton County
127	3935	0.1	**Forestville** (CDP) Hamilton County
127	3935	0.1	**Fostoria** (city) Seneca County
127	3935	0.1	**Galion** (city) Crawford County
127	3935	0.1	**Hudson** (city) Summit County
127	3935	0.1	**Loveland** (city) Hamilton County
127	3935	0.1	**Macedonia** (city) Summit County
127	3935	0.1	**Mack** (CDP) Hamilton County

Note: *The state column ranks the top/bottom 150 places from all places in the state with population of 10,000 or more. The national column ranks the top/bottom 150 places from all places in the country with population of 10,000 or more. Places that are unincorporated were not considered in the rankings. Please refer to the User Guide for additional information.*

American Indian/Alaska Native Population

Top 150 Places Ranked in *Ascending* Order

State Rank	Nat'l Rank	Percent	Place
1	1	0.0	**Beachwood** (city) Cuyahoga County
1	1	0.0	**Lyndhurst** (city) Cuyahoga County
1	1	0.0	**Worthington** (city) Franklin County
4	61	0.1	**Ashland** (city) Ashland County
4	61	0.1	**Aurora** (city) Portage County
4	61	0.1	**Avon** (city) Lorain County
4	61	0.1	**Avon Lake** (city) Lorain County
4	61	0.1	**Bay Village** (city) Cuyahoga County
4	61	0.1	**Bedford Heights** (city) Cuyahoga County
4	61	0.1	**Bexley** (city) Franklin County
4	61	0.1	**Boardman** (CDP) Mahoning County
4	61	0.1	**Brecksville** (city) Cuyahoga County
4	61	0.1	**Bridgetown** (CDP) Hamilton County
4	61	0.1	**Broadview Heights** (city) Cuyahoga County
4	61	0.1	**Brunswick** (city) Medina County
4	61	0.1	**Dent** (CDP) Hamilton County
4	61	0.1	**Dublin** (city) Franklin County
4	61	0.1	**Eastlake** (city) Lake County
4	61	0.1	**Fairview Park** (city) Cuyahoga County
4	61	0.1	**Finneytown** (CDP) Hamilton County
4	61	0.1	**Forestville** (CDP) Hamilton County
4	61	0.1	**Fostoria** (city) Seneca County
4	61	0.1	**Galion** (city) Crawford County
4	61	0.1	**Hudson** (city) Summit County
4	61	0.1	**Loveland** (city) Hamilton County
4	61	0.1	**Macedonia** (city) Summit County
4	61	0.1	**Mack** (CDP) Hamilton County
4	61	0.1	**Mayfield Heights** (city) Cuyahoga County
4	61	0.1	**Medina** (city) Medina County
4	61	0.1	**Mentor** (city) Lake County
4	61	0.1	**Monfort Heights** (CDP) Hamilton County
4	61	0.1	**Montgomery** (city) Hamilton County
4	61	0.1	**New Franklin** (city) Summit County
4	61	0.1	**North Olmsted** (city) Cuyahoga County
4	61	0.1	**North Royalton** (city) Cuyahoga County
4	61	0.1	**Perrysburg** (city) Wood County
4	61	0.1	**Powell** (city) Delaware County
4	61	0.1	**Reading** (city) Hamilton County
4	61	0.1	**Richmond Heights** (city) Cuyahoga County
4	61	0.1	**Rocky River** (city) Cuyahoga County
4	61	0.1	**Seven Hills** (city) Cuyahoga County
4	61	0.1	**Shaker Heights** (city) Cuyahoga County
4	61	0.1	**Solon** (city) Cuyahoga County
4	61	0.1	**South Euclid** (city) Cuyahoga County
4	61	0.1	**Springboro** (city) Warren County
4	61	0.1	**Stow** (city) Summit County
4	61	0.1	**Strongsville** (city) Cuyahoga County
4	61	0.1	**Sylvania** (city) Lucas County
4	61	0.1	**Twinsburg** (city) Summit County
4	61	0.1	**University Heights** (city) Cuyahoga County
4	61	0.1	**Upper Arlington** (city) Franklin County
4	61	0.1	**Van Wert** (city) Van Wert County
4	61	0.1	**Vandalia** (city) Montgomery County
4	61	0.1	**Westlake** (city) Cuyahoga County
4	61	0.1	**Wickliffe** (city) Lake County
4	61	0.1	**Willoughby** (city) Lake County
4	61	0.1	**Willowick** (city) Lake County
58	722	0.2	**Akron** (city) Summit County
58	722	0.2	**Alliance** (city) Stark County
58	722	0.2	**Amherst** (city) Lorain County
58	722	0.2	**Athens** (city) Athens County
58	722	0.2	**Austintown** (CDP) Mahoning County
58	722	0.2	**Beavercreek** (city) Greene County
58	722	0.2	**Bedford** (city) Cuyahoga County
58	722	0.2	**Bellefontaine** (city) Logan County
58	722	0.2	**Berea** (city) Cuyahoga County
58	722	0.2	**Blue Ash** (city) Hamilton County
58	722	0.2	**Bowling Green** (city) Wood County
58	722	0.2	**Brook Park** (city) Cuyahoga County
58	722	0.2	**Brooklyn** (city) Cuyahoga County
58	722	0.2	**Bucyrus** (city) Crawford County
58	722	0.2	**Centerville** (city) Montgomery County
58	722	0.2	**Circleville** (city) Pickaway County
58	722	0.2	**Clayton** (city) Montgomery County
58	722	0.2	**Cleveland Heights** (city) Cuyahoga County
58	722	0.2	**Conneaut** (city) Ashtabula County
58	722	0.2	**Coshocton** (city) Coshocton County
58	722	0.2	**Cuyahoga Falls** (city) Summit County
58	722	0.2	**Delaware** (city) Delaware County
58	722	0.2	**East Cleveland** (city) Cuyahoga County
58	722	0.2	**East Liverpool** (city) Columbiana County
58	722	0.2	**Englewood** (city) Montgomery County
58	722	0.2	**Euclid** (city) Cuyahoga County
58	722	0.2	**Forest Park** (city) Hamilton County
58	722	0.2	**Franklin** (city) Warren County
58	722	0.2	**Fremont** (city) Sandusky County
58	722	0.2	**Gahanna** (city) Franklin County
58	722	0.2	**Garfield Heights** (city) Cuyahoga County
58	722	0.2	**Green** (city) Summit County
58	722	0.2	**Greenville** (city) Darke County
58	722	0.2	**Grove City** (city) Franklin County
58	722	0.2	**Hamilton** (city) Butler County
58	722	0.2	**Heath** (city) Licking County
58	722	0.2	**Hilliard** (city) Franklin County
58	722	0.2	**Ironton** (city) Lawrence County
58	722	0.2	**Kent** (city) Portage County
58	722	0.2	**Kettering** (city) Montgomery County
58	722	0.2	**Lebanon** (city) Warren County
58	722	0.2	**Mansfield** (city) Richland County
58	722	0.2	**Maple Heights** (city) Cuyahoga County
58	722	0.2	**Marion** (city) Marion County
58	722	0.2	**Mason** (city) Warren County
58	722	0.2	**Maumee** (city) Lucas County
58	722	0.2	**Miamisburg** (city) Montgomery County
58	722	0.2	**Middleburg Heights** (city) Cuyahoga County
58	722	0.2	**Middletown** (city) Butler County
58	722	0.2	**Monroe** (city) Butler County
58	722	0.2	**Mount Vernon** (city) Knox County
58	722	0.2	**Niles** (city) Trumbull County
58	722	0.2	**North Canton** (city) Stark County
58	722	0.2	**North Ridgeville** (city) Lorain County
58	722	0.2	**Norton** (city) Summit County
58	722	0.2	**Norwalk** (city) Huron County
58	722	0.2	**Oregon** (city) Lucas County
58	722	0.2	**Oxford** (city) Butler County
58	722	0.2	**Parma** (city) Cuyahoga County
58	722	0.2	**Parma Heights** (city) Cuyahoga County
58	722	0.2	**Pickerington** (city) Fairfield County
58	722	0.2	**Piqua** (city) Miami County
58	722	0.2	**Ravenna** (city) Portage County
58	722	0.2	**Reynoldsburg** (city) Franklin County
58	722	0.2	**Salem** (city) Columbiana County
58	722	0.2	**Sharonville** (city) Hamilton County
58	722	0.2	**Sidney** (city) Shelby County
58	722	0.2	**Steubenville** (city) Jefferson County
58	722	0.2	**Streetsboro** (city) Portage County
58	722	0.2	**Struthers** (city) Mahoning County
58	722	0.2	**Tiffin** (city) Seneca County
58	722	0.2	**Trenton** (city) Butler County
58	722	0.2	**Trotwood** (city) Montgomery County
58	722	0.2	**Troy** (city) Miami County
58	722	0.2	**Vermilion** (city) Lorain County
58	722	0.2	**Wadsworth** (city) Medina County
58	722	0.2	**Warren** (city) Trumbull County
58	722	0.2	**Warrensville Heights** (city) Cuyahoga County
58	722	0.2	**Westerville** (city) Franklin County
58	722	0.2	**White Oak** (CDP) Hamilton County
58	722	0.2	**Wilmington** (city) Clinton County
139	1626	0.3	**Barberton** (city) Summit County
139	1626	0.3	**Cambridge** (city) Guernsey County
139	1626	0.3	**Chillicothe** (city) Ross County
139	1626	0.3	**Cincinnati** (city) Hamilton County
139	1626	0.3	**Cleveland** (city) Cuyahoga County
139	1626	0.3	**Columbus** (city) Franklin County
139	1626	0.3	**Dayton** (city) Montgomery County
139	1626	0.3	**Defiance** (city) Defiance County
139	1626	0.3	**Elyria** (city) Lorain County
139	1626	0.3	**Fairborn** (city) Greene County
139	1626	0.3	**Fairfield** (city) Butler County
139	1626	0.3	**Findlay** (city) Hancock County

Note: *The state column ranks the top/bottom 150 places from all places in the state with population of 10,000 or more. The national column ranks the top/bottom 150 places from all places in the country with population of 10,000 or more. Places that are unincorporated were not considered in the rankings. Please refer to the User Guide for additional information.*

Native Hawaiian/Other Pacific Islander Population

Top 150 Places Ranked in *Descending* Order

State Rank	Nat'l Rank	Percent	Place
1	176	0.7	**Dover** (city) Tuscarawas County
2	288	0.4	**Celina** (city) Mercer County
2	288	0.4	**New Philadelphia** (city) Tuscarawas County
2	288	0.4	**Springdale** (city) Hamilton County
5	374	0.3	**Sharonville** (city) Hamilton County
6	510	0.2	**Forest Park** (city) Hamilton County
6	510	0.2	**Sidney** (city) Shelby County
8	820	0.1	**Ashland** (city) Ashland County
8	820	0.1	**Bridgetown** (CDP) Hamilton County
8	820	0.1	**Cincinnati** (city) Hamilton County
8	820	0.1	**Columbus** (city) Franklin County
8	820	0.1	**Englewood** (city) Montgomery County
8	820	0.1	**Fairborn** (city) Greene County
8	820	0.1	**Fairfield** (city) Butler County
8	820	0.1	**Finneytown** (CDP) Hamilton County
8	820	0.1	**Forestville** (CDP) Hamilton County
8	820	0.1	**Hamilton** (city) Butler County
8	820	0.1	**Huber Heights** (city) Montgomery County
8	820	0.1	**Kent** (city) Portage County
8	820	0.1	**Loveland** (city) Hamilton County
8	820	0.1	**Mansfield** (city) Richland County
8	820	0.1	**Marysville** (city) Union County
8	820	0.1	**Mason** (city) Warren County
8	820	0.1	**Northbrook** (CDP) Hamilton County
8	820	0.1	**Norton** (city) Summit County
8	820	0.1	**Norwood** (city) Hamilton County
8	820	0.1	**Reynoldsburg** (city) Franklin County
8	820	0.1	**Sylvania** (city) Lucas County
8	820	0.1	**Tallmadge** (city) Summit County
8	820	0.1	**Westlake** (city) Cuyahoga County
8	820	0.1	**Wilmington** (city) Clinton County
32	2061	0.0	**Akron** (city) Summit County
32	2061	0.0	**Alliance** (city) Stark County
32	2061	0.0	**Amherst** (city) Lorain County
32	2061	0.0	**Ashtabula** (city) Ashtabula County
32	2061	0.0	**Athens** (city) Athens County
32	2061	0.0	**Aurora** (city) Portage County
32	2061	0.0	**Austintown** (CDP) Mahoning County
32	2061	0.0	**Avon** (city) Lorain County
32	2061	0.0	**Avon Lake** (city) Lorain County
32	2061	0.0	**Barberton** (city) Summit County
32	2061	0.0	**Bay Village** (city) Cuyahoga County
32	2061	0.0	**Beachwood** (city) Cuyahoga County
32	2061	0.0	**Beavercreek** (city) Greene County
32	2061	0.0	**Bedford** (city) Cuyahoga County
32	2061	0.0	**Bedford Heights** (city) Cuyahoga County
32	2061	0.0	**Bellefontaine** (city) Logan County
32	2061	0.0	**Berea** (city) Cuyahoga County
32	2061	0.0	**Bexley** (city) Franklin County
32	2061	0.0	**Blue Ash** (city) Hamilton County
32	2061	0.0	**Boardman** (CDP) Mahoning County
32	2061	0.0	**Bowling Green** (city) Wood County
32	2061	0.0	**Brecksville** (city) Cuyahoga County
32	2061	0.0	**Broadview Heights** (city) Cuyahoga County
32	2061	0.0	**Brook Park** (city) Cuyahoga County
32	2061	0.0	**Brooklyn** (city) Cuyahoga County
32	2061	0.0	**Brunswick** (city) Medina County
32	2061	0.0	**Bucyrus** (city) Crawford County
32	2061	0.0	**Cambridge** (city) Guernsey County
32	2061	0.0	**Canton** (city) Stark County
32	2061	0.0	**Centerville** (city) Montgomery County
32	2061	0.0	**Chillicothe** (city) Ross County
32	2061	0.0	**Circleville** (city) Pickaway County
32	2061	0.0	**Clayton** (city) Montgomery County
32	2061	0.0	**Cleveland** (city) Cuyahoga County
32	2061	0.0	**Cleveland Heights** (city) Cuyahoga County
32	2061	0.0	**Conneaut** (city) Ashtabula County
32	2061	0.0	**Coshocton** (city) Coshocton County
32	2061	0.0	**Cuyahoga Falls** (city) Summit County
32	2061	0.0	**Dayton** (city) Montgomery County
32	2061	0.0	**Defiance** (city) Defiance County
32	2061	0.0	**Delaware** (city) Delaware County
32	2061	0.0	**Dent** (CDP) Hamilton County
32	2061	0.0	**Dublin** (city) Franklin County
32	2061	0.0	**East Cleveland** (city) Cuyahoga County
32	2061	0.0	**East Liverpool** (city) Columbiana County
32	2061	0.0	**Eastlake** (city) Lake County
32	2061	0.0	**Elyria** (city) Lorain County
32	2061	0.0	**Euclid** (city) Cuyahoga County
32	2061	0.0	**Fairview Park** (city) Cuyahoga County
32	2061	0.0	**Findlay** (city) Hancock County
32	2061	0.0	**Fostoria** (city) Seneca County
32	2061	0.0	**Franklin** (city) Warren County
32	2061	0.0	**Fremont** (city) Sandusky County
32	2061	0.0	**Gahanna** (city) Franklin County
32	2061	0.0	**Galion** (city) Crawford County
32	2061	0.0	**Garfield Heights** (city) Cuyahoga County
32	2061	0.0	**Green** (city) Summit County
32	2061	0.0	**Greenville** (city) Darke County
32	2061	0.0	**Grove City** (city) Franklin County
32	2061	0.0	**Heath** (city) Licking County
32	2061	0.0	**Hilliard** (city) Franklin County
32	2061	0.0	**Hudson** (city) Summit County
32	2061	0.0	**Ironton** (city) Lawrence County
32	2061	0.0	**Kettering** (city) Montgomery County
32	2061	0.0	**Lakewood** (city) Cuyahoga County
32	2061	0.0	**Lancaster** (city) Fairfield County
32	2061	0.0	**Lebanon** (city) Warren County
32	2061	0.0	**Lima** (city) Allen County
32	2061	0.0	**Lorain** (city) Lorain County
32	2061	0.0	**Lyndhurst** (city) Cuyahoga County
32	2061	0.0	**Macedonia** (city) Summit County
32	2061	0.0	**Mack** (CDP) Hamilton County
32	2061	0.0	**Maple Heights** (city) Cuyahoga County
32	2061	0.0	**Marietta** (city) Washington County
32	2061	0.0	**Marion** (city) Marion County
32	2061	0.0	**Massillon** (city) Stark County
32	2061	0.0	**Maumee** (city) Lucas County
32	2061	0.0	**Mayfield Heights** (city) Cuyahoga County
32	2061	0.0	**Medina** (city) Medina County
32	2061	0.0	**Mentor** (city) Lake County
32	2061	0.0	**Miamisburg** (city) Montgomery County
32	2061	0.0	**Middleburg Heights** (city) Cuyahoga County
32	2061	0.0	**Middletown** (city) Butler County
32	2061	0.0	**Monfort Heights** (CDP) Hamilton County
32	2061	0.0	**Monroe** (city) Butler County
32	2061	0.0	**Montgomery** (city) Hamilton County
32	2061	0.0	**Mount Vernon** (city) Knox County
32	2061	0.0	**New Franklin** (city) Summit County
32	2061	0.0	**Newark** (city) Licking County
32	2061	0.0	**Niles** (city) Trumbull County
32	2061	0.0	**North Canton** (city) Stark County
32	2061	0.0	**North Olmsted** (city) Cuyahoga County
32	2061	0.0	**North Ridgeville** (city) Lorain County
32	2061	0.0	**North Royalton** (city) Cuyahoga County
32	2061	0.0	**Norwalk** (city) Huron County
32	2061	0.0	**Oregon** (city) Lucas County
32	2061	0.0	**Oxford** (city) Butler County
32	2061	0.0	**Painesville** (city) Lake County
32	2061	0.0	**Parma** (city) Cuyahoga County
32	2061	0.0	**Parma Heights** (city) Cuyahoga County
32	2061	0.0	**Pataskala** (city) Licking County
32	2061	0.0	**Perrysburg** (city) Wood County
32	2061	0.0	**Pickerington** (city) Fairfield County
32	2061	0.0	**Piqua** (city) Miami County
32	2061	0.0	**Portsmouth** (city) Scioto County
32	2061	0.0	**Powell** (city) Delaware County
32	2061	0.0	**Ravenna** (city) Portage County
32	2061	0.0	**Reading** (city) Hamilton County
32	2061	0.0	**Richmond Heights** (city) Cuyahoga County
32	2061	0.0	**Riverside** (city) Montgomery County
32	2061	0.0	**Rocky River** (city) Cuyahoga County
32	2061	0.0	**Salem** (city) Columbiana County
32	2061	0.0	**Sandusky** (city) Erie County
32	2061	0.0	**Seven Hills** (city) Cuyahoga County
32	2061	0.0	**Shaker Heights** (city) Cuyahoga County
32	2061	0.0	**Solon** (city) Cuyahoga County
32	2061	0.0	**South Euclid** (city) Cuyahoga County
32	2061	0.0	**Springboro** (city) Warren County
32	2061	0.0	**Springfield** (city) Clark County

Note: *The state column ranks the top/bottom 150 places from all places in the state with population of 10,000 or more. The national column ranks the top/bottom 150 places from all places in the country with population of 10,000 or more. Places that are unincorporated were not considered in the rankings. Please refer to the User Guide for additional information.*

Two or More Races

Top 150 Places Ranked in *Descending* Order

State Rank	Nat'l Rank	Percent	Place
1	259	5.5	**Sandusky** (city) Erie County
2	281	5.4	**Lorain** (city) Lorain County
3	351	5.1	**Fremont** (city) Sandusky County
4	391	5.0	**Ashtabula** (city) Ashtabula County
5	461	4.8	**Canton** (city) Stark County
6	496	4.7	**Fostoria** (city) Seneca County
6	496	4.7	**Zanesville** (city) Muskingum County
8	577	4.5	**Painesville** (city) Lake County
9	625	4.4	**Lima** (city) Allen County
9	625	4.4	**Whitehall** (city) Franklin County
11	790	4.1	**Elyria** (city) Lorain County
12	854	4.0	**Springfield** (city) Clark County
13	915	3.9	**Toledo** (city) Lucas County
14	1030	3.7	**Bellefontaine** (city) Logan County
14	1030	3.7	**Youngstown** (city) Mahoning County
16	1109	3.6	**Forest Park** (city) Hamilton County
16	1109	3.6	**Northbrook** (CDP) Hamilton County
18	1191	3.5	**Huber Heights** (city) Montgomery County
18	1191	3.5	**Reynoldsburg** (city) Franklin County
18	1191	3.5	**Steubenville** (city) Jefferson County
18	1191	3.5	**Wilmington** (city) Clinton County
22	1272	3.4	**Alliance** (city) Stark County
22	1272	3.4	**Chillicothe** (city) Ross County
24	1354	3.3	**Columbus** (city) Franklin County
24	1354	3.3	**Sidney** (city) Shelby County
24	1354	3.3	**Warren** (city) Trumbull County
27	1439	3.2	**Akron** (city) Summit County
27	1439	3.2	**Xenia** (city) Greene County
29	1517	3.1	**Fairborn** (city) Greene County
29	1517	3.1	**Pickerington** (city) Fairfield County
29	1517	3.1	**Urbana** (city) Champaign County
32	1610	3.0	**Cambridge** (city) Guernsey County
32	1610	3.0	**East Liverpool** (city) Columbiana County
32	1610	3.0	**Mansfield** (city) Richland County
32	1610	3.0	**Portsmouth** (city) Scioto County
32	1610	3.0	**Sharonville** (city) Hamilton County
37	1717	2.9	**Dayton** (city) Montgomery County
37	1717	2.9	**Hamilton** (city) Butler County
37	1717	2.9	**Kent** (city) Portage County
37	1717	2.9	**Piqua** (city) Miami County
37	1717	2.9	**Springdale** (city) Hamilton County
42	1828	2.8	**Cleveland** (city) Cuyahoga County
42	1828	2.8	**Cleveland Heights** (city) Cuyahoga County
42	1828	2.8	**Defiance** (city) Defiance County
42	1828	2.8	**Riverside** (city) Montgomery County
46	1935	2.7	**Lakewood** (city) Cuyahoga County
46	1935	2.7	**Middletown** (city) Butler County
46	1935	2.7	**Shaker Heights** (city) Cuyahoga County
49	2062	2.6	**Massillon** (city) Stark County
49	2062	2.6	**Newark** (city) Licking County
49	2062	2.6	**Trotwood** (city) Montgomery County
52	2209	2.5	**Bedford** (city) Cuyahoga County
52	2209	2.5	**Bexley** (city) Franklin County
52	2209	2.5	**Cincinnati** (city) Hamilton County
52	2209	2.5	**Clayton** (city) Montgomery County
52	2209	2.5	**Delaware** (city) Delaware County
52	2209	2.5	**Norwood** (city) Hamilton County
52	2209	2.5	**Pataskala** (city) Licking County
52	2209	2.5	**South Euclid** (city) Cuyahoga County
60	2357	2.4	**Brooklyn** (city) Cuyahoga County
60	2357	2.4	**Fairfield** (city) Butler County
60	2357	2.4	**Gahanna** (city) Franklin County
60	2357	2.4	**Troy** (city) Miami County
60	2357	2.4	**Wooster** (city) Wayne County
65	2489	2.3	**Athens** (city) Athens County
65	2489	2.3	**Beavercreek** (city) Greene County
65	2489	2.3	**Berea** (city) Cuyahoga County
65	2489	2.3	**Englewood** (city) Montgomery County
65	2489	2.3	**Euclid** (city) Cuyahoga County
65	2489	2.3	**Finneytown** (CDP) Hamilton County
65	2489	2.3	**Ravenna** (city) Portage County
72	2642	2.2	**Barberton** (city) Summit County
72	2642	2.2	**Bowling Green** (city) Wood County
72	2642	2.2	**Heath** (city) Licking County
72	2642	2.2	**Niles** (city) Trumbull County
72	2642	2.2	**Oxford** (city) Butler County
77	2791	2.1	**Bedford Heights** (city) Cuyahoga County
77	2791	2.1	**Blue Ash** (city) Hamilton County
77	2791	2.1	**Findlay** (city) Hancock County
77	2791	2.1	**Garfield Heights** (city) Cuyahoga County
77	2791	2.1	**Grove City** (city) Franklin County
77	2791	2.1	**Ironton** (city) Lawrence County
77	2791	2.1	**Kettering** (city) Montgomery County
77	2791	2.1	**Maple Heights** (city) Cuyahoga County
77	2791	2.1	**Marion** (city) Marion County
77	2791	2.1	**Medina** (city) Medina County
77	2791	2.1	**Norwalk** (city) Huron County
77	2791	2.1	**Vandalia** (city) Montgomery County
77	2791	2.1	**Washington Court House** (city) Fayette County
77	2791	2.1	**Westerville** (city) Franklin County
91	2950	2.0	**Forestville** (CDP) Hamilton County
91	2950	2.0	**Lebanon** (city) Warren County
91	2950	2.0	**Van Wert** (city) Van Wert County
91	2950	2.0	**Warrensville Heights** (city) Cuyahoga County
91	2950	2.0	**West Carrollton** (city) Montgomery County
91	2950	2.0	**Worthington** (city) Franklin County
97	3098	1.9	**Brook Park** (city) Cuyahoga County
97	3098	1.9	**Centerville** (city) Montgomery County
97	3098	1.9	**Hilliard** (city) Franklin County
97	3098	1.9	**Loveland** (city) Hamilton County
97	3098	1.9	**Oregon** (city) Lucas County
97	3098	1.9	**Reading** (city) Hamilton County
97	3098	1.9	**Struthers** (city) Mahoning County
97	3098	1.9	**Trenton** (city) Butler County
97	3098	1.9	**Twinsburg** (city) Summit County
106	3250	1.8	**Austintown** (CDP) Mahoning County
106	3250	1.8	**Conneaut** (city) Ashtabula County
106	3250	1.8	**Dublin** (city) Franklin County
106	3250	1.8	**Marysville** (city) Union County
106	3250	1.8	**New Philadelphia** (city) Tuscarawas County
106	3250	1.8	**Parma Heights** (city) Cuyahoga County
106	3250	1.8	**Richmond Heights** (city) Cuyahoga County
106	3250	1.8	**Streetsboro** (city) Portage County
106	3250	1.8	**Vermilion** (city) Lorain County
106	3250	1.8	**White Oak** (CDP) Hamilton County
116	3438	1.7	**Amherst** (city) Lorain County
116	3438	1.7	**Boardman** (CDP) Mahoning County
116	3438	1.7	**Circleville** (city) Pickaway County
116	3438	1.7	**Franklin** (city) Warren County
116	3438	1.7	**Lancaster** (city) Fairfield County
116	3438	1.7	**Maumee** (city) Lucas County
116	3438	1.7	**Mayfield Heights** (city) Cuyahoga County
116	3438	1.7	**North Olmsted** (city) Cuyahoga County
116	3438	1.7	**Powell** (city) Delaware County
116	3438	1.7	**Springboro** (city) Warren County
116	3438	1.7	**Sylvania** (city) Lucas County
127	3607	1.6	**Celina** (city) Mercer County
127	3607	1.6	**Coshocton** (city) Coshocton County
127	3607	1.6	**Cuyahoga Falls** (city) Summit County
127	3607	1.6	**Macedonia** (city) Summit County
127	3607	1.6	**North Ridgeville** (city) Lorain County
127	3607	1.6	**Parma** (city) Cuyahoga County
127	3607	1.6	**Perrysburg** (city) Wood County
127	3607	1.6	**Tiffin** (city) Seneca County
127	3607	1.6	**University Heights** (city) Cuyahoga County
127	3607	1.6	**Upper Arlington** (city) Franklin County
127	3607	1.6	**Westlake** (city) Cuyahoga County
127	3607	1.6	**Wickliffe** (city) Lake County
139	3796	1.5	**East Cleveland** (city) Cuyahoga County
139	3796	1.5	**Marietta** (city) Washington County
139	3796	1.5	**Mason** (city) Warren County
139	3796	1.5	**Miamisburg** (city) Montgomery County
139	3796	1.5	**Monfort Heights** (CDP) Hamilton County
139	3796	1.5	**Mount Vernon** (city) Knox County
139	3796	1.5	**North Canton** (city) Stark County
139	3796	1.5	**Tallmadge** (city) Summit County
139	3796	1.5	**Willoughby** (city) Lake County
148	3933	1.4	**Avon** (city) Lorain County
148	3933	1.4	**Avon Lake** (city) Lorain County
148	3933	1.4	**Dover** (city) Tuscarawas County

Note: *The state column ranks the top/bottom 150 places from all places in the state with population of 10,000 or more. The national column ranks the top/bottom 150 places from all places in the country with population of 10,000 or more. Places that are unincorporated were not considered in the rankings. Please refer to the User Guide for additional information.*

Two or More Races

Top 150 Places Ranked in *Ascending* Order

State Rank	Nat'l Rank	Percent	Place
1	27	0.7	**Mack** (CDP) Hamilton County
1	27	0.7	**Seven Hills** (city) Cuyahoga County
3	90	0.9	**Middleburg Heights** (city) Cuyahoga County
4	124	1.0	**Aurora** (city) Portage County
4	124	1.0	**Dent** (CDP) Hamilton County
4	124	1.0	**Mentor** (city) Lake County
4	124	1.0	**New Franklin** (city) Summit County
4	124	1.0	**Norton** (city) Summit County
9	192	1.1	**Bay Village** (city) Cuyahoga County
9	192	1.1	**Brecksville** (city) Cuyahoga County
9	192	1.1	**Bridgetown** (CDP) Hamilton County
9	192	1.1	**Galion** (city) Crawford County
9	192	1.1	**Greenville** (city) Darke County
9	192	1.1	**North Royalton** (city) Cuyahoga County
9	192	1.1	**Wadsworth** (city) Medina County
16	295	1.2	**Beachwood** (city) Cuyahoga County
16	295	1.2	**Eastlake** (city) Lake County
16	295	1.2	**Fairview Park** (city) Cuyahoga County
16	295	1.2	**Green** (city) Summit County
16	295	1.2	**Lyndhurst** (city) Cuyahoga County
16	295	1.2	**Salem** (city) Columbiana County
22	415	1.3	**Ashland** (city) Ashland County
22	415	1.3	**Broadview Heights** (city) Cuyahoga County
22	415	1.3	**Brunswick** (city) Medina County
22	415	1.3	**Bucyrus** (city) Crawford County
22	415	1.3	**Hudson** (city) Summit County
22	415	1.3	**Monroe** (city) Butler County
22	415	1.3	**Rocky River** (city) Cuyahoga County
22	415	1.3	**Willowick** (city) Lake County
30	549	1.4	**Avon** (city) Lorain County
30	549	1.4	**Avon Lake** (city) Lorain County
30	549	1.4	**Dover** (city) Tuscarawas County
30	549	1.4	**Montgomery** (city) Hamilton County
30	549	1.4	**Solon** (city) Cuyahoga County
30	549	1.4	**Stow** (city) Summit County
30	549	1.4	**Strongsville** (city) Cuyahoga County
37	724	1.5	**East Cleveland** (city) Cuyahoga County
37	724	1.5	**Marietta** (city) Washington County
37	724	1.5	**Mason** (city) Warren County
37	724	1.5	**Miamisburg** (city) Montgomery County
37	724	1.5	**Monfort Heights** (CDP) Hamilton County
37	724	1.5	**Mount Vernon** (city) Knox County
37	724	1.5	**North Canton** (city) Stark County
37	724	1.5	**Tallmadge** (city) Summit County
37	724	1.5	**Willoughby** (city) Lake County
46	861	1.6	**Celina** (city) Mercer County
46	861	1.6	**Coshocton** (city) Coshocton County
46	861	1.6	**Cuyahoga Falls** (city) Summit County
46	861	1.6	**Macedonia** (city) Summit County
46	861	1.6	**North Ridgeville** (city) Lorain County
46	861	1.6	**Parma** (city) Cuyahoga County
46	861	1.6	**Perrysburg** (city) Wood County
46	861	1.6	**Tiffin** (city) Seneca County
46	861	1.6	**University Heights** (city) Cuyahoga County
46	861	1.6	**Upper Arlington** (city) Franklin County
46	861	1.6	**Westlake** (city) Cuyahoga County
46	861	1.6	**Wickliffe** (city) Lake County
58	1050	1.7	**Amherst** (city) Lorain County
58	1050	1.7	**Boardman** (CDP) Mahoning County
58	1050	1.7	**Circleville** (city) Pickaway County
58	1050	1.7	**Franklin** (city) Warren County
58	1050	1.7	**Lancaster** (city) Fairfield County
58	1050	1.7	**Maumee** (city) Lucas County
58	1050	1.7	**Mayfield Heights** (city) Cuyahoga County
58	1050	1.7	**North Olmsted** (city) Cuyahoga County
58	1050	1.7	**Powell** (city) Delaware County
58	1050	1.7	**Springboro** (city) Warren County
58	1050	1.7	**Sylvania** (city) Lucas County
69	1219	1.8	**Austintown** (CDP) Mahoning County
69	1219	1.8	**Conneaut** (city) Ashtabula County
69	1219	1.8	**Dublin** (city) Franklin County
69	1219	1.8	**Marysville** (city) Union County
69	1219	1.8	**New Philadelphia** (city) Tuscarawas County
69	1219	1.8	**Parma Heights** (city) Cuyahoga County
69	1219	1.8	**Richmond Heights** (city) Cuyahoga County
69	1219	1.8	**Streetsboro** (city) Portage County
69	1219	1.8	**Vermilion** (city) Lorain County
69	1219	1.8	**White Oak** (CDP) Hamilton County
79	1407	1.9	**Brook Park** (city) Cuyahoga County
79	1407	1.9	**Centerville** (city) Montgomery County
79	1407	1.9	**Hilliard** (city) Franklin County
79	1407	1.9	**Loveland** (city) Hamilton County
79	1407	1.9	**Oregon** (city) Lucas County
79	1407	1.9	**Reading** (city) Hamilton County
79	1407	1.9	**Struthers** (city) Mahoning County
79	1407	1.9	**Trenton** (city) Butler County
79	1407	1.9	**Twinsburg** (city) Summit County
88	1559	2.0	**Forestville** (CDP) Hamilton County
88	1559	2.0	**Lebanon** (city) Warren County
88	1559	2.0	**Van Wert** (city) Van Wert County
88	1559	2.0	**Warrensville Heights** (city) Cuyahoga County
88	1559	2.0	**West Carrollton** (city) Montgomery County
88	1559	2.0	**Worthington** (city) Franklin County
94	1707	2.1	**Bedford Heights** (city) Cuyahoga County
94	1707	2.1	**Blue Ash** (city) Hamilton County
94	1707	2.1	**Findlay** (city) Hancock County
94	1707	2.1	**Garfield Heights** (city) Cuyahoga County
94	1707	2.1	**Grove City** (city) Franklin County
94	1707	2.1	**Ironton** (city) Lawrence County
94	1707	2.1	**Kettering** (city) Montgomery County
94	1707	2.1	**Maple Heights** (city) Cuyahoga County
94	1707	2.1	**Marion** (city) Marion County
94	1707	2.1	**Medina** (city) Medina County
94	1707	2.1	**Norwalk** (city) Huron County
94	1707	2.1	**Vandalia** (city) Montgomery County
94	1707	2.1	**Washington Court House** (city) Fayette County
94	1707	2.1	**Westerville** (city) Franklin County
108	1866	2.2	**Barberton** (city) Summit County
108	1866	2.2	**Bowling Green** (city) Wood County
108	1866	2.2	**Heath** (city) Licking County
108	1866	2.2	**Niles** (city) Trumbull County
108	1866	2.2	**Oxford** (city) Butler County
113	2015	2.3	**Athens** (city) Athens County
113	2015	2.3	**Beavercreek** (city) Greene County
113	2015	2.3	**Berea** (city) Cuyahoga County
113	2015	2.3	**Englewood** (city) Montgomery County
113	2015	2.3	**Euclid** (city) Cuyahoga County
113	2015	2.3	**Finneytown** (CDP) Hamilton County
113	2015	2.3	**Ravenna** (city) Portage County
120	2168	2.4	**Brooklyn** (city) Cuyahoga County
120	2168	2.4	**Fairfield** (city) Butler County
120	2168	2.4	**Gahanna** (city) Franklin County
120	2168	2.4	**Troy** (city) Miami County
120	2168	2.4	**Wooster** (city) Wayne County
125	2300	2.5	**Bedford** (city) Cuyahoga County
125	2300	2.5	**Bexley** (city) Franklin County
125	2300	2.5	**Cincinnati** (city) Hamilton County
125	2300	2.5	**Clayton** (city) Montgomery County
125	2300	2.5	**Delaware** (city) Delaware County
125	2300	2.5	**Norwood** (city) Hamilton County
125	2300	2.5	**Pataskala** (city) Licking County
125	2300	2.5	**South Euclid** (city) Cuyahoga County
133	2448	2.6	**Massillon** (city) Stark County
133	2448	2.6	**Newark** (city) Licking County
133	2448	2.6	**Trotwood** (city) Montgomery County
136	2595	2.7	**Lakewood** (city) Cuyahoga County
136	2595	2.7	**Middletown** (city) Butler County
136	2595	2.7	**Shaker Heights** (city) Cuyahoga County
139	2722	2.8	**Cleveland** (city) Cuyahoga County
139	2722	2.8	**Cleveland Heights** (city) Cuyahoga County
139	2722	2.8	**Defiance** (city) Defiance County
139	2722	2.8	**Riverside** (city) Montgomery County
143	2829	2.9	**Dayton** (city) Montgomery County
143	2829	2.9	**Hamilton** (city) Butler County
143	2829	2.9	**Kent** (city) Portage County
143	2829	2.9	**Piqua** (city) Miami County
143	2829	2.9	**Springdale** (city) Hamilton County
148	2940	3.0	**Cambridge** (city) Guernsey County
148	2940	3.0	**East Liverpool** (city) Columbiana County
148	2940	3.0	**Mansfield** (city) Richland County

Note: *The state column ranks the top/bottom 150 places from all places in the state with population of 10,000 or more. The national column ranks the top/bottom 150 places from all places in the country with population of 10,000 or more. Places that are unincorporated were not considered in the rankings. Please refer to the User Guide for additional information.*

Hispanic Population

Top 150 Places Ranked in *Descending* Order

State Rank	Nat'l Rank	Percent	Place
1	793	25.2	**Lorain** (city) Lorain County
2	909	22.0	**Painesville** (city) Lake County
3	1131	17.5	**Springdale** (city) Hamilton County
4	1226	16.1	**Fremont** (city) Sandusky County
5	1361	14.4	**Defiance** (city) Defiance County
6	1652	11.5	**Fostoria** (city) Seneca County
7	1786	10.4	**Brooklyn** (city) Cuyahoga County
8	1829	10.0	**Cleveland** (city) Cuyahoga County
9	1846	9.9	**Whitehall** (city) Franklin County
10	1921	9.3	**Ashtabula** (city) Ashtabula County
10	1921	9.3	**Youngstown** (city) Mahoning County
12	2200	7.5	**Oregon** (city) Lucas County
13	2225	7.4	**Toledo** (city) Lucas County
14	2269	7.2	**Norwalk** (city) Huron County
15	2312	7.0	**Sharonville** (city) Hamilton County
16	2462	6.4	**Forest Park** (city) Hamilton County
16	2462	6.4	**Hamilton** (city) Butler County
18	2640	5.7	**Findlay** (city) Hancock County
19	2661	5.6	**Columbus** (city) Franklin County
20	2687	5.5	**Fairfield** (city) Butler County
21	2736	5.3	**Amherst** (city) Lorain County
22	2801	5.1	**Norwood** (city) Hamilton County
23	2870	4.9	**Elyria** (city) Lorain County
23	2870	4.9	**Sandusky** (city) Erie County
25	2904	4.8	**Bowling Green** (city) Wood County
26	3098	4.2	**New Philadelphia** (city) Tuscarawas County
27	3122	4.1	**Dover** (city) Tuscarawas County
27	3122	4.1	**Lakewood** (city) Cuyahoga County
29	3169	4.0	**Van Wert** (city) Van Wert County
30	3229	3.8	**Middletown** (city) Butler County
30	3229	3.8	**Parma Heights** (city) Cuyahoga County
32	3261	3.7	**Lima** (city) Allen County
33	3297	3.6	**Parma** (city) Cuyahoga County
34	3334	3.5	**Lebanon** (city) Warren County
34	3334	3.5	**North Olmsted** (city) Cuyahoga County
34	3334	3.5	**Northbrook** (CDP) Hamilton County
37	3377	3.4	**Avon** (city) Lorain County
37	3377	3.4	**Brook Park** (city) Cuyahoga County
37	3377	3.4	**Maumee** (city) Lucas County
37	3377	3.4	**Reynoldsburg** (city) Franklin County
41	3421	3.3	**Boardman** (CDP) Mahoning County
41	3421	3.3	**Fairview Park** (city) Cuyahoga County
41	3421	3.3	**North Ridgeville** (city) Lorain County
41	3421	3.3	**Riverside** (city) Montgomery County
45	3462	3.2	**Mason** (city) Warren County
45	3462	3.2	**Perrysburg** (city) Wood County
47	3505	3.1	**Huber Heights** (city) Montgomery County
47	3505	3.1	**Struthers** (city) Mahoning County
47	3505	3.1	**Tiffin** (city) Seneca County
50	3560	3.0	**Dayton** (city) Montgomery County
50	3560	3.0	**Marion** (city) Marion County
50	3560	3.0	**Springfield** (city) Clark County
53	3607	2.9	**Sylvania** (city) Lucas County
54	3660	2.8	**Berea** (city) Cuyahoga County
54	3660	2.8	**Celina** (city) Mercer County
54	3660	2.8	**Cincinnati** (city) Hamilton County
54	3660	2.8	**University Heights** (city) Cuyahoga County
54	3660	2.8	**Vermilion** (city) Lorain County
59	3711	2.7	**Austintown** (CDP) Mahoning County
60	3754	2.6	**Beavercreek** (city) Greene County
60	3754	2.6	**Bedford Heights** (city) Cuyahoga County
60	3754	2.6	**Canton** (city) Stark County
60	3754	2.6	**Gahanna** (city) Franklin County
60	3754	2.6	**Grove City** (city) Franklin County
60	3754	2.6	**West Carrollton** (city) Montgomery County
60	3754	2.6	**Wilmington** (city) Clinton County
67	3812	2.5	**Blue Ash** (city) Hamilton County
67	3812	2.5	**Delaware** (city) Delaware County
67	3812	2.5	**Pickerington** (city) Fairfield County
67	3812	2.5	**Salem** (city) Columbiana County
67	3812	2.5	**Westlake** (city) Cuyahoga County
72	3857	2.4	**Athens** (city) Athens County
72	3857	2.4	**Avon Lake** (city) Lorain County
72	3857	2.4	**Fairborn** (city) Greene County
72	3857	2.4	**Loveland** (city) Hamilton County
72	3857	2.4	**Steubenville** (city) Jefferson County
77	3931	2.3	**Brunswick** (city) Medina County
77	3931	2.3	**Garfield Heights** (city) Cuyahoga County
77	3931	2.3	**Hilliard** (city) Franklin County
77	3931	2.3	**Oxford** (city) Butler County
81	3988	2.2	**Kent** (city) Portage County
81	3988	2.2	**Middleburg Heights** (city) Cuyahoga County
81	3988	2.2	**Portsmouth** (city) Scioto County
81	3988	2.2	**Shaker Heights** (city) Cuyahoga County
81	3988	2.2	**Sidney** (city) Shelby County
81	3988	2.2	**Wooster** (city) Wayne County
87	4045	2.1	**Akron** (city) Summit County
87	4045	2.1	**Kettering** (city) Montgomery County
89	4094	2.0	**Bedford** (city) Cuyahoga County
89	4094	2.0	**Cleveland Heights** (city) Cuyahoga County
89	4094	2.0	**Massillon** (city) Stark County
89	4094	2.0	**Mayfield Heights** (city) Cuyahoga County
89	4094	2.0	**Pataskala** (city) Licking County
89	4094	2.0	**South Euclid** (city) Cuyahoga County
89	4094	2.0	**Strongsville** (city) Cuyahoga County
89	4094	2.0	**Urbana** (city) Champaign County
97	4156	1.9	**Alliance** (city) Stark County
97	4156	1.9	**Beachwood** (city) Cuyahoga County
97	4156	1.9	**Bellefontaine** (city) Logan County
97	4156	1.9	**Finneytown** (CDP) Hamilton County
97	4156	1.9	**Mansfield** (city) Richland County
97	4156	1.9	**Warren** (city) Trumbull County
97	4156	1.9	**Westerville** (city) Franklin County
104	4213	1.8	**Bexley** (city) Franklin County
104	4213	1.8	**Broadview Heights** (city) Cuyahoga County
104	4213	1.8	**Centerville** (city) Montgomery County
104	4213	1.8	**Conneaut** (city) Ashtabula County
104	4213	1.8	**Dublin** (city) Franklin County
104	4213	1.8	**Marysville** (city) Union County
104	4213	1.8	**Medina** (city) Medina County
104	4213	1.8	**Monroe** (city) Butler County
104	4213	1.8	**Montgomery** (city) Hamilton County
104	4213	1.8	**Mount Vernon** (city) Knox County
104	4213	1.8	**Richmond Heights** (city) Cuyahoga County
104	4213	1.8	**Rocky River** (city) Cuyahoga County
104	4213	1.8	**Springboro** (city) Warren County
104	4213	1.8	**Troy** (city) Miami County
104	4213	1.8	**Washington Court House** (city) Fayette County
119	4287	1.7	**Hudson** (city) Summit County
119	4287	1.7	**Reading** (city) Hamilton County
119	4287	1.7	**Streetsboro** (city) Portage County
119	4287	1.7	**Trenton** (city) Butler County
119	4287	1.7	**Worthington** (city) Franklin County
119	4287	1.7	**Xenia** (city) Greene County
125	4340	1.6	**Bay Village** (city) Cuyahoga County
125	4340	1.6	**Bucyrus** (city) Crawford County
125	4340	1.6	**Euclid** (city) Cuyahoga County
125	4340	1.6	**Franklin** (city) Warren County
125	4340	1.6	**Lancaster** (city) Fairfield County
125	4340	1.6	**Miamisburg** (city) Montgomery County
125	4340	1.6	**North Royalton** (city) Cuyahoga County
125	4340	1.6	**Upper Arlington** (city) Franklin County
125	4340	1.6	**Vandalia** (city) Montgomery County
134	4394	1.5	**Forestville** (CDP) Hamilton County
134	4394	1.5	**Heath** (city) Licking County
134	4394	1.5	**Maple Heights** (city) Cuyahoga County
134	4394	1.5	**North Canton** (city) Stark County
134	4394	1.5	**Solon** (city) Cuyahoga County
134	4394	1.5	**Stow** (city) Summit County
140	4442	1.4	**Barberton** (city) Summit County
140	4442	1.4	**Brecksville** (city) Cuyahoga County
140	4442	1.4	**Clayton** (city) Montgomery County
140	4442	1.4	**Cuyahoga Falls** (city) Summit County
140	4442	1.4	**Eastlake** (city) Lake County
140	4442	1.4	**Greenville** (city) Darke County
140	4442	1.4	**Piqua** (city) Miami County
140	4442	1.4	**Powell** (city) Delaware County
140	4442	1.4	**Ravenna** (city) Portage County
140	4442	1.4	**Warrensville Heights** (city) Cuyahoga County
140	4442	1.4	**White Oak** (CDP) Hamilton County

Note: *The state column ranks the top/bottom 150 places from all places in the state with population of 10,000 or more. The national column ranks the top/bottom 150 places from all places in the country with population of 10,000 or more. Places that are unincorporated were not considered in the rankings. Please refer to the User Guide for additional information.*

Hispanic Population

Top 150 Places Ranked in *Ascending* Order

State Rank	Nat'l Rank	Percent	Place
1	2	0.5	**Ironton** (city) Lawrence County
2	7	0.6	**Mack** (CDP) Hamilton County
3	20	0.8	**Bridgetown** (CDP) Hamilton County
3	20	0.8	**New Franklin** (city) Summit County
5	32	0.9	**Monfort Heights** (CDP) Hamilton County
5	32	0.9	**Norton** (city) Summit County
5	32	0.9	**Trotwood** (city) Montgomery County
8	58	1.0	**East Cleveland** (city) Cuyahoga County
8	58	1.0	**Tallmadge** (city) Summit County
10	80	1.1	**Circleville** (city) Pickaway County
10	80	1.1	**Coshocton** (city) Coshocton County
10	80	1.1	**Dent** (CDP) Hamilton County
10	80	1.1	**East Liverpool** (city) Columbiana County
10	80	1.1	**Englewood** (city) Montgomery County
10	80	1.1	**Marietta** (city) Washington County
16	107	1.2	**Ashland** (city) Ashland County
16	107	1.2	**Cambridge** (city) Guernsey County
16	107	1.2	**Green** (city) Summit County
16	107	1.2	**Newark** (city) Licking County
16	107	1.2	**Twinsburg** (city) Summit County
16	107	1.2	**Wadsworth** (city) Medina County
16	107	1.2	**Wickliffe** (city) Lake County
16	107	1.2	**Zanesville** (city) Muskingum County
24	144	1.3	**Aurora** (city) Portage County
24	144	1.3	**Chillicothe** (city) Ross County
24	144	1.3	**Galion** (city) Crawford County
24	144	1.3	**Lyndhurst** (city) Cuyahoga County
24	144	1.3	**Macedonia** (city) Summit County
24	144	1.3	**Mentor** (city) Lake County
24	144	1.3	**Niles** (city) Trumbull County
24	144	1.3	**Seven Hills** (city) Cuyahoga County
24	144	1.3	**Willoughby** (city) Lake County
24	144	1.3	**Willowick** (city) Lake County
34	172	1.4	**Barberton** (city) Summit County
34	172	1.4	**Brecksville** (city) Cuyahoga County
34	172	1.4	**Clayton** (city) Montgomery County
34	172	1.4	**Cuyahoga Falls** (city) Summit County
34	172	1.4	**Eastlake** (city) Lake County
34	172	1.4	**Greenville** (city) Darke County
34	172	1.4	**Piqua** (city) Miami County
34	172	1.4	**Powell** (city) Delaware County
34	172	1.4	**Ravenna** (city) Portage County
34	172	1.4	**Warrensville Heights** (city) Cuyahoga County
34	172	1.4	**White Oak** (CDP) Hamilton County
45	215	1.5	**Forestville** (CDP) Hamilton County
45	215	1.5	**Heath** (city) Licking County
45	215	1.5	**Maple Heights** (city) Cuyahoga County
45	215	1.5	**North Canton** (city) Stark County
45	215	1.5	**Solon** (city) Cuyahoga County
45	215	1.5	**Stow** (city) Summit County
51	263	1.6	**Bay Village** (city) Cuyahoga County
51	263	1.6	**Bucyrus** (city) Crawford County
51	263	1.6	**Euclid** (city) Cuyahoga County
51	263	1.6	**Franklin** (city) Warren County
51	263	1.6	**Lancaster** (city) Fairfield County
51	263	1.6	**Miamisburg** (city) Montgomery County
51	263	1.6	**North Royalton** (city) Cuyahoga County
51	263	1.6	**Upper Arlington** (city) Franklin County
51	263	1.6	**Vandalia** (city) Montgomery County
60	317	1.7	**Hudson** (city) Summit County
60	317	1.7	**Reading** (city) Hamilton County
60	317	1.7	**Streetsboro** (city) Portage County
60	317	1.7	**Trenton** (city) Butler County
60	317	1.7	**Worthington** (city) Franklin County
60	317	1.7	**Xenia** (city) Greene County
66	370	1.8	**Bexley** (city) Franklin County
66	370	1.8	**Broadview Heights** (city) Cuyahoga County
66	370	1.8	**Centerville** (city) Montgomery County
66	370	1.8	**Conneaut** (city) Ashtabula County
66	370	1.8	**Dublin** (city) Franklin County
66	370	1.8	**Marysville** (city) Union County
66	370	1.8	**Medina** (city) Medina County
66	370	1.8	**Monroe** (city) Butler County
66	370	1.8	**Montgomery** (city) Hamilton County
66	370	1.8	**Mount Vernon** (city) Knox County
66	370	1.8	**Richmond Heights** (city) Cuyahoga County
66	370	1.8	**Rocky River** (city) Cuyahoga County
66	370	1.8	**Springboro** (city) Warren County
66	370	1.8	**Troy** (city) Miami County
66	370	1.8	**Washington Court House** (city) Fayette County
81	444	1.9	**Alliance** (city) Stark County
81	444	1.9	**Beachwood** (city) Cuyahoga County
81	444	1.9	**Bellefontaine** (city) Logan County
81	444	1.9	**Finneytown** (CDP) Hamilton County
81	444	1.9	**Mansfield** (city) Richland County
81	444	1.9	**Warren** (city) Trumbull County
81	444	1.9	**Westerville** (city) Franklin County
88	501	2.0	**Bedford** (city) Cuyahoga County
88	501	2.0	**Cleveland Heights** (city) Cuyahoga County
88	501	2.0	**Massillon** (city) Stark County
88	501	2.0	**Mayfield Heights** (city) Cuyahoga County
88	501	2.0	**Pataskala** (city) Licking County
88	501	2.0	**South Euclid** (city) Cuyahoga County
88	501	2.0	**Strongsville** (city) Cuyahoga County
88	501	2.0	**Urbana** (city) Champaign County
96	563	2.1	**Akron** (city) Summit County
96	563	2.1	**Kettering** (city) Montgomery County
98	612	2.2	**Kent** (city) Portage County
98	612	2.2	**Middleburg Heights** (city) Cuyahoga County
98	612	2.2	**Portsmouth** (city) Scioto County
98	612	2.2	**Shaker Heights** (city) Cuyahoga County
98	612	2.2	**Sidney** (city) Shelby County
98	612	2.2	**Wooster** (city) Wayne County
104	669	2.3	**Brunswick** (city) Medina County
104	669	2.3	**Garfield Heights** (city) Cuyahoga County
104	669	2.3	**Hilliard** (city) Franklin County
104	669	2.3	**Oxford** (city) Butler County
108	726	2.4	**Athens** (city) Athens County
108	726	2.4	**Avon Lake** (city) Lorain County
108	726	2.4	**Fairborn** (city) Greene County
108	726	2.4	**Loveland** (city) Hamilton County
108	726	2.4	**Steubenville** (city) Jefferson County
113	800	2.5	**Blue Ash** (city) Hamilton County
113	800	2.5	**Delaware** (city) Delaware County
113	800	2.5	**Pickerington** (city) Fairfield County
113	800	2.5	**Salem** (city) Columbiana County
113	800	2.5	**Westlake** (city) Cuyahoga County
118	845	2.6	**Beavercreek** (city) Greene County
118	845	2.6	**Bedford Heights** (city) Cuyahoga County
118	845	2.6	**Canton** (city) Stark County
118	845	2.6	**Gahanna** (city) Franklin County
118	845	2.6	**Grove City** (city) Franklin County
118	845	2.6	**West Carrollton** (city) Montgomery County
118	845	2.6	**Wilmington** (city) Clinton County
125	903	2.7	**Austintown** (CDP) Mahoning County
126	946	2.8	**Berea** (city) Cuyahoga County
126	946	2.8	**Celina** (city) Mercer County
126	946	2.8	**Cincinnati** (city) Hamilton County
126	946	2.8	**University Heights** (city) Cuyahoga County
126	946	2.8	**Vermilion** (city) Lorain County
131	997	2.9	**Sylvania** (city) Lucas County
132	1050	3.0	**Dayton** (city) Montgomery County
132	1050	3.0	**Marion** (city) Marion County
132	1050	3.0	**Springfield** (city) Clark County
135	1097	3.1	**Huber Heights** (city) Montgomery County
135	1097	3.1	**Struthers** (city) Mahoning County
135	1097	3.1	**Tiffin** (city) Seneca County
138	1152	3.2	**Mason** (city) Warren County
138	1152	3.2	**Perrysburg** (city) Wood County
140	1195	3.3	**Boardman** (CDP) Mahoning County
140	1195	3.3	**Fairview Park** (city) Cuyahoga County
140	1195	3.3	**North Ridgeville** (city) Lorain County
140	1195	3.3	**Riverside** (city) Montgomery County
144	1236	3.4	**Avon** (city) Lorain County
144	1236	3.4	**Brook Park** (city) Cuyahoga County
144	1236	3.4	**Maumee** (city) Lucas County
144	1236	3.4	**Reynoldsburg** (city) Franklin County
148	1280	3.5	**Lebanon** (city) Warren County
148	1280	3.5	**North Olmsted** (city) Cuyahoga County
148	1280	3.5	**Northbrook** (CDP) Hamilton County

Note: *The state column ranks the top/bottom 150 places from all places in the state with population of 10,000 or more. The national column ranks the top/bottom 150 places from all places in the country with population of 10,000 or more. Places that are unincorporated were not considered in the rankings. Please refer to the User Guide for additional information.*

Average Household Size

Top 150 Places Ranked in *Descending* Order

State Rank	Nat'l Rank	Persons	Place
1	532	3.0	**Powell** (city) Delaware County
2	796	2.9	**Pickerington** (city) Fairfield County
3	863	2.8	**Springboro** (city) Warren County
4	931	2.8	**Hudson** (city) Summit County
4	931	2.8	**Mack** (CDP) Hamilton County
6	989	2.8	**Trenton** (city) Butler County
7	1213	2.7	**Dublin** (city) Franklin County
7	1213	2.7	**Solon** (city) Cuyahoga County
9	1246	2.7	**Hilliard** (city) Franklin County
9	1246	2.7	**Mason** (city) Warren County
11	1283	2.7	**Avon** (city) Lorain County
12	1738	2.6	**Pataskala** (city) Licking County
13	1788	2.6	**Northbrook** (CDP) Hamilton County
14	1833	2.6	**Painesville** (city) Lake County
15	1900	2.6	**Brunswick** (city) Medina County
15	1900	2.6	**Monroe** (city) Butler County
17	1961	2.6	**Lebanon** (city) Warren County
17	1961	2.6	**Marysville** (city) Union County
19	2049	2.6	**Montgomery** (city) Hamilton County
20	2093	2.5	**Bexley** (city) Franklin County
20	2093	2.5	**Forest Park** (city) Hamilton County
22	2136	2.5	**Huber Heights** (city) Montgomery County
22	2136	2.5	**Macedonia** (city) Summit County
24	2234	2.5	**Clayton** (city) Montgomery County
25	2282	2.5	**Loveland** (city) Hamilton County
26	2334	2.5	**Aurora** (city) Portage County
26	2334	2.5	**Gahanna** (city) Franklin County
26	2334	2.5	**Green** (city) Summit County
26	2334	2.5	**North Ridgeville** (city) Lorain County
30	2398	2.5	**Avon Lake** (city) Lorain County
30	2398	2.5	**Finneytown** (CDP) Hamilton County
30	2398	2.5	**Grove City** (city) Franklin County
30	2398	2.5	**Medina** (city) Medina County
30	2398	2.5	**Norton** (city) Summit County
35	2464	2.5	**Strongsville** (city) Cuyahoga County
36	2518	2.5	**New Franklin** (city) Summit County
36	2518	2.5	**Sidney** (city) Shelby County
38	2568	2.5	**Amherst** (city) Lorain County
38	2568	2.5	**Bay Village** (city) Cuyahoga County
38	2568	2.5	**Brecksville** (city) Cuyahoga County
38	2568	2.5	**Broadview Heights** (city) Cuyahoga County
38	2568	2.5	**Miamisburg** (city) Montgomery County
38	2568	2.5	**Vermilion** (city) Lorain County
44	2630	2.4	**Franklin** (city) Warren County
44	2630	2.4	**Reynoldsburg** (city) Franklin County
44	2630	2.4	**Twinsburg** (city) Summit County
47	2698	2.4	**Lorain** (city) Lorain County
47	2698	2.4	**Monfort Heights** (CDP) Hamilton County
47	2698	2.4	**Perrysburg** (city) Wood County
47	2698	2.4	**University Heights** (city) Cuyahoga County
47	2698	2.4	**Wadsworth** (city) Medina County
47	2698	2.4	**Westerville** (city) Franklin County
53	2768	2.4	**Beavercreek** (city) Greene County
53	2768	2.4	**Delaware** (city) Delaware County
53	2768	2.4	**Hamilton** (city) Butler County
56	2829	2.4	**Bridgetown** (CDP) Hamilton County
56	2829	2.4	**Norwalk** (city) Huron County
58	2893	2.4	**Brook Park** (city) Cuyahoga County
58	2893	2.4	**Heath** (city) Licking County
58	2893	2.4	**Marion** (city) Marion County
58	2893	2.4	**Riverside** (city) Montgomery County
58	2893	2.4	**Tallmadge** (city) Summit County
63	2968	2.4	**Bellefontaine** (city) Logan County
63	2968	2.4	**Mentor** (city) Lake County
63	2968	2.4	**Oregon** (city) Lucas County
63	2968	2.4	**Piqua** (city) Miami County
63	2968	2.4	**Upper Arlington** (city) Franklin County
68	3032	2.4	**Forestville** (CDP) Hamilton County
68	3032	2.4	**Garfield Heights** (city) Cuyahoga County
68	3032	2.4	**South Euclid** (city) Cuyahoga County
68	3032	2.4	**Streetsboro** (city) Portage County
68	3032	2.4	**Struthers** (city) Mahoning County
68	3032	2.4	**Sylvania** (city) Lucas County
68	3032	2.4	**White Oak** (CDP) Hamilton County
75	3107	2.4	**Ashtabula** (city) Ashtabula County
75	3107	2.4	**Fostoria** (city) Seneca County
75	3107	2.4	**Fremont** (city) Sandusky County
75	3107	2.4	**Lima** (city) Allen County
75	3107	2.4	**Stow** (city) Summit County
80	3179	2.4	**Fairfield** (city) Butler County
80	3179	2.4	**Maple Heights** (city) Cuyahoga County
82	3241	2.4	**Blue Ash** (city) Hamilton County
82	3241	2.4	**Oxford** (city) Butler County
82	3241	2.4	**Whitehall** (city) Franklin County
85	3296	2.3	**Dent** (CDP) Hamilton County
85	3296	2.3	**East Liverpool** (city) Columbiana County
85	3296	2.3	**Elyria** (city) Lorain County
85	3296	2.3	**Shaker Heights** (city) Cuyahoga County
85	3296	2.3	**Xenia** (city) Greene County
90	3347	2.3	**Alliance** (city) Stark County
90	3347	2.3	**Defiance** (city) Defiance County
90	3347	2.3	**Middletown** (city) Butler County
90	3347	2.3	**Springdale** (city) Hamilton County
90	3347	2.3	**Springfield** (city) Clark County
90	3347	2.3	**Troy** (city) Miami County
96	3423	2.3	**Barberton** (city) Summit County
96	3423	2.3	**Celina** (city) Mercer County
96	3423	2.3	**Conneaut** (city) Ashtabula County
96	3423	2.3	**Dover** (city) Tuscarawas County
96	3423	2.3	**Eastlake** (city) Lake County
96	3423	2.3	**Englewood** (city) Montgomery County
96	3423	2.3	**Massillon** (city) Stark County
96	3423	2.3	**Maumee** (city) Lucas County
96	3423	2.3	**North Olmsted** (city) Cuyahoga County
96	3423	2.3	**Washington Court House** (city) Fayette County
106	3485	2.3	**Circleville** (city) Pickaway County
106	3485	2.3	**Lancaster** (city) Fairfield County
106	3485	2.3	**Seven Hills** (city) Cuyahoga County
109	3550	2.3	**Canton** (city) Stark County
109	3550	2.3	**Newark** (city) Licking County
109	3550	2.3	**Worthington** (city) Franklin County
112	3608	2.3	**Parma** (city) Cuyahoga County
112	3608	2.3	**Urbana** (city) Champaign County
114	3660	2.3	**North Royalton** (city) Cuyahoga County
114	3660	2.3	**Toledo** (city) Lucas County
114	3660	2.3	**Van Wert** (city) Van Wert County
117	3713	2.3	**Galion** (city) Crawford County
117	3713	2.3	**New Philadelphia** (city) Tuscarawas County
117	3713	2.3	**Willowick** (city) Lake County
120	3765	2.3	**Akron** (city) Summit County
120	3765	2.3	**Columbus** (city) Franklin County
122	3820	2.3	**Vandalia** (city) Montgomery County
122	3820	2.3	**Warren** (city) Trumbull County
122	3820	2.3	**Westlake** (city) Cuyahoga County
125	3879	2.2	**Cleveland** (city) Cuyahoga County
125	3879	2.2	**Findlay** (city) Hancock County
125	3879	2.2	**Tiffin** (city) Seneca County
125	3879	2.2	**Trotwood** (city) Montgomery County
125	3879	2.2	**Wickliffe** (city) Lake County
125	3879	2.2	**Zanesville** (city) Muskingum County
131	3937	2.2	**Ashland** (city) Ashland County
131	3937	2.2	**Athens** (city) Athens County
131	3937	2.2	**Norwood** (city) Hamilton County
131	3937	2.2	**Portsmouth** (city) Scioto County
131	3937	2.2	**Ravenna** (city) Portage County
131	3937	2.2	**Sandusky** (city) Erie County
131	3937	2.2	**Youngstown** (city) Mahoning County
138	3984	2.2	**Cleveland Heights** (city) Cuyahoga County
138	3984	2.2	**Wilmington** (city) Clinton County
140	4034	2.2	**Berea** (city) Cuyahoga County
140	4034	2.2	**Bucyrus** (city) Crawford County
140	4034	2.2	**Dayton** (city) Montgomery County
140	4034	2.2	**Reading** (city) Hamilton County
144	4084	2.2	**Chillicothe** (city) Ross County
144	4084	2.2	**Coshocton** (city) Coshocton County
144	4084	2.2	**Salem** (city) Columbiana County
147	4126	2.2	**Fairborn** (city) Greene County
147	4126	2.2	**Niles** (city) Trumbull County
149	4164	2.2	**Boardman** (CDP) Mahoning County
149	4164	2.2	**Cambridge** (city) Guernsey County

Note: *The state column ranks the top/bottom 150 places from all places in the state with population of 10,000 or more. The national column ranks the top/bottom 150 places from all places in the country with population of 10,000 or more. Places that are unincorporated were not considered in the rankings. Please refer to the User Guide for additional information.*

Average Household Size

Top 150 Places Ranked in *Ascending* Order

State Rank	Nat'l Rank	Persons	Place
1	40	1.9	**Mayfield Heights** (city) Cuyahoga County
2	80	2.0	**Lakewood** (city) Cuyahoga County
3	102	2.0	**Bedford** (city) Cuyahoga County
4	114	2.0	**Bedford Heights** (city) Cuyahoga County
5	144	2.1	**East Cleveland** (city) Cuyahoga County
6	159	2.1	**Cincinnati** (city) Hamilton County
6	159	2.1	**Willoughby** (city) Lake County
8	170	2.1	**Euclid** (city) Cuyahoga County
9	183	2.1	**Marietta** (city) Washington County
10	199	2.1	**Lyndhurst** (city) Cuyahoga County
10	199	2.1	**North Canton** (city) Stark County
10	199	2.1	**Parma Heights** (city) Cuyahoga County
13	223	2.1	**Beachwood** (city) Cuyahoga County
13	223	2.1	**Bowling Green** (city) Wood County
13	223	2.1	**Rocky River** (city) Cuyahoga County
16	244	2.1	**Brooklyn** (city) Cuyahoga County
16	244	2.1	**Greenville** (city) Darke County
16	244	2.1	**Richmond Heights** (city) Cuyahoga County
16	244	2.1	**Sharonville** (city) Hamilton County
20	278	2.1	**Middleburg Heights** (city) Cuyahoga County
20	278	2.1	**West Carrollton** (city) Montgomery County
22	312	2.1	**Centerville** (city) Montgomery County
22	312	2.1	**Kettering** (city) Montgomery County
22	312	2.1	**Mount Vernon** (city) Knox County
25	364	2.2	**Cuyahoga Falls** (city) Summit County
25	364	2.2	**Mansfield** (city) Richland County
25	364	2.2	**Wooster** (city) Wayne County
28	405	2.2	**Austintown** (CDP) Mahoning County
28	405	2.2	**Fairview Park** (city) Cuyahoga County
28	405	2.2	**Kent** (city) Portage County
28	405	2.2	**Steubenville** (city) Jefferson County
28	405	2.2	**Warrensville Heights** (city) Cuyahoga County
33	453	2.2	**Boardman** (CDP) Mahoning County
33	453	2.2	**Cambridge** (city) Guernsey County
33	453	2.2	**Ironton** (city) Lawrence County
36	493	2.2	**Fairborn** (city) Greene County
36	493	2.2	**Niles** (city) Trumbull County
38	531	2.2	**Chillicothe** (city) Ross County
38	531	2.2	**Coshocton** (city) Coshocton County
38	531	2.2	**Salem** (city) Columbiana County
41	573	2.2	**Berea** (city) Cuyahoga County
41	573	2.2	**Bucyrus** (city) Crawford County
41	573	2.2	**Dayton** (city) Montgomery County
41	573	2.2	**Reading** (city) Hamilton County
45	623	2.2	**Cleveland Heights** (city) Cuyahoga County
45	623	2.2	**Wilmington** (city) Clinton County
47	673	2.2	**Ashland** (city) Ashland County
47	673	2.2	**Athens** (city) Athens County
47	673	2.2	**Norwood** (city) Hamilton County
47	673	2.2	**Portsmouth** (city) Scioto County
47	673	2.2	**Ravenna** (city) Portage County
47	673	2.2	**Sandusky** (city) Erie County
47	673	2.2	**Youngstown** (city) Mahoning County
54	720	2.2	**Cleveland** (city) Cuyahoga County
54	720	2.2	**Findlay** (city) Hancock County
54	720	2.2	**Tiffin** (city) Seneca County
54	720	2.2	**Trotwood** (city) Montgomery County
54	720	2.2	**Wickliffe** (city) Lake County
54	720	2.2	**Zanesville** (city) Muskingum County
60	778	2.3	**Vandalia** (city) Montgomery County
60	778	2.3	**Warren** (city) Trumbull County
60	778	2.3	**Westlake** (city) Cuyahoga County
63	837	2.3	**Akron** (city) Summit County
63	837	2.3	**Columbus** (city) Franklin County
65	892	2.3	**Galion** (city) Crawford County
65	892	2.3	**New Philadelphia** (city) Tuscarawas County
65	892	2.3	**Willowick** (city) Lake County
68	944	2.3	**North Royalton** (city) Cuyahoga County
68	944	2.3	**Toledo** (city) Lucas County
68	944	2.3	**Van Wert** (city) Van Wert County
71	997	2.3	**Parma** (city) Cuyahoga County
71	997	2.3	**Urbana** (city) Champaign County
73	1049	2.3	**Canton** (city) Stark County
73	1049	2.3	**Newark** (city) Licking County
73	1049	2.3	**Worthington** (city) Franklin County
76	1107	2.3	**Circleville** (city) Pickaway County
76	1107	2.3	**Lancaster** (city) Fairfield County
76	1107	2.3	**Seven Hills** (city) Cuyahoga County
79	1172	2.3	**Barberton** (city) Summit County
79	1172	2.3	**Celina** (city) Mercer County
79	1172	2.3	**Conneaut** (city) Ashtabula County
79	1172	2.3	**Dover** (city) Tuscarawas County
79	1172	2.3	**Eastlake** (city) Lake County
79	1172	2.3	**Englewood** (city) Montgomery County
79	1172	2.3	**Massillon** (city) Stark County
79	1172	2.3	**Maumee** (city) Lucas County
79	1172	2.3	**North Olmsted** (city) Cuyahoga County
79	1172	2.3	**Washington Court House** (city) Fayette County
89	1234	2.3	**Alliance** (city) Stark County
89	1234	2.3	**Defiance** (city) Defiance County
89	1234	2.3	**Middletown** (city) Butler County
89	1234	2.3	**Springdale** (city) Hamilton County
89	1234	2.3	**Springfield** (city) Clark County
89	1234	2.3	**Troy** (city) Miami County
95	1310	2.3	**Dent** (CDP) Hamilton County
95	1310	2.3	**East Liverpool** (city) Columbiana County
95	1310	2.3	**Elyria** (city) Lorain County
95	1310	2.3	**Shaker Heights** (city) Cuyahoga County
95	1310	2.3	**Xenia** (city) Greene County
100	1361	2.4	**Blue Ash** (city) Hamilton County
100	1361	2.4	**Oxford** (city) Butler County
100	1361	2.4	**Whitehall** (city) Franklin County
103	1416	2.4	**Fairfield** (city) Butler County
103	1416	2.4	**Maple Heights** (city) Cuyahoga County
105	1478	2.4	**Ashtabula** (city) Ashtabula County
105	1478	2.4	**Fostoria** (city) Seneca County
105	1478	2.4	**Fremont** (city) Sandusky County
105	1478	2.4	**Lima** (city) Allen County
105	1478	2.4	**Stow** (city) Summit County
110	1550	2.4	**Forestville** (CDP) Hamilton County
110	1550	2.4	**Garfield Heights** (city) Cuyahoga County
110	1550	2.4	**South Euclid** (city) Cuyahoga County
110	1550	2.4	**Streetsboro** (city) Portage County
110	1550	2.4	**Struthers** (city) Mahoning County
110	1550	2.4	**Sylvania** (city) Lucas County
110	1550	2.4	**White Oak** (CDP) Hamilton County
117	1625	2.4	**Bellefontaine** (city) Logan County
117	1625	2.4	**Mentor** (city) Lake County
117	1625	2.4	**Oregon** (city) Lucas County
117	1625	2.4	**Piqua** (city) Miami County
117	1625	2.4	**Upper Arlington** (city) Franklin County
122	1689	2.4	**Brook Park** (city) Cuyahoga County
122	1689	2.4	**Heath** (city) Licking County
122	1689	2.4	**Marion** (city) Marion County
122	1689	2.4	**Riverside** (city) Montgomery County
122	1689	2.4	**Tallmadge** (city) Summit County
127	1764	2.4	**Bridgetown** (CDP) Hamilton County
127	1764	2.4	**Norwalk** (city) Huron County
129	1828	2.4	**Beavercreek** (city) Greene County
129	1828	2.4	**Delaware** (city) Delaware County
129	1828	2.4	**Hamilton** (city) Butler County
132	1889	2.4	**Lorain** (city) Lorain County
132	1889	2.4	**Monfort Heights** (CDP) Hamilton County
132	1889	2.4	**Perrysburg** (city) Wood County
132	1889	2.4	**University Heights** (city) Cuyahoga County
132	1889	2.4	**Wadsworth** (city) Medina County
132	1889	2.4	**Westerville** (city) Franklin County
138	1959	2.4	**Franklin** (city) Warren County
138	1959	2.4	**Reynoldsburg** (city) Franklin County
138	1959	2.4	**Twinsburg** (city) Summit County
141	2027	2.5	**Amherst** (city) Lorain County
141	2027	2.5	**Bay Village** (city) Cuyahoga County
141	2027	2.5	**Brecksville** (city) Cuyahoga County
141	2027	2.5	**Broadview Heights** (city) Cuyahoga County
141	2027	2.5	**Miamisburg** (city) Montgomery County
141	2027	2.5	**Vermilion** (city) Lorain County
147	2089	2.5	**New Franklin** (city) Summit County
147	2089	2.5	**Sidney** (city) Shelby County
149	2139	2.5	**Strongsville** (city) Cuyahoga County
150	2193	2.5	**Avon Lake** (city) Lorain County

Note: *The state column ranks the top/bottom 150 places from all places in the state with population of 10,000 or more. The national column ranks the top/bottom 150 places from all places in the country with population of 10,000 or more. Places that are unincorporated were not considered in the rankings. Please refer to the User Guide for additional information.*

Median Age

Top 150 Places Ranked in *Descending* Order

State Rank	Nat'l Rank	Years	Place
1	44	52.5	**Beachwood** (city) Cuyahoga County
2	73	50.0	**Seven Hills** (city) Cuyahoga County
3	146	47.4	**Brecksville** (city) Cuyahoga County
4	167	47.0	**Lyndhurst** (city) Cuyahoga County
5	173	46.9	**Centerville** (city) Montgomery County
5	173	46.9	**Montgomery** (city) Hamilton County
7	194	46.6	**Middleburg Heights** (city) Cuyahoga County
8	225	46.1	**Richmond Heights** (city) Cuyahoga County
9	262	45.6	**Rocky River** (city) Cuyahoga County
10	274	45.5	**New Franklin** (city) Summit County
11	291	45.4	**Aurora** (city) Portage County
12	335	45.1	**Tallmadge** (city) Summit County
13	351	45.0	**Amherst** (city) Lorain County
13	351	45.0	**Westlake** (city) Cuyahoga County
15	367	44.9	**Worthington** (city) Franklin County
16	380	44.8	**Mentor** (city) Lake County
17	440	44.4	**Mack** (CDP) Hamilton County
18	471	44.2	**Strongsville** (city) Cuyahoga County
19	494	44.0	**Wickliffe** (city) Lake County
20	533	43.8	**Boardman** (CDP) Mahoning County
20	533	43.8	**Brook Park** (city) Cuyahoga County
22	552	43.7	**Norton** (city) Summit County
23	569	43.6	**Willoughby** (city) Lake County
24	588	43.5	**North Olmsted** (city) Cuyahoga County
24	588	43.5	**North Royalton** (city) Cuyahoga County
24	588	43.5	**Vermilion** (city) Lorain County
27	613	43.4	**Bay Village** (city) Cuyahoga County
27	613	43.4	**Greenville** (city) Darke County
27	613	43.4	**Macedonia** (city) Summit County
30	632	43.3	**Bedford Heights** (city) Cuyahoga County
31	659	43.2	**Parma Heights** (city) Cuyahoga County
32	677	43.1	**Solon** (city) Cuyahoga County
33	720	42.9	**Brooklyn** (city) Cuyahoga County
33	720	42.9	**Coshocton** (city) Coshocton County
33	720	42.9	**Dover** (city) Tuscarawas County
33	720	42.9	**Mayfield Heights** (city) Cuyahoga County
37	755	42.8	**Austintown** (CDP) Mahoning County
37	755	42.8	**Salem** (city) Columbiana County
37	755	42.8	**Upper Arlington** (city) Franklin County
40	787	42.7	**Eastlake** (city) Lake County
40	787	42.7	**Sylvania** (city) Lucas County
42	810	42.6	**Clayton** (city) Montgomery County
42	810	42.6	**East Cleveland** (city) Cuyahoga County
44	843	42.5	**Hudson** (city) Summit County
44	843	42.5	**North Canton** (city) Stark County
46	905	42.3	**Fairview Park** (city) Cuyahoga County
46	905	42.3	**Oregon** (city) Lucas County
48	955	42.1	**Englewood** (city) Montgomery County
48	955	42.1	**Ironton** (city) Lawrence County
50	980	42.0	**Forestville** (CDP) Hamilton County
50	980	42.0	**Niles** (city) Trumbull County
52	1008	41.9	**Avon Lake** (city) Lorain County
52	1008	41.9	**Bedford** (city) Cuyahoga County
54	1043	41.8	**Green** (city) Summit County
54	1043	41.8	**Trotwood** (city) Montgomery County
56	1100	41.6	**Blue Ash** (city) Hamilton County
56	1100	41.6	**Monfort Heights** (CDP) Hamilton County
58	1132	41.5	**Broadview Heights** (city) Cuyahoga County
58	1132	41.5	**Chillicothe** (city) Ross County
58	1132	41.5	**Parma** (city) Cuyahoga County
58	1132	41.5	**Willowick** (city) Lake County
62	1167	41.4	**Struthers** (city) Mahoning County
62	1167	41.4	**Twinsburg** (city) Summit County
64	1244	41.2	**Westerville** (city) Franklin County
65	1274	41.1	**Bucyrus** (city) Crawford County
66	1296	41.0	**Euclid** (city) Cuyahoga County
67	1321	40.9	**Kettering** (city) Montgomery County
67	1321	40.9	**Shaker Heights** (city) Cuyahoga County
69	1349	40.8	**Sharonville** (city) Hamilton County
70	1373	40.7	**North Ridgeville** (city) Lorain County
71	1404	40.6	**Vandalia** (city) Montgomery County
72	1472	40.4	**Beavercreek** (city) Greene County
72	1472	40.4	**New Philadelphia** (city) Tuscarawas County
74	1538	40.2	**Bridgetown** (CDP) Hamilton County
74	1538	40.2	**Dent** (CDP) Hamilton County
74	1538	40.2	**Miamisburg** (city) Montgomery County
74	1538	40.2	**White Oak** (CDP) Hamilton County
78	1576	40.1	**Heath** (city) Licking County
78	1576	40.1	**Massillon** (city) Stark County
80	1673	39.8	**Barberton** (city) Summit County
81	1710	39.7	**Galion** (city) Crawford County
81	1710	39.7	**Maumee** (city) Lucas County
81	1710	39.7	**Stow** (city) Summit County
84	1736	39.6	**Conneaut** (city) Ashtabula County
84	1736	39.6	**Van Wert** (city) Van Wert County
86	1770	39.5	**Finneytown** (CDP) Hamilton County
86	1770	39.5	**Reading** (city) Hamilton County
88	1808	39.4	**Cuyahoga Falls** (city) Summit County
88	1808	39.4	**Gahanna** (city) Franklin County
90	1839	39.3	**Circleville** (city) Pickaway County
91	1872	39.2	**Maple Heights** (city) Cuyahoga County
91	1872	39.2	**Warrensville Heights** (city) Cuyahoga County
93	1904	39.1	**Brunswick** (city) Medina County
94	1934	39.0	**Marietta** (city) Washington County
95	1994	38.8	**Cambridge** (city) Guernsey County
95	1994	38.8	**Steubenville** (city) Jefferson County
97	2018	38.7	**Springdale** (city) Hamilton County
97	2018	38.7	**Wadsworth** (city) Medina County
99	2066	38.5	**Garfield Heights** (city) Cuyahoga County
99	2066	38.5	**Mansfield** (city) Richland County
99	2066	38.5	**Sandusky** (city) Erie County
102	2107	38.4	**Avon** (city) Lorain County
102	2107	38.4	**Mason** (city) Warren County
102	2107	38.4	**Perrysburg** (city) Wood County
102	2107	38.4	**Washington Court House** (city) Fayette County
106	2137	38.3	**Celina** (city) Mercer County
106	2137	38.3	**Dublin** (city) Franklin County
106	2137	38.3	**Fairfield** (city) Butler County
106	2137	38.3	**Middletown** (city) Butler County
106	2137	38.3	**Warren** (city) Trumbull County
111	2175	38.2	**Urbana** (city) Champaign County
112	2205	38.1	**Elyria** (city) Lorain County
112	2205	38.1	**Piqua** (city) Miami County
114	2234	38.0	**Loveland** (city) Hamilton County
114	2234	38.0	**Youngstown** (city) Mahoning County
116	2272	37.9	**Fostoria** (city) Seneca County
116	2272	37.9	**Ravenna** (city) Portage County
116	2272	37.9	**South Euclid** (city) Cuyahoga County
116	2272	37.9	**Streetsboro** (city) Portage County
120	2309	37.8	**Grove City** (city) Franklin County
121	2367	37.6	**East Liverpool** (city) Columbiana County
122	2398	37.5	**Lancaster** (city) Fairfield County
122	2398	37.5	**West Carrollton** (city) Montgomery County
124	2432	37.4	**Huber Heights** (city) Montgomery County
124	2432	37.4	**Powell** (city) Delaware County
126	2466	37.3	**Marion** (city) Marion County
126	2466	37.3	**Newark** (city) Licking County
126	2466	37.3	**Reynoldsburg** (city) Franklin County
126	2466	37.3	**Wooster** (city) Wayne County
130	2496	37.2	**Mount Vernon** (city) Knox County
131	2534	37.1	**Berea** (city) Cuyahoga County
131	2534	37.1	**Defiance** (city) Defiance County
131	2534	37.1	**Xenia** (city) Greene County
134	2575	37.0	**Ashtabula** (city) Ashtabula County
134	2575	37.0	**Norwalk** (city) Huron County
136	2615	36.9	**Monroe** (city) Butler County
136	2615	36.9	**Troy** (city) Miami County
138	2641	36.8	**Lorain** (city) Lorain County
139	2681	36.7	**Franklin** (city) Warren County
140	2768	36.4	**Medina** (city) Medina County
140	2768	36.4	**Springboro** (city) Warren County
142	2802	36.3	**Zanesville** (city) Muskingum County
143	2861	36.1	**Ashland** (city) Ashland County
143	2861	36.1	**Portsmouth** (city) Scioto County
143	2861	36.1	**Sidney** (city) Shelby County
146	2893	36.0	**Springfield** (city) Clark County
147	2929	35.9	**Findlay** (city) Hancock County
147	2929	35.9	**Hilliard** (city) Franklin County
149	2956	35.8	**Cleveland Heights** (city) Cuyahoga County
149	2956	35.8	**Forest Park** (city) Hamilton County

Note: *The state column ranks the top/bottom 150 places from all places in the state with population of 10,000 or more. The national column ranks the top/bottom 150 places from all places in the country with population of 10,000 or more. Places that are unincorporated were not considered in the rankings. Please refer to the User Guide for additional information.*

Median Age

Top 150 Places Ranked in *Ascending* Order

State Rank	Nat'l Rank	Years	Place
1	18	21.4	**Oxford** (city) Butler County
2	22	21.6	**Athens** (city) Athens County
3	54	22.7	**Kent** (city) Portage County
4	69	23.2	**Bowling Green** (city) Wood County
5	430	30.2	**Painesville** (city) Lake County
6	493	30.7	**University Heights** (city) Cuyahoga County
7	572	31.2	**Columbus** (city) Franklin County
8	755	32.2	**Trenton** (city) Butler County
9	799	32.4	**Fairborn** (city) Greene County
10	818	32.5	**Cincinnati** (city) Hamilton County
11	910	32.9	**Lima** (city) Allen County
11	910	32.9	**Pickerington** (city) Fairfield County
13	959	33.1	**Marysville** (city) Union County
14	982	33.2	**Delaware** (city) Delaware County
15	1027	33.4	**Norwood** (city) Hamilton County
16	1080	33.6	**Northbrook** (CDP) Hamilton County
17	1103	33.7	**Wilmington** (city) Clinton County
18	1249	34.2	**Toledo** (city) Lucas County
19	1296	34.4	**Dayton** (city) Montgomery County
20	1377	34.7	**Lebanon** (city) Warren County
21	1410	34.8	**Bellefontaine** (city) Logan County
21	1410	34.8	**Riverside** (city) Montgomery County
23	1465	35.0	**Whitehall** (city) Franklin County
24	1512	35.2	**Tiffin** (city) Seneca County
25	1533	35.3	**Alliance** (city) Stark County
25	1533	35.3	**Fremont** (city) Sandusky County
25	1533	35.3	**Hamilton** (city) Butler County
28	1556	35.4	**Lakewood** (city) Cuyahoga County
29	1588	35.5	**Bexley** (city) Franklin County
30	1618	35.6	**Canton** (city) Stark County
31	1652	35.7	**Akron** (city) Summit County
31	1652	35.7	**Cleveland** (city) Cuyahoga County
33	1679	35.8	**Cleveland Heights** (city) Cuyahoga County
33	1679	35.8	**Forest Park** (city) Hamilton County
33	1679	35.8	**Pataskala** (city) Licking County
36	1701	35.9	**Findlay** (city) Hancock County
36	1701	35.9	**Hilliard** (city) Franklin County
38	1728	36.0	**Springfield** (city) Clark County
39	1764	36.1	**Ashland** (city) Ashland County
39	1764	36.1	**Portsmouth** (city) Scioto County
39	1764	36.1	**Sidney** (city) Shelby County
42	1831	36.3	**Zanesville** (city) Muskingum County
43	1855	36.4	**Medina** (city) Medina County
43	1855	36.4	**Springboro** (city) Warren County
45	1941	36.7	**Franklin** (city) Warren County
46	1976	36.8	**Lorain** (city) Lorain County
47	2016	36.9	**Monroe** (city) Butler County
47	2016	36.9	**Troy** (city) Miami County
49	2042	37.0	**Ashtabula** (city) Ashtabula County
49	2042	37.0	**Norwalk** (city) Huron County
51	2082	37.1	**Berea** (city) Cuyahoga County
51	2082	37.1	**Defiance** (city) Defiance County
51	2082	37.1	**Xenia** (city) Greene County
54	2123	37.2	**Mount Vernon** (city) Knox County
55	2161	37.3	**Marion** (city) Marion County
55	2161	37.3	**Newark** (city) Licking County
55	2161	37.3	**Reynoldsburg** (city) Franklin County
55	2161	37.3	**Wooster** (city) Wayne County
59	2191	37.4	**Huber Heights** (city) Montgomery County
59	2191	37.4	**Powell** (city) Delaware County
61	2225	37.5	**Lancaster** (city) Fairfield County
61	2225	37.5	**West Carrollton** (city) Montgomery County
63	2259	37.6	**East Liverpool** (city) Columbiana County
64	2315	37.8	**Grove City** (city) Franklin County
65	2348	37.9	**Fostoria** (city) Seneca County
65	2348	37.9	**Ravenna** (city) Portage County
65	2348	37.9	**South Euclid** (city) Cuyahoga County
65	2348	37.9	**Streetsboro** (city) Portage County
69	2385	38.0	**Loveland** (city) Hamilton County
69	2385	38.0	**Youngstown** (city) Mahoning County
71	2423	38.1	**Elyria** (city) Lorain County
71	2423	38.1	**Piqua** (city) Miami County
73	2452	38.2	**Urbana** (city) Champaign County
74	2482	38.3	**Celina** (city) Mercer County
74	2482	38.3	**Dublin** (city) Franklin County
74	2482	38.3	**Fairfield** (city) Butler County
74	2482	38.3	**Middletown** (city) Butler County
74	2482	38.3	**Warren** (city) Trumbull County
79	2520	38.4	**Avon** (city) Lorain County
79	2520	38.4	**Mason** (city) Warren County
79	2520	38.4	**Perrysburg** (city) Wood County
79	2520	38.4	**Washington Court House** (city) Fayette County
83	2550	38.5	**Garfield Heights** (city) Cuyahoga County
83	2550	38.5	**Mansfield** (city) Richland County
83	2550	38.5	**Sandusky** (city) Erie County
86	2615	38.7	**Springdale** (city) Hamilton County
86	2615	38.7	**Wadsworth** (city) Medina County
88	2639	38.8	**Cambridge** (city) Guernsey County
88	2639	38.8	**Steubenville** (city) Jefferson County
90	2696	39.0	**Marietta** (city) Washington County
91	2723	39.1	**Brunswick** (city) Medina County
92	2753	39.2	**Maple Heights** (city) Cuyahoga County
92	2753	39.2	**Warrensville Heights** (city) Cuyahoga County
94	2785	39.3	**Circleville** (city) Pickaway County
95	2818	39.4	**Cuyahoga Falls** (city) Summit County
95	2818	39.4	**Gahanna** (city) Franklin County
97	2849	39.5	**Finneytown** (CDP) Hamilton County
97	2849	39.5	**Reading** (city) Hamilton County
99	2887	39.6	**Conneaut** (city) Ashtabula County
99	2887	39.6	**Van Wert** (city) Van Wert County
101	2921	39.7	**Galion** (city) Crawford County
101	2921	39.7	**Maumee** (city) Lucas County
101	2921	39.7	**Stow** (city) Summit County
104	2947	39.8	**Barberton** (city) Summit County
105	3047	40.1	**Heath** (city) Licking County
105	3047	40.1	**Massillon** (city) Stark County
107	3081	40.2	**Bridgetown** (CDP) Hamilton County
107	3081	40.2	**Dent** (CDP) Hamilton County
107	3081	40.2	**Miamisburg** (city) Montgomery County
107	3081	40.2	**White Oak** (CDP) Hamilton County
111	3152	40.4	**Beavercreek** (city) Greene County
111	3152	40.4	**New Philadelphia** (city) Tuscarawas County
113	3220	40.6	**Vandalia** (city) Montgomery County
114	3253	40.7	**North Ridgeville** (city) Lorain County
115	3284	40.8	**Sharonville** (city) Hamilton County
116	3308	40.9	**Kettering** (city) Montgomery County
116	3308	40.9	**Shaker Heights** (city) Cuyahoga County
118	3336	41.0	**Euclid** (city) Cuyahoga County
119	3361	41.1	**Bucyrus** (city) Crawford County
120	3383	41.2	**Westerville** (city) Franklin County
121	3453	41.4	**Struthers** (city) Mahoning County
121	3453	41.4	**Twinsburg** (city) Summit County
123	3490	41.5	**Broadview Heights** (city) Cuyahoga County
123	3490	41.5	**Chillicothe** (city) Ross County
123	3490	41.5	**Parma** (city) Cuyahoga County
123	3490	41.5	**Willowick** (city) Lake County
127	3525	41.6	**Blue Ash** (city) Hamilton County
127	3525	41.6	**Monfort Heights** (CDP) Hamilton County
129	3584	41.8	**Green** (city) Summit County
129	3584	41.8	**Trotwood** (city) Montgomery County
131	3614	41.9	**Avon Lake** (city) Lorain County
131	3614	41.9	**Bedford** (city) Cuyahoga County
133	3649	42.0	**Forestville** (CDP) Hamilton County
133	3649	42.0	**Niles** (city) Trumbull County
135	3677	42.1	**Englewood** (city) Montgomery County
135	3677	42.1	**Ironton** (city) Lawrence County
137	3725	42.3	**Fairview Park** (city) Cuyahoga County
137	3725	42.3	**Oregon** (city) Lucas County
139	3781	42.5	**Hudson** (city) Summit County
139	3781	42.5	**North Canton** (city) Stark County
141	3814	42.6	**Clayton** (city) Montgomery County
141	3814	42.6	**East Cleveland** (city) Cuyahoga County
143	3847	42.7	**Eastlake** (city) Lake County
143	3847	42.7	**Sylvania** (city) Lucas County
145	3870	42.8	**Austintown** (CDP) Mahoning County
145	3870	42.8	**Salem** (city) Columbiana County
145	3870	42.8	**Upper Arlington** (city) Franklin County
148	3902	42.9	**Brooklyn** (city) Cuyahoga County
148	3902	42.9	**Coshocton** (city) Coshocton County
148	3902	42.9	**Dover** (city) Tuscarawas County

Note: *The state column ranks the top/bottom 150 places from all places in the state with population of 10,000 or more. The national column ranks the top/bottom 150 places from all places in the country with population of 10,000 or more. Places that are unincorporated were not considered in the rankings. Please refer to the User Guide for additional information.*

Population Under Age 18

Top 150 Places Ranked in *Descending* Order

State Rank	Nat'l Rank	Percent	Place
1	93	34.7	**Powell** (city) Delaware County
2	149	33.3	**Pickerington** (city) Fairfield County
3	233	32.2	**Springboro** (city) Warren County
4	347	31.0	**Trenton** (city) Butler County
5	368	30.8	**Mason** (city) Warren County
6	408	30.5	**Avon** (city) Lorain County
7	424	30.4	**Dublin** (city) Franklin County
8	468	30.1	**Hilliard** (city) Franklin County
8	468	30.1	**Hudson** (city) Summit County
10	618	29.2	**Lebanon** (city) Warren County
11	784	28.3	**Medina** (city) Medina County
11	784	28.3	**Painesville** (city) Lake County
13	812	28.2	**Northbrook** (CDP) Hamilton County
14	889	27.9	**Loveland** (city) Hamilton County
15	925	27.8	**Solon** (city) Cuyahoga County
16	972	27.6	**Pataskala** (city) Licking County
17	1069	27.2	**Fremont** (city) Sandusky County
17	1069	27.2	**Sidney** (city) Shelby County
19	1097	27.1	**Bellefontaine** (city) Logan County
20	1125	27.0	**Monroe** (city) Butler County
21	1156	26.9	**Forest Park** (city) Hamilton County
22	1221	26.7	**Lorain** (city) Lorain County
22	1221	26.7	**Shaker Heights** (city) Cuyahoga County
24	1251	26.6	**Marysville** (city) Union County
25	1290	26.5	**Perrysburg** (city) Wood County
26	1328	26.4	**Ashtabula** (city) Ashtabula County
27	1371	26.3	**Reynoldsburg** (city) Franklin County
28	1403	26.2	**Avon Lake** (city) Lorain County
28	1403	26.2	**Norwalk** (city) Huron County
30	1461	26.0	**Fostoria** (city) Seneca County
31	1530	25.8	**Finneytown** (CDP) Hamilton County
31	1530	25.8	**Whitehall** (city) Franklin County
33	1567	25.7	**Bexley** (city) Franklin County
34	1602	25.6	**Celina** (city) Mercer County
34	1602	25.6	**Wadsworth** (city) Medina County
36	1643	25.5	**Delaware** (city) Delaware County
36	1643	25.5	**Franklin** (city) Warren County
38	1682	25.4	**Bay Village** (city) Cuyahoga County
38	1682	25.4	**East Liverpool** (city) Columbiana County
38	1682	25.4	**Grove City** (city) Franklin County
38	1682	25.4	**Huber Heights** (city) Montgomery County
38	1682	25.4	**Twinsburg** (city) Summit County
43	1718	25.3	**Gahanna** (city) Franklin County
43	1718	25.3	**Montgomery** (city) Hamilton County
45	1762	25.2	**Brunswick** (city) Medina County
45	1762	25.2	**Troy** (city) Miami County
47	1797	25.1	**Canton** (city) Stark County
47	1797	25.1	**Forestville** (CDP) Hamilton County
47	1797	25.1	**Maple Heights** (city) Cuyahoga County
47	1797	25.1	**Miamisburg** (city) Montgomery County
47	1797	25.1	**Upper Arlington** (city) Franklin County
47	1797	25.1	**Zanesville** (city) Muskingum County
53	1841	25.0	**Garfield Heights** (city) Cuyahoga County
53	1841	25.0	**Washington Court House** (city) Fayette County
55	1891	24.9	**Hamilton** (city) Butler County
56	1934	24.8	**Lima** (city) Allen County
56	1934	24.8	**Piqua** (city) Miami County
56	1934	24.8	**Xenia** (city) Greene County
59	1977	24.7	**Riverside** (city) Montgomery County
60	2025	24.6	**Aurora** (city) Portage County
60	2025	24.6	**Broadview Heights** (city) Cuyahoga County
60	2025	24.6	**Cambridge** (city) Guernsey County
60	2025	24.6	**Cleveland** (city) Cuyahoga County
60	2025	24.6	**Mack** (CDP) Hamilton County
65	2075	24.5	**Warrensville Heights** (city) Cuyahoga County
66	2122	24.4	**Springfield** (city) Clark County
66	2122	24.4	**Van Wert** (city) Van Wert County
68	2158	24.3	**Galion** (city) Crawford County
68	2158	24.3	**Heath** (city) Licking County
68	2158	24.3	**Middletown** (city) Butler County
71	2205	24.2	**Elyria** (city) Lorain County
72	2255	24.1	**Defiance** (city) Defiance County
72	2255	24.1	**Green** (city) Summit County
74	2302	24.0	**Lancaster** (city) Fairfield County
74	2302	24.0	**Newark** (city) Licking County
74	2302	24.0	**South Euclid** (city) Cuyahoga County
74	2302	24.0	**Toledo** (city) Lucas County
78	2343	23.9	**Sandusky** (city) Erie County
79	2423	23.7	**Bridgetown** (CDP) Hamilton County
79	2423	23.7	**Urbana** (city) Champaign County
79	2423	23.7	**Warren** (city) Trumbull County
82	2483	23.6	**Sylvania** (city) Lucas County
82	2483	23.6	**Trotwood** (city) Montgomery County
84	2525	23.5	**Barberton** (city) Summit County
84	2525	23.5	**Monfort Heights** (CDP) Hamilton County
84	2525	23.5	**Wilmington** (city) Clinton County
87	2577	23.4	**Clayton** (city) Montgomery County
88	2624	23.3	**Circleville** (city) Pickaway County
88	2624	23.3	**Strongsville** (city) Cuyahoga County
90	2676	23.2	**Columbus** (city) Franklin County
90	2676	23.2	**Fairfield** (city) Butler County
90	2676	23.2	**White Oak** (CDP) Hamilton County
90	2676	23.2	**Worthington** (city) Franklin County
94	2724	23.1	**North Ridgeville** (city) Lorain County
94	2724	23.1	**Vandalia** (city) Montgomery County
96	2776	23.0	**Dent** (CDP) Hamilton County
96	2776	23.0	**Englewood** (city) Montgomery County
98	2824	22.9	**Akron** (city) Summit County
98	2824	22.9	**Dayton** (city) Montgomery County
98	2824	22.9	**Euclid** (city) Cuyahoga County
98	2824	22.9	**Massillon** (city) Stark County
102	2870	22.8	**Brecksville** (city) Cuyahoga County
102	2870	22.8	**Youngstown** (city) Mahoning County
104	2913	22.7	**Blue Ash** (city) Hamilton County
104	2913	22.7	**Stow** (city) Summit County
104	2913	22.7	**University Heights** (city) Cuyahoga County
107	2957	22.6	**Beavercreek** (city) Greene County
107	2957	22.6	**Maumee** (city) Lucas County
107	2957	22.6	**Oregon** (city) Lucas County
107	2957	22.6	**Springdale** (city) Hamilton County
107	2957	22.6	**Vermilion** (city) Lorain County
112	3007	22.5	**Ravenna** (city) Portage County
113	3047	22.4	**Westerville** (city) Franklin County
114	3092	22.3	**Cleveland Heights** (city) Cuyahoga County
114	3092	22.3	**Dover** (city) Tuscarawas County
114	3092	22.3	**Macedonia** (city) Summit County
114	3092	22.3	**Streetsboro** (city) Portage County
118	3141	22.2	**East Cleveland** (city) Cuyahoga County
118	3141	22.2	**Findlay** (city) Hancock County
118	3141	22.2	**Marion** (city) Marion County
118	3141	22.2	**Struthers** (city) Mahoning County
122	3185	22.1	**Amherst** (city) Lorain County
122	3185	22.1	**Cincinnati** (city) Hamilton County
124	3222	22.0	**Alliance** (city) Stark County
124	3222	22.0	**Bucyrus** (city) Crawford County
126	3267	21.9	**New Philadelphia** (city) Tuscarawas County
127	3308	21.8	**Chillicothe** (city) Ross County
127	3308	21.8	**Mount Vernon** (city) Knox County
127	3308	21.8	**Norton** (city) Summit County
127	3308	21.8	**Rocky River** (city) Cuyahoga County
131	3342	21.7	**Coshocton** (city) Coshocton County
132	3386	21.6	**Portsmouth** (city) Scioto County
132	3386	21.6	**Reading** (city) Hamilton County
132	3386	21.6	**Tallmadge** (city) Summit County
135	3422	21.5	**Greenville** (city) Darke County
135	3422	21.5	**Westlake** (city) Cuyahoga County
137	3536	21.2	**Bedford** (city) Cuyahoga County
137	3536	21.2	**Mentor** (city) Lake County
137	3536	21.2	**New Franklin** (city) Summit County
137	3536	21.2	**Salem** (city) Columbiana County
141	3570	21.1	**Fairview Park** (city) Cuyahoga County
141	3570	21.1	**Ironton** (city) Lawrence County
141	3570	21.1	**West Carrollton** (city) Montgomery County
144	3606	21.0	**Ashland** (city) Ashland County
144	3606	21.0	**Brook Park** (city) Cuyahoga County
144	3606	21.0	**Kettering** (city) Montgomery County
147	3650	20.9	**Cuyahoga Falls** (city) Summit County
147	3650	20.9	**Willowick** (city) Lake County
149	3729	20.7	**Niles** (city) Trumbull County
149	3729	20.7	**North Olmsted** (city) Cuyahoga County

***Note:** The state column ranks the top/bottom 150 places from all places in the state with population of 10,000 or more. The national column ranks the top/bottom 150 places from all places in the country with population of 10,000 or more. Places that are unincorporated were not considered in the rankings. Please refer to the User Guide for additional information.*

Population Under Age 18

Top 150 Places Ranked in *Ascending* Order

State Rank	Nat'l Rank	Percent	Place
1	17	5.8	**Athens** (city) Athens County
2	20	6.8	**Oxford** (city) Butler County
3	78	12.8	**Bowling Green** (city) Wood County
4	112	14.1	**Kent** (city) Portage County
5	197	16.3	**Seven Hills** (city) Cuyahoga County
6	276	17.4	**Lyndhurst** (city) Cuyahoga County
7	284	17.5	**Middleburg Heights** (city) Cuyahoga County
8	294	17.6	**Mayfield Heights** (city) Cuyahoga County
9	355	18.3	**Berea** (city) Cuyahoga County
10	368	18.4	**Richmond Heights** (city) Cuyahoga County
11	398	18.6	**North Canton** (city) Stark County
12	453	18.9	**Marietta** (city) Washington County
12	453	18.9	**Parma Heights** (city) Cuyahoga County
14	487	19.1	**Brooklyn** (city) Cuyahoga County
14	487	19.1	**Willoughby** (city) Lake County
16	605	19.6	**Beachwood** (city) Cuyahoga County
16	605	19.6	**Lakewood** (city) Cuyahoga County
18	680	19.9	**Bedford Heights** (city) Cuyahoga County
19	696	20.0	**Austintown** (CDP) Mahoning County
19	696	20.0	**Boardman** (CDP) Mahoning County
19	696	20.0	**Sharonville** (city) Hamilton County
22	719	20.1	**Centerville** (city) Montgomery County
22	719	20.1	**North Royalton** (city) Cuyahoga County
24	749	20.2	**Conneaut** (city) Ashtabula County
24	749	20.2	**Mansfield** (city) Richland County
24	749	20.2	**Norwood** (city) Hamilton County
27	776	20.3	**Steubenville** (city) Jefferson County
28	807	20.4	**Fairborn** (city) Greene County
28	807	20.4	**Parma** (city) Cuyahoga County
28	807	20.4	**Wickliffe** (city) Lake County
28	807	20.4	**Wooster** (city) Wayne County
32	867	20.6	**Eastlake** (city) Lake County
33	891	20.7	**Niles** (city) Trumbull County
33	891	20.7	**North Olmsted** (city) Cuyahoga County
33	891	20.7	**Tiffin** (city) Seneca County
36	967	20.9	**Cuyahoga Falls** (city) Summit County
36	967	20.9	**Willowick** (city) Lake County
38	1007	21.0	**Ashland** (city) Ashland County
38	1007	21.0	**Brook Park** (city) Cuyahoga County
38	1007	21.0	**Kettering** (city) Montgomery County
41	1051	21.1	**Fairview Park** (city) Cuyahoga County
41	1051	21.1	**Ironton** (city) Lawrence County
41	1051	21.1	**West Carrollton** (city) Montgomery County
44	1087	21.2	**Bedford** (city) Cuyahoga County
44	1087	21.2	**Mentor** (city) Lake County
44	1087	21.2	**New Franklin** (city) Summit County
44	1087	21.2	**Salem** (city) Columbiana County
48	1195	21.5	**Greenville** (city) Darke County
48	1195	21.5	**Westlake** (city) Cuyahoga County
50	1235	21.6	**Portsmouth** (city) Scioto County
50	1235	21.6	**Reading** (city) Hamilton County
50	1235	21.6	**Tallmadge** (city) Summit County
53	1271	21.7	**Coshocton** (city) Coshocton County
54	1315	21.8	**Chillicothe** (city) Ross County
54	1315	21.8	**Mount Vernon** (city) Knox County
54	1315	21.8	**Norton** (city) Summit County
54	1315	21.8	**Rocky River** (city) Cuyahoga County
58	1349	21.9	**New Philadelphia** (city) Tuscarawas County
59	1390	22.0	**Alliance** (city) Stark County
59	1390	22.0	**Bucyrus** (city) Crawford County
61	1435	22.1	**Amherst** (city) Lorain County
61	1435	22.1	**Cincinnati** (city) Hamilton County
63	1472	22.2	**East Cleveland** (city) Cuyahoga County
63	1472	22.2	**Findlay** (city) Hancock County
63	1472	22.2	**Marion** (city) Marion County
63	1472	22.2	**Struthers** (city) Mahoning County
67	1516	22.3	**Cleveland Heights** (city) Cuyahoga County
67	1516	22.3	**Dover** (city) Tuscarawas County
67	1516	22.3	**Macedonia** (city) Summit County
67	1516	22.3	**Streetsboro** (city) Portage County
71	1565	22.4	**Westerville** (city) Franklin County
72	1610	22.5	**Ravenna** (city) Portage County
73	1650	22.6	**Beavercreek** (city) Greene County
73	1650	22.6	**Maumee** (city) Lucas County
73	1650	22.6	**Oregon** (city) Lucas County
73	1650	22.6	**Springdale** (city) Hamilton County
73	1650	22.6	**Vermilion** (city) Lorain County
78	1700	22.7	**Blue Ash** (city) Hamilton County
78	1700	22.7	**Stow** (city) Summit County
78	1700	22.7	**University Heights** (city) Cuyahoga County
81	1744	22.8	**Brecksville** (city) Cuyahoga County
81	1744	22.8	**Youngstown** (city) Mahoning County
83	1787	22.9	**Akron** (city) Summit County
83	1787	22.9	**Dayton** (city) Montgomery County
83	1787	22.9	**Euclid** (city) Cuyahoga County
83	1787	22.9	**Massillon** (city) Stark County
87	1833	23.0	**Dent** (CDP) Hamilton County
87	1833	23.0	**Englewood** (city) Montgomery County
89	1881	23.1	**North Ridgeville** (city) Lorain County
89	1881	23.1	**Vandalia** (city) Montgomery County
91	1933	23.2	**Columbus** (city) Franklin County
91	1933	23.2	**Fairfield** (city) Butler County
91	1933	23.2	**White Oak** (CDP) Hamilton County
91	1933	23.2	**Worthington** (city) Franklin County
95	1981	23.3	**Circleville** (city) Pickaway County
95	1981	23.3	**Strongsville** (city) Cuyahoga County
97	2033	23.4	**Clayton** (city) Montgomery County
98	2080	23.5	**Barberton** (city) Summit County
98	2080	23.5	**Monfort Heights** (CDP) Hamilton County
98	2080	23.5	**Wilmington** (city) Clinton County
101	2132	23.6	**Sylvania** (city) Lucas County
101	2132	23.6	**Trotwood** (city) Montgomery County
103	2174	23.7	**Bridgetown** (CDP) Hamilton County
103	2174	23.7	**Urbana** (city) Champaign County
103	2174	23.7	**Warren** (city) Trumbull County
106	2268	23.9	**Sandusky** (city) Erie County
107	2314	24.0	**Lancaster** (city) Fairfield County
107	2314	24.0	**Newark** (city) Licking County
107	2314	24.0	**South Euclid** (city) Cuyahoga County
107	2314	24.0	**Toledo** (city) Lucas County
111	2355	24.1	**Defiance** (city) Defiance County
111	2355	24.1	**Green** (city) Summit County
113	2402	24.2	**Elyria** (city) Lorain County
114	2452	24.3	**Galion** (city) Crawford County
114	2452	24.3	**Heath** (city) Licking County
114	2452	24.3	**Middletown** (city) Butler County
117	2499	24.4	**Springfield** (city) Clark County
117	2499	24.4	**Van Wert** (city) Van Wert County
119	2535	24.5	**Warrensville Heights** (city) Cuyahoga County
120	2582	24.6	**Aurora** (city) Portage County
120	2582	24.6	**Broadview Heights** (city) Cuyahoga County
120	2582	24.6	**Cambridge** (city) Guernsey County
120	2582	24.6	**Cleveland** (city) Cuyahoga County
120	2582	24.6	**Mack** (CDP) Hamilton County
125	2632	24.7	**Riverside** (city) Montgomery County
126	2680	24.8	**Lima** (city) Allen County
126	2680	24.8	**Piqua** (city) Miami County
126	2680	24.8	**Xenia** (city) Greene County
129	2723	24.9	**Hamilton** (city) Butler County
130	2766	25.0	**Garfield Heights** (city) Cuyahoga County
130	2766	25.0	**Washington Court House** (city) Fayette County
132	2816	25.1	**Canton** (city) Stark County
132	2816	25.1	**Forestville** (CDP) Hamilton County
132	2816	25.1	**Maple Heights** (city) Cuyahoga County
132	2816	25.1	**Miamisburg** (city) Montgomery County
132	2816	25.1	**Upper Arlington** (city) Franklin County
132	2816	25.1	**Zanesville** (city) Muskingum County
138	2860	25.2	**Brunswick** (city) Medina County
138	2860	25.2	**Troy** (city) Miami County
140	2895	25.3	**Gahanna** (city) Franklin County
140	2895	25.3	**Montgomery** (city) Hamilton County
142	2939	25.4	**Bay Village** (city) Cuyahoga County
142	2939	25.4	**East Liverpool** (city) Columbiana County
142	2939	25.4	**Grove City** (city) Franklin County
142	2939	25.4	**Huber Heights** (city) Montgomery County
142	2939	25.4	**Twinsburg** (city) Summit County
147	2975	25.5	**Delaware** (city) Delaware County
147	2975	25.5	**Franklin** (city) Warren County
149	3014	25.6	**Celina** (city) Mercer County
149	3014	25.6	**Wadsworth** (city) Medina County

Note: *The state column ranks the top/bottom 150 places from all places in the state with population of 10,000 or more. The national column ranks the top/bottom 150 places from all places in the country with population of 10,000 or more. Places that are unincorporated were not considered in the rankings. Please refer to the User Guide for additional information.*

Population Age 65 and Over

Top 150 Places Ranked in *Descending* Order

State Rank	Nat'l Rank	Percent	Place
1	33	32.3	**Beachwood** (city) Cuyahoga County
2	84	26.3	**Seven Hills** (city) Cuyahoga County
3	121	24.4	**Centerville** (city) Montgomery County
4	122	24.3	**Lyndhurst** (city) Cuyahoga County
5	130	23.8	**Mayfield Heights** (city) Cuyahoga County
6	147	23.1	**Middleburg Heights** (city) Cuyahoga County
7	168	22.5	**Greenville** (city) Darke County
8	169	22.4	**Rocky River** (city) Cuyahoga County
9	191	22.0	**Dover** (city) Tuscarawas County
10	204	21.7	**Wickliffe** (city) Lake County
11	209	21.5	**North Canton** (city) Stark County
12	260	20.5	**Coshocton** (city) Coshocton County
12	260	20.5	**Parma Heights** (city) Cuyahoga County
12	260	20.5	**Richmond Heights** (city) Cuyahoga County
15	307	20.0	**Springdale** (city) Hamilton County
16	320	19.9	**Montgomery** (city) Hamilton County
17	331	19.8	**Brook Park** (city) Cuyahoga County
18	361	19.5	**Tallmadge** (city) Summit County
19	392	19.2	**Brooklyn** (city) Cuyahoga County
19	392	19.2	**Englewood** (city) Montgomery County
19	392	19.2	**Ironton** (city) Lawrence County
22	404	19.1	**Aurora** (city) Portage County
22	404	19.1	**Salem** (city) Columbiana County
22	404	19.1	**Willoughby** (city) Lake County
22	404	19.1	**Willowick** (city) Lake County
22	404	19.1	**Worthington** (city) Franklin County
27	435	19.0	**Westlake** (city) Cuyahoga County
28	467	18.8	**Austintown** (CDP) Mahoning County
28	467	18.8	**Bridgetown** (CDP) Hamilton County
28	467	18.8	**East Cleveland** (city) Cuyahoga County
31	525	18.4	**Boardman** (CDP) Mahoning County
31	525	18.4	**Marietta** (city) Washington County
33	556	18.2	**Bucyrus** (city) Crawford County
34	574	18.1	**Van Wert** (city) Van Wert County
35	595	18.0	**Kettering** (city) Montgomery County
35	595	18.0	**Struthers** (city) Mahoning County
37	616	17.9	**Chillicothe** (city) Ross County
38	635	17.8	**Amherst** (city) Lorain County
38	635	17.8	**Brecksville** (city) Cuyahoga County
38	635	17.8	**Niles** (city) Trumbull County
38	635	17.8	**North Olmsted** (city) Cuyahoga County
38	635	17.8	**Trotwood** (city) Montgomery County
43	659	17.7	**Ashland** (city) Ashland County
43	659	17.7	**Circleville** (city) Pickaway County
43	659	17.7	**New Franklin** (city) Summit County
43	659	17.7	**Parma** (city) Cuyahoga County
47	688	17.6	**Oregon** (city) Lucas County
47	688	17.6	**Sharonville** (city) Hamilton County
49	718	17.5	**Forestville** (CDP) Hamilton County
49	718	17.5	**Steubenville** (city) Jefferson County
49	718	17.5	**Warrensville Heights** (city) Cuyahoga County
52	762	17.3	**Cambridge** (city) Guernsey County
52	762	17.3	**Galion** (city) Crawford County
52	762	17.3	**Mount Vernon** (city) Knox County
55	786	17.2	**Sylvania** (city) Lucas County
56	848	17.0	**Bedford** (city) Cuyahoga County
57	874	16.9	**Heath** (city) Licking County
57	874	16.9	**Monfort Heights** (CDP) Hamilton County
59	892	16.8	**Bedford Heights** (city) Cuyahoga County
59	892	16.8	**Fairview Park** (city) Cuyahoga County
59	892	16.8	**New Philadelphia** (city) Tuscarawas County
59	892	16.8	**Vermilion** (city) Lorain County
63	918	16.7	**Massillon** (city) Stark County
63	918	16.7	**Upper Arlington** (city) Franklin County
65	939	16.6	**Wooster** (city) Wayne County
66	971	16.5	**Barberton** (city) Summit County
66	971	16.5	**Mentor** (city) Lake County
68	1004	16.4	**Portsmouth** (city) Scioto County
68	1004	16.4	**Urbana** (city) Champaign County
70	1062	16.2	**Celina** (city) Mercer County
70	1062	16.2	**Finneytown** (CDP) Hamilton County
70	1062	16.2	**Miamisburg** (city) Montgomery County
73	1091	16.1	**Norton** (city) Summit County
73	1091	16.1	**Strongsville** (city) Cuyahoga County
75	1124	16.0	**Fostoria** (city) Seneca County
75	1124	16.0	**Warren** (city) Trumbull County
77	1150	15.9	**Euclid** (city) Cuyahoga County
77	1150	15.9	**Washington Court House** (city) Fayette County
79	1180	15.8	**Tiffin** (city) Seneca County
79	1180	15.8	**Wadsworth** (city) Medina County
79	1180	15.8	**Youngstown** (city) Mahoning County
82	1222	15.7	**Alliance** (city) Stark County
82	1222	15.7	**Conneaut** (city) Ashtabula County
82	1222	15.7	**Dent** (CDP) Hamilton County
82	1222	15.7	**Lancaster** (city) Fairfield County
82	1222	15.7	**Mansfield** (city) Richland County
82	1222	15.7	**Vandalia** (city) Montgomery County
82	1222	15.7	**Xenia** (city) Greene County
89	1295	15.5	**Bay Village** (city) Cuyahoga County
89	1295	15.5	**Shaker Heights** (city) Cuyahoga County
89	1295	15.5	**White Oak** (CDP) Hamilton County
92	1326	15.4	**Blue Ash** (city) Hamilton County
92	1326	15.4	**Eastlake** (city) Lake County
92	1326	15.4	**Garfield Heights** (city) Cuyahoga County
95	1355	15.3	**Cuyahoga Falls** (city) Summit County
95	1355	15.3	**Defiance** (city) Defiance County
95	1355	15.3	**Springfield** (city) Clark County
98	1386	15.2	**Zanesville** (city) Muskingum County
99	1433	15.1	**North Royalton** (city) Cuyahoga County
100	1466	15.0	**North Ridgeville** (city) Lorain County
100	1466	15.0	**Sandusky** (city) Erie County
102	1502	14.9	**Middletown** (city) Butler County
102	1502	14.9	**Ravenna** (city) Portage County
102	1502	14.9	**Reading** (city) Hamilton County
105	1532	14.8	**Broadview Heights** (city) Cuyahoga County
106	1574	14.7	**Ashtabula** (city) Ashtabula County
106	1574	14.7	**Macedonia** (city) Summit County
106	1574	14.7	**Piqua** (city) Miami County
109	1615	14.6	**East Liverpool** (city) Columbiana County
109	1615	14.6	**Norwalk** (city) Huron County
111	1653	14.5	**Avon Lake** (city) Lorain County
111	1653	14.5	**Findlay** (city) Hancock County
111	1653	14.5	**Green** (city) Summit County
111	1653	14.5	**Newark** (city) Licking County
111	1653	14.5	**Twinsburg** (city) Summit County
111	1653	14.5	**West Carrollton** (city) Montgomery County
111	1653	14.5	**Wilmington** (city) Clinton County
118	1740	14.3	**Beavercreek** (city) Greene County
118	1740	14.3	**Elyria** (city) Lorain County
118	1740	14.3	**Monroe** (city) Butler County
118	1740	14.3	**Westerville** (city) Franklin County
122	1865	14.0	**Clayton** (city) Montgomery County
123	1911	13.9	**Berea** (city) Cuyahoga County
123	1911	13.9	**Fremont** (city) Sandusky County
123	1911	13.9	**Lorain** (city) Lorain County
126	1964	13.8	**Mack** (CDP) Hamilton County
126	1964	13.8	**Riverside** (city) Montgomery County
126	1964	13.8	**Stow** (city) Summit County
129	2011	13.7	**Maumee** (city) Lucas County
130	2095	13.5	**Cleveland Heights** (city) Cuyahoga County
131	2220	13.2	**Fairborn** (city) Greene County
131	2220	13.2	**Hamilton** (city) Butler County
131	2220	13.2	**Maple Heights** (city) Cuyahoga County
134	2260	13.1	**Troy** (city) Miami County
135	2304	13.0	**Fairfield** (city) Butler County
136	2344	12.9	**Huber Heights** (city) Montgomery County
136	2344	12.9	**South Euclid** (city) Cuyahoga County
138	2390	12.8	**Bellefontaine** (city) Logan County
138	2390	12.8	**Canton** (city) Stark County
138	2390	12.8	**Loveland** (city) Hamilton County
141	2486	12.6	**Akron** (city) Summit County
141	2486	12.6	**Avon** (city) Lorain County
141	2486	12.6	**Marion** (city) Marion County
144	2538	12.5	**Franklin** (city) Warren County
145	2582	12.4	**Sidney** (city) Shelby County
145	2582	12.4	**Solon** (city) Cuyahoga County
147	2628	12.3	**Perrysburg** (city) Wood County
148	2665	12.2	**Grove City** (city) Franklin County
149	2699	12.1	**Toledo** (city) Lucas County
150	2738	12.0	**Cleveland** (city) Cuyahoga County

***Note:** The state column ranks the top/bottom 150 places from all places in the state with population of 10,000 or more. The national column ranks the top/bottom 150 places from all places in the country with population of 10,000 or more. Places that are unincorporated were not considered in the rankings. Please refer to the User Guide for additional information.*

Population Age 65 and Over

Top 150 Places Ranked in *Ascending* Order

State Rank	Nat'l Rank	Percent	Place
1	46	4.3	**Athens** (city) Athens County
2	157	5.6	**Oxford** (city) Butler County
3	312	6.8	**Pickerington** (city) Fairfield County
4	425	7.4	**Kent** (city) Portage County
5	481	7.7	**Powell** (city) Delaware County
6	506	7.8	**Dublin** (city) Franklin County
7	570	8.1	**Marysville** (city) Union County
8	699	8.6	**Columbus** (city) Franklin County
8	699	8.6	**Hilliard** (city) Franklin County
10	733	8.7	**Painesville** (city) Lake County
11	801	8.9	**Bowling Green** (city) Wood County
12	912	9.3	**Springboro** (city) Warren County
13	944	9.4	**Trenton** (city) Butler County
14	1072	9.9	**Mason** (city) Warren County
15	1137	10.1	**Bexley** (city) Franklin County
15	1137	10.1	**Lebanon** (city) Warren County
17	1306	10.6	**Pataskala** (city) Licking County
18	1391	10.8	**Cincinnati** (city) Hamilton County
19	1467	11.0	**Lakewood** (city) Cuyahoga County
20	1498	11.1	**Delaware** (city) Delaware County
20	1498	11.1	**Norwood** (city) Hamilton County
22	1532	11.2	**Whitehall** (city) Franklin County
23	1626	11.4	**Lima** (city) Allen County
23	1626	11.4	**Northbrook** (CDP) Hamilton County
25	1700	11.6	**Medina** (city) Medina County
25	1700	11.6	**Reynoldsburg** (city) Franklin County
27	1733	11.7	**Forest Park** (city) Hamilton County
27	1733	11.7	**Gahanna** (city) Franklin County
27	1733	11.7	**Streetsboro** (city) Portage County
27	1733	11.7	**University Heights** (city) Cuyahoga County
31	1789	11.8	**Dayton** (city) Montgomery County
31	1789	11.8	**Hudson** (city) Summit County
33	1834	11.9	**Brunswick** (city) Medina County
34	1877	12.0	**Cleveland** (city) Cuyahoga County
35	1919	12.1	**Toledo** (city) Lucas County
36	1958	12.2	**Grove City** (city) Franklin County
37	1992	12.3	**Perrysburg** (city) Wood County
38	2029	12.4	**Sidney** (city) Shelby County
38	2029	12.4	**Solon** (city) Cuyahoga County
40	2075	12.5	**Franklin** (city) Warren County
41	2119	12.6	**Akron** (city) Summit County
41	2119	12.6	**Avon** (city) Lorain County
41	2119	12.6	**Marion** (city) Marion County
44	2221	12.8	**Bellefontaine** (city) Logan County
44	2221	12.8	**Canton** (city) Stark County
44	2221	12.8	**Loveland** (city) Hamilton County
47	2267	12.9	**Huber Heights** (city) Montgomery County
47	2267	12.9	**South Euclid** (city) Cuyahoga County
49	2313	13.0	**Fairfield** (city) Butler County
50	2353	13.1	**Troy** (city) Miami County
51	2397	13.2	**Fairborn** (city) Greene County
51	2397	13.2	**Hamilton** (city) Butler County
51	2397	13.2	**Maple Heights** (city) Cuyahoga County
54	2514	13.5	**Cleveland Heights** (city) Cuyahoga County
55	2605	13.7	**Maumee** (city) Lucas County
56	2646	13.8	**Mack** (CDP) Hamilton County
56	2646	13.8	**Riverside** (city) Montgomery County
56	2646	13.8	**Stow** (city) Summit County
59	2693	13.9	**Berea** (city) Cuyahoga County
59	2693	13.9	**Fremont** (city) Sandusky County
59	2693	13.9	**Lorain** (city) Lorain County
62	2746	14.0	**Clayton** (city) Montgomery County
63	2876	14.3	**Beavercreek** (city) Greene County
63	2876	14.3	**Elyria** (city) Lorain County
63	2876	14.3	**Monroe** (city) Butler County
63	2876	14.3	**Westerville** (city) Franklin County
67	2966	14.5	**Avon Lake** (city) Lorain County
67	2966	14.5	**Findlay** (city) Hancock County
67	2966	14.5	**Green** (city) Summit County
67	2966	14.5	**Newark** (city) Licking County
67	2966	14.5	**Twinsburg** (city) Summit County
67	2966	14.5	**West Carrollton** (city) Montgomery County
67	2966	14.5	**Wilmington** (city) Clinton County
74	3004	14.6	**East Liverpool** (city) Columbiana County
74	3004	14.6	**Norwalk** (city) Huron County
76	3042	14.7	**Ashtabula** (city) Ashtabula County
76	3042	14.7	**Macedonia** (city) Summit County
76	3042	14.7	**Piqua** (city) Miami County
79	3083	14.8	**Broadview Heights** (city) Cuyahoga County
80	3125	14.9	**Middletown** (city) Butler County
80	3125	14.9	**Ravenna** (city) Portage County
80	3125	14.9	**Reading** (city) Hamilton County
83	3155	15.0	**North Ridgeville** (city) Lorain County
83	3155	15.0	**Sandusky** (city) Erie County
85	3191	15.1	**North Royalton** (city) Cuyahoga County
86	3224	15.2	**Zanesville** (city) Muskingum County
87	3271	15.3	**Cuyahoga Falls** (city) Summit County
87	3271	15.3	**Defiance** (city) Defiance County
87	3271	15.3	**Springfield** (city) Clark County
90	3302	15.4	**Blue Ash** (city) Hamilton County
90	3302	15.4	**Eastlake** (city) Lake County
90	3302	15.4	**Garfield Heights** (city) Cuyahoga County
93	3331	15.5	**Bay Village** (city) Cuyahoga County
93	3331	15.5	**Shaker Heights** (city) Cuyahoga County
93	3331	15.5	**White Oak** (CDP) Hamilton County
96	3399	15.7	**Alliance** (city) Stark County
96	3399	15.7	**Conneaut** (city) Ashtabula County
96	3399	15.7	**Dent** (CDP) Hamilton County
96	3399	15.7	**Lancaster** (city) Fairfield County
96	3399	15.7	**Mansfield** (city) Richland County
96	3399	15.7	**Vandalia** (city) Montgomery County
96	3399	15.7	**Xenia** (city) Greene County
103	3435	15.8	**Tiffin** (city) Seneca County
103	3435	15.8	**Wadsworth** (city) Medina County
103	3435	15.8	**Youngstown** (city) Mahoning County
106	3477	15.9	**Euclid** (city) Cuyahoga County
106	3477	15.9	**Washington Court House** (city) Fayette County
108	3507	16.0	**Fostoria** (city) Seneca County
108	3507	16.0	**Warren** (city) Trumbull County
110	3533	16.1	**Norton** (city) Summit County
110	3533	16.1	**Strongsville** (city) Cuyahoga County
112	3566	16.2	**Celina** (city) Mercer County
112	3566	16.2	**Finneytown** (CDP) Hamilton County
112	3566	16.2	**Miamisburg** (city) Montgomery County
115	3624	16.4	**Portsmouth** (city) Scioto County
115	3624	16.4	**Urbana** (city) Champaign County
117	3653	16.5	**Barberton** (city) Summit County
117	3653	16.5	**Mentor** (city) Lake County
119	3686	16.6	**Wooster** (city) Wayne County
120	3718	16.7	**Massillon** (city) Stark County
120	3718	16.7	**Upper Arlington** (city) Franklin County
122	3739	16.8	**Bedford Heights** (city) Cuyahoga County
122	3739	16.8	**Fairview Park** (city) Cuyahoga County
122	3739	16.8	**New Philadelphia** (city) Tuscarawas County
122	3739	16.8	**Vermilion** (city) Lorain County
126	3765	16.9	**Heath** (city) Licking County
126	3765	16.9	**Monfort Heights** (CDP) Hamilton County
128	3783	17.0	**Bedford** (city) Cuyahoga County
129	3837	17.2	**Sylvania** (city) Lucas County
130	3871	17.3	**Cambridge** (city) Guernsey County
130	3871	17.3	**Galion** (city) Crawford County
130	3871	17.3	**Mount Vernon** (city) Knox County
133	3916	17.5	**Forestville** (CDP) Hamilton County
133	3916	17.5	**Steubenville** (city) Jefferson County
133	3916	17.5	**Warrensville Heights** (city) Cuyahoga County
136	3939	17.6	**Oregon** (city) Lucas County
136	3939	17.6	**Sharonville** (city) Hamilton County
138	3969	17.7	**Ashland** (city) Ashland County
138	3969	17.7	**Circleville** (city) Pickaway County
138	3969	17.7	**New Franklin** (city) Summit County
138	3969	17.7	**Parma** (city) Cuyahoga County
142	3998	17.8	**Amherst** (city) Lorain County
142	3998	17.8	**Brecksville** (city) Cuyahoga County
142	3998	17.8	**Niles** (city) Trumbull County
142	3998	17.8	**North Olmsted** (city) Cuyahoga County
142	3998	17.8	**Trotwood** (city) Montgomery County
147	4022	17.9	**Chillicothe** (city) Ross County
148	4041	18.0	**Kettering** (city) Montgomery County
148	4041	18.0	**Struthers** (city) Mahoning County
150	4062	18.1	**Van Wert** (city) Van Wert County

Note: *The state column ranks the top/bottom 150 places from all places in the state with population of 10,000 or more. The national column ranks the top/bottom 150 places from all places in the country with population of 10,000 or more. Places that are unincorporated were not considered in the rankings. Please refer to the User Guide for additional information.*

Males per 100 Females

Top 150 Places Ranked in *Descending* Order

State Rank	Nat'l Rank	Ratio	Place
1	76	121.6	**Marion** (city) Marion County
2	85	119.5	**Conneaut** (city) Ashtabula County
3	117	112.6	**Mansfield** (city) Richland County
4	120	112.0	**Lima** (city) Allen County
5	490	101.2	**Painesville** (city) Lake County
6	638	100.1	**Mack** (CDP) Hamilton County
7	653	100.0	**Athens** (city) Athens County
8	697	99.7	**Beavercreek** (city) Greene County
9	736	99.5	**Brecksville** (city) Cuyahoga County
9	736	99.5	**Norwood** (city) Hamilton County
11	1070	98.0	**New Franklin** (city) Summit County
12	1165	97.6	**Dublin** (city) Franklin County
13	1281	97.2	**Eastlake** (city) Lake County
13	1281	97.2	**Norton** (city) Summit County
15	1345	97.0	**Powell** (city) Delaware County
16	1382	96.9	**Youngstown** (city) Mahoning County
17	1471	96.6	**Brunswick** (city) Medina County
17	1471	96.6	**Lakewood** (city) Cuyahoga County
19	1504	96.5	**Pataskala** (city) Licking County
20	1532	96.4	**Hudson** (city) Summit County
20	1532	96.4	**Reading** (city) Hamilton County
20	1532	96.4	**Sidney** (city) Shelby County
23	1574	96.3	**North Ridgeville** (city) Lorain County
24	1598	96.2	**Lebanon** (city) Warren County
25	1685	96.0	**Blue Ash** (city) Hamilton County
26	1730	95.9	**Clayton** (city) Montgomery County
26	1730	95.9	**Maumee** (city) Lucas County
28	1769	95.8	**Fairborn** (city) Greene County
28	1769	95.8	**Tiffin** (city) Seneca County
30	1839	95.6	**Springboro** (city) Warren County
31	1882	95.5	**Hilliard** (city) Franklin County
32	1923	95.4	**Columbus** (city) Franklin County
32	1923	95.4	**Hamilton** (city) Butler County
34	1954	95.3	**North Royalton** (city) Cuyahoga County
35	2048	95.1	**Green** (city) Summit County
35	2048	95.1	**Monroe** (city) Butler County
35	2048	95.1	**Solon** (city) Cuyahoga County
38	2089	95.0	**Dayton** (city) Montgomery County
38	2089	95.0	**Seven Hills** (city) Cuyahoga County
40	2117	94.9	**Troy** (city) Miami County
41	2207	94.7	**Pickerington** (city) Fairfield County
41	2207	94.7	**Strongsville** (city) Cuyahoga County
43	2254	94.6	**Trenton** (city) Butler County
43	2254	94.6	**Whitehall** (city) Franklin County
45	2299	94.5	**Vermilion** (city) Lorain County
46	2399	94.2	**Riverside** (city) Montgomery County
46	2399	94.2	**Streetsboro** (city) Portage County
48	2431	94.1	**Macedonia** (city) Summit County
48	2431	94.1	**Mason** (city) Warren County
48	2431	94.1	**New Philadelphia** (city) Tuscarawas County
51	2475	94.0	**Massillon** (city) Stark County
51	2475	94.0	**Perrysburg** (city) Wood County
53	2526	93.9	**Bellefontaine** (city) Logan County
53	2526	93.9	**Vandalia** (city) Montgomery County
55	2575	93.8	**Avon** (city) Lorain County
55	2575	93.8	**Toledo** (city) Lucas County
55	2575	93.8	**Willowick** (city) Lake County
58	2620	93.7	**Mentor** (city) Lake County
58	2620	93.7	**Wickliffe** (city) Lake County
60	2672	93.6	**Akron** (city) Summit County
61	2717	93.5	**Grove City** (city) Franklin County
62	2760	93.4	**Amherst** (city) Lorain County
62	2760	93.4	**Defiance** (city) Defiance County
62	2760	93.4	**Huber Heights** (city) Montgomery County
62	2760	93.4	**North Olmsted** (city) Cuyahoga County
66	2806	93.3	**Avon Lake** (city) Lorain County
66	2806	93.3	**Celina** (city) Mercer County
68	2894	93.1	**Brooklyn** (city) Cuyahoga County
68	2894	93.1	**Franklin** (city) Warren County
70	2929	93.0	**Stow** (city) Summit County
70	2929	93.0	**West Carrollton** (city) Montgomery County
70	2929	93.0	**White Oak** (CDP) Hamilton County
73	2962	92.9	**Fairfield** (city) Butler County
74	2989	92.8	**Parma** (city) Cuyahoga County
74	2989	92.8	**Ravenna** (city) Portage County
76	3028	92.7	**Broadview Heights** (city) Cuyahoga County
76	3028	92.7	**Monfort Heights** (CDP) Hamilton County
76	3028	92.7	**Montgomery** (city) Hamilton County
76	3028	92.7	**Oregon** (city) Lucas County
80	3076	92.6	**Warren** (city) Trumbull County
81	3111	92.5	**Cincinnati** (city) Hamilton County
81	3111	92.5	**Medina** (city) Medina County
81	3111	92.5	**Wadsworth** (city) Medina County
84	3144	92.4	**Brook Park** (city) Cuyahoga County
85	3199	92.2	**Delaware** (city) Delaware County
85	3199	92.2	**Lancaster** (city) Fairfield County
85	3199	92.2	**Piqua** (city) Miami County
88	3243	92.1	**Bowling Green** (city) Wood County
88	3243	92.1	**Cleveland** (city) Cuyahoga County
88	3243	92.1	**Fairview Park** (city) Cuyahoga County
91	3276	92.0	**Aurora** (city) Portage County
91	3276	92.0	**Barberton** (city) Summit County
91	3276	92.0	**Circleville** (city) Pickaway County
94	3314	91.9	**Alliance** (city) Stark County
94	3314	91.9	**Dent** (CDP) Hamilton County
94	3314	91.9	**Gahanna** (city) Franklin County
94	3314	91.9	**Heath** (city) Licking County
98	3357	91.8	**Loveland** (city) Hamilton County
98	3357	91.8	**Salem** (city) Columbiana County
100	3393	91.7	**Fremont** (city) Sandusky County
100	3393	91.7	**Norwalk** (city) Huron County
100	3393	91.7	**Upper Arlington** (city) Franklin County
103	3424	91.6	**Elyria** (city) Lorain County
104	3451	91.5	**Newark** (city) Licking County
104	3451	91.5	**Sharonville** (city) Hamilton County
104	3451	91.5	**Tallmadge** (city) Summit County
107	3481	91.4	**Bucyrus** (city) Crawford County
108	3515	91.3	**Berea** (city) Cuyahoga County
109	3540	91.2	**Kettering** (city) Montgomery County
110	3566	91.1	**Washington Court House** (city) Fayette County
111	3598	91.0	**Sandusky** (city) Erie County
111	3598	91.0	**University Heights** (city) Cuyahoga County
111	3598	91.0	**Wooster** (city) Wayne County
114	3633	90.9	**Ashtabula** (city) Ashtabula County
114	3633	90.9	**Niles** (city) Trumbull County
114	3633	90.9	**Springfield** (city) Clark County
114	3633	90.9	**Struthers** (city) Mahoning County
118	3658	90.8	**Chillicothe** (city) Ross County
119	3682	90.7	**Boardman** (CDP) Mahoning County
119	3682	90.7	**East Liverpool** (city) Columbiana County
119	3682	90.7	**Findlay** (city) Hancock County
119	3682	90.7	**Miamisburg** (city) Montgomery County
119	3682	90.7	**Oxford** (city) Butler County
124	3706	90.6	**Austintown** (CDP) Mahoning County
124	3706	90.6	**Middletown** (city) Butler County
126	3736	90.5	**Lorain** (city) Lorain County
127	3764	90.4	**Bay Village** (city) Cuyahoga County
128	3788	90.3	**Dover** (city) Tuscarawas County
129	3819	90.2	**Westlake** (city) Cuyahoga County
130	3859	90.0	**Bridgetown** (CDP) Hamilton County
130	3859	90.0	**Canton** (city) Stark County
130	3859	90.0	**Reynoldsburg** (city) Franklin County
133	3923	89.7	**Cuyahoga Falls** (city) Summit County
133	3923	89.7	**Fostoria** (city) Seneca County
133	3923	89.7	**Sylvania** (city) Lucas County
136	3944	89.6	**Middleburg Heights** (city) Cuyahoga County
137	4002	89.3	**Worthington** (city) Franklin County
137	4002	89.3	**Xenia** (city) Greene County
139	4026	89.1	**Ironton** (city) Lawrence County
139	4026	89.1	**Urbana** (city) Champaign County
141	4070	88.9	**Galion** (city) Crawford County
142	4136	88.5	**Westerville** (city) Franklin County
143	4153	88.4	**Bexley** (city) Franklin County
143	4153	88.4	**Marietta** (city) Washington County
143	4153	88.4	**Northbrook** (CDP) Hamilton County
146	4190	88.1	**Ashland** (city) Ashland County
146	4190	88.1	**Willoughby** (city) Lake County
148	4205	88.0	**Coshocton** (city) Coshocton County
148	4205	88.0	**Twinsburg** (city) Summit County
148	4205	88.0	**Van Wert** (city) Van Wert County

Note: *The state column ranks the top/bottom 150 places from all places in the state with population of 10,000 or more. The national column ranks the top/bottom 150 places from all places in the country with population of 10,000 or more. Places that are unincorporated were not considered in the rankings. Please refer to the User Guide for additional information.*

Males per 100 Females

Top 150 Places Ranked in *Ascending* Order

State Rank	Nat'l Rank	Ratio	Place
1	8	74.4	**Warrensville Heights** (city) Cuyahoga County
2	10	74.9	**Marysville** (city) Union County
3	25	79.6	**Beachwood** (city) Cuyahoga County
4	27	79.9	**Trotwood** (city) Montgomery County
5	47	81.1	**Euclid** (city) Cuyahoga County
6	56	81.5	**Richmond Heights** (city) Cuyahoga County
7	69	82.1	**East Cleveland** (city) Cuyahoga County
8	77	82.5	**Shaker Heights** (city) Cuyahoga County
9	80	82.7	**Mayfield Heights** (city) Cuyahoga County
10	116	83.9	**South Euclid** (city) Cuyahoga County
11	137	84.4	**Bedford** (city) Cuyahoga County
12	173	84.9	**Bedford Heights** (city) Cuyahoga County
13	186	85.2	**Garfield Heights** (city) Cuyahoga County
14	197	85.3	**Lyndhurst** (city) Cuyahoga County
15	205	85.4	**Greenville** (city) Darke County
16	210	85.5	**Rocky River** (city) Cuyahoga County
17	223	85.7	**Steubenville** (city) Jefferson County
18	245	86.0	**Centerville** (city) Montgomery County
19	253	86.1	**Forestville** (CDP) Hamilton County
19	253	86.1	**Maple Heights** (city) Cuyahoga County
19	253	86.1	**North Canton** (city) Stark County
22	261	86.2	**Kent** (city) Portage County
23	286	86.6	**Forest Park** (city) Hamilton County
23	286	86.6	**Portsmouth** (city) Scioto County
25	313	86.8	**Springdale** (city) Hamilton County
26	328	86.9	**Mount Vernon** (city) Knox County
27	336	87.0	**Parma Heights** (city) Cuyahoga County
28	344	87.1	**Finneytown** (CDP) Hamilton County
29	353	87.2	**Cleveland Heights** (city) Cuyahoga County
29	353	87.2	**Englewood** (city) Montgomery County
31	364	87.3	**Zanesville** (city) Muskingum County
32	371	87.4	**Cambridge** (city) Guernsey County
33	401	87.7	**Wilmington** (city) Clinton County
34	435	88.0	**Coshocton** (city) Coshocton County
34	435	88.0	**Twinsburg** (city) Summit County
34	435	88.0	**Van Wert** (city) Van Wert County
37	452	88.1	**Ashland** (city) Ashland County
37	452	88.1	**Willoughby** (city) Lake County
39	494	88.4	**Bexley** (city) Franklin County
39	494	88.4	**Marietta** (city) Washington County
39	494	88.4	**Northbrook** (CDP) Hamilton County
42	504	88.5	**Westerville** (city) Franklin County
43	568	88.9	**Galion** (city) Crawford County
44	606	89.1	**Ironton** (city) Lawrence County
44	606	89.1	**Urbana** (city) Champaign County
46	641	89.3	**Worthington** (city) Franklin County
46	641	89.3	**Xenia** (city) Greene County
48	689	89.6	**Middleburg Heights** (city) Cuyahoga County
49	713	89.7	**Cuyahoga Falls** (city) Summit County
49	713	89.7	**Fostoria** (city) Seneca County
49	713	89.7	**Sylvania** (city) Lucas County
52	774	90.0	**Bridgetown** (CDP) Hamilton County
52	774	90.0	**Canton** (city) Stark County
52	774	90.0	**Reynoldsburg** (city) Franklin County
55	822	90.2	**Westlake** (city) Cuyahoga County
56	838	90.3	**Dover** (city) Tuscarawas County
57	869	90.4	**Bay Village** (city) Cuyahoga County
58	893	90.5	**Lorain** (city) Lorain County
59	921	90.6	**Austintown** (CDP) Mahoning County
59	921	90.6	**Middletown** (city) Butler County
61	951	90.7	**Boardman** (CDP) Mahoning County
61	951	90.7	**East Liverpool** (city) Columbiana County
61	951	90.7	**Findlay** (city) Hancock County
61	951	90.7	**Miamisburg** (city) Montgomery County
61	951	90.7	**Oxford** (city) Butler County
66	975	90.8	**Chillicothe** (city) Ross County
67	999	90.9	**Ashtabula** (city) Ashtabula County
67	999	90.9	**Niles** (city) Trumbull County
67	999	90.9	**Springfield** (city) Clark County
67	999	90.9	**Struthers** (city) Mahoning County
71	1024	91.0	**Sandusky** (city) Erie County
71	1024	91.0	**University Heights** (city) Cuyahoga County
71	1024	91.0	**Wooster** (city) Wayne County
74	1059	91.1	**Washington Court House** (city) Fayette County
75	1091	91.2	**Kettering** (city) Montgomery County
76	1117	91.3	**Berea** (city) Cuyahoga County
77	1142	91.4	**Bucyrus** (city) Crawford County
78	1176	91.5	**Newark** (city) Licking County
78	1176	91.5	**Sharonville** (city) Hamilton County
78	1176	91.5	**Tallmadge** (city) Summit County
81	1206	91.6	**Elyria** (city) Lorain County
82	1233	91.7	**Fremont** (city) Sandusky County
82	1233	91.7	**Norwalk** (city) Huron County
82	1233	91.7	**Upper Arlington** (city) Franklin County
85	1264	91.8	**Loveland** (city) Hamilton County
85	1264	91.8	**Salem** (city) Columbiana County
87	1300	91.9	**Alliance** (city) Stark County
87	1300	91.9	**Dent** (CDP) Hamilton County
87	1300	91.9	**Gahanna** (city) Franklin County
87	1300	91.9	**Heath** (city) Licking County
91	1343	92.0	**Aurora** (city) Portage County
91	1343	92.0	**Barberton** (city) Summit County
91	1343	92.0	**Circleville** (city) Pickaway County
94	1381	92.1	**Bowling Green** (city) Wood County
94	1381	92.1	**Cleveland** (city) Cuyahoga County
94	1381	92.1	**Fairview Park** (city) Cuyahoga County
97	1414	92.2	**Delaware** (city) Delaware County
97	1414	92.2	**Lancaster** (city) Fairfield County
97	1414	92.2	**Piqua** (city) Miami County
100	1487	92.4	**Brook Park** (city) Cuyahoga County
101	1513	92.5	**Cincinnati** (city) Hamilton County
101	1513	92.5	**Medina** (city) Medina County
101	1513	92.5	**Wadsworth** (city) Medina County
104	1546	92.6	**Warren** (city) Trumbull County
105	1581	92.7	**Broadview Heights** (city) Cuyahoga County
105	1581	92.7	**Monfort Heights** (CDP) Hamilton County
105	1581	92.7	**Montgomery** (city) Hamilton County
105	1581	92.7	**Oregon** (city) Lucas County
109	1629	92.8	**Parma** (city) Cuyahoga County
109	1629	92.8	**Ravenna** (city) Portage County
111	1668	92.9	**Fairfield** (city) Butler County
112	1695	93.0	**Stow** (city) Summit County
112	1695	93.0	**West Carrollton** (city) Montgomery County
112	1695	93.0	**White Oak** (CDP) Hamilton County
115	1728	93.1	**Brooklyn** (city) Cuyahoga County
115	1728	93.1	**Franklin** (city) Warren County
117	1811	93.3	**Avon Lake** (city) Lorain County
117	1811	93.3	**Celina** (city) Mercer County
119	1851	93.4	**Amherst** (city) Lorain County
119	1851	93.4	**Defiance** (city) Defiance County
119	1851	93.4	**Huber Heights** (city) Montgomery County
119	1851	93.4	**North Olmsted** (city) Cuyahoga County
123	1897	93.5	**Grove City** (city) Franklin County
124	1940	93.6	**Akron** (city) Summit County
125	1985	93.7	**Mentor** (city) Lake County
125	1985	93.7	**Wickliffe** (city) Lake County
127	2037	93.8	**Avon** (city) Lorain County
127	2037	93.8	**Toledo** (city) Lucas County
127	2037	93.8	**Willowick** (city) Lake County
130	2082	93.9	**Bellefontaine** (city) Logan County
130	2082	93.9	**Vandalia** (city) Montgomery County
132	2131	94.0	**Massillon** (city) Stark County
132	2131	94.0	**Perrysburg** (city) Wood County
134	2182	94.1	**Macedonia** (city) Summit County
134	2182	94.1	**Mason** (city) Warren County
134	2182	94.1	**New Philadelphia** (city) Tuscarawas County
137	2226	94.2	**Riverside** (city) Montgomery County
137	2226	94.2	**Streetsboro** (city) Portage County
139	2327	94.5	**Vermilion** (city) Lorain County
140	2358	94.6	**Trenton** (city) Butler County
140	2358	94.6	**Whitehall** (city) Franklin County
142	2403	94.7	**Pickerington** (city) Fairfield County
142	2403	94.7	**Strongsville** (city) Cuyahoga County
144	2486	94.9	**Troy** (city) Miami County
145	2540	95.0	**Dayton** (city) Montgomery County
145	2540	95.0	**Seven Hills** (city) Cuyahoga County
147	2568	95.1	**Green** (city) Summit County
147	2568	95.1	**Monroe** (city) Butler County
147	2568	95.1	**Solon** (city) Cuyahoga County
150	2656	95.3	**North Royalton** (city) Cuyahoga County

Note: *The state column ranks the top/bottom 150 places from all places in the state with population of 10,000 or more. The national column ranks the top/bottom 150 places from all places in the country with population of 10,000 or more. Places that are unincorporated were not considered in the rankings. Please refer to the User Guide for additional information.*

Marriage Status: Never Married

Top 150 Places Ranked in *Descending* Order

State Rank	Nat'l Rank	Percent	Place
1	8	81.3	**Athens** (city) Athens County
2	9	77.6	**Oxford** (city) Butler County
3	47	61.1	**Kent** (city) Portage County
4	50	60.6	**Bowling Green** (city) Wood County
5	171	50.9	**Cincinnati** (city) Hamilton County
6	213	48.7	**Dayton** (city) Montgomery County
7	217	48.6	**Cleveland** (city) Cuyahoga County
8	286	46.4	**East Cleveland** (city) Cuyahoga County
9	368	44.1	**Norwood** (city) Hamilton County
10	380	43.8	**Youngstown** (city) Mahoning County
11	401	43.5	**Lakewood** (city) Cuyahoga County
12	406	43.4	**Euclid** (city) Cuyahoga County
13	412	43.3	**Columbus** (city) Franklin County
14	504	41.8	**Cleveland Heights** (city) Cuyahoga County
15	511	41.6	**University Heights** (city) Cuyahoga County
16	520	41.5	**Akron** (city) Summit County
17	532	41.3	**Lima** (city) Allen County
18	546	41.1	**Painesville** (city) Lake County
19	553	41.0	**South Euclid** (city) Cuyahoga County
19	553	41.0	**Toledo** (city) Lucas County
21	583	40.7	**Warrensville Heights** (city) Cuyahoga County
22	627	40.2	**Berea** (city) Cuyahoga County
23	654	39.8	**Maple Heights** (city) Cuyahoga County
24	754	38.7	**Steubenville** (city) Jefferson County
25	767	38.6	**Garfield Heights** (city) Cuyahoga County
26	783	38.4	**Alliance** (city) Stark County
27	793	38.3	**Fairborn** (city) Greene County
28	810	38.1	**Trotwood** (city) Montgomery County
29	829	37.9	**Canton** (city) Stark County
30	847	37.7	**Tiffin** (city) Seneca County
31	866	37.6	**Bedford Heights** (city) Cuyahoga County
32	900	37.3	**Richmond Heights** (city) Cuyahoga County
32	900	37.3	**Whitehall** (city) Franklin County
34	924	37.1	**Warren** (city) Trumbull County
35	1029	36.3	**Wooster** (city) Wayne County
36	1040	36.2	**Sandusky** (city) Erie County
37	1070	36.0	**Bexley** (city) Franklin County
38	1095	35.8	**Mansfield** (city) Richland County
39	1116	35.6	**Lorain** (city) Lorain County
40	1124	35.5	**Ravenna** (city) Portage County
40	1124	35.5	**Reading** (city) Hamilton County
42	1158	35.3	**Springfield** (city) Clark County
43	1312	34.4	**Elyria** (city) Lorain County
44	1388	34.1	**Forest Park** (city) Hamilton County
45	1426	33.9	**Portsmouth** (city) Scioto County
46	1439	33.8	**Bedford** (city) Cuyahoga County
47	1471	33.6	**Zanesville** (city) Muskingum County
48	1509	33.4	**Barberton** (city) Summit County
49	1526	33.3	**Fremont** (city) Sandusky County
50	1544	33.2	**Springdale** (city) Hamilton County
51	1578	33.0	**Ashland** (city) Ashland County
51	1578	33.0	**Marietta** (city) Washington County
53	1619	32.8	**Northbrook** (CDP) Hamilton County
54	1661	32.6	**Marion** (city) Marion County
55	1679	32.5	**Conneaut** (city) Ashtabula County
55	1679	32.5	**Mayfield Heights** (city) Cuyahoga County
57	1724	32.3	**Mount Vernon** (city) Knox County
58	1768	32.1	**Findlay** (city) Hancock County
58	1768	32.1	**Reynoldsburg** (city) Franklin County
60	1810	31.9	**Hamilton** (city) Butler County
60	1810	31.9	**Streetsboro** (city) Portage County
62	1847	31.8	**Delaware** (city) Delaware County
62	1847	31.8	**Fairview Park** (city) Cuyahoga County
64	1876	31.7	**Defiance** (city) Defiance County
65	1905	31.6	**Ashtabula** (city) Ashtabula County
66	1929	31.5	**Parma** (city) Cuyahoga County
66	1929	31.5	**Sharonville** (city) Hamilton County
68	1984	31.3	**Massillon** (city) Stark County
69	2012	31.2	**Brooklyn** (city) Cuyahoga County
70	2030	31.1	**East Liverpool** (city) Columbiana County
71	2102	30.8	**Struthers** (city) Mahoning County
71	2102	30.8	**Wilmington** (city) Clinton County
73	2130	30.7	**Chillicothe** (city) Ross County
73	2130	30.7	**Eastlake** (city) Lake County
75	2192	30.4	**Brook Park** (city) Cuyahoga County
76	2241	30.2	**Cuyahoga Falls** (city) Summit County
76	2241	30.2	**Finneytown** (CDP) Hamilton County
78	2277	30.1	**Willowick** (city) Lake County
79	2307	30.0	**Niles** (city) Trumbull County
80	2380	29.7	**Willoughby** (city) Lake County
81	2399	29.6	**Marysville** (city) Union County
81	2399	29.6	**Middletown** (city) Butler County
81	2399	29.6	**North Canton** (city) Stark County
84	2459	29.4	**Ironton** (city) Lawrence County
85	2512	29.2	**Parma Heights** (city) Cuyahoga County
86	2567	29.0	**Newark** (city) Licking County
87	2587	28.9	**North Royalton** (city) Cuyahoga County
87	2587	28.9	**West Carrollton** (city) Montgomery County
89	2618	28.8	**Gahanna** (city) Franklin County
90	2646	28.7	**Boardman** (CDP) Mahoning County
90	2646	28.7	**Brunswick** (city) Medina County
90	2646	28.7	**Shaker Heights** (city) Cuyahoga County
93	2681	28.6	**Fostoria** (city) Seneca County
93	2681	28.6	**Lebanon** (city) Warren County
95	2713	28.5	**Austintown** (CDP) Mahoning County
95	2713	28.5	**Kettering** (city) Montgomery County
95	2713	28.5	**Lancaster** (city) Fairfield County
98	2776	28.3	**Cambridge** (city) Guernsey County
99	2834	28.1	**Piqua** (city) Miami County
100	2866	28.0	**Fairfield** (city) Butler County
101	2901	27.9	**Bridgetown** (CDP) Hamilton County
101	2901	27.9	**New Philadelphia** (city) Tuscarawas County
103	2929	27.8	**Sidney** (city) Shelby County
103	2929	27.8	**Troy** (city) Miami County
105	2954	27.7	**Sylvania** (city) Lucas County
105	2954	27.7	**Xenia** (city) Greene County
107	2984	27.6	**Medina** (city) Medina County
107	2984	27.6	**Urbana** (city) Champaign County
109	3022	27.5	**Riverside** (city) Montgomery County
110	3042	27.4	**Bellefontaine** (city) Logan County
111	3068	27.3	**Westerville** (city) Franklin County
112	3100	27.2	**Circleville** (city) Pickaway County
112	3100	27.2	**White Oak** (CDP) Hamilton County
112	3100	27.2	**Wickliffe** (city) Lake County
115	3134	27.1	**Norwalk** (city) Huron County
116	3174	26.9	**Huber Heights** (city) Montgomery County
116	3174	26.9	**Vandalia** (city) Montgomery County
118	3201	26.8	**Greenville** (city) Darke County
118	3201	26.8	**North Olmsted** (city) Cuyahoga County
118	3201	26.8	**Rocky River** (city) Cuyahoga County
121	3238	26.7	**Broadview Heights** (city) Cuyahoga County
122	3265	26.6	**Pataskala** (city) Licking County
123	3302	26.5	**Stow** (city) Summit County
124	3359	26.3	**Beavercreek** (city) Greene County
125	3376	26.2	**Dent** (CDP) Hamilton County
126	3403	26.1	**Brecksville** (city) Cuyahoga County
126	3403	26.1	**Grove City** (city) Franklin County
126	3403	26.1	**Loveland** (city) Hamilton County
129	3430	26.0	**Monfort Heights** (CDP) Hamilton County
130	3469	25.8	**Maumee** (city) Lucas County
130	3469	25.8	**Tallmadge** (city) Summit County
132	3493	25.7	**Salem** (city) Columbiana County
133	3551	25.5	**Middleburg Heights** (city) Cuyahoga County
134	3602	25.3	**Clayton** (city) Montgomery County
135	3632	25.2	**Oregon** (city) Lucas County
135	3632	25.2	**Washington Court House** (city) Fayette County
137	3650	25.1	**Amherst** (city) Lorain County
137	3650	25.1	**Blue Ash** (city) Hamilton County
137	3650	25.1	**Lyndhurst** (city) Cuyahoga County
140	3668	25.0	**Seven Hills** (city) Cuyahoga County
141	3710	24.8	**Twinsburg** (city) Summit County
141	3710	24.8	**Van Wert** (city) Van Wert County
141	3710	24.8	**Westlake** (city) Cuyahoga County
144	3729	24.7	**Heath** (city) Licking County
145	3751	24.6	**Bucyrus** (city) Crawford County
145	3751	24.6	**Mentor** (city) Lake County
147	3773	24.5	**Coshocton** (city) Coshocton County
147	3773	24.5	**Pickerington** (city) Fairfield County
149	3863	24.1	**Englewood** (city) Montgomery County
150	3891	24.0	**Galion** (city) Crawford County

Note: *The state column ranks the top/bottom 150 places from all places in the state with population of 10,000 or more. The national column ranks the top/bottom 150 places from all places in the country with population of 10,000 or more. Places that are unincorporated were not considered in the rankings. Please refer to the User Guide for additional information.*

Marriage Status: Never Married

Top 150 Places Ranked in *Ascending* Order

State Rank	Nat'l Rank	Percent	Place
1	60	18.2	**Beachwood** (city) Cuyahoga County
2	65	18.3	**Montgomery** (city) Hamilton County
3	71	18.4	**Springboro** (city) Warren County
4	87	19.0	**Powell** (city) Delaware County
5	111	19.5	**Avon** (city) Lorain County
6	168	20.3	**Worthington** (city) Franklin County
7	172	20.4	**Hudson** (city) Summit County
8	176	20.5	**Forestville** (CDP) Hamilton County
8	176	20.5	**Norton** (city) Summit County
10	187	20.6	**Dover** (city) Tuscarawas County
11	213	20.9	**Bay Village** (city) Cuyahoga County
11	213	20.9	**Solon** (city) Cuyahoga County
13	253	21.3	**Wadsworth** (city) Medina County
14	262	21.4	**Miamisburg** (city) Montgomery County
15	280	21.5	**New Franklin** (city) Summit County
16	313	21.8	**Aurora** (city) Portage County
17	325	21.9	**North Ridgeville** (city) Lorain County
18	347	22.1	**Avon Lake** (city) Lorain County
19	385	22.3	**Centerville** (city) Montgomery County
20	401	22.4	**Hilliard** (city) Franklin County
21	459	22.7	**Dublin** (city) Franklin County
21	459	22.7	**Franklin** (city) Warren County
23	482	22.8	**Trenton** (city) Butler County
24	540	23.1	**Macedonia** (city) Summit County
25	593	23.3	**Mason** (city) Warren County
26	613	23.4	**Perrysburg** (city) Wood County
26	613	23.4	**Strongsville** (city) Cuyahoga County
26	613	23.4	**Vermilion** (city) Lorain County
29	648	23.5	**Green** (city) Summit County
29	648	23.5	**Monroe** (city) Butler County
31	691	23.7	**Celina** (city) Mercer County
32	733	23.9	**Mack** (CDP) Hamilton County
33	748	24.0	**Galion** (city) Crawford County
33	748	24.0	**Upper Arlington** (city) Franklin County
35	766	24.1	**Englewood** (city) Montgomery County
36	862	24.5	**Coshocton** (city) Coshocton County
36	862	24.5	**Pickerington** (city) Fairfield County
38	884	24.6	**Bucyrus** (city) Crawford County
38	884	24.6	**Mentor** (city) Lake County
40	906	24.7	**Heath** (city) Licking County
41	928	24.8	**Twinsburg** (city) Summit County
41	928	24.8	**Van Wert** (city) Van Wert County
41	928	24.8	**Westlake** (city) Cuyahoga County
44	965	25.0	**Seven Hills** (city) Cuyahoga County
45	989	25.1	**Amherst** (city) Lorain County
45	989	25.1	**Blue Ash** (city) Hamilton County
45	989	25.1	**Lyndhurst** (city) Cuyahoga County
48	1007	25.2	**Oregon** (city) Lucas County
48	1007	25.2	**Washington Court House** (city) Fayette County
50	1025	25.3	**Clayton** (city) Montgomery County
51	1083	25.5	**Middleburg Heights** (city) Cuyahoga County
52	1141	25.7	**Salem** (city) Columbiana County
53	1164	25.8	**Maumee** (city) Lucas County
53	1164	25.8	**Tallmadge** (city) Summit County
55	1203	26.0	**Monfort Heights** (CDP) Hamilton County
56	1227	26.1	**Brecksville** (city) Cuyahoga County
56	1227	26.1	**Grove City** (city) Franklin County
56	1227	26.1	**Loveland** (city) Hamilton County
59	1254	26.2	**Dent** (CDP) Hamilton County
60	1281	26.3	**Beavercreek** (city) Greene County
61	1327	26.5	**Stow** (city) Summit County
62	1355	26.6	**Pataskala** (city) Licking County
63	1392	26.7	**Broadview Heights** (city) Cuyahoga County
64	1419	26.8	**Greenville** (city) Darke County
64	1419	26.8	**North Olmsted** (city) Cuyahoga County
64	1419	26.8	**Rocky River** (city) Cuyahoga County
67	1456	26.9	**Huber Heights** (city) Montgomery County
67	1456	26.9	**Vandalia** (city) Montgomery County
69	1502	27.1	**Norwalk** (city) Huron County
70	1523	27.2	**Circleville** (city) Pickaway County
70	1523	27.2	**White Oak** (CDP) Hamilton County
70	1523	27.2	**Wickliffe** (city) Lake County
73	1557	27.3	**Westerville** (city) Franklin County
74	1589	27.4	**Bellefontaine** (city) Logan County
75	1615	27.5	**Riverside** (city) Montgomery County
76	1635	27.6	**Medina** (city) Medina County
76	1635	27.6	**Urbana** (city) Champaign County
78	1673	27.7	**Sylvania** (city) Lucas County
78	1673	27.7	**Xenia** (city) Greene County
80	1703	27.8	**Sidney** (city) Shelby County
80	1703	27.8	**Troy** (city) Miami County
82	1728	27.9	**Bridgetown** (CDP) Hamilton County
82	1728	27.9	**New Philadelphia** (city) Tuscarawas County
84	1756	28.0	**Fairfield** (city) Butler County
85	1791	28.1	**Piqua** (city) Miami County
86	1855	28.3	**Cambridge** (city) Guernsey County
87	1911	28.5	**Austintown** (CDP) Mahoning County
87	1911	28.5	**Kettering** (city) Montgomery County
87	1911	28.5	**Lancaster** (city) Fairfield County
90	1944	28.6	**Fostoria** (city) Seneca County
90	1944	28.6	**Lebanon** (city) Warren County
92	1976	28.7	**Boardman** (CDP) Mahoning County
92	1976	28.7	**Brunswick** (city) Medina County
92	1976	28.7	**Shaker Heights** (city) Cuyahoga County
95	2011	28.8	**Gahanna** (city) Franklin County
96	2039	28.9	**North Royalton** (city) Cuyahoga County
96	2039	28.9	**West Carrollton** (city) Montgomery County
98	2070	29.0	**Newark** (city) Licking County
99	2116	29.2	**Parma Heights** (city) Cuyahoga County
100	2166	29.4	**Ironton** (city) Lawrence County
101	2234	29.6	**Marysville** (city) Union County
101	2234	29.6	**Middletown** (city) Butler County
101	2234	29.6	**North Canton** (city) Stark County
104	2258	29.7	**Willoughby** (city) Lake County
105	2320	30.0	**Niles** (city) Trumbull County
106	2350	30.1	**Willowick** (city) Lake County
107	2380	30.2	**Cuyahoga Falls** (city) Summit County
107	2380	30.2	**Finneytown** (CDP) Hamilton County
109	2438	30.4	**Brook Park** (city) Cuyahoga County
110	2499	30.7	**Chillicothe** (city) Ross County
110	2499	30.7	**Eastlake** (city) Lake County
112	2527	30.8	**Struthers** (city) Mahoning County
112	2527	30.8	**Wilmington** (city) Clinton County
114	2609	31.1	**East Liverpool** (city) Columbiana County
115	2627	31.2	**Brooklyn** (city) Cuyahoga County
116	2645	31.3	**Massillon** (city) Stark County
117	2694	31.5	**Parma** (city) Cuyahoga County
117	2694	31.5	**Sharonville** (city) Hamilton County
119	2728	31.6	**Ashtabula** (city) Ashtabula County
120	2752	31.7	**Defiance** (city) Defiance County
121	2781	31.8	**Delaware** (city) Delaware County
121	2781	31.8	**Fairview Park** (city) Cuyahoga County
123	2810	31.9	**Hamilton** (city) Butler County
123	2810	31.9	**Streetsboro** (city) Portage County
125	2864	32.1	**Findlay** (city) Hancock County
125	2864	32.1	**Reynoldsburg** (city) Franklin County
127	2915	32.3	**Mount Vernon** (city) Knox County
128	2951	32.5	**Conneaut** (city) Ashtabula County
128	2951	32.5	**Mayfield Heights** (city) Cuyahoga County
130	2978	32.6	**Marion** (city) Marion County
131	3018	32.8	**Northbrook** (CDP) Hamilton County
132	3060	33.0	**Ashland** (city) Ashland County
132	3060	33.0	**Marietta** (city) Washington County
134	3095	33.2	**Springdale** (city) Hamilton County
135	3113	33.3	**Fremont** (city) Sandusky County
136	3131	33.4	**Barberton** (city) Summit County
137	3169	33.6	**Zanesville** (city) Muskingum County
138	3204	33.8	**Bedford** (city) Cuyahoga County
139	3218	33.9	**Portsmouth** (city) Scioto County
140	3249	34.1	**Forest Park** (city) Hamilton County
141	3315	34.4	**Elyria** (city) Lorain County
142	3477	35.3	**Springfield** (city) Clark County
143	3516	35.5	**Ravenna** (city) Portage County
143	3516	35.5	**Reading** (city) Hamilton County
145	3533	35.6	**Lorain** (city) Lorain County
146	3551	35.8	**Mansfield** (city) Richland County
147	3575	36.0	**Bexley** (city) Franklin County
148	3599	36.2	**Sandusky** (city) Erie County
149	3617	36.3	**Wooster** (city) Wayne County
150	3721	37.1	**Warren** (city) Trumbull County

***Note:** The state column ranks the top/bottom 150 places from all places in the state with population of 10,000 or more. The national column ranks the top/bottom 150 places from all places in the country with population of 10,000 or more. Places that are unincorporated were not considered in the rankings. Please refer to the User Guide for additional information.*

Marriage Status: Now Married

Top 150 Places Ranked in *Descending* Order

State Rank	Nat'l Rank	Percent	Place
1	37	71.4	**Powell** (city) Delaware County
2	66	69.3	**Springboro** (city) Warren County
3	86	68.7	**Hudson** (city) Summit County
3	86	68.7	**Montgomery** (city) Hamilton County
5	145	67.4	**Dublin** (city) Franklin County
6	196	66.4	**Solon** (city) Cuyahoga County
7	246	65.6	**Mack** (CDP) Hamilton County
8	336	64.4	**Avon** (city) Lorain County
9	378	64.0	**New Franklin** (city) Summit County
10	438	63.3	**Upper Arlington** (city) Franklin County
11	452	63.1	**Worthington** (city) Franklin County
12	466	62.9	**Pickerington** (city) Fairfield County
13	479	62.8	**Hilliard** (city) Franklin County
14	485	62.7	**Norton** (city) Summit County
15	502	62.6	**Mason** (city) Warren County
16	548	62.1	**North Ridgeville** (city) Lorain County
16	548	62.1	**Strongsville** (city) Cuyahoga County
18	581	61.9	**Bay Village** (city) Cuyahoga County
19	596	61.8	**Aurora** (city) Portage County
20	643	61.4	**Avon Lake** (city) Lorain County
21	654	61.3	**Macedonia** (city) Summit County
22	752	60.6	**Monfort Heights** (CDP) Hamilton County
23	783	60.4	**Green** (city) Summit County
23	783	60.4	**Trenton** (city) Butler County
23	783	60.4	**Twinsburg** (city) Summit County
26	854	59.9	**Perrysburg** (city) Wood County
27	901	59.6	**Beavercreek** (city) Greene County
28	1025	58.8	**Forestville** (CDP) Hamilton County
28	1025	58.8	**Seven Hills** (city) Cuyahoga County
30	1046	58.7	**Blue Ash** (city) Hamilton County
31	1073	58.5	**Mentor** (city) Lake County
32	1121	58.2	**Brecksville** (city) Cuyahoga County
33	1129	58.1	**Lyndhurst** (city) Cuyahoga County
34	1145	58.0	**Beachwood** (city) Cuyahoga County
34	1145	58.0	**Monroe** (city) Butler County
34	1145	58.0	**Westerville** (city) Franklin County
37	1245	57.4	**Clayton** (city) Montgomery County
38	1260	57.3	**Sylvania** (city) Lucas County
39	1311	57.0	**Dent** (CDP) Hamilton County
40	1323	56.9	**Westlake** (city) Cuyahoga County
41	1339	56.8	**Centerville** (city) Montgomery County
42	1352	56.7	**Amherst** (city) Lorain County
43	1399	56.5	**Grove City** (city) Franklin County
44	1424	56.4	**Tallmadge** (city) Summit County
45	1443	56.3	**Broadview Heights** (city) Cuyahoga County
46	1476	56.1	**Brunswick** (city) Medina County
47	1554	55.7	**North Olmsted** (city) Cuyahoga County
47	1554	55.7	**Stow** (city) Summit County
47	1554	55.7	**Wadsworth** (city) Medina County
50	1595	55.5	**Huber Heights** (city) Montgomery County
50	1595	55.5	**Vermilion** (city) Lorain County
52	1618	55.4	**Englewood** (city) Montgomery County
53	1638	55.3	**Oregon** (city) Lucas County
53	1638	55.3	**Pataskala** (city) Licking County
53	1638	55.3	**White Oak** (CDP) Hamilton County
56	1650	55.2	**Gahanna** (city) Franklin County
57	1671	55.1	**Maumee** (city) Lucas County
58	1733	54.8	**Dover** (city) Tuscarawas County
58	1733	54.8	**Vandalia** (city) Montgomery County
60	1756	54.7	**Franklin** (city) Warren County
60	1756	54.7	**Rocky River** (city) Cuyahoga County
62	1792	54.5	**Miamisburg** (city) Montgomery County
63	1809	54.4	**Shaker Heights** (city) Cuyahoga County
64	1895	54.0	**North Royalton** (city) Cuyahoga County
65	2003	53.5	**Heath** (city) Licking County
66	2032	53.4	**Medina** (city) Medina County
67	2087	53.1	**Galion** (city) Crawford County
68	2131	52.9	**Finneytown** (CDP) Hamilton County
69	2148	52.8	**Fairfield** (city) Butler County
70	2170	52.7	**Lebanon** (city) Warren County
71	2190	52.6	**Bexley** (city) Franklin County
71	2190	52.6	**Celina** (city) Mercer County
73	2220	52.4	**New Philadelphia** (city) Tuscarawas County
74	2306	52.0	**Bridgetown** (CDP) Hamilton County
75	2325	51.9	**Coshocton** (city) Coshocton County

State Rank	Nat'l Rank	Percent	Place
76	2375	51.7	**Bucyrus** (city) Crawford County
77	2385	51.6	**Van Wert** (city) Van Wert County
78	2518	50.9	**Middleburg Heights** (city) Cuyahoga County
79	2535	50.8	**Delaware** (city) Delaware County
79	2535	50.8	**Loveland** (city) Hamilton County
81	2582	50.6	**Riverside** (city) Montgomery County
81	2582	50.6	**Troy** (city) Miami County
83	2631	50.4	**Norwalk** (city) Huron County
84	2697	50.1	**Streetsboro** (city) Portage County
85	2720	50.0	**Fairview Park** (city) Cuyahoga County
86	2753	49.8	**Eastlake** (city) Lake County
87	2774	49.7	**Kettering** (city) Montgomery County
87	2774	49.7	**Xenia** (city) Greene County
89	2803	49.6	**Marysville** (city) Union County
90	2820	49.5	**Boardman** (CDP) Mahoning County
90	2820	49.5	**Sidney** (city) Shelby County
92	2849	49.4	**Wickliffe** (city) Lake County
92	2849	49.4	**Willowick** (city) Lake County
94	2884	49.2	**Cuyahoga Falls** (city) Summit County
95	2924	49.0	**Brook Park** (city) Cuyahoga County
95	2924	49.0	**Defiance** (city) Defiance County
97	2940	48.9	**Salem** (city) Columbiana County
98	2982	48.7	**Urbana** (city) Champaign County
99	3005	48.6	**Parma** (city) Cuyahoga County
99	3005	48.6	**Washington Court House** (city) Fayette County
101	3023	48.5	**Austintown** (CDP) Mahoning County
102	3042	48.4	**Circleville** (city) Pickaway County
102	3042	48.4	**Forest Park** (city) Hamilton County
102	3042	48.4	**Parma Heights** (city) Cuyahoga County
102	3042	48.4	**Piqua** (city) Miami County
106	3067	48.3	**Bellefontaine** (city) Logan County
107	3087	48.2	**Reynoldsburg** (city) Franklin County
108	3138	47.9	**Newark** (city) Licking County
109	3153	47.8	**University Heights** (city) Cuyahoga County
109	3153	47.8	**Willoughby** (city) Lake County
111	3172	47.7	**Findlay** (city) Hancock County
111	3172	47.7	**North Canton** (city) Stark County
113	3220	47.5	**Ashland** (city) Ashland County
114	3253	47.3	**Elyria** (city) Lorain County
115	3268	47.2	**Middletown** (city) Butler County
116	3370	46.6	**Greenville** (city) Darke County
117	3426	46.3	**Brooklyn** (city) Cuyahoga County
118	3444	46.2	**Lancaster** (city) Fairfield County
118	3444	46.2	**West Carrollton** (city) Montgomery County
120	3459	46.1	**Massillon** (city) Stark County
120	3459	46.1	**Sharonville** (city) Hamilton County
120	3459	46.1	**Wooster** (city) Wayne County
123	3478	46.0	**East Liverpool** (city) Columbiana County
124	3538	45.6	**Conneaut** (city) Ashtabula County
124	3538	45.6	**Fremont** (city) Sandusky County
126	3558	45.5	**Wilmington** (city) Clinton County
127	3579	45.4	**Mayfield Heights** (city) Cuyahoga County
128	3590	45.3	**Chillicothe** (city) Ross County
128	3590	45.3	**Hamilton** (city) Butler County
130	3614	45.1	**Mount Vernon** (city) Knox County
130	3614	45.1	**Northbrook** (CDP) Hamilton County
132	3626	45.0	**Reading** (city) Hamilton County
133	3638	44.9	**Springdale** (city) Hamilton County
134	3659	44.7	**Cambridge** (city) Guernsey County
134	3659	44.7	**Fostoria** (city) Seneca County
134	3659	44.7	**Tiffin** (city) Seneca County
137	3738	44.2	**Richmond Heights** (city) Cuyahoga County
138	3799	43.7	**Bedford** (city) Cuyahoga County
138	3799	43.7	**Niles** (city) Trumbull County
140	3809	43.6	**Marion** (city) Marion County
141	3839	43.4	**Ashtabula** (city) Ashtabula County
142	3853	43.3	**Ironton** (city) Lawrence County
143	3869	43.2	**Lorain** (city) Lorain County
144	3897	42.9	**Struthers** (city) Mahoning County
145	3911	42.8	**Marietta** (city) Washington County
146	3956	42.4	**Berea** (city) Cuyahoga County
147	3965	42.3	**Fairborn** (city) Greene County
148	4009	41.9	**Sandusky** (city) Erie County
149	4045	41.4	**Ravenna** (city) Portage County
150	4058	41.3	**Barberton** (city) Summit County

Note: *The state column ranks the top/bottom 150 places from all places in the state with population of 10,000 or more. The national column ranks the top/bottom 150 places from all places in the country with population of 10,000 or more. Places that are unincorporated were not considered in the rankings. Please refer to the User Guide for additional information.*

Marriage Status: Now Married

Top 150 Places Ranked in *Ascending* Order

State Rank	Nat'l Rank	Percent	Place
1	7	13.9	**Athens** (city) Athens County
2	11	17.2	**Oxford** (city) Butler County
3	47	26.0	**East Cleveland** (city) Cuyahoga County
4	65	28.5	**Kent** (city) Portage County
5	74	29.0	**Dayton** (city) Montgomery County
6	76	29.1	**Cleveland** (city) Cuyahoga County
7	84	29.6	**Bowling Green** (city) Wood County
8	111	31.0	**Cincinnati** (city) Hamilton County
9	126	31.6	**Youngstown** (city) Mahoning County
10	220	34.8	**Euclid** (city) Cuyahoga County
11	226	34.9	**Warrensville Heights** (city) Cuyahoga County
12	241	35.2	**Lima** (city) Allen County
13	275	36.2	**Bedford Heights** (city) Cuyahoga County
14	313	37.0	**Trotwood** (city) Montgomery County
15	326	37.3	**Whitehall** (city) Franklin County
16	337	37.6	**Akron** (city) Summit County
17	344	37.7	**Toledo** (city) Lucas County
18	353	37.9	**Lakewood** (city) Cuyahoga County
19	368	38.1	**Norwood** (city) Hamilton County
20	381	38.3	**Warren** (city) Trumbull County
21	423	38.9	**Alliance** (city) Stark County
22	427	39.0	**Maple Heights** (city) Cuyahoga County
23	442	39.3	**Canton** (city) Stark County
24	447	39.4	**Columbus** (city) Franklin County
25	466	39.7	**Mansfield** (city) Richland County
26	474	39.8	**Zanesville** (city) Muskingum County
27	481	39.9	**South Euclid** (city) Cuyahoga County
28	511	40.3	**Garfield Heights** (city) Cuyahoga County
28	511	40.3	**Springfield** (city) Clark County
30	526	40.4	**Portsmouth** (city) Scioto County
31	546	40.7	**Cleveland Heights** (city) Cuyahoga County
32	571	41.0	**Painesville** (city) Lake County
32	571	41.0	**Steubenville** (city) Jefferson County
34	588	41.3	**Barberton** (city) Summit County
35	599	41.4	**Ravenna** (city) Portage County
36	638	41.9	**Sandusky** (city) Erie County
37	676	42.3	**Fairborn** (city) Greene County
38	692	42.4	**Berea** (city) Cuyahoga County
39	735	42.8	**Marietta** (city) Washington County
40	746	42.9	**Struthers** (city) Mahoning County
41	777	43.2	**Lorain** (city) Lorain County
42	788	43.3	**Ironton** (city) Lawrence County
43	804	43.4	**Ashtabula** (city) Ashtabula County
44	830	43.6	**Marion** (city) Marion County
45	848	43.7	**Bedford** (city) Cuyahoga County
45	848	43.7	**Niles** (city) Trumbull County
47	910	44.2	**Richmond Heights** (city) Cuyahoga County
48	975	44.7	**Cambridge** (city) Guernsey County
48	975	44.7	**Fostoria** (city) Seneca County
48	975	44.7	**Tiffin** (city) Seneca County
51	1006	44.9	**Springdale** (city) Hamilton County
52	1019	45.0	**Reading** (city) Hamilton County
53	1031	45.1	**Mount Vernon** (city) Knox County
53	1031	45.1	**Northbrook** (CDP) Hamilton County
55	1051	45.3	**Chillicothe** (city) Ross County
55	1051	45.3	**Hamilton** (city) Butler County
57	1067	45.4	**Mayfield Heights** (city) Cuyahoga County
58	1078	45.5	**Wilmington** (city) Clinton County
59	1099	45.6	**Conneaut** (city) Ashtabula County
59	1099	45.6	**Fremont** (city) Sandusky County
61	1167	46.0	**East Liverpool** (city) Columbiana County
62	1179	46.1	**Massillon** (city) Stark County
62	1179	46.1	**Sharonville** (city) Hamilton County
62	1179	46.1	**Wooster** (city) Wayne County
65	1198	46.2	**Lancaster** (city) Fairfield County
65	1198	46.2	**West Carrollton** (city) Montgomery County
67	1213	46.3	**Brooklyn** (city) Cuyahoga County
68	1264	46.6	**Greenville** (city) Darke County
69	1371	47.2	**Middletown** (city) Butler County
70	1389	47.3	**Elyria** (city) Lorain County
71	1420	47.5	**Ashland** (city) Ashland County
72	1458	47.7	**Findlay** (city) Hancock County
72	1458	47.7	**North Canton** (city) Stark County
74	1485	47.8	**University Heights** (city) Cuyahoga County
74	1485	47.8	**Willoughby** (city) Lake County
76	1504	47.9	**Newark** (city) Licking County
77	1553	48.2	**Reynoldsburg** (city) Franklin County
78	1570	48.3	**Bellefontaine** (city) Logan County
79	1590	48.4	**Circleville** (city) Pickaway County
79	1590	48.4	**Forest Park** (city) Hamilton County
79	1590	48.4	**Parma Heights** (city) Cuyahoga County
79	1590	48.4	**Piqua** (city) Miami County
83	1615	48.5	**Austintown** (CDP) Mahoning County
84	1634	48.6	**Parma** (city) Cuyahoga County
84	1634	48.6	**Washington Court House** (city) Fayette County
86	1652	48.7	**Urbana** (city) Champaign County
87	1696	48.9	**Salem** (city) Columbiana County
88	1717	49.0	**Brook Park** (city) Cuyahoga County
88	1717	49.0	**Defiance** (city) Defiance County
90	1756	49.2	**Cuyahoga Falls** (city) Summit County
91	1788	49.4	**Wickliffe** (city) Lake County
91	1788	49.4	**Willowick** (city) Lake County
93	1808	49.5	**Boardman** (CDP) Mahoning County
93	1808	49.5	**Sidney** (city) Shelby County
95	1837	49.6	**Marysville** (city) Union County
96	1854	49.7	**Kettering** (city) Montgomery County
96	1854	49.7	**Xenia** (city) Greene County
98	1883	49.8	**Eastlake** (city) Lake County
99	1918	50.0	**Fairview Park** (city) Cuyahoga County
100	1937	50.1	**Streetsboro** (city) Portage County
101	2006	50.4	**Norwalk** (city) Huron County
102	2050	50.6	**Riverside** (city) Montgomery County
102	2050	50.6	**Troy** (city) Miami County
104	2100	50.8	**Delaware** (city) Delaware County
104	2100	50.8	**Loveland** (city) Hamilton County
106	2122	50.9	**Middleburg Heights** (city) Cuyahoga County
107	2250	51.6	**Van Wert** (city) Van Wert County
108	2272	51.7	**Bucyrus** (city) Crawford County
109	2310	51.9	**Coshocton** (city) Coshocton County
110	2332	52.0	**Bridgetown** (CDP) Hamilton County
111	2415	52.4	**New Philadelphia** (city) Tuscarawas County
112	2451	52.6	**Bexley** (city) Franklin County
112	2451	52.6	**Celina** (city) Mercer County
114	2467	52.7	**Lebanon** (city) Warren County
115	2487	52.8	**Fairfield** (city) Butler County
116	2509	52.9	**Finneytown** (CDP) Hamilton County
117	2548	53.1	**Galion** (city) Crawford County
118	2604	53.4	**Medina** (city) Medina County
119	2625	53.5	**Heath** (city) Licking County
120	2741	54.0	**North Royalton** (city) Cuyahoga County
121	2828	54.4	**Shaker Heights** (city) Cuyahoga County
122	2848	54.5	**Miamisburg** (city) Montgomery County
123	2884	54.7	**Franklin** (city) Warren County
123	2884	54.7	**Rocky River** (city) Cuyahoga County
125	2901	54.8	**Dover** (city) Tuscarawas County
125	2901	54.8	**Vandalia** (city) Montgomery County
127	2960	55.1	**Maumee** (city) Lucas County
128	2986	55.2	**Gahanna** (city) Franklin County
129	3007	55.3	**Oregon** (city) Lucas County
129	3007	55.3	**Pataskala** (city) Licking County
129	3007	55.3	**White Oak** (CDP) Hamilton County
132	3019	55.4	**Englewood** (city) Montgomery County
133	3039	55.5	**Huber Heights** (city) Montgomery County
133	3039	55.5	**Vermilion** (city) Lorain County
135	3070	55.7	**North Olmsted** (city) Cuyahoga County
135	3070	55.7	**Stow** (city) Summit County
135	3070	55.7	**Wadsworth** (city) Medina County
138	3162	56.1	**Brunswick** (city) Medina County
139	3193	56.3	**Broadview Heights** (city) Cuyahoga County
140	3214	56.4	**Tallmadge** (city) Summit County
141	3233	56.5	**Grove City** (city) Franklin County
142	3281	56.7	**Amherst** (city) Lorain County
143	3305	56.8	**Centerville** (city) Montgomery County
144	3318	56.9	**Westlake** (city) Cuyahoga County
145	3334	57.0	**Dent** (CDP) Hamilton County
146	3381	57.3	**Sylvania** (city) Lucas County
147	3397	57.4	**Clayton** (city) Montgomery County
148	3491	58.0	**Beachwood** (city) Cuyahoga County
148	3491	58.0	**Monroe** (city) Butler County
148	3491	58.0	**Westerville** (city) Franklin County

***Note:** The state column ranks the top/bottom 150 places from all places in the state with population of 10,000 or more. The national column ranks the top/bottom 150 places from all places in the country with population of 10,000 or more. Places that are unincorporated were not considered in the rankings. Please refer to the User Guide for additional information.*

Marriage Status: Separated

Top 150 Places Ranked in *Descending* Order

State Rank	Nat'l Rank	Percent	Place
1	47	5.3	**Bellefontaine** (city) Logan County
2	185	4.3	**Trenton** (city) Butler County
3	212	4.2	**Washington Court House** (city) Fayette County
4	267	4.0	**Bedford Heights** (city) Cuyahoga County
5	342	3.8	**East Cleveland** (city) Cuyahoga County
5	342	3.8	**East Liverpool** (city) Columbiana County
5	342	3.8	**Forest Park** (city) Hamilton County
8	387	3.7	**Fostoria** (city) Seneca County
8	387	3.7	**Franklin** (city) Warren County
8	387	3.7	**Mansfield** (city) Richland County
8	387	3.7	**Northbrook** (CDP) Hamilton County
8	387	3.7	**Warrensville Heights** (city) Cuyahoga County
13	487	3.5	**Bedford** (city) Cuyahoga County
13	487	3.5	**Cambridge** (city) Guernsey County
13	487	3.5	**Cleveland** (city) Cuyahoga County
13	487	3.5	**Mount Vernon** (city) Knox County
17	554	3.4	**Englewood** (city) Montgomery County
17	554	3.4	**Marion** (city) Marion County
17	554	3.4	**Urbana** (city) Champaign County
20	615	3.3	**Whitehall** (city) Franklin County
20	615	3.3	**Youngstown** (city) Mahoning County
20	615	3.3	**Zanesville** (city) Muskingum County
23	686	3.2	**Hamilton** (city) Butler County
23	686	3.2	**Lima** (city) Allen County
25	747	3.1	**Canton** (city) Stark County
25	747	3.1	**Chillicothe** (city) Ross County
25	747	3.1	**Cincinnati** (city) Hamilton County
25	747	3.1	**Springfield** (city) Clark County
29	815	3.0	**Dayton** (city) Montgomery County
29	815	3.0	**Huber Heights** (city) Montgomery County
29	815	3.0	**Warren** (city) Trumbull County
32	906	2.9	**Lorain** (city) Lorain County
32	906	2.9	**Marysville** (city) Union County
32	906	2.9	**Sandusky** (city) Erie County
32	906	2.9	**Wilmington** (city) Clinton County
36	1005	2.8	**Norwood** (city) Hamilton County
37	1100	2.7	**Lancaster** (city) Fairfield County
37	1100	2.7	**Middletown** (city) Butler County
37	1100	2.7	**Painesville** (city) Lake County
37	1100	2.7	**Struthers** (city) Mahoning County
41	1195	2.6	**Elyria** (city) Lorain County
41	1195	2.6	**Euclid** (city) Cuyahoga County
41	1195	2.6	**Maple Heights** (city) Cuyahoga County
41	1195	2.6	**Marietta** (city) Washington County
41	1195	2.6	**Trotwood** (city) Montgomery County
46	1300	2.5	**Akron** (city) Summit County
46	1300	2.5	**Columbus** (city) Franklin County
46	1300	2.5	**Steubenville** (city) Jefferson County
49	1419	2.4	**Finneytown** (CDP) Hamilton County
49	1419	2.4	**Toledo** (city) Lucas County
49	1419	2.4	**Xenia** (city) Greene County
52	1550	2.3	**Alliance** (city) Stark County
52	1550	2.3	**Fremont** (city) Sandusky County
52	1550	2.3	**Ironton** (city) Lawrence County
52	1550	2.3	**Newark** (city) Licking County
52	1550	2.3	**Niles** (city) Trumbull County
52	1550	2.3	**Portsmouth** (city) Scioto County
58	1676	2.2	**Barberton** (city) Summit County
58	1676	2.2	**Lebanon** (city) Warren County
58	1676	2.2	**Riverside** (city) Montgomery County
58	1676	2.2	**Vandalia** (city) Montgomery County
62	1816	2.1	**Bucyrus** (city) Crawford County
62	1816	2.1	**Circleville** (city) Pickaway County
62	1816	2.1	**Heath** (city) Licking County
62	1816	2.1	**New Philadelphia** (city) Tuscarawas County
62	1816	2.1	**Sidney** (city) Shelby County
67	1961	2.0	**North Ridgeville** (city) Lorain County
67	1961	2.0	**Pataskala** (city) Licking County
69	2118	1.9	**Aurora** (city) Portage County
69	2118	1.9	**Fairfield** (city) Butler County
69	2118	1.9	**Galion** (city) Crawford County
69	2118	1.9	**Grove City** (city) Franklin County
69	2118	1.9	**Pickerington** (city) Fairfield County
69	2118	1.9	**Piqua** (city) Miami County
69	2118	1.9	**Reynoldsburg** (city) Franklin County
69	2118	1.9	**Salem** (city) Columbiana County
69	2118	1.9	**Van Wert** (city) Van Wert County
69	2118	1.9	**West Carrollton** (city) Montgomery County
79	2275	1.8	**Boardman** (CDP) Mahoning County
79	2275	1.8	**Dover** (city) Tuscarawas County
79	2275	1.8	**Fairborn** (city) Greene County
79	2275	1.8	**Findlay** (city) Hancock County
79	2275	1.8	**Gahanna** (city) Franklin County
79	2275	1.8	**Massillon** (city) Stark County
85	2422	1.7	**Ashtabula** (city) Ashtabula County
85	2422	1.7	**Cleveland Heights** (city) Cuyahoga County
85	2422	1.7	**Coshocton** (city) Coshocton County
85	2422	1.7	**Oregon** (city) Lucas County
85	2422	1.7	**Reading** (city) Hamilton County
85	2422	1.7	**White Oak** (CDP) Hamilton County
91	2603	1.6	**Celina** (city) Mercer County
91	2603	1.6	**Garfield Heights** (city) Cuyahoga County
91	2603	1.6	**Greenville** (city) Darke County
91	2603	1.6	**Lakewood** (city) Cuyahoga County
91	2603	1.6	**Ravenna** (city) Portage County
91	2603	1.6	**South Euclid** (city) Cuyahoga County
91	2603	1.6	**Willowick** (city) Lake County
98	2791	1.5	**Conneaut** (city) Ashtabula County
98	2791	1.5	**Defiance** (city) Defiance County
98	2791	1.5	**Delaware** (city) Delaware County
98	2791	1.5	**Dent** (CDP) Hamilton County
98	2791	1.5	**Kettering** (city) Montgomery County
98	2791	1.5	**Perrysburg** (city) Wood County
98	2791	1.5	**Springdale** (city) Hamilton County
105	2983	1.4	**Bowling Green** (city) Wood County
105	2983	1.4	**Maumee** (city) Lucas County
105	2983	1.4	**Norwalk** (city) Huron County
105	2983	1.4	**Sharonville** (city) Hamilton County
105	2983	1.4	**Troy** (city) Miami County
110	3167	1.3	**Beavercreek** (city) Greene County
110	3167	1.3	**Brooklyn** (city) Cuyahoga County
110	3167	1.3	**Cuyahoga Falls** (city) Summit County
110	3167	1.3	**Mason** (city) Warren County
110	3167	1.3	**Medina** (city) Medina County
110	3167	1.3	**Miamisburg** (city) Montgomery County
110	3167	1.3	**Norton** (city) Summit County
110	3167	1.3	**Stow** (city) Summit County
118	3376	1.2	**Ashland** (city) Ashland County
118	3376	1.2	**Berea** (city) Cuyahoga County
118	3376	1.2	**Broadview Heights** (city) Cuyahoga County
118	3376	1.2	**Brook Park** (city) Cuyahoga County
118	3376	1.2	**Clayton** (city) Montgomery County
118	3376	1.2	**North Canton** (city) Stark County
118	3376	1.2	**Parma** (city) Cuyahoga County
118	3376	1.2	**Tiffin** (city) Seneca County
118	3376	1.2	**Vermilion** (city) Lorain County
118	3376	1.2	**Wickliffe** (city) Lake County
118	3376	1.2	**Worthington** (city) Franklin County
129	3561	1.1	**Austintown** (CDP) Mahoning County
129	3561	1.1	**Centerville** (city) Montgomery County
129	3561	1.1	**Forestville** (CDP) Hamilton County
129	3561	1.1	**Kent** (city) Portage County
129	3561	1.1	**Macedonia** (city) Summit County
129	3561	1.1	**Monfort Heights** (CDP) Hamilton County
129	3561	1.1	**Monroe** (city) Butler County
129	3561	1.1	**Shaker Heights** (city) Cuyahoga County
129	3561	1.1	**Wooster** (city) Wayne County
138	3734	1.0	**Blue Ash** (city) Hamilton County
138	3734	1.0	**North Olmsted** (city) Cuyahoga County
138	3734	1.0	**Richmond Heights** (city) Cuyahoga County
138	3734	1.0	**Streetsboro** (city) Portage County
138	3734	1.0	**Upper Arlington** (city) Franklin County
143	3894	0.9	**Bexley** (city) Franklin County
143	3894	0.9	**Mayfield Heights** (city) Cuyahoga County
143	3894	0.9	**Oxford** (city) Butler County
143	3894	0.9	**Sylvania** (city) Lucas County
147	4037	0.8	**Beachwood** (city) Cuyahoga County
147	4037	0.8	**Brunswick** (city) Medina County
147	4037	0.8	**Hilliard** (city) Franklin County
147	4037	0.8	**Middleburg Heights** (city) Cuyahoga County

Note: *The state column ranks the top/bottom 150 places from all places in the state with population of 10,000 or more. The national column ranks the top/bottom 150 places from all places in the country with population of 10,000 or more. Places that are unincorporated were not considered in the rankings. Please refer to the User Guide for additional information.*

Marriage Status: Separated

Top 150 Places Ranked in *Ascending* Order

State Rank	Nat'l Rank	Percent	Place
1	6	0.1	**Mack** (CDP) Hamilton County
2	80	0.4	**Bay Village** (city) Cuyahoga County
3	133	0.5	**Avon Lake** (city) Lorain County
3	133	0.5	**Dublin** (city) Franklin County
3	133	0.5	**Green** (city) Summit County
3	133	0.5	**Hudson** (city) Summit County
7	212	0.6	**Amherst** (city) Lorain County
7	212	0.6	**Athens** (city) Athens County
7	212	0.6	**Bridgetown** (CDP) Hamilton County
7	212	0.6	**Fairview Park** (city) Cuyahoga County
7	212	0.6	**Loveland** (city) Hamilton County
7	212	0.6	**Powell** (city) Delaware County
7	212	0.6	**Seven Hills** (city) Cuyahoga County
7	212	0.6	**Twinsburg** (city) Summit County
7	212	0.6	**Wadsworth** (city) Medina County
7	212	0.6	**Westerville** (city) Franklin County
7	212	0.6	**Westlake** (city) Cuyahoga County
18	344	0.7	**Avon** (city) Lorain County
18	344	0.7	**Brecksville** (city) Cuyahoga County
18	344	0.7	**Eastlake** (city) Lake County
18	344	0.7	**Lyndhurst** (city) Cuyahoga County
18	344	0.7	**Mentor** (city) Lake County
18	344	0.7	**Montgomery** (city) Hamilton County
18	344	0.7	**Solon** (city) Cuyahoga County
25	467	0.8	**Beachwood** (city) Cuyahoga County
25	467	0.8	**Brunswick** (city) Medina County
25	467	0.8	**Hilliard** (city) Franklin County
25	467	0.8	**Middleburg Heights** (city) Cuyahoga County
25	467	0.8	**New Franklin** (city) Summit County
25	467	0.8	**North Royalton** (city) Cuyahoga County
25	467	0.8	**Parma Heights** (city) Cuyahoga County
25	467	0.8	**Rocky River** (city) Cuyahoga County
25	467	0.8	**Springboro** (city) Warren County
25	467	0.8	**Strongsville** (city) Cuyahoga County
25	467	0.8	**Tallmadge** (city) Summit County
25	467	0.8	**University Heights** (city) Cuyahoga County
25	467	0.8	**Willoughby** (city) Lake County
38	620	0.9	**Bexley** (city) Franklin County
38	620	0.9	**Mayfield Heights** (city) Cuyahoga County
38	620	0.9	**Oxford** (city) Butler County
38	620	0.9	**Sylvania** (city) Lucas County
42	763	1.0	**Blue Ash** (city) Hamilton County
42	763	1.0	**North Olmsted** (city) Cuyahoga County
42	763	1.0	**Richmond Heights** (city) Cuyahoga County
42	763	1.0	**Streetsboro** (city) Portage County
42	763	1.0	**Upper Arlington** (city) Franklin County
47	923	1.1	**Austintown** (CDP) Mahoning County
47	923	1.1	**Centerville** (city) Montgomery County
47	923	1.1	**Forestville** (CDP) Hamilton County
47	923	1.1	**Kent** (city) Portage County
47	923	1.1	**Macedonia** (city) Summit County
47	923	1.1	**Monfort Heights** (CDP) Hamilton County
47	923	1.1	**Monroe** (city) Butler County
47	923	1.1	**Shaker Heights** (city) Cuyahoga County
47	923	1.1	**Wooster** (city) Wayne County
56	1096	1.2	**Ashland** (city) Ashland County
56	1096	1.2	**Berea** (city) Cuyahoga County
56	1096	1.2	**Broadview Heights** (city) Cuyahoga County
56	1096	1.2	**Brook Park** (city) Cuyahoga County
56	1096	1.2	**Clayton** (city) Montgomery County
56	1096	1.2	**North Canton** (city) Stark County
56	1096	1.2	**Parma** (city) Cuyahoga County
56	1096	1.2	**Tiffin** (city) Seneca County
56	1096	1.2	**Vermilion** (city) Lorain County
56	1096	1.2	**Wickliffe** (city) Lake County
56	1096	1.2	**Worthington** (city) Franklin County
67	1281	1.3	**Beavercreek** (city) Greene County
67	1281	1.3	**Brooklyn** (city) Cuyahoga County
67	1281	1.3	**Cuyahoga Falls** (city) Summit County
67	1281	1.3	**Mason** (city) Warren County
67	1281	1.3	**Medina** (city) Medina County
67	1281	1.3	**Miamisburg** (city) Montgomery County
67	1281	1.3	**Norton** (city) Summit County
67	1281	1.3	**Stow** (city) Summit County
75	1490	1.4	**Bowling Green** (city) Wood County
75	1490	1.4	**Maumee** (city) Lucas County
75	1490	1.4	**Norwalk** (city) Huron County
75	1490	1.4	**Sharonville** (city) Hamilton County
75	1490	1.4	**Troy** (city) Miami County
80	1674	1.5	**Conneaut** (city) Ashtabula County
80	1674	1.5	**Defiance** (city) Defiance County
80	1674	1.5	**Delaware** (city) Delaware County
80	1674	1.5	**Dent** (CDP) Hamilton County
80	1674	1.5	**Kettering** (city) Montgomery County
80	1674	1.5	**Perrysburg** (city) Wood County
80	1674	1.5	**Springdale** (city) Hamilton County
87	1866	1.6	**Celina** (city) Mercer County
87	1866	1.6	**Garfield Heights** (city) Cuyahoga County
87	1866	1.6	**Greenville** (city) Darke County
87	1866	1.6	**Lakewood** (city) Cuyahoga County
87	1866	1.6	**Ravenna** (city) Portage County
87	1866	1.6	**South Euclid** (city) Cuyahoga County
87	1866	1.6	**Willowick** (city) Lake County
94	2054	1.7	**Ashtabula** (city) Ashtabula County
94	2054	1.7	**Cleveland Heights** (city) Cuyahoga County
94	2054	1.7	**Coshocton** (city) Coshocton County
94	2054	1.7	**Oregon** (city) Lucas County
94	2054	1.7	**Reading** (city) Hamilton County
94	2054	1.7	**White Oak** (CDP) Hamilton County
100	2235	1.8	**Boardman** (CDP) Mahoning County
100	2235	1.8	**Dover** (city) Tuscarawas County
100	2235	1.8	**Fairborn** (city) Greene County
100	2235	1.8	**Findlay** (city) Hancock County
100	2235	1.8	**Gahanna** (city) Franklin County
100	2235	1.8	**Massillon** (city) Stark County
106	2382	1.9	**Aurora** (city) Portage County
106	2382	1.9	**Fairfield** (city) Butler County
106	2382	1.9	**Galion** (city) Crawford County
106	2382	1.9	**Grove City** (city) Franklin County
106	2382	1.9	**Pickerington** (city) Fairfield County
106	2382	1.9	**Piqua** (city) Miami County
106	2382	1.9	**Reynoldsburg** (city) Franklin County
106	2382	1.9	**Salem** (city) Columbiana County
106	2382	1.9	**Van Wert** (city) Van Wert County
106	2382	1.9	**West Carrollton** (city) Montgomery County
116	2539	2.0	**North Ridgeville** (city) Lorain County
116	2539	2.0	**Pataskala** (city) Licking County
118	2696	2.1	**Bucyrus** (city) Crawford County
118	2696	2.1	**Circleville** (city) Pickaway County
118	2696	2.1	**Heath** (city) Licking County
118	2696	2.1	**New Philadelphia** (city) Tuscarawas County
118	2696	2.1	**Sidney** (city) Shelby County
123	2841	2.2	**Barberton** (city) Summit County
123	2841	2.2	**Lebanon** (city) Warren County
123	2841	2.2	**Riverside** (city) Montgomery County
123	2841	2.2	**Vandalia** (city) Montgomery County
127	2981	2.3	**Alliance** (city) Stark County
127	2981	2.3	**Fremont** (city) Sandusky County
127	2981	2.3	**Ironton** (city) Lawrence County
127	2981	2.3	**Newark** (city) Licking County
127	2981	2.3	**Niles** (city) Trumbull County
127	2981	2.3	**Portsmouth** (city) Scioto County
133	3107	2.4	**Finneytown** (CDP) Hamilton County
133	3107	2.4	**Toledo** (city) Lucas County
133	3107	2.4	**Xenia** (city) Greene County
136	3238	2.5	**Akron** (city) Summit County
136	3238	2.5	**Columbus** (city) Franklin County
136	3238	2.5	**Steubenville** (city) Jefferson County
139	3357	2.6	**Elyria** (city) Lorain County
139	3357	2.6	**Euclid** (city) Cuyahoga County
139	3357	2.6	**Maple Heights** (city) Cuyahoga County
139	3357	2.6	**Marietta** (city) Washington County
139	3357	2.6	**Trotwood** (city) Montgomery County
144	3462	2.7	**Lancaster** (city) Fairfield County
144	3462	2.7	**Middletown** (city) Butler County
144	3462	2.7	**Painesville** (city) Lake County
144	3462	2.7	**Struthers** (city) Mahoning County
148	3557	2.8	**Norwood** (city) Hamilton County
149	3652	2.9	**Lorain** (city) Lorain County
149	3652	2.9	**Marysville** (city) Union County

Note: *The state column ranks the top/bottom 150 places from all places in the state with population of 10,000 or more. The national column ranks the top/bottom 150 places from all places in the country with population of 10,000 or more. Places that are unincorporated were not considered in the rankings. Please refer to the User Guide for additional information.*

Marriage Status: Widowed

Top 150 Places Ranked in *Descending* Order

State Rank	Nat'l Rank	Percent	Place
1	15	15.2	**Beachwood** (city) Cuyahoga County
2	59	11.5	**Mayfield Heights** (city) Cuyahoga County
3	64	11.4	**Greenville** (city) Darke County
4	75	11.0	**Wickliffe** (city) Lake County
5	90	10.8	**Bridgetown** (CDP) Hamilton County
6	99	10.7	**Coshocton** (city) Coshocton County
7	122	10.5	**Fostoria** (city) Seneca County
7	122	10.5	**Miamisburg** (city) Montgomery County
7	122	10.5	**Struthers** (city) Mahoning County
10	132	10.4	**East Cleveland** (city) Cuyahoga County
10	132	10.4	**Ironton** (city) Lawrence County
12	144	10.3	**Willowick** (city) Lake County
13	160	10.2	**Barberton** (city) Summit County
13	160	10.2	**Cambridge** (city) Guernsey County
13	160	10.2	**Forestville** (CDP) Hamilton County
16	179	10.1	**Austintown** (CDP) Mahoning County
16	179	10.1	**Niles** (city) Trumbull County
18	197	10.0	**Springdale** (city) Hamilton County
19	217	9.9	**Galion** (city) Crawford County
20	234	9.8	**Centerville** (city) Montgomery County
21	250	9.7	**Parma Heights** (city) Cuyahoga County
21	250	9.7	**Rocky River** (city) Cuyahoga County
23	282	9.6	**Celina** (city) Mercer County
24	304	9.5	**Circleville** (city) Pickaway County
24	304	9.5	**Marietta** (city) Washington County
26	323	9.4	**Garfield Heights** (city) Cuyahoga County
27	348	9.3	**Middleburg Heights** (city) Cuyahoga County
27	348	9.3	**Wilmington** (city) Clinton County
29	373	9.2	**Trotwood** (city) Montgomery County
29	373	9.2	**Warren** (city) Trumbull County
29	373	9.2	**Youngstown** (city) Mahoning County
32	403	9.1	**Brook Park** (city) Cuyahoga County
32	403	9.1	**Dover** (city) Tuscarawas County
32	403	9.1	**Mount Vernon** (city) Knox County
32	403	9.1	**North Canton** (city) Stark County
32	403	9.1	**Portsmouth** (city) Scioto County
37	433	9.0	**Bedford** (city) Cuyahoga County
37	433	9.0	**Chillicothe** (city) Ross County
39	452	8.9	**Boardman** (CDP) Mahoning County
39	452	8.9	**Loveland** (city) Hamilton County
39	452	8.9	**Monroe** (city) Butler County
39	452	8.9	**Zanesville** (city) Muskingum County
43	514	8.7	**Wadsworth** (city) Medina County
43	514	8.7	**Willoughby** (city) Lake County
43	514	8.7	**Xenia** (city) Greene County
46	560	8.6	**Bucyrus** (city) Crawford County
46	560	8.6	**Piqua** (city) Miami County
48	602	8.5	**East Liverpool** (city) Columbiana County
48	602	8.5	**Mansfield** (city) Richland County
48	602	8.5	**Richmond Heights** (city) Cuyahoga County
51	648	8.4	**Van Wert** (city) Van Wert County
52	696	8.3	**Bellefontaine** (city) Logan County
52	696	8.3	**Lyndhurst** (city) Cuyahoga County
52	696	8.3	**Sharonville** (city) Hamilton County
52	696	8.3	**West Carrollton** (city) Montgomery County
56	743	8.2	**Parma** (city) Cuyahoga County
56	743	8.2	**Seven Hills** (city) Cuyahoga County
56	743	8.2	**Springfield** (city) Clark County
56	743	8.2	**Steubenville** (city) Jefferson County
56	743	8.2	**Westlake** (city) Cuyahoga County
61	786	8.1	**Brooklyn** (city) Cuyahoga County
61	786	8.1	**Heath** (city) Licking County
63	833	8.0	**Euclid** (city) Cuyahoga County
63	833	8.0	**Vermilion** (city) Lorain County
63	833	8.0	**Warrensville Heights** (city) Cuyahoga County
66	881	7.9	**Ashtabula** (city) Ashtabula County
66	881	7.9	**Aurora** (city) Portage County
66	881	7.9	**Montgomery** (city) Hamilton County
66	881	7.9	**Reading** (city) Hamilton County
66	881	7.9	**Twinsburg** (city) Summit County
66	881	7.9	**Washington Court House** (city) Fayette County
72	942	7.8	**Bedford Heights** (city) Cuyahoga County
72	942	7.8	**Englewood** (city) Montgomery County
72	942	7.8	**Lancaster** (city) Fairfield County
72	942	7.8	**Lorain** (city) Lorain County
76	986	7.7	**Alliance** (city) Stark County
76	986	7.7	**Findlay** (city) Hancock County
76	986	7.7	**Newark** (city) Licking County
76	986	7.7	**Oregon** (city) Lucas County
76	986	7.7	**Riverside** (city) Montgomery County
81	1110	7.5	**Ashland** (city) Ashland County
81	1110	7.5	**Green** (city) Summit County
81	1110	7.5	**Maple Heights** (city) Cuyahoga County
81	1110	7.5	**Sandusky** (city) Erie County
81	1110	7.5	**Tallmadge** (city) Summit County
86	1177	7.4	**Cleveland** (city) Cuyahoga County
86	1177	7.4	**Eastlake** (city) Lake County
86	1177	7.4	**Massillon** (city) Stark County
86	1177	7.4	**Salem** (city) Columbiana County
90	1250	7.3	**Kettering** (city) Montgomery County
91	1323	7.2	**Defiance** (city) Defiance County
91	1323	7.2	**Finneytown** (CDP) Hamilton County
91	1323	7.2	**Macedonia** (city) Summit County
91	1323	7.2	**North Olmsted** (city) Cuyahoga County
91	1323	7.2	**Perrysburg** (city) Wood County
96	1398	7.1	**Conneaut** (city) Ashtabula County
96	1398	7.1	**Marion** (city) Marion County
96	1398	7.1	**Middletown** (city) Butler County
96	1398	7.1	**Norton** (city) Summit County
96	1398	7.1	**South Euclid** (city) Cuyahoga County
96	1398	7.1	**Strongsville** (city) Cuyahoga County
102	1478	7.0	**Amherst** (city) Lorain County
102	1478	7.0	**Fremont** (city) Sandusky County
102	1478	7.0	**Hamilton** (city) Butler County
102	1478	7.0	**Monfort Heights** (CDP) Hamilton County
102	1478	7.0	**Sidney** (city) Shelby County
102	1478	7.0	**Urbana** (city) Champaign County
108	1553	6.9	**Avon Lake** (city) Lorain County
108	1553	6.9	**Canton** (city) Stark County
110	1628	6.8	**Mentor** (city) Lake County
110	1628	6.8	**North Royalton** (city) Cuyahoga County
110	1628	6.8	**Norwalk** (city) Huron County
113	1706	6.7	**Cuyahoga Falls** (city) Summit County
113	1706	6.7	**Stow** (city) Summit County
115	1779	6.6	**Akron** (city) Summit County
115	1779	6.6	**Broadview Heights** (city) Cuyahoga County
117	1858	6.5	**Berea** (city) Cuyahoga County
117	1858	6.5	**Dayton** (city) Montgomery County
117	1858	6.5	**Fairview Park** (city) Cuyahoga County
117	1858	6.5	**Toledo** (city) Lucas County
117	1858	6.5	**Troy** (city) Miami County
117	1858	6.5	**Vandalia** (city) Montgomery County
123	1936	6.4	**Maumee** (city) Lucas County
123	1936	6.4	**Shaker Heights** (city) Cuyahoga County
123	1936	6.4	**Tiffin** (city) Seneca County
126	2038	6.3	**Lima** (city) Allen County
126	2038	6.3	**Worthington** (city) Franklin County
128	2119	6.2	**Avon** (city) Lorain County
128	2119	6.2	**Beavercreek** (city) Greene County
128	2119	6.2	**Dent** (CDP) Hamilton County
128	2119	6.2	**Elyria** (city) Lorain County
128	2119	6.2	**Ravenna** (city) Portage County
128	2119	6.2	**White Oak** (CDP) Hamilton County
128	2119	6.2	**Whitehall** (city) Franklin County
135	2198	6.1	**Medina** (city) Medina County
135	2198	6.1	**New Philadelphia** (city) Tuscarawas County
135	2198	6.1	**Northbrook** (CDP) Hamilton County
135	2198	6.1	**Sylvania** (city) Lucas County
139	2296	6.0	**Bay Village** (city) Cuyahoga County
139	2296	6.0	**Blue Ash** (city) Hamilton County
139	2296	6.0	**Norwood** (city) Hamilton County
139	2296	6.0	**Wooster** (city) Wayne County
143	2383	5.9	**Cincinnati** (city) Hamilton County
143	2383	5.9	**Pataskala** (city) Licking County
143	2383	5.9	**Streetsboro** (city) Portage County
143	2383	5.9	**Westerville** (city) Franklin County
147	2479	5.8	**Fairfield** (city) Butler County
147	2479	5.8	**Trenton** (city) Butler County
149	2574	5.7	**Cleveland Heights** (city) Cuyahoga County
149	2574	5.7	**Fairborn** (city) Greene County

Note: *The state column ranks the top/bottom 150 places from all places in the state with population of 10,000 or more. The national column ranks the top/bottom 150 places from all places in the country with population of 10,000 or more. Places that are unincorporated were not considered in the rankings. Please refer to the User Guide for additional information.*

Marriage Status: Widowed

Top 150 Places Ranked in *Ascending* Order

State Rank	Nat'l Rank	Percent	Place
1	28	1.6	**Athens** (city) Athens County
2	57	2.0	**Oxford** (city) Butler County
3	117	2.5	**Powell** (city) Delaware County
4	187	2.8	**Bowling Green** (city) Wood County
4	187	2.8	**Springboro** (city) Warren County
6	220	2.9	**Kent** (city) Portage County
7	281	3.1	**Bexley** (city) Franklin County
8	307	3.2	**Pickerington** (city) Fairfield County
9	382	3.4	**Dublin** (city) Franklin County
10	768	4.2	**University Heights** (city) Cuyahoga County
11	840	4.3	**Marysville** (city) Union County
12	965	4.5	**Mason** (city) Warren County
12	965	4.5	**Painesville** (city) Lake County
14	1132	4.7	**Columbus** (city) Franklin County
15	1218	4.8	**Delaware** (city) Delaware County
16	1295	4.9	**Forest Park** (city) Hamilton County
16	1295	4.9	**Gahanna** (city) Franklin County
16	1295	4.9	**Hudson** (city) Summit County
19	1384	5.0	**Huber Heights** (city) Montgomery County
19	1384	5.0	**Mack** (CDP) Hamilton County
21	1457	5.1	**Solon** (city) Cuyahoga County
22	1606	5.3	**Franklin** (city) Warren County
22	1606	5.3	**Hilliard** (city) Franklin County
22	1606	5.3	**Reynoldsburg** (city) Franklin County
22	1606	5.3	**Upper Arlington** (city) Franklin County
26	1704	5.4	**Brecksville** (city) Cuyahoga County
26	1704	5.4	**Clayton** (city) Montgomery County
26	1704	5.4	**Lakewood** (city) Cuyahoga County
26	1704	5.4	**New Franklin** (city) Summit County
30	1794	5.5	**North Ridgeville** (city) Lorain County
31	1891	5.6	**Brunswick** (city) Medina County
31	1891	5.6	**Grove City** (city) Franklin County
31	1891	5.6	**Lebanon** (city) Warren County
34	1974	5.7	**Cleveland Heights** (city) Cuyahoga County
34	1974	5.7	**Fairborn** (city) Greene County
36	2083	5.8	**Fairfield** (city) Butler County
36	2083	5.8	**Trenton** (city) Butler County
38	2178	5.9	**Cincinnati** (city) Hamilton County
38	2178	5.9	**Pataskala** (city) Licking County
38	2178	5.9	**Streetsboro** (city) Portage County
38	2178	5.9	**Westerville** (city) Franklin County
42	2274	6.0	**Bay Village** (city) Cuyahoga County
42	2274	6.0	**Blue Ash** (city) Hamilton County
42	2274	6.0	**Norwood** (city) Hamilton County
42	2274	6.0	**Wooster** (city) Wayne County
46	2361	6.1	**Medina** (city) Medina County
46	2361	6.1	**New Philadelphia** (city) Tuscarawas County
46	2361	6.1	**Northbrook** (CDP) Hamilton County
46	2361	6.1	**Sylvania** (city) Lucas County
50	2459	6.2	**Avon** (city) Lorain County
50	2459	6.2	**Beavercreek** (city) Greene County
50	2459	6.2	**Dent** (CDP) Hamilton County
50	2459	6.2	**Elyria** (city) Lorain County
50	2459	6.2	**Ravenna** (city) Portage County
50	2459	6.2	**White Oak** (CDP) Hamilton County
50	2459	6.2	**Whitehall** (city) Franklin County
57	2538	6.3	**Lima** (city) Allen County
57	2538	6.3	**Worthington** (city) Franklin County
59	2619	6.4	**Maumee** (city) Lucas County
59	2619	6.4	**Shaker Heights** (city) Cuyahoga County
59	2619	6.4	**Tiffin** (city) Seneca County
62	2721	6.5	**Berea** (city) Cuyahoga County
62	2721	6.5	**Dayton** (city) Montgomery County
62	2721	6.5	**Fairview Park** (city) Cuyahoga County
62	2721	6.5	**Toledo** (city) Lucas County
62	2721	6.5	**Troy** (city) Miami County
62	2721	6.5	**Vandalia** (city) Montgomery County
68	2799	6.6	**Akron** (city) Summit County
68	2799	6.6	**Broadview Heights** (city) Cuyahoga County
70	2878	6.7	**Cuyahoga Falls** (city) Summit County
70	2878	6.7	**Stow** (city) Summit County
72	2951	6.8	**Mentor** (city) Lake County
72	2951	6.8	**North Royalton** (city) Cuyahoga County
72	2951	6.8	**Norwalk** (city) Huron County
75	3029	6.9	**Avon Lake** (city) Lorain County
75	3029	6.9	**Canton** (city) Stark County
77	3104	7.0	**Amherst** (city) Lorain County
77	3104	7.0	**Fremont** (city) Sandusky County
77	3104	7.0	**Hamilton** (city) Butler County
77	3104	7.0	**Monfort Heights** (CDP) Hamilton County
77	3104	7.0	**Sidney** (city) Shelby County
77	3104	7.0	**Urbana** (city) Champaign County
83	3179	7.1	**Conneaut** (city) Ashtabula County
83	3179	7.1	**Marion** (city) Marion County
83	3179	7.1	**Middletown** (city) Butler County
83	3179	7.1	**Norton** (city) Summit County
83	3179	7.1	**South Euclid** (city) Cuyahoga County
83	3179	7.1	**Strongsville** (city) Cuyahoga County
89	3259	7.2	**Defiance** (city) Defiance County
89	3259	7.2	**Finneytown** (CDP) Hamilton County
89	3259	7.2	**Macedonia** (city) Summit County
89	3259	7.2	**North Olmsted** (city) Cuyahoga County
89	3259	7.2	**Perrysburg** (city) Wood County
94	3334	7.3	**Kettering** (city) Montgomery County
95	3407	7.4	**Cleveland** (city) Cuyahoga County
95	3407	7.4	**Eastlake** (city) Lake County
95	3407	7.4	**Massillon** (city) Stark County
95	3407	7.4	**Salem** (city) Columbiana County
99	3480	7.5	**Ashland** (city) Ashland County
99	3480	7.5	**Green** (city) Summit County
99	3480	7.5	**Maple Heights** (city) Cuyahoga County
99	3480	7.5	**Sandusky** (city) Erie County
99	3480	7.5	**Tallmadge** (city) Summit County
104	3609	7.7	**Alliance** (city) Stark County
104	3609	7.7	**Findlay** (city) Hancock County
104	3609	7.7	**Newark** (city) Licking County
104	3609	7.7	**Oregon** (city) Lucas County
104	3609	7.7	**Riverside** (city) Montgomery County
109	3671	7.8	**Bedford Heights** (city) Cuyahoga County
109	3671	7.8	**Englewood** (city) Montgomery County
109	3671	7.8	**Lancaster** (city) Fairfield County
109	3671	7.8	**Lorain** (city) Lorain County
113	3715	7.9	**Ashtabula** (city) Ashtabula County
113	3715	7.9	**Aurora** (city) Portage County
113	3715	7.9	**Montgomery** (city) Hamilton County
113	3715	7.9	**Reading** (city) Hamilton County
113	3715	7.9	**Twinsburg** (city) Summit County
113	3715	7.9	**Washington Court House** (city) Fayette County
119	3776	8.0	**Euclid** (city) Cuyahoga County
119	3776	8.0	**Vermilion** (city) Lorain County
119	3776	8.0	**Warrensville Heights** (city) Cuyahoga County
122	3824	8.1	**Brooklyn** (city) Cuyahoga County
122	3824	8.1	**Heath** (city) Licking County
124	3871	8.2	**Parma** (city) Cuyahoga County
124	3871	8.2	**Seven Hills** (city) Cuyahoga County
124	3871	8.2	**Springfield** (city) Clark County
124	3871	8.2	**Steubenville** (city) Jefferson County
124	3871	8.2	**Westlake** (city) Cuyahoga County
129	3914	8.3	**Bellefontaine** (city) Logan County
129	3914	8.3	**Lyndhurst** (city) Cuyahoga County
129	3914	8.3	**Sharonville** (city) Hamilton County
129	3914	8.3	**West Carrollton** (city) Montgomery County
133	3961	8.4	**Van Wert** (city) Van Wert County
134	4009	8.5	**East Liverpool** (city) Columbiana County
134	4009	8.5	**Mansfield** (city) Richland County
134	4009	8.5	**Richmond Heights** (city) Cuyahoga County
137	4055	8.6	**Bucyrus** (city) Crawford County
137	4055	8.6	**Piqua** (city) Miami County
139	4097	8.7	**Wadsworth** (city) Medina County
139	4097	8.7	**Willoughby** (city) Lake County
139	4097	8.7	**Xenia** (city) Greene County
142	4177	8.9	**Boardman** (CDP) Mahoning County
142	4177	8.9	**Loveland** (city) Hamilton County
142	4177	8.9	**Monroe** (city) Butler County
142	4177	8.9	**Zanesville** (city) Muskingum County
146	4205	9.0	**Bedford** (city) Cuyahoga County
146	4205	9.0	**Chillicothe** (city) Ross County
148	4224	9.1	**Brook Park** (city) Cuyahoga County
148	4224	9.1	**Dover** (city) Tuscarawas County
148	4224	9.1	**Mount Vernon** (city) Knox County

***Note:** The state column ranks the top/bottom 150 places from all places in the state with population of 10,000 or more. The national column ranks the top/bottom 150 places from all places in the country with population of 10,000 or more. Places that are unincorporated were not considered in the rankings. Please refer to the User Guide for additional information.*

Marriage Status: Divorced

Top 150 Places Ranked in *Descending* Order

State Rank	Nat'l Rank	Percent	Place
1	23	19.3	**Whitehall** (city) Franklin County
2	41	18.4	**Bedford Heights** (city) Cuyahoga County
3	43	18.3	**Washington Court House** (city) Fayette County
4	53	18.0	**Salem** (city) Columbiana County
5	68	17.7	**Zanesville** (city) Muskingum County
6	85	17.4	**Lancaster** (city) Fairfield County
7	89	17.3	**East Cleveland** (city) Cuyahoga County
8	98	17.2	**Franklin** (city) Warren County
8	98	17.2	**Lima** (city) Allen County
10	106	17.1	**Ashtabula** (city) Ashtabula County
11	115	17.0	**Ironton** (city) Lawrence County
12	127	16.9	**Ravenna** (city) Portage County
13	137	16.8	**Cambridge** (city) Guernsey County
14	149	16.7	**Marion** (city) Marion County
14	149	16.7	**Urbana** (city) Champaign County
16	159	16.6	**Portsmouth** (city) Scioto County
16	159	16.6	**West Carrollton** (city) Montgomery County
18	172	16.5	**Marysville** (city) Union County
19	184	16.4	**Warrensville Heights** (city) Cuyahoga County
20	194	16.3	**Niles** (city) Trumbull County
21	204	16.2	**Fostoria** (city) Seneca County
21	204	16.2	**Springfield** (city) Clark County
23	222	16.1	**Middletown** (city) Butler County
24	241	16.0	**Bellefontaine** (city) Logan County
24	241	16.0	**Canton** (city) Stark County
24	241	16.0	**Mansfield** (city) Richland County
24	241	16.0	**Northbrook** (CDP) Hamilton County
28	270	15.8	**Hamilton** (city) Butler County
28	270	15.8	**Sidney** (city) Shelby County
28	270	15.8	**Struthers** (city) Mahoning County
31	285	15.7	**Dayton** (city) Montgomery County
31	285	15.7	**Norwalk** (city) Huron County
31	285	15.7	**Trotwood** (city) Montgomery County
34	321	15.5	**Dover** (city) Tuscarawas County
35	339	15.4	**Newark** (city) Licking County
35	339	15.4	**Warren** (city) Trumbull County
35	339	15.4	**Youngstown** (city) Mahoning County
38	366	15.3	**Massillon** (city) Stark County
39	386	15.2	**Greenville** (city) Darke County
39	386	15.2	**Troy** (city) Miami County
41	413	15.1	**Barberton** (city) Summit County
41	413	15.1	**Bucyrus** (city) Crawford County
41	413	15.1	**Van Wert** (city) Van Wert County
44	437	15.0	**Alliance** (city) Stark County
44	437	15.0	**Chillicothe** (city) Ross County
46	464	14.9	**Circleville** (city) Pickaway County
46	464	14.9	**Cleveland** (city) Cuyahoga County
46	464	14.9	**Piqua** (city) Miami County
49	494	14.8	**Conneaut** (city) Ashtabula County
49	494	14.8	**Toledo** (city) Lucas County
51	543	14.6	**Kettering** (city) Montgomery County
51	543	14.6	**Marietta** (city) Washington County
53	573	14.5	**Wilmington** (city) Clinton County
54	613	14.4	**Brooklyn** (city) Cuyahoga County
54	613	14.4	**East Liverpool** (city) Columbiana County
54	613	14.4	**Sandusky** (city) Erie County
57	637	14.3	**Akron** (city) Summit County
57	637	14.3	**Middleburg Heights** (city) Cuyahoga County
57	637	14.3	**Reynoldsburg** (city) Franklin County
57	637	14.3	**Wadsworth** (city) Medina County
61	667	14.2	**Loveland** (city) Hamilton County
61	667	14.2	**Riverside** (city) Montgomery County
63	698	14.1	**Fremont** (city) Sandusky County
63	698	14.1	**Sharonville** (city) Hamilton County
65	738	14.0	**Celina** (city) Mercer County
66	766	13.9	**Cuyahoga Falls** (city) Summit County
66	766	13.9	**Euclid** (city) Cuyahoga County
66	766	13.9	**Xenia** (city) Greene County
69	809	13.8	**Willoughby** (city) Lake County
70	850	13.7	**Fairborn** (city) Greene County
70	850	13.7	**Heath** (city) Licking County
70	850	13.7	**Maple Heights** (city) Cuyahoga County
73	889	13.6	**Bedford** (city) Cuyahoga County
73	889	13.6	**Miamisburg** (city) Montgomery County
73	889	13.6	**New Philadelphia** (city) Tuscarawas County

State Rank	Nat'l Rank	Percent	Place
73	889	13.6	**North Canton** (city) Stark County
77	920	13.5	**Mount Vernon** (city) Knox County
78	969	13.4	**Fairfield** (city) Butler County
78	969	13.4	**Lorain** (city) Lorain County
78	969	13.4	**Painesville** (city) Lake County
81	1025	13.3	**Lakewood** (city) Cuyahoga County
82	1090	13.1	**Lebanon** (city) Warren County
82	1090	13.1	**Vermilion** (city) Lorain County
84	1134	13.0	**Austintown** (CDP) Mahoning County
84	1134	13.0	**Boardman** (CDP) Mahoning County
84	1134	13.0	**Galion** (city) Crawford County
87	1186	12.9	**Coshocton** (city) Coshocton County
87	1186	12.9	**Medina** (city) Medina County
89	1223	12.8	**Parma Heights** (city) Cuyahoga County
90	1270	12.7	**Delaware** (city) Delaware County
91	1312	12.6	**Columbus** (city) Franklin County
91	1312	12.6	**Englewood** (city) Montgomery County
91	1312	12.6	**Huber Heights** (city) Montgomery County
91	1312	12.6	**Maumee** (city) Lucas County
95	1361	12.5	**Forest Park** (city) Hamilton County
96	1398	12.4	**Findlay** (city) Hancock County
96	1398	12.4	**Wickliffe** (city) Lake County
98	1444	12.3	**Pataskala** (city) Licking County
99	1497	12.2	**Cincinnati** (city) Hamilton County
99	1497	12.2	**Defiance** (city) Defiance County
101	1545	12.1	**Eastlake** (city) Lake County
101	1545	12.1	**Elyria** (city) Lorain County
101	1545	12.1	**South Euclid** (city) Cuyahoga County
101	1545	12.1	**Steubenville** (city) Jefferson County
101	1545	12.1	**Streetsboro** (city) Portage County
106	1646	11.9	**Ashland** (city) Ashland County
107	1695	11.8	**Clayton** (city) Montgomery County
107	1695	11.8	**Cleveland Heights** (city) Cuyahoga County
107	1695	11.8	**Grove City** (city) Franklin County
107	1695	11.8	**Norwood** (city) Hamilton County
107	1695	11.8	**Oregon** (city) Lucas County
107	1695	11.8	**Parma** (city) Cuyahoga County
107	1695	11.8	**Springdale** (city) Hamilton County
107	1695	11.8	**Vandalia** (city) Montgomery County
115	1750	11.7	**Fairview Park** (city) Cuyahoga County
115	1750	11.7	**Garfield Heights** (city) Cuyahoga County
115	1750	11.7	**Reading** (city) Hamilton County
115	1750	11.7	**Wooster** (city) Wayne County
119	1804	11.6	**Brook Park** (city) Cuyahoga County
120	1954	11.3	**White Oak** (CDP) Hamilton County
121	2009	11.2	**Amherst** (city) Lorain County
121	2009	11.2	**Bay Village** (city) Cuyahoga County
121	2009	11.2	**Tiffin** (city) Seneca County
124	2066	11.1	**Centerville** (city) Montgomery County
124	2066	11.1	**Gahanna** (city) Franklin County
124	2066	11.1	**Stow** (city) Summit County
124	2066	11.1	**Trenton** (city) Butler County
128	2111	11.0	**Berea** (city) Cuyahoga County
129	2277	10.7	**Mayfield Heights** (city) Cuyahoga County
130	2339	10.6	**Dent** (CDP) Hamilton County
131	2394	10.5	**Forestville** (CDP) Hamilton County
131	2394	10.5	**North Ridgeville** (city) Lorain County
131	2394	10.5	**Shaker Heights** (city) Cuyahoga County
134	2441	10.4	**Broadview Heights** (city) Cuyahoga County
135	2487	10.3	**Brecksville** (city) Cuyahoga County
135	2487	10.3	**North Olmsted** (city) Cuyahoga County
137	2536	10.2	**Blue Ash** (city) Hamilton County
137	2536	10.2	**North Royalton** (city) Cuyahoga County
137	2536	10.2	**Tallmadge** (city) Summit County
137	2536	10.2	**Worthington** (city) Franklin County
141	2602	10.1	**Mentor** (city) Lake County
141	2602	10.1	**Westlake** (city) Cuyahoga County
141	2602	10.1	**Willowick** (city) Lake County
144	2675	10.0	**Richmond Heights** (city) Cuyahoga County
145	2726	9.9	**Avon** (city) Lorain County
146	2834	9.7	**Brunswick** (city) Medina County
146	2834	9.7	**Finneytown** (CDP) Hamilton County
146	2834	9.7	**Mason** (city) Warren County
146	2834	9.7	**Norton** (city) Summit County
150	2882	9.6	**Avon Lake** (city) Lorain County

Note: *The state column ranks the top/bottom 150 places from all places in the state with population of 10,000 or more. The national column ranks the top/bottom 150 places from all places in the country with population of 10,000 or more. Places that are unincorporated were not considered in the rankings. Please refer to the User Guide for additional information.*

Marriage Status: Divorced

Top 150 Places Ranked in *Ascending* Order

State Rank	Nat'l Rank	Percent	Place
1	27	3.2	**Athens** (city) Athens County
1	27	3.2	**Oxford** (city) Butler County
3	156	5.2	**Montgomery** (city) Hamilton County
4	199	5.5	**Mack** (CDP) Hamilton County
5	294	6.0	**Hudson** (city) Summit County
6	395	6.4	**Monfort Heights** (CDP) Hamilton County
6	395	6.4	**University Heights** (city) Cuyahoga County
8	442	6.6	**Dublin** (city) Franklin County
9	525	6.9	**Twinsburg** (city) Summit County
10	554	7.0	**Bowling Green** (city) Wood County
11	587	7.1	**Powell** (city) Delaware County
12	689	7.4	**Kent** (city) Portage County
12	689	7.4	**Upper Arlington** (city) Franklin County
14	729	7.5	**Strongsville** (city) Cuyahoga County
15	770	7.6	**Solon** (city) Cuyahoga County
16	902	7.9	**Beavercreek** (city) Greene County
17	949	8.0	**Seven Hills** (city) Cuyahoga County
18	1092	8.3	**Bexley** (city) Franklin County
19	1135	8.4	**Lyndhurst** (city) Cuyahoga County
19	1135	8.4	**Macedonia** (city) Summit County
21	1178	8.5	**Aurora** (city) Portage County
22	1228	8.6	**Beachwood** (city) Cuyahoga County
22	1228	8.6	**Green** (city) Summit County
24	1324	8.8	**Rocky River** (city) Cuyahoga County
24	1324	8.8	**Westerville** (city) Franklin County
26	1426	9.0	**New Franklin** (city) Summit County
26	1426	9.0	**Sylvania** (city) Lucas County
28	1512	9.2	**Bridgetown** (CDP) Hamilton County
29	1625	9.4	**Pickerington** (city) Fairfield County
29	1625	9.4	**Springboro** (city) Warren County
31	1677	9.5	**Hilliard** (city) Franklin County
31	1677	9.5	**Perrysburg** (city) Wood County
33	1730	9.6	**Avon Lake** (city) Lorain County
33	1730	9.6	**Monroe** (city) Butler County
35	1775	9.7	**Brunswick** (city) Medina County
35	1775	9.7	**Finneytown** (CDP) Hamilton County
35	1775	9.7	**Mason** (city) Warren County
35	1775	9.7	**Norton** (city) Summit County
39	1878	9.9	**Avon** (city) Lorain County
40	1931	10.0	**Richmond Heights** (city) Cuyahoga County
41	1982	10.1	**Mentor** (city) Lake County
41	1982	10.1	**Westlake** (city) Cuyahoga County
41	1982	10.1	**Willowick** (city) Lake County
44	2055	10.2	**Blue Ash** (city) Hamilton County
44	2055	10.2	**North Royalton** (city) Cuyahoga County
44	2055	10.2	**Tallmadge** (city) Summit County
44	2055	10.2	**Worthington** (city) Franklin County
48	2121	10.3	**Brecksville** (city) Cuyahoga County
48	2121	10.3	**North Olmsted** (city) Cuyahoga County
50	2170	10.4	**Broadview Heights** (city) Cuyahoga County
51	2216	10.5	**Forestville** (CDP) Hamilton County
51	2216	10.5	**North Ridgeville** (city) Lorain County
51	2216	10.5	**Shaker Heights** (city) Cuyahoga County
54	2263	10.6	**Dent** (CDP) Hamilton County
55	2318	10.7	**Mayfield Heights** (city) Cuyahoga County
56	2489	11.0	**Berea** (city) Cuyahoga County
57	2546	11.1	**Centerville** (city) Montgomery County
57	2546	11.1	**Gahanna** (city) Franklin County
57	2546	11.1	**Stow** (city) Summit County
57	2546	11.1	**Trenton** (city) Butler County
61	2591	11.2	**Amherst** (city) Lorain County
61	2591	11.2	**Bay Village** (city) Cuyahoga County
61	2591	11.2	**Tiffin** (city) Seneca County
64	2648	11.3	**White Oak** (CDP) Hamilton County
65	2798	11.6	**Brook Park** (city) Cuyahoga County
66	2853	11.7	**Fairview Park** (city) Cuyahoga County
66	2853	11.7	**Garfield Heights** (city) Cuyahoga County
66	2853	11.7	**Reading** (city) Hamilton County
66	2853	11.7	**Wooster** (city) Wayne County
70	2907	11.8	**Clayton** (city) Montgomery County
70	2907	11.8	**Cleveland Heights** (city) Cuyahoga County
70	2907	11.8	**Grove City** (city) Franklin County
70	2907	11.8	**Norwood** (city) Hamilton County
70	2907	11.8	**Oregon** (city) Lucas County
70	2907	11.8	**Parma** (city) Cuyahoga County
70	2907	11.8	**Springdale** (city) Hamilton County
70	2907	11.8	**Vandalia** (city) Montgomery County
78	2962	11.9	**Ashland** (city) Ashland County
79	3053	12.1	**Eastlake** (city) Lake County
79	3053	12.1	**Elyria** (city) Lorain County
79	3053	12.1	**South Euclid** (city) Cuyahoga County
79	3053	12.1	**Steubenville** (city) Jefferson County
79	3053	12.1	**Streetsboro** (city) Portage County
84	3112	12.2	**Cincinnati** (city) Hamilton County
84	3112	12.2	**Defiance** (city) Defiance County
86	3160	12.3	**Pataskala** (city) Licking County
87	3213	12.4	**Findlay** (city) Hancock County
87	3213	12.4	**Wickliffe** (city) Lake County
89	3259	12.5	**Forest Park** (city) Hamilton County
90	3296	12.6	**Columbus** (city) Franklin County
90	3296	12.6	**Englewood** (city) Montgomery County
90	3296	12.6	**Huber Heights** (city) Montgomery County
90	3296	12.6	**Maumee** (city) Lucas County
94	3345	12.7	**Delaware** (city) Delaware County
95	3387	12.8	**Parma Heights** (city) Cuyahoga County
96	3434	12.9	**Coshocton** (city) Coshocton County
96	3434	12.9	**Medina** (city) Medina County
98	3471	13.0	**Austintown** (CDP) Mahoning County
98	3471	13.0	**Boardman** (CDP) Mahoning County
98	3471	13.0	**Galion** (city) Crawford County
101	3523	13.1	**Lebanon** (city) Warren County
101	3523	13.1	**Vermilion** (city) Lorain County
103	3606	13.3	**Lakewood** (city) Cuyahoga County
104	3632	13.4	**Fairfield** (city) Butler County
104	3632	13.4	**Lorain** (city) Lorain County
104	3632	13.4	**Painesville** (city) Lake County
107	3688	13.5	**Mount Vernon** (city) Knox County
108	3737	13.6	**Bedford** (city) Cuyahoga County
108	3737	13.6	**Miamisburg** (city) Montgomery County
108	3737	13.6	**New Philadelphia** (city) Tuscarawas County
108	3737	13.6	**North Canton** (city) Stark County
112	3768	13.7	**Fairborn** (city) Greene County
112	3768	13.7	**Heath** (city) Licking County
112	3768	13.7	**Maple Heights** (city) Cuyahoga County
115	3807	13.8	**Willoughby** (city) Lake County
116	3848	13.9	**Cuyahoga Falls** (city) Summit County
116	3848	13.9	**Euclid** (city) Cuyahoga County
116	3848	13.9	**Xenia** (city) Greene County
119	3891	14.0	**Celina** (city) Mercer County
120	3919	14.1	**Fremont** (city) Sandusky County
120	3919	14.1	**Sharonville** (city) Hamilton County
122	3959	14.2	**Loveland** (city) Hamilton County
122	3959	14.2	**Riverside** (city) Montgomery County
124	3990	14.3	**Akron** (city) Summit County
124	3990	14.3	**Middleburg Heights** (city) Cuyahoga County
124	3990	14.3	**Reynoldsburg** (city) Franklin County
124	3990	14.3	**Wadsworth** (city) Medina County
128	4020	14.4	**Brooklyn** (city) Cuyahoga County
128	4020	14.4	**East Liverpool** (city) Columbiana County
128	4020	14.4	**Sandusky** (city) Erie County
131	4044	14.5	**Wilmington** (city) Clinton County
132	4084	14.6	**Kettering** (city) Montgomery County
132	4084	14.6	**Marietta** (city) Washington County
134	4143	14.8	**Conneaut** (city) Ashtabula County
134	4143	14.8	**Toledo** (city) Lucas County
136	4163	14.9	**Circleville** (city) Pickaway County
136	4163	14.9	**Cleveland** (city) Cuyahoga County
136	4163	14.9	**Piqua** (city) Miami County
139	4193	15.0	**Alliance** (city) Stark County
139	4193	15.0	**Chillicothe** (city) Ross County
141	4220	15.1	**Barberton** (city) Summit County
141	4220	15.1	**Bucyrus** (city) Crawford County
141	4220	15.1	**Van Wert** (city) Van Wert County
144	4244	15.2	**Greenville** (city) Darke County
144	4244	15.2	**Troy** (city) Miami County
146	4271	15.3	**Massillon** (city) Stark County
147	4291	15.4	**Newark** (city) Licking County
147	4291	15.4	**Warren** (city) Trumbull County
147	4291	15.4	**Youngstown** (city) Mahoning County
150	4318	15.5	**Dover** (city) Tuscarawas County

Note: *The state column ranks the top/bottom 150 places from all places in the state with population of 10,000 or more. The national column ranks the top/bottom 150 places from all places in the country with population of 10,000 or more. Places that are unincorporated were not considered in the rankings. Please refer to the User Guide for additional information.*

Foreign Born

Top 150 Places Ranked in *Descending* Order

State Rank	Nat'l Rank	Percent	Place
1	1090	17.6	**Beachwood** (city) Cuyahoga County
2	1112	17.3	**Mayfield Heights** (city) Cuyahoga County
3	1250	15.5	**Blue Ash** (city) Hamilton County
4	1309	15.0	**Dublin** (city) Franklin County
5	1392	14.3	**Middleburg Heights** (city) Cuyahoga County
5	1392	14.3	**Seven Hills** (city) Cuyahoga County
7	1400	14.2	**Springdale** (city) Hamilton County
8	1438	13.8	**Solon** (city) Cuyahoga County
9	1538	13.0	**Painesville** (city) Lake County
9	1538	13.0	**Parma Heights** (city) Cuyahoga County
11	1707	11.7	**Whitehall** (city) Franklin County
12	1776	11.2	**Rocky River** (city) Cuyahoga County
12	1776	11.2	**Westlake** (city) Cuyahoga County
14	1819	11.0	**Richmond Heights** (city) Cuyahoga County
15	1842	10.9	**Brooklyn** (city) Cuyahoga County
15	1842	10.9	**Columbus** (city) Franklin County
15	1842	10.9	**Mason** (city) Warren County
18	1931	10.4	**Sharonville** (city) Hamilton County
19	2031	9.9	**Powell** (city) Delaware County
20	2066	9.8	**Forest Park** (city) Hamilton County
20	2066	9.8	**Parma** (city) Cuyahoga County
22	2178	9.2	**North Royalton** (city) Cuyahoga County
23	2264	8.8	**Shaker Heights** (city) Cuyahoga County
24	2283	8.7	**Broadview Heights** (city) Cuyahoga County
25	2302	8.6	**North Olmsted** (city) Cuyahoga County
26	2324	8.5	**Cleveland Heights** (city) Cuyahoga County
27	2346	8.4	**Strongsville** (city) Cuyahoga County
28	2364	8.3	**Athens** (city) Athens County
29	2402	8.1	**Hudson** (city) Summit County
30	2429	8.0	**Lakewood** (city) Cuyahoga County
31	2455	7.9	**Fairview Park** (city) Cuyahoga County
31	2455	7.9	**University Heights** (city) Cuyahoga County
33	2475	7.8	**Lyndhurst** (city) Cuyahoga County
34	2497	7.7	**Montgomery** (city) Hamilton County
34	2497	7.7	**Twinsburg** (city) Summit County
36	2528	7.6	**Upper Arlington** (city) Franklin County
37	2588	7.4	**Brecksville** (city) Cuyahoga County
38	2648	7.2	**Beavercreek** (city) Greene County
39	2696	7.0	**Fairfield** (city) Butler County
40	2755	6.8	**Oxford** (city) Butler County
41	2806	6.6	**Aurora** (city) Portage County
42	2839	6.5	**Macedonia** (city) Summit County
43	2869	6.4	**Bexley** (city) Franklin County
43	2869	6.4	**Westerville** (city) Franklin County
45	2904	6.3	**South Euclid** (city) Cuyahoga County
45	2904	6.3	**Willoughby** (city) Lake County
47	2929	6.2	**Eastlake** (city) Lake County
47	2929	6.2	**Kent** (city) Portage County
49	2955	6.1	**Sylvania** (city) Lucas County
50	3011	5.9	**Reynoldsburg** (city) Franklin County
50	3011	5.9	**Springboro** (city) Warren County
52	3070	5.7	**Hilliard** (city) Franklin County
53	3093	5.6	**Gahanna** (city) Franklin County
54	3128	5.5	**Avon** (city) Lorain County
55	3191	5.3	**Centerville** (city) Montgomery County
56	3225	5.2	**Bowling Green** (city) Wood County
56	3225	5.2	**Cincinnati** (city) Hamilton County
56	3225	5.2	**Perrysburg** (city) Wood County
59	3257	5.1	**Willowick** (city) Lake County
60	3295	5.0	**Fairborn** (city) Greene County
61	3329	4.9	**Finneytown** (CDP) Hamilton County
61	3329	4.9	**Forestville** (CDP) Hamilton County
61	3329	4.9	**Huber Heights** (city) Montgomery County
64	3363	4.8	**Loveland** (city) Hamilton County
64	3363	4.8	**Pickerington** (city) Fairfield County
66	3401	4.7	**North Ridgeville** (city) Lorain County
67	3433	4.6	**Bedford Heights** (city) Cuyahoga County
67	3433	4.6	**Cleveland** (city) Cuyahoga County
67	3433	4.6	**Worthington** (city) Franklin County
70	3455	4.5	**Akron** (city) Summit County
71	3489	4.4	**Berea** (city) Cuyahoga County
71	3489	4.4	**Englewood** (city) Montgomery County
71	3489	4.4	**Stow** (city) Summit County
71	3489	4.4	**West Carrollton** (city) Montgomery County
75	3522	4.3	**Brook Park** (city) Cuyahoga County
75	3522	4.3	**Youngstown** (city) Mahoning County
77	3554	4.2	**Avon Lake** (city) Lorain County
78	3592	4.1	**Reading** (city) Hamilton County
79	3625	4.0	**Wickliffe** (city) Lake County
80	3661	3.9	**Ashland** (city) Ashland County
80	3661	3.9	**Wooster** (city) Wayne County
82	3689	3.8	**Dayton** (city) Montgomery County
82	3689	3.8	**Hamilton** (city) Butler County
84	3792	3.5	**East Cleveland** (city) Cuyahoga County
84	3792	3.5	**Garfield Heights** (city) Cuyahoga County
84	3792	3.5	**Lebanon** (city) Warren County
84	3792	3.5	**Mentor** (city) Lake County
84	3792	3.5	**Streetsboro** (city) Portage County
89	3831	3.4	**Delaware** (city) Delaware County
89	3831	3.4	**Findlay** (city) Hancock County
89	3831	3.4	**Norwalk** (city) Huron County
92	3896	3.2	**Bay Village** (city) Cuyahoga County
92	3896	3.2	**Euclid** (city) Cuyahoga County
92	3896	3.2	**Green** (city) Summit County
92	3896	3.2	**Lorain** (city) Lorain County
92	3896	3.2	**Toledo** (city) Lucas County
97	3933	3.1	**Barberton** (city) Summit County
97	3933	3.1	**Brunswick** (city) Medina County
97	3933	3.1	**Dover** (city) Tuscarawas County
97	3933	3.1	**Marysville** (city) Union County
101	3969	3.0	**Cuyahoga Falls** (city) Summit County
101	3969	3.0	**Kettering** (city) Montgomery County
101	3969	3.0	**Maple Heights** (city) Cuyahoga County
101	3969	3.0	**Middletown** (city) Butler County
101	3969	3.0	**Riverside** (city) Montgomery County
101	3969	3.0	**White Oak** (CDP) Hamilton County
107	4009	2.9	**Boardman** (CDP) Mahoning County
107	4009	2.9	**Tiffin** (city) Seneca County
107	4009	2.9	**Troy** (city) Miami County
110	4035	2.8	**Fremont** (city) Sandusky County
110	4035	2.8	**Marietta** (city) Washington County
112	4085	2.7	**Monroe** (city) Butler County
112	4085	2.7	**North Canton** (city) Stark County
112	4085	2.7	**Northbrook** (CDP) Hamilton County
112	4085	2.7	**Tallmadge** (city) Summit County
116	4119	2.6	**Medina** (city) Medina County
116	4119	2.6	**Norwood** (city) Hamilton County
116	4119	2.6	**Springfield** (city) Clark County
119	4151	2.5	**Amherst** (city) Lorain County
119	4151	2.5	**Dent** (CDP) Hamilton County
119	4151	2.5	**Oregon** (city) Lucas County
119	4151	2.5	**Sidney** (city) Shelby County
123	4176	2.4	**Grove City** (city) Franklin County
123	4176	2.4	**New Franklin** (city) Summit County
125	4198	2.3	**Maumee** (city) Lucas County
125	4198	2.3	**Portsmouth** (city) Scioto County
125	4198	2.3	**Warrensville Heights** (city) Cuyahoga County
128	4239	2.2	**Bedford** (city) Cuyahoga County
128	4239	2.2	**Canton** (city) Stark County
128	4239	2.2	**Monfort Heights** (CDP) Hamilton County
128	4239	2.2	**Vandalia** (city) Montgomery County
132	4305	2.0	**Bellefontaine** (city) Logan County
132	4305	2.0	**Clayton** (city) Montgomery County
132	4305	2.0	**Heath** (city) Licking County
132	4305	2.0	**Norton** (city) Summit County
132	4305	2.0	**Wadsworth** (city) Medina County
137	4338	1.9	**Mack** (CDP) Hamilton County
137	4338	1.9	**Washington Court House** (city) Fayette County
137	4338	1.9	**Wilmington** (city) Clinton County
140	4365	1.8	**Austintown** (CDP) Mahoning County
140	4365	1.8	**Sandusky** (city) Erie County
140	4365	1.8	**Trotwood** (city) Montgomery County
143	4396	1.7	**Alliance** (city) Stark County
143	4396	1.7	**Mansfield** (city) Richland County
143	4396	1.7	**Steubenville** (city) Jefferson County
143	4396	1.7	**Warren** (city) Trumbull County
147	4421	1.6	**Elyria** (city) Lorain County
147	4421	1.6	**Xenia** (city) Greene County
149	4445	1.5	**Pataskala** (city) Licking County
150	4475	1.4	**Celina** (city) Mercer County

Note: *The state column ranks the top/bottom 150 places from all places in the state with population of 10,000 or more. The national column ranks the top/bottom 150 places from all places in the country with population of 10,000 or more. Places that are unincorporated were not considered in the rankings. Please refer to the User Guide for additional information.*

Foreign Born

Top 150 Places Ranked in *Ascending* Order

State Rank	Nat'l Rank	Percent	Place
1	1	0.1	**Circleville** (city) Pickaway County
1	1	0.1	**Trenton** (city) Butler County
3	4	0.3	**Ironton** (city) Lawrence County
4	17	0.6	**Coshocton** (city) Coshocton County
5	30	0.7	**Bucyrus** (city) Crawford County
5	30	0.7	**Fostoria** (city) Seneca County
5	30	0.7	**Franklin** (city) Warren County
8	41	0.8	**Galion** (city) Crawford County
8	41	0.8	**Struthers** (city) Mahoning County
10	58	0.9	**Chillicothe** (city) Ross County
10	58	0.9	**East Liverpool** (city) Columbiana County
10	58	0.9	**Greenville** (city) Darke County
13	75	1.0	**Cambridge** (city) Guernsey County
13	75	1.0	**Conneaut** (city) Ashtabula County
13	75	1.0	**Piqua** (city) Miami County
13	75	1.0	**Ravenna** (city) Portage County
13	75	1.0	**Vermilion** (city) Lorain County
18	96	1.1	**Ashtabula** (city) Ashtabula County
18	96	1.1	**Massillon** (city) Stark County
18	96	1.1	**Newark** (city) Licking County
18	96	1.1	**Urbana** (city) Champaign County
22	119	1.2	**Bridgetown** (CDP) Hamilton County
22	119	1.2	**Lancaster** (city) Fairfield County
22	119	1.2	**Marion** (city) Marion County
22	119	1.2	**Mount Vernon** (city) Knox County
22	119	1.2	**New Philadelphia** (city) Tuscarawas County
22	119	1.2	**Van Wert** (city) Van Wert County
28	141	1.3	**Defiance** (city) Defiance County
28	141	1.3	**Miamisburg** (city) Montgomery County
28	141	1.3	**Salem** (city) Columbiana County
28	141	1.3	**Zanesville** (city) Muskingum County
32	162	1.4	**Celina** (city) Mercer County
32	162	1.4	**Lima** (city) Allen County
32	162	1.4	**Niles** (city) Trumbull County
35	182	1.5	**Pataskala** (city) Licking County
36	212	1.6	**Elyria** (city) Lorain County
36	212	1.6	**Xenia** (city) Greene County
38	236	1.7	**Alliance** (city) Stark County
38	236	1.7	**Mansfield** (city) Richland County
38	236	1.7	**Steubenville** (city) Jefferson County
38	236	1.7	**Warren** (city) Trumbull County
42	261	1.8	**Austintown** (CDP) Mahoning County
42	261	1.8	**Sandusky** (city) Erie County
42	261	1.8	**Trotwood** (city) Montgomery County
45	292	1.9	**Mack** (CDP) Hamilton County
45	292	1.9	**Washington Court House** (city) Fayette County
45	292	1.9	**Wilmington** (city) Clinton County
48	319	2.0	**Bellefontaine** (city) Logan County
48	319	2.0	**Clayton** (city) Montgomery County
48	319	2.0	**Heath** (city) Licking County
48	319	2.0	**Norton** (city) Summit County
48	319	2.0	**Wadsworth** (city) Medina County
53	381	2.2	**Bedford** (city) Cuyahoga County
53	381	2.2	**Canton** (city) Stark County
53	381	2.2	**Monfort Heights** (CDP) Hamilton County
53	381	2.2	**Vandalia** (city) Montgomery County
57	418	2.3	**Maumee** (city) Lucas County
57	418	2.3	**Portsmouth** (city) Scioto County
57	418	2.3	**Warrensville Heights** (city) Cuyahoga County
60	459	2.4	**Grove City** (city) Franklin County
60	459	2.4	**New Franklin** (city) Summit County
62	481	2.5	**Amherst** (city) Lorain County
62	481	2.5	**Dent** (CDP) Hamilton County
62	481	2.5	**Oregon** (city) Lucas County
62	481	2.5	**Sidney** (city) Shelby County
66	506	2.6	**Medina** (city) Medina County
66	506	2.6	**Norwood** (city) Hamilton County
66	506	2.6	**Springfield** (city) Clark County
69	538	2.7	**Monroe** (city) Butler County
69	538	2.7	**North Canton** (city) Stark County
69	538	2.7	**Northbrook** (CDP) Hamilton County
69	538	2.7	**Tallmadge** (city) Summit County
73	572	2.8	**Fremont** (city) Sandusky County
73	572	2.8	**Marietta** (city) Washington County
75	622	2.9	**Boardman** (CDP) Mahoning County
75	622	2.9	**Tiffin** (city) Seneca County
75	622	2.9	**Troy** (city) Miami County
78	648	3.0	**Cuyahoga Falls** (city) Summit County
78	648	3.0	**Kettering** (city) Montgomery County
78	648	3.0	**Maple Heights** (city) Cuyahoga County
78	648	3.0	**Middletown** (city) Butler County
78	648	3.0	**Riverside** (city) Montgomery County
78	648	3.0	**White Oak** (CDP) Hamilton County
84	688	3.1	**Barberton** (city) Summit County
84	688	3.1	**Brunswick** (city) Medina County
84	688	3.1	**Dover** (city) Tuscarawas County
84	688	3.1	**Marysville** (city) Union County
88	724	3.2	**Bay Village** (city) Cuyahoga County
88	724	3.2	**Euclid** (city) Cuyahoga County
88	724	3.2	**Green** (city) Summit County
88	724	3.2	**Lorain** (city) Lorain County
88	724	3.2	**Toledo** (city) Lucas County
93	791	3.4	**Delaware** (city) Delaware County
93	791	3.4	**Findlay** (city) Hancock County
93	791	3.4	**Norwalk** (city) Huron County
96	826	3.5	**East Cleveland** (city) Cuyahoga County
96	826	3.5	**Garfield Heights** (city) Cuyahoga County
96	826	3.5	**Lebanon** (city) Warren County
96	826	3.5	**Mentor** (city) Lake County
96	826	3.5	**Streetsboro** (city) Portage County
101	934	3.8	**Dayton** (city) Montgomery County
101	934	3.8	**Hamilton** (city) Butler County
103	968	3.9	**Ashland** (city) Ashland County
103	968	3.9	**Wooster** (city) Wayne County
105	996	4.0	**Wickliffe** (city) Lake County
106	1032	4.1	**Reading** (city) Hamilton County
107	1065	4.2	**Avon Lake** (city) Lorain County
108	1103	4.3	**Brook Park** (city) Cuyahoga County
108	1103	4.3	**Youngstown** (city) Mahoning County
110	1135	4.4	**Berea** (city) Cuyahoga County
110	1135	4.4	**Englewood** (city) Montgomery County
110	1135	4.4	**Stow** (city) Summit County
110	1135	4.4	**West Carrollton** (city) Montgomery County
114	1168	4.5	**Akron** (city) Summit County
115	1202	4.6	**Bedford Heights** (city) Cuyahoga County
115	1202	4.6	**Cleveland** (city) Cuyahoga County
115	1202	4.6	**Worthington** (city) Franklin County
118	1224	4.7	**North Ridgeville** (city) Lorain County
119	1256	4.8	**Loveland** (city) Hamilton County
119	1256	4.8	**Pickerington** (city) Fairfield County
121	1294	4.9	**Finneytown** (CDP) Hamilton County
121	1294	4.9	**Forestville** (CDP) Hamilton County
121	1294	4.9	**Huber Heights** (city) Montgomery County
124	1328	5.0	**Fairborn** (city) Greene County
125	1362	5.1	**Willowick** (city) Lake County
126	1400	5.2	**Bowling Green** (city) Wood County
126	1400	5.2	**Cincinnati** (city) Hamilton County
126	1400	5.2	**Perrysburg** (city) Wood County
129	1432	5.3	**Centerville** (city) Montgomery County
130	1492	5.5	**Avon** (city) Lorain County
131	1529	5.6	**Gahanna** (city) Franklin County
132	1564	5.7	**Hilliard** (city) Franklin County
133	1618	5.9	**Reynoldsburg** (city) Franklin County
133	1618	5.9	**Springboro** (city) Warren County
135	1667	6.1	**Sylvania** (city) Lucas County
136	1702	6.2	**Eastlake** (city) Lake County
136	1702	6.2	**Kent** (city) Portage County
138	1728	6.3	**South Euclid** (city) Cuyahoga County
138	1728	6.3	**Willoughby** (city) Lake County
140	1753	6.4	**Bexley** (city) Franklin County
140	1753	6.4	**Westerville** (city) Franklin County
142	1788	6.5	**Macedonia** (city) Summit County
143	1818	6.6	**Aurora** (city) Portage County
144	1875	6.8	**Oxford** (city) Butler County
145	1928	7.0	**Fairfield** (city) Butler County
146	1988	7.2	**Beavercreek** (city) Greene County
147	2042	7.4	**Brecksville** (city) Cuyahoga County
148	2092	7.6	**Upper Arlington** (city) Franklin County
149	2129	7.7	**Montgomery** (city) Hamilton County
149	2129	7.7	**Twinsburg** (city) Summit County

Note: *The state column ranks the top/bottom 150 places from all places in the state with population of 10,000 or more. The national column ranks the top/bottom 150 places from all places in the country with population of 10,000 or more. Places that are unincorporated were not considered in the rankings. Please refer to the User Guide for additional information.*

Speak English Only at Home

Top 150 Places Ranked in *Descending* Order

State Rank	Nat'l Rank	Percent	Place
1	6	98.9	**Bucyrus** (city) Crawford County
2	8	98.8	**Coshocton** (city) Coshocton County
2	8	98.8	**Franklin** (city) Warren County
2	8	98.8	**Galion** (city) Crawford County
2	8	98.8	**Trenton** (city) Butler County
6	15	98.7	**East Liverpool** (city) Columbiana County
6	15	98.7	**Ironton** (city) Lawrence County
8	31	98.4	**Circleville** (city) Pickaway County
8	31	98.4	**Lancaster** (city) Fairfield County
8	31	98.4	**Mount Vernon** (city) Knox County
11	36	98.3	**Miamisburg** (city) Montgomery County
12	42	98.2	**Greenville** (city) Darke County
12	42	98.2	**Ravenna** (city) Portage County
12	42	98.2	**Vermilion** (city) Lorain County
15	65	97.9	**Salem** (city) Columbiana County
16	79	97.8	**Cambridge** (city) Guernsey County
17	89	97.7	**Newark** (city) Licking County
17	89	97.7	**Urbana** (city) Champaign County
17	89	97.7	**Van Wert** (city) Van Wert County
20	126	97.4	**Piqua** (city) Miami County
21	144	97.3	**Mack** (CDP) Hamilton County
21	144	97.3	**Zanesville** (city) Muskingum County
23	162	97.2	**Alliance** (city) Stark County
23	162	97.2	**Xenia** (city) Greene County
25	179	97.1	**Austintown** (CDP) Mahoning County
25	179	97.1	**Lima** (city) Allen County
27	191	97.0	**Massillon** (city) Stark County
27	191	97.0	**New Franklin** (city) Summit County
27	191	97.0	**Trotwood** (city) Montgomery County
30	210	96.9	**Celina** (city) Mercer County
30	210	96.9	**Heath** (city) Licking County
30	210	96.9	**Vandalia** (city) Montgomery County
33	240	96.8	**Conneaut** (city) Ashtabula County
33	240	96.8	**Marietta** (city) Washington County
33	240	96.8	**Northbrook** (CDP) Hamilton County
33	240	96.8	**Norton** (city) Summit County
37	254	96.7	**Bridgetown** (CDP) Hamilton County
37	254	96.7	**Fostoria** (city) Seneca County
37	254	96.7	**Mansfield** (city) Richland County
37	254	96.7	**Maple Heights** (city) Cuyahoga County
37	254	96.7	**Pataskala** (city) Licking County
37	254	96.7	**Wilmington** (city) Clinton County
43	282	96.6	**Chillicothe** (city) Ross County
44	301	96.5	**Dent** (CDP) Hamilton County
44	301	96.5	**North Canton** (city) Stark County
46	318	96.4	**Maumee** (city) Lucas County
46	318	96.4	**Washington Court House** (city) Fayette County
48	338	96.3	**Amherst** (city) Lorain County
48	338	96.3	**Elyria** (city) Lorain County
48	338	96.3	**Monfort Heights** (CDP) Hamilton County
48	338	96.3	**New Philadelphia** (city) Tuscarawas County
48	338	96.3	**Niles** (city) Trumbull County
48	338	96.3	**Sidney** (city) Shelby County
54	363	96.2	**Tallmadge** (city) Summit County
54	363	96.2	**Tiffin** (city) Seneca County
54	363	96.2	**White Oak** (CDP) Hamilton County
57	386	96.1	**Bellefontaine** (city) Logan County
57	386	96.1	**Portsmouth** (city) Scioto County
57	386	96.1	**Streetsboro** (city) Portage County
60	412	96.0	**Delaware** (city) Delaware County
60	412	96.0	**Sandusky** (city) Erie County
60	412	96.0	**Wadsworth** (city) Medina County
63	436	95.9	**Cuyahoga Falls** (city) Summit County
64	456	95.8	**Warrensville Heights** (city) Cuyahoga County
65	492	95.7	**Clayton** (city) Montgomery County
65	492	95.7	**Euclid** (city) Cuyahoga County
65	492	95.7	**Warren** (city) Trumbull County
68	520	95.6	**Barberton** (city) Summit County
68	520	95.6	**Grove City** (city) Franklin County
68	520	95.6	**Marysville** (city) Union County
68	520	95.6	**Stow** (city) Summit County
72	579	95.4	**Bedford** (city) Cuyahoga County
72	579	95.4	**Marion** (city) Marion County
72	579	95.4	**Medina** (city) Medina County
72	579	95.4	**Troy** (city) Miami County
76	594	95.3	**Canton** (city) Stark County
76	594	95.3	**Steubenville** (city) Jefferson County
78	658	95.1	**Ashland** (city) Ashland County
78	658	95.1	**Finneytown** (CDP) Hamilton County
78	658	95.1	**Oregon** (city) Lucas County
78	658	95.1	**Springfield** (city) Clark County
82	688	95.0	**East Cleveland** (city) Cuyahoga County
82	688	95.0	**Riverside** (city) Montgomery County
84	714	94.9	**Bay Village** (city) Cuyahoga County
84	714	94.9	**Mentor** (city) Lake County
84	714	94.9	**Middletown** (city) Butler County
84	714	94.9	**Norwood** (city) Hamilton County
88	742	94.8	**Englewood** (city) Montgomery County
88	742	94.8	**Kettering** (city) Montgomery County
88	742	94.8	**Lebanon** (city) Warren County
88	742	94.8	**Reading** (city) Hamilton County
88	742	94.8	**West Carrollton** (city) Montgomery County
93	768	94.7	**Worthington** (city) Franklin County
94	794	94.6	**Findlay** (city) Hancock County
94	794	94.6	**Monroe** (city) Butler County
96	832	94.4	**Dover** (city) Tuscarawas County
96	832	94.4	**North Ridgeville** (city) Lorain County
96	832	94.4	**Pickerington** (city) Fairfield County
99	854	94.3	**Dayton** (city) Montgomery County
99	854	94.3	**Hamilton** (city) Butler County
99	854	94.3	**Norwalk** (city) Huron County
102	882	94.2	**Garfield Heights** (city) Cuyahoga County
103	904	94.1	**Brunswick** (city) Medina County
103	904	94.1	**Gahanna** (city) Franklin County
105	954	93.9	**Toledo** (city) Lucas County
106	998	93.7	**Avon Lake** (city) Lorain County
106	998	93.7	**Boardman** (CDP) Mahoning County
106	998	93.7	**Green** (city) Summit County
109	1025	93.6	**Akron** (city) Summit County
109	1025	93.6	**Wickliffe** (city) Lake County
111	1047	93.5	**Struthers** (city) Mahoning County
112	1071	93.4	**Willowick** (city) Lake County
112	1071	93.4	**Wooster** (city) Wayne County
114	1097	93.3	**Ashtabula** (city) Ashtabula County
114	1097	93.3	**Brook Park** (city) Cuyahoga County
116	1144	93.1	**Centerville** (city) Montgomery County
116	1144	93.1	**Fairborn** (city) Greene County
116	1144	93.1	**Montgomery** (city) Hamilton County
116	1144	93.1	**Perrysburg** (city) Wood County
120	1168	93.0	**Forestville** (CDP) Hamilton County
120	1168	93.0	**Sylvania** (city) Lucas County
122	1194	92.9	**Bowling Green** (city) Wood County
123	1210	92.8	**Bedford Heights** (city) Cuyahoga County
123	1210	92.8	**Berea** (city) Cuyahoga County
123	1210	92.8	**Springboro** (city) Warren County
126	1240	92.7	**Huber Heights** (city) Montgomery County
127	1296	92.5	**Bexley** (city) Franklin County
128	1325	92.4	**Cincinnati** (city) Hamilton County
128	1325	92.4	**Kent** (city) Portage County
128	1325	92.4	**Macedonia** (city) Summit County
128	1325	92.4	**Willoughby** (city) Lake County
132	1346	92.3	**Westerville** (city) Franklin County
133	1370	92.2	**Loveland** (city) Hamilton County
134	1395	92.1	**Defiance** (city) Defiance County
134	1395	92.1	**Eastlake** (city) Lake County
134	1395	92.1	**Reynoldsburg** (city) Franklin County
137	1457	91.8	**Oxford** (city) Butler County
138	1481	91.7	**Hilliard** (city) Franklin County
138	1481	91.7	**Hudson** (city) Summit County
140	1502	91.6	**Fairfield** (city) Butler County
141	1583	91.2	**Lyndhurst** (city) Cuyahoga County
142	1605	91.1	**South Euclid** (city) Cuyahoga County
143	1639	90.9	**Athens** (city) Athens County
143	1639	90.9	**Twinsburg** (city) Summit County
145	1674	90.7	**Aurora** (city) Portage County
145	1674	90.7	**Avon** (city) Lorain County
147	1694	90.6	**Beavercreek** (city) Greene County
147	1694	90.6	**Brecksville** (city) Cuyahoga County
149	1760	90.3	**Youngstown** (city) Mahoning County
150	1808	90.1	**Fremont** (city) Sandusky County

Note: *The state column ranks the top/bottom 150 places from all places in the state with population of 10,000 or more. The national column ranks the top/bottom 150 places from all places in the country with population of 10,000 or more. Places that are unincorporated were not considered in the rankings. Please refer to the User Guide for additional information.*

Speak English Only at Home

Top 150 Places Ranked in *Ascending* Order

State Rank	Nat'l Rank	Percent	Place
1	1381	78.3	**Springdale** (city) Hamilton County
2	1440	79.1	**Mayfield Heights** (city) Cuyahoga County
3	1480	79.6	**Seven Hills** (city) Cuyahoga County
4	1539	80.4	**Beachwood** (city) Cuyahoga County
5	1551	80.5	**Painesville** (city) Lake County
6	1648	81.5	**Middleburg Heights** (city) Cuyahoga County
7	1679	81.8	**Lorain** (city) Lorain County
8	1724	82.3	**Brooklyn** (city) Cuyahoga County
9	1748	82.5	**Solon** (city) Cuyahoga County
10	1787	82.8	**Whitehall** (city) Franklin County
11	1817	83.0	**Blue Ash** (city) Hamilton County
12	1823	83.1	**Dublin** (city) Franklin County
13	1853	83.4	**Parma Heights** (city) Cuyahoga County
14	1935	84.2	**Westlake** (city) Cuyahoga County
15	2032	85.0	**Mason** (city) Warren County
16	2052	85.1	**Richmond Heights** (city) Cuyahoga County
17	2157	85.9	**Parma** (city) Cuyahoga County
18	2172	86.0	**Columbus** (city) Franklin County
19	2238	86.4	**Broadview Heights** (city) Cuyahoga County
20	2266	86.6	**North Olmsted** (city) Cuyahoga County
20	2266	86.6	**Rocky River** (city) Cuyahoga County
22	2282	86.7	**North Royalton** (city) Cuyahoga County
22	2282	86.7	**Sharonville** (city) Hamilton County
24	2396	87.6	**Powell** (city) Delaware County
25	2492	88.2	**Cleveland** (city) Cuyahoga County
25	2492	88.2	**Fairview Park** (city) Cuyahoga County
25	2492	88.2	**Forest Park** (city) Hamilton County
28	2598	88.8	**University Heights** (city) Cuyahoga County
29	2657	89.1	**Lakewood** (city) Cuyahoga County
30	2708	89.4	**Shaker Heights** (city) Cuyahoga County
30	2708	89.4	**Strongsville** (city) Cuyahoga County
32	2726	89.5	**Upper Arlington** (city) Franklin County
33	2753	89.7	**Cleveland Heights** (city) Cuyahoga County
34	2829	90.1	**Fremont** (city) Sandusky County
35	2877	90.3	**Youngstown** (city) Mahoning County
36	2938	90.6	**Beavercreek** (city) Greene County
36	2938	90.6	**Brecksville** (city) Cuyahoga County
38	2963	90.7	**Aurora** (city) Portage County
38	2963	90.7	**Avon** (city) Lorain County
40	2998	90.9	**Athens** (city) Athens County
40	2998	90.9	**Twinsburg** (city) Summit County
42	3035	91.1	**South Euclid** (city) Cuyahoga County
43	3052	91.2	**Lyndhurst** (city) Cuyahoga County
44	3128	91.6	**Fairfield** (city) Butler County
45	3155	91.7	**Hilliard** (city) Franklin County
45	3155	91.7	**Hudson** (city) Summit County
47	3176	91.8	**Oxford** (city) Butler County
48	3241	92.1	**Defiance** (city) Defiance County
48	3241	92.1	**Eastlake** (city) Lake County
48	3241	92.1	**Reynoldsburg** (city) Franklin County
51	3262	92.2	**Loveland** (city) Hamilton County
52	3287	92.3	**Westerville** (city) Franklin County
53	3311	92.4	**Cincinnati** (city) Hamilton County
53	3311	92.4	**Kent** (city) Portage County
53	3311	92.4	**Macedonia** (city) Summit County
53	3311	92.4	**Willoughby** (city) Lake County
57	3332	92.5	**Bexley** (city) Franklin County
58	3386	92.7	**Huber Heights** (city) Montgomery County
59	3417	92.8	**Bedford Heights** (city) Cuyahoga County
59	3417	92.8	**Berea** (city) Cuyahoga County
59	3417	92.8	**Springboro** (city) Warren County
62	3447	92.9	**Bowling Green** (city) Wood County
63	3463	93.0	**Forestville** (CDP) Hamilton County
63	3463	93.0	**Sylvania** (city) Lucas County
65	3489	93.1	**Centerville** (city) Montgomery County
65	3489	93.1	**Fairborn** (city) Greene County
65	3489	93.1	**Montgomery** (city) Hamilton County
65	3489	93.1	**Perrysburg** (city) Wood County
69	3533	93.3	**Ashtabula** (city) Ashtabula County
69	3533	93.3	**Brook Park** (city) Cuyahoga County
71	3560	93.4	**Willowick** (city) Lake County
71	3560	93.4	**Wooster** (city) Wayne County
73	3586	93.5	**Struthers** (city) Mahoning County
74	3610	93.6	**Akron** (city) Summit County
74	3610	93.6	**Wickliffe** (city) Lake County
76	3632	93.7	**Avon Lake** (city) Lorain County
76	3632	93.7	**Boardman** (CDP) Mahoning County
76	3632	93.7	**Green** (city) Summit County
79	3682	93.9	**Toledo** (city) Lucas County
80	3726	94.1	**Brunswick** (city) Medina County
80	3726	94.1	**Gahanna** (city) Franklin County
82	3753	94.2	**Garfield Heights** (city) Cuyahoga County
83	3775	94.3	**Dayton** (city) Montgomery County
83	3775	94.3	**Hamilton** (city) Butler County
83	3775	94.3	**Norwalk** (city) Huron County
86	3803	94.4	**Dover** (city) Tuscarawas County
86	3803	94.4	**North Ridgeville** (city) Lorain County
86	3803	94.4	**Pickerington** (city) Fairfield County
89	3843	94.6	**Findlay** (city) Hancock County
89	3843	94.6	**Monroe** (city) Butler County
91	3863	94.7	**Worthington** (city) Franklin County
92	3889	94.8	**Englewood** (city) Montgomery County
92	3889	94.8	**Kettering** (city) Montgomery County
92	3889	94.8	**Lebanon** (city) Warren County
92	3889	94.8	**Reading** (city) Hamilton County
92	3889	94.8	**West Carrollton** (city) Montgomery County
97	3915	94.9	**Bay Village** (city) Cuyahoga County
97	3915	94.9	**Mentor** (city) Lake County
97	3915	94.9	**Middletown** (city) Butler County
97	3915	94.9	**Norwood** (city) Hamilton County
101	3943	95.0	**East Cleveland** (city) Cuyahoga County
101	3943	95.0	**Riverside** (city) Montgomery County
103	3969	95.1	**Ashland** (city) Ashland County
103	3969	95.1	**Finneytown** (CDP) Hamilton County
103	3969	95.1	**Oregon** (city) Lucas County
103	3969	95.1	**Springfield** (city) Clark County
107	4028	95.3	**Canton** (city) Stark County
107	4028	95.3	**Steubenville** (city) Jefferson County
109	4063	95.4	**Bedford** (city) Cuyahoga County
109	4063	95.4	**Marion** (city) Marion County
109	4063	95.4	**Medina** (city) Medina County
109	4063	95.4	**Troy** (city) Miami County
113	4106	95.6	**Barberton** (city) Summit County
113	4106	95.6	**Grove City** (city) Franklin County
113	4106	95.6	**Marysville** (city) Union County
113	4106	95.6	**Stow** (city) Summit County
117	4137	95.7	**Clayton** (city) Montgomery County
117	4137	95.7	**Euclid** (city) Cuyahoga County
117	4137	95.7	**Warren** (city) Trumbull County
120	4165	95.8	**Warrensville Heights** (city) Cuyahoga County
121	4201	95.9	**Cuyahoga Falls** (city) Summit County
122	4221	96.0	**Delaware** (city) Delaware County
122	4221	96.0	**Sandusky** (city) Erie County
122	4221	96.0	**Wadsworth** (city) Medina County
125	4245	96.1	**Bellefontaine** (city) Logan County
125	4245	96.1	**Portsmouth** (city) Scioto County
125	4245	96.1	**Streetsboro** (city) Portage County
128	4271	96.2	**Tallmadge** (city) Summit County
128	4271	96.2	**Tiffin** (city) Seneca County
128	4271	96.2	**White Oak** (CDP) Hamilton County
131	4294	96.3	**Amherst** (city) Lorain County
131	4294	96.3	**Elyria** (city) Lorain County
131	4294	96.3	**Monfort Heights** (CDP) Hamilton County
131	4294	96.3	**New Philadelphia** (city) Tuscarawas County
131	4294	96.3	**Niles** (city) Trumbull County
131	4294	96.3	**Sidney** (city) Shelby County
137	4319	96.4	**Maumee** (city) Lucas County
137	4319	96.4	**Washington Court House** (city) Fayette County
139	4339	96.5	**Dent** (CDP) Hamilton County
139	4339	96.5	**North Canton** (city) Stark County
141	4356	96.6	**Chillicothe** (city) Ross County
142	4375	96.7	**Bridgetown** (CDP) Hamilton County
142	4375	96.7	**Fostoria** (city) Seneca County
142	4375	96.7	**Mansfield** (city) Richland County
142	4375	96.7	**Maple Heights** (city) Cuyahoga County
142	4375	96.7	**Pataskala** (city) Licking County
142	4375	96.7	**Wilmington** (city) Clinton County
148	4403	96.8	**Conneaut** (city) Ashtabula County
148	4403	96.8	**Marietta** (city) Washington County
148	4403	96.8	**Northbrook** (CDP) Hamilton County

Note: *The state column ranks the top/bottom 150 places from all places in the state with population of 10,000 or more. The national column ranks the top/bottom 150 places from all places in the country with population of 10,000 or more. Places that are unincorporated were not considered in the rankings. Please refer to the User Guide for additional information.*

Population with a Disability

Top 150 Places Ranked in *Descending* Order

State Rank	Nat'l Rank	Percent	Place
1	16	25.0	**Ironton** (city) Lawrence County
2	23	23.9	**Portsmouth** (city) Scioto County
3	58	22.0	**Zanesville** (city) Muskingum County
4	61	21.8	**East Cleveland** (city) Cuyahoga County
4	61	21.8	**East Liverpool** (city) Columbiana County
6	74	21.6	**Chillicothe** (city) Ross County
7	96	20.9	**Youngstown** (city) Mahoning County
8	103	20.7	**Cambridge** (city) Guernsey County
9	118	20.4	**Circleville** (city) Pickaway County
10	148	20.0	**Washington Court House** (city) Fayette County
11	157	19.9	**Marietta** (city) Washington County
12	176	19.7	**Galion** (city) Crawford County
13	195	19.5	**Bellefontaine** (city) Logan County
13	195	19.5	**Marion** (city) Marion County
15	211	19.3	**Middletown** (city) Butler County
15	211	19.3	**Ravenna** (city) Portage County
17	220	19.2	**Greenville** (city) Darke County
18	228	19.1	**Cleveland** (city) Cuyahoga County
19	239	19.0	**Dayton** (city) Montgomery County
19	239	19.0	**Trotwood** (city) Montgomery County
21	258	18.8	**Lancaster** (city) Fairfield County
22	280	18.6	**Lorain** (city) Lorain County
22	280	18.6	**Mount Vernon** (city) Knox County
22	280	18.6	**Struthers** (city) Mahoning County
25	310	18.3	**Franklin** (city) Warren County
25	310	18.3	**Springfield** (city) Clark County
27	327	18.1	**Mansfield** (city) Richland County
28	332	18.0	**Sandusky** (city) Erie County
29	349	17.9	**Niles** (city) Trumbull County
30	357	17.8	**Salem** (city) Columbiana County
31	377	17.7	**Lima** (city) Allen County
32	384	17.6	**Bucyrus** (city) Crawford County
33	399	17.5	**Newark** (city) Licking County
33	399	17.5	**Urbana** (city) Champaign County
35	425	17.3	**Toledo** (city) Lucas County
36	466	17.0	**Ashtabula** (city) Ashtabula County
36	466	17.0	**Fostoria** (city) Seneca County
38	481	16.9	**Whitehall** (city) Franklin County
39	499	16.8	**Canton** (city) Stark County
39	499	16.8	**Heath** (city) Licking County
41	515	16.7	**Warren** (city) Trumbull County
42	536	16.6	**Steubenville** (city) Jefferson County
43	555	16.5	**Massillon** (city) Stark County
44	576	16.4	**Van Wert** (city) Van Wert County
45	593	16.3	**Alliance** (city) Stark County
45	593	16.3	**Riverside** (city) Montgomery County
47	610	16.2	**Maple Heights** (city) Cuyahoga County
47	610	16.2	**Xenia** (city) Greene County
49	632	16.1	**Parma Heights** (city) Cuyahoga County
50	658	16.0	**Barberton** (city) Summit County
50	658	16.0	**Norwood** (city) Hamilton County
50	658	16.0	**Piqua** (city) Miami County
53	699	15.8	**Elyria** (city) Lorain County
53	699	15.8	**Reading** (city) Hamilton County
55	774	15.5	**Euclid** (city) Cuyahoga County
56	791	15.4	**Bedford Heights** (city) Cuyahoga County
56	791	15.4	**Brook Park** (city) Cuyahoga County
56	791	15.4	**Defiance** (city) Defiance County
56	791	15.4	**Fairborn** (city) Greene County
56	791	15.4	**West Carrollton** (city) Montgomery County
56	791	15.4	**Wilmington** (city) Clinton County
62	839	15.2	**Austintown** (CDP) Mahoning County
62	839	15.2	**Coshocton** (city) Coshocton County
62	839	15.2	**Fremont** (city) Sandusky County
62	839	15.2	**Hamilton** (city) Butler County
66	869	15.1	**Akron** (city) Summit County
66	869	15.1	**Tiffin** (city) Seneca County
68	899	15.0	**Sidney** (city) Shelby County
69	920	14.9	**Celina** (city) Mercer County
69	920	14.9	**Norwalk** (city) Huron County
71	1007	14.5	**Garfield Heights** (city) Cuyahoga County
71	1007	14.5	**Huber Heights** (city) Montgomery County
73	1031	14.4	**Oregon** (city) Lucas County
74	1058	14.3	**Wickliffe** (city) Lake County
75	1086	14.2	**Centerville** (city) Montgomery County
75	1086	14.2	**Parma** (city) Cuyahoga County
77	1119	14.1	**Brooklyn** (city) Cuyahoga County
77	1119	14.1	**Conneaut** (city) Ashtabula County
77	1119	14.1	**Miamisburg** (city) Montgomery County
80	1145	14.0	**Cincinnati** (city) Hamilton County
80	1145	14.0	**Painesville** (city) Lake County
82	1177	13.9	**Bedford** (city) Cuyahoga County
83	1201	13.8	**Englewood** (city) Montgomery County
84	1298	13.5	**Seven Hills** (city) Cuyahoga County
85	1324	13.4	**Sharonville** (city) Hamilton County
86	1347	13.3	**Ashland** (city) Ashland County
86	1347	13.3	**Forestville** (CDP) Hamilton County
86	1347	13.3	**New Philadelphia** (city) Tuscarawas County
86	1347	13.3	**Northbrook** (CDP) Hamilton County
90	1393	13.2	**Berea** (city) Cuyahoga County
91	1426	13.1	**Dover** (city) Tuscarawas County
92	1458	13.0	**Boardman** (CDP) Mahoning County
92	1458	13.0	**Findlay** (city) Hancock County
92	1458	13.0	**Mayfield Heights** (city) Cuyahoga County
92	1458	13.0	**Trenton** (city) Butler County
96	1489	12.9	**Cuyahoga Falls** (city) Summit County
97	1522	12.8	**Grove City** (city) Franklin County
97	1522	12.8	**Troy** (city) Miami County
97	1522	12.8	**Warrensville Heights** (city) Cuyahoga County
100	1554	12.7	**Forest Park** (city) Hamilton County
100	1554	12.7	**Kettering** (city) Montgomery County
100	1554	12.7	**Willowick** (city) Lake County
103	1580	12.6	**Norton** (city) Summit County
103	1580	12.6	**Vermilion** (city) Lorain County
105	1655	12.4	**Eastlake** (city) Lake County
105	1655	12.4	**Middleburg Heights** (city) Cuyahoga County
105	1655	12.4	**North Olmsted** (city) Cuyahoga County
105	1655	12.4	**Pataskala** (city) Licking County
105	1655	12.4	**Springdale** (city) Hamilton County
110	1705	12.3	**Wooster** (city) Wayne County
111	1744	12.2	**Clayton** (city) Montgomery County
112	1788	12.1	**Bridgetown** (CDP) Hamilton County
112	1788	12.1	**Tallmadge** (city) Summit County
112	1788	12.1	**Vandalia** (city) Montgomery County
115	1824	12.0	**Lakewood** (city) Cuyahoga County
115	1824	12.0	**New Franklin** (city) Summit County
115	1824	12.0	**North Canton** (city) Stark County
118	1912	11.8	**Columbus** (city) Franklin County
118	1912	11.8	**Richmond Heights** (city) Cuyahoga County
120	1952	11.7	**Marysville** (city) Union County
120	1952	11.7	**Willoughby** (city) Lake County
122	2049	11.5	**White Oak** (CDP) Hamilton County
123	2082	11.4	**Amherst** (city) Lorain County
124	2134	11.3	**Mentor** (city) Lake County
125	2178	11.2	**North Royalton** (city) Cuyahoga County
125	2178	11.2	**Reynoldsburg** (city) Franklin County
127	2220	11.1	**Beachwood** (city) Cuyahoga County
127	2220	11.1	**Cleveland Heights** (city) Cuyahoga County
127	2220	11.1	**Mack** (CDP) Hamilton County
127	2220	11.1	**Monfort Heights** (CDP) Hamilton County
131	2256	11.0	**Brecksville** (city) Cuyahoga County
132	2307	10.9	**Medina** (city) Medina County
133	2395	10.7	**Green** (city) Summit County
134	2439	10.6	**Maumee** (city) Lucas County
134	2439	10.6	**Monroe** (city) Butler County
136	2495	10.5	**Delaware** (city) Delaware County
136	2495	10.5	**Gahanna** (city) Franklin County
136	2495	10.5	**Lyndhurst** (city) Cuyahoga County
139	2544	10.4	**Fairview Park** (city) Cuyahoga County
140	2599	10.3	**Dent** (CDP) Hamilton County
140	2599	10.3	**Finneytown** (CDP) Hamilton County
142	2684	10.1	**Avon Lake** (city) Lorain County
142	2684	10.1	**Sylvania** (city) Lucas County
144	2731	10.0	**Aurora** (city) Portage County
144	2731	10.0	**South Euclid** (city) Cuyahoga County
146	2772	9.9	**Lebanon** (city) Warren County
147	2831	9.8	**Beavercreek** (city) Greene County
147	2831	9.8	**Macedonia** (city) Summit County
149	2917	9.6	**North Ridgeville** (city) Lorain County
149	2917	9.6	**Streetsboro** (city) Portage County

Note: *The state column ranks the top/bottom 150 places from all places in the state with population of 10,000 or more. The national column ranks the top/bottom 150 places from all places in the country with population of 10,000 or more. Places that are unincorporated were not considered in the rankings. Please refer to the User Guide for additional information.*

Population with a Disability

Top 150 Places Ranked in *Ascending* Order

State Rank	Nat'l Rank	Percent	Place
1	54	4.6	**Powell** (city) Delaware County
2	128	5.3	**Dublin** (city) Franklin County
3	159	5.5	**Athens** (city) Athens County
3	159	5.5	**Pickerington** (city) Fairfield County
5	305	6.3	**Hudson** (city) Summit County
6	358	6.5	**Oxford** (city) Butler County
7	386	6.6	**Springboro** (city) Warren County
8	435	6.8	**Bowling Green** (city) Wood County
9	550	7.2	**Bexley** (city) Franklin County
9	550	7.2	**Hilliard** (city) Franklin County
9	550	7.2	**Mason** (city) Warren County
12	624	7.4	**Worthington** (city) Franklin County
13	669	7.5	**Solon** (city) Cuyahoga County
14	903	8.0	**Upper Arlington** (city) Franklin County
15	953	8.1	**Avon** (city) Lorain County
16	1041	8.3	**Bay Village** (city) Cuyahoga County
16	1041	8.3	**Broadview Heights** (city) Cuyahoga County
16	1041	8.3	**Perrysburg** (city) Wood County
19	1127	8.5	**Shaker Heights** (city) Cuyahoga County
19	1127	8.5	**University Heights** (city) Cuyahoga County
21	1168	8.6	**Blue Ash** (city) Hamilton County
21	1168	8.6	**Loveland** (city) Hamilton County
21	1168	8.6	**Montgomery** (city) Hamilton County
21	1168	8.6	**Twinsburg** (city) Summit County
25	1373	9.0	**Fairfield** (city) Butler County
26	1468	9.2	**Brunswick** (city) Medina County
26	1468	9.2	**Strongsville** (city) Cuyahoga County
28	1527	9.3	**Kent** (city) Portage County
29	1567	9.4	**Stow** (city) Summit County
29	1567	9.4	**Wadsworth** (city) Medina County
31	1625	9.5	**Rocky River** (city) Cuyahoga County
31	1625	9.5	**Westerville** (city) Franklin County
33	1680	9.6	**North Ridgeville** (city) Lorain County
33	1680	9.6	**Streetsboro** (city) Portage County
33	1680	9.6	**Westlake** (city) Cuyahoga County
36	1773	9.8	**Beavercreek** (city) Greene County
36	1773	9.8	**Macedonia** (city) Summit County
38	1826	9.9	**Lebanon** (city) Warren County
39	1885	10.0	**Aurora** (city) Portage County
39	1885	10.0	**South Euclid** (city) Cuyahoga County
41	1926	10.1	**Avon Lake** (city) Lorain County
41	1926	10.1	**Sylvania** (city) Lucas County
43	2012	10.3	**Dent** (CDP) Hamilton County
43	2012	10.3	**Finneytown** (CDP) Hamilton County
45	2058	10.4	**Fairview Park** (city) Cuyahoga County
46	2113	10.5	**Delaware** (city) Delaware County
46	2113	10.5	**Gahanna** (city) Franklin County
46	2113	10.5	**Lyndhurst** (city) Cuyahoga County
49	2162	10.6	**Maumee** (city) Lucas County
49	2162	10.6	**Monroe** (city) Butler County
51	2218	10.7	**Green** (city) Summit County
52	2305	10.9	**Medina** (city) Medina County
53	2350	11.0	**Brecksville** (city) Cuyahoga County
54	2401	11.1	**Beachwood** (city) Cuyahoga County
54	2401	11.1	**Cleveland Heights** (city) Cuyahoga County
54	2401	11.1	**Mack** (CDP) Hamilton County
54	2401	11.1	**Monfort Heights** (CDP) Hamilton County
58	2437	11.2	**North Royalton** (city) Cuyahoga County
58	2437	11.2	**Reynoldsburg** (city) Franklin County
60	2479	11.3	**Mentor** (city) Lake County
61	2523	11.4	**Amherst** (city) Lorain County
62	2575	11.5	**White Oak** (CDP) Hamilton County
63	2661	11.7	**Marysville** (city) Union County
63	2661	11.7	**Willoughby** (city) Lake County
65	2705	11.8	**Columbus** (city) Franklin County
65	2705	11.8	**Richmond Heights** (city) Cuyahoga County
67	2785	12.0	**Lakewood** (city) Cuyahoga County
67	2785	12.0	**New Franklin** (city) Summit County
67	2785	12.0	**North Canton** (city) Stark County
70	2833	12.1	**Bridgetown** (CDP) Hamilton County
70	2833	12.1	**Tallmadge** (city) Summit County
70	2833	12.1	**Vandalia** (city) Montgomery County
73	2869	12.2	**Clayton** (city) Montgomery County
74	2913	12.3	**Wooster** (city) Wayne County
75	2952	12.4	**Eastlake** (city) Lake County
75	2952	12.4	**Middleburg Heights** (city) Cuyahoga County
75	2952	12.4	**North Olmsted** (city) Cuyahoga County
75	2952	12.4	**Pataskala** (city) Licking County
75	2952	12.4	**Springdale** (city) Hamilton County
80	3039	12.6	**Norton** (city) Summit County
80	3039	12.6	**Vermilion** (city) Lorain County
82	3077	12.7	**Forest Park** (city) Hamilton County
82	3077	12.7	**Kettering** (city) Montgomery County
82	3077	12.7	**Willowick** (city) Lake County
85	3103	12.8	**Grove City** (city) Franklin County
85	3103	12.8	**Troy** (city) Miami County
85	3103	12.8	**Warrensville Heights** (city) Cuyahoga County
88	3135	12.9	**Cuyahoga Falls** (city) Summit County
89	3168	13.0	**Boardman** (CDP) Mahoning County
89	3168	13.0	**Findlay** (city) Hancock County
89	3168	13.0	**Mayfield Heights** (city) Cuyahoga County
89	3168	13.0	**Trenton** (city) Butler County
93	3199	13.1	**Dover** (city) Tuscarawas County
94	3231	13.2	**Berea** (city) Cuyahoga County
95	3264	13.3	**Ashland** (city) Ashland County
95	3264	13.3	**Forestville** (CDP) Hamilton County
95	3264	13.3	**New Philadelphia** (city) Tuscarawas County
95	3264	13.3	**Northbrook** (CDP) Hamilton County
99	3310	13.4	**Sharonville** (city) Hamilton County
100	3333	13.5	**Seven Hills** (city) Cuyahoga County
101	3429	13.8	**Englewood** (city) Montgomery County
102	3456	13.9	**Bedford** (city) Cuyahoga County
103	3480	14.0	**Cincinnati** (city) Hamilton County
103	3480	14.0	**Painesville** (city) Lake County
105	3512	14.1	**Brooklyn** (city) Cuyahoga County
105	3512	14.1	**Conneaut** (city) Ashtabula County
105	3512	14.1	**Miamisburg** (city) Montgomery County
108	3538	14.2	**Centerville** (city) Montgomery County
108	3538	14.2	**Parma** (city) Cuyahoga County
110	3571	14.3	**Wickliffe** (city) Lake County
111	3599	14.4	**Oregon** (city) Lucas County
112	3626	14.5	**Garfield Heights** (city) Cuyahoga County
112	3626	14.5	**Huber Heights** (city) Montgomery County
114	3714	14.9	**Celina** (city) Mercer County
114	3714	14.9	**Norwalk** (city) Huron County
116	3737	15.0	**Sidney** (city) Shelby County
117	3758	15.1	**Akron** (city) Summit County
117	3758	15.1	**Tiffin** (city) Seneca County
119	3788	15.2	**Austintown** (CDP) Mahoning County
119	3788	15.2	**Coshocton** (city) Coshocton County
119	3788	15.2	**Fremont** (city) Sandusky County
119	3788	15.2	**Hamilton** (city) Butler County
123	3837	15.4	**Bedford Heights** (city) Cuyahoga County
123	3837	15.4	**Brook Park** (city) Cuyahoga County
123	3837	15.4	**Defiance** (city) Defiance County
123	3837	15.4	**Fairborn** (city) Greene County
123	3837	15.4	**West Carrollton** (city) Montgomery County
123	3837	15.4	**Wilmington** (city) Clinton County
129	3866	15.5	**Euclid** (city) Cuyahoga County
130	3940	15.8	**Elyria** (city) Lorain County
130	3940	15.8	**Reading** (city) Hamilton County
132	3976	16.0	**Barberton** (city) Summit County
132	3976	16.0	**Norwood** (city) Hamilton County
132	3976	16.0	**Piqua** (city) Miami County
135	3999	16.1	**Parma Heights** (city) Cuyahoga County
136	4025	16.2	**Maple Heights** (city) Cuyahoga County
136	4025	16.2	**Xenia** (city) Greene County
138	4047	16.3	**Alliance** (city) Stark County
138	4047	16.3	**Riverside** (city) Montgomery County
140	4064	16.4	**Van Wert** (city) Van Wert County
141	4081	16.5	**Massillon** (city) Stark County
142	4102	16.6	**Steubenville** (city) Jefferson County
143	4121	16.7	**Warren** (city) Trumbull County
144	4142	16.8	**Canton** (city) Stark County
144	4142	16.8	**Heath** (city) Licking County
146	4158	16.9	**Whitehall** (city) Franklin County
147	4176	17.0	**Ashtabula** (city) Ashtabula County
147	4176	17.0	**Fostoria** (city) Seneca County
149	4221	17.3	**Toledo** (city) Lucas County
150	4243	17.5	**Newark** (city) Licking County

***Note:** The state column ranks the top/bottom 150 places from all places in the state with population of 10,000 or more. The national column ranks the top/bottom 150 places from all places in the country with population of 10,000 or more. Places that are unincorporated were not considered in the rankings. Please refer to the User Guide for additional information.*

Veterans

Top 150 Places Ranked in *Descending* Order

State Rank	Nat'l Rank	Percent	Place
1	86	19.1	**Beavercreek** (city) Greene County
2	194	15.9	**Riverside** (city) Montgomery County
3	214	15.5	**Huber Heights** (city) Montgomery County
4	307	14.2	**Fairborn** (city) Greene County
5	401	13.3	**Englewood** (city) Montgomery County
6	416	13.2	**Austintown** (CDP) Mahoning County
6	416	13.2	**Monroe** (city) Butler County
8	429	13.1	**Dover** (city) Tuscarawas County
9	482	12.8	**Cambridge** (city) Guernsey County
9	482	12.8	**Fostoria** (city) Seneca County
11	499	12.7	**Wickliffe** (city) Lake County
12	518	12.6	**Franklin** (city) Warren County
12	518	12.6	**Heath** (city) Licking County
12	518	12.6	**Salem** (city) Columbiana County
12	518	12.6	**Vermilion** (city) Lorain County
16	566	12.4	**Centerville** (city) Montgomery County
16	566	12.4	**Conneaut** (city) Ashtabula County
16	566	12.4	**Northbrook** (CDP) Hamilton County
19	586	12.3	**Chillicothe** (city) Ross County
20	603	12.2	**Bedford** (city) Cuyahoga County
20	603	12.2	**Bedford Heights** (city) Cuyahoga County
20	603	12.2	**Clayton** (city) Montgomery County
20	603	12.2	**Coshocton** (city) Coshocton County
20	603	12.2	**New Philadelphia** (city) Tuscarawas County
25	629	12.1	**Brooklyn** (city) Cuyahoga County
25	629	12.1	**New Franklin** (city) Summit County
25	629	12.1	**Norwalk** (city) Huron County
28	652	12.0	**Pataskala** (city) Licking County
29	675	11.9	**East Liverpool** (city) Columbiana County
29	675	11.9	**Springboro** (city) Warren County
31	720	11.7	**Miamisburg** (city) Montgomery County
32	756	11.6	**Brook Park** (city) Cuyahoga County
32	756	11.6	**Bucyrus** (city) Crawford County
32	756	11.6	**Lancaster** (city) Fairfield County
32	756	11.6	**Massillon** (city) Stark County
32	756	11.6	**Trotwood** (city) Montgomery County
37	796	11.5	**Marietta** (city) Washington County
37	796	11.5	**Sharonville** (city) Hamilton County
39	831	11.4	**Celina** (city) Mercer County
39	831	11.4	**Circleville** (city) Pickaway County
39	831	11.4	**Mansfield** (city) Richland County
39	831	11.4	**Tallmadge** (city) Summit County
43	900	11.2	**Amherst** (city) Lorain County
43	900	11.2	**North Canton** (city) Stark County
45	933	11.1	**Springfield** (city) Clark County
45	933	11.1	**Xenia** (city) Greene County
47	976	11.0	**Finneytown** (CDP) Hamilton County
47	976	11.0	**Newark** (city) Licking County
47	976	11.0	**Wadsworth** (city) Medina County
50	1016	10.9	**Aurora** (city) Portage County
50	1016	10.9	**Forestville** (CDP) Hamilton County
50	1016	10.9	**Macedonia** (city) Summit County
50	1016	10.9	**Rocky River** (city) Cuyahoga County
50	1016	10.9	**Seven Hills** (city) Cuyahoga County
50	1016	10.9	**Urbana** (city) Champaign County
50	1016	10.9	**Vandalia** (city) Montgomery County
57	1065	10.8	**Troy** (city) Miami County
58	1118	10.7	**Elyria** (city) Lorain County
58	1118	10.7	**Garfield Heights** (city) Cuyahoga County
58	1118	10.7	**Marion** (city) Marion County
58	1118	10.7	**Medina** (city) Medina County
58	1118	10.7	**Sandusky** (city) Erie County
58	1118	10.7	**Van Wert** (city) Van Wert County
64	1169	10.6	**Boardman** (CDP) Mahoning County
64	1169	10.6	**Kettering** (city) Montgomery County
64	1169	10.6	**Niles** (city) Trumbull County
67	1222	10.5	**Brecksville** (city) Cuyahoga County
67	1222	10.5	**Eastlake** (city) Lake County
67	1222	10.5	**Piqua** (city) Miami County
70	1272	10.4	**Canton** (city) Stark County
70	1272	10.4	**Mentor** (city) Lake County
70	1272	10.4	**Springdale** (city) Hamilton County
70	1272	10.4	**Warren** (city) Trumbull County
74	1328	10.3	**Defiance** (city) Defiance County
74	1328	10.3	**Maple Heights** (city) Cuyahoga County
74	1328	10.3	**Norton** (city) Summit County
74	1328	10.3	**Reading** (city) Hamilton County
78	1386	10.2	**Avon Lake** (city) Lorain County
78	1386	10.2	**Bridgetown** (CDP) Hamilton County
78	1386	10.2	**Pickerington** (city) Fairfield County
78	1386	10.2	**Tiffin** (city) Seneca County
78	1386	10.2	**Washington Court House** (city) Fayette County
83	1445	10.1	**Steubenville** (city) Jefferson County
84	1492	10.0	**Forest Park** (city) Hamilton County
84	1492	10.0	**Hamilton** (city) Butler County
84	1492	10.0	**Middleburg Heights** (city) Cuyahoga County
84	1492	10.0	**Portsmouth** (city) Scioto County
84	1492	10.0	**Reynoldsburg** (city) Franklin County
84	1492	10.0	**Warrensville Heights** (city) Cuyahoga County
84	1492	10.0	**White Oak** (CDP) Hamilton County
84	1492	10.0	**Wilmington** (city) Clinton County
92	1565	9.9	**Ashtabula** (city) Ashtabula County
92	1565	9.9	**Bay Village** (city) Cuyahoga County
92	1565	9.9	**Blue Ash** (city) Hamilton County
92	1565	9.9	**Cuyahoga Falls** (city) Summit County
92	1565	9.9	**Delaware** (city) Delaware County
92	1565	9.9	**Ironton** (city) Lawrence County
92	1565	9.9	**Middletown** (city) Butler County
92	1565	9.9	**Richmond Heights** (city) Cuyahoga County
92	1565	9.9	**Trenton** (city) Butler County
101	1640	9.8	**Findlay** (city) Hancock County
101	1640	9.8	**Streetsboro** (city) Portage County
101	1640	9.8	**Willowick** (city) Lake County
101	1640	9.8	**Youngstown** (city) Mahoning County
105	1706	9.7	**Mount Vernon** (city) Knox County
106	1770	9.6	**Akron** (city) Summit County
106	1770	9.6	**Barberton** (city) Summit County
106	1770	9.6	**Green** (city) Summit County
106	1770	9.6	**North Ridgeville** (city) Lorain County
106	1770	9.6	**Sidney** (city) Shelby County
106	1770	9.6	**Stow** (city) Summit County
112	1832	9.5	**Alliance** (city) Stark County
112	1832	9.5	**Brunswick** (city) Medina County
112	1832	9.5	**Grove City** (city) Franklin County
112	1832	9.5	**Oregon** (city) Lucas County
116	1897	9.4	**Ashland** (city) Ashland County
116	1897	9.4	**Euclid** (city) Cuyahoga County
116	1897	9.4	**Lebanon** (city) Warren County
116	1897	9.4	**Lorain** (city) Lorain County
116	1897	9.4	**Parma** (city) Cuyahoga County
116	1897	9.4	**Willoughby** (city) Lake County
122	1977	9.3	**East Cleveland** (city) Cuyahoga County
122	1977	9.3	**Monfort Heights** (CDP) Hamilton County
122	1977	9.3	**North Olmsted** (city) Cuyahoga County
122	1977	9.3	**Parma Heights** (city) Cuyahoga County
122	1977	9.3	**West Carrollton** (city) Montgomery County
127	2103	9.1	**Avon** (city) Lorain County
127	2103	9.1	**Fairfield** (city) Butler County
127	2103	9.1	**Lima** (city) Allen County
127	2103	9.1	**Maumee** (city) Lucas County
131	2178	9.0	**Beachwood** (city) Cuyahoga County
131	2178	9.0	**Dayton** (city) Montgomery County
131	2178	9.0	**Fremont** (city) Sandusky County
131	2178	9.0	**Westerville** (city) Franklin County
135	2253	8.9	**Dent** (CDP) Hamilton County
135	2253	8.9	**Galion** (city) Crawford County
135	2253	8.9	**Sylvania** (city) Lucas County
135	2253	8.9	**Wooster** (city) Wayne County
139	2312	8.8	**Marysville** (city) Union County
139	2312	8.8	**North Royalton** (city) Cuyahoga County
139	2312	8.8	**Westlake** (city) Cuyahoga County
139	2312	8.8	**Zanesville** (city) Muskingum County
143	2383	8.7	**Norwood** (city) Hamilton County
144	2468	8.6	**Lyndhurst** (city) Cuyahoga County
145	2535	8.5	**Struthers** (city) Mahoning County
146	2599	8.4	**Gahanna** (city) Franklin County
146	2599	8.4	**Loveland** (city) Hamilton County
146	2599	8.4	**Ravenna** (city) Portage County
146	2599	8.4	**Strongsville** (city) Cuyahoga County
146	2599	8.4	**Toledo** (city) Lucas County

Note: *The state column ranks the top/bottom 150 places from all places in the state with population of 10,000 or more. The national column ranks the top/bottom 150 places from all places in the country with population of 10,000 or more. Places that are unincorporated were not considered in the rankings. Please refer to the User Guide for additional information.*

Veterans

Top 150 Places Ranked in *Ascending* Order

State Rank	Nat'l Rank	Percent	Place
1	60	2.3	**Athens** (city) Athens County
2	92	2.8	**Oxford** (city) Butler County
3	360	4.7	**Bexley** (city) Franklin County
4	382	4.8	**Kent** (city) Portage County
5	399	4.9	**Bowling Green** (city) Wood County
6	429	5.0	**University Heights** (city) Cuyahoga County
7	482	5.2	**Powell** (city) Delaware County
8	868	6.2	**South Euclid** (city) Cuyahoga County
9	1064	6.7	**Shaker Heights** (city) Cuyahoga County
10	1119	6.8	**Dublin** (city) Franklin County
11	1179	6.9	**Cleveland Heights** (city) Cuyahoga County
11	1179	6.9	**Solon** (city) Cuyahoga County
13	1230	7.0	**Cincinnati** (city) Hamilton County
14	1286	7.1	**Twinsburg** (city) Summit County
15	1344	7.2	**Columbus** (city) Franklin County
15	1344	7.2	**Painesville** (city) Lake County
17	1443	7.4	**Bellefontaine** (city) Logan County
17	1443	7.4	**Upper Arlington** (city) Franklin County
19	1507	7.5	**Hudson** (city) Summit County
20	1599	7.7	**Hilliard** (city) Franklin County
20	1599	7.7	**Mayfield Heights** (city) Cuyahoga County
22	1661	7.8	**Mason** (city) Warren County
23	1710	7.9	**Montgomery** (city) Hamilton County
23	1710	7.9	**Perrysburg** (city) Wood County
25	1763	8.0	**Berea** (city) Cuyahoga County
25	1763	8.0	**Worthington** (city) Franklin County
27	1822	8.1	**Broadview Heights** (city) Cuyahoga County
27	1822	8.1	**Lakewood** (city) Cuyahoga County
29	1876	8.2	**Whitehall** (city) Franklin County
30	1930	8.3	**Cleveland** (city) Cuyahoga County
30	1930	8.3	**Fairview Park** (city) Cuyahoga County
30	1930	8.3	**Greenville** (city) Darke County
30	1930	8.3	**Mack** (CDP) Hamilton County
34	1991	8.4	**Gahanna** (city) Franklin County
34	1991	8.4	**Loveland** (city) Hamilton County
34	1991	8.4	**Ravenna** (city) Portage County
34	1991	8.4	**Strongsville** (city) Cuyahoga County
34	1991	8.4	**Toledo** (city) Lucas County
39	2058	8.5	**Struthers** (city) Mahoning County
40	2122	8.6	**Lyndhurst** (city) Cuyahoga County
41	2189	8.7	**Norwood** (city) Hamilton County
42	2274	8.8	**Marysville** (city) Union County
42	2274	8.8	**North Royalton** (city) Cuyahoga County
42	2274	8.8	**Westlake** (city) Cuyahoga County
42	2274	8.8	**Zanesville** (city) Muskingum County
46	2345	8.9	**Dent** (CDP) Hamilton County
46	2345	8.9	**Galion** (city) Crawford County
46	2345	8.9	**Sylvania** (city) Lucas County
46	2345	8.9	**Wooster** (city) Wayne County
50	2404	9.0	**Beachwood** (city) Cuyahoga County
50	2404	9.0	**Dayton** (city) Montgomery County
50	2404	9.0	**Fremont** (city) Sandusky County
50	2404	9.0	**Westerville** (city) Franklin County
54	2479	9.1	**Avon** (city) Lorain County
54	2479	9.1	**Fairfield** (city) Butler County
54	2479	9.1	**Lima** (city) Allen County
54	2479	9.1	**Maumee** (city) Lucas County
58	2615	9.3	**East Cleveland** (city) Cuyahoga County
58	2615	9.3	**Monfort Heights** (CDP) Hamilton County
58	2615	9.3	**North Olmsted** (city) Cuyahoga County
58	2615	9.3	**Parma Heights** (city) Cuyahoga County
58	2615	9.3	**West Carrollton** (city) Montgomery County
63	2680	9.4	**Ashland** (city) Ashland County
63	2680	9.4	**Euclid** (city) Cuyahoga County
63	2680	9.4	**Lebanon** (city) Warren County
63	2680	9.4	**Lorain** (city) Lorain County
63	2680	9.4	**Parma** (city) Cuyahoga County
63	2680	9.4	**Willoughby** (city) Lake County
69	2760	9.5	**Alliance** (city) Stark County
69	2760	9.5	**Brunswick** (city) Medina County
69	2760	9.5	**Grove City** (city) Franklin County
69	2760	9.5	**Oregon** (city) Lucas County
73	2825	9.6	**Akron** (city) Summit County
73	2825	9.6	**Barberton** (city) Summit County
73	2825	9.6	**Green** (city) Summit County
73	2825	9.6	**North Ridgeville** (city) Lorain County
73	2825	9.6	**Sidney** (city) Shelby County
73	2825	9.6	**Stow** (city) Summit County
79	2887	9.7	**Mount Vernon** (city) Knox County
80	2951	9.8	**Findlay** (city) Hancock County
80	2951	9.8	**Streetsboro** (city) Portage County
80	2951	9.8	**Willowick** (city) Lake County
80	2951	9.8	**Youngstown** (city) Mahoning County
84	3017	9.9	**Ashtabula** (city) Ashtabula County
84	3017	9.9	**Bay Village** (city) Cuyahoga County
84	3017	9.9	**Blue Ash** (city) Hamilton County
84	3017	9.9	**Cuyahoga Falls** (city) Summit County
84	3017	9.9	**Delaware** (city) Delaware County
84	3017	9.9	**Ironton** (city) Lawrence County
84	3017	9.9	**Middletown** (city) Butler County
84	3017	9.9	**Richmond Heights** (city) Cuyahoga County
84	3017	9.9	**Trenton** (city) Butler County
93	3092	10.0	**Forest Park** (city) Hamilton County
93	3092	10.0	**Hamilton** (city) Butler County
93	3092	10.0	**Middleburg Heights** (city) Cuyahoga County
93	3092	10.0	**Portsmouth** (city) Scioto County
93	3092	10.0	**Reynoldsburg** (city) Franklin County
93	3092	10.0	**Warrensville Heights** (city) Cuyahoga County
93	3092	10.0	**White Oak** (CDP) Hamilton County
93	3092	10.0	**Wilmington** (city) Clinton County
101	3165	10.1	**Steubenville** (city) Jefferson County
102	3212	10.2	**Avon Lake** (city) Lorain County
102	3212	10.2	**Bridgetown** (CDP) Hamilton County
102	3212	10.2	**Pickerington** (city) Fairfield County
102	3212	10.2	**Tiffin** (city) Seneca County
102	3212	10.2	**Washington Court House** (city) Fayette County
107	3271	10.3	**Defiance** (city) Defiance County
107	3271	10.3	**Maple Heights** (city) Cuyahoga County
107	3271	10.3	**Norton** (city) Summit County
107	3271	10.3	**Reading** (city) Hamilton County
111	3329	10.4	**Canton** (city) Stark County
111	3329	10.4	**Mentor** (city) Lake County
111	3329	10.4	**Springdale** (city) Hamilton County
111	3329	10.4	**Warren** (city) Trumbull County
115	3385	10.5	**Brecksville** (city) Cuyahoga County
115	3385	10.5	**Eastlake** (city) Lake County
115	3385	10.5	**Piqua** (city) Miami County
118	3435	10.6	**Boardman** (CDP) Mahoning County
118	3435	10.6	**Kettering** (city) Montgomery County
118	3435	10.6	**Niles** (city) Trumbull County
121	3488	10.7	**Elyria** (city) Lorain County
121	3488	10.7	**Garfield Heights** (city) Cuyahoga County
121	3488	10.7	**Marion** (city) Marion County
121	3488	10.7	**Medina** (city) Medina County
121	3488	10.7	**Sandusky** (city) Erie County
121	3488	10.7	**Van Wert** (city) Van Wert County
127	3539	10.8	**Troy** (city) Miami County
128	3592	10.9	**Aurora** (city) Portage County
128	3592	10.9	**Forestville** (CDP) Hamilton County
128	3592	10.9	**Macedonia** (city) Summit County
128	3592	10.9	**Rocky River** (city) Cuyahoga County
128	3592	10.9	**Seven Hills** (city) Cuyahoga County
128	3592	10.9	**Urbana** (city) Champaign County
128	3592	10.9	**Vandalia** (city) Montgomery County
135	3641	11.0	**Finneytown** (CDP) Hamilton County
135	3641	11.0	**Newark** (city) Licking County
135	3641	11.0	**Wadsworth** (city) Medina County
138	3681	11.1	**Springfield** (city) Clark County
138	3681	11.1	**Xenia** (city) Greene County
140	3724	11.2	**Amherst** (city) Lorain County
140	3724	11.2	**North Canton** (city) Stark County
142	3799	11.4	**Celina** (city) Mercer County
142	3799	11.4	**Circleville** (city) Pickaway County
142	3799	11.4	**Mansfield** (city) Richland County
142	3799	11.4	**Tallmadge** (city) Summit County
146	3826	11.5	**Marietta** (city) Washington County
146	3826	11.5	**Sharonville** (city) Hamilton County
148	3861	11.6	**Brook Park** (city) Cuyahoga County
148	3861	11.6	**Bucyrus** (city) Crawford County
148	3861	11.6	**Lancaster** (city) Fairfield County

Note: *The state column ranks the top/bottom 150 places from all places in the state with population of 10,000 or more. The national column ranks the top/bottom 150 places from all places in the country with population of 10,000 or more. Places that are unincorporated were not considered in the rankings. Please refer to the User Guide for additional information.*

Ancestry: German

Top 150 Places Ranked in *Descending* Order

State Rank	Nat'l Rank	Percent	Place
1	1	76.8	**Chilton** (city) Calumet County
2	2	73.3	**Barton** (town) Washington County
3	3	73.0	**Addison** (town) Washington County
4	4	72.6	**Dyersville** (city) Dubuque County
5	5	70.9	**Jackson** (town) Washington County
6	6	70.5	**Howards Grove** (village) Sheboygan County
7	7	70.3	**Mayville** (city) Dodge County
8	8	69.9	**Minster** (village) Auglaize County
9	9	69.1	**Hartford** (town) Washington County
9	9	69.1	**Polk** (town) Washington County
11	11	68.4	**Medford** (town) Taylor County
12	12	68.1	**Brillion** (city) Calumet County
13	13	67.8	**Kiel** (city) Manitowoc County
14	14	67.7	**Hortonville** (village) Outagamie County
15	15	66.9	**Wakefield** (township) Stearns County
16	16	66.1	**Center** (town) Outagamie County
17	17	66.0	**Plymouth** (town) Sheboygan County
17	17	66.0	**Sheboygan** (town) Sheboygan County
17	17	66.0	**Trenton** (town) Washington County
20	20	65.8	**Fayette** (township) Juniata County
20	20	65.8	**Wheatland** (town) Kenosha County
22	22	65.5	**Kewaskum** (village) Washington County
23	23	65.4	**Springfield** (town) Dane County
24	24	65.2	**Empire** (town) Fond du Lac County
25	25	64.8	**Mukwa** (town) Waupaca County
26	26	64.2	**Albany** (city) Stearns County
27	27	64.0	**Jackson** (village) Washington County
28	28	63.9	**New Bremen** (village) Auglaize County
29	29	63.8	**New Ulm** (city) Brown County
30	30	63.0	**Coldwater** (village) Mercer County
30	30	63.0	**West Bend** (town) Washington County
32	32	62.3	**Breese** (city) Clinton County
33	33	61.9	**Taycheedah** (town) Fond du Lac County
34	34	61.4	**Merrill** (town) Lincoln County
34	34	61.4	**New Holstein** (city) Calumet County
36	36	60.9	**Beaver Dam** (town) Dodge County
36	36	60.9	**Friendship** (town) Fond du Lac County
36	36	60.9	**Mandan** (city) Morton County
39	39	60.8	**Miami Heights** (CDP) Hamilton County
40	40	60.6	**Plymouth** (city) Sheboygan County
40	40	60.6	**Sheboygan Falls** (city) Sheboygan County
42	42	60.4	**Medford** (city) Taylor County
43	43	60.3	**Merrill** (city) Lincoln County
43	43	60.3	**Saint Marys** (city) Elk County
45	45	60.2	**Elizabeth** (township) Lancaster County
46	46	59.7	**Stettin** (town) Marathon County
47	47	59.6	**Merton** (village) Waukesha County
48	48	59.5	**Wales** (village) Waukesha County
49	49	59.4	**Dale** (town) Outagamie County
49	49	59.4	**Germantown** (village) Washington County
49	49	59.4	**Grundy Center** (city) Grundy County
49	49	59.4	**Saint Augusta** (city) Stearns County
53	53	59.3	**Columbus** (city) Columbia County
53	53	59.3	**Farmington** (town) Washington County
55	55	59.2	**Fond du Lac** (town) Fond du Lac County
55	55	59.2	**Wayne** (city) Wayne County
57	57	59.1	**Caledonia** (city) Houston County
58	58	58.9	**Ixonia** (town) Jefferson County
58	58	58.9	**Lodi** (town) Columbia County
60	60	58.3	**Horicon** (city) Dodge County
61	61	58.2	**Johnson Creek** (village) Jefferson County
62	62	58.0	**Oakland** (town) Jefferson County
62	62	58.0	**Sauk Centre** (city) Stearns County
64	64	57.8	**Richfield** (village) Washington County
65	65	57.7	**Harrison** (town) Calumet County
65	65	57.7	**Sebewaing** (township) Huron County
67	67	57.6	**Fox** (township) Elk County
67	67	57.6	**West Bend** (city) Washington County
69	69	57.4	**Grafton** (town) Ozaukee County
69	69	57.4	**Ripon** (city) Fond du Lac County
71	71	57.3	**Harrison** (city) Hamilton County
72	72	57.2	**Carroll** (city) Carroll County
72	72	57.2	**Washington** (township) Schuylkill County
74	74	57.1	**Kronenwetter** (village) Marathon County
75	75	56.9	**Ellington** (town) Outagamie County
76	76	56.8	**Norwood Young America** (city) Carver County
76	76	56.8	**Saukville** (village) Ozaukee County
78	78	56.5	**Sherwood** (village) Calumet County
78	78	56.5	**Slinger** (village) Washington County
80	80	56.4	**Delphos** (city) Allen County
80	80	56.4	**Oregon** (town) Dane County
80	80	56.4	**Shelby** (town) La Crosse County
83	83	56.3	**Lisbon** (town) Waukesha County
83	83	56.3	**Sussex** (village) Waukesha County
85	85	56.2	**Bismarck** (city) Burleigh County
85	85	56.2	**Poynette** (village) Columbia County
87	87	56.0	**Alsace** (township) Berks County
87	87	56.0	**Jordan** (city) Scott County
89	89	55.9	**Eagle** (town) Waukesha County
90	90	55.8	**Waukesha** (town) Waukesha County
91	91	55.7	**Clayton** (town) Winnebago County
91	91	55.7	**Pine Grove** (township) Schuylkill County
93	93	55.6	**Ashippun** (town) Dodge County
93	93	55.6	**Rockland** (township) Berks County
95	95	55.5	**Clintonville** (city) Waupaca County
95	95	55.5	**Pewaukee** (city) Waukesha County
95	95	55.5	**Sevastopol** (town) Door County
98	98	55.3	**Lake Crystal** (city) Blue Earth County
98	98	55.3	**Plainview** (city) Wabasha County
98	98	55.3	**Rock Rapids** (city) Lyon County
101	101	55.2	**De Witt** (city) Clinton County
101	101	55.2	**Merton** (town) Waukesha County
101	101	55.2	**Watertown** (city) Jefferson County
104	104	55.1	**Hartford** (city) Washington County
105	105	55.0	**Upper Augusta** (township) Northumberland County
106	106	54.9	**Delhi Hills** (CDP) Hamilton County
107	107	54.8	**Aberdeen** (city) Brown County
107	107	54.8	**Delafield** (town) Waukesha County
109	109	54.7	**Jamestown** (city) Stutsman County
110	110	54.6	**Cottage Grove** (town) Dane County
110	110	54.6	**Hallam** (borough) York County
110	110	54.6	**Vernon** (town) Waukesha County
113	113	54.5	**Monticello** (city) Jones County
113	113	54.5	**Mukwonago** (town) Waukesha County
115	115	54.4	**Milbank** (city) Grant County
116	116	54.3	**Beulah** (city) Mercer County
116	116	54.3	**Cross Plains** (village) Dane County
116	116	54.3	**Lima** (town) Sheboygan County
119	119	54.2	**Algoma** (city) Kewaunee County
119	119	54.2	**Cold Spring** (city) Stearns County
119	119	54.2	**Lodi** (city) Columbia County
119	119	54.2	**Monfort Heights** (CDP) Hamilton County
123	123	54.1	**Mack** (CDP) Hamilton County
123	123	54.1	**North Mankato** (city) Nicollet County
125	125	54.0	**Menasha** (town) Winnebago County
125	125	54.0	**Rome** (town) Adams County
127	127	53.9	**Hays** (city) Ellis County
128	128	53.8	**Brockway** (township) Stearns County
128	128	53.8	**Dent** (CDP) Hamilton County
128	128	53.8	**Lake Wazeecha** (CDP) Wood County
128	128	53.8	**Sleepy Eye** (city) Brown County
132	132	53.7	**Zumbrota** (city) Goodhue County
133	133	53.6	**Dickinson** (city) Stark County
134	134	53.5	**Beaver Dam** (city) Dodge County
134	134	53.5	**Fond du Lac** (city) Fond du Lac County
134	134	53.5	**Wescott** (town) Shawano County
137	137	53.4	**Eagle Point** (town) Chippewa County
137	137	53.4	**Grafton** (village) Ozaukee County
139	139	53.3	**Freeburg** (village) Saint Clair County
140	140	53.2	**Lake Wisconsin** (CDP) Columbia County
140	140	53.2	**Marshfield** (city) Wood County
142	142	53.1	**Dell Rapids** (city) Minnehaha County
142	142	53.1	**Lake Mills** (city) Jefferson County
142	142	53.1	**Muskego** (city) Waukesha County
142	142	53.1	**Oregon** (village) Dane County
142	142	53.1	**Portage** (city) Columbia County
147	147	53.0	**Hereford** (township) Berks County
147	147	53.0	**Marysville** (city) Marshall County
147	147	53.0	**North Fond du Lac** (village) Fond du Lac County
150	150	52.9	**Blackhawk** (CDP) Meade County

Note: *The state column ranks the top/bottom 150 places from all places in the state with population of 10,000 or more. The national column ranks the top/bottom 150 places from all places in the country with population of 10,000 or more. Places that are unincorporated were not considered in the rankings. Please refer to the User Guide for additional information.*

Ancestry: English

Top 150 Places Ranked in *Descending* Order

State Rank	Nat'l Rank	Percent	Place
1	1	84.4	**Hildale** (city) Washington County
2	2	66.2	**Colorado City** (town) Mohave County
3	3	42.2	**Alpine** (city) Utah County
4	4	41.5	**Fruit Heights** (city) Davis County
4	4	41.5	**Manti** (city) Sanpete County
6	6	40.8	**Highland** (city) Utah County
7	7	40.5	**Mapleton** (city) Utah County
8	8	39.1	**Beaver** (city) Beaver County
9	9	38.4	**Centerville** (city) Davis County
10	10	38.2	**Hooper** (city) Weber County
10	10	38.2	**Hopkinton** (town) Merrimack County
12	12	37.8	**Sheridan** (city) Grant County
13	13	36.9	**Santa Clara** (city) Washington County
14	14	36.0	**Saint George** (town) Knox County
15	15	35.9	**Farmingdale** (town) Kennebec County
16	16	35.7	**Bountiful** (city) Davis County
17	17	35.6	**Rockport** (town) Knox County
18	18	35.4	**Kanab** (city) Kane County
18	18	35.4	**McCall** (city) Valley County
20	20	35.0	**Wolfeboro** (CDP) Carroll County
21	21	34.8	**Farr West** (city) Weber County
21	21	34.8	**Providence** (city) Cache County
23	23	34.6	**Bristol** (town) Lincoln County
23	23	34.6	**Rexburg** (city) Madison County
25	25	34.5	**North Logan** (city) Cache County
26	26	34.3	**Boothbay** (town) Lincoln County
26	26	34.3	**Parowan** (city) Iron County
28	28	34.2	**Pleasant View** (city) Weber County
29	29	33.8	**Wellsville** (city) Cache County
30	30	33.6	**Monmouth** (town) Kennebec County
31	31	33.5	**Holladay** (city) Salt Lake County
32	32	33.4	**Hyde Park** (city) Cache County
32	32	33.4	**Trent Woods** (town) Craven County
34	34	33.0	**Salem** (city) Utah County
35	35	32.9	**Delta** (city) Millard County
36	36	32.8	**Freeport** (town) Cumberland County
36	36	32.8	**Midway** (city) Wasatch County
36	36	32.8	**West Bountiful** (city) Davis County
39	39	32.6	**Farmington** (city) Davis County
39	39	32.6	**Kaysville** (city) Davis County
41	41	32.5	**Kennebunkport** (town) York County
42	42	32.4	**Wolfeboro** (town) Carroll County
43	43	32.2	**Woodstock** (town) Windsor County
44	44	32.0	**Santaquin** (city) Utah County
45	45	31.9	**Chichester** (town) Merrimack County
46	46	31.8	**American Fork** (city) Utah County
46	46	31.8	**Anson** (town) Somerset County
46	46	31.8	**Camden** (town) Knox County
46	46	31.8	**Hyrum** (city) Cache County
50	50	31.6	**Spring Arbor** (township) Jackson County
51	51	31.5	**Poland** (town) Androscoggin County
52	52	31.4	**Herriman** (city) Salt Lake County
53	53	31.3	**Morgan** (city) Morgan County
54	54	31.1	**Alamo** (town) Wheeler County
54	54	31.1	**Charlestown** (town) Sullivan County
56	56	31.0	**Spanish Fork** (city) Utah County
56	56	31.0	**Waldoboro** (town) Lincoln County
58	58	30.9	**Ivins** (city) Washington County
59	59	30.8	**Yarmouth** (town) Cumberland County
60	60	30.7	**Cedar Hills** (city) Utah County
61	61	30.6	**Bethel** (town) Oxford County
61	61	30.6	**Bridgton** (town) Cumberland County
61	61	30.6	**Lake San Marcos** (CDP) San Diego County
61	61	30.6	**Rockland** (city) Knox County
61	61	30.6	**Saint George** (city) Washington County
61	61	30.6	**Woods Cross** (city) Davis County
67	67	30.5	**Cedar City** (city) Iron County
68	68	30.3	**North Salt Lake** (city) Davis County
68	68	30.3	**South Jordan** (city) Salt Lake County
70	70	30.2	**Eagle Mountain** (city) Utah County
71	71	30.1	**Preston** (city) Franklin County
72	72	29.9	**Camden** (CDP) Knox County
73	73	29.8	**South Beach** (CDP) Indian River County
74	74	29.7	**Harpswell** (town) Cumberland County
74	74	29.7	**Indian River Shores** (town) Indian River County
76	76	29.5	**Helena** (city) Telfair County
76	76	29.5	**Manchester** (town) Kennebec County
76	76	29.5	**Nephi** (city) Juab County
76	76	29.5	**Washington Terrace** (city) Weber County
80	80	29.4	**Yarmouth** (CDP) Cumberland County
81	81	29.3	**Springville** (city) Utah County
82	82	29.2	**Clinton** (town) Kennebec County
82	82	29.2	**Grantsville** (city) Tooele County
84	84	29.1	**Little Compton** (town) Newport County
84	84	29.1	**Plain City** (city) Weber County
86	86	29.0	**Cottonwood Heights** (city) Salt Lake County
86	86	29.0	**Warren** (town) Knox County
88	88	28.9	**Madison** (town) Carroll County
88	88	28.9	**Washington** (city) Washington County
90	90	28.8	**Lindon** (city) Utah County
90	90	28.8	**Livermore Falls** (town) Androscoggin County
90	90	28.8	**Nibley** (city) Cache County
93	93	28.7	**Orem** (city) Utah County
93	93	28.7	**Woolwich** (town) Sagadahoc County
95	95	28.6	**Pleasant Grove** (city) Utah County
96	96	28.5	**Arundel** (town) York County
96	96	28.5	**China** (town) Kennebec County
98	98	28.4	**Lehi** (city) Utah County
98	98	28.4	**Tamworth** (town) Carroll County
100	100	28.3	**Bradford** (town) Orange County
100	100	28.3	**Enoch** (city) Iron County
102	102	28.2	**Oneida** (town) Scott County
102	102	28.2	**Oxford** (town) Oxford County
102	102	28.2	**South Weber** (city) Davis County
105	105	28.1	**Maeser** (CDP) Uintah County
105	105	28.1	**Walpole** (town) Cheshire County
107	107	28.0	**Hampden** (CDP) Penobscot County
107	107	28.0	**Sandy** (city) Salt Lake County
109	109	27.9	**Northfield** (town) Franklin County
109	109	27.9	**Perry** (city) Box Elder County
111	111	27.8	**Limerick** (town) York County
111	111	27.8	**Orleans** (town) Barnstable County
111	111	27.8	**Riverton** (city) Salt Lake County
114	114	27.7	**Draper** (city) Salt Lake County
114	114	27.7	**Hartland** (town) Windsor County
114	114	27.7	**Otisco** (town) Onondaga County
114	114	27.7	**Saratoga Springs** (city) Utah County
114	114	27.7	**Smithfield** (city) Cache County
119	119	27.6	**Bluffdale** (city) Salt Lake County
119	119	27.6	**Bowdoin** (town) Sagadahoc County
119	119	27.6	**East Bloomfield** (town) Ontario County
119	119	27.6	**North Yarmouth** (town) Cumberland County
119	119	27.6	**Syracuse** (city) Davis County
124	124	27.5	**Harrison** (town) Cumberland County
124	124	27.5	**Highland Park** (town) Dallas County
124	124	27.5	**South Eliot** (CDP) York County
127	127	27.4	**Hampden** (town) Penobscot County
127	127	27.4	**Montpelier** (city) Bear Lake County
127	127	27.4	**Winston** (city) Douglas County
130	130	27.3	**Buxton** (town) York County
130	130	27.3	**North Ogden** (city) Weber County
130	130	27.3	**White Hall** (city) Jefferson County
133	133	27.2	**Thetford** (town) Orange County
134	134	27.1	**Greene** (town) Chenango County
134	134	27.1	**Wakefield** (town) Carroll County
136	136	26.9	**New Durham** (town) Strafford County
136	136	26.9	**Stansbury Park** (CDP) Tooele County
136	136	26.9	**Surfside Beach** (town) Horry County
139	139	26.8	**Stratham** (town) Rockingham County
140	140	26.6	**Concord** (township) Jackson County
140	140	26.6	**Millcreek** (CDP) Salt Lake County
140	140	26.6	**Peterborough** (CDP) Hillsborough County
140	140	26.6	**Turner** (town) Androscoggin County
144	144	26.5	**Foster** (town) Providence County
144	144	26.5	**Hope** (township) Barry County
144	144	26.5	**Norwich** (town) Windsor County
147	147	26.4	**Belle Meade** (city) Davidson County
148	148	26.3	**Belfast** (city) Waldo County
149	149	26.2	**Richfield** (city) Sevier County
149	149	26.2	**South Duxbury** (CDP) Plymouth County

Note: *The state column ranks the top/bottom 150 places from all places in the state with population of 10,000 or more. The national column ranks the top/bottom 150 places from all places in the country with population of 10,000 or more. Places that are unincorporated were not considered in the rankings. Please refer to the User Guide for additional information.*

Ancestry: American

Top 150 Places Ranked in *Descending* Order

State Rank	Nat'l Rank	Percent	Place
1	1	66.4	**La Follette** (city) Campbell County
2	2	60.0	**Gloverville** (CDP) Aiken County
3	3	54.6	**Clearwater** (CDP) Aiken County
4	4	54.4	**Treasure Lake** (CDP) Clearfield County
5	5	51.7	**Healdton** (city) Carter County
6	6	45.9	**Bonifay** (city) Holmes County
7	7	45.8	**Harlem** (CDP) Hendry County
8	8	45.5	**Bean Station** (city) Grainger County
8	8	45.5	**Stanford** (city) Lincoln County
10	10	44.5	**Pell City** (city) Saint Clair County
11	11	44.3	**New Tazewell** (town) Claiborne County
12	12	43.9	**Dresden** (town) Weakley County
13	13	43.6	**Hartford** (city) Ohio County
14	14	43.2	**Blue Hill** (town) Hancock County
15	15	43.1	**Eaton** (town) Madison County
16	16	43.0	**Church Hill** (city) Hawkins County
17	17	42.6	**Middlesborough** (city) Bell County
18	18	42.1	**Temple** (city) Carroll County
19	19	41.1	**Georgetown** (city) Vermilion County
20	20	40.9	**Grantville** (city) Coweta County
20	20	40.9	**Summerville** (city) Chattooga County
22	22	40.6	**Morehead** (city) Rowan County
23	23	40.5	**Bayou Vista** (CDP) Saint Mary Parish
24	24	40.4	**Lone Grove** (city) Carter County
24	24	40.4	**Wilkesboro** (town) Wilkes County
26	26	39.9	**Chincoteague** (town) Accomack County
27	27	39.8	**Bremen** (city) Haralson County
28	28	39.7	**Cullowhee** (CDP) Jackson County
29	29	39.4	**Nassau Village-Ratliff** (CDP) Nassau County
30	30	38.8	**Crab Orchard** (CDP) Raleigh County
31	31	38.7	**Stanton** (city) Powell County
32	32	38.4	**Rogersville** (town) Hawkins County
33	33	38.2	**Cookeville** (city) Putnam County
34	34	38.0	**Livingston** (town) Overton County
35	35	37.6	**Gray Summit** (CDP) Franklin County
35	35	37.6	**Harrogate** (city) Claiborne County
37	37	37.4	**North Terre Haute** (CDP) Vigo County
38	38	37.3	**Mount Carmel** (CDP) Clermont County
39	39	36.9	**Atkins** (city) Pope County
39	39	36.9	**Burnettown** (town) Aiken County
39	39	36.9	**De Funiak Springs** (city) Walton County
42	42	36.8	**Lake of the Woods** (CDP) Champaign County
42	42	36.8	**Suncoast Estates** (CDP) Lee County
44	44	36.7	**Lancaster** (city) Garrard County
44	44	36.7	**Sandy** (township) Clearfield County
46	46	36.6	**Donalsonville** (city) Seminole County
47	47	36.3	**Bradford** (township) Clearfield County
47	47	36.3	**Broadway** (town) Rockingham County
47	47	36.3	**Jena** (town) La Salle Parish
50	50	36.2	**Algood** (city) Putnam County
50	50	36.2	**Sylva** (town) Jackson County
52	52	36.0	**Unicoi** (town) Unicoi County
53	53	35.6	**Bloomingdale** (CDP) Sullivan County
53	53	35.6	**Somerset** (city) Pulaski County
53	53	35.6	**Timberville** (town) Rockingham County
56	56	35.5	**Beaver Dam** (city) Ohio County
56	56	35.5	**Oliver Springs** (town) Anderson County
58	58	35.4	**Bucksport** (CDP) Hancock County
59	59	35.1	**England** (city) Lonoke County
59	59	35.1	**Fairview** (CDP) Walker County
59	59	35.1	**LaFayette** (city) Walker County
62	62	34.9	**Bucksport** (town) Hancock County
62	62	34.9	**Mountain City** (town) Johnson County
62	62	34.9	**Shepherdsville** (city) Bullitt County
65	65	34.8	**Blennerhassett** (CDP) Wood County
66	66	34.7	**South Lebanon** (village) Warren County
67	67	34.5	**Mount Carmel** (town) Hawkins County
68	68	34.3	**Hannahs Mill** (CDP) Upson County
69	69	34.2	**Mills** (town) Natrona County
69	69	34.2	**Rockwood** (city) Roane County
71	71	33.5	**North Wilkesboro** (town) Wilkes County
71	71	33.5	**Odenville** (town) Saint Clair County
73	73	33.3	**Ward** (city) Lonoke County
74	74	33.2	**Bawcomville** (CDP) Ouachita Parish
75	75	33.1	**Bethel** (village) Clermont County
75	75	33.1	**Grottoes** (town) Rockingham County
77	77	33.0	**Shelbyville** (city) Bedford County
78	78	32.7	**Dawson Springs** (city) Hopkins County
78	78	32.7	**Galena** (city) Cherokee County
78	78	32.7	**Pike Road** (town) Montgomery County
81	81	32.6	**Erwin** (town) Unicoi County
81	81	32.6	**Honea Path** (town) Anderson County
83	83	32.5	**West Tisbury** (town) Dukes County
84	84	32.3	**Pearisburg** (town) Giles County
85	85	32.2	**Evansville** (town) Natrona County
86	86	32.0	**Moody** (city) Saint Clair County
86	86	32.0	**Pittsburg** (city) Crawford County
88	88	31.9	**Woodbury** (town) Cannon County
89	89	31.8	**Dandridge** (town) Jefferson County
90	90	31.7	**Withamsville** (CDP) Clermont County
91	91	31.5	**Margaret** (town) Saint Clair County
92	92	31.4	**Pigeon Forge** (city) Sevier County
93	93	31.3	**Alva** (CDP) Lee County
94	94	31.1	**Hilliard** (town) Nassau County
95	95	30.8	**Monterey** (town) Putnam County
96	96	30.7	**Icard** (CDP) Burke County
97	97	30.5	**Flemingsburg** (city) Fleming County
97	97	30.5	**Shady Spring** (CDP) Raleigh County
99	99	30.4	**Irvine** (city) Estill County
100	100	30.3	**Cloverdale** (CDP) Botetourt County
100	100	30.3	**Hamilton** (town) Madison County
100	100	30.3	**Sylacauga** (city) Talladega County
100	100	30.3	**Underwood-Petersville** (CDP) Lauderdale County
104	104	30.2	**Central City** (city) Muhlenberg County
104	104	30.2	**Harriman** (city) Roane County
104	104	30.2	**Prestonsburg** (city) Floyd County
107	107	30.1	**Stuarts Draft** (CDP) Augusta County
108	108	30.0	**Madison** (town) Madison County
108	108	30.0	**Verona** (CDP) Augusta County
108	108	30.0	**Waynesville** (town) Haywood County
111	111	29.8	**Granville** (town) Washington County
111	111	29.8	**Paris** (city) Bourbon County
111	111	29.8	**Winchester** (city) Clark County
114	114	29.7	**Byron** (city) Peach County
114	114	29.7	**Emmett** (city) Gem County
114	114	29.7	**Hillview** (city) Bullitt County
114	114	29.7	**Oak Grove** (CDP) Washington County
114	114	29.7	**Sunnyvale** (town) Dallas County
114	114	29.7	**Wickenburg** (town) Maricopa County
120	120	29.6	**Jefferson City** (city) Jefferson County
121	121	29.5	**Ball** (town) Rapides Parish
121	121	29.5	**Corinth** (town) Penobscot County
121	121	29.5	**Lincoln** (city) Talladega County
124	124	29.4	**Manchester** (city) Coffee County
124	124	29.4	**Owensboro** (city) Daviess County
126	126	29.3	**Kings Mountain** (city) Cleveland County
127	127	29.2	**Buckner** (CDP) Oldham County
127	127	29.2	**Malabar** (town) Brevard County
129	129	29.1	**Baxter Springs** (city) Cherokee County
130	130	28.9	**Kingston** (city) Roane County
130	130	28.9	**Morristown** (city) Hamblen County
132	132	28.8	**Bayshore** (CDP) New Hanover County
132	132	28.8	**Buena Vista** (independent city)
134	134	28.7	**Grissom AFB** (CDP) Miami County
134	134	28.7	**Hodgenville** (city) Larue County
136	136	28.5	**Claiborne** (CDP) Ouachita Parish
136	136	28.5	**Inwood** (CDP) Polk County
136	136	28.5	**Moyock** (CDP) Currituck County
136	136	28.5	**Richlands** (town) Tazewell County
136	136	28.5	**Tabor City** (town) Columbus County
141	141	28.4	**Dundee** (town) Polk County
141	141	28.4	**Jan Phyl Village** (CDP) Polk County
141	141	28.4	**Morgan** (city) Morgan County
144	144	28.3	**West Liberty** (city) Morgan County
145	145	28.2	**Bicknell** (city) Knox County
145	145	28.2	**Fort Scott** (city) Bourbon County
145	145	28.2	**Putney** (CDP) Dougherty County
148	148	28.1	**Berwick** (town) Saint Mary Parish
148	148	28.1	**Corinth** (town) Saratoga County
148	148	28.1	**Middleton** (city) Canyon County

Note: *The state column ranks the top/bottom 150 places from all places in the state with population of 10,000 or more. The national column ranks the top/bottom 150 places from all places in the country with population of 10,000 or more. Places that are unincorporated were not considered in the rankings. Please refer to the User Guide for additional information.*

Ancestry: Irish

Top 150 Places Ranked in *Descending* Order

State Rank	Nat'l Rank	Percent	Place
1	1	52.0	**Pearl River** (CDP) Rockland County
2	2	51.7	**Ocean Bluff-Brant Rock** (CDP) Plymouth County
3	3	50.6	**Green Harbor-Cedar Crest** (CDP) Plymouth County
4	4	49.4	**Rockledge** (borough) Montgomery County
5	5	48.3	**Walpole** (CDP) Norfolk County
6	6	47.4	**North Scituate** (CDP) Plymouth County
7	7	47.0	**Scituate** (CDP) Plymouth County
8	8	46.9	**Marshfield** (town) Plymouth County
9	9	46.2	**Scituate** (town) Plymouth County
10	10	45.8	**Ridley Park** (borough) Delaware County
11	11	45.5	**Spring Lake Heights** (borough) Monmouth County
12	12	45.3	**Oak Valley** (CDP) Gloucester County
13	13	45.2	**Hanover** (town) Plymouth County
14	14	44.7	**Norwell** (town) Plymouth County
15	15	44.2	**Glenside** (CDP) Montgomery County
15	15	44.2	**Manasquan** (borough) Monmouth County
17	17	43.8	**Norwood** (borough) Delaware County
18	18	42.9	**Walpole** (town) Norfolk County
18	18	42.9	**Wynantskill** (CDP) Rensselaer County
20	20	42.8	**Springfield** (township) Delaware County
21	21	42.6	**Folsom** (CDP) Delaware County
21	21	42.6	**Glenolden** (borough) Delaware County
21	21	42.6	**Highlands** (borough) Monmouth County
24	24	42.2	**Marshfield** (CDP) Plymouth County
25	25	41.7	**North Middletown** (CDP) Monmouth County
26	26	41.6	**Braintree Town** (city) Norfolk County
27	27	41.4	**Weymouth Town** (city) Norfolk County
28	28	41.1	**Littleton Common** (CDP) Middlesex County
28	28	41.1	**North Wildwood** (city) Cape May County
30	30	41.0	**Bridgewater** (CDP) Plymouth County
31	31	40.9	**Abington** (cdp/town) Plymouth County
31	31	40.9	**Nahant** (cdp/town) Essex County
31	31	40.9	**Spring Lake** (borough) Monmouth County
34	34	40.6	**Whitman** (town) Plymouth County
35	35	40.5	**Cohasset** (town) Norfolk County
35	35	40.5	**Hopedale** (CDP) Worcester County
35	35	40.5	**Sayville** (CDP) Suffolk County
38	38	40.4	**Brielle** (borough) Monmouth County
39	39	40.3	**Hull** (cdp/town) Plymouth County
40	40	40.2	**Gloucester City** (city) Camden County
41	41	39.9	**Churchville** (CDP) Bucks County
42	42	39.7	**Haddon Heights** (borough) Camden County
43	43	39.6	**Notre Dame** (CDP) Saint Joseph County
44	44	39.5	**Ashland** (borough) Schuylkill County
44	44	39.5	**Hingham** (town) Plymouth County
46	46	39.4	**Avon** (town) Norfolk County
47	47	39.3	**Garden City** (village) Nassau County
47	47	39.3	**Tinicum** (township) Delaware County
49	49	39.2	**Milton** (cdp/town) Norfolk County
49	49	39.2	**Ramtown** (CDP) Monmouth County
51	51	39.1	**Ridley** (township) Delaware County
52	52	38.8	**Bridgewater** (town) Plymouth County
53	53	38.5	**Hanson** (town) Plymouth County
53	53	38.5	**North Reading** (town) Middlesex County
53	53	38.5	**Prospect Park** (borough) Delaware County
53	53	38.5	**Rockland** (town) Plymouth County
57	57	38.4	**Hingham** (CDP) Plymouth County
58	58	38.3	**Foxborough** (town) Norfolk County
59	59	38.1	**Foxborough** (CDP) Norfolk County
60	60	38.0	**Barrington** (borough) Camden County
61	61	37.9	**Aldan** (borough) Delaware County
61	61	37.9	**Mansfield Center** (CDP) Bristol County
61	61	37.9	**National Park** (borough) Gloucester County
64	64	37.8	**East Sandwich** (CDP) Barnstable County
65	65	37.6	**Haverford** (township) Delaware County
65	65	37.6	**West Brandywine** (township) Chester County
67	67	37.5	**East Bridgewater** (town) Plymouth County
68	68	37.4	**Buzzards Bay** (CDP) Barnstable County
69	69	37.3	**Blauvelt** (CDP) Rockland County
69	69	37.3	**East Quogue** (CDP) Suffolk County
71	71	37.2	**Canton** (town) Norfolk County
71	71	37.2	**North Falmouth** (CDP) Barnstable County
73	73	37.1	**Pembroke** (town) Plymouth County
73	73	37.1	**Upton** (CDP) Worcester County
73	73	37.1	**Woodbury Heights** (borough) Gloucester County
76	76	36.9	**Fair Haven** (borough) Monmouth County
77	77	36.8	**Clementon** (borough) Camden County
77	77	36.8	**Duxbury** (town) Plymouth County
79	79	36.7	**Fairview** (CDP) Monmouth County
79	79	36.7	**Folcroft** (borough) Delaware County
79	79	36.7	**Newtown** (township) Delaware County
82	82	36.6	**Rockville Centre** (village) Nassau County
83	83	36.5	**Oceanport** (borough) Monmouth County
83	83	36.5	**West Bridgewater** (town) Plymouth County
85	85	36.2	**Audubon** (borough) Camden County
85	85	36.2	**Campo** (CDP) San Diego County
87	87	36.0	**Orleans** (town) Jefferson County
87	87	36.0	**Shark River Hills** (CDP) Monmouth County
89	89	35.8	**Drexel Hill** (CDP) Delaware County
89	89	35.8	**Trappe** (borough) Montgomery County
89	89	35.8	**West Sayville** (CDP) Suffolk County
92	92	35.5	**Leonardo** (CDP) Monmouth County
92	92	35.5	**Little Silver** (borough) Monmouth County
94	94	35.3	**Bethlehem** (township) Hunterdon County
95	95	35.2	**East Islip** (CDP) Suffolk County
95	95	35.2	**Kingston** (town) Plymouth County
97	97	35.1	**Dedham** (cdp/town) Norfolk County
97	97	35.1	**Hopedale** (town) Worcester County
97	97	35.1	**Wilmington** (cdp/town) Middlesex County
100	100	35.0	**Green Island** (town/village) Albany County
100	100	35.0	**Medford Lakes** (borough) Burlington County
102	102	34.9	**Holbrook** (cdp/town) Norfolk County
102	102	34.9	**Mansfield** (town) Bristol County
104	104	34.8	**LaFayette** (town) Onondaga County
104	104	34.8	**North Plymouth** (CDP) Plymouth County
104	104	34.8	**Norton** (town) Bristol County
104	104	34.8	**Tuckerton** (borough) Ocean County
104	104	34.8	**Wakefield** (cdp/town) Middlesex County
109	109	34.7	**Cape Neddick** (CDP) York County
109	109	34.7	**Tewksbury** (town) Middlesex County
109	109	34.7	**Woodlyn** (CDP) Delaware County
109	109	34.7	**Woolwich** (township) Gloucester County
113	113	34.6	**Wanamassa** (CDP) Monmouth County
114	114	34.5	**East Shoreham** (CDP) Suffolk County
114	114	34.5	**Horsham** (CDP) Montgomery County
114	114	34.5	**Skippack** (CDP) Montgomery County
117	117	34.4	**Plymouth** (town) Plymouth County
117	117	34.4	**Western Springs** (village) Cook County
119	119	34.3	**Bethel** (township) Delaware County
119	119	34.3	**Melrose** (city) Middlesex County
119	119	34.3	**Point Pleasant** (borough) Ocean County
122	122	34.2	**Aston** (township) Delaware County
122	122	34.2	**North Seekonk** (CDP) Bristol County
122	122	34.2	**Wanakah** (CDP) Erie County
122	122	34.2	**Westvale** (CDP) Onondaga County
126	126	34.1	**Reading** (cdp/town) Middlesex County
126	126	34.1	**Winthrop Town** (city) Suffolk County
128	128	34.0	**Atkinson** (town) Rockingham County
128	128	34.0	**Bella Vista** (CDP) Shasta County
128	128	34.0	**Hopkinton** (CDP) Middlesex County
128	128	34.0	**Plymouth** (CDP) Plymouth County
128	128	34.0	**Washington** (town) Dutchess County
128	128	34.0	**Williston Park** (village) Nassau County
134	134	33.9	**Norwood** (cdp/town) Norfolk County
135	135	33.8	**Clinton** (town) Worcester County
135	135	33.8	**Halifax** (town) Plymouth County
135	135	33.8	**Mystic Island** (CDP) Ocean County
135	135	33.8	**Wall** (township) Monmouth County
139	139	33.7	**Massapequa Park** (village) Nassau County
140	140	33.6	**Cold Spring Harbor** (CDP) Suffolk County
140	140	33.6	**Dalton** (town) Berkshire County
142	142	33.5	**Colonie** (village) Albany County
142	142	33.5	**Middletown** (township) Monmouth County
142	142	33.5	**Seabrook** (town) Rockingham County
142	142	33.5	**Waterford** (township) Camden County
146	146	33.4	**Medfield** (CDP) Norfolk County
146	146	33.4	**Montgomery** (village) Orange County
146	146	33.4	**Mount Ephraim** (borough) Camden County
149	149	33.3	**Dover** (town) Dutchess County
149	149	33.3	**Fort Salonga** (CDP) Suffolk County

Note: *The state column ranks the top/bottom 150 places from all places in the state with population of 10,000 or more. The national column ranks the top/bottom 150 places from all places in the country with population of 10,000 or more. Places that are unincorporated were not considered in the rankings. Please refer to the User Guide for additional information.*

Ancestry: Italian

Top 150 Places Ranked in *Descending* Order

State Rank	Nat'l Rank	Percent	Place
1	1	51.2	**Johnston** (town) Providence County
2	2	50.9	**Fairfield** (township) Essex County
3	3	49.0	**North Massapequa** (CDP) Nassau County
4	4	47.7	**East Haven** (cdp/town) New Haven County
5	5	47.3	**Watertown** (CDP) Litchfield County
6	6	46.3	**Massapequa** (CDP) Nassau County
7	7	45.4	**Eastchester** (CDP) Westchester County
8	8	45.3	**Thornwood** (CDP) Westchester County
9	9	44.4	**Glendora** (CDP) Camden County
10	10	44.0	**Frankfort** (village) Herkimer County
11	11	43.5	**Hawthorne** (CDP) Westchester County
12	12	43.4	**Hammonton** (town) Atlantic County
13	13	43.3	**North Branford** (town) New Haven County
13	13	43.3	**Turnersville** (CDP) Gloucester County
15	15	42.8	**West Islip** (CDP) Suffolk County
16	16	42.6	**Massapequa Park** (village) Nassau County
17	17	42.1	**Franklin Square** (CDP) Nassau County
18	18	41.9	**Islip Terrace** (CDP) Suffolk County
19	19	41.6	**Watertown** (town) Litchfield County
20	20	41.4	**Nesconset** (CDP) Suffolk County
21	21	41.1	**Lake Grove** (village) Suffolk County
22	22	40.4	**North Haven** (cdp/town) New Haven County
23	23	40.3	**Gibbstown** (CDP) Gloucester County
24	24	40.2	**Saint James** (CDP) Suffolk County
24	24	40.2	**Seaford** (CDP) Nassau County
26	26	40.1	**East Hanover** (township) Morris County
26	26	40.1	**Saugus** (cdp/town) Essex County
28	28	39.9	**Marlboro** (CDP) Ulster County
29	29	39.7	**Beach Haven West** (CDP) Ocean County
30	30	39.5	**East Islip** (CDP) Suffolk County
30	30	39.5	**Smithtown** (CDP) Suffolk County
32	32	39.3	**Jefferson Valley-Yorktown** (CDP) Westchester County
33	33	39.2	**Jessup** (borough) Lackawanna County
33	33	39.2	**Monmouth Beach** (borough) Monmouth County
35	35	39.0	**Brightwaters** (village) Suffolk County
36	36	38.7	**South Farmingdale** (CDP) Nassau County
37	37	38.1	**Frankfort** (town) Herkimer County
37	37	38.1	**Richwood** (CDP) Gloucester County
39	39	38.0	**Bayville** (village) Nassau County
39	39	38.0	**Malverne** (village) Nassau County
39	39	38.0	**North Providence** (town) Providence County
42	42	37.9	**Cedar Grove** (township) Essex County
43	43	37.8	**Plainedge** (CDP) Nassau County
44	44	37.7	**Holtsville** (CDP) Suffolk County
44	44	37.7	**Oakville** (CDP) Litchfield County
46	46	37.6	**Blackwood** (CDP) Camden County
46	46	37.6	**Holbrook** (CDP) Suffolk County
48	48	37.4	**Center Moriches** (CDP) Suffolk County
48	48	37.4	**Dunmore** (borough) Lackawanna County
48	48	37.4	**Smithtown** (town) Suffolk County
51	51	37.2	**North Great River** (CDP) Suffolk County
52	52	37.1	**Blue Point** (CDP) Suffolk County
52	52	37.1	**East Norwich** (CDP) Nassau County
52	52	37.1	**Ronkonkoma** (CDP) Suffolk County
52	52	37.1	**West Pittston** (borough) Luzerne County
56	56	36.9	**Hauppauge** (CDP) Suffolk County
57	57	36.8	**Bohemia** (CDP) Suffolk County
57	57	36.8	**Farmingville** (CDP) Suffolk County
57	57	36.8	**Old Forge** (borough) Lackawanna County
57	57	36.8	**Pemberwick** (CDP) Fairfield County
61	61	36.7	**Mechanicville** (city) Saratoga County
61	61	36.7	**Miller Place** (CDP) Suffolk County
61	61	36.7	**Nutley** (township) Essex County
61	61	36.7	**Selden** (CDP) Suffolk County
61	61	36.7	**Wood-Ridge** (borough) Bergen County
66	66	36.6	**Glen Head** (CDP) Nassau County
67	67	36.5	**Pittston** (city) Luzerne County
68	68	36.4	**Centerport** (CDP) Suffolk County
69	69	36.2	**Barnegat** (CDP) Ocean County
70	70	36.1	**Mahopac** (CDP) Putnam County
70	70	36.1	**Ocean Acres** (CDP) Ocean County
72	72	36.0	**Lindenhurst** (village) Suffolk County
72	72	36.0	**Lyncourt** (CDP) Onondaga County
72	72	36.0	**Union Vale** (town) Dutchess County
72	72	36.0	**Washington** (township) Gloucester County
76	76	35.9	**Eastchester** (town) Westchester County
77	77	35.8	**Garden City South** (CDP) Nassau County
77	77	35.8	**Greenwich** (township) Gloucester County
77	77	35.8	**Manorville** (CDP) Suffolk County
80	80	35.7	**Lake Pocotopaug** (CDP) Middlesex County
80	80	35.7	**Moonachie** (borough) Bergen County
80	80	35.7	**Oyster Bay** (CDP) Nassau County
83	83	35.6	**East Freehold** (CDP) Monmouth County
83	83	35.6	**Oakdale** (CDP) Suffolk County
83	83	35.6	**Ramtown** (CDP) Monmouth County
86	86	35.5	**Kensington** (CDP) Hartford County
86	86	35.5	**Pelham Manor** (village) Westchester County
88	88	35.4	**Holiday City-Berkeley** (CDP) Ocean County
88	88	35.4	**Yaphank** (CDP) Suffolk County
90	90	35.2	**Carmel** (town) Putnam County
91	91	35.1	**Commack** (CDP) Suffolk County
92	92	34.9	**Hazlet** (township) Monmouth County
92	92	34.9	**Somers** (town) Westchester County
94	94	34.5	**Bethpage** (CDP) Nassau County
94	94	34.5	**Middle Island** (CDP) Suffolk County
94	94	34.5	**Port Jefferson Station** (CDP) Suffolk County
97	97	34.4	**Lynnfield** (cdp/town) Essex County
98	98	34.3	**Kings Park** (CDP) Suffolk County
98	98	34.3	**North Babylon** (CDP) Suffolk County
98	98	34.3	**West Babylon** (CDP) Suffolk County
101	101	34.2	**Totowa** (borough) Passaic County
102	102	34.1	**Ellwood City** (borough) Lawrence County
102	102	34.1	**Stoneham** (cdp/town) Middlesex County
104	104	34.0	**Cranston** (city) Providence County
104	104	34.0	**Shirley** (CDP) Suffolk County
106	106	33.9	**Pequannock** (township) Morris County
106	106	33.9	**Pine Lake Park** (CDP) Ocean County
108	108	33.8	**East Fishkill** (town) Dutchess County
108	108	33.8	**Montrose** (CDP) Westchester County
110	110	33.7	**Locust Valley** (CDP) Nassau County
110	110	33.7	**Neshannock** (township) Lawrence County
110	110	33.7	**West Bay Shore** (CDP) Suffolk County
110	110	33.7	**Yorktown** (town) Westchester County
114	114	33.6	**Holiday City South** (CDP) Ocean County
114	114	33.6	**Kenmore** (village) Erie County
114	114	33.6	**Lacey** (township) Ocean County
114	114	33.6	**Prospect** (town) New Haven County
114	114	33.6	**Roseland** (borough) Essex County
114	114	33.6	**Wantagh** (CDP) Nassau County
120	120	33.5	**Waldwick** (borough) Bergen County
120	120	33.5	**Wolcott** (town) New Haven County
122	122	33.4	**East Shoreham** (CDP) Suffolk County
122	122	33.4	**South Huntington** (CDP) Suffolk County
122	122	33.4	**West Sayville** (CDP) Suffolk County
125	125	33.3	**Exeter** (borough) Luzerne County
125	125	33.3	**Toms River** (township) Ocean County
127	127	33.2	**East Williston** (village) Nassau County
127	127	33.2	**Lyndhurst** (township) Bergen County
129	129	33.1	**Lake Ronkonkoma** (CDP) Suffolk County
129	129	33.1	**Toms River** (CDP) Ocean County
129	129	33.1	**Westerly** (CDP) Washington County
132	132	33.0	**Cold Spring Harbor** (CDP) Suffolk County
132	132	33.0	**Mount Sinai** (CDP) Suffolk County
134	134	32.9	**Hasbrouck Heights** (borough) Bergen County
134	134	32.9	**Stafford** (township) Ocean County
136	136	32.8	**Berlin** (town) Hartford County
136	136	32.8	**Galeville** (CDP) Onondaga County
136	136	32.8	**West Caldwell** (township) Essex County
139	139	32.7	**Putnam Valley** (town) Putnam County
139	139	32.7	**Sound Beach** (CDP) Suffolk County
141	141	32.6	**Babylon** (village) Suffolk County
141	141	32.6	**Centereach** (CDP) Suffolk County
141	141	32.6	**Elwood** (CDP) Suffolk County
141	141	32.6	**Middletown** (township) Monmouth County
141	141	32.6	**North Patchogue** (CDP) Suffolk County
146	146	32.5	**Lincroft** (CDP) Monmouth County
147	147	32.4	**Barnegat** (township) Ocean County
147	147	32.4	**Caldwell** (borough) Essex County
147	147	32.4	**Levittown** (CDP) Nassau County
147	147	32.4	**Oceanport** (borough) Monmouth County

Note: *The state column ranks the top/bottom 150 places from all places in the state with population of 10,000 or more. The national column ranks the top/bottom 150 places from all places in the country with population of 10,000 or more. Places that are unincorporated were not considered in the rankings. Please refer to the User Guide for additional information.*

Employment: Management, Business, and Financial Occupations

Top 150 Places Ranked in *Descending* Order

State Rank	Nat'l Rank	Percent	Place
1	92	30.1	**Dublin** (city) Franklin County
2	119	29.0	**Hudson** (city) Summit County
3	163	27.9	**Montgomery** (city) Hamilton County
4	194	27.2	**Powell** (city) Delaware County
5	210	26.8	**Aurora** (city) Portage County
6	220	26.7	**Brecksville** (city) Cuyahoga County
6	220	26.7	**Rocky River** (city) Cuyahoga County
8	307	25.4	**Springboro** (city) Warren County
9	354	24.7	**Bay Village** (city) Cuyahoga County
10	381	24.4	**Westlake** (city) Cuyahoga County
11	388	24.3	**Bexley** (city) Franklin County
12	396	24.2	**Avon Lake** (city) Lorain County
13	405	24.1	**Worthington** (city) Franklin County
14	413	24.0	**Avon** (city) Lorain County
15	435	23.8	**Solon** (city) Cuyahoga County
16	453	23.6	**Beavercreek** (city) Greene County
16	453	23.6	**Upper Arlington** (city) Franklin County
18	466	23.4	**Beachwood** (city) Cuyahoga County
19	477	23.3	**Mason** (city) Warren County
20	487	23.2	**Perrysburg** (city) Wood County
21	495	23.1	**Twinsburg** (city) Summit County
22	528	22.8	**Gahanna** (city) Franklin County
23	546	22.7	**Westerville** (city) Franklin County
24	597	22.1	**Hilliard** (city) Franklin County
25	619	21.9	**University Heights** (city) Cuyahoga County
26	634	21.8	**Mack** (CDP) Hamilton County
27	671	21.5	**Shaker Heights** (city) Cuyahoga County
28	718	21.1	**Pickerington** (city) Fairfield County
29	725	21.0	**Forestville** (CDP) Hamilton County
30	740	20.9	**Lyndhurst** (city) Cuyahoga County
30	740	20.9	**Strongsville** (city) Cuyahoga County
32	869	20.0	**North Royalton** (city) Cuyahoga County
33	888	19.8	**Broadview Heights** (city) Cuyahoga County
34	929	19.6	**Blue Ash** (city) Hamilton County
35	959	19.4	**Dent** (CDP) Hamilton County
36	1036	18.9	**Macedonia** (city) Summit County
37	1072	18.7	**Centerville** (city) Montgomery County
38	1156	18.3	**Loveland** (city) Hamilton County
39	1176	18.2	**Monfort Heights** (CDP) Hamilton County
40	1194	18.1	**Seven Hills** (city) Cuyahoga County
41	1214	18.0	**Middleburg Heights** (city) Cuyahoga County
42	1293	17.6	**Sharonville** (city) Hamilton County
43	1361	17.3	**Wadsworth** (city) Medina County
44	1375	17.2	**Stow** (city) Summit County
45	1401	17.1	**Green** (city) Summit County
46	1419	17.0	**North Ridgeville** (city) Lorain County
46	1419	17.0	**Streetsboro** (city) Portage County
48	1507	16.6	**Mentor** (city) Lake County
49	1535	16.5	**Lakewood** (city) Cuyahoga County
50	1559	16.4	**Delaware** (city) Delaware County
50	1559	16.4	**Reynoldsburg** (city) Franklin County
52	1577	16.3	**North Olmsted** (city) Cuyahoga County
53	1618	16.1	**Clayton** (city) Montgomery County
53	1618	16.1	**Sylvania** (city) Lucas County
55	1671	15.9	**Pataskala** (city) Licking County
56	1722	15.7	**Findlay** (city) Hancock County
56	1722	15.7	**Miamisburg** (city) Montgomery County
58	1749	15.6	**Grove City** (city) Franklin County
59	1802	15.4	**South Euclid** (city) Cuyahoga County
60	1870	15.2	**Columbus** (city) Franklin County
60	1870	15.2	**Fairview Park** (city) Cuyahoga County
62	1934	14.9	**Monroe** (city) Butler County
63	1957	14.8	**Mayfield Heights** (city) Cuyahoga County
63	1957	14.8	**White Oak** (CDP) Hamilton County
65	2008	14.6	**Cleveland Heights** (city) Cuyahoga County
65	2008	14.6	**North Canton** (city) Stark County
67	2028	14.5	**Vandalia** (city) Montgomery County
68	2085	14.3	**Cincinnati** (city) Hamilton County
69	2126	14.2	**Boardman** (CDP) Mahoning County
69	2126	14.2	**Bridgetown** (CDP) Hamilton County
71	2155	14.1	**Lebanon** (city) Warren County
72	2195	14.0	**Cuyahoga Falls** (city) Summit County
72	2195	14.0	**Medina** (city) Medina County
74	2274	13.7	**Tallmadge** (city) Summit County
75	2341	13.5	**Franklin** (city) Warren County
76	2393	13.3	**Fairfield** (city) Butler County
77	2436	13.2	**Norton** (city) Summit County
78	2476	13.1	**Heath** (city) Licking County
78	2476	13.1	**Kettering** (city) Montgomery County
78	2476	13.1	**Marysville** (city) Union County
78	2476	13.1	**Norwood** (city) Hamilton County
82	2520	13.0	**Brunswick** (city) Medina County
83	2551	12.9	**Eastlake** (city) Lake County
83	2551	12.9	**Troy** (city) Miami County
85	2579	12.8	**Amherst** (city) Lorain County
86	2697	12.4	**Willowick** (city) Lake County
87	2733	12.3	**Ashland** (city) Ashland County
87	2733	12.3	**Berea** (city) Cuyahoga County
89	2927	11.8	**Englewood** (city) Montgomery County
89	2927	11.8	**Huber Heights** (city) Montgomery County
89	2927	11.8	**Maumee** (city) Lucas County
89	2927	11.8	**Reading** (city) Hamilton County
93	2963	11.7	**New Franklin** (city) Summit County
93	2963	11.7	**Parma** (city) Cuyahoga County
93	2963	11.7	**Sidney** (city) Shelby County
93	2963	11.7	**Willoughby** (city) Lake County
97	3001	11.6	**Finneytown** (CDP) Hamilton County
98	3023	11.5	**New Philadelphia** (city) Tuscarawas County
98	3023	11.5	**Riverside** (city) Montgomery County
100	3061	11.4	**Circleville** (city) Pickaway County
100	3061	11.4	**Steubenville** (city) Jefferson County
102	3101	11.3	**Euclid** (city) Cuyahoga County
103	3167	11.1	**Mount Vernon** (city) Knox County
103	3167	11.1	**Washington Court House** (city) Fayette County
103	3167	11.1	**West Carrollton** (city) Montgomery County
106	3202	11.0	**Oxford** (city) Butler County
106	3202	11.0	**Urbana** (city) Champaign County
108	3235	10.9	**Dover** (city) Tuscarawas County
108	3235	10.9	**Trotwood** (city) Montgomery County
110	3270	10.8	**Celina** (city) Mercer County
110	3270	10.8	**Middletown** (city) Butler County
112	3303	10.7	**Parma Heights** (city) Cuyahoga County
112	3303	10.7	**Richmond Heights** (city) Cuyahoga County
114	3372	10.5	**Portsmouth** (city) Scioto County
115	3397	10.4	**Fairborn** (city) Greene County
115	3397	10.4	**Xenia** (city) Greene County
117	3512	10.1	**Akron** (city) Summit County
117	3512	10.1	**Wickliffe** (city) Lake County
119	3549	10.0	**Bedford** (city) Cuyahoga County
119	3549	10.0	**Bedford Heights** (city) Cuyahoga County
119	3549	10.0	**Newark** (city) Licking County
122	3616	9.8	**Lancaster** (city) Fairfield County
122	3616	9.8	**Trenton** (city) Butler County
124	3653	9.7	**Springfield** (city) Clark County
125	3680	9.6	**Elyria** (city) Lorain County
125	3680	9.6	**Ironton** (city) Lawrence County
125	3680	9.6	**Wilmington** (city) Clinton County
128	3717	9.5	**Marietta** (city) Washington County
129	3753	9.4	**Austintown** (CDP) Mahoning County
129	3753	9.4	**Bowling Green** (city) Wood County
129	3753	9.4	**Chillicothe** (city) Ross County
129	3753	9.4	**Garfield Heights** (city) Cuyahoga County
129	3753	9.4	**Sandusky** (city) Erie County
134	3794	9.3	**Bucyrus** (city) Crawford County
135	3825	9.2	**Coshocton** (city) Coshocton County
135	3825	9.2	**Greenville** (city) Darke County
135	3825	9.2	**Norwalk** (city) Huron County
138	3868	9.1	**Cleveland** (city) Cuyahoga County
138	3868	9.1	**Dayton** (city) Montgomery County
138	3868	9.1	**Kent** (city) Portage County
141	3900	9.0	**Brooklyn** (city) Cuyahoga County
141	3900	9.0	**Springdale** (city) Hamilton County
143	3934	8.9	**Forest Park** (city) Hamilton County
143	3934	8.9	**Lorain** (city) Lorain County
143	3934	8.9	**Toledo** (city) Lucas County
146	3973	8.8	**East Liverpool** (city) Columbiana County
147	4004	8.7	**Cambridge** (city) Guernsey County
147	4004	8.7	**Ravenna** (city) Portage County
147	4004	8.7	**Wooster** (city) Wayne County
150	4030	8.6	**Brook Park** (city) Cuyahoga County

Note: *The state column ranks the top/bottom 150 places from all places in the state with population of 10,000 or more. The national column ranks the top/bottom 150 places from all places in the country with population of 10,000 or more. Places that are unincorporated were not considered in the rankings. Please refer to the User Guide for additional information.*

Employment: Management, Business, and Financial Occupations

Top 150 Places Ranked in *Ascending* Order

State Rank	Nat'l Rank	Percent	Place
1	45	4.1	**East Cleveland** (city) Cuyahoga County
2	103	5.5	**Fremont** (city) Sandusky County
3	110	5.6	**Fostoria** (city) Seneca County
3	110	5.6	**Marion** (city) Marion County
5	157	6.1	**Van Wert** (city) Van Wert County
6	166	6.2	**Northbrook** (CDP) Hamilton County
7	205	6.5	**Salem** (city) Columbiana County
8	224	6.7	**Ashtabula** (city) Ashtabula County
9	268	7.0	**Niles** (city) Trumbull County
9	268	7.0	**Youngstown** (city) Mahoning County
11	288	7.1	**Athens** (city) Athens County
11	288	7.1	**Tiffin** (city) Seneca County
13	311	7.2	**Barberton** (city) Summit County
14	344	7.4	**Lima** (city) Allen County
15	357	7.5	**Conneaut** (city) Ashtabula County
15	357	7.5	**Galion** (city) Crawford County
15	357	7.5	**Piqua** (city) Miami County
15	357	7.5	**Zanesville** (city) Muskingum County
19	380	7.6	**Painesville** (city) Lake County
20	406	7.7	**Alliance** (city) Stark County
21	419	7.8	**Warrensville Heights** (city) Cuyahoga County
22	439	7.9	**Canton** (city) Stark County
23	456	8.0	**Hamilton** (city) Butler County
23	456	8.0	**Warren** (city) Trumbull County
25	497	8.2	**Bellefontaine** (city) Logan County
26	519	8.3	**Mansfield** (city) Richland County
26	519	8.3	**Maple Heights** (city) Cuyahoga County
26	519	8.3	**Massillon** (city) Stark County
26	519	8.3	**Struthers** (city) Mahoning County
26	519	8.3	**Vermilion** (city) Lorain County
31	546	8.4	**Defiance** (city) Defiance County
31	546	8.4	**Oregon** (city) Lucas County
33	569	8.5	**Whitehall** (city) Franklin County
34	602	8.6	**Brook Park** (city) Cuyahoga County
35	627	8.7	**Cambridge** (city) Guernsey County
35	627	8.7	**Ravenna** (city) Portage County
35	627	8.7	**Wooster** (city) Wayne County
38	653	8.8	**East Liverpool** (city) Columbiana County
39	684	8.9	**Forest Park** (city) Hamilton County
39	684	8.9	**Lorain** (city) Lorain County
39	684	8.9	**Toledo** (city) Lucas County
42	723	9.0	**Brooklyn** (city) Cuyahoga County
42	723	9.0	**Springdale** (city) Hamilton County
44	757	9.1	**Cleveland** (city) Cuyahoga County
44	757	9.1	**Dayton** (city) Montgomery County
44	757	9.1	**Kent** (city) Portage County
47	789	9.2	**Coshocton** (city) Coshocton County
47	789	9.2	**Greenville** (city) Darke County
47	789	9.2	**Norwalk** (city) Huron County
50	832	9.3	**Bucyrus** (city) Crawford County
51	863	9.4	**Austintown** (CDP) Mahoning County
51	863	9.4	**Bowling Green** (city) Wood County
51	863	9.4	**Chillicothe** (city) Ross County
51	863	9.4	**Garfield Heights** (city) Cuyahoga County
51	863	9.4	**Sandusky** (city) Erie County
56	904	9.5	**Marietta** (city) Washington County
57	940	9.6	**Elyria** (city) Lorain County
57	940	9.6	**Ironton** (city) Lawrence County
57	940	9.6	**Wilmington** (city) Clinton County
60	977	9.7	**Springfield** (city) Clark County
61	1004	9.8	**Lancaster** (city) Fairfield County
61	1004	9.8	**Trenton** (city) Butler County
63	1067	10.0	**Bedford** (city) Cuyahoga County
63	1067	10.0	**Bedford Heights** (city) Cuyahoga County
63	1067	10.0	**Newark** (city) Licking County
66	1108	10.1	**Akron** (city) Summit County
66	1108	10.1	**Wickliffe** (city) Lake County
68	1224	10.4	**Fairborn** (city) Greene County
68	1224	10.4	**Xenia** (city) Greene County
70	1260	10.5	**Portsmouth** (city) Scioto County
71	1321	10.7	**Parma Heights** (city) Cuyahoga County
71	1321	10.7	**Richmond Heights** (city) Cuyahoga County
73	1354	10.8	**Celina** (city) Mercer County
73	1354	10.8	**Middletown** (city) Butler County
75	1387	10.9	**Dover** (city) Tuscarawas County
75	1387	10.9	**Trotwood** (city) Montgomery County
77	1422	11.0	**Oxford** (city) Butler County
77	1422	11.0	**Urbana** (city) Champaign County
79	1455	11.1	**Mount Vernon** (city) Knox County
79	1455	11.1	**Washington Court House** (city) Fayette County
79	1455	11.1	**West Carrollton** (city) Montgomery County
82	1524	11.3	**Euclid** (city) Cuyahoga County
83	1556	11.4	**Circleville** (city) Pickaway County
83	1556	11.4	**Steubenville** (city) Jefferson County
85	1596	11.5	**New Philadelphia** (city) Tuscarawas County
85	1596	11.5	**Riverside** (city) Montgomery County
87	1634	11.6	**Finneytown** (CDP) Hamilton County
88	1656	11.7	**New Franklin** (city) Summit County
88	1656	11.7	**Parma** (city) Cuyahoga County
88	1656	11.7	**Sidney** (city) Shelby County
88	1656	11.7	**Willoughby** (city) Lake County
92	1694	11.8	**Englewood** (city) Montgomery County
92	1694	11.8	**Huber Heights** (city) Montgomery County
92	1694	11.8	**Maumee** (city) Lucas County
92	1694	11.8	**Reading** (city) Hamilton County
96	1886	12.3	**Ashland** (city) Ashland County
96	1886	12.3	**Berea** (city) Cuyahoga County
98	1924	12.4	**Willowick** (city) Lake County
99	2044	12.8	**Amherst** (city) Lorain County
100	2078	12.9	**Eastlake** (city) Lake County
100	2078	12.9	**Troy** (city) Miami County
102	2106	13.0	**Brunswick** (city) Medina County
103	2137	13.1	**Heath** (city) Licking County
103	2137	13.1	**Kettering** (city) Montgomery County
103	2137	13.1	**Marysville** (city) Union County
103	2137	13.1	**Norwood** (city) Hamilton County
107	2181	13.2	**Norton** (city) Summit County
108	2221	13.3	**Fairfield** (city) Butler County
109	2294	13.5	**Franklin** (city) Warren County
110	2346	13.7	**Tallmadge** (city) Summit County
111	2433	14.0	**Cuyahoga Falls** (city) Summit County
111	2433	14.0	**Medina** (city) Medina County
113	2462	14.1	**Lebanon** (city) Warren County
114	2502	14.2	**Boardman** (CDP) Mahoning County
114	2502	14.2	**Bridgetown** (CDP) Hamilton County
116	2531	14.3	**Cincinnati** (city) Hamilton County
117	2596	14.5	**Vandalia** (city) Montgomery County
118	2629	14.6	**Cleveland Heights** (city) Cuyahoga County
118	2629	14.6	**North Canton** (city) Stark County
120	2674	14.8	**Mayfield Heights** (city) Cuyahoga County
120	2674	14.8	**White Oak** (CDP) Hamilton County
122	2700	14.9	**Monroe** (city) Butler County
123	2763	15.2	**Columbus** (city) Franklin County
123	2763	15.2	**Fairview Park** (city) Cuyahoga County
125	2816	15.4	**South Euclid** (city) Cuyahoga County
126	2885	15.6	**Grove City** (city) Franklin County
127	2908	15.7	**Findlay** (city) Hancock County
127	2908	15.7	**Miamisburg** (city) Montgomery County
129	2962	15.9	**Pataskala** (city) Licking County
130	3013	16.1	**Clayton** (city) Montgomery County
130	3013	16.1	**Sylvania** (city) Lucas County
132	3057	16.3	**North Olmsted** (city) Cuyahoga County
133	3080	16.4	**Delaware** (city) Delaware County
133	3080	16.4	**Reynoldsburg** (city) Franklin County
135	3098	16.5	**Lakewood** (city) Cuyahoga County
136	3122	16.6	**Mentor** (city) Lake County
137	3217	17.0	**North Ridgeville** (city) Lorain County
137	3217	17.0	**Streetsboro** (city) Portage County
139	3238	17.1	**Green** (city) Summit County
140	3256	17.2	**Stow** (city) Summit County
141	3282	17.3	**Wadsworth** (city) Medina County
142	3346	17.6	**Sharonville** (city) Hamilton County
143	3426	18.0	**Middleburg Heights** (city) Cuyahoga County
144	3443	18.1	**Seven Hills** (city) Cuyahoga County
145	3463	18.2	**Monfort Heights** (CDP) Hamilton County
146	3481	18.3	**Loveland** (city) Hamilton County
147	3559	18.7	**Centerville** (city) Montgomery County
148	3599	18.9	**Macedonia** (city) Summit County
149	3681	19.4	**Dent** (CDP) Hamilton County
150	3717	19.6	**Blue Ash** (city) Hamilton County

Note: *The state column ranks the top/bottom 150 places from all places in the state with population of 10,000 or more. The national column ranks the top/bottom 150 places from all places in the country with population of 10,000 or more. Places that are unincorporated were not considered in the rankings. Please refer to the User Guide for additional information.*

Employment: Computer, Engineering, and Science Occupations

Top 150 Places Ranked in *Descending* Order

State Rank	Nat'l Rank	Percent	Place
1	120	14.4	**Dublin** (city) Franklin County
2	152	13.4	**Mayfield Heights** (city) Cuyahoga County
3	190	12.8	**Beavercreek** (city) Greene County
4	229	12.2	**Powell** (city) Delaware County
5	342	10.8	**Upper Arlington** (city) Franklin County
6	363	10.6	**Montgomery** (city) Hamilton County
7	374	10.5	**Middleburg Heights** (city) Cuyahoga County
8	424	10.2	**Springboro** (city) Warren County
9	514	9.6	**Twinsburg** (city) Summit County
10	524	9.5	**Marysville** (city) Union County
11	550	9.3	**Hilliard** (city) Franklin County
11	550	9.3	**Mason** (city) Warren County
13	566	9.2	**Seven Hills** (city) Cuyahoga County
14	581	9.1	**Springdale** (city) Hamilton County
15	642	8.8	**Broadview Heights** (city) Cuyahoga County
15	642	8.8	**Hudson** (city) Summit County
15	642	8.8	**Sharonville** (city) Hamilton County
18	695	8.6	**Beachwood** (city) Cuyahoga County
19	715	8.5	**Strongsville** (city) Cuyahoga County
19	715	8.5	**Westlake** (city) Cuyahoga County
21	744	8.4	**University Heights** (city) Cuyahoga County
22	767	8.3	**Loveland** (city) Hamilton County
23	821	8.1	**Cleveland Heights** (city) Cuyahoga County
24	874	7.9	**Blue Ash** (city) Hamilton County
24	874	7.9	**Gahanna** (city) Franklin County
26	924	7.7	**Avon** (city) Lorain County
26	924	7.7	**Macedonia** (city) Summit County
28	957	7.6	**Fairborn** (city) Greene County
28	957	7.6	**Rocky River** (city) Cuyahoga County
30	992	7.5	**Stow** (city) Summit County
31	1022	7.4	**Shaker Heights** (city) Cuyahoga County
32	1061	7.3	**Worthington** (city) Franklin County
33	1097	7.2	**Centerville** (city) Montgomery County
33	1097	7.2	**Kettering** (city) Montgomery County
35	1137	7.1	**Richmond Heights** (city) Cuyahoga County
35	1137	7.1	**Solon** (city) Cuyahoga County
37	1190	7.0	**Delaware** (city) Delaware County
38	1224	6.9	**Perrysburg** (city) Wood County
39	1267	6.8	**Bexley** (city) Franklin County
39	1267	6.8	**South Euclid** (city) Cuyahoga County
39	1267	6.8	**Wooster** (city) Wayne County
42	1303	6.7	**Brecksville** (city) Cuyahoga County
43	1354	6.6	**Mack** (CDP) Hamilton County
43	1354	6.6	**North Royalton** (city) Cuyahoga County
43	1354	6.6	**Riverside** (city) Montgomery County
43	1354	6.6	**Westerville** (city) Franklin County
47	1402	6.5	**Reynoldsburg** (city) Franklin County
48	1445	6.4	**Fairview Park** (city) Cuyahoga County
48	1445	6.4	**Finneytown** (CDP) Hamilton County
48	1445	6.4	**Huber Heights** (city) Montgomery County
48	1445	6.4	**Mentor** (city) Lake County
52	1484	6.3	**Cincinnati** (city) Hamilton County
53	1535	6.2	**Columbus** (city) Franklin County
53	1535	6.2	**Cuyahoga Falls** (city) Summit County
53	1535	6.2	**Lyndhurst** (city) Cuyahoga County
56	1579	6.1	**North Olmsted** (city) Cuyahoga County
56	1579	6.1	**Sylvania** (city) Lucas County
58	1682	5.9	**Berea** (city) Cuyahoga County
58	1682	5.9	**Monroe** (city) Butler County
60	1735	5.8	**Dent** (CDP) Hamilton County
60	1735	5.8	**Fairfield** (city) Butler County
60	1735	5.8	**Miamisburg** (city) Montgomery County
63	1790	5.7	**Norton** (city) Summit County
64	1837	5.6	**Amherst** (city) Lorain County
64	1837	5.6	**Brooklyn** (city) Cuyahoga County
64	1837	5.6	**New Franklin** (city) Summit County
64	1837	5.6	**Wadsworth** (city) Medina County
64	1837	5.6	**Willoughby** (city) Lake County
69	1895	5.5	**Englewood** (city) Montgomery County
69	1895	5.5	**Lakewood** (city) Cuyahoga County
69	1895	5.5	**North Ridgeville** (city) Lorain County
69	1895	5.5	**Wickliffe** (city) Lake County
73	2011	5.3	**Aurora** (city) Portage County
73	2011	5.3	**Parma Heights** (city) Cuyahoga County
73	2011	5.3	**Troy** (city) Miami County
76	2067	5.2	**North Canton** (city) Stark County
77	2126	5.1	**Athens** (city) Athens County
77	2126	5.1	**Eastlake** (city) Lake County
77	2126	5.1	**Findlay** (city) Hancock County
77	2126	5.1	**Grove City** (city) Franklin County
77	2126	5.1	**Norwood** (city) Hamilton County
82	2178	5.0	**Forestville** (CDP) Hamilton County
82	2178	5.0	**Lebanon** (city) Warren County
82	2178	5.0	**Reading** (city) Hamilton County
85	2244	4.9	**Kent** (city) Portage County
85	2244	4.9	**West Carrollton** (city) Montgomery County
87	2311	4.8	**Medina** (city) Medina County
87	2311	4.8	**Pickerington** (city) Fairfield County
87	2311	4.8	**Tallmadge** (city) Summit County
90	2376	4.7	**Green** (city) Summit County
90	2376	4.7	**Trenton** (city) Butler County
92	2496	4.5	**Brunswick** (city) Medina County
92	2496	4.5	**White Oak** (CDP) Hamilton County
94	2583	4.4	**Franklin** (city) Warren County
95	2627	4.3	**Clayton** (city) Montgomery County
95	2627	4.3	**Marietta** (city) Washington County
97	2703	4.2	**Bay Village** (city) Cuyahoga County
97	2703	4.2	**Urbana** (city) Champaign County
99	2777	4.1	**Norwalk** (city) Huron County
99	2777	4.1	**Parma** (city) Cuyahoga County
101	2835	4.0	**Euclid** (city) Cuyahoga County
101	2835	4.0	**Vandalia** (city) Montgomery County
103	2899	3.9	**Barberton** (city) Summit County
103	2899	3.9	**Bridgetown** (CDP) Hamilton County
103	2899	3.9	**Elyria** (city) Lorain County
103	2899	3.9	**Newark** (city) Licking County
103	2899	3.9	**Willowick** (city) Lake County
108	2972	3.8	**Chillicothe** (city) Ross County
108	2972	3.8	**Dayton** (city) Montgomery County
108	2972	3.8	**Fremont** (city) Sandusky County
108	2972	3.8	**Oregon** (city) Lucas County
112	3030	3.7	**Bellefontaine** (city) Logan County
112	3030	3.7	**Maumee** (city) Lucas County
112	3030	3.7	**Oxford** (city) Butler County
115	3093	3.6	**Forest Park** (city) Hamilton County
115	3093	3.6	**Steubenville** (city) Jefferson County
117	3157	3.5	**Akron** (city) Summit County
117	3157	3.5	**Avon Lake** (city) Lorain County
119	3220	3.4	**Hamilton** (city) Butler County
119	3220	3.4	**Maple Heights** (city) Cuyahoga County
119	3220	3.4	**Middletown** (city) Butler County
119	3220	3.4	**Pataskala** (city) Licking County
119	3220	3.4	**Trotwood** (city) Montgomery County
119	3220	3.4	**Van Wert** (city) Van Wert County
119	3220	3.4	**Vermilion** (city) Lorain County
126	3297	3.3	**Bedford** (city) Cuyahoga County
126	3297	3.3	**Boardman** (CDP) Mahoning County
126	3297	3.3	**Wilmington** (city) Clinton County
129	3358	3.2	**Monfort Heights** (CDP) Hamilton County
129	3358	3.2	**Piqua** (city) Miami County
129	3358	3.2	**Zanesville** (city) Muskingum County
132	3435	3.1	**Dover** (city) Tuscarawas County
133	3489	3.0	**Ashland** (city) Ashland County
133	3489	3.0	**Brook Park** (city) Cuyahoga County
133	3489	3.0	**Cleveland** (city) Cuyahoga County
133	3489	3.0	**Garfield Heights** (city) Cuyahoga County
137	3568	2.9	**Mount Vernon** (city) Knox County
137	3568	2.9	**Streetsboro** (city) Portage County
139	3632	2.8	**Bowling Green** (city) Wood County
139	3632	2.8	**Lancaster** (city) Fairfield County
139	3632	2.8	**Mansfield** (city) Richland County
139	3632	2.8	**New Philadelphia** (city) Tuscarawas County
139	3632	2.8	**Toledo** (city) Lucas County
144	3705	2.7	**Austintown** (CDP) Mahoning County
144	3705	2.7	**Celina** (city) Mercer County
144	3705	2.7	**Painesville** (city) Lake County
147	3764	2.6	**Ravenna** (city) Portage County
147	3764	2.6	**Xenia** (city) Greene County
149	3837	2.5	**Canton** (city) Stark County
149	3837	2.5	**Lorain** (city) Lorain County

Note: *The state column ranks the top/bottom 150 places from all places in the state with population of 10,000 or more. The national column ranks the top/bottom 150 places from all places in the country with population of 10,000 or more. Places that are unincorporated were not considered in the rankings. Please refer to the User Guide for additional information.*

Employment: Computer, Engineering, and Science Occupations

Top 150 Places Ranked in *Ascending* Order

State Rank	Nat'l Rank	Percent	Place
1	80	0.9	**East Cleveland** (city) Cuyahoga County
1	80	0.9	**Struthers** (city) Mahoning County
3	101	1.0	**East Liverpool** (city) Columbiana County
4	172	1.3	**Fostoria** (city) Seneca County
4	172	1.3	**Lima** (city) Allen County
6	202	1.4	**Ashtabula** (city) Ashtabula County
6	202	1.4	**Portsmouth** (city) Scioto County
6	202	1.4	**Salem** (city) Columbiana County
9	239	1.5	**Defiance** (city) Defiance County
9	239	1.5	**Niles** (city) Trumbull County
11	283	1.6	**Northbrook** (CDP) Hamilton County
11	283	1.6	**Washington Court House** (city) Fayette County
13	325	1.7	**Cambridge** (city) Guernsey County
13	325	1.7	**Greenville** (city) Darke County
13	325	1.7	**Ironton** (city) Lawrence County
16	360	1.8	**Bucyrus** (city) Crawford County
16	360	1.8	**Conneaut** (city) Ashtabula County
16	360	1.8	**Sandusky** (city) Erie County
16	360	1.8	**Tiffin** (city) Seneca County
16	360	1.8	**Youngstown** (city) Mahoning County
21	425	1.9	**Circleville** (city) Pickaway County
21	425	1.9	**Warren** (city) Trumbull County
23	479	2.0	**Coshocton** (city) Coshocton County
24	536	2.1	**Galion** (city) Crawford County
24	536	2.1	**Massillon** (city) Stark County
26	586	2.2	**Sidney** (city) Shelby County
26	586	2.2	**Springfield** (city) Clark County
28	649	2.3	**Alliance** (city) Stark County
28	649	2.3	**Heath** (city) Licking County
28	649	2.3	**Whitehall** (city) Franklin County
31	704	2.4	**Bedford Heights** (city) Cuyahoga County
32	754	2.5	**Canton** (city) Stark County
32	754	2.5	**Lorain** (city) Lorain County
32	754	2.5	**Marion** (city) Marion County
32	754	2.5	**Warrensville Heights** (city) Cuyahoga County
36	820	2.6	**Ravenna** (city) Portage County
36	820	2.6	**Xenia** (city) Greene County
38	893	2.7	**Austintown** (CDP) Mahoning County
38	893	2.7	**Celina** (city) Mercer County
38	893	2.7	**Painesville** (city) Lake County
41	952	2.8	**Bowling Green** (city) Wood County
41	952	2.8	**Lancaster** (city) Fairfield County
41	952	2.8	**Mansfield** (city) Richland County
41	952	2.8	**New Philadelphia** (city) Tuscarawas County
41	952	2.8	**Toledo** (city) Lucas County
46	1025	2.9	**Mount Vernon** (city) Knox County
46	1025	2.9	**Streetsboro** (city) Portage County
48	1089	3.0	**Ashland** (city) Ashland County
48	1089	3.0	**Brook Park** (city) Cuyahoga County
48	1089	3.0	**Cleveland** (city) Cuyahoga County
48	1089	3.0	**Garfield Heights** (city) Cuyahoga County
52	1168	3.1	**Dover** (city) Tuscarawas County
53	1222	3.2	**Monfort Heights** (CDP) Hamilton County
53	1222	3.2	**Piqua** (city) Miami County
53	1222	3.2	**Zanesville** (city) Muskingum County
56	1299	3.3	**Bedford** (city) Cuyahoga County
56	1299	3.3	**Boardman** (CDP) Mahoning County
56	1299	3.3	**Wilmington** (city) Clinton County
59	1360	3.4	**Hamilton** (city) Butler County
59	1360	3.4	**Maple Heights** (city) Cuyahoga County
59	1360	3.4	**Middletown** (city) Butler County
59	1360	3.4	**Pataskala** (city) Licking County
59	1360	3.4	**Trotwood** (city) Montgomery County
59	1360	3.4	**Van Wert** (city) Van Wert County
59	1360	3.4	**Vermilion** (city) Lorain County
66	1437	3.5	**Akron** (city) Summit County
66	1437	3.5	**Avon Lake** (city) Lorain County
68	1500	3.6	**Forest Park** (city) Hamilton County
68	1500	3.6	**Steubenville** (city) Jefferson County
70	1564	3.7	**Bellefontaine** (city) Logan County
70	1564	3.7	**Maumee** (city) Lucas County
70	1564	3.7	**Oxford** (city) Butler County
73	1627	3.8	**Chillicothe** (city) Ross County
73	1627	3.8	**Dayton** (city) Montgomery County
73	1627	3.8	**Fremont** (city) Sandusky County
73	1627	3.8	**Oregon** (city) Lucas County
77	1685	3.9	**Barberton** (city) Summit County
77	1685	3.9	**Bridgetown** (CDP) Hamilton County
77	1685	3.9	**Elyria** (city) Lorain County
77	1685	3.9	**Newark** (city) Licking County
77	1685	3.9	**Willowick** (city) Lake County
82	1758	4.0	**Euclid** (city) Cuyahoga County
82	1758	4.0	**Vandalia** (city) Montgomery County
84	1822	4.1	**Norwalk** (city) Huron County
84	1822	4.1	**Parma** (city) Cuyahoga County
86	1880	4.2	**Bay Village** (city) Cuyahoga County
86	1880	4.2	**Urbana** (city) Champaign County
88	1954	4.3	**Clayton** (city) Montgomery County
88	1954	4.3	**Marietta** (city) Washington County
90	2030	4.4	**Franklin** (city) Warren County
91	2074	4.5	**Brunswick** (city) Medina County
91	2074	4.5	**White Oak** (CDP) Hamilton County
93	2229	4.7	**Green** (city) Summit County
93	2229	4.7	**Trenton** (city) Butler County
95	2281	4.8	**Medina** (city) Medina County
95	2281	4.8	**Pickerington** (city) Fairfield County
95	2281	4.8	**Tallmadge** (city) Summit County
98	2346	4.9	**Kent** (city) Portage County
98	2346	4.9	**West Carrollton** (city) Montgomery County
100	2413	5.0	**Forestville** (CDP) Hamilton County
100	2413	5.0	**Lebanon** (city) Warren County
100	2413	5.0	**Reading** (city) Hamilton County
103	2479	5.1	**Athens** (city) Athens County
103	2479	5.1	**Eastlake** (city) Lake County
103	2479	5.1	**Findlay** (city) Hancock County
103	2479	5.1	**Grove City** (city) Franklin County
103	2479	5.1	**Norwood** (city) Hamilton County
108	2531	5.2	**North Canton** (city) Stark County
109	2590	5.3	**Aurora** (city) Portage County
109	2590	5.3	**Parma Heights** (city) Cuyahoga County
109	2590	5.3	**Troy** (city) Miami County
112	2705	5.5	**Englewood** (city) Montgomery County
112	2705	5.5	**Lakewood** (city) Cuyahoga County
112	2705	5.5	**North Ridgeville** (city) Lorain County
112	2705	5.5	**Wickliffe** (city) Lake County
116	2762	5.6	**Amherst** (city) Lorain County
116	2762	5.6	**Brooklyn** (city) Cuyahoga County
116	2762	5.6	**New Franklin** (city) Summit County
116	2762	5.6	**Wadsworth** (city) Medina County
116	2762	5.6	**Willoughby** (city) Lake County
121	2820	5.7	**Norton** (city) Summit County
122	2867	5.8	**Dent** (CDP) Hamilton County
122	2867	5.8	**Fairfield** (city) Butler County
122	2867	5.8	**Miamisburg** (city) Montgomery County
125	2922	5.9	**Berea** (city) Cuyahoga County
125	2922	5.9	**Monroe** (city) Butler County
127	3033	6.1	**North Olmsted** (city) Cuyahoga County
127	3033	6.1	**Sylvania** (city) Lucas County
129	3078	6.2	**Columbus** (city) Franklin County
129	3078	6.2	**Cuyahoga Falls** (city) Summit County
129	3078	6.2	**Lyndhurst** (city) Cuyahoga County
132	3122	6.3	**Cincinnati** (city) Hamilton County
133	3173	6.4	**Fairview Park** (city) Cuyahoga County
133	3173	6.4	**Finneytown** (CDP) Hamilton County
133	3173	6.4	**Huber Heights** (city) Montgomery County
133	3173	6.4	**Mentor** (city) Lake County
137	3212	6.5	**Reynoldsburg** (city) Franklin County
138	3255	6.6	**Mack** (CDP) Hamilton County
138	3255	6.6	**North Royalton** (city) Cuyahoga County
138	3255	6.6	**Riverside** (city) Montgomery County
138	3255	6.6	**Westerville** (city) Franklin County
142	3303	6.7	**Brecksville** (city) Cuyahoga County
143	3354	6.8	**Bexley** (city) Franklin County
143	3354	6.8	**South Euclid** (city) Cuyahoga County
143	3354	6.8	**Wooster** (city) Wayne County
146	3390	6.9	**Perrysburg** (city) Wood County
147	3433	7.0	**Delaware** (city) Delaware County
148	3467	7.1	**Richmond Heights** (city) Cuyahoga County
148	3467	7.1	**Solon** (city) Cuyahoga County
150	3520	7.2	**Centerville** (city) Montgomery County

Note: *The state column ranks the top/bottom 150 places from all places in the state with population of 10,000 or more. The national column ranks the top/bottom 150 places from all places in the country with population of 10,000 or more. Places that are unincorporated were not considered in the rankings. Please refer to the User Guide for additional information.*

Employment: Education, Legal, Community Service, Arts, and Media Occupations

Top 150 Places Ranked in *Descending* Order

State Rank	Nat'l Rank	Percent	Place
1	43	24.6	**Shaker Heights** (city) Cuyahoga County
2	45	24.5	**Athens** (city) Athens County
3	55	23.7	**Bexley** (city) Franklin County
4	64	23.4	**Worthington** (city) Franklin County
5	108	21.5	**Oxford** (city) Butler County
6	145	20.3	**Bowling Green** (city) Wood County
7	162	19.9	**Cleveland Heights** (city) Cuyahoga County
8	175	19.6	**Bay Village** (city) Cuyahoga County
8	175	19.6	**Montgomery** (city) Hamilton County
8	175	19.6	**Upper Arlington** (city) Franklin County
11	180	19.5	**Beachwood** (city) Cuyahoga County
12	193	19.4	**University Heights** (city) Cuyahoga County
13	205	19.2	**Forestville** (CDP) Hamilton County
14	376	16.7	**Blue Ash** (city) Hamilton County
15	447	16.1	**Kent** (city) Portage County
16	462	16.0	**Sylvania** (city) Lucas County
17	550	15.4	**Hudson** (city) Summit County
18	604	15.1	**Wooster** (city) Wayne County
19	680	14.7	**Centerville** (city) Montgomery County
19	680	14.7	**North Canton** (city) Stark County
21	701	14.6	**Westerville** (city) Franklin County
22	744	14.4	**Rocky River** (city) Cuyahoga County
23	771	14.3	**Lyndhurst** (city) Cuyahoga County
23	771	14.3	**Solon** (city) Cuyahoga County
25	795	14.2	**Lakewood** (city) Cuyahoga County
26	824	14.1	**Brecksville** (city) Cuyahoga County
27	904	13.8	**Avon Lake** (city) Lorain County
28	931	13.7	**Richmond Heights** (city) Cuyahoga County
29	993	13.5	**Perrysburg** (city) Wood County
30	1079	13.2	**Avon** (city) Lorain County
30	1079	13.2	**Defiance** (city) Defiance County
30	1079	13.2	**Gahanna** (city) Franklin County
33	1117	13.1	**South Euclid** (city) Cuyahoga County
34	1147	13.0	**Hilliard** (city) Franklin County
35	1188	12.9	**Loveland** (city) Hamilton County
36	1307	12.6	**Berea** (city) Cuyahoga County
36	1307	12.6	**Portsmouth** (city) Scioto County
38	1346	12.5	**Ashland** (city) Ashland County
38	1346	12.5	**Westlake** (city) Cuyahoga County
40	1460	12.2	**Cincinnati** (city) Hamilton County
41	1505	12.1	**Mayfield Heights** (city) Cuyahoga County
42	1586	11.9	**Tallmadge** (city) Summit County
42	1586	11.9	**Twinsburg** (city) Summit County
42	1586	11.9	**Warrensville Heights** (city) Cuyahoga County
45	1642	11.8	**Delaware** (city) Delaware County
45	1642	11.8	**Dublin** (city) Franklin County
47	1698	11.7	**Green** (city) Summit County
47	1698	11.7	**Seven Hills** (city) Cuyahoga County
49	1745	11.6	**Bellefontaine** (city) Logan County
49	1745	11.6	**Ironton** (city) Lawrence County
51	1803	11.5	**Beavercreek** (city) Greene County
51	1803	11.5	**Broadview Heights** (city) Cuyahoga County
53	1897	11.3	**Columbus** (city) Franklin County
53	1897	11.3	**Mount Vernon** (city) Knox County
53	1897	11.3	**Powell** (city) Delaware County
53	1897	11.3	**Stow** (city) Summit County
53	1897	11.3	**Tiffin** (city) Seneca County
58	1945	11.2	**Kettering** (city) Montgomery County
59	1998	11.1	**Norton** (city) Summit County
60	2048	11.0	**Clayton** (city) Montgomery County
60	2048	11.0	**Cuyahoga Falls** (city) Summit County
60	2048	11.0	**Fairview Park** (city) Cuyahoga County
60	2048	11.0	**Marietta** (city) Washington County
60	2048	11.0	**Springboro** (city) Warren County
65	2158	10.8	**Boardman** (CDP) Mahoning County
65	2158	10.8	**Springdale** (city) Hamilton County
67	2211	10.7	**Aurora** (city) Portage County
67	2211	10.7	**Englewood** (city) Montgomery County
69	2283	10.6	**Dayton** (city) Montgomery County
69	2283	10.6	**Finneytown** (CDP) Hamilton County
69	2283	10.6	**Pickerington** (city) Fairfield County
72	2350	10.5	**Dover** (city) Tuscarawas County
73	2414	10.4	**Macedonia** (city) Summit County
73	2414	10.4	**Maumee** (city) Lucas County
73	2414	10.4	**Wadsworth** (city) Medina County
76	2466	10.3	**Steubenville** (city) Jefferson County
76	2466	10.3	**Strongsville** (city) Cuyahoga County
76	2466	10.3	**Xenia** (city) Greene County
79	2529	10.2	**Springfield** (city) Clark County
80	2588	10.1	**Mason** (city) Warren County
80	2588	10.1	**Norwood** (city) Hamilton County
82	2650	10.0	**Heath** (city) Licking County
82	2650	10.0	**North Olmsted** (city) Cuyahoga County
82	2650	10.0	**Wilmington** (city) Clinton County
85	2719	9.9	**Amherst** (city) Lorain County
85	2719	9.9	**Bedford Heights** (city) Cuyahoga County
85	2719	9.9	**Miamisburg** (city) Montgomery County
85	2719	9.9	**Willoughby** (city) Lake County
89	2775	9.8	**Galion** (city) Crawford County
90	2888	9.6	**Akron** (city) Summit County
90	2888	9.6	**Circleville** (city) Pickaway County
90	2888	9.6	**North Ridgeville** (city) Lorain County
90	2888	9.6	**Wickliffe** (city) Lake County
94	2942	9.5	**Austintown** (CDP) Mahoning County
94	2942	9.5	**Reynoldsburg** (city) Franklin County
96	2993	9.4	**Troy** (city) Miami County
97	3049	9.3	**Coshocton** (city) Coshocton County
97	3049	9.3	**Toledo** (city) Lucas County
99	3111	9.2	**Lebanon** (city) Warren County
99	3111	9.2	**Sandusky** (city) Erie County
101	3168	9.1	**Newark** (city) Licking County
102	3217	9.0	**Cambridge** (city) Guernsey County
102	3217	9.0	**Findlay** (city) Hancock County
104	3269	8.9	**Norwalk** (city) Huron County
104	3269	8.9	**Van Wert** (city) Van Wert County
106	3328	8.8	**Fairfield** (city) Butler County
106	3328	8.8	**Forest Park** (city) Hamilton County
106	3328	8.8	**Oregon** (city) Lucas County
106	3328	8.8	**Vermilion** (city) Lorain County
110	3397	8.7	**Fairborn** (city) Greene County
110	3397	8.7	**Medina** (city) Medina County
112	3441	8.6	**Cleveland** (city) Cuyahoga County
112	3441	8.6	**North Royalton** (city) Cuyahoga County
114	3485	8.5	**Reading** (city) Hamilton County
115	3539	8.4	**Celina** (city) Mercer County
115	3539	8.4	**Hamilton** (city) Butler County
115	3539	8.4	**Monfort Heights** (CDP) Hamilton County
115	3539	8.4	**New Philadelphia** (city) Tuscarawas County
115	3539	8.4	**White Oak** (CDP) Hamilton County
115	3539	8.4	**Zanesville** (city) Muskingum County
121	3590	8.3	**Huber Heights** (city) Montgomery County
121	3590	8.3	**Mentor** (city) Lake County
121	3590	8.3	**Willowick** (city) Lake County
124	3634	8.2	**Elyria** (city) Lorain County
124	3634	8.2	**Painesville** (city) Lake County
126	3680	8.1	**Canton** (city) Stark County
126	3680	8.1	**Lima** (city) Allen County
126	3680	8.1	**Mack** (CDP) Hamilton County
126	3680	8.1	**Vandalia** (city) Montgomery County
130	3721	8.0	**Bridgetown** (CDP) Hamilton County
130	3721	8.0	**Conneaut** (city) Ashtabula County
132	3764	7.9	**Bedford** (city) Cuyahoga County
132	3764	7.9	**Monroe** (city) Butler County
132	3764	7.9	**Pataskala** (city) Licking County
135	3863	7.7	**Lancaster** (city) Fairfield County
135	3863	7.7	**Parma** (city) Cuyahoga County
135	3863	7.7	**Trotwood** (city) Montgomery County
135	3863	7.7	**Youngstown** (city) Mahoning County
139	3898	7.6	**Urbana** (city) Champaign County
140	3941	7.5	**Dent** (CDP) Hamilton County
140	3941	7.5	**Lorain** (city) Lorain County
140	3941	7.5	**Mansfield** (city) Richland County
140	3941	7.5	**Middleburg Heights** (city) Cuyahoga County
144	3975	7.4	**Marion** (city) Marion County
144	3975	7.4	**New Franklin** (city) Summit County
146	4011	7.3	**Brunswick** (city) Medina County
146	4011	7.3	**East Liverpool** (city) Columbiana County
146	4011	7.3	**Euclid** (city) Cuyahoga County
149	4051	7.2	**East Cleveland** (city) Cuyahoga County
150	4084	7.1	**Greenville** (city) Darke County

Note: *The state column ranks the top/bottom 150 places from all places in the state with population of 10,000 or more. The national column ranks the top/bottom 150 places from all places in the country with population of 10,000 or more. Places that are unincorporated were not considered in the rankings. Please refer to the User Guide for additional information.*

Employment: Education, Legal, Community Service, Arts, and Media Occupations

Top 150 Places Ranked in *Ascending* Order

State Rank	Nat'l Rank	Percent	Place
1	48	4.3	**Franklin** (city) Warren County
2	67	4.6	**Sidney** (city) Shelby County
3	97	5.0	**Barberton** (city) Summit County
4	110	5.1	**Whitehall** (city) Franklin County
5	122	5.2	**Riverside** (city) Montgomery County
6	175	5.6	**Niles** (city) Trumbull County
6	175	5.6	**Ravenna** (city) Portage County
8	203	5.8	**Fostoria** (city) Seneca County
9	235	6.0	**Sharonville** (city) Hamilton County
10	257	6.1	**Chillicothe** (city) Ross County
10	257	6.1	**Fremont** (city) Sandusky County
12	292	6.2	**Eastlake** (city) Lake County
12	292	6.2	**Trenton** (city) Butler County
12	292	6.2	**West Carrollton** (city) Montgomery County
15	384	6.6	**Ashtabula** (city) Ashtabula County
15	384	6.6	**Brook Park** (city) Cuyahoga County
15	384	6.6	**Maple Heights** (city) Cuyahoga County
18	409	6.7	**Massillon** (city) Stark County
18	409	6.7	**Parma Heights** (city) Cuyahoga County
20	433	6.8	**Struthers** (city) Mahoning County
21	461	6.9	**Alliance** (city) Stark County
21	461	6.9	**Marysville** (city) Union County
21	461	6.9	**Middletown** (city) Butler County
21	461	6.9	**Northbrook** (CDP) Hamilton County
21	461	6.9	**Piqua** (city) Miami County
26	507	7.0	**Brooklyn** (city) Cuyahoga County
26	507	7.0	**Bucyrus** (city) Crawford County
26	507	7.0	**Garfield Heights** (city) Cuyahoga County
26	507	7.0	**Salem** (city) Columbiana County
30	547	7.1	**Greenville** (city) Darke County
30	547	7.1	**Grove City** (city) Franklin County
30	547	7.1	**Streetsboro** (city) Portage County
30	547	7.1	**Warren** (city) Trumbull County
30	547	7.1	**Washington Court House** (city) Fayette County
35	573	7.2	**East Cleveland** (city) Cuyahoga County
36	606	7.3	**Brunswick** (city) Medina County
36	606	7.3	**East Liverpool** (city) Columbiana County
36	606	7.3	**Euclid** (city) Cuyahoga County
39	646	7.4	**Marion** (city) Marion County
39	646	7.4	**New Franklin** (city) Summit County
41	682	7.5	**Dent** (CDP) Hamilton County
41	682	7.5	**Lorain** (city) Lorain County
41	682	7.5	**Mansfield** (city) Richland County
41	682	7.5	**Middleburg Heights** (city) Cuyahoga County
45	716	7.6	**Urbana** (city) Champaign County
46	759	7.7	**Lancaster** (city) Fairfield County
46	759	7.7	**Parma** (city) Cuyahoga County
46	759	7.7	**Trotwood** (city) Montgomery County
46	759	7.7	**Youngstown** (city) Mahoning County
50	845	7.9	**Bedford** (city) Cuyahoga County
50	845	7.9	**Monroe** (city) Butler County
50	845	7.9	**Pataskala** (city) Licking County
53	893	8.0	**Bridgetown** (CDP) Hamilton County
53	893	8.0	**Conneaut** (city) Ashtabula County
55	936	8.1	**Canton** (city) Stark County
55	936	8.1	**Lima** (city) Allen County
55	936	8.1	**Mack** (CDP) Hamilton County
55	936	8.1	**Vandalia** (city) Montgomery County
59	977	8.2	**Elyria** (city) Lorain County
59	977	8.2	**Painesville** (city) Lake County
61	1023	8.3	**Huber Heights** (city) Montgomery County
61	1023	8.3	**Mentor** (city) Lake County
61	1023	8.3	**Willowick** (city) Lake County
64	1067	8.4	**Celina** (city) Mercer County
64	1067	8.4	**Hamilton** (city) Butler County
64	1067	8.4	**Monfort Heights** (CDP) Hamilton County
64	1067	8.4	**New Philadelphia** (city) Tuscarawas County
64	1067	8.4	**White Oak** (CDP) Hamilton County
64	1067	8.4	**Zanesville** (city) Muskingum County
70	1118	8.5	**Reading** (city) Hamilton County
71	1172	8.6	**Cleveland** (city) Cuyahoga County
71	1172	8.6	**North Royalton** (city) Cuyahoga County
73	1216	8.7	**Fairborn** (city) Greene County
73	1216	8.7	**Medina** (city) Medina County
75	1260	8.8	**Fairfield** (city) Butler County
75	1260	8.8	**Forest Park** (city) Hamilton County
75	1260	8.8	**Oregon** (city) Lucas County
75	1260	8.8	**Vermilion** (city) Lorain County
79	1329	8.9	**Norwalk** (city) Huron County
79	1329	8.9	**Van Wert** (city) Van Wert County
81	1388	9.0	**Cambridge** (city) Guernsey County
81	1388	9.0	**Findlay** (city) Hancock County
83	1440	9.1	**Newark** (city) Licking County
84	1489	9.2	**Lebanon** (city) Warren County
84	1489	9.2	**Sandusky** (city) Erie County
86	1546	9.3	**Coshocton** (city) Coshocton County
86	1546	9.3	**Toledo** (city) Lucas County
88	1608	9.4	**Troy** (city) Miami County
89	1664	9.5	**Austintown** (CDP) Mahoning County
89	1664	9.5	**Reynoldsburg** (city) Franklin County
91	1715	9.6	**Akron** (city) Summit County
91	1715	9.6	**Circleville** (city) Pickaway County
91	1715	9.6	**North Ridgeville** (city) Lorain County
91	1715	9.6	**Wickliffe** (city) Lake County
95	1834	9.8	**Galion** (city) Crawford County
96	1882	9.9	**Amherst** (city) Lorain County
96	1882	9.9	**Bedford Heights** (city) Cuyahoga County
96	1882	9.9	**Miamisburg** (city) Montgomery County
96	1882	9.9	**Willoughby** (city) Lake County
100	1938	10.0	**Heath** (city) Licking County
100	1938	10.0	**North Olmsted** (city) Cuyahoga County
100	1938	10.0	**Wilmington** (city) Clinton County
103	2007	10.1	**Mason** (city) Warren County
103	2007	10.1	**Norwood** (city) Hamilton County
105	2069	10.2	**Springfield** (city) Clark County
106	2128	10.3	**Steubenville** (city) Jefferson County
106	2128	10.3	**Strongsville** (city) Cuyahoga County
106	2128	10.3	**Xenia** (city) Greene County
109	2191	10.4	**Macedonia** (city) Summit County
109	2191	10.4	**Maumee** (city) Lucas County
109	2191	10.4	**Wadsworth** (city) Medina County
112	2243	10.5	**Dover** (city) Tuscarawas County
113	2307	10.6	**Dayton** (city) Montgomery County
113	2307	10.6	**Finneytown** (CDP) Hamilton County
113	2307	10.6	**Pickerington** (city) Fairfield County
116	2374	10.7	**Aurora** (city) Portage County
116	2374	10.7	**Englewood** (city) Montgomery County
118	2446	10.8	**Boardman** (CDP) Mahoning County
118	2446	10.8	**Springdale** (city) Hamilton County
120	2553	11.0	**Clayton** (city) Montgomery County
120	2553	11.0	**Cuyahoga Falls** (city) Summit County
120	2553	11.0	**Fairview Park** (city) Cuyahoga County
120	2553	11.0	**Marietta** (city) Washington County
120	2553	11.0	**Springboro** (city) Warren County
125	2609	11.1	**Norton** (city) Summit County
126	2659	11.2	**Kettering** (city) Montgomery County
127	2712	11.3	**Columbus** (city) Franklin County
127	2712	11.3	**Mount Vernon** (city) Knox County
127	2712	11.3	**Powell** (city) Delaware County
127	2712	11.3	**Stow** (city) Summit County
127	2712	11.3	**Tiffin** (city) Seneca County
132	2816	11.5	**Beavercreek** (city) Greene County
132	2816	11.5	**Broadview Heights** (city) Cuyahoga County
134	2854	11.6	**Bellefontaine** (city) Logan County
134	2854	11.6	**Ironton** (city) Lawrence County
136	2912	11.7	**Green** (city) Summit County
136	2912	11.7	**Seven Hills** (city) Cuyahoga County
138	2959	11.8	**Delaware** (city) Delaware County
138	2959	11.8	**Dublin** (city) Franklin County
140	3015	11.9	**Tallmadge** (city) Summit County
140	3015	11.9	**Twinsburg** (city) Summit County
140	3015	11.9	**Warrensville Heights** (city) Cuyahoga County
143	3105	12.1	**Mayfield Heights** (city) Cuyahoga County
144	3152	12.2	**Cincinnati** (city) Hamilton County
145	3277	12.5	**Ashland** (city) Ashland County
145	3277	12.5	**Westlake** (city) Cuyahoga County
147	3311	12.6	**Berea** (city) Cuyahoga County
147	3311	12.6	**Portsmouth** (city) Scioto County
149	3429	12.9	**Loveland** (city) Hamilton County
150	3469	13.0	**Hilliard** (city) Franklin County

Note: *The state column ranks the top/bottom 150 places from all places in the state with population of 10,000 or more. The national column ranks the top/bottom 150 places from all places in the country with population of 10,000 or more. Places that are unincorporated were not considered in the rankings. Please refer to the User Guide for additional information.*

Employment: Healthcare Practitioners

Top 150 Places Ranked in *Descending* Order

State Rank	Nat'l Rank	Percent	Place
1	40	12.5	**Cleveland Heights** (city) Cuyahoga County
1	40	12.5	**Shaker Heights** (city) Cuyahoga County
3	43	12.4	**Powell** (city) Delaware County
4	67	11.6	**University Heights** (city) Cuyahoga County
5	73	11.5	**White Oak** (CDP) Hamilton County
6	92	11.2	**Beachwood** (city) Cuyahoga County
6	92	11.2	**Westlake** (city) Cuyahoga County
8	99	11.1	**Monfort Heights** (CDP) Hamilton County
9	106	10.8	**Brecksville** (city) Cuyahoga County
10	118	10.7	**Blue Ash** (city) Hamilton County
11	129	10.6	**Upper Arlington** (city) Franklin County
12	180	10.0	**Portsmouth** (city) Scioto County
13	206	9.8	**Solon** (city) Cuyahoga County
14	279	9.4	**Vermilion** (city) Lorain County
15	315	9.2	**Perrysburg** (city) Wood County
16	336	9.1	**Bridgetown** (CDP) Hamilton County
16	336	9.1	**Cambridge** (city) Guernsey County
16	336	9.1	**Mack** (CDP) Hamilton County
16	336	9.1	**North Royalton** (city) Cuyahoga County
20	356	9.0	**Beavercreek** (city) Greene County
20	356	9.0	**Centerville** (city) Montgomery County
20	356	9.0	**Lyndhurst** (city) Cuyahoga County
20	356	9.0	**Maumee** (city) Lucas County
24	377	8.9	**Broadview Heights** (city) Cuyahoga County
24	377	8.9	**Springboro** (city) Warren County
26	412	8.7	**Niles** (city) Trumbull County
26	412	8.7	**Rocky River** (city) Cuyahoga County
28	441	8.6	**Dublin** (city) Franklin County
29	465	8.5	**Dover** (city) Tuscarawas County
30	491	8.4	**Englewood** (city) Montgomery County
30	491	8.4	**Steubenville** (city) Jefferson County
32	519	8.3	**Avon** (city) Lorain County
32	519	8.3	**Sylvania** (city) Lucas County
34	559	8.2	**Seven Hills** (city) Cuyahoga County
35	597	8.1	**Grove City** (city) Franklin County
35	597	8.1	**Montgomery** (city) Hamilton County
35	597	8.1	**South Euclid** (city) Cuyahoga County
38	718	7.8	**Bay Village** (city) Cuyahoga County
38	718	7.8	**Fairview Park** (city) Cuyahoga County
40	755	7.7	**Hudson** (city) Summit County
40	755	7.7	**Macedonia** (city) Summit County
40	755	7.7	**Strongsville** (city) Cuyahoga County
43	804	7.6	**Mayfield Heights** (city) Cuyahoga County
43	804	7.6	**Oregon** (city) Lucas County
43	804	7.6	**Pickerington** (city) Fairfield County
46	848	7.5	**Austintown** (CDP) Mahoning County
46	848	7.5	**Euclid** (city) Cuyahoga County
46	848	7.5	**Willoughby** (city) Lake County
49	903	7.4	**Avon Lake** (city) Lorain County
49	903	7.4	**Lakewood** (city) Cuyahoga County
51	954	7.3	**Aurora** (city) Portage County
51	954	7.3	**Boardman** (CDP) Mahoning County
51	954	7.3	**Clayton** (city) Montgomery County
54	1026	7.2	**Marietta** (city) Washington County
54	1026	7.2	**Mentor** (city) Lake County
54	1026	7.2	**Worthington** (city) Franklin County
57	1083	7.1	**Brunswick** (city) Medina County
57	1083	7.1	**North Olmsted** (city) Cuyahoga County
57	1083	7.1	**Wickliffe** (city) Lake County
60	1138	7.0	**Kettering** (city) Montgomery County
60	1138	7.0	**Mason** (city) Warren County
60	1138	7.0	**Stow** (city) Summit County
60	1138	7.0	**Tallmadge** (city) Summit County
60	1138	7.0	**Vandalia** (city) Montgomery County
65	1192	6.9	**Hilliard** (city) Franklin County
65	1192	6.9	**Norton** (city) Summit County
67	1253	6.8	**Dent** (CDP) Hamilton County
67	1253	6.8	**East Liverpool** (city) Columbiana County
67	1253	6.8	**Middleburg Heights** (city) Cuyahoga County
67	1253	6.8	**New Franklin** (city) Summit County
71	1404	6.6	**Amherst** (city) Lorain County
71	1404	6.6	**Cuyahoga Falls** (city) Summit County
71	1404	6.6	**Ironton** (city) Lawrence County
71	1404	6.6	**Lancaster** (city) Fairfield County
71	1404	6.6	**Monroe** (city) Butler County
71	1404	6.6	**North Ridgeville** (city) Lorain County
71	1404	6.6	**Springdale** (city) Hamilton County
78	1488	6.5	**Green** (city) Summit County
79	1625	6.3	**Bellefontaine** (city) Logan County
79	1625	6.3	**Eastlake** (city) Lake County
79	1625	6.3	**Heath** (city) Licking County
79	1625	6.3	**Loveland** (city) Hamilton County
79	1625	6.3	**West Carrollton** (city) Montgomery County
84	1723	6.2	**Chillicothe** (city) Ross County
84	1723	6.2	**Finneytown** (CDP) Hamilton County
84	1723	6.2	**Sharonville** (city) Hamilton County
87	1812	6.1	**Richmond Heights** (city) Cuyahoga County
87	1812	6.1	**Van Wert** (city) Van Wert County
87	1812	6.1	**Warren** (city) Trumbull County
90	1919	6.0	**Fairfield** (city) Butler County
90	1919	6.0	**Twinsburg** (city) Summit County
92	2017	5.9	**Parma** (city) Cuyahoga County
92	2017	5.9	**Parma Heights** (city) Cuyahoga County
92	2017	5.9	**Riverside** (city) Montgomery County
95	2114	5.8	**Bexley** (city) Franklin County
95	2114	5.8	**Findlay** (city) Hancock County
95	2114	5.8	**Huber Heights** (city) Montgomery County
95	2114	5.8	**Pataskala** (city) Licking County
95	2114	5.8	**Trotwood** (city) Montgomery County
100	2211	5.7	**Cincinnati** (city) Hamilton County
100	2211	5.7	**East Cleveland** (city) Cuyahoga County
100	2211	5.7	**Medina** (city) Medina County
100	2211	5.7	**Miamisburg** (city) Montgomery County
100	2211	5.7	**North Canton** (city) Stark County
105	2328	5.6	**Berea** (city) Cuyahoga County
105	2328	5.6	**Canton** (city) Stark County
105	2328	5.6	**Elyria** (city) Lorain County
105	2328	5.6	**Fairborn** (city) Greene County
105	2328	5.6	**Forestville** (CDP) Hamilton County
105	2328	5.6	**Salem** (city) Columbiana County
105	2328	5.6	**Toledo** (city) Lucas County
105	2328	5.6	**Westerville** (city) Franklin County
113	2423	5.5	**Franklin** (city) Warren County
113	2423	5.5	**Gahanna** (city) Franklin County
113	2423	5.5	**Mansfield** (city) Richland County
113	2423	5.5	**Newark** (city) Licking County
113	2423	5.5	**Wadsworth** (city) Medina County
113	2423	5.5	**Youngstown** (city) Mahoning County
119	2519	5.4	**Cleveland** (city) Cuyahoga County
119	2519	5.4	**Forest Park** (city) Hamilton County
121	2614	5.3	**Columbus** (city) Franklin County
121	2614	5.3	**Middletown** (city) Butler County
121	2614	5.3	**New Philadelphia** (city) Tuscarawas County
124	2696	5.2	**Akron** (city) Summit County
124	2696	5.2	**Delaware** (city) Delaware County
124	2696	5.2	**Lebanon** (city) Warren County
124	2696	5.2	**Urbana** (city) Champaign County
128	2789	5.1	**Greenville** (city) Darke County
128	2789	5.1	**Xenia** (city) Greene County
128	2789	5.1	**Zanesville** (city) Muskingum County
131	2895	5.0	**Marysville** (city) Union County
131	2895	5.0	**Reynoldsburg** (city) Franklin County
131	2895	5.0	**Springfield** (city) Clark County
131	2895	5.0	**Willowick** (city) Lake County
135	2977	4.9	**Hamilton** (city) Butler County
135	2977	4.9	**Massillon** (city) Stark County
137	3071	4.8	**Ashland** (city) Ashland County
137	3071	4.8	**Barberton** (city) Summit County
139	3155	4.7	**Ashtabula** (city) Ashtabula County
139	3155	4.7	**Brooklyn** (city) Cuyahoga County
141	3239	4.6	**Garfield Heights** (city) Cuyahoga County
141	3239	4.6	**Lorain** (city) Lorain County
143	3312	4.5	**Fostoria** (city) Seneca County
143	3312	4.5	**Tiffin** (city) Seneca County
145	3409	4.4	**Brook Park** (city) Cuyahoga County
145	3409	4.4	**Sandusky** (city) Erie County
145	3409	4.4	**Troy** (city) Miami County
148	3506	4.3	**Dayton** (city) Montgomery County
148	3506	4.3	**Maple Heights** (city) Cuyahoga County
150	3581	4.2	**Bucyrus** (city) Crawford County

Note: *The state column ranks the top/bottom 150 places from all places in the state with population of 10,000 or more. The national column ranks the top/bottom 150 places from all places in the country with population of 10,000 or more. Places that are unincorporated were not considered in the rankings. Please refer to the User Guide for additional information.*

Employment: Healthcare Practitioners

Top 150 Places Ranked in *Ascending* Order

State Rank	Nat'l Rank	Percent	Place
1	80	1.8	**Whitehall** (city) Franklin County
2	156	2.3	**Oxford** (city) Butler County
3	370	3.0	**Streetsboro** (city) Portage County
4	396	3.1	**Celina** (city) Mercer County
4	396	3.1	**Warrensville Heights** (city) Cuyahoga County
6	437	3.2	**Bedford** (city) Cuyahoga County
6	437	3.2	**Bedford Heights** (city) Cuyahoga County
8	480	3.3	**Athens** (city) Athens County
8	480	3.3	**Wilmington** (city) Clinton County
10	529	3.4	**Bowling Green** (city) Wood County
10	529	3.4	**Norwood** (city) Hamilton County
10	529	3.4	**Painesville** (city) Lake County
10	529	3.4	**Piqua** (city) Miami County
10	529	3.4	**Trenton** (city) Butler County
15	595	3.5	**Conneaut** (city) Ashtabula County
16	655	3.6	**Marion** (city) Marion County
16	655	3.6	**Norwalk** (city) Huron County
18	706	3.7	**Alliance** (city) Stark County
18	706	3.7	**Circleville** (city) Pickaway County
20	760	3.8	**Coshocton** (city) Coshocton County
20	760	3.8	**Mount Vernon** (city) Knox County
20	760	3.8	**Sidney** (city) Shelby County
20	760	3.8	**Struthers** (city) Mahoning County
20	760	3.8	**Washington Court House** (city) Fayette County
25	876	4.0	**Fremont** (city) Sandusky County
25	876	4.0	**Ravenna** (city) Portage County
27	935	4.1	**Defiance** (city) Defiance County
27	935	4.1	**Galion** (city) Crawford County
27	935	4.1	**Kent** (city) Portage County
27	935	4.1	**Northbrook** (CDP) Hamilton County
27	935	4.1	**Reading** (city) Hamilton County
32	1004	4.2	**Bucyrus** (city) Crawford County
32	1004	4.2	**Lima** (city) Allen County
32	1004	4.2	**Wooster** (city) Wayne County
35	1076	4.3	**Dayton** (city) Montgomery County
35	1076	4.3	**Maple Heights** (city) Cuyahoga County
37	1151	4.4	**Brook Park** (city) Cuyahoga County
37	1151	4.4	**Sandusky** (city) Erie County
37	1151	4.4	**Troy** (city) Miami County
40	1248	4.5	**Fostoria** (city) Seneca County
40	1248	4.5	**Tiffin** (city) Seneca County
42	1345	4.6	**Garfield Heights** (city) Cuyahoga County
42	1345	4.6	**Lorain** (city) Lorain County
44	1418	4.7	**Ashtabula** (city) Ashtabula County
44	1418	4.7	**Brooklyn** (city) Cuyahoga County
46	1502	4.8	**Ashland** (city) Ashland County
46	1502	4.8	**Barberton** (city) Summit County
48	1586	4.9	**Hamilton** (city) Butler County
48	1586	4.9	**Massillon** (city) Stark County
50	1680	5.0	**Marysville** (city) Union County
50	1680	5.0	**Reynoldsburg** (city) Franklin County
50	1680	5.0	**Springfield** (city) Clark County
50	1680	5.0	**Willowick** (city) Lake County
54	1762	5.1	**Greenville** (city) Darke County
54	1762	5.1	**Xenia** (city) Greene County
54	1762	5.1	**Zanesville** (city) Muskingum County
57	1868	5.2	**Akron** (city) Summit County
57	1868	5.2	**Delaware** (city) Delaware County
57	1868	5.2	**Lebanon** (city) Warren County
57	1868	5.2	**Urbana** (city) Champaign County
61	1961	5.3	**Columbus** (city) Franklin County
61	1961	5.3	**Middletown** (city) Butler County
61	1961	5.3	**New Philadelphia** (city) Tuscarawas County
64	2043	5.4	**Cleveland** (city) Cuyahoga County
64	2043	5.4	**Forest Park** (city) Hamilton County
66	2138	5.5	**Franklin** (city) Warren County
66	2138	5.5	**Gahanna** (city) Franklin County
66	2138	5.5	**Mansfield** (city) Richland County
66	2138	5.5	**Newark** (city) Licking County
66	2138	5.5	**Wadsworth** (city) Medina County
66	2138	5.5	**Youngstown** (city) Mahoning County
72	2234	5.6	**Berea** (city) Cuyahoga County
72	2234	5.6	**Canton** (city) Stark County
72	2234	5.6	**Elyria** (city) Lorain County
72	2234	5.6	**Fairborn** (city) Greene County
72	2234	5.6	**Forestville** (CDP) Hamilton County
72	2234	5.6	**Salem** (city) Columbiana County
72	2234	5.6	**Toledo** (city) Lucas County
72	2234	5.6	**Westerville** (city) Franklin County
80	2329	5.7	**Cincinnati** (city) Hamilton County
80	2329	5.7	**East Cleveland** (city) Cuyahoga County
80	2329	5.7	**Medina** (city) Medina County
80	2329	5.7	**Miamisburg** (city) Montgomery County
80	2329	5.7	**North Canton** (city) Stark County
85	2446	5.8	**Bexley** (city) Franklin County
85	2446	5.8	**Findlay** (city) Hancock County
85	2446	5.8	**Huber Heights** (city) Montgomery County
85	2446	5.8	**Pataskala** (city) Licking County
85	2446	5.8	**Trotwood** (city) Montgomery County
90	2543	5.9	**Parma** (city) Cuyahoga County
90	2543	5.9	**Parma Heights** (city) Cuyahoga County
90	2543	5.9	**Riverside** (city) Montgomery County
93	2640	6.0	**Fairfield** (city) Butler County
93	2640	6.0	**Twinsburg** (city) Summit County
95	2738	6.1	**Richmond Heights** (city) Cuyahoga County
95	2738	6.1	**Van Wert** (city) Van Wert County
95	2738	6.1	**Warren** (city) Trumbull County
98	2845	6.2	**Chillicothe** (city) Ross County
98	2845	6.2	**Finneytown** (CDP) Hamilton County
98	2845	6.2	**Sharonville** (city) Hamilton County
101	2934	6.3	**Bellefontaine** (city) Logan County
101	2934	6.3	**Eastlake** (city) Lake County
101	2934	6.3	**Heath** (city) Licking County
101	2934	6.3	**Loveland** (city) Hamilton County
101	2934	6.3	**West Carrollton** (city) Montgomery County
106	3097	6.5	**Green** (city) Summit County
107	3169	6.6	**Amherst** (city) Lorain County
107	3169	6.6	**Cuyahoga Falls** (city) Summit County
107	3169	6.6	**Ironton** (city) Lawrence County
107	3169	6.6	**Lancaster** (city) Fairfield County
107	3169	6.6	**Monroe** (city) Butler County
107	3169	6.6	**North Ridgeville** (city) Lorain County
107	3169	6.6	**Springdale** (city) Hamilton County
114	3318	6.8	**Dent** (CDP) Hamilton County
114	3318	6.8	**East Liverpool** (city) Columbiana County
114	3318	6.8	**Middleburg Heights** (city) Cuyahoga County
114	3318	6.8	**New Franklin** (city) Summit County
118	3404	6.9	**Hilliard** (city) Franklin County
118	3404	6.9	**Norton** (city) Summit County
120	3465	7.0	**Kettering** (city) Montgomery County
120	3465	7.0	**Mason** (city) Warren County
120	3465	7.0	**Stow** (city) Summit County
120	3465	7.0	**Tallmadge** (city) Summit County
120	3465	7.0	**Vandalia** (city) Montgomery County
125	3519	7.1	**Brunswick** (city) Medina County
125	3519	7.1	**North Olmsted** (city) Cuyahoga County
125	3519	7.1	**Wickliffe** (city) Lake County
128	3574	7.2	**Marietta** (city) Washington County
128	3574	7.2	**Mentor** (city) Lake County
128	3574	7.2	**Worthington** (city) Franklin County
131	3631	7.3	**Aurora** (city) Portage County
131	3631	7.3	**Boardman** (CDP) Mahoning County
131	3631	7.3	**Clayton** (city) Montgomery County
134	3703	7.4	**Avon Lake** (city) Lorain County
134	3703	7.4	**Lakewood** (city) Cuyahoga County
136	3754	7.5	**Austintown** (CDP) Mahoning County
136	3754	7.5	**Euclid** (city) Cuyahoga County
136	3754	7.5	**Willoughby** (city) Lake County
139	3809	7.6	**Mayfield Heights** (city) Cuyahoga County
139	3809	7.6	**Oregon** (city) Lucas County
139	3809	7.6	**Pickerington** (city) Fairfield County
142	3853	7.7	**Hudson** (city) Summit County
142	3853	7.7	**Macedonia** (city) Summit County
142	3853	7.7	**Strongsville** (city) Cuyahoga County
145	3902	7.8	**Bay Village** (city) Cuyahoga County
145	3902	7.8	**Fairview Park** (city) Cuyahoga County
147	4021	8.1	**Grove City** (city) Franklin County
147	4021	8.1	**Montgomery** (city) Hamilton County
147	4021	8.1	**South Euclid** (city) Cuyahoga County
150	4060	8.2	**Seven Hills** (city) Cuyahoga County

Note: *The state column ranks the top/bottom 150 places from all places in the state with population of 10,000 or more. The national column ranks the top/bottom 150 places from all places in the country with population of 10,000 or more. Places that are unincorporated were not considered in the rankings. Please refer to the User Guide for additional information.*

Employment: Service Occupations

Top 150 Places Ranked in *Descending* Order

State Rank	Nat'l Rank	Percent	Place
1	15	38.8	**East Cleveland** (city) Cuyahoga County
2	123	29.9	**Oxford** (city) Butler County
3	149	29.3	**Youngstown** (city) Mahoning County
4	167	28.8	**Athens** (city) Athens County
5	171	28.7	**Canton** (city) Stark County
6	215	27.9	**Kent** (city) Portage County
7	224	27.7	**Lima** (city) Allen County
8	238	27.5	**Ravenna** (city) Portage County
9	248	27.3	**Cleveland** (city) Cuyahoga County
10	347	25.9	**Warren** (city) Trumbull County
11	367	25.7	**Painesville** (city) Lake County
12	384	25.5	**Dayton** (city) Montgomery County
12	384	25.5	**Sandusky** (city) Erie County
14	407	25.3	**Zanesville** (city) Muskingum County
15	421	25.2	**Bowling Green** (city) Wood County
16	460	24.9	**Chillicothe** (city) Ross County
17	476	24.8	**Fostoria** (city) Seneca County
18	495	24.7	**Marietta** (city) Washington County
19	522	24.5	**Ashtabula** (city) Ashtabula County
20	536	24.4	**Portsmouth** (city) Scioto County
21	572	24.2	**Cambridge** (city) Guernsey County
22	617	23.9	**Lorain** (city) Lorain County
22	617	23.9	**Springfield** (city) Clark County
24	667	23.6	**New Philadelphia** (city) Tuscarawas County
25	676	23.5	**Coshocton** (city) Coshocton County
26	710	23.3	**Struthers** (city) Mahoning County
26	710	23.3	**Toledo** (city) Lucas County
28	734	23.2	**Circleville** (city) Pickaway County
28	734	23.2	**Niles** (city) Trumbull County
28	734	23.2	**Whitehall** (city) Franklin County
31	752	23.1	**Alliance** (city) Stark County
31	752	23.1	**Washington Court House** (city) Fayette County
33	778	23.0	**Barberton** (city) Summit County
33	778	23.0	**Celina** (city) Mercer County
35	794	22.9	**Brook Park** (city) Cuyahoga County
35	794	22.9	**Reading** (city) Hamilton County
37	822	22.8	**Northbrook** (CDP) Hamilton County
38	892	22.4	**Mount Vernon** (city) Knox County
39	940	22.2	**Lancaster** (city) Fairfield County
39	940	22.2	**Marion** (city) Marion County
41	963	22.1	**East Liverpool** (city) Columbiana County
41	963	22.1	**Mansfield** (city) Richland County
43	983	22.0	**Akron** (city) Summit County
43	983	22.0	**Brooklyn** (city) Cuyahoga County
43	983	22.0	**Cincinnati** (city) Hamilton County
43	983	22.0	**Galion** (city) Crawford County
43	983	22.0	**Massillon** (city) Stark County
48	1035	21.8	**Salem** (city) Columbiana County
49	1060	21.7	**Elyria** (city) Lorain County
49	1060	21.7	**Warrensville Heights** (city) Cuyahoga County
51	1083	21.6	**Tiffin** (city) Seneca County
52	1108	21.5	**Hamilton** (city) Butler County
53	1138	21.4	**Middletown** (city) Butler County
54	1162	21.3	**Euclid** (city) Cuyahoga County
55	1192	21.2	**Newark** (city) Licking County
55	1192	21.2	**Sidney** (city) Shelby County
55	1192	21.2	**Wooster** (city) Wayne County
58	1252	21.0	**Bedford Heights** (city) Cuyahoga County
59	1272	20.9	**Forest Park** (city) Hamilton County
59	1272	20.9	**Trotwood** (city) Montgomery County
61	1307	20.8	**Ironton** (city) Lawrence County
61	1307	20.8	**Steubenville** (city) Jefferson County
61	1307	20.8	**Vandalia** (city) Montgomery County
61	1307	20.8	**Vermilion** (city) Lorain County
65	1386	20.5	**Fairborn** (city) Greene County
66	1505	20.1	**Maple Heights** (city) Cuyahoga County
66	1505	20.1	**Van Wert** (city) Van Wert County
68	1530	20.0	**Riverside** (city) Montgomery County
69	1565	19.9	**Parma Heights** (city) Cuyahoga County
69	1565	19.9	**Wilmington** (city) Clinton County
71	1592	19.8	**Ashland** (city) Ashland County
72	1626	19.7	**Englewood** (city) Montgomery County
72	1626	19.7	**Springdale** (city) Hamilton County
74	1662	19.6	**Conneaut** (city) Ashtabula County
74	1662	19.6	**Xenia** (city) Greene County
76	1696	19.5	**Lebanon** (city) Warren County
77	1792	19.2	**Defiance** (city) Defiance County
77	1792	19.2	**Findlay** (city) Hancock County
79	1833	19.1	**Bucyrus** (city) Crawford County
80	1875	19.0	**Finneytown** (CDP) Hamilton County
80	1875	19.0	**Huber Heights** (city) Montgomery County
80	1875	19.0	**Parma** (city) Cuyahoga County
80	1875	19.0	**West Carrollton** (city) Montgomery County
84	1910	18.9	**Streetsboro** (city) Portage County
85	1971	18.7	**Garfield Heights** (city) Cuyahoga County
86	2005	18.6	**Austintown** (CDP) Mahoning County
86	2005	18.6	**North Canton** (city) Stark County
88	2067	18.4	**Wickliffe** (city) Lake County
89	2095	18.3	**Bedford** (city) Cuyahoga County
89	2095	18.3	**Columbus** (city) Franklin County
89	2095	18.3	**Fremont** (city) Sandusky County
89	2095	18.3	**Mayfield Heights** (city) Cuyahoga County
93	2185	18.0	**Delaware** (city) Delaware County
93	2185	18.0	**New Franklin** (city) Summit County
95	2221	17.9	**Norwood** (city) Hamilton County
95	2221	17.9	**Willowick** (city) Lake County
97	2291	17.7	**Urbana** (city) Champaign County
97	2291	17.7	**Wadsworth** (city) Medina County
99	2317	17.6	**Eastlake** (city) Lake County
99	2317	17.6	**Greenville** (city) Darke County
101	2396	17.4	**Lakewood** (city) Cuyahoga County
101	2396	17.4	**Norwalk** (city) Huron County
103	2496	17.1	**Kettering** (city) Montgomery County
104	2519	17.0	**Berea** (city) Cuyahoga County
104	2519	17.0	**Bridgetown** (CDP) Hamilton County
104	2519	17.0	**Heath** (city) Licking County
104	2519	17.0	**Medina** (city) Medina County
104	2519	17.0	**Pataskala** (city) Licking County
109	2607	16.7	**Oregon** (city) Lucas County
109	2607	16.7	**White Oak** (CDP) Hamilton County
111	2651	16.6	**Boardman** (CDP) Mahoning County
111	2651	16.6	**Brunswick** (city) Medina County
111	2651	16.6	**Grove City** (city) Franklin County
111	2651	16.6	**Reynoldsburg** (city) Franklin County
111	2651	16.6	**South Euclid** (city) Cuyahoga County
111	2651	16.6	**Sylvania** (city) Lucas County
117	2692	16.5	**Piqua** (city) Miami County
118	2722	16.4	**Dover** (city) Tuscarawas County
118	2722	16.4	**Pickerington** (city) Fairfield County
118	2722	16.4	**Willoughby** (city) Lake County
121	2763	16.3	**Maumee** (city) Lucas County
122	2797	16.2	**Bellefontaine** (city) Logan County
123	2828	16.1	**Tallmadge** (city) Summit County
124	2929	15.8	**Cleveland Heights** (city) Cuyahoga County
125	2962	15.7	**Amherst** (city) Lorain County
125	2962	15.7	**Fairfield** (city) Butler County
125	2962	15.7	**Gahanna** (city) Franklin County
125	2962	15.7	**Norton** (city) Summit County
125	2962	15.7	**Sharonville** (city) Hamilton County
130	3032	15.5	**Trenton** (city) Butler County
131	3090	15.3	**Miamisburg** (city) Montgomery County
132	3128	15.2	**Fairview Park** (city) Cuyahoga County
132	3128	15.2	**Monfort Heights** (CDP) Hamilton County
134	3182	15.0	**Centerville** (city) Montgomery County
134	3182	15.0	**Marysville** (city) Union County
136	3215	14.9	**Aurora** (city) Portage County
136	3215	14.9	**Clayton** (city) Montgomery County
136	3215	14.9	**Richmond Heights** (city) Cuyahoga County
136	3215	14.9	**Troy** (city) Miami County
140	3250	14.8	**Lyndhurst** (city) Cuyahoga County
140	3250	14.8	**Monroe** (city) Butler County
142	3312	14.6	**Middleburg Heights** (city) Cuyahoga County
143	3345	14.5	**Cuyahoga Falls** (city) Summit County
143	3345	14.5	**Mentor** (city) Lake County
143	3345	14.5	**North Ridgeville** (city) Lorain County
146	3376	14.4	**Stow** (city) Summit County
147	3434	14.2	**Green** (city) Summit County
147	3434	14.2	**North Royalton** (city) Cuyahoga County
149	3458	14.1	**Forestville** (CDP) Hamilton County
150	3514	13.9	**Blue Ash** (city) Hamilton County

Note: *The state column ranks the top/bottom 150 places from all places in the state with population of 10,000 or more. The national column ranks the top/bottom 150 places from all places in the country with population of 10,000 or more. Places that are unincorporated were not considered in the rankings. Please refer to the User Guide for additional information.*

Employment: Service Occupations

Top 150 Places Ranked in *Ascending* Order

State Rank	Nat'l Rank	Percent	Place
1	17	5.2	**Powell** (city) Delaware County
2	80	7.2	**Beachwood** (city) Cuyahoga County
3	96	7.5	**Worthington** (city) Franklin County
4	120	7.9	**Hudson** (city) Summit County
5	180	8.7	**Dublin** (city) Franklin County
5	180	8.7	**Upper Arlington** (city) Franklin County
7	246	9.3	**Brecksville** (city) Cuyahoga County
8	276	9.6	**Broadview Heights** (city) Cuyahoga County
8	276	9.6	**Springboro** (city) Warren County
10	322	10.0	**Shaker Heights** (city) Cuyahoga County
11	360	10.3	**Bay Village** (city) Cuyahoga County
11	360	10.3	**Montgomery** (city) Hamilton County
13	378	10.4	**Seven Hills** (city) Cuyahoga County
14	468	11.0	**Strongsville** (city) Cuyahoga County
14	468	11.0	**University Heights** (city) Cuyahoga County
16	509	11.2	**Perrysburg** (city) Wood County
16	509	11.2	**Westlake** (city) Cuyahoga County
18	535	11.3	**Rocky River** (city) Cuyahoga County
19	651	11.9	**Loveland** (city) Hamilton County
20	680	12.0	**Twinsburg** (city) Summit County
21	701	12.1	**Solon** (city) Cuyahoga County
22	722	12.2	**Avon Lake** (city) Lorain County
23	775	12.5	**Hilliard** (city) Franklin County
24	796	12.6	**Beavercreek** (city) Greene County
25	895	13.0	**Dent** (CDP) Hamilton County
26	947	13.2	**Mack** (CDP) Hamilton County
27	970	13.3	**Westerville** (city) Franklin County
28	1040	13.6	**Bexley** (city) Franklin County
28	1040	13.6	**Macedonia** (city) Summit County
30	1061	13.7	**Avon** (city) Lorain County
31	1114	13.9	**Blue Ash** (city) Hamilton County
31	1114	13.9	**Franklin** (city) Warren County
31	1114	13.9	**Mason** (city) Warren County
31	1114	13.9	**North Olmsted** (city) Cuyahoga County
35	1167	14.1	**Forestville** (CDP) Hamilton County
36	1199	14.2	**Green** (city) Summit County
36	1199	14.2	**North Royalton** (city) Cuyahoga County
38	1246	14.4	**Stow** (city) Summit County
39	1281	14.5	**Cuyahoga Falls** (city) Summit County
39	1281	14.5	**Mentor** (city) Lake County
39	1281	14.5	**North Ridgeville** (city) Lorain County
42	1312	14.6	**Middleburg Heights** (city) Cuyahoga County
43	1375	14.8	**Lyndhurst** (city) Cuyahoga County
43	1375	14.8	**Monroe** (city) Butler County
45	1407	14.9	**Aurora** (city) Portage County
45	1407	14.9	**Clayton** (city) Montgomery County
45	1407	14.9	**Richmond Heights** (city) Cuyahoga County
45	1407	14.9	**Troy** (city) Miami County
49	1442	15.0	**Centerville** (city) Montgomery County
49	1442	15.0	**Marysville** (city) Union County
51	1506	15.2	**Fairview Park** (city) Cuyahoga County
51	1506	15.2	**Monfort Heights** (CDP) Hamilton County
53	1529	15.3	**Miamisburg** (city) Montgomery County
54	1592	15.5	**Trenton** (city) Butler County
55	1657	15.7	**Amherst** (city) Lorain County
55	1657	15.7	**Fairfield** (city) Butler County
55	1657	15.7	**Gahanna** (city) Franklin County
55	1657	15.7	**Norton** (city) Summit County
55	1657	15.7	**Sharonville** (city) Hamilton County
60	1695	15.8	**Cleveland Heights** (city) Cuyahoga County
61	1792	16.1	**Tallmadge** (city) Summit County
62	1829	16.2	**Bellefontaine** (city) Logan County
63	1860	16.3	**Maumee** (city) Lucas County
64	1894	16.4	**Dover** (city) Tuscarawas County
64	1894	16.4	**Pickerington** (city) Fairfield County
64	1894	16.4	**Willoughby** (city) Lake County
67	1935	16.5	**Piqua** (city) Miami County
68	1965	16.6	**Boardman** (CDP) Mahoning County
68	1965	16.6	**Brunswick** (city) Medina County
68	1965	16.6	**Grove City** (city) Franklin County
68	1965	16.6	**Reynoldsburg** (city) Franklin County
68	1965	16.6	**South Euclid** (city) Cuyahoga County
68	1965	16.6	**Sylvania** (city) Lucas County
74	2006	16.7	**Oregon** (city) Lucas County
74	2006	16.7	**White Oak** (CDP) Hamilton County
76	2103	17.0	**Berea** (city) Cuyahoga County
76	2103	17.0	**Bridgetown** (CDP) Hamilton County
76	2103	17.0	**Heath** (city) Licking County
76	2103	17.0	**Medina** (city) Medina County
76	2103	17.0	**Pataskala** (city) Licking County
81	2138	17.1	**Kettering** (city) Montgomery County
82	2228	17.4	**Lakewood** (city) Cuyahoga County
82	2228	17.4	**Norwalk** (city) Huron County
84	2296	17.6	**Eastlake** (city) Lake County
84	2296	17.6	**Greenville** (city) Darke County
86	2340	17.7	**Urbana** (city) Champaign County
86	2340	17.7	**Wadsworth** (city) Medina County
88	2397	17.9	**Norwood** (city) Hamilton County
88	2397	17.9	**Willowick** (city) Lake County
90	2436	18.0	**Delaware** (city) Delaware County
90	2436	18.0	**New Franklin** (city) Summit County
92	2523	18.3	**Bedford** (city) Cuyahoga County
92	2523	18.3	**Columbus** (city) Franklin County
92	2523	18.3	**Fremont** (city) Sandusky County
92	2523	18.3	**Mayfield Heights** (city) Cuyahoga County
96	2562	18.4	**Wickliffe** (city) Lake County
97	2620	18.6	**Austintown** (CDP) Mahoning County
97	2620	18.6	**North Canton** (city) Stark County
99	2652	18.7	**Garfield Heights** (city) Cuyahoga County
100	2717	18.9	**Streetsboro** (city) Portage County
101	2747	19.0	**Finneytown** (CDP) Hamilton County
101	2747	19.0	**Huber Heights** (city) Montgomery County
101	2747	19.0	**Parma** (city) Cuyahoga County
101	2747	19.0	**West Carrollton** (city) Montgomery County
105	2782	19.1	**Bucyrus** (city) Crawford County
106	2824	19.2	**Defiance** (city) Defiance County
106	2824	19.2	**Findlay** (city) Hancock County
108	2925	19.5	**Lebanon** (city) Warren County
109	2961	19.6	**Conneaut** (city) Ashtabula County
109	2961	19.6	**Xenia** (city) Greene County
111	2995	19.7	**Englewood** (city) Montgomery County
111	2995	19.7	**Springdale** (city) Hamilton County
113	3031	19.8	**Ashland** (city) Ashland County
114	3065	19.9	**Parma Heights** (city) Cuyahoga County
114	3065	19.9	**Wilmington** (city) Clinton County
116	3092	20.0	**Riverside** (city) Montgomery County
117	3127	20.1	**Maple Heights** (city) Cuyahoga County
117	3127	20.1	**Van Wert** (city) Van Wert County
119	3244	20.5	**Fairborn** (city) Greene County
120	3325	20.8	**Ironton** (city) Lawrence County
120	3325	20.8	**Steubenville** (city) Jefferson County
120	3325	20.8	**Vandalia** (city) Montgomery County
120	3325	20.8	**Vermilion** (city) Lorain County
124	3350	20.9	**Forest Park** (city) Hamilton County
124	3350	20.9	**Trotwood** (city) Montgomery County
126	3385	21.0	**Bedford Heights** (city) Cuyahoga County
127	3435	21.2	**Newark** (city) Licking County
127	3435	21.2	**Sidney** (city) Shelby County
127	3435	21.2	**Wooster** (city) Wayne County
130	3465	21.3	**Euclid** (city) Cuyahoga County
131	3495	21.4	**Middletown** (city) Butler County
132	3519	21.5	**Hamilton** (city) Butler County
133	3549	21.6	**Tiffin** (city) Seneca County
134	3574	21.7	**Elyria** (city) Lorain County
134	3574	21.7	**Warrensville Heights** (city) Cuyahoga County
136	3597	21.8	**Salem** (city) Columbiana County
137	3650	22.0	**Akron** (city) Summit County
137	3650	22.0	**Brooklyn** (city) Cuyahoga County
137	3650	22.0	**Cincinnati** (city) Hamilton County
137	3650	22.0	**Galion** (city) Crawford County
137	3650	22.0	**Massillon** (city) Stark County
142	3674	22.1	**East Liverpool** (city) Columbiana County
142	3674	22.1	**Mansfield** (city) Richland County
144	3694	22.2	**Lancaster** (city) Fairfield County
144	3694	22.2	**Marion** (city) Marion County
146	3742	22.4	**Mount Vernon** (city) Knox County
147	3816	22.8	**Northbrook** (CDP) Hamilton County
148	3835	22.9	**Brook Park** (city) Cuyahoga County
148	3835	22.9	**Reading** (city) Hamilton County
150	3863	23.0	**Barberton** (city) Summit County

Note: *The state column ranks the top/bottom 150 places from all places in the state with population of 10,000 or more. The national column ranks the top/bottom 150 places from all places in the country with population of 10,000 or more. Places that are unincorporated were not considered in the rankings. Please refer to the User Guide for additional information.*

Employment: Sales and Office Occupations

Top 150 Places Ranked in *Descending* Order

State Rank	Nat'l Rank	Percent	Place
1	13	36.5	**Dent** (CDP) Hamilton County
2	19	35.3	**Northbrook** (CDP) Hamilton County
3	43	34.2	**Bedford** (city) Cuyahoga County
4	46	34.0	**Garfield Heights** (city) Cuyahoga County
5	49	33.8	**Maple Heights** (city) Cuyahoga County
6	96	32.4	**Lebanon** (city) Warren County
7	132	31.9	**Trenton** (city) Butler County
8	294	30.5	**Warrensville Heights** (city) Cuyahoga County
9	329	30.2	**Amherst** (city) Lorain County
9	329	30.2	**Bedford Heights** (city) Cuyahoga County
9	329	30.2	**Boardman** (CDP) Mahoning County
9	329	30.2	**Richmond Heights** (city) Cuyahoga County
13	344	30.1	**Struthers** (city) Mahoning County
14	363	30.0	**Monroe** (city) Butler County
15	376	29.9	**North Olmsted** (city) Cuyahoga County
16	395	29.8	**Medina** (city) Medina County
17	422	29.7	**Reynoldsburg** (city) Franklin County
18	448	29.6	**Bridgetown** (CDP) Hamilton County
19	469	29.5	**Clayton** (city) Montgomery County
20	492	29.4	**Finneytown** (CDP) Hamilton County
20	492	29.4	**Streetsboro** (city) Portage County
22	524	29.3	**Norwood** (city) Hamilton County
23	558	29.2	**Pataskala** (city) Licking County
24	800	28.3	**Trotwood** (city) Montgomery County
24	800	28.3	**Westerville** (city) Franklin County
26	827	28.2	**Avon Lake** (city) Lorain County
26	827	28.2	**Strongsville** (city) Cuyahoga County
28	860	28.1	**Fairborn** (city) Greene County
28	860	28.1	**Fairfield** (city) Butler County
30	972	27.8	**Lyndhurst** (city) Cuyahoga County
30	972	27.8	**Mentor** (city) Lake County
32	1015	27.7	**Englewood** (city) Montgomery County
32	1015	27.7	**Lancaster** (city) Fairfield County
32	1015	27.7	**Miamisburg** (city) Montgomery County
32	1015	27.7	**Steubenville** (city) Jefferson County
36	1062	27.6	**Cuyahoga Falls** (city) Summit County
36	1062	27.6	**Fairview Park** (city) Cuyahoga County
36	1062	27.6	**North Canton** (city) Stark County
36	1062	27.6	**Parma** (city) Cuyahoga County
40	1156	27.4	**Loveland** (city) Hamilton County
40	1156	27.4	**Parma Heights** (city) Cuyahoga County
42	1198	27.3	**Willoughby** (city) Lake County
43	1236	27.2	**Heath** (city) Licking County
43	1236	27.2	**Kettering** (city) Montgomery County
45	1286	27.1	**Akron** (city) Summit County
45	1286	27.1	**Brunswick** (city) Medina County
45	1286	27.1	**Euclid** (city) Cuyahoga County
45	1286	27.1	**Ironton** (city) Lawrence County
49	1337	27.0	**Beachwood** (city) Cuyahoga County
49	1337	27.0	**Oregon** (city) Lucas County
49	1337	27.0	**South Euclid** (city) Cuyahoga County
49	1337	27.0	**Stow** (city) Summit County
53	1394	26.9	**Grove City** (city) Franklin County
54	1464	26.8	**Columbus** (city) Franklin County
54	1464	26.8	**Newark** (city) Licking County
54	1464	26.8	**White Oak** (CDP) Hamilton County
57	1515	26.7	**Forest Park** (city) Hamilton County
57	1515	26.7	**Monfort Heights** (CDP) Hamilton County
59	1565	26.6	**Berea** (city) Cuyahoga County
59	1565	26.6	**Wickliffe** (city) Lake County
59	1565	26.6	**Xenia** (city) Greene County
62	1625	26.5	**Barberton** (city) Summit County
62	1625	26.5	**Brook Park** (city) Cuyahoga County
62	1625	26.5	**Massillon** (city) Stark County
62	1625	26.5	**Whitehall** (city) Franklin County
66	1738	26.3	**Green** (city) Summit County
66	1738	26.3	**Hamilton** (city) Butler County
68	1799	26.2	**Austintown** (CDP) Mahoning County
68	1799	26.2	**Broadview Heights** (city) Cuyahoga County
68	1799	26.2	**Mason** (city) Warren County
71	1873	26.1	**Huber Heights** (city) Montgomery County
71	1873	26.1	**Mack** (CDP) Hamilton County
71	1873	26.1	**Maumee** (city) Lucas County
71	1873	26.1	**Wadsworth** (city) Medina County
75	1930	26.0	**Conneaut** (city) Ashtabula County
75	1930	26.0	**Middletown** (city) Butler County
75	1930	26.0	**West Carrollton** (city) Montgomery County
78	1997	25.9	**Ashland** (city) Ashland County
78	1997	25.9	**Middleburg Heights** (city) Cuyahoga County
80	2060	25.8	**Dover** (city) Tuscarawas County
81	2116	25.7	**Mansfield** (city) Richland County
82	2172	25.6	**Forestville** (CDP) Hamilton County
83	2226	25.5	**Seven Hills** (city) Cuyahoga County
83	2226	25.5	**Willowick** (city) Lake County
85	2276	25.4	**Marietta** (city) Washington County
85	2276	25.4	**Vandalia** (city) Montgomery County
87	2385	25.2	**Niles** (city) Trumbull County
88	2441	25.1	**Delaware** (city) Delaware County
88	2441	25.1	**Lakewood** (city) Cuyahoga County
90	2489	25.0	**Piqua** (city) Miami County
90	2489	25.0	**Powell** (city) Delaware County
92	2554	24.9	**Alliance** (city) Stark County
92	2554	24.9	**Chillicothe** (city) Ross County
92	2554	24.9	**Eastlake** (city) Lake County
92	2554	24.9	**Warren** (city) Trumbull County
96	2612	24.8	**North Ridgeville** (city) Lorain County
96	2612	24.8	**Wilmington** (city) Clinton County
98	2671	24.7	**Centerville** (city) Montgomery County
98	2671	24.7	**Greenville** (city) Darke County
98	2671	24.7	**North Royalton** (city) Cuyahoga County
98	2671	24.7	**Pickerington** (city) Fairfield County
102	2790	24.5	**Circleville** (city) Pickaway County
102	2790	24.5	**Hilliard** (city) Franklin County
102	2790	24.5	**Hudson** (city) Summit County
102	2790	24.5	**Marysville** (city) Union County
102	2790	24.5	**Reading** (city) Hamilton County
102	2790	24.5	**Solon** (city) Cuyahoga County
102	2790	24.5	**Washington Court House** (city) Fayette County
102	2790	24.5	**Zanesville** (city) Muskingum County
110	2857	24.4	**Dayton** (city) Montgomery County
110	2857	24.4	**Toledo** (city) Lucas County
112	2911	24.3	**Ashtabula** (city) Ashtabula County
112	2911	24.3	**Kent** (city) Portage County
112	2911	24.3	**Mount Vernon** (city) Knox County
115	3009	24.1	**Brooklyn** (city) Cuyahoga County
115	3009	24.1	**Gahanna** (city) Franklin County
115	3009	24.1	**Springfield** (city) Clark County
118	3051	24.0	**Athens** (city) Athens County
118	3051	24.0	**Bucyrus** (city) Crawford County
118	3051	24.0	**Cincinnati** (city) Hamilton County
118	3051	24.0	**Defiance** (city) Defiance County
118	3051	24.0	**Tallmadge** (city) Summit County
123	3102	23.9	**Elyria** (city) Lorain County
123	3102	23.9	**Lima** (city) Allen County
123	3102	23.9	**Lorain** (city) Lorain County
123	3102	23.9	**Troy** (city) Miami County
123	3102	23.9	**Youngstown** (city) Mahoning County
128	3142	23.8	**Galion** (city) Crawford County
128	3142	23.8	**Portsmouth** (city) Scioto County
130	3190	23.7	**Bay Village** (city) Cuyahoga County
131	3236	23.6	**Cleveland** (city) Cuyahoga County
131	3236	23.6	**Franklin** (city) Warren County
131	3236	23.6	**Norwalk** (city) Huron County
131	3236	23.6	**Rocky River** (city) Cuyahoga County
135	3282	23.5	**Avon** (city) Lorain County
135	3282	23.5	**Brecksville** (city) Cuyahoga County
135	3282	23.5	**Oxford** (city) Butler County
138	3337	23.4	**Perrysburg** (city) Wood County
138	3337	23.4	**Riverside** (city) Montgomery County
138	3337	23.4	**Springboro** (city) Warren County
141	3382	23.3	**Ravenna** (city) Portage County
142	3418	23.2	**New Philadelphia** (city) Tuscarawas County
143	3495	23.0	**Vermilion** (city) Lorain County
144	3531	22.9	**Norton** (city) Summit County
144	3531	22.9	**Worthington** (city) Franklin County
146	3577	22.8	**Canton** (city) Stark County
147	3616	22.7	**Aurora** (city) Portage County
147	3616	22.7	**Macedonia** (city) Summit County
147	3616	22.7	**Mayfield Heights** (city) Cuyahoga County
147	3616	22.7	**Sandusky** (city) Erie County

Note: *The state column ranks the top/bottom 150 places from all places in the state with population of 10,000 or more. The national column ranks the top/bottom 150 places from all places in the country with population of 10,000 or more. Places that are unincorporated were not considered in the rankings. Please refer to the User Guide for additional information.*

Employment: Sales and Office Occupations

Top 150 Places Ranked in *Ascending* Order

State Rank	Nat'l Rank	Percent	Place
1	69	16.6	**Sidney** (city) Shelby County
2	86	17.1	**Shaker Heights** (city) Cuyahoga County
3	98	17.3	**Blue Ash** (city) Hamilton County
4	134	17.9	**Coshocton** (city) Coshocton County
5	157	18.3	**Fostoria** (city) Seneca County
5	157	18.3	**Montgomery** (city) Hamilton County
7	167	18.4	**Bellefontaine** (city) Logan County
8	199	18.8	**Celina** (city) Mercer County
9	212	19.0	**Beavercreek** (city) Greene County
10	299	19.7	**Findlay** (city) Hancock County
11	309	19.8	**Cleveland Heights** (city) Cuyahoga County
12	321	19.9	**Urbana** (city) Champaign County
13	380	20.3	**Van Wert** (city) Van Wert County
14	401	20.4	**Bexley** (city) Franklin County
15	418	20.5	**East Liverpool** (city) Columbiana County
16	482	20.8	**Cambridge** (city) Guernsey County
17	618	21.4	**Upper Arlington** (city) Franklin County
18	643	21.5	**East Cleveland** (city) Cuyahoga County
19	729	21.8	**Fremont** (city) Sandusky County
20	762	21.9	**Springdale** (city) Hamilton County
21	787	22.0	**New Franklin** (city) Summit County
22	836	22.2	**Marion** (city) Marion County
22	836	22.2	**Twinsburg** (city) Summit County
22	836	22.2	**University Heights** (city) Cuyahoga County
25	881	22.3	**Sylvania** (city) Lucas County
26	906	22.4	**Painesville** (city) Lake County
26	906	22.4	**Sharonville** (city) Hamilton County
28	940	22.5	**Bowling Green** (city) Wood County
28	940	22.5	**Wooster** (city) Wayne County
30	974	22.6	**Dublin** (city) Franklin County
30	974	22.6	**Salem** (city) Columbiana County
30	974	22.6	**Tiffin** (city) Seneca County
30	974	22.6	**Westlake** (city) Cuyahoga County
34	1004	22.7	**Aurora** (city) Portage County
34	1004	22.7	**Macedonia** (city) Summit County
34	1004	22.7	**Mayfield Heights** (city) Cuyahoga County
34	1004	22.7	**Sandusky** (city) Erie County
38	1041	22.8	**Canton** (city) Stark County
39	1080	22.9	**Norton** (city) Summit County
39	1080	22.9	**Worthington** (city) Franklin County
41	1126	23.0	**Vermilion** (city) Lorain County
42	1198	23.2	**New Philadelphia** (city) Tuscarawas County
43	1239	23.3	**Ravenna** (city) Portage County
44	1275	23.4	**Perrysburg** (city) Wood County
44	1275	23.4	**Riverside** (city) Montgomery County
44	1275	23.4	**Springboro** (city) Warren County
47	1320	23.5	**Avon** (city) Lorain County
47	1320	23.5	**Brecksville** (city) Cuyahoga County
47	1320	23.5	**Oxford** (city) Butler County
50	1375	23.6	**Cleveland** (city) Cuyahoga County
50	1375	23.6	**Franklin** (city) Warren County
50	1375	23.6	**Norwalk** (city) Huron County
50	1375	23.6	**Rocky River** (city) Cuyahoga County
54	1421	23.7	**Bay Village** (city) Cuyahoga County
55	1467	23.8	**Galion** (city) Crawford County
55	1467	23.8	**Portsmouth** (city) Scioto County
57	1515	23.9	**Elyria** (city) Lorain County
57	1515	23.9	**Lima** (city) Allen County
57	1515	23.9	**Lorain** (city) Lorain County
57	1515	23.9	**Troy** (city) Miami County
57	1515	23.9	**Youngstown** (city) Mahoning County
62	1555	24.0	**Athens** (city) Athens County
62	1555	24.0	**Bucyrus** (city) Crawford County
62	1555	24.0	**Cincinnati** (city) Hamilton County
62	1555	24.0	**Defiance** (city) Defiance County
62	1555	24.0	**Tallmadge** (city) Summit County
67	1606	24.1	**Brooklyn** (city) Cuyahoga County
67	1606	24.1	**Gahanna** (city) Franklin County
67	1606	24.1	**Springfield** (city) Clark County
70	1693	24.3	**Ashtabula** (city) Ashtabula County
70	1693	24.3	**Kent** (city) Portage County
70	1693	24.3	**Mount Vernon** (city) Knox County
73	1746	24.4	**Dayton** (city) Montgomery County
73	1746	24.4	**Toledo** (city) Lucas County
75	1800	24.5	**Circleville** (city) Pickaway County
75	1800	24.5	**Hilliard** (city) Franklin County
75	1800	24.5	**Hudson** (city) Summit County
75	1800	24.5	**Marysville** (city) Union County
75	1800	24.5	**Reading** (city) Hamilton County
75	1800	24.5	**Solon** (city) Cuyahoga County
75	1800	24.5	**Washington Court House** (city) Fayette County
75	1800	24.5	**Zanesville** (city) Muskingum County
83	1933	24.7	**Centerville** (city) Montgomery County
83	1933	24.7	**Greenville** (city) Darke County
83	1933	24.7	**North Royalton** (city) Cuyahoga County
83	1933	24.7	**Pickerington** (city) Fairfield County
87	1986	24.8	**North Ridgeville** (city) Lorain County
87	1986	24.8	**Wilmington** (city) Clinton County
89	2045	24.9	**Alliance** (city) Stark County
89	2045	24.9	**Chillicothe** (city) Ross County
89	2045	24.9	**Eastlake** (city) Lake County
89	2045	24.9	**Warren** (city) Trumbull County
93	2103	25.0	**Piqua** (city) Miami County
93	2103	25.0	**Powell** (city) Delaware County
95	2168	25.1	**Delaware** (city) Delaware County
95	2168	25.1	**Lakewood** (city) Cuyahoga County
97	2216	25.2	**Niles** (city) Trumbull County
98	2330	25.4	**Marietta** (city) Washington County
98	2330	25.4	**Vandalia** (city) Montgomery County
100	2381	25.5	**Seven Hills** (city) Cuyahoga County
100	2381	25.5	**Willowick** (city) Lake County
102	2431	25.6	**Forestville** (CDP) Hamilton County
103	2485	25.7	**Mansfield** (city) Richland County
104	2541	25.8	**Dover** (city) Tuscarawas County
105	2597	25.9	**Ashland** (city) Ashland County
105	2597	25.9	**Middleburg Heights** (city) Cuyahoga County
107	2660	26.0	**Conneaut** (city) Ashtabula County
107	2660	26.0	**Middletown** (city) Butler County
107	2660	26.0	**West Carrollton** (city) Montgomery County
110	2727	26.1	**Huber Heights** (city) Montgomery County
110	2727	26.1	**Mack** (CDP) Hamilton County
110	2727	26.1	**Maumee** (city) Lucas County
110	2727	26.1	**Wadsworth** (city) Medina County
114	2784	26.2	**Austintown** (CDP) Mahoning County
114	2784	26.2	**Broadview Heights** (city) Cuyahoga County
114	2784	26.2	**Mason** (city) Warren County
117	2858	26.3	**Green** (city) Summit County
117	2858	26.3	**Hamilton** (city) Butler County
119	2976	26.5	**Barberton** (city) Summit County
119	2976	26.5	**Brook Park** (city) Cuyahoga County
119	2976	26.5	**Massillon** (city) Stark County
119	2976	26.5	**Whitehall** (city) Franklin County
123	3032	26.6	**Berea** (city) Cuyahoga County
123	3032	26.6	**Wickliffe** (city) Lake County
123	3032	26.6	**Xenia** (city) Greene County
126	3092	26.7	**Forest Park** (city) Hamilton County
126	3092	26.7	**Monfort Heights** (CDP) Hamilton County
128	3142	26.8	**Columbus** (city) Franklin County
128	3142	26.8	**Newark** (city) Licking County
128	3142	26.8	**White Oak** (CDP) Hamilton County
131	3193	26.9	**Grove City** (city) Franklin County
132	3263	27.0	**Beachwood** (city) Cuyahoga County
132	3263	27.0	**Oregon** (city) Lucas County
132	3263	27.0	**South Euclid** (city) Cuyahoga County
132	3263	27.0	**Stow** (city) Summit County
136	3320	27.1	**Akron** (city) Summit County
136	3320	27.1	**Brunswick** (city) Medina County
136	3320	27.1	**Euclid** (city) Cuyahoga County
136	3320	27.1	**Ironton** (city) Lawrence County
140	3371	27.2	**Heath** (city) Licking County
140	3371	27.2	**Kettering** (city) Montgomery County
142	3421	27.3	**Willoughby** (city) Lake County
143	3459	27.4	**Loveland** (city) Hamilton County
143	3459	27.4	**Parma Heights** (city) Cuyahoga County
145	3547	27.6	**Cuyahoga Falls** (city) Summit County
145	3547	27.6	**Fairview Park** (city) Cuyahoga County
145	3547	27.6	**North Canton** (city) Stark County
145	3547	27.6	**Parma** (city) Cuyahoga County
149	3595	27.7	**Englewood** (city) Montgomery County
149	3595	27.7	**Lancaster** (city) Fairfield County

Note: *The state column ranks the top/bottom 150 places from all places in the state with population of 10,000 or more. The national column ranks the top/bottom 150 places from all places in the country with population of 10,000 or more. Places that are unincorporated were not considered in the rankings. Please refer to the User Guide for additional information.*

Employment: Natural Resources, Construction, and Maintenance Occupations

Top 150 Places Ranked in *Descending* Order

State Rank	Nat'l Rank	Percent	Place
1	305	14.0	**New Franklin** (city) Summit County
2	524	12.2	**Xenia** (city) Greene County
3	880	10.7	**Norton** (city) Summit County
4	938	10.5	**West Carrollton** (city) Montgomery County
5	977	10.4	**Vermilion** (city) Lorain County
6	1044	10.2	**Struthers** (city) Mahoning County
7	1078	10.1	**Brook Park** (city) Cuyahoga County
8	1124	10.0	**Brooklyn** (city) Cuyahoga County
9	1163	9.9	**Norwalk** (city) Huron County
10	1202	9.8	**Barberton** (city) Summit County
11	1245	9.7	**Tallmadge** (city) Summit County
12	1289	9.6	**Conneaut** (city) Ashtabula County
12	1289	9.6	**Niles** (city) Trumbull County
14	1329	9.5	**Hamilton** (city) Butler County
15	1418	9.3	**Eastlake** (city) Lake County
15	1418	9.3	**Oregon** (city) Lucas County
15	1418	9.3	**Riverside** (city) Montgomery County
18	1465	9.2	**Bellefontaine** (city) Logan County
18	1465	9.2	**Bridgetown** (CDP) Hamilton County
20	1514	9.1	**Willowick** (city) Lake County
21	1683	8.8	**Coshocton** (city) Coshocton County
21	1683	8.8	**Piqua** (city) Miami County
23	1748	8.7	**Pataskala** (city) Licking County
24	1791	8.6	**Franklin** (city) Warren County
25	1835	8.5	**Brunswick** (city) Medina County
25	1835	8.5	**Celina** (city) Mercer County
25	1835	8.5	**Chillicothe** (city) Ross County
25	1835	8.5	**Maumee** (city) Lucas County
25	1835	8.5	**Salem** (city) Columbiana County
30	1887	8.4	**Marion** (city) Marion County
30	1887	8.4	**Painesville** (city) Lake County
30	1887	8.4	**Parma** (city) Cuyahoga County
33	1931	8.3	**Massillon** (city) Stark County
33	1931	8.3	**Northbrook** (CDP) Hamilton County
35	1984	8.2	**Medina** (city) Medina County
36	2041	8.1	**East Liverpool** (city) Columbiana County
37	2093	8.0	**Fremont** (city) Sandusky County
37	2093	8.0	**Middletown** (city) Butler County
37	2093	8.0	**Parma Heights** (city) Cuyahoga County
40	2142	7.9	**Bucyrus** (city) Crawford County
40	2142	7.9	**Maple Heights** (city) Cuyahoga County
40	2142	7.9	**Trenton** (city) Butler County
40	2142	7.9	**Whitehall** (city) Franklin County
44	2189	7.8	**Fairview Park** (city) Cuyahoga County
44	2189	7.8	**Garfield Heights** (city) Cuyahoga County
44	2189	7.8	**Ironton** (city) Lawrence County
44	2189	7.8	**North Ridgeville** (city) Lorain County
44	2189	7.8	**Springdale** (city) Hamilton County
44	2189	7.8	**Zanesville** (city) Muskingum County
50	2240	7.7	**Ashtabula** (city) Ashtabula County
50	2240	7.7	**Grove City** (city) Franklin County
50	2240	7.7	**Newark** (city) Licking County
50	2240	7.7	**Norwood** (city) Hamilton County
50	2240	7.7	**Wickliffe** (city) Lake County
55	2306	7.6	**Elyria** (city) Lorain County
55	2306	7.6	**Ravenna** (city) Portage County
55	2306	7.6	**Reading** (city) Hamilton County
55	2306	7.6	**Warren** (city) Trumbull County
55	2306	7.6	**Willoughby** (city) Lake County
60	2372	7.5	**Amherst** (city) Lorain County
60	2372	7.5	**Austintown** (CDP) Mahoning County
60	2372	7.5	**Cuyahoga Falls** (city) Summit County
60	2372	7.5	**Seven Hills** (city) Cuyahoga County
64	2439	7.4	**Heath** (city) Licking County
64	2439	7.4	**Lorain** (city) Lorain County
66	2512	7.3	**Dayton** (city) Montgomery County
66	2512	7.3	**Green** (city) Summit County
66	2512	7.3	**Marietta** (city) Washington County
66	2512	7.3	**Toledo** (city) Lucas County
66	2512	7.3	**Washington Court House** (city) Fayette County
71	2570	7.2	**Berea** (city) Cuyahoga County
71	2570	7.2	**Bowling Green** (city) Wood County
71	2570	7.2	**Defiance** (city) Defiance County
74	2639	7.1	**Huber Heights** (city) Montgomery County
74	2639	7.1	**Youngstown** (city) Mahoning County
76	2692	7.0	**Urbana** (city) Champaign County
77	2750	6.9	**Alliance** (city) Stark County
77	2750	6.9	**Bedford Heights** (city) Cuyahoga County
77	2750	6.9	**Findlay** (city) Hancock County
77	2750	6.9	**Macedonia** (city) Summit County
77	2750	6.9	**Sandusky** (city) Erie County
82	2807	6.8	**Lancaster** (city) Fairfield County
83	2855	6.7	**Fairfield** (city) Butler County
83	2855	6.7	**Galion** (city) Crawford County
83	2855	6.7	**Marysville** (city) Union County
83	2855	6.7	**Monfort Heights** (CDP) Hamilton County
87	2904	6.6	**Akron** (city) Summit County
87	2904	6.6	**Canton** (city) Stark County
87	2904	6.6	**Dover** (city) Tuscarawas County
87	2904	6.6	**North Royalton** (city) Cuyahoga County
87	2904	6.6	**Tiffin** (city) Seneca County
92	2974	6.5	**Greenville** (city) Darke County
92	2974	6.5	**Pickerington** (city) Fairfield County
94	3035	6.4	**Boardman** (CDP) Mahoning County
94	3035	6.4	**Cambridge** (city) Guernsey County
94	3035	6.4	**Dent** (CDP) Hamilton County
94	3035	6.4	**Reynoldsburg** (city) Franklin County
94	3035	6.4	**Wilmington** (city) Clinton County
99	3112	6.3	**Mount Vernon** (city) Knox County
100	3158	6.2	**Cleveland** (city) Cuyahoga County
100	3158	6.2	**Fairborn** (city) Greene County
100	3158	6.2	**North Olmsted** (city) Cuyahoga County
100	3158	6.2	**Van Wert** (city) Van Wert County
104	3207	6.1	**Ashland** (city) Ashland County
104	3207	6.1	**Monroe** (city) Butler County
104	3207	6.1	**Troy** (city) Miami County
107	3276	6.0	**Lima** (city) Allen County
107	3276	6.0	**Miamisburg** (city) Montgomery County
107	3276	6.0	**Portsmouth** (city) Scioto County
110	3341	5.9	**Bedford** (city) Cuyahoga County
110	3341	5.9	**Clayton** (city) Montgomery County
110	3341	5.9	**Streetsboro** (city) Portage County
110	3341	5.9	**Trotwood** (city) Montgomery County
110	3341	5.9	**Vandalia** (city) Montgomery County
115	3411	5.8	**Forest Park** (city) Hamilton County
115	3411	5.8	**Loveland** (city) Hamilton County
115	3411	5.8	**Mentor** (city) Lake County
115	3411	5.8	**Sidney** (city) Shelby County
115	3411	5.8	**White Oak** (CDP) Hamilton County
120	3458	5.7	**Fostoria** (city) Seneca County
120	3458	5.7	**Middleburg Heights** (city) Cuyahoga County
120	3458	5.7	**Wooster** (city) Wayne County
123	3508	5.6	**Euclid** (city) Cuyahoga County
123	3508	5.6	**Kettering** (city) Montgomery County
123	3508	5.6	**Mack** (CDP) Hamilton County
123	3508	5.6	**Springfield** (city) Clark County
123	3508	5.6	**Stow** (city) Summit County
128	3548	5.5	**Columbus** (city) Franklin County
129	3584	5.4	**New Philadelphia** (city) Tuscarawas County
129	3584	5.4	**Steubenville** (city) Jefferson County
131	3634	5.3	**Delaware** (city) Delaware County
131	3634	5.3	**South Euclid** (city) Cuyahoga County
133	3670	5.2	**Lakewood** (city) Cuyahoga County
134	3766	5.0	**Englewood** (city) Montgomery County
134	3766	5.0	**Wadsworth** (city) Medina County
136	3811	4.9	**Brecksville** (city) Cuyahoga County
136	3811	4.9	**Perrysburg** (city) Wood County
138	3844	4.8	**Warrensville Heights** (city) Cuyahoga County
139	3892	4.7	**North Canton** (city) Stark County
140	3928	4.6	**Blue Ash** (city) Hamilton County
140	3928	4.6	**Cincinnati** (city) Hamilton County
142	3965	4.5	**Avon Lake** (city) Lorain County
142	3965	4.5	**Bay Village** (city) Cuyahoga County
142	3965	4.5	**Mansfield** (city) Richland County
142	3965	4.5	**Strongsville** (city) Cuyahoga County
146	4049	4.3	**Sharonville** (city) Hamilton County
147	4073	4.2	**Circleville** (city) Pickaway County
147	4073	4.2	**Forestville** (CDP) Hamilton County
149	4104	4.1	**Mayfield Heights** (city) Cuyahoga County
149	4104	4.1	**Springboro** (city) Warren County

Note: *The state column ranks the top/bottom 150 places from all places in the state with population of 10,000 or more. The national column ranks the top/bottom 150 places from all places in the country with population of 10,000 or more. Places that are unincorporated were not considered in the rankings. Please refer to the User Guide for additional information.*

Employment: Natural Resources, Construction, and Maintenance Occupations

Top 150 Places Ranked in *Ascending* Order

State Rank	Nat'l Rank	Percent	Place
1	6	0.7	**Beachwood** (city) Cuyahoga County
2	24	1.3	**Athens** (city) Athens County
2	24	1.3	**Dublin** (city) Franklin County
4	83	2.0	**Hudson** (city) Summit County
4	83	2.0	**University Heights** (city) Cuyahoga County
6	99	2.1	**Oxford** (city) Butler County
6	99	2.1	**Powell** (city) Delaware County
8	127	2.3	**Shaker Heights** (city) Cuyahoga County
9	138	2.4	**Upper Arlington** (city) Franklin County
10	151	2.5	**Cleveland Heights** (city) Cuyahoga County
10	151	2.5	**Montgomery** (city) Hamilton County
12	169	2.6	**Lyndhurst** (city) Cuyahoga County
13	203	2.8	**Bexley** (city) Franklin County
14	219	2.9	**Avon** (city) Lorain County
14	219	2.9	**Sylvania** (city) Lucas County
16	257	3.1	**Worthington** (city) Franklin County
17	281	3.2	**Centerville** (city) Montgomery County
17	281	3.2	**Rocky River** (city) Cuyahoga County
19	308	3.3	**Beavercreek** (city) Greene County
20	324	3.4	**Aurora** (city) Portage County
20	324	3.4	**Finneytown** (CDP) Hamilton County
20	324	3.4	**Hilliard** (city) Franklin County
20	324	3.4	**Lebanon** (city) Warren County
20	324	3.4	**Mason** (city) Warren County
25	355	3.5	**East Cleveland** (city) Cuyahoga County
25	355	3.5	**Solon** (city) Cuyahoga County
25	355	3.5	**Twinsburg** (city) Summit County
25	355	3.5	**Westlake** (city) Cuyahoga County
29	377	3.6	**Broadview Heights** (city) Cuyahoga County
29	377	3.6	**Gahanna** (city) Franklin County
31	407	3.7	**Kent** (city) Portage County
32	466	3.9	**Westerville** (city) Franklin County
33	500	4.0	**Richmond Heights** (city) Cuyahoga County
34	518	4.1	**Mayfield Heights** (city) Cuyahoga County
34	518	4.1	**Springboro** (city) Warren County
36	553	4.2	**Circleville** (city) Pickaway County
36	553	4.2	**Forestville** (CDP) Hamilton County
38	584	4.3	**Sharonville** (city) Hamilton County
39	641	4.5	**Avon Lake** (city) Lorain County
39	641	4.5	**Bay Village** (city) Cuyahoga County
39	641	4.5	**Mansfield** (city) Richland County
39	641	4.5	**Strongsville** (city) Cuyahoga County
43	692	4.6	**Blue Ash** (city) Hamilton County
43	692	4.6	**Cincinnati** (city) Hamilton County
45	729	4.7	**North Canton** (city) Stark County
46	765	4.8	**Warrensville Heights** (city) Cuyahoga County
47	813	4.9	**Brecksville** (city) Cuyahoga County
47	813	4.9	**Perrysburg** (city) Wood County
49	846	5.0	**Englewood** (city) Montgomery County
49	846	5.0	**Wadsworth** (city) Medina County
51	947	5.2	**Lakewood** (city) Cuyahoga County
52	987	5.3	**Delaware** (city) Delaware County
52	987	5.3	**South Euclid** (city) Cuyahoga County
54	1023	5.4	**New Philadelphia** (city) Tuscarawas County
54	1023	5.4	**Steubenville** (city) Jefferson County
56	1073	5.5	**Columbus** (city) Franklin County
57	1109	5.6	**Euclid** (city) Cuyahoga County
57	1109	5.6	**Kettering** (city) Montgomery County
57	1109	5.6	**Mack** (CDP) Hamilton County
57	1109	5.6	**Springfield** (city) Clark County
57	1109	5.6	**Stow** (city) Summit County
62	1149	5.7	**Fostoria** (city) Seneca County
62	1149	5.7	**Middleburg Heights** (city) Cuyahoga County
62	1149	5.7	**Wooster** (city) Wayne County
65	1199	5.8	**Forest Park** (city) Hamilton County
65	1199	5.8	**Loveland** (city) Hamilton County
65	1199	5.8	**Mentor** (city) Lake County
65	1199	5.8	**Sidney** (city) Shelby County
65	1199	5.8	**White Oak** (CDP) Hamilton County
70	1246	5.9	**Bedford** (city) Cuyahoga County
70	1246	5.9	**Clayton** (city) Montgomery County
70	1246	5.9	**Streetsboro** (city) Portage County
70	1246	5.9	**Trotwood** (city) Montgomery County
70	1246	5.9	**Vandalia** (city) Montgomery County
75	1316	6.0	**Lima** (city) Allen County
75	1316	6.0	**Miamisburg** (city) Montgomery County
75	1316	6.0	**Portsmouth** (city) Scioto County
78	1381	6.1	**Ashland** (city) Ashland County
78	1381	6.1	**Monroe** (city) Butler County
78	1381	6.1	**Troy** (city) Miami County
81	1450	6.2	**Cleveland** (city) Cuyahoga County
81	1450	6.2	**Fairborn** (city) Greene County
81	1450	6.2	**North Olmsted** (city) Cuyahoga County
81	1450	6.2	**Van Wert** (city) Van Wert County
85	1499	6.3	**Mount Vernon** (city) Knox County
86	1545	6.4	**Boardman** (CDP) Mahoning County
86	1545	6.4	**Cambridge** (city) Guernsey County
86	1545	6.4	**Dent** (CDP) Hamilton County
86	1545	6.4	**Reynoldsburg** (city) Franklin County
86	1545	6.4	**Wilmington** (city) Clinton County
91	1622	6.5	**Greenville** (city) Darke County
91	1622	6.5	**Pickerington** (city) Fairfield County
93	1683	6.6	**Akron** (city) Summit County
93	1683	6.6	**Canton** (city) Stark County
93	1683	6.6	**Dover** (city) Tuscarawas County
93	1683	6.6	**North Royalton** (city) Cuyahoga County
93	1683	6.6	**Tiffin** (city) Seneca County
98	1753	6.7	**Fairfield** (city) Butler County
98	1753	6.7	**Galion** (city) Crawford County
98	1753	6.7	**Marysville** (city) Union County
98	1753	6.7	**Monfort Heights** (CDP) Hamilton County
102	1802	6.8	**Lancaster** (city) Fairfield County
103	1850	6.9	**Alliance** (city) Stark County
103	1850	6.9	**Bedford Heights** (city) Cuyahoga County
103	1850	6.9	**Findlay** (city) Hancock County
103	1850	6.9	**Macedonia** (city) Summit County
103	1850	6.9	**Sandusky** (city) Erie County
108	1907	7.0	**Urbana** (city) Champaign County
109	1965	7.1	**Huber Heights** (city) Montgomery County
109	1965	7.1	**Youngstown** (city) Mahoning County
111	2018	7.2	**Berea** (city) Cuyahoga County
111	2018	7.2	**Bowling Green** (city) Wood County
111	2018	7.2	**Defiance** (city) Defiance County
114	2087	7.3	**Dayton** (city) Montgomery County
114	2087	7.3	**Green** (city) Summit County
114	2087	7.3	**Marietta** (city) Washington County
114	2087	7.3	**Toledo** (city) Lucas County
114	2087	7.3	**Washington Court House** (city) Fayette County
119	2145	7.4	**Heath** (city) Licking County
119	2145	7.4	**Lorain** (city) Lorain County
121	2218	7.5	**Amherst** (city) Lorain County
121	2218	7.5	**Austintown** (CDP) Mahoning County
121	2218	7.5	**Cuyahoga Falls** (city) Summit County
121	2218	7.5	**Seven Hills** (city) Cuyahoga County
125	2285	7.6	**Elyria** (city) Lorain County
125	2285	7.6	**Ravenna** (city) Portage County
125	2285	7.6	**Reading** (city) Hamilton County
125	2285	7.6	**Warren** (city) Trumbull County
125	2285	7.6	**Willoughby** (city) Lake County
130	2351	7.7	**Ashtabula** (city) Ashtabula County
130	2351	7.7	**Grove City** (city) Franklin County
130	2351	7.7	**Newark** (city) Licking County
130	2351	7.7	**Norwood** (city) Hamilton County
130	2351	7.7	**Wickliffe** (city) Lake County
135	2417	7.8	**Fairview Park** (city) Cuyahoga County
135	2417	7.8	**Garfield Heights** (city) Cuyahoga County
135	2417	7.8	**Ironton** (city) Lawrence County
135	2417	7.8	**North Ridgeville** (city) Lorain County
135	2417	7.8	**Springdale** (city) Hamilton County
135	2417	7.8	**Zanesville** (city) Muskingum County
141	2468	7.9	**Bucyrus** (city) Crawford County
141	2468	7.9	**Maple Heights** (city) Cuyahoga County
141	2468	7.9	**Trenton** (city) Butler County
141	2468	7.9	**Whitehall** (city) Franklin County
145	2515	8.0	**Fremont** (city) Sandusky County
145	2515	8.0	**Middletown** (city) Butler County
145	2515	8.0	**Parma Heights** (city) Cuyahoga County
148	2564	8.1	**East Liverpool** (city) Columbiana County
149	2616	8.2	**Medina** (city) Medina County
150	2673	8.3	**Massillon** (city) Stark County

Note: *The state column ranks the top/bottom 150 places from all places in the state with population of 10,000 or more. The national column ranks the top/bottom 150 places from all places in the country with population of 10,000 or more. Places that are unincorporated were not considered in the rankings. Please refer to the User Guide for additional information.*

Employment: Production, Transportation, and Material Moving Occupations

Top 150 Places Ranked in *Descending* Order

State Rank	Nat'l Rank	Percent	Place
1	10	34.3	**Sidney** (city) Shelby County
2	12	33.9	**Fostoria** (city) Seneca County
3	20	32.6	**Fremont** (city) Sandusky County
4	57	28.8	**Piqua** (city) Miami County
4	57	28.8	**Van Wert** (city) Van Wert County
6	63	28.1	**Greenville** (city) Darke County
6	63	28.1	**Marion** (city) Marion County
8	75	27.5	**Urbana** (city) Champaign County
9	90	26.7	**Bucyrus** (city) Crawford County
10	92	26.6	**Salem** (city) Columbiana County
11	97	26.4	**Bellefontaine** (city) Logan County
12	101	26.2	**Franklin** (city) Warren County
13	122	25.4	**Coshocton** (city) Coshocton County
13	122	25.4	**East Liverpool** (city) Columbiana County
15	134	24.7	**Celina** (city) Mercer County
15	134	24.7	**Whitehall** (city) Franklin County
17	147	24.5	**Alliance** (city) Stark County
18	152	24.4	**Tiffin** (city) Seneca County
19	163	24.1	**Galion** (city) Crawford County
20	168	24.0	**Ashtabula** (city) Ashtabula County
20	168	24.0	**Conneaut** (city) Ashtabula County
22	181	23.6	**Mansfield** (city) Richland County
23	193	23.2	**Norwalk** (city) Huron County
24	201	23.0	**Troy** (city) Miami County
25	219	22.6	**Wilmington** (city) Clinton County
26	230	22.3	**Defiance** (city) Defiance County
27	270	21.5	**Circleville** (city) Pickaway County
27	270	21.5	**Painesville** (city) Lake County
27	270	21.5	**Washington Court House** (city) Fayette County
30	278	21.4	**Lima** (city) Allen County
31	296	21.2	**Lorain** (city) Lorain County
32	301	21.1	**Massillon** (city) Stark County
33	332	20.7	**Ravenna** (city) Portage County
34	356	20.5	**Trenton** (city) Butler County
35	400	20.0	**Cambridge** (city) Guernsey County
35	400	20.0	**Sandusky** (city) Erie County
37	408	19.9	**Forest Park** (city) Hamilton County
38	415	19.8	**Barberton** (city) Summit County
38	415	19.8	**New Philadelphia** (city) Tuscarawas County
40	438	19.5	**Elyria** (city) Lorain County
41	453	19.4	**Marysville** (city) Union County
41	453	19.4	**Springfield** (city) Clark County
43	468	19.2	**Niles** (city) Trumbull County
44	488	19.0	**Sharonville** (city) Hamilton County
45	512	18.7	**Warren** (city) Trumbull County
46	522	18.6	**Austintown** (CDP) Mahoning County
46	522	18.6	**Toledo** (city) Lucas County
48	541	18.5	**Findlay** (city) Hancock County
49	556	18.3	**East Cleveland** (city) Cuyahoga County
49	556	18.3	**Oregon** (city) Lucas County
49	556	18.3	**Riverside** (city) Montgomery County
49	556	18.3	**Zanesville** (city) Muskingum County
53	573	18.2	**Dover** (city) Tuscarawas County
53	573	18.2	**Middletown** (city) Butler County
55	610	18.0	**Hamilton** (city) Butler County
56	627	17.9	**Canton** (city) Stark County
56	627	17.9	**Mount Vernon** (city) Knox County
56	627	17.9	**Willowick** (city) Lake County
59	639	17.8	**Brook Park** (city) Cuyahoga County
60	651	17.7	**Eastlake** (city) Lake County
60	651	17.7	**Youngstown** (city) Mahoning County
62	668	17.6	**Warrensville Heights** (city) Cuyahoga County
63	676	17.5	**Brooklyn** (city) Cuyahoga County
64	691	17.4	**Bedford** (city) Cuyahoga County
65	739	17.1	**Trotwood** (city) Montgomery County
66	787	16.8	**Cleveland** (city) Cuyahoga County
67	808	16.6	**Heath** (city) Licking County
67	808	16.6	**Struthers** (city) Mahoning County
69	839	16.4	**Bedford Heights** (city) Cuyahoga County
69	839	16.4	**Lancaster** (city) Fairfield County
71	890	16.1	**Parma Heights** (city) Cuyahoga County
72	909	16.0	**Chillicothe** (city) Ross County
72	909	16.0	**Euclid** (city) Cuyahoga County
74	929	15.9	**Newark** (city) Licking County
74	929	15.9	**West Carrollton** (city) Montgomery County
76	949	15.8	**Akron** (city) Summit County
76	949	15.8	**Brunswick** (city) Medina County
76	949	15.8	**Streetsboro** (city) Portage County
76	949	15.8	**Vermilion** (city) Lorain County
76	949	15.8	**Wooster** (city) Wayne County
81	972	15.7	**Fairfield** (city) Butler County
81	972	15.7	**Maple Heights** (city) Cuyahoga County
83	996	15.6	**Ashland** (city) Ashland County
83	996	15.6	**Reading** (city) Hamilton County
85	1017	15.5	**Garfield Heights** (city) Cuyahoga County
85	1017	15.5	**Huber Heights** (city) Montgomery County
85	1017	15.5	**Parma** (city) Cuyahoga County
88	1107	15.0	**Dayton** (city) Montgomery County
88	1107	15.0	**Springdale** (city) Hamilton County
90	1128	14.9	**Wickliffe** (city) Lake County
91	1152	14.8	**Northbrook** (CDP) Hamilton County
92	1163	14.7	**Ironton** (city) Lawrence County
93	1224	14.4	**New Franklin** (city) Summit County
94	1249	14.3	**Maumee** (city) Lucas County
95	1269	14.2	**North Ridgeville** (city) Lorain County
95	1269	14.2	**Vandalia** (city) Montgomery County
97	1316	14.0	**Willoughby** (city) Lake County
98	1337	13.9	**Miamisburg** (city) Montgomery County
98	1337	13.9	**Monroe** (city) Butler County
100	1416	13.6	**Mentor** (city) Lake County
100	1416	13.6	**Norton** (city) Summit County
102	1442	13.5	**Finneytown** (CDP) Hamilton County
103	1457	13.4	**Norwood** (city) Hamilton County
104	1483	13.3	**Richmond Heights** (city) Cuyahoga County
105	1508	13.2	**Xenia** (city) Greene County
106	1552	13.0	**Grove City** (city) Franklin County
106	1552	13.0	**Tallmadge** (city) Summit County
108	1582	12.9	**Fairborn** (city) Greene County
109	1633	12.7	**Berea** (city) Cuyahoga County
110	1693	12.5	**Cuyahoga Falls** (city) Summit County
111	1723	12.4	**Steubenville** (city) Jefferson County
112	1778	12.2	**Green** (city) Summit County
112	1778	12.2	**Pataskala** (city) Licking County
112	1778	12.2	**Wadsworth** (city) Medina County
115	1841	12.0	**Macedonia** (city) Summit County
116	1893	11.8	**Medina** (city) Medina County
117	1923	11.7	**Kettering** (city) Montgomery County
117	1923	11.7	**Sylvania** (city) Lucas County
117	1923	11.7	**Twinsburg** (city) Summit County
120	1958	11.6	**Amherst** (city) Lorain County
120	1958	11.6	**Broadview Heights** (city) Cuyahoga County
122	1994	11.5	**White Oak** (CDP) Hamilton County
123	2015	11.4	**Columbus** (city) Franklin County
124	2043	11.3	**Boardman** (CDP) Mahoning County
124	2043	11.3	**Lebanon** (city) Warren County
124	2043	11.3	**Portsmouth** (city) Scioto County
127	2115	11.1	**Delaware** (city) Delaware County
127	2115	11.1	**Englewood** (city) Montgomery County
129	2146	11.0	**Clayton** (city) Montgomery County
130	2180	10.9	**Cincinnati** (city) Hamilton County
130	2180	10.9	**Middleburg Heights** (city) Cuyahoga County
132	2335	10.5	**Marietta** (city) Washington County
132	2335	10.5	**Monfort Heights** (CDP) Hamilton County
134	2365	10.4	**North Olmsted** (city) Cuyahoga County
134	2365	10.4	**North Royalton** (city) Cuyahoga County
136	2484	10.0	**Reynoldsburg** (city) Franklin County
136	2484	10.0	**Stow** (city) Summit County
138	2523	9.9	**Kent** (city) Portage County
139	2581	9.7	**Mack** (CDP) Hamilton County
140	2700	9.4	**Seven Hills** (city) Cuyahoga County
141	2731	9.3	**Blue Ash** (city) Hamilton County
141	2731	9.3	**Bowling Green** (city) Wood County
143	2795	9.1	**Loveland** (city) Hamilton County
144	2827	9.0	**Bridgetown** (CDP) Hamilton County
144	2827	9.0	**Fairview Park** (city) Cuyahoga County
144	2827	9.0	**North Canton** (city) Stark County
147	2868	8.9	**Aurora** (city) Portage County
148	2902	8.8	**Lakewood** (city) Cuyahoga County
148	2902	8.8	**Strongsville** (city) Cuyahoga County
150	3071	8.3	**Hilliard** (city) Franklin County

Note: *The state column ranks the top/bottom 150 places from all places in the state with population of 10,000 or more. The national column ranks the top/bottom 150 places from all places in the country with population of 10,000 or more. Places that are unincorporated were not considered in the rankings. Please refer to the User Guide for additional information.*

Employment: Production, Transportation, and Material Moving Occupations

Top 150 Places Ranked in *Ascending* Order

State Rank	Nat'l Rank	Percent	Place
1	61	2.3	**Beachwood** (city) Cuyahoga County
2	81	2.5	**Bexley** (city) Franklin County
2	81	2.5	**Dublin** (city) Franklin County
4	115	2.8	**Montgomery** (city) Hamilton County
5	151	3.1	**Upper Arlington** (city) Franklin County
6	214	3.5	**University Heights** (city) Cuyahoga County
7	289	3.9	**Brecksville** (city) Cuyahoga County
8	373	4.3	**Lyndhurst** (city) Cuyahoga County
9	398	4.4	**Worthington** (city) Franklin County
10	424	4.5	**Rocky River** (city) Cuyahoga County
10	424	4.5	**Shaker Heights** (city) Cuyahoga County
12	450	4.6	**Dent** (CDP) Hamilton County
13	470	4.7	**Powell** (city) Delaware County
14	491	4.8	**Hudson** (city) Summit County
15	524	4.9	**Solon** (city) Cuyahoga County
16	548	5.0	**Bay Village** (city) Cuyahoga County
17	602	5.2	**Forestville** (CDP) Hamilton County
17	602	5.2	**Westerville** (city) Franklin County
19	792	5.9	**Athens** (city) Athens County
20	817	6.0	**Oxford** (city) Butler County
20	817	6.0	**Westlake** (city) Cuyahoga County
22	886	6.2	**Avon Lake** (city) Lorain County
23	993	6.6	**Avon** (city) Lorain County
24	1049	6.8	**Cleveland Heights** (city) Cuyahoga County
24	1049	6.8	**Mason** (city) Warren County
26	1081	6.9	**Mayfield Heights** (city) Cuyahoga County
27	1193	7.3	**Gahanna** (city) Franklin County
28	1265	7.5	**Centerville** (city) Montgomery County
28	1265	7.5	**Springboro** (city) Warren County
30	1325	7.7	**Perrysburg** (city) Wood County
31	1362	7.8	**South Euclid** (city) Cuyahoga County
32	1515	8.2	**Beavercreek** (city) Greene County
32	1515	8.2	**Pickerington** (city) Fairfield County
34	1547	8.3	**Hilliard** (city) Franklin County
35	1718	8.8	**Lakewood** (city) Cuyahoga County
35	1718	8.8	**Strongsville** (city) Cuyahoga County
37	1755	8.9	**Aurora** (city) Portage County
38	1789	9.0	**Bridgetown** (CDP) Hamilton County
38	1789	9.0	**Fairview Park** (city) Cuyahoga County
38	1789	9.0	**North Canton** (city) Stark County
41	1830	9.1	**Loveland** (city) Hamilton County
42	1898	9.3	**Blue Ash** (city) Hamilton County
42	1898	9.3	**Bowling Green** (city) Wood County
44	1926	9.4	**Seven Hills** (city) Cuyahoga County
45	2032	9.7	**Mack** (CDP) Hamilton County
46	2106	9.9	**Kent** (city) Portage County
47	2134	10.0	**Reynoldsburg** (city) Franklin County
47	2134	10.0	**Stow** (city) Summit County
49	2268	10.4	**North Olmsted** (city) Cuyahoga County
49	2268	10.4	**North Royalton** (city) Cuyahoga County
51	2292	10.5	**Marietta** (city) Washington County
51	2292	10.5	**Monfort Heights** (CDP) Hamilton County
53	2446	10.9	**Cincinnati** (city) Hamilton County
53	2446	10.9	**Middleburg Heights** (city) Cuyahoga County
55	2477	11.0	**Clayton** (city) Montgomery County
56	2511	11.1	**Delaware** (city) Delaware County
56	2511	11.1	**Englewood** (city) Montgomery County
58	2577	11.3	**Boardman** (CDP) Mahoning County
58	2577	11.3	**Lebanon** (city) Warren County
58	2577	11.3	**Portsmouth** (city) Scioto County
61	2614	11.4	**Columbus** (city) Franklin County
62	2642	11.5	**White Oak** (CDP) Hamilton County
63	2663	11.6	**Amherst** (city) Lorain County
63	2663	11.6	**Broadview Heights** (city) Cuyahoga County
65	2699	11.7	**Kettering** (city) Montgomery County
65	2699	11.7	**Sylvania** (city) Lucas County
65	2699	11.7	**Twinsburg** (city) Summit County
68	2734	11.8	**Medina** (city) Medina County
69	2789	12.0	**Macedonia** (city) Summit County
70	2842	12.2	**Green** (city) Summit County
70	2842	12.2	**Pataskala** (city) Licking County
70	2842	12.2	**Wadsworth** (city) Medina County
73	2898	12.4	**Steubenville** (city) Jefferson County
74	2934	12.5	**Cuyahoga Falls** (city) Summit County
75	2992	12.7	**Berea** (city) Cuyahoga County
76	3049	12.9	**Fairborn** (city) Greene County
77	3075	13.0	**Grove City** (city) Franklin County
77	3075	13.0	**Tallmadge** (city) Summit County
79	3128	13.2	**Xenia** (city) Greene County
80	3149	13.3	**Richmond Heights** (city) Cuyahoga County
81	3174	13.4	**Norwood** (city) Hamilton County
82	3200	13.5	**Finneytown** (CDP) Hamilton County
83	3215	13.6	**Mentor** (city) Lake County
83	3215	13.6	**Norton** (city) Summit County
85	3294	13.9	**Miamisburg** (city) Montgomery County
85	3294	13.9	**Monroe** (city) Butler County
87	3320	14.0	**Willoughby** (city) Lake County
88	3369	14.2	**North Ridgeville** (city) Lorain County
88	3369	14.2	**Vandalia** (city) Montgomery County
90	3388	14.3	**Maumee** (city) Lucas County
91	3408	14.4	**New Franklin** (city) Summit County
92	3473	14.7	**Ironton** (city) Lawrence County
93	3494	14.8	**Northbrook** (CDP) Hamilton County
94	3505	14.9	**Wickliffe** (city) Lake County
95	3529	15.0	**Dayton** (city) Montgomery County
95	3529	15.0	**Springdale** (city) Hamilton County
97	3622	15.5	**Garfield Heights** (city) Cuyahoga County
97	3622	15.5	**Huber Heights** (city) Montgomery County
97	3622	15.5	**Parma** (city) Cuyahoga County
100	3640	15.6	**Ashland** (city) Ashland County
100	3640	15.6	**Reading** (city) Hamilton County
102	3661	15.7	**Fairfield** (city) Butler County
102	3661	15.7	**Maple Heights** (city) Cuyahoga County
104	3685	15.8	**Akron** (city) Summit County
104	3685	15.8	**Brunswick** (city) Medina County
104	3685	15.8	**Streetsboro** (city) Portage County
104	3685	15.8	**Vermilion** (city) Lorain County
104	3685	15.8	**Wooster** (city) Wayne County
109	3708	15.9	**Newark** (city) Licking County
109	3708	15.9	**West Carrollton** (city) Montgomery County
111	3728	16.0	**Chillicothe** (city) Ross County
111	3728	16.0	**Euclid** (city) Cuyahoga County
113	3748	16.1	**Parma Heights** (city) Cuyahoga County
114	3797	16.4	**Bedford Heights** (city) Cuyahoga County
114	3797	16.4	**Lancaster** (city) Fairfield County
116	3832	16.6	**Heath** (city) Licking County
116	3832	16.6	**Struthers** (city) Mahoning County
118	3860	16.8	**Cleveland** (city) Cuyahoga County
119	3903	17.1	**Trotwood** (city) Montgomery County
120	3950	17.4	**Bedford** (city) Cuyahoga County
121	3966	17.5	**Brooklyn** (city) Cuyahoga County
122	3981	17.6	**Warrensville Heights** (city) Cuyahoga County
123	3989	17.7	**Eastlake** (city) Lake County
123	3989	17.7	**Youngstown** (city) Mahoning County
125	4006	17.8	**Brook Park** (city) Cuyahoga County
126	4018	17.9	**Canton** (city) Stark County
126	4018	17.9	**Mount Vernon** (city) Knox County
126	4018	17.9	**Willowick** (city) Lake County
129	4030	18.0	**Hamilton** (city) Butler County
130	4066	18.2	**Dover** (city) Tuscarawas County
130	4066	18.2	**Middletown** (city) Butler County
132	4084	18.3	**East Cleveland** (city) Cuyahoga County
132	4084	18.3	**Oregon** (city) Lucas County
132	4084	18.3	**Riverside** (city) Montgomery County
132	4084	18.3	**Zanesville** (city) Muskingum County
136	4105	18.5	**Findlay** (city) Hancock County
137	4116	18.6	**Austintown** (CDP) Mahoning County
137	4116	18.6	**Toledo** (city) Lucas County
139	4135	18.7	**Warren** (city) Trumbull County
140	4159	19.0	**Sharonville** (city) Hamilton County
141	4181	19.2	**Niles** (city) Trumbull County
142	4198	19.4	**Marysville** (city) Union County
142	4198	19.4	**Springfield** (city) Clark County
144	4204	19.5	**Elyria** (city) Lorain County
145	4234	19.8	**Barberton** (city) Summit County
145	4234	19.8	**New Philadelphia** (city) Tuscarawas County
147	4242	19.9	**Forest Park** (city) Hamilton County
148	4249	20.0	**Cambridge** (city) Guernsey County
148	4249	20.0	**Sandusky** (city) Erie County
150	4289	20.5	**Trenton** (city) Butler County

Note: *The state column ranks the top/bottom 150 places from all places in the state with population of 10,000 or more. The national column ranks the top/bottom 150 places from all places in the country with population of 10,000 or more. Places that are unincorporated were not considered in the rankings. Please refer to the User Guide for additional information.*

Per Capita Income

Top 150 Places Ranked in *Descending* Order

State Rank	Nat'l Rank	Dollars	Place
1	216	54,099	**Beachwood** (city) Cuyahoga County
2	236	53,322	**Montgomery** (city) Hamilton County
3	243	52,906	**Dublin** (city) Franklin County
4	265	51,932	**Upper Arlington** (city) Franklin County
5	307	49,903	**Hudson** (city) Summit County
6	312	49,686	**Brecksville** (city) Cuyahoga County
7	330	48,868	**Shaker Heights** (city) Cuyahoga County
8	353	48,246	**Powell** (city) Delaware County
9	392	47,332	**Solon** (city) Cuyahoga County
10	415	46,684	**Westlake** (city) Cuyahoga County
11	432	46,147	**Bexley** (city) Franklin County
12	464	45,272	**Worthington** (city) Franklin County
13	468	45,176	**Rocky River** (city) Cuyahoga County
14	529	44,114	**Blue Ash** (city) Hamilton County
15	566	43,498	**Bay Village** (city) Cuyahoga County
16	624	42,549	**Aurora** (city) Portage County
17	659	41,876	**Avon** (city) Lorain County
18	773	40,049	**Avon Lake** (city) Lorain County
19	843	39,212	**Beavercreek** (city) Greene County
20	851	39,132	**Macedonia** (city) Summit County
21	950	37,896	**Mack** (CDP) Hamilton County
22	955	37,849	**Mason** (city) Warren County
23	987	37,484	**Twinsburg** (city) Summit County
24	998	37,431	**Westerville** (city) Franklin County
25	1001	37,401	**Strongsville** (city) Cuyahoga County
26	1021	37,115	**Broadview Heights** (city) Cuyahoga County
27	1079	36,432	**Lyndhurst** (city) Cuyahoga County
28	1097	36,227	**Monfort Heights** (CDP) Hamilton County
29	1106	36,192	**Perrysburg** (city) Wood County
30	1111	36,157	**Springboro** (city) Warren County
31	1146	35,825	**Centerville** (city) Montgomery County
32	1170	35,604	**Hilliard** (city) Franklin County
33	1234	35,037	**Gahanna** (city) Franklin County
34	1250	34,896	**Loveland** (city) Hamilton County
35	1296	34,559	**Seven Hills** (city) Cuyahoga County
36	1304	34,478	**Sylvania** (city) Lucas County
37	1323	34,352	**North Royalton** (city) Cuyahoga County
38	1383	33,853	**Forestville** (CDP) Hamilton County
39	1405	33,694	**Dent** (CDP) Hamilton County
40	1557	32,485	**Mentor** (city) Lake County
41	1643	31,909	**Green** (city) Summit County
42	1720	31,365	**Stow** (city) Summit County
43	1724	31,347	**Pickerington** (city) Fairfield County
44	1831	30,638	**Grove City** (city) Franklin County
45	1849	30,541	**University Heights** (city) Cuyahoga County
46	1857	30,503	**Fairview Park** (city) Cuyahoga County
47	1867	30,471	**Clayton** (city) Montgomery County
48	1869	30,468	**North Ridgeville** (city) Lorain County
49	1907	30,167	**Cleveland Heights** (city) Cuyahoga County
50	1908	30,152	**North Olmsted** (city) Cuyahoga County
51	1933	29,989	**White Oak** (CDP) Hamilton County
52	1941	29,925	**Richmond Heights** (city) Cuyahoga County
53	1949	29,808	**New Franklin** (city) Summit County
54	1966	29,712	**Sharonville** (city) Hamilton County
55	2003	29,489	**Kettering** (city) Montgomery County
56	2017	29,383	**Willoughby** (city) Lake County
57	2051	29,202	**Middleburg Heights** (city) Cuyahoga County
58	2095	28,959	**Reynoldsburg** (city) Franklin County
59	2125	28,792	**Maumee** (city) Lucas County
60	2142	28,708	**Amherst** (city) Lorain County
61	2147	28,663	**Fairfield** (city) Butler County
62	2196	28,450	**Bridgetown** (CDP) Hamilton County
63	2225	28,256	**North Canton** (city) Stark County
64	2231	28,225	**Brunswick** (city) Medina County
65	2254	28,072	**Tallmadge** (city) Summit County
66	2255	28,062	**Oregon** (city) Lucas County
67	2261	28,039	**Boardman** (CDP) Mahoning County
68	2291	27,873	**Willowick** (city) Lake County
69	2294	27,858	**Lakewood** (city) Cuyahoga County
70	2319	27,730	**Miamisburg** (city) Montgomery County
71	2329	27,704	**South Euclid** (city) Cuyahoga County
72	2346	27,586	**Pataskala** (city) Licking County
73	2356	27,533	**Streetsboro** (city) Portage County
74	2387	27,279	**Mayfield Heights** (city) Cuyahoga County
75	2411	27,149	**Monroe** (city) Butler County
76	2435	26,999	**Wadsworth** (city) Medina County
77	2437	26,992	**Delaware** (city) Delaware County
78	2474	26,856	**Vermilion** (city) Lorain County
79	2488	26,774	**Vandalia** (city) Montgomery County
80	2510	26,648	**Norton** (city) Summit County
81	2556	26,402	**Cuyahoga Falls** (city) Summit County
82	2565	26,352	**Medina** (city) Medina County
83	2573	26,299	**Finneytown** (CDP) Hamilton County
84	2672	25,732	**Berea** (city) Cuyahoga County
85	2696	25,624	**Eastlake** (city) Lake County
86	2704	25,563	**Lebanon** (city) Warren County
87	2741	25,418	**Wickliffe** (city) Lake County
88	2749	25,377	**Englewood** (city) Montgomery County
89	2804	25,013	**Huber Heights** (city) Montgomery County
90	2853	24,810	**Reading** (city) Hamilton County
91	2860	24,783	**Findlay** (city) Hancock County
92	2864	24,779	**Cincinnati** (city) Hamilton County
93	2879	24,713	**Parma** (city) Cuyahoga County
94	2899	24,598	**Heath** (city) Licking County
95	2932	24,351	**Columbus** (city) Franklin County
96	2936	24,331	**Parma Heights** (city) Cuyahoga County
97	2961	24,221	**Wooster** (city) Wayne County
98	2983	24,101	**Marietta** (city) Washington County
99	3027	23,893	**Brook Park** (city) Cuyahoga County
100	3049	23,779	**Troy** (city) Miami County
101	3164	23,216	**Bedford** (city) Cuyahoga County
102	3196	23,055	**Dover** (city) Tuscarawas County
103	3221	22,959	**Fairborn** (city) Greene County
104	3236	22,888	**Marysville** (city) Union County
105	3239	22,861	**Austintown** (CDP) Mahoning County
106	3272	22,668	**Brooklyn** (city) Cuyahoga County
107	3306	22,534	**West Carrollton** (city) Montgomery County
108	3314	22,503	**Norwood** (city) Hamilton County
109	3321	22,474	**Trenton** (city) Butler County
110	3338	22,381	**Springdale** (city) Hamilton County
111	3339	22,378	**Euclid** (city) Cuyahoga County
112	3345	22,367	**Forest Park** (city) Hamilton County
113	3424	21,962	**Defiance** (city) Defiance County
114	3434	21,911	**Norwalk** (city) Huron County
115	3435	21,899	**Celina** (city) Mercer County
116	3456	21,776	**Chillicothe** (city) Ross County
117	3484	21,654	**Newark** (city) Licking County
118	3487	21,649	**Bedford Heights** (city) Cuyahoga County
119	3495	21,616	**New Philadelphia** (city) Tuscarawas County
120	3523	21,494	**Sidney** (city) Shelby County
121	3539	21,397	**Lancaster** (city) Fairfield County
122	3560	21,276	**Elyria** (city) Lorain County
123	3577	21,247	**Riverside** (city) Montgomery County
124	3605	21,115	**Coshocton** (city) Coshocton County
125	3613	21,081	**Franklin** (city) Warren County
126	3632	20,993	**Garfield Heights** (city) Cuyahoga County
127	3636	20,983	**Ashland** (city) Ashland County
128	3651	20,883	**Sandusky** (city) Erie County
129	3691	20,701	**Massillon** (city) Stark County
130	3698	20,669	**Bellefontaine** (city) Logan County
131	3730	20,514	**Xenia** (city) Greene County
132	3731	20,507	**Niles** (city) Trumbull County
133	3732	20,506	**Barberton** (city) Summit County
134	3747	20,453	**Circleville** (city) Pickaway County
135	3749	20,433	**Van Wert** (city) Van Wert County
136	3755	20,396	**Trotwood** (city) Montgomery County
137	3762	20,359	**Steubenville** (city) Jefferson County
138	3775	20,286	**Greenville** (city) Darke County
139	3777	20,283	**Hamilton** (city) Butler County
140	3790	20,199	**Middletown** (city) Butler County
141	3817	20,084	**Ravenna** (city) Portage County
142	3834	19,997	**Salem** (city) Columbiana County
143	3839	19,968	**Akron** (city) Summit County
144	3850	19,902	**Ironton** (city) Lawrence County
145	3868	19,843	**Mount Vernon** (city) Knox County
146	3869	19,831	**Warrensville Heights** (city) Cuyahoga County
147	3894	19,696	**Washington Court House** (city) Fayette County
148	3930	19,517	**Urbana** (city) Champaign County
149	3940	19,471	**Maple Heights** (city) Cuyahoga County
150	3950	19,419	**Piqua** (city) Miami County

Note: *The state column ranks the top/bottom 150 places from all places in the state with population of 10,000 or more. The national column ranks the top/bottom 150 places from all places in the country with population of 10,000 or more. Places that are unincorporated were not considered in the rankings. Please refer to the User Guide for additional information.*

Per Capita Income

Top 150 Places Ranked in *Ascending* Order

State Rank	Nat'l Rank	Dollars	Place
1	53	11,929	**Athens** (city) Athens County
2	111	13,902	**East Cleveland** (city) Cuyahoga County
3	158	14,876	**Youngstown** (city) Mahoning County
4	164	14,950	**Oxford** (city) Butler County
5	177	15,266	**Lima** (city) Allen County
6	207	15,815	**Marion** (city) Marion County
7	246	16,212	**Conneaut** (city) Ashtabula County
8	258	16,356	**Ashtabula** (city) Ashtabula County
9	271	16,494	**Dayton** (city) Montgomery County
10	283	16,584	**East Liverpool** (city) Columbiana County
11	291	16,669	**Canton** (city) Stark County
12	292	16,690	**Galion** (city) Crawford County
13	311	16,876	**Zanesville** (city) Muskingum County
14	316	16,939	**Warren** (city) Trumbull County
15	323	16,992	**Cleveland** (city) Cuyahoga County
16	352	17,205	**Alliance** (city) Stark County
17	438	17,818	**Portsmouth** (city) Scioto County
18	473	18,004	**Fostoria** (city) Seneca County
19	488	18,117	**Northbrook** (CDP) Hamilton County
20	510	18,230	**Fremont** (city) Sandusky County
21	514	18,259	**Whitehall** (city) Franklin County
22	518	18,279	**Mansfield** (city) Richland County
23	553	18,550	**Cambridge** (city) Guernsey County
24	572	18,633	**Springfield** (city) Clark County
25	575	18,643	**Struthers** (city) Mahoning County
26	588	18,698	**Lorain** (city) Lorain County
27	594	18,760	**Toledo** (city) Lucas County
28	601	18,797	**Painesville** (city) Lake County
29	604	18,801	**Tiffin** (city) Seneca County
30	621	18,887	**Wilmington** (city) Clinton County
31	655	19,143	**Kent** (city) Portage County
32	667	19,189	**Bucyrus** (city) Crawford County
33	684	19,266	**Bowling Green** (city) Wood County
34	706	19,419	**Piqua** (city) Miami County
35	716	19,471	**Maple Heights** (city) Cuyahoga County
36	724	19,517	**Urbana** (city) Champaign County
37	762	19,696	**Washington Court House** (city) Fayette County
38	787	19,831	**Warrensville Heights** (city) Cuyahoga County
39	788	19,843	**Mount Vernon** (city) Knox County
40	806	19,902	**Ironton** (city) Lawrence County
41	816	19,968	**Akron** (city) Summit County
42	821	19,997	**Salem** (city) Columbiana County
43	839	20,084	**Ravenna** (city) Portage County
44	866	20,199	**Middletown** (city) Butler County
45	879	20,283	**Hamilton** (city) Butler County
46	881	20,286	**Greenville** (city) Darke County
47	894	20,359	**Steubenville** (city) Jefferson County
48	901	20,396	**Trotwood** (city) Montgomery County
49	907	20,433	**Van Wert** (city) Van Wert County
50	909	20,453	**Circleville** (city) Pickaway County
51	924	20,506	**Barberton** (city) Summit County
52	925	20,507	**Niles** (city) Trumbull County
53	926	20,514	**Xenia** (city) Greene County
54	958	20,669	**Bellefontaine** (city) Logan County
55	965	20,701	**Massillon** (city) Stark County
56	1005	20,883	**Sandusky** (city) Erie County
57	1020	20,983	**Ashland** (city) Ashland County
58	1024	20,993	**Garfield Heights** (city) Cuyahoga County
59	1042	21,081	**Franklin** (city) Warren County
60	1050	21,115	**Coshocton** (city) Coshocton County
61	1079	21,247	**Riverside** (city) Montgomery County
62	1096	21,276	**Elyria** (city) Lorain County
63	1117	21,397	**Lancaster** (city) Fairfield County
64	1133	21,494	**Sidney** (city) Shelby County
65	1161	21,616	**New Philadelphia** (city) Tuscarawas County
66	1169	21,649	**Bedford Heights** (city) Cuyahoga County
67	1172	21,654	**Newark** (city) Licking County
68	1200	21,776	**Chillicothe** (city) Ross County
69	1221	21,899	**Celina** (city) Mercer County
70	1222	21,911	**Norwalk** (city) Huron County
71	1231	21,962	**Defiance** (city) Defiance County
72	1311	22,367	**Forest Park** (city) Hamilton County
73	1317	22,378	**Euclid** (city) Cuyahoga County
74	1318	22,381	**Springdale** (city) Hamilton County
75	1335	22,474	**Trenton** (city) Butler County
76	1342	22,503	**Norwood** (city) Hamilton County
77	1350	22,534	**West Carrollton** (city) Montgomery County
78	1384	22,668	**Brooklyn** (city) Cuyahoga County
79	1417	22,861	**Austintown** (CDP) Mahoning County
80	1420	22,888	**Marysville** (city) Union County
81	1435	22,959	**Fairborn** (city) Greene County
82	1458	23,055	**Dover** (city) Tuscarawas County
83	1492	23,216	**Bedford** (city) Cuyahoga County
84	1607	23,779	**Troy** (city) Miami County
85	1629	23,893	**Brook Park** (city) Cuyahoga County
86	1673	24,101	**Marietta** (city) Washington County
87	1694	24,221	**Wooster** (city) Wayne County
88	1720	24,331	**Parma Heights** (city) Cuyahoga County
89	1724	24,351	**Columbus** (city) Franklin County
90	1757	24,598	**Heath** (city) Licking County
91	1777	24,713	**Parma** (city) Cuyahoga County
92	1791	24,779	**Cincinnati** (city) Hamilton County
93	1796	24,783	**Findlay** (city) Hancock County
94	1802	24,810	**Reading** (city) Hamilton County
95	1852	25,013	**Huber Heights** (city) Montgomery County
96	1907	25,377	**Englewood** (city) Montgomery County
97	1915	25,418	**Wickliffe** (city) Lake County
98	1951	25,563	**Lebanon** (city) Warren County
99	1960	25,624	**Eastlake** (city) Lake County
100	1983	25,732	**Berea** (city) Cuyahoga County
101	2083	26,299	**Finneytown** (CDP) Hamilton County
102	2091	26,352	**Medina** (city) Medina County
103	2100	26,402	**Cuyahoga Falls** (city) Summit County
104	2146	26,648	**Norton** (city) Summit County
105	2167	26,774	**Vandalia** (city) Montgomery County
106	2182	26,856	**Vermilion** (city) Lorain County
107	2219	26,992	**Delaware** (city) Delaware County
108	2221	26,999	**Wadsworth** (city) Medina County
109	2245	27,149	**Monroe** (city) Butler County
110	2269	27,279	**Mayfield Heights** (city) Cuyahoga County
111	2300	27,533	**Streetsboro** (city) Portage County
112	2310	27,586	**Pataskala** (city) Licking County
113	2327	27,704	**South Euclid** (city) Cuyahoga County
114	2337	27,730	**Miamisburg** (city) Montgomery County
115	2362	27,858	**Lakewood** (city) Cuyahoga County
116	2365	27,873	**Willowick** (city) Lake County
117	2395	28,039	**Boardman** (CDP) Mahoning County
118	2401	28,062	**Oregon** (city) Lucas County
119	2402	28,072	**Tallmadge** (city) Summit County
120	2425	28,225	**Brunswick** (city) Medina County
121	2430	28,256	**North Canton** (city) Stark County
122	2460	28,450	**Bridgetown** (CDP) Hamilton County
123	2509	28,663	**Fairfield** (city) Butler County
124	2514	28,708	**Amherst** (city) Lorain County
125	2530	28,792	**Maumee** (city) Lucas County
126	2561	28,959	**Reynoldsburg** (city) Franklin County
127	2605	29,202	**Middleburg Heights** (city) Cuyahoga County
128	2639	29,383	**Willoughby** (city) Lake County
129	2653	29,409	**Kettering** (city) Montgomery County
130	2689	29,712	**Sharonville** (city) Hamilton County
131	2707	29,808	**New Franklin** (city) Summit County
132	2714	29,925	**Richmond Heights** (city) Cuyahoga County
133	2723	29,989	**White Oak** (CDP) Hamilton County
134	2748	30,152	**North Olmsted** (city) Cuyahoga County
135	2749	30,167	**Cleveland Heights** (city) Cuyahoga County
136	2787	30,468	**North Ridgeville** (city) Lorain County
137	2789	30,471	**Clayton** (city) Montgomery County
138	2799	30,503	**Fairview Park** (city) Cuyahoga County
139	2807	30,541	**University Heights** (city) Cuyahoga County
140	2825	30,638	**Grove City** (city) Franklin County
141	2932	31,347	**Pickerington** (city) Fairfield County
142	2936	31,365	**Stow** (city) Summit County
143	3013	31,909	**Green** (city) Summit County
144	3098	32,485	**Mentor** (city) Lake County
145	3251	33,694	**Dent** (CDP) Hamilton County
146	3273	33,853	**Forestville** (CDP) Hamilton County
147	3333	34,352	**North Royalton** (city) Cuyahoga County
148	3352	34,478	**Sylvania** (city) Lucas County
149	3360	34,559	**Seven Hills** (city) Cuyahoga County
150	3405	34,896	**Loveland** (city) Hamilton County

Note: *The state column ranks the top/bottom 150 places from all places in the state with population of 10,000 or more. The national column ranks the top/bottom 150 places from all places in the country with population of 10,000 or more. Places that are unincorporated were not considered in the rankings. Please refer to the User Guide for additional information.*

Median Household Income

Top 150 Places Ranked in *Descending* Order

State Rank	Nat'l Rank	Dollars	Place
1	94	132,598	**Powell** (city) Delaware County
2	176	119,212	**Hudson** (city) Summit County
3	231	113,182	**Dublin** (city) Franklin County
4	315	107,620	**Montgomery** (city) Hamilton County
5	491	97,829	**Upper Arlington** (city) Franklin County
6	501	97,181	**Solon** (city) Cuyahoga County
7	533	96,094	**Springboro** (city) Warren County
8	597	93,478	**Bexley** (city) Franklin County
9	662	90,924	**Brecksville** (city) Cuyahoga County
10	788	86,855	**Worthington** (city) Franklin County
11	838	85,697	**Mason** (city) Warren County
12	856	85,052	**Hilliard** (city) Franklin County
13	898	83,861	**Mack** (CDP) Hamilton County
14	902	83,679	**Bay Village** (city) Cuyahoga County
15	929	82,603	**Avon** (city) Lorain County
16	941	82,146	**Westerville** (city) Franklin County
17	970	81,540	**Pickerington** (city) Fairfield County
18	994	80,930	**Macedonia** (city) Summit County
19	1020	80,400	**Aurora** (city) Portage County
20	1032	80,271	**Avon Lake** (city) Lorain County
21	1059	79,722	**Beachwood** (city) Cuyahoga County
22	1126	77,951	**Shaker Heights** (city) Cuyahoga County
23	1198	76,397	**Strongsville** (city) Cuyahoga County
24	1200	76,358	**Westlake** (city) Cuyahoga County
25	1206	76,162	**Beavercreek** (city) Greene County
26	1223	75,882	**Broadview Heights** (city) Cuyahoga County
27	1299	74,020	**Loveland** (city) Hamilton County
28	1450	71,220	**Perrysburg** (city) Wood County
29	1452	71,201	**Gahanna** (city) Franklin County
30	1468	70,958	**Twinsburg** (city) Summit County
31	1474	70,787	**Blue Ash** (city) Hamilton County
32	1569	69,000	**Monfort Heights** (CDP) Hamilton County
33	1618	67,926	**Rocky River** (city) Cuyahoga County
34	1627	67,826	**University Heights** (city) Cuyahoga County
35	1628	67,817	**Sylvania** (city) Lucas County
36	1666	67,156	**North Ridgeville** (city) Lorain County
37	1672	67,046	**Monroe** (city) Butler County
38	1683	66,794	**Seven Hills** (city) Cuyahoga County
39	1691	66,683	**North Royalton** (city) Cuyahoga County
40	1716	66,299	**Grove City** (city) Franklin County
41	1740	65,892	**New Franklin** (city) Summit County
42	1741	65,888	**Mentor** (city) Lake County
43	1759	65,593	**Pataskala** (city) Licking County
44	1787	65,187	**Clayton** (city) Montgomery County
45	1813	64,878	**Dent** (CDP) Hamilton County
46	1849	64,250	**Forestville** (CDP) Hamilton County
47	1871	63,924	**Brunswick** (city) Medina County
48	1873	63,895	**Amherst** (city) Lorain County
49	1886	63,593	**Lyndhurst** (city) Cuyahoga County
50	1915	63,085	**Stow** (city) Summit County
51	2001	61,940	**Streetsboro** (city) Portage County
52	2057	61,150	**Green** (city) Summit County
53	2135	60,162	**Centerville** (city) Montgomery County
54	2149	59,968	**South Euclid** (city) Cuyahoga County
55	2175	59,411	**North Olmsted** (city) Cuyahoga County
56	2184	59,261	**Norton** (city) Summit County
57	2221	58,649	**Lebanon** (city) Warren County
58	2248	58,257	**Reynoldsburg** (city) Franklin County
59	2257	58,181	**Trenton** (city) Butler County
60	2301	57,539	**Wadsworth** (city) Medina County
61	2310	57,424	**Bridgetown** (CDP) Hamilton County
62	2336	56,963	**Delaware** (city) Delaware County
63	2383	56,318	**Fairfield** (city) Butler County
64	2398	56,066	**White Oak** (CDP) Hamilton County
65	2401	56,002	**Middleburg Heights** (city) Cuyahoga County
66	2406	55,942	**Berea** (city) Cuyahoga County
67	2527	54,225	**Tallmadge** (city) Summit County
68	2528	54,191	**Oregon** (city) Lucas County
69	2535	54,128	**Maumee** (city) Lucas County
70	2559	53,880	**Marysville** (city) Union County
71	2591	53,586	**Medina** (city) Medina County
72	2619	53,165	**Finneytown** (CDP) Hamilton County
73	2654	52,844	**Fairview Park** (city) Cuyahoga County
74	2686	52,441	**Eastlake** (city) Lake County
75	2701	52,261	**Huber Heights** (city) Montgomery County
76	2711	52,164	**Vandalia** (city) Montgomery County
77	2722	52,007	**Miamisburg** (city) Montgomery County
78	2729	51,899	**Vermilion** (city) Lorain County
79	2730	51,892	**Sharonville** (city) Hamilton County
80	2772	51,245	**Willoughby** (city) Lake County
81	2787	51,042	**Englewood** (city) Montgomery County
82	2814	50,728	**North Canton** (city) Stark County
83	2862	50,109	**Cleveland Heights** (city) Cuyahoga County
84	2899	49,654	**Parma** (city) Cuyahoga County
85	2909	49,522	**Kettering** (city) Montgomery County
86	2916	49,438	**Cuyahoga Falls** (city) Summit County
87	2933	49,222	**Springdale** (city) Hamilton County
88	2952	49,010	**Brook Park** (city) Cuyahoga County
89	2991	48,570	**Troy** (city) Miami County
90	3024	48,233	**Richmond Heights** (city) Cuyahoga County
91	3099	47,381	**Boardman** (CDP) Mahoning County
92	3116	47,155	**Wickliffe** (city) Lake County
93	3127	47,071	**Willowick** (city) Lake County
94	3140	46,949	**Forest Park** (city) Hamilton County
95	3376	44,072	**Columbus** (city) Franklin County
96	3404	43,657	**Heath** (city) Licking County
97	3411	43,615	**Mayfield Heights** (city) Cuyahoga County
98	3416	43,502	**Parma Heights** (city) Cuyahoga County
99	3436	43,347	**Sidney** (city) Shelby County
100	3459	43,220	**Franklin** (city) Warren County
101	3462	43,218	**Lakewood** (city) Cuyahoga County
102	3490	42,901	**Findlay** (city) Hancock County
103	3522	42,511	**Garfield Heights** (city) Cuyahoga County
104	3538	42,395	**Defiance** (city) Defiance County
105	3561	42,142	**Norwalk** (city) Huron County
106	3599	41,732	**Dover** (city) Tuscarawas County
107	3600	41,720	**Fairborn** (city) Greene County
108	3603	41,713	**Austintown** (CDP) Mahoning County
109	3610	41,637	**Brooklyn** (city) Cuyahoga County
110	3613	41,600	**Elyria** (city) Lorain County
111	3663	41,104	**Riverside** (city) Montgomery County
112	3712	40,665	**Celina** (city) Mercer County
113	3717	40,633	**Wooster** (city) Wayne County
114	3732	40,426	**Hamilton** (city) Butler County
115	3734	40,417	**Bedford** (city) Cuyahoga County
116	3753	40,219	**Ashland** (city) Ashland County
117	3777	39,905	**New Philadelphia** (city) Tuscarawas County
118	3783	39,821	**Bellefontaine** (city) Logan County
119	3784	39,756	**Xenia** (city) Greene County
120	3793	39,662	**Reading** (city) Hamilton County
121	3877	38,807	**Northbrook** (CDP) Hamilton County
122	3901	38,480	**Circleville** (city) Pickaway County
123	3923	38,295	**Newark** (city) Licking County
124	3927	38,255	**West Carrollton** (city) Montgomery County
125	3933	38,142	**Massillon** (city) Stark County
126	3947	37,948	**Fremont** (city) Sandusky County
127	3962	37,819	**Barberton** (city) Summit County
128	4006	37,303	**Norwood** (city) Hamilton County
129	4012	37,205	**Van Wert** (city) Van Wert County
130	4016	37,169	**Niles** (city) Trumbull County
131	4022	37,087	**Lancaster** (city) Fairfield County
132	4031	37,010	**Urbana** (city) Champaign County
133	4037	36,927	**Chillicothe** (city) Ross County
134	4053	36,664	**Maple Heights** (city) Cuyahoga County
135	4057	36,628	**Struthers** (city) Mahoning County
136	4079	36,277	**Trotwood** (city) Montgomery County
137	4080	36,272	**Euclid** (city) Cuyahoga County
138	4081	36,260	**Piqua** (city) Miami County
139	4094	36,122	**Salem** (city) Columbiana County
140	4111	35,853	**Middletown** (city) Butler County
141	4116	35,776	**Sandusky** (city) Erie County
142	4118	35,756	**Ravenna** (city) Portage County
143	4135	35,536	**Painesville** (city) Lake County
144	4142	35,461	**Warrensville Heights** (city) Cuyahoga County
145	4153	35,280	**Bucyrus** (city) Crawford County
146	4161	35,179	**Tiffin** (city) Seneca County
147	4165	35,162	**Mount Vernon** (city) Knox County
148	4171	35,090	**Fostoria** (city) Seneca County
149	4200	34,663	**Coshocton** (city) Coshocton County
150	4202	34,662	**Bedford Heights** (city) Cuyahoga County

Note: *The state column ranks the top/bottom 150 places from all places in the state with population of 10,000 or more. The national column ranks the top/bottom 150 places from all places in the country with population of 10,000 or more. Places that are unincorporated were not considered in the rankings. Please refer to the User Guide for additional information.*

Median Household Income

Top 150 Places Ranked in *Ascending* Order

State Rank	Nat'l Rank	Dollars	Place
1	3	17,933	**Athens** (city) Athens County
2	13	20,577	**East Cleveland** (city) Cuyahoga County
3	29	24,454	**Youngstown** (city) Mahoning County
4	64	26,217	**Cleveland** (city) Cuyahoga County
5	81	26,986	**Zanesville** (city) Muskingum County
6	82	26,987	**Cambridge** (city) Guernsey County
7	118	27,876	**Ashtabula** (city) Ashtabula County
8	119	27,886	**East Liverpool** (city) Columbiana County
9	122	27,976	**Portsmouth** (city) Scioto County
10	124	28,050	**Lima** (city) Allen County
11	136	28,429	**Oxford** (city) Butler County
12	138	28,456	**Dayton** (city) Montgomery County
13	163	29,317	**Warren** (city) Trumbull County
14	179	29,828	**Wilmington** (city) Clinton County
15	194	30,209	**Canton** (city) Stark County
16	234	31,035	**Kent** (city) Portage County
17	242	31,152	**Alliance** (city) Stark County
18	269	31,635	**Springfield** (city) Clark County
19	274	31,739	**Marietta** (city) Washington County
20	275	31,758	**Greenville** (city) Darke County
21	294	32,092	**Steubenville** (city) Jefferson County
22	301	32,186	**Washington Court House** (city) Fayette County
23	334	32,722	**Mansfield** (city) Richland County
24	356	33,065	**Conneaut** (city) Ashtabula County
25	372	33,311	**Whitehall** (city) Franklin County
26	374	33,317	**Toledo** (city) Lucas County
27	377	33,414	**Galion** (city) Crawford County
28	390	33,586	**Marion** (city) Marion County
29	392	33,610	**Lorain** (city) Lorain County
30	414	33,909	**Akron** (city) Summit County
31	420	34,116	**Cincinnati** (city) Hamilton County
32	438	34,448	**Ironton** (city) Lawrence County
33	445	34,550	**Bowling Green** (city) Wood County
34	454	34,662	**Bedford Heights** (city) Cuyahoga County
35	455	34,663	**Coshocton** (city) Coshocton County
36	485	35,090	**Fostoria** (city) Seneca County
37	491	35,162	**Mount Vernon** (city) Knox County
38	495	35,179	**Tiffin** (city) Seneca County
39	503	35,280	**Bucyrus** (city) Crawford County
40	514	35,461	**Warrensville Heights** (city) Cuyahoga County
41	521	35,536	**Painesville** (city) Lake County
42	538	35,756	**Ravenna** (city) Portage County
43	540	35,776	**Sandusky** (city) Erie County
44	545	35,853	**Middletown** (city) Butler County
45	562	36,122	**Salem** (city) Columbiana County
46	575	36,260	**Piqua** (city) Miami County
47	576	36,272	**Euclid** (city) Cuyahoga County
48	577	36,277	**Trotwood** (city) Montgomery County
49	599	36,628	**Struthers** (city) Mahoning County
50	603	36,664	**Maple Heights** (city) Cuyahoga County
51	619	36,927	**Chillicothe** (city) Ross County
52	625	37,010	**Urbana** (city) Champaign County
53	634	37,087	**Lancaster** (city) Fairfield County
54	640	37,169	**Niles** (city) Trumbull County
55	644	37,205	**Van Wert** (city) Van Wert County
56	650	37,303	**Norwood** (city) Hamilton County
57	694	37,819	**Barberton** (city) Summit County
58	709	37,948	**Fremont** (city) Sandusky County
59	723	38,142	**Massillon** (city) Stark County
60	729	38,255	**West Carrollton** (city) Montgomery County
61	733	38,295	**Newark** (city) Licking County
62	755	38,480	**Circleville** (city) Pickaway County
63	779	38,807	**Northbrook** (CDP) Hamilton County
64	863	39,662	**Reading** (city) Hamilton County
65	872	39,756	**Xenia** (city) Greene County
66	873	39,821	**Bellefontaine** (city) Logan County
67	879	39,905	**New Philadelphia** (city) Tuscarawas County
68	903	40,219	**Ashland** (city) Ashland County
69	921	40,417	**Bedford** (city) Cuyahoga County
70	924	40,426	**Hamilton** (city) Butler County
71	939	40,633	**Wooster** (city) Wayne County
72	944	40,665	**Celina** (city) Mercer County
73	993	41,104	**Riverside** (city) Montgomery County
74	1043	41,600	**Elyria** (city) Lorain County
75	1046	41,637	**Brooklyn** (city) Cuyahoga County
76	1053	41,713	**Austintown** (CDP) Mahoning County
77	1056	41,720	**Fairborn** (city) Greene County
78	1057	41,732	**Dover** (city) Tuscarawas County
79	1095	42,142	**Norwalk** (city) Huron County
80	1118	42,395	**Defiance** (city) Defiance County
81	1134	42,511	**Garfield Heights** (city) Cuyahoga County
82	1166	42,901	**Findlay** (city) Hancock County
83	1194	43,218	**Lakewood** (city) Cuyahoga County
84	1195	43,220	**Franklin** (city) Warren County
85	1220	43,347	**Sidney** (city) Shelby County
86	1240	43,502	**Parma Heights** (city) Cuyahoga County
87	1245	43,615	**Mayfield Heights** (city) Cuyahoga County
88	1252	43,657	**Heath** (city) Licking County
89	1280	44,072	**Columbus** (city) Franklin County
90	1516	46,949	**Forest Park** (city) Hamilton County
91	1529	47,071	**Willowick** (city) Lake County
92	1540	47,155	**Wickliffe** (city) Lake County
93	1557	47,381	**Boardman** (CDP) Mahoning County
94	1632	48,233	**Richmond Heights** (city) Cuyahoga County
95	1665	48,570	**Troy** (city) Miami County
96	1704	49,010	**Brook Park** (city) Cuyahoga County
97	1723	49,222	**Springdale** (city) Hamilton County
98	1740	49,438	**Cuyahoga Falls** (city) Summit County
99	1747	49,522	**Kettering** (city) Montgomery County
100	1757	49,654	**Parma** (city) Cuyahoga County
101	1794	50,109	**Cleveland Heights** (city) Cuyahoga County
102	1842	50,728	**North Canton** (city) Stark County
103	1869	51,042	**Englewood** (city) Montgomery County
104	1884	51,245	**Willoughby** (city) Lake County
105	1926	51,892	**Sharonville** (city) Hamilton County
106	1927	51,899	**Vermilion** (city) Lorain County
107	1934	52,007	**Miamisburg** (city) Montgomery County
108	1945	52,164	**Vandalia** (city) Montgomery County
109	1955	52,261	**Huber Heights** (city) Montgomery County
110	1970	52,441	**Eastlake** (city) Lake County
111	2002	52,844	**Fairview Park** (city) Cuyahoga County
112	2036	53,165	**Finneytown** (CDP) Hamilton County
113	2065	53,586	**Medina** (city) Medina County
114	2097	53,880	**Marysville** (city) Union County
115	2121	54,128	**Maumee** (city) Lucas County
116	2128	54,191	**Oregon** (city) Lucas County
117	2129	54,225	**Tallmadge** (city) Summit County
118	2250	55,942	**Berea** (city) Cuyahoga County
119	2255	56,002	**Middleburg Heights** (city) Cuyahoga County
120	2258	56,066	**White Oak** (CDP) Hamilton County
121	2273	56,318	**Fairfield** (city) Butler County
122	2320	56,963	**Delaware** (city) Delaware County
123	2346	57,424	**Bridgetown** (CDP) Hamilton County
124	2355	57,539	**Wadsworth** (city) Medina County
125	2399	58,181	**Trenton** (city) Butler County
126	2408	58,257	**Reynoldsburg** (city) Franklin County
127	2435	58,649	**Lebanon** (city) Warren County
128	2472	59,261	**Norton** (city) Summit County
129	2481	59,411	**North Olmsted** (city) Cuyahoga County
130	2507	59,968	**South Euclid** (city) Cuyahoga County
131	2521	60,162	**Centerville** (city) Montgomery County
132	2599	61,150	**Green** (city) Summit County
133	2655	61,940	**Streetsboro** (city) Portage County
134	2741	63,085	**Stow** (city) Summit County
135	2770	63,593	**Lyndhurst** (city) Cuyahoga County
136	2783	63,895	**Amherst** (city) Lorain County
137	2785	63,924	**Brunswick** (city) Medina County
138	2807	64,250	**Forestville** (CDP) Hamilton County
139	2843	64,878	**Dent** (CDP) Hamilton County
140	2869	65,187	**Clayton** (city) Montgomery County
141	2897	65,593	**Pataskala** (city) Licking County
142	2915	65,888	**Mentor** (city) Lake County
143	2916	65,892	**New Franklin** (city) Summit County
144	2940	66,299	**Grove City** (city) Franklin County
145	2965	66,683	**North Royalton** (city) Cuyahoga County
146	2973	66,794	**Seven Hills** (city) Cuyahoga County
147	2984	67,046	**Monroe** (city) Butler County
148	2990	67,156	**North Ridgeville** (city) Lorain County
149	3028	67,817	**Sylvania** (city) Lucas County
150	3029	67,826	**University Heights** (city) Cuyahoga County

Note: *The state column ranks the top/bottom 150 places from all places in the state with population of 10,000 or more. The national column ranks the top/bottom 150 places from all places in the country with population of 10,000 or more. Places that are unincorporated were not considered in the rankings. Please refer to the User Guide for additional information.*

Average Household Income

Top 150 Places Ranked in *Descending* Order

State Rank	Nat'l Rank	Dollars	Place
1	222	146,145	**Dublin** (city) Franklin County
2	234	144,323	**Hudson** (city) Summit County
3	236	143,390	**Montgomery** (city) Hamilton County
4	243	142,845	**Powell** (city) Delaware County
5	333	133,209	**Solon** (city) Cuyahoga County
6	338	132,664	**Bexley** (city) Franklin County
7	357	130,971	**Upper Arlington** (city) Franklin County
8	410	126,291	**Beachwood** (city) Cuyahoga County
9	424	125,171	**Brecksville** (city) Cuyahoga County
10	465	122,111	**Shaker Heights** (city) Cuyahoga County
11	600	113,883	**Avon** (city) Lorain County
12	680	110,717	**Westlake** (city) Cuyahoga County
13	683	110,528	**Worthington** (city) Franklin County
14	692	110,102	**Bay Village** (city) Cuyahoga County
15	747	107,678	**Springboro** (city) Warren County
16	753	107,375	**Aurora** (city) Portage County
17	772	106,386	**Mack** (CDP) Hamilton County
18	788	105,916	**Mason** (city) Warren County
19	837	103,933	**Blue Ash** (city) Hamilton County
20	864	103,122	**Rocky River** (city) Cuyahoga County
21	938	100,905	**Avon Lake** (city) Lorain County
22	952	100,586	**Macedonia** (city) Summit County
23	1002	99,206	**Westerville** (city) Franklin County
24	1017	98,726	**Hilliard** (city) Franklin County
25	1128	95,686	**Beavercreek** (city) Greene County
26	1159	94,668	**Strongsville** (city) Cuyahoga County
27	1224	93,154	**Twinsburg** (city) Summit County
28	1270	92,040	**Broadview Heights** (city) Cuyahoga County
29	1346	90,053	**Loveland** (city) Hamilton County
30	1370	89,591	**Gahanna** (city) Franklin County
31	1382	89,339	**Monfort Heights** (CDP) Hamilton County
32	1415	88,418	**Perrysburg** (city) Wood County
33	1434	87,917	**Pickerington** (city) Fairfield County
34	1542	85,088	**Sylvania** (city) Lucas County
35	1563	84,553	**University Heights** (city) Cuyahoga County
36	1657	82,526	**North Royalton** (city) Cuyahoga County
37	1670	82,262	**Seven Hills** (city) Cuyahoga County
38	1697	81,818	**Lyndhurst** (city) Cuyahoga County
39	1794	79,987	**Forestville** (CDP) Hamilton County
40	1826	79,468	**Mentor** (city) Lake County
41	1865	78,756	**Green** (city) Summit County
42	1890	78,409	**Dent** (CDP) Hamilton County
43	1926	77,809	**Grove City** (city) Franklin County
44	1940	77,576	**Centerville** (city) Montgomery County
45	1941	77,534	**Stow** (city) Summit County
46	1983	76,941	**Clayton** (city) Montgomery County
47	2009	76,535	**New Franklin** (city) Summit County
48	2029	76,027	**North Ridgeville** (city) Lorain County
49	2066	75,310	**Amherst** (city) Lorain County
50	2191	73,250	**Pataskala** (city) Licking County
51	2218	72,755	**Brunswick** (city) Medina County
52	2219	72,716	**Monroe** (city) Butler County
53	2273	71,824	**White Oak** (CDP) Hamilton County
54	2301	71,357	**Reynoldsburg** (city) Franklin County
55	2327	70,979	**Lebanon** (city) Warren County
56	2364	70,525	**North Olmsted** (city) Cuyahoga County
57	2391	70,158	**Tallmadge** (city) Summit County
58	2430	69,488	**Fairfield** (city) Butler County
59	2437	69,356	**Delaware** (city) Delaware County
60	2453	69,089	**Cleveland Heights** (city) Cuyahoga County
61	2460	68,991	**Wadsworth** (city) Medina County
62	2468	68,912	**Bridgetown** (CDP) Hamilton County
63	2471	68,887	**Medina** (city) Medina County
64	2526	68,039	**South Euclid** (city) Cuyahoga County
65	2540	67,778	**Fairview Park** (city) Cuyahoga County
66	2563	67,570	**Streetsboro** (city) Portage County
67	2582	67,291	**Maumee** (city) Lucas County
68	2618	66,921	**Norton** (city) Summit County
69	2677	66,236	**Oregon** (city) Lucas County
70	2701	65,960	**Marysville** (city) Union County
71	2707	65,886	**Berea** (city) Cuyahoga County
72	2729	65,598	**Miamisburg** (city) Montgomery County
73	2780	64,817	**Middleburg Heights** (city) Cuyahoga County
74	2798	64,572	**North Canton** (city) Stark County
75	2800	64,557	**Kettering** (city) Montgomery County
76	2805	64,486	**Finneytown** (CDP) Hamilton County
77	2806	64,422	**Sharonville** (city) Hamilton County
78	2832	64,033	**Vermilion** (city) Lorain County
79	2844	63,887	**Richmond Heights** (city) Cuyahoga County
80	2870	63,383	**Huber Heights** (city) Montgomery County
81	2874	63,367	**Vandalia** (city) Montgomery County
82	2894	63,031	**Willoughby** (city) Lake County
83	2917	62,718	**Trenton** (city) Butler County
84	2943	62,468	**Willowick** (city) Lake County
85	3018	61,583	**Boardman** (CDP) Mahoning County
86	3066	60,989	**Englewood** (city) Montgomery County
87	3173	59,474	**Eastlake** (city) Lake County
88	3201	59,147	**Springdale** (city) Hamilton County
89	3249	58,530	**Parma** (city) Cuyahoga County
89	3249	58,530	**Wooster** (city) Wayne County
91	3251	58,490	**Cuyahoga Falls** (city) Summit County
92	3322	57,741	**Wickliffe** (city) Lake County
93	3323	57,740	**Brook Park** (city) Cuyahoga County
94	3333	57,570	**Columbus** (city) Franklin County
95	3340	57,491	**Findlay** (city) Hancock County
96	3371	57,172	**Heath** (city) Licking County
97	3403	56,813	**Lakewood** (city) Cuyahoga County
98	3410	56,728	**Troy** (city) Miami County
99	3447	56,240	**Forest Park** (city) Hamilton County
100	3538	55,259	**Mayfield Heights** (city) Cuyahoga County
101	3555	55,034	**Dover** (city) Tuscarawas County
102	3577	54,701	**Reading** (city) Hamilton County
103	3638	54,204	**Cincinnati** (city) Hamilton County
104	3642	54,156	**Parma Heights** (city) Cuyahoga County
105	3647	54,121	**Sidney** (city) Shelby County
106	3679	53,647	**Norwalk** (city) Huron County
107	3736	52,985	**Marietta** (city) Washington County
108	3743	52,910	**Defiance** (city) Defiance County
109	3756	52,770	**Fairborn** (city) Greene County
110	3798	52,194	**Ashland** (city) Ashland County
111	3845	51,643	**New Philadelphia** (city) Tuscarawas County
112	3852	51,507	**Kent** (city) Portage County
113	3867	51,331	**Newark** (city) Licking County
114	3874	51,242	**Franklin** (city) Warren County
115	3880	51,136	**Oxford** (city) Butler County
116	3885	51,085	**Bellefontaine** (city) Logan County
117	3887	51,072	**Bowling Green** (city) Wood County
118	3894	50,984	**Riverside** (city) Montgomery County
119	3907	50,756	**Painesville** (city) Lake County
120	3914	50,619	**Brooklyn** (city) Cuyahoga County
121	3918	50,576	**Austintown** (CDP) Mahoning County
122	3929	50,466	**Hamilton** (city) Butler County
123	3963	49,988	**Lancaster** (city) Fairfield County
124	3968	49,944	**Circleville** (city) Pickaway County
125	3971	49,922	**Celina** (city) Mercer County
126	3974	49,873	**Elyria** (city) Lorain County
127	3982	49,767	**Chillicothe** (city) Ross County
128	3993	49,619	**Garfield Heights** (city) Cuyahoga County
129	3996	49,599	**Van Wert** (city) Van Wert County
130	4009	49,369	**Norwood** (city) Hamilton County
131	4020	49,228	**Xenia** (city) Greene County
132	4044	48,925	**Bedford** (city) Cuyahoga County
133	4056	48,830	**Steubenville** (city) Jefferson County
134	4100	48,390	**Massillon** (city) Stark County
135	4112	48,233	**Barberton** (city) Summit County
136	4113	48,231	**Coshocton** (city) Coshocton County
137	4117	48,185	**Middletown** (city) Butler County
138	4123	48,102	**Urbana** (city) Champaign County
139	4134	47,878	**Euclid** (city) Cuyahoga County
140	4140	47,763	**West Carrollton** (city) Montgomery County
141	4158	47,517	**Tiffin** (city) Seneca County
142	4177	47,309	**Mount Vernon** (city) Knox County
143	4205	46,922	**Sandusky** (city) Erie County
144	4212	46,844	**Northbrook** (CDP) Hamilton County
145	4231	46,623	**Trotwood** (city) Montgomery County
146	4269	46,184	**Niles** (city) Trumbull County
147	4285	45,886	**Ironton** (city) Lawrence County
148	4288	45,847	**Akron** (city) Summit County
149	4296	45,689	**Salem** (city) Columbiana County
150	4303	45,623	**Ravenna** (city) Portage County

Note: *The state column ranks the top/bottom 150 places from all places in the state with population of 10,000 or more. The national column ranks the top/bottom 150 places from all places in the country with population of 10,000 or more. Places that are unincorporated were not considered in the rankings. Please refer to the User Guide for additional information.*

Average Household Income

Top 150 Places Ranked in *Ascending* Order

State Rank	Nat'l Rank	Dollars	Place
1	7	29,297	**East Cleveland** (city) Cuyahoga County
2	28	34,894	**Youngstown** (city) Mahoning County
3	63	38,007	**Ashtabula** (city) Ashtabula County
4	71	38,274	**Cleveland** (city) Cuyahoga County
5	75	38,568	**East Liverpool** (city) Columbiana County
6	85	38,989	**Zanesville** (city) Muskingum County
7	86	38,996	**Lima** (city) Allen County
8	89	39,105	**Dayton** (city) Montgomery County
9	94	39,453	**Warren** (city) Trumbull County
10	97	39,622	**Athens** (city) Athens County
11	99	39,690	**Cambridge** (city) Guernsey County
12	103	39,787	**Canton** (city) Stark County
13	137	40,847	**Galion** (city) Crawford County
14	146	41,085	**Conneaut** (city) Ashtabula County
15	168	41,900	**Alliance** (city) Stark County
16	185	42,326	**Fostoria** (city) Seneca County
17	196	42,528	**Portsmouth** (city) Scioto County
18	198	42,594	**Whitehall** (city) Franklin County
19	205	42,742	**Greenville** (city) Darke County
20	219	43,161	**Wilmington** (city) Clinton County
21	221	43,183	**Warrensville Heights** (city) Cuyahoga County
22	226	43,389	**Bucyrus** (city) Crawford County
23	233	43,543	**Toledo** (city) Lucas County
24	274	44,420	**Mansfield** (city) Richland County
25	285	44,647	**Marion** (city) Marion County
26	292	44,755	**Maple Heights** (city) Cuyahoga County
27	295	44,778	**Springfield** (city) Clark County
28	297	44,790	**Struthers** (city) Mahoning County
29	321	45,080	**Fremont** (city) Sandusky County
30	332	45,347	**Lorain** (city) Lorain County
31	343	45,503	**Piqua** (city) Miami County
32	345	45,521	**Washington Court House** (city) Fayette County
33	347	45,553	**Bedford Heights** (city) Cuyahoga County
34	353	45,623	**Ravenna** (city) Portage County
35	360	45,689	**Salem** (city) Columbiana County
36	368	45,847	**Akron** (city) Summit County
37	370	45,886	**Ironton** (city) Lawrence County
38	387	46,184	**Niles** (city) Trumbull County
39	425	46,623	**Trotwood** (city) Montgomery County
40	444	46,844	**Northbrook** (CDP) Hamilton County
41	451	46,922	**Sandusky** (city) Erie County
42	479	47,309	**Mount Vernon** (city) Knox County
43	498	47,517	**Tiffin** (city) Seneca County
44	516	47,763	**West Carrollton** (city) Montgomery County
45	522	47,878	**Euclid** (city) Cuyahoga County
46	533	48,102	**Urbana** (city) Champaign County
47	539	48,185	**Middletown** (city) Butler County
48	543	48,231	**Coshocton** (city) Coshocton County
49	544	48,233	**Barberton** (city) Summit County
50	556	48,390	**Massillon** (city) Stark County
51	600	48,830	**Steubenville** (city) Jefferson County
52	612	48,925	**Bedford** (city) Cuyahoga County
53	636	49,228	**Xenia** (city) Greene County
54	647	49,369	**Norwood** (city) Hamilton County
55	660	49,599	**Van Wert** (city) Van Wert County
56	663	49,619	**Garfield Heights** (city) Cuyahoga County
57	674	49,767	**Chillicothe** (city) Ross County
58	682	49,873	**Elyria** (city) Lorain County
59	685	49,922	**Celina** (city) Mercer County
60	687	49,944	**Circleville** (city) Pickaway County
61	693	49,988	**Lancaster** (city) Fairfield County
62	727	50,466	**Hamilton** (city) Butler County
63	738	50,576	**Austintown** (CDP) Mahoning County
64	742	50,619	**Brooklyn** (city) Cuyahoga County
65	749	50,756	**Painesville** (city) Lake County
66	762	50,984	**Riverside** (city) Montgomery County
67	769	51,072	**Bowling Green** (city) Wood County
68	771	51,085	**Bellefontaine** (city) Logan County
69	775	51,136	**Oxford** (city) Butler County
70	782	51,242	**Franklin** (city) Warren County
71	789	51,331	**Newark** (city) Licking County
72	804	51,507	**Kent** (city) Portage County
73	811	51,643	**New Philadelphia** (city) Tuscarawas County
74	858	52,194	**Ashland** (city) Ashland County
75	900	52,770	**Fairborn** (city) Greene County
76	913	52,910	**Defiance** (city) Defiance County
77	920	52,985	**Marietta** (city) Washington County
78	977	53,647	**Norwalk** (city) Huron County
79	1009	54,121	**Sidney** (city) Shelby County
80	1014	54,156	**Parma Heights** (city) Cuyahoga County
81	1018	54,204	**Cincinnati** (city) Hamilton County
82	1079	54,701	**Reading** (city) Hamilton County
83	1101	55,034	**Dover** (city) Tuscarawas County
84	1118	55,259	**Mayfield Heights** (city) Cuyahoga County
85	1209	56,240	**Forest Park** (city) Hamilton County
86	1246	56,728	**Troy** (city) Miami County
87	1253	56,813	**Lakewood** (city) Cuyahoga County
88	1285	57,172	**Heath** (city) Licking County
89	1316	57,491	**Findlay** (city) Hancock County
90	1323	57,570	**Columbus** (city) Franklin County
91	1333	57,740	**Brook Park** (city) Cuyahoga County
92	1334	57,741	**Wickliffe** (city) Lake County
93	1404	58,490	**Cuyahoga Falls** (city) Summit County
94	1406	58,530	**Parma** (city) Cuyahoga County
94	1406	58,530	**Wooster** (city) Wayne County
96	1455	59,147	**Springdale** (city) Hamilton County
97	1483	59,474	**Eastlake** (city) Lake County
98	1590	60,989	**Englewood** (city) Montgomery County
99	1638	61,583	**Boardman** (CDP) Mahoning County
100	1713	62,468	**Willowick** (city) Lake County
101	1739	62,718	**Trenton** (city) Butler County
102	1762	63,031	**Willoughby** (city) Lake County
103	1782	63,367	**Vandalia** (city) Montgomery County
104	1786	63,383	**Huber Heights** (city) Montgomery County
105	1812	63,887	**Richmond Heights** (city) Cuyahoga County
106	1824	64,033	**Vermilion** (city) Lorain County
107	1850	64,422	**Sharonville** (city) Hamilton County
108	1851	64,486	**Finneytown** (CDP) Hamilton County
109	1856	64,557	**Kettering** (city) Montgomery County
110	1858	64,572	**North Canton** (city) Stark County
111	1876	64,817	**Middleburg Heights** (city) Cuyahoga County
112	1927	65,598	**Miamisburg** (city) Montgomery County
113	1949	65,886	**Berea** (city) Cuyahoga County
114	1955	65,960	**Marysville** (city) Union County
115	1979	66,236	**Oregon** (city) Lucas County
116	2038	66,921	**Norton** (city) Summit County
117	2074	67,291	**Maumee** (city) Lucas County
118	2093	67,570	**Streetsboro** (city) Portage County
119	2116	67,778	**Fairview Park** (city) Cuyahoga County
120	2130	68,039	**South Euclid** (city) Cuyahoga County
121	2185	68,887	**Medina** (city) Medina County
122	2188	68,912	**Bridgetown** (CDP) Hamilton County
123	2196	68,991	**Wadsworth** (city) Medina County
124	2203	69,089	**Cleveland Heights** (city) Cuyahoga County
125	2219	69,356	**Delaware** (city) Delaware County
126	2226	69,488	**Fairfield** (city) Butler County
127	2264	70,158	**Tallmadge** (city) Summit County
128	2292	70,525	**North Olmsted** (city) Cuyahoga County
129	2329	70,979	**Lebanon** (city) Warren County
130	2355	71,357	**Reynoldsburg** (city) Franklin County
131	2383	71,824	**White Oak** (CDP) Hamilton County
132	2437	72,716	**Monroe** (city) Butler County
133	2438	72,755	**Brunswick** (city) Medina County
134	2465	73,250	**Pataskala** (city) Licking County
135	2590	75,310	**Amherst** (city) Lorain County
136	2627	76,027	**North Ridgeville** (city) Lorain County
137	2647	76,535	**New Franklin** (city) Summit County
138	2673	76,941	**Clayton** (city) Montgomery County
139	2715	77,534	**Stow** (city) Summit County
140	2716	77,576	**Centerville** (city) Montgomery County
141	2730	77,809	**Grove City** (city) Franklin County
142	2766	78,409	**Dent** (CDP) Hamilton County
143	2791	78,756	**Green** (city) Summit County
144	2830	79,468	**Mentor** (city) Lake County
145	2861	79,987	**Forestville** (CDP) Hamilton County
146	2959	81,818	**Lyndhurst** (city) Cuyahoga County
147	2986	82,262	**Seven Hills** (city) Cuyahoga County
148	2999	82,526	**North Royalton** (city) Cuyahoga County
149	3093	84,553	**University Heights** (city) Cuyahoga County
150	3114	85,088	**Sylvania** (city) Lucas County

Note: *The state column ranks the top/bottom 150 places from all places in the state with population of 10,000 or more. The national column ranks the top/bottom 150 places from all places in the country with population of 10,000 or more. Places that are unincorporated were not considered in the rankings. Please refer to the User Guide for additional information.*

Households with Income of $100,000 or More

Top 150 Places Ranked in *Descending* Order

State Rank	Nat'l Rank	Percent	Place
1	58	67.4	**Powell** (city) Delaware County
2	168	59.1	**Dublin** (city) Franklin County
3	203	57.6	**Hudson** (city) Summit County
4	358	52.6	**Montgomery** (city) Hamilton County
5	493	48.8	**Upper Arlington** (city) Franklin County
6	510	48.4	**Solon** (city) Cuyahoga County
7	545	47.8	**Springboro** (city) Warren County
8	594	46.5	**Bexley** (city) Franklin County
9	606	46.2	**Brecksville** (city) Cuyahoga County
10	712	43.8	**Mack** (CDP) Hamilton County
11	717	43.7	**Worthington** (city) Franklin County
12	753	42.9	**Mason** (city) Warren County
13	789	42.4	**Beachwood** (city) Cuyahoga County
14	815	42.0	**Avon** (city) Lorain County
14	815	42.0	**Hilliard** (city) Franklin County
16	923	40.0	**Westerville** (city) Franklin County
17	937	39.7	**Shaker Heights** (city) Cuyahoga County
18	956	39.4	**Aurora** (city) Portage County
19	977	39.1	**Bay Village** (city) Cuyahoga County
20	1029	38.3	**Avon Lake** (city) Lorain County
21	1056	37.9	**Strongsville** (city) Cuyahoga County
22	1071	37.7	**Westlake** (city) Cuyahoga County
23	1092	37.4	**Loveland** (city) Hamilton County
24	1245	35.4	**Macedonia** (city) Summit County
25	1249	35.3	**Beavercreek** (city) Greene County
25	1249	35.3	**Blue Ash** (city) Hamilton County
27	1257	35.2	**Pickerington** (city) Fairfield County
28	1297	34.7	**Broadview Heights** (city) Cuyahoga County
29	1310	34.5	**Gahanna** (city) Franklin County
30	1379	33.4	**Perrysburg** (city) Wood County
30	1379	33.4	**Rocky River** (city) Cuyahoga County
32	1387	33.3	**Sylvania** (city) Lucas County
33	1430	32.7	**Twinsburg** (city) Summit County
34	1435	32.6	**University Heights** (city) Cuyahoga County
35	1499	31.5	**Forestville** (CDP) Hamilton County
36	1602	30.0	**Amherst** (city) Lorain County
37	1653	29.3	**Monfort Heights** (CDP) Hamilton County
38	1717	28.6	**Dent** (CDP) Hamilton County
38	1717	28.6	**Seven Hills** (city) Cuyahoga County
40	1741	28.3	**Lyndhurst** (city) Cuyahoga County
41	1768	28.0	**North Royalton** (city) Cuyahoga County
42	1822	27.3	**Mentor** (city) Lake County
42	1822	27.3	**Stow** (city) Summit County
44	1853	26.9	**Grove City** (city) Franklin County
45	1895	26.4	**North Ridgeville** (city) Lorain County
46	1974	25.7	**Centerville** (city) Montgomery County
47	1986	25.6	**Clayton** (city) Montgomery County
48	2022	25.3	**Green** (city) Summit County
49	2123	24.2	**White Oak** (CDP) Hamilton County
50	2133	24.1	**Lebanon** (city) Warren County
51	2165	23.7	**Monroe** (city) Butler County
52	2219	23.1	**Reynoldsburg** (city) Franklin County
53	2240	22.9	**Miamisburg** (city) Montgomery County
54	2331	22.0	**Wadsworth** (city) Medina County
55	2362	21.7	**Delaware** (city) Delaware County
55	2362	21.7	**North Olmsted** (city) Cuyahoga County
57	2371	21.6	**Marysville** (city) Union County
58	2399	21.3	**Medina** (city) Medina County
58	2399	21.3	**Norton** (city) Summit County
60	2417	21.2	**Tallmadge** (city) Summit County
61	2466	20.7	**South Euclid** (city) Cuyahoga County
62	2492	20.5	**New Franklin** (city) Summit County
63	2504	20.4	**Bridgetown** (CDP) Hamilton County
64	2531	20.2	**Fairfield** (city) Butler County
65	2562	20.0	**Cleveland Heights** (city) Cuyahoga County
65	2562	20.0	**Streetsboro** (city) Portage County
67	2579	19.9	**Fairview Park** (city) Cuyahoga County
67	2579	19.9	**Finneytown** (CDP) Hamilton County
67	2579	19.9	**Oregon** (city) Lucas County
70	2609	19.7	**Middleburg Heights** (city) Cuyahoga County
71	2633	19.5	**Brunswick** (city) Medina County
72	2666	19.2	**Pataskala** (city) Licking County
73	2684	19.0	**Vermilion** (city) Lorain County
74	2697	18.9	**Vandalia** (city) Montgomery County
75	2760	18.4	**Berea** (city) Cuyahoga County
76	2823	17.9	**Richmond Heights** (city) Cuyahoga County
77	2865	17.6	**Maumee** (city) Lucas County
77	2865	17.6	**Sharonville** (city) Hamilton County
79	2901	17.3	**Springdale** (city) Hamilton County
80	2938	17.0	**Kettering** (city) Montgomery County
81	2950	16.9	**North Canton** (city) Stark County
82	2964	16.8	**Trenton** (city) Butler County
83	3031	16.2	**Englewood** (city) Montgomery County
84	3057	16.0	**Huber Heights** (city) Montgomery County
85	3103	15.7	**Reading** (city) Hamilton County
86	3126	15.5	**Willoughby** (city) Lake County
87	3136	15.4	**Boardman** (CDP) Mahoning County
88	3153	15.3	**Wickliffe** (city) Lake County
89	3178	15.1	**Bowling Green** (city) Wood County
90	3205	14.9	**Oxford** (city) Butler County
91	3234	14.7	**Columbus** (city) Franklin County
91	3234	14.7	**Lakewood** (city) Cuyahoga County
93	3268	14.5	**Eastlake** (city) Lake County
93	3268	14.5	**Heath** (city) Licking County
95	3280	14.4	**Cuyahoga Falls** (city) Summit County
96	3317	14.1	**Findlay** (city) Hancock County
97	3333	14.0	**Parma** (city) Cuyahoga County
98	3414	13.4	**Cincinnati** (city) Hamilton County
99	3434	13.3	**Mayfield Heights** (city) Cuyahoga County
100	3463	13.1	**Troy** (city) Miami County
101	3494	12.9	**Parma Heights** (city) Cuyahoga County
102	3512	12.7	**Steubenville** (city) Jefferson County
102	3512	12.7	**Wooster** (city) Wayne County
104	3552	12.5	**Forest Park** (city) Hamilton County
105	3565	12.4	**Fairborn** (city) Greene County
106	3581	12.3	**Kent** (city) Portage County
107	3602	12.2	**Ashland** (city) Ashland County
107	3602	12.2	**Brook Park** (city) Cuyahoga County
109	3632	12.1	**Marietta** (city) Washington County
110	3691	11.8	**Dover** (city) Tuscarawas County
111	3706	11.7	**Willowick** (city) Lake County
112	3720	11.6	**Norwalk** (city) Huron County
113	3738	11.5	**Riverside** (city) Montgomery County
114	3831	11.0	**Athens** (city) Athens County
115	3842	10.9	**Franklin** (city) Warren County
115	3842	10.9	**Norwood** (city) Hamilton County
117	3854	10.8	**Bellefontaine** (city) Logan County
117	3854	10.8	**Circleville** (city) Pickaway County
119	3893	10.6	**Newark** (city) Licking County
120	3938	10.4	**Defiance** (city) Defiance County
120	3938	10.4	**Lancaster** (city) Fairfield County
120	3938	10.4	**Trotwood** (city) Montgomery County
123	3953	10.3	**Ironton** (city) Lawrence County
124	3968	10.2	**Austintown** (CDP) Mahoning County
124	3968	10.2	**Hamilton** (city) Butler County
124	3968	10.2	**New Philadelphia** (city) Tuscarawas County
127	3991	10.1	**Chillicothe** (city) Ross County
128	4007	10.0	**Xenia** (city) Greene County
129	4024	9.9	**Coshocton** (city) Coshocton County
130	4058	9.7	**Elyria** (city) Lorain County
131	4090	9.5	**West Carrollton** (city) Montgomery County
132	4105	9.4	**Painesville** (city) Lake County
133	4119	9.3	**Euclid** (city) Cuyahoga County
133	4119	9.3	**Sandusky** (city) Erie County
135	4153	9.1	**Lorain** (city) Lorain County
136	4179	8.9	**Portsmouth** (city) Scioto County
137	4195	8.8	**Massillon** (city) Stark County
137	4195	8.8	**Van Wert** (city) Van Wert County
139	4208	8.7	**Akron** (city) Summit County
139	4208	8.7	**Middletown** (city) Butler County
141	4226	8.6	**Garfield Heights** (city) Cuyahoga County
142	4256	8.4	**Celina** (city) Mercer County
142	4256	8.4	**Fremont** (city) Sandusky County
142	4256	8.4	**Springfield** (city) Clark County
145	4271	8.3	**Bedford** (city) Cuyahoga County
146	4282	8.2	**Bedford Heights** (city) Cuyahoga County
146	4282	8.2	**Sidney** (city) Shelby County
148	4313	8.0	**Niles** (city) Trumbull County
149	4323	7.9	**Mount Vernon** (city) Knox County
150	4352	7.7	**Mansfield** (city) Richland County

Note: *The state column ranks the top/bottom 150 places from all places in the state with population of 10,000 or more. The national column ranks the top/bottom 150 places from all places in the country with population of 10,000 or more. Places that are unincorporated were not considered in the rankings. Please refer to the User Guide for additional information.*

Households with Income of $100,000 or More

Top 150 Places Ranked in *Ascending* Order

State Rank	Nat'l Rank	Percent	Place
1	16	2.8	**East Cleveland** (city) Cuyahoga County
2	28	3.5	**Bucyrus** (city) Crawford County
3	41	4.2	**Youngstown** (city) Mahoning County
4	72	5.0	**Warrensville Heights** (city) Cuyahoga County
4	72	5.0	**Whitehall** (city) Franklin County
6	74	5.1	**Ashtabula** (city) Ashtabula County
6	74	5.1	**Galion** (city) Crawford County
6	74	5.1	**Struthers** (city) Mahoning County
6	74	5.1	**Wilmington** (city) Clinton County
10	87	5.3	**Zanesville** (city) Muskingum County
11	94	5.4	**Fostoria** (city) Seneca County
12	99	5.5	**Northbrook** (CDP) Hamilton County
13	128	5.9	**Canton** (city) Stark County
13	128	5.9	**Dayton** (city) Montgomery County
15	141	6.1	**East Liverpool** (city) Columbiana County
15	141	6.1	**Lima** (city) Allen County
17	146	6.2	**Washington Court House** (city) Fayette County
18	154	6.3	**Conneaut** (city) Ashtabula County
19	167	6.4	**Warren** (city) Trumbull County
20	173	6.5	**Tiffin** (city) Seneca County
21	182	6.6	**Cleveland** (city) Cuyahoga County
22	227	7.1	**Greenville** (city) Darke County
22	227	7.1	**Ravenna** (city) Portage County
24	238	7.2	**Cambridge** (city) Guernsey County
24	238	7.2	**Maple Heights** (city) Cuyahoga County
24	238	7.2	**Piqua** (city) Miami County
27	245	7.3	**Marion** (city) Marion County
28	257	7.4	**Alliance** (city) Stark County
28	257	7.4	**Salem** (city) Columbiana County
28	257	7.4	**Toledo** (city) Lucas County
31	281	7.6	**Barberton** (city) Summit County
31	281	7.6	**Brooklyn** (city) Cuyahoga County
31	281	7.6	**Urbana** (city) Champaign County
34	294	7.7	**Mansfield** (city) Richland County
35	317	7.9	**Mount Vernon** (city) Knox County
36	334	8.0	**Niles** (city) Trumbull County
37	362	8.2	**Bedford Heights** (city) Cuyahoga County
37	362	8.2	**Sidney** (city) Shelby County
39	375	8.3	**Bedford** (city) Cuyahoga County
40	386	8.4	**Celina** (city) Mercer County
40	386	8.4	**Fremont** (city) Sandusky County
40	386	8.4	**Springfield** (city) Clark County
43	414	8.6	**Garfield Heights** (city) Cuyahoga County
44	431	8.7	**Akron** (city) Summit County
44	431	8.7	**Middletown** (city) Butler County
46	449	8.8	**Massillon** (city) Stark County
46	449	8.8	**Van Wert** (city) Van Wert County
48	462	8.9	**Portsmouth** (city) Scioto County
49	488	9.1	**Lorain** (city) Lorain County
50	519	9.3	**Euclid** (city) Cuyahoga County
50	519	9.3	**Sandusky** (city) Erie County
52	538	9.4	**Painesville** (city) Lake County
53	552	9.5	**West Carrollton** (city) Montgomery County
54	586	9.7	**Elyria** (city) Lorain County
55	621	9.9	**Coshocton** (city) Coshocton County
56	633	10.0	**Xenia** (city) Greene County
57	650	10.1	**Chillicothe** (city) Ross County
58	666	10.2	**Austintown** (CDP) Mahoning County
58	666	10.2	**Hamilton** (city) Butler County
58	666	10.2	**New Philadelphia** (city) Tuscarawas County
61	689	10.3	**Ironton** (city) Lawrence County
62	704	10.4	**Defiance** (city) Defiance County
62	704	10.4	**Lancaster** (city) Fairfield County
62	704	10.4	**Trotwood** (city) Montgomery County
65	741	10.6	**Newark** (city) Licking County
66	779	10.8	**Bellefontaine** (city) Logan County
66	779	10.8	**Circleville** (city) Pickaway County
68	803	10.9	**Franklin** (city) Warren County
68	803	10.9	**Norwood** (city) Hamilton County
70	815	11.0	**Athens** (city) Athens County
71	894	11.5	**Riverside** (city) Montgomery County
72	919	11.6	**Norwalk** (city) Huron County
73	937	11.7	**Willowick** (city) Lake County
74	951	11.8	**Dover** (city) Tuscarawas County
75	1004	12.1	**Marietta** (city) Washington County
76	1025	12.2	**Ashland** (city) Ashland County
76	1025	12.2	**Brook Park** (city) Cuyahoga County
78	1055	12.3	**Kent** (city) Portage County
79	1076	12.4	**Fairborn** (city) Greene County
80	1092	12.5	**Forest Park** (city) Hamilton County
81	1126	12.7	**Steubenville** (city) Jefferson County
81	1126	12.7	**Wooster** (city) Wayne County
83	1149	12.9	**Parma Heights** (city) Cuyahoga County
84	1179	13.1	**Troy** (city) Miami County
85	1209	13.3	**Mayfield Heights** (city) Cuyahoga County
86	1223	13.4	**Cincinnati** (city) Hamilton County
87	1310	14.0	**Parma** (city) Cuyahoga County
88	1324	14.1	**Findlay** (city) Hancock County
89	1362	14.4	**Cuyahoga Falls** (city) Summit County
90	1377	14.5	**Eastlake** (city) Lake County
90	1377	14.5	**Heath** (city) Licking County
92	1403	14.7	**Columbus** (city) Franklin County
92	1403	14.7	**Lakewood** (city) Cuyahoga County
94	1437	14.9	**Oxford** (city) Butler County
95	1465	15.1	**Bowling Green** (city) Wood County
96	1490	15.3	**Wickliffe** (city) Lake County
97	1504	15.4	**Boardman** (CDP) Mahoning County
98	1521	15.5	**Willoughby** (city) Lake County
99	1545	15.7	**Reading** (city) Hamilton County
100	1583	16.0	**Huber Heights** (city) Montgomery County
101	1610	16.2	**Englewood** (city) Montgomery County
102	1682	16.8	**Trenton** (city) Butler County
103	1693	16.9	**North Canton** (city) Stark County
104	1707	17.0	**Kettering** (city) Montgomery County
105	1743	17.3	**Springdale** (city) Hamilton County
106	1781	17.6	**Maumee** (city) Lucas County
106	1781	17.6	**Sharonville** (city) Hamilton County
108	1815	17.9	**Richmond Heights** (city) Cuyahoga County
109	1885	18.4	**Berea** (city) Cuyahoga County
110	1947	18.9	**Vandalia** (city) Montgomery County
111	1960	19.0	**Vermilion** (city) Lorain County
112	1981	19.2	**Pataskala** (city) Licking County
113	2013	19.5	**Brunswick** (city) Medina County
114	2034	19.7	**Middleburg Heights** (city) Cuyahoga County
115	2062	19.9	**Fairview Park** (city) Cuyahoga County
115	2062	19.9	**Finneytown** (CDP) Hamilton County
115	2062	19.9	**Oregon** (city) Lucas County
118	2078	20.0	**Cleveland Heights** (city) Cuyahoga County
118	2078	20.0	**Streetsboro** (city) Portage County
120	2110	20.2	**Fairfield** (city) Butler County
121	2141	20.4	**Bridgetown** (CDP) Hamilton County
122	2153	20.5	**New Franklin** (city) Summit County
123	2178	20.7	**South Euclid** (city) Cuyahoga County
124	2231	21.2	**Tallmadge** (city) Summit County
125	2240	21.3	**Medina** (city) Medina County
125	2240	21.3	**Norton** (city) Summit County
127	2274	21.6	**Marysville** (city) Union County
128	2286	21.7	**Delaware** (city) Delaware County
128	2286	21.7	**North Olmsted** (city) Cuyahoga County
130	2313	22.0	**Wadsworth** (city) Medina County
131	2403	22.9	**Miamisburg** (city) Montgomery County
132	2424	23.1	**Reynoldsburg** (city) Franklin County
133	2482	23.7	**Monroe** (city) Butler County
134	2515	24.1	**Lebanon** (city) Warren County
135	2524	24.2	**White Oak** (CDP) Hamilton County
136	2623	25.3	**Green** (city) Summit County
137	2654	25.6	**Clayton** (city) Montgomery County
138	2671	25.7	**Centerville** (city) Montgomery County
139	2750	26.4	**North Ridgeville** (city) Lorain County
140	2796	26.9	**Grove City** (city) Franklin County
141	2826	27.3	**Mentor** (city) Lake County
141	2826	27.3	**Stow** (city) Summit County
143	2880	28.0	**North Royalton** (city) Cuyahoga County
144	2901	28.3	**Lyndhurst** (city) Cuyahoga County
145	2933	28.6	**Dent** (CDP) Hamilton County
145	2933	28.6	**Seven Hills** (city) Cuyahoga County
147	2991	29.3	**Monfort Heights** (CDP) Hamilton County
148	3047	30.0	**Amherst** (city) Lorain County
149	3149	31.5	**Forestville** (CDP) Hamilton County
150	3215	32.6	**University Heights** (city) Cuyahoga County

Note: *The state column ranks the top/bottom 150 places from all places in the state with population of 10,000 or more. The national column ranks the top/bottom 150 places from all places in the country with population of 10,000 or more. Places that are unincorporated were not considered in the rankings. Please refer to the User Guide for additional information.*

Poverty Rate

Top 150 Places Ranked in *Descending* Order

State Rank	Nat'l Rank	Percent	Place
1	4	57.4	**Athens** (city) Athens County
2	22	46.0	**Oxford** (city) Butler County
3	34	42.6	**East Cleveland** (city) Cuyahoga County
4	93	36.4	**Youngstown** (city) Mahoning County
5	113	35.4	**Cleveland** (city) Cuyahoga County
6	117	35.3	**Kent** (city) Portage County
7	127	34.7	**Dayton** (city) Montgomery County
8	152	33.9	**Lima** (city) Allen County
9	171	32.9	**Ashtabula** (city) Ashtabula County
10	189	32.5	**Bowling Green** (city) Wood County
11	194	32.3	**Warren** (city) Trumbull County
12	219	31.7	**Canton** (city) Stark County
13	246	30.6	**Portsmouth** (city) Scioto County
14	253	30.4	**Cincinnati** (city) Hamilton County
14	253	30.4	**Lorain** (city) Lorain County
14	253	30.4	**Springfield** (city) Clark County
17	273	30.1	**East Liverpool** (city) Columbiana County
18	287	29.7	**Zanesville** (city) Muskingum County
19	341	28.6	**Cambridge** (city) Guernsey County
19	341	28.6	**Steubenville** (city) Jefferson County
21	366	27.9	**Marion** (city) Marion County
22	391	27.5	**Akron** (city) Summit County
23	411	27.2	**Toledo** (city) Lucas County
24	427	26.9	**Alliance** (city) Stark County
25	514	25.6	**Painesville** (city) Lake County
26	556	25.1	**Ravenna** (city) Portage County
27	574	24.8	**Wilmington** (city) Clinton County
28	578	24.7	**Fostoria** (city) Seneca County
29	589	24.5	**Xenia** (city) Greene County
30	601	24.4	**Mansfield** (city) Richland County
31	614	24.3	**Bellefontaine** (city) Logan County
31	614	24.3	**Fairborn** (city) Greene County
31	614	24.3	**Whitehall** (city) Franklin County
34	681	23.6	**Chillicothe** (city) Ross County
35	690	23.5	**Springdale** (city) Hamilton County
36	700	23.4	**Piqua** (city) Miami County
37	732	23.1	**Sandusky** (city) Erie County
37	732	23.1	**Washington Court House** (city) Fayette County
39	745	23.0	**Middletown** (city) Butler County
40	752	22.9	**Hamilton** (city) Butler County
41	762	22.8	**Conneaut** (city) Ashtabula County
41	762	22.8	**Fremont** (city) Sandusky County
41	762	22.8	**Marietta** (city) Washington County
41	762	22.8	**Salem** (city) Columbiana County
45	797	22.4	**Columbus** (city) Franklin County
46	844	22.0	**Galion** (city) Crawford County
47	905	21.4	**Bucyrus** (city) Crawford County
48	924	21.2	**Trotwood** (city) Montgomery County
49	935	21.1	**Lancaster** (city) Fairfield County
50	947	21.0	**Newark** (city) Licking County
51	975	20.7	**Norwood** (city) Hamilton County
52	982	20.6	**Reading** (city) Hamilton County
53	993	20.5	**Barberton** (city) Summit County
54	1028	20.2	**Findlay** (city) Hancock County
54	1028	20.2	**Mount Vernon** (city) Knox County
56	1052	20.0	**Cleveland Heights** (city) Cuyahoga County
57	1065	19.9	**Euclid** (city) Cuyahoga County
58	1081	19.8	**Circleville** (city) Pickaway County
58	1081	19.8	**Struthers** (city) Mahoning County
58	1081	19.8	**Van Wert** (city) Van Wert County
61	1115	19.5	**Coshocton** (city) Coshocton County
61	1115	19.5	**Maple Heights** (city) Cuyahoga County
63	1131	19.4	**Niles** (city) Trumbull County
64	1145	19.3	**Urbana** (city) Champaign County
64	1145	19.3	**Warrensville Heights** (city) Cuyahoga County
66	1193	19.0	**Massillon** (city) Stark County
67	1215	18.8	**Elyria** (city) Lorain County
68	1257	18.4	**Defiance** (city) Defiance County
68	1257	18.4	**Greenville** (city) Darke County
70	1273	18.3	**New Philadelphia** (city) Tuscarawas County
71	1295	18.1	**Ironton** (city) Lawrence County
72	1368	17.6	**Riverside** (city) Montgomery County
73	1399	17.4	**Wooster** (city) Wayne County
74	1424	17.2	**Forest Park** (city) Hamilton County
74	1424	17.2	**Tiffin** (city) Seneca County
76	1532	16.4	**Lakewood** (city) Cuyahoga County
76	1532	16.4	**Sidney** (city) Shelby County
78	1545	16.3	**Ashland** (city) Ashland County
79	1561	16.2	**Norwalk** (city) Huron County
79	1561	16.2	**Troy** (city) Miami County
79	1561	16.2	**West Carrollton** (city) Montgomery County
82	1619	15.8	**Franklin** (city) Warren County
83	1670	15.4	**Brooklyn** (city) Cuyahoga County
84	1696	15.2	**Northbrook** (CDP) Hamilton County
85	1758	14.8	**Celina** (city) Mercer County
85	1758	14.8	**Garfield Heights** (city) Cuyahoga County
87	1886	14.0	**Bedford Heights** (city) Cuyahoga County
88	1901	13.9	**Dover** (city) Tuscarawas County
89	1924	13.7	**Lebanon** (city) Warren County
90	1954	13.5	**Bedford** (city) Cuyahoga County
91	1995	13.3	**Medina** (city) Medina County
92	2055	12.8	**Heath** (city) Licking County
92	2055	12.8	**Reynoldsburg** (city) Franklin County
94	2083	12.6	**White Oak** (CDP) Hamilton County
95	2092	12.5	**Vermilion** (city) Lorain County
96	2140	12.2	**Austintown** (CDP) Mahoning County
97	2161	12.1	**Finneytown** (CDP) Hamilton County
97	2161	12.1	**Parma Heights** (city) Cuyahoga County
99	2185	12.0	**Cuyahoga Falls** (city) Summit County
100	2255	11.6	**Miamisburg** (city) Montgomery County
101	2327	11.2	**Berea** (city) Cuyahoga County
101	2327	11.2	**Sharonville** (city) Hamilton County
103	2349	11.1	**Kettering** (city) Montgomery County
104	2369	11.0	**Huber Heights** (city) Montgomery County
105	2384	10.9	**Parma** (city) Cuyahoga County
105	2384	10.9	**Vandalia** (city) Montgomery County
107	2498	10.3	**Boardman** (CDP) Mahoning County
108	2540	10.1	**Tallmadge** (city) Summit County
109	2648	9.6	**Delaware** (city) Delaware County
109	2648	9.6	**Trenton** (city) Butler County
111	2691	9.4	**Marysville** (city) Union County
111	2691	9.4	**Oregon** (city) Lucas County
111	2691	9.4	**Pataskala** (city) Licking County
114	2711	9.3	**Englewood** (city) Montgomery County
115	2730	9.2	**Shaker Heights** (city) Cuyahoga County
116	2792	8.9	**University Heights** (city) Cuyahoga County
117	2816	8.8	**Bexley** (city) Franklin County
117	2816	8.8	**Wickliffe** (city) Lake County
119	2834	8.7	**Brook Park** (city) Cuyahoga County
119	2834	8.7	**Grove City** (city) Franklin County
121	2903	8.4	**Willowick** (city) Lake County
122	2927	8.3	**Green** (city) Summit County
122	2927	8.3	**South Euclid** (city) Cuyahoga County
124	2952	8.2	**Fairview Park** (city) Cuyahoga County
124	2952	8.2	**Maumee** (city) Lucas County
126	2973	8.1	**Fairfield** (city) Butler County
127	3006	8.0	**Loveland** (city) Hamilton County
127	3006	8.0	**Monroe** (city) Butler County
129	3028	7.9	**Amherst** (city) Lorain County
130	3056	7.8	**Middleburg Heights** (city) Cuyahoga County
130	3056	7.8	**Willoughby** (city) Lake County
132	3124	7.6	**Clayton** (city) Montgomery County
132	3124	7.6	**Mayfield Heights** (city) Cuyahoga County
132	3124	7.6	**Stow** (city) Summit County
135	3148	7.5	**Centerville** (city) Montgomery County
135	3148	7.5	**Forestville** (CDP) Hamilton County
135	3148	7.5	**Streetsboro** (city) Portage County
138	3204	7.3	**Eastlake** (city) Lake County
138	3204	7.3	**Wadsworth** (city) Medina County
140	3225	7.2	**North Olmsted** (city) Cuyahoga County
141	3250	7.1	**Sylvania** (city) Lucas County
142	3274	7.0	**Richmond Heights** (city) Cuyahoga County
143	3328	6.8	**Mentor** (city) Lake County
143	3328	6.8	**North Canton** (city) Stark County
145	3354	6.7	**Brunswick** (city) Medina County
146	3382	6.6	**Broadview Heights** (city) Cuyahoga County
146	3382	6.6	**New Franklin** (city) Summit County
146	3382	6.6	**North Ridgeville** (city) Lorain County
146	3382	6.6	**Westerville** (city) Franklin County
150	3445	6.4	**Bridgetown** (CDP) Hamilton County

Note: *The state column ranks the top/bottom 150 places from all places in the state with population of 10,000 or more. The national column ranks the top/bottom 150 places from all places in the country with population of 10,000 or more. Places that are unincorporated were not considered in the rankings. Please refer to the User Guide for additional information.*

Poverty Rate

Top 150 Places Ranked in *Ascending* Order

State Rank	Nat'l Rank	Percent	Place
1	2	1.0	**Macedonia** (city) Summit County
2	3	1.2	**Powell** (city) Delaware County
3	105	2.5	**Brecksville** (city) Cuyahoga County
4	197	3.0	**Dublin** (city) Franklin County
4	197	3.0	**Montgomery** (city) Hamilton County
6	247	3.2	**Beachwood** (city) Cuyahoga County
7	330	3.5	**Worthington** (city) Franklin County
8	365	3.6	**Hudson** (city) Summit County
9	391	3.7	**Twinsburg** (city) Summit County
10	428	3.8	**Solon** (city) Cuyahoga County
11	453	3.9	**Mack** (CDP) Hamilton County
11	453	3.9	**Mason** (city) Warren County
11	453	3.9	**Monfort Heights** (CDP) Hamilton County
11	453	3.9	**Springboro** (city) Warren County
15	478	4.0	**Bay Village** (city) Cuyahoga County
16	520	4.1	**Seven Hills** (city) Cuyahoga County
17	546	4.2	**Westlake** (city) Cuyahoga County
18	578	4.3	**Lyndhurst** (city) Cuyahoga County
18	578	4.3	**North Royalton** (city) Cuyahoga County
20	618	4.4	**Pickerington** (city) Fairfield County
21	656	4.5	**Avon** (city) Lorain County
22	680	4.6	**Avon Lake** (city) Lorain County
22	680	4.6	**Upper Arlington** (city) Franklin County
24	710	4.7	**Hilliard** (city) Franklin County
25	745	4.8	**Dent** (CDP) Hamilton County
26	800	5.0	**Aurora** (city) Portage County
26	800	5.0	**Rocky River** (city) Cuyahoga County
26	800	5.0	**Strongsville** (city) Cuyahoga County
29	883	5.3	**Perrysburg** (city) Wood County
30	937	5.5	**Beavercreek** (city) Greene County
30	937	5.5	**Gahanna** (city) Franklin County
32	964	5.6	**Blue Ash** (city) Hamilton County
33	1134	6.2	**Norton** (city) Summit County
34	1184	6.4	**Bridgetown** (CDP) Hamilton County
35	1235	6.6	**Broadview Heights** (city) Cuyahoga County
35	1235	6.6	**New Franklin** (city) Summit County
35	1235	6.6	**North Ridgeville** (city) Lorain County
35	1235	6.6	**Westerville** (city) Franklin County
39	1275	6.7	**Brunswick** (city) Medina County
40	1303	6.8	**Mentor** (city) Lake County
40	1303	6.8	**North Canton** (city) Stark County
42	1355	7.0	**Richmond Heights** (city) Cuyahoga County
43	1383	7.1	**Sylvania** (city) Lucas County
44	1407	7.2	**North Olmsted** (city) Cuyahoga County
45	1432	7.3	**Eastlake** (city) Lake County
45	1432	7.3	**Wadsworth** (city) Medina County
47	1482	7.5	**Centerville** (city) Montgomery County
47	1482	7.5	**Forestville** (CDP) Hamilton County
47	1482	7.5	**Streetsboro** (city) Portage County
50	1509	7.6	**Clayton** (city) Montgomery County
50	1509	7.6	**Mayfield Heights** (city) Cuyahoga County
50	1509	7.6	**Stow** (city) Summit County
53	1572	7.8	**Middleburg Heights** (city) Cuyahoga County
53	1572	7.8	**Willoughby** (city) Lake County
55	1601	7.9	**Amherst** (city) Lorain County
56	1629	8.0	**Loveland** (city) Hamilton County
56	1629	8.0	**Monroe** (city) Butler County
58	1651	8.1	**Fairfield** (city) Butler County
59	1684	8.2	**Fairview Park** (city) Cuyahoga County
59	1684	8.2	**Maumee** (city) Lucas County
61	1705	8.3	**Green** (city) Summit County
61	1705	8.3	**South Euclid** (city) Cuyahoga County
63	1730	8.4	**Willowick** (city) Lake County
64	1804	8.7	**Brook Park** (city) Cuyahoga County
64	1804	8.7	**Grove City** (city) Franklin County
66	1823	8.8	**Bexley** (city) Franklin County
66	1823	8.8	**Wickliffe** (city) Lake County
68	1841	8.9	**University Heights** (city) Cuyahoga County
69	1910	9.2	**Shaker Heights** (city) Cuyahoga County
70	1927	9.3	**Englewood** (city) Montgomery County
71	1946	9.4	**Marysville** (city) Union County
71	1946	9.4	**Oregon** (city) Lucas County
71	1946	9.4	**Pataskala** (city) Licking County
74	1982	9.6	**Delaware** (city) Delaware County
74	1982	9.6	**Trenton** (city) Butler County
76	2104	10.1	**Tallmadge** (city) Summit County
77	2136	10.3	**Boardman** (CDP) Mahoning County
78	2260	10.9	**Parma** (city) Cuyahoga County
78	2260	10.9	**Vandalia** (city) Montgomery County
80	2273	11.0	**Huber Heights** (city) Montgomery County
81	2288	11.1	**Kettering** (city) Montgomery County
82	2308	11.2	**Berea** (city) Cuyahoga County
82	2308	11.2	**Sharonville** (city) Hamilton County
84	2383	11.6	**Miamisburg** (city) Montgomery County
85	2455	12.0	**Cuyahoga Falls** (city) Summit County
86	2472	12.1	**Finneytown** (CDP) Hamilton County
86	2472	12.1	**Parma Heights** (city) Cuyahoga County
88	2496	12.2	**Austintown** (CDP) Mahoning County
89	2548	12.5	**Vermilion** (city) Lorain County
90	2565	12.6	**White Oak** (CDP) Hamilton County
91	2586	12.8	**Heath** (city) Licking County
91	2586	12.8	**Reynoldsburg** (city) Franklin County
93	2649	13.3	**Medina** (city) Medina County
94	2678	13.5	**Bedford** (city) Cuyahoga County
95	2714	13.7	**Lebanon** (city) Warren County
96	2743	13.9	**Dover** (city) Tuscarawas County
97	2756	14.0	**Bedford Heights** (city) Cuyahoga County
98	2884	14.8	**Celina** (city) Mercer County
98	2884	14.8	**Garfield Heights** (city) Cuyahoga County
100	2942	15.2	**Northbrook** (CDP) Hamilton County
101	2972	15.4	**Brooklyn** (city) Cuyahoga County
102	3027	15.8	**Franklin** (city) Warren County
103	3084	16.2	**Norwalk** (city) Huron County
103	3084	16.2	**Troy** (city) Miami County
103	3084	16.2	**West Carrollton** (city) Montgomery County
106	3096	16.3	**Ashland** (city) Ashland County
107	3112	16.4	**Lakewood** (city) Cuyahoga County
107	3112	16.4	**Sidney** (city) Shelby County
109	3220	17.2	**Forest Park** (city) Hamilton County
109	3220	17.2	**Tiffin** (city) Seneca County
111	3248	17.4	**Wooster** (city) Wayne County
112	3270	17.6	**Riverside** (city) Montgomery County
113	3348	18.1	**Ironton** (city) Lawrence County
114	3375	18.3	**New Philadelphia** (city) Tuscarawas County
115	3384	18.4	**Defiance** (city) Defiance County
115	3384	18.4	**Greenville** (city) Darke County
117	3435	18.8	**Elyria** (city) Lorain County
118	3452	19.0	**Massillon** (city) Stark County
119	3500	19.3	**Urbana** (city) Champaign County
119	3500	19.3	**Warrensville Heights** (city) Cuyahoga County
121	3512	19.4	**Niles** (city) Trumbull County
122	3526	19.5	**Coshocton** (city) Coshocton County
122	3526	19.5	**Maple Heights** (city) Cuyahoga County
124	3566	19.8	**Circleville** (city) Pickaway County
124	3566	19.8	**Struthers** (city) Mahoning County
124	3566	19.8	**Van Wert** (city) Van Wert County
127	3576	19.9	**Euclid** (city) Cuyahoga County
128	3592	20.0	**Cleveland Heights** (city) Cuyahoga County
129	3616	20.2	**Findlay** (city) Hancock County
129	3616	20.2	**Mount Vernon** (city) Knox County
131	3643	20.5	**Barberton** (city) Summit County
132	3664	20.6	**Reading** (city) Hamilton County
133	3675	20.7	**Norwood** (city) Hamilton County
134	3702	21.0	**Newark** (city) Licking County
135	3710	21.1	**Lancaster** (city) Fairfield County
136	3722	21.2	**Trotwood** (city) Montgomery County
137	3739	21.4	**Bucyrus** (city) Crawford County
138	3804	22.0	**Galion** (city) Crawford County
139	3843	22.4	**Columbus** (city) Franklin County
140	3882	22.8	**Conneaut** (city) Ashtabula County
140	3882	22.8	**Fremont** (city) Sandusky County
140	3882	22.8	**Marietta** (city) Washington County
140	3882	22.8	**Salem** (city) Columbiana County
144	3895	22.9	**Hamilton** (city) Butler County
145	3905	23.0	**Middletown** (city) Butler County
146	3912	23.1	**Sandusky** (city) Erie County
146	3912	23.1	**Washington Court House** (city) Fayette County
148	3947	23.4	**Piqua** (city) Miami County
149	3957	23.5	**Springdale** (city) Hamilton County
150	3967	23.6	**Chillicothe** (city) Ross County

Note: *The state column ranks the top/bottom 150 places from all places in the state with population of 10,000 or more. The national column ranks the top/bottom 150 places from all places in the country with population of 10,000 or more. Places that are unincorporated were not considered in the rankings. Please refer to the User Guide for additional information.*

Educational Attainment: High School Diploma or Higher

Top 150 Places Ranked in *Descending* Order

State Rank	Nat'l Rank	Percent	Place
1	17	98.8	**Powell** (city) Delaware County
2	37	98.5	**Dublin** (city) Franklin County
2	37	98.5	**Hudson** (city) Summit County
4	43	98.4	**Bexley** (city) Franklin County
4	43	98.4	**Upper Arlington** (city) Franklin County
6	61	98.2	**Springboro** (city) Warren County
6	61	98.2	**Worthington** (city) Franklin County
8	78	98.1	**Bay Village** (city) Cuyahoga County
9	131	97.7	**Montgomery** (city) Hamilton County
10	306	96.8	**Pickerington** (city) Fairfield County
11	332	96.7	**Avon Lake** (city) Lorain County
12	391	96.4	**Beavercreek** (city) Greene County
12	391	96.4	**Perrysburg** (city) Wood County
14	423	96.3	**Solon** (city) Cuyahoga County
14	423	96.3	**University Heights** (city) Cuyahoga County
16	474	96.1	**Mason** (city) Warren County
17	501	96.0	**Avon** (city) Lorain County
17	501	96.0	**Macedonia** (city) Summit County
19	524	95.9	**Shaker Heights** (city) Cuyahoga County
19	524	95.9	**Westerville** (city) Franklin County
21	580	95.7	**Aurora** (city) Portage County
21	580	95.7	**Hilliard** (city) Franklin County
23	766	95.1	**Gahanna** (city) Franklin County
23	766	95.1	**Westlake** (city) Cuyahoga County
25	790	95.0	**Fairview Park** (city) Cuyahoga County
25	790	95.0	**Monfort Heights** (CDP) Hamilton County
27	852	94.8	**Forestville** (CDP) Hamilton County
27	852	94.8	**Maumee** (city) Lucas County
29	881	94.7	**Centerville** (city) Montgomery County
30	910	94.6	**Rocky River** (city) Cuyahoga County
30	910	94.6	**Sylvania** (city) Lucas County
32	937	94.5	**Broadview Heights** (city) Cuyahoga County
32	937	94.5	**Mentor** (city) Lake County
32	937	94.5	**Strongsville** (city) Cuyahoga County
35	970	94.4	**Brecksville** (city) Cuyahoga County
35	970	94.4	**Englewood** (city) Montgomery County
37	1004	94.3	**Athens** (city) Athens County
37	1004	94.3	**Beachwood** (city) Cuyahoga County
37	1004	94.3	**North Royalton** (city) Cuyahoga County
40	1077	94.1	**Grove City** (city) Franklin County
40	1077	94.1	**Stow** (city) Summit County
42	1118	94.0	**Cleveland Heights** (city) Cuyahoga County
42	1118	94.0	**Loveland** (city) Hamilton County
42	1118	94.0	**Mack** (CDP) Hamilton County
45	1160	93.9	**Kettering** (city) Montgomery County
45	1160	93.9	**Lyndhurst** (city) Cuyahoga County
47	1192	93.8	**Clayton** (city) Montgomery County
47	1192	93.8	**North Canton** (city) Stark County
49	1224	93.7	**Bowling Green** (city) Wood County
49	1224	93.7	**South Euclid** (city) Cuyahoga County
51	1264	93.6	**Medina** (city) Medina County
52	1330	93.4	**Cuyahoga Falls** (city) Summit County
53	1369	93.3	**Twinsburg** (city) Summit County
54	1431	93.1	**Willoughby** (city) Lake County
55	1468	93.0	**North Ridgeville** (city) Lorain County
56	1494	92.9	**Dent** (CDP) Hamilton County
56	1494	92.9	**Monroe** (city) Butler County
58	1569	92.7	**Boardman** (CDP) Mahoning County
58	1569	92.7	**North Olmsted** (city) Cuyahoga County
60	1595	92.6	**Amherst** (city) Lorain County
61	1629	92.5	**Bridgetown** (CDP) Hamilton County
61	1629	92.5	**Streetsboro** (city) Portage County
61	1629	92.5	**Tallmadge** (city) Summit County
64	1670	92.4	**Blue Ash** (city) Hamilton County
64	1670	92.4	**Delaware** (city) Delaware County
64	1670	92.4	**New Franklin** (city) Summit County
64	1670	92.4	**Wadsworth** (city) Medina County
68	1702	92.3	**Finneytown** (CDP) Hamilton County
68	1702	92.3	**Green** (city) Summit County
68	1702	92.3	**Oxford** (city) Butler County
71	1734	92.2	**Lakewood** (city) Cuyahoga County
71	1734	92.2	**Richmond Heights** (city) Cuyahoga County
73	1768	92.1	**Brunswick** (city) Medina County
73	1768	92.1	**Reynoldsburg** (city) Franklin County
75	1856	91.8	**Berea** (city) Cuyahoga County
76	1884	91.7	**Fairfield** (city) Butler County
76	1884	91.7	**Kent** (city) Portage County
76	1884	91.7	**Wickliffe** (city) Lake County
79	1906	91.6	**Huber Heights** (city) Montgomery County
80	1944	91.5	**Lebanon** (city) Warren County
81	1965	91.4	**Norton** (city) Summit County
82	1992	91.3	**Pataskala** (city) Licking County
83	2050	91.1	**Austintown** (CDP) Mahoning County
83	2050	91.1	**White Oak** (CDP) Hamilton County
85	2071	91.0	**Dover** (city) Tuscarawas County
85	2071	91.0	**Middleburg Heights** (city) Cuyahoga County
87	2102	90.9	**Vandalia** (city) Montgomery County
88	2137	90.8	**Mayfield Heights** (city) Cuyahoga County
89	2160	90.7	**Wooster** (city) Wayne County
90	2293	90.2	**Findlay** (city) Hancock County
91	2342	90.0	**Marysville** (city) Union County
91	2342	90.0	**Miamisburg** (city) Montgomery County
91	2342	90.0	**Struthers** (city) Mahoning County
91	2342	90.0	**Willowick** (city) Lake County
95	2369	89.9	**Sharonville** (city) Hamilton County
96	2430	89.6	**Trenton** (city) Butler County
97	2501	89.3	**Seven Hills** (city) Cuyahoga County
98	2525	89.2	**Parma Heights** (city) Cuyahoga County
99	2551	89.1	**Parma** (city) Cuyahoga County
100	2571	89.0	**Vermilion** (city) Lorain County
101	2614	88.8	**Eastlake** (city) Lake County
102	2654	88.6	**Bedford Heights** (city) Cuyahoga County
103	2684	88.5	**Celina** (city) Mercer County
103	2684	88.5	**Troy** (city) Miami County
105	2710	88.4	**Oregon** (city) Lucas County
106	2739	88.3	**Columbus** (city) Franklin County
107	2764	88.2	**Maple Heights** (city) Cuyahoga County
108	2785	88.1	**Mount Vernon** (city) Knox County
108	2785	88.1	**Van Wert** (city) Van Wert County
108	2785	88.1	**Xenia** (city) Greene County
111	2805	88.0	**Euclid** (city) Cuyahoga County
112	2830	87.9	**Elyria** (city) Lorain County
112	2830	87.9	**Tiffin** (city) Seneca County
114	2856	87.8	**Ironton** (city) Lawrence County
114	2856	87.8	**New Philadelphia** (city) Tuscarawas County
114	2856	87.8	**West Carrollton** (city) Montgomery County
117	2873	87.7	**Ashland** (city) Ashland County
117	2873	87.7	**Bedford** (city) Cuyahoga County
117	2873	87.7	**Forest Park** (city) Hamilton County
117	2873	87.7	**Heath** (city) Licking County
121	2899	87.6	**Norwalk** (city) Huron County
121	2899	87.6	**Steubenville** (city) Jefferson County
123	2911	87.5	**Marietta** (city) Washington County
124	2968	87.2	**Warrensville Heights** (city) Cuyahoga County
125	2987	87.1	**Defiance** (city) Defiance County
126	3057	86.7	**Fairborn** (city) Greene County
126	3057	86.7	**Fostoria** (city) Seneca County
128	3077	86.6	**Massillon** (city) Stark County
129	3102	86.4	**Lancaster** (city) Fairfield County
130	3135	86.2	**Garfield Heights** (city) Cuyahoga County
130	3135	86.2	**Salem** (city) Columbiana County
132	3155	86.1	**Bucyrus** (city) Crawford County
132	3155	86.1	**Newark** (city) Licking County
134	3194	85.9	**Niles** (city) Trumbull County
135	3212	85.8	**Coshocton** (city) Coshocton County
136	3233	85.7	**Riverside** (city) Montgomery County
137	3285	85.4	**Akron** (city) Summit County
137	3285	85.4	**Brooklyn** (city) Cuyahoga County
139	3307	85.3	**Brook Park** (city) Cuyahoga County
140	3324	85.2	**Barberton** (city) Summit County
140	3324	85.2	**Wilmington** (city) Clinton County
142	3374	84.9	**Reading** (city) Hamilton County
143	3385	84.8	**Greenville** (city) Darke County
143	3385	84.8	**Toledo** (city) Lucas County
145	3407	84.7	**Fremont** (city) Sandusky County
145	3407	84.7	**Urbana** (city) Champaign County
147	3422	84.6	**Cambridge** (city) Guernsey County
147	3422	84.6	**Conneaut** (city) Ashtabula County
149	3461	84.3	**Cincinnati** (city) Hamilton County
150	3476	84.2	**Springdale** (city) Hamilton County

Note: *The state column ranks the top/bottom 150 places from all places in the state with population of 10,000 or more. The national column ranks the top/bottom 150 places from all places in the country with population of 10,000 or more. Places that are unincorporated were not considered in the rankings. Please refer to the User Guide for additional information.*

Educational Attainment: High School Diploma or Higher

Top 150 Places Ranked in *Ascending* Order

State Rank	Nat'l Rank	Percent	Place
1	486	77.4	**Cleveland** (city) Cuyahoga County
2	510	77.8	**Portsmouth** (city) Scioto County
3	538	78.3	**East Cleveland** (city) Cuyahoga County
4	595	79.0	**Painesville** (city) Lake County
5	612	79.2	**Whitehall** (city) Franklin County
6	651	79.7	**Zanesville** (city) Muskingum County
7	710	80.4	**Youngstown** (city) Mahoning County
8	749	80.8	**Dayton** (city) Montgomery County
9	755	80.9	**Norwood** (city) Hamilton County
10	762	81.0	**Washington Court House** (city) Fayette County
11	774	81.1	**Lorain** (city) Lorain County
12	787	81.2	**East Liverpool** (city) Columbiana County
13	855	81.8	**Marion** (city) Marion County
14	870	82.0	**Mansfield** (city) Richland County
15	882	82.1	**Springfield** (city) Clark County
16	911	82.4	**Middletown** (city) Butler County
16	911	82.4	**Piqua** (city) Miami County
18	929	82.5	**Lima** (city) Allen County
19	951	82.7	**Canton** (city) Stark County
20	993	83.1	**Hamilton** (city) Butler County
20	993	83.1	**Sandusky** (city) Erie County
22	1007	83.2	**Bellefontaine** (city) Logan County
22	1007	83.2	**Chillicothe** (city) Ross County
22	1007	83.2	**Franklin** (city) Warren County
22	1007	83.2	**Warren** (city) Trumbull County
26	1020	83.3	**Galion** (city) Crawford County
27	1027	83.4	**Northbrook** (CDP) Hamilton County
28	1048	83.5	**Ashtabula** (city) Ashtabula County
28	1048	83.5	**Trotwood** (city) Montgomery County
30	1065	83.6	**Circleville** (city) Pickaway County
31	1086	83.7	**Alliance** (city) Stark County
32	1121	83.9	**Sidney** (city) Shelby County
33	1141	84.0	**Ravenna** (city) Portage County
34	1171	84.2	**Springdale** (city) Hamilton County
35	1181	84.3	**Cincinnati** (city) Hamilton County
36	1219	84.6	**Cambridge** (city) Guernsey County
36	1219	84.6	**Conneaut** (city) Ashtabula County
38	1235	84.7	**Fremont** (city) Sandusky County
38	1235	84.7	**Urbana** (city) Champaign County
40	1250	84.8	**Greenville** (city) Darke County
40	1250	84.8	**Toledo** (city) Lucas County
42	1272	84.9	**Reading** (city) Hamilton County
43	1307	85.2	**Barberton** (city) Summit County
43	1307	85.2	**Wilmington** (city) Clinton County
45	1333	85.3	**Brook Park** (city) Cuyahoga County
46	1350	85.4	**Akron** (city) Summit County
46	1350	85.4	**Brooklyn** (city) Cuyahoga County
48	1403	85.7	**Riverside** (city) Montgomery County
49	1424	85.8	**Coshocton** (city) Coshocton County
50	1445	85.9	**Niles** (city) Trumbull County
51	1486	86.1	**Bucyrus** (city) Crawford County
51	1486	86.1	**Newark** (city) Licking County
53	1502	86.2	**Garfield Heights** (city) Cuyahoga County
53	1502	86.2	**Salem** (city) Columbiana County
55	1537	86.4	**Lancaster** (city) Fairfield County
56	1569	86.6	**Massillon** (city) Stark County
57	1580	86.7	**Fairborn** (city) Greene County
57	1580	86.7	**Fostoria** (city) Seneca County
59	1649	87.1	**Defiance** (city) Defiance County
60	1670	87.2	**Warrensville Heights** (city) Cuyahoga County
61	1724	87.5	**Marietta** (city) Washington County
62	1746	87.6	**Norwalk** (city) Huron County
62	1746	87.6	**Steubenville** (city) Jefferson County
64	1758	87.7	**Ashland** (city) Ashland County
64	1758	87.7	**Bedford** (city) Cuyahoga County
64	1758	87.7	**Forest Park** (city) Hamilton County
64	1758	87.7	**Heath** (city) Licking County
68	1784	87.8	**Ironton** (city) Lawrence County
68	1784	87.8	**New Philadelphia** (city) Tuscarawas County
68	1784	87.8	**West Carrollton** (city) Montgomery County
71	1801	87.9	**Elyria** (city) Lorain County
71	1801	87.9	**Tiffin** (city) Seneca County
73	1827	88.0	**Euclid** (city) Cuyahoga County
74	1852	88.1	**Mount Vernon** (city) Knox County
74	1852	88.1	**Van Wert** (city) Van Wert County
74	1852	88.1	**Xenia** (city) Greene County
77	1872	88.2	**Maple Heights** (city) Cuyahoga County
78	1893	88.3	**Columbus** (city) Franklin County
79	1918	88.4	**Oregon** (city) Lucas County
80	1947	88.5	**Celina** (city) Mercer County
80	1947	88.5	**Troy** (city) Miami County
82	1973	88.6	**Bedford Heights** (city) Cuyahoga County
83	2021	88.8	**Eastlake** (city) Lake County
84	2061	89.0	**Vermilion** (city) Lorain County
85	2086	89.1	**Parma** (city) Cuyahoga County
86	2106	89.2	**Parma Heights** (city) Cuyahoga County
87	2132	89.3	**Seven Hills** (city) Cuyahoga County
88	2203	89.6	**Trenton** (city) Butler County
89	2268	89.9	**Sharonville** (city) Hamilton County
90	2288	90.0	**Marysville** (city) Union County
90	2288	90.0	**Miamisburg** (city) Montgomery County
90	2288	90.0	**Struthers** (city) Mahoning County
90	2288	90.0	**Willowick** (city) Lake County
94	2336	90.2	**Findlay** (city) Hancock County
95	2473	90.7	**Wooster** (city) Wayne County
96	2497	90.8	**Mayfield Heights** (city) Cuyahoga County
97	2520	90.9	**Vandalia** (city) Montgomery County
98	2555	91.0	**Dover** (city) Tuscarawas County
98	2555	91.0	**Middleburg Heights** (city) Cuyahoga County
100	2586	91.1	**Austintown** (CDP) Mahoning County
100	2586	91.1	**White Oak** (CDP) Hamilton County
102	2633	91.3	**Pataskala** (city) Licking County
103	2665	91.4	**Norton** (city) Summit County
104	2692	91.5	**Lebanon** (city) Warren County
105	2713	91.6	**Huber Heights** (city) Montgomery County
106	2751	91.7	**Fairfield** (city) Butler County
106	2751	91.7	**Kent** (city) Portage County
106	2751	91.7	**Wickliffe** (city) Lake County
109	2773	91.8	**Berea** (city) Cuyahoga County
110	2858	92.1	**Brunswick** (city) Medina County
110	2858	92.1	**Reynoldsburg** (city) Franklin County
112	2889	92.2	**Lakewood** (city) Cuyahoga County
112	2889	92.2	**Richmond Heights** (city) Cuyahoga County
114	2923	92.3	**Finneytown** (CDP) Hamilton County
114	2923	92.3	**Green** (city) Summit County
114	2923	92.3	**Oxford** (city) Butler County
117	2955	92.4	**Blue Ash** (city) Hamilton County
117	2955	92.4	**Delaware** (city) Delaware County
117	2955	92.4	**New Franklin** (city) Summit County
117	2955	92.4	**Wadsworth** (city) Medina County
121	2987	92.5	**Bridgetown** (CDP) Hamilton County
121	2987	92.5	**Streetsboro** (city) Portage County
121	2987	92.5	**Tallmadge** (city) Summit County
124	3028	92.6	**Amherst** (city) Lorain County
125	3062	92.7	**Boardman** (CDP) Mahoning County
125	3062	92.7	**North Olmsted** (city) Cuyahoga County
127	3125	92.9	**Dent** (CDP) Hamilton County
127	3125	92.9	**Monroe** (city) Butler County
129	3163	93.0	**North Ridgeville** (city) Lorain County
130	3189	93.1	**Willoughby** (city) Lake County
131	3258	93.3	**Twinsburg** (city) Summit County
132	3288	93.4	**Cuyahoga Falls** (city) Summit County
133	3356	93.6	**Medina** (city) Medina County
134	3393	93.7	**Bowling Green** (city) Wood County
134	3393	93.7	**South Euclid** (city) Cuyahoga County
136	3433	93.8	**Clayton** (city) Montgomery County
136	3433	93.8	**North Canton** (city) Stark County
138	3465	93.9	**Kettering** (city) Montgomery County
138	3465	93.9	**Lyndhurst** (city) Cuyahoga County
140	3497	94.0	**Cleveland Heights** (city) Cuyahoga County
140	3497	94.0	**Loveland** (city) Hamilton County
140	3497	94.0	**Mack** (CDP) Hamilton County
143	3539	94.1	**Grove City** (city) Franklin County
143	3539	94.1	**Stow** (city) Summit County
145	3614	94.3	**Athens** (city) Athens County
145	3614	94.3	**Beachwood** (city) Cuyahoga County
145	3614	94.3	**North Royalton** (city) Cuyahoga County
148	3653	94.4	**Brecksville** (city) Cuyahoga County
148	3653	94.4	**Englewood** (city) Montgomery County
150	3687	94.5	**Broadview Heights** (city) Cuyahoga County

Note: *The state column ranks the top/bottom 150 places from all places in the state with population of 10,000 or more. The national column ranks the top/bottom 150 places from all places in the country with population of 10,000 or more. Places that are unincorporated were not considered in the rankings. Please refer to the User Guide for additional information.*

Educational Attainment: Bachelor's Degree or Higher

Top 150 Places Ranked in *Descending* Order

State Rank	Nat'l Rank	Percent	Place
1	80	73.4	**Dublin** (city) Franklin County
2	85	72.9	**Upper Arlington** (city) Franklin County
3	113	70.6	**Powell** (city) Delaware County
4	117	70.4	**Montgomery** (city) Hamilton County
5	129	69.2	**Bexley** (city) Franklin County
6	141	68.4	**Hudson** (city) Summit County
7	175	66.5	**Worthington** (city) Franklin County
8	202	65.3	**Shaker Heights** (city) Cuyahoga County
9	230	64.1	**University Heights** (city) Cuyahoga County
10	242	63.7	**Athens** (city) Athens County
11	337	59.8	**Oxford** (city) Butler County
12	381	57.9	**Beachwood** (city) Cuyahoga County
13	420	56.6	**Solon** (city) Cuyahoga County
14	437	56.2	**Bay Village** (city) Cuyahoga County
15	488	55.1	**Rocky River** (city) Cuyahoga County
16	511	54.5	**Blue Ash** (city) Hamilton County
17	534	54.0	**Mason** (city) Warren County
18	585	52.4	**Westlake** (city) Cuyahoga County
19	611	51.8	**Westerville** (city) Franklin County
20	636	51.3	**Avon** (city) Lorain County
20	636	51.3	**Brecksville** (city) Cuyahoga County
22	675	50.3	**Springboro** (city) Warren County
23	678	50.2	**Cleveland Heights** (city) Cuyahoga County
24	683	50.1	**Avon Lake** (city) Lorain County
25	710	49.5	**Beavercreek** (city) Greene County
25	710	49.5	**Forestville** (CDP) Hamilton County
27	792	47.9	**Aurora** (city) Portage County
28	835	47.0	**Gahanna** (city) Franklin County
29	883	46.0	**Hilliard** (city) Franklin County
29	883	46.0	**Perrysburg** (city) Wood County
31	928	45.2	**Centerville** (city) Montgomery County
31	928	45.2	**Lyndhurst** (city) Cuyahoga County
33	977	44.3	**Twinsburg** (city) Summit County
34	989	44.1	**Broadview Heights** (city) Cuyahoga County
35	1035	43.3	**Loveland** (city) Hamilton County
36	1055	43.0	**Strongsville** (city) Cuyahoga County
37	1108	42.0	**Bowling Green** (city) Wood County
37	1108	42.0	**Kent** (city) Portage County
39	1187	40.7	**Lakewood** (city) Cuyahoga County
40	1209	40.4	**Sylvania** (city) Lucas County
41	1219	40.3	**Richmond Heights** (city) Cuyahoga County
42	1245	40.0	**Stow** (city) Summit County
43	1281	39.5	**Macedonia** (city) Summit County
44	1330	38.8	**Pickerington** (city) Fairfield County
44	1330	38.8	**South Euclid** (city) Cuyahoga County
46	1374	38.2	**Mayfield Heights** (city) Cuyahoga County
46	1374	38.2	**Monfort Heights** (CDP) Hamilton County
48	1408	37.8	**Fairview Park** (city) Cuyahoga County
49	1649	35.0	**Dent** (CDP) Hamilton County
49	1649	35.0	**Mack** (CDP) Hamilton County
51	1705	34.4	**North Royalton** (city) Cuyahoga County
52	1723	34.2	**Delaware** (city) Delaware County
52	1723	34.2	**Seven Hills** (city) Cuyahoga County
54	1800	33.5	**Green** (city) Summit County
55	1807	33.3	**Clayton** (city) Montgomery County
56	1831	33.1	**Columbus** (city) Franklin County
57	1874	32.7	**North Canton** (city) Stark County
58	1913	32.3	**Maumee** (city) Lucas County
59	1926	32.1	**Middleburg Heights** (city) Cuyahoga County
60	1935	32.0	**Wadsworth** (city) Medina County
61	1972	31.7	**Medina** (city) Medina County
62	1976	31.6	**Finneytown** (CDP) Hamilton County
63	1989	31.5	**Cincinnati** (city) Hamilton County
64	2022	31.1	**Kettering** (city) Montgomery County
65	2065	30.7	**Berea** (city) Cuyahoga County
65	2065	30.7	**Sharonville** (city) Hamilton County
67	2074	30.6	**Monroe** (city) Butler County
68	2090	30.5	**North Olmsted** (city) Cuyahoga County
69	2103	30.4	**Cuyahoga Falls** (city) Summit County
70	2144	30.0	**Lebanon** (city) Warren County
71	2158	29.9	**Reynoldsburg** (city) Franklin County
72	2275	28.9	**Mentor** (city) Lake County
72	2275	28.9	**Wooster** (city) Wayne County
74	2316	28.5	**Tallmadge** (city) Summit County
75	2327	28.4	**Springdale** (city) Hamilton County
76	2359	28.1	**Pataskala** (city) Licking County
77	2404	27.7	**Ashland** (city) Ashland County
77	2404	27.7	**Englewood** (city) Montgomery County
77	2404	27.7	**White Oak** (CDP) Hamilton County
80	2418	27.6	**Willoughby** (city) Lake County
81	2442	27.3	**Grove City** (city) Franklin County
81	2442	27.3	**North Ridgeville** (city) Lorain County
83	2467	27.1	**Boardman** (CDP) Mahoning County
83	2467	27.1	**Findlay** (city) Hancock County
85	2542	26.5	**Fairfield** (city) Butler County
86	2605	26.0	**Amherst** (city) Lorain County
87	2698	25.2	**Fairborn** (city) Greene County
88	2711	25.1	**Bridgetown** (CDP) Hamilton County
89	2722	25.0	**Marysville** (city) Union County
90	2795	24.4	**Forest Park** (city) Hamilton County
91	2807	24.3	**Streetsboro** (city) Portage County
92	2819	24.2	**Norwood** (city) Hamilton County
93	2922	23.4	**Dover** (city) Tuscarawas County
94	2932	23.3	**Marietta** (city) Washington County
95	3025	22.5	**Miamisburg** (city) Montgomery County
95	3025	22.5	**Troy** (city) Miami County
97	3069	22.1	**Huber Heights** (city) Montgomery County
98	3111	21.8	**New Franklin** (city) Summit County
99	3176	21.3	**Norton** (city) Summit County
99	3176	21.3	**Vandalia** (city) Montgomery County
101	3218	21.0	**Parma Heights** (city) Cuyahoga County
102	3229	20.9	**Wickliffe** (city) Lake County
103	3253	20.8	**Brunswick** (city) Medina County
104	3282	20.6	**Steubenville** (city) Jefferson County
105	3325	20.3	**Mount Vernon** (city) Knox County
106	3339	20.2	**Akron** (city) Summit County
107	3412	19.6	**Parma** (city) Cuyahoga County
108	3429	19.5	**Defiance** (city) Defiance County
108	3429	19.5	**Euclid** (city) Cuyahoga County
110	3472	19.2	**Bedford** (city) Cuyahoga County
111	3507	19.0	**Willowick** (city) Lake County
112	3541	18.7	**Oregon** (city) Lucas County
113	3590	18.4	**Chillicothe** (city) Ross County
113	3590	18.4	**Vermilion** (city) Lorain County
115	3606	18.3	**Austintown** (CDP) Mahoning County
115	3606	18.3	**Xenia** (city) Greene County
117	3672	17.9	**Heath** (city) Licking County
118	3735	17.4	**New Philadelphia** (city) Tuscarawas County
118	3735	17.4	**Portsmouth** (city) Scioto County
120	3752	17.3	**Tiffin** (city) Seneca County
121	3762	17.2	**Toledo** (city) Lucas County
122	3815	16.8	**Celina** (city) Mercer County
122	3815	16.8	**Ironton** (city) Lawrence County
124	3837	16.6	**Bedford Heights** (city) Cuyahoga County
125	3845	16.5	**Eastlake** (city) Lake County
125	3845	16.5	**Lancaster** (city) Fairfield County
127	3858	16.4	**Dayton** (city) Montgomery County
128	3870	16.3	**Warrensville Heights** (city) Cuyahoga County
129	3895	16.1	**Urbana** (city) Champaign County
130	3907	16.0	**Bellefontaine** (city) Logan County
131	3938	15.8	**Niles** (city) Trumbull County
132	3963	15.6	**Brooklyn** (city) Cuyahoga County
132	3963	15.6	**Reading** (city) Hamilton County
134	3977	15.5	**Middletown** (city) Butler County
134	3977	15.5	**West Carrollton** (city) Montgomery County
136	3989	15.4	**Newark** (city) Licking County
137	4021	15.2	**Riverside** (city) Montgomery County
137	4021	15.2	**Van Wert** (city) Van Wert County
139	4038	15.0	**Elyria** (city) Lorain County
139	4038	15.0	**Washington Court House** (city) Fayette County
141	4054	14.9	**Cleveland** (city) Cuyahoga County
141	4054	14.9	**Coshocton** (city) Coshocton County
141	4054	14.9	**Painesville** (city) Lake County
141	4054	14.9	**Springfield** (city) Clark County
145	4075	14.8	**Hamilton** (city) Butler County
146	4108	14.6	**Sandusky** (city) Erie County
147	4132	14.4	**Norwalk** (city) Huron County
147	4132	14.4	**Trotwood** (city) Montgomery County
149	4140	14.3	**Massillon** (city) Stark County
150	4158	14.1	**Wilmington** (city) Clinton County

Note: *The state column ranks the top/bottom 150 places from all places in the state with population of 10,000 or more. The national column ranks the top/bottom 150 places from all places in the country with population of 10,000 or more. Places that are unincorporated were not considered in the rankings. Please refer to the User Guide for additional information.*

Educational Attainment: Bachelor's Degree or Higher

Top 150 Places Ranked in *Ascending* Order

State Rank	Nat'l Rank	Percent	Place
1	52	6.6	**East Liverpool** (city) Columbiana County
2	105	8.9	**Ashtabula** (city) Ashtabula County
3	128	9.4	**Fostoria** (city) Seneca County
4	138	9.7	**Conneaut** (city) Ashtabula County
5	143	9.8	**Whitehall** (city) Franklin County
6	149	9.9	**Galion** (city) Crawford County
6	149	9.9	**Marion** (city) Marion County
8	165	10.1	**Bucyrus** (city) Crawford County
9	193	10.4	**Northbrook** (CDP) Hamilton County
9	193	10.4	**Piqua** (city) Miami County
11	218	10.8	**Lima** (city) Allen County
12	231	11.0	**Greenville** (city) Darke County
12	231	11.0	**Trenton** (city) Butler County
12	231	11.0	**Youngstown** (city) Mahoning County
15	240	11.1	**East Cleveland** (city) Cuyahoga County
15	240	11.1	**Zanesville** (city) Muskingum County
17	254	11.3	**Brook Park** (city) Cuyahoga County
18	260	11.4	**Barberton** (city) Summit County
18	260	11.4	**Franklin** (city) Warren County
20	276	11.6	**Sidney** (city) Shelby County
21	295	11.8	**Lorain** (city) Lorain County
22	308	12.0	**Fremont** (city) Sandusky County
23	314	12.1	**Warren** (city) Trumbull County
24	328	12.3	**Salem** (city) Columbiana County
25	340	12.4	**Mansfield** (city) Richland County
26	378	12.8	**Struthers** (city) Mahoning County
27	414	13.2	**Ravenna** (city) Portage County
28	426	13.3	**Cambridge** (city) Guernsey County
29	430	13.4	**Circleville** (city) Pickaway County
30	440	13.5	**Alliance** (city) Stark County
31	456	13.7	**Garfield Heights** (city) Cuyahoga County
32	461	13.8	**Canton** (city) Stark County
33	480	14.0	**Maple Heights** (city) Cuyahoga County
34	492	14.1	**Wilmington** (city) Clinton County
35	510	14.3	**Massillon** (city) Stark County
36	517	14.4	**Norwalk** (city) Huron County
36	517	14.4	**Trotwood** (city) Montgomery County
38	536	14.6	**Sandusky** (city) Erie County
39	564	14.8	**Hamilton** (city) Butler County
40	582	14.9	**Cleveland** (city) Cuyahoga County
40	582	14.9	**Coshocton** (city) Coshocton County
40	582	14.9	**Painesville** (city) Lake County
40	582	14.9	**Springfield** (city) Clark County
44	603	15.0	**Elyria** (city) Lorain County
44	603	15.0	**Washington Court House** (city) Fayette County
46	629	15.2	**Riverside** (city) Montgomery County
46	629	15.2	**Van Wert** (city) Van Wert County
48	649	15.4	**Newark** (city) Licking County
49	668	15.5	**Middletown** (city) Butler County
49	668	15.5	**West Carrollton** (city) Montgomery County
51	680	15.6	**Brooklyn** (city) Cuyahoga County
51	680	15.6	**Reading** (city) Hamilton County
53	703	15.8	**Niles** (city) Trumbull County
54	733	16.0	**Bellefontaine** (city) Logan County
55	750	16.1	**Urbana** (city) Champaign County
56	774	16.3	**Warrensville Heights** (city) Cuyahoga County
57	787	16.4	**Dayton** (city) Montgomery County
58	799	16.5	**Eastlake** (city) Lake County
58	799	16.5	**Lancaster** (city) Fairfield County
60	812	16.6	**Bedford Heights** (city) Cuyahoga County
61	829	16.8	**Celina** (city) Mercer County
61	829	16.8	**Ironton** (city) Lawrence County
63	881	17.2	**Toledo** (city) Lucas County
64	895	17.3	**Tiffin** (city) Seneca County
65	905	17.4	**New Philadelphia** (city) Tuscarawas County
65	905	17.4	**Portsmouth** (city) Scioto County
67	972	17.9	**Heath** (city) Licking County
68	1042	18.3	**Austintown** (CDP) Mahoning County
68	1042	18.3	**Xenia** (city) Greene County
70	1051	18.4	**Chillicothe** (city) Ross County
70	1051	18.4	**Vermilion** (city) Lorain County
72	1100	18.7	**Oregon** (city) Lucas County
73	1141	19.0	**Willowick** (city) Lake County
74	1169	19.2	**Bedford** (city) Cuyahoga County
75	1212	19.5	**Defiance** (city) Defiance County
75	1212	19.5	**Euclid** (city) Cuyahoga County
77	1228	19.6	**Parma** (city) Cuyahoga County
78	1304	20.2	**Akron** (city) Summit County
79	1318	20.3	**Mount Vernon** (city) Knox County
80	1356	20.6	**Steubenville** (city) Jefferson County
81	1385	20.8	**Brunswick** (city) Medina County
82	1404	20.9	**Wickliffe** (city) Lake County
83	1428	21.0	**Parma Heights** (city) Cuyahoga County
84	1470	21.3	**Norton** (city) Summit County
84	1470	21.3	**Vandalia** (city) Montgomery County
86	1537	21.8	**New Franklin** (city) Summit County
87	1571	22.1	**Huber Heights** (city) Montgomery County
88	1619	22.5	**Miamisburg** (city) Montgomery County
88	1619	22.5	**Troy** (city) Miami County
90	1711	23.3	**Marietta** (city) Washington County
91	1725	23.4	**Dover** (city) Tuscarawas County
92	1822	24.2	**Norwood** (city) Hamilton County
93	1838	24.3	**Streetsboro** (city) Portage County
94	1850	24.4	**Forest Park** (city) Hamilton County
95	1920	25.0	**Marysville** (city) Union County
96	1935	25.1	**Bridgetown** (CDP) Hamilton County
97	1946	25.2	**Fairborn** (city) Greene County
98	2039	26.0	**Amherst** (city) Lorain County
99	2095	26.5	**Fairfield** (city) Butler County
100	2173	27.1	**Boardman** (CDP) Mahoning County
100	2173	27.1	**Findlay** (city) Hancock County
102	2197	27.3	**Grove City** (city) Franklin County
102	2197	27.3	**North Ridgeville** (city) Lorain County
104	2232	27.6	**Willoughby** (city) Lake County
105	2239	27.7	**Ashland** (city) Ashland County
105	2239	27.7	**Englewood** (city) Montgomery County
105	2239	27.7	**White Oak** (CDP) Hamilton County
108	2291	28.1	**Pataskala** (city) Licking County
109	2318	28.4	**Springdale** (city) Hamilton County
110	2330	28.5	**Tallmadge** (city) Summit County
111	2366	28.9	**Mentor** (city) Lake County
111	2366	28.9	**Wooster** (city) Wayne County
113	2483	29.9	**Reynoldsburg** (city) Franklin County
114	2499	30.0	**Lebanon** (city) Warren County
115	2548	30.4	**Cuyahoga Falls** (city) Summit County
116	2554	30.5	**North Olmsted** (city) Cuyahoga County
117	2567	30.6	**Monroe** (city) Butler County
118	2583	30.7	**Berea** (city) Cuyahoga County
118	2583	30.7	**Sharonville** (city) Hamilton County
120	2625	31.1	**Kettering** (city) Montgomery County
121	2664	31.5	**Cincinnati** (city) Hamilton County
122	2668	31.6	**Finneytown** (CDP) Hamilton County
123	2681	31.7	**Medina** (city) Medina County
124	2709	32.0	**Wadsworth** (city) Medina County
125	2722	32.1	**Middleburg Heights** (city) Cuyahoga County
126	2738	32.3	**Maumee** (city) Lucas County
127	2768	32.7	**North Canton** (city) Stark County
128	2816	33.1	**Columbus** (city) Franklin County
129	2840	33.3	**Clayton** (city) Montgomery County
130	2854	33.5	**Green** (city) Summit County
131	2922	34.2	**Delaware** (city) Delaware County
131	2922	34.2	**Seven Hills** (city) Cuyahoga County
133	2942	34.4	**North Royalton** (city) Cuyahoga County
134	2999	35.0	**Dent** (CDP) Hamilton County
134	2999	35.0	**Mack** (CDP) Hamilton County
136	3239	37.8	**Fairview Park** (city) Cuyahoga County
137	3274	38.2	**Mayfield Heights** (city) Cuyahoga County
137	3274	38.2	**Monfort Heights** (CDP) Hamilton County
139	3320	38.8	**Pickerington** (city) Fairfield County
139	3320	38.8	**South Euclid** (city) Cuyahoga County
141	3369	39.5	**Macedonia** (city) Summit County
142	3405	40.0	**Stow** (city) Summit County
143	3428	40.3	**Richmond Heights** (city) Cuyahoga County
144	3438	40.4	**Sylvania** (city) Lucas County
145	3461	40.7	**Lakewood** (city) Cuyahoga County
146	3540	42.0	**Bowling Green** (city) Wood County
146	3540	42.0	**Kent** (city) Portage County
148	3599	43.0	**Strongsville** (city) Cuyahoga County
149	3615	43.3	**Loveland** (city) Hamilton County
150	3663	44.1	**Broadview Heights** (city) Cuyahoga County

Note: *The state column ranks the top/bottom 150 places from all places in the state with population of 10,000 or more. The national column ranks the top/bottom 150 places from all places in the country with population of 10,000 or more. Places that are unincorporated were not considered in the rankings. Please refer to the User Guide for additional information.*

Educational Attainment: Graduate/Professional Degree or Higher

Top 150 Places Ranked in *Descending* Order

State Rank	Nat'l Rank	Percent	Place
1	58	40.1	**Athens** (city) Athens County
2	68	38.7	**Shaker Heights** (city) Cuyahoga County
3	145	33.9	**University Heights** (city) Cuyahoga County
4	151	33.7	**Upper Arlington** (city) Franklin County
5	191	31.8	**Oxford** (city) Butler County
6	209	31.1	**Montgomery** (city) Hamilton County
7	218	30.7	**Bexley** (city) Franklin County
8	220	30.6	**Beachwood** (city) Cuyahoga County
9	248	29.7	**Worthington** (city) Franklin County
10	288	28.5	**Dublin** (city) Franklin County
11	295	28.3	**Hudson** (city) Summit County
12	300	28.1	**Powell** (city) Delaware County
13	331	27.5	**Blue Ash** (city) Hamilton County
14	334	27.4	**Solon** (city) Cuyahoga County
15	369	26.4	**Cleveland Heights** (city) Cuyahoga County
16	382	26.0	**Beavercreek** (city) Greene County
17	489	23.3	**Mason** (city) Warren County
18	497	23.1	**Brecksville** (city) Cuyahoga County
19	555	21.9	**Bay Village** (city) Cuyahoga County
20	586	21.5	**Bowling Green** (city) Wood County
21	624	21.0	**Avon** (city) Lorain County
22	634	20.9	**Westlake** (city) Cuyahoga County
23	643	20.8	**Rocky River** (city) Cuyahoga County
24	734	19.8	**Forestville** (CDP) Hamilton County
25	753	19.6	**Springboro** (city) Warren County
26	771	19.4	**Centerville** (city) Montgomery County
27	792	19.1	**Broadview Heights** (city) Cuyahoga County
28	825	18.8	**Avon Lake** (city) Lorain County
29	850	18.5	**Aurora** (city) Portage County
30	900	18.0	**Westerville** (city) Franklin County
31	919	17.8	**Kent** (city) Portage County
32	938	17.6	**Perrysburg** (city) Wood County
33	1071	16.5	**Hilliard** (city) Franklin County
34	1122	16.1	**Gahanna** (city) Franklin County
34	1122	16.1	**Strongsville** (city) Cuyahoga County
36	1134	16.0	**South Euclid** (city) Cuyahoga County
36	1134	16.0	**Sylvania** (city) Lucas County
38	1170	15.7	**Loveland** (city) Hamilton County
39	1199	15.5	**Mayfield Heights** (city) Cuyahoga County
40	1218	15.3	**Richmond Heights** (city) Cuyahoga County
40	1218	15.3	**Twinsburg** (city) Summit County
42	1232	15.2	**Lyndhurst** (city) Cuyahoga County
42	1232	15.2	**Macedonia** (city) Summit County
44	1342	14.3	**Clayton** (city) Montgomery County
45	1389	14.0	**Lakewood** (city) Cuyahoga County
46	1428	13.8	**Middleburg Heights** (city) Cuyahoga County
47	1460	13.6	**Pickerington** (city) Fairfield County
48	1476	13.5	**Fairview Park** (city) Cuyahoga County
48	1476	13.5	**North Royalton** (city) Cuyahoga County
50	1497	13.4	**Stow** (city) Summit County
51	1510	13.3	**Monfort Heights** (CDP) Hamilton County
52	1579	12.9	**Cincinnati** (city) Hamilton County
53	1598	12.8	**Ashland** (city) Ashland County
54	1617	12.7	**Sharonville** (city) Hamilton County
55	1643	12.6	**Kettering** (city) Montgomery County
56	1692	12.3	**Delaware** (city) Delaware County
57	1791	11.9	**Maumee** (city) Lucas County
58	1853	11.6	**Wooster** (city) Wayne County
59	1870	11.5	**Green** (city) Summit County
59	1870	11.5	**North Canton** (city) Stark County
61	1960	11.1	**Columbus** (city) Franklin County
62	1985	11.0	**Amherst** (city) Lorain County
63	2008	10.9	**Fairborn** (city) Greene County
64	2028	10.8	**Seven Hills** (city) Cuyahoga County
65	2082	10.6	**Berea** (city) Cuyahoga County
65	2082	10.6	**Mack** (CDP) Hamilton County
67	2127	10.4	**Wadsworth** (city) Medina County
68	2213	10.1	**Englewood** (city) Montgomery County
68	2213	10.1	**Findlay** (city) Hancock County
70	2241	10.0	**Finneytown** (CDP) Hamilton County
71	2271	9.9	**Lebanon** (city) Warren County
72	2317	9.7	**North Olmsted** (city) Cuyahoga County
73	2345	9.6	**Cuyahoga Falls** (city) Summit County
73	2345	9.6	**Mentor** (city) Lake County
73	2345	9.6	**Tallmadge** (city) Summit County
76	2374	9.5	**Dent** (CDP) Hamilton County
77	2445	9.3	**Medina** (city) Medina County
78	2501	9.1	**Boardman** (CDP) Mahoning County
78	2501	9.1	**White Oak** (CDP) Hamilton County
78	2501	9.1	**Willoughby** (city) Lake County
81	2534	9.0	**Vandalia** (city) Montgomery County
82	2565	8.9	**Pataskala** (city) Licking County
83	2586	8.8	**Miamisburg** (city) Montgomery County
83	2586	8.8	**Springdale** (city) Hamilton County
85	2615	8.7	**Celina** (city) Mercer County
85	2615	8.7	**North Ridgeville** (city) Lorain County
87	2646	8.6	**Grove City** (city) Franklin County
87	2646	8.6	**Huber Heights** (city) Montgomery County
87	2646	8.6	**Mount Vernon** (city) Knox County
90	2683	8.5	**Fairfield** (city) Butler County
91	2716	8.4	**Reynoldsburg** (city) Franklin County
92	2814	8.1	**Vermilion** (city) Lorain County
93	2851	8.0	**Dover** (city) Tuscarawas County
93	2851	8.0	**Forest Park** (city) Hamilton County
95	2917	7.8	**Marietta** (city) Washington County
96	2960	7.7	**Bridgetown** (CDP) Hamilton County
96	2960	7.7	**Steubenville** (city) Jefferson County
98	3022	7.5	**Streetsboro** (city) Portage County
99	3128	7.2	**Chillicothe** (city) Ross County
99	3128	7.2	**Defiance** (city) Defiance County
99	3128	7.2	**Troy** (city) Miami County
102	3171	7.1	**Norwood** (city) Hamilton County
102	3171	7.1	**Oregon** (city) Lucas County
104	3197	7.0	**Bellefontaine** (city) Logan County
105	3266	6.8	**New Philadelphia** (city) Tuscarawas County
105	3266	6.8	**Reading** (city) Hamilton County
105	3266	6.8	**Xenia** (city) Greene County
108	3297	6.7	**Monroe** (city) Butler County
108	3297	6.7	**Norton** (city) Summit County
110	3330	6.6	**Akron** (city) Summit County
110	3330	6.6	**Euclid** (city) Cuyahoga County
110	3330	6.6	**Portsmouth** (city) Scioto County
113	3373	6.5	**Dayton** (city) Montgomery County
113	3373	6.5	**Ironton** (city) Lawrence County
113	3373	6.5	**Wickliffe** (city) Lake County
116	3449	6.3	**Marysville** (city) Union County
117	3486	6.2	**Austintown** (CDP) Mahoning County
117	3486	6.2	**Tiffin** (city) Seneca County
117	3486	6.2	**Van Wert** (city) Van Wert County
120	3519	6.1	**Bedford Heights** (city) Cuyahoga County
120	3519	6.1	**Norwalk** (city) Huron County
120	3519	6.1	**Ravenna** (city) Portage County
123	3558	6.0	**Parma** (city) Cuyahoga County
124	3593	5.9	**Toledo** (city) Lucas County
125	3629	5.8	**Brunswick** (city) Medina County
125	3629	5.8	**Eastlake** (city) Lake County
125	3629	5.8	**Parma Heights** (city) Cuyahoga County
125	3629	5.8	**Riverside** (city) Montgomery County
129	3666	5.7	**New Franklin** (city) Summit County
130	3697	5.6	**Cleveland** (city) Cuyahoga County
130	3697	5.6	**Lancaster** (city) Fairfield County
130	3697	5.6	**Springfield** (city) Clark County
130	3697	5.6	**Trotwood** (city) Montgomery County
134	3765	5.4	**Bedford** (city) Cuyahoga County
134	3765	5.4	**Elyria** (city) Lorain County
134	3765	5.4	**Sidney** (city) Shelby County
137	3794	5.3	**Coshocton** (city) Coshocton County
137	3794	5.3	**Heath** (city) Licking County
137	3794	5.3	**Willowick** (city) Lake County
140	3829	5.2	**Cambridge** (city) Guernsey County
140	3829	5.2	**Sandusky** (city) Erie County
142	3866	5.1	**Wilmington** (city) Clinton County
143	3899	5.0	**Circleville** (city) Pickaway County
144	3931	4.9	**Brooklyn** (city) Cuyahoga County
144	3931	4.9	**Garfield Heights** (city) Cuyahoga County
146	3978	4.8	**Washington Court House** (city) Fayette County
147	4011	4.7	**Massillon** (city) Stark County
148	4037	4.6	**Galion** (city) Crawford County
148	4037	4.6	**Greenville** (city) Darke County
148	4037	4.6	**Hamilton** (city) Butler County

Note: *The state column ranks the top/bottom 150 places from all places in the state with population of 10,000 or more. The national column ranks the top/bottom 150 places from all places in the country with population of 10,000 or more. Places that are unincorporated were not considered in the rankings. Please refer to the User Guide for additional information.*

Educational Attainment: Graduate/Professional Degree or Higher

Top 150 Places Ranked in *Ascending* Order

State Rank	Nat'l Rank	Percent	Place
1	86	2.1	**Northbrook** (CDP) Hamilton County
2	120	2.4	**Barberton** (city) Summit County
3	133	2.5	**Whitehall** (city) Franklin County
4	163	2.7	**Franklin** (city) Warren County
5	180	2.8	**Brook Park** (city) Cuyahoga County
6	205	3.0	**Bucyrus** (city) Crawford County
6	205	3.0	**Fostoria** (city) Seneca County
8	304	3.5	**Conneaut** (city) Ashtabula County
8	304	3.5	**East Liverpool** (city) Columbiana County
8	304	3.5	**Warren** (city) Trumbull County
11	326	3.6	**Trenton** (city) Butler County
11	326	3.6	**West Carrollton** (city) Montgomery County
13	378	3.8	**Piqua** (city) Miami County
14	398	3.9	**Marion** (city) Marion County
14	398	3.9	**Struthers** (city) Mahoning County
16	415	4.0	**Alliance** (city) Stark County
16	415	4.0	**Lorain** (city) Lorain County
16	415	4.0	**Youngstown** (city) Mahoning County
19	456	4.1	**Canton** (city) Stark County
19	456	4.1	**Maple Heights** (city) Cuyahoga County
19	456	4.1	**Newark** (city) Licking County
19	456	4.1	**Salem** (city) Columbiana County
19	456	4.1	**Zanesville** (city) Muskingum County
24	481	4.2	**Fremont** (city) Sandusky County
24	481	4.2	**Warrensville Heights** (city) Cuyahoga County
26	497	4.3	**Urbana** (city) Champaign County
27	551	4.5	**Ashtabula** (city) Ashtabula County
27	551	4.5	**East Cleveland** (city) Cuyahoga County
27	551	4.5	**Lima** (city) Allen County
27	551	4.5	**Painesville** (city) Lake County
31	590	4.6	**Galion** (city) Crawford County
31	590	4.6	**Greenville** (city) Darke County
31	590	4.6	**Hamilton** (city) Butler County
31	590	4.6	**Mansfield** (city) Richland County
31	590	4.6	**Middletown** (city) Butler County
31	590	4.6	**Niles** (city) Trumbull County
37	620	4.7	**Massillon** (city) Stark County
38	646	4.8	**Washington Court House** (city) Fayette County
39	679	4.9	**Brooklyn** (city) Cuyahoga County
39	679	4.9	**Garfield Heights** (city) Cuyahoga County
41	726	5.0	**Circleville** (city) Pickaway County
42	758	5.1	**Wilmington** (city) Clinton County
43	791	5.2	**Cambridge** (city) Guernsey County
43	791	5.2	**Sandusky** (city) Erie County
45	828	5.3	**Coshocton** (city) Coshocton County
45	828	5.3	**Heath** (city) Licking County
45	828	5.3	**Willowick** (city) Lake County
48	863	5.4	**Bedford** (city) Cuyahoga County
48	863	5.4	**Elyria** (city) Lorain County
48	863	5.4	**Sidney** (city) Shelby County
51	922	5.6	**Cleveland** (city) Cuyahoga County
51	922	5.6	**Lancaster** (city) Fairfield County
51	922	5.6	**Springfield** (city) Clark County
51	922	5.6	**Trotwood** (city) Montgomery County
55	960	5.7	**New Franklin** (city) Summit County
56	991	5.8	**Brunswick** (city) Medina County
56	991	5.8	**Eastlake** (city) Lake County
56	991	5.8	**Parma Heights** (city) Cuyahoga County
56	991	5.8	**Riverside** (city) Montgomery County
60	1028	5.9	**Toledo** (city) Lucas County
61	1064	6.0	**Parma** (city) Cuyahoga County
62	1099	6.1	**Bedford Heights** (city) Cuyahoga County
62	1099	6.1	**Norwalk** (city) Huron County
62	1099	6.1	**Ravenna** (city) Portage County
65	1138	6.2	**Austintown** (CDP) Mahoning County
65	1138	6.2	**Tiffin** (city) Seneca County
65	1138	6.2	**Van Wert** (city) Van Wert County
68	1171	6.3	**Marysville** (city) Union County
69	1246	6.5	**Dayton** (city) Montgomery County
69	1246	6.5	**Ironton** (city) Lawrence County
69	1246	6.5	**Wickliffe** (city) Lake County
72	1284	6.6	**Akron** (city) Summit County
72	1284	6.6	**Euclid** (city) Cuyahoga County
72	1284	6.6	**Portsmouth** (city) Scioto County
75	1327	6.7	**Monroe** (city) Butler County
75	1327	6.7	**Norton** (city) Summit County
77	1360	6.8	**New Philadelphia** (city) Tuscarawas County
77	1360	6.8	**Reading** (city) Hamilton County
77	1360	6.8	**Xenia** (city) Greene County
80	1426	7.0	**Bellefontaine** (city) Logan County
81	1460	7.1	**Norwood** (city) Hamilton County
81	1460	7.1	**Oregon** (city) Lucas County
83	1486	7.2	**Chillicothe** (city) Ross County
83	1486	7.2	**Defiance** (city) Defiance County
83	1486	7.2	**Troy** (city) Miami County
86	1602	7.5	**Streetsboro** (city) Portage County
87	1660	7.7	**Bridgetown** (CDP) Hamilton County
87	1660	7.7	**Steubenville** (city) Jefferson County
89	1697	7.8	**Marietta** (city) Washington County
90	1775	8.0	**Dover** (city) Tuscarawas County
90	1775	8.0	**Forest Park** (city) Hamilton County
92	1806	8.1	**Vermilion** (city) Lorain County
93	1908	8.4	**Reynoldsburg** (city) Franklin County
94	1941	8.5	**Fairfield** (city) Butler County
95	1974	8.6	**Grove City** (city) Franklin County
95	1974	8.6	**Huber Heights** (city) Montgomery County
95	1974	8.6	**Mount Vernon** (city) Knox County
98	2011	8.7	**Celina** (city) Mercer County
98	2011	8.7	**North Ridgeville** (city) Lorain County
100	2042	8.8	**Miamisburg** (city) Montgomery County
100	2042	8.8	**Springdale** (city) Hamilton County
102	2071	8.9	**Pataskala** (city) Licking County
103	2092	9.0	**Vandalia** (city) Montgomery County
104	2123	9.1	**Boardman** (CDP) Mahoning County
104	2123	9.1	**White Oak** (CDP) Hamilton County
104	2123	9.1	**Willoughby** (city) Lake County
107	2186	9.3	**Medina** (city) Medina County
108	2245	9.5	**Dent** (CDP) Hamilton County
109	2283	9.6	**Cuyahoga Falls** (city) Summit County
109	2283	9.6	**Mentor** (city) Lake County
109	2283	9.6	**Tallmadge** (city) Summit County
112	2312	9.7	**North Olmsted** (city) Cuyahoga County
113	2363	9.9	**Lebanon** (city) Warren County
114	2386	10.0	**Finneytown** (CDP) Hamilton County
115	2416	10.1	**Englewood** (city) Montgomery County
115	2416	10.1	**Findlay** (city) Hancock County
117	2509	10.4	**Wadsworth** (city) Medina County
118	2556	10.6	**Berea** (city) Cuyahoga County
118	2556	10.6	**Mack** (CDP) Hamilton County
120	2598	10.8	**Seven Hills** (city) Cuyahoga County
121	2629	10.9	**Fairborn** (city) Greene County
122	2649	11.0	**Amherst** (city) Lorain County
123	2672	11.1	**Columbus** (city) Franklin County
124	2760	11.5	**Green** (city) Summit County
124	2760	11.5	**North Canton** (city) Stark County
126	2787	11.6	**Wooster** (city) Wayne County
127	2844	11.9	**Maumee** (city) Lucas County
128	2938	12.3	**Delaware** (city) Delaware County
129	2991	12.6	**Kettering** (city) Montgomery County
130	3014	12.7	**Sharonville** (city) Hamilton County
131	3040	12.8	**Ashland** (city) Ashland County
132	3059	12.9	**Cincinnati** (city) Hamilton County
133	3130	13.3	**Monfort Heights** (CDP) Hamilton County
134	3147	13.4	**Stow** (city) Summit County
135	3160	13.5	**Fairview Park** (city) Cuyahoga County
135	3160	13.5	**North Royalton** (city) Cuyahoga County
137	3181	13.6	**Pickerington** (city) Fairfield County
138	3214	13.8	**Middleburg Heights** (city) Cuyahoga County
139	3245	14.0	**Lakewood** (city) Cuyahoga County
140	3297	14.3	**Clayton** (city) Montgomery County
141	3411	15.2	**Lyndhurst** (city) Cuyahoga County
141	3411	15.2	**Macedonia** (city) Summit County
143	3425	15.3	**Richmond Heights** (city) Cuyahoga County
143	3425	15.3	**Twinsburg** (city) Summit County
145	3448	15.5	**Mayfield Heights** (city) Cuyahoga County
146	3475	15.7	**Loveland** (city) Hamilton County
147	3512	16.0	**South Euclid** (city) Cuyahoga County
147	3512	16.0	**Sylvania** (city) Lucas County
149	3523	16.1	**Gahanna** (city) Franklin County
149	3523	16.1	**Strongsville** (city) Cuyahoga County

Note: *The state column ranks the top/bottom 150 places from all places in the state with population of 10,000 or more. The national column ranks the top/bottom 150 places from all places in the country with population of 10,000 or more. Places that are unincorporated were not considered in the rankings. Please refer to the User Guide for additional information.*

Homeownership Rate

Top 150 Places Ranked in *Descending* Order

State Rank	Nat'l Rank	Percent	Place
1	5	96.4	**Mack** (CDP) Hamilton County
2	23	94.7	**Seven Hills** (city) Cuyahoga County
3	36	94.1	**Powell** (city) Delaware County
4	91	92.2	**Macedonia** (city) Summit County
5	125	91.5	**Bay Village** (city) Cuyahoga County
6	204	90.0	**North Ridgeville** (city) Lorain County
7	217	89.7	**Hudson** (city) Summit County
8	344	87.7	**Brecksville** (city) Cuyahoga County
9	389	87.2	**New Franklin** (city) Summit County
10	405	86.9	**Solon** (city) Cuyahoga County
11	430	86.5	**Montgomery** (city) Hamilton County
12	470	85.9	**Lyndhurst** (city) Cuyahoga County
13	474	85.8	**Springboro** (city) Warren County
14	496	85.5	**Mentor** (city) Lake County
15	505	85.3	**Bridgetown** (CDP) Hamilton County
16	520	85.1	**Monfort Heights** (CDP) Hamilton County
17	537	84.9	**Norton** (city) Summit County
18	572	84.5	**Amherst** (city) Lorain County
19	594	84.2	**Avon** (city) Lorain County
20	656	83.5	**Mason** (city) Warren County
21	709	82.8	**Clayton** (city) Montgomery County
22	753	82.3	**Worthington** (city) Franklin County
23	763	82.2	**Avon Lake** (city) Lorain County
23	763	82.2	**Broadview Heights** (city) Cuyahoga County
25	874	81.0	**Brook Park** (city) Cuyahoga County
26	893	80.8	**Strongsville** (city) Cuyahoga County
26	893	80.8	**Upper Arlington** (city) Franklin County
28	931	80.3	**Aurora** (city) Portage County
29	950	80.2	**South Euclid** (city) Cuyahoga County
30	959	80.1	**Willowick** (city) Lake County
31	1024	79.4	**Finneytown** (CDP) Hamilton County
31	1024	79.4	**Wickliffe** (city) Lake County
33	1040	79.2	**Hilliard** (city) Franklin County
34	1046	79.1	**Dublin** (city) Franklin County
35	1101	78.6	**Green** (city) Summit County
36	1107	78.5	**Brunswick** (city) Medina County
37	1114	78.4	**Monroe** (city) Butler County
38	1143	78.1	**Vermilion** (city) Lorain County
39	1156	78.0	**Tallmadge** (city) Summit County
40	1193	77.6	**Dent** (CDP) Hamilton County
41	1204	77.4	**Pickerington** (city) Fairfield County
42	1226	77.2	**Pataskala** (city) Licking County
43	1248	77.0	**Westerville** (city) Franklin County
44	1287	76.7	**Twinsburg** (city) Summit County
45	1323	76.3	**North Olmsted** (city) Cuyahoga County
46	1390	75.6	**Bexley** (city) Franklin County
47	1442	75.0	**Gahanna** (city) Franklin County
48	1480	74.6	**Eastlake** (city) Lake County
49	1533	74.1	**Parma** (city) Cuyahoga County
50	1546	74.0	**Beavercreek** (city) Greene County
51	1559	73.8	**Englewood** (city) Montgomery County
52	1567	73.7	**Maple Heights** (city) Cuyahoga County
53	1594	73.4	**Fairview Park** (city) Cuyahoga County
54	1605	73.3	**Loveland** (city) Hamilton County
55	1638	73.0	**Struthers** (city) Mahoning County
56	1655	72.8	**Forestville** (CDP) Hamilton County
56	1655	72.8	**Maumee** (city) Lucas County
56	1655	72.8	**Middleburg Heights** (city) Cuyahoga County
59	1668	72.7	**White Oak** (CDP) Hamilton County
60	1678	72.6	**Trenton** (city) Butler County
61	1690	72.5	**Westlake** (city) Cuyahoga County
62	1700	72.4	**Wadsworth** (city) Medina County
63	1748	72.1	**Centerville** (city) Montgomery County
63	1748	72.1	**Rocky River** (city) Cuyahoga County
65	1768	72.0	**Huber Heights** (city) Montgomery County
66	1809	71.6	**North Royalton** (city) Cuyahoga County
67	1823	71.5	**Miamisburg** (city) Montgomery County
67	1823	71.5	**Oregon** (city) Lucas County
67	1823	71.5	**Sylvania** (city) Lucas County
70	1865	71.1	**Blue Ash** (city) Hamilton County
71	1923	70.5	**Perrysburg** (city) Wood County
72	1947	70.2	**Berea** (city) Cuyahoga County
73	1958	70.1	**Streetsboro** (city) Portage County
74	1987	69.8	**Northbrook** (CDP) Hamilton County
74	1987	69.8	**University Heights** (city) Cuyahoga County
76	1998	69.7	**Grove City** (city) Franklin County
77	2007	69.6	**Garfield Heights** (city) Cuyahoga County
77	2007	69.6	**Stow** (city) Summit County
79	2032	69.4	**Dover** (city) Tuscarawas County
80	2132	68.5	**Boardman** (CDP) Mahoning County
81	2215	67.7	**North Canton** (city) Stark County
82	2278	67.1	**Defiance** (city) Defiance County
83	2334	66.6	**Massillon** (city) Stark County
84	2373	66.3	**Medina** (city) Medina County
85	2381	66.2	**Celina** (city) Mercer County
85	2381	66.2	**Conneaut** (city) Ashtabula County
87	2404	66.0	**Van Wert** (city) Van Wert County
88	2416	65.9	**Austintown** (CDP) Mahoning County
89	2427	65.8	**Heath** (city) Licking County
90	2512	65.1	**Marysville** (city) Union County
91	2534	64.8	**Kettering** (city) Montgomery County
92	2577	64.3	**Vandalia** (city) Montgomery County
93	2591	64.1	**Richmond Heights** (city) Cuyahoga County
94	2611	63.9	**Shaker Heights** (city) Cuyahoga County
95	2620	63.8	**Fairfield** (city) Butler County
95	2620	63.8	**Fostoria** (city) Seneca County
97	2628	63.7	**Cuyahoga Falls** (city) Summit County
98	2647	63.5	**New Philadelphia** (city) Tuscarawas County
98	2647	63.5	**Reynoldsburg** (city) Franklin County
100	2747	62.6	**Tiffin** (city) Seneca County
101	2775	62.4	**Barberton** (city) Summit County
102	2784	62.3	**Beachwood** (city) Cuyahoga County
103	2825	61.9	**Ashland** (city) Ashland County
104	2836	61.8	**Lebanon** (city) Warren County
105	2854	61.6	**Xenia** (city) Greene County
106	2884	61.3	**Salem** (city) Columbiana County
107	2905	61.1	**Piqua** (city) Miami County
107	2905	61.1	**Willoughby** (city) Lake County
109	2923	61.0	**Sharonville** (city) Hamilton County
110	2932	60.9	**Delaware** (city) Delaware County
110	2932	60.9	**Elyria** (city) Lorain County
112	2944	60.8	**Galion** (city) Crawford County
113	2961	60.7	**Coshocton** (city) Coshocton County
114	3007	60.4	**Findlay** (city) Hancock County
115	3053	60.1	**Norwalk** (city) Huron County
116	3062	60.0	**Niles** (city) Trumbull County
117	3122	59.4	**Ironton** (city) Lawrence County
117	3122	59.4	**Parma Heights** (city) Cuyahoga County
119	3134	59.3	**Forest Park** (city) Hamilton County
119	3134	59.3	**Sidney** (city) Shelby County
121	3153	59.2	**Bucyrus** (city) Crawford County
121	3153	59.2	**Troy** (city) Miami County
123	3164	59.1	**Chillicothe** (city) Ross County
124	3174	59.0	**Greenville** (city) Darke County
125	3187	58.9	**Wooster** (city) Wayne County
126	3214	58.7	**Brooklyn** (city) Cuyahoga County
127	3279	58.2	**Youngstown** (city) Mahoning County
128	3290	58.1	**Fremont** (city) Sandusky County
129	3301	58.0	**Circleville** (city) Pickaway County
130	3323	57.8	**Lorain** (city) Lorain County
131	3335	57.7	**Lancaster** (city) Fairfield County
132	3340	57.6	**Franklin** (city) Warren County
133	3355	57.5	**Trotwood** (city) Montgomery County
134	3368	57.4	**Marion** (city) Marion County
134	3368	57.4	**Reading** (city) Hamilton County
136	3395	57.2	**Urbana** (city) Champaign County
137	3406	57.1	**Riverside** (city) Montgomery County
138	3432	56.8	**West Carrollton** (city) Montgomery County
139	3449	56.6	**Warren** (city) Trumbull County
140	3479	56.4	**Newark** (city) Licking County
141	3495	56.3	**Bedford** (city) Cuyahoga County
141	3495	56.3	**Cleveland Heights** (city) Cuyahoga County
143	3533	56.0	**Bellefontaine** (city) Logan County
143	3533	56.0	**Steubenville** (city) Jefferson County
145	3545	55.9	**Hamilton** (city) Butler County
146	3582	55.5	**Toledo** (city) Lucas County
147	3650	54.9	**Alliance** (city) Stark County
148	3666	54.7	**East Liverpool** (city) Columbiana County
148	3666	54.7	**Marietta** (city) Washington County
150	3684	54.5	**Akron** (city) Summit County

Note: *The state column ranks the top/bottom 150 places from all places in the state with population of 10,000 or more. The national column ranks the top/bottom 150 places from all places in the country with population of 10,000 or more. Places that are unincorporated were not considered in the rankings. Please refer to the User Guide for additional information.*

Homeownership Rate

Top 150 Places Ranked in *Ascending* Order

State Rank	Nat'l Rank	Percent	Place
1	44	27.5	**Athens** (city) Athens County
2	64	30.5	**Oxford** (city) Butler County
3	86	33.5	**East Cleveland** (city) Cuyahoga County
4	132	37.0	**Kent** (city) Portage County
5	178	38.9	**Cincinnati** (city) Hamilton County
6	200	39.9	**Bowling Green** (city) Wood County
7	236	41.6	**Whitehall** (city) Franklin County
8	301	43.3	**Lakewood** (city) Cuyahoga County
8	301	43.3	**Warrensville Heights** (city) Cuyahoga County
10	338	44.1	**Cleveland** (city) Cuyahoga County
11	441	47.0	**Columbus** (city) Franklin County
11	441	47.0	**Zanesville** (city) Muskingum County
13	470	47.7	**Wilmington** (city) Clinton County
14	548	49.0	**Norwood** (city) Hamilton County
15	586	49.5	**Cambridge** (city) Guernsey County
16	604	49.9	**Dayton** (city) Montgomery County
17	617	50.1	**Portsmouth** (city) Scioto County
18	626	50.2	**Painesville** (city) Lake County
19	645	50.6	**Lima** (city) Allen County
20	655	50.7	**Fairborn** (city) Greene County
21	661	50.8	**Mayfield Heights** (city) Cuyahoga County
22	676	51.0	**Bedford Heights** (city) Cuyahoga County
23	759	52.2	**Ashtabula** (city) Ashtabula County
24	767	52.3	**Washington Court House** (city) Fayette County
25	823	52.8	**Springfield** (city) Clark County
26	853	53.3	**Canton** (city) Stark County
26	853	53.3	**Mount Vernon** (city) Knox County
28	864	53.4	**Sandusky** (city) Erie County
29	907	53.8	**Middletown** (city) Butler County
30	920	54.0	**Euclid** (city) Cuyahoga County
30	920	54.0	**Mansfield** (city) Richland County
32	945	54.2	**Ravenna** (city) Portage County
33	964	54.5	**Akron** (city) Summit County
33	964	54.5	**Springdale** (city) Hamilton County
35	983	54.7	**East Liverpool** (city) Columbiana County
35	983	54.7	**Marietta** (city) Washington County
37	999	54.9	**Alliance** (city) Stark County
38	1063	55.5	**Toledo** (city) Lucas County
39	1104	55.9	**Hamilton** (city) Butler County
40	1112	56.0	**Bellefontaine** (city) Logan County
40	1112	56.0	**Steubenville** (city) Jefferson County
42	1151	56.3	**Bedford** (city) Cuyahoga County
42	1151	56.3	**Cleveland Heights** (city) Cuyahoga County
44	1162	56.4	**Newark** (city) Licking County
45	1192	56.6	**Warren** (city) Trumbull County
46	1218	56.8	**West Carrollton** (city) Montgomery County
47	1236	57.1	**Riverside** (city) Montgomery County
48	1251	57.2	**Urbana** (city) Champaign County
49	1274	57.4	**Marion** (city) Marion County
49	1274	57.4	**Reading** (city) Hamilton County
51	1289	57.5	**Trotwood** (city) Montgomery County
52	1302	57.6	**Franklin** (city) Warren County
53	1317	57.7	**Lancaster** (city) Fairfield County
54	1322	57.8	**Lorain** (city) Lorain County
55	1345	58.0	**Circleville** (city) Pickaway County
56	1356	58.1	**Fremont** (city) Sandusky County
57	1367	58.2	**Youngstown** (city) Mahoning County
58	1427	58.7	**Brooklyn** (city) Cuyahoga County
59	1457	58.9	**Wooster** (city) Wayne County
60	1470	59.0	**Greenville** (city) Darke County
61	1483	59.1	**Chillicothe** (city) Ross County
62	1493	59.2	**Bucyrus** (city) Crawford County
62	1493	59.2	**Troy** (city) Miami County
64	1504	59.3	**Forest Park** (city) Hamilton County
64	1504	59.3	**Sidney** (city) Shelby County
66	1523	59.4	**Ironton** (city) Lawrence County
66	1523	59.4	**Parma Heights** (city) Cuyahoga County
68	1583	60.0	**Niles** (city) Trumbull County
69	1595	60.1	**Norwalk** (city) Huron County
70	1633	60.4	**Findlay** (city) Hancock County
71	1674	60.7	**Coshocton** (city) Coshocton County
72	1696	60.8	**Galion** (city) Crawford County
73	1713	60.9	**Delaware** (city) Delaware County
73	1713	60.9	**Elyria** (city) Lorain County
75	1725	61.0	**Sharonville** (city) Hamilton County
76	1734	61.1	**Piqua** (city) Miami County
76	1734	61.1	**Willoughby** (city) Lake County
78	1757	61.3	**Salem** (city) Columbiana County
79	1792	61.6	**Xenia** (city) Greene County
80	1811	61.8	**Lebanon** (city) Warren County
81	1821	61.9	**Ashland** (city) Ashland County
82	1862	62.3	**Beachwood** (city) Cuyahoga County
83	1873	62.4	**Barberton** (city) Summit County
84	1896	62.6	**Tiffin** (city) Seneca County
85	1996	63.5	**New Philadelphia** (city) Tuscarawas County
85	1996	63.5	**Reynoldsburg** (city) Franklin County
87	2018	63.7	**Cuyahoga Falls** (city) Summit County
88	2029	63.8	**Fairfield** (city) Butler County
88	2029	63.8	**Fostoria** (city) Seneca County
90	2037	63.9	**Shaker Heights** (city) Cuyahoga County
91	2055	64.1	**Richmond Heights** (city) Cuyahoga County
92	2075	64.3	**Vandalia** (city) Montgomery County
93	2111	64.8	**Kettering** (city) Montgomery County
94	2136	65.1	**Marysville** (city) Union County
95	2222	65.8	**Heath** (city) Licking County
96	2230	65.9	**Austintown** (CDP) Mahoning County
97	2241	66.0	**Van Wert** (city) Van Wert County
98	2264	66.2	**Celina** (city) Mercer County
98	2264	66.2	**Conneaut** (city) Ashtabula County
100	2276	66.3	**Medina** (city) Medina County
101	2307	66.6	**Massillon** (city) Stark County
102	2365	67.1	**Defiance** (city) Defiance County
103	2432	67.7	**North Canton** (city) Stark County
104	2514	68.5	**Boardman** (CDP) Mahoning County
105	2615	69.4	**Dover** (city) Tuscarawas County
106	2638	69.6	**Garfield Heights** (city) Cuyahoga County
106	2638	69.6	**Stow** (city) Summit County
108	2650	69.7	**Grove City** (city) Franklin County
109	2659	69.8	**Northbrook** (CDP) Hamilton County
109	2659	69.8	**University Heights** (city) Cuyahoga County
111	2691	70.1	**Streetsboro** (city) Portage County
112	2699	70.2	**Berea** (city) Cuyahoga County
113	2720	70.5	**Perrysburg** (city) Wood County
114	2779	71.1	**Blue Ash** (city) Hamilton County
115	2822	71.5	**Miamisburg** (city) Montgomery County
115	2822	71.5	**Oregon** (city) Lucas County
115	2822	71.5	**Sylvania** (city) Lucas County
118	2834	71.6	**North Royalton** (city) Cuyahoga County
119	2881	72.0	**Huber Heights** (city) Montgomery County
120	2889	72.1	**Centerville** (city) Montgomery County
120	2889	72.1	**Rocky River** (city) Cuyahoga County
122	2942	72.4	**Wadsworth** (city) Medina County
123	2957	72.5	**Westlake** (city) Cuyahoga County
124	2967	72.6	**Trenton** (city) Butler County
125	2979	72.7	**White Oak** (CDP) Hamilton County
126	2989	72.8	**Forestville** (CDP) Hamilton County
126	2989	72.8	**Maumee** (city) Lucas County
126	2989	72.8	**Middleburg Heights** (city) Cuyahoga County
129	3007	73.0	**Struthers** (city) Mahoning County
130	3038	73.3	**Loveland** (city) Hamilton County
131	3052	73.4	**Fairview Park** (city) Cuyahoga County
132	3081	73.7	**Maple Heights** (city) Cuyahoga County
133	3090	73.8	**Englewood** (city) Montgomery County
134	3105	74.0	**Beavercreek** (city) Greene County
135	3111	74.1	**Parma** (city) Cuyahoga County
136	3165	74.6	**Eastlake** (city) Lake County
137	3205	75.0	**Gahanna** (city) Franklin County
138	3256	75.6	**Bexley** (city) Franklin County
139	3320	76.3	**North Olmsted** (city) Cuyahoga County
140	3364	76.7	**Twinsburg** (city) Summit County
141	3396	77.0	**Westerville** (city) Franklin County
142	3419	77.2	**Pataskala** (city) Licking County
143	3440	77.4	**Pickerington** (city) Fairfield County
144	3460	77.6	**Dent** (CDP) Hamilton County
145	3488	78.0	**Tallmadge** (city) Summit County
146	3501	78.1	**Vermilion** (city) Lorain County
147	3533	78.4	**Monroe** (city) Butler County
148	3543	78.5	**Brunswick** (city) Medina County
149	3550	78.6	**Green** (city) Summit County
150	3601	79.1	**Dublin** (city) Franklin County

Note: *The state column ranks the top/bottom 150 places from all places in the state with population of 10,000 or more. The national column ranks the top/bottom 150 places from all places in the country with population of 10,000 or more. Places that are unincorporated were not considered in the rankings. Please refer to the User Guide for additional information.*

Median Home Value

Top 150 Places Ranked in *Descending* Order

State Rank	Nat'l Rank	Dollars	Place
1	942	330,900	**Dublin** (city) Franklin County
2	1004	324,400	**Powell** (city) Delaware County
3	1104	309,200	**Montgomery** (city) Hamilton County
4	1121	306,800	**Upper Arlington** (city) Franklin County
5	1231	289,900	**Hudson** (city) Summit County
6	1305	280,800	**Beachwood** (city) Cuyahoga County
7	1376	274,600	**Bexley** (city) Franklin County
8	1444	266,300	**Solon** (city) Cuyahoga County
9	1601	249,100	**Avon** (city) Lorain County
10	1616	247,600	**Aurora** (city) Portage County
11	1661	243,800	**Brecksville** (city) Cuyahoga County
12	1721	239,100	**Worthington** (city) Franklin County
13	1841	228,800	**Westlake** (city) Cuyahoga County
14	1890	223,800	**Shaker Heights** (city) Cuyahoga County
15	1911	221,500	**Mason** (city) Warren County
16	1998	214,500	**Blue Ash** (city) Hamilton County
17	2007	213,700	**Broadview Heights** (city) Cuyahoga County
18	2013	213,300	**Avon Lake** (city) Lorain County
19	2062	209,800	**Mack** (CDP) Hamilton County
20	2098	207,600	**Forestville** (CDP) Hamilton County
21	2112	206,700	**Twinsburg** (city) Summit County
22	2129	205,000	**Hilliard** (city) Franklin County
23	2130	204,900	**Westerville** (city) Franklin County
24	2158	201,900	**Springboro** (city) Warren County
25	2199	199,100	**Rocky River** (city) Cuyahoga County
26	2220	197,800	**Bay Village** (city) Cuyahoga County
27	2274	193,700	**North Royalton** (city) Cuyahoga County
27	2274	193,700	**Strongsville** (city) Cuyahoga County
29	2333	189,300	**Perrysburg** (city) Wood County
30	2351	188,100	**Oxford** (city) Butler County
31	2354	188,000	**Dent** (CDP) Hamilton County
32	2356	187,900	**Macedonia** (city) Summit County
33	2391	186,300	**Gahanna** (city) Franklin County
34	2426	183,200	**Pickerington** (city) Fairfield County
35	2567	174,300	**Green** (city) Summit County
36	2570	174,100	**Beavercreek** (city) Greene County
37	2614	171,800	**Sylvania** (city) Lucas County
38	2654	169,500	**Centerville** (city) Montgomery County
39	2663	169,000	**Mentor** (city) Lake County
40	2708	167,300	**Loveland** (city) Hamilton County
41	2727	166,000	**Seven Hills** (city) Cuyahoga County
42	2731	165,900	**Stow** (city) Summit County
43	2753	165,200	**Monfort Heights** (CDP) Hamilton County
44	2805	162,300	**Athens** (city) Athens County
45	2811	161,900	**North Ridgeville** (city) Lorain County
46	2816	161,700	**Medina** (city) Medina County
47	2825	161,200	**Pataskala** (city) Licking County
48	2843	160,300	**Middleburg Heights** (city) Cuyahoga County
49	2848	160,100	**Grove City** (city) Franklin County
50	2852	159,900	**Bowling Green** (city) Wood County
51	2864	159,500	**Marysville** (city) Union County
52	2870	159,200	**Lebanon** (city) Warren County
52	2870	159,200	**Wadsworth** (city) Medina County
54	2876	159,100	**University Heights** (city) Cuyahoga County
55	2888	158,500	**Delaware** (city) Delaware County
56	2898	158,100	**Monroe** (city) Butler County
57	2915	157,400	**Brunswick** (city) Medina County
58	2959	155,400	**Richmond Heights** (city) Cuyahoga County
59	2962	155,200	**Tallmadge** (city) Summit County
60	2989	153,700	**Amherst** (city) Lorain County
61	3092	149,500	**Streetsboro** (city) Portage County
62	3143	147,400	**North Olmsted** (city) Cuyahoga County
62	3143	147,400	**Willoughby** (city) Lake County
64	3149	147,100	**Fairfield** (city) Butler County
65	3178	145,200	**Reynoldsburg** (city) Franklin County
66	3187	144,600	**Fairview Park** (city) Cuyahoga County
67	3202	143,900	**Lyndhurst** (city) Cuyahoga County
68	3214	143,300	**Sharonville** (city) Hamilton County
69	3225	142,700	**Mayfield Heights** (city) Cuyahoga County
70	3289	139,200	**New Franklin** (city) Summit County
71	3297	138,600	**Kent** (city) Portage County
72	3319	137,800	**Norton** (city) Summit County
73	3320	137,700	**Vandalia** (city) Montgomery County
74	3330	137,300	**North Canton** (city) Stark County
75	3339	136,800	**Miamisburg** (city) Montgomery County
76	3357	135,800	**Clayton** (city) Montgomery County
77	3408	133,100	**Oregon** (city) Lucas County
78	3423	132,600	**Cleveland Heights** (city) Cuyahoga County
79	3425	132,500	**White Oak** (CDP) Hamilton County
80	3461	130,700	**Columbus** (city) Franklin County
81	3470	130,300	**Vermilion** (city) Lorain County
82	3473	130,100	**Kettering** (city) Montgomery County
83	3488	129,600	**Heath** (city) Licking County
84	3494	129,400	**Lakewood** (city) Cuyahoga County
85	3522	128,300	**Bridgetown** (CDP) Hamilton County
85	3522	128,300	**Finneytown** (CDP) Hamilton County
87	3525	128,100	**Berea** (city) Cuyahoga County
88	3527	128,000	**Eastlake** (city) Lake County
89	3536	127,600	**Springdale** (city) Hamilton County
90	3538	127,400	**Reading** (city) Hamilton County
91	3544	127,000	**Maumee** (city) Lucas County
92	3556	126,200	**Wickliffe** (city) Lake County
93	3575	125,100	**Trenton** (city) Butler County
94	3595	123,800	**Troy** (city) Miami County
95	3600	123,600	**Cincinnati** (city) Hamilton County
96	3605	123,300	**Findlay** (city) Hancock County
97	3607	123,100	**Wooster** (city) Wayne County
98	3632	121,900	**Norwood** (city) Hamilton County
99	3654	121,000	**Willowick** (city) Lake County
100	3666	120,400	**Cuyahoga Falls** (city) Summit County
101	3671	120,200	**Englewood** (city) Montgomery County
102	3688	119,100	**Circleville** (city) Pickaway County
103	3719	118,100	**Norwalk** (city) Huron County
104	3738	117,700	**Brook Park** (city) Cuyahoga County
104	3738	117,700	**Parma Heights** (city) Cuyahoga County
106	3772	115,900	**Lancaster** (city) Fairfield County
107	3776	115,700	**Parma** (city) Cuyahoga County
108	3792	115,100	**Brooklyn** (city) Cuyahoga County
109	3821	114,100	**South Euclid** (city) Cuyahoga County
110	3826	113,900	**Newark** (city) Licking County
111	3869	111,700	**Dover** (city) Tuscarawas County
112	3873	111,500	**Bedford Heights** (city) Cuyahoga County
112	3873	111,500	**Boardman** (CDP) Mahoning County
114	3887	110,800	**Forest Park** (city) Hamilton County
115	3895	110,500	**Painesville** (city) Lake County
116	3913	109,400	**Franklin** (city) Warren County
117	3919	109,100	**Fairborn** (city) Greene County
118	3936	108,000	**Huber Heights** (city) Montgomery County
119	3969	106,100	**Ravenna** (city) Portage County
120	3987	105,200	**Sidney** (city) Shelby County
121	4004	104,300	**Hamilton** (city) Butler County
122	4019	103,000	**Celina** (city) Mercer County
123	4022	102,800	**New Philadelphia** (city) Tuscarawas County
124	4028	102,600	**Mount Vernon** (city) Knox County
125	4035	102,200	**West Carrollton** (city) Montgomery County
126	4045	101,600	**Ashland** (city) Ashland County
127	4065	100,500	**Bellefontaine** (city) Logan County
128	4070	100,400	**Elyria** (city) Lorain County
129	4074	100,000	**Marietta** (city) Washington County
130	4100	98,500	**Washington Court House** (city) Fayette County
131	4104	98,400	**Defiance** (city) Defiance County
131	4104	98,400	**Xenia** (city) Greene County
133	4106	98,300	**Urbana** (city) Champaign County
134	4111	98,100	**Massillon** (city) Stark County
135	4115	97,800	**Chillicothe** (city) Ross County
136	4116	97,700	**Wilmington** (city) Clinton County
137	4129	97,200	**Middletown** (city) Butler County
138	4162	95,000	**Bedford** (city) Cuyahoga County
139	4184	93,600	**Warrensville Heights** (city) Cuyahoga County
140	4189	93,400	**Lorain** (city) Lorain County
141	4190	93,300	**Steubenville** (city) Jefferson County
142	4206	92,800	**Riverside** (city) Montgomery County
143	4235	91,400	**Austintown** (CDP) Mahoning County
143	4235	91,400	**Tiffin** (city) Seneca County
145	4238	91,200	**Euclid** (city) Cuyahoga County
146	4247	90,900	**Whitehall** (city) Franklin County
147	4315	87,400	**Piqua** (city) Miami County
148	4318	87,300	**Ironton** (city) Lawrence County
149	4320	87,200	**Conneaut** (city) Ashtabula County
150	4323	87,000	**Coshocton** (city) Coshocton County

Note: *The state column ranks the top/bottom 150 places from all places in the state with population of 10,000 or more. The national column ranks the top/bottom 150 places from all places in the country with population of 10,000 or more. Places that are unincorporated were not considered in the rankings. Please refer to the User Guide for additional information.*

Median Home Value

Top 150 Places Ranked in *Ascending* Order

State Rank	Nat'l Rank	Dollars	Place
1	9	46,600	**Youngstown** (city) Mahoning County
2	17	54,700	**East Liverpool** (city) Columbiana County
3	64	65,600	**Warren** (city) Trumbull County
4	82	68,100	**Fostoria** (city) Seneca County
5	88	68,900	**East Cleveland** (city) Cuyahoga County
6	96	69,600	**Dayton** (city) Montgomery County
7	102	70,500	**Lima** (city) Allen County
8	104	71,100	**Galion** (city) Crawford County
8	104	71,100	**Struthers** (city) Mahoning County
10	127	74,200	**Portsmouth** (city) Scioto County
11	151	76,200	**Zanesville** (city) Muskingum County
12	154	76,700	**Cleveland** (city) Cuyahoga County
13	163	77,200	**Canton** (city) Stark County
14	165	77,500	**Marion** (city) Marion County
15	180	78,700	**Ashtabula** (city) Ashtabula County
16	199	79,900	**Mansfield** (city) Richland County
17	212	80,700	**Bucyrus** (city) Crawford County
18	216	81,200	**Alliance** (city) Stark County
19	219	81,300	**Trotwood** (city) Montgomery County
20	229	81,600	**Niles** (city) Trumbull County
21	238	82,100	**Springfield** (city) Clark County
21	238	82,100	**Van Wert** (city) Van Wert County
23	257	83,600	**Toledo** (city) Lucas County
24	262	83,900	**Akron** (city) Summit County
25	271	84,300	**Cambridge** (city) Guernsey County
26	272	84,400	**Maple Heights** (city) Cuyahoga County
27	283	85,000	**Sandusky** (city) Erie County
28	295	85,600	**Salem** (city) Columbiana County
29	300	85,800	**Fremont** (city) Sandusky County
30	305	85,900	**Garfield Heights** (city) Cuyahoga County
31	318	86,600	**Northbrook** (CDP) Hamilton County
32	320	86,800	**Barberton** (city) Summit County
33	324	87,000	**Coshocton** (city) Coshocton County
33	324	87,000	**Greenville** (city) Darke County
35	328	87,200	**Conneaut** (city) Ashtabula County
36	329	87,300	**Ironton** (city) Lawrence County
37	331	87,400	**Piqua** (city) Miami County
38	401	90,900	**Whitehall** (city) Franklin County
39	405	91,200	**Euclid** (city) Cuyahoga County
40	411	91,400	**Austintown** (CDP) Mahoning County
40	411	91,400	**Tiffin** (city) Seneca County
42	440	92,800	**Riverside** (city) Montgomery County
43	454	93,300	**Steubenville** (city) Jefferson County
44	459	93,400	**Lorain** (city) Lorain County
45	462	93,600	**Warrensville Heights** (city) Cuyahoga County
46	485	95,000	**Bedford** (city) Cuyahoga County
47	519	97,200	**Middletown** (city) Butler County
48	532	97,700	**Wilmington** (city) Clinton County
49	533	97,800	**Chillicothe** (city) Ross County
50	534	98,100	**Massillon** (city) Stark County
51	542	98,300	**Urbana** (city) Champaign County
52	543	98,400	**Defiance** (city) Defiance County
52	543	98,400	**Xenia** (city) Greene County
54	545	98,500	**Washington Court House** (city) Fayette County
55	572	100,000	**Marietta** (city) Washington County
56	577	100,400	**Elyria** (city) Lorain County
57	579	100,500	**Bellefontaine** (city) Logan County
58	601	101,600	**Ashland** (city) Ashland County
59	611	102,200	**West Carrollton** (city) Montgomery County
60	620	102,600	**Mount Vernon** (city) Knox County
61	625	102,800	**New Philadelphia** (city) Tuscarawas County
62	628	103,000	**Celina** (city) Mercer County
63	644	104,300	**Hamilton** (city) Butler County
64	659	105,200	**Sidney** (city) Shelby County
65	677	106,100	**Ravenna** (city) Portage County
66	711	108,000	**Huber Heights** (city) Montgomery County
67	728	109,100	**Fairborn** (city) Greene County
68	731	109,400	**Franklin** (city) Warren County
69	753	110,500	**Painesville** (city) Lake County
70	759	110,800	**Forest Park** (city) Hamilton County
71	771	111,500	**Bedford Heights** (city) Cuyahoga County
71	771	111,500	**Boardman** (CDP) Mahoning County
73	778	111,700	**Dover** (city) Tuscarawas County
74	821	113,900	**Newark** (city) Licking County
75	826	114,100	**South Euclid** (city) Cuyahoga County
76	854	115,100	**Brooklyn** (city) Cuyahoga County
77	869	115,700	**Parma** (city) Cuyahoga County
78	874	115,900	**Lancaster** (city) Fairfield County
79	908	117,700	**Brook Park** (city) Cuyahoga County
79	908	117,700	**Parma Heights** (city) Cuyahoga County
81	922	118,100	**Norwalk** (city) Huron County
82	956	119,100	**Circleville** (city) Pickaway County
83	974	120,200	**Englewood** (city) Montgomery County
84	979	120,400	**Cuyahoga Falls** (city) Summit County
85	991	121,000	**Willowick** (city) Lake County
86	1013	121,900	**Norwood** (city) Hamilton County
87	1039	123,100	**Wooster** (city) Wayne County
88	1043	123,300	**Findlay** (city) Hancock County
89	1047	123,600	**Cincinnati** (city) Hamilton County
90	1052	123,800	**Troy** (city) Miami County
91	1073	125,100	**Trenton** (city) Butler County
92	1090	126,200	**Wickliffe** (city) Lake County
93	1101	127,000	**Maumee** (city) Lucas County
94	1108	127,400	**Reading** (city) Hamilton County
95	1111	127,600	**Springdale** (city) Hamilton County
96	1121	128,000	**Eastlake** (city) Lake County
97	1122	128,100	**Berea** (city) Cuyahoga County
98	1125	128,300	**Bridgetown** (CDP) Hamilton County
98	1125	128,300	**Finneytown** (CDP) Hamilton County
100	1151	129,400	**Lakewood** (city) Cuyahoga County
101	1157	129,600	**Heath** (city) Licking County
102	1175	130,100	**Kettering** (city) Montgomery County
103	1178	130,300	**Vermilion** (city) Lorain County
104	1185	130,700	**Columbus** (city) Franklin County
105	1223	132,500	**White Oak** (CDP) Hamilton County
106	1224	132,600	**Cleveland Heights** (city) Cuyahoga County
107	1237	133,100	**Oregon** (city) Lucas County
108	1291	135,800	**Clayton** (city) Montgomery County
109	1309	136,800	**Miamisburg** (city) Montgomery County
110	1317	137,300	**North Canton** (city) Stark County
111	1325	137,700	**Vandalia** (city) Montgomery County
112	1329	137,800	**Norton** (city) Summit County
113	1349	138,600	**Kent** (city) Portage County
114	1357	139,200	**New Franklin** (city) Summit County
115	1420	142,700	**Mayfield Heights** (city) Cuyahoga County
116	1432	143,300	**Sharonville** (city) Hamilton County
117	1445	143,900	**Lyndhurst** (city) Cuyahoga County
118	1459	144,600	**Fairview Park** (city) Cuyahoga County
119	1469	145,200	**Reynoldsburg** (city) Franklin County
120	1498	147,100	**Fairfield** (city) Butler County
121	1502	147,400	**North Olmsted** (city) Cuyahoga County
121	1502	147,400	**Willoughby** (city) Lake County
123	1554	149,500	**Streetsboro** (city) Portage County
124	1656	153,700	**Amherst** (city) Lorain County
125	1685	155,200	**Tallmadge** (city) Summit County
126	1688	155,400	**Richmond Heights** (city) Cuyahoga County
127	1732	157,400	**Brunswick** (city) Medina County
128	1747	158,100	**Monroe** (city) Butler County
129	1758	158,500	**Delaware** (city) Delaware County
130	1771	159,100	**University Heights** (city) Cuyahoga County
131	1773	159,200	**Lebanon** (city) Warren County
131	1773	159,200	**Wadsworth** (city) Medina County
133	1783	159,500	**Marysville** (city) Union County
134	1793	159,900	**Bowling Green** (city) Wood County
135	1797	160,100	**Grove City** (city) Franklin County
136	1804	160,300	**Middleburg Heights** (city) Cuyahoga County
137	1817	161,200	**Pataskala** (city) Licking County
138	1831	161,700	**Medina** (city) Medina County
139	1835	161,900	**North Ridgeville** (city) Lorain County
140	1843	162,300	**Athens** (city) Athens County
141	1893	165,200	**Monfort Heights** (CDP) Hamilton County
142	1915	165,900	**Stow** (city) Summit County
143	1918	166,000	**Seven Hills** (city) Cuyahoga County
144	1938	167,300	**Loveland** (city) Hamilton County
145	1983	169,000	**Mentor** (city) Lake County
146	1993	169,500	**Centerville** (city) Montgomery County
147	2030	171,800	**Sylvania** (city) Lucas County
148	2076	174,100	**Beavercreek** (city) Greene County
149	2080	174,300	**Green** (city) Summit County
150	2221	183,200	**Pickerington** (city) Fairfield County

Note: *The state column ranks the top/bottom 150 places from all places in the state with population of 10,000 or more. The national column ranks the top/bottom 150 places from all places in the country with population of 10,000 or more. Places that are unincorporated were not considered in the rankings. Please refer to the User Guide for additional information.*

Median Year Structure Built

Top 150 Places Ranked in *Descending* Order

State Rank	Nat'l Rank	Year	Place
1	153	1999	**Monroe** (city) Butler County
1	153	1999	**Pickerington** (city) Fairfield County
1	153	1999	**Powell** (city) Delaware County
4	181	1998	**Avon** (city) Lorain County
5	369	1994	**Mason** (city) Warren County
5	369	1994	**Springboro** (city) Warren County
7	435	1993	**Dublin** (city) Franklin County
8	501	1992	**Hilliard** (city) Franklin County
8	501	1992	**Marysville** (city) Union County
8	501	1992	**Pataskala** (city) Licking County
11	566	1991	**Twinsburg** (city) Summit County
12	715	1989	**Dent** (CDP) Hamilton County
12	715	1989	**Lebanon** (city) Warren County
12	715	1989	**Streetsboro** (city) Portage County
15	778	1988	**Delaware** (city) Delaware County
15	778	1988	**Grove City** (city) Franklin County
17	933	1986	**Aurora** (city) Portage County
17	933	1986	**Avon Lake** (city) Lorain County
19	1031	1985	**Macedonia** (city) Summit County
20	1133	1984	**Gahanna** (city) Franklin County
21	1344	1982	**North Royalton** (city) Cuyahoga County
21	1344	1982	**Reynoldsburg** (city) Franklin County
21	1344	1982	**Solon** (city) Cuyahoga County
24	1463	1981	**Perrysburg** (city) Wood County
24	1463	1981	**Westlake** (city) Cuyahoga County
26	1563	1980	**Broadview Heights** (city) Cuyahoga County
26	1563	1980	**Green** (city) Summit County
26	1563	1980	**Hudson** (city) Summit County
26	1563	1980	**Strongsville** (city) Cuyahoga County
26	1563	1980	**Westerville** (city) Franklin County
31	1668	1979	**Beavercreek** (city) Greene County
31	1668	1979	**Forestville** (CDP) Hamilton County
31	1668	1979	**Medina** (city) Medina County
31	1668	1979	**North Ridgeville** (city) Lorain County
31	1668	1979	**Oxford** (city) Butler County
31	1668	1979	**Stow** (city) Summit County
37	1795	1978	**Blue Ash** (city) Hamilton County
37	1795	1978	**Fairfield** (city) Butler County
37	1795	1978	**Heath** (city) Licking County
37	1795	1978	**Sharonville** (city) Hamilton County
41	1932	1977	**Bowling Green** (city) Wood County
41	1932	1977	**Brunswick** (city) Medina County
41	1932	1977	**Loveland** (city) Hamilton County
41	1932	1977	**Trenton** (city) Butler County
45	2051	1976	**Brecksville** (city) Cuyahoga County
45	2051	1976	**Centerville** (city) Montgomery County
45	2051	1976	**Mack** (CDP) Hamilton County
48	2191	1975	**Montgomery** (city) Hamilton County
48	2191	1975	**Sylvania** (city) Lucas County
50	2330	1974	**Columbus** (city) Franklin County
50	2330	1974	**Englewood** (city) Montgomery County
50	2330	1974	**Monfort Heights** (CDP) Hamilton County
53	2449	1973	**Huber Heights** (city) Montgomery County
53	2449	1973	**Wadsworth** (city) Medina County
55	2560	1972	**Mentor** (city) Lake County
55	2560	1972	**Springdale** (city) Hamilton County
55	2560	1972	**Vandalia** (city) Montgomery County
55	2560	1972	**Wooster** (city) Wayne County
59	2668	1971	**Clayton** (city) Montgomery County
59	2668	1971	**Forest Park** (city) Hamilton County
59	2668	1971	**Miamisburg** (city) Montgomery County
59	2668	1971	**Middleburg Heights** (city) Cuyahoga County
59	2668	1971	**West Carrollton** (city) Montgomery County
59	2668	1971	**Willoughby** (city) Lake County
65	2810	1970	**Athens** (city) Athens County
65	2810	1970	**Kent** (city) Portage County
67	2903	1969	**Amherst** (city) Lorain County
67	2903	1969	**Beachwood** (city) Cuyahoga County
67	2903	1969	**Celina** (city) Mercer County
67	2903	1969	**Fairborn** (city) Greene County
67	2903	1969	**Oregon** (city) Lucas County
67	2903	1969	**Troy** (city) Miami County
67	2903	1969	**Xenia** (city) Greene County
74	3015	1968	**North Canton** (city) Stark County
74	3015	1968	**Sidney** (city) Shelby County
74	3015	1968	**Tallmadge** (city) Summit County
74	3015	1968	**Wilmington** (city) Clinton County
78	3117	1967	**Franklin** (city) Warren County
78	3117	1967	**Richmond Heights** (city) Cuyahoga County
78	3117	1967	**White Oak** (CDP) Hamilton County
81	3213	1966	**Austintown** (CDP) Mahoning County
81	3213	1966	**Bedford Heights** (city) Cuyahoga County
81	3213	1966	**Findlay** (city) Hancock County
81	3213	1966	**North Olmsted** (city) Cuyahoga County
81	3213	1966	**Northbrook** (CDP) Hamilton County
81	3213	1966	**Norwalk** (city) Huron County
81	3213	1966	**Seven Hills** (city) Cuyahoga County
81	3213	1966	**Vermilion** (city) Lorain County
81	3213	1966	**Washington Court House** (city) Fayette County
90	3323	1965	**Eastlake** (city) Lake County
90	3323	1965	**Elyria** (city) Lorain County
90	3323	1965	**Trotwood** (city) Montgomery County
93	3399	1964	**Boardman** (CDP) Mahoning County
93	3399	1964	**Mayfield Heights** (city) Cuyahoga County
93	3399	1964	**New Franklin** (city) Summit County
96	3485	1963	**Circleville** (city) Pickaway County
96	3485	1963	**Norton** (city) Summit County
96	3485	1963	**Riverside** (city) Montgomery County
96	3485	1963	**Worthington** (city) Franklin County
100	3560	1962	**Ashland** (city) Ashland County
100	3560	1962	**Bellefontaine** (city) Logan County
100	3560	1962	**Lancaster** (city) Fairfield County
100	3560	1962	**New Philadelphia** (city) Tuscarawas County
104	3639	1961	**Brook Park** (city) Cuyahoga County
104	3639	1961	**Maumee** (city) Lucas County
104	3639	1961	**Newark** (city) Licking County
107	3696	1960	**Bridgetown** (CDP) Hamilton County
107	3696	1960	**Defiance** (city) Defiance County
107	3696	1960	**Kettering** (city) Montgomery County
107	3696	1960	**Painesville** (city) Lake County
107	3696	1960	**Parma Heights** (city) Cuyahoga County
107	3696	1960	**Warrensville Heights** (city) Cuyahoga County
107	3696	1960	**Whitehall** (city) Franklin County
114	3771	1959	**Berea** (city) Cuyahoga County
115	3849	1958	**Brooklyn** (city) Cuyahoga County
115	3849	1958	**Cuyahoga Falls** (city) Summit County
115	3849	1958	**Finneytown** (CDP) Hamilton County
115	3849	1958	**Lorain** (city) Lorain County
115	3849	1958	**Middletown** (city) Butler County
115	3849	1958	**Mount Vernon** (city) Knox County
115	3849	1958	**Parma** (city) Cuyahoga County
115	3849	1958	**Rocky River** (city) Cuyahoga County
115	3849	1958	**Upper Arlington** (city) Franklin County
115	3849	1958	**Urbana** (city) Champaign County
125	3932	1957	**Bay Village** (city) Cuyahoga County
125	3932	1957	**Bedford** (city) Cuyahoga County
125	3932	1957	**Greenville** (city) Darke County
125	3932	1957	**Reading** (city) Hamilton County
125	3932	1957	**Wickliffe** (city) Lake County
125	3932	1957	**Willowick** (city) Lake County
131	4027	1956	**Dover** (city) Tuscarawas County
131	4027	1956	**Euclid** (city) Cuyahoga County
131	4027	1956	**Fairview Park** (city) Cuyahoga County
131	4027	1956	**Lyndhurst** (city) Cuyahoga County
131	4027	1956	**Mansfield** (city) Richland County
131	4027	1956	**Maple Heights** (city) Cuyahoga County
131	4027	1956	**Niles** (city) Trumbull County
138	4113	1955	**Massillon** (city) Stark County
138	4113	1955	**Van Wert** (city) Van Wert County
138	4113	1955	**Warren** (city) Trumbull County
141	4175	1954	**Bucyrus** (city) Crawford County
141	4175	1954	**Garfield Heights** (city) Cuyahoga County
141	4175	1954	**Hamilton** (city) Butler County
141	4175	1954	**Piqua** (city) Miami County
141	4175	1954	**Ravenna** (city) Portage County
141	4175	1954	**South Euclid** (city) Cuyahoga County
141	4175	1954	**Steubenville** (city) Jefferson County
141	4175	1954	**Struthers** (city) Mahoning County
149	4232	1953	**Akron** (city) Summit County
149	4232	1953	**Barberton** (city) Summit County

Note: *The state column ranks the top/bottom 150 places from all places in the state with population of 10,000 or more. The national column ranks the top/bottom 150 places from all places in the country with population of 10,000 or more. Places that are unincorporated were not considered in the rankings. Please refer to the User Guide for additional information.*

Median Year Structure Built

Top 150 Places Ranked in *Ascending* Order

State Rank	Nat'l Rank	Year	Place
1	1	<1940	**Cleveland** (city) Cuyahoga County
1	1	<1940	**Cleveland Heights** (city) Cuyahoga County
1	1	<1940	**East Cleveland** (city) Cuyahoga County
1	1	<1940	**Lakewood** (city) Cuyahoga County
1	1	<1940	**Norwood** (city) Hamilton County
1	1	<1940	**Portsmouth** (city) Scioto County
7	144	1943	**Bexley** (city) Franklin County
7	144	1943	**East Liverpool** (city) Columbiana County
9	156	1944	**Conneaut** (city) Ashtabula County
10	168	1945	**Shaker Heights** (city) Cuyahoga County
11	179	1946	**Canton** (city) Stark County
11	179	1946	**Coshocton** (city) Coshocton County
11	179	1946	**Fremont** (city) Sandusky County
14	202	1947	**Cambridge** (city) Guernsey County
14	202	1947	**Cincinnati** (city) Hamilton County
16	224	1948	**University Heights** (city) Cuyahoga County
16	224	1948	**Youngstown** (city) Mahoning County
16	224	1948	**Zanesville** (city) Muskingum County
19	270	1950	**Ashtabula** (city) Ashtabula County
19	270	1950	**Dayton** (city) Montgomery County
19	270	1950	**Marion** (city) Marion County
22	306	1951	**Alliance** (city) Stark County
22	306	1951	**Ironton** (city) Lawrence County
22	306	1951	**Marietta** (city) Washington County
22	306	1951	**Springfield** (city) Clark County
22	306	1951	**Tiffin** (city) Seneca County
27	344	1952	**Fostoria** (city) Seneca County
27	344	1952	**Galion** (city) Crawford County
27	344	1952	**Sandusky** (city) Erie County
30	383	1953	**Akron** (city) Summit County
30	383	1953	**Barberton** (city) Summit County
30	383	1953	**Chillicothe** (city) Ross County
30	383	1953	**Lima** (city) Allen County
30	383	1953	**Salem** (city) Columbiana County
30	383	1953	**Toledo** (city) Lucas County
36	425	1954	**Bucyrus** (city) Crawford County
36	425	1954	**Garfield Heights** (city) Cuyahoga County
36	425	1954	**Hamilton** (city) Butler County
36	425	1954	**Piqua** (city) Miami County
36	425	1954	**Ravenna** (city) Portage County
36	425	1954	**South Euclid** (city) Cuyahoga County
36	425	1954	**Steubenville** (city) Jefferson County
36	425	1954	**Struthers** (city) Mahoning County
44	482	1955	**Massillon** (city) Stark County
44	482	1955	**Van Wert** (city) Van Wert County
44	482	1955	**Warren** (city) Trumbull County
47	544	1956	**Dover** (city) Tuscarawas County
47	544	1956	**Euclid** (city) Cuyahoga County
47	544	1956	**Fairview Park** (city) Cuyahoga County
47	544	1956	**Lyndhurst** (city) Cuyahoga County
47	544	1956	**Mansfield** (city) Richland County
47	544	1956	**Maple Heights** (city) Cuyahoga County
47	544	1956	**Niles** (city) Trumbull County
54	630	1957	**Bay Village** (city) Cuyahoga County
54	630	1957	**Bedford** (city) Cuyahoga County
54	630	1957	**Greenville** (city) Darke County
54	630	1957	**Reading** (city) Hamilton County
54	630	1957	**Wickliffe** (city) Lake County
54	630	1957	**Willowick** (city) Lake County
60	725	1958	**Brooklyn** (city) Cuyahoga County
60	725	1958	**Cuyahoga Falls** (city) Summit County
60	725	1958	**Finneytown** (CDP) Hamilton County
60	725	1958	**Lorain** (city) Lorain County
60	725	1958	**Middletown** (city) Butler County
60	725	1958	**Mount Vernon** (city) Knox County
60	725	1958	**Parma** (city) Cuyahoga County
60	725	1958	**Rocky River** (city) Cuyahoga County
60	725	1958	**Upper Arlington** (city) Franklin County
60	725	1958	**Urbana** (city) Champaign County
70	808	1959	**Berea** (city) Cuyahoga County
71	886	1960	**Bridgetown** (CDP) Hamilton County
71	886	1960	**Defiance** (city) Defiance County
71	886	1960	**Kettering** (city) Montgomery County
71	886	1960	**Painesville** (city) Lake County
71	886	1960	**Parma Heights** (city) Cuyahoga County
71	886	1960	**Warrensville Heights** (city) Cuyahoga County
71	886	1960	**Whitehall** (city) Franklin County
78	961	1961	**Brook Park** (city) Cuyahoga County
78	961	1961	**Maumee** (city) Lucas County
78	961	1961	**Newark** (city) Licking County
81	1018	1962	**Ashland** (city) Ashland County
81	1018	1962	**Bellefontaine** (city) Logan County
81	1018	1962	**Lancaster** (city) Fairfield County
81	1018	1962	**New Philadelphia** (city) Tuscarawas County
85	1097	1963	**Circleville** (city) Pickaway County
85	1097	1963	**Norton** (city) Summit County
85	1097	1963	**Riverside** (city) Montgomery County
85	1097	1963	**Worthington** (city) Franklin County
89	1172	1964	**Boardman** (CDP) Mahoning County
89	1172	1964	**Mayfield Heights** (city) Cuyahoga County
89	1172	1964	**New Franklin** (city) Summit County
92	1258	1965	**Eastlake** (city) Lake County
92	1258	1965	**Elyria** (city) Lorain County
92	1258	1965	**Trotwood** (city) Montgomery County
95	1334	1966	**Austintown** (CDP) Mahoning County
95	1334	1966	**Bedford Heights** (city) Cuyahoga County
95	1334	1966	**Findlay** (city) Hancock County
95	1334	1966	**North Olmsted** (city) Cuyahoga County
95	1334	1966	**Northbrook** (CDP) Hamilton County
95	1334	1966	**Norwalk** (city) Huron County
95	1334	1966	**Seven Hills** (city) Cuyahoga County
95	1334	1966	**Vermilion** (city) Lorain County
95	1334	1966	**Washington Court House** (city) Fayette County
104	1444	1967	**Franklin** (city) Warren County
104	1444	1967	**Richmond Heights** (city) Cuyahoga County
104	1444	1967	**White Oak** (CDP) Hamilton County
107	1540	1968	**North Canton** (city) Stark County
107	1540	1968	**Sidney** (city) Shelby County
107	1540	1968	**Tallmadge** (city) Summit County
107	1540	1968	**Wilmington** (city) Clinton County
111	1642	1969	**Amherst** (city) Lorain County
111	1642	1969	**Beachwood** (city) Cuyahoga County
111	1642	1969	**Celina** (city) Mercer County
111	1642	1969	**Fairborn** (city) Greene County
111	1642	1969	**Oregon** (city) Lucas County
111	1642	1969	**Troy** (city) Miami County
111	1642	1969	**Xenia** (city) Greene County
118	1754	1970	**Athens** (city) Athens County
118	1754	1970	**Kent** (city) Portage County
120	1847	1971	**Clayton** (city) Montgomery County
120	1847	1971	**Forest Park** (city) Hamilton County
120	1847	1971	**Miamisburg** (city) Montgomery County
120	1847	1971	**Middleburg Heights** (city) Cuyahoga County
120	1847	1971	**West Carrollton** (city) Montgomery County
120	1847	1971	**Willoughby** (city) Lake County
126	1989	1972	**Mentor** (city) Lake County
126	1989	1972	**Springdale** (city) Hamilton County
126	1989	1972	**Vandalia** (city) Montgomery County
126	1989	1972	**Wooster** (city) Wayne County
130	2097	1973	**Huber Heights** (city) Montgomery County
130	2097	1973	**Wadsworth** (city) Medina County
132	2208	1974	**Columbus** (city) Franklin County
132	2208	1974	**Englewood** (city) Montgomery County
132	2208	1974	**Monfort Heights** (CDP) Hamilton County
135	2327	1975	**Montgomery** (city) Hamilton County
135	2327	1975	**Sylvania** (city) Lucas County
137	2466	1976	**Brecksville** (city) Cuyahoga County
137	2466	1976	**Centerville** (city) Montgomery County
137	2466	1976	**Mack** (CDP) Hamilton County
140	2606	1977	**Bowling Green** (city) Wood County
140	2606	1977	**Brunswick** (city) Medina County
140	2606	1977	**Loveland** (city) Hamilton County
140	2606	1977	**Trenton** (city) Butler County
144	2725	1978	**Blue Ash** (city) Hamilton County
144	2725	1978	**Fairfield** (city) Butler County
144	2725	1978	**Heath** (city) Licking County
144	2725	1978	**Sharonville** (city) Hamilton County
148	2862	1979	**Beavercreek** (city) Greene County
148	2862	1979	**Forestville** (CDP) Hamilton County
148	2862	1979	**Medina** (city) Medina County

Note: *The state column ranks the top/bottom 150 places from all places in the state with population of 10,000 or more. The national column ranks the top/bottom 150 places from all places in the country with population of 10,000 or more. Places that are unincorporated were not considered in the rankings. Please refer to the User Guide for additional information.*

Homeowner Vacancy Rate

Top 150 Places Ranked in *Descending* Order

State Rank	Nat'l Rank	Percent	Place
1	4	11.4	**East Cleveland** (city) Cuyahoga County
2	147	5.3	**Zanesville** (city) Muskingum County
3	169	5.1	**Cincinnati** (city) Hamilton County
4	206	4.9	**Ashtabula** (city) Ashtabula County
5	263	4.6	**Dayton** (city) Montgomery County
5	263	4.6	**Washington Court House** (city) Fayette County
7	287	4.5	**Fostoria** (city) Seneca County
7	287	4.5	**Maple Heights** (city) Cuyahoga County
9	340	4.3	**Canton** (city) Stark County
10	367	4.2	**Chillicothe** (city) Ross County
10	367	4.2	**Conneaut** (city) Ashtabula County
10	367	4.2	**Garfield Heights** (city) Cuyahoga County
10	367	4.2	**Piqua** (city) Miami County
10	367	4.2	**Sandusky** (city) Erie County
15	403	4.1	**Euclid** (city) Cuyahoga County
15	403	4.1	**Wilmington** (city) Clinton County
17	444	4.0	**Middletown** (city) Butler County
17	444	4.0	**Shaker Heights** (city) Cuyahoga County
17	444	4.0	**Steubenville** (city) Jefferson County
17	444	4.0	**Warren** (city) Trumbull County
21	485	3.9	**Cleveland** (city) Cuyahoga County
21	485	3.9	**Cleveland Heights** (city) Cuyahoga County
23	539	3.8	**Painesville** (city) Lake County
23	539	3.8	**Tiffin** (city) Seneca County
25	589	3.7	**Akron** (city) Summit County
25	589	3.7	**Bedford** (city) Cuyahoga County
25	589	3.7	**Springfield** (city) Clark County
25	589	3.7	**Urbana** (city) Champaign County
29	641	3.6	**Cambridge** (city) Guernsey County
29	641	3.6	**Dent** (CDP) Hamilton County
29	641	3.6	**Lorain** (city) Lorain County
29	641	3.6	**Trotwood** (city) Montgomery County
33	702	3.5	**East Liverpool** (city) Columbiana County
33	702	3.5	**Norwood** (city) Hamilton County
33	702	3.5	**Sidney** (city) Shelby County
36	765	3.4	**Lima** (city) Allen County
36	765	3.4	**Mansfield** (city) Richland County
36	765	3.4	**Marion** (city) Marion County
36	765	3.4	**Pickerington** (city) Fairfield County
36	765	3.4	**University Heights** (city) Cuyahoga County
36	765	3.4	**Van Wert** (city) Van Wert County
36	765	3.4	**Willoughby** (city) Lake County
43	841	3.3	**Barberton** (city) Summit County
43	841	3.3	**Bellefontaine** (city) Logan County
43	841	3.3	**Bucyrus** (city) Crawford County
43	841	3.3	**Columbus** (city) Franklin County
43	841	3.3	**Defiance** (city) Defiance County
43	841	3.3	**Marysville** (city) Union County
43	841	3.3	**South Euclid** (city) Cuyahoga County
50	932	3.2	**Ashland** (city) Ashland County
50	932	3.2	**Coshocton** (city) Coshocton County
50	932	3.2	**Toledo** (city) Lucas County
50	932	3.2	**Youngstown** (city) Mahoning County
54	1014	3.1	**Alliance** (city) Stark County
54	1014	3.1	**Galion** (city) Crawford County
54	1014	3.1	**Niles** (city) Trumbull County
54	1014	3.1	**West Carrollton** (city) Montgomery County
58	1083	3.0	**Bedford Heights** (city) Cuyahoga County
58	1083	3.0	**Elyria** (city) Lorain County
58	1083	3.0	**Massillon** (city) Stark County
58	1083	3.0	**Richmond Heights** (city) Cuyahoga County
62	1191	2.9	**Forest Park** (city) Hamilton County
62	1191	2.9	**Hamilton** (city) Butler County
62	1191	2.9	**Portsmouth** (city) Scioto County
62	1191	2.9	**Warrensville Heights** (city) Cuyahoga County
62	1191	2.9	**Xenia** (city) Greene County
67	1296	2.8	**Celina** (city) Mercer County
67	1296	2.8	**Circleville** (city) Pickaway County
67	1296	2.8	**Heath** (city) Licking County
67	1296	2.8	**Marietta** (city) Washington County
67	1296	2.8	**Newark** (city) Licking County
67	1296	2.8	**Norwalk** (city) Huron County
67	1296	2.8	**Oxford** (city) Butler County
74	1413	2.7	**Findlay** (city) Hancock County
74	1413	2.7	**Lakewood** (city) Cuyahoga County
74	1413	2.7	**Lancaster** (city) Fairfield County
74	1413	2.7	**Lyndhurst** (city) Cuyahoga County
74	1413	2.7	**Northbrook** (CDP) Hamilton County
74	1413	2.7	**Reynoldsburg** (city) Franklin County
74	1413	2.7	**Vermilion** (city) Lorain County
81	1548	2.6	**Avon Lake** (city) Lorain County
81	1548	2.6	**Beachwood** (city) Cuyahoga County
81	1548	2.6	**Boardman** (CDP) Mahoning County
81	1548	2.6	**Bowling Green** (city) Wood County
81	1548	2.6	**Fairborn** (city) Greene County
81	1548	2.6	**Whitehall** (city) Franklin County
81	1548	2.6	**Wooster** (city) Wayne County
88	1665	2.5	**Delaware** (city) Delaware County
88	1665	2.5	**Fremont** (city) Sandusky County
88	1665	2.5	**Greenville** (city) Darke County
88	1665	2.5	**Ironton** (city) Lawrence County
88	1665	2.5	**Mount Vernon** (city) Knox County
88	1665	2.5	**Ravenna** (city) Portage County
88	1665	2.5	**Springdale** (city) Hamilton County
95	1799	2.4	**Clayton** (city) Montgomery County
95	1799	2.4	**Kettering** (city) Montgomery County
95	1799	2.4	**Rocky River** (city) Cuyahoga County
95	1799	2.4	**Salem** (city) Columbiana County
95	1799	2.4	**Struthers** (city) Mahoning County
95	1799	2.4	**Trenton** (city) Butler County
101	1955	2.3	**Athens** (city) Athens County
101	1955	2.3	**Englewood** (city) Montgomery County
101	1955	2.3	**Finneytown** (CDP) Hamilton County
101	1955	2.3	**Franklin** (city) Warren County
101	1955	2.3	**Kent** (city) Portage County
101	1955	2.3	**Lebanon** (city) Warren County
101	1955	2.3	**Miamisburg** (city) Montgomery County
101	1955	2.3	**Streetsboro** (city) Portage County
101	1955	2.3	**Troy** (city) Miami County
101	1955	2.3	**Upper Arlington** (city) Franklin County
111	2126	2.2	**Dublin** (city) Franklin County
111	2126	2.2	**Green** (city) Summit County
111	2126	2.2	**Huber Heights** (city) Montgomery County
111	2126	2.2	**Mayfield Heights** (city) Cuyahoga County
111	2126	2.2	**Perrysburg** (city) Wood County
111	2126	2.2	**Wadsworth** (city) Medina County
117	2268	2.1	**Aurora** (city) Portage County
117	2268	2.1	**Berea** (city) Cuyahoga County
117	2268	2.1	**Blue Ash** (city) Hamilton County
117	2268	2.1	**Middleburg Heights** (city) Cuyahoga County
117	2268	2.1	**Oregon** (city) Lucas County
117	2268	2.1	**Pataskala** (city) Licking County
117	2268	2.1	**Sylvania** (city) Lucas County
117	2268	2.1	**Westlake** (city) Cuyahoga County
125	2443	2.0	**Austintown** (CDP) Mahoning County
125	2443	2.0	**Bridgetown** (CDP) Hamilton County
125	2443	2.0	**Forestville** (CDP) Hamilton County
125	2443	2.0	**North Ridgeville** (city) Lorain County
125	2443	2.0	**Powell** (city) Delaware County
125	2443	2.0	**Riverside** (city) Montgomery County
125	2443	2.0	**White Oak** (CDP) Hamilton County
132	2621	1.9	**Amherst** (city) Lorain County
132	2621	1.9	**Centerville** (city) Montgomery County
132	2621	1.9	**Dover** (city) Tuscarawas County
132	2621	1.9	**Grove City** (city) Franklin County
132	2621	1.9	**Macedonia** (city) Summit County
132	2621	1.9	**Medina** (city) Medina County
132	2621	1.9	**New Philadelphia** (city) Tuscarawas County
132	2621	1.9	**Reading** (city) Hamilton County
140	2810	1.8	**Brooklyn** (city) Cuyahoga County
140	2810	1.8	**Loveland** (city) Hamilton County
140	2810	1.8	**Monfort Heights** (CDP) Hamilton County
140	2810	1.8	**Montgomery** (city) Hamilton County
140	2810	1.8	**Parma Heights** (city) Cuyahoga County
145	2963	1.7	**Beavercreek** (city) Greene County
145	2963	1.7	**Cuyahoga Falls** (city) Summit County
145	2963	1.7	**Fairfield** (city) Butler County
145	2963	1.7	**Hilliard** (city) Franklin County
145	2963	1.7	**Maumee** (city) Lucas County
145	2963	1.7	**North Canton** (city) Stark County

Note: *The state column ranks the top/bottom 150 places from all places in the state with population of 10,000 or more. The national column ranks the top/bottom 150 places from all places in the country with population of 10,000 or more. Places that are unincorporated were not considered in the rankings. Please refer to the User Guide for additional information.*

Homeowner Vacancy Rate

Top 150 Places Ranked in *Ascending* Order

State Rank	Nat'l Rank	Percent	Place
1	248	0.9	**Mack** (CDP) Hamilton County
2	519	1.1	**Bay Village** (city) Cuyahoga County
3	672	1.2	**Brook Park** (city) Cuyahoga County
3	672	1.2	**Gahanna** (city) Franklin County
3	672	1.2	**Twinsburg** (city) Summit County
6	842	1.3	**Broadview Heights** (city) Cuyahoga County
6	842	1.3	**Brunswick** (city) Medina County
6	842	1.3	**Seven Hills** (city) Cuyahoga County
6	842	1.3	**Solon** (city) Cuyahoga County
10	1011	1.4	**New Franklin** (city) Summit County
10	1011	1.4	**Norton** (city) Summit County
10	1011	1.4	**Sharonville** (city) Hamilton County
10	1011	1.4	**Strongsville** (city) Cuyahoga County
10	1011	1.4	**Westerville** (city) Franklin County
15	1168	1.5	**Bexley** (city) Franklin County
15	1168	1.5	**Brecksville** (city) Cuyahoga County
15	1168	1.5	**Mason** (city) Warren County
15	1168	1.5	**North Royalton** (city) Cuyahoga County
15	1168	1.5	**Worthington** (city) Franklin County
20	1342	1.6	**Avon** (city) Lorain County
20	1342	1.6	**Eastlake** (city) Lake County
20	1342	1.6	**Fairview Park** (city) Cuyahoga County
20	1342	1.6	**Hudson** (city) Summit County
20	1342	1.6	**Mentor** (city) Lake County
20	1342	1.6	**Monroe** (city) Butler County
20	1342	1.6	**North Olmsted** (city) Cuyahoga County
20	1342	1.6	**Springboro** (city) Warren County
20	1342	1.6	**Stow** (city) Summit County
20	1342	1.6	**Wickliffe** (city) Lake County
30	1503	1.7	**Beavercreek** (city) Greene County
30	1503	1.7	**Cuyahoga Falls** (city) Summit County
30	1503	1.7	**Fairfield** (city) Butler County
30	1503	1.7	**Hilliard** (city) Franklin County
30	1503	1.7	**Maumee** (city) Lucas County
30	1503	1.7	**North Canton** (city) Stark County
30	1503	1.7	**Parma** (city) Cuyahoga County
30	1503	1.7	**Tallmadge** (city) Summit County
30	1503	1.7	**Vandalia** (city) Montgomery County
30	1503	1.7	**Willowick** (city) Lake County
40	1694	1.8	**Brooklyn** (city) Cuyahoga County
40	1694	1.8	**Loveland** (city) Hamilton County
40	1694	1.8	**Monfort Heights** (CDP) Hamilton County
40	1694	1.8	**Montgomery** (city) Hamilton County
40	1694	1.8	**Parma Heights** (city) Cuyahoga County
45	1847	1.9	**Amherst** (city) Lorain County
45	1847	1.9	**Centerville** (city) Montgomery County
45	1847	1.9	**Dover** (city) Tuscarawas County
45	1847	1.9	**Grove City** (city) Franklin County
45	1847	1.9	**Macedonia** (city) Summit County
45	1847	1.9	**Medina** (city) Medina County
45	1847	1.9	**New Philadelphia** (city) Tuscarawas County
45	1847	1.9	**Reading** (city) Hamilton County
53	2036	2.0	**Austintown** (CDP) Mahoning County
53	2036	2.0	**Bridgetown** (CDP) Hamilton County
53	2036	2.0	**Forestville** (CDP) Hamilton County
53	2036	2.0	**North Ridgeville** (city) Lorain County
53	2036	2.0	**Powell** (city) Delaware County
53	2036	2.0	**Riverside** (city) Montgomery County
53	2036	2.0	**White Oak** (CDP) Hamilton County
60	2214	2.1	**Aurora** (city) Portage County
60	2214	2.1	**Berea** (city) Cuyahoga County
60	2214	2.1	**Blue Ash** (city) Hamilton County
60	2214	2.1	**Middleburg Heights** (city) Cuyahoga County
60	2214	2.1	**Oregon** (city) Lucas County
60	2214	2.1	**Pataskala** (city) Licking County
60	2214	2.1	**Sylvania** (city) Lucas County
60	2214	2.1	**Westlake** (city) Cuyahoga County
68	2389	2.2	**Dublin** (city) Franklin County
68	2389	2.2	**Green** (city) Summit County
68	2389	2.2	**Huber Heights** (city) Montgomery County
68	2389	2.2	**Mayfield Heights** (city) Cuyahoga County
68	2389	2.2	**Perrysburg** (city) Wood County
68	2389	2.2	**Wadsworth** (city) Medina County
74	2531	2.3	**Athens** (city) Athens County
74	2531	2.3	**Englewood** (city) Montgomery County
74	2531	2.3	**Finneytown** (CDP) Hamilton County
74	2531	2.3	**Franklin** (city) Warren County
74	2531	2.3	**Kent** (city) Portage County
74	2531	2.3	**Lebanon** (city) Warren County
74	2531	2.3	**Miamisburg** (city) Montgomery County
74	2531	2.3	**Streetsboro** (city) Portage County
74	2531	2.3	**Troy** (city) Miami County
74	2531	2.3	**Upper Arlington** (city) Franklin County
84	2702	2.4	**Clayton** (city) Montgomery County
84	2702	2.4	**Kettering** (city) Montgomery County
84	2702	2.4	**Rocky River** (city) Cuyahoga County
84	2702	2.4	**Salem** (city) Columbiana County
84	2702	2.4	**Struthers** (city) Mahoning County
84	2702	2.4	**Trenton** (city) Butler County
90	2858	2.5	**Delaware** (city) Delaware County
90	2858	2.5	**Fremont** (city) Sandusky County
90	2858	2.5	**Greenville** (city) Darke County
90	2858	2.5	**Ironton** (city) Lawrence County
90	2858	2.5	**Mount Vernon** (city) Knox County
90	2858	2.5	**Ravenna** (city) Portage County
90	2858	2.5	**Springdale** (city) Hamilton County
97	2992	2.6	**Avon Lake** (city) Lorain County
97	2992	2.6	**Beachwood** (city) Cuyahoga County
97	2992	2.6	**Boardman** (CDP) Mahoning County
97	2992	2.6	**Bowling Green** (city) Wood County
97	2992	2.6	**Fairborn** (city) Greene County
97	2992	2.6	**Whitehall** (city) Franklin County
97	2992	2.6	**Wooster** (city) Wayne County
104	3109	2.7	**Findlay** (city) Hancock County
104	3109	2.7	**Lakewood** (city) Cuyahoga County
104	3109	2.7	**Lancaster** (city) Fairfield County
104	3109	2.7	**Lyndhurst** (city) Cuyahoga County
104	3109	2.7	**Northbrook** (CDP) Hamilton County
104	3109	2.7	**Reynoldsburg** (city) Franklin County
104	3109	2.7	**Vermilion** (city) Lorain County
111	3244	2.8	**Celina** (city) Mercer County
111	3244	2.8	**Circleville** (city) Pickaway County
111	3244	2.8	**Heath** (city) Licking County
111	3244	2.8	**Marietta** (city) Washington County
111	3244	2.8	**Newark** (city) Licking County
111	3244	2.8	**Norwalk** (city) Huron County
111	3244	2.8	**Oxford** (city) Butler County
118	3361	2.9	**Forest Park** (city) Hamilton County
118	3361	2.9	**Hamilton** (city) Butler County
118	3361	2.9	**Portsmouth** (city) Scioto County
118	3361	2.9	**Warrensville Heights** (city) Cuyahoga County
118	3361	2.9	**Xenia** (city) Greene County
123	3466	3.0	**Bedford Heights** (city) Cuyahoga County
123	3466	3.0	**Elyria** (city) Lorain County
123	3466	3.0	**Massillon** (city) Stark County
123	3466	3.0	**Richmond Heights** (city) Cuyahoga County
127	3574	3.1	**Alliance** (city) Stark County
127	3574	3.1	**Galion** (city) Crawford County
127	3574	3.1	**Niles** (city) Trumbull County
127	3574	3.1	**West Carrollton** (city) Montgomery County
131	3643	3.2	**Ashland** (city) Ashland County
131	3643	3.2	**Coshocton** (city) Coshocton County
131	3643	3.2	**Toledo** (city) Lucas County
131	3643	3.2	**Youngstown** (city) Mahoning County
135	3725	3.3	**Barberton** (city) Summit County
135	3725	3.3	**Bellefontaine** (city) Logan County
135	3725	3.3	**Bucyrus** (city) Crawford County
135	3725	3.3	**Columbus** (city) Franklin County
135	3725	3.3	**Defiance** (city) Defiance County
135	3725	3.3	**Marysville** (city) Union County
135	3725	3.3	**South Euclid** (city) Cuyahoga County
142	3816	3.4	**Lima** (city) Allen County
142	3816	3.4	**Mansfield** (city) Richland County
142	3816	3.4	**Marion** (city) Marion County
142	3816	3.4	**Pickerington** (city) Fairfield County
142	3816	3.4	**University Heights** (city) Cuyahoga County
142	3816	3.4	**Van Wert** (city) Van Wert County
142	3816	3.4	**Willoughby** (city) Lake County
149	3892	3.5	**East Liverpool** (city) Columbiana County
149	3892	3.5	**Norwood** (city) Hamilton County

Note: *The state column ranks the top/bottom 150 places from all places in the state with population of 10,000 or more. The national column ranks the top/bottom 150 places from all places in the country with population of 10,000 or more. Places that are unincorporated were not considered in the rankings. Please refer to the User Guide for additional information.*

Median Gross Rent

Top 150 Places Ranked in *Descending* Order

State Rank	Nat'l Rank	Dollars	Place
1	80	1,972	**Hudson** (city) Summit County
2	106	1,897	**Powell** (city) Delaware County
3	381	1,580	**Beachwood** (city) Cuyahoga County
4	572	1,442	**Aurora** (city) Portage County
5	718	1,378	**Brecksville** (city) Cuyahoga County
6	799	1,348	**Mack** (CDP) Hamilton County
7	1148	1,221	**Montgomery** (city) Hamilton County
8	1346	1,165	**Macedonia** (city) Summit County
9	1361	1,161	**Dublin** (city) Franklin County
10	1426	1,145	**Avon** (city) Lorain County
11	1580	1,110	**Seven Hills** (city) Cuyahoga County
12	1649	1,092	**Lyndhurst** (city) Cuyahoga County
13	1714	1,080	**Beavercreek** (city) Greene County
14	1726	1,077	**Springboro** (city) Warren County
15	1850	1,052	**Avon Lake** (city) Lorain County
16	1865	1,047	**Solon** (city) Cuyahoga County
17	1907	1,034	**Blue Ash** (city) Hamilton County
18	1983	1,012	**Bay Village** (city) Cuyahoga County
19	1988	1,011	**University Heights** (city) Cuyahoga County
20	1994	1,009	**Mason** (city) Warren County
21	2044	997	**Westlake** (city) Cuyahoga County
22	2105	989	**Upper Arlington** (city) Franklin County
23	2250	968	**Hilliard** (city) Franklin County
23	2250	968	**Monroe** (city) Butler County
25	2270	966	**South Euclid** (city) Cuyahoga County
26	2346	955	**Gahanna** (city) Franklin County
27	2355	954	**Twinsburg** (city) Summit County
28	2378	949	**Pickerington** (city) Fairfield County
29	2403	945	**Northbrook** (CDP) Hamilton County
30	2416	943	**Shaker Heights** (city) Cuyahoga County
31	2552	920	**Norton** (city) Summit County
32	2563	918	**Streetsboro** (city) Portage County
33	2622	907	**Forestville** (CDP) Hamilton County
34	2641	904	**Westerville** (city) Franklin County
35	2668	900	**Forest Park** (city) Hamilton County
36	2706	895	**Bexley** (city) Franklin County
37	2754	887	**Pataskala** (city) Licking County
38	2766	885	**Mentor** (city) Lake County
39	2805	879	**Monfort Heights** (CDP) Hamilton County
40	2847	873	**Clayton** (city) Montgomery County
41	2858	871	**Bridgetown** (CDP) Hamilton County
42	2882	868	**Springdale** (city) Hamilton County
43	2913	862	**Loveland** (city) Hamilton County
44	2936	858	**Broadview Heights** (city) Cuyahoga County
45	2961	855	**Fairfield** (city) Butler County
46	2979	852	**Huber Heights** (city) Montgomery County
47	3006	848	**Finneytown** (CDP) Hamilton County
48	3016	847	**Grove City** (city) Franklin County
49	3035	845	**Perrysburg** (city) Wood County
50	3042	843	**Stow** (city) Summit County
51	3055	841	**Centerville** (city) Montgomery County
52	3075	838	**New Franklin** (city) Summit County
53	3087	836	**Worthington** (city) Franklin County
54	3104	833	**Marysville** (city) Union County
55	3115	831	**Brook Park** (city) Cuyahoga County
55	3115	831	**Cleveland Heights** (city) Cuyahoga County
57	3127	829	**North Ridgeville** (city) Lorain County
58	3140	827	**Reynoldsburg** (city) Franklin County
59	3145	826	**Dent** (CDP) Hamilton County
59	3145	826	**Willoughby** (city) Lake County
61	3156	824	**Sharonville** (city) Hamilton County
62	3177	821	**Mayfield Heights** (city) Cuyahoga County
63	3229	811	**Green** (city) Summit County
64	3234	810	**Brunswick** (city) Medina County
64	3234	810	**Strongsville** (city) Cuyahoga County
66	3239	809	**Columbus** (city) Franklin County
67	3253	807	**Delaware** (city) Delaware County
68	3279	802	**Medina** (city) Medina County
68	3279	802	**Rocky River** (city) Cuyahoga County
70	3309	796	**North Olmsted** (city) Cuyahoga County
71	3320	794	**Heath** (city) Licking County
71	3320	794	**Lebanon** (city) Warren County
73	3357	788	**Middleburg Heights** (city) Cuyahoga County
74	3365	787	**Wadsworth** (city) Medina County
75	3398	781	**Sylvania** (city) Lucas County
76	3405	780	**Trenton** (city) Butler County
77	3419	778	**Wickliffe** (city) Lake County
78	3423	777	**Maple Heights** (city) Cuyahoga County
79	3452	773	**Warrensville Heights** (city) Cuyahoga County
80	3460	771	**Vermilion** (city) Lorain County
81	3473	769	**Bedford** (city) Cuyahoga County
82	3479	768	**Eastlake** (city) Lake County
82	3479	768	**Oxford** (city) Butler County
84	3501	764	**North Royalton** (city) Cuyahoga County
85	3511	762	**Athens** (city) Athens County
86	3517	761	**Cuyahoga Falls** (city) Summit County
87	3522	760	**Fairborn** (city) Greene County
87	3522	760	**Franklin** (city) Warren County
89	3536	758	**Parma** (city) Cuyahoga County
90	3540	757	**North Canton** (city) Stark County
91	3611	746	**Amherst** (city) Lorain County
92	3617	745	**Garfield Heights** (city) Cuyahoga County
93	3624	744	**Whitehall** (city) Franklin County
94	3638	742	**Riverside** (city) Montgomery County
95	3652	741	**Kettering** (city) Montgomery County
96	3665	738	**West Carrollton** (city) Montgomery County
97	3675	736	**Parma Heights** (city) Cuyahoga County
98	3682	735	**Maumee** (city) Lucas County
99	3687	734	**Willowick** (city) Lake County
100	3695	733	**Euclid** (city) Cuyahoga County
101	3700	732	**Middletown** (city) Butler County
102	3712	731	**Circleville** (city) Pickaway County
103	3740	726	**Painesville** (city) Lake County
104	3787	718	**Elyria** (city) Lorain County
105	3797	716	**Kent** (city) Portage County
106	3808	714	**Bedford Heights** (city) Cuyahoga County
107	3819	712	**Lancaster** (city) Fairfield County
108	3827	711	**Bellefontaine** (city) Logan County
109	3833	710	**Richmond Heights** (city) Cuyahoga County
110	3845	708	**Trotwood** (city) Montgomery County
111	3851	707	**Hamilton** (city) Butler County
112	3869	704	**Fairview Park** (city) Cuyahoga County
112	3869	704	**Troy** (city) Miami County
114	3895	699	**Lakewood** (city) Cuyahoga County
115	3929	693	**Berea** (city) Cuyahoga County
116	3935	692	**Washington Court House** (city) Fayette County
117	3947	690	**Englewood** (city) Montgomery County
118	3959	688	**Ashland** (city) Ashland County
119	3986	684	**Brooklyn** (city) Cuyahoga County
120	3994	683	**Barberton** (city) Summit County
121	3995	682	**White Oak** (CDP) Hamilton County
122	4007	680	**Akron** (city) Summit County
122	4007	680	**Miamisburg** (city) Montgomery County
124	4041	674	**Tallmadge** (city) Summit County
125	4049	673	**Sidney** (city) Shelby County
126	4069	670	**Marion** (city) Marion County
126	4069	670	**Wilmington** (city) Clinton County
128	4073	669	**Celina** (city) Mercer County
129	4083	667	**Newark** (city) Licking County
130	4106	662	**Galion** (city) Crawford County
130	4106	662	**Vandalia** (city) Montgomery County
132	4116	659	**Cleveland** (city) Cuyahoga County
132	4116	659	**Urbana** (city) Champaign County
134	4120	658	**Mount Vernon** (city) Knox County
135	4129	656	**Wooster** (city) Wayne County
136	4151	652	**Piqua** (city) Miami County
137	4159	651	**Xenia** (city) Greene County
138	4209	642	**Bowling Green** (city) Wood County
138	4209	642	**Findlay** (city) Hancock County
140	4224	640	**Chillicothe** (city) Ross County
140	4224	640	**Cincinnati** (city) Hamilton County
142	4232	639	**Defiance** (city) Defiance County
143	4239	638	**Massillon** (city) Stark County
143	4239	638	**Springfield** (city) Clark County
145	4246	637	**Dayton** (city) Montgomery County
146	4251	636	**Norwood** (city) Hamilton County
147	4264	634	**New Philadelphia** (city) Tuscarawas County
148	4276	632	**Bucyrus** (city) Crawford County
149	4286	630	**Lorain** (city) Lorain County
150	4291	629	**Dover** (city) Tuscarawas County

Note: *The state column ranks the top/bottom 150 places from all places in the state with population of 10,000 or more. The national column ranks the top/bottom 150 places from all places in the country with population of 10,000 or more. Places that are unincorporated were not considered in the rankings. Please refer to the User Guide for additional information.*

Median Gross Rent

Top 150 Places Ranked in *Ascending* Order

State Rank	Nat'l Rank	Dollars	Place
1	30	536	**Portsmouth** (city) Scioto County
2	35	537	**Ironton** (city) Lawrence County
3	58	554	**Cambridge** (city) Guernsey County
4	62	557	**East Liverpool** (city) Columbiana County
5	68	558	**Greenville** (city) Darke County
6	77	561	**Steubenville** (city) Jefferson County
7	100	568	**Marietta** (city) Washington County
8	103	569	**Coshocton** (city) Coshocton County
9	116	573	**Mansfield** (city) Richland County
10	136	579	**Fostoria** (city) Seneca County
11	149	582	**Canton** (city) Stark County
11	149	582	**Conneaut** (city) Ashtabula County
13	160	585	**Youngstown** (city) Mahoning County
14	165	586	**Salem** (city) Columbiana County
15	183	591	**Austintown** (CDP) Mahoning County
16	205	596	**Warren** (city) Trumbull County
17	213	598	**Norwalk** (city) Huron County
18	223	600	**Fremont** (city) Sandusky County
19	249	605	**Zanesville** (city) Muskingum County
20	258	608	**East Cleveland** (city) Cuyahoga County
20	258	608	**Niles** (city) Trumbull County
22	267	611	**Alliance** (city) Stark County
23	274	612	**Boardman** (CDP) Mahoning County
24	296	615	**Van Wert** (city) Van Wert County
25	303	617	**Oregon** (city) Lucas County
26	323	621	**Ashtabula** (city) Ashtabula County
27	327	622	**Sandusky** (city) Erie County
27	327	622	**Tiffin** (city) Seneca County
29	331	623	**Lima** (city) Allen County
29	331	623	**Reading** (city) Hamilton County
29	331	623	**Struthers** (city) Mahoning County
32	346	626	**Ravenna** (city) Portage County
33	361	629	**Dover** (city) Tuscarawas County
33	361	629	**Toledo** (city) Lucas County
35	366	630	**Lorain** (city) Lorain County
36	374	632	**Bucyrus** (city) Crawford County
37	389	634	**New Philadelphia** (city) Tuscarawas County
38	398	636	**Norwood** (city) Hamilton County
39	406	637	**Dayton** (city) Montgomery County
40	411	638	**Massillon** (city) Stark County
40	411	638	**Springfield** (city) Clark County
42	418	639	**Defiance** (city) Defiance County
43	425	640	**Chillicothe** (city) Ross County
43	425	640	**Cincinnati** (city) Hamilton County
45	439	642	**Bowling Green** (city) Wood County
45	439	642	**Findlay** (city) Hancock County
47	494	651	**Xenia** (city) Greene County
48	498	652	**Piqua** (city) Miami County
49	524	656	**Wooster** (city) Wayne County
50	532	658	**Mount Vernon** (city) Knox County
51	537	659	**Cleveland** (city) Cuyahoga County
51	537	659	**Urbana** (city) Champaign County
53	545	662	**Galion** (city) Crawford County
53	545	662	**Vandalia** (city) Montgomery County
55	571	667	**Newark** (city) Licking County
56	580	669	**Celina** (city) Mercer County
57	584	670	**Marion** (city) Marion County
57	584	670	**Wilmington** (city) Clinton County
59	601	673	**Sidney** (city) Shelby County
60	608	674	**Tallmadge** (city) Summit County
61	646	680	**Akron** (city) Summit County
61	646	680	**Miamisburg** (city) Montgomery County
63	656	682	**White Oak** (CDP) Hamilton County
64	662	683	**Barberton** (city) Summit County
65	663	684	**Brooklyn** (city) Cuyahoga County
66	691	688	**Ashland** (city) Ashland County
67	705	690	**Englewood** (city) Montgomery County
68	714	692	**Washington Court House** (city) Fayette County
69	722	693	**Berea** (city) Cuyahoga County
70	757	699	**Lakewood** (city) Cuyahoga County
71	782	704	**Fairview Park** (city) Cuyahoga County
71	782	704	**Troy** (city) Miami County
73	798	707	**Hamilton** (city) Butler County
74	806	708	**Trotwood** (city) Montgomery County
75	818	710	**Richmond Heights** (city) Cuyahoga County
76	824	711	**Bellefontaine** (city) Logan County
77	830	712	**Lancaster** (city) Fairfield County
78	845	714	**Bedford Heights** (city) Cuyahoga County
79	853	716	**Kent** (city) Portage County
80	864	718	**Elyria** (city) Lorain County
81	910	726	**Painesville** (city) Lake County
82	942	731	**Circleville** (city) Pickaway County
83	945	732	**Middletown** (city) Butler County
84	957	733	**Euclid** (city) Cuyahoga County
85	962	734	**Willowick** (city) Lake County
86	970	735	**Maumee** (city) Lucas County
87	975	736	**Parma Heights** (city) Cuyahoga County
88	987	738	**West Carrollton** (city) Montgomery County
89	998	741	**Kettering** (city) Montgomery County
90	1005	742	**Riverside** (city) Montgomery County
91	1026	744	**Whitehall** (city) Franklin County
92	1033	745	**Garfield Heights** (city) Cuyahoga County
93	1040	746	**Amherst** (city) Lorain County
94	1112	757	**North Canton** (city) Stark County
95	1117	758	**Parma** (city) Cuyahoga County
96	1126	760	**Fairborn** (city) Greene County
96	1126	760	**Franklin** (city) Warren County
98	1135	761	**Cuyahoga Falls** (city) Summit County
99	1140	762	**Athens** (city) Athens County
100	1152	764	**North Royalton** (city) Cuyahoga County
101	1172	768	**Eastlake** (city) Lake County
101	1172	768	**Oxford** (city) Butler County
103	1178	769	**Bedford** (city) Cuyahoga County
104	1194	771	**Vermilion** (city) Lorain County
105	1201	773	**Warrensville Heights** (city) Cuyahoga County
106	1224	777	**Maple Heights** (city) Cuyahoga County
107	1234	778	**Wickliffe** (city) Lake County
108	1245	780	**Trenton** (city) Butler County
109	1252	781	**Sylvania** (city) Lucas County
110	1285	787	**Wadsworth** (city) Medina County
111	1292	788	**Middleburg Heights** (city) Cuyahoga County
112	1326	794	**Heath** (city) Licking County
112	1326	794	**Lebanon** (city) Warren County
114	1341	796	**North Olmsted** (city) Cuyahoga County
115	1372	802	**Medina** (city) Medina County
115	1372	802	**Rocky River** (city) Cuyahoga County
117	1398	807	**Delaware** (city) Delaware County
118	1412	809	**Columbus** (city) Franklin County
119	1418	810	**Brunswick** (city) Medina County
119	1418	810	**Strongsville** (city) Cuyahoga County
121	1423	811	**Green** (city) Summit County
122	1473	821	**Mayfield Heights** (city) Cuyahoga County
123	1494	824	**Sharonville** (city) Hamilton County
124	1506	826	**Dent** (CDP) Hamilton County
124	1506	826	**Willoughby** (city) Lake County
126	1512	827	**Reynoldsburg** (city) Franklin County
127	1523	829	**North Ridgeville** (city) Lorain County
128	1537	831	**Brook Park** (city) Cuyahoga County
128	1537	831	**Cleveland Heights** (city) Cuyahoga County
130	1548	833	**Marysville** (city) Union County
131	1565	836	**Worthington** (city) Franklin County
132	1573	838	**New Franklin** (city) Summit County
133	1595	841	**Centerville** (city) Montgomery County
134	1605	843	**Stow** (city) Summit County
135	1621	845	**Perrysburg** (city) Wood County
136	1631	847	**Grove City** (city) Franklin County
137	1641	848	**Finneytown** (CDP) Hamilton County
138	1670	852	**Huber Heights** (city) Montgomery County
139	1689	855	**Fairfield** (city) Butler County
140	1713	858	**Broadview Heights** (city) Cuyahoga County
141	1741	862	**Loveland** (city) Hamilton County
142	1773	868	**Springdale** (city) Hamilton County
143	1794	871	**Bridgetown** (CDP) Hamilton County
144	1807	873	**Clayton** (city) Montgomery County
145	1843	879	**Monfort Heights** (CDP) Hamilton County
146	1887	885	**Mentor** (city) Lake County
147	1897	887	**Pataskala** (city) Licking County
148	1945	895	**Bexley** (city) Franklin County
149	1979	900	**Forest Park** (city) Hamilton County
150	2010	904	**Westerville** (city) Franklin County

Note: *The state column ranks the top/bottom 150 places from all places in the state with population of 10,000 or more. The national column ranks the top/bottom 150 places from all places in the country with population of 10,000 or more. Places that are unincorporated were not considered in the rankings. Please refer to the User Guide for additional information.*

Rental Vacancy Rate

Top 150 Places Ranked in *Descending* Order

State Rank	Nat'l Rank	Percent	Place
1	30	22.1	**East Cleveland** (city) Cuyahoga County
2	66	19.0	**Richmond Heights** (city) Cuyahoga County
3	96	17.7	**Broadview Heights** (city) Cuyahoga County
3	96	17.7	**Whitehall** (city) Franklin County
5	145	16.3	**Bexley** (city) Franklin County
6	174	15.8	**Mansfield** (city) Richland County
6	174	15.8	**Monfort Heights** (CDP) Hamilton County
8	181	15.7	**Dayton** (city) Montgomery County
9	202	15.4	**Bedford Heights** (city) Cuyahoga County
10	219	15.0	**Cleveland** (city) Cuyahoga County
11	239	14.7	**Cincinnati** (city) Hamilton County
12	246	14.6	**Euclid** (city) Cuyahoga County
13	283	14.2	**Trotwood** (city) Montgomery County
14	295	14.1	**Middletown** (city) Butler County
14	295	14.1	**Wilmington** (city) Clinton County
16	316	13.9	**Tiffin** (city) Seneca County
17	321	13.8	**Oxford** (city) Butler County
18	335	13.7	**Maple Heights** (city) Cuyahoga County
18	335	13.7	**Shaker Heights** (city) Cuyahoga County
20	370	13.4	**Celina** (city) Mercer County
20	370	13.4	**Green** (city) Summit County
22	385	13.3	**Elyria** (city) Lorain County
22	385	13.3	**Sandusky** (city) Erie County
22	385	13.3	**Warren** (city) Trumbull County
25	400	13.2	**Lorain** (city) Lorain County
26	409	13.1	**Rocky River** (city) Cuyahoga County
27	446	12.9	**Marion** (city) Marion County
28	459	12.8	**Alliance** (city) Stark County
29	480	12.7	**Piqua** (city) Miami County
30	493	12.6	**Miamisburg** (city) Montgomery County
31	543	12.3	**Austintown** (CDP) Mahoning County
31	543	12.3	**Fairview Park** (city) Cuyahoga County
33	561	12.2	**Fairborn** (city) Greene County
34	582	12.1	**Galion** (city) Crawford County
35	605	12.0	**Fairfield** (city) Butler County
35	605	12.0	**Findlay** (city) Hancock County
35	605	12.0	**Lakewood** (city) Cuyahoga County
35	605	12.0	**Lima** (city) Allen County
35	605	12.0	**Toledo** (city) Lucas County
40	635	11.9	**Circleville** (city) Pickaway County
40	635	11.9	**Hamilton** (city) Butler County
42	656	11.8	**East Liverpool** (city) Columbiana County
43	682	11.7	**Pickerington** (city) Fairfield County
44	706	11.6	**Ashtabula** (city) Ashtabula County
44	706	11.6	**Reynoldsburg** (city) Franklin County
44	706	11.6	**Springfield** (city) Clark County
47	731	11.5	**Huber Heights** (city) Montgomery County
47	731	11.5	**Reading** (city) Hamilton County
49	778	11.3	**Fostoria** (city) Seneca County
49	778	11.3	**North Olmsted** (city) Cuyahoga County
49	778	11.3	**Streetsboro** (city) Portage County
49	778	11.3	**Vermilion** (city) Lorain County
53	805	11.2	**Lyndhurst** (city) Cuyahoga County
53	805	11.2	**Mentor** (city) Lake County
55	831	11.1	**Conneaut** (city) Ashtabula County
55	831	11.1	**Forest Park** (city) Hamilton County
55	831	11.1	**Perrysburg** (city) Wood County
55	831	11.1	**Urbana** (city) Champaign County
55	831	11.1	**Willoughby** (city) Lake County
55	831	11.1	**Youngstown** (city) Mahoning County
61	860	11.0	**New Philadelphia** (city) Tuscarawas County
61	860	11.0	**Van Wert** (city) Van Wert County
63	896	10.9	**Boardman** (CDP) Mahoning County
63	896	10.9	**Centerville** (city) Montgomery County
63	896	10.9	**Marietta** (city) Washington County
63	896	10.9	**Norwood** (city) Hamilton County
67	930	10.8	**Bedford** (city) Cuyahoga County
67	930	10.8	**Bellefontaine** (city) Logan County
67	930	10.8	**Wadsworth** (city) Medina County
70	960	10.7	**Riverside** (city) Montgomery County
71	991	10.6	**Bucyrus** (city) Crawford County
71	991	10.6	**Coshocton** (city) Coshocton County
71	991	10.6	**Sharonville** (city) Hamilton County
74	1024	10.5	**Akron** (city) Summit County
74	1024	10.5	**Dover** (city) Tuscarawas County
74	1024	10.5	**Fremont** (city) Sandusky County
74	1024	10.5	**Niles** (city) Trumbull County
74	1024	10.5	**Parma Heights** (city) Cuyahoga County
74	1024	10.5	**Powell** (city) Delaware County
74	1024	10.5	**Steubenville** (city) Jefferson County
81	1061	10.4	**Brunswick** (city) Medina County
81	1061	10.4	**Canton** (city) Stark County
81	1061	10.4	**Massillon** (city) Stark County
81	1061	10.4	**Middleburg Heights** (city) Cuyahoga County
81	1061	10.4	**West Carrollton** (city) Montgomery County
86	1107	10.3	**Beavercreek** (city) Greene County
86	1107	10.3	**Medina** (city) Medina County
86	1107	10.3	**Newark** (city) Licking County
86	1107	10.3	**Vandalia** (city) Montgomery County
90	1151	10.2	**Kettering** (city) Montgomery County
90	1151	10.2	**Mayfield Heights** (city) Cuyahoga County
90	1151	10.2	**Monroe** (city) Butler County
90	1151	10.2	**Wooster** (city) Wayne County
94	1185	10.1	**Ashland** (city) Ashland County
95	1220	10.0	**Cleveland Heights** (city) Cuyahoga County
95	1220	10.0	**Hudson** (city) Summit County
95	1220	10.0	**Ravenna** (city) Portage County
95	1220	10.0	**Warrensville Heights** (city) Cuyahoga County
99	1258	9.9	**Brecksville** (city) Cuyahoga County
99	1258	9.9	**Chillicothe** (city) Ross County
101	1291	9.8	**Defiance** (city) Defiance County
102	1340	9.7	**Bridgetown** (CDP) Hamilton County
102	1340	9.7	**Maumee** (city) Lucas County
104	1384	9.6	**Columbus** (city) Franklin County
105	1415	9.5	**Garfield Heights** (city) Cuyahoga County
105	1415	9.5	**University Heights** (city) Cuyahoga County
107	1496	9.3	**Amherst** (city) Lorain County
107	1496	9.3	**Brook Park** (city) Cuyahoga County
107	1496	9.3	**North Ridgeville** (city) Lorain County
107	1496	9.3	**North Royalton** (city) Cuyahoga County
107	1496	9.3	**Norwalk** (city) Huron County
107	1496	9.3	**Stow** (city) Summit County
113	1541	9.2	**Xenia** (city) Greene County
114	1583	9.1	**Sylvania** (city) Lucas County
114	1583	9.1	**Twinsburg** (city) Summit County
114	1583	9.1	**Westlake** (city) Cuyahoga County
117	1625	9.0	**Forestville** (CDP) Hamilton County
117	1625	9.0	**Marysville** (city) Union County
117	1625	9.0	**Mount Vernon** (city) Knox County
117	1625	9.0	**Troy** (city) Miami County
117	1625	9.0	**White Oak** (CDP) Hamilton County
122	1674	8.9	**Avon** (city) Lorain County
122	1674	8.9	**Cambridge** (city) Guernsey County
122	1674	8.9	**Englewood** (city) Montgomery County
122	1674	8.9	**Zanesville** (city) Muskingum County
126	1710	8.8	**Painesville** (city) Lake County
127	1755	8.7	**Lancaster** (city) Fairfield County
127	1755	8.7	**Parma** (city) Cuyahoga County
129	1792	8.6	**Clayton** (city) Montgomery County
129	1792	8.6	**Greenville** (city) Darke County
129	1792	8.6	**Sidney** (city) Shelby County
132	1833	8.5	**Bowling Green** (city) Wood County
132	1833	8.5	**North Canton** (city) Stark County
132	1833	8.5	**Strongsville** (city) Cuyahoga County
135	1892	8.4	**Delaware** (city) Delaware County
136	1940	8.3	**Cuyahoga Falls** (city) Summit County
137	1993	8.2	**Macedonia** (city) Summit County
138	2058	8.1	**New Franklin** (city) Summit County
139	2115	8.0	**Kent** (city) Portage County
139	2115	8.0	**Portsmouth** (city) Scioto County
139	2115	8.0	**Washington Court House** (city) Fayette County
142	2176	7.9	**Solon** (city) Cuyahoga County
143	2225	7.8	**Tallmadge** (city) Summit County
143	2225	7.8	**Trenton** (city) Butler County
143	2225	7.8	**Willowick** (city) Lake County
146	2285	7.7	**Pataskala** (city) Licking County
146	2285	7.7	**Springboro** (city) Warren County
148	2325	7.6	**Brooklyn** (city) Cuyahoga County
148	2325	7.6	**Dent** (CDP) Hamilton County
148	2325	7.6	**Oregon** (city) Lucas County

Note: *The state column ranks the top/bottom 150 places from all places in the state with population of 10,000 or more. The national column ranks the top/bottom 150 places from all places in the country with population of 10,000 or more. Places that are unincorporated were not considered in the rankings. Please refer to the User Guide for additional information.*

Rental Vacancy Rate

Top 150 Places Ranked in *Ascending* Order

State Rank	Nat'l Rank	Percent	Place
1	43	2.6	**Mack** (CDP) Hamilton County
1	43	2.6	**Seven Hills** (city) Cuyahoga County
3	304	4.0	**Northbrook** (CDP) Hamilton County
4	419	4.3	**Bay Village** (city) Cuyahoga County
5	593	4.7	**Athens** (city) Athens County
6	1198	5.8	**Norton** (city) Summit County
7	1255	5.9	**Beachwood** (city) Cuyahoga County
7	1255	5.9	**Worthington** (city) Franklin County
9	1364	6.1	**Eastlake** (city) Lake County
9	1364	6.1	**Salem** (city) Columbiana County
11	1480	6.3	**Aurora** (city) Portage County
11	1480	6.3	**Finneytown** (CDP) Hamilton County
13	1540	6.4	**Springdale** (city) Hamilton County
14	1614	6.5	**Gahanna** (city) Franklin County
14	1614	6.5	**Struthers** (city) Mahoning County
16	1680	6.6	**Avon Lake** (city) Lorain County
16	1680	6.6	**Blue Ash** (city) Hamilton County
18	1792	6.8	**Franklin** (city) Warren County
18	1792	6.8	**Westerville** (city) Franklin County
20	1847	6.9	**Grove City** (city) Franklin County
20	1847	6.9	**South Euclid** (city) Cuyahoga County
22	1894	7.0	**Dublin** (city) Franklin County
22	1894	7.0	**Ironton** (city) Lawrence County
22	1894	7.0	**Lebanon** (city) Warren County
22	1894	7.0	**Loveland** (city) Hamilton County
22	1894	7.0	**Upper Arlington** (city) Franklin County
22	1894	7.0	**Wickliffe** (city) Lake County
28	2099	7.3	**Hilliard** (city) Franklin County
28	2099	7.3	**Mason** (city) Warren County
30	2153	7.4	**Barberton** (city) Summit County
30	2153	7.4	**Heath** (city) Licking County
32	2217	7.5	**Berea** (city) Cuyahoga County
32	2217	7.5	**Montgomery** (city) Hamilton County
34	2268	7.6	**Brooklyn** (city) Cuyahoga County
34	2268	7.6	**Dent** (CDP) Hamilton County
34	2268	7.6	**Oregon** (city) Lucas County
37	2332	7.7	**Pataskala** (city) Licking County
37	2332	7.7	**Springboro** (city) Warren County
39	2372	7.8	**Tallmadge** (city) Summit County
39	2372	7.8	**Trenton** (city) Butler County
39	2372	7.8	**Willowick** (city) Lake County
42	2432	7.9	**Solon** (city) Cuyahoga County
43	2481	8.0	**Kent** (city) Portage County
43	2481	8.0	**Portsmouth** (city) Scioto County
43	2481	8.0	**Washington Court House** (city) Fayette County
46	2542	8.1	**New Franklin** (city) Summit County
47	2599	8.2	**Macedonia** (city) Summit County
48	2664	8.3	**Cuyahoga Falls** (city) Summit County
49	2717	8.4	**Delaware** (city) Delaware County
50	2765	8.5	**Bowling Green** (city) Wood County
50	2765	8.5	**North Canton** (city) Stark County
50	2765	8.5	**Strongsville** (city) Cuyahoga County
53	2824	8.6	**Clayton** (city) Montgomery County
53	2824	8.6	**Greenville** (city) Darke County
53	2824	8.6	**Sidney** (city) Shelby County
56	2865	8.7	**Lancaster** (city) Fairfield County
56	2865	8.7	**Parma** (city) Cuyahoga County
58	2902	8.8	**Painesville** (city) Lake County
59	2947	8.9	**Avon** (city) Lorain County
59	2947	8.9	**Cambridge** (city) Guernsey County
59	2947	8.9	**Englewood** (city) Montgomery County
59	2947	8.9	**Zanesville** (city) Muskingum County
63	2983	9.0	**Forestville** (CDP) Hamilton County
63	2983	9.0	**Marysville** (city) Union County
63	2983	9.0	**Mount Vernon** (city) Knox County
63	2983	9.0	**Troy** (city) Miami County
63	2983	9.0	**White Oak** (CDP) Hamilton County
68	3032	9.1	**Sylvania** (city) Lucas County
68	3032	9.1	**Twinsburg** (city) Summit County
68	3032	9.1	**Westlake** (city) Cuyahoga County
71	3074	9.2	**Xenia** (city) Greene County
72	3116	9.3	**Amherst** (city) Lorain County
72	3116	9.3	**Brook Park** (city) Cuyahoga County
72	3116	9.3	**North Ridgeville** (city) Lorain County
72	3116	9.3	**North Royalton** (city) Cuyahoga County
72	3116	9.3	**Norwalk** (city) Huron County
72	3116	9.3	**Stow** (city) Summit County
78	3202	9.5	**Garfield Heights** (city) Cuyahoga County
78	3202	9.5	**University Heights** (city) Cuyahoga County
80	3242	9.6	**Columbus** (city) Franklin County
81	3273	9.7	**Bridgetown** (CDP) Hamilton County
81	3273	9.7	**Maumee** (city) Lucas County
83	3317	9.8	**Defiance** (city) Defiance County
84	3366	9.9	**Brecksville** (city) Cuyahoga County
84	3366	9.9	**Chillicothe** (city) Ross County
86	3399	10.0	**Cleveland Heights** (city) Cuyahoga County
86	3399	10.0	**Hudson** (city) Summit County
86	3399	10.0	**Ravenna** (city) Portage County
86	3399	10.0	**Warrensville Heights** (city) Cuyahoga County
90	3437	10.1	**Ashland** (city) Ashland County
91	3472	10.2	**Kettering** (city) Montgomery County
91	3472	10.2	**Mayfield Heights** (city) Cuyahoga County
91	3472	10.2	**Monroe** (city) Butler County
91	3472	10.2	**Wooster** (city) Wayne County
95	3506	10.3	**Beavercreek** (city) Greene County
95	3506	10.3	**Medina** (city) Medina County
95	3506	10.3	**Newark** (city) Licking County
95	3506	10.3	**Vandalia** (city) Montgomery County
99	3550	10.4	**Brunswick** (city) Medina County
99	3550	10.4	**Canton** (city) Stark County
99	3550	10.4	**Massillon** (city) Stark County
99	3550	10.4	**Middleburg Heights** (city) Cuyahoga County
99	3550	10.4	**West Carrollton** (city) Montgomery County
104	3596	10.5	**Akron** (city) Summit County
104	3596	10.5	**Dover** (city) Tuscarawas County
104	3596	10.5	**Fremont** (city) Sandusky County
104	3596	10.5	**Niles** (city) Trumbull County
104	3596	10.5	**Parma Heights** (city) Cuyahoga County
104	3596	10.5	**Powell** (city) Delaware County
104	3596	10.5	**Steubenville** (city) Jefferson County
111	3633	10.6	**Bucyrus** (city) Crawford County
111	3633	10.6	**Coshocton** (city) Coshocton County
111	3633	10.6	**Sharonville** (city) Hamilton County
114	3666	10.7	**Riverside** (city) Montgomery County
115	3697	10.8	**Bedford** (city) Cuyahoga County
115	3697	10.8	**Bellefontaine** (city) Logan County
115	3697	10.8	**Wadsworth** (city) Medina County
118	3727	10.9	**Boardman** (CDP) Mahoning County
118	3727	10.9	**Centerville** (city) Montgomery County
118	3727	10.9	**Marietta** (city) Washington County
118	3727	10.9	**Norwood** (city) Hamilton County
122	3761	11.0	**New Philadelphia** (city) Tuscarawas County
122	3761	11.0	**Van Wert** (city) Van Wert County
124	3797	11.1	**Conneaut** (city) Ashtabula County
124	3797	11.1	**Forest Park** (city) Hamilton County
124	3797	11.1	**Perrysburg** (city) Wood County
124	3797	11.1	**Urbana** (city) Champaign County
124	3797	11.1	**Willoughby** (city) Lake County
124	3797	11.1	**Youngstown** (city) Mahoning County
130	3826	11.2	**Lyndhurst** (city) Cuyahoga County
130	3826	11.2	**Mentor** (city) Lake County
132	3852	11.3	**Fostoria** (city) Seneca County
132	3852	11.3	**North Olmsted** (city) Cuyahoga County
132	3852	11.3	**Streetsboro** (city) Portage County
132	3852	11.3	**Vermilion** (city) Lorain County
136	3901	11.5	**Huber Heights** (city) Montgomery County
136	3901	11.5	**Reading** (city) Hamilton County
138	3926	11.6	**Ashtabula** (city) Ashtabula County
138	3926	11.6	**Reynoldsburg** (city) Franklin County
138	3926	11.6	**Springfield** (city) Clark County
141	3951	11.7	**Pickerington** (city) Fairfield County
142	3975	11.8	**East Liverpool** (city) Columbiana County
143	4001	11.9	**Circleville** (city) Pickaway County
143	4001	11.9	**Hamilton** (city) Butler County
145	4022	12.0	**Fairfield** (city) Butler County
145	4022	12.0	**Findlay** (city) Hancock County
145	4022	12.0	**Lakewood** (city) Cuyahoga County
145	4022	12.0	**Lima** (city) Allen County
145	4022	12.0	**Toledo** (city) Lucas County
150	4052	12.1	**Galion** (city) Crawford County

Note: *The state column ranks the top/bottom 150 places from all places in the state with population of 10,000 or more. The national column ranks the top/bottom 150 places from all places in the country with population of 10,000 or more. Places that are unincorporated were not considered in the rankings. Please refer to the User Guide for additional information.*

Population with Health Insurance

Top 150 Places Ranked in *Descending* Order

State Rank	Nat'l Rank	Percent	Place
1	37	98.4	**Powell** (city) Delaware County
2	108	97.5	**Beachwood** (city) Cuyahoga County
3	190	96.9	**Dublin** (city) Franklin County
4	227	96.7	**Montgomery** (city) Hamilton County
5	245	96.6	**Dent** (CDP) Hamilton County
6	276	96.4	**Monfort Heights** (CDP) Hamilton County
6	276	96.4	**Twinsburg** (city) Summit County
8	291	96.3	**Bay Village** (city) Cuyahoga County
9	314	96.2	**Hudson** (city) Summit County
9	314	96.2	**Macedonia** (city) Summit County
11	361	96.0	**Avon** (city) Lorain County
12	387	95.9	**Mack** (CDP) Hamilton County
12	387	95.9	**University Heights** (city) Cuyahoga County
14	412	95.8	**Avon Lake** (city) Lorain County
14	412	95.8	**Springboro** (city) Warren County
16	456	95.6	**Lyndhurst** (city) Cuyahoga County
17	542	95.3	**Athens** (city) Athens County
17	542	95.3	**Forestville** (CDP) Hamilton County
19	559	95.2	**Seven Hills** (city) Cuyahoga County
19	559	95.2	**Upper Arlington** (city) Franklin County
21	597	95.0	**Solon** (city) Cuyahoga County
21	597	95.0	**Westlake** (city) Cuyahoga County
21	597	95.0	**Worthington** (city) Franklin County
24	651	94.8	**Brecksville** (city) Cuyahoga County
25	680	94.7	**Mason** (city) Warren County
26	702	94.6	**Strongsville** (city) Cuyahoga County
26	702	94.6	**Westerville** (city) Franklin County
28	746	94.4	**Gahanna** (city) Franklin County
29	779	94.3	**Tallmadge** (city) Summit County
30	801	94.2	**Beavercreek** (city) Greene County
30	801	94.2	**Bexley** (city) Franklin County
30	801	94.2	**Oxford** (city) Butler County
30	801	94.2	**Perrysburg** (city) Wood County
34	828	94.1	**Blue Ash** (city) Hamilton County
34	828	94.1	**Pickerington** (city) Fairfield County
36	864	94.0	**Loveland** (city) Hamilton County
36	864	94.0	**Mentor** (city) Lake County
36	864	94.0	**Rocky River** (city) Cuyahoga County
39	886	93.9	**Amherst** (city) Lorain County
40	902	93.8	**Aurora** (city) Portage County
41	926	93.7	**Broadview Heights** (city) Cuyahoga County
41	926	93.7	**Shaker Heights** (city) Cuyahoga County
43	989	93.5	**Sylvania** (city) Lucas County
44	1023	93.4	**Centerville** (city) Montgomery County
44	1023	93.4	**Clayton** (city) Montgomery County
46	1063	93.2	**Bridgetown** (CDP) Hamilton County
47	1109	93.0	**Stow** (city) Summit County
48	1199	92.7	**Monroe** (city) Butler County
49	1236	92.6	**Hilliard** (city) Franklin County
49	1236	92.6	**North Ridgeville** (city) Lorain County
51	1266	92.5	**Delaware** (city) Delaware County
52	1286	92.4	**Maumee** (city) Lucas County
52	1286	92.4	**New Franklin** (city) Summit County
54	1343	92.2	**North Olmsted** (city) Cuyahoga County
55	1366	92.1	**North Canton** (city) Stark County
56	1391	92.0	**Berea** (city) Cuyahoga County
56	1391	92.0	**Englewood** (city) Montgomery County
56	1391	92.0	**Middleburg Heights** (city) Cuyahoga County
56	1391	92.0	**Norton** (city) Summit County
60	1428	91.9	**Wickliffe** (city) Lake County
61	1454	91.8	**Bowling Green** (city) Wood County
61	1454	91.8	**Finneytown** (CDP) Hamilton County
63	1478	91.7	**Willowick** (city) Lake County
64	1499	91.6	**North Royalton** (city) Cuyahoga County
65	1552	91.4	**Mayfield Heights** (city) Cuyahoga County
66	1634	91.1	**Brunswick** (city) Medina County
66	1634	91.1	**Wooster** (city) Wayne County
68	1655	91.0	**Miamisburg** (city) Montgomery County
69	1675	90.9	**Marysville** (city) Union County
70	1703	90.8	**Medina** (city) Medina County
71	1728	90.7	**Wadsworth** (city) Medina County
72	1759	90.6	**Green** (city) Summit County
72	1759	90.6	**Oregon** (city) Lucas County
74	1781	90.5	**White Oak** (CDP) Hamilton County
75	1807	90.4	**Celina** (city) Mercer County
75	1807	90.4	**Kettering** (city) Montgomery County
75	1807	90.4	**Lebanon** (city) Warren County
78	1830	90.3	**Fairview Park** (city) Cuyahoga County
78	1830	90.3	**Reynoldsburg** (city) Franklin County
78	1830	90.3	**South Euclid** (city) Cuyahoga County
81	1847	90.2	**Grove City** (city) Franklin County
82	1919	89.9	**Boardman** (CDP) Mahoning County
83	1948	89.8	**Cuyahoga Falls** (city) Summit County
83	1948	89.8	**Vandalia** (city) Montgomery County
85	1978	89.7	**Cleveland Heights** (city) Cuyahoga County
86	2021	89.5	**Franklin** (city) Warren County
86	2021	89.5	**Garfield Heights** (city) Cuyahoga County
86	2021	89.5	**Heath** (city) Licking County
86	2021	89.5	**Streetsboro** (city) Portage County
86	2021	89.5	**Willoughby** (city) Lake County
91	2044	89.4	**Norwalk** (city) Huron County
91	2044	89.4	**Trenton** (city) Butler County
93	2068	89.3	**Steubenville** (city) Jefferson County
94	2091	89.2	**Brook Park** (city) Cuyahoga County
94	2091	89.2	**Pataskala** (city) Licking County
96	2117	89.1	**Bedford** (city) Cuyahoga County
96	2117	89.1	**Parma** (city) Cuyahoga County
98	2144	89.0	**New Philadelphia** (city) Tuscarawas County
99	2194	88.8	**Fairborn** (city) Greene County
99	2194	88.8	**Ravenna** (city) Portage County
99	2194	88.8	**Troy** (city) Miami County
102	2223	88.7	**Austintown** (CDP) Mahoning County
102	2223	88.7	**Wilmington** (city) Clinton County
104	2245	88.6	**Vermilion** (city) Lorain County
105	2264	88.5	**Massillon** (city) Stark County
106	2285	88.4	**Van Wert** (city) Van Wert County
107	2303	88.3	**Coshocton** (city) Coshocton County
107	2303	88.3	**Xenia** (city) Greene County
109	2326	88.2	**Maple Heights** (city) Cuyahoga County
110	2351	88.1	**Galion** (city) Crawford County
110	2351	88.1	**Parma Heights** (city) Cuyahoga County
112	2375	88.0	**Defiance** (city) Defiance County
112	2375	88.0	**Eastlake** (city) Lake County
112	2375	88.0	**Fairfield** (city) Butler County
115	2405	87.9	**Bucyrus** (city) Crawford County
116	2425	87.8	**Elyria** (city) Lorain County
116	2425	87.8	**Findlay** (city) Hancock County
116	2425	87.8	**Huber Heights** (city) Montgomery County
116	2425	87.8	**Kent** (city) Portage County
120	2482	87.6	**Brooklyn** (city) Cuyahoga County
120	2482	87.6	**Lancaster** (city) Fairfield County
120	2482	87.6	**Tiffin** (city) Seneca County
120	2482	87.6	**Warrensville Heights** (city) Cuyahoga County
124	2527	87.4	**Cambridge** (city) Guernsey County
125	2546	87.3	**East Liverpool** (city) Columbiana County
126	2574	87.2	**Sharonville** (city) Hamilton County
127	2638	86.9	**Circleville** (city) Pickaway County
127	2638	86.9	**Marietta** (city) Washington County
127	2638	86.9	**Warren** (city) Trumbull County
130	2666	86.8	**Lorain** (city) Lorain County
130	2666	86.8	**Mount Vernon** (city) Knox County
132	2685	86.7	**Conneaut** (city) Ashtabula County
132	2685	86.7	**Mansfield** (city) Richland County
134	2715	86.6	**Reading** (city) Hamilton County
134	2715	86.6	**Sidney** (city) Shelby County
136	2739	86.5	**Bellefontaine** (city) Logan County
137	2773	86.3	**Ashland** (city) Ashland County
137	2773	86.3	**Riverside** (city) Montgomery County
139	2802	86.2	**Struthers** (city) Mahoning County
140	2822	86.1	**Urbana** (city) Champaign County
141	2844	86.0	**Newark** (city) Licking County
141	2844	86.0	**Richmond Heights** (city) Cuyahoga County
143	2876	85.9	**Dover** (city) Tuscarawas County
143	2876	85.9	**Ironton** (city) Lawrence County
145	2899	85.8	**Barberton** (city) Summit County
145	2899	85.8	**Greenville** (city) Darke County
147	2921	85.7	**Ashtabula** (city) Ashtabula County
147	2921	85.7	**Lakewood** (city) Cuyahoga County
149	2944	85.6	**Northbrook** (CDP) Hamilton County
149	2944	85.6	**Springfield** (city) Clark County

Note: *The state column ranks the top/bottom 150 places from all places in the state with population of 10,000 or more. The national column ranks the top/bottom 150 places from all places in the country with population of 10,000 or more. Places that are unincorporated were not considered in the rankings. Please refer to the User Guide for additional information.*

Population with Health Insurance

Top 150 Places Ranked in *Ascending* Order

State Rank	Nat'l Rank	Percent	Place
1	458	77.4	**Whitehall** (city) Franklin County
2	774	80.4	**East Cleveland** (city) Cuyahoga County
3	822	80.8	**Painesville** (city) Lake County
4	983	81.8	**Forest Park** (city) Hamilton County
5	1074	82.4	**Portsmouth** (city) Scioto County
6	1115	82.6	**Lima** (city) Allen County
7	1137	82.7	**Norwood** (city) Hamilton County
8	1191	83.0	**Springdale** (city) Hamilton County
9	1209	83.1	**Cleveland** (city) Cuyahoga County
9	1209	83.1	**Dayton** (city) Montgomery County
11	1265	83.4	**Canton** (city) Stark County
12	1286	83.5	**Niles** (city) Trumbull County
13	1311	83.6	**Sandusky** (city) Erie County
14	1355	83.8	**Fremont** (city) Sandusky County
14	1355	83.8	**Washington Court House** (city) Fayette County
16	1394	84.0	**Akron** (city) Summit County
17	1429	84.2	**Fostoria** (city) Seneca County
17	1429	84.2	**Marion** (city) Marion County
19	1452	84.3	**Salem** (city) Columbiana County
19	1452	84.3	**Trotwood** (city) Montgomery County
21	1490	84.5	**Hamilton** (city) Butler County
22	1511	84.6	**Bedford Heights** (city) Cuyahoga County
23	1529	84.7	**Columbus** (city) Franklin County
23	1529	84.7	**Toledo** (city) Lucas County
25	1557	84.9	**Cincinnati** (city) Hamilton County
25	1557	84.9	**Youngstown** (city) Mahoning County
27	1578	85.0	**Middletown** (city) Butler County
28	1588	85.1	**West Carrollton** (city) Montgomery County
29	1624	85.3	**Chillicothe** (city) Ross County
30	1643	85.4	**Euclid** (city) Cuyahoga County
31	1663	85.5	**Alliance** (city) Stark County
31	1663	85.5	**Piqua** (city) Miami County
33	1683	85.6	**Northbrook** (CDP) Hamilton County
33	1683	85.6	**Springfield** (city) Clark County
33	1683	85.6	**Zanesville** (city) Muskingum County
36	1713	85.7	**Ashtabula** (city) Ashtabula County
36	1713	85.7	**Lakewood** (city) Cuyahoga County
38	1736	85.8	**Barberton** (city) Summit County
38	1736	85.8	**Greenville** (city) Darke County
40	1758	85.9	**Dover** (city) Tuscarawas County
40	1758	85.9	**Ironton** (city) Lawrence County
42	1781	86.0	**Newark** (city) Licking County
42	1781	86.0	**Richmond Heights** (city) Cuyahoga County
44	1813	86.1	**Urbana** (city) Champaign County
45	1835	86.2	**Struthers** (city) Mahoning County
46	1855	86.3	**Ashland** (city) Ashland County
46	1855	86.3	**Riverside** (city) Montgomery County
48	1897	86.5	**Bellefontaine** (city) Logan County
49	1918	86.6	**Reading** (city) Hamilton County
49	1918	86.6	**Sidney** (city) Shelby County
51	1942	86.7	**Conneaut** (city) Ashtabula County
51	1942	86.7	**Mansfield** (city) Richland County
53	1972	86.8	**Lorain** (city) Lorain County
53	1972	86.8	**Mount Vernon** (city) Knox County
55	1991	86.9	**Circleville** (city) Pickaway County
55	1991	86.9	**Marietta** (city) Washington County
55	1991	86.9	**Warren** (city) Trumbull County
58	2063	87.2	**Sharonville** (city) Hamilton County
59	2083	87.3	**East Liverpool** (city) Columbiana County
60	2111	87.4	**Cambridge** (city) Guernsey County
61	2153	87.6	**Brooklyn** (city) Cuyahoga County
61	2153	87.6	**Lancaster** (city) Fairfield County
61	2153	87.6	**Tiffin** (city) Seneca County
61	2153	87.6	**Warrensville Heights** (city) Cuyahoga County
65	2201	87.8	**Elyria** (city) Lorain County
65	2201	87.8	**Findlay** (city) Hancock County
65	2201	87.8	**Huber Heights** (city) Montgomery County
65	2201	87.8	**Kent** (city) Portage County
69	2232	87.9	**Bucyrus** (city) Crawford County
70	2252	88.0	**Defiance** (city) Defiance County
70	2252	88.0	**Eastlake** (city) Lake County
70	2252	88.0	**Fairfield** (city) Butler County
73	2282	88.1	**Galion** (city) Crawford County
73	2282	88.1	**Parma Heights** (city) Cuyahoga County
75	2306	88.2	**Maple Heights** (city) Cuyahoga County
76	2331	88.3	**Coshocton** (city) Coshocton County
76	2331	88.3	**Xenia** (city) Greene County
78	2354	88.4	**Van Wert** (city) Van Wert County
79	2372	88.5	**Massillon** (city) Stark County
80	2393	88.6	**Vermilion** (city) Lorain County
81	2412	88.7	**Austintown** (CDP) Mahoning County
81	2412	88.7	**Wilmington** (city) Clinton County
83	2434	88.8	**Fairborn** (city) Greene County
83	2434	88.8	**Ravenna** (city) Portage County
83	2434	88.8	**Troy** (city) Miami County
86	2486	89.0	**New Philadelphia** (city) Tuscarawas County
87	2513	89.1	**Bedford** (city) Cuyahoga County
87	2513	89.1	**Parma** (city) Cuyahoga County
89	2540	89.2	**Brook Park** (city) Cuyahoga County
89	2540	89.2	**Pataskala** (city) Licking County
91	2566	89.3	**Steubenville** (city) Jefferson County
92	2589	89.4	**Norwalk** (city) Huron County
92	2589	89.4	**Trenton** (city) Butler County
94	2613	89.5	**Franklin** (city) Warren County
94	2613	89.5	**Garfield Heights** (city) Cuyahoga County
94	2613	89.5	**Heath** (city) Licking County
94	2613	89.5	**Streetsboro** (city) Portage County
94	2613	89.5	**Willoughby** (city) Lake County
99	2653	89.7	**Cleveland Heights** (city) Cuyahoga County
100	2679	89.8	**Cuyahoga Falls** (city) Summit County
100	2679	89.8	**Vandalia** (city) Montgomery County
102	2709	89.9	**Boardman** (CDP) Mahoning County
103	2781	90.2	**Grove City** (city) Franklin County
104	2810	90.3	**Fairview Park** (city) Cuyahoga County
104	2810	90.3	**Reynoldsburg** (city) Franklin County
104	2810	90.3	**South Euclid** (city) Cuyahoga County
107	2827	90.4	**Celina** (city) Mercer County
107	2827	90.4	**Kettering** (city) Montgomery County
107	2827	90.4	**Lebanon** (city) Warren County
110	2850	90.5	**White Oak** (CDP) Hamilton County
111	2876	90.6	**Green** (city) Summit County
111	2876	90.6	**Oregon** (city) Lucas County
113	2898	90.7	**Wadsworth** (city) Medina County
114	2929	90.8	**Medina** (city) Medina County
115	2954	90.9	**Marysville** (city) Union County
116	2982	91.0	**Miamisburg** (city) Montgomery County
117	3002	91.1	**Brunswick** (city) Medina County
117	3002	91.1	**Wooster** (city) Wayne County
119	3078	91.4	**Mayfield Heights** (city) Cuyahoga County
120	3132	91.6	**North Royalton** (city) Cuyahoga County
121	3158	91.7	**Willowick** (city) Lake County
122	3179	91.8	**Bowling Green** (city) Wood County
122	3179	91.8	**Finneytown** (CDP) Hamilton County
124	3203	91.9	**Wickliffe** (city) Lake County
125	3229	92.0	**Berea** (city) Cuyahoga County
125	3229	92.0	**Englewood** (city) Montgomery County
125	3229	92.0	**Middleburg Heights** (city) Cuyahoga County
125	3229	92.0	**Norton** (city) Summit County
129	3266	92.1	**North Canton** (city) Stark County
130	3291	92.2	**North Olmsted** (city) Cuyahoga County
131	3342	92.4	**Maumee** (city) Lucas County
131	3342	92.4	**New Franklin** (city) Summit County
133	3371	92.5	**Delaware** (city) Delaware County
134	3391	92.6	**Hilliard** (city) Franklin County
134	3391	92.6	**North Ridgeville** (city) Lorain County
136	3421	92.7	**Monroe** (city) Butler County
137	3523	93.0	**Stow** (city) Summit County
138	3570	93.2	**Bridgetown** (CDP) Hamilton County
139	3611	93.4	**Centerville** (city) Montgomery County
139	3611	93.4	**Clayton** (city) Montgomery County
141	3634	93.5	**Sylvania** (city) Lucas County
142	3698	93.7	**Broadview Heights** (city) Cuyahoga County
142	3698	93.7	**Shaker Heights** (city) Cuyahoga County
144	3731	93.8	**Aurora** (city) Portage County
145	3755	93.9	**Amherst** (city) Lorain County
146	3771	94.0	**Loveland** (city) Hamilton County
146	3771	94.0	**Mentor** (city) Lake County
146	3771	94.0	**Rocky River** (city) Cuyahoga County
149	3793	94.1	**Blue Ash** (city) Hamilton County
149	3793	94.1	**Pickerington** (city) Fairfield County

Note: *The state column ranks the top/bottom 150 places from all places in the state with population of 10,000 or more. The national column ranks the top/bottom 150 places from all places in the country with population of 10,000 or more. Places that are unincorporated were not considered in the rankings. Please refer to the User Guide for additional information.*

Population with Private Health Insurance

Top 150 Places Ranked in *Descending* Order

State Rank	Nat'l Rank	Percent	Place
1	15	94.9	**Powell** (city) Delaware County
2	44	93.4	**Dublin** (city) Franklin County
3	76	92.5	**Hudson** (city) Summit County
4	174	90.7	**Montgomery** (city) Hamilton County
5	207	90.4	**Avon** (city) Lorain County
6	250	89.9	**Mason** (city) Warren County
7	257	89.8	**Avon Lake** (city) Lorain County
8	315	89.1	**Bay Village** (city) Cuyahoga County
8	315	89.1	**Macedonia** (city) Summit County
10	343	88.8	**Athens** (city) Athens County
11	353	88.7	**Beachwood** (city) Cuyahoga County
12	361	88.6	**Pickerington** (city) Fairfield County
12	361	88.6	**Springboro** (city) Warren County
12	361	88.6	**Worthington** (city) Franklin County
15	389	88.4	**Dent** (CDP) Hamilton County
15	389	88.4	**Upper Arlington** (city) Franklin County
17	403	88.3	**Oxford** (city) Butler County
18	437	88.0	**Bexley** (city) Franklin County
18	437	88.0	**Twinsburg** (city) Summit County
20	493	87.6	**Perrysburg** (city) Wood County
21	520	87.4	**Brecksville** (city) Cuyahoga County
22	559	87.0	**Lyndhurst** (city) Cuyahoga County
22	559	87.0	**Solon** (city) Cuyahoga County
24	577	86.9	**Mack** (CDP) Hamilton County
25	592	86.8	**Broadview Heights** (city) Cuyahoga County
26	600	86.7	**Westlake** (city) Cuyahoga County
27	649	86.3	**Beavercreek** (city) Greene County
28	655	86.2	**Aurora** (city) Portage County
29	696	85.9	**Westerville** (city) Franklin County
30	733	85.7	**Gahanna** (city) Franklin County
31	764	85.4	**Strongsville** (city) Cuyahoga County
32	816	85.0	**Blue Ash** (city) Hamilton County
33	890	84.4	**Stow** (city) Summit County
34	938	84.0	**Sylvania** (city) Lucas County
35	979	83.7	**Forestville** (CDP) Hamilton County
35	979	83.7	**Mentor** (city) Lake County
37	991	83.6	**Monfort Heights** (CDP) Hamilton County
38	1030	83.3	**Hilliard** (city) Franklin County
38	1030	83.3	**Maumee** (city) Lucas County
38	1030	83.3	**Shaker Heights** (city) Cuyahoga County
41	1060	83.1	**Rocky River** (city) Cuyahoga County
42	1080	82.9	**Bowling Green** (city) Wood County
43	1096	82.8	**North Ridgeville** (city) Lorain County
43	1096	82.8	**Seven Hills** (city) Cuyahoga County
45	1143	82.4	**University Heights** (city) Cuyahoga County
46	1170	82.2	**North Royalton** (city) Cuyahoga County
47	1306	81.0	**Centerville** (city) Montgomery County
47	1306	81.0	**Monroe** (city) Butler County
49	1321	80.9	**Amherst** (city) Lorain County
49	1321	80.9	**Loveland** (city) Hamilton County
51	1384	80.5	**Tallmadge** (city) Summit County
52	1405	80.3	**New Franklin** (city) Summit County
52	1405	80.3	**North Canton** (city) Stark County
54	1419	80.2	**Bridgetown** (CDP) Hamilton County
55	1440	80.1	**Middleburg Heights** (city) Cuyahoga County
56	1462	79.9	**Brunswick** (city) Medina County
57	1533	79.4	**Mayfield Heights** (city) Cuyahoga County
58	1544	79.3	**Norton** (city) Summit County
59	1553	79.2	**Clayton** (city) Montgomery County
59	1553	79.2	**Delaware** (city) Delaware County
61	1594	78.9	**Grove City** (city) Franklin County
62	1638	78.5	**North Olmsted** (city) Cuyahoga County
62	1638	78.5	**Oregon** (city) Lucas County
64	1662	78.3	**Berea** (city) Cuyahoga County
65	1682	78.1	**Green** (city) Summit County
66	1761	77.2	**Fairview Park** (city) Cuyahoga County
66	1761	77.2	**Marysville** (city) Union County
66	1761	77.2	**Wadsworth** (city) Medina County
69	1777	77.1	**Willoughby** (city) Lake County
70	1796	77.0	**Streetsboro** (city) Portage County
71	1825	76.7	**Medina** (city) Medina County
72	1847	76.5	**Fairfield** (city) Butler County
73	1857	76.4	**Willowick** (city) Lake County
74	1887	76.2	**Wickliffe** (city) Lake County
75	1921	75.9	**Cuyahoga Falls** (city) Summit County
76	1943	75.7	**Pataskala** (city) Licking County
77	1955	75.6	**Trenton** (city) Butler County
78	1970	75.5	**Kettering** (city) Montgomery County
79	2055	74.7	**Reynoldsburg** (city) Franklin County
79	2055	74.7	**Richmond Heights** (city) Cuyahoga County
81	2120	74.2	**Englewood** (city) Montgomery County
82	2133	74.1	**South Euclid** (city) Cuyahoga County
83	2162	73.8	**White Oak** (CDP) Hamilton County
84	2195	73.5	**Vermilion** (city) Lorain County
85	2237	73.0	**Eastlake** (city) Lake County
86	2263	72.7	**Vandalia** (city) Montgomery County
87	2272	72.6	**Celina** (city) Mercer County
87	2272	72.6	**Kent** (city) Portage County
89	2306	72.3	**Bedford** (city) Cuyahoga County
89	2306	72.3	**Boardman** (CDP) Mahoning County
91	2319	72.1	**Miamisburg** (city) Montgomery County
91	2319	72.1	**Wooster** (city) Wayne County
93	2354	71.7	**Dover** (city) Tuscarawas County
93	2354	71.7	**Troy** (city) Miami County
95	2374	71.6	**Lebanon** (city) Warren County
96	2394	71.4	**Parma** (city) Cuyahoga County
97	2452	70.8	**Huber Heights** (city) Montgomery County
98	2462	70.7	**Cleveland Heights** (city) Cuyahoga County
99	2471	70.6	**Brook Park** (city) Cuyahoga County
100	2494	70.4	**Heath** (city) Licking County
101	2538	70.0	**Findlay** (city) Hancock County
102	2553	69.9	**Sharonville** (city) Hamilton County
103	2594	69.6	**Ashland** (city) Ashland County
104	2678	68.7	**Parma Heights** (city) Cuyahoga County
105	2702	68.4	**Defiance** (city) Defiance County
106	2726	68.2	**Austintown** (CDP) Mahoning County
107	2757	67.8	**Finneytown** (CDP) Hamilton County
108	2799	67.4	**Fairborn** (city) Greene County
109	2811	67.3	**Norwalk** (city) Huron County
110	2828	67.1	**West Carrollton** (city) Montgomery County
111	2865	66.8	**Brooklyn** (city) Cuyahoga County
111	2865	66.8	**Garfield Heights** (city) Cuyahoga County
111	2865	66.8	**Lakewood** (city) Cuyahoga County
114	2883	66.6	**Tiffin** (city) Seneca County
115	2941	65.9	**Franklin** (city) Warren County
116	3064	64.6	**Massillon** (city) Stark County
117	3120	64.0	**Sidney** (city) Shelby County
118	3132	63.9	**Elyria** (city) Lorain County
118	3132	63.9	**New Philadelphia** (city) Tuscarawas County
120	3142	63.8	**Steubenville** (city) Jefferson County
121	3150	63.7	**Columbus** (city) Franklin County
122	3169	63.5	**Van Wert** (city) Van Wert County
123	3194	63.3	**Bucyrus** (city) Crawford County
123	3194	63.3	**Euclid** (city) Cuyahoga County
125	3207	63.2	**Marietta** (city) Washington County
126	3216	63.1	**Xenia** (city) Greene County
127	3228	63.0	**Forest Park** (city) Hamilton County
128	3240	62.8	**Bedford Heights** (city) Cuyahoga County
128	3240	62.8	**Riverside** (city) Montgomery County
130	3261	62.6	**Conneaut** (city) Ashtabula County
131	3301	62.2	**Ironton** (city) Lawrence County
132	3316	62.0	**Norwood** (city) Hamilton County
133	3325	61.8	**Piqua** (city) Miami County
133	3325	61.8	**Urbana** (city) Champaign County
135	3341	61.6	**Coshocton** (city) Coshocton County
136	3359	61.4	**Maple Heights** (city) Cuyahoga County
136	3359	61.4	**Mount Vernon** (city) Knox County
138	3392	61.0	**Northbrook** (CDP) Hamilton County
139	3419	60.6	**Niles** (city) Trumbull County
139	3419	60.6	**Salem** (city) Columbiana County
141	3426	60.5	**Springdale** (city) Hamilton County
142	3438	60.3	**Fremont** (city) Sandusky County
143	3451	60.2	**Newark** (city) Licking County
144	3479	59.9	**Hamilton** (city) Butler County
144	3479	59.9	**Reading** (city) Hamilton County
144	3479	59.9	**Wilmington** (city) Clinton County
147	3498	59.7	**Circleville** (city) Pickaway County
148	3505	59.6	**Barberton** (city) Summit County
149	3511	59.5	**Greenville** (city) Darke County
150	3518	59.4	**Fostoria** (city) Seneca County

Note: *The state column ranks the top/bottom 150 places from all places in the state with population of 10,000 or more. The national column ranks the top/bottom 150 places from all places in the country with population of 10,000 or more. Places that are unincorporated were not considered in the rankings. Please refer to the User Guide for additional information.*

Population with Private Health Insurance

Top 150 Places Ranked in *Ascending* Order

State Rank	Nat'l Rank	Percent	Place
1	111	36.5	**East Cleveland** (city) Cuyahoga County
2	198	42.0	**Youngstown** (city) Mahoning County
3	232	43.3	**Zanesville** (city) Muskingum County
4	296	45.3	**Cleveland** (city) Cuyahoga County
5	389	47.7	**Whitehall** (city) Franklin County
6	475	49.6	**Canton** (city) Stark County
7	492	50.0	**Ashtabula** (city) Ashtabula County
7	492	50.0	**Warren** (city) Trumbull County
9	500	50.1	**Portsmouth** (city) Scioto County
10	512	50.3	**Lima** (city) Allen County
11	547	51.1	**Dayton** (city) Montgomery County
12	590	51.9	**East Liverpool** (city) Columbiana County
13	644	53.1	**Lorain** (city) Lorain County
13	644	53.1	**Marion** (city) Marion County
15	653	53.2	**Springfield** (city) Clark County
16	675	53.6	**Cambridge** (city) Guernsey County
17	744	54.7	**Mansfield** (city) Richland County
18	785	55.2	**Galion** (city) Crawford County
18	785	55.2	**Painesville** (city) Lake County
20	805	55.4	**Middletown** (city) Butler County
21	814	55.5	**Washington Court House** (city) Fayette County
22	826	55.7	**Sandusky** (city) Erie County
23	843	56.0	**Akron** (city) Summit County
24	879	56.4	**Alliance** (city) Stark County
25	889	56.5	**Struthers** (city) Mahoning County
26	909	56.7	**Ravenna** (city) Portage County
27	918	56.8	**Chillicothe** (city) Ross County
28	925	56.9	**Toledo** (city) Lucas County
29	935	57.1	**Trotwood** (city) Montgomery County
30	983	57.6	**Cincinnati** (city) Hamilton County
31	988	57.7	**Bellefontaine** (city) Logan County
32	1085	58.9	**Warrensville Heights** (city) Cuyahoga County
33	1126	59.4	**Fostoria** (city) Seneca County
33	1126	59.4	**Lancaster** (city) Fairfield County
35	1139	59.5	**Greenville** (city) Darke County
36	1146	59.6	**Barberton** (city) Summit County
37	1152	59.7	**Circleville** (city) Pickaway County
38	1166	59.9	**Hamilton** (city) Butler County
38	1166	59.9	**Reading** (city) Hamilton County
38	1166	59.9	**Wilmington** (city) Clinton County
41	1199	60.2	**Newark** (city) Licking County
42	1206	60.3	**Fremont** (city) Sandusky County
43	1225	60.5	**Springdale** (city) Hamilton County
44	1231	60.6	**Niles** (city) Trumbull County
44	1231	60.6	**Salem** (city) Columbiana County
46	1257	61.0	**Northbrook** (CDP) Hamilton County
47	1290	61.4	**Maple Heights** (city) Cuyahoga County
47	1290	61.4	**Mount Vernon** (city) Knox County
49	1309	61.6	**Coshocton** (city) Coshocton County
50	1326	61.8	**Piqua** (city) Miami County
50	1326	61.8	**Urbana** (city) Champaign County
52	1338	62.0	**Norwood** (city) Hamilton County
53	1345	62.2	**Ironton** (city) Lawrence County
54	1385	62.6	**Conneaut** (city) Ashtabula County
55	1405	62.8	**Bedford Heights** (city) Cuyahoga County
55	1405	62.8	**Riverside** (city) Montgomery County
57	1421	63.0	**Forest Park** (city) Hamilton County
58	1429	63.1	**Xenia** (city) Greene County
59	1441	63.2	**Marietta** (city) Washington County
60	1450	63.3	**Bucyrus** (city) Crawford County
60	1450	63.3	**Euclid** (city) Cuyahoga County
62	1475	63.5	**Van Wert** (city) Van Wert County
63	1498	63.7	**Columbus** (city) Franklin County
64	1507	63.8	**Steubenville** (city) Jefferson County
65	1515	63.9	**Elyria** (city) Lorain County
65	1515	63.9	**New Philadelphia** (city) Tuscarawas County
67	1525	64.0	**Sidney** (city) Shelby County
68	1583	64.6	**Massillon** (city) Stark County
69	1708	65.9	**Franklin** (city) Warren County
70	1764	66.6	**Tiffin** (city) Seneca County
71	1779	66.8	**Brooklyn** (city) Cuyahoga County
71	1779	66.8	**Garfield Heights** (city) Cuyahoga County
71	1779	66.8	**Lakewood** (city) Cuyahoga County
74	1821	67.1	**West Carrollton** (city) Montgomery County
75	1840	67.3	**Norwalk** (city) Huron County
76	1846	67.4	**Fairborn** (city) Greene County
77	1889	67.8	**Finneytown** (CDP) Hamilton County
78	1922	68.2	**Austintown** (CDP) Mahoning County
79	1939	68.4	**Defiance** (city) Defiance County
80	1972	68.7	**Parma Heights** (city) Cuyahoga County
81	2056	69.6	**Ashland** (city) Ashland County
82	2090	69.9	**Sharonville** (city) Hamilton County
83	2104	70.0	**Findlay** (city) Hancock County
84	2153	70.4	**Heath** (city) Licking County
85	2174	70.6	**Brook Park** (city) Cuyahoga County
86	2186	70.7	**Cleveland Heights** (city) Cuyahoga County
87	2195	70.8	**Huber Heights** (city) Montgomery County
88	2256	71.4	**Parma** (city) Cuyahoga County
89	2273	71.6	**Lebanon** (city) Warren County
90	2283	71.7	**Dover** (city) Tuscarawas County
90	2283	71.7	**Troy** (city) Miami County
92	2328	72.1	**Miamisburg** (city) Montgomery County
92	2328	72.1	**Wooster** (city) Wayne County
94	2344	72.3	**Bedford** (city) Cuyahoga County
94	2344	72.3	**Boardman** (CDP) Mahoning County
96	2368	72.6	**Celina** (city) Mercer County
96	2368	72.6	**Kent** (city) Portage County
98	2385	72.7	**Vandalia** (city) Montgomery County
99	2410	73.0	**Eastlake** (city) Lake County
100	2456	73.5	**Vermilion** (city) Lorain County
101	2485	73.8	**White Oak** (CDP) Hamilton County
102	2514	74.1	**South Euclid** (city) Cuyahoga County
103	2524	74.2	**Englewood** (city) Montgomery County
104	2589	74.7	**Reynoldsburg** (city) Franklin County
104	2589	74.7	**Richmond Heights** (city) Cuyahoga County
106	2679	75.5	**Kettering** (city) Montgomery County
107	2687	75.6	**Trenton** (city) Butler County
108	2702	75.7	**Pataskala** (city) Licking County
109	2720	75.9	**Cuyahoga Falls** (city) Summit County
110	2756	76.2	**Wickliffe** (city) Lake County
111	2786	76.4	**Willowick** (city) Lake County
112	2800	76.5	**Fairfield** (city) Butler County
113	2821	76.7	**Medina** (city) Medina County
114	2852	77.0	**Streetsboro** (city) Portage County
115	2861	77.1	**Willoughby** (city) Lake County
116	2880	77.2	**Fairview Park** (city) Cuyahoga County
116	2880	77.2	**Marysville** (city) Union County
116	2880	77.2	**Wadsworth** (city) Medina County
119	2968	78.1	**Green** (city) Summit County
120	2986	78.3	**Berea** (city) Cuyahoga County
121	3007	78.5	**North Olmsted** (city) Cuyahoga County
121	3007	78.5	**Oregon** (city) Lucas County
123	3054	78.9	**Grove City** (city) Franklin County
124	3091	79.2	**Clayton** (city) Montgomery County
124	3091	79.2	**Delaware** (city) Delaware County
126	3104	79.3	**Norton** (city) Summit County
127	3113	79.4	**Mayfield Heights** (city) Cuyahoga County
128	3183	79.9	**Brunswick** (city) Medina County
129	3206	80.1	**Middleburg Heights** (city) Cuyahoga County
130	3217	80.2	**Bridgetown** (CDP) Hamilton County
131	3238	80.3	**New Franklin** (city) Summit County
131	3238	80.3	**North Canton** (city) Stark County
133	3258	80.5	**Tallmadge** (city) Summit County
134	3323	80.9	**Amherst** (city) Lorain County
134	3323	80.9	**Loveland** (city) Hamilton County
136	3336	81.0	**Centerville** (city) Montgomery County
136	3336	81.0	**Monroe** (city) Butler County
138	3477	82.2	**North Royalton** (city) Cuyahoga County
139	3502	82.4	**University Heights** (city) Cuyahoga County
140	3547	82.8	**North Ridgeville** (city) Lorain County
140	3547	82.8	**Seven Hills** (city) Cuyahoga County
142	3561	82.9	**Bowling Green** (city) Wood County
143	3587	83.1	**Rocky River** (city) Cuyahoga County
144	3610	83.3	**Hilliard** (city) Franklin County
144	3610	83.3	**Maumee** (city) Lucas County
144	3610	83.3	**Shaker Heights** (city) Cuyahoga County
147	3655	83.6	**Monfort Heights** (CDP) Hamilton County
148	3666	83.7	**Forestville** (CDP) Hamilton County
148	3666	83.7	**Mentor** (city) Lake County
150	3700	84.0	**Sylvania** (city) Lucas County

Note: *The state column ranks the top/bottom 150 places from all places in the state with population of 10,000 or more. The national column ranks the top/bottom 150 places from all places in the country with population of 10,000 or more. Places that are unincorporated were not considered in the rankings. Please refer to the User Guide for additional information.*

Population with Public Health Insurance

Top 150 Places Ranked in *Descending* Order

State Rank	Nat'l Rank	Percent	Place
1	26	56.9	**East Cleveland** (city) Cuyahoga County
2	32	55.9	**Zanesville** (city) Muskingum County
3	41	54.4	**Youngstown** (city) Mahoning County
4	120	49.4	**Warren** (city) Trumbull County
5	130	49.0	**Galion** (city) Crawford County
6	133	48.8	**East Liverpool** (city) Columbiana County
7	136	48.7	**Cambridge** (city) Guernsey County
8	141	48.4	**Ashtabula** (city) Ashtabula County
9	170	47.6	**Mansfield** (city) Richland County
10	184	47.2	**Cleveland** (city) Cuyahoga County
11	232	46.0	**Lorain** (city) Lorain County
12	240	45.8	**Springfield** (city) Clark County
13	256	45.4	**Portsmouth** (city) Scioto County
14	263	45.2	**Canton** (city) Stark County
15	287	44.7	**Coshocton** (city) Coshocton County
16	291	44.6	**Lima** (city) Allen County
17	307	44.3	**Chillicothe** (city) Ross County
17	307	44.3	**Greenville** (city) Darke County
19	320	44.2	**Marion** (city) Marion County
20	336	44.0	**Wilmington** (city) Clinton County
21	354	43.7	**Ravenna** (city) Portage County
22	369	43.5	**Lancaster** (city) Fairfield County
23	380	43.3	**Middletown** (city) Butler County
24	391	43.2	**Bucyrus** (city) Crawford County
25	414	42.8	**Warrensville Heights** (city) Cuyahoga County
26	419	42.7	**Fostoria** (city) Seneca County
27	428	42.6	**Sandusky** (city) Erie County
28	457	42.1	**Bellefontaine** (city) Logan County
29	468	42.0	**Dayton** (city) Montgomery County
30	481	41.8	**Alliance** (city) Stark County
31	493	41.6	**Massillon** (city) Stark County
32	499	41.5	**Washington Court House** (city) Fayette County
33	512	41.4	**Circleville** (city) Pickaway County
34	538	41.1	**Struthers** (city) Mahoning County
35	543	41.0	**Conneaut** (city) Ashtabula County
35	543	41.0	**Steubenville** (city) Jefferson County
37	575	40.5	**Mount Vernon** (city) Knox County
38	595	40.2	**Trotwood** (city) Montgomery County
39	629	39.8	**Urbana** (city) Champaign County
40	647	39.6	**Van Wert** (city) Van Wert County
41	655	39.5	**Xenia** (city) Greene County
42	666	39.4	**Maple Heights** (city) Cuyahoga County
42	666	39.4	**Salem** (city) Columbiana County
42	666	39.4	**Toledo** (city) Lucas County
45	686	39.2	**Akron** (city) Summit County
46	736	38.6	**Marietta** (city) Washington County
47	746	38.5	**Barberton** (city) Summit County
48	754	38.4	**Whitehall** (city) Franklin County
49	768	38.2	**Elyria** (city) Lorain County
49	768	38.2	**Niles** (city) Trumbull County
51	779	38.1	**Newark** (city) Licking County
51	779	38.1	**Norwalk** (city) Huron County
53	803	37.9	**Ironton** (city) Lawrence County
54	813	37.8	**Piqua** (city) Miami County
55	834	37.6	**New Philadelphia** (city) Tuscarawas County
56	847	37.5	**Garfield Heights** (city) Cuyahoga County
57	891	37.1	**Franklin** (city) Warren County
58	907	37.0	**Fremont** (city) Sandusky County
59	914	36.9	**Reading** (city) Hamilton County
60	959	36.4	**Brooklyn** (city) Cuyahoga County
61	966	36.3	**Finneytown** (CDP) Hamilton County
62	980	36.2	**Hamilton** (city) Butler County
63	994	36.1	**Bedford Heights** (city) Cuyahoga County
63	994	36.1	**Riverside** (city) Montgomery County
65	1066	35.6	**Fairborn** (city) Greene County
66	1085	35.4	**Austintown** (CDP) Mahoning County
67	1095	35.3	**Cincinnati** (city) Hamilton County
67	1095	35.3	**Sidney** (city) Shelby County
69	1151	34.9	**Tiffin** (city) Seneca County
69	1151	34.9	**Wooster** (city) Wayne County
71	1218	34.4	**Defiance** (city) Defiance County
71	1218	34.4	**Miamisburg** (city) Montgomery County
71	1218	34.4	**Northbrook** (CDP) Hamilton County
74	1235	34.3	**Euclid** (city) Cuyahoga County
74	1235	34.3	**Springdale** (city) Hamilton County
76	1263	34.1	**Heath** (city) Licking County
76	1263	34.1	**Painesville** (city) Lake County
76	1263	34.1	**Parma Heights** (city) Cuyahoga County
79	1330	33.7	**Englewood** (city) Montgomery County
80	1441	33.0	**Brook Park** (city) Cuyahoga County
80	1441	33.0	**Vermilion** (city) Lorain County
82	1557	32.2	**Bedford** (city) Cuyahoga County
83	1605	31.8	**Parma** (city) Cuyahoga County
83	1605	31.8	**Wickliffe** (city) Lake County
85	1627	31.7	**Centerville** (city) Montgomery County
86	1639	31.6	**Celina** (city) Mercer County
86	1639	31.6	**Findlay** (city) Hancock County
88	1702	31.2	**Ashland** (city) Ashland County
89	1727	31.0	**Boardman** (CDP) Mahoning County
90	1740	30.9	**Huber Heights** (city) Montgomery County
91	1757	30.8	**Tallmadge** (city) Summit County
92	1776	30.7	**Dover** (city) Tuscarawas County
93	1795	30.6	**Seven Hills** (city) Cuyahoga County
94	1830	30.4	**Cleveland Heights** (city) Cuyahoga County
95	1878	30.1	**Willowick** (city) Lake County
96	1896	30.0	**Norwood** (city) Hamilton County
97	1934	29.8	**West Carrollton** (city) Montgomery County
98	1949	29.7	**Forest Park** (city) Hamilton County
99	1999	29.4	**Amherst** (city) Lorain County
100	2010	29.3	**Troy** (city) Miami County
101	2040	29.1	**Bridgetown** (CDP) Hamilton County
102	2056	29.0	**North Canton** (city) Stark County
103	2078	28.9	**Kettering** (city) Montgomery County
103	2078	28.9	**Sharonville** (city) Hamilton County
105	2127	28.6	**Columbus** (city) Franklin County
106	2155	28.4	**Oregon** (city) Lucas County
107	2176	28.3	**Vandalia** (city) Montgomery County
107	2176	28.3	**White Oak** (CDP) Hamilton County
109	2195	28.2	**Middleburg Heights** (city) Cuyahoga County
110	2211	28.1	**New Franklin** (city) Summit County
110	2211	28.1	**North Olmsted** (city) Cuyahoga County
110	2211	28.1	**Rocky River** (city) Cuyahoga County
113	2262	27.8	**Forestville** (CDP) Hamilton County
114	2283	27.7	**Eastlake** (city) Lake County
114	2283	27.7	**Monfort Heights** (CDP) Hamilton County
116	2352	27.3	**Mayfield Heights** (city) Cuyahoga County
117	2371	27.2	**Beachwood** (city) Cuyahoga County
117	2371	27.2	**Fairview Park** (city) Cuyahoga County
119	2395	27.1	**Lakewood** (city) Cuyahoga County
119	2395	27.1	**Reynoldsburg** (city) Franklin County
121	2451	26.8	**Lebanon** (city) Warren County
122	2504	26.6	**Norton** (city) Summit County
123	2543	26.4	**Wadsworth** (city) Medina County
124	2569	26.3	**Cuyahoga Falls** (city) Summit County
125	2602	26.1	**Willoughby** (city) Lake County
126	2643	25.9	**Richmond Heights** (city) Cuyahoga County
127	2674	25.7	**Berea** (city) Cuyahoga County
127	2674	25.7	**Lyndhurst** (city) Cuyahoga County
129	2692	25.6	**Pataskala** (city) Licking County
130	2730	25.4	**Clayton** (city) Montgomery County
131	2791	25.1	**South Euclid** (city) Cuyahoga County
132	2843	24.8	**Medina** (city) Medina County
133	2865	24.7	**Mentor** (city) Lake County
134	2889	24.6	**Sylvania** (city) Lucas County
135	2917	24.4	**Green** (city) Summit County
136	2954	24.2	**Shaker Heights** (city) Cuyahoga County
137	3034	23.8	**University Heights** (city) Cuyahoga County
138	3057	23.7	**Loveland** (city) Hamilton County
139	3090	23.5	**Kent** (city) Portage County
139	3090	23.5	**North Ridgeville** (city) Lorain County
141	3142	23.3	**Delaware** (city) Delaware County
141	3142	23.3	**Grove City** (city) Franklin County
143	3166	23.2	**Maumee** (city) Lucas County
144	3191	23.1	**Brunswick** (city) Medina County
144	3191	23.1	**Streetsboro** (city) Portage County
146	3293	22.5	**Trenton** (city) Butler County
147	3305	22.4	**Beavercreek** (city) Greene County
148	3321	22.3	**North Royalton** (city) Cuyahoga County
149	3360	22.1	**Brecksville** (city) Cuyahoga County
150	3403	21.9	**Monroe** (city) Butler County

Note: *The state column ranks the top/bottom 150 places from all places in the state with population of 10,000 or more. The national column ranks the top/bottom 150 places from all places in the country with population of 10,000 or more. Places that are unincorporated were not considered in the rankings. Please refer to the User Guide for additional information.*

Population with Public Health Insurance

Top 150 Places Ranked in *Ascending* Order

State Rank	Nat'l Rank	Percent	Place
1	56	10.2	**Dublin** (city) Franklin County
2	88	11.3	**Athens** (city) Athens County
3	102	11.7	**Oxford** (city) Butler County
4	117	12.1	**Powell** (city) Delaware County
5	172	13.4	**Pickerington** (city) Fairfield County
6	193	13.8	**Mason** (city) Warren County
7	282	15.0	**Bexley** (city) Franklin County
8	336	15.7	**Hudson** (city) Summit County
9	358	15.9	**Springboro** (city) Warren County
10	478	17.1	**Perrysburg** (city) Wood County
11	553	17.8	**Hilliard** (city) Franklin County
12	588	18.1	**Bowling Green** (city) Wood County
13	681	18.7	**Avon** (city) Lorain County
13	681	18.7	**Solon** (city) Cuyahoga County
15	713	18.9	**Gahanna** (city) Franklin County
16	737	19.0	**Upper Arlington** (city) Franklin County
17	779	19.3	**Macedonia** (city) Summit County
17	779	19.3	**Montgomery** (city) Hamilton County
19	817	19.5	**Avon Lake** (city) Lorain County
20	834	19.6	**Westerville** (city) Franklin County
21	913	20.1	**Twinsburg** (city) Summit County
22	936	20.2	**Broadview Heights** (city) Cuyahoga County
23	954	20.3	**Stow** (city) Summit County
24	973	20.4	**Dent** (CDP) Hamilton County
25	989	20.5	**Bay Village** (city) Cuyahoga County
26	1007	20.6	**Worthington** (city) Franklin County
27	1091	21.1	**Fairfield** (city) Butler County
28	1133	21.3	**Mack** (CDP) Hamilton County
29	1187	21.6	**Blue Ash** (city) Hamilton County
29	1187	21.6	**Marysville** (city) Union County
29	1187	21.6	**Strongsville** (city) Cuyahoga County
32	1206	21.7	**Aurora** (city) Portage County
33	1219	21.8	**Westlake** (city) Cuyahoga County
34	1242	21.9	**Monroe** (city) Butler County
35	1272	22.1	**Brecksville** (city) Cuyahoga County
36	1321	22.3	**North Royalton** (city) Cuyahoga County
37	1336	22.4	**Beavercreek** (city) Greene County
38	1352	22.5	**Trenton** (city) Butler County
39	1451	23.1	**Brunswick** (city) Medina County
39	1451	23.1	**Streetsboro** (city) Portage County
41	1466	23.2	**Maumee** (city) Lucas County
42	1491	23.3	**Delaware** (city) Delaware County
42	1491	23.3	**Grove City** (city) Franklin County
44	1540	23.5	**Kent** (city) Portage County
44	1540	23.5	**North Ridgeville** (city) Lorain County
46	1588	23.7	**Loveland** (city) Hamilton County
47	1600	23.8	**University Heights** (city) Cuyahoga County
48	1683	24.2	**Shaker Heights** (city) Cuyahoga County
49	1723	24.4	**Green** (city) Summit County
50	1751	24.6	**Sylvania** (city) Lucas County
51	1768	24.7	**Mentor** (city) Lake County
52	1792	24.8	**Medina** (city) Medina County
53	1848	25.1	**South Euclid** (city) Cuyahoga County
54	1909	25.4	**Clayton** (city) Montgomery County
55	1944	25.6	**Pataskala** (city) Licking County
56	1965	25.7	**Berea** (city) Cuyahoga County
56	1965	25.7	**Lyndhurst** (city) Cuyahoga County
58	1997	25.9	**Richmond Heights** (city) Cuyahoga County
59	2035	26.1	**Willoughby** (city) Lake County
60	2075	26.3	**Cuyahoga Falls** (city) Summit County
61	2088	26.4	**Wadsworth** (city) Medina County
62	2128	26.6	**Norton** (city) Summit County
63	2174	26.8	**Lebanon** (city) Warren County
64	2247	27.1	**Lakewood** (city) Cuyahoga County
64	2247	27.1	**Reynoldsburg** (city) Franklin County
66	2262	27.2	**Beachwood** (city) Cuyahoga County
66	2262	27.2	**Fairview Park** (city) Cuyahoga County
68	2286	27.3	**Mayfield Heights** (city) Cuyahoga County
69	2358	27.7	**Eastlake** (city) Lake County
69	2358	27.7	**Monfort Heights** (CDP) Hamilton County
71	2374	27.8	**Forestville** (CDP) Hamilton County
72	2433	28.1	**New Franklin** (city) Summit County
72	2433	28.1	**North Olmsted** (city) Cuyahoga County
72	2433	28.1	**Rocky River** (city) Cuyahoga County
75	2446	28.2	**Middleburg Heights** (city) Cuyahoga County
76	2462	28.3	**Vandalia** (city) Montgomery County
76	2462	28.3	**White Oak** (CDP) Hamilton County
78	2481	28.4	**Oregon** (city) Lucas County
79	2515	28.6	**Columbus** (city) Franklin County
80	2563	28.9	**Kettering** (city) Montgomery County
80	2563	28.9	**Sharonville** (city) Hamilton County
82	2579	29.0	**North Canton** (city) Stark County
83	2601	29.1	**Bridgetown** (CDP) Hamilton County
84	2636	29.3	**Troy** (city) Miami County
85	2647	29.4	**Amherst** (city) Lorain County
86	2691	29.7	**Forest Park** (city) Hamilton County
87	2708	29.8	**West Carrollton** (city) Montgomery County
88	2736	30.0	**Norwood** (city) Hamilton County
89	2761	30.1	**Willowick** (city) Lake County
90	2813	30.4	**Cleveland Heights** (city) Cuyahoga County
91	2841	30.6	**Seven Hills** (city) Cuyahoga County
92	2862	30.7	**Dover** (city) Tuscarawas County
93	2881	30.8	**Tallmadge** (city) Summit County
94	2900	30.9	**Huber Heights** (city) Montgomery County
95	2917	31.0	**Boardman** (CDP) Mahoning County
96	2944	31.2	**Ashland** (city) Ashland County
97	3004	31.6	**Celina** (city) Mercer County
97	3004	31.6	**Findlay** (city) Hancock County
99	3018	31.7	**Centerville** (city) Montgomery County
100	3030	31.8	**Parma** (city) Cuyahoga County
100	3030	31.8	**Wickliffe** (city) Lake County
102	3086	32.2	**Bedford** (city) Cuyahoga County
103	3201	33.0	**Brook Park** (city) Cuyahoga County
103	3201	33.0	**Vermilion** (city) Lorain County
105	3309	33.7	**Englewood** (city) Montgomery County
106	3378	34.1	**Heath** (city) Licking County
106	3378	34.1	**Painesville** (city) Lake County
106	3378	34.1	**Parma Heights** (city) Cuyahoga County
109	3404	34.3	**Euclid** (city) Cuyahoga County
109	3404	34.3	**Springdale** (city) Hamilton County
111	3422	34.4	**Defiance** (city) Defiance County
111	3422	34.4	**Miamisburg** (city) Montgomery County
111	3422	34.4	**Northbrook** (CDP) Hamilton County
114	3487	34.9	**Tiffin** (city) Seneca County
114	3487	34.9	**Wooster** (city) Wayne County
116	3545	35.3	**Cincinnati** (city) Hamilton County
116	3545	35.3	**Sidney** (city) Shelby County
118	3562	35.4	**Austintown** (CDP) Mahoning County
119	3580	35.6	**Fairborn** (city) Greene County
120	3647	36.1	**Bedford Heights** (city) Cuyahoga County
120	3647	36.1	**Riverside** (city) Montgomery County
122	3663	36.2	**Hamilton** (city) Butler County
123	3677	36.3	**Finneytown** (CDP) Hamilton County
124	3691	36.4	**Brooklyn** (city) Cuyahoga County
125	3733	36.9	**Reading** (city) Hamilton County
126	3743	37.0	**Fremont** (city) Sandusky County
127	3750	37.1	**Franklin** (city) Warren County
128	3800	37.5	**Garfield Heights** (city) Cuyahoga County
129	3810	37.6	**New Philadelphia** (city) Tuscarawas County
130	3832	37.8	**Piqua** (city) Miami County
131	3844	37.9	**Ironton** (city) Lawrence County
132	3866	38.1	**Newark** (city) Licking County
132	3866	38.1	**Norwalk** (city) Huron County
134	3878	38.2	**Elyria** (city) Lorain County
134	3878	38.2	**Niles** (city) Trumbull County
136	3892	38.4	**Whitehall** (city) Franklin County
137	3903	38.5	**Barberton** (city) Summit County
138	3911	38.6	**Marietta** (city) Washington County
139	3962	39.2	**Akron** (city) Summit County
140	3980	39.4	**Maple Heights** (city) Cuyahoga County
140	3980	39.4	**Salem** (city) Columbiana County
140	3980	39.4	**Toledo** (city) Lucas County
143	3991	39.5	**Xenia** (city) Greene County
144	4002	39.6	**Van Wert** (city) Van Wert County
145	4017	39.8	**Urbana** (city) Champaign County
146	4049	40.2	**Trotwood** (city) Montgomery County
147	4071	40.5	**Mount Vernon** (city) Knox County
148	4107	41.0	**Conneaut** (city) Ashtabula County
148	4107	41.0	**Steubenville** (city) Jefferson County
150	4114	41.1	**Struthers** (city) Mahoning County

Note: *The state column ranks the top/bottom 150 places from all places in the state with population of 10,000 or more. The national column ranks the top/bottom 150 places from all places in the country with population of 10,000 or more. Places that are unincorporated were not considered in the rankings. Please refer to the User Guide for additional information.*

Population with No Health Insurance

Top 150 Places Ranked in *Descending* Order

State Rank	Nat'l Rank	Percent	Place
1	458	22.6	**Whitehall** (city) Franklin County
2	774	19.6	**East Cleveland** (city) Cuyahoga County
3	822	19.2	**Painesville** (city) Lake County
4	983	18.2	**Forest Park** (city) Hamilton County
5	1074	17.6	**Portsmouth** (city) Scioto County
6	1115	17.4	**Lima** (city) Allen County
7	1137	17.3	**Norwood** (city) Hamilton County
8	1191	17.0	**Springdale** (city) Hamilton County
9	1209	16.9	**Cleveland** (city) Cuyahoga County
9	1209	16.9	**Dayton** (city) Montgomery County
11	1265	16.6	**Canton** (city) Stark County
12	1286	16.5	**Niles** (city) Trumbull County
13	1311	16.4	**Sandusky** (city) Erie County
14	1355	16.2	**Fremont** (city) Sandusky County
14	1355	16.2	**Washington Court House** (city) Fayette County
16	1394	16.0	**Akron** (city) Summit County
17	1429	15.8	**Fostoria** (city) Seneca County
17	1429	15.8	**Marion** (city) Marion County
19	1452	15.7	**Salem** (city) Columbiana County
19	1452	15.7	**Trotwood** (city) Montgomery County
21	1490	15.5	**Hamilton** (city) Butler County
22	1511	15.4	**Bedford Heights** (city) Cuyahoga County
23	1529	15.3	**Columbus** (city) Franklin County
23	1529	15.3	**Toledo** (city) Lucas County
25	1557	15.1	**Cincinnati** (city) Hamilton County
25	1557	15.1	**Youngstown** (city) Mahoning County
27	1578	15.0	**Middletown** (city) Butler County
28	1588	14.9	**West Carrollton** (city) Montgomery County
29	1624	14.7	**Chillicothe** (city) Ross County
30	1643	14.6	**Euclid** (city) Cuyahoga County
31	1663	14.5	**Alliance** (city) Stark County
31	1663	14.5	**Piqua** (city) Miami County
33	1683	14.4	**Northbrook** (CDP) Hamilton County
33	1683	14.4	**Springfield** (city) Clark County
33	1683	14.4	**Zanesville** (city) Muskingum County
36	1713	14.3	**Ashtabula** (city) Ashtabula County
36	1713	14.3	**Lakewood** (city) Cuyahoga County
38	1736	14.2	**Barberton** (city) Summit County
38	1736	14.2	**Greenville** (city) Darke County
40	1758	14.1	**Dover** (city) Tuscarawas County
40	1758	14.1	**Ironton** (city) Lawrence County
42	1781	14.0	**Newark** (city) Licking County
42	1781	14.0	**Richmond Heights** (city) Cuyahoga County
44	1813	13.9	**Urbana** (city) Champaign County
45	1835	13.8	**Struthers** (city) Mahoning County
46	1855	13.7	**Ashland** (city) Ashland County
46	1855	13.7	**Riverside** (city) Montgomery County
48	1897	13.5	**Bellefontaine** (city) Logan County
49	1918	13.4	**Reading** (city) Hamilton County
49	1918	13.4	**Sidney** (city) Shelby County
51	1942	13.3	**Conneaut** (city) Ashtabula County
51	1942	13.3	**Mansfield** (city) Richland County
53	1972	13.2	**Lorain** (city) Lorain County
53	1972	13.2	**Mount Vernon** (city) Knox County
55	1991	13.1	**Circleville** (city) Pickaway County
55	1991	13.1	**Marietta** (city) Washington County
55	1991	13.1	**Warren** (city) Trumbull County
58	2063	12.8	**Sharonville** (city) Hamilton County
59	2083	12.7	**East Liverpool** (city) Columbiana County
60	2111	12.6	**Cambridge** (city) Guernsey County
61	2153	12.4	**Brooklyn** (city) Cuyahoga County
61	2153	12.4	**Lancaster** (city) Fairfield County
61	2153	12.4	**Tiffin** (city) Seneca County
61	2153	12.4	**Warrensville Heights** (city) Cuyahoga County
65	2201	12.2	**Elyria** (city) Lorain County
65	2201	12.2	**Findlay** (city) Hancock County
65	2201	12.2	**Huber Heights** (city) Montgomery County
65	2201	12.2	**Kent** (city) Portage County
69	2232	12.1	**Bucyrus** (city) Crawford County
70	2252	12.0	**Defiance** (city) Defiance County
70	2252	12.0	**Eastlake** (city) Lake County
70	2252	12.0	**Fairfield** (city) Butler County
73	2282	11.9	**Galion** (city) Crawford County
73	2282	11.9	**Parma Heights** (city) Cuyahoga County
75	2306	11.8	**Maple Heights** (city) Cuyahoga County
76	2331	11.7	**Coshocton** (city) Coshocton County
76	2331	11.7	**Xenia** (city) Greene County
78	2354	11.6	**Van Wert** (city) Van Wert County
79	2372	11.5	**Massillon** (city) Stark County
80	2393	11.4	**Vermilion** (city) Lorain County
81	2412	11.3	**Austintown** (CDP) Mahoning County
81	2412	11.3	**Wilmington** (city) Clinton County
83	2434	11.2	**Fairborn** (city) Greene County
83	2434	11.2	**Ravenna** (city) Portage County
83	2434	11.2	**Troy** (city) Miami County
86	2486	11.0	**New Philadelphia** (city) Tuscarawas County
87	2513	10.9	**Bedford** (city) Cuyahoga County
87	2513	10.9	**Parma** (city) Cuyahoga County
89	2540	10.8	**Brook Park** (city) Cuyahoga County
89	2540	10.8	**Pataskala** (city) Licking County
91	2566	10.7	**Steubenville** (city) Jefferson County
92	2589	10.6	**Norwalk** (city) Huron County
92	2589	10.6	**Trenton** (city) Butler County
94	2613	10.5	**Franklin** (city) Warren County
94	2613	10.5	**Garfield Heights** (city) Cuyahoga County
94	2613	10.5	**Heath** (city) Licking County
94	2613	10.5	**Streetsboro** (city) Portage County
94	2613	10.5	**Willoughby** (city) Lake County
99	2653	10.3	**Cleveland Heights** (city) Cuyahoga County
100	2679	10.2	**Cuyahoga Falls** (city) Summit County
100	2679	10.2	**Vandalia** (city) Montgomery County
102	2709	10.1	**Boardman** (CDP) Mahoning County
103	2781	9.8	**Grove City** (city) Franklin County
104	2810	9.7	**Fairview Park** (city) Cuyahoga County
104	2810	9.7	**Reynoldsburg** (city) Franklin County
104	2810	9.7	**South Euclid** (city) Cuyahoga County
107	2827	9.6	**Celina** (city) Mercer County
107	2827	9.6	**Kettering** (city) Montgomery County
107	2827	9.6	**Lebanon** (city) Warren County
110	2850	9.5	**White Oak** (CDP) Hamilton County
111	2876	9.4	**Green** (city) Summit County
111	2876	9.4	**Oregon** (city) Lucas County
113	2898	9.3	**Wadsworth** (city) Medina County
114	2929	9.2	**Medina** (city) Medina County
115	2954	9.1	**Marysville** (city) Union County
116	2982	9.0	**Miamisburg** (city) Montgomery County
117	3002	8.9	**Brunswick** (city) Medina County
117	3002	8.9	**Wooster** (city) Wayne County
119	3078	8.6	**Mayfield Heights** (city) Cuyahoga County
120	3132	8.4	**North Royalton** (city) Cuyahoga County
121	3158	8.3	**Willowick** (city) Lake County
122	3179	8.2	**Bowling Green** (city) Wood County
122	3179	8.2	**Finneytown** (CDP) Hamilton County
124	3203	8.1	**Wickliffe** (city) Lake County
125	3229	8.0	**Berea** (city) Cuyahoga County
125	3229	8.0	**Englewood** (city) Montgomery County
125	3229	8.0	**Middleburg Heights** (city) Cuyahoga County
125	3229	8.0	**Norton** (city) Summit County
129	3266	7.9	**North Canton** (city) Stark County
130	3291	7.8	**North Olmsted** (city) Cuyahoga County
131	3342	7.6	**Maumee** (city) Lucas County
131	3342	7.6	**New Franklin** (city) Summit County
133	3371	7.5	**Delaware** (city) Delaware County
134	3391	7.4	**Hilliard** (city) Franklin County
134	3391	7.4	**North Ridgeville** (city) Lorain County
136	3421	7.3	**Monroe** (city) Butler County
137	3523	7.0	**Stow** (city) Summit County
138	3570	6.8	**Bridgetown** (CDP) Hamilton County
139	3611	6.6	**Centerville** (city) Montgomery County
139	3611	6.6	**Clayton** (city) Montgomery County
141	3634	6.5	**Sylvania** (city) Lucas County
142	3698	6.3	**Broadview Heights** (city) Cuyahoga County
142	3698	6.3	**Shaker Heights** (city) Cuyahoga County
144	3731	6.2	**Aurora** (city) Portage County
145	3755	6.1	**Amherst** (city) Lorain County
146	3771	6.0	**Loveland** (city) Hamilton County
146	3771	6.0	**Mentor** (city) Lake County
146	3771	6.0	**Rocky River** (city) Cuyahoga County
149	3793	5.9	**Blue Ash** (city) Hamilton County
149	3793	5.9	**Pickerington** (city) Fairfield County

Note: *The state column ranks the top/bottom 150 places from all places in the state with population of 10,000 or more. The national column ranks the top/bottom 150 places from all places in the country with population of 10,000 or more. Places that are unincorporated were not considered in the rankings. Please refer to the User Guide for additional information.*

Population with No Health Insurance

Top 150 Places Ranked in *Ascending* Order

State Rank	Nat'l Rank	Percent	Place
1	37	1.6	**Powell** (city) Delaware County
2	108	2.5	**Beachwood** (city) Cuyahoga County
3	190	3.1	**Dublin** (city) Franklin County
4	227	3.3	**Montgomery** (city) Hamilton County
5	245	3.4	**Dent** (CDP) Hamilton County
6	276	3.6	**Monfort Heights** (CDP) Hamilton County
6	276	3.6	**Twinsburg** (city) Summit County
8	291	3.7	**Bay Village** (city) Cuyahoga County
9	314	3.8	**Hudson** (city) Summit County
9	314	3.8	**Macedonia** (city) Summit County
11	361	4.0	**Avon** (city) Lorain County
12	387	4.1	**Mack** (CDP) Hamilton County
12	387	4.1	**University Heights** (city) Cuyahoga County
14	412	4.2	**Avon Lake** (city) Lorain County
14	412	4.2	**Springboro** (city) Warren County
16	456	4.4	**Lyndhurst** (city) Cuyahoga County
17	542	4.7	**Athens** (city) Athens County
17	542	4.7	**Forestville** (CDP) Hamilton County
19	559	4.8	**Seven Hills** (city) Cuyahoga County
19	559	4.8	**Upper Arlington** (city) Franklin County
21	597	5.0	**Solon** (city) Cuyahoga County
21	597	5.0	**Westlake** (city) Cuyahoga County
21	597	5.0	**Worthington** (city) Franklin County
24	651	5.2	**Brecksville** (city) Cuyahoga County
25	680	5.3	**Mason** (city) Warren County
26	702	5.4	**Strongsville** (city) Cuyahoga County
26	702	5.4	**Westerville** (city) Franklin County
28	746	5.6	**Gahanna** (city) Franklin County
29	779	5.7	**Tallmadge** (city) Summit County
30	801	5.8	**Beavercreek** (city) Greene County
30	801	5.8	**Bexley** (city) Franklin County
30	801	5.8	**Oxford** (city) Butler County
30	801	5.8	**Perrysburg** (city) Wood County
34	828	5.9	**Blue Ash** (city) Hamilton County
34	828	5.9	**Pickerington** (city) Fairfield County
36	864	6.0	**Loveland** (city) Hamilton County
36	864	6.0	**Mentor** (city) Lake County
36	864	6.0	**Rocky River** (city) Cuyahoga County
39	886	6.1	**Amherst** (city) Lorain County
40	902	6.2	**Aurora** (city) Portage County
41	926	6.3	**Broadview Heights** (city) Cuyahoga County
41	926	6.3	**Shaker Heights** (city) Cuyahoga County
43	989	6.5	**Sylvania** (city) Lucas County
44	1023	6.6	**Centerville** (city) Montgomery County
44	1023	6.6	**Clayton** (city) Montgomery County
46	1063	6.8	**Bridgetown** (CDP) Hamilton County
47	1109	7.0	**Stow** (city) Summit County
48	1199	7.3	**Monroe** (city) Butler County
49	1236	7.4	**Hilliard** (city) Franklin County
49	1236	7.4	**North Ridgeville** (city) Lorain County
51	1266	7.5	**Delaware** (city) Delaware County
52	1286	7.6	**Maumee** (city) Lucas County
52	1286	7.6	**New Franklin** (city) Summit County
54	1343	7.8	**North Olmsted** (city) Cuyahoga County
55	1366	7.9	**North Canton** (city) Stark County
56	1391	8.0	**Berea** (city) Cuyahoga County
56	1391	8.0	**Englewood** (city) Montgomery County
56	1391	8.0	**Middleburg Heights** (city) Cuyahoga County
56	1391	8.0	**Norton** (city) Summit County
60	1428	8.1	**Wickliffe** (city) Lake County
61	1454	8.2	**Bowling Green** (city) Wood County
61	1454	8.2	**Finneytown** (CDP) Hamilton County
63	1478	8.3	**Willowick** (city) Lake County
64	1499	8.4	**North Royalton** (city) Cuyahoga County
65	1552	8.6	**Mayfield Heights** (city) Cuyahoga County
66	1634	8.9	**Brunswick** (city) Medina County
66	1634	8.9	**Wooster** (city) Wayne County
68	1655	9.0	**Miamisburg** (city) Montgomery County
69	1675	9.1	**Marysville** (city) Union County
70	1703	9.2	**Medina** (city) Medina County
71	1728	9.3	**Wadsworth** (city) Medina County
72	1759	9.4	**Green** (city) Summit County
72	1759	9.4	**Oregon** (city) Lucas County
74	1781	9.5	**White Oak** (CDP) Hamilton County
75	1807	9.6	**Celina** (city) Mercer County
75	1807	9.6	**Kettering** (city) Montgomery County
75	1807	9.6	**Lebanon** (city) Warren County
78	1830	9.7	**Fairview Park** (city) Cuyahoga County
78	1830	9.7	**Reynoldsburg** (city) Franklin County
78	1830	9.7	**South Euclid** (city) Cuyahoga County
81	1847	9.8	**Grove City** (city) Franklin County
82	1919	10.1	**Boardman** (CDP) Mahoning County
83	1948	10.2	**Cuyahoga Falls** (city) Summit County
83	1948	10.2	**Vandalia** (city) Montgomery County
85	1978	10.3	**Cleveland Heights** (city) Cuyahoga County
86	2021	10.5	**Franklin** (city) Warren County
86	2021	10.5	**Garfield Heights** (city) Cuyahoga County
86	2021	10.5	**Heath** (city) Licking County
86	2021	10.5	**Streetsboro** (city) Portage County
86	2021	10.5	**Willoughby** (city) Lake County
91	2044	10.6	**Norwalk** (city) Huron County
91	2044	10.6	**Trenton** (city) Butler County
93	2068	10.7	**Steubenville** (city) Jefferson County
94	2091	10.8	**Brook Park** (city) Cuyahoga County
94	2091	10.8	**Pataskala** (city) Licking County
96	2117	10.9	**Bedford** (city) Cuyahoga County
96	2117	10.9	**Parma** (city) Cuyahoga County
98	2144	11.0	**New Philadelphia** (city) Tuscarawas County
99	2194	11.2	**Fairborn** (city) Greene County
99	2194	11.2	**Ravenna** (city) Portage County
99	2194	11.2	**Troy** (city) Miami County
102	2223	11.3	**Austintown** (CDP) Mahoning County
102	2223	11.3	**Wilmington** (city) Clinton County
104	2245	11.4	**Vermilion** (city) Lorain County
105	2264	11.5	**Massillon** (city) Stark County
106	2285	11.6	**Van Wert** (city) Van Wert County
107	2303	11.7	**Coshocton** (city) Coshocton County
107	2303	11.7	**Xenia** (city) Greene County
109	2326	11.8	**Maple Heights** (city) Cuyahoga County
110	2351	11.9	**Galion** (city) Crawford County
110	2351	11.9	**Parma Heights** (city) Cuyahoga County
112	2375	12.0	**Defiance** (city) Defiance County
112	2375	12.0	**Eastlake** (city) Lake County
112	2375	12.0	**Fairfield** (city) Butler County
115	2405	12.1	**Bucyrus** (city) Crawford County
116	2425	12.2	**Elyria** (city) Lorain County
116	2425	12.2	**Findlay** (city) Hancock County
116	2425	12.2	**Huber Heights** (city) Montgomery County
116	2425	12.2	**Kent** (city) Portage County
120	2482	12.4	**Brooklyn** (city) Cuyahoga County
120	2482	12.4	**Lancaster** (city) Fairfield County
120	2482	12.4	**Tiffin** (city) Seneca County
120	2482	12.4	**Warrensville Heights** (city) Cuyahoga County
124	2527	12.6	**Cambridge** (city) Guernsey County
125	2546	12.7	**East Liverpool** (city) Columbiana County
126	2574	12.8	**Sharonville** (city) Hamilton County
127	2638	13.1	**Circleville** (city) Pickaway County
127	2638	13.1	**Marietta** (city) Washington County
127	2638	13.1	**Warren** (city) Trumbull County
130	2666	13.2	**Lorain** (city) Lorain County
130	2666	13.2	**Mount Vernon** (city) Knox County
132	2685	13.3	**Conneaut** (city) Ashtabula County
132	2685	13.3	**Mansfield** (city) Richland County
134	2715	13.4	**Reading** (city) Hamilton County
134	2715	13.4	**Sidney** (city) Shelby County
136	2739	13.5	**Bellefontaine** (city) Logan County
137	2773	13.7	**Ashland** (city) Ashland County
137	2773	13.7	**Riverside** (city) Montgomery County
139	2802	13.8	**Struthers** (city) Mahoning County
140	2822	13.9	**Urbana** (city) Champaign County
141	2844	14.0	**Newark** (city) Licking County
141	2844	14.0	**Richmond Heights** (city) Cuyahoga County
143	2876	14.1	**Dover** (city) Tuscarawas County
143	2876	14.1	**Ironton** (city) Lawrence County
145	2899	14.2	**Barberton** (city) Summit County
145	2899	14.2	**Greenville** (city) Darke County
147	2921	14.3	**Ashtabula** (city) Ashtabula County
147	2921	14.3	**Lakewood** (city) Cuyahoga County
149	2944	14.4	**Northbrook** (CDP) Hamilton County
149	2944	14.4	**Springfield** (city) Clark County

***Note:** The state column ranks the top/bottom 150 places from all places in the state with population of 10,000 or more. The national column ranks the top/bottom 150 places from all places in the country with population of 10,000 or more. Places that are unincorporated were not considered in the rankings. Please refer to the User Guide for additional information.*

Population Under 18 Years Old with No Health Insurance

Top 150 Places Ranked in *Descending* Order

State Rank	Nat'l Rank	Percent	Place
1	384	13.7	**Richmond Heights** (city) Cuyahoga County
2	478	12.6	**Niles** (city) Trumbull County
2	478	12.6	**Painesville** (city) Lake County
4	598	11.6	**Marietta** (city) Washington County
5	761	10.5	**Northbrook** (CDP) Hamilton County
6	806	10.2	**Eastlake** (city) Lake County
6	806	10.2	**Norwood** (city) Hamilton County
8	933	9.6	**Whitehall** (city) Franklin County
9	1024	9.2	**Forest Park** (city) Hamilton County
10	1040	9.1	**Mayfield Heights** (city) Cuyahoga County
11	1083	8.9	**West Carrollton** (city) Montgomery County
12	1098	8.8	**East Cleveland** (city) Cuyahoga County
13	1138	8.6	**Sharonville** (city) Hamilton County
14	1164	8.5	**Willoughby** (city) Lake County
15	1205	8.3	**Ashland** (city) Ashland County
16	1227	8.2	**Bedford Heights** (city) Cuyahoga County
16	1227	8.2	**Huber Heights** (city) Montgomery County
16	1227	8.2	**Trenton** (city) Butler County
19	1279	8.0	**Troy** (city) Miami County
20	1335	7.8	**Euclid** (city) Cuyahoga County
21	1429	7.5	**Fremont** (city) Sandusky County
22	1456	7.4	**Alliance** (city) Stark County
22	1456	7.4	**Brooklyn** (city) Cuyahoga County
22	1456	7.4	**Parma Heights** (city) Cuyahoga County
25	1484	7.3	**Akron** (city) Summit County
25	1484	7.3	**Barberton** (city) Summit County
25	1484	7.3	**Greenville** (city) Darke County
25	1484	7.3	**Piqua** (city) Miami County
29	1551	7.1	**Canton** (city) Stark County
29	1551	7.1	**Sandusky** (city) Erie County
31	1595	7.0	**Columbus** (city) Franklin County
31	1595	7.0	**Hamilton** (city) Butler County
33	1650	6.8	**Ashtabula** (city) Ashtabula County
33	1650	6.8	**Trotwood** (city) Montgomery County
35	1752	6.5	**White Oak** (CDP) Hamilton County
36	1785	6.4	**Austintown** (CDP) Mahoning County
37	1822	6.3	**Urbana** (city) Champaign County
38	1882	6.1	**Van Wert** (city) Van Wert County
39	1955	5.9	**Boardman** (CDP) Mahoning County
39	1955	5.9	**Findlay** (city) Hancock County
39	1955	5.9	**Oxford** (city) Butler County
39	1955	5.9	**Stow** (city) Summit County
43	1989	5.8	**Chillicothe** (city) Ross County
43	1989	5.8	**Riverside** (city) Montgomery County
43	1989	5.8	**Springdale** (city) Hamilton County
46	2093	5.5	**Cincinnati** (city) Hamilton County
46	2093	5.5	**Fairview Park** (city) Cuyahoga County
48	2147	5.4	**Toledo** (city) Lucas County
48	2147	5.4	**Wadsworth** (city) Medina County
50	2193	5.3	**Cuyahoga Falls** (city) Summit County
50	2193	5.3	**Green** (city) Summit County
50	2193	5.3	**Grove City** (city) Franklin County
50	2193	5.3	**Kettering** (city) Montgomery County
50	2193	5.3	**Lakewood** (city) Cuyahoga County
50	2193	5.3	**Streetsboro** (city) Portage County
50	2193	5.3	**Vermilion** (city) Lorain County
50	2193	5.3	**Zanesville** (city) Muskingum County
58	2239	5.2	**Cleveland Heights** (city) Cuyahoga County
58	2239	5.2	**Dayton** (city) Montgomery County
60	2289	5.1	**Middletown** (city) Butler County
60	2289	5.1	**Sidney** (city) Shelby County
62	2330	5.0	**Marion** (city) Marion County
62	2330	5.0	**Massillon** (city) Stark County
62	2330	5.0	**Medina** (city) Medina County
62	2330	5.0	**Mount Vernon** (city) Knox County
62	2330	5.0	**Parma** (city) Cuyahoga County
67	2378	4.9	**Finneytown** (CDP) Hamilton County
67	2378	4.9	**Portsmouth** (city) Scioto County
67	2378	4.9	**South Euclid** (city) Cuyahoga County
67	2378	4.9	**Springfield** (city) Clark County
71	2419	4.8	**Circleville** (city) Pickaway County
72	2465	4.7	**Brecksville** (city) Cuyahoga County
73	2540	4.5	**Heath** (city) Licking County
73	2540	4.5	**Lebanon** (city) Warren County
75	2616	4.3	**Lancaster** (city) Fairfield County
75	2616	4.3	**North Royalton** (city) Cuyahoga County
77	2675	4.2	**Bridgetown** (CDP) Hamilton County
77	2675	4.2	**Franklin** (city) Warren County
77	2675	4.2	**Ironton** (city) Lawrence County
77	2675	4.2	**Newark** (city) Licking County
81	2719	4.1	**Garfield Heights** (city) Cuyahoga County
81	2719	4.1	**Mansfield** (city) Richland County
81	2719	4.1	**Marysville** (city) Union County
84	2765	4.0	**Aurora** (city) Portage County
84	2765	4.0	**Kent** (city) Portage County
84	2765	4.0	**New Philadelphia** (city) Tuscarawas County
84	2765	4.0	**Oregon** (city) Lucas County
84	2765	4.0	**Washington Court House** (city) Fayette County
89	2825	3.9	**Brunswick** (city) Medina County
89	2825	3.9	**Cleveland** (city) Cuyahoga County
89	2825	3.9	**Delaware** (city) Delaware County
89	2825	3.9	**Montgomery** (city) Hamilton County
89	2825	3.9	**Steubenville** (city) Jefferson County
94	2871	3.8	**Centerville** (city) Montgomery County
94	2871	3.8	**Monroe** (city) Butler County
94	2871	3.8	**Perrysburg** (city) Wood County
94	2871	3.8	**Reading** (city) Hamilton County
94	2871	3.8	**Reynoldsburg** (city) Franklin County
99	2926	3.7	**Englewood** (city) Montgomery County
99	2926	3.7	**Middleburg Heights** (city) Cuyahoga County
99	2926	3.7	**Salem** (city) Columbiana County
99	2926	3.7	**Upper Arlington** (city) Franklin County
99	2926	3.7	**Wooster** (city) Wayne County
104	2975	3.6	**Beavercreek** (city) Greene County
104	2975	3.6	**Lima** (city) Allen County
104	2975	3.6	**Lorain** (city) Lorain County
104	2975	3.6	**Westlake** (city) Cuyahoga County
108	3036	3.5	**Fairfield** (city) Butler County
108	3036	3.5	**Norwalk** (city) Huron County
108	3036	3.5	**Tiffin** (city) Seneca County
108	3036	3.5	**Wickliffe** (city) Lake County
112	3084	3.4	**Amherst** (city) Lorain County
113	3151	3.3	**Bedford** (city) Cuyahoga County
113	3151	3.3	**Mentor** (city) Lake County
113	3151	3.3	**Youngstown** (city) Mahoning County
116	3196	3.2	**Brook Park** (city) Cuyahoga County
116	3196	3.2	**East Liverpool** (city) Columbiana County
116	3196	3.2	**Fairborn** (city) Greene County
119	3246	3.1	**Broadview Heights** (city) Cuyahoga County
119	3246	3.1	**Conneaut** (city) Ashtabula County
119	3246	3.1	**Fostoria** (city) Seneca County
119	3246	3.1	**Strongsville** (city) Cuyahoga County
123	3306	3.0	**Elyria** (city) Lorain County
123	3306	3.0	**Maumee** (city) Lucas County
123	3306	3.0	**Ravenna** (city) Portage County
126	3371	2.9	**Galion** (city) Crawford County
126	3371	2.9	**Hilliard** (city) Franklin County
126	3371	2.9	**Solon** (city) Cuyahoga County
129	3429	2.8	**Dover** (city) Tuscarawas County
129	3429	2.8	**Hudson** (city) Summit County
129	3429	2.8	**Vandalia** (city) Montgomery County
129	3429	2.8	**Warrensville Heights** (city) Cuyahoga County
129	3429	2.8	**Wilmington** (city) Clinton County
134	3524	2.6	**Pickerington** (city) Fairfield County
134	3524	2.6	**Sylvania** (city) Lucas County
136	3571	2.5	**Bowling Green** (city) Wood County
136	3571	2.5	**North Olmsted** (city) Cuyahoga County
138	3623	2.4	**Bucyrus** (city) Crawford County
138	3623	2.4	**Seven Hills** (city) Cuyahoga County
138	3623	2.4	**Struthers** (city) Mahoning County
138	3623	2.4	**Willowick** (city) Lake County
138	3623	2.4	**Xenia** (city) Greene County
143	3677	2.3	**Warren** (city) Trumbull County
144	3730	2.2	**Loveland** (city) Hamilton County
145	3781	2.1	**Blue Ash** (city) Hamilton County
145	3781	2.1	**Gahanna** (city) Franklin County
145	3781	2.1	**Shaker Heights** (city) Cuyahoga County
148	3822	2.0	**Bexley** (city) Franklin County
149	3874	1.9	**Bay Village** (city) Cuyahoga County
149	3874	1.9	**Berea** (city) Cuyahoga County

Note: *The state column ranks the top/bottom 150 places from all places in the state with population of 10,000 or more. The national column ranks the top/bottom 150 places from all places in the country with population of 10,000 or more. Places that are unincorporated were not considered in the rankings. Please refer to the User Guide for additional information.*

Population Under 18 Years Old with No Health Insurance

Top 150 Places Ranked in *Ascending* Order

State Rank	Nat'l Rank	Percent	Place
1	1	0.0	**Monfort Heights** (CDP) Hamilton County
1	1	0.0	**Powell** (city) Delaware County
3	153	0.5	**Athens** (city) Athens County
3	153	0.5	**Macedonia** (city) Summit County
5	210	0.7	**Avon** (city) Lorain County
5	210	0.7	**Maple Heights** (city) Cuyahoga County
7	264	0.9	**Cambridge** (city) Guernsey County
7	264	0.9	**Celina** (city) Mercer County
9	300	1.0	**Bellefontaine** (city) Logan County
9	300	1.0	**Tallmadge** (city) Summit County
11	344	1.1	**Avon Lake** (city) Lorain County
11	344	1.1	**Dent** (CDP) Hamilton County
13	382	1.2	**Lyndhurst** (city) Cuyahoga County
13	382	1.2	**Pataskala** (city) Licking County
15	424	1.3	**Beachwood** (city) Cuyahoga County
15	424	1.3	**Springboro** (city) Warren County
15	424	1.3	**Twinsburg** (city) Summit County
15	424	1.3	**Worthington** (city) Franklin County
19	469	1.4	**Defiance** (city) Defiance County
19	469	1.4	**Dublin** (city) Franklin County
19	469	1.4	**Norton** (city) Summit County
22	528	1.5	**Clayton** (city) Montgomery County
22	528	1.5	**University Heights** (city) Cuyahoga County
24	577	1.6	**New Franklin** (city) Summit County
24	577	1.6	**North Ridgeville** (city) Lorain County
26	627	1.7	**Coshocton** (city) Coshocton County
26	627	1.7	**Miamisburg** (city) Montgomery County
26	627	1.7	**North Canton** (city) Stark County
26	627	1.7	**Westerville** (city) Franklin County
30	729	1.9	**Bay Village** (city) Cuyahoga County
30	729	1.9	**Berea** (city) Cuyahoga County
30	729	1.9	**Forestville** (CDP) Hamilton County
30	729	1.9	**Mack** (CDP) Hamilton County
30	729	1.9	**Mason** (city) Warren County
30	729	1.9	**Rocky River** (city) Cuyahoga County
36	783	2.0	**Bexley** (city) Franklin County
37	835	2.1	**Blue Ash** (city) Hamilton County
37	835	2.1	**Gahanna** (city) Franklin County
37	835	2.1	**Shaker Heights** (city) Cuyahoga County
40	876	2.2	**Loveland** (city) Hamilton County
41	927	2.3	**Warren** (city) Trumbull County
42	980	2.4	**Bucyrus** (city) Crawford County
42	980	2.4	**Seven Hills** (city) Cuyahoga County
42	980	2.4	**Struthers** (city) Mahoning County
42	980	2.4	**Willowick** (city) Lake County
42	980	2.4	**Xenia** (city) Greene County
47	1034	2.5	**Bowling Green** (city) Wood County
47	1034	2.5	**North Olmsted** (city) Cuyahoga County
49	1086	2.6	**Pickerington** (city) Fairfield County
49	1086	2.6	**Sylvania** (city) Lucas County
51	1185	2.8	**Dover** (city) Tuscarawas County
51	1185	2.8	**Hudson** (city) Summit County
51	1185	2.8	**Vandalia** (city) Montgomery County
51	1185	2.8	**Warrensville Heights** (city) Cuyahoga County
51	1185	2.8	**Wilmington** (city) Clinton County
56	1228	2.9	**Galion** (city) Crawford County
56	1228	2.9	**Hilliard** (city) Franklin County
56	1228	2.9	**Solon** (city) Cuyahoga County
59	1286	3.0	**Elyria** (city) Lorain County
59	1286	3.0	**Maumee** (city) Lucas County
59	1286	3.0	**Ravenna** (city) Portage County
62	1351	3.1	**Broadview Heights** (city) Cuyahoga County
62	1351	3.1	**Conneaut** (city) Ashtabula County
62	1351	3.1	**Fostoria** (city) Seneca County
62	1351	3.1	**Strongsville** (city) Cuyahoga County
66	1411	3.2	**Brook Park** (city) Cuyahoga County
66	1411	3.2	**East Liverpool** (city) Columbiana County
66	1411	3.2	**Fairborn** (city) Greene County
69	1461	3.3	**Bedford** (city) Cuyahoga County
69	1461	3.3	**Mentor** (city) Lake County
69	1461	3.3	**Youngstown** (city) Mahoning County
72	1506	3.4	**Amherst** (city) Lorain County
73	1573	3.5	**Fairfield** (city) Butler County
73	1573	3.5	**Norwalk** (city) Huron County
73	1573	3.5	**Tiffin** (city) Seneca County
73	1573	3.5	**Wickliffe** (city) Lake County
77	1621	3.6	**Beavercreek** (city) Greene County
77	1621	3.6	**Lima** (city) Allen County
77	1621	3.6	**Lorain** (city) Lorain County
77	1621	3.6	**Westlake** (city) Cuyahoga County
81	1682	3.7	**Englewood** (city) Montgomery County
81	1682	3.7	**Middleburg Heights** (city) Cuyahoga County
81	1682	3.7	**Salem** (city) Columbiana County
81	1682	3.7	**Upper Arlington** (city) Franklin County
81	1682	3.7	**Wooster** (city) Wayne County
86	1731	3.8	**Centerville** (city) Montgomery County
86	1731	3.8	**Monroe** (city) Butler County
86	1731	3.8	**Perrysburg** (city) Wood County
86	1731	3.8	**Reading** (city) Hamilton County
86	1731	3.8	**Reynoldsburg** (city) Franklin County
91	1786	3.9	**Brunswick** (city) Medina County
91	1786	3.9	**Cleveland** (city) Cuyahoga County
91	1786	3.9	**Delaware** (city) Delaware County
91	1786	3.9	**Montgomery** (city) Hamilton County
91	1786	3.9	**Steubenville** (city) Jefferson County
96	1832	4.0	**Aurora** (city) Portage County
96	1832	4.0	**Kent** (city) Portage County
96	1832	4.0	**New Philadelphia** (city) Tuscarawas County
96	1832	4.0	**Oregon** (city) Lucas County
96	1832	4.0	**Washington Court House** (city) Fayette County
101	1892	4.1	**Garfield Heights** (city) Cuyahoga County
101	1892	4.1	**Mansfield** (city) Richland County
101	1892	4.1	**Marysville** (city) Union County
104	1938	4.2	**Bridgetown** (CDP) Hamilton County
104	1938	4.2	**Franklin** (city) Warren County
104	1938	4.2	**Ironton** (city) Lawrence County
104	1938	4.2	**Newark** (city) Licking County
108	1982	4.3	**Lancaster** (city) Fairfield County
108	1982	4.3	**North Royalton** (city) Cuyahoga County
110	2079	4.5	**Heath** (city) Licking County
110	2079	4.5	**Lebanon** (city) Warren County
112	2154	4.7	**Brecksville** (city) Cuyahoga County
113	2192	4.8	**Circleville** (city) Pickaway County
114	2238	4.9	**Finneytown** (CDP) Hamilton County
114	2238	4.9	**Portsmouth** (city) Scioto County
114	2238	4.9	**South Euclid** (city) Cuyahoga County
114	2238	4.9	**Springfield** (city) Clark County
118	2279	5.0	**Marion** (city) Marion County
118	2279	5.0	**Massillon** (city) Stark County
118	2279	5.0	**Medina** (city) Medina County
118	2279	5.0	**Mount Vernon** (city) Knox County
118	2279	5.0	**Parma** (city) Cuyahoga County
123	2327	5.1	**Middletown** (city) Butler County
123	2327	5.1	**Sidney** (city) Shelby County
125	2368	5.2	**Cleveland Heights** (city) Cuyahoga County
125	2368	5.2	**Dayton** (city) Montgomery County
127	2418	5.3	**Cuyahoga Falls** (city) Summit County
127	2418	5.3	**Green** (city) Summit County
127	2418	5.3	**Grove City** (city) Franklin County
127	2418	5.3	**Kettering** (city) Montgomery County
127	2418	5.3	**Lakewood** (city) Cuyahoga County
127	2418	5.3	**Streetsboro** (city) Portage County
127	2418	5.3	**Vermilion** (city) Lorain County
127	2418	5.3	**Zanesville** (city) Muskingum County
135	2464	5.4	**Toledo** (city) Lucas County
135	2464	5.4	**Wadsworth** (city) Medina County
137	2510	5.5	**Cincinnati** (city) Hamilton County
137	2510	5.5	**Fairview Park** (city) Cuyahoga County
139	2632	5.8	**Chillicothe** (city) Ross County
139	2632	5.8	**Riverside** (city) Montgomery County
139	2632	5.8	**Springdale** (city) Hamilton County
142	2668	5.9	**Boardman** (CDP) Mahoning County
142	2668	5.9	**Findlay** (city) Hancock County
142	2668	5.9	**Oxford** (city) Butler County
142	2668	5.9	**Stow** (city) Summit County
146	2735	6.1	**Van Wert** (city) Van Wert County
147	2808	6.3	**Urbana** (city) Champaign County
148	2835	6.4	**Austintown** (CDP) Mahoning County
149	2872	6.5	**White Oak** (CDP) Hamilton County
150	2970	6.8	**Ashtabula** (city) Ashtabula County

Note: *The state column ranks the top/bottom 150 places from all places in the state with population of 10,000 or more. The national column ranks the top/bottom 150 places from all places in the country with population of 10,000 or more. Places that are unincorporated were not considered in the rankings. Please refer to the User Guide for additional information.*

Commute to Work: Car

Top 150 Places Ranked in *Descending* Order

State Rank	Nat'l Rank	Percent	Place
1	15	97.7	**Franklin** (city) Warren County
2	34	97.2	**Trenton** (city) Butler County
3	53	96.9	**Austintown** (CDP) Mahoning County
4	73	96.7	**Tallmadge** (city) Summit County
5	86	96.6	**Fairfield** (city) Butler County
5	86	96.6	**New Franklin** (city) Summit County
5	86	96.6	**Niles** (city) Trumbull County
5	86	96.6	**Oregon** (city) Lucas County
9	115	96.4	**Clayton** (city) Montgomery County
9	115	96.4	**White Oak** (CDP) Hamilton County
11	123	96.3	**Bridgetown** (CDP) Hamilton County
11	123	96.3	**Riverside** (city) Montgomery County
13	138	96.2	**Salem** (city) Columbiana County
14	150	96.1	**Mayfield Heights** (city) Cuyahoga County
14	150	96.1	**Springdale** (city) Hamilton County
16	177	95.9	**Sidney** (city) Shelby County
17	198	95.8	**Green** (city) Summit County
17	198	95.8	**Struthers** (city) Mahoning County
17	198	95.8	**Wickliffe** (city) Lake County
20	228	95.7	**Macedonia** (city) Summit County
21	278	95.5	**Boardman** (CDP) Mahoning County
21	278	95.5	**Streetsboro** (city) Portage County
23	306	95.4	**Maumee** (city) Lucas County
23	306	95.4	**Norton** (city) Summit County
25	333	95.3	**East Liverpool** (city) Columbiana County
26	365	95.2	**Lorain** (city) Lorain County
26	365	95.2	**Piqua** (city) Miami County
28	390	95.1	**Springboro** (city) Warren County
28	390	95.1	**Willoughby** (city) Lake County
30	412	95.0	**Middletown** (city) Butler County
31	437	94.9	**Dent** (CDP) Hamilton County
31	437	94.9	**Eastlake** (city) Lake County
31	437	94.9	**Englewood** (city) Montgomery County
31	437	94.9	**Marion** (city) Marion County
35	469	94.8	**Fairborn** (city) Greene County
35	469	94.8	**Massillon** (city) Stark County
37	500	94.7	**Cuyahoga Falls** (city) Summit County
37	500	94.7	**Fostoria** (city) Seneca County
37	500	94.7	**Urbana** (city) Champaign County
40	539	94.6	**Amherst** (city) Lorain County
40	539	94.6	**Elyria** (city) Lorain County
40	539	94.6	**Monroe** (city) Butler County
40	539	94.6	**Ravenna** (city) Portage County
40	539	94.6	**Sylvania** (city) Lucas County
40	539	94.6	**Vandalia** (city) Montgomery County
46	574	94.5	**Barberton** (city) Summit County
46	574	94.5	**Defiance** (city) Defiance County
46	574	94.5	**Norwalk** (city) Huron County
49	609	94.4	**Mentor** (city) Lake County
49	609	94.4	**North Ridgeville** (city) Lorain County
49	609	94.4	**Seven Hills** (city) Cuyahoga County
49	609	94.4	**Troy** (city) Miami County
49	609	94.4	**Twinsburg** (city) Summit County
54	649	94.3	**Bellefontaine** (city) Logan County
55	678	94.2	**Chillicothe** (city) Ross County
55	678	94.2	**Parma Heights** (city) Cuyahoga County
55	678	94.2	**Pataskala** (city) Licking County
58	722	94.1	**Brooklyn** (city) Cuyahoga County
58	722	94.1	**Hamilton** (city) Butler County
58	722	94.1	**Stow** (city) Summit County
58	722	94.1	**Willowick** (city) Lake County
62	767	94.0	**Brunswick** (city) Medina County
62	767	94.0	**Mason** (city) Warren County
62	767	94.0	**Northbrook** (CDP) Hamilton County
62	767	94.0	**Parma** (city) Cuyahoga County
66	816	93.9	**Lima** (city) Allen County
66	816	93.9	**Washington Court House** (city) Fayette County
68	865	93.8	**Huber Heights** (city) Montgomery County
69	917	93.7	**Bucyrus** (city) Crawford County
69	917	93.7	**Galion** (city) Crawford County
69	917	93.7	**Ironton** (city) Lawrence County
69	917	93.7	**Medina** (city) Medina County
69	917	93.7	**Warren** (city) Trumbull County
74	964	93.6	**Blue Ash** (city) Hamilton County
74	964	93.6	**Lancaster** (city) Fairfield County
76	1000	93.5	**Grove City** (city) Franklin County
76	1000	93.5	**Marysville** (city) Union County
76	1000	93.5	**Sharonville** (city) Hamilton County
76	1000	93.5	**Xenia** (city) Greene County
80	1043	93.4	**Celina** (city) Mercer County
80	1043	93.4	**Circleville** (city) Pickaway County
80	1043	93.4	**Heath** (city) Licking County
80	1043	93.4	**Middleburg Heights** (city) Cuyahoga County
80	1043	93.4	**Newark** (city) Licking County
80	1043	93.4	**Wadsworth** (city) Medina County
86	1086	93.3	**Bedford Heights** (city) Cuyahoga County
86	1086	93.3	**Brook Park** (city) Cuyahoga County
86	1086	93.3	**Dover** (city) Tuscarawas County
86	1086	93.3	**Forest Park** (city) Hamilton County
86	1086	93.3	**Miamisburg** (city) Montgomery County
86	1086	93.3	**Solon** (city) Cuyahoga County
92	1147	93.2	**Perrysburg** (city) Wood County
93	1193	93.1	**Centerville** (city) Montgomery County
93	1193	93.1	**Mansfield** (city) Richland County
95	1277	92.9	**Hilliard** (city) Franklin County
95	1277	92.9	**New Philadelphia** (city) Tuscarawas County
97	1322	92.8	**Fremont** (city) Sandusky County
97	1322	92.8	**Montgomery** (city) Hamilton County
99	1416	92.6	**Monfort Heights** (CDP) Hamilton County
99	1416	92.6	**North Royalton** (city) Cuyahoga County
99	1416	92.6	**Trotwood** (city) Montgomery County
102	1466	92.5	**Alliance** (city) Stark County
102	1466	92.5	**Pickerington** (city) Fairfield County
104	1514	92.4	**Beavercreek** (city) Greene County
104	1514	92.4	**Loveland** (city) Hamilton County
104	1514	92.4	**North Olmsted** (city) Cuyahoga County
104	1514	92.4	**Richmond Heights** (city) Cuyahoga County
108	1608	92.2	**Finneytown** (CDP) Hamilton County
108	1608	92.2	**Zanesville** (city) Muskingum County
110	1644	92.1	**Avon Lake** (city) Lorain County
111	1695	92.0	**Reading** (city) Hamilton County
111	1695	92.0	**Vermilion** (city) Lorain County
111	1695	92.0	**Westlake** (city) Cuyahoga County
114	1744	91.9	**Brecksville** (city) Cuyahoga County
115	1782	91.8	**Broadview Heights** (city) Cuyahoga County
115	1782	91.8	**Conneaut** (city) Ashtabula County
115	1782	91.8	**Strongsville** (city) Cuyahoga County
118	1819	91.7	**Avon** (city) Lorain County
118	1819	91.7	**Kettering** (city) Montgomery County
118	1819	91.7	**Lebanon** (city) Warren County
118	1819	91.7	**Mack** (CDP) Hamilton County
122	1892	91.5	**Bedford** (city) Cuyahoga County
122	1892	91.5	**Fairview Park** (city) Cuyahoga County
122	1892	91.5	**Findlay** (city) Hancock County
122	1892	91.5	**Toledo** (city) Lucas County
126	1937	91.4	**Reynoldsburg** (city) Franklin County
127	1981	91.3	**Ashtabula** (city) Ashtabula County
127	1981	91.3	**Canton** (city) Stark County
127	1981	91.3	**Gahanna** (city) Franklin County
127	1981	91.3	**Van Wert** (city) Van Wert County
127	1981	91.3	**West Carrollton** (city) Montgomery County
132	2023	91.2	**Akron** (city) Summit County
132	2023	91.2	**Aurora** (city) Portage County
132	2023	91.2	**Garfield Heights** (city) Cuyahoga County
132	2023	91.2	**Greenville** (city) Darke County
136	2149	90.9	**Coshocton** (city) Coshocton County
136	2149	90.9	**Painesville** (city) Lake County
138	2200	90.8	**Sandusky** (city) Erie County
139	2240	90.7	**Norwood** (city) Hamilton County
140	2276	90.6	**Lyndhurst** (city) Cuyahoga County
141	2308	90.5	**Dublin** (city) Franklin County
141	2308	90.5	**Rocky River** (city) Cuyahoga County
141	2308	90.5	**Westerville** (city) Franklin County
144	2383	90.3	**North Canton** (city) Stark County
144	2383	90.3	**Worthington** (city) Franklin County
146	2423	90.2	**Maple Heights** (city) Cuyahoga County
146	2423	90.2	**Springfield** (city) Clark County
148	2487	90.0	**Delaware** (city) Delaware County
148	2487	90.0	**Forestville** (CDP) Hamilton County
150	2530	89.9	**Bay Village** (city) Cuyahoga County

Note: *The state column ranks the top/bottom 150 places from all places in the state with population of 10,000 or more. The national column ranks the top/bottom 150 places from all places in the country with population of 10,000 or more. Places that are unincorporated were not considered in the rankings. Please refer to the User Guide for additional information.*

Commute to Work: Car

Top 150 Places Ranked in *Ascending* Order

State Rank	Nat'l Rank	Percent	Place
1	35	51.9	**Athens** (city) Athens County
2	40	54.8	**Oxford** (city) Butler County
3	175	69.2	**East Cleveland** (city) Cuyahoga County
4	421	78.4	**Bowling Green** (city) Wood County
5	487	80.0	**Cleveland** (city) Cuyahoga County
6	569	81.3	**Cincinnati** (city) Hamilton County
7	588	81.5	**Kent** (city) Portage County
8	611	81.8	**Steubenville** (city) Jefferson County
9	667	82.5	**Dayton** (city) Montgomery County
9	667	82.5	**University Heights** (city) Cuyahoga County
11	692	82.7	**Cleveland Heights** (city) Cuyahoga County
12	796	83.7	**Shaker Heights** (city) Cuyahoga County
13	809	83.8	**Wooster** (city) Wayne County
14	946	84.9	**Bexley** (city) Franklin County
15	972	85.1	**Berea** (city) Cuyahoga County
16	1241	86.7	**Beachwood** (city) Cuyahoga County
16	1241	86.7	**Lakewood** (city) Cuyahoga County
18	1260	86.8	**Wilmington** (city) Clinton County
19	1313	87.1	**Warrensville Heights** (city) Cuyahoga County
20	1436	87.7	**Tiffin** (city) Seneca County
21	1459	87.8	**Mount Vernon** (city) Knox County
22	1565	88.2	**Hudson** (city) Summit County
22	1565	88.2	**Marietta** (city) Washington County
24	1625	88.4	**Euclid** (city) Cuyahoga County
24	1625	88.4	**Youngstown** (city) Mahoning County
26	1736	88.8	**Upper Arlington** (city) Franklin County
27	1826	89.1	**Columbus** (city) Franklin County
28	1859	89.2	**Powell** (city) Delaware County
29	1916	89.4	**Ashland** (city) Ashland County
29	1916	89.4	**Portsmouth** (city) Scioto County
31	2000	89.6	**Cambridge** (city) Guernsey County
31	2000	89.6	**Whitehall** (city) Franklin County
33	2086	89.9	**Bay Village** (city) Cuyahoga County
33	2086	89.9	**South Euclid** (city) Cuyahoga County
35	2127	90.0	**Delaware** (city) Delaware County
35	2127	90.0	**Forestville** (CDP) Hamilton County
37	2204	90.2	**Maple Heights** (city) Cuyahoga County
37	2204	90.2	**Springfield** (city) Clark County
39	2234	90.3	**North Canton** (city) Stark County
39	2234	90.3	**Worthington** (city) Franklin County
41	2310	90.5	**Dublin** (city) Franklin County
41	2310	90.5	**Rocky River** (city) Cuyahoga County
41	2310	90.5	**Westerville** (city) Franklin County
44	2349	90.6	**Lyndhurst** (city) Cuyahoga County
45	2381	90.7	**Norwood** (city) Hamilton County
46	2417	90.8	**Sandusky** (city) Erie County
47	2457	90.9	**Coshocton** (city) Coshocton County
47	2457	90.9	**Painesville** (city) Lake County
49	2590	91.2	**Akron** (city) Summit County
49	2590	91.2	**Aurora** (city) Portage County
49	2590	91.2	**Garfield Heights** (city) Cuyahoga County
49	2590	91.2	**Greenville** (city) Darke County
53	2634	91.3	**Ashtabula** (city) Ashtabula County
53	2634	91.3	**Canton** (city) Stark County
53	2634	91.3	**Gahanna** (city) Franklin County
53	2634	91.3	**Van Wert** (city) Van Wert County
53	2634	91.3	**West Carrollton** (city) Montgomery County
58	2676	91.4	**Reynoldsburg** (city) Franklin County
59	2720	91.5	**Bedford** (city) Cuyahoga County
59	2720	91.5	**Fairview Park** (city) Cuyahoga County
59	2720	91.5	**Findlay** (city) Hancock County
59	2720	91.5	**Toledo** (city) Lucas County
63	2800	91.7	**Avon** (city) Lorain County
63	2800	91.7	**Kettering** (city) Montgomery County
63	2800	91.7	**Lebanon** (city) Warren County
63	2800	91.7	**Mack** (CDP) Hamilton County
67	2838	91.8	**Broadview Heights** (city) Cuyahoga County
67	2838	91.8	**Conneaut** (city) Ashtabula County
67	2838	91.8	**Strongsville** (city) Cuyahoga County
70	2875	91.9	**Brecksville** (city) Cuyahoga County
71	2913	92.0	**Reading** (city) Hamilton County
71	2913	92.0	**Vermilion** (city) Lorain County
71	2913	92.0	**Westlake** (city) Cuyahoga County
74	2962	92.1	**Avon Lake** (city) Lorain County
75	3013	92.2	**Finneytown** (CDP) Hamilton County
75	3013	92.2	**Zanesville** (city) Muskingum County
77	3094	92.4	**Beavercreek** (city) Greene County
77	3094	92.4	**Loveland** (city) Hamilton County
77	3094	92.4	**North Olmsted** (city) Cuyahoga County
77	3094	92.4	**Richmond Heights** (city) Cuyahoga County
81	3143	92.5	**Alliance** (city) Stark County
81	3143	92.5	**Pickerington** (city) Fairfield County
83	3191	92.6	**Monfort Heights** (CDP) Hamilton County
83	3191	92.6	**North Royalton** (city) Cuyahoga County
83	3191	92.6	**Trotwood** (city) Montgomery County
86	3286	92.8	**Fremont** (city) Sandusky County
86	3286	92.8	**Montgomery** (city) Hamilton County
88	3335	92.9	**Hilliard** (city) Franklin County
88	3335	92.9	**New Philadelphia** (city) Tuscarawas County
90	3420	93.1	**Centerville** (city) Montgomery County
90	3420	93.1	**Mansfield** (city) Richland County
92	3464	93.2	**Perrysburg** (city) Wood County
93	3510	93.3	**Bedford Heights** (city) Cuyahoga County
93	3510	93.3	**Brook Park** (city) Cuyahoga County
93	3510	93.3	**Dover** (city) Tuscarawas County
93	3510	93.3	**Forest Park** (city) Hamilton County
93	3510	93.3	**Miamisburg** (city) Montgomery County
93	3510	93.3	**Solon** (city) Cuyahoga County
99	3571	93.4	**Celina** (city) Mercer County
99	3571	93.4	**Circleville** (city) Pickaway County
99	3571	93.4	**Heath** (city) Licking County
99	3571	93.4	**Middleburg Heights** (city) Cuyahoga County
99	3571	93.4	**Newark** (city) Licking County
99	3571	93.4	**Wadsworth** (city) Medina County
105	3614	93.5	**Grove City** (city) Franklin County
105	3614	93.5	**Marysville** (city) Union County
105	3614	93.5	**Sharonville** (city) Hamilton County
105	3614	93.5	**Xenia** (city) Greene County
109	3657	93.6	**Blue Ash** (city) Hamilton County
109	3657	93.6	**Lancaster** (city) Fairfield County
111	3693	93.7	**Bucyrus** (city) Crawford County
111	3693	93.7	**Galion** (city) Crawford County
111	3693	93.7	**Ironton** (city) Lawrence County
111	3693	93.7	**Medina** (city) Medina County
111	3693	93.7	**Warren** (city) Trumbull County
116	3740	93.8	**Huber Heights** (city) Montgomery County
117	3792	93.9	**Lima** (city) Allen County
117	3792	93.9	**Washington Court House** (city) Fayette County
119	3841	94.0	**Brunswick** (city) Medina County
119	3841	94.0	**Mason** (city) Warren County
119	3841	94.0	**Northbrook** (CDP) Hamilton County
119	3841	94.0	**Parma** (city) Cuyahoga County
123	3890	94.1	**Brooklyn** (city) Cuyahoga County
123	3890	94.1	**Hamilton** (city) Butler County
123	3890	94.1	**Stow** (city) Summit County
123	3890	94.1	**Willowick** (city) Lake County
127	3935	94.2	**Chillicothe** (city) Ross County
127	3935	94.2	**Parma Heights** (city) Cuyahoga County
127	3935	94.2	**Pataskala** (city) Licking County
130	3979	94.3	**Bellefontaine** (city) Logan County
131	4008	94.4	**Mentor** (city) Lake County
131	4008	94.4	**North Ridgeville** (city) Lorain County
131	4008	94.4	**Seven Hills** (city) Cuyahoga County
131	4008	94.4	**Troy** (city) Miami County
131	4008	94.4	**Twinsburg** (city) Summit County
136	4048	94.5	**Barberton** (city) Summit County
136	4048	94.5	**Defiance** (city) Defiance County
136	4048	94.5	**Norwalk** (city) Huron County
139	4083	94.6	**Amherst** (city) Lorain County
139	4083	94.6	**Elyria** (city) Lorain County
139	4083	94.6	**Monroe** (city) Butler County
139	4083	94.6	**Ravenna** (city) Portage County
139	4083	94.6	**Sylvania** (city) Lucas County
139	4083	94.6	**Vandalia** (city) Montgomery County
145	4118	94.7	**Cuyahoga Falls** (city) Summit County
145	4118	94.7	**Fostoria** (city) Seneca County
145	4118	94.7	**Urbana** (city) Champaign County
148	4157	94.8	**Fairborn** (city) Greene County
148	4157	94.8	**Massillon** (city) Stark County
150	4188	94.9	**Dent** (CDP) Hamilton County

Note: *The state column ranks the top/bottom 150 places from all places in the state with population of 10,000 or more. The national column ranks the top/bottom 150 places from all places in the country with population of 10,000 or more. Places that are unincorporated were not considered in the rankings. Please refer to the User Guide for additional information.*

Commute to Work: Public Transportation

Top 150 Places Ranked in *Descending* Order

State Rank	Nat'l Rank	Percent	Place
1	68	23.7	**East Cleveland** (city) Cuyahoga County
2	352	10.9	**Cleveland** (city) Cuyahoga County
3	444	9.4	**Warrensville Heights** (city) Cuyahoga County
4	562	7.9	**Cincinnati** (city) Hamilton County
5	665	7.0	**Euclid** (city) Cuyahoga County
6	756	6.3	**Lakewood** (city) Cuyahoga County
7	791	6.0	**Whitehall** (city) Franklin County
8	803	5.9	**Cleveland Heights** (city) Cuyahoga County
9	812	5.8	**Shaker Heights** (city) Cuyahoga County
10	831	5.7	**Oxford** (city) Butler County
11	884	5.3	**Dayton** (city) Montgomery County
12	983	4.8	**Maple Heights** (city) Cuyahoga County
13	1126	4.1	**Garfield Heights** (city) Cuyahoga County
13	1126	4.1	**Trotwood** (city) Montgomery County
15	1208	3.8	**Akron** (city) Summit County
15	1208	3.8	**Bedford** (city) Cuyahoga County
17	1411	3.2	**Forestville** (CDP) Hamilton County
17	1411	3.2	**Youngstown** (city) Mahoning County
19	1476	3.0	**Canton** (city) Stark County
19	1476	3.0	**Columbus** (city) Franklin County
21	1596	2.7	**South Euclid** (city) Cuyahoga County
22	1635	2.6	**Brooklyn** (city) Cuyahoga County
22	1635	2.6	**Forest Park** (city) Hamilton County
22	1635	2.6	**University Heights** (city) Cuyahoga County
25	1685	2.5	**Beachwood** (city) Cuyahoga County
25	1685	2.5	**North Olmsted** (city) Cuyahoga County
25	1685	2.5	**Rocky River** (city) Cuyahoga County
28	1739	2.4	**Kent** (city) Portage County
29	1801	2.3	**Bedford Heights** (city) Cuyahoga County
29	1801	2.3	**Toledo** (city) Lucas County
29	1801	2.3	**West Carrollton** (city) Montgomery County
32	1855	2.2	**Fairview Park** (city) Cuyahoga County
32	1855	2.2	**Greenville** (city) Darke County
32	1855	2.2	**Lyndhurst** (city) Cuyahoga County
32	1855	2.2	**Parma Heights** (city) Cuyahoga County
36	1897	2.1	**Norwood** (city) Hamilton County
36	1897	2.1	**Steubenville** (city) Jefferson County
38	1948	2.0	**Athens** (city) Athens County
38	1948	2.0	**Bay Village** (city) Cuyahoga County
38	1948	2.0	**Brook Park** (city) Cuyahoga County
38	1948	2.0	**Parma** (city) Cuyahoga County
38	1948	2.0	**Strongsville** (city) Cuyahoga County
43	2005	1.9	**Finneytown** (CDP) Hamilton County
44	2054	1.8	**Centerville** (city) Montgomery County
44	2054	1.8	**Reynoldsburg** (city) Franklin County
44	2054	1.8	**Richmond Heights** (city) Cuyahoga County
47	2111	1.7	**Berea** (city) Cuyahoga County
47	2111	1.7	**Painesville** (city) Lake County
49	2157	1.6	**Huber Heights** (city) Montgomery County
49	2157	1.6	**Mansfield** (city) Richland County
51	2239	1.5	**Broadview Heights** (city) Cuyahoga County
51	2239	1.5	**Reading** (city) Hamilton County
53	2324	1.4	**Cambridge** (city) Guernsey County
53	2324	1.4	**Lebanon** (city) Warren County
53	2324	1.4	**Middleburg Heights** (city) Cuyahoga County
53	2324	1.4	**North Ridgeville** (city) Lorain County
53	2324	1.4	**Northbrook** (CDP) Hamilton County
53	2324	1.4	**Upper Arlington** (city) Franklin County
53	2324	1.4	**Westlake** (city) Cuyahoga County
60	2411	1.3	**Avon** (city) Lorain County
60	2411	1.3	**Conneaut** (city) Ashtabula County
60	2411	1.3	**Montgomery** (city) Hamilton County
60	2411	1.3	**Sandusky** (city) Erie County
60	2411	1.3	**Seven Hills** (city) Cuyahoga County
60	2411	1.3	**Springfield** (city) Clark County
66	2496	1.2	**Kettering** (city) Montgomery County
67	2599	1.1	**Avon Lake** (city) Lorain County
67	2599	1.1	**Brecksville** (city) Cuyahoga County
67	2599	1.1	**Brunswick** (city) Medina County
67	2599	1.1	**Dent** (CDP) Hamilton County
67	2599	1.1	**Lima** (city) Allen County
67	2599	1.1	**Mayfield Heights** (city) Cuyahoga County
67	2599	1.1	**Sylvania** (city) Lucas County
67	2599	1.1	**Willoughby** (city) Lake County
67	2599	1.1	**Willowick** (city) Lake County
67	2599	1.1	**Xenia** (city) Greene County
77	2684	1.0	**Barberton** (city) Summit County
77	2684	1.0	**Blue Ash** (city) Hamilton County
77	2684	1.0	**East Liverpool** (city) Columbiana County
77	2684	1.0	**Eastlake** (city) Lake County
77	2684	1.0	**Massillon** (city) Stark County
77	2684	1.0	**Mentor** (city) Lake County
77	2684	1.0	**Stow** (city) Summit County
77	2684	1.0	**Wickliffe** (city) Lake County
85	2793	0.9	**Bexley** (city) Franklin County
85	2793	0.9	**Lorain** (city) Lorain County
85	2793	0.9	**Middletown** (city) Butler County
85	2793	0.9	**Warren** (city) Trumbull County
85	2793	0.9	**White Oak** (CDP) Hamilton County
85	2793	0.9	**Worthington** (city) Franklin County
91	2912	0.8	**Ashtabula** (city) Ashtabula County
91	2912	0.8	**Cuyahoga Falls** (city) Summit County
91	2912	0.8	**Hudson** (city) Summit County
91	2912	0.8	**Marion** (city) Marion County
91	2912	0.8	**Miamisburg** (city) Montgomery County
91	2912	0.8	**Monfort Heights** (CDP) Hamilton County
91	2912	0.8	**North Canton** (city) Stark County
91	2912	0.8	**Powell** (city) Delaware County
91	2912	0.8	**Ravenna** (city) Portage County
91	2912	0.8	**Troy** (city) Miami County
101	3031	0.7	**Boardman** (CDP) Mahoning County
101	3031	0.7	**Chillicothe** (city) Ross County
101	3031	0.7	**Elyria** (city) Lorain County
101	3031	0.7	**Grove City** (city) Franklin County
101	3031	0.7	**Heath** (city) Licking County
101	3031	0.7	**Mason** (city) Warren County
107	3184	0.6	**Clayton** (city) Montgomery County
107	3184	0.6	**Mack** (CDP) Hamilton County
107	3184	0.6	**Maumee** (city) Lucas County
107	3184	0.6	**Medina** (city) Medina County
107	3184	0.6	**Niles** (city) Trumbull County
107	3184	0.6	**Riverside** (city) Montgomery County
107	3184	0.6	**Springdale** (city) Hamilton County
114	3338	0.5	**Aurora** (city) Portage County
114	3338	0.5	**Bellefontaine** (city) Logan County
114	3338	0.5	**Bridgetown** (CDP) Hamilton County
114	3338	0.5	**Bucyrus** (city) Crawford County
114	3338	0.5	**Circleville** (city) Pickaway County
114	3338	0.5	**North Royalton** (city) Cuyahoga County
114	3338	0.5	**Streetsboro** (city) Portage County
114	3338	0.5	**Struthers** (city) Mahoning County
114	3338	0.5	**Vandalia** (city) Montgomery County
114	3338	0.5	**Washington Court House** (city) Fayette County
114	3338	0.5	**Zanesville** (city) Muskingum County
125	3488	0.4	**Defiance** (city) Defiance County
125	3488	0.4	**Englewood** (city) Montgomery County
125	3488	0.4	**Fremont** (city) Sandusky County
125	3488	0.4	**Macedonia** (city) Summit County
125	3488	0.4	**Marysville** (city) Union County
125	3488	0.4	**Piqua** (city) Miami County
125	3488	0.4	**Tallmadge** (city) Summit County
125	3488	0.4	**Tiffin** (city) Seneca County
125	3488	0.4	**Westerville** (city) Franklin County
125	3488	0.4	**Wooster** (city) Wayne County
135	3669	0.3	**Austintown** (CDP) Mahoning County
135	3669	0.3	**Coshocton** (city) Coshocton County
135	3669	0.3	**Delaware** (city) Delaware County
135	3669	0.3	**Dublin** (city) Franklin County
135	3669	0.3	**Fairborn** (city) Greene County
135	3669	0.3	**Fairfield** (city) Butler County
135	3669	0.3	**Fostoria** (city) Seneca County
135	3669	0.3	**Franklin** (city) Warren County
135	3669	0.3	**Gahanna** (city) Franklin County
135	3669	0.3	**Galion** (city) Crawford County
135	3669	0.3	**New Franklin** (city) Summit County
135	3669	0.3	**Norwalk** (city) Huron County
135	3669	0.3	**Trenton** (city) Butler County
135	3669	0.3	**Urbana** (city) Champaign County
135	3669	0.3	**Van Wert** (city) Van Wert County
135	3669	0.3	**Wilmington** (city) Clinton County

Note: *The state column ranks the top/bottom 150 places from all places in the state with population of 10,000 or more. The national column ranks the top/bottom 150 places from all places in the country with population of 10,000 or more. Places that are unincorporated were not considered in the rankings. Please refer to the User Guide for additional information.*

Commute to Work: Walk

Top 150 Places Ranked in *Descending* Order

State Rank	Nat'l Rank	Percent	Place
1	5	36.9	**Athens** (city) Athens County
2	15	26.9	**Oxford** (city) Butler County
3	68	15.0	**Bowling Green** (city) Wood County
4	130	10.7	**Wooster** (city) Wayne County
5	134	10.6	**Kent** (city) Portage County
6	173	9.5	**Mount Vernon** (city) Knox County
6	173	9.5	**Steubenville** (city) Jefferson County
8	227	8.1	**Dayton** (city) Montgomery County
9	256	7.6	**Marietta** (city) Washington County
10	261	7.5	**Portsmouth** (city) Scioto County
10	261	7.5	**Wilmington** (city) Clinton County
12	285	7.2	**University Heights** (city) Cuyahoga County
13	292	7.1	**Bexley** (city) Franklin County
14	307	6.9	**Tiffin** (city) Seneca County
15	345	6.4	**Ashland** (city) Ashland County
16	403	5.7	**Berea** (city) Cuyahoga County
17	413	5.6	**Cincinnati** (city) Hamilton County
17	413	5.6	**Springfield** (city) Clark County
19	483	5.1	**Vermilion** (city) Lorain County
20	493	5.0	**Cleveland Heights** (city) Cuyahoga County
21	538	4.7	**Reading** (city) Hamilton County
22	560	4.6	**Cleveland** (city) Cuyahoga County
23	678	4.0	**Painesville** (city) Lake County
24	707	3.9	**Coshocton** (city) Coshocton County
24	707	3.9	**East Cleveland** (city) Cuyahoga County
26	799	3.6	**Delaware** (city) Delaware County
26	799	3.6	**Van Wert** (city) Van Wert County
28	839	3.5	**Alliance** (city) Stark County
28	839	3.5	**Galion** (city) Crawford County
30	925	3.3	**Lancaster** (city) Fairfield County
31	965	3.2	**Fostoria** (city) Seneca County
32	1009	3.1	**Washington Court House** (city) Fayette County
32	1009	3.1	**Westerville** (city) Franklin County
34	1053	3.0	**Ashtabula** (city) Ashtabula County
34	1053	3.0	**Findlay** (city) Hancock County
34	1053	3.0	**Toledo** (city) Lucas County
37	1105	2.9	**Cambridge** (city) Guernsey County
37	1105	2.9	**Canton** (city) Stark County
37	1105	2.9	**Lima** (city) Allen County
37	1105	2.9	**Youngstown** (city) Mahoning County
41	1164	2.8	**Columbus** (city) Franklin County
41	1164	2.8	**Norwalk** (city) Huron County
43	1218	2.7	**Sandusky** (city) Erie County
43	1218	2.7	**Sharonville** (city) Hamilton County
45	1289	2.6	**Forestville** (CDP) Hamilton County
45	1289	2.6	**Mansfield** (city) Richland County
45	1289	2.6	**Norwood** (city) Hamilton County
45	1289	2.6	**Zanesville** (city) Muskingum County
49	1347	2.5	**Fremont** (city) Sandusky County
49	1347	2.5	**Lebanon** (city) Warren County
49	1347	2.5	**New Philadelphia** (city) Tuscarawas County
49	1347	2.5	**North Canton** (city) Stark County
49	1347	2.5	**Xenia** (city) Greene County
54	1439	2.4	**Hamilton** (city) Butler County
54	1439	2.4	**Ravenna** (city) Portage County
56	1513	2.3	**Bucyrus** (city) Crawford County
56	1513	2.3	**Finneytown** (CDP) Hamilton County
56	1513	2.3	**Lakewood** (city) Cuyahoga County
59	1584	2.2	**Akron** (city) Summit County
59	1584	2.2	**Beachwood** (city) Cuyahoga County
59	1584	2.2	**Fairborn** (city) Greene County
59	1584	2.2	**Massillon** (city) Stark County
59	1584	2.2	**Newark** (city) Licking County
64	1686	2.1	**Brook Park** (city) Cuyahoga County
64	1686	2.1	**Conneaut** (city) Ashtabula County
64	1686	2.1	**Piqua** (city) Miami County
64	1686	2.1	**Troy** (city) Miami County
68	1781	2.0	**Avon Lake** (city) Lorain County
68	1781	2.0	**Bedford Heights** (city) Cuyahoga County
68	1781	2.0	**Salem** (city) Columbiana County
68	1781	2.0	**Shaker Heights** (city) Cuyahoga County
68	1781	2.0	**South Euclid** (city) Cuyahoga County
73	1886	1.9	**Barberton** (city) Summit County
73	1886	1.9	**Circleville** (city) Pickaway County
73	1886	1.9	**Dover** (city) Tuscarawas County
73	1886	1.9	**Warrensville Heights** (city) Cuyahoga County
77	1994	1.8	**Bellefontaine** (city) Logan County
77	1994	1.8	**Chillicothe** (city) Ross County
77	1994	1.8	**East Liverpool** (city) Columbiana County
77	1994	1.8	**Garfield Heights** (city) Cuyahoga County
77	1994	1.8	**Maple Heights** (city) Cuyahoga County
77	1994	1.8	**Reynoldsburg** (city) Franklin County
77	1994	1.8	**Whitehall** (city) Franklin County
84	2120	1.7	**Bedford** (city) Cuyahoga County
84	2120	1.7	**Eastlake** (city) Lake County
84	2120	1.7	**Kettering** (city) Montgomery County
87	2230	1.6	**Beavercreek** (city) Greene County
87	2230	1.6	**Brunswick** (city) Medina County
87	2230	1.6	**Defiance** (city) Defiance County
90	2367	1.5	**Hudson** (city) Summit County
90	2367	1.5	**Ironton** (city) Lawrence County
90	2367	1.5	**Loveland** (city) Hamilton County
90	2367	1.5	**Lyndhurst** (city) Cuyahoga County
90	2367	1.5	**Marion** (city) Marion County
90	2367	1.5	**Monfort Heights** (CDP) Hamilton County
90	2367	1.5	**Upper Arlington** (city) Franklin County
97	2500	1.4	**Broadview Heights** (city) Cuyahoga County
97	2500	1.4	**Celina** (city) Mercer County
97	2500	1.4	**Euclid** (city) Cuyahoga County
97	2500	1.4	**Heath** (city) Licking County
97	2500	1.4	**Lorain** (city) Lorain County
97	2500	1.4	**Marysville** (city) Union County
97	2500	1.4	**Parma** (city) Cuyahoga County
97	2500	1.4	**Springdale** (city) Hamilton County
97	2500	1.4	**Trotwood** (city) Montgomery County
97	2500	1.4	**Urbana** (city) Champaign County
107	2661	1.3	**Dent** (CDP) Hamilton County
107	2661	1.3	**Greenville** (city) Darke County
107	2661	1.3	**Miamisburg** (city) Montgomery County
107	2661	1.3	**Northbrook** (CDP) Hamilton County
107	2661	1.3	**Norton** (city) Summit County
107	2661	1.3	**Perrysburg** (city) Wood County
107	2661	1.3	**Stow** (city) Summit County
107	2661	1.3	**Trenton** (city) Butler County
107	2661	1.3	**Wadsworth** (city) Medina County
107	2661	1.3	**Willoughby** (city) Lake County
117	2817	1.2	**Brecksville** (city) Cuyahoga County
117	2817	1.2	**Mayfield Heights** (city) Cuyahoga County
117	2817	1.2	**Medina** (city) Medina County
117	2817	1.2	**North Olmsted** (city) Cuyahoga County
117	2817	1.2	**Riverside** (city) Montgomery County
117	2817	1.2	**Strongsville** (city) Cuyahoga County
117	2817	1.2	**Warren** (city) Trumbull County
124	2976	1.1	**Englewood** (city) Montgomery County
124	2976	1.1	**Huber Heights** (city) Montgomery County
124	2976	1.1	**Mentor** (city) Lake County
124	2976	1.1	**Parma Heights** (city) Cuyahoga County
124	2976	1.1	**White Oak** (CDP) Hamilton County
129	3154	1.0	**Boardman** (CDP) Mahoning County
129	3154	1.0	**Cuyahoga Falls** (city) Summit County
129	3154	1.0	**Elyria** (city) Lorain County
129	3154	1.0	**Middletown** (city) Butler County
129	3154	1.0	**Niles** (city) Trumbull County
129	3154	1.0	**Powell** (city) Delaware County
129	3154	1.0	**Sidney** (city) Shelby County
129	3154	1.0	**Westlake** (city) Cuyahoga County
129	3154	1.0	**Willowick** (city) Lake County
138	3333	0.9	**Aurora** (city) Portage County
138	3333	0.9	**Blue Ash** (city) Hamilton County
138	3333	0.9	**Brooklyn** (city) Cuyahoga County
138	3333	0.9	**Fairview Park** (city) Cuyahoga County
138	3333	0.9	**Hilliard** (city) Franklin County
138	3333	0.9	**Rocky River** (city) Cuyahoga County
138	3333	0.9	**Streetsboro** (city) Portage County
138	3333	0.9	**Struthers** (city) Mahoning County
138	3333	0.9	**West Carrollton** (city) Montgomery County
147	3503	0.8	**Bay Village** (city) Cuyahoga County
147	3503	0.8	**Bridgetown** (CDP) Hamilton County
147	3503	0.8	**Macedonia** (city) Summit County
147	3503	0.8	**Maumee** (city) Lucas County

Note: *The state column ranks the top/bottom 150 places from all places in the state with population of 10,000 or more. The national column ranks the top/bottom 150 places from all places in the country with population of 10,000 or more. Places that are unincorporated were not considered in the rankings. Please refer to the User Guide for additional information.*

Commute to Work: Walk

Top 150 Places Ranked in *Ascending* Order

State Rank	Nat'l Rank	Percent	Place
1	1	0.0	**Springboro** (city) Warren County
2	93	0.1	**Austintown** (CDP) Mahoning County
2	93	0.1	**Centerville** (city) Montgomery County
4	151	0.2	**New Franklin** (city) Summit County
5	246	0.3	**Green** (city) Summit County
5	246	0.3	**Grove City** (city) Franklin County
5	246	0.3	**Pickerington** (city) Fairfield County
5	246	0.3	**Vandalia** (city) Montgomery County
9	358	0.4	**Amherst** (city) Lorain County
9	358	0.4	**Mack** (CDP) Hamilton County
9	358	0.4	**North Ridgeville** (city) Lorain County
9	358	0.4	**North Royalton** (city) Cuyahoga County
9	358	0.4	**Seven Hills** (city) Cuyahoga County
14	497	0.5	**Dublin** (city) Franklin County
14	497	0.5	**Fairfield** (city) Butler County
14	497	0.5	**Franklin** (city) Warren County
14	497	0.5	**Mason** (city) Warren County
14	497	0.5	**Oregon** (city) Lucas County
14	497	0.5	**Sylvania** (city) Lucas County
14	497	0.5	**Wickliffe** (city) Lake County
21	651	0.6	**Clayton** (city) Montgomery County
21	651	0.6	**Forest Park** (city) Hamilton County
21	651	0.6	**Montgomery** (city) Hamilton County
21	651	0.6	**Solon** (city) Cuyahoga County
25	802	0.7	**Avon** (city) Lorain County
25	802	0.7	**Gahanna** (city) Franklin County
25	802	0.7	**Twinsburg** (city) Summit County
25	802	0.7	**Worthington** (city) Franklin County
29	970	0.8	**Bay Village** (city) Cuyahoga County
29	970	0.8	**Bridgetown** (CDP) Hamilton County
29	970	0.8	**Macedonia** (city) Summit County
29	970	0.8	**Maumee** (city) Lucas County
29	970	0.8	**Middleburg Heights** (city) Cuyahoga County
29	970	0.8	**Monroe** (city) Butler County
29	970	0.8	**Pataskala** (city) Licking County
29	970	0.8	**Richmond Heights** (city) Cuyahoga County
29	970	0.8	**Tallmadge** (city) Summit County
38	1154	0.9	**Aurora** (city) Portage County
38	1154	0.9	**Blue Ash** (city) Hamilton County
38	1154	0.9	**Brooklyn** (city) Cuyahoga County
38	1154	0.9	**Fairview Park** (city) Cuyahoga County
38	1154	0.9	**Hilliard** (city) Franklin County
38	1154	0.9	**Rocky River** (city) Cuyahoga County
38	1154	0.9	**Streetsboro** (city) Portage County
38	1154	0.9	**Struthers** (city) Mahoning County
38	1154	0.9	**West Carrollton** (city) Montgomery County
47	1324	1.0	**Boardman** (CDP) Mahoning County
47	1324	1.0	**Cuyahoga Falls** (city) Summit County
47	1324	1.0	**Elyria** (city) Lorain County
47	1324	1.0	**Middletown** (city) Butler County
47	1324	1.0	**Niles** (city) Trumbull County
47	1324	1.0	**Powell** (city) Delaware County
47	1324	1.0	**Sidney** (city) Shelby County
47	1324	1.0	**Westlake** (city) Cuyahoga County
47	1324	1.0	**Willowick** (city) Lake County
56	1503	1.1	**Englewood** (city) Montgomery County
56	1503	1.1	**Huber Heights** (city) Montgomery County
56	1503	1.1	**Mentor** (city) Lake County
56	1503	1.1	**Parma Heights** (city) Cuyahoga County
56	1503	1.1	**White Oak** (CDP) Hamilton County
61	1681	1.2	**Brecksville** (city) Cuyahoga County
61	1681	1.2	**Mayfield Heights** (city) Cuyahoga County
61	1681	1.2	**Medina** (city) Medina County
61	1681	1.2	**North Olmsted** (city) Cuyahoga County
61	1681	1.2	**Riverside** (city) Montgomery County
61	1681	1.2	**Strongsville** (city) Cuyahoga County
61	1681	1.2	**Warren** (city) Trumbull County
68	1840	1.3	**Dent** (CDP) Hamilton County
68	1840	1.3	**Greenville** (city) Darke County
68	1840	1.3	**Miamisburg** (city) Montgomery County
68	1840	1.3	**Northbrook** (CDP) Hamilton County
68	1840	1.3	**Norton** (city) Summit County
68	1840	1.3	**Perrysburg** (city) Wood County
68	1840	1.3	**Stow** (city) Summit County
68	1840	1.3	**Trenton** (city) Butler County
68	1840	1.3	**Wadsworth** (city) Medina County
68	1840	1.3	**Willoughby** (city) Lake County
78	1996	1.4	**Broadview Heights** (city) Cuyahoga County
78	1996	1.4	**Celina** (city) Mercer County
78	1996	1.4	**Euclid** (city) Cuyahoga County
78	1996	1.4	**Heath** (city) Licking County
78	1996	1.4	**Lorain** (city) Lorain County
78	1996	1.4	**Marysville** (city) Union County
78	1996	1.4	**Parma** (city) Cuyahoga County
78	1996	1.4	**Springdale** (city) Hamilton County
78	1996	1.4	**Trotwood** (city) Montgomery County
78	1996	1.4	**Urbana** (city) Champaign County
88	2157	1.5	**Hudson** (city) Summit County
88	2157	1.5	**Ironton** (city) Lawrence County
88	2157	1.5	**Loveland** (city) Hamilton County
88	2157	1.5	**Lyndhurst** (city) Cuyahoga County
88	2157	1.5	**Marion** (city) Marion County
88	2157	1.5	**Monfort Heights** (CDP) Hamilton County
88	2157	1.5	**Upper Arlington** (city) Franklin County
95	2290	1.6	**Beavercreek** (city) Greene County
95	2290	1.6	**Brunswick** (city) Medina County
95	2290	1.6	**Defiance** (city) Defiance County
98	2427	1.7	**Bedford** (city) Cuyahoga County
98	2427	1.7	**Eastlake** (city) Lake County
98	2427	1.7	**Kettering** (city) Montgomery County
101	2537	1.8	**Bellefontaine** (city) Logan County
101	2537	1.8	**Chillicothe** (city) Ross County
101	2537	1.8	**East Liverpool** (city) Columbiana County
101	2537	1.8	**Garfield Heights** (city) Cuyahoga County
101	2537	1.8	**Maple Heights** (city) Cuyahoga County
101	2537	1.8	**Reynoldsburg** (city) Franklin County
101	2537	1.8	**Whitehall** (city) Franklin County
108	2663	1.9	**Barberton** (city) Summit County
108	2663	1.9	**Circleville** (city) Pickaway County
108	2663	1.9	**Dover** (city) Tuscarawas County
108	2663	1.9	**Warrensville Heights** (city) Cuyahoga County
112	2771	2.0	**Avon Lake** (city) Lorain County
112	2771	2.0	**Bedford Heights** (city) Cuyahoga County
112	2771	2.0	**Salem** (city) Columbiana County
112	2771	2.0	**Shaker Heights** (city) Cuyahoga County
112	2771	2.0	**South Euclid** (city) Cuyahoga County
117	2876	2.1	**Brook Park** (city) Cuyahoga County
117	2876	2.1	**Conneaut** (city) Ashtabula County
117	2876	2.1	**Piqua** (city) Miami County
117	2876	2.1	**Troy** (city) Miami County
121	2971	2.2	**Akron** (city) Summit County
121	2971	2.2	**Beachwood** (city) Cuyahoga County
121	2971	2.2	**Fairborn** (city) Greene County
121	2971	2.2	**Massillon** (city) Stark County
121	2971	2.2	**Newark** (city) Licking County
126	3073	2.3	**Bucyrus** (city) Crawford County
126	3073	2.3	**Finneytown** (CDP) Hamilton County
126	3073	2.3	**Lakewood** (city) Cuyahoga County
129	3144	2.4	**Hamilton** (city) Butler County
129	3144	2.4	**Ravenna** (city) Portage County
131	3218	2.5	**Fremont** (city) Sandusky County
131	3218	2.5	**Lebanon** (city) Warren County
131	3218	2.5	**New Philadelphia** (city) Tuscarawas County
131	3218	2.5	**North Canton** (city) Stark County
131	3218	2.5	**Xenia** (city) Greene County
136	3310	2.6	**Forestville** (CDP) Hamilton County
136	3310	2.6	**Mansfield** (city) Richland County
136	3310	2.6	**Norwood** (city) Hamilton County
136	3310	2.6	**Zanesville** (city) Muskingum County
140	3368	2.7	**Sandusky** (city) Erie County
140	3368	2.7	**Sharonville** (city) Hamilton County
142	3439	2.8	**Columbus** (city) Franklin County
142	3439	2.8	**Norwalk** (city) Huron County
144	3493	2.9	**Cambridge** (city) Guernsey County
144	3493	2.9	**Canton** (city) Stark County
144	3493	2.9	**Lima** (city) Allen County
144	3493	2.9	**Youngstown** (city) Mahoning County
148	3552	3.0	**Ashtabula** (city) Ashtabula County
148	3552	3.0	**Findlay** (city) Hancock County
148	3552	3.0	**Toledo** (city) Lucas County

Note: *The state column ranks the top/bottom 150 places from all places in the state with population of 10,000 or more. The national column ranks the top/bottom 150 places from all places in the country with population of 10,000 or more. Places that are unincorporated were not considered in the rankings. Please refer to the User Guide for additional information.*

Commute to Work: Work from Home

Top 150 Places Ranked in *Descending* Order

State Rank	Nat'l Rank	Percent	Place
1	87	11.0	**Oxford** (city) Butler County
2	200	9.0	**Powell** (city) Delaware County
3	288	8.1	**Hudson** (city) Summit County
4	304	8.0	**Beachwood** (city) Cuyahoga County
5	351	7.7	**Dublin** (city) Franklin County
6	475	7.1	**Gahanna** (city) Franklin County
6	475	7.1	**University Heights** (city) Cuyahoga County
6	475	7.1	**Worthington** (city) Franklin County
9	548	6.8	**Upper Arlington** (city) Franklin County
10	600	6.6	**Mack** (CDP) Hamilton County
10	600	6.6	**Shaker Heights** (city) Cuyahoga County
12	649	6.4	**Athens** (city) Athens County
12	649	6.4	**Aurora** (city) Portage County
14	739	6.1	**Bay Village** (city) Cuyahoga County
15	769	6.0	**North Canton** (city) Stark County
16	809	5.9	**Steubenville** (city) Jefferson County
17	845	5.8	**Cambridge** (city) Guernsey County
18	931	5.6	**Avon** (city) Lorain County
18	931	5.6	**North Royalton** (city) Cuyahoga County
20	1010	5.4	**Rocky River** (city) Cuyahoga County
20	1010	5.4	**Solon** (city) Cuyahoga County
20	1010	5.4	**Westerville** (city) Franklin County
23	1060	5.3	**Berea** (city) Cuyahoga County
23	1060	5.3	**Delaware** (city) Delaware County
23	1060	5.3	**Pickerington** (city) Fairfield County
26	1109	5.2	**Brecksville** (city) Cuyahoga County
27	1163	5.1	**Loveland** (city) Hamilton County
28	1209	5.0	**Beavercreek** (city) Greene County
28	1209	5.0	**Broadview Heights** (city) Cuyahoga County
30	1254	4.9	**Lyndhurst** (city) Cuyahoga County
30	1254	4.9	**Perrysburg** (city) Wood County
32	1316	4.8	**Bexley** (city) Franklin County
32	1316	4.8	**Hilliard** (city) Franklin County
34	1372	4.7	**Centerville** (city) Montgomery County
35	1429	4.6	**Cleveland Heights** (city) Cuyahoga County
35	1429	4.6	**Mason** (city) Warren County
35	1429	4.6	**Montgomery** (city) Hamilton County
35	1429	4.6	**Westlake** (city) Cuyahoga County
39	1495	4.5	**Monfort Heights** (CDP) Hamilton County
39	1495	4.5	**Pataskala** (city) Licking County
39	1495	4.5	**Richmond Heights** (city) Cuyahoga County
42	1566	4.4	**Springboro** (city) Warren County
42	1566	4.4	**Zanesville** (city) Muskingum County
44	1650	4.3	**Strongsville** (city) Cuyahoga County
44	1650	4.3	**Wadsworth** (city) Medina County
46	1720	4.2	**Kent** (city) Portage County
46	1720	4.2	**Marysville** (city) Union County
46	1720	4.2	**Monroe** (city) Butler County
49	1790	4.1	**Amherst** (city) Lorain County
49	1790	4.1	**Dover** (city) Tuscarawas County
49	1790	4.1	**Forestville** (CDP) Hamilton County
49	1790	4.1	**Greenville** (city) Darke County
49	1790	4.1	**Miamisburg** (city) Montgomery County
49	1790	4.1	**Reynoldsburg** (city) Franklin County
49	1790	4.1	**Twinsburg** (city) Summit County
56	1884	4.0	**Cincinnati** (city) Hamilton County
56	1884	4.0	**Kettering** (city) Montgomery County
56	1884	4.0	**South Euclid** (city) Cuyahoga County
59	1952	3.9	**Lebanon** (city) Warren County
60	2046	3.8	**Blue Ash** (city) Hamilton County
60	2046	3.8	**Findlay** (city) Hancock County
60	2046	3.8	**Grove City** (city) Franklin County
63	2227	3.6	**Avon Lake** (city) Lorain County
63	2227	3.6	**Conneaut** (city) Ashtabula County
63	2227	3.6	**Fairview Park** (city) Cuyahoga County
63	2227	3.6	**Green** (city) Summit County
67	2321	3.5	**Circleville** (city) Pickaway County
68	2433	3.4	**Ashland** (city) Ashland County
68	2433	3.4	**Columbus** (city) Franklin County
68	2433	3.4	**North Ridgeville** (city) Lorain County
68	2433	3.4	**Stow** (city) Summit County
68	2433	3.4	**Sylvania** (city) Lucas County
68	2433	3.4	**Wilmington** (city) Clinton County
74	2522	3.3	**Marietta** (city) Washington County
75	2621	3.2	**Bowling Green** (city) Wood County
75	2621	3.2	**Coshocton** (city) Coshocton County
75	2621	3.2	**Medina** (city) Medina County
75	2621	3.2	**North Olmsted** (city) Cuyahoga County
79	2729	3.1	**Lakewood** (city) Cuyahoga County
79	2729	3.1	**Macedonia** (city) Summit County
79	2729	3.1	**West Carrollton** (city) Montgomery County
79	2729	3.1	**Willowick** (city) Lake County
79	2729	3.1	**Wooster** (city) Wayne County
84	2821	3.0	**Forest Park** (city) Hamilton County
84	2821	3.0	**Mentor** (city) Lake County
84	2821	3.0	**Seven Hills** (city) Cuyahoga County
87	2913	2.9	**Cuyahoga Falls** (city) Summit County
87	2913	2.9	**Englewood** (city) Montgomery County
87	2913	2.9	**Middleburg Heights** (city) Cuyahoga County
87	2913	2.9	**Northbrook** (CDP) Hamilton County
87	2913	2.9	**Norwood** (city) Hamilton County
92	3026	2.8	**Cleveland** (city) Cuyahoga County
92	3026	2.8	**Warren** (city) Trumbull County
94	3110	2.7	**Alliance** (city) Stark County
94	3110	2.7	**Bellefontaine** (city) Logan County
94	3110	2.7	**Brunswick** (city) Medina County
94	3110	2.7	**Chillicothe** (city) Ross County
94	3110	2.7	**Dent** (CDP) Hamilton County
94	3110	2.7	**East Cleveland** (city) Cuyahoga County
94	3110	2.7	**Heath** (city) Licking County
94	3110	2.7	**Sandusky** (city) Erie County
94	3110	2.7	**Youngstown** (city) Mahoning County
103	3231	2.6	**Euclid** (city) Cuyahoga County
103	3231	2.6	**Finneytown** (CDP) Hamilton County
103	3231	2.6	**Maumee** (city) Lucas County
103	3231	2.6	**Newark** (city) Licking County
103	3231	2.6	**Streetsboro** (city) Portage County
103	3231	2.6	**Vandalia** (city) Montgomery County
109	3336	2.5	**Fremont** (city) Sandusky County
110	3451	2.4	**Ashtabula** (city) Ashtabula County
110	3451	2.4	**New Franklin** (city) Summit County
110	3451	2.4	**Norton** (city) Summit County
110	3451	2.4	**Oregon** (city) Lucas County
110	3451	2.4	**Sharonville** (city) Hamilton County
115	3553	2.3	**Celina** (city) Mercer County
115	3553	2.3	**Troy** (city) Miami County
115	3553	2.3	**Wickliffe** (city) Lake County
118	3645	2.2	**Dayton** (city) Montgomery County
118	3645	2.2	**Ironton** (city) Lawrence County
118	3645	2.2	**Vermilion** (city) Lorain County
121	3752	2.1	**Akron** (city) Summit County
121	3752	2.1	**Elyria** (city) Lorain County
121	3752	2.1	**Sidney** (city) Shelby County
121	3752	2.1	**Springfield** (city) Clark County
121	3752	2.1	**Toledo** (city) Lucas County
121	3752	2.1	**Willoughby** (city) Lake County
127	3839	2.0	**Austintown** (CDP) Mahoning County
127	3839	2.0	**Boardman** (CDP) Mahoning County
127	3839	2.0	**Bridgetown** (CDP) Hamilton County
127	3839	2.0	**Canton** (city) Stark County
127	3839	2.0	**Eastlake** (city) Lake County
127	3839	2.0	**Fairfield** (city) Butler County
127	3839	2.0	**Middletown** (city) Butler County
127	3839	2.0	**Ravenna** (city) Portage County
127	3839	2.0	**Xenia** (city) Greene County
136	3947	1.9	**Galion** (city) Crawford County
136	3947	1.9	**Garfield Heights** (city) Cuyahoga County
136	3947	1.9	**Mount Vernon** (city) Knox County
139	4023	1.8	**Clayton** (city) Montgomery County
139	4023	1.8	**Fairborn** (city) Greene County
139	4023	1.8	**Marion** (city) Marion County
139	4023	1.8	**Parma** (city) Cuyahoga County
139	4023	1.8	**Portsmouth** (city) Scioto County
144	4118	1.7	**Brooklyn** (city) Cuyahoga County
144	4118	1.7	**Defiance** (city) Defiance County
144	4118	1.7	**Lorain** (city) Lorain County
144	4118	1.7	**Mansfield** (city) Richland County
144	4118	1.7	**Parma Heights** (city) Cuyahoga County
144	4118	1.7	**Urbana** (city) Champaign County
150	4190	1.6	**Hamilton** (city) Butler County

Note: *The state column ranks the top/bottom 150 places from all places in the state with population of 10,000 or more. The national column ranks the top/bottom 150 places from all places in the country with population of 10,000 or more. Places that are unincorporated were not considered in the rankings. Please refer to the User Guide for additional information.*

Commute to Work: Work from Home

Top 150 Places Ranked in *Ascending* Order

State Rank	Nat'l Rank	Percent	Place
1	13	0.4	**Bedford Heights** (city) Cuyahoga County
2	40	0.7	**Struthers** (city) Mahoning County
3	59	0.8	**Bedford** (city) Cuyahoga County
4	110	1.0	**East Liverpool** (city) Columbiana County
5	139	1.1	**Niles** (city) Trumbull County
5	139	1.1	**Trotwood** (city) Montgomery County
7	180	1.2	**Fostoria** (city) Seneca County
7	180	1.2	**Norwalk** (city) Huron County
7	180	1.2	**Piqua** (city) Miami County
7	180	1.2	**Trenton** (city) Butler County
7	180	1.2	**White Oak** (CDP) Hamilton County
12	225	1.3	**Barberton** (city) Summit County
12	225	1.3	**Lima** (city) Allen County
12	225	1.3	**Riverside** (city) Montgomery County
12	225	1.3	**Warrensville Heights** (city) Cuyahoga County
12	225	1.3	**Whitehall** (city) Franklin County
17	272	1.4	**Brook Park** (city) Cuyahoga County
17	272	1.4	**Lancaster** (city) Fairfield County
17	272	1.4	**Reading** (city) Hamilton County
17	272	1.4	**Tiffin** (city) Seneca County
17	272	1.4	**Van Wert** (city) Van Wert County
17	272	1.4	**Washington Court House** (city) Fayette County
23	327	1.5	**Bucyrus** (city) Crawford County
23	327	1.5	**Franklin** (city) Warren County
23	327	1.5	**Maple Heights** (city) Cuyahoga County
23	327	1.5	**Massillon** (city) Stark County
23	327	1.5	**Mayfield Heights** (city) Cuyahoga County
23	327	1.5	**New Philadelphia** (city) Tuscarawas County
23	327	1.5	**Springdale** (city) Hamilton County
30	398	1.6	**Hamilton** (city) Butler County
30	398	1.6	**Huber Heights** (city) Montgomery County
30	398	1.6	**Painesville** (city) Lake County
30	398	1.6	**Salem** (city) Columbiana County
30	398	1.6	**Tallmadge** (city) Summit County
35	467	1.7	**Brooklyn** (city) Cuyahoga County
35	467	1.7	**Defiance** (city) Defiance County
35	467	1.7	**Lorain** (city) Lorain County
35	467	1.7	**Mansfield** (city) Richland County
35	467	1.7	**Parma Heights** (city) Cuyahoga County
35	467	1.7	**Urbana** (city) Champaign County
41	539	1.8	**Clayton** (city) Montgomery County
41	539	1.8	**Fairborn** (city) Greene County
41	539	1.8	**Marion** (city) Marion County
41	539	1.8	**Parma** (city) Cuyahoga County
41	539	1.8	**Portsmouth** (city) Scioto County
46	634	1.9	**Galion** (city) Crawford County
46	634	1.9	**Garfield Heights** (city) Cuyahoga County
46	634	1.9	**Mount Vernon** (city) Knox County
49	710	2.0	**Austintown** (CDP) Mahoning County
49	710	2.0	**Boardman** (CDP) Mahoning County
49	710	2.0	**Bridgetown** (CDP) Hamilton County
49	710	2.0	**Canton** (city) Stark County
49	710	2.0	**Eastlake** (city) Lake County
49	710	2.0	**Fairfield** (city) Butler County
49	710	2.0	**Middletown** (city) Butler County
49	710	2.0	**Ravenna** (city) Portage County
49	710	2.0	**Xenia** (city) Greene County
58	818	2.1	**Akron** (city) Summit County
58	818	2.1	**Elyria** (city) Lorain County
58	818	2.1	**Sidney** (city) Shelby County
58	818	2.1	**Springfield** (city) Clark County
58	818	2.1	**Toledo** (city) Lucas County
58	818	2.1	**Willoughby** (city) Lake County
64	905	2.2	**Dayton** (city) Montgomery County
64	905	2.2	**Ironton** (city) Lawrence County
64	905	2.2	**Vermilion** (city) Lorain County
67	1012	2.3	**Celina** (city) Mercer County
67	1012	2.3	**Troy** (city) Miami County
67	1012	2.3	**Wickliffe** (city) Lake County
70	1104	2.4	**Ashtabula** (city) Ashtabula County
70	1104	2.4	**New Franklin** (city) Summit County
70	1104	2.4	**Norton** (city) Summit County
70	1104	2.4	**Oregon** (city) Lucas County
70	1104	2.4	**Sharonville** (city) Hamilton County
75	1206	2.5	**Fremont** (city) Sandusky County
76	1321	2.6	**Euclid** (city) Cuyahoga County
76	1321	2.6	**Finneytown** (CDP) Hamilton County
76	1321	2.6	**Maumee** (city) Lucas County
76	1321	2.6	**Newark** (city) Licking County
76	1321	2.6	**Streetsboro** (city) Portage County
76	1321	2.6	**Vandalia** (city) Montgomery County
82	1426	2.7	**Alliance** (city) Stark County
82	1426	2.7	**Bellefontaine** (city) Logan County
82	1426	2.7	**Brunswick** (city) Medina County
82	1426	2.7	**Chillicothe** (city) Ross County
82	1426	2.7	**Dent** (CDP) Hamilton County
82	1426	2.7	**East Cleveland** (city) Cuyahoga County
82	1426	2.7	**Heath** (city) Licking County
82	1426	2.7	**Sandusky** (city) Erie County
82	1426	2.7	**Youngstown** (city) Mahoning County
91	1547	2.8	**Cleveland** (city) Cuyahoga County
91	1547	2.8	**Warren** (city) Trumbull County
93	1631	2.9	**Cuyahoga Falls** (city) Summit County
93	1631	2.9	**Englewood** (city) Montgomery County
93	1631	2.9	**Middleburg Heights** (city) Cuyahoga County
93	1631	2.9	**Northbrook** (CDP) Hamilton County
93	1631	2.9	**Norwood** (city) Hamilton County
98	1744	3.0	**Forest Park** (city) Hamilton County
98	1744	3.0	**Mentor** (city) Lake County
98	1744	3.0	**Seven Hills** (city) Cuyahoga County
101	1836	3.1	**Lakewood** (city) Cuyahoga County
101	1836	3.1	**Macedonia** (city) Summit County
101	1836	3.1	**West Carrollton** (city) Montgomery County
101	1836	3.1	**Willowick** (city) Lake County
101	1836	3.1	**Wooster** (city) Wayne County
106	1928	3.2	**Bowling Green** (city) Wood County
106	1928	3.2	**Coshocton** (city) Coshocton County
106	1928	3.2	**Medina** (city) Medina County
106	1928	3.2	**North Olmsted** (city) Cuyahoga County
110	2036	3.3	**Marietta** (city) Washington County
111	2135	3.4	**Ashland** (city) Ashland County
111	2135	3.4	**Columbus** (city) Franklin County
111	2135	3.4	**North Ridgeville** (city) Lorain County
111	2135	3.4	**Stow** (city) Summit County
111	2135	3.4	**Sylvania** (city) Lucas County
111	2135	3.4	**Wilmington** (city) Clinton County
117	2224	3.5	**Circleville** (city) Pickaway County
118	2336	3.6	**Avon Lake** (city) Lorain County
118	2336	3.6	**Conneaut** (city) Ashtabula County
118	2336	3.6	**Fairview Park** (city) Cuyahoga County
118	2336	3.6	**Green** (city) Summit County
122	2520	3.8	**Blue Ash** (city) Hamilton County
122	2520	3.8	**Findlay** (city) Hancock County
122	2520	3.8	**Grove City** (city) Franklin County
125	2611	3.9	**Lebanon** (city) Warren County
126	2705	4.0	**Cincinnati** (city) Hamilton County
126	2705	4.0	**Kettering** (city) Montgomery County
126	2705	4.0	**South Euclid** (city) Cuyahoga County
129	2773	4.1	**Amherst** (city) Lorain County
129	2773	4.1	**Dover** (city) Tuscarawas County
129	2773	4.1	**Forestville** (CDP) Hamilton County
129	2773	4.1	**Greenville** (city) Darke County
129	2773	4.1	**Miamisburg** (city) Montgomery County
129	2773	4.1	**Reynoldsburg** (city) Franklin County
129	2773	4.1	**Twinsburg** (city) Summit County
136	2867	4.2	**Kent** (city) Portage County
136	2867	4.2	**Marysville** (city) Union County
136	2867	4.2	**Monroe** (city) Butler County
139	2937	4.3	**Strongsville** (city) Cuyahoga County
139	2937	4.3	**Wadsworth** (city) Medina County
141	3007	4.4	**Springboro** (city) Warren County
141	3007	4.4	**Zanesville** (city) Muskingum County
143	3091	4.5	**Monfort Heights** (CDP) Hamilton County
143	3091	4.5	**Pataskala** (city) Licking County
143	3091	4.5	**Richmond Heights** (city) Cuyahoga County
146	3162	4.6	**Cleveland Heights** (city) Cuyahoga County
146	3162	4.6	**Mason** (city) Warren County
146	3162	4.6	**Montgomery** (city) Hamilton County
146	3162	4.6	**Westlake** (city) Cuyahoga County
150	3228	4.7	**Centerville** (city) Montgomery County

Note: *The state column ranks the top/bottom 150 places from all places in the state with population of 10,000 or more. The national column ranks the top/bottom 150 places from all places in the country with population of 10,000 or more. Places that are unincorporated were not considered in the rankings. Please refer to the User Guide for additional information.*

Median Travel Time to Work

Top 150 Places Ranked in *Descending* Order

State Rank	Nat'l Rank	Minutes	Place
1	1189	28.9	**Brunswick** (city) Medina County
2	1335	28.3	**Hudson** (city) Summit County
3	1357	28.2	**Mack** (CDP) Hamilton County
4	1399	28.0	**Broadview Heights** (city) Cuyahoga County
5	1461	27.7	**Vermilion** (city) Lorain County
6	1519	27.5	**North Royalton** (city) Cuyahoga County
7	1559	27.3	**Strongsville** (city) Cuyahoga County
8	1606	27.1	**North Ridgeville** (city) Lorain County
9	1622	27.0	**Monroe** (city) Butler County
10	1656	26.9	**Trenton** (city) Butler County
11	1696	26.7	**Pickerington** (city) Fairfield County
12	1776	26.4	**Delaware** (city) Delaware County
13	1799	26.3	**Aurora** (city) Portage County
13	1799	26.3	**Avon Lake** (city) Lorain County
13	1799	26.3	**Twinsburg** (city) Summit County
16	1824	26.2	**East Cleveland** (city) Cuyahoga County
16	1824	26.2	**Warrensville Heights** (city) Cuyahoga County
18	1851	26.1	**Medina** (city) Medina County
19	1910	25.9	**Avon** (city) Lorain County
20	1966	25.7	**Seven Hills** (city) Cuyahoga County
21	2014	25.5	**Solon** (city) Cuyahoga County
22	2067	25.3	**Pataskala** (city) Licking County
23	2097	25.2	**Parma Heights** (city) Cuyahoga County
24	2149	25.0	**Fairview Park** (city) Cuyahoga County
24	2149	25.0	**Forestville** (CDP) Hamilton County
24	2149	25.0	**Lebanon** (city) Warren County
27	2239	24.7	**Powell** (city) Delaware County
28	2284	24.5	**Bridgetown** (CDP) Hamilton County
29	2313	24.4	**East Liverpool** (city) Columbiana County
29	2313	24.4	**Forest Park** (city) Hamilton County
29	2313	24.4	**Richmond Heights** (city) Cuyahoga County
32	2350	24.3	**Cleveland** (city) Cuyahoga County
32	2350	24.3	**Euclid** (city) Cuyahoga County
32	2350	24.3	**Lakewood** (city) Cuyahoga County
32	2350	24.3	**Parma** (city) Cuyahoga County
32	2350	24.3	**Stow** (city) Summit County
32	2350	24.3	**Trotwood** (city) Montgomery County
32	2350	24.3	**Westlake** (city) Cuyahoga County
39	2386	24.2	**Hamilton** (city) Butler County
39	2386	24.2	**New Franklin** (city) Summit County
39	2386	24.2	**South Euclid** (city) Cuyahoga County
42	2421	24.1	**Clayton** (city) Montgomery County
42	2421	24.1	**Mentor** (city) Lake County
44	2445	24.0	**Circleville** (city) Pickaway County
44	2445	24.0	**Dent** (CDP) Hamilton County
46	2483	23.9	**Lancaster** (city) Fairfield County
46	2483	23.9	**Montgomery** (city) Hamilton County
48	2510	23.8	**Streetsboro** (city) Portage County
49	2543	23.7	**Brecksville** (city) Cuyahoga County
50	2577	23.6	**Bay Village** (city) Cuyahoga County
50	2577	23.6	**Rocky River** (city) Cuyahoga County
52	2614	23.5	**Reynoldsburg** (city) Franklin County
53	2641	23.4	**Eastlake** (city) Lake County
53	2641	23.4	**Loveland** (city) Hamilton County
53	2641	23.4	**Macedonia** (city) Summit County
56	2697	23.2	**Mason** (city) Warren County
57	2725	23.1	**North Olmsted** (city) Cuyahoga County
58	2741	23.0	**Fairfield** (city) Butler County
58	2741	23.0	**Shaker Heights** (city) Cuyahoga County
60	2760	22.9	**Bedford Heights** (city) Cuyahoga County
60	2760	22.9	**Lorain** (city) Lorain County
62	2818	22.7	**Maple Heights** (city) Cuyahoga County
63	2845	22.6	**Cuyahoga Falls** (city) Summit County
63	2845	22.6	**Wadsworth** (city) Medina County
65	2871	22.5	**Green** (city) Summit County
66	2911	22.4	**Cincinnati** (city) Hamilton County
66	2911	22.4	**Conneaut** (city) Ashtabula County
66	2911	22.4	**Dublin** (city) Franklin County
66	2911	22.4	**Garfield Heights** (city) Cuyahoga County
66	2911	22.4	**Springboro** (city) Warren County
66	2911	22.4	**White Oak** (CDP) Hamilton County
72	2943	22.3	**Cleveland Heights** (city) Cuyahoga County
72	2943	22.3	**Finneytown** (CDP) Hamilton County
72	2943	22.3	**Huber Heights** (city) Montgomery County
72	2943	22.3	**Lyndhurst** (city) Cuyahoga County
76	2977	22.2	**Bucyrus** (city) Crawford County
76	2977	22.2	**University Heights** (city) Cuyahoga County
78	3005	22.1	**Franklin** (city) Warren County
78	3005	22.1	**Hilliard** (city) Franklin County
78	3005	22.1	**Xenia** (city) Greene County
81	3038	22.0	**Bedford** (city) Cuyahoga County
82	3064	21.9	**Elyria** (city) Lorain County
82	3064	21.9	**Grove City** (city) Franklin County
82	3064	21.9	**Norton** (city) Summit County
85	3095	21.8	**Centerville** (city) Montgomery County
85	3095	21.8	**Englewood** (city) Montgomery County
87	3114	21.7	**Marysville** (city) Union County
87	3114	21.7	**Middleburg Heights** (city) Cuyahoga County
89	3142	21.6	**Northbrook** (CDP) Hamilton County
90	3166	21.5	**Chillicothe** (city) Ross County
90	3166	21.5	**Galion** (city) Crawford County
90	3166	21.5	**Heath** (city) Licking County
93	3200	21.4	**Berea** (city) Cuyahoga County
93	3200	21.4	**Willoughby** (city) Lake County
95	3222	21.3	**Barberton** (city) Summit County
95	3222	21.3	**Columbus** (city) Franklin County
95	3222	21.3	**Kent** (city) Portage County
95	3222	21.3	**Springdale** (city) Hamilton County
99	3251	21.2	**Brook Park** (city) Cuyahoga County
99	3251	21.2	**Brooklyn** (city) Cuyahoga County
99	3251	21.2	**Mayfield Heights** (city) Cuyahoga County
99	3251	21.2	**Middletown** (city) Butler County
99	3251	21.2	**Ravenna** (city) Portage County
104	3272	21.1	**Beachwood** (city) Cuyahoga County
104	3272	21.1	**Newark** (city) Licking County
104	3272	21.1	**Whitehall** (city) Franklin County
107	3309	21.0	**Gahanna** (city) Franklin County
107	3309	21.0	**Worthington** (city) Franklin County
107	3309	21.0	**Zanesville** (city) Muskingum County
110	3334	20.9	**Miamisburg** (city) Montgomery County
110	3334	20.9	**Monfort Heights** (CDP) Hamilton County
110	3334	20.9	**Tallmadge** (city) Summit County
113	3359	20.8	**Urbana** (city) Champaign County
113	3359	20.8	**Vandalia** (city) Montgomery County
115	3391	20.7	**West Carrollton** (city) Montgomery County
115	3391	20.7	**Westerville** (city) Franklin County
117	3410	20.6	**Amherst** (city) Lorain County
117	3410	20.6	**Massillon** (city) Stark County
119	3434	20.5	**Akron** (city) Summit County
120	3453	20.4	**Boardman** (CDP) Mahoning County
121	3478	20.3	**Salem** (city) Columbiana County
121	3478	20.3	**Youngstown** (city) Mahoning County
123	3506	20.2	**Bellefontaine** (city) Logan County
123	3506	20.2	**Blue Ash** (city) Hamilton County
123	3506	20.2	**Dayton** (city) Montgomery County
123	3506	20.2	**Fostoria** (city) Seneca County
123	3506	20.2	**Kettering** (city) Montgomery County
128	3541	20.1	**Perrysburg** (city) Wood County
128	3541	20.1	**Washington Court House** (city) Fayette County
128	3541	20.1	**Willowick** (city) Lake County
131	3572	20.0	**Sylvania** (city) Lucas County
131	3572	20.0	**Wilmington** (city) Clinton County
133	3592	19.9	**Wickliffe** (city) Lake County
134	3661	19.6	**Dover** (city) Tuscarawas County
135	3684	19.5	**Austintown** (CDP) Mahoning County
135	3684	19.5	**Fairborn** (city) Greene County
135	3684	19.5	**Marion** (city) Marion County
135	3684	19.5	**Oregon** (city) Lucas County
135	3684	19.5	**Reading** (city) Hamilton County
135	3684	19.5	**Warren** (city) Trumbull County
141	3720	19.4	**Ashtabula** (city) Ashtabula County
141	3720	19.4	**Canton** (city) Stark County
141	3720	19.4	**Springfield** (city) Clark County
144	3774	19.2	**Painesville** (city) Lake County
144	3774	19.2	**Struthers** (city) Mahoning County
146	3795	19.1	**Maumee** (city) Lucas County
146	3795	19.1	**Mount Vernon** (city) Knox County
146	3795	19.1	**Norwood** (city) Hamilton County
146	3795	19.1	**Upper Arlington** (city) Franklin County
150	3824	19.0	**Toledo** (city) Lucas County

Note: *The state column ranks the top/bottom 150 places from all places in the state with population of 10,000 or more. The national column ranks the top/bottom 150 places from all places in the country with population of 10,000 or more. Places that are unincorporated were not considered in the rankings. Please refer to the User Guide for additional information.*

Median Travel Time to Work

Top 150 Places Ranked in *Ascending* Order

State Rank	Nat'l Rank	Minutes	Place
1	99	14.0	**Athens** (city) Athens County
1	99	14.0	**Oxford** (city) Butler County
3	131	14.5	**Findlay** (city) Hancock County
3	131	14.5	**Van Wert** (city) Van Wert County
5	139	14.6	**Coshocton** (city) Coshocton County
6	195	15.1	**Marietta** (city) Washington County
7	241	15.5	**Bowling Green** (city) Wood County
8	350	16.3	**Tiffin** (city) Seneca County
9	361	16.4	**Wooster** (city) Wayne County
10	384	16.6	**Fremont** (city) Sandusky County
10	384	16.6	**Sandusky** (city) Erie County
10	384	16.6	**Sidney** (city) Shelby County
13	397	16.7	**Bexley** (city) Franklin County
13	397	16.7	**Ironton** (city) Lawrence County
15	419	16.8	**Celina** (city) Mercer County
16	468	17.1	**Niles** (city) Trumbull County
16	468	17.1	**Steubenville** (city) Jefferson County
18	522	17.4	**New Philadelphia** (city) Tuscarawas County
19	536	17.5	**Defiance** (city) Defiance County
20	551	17.6	**Riverside** (city) Montgomery County
21	568	17.7	**Ashland** (city) Ashland County
21	568	17.7	**Lima** (city) Allen County
23	590	17.8	**Alliance** (city) Stark County
24	611	17.9	**Cambridge** (city) Guernsey County
24	611	17.9	**Piqua** (city) Miami County
26	643	18.1	**Troy** (city) Miami County
27	686	18.3	**Greenville** (city) Darke County
27	686	18.3	**North Canton** (city) Stark County
29	756	18.7	**Beavercreek** (city) Greene County
29	756	18.7	**Mansfield** (city) Richland County
29	756	18.7	**Norwalk** (city) Huron County
29	756	18.7	**Portsmouth** (city) Scioto County
33	781	18.8	**Sharonville** (city) Hamilton County
34	811	19.0	**Toledo** (city) Lucas County
35	833	19.1	**Maumee** (city) Lucas County
35	833	19.1	**Mount Vernon** (city) Knox County
35	833	19.1	**Norwood** (city) Hamilton County
35	833	19.1	**Upper Arlington** (city) Franklin County
39	862	19.2	**Painesville** (city) Lake County
39	862	19.2	**Struthers** (city) Mahoning County
41	909	19.4	**Ashtabula** (city) Ashtabula County
41	909	19.4	**Canton** (city) Stark County
41	909	19.4	**Springfield** (city) Clark County
44	937	19.5	**Austintown** (CDP) Mahoning County
44	937	19.5	**Fairborn** (city) Greene County
44	937	19.5	**Marion** (city) Marion County
44	937	19.5	**Oregon** (city) Lucas County
44	937	19.5	**Reading** (city) Hamilton County
44	937	19.5	**Warren** (city) Trumbull County
50	973	19.6	**Dover** (city) Tuscarawas County
51	1045	19.9	**Wickliffe** (city) Lake County
52	1065	20.0	**Sylvania** (city) Lucas County
52	1065	20.0	**Wilmington** (city) Clinton County
54	1085	20.1	**Perrysburg** (city) Wood County
54	1085	20.1	**Washington Court House** (city) Fayette County
54	1085	20.1	**Willowick** (city) Lake County
57	1116	20.2	**Bellefontaine** (city) Logan County
57	1116	20.2	**Blue Ash** (city) Hamilton County
57	1116	20.2	**Dayton** (city) Montgomery County
57	1116	20.2	**Fostoria** (city) Seneca County
57	1116	20.2	**Kettering** (city) Montgomery County
62	1151	20.3	**Salem** (city) Columbiana County
62	1151	20.3	**Youngstown** (city) Mahoning County
64	1179	20.4	**Boardman** (CDP) Mahoning County
65	1204	20.5	**Akron** (city) Summit County
66	1223	20.6	**Amherst** (city) Lorain County
66	1223	20.6	**Massillon** (city) Stark County
68	1247	20.7	**West Carrollton** (city) Montgomery County
68	1247	20.7	**Westerville** (city) Franklin County
70	1266	20.8	**Urbana** (city) Champaign County
70	1266	20.8	**Vandalia** (city) Montgomery County
72	1298	20.9	**Miamisburg** (city) Montgomery County
72	1298	20.9	**Monfort Heights** (CDP) Hamilton County
72	1298	20.9	**Tallmadge** (city) Summit County
75	1323	21.0	**Gahanna** (city) Franklin County
75	1323	21.0	**Worthington** (city) Franklin County
75	1323	21.0	**Zanesville** (city) Muskingum County
78	1348	21.1	**Beachwood** (city) Cuyahoga County
78	1348	21.1	**Newark** (city) Licking County
78	1348	21.1	**Whitehall** (city) Franklin County
81	1385	21.2	**Brook Park** (city) Cuyahoga County
81	1385	21.2	**Brooklyn** (city) Cuyahoga County
81	1385	21.2	**Mayfield Heights** (city) Cuyahoga County
81	1385	21.2	**Middletown** (city) Butler County
81	1385	21.2	**Ravenna** (city) Portage County
86	1406	21.3	**Barberton** (city) Summit County
86	1406	21.3	**Columbus** (city) Franklin County
86	1406	21.3	**Kent** (city) Portage County
86	1406	21.3	**Springdale** (city) Hamilton County
90	1435	21.4	**Berea** (city) Cuyahoga County
90	1435	21.4	**Willoughby** (city) Lake County
92	1457	21.5	**Chillicothe** (city) Ross County
92	1457	21.5	**Galion** (city) Crawford County
92	1457	21.5	**Heath** (city) Licking County
95	1491	21.6	**Northbrook** (CDP) Hamilton County
96	1515	21.7	**Marysville** (city) Union County
96	1515	21.7	**Middleburg Heights** (city) Cuyahoga County
98	1543	21.8	**Centerville** (city) Montgomery County
98	1543	21.8	**Englewood** (city) Montgomery County
100	1562	21.9	**Elyria** (city) Lorain County
100	1562	21.9	**Grove City** (city) Franklin County
100	1562	21.9	**Norton** (city) Summit County
103	1593	22.0	**Bedford** (city) Cuyahoga County
104	1619	22.1	**Franklin** (city) Warren County
104	1619	22.1	**Hilliard** (city) Franklin County
104	1619	22.1	**Xenia** (city) Greene County
107	1652	22.2	**Bucyrus** (city) Crawford County
107	1652	22.2	**University Heights** (city) Cuyahoga County
109	1680	22.3	**Cleveland Heights** (city) Cuyahoga County
109	1680	22.3	**Finneytown** (CDP) Hamilton County
109	1680	22.3	**Huber Heights** (city) Montgomery County
109	1680	22.3	**Lyndhurst** (city) Cuyahoga County
113	1714	22.4	**Cincinnati** (city) Hamilton County
113	1714	22.4	**Conneaut** (city) Ashtabula County
113	1714	22.4	**Dublin** (city) Franklin County
113	1714	22.4	**Garfield Heights** (city) Cuyahoga County
113	1714	22.4	**Springboro** (city) Warren County
113	1714	22.4	**White Oak** (CDP) Hamilton County
119	1746	22.5	**Green** (city) Summit County
120	1786	22.6	**Cuyahoga Falls** (city) Summit County
120	1786	22.6	**Wadsworth** (city) Medina County
122	1812	22.7	**Maple Heights** (city) Cuyahoga County
123	1861	22.9	**Bedford Heights** (city) Cuyahoga County
123	1861	22.9	**Lorain** (city) Lorain County
125	1897	23.0	**Fairfield** (city) Butler County
125	1897	23.0	**Shaker Heights** (city) Cuyahoga County
127	1916	23.1	**North Olmsted** (city) Cuyahoga County
128	1932	23.2	**Mason** (city) Warren County
129	1993	23.4	**Eastlake** (city) Lake County
129	1993	23.4	**Loveland** (city) Hamilton County
129	1993	23.4	**Macedonia** (city) Summit County
132	2016	23.5	**Reynoldsburg** (city) Franklin County
133	2043	23.6	**Bay Village** (city) Cuyahoga County
133	2043	23.6	**Rocky River** (city) Cuyahoga County
135	2080	23.7	**Brecksville** (city) Cuyahoga County
136	2114	23.8	**Streetsboro** (city) Portage County
137	2147	23.9	**Lancaster** (city) Fairfield County
137	2147	23.9	**Montgomery** (city) Hamilton County
139	2174	24.0	**Circleville** (city) Pickaway County
139	2174	24.0	**Dent** (CDP) Hamilton County
141	2212	24.1	**Clayton** (city) Montgomery County
141	2212	24.1	**Mentor** (city) Lake County
143	2236	24.2	**Hamilton** (city) Butler County
143	2236	24.2	**New Franklin** (city) Summit County
143	2236	24.2	**South Euclid** (city) Cuyahoga County
146	2271	24.3	**Cleveland** (city) Cuyahoga County
146	2271	24.3	**Euclid** (city) Cuyahoga County
146	2271	24.3	**Lakewood** (city) Cuyahoga County
146	2271	24.3	**Parma** (city) Cuyahoga County
146	2271	24.3	**Stow** (city) Summit County

Note: *The state column ranks the top/bottom 150 places from all places in the state with population of 10,000 or more. The national column ranks the top/bottom 150 places from all places in the country with population of 10,000 or more. Places that are unincorporated were not considered in the rankings. Please refer to the User Guide for additional information.*

Violent Crime Rate per 10,000 Population

Top 150 Places Ranked in *Descending* Order

State Rank	Nat'l Rank	Rate	Place
1	41	147.8	**Cleveland** (city) Cuyahoga County
2	124	102.5	**Toledo** (city) Lucas County
3	151	95.8	**Lima** (city) Allen County
4	153	95.3	**Cincinnati** (city) Hamilton County
5	167	92.7	**Canton** (city) Stark County
6	190	87.1	**Dayton** (city) Montgomery County
7	229	81.0	**Youngstown** (city) Mahoning County
8	243	79.1	**Akron** (city) Summit County
9	306	71.2	**Springfield** (city) Clark County
10	334	68.7	**Whitehall** (city) Franklin County
11	375	65.0	**Warren** (city) Trumbull County
12	416	61.8	**Middletown** (city) Butler County
13	438	60.7	**Hamilton** (city) Butler County
14	641	47.8	**Lorain** (city) Lorain County
15	712	45.3	**Trotwood** (city) Montgomery County
16	742	43.8	**Portsmouth** (city) Scioto County
17	819	40.6	**Zanesville** (city) Muskingum County
18	837	39.9	**Monroe** (city) Butler County
19	906	37.5	**Alliance** (city) Stark County
20	937	36.6	**Springdale** (city) Hamilton County
21	951	36.1	**Mansfield** (city) Richland County
22	989	35.1	**Cambridge** (city) Guernsey County
23	1021	34.2	**Bellefontaine** (city) Logan County
24	1034	33.7	**Chillicothe** (city) Ross County
25	1059	33.1	**Barberton** (city) Summit County
26	1080	32.5	**Norwood** (city) Hamilton County
27	1144	31.1	**Cleveland Heights** (city) Cuyahoga County
28	1156	30.7	**Sandusky** (city) Erie County
29	1266	28.1	**Fairfield** (city) Butler County
30	1328	26.9	**Niles** (city) Trumbull County
31	1359	26.0	**Greenville** (city) Darke County
32	1386	25.4	**Fremont** (city) Sandusky County
33	1451	24.1	**Bedford** (city) Cuyahoga County
34	1503	22.9	**Painesville** (city) Lake County
35	1531	22.2	**West Carrollton** (city) Montgomery County
36	1542	22.0	**Oxford** (city) Butler County
37	1565	21.6	**Galion** (city) Crawford County
38	1572	21.5	**Massillon** (city) Stark County
39	1606	21.1	**Xenia** (city) Greene County
40	1707	19.4	**Van Wert** (city) Van Wert County
41	1715	19.2	**Heath** (city) Licking County
42	1741	18.9	**Fairborn** (city) Greene County
43	1764	18.6	**Kent** (city) Portage County
44	1769	18.5	**Defiance** (city) Defiance County
45	1796	18.2	**Brooklyn** (city) Cuyahoga County
46	1806	18.0	**Findlay** (city) Hancock County
47	1831	17.5	**Riverside** (city) Montgomery County
48	1848	17.2	**Urbana** (city) Champaign County
49	1855	17.1	**University Heights** (city) Cuyahoga County
50	1868	17.0	**Circleville** (city) Pickaway County
50	1868	17.0	**Washington Court House** (city) Fayette County
52	1924	16.2	**Sidney** (city) Shelby County
53	1935	16.1	**Forest Park** (city) Hamilton County
54	1940	16.0	**Huber Heights** (city) Montgomery County
54	1940	16.0	**Piqua** (city) Miami County
56	1951	15.9	**Wooster** (city) Wayne County
57	1992	15.4	**Bowling Green** (city) Wood County
58	2021	15.0	**Bexley** (city) Franklin County
59	2041	14.7	**Shaker Heights** (city) Cuyahoga County
60	2050	14.6	**Austintown** (CDP) Mahoning County
60	2050	14.6	**Delaware** (city) Delaware County
62	2063	14.5	**Vandalia** (city) Montgomery County
63	2096	14.1	**South Euclid** (city) Cuyahoga County
64	2110	14.0	**Cuyahoga Falls** (city) Summit County
64	2110	14.0	**Newark** (city) Licking County
66	2138	13.6	**Marietta** (city) Washington County
67	2196	12.9	**Oregon** (city) Lucas County
68	2232	12.4	**Richmond Heights** (city) Cuyahoga County
69	2269	12.0	**Tallmadge** (city) Summit County
70	2325	11.2	**Norwalk** (city) Huron County
71	2332	11.1	**Englewood** (city) Montgomery County
72	2345	10.9	**Dover** (city) Tuscarawas County
73	2352	10.8	**Grove City** (city) Franklin County
74	2363	10.6	**Celina** (city) Mercer County
75	2372	10.5	**Struthers** (city) Mahoning County
75	2372	10.5	**Vermilion** (city) Lorain County
77	2430	9.8	**Lebanon** (city) Warren County
78	2455	9.5	**Berea** (city) Cuyahoga County
78	2455	9.5	**Kettering** (city) Montgomery County
80	2467	9.4	**Miamisburg** (city) Montgomery County
81	2486	9.2	**Mentor** (city) Lake County
82	2529	8.7	**Eastlake** (city) Lake County
83	2557	8.4	**Mount Vernon** (city) Knox County
84	2568	8.3	**Hilliard** (city) Franklin County
84	2568	8.3	**Parma Heights** (city) Cuyahoga County
84	2568	8.3	**Wadsworth** (city) Medina County
87	2606	7.9	**Centerville** (city) Montgomery County
88	2621	7.8	**Conneaut** (city) Ashtabula County
88	2621	7.8	**Maumee** (city) Lucas County
90	2656	7.5	**Amherst** (city) Lorain County
90	2656	7.5	**Troy** (city) Miami County
92	2693	7.2	**Athens** (city) Athens County
92	2693	7.2	**Medina** (city) Medina County
94	2730	6.9	**Ashland** (city) Ashland County
94	2730	6.9	**North Canton** (city) Stark County
96	2741	6.8	**Gahanna** (city) Franklin County
97	2770	6.6	**Stow** (city) Summit County
98	2798	6.3	**Willoughby** (city) Lake County
99	2810	6.2	**Springboro** (city) Warren County
99	2810	6.2	**Streetsboro** (city) Portage County
101	2821	6.1	**Strongsville** (city) Cuyahoga County
102	2855	5.8	**Aurora** (city) Portage County
102	2855	5.8	**Blue Ash** (city) Hamilton County
102	2855	5.8	**Norton** (city) Summit County
105	2865	5.7	**Broadview Heights** (city) Cuyahoga County
105	2865	5.7	**Loveland** (city) Hamilton County
107	2899	5.4	**Marysville** (city) Union County
108	2937	5.0	**Salem** (city) Columbiana County
109	2957	4.8	**Twinsburg** (city) Summit County
110	2965	4.7	**Brunswick** (city) Medina County
111	2973	4.6	**New Philadelphia** (city) Tuscarawas County
112	2983	4.5	**North Ridgeville** (city) Lorain County
113	3006	4.3	**Seven Hills** (city) Cuyahoga County
114	3052	3.8	**Clayton** (city) Montgomery County
115	3063	3.6	**Lyndhurst** (city) Cuyahoga County
115	3063	3.6	**Worthington** (city) Franklin County
117	3072	3.5	**Mason** (city) Warren County
117	3072	3.5	**New Franklin** (city) Summit County
117	3072	3.5	**Westerville** (city) Franklin County
120	3101	3.0	**Solon** (city) Cuyahoga County
121	3110	2.9	**Montgomery** (city) Hamilton County
121	3110	2.9	**Upper Arlington** (city) Franklin County
123	3129	2.6	**Beavercreek** (city) Greene County
124	3149	2.4	**Perrysburg** (city) Wood County
125	3159	2.3	**Dublin** (city) Franklin County
126	3202	1.7	**Powell** (city) Delaware County
127	3216	1.3	**Hudson** (city) Summit County
128	3246	0.7	**Brecksville** (city) Cuyahoga County

Note: *The state column ranks the top/bottom 150 places from all places in the state with population of 10,000 or more. The national column ranks the top/bottom 150 places from all places in the country with population of 10,000 or more. Places that are unincorporated were not considered in the rankings. Please refer to the User Guide for additional information.*

Violent Crime Rate per 10,000 Population

Top 150 Places Ranked in *Ascending* Order

State Rank	Nat'l Rank	Rate	Place
1	18	0.7	**Brecksville** (city) Cuyahoga County
2	52	1.3	**Hudson** (city) Summit County
3	64	1.7	**Powell** (city) Delaware County
4	107	2.3	**Dublin** (city) Franklin County
5	113	2.4	**Perrysburg** (city) Wood County
6	136	2.6	**Beavercreek** (city) Greene County
7	153	2.9	**Montgomery** (city) Hamilton County
7	153	2.9	**Upper Arlington** (city) Franklin County
9	162	3.0	**Solon** (city) Cuyahoga County
10	189	3.5	**Mason** (city) Warren County
10	189	3.5	**New Franklin** (city) Summit County
10	189	3.5	**Westerville** (city) Franklin County
13	200	3.6	**Lyndhurst** (city) Cuyahoga County
13	200	3.6	**Worthington** (city) Franklin County
15	213	3.8	**Clayton** (city) Montgomery County
16	257	4.3	**Seven Hills** (city) Cuyahoga County
17	280	4.5	**North Ridgeville** (city) Lorain County
18	289	4.6	**New Philadelphia** (city) Tuscarawas County
19	299	4.7	**Brunswick** (city) Medina County
20	307	4.8	**Twinsburg** (city) Summit County
21	326	5.0	**Salem** (city) Columbiana County
22	362	5.4	**Marysville** (city) Union County
23	392	5.7	**Broadview Heights** (city) Cuyahoga County
23	392	5.7	**Loveland** (city) Hamilton County
25	407	5.8	**Aurora** (city) Portage County
25	407	5.8	**Blue Ash** (city) Hamilton County
25	407	5.8	**Norton** (city) Summit County
28	444	6.1	**Strongsville** (city) Cuyahoga County
29	451	6.2	**Springboro** (city) Warren County
29	451	6.2	**Streetsboro** (city) Portage County
31	462	6.3	**Willoughby** (city) Lake County
32	492	6.6	**Stow** (city) Summit County
33	516	6.8	**Gahanna** (city) Franklin County
34	531	6.9	**Ashland** (city) Ashland County
34	531	6.9	**North Canton** (city) Stark County
36	564	7.2	**Athens** (city) Athens County
36	564	7.2	**Medina** (city) Medina County
38	603	7.5	**Amherst** (city) Lorain County
38	603	7.5	**Troy** (city) Miami County
40	638	7.8	**Conneaut** (city) Ashtabula County
40	638	7.8	**Maumee** (city) Lucas County
42	651	7.9	**Centerville** (city) Montgomery County
43	689	8.3	**Hilliard** (city) Franklin County
43	689	8.3	**Parma Heights** (city) Cuyahoga County
43	689	8.3	**Wadsworth** (city) Medina County
46	704	8.4	**Mount Vernon** (city) Knox County
47	736	8.7	**Eastlake** (city) Lake County
48	777	9.2	**Mentor** (city) Lake County
49	793	9.4	**Miamisburg** (city) Montgomery County
50	805	9.5	**Berea** (city) Cuyahoga County
50	805	9.5	**Kettering** (city) Montgomery County
52	835	9.8	**Lebanon** (city) Warren County
53	887	10.5	**Struthers** (city) Mahoning County
53	887	10.5	**Vermilion** (city) Lorain County
55	900	10.6	**Celina** (city) Mercer County
56	914	10.8	**Grove City** (city) Franklin County
57	920	10.9	**Dover** (city) Tuscarawas County
58	933	11.1	**Englewood** (city) Montgomery County
59	940	11.2	**Norwalk** (city) Huron County
60	996	12.0	**Tallmadge** (city) Summit County
61	1032	12.4	**Richmond Heights** (city) Cuyahoga County
62	1067	12.9	**Oregon** (city) Lucas County
63	1128	13.6	**Marietta** (city) Washington County
64	1156	14.0	**Cuyahoga Falls** (city) Summit County
64	1156	14.0	**Newark** (city) Licking County
66	1162	14.1	**South Euclid** (city) Cuyahoga County
67	1205	14.5	**Vandalia** (city) Montgomery County
68	1209	14.6	**Austintown** (CDP) Mahoning County
68	1209	14.6	**Delaware** (city) Delaware County
70	1222	14.7	**Shaker Heights** (city) Cuyahoga County
71	1243	15.0	**Bexley** (city) Franklin County
72	1270	15.4	**Bowling Green** (city) Wood County
73	1315	15.9	**Wooster** (city) Wayne County
74	1321	16.0	**Huber Heights** (city) Montgomery County
74	1321	16.0	**Piqua** (city) Miami County
76	1332	16.1	**Forest Park** (city) Hamilton County
77	1337	16.2	**Sidney** (city) Shelby County
78	1392	17.0	**Circleville** (city) Pickaway County
78	1392	17.0	**Washington Court House** (city) Fayette County
80	1404	17.1	**University Heights** (city) Cuyahoga County
81	1417	17.2	**Urbana** (city) Champaign County
82	1437	17.5	**Riverside** (city) Montgomery County
83	1460	18.0	**Findlay** (city) Hancock County
84	1469	18.2	**Brooklyn** (city) Cuyahoga County
85	1492	18.5	**Defiance** (city) Defiance County
86	1503	18.6	**Kent** (city) Portage County
87	1524	18.9	**Fairborn** (city) Greene County
88	1548	19.2	**Heath** (city) Licking County
89	1560	19.4	**Van Wert** (city) Van Wert County
90	1657	21.1	**Xenia** (city) Greene County
91	1693	21.5	**Massillon** (city) Stark County
92	1700	21.6	**Galion** (city) Crawford County
93	1726	22.0	**Oxford** (city) Butler County
94	1737	22.2	**West Carrollton** (city) Montgomery County
95	1765	22.9	**Painesville** (city) Lake County
96	1813	24.1	**Bedford** (city) Cuyahoga County
97	1880	25.4	**Fremont** (city) Sandusky County
98	1906	26.0	**Greenville** (city) Darke County
99	1938	26.9	**Niles** (city) Trumbull County
100	1999	28.1	**Fairfield** (city) Butler County
101	2113	30.7	**Sandusky** (city) Erie County
102	2125	31.1	**Cleveland Heights** (city) Cuyahoga County
103	2187	32.5	**Norwood** (city) Hamilton County
104	2209	33.1	**Barberton** (city) Summit County
105	2232	33.7	**Chillicothe** (city) Ross County
106	2247	34.2	**Bellefontaine** (city) Logan County
107	2275	35.1	**Cambridge** (city) Guernsey County
108	2315	36.1	**Mansfield** (city) Richland County
109	2332	36.6	**Springdale** (city) Hamilton County
110	2361	37.5	**Alliance** (city) Stark County
111	2433	39.9	**Monroe** (city) Butler County
112	2452	40.6	**Zanesville** (city) Muskingum County
113	2529	43.8	**Portsmouth** (city) Scioto County
114	2556	45.3	**Trotwood** (city) Montgomery County
115	2626	47.8	**Lorain** (city) Lorain County
116	2833	60.7	**Hamilton** (city) Butler County
117	2855	61.8	**Middletown** (city) Butler County
118	2896	65.0	**Warren** (city) Trumbull County
119	2936	68.7	**Whitehall** (city) Franklin County
120	2964	71.2	**Springfield** (city) Clark County
121	3028	79.1	**Akron** (city) Summit County
122	3041	81.0	**Youngstown** (city) Mahoning County
123	3081	87.1	**Dayton** (city) Montgomery County
124	3103	92.7	**Canton** (city) Stark County
125	3118	95.3	**Cincinnati** (city) Hamilton County
126	3120	95.8	**Lima** (city) Allen County
127	3147	102.5	**Toledo** (city) Lucas County
128	3230	147.8	**Cleveland** (city) Cuyahoga County

Note: *The state column ranks the top/bottom 150 places from all places in the state with population of 10,000 or more. The national column ranks the top/bottom 150 places from all places in the country with population of 10,000 or more. Places that are unincorporated were not considered in the rankings. Please refer to the User Guide for additional information.*

Property Crime Rate per 10,000 Population

Top 150 Places Ranked in *Descending* Order

State Rank	Nat'l Rank	Rate	Place
1	24	896.3	**Chillicothe** (city) Ross County
2	37	816.2	**Middletown** (city) Butler County
3	53	776.5	**Portsmouth** (city) Scioto County
4	63	743.7	**Springfield** (city) Clark County
5	71	725.6	**Whitehall** (city) Franklin County
6	88	691.6	**Springdale** (city) Hamilton County
7	97	676.2	**Mansfield** (city) Richland County
8	111	661.9	**Norwood** (city) Hamilton County
9	124	645.4	**Brooklyn** (city) Cuyahoga County
10	143	630.9	**Zanesville** (city) Muskingum County
11	145	630.3	**Hamilton** (city) Butler County
12	167	613.7	**Circleville** (city) Pickaway County
13	187	595.3	**Cleveland** (city) Cuyahoga County
14	192	588.7	**Sidney** (city) Shelby County
15	197	585.8	**Canton** (city) Stark County
16	204	581.2	**Cincinnati** (city) Hamilton County
17	205	580.7	**Fremont** (city) Sandusky County
18	209	577.3	**Galion** (city) Crawford County
19	213	575.4	**Heath** (city) Licking County
20	254	549.8	**Youngstown** (city) Mahoning County
21	267	542.3	**Dayton** (city) Montgomery County
22	284	534.4	**Mount Vernon** (city) Knox County
23	314	520.2	**Cambridge** (city) Guernsey County
24	336	511.5	**Trotwood** (city) Montgomery County
25	352	505.6	**Lima** (city) Allen County
26	356	504.0	**Piqua** (city) Miami County
27	380	496.8	**Newark** (city) Licking County
28	389	493.9	**Niles** (city) Trumbull County
29	418	486.3	**Akron** (city) Summit County
30	430	484.3	**Washington Court House** (city) Fayette County
31	461	472.2	**Warren** (city) Trumbull County
32	533	450.0	**Sandusky** (city) Erie County
33	560	442.7	**Bellefontaine** (city) Logan County
34	564	441.7	**Alliance** (city) Stark County
35	570	439.0	**Lorain** (city) Lorain County
36	640	421.8	**Greenville** (city) Darke County
37	684	410.2	**Monroe** (city) Butler County
38	712	402.9	**Xenia** (city) Greene County
39	768	389.3	**Oregon** (city) Lucas County
40	841	372.1	**Maumee** (city) Lucas County
41	848	370.6	**Wooster** (city) Wayne County
42	859	368.1	**Barberton** (city) Summit County
43	898	361.2	**Van Wert** (city) Van Wert County
44	901	361.0	**Huber Heights** (city) Montgomery County
45	909	358.9	**Celina** (city) Mercer County
46	960	348.5	**Findlay** (city) Hancock County
47	988	341.3	**Grove City** (city) Franklin County
48	1021	336.0	**Cleveland Heights** (city) Cuyahoga County
49	1039	333.5	**Miamisburg** (city) Montgomery County
50	1060	329.3	**Urbana** (city) Champaign County
51	1064	328.5	**Englewood** (city) Montgomery County
52	1112	321.4	**Blue Ash** (city) Hamilton County
53	1119	320.6	**Norwalk** (city) Huron County
54	1166	312.3	**Richmond Heights** (city) Cuyahoga County
55	1170	311.1	**Troy** (city) Miami County
56	1193	308.0	**Bedford** (city) Cuyahoga County
57	1225	303.2	**Massillon** (city) Stark County
58	1242	300.5	**West Carrollton** (city) Montgomery County
59	1367	281.8	**Fairborn** (city) Greene County
60	1370	281.7	**Defiance** (city) Defiance County
61	1403	277.9	**Worthington** (city) Franklin County
62	1452	271.9	**Bexley** (city) Franklin County
63	1463	270.9	**Oxford** (city) Butler County
64	1527	262.8	**Austintown** (CDP) Mahoning County
65	1538	261.9	**Cuyahoga Falls** (city) Summit County
66	1560	259.0	**Painesville** (city) Lake County
67	1574	257.8	**Fairfield** (city) Butler County
68	1594	255.9	**Delaware** (city) Delaware County
69	1599	255.6	**Ashland** (city) Ashland County
70	1637	250.6	**Forest Park** (city) Hamilton County
71	1657	248.4	**Beavercreek** (city) Greene County
72	1671	246.5	**Riverside** (city) Montgomery County
73	1678	245.3	**Bowling Green** (city) Wood County
74	1767	234.5	**Eastlake** (city) Lake County
75	1798	230.7	**Shaker Heights** (city) Cuyahoga County
76	1800	230.2	**Kettering** (city) Montgomery County
77	1804	229.3	**Hilliard** (city) Franklin County
78	1824	226.4	**Westerville** (city) Franklin County
79	1833	225.4	**Mentor** (city) Lake County
80	1857	223.3	**Vandalia** (city) Montgomery County
81	1886	220.2	**Conneaut** (city) Ashtabula County
82	1888	219.9	**Willoughby** (city) Lake County
83	1890	219.4	**Kent** (city) Portage County
84	1937	215.2	**South Euclid** (city) Cuyahoga County
85	1945	214.3	**Parma Heights** (city) Cuyahoga County
86	1963	212.8	**Wadsworth** (city) Medina County
87	1993	209.9	**Gahanna** (city) Franklin County
88	2001	208.7	**University Heights** (city) Cuyahoga County
89	2039	205.1	**Stow** (city) Summit County
90	2049	203.9	**Salem** (city) Columbiana County
91	2061	202.8	**Tallmadge** (city) Summit County
92	2081	201.4	**North Canton** (city) Stark County
93	2108	198.7	**Lebanon** (city) Warren County
94	2145	193.4	**Marysville** (city) Union County
95	2198	188.1	**Norton** (city) Summit County
96	2260	181.9	**Amherst** (city) Lorain County
97	2263	181.6	**Centerville** (city) Montgomery County
98	2337	171.2	**Athens** (city) Athens County
99	2374	167.3	**Strongsville** (city) Cuyahoga County
100	2394	165.4	**New Philadelphia** (city) Tuscarawas County
101	2403	164.6	**Medina** (city) Medina County
102	2440	159.1	**Montgomery** (city) Hamilton County
103	2443	159.0	**Clayton** (city) Montgomery County
104	2445	158.7	**Struthers** (city) Mahoning County
105	2538	148.0	**Perrysburg** (city) Wood County
106	2640	134.9	**Mason** (city) Warren County
107	2661	132.7	**Marietta** (city) Washington County
108	2669	131.7	**Vermilion** (city) Lorain County
109	2678	130.9	**Berea** (city) Cuyahoga County
110	2690	129.5	**Upper Arlington** (city) Franklin County
111	2698	129.1	**Dublin** (city) Franklin County
112	2830	111.8	**Springboro** (city) Warren County
113	2839	111.2	**Solon** (city) Cuyahoga County
114	2914	103.0	**Loveland** (city) Hamilton County
115	2921	102.2	**Aurora** (city) Portage County
116	3043	86.1	**North Ridgeville** (city) Lorain County
117	3062	83.7	**Brunswick** (city) Medina County
118	3143	70.4	**Twinsburg** (city) Summit County
119	3151	68.6	**Powell** (city) Delaware County
120	3185	59.1	**Hudson** (city) Summit County
121	3219	49.2	**New Franklin** (city) Summit County
122	3224	47.4	**Brecksville** (city) Cuyahoga County
123	3231	45.4	**Dover** (city) Tuscarawas County
124	3237	43.4	**Streetsboro** (city) Portage County
125	3245	41.0	**Seven Hills** (city) Cuyahoga County
126	3268	0.0	**Broadview Heights** (city) Cuyahoga County
126	3268	0.0	**Lyndhurst** (city) Cuyahoga County

Note: *The state column ranks the top/bottom 150 places from all places in the state with population of 10,000 or more. The national column ranks the top/bottom 150 places from all places in the country with population of 10,000 or more. Places that are unincorporated were not considered in the rankings. Please refer to the User Guide for additional information.*

Property Crime Rate per 10,000 Population

Top 150 Places Ranked in *Ascending* Order

State Rank	Nat'l Rank	Rate	Place
1	1	0.0	**Broadview Heights** (city) Cuyahoga County
1	1	0.0	**Lyndhurst** (city) Cuyahoga County
3	25	41.0	**Seven Hills** (city) Cuyahoga County
4	33	43.4	**Streetsboro** (city) Portage County
5	39	45.4	**Dover** (city) Tuscarawas County
6	46	47.4	**Brecksville** (city) Cuyahoga County
7	51	49.2	**New Franklin** (city) Summit County
8	85	59.1	**Hudson** (city) Summit County
9	118	68.6	**Powell** (city) Delaware County
10	127	70.4	**Twinsburg** (city) Summit County
11	208	83.7	**Brunswick** (city) Medina County
12	227	86.1	**North Ridgeville** (city) Lorain County
13	347	102.2	**Aurora** (city) Portage County
14	355	103.0	**Loveland** (city) Hamilton County
15	430	111.2	**Solon** (city) Cuyahoga County
16	437	111.8	**Springboro** (city) Warren County
17	569	129.1	**Dublin** (city) Franklin County
18	579	129.5	**Upper Arlington** (city) Franklin County
19	591	130.9	**Berea** (city) Cuyahoga County
20	601	131.7	**Vermilion** (city) Lorain County
21	608	132.7	**Marietta** (city) Washington County
22	630	134.9	**Mason** (city) Warren County
23	731	148.0	**Perrysburg** (city) Wood County
24	823	158.7	**Struthers** (city) Mahoning County
25	826	159.0	**Clayton** (city) Montgomery County
26	828	159.1	**Montgomery** (city) Hamilton County
27	866	164.6	**Medina** (city) Medina County
28	874	165.4	**New Philadelphia** (city) Tuscarawas County
29	892	167.3	**Strongsville** (city) Cuyahoga County
30	932	171.2	**Athens** (city) Athens County
31	1006	181.6	**Centerville** (city) Montgomery County
32	1009	181.9	**Amherst** (city) Lorain County
33	1071	188.1	**Norton** (city) Summit County
34	1124	193.4	**Marysville** (city) Union County
35	1162	198.7	**Lebanon** (city) Warren County
36	1189	201.4	**North Canton** (city) Stark County
37	1208	202.8	**Tallmadge** (city) Summit County
38	1221	203.9	**Salem** (city) Columbiana County
39	1231	205.1	**Stow** (city) Summit County
40	1266	208.7	**University Heights** (city) Cuyahoga County
41	1277	209.9	**Gahanna** (city) Franklin County
42	1306	212.8	**Wadsworth** (city) Medina County
43	1324	214.3	**Parma Heights** (city) Cuyahoga County
44	1333	215.2	**South Euclid** (city) Cuyahoga County
45	1380	219.4	**Kent** (city) Portage County
46	1381	219.9	**Willoughby** (city) Lake County
47	1383	220.2	**Conneaut** (city) Ashtabula County
48	1413	223.3	**Vandalia** (city) Montgomery County
49	1434	225.4	**Mentor** (city) Lake County
50	1445	226.4	**Westerville** (city) Franklin County
51	1463	229.3	**Hilliard** (city) Franklin County
52	1470	230.2	**Kettering** (city) Montgomery County
53	1472	230.7	**Shaker Heights** (city) Cuyahoga County
54	1502	234.5	**Eastlake** (city) Lake County
55	1591	245.3	**Bowling Green** (city) Wood County
56	1599	246.5	**Riverside** (city) Montgomery County
57	1612	248.4	**Beavercreek** (city) Greene County
58	1631	250.6	**Forest Park** (city) Hamilton County
59	1671	255.6	**Ashland** (city) Ashland County
60	1674	255.9	**Delaware** (city) Delaware County
61	1694	257.8	**Fairfield** (city) Butler County
62	1710	259.0	**Painesville** (city) Lake County
63	1732	261.9	**Cuyahoga Falls** (city) Summit County
64	1742	262.8	**Austintown** (CDP) Mahoning County
65	1807	270.9	**Oxford** (city) Butler County
66	1816	271.9	**Bexley** (city) Franklin County
67	1867	277.9	**Worthington** (city) Franklin County
68	1900	281.7	**Defiance** (city) Defiance County
69	1901	281.8	**Fairborn** (city) Greene County
70	2028	300.5	**West Carrollton** (city) Montgomery County
71	2045	303.2	**Massillon** (city) Stark County
72	2076	308.0	**Bedford** (city) Cuyahoga County
73	2100	311.1	**Troy** (city) Miami County
74	2104	312.3	**Richmond Heights** (city) Cuyahoga County
75	2151	320.6	**Norwalk** (city) Huron County
76	2157	321.4	**Blue Ash** (city) Hamilton County
77	2206	328.5	**Englewood** (city) Montgomery County
78	2210	329.3	**Urbana** (city) Champaign County
79	2231	333.5	**Miamisburg** (city) Montgomery County
80	2249	336.0	**Cleveland Heights** (city) Cuyahoga County
81	2281	341.3	**Grove City** (city) Franklin County
82	2309	348.5	**Findlay** (city) Hancock County
83	2361	358.9	**Celina** (city) Mercer County
84	2369	361.0	**Huber Heights** (city) Montgomery County
85	2370	361.2	**Van Wert** (city) Van Wert County
86	2411	368.1	**Barberton** (city) Summit County
87	2422	370.6	**Wooster** (city) Wayne County
88	2428	372.1	**Maumee** (city) Lucas County
89	2502	389.3	**Oregon** (city) Lucas County
90	2558	402.9	**Xenia** (city) Greene County
91	2584	410.2	**Monroe** (city) Butler County
92	2629	421.8	**Greenville** (city) Darke County
93	2699	439.0	**Lorain** (city) Lorain County
94	2706	441.7	**Alliance** (city) Stark County
95	2710	442.7	**Bellefontaine** (city) Logan County
96	2736	450.0	**Sandusky** (city) Erie County
97	2809	472.2	**Warren** (city) Trumbull County
98	2840	484.3	**Washington Court House** (city) Fayette County
99	2852	486.3	**Akron** (city) Summit County
100	2880	493.9	**Niles** (city) Trumbull County
101	2889	496.8	**Newark** (city) Licking County
102	2914	504.0	**Piqua** (city) Miami County
103	2917	505.6	**Lima** (city) Allen County
104	2934	511.5	**Trotwood** (city) Montgomery County
105	2956	520.2	**Cambridge** (city) Guernsey County
106	2985	534.4	**Mount Vernon** (city) Knox County
107	3003	542.3	**Dayton** (city) Montgomery County
108	3016	549.8	**Youngstown** (city) Mahoning County
109	3057	575.4	**Heath** (city) Licking County
110	3061	577.3	**Galion** (city) Crawford County
111	3065	580.7	**Fremont** (city) Sandusky County
112	3066	581.2	**Cincinnati** (city) Hamilton County
113	3073	585.8	**Canton** (city) Stark County
114	3078	588.7	**Sidney** (city) Shelby County
115	3082	595.3	**Cleveland** (city) Cuyahoga County
116	3103	613.7	**Circleville** (city) Pickaway County
117	3125	630.3	**Hamilton** (city) Butler County
118	3127	630.9	**Zanesville** (city) Muskingum County
119	3146	645.4	**Brooklyn** (city) Cuyahoga County
120	3158	661.9	**Norwood** (city) Hamilton County
121	3173	676.2	**Mansfield** (city) Richland County
122	3181	691.6	**Springdale** (city) Hamilton County
123	3199	725.6	**Whitehall** (city) Franklin County
124	3207	743.7	**Springfield** (city) Clark County
125	3217	776.5	**Portsmouth** (city) Scioto County
126	3233	816.2	**Middletown** (city) Butler County
127	3246	896.3	**Chillicothe** (city) Ross County

Note: *The state column ranks the top/bottom 150 places from all places in the state with population of 10,000 or more. The national column ranks the top/bottom 150 places from all places in the country with population of 10,000 or more. Places that are unincorporated were not considered in the rankings. Please refer to the User Guide for additional information.*

Education

Ohio Public School Educational Profile

Category	Value	Category	Value
Schools *(2011-2012)*	3,741	**Diploma Recipients** *(2009-2010)*	123,437
Instructional Level		White, Non-Hispanic	99,925
Primary	1,961	Black, Non-Hispanic	16,574
Middle	723	Asian/Pacific Islander, Non-Hispanic	1,695
High	854	American Indian/Alaskan Native, Non-Hispanic	165
Other/Not Reported	203	Hawaiian Native/Pacific Islander, Non-Hispanic	n/a
Curriculum		Two or More Races, Non-Hispanic	n/a
Regular	3,606	Hispanic of Any Race	2,314
Special Education	57	**Staff** *(2011-2012)*	
Vocational	72	Teachers (FTE)	107,869.2
Alternative	6	Salary[1] ($)	57,270
Type		Librarians/Media Specialists (FTE)	1,116.1
Magnet	0	Guidance Counselors (FTE)	3,674.7
Charter	378	**Ratios** *(2011-2012)*	
Title I Eligible	2,925	Number of Students per Teacher	16.1 to 1
School-wide Title I	2,185	Number of Students per Librarian	1,559.0 to 1
Students *(2011-2012)*	1,739,994	Number of Students per Guidance Counselor	473.5 to 1
Gender (%)		**Finances** *(2010-2011)*	
Male	51.4	Current Expenditures ($ per student)	
Female	48.6	Total	11,395
Race/Ethnicity (%)		Instruction	6,483
White, Non-Hispanic	73.7	Support Services	4,536
Black, Non-Hispanic	16.2	Other	376
Asian, Non-Hispanic	1.8	General Revenue ($ per student)	
American Indian/Alaskan Native, Non-Hisp.	0.1	Total	13,096
Hawaiian Native/Pacific Islander, Non-Hisp.	0.0	From Federal Sources	1,541
Two or More Races, Non-Hispanic	4.3	From State Sources	5,656
Hispanic of Any Race	3.8	From Local Sources	5,899
Special Programs (%)		Long-Term Debt Outstanding ($ per student)	
Individual Education Program (IEP)	14.9	At Beginning of Fiscal Year	4,670
English Language Learner (ELL)	2.2	Issued During Fiscal Year	312
Eligible for Free Lunch Program	37.6	Retired During Fiscal Year	487
Eligible for Reduced-Price Lunch Program	6.0	At End of Fiscal Year	4,726
Average Freshman Grad. Rate (%) *(2009-2010)*	81.4	**College Entrance Exam Scores**	
White, Non-Hispanic	86.5	SAT Reasoning Test™ *(2013)*	
Black, Non-Hispanic	60.2	Participation Rate (%)	17
Asian/Pacific Islander, Non-Hispanic	97.7	Mean Critical Reading Score	548
American Indian/Alaskan Native, Non-Hispanic	80.9	Mean Math Score	556
Hispanic of Any Race	67.7	Mean Writing Score	531
High School Drop-out Rate (%) *(2009-2010)*	4.2	ACT *(2013)*	
White, Non-Hispanic	2.8	Participation Rate (%)	72
Black, Non-Hispanic	9.4	Mean Composite Score	21.8
Asian/Pacific Islander, Non-Hispanic	1.4	Mean English Score	21.2
American Indian/Alaskan Native, Non-Hispanic	7.8	Mean Math Score	21.5
Hawaiian Native/Pacific Islander, Non-Hispanic	n/a	Mean Reading Score	22.2
Two or More Races, Non-Hispanic	n/a	Mean Science Score	21.8
Hispanic of Any Race	7.4		

Note: *For an explanation of data, please refer to the User Guide in the front of the book; (1) Average salary for classroom teachers in 2013-14*

Number of Schools

Rank	Number	District Name	City
1	119	Columbus City SD	Columbus
2	100	Cleveland Municipal	Cleveland
3	57	Cincinnati City	Cincinnati
4	53	Akron City	Akron
5	51	Toledo City	Toledo
6	33	South-Western City	Grove City
7	30	Dayton City	Dayton
8	24	Canton City	Canton
8	24	Westerville City	Westerville
10	23	Hilliard City	Hilliard
10	23	Olentangy Local	Lewis Center
12	20	Lakota Local	Liberty Twp
13	19	Dublin City	Dublin
13	19	Parma City	Parma
15	18	Worthington City	Worthington
16	17	Youngstown City Schools	Youngstown
17	16	Lorain City	Lorain
17	16	Springfield City	Springfield
19	15	Reynoldsburg City	Reynoldsburg
20	14	Northwest Local	Cincinnati
20	14	Pickerington Local	Pickerington
22	13	Centerville City	Centerville
22	13	Elyria City Schools	Elyria
22	13	Mentor Exempted Village	Mentor
22	13	Willoughby-Eastlake City	Willoughby
26	12	Cleveland Hgts-University Hgts City	University Hgts
26	12	Findlay City	Findlay
26	12	Hamilton City	Hamilton
26	12	Kettering City	Kettering
26	12	Lima City	Lima
26	12	Sylvania City	Sylvania
26	12	West Clermont Local	Cincinnati
33	11	Brunswick City	Brunswick
33	11	Gahanna-Jefferson City	Gahanna
33	11	Lancaster City	Lancaster
33	11	Medina City SD	Medina
33	11	Newark City	Newark
33	11	Princeton City	Cincinnati
33	11	Strongsville City	Strongsville
33	11	Washington Local	Toledo
41	10	Groveport Madison Local	Groveport
41	10	Lakewood City	Lakewood
41	10	Miamisburg City	Miamisburg
41	10	Middletown City	Middletown
41	10	Switzerland of Ohio Local	Woodsfield
46	9	Cuyahoga Falls City	Cuyahoga Falls
46	9	East Holmes Local	Berlin
46	9	Euclid City	Euclid
46	9	Fairfield City	Fairfield
46	9	Forest Hills Local	Cincinnati
46	9	Fremont City	Fremont
46	9	Mansfield City	Mansfield
46	9	Milford Exempted Village	Milford
46	9	North Olmsted City	North Olmsted
46	9	Oak Hills Local	Cincinnati
46	9	Piqua City	Piqua
46	9	Plain Local	Canton
46	9	Ravenna City	Ravenna
46	9	Stow-Munroe Falls City SD	Stow
46	9	Troy City	Troy
46	9	Wooster City	Wooster
62	8	Ashtabula Area City	Ashtabula
62	8	Beavercreek City	Beavercreek
62	8	Berea City	Berea
62	8	Delaware City	Delaware
62	8	Franklin City	Franklin
62	8	Gallia County Local	Gallipolis
62	8	Huber Heights City	Huber Heights
62	8	Mad River Local	Dayton
62	8	Marion City	Marion
62	8	Marysville Exempted Village	Marysville
62	8	Massillon City	Massillon
62	8	Mount Vernon City	Mount Vernon
62	8	Northmont City	Englewood
62	8	Perry Local	Massillon
62	8	Riverside Local	Painesville
62	8	Sandusky City	Sandusky
62	8	Shaker Heights City	Shaker Heights
62	8	Springboro Community City	Springboro
62	8	Wadsworth City	Wadsworth
62	8	Xenia Community City	Xenia
82	7	Adams County/ohio Valley Local	West Union
82	7	Ashland City	Ashland
82	7	Athens City	The Plains
82	7	Austintown Local	Youngstown
82	7	Avon Lake City	Avon Lake
82	7	Barberton City	Barberton
82	7	Boardman Local	Youngstown
82	7	Bowling Green City SD	Bowling Green
82	7	Celina City	Celina
82	7	Chillicothe City	Chillicothe
82	7	Clark-Shawnee Local	Springfield
82	7	Claymont City	Dennison
82	7	East Cleveland City SD	East Cleveland
82	7	Kent City	Kent
82	7	Logan-Hocking Local	Logan
82	7	Mayfield City	Mayfield Hgts
82	7	New Philadel. City	New Philadel.
82	7	North Canton City	North Canton
82	7	N Ridgeville City	N Ridgeville
82	7	Northeastern Local	Springfield
82	7	Norwalk City	Norwalk
82	7	Oregon City	Oregon
82	7	Solon City	Solon
82	7	Sycamore Community City	Cincinnati
82	7	Teays Valley Local	Ashville
82	7	Tiffin City	Tiffin
82	7	Upper Arlington City	Upper Arlington
82	7	Van Wert City	Van Wert
82	7	West Carrollton City	West Carrollton
82	7	West Holmes Local	Millersburg
82	7	Westlake City	Westlake
113	6	Alliance City	Alliance
113	6	Amherst Exempted Village	Amherst
113	6	Anthony Wayne Local	Whitehouse
113	6	Avon Local	Avon
113	6	Bedford City	Bedford
113	6	Big Walnut Local	Galena
113	6	Brecksville-Broadview Hghts City	Brecksville
113	6	Chardon Local	Chardon
113	6	Circleville City	Circleville
113	6	East Muskingum Local	New Concord
113	6	Howland Local	Warren
113	6	Hudson City	Hudson
113	6	Indian Creek Local	Wintersville
113	6	Jackson Local	Massillon
113	6	Kenton City	Kenton
113	6	Kings Local	Kings Mills
113	6	Lebanon City	Lebanon
113	6	Logan Elm Local	Circleville
113	6	Loveland City	Loveland
113	6	Madison Local	Mansfield
113	6	Madison Local	Madison
113	6	Marietta City	Marietta
113	6	Mason City SD	Mason
113	6	Nordonia Hills City	Northfield
113	6	North Royalton City	North Royalton
113	6	Norwood City	Norwood
113	6	Perrysburg Exempted Village	Perrysburg
113	6	Poland Local	Poland
113	6	River View Local	Warsaw
113	6	Sheffield-Sheffield Lake City	Sheffield Vllg
113	6	Sidney City	Sidney
113	6	South Euclid-Lyndhurst City	Lyndhurst
113	6	Southeast Local	Apple Creek
113	6	Southwest Licking Local	Pataskala
113	6	Southwest Local	Harrison
113	6	Springfield Local	Holland
113	6	Tecumseh Local	New Carlisle
113	6	Tri-Valley Local	Dresden
113	6	Urbana City	Urbana
113	6	Vandalia-Butler City	Vandalia
113	6	Whitehall City	Whitehall
113	6	Winton Woods City	Cincinnati
113	6	Zanesville City	Zanesville
156	5	Beachwood City	Beachwood
156	5	Beaver Local	Lisbon
156	5	Bellbrook-Sugarcreek Local SD	Bellbrook
156	5	Bellefontaine City	Bellefontaine
156	5	Bellevue City	Bellevue
156	5	Benton Carroll Salem Local	Oak Harbor
156	5	Bexley City	Bexley
156	5	Bryan City	Bryan
156	5	Buckeye Local	Dillonvale
156	5	Buckeye Valley Local	Delaware
156	5	Cambridge City	Cambridge
156	5	Carrollton Exempted Village	Carrollton
156	5	Copley-Fairlawn City	Copley
156	5	Crestwood Local	Mantua
156	5	Dover City	Dover
156	5	East Liverpool City	East Liverpool
156	5	Edgewood City	Trenton
156	5	Edison Local	Hammondsville
156	5	Gallipolis City	Gallipolis
156	5	Garfield Hgts City Schools	Garfield Hgts
156	5	Geneva Area City	Geneva
156	5	Green Local	Uniontown
156	5	Greenfield Exempted Village	Greenfield
156	5	Greenville City	Greenville
156	5	Highland Local	Medina
156	5	Hillsboro City	Hillsboro
156	5	Jackson City	Jackson
156	5	Jonathan Alder Local	Plain City
156	5	Kenston Local	Chagrin Falls
156	5	Lake Local	Uniontown
156	5	Lexington Local	Lexington
156	5	Licking Heights Local	Pataskala
156	5	Louisville City	Louisville
156	5	Maple Heights City	Maple Heights
156	5	Marlington Local	Alliance
156	5	Maumee City	Maumee
156	5	Midview Local	Grafton
156	5	Morgan Local	Mc Connelsville
156	5	Mt Healthy City	Cincinnati
156	5	Napoleon Area City	Napoleon
156	5	New Albany-Plain Local	New Albany
156	5	New Richmond Exempted Village	New Richmond
156	5	Niles City	Niles
156	5	Northern Local	Thornville
156	5	Northridge Local	Dayton
156	5	Norton City	Norton
156	5	Oakwood City	Dayton
156	5	Olmsted Falls City	Olmsted Falls
156	5	Painesville City Local	Painesville
156	5	Rolling Hills Local	Cambridge
156	5	Rossford Exempted Village	Rossford
156	5	Salem City	Salem
156	5	Shelby City	Shelby
156	5	Southeast Local	Ravenna
156	5	Springfield Local	Akron
156	5	Steubenville City	Steubenville
156	5	Streetsboro City	Streetsboro
156	5	Talawanda City	Oxford
156	5	Tipp City Exempted Village	Tipp City
156	5	Triway Local	Wooster
156	5	Twinsburg City	Twinsburg
156	5	Upper Sandusky Exempted Village	Upper Sandusky
156	5	Vinton County Local	Mc Arthur
156	5	Wapakoneta City	Wapakoneta
156	5	Warren City	Warren
156	5	Warrensville Hgts City	Warrensville Hgts
156	5	West Branch Local	Beloit
156	5	Willard City	Willard
156	5	Wilmington City	Wilmington
156	5	Wyoming City	Wyoming
226	4	Amanda-Clearcreek Local	Amanda
226	4	Aurora City	Aurora
226	4	Bay Village City	Bay Village
226	4	Bethel-Tate Local	Bethel
226	4	Blanchester Local	Blanchester
226	4	Bloom-Carroll Local	Carroll
226	4	Buckeye Local	Ashtabula
226	4	Buckeye Local	Medina
226	4	Canal Wnchstr Local	Canal Wnchstr
226	4	Canfield Local	Canfield
226	4	Carlisle Local	Carlisle
226	4	Chagrin Falls Exempted Village	Chagrin Falls
226	4	Clear Fork Valley Local	Bellville
226	4	Clyde-Green Springs Ex. Village	Clyde
226	4	Conneaut Area City	Conneaut
226	4	Coshocton City	Coshocton
226	4	Coventry Local	Akron
226	4	Eastwood Local	Pemberville
226	4	Eaton Community City	Eaton
226	4	Elida Local	Elida
226	4	Fairborn City	Fairborn
226	4	Fairfield Union Local	Lancaster
226	4	Fairland Local	Proctorville
226	4	Fairview Park City	Fairview Park

Note: This section only includes districts with 1,500 or more students; All categories are ranked from high to low

Rank	Number	District Name	City
226	4	Field Local	Mogadore
226	4	Fostoria City	Fostoria
226	4	Franklin Local	Duncan Falls
226	4	Galion City	Galion
226	4	Girard City SD	Girard
226	4	Goshen Local	Goshen
226	4	Granville Exempted Village	Granville
226	4	Greenon Local	Enon
226	4	Hamilton Local	Columbus
226	4	Heath City	Heath
226	4	Indian Hill Exempted Village	Cincinnati
226	4	Indian Valley Local Schools	Gnadenhutten
226	4	Jefferson Area Local	Jefferson
226	4	Johnstown-Monroe Local	Johnstown
226	4	Lake Local	Millbury
226	4	Lakewood Local	Hebron
226	4	Little Miami Local	Maineville
226	4	Mariemont City	Cincinnati
226	4	Meigs Local	Pomeroy
226	4	Monroe Local SD	Monroe
226	4	New Lexington City	New Lexington
226	4	North Fork Local	Utica
226	4	Northwest Local	Canal Fulton
226	4	Ontario Local	Mansfield
226	4	Orange City	Cleveland
226	4	Otsego Local	Tontogany
226	4	Ottawa-Glandorf Local	Ottawa
226	4	Paulding Exempted Village	Paulding
226	4	Perkins Local	Sandusky
226	4	Perry Local	Perry
226	4	Port Clinton City	Port Clinton
226	4	Reading Community City	Reading
226	4	Revere Local	Bath
226	4	River Valley Local	Caledonia
226	4	Rocky River City	Rocky River
226	4	Ross Local	Hamilton
226	4	Saint Marys City	Saint Marys
226	4	Shawnee Local	Lima
226	4	South Point Local	South Point
226	4	Struthers City	Struthers
226	4	Tallmadge City	Tallmadge
226	4	Three Rivers Local	Cleves
226	4	Valley View Local	Germantown
226	4	Warren Local	Vincent
226	4	Washington CH City	Washington CH
226	4	Wauseon Exempted Village	Wauseon
226	4	Waverly City	Waverly
226	4	Wellston City	Wellston
226	4	West Geauga Local	Chesterland
226	4	Western Brown Local	Mount Orab
226	4	Woodridge Local	Peninsula
301	3	Alexander Local	Albany
301	3	Batavia Local	Batavia
301	3	Bath Local	Lima
301	3	Benjamin Logan Local	Bellefontaine
301	3	Canton Local	Canton
301	3	Clearview Local	Lorain
301	3	Clermont Northeastern Local	Batavia
301	3	Clinton-Massie Local	Clarksville
301	3	Cloverleaf Local	Lodi
301	3	Defiance City	Defiance
301	3	Edison Local (Formerly Berlin-Milan)	Milan
301	3	Fairless Local	Navarre
301	3	Firelands Local	South Amherst
301	3	Graham Local	Saint Paris
301	3	Harrison Hills City	Cadiz
301	3	Highland Local	Sparta
301	3	Hubbard Exempted Village	Hubbard
301	3	Indian Lake Local	Lewistown
301	3	Keystone Local	Lagrange
301	3	Lakeview Local	Cortland
301	3	Licking Valley Local	Newark
301	3	London City	London
301	3	Madison Local	Middletown
301	3	Maysville Local	Zanesville
301	3	Miami Trace Local	Washington CH
301	3	Minerva Local	Minerva
301	3	Minford Local	Minford
301	3	North College Hill City	Cincinnati
301	3	Northwest Local	Mc Dermott
301	3	Northwestern Local	Springfield
301	3	Orrville City	Orrville
301	3	Portsmouth City	Portsmouth
301	3	Saint Clairsville-Richland City	Saint Clairsville
301	3	Trotwood-Madison City	Trotwood
301	3	Union-Scioto Local	Chillicothe
301	3	Vermilion Local	Vermilion
301	3	Washington-Nile Local	West Portsmouth
301	3	Westfall Local	Williamsport
301	3	Wheelersburg Local	Wheelersburg
301	3	Wickliffe City	Wickliffe
301	3	Zane Trace Local	Chillicothe
342	2	Bucyrus City	Bucyrus
343	1	Alternative Education Academy	Toledo
343	1	Electronic Classroom of Tomorrow	Columbus
343	1	Ohio Connections Academy Inc	Cleveland
343	1	Ohio Virtual Academy	Maumee
343	1	Treca Digital Academy	Marion

Number of Teachers

Rank	Number	District Name	City
1	3,515.9	Cleveland Municipal	Cleveland
2	3,186.9	Columbus City SD	Columbus
3	1,681.3	Cincinnati City	Cincinnati
4	1,569.0	Akron City	Akron
5	1,437.8	Toledo City	Toledo
6	1,107.7	South-Western City	Grove City
7	913.5	Dayton City	Dayton
8	878.7	Olentangy Local	Lewis Center
9	867.1	Dublin City	Dublin
10	844.7	Hilliard City	Hilliard
11	844.4	Lakota Local	Liberty Twp
12	783.9	Westerville City	Westerville
13	694.8	Parma City	Parma
14	606.9	Worthington City	Worthington
15	599.7	Canton City	Canton
16	549.9	Mason City SD	Mason
17	539.8	Willoughby-Eastlake City	Willoughby
18	530.0	Pickerington Local	Pickerington
19	511.4	Fairfield City	Fairfield
20	507.2	Hamilton City	Hamilton
21	495.7	Springfield City	Springfield
22	494.1	Cleveland Hgts-University Hgts City	University Hgts
23	472.0	Northwest Local	Cincinnati
24	469.7	Centerville City	Centerville
25	464.4	Mentor Exempted Village	Mentor
26	461.8	West Clermont Local	Cincinnati
27	460.2	Youngstown City Schools	Youngstown
28	447.3	Sylvania City	Sylvania
29	440.1	Kettering City	Kettering
30	436.7	Elyria City Schools	Elyria
31	429.9	Gahanna-Jefferson City	Gahanna
32	426.3	Lorain City	Lorain
33	422.7	Beavercreek City	Beavercreek
34	415.5	Berea City	Berea
35	413.7	Brunswick City	Brunswick
36	410.2	Oak Hills Local	Cincinnati
37	409.5	Washington Local	Toledo
38	405.7	Upper Arlington City	Upper Arlington
39	396.6	Middletown City	Middletown
40	380.3	Newark City	Newark
41	379.6	Forest Hills Local	Cincinnati
42	376.0	Huber Heights City	Huber Heights
43	374.6	Strongsville City	Strongsville
44	362.6	Euclid City	Euclid
45	360.0	Shaker Heights City	Shaker Heights
46	340.8	Lakewood City	Lakewood
47	338.3	Findlay City	Findlay
48	335.8	Groveport Madison Local	Groveport
49	333.8	Medina City SD	Medina
50	330.0	Lancaster City	Lancaster
51	319.9	Sycamore Community City	Cincinnati
52	319.7	Miamisburg City	Miamisburg
53	311.7	Milford Exempted Village	Milford
54	305.3	Warren City	Warren
55	300.2	Marysville Exempted Village	Marysville
56	299.3	Cuyahoga Falls City	Cuyahoga Falls
57	297.5	Plain Local	Canton
58	295.4	Princeton City	Cincinnati
59	295.1	Jackson Local	Massillon
60	294.5	Lima City	Lima
61	294.2	Mayfield City	Mayfield Hgts
62	289.7	Springboro Community City	Springboro
63	289.3	Stow-Munroe Falls City SD	Stow
64	288.0	Electronic Classroom of Tomorrow	Columbus
65	287.1	Reynoldsburg City	Reynoldsburg
66	284.9	Austintown Local	Youngstown
67	284.7	Northmont City	Englewood
68	282.6	Marion City	Marion
69	282.5	Hudson City	Hudson
70	281.0	New Albany-Plain Local	New Albany
71	278.0	Solon City	Solon
72	276.3	Delaware City	Delaware
73	275.0	Mansfield City	Mansfield
74	270.0	Perry Local	Massillon
75	264.5	North Canton City	North Canton
76	262.9	Westlake City	Westlake
77	262.6	Massillon City	Massillon
78	261.4	Kent City	Kent
79	258.5	Riverside Local	Painesville
80	258.1	Xenia Community City	Xenia
81	255.4	South Euclid-Lyndhurst City	Lyndhurst
82	253.5	Fairborn City	Fairborn
83	252.9	Lebanon City	Lebanon
84	252.7	Barberton City	Barberton
85	251.0	Boardman Local	Youngstown
86	245.1	Wadsworth City	Wadsworth
87	244.2	Adams County/ohio Valley Local	West Union
88	238.4	Wooster City	Wooster
89	237.5	Troy City	Troy
90	236.9	Perrysburg Exempted Village	Perrysburg
91	235.3	North Royalton City	North Royalton
92	233.4	Mount Vernon City	Mount Vernon
93	233.2	East Cleveland City SD	East Cleveland
94	233.1	North Olmsted City	North Olmsted
95	231.9	Loveland City	Loveland
96	228.3	Green Local	Uniontown
97	228.1	Oregon City	Oregon
98	227.5	N Ridgeville City	N Ridgeville
99	227.0	Madison Local	Mansfield
100	226.5	Fremont City	Fremont
101	226.0	Amherst Exempted Village	Amherst
102	225.9	Logan-Hocking Local	Logan
103	224.4	Bedford City	Bedford
104	223.1	Maple Heights City	Maple Heights
105	221.7	Ashtabula Area City	Ashtabula
106	221.3	Mad River Local	Dayton
107	216.5	Anthony Wayne Local	Whitehouse
108	216.0	Greenville City	Greenville
109	213.0	Ohio Virtual Academy	Maumee
110	211.3	Southwest Licking Local	Pataskala
111	209.9	Avon Lake City	Avon Lake
112	209.7	Twinsburg City	Twinsburg
113	209.6	Northeastern Local	Springfield
114	209.3	Kings Local	Kings Mills
115	207.4	Sandusky City	Sandusky
116	207.3	Brecksville-Broadview Hghts City	Brecksville
117	206.7	West Carrollton City	West Carrollton
118	205.1	Athens City	The Plains
119	200.8	Ashland City	Ashland
120	200.0	Teays Valley Local	Ashville
121	199.8	Mt Healthy City	Cincinnati
122	198.1	Springfield Local	Holland
123	198.0	Alliance City	Alliance
124	197.2	Avon Local	Avon
125	197.1	Kenston Local	Chagrin Falls
126	196.8	Olmsted Falls City	Olmsted Falls
127	196.3	Vandalia-Butler City	Vandalia
128	195.4	Garfield Hgts City Schools	Garfield Hgts
129	193.7	Piqua City	Piqua
130	191.1	Licking Heights Local	Pataskala
131	191.0	Talawanda City	Oxford
132	190.8	Lake Local	Uniontown
133	187.8	Nordonia Hills City	Northfield
134	187.6	Switzerland of Ohio Local	Woodsfield
135	187.3	Canal Wnchstr Local	Canal Wnchstr
136	186.6	Celina City	Celina
137	186.4	Winton Woods City	Cincinnati
138	180.8	Copley-Fairlawn City	Copley
139	180.2	Little Miami Local	Maineville
140	178.6	New Philadel. City	New Philadel.
141	178.1	Chardon Local	Chardon
142	177.3	Chillicothe City	Chillicothe
143	176.1	Bellefontaine City	Bellefontaine
143	176.1	Zanesville City	Zanesville
145	174.5	Vinton County Local	Mc Arthur
146	173.9	Edgewood City	Trenton
147	172.7	Ravenna City	Ravenna
148	171.9	Howland Local	Warren
149	171.1	Whitehall City	Whitehall

Note: This section only includes districts with 1,500 or more students; All categories are ranked from high to low

150	170.4	Louisville City	Louisville
151	169.5	Madison Local	Madison
152	169.3	Southwest Local	Harrison
153	168.4	Midview Local	Grafton
154	167.7	Franklin City	Franklin
154	167.7	Tecumseh Local	New Carlisle
156	167.2	Painesville City Local	Painesville
157	166.9	Sidney City	Sidney
158	166.0	Marietta City	Marietta
158	166.0	Rocky River City	Rocky River
160	164.7	Revere Local	Bath
161	164.4	Jackson City	Jackson
162	164.3	Steubenville City	Steubenville
163	162.6	Canfield Local	Canfield
163	162.6	Orange City	Cleveland
165	162.4	Bowling Green City SD	Bowling Green
166	161.0	Highland Local	Medina
167	160.2	Norwalk City	Norwalk
168	159.3	Aurora City	Aurora
169	158.5	East Liverpool City	East Liverpool
170	157.6	Maumee City	Maumee
171	155.5	Hamilton Local	Columbus
171	155.5	Lakewood Local	Hebron
173	154.4	Norwood City	Norwood
174	154.0	Indian Creek Local	Wintersville
175	153.8	Western Brown Local	Mount Orab
176	152.7	Defiance City	Defiance
177	152.6	Big Walnut Local	Galena
178	152.3	Niles City	Niles
179	150.5	Tallmadge City	Tallmadge
180	150.0	Bay Village City	Bay Village
180	150.0	Trotwood-Madison City	Trotwood
182	149.9	Wilmington City	Wilmington
183	149.6	Shawnee Local	Lima
184	149.0	Tipp City Exempted Village	Tipp City
185	148.2	Perkins Local	Sandusky
186	147.8	Buckeye Local	Dillonvale
187	147.7	Wapakoneta City	Wapakoneta
188	146.1	Hillsboro City	Hillsboro
189	145.7	New Richmond Exempted Village	New Richmond
190	145.4	Tiffin City	Tiffin
191	145.1	Lexington Local	Lexington
192	144.2	Indian Hill Exempted Village	Cincinnati
193	141.5	Bexley City	Bexley
194	141.4	Tri-Valley Local	Dresden
195	141.2	Circleville City	Circleville
195	141.2	Miami Trace Local	Washington CH
197	141.0	Maysville Local	Zanesville
198	139.1	Marlington Local	Alliance
199	139.0	Ross Local	Hamilton
200	138.7	Northern Local	Thornville
201	138.5	Clyde-Green Springs Ex. Village	Clyde
202	138.1	West Branch Local	Beloit
203	137.8	Coventry Local	Akron
203	137.8	Granville Exempted Village	Granville
205	137.5	Gallia County Local	Gallipolis
206	136.7	Springfield Local	Akron
207	136.5	Morgan Local	Mc Connelsville
208	136.3	Goshen Local	Goshen
208	136.3	Norton City	Norton
208	136.3	Urbana City	Urbana
211	135.8	Cloverleaf Local	Lodi
211	135.8	Oakwood City	Dayton
213	135.6	Buckeye Valley Local	Delaware
214	135.4	Beachwood City	Beachwood
215	135.2	Cambridge City	Cambridge
215	135.2	Claymont City	Dennison
217	135.0	West Holmes Local	Millersburg
218	134.6	Logan Elm Local	Circleville
219	134.2	Gallipolis City	Gallipolis
219	134.2	Wyoming City	Wyoming
221	133.6	Van Wert City	Van Wert
222	133.5	Dover City	Dover
222	133.5	Field Local	Mogadore
224	133.2	Elida Local	Elida
225	132.0	Carrollton Exempted Village	Carrollton
226	128.6	Portsmouth City	Portsmouth
227	127.9	Chagrin Falls Exempted Village	Chagrin Falls
228	127.6	Poland Local	Poland
229	127.3	Bellbrook-Sugarcreek Local SD	Bellbrook
230	126.5	East Muskingum Local	New Concord
231	126.0	Geneva Area City	Geneva
231	126.0	Streetsboro City	Streetsboro
233	125.9	Salem City	Salem
234	125.7	Franklin Local	Duncan Falls
235	125.3	Bellevue City	Bellevue
236	125.2	River View Local	Warsaw
237	124.8	Bryan City	Bryan
238	124.7	Washington CH City	Washington CH
239	124.0	Warrensville Hgts City	Warrensville Hgts
240	123.9	Napoleon Area City	Napoleon
241	123.5	Saint Marys City	Saint Marys
242	123.2	Warren Local	Vincent
243	123.1	New Lexington City	New Lexington
244	122.8	Valley View Local	Germantown
245	122.3	Woodridge Local	Peninsula
246	122.0	Batavia Local	Batavia
247	121.2	Vermilion Local	Vermilion
248	120.7	Buckeye Local	Medina
249	120.1	Jonathan Alder Local	Plain City
250	119.8	Canton Local	Canton
251	118.7	Rossford Exempted Village	Rossford
252	118.6	Monroe Local SD	Monroe
253	118.3	Beaver Local	Lisbon
253	118.3	Rolling Hills Local	Cambridge
253	118.3	West Geauga Local	Chesterland
256	118.2	Triway Local	Wooster
257	118.1	Crestwood Local	Mantua
258	117.6	Conneaut Area City	Conneaut
259	116.5	Meigs Local	Pomeroy
260	116.4	Coshocton City	Coshocton
261	116.1	East Holmes Local	Berlin
262	116.0	Jefferson Area Local	Jefferson
263	115.8	Shelby City	Shelby
264	115.5	Kenton City	Kenton
264	115.5	Struthers City	Struthers
266	115.2	Eaton Community City	Eaton
267	114.6	Licking Valley Local	Newark
268	114.2	Fostoria City	Fostoria
269	114.1	Willard City	Willard
270	113.4	Hubbard Exempted Village	Hubbard
271	113.2	Port Clinton City	Port Clinton
272	112.6	Southeast Local	Ravenna
273	112.4	Benjamin Logan Local	Bellefontaine
274	111.8	Firelands Local	South Amherst
275	111.7	Sheffield-Sheffield Lake City	Sheffield Vllg
276	111.5	Greenfield Exempted Village	Greenfield
277	111.0	Union-Scioto Local	Chillicothe
278	110.7	Indian Lake Local	Lewistown
279	110.0	South Point Local	South Point
280	109.2	London City	London
281	109.1	Northwest Local	Canal Fulton
282	108.9	Northridge Local	Dayton
283	108.3	Bethel-Tate Local	Bethel
284	107.9	Clark-Shawnee Local	Springfield
285	107.0	Northwest Local	Mc Dermott
286	106.5	Carlisle Local	Carlisle
287	106.3	Perry Local	Perry
288	106.2	Clear Fork Valley Local	Bellville
289	106.1	Minerva Local	Minerva
290	106.0	Highland Local	Sparta
290	106.0	Indian Valley Local Schools	Gnadenhutten
292	105.6	Wauseon Exempted Village	Wauseon
293	105.3	Three Rivers Local	Cleves
294	105.1	Buckeye Local	Ashtabula
295	104.7	Galion City	Galion
295	104.7	Paulding Exempted Village	Paulding
297	104.6	Wickliffe City	Wickliffe
298	102.9	Girard City SD	Girard
299	102.8	Graham Local	Saint Paris
300	102.1	Fairfield Union Local	Lancaster
300	102.1	Fairview Park City	Fairview Park
302	102.0	Clinton-Massie Local	Clarksville
303	101.6	Saint Clairsville-Richland City	Saint Clairsville
304	100.8	Alexander Local	Albany
305	100.3	Mariemont City	Cincinnati
306	100.1	Bath Local	Lima
307	100.0	Keystone Local	Lagrange
308	99.7	Edison Local	Hammondsville
308	99.7	Southeast Local	Apple Creek
310	98.6	Northwestern Local	Springfield
311	97.2	Bucyrus City	Bucyrus
312	97.0	Fairland Local	Proctorville
313	96.1	Lakeview Local	Cortland
314	96.0	Waverly City	Waverly
315	95.7	Lake Local	Millbury
316	94.1	Ontario Local	Mansfield
317	94.0	Orrville City	Orrville
318	93.4	Upper Sandusky Exempted Village	Upper Sandusky
319	92.5	Westfall Local	Williamsport
320	92.0	Greenon Local	Enon
320	92.0	North Fork Local	Utica
322	91.5	Benton Carroll Salem Local	Oak Harbor
323	91.1	Fairless Local	Navarre
324	90.9	Reading Community City	Reading
325	90.7	Wellston City	Wellston
326	90.2	Edison Local (Formerly Berlin-Milan)	Milan
327	89.8	River Valley Local	Caledonia
328	88.4	Heath City	Heath
329	88.2	Blanchester Local	Blanchester
330	88.0	Clearview Local	Lorain
331	87.8	Johnstown-Monroe Local	Johnstown
332	84.7	Bloom-Carroll Local	Carroll
333	84.5	Madison Local	Middletown
334	84.0	Washington-Nile Local	West Portsmouth
335	83.6	Eastwood Local	Pemberville
336	82.9	Wheelersburg Local	Wheelersburg
337	81.8	Clermont Northeastern Local	Batavia
338	80.6	Ottawa-Glandorf Local	Ottawa
339	80.0	Zane Trace Local	Chillicothe
340	78.7	Harrison Hills City	Cadiz
341	78.1	Minford Local	Minford
342	77.4	Amanda-Clearcreek Local	Amanda
343	75.4	Otsego Local	Tontogany
344	74.4	Ohio Connections Academy Inc	Cleveland
345	68.7	North College Hill City	Cincinnati
346	63.0	Alternative Education Academy	Toledo
347	16.2	Treca Digital Academy	Marion

Number of Students

Rank	Number	District Name	City
1	50,488	Columbus City SD	Columbus
2	42,805	Cleveland Municipal	Cleveland
3	32,154	Cincinnati City	Cincinnati
4	23,115	Toledo City	Toledo
5	22,678	Akron City	Akron
6	20,895	South-Western City	Grove City
7	17,364	Lakota Local	Liberty Twp
8	16,690	Olentangy Local	Lewis Center
9	15,464	Hilliard City	Hilliard
10	14,940	Westerville City	Westerville
11	14,795	Dayton City	Dayton
12	14,453	Dublin City	Dublin
13	11,640	Ohio Virtual Academy	Maumee
14	11,569	Parma City	Parma
15	10,931	Mason City SD	Mason
16	10,840	Electronic Classroom of Tomorrow	Columbus
17	10,166	Pickerington Local	Pickerington
18	9,911	Canton City	Canton
19	9,796	Fairfield City	Fairfield
20	9,745	Hamilton City	Hamilton
21	9,317	Worthington City	Worthington
22	9,212	Northwest Local	Cincinnati
23	8,717	West Clermont Local	Cincinnati
24	8,524	Willoughby-Eastlake City	Willoughby
25	8,452	Centerville City	Centerville
26	8,174	Mentor Exempted Village	Mentor
27	7,938	Oak Hills Local	Cincinnati
28	7,915	Beavercreek City	Beavercreek
29	7,768	Kettering City	Kettering
30	7,596	Sylvania City	Sylvania
31	7,505	Lorain City	Lorain
32	7,484	Forest Hills Local	Cincinnati
33	7,435	Springfield City	Springfield
34	7,329	Brunswick City	Brunswick
35	7,321	Medina City SD	Medina
36	7,163	Berea City	Berea
37	7,029	Gahanna-Jefferson City	Gahanna
38	6,736	Washington Local	Toledo
39	6,616	Elyria City Schools	Elyria
40	6,523	Strongsville City	Strongsville
41	6,518	Milford Exempted Village	Milford
42	6,351	Middletown City	Middletown
43	6,331	Huber Heights City	Huber Heights
44	6,181	Newark City	Newark
45	6,044	Lancaster City	Lancaster
46	6,017	Plain Local	Canton
47	5,923	Cleveland Hgts-University Hgts City	University Hgts
48	5,906	Reynoldsburg City	Reynoldsburg
49	5,875	Findlay City	Findlay

Note: This section only includes districts with 1,500 or more students; All categories are ranked from high to low

Rank	Number	District Name	City
50	5,849	Youngstown City Schools	Youngstown
51	5,844	Lakewood City	Lakewood
52	5,824	Jackson Local	Massillon
53	5,737	Euclid City	Euclid
54	5,661	Springboro Community City	Springboro
55	5,650	Groveport Madison Local	Groveport
56	5,551	Miamisburg City	Miamisburg
57	5,438	Shaker Heights City	Shaker Heights
58	5,414	Lebanon City	Lebanon
59	5,410	Stow-Munroe Falls City SD	Stow
60	5,390	Warren City	Warren
61	5,336	Princeton City	Cincinnati
62	5,306	Sycamore Community City	Cincinnati
63	5,278	Marysville Exempted Village	Marysville
64	5,250	Austintown Local	Youngstown
65	5,223	Upper Arlington City	Upper Arlington
66	5,204	Northmont City	Englewood
67	5,123	Delaware City	Delaware
68	5,068	Solon City	Solon
69	4,898	Perry Local	Massillon
70	4,888	Wadsworth City	Wadsworth
71	4,886	Cuyahoga Falls City	Cuyahoga Falls
72	4,879	Riverside Local	Painesville
73	4,725	North Canton City	North Canton
74	4,685	Hudson City	Hudson
75	4,677	Loveland City	Loveland
76	4,674	North Royalton City	North Royalton
77	4,571	Perrysburg Exempted Village	Perrysburg
78	4,561	Mayfield City	Mayfield Hgts
79	4,559	Boardman Local	Youngstown
80	4,540	Xenia Community City	Xenia
81	4,416	New Albany-Plain Local	New Albany
82	4,413	Fairborn City	Fairborn
83	4,399	Troy City	Troy
84	4,359	Twinsburg City	Twinsburg
85	4,288	Brecksville-Broadview Hghts City	Brecksville
86	4,266	Anthony Wayne Local	Whitehouse
87	4,234	Marion City	Marion
88	4,164	Massillon City	Massillon
89	4,153	South Euclid-Lyndhurst City	Lyndhurst
90	4,137	Amherst Exempted Village	Amherst
91	4,136	Green Local	Uniontown
92	4,118	Fremont City	Fremont
93	4,109	North Olmsted City	North Olmsted
94	4,101	Barberton City	Barberton
95	4,018	Avon Local	Avon
96	4,016	N Ridgeville City	N Ridgeville
97	3,997	Westlake City	Westlake
98	3,990	Adams County/ohio Valley Local	West Union
99	3,968	Kings Local	Kings Mills
100	3,946	Logan-Hocking Local	Logan
101	3,934	Lima City	Lima
102	3,907	Springfield Local	Holland
103	3,892	Mount Vernon City	Mount Vernon
104	3,882	Ashtabula Area City	Ashtabula
104	3,882	Nordonia Hills City	Northfield
106	3,880	Garfield Hgts City Schools	Garfield Hgts
107	3,834	West Carrollton City	West Carrollton
108	3,814	Oregon City	Oregon
109	3,808	Avon Lake City	Avon Lake
110	3,782	Maple Heights City	Maple Heights
110	3,782	Olmsted Falls City	Olmsted Falls
112	3,776	Southwest Licking Local	Pataskala
113	3,700	Mad River Local	Dayton
114	3,682	Wooster City	Wooster
115	3,672	Teays Valley Local	Ashville
116	3,647	Little Miami Local	Maineville
117	3,600	Kent City	Kent
118	3,593	Edgewood City	Trenton
119	3,581	Mansfield City	Mansfield
120	3,553	Canal Wnchstr Local	Canal Wnchstr
121	3,547	Lake Local	Uniontown
122	3,531	Bedford City	Bedford
123	3,525	Zanesville City	Zanesville
124	3,513	Northeastern Local	Springfield
125	3,505	Sidney City	Sidney
126	3,494	Piqua City	Piqua
127	3,470	Licking Heights Local	Pataskala
128	3,419	Winton Woods City	Cincinnati
129	3,413	Sandusky City	Sandusky
130	3,403	Madison Local	Madison
131	3,396	Mt Healthy City	Cincinnati
132	3,390	Southwest Local	Harrison
133	3,321	Ashland City	Ashland
134	3,298	Copley-Fairlawn City	Copley
135	3,244	Vandalia-Butler City	Vandalia
136	3,201	Highland Local	Medina
137	3,192	Madison Local	Mansfield
138	3,189	Painesville City Local	Painesville
139	3,186	Western Brown Local	Mount Orab
140	3,148	Midview Local	Grafton
141	3,125	Wilmington City	Wilmington
142	3,107	Tecumseh Local	New Carlisle
143	3,094	Hamilton Local	Columbus
144	3,085	East Cleveland City SD	East Cleveland
145	3,073	Louisville City	Louisville
146	3,070	Chardon Local	Chardon
146	3,070	Kenston Local	Chagrin Falls
148	3,047	Alliance City	Alliance
149	3,039	Talawanda City	Oxford
150	2,995	Tri-Valley Local	Dresden
151	2,990	Bowling Green City SD	Bowling Green
152	2,979	Howland Local	Warren
153	2,970	Big Walnut Local	Galena
154	2,964	Aurora City	Aurora
155	2,955	Ohio Connections Academy Inc	Cleveland
156	2,941	Norwalk City	Norwalk
157	2,931	Wapakoneta City	Wapakoneta
158	2,925	New Philadel. City	New Philadel.
159	2,900	Whitehall City	Whitehall
160	2,898	Canfield Local	Canfield
161	2,874	Franklin City	Franklin
162	2,835	Ross Local	Hamilton
163	2,833	Ravenna City	Ravenna
164	2,832	Chillicothe City	Chillicothe
165	2,787	Tiffin City	Tiffin
166	2,786	Marietta City	Marietta
167	2,770	Celina City	Celina
168	2,718	Dover City	Dover
169	2,715	Cloverleaf Local	Lodi
170	2,687	Revere Local	Bath
171	2,680	Greenville City	Greenville
172	2,654	Athens City	The Plains
173	2,650	Hillsboro City	Hillsboro
174	2,633	Geneva Area City	Geneva
175	2,628	Rocky River City	Rocky River
176	2,603	Niles City	Niles
177	2,600	Trotwood-Madison City	Trotwood
178	2,599	Bellbrook-Sugarcreek Local SD	Bellbrook
179	2,598	Bellefontaine City	Bellefontaine
180	2,591	Maumee City	Maumee
181	2,580	Bay Village City	Bay Village
182	2,571	Norton City	Norton
183	2,567	Tallmadge City	Tallmadge
184	2,530	Goshen Local	Goshen
185	2,526	Tipp City Exempted Village	Tipp City
186	2,500	Shawnee Local	Lima
187	2,498	Defiance City	Defiance
188	2,481	Granville Exempted Village	Granville
189	2,471	Steubenville City	Steubenville
190	2,465	Switzerland of Ohio Local	Woodsfield
191	2,461	Lexington Local	Lexington
192	2,451	Miami Trace Local	Washington CH
193	2,419	Elida Local	Elida
193	2,419	Jackson City	Jackson
195	2,416	West Holmes Local	Millersburg
196	2,410	Monroe Local SD	Monroe
197	2,403	Marlington Local	Alliance
198	2,348	Carrollton Exempted Village	Carrollton
199	2,332	Washington CH City	Washington CH
200	2,327	Perkins Local	Sandusky
201	2,320	Vinton County Local	Mc Arthur
202	2,310	New Richmond Exempted Village	New Richmond
203	2,309	Springfield Local	Akron
204	2,302	Buckeye Local	Medina
205	2,289	Buckeye Valley Local	Delaware
206	2,270	Clyde-Green Springs Ex. Village	Clyde
207	2,256	Warren Local	Vincent
208	2,251	West Geauga Local	Chesterland
209	2,250	Coventry Local	Akron
210	2,246	East Liverpool City	East Liverpool
211	2,245	Maysville Local	Zanesville
212	2,239	Saint Marys City	Saint Marys
213	2,235	Orange City	Cleveland
214	2,232	Canton Local	Canton
215	2,223	Union-Scioto Local	Chillicothe
216	2,220	Poland Local	Poland
217	2,218	Cambridge City	Cambridge
218	2,214	Gallia County Local	Gallipolis
219	2,210	Gallipolis City	Gallipolis
220	2,207	Indian Creek Local	Wintersville
220	2,207	Northern Local	Thornville
222	2,197	Jonathan Alder Local	Plain City
223	2,190	West Branch Local	Beloit
224	2,182	Circleville City	Circleville
225	2,171	Eaton Community City	Eaton
225	2,171	Field Local	Mogadore
227	2,139	Greenfield Exempted Village	Greenfield
228	2,121	Bexley City	Bexley
229	2,116	Clark-Shawnee Local	Springfield
230	2,115	Claymont City	Dennison
231	2,113	Salem City	Salem
232	2,111	Urbana City	Urbana
233	2,107	Graham Local	Saint Paris
234	2,096	East Muskingum Local	New Concord
235	2,085	Vermilion Local	Vermilion
236	2,081	Morgan Local	Mc Connelsville
237	2,077	Van Wert City	Van Wert
238	2,076	Bellevue City	Bellevue
239	2,074	Franklin Local	Duncan Falls
240	2,066	Oakwood City	Dayton
241	2,062	River View Local	Warsaw
242	2,061	Logan Elm Local	Circleville
243	2,058	Crestwood Local	Mantua
244	2,050	Woodridge Local	Peninsula
245	2,043	Norwood City	Norwood
246	2,040	Streetsboro City	Streetsboro
247	2,036	London City	London
248	2,034	Batavia Local	Batavia
249	2,025	Chagrin Falls Exempted Village	Chagrin Falls
250	2,008	Hubbard Exempted Village	Hubbard
251	2,004	Indian Hill Exempted Village	Cincinnati
252	1,998	Buckeye Local	Dillonvale
253	1,996	Lakewood Local	Hebron
253	1,996	Licking Valley Local	Newark
255	1,995	Fairfield Union Local	Lancaster
256	1,989	Northwest Local	Canal Fulton
257	1,986	River Valley Local	Caledonia
258	1,985	Portsmouth City	Portsmouth
259	1,964	Bryan City	Bryan
260	1,955	Valley View Local	Germantown
261	1,943	Beaver Local	Lisbon
261	1,943	Edison Local	Hammondsville
263	1,931	Three Rivers Local	Cleves
264	1,927	Wyoming City	Wyoming
265	1,924	Napoleon Area City	Napoleon
266	1,920	Struthers City	Struthers
267	1,911	Shelby City	Shelby
268	1,895	Waverly City	Waverly
269	1,887	Treca Digital Academy	Marion
270	1,873	Wauseon Exempted Village	Wauseon
271	1,870	Kenton City	Kenton
272	1,864	Alternative Education Academy	Toledo
273	1,854	Sheffield-Sheffield Lake City	Sheffield Vllg
274	1,852	Jefferson Area Local	Jefferson
275	1,850	Clinton-Massie Local	Clarksville
275	1,850	Highland Local	Sparta
277	1,845	Minerva Local	Minerva
278	1,838	Conneaut Area City	Conneaut
278	1,838	Greenon Local	Enon
280	1,836	Fostoria City	Fostoria
281	1,832	New Lexington City	New Lexington
282	1,831	Meigs Local	Pomeroy
283	1,828	Buckeye Local	Ashtabula
284	1,827	South Point Local	South Point
285	1,825	East Holmes Local	Berlin
286	1,823	Clear Fork Valley Local	Bellville
287	1,810	Indian Valley Local Schools	Gnadenhutten
288	1,809	Bath Local	Lima
289	1,807	Northridge Local	Dayton
290	1,802	Southeast Local	Ravenna
291	1,794	Lakeview Local	Cortland
292	1,779	Galion City	Galion
293	1,768	Triway Local	Wooster
294	1,762	Rossford Exempted Village	Rossford
295	1,761	Fairland Local	Proctorville
296	1,757	Fairview Park City	Fairview Park
297	1,752	Firelands Local	South Amherst
298	1,751	Bethel-Tate Local	Bethel
299	1,748	Northwestern Local	Springfield
300	1,746	Port Clinton City	Port Clinton
301	1,745	Ontario Local	Mansfield

Note: This section only includes districts with 1,500 or more students; All categories are ranked from high to low

302	1,743	Perry Local	Perry
303	1,733	Rolling Hills Local	Cambridge
304	1,732	Willard City	Willard
305	1,731	Indian Lake Local	Lewistown
305	1,731	Warrensville Hgts City	Warrensville Hgts
307	1,729	Saint Clairsville-Richland City	Saint Clairsville
308	1,728	Benjamin Logan Local	Bellefontaine
309	1,712	Upper Sandusky Exempted Village	Upper Sandusky
310	1,701	Benton Carroll Salem Local	Oak Harbor
311	1,694	Blanchester Local	Blanchester
312	1,692	Bloom-Carroll Local	Carroll
313	1,681	Girard City SD	Girard
314	1,669	Coshocton City	Coshocton
315	1,667	Northwest Local	Mc Dermott
316	1,666	North Fork Local	Utica
317	1,662	Carlisle Local	Carlisle
318	1,656	Clearview Local	Lorain
319	1,630	Amanda-Clearcreek Local	Amanda
320	1,628	Keystone Local	Lagrange
321	1,623	Clermont Northeastern Local	Batavia
322	1,615	Beachwood City	Beachwood
322	1,615	Edison Local (Formerly Berlin-Milan)	Milan
324	1,612	Heath City	Heath
325	1,596	Westfall Local	Williamsport
326	1,590	Mariemont City	Cincinnati
327	1,582	Reading Community City	Reading
328	1,581	Lake Local	Millbury
329	1,580	North College Hill City	Cincinnati
330	1,566	Fairless Local	Navarre
331	1,565	Alexander Local	Albany
332	1,558	Johnstown-Monroe Local	Johnstown
333	1,556	Orrville City	Orrville
334	1,550	Minford Local	Minford
335	1,546	Otsego Local	Tontogany
336	1,540	Washington-Nile Local	West Portsmouth
337	1,534	Zane Trace Local	Chillicothe
338	1,532	Wellston City	Wellston
339	1,531	Wheelersburg Local	Wheelersburg
340	1,519	Bucyrus City	Bucyrus
341	1,512	Eastwood Local	Pemberville
341	1,512	Madison Local	Middletown
341	1,512	Ottawa-Glandorf Local	Ottawa
344	1,510	Harrison Hills City	Cadiz
345	1,508	Wickliffe City	Wickliffe
346	1,506	Paulding Exempted Village	Paulding
346	1,506	Southeast Local	Apple Creek

Male Students

Rank	Percent	District Name	City
1	54.8	North College Hill City	Cincinnati
2	54.4	Morgan Local	Mc Connelsville
3	54.0	Wauseon Exempted Village	Wauseon
4	53.9	Southeast Local	Apple Creek
5	53.7	Minford Local	Minford
5	53.7	N Ridgeville City	N Ridgeville
5	53.7	Saint Marys City	Saint Marys
8	53.6	Mansfield City	Mansfield
8	53.6	Southeast Local	Ravenna
10	53.5	Canton Local	Canton
10	53.5	Dover City	Dover
10	53.5	Massillon City	Massillon
10	53.5	Mayfield City	Mayfield Hgts
10	53.5	Otsego Local	Tontogany
15	53.4	Bellefontaine City	Bellefontaine
15	53.4	Coventry Local	Akron
15	53.4	Indian Valley Local Schools	Gnadenhutten
15	53.4	Maple Heights City	Maple Heights
15	53.4	Monroe Local SD	Monroe
15	53.4	Norwood City	Norwood
15	53.4	Warrensville Hgts City	Warrensville Hgts
22	53.3	Claymont City	Dennison
22	53.3	Clyde-Green Springs Ex. Village	Clyde
22	53.3	Garfield Hgts City Schools	Garfield Hgts
25	53.2	Highland Local	Sparta
25	53.2	Three Rivers Local	Cleves
27	53.1	Fairborn City	Fairborn
27	53.1	Lake Local	Uniontown
27	53.1	Marysville Exempted Village	Marysville
27	53.1	Springfield Local	Akron
31	53.0	Mt Healthy City	Cincinnati
32	52.9	Amanda-Clearcreek Local	Amanda
32	52.9	Clinton-Massie Local	Clarksville
32	52.9	Miami Trace Local	Washington CH
32	52.9	Waverly City	Waverly
32	52.9	Zane Trace Local	Chillicothe
37	52.8	Big Walnut Local	Galena
37	52.8	Elida Local	Elida
37	52.8	Huber Heights City	Huber Heights
37	52.8	Reynoldsburg City	Reynoldsburg
37	52.8	River View Local	Warsaw
42	52.7	Gallipolis City	Gallipolis
42	52.7	Graham Local	Saint Paris
42	52.7	Groveport Madison Local	Groveport
42	52.7	Painesville City Local	Painesville
42	52.7	Rossford Exempted Village	Rossford
42	52.7	Willoughby-Eastlake City	Willoughby
48	52.6	Alliance City	Alliance
48	52.6	Buckeye Local	Medina
48	52.6	Copley-Fairlawn City	Copley
48	52.6	Jackson City	Jackson
48	52.6	Licking Heights Local	Pataskala
48	52.6	Revere Local	Bath
54	52.5	Defiance City	Defiance
54	52.5	Dublin City	Dublin
54	52.5	Euclid City	Euclid
54	52.5	Marlington Local	Alliance
54	52.5	Milford Exempted Village	Milford
54	52.5	Toledo City	Toledo
60	52.4	Blanchester Local	Blanchester
60	52.4	Coshocton City	Coshocton
60	52.4	Greenville City	Greenville
60	52.4	Hamilton Local	Columbus
60	52.4	Marion City	Marion
60	52.4	Northmont City	Englewood
60	52.4	Piqua City	Piqua
60	52.4	River Valley Local	Caledonia
60	52.4	Ross Local	Hamilton
60	52.4	Saint Clairsville-Richland City	Saint Clairsville
60	52.4	Talawanda City	Oxford
60	52.4	Tecumseh Local	New Carlisle
60	52.4	Wheelersburg Local	Wheelersburg
73	52.3	Alexander Local	Albany
73	52.3	Eaton Community City	Eaton
73	52.3	Goshen Local	Goshen
73	52.3	Kenton City	Kenton
73	52.3	Kings Local	Kings Mills
73	52.3	Napoleon Area City	Napoleon
73	52.3	North Royalton City	North Royalton
73	52.3	Northern Local	Thornville
73	52.3	Shaker Heights City	Shaker Heights
73	52.3	Springfield City	Springfield
73	52.3	Tiffin City	Tiffin
73	52.3	West Clermont Local	Cincinnati
73	52.3	Whitehall City	Whitehall
86	52.2	Boardman Local	Youngstown
86	52.2	Bryan City	Bryan
86	52.2	Cloverleaf Local	Lodi
86	52.2	Fostoria City	Fostoria
86	52.2	Jefferson Area Local	Jefferson
86	52.2	Lancaster City	Lancaster
86	52.2	Orrville City	Orrville
86	52.2	Parma City	Parma
86	52.2	Portsmouth City	Portsmouth
86	52.2	Shelby City	Shelby
86	52.2	Southwest Local	Harrison
86	52.2	Wooster City	Wooster
98	52.1	Batavia Local	Batavia
98	52.1	Beavercreek City	Beavercreek
98	52.1	Bethel-Tate Local	Bethel
98	52.1	Brecksville-Broadview Hghts City	Brecksville
98	52.1	Greenfield Exempted Village	Greenfield
98	52.1	Licking Valley Local	Newark
98	52.1	Loveland City	Loveland
98	52.1	Teays Valley Local	Ashville
98	52.1	Tipp City Exempted Village	Tipp City
98	52.1	Washington CH City	Washington CH
108	52.0	Beaver Local	Lisbon
108	52.0	Hilliard City	Hilliard
108	52.0	Ontario Local	Mansfield
108	52.0	Perkins Local	Sandusky
108	52.0	Ravenna City	Ravenna
108	52.0	Streetsboro City	Streetsboro
108	52.0	Upper Sandusky Exempted Village	Upper Sandusky
108	52.0	Wadsworth City	Wadsworth
116	51.9	Aurora City	Aurora
116	51.9	Celina City	Celina
116	51.9	Centerville City	Centerville
116	51.9	Elyria City Schools	Elyria
116	51.9	Fairfield Union Local	Lancaster
116	51.9	Field Local	Mogadore
116	51.9	Lima City	Lima
116	51.9	Maumee City	Maumee
116	51.9	Newark City	Newark
116	51.9	Niles City	Niles
116	51.9	North Canton City	North Canton
116	51.9	Salem City	Salem
116	51.9	Triway Local	Wooster
116	51.9	Trotwood-Madison City	Trotwood
116	51.9	Washington-Nile Local	West Portsmouth
116	51.9	West Carrollton City	West Carrollton
132	51.8	Benjamin Logan Local	Bellefontaine
132	51.8	Berea City	Berea
132	51.8	Bexley City	Bexley
132	51.8	Clermont Northeastern Local	Batavia
132	51.8	Fairless Local	Navarre
132	51.8	Lebanon City	Lebanon
132	51.8	Northwest Local	Cincinnati
132	51.8	Reading Community City	Reading
132	51.8	Southwest Licking Local	Pataskala
132	51.8	Tri-Valley Local	Dresden
132	51.8	Vermilion Local	Vermilion
143	51.7	Dayton City	Dayton
143	51.7	Edgewood City	Trenton
143	51.7	Findlay City	Findlay
143	51.7	Hudson City	Hudson
143	51.7	Kettering City	Kettering
143	51.7	Lakewood City	Lakewood
143	51.7	Perrysburg Exempted Village	Perrysburg
143	51.7	Riverside Local	Painesville
143	51.7	Sidney City	Sidney
143	51.7	Sycamore Community City	Cincinnati
143	51.7	Vandalia-Butler City	Vandalia
143	51.7	West Geauga Local	Chesterland
143	51.7	Westerville City	Westerville
156	51.6	Bloom-Carroll Local	Carroll
156	51.6	Canton City	Canton
156	51.6	Heath City	Heath
156	51.6	Lakewood Local	Hebron
156	51.6	Lorain City	Lorain
156	51.6	Mariemont City	Cincinnati
156	51.6	New Richmond Exempted Village	New Richmond
156	51.6	North Fork Local	Utica
156	51.6	Olmsted Falls City	Olmsted Falls
156	51.6	Perry Local	Massillon
156	51.6	Struthers City	Struthers
156	51.6	Sylvania City	Sylvania
156	51.6	Twinsburg City	Twinsburg
156	51.6	Woodridge Local	Peninsula
170	51.5	Barberton City	Barberton
170	51.5	Cleveland Municipal	Cleveland
170	51.5	East Liverpool City	East Liverpool
170	51.5	Geneva Area City	Geneva
170	51.5	Green Local	Uniontown
170	51.5	Highland Local	Medina
170	51.5	Johnstown-Monroe Local	Johnstown
170	51.5	Logan-Hocking Local	Logan
170	51.5	Mad River Local	Dayton
170	51.5	New Lexington City	New Lexington
170	51.5	Stow-Munroe Falls City SD	Stow
170	51.5	Troy City	Troy
170	51.5	Vinton County Local	Mc Arthur
170	51.5	West Holmes Local	Millersburg
170	51.5	Wickliffe City	Wickliffe
185	51.4	Chillicothe City	Chillicothe
185	51.4	Clear Fork Valley Local	Bellville
185	51.4	Lakeview Local	Cortland
185	51.4	Northridge Local	Dayton
185	51.4	Orange City	Cleveland
185	51.4	Pickerington Local	Pickerington
185	51.4	Princeton City	Cincinnati
185	51.4	Sheffield-Sheffield Lake City	Sheffield Vllg
185	51.4	Solon City	Solon
185	51.4	Urbana City	Urbana
185	51.4	Wapakoneta City	Wapakoneta
185	51.4	Westfall Local	Williamsport
197	51.3	Cuyahoga Falls City	Cuyahoga Falls
197	51.3	Kenston Local	Chagrin Falls
197	51.3	London City	London
197	51.3	New Albany-Plain Local	New Albany
197	51.3	North Olmsted City	North Olmsted

Note: This section only includes districts with 1,500 or more students; All categories are ranked from high to low

197	51.3	Norwalk City	Norwalk
197	51.3	Olentangy Local	Lewis Center
197	51.3	Zanesville City	Zanesville
205	51.2	Bellevue City	Bellevue
205	51.2	Buckeye Valley Local	Delaware
205	51.2	Hamilton City	Hamilton
205	51.2	Harrison Hills City	Cadiz
205	51.2	Indian Lake Local	Lewistown
205	51.2	Little Miami Local	Maineville
205	51.2	Mentor Exempted Village	Mentor
205	51.2	Northeastern Local	Springfield
205	51.2	Poland Local	Poland
205	51.2	Rolling Hills Local	Cambridge
205	51.2	South-Western City	Grove City
205	51.2	Upper Arlington City	Upper Arlington
205	51.2	Western Brown Local	Mount Orab
205	51.2	Xenia Community City	Xenia
219	51.1	Akron City	Akron
219	51.1	Ashtabula Area City	Ashtabula
219	51.1	Avon Lake City	Avon Lake
219	51.1	Bedford City	Bedford
219	51.1	Carlisle Local	Carlisle
219	51.1	Columbus City SD	Columbus
219	51.1	Fairview Park City	Fairview Park
219	51.1	Hubbard Exempted Village	Hubbard
219	51.1	Kent City	Kent
219	51.1	Madison Local	Mansfield
219	51.1	Mason City SD	Mason
219	51.1	Strongsville City	Strongsville
219	51.1	Tallmadge City	Tallmadge
219	51.1	Washington Local	Toledo
233	51.0	Ashland City	Ashland
233	51.0	Brunswick City	Brunswick
233	51.0	Bucyrus City	Bucyrus
233	51.0	East Muskingum Local	New Concord
233	51.0	Forest Hills Local	Cincinnati
233	51.0	Gahanna-Jefferson City	Gahanna
233	51.0	Granville Exempted Village	Granville
233	51.0	Indian Creek Local	Wintersville
233	51.0	Madison Local	Madison
233	51.0	Meigs Local	Pomeroy
233	51.0	Oregon City	Oregon
233	51.0	Winton Woods City	Cincinnati
233	51.0	Youngstown City Schools	Youngstown
246	50.9	Cambridge City	Cambridge
246	50.9	Carrollton Exempted Village	Carrollton
246	50.9	Fairfield City	Fairfield
246	50.9	Howland Local	Warren
246	50.9	Middletown City	Middletown
246	50.9	Mount Vernon City	Mount Vernon
246	50.9	Nordonia Hills City	Northfield
246	50.9	Northwest Local	Mc Dermott
246	50.9	Warren Local	Vincent
255	50.8	Chagrin Falls Exempted Village	Chagrin Falls
255	50.8	Clark-Shawnee Local	Springfield
255	50.8	Cleveland Hgts-University Hgts City	University Hgts
255	50.8	Delaware City	Delaware
255	50.8	Greenon Local	Enon
255	50.8	Jackson Local	Massillon
255	50.8	Lakota Local	Liberty Twp
255	50.8	Lexington Local	Lexington
255	50.8	Plain Local	Canton
255	50.8	Springboro Community City	Springboro
255	50.8	Worthington City	Worthington
266	50.7	Buckeye Local	Dillonvale
266	50.7	Conneaut Area City	Conneaut
266	50.7	East Cleveland City SD	East Cleveland
266	50.7	Fairland Local	Proctorville
266	50.7	Firelands Local	South Amherst
266	50.7	Fremont City	Fremont
266	50.7	Galion City	Galion
266	50.7	Lake Local	Millbury
266	50.7	Oak Hills Local	Cincinnati
275	50.6	Benton Carroll Salem Local	Oak Harbor
275	50.6	Bowling Green City SD	Bowling Green
275	50.6	Edison Local (Formerly Berlin-Milan)	Milan
275	50.6	Franklin Local	Duncan Falls
275	50.6	Sandusky City	Sandusky
280	50.5	Athens City	The Plains
280	50.5	Avon Local	Avon
280	50.5	Switzerland of Ohio Local	Woodsfield
283	50.4	Girard City SD	Girard
283	50.4	Medina City SD	Medina
283	50.4	Midview Local	Grafton
283	50.4	Norton City	Norton
283	50.4	Paulding Exempted Village	Paulding
283	50.4	Steubenville City	Steubenville
283	50.4	Wilmington City	Wilmington
290	50.3	Canal Wnchstr Local	Canal Wnchstr
290	50.3	East Holmes Local	Berlin
290	50.3	Franklin City	Franklin
290	50.3	Hillsboro City	Hillsboro
290	50.3	Jonathan Alder Local	Plain City
290	50.3	Maysville Local	Zanesville
290	50.3	Northwestern Local	Springfield
290	50.3	Ottawa-Glandorf Local	Ottawa
290	50.3	Perry Local	Perry
290	50.3	West Branch Local	Beloit
300	50.2	Beachwood City	Beachwood
300	50.2	Cincinnati City	Cincinnati
300	50.2	Crestwood Local	Mantua
300	50.2	New Philadel. City	New Philadel.
300	50.2	Springfield Local	Holland
300	50.2	Union-Scioto Local	Chillicothe
300	50.2	Wyoming City	Wyoming
307	50.1	Austintown Local	Youngstown
307	50.1	Bellbrook-Sugarcreek Local SD	Bellbrook
307	50.1	Canfield Local	Canfield
307	50.1	Keystone Local	Lagrange
307	50.1	South Point Local	South Point
307	50.1	Valley View Local	Germantown
307	50.1	Westlake City	Westlake
314	50.0	Amherst Exempted Village	Amherst
314	50.0	Buckeye Local	Ashtabula
314	50.0	Marietta City	Marietta
314	50.0	Oakwood City	Dayton
314	50.0	South Euclid-Lyndhurst City	Lyndhurst
314	50.0	Van Wert City	Van Wert
314	50.0	Warren City	Warren
321	49.9	Edison Local	Hammondsville
321	49.9	Willard City	Willard
323	49.8	Adams County/ohio Valley Local	West Union
323	49.8	Eastwood Local	Pemberville
323	49.8	Northwest Local	Canal Fulton
326	49.6	Gallia County Local	Gallipolis
326	49.6	Minerva Local	Minerva
328	49.5	Chardon Local	Chardon
328	49.5	Louisville City	Louisville
328	49.5	Rocky River City	Rocky River
331	49.4	Anthony Wayne Local	Whitehouse
331	49.4	Bath Local	Lima
333	49.3	Circleville City	Circleville
333	49.3	Madison Local	Middletown
333	49.3	Miamisburg City	Miamisburg
336	49.2	Logan Elm Local	Circleville
336	49.2	Port Clinton City	Port Clinton
336	49.2	Wellston City	Wellston
339	48.6	Clearview Local	Lorain
340	48.5	Shawnee Local	Lima
341	48.2	Ohio Virtual Academy	Maumee
342	48.0	Bay Village City	Bay Village
342	48.0	Indian Hill Exempted Village	Cincinnati
344	47.9	Treca Digital Academy	Marion
345	47.4	Ohio Connections Academy Inc	Cleveland
346	46.3	Electronic Classroom of Tomorrow	Columbus
347	44.5	Alternative Education Academy	Toledo

Female Students

Rank	Percent	District Name	City
1	55.5	Alternative Education Academy	Toledo
2	53.7	Electronic Classroom of Tomorrow	Columbus
3	52.6	Ohio Connections Academy Inc	Cleveland
4	52.1	Treca Digital Academy	Marion
5	52.0	Bay Village City	Bay Village
5	52.0	Indian Hill Exempted Village	Cincinnati
7	51.8	Ohio Virtual Academy	Maumee
8	51.5	Shawnee Local	Lima
9	51.4	Clearview Local	Lorain
10	50.8	Logan Elm Local	Circleville
10	50.8	Port Clinton City	Port Clinton
10	50.8	Wellston City	Wellston
13	50.7	Circleville City	Circleville
13	50.7	Madison Local	Middletown
13	50.7	Miamisburg City	Miamisburg
16	50.6	Anthony Wayne Local	Whitehouse
16	50.6	Bath Local	Lima
18	50.5	Chardon Local	Chardon
18	50.5	Louisville City	Louisville
18	50.5	Rocky River City	Rocky River
21	50.4	Gallia County Local	Gallipolis
21	50.4	Minerva Local	Minerva
23	50.2	Adams County/ohio Valley Local	West Union
23	50.2	Eastwood Local	Pemberville
23	50.2	Northwest Local	Canal Fulton
26	50.1	Edison Local	Hammondsville
26	50.1	Willard City	Willard
28	50.0	Amherst Exempted Village	Amherst
28	50.0	Buckeye Local	Ashtabula
28	50.0	Marietta City	Marietta
28	50.0	Oakwood City	Dayton
28	50.0	South Euclid-Lyndhurst City	Lyndhurst
28	50.0	Van Wert City	Van Wert
28	50.0	Warren City	Warren
35	49.9	Austintown Local	Youngstown
35	49.9	Bellbrook-Sugarcreek Local SD	Bellbrook
35	49.9	Canfield Local	Canfield
35	49.9	Keystone Local	Lagrange
35	49.9	South Point Local	South Point
35	49.9	Valley View Local	Germantown
35	49.9	Westlake City	Westlake
42	49.8	Beachwood City	Beachwood
42	49.8	Cincinnati City	Cincinnati
42	49.8	Crestwood Local	Mantua
42	49.8	New Philadel. City	New Philadel.
42	49.8	Springfield Local	Holland
42	49.8	Union-Scioto Local	Chillicothe
42	49.8	Wyoming City	Wyoming
49	49.7	Canal Wnchstr Local	Canal Wnchstr
49	49.7	East Holmes Local	Berlin
49	49.7	Franklin City	Franklin
49	49.7	Hillsboro City	Hillsboro
49	49.7	Jonathan Alder Local	Plain City
49	49.7	Maysville Local	Zanesville
49	49.7	Northwestern Local	Springfield
49	49.7	Ottawa-Glandorf Local	Ottawa
49	49.7	Perry Local	Perry
49	49.7	West Branch Local	Beloit
59	49.6	Girard City SD	Girard
59	49.6	Medina City SD	Medina
59	49.6	Midview Local	Grafton
59	49.6	Norton City	Norton
59	49.6	Paulding Exempted Village	Paulding
59	49.6	Steubenville City	Steubenville
59	49.6	Wilmington City	Wilmington
66	49.5	Athens City	The Plains
66	49.5	Avon Local	Avon
66	49.5	Switzerland of Ohio Local	Woodsfield
69	49.4	Benton Carroll Salem Local	Oak Harbor
69	49.4	Bowling Green City SD	Bowling Green
69	49.4	Edison Local (Formerly Berlin-Milan)	Milan
69	49.4	Franklin Local	Duncan Falls
69	49.4	Sandusky City	Sandusky
74	49.3	Buckeye Local	Dillonvale
74	49.3	Conneaut Area City	Conneaut
74	49.3	East Cleveland City SD	East Cleveland
74	49.3	Fairland Local	Proctorville
74	49.3	Firelands Local	South Amherst
74	49.3	Fremont City	Fremont
74	49.3	Galion City	Galion
74	49.3	Lake Local	Millbury
74	49.3	Oak Hills Local	Cincinnati
83	49.2	Chagrin Falls Exempted Village	Chagrin Falls
83	49.2	Clark-Shawnee Local	Springfield
83	49.2	Cleveland Hgts-University Hgts City	University Hgts
83	49.2	Delaware City	Delaware
83	49.2	Greenon Local	Enon
83	49.2	Jackson Local	Massillon
83	49.2	Lakota Local	Liberty Twp
83	49.2	Lexington Local	Lexington
83	49.2	Plain Local	Canton
83	49.2	Springboro Community City	Springboro
83	49.2	Worthington City	Worthington
94	49.1	Cambridge City	Cambridge
94	49.1	Carrollton Exempted Village	Carrollton
94	49.1	Fairfield City	Fairfield
94	49.1	Howland Local	Warren
94	49.1	Middletown City	Middletown
94	49.1	Mount Vernon City	Mount Vernon
94	49.1	Nordonia Hills City	Northfield
94	49.1	Northwest Local	Mc Dermott

Note: This section only includes districts with 1,500 or more students; All categories are ranked from high to low

Rank	Percent	District Name	City
94	49.1	Warren Local	Vincent
103	49.0	Ashland City	Ashland
103	49.0	Brunswick City	Brunswick
103	49.0	Bucyrus City	Bucyrus
103	49.0	East Muskingum Local	New Concord
103	49.0	Forest Hills Local	Cincinnati
103	49.0	Gahanna-Jefferson City	Gahanna
103	49.0	Granville Exempted Village	Granville
103	49.0	Indian Creek Local	Wintersville
103	49.0	Madison Local	Madison
103	49.0	Meigs Local	Pomeroy
103	49.0	Oregon City	Oregon
103	49.0	Winton Woods City	Cincinnati
103	49.0	Youngstown City Schools	Youngstown
116	48.9	Akron City	Akron
116	48.9	Ashtabula Area City	Ashtabula
116	48.9	Avon Lake City	Avon Lake
116	48.9	Bedford City	Bedford
116	48.9	Carlisle Local	Carlisle
116	48.9	Columbus City SD	Columbus
116	48.9	Fairview Park City	Fairview Park
116	48.9	Hubbard Exempted Village	Hubbard
116	48.9	Kent City	Kent
116	48.9	Madison Local	Mansfield
116	48.9	Mason City SD	Mason
116	48.9	Strongsville City	Strongsville
116	48.9	Tallmadge City	Tallmadge
116	48.9	Washington Local	Toledo
130	48.8	Bellevue City	Bellevue
130	48.8	Buckeye Valley Local	Delaware
130	48.8	Hamilton City	Hamilton
130	48.8	Harrison Hills City	Cadiz
130	48.8	Indian Lake Local	Lewistown
130	48.8	Little Miami Local	Maineville
130	48.8	Mentor Exempted Village	Mentor
130	48.8	Northeastern Local	Springfield
130	48.8	Poland Local	Poland
130	48.8	Rolling Hills Local	Cambridge
130	48.8	South-Western City	Grove City
130	48.8	Upper Arlington City	Upper Arlington
130	48.8	Western Brown Local	Mount Orab
130	48.8	Xenia Community City	Xenia
144	48.7	Cuyahoga Falls City	Cuyahoga Falls
144	48.7	Kenston Local	Chagrin Falls
144	48.7	London City	London
144	48.7	New Albany-Plain Local	New Albany
144	48.7	North Olmsted City	North Olmsted
144	48.7	Norwalk City	Norwalk
144	48.7	Olentangy Local	Lewis Center
144	48.7	Zanesville City	Zanesville
152	48.6	Chillicothe City	Chillicothe
152	48.6	Clear Fork Valley Local	Bellville
152	48.6	Lakeview Local	Cortland
152	48.6	Northridge Local	Dayton
152	48.6	Orange City	Cleveland
152	48.6	Pickerington Local	Pickerington
152	48.6	Princeton City	Cincinnati
152	48.6	Sheffield-Sheffield Lake City	Sheffield Vllg
152	48.6	Solon City	Solon
152	48.6	Urbana City	Urbana
152	48.6	Wapakoneta City	Wapakoneta
152	48.6	Westfall Local	Williamsport
164	48.5	Barberton City	Barberton
164	48.5	Cleveland Municipal	Cleveland
164	48.5	East Liverpool City	East Liverpool
164	48.5	Geneva Area City	Geneva
164	48.5	Green Local	Uniontown
164	48.5	Highland Local	Medina
164	48.5	Johnstown-Monroe Local	Johnstown
164	48.5	Logan-Hocking Local	Logan
164	48.5	Mad River Local	Dayton
164	48.5	New Lexington City	New Lexington
164	48.5	Stow-Munroe Falls City SD	Stow
164	48.5	Troy City	Troy
164	48.5	Vinton County Local	Mc Arthur
164	48.5	West Holmes Local	Millersburg
164	48.5	Wickliffe City	Wickliffe
179	48.4	Bloom-Carroll Local	Carroll
179	48.4	Canton City	Canton
179	48.4	Heath City	Heath
179	48.4	Lakewood Local	Hebron
179	48.4	Lorain City	Lorain
179	48.4	Mariemont City	Cincinnati
179	48.4	New Richmond Exempted Village	New Richmond
179	48.4	North Fork Local	Utica
179	48.4	Olmsted Falls City	Olmsted Falls
179	48.4	Perry Local	Massillon
179	48.4	Struthers City	Struthers
179	48.4	Sylvania City	Sylvania
179	48.4	Twinsburg City	Twinsburg
179	48.4	Woodridge Local	Peninsula
193	48.3	Dayton City	Dayton
193	48.3	Edgewood City	Trenton
193	48.3	Findlay City	Findlay
193	48.3	Hudson City	Hudson
193	48.3	Kettering City	Kettering
193	48.3	Lakewood City	Lakewood
193	48.3	Perrysburg Exempted Village	Perrysburg
193	48.3	Riverside Local	Painesville
193	48.3	Sidney City	Sidney
193	48.3	Sycamore Community City	Cincinnati
193	48.3	Vandalia-Butler City	Vandalia
193	48.3	West Geauga Local	Chesterland
193	48.3	Westerville City	Westerville
206	48.2	Benjamin Logan Local	Bellefontaine
206	48.2	Berea City	Berea
206	48.2	Bexley City	Bexley
206	48.2	Clermont Northeastern Local	Batavia
206	48.2	Fairless Local	Navarre
206	48.2	Lebanon City	Lebanon
206	48.2	Northwest Local	Cincinnati
206	48.2	Reading Community City	Reading
206	48.2	Southwest Licking Local	Pataskala
206	48.2	Tri-Valley Local	Dresden
206	48.2	Vermilion Local	Vermilion
217	48.1	Aurora City	Aurora
217	48.1	Celina City	Celina
217	48.1	Centerville City	Centerville
217	48.1	Elyria City Schools	Elyria
217	48.1	Fairfield Union Local	Lancaster
217	48.1	Field Local	Mogadore
217	48.1	Lima City	Lima
217	48.1	Maumee City	Maumee
217	48.1	Newark City	Newark
217	48.1	Niles City	Niles
217	48.1	North Canton City	North Canton
217	48.1	Salem City	Salem
217	48.1	Triway Local	Wooster
217	48.1	Trotwood-Madison City	Trotwood
217	48.1	Washington-Nile Local	West Portsmouth
217	48.1	West Carrollton City	West Carrollton
233	48.0	Beaver Local	Lisbon
233	48.0	Hilliard City	Hilliard
233	48.0	Ontario Local	Mansfield
233	48.0	Perkins Local	Sandusky
233	48.0	Ravenna City	Ravenna
233	48.0	Streetsboro City	Streetsboro
233	48.0	Upper Sandusky Exempted Village	Upper Sandusky
233	48.0	Wadsworth City	Wadsworth
241	47.9	Batavia Local	Batavia
241	47.9	Beavercreek City	Beavercreek
241	47.9	Bethel-Tate Local	Bethel
241	47.9	Brecksville-Broadview Hghts City	Brecksville
241	47.9	Greenfield Exempted Village	Greenfield
241	47.9	Licking Valley Local	Newark
241	47.0	Loveland City	Loveland
241	47.9	Teays Valley Local	Ashville
241	47.9	Tipp City Exempted Village	Tipp City
241	47.9	Washington CH City	Washington CH
251	47.8	Boardman Local	Youngstown
251	47.8	Bryan City	Bryan
251	47.8	Cloverleaf Local	Lodi
251	47.8	Fostoria City	Fostoria
251	47.8	Jefferson Area Local	Jefferson
251	47.8	Lancaster City	Lancaster
251	47.8	Orrville City	Orrville
251	47.8	Parma City	Parma
251	47.8	Portsmouth City	Portsmouth
251	47.8	Shelby City	Shelby
251	47.8	Southwest Local	Harrison
251	47.8	Wooster City	Wooster
263	47.7	Alexander Local	Albany
263	47.7	Eaton Community City	Eaton
263	47.7	Goshen Local	Goshen
263	47.7	Kenton City	Kenton
263	47.7	Kings Local	Kings Mills
263	47.7	Napoleon Area City	Napoleon
263	47.7	North Royalton City	North Royalton
263	47.7	Northern Local	Thornville
263	47.7	Shaker Heights City	Shaker Heights
263	47.7	Springfield City	Springfield
263	47.7	Tiffin City	Tiffin
263	47.7	West Clermont Local	Cincinnati
263	47.7	Whitehall City	Whitehall
276	47.6	Blanchester Local	Blanchester
276	47.6	Coshocton City	Coshocton
276	47.6	Greenville City	Greenville
276	47.6	Hamilton Local	Columbus
276	47.6	Marion City	Marion
276	47.6	Northmont City	Englewood
276	47.6	Piqua City	Piqua
276	47.6	River Valley Local	Caledonia
276	47.6	Ross Local	Hamilton
276	47.6	Saint Clairsville-Richland City	Saint Clairsville
276	47.6	Talawanda City	Oxford
276	47.6	Tecumseh Local	New Carlisle
276	47.6	Wheelersburg Local	Wheelersburg
289	47.5	Defiance City	Defiance
289	47.5	Dublin City	Dublin
289	47.5	Euclid City	Euclid
289	47.5	Marlington Local	Alliance
289	47.5	Milford Exempted Village	Milford
289	47.5	Toledo City	Toledo
295	47.4	Alliance City	Alliance
295	47.4	Buckeye Local	Medina
295	47.4	Copley-Fairlawn City	Copley
295	47.4	Jackson City	Jackson
295	47.4	Licking Heights Local	Pataskala
295	47.4	Revere Local	Bath
301	47.3	Gallipolis City	Gallipolis
301	47.3	Graham Local	Saint Paris
301	47.3	Groveport Madison Local	Groveport
301	47.3	Painesville City Local	Painesville
301	47.3	Rossford Exempted Village	Rossford
301	47.3	Willoughby-Eastlake City	Willoughby
307	47.2	Big Walnut Local	Galena
307	47.2	Elida Local	Elida
307	47.2	Huber Heights City	Huber Heights
307	47.2	Reynoldsburg City	Reynoldsburg
307	47.2	River View Local	Warsaw
312	47.1	Amanda-Clearcreek Local	Amanda
312	47.1	Clinton-Massie Local	Clarksville
312	47.1	Miami Trace Local	Washington CH
312	47.1	Waverly City	Waverly
312	47.1	Zane Trace Local	Chillicothe
317	47.0	Mt Healthy City	Cincinnati
318	46.9	Fairborn City	Fairborn
318	46.9	Lake Local	Uniontown
318	46.9	Marysville Exempted Village	Marysville
318	46.9	Springfield Local	Akron
322	46.8	Highland Local	Sparta
322	46.8	Three Rivers Local	Cleves
324	46.7	Claymont City	Dennison
324	46.7	Clyde-Green Springs Ex. Village	Clyde
324	46.7	Garfield Hgts City Schools	Garfield Hgts
327	46.6	Bellefontaine City	Bellefontaine
327	46.6	Coventry Local	Akron
327	46.6	Indian Valley Local Schools	Gnadenhutten
327	46.6	Maple Heights City	Maple Heights
327	46.6	Monroe Local SD	Monroe
327	46.6	Norwood City	Norwood
327	46.6	Warrensville Hgts City	Warrensville Hgts
334	46.5	Canton Local	Canton
334	46.5	Dover City	Dover
334	46.5	Massillon City	Massillon
334	46.5	Mayfield City	Mayfield Hgts
334	46.5	Otsego Local	Tontogany
339	46.4	Mansfield City	Mansfield
339	46.4	Southeast Local	Ravenna
341	46.3	Minford Local	Minford
341	46.3	N Ridgeville City	N Ridgeville
341	46.3	Saint Marys City	Saint Marys
344	46.1	Southeast Local	Apple Creek
345	46.0	Wauseon Exempted Village	Wauseon
346	45.6	Morgan Local	Mc Connelsville
347	45.2	North College Hill City	Cincinnati

Individual Education Program Students

Rank	Percent	District Name	City
1	27.3	Portsmouth City	Portsmouth

Note: This section only includes districts with 1,500 or more students; All categories are ranked from high to low

2	25.7	Coshocton City	Coshocton
3	24.5	Mansfield City	Mansfield
4	23.7	Lima City	Lima
5	23.3	Sidney City	Sidney
6	22.9	Cambridge City	Cambridge
6	22.9	Urbana City	Urbana
8	22.8	Gallipolis City	Gallipolis
9	22.7	Harrison Hills City	Cadiz
10	22.5	Youngstown City Schools	Youngstown
11	22.2	Paulding Exempted Village	Paulding
12	22.1	Marion City	Marion
13	21.9	Zanesville City	Zanesville
14	21.8	Claymont City	Dennison
15	21.5	Electronic Classroom of Tomorrow	Columbus
16	21.4	Port Clinton City	Port Clinton
16	21.4	Sandusky City	Sandusky
18	21.3	Ashtabula Area City	Ashtabula
18	21.3	Bucyrus City	Bucyrus
18	21.3	Cincinnati City	Cincinnati
18	21.3	Switzerland of Ohio Local	Woodsfield
22	21.2	Alexander Local	Albany
22	21.2	Cleveland Municipal	Cleveland
22	21.2	Napoleon Area City	Napoleon
25	21.0	East Liverpool City	East Liverpool
26	20.7	Rolling Hills Local	Cambridge
27	20.6	Galion City	Galion
27	20.6	Ravenna City	Ravenna
29	20.4	Warrensville Hgts City	Warrensville Hgts
30	20.1	Orrville City	Orrville
31	20.0	Lorain City	Lorain
31	20.0	Mt Healthy City	Cincinnati
33	19.9	Warren City	Warren
34	19.7	Fairless Local	Navarre
34	19.7	River View Local	Warsaw
34	19.7	Tiffin City	Tiffin
37	19.6	Defiance City	Defiance
38	19.5	Wellston City	Wellston
39	19.4	Clermont Northeastern Local	Batavia
40	19.3	Parma City	Parma
41	19.2	Akron City	Akron
41	19.2	Alliance City	Alliance
43	19.1	Van Wert City	Van Wert
44	18.9	West Holmes Local	Millersburg
45	18.8	Celina City	Celina
45	18.8	Conneaut Area City	Conneaut
45	18.8	Euclid City	Euclid
45	18.8	Saint Marys City	Saint Marys
45	18.8	Wooster City	Wooster
50	18.7	Goshen Local	Goshen
50	18.7	Middletown City	Middletown
52	18.6	Piqua City	Piqua
52	18.6	South Point Local	South Point
54	18.5	Dayton City	Dayton
54	18.5	Massillon City	Massillon
54	18.5	Maumee City	Maumee
54	18.5	Springfield Local	Akron
58	18.2	New Philadel. City	New Philadel.
59	18.1	Adams County/ohio Valley Local	West Union
59	18.1	Bellefontaine City	Bellefontaine
59	18.1	Logan Elm Local	Circleville
59	18.1	Southeast Local	Ravenna
63	18.0	Franklin City	Franklin
63	18.0	Greenville City	Greenville
63	18.0	Northwest Local	Mc Dermott
66	17.9	Gallia County Local	Gallipolis
66	17.9	Reading Community City	Reading
66	17.9	Springfield City	Springfield
66	17.9	Three Rivers Local	Cleves
66	17.9	Winton Woods City	Cincinnati
71	17.8	Cleveland Hgts-University Hgts City	University Hgts
72	17.7	Carrollton Exempted Village	Carrollton
72	17.7	Southwest Local	Harrison
74	17.6	Marietta City	Marietta
74	17.6	Mount Vernon City	Mount Vernon
74	17.6	Newark City	Newark
74	17.6	Vermilion Local	Vermilion
78	17.5	Columbus City SD	Columbus
79	17.3	Circleville City	Circleville
79	17.3	Elyria City Schools	Elyria
81	17.2	Bedford City	Bedford
81	17.2	Kenton City	Kenton
81	17.2	Washington CH City	Washington CH
84	17.1	Bryan City	Bryan
85	17.0	Athens City	The Plains
85	17.0	Findlay City	Findlay
85	17.0	Fremont City	Fremont
85	17.0	Hamilton City	Hamilton
85	17.0	Northwest Local	Canal Fulton
85	17.0	South Euclid-Lyndhurst City	Lyndhurst
85	17.0	Upper Sandusky Exempted Village	Upper Sandusky
92	16.9	Alternative Education Academy	Toledo
92	16.9	Springfield Local	Holland
94	16.8	Barberton City	Barberton
94	16.8	Edgewood City	Trenton
94	16.8	Marysville Exempted Village	Marysville
97	16.7	Canton City	Canton
97	16.7	Fostoria City	Fostoria
97	16.7	North Fork Local	Utica
100	16.6	Beaver Local	Lisbon
100	16.6	Bellevue City	Bellevue
100	16.6	Clyde-Green Springs Ex. Village	Clyde
100	16.6	Minerva Local	Minerva
100	16.6	Norwood City	Norwood
100	16.6	Vinton County Local	Mc Arthur
106	16.5	Northwest Local	Cincinnati
107	16.4	Amherst Exempted Village	Amherst
107	16.4	East Cleveland City SD	East Cleveland
107	16.4	Hudson City	Hudson
107	16.4	Indian Creek Local	Wintersville
111	16.3	Edison Local	Hammondsville
111	16.3	Logan-Hocking Local	Logan
113	16.2	Benton Carroll Salem Local	Oak Harbor
113	16.2	Groveport Madison Local	Groveport
113	16.2	Meigs Local	Pomeroy
113	16.2	New Richmond Exempted Village	New Richmond
113	16.2	North College Hill City	Cincinnati
118	16.1	Marlington Local	Alliance
118	16.1	Xenia Community City	Xenia
120	16.0	Fairland Local	Proctorville
121	15.9	Lakewood Local	Hebron
121	15.9	Treca Digital Academy	Marion
121	15.9	Waverly City	Waverly
124	15.8	Kettering City	Kettering
124	15.8	Westlake City	Westlake
124	15.8	Willard City	Willard
127	15.7	Indian Valley Local Schools	Gnadenhutten
127	15.7	Shelby City	Shelby
127	15.7	Southeast Local	Apple Creek
130	15.6	Dover City	Dover
131	15.5	Buckeye Local	Dillonvale
131	15.5	Huber Heights City	Huber Heights
131	15.5	Wapakoneta City	Wapakoneta
134	15.4	Lancaster City	Lancaster
134	15.4	Vandalia-Butler City	Vandalia
136	15.3	Clear Fork Valley Local	Bellville
136	15.3	Graham Local	Saint Paris
136	15.3	Princeton City	Cincinnati
136	15.3	Tri-Valley Local	Dresden
136	15.3	Washington-Nile Local	West Portsmouth
141	15.2	Jackson City	Jackson
141	15.2	Oak Hills Local	Cincinnati
141	15.2	Southwest Licking Local	Pataskala
144	15.1	Ashland City	Ashland
144	15.1	Girard City SD	Girard
144	15.1	New Lexington City	New Lexington
144	15.1	West Clermont Local	Cincinnati
148	15.0	Benjamin Logan Local	Bellefontaine
148	15.0	Geneva Area City	Geneva
148	15.0	Niles City	Niles
148	15.0	Streetsboro City	Streetsboro
152	14.9	Batavia Local	Batavia
152	14.9	Salem City	Salem
152	14.9	Struthers City	Struthers
152	14.9	Western Brown Local	Mount Orab
156	14.8	Cuyahoga Falls City	Cuyahoga Falls
156	14.8	West Carrollton City	West Carrollton
158	14.7	Berea City	Berea
158	14.7	Delaware City	Delaware
158	14.7	Garfield Hgts City Schools	Garfield Hgts
158	14.7	Indian Lake Local	Lewistown
162	14.6	Fairborn City	Fairborn
162	14.6	Franklin Local	Duncan Falls
162	14.6	Miamisburg City	Miamisburg
162	14.6	South-Western City	Grove City
162	14.6	Tecumseh Local	New Carlisle
162	14.6	Trotwood-Madison City	Trotwood
162	14.6	Whitehall City	Whitehall
169	14.5	Austintown Local	Youngstown
169	14.5	Maysville Local	Zanesville
169	14.5	Northmont City	Englewood
169	14.5	Steubenville City	Steubenville
173	14.4	Miami Trace Local	Washington CH
173	14.4	Painesville City Local	Painesville
173	14.4	Plain Local	Canton
173	14.4	Tipp City Exempted Village	Tipp City
177	14.3	Beavercreek City	Beavercreek
177	14.3	Boardman Local	Youngstown
177	14.3	Milford Exempted Village	Milford
177	14.3	Toledo City	Toledo
177	14.3	Willoughby-Eastlake City	Willoughby
182	14.2	Madison Local	Mansfield
182	14.2	North Olmsted City	North Olmsted
182	14.2	Reynoldsburg City	Reynoldsburg
185	14.1	Buckeye Local	Ashtabula
185	14.1	Gahanna-Jefferson City	Gahanna
187	14.0	Bay Village City	Bay Village
187	14.0	Maple Heights City	Maple Heights
187	14.0	Shaker Heights City	Shaker Heights
190	13.9	Jefferson Area Local	Jefferson
190	13.9	Lakewood City	Lakewood
190	13.9	Mayfield City	Mayfield Hgts
190	13.9	N Ridgeville City	N Ridgeville
194	13.8	Cloverleaf Local	Lodi
194	13.8	East Muskingum Local	New Concord
194	13.8	Lexington Local	Lexington
194	13.8	Orange City	Cleveland
198	13.7	Morgan Local	Mc Connelsville
199	13.6	Bowling Green City SD	Bowling Green
199	13.6	Northern Local	Thornville
199	13.6	Norwalk City	Norwalk
199	13.6	Westerville City	Westerville
203	13.5	Lake Local	Millbury
203	13.5	Otsego Local	Tontogany
203	13.5	Washington Local	Toledo
203	13.5	Wickliffe City	Wickliffe
203	13.5	Zane Trace Local	Chillicothe
208	13.4	Field Local	Mogadore
208	13.4	Medina City SD	Medina
208	13.4	Sylvania City	Sylvania
208	13.4	West Geauga Local	Chesterland
208	13.4	Woodridge Local	Peninsula
213	13.2	Chillicothe City	Chillicothe
213	13.2	Crestwood Local	Mantua
213	13.2	Kings Local	Kings Mills
216	13.1	Canal Wnchstr Local	Canal Wnchstr
216	13.1	Green Local	Uniontown
216	13.1	Hillsboro City	Hillsboro
216	13.1	Little Miami Local	Maineville
216	13.1	Mentor Exempted Village	Mentor
221	13.0	Centerville City	Centerville
221	13.0	Wilmington City	Wilmington
223	12.9	Beachwood City	Beachwood
223	12.9	Northridge Local	Dayton
225	12.8	Olmsted Falls City	Olmsted Falls
225	12.8	West Branch Local	Beloit
227	12.7	Big Walnut Local	Galena
227	12.7	Blanchester Local	Blanchester
227	12.7	Edison Local (Formerly Berlin-Milan)	Milan
227	12.7	Fairview Park City	Fairview Park
227	12.7	Kent City	Kent
227	12.7	Mad River Local	Dayton
227	12.7	Rocky River City	Rocky River
234	12.6	Chardon Local	Chardon
234	12.6	Ottawa-Glandorf Local	Ottawa
234	12.6	Sheffield-Sheffield Lake City	Sheffield Vllg
234	12.6	Troy City	Troy
238	12.5	Fairfield City	Fairfield
238	12.5	Lebanon City	Lebanon
238	12.5	Pickerington Local	Pickerington
238	12.5	Springboro Community City	Springboro
238	12.5	Tallmadge City	Tallmadge
238	12.5	Valley View Local	Germantown
244	12.4	Canton Local	Canton
244	12.4	Coventry Local	Akron
244	12.4	Granville Exempted Village	Granville
244	12.4	Rossford Exempted Village	Rossford
244	12.4	Triway Local	Wooster
249	12.3	Eaton Community City	Eaton
249	12.3	Sycamore Community City	Cincinnati
249	12.3	Teays Valley Local	Ashville
252	12.2	Highland Local	Sparta
252	12.2	Hilliard City	Hilliard

Note: This section only includes districts with 1,500 or more students; All categories are ranked from high to low

252	12.2	Ohio Virtual Academy	Maumee
255	12.1	Bethel-Tate Local	Bethel
255	12.1	Keystone Local	Lagrange
257	12.0	Avon Local	Avon
257	12.0	Minford Local	Minford
259	11.9	Highland Local	Medina
259	11.9	Johnstown-Monroe Local	Johnstown
259	11.9	Lakeview Local	Cortland
259	11.9	Perkins Local	Sandusky
263	11.8	Louisville City	Louisville
263	11.8	Worthington City	Worthington
265	11.7	Bath Local	Lima
265	11.7	Lake Local	Uniontown
265	11.7	Loveland City	Loveland
265	11.7	Northwestern Local	Springfield
265	11.7	Westfall Local	Williamsport
270	11.6	London City	London
270	11.6	Riverside Local	Painesville
272	11.5	Wadsworth City	Wadsworth
273	11.4	Brunswick City	Brunswick
273	11.4	Buckeye Valley Local	Delaware
273	11.4	Chagrin Falls Exempted Village	Chagrin Falls
273	11.4	Clinton-Massie Local	Clarksville
273	11.4	East Holmes Local	Berlin
273	11.4	North Canton City	North Canton
273	11.4	Warren Local	Vincent
280	11.3	Saint Clairsville-Richland City	Saint Clairsville
280	11.3	Wheelersburg Local	Wheelersburg
282	11.2	Elida Local	Elida
282	11.2	Howland Local	Warren
282	11.2	Midview Local	Grafton
282	11.2	Oakwood City	Dayton
282	11.2	Oregon City	Oregon
282	11.2	Perry Local	Massillon
282	11.2	River Valley Local	Caledonia
289	11.1	Madison Local	Middletown
289	11.1	Stow-Munroe Falls City SD	Stow
291	11.0	Carlisle Local	Carlisle
291	11.0	Monroe Local SD	Monroe
291	11.0	Perry Local	Perry
294	10.9	Clark-Shawnee Local	Springfield
294	10.9	Hamilton Local	Columbus
296	10.8	Copley-Fairlawn City	Copley
296	10.8	Licking Heights Local	Pataskala
298	10.7	Buckeye Local	Medina
298	10.7	Canfield Local	Canfield
298	10.7	Hubbard Exempted Village	Hubbard
298	10.7	Ross Local	Hamilton
302	10.6	Fairfield Union Local	Lancaster
302	10.6	Greenfield Exempted Village	Greenfield
302	10.6	Mariemont City	Cincinnati
302	10.6	New Albany-Plain Local	New Albany
306	10.5	Clearview Local	Lorain
306	10.5	Jonathan Alder Local	Plain City
308	10.4	Olentangy Local	Lewis Center
308	10.4	Union-Scioto Local	Chillicothe
310	10.3	Forest Hills Local	Cincinnati
310	10.3	Perrysburg Exempted Village	Perrysburg
310	10.3	Solon City	Solon
310	10.3	Strongsville City	Strongsville
314	10.2	Bellbrook-Sugarcreek Local SD	Bellbrook
314	10.2	Bloom-Carroll Local	Carroll
314	10.2	Brecksville-Broadview Hghts City	Brecksville
314	10.2	Ohio Connections Academy Inc	Cleveland
314	10.2	Ontario Local	Mansfield
319	10.1	Indian Hill Exempted Village	Cincinnati
320	10.0	Avon Lake City	Avon Lake
320	10.0	Firelands Local	South Amherst
320	10.0	North Royalton City	North Royalton
323	9.8	Eastwood Local	Pemberville
323	9.8	Heath City	Heath
323	9.8	Lakota Local	Liberty Twp
323	9.8	Nordonia Hills City	Northfield
327	9.7	Norton City	Norton
327	9.7	Wauseon Exempted Village	Wauseon
329	9.6	Jackson Local	Massillon
329	9.6	Upper Arlington City	Upper Arlington
331	9.5	Anthony Wayne Local	Whitehouse
331	9.5	Bexley City	Bexley
331	9.5	Greenon Local	Enon
331	9.5	Madison Local	Madison
331	9.5	Talawanda City	Oxford
336	9.4	Kenston Local	Chagrin Falls
337	9.3	Amanda-Clearcreek Local	Amanda
337	9.3	Aurora City	Aurora
337	9.3	Dublin City	Dublin
340	9.1	Poland Local	Poland
341	9.0	Licking Valley Local	Newark
341	9.0	Mason City SD	Mason
343	8.9	Northeastern Local	Springfield
343	8.9	Twinsburg City	Twinsburg
345	8.5	Shawnee Local	Lima
346	8.4	Revere Local	Bath
347	8.2	Wyoming City	Wyoming

English Language Learner Students

Rank	Percent	District Name	City
1	36.8	East Holmes Local	Berlin
2	27.5	Painesville City Local	Painesville
3	14.3	Whitehall City	Whitehall
4	12.6	Southeast Local	Apple Creek
5	12.3	Princeton City	Cincinnati
6	11.8	South-Western City	Grove City
7	9.8	Columbus City SD	Columbus
8	8.5	Winton Woods City	Cincinnati
9	8.1	Dublin City	Dublin
10	8.0	Westerville City	Westerville
11	7.7	Lakewood City	Lakewood
11	7.7	Licking Heights Local	Pataskala
13	6.8	Hilliard City	Hilliard
14	6.2	Willard City	Willard
15	6.1	Cleveland Municipal	Cleveland
16	5.6	North Olmsted City	North Olmsted
17	5.3	Reynoldsburg City	Reynoldsburg
18	5.2	Ashtabula Area City	Ashtabula
18	5.2	Fremont City	Fremont
20	5.0	Fairfield City	Fairfield
20	5.0	Lakota Local	Liberty Twp
20	5.0	Norwood City	Norwood
23	4.8	West Carrollton City	West Carrollton
23	4.8	Worthington City	Worthington
25	4.7	Hamilton City	Hamilton
26	4.6	Fairview Park City	Fairview Park
27	4.5	Sycamore Community City	Cincinnati
28	4.4	Tecumseh Local	New Carlisle
29	4.1	Beachwood City	Beachwood
29	4.1	Copley-Fairlawn City	Copley
31	3.9	Cincinnati City	Cincinnati
31	3.9	Lorain City	Lorain
31	3.9	Westlake City	Westlake
34	3.8	Akron City	Akron
34	3.8	Middletown City	Middletown
36	3.7	Norwalk City	Norwalk
37	3.6	Youngstown City Schools	Youngstown
38	3.4	Mayfield City	Mayfield Hgts
38	3.4	Perry Local	Perry
40	3.2	Dayton City	Dayton
40	3.2	Monroe Local SD	Monroe
40	3.2	Orrville City	Orrville
43	3.1	Mason City SD	Mason
43	3.1	Solon City	Solon
45	3.0	Groveport Madison Local	Groveport
45	3.0	New Philadel. City	New Philadel.
47	2.9	Huber Heights City	Huber Heights
48	2.8	Geneva Area City	Geneva
48	2.8	Pickerington Local	Pickerington
48	2.8	Talawanda City	Oxford
51	2.7	Marlington Local	Alliance
51	2.7	North Royalton City	North Royalton
51	2.7	Strongsville City	Strongsville
54	2.6	Shaker Heights City	Shaker Heights
55	2.5	Gahanna-Jefferson City	Gahanna
55	2.5	Twinsburg City	Twinsburg
57	2.3	Canal Wnchstr Local	Canal Wnchstr
57	2.3	Northwest Local	Cincinnati
57	2.3	Rocky River City	Rocky River
57	2.3	Wauseon Exempted Village	Wauseon
61	2.2	Beavercreek City	Beavercreek
61	2.2	Dover City	Dover
61	2.2	Kings Local	Kings Mills
61	2.2	New Albany-Plain Local	New Albany
65	2.1	Boardman Local	Youngstown
65	2.1	Woodridge Local	Peninsula
67	2.0	Fostoria City	Fostoria
67	2.0	Sidney City	Sidney
69	1.9	Athens City	The Plains
69	1.9	Centerville City	Centerville
69	1.9	Parma City	Parma
69	1.9	Riverside Local	Painesville
73	1.8	Brecksville-Broadview Hghts City	Brecksville
73	1.8	Lebanon City	Lebanon
73	1.8	Olentangy Local	Lewis Center
73	1.8	Sylvania City	Sylvania
73	1.8	Tipp City Exempted Village	Tipp City
73	1.8	Willoughby-Eastlake City	Willoughby
79	1.7	Avon Local	Avon
79	1.7	Northmont City	Englewood
81	1.6	Kettering City	Kettering
81	1.6	Troy City	Troy
81	1.6	Upper Sandusky Exempted Village	Upper Sandusky
84	1.5	Cuyahoga Falls City	Cuyahoga Falls
84	1.5	Granville Exempted Village	Granville
84	1.5	Mentor Exempted Village	Mentor
87	1.4	Bellbrook-Sugarcreek Local SD	Bellbrook
87	1.4	Cleveland Hgts-University Hgts City	University Hgts
87	1.4	Maumee City	Maumee
87	1.4	Miamisburg City	Miamisburg
87	1.4	Springfield City	Springfield
87	1.4	Tallmadge City	Tallmadge
87	1.4	Toledo City	Toledo
94	1.3	Bedford City	Bedford
94	1.3	Berea City	Berea
94	1.3	Fairborn City	Fairborn
94	1.3	Findlay City	Findlay
94	1.3	Lake Local	Millbury
94	1.3	Springfield Local	Holland
94	1.3	Upper Arlington City	Upper Arlington
94	1.3	Washington Local	Toledo
102	1.2	Field Local	Mogadore
102	1.2	Marion City	Marion
102	1.2	N Ridgeville City	N Ridgeville
102	1.2	Salem City	Salem
102	1.2	South Euclid-Lyndhurst City	Lyndhurst
102	1.2	West Clermont Local	Cincinnati
108	1.1	Bowling Green City SD	Bowling Green
108	1.1	Clearview Local	Lorain
108	1.1	Coventry Local	Akron
108	1.1	Elyria City Schools	Elyria
108	1.1	Madison Local	Madison
108	1.1	Milford Exempted Village	Milford
108	1.1	Mt Healthy City	Cincinnati
108	1.1	Napoleon Area City	Napoleon
108	1.1	Nordonia Hills City	Northfield
108	1.1	Ottawa-Glandorf Local	Ottawa
108	1.1	Sandusky City	Sandusky
108	1.1	Triway Local	Wooster
120	1.0	Bexley City	Bexley
120	1.0	Delaware City	Delaware
120	1.0	Highland Local	Medina
120	1.0	Jonathan Alder Local	Plain City
120	1.0	Loveland City	Loveland
120	1.0	Revere Local	Bath
120	1.0	Streetsboro City	Streetsboro
127	0.9	Eaton Community City	Eaton
127	0.9	Johnstown-Monroe Local	Johnstown
127	0.9	Kent City	Kent
127	0.9	Lexington Local	Lexington
127	0.9	London City	London
127	0.9	North College Hill City	Cincinnati
127	0.9	Ontario Local	Mansfield
127	0.9	Orange City	Cleveland
127	0.9	Perrysburg Exempted Village	Perrysburg
127	0.9	Stow-Munroe Falls City SD	Stow
127	0.9	Wilmington City	Wilmington
127	0.9	Wooster City	Wooster
139	0.8	Austintown Local	Youngstown
139	0.8	Bellefontaine City	Bellefontaine
139	0.8	Canton City	Canton
139	0.8	Chagrin Falls Exempted Village	Chagrin Falls
139	0.8	Green Local	Uniontown
139	0.8	Hudson City	Hudson
139	0.8	Indian Hill Exempted Village	Cincinnati
139	0.8	Little Miami Local	Maineville
139	0.8	Mad River Local	Dayton
139	0.8	Mount Vernon City	Mount Vernon
139	0.8	Vandalia-Butler City	Vandalia
150	0.7	Bath Local	Lima
150	0.7	Brunswick City	Brunswick
150	0.7	Coshocton City	Coshocton
150	0.7	Defiance City	Defiance

Note: This section only includes districts with 1,500 or more students; All categories are ranked from high to low

150	0.7	Edison Local (Formerly Berlin-Milan)	Milan
150	0.7	Forest Hills Local	Cincinnati
150	0.7	Goshen Local	Goshen
150	0.7	Hamilton Local	Columbus
150	0.7	Jackson Local	Massillon
150	0.7	Lake Local	Uniontown
150	0.7	Perry Local	Massillon
150	0.7	Plain Local	Canton
150	0.7	West Geauga Local	Chesterland
163	0.6	Aurora City	Aurora
163	0.6	Avon Lake City	Avon Lake
163	0.6	Bucyrus City	Bucyrus
163	0.6	Celina City	Celina
163	0.6	Chardon Local	Chardon
163	0.6	Garfield Hgts City Schools	Garfield Hgts
163	0.6	Greenville City	Greenville
163	0.6	Heath City	Heath
163	0.6	Marysville Exempted Village	Marysville
163	0.6	Miami Trace Local	Washington CH
163	0.6	Reading Community City	Reading
163	0.6	Springfield Local	Akron
175	0.5	Amherst Exempted Village	Amherst
175	0.5	Ashland City	Ashland
175	0.5	Barberton City	Barberton
175	0.5	Batavia Local	Batavia
175	0.5	Elida Local	Elida
175	0.5	Euclid City	Euclid
175	0.5	Mariemont City	Cincinnati
175	0.5	North Canton City	North Canton
175	0.5	Northwest Local	Canal Fulton
175	0.5	Norton City	Norton
175	0.5	Oregon City	Oregon
175	0.5	Perkins Local	Sandusky
175	0.5	Poland Local	Poland
175	0.5	Southwest Licking Local	Pataskala
175	0.5	Westfall Local	Williamsport
175	0.5	Wyoming City	Wyoming
175	0.5	Xenia Community City	Xenia
192	0.4	Alliance City	Alliance
192	0.4	Bay Village City	Bay Village
192	0.4	Big Walnut Local	Galena
192	0.4	Buckeye Local	Ashtabula
192	0.4	Buckeye Valley Local	Delaware
192	0.4	Howland Local	Warren
192	0.4	Mansfield City	Mansfield
192	0.4	Massillon City	Massillon
192	0.4	Medina City SD	Medina
192	0.4	Midview Local	Grafton
192	0.4	Olmsted Falls City	Olmsted Falls
192	0.4	Ravenna City	Ravenna
192	0.4	River Valley Local	Caledonia
192	0.4	Springboro Community City	Springboro
192	0.4	Tiffin City	Tiffin
192	0.4	Valley View Local	Germantown
192	0.4	West Holmes Local	Millersburg
192	0.4	Wickliffe City	Wickliffe
210	0.3	Anthony Wayne Local	Whitehouse
210	0.3	Bryan City	Bryan
210	0.3	Cambridge City	Cambridge
210	0.3	Canfield Local	Canfield
210	0.3	Clyde-Green Springs Ex. Village	Clyde
210	0.3	Conneaut Area City	Conneaut
210	0.3	Kenston Local	Chagrin Falls
210	0.3	Lakeview Local	Cortland
210	0.3	Lima City	Lima
210	0.3	Maple Heights City	Maple Heights
210	0.3	Newark City	Newark
210	0.3	Niles City	Niles
210	0.3	Piqua City	Piqua
210	0.3	Ross Local	Hamilton
210	0.3	Rossford Exempted Village	Rossford
210	0.3	Saint Marys City	Saint Marys
210	0.3	Southwest Local	Harrison
210	0.3	Three Rivers Local	Cleves
210	0.3	Treca Digital Academy	Marion
210	0.3	Trotwood-Madison City	Trotwood
210	0.3	Van Wert City	Van Wert
210	0.3	Wapakoneta City	Wapakoneta
210	0.3	Washington CH City	Washington CH
233	0.2	Canton Local	Canton
233	0.2	Clear Fork Valley Local	Bellville
233	0.2	Crestwood Local	Mantua
233	0.2	East Cleveland City SD	East Cleveland
233	0.2	Edgewood City	Trenton
233	0.2	Franklin City	Franklin
233	0.2	Galion City	Galion
233	0.2	Greenon Local	Enon
233	0.2	Hillsboro City	Hillsboro
233	0.2	Lancaster City	Lancaster
233	0.2	Louisville City	Louisville
233	0.2	Madison Local	Mansfield
233	0.2	Northridge Local	Dayton
233	0.2	Port Clinton City	Port Clinton
233	0.2	Saint Clairsville-Richland City	Saint Clairsville
233	0.2	Shawnee Local	Lima
233	0.2	South Point Local	South Point
233	0.2	Struthers City	Struthers
233	0.2	Union-Scioto Local	Chillicothe
233	0.2	Vermilion Local	Vermilion
233	0.2	Wadsworth City	Wadsworth
233	0.2	Warren City	Warren
233	0.2	Warrensville Hgts City	Warrensville Hgts
256	0.1	Bethel-Tate Local	Bethel
256	0.1	Buckeye Local	Dillonvale
256	0.1	Carrollton Exempted Village	Carrollton
256	0.1	Chillicothe City	Chillicothe
256	0.1	Circleville City	Circleville
256	0.1	Clark-Shawnee Local	Springfield
256	0.1	Claymont City	Dennison
256	0.1	Clinton-Massie Local	Clarksville
256	0.1	Cloverleaf Local	Lodi
256	0.1	Electronic Classroom of Tomorrow	Columbus
256	0.1	Fairfield Union Local	Lancaster
256	0.1	Fairland Local	Proctorville
256	0.1	Firelands Local	South Amherst
256	0.1	Highland Local	Sparta
256	0.1	Hubbard Exempted Village	Hubbard
256	0.1	Indian Lake Local	Lewistown
256	0.1	Marietta City	Marietta
256	0.1	Minerva Local	Minerva
256	0.1	New Lexington City	New Lexington
256	0.1	New Richmond Exempted Village	New Richmond
256	0.1	Northwestern Local	Springfield
256	0.1	Oak Hills Local	Cincinnati
256	0.1	Ohio Virtual Academy	Maumee
256	0.1	Portsmouth City	Portsmouth
256	0.1	Sheffield-Sheffield Lake City	Sheffield Vllg
256	0.1	Steubenville City	Steubenville
256	0.1	Teays Valley Local	Ashville
256	0.1	West Branch Local	Beloit
256	0.1	Zanesville City	Zanesville
285	0.0	Adams County/ohio Valley Local	West Union
285	0.0	Alexander Local	Albany
285	0.0	Alternative Education Academy	Toledo
285	0.0	Amanda-Clearcreek Local	Amanda
285	0.0	Beaver Local	Lisbon
285	0.0	Bellevue City	Bellevue
285	0.0	Benjamin Logan Local	Bellefontaine
285	0.0	Benton Carroll Salem Local	Oak Harbor
285	0.0	Blanchester Local	Blanchester
285	0.0	Bloom-Carroll Local	Carroll
285	0.0	Buckeye Local	Medina
285	0.0	Carlisle Local	Carlisle
285	0.0	Clermont Northeastern Local	Batavia
285	0.0	East Liverpool City	East Liverpool
285	0.0	East Muskingum Local	New Concord
285	0.0	Eastwood Local	Pemberville
285	0.0	Edison Local	Hammondsville
285	0.0	Fairless Local	Navarre
285	0.0	Franklin Local	Duncan Falls
285	0.0	Gallia County Local	Gallipolis
285	0.0	Gallipolis City	Gallipolis
285	0.0	Girard City SD	Girard
285	0.0	Graham Local	Saint Paris
285	0.0	Greenfield Exempted Village	Greenfield
285	0.0	Harrison Hills City	Cadiz
285	0.0	Indian Creek Local	Wintersville
285	0.0	Indian Valley Local Schools	Gnadenhutten
285	0.0	Jackson City	Jackson
285	0.0	Jefferson Area Local	Jefferson
285	0.0	Kenton City	Kenton
285	0.0	Keystone Local	Lagrange
285	0.0	Lakewood Local	Hebron
285	0.0	Licking Valley Local	Newark
285	0.0	Logan Elm Local	Circleville
285	0.0	Logan-Hocking Local	Logan
285	0.0	Madison Local	Middletown
285	0.0	Maysville Local	Zanesville
285	0.0	Meigs Local	Pomeroy
285	0.0	Minford Local	Minford
285	0.0	Morgan Local	Mc Connelsville
285	0.0	North Fork Local	Utica
285	0.0	Northeastern Local	Springfield
285	0.0	Northern Local	Thornville
285	0.0	Northwest Local	Mc Dermott
285	0.0	Oakwood City	Dayton
285	0.0	Ohio Connections Academy Inc	Cleveland
285	0.0	Otsego Local	Tontogany
285	0.0	Paulding Exempted Village	Paulding
285	0.0	River View Local	Warsaw
285	0.0	Rolling Hills Local	Cambridge
285	0.0	Shelby City	Shelby
285	0.0	Southeast Local	Ravenna
285	0.0	Switzerland of Ohio Local	Woodsfield
285	0.0	Tri-Valley Local	Dresden
285	0.0	Urbana City	Urbana
285	0.0	Vinton County Local	Mc Arthur
285	0.0	Warren Local	Vincent
285	0.0	Washington-Nile Local	West Portsmouth
285	0.0	Waverly City	Waverly
285	0.0	Wellston City	Wellston
285	0.0	Western Brown Local	Mount Orab
285	0.0	Wheelersburg Local	Wheelersburg
285	0.0	Zane Trace Local	Chillicothe

Students Eligible for Free Lunch

Rank	Percent	District Name	City
1	90.3	East Cleveland City SD	East Cleveland
2	85.4	Northridge Local	Dayton
3	85.1	Youngstown City Schools	Youngstown
4	81.2	Lima City	Lima
5	80.3	Cleveland Municipal	Cleveland
6	78.3	Portsmouth City	Portsmouth
7	77.4	Painesville City Local	Painesville
8	76.3	Mansfield City	Mansfield
9	76.2	Warren City	Warren
10	74.8	Lorain City	Lorain
11	73.7	Springfield City	Springfield
11	73.7	Zanesville City	Zanesville
13	72.9	Canton City	Canton
14	71.9	Trotwood-Madison City	Trotwood
15	71.4	Whitehall City	Whitehall
16	70.4	Mt Healthy City	Cincinnati
17	69.1	Fostoria City	Fostoria
18	68.8	Columbus City SD	Columbus
19	68.4	Sandusky City	Sandusky
20	67.7	Dayton City	Dayton
21	67.0	Alliance City	Alliance
22	66.9	Clearview Local	Lorain
23	65.6	Marion City	Marion
24	65.0	Toledo City	Toledo
25	64.8	Euclid City	Euclid
26	63.9	East Liverpool City	East Liverpool
27	63.5	Cincinnati City	Cincinnati
27	63.5	Massillon City	Massillon
29	62.4	Northwest Local	Mc Dermott
30	62.0	Coshocton City	Coshocton
31	61.8	Akron City	Akron
32	61.1	Hamilton City	Hamilton
33	60.6	Barberton City	Barberton
34	59.8	Ashtabula Area City	Ashtabula
35	59.2	Vinton County Local	Mc Arthur
36	58.9	Ravenna City	Ravenna
37	58.3	Groveport Madison Local	Groveport
38	58.0	Niles City	Niles
39	57.8	Washington-Nile Local	West Portsmouth
40	57.0	Wellston City	Wellston
41	56.7	Middletown City	Middletown
42	56.6	Elyria City Schools	Elyria
43	56.5	Bucyrus City	Bucyrus
43	56.5	Goshen Local	Goshen
45	56.4	Struthers City	Struthers
46	56.1	Circleville City	Circleville
47	56.0	Cambridge City	Cambridge
48	55.5	Princeton City	Cincinnati
49	54.7	Gallia County Local	Gallipolis
49	54.7	New Lexington City	New Lexington
51	54.5	Winton Woods City	Cincinnati
52	54.4	Bedford City	Bedford
52	54.4	Cleveland Hgts-University Hgts City	University Hgts

Note: This section only includes districts with 1,500 or more students; All categories are ranked from high to low

52	54.4	Piqua City	Piqua
52	54.4	Rolling Hills Local	Cambridge
56	54.3	Norwood City	Norwood
57	54.2	Garfield Hgts City Schools	Garfield Hgts
58	53.9	Steubenville City	Steubenville
59	53.8	Chillicothe City	Chillicothe
60	53.7	South Point Local	South Point
61	52.9	West Carrollton City	West Carrollton
62	52.6	Hamilton Local	Columbus
63	52.4	Madison Local	Mansfield
64	52.0	Buckeye Local	Dillonvale
65	51.9	Newark City	Newark
66	51.6	Conneaut Area City	Conneaut
66	51.6	North College Hill City	Cincinnati
68	51.3	Tecumseh Local	New Carlisle
69	51.0	Fremont City	Fremont
70	50.8	Willard City	Willard
71	50.4	Lakewood City	Lakewood
72	50.0	Meigs Local	Pomeroy
73	49.7	Girard City SD	Girard
74	49.5	Fairborn City	Fairborn
74	49.5	Kenton City	Kenton
74	49.5	Washington CH City	Washington CH
77	49.3	Claymont City	Dennison
77	49.3	Harrison Hills City	Cadiz
79	48.9	Jackson City	Jackson
80	48.7	Minerva Local	Minerva
80	48.7	Sidney City	Sidney
82	48.4	Wilmington City	Wilmington
83	48.3	Galion City	Galion
83	48.3	Morgan Local	Mc Connelsville
85	48.1	Indian Creek Local	Wintersville
85	48.1	Springfield Local	Akron
87	48.0	Lancaster City	Lancaster
88	47.9	Logan-Hocking Local	Logan
89	47.8	Urbana City	Urbana
90	47.4	Mad River Local	Dayton
91	47.2	Defiance City	Defiance
92	46.9	Adams County/ohio Valley Local	West Union
93	46.5	Union-Scioto Local	Chillicothe
94	46.0	Indian Lake Local	Lewistown
95	45.9	Mount Vernon City	Mount Vernon
96	45.8	Bellefontaine City	Bellefontaine
96	45.8	South-Western City	Grove City
98	45.4	Gallipolis City	Gallipolis
99	45.3	Washington Local	Toledo
99	45.3	Xenia Community City	Xenia
101	45.2	Norwalk City	Norwalk
102	44.8	River View Local	Warsaw
103	44.1	Batavia Local	Batavia
104	43.9	Canton Local	Canton
104	43.9	Western Brown Local	Mount Orab
106	43.8	Fairland Local	Proctorville
107	43.5	Miami Trace Local	Washington CH
108	43.3	Beaver Local	Lisbon
109	42.9	New Richmond Exempted Village	New Richmond
110	42.8	Marietta City	Marietta
111	42.7	Buckeye Local	Ashtabula
111	42.7	Orrville City	Orrville
111	42.7	Waverly City	Waverly
114	42.4	Lake Local	Millbury
114	42.4	Reading Community City	Reading
116	42.1	Clear Fork Valley Local	Bellville
117	41.9	Edison Local	Hammondsville
117	41.9	Salem City	Salem
119	41.7	Switzerland of Ohio Local	Woodsfield
120	41.6	Port Clinton City	Port Clinton
121	41.4	Paulding Exempted Village	Paulding
121	41.4	Wooster City	Wooster
123	41.3	Franklin Local	Duncan Falls
124	41.1	Sheffield-Sheffield Lake City	Sheffield Vllg
125	41.0	London City	London
126	40.9	Blanchester Local	Blanchester
126	40.9	Maysville Local	Zanesville
128	40.8	Carrollton Exempted Village	Carrollton
129	40.5	Clermont Northeastern Local	Batavia
130	40.0	Minford Local	Minford
131	39.8	Elida Local	Elida
132	39.7	Austintown Local	Youngstown
133	39.6	Athens City	The Plains
133	39.6	Northwest Local	Cincinnati
135	39.5	Westfall Local	Williamsport
136	39.4	Lakewood Local	Hebron
137	39.2	Tri-Valley Local	Dresden
138	39.1	South Euclid-Lyndhurst City	Lyndhurst
139	39.0	Rossford Exempted Village	Rossford
140	38.8	Northern Local	Thornville
140	38.8	Wheelersburg Local	Wheelersburg
142	38.6	Warrensville Hgts City	Warrensville Hgts
143	38.5	Franklin City	Franklin
144	38.0	Eaton Community City	Eaton
145	37.9	Huber Heights City	Huber Heights
146	37.8	Tiffin City	Tiffin
147	37.7	Fairless Local	Navarre
148	37.6	Clark-Shawnee Local	Springfield
148	37.6	Highland Local	Sparta
148	37.6	Indian Valley Local Schools	Gnadenhutten
151	37.5	Parma City	Parma
152	37.3	Shelby City	Shelby
153	37.2	Springfield Local	Holland
154	37.1	Kent City	Kent
155	36.8	Van Wert City	Van Wert
156	36.7	Ashland City	Ashland
156	36.7	Bethel-Tate Local	Bethel
158	36.5	Geneva Area City	Geneva
158	36.5	Marlington Local	Alliance
160	36.4	North Fork Local	Utica
161	36.3	Hillsboro City	Hillsboro
162	36.1	Southwest Local	Harrison
163	36.0	Logan Elm Local	Circleville
163	36.0	Plain Local	Canton
165	35.9	Oregon City	Oregon
166	35.7	Three Rivers Local	Cleves
167	35.6	Amanda-Clearcreek Local	Amanda
168	35.5	Southeast Local	Apple Creek
169	34.9	Bath Local	Lima
170	34.5	Reynoldsburg City	Reynoldsburg
171	34.2	Jefferson Area Local	Jefferson
172	34.1	Miamisburg City	Miamisburg
173	33.8	Greenfield Exempted Village	Greenfield
174	33.6	Hubbard Exempted Village	Hubbard
175	33.5	Wapakoneta City	Wapakoneta
176	33.3	Graham Local	Saint Paris
177	33.2	Celina City	Celina
177	33.2	Greenon Local	Enon
179	32.7	Bellevue City	Bellevue
179	32.7	Clyde-Green Springs Ex. Village	Clyde
179	32.7	Findlay City	Findlay
179	32.7	Wauseon Exempted Village	Wauseon
179	32.7	West Holmes Local	Millersburg
184	32.6	New Philadel. City	New Philadel.
185	32.3	Madison Local	Middletown
185	32.3	Vermilion Local	Vermilion
187	32.1	Fairfield Union Local	Lancaster
187	32.1	Greenville City	Greenville
189	31.9	Bryan City	Bryan
189	31.9	Cuyahoga Falls City	Cuyahoga Falls
191	31.7	Licking Heights Local	Pataskala
191	31.7	Napoleon Area City	Napoleon
191	31.7	Saint Marys City	Saint Marys
194	31.6	Shaker Heights City	Shaker Heights
194	31.6	Troy City	Troy
196	31.4	Madison Local	Madison
197	31.2	Licking Valley Local	Newark
197	31.2	Northwestern Local	Springfield
199	30.8	Woodridge Local	Peninsula
200	30.5	North Olmsted City	North Olmsted
201	30.4	Kettering City	Kettering
202	30.1	East Muskingum Local	New Concord
203	30.0	Heath City	Heath
203	30.0	Southeast Local	Ravenna
205	29.8	Perry Local	Massillon
206	29.6	Howland Local	Warren
206	29.6	West Branch Local	Beloit
208	29.5	Midview Local	Grafton
209	29.4	Boardman Local	Youngstown
209	29.4	Delaware City	Delaware
211	29.2	Edgewood City	Trenton
212	29.0	West Clermont Local	Cincinnati
213	28.9	Wickliffe City	Wickliffe
214	28.8	Talawanda City	Oxford
215	28.7	Bowling Green City SD	Bowling Green
215	28.7	Jonathan Alder Local	Plain City
217	28.4	Maple Heights City	Maple Heights
218	28.3	River Valley Local	Caledonia
219	28.0	Upper Sandusky Exempted Village	Upper Sandusky
220	27.8	Coventry Local	Akron
221	27.5	Triway Local	Wooster
222	27.4	Edison Local (Formerly Berlin-Milan)	Milan
222	27.4	Perkins Local	Sandusky
222	27.4	Saint Clairsville-Richland City	Saint Clairsville
225	27.3	Dover City	Dover
226	27.0	Southwest Licking Local	Pataskala
226	27.0	Zane Trace Local	Chillicothe
228	26.9	Berea City	Berea
228	26.9	Willoughby-Eastlake City	Willoughby
230	26.8	Benton Carroll Salem Local	Oak Harbor
231	26.7	Fairfield City	Fairfield
232	26.5	Monroe Local SD	Monroe
233	26.3	Maumee City	Maumee
233	26.3	Teays Valley Local	Ashville
235	26.2	Streetsboro City	Streetsboro
236	25.7	Otsego Local	Tontogany
237	25.6	Canal Wnchstr Local	Canal Wnchstr
238	25.5	Carlisle Local	Carlisle
239	24.9	Louisville City	Louisville
239	24.9	Warren Local	Vincent
241	24.6	Shawnee Local	Lima
242	24.5	Vandalia-Butler City	Vandalia
243	24.4	Crestwood Local	Mantua
243	24.4	Westerville City	Westerville
245	24.2	Norton City	Norton
246	24.1	Alexander Local	Albany
247	23.8	Ontario Local	Mansfield
248	23.6	Northmont City	Englewood
249	23.1	Buckeye Valley Local	Delaware
249	23.1	Field Local	Mogadore
249	23.1	Johnstown-Monroe Local	Johnstown
252	22.9	Lebanon City	Lebanon
253	22.8	Northwest Local	Canal Fulton
254	22.7	Buckeye Local	Medina
255	22.3	Lakeview Local	Cortland
256	22.1	Marysville Exempted Village	Marysville
257	21.9	Clinton-Massie Local	Clarksville
258	21.8	Northeastern Local	Springfield
259	21.7	Firelands Local	South Amherst
259	21.7	Perry Local	Perry
261	21.6	Keystone Local	Lagrange
262	21.4	Cloverleaf Local	Lodi
262	21.4	Gahanna-Jefferson City	Gahanna
262	21.4	Ross Local	Hamilton
265	21.1	Nordonia Hills City	Northfield
266	20.5	Fairview Park City	Fairview Park
267	20.4	Benjamin Logan Local	Bellefontaine
268	20.3	Worthington City	Worthington
269	20.2	Milford Exempted Village	Milford
270	19.9	East Holmes Local	Berlin
270	19.9	Valley View Local	Germantown
272	19.8	Ottawa-Glandorf Local	Ottawa
273	19.7	Lexington Local	Lexington
274	19.3	Tallmadge City	Tallmadge
275	18.8	Green Local	Uniontown
275	18.8	Hilliard City	Hilliard
277	18.7	Little Miami Local	Maineville
278	18.3	Pickerington Local	Pickerington
279	18.1	Big Walnut Local	Galena
280	17.9	N Ridgeville City	N Ridgeville
281	17.7	Mentor Exempted Village	Mentor
282	17.6	Eastwood Local	Pemberville
283	17.3	Sylvania City	Sylvania
284	16.8	Bloom-Carroll Local	Carroll
285	16.7	Brunswick City	Brunswick
286	16.5	Chardon Local	Chardon
287	16.3	Kings Local	Kings Mills
288	16.1	Riverside Local	Painesville
289	15.9	Amherst Exempted Village	Amherst
290	15.6	Mayfield City	Mayfield Hgts
291	15.4	Bellbrook-Sugarcreek Local SD	Bellbrook
292	14.8	Lake Local	Uniontown
293	14.6	Stow-Munroe Falls City SD	Stow
294	14.5	Medina City SD	Medina
294	14.5	Poland Local	Poland
296	14.2	Sycamore Community City	Cincinnati
296	14.2	Westlake City	Westlake
298	14.1	Twinsburg City	Twinsburg
299	14.0	Copley-Fairlawn City	Copley
299	14.0	Wadsworth City	Wadsworth
301	13.5	Lakota Local	Liberty Twp
302	13.4	North Royalton City	North Royalton
303	13.3	Tipp City Exempted Village	Tipp City
304	13.0	Jackson Local	Massillon
305	12.9	Olmsted Falls City	Olmsted Falls

Note: This section only includes districts with 1,500 or more students; All categories are ranked from high to low

Rank	Percent	District Name	City
306	12.6	North Canton City	North Canton
307	12.1	Canfield Local	Canfield
308	12.0	Dublin City	Dublin
309	11.4	Loveland City	Loveland
310	11.1	West Geauga Local	Chesterland
311	10.9	Orange City	Cleveland
312	10.8	Beavercreek City	Beavercreek
313	10.7	Centerville City	Centerville
314	10.2	Avon Lake City	Avon Lake
315	10.1	Wyoming City	Wyoming
316	10.0	Bexley City	Bexley
317	9.7	Brecksville-Broadview Hghts City	Brecksville
318	9.5	Kenston Local	Chagrin Falls
319	9.4	Anthony Wayne Local	Whitehouse
320	9.3	Avon Local	Avon
320	9.3	Forest Hills Local	Cincinnati
320	9.3	Perrysburg Exempted Village	Perrysburg
323	8.9	Strongsville City	Strongsville
324	8.7	Beachwood City	Beachwood
325	8.1	Highland Local	Medina
325	8.1	Mariemont City	Cincinnati
325	8.1	Solon City	Solon
328	7.0	New Albany-Plain Local	New Albany
329	6.9	Aurora City	Aurora
329	6.9	Springboro Community City	Springboro
331	6.5	Bay Village City	Bay Village
332	6.4	Olentangy Local	Lewis Center
333	5.9	Rocky River City	Rocky River
334	5.2	Oak Hills Local	Cincinnati
335	5.1	Indian Hill Exempted Village	Cincinnati
336	4.9	Revere Local	Bath
337	4.7	Mason City SD	Mason
338	3.8	Hudson City	Hudson
339	3.4	Chagrin Falls Exempted Village	Chagrin Falls
340	3.1	Granville Exempted Village	Granville
341	2.1	Oakwood City	Dayton
342	1.2	Upper Arlington City	Upper Arlington
343	0.0	Alternative Education Academy	Toledo
343	0.0	Electronic Classroom of Tomorrow	Columbus
343	0.0	Ohio Connections Academy Inc	Cleveland
343	0.0	Ohio Virtual Academy	Maumee
343	0.0	Treca Digital Academy	Marion

Students Eligible for Reduced-Price Lunch

Rank	Percent	District Name	City
1	15.7	Clark-Shawnee Local	Springfield
1	15.7	East Holmes Local	Berlin
3	14.4	Fairless Local	Navarre
4	13.5	Hamilton Local	Columbus
5	13.0	North Fork Local	Utica
6	12.7	West Holmes Local	Millersburg
7	12.5	Bucyrus City	Bucyrus
8	12.3	Clearview Local	Lorain
9	11.5	Galion City	Galion
9	11.5	Indian Valley Local Schools	Gnadenhutten
11	11.3	Buckeye Local	Ashtabula
12	11.2	Southeast Local	Apple Creek
13	11.1	Sheffield-Sheffield Lake City	Sheffield Vllg
14	11.0	Bedford City	Bedford
14	11.0	Wheelersburg Local	Wheelersburg
16	10.9	Elida Local	Elida
16	10.9	Wauseon Exempted Village	Wauseon
18	10.8	Marlington Local	Alliance
18	10.8	Minerva Local	Minerva
20	10.7	Madison Local	Mansfield
20	10.7	Springfield Local	Akron
22	10.6	Kenton City	Kenton
22	10.6	Rossford Exempted Village	Rossford
22	10.6	Shelby City	Shelby
25	10.5	Rolling Hills Local	Cambridge
26	10.4	Clyde-Green Springs Ex. Village	Clyde
27	10.2	Fremont City	Fremont
27	10.2	Struthers City	Struthers
29	10.0	Clear Fork Valley Local	Bellville
29	10.0	Fostoria City	Fostoria
29	10.0	Switzerland of Ohio Local	Woodsfield
32	9.9	Mad River Local	Dayton
33	9.8	Akron City	Akron
34	9.7	Bellevue City	Bellevue
34	9.7	Upper Sandusky Exempted Village	Upper Sandusky
36	9.5	Ashland City	Ashland
36	9.5	Celina City	Celina
36	9.5	Hubbard Exempted Village	Hubbard
36	9.5	Logan-Hocking Local	Logan
36	9.5	Morgan Local	Mc Connelsville
36	9.5	Parma City	Parma
42	9.4	Conneaut Area City	Conneaut
42	9.4	Cuyahoga Falls City	Cuyahoga Falls
42	9.4	Northern Local	Thornville
45	9.3	Garfield Hgts City Schools	Garfield Hgts
45	9.3	Geneva Area City	Geneva
45	9.3	Sandusky City	Sandusky
45	9.3	Triway Local	Wooster
49	9.2	Defiance City	Defiance
49	9.2	Maumee City	Maumee
49	9.2	Northwest Local	Mc Dermott
49	9.2	Paulding Exempted Village	Paulding
53	9.1	Edison Local	Hammondsville
53	9.1	Highland Local	Sparta
53	9.1	Orrville City	Orrville
53	9.1	Piqua City	Piqua
53	9.1	Wapakoneta City	Wapakoneta
58	9.0	Elyria City Schools	Elyria
58	9.0	Midview Local	Grafton
60	8.8	Marion City	Marion
60	8.8	Perry Local	Massillon
62	8.7	Beaver Local	Lisbon
62	8.7	Lake Local	Millbury
64	8.6	Bethel-Tate Local	Bethel
64	8.6	Euclid City	Euclid
64	8.6	Whitehall City	Whitehall
67	8.5	Licking Valley Local	Newark
67	8.5	Norwalk City	Norwalk
67	8.5	Ontario Local	Mansfield
70	8.4	Barberton City	Barberton
70	8.4	Buckeye Local	Dillonvale
70	8.4	Huber Heights City	Huber Heights
70	8.4	Indian Creek Local	Wintersville
70	8.4	Massillon City	Massillon
70	8.4	Saint Marys City	Saint Marys
70	8.4	South Euclid-Lyndhurst City	Lyndhurst
70	8.4	Tiffin City	Tiffin
70	8.4	Wooster City	Wooster
79	8.3	Keystone Local	Lagrange
79	8.3	Lakewood Local	Hebron
79	8.3	Washington Local	Toledo
79	8.3	Western Brown Local	Mount Orab
83	8.2	Austintown Local	Youngstown
83	8.2	East Muskingum Local	New Concord
83	8.2	Eaton Community City	Eaton
83	8.2	Fairland Local	Proctorville
83	8.2	Maysville Local	Zanesville
83	8.2	Ravenna City	Ravenna
83	8.2	Sidney City	Sidney
83	8.2	Trotwood-Madison City	Trotwood
91	8.1	Alliance City	Alliance
91	8.1	Franklin Local	Duncan Falls
91	8.1	Nordonia Hills City	Northfield
91	8.1	Northmont City	Englewood
91	8.1	Painesville City Local	Painesville
91	8.1	Princeton City	Cincinnati
91	8.1	Willard City	Willard
98	8.0	Bath Local	Lima
98	8.0	Cambridge City	Cambridge
98	8.0	Canton Local	Canton
98	8.0	Kettering City	Kettering
98	8.0	New Lexington City	New Lexington
98	8.0	Northwest Local	Cincinnati
104	7.9	Carlisle Local	Carlisle
104	7.9	Gallia County Local	Gallipolis
104	7.9	Groveport Madison Local	Groveport
104	7.9	Hamilton City	Hamilton
104	7.9	Jackson City	Jackson
104	7.9	Niles City	Niles
104	7.9	Oregon City	Oregon
104	7.9	Vermilion Local	Vermilion
112	7.8	Adams County/ohio Valley Local	West Union
112	7.8	Carrollton Exempted Village	Carrollton
112	7.8	Claymont City	Dennison
112	7.8	Fairfield Union Local	Lancaster
112	7.8	Shawnee Local	Lima
117	7.7	Clermont Northeastern Local	Batavia
117	7.7	Girard City SD	Girard
117	7.7	Harrison Hills City	Cadiz
117	7.7	Union-Scioto Local	Chillicothe
121	7.6	Coshocton City	Coshocton
121	7.6	Crestwood Local	Mantua
121	7.6	Perkins Local	Sandusky
121	7.6	Van Wert City	Van Wert
121	7.6	West Carrollton City	West Carrollton
121	7.6	Wilmington City	Wilmington
127	7.5	Bryan City	Bryan
127	7.5	Mt Healthy City	Cincinnati
127	7.5	Northwest Local	Canal Fulton
127	7.5	Norton City	Norton
127	7.5	Winton Woods City	Cincinnati
132	7.4	Benton Carroll Salem Local	Oak Harbor
132	7.4	Tecumseh Local	New Carlisle
132	7.4	West Branch Local	Beloit
135	7.3	Blanchester Local	Blanchester
135	7.3	Edgewood City	Trenton
135	7.3	Franklin City	Franklin
135	7.3	Miami Trace Local	Washington CH
135	7.3	New Richmond Exempted Village	New Richmond
135	7.3	Newark City	Newark
135	7.3	River Valley Local	Caledonia
135	7.3	Troy City	Troy
135	7.3	Urbana City	Urbana
144	7.2	Fairborn City	Fairborn
144	7.2	Lexington Local	Lexington
144	7.2	Logan Elm Local	Circleville
144	7.2	Mount Vernon City	Mount Vernon
144	7.2	North College Hill City	Cincinnati
144	7.2	Salem City	Salem
144	7.2	Southeast Local	Ravenna
144	7.2	Vinton County Local	Mc Arthur
144	7.2	Warren Local	Vincent
153	7.1	Bellefontaine City	Bellefontaine
153	7.1	North Olmsted City	North Olmsted
153	7.1	Xenia Community City	Xenia
156	7.0	Greenville City	Greenville
156	7.0	River View Local	Warsaw
156	7.0	Saint Clairsville-Richland City	Saint Clairsville
159	6.9	East Liverpool City	East Liverpool
159	6.9	Marietta City	Marietta
159	6.9	Meigs Local	Pomeroy
159	6.9	Streetsboro City	Streetsboro
159	6.9	Willoughby-Eastlake City	Willoughby
164	6.8	Benjamin Logan Local	Bellefontaine
164	6.8	Berea City	Berea
164	6.8	Field Local	Mogadore
164	6.8	Lancaster City	Lancaster
164	6.8	Napoleon Area City	Napoleon
164	6.8	Vandalia-Butler City	Vandalia
164	6.8	Zanesville City	Zanesville
171	6.7	Bowling Green City SD	Bowling Green
171	6.7	Coventry Local	Akron
171	6.7	New Philadel. City	New Philadel.
171	6.7	Port Clinton City	Port Clinton
171	6.7	South Point Local	South Point
171	6.7	Talawanda City	Oxford
177	6.6	Ashtabula Area City	Ashtabula
177	6.6	Edison Local (Formerly Berlin-Milan)	Milan
177	6.6	Licking Heights Local	Pataskala
177	6.6	Poland Local	Poland
177	6.6	Washington CH City	Washington CH
177	6.6	Wickliffe City	Wickliffe
183	6.5	Cloverleaf Local	Lodi
183	6.5	Delaware City	Delaware
183	6.5	Dover City	Dover
183	6.5	Fairview Park City	Fairview Park
183	6.5	Jefferson Area Local	Jefferson
183	6.5	Otsego Local	Tontogany
183	6.5	Plain Local	Canton
190	6.4	Canton City	Canton
190	6.4	Minford Local	Minford
190	6.4	West Clermont Local	Cincinnati
190	6.4	Woodridge Local	Peninsula
194	6.3	Dayton City	Dayton
194	6.3	Eastwood Local	Pemberville
194	6.3	Lorain City	Lorain
194	6.3	Mansfield City	Mansfield
194	6.3	South-Western City	Grove City
194	6.3	Warren City	Warren
194	6.3	Washington-Nile Local	West Portsmouth
201	6.2	Chillicothe City	Chillicothe
201	6.2	Heath City	Heath
201	6.2	Lakewood City	Lakewood
201	6.2	Madison Local	Madison

Note: This section only includes districts with 1,500 or more students; All categories are ranked from high to low

Rank	Number	District Name	City
205	6.1	Greenon Local	Enon
205	6.1	Louisville City	Louisville
205	6.1	Norwood City	Norwood
205	6.1	Reading Community City	Reading
205	6.1	Tri-Valley Local	Dresden
205	6.1	Westfall Local	Williamsport
211	6.0	Cleveland Hgts-University Hgts City	University Hgts
211	6.0	Howland Local	Warren
211	6.0	Southwest Licking Local	Pataskala
214	5.9	Boardman Local	Youngstown
214	5.9	Graham Local	Saint Paris
214	5.9	Middletown City	Middletown
214	5.9	Reynoldsburg City	Reynoldsburg
214	5.9	Wellston City	Wellston
219	5.8	Batavia Local	Batavia
219	5.8	Goshen Local	Goshen
221	5.7	Lakeview Local	Cortland
221	5.7	Teays Valley Local	Ashville
223	5.6	Buckeye Local	Medina
223	5.6	Jonathan Alder Local	Plain City
223	5.6	Lima City	Lima
223	5.6	Southwest Local	Harrison
227	5.5	Amherst Exempted Village	Amherst
227	5.5	Circleville City	Circleville
227	5.5	Findlay City	Findlay
227	5.5	Hillsboro City	Hillsboro
227	5.5	Indian Lake Local	Lewistown
227	5.5	Northwestern Local	Springfield
227	5.5	Valley View Local	Germantown
227	5.5	Wadsworth City	Wadsworth
227	5.5	Waverly City	Waverly
236	5.4	Clinton-Massie Local	Clarksville
236	5.4	Kent City	Kent
236	5.4	London City	London
236	5.4	Ottawa-Glandorf Local	Ottawa
240	5.3	Bloom-Carroll Local	Carroll
240	5.3	Firelands Local	South Amherst
240	5.3	Mayfield City	Mayfield Hgts
240	5.3	N Ridgeville City	N Ridgeville
240	5.3	Northridge Local	Dayton
245	5.2	Gallipolis City	Gallipolis
246	5.1	Athens City	The Plains
246	5.1	Johnstown-Monroe Local	Johnstown
246	5.1	Miamisburg City	Miamisburg
246	5.1	Steubenville City	Steubenville
250	5.0	Brunswick City	Brunswick
250	5.0	Gahanna-Jefferson City	Gahanna
250	5.0	Mentor Exempted Village	Mentor
250	5.0	Portsmouth City	Portsmouth
250	5.0	Toledo City	Toledo
250	5.0	Worthington City	Worthington
256	4.9	Madison Local	Middletown
257	4.7	Buckeye Valley Local	Delaware
257	4.7	Canal Wnchstr Local	Canal Wnchstr
257	4.7	Fairfield City	Fairfield
257	4.7	Greenfield Exempted Village	Greenfield
257	4.7	Lebanon City	Lebanon
257	4.7	Milford Exempted Village	Milford
257	4.7	Stow-Munroe Falls City SD	Stow
264	4.6	Chardon Local	Chardon
264	4.6	Ross Local	Hamilton
266	4.5	Columbus City SD	Columbus
266	4.5	Monroe Local SD	Monroe
266	4.5	Springfield Local	Holland
266	4.5	West Geauga Local	Chesterland
270	4.4	Little Miami Local	Maineville
270	4.4	Marysville Exempted Village	Marysville
270	4.4	Northeastern Local	Springfield
273	4.3	Pickerington Local	Pickerington
273	4.3	Westerville City	Westerville
275	4.2	Beavercreek City	Beavercreek
276	4.1	Perry Local	Perry
276	4.1	Tallmadge City	Tallmadge
276	4.1	Youngstown City Schools	Youngstown
276	4.1	Zane Trace Local	Chillicothe
280	4.0	Amanda-Clearcreek Local	Amanda
280	4.0	North Canton City	North Canton
280	4.0	Twinsburg City	Twinsburg
283	3.9	Lake Local	Uniontown
283	3.9	Olmsted Falls City	Olmsted Falls
283	3.9	Perrysburg Exempted Village	Perrysburg
283	3.9	Springfield City	Springfield
283	3.9	Three Rivers Local	Cleves
288	3.8	Bellbrook-Sugarcreek Local SD	Bellbrook
288	3.8	Riverside Local	Painesville
290	3.7	Brecksville-Broadview Hghts City	Brecksville
290	3.7	Green Local	Uniontown
290	3.7	Shaker Heights City	Shaker Heights
290	3.7	Tipp City Exempted Village	Tipp City
294	3.6	Alexander Local	Albany
294	3.6	Canfield Local	Canfield
294	3.6	Copley-Fairlawn City	Copley
294	3.6	Hilliard City	Hilliard
294	3.6	Kenston Local	Chagrin Falls
294	3.6	Kings Local	Kings Mills
294	3.6	Sycamore Community City	Cincinnati
301	3.5	Jackson Local	Massillon
301	3.5	Sylvania City	Sylvania
303	3.3	Beachwood City	Beachwood
303	3.3	Big Walnut Local	Galena
303	3.3	Loveland City	Loveland
306	3.1	Maple Heights City	Maple Heights
307	3.0	Avon Lake City	Avon Lake
307	3.0	North Royalton City	North Royalton
309	2.9	Bay Village City	Bay Village
309	2.9	Medina City SD	Medina
309	2.9	Strongsville City	Strongsville
309	2.9	Warrensville Hgts City	Warrensville Hgts
313	2.8	Cincinnati City	Cincinnati
313	2.8	East Cleveland City SD	East Cleveland
313	2.8	Orange City	Cleveland
316	2.7	Westlake City	Westlake
317	2.5	Cleveland Municipal	Cleveland
318	2.3	Forest Hills Local	Cincinnati
318	2.3	Revere Local	Bath
320	2.2	Aurora City	Aurora
320	2.2	Bexley City	Bexley
320	2.2	Dublin City	Dublin
320	2.2	Highland Local	Medina
324	2.1	Centerville City	Centerville
325	2.0	Anthony Wayne Local	Whitehouse
325	2.0	Lakota Local	Liberty Twp
325	2.0	Springboro Community City	Springboro
328	1.8	Chagrin Falls Exempted Village	Chagrin Falls
328	1.8	Solon City	Solon
330	1.6	Mason City SD	Mason
330	1.6	Olentangy Local	Lewis Center
332	1.5	Granville Exempted Village	Granville
333	1.4	Avon Local	Avon
333	1.4	Hudson City	Hudson
333	1.4	Mariemont City	Cincinnati
336	1.3	New Albany-Plain Local	New Albany
337	0.9	Indian Hill Exempted Village	Cincinnati
337	0.9	Wyoming City	Wyoming
339	0.8	Oak Hills Local	Cincinnati
339	0.8	Rocky River City	Rocky River
341	0.5	Oakwood City	Dayton
342	0.2	Upper Arlington City	Upper Arlington
343	0.0	Alternative Education Academy	Toledo
343	0.0	Electronic Classroom of Tomorrow	Columbus
343	0.0	Ohio Connections Academy Inc	Cleveland
343	0.0	Ohio Virtual Academy	Maumee
343	0.0	Treca Digital Academy	Marion

Student/Teacher Ratio

(number of students per teacher)

Rank	Number	District Name	City
1	11.9	Beachwood City	Beachwood
2	12.0	Cleveland Hgts-University Hgts City	University Hgts
3	12.2	Cleveland Municipal	Cleveland
4	12.4	Greenville City	Greenville
5	12.7	Youngstown City Schools	Youngstown
6	12.8	Lakewood Local	Hebron
7	12.9	Athens City	The Plains
7	12.9	Upper Arlington City	Upper Arlington
9	13.0	Mansfield City	Mansfield
10	13.1	Switzerland of Ohio Local	Woodsfield
11	13.2	East Cleveland City SD	East Cleveland
11	13.2	Norwood City	Norwood
13	13.3	Vinton County Local	Mc Arthur
14	13.4	Lima City	Lima
15	13.5	Buckeye Local	Dillonvale
16	13.7	Orange City	Cleveland
17	13.8	Kent City	Kent
18	13.9	Indian Hill Exempted Village	Cincinnati
19	14.0	Warrensville Hgts City	Warrensville Hgts
20	14.1	Madison Local	Mansfield
21	14.2	East Liverpool City	East Liverpool
22	14.3	Coshocton City	Coshocton
22	14.3	Indian Creek Local	Wintersville
24	14.4	Paulding Exempted Village	Paulding
24	14.4	Wickliffe City	Wickliffe
24	14.4	Wyoming City	Wyoming
27	14.5	Akron City	Akron
28	14.7	Jackson City	Jackson
28	14.7	Rolling Hills Local	Cambridge
30	14.8	Bellefontaine City	Bellefontaine
30	14.8	Celina City	Celina
30	14.8	Rossford Exempted Village	Rossford
33	14.9	New Lexington City	New Lexington
34	15.0	Bexley City	Bexley
34	15.0	Marion City	Marion
34	15.0	Springfield City	Springfield
34	15.0	Steubenville City	Steubenville
34	15.0	Triway Local	Wooster
39	15.1	Elyria City Schools	Elyria
39	15.1	Shaker Heights City	Shaker Heights
39	15.1	Southeast Local	Apple Creek
42	15.2	Morgan Local	Mc Connelsville
42	15.2	Oakwood City	Dayton
42	15.2	Westlake City	Westlake
42	15.2	Willard City	Willard
46	15.3	Logan Elm Local	Circleville
47	15.4	Alliance City	Alliance
47	15.4	Benjamin Logan Local	Bellefontaine
47	15.4	Port Clinton City	Port Clinton
47	15.4	Portsmouth City	Portsmouth
47	15.4	Wooster City	Wooster
47	15.4	Worthington City	Worthington
53	15.5	Alexander Local	Albany
53	15.5	Circleville City	Circleville
53	15.5	Mayfield City	Mayfield Hgts
53	15.5	Napoleon Area City	Napoleon
53	15.5	Urbana City	Urbana
58	15.6	Bucyrus City	Bucyrus
58	15.6	Carlisle Local	Carlisle
58	15.6	Claymont City	Dennison
58	15.6	Conneaut Area City	Conneaut
58	15.6	Indian Lake Local	Lewistown
58	15.6	Kenston Local	Chagrin Falls
58	15.6	Northwest Local	Mc Dermott
58	15.6	Van Wert City	Van Wert
66	15.7	Bedford City	Bedford
66	15.7	Bryan City	Bryan
66	15.7	East Holmes Local	Berlin
66	15.7	Firelands Local	South Amherst
66	15.7	Meigs Local	Pomeroy
66	15.7	New Albany-Plain Local	New Albany
66	15.7	Perkins Local	Sandusky
73	15.8	Chagrin Falls Exempted Village	Chagrin Falls
73	15.8	Columbus City SD	Columbus
73	15.8	Euclid City	Euclid
73	15.8	Rocky River City	Rocky River
73	15.8	Willoughby-Eastlake City	Willoughby
78	15.9	Mariemont City	Cincinnati
78	15.9	Massillon City	Massillon
78	15.9	Maysville Local	Zanesville
78	15.9	New Richmond Exempted Village	New Richmond
78	15.9	Northern Local	Thornville
78	15.9	Talawanda City	Oxford
78	15.9	Valley View Local	Germantown
78	15.9	West Branch Local	Beloit
86	16.0	Chillicothe City	Chillicothe
86	16.0	Jefferson Area Local	Jefferson
86	16.0	Middletown City	Middletown
86	16.0	Southeast Local	Ravenna
90	16.1	Fostoria City	Fostoria
90	16.1	Gallia County Local	Gallipolis
90	16.1	Toledo City	Toledo
93	16.2	Barberton City	Barberton
93	16.2	Bethel-Tate Local	Bethel
93	16.2	Dayton City	Dayton
93	16.2	Kenton City	Kenton
93	16.2	Streetsboro City	Streetsboro
98	16.3	Adams County/ohio Valley Local	West Union
98	16.3	Coventry Local	Akron
98	16.3	Cuyahoga Falls City	Cuyahoga Falls
98	16.3	Field Local	Mogadore
98	16.3	Gahanna-Jefferson City	Gahanna
98	16.3	Girard City SD	Girard

Note: This section only includes districts with 1,500 or more students; All categories are ranked from high to low

98	16.3	Keystone Local	Lagrange
98	16.3	Newark City	Newark
98	16.3	Revere Local	Bath
98	16.3	South Euclid-Lyndhurst City	Lyndhurst
108	16.4	Beaver Local	Lisbon
108	16.4	Cambridge City	Cambridge
108	16.4	Clyde-Green Springs Ex. Village	Clyde
108	16.4	Defiance City	Defiance
108	16.4	Maumee City	Maumee
108	16.4	New Philadel. City	New Philadel.
108	16.4	Perry Local	Perry
108	16.4	Ravenna City	Ravenna
108	16.4	Washington Local	Toledo
117	16.5	Ashland City	Ashland
117	16.5	Canton City	Canton
117	16.5	Franklin Local	Duncan Falls
117	16.5	Gallipolis City	Gallipolis
117	16.5	Lake Local	Millbury
117	16.5	River View Local	Warsaw
117	16.5	Sandusky City	Sandusky
117	16.5	Shelby City	Shelby
117	16.5	Vandalia-Butler City	Vandalia
126	16.6	Bellevue City	Bellevue
126	16.6	East Muskingum Local	New Concord
126	16.6	Hudson City	Hudson
126	16.6	Northridge Local	Dayton
126	16.6	Orrville City	Orrville
126	16.6	Sheffield-Sheffield Lake City	Sheffield Vlg
126	16.6	South Point Local	South Point
126	16.6	Struthers City	Struthers
126	16.6	Sycamore Community City	Cincinnati
135	16.7	Batavia Local	Batavia
135	16.7	Dublin City	Dublin
135	16.7	Mad River Local	Dayton
135	16.7	Mount Vernon City	Mount Vernon
135	16.7	Oregon City	Oregon
135	16.7	Parma City	Parma
135	16.7	Shawnee Local	Lima
142	16.8	Groveport Madison Local	Groveport
142	16.8	Huber Heights City	Huber Heights
142	16.8	Marietta City	Marietta
142	16.8	Northeastern Local	Springfield
142	16.8	Salem City	Salem
142	16.8	Woodridge Local	Peninsula
148	16.9	Buckeye Valley Local	Delaware
148	16.9	Maple Heights City	Maple Heights
148	16.9	Springfield Local	Akron
148	16.9	Wellston City	Wellston
148	16.9	Whitehall City	Whitehall
153	17.0	Galion City	Galion
153	17.0	Lexington Local	Lexington
153	17.0	Mt Healthy City	Cincinnati
153	17.0	Saint Clairsville-Richland City	Saint Clairsville
153	17.0	Sylvania City	Sylvania
153	17.0	Tipp City Exempted Village	Tipp City
159	17.1	Franklin City	Franklin
159	17.1	Indian Valley Local Schools	Gnadenhutten
159	17.1	Lakewood City	Lakewood
159	17.1	Niles City	Niles
159	17.1	Tallmadge City	Tallmadge
164	17.2	Bay Village City	Bay Village
164	17.2	Berea City	Berea
164	17.2	Chardon Local	Chardon
164	17.2	Clear Fork Valley Local	Bellville
164	17.2	Fairless Local	Navarre
164	17.2	Fairview Park City	Fairview Park
164	17.2	Vermilion Local	Vermilion
171	17.3	Howland Local	Warren
171	17.3	Marlington Local	Alliance
171	17.3	Trotwood-Madison City	Trotwood
171	17.3	Westfall Local	Williamsport
175	17.4	Buckeye Local	Ashtabula
175	17.4	Crestwood Local	Mantua
175	17.4	Fairborn City	Fairborn
175	17.4	Findlay City	Findlay
175	17.4	Licking Valley Local	Newark
175	17.4	Miami Trace Local	Washington CH
175	17.4	Miamisburg City	Miamisburg
175	17.4	Minerva Local	Minerva
175	17.4	Poland Local	Poland
175	17.4	Reading Community City	Reading
175	17.4	Strongsville City	Strongsville
186	17.5	Ashtabula Area City	Ashtabula
186	17.5	Highland Local	Sparta
186	17.5	Logan-Hocking Local	Logan
189	17.6	Lorain City	Lorain
189	17.6	Marysville Exempted Village	Marysville
189	17.6	Mentor Exempted Village	Mentor
189	17.6	North Olmsted City	North Olmsted
189	17.6	Xenia Community City	Xenia
194	17.7	Brunswick City	Brunswick
194	17.7	Hubbard Exempted Village	Hubbard
194	17.7	Johnstown-Monroe Local	Johnstown
194	17.7	Kettering City	Kettering
194	17.7	N Ridgeville City	N Ridgeville
194	17.7	Northwestern Local	Springfield
194	17.7	Warren City	Warren
194	17.7	Wauseon Exempted Village	Wauseon
202	17.8	Canfield Local	Canfield
202	17.8	Carrollton Exempted Village	Carrollton
204	17.9	Edison Local (Formerly Berlin-Milan)	Milan
204	17.9	Madison Local	Middletown
204	17.9	North Canton City	North Canton
204	17.9	Southwest Licking Local	Pataskala
204	17.9	West Holmes Local	Millersburg
209	18.0	Centerville City	Centerville
209	18.0	Granville Exempted Village	Granville
209	18.0	Louisville City	Louisville
209	18.0	Piqua City	Piqua
213	18.1	Avon Lake City	Avon Lake
213	18.1	Bath Local	Lima
213	18.1	Clinton-Massie Local	Clarksville
213	18.1	Eastwood Local	Pemberville
213	18.1	Green Local	Uniontown
213	18.1	Hillsboro City	Hillsboro
213	18.1	North Fork Local	Utica
213	18.1	Perry Local	Massillon
213	18.1	Princeton City	Cincinnati
213	18.1	Saint Marys City	Saint Marys
223	18.2	Boardman Local	Youngstown
223	18.2	Copley-Fairlawn City	Copley
223	18.2	Elida Local	Elida
223	18.2	Fairland Local	Proctorville
223	18.2	Fremont City	Fremont
223	18.2	Heath City	Heath
223	18.2	Licking Heights Local	Pataskala
223	18.2	Northwest Local	Canal Fulton
223	18.2	Solon City	Solon
232	18.3	Amherst Exempted Village	Amherst
232	18.3	Hilliard City	Hilliard
232	18.3	Jonathan Alder Local	Plain City
232	18.3	Lancaster City	Lancaster
232	18.3	Northmont City	Englewood
232	18.3	Three Rivers Local	Cleves
232	18.3	Upper Sandusky Exempted Village	Upper Sandusky
232	18.3	Warren Local	Vincent
232	18.3	Washington-Nile Local	West Portsmouth
232	18.3	Winton Woods City	Cincinnati
242	18.4	Austintown Local	Youngstown
242	18.4	Bowling Green City SD	Bowling Green
242	18.4	Norwalk City	Norwalk
242	18.4	Teays Valley Local	Ashville
246	18.5	Delaware City	Delaware
246	18.5	Ontario Local	Mansfield
246	18.5	Tecumseh Local	New Carlisle
246	18.5	Troy City	Troy
246	18.5	West Carrollton City	West Carrollton
246	18.5	Wheelersburg Local	Wheelersburg
252	18.6	Aurora City	Aurora
252	18.6	Benton Carroll Salem Local	Oak Harbor
252	18.6	Canton Local	Canton
252	18.6	Goshen Local	Goshen
252	18.6	Lake Local	Uniontown
252	18.6	London City	London
258	18.7	Beavercreek City	Beavercreek
258	18.7	Lakeview Local	Cortland
258	18.7	Midview Local	Grafton
258	18.7	Stow-Munroe Falls City SD	Stow
258	18.7	Washington CH City	Washington CH
263	18.8	Clearview Local	Lorain
263	18.8	Eaton Community City	Eaton
263	18.8	Ottawa-Glandorf Local	Ottawa
266	18.9	Norton City	Norton
266	18.9	Riverside Local	Painesville
266	18.9	South-Western City	Grove City
266	18.9	West Clermont Local	Cincinnati
270	19.0	Canal Wnchstr Local	Canal Wnchstr
270	19.0	Kings Local	Kings Mills
270	19.0	Olentangy Local	Lewis Center
270	19.0	West Geauga Local	Chesterland
274	19.1	Buckeye Local	Medina
274	19.1	Cincinnati City	Cincinnati
274	19.1	Painesville City Local	Painesville
274	19.1	Westerville City	Westerville
278	19.2	Blanchester Local	Blanchester
278	19.2	Fairfield City	Fairfield
278	19.2	Greenfield Exempted Village	Greenfield
278	19.2	Hamilton City	Hamilton
278	19.2	Harrison Hills City	Cadiz
278	19.2	Olmsted Falls City	Olmsted Falls
278	19.2	Pickerington Local	Pickerington
278	19.2	Tiffin City	Tiffin
278	19.2	Zane Trace Local	Chillicothe
287	19.3	Perrysburg Exempted Village	Perrysburg
288	19.4	Oak Hills Local	Cincinnati
289	19.5	Big Walnut Local	Galena
289	19.5	Edison Local	Hammondsville
289	19.5	Fairfield Union Local	Lancaster
289	19.5	Northwest Local	Cincinnati
289	19.5	Springboro Community City	Springboro
294	19.6	Clark-Shawnee Local	Springfield
295	19.7	Anthony Wayne Local	Whitehouse
295	19.7	Forest Hills Local	Cincinnati
295	19.7	Jackson Local	Massillon
295	19.7	Springfield Local	Holland
295	19.7	Waverly City	Waverly
300	19.8	Clermont Northeastern Local	Batavia
300	19.8	Minford Local	Minford
302	19.9	Garfield Hgts City Schools	Garfield Hgts
302	19.9	Hamilton Local	Columbus
302	19.9	Highland Local	Medina
302	19.9	Mason City SD	Mason
302	19.9	North Royalton City	North Royalton
302	19.9	Wadsworth City	Wadsworth
302	19.9	Wapakoneta City	Wapakoneta
309	20.0	Bloom-Carroll Local	Carroll
309	20.0	Cloverleaf Local	Lodi
309	20.0	Greenon Local	Enon
309	20.0	Southwest Local	Harrison
309	20.0	Union-Scioto Local	Chillicothe
309	20.0	Zanesville City	Zanesville
315	20.1	Madison Local	Madison
316	20.2	Little Miami Local	Maineville
316	20.2	Loveland City	Loveland
316	20.2	Plain Local	Canton
319	20.3	Monroe Local SD	Monroe
320	20.4	Avon Local	Avon
320	20.4	Bellbrook-Sugarcreek Local SD	Bellbrook
320	20.4	Dover City	Dover
320	20.4	Ross Local	Hamilton
324	20.5	Graham Local	Saint Paris
324	20.5	Otsego Local	Tontogany
326	20.6	Lakota Local	Liberty Twp
326	20.6	Reynoldsburg City	Reynoldsburg
328	20.7	Brecksville-Broadview Hghts City	Brecksville
328	20.7	Edgewood City	Trenton
328	20.7	Nordonia Hills City	Northfield
328	20.7	Western Brown Local	Mount Orab
332	20.8	Twinsburg City	Twinsburg
332	20.8	Wilmington City	Wilmington
334	20.9	Geneva Area City	Geneva
334	20.9	Milford Exempted Village	Milford
336	21.0	Amanda-Clearcreek Local	Amanda
336	21.0	Sidney City	Sidney
338	21.2	Tri-Valley Local	Dresden
339	21.4	Lebanon City	Lebanon
340	21.9	Medina City SD	Medina
341	22.1	River Valley Local	Caledonia
342	23.0	North College Hill City	Cincinnati
343	29.6	Alternative Education Academy	Toledo
344	37.6	Electronic Classroom of Tomorrow	Columbus
345	39.7	Ohio Connections Academy Inc	Cleveland
346	54.6	Ohio Virtual Academy	Maumee
347	116.6	Treca Digital Academy	Marion

Student/Librarian Ratio

(number of students per librarian)

Rank	Number	District Name	City
1	323.0	Beachwood City	Beachwood
2	372.5	Orange City	Cleveland

Note: This section only includes districts with 1,500 or more students; All categories are ranked from high to low

Rank	Value	District	City
3	431.6	Shaker Heights City	Shaker Heights
4	441.6	New Albany-Plain Local	New Albany
5	465.2	Chardon Local	Chardon
6	501.0	Indian Hill Exempted Village	Cincinnati
7	513.6	Groveport Madison Local	Groveport
8	522.3	Upper Arlington City	Upper Arlington
9	530.3	Bexley City	Bexley
10	552.3	Shelby City	Shelby
11	555.0	Poland Local	Poland
12	577.0	Warrensville Hgts City	Warrensville Hgts
13	580.0	Whitehall City	Whitehall
14	602.9	Cleveland Municipal	Cleveland
15	607.8	Talawanda City	Oxford
16	610.3	Meigs Local	Pomeroy
17	610.7	New Lexington City	New Lexington
18	620.3	Granville Exempted Village	Granville
19	621.1	Worthington City	Worthington
20	628.4	Dublin City	Dublin
21	658.1	Cleveland Hgts-University Hgts City	University Hgts
22	668.4	Westlake City	Westlake
23	695.4	Olentangy Local	Lewis Center
24	702.9	Gahanna-Jefferson City	Gahanna
25	765.5	Wheelersburg Local	Wheelersburg
26	770.0	Washington-Nile Local	West Portsmouth
27	774.1	Maysville Local	Zanesville
28	775.0	Minford Local	Minford
29	778.4	Elyria City Schools	Elyria
30	790.5	Lake Local	Millbury
31	806.3	Jackson City	Jackson
32	831.0	Carlisle Local	Carlisle
33	834.9	Lakewood City	Lakewood
34	857.4	Heath City	Heath
35	868.3	Benjamin Logan Local	Bellefontaine
36	872.5	Ontario Local	Mansfield
37	878.3	Northeastern Local	Springfield
38	878.5	Fairview Park City	Fairview Park
39	880.5	Fairland Local	Proctorville
40	881.0	Rossford Exempted Village	Rossford
41	884.3	Sycamore Community City	Cincinnati
42	897.0	Lakeview Local	Cortland
43	900.0	Kent City	Kent
44	909.6	Hilliard City	Hilliard
45	935.5	Forest Hills Local	Cincinnati
46	937.0	Hudson City	Hudson
47	955.0	Licking Valley Local	Newark
48	960.0	Struthers City	Struthers
49	962.0	Napoleon Area City	Napoleon
50	963.5	Wyoming City	Wyoming
51	966.5	Union-Scioto Local	Chillicothe
52	977.5	Valley View Local	Germantown
53	980.3	Norwalk City	Norwalk
54	980.4	Miami Trace Local	Washington CH
55	992.5	Portsmouth City	Portsmouth
56	996.7	Bowling Green City SD	Bowling Green
57	1,004.0	Hubbard Exempted Village	Hubbard
58	1,012.5	Chagrin Falls Exempted Village	Chagrin Falls
59	1,033.0	Oakwood City	Dayton
60	1,042.5	Vermilion Local	Vermilion
61	1,048.0	East Muskingum Local	New Concord
62	1,066.9	Sylvania City	Sylvania
63	1,082.8	Lebanon City	Lebanon
04	1,009.8	Twinsburg City	Twinsburg
65	1,103.5	Indian Creek Local	Wintersville
65	1,103.5	Northern Local	Thornville
67	1,107.0	Gallia County Local	Gallipolis
68	1,110.5	Washington CH City	Washington CH
69	1,117.5	Berea City	Berea
70	1,125.5	West Geauga Local	Chesterland
71	1,158.1	Westerville City	Westerville
72	1,162.4	Solon City	Solon
73	1,169.8	Youngstown City Schools	Youngstown
74	1,188.3	Canal Wnchstr Local	Canal Wnchstr
75	1,193.7	Mansfield City	Mansfield
76	1,201.5	Marlington Local	Alliance
77	1,221.5	Cuyahoga Falls City	Cuyahoga Falls
78	1,230.5	Lexington Local	Lexington
79	1,249.0	Defiance City	Defiance
80	1,259.9	Akron City	Akron
81	1,263.0	Tipp City Exempted Village	Tipp City
82	1,290.0	Bay Village City	Bay Village
83	1,295.5	Maumee City	Maumee
84	1,300.0	Trotwood-Madison City	Trotwood
85	1,304.6	Strongsville City	Strongsville
86	1,308.6	Avon Lake City	Avon Lake
87	1,319.2	Beavercreek City	Beavercreek
88	1,322.7	Kings Local	Kings Mills
89	1,324.3	Warren City	Warren
90	1,342.9	Wadsworth City	Wadsworth
91	1,343.5	Revere Local	Bath
92	1,367.0	Barberton City	Barberton
93	1,405.5	Otsego Local	Tontogany
94	1,437.0	Franklin City	Franklin
95	1,449.0	Canfield Local	Canfield
96	1,487.0	Springfield City	Springfield
97	1,493.7	Columbus City SD	Columbus
98	1,506.0	Paulding Exempted Village	Paulding
99	1,509.6	Cincinnati City	Cincinnati
100	1,512.0	Eastwood Local	Pemberville
100	1,512.0	Madison Local	Middletown
102	1,513.3	Xenia Community City	Xenia
103	1,523.5	Alliance City	Alliance
104	1,532.0	Wellston City	Wellston
105	1,536.5	Louisville City	Louisville
106	1,541.0	Toledo City	Toledo
107	1,542.5	East Cleveland City SD	East Cleveland
108	1,558.0	Johnstown-Monroe Local	Johnstown
109	1,566.0	Fairless Local	Navarre
110	1,574.0	Midview Local	Grafton
111	1,577.1	Clearview Local	Lorain
112	1,580.0	North College Hill City	Cincinnati
113	1,590.0	Mariemont City	Cincinnati
114	1,594.5	Painesville City Local	Painesville
115	1,596.0	Madison Local	Mansfield
115	1,596.0	Westfall Local	Williamsport
117	1,628.0	Keystone Local	Lagrange
118	1,632.7	Perry Local	Massillon
119	1,649.0	Copley-Fairlawn City	Copley
120	1,660.5	Ashland City	Ashland
121	1,667.0	Northwest Local	Mc Dermott
122	1,669.0	Coshocton City	Coshocton
123	1,670.4	Tecumseh Local	New Carlisle
124	1,680.1	Wilmington City	Wilmington
125	1,692.0	Bloom-Carroll Local	Carroll
126	1,694.0	Blanchester Local	Blanchester
127	1,694.3	Pickerington Local	Pickerington
128	1,701.0	Benton Carroll Salem Local	Oak Harbor
129	1,704.8	Willoughby-Eastlake City	Willoughby
130	1,709.5	Winton Woods City	Cincinnati
131	1,712.0	Upper Sandusky Exempted Village	Upper Sandusky
132	1,717.5	Stow-Munroe Falls City SD	Stow
133	1,732.0	Willard City	Willard
134	1,736.4	Lakota Local	Liberty Twp
135	1,738.1	West Holmes Local	Millersburg
136	1,743.0	Perry Local	Perry
137	1,748.0	Northwestern Local	Springfield
138	1,752.0	Firelands Local	South Amherst
139	1,752.5	Sidney City	Sidney
140	1,768.0	Triway Local	Wooster
141	1,768.2	Orrville City	Orrville
142	1,773.5	Lake Local	Uniontown
143	1,802.0	Southeast Local	Ravenna
144	1,809.0	Bath Local	Lima
145	1,823.0	Clear Fork Valley Local	Bellville
146	1,827.0	South Point Local	South Point
147	1,828.0	Buckeye Local	Ashtabula
148	1,832.3	Brunswick City	Brunswick
149	1,836.0	Fostoria City	Fostoria
149	1,836.0	Teays Valley Local	Ashville
151	1,845.0	Minerva Local	Minerva
152	1,850.0	Clinton-Massie Local	Clarksville
152	1,850.0	Highland Local	Sparta
152	1,850.0	Mad River Local	Dayton
155	1,852.0	Jefferson Area Local	Jefferson
156	1,854.0	Sheffield-Sheffield Lake City	Sheffield Vllg
157	1,857.3	Marietta City	Marietta
158	1,873.0	Newark City	Newark
159	1,891.0	Maple Heights City	Maple Heights
160	1,903.3	Bethel-Tate Local	Bethel
161	1,931.0	Three Rivers Local	Cleves
162	1,943.0	Edison Local	Hammondsville
163	1,946.0	Mount Vernon City	Mount Vernon
164	1,949.0	Hamilton City	Hamilton
165	1,973.0	Logan-Hocking Local	Logan
166	1,995.0	Fairfield Union Local	Lancaster
167	2,014.7	Lancaster City	Lancaster
168	2,040.0	Streetsboro City	Streetsboro
169	2,050.0	Woodridge Local	Peninsula
170	2,058.0	Crestwood Local	Mantua
171	2,059.0	Fremont City	Fremont
172	2,061.0	Logan Elm Local	Circleville
173	2,076.0	Bellevue City	Bellevue
174	2,076.5	South Euclid-Lyndhurst City	Lyndhurst
175	2,077.0	Van Wert City	Van Wert
176	2,081.0	Morgan Local	Mc Connelsville
177	2,082.0	Massillon City	Massillon
178	2,091.7	Medina City SD	Medina
179	2,101.1	Lakewood Local	Hebron
180	2,107.0	Graham Local	Saint Paris
181	2,110.3	Huber Heights City	Huber Heights
182	2,113.0	Salem City	Salem
183	2,113.6	Dayton City	Dayton
184	2,115.0	Claymont City	Dennison
185	2,116.0	Clark-Shawnee Local	Springfield
186	2,117.0	Marion City	Marion
187	2,133.0	Anthony Wayne Local	Whitehouse
188	2,139.0	Greenfield Exempted Village	Greenfield
189	2,171.0	Field Local	Mogadore
190	2,182.0	Circleville City	Circleville
191	2,190.0	West Branch Local	Beloit
192	2,197.0	Jonathan Alder Local	Plain City
193	2,218.0	Cambridge City	Cambridge
194	2,239.0	Saint Marys City	Saint Marys
195	2,246.0	East Liverpool City	East Liverpool
196	2,256.0	Warren Local	Vincent
197	2,270.0	Clyde-Green Springs Ex. Village	Clyde
198	2,279.5	Boardman Local	Youngstown
199	2,280.5	Mayfield City	Mayfield Hgts
200	2,286.2	Northwest Local	Canal Fulton
201	2,289.0	Buckeye Valley Local	Delaware
202	2,291.1	River View Local	Warsaw
203	2,303.0	Northwest Local	Cincinnati
204	2,309.0	Springfield Local	Akron
205	2,320.0	Vinton County Local	Mc Arthur
206	2,337.0	North Royalton City	North Royalton
207	2,410.0	Monroe Local SD	Monroe
208	2,419.0	Elida Local	Elida
209	2,465.0	Switzerland of Ohio Local	Woodsfield
210	2,530.0	Goshen Local	Goshen
211	2,540.2	Gallipolis City	Gallipolis
212	2,561.5	Delaware City	Delaware
213	2,567.0	Tallmadge City	Tallmadge
214	2,592.5	Franklin Local	Duncan Falls
215	2,598.0	Bellefontaine City	Bellefontaine
216	2,603.0	Niles City	Niles
217	2,628.0	Rocky River City	Rocky River
218	2,639.0	Marysville Exempted Village	Marysville
219	2,650.0	Hillsboro City	Hillsboro
220	2,654.0	Athens City	The Plains
221	2,654.3	Tiffin City	Tiffin
222	2,668.0	Princeton City	Cincinnati
223	2,677.3	N Ridgeville City	N Ridgeville
224	2,680.0	Greenville City	Greenville
225	2,715.0	Cloverleaf Local	Lodi
226	2,718.0	Dover City	Dover
227	2,770.0	Celina City	Celina
228	2,807.7	East Holmes Local	Berlin
229	2,830.5	Springboro Community City	Springboro
230	2,832.0	Chillicothe City	Chillicothe
231	2,833.0	Ravenna City	Ravenna
232	2,835.0	Ross Local	Hamilton
233	2,858.7	Brecksville-Broadview Hghts City	Brecksville
234	2,892.3	Parma City	Parma
235	2,905.7	West Clermont Local	Cincinnati
236	2,912.0	Jackson Local	Massillon
237	2,913.9	Buckeye Local	Medina
238	2,925.0	New Philadel. City	New Philadel.
239	2,931.0	Wapakoneta City	Wapakoneta
240	2,943.9	Beaver Local	Lisbon
241	2,953.0	Reynoldsburg City	Reynoldsburg
242	2,964.0	Aurora City	Aurora
243	2,970.0	Big Walnut Local	Galena
244	2,979.0	Howland Local	Warren
245	3,070.0	Kenston Local	Chagrin Falls
246	3,175.5	Middletown City	Middletown
247	3,186.0	Western Brown Local	Mount Orab
248	3,246.0	Clermont Northeastern Local	Batavia
249	3,259.0	Milford Exempted Village	Milford
250	3,368.0	Washington Local	Toledo
251	3,390.0	Southwest Local	Harrison
252	3,396.0	Mt Healthy City	Cincinnati
253	3,413.0	Sandusky City	Sandusky
254	3,493.9	Avon Local	Avon

Note: This section only includes districts with 1,500 or more students; All categories are ranked from high to low

Rank	Number	District Name	City
255	3,525.0	Zanesville City	Zanesville
256	3,531.0	Bedford City	Bedford
257	3,558.0	Galion City	Galion
258	3,593.0	Edgewood City	Trenton
259	3,647.0	Little Miami Local	Maineville
260	3,682.0	Wooster City	Wooster
261	3,776.0	Southwest Licking Local	Pataskala
262	3,782.0	Olmsted Falls City	Olmsted Falls
263	3,814.0	Oregon City	Oregon
264	3,834.0	West Carrollton City	West Carrollton
265	3,882.0	Nordonia Hills City	Northfield
266	3,884.0	Kettering City	Kettering
267	3,907.0	Springfield Local	Holland
268	4,109.0	North Olmsted City	North Olmsted
269	4,118.3	Steubenville City	Steubenville
270	4,136.0	Green Local	Uniontown
271	4,137.0	Amherst Exempted Village	Amherst
272	4,189.5	Troy City	Troy
273	4,226.0	Centerville City	Centerville
274	4,413.0	Fairborn City	Fairborn
275	4,571.0	Perrysburg Exempted Village	Perrysburg
276	4,626.7	Licking Heights Local	Pataskala
277	4,628.2	Lima City	Lima
278	4,677.0	Loveland City	Loveland
279	4,725.0	North Canton City	North Canton
280	4,879.0	Riverside Local	Painesville
281	4,898.0	Fairfield City	Fairfield
282	4,955.5	Canton City	Canton
283	5,204.0	Northmont City	Englewood
284	5,223.8	South-Western City	Grove City
285	5,250.0	Austintown Local	Youngstown
286	5,266.0	Geneva Area City	Geneva
287	5,465.5	Mason City SD	Mason
288	5,551.0	Miamisburg City	Miamisburg
289	5,737.0	Euclid City	Euclid
290	5,875.0	Findlay City	Findlay
291	5,962.1	Saint Clairsville-Richland City	Saint Clairsville
292	7,505.0	Lorain City	Lorain
293	7,760.0	Garfield Hgts City Schools	Garfield Hgts
294	7,938.0	Oak Hills Local	Cincinnati
295	8,174.0	Mentor Exempted Village	Mentor
296	8,651.4	Highland Local	Medina
297	10,840.0	Electronic Classroom of Tomorrow	Columbus
298	173,100.0	Indian Lake Local	Lewistown
n/a	n/a	Adams County/ohio Valley Local	West Union
n/a	n/a	Alexander Local	Albany
n/a	n/a	Alternative Education Academy	Toledo
n/a	n/a	Amanda-Clearcreek Local	Amanda
n/a	n/a	Ashtabula Area City	Ashtabula
n/a	n/a	Batavia Local	Batavia
n/a	n/a	Bellbrook-Sugarcreek Local SD	Bellbrook
n/a	n/a	Bryan City	Bryan
n/a	n/a	Buckeye Local	Dillonvale
n/a	n/a	Bucyrus City	Bucyrus
n/a	n/a	Canton Local	Canton
n/a	n/a	Carrollton Exempted Village	Carrollton
n/a	n/a	Conneaut Area City	Conneaut
n/a	n/a	Coventry Local	Akron
n/a	n/a	Eaton Community City	Eaton
n/a	n/a	Edison Local (Formerly Berlin-Milan)	Milan
n/a	n/a	Girard City SD	Girard
n/a	n/a	Greenon Local	Enon
n/a	n/a	Hamilton Local	Columbus
n/a	n/a	Harrison Hills City	Cadiz
n/a	n/a	Indian Valley Local Schools	Gnadenhutten
n/a	n/a	Kenton City	Kenton
n/a	n/a	London City	London
n/a	n/a	Madison Local	Madison
n/a	n/a	New Richmond Exempted Village	New Richmond
n/a	n/a	North Fork Local	Utica
n/a	n/a	Northridge Local	Dayton
n/a	n/a	Norton City	Norton
n/a	n/a	Norwood City	Norwood
n/a	n/a	Ohio Connections Academy Inc	Cleveland
n/a	n/a	Ohio Virtual Academy	Maumee
n/a	n/a	Ottawa-Glandorf Local	Ottawa
n/a	n/a	Perkins Local	Sandusky
n/a	n/a	Piqua City	Piqua
n/a	n/a	Plain Local	Canton
n/a	n/a	Port Clinton City	Port Clinton
n/a	n/a	Reading Community City	Reading
n/a	n/a	River Valley Local	Caledonia
n/a	n/a	Rolling Hills Local	Cambridge
n/a	n/a	Shawnee Local	Lima
n/a	n/a	Southeast Local	Apple Creek
n/a	n/a	Treca Digital Academy	Marion
n/a	n/a	Tri-Valley Local	Dresden
n/a	n/a	Urbana City	Urbana
n/a	n/a	Vandalia-Butler City	Vandalia
n/a	n/a	Wauseon Exempted Village	Wauseon
n/a	n/a	Waverly City	Waverly
n/a	n/a	Wickliffe City	Wickliffe
n/a	n/a	Zane Trace Local	Chillicothe

Student/Counselor Ratio

(number of students per counselor)

Rank	Number	District Name	City
1	155.8	Talawanda City	Oxford
2	193.3	Whitehall City	Whitehall
3	210.8	Orange City	Cleveland
4	212.3	Shelby City	Shelby
5	215.4	Wickliffe City	Wickliffe
6	219.6	Bay Village City	Bay Village
7	223.4	Indian Hill Exempted Village	Cincinnati
8	230.4	Solon City	Solon
9	233.4	Tallmadge City	Tallmadge
10	234.1	Cleveland Hgts-University Hgts City	University Hgts
11	234.4	Alliance City	Alliance
12	240.0	Struthers City	Struthers
13	240.5	Napoleon Area City	Napoleon
14	243.6	Greenville City	Greenville
15	253.1	Chagrin Falls Exempted Village	Chagrin Falls
16	262.3	Fostoria City	Fostoria
17	264.6	Barberton City	Barberton
18	266.1	Kings Local	Kings Mills
19	269.2	Beachwood City	Beachwood
20	271.3	Keystone Local	Lagrange
21	274.6	Shaker Heights City	Shaker Heights
22	282.2	Shawnee Local	Lima
23	286.3	Bryan City	Bryan
24	291.9	Norwood City	Norwood
25	292.6	Bexley City	Bexley
26	294.2	Fairborn City	Fairborn
27	299.8	Copley-Fairlawn City	Copley
28	307.8	Youngstown City Schools	Youngstown
29	308.1	Upper Arlington City	Upper Arlington
30	315.4	Western Brown Local	Mount Orab
31	316.4	Reading Community City	Reading
32	317.6	Union-Scioto Local	Chillicothe
33	318.6	Sidney City	Sidney
34	320.9	East Liverpool City	East Liverpool
35	321.0	Bedford City	Bedford
36	324.2	Lake Local	Uniontown
37	330.0	Elyria City Schools	Elyria
38	339.9	Fairfield Union Local	Lancaster
39	341.5	Poland Local	Poland
40	347.0	Licking Heights Local	Pataskala
41	348.4	Oakwood City	Dayton
42	349.9	Perry Local	Massillon
43	351.4	Fairview Park City	Fairview Park
44	352.4	Rossford Exempted Village	Rossford
45	353.7	Sycamore Community City	Cincinnati
46	358.8	Lakeview Local	Cortland
47	360.0	Kent City	Kent
48	361.6	Washington CH City	Washington CH
49	363.8	Kettering City	Kettering
50	369.0	Ashland City	Ashland
51	369.8	Benton Carroll Salem Local	Oak Harbor
52	370.6	Dublin City	Dublin
53	373.5	North Olmsted City	North Olmsted
54	374.0	Kenton City	Kenton
55	374.2	Washington Local	Toledo
56	374.8	Hudson City	Hudson
57	375.2	West Geauga Local	Chesterland
58	375.4	Rocky River City	Rocky River
59	375.8	Cuyahoga Falls City	Cuyahoga Falls
60	376.5	Paulding Exempted Village	Paulding
61	378.3	Bellbrook-Sugarcreek Local SD	Bellbrook
62	378.4	Perkins Local	Sandusky
63	378.5	Westlake City	Westlake
64	381.8	Tiffin City	Tiffin
65	384.7	Clark-Shawnee Local	Springfield
66	385.0	Washington-Nile Local	West Portsmouth
67	386.5	Otsego Local	Tontogany
68	388.2	Nordonia Hills City	Northfield
69	388.6	Edison Local	Hammondsville
70	389.5	North Royalton City	North Royalton
71	392.9	Columbus City SD	Columbus
72	395.3	Lake Local	Millbury
73	395.5	South Euclid-Lyndhurst City	Lyndhurst
74	395.7	Huber Heights City	Huber Heights
75	397.0	Portsmouth City	Portsmouth
76	399.2	Northeastern Local	Springfield
77	400.5	Marlington Local	Alliance
78	402.8	Revere Local	Bath
79	403.3	Cambridge City	Cambridge
80	404.5	Sylvania City	Sylvania
81	409.7	Louisville City	Louisville
82	410.0	Woodridge Local	Peninsula
83	410.6	Franklin City	Franklin
84	411.6	Crestwood Local	Mantua
85	411.8	Steubenville City	Steubenville
86	413.0	Canton City	Canton
87	413.5	Granville Exempted Village	Granville
88	413.6	Green Local	Uniontown
89	415.0	Mayfield City	Mayfield Hgts
90	415.2	Bellevue City	Bellevue
91	415.5	Perrysburg Exempted Village	Perrysburg
92	416.8	Northwest Local	Mc Dermott
93	421.0	Tipp City Exempted Village	Tipp City
94	422.2	Urbana City	Urbana
95	422.6	Centerville City	Centerville
96	423.0	Claymont City	Dennison
97	423.4	Aurora City	Aurora
97	423.4	Kenston Local	Chagrin Falls
99	424.8	Groveport Madison Local	Groveport
100	425.6	Howland Local	Warren
101	425.8	Brecksville-Broadview Hghts City	Brecksville
102	426.6	Anthony Wayne Local	Whitehouse
102	426.6	Sandusky City	Sandusky
104	426.9	Delaware City	Delaware
105	427.1	Bowling Green City SD	Bowling Green
106	428.0	Saint Clairsville-Richland City	Saint Clairsville
107	429.2	Ravenna City	Ravenna
108	429.8	Plain Local	Canton
109	431.8	Maumee City	Maumee
110	432.0	Benjamin Logan Local	Bellefontaine
110	432.0	Ottawa-Glandorf Local	Ottawa
112	432.2	Defiance City	Defiance
113	432.8	Indian Lake Local	Lewistown
114	433.0	Bellefontaine City	Bellefontaine
114	433.0	Willard City	Willard
116	433.2	Wooster City	Wooster
117	433.3	Trotwood-Madison City	Trotwood
118	434.2	Eaton Community City	Eaton
119	435.8	Perry Local	Perry
120	436.3	Ontario Local	Mansfield
121	436.5	Port Clinton City	Port Clinton
122	436.8	Berea City	Berea
123	437.5	Austintown Local	Youngstown
124	438.0	West Branch Local	Beloit
125	439.9	Troy City	Troy
126	440.9	Oregon City	Oregon
127	442.0	Northwest Local	Canal Fulton
127	442.0	Triway Local	Wooster
129	443.6	Forest Hills Local	Cincinnati
130	447.8	Saint Marys City	Saint Marys
131	448.6	Olmsted Falls City	Olmsted Falls
132	449.2	Warren City	Warren
133	450.5	Southeast Local	Ravenna
134	452.5	Cloverleaf Local	Lodi
135	454.0	Clyde-Green Springs Ex. Village	Clyde
135	454.0	Xenia Community City	Xenia
137	454.3	North Canton City	North Canton
138	455.9	Boardman Local	Youngstown
139	456.0	Madison Local	Mansfield
140	457.6	Fremont City	Fremont
141	458.2	Avon Lake City	Avon Lake
142	461.3	Minerva Local	Minerva
143	462.1	Pickerington Local	Pickerington
144	462.5	Clinton-Massie Local	Clarksville
145	463.5	Sheffield-Sheffield Lake City	Sheffield Vllg
146	463.7	Massillon City	Massillon
147	464.0	Vinton County Local	Mc Arthur
148	465.6	Beavercreek City	Beavercreek
149	468.3	Wauseon Exempted Village	Wauseon
150	469.6	Licking Valley Local	Newark
151	470.4	Marion City	Marion
152	472.3	Chardon Local	Chardon

Note: This section only includes districts with 1,500 or more students; All categories are ranked from high to low

153	472.5	Ross Local	Hamilton
154	476.9	Olentangy Local	Lewis Center
155	479.8	Marysville Exempted Village	Marysville
156	480.3	Girard City SD	Girard
156	480.3	Worthington City	Worthington
158	481.6	Toledo City	Toledo
159	481.8	Wyoming City	Wyoming
160	481.9	Northmont City	Englewood
161	482.2	West Holmes Local	Millersburg
162	482.5	Akron City	Akron
163	484.3	Southwest Local	Harrison
164	485.3	Jackson Local	Massillon
165	488.2	Jonathan Alder Local	Plain City
166	490.2	Miami Trace Local	Washington CH
167	490.4	Indian Creek Local	Wintersville
168	490.7	New Albany-Plain Local	New Albany
169	491.4	Treca Digital Academy	Marion
170	496.5	River Valley Local	Caledonia
171	496.9	Mariemont City	Cincinnati
172	499.1	Piqua City	Piqua
173	499.5	Buckeye Local	Dillonvale
174	500.0	Findlay City	Findlay
175	500.6	Firelands Local	South Amherst
176	502.0	Hubbard Exempted Village	Hubbard
176	502.0	Southeast Local	Apple Creek
178	503.5	Southwest Licking Local	Pataskala
179	504.0	Eastwood Local	Pemberville
179	504.0	Madison Local	Middletown
181	506.0	Goshen Local	Goshen
182	506.3	Bucyrus City	Bucyrus
183	509.3	Miamisburg City	Miamisburg
184	510.3	Wheelersburg Local	Wheelersburg
185	510.9	Mentor Exempted Village	Mentor
186	511.3	Zane Trace Local	Chillicothe
187	511.6	Mansfield City	Mansfield
188	511.8	Northwest Local	Cincinnati
189	513.3	Edgewood City	Trenton
190	514.2	East Cleveland City SD	East Cleveland
191	514.6	Springboro Community City	Springboro
192	516.7	Minford Local	Minford
193	519.3	Johnstown-Monroe Local	Johnstown
193	519.3	Van Wert City	Van Wert
195	520.5	Mason City SD	Mason
196	521.7	Alexander Local	Albany
197	521.8	Strongsville City	Strongsville
198	522.4	Westerville City	Westerville
199	522.5	Mt Healthy City	Cincinnati
200	522.6	Vermilion Local	Vermilion
201	526.6	Geneva Area City	Geneva
202	528.8	Electronic Classroom of Tomorrow	Columbus
203	530.0	Hillsboro City	Hillsboro
204	530.8	Athens City	The Plains
205	531.1	Springfield City	Springfield
206	531.5	Painesville City Local	Painesville
207	533.5	Highland Local	Medina
208	538.9	Lima City	Lima
209	540.3	Maple Heights City	Maple Heights
209	540.3	Orrville City	Orrville
211	540.7	Vandalia-Butler City	Vandalia
212	541.0	Clermont Northeastern Local	Batavia
213	543.0	Clearview Local	Lorain
214	543.1	Wadsworth City	Wadsworth
215	543.3	Amanda-Clearcreek Local	Amanda
216	543.6	Dover City	Dover
217	543.9	Lakewood Local	Hebron
218	544.9	Twinsburg City	Twinsburg
219	545.5	Circleville City	Circleville
220	545.8	Wapakoneta City	Wapakoneta
221	550.4	Parma City	Parma
222	554.0	Carlisle Local	Carlisle
222	554.0	Celina City	Celina
224	555.3	North Fork Local	Utica
225	556.6	Stow-Munroe Falls City SD	Stow
226	557.2	Marietta City	Marietta
227	558.0	Canton Local	Canton
228	558.1	Springfield Local	Holland
229	558.6	Valley View Local	Germantown
230	561.3	Maysville Local	Zanesville
231	562.3	Hilliard City	Hilliard
232	562.5	Coventry Local	Akron
233	566.5	Lakota Local	Liberty Twp
234	570.7	Upper Sandusky Exempted Village	Upper Sandusky
235	573.7	Euclid City	Euclid
236	577.0	Warrensville Hgts City	Warrensville Hgts
237	577.3	Springfield Local	Akron
238	577.5	New Richmond Exempted Village	New Richmond
239	577.7	Rolling Hills Local	Cambridge
240	579.6	Canfield Local	Canfield
241	582.7	Northwestern Local	Springfield
242	584.3	Middletown City	Middletown
243	584.6	Loveland City	Loveland
244	585.8	Gahanna-Jefferson City	Gahanna
245	587.0	Fairland Local	Proctorville
246	601.6	Lebanon City	Lebanon
247	602.5	Monroe Local SD	Monroe
248	603.0	Bath Local	Lima
249	607.8	Little Miami Local	Maineville
250	609.3	Buckeye Local	Ashtabula
251	610.3	Meigs Local	Pomeroy
252	611.5	Cleveland Municipal	Cleveland
253	612.0	Teays Valley Local	Ashville
254	612.7	Greenon Local	Enon
255	615.3	Lexington Local	Lexington
256	616.3	Switzerland of Ohio Local	Woodsfield
257	618.8	Hamilton Local	Columbus
258	625.0	Wilmington City	Wilmington
259	627.5	N Ridgeville City	N Ridgeville
260	631.7	Waverly City	Waverly
261	637.3	Brunswick City	Brunswick
262	642.8	Norton City	Norton
263	643.7	Three Rivers Local	Cleves
264	644.8	Heath City	Heath
265	647.0	Ashtabula Area City	Ashtabula
266	647.7	Beaver Local	Lisbon
267	649.3	Lakewood City	Lakewood
268	649.7	Hamilton City	Hamilton
269	650.5	Riverside Local	Painesville
270	655.7	Willoughby-Eastlake City	Willoughby
271	657.7	Logan-Hocking Local	Logan
272	671.1	Reynoldsburg City	Reynoldsburg
273	675.2	Mad River Local	Dayton
274	680.0	Streetsboro City	Streetsboro
275	683.8	Winton Woods City	Cincinnati
276	687.0	Logan Elm Local	Circleville
277	689.5	Amherst Exempted Village	Amherst
278	691.3	Franklin Local	Duncan Falls
278	691.3	New Lexington City	New Lexington
280	699.6	Midview Local	Grafton
281	702.3	Graham Local	Saint Paris
282	704.3	Salem City	Salem
283	708.0	Chillicothe City	Chillicothe
284	708.1	East Muskingum Local	New Concord
285	710.6	Canal Wnchstr Local	Canal Wnchstr
286	711.5	Princeton City	Cincinnati
287	713.0	Greenfield Exempted Village	Greenfield
288	735.3	Norwalk City	Norwalk
289	735.7	Northern Local	Thornville
290	738.0	Gallia County Local	Gallipolis
291	742.5	Big Walnut Local	Galena
292	750.5	Lorain City	Lorain
293	753.5	Fairfield City	Fairfield
294	755.5	Lancaster City	Lancaster
295	766.0	Wellston City	Wellston
296	766.8	West Carrollton City	West Carrollton
297	767.3	Buckeye Local	Medina
298	776.0	Garfield Hgts City Schools	Garfield Hgts
299	776.8	Tecumseh Local	New Carlisle
300	778.4	Mount Vernon City	Mount Vernon
301	782.7	Carrollton Exempted Village	Carrollton
302	783.0	Fairless Local	Navarre
303	798.0	Adams County/ohio Valley Local	West Union
303	798.0	Westfall Local	Williamsport
305	802.0	North College Hill City	Cincinnati
306	803.7	South-Western City	Grove City
307	806.3	Elida Local	Elida
307	806.3	Jackson City	Jackson
309	807.5	Edison Local (Formerly Berlin-Milan)	Milan
310	834.5	Coshocton City	Coshocton
311	846.0	Bloom-Carroll Local	Carroll
312	850.8	Madison Local	Madison
313	867.7	Niles City	Niles
314	875.5	Bethel-Tate Local	Bethel
315	881.3	Zanesville City	Zanesville
316	889.5	Galion City	Galion
317	902.0	Oak Hills Local	Cincinnati
318	903.5	Northridge Local	Dayton
319	905.0	Indian Valley Local Schools	Gnadenhutten
320	912.5	East Holmes Local	Berlin
321	913.5	South Point Local	South Point
322	919.0	Conneaut Area City	Conneaut
323	925.0	Highland Local	Sparta
324	926.0	Jefferson Area Local	Jefferson
325	932.0	Alternative Education Academy	Toledo
326	946.6	Newark City	Newark
327	968.6	West Clermont Local	Cincinnati
328	975.0	New Philadel. City	New Philadel.
329	985.0	Ohio Connections Academy Inc	Cleveland
330	998.3	Tri-Valley Local	Dresden
331	1,017.0	Batavia Local	Batavia
332	1,018.0	London City	London
333	1,031.0	River View Local	Warsaw
334	1,040.5	Morgan Local	Mc Connelsville
335	1,085.5	Field Local	Mogadore
336	1,086.3	Milford Exempted Village	Milford
337	1,105.0	Gallipolis City	Gallipolis
338	1,128.0	Warren Local	Vincent
339	1,144.5	Buckeye Valley Local	Delaware
340	1,176.1	Clear Fork Valley Local	Bellville
341	1,232.9	Dayton City	Dayton
342	1,273.2	Medina City SD	Medina
343	1,339.3	Avon Local	Avon
344	1,510.0	Harrison Hills City	Cadiz
345	1,662.9	Ohio Virtual Academy	Maumee
346	1,694.0	Blanchester Local	Blanchester
347	2,296.7	Cincinnati City	Cincinnati

Current Expenditures per Student

Rank	Dollars	District Name	City
1	19,881	Orange City	Cleveland
2	18,414	Beachwood City	Beachwood
3	16,992	Cleveland Hgts-University Hgts City	University Hgts
4	16,402	Shaker Heights City	Shaker Heights
5	15,937	East Cleveland City SD	East Cleveland
6	15,518	Upper Arlington City	Upper Arlington
7	15,515	Indian Hill Exempted Village	Cincinnati
8	14,393	Rossford Exempted Village	Rossford
9	14,387	Bexley City	Bexley
10	14,358	Cleveland Municipal	Cleveland
11	14,245	Sycamore Community City	Cincinnati
12	14,213	Columbus City SD	Columbus
13	14,202	Warrensville Hgts City	Warrensville Hgts
14	14,139	Youngstown City Schools	Youngstown
15	14,063	Princeton City	Cincinnati
16	13,960	Mansfield City	Mansfield
17	13,466	Akron City	Akron
18	13,324	Perry Local	Perry
19	13,320	Euclid City	Euclid
20	13,282	South Euclid-Lyndhurst City	Lyndhurst
21	13,280	Cincinnati City	Cincinnati
22	13,274	Hudson City	Hudson
23	13,141	Solon City	Solon
24	13,093	Toledo City	Toledo
25	13,016	Winton Woods City	Cincinnati
26	12,921	Dayton City	Dayton
27	12,844	Worthington City	Worthington
28	12,610	Westlake City	Westlake
29	12,604	Mariemont City	Cincinnati
30	12,561	Sandusky City	Sandusky
31	12,430	Fostoria City	Fostoria
32	12,426	Dublin City	Dublin
33	12,424	Warren City	Warren
34	12,286	North Olmsted City	North Olmsted
35	12,202	Berea City	Berea
36	12,170	Mayfield City	Mayfield Hgts
37	12,096	Benton Carroll Salem Local	Oak Harbor
38	12,069	Chagrin Falls Exempted Village	Chagrin Falls
39	11,977	Rocky River City	Rocky River
40	11,931	Wickliffe City	Wickliffe
41	11,906	Lima City	Lima
42	11,847	Mentor Exempted Village	Mentor
43	11,837	Bedford City	Bedford
44	11,799	New Albany-Plain Local	New Albany
45	11,727	Kent City	Kent
46	11,719	Norwood City	Norwood
47	11,662	Lorain City	Lorain
48	11,633	Port Clinton City	Port Clinton
49	11,598	Vandalia-Butler City	Vandalia
50	11,561	Athens City	The Plains
51	11,557	Lakewood City	Lakewood
52	11,471	Xenia Community City	Xenia

Note: This section only includes districts with 1,500 or more students; All categories are ranked from high to low

Rank	Number	District Name	City
53	11,301	Brecksville-Broadview Hghts City	Brecksville
54	11,231	Kenston Local	Chagrin Falls
55	11,215	Northridge Local	Dayton
56	11,205	Woodridge Local	Peninsula
57	11,196	Sylvania City	Sylvania
58	11,180	Gahanna-Jefferson City	Gahanna
59	11,163	Celina City	Celina
60	11,145	Urbana City	Urbana
61	11,127	Portsmouth City	Portsmouth
62	11,117	Fairview Park City	Fairview Park
63	11,113	Three Rivers Local	Cleves
64	11,075	Strongsville City	Strongsville
65	11,064	Trotwood-Madison City	Trotwood
66	11,051	New Richmond Exempted Village	New Richmond
67	11,025	Mt Healthy City	Cincinnati
68	11,019	Kettering City	Kettering
69	11,015	Wyoming City	Wyoming
70	11,010	Hilliard City	Hilliard
71	11,001	Revere Local	Bath
72	10,991	West Geauga Local	Chesterland
73	10,987	Washington Local	Toledo
74	10,975	Oakwood City	Dayton
75	10,946	Canton City	Canton
76	10,899	Mad River Local	Dayton
77	10,887	Circleville City	Circleville
78	10,882	Bay Village City	Bay Village
79	10,862	Maumee City	Maumee
80	10,856	Whitehall City	Whitehall
81	10,836	Parma City	Parma
82	10,809	Middletown City	Middletown
83	10,805	Avon Lake City	Avon Lake
84	10,783	Massillon City	Massillon
85	10,735	Wooster City	Wooster
86	10,726	Springfield City	Springfield
87	10,679	Canton Local	Canton
88	10,672	London City	London
89	10,593	New Lexington City	New Lexington
90	10,525	Nordonia Hills City	Northfield
91	10,514	Willoughby-Eastlake City	Willoughby
92	10,513	Meigs Local	Pomeroy
93	10,501	East Liverpool City	East Liverpool
94	10,485	Eastwood Local	Pemberville
95	10,469	Switzerland of Ohio Local	Woodsfield
96	10,451	West Carrollton City	West Carrollton
97	10,438	Marion City	Marion
98	10,410	Bowling Green City SD	Bowling Green
98	10,410	Napoleon Area City	Napoleon
100	10,409	Centerville City	Centerville
101	10,407	Kings Local	Kings Mills
102	10,399	Twinsburg City	Twinsburg
103	10,352	Huber Heights City	Huber Heights
104	10,350	Aurora City	Aurora
105	10,341	Bucyrus City	Bucyrus
106	10,316	Vinton County Local	Mc Arthur
107	10,283	Southeast Local	Apple Creek
108	10,267	Wellston City	Wellston
109	10,259	Elyria City Schools	Elyria
110	10,245	Talawanda City	Oxford
111	10,244	Northwest Local	Mc Dermott
112	10,225	Maple Heights City	Maple Heights
113	10,221	Barberton City	Barberton
114	10,210	Valley View Local	Germantown
115	10,202	Goshen Local	Goshen
116	10,187	Westerville City	Westerville
117	10,164	Beavercreek City	Beavercreek
118	10,163	Oregon City	Oregon
119	10,154	Painesville City Local	Painesville
120	10,116	Benjamin Logan Local	Bellefontaine
121	10,114	Perkins Local	Sandusky
122	10,101	Canal Wnchstr Local	Canal Wnchstr
123	10,095	Forest Hills Local	Cincinnati
124	10,072	Granville Exempted Village	Granville
125	10,057	Buckeye Local	Dillonvale
126	10,023	Harrison Hills City	Cadiz
126	10,023	Indian Lake Local	Lewistown
128	10,019	Alexander Local	Albany
128	10,019	Shelby City	Shelby
130	10,009	Alliance City	Alliance
131	10,007	Buckeye Valley Local	Delaware
132	10,005	Orrville City	Orrville
133	10,003	Sheffield-Sheffield Lake City	Sheffield Vllg
134	9,992	Gallia County Local	Gallipolis
135	9,971	Northmont City	Englewood
136	9,965	Ashtabula Area City	Ashtabula
137	9,962	Cambridge City	Cambridge
138	9,958	Crestwood Local	Mantua
139	9,956	Gallipolis City	Gallipolis
140	9,954	North Royalton City	North Royalton
141	9,928	Willard City	Willard
142	9,916	Madison Local	Mansfield
143	9,891	River View Local	Warsaw
144	9,877	Howland Local	Warren
145	9,873	Franklin City	Franklin
146	9,872	Lakewood Local	Hebron
147	9,840	Logan Elm Local	Circleville
147	9,840	Southwest Local	Harrison
149	9,833	Olentangy Local	Lewis Center
149	9,833	Zanesville City	Zanesville
151	9,826	Washington-Nile Local	West Portsmouth
152	9,819	Triway Local	Wooster
153	9,802	Bellbrook-Sugarcreek Local SD	Bellbrook
154	9,786	Streetsboro City	Streetsboro
155	9,784	Coshocton City	Coshocton
156	9,762	Cloverleaf Local	Lodi
157	9,750	Adams County/ohio Valley Local	West Union
158	9,740	Fairborn City	Fairborn
159	9,726	East Holmes Local	Berlin
159	9,726	Northern Local	Thornville
161	9,725	Galion City	Galion
162	9,721	Chardon Local	Chardon
163	9,720	Firelands Local	South Amherst
164	9,699	Carlisle Local	Carlisle
165	9,697	Chillicothe City	Chillicothe
166	9,695	Springfield Local	Akron
167	9,680	Tallmadge City	Tallmadge
168	9,676	Vermilion Local	Vermilion
169	9,659	South-Western City	Grove City
170	9,649	Bryan City	Bryan
171	9,643	Ravenna City	Ravenna
172	9,639	Olmsted Falls City	Olmsted Falls
172	9,639	Troy City	Troy
174	9,632	Copley-Fairlawn City	Copley
175	9,628	Groveport Madison Local	Groveport
175	9,628	Mason City SD	Mason
177	9,603	Morgan Local	Mc Connelsville
178	9,602	Fairless Local	Navarre
179	9,592	Newark City	Newark
180	9,590	Van Wert City	Van Wert
181	9,574	Pickerington Local	Pickerington
182	9,571	Ashland City	Ashland
183	9,566	Logan-Hocking Local	Logan
184	9,555	North Fork Local	Utica
185	9,547	Perry Local	Massillon
186	9,544	Medina City SD	Medina
187	9,538	Bath Local	Lima
188	9,528	Salem City	Salem
189	9,520	Lake Local	Millbury
190	9,485	Brunswick City	Brunswick
191	9,481	Springfield Local	Holland
191	9,481	Teays Valley Local	Ashville
193	9,470	Findlay City	Findlay
193	9,470	Poland Local	Poland
195	9,462	Franklin Local	Duncan Falls
196	9,457	Stow-Munroe Falls City SD	Stow
197	9,442	Piqua City	Piqua
198	9,431	Marysville Exempted Village	Marysville
199	9,396	Ontario Local	Mansfield
200	9,393	Tipp City Exempted Village	Tipp City
201	9,383	Electronic Classroom of Tomorrow	Columbus
202	9,382	Conneaut Area City	Conneaut
203	9,368	Perrysburg Exempted Village	Perrysburg
204	9,367	Edison Local	Hammondsville
204	9,367	Waverly City	Waverly
206	9,342	Kenton City	Kenton
207	9,339	Delaware City	Delaware
208	9,325	Saint Marys City	Saint Marys
209	9,320	Jackson City	Jackson
210	9,315	Buckeye Local	Ashtabula
211	9,306	Loveland City	Loveland
211	9,306	Northwest Local	Cincinnati
213	9,304	Reading Community City	Reading
214	9,303	Oak Hills Local	Cincinnati
215	9,300	Paulding Exempted Village	Paulding
216	9,284	Miami Trace Local	Washington CH
217	9,241	Boardman Local	Youngstown
218	9,220	Claymont City	Dennison
218	9,220	Coventry Local	Akron
220	9,218	Rolling Hills Local	Cambridge
221	9,205	Milford Exempted Village	Milford
222	9,170	Edison Local (Formerly Berlin-Milan)	Milan
223	9,156	Northwest Local	Canal Fulton
224	9,138	Jefferson Area Local	Jefferson
225	9,131	Bellefontaine City	Bellefontaine
226	9,117	Niles City	Niles
227	9,116	Shawnee Local	Lima
228	9,115	West Holmes Local	Millersburg
229	9,105	Highland Local	Sparta
230	9,103	Tecumseh Local	New Carlisle
231	9,095	Clermont Northeastern Local	Batavia
232	9,089	Big Walnut Local	Galena
232	9,089	Reynoldsburg City	Reynoldsburg
234	9,083	North Canton City	North Canton
235	9,059	Lakota Local	Liberty Twp
236	9,051	Clark-Shawnee Local	Springfield
237	9,040	Eaton Community City	Eaton
238	9,029	Southeast Local	Ravenna
239	9,015	Cuyahoga Falls City	Cuyahoga Falls
240	9,002	Monroe Local SD	Monroe
241	8,997	Hubbard Exempted Village	Hubbard
242	8,991	Hamilton City	Hamilton
242	8,991	North College Hill City	Cincinnati
244	8,988	Maysville Local	Zanesville
245	8,967	Bellevue City	Bellevue
246	8,965	Southwest Licking Local	Pataskala
247	8,962	Heath City	Heath
248	8,961	Mount Vernon City	Mount Vernon
249	8,953	Lexington Local	Lexington
249	8,953	Minerva Local	Minerva
251	8,949	Field Local	Mogadore
252	8,948	Fairfield Union Local	Lancaster
253	8,941	Clyde-Green Springs Ex. Village	Clyde
254	8,917	Madison Local	Middletown
255	8,878	Canfield Local	Canfield
256	8,875	Fremont City	Fremont
257	8,843	Greenville City	Greenville
258	8,814	Steubenville City	Steubenville
259	8,813	Licking Valley Local	Newark
260	8,796	East Muskingum Local	New Concord
261	8,795	Defiance City	Defiance
262	8,787	Garfield Hgts City Schools	Garfield Hgts
263	8,778	Geneva Area City	Geneva
264	8,771	Green Local	Uniontown
265	8,770	Bloom-Carroll Local	Carroll
266	8,769	Alternative Education Academy	Toledo
267	8,767	Keystone Local	Lagrange
268	8,761	Wapakoneta City	Wapakoneta
269	8,754	Miamisburg City	Miamisburg
270	8,748	Saint Clairsville-Richland City	Saint Clairsville
271	8,742	Clearview Local	Lorain
272	8,720	Lancaster City	Lancaster
273	8,712	Edgewood City	Trenton
274	8,697	Struthers City	Struthers
275	8,691	Minford Local	Minford
276	8,690	Girard City SD	Girard
277	8,684	Sidney City	Sidney
278	8,671	Elida Local	Elida
279	8,669	South Point Local	South Point
280	8,666	Riverside Local	Painesville
281	8,655	Upper Sandusky Exempted Village	Upper Sandusky
282	8,648	Beaver Local	Lisbon
282	8,648	West Branch Local	Beloit
284	8,642	Louisville City	Louisville
285	8,633	Amherst Exempted Village	Amherst
286	8,615	Hillsboro City	Hillsboro
287	8,612	Amanda-Clearcreek Local	Amanda
287	8,612	Otsego Local	Tontogany
289	8,611	Blanchester Local	Blanchester
290	8,579	Plain Local	Canton
291	8,566	Marietta City	Marietta
292	8,563	Northeastern Local	Springfield
293	8,551	Madison Local	Madison
294	8,536	Fairland Local	Proctorville
295	8,525	Dover City	Dover
296	8,513	Tri-Valley Local	Dresden
297	8,503	West Clermont Local	Cincinnati
298	8,496	Northwestern Local	Springfield
299	8,487	Washington CH City	Washington CH
300	8,483	Lake Local	Uniontown
301	8,482	Greenfield Exempted Village	Greenfield
302	8,469	Wauseon Exempted Village	Wauseon
303	8,455	Zane Trace Local	Chillicothe
304	8,449	New Philadel. City	New Philadel.

Note: This section only includes districts with 1,500 or more students; All categories are ranked from high to low

Rank	Dollars	District Name	City
305	8,423	Indian Creek Local	Wintersville
305	8,423	Jackson Local	Massillon
307	8,414	Licking Heights Local	Pataskala
308	8,402	Clinton-Massie Local	Clarksville
309	8,359	Ross Local	Hamilton
310	8,314	Lakeview Local	Cortland
311	8,308	Carrollton Exempted Village	Carrollton
312	8,300	Buckeye Local	Medina
313	8,298	Westfall Local	Williamsport
314	8,289	Batavia Local	Batavia
315	8,288	N Ridgeville City	N Ridgeville
316	8,239	Western Brown Local	Mount Orab
317	8,234	Warren Local	Vincent
318	8,229	Jonathan Alder Local	Plain City
319	8,224	Anthony Wayne Local	Whitehouse
320	8,206	Fairfield City	Fairfield
321	8,181	Norwalk City	Norwalk
322	8,178	Highland Local	Medina
323	8,165	Wheelersburg Local	Wheelersburg
324	8,160	Marlington Local	Alliance
325	8,155	Austintown Local	Youngstown
325	8,155	Norton City	Norton
327	8,144	Clear Fork Valley Local	Bellville
328	8,125	Ottawa-Glandorf Local	Ottawa
329	8,113	Wilmington City	Wilmington
330	8,083	Wadsworth City	Wadsworth
331	8,072	Tiffin City	Tiffin
332	8,055	Greenon Local	Enon
333	8,051	Indian Valley Local Schools	Gnadenhutten
334	7,990	Bethel-Tate Local	Bethel
335	7,904	Graham Local	Saint Paris
336	7,894	River Valley Local	Caledonia
337	7,877	Union-Scioto Local	Chillicothe
338	7,866	Lebanon City	Lebanon
339	7,831	Hamilton Local	Columbus
340	7,800	Springboro Community City	Springboro
341	7,793	Midview Local	Grafton
342	7,650	Little Miami Local	Maineville
343	7,582	Johnstown-Monroe Local	Johnstown
344	7,096	Avon Local	Avon
345	6,802	Ohio Virtual Academy	Maumee
346	6,453	Ohio Connections Academy Inc	Cleveland
347	5,979	Treca Digital Academy	Marion

Total General Revenue per Student

Rank	Dollars	District Name	City
1	24,101	Whitehall City	Whitehall
2	23,285	Orange City	Cleveland
3	22,942	Lake Local	Millbury
4	22,291	Beachwood City	Beachwood
5	22,096	Switzerland of Ohio Local	Woodsfield
6	21,041	Youngstown City Schools	Youngstown
7	21,019	East Cleveland City SD	East Cleveland
8	20,168	Cleveland Municipal	Cleveland
9	19,985	Indian Hill Exempted Village	Cincinnati
10	19,941	Dayton City	Dayton
11	19,867	Cincinnati City	Cincinnati
12	19,783	Warrensville Hgts City	Warrensville Hgts
13	19,435	Cleveland Hgts-University Hgts City	University Hgts
14	19,420	Maple Heights City	Maple Heights
15	19,396	London City	London
16	19,327	Bexley City	Bexley
17	19,166	Columbus City SD	Columbus
18	19,097	Ashtabula Area City	Ashtabula
19	18,849	Toledo City	Toledo
20	18,746	Huber Heights City	Huber Heights
21	18,499	Mansfield City	Mansfield
22	18,209	Northwest Local	Canal Fulton
23	18,050	Shaker Heights City	Shaker Heights
24	17,955	Akron City	Akron
25	17,760	Upper Arlington City	Upper Arlington
26	17,572	Lorain City	Lorain
27	17,523	Barberton City	Barberton
28	16,956	Newark City	Newark
29	16,843	Princeton City	Cincinnati
30	16,822	Washington-Nile Local	West Portsmouth
31	16,790	Xenia Community City	Xenia
32	16,622	Bellevue City	Bellevue
33	16,470	Van Wert City	Van Wert
34	16,256	Louisville City	Louisville
35	16,249	Euclid City	Euclid
36	15,907	Mayfield City	Mayfield Hgts
37	15,875	Sycamore Community City	Cincinnati
38	15,851	Perry Local	Perry
39	15,843	Westlake City	Westlake
40	15,763	Portsmouth City	Portsmouth
41	15,709	Trotwood-Madison City	Trotwood
42	15,666	Orrville City	Orrville
43	15,542	Port Clinton City	Port Clinton
44	15,412	Three Rivers Local	Cleves
45	15,303	Mariemont City	Cincinnati
46	15,246	Rocky River City	Rocky River
47	15,220	South Euclid-Lyndhurst City	Lyndhurst
48	15,128	Garfield Hgts City Schools	Garfield Hgts
49	15,105	Springfield Local	Akron
50	15,089	Solon City	Solon
51	15,056	Bedford City	Bedford
52	15,041	Gallia County Local	Gallipolis
53	15,005	Ottawa-Glandorf Local	Ottawa
54	14,992	Jonathan Alder Local	Plain City
55	14,799	Circleville City	Circleville
56	14,796	Lakewood City	Lakewood
57	14,735	Chagrin Falls Exempted Village	Chagrin Falls
58	14,655	Worthington City	Worthington
59	14,637	Hudson City	Hudson
60	14,562	Sandusky City	Sandusky
61	14,483	Reynoldsburg City	Reynoldsburg
62	14,434	Lima City	Lima
63	14,428	Bellefontaine City	Bellefontaine
64	14,411	Winton Woods City	Cincinnati
65	14,380	Warren City	Warren
66	14,336	Coshocton City	Coshocton
67	14,308	Niles City	Niles
68	14,294	Fairview Park City	Fairview Park
69	14,212	Rossford Exempted Village	Rossford
70	14,209	Streetsboro City	Streetsboro
71	14,190	Gallipolis City	Gallipolis
72	14,138	Ross Local	Hamilton
73	14,112	Springfield City	Springfield
74	14,097	New Albany-Plain Local	New Albany
75	14,068	North Olmsted City	North Olmsted
76	13,989	Zanesville City	Zanesville
77	13,967	Dublin City	Dublin
78	13,965	Findlay City	Findlay
79	13,909	Groveport Madison Local	Groveport
80	13,812	Wadsworth City	Wadsworth
81	13,775	Harrison Hills City	Cadiz
82	13,715	Canton City	Canton
83	13,664	West Geauga Local	Chesterland
84	13,619	Northridge Local	Dayton
85	13,588	Kenston Local	Chagrin Falls
86	13,580	Otsego Local	Tontogany
87	13,579	Mt Healthy City	Cincinnati
88	13,569	Wooster City	Wooster
89	13,551	Kent City	Kent
90	13,524	Geneva Area City	Geneva
91	13,487	Athens City	The Plains
92	13,442	Mentor Exempted Village	Mentor
93	13,400	Northwestern Local	Springfield
94	13,377	Maumee City	Maumee
95	13,355	Eaton Community City	Eaton
96	13,353	Norwood City	Norwood
97	13,316	East Liverpool City	East Liverpool
98	13,313	Middletown City	Middletown
99	13,299	Fostoria City	Fostoria
100	13,261	Wellston City	Wellston
101	13,219	Elyria City Schools	Elyria
102	13,180	Buckeye Local	Medina
103	13,151	New Richmond Exempted Village	New Richmond
104	13,144	Talawanda City	Oxford
105	13,117	Pickerington Local	Pickerington
106	13,067	Parma City	Parma
107	13,066	Marion City	Marion
108	12,904	South-Western City	Grove City
109	12,900	Bay Village City	Bay Village
110	12,884	Revere Local	Bath
111	12,787	Napoleon Area City	Napoleon
112	12,751	Wyoming City	Wyoming
113	12,742	Kettering City	Kettering
114	12,670	Brecksville-Broadview Hghts City	Brecksville
115	12,607	Madison Local	Mansfield
116	12,561	Alexander Local	Albany
117	12,530	Berea City	Berea
118	12,505	Vermilion Local	Vermilion
119	12,494	Indian Lake Local	Lewistown
120	12,491	Canton Local	Canton
121	12,370	Hilliard City	Hilliard
122	12,349	Westerville City	Westerville
123	12,329	Oregon City	Oregon
124	12,321	Washington Local	Toledo
125	12,301	Oakwood City	Dayton
126	12,277	Wickliffe City	Wickliffe
127	12,252	Celina City	Celina
128	12,223	North Royalton City	North Royalton
129	12,215	Sylvania City	Sylvania
130	12,213	Woodridge Local	Peninsula
131	12,192	Bucyrus City	Bucyrus
132	12,191	Strongsville City	Strongsville
133	12,189	Meigs Local	Pomeroy
134	12,167	Vandalia-Butler City	Vandalia
135	12,151	Gahanna-Jefferson City	Gahanna
136	12,124	Miami Trace Local	Washington CH
137	12,061	Painesville City Local	Painesville
138	12,057	Centerville City	Centerville
139	12,034	Fairfield Union Local	Lancaster
140	12,033	Benton Carroll Salem Local	Oak Harbor
141	12,007	Avon Lake City	Avon Lake
141	12,007	Canal Wnchstr Local	Canal Wnchstr
143	11,943	Bellbrook-Sugarcreek Local SD	Bellbrook
144	11,910	Morgan Local	Mc Connelsville
145	11,905	Massillon City	Massillon
146	11,904	Bowling Green City SD	Bowling Green
147	11,869	Chillicothe City	Chillicothe
148	11,863	Aurora City	Aurora
149	11,852	Willard City	Willard
150	11,844	Big Walnut Local	Galena
151	11,840	Paulding Exempted Village	Paulding
152	11,839	Southeast Local	Ravenna
153	11,793	Tallmadge City	Tallmadge
154	11,777	North College Hill City	Cincinnati
155	11,759	Clermont Northeastern Local	Batavia
156	11,743	Medina City SD	Medina
157	11,732	Edgewood City	Trenton
158	11,719	Marysville Exempted Village	Marysville
159	11,717	Troy City	Troy
160	11,711	Urbana City	Urbana
161	11,708	Saint Marys City	Saint Marys
162	11,707	Crestwood Local	Mantua
163	11,701	Sidney City	Sidney
164	11,685	Kings Local	Kings Mills
165	11,642	Cloverleaf Local	Lodi
166	11,622	River View Local	Warsaw
166	11,622	Vinton County Local	Mc Arthur
168	11,611	Lakewood Local	Hebron
169	11,608	Mad River Local	Dayton
170	11,555	Willoughby-Eastlake City	Willoughby
171	11,549	Rolling Hills Local	Cambridge
172	11,545	Galion City	Galion
173	11,536	Alliance City	Alliance
174	11,527	Springfield Local	Holland
175	11,513	Hubbard Exempted Village	Hubbard
176	11,497	Reading Community City	Reading
177	11,483	Fairless Local	Navarre
178	11,482	New Lexington City	New Lexington
179	11,477	Olmsted Falls City	Olmsted Falls
180	11,468	Jackson City	Jackson
181	11,433	Shelby City	Shelby
182	11,430	Olentangy Local	Lewis Center
183	11,420	Bloom-Carroll Local	Carroll
183	11,420	West Carrollton City	West Carrollton
185	11,408	Bryan City	Bryan
186	11,403	Copley-Fairlawn City	Copley
187	11,401	Cambridge City	Cambridge
188	11,397	Chardon Local	Chardon
189	11,395	Buckeye Valley Local	Delaware
190	11,392	Perkins Local	Sandusky
191	11,368	Conneaut Area City	Conneaut
192	11,366	Miamisburg City	Miamisburg
193	11,356	Ravenna City	Ravenna
194	11,349	Struthers City	Struthers
195	11,333	Granville Exempted Village	Granville
196	11,328	Benjamin Logan Local	Bellefontaine
197	11,325	Eastwood Local	Pemberville
198	11,322	Beavercreek City	Beavercreek
199	11,310	Mason City SD	Mason
200	11,299	Buckeye Local	Dillonvale
201	11,250	Fairborn City	Fairborn
202	11,249	Jackson Local	Massillon
203	11,248	Nordonia Hills City	Northfield
204	11,224	Salem City	Salem

Note: This section only includes districts with 1,500 or more students; All categories are ranked from high to low

Rank	Dollars	District Name	City
205	11,202	Austintown Local	Youngstown
206	11,197	Franklin Local	Duncan Falls
207	11,188	Edison Local	Hammondsville
208	11,185	Clyde-Green Springs Ex. Village	Clyde
209	11,170	Lancaster City	Lancaster
210	11,169	Elida Local	Elida
211	11,164	Southeast Local	Apple Creek
212	11,149	Twinsburg City	Twinsburg
213	11,143	Adams County/ohio Valley Local	West Union
214	11,126	Logan-Hocking Local	Logan
215	11,119	Highland Local	Sparta
216	11,113	North Fork Local	Utica
217	11,111	Greenfield Exempted Village	Greenfield
218	11,064	Goshen Local	Goshen
219	11,062	Greenville City	Greenville
220	11,054	Howland Local	Warren
221	11,041	Franklin City	Franklin
222	11,031	Perrysburg Exempted Village	Perrysburg
223	11,019	Midview Local	Grafton
224	11,001	Steubenville City	Steubenville
225	10,995	Sheffield-Sheffield Lake City	Sheffield Vllg
226	10,988	Fremont City	Fremont
227	10,984	Hillsboro City	Hillsboro
228	10,947	Ashland City	Ashland
229	10,944	Ontario Local	Mansfield
230	10,936	Jefferson Area Local	Jefferson
231	10,928	Indian Creek Local	Wintersville
232	10,919	Defiance City	Defiance
233	10,893	South Point Local	South Point
234	10,880	Minerva Local	Minerva
235	10,846	Northwest Local	Mc Dermott
236	10,828	Southwest Local	Harrison
237	10,826	Madison Local	Middletown
238	10,752	Buckeye Local	Ashtabula
239	10,738	Keystone Local	Lagrange
240	10,730	Waverly City	Waverly
241	10,723	Plain Local	Canton
242	10,713	Piqua City	Piqua
243	10,706	Heath City	Heath
243	10,706	Northmont City	Englewood
245	10,699	Minford Local	Minford
246	10,671	Milford Exempted Village	Milford
247	10,654	Loveland City	Loveland
248	10,630	Delaware City	Delaware
249	10,621	Cuyahoga Falls City	Cuyahoga Falls
250	10,605	Westfall Local	Williamsport
251	10,594	Firelands Local	South Amherst
252	10,588	West Holmes Local	Millersburg
253	10,584	Edison Local (Formerly Berlin-Milan)	Milan
254	10,564	Brunswick City	Brunswick
255	10,562	Girard City SD	Girard
256	10,545	Tipp City Exempted Village	Tipp City
257	10,540	Wauseon Exempted Village	Wauseon
258	10,502	Madison Local	Madison
259	10,493	Indian Valley Local Schools	Gnadenhutten
260	10,487	Hamilton City	Hamilton
261	10,481	Shawnee Local	Lima
262	10,468	Triway Local	Wooster
263	10,452	Logan Elm Local	Circleville
264	10,444	East Holmes Local	Berlin
265	10,382	Wapakoneta City	Wapakoneta
266	10,356	Tecumseh Local	New Carlisle
267	10,342	Northern Local	Thornville
267	10,342	Stow-Munroe Falls City SD	Stow
269	10,327	Johnstown-Monroe Local	Johnstown
270	10,322	Bath Local	Lima
271	10,317	Southwest Licking Local	Pataskala
272	10,274	Beaver Local	Lisbon
273	10,266	Claymont City	Dennison
274	10,218	Northwest Local	Cincinnati
275	10,185	Little Miami Local	Maineville
276	10,180	Licking Valley Local	Newark
277	10,168	Kenton City	Kenton
278	10,161	Coventry Local	Akron
279	10,158	North Canton City	North Canton
280	10,137	Lakeview Local	Cortland
281	10,128	East Muskingum Local	New Concord
282	10,127	Wheelersburg Local	Wheelersburg
283	10,124	Maysville Local	Zanesville
284	10,123	Clark-Shawnee Local	Springfield
285	10,118	Field Local	Mogadore
286	10,090	Licking Heights Local	Pataskala
287	10,047	Washington CH City	Washington CH
288	10,041	Boardman Local	Youngstown
289	10,024	Lake Local	Uniontown
290	9,987	Blanchester Local	Blanchester
291	9,980	Perry Local	Massillon
292	9,972	Monroe Local SD	Monroe
293	9,950	Poland Local	Poland
294	9,948	Batavia Local	Batavia
295	9,944	Marlington Local	Alliance
296	9,942	Graham Local	Saint Paris
297	9,932	Amherst Exempted Village	Amherst
298	9,924	Anthony Wayne Local	Whitehouse
299	9,922	Western Brown Local	Mount Orab
300	9,909	Teays Valley Local	Ashville
301	9,902	Carlisle Local	Carlisle
302	9,813	Clinton-Massie Local	Clarksville
303	9,798	Upper Sandusky Exempted Village	Upper Sandusky
304	9,792	Tri-Valley Local	Dresden
305	9,763	Valley View Local	Germantown
306	9,754	Forest Hills Local	Cincinnati
307	9,717	Electronic Classroom of Tomorrow	Columbus
308	9,711	River Valley Local	Caledonia
309	9,695	Amanda-Clearcreek Local	Amanda
310	9,687	West Branch Local	Beloit
311	9,656	Carrollton Exempted Village	Carrollton
312	9,655	Dover City	Dover
313	9,653	Bethel-Tate Local	Bethel
314	9,644	Hamilton Local	Columbus
315	9,631	Clearview Local	Lorain
316	9,629	Green Local	Uniontown
317	9,627	Warren Local	Vincent
318	9,624	Springboro Community City	Springboro
319	9,620	Union-Scioto Local	Chillicothe
320	9,618	Tiffin City	Tiffin
321	9,562	Marietta City	Marietta
322	9,557	Canfield Local	Canfield
323	9,539	Lebanon City	Lebanon
324	9,513	Highland Local	Medina
325	9,509	Saint Clairsville-Richland City	Saint Clairsville
326	9,494	Clear Fork Valley Local	Bellville
327	9,484	Norwalk City	Norwalk
328	9,437	Mount Vernon City	Mount Vernon
329	9,385	Avon Local	Avon
330	9,330	West Clermont Local	Cincinnati
331	9,300	Fairland Local	Proctorville
332	9,270	Zane Trace Local	Chillicothe
333	9,265	Greenon Local	Enon
334	9,220	New Philadel. City	New Philadel.
335	9,181	Northeastern Local	Springfield
336	9,165	Wilmington City	Wilmington
337	9,133	Lexington Local	Lexington
338	9,076	Lakota Local	Liberty Twp
339	8,946	N Ridgeville City	N Ridgeville
340	8,877	Fairfield City	Fairfield
341	8,847	Oak Hills Local	Cincinnati
342	8,819	Riverside Local	Painesville
343	8,795	Norton City	Norton
344	8,514	Alternative Education Academy	Toledo
345	7,552	Treca Digital Academy	Marion
346	7,009	Ohio Virtual Academy	Maumee
347	6,458	Ohio Connections Academy Inc	Cleveland

Long-Term Debt per Student (end of FY)

Rank	Dollars	District Name	City
1	27,809	Beachwood City	Beachwood
2	25,788	Indian Lake Local	Lewistown
3	23,345	Olentangy Local	Lewis Center
4	21,142	Cincinnati City	Cincinnati
5	20,966	Wadsworth City	Wadsworth
6	20,890	Three Rivers Local	Cleves
7	20,782	Rocky River City	Rocky River
8	20,506	Lakewood City	Lakewood
9	18,947	Licking Heights Local	Pataskala
10	17,409	Gallia County Local	Gallipolis
11	17,307	Marysville Exempted Village	Marysville
12	17,123	Vandalia-Butler City	Vandalia
13	16,700	Northwestern Local	Springfield
14	15,611	Bellbrook-Sugarcreek Local SD	Bellbrook
15	15,423	Bloom-Carroll Local	Carroll
16	15,341	Elida Local	Elida
17	15,258	Fairview Park City	Fairview Park
18	15,030	Keystone Local	Lagrange
19	14,241	Trotwood-Madison City	Trotwood
20	13,707	Monroe Local SD	Monroe
21	13,667	Switzerland of Ohio Local	Woodsfield
22	13,657	Otsego Local	Tontogany
23	13,420	Kenston Local	Chagrin Falls
24	13,343	Beavercreek City	Beavercreek
25	13,285	Barberton City	Barberton
26	13,185	Huber Heights City	Huber Heights
27	13,130	Fairfield Union Local	Lancaster
28	12,943	Lake Local	Millbury
29	12,859	Willard City	Willard
30	12,830	Maumee City	Maumee
31	12,826	Sylvania City	Sylvania
32	12,807	Sycamore Community City	Cincinnati
33	12,792	Wauseon Exempted Village	Wauseon
34	12,629	Northwest Local	Canal Fulton
35	12,456	Bucyrus City	Bucyrus
36	12,429	Dublin City	Dublin
37	12,414	Springboro Community City	Springboro
38	11,943	Granville Exempted Village	Granville
39	11,887	Bexley City	Bexley
40	11,875	New Albany-Plain Local	New Albany
41	11,679	Van Wert City	Van Wert
42	11,555	Bellevue City	Bellevue
43	11,245	Garfield Hgts City Schools	Garfield Hgts
44	11,217	Miami Trace Local	Washington CH
45	11,206	Hilliard City	Hilliard
46	11,183	London City	London
47	11,169	Jackson Local	Massillon
48	10,977	Aurora City	Aurora
49	10,948	Saint Marys City	Saint Marys
50	10,824	Newark City	Newark
51	10,752	Clyde-Green Springs Ex. Village	Clyde
52	10,688	Ross Local	Hamilton
53	10,671	Orange City	Cleveland
54	10,451	Ottawa-Glandorf Local	Ottawa
55	10,450	Louisville City	Louisville
56	10,395	Whitehall City	Whitehall
57	10,227	Chillicothe City	Chillicothe
58	10,102	Teays Valley Local	Ashville
59	10,056	Jonathan Alder Local	Plain City
60	9,984	Milford Exempted Village	Milford
61	9,869	Warrensville Hgts City	Warrensville Hgts
62	9,868	Jefferson Area Local	Jefferson
63	9,728	Tallmadge City	Tallmadge
64	9,721	Edgewood City	Trenton
65	9,717	Buckeye Valley Local	Delaware
66	9,650	Mayfield City	Mayfield Hgts
67	9,186	Buckeye Local	Medina
68	9,099	Columbus City SD	Columbus
69	9,029	Highland Local	Medina
70	9,004	Painesville City Local	Painesville
71	8,983	Xenia Community City	Xenia
72	8,980	Mt Healthy City	Cincinnati
73	8,859	Findlay City	Findlay
74	8,797	Middletown City	Middletown
75	8,655	Bowling Green City SD	Bowling Green
76	8,579	Avon Local	Avon
77	8,383	Ontario Local	Mansfield
78	8,332	Bellefontaine City	Bellefontaine
79	8,279	Wapakoneta City	Wapakoneta
80	8,252	Zanesville City	Zanesville
81	8,233	Washington CH City	Washington CH
82	8,191	Highland Local	Sparta
83	8,165	Ashtabula Area City	Ashtabula
84	8,149	Graham Local	Saint Paris
85	8,065	Madison Local	Mansfield
86	8,049	Clark-Shawnee Local	Springfield
87	7,982	Hamilton Local	Columbus
88	7,940	Medina City SD	Medina
89	7,921	Adams County/ohio Valley Local	West Union
90	7,832	Madison Local	Madison
91	7,726	Nordonia Hills City	Northfield
92	7,709	Westerville City	Westerville
93	7,609	Fairless Local	Navarre
94	7,505	Heath City	Heath
95	7,396	Loveland City	Loveland
96	7,302	Centerville City	Centerville
97	6,931	Madison Local	Middletown
98	6,848	Toledo City	Toledo
99	6,833	River Valley Local	Caledonia
100	6,782	Geneva Area City	Geneva
101	6,656	Girard City SD	Girard
102	6,613	Portsmouth City	Portsmouth
103	6,528	Minerva Local	Minerva
104	6,493	Tipp City Exempted Village	Tipp City

Note: This section only includes districts with 1,500 or more students; All categories are ranked from high to low

Rank	Number	District Name	City
105	6,483	Warren City	Warren
106	6,379	Elyria City Schools	Elyria
107	6,332	Hudson City	Hudson
108	6,254	Licking Valley Local	Newark
109	6,183	Waverly City	Waverly
110	6,171	Hillsboro City	Hillsboro
111	6,131	Delaware City	Delaware
112	5,977	Defiance City	Defiance
113	5,885	Woodridge Local	Peninsula
114	5,884	Worthington City	Worthington
115	5,859	Lorain City	Lorain
116	5,856	Wheelersburg Local	Wheelersburg
117	5,639	Lakewood Local	Hebron
118	5,618	Streetsboro City	Streetsboro
119	5,553	Coshocton City	Coshocton
120	5,455	Olmsted Falls City	Olmsted Falls
121	5,425	Tecumseh Local	New Carlisle
122	5,364	South Point Local	South Point
123	5,324	Jackson City	Jackson
124	5,311	Brunswick City	Brunswick
125	5,269	Tri-Valley Local	Dresden
126	5,266	Youngstown City Schools	Youngstown
127	5,219	Bay Village City	Bay Village
128	5,195	Upper Arlington City	Upper Arlington
129	5,152	Norwalk City	Norwalk
130	5,130	Gahanna-Jefferson City	Gahanna
131	5,086	Sidney City	Sidney
132	4,955	Gallipolis City	Gallipolis
133	4,953	Fairborn City	Fairborn
134	4,907	Brecksville-Broadview Hghts City	Brecksville
135	4,896	Northridge Local	Dayton
136	4,727	Alliance City	Alliance
137	4,661	Logan-Hocking Local	Logan
138	4,563	Anthony Wayne Local	Whitehouse
139	4,494	Mad River Local	Dayton
140	4,402	Troy City	Troy
141	4,379	Springfield City	Springfield
142	4,317	Shaker Heights City	Shaker Heights
143	4,314	Fremont City	Fremont
144	4,216	Clinton-Massie Local	Clarksville
145	4,094	South-Western City	Grove City
146	4,075	Canton City	Canton
147	3,943	Alexander Local	Albany
148	3,904	Morgan Local	Mc Connelsville
149	3,656	Clear Fork Valley Local	Bellville
150	3,467	Celina City	Celina
151	3,447	Solon City	Solon
152	3,411	Lima City	Lima
153	3,336	Goshen Local	Goshen
154	3,310	West Branch Local	Beloit
155	3,269	Conneaut Area City	Conneaut
156	3,220	Strongsville City	Strongsville
157	3,163	Paulding Exempted Village	Paulding
158	3,153	South Euclid-Lyndhurst City	Lyndhurst
159	3,081	Parma City	Parma
160	3,009	Fairfield City	Fairfield
161	2,970	North Canton City	North Canton
162	2,906	Piqua City	Piqua
163	2,835	Coventry Local	Akron
164	2,766	Southeast Local	Ravenna
165	2,749	Crestwood Local	Mantua
166	2,729	North Royalton City	North Royalton
167	2,692	Tiffin City	Tiffin
168	2,666	Vermilion Local	Vermilion
169	2,649	Meigs Local	Pomeroy
170	2,589	Willoughby-Eastlake City	Willoughby
171	2,585	Franklin Local	Duncan Falls
172	2,510	Vinton County Local	Mc Arthur
173	2,469	Cleveland Hgts-University Hgts City	University Hgts
174	2,405	Revere Local	Bath
175	2,370	Bethel-Tate Local	Bethel
176	2,368	East Muskingum Local	New Concord
177	2,291	Marion City	Marion
178	2,196	Napoleon Area City	Napoleon
179	2,187	Lakeview Local	Cortland
180	2,137	East Liverpool City	East Liverpool
181	2,080	Wilmington City	Wilmington
182	2,051	Eastwood Local	Pemberville
183	2,046	Forest Hills Local	Cincinnati
184	1,849	Northwest Local	Cincinnati
185	1,756	East Cleveland City SD	East Cleveland
186	1,672	Blanchester Local	Blanchester
187	1,388	Fairland Local	Proctorville
188	1,323	Maysville Local	Zanesville
189	1,313	New Lexington City	New Lexington
190	1,288	Franklin City	Franklin
191	1,260	Copley-Fairlawn City	Copley
192	1,203	Saint Clairsville-Richland City	Saint Clairsville
193	1,187	Union-Scioto Local	Chillicothe
194	1,179	Dover City	Dover
195	1,144	New Philadel. City	New Philadel.
196	1,119	Perry Local	Massillon
197	1,113	Greenfield Exempted Village	Greenfield
198	1,050	Northwest Local	Mc Dermott
199	965	East Holmes Local	Berlin
200	859	Riverside Local	Painesville
201	836	Cuyahoga Falls City	Cuyahoga Falls
202	835	Salem City	Salem
203	612	Perkins Local	Sandusky
204	601	River View Local	Warsaw
205	561	Firelands Local	South Amherst
206	543	Minford Local	Minford
207	526	Perry Local	Perry
208	523	West Carrollton City	West Carrollton
209	511	Stow-Munroe Falls City SD	Stow
210	490	Urbana City	Urbana
211	480	Bath Local	Lima
211	480	N Ridgeville City	N Ridgeville
213	473	Mansfield City	Mansfield
214	436	Howland Local	Warren
215	402	Benjamin Logan Local	Bellefontaine
216	381	Washington-Nile Local	West Portsmouth
217	376	Rolling Hills Local	Cambridge
218	333	Harrison Hills City	Cadiz
219	280	Johnstown-Monroe Local	Johnstown
220	243	Mentor Exempted Village	Mentor
221	220	Valley View Local	Germantown
222	201	Sheffield-Sheffield Lake City	Sheffield Vllg
223	180	Washington Local	Toledo
224	130	Reading Community City	Reading
225	81	North Olmsted City	North Olmsted
226	79	Beaver Local	Lisbon
227	29	Buckeye Local	Ashtabula
228	0	Akron City	Akron
228	0	Alternative Education Academy	Toledo
228	0	Amanda-Clearcreek Local	Amanda
228	0	Amherst Exempted Village	Amherst
228	0	Ashland City	Ashland
228	0	Athens City	The Plains
228	0	Austintown Local	Youngstown
228	0	Avon Lake City	Avon Lake
228	0	Batavia Local	Batavia
228	0	Bedford City	Bedford
228	0	Benton Carroll Salem Local	Oak Harbor
228	0	Berea City	Berea
228	0	Big Walnut Local	Galena
228	0	Boardman Local	Youngstown
228	0	Bryan City	Bryan
228	0	Buckeye Local	Dillonvale
228	0	Cambridge City	Cambridge
228	0	Canal Wnchstr Local	Canal Wnchstr
228	0	Canfield Local	Canfield
228	0	Canton Local	Canton
228	0	Carlisle Local	Carlisle
228	0	Carrollton Exempted Village	Carrollton
228	0	Chagrin Falls Exempted Village	Chagrin Falls
228	0	Chardon Local	Chardon
228	0	Circleville City	Circleville
228	0	Claymont City	Dennison
228	0	Clearview Local	Lorain
228	0	Clermont Northeastern Local	Batavia
228	0	Cleveland Municipal	Cleveland
228	0	Cloverleaf Local	Lodi
228	0	Dayton City	Dayton
228	0	Eaton Community City	Eaton
228	0	Edison Local	Hammondsville
228	0	Edison Local (Formerly Berlin-Milan)	Milan
228	0	Electronic Classroom of Tomorrow	Columbus
228	0	Euclid City	Euclid
228	0	Field Local	Mogadore
228	0	Fostoria City	Fostoria
228	0	Galion City	Galion
228	0	Green Local	Uniontown
228	0	Greenon Local	Enon
228	0	Greenville City	Greenville
228	0	Groveport Madison Local	Groveport
228	0	Hamilton City	Hamilton
228	0	Hubbard Exempted Village	Hubbard
228	0	Indian Creek Local	Wintersville
228	0	Indian Hill Exempted Village	Cincinnati
228	0	Indian Valley Local Schools	Gnadenhutten
228	0	Kent City	Kent
228	0	Kenton City	Kenton
228	0	Kettering City	Kettering
228	0	Kings Local	Kings Mills
228	0	Lake Local	Uniontown
228	0	Lakota Local	Liberty Twp
228	0	Lancaster City	Lancaster
228	0	Lebanon City	Lebanon
228	0	Lexington Local	Lexington
228	0	Little Miami Local	Maineville
228	0	Logan Elm Local	Circleville
228	0	Maple Heights City	Maple Heights
228	0	Mariemont City	Cincinnati
228	0	Marietta City	Marietta
228	0	Marlington Local	Alliance
228	0	Mason City SD	Mason
228	0	Massillon City	Massillon
228	0	Miamisburg City	Miamisburg
228	0	Midview Local	Grafton
228	0	Mount Vernon City	Mount Vernon
228	0	New Richmond Exempted Village	New Richmond
228	0	Niles City	Niles
228	0	North College Hill City	Cincinnati
228	0	North Fork Local	Utica
228	0	Northeastern Local	Springfield
228	0	Northern Local	Thornville
228	0	Northmont City	Englewood
228	0	Norton City	Norton
228	0	Norwood City	Norwood
228	0	Oak Hills Local	Cincinnati
228	0	Oakwood City	Dayton
228	0	Ohio Connections Academy Inc	Cleveland
228	0	Ohio Virtual Academy	Maumee
228	0	Oregon City	Oregon
228	0	Orrville City	Orrville
228	0	Perrysburg Exempted Village	Perrysburg
228	0	Pickerington Local	Pickerington
228	0	Plain Local	Canton
228	0	Poland Local	Poland
228	0	Port Clinton City	Port Clinton
228	0	Princeton City	Cincinnati
228	0	Ravenna City	Ravenna
228	0	Reynoldsburg City	Reynoldsburg
228	0	Rossford Exempted Village	Rossford
228	0	Sandusky City	Sandusky
228	0	Shawnee Local	Lima
228	0	Shelby City	Shelby
228	0	Southeast Local	Apple Creek
228	0	Southwest Licking Local	Pataskala
228	0	Southwest Local	Harrison
228	0	Springfield Local	Holland
228	0	Springfield Local	Akron
228	0	Steubenville City	Steubenville
228	0	Struthers City	Struthers
228	0	Talawanda City	Oxford
228	0	Treca Digital Academy	Marion
228	0	Triway Local	Wooster
228	0	Twinsburg City	Twinsburg
228	0	Upper Sandusky Exempted Village	Upper Sandusky
228	0	Warren Local	Vincent
228	0	Wellston City	Wellston
228	0	West Clermont Local	Cincinnati
228	0	West Geauga Local	Chesterland
228	0	West Holmes Local	Millersburg
228	0	Western Brown Local	Mount Orab
228	0	Westfall Local	Williamsport
228	0	Westlake City	Westlake
228	0	Wickliffe City	Wickliffe
228	0	Winton Woods City	Cincinnati
228	0	Wooster City	Wooster
228	0	Wyoming City	Wyoming
228	0	Zane Trace Local	Chillicothe

Number of Diploma Recipients

Rank	Number	District Name	City
1	2,709	Columbus City SD	Columbus
2	2,187	Cleveland Municipal	Cleveland
3	1,723	Cincinnati City	Cincinnati
4	1,484	Akron City	Akron

Note: This section only includes districts with 1,500 or more students; All categories are ranked from high to low

Rank	Number	District Name	City
5	1,276	Toledo City	Toledo
6	1,232	Lakota Local	Liberty Twp
7	1,231	Electronic Classroom of Tomorrow	Columbus
8	1,220	South-Western City	Grove City
9	1,040	Parma City	Parma
10	1,035	Dublin City	Dublin
11	980	Westerville City	Westerville
12	968	Hilliard City	Hilliard
13	782	Willoughby-Eastlake City	Willoughby
14	781	Worthington City	Worthington
15	751	Mentor Exempted Village	Mentor
16	748	Fairfield City	Fairfield
17	733	Olentangy Local	Lewis Center
18	722	Pickerington Local	Pickerington
19	715	Northwest Local	Cincinnati
20	712	Oak Hills Local	Cincinnati
21	692	Dayton City	Dayton
22	676	Mason City SD	Mason
23	673	Centerville City	Centerville
24	671	Canton City	Canton
25	667	West Clermont Local	Cincinnati
26	631	Beavercreek City	Beavercreek
27	623	Sylvania City	Sylvania
28	608	Berea City	Berea
29	582	Strongsville City	Strongsville
30	553	Forest Hills Local	Cincinnati
31	542	Kettering City	Kettering
32	541	Brunswick City	Brunswick
33	540	Medina City SD	Medina
34	503	Gahanna-Jefferson City	Gahanna
35	493	Sycamore Community City	Cincinnati
36	489	Lorain City	Lorain
37	475	Huber Heights City	Huber Heights
38	464	Washington Local	Toledo
39	460	Reynoldsburg City	Reynoldsburg
40	456	Jackson Local	Massillon
41	452	Upper Arlington City	Upper Arlington
42	450	Stow-Munroe Falls City SD	Stow
43	446	Elyria City Schools	Elyria
43	446	Milford Exempted Village	Milford
45	440	Northmont City	Englewood
46	437	Findlay City	Findlay
47	435	Plain Local	Canton
48	432	Solon City	Solon
49	430	Hamilton City	Hamilton
50	423	Lakewood City	Lakewood
51	418	North Royalton City	North Royalton
52	415	Lancaster City	Lancaster
53	414	North Canton City	North Canton
54	412	Hudson City	Hudson
55	407	Springfield City	Springfield
56	406	Brecksville-Broadview Hghts City	Brecksville
57	402	Shaker Heights City	Shaker Heights
58	396	Miamisburg City	Miamisburg
59	391	Princeton City	Cincinnati
60	385	Boardman Local	Youngstown
61	381	North Olmsted City	North Olmsted
62	378	Euclid City	Euclid
63	372	Austintown Local	Youngstown
64	371	Marysville Exempted Village	Marysville
65	370	Perrysburg Exempted Village	Perrysburg
66	364	Riverside Local	Painesville
67	363	Amherst Exempted Village	Amherst
67	363	Lebanon City	Lebanon
69	355	Perry Local	Massillon
70	354	Wadsworth City	Wadsworth
71	353	Troy City	Troy
72	351	Groveport Madison Local	Groveport
73	346	Nordonia Hills City	Northfield
74	344	Cuyahoga Falls City	Cuyahoga Falls
75	340	Newark City	Newark
76	339	Cleveland Hgts-University Hgts City	University Hgts
77	338	Anthony Wayne Local	Whitehouse
77	338	Green Local	Uniontown
77	338	Springboro Community City	Springboro
80	333	Middletown City	Middletown
81	317	Twinsburg City	Twinsburg
81	317	Youngstown City Schools	Youngstown
83	316	Mayfield City	Mayfield Hgts
83	316	Xenia Community City	Xenia
85	315	Northeastern Local	Springfield
86	312	South Euclid-Lyndhurst City	Lyndhurst
86	312	Westlake City	Westlake
88	309	Lake Local	Uniontown
89	307	Loveland City	Loveland
90	303	Logan-Hocking Local	Logan
91	302	Kent City	Kent
92	296	Warren City	Warren
93	293	Mount Vernon City	Mount Vernon
94	291	Delaware City	Delaware
95	290	Wooster City	Wooster
96	288	Adams County/ohio Valley Local	West Union
97	287	Fremont City	Fremont
98	286	Piqua City	Piqua
99	285	Olmsted Falls City	Olmsted Falls
100	284	Fairborn City	Fairborn
101	280	Celina City	Celina
102	279	Avon Lake City	Avon Lake
102	279	Garfield Hgts City Schools	Garfield Hgts
102	279	Vandalia-Butler City	Vandalia
105	278	Oregon City	Oregon
106	277	Marion City	Marion
106	277	Southwest Licking Local	Pataskala
108	275	Little Miami Local	Maineville
109	273	Southwest Local	Harrison
109	273	Talawanda City	Oxford
111	269	Sidney City	Sidney
112	266	Edgewood City	Trenton
112	266	Maumee City	Maumee
114	264	Ashland City	Ashland
114	264	Massillon City	Massillon
116	262	Highland Local	Medina
117	261	Bowling Green City SD	Bowling Green
118	260	Louisville City	Louisville
119	258	Winton Woods City	Cincinnati
120	257	Canfield Local	Canfield
121	256	N Ridgeville City	N Ridgeville
122	254	Chardon Local	Chardon
123	250	Teays Valley Local	Ashville
123	250	Tecumseh Local	New Carlisle
123	250	Tri-Valley Local	Dresden
126	248	Kings Local	Kings Mills
127	246	Maple Heights City	Maple Heights
128	245	Madison Local	Madison
128	245	Midview Local	Grafton
130	244	New Philadel. City	New Philadel.
130	244	Rocky River City	Rocky River
130	244	Wapakoneta City	Wapakoneta
133	242	Barberton City	Barberton
133	242	Greenville City	Greenville
135	241	Cloverleaf Local	Lodi
136	240	Springfield Local	Holland
137	238	Bedford City	Bedford
137	238	Geneva Area City	Geneva
139	237	Western Brown Local	Mount Orab
140	235	Copley-Fairlawn City	Copley
141	234	New Albany-Plain Local	New Albany
142	232	Kenston Local	Chagrin Falls
143	231	Big Walnut Local	Galena
144	230	Bellbrook-Sugarcreek Local SD	Bellbrook
145	228	Madison Local	Mansfield
145	228	West Carrollton City	West Carrollton
147	226	Sandusky City	Sandusky
148	225	Ashtabula Area City	Ashtabula
149	224	Mt Healthy City	Cincinnati
150	223	Shawnee Local	Lima
151	222	Poland Local	Poland
152	221	Revere Local	Bath
153	220	Carrollton Exempted Village	Carrollton
154	219	Howland Local	Warren
154	219	Lima City	Lima
156	216	Tallmadge City	Tallmadge
157	215	Mad River Local	Dayton
158	212	Crestwood Local	Mantua
158	212	West Geauga Local	Chesterland
160	209	Bellefontaine City	Bellefontaine
161	207	Chillicothe City	Chillicothe
161	207	Marlington Local	Alliance
163	205	Ross Local	Hamilton
164	204	Logan Elm Local	Circleville
164	204	Springfield Local	Akron
166	203	Aurora City	Aurora
167	202	Lexington Local	Lexington
167	202	Marietta City	Marietta
167	202	Northwest Local	Canal Fulton
167	202	Saint Marys City	Saint Marys
171	200	Mansfield City	Mansfield
172	199	Ravenna City	Ravenna
172	199	Tiffin City	Tiffin
174	195	Buckeye Local	Dillonvale
174	195	Canal Wnchstr Local	Canal Wnchstr
174	195	Napoleon Area City	Napoleon
174	195	Switzerland of Ohio Local	Woodsfield
178	194	Tipp City Exempted Village	Tipp City
178	194	Vermilion Local	Vermilion
180	193	Trotwood-Madison City	Trotwood
181	192	Canton Local	Canton
182	191	Bellevue City	Bellevue
182	191	Hillsboro City	Hillsboro
182	191	Jackson City	Jackson
185	190	Avon Local	Avon
186	189	New Richmond Exempted Village	New Richmond
187	186	Bexley City	Bexley
187	186	Elida Local	Elida
189	185	Bay Village City	Bay Village
190	184	Niles City	Niles
190	184	River View Local	Warsaw
190	184	West Branch Local	Beloit
193	183	Alliance City	Alliance
193	183	Athens City	The Plains
193	183	Clark-Shawnee Local	Springfield
193	183	Minerva Local	Minerva
197	182	Valley View Local	Germantown
198	181	Defiance City	Defiance
199	180	Shelby City	Shelby
200	179	West Holmes Local	Millersburg
201	178	Buckeye Valley Local	Delaware
202	175	Buckeye Local	Medina
202	175	Miami Trace Local	Washington CH
204	174	Beaver Local	Lisbon
205	173	Coventry Local	Akron
205	173	East Cleveland City SD	East Cleveland
207	172	Granville Exempted Village	Granville
207	172	Northern Local	Thornville
207	172	Norwalk City	Norwalk
207	172	Van Wert City	Van Wert
211	171	Hubbard Exempted Village	Hubbard
212	170	Fairless Local	Navarre
212	170	Franklin City	Franklin
212	170	Zanesville City	Zanesville
215	169	Buckeye Local	Ashtabula
215	169	Field Local	Mogadore
215	169	Warren Local	Vincent
218	168	Vinton County Local	Mc Arthur
219	167	Indian Hill Exempted Village	Cincinnati
219	167	Oakwood City	Dayton
219	167	Wyoming City	Wyoming
222	165	Edison Local	Hammondsville
222	165	Firelands Local	South Amherst
224	163	Franklin Local	Duncan Falls
225	162	Hamilton Local	Columbus
225	162	Lakewood Local	Hebron
227	161	Dover City	Dover
227	161	Morgan Local	Mc Connelsville
227	161	Wilmington City	Wilmington
230	160	Perkins Local	Sandusky
231	159	Clyde-Green Springs Ex. Village	Clyde
231	159	Gallia County Local	Gallipolis
231	159	Licking Heights Local	Pataskala
234	158	Struthers City	Struthers
234	158	Wauseon Exempted Village	Wauseon
236	157	Benton Carroll Salem Local	Oak Harbor
236	157	Circleville City	Circleville
236	157	Goshen Local	Goshen
236	157	Streetsboro City	Streetsboro
240	156	Greenon Local	Enon
240	156	Southeast Local	Ravenna
242	155	Ottawa-Glandorf Local	Ottawa
242	155	Whitehall City	Whitehall
244	154	Conneaut Area City	Conneaut
244	154	Eaton Community City	Eaton
246	153	Meigs Local	Pomeroy
247	152	Bryan City	Bryan
247	152	East Muskingum Local	New Concord
247	152	Jonathan Alder Local	Plain City
250	151	Monroe Local SD	Monroe
250	151	Norton City	Norton
252	150	East Liverpool City	East Liverpool
252	150	Greenfield Exempted Village	Greenfield
254	149	Blanchester Local	Blanchester
254	149	Chagrin Falls Exempted Village	Chagrin Falls
254	149	Fairfield Union Local	Lancaster

Note: This section only includes districts with 1,500 or more students; All categories are ranked from high to low

Rank	Number	District Name	City
254	149	Indian Lake Local	Lewistown
254	149	Lakeview Local	Cortland
254	149	Upper Sandusky Exempted Village	Upper Sandusky
260	148	Harrison Hills City	Cadiz
260	148	Orange City	Cleveland
260	148	Rossford Exempted Village	Rossford
260	148	Salem City	Salem
264	146	Cambridge City	Cambridge
264	146	Licking Valley Local	Newark
264	146	Woodridge Local	Peninsula
267	145	Willard City	Willard
268	144	Bloom-Carroll Local	Carroll
268	144	Indian Creek Local	Wintersville
270	143	Graham Local	Saint Paris
270	143	Norwood City	Norwood
272	142	Clermont Northeastern Local	Batavia
272	142	Steubenville City	Steubenville
274	140	Benjamin Logan Local	Bellefontaine
274	140	Claymont City	Dennison
274	140	Sheffield-Sheffield Lake City	Sheffield Vllg
277	139	Bath Local	Lima
277	139	London City	London
277	139	Ontario Local	Mansfield
280	138	Fairview Park City	Fairview Park
280	138	Keystone Local	Lagrange
280	138	Waverly City	Waverly
283	137	Warrensville Hgts City	Warrensville Hgts
284	136	Beachwood City	Beachwood
284	136	Maysville Local	Zanesville
286	135	Batavia Local	Batavia
286	135	Clear Fork Valley Local	Bellville
286	135	Eastwood Local	Pemberville
286	135	North Fork Local	Utica
286	135	Northwestern Local	Springfield
286	135	Perry Local	Perry
292	134	Heath City	Heath
292	134	Kenton City	Kenton
292	134	Triway Local	Wooster
295	133	Bethel-Tate Local	Bethel
295	133	Three Rivers Local	Cleves
297	132	Jefferson Area Local	Jefferson
298	131	Carlisle Local	Carlisle
298	131	Clinton-Massie Local	Clarksville
298	131	Lake Local	Millbury
298	131	Treca Digital Academy	Marion
302	130	Port Clinton City	Port Clinton
302	130	Rolling Hills Local	Cambridge
302	130	Union-Scioto Local	Chillicothe
302	130	Washington CH City	Washington CH
306	129	Coshocton City	Coshocton
307	127	Clearview Local	Lorain
307	127	Otsego Local	Tontogany
309	126	Paulding Exempted Village	Paulding
310	125	New Lexington City	New Lexington
311	124	Johnstown-Monroe Local	Johnstown
311	124	Northridge Local	Dayton
313	123	Fairland Local	Proctorville
314	122	River Valley Local	Caledonia
315	121	Bucyrus City	Bucyrus
315	121	Edison Local (Formerly Berlin-Milan)	Milan
317	119	Minford Local	Minford
318	118	North College Hill City	Cincinnati
319	117	Alexander Local	Albany
319	117	Painesville City Local	Painesville
321	116	Galion City	Galion
321	116	Orrville City	Orrville
323	114	Indian Valley Local Schools	Gnadenhutten
323	114	Saint Clairsville-Richland City	Saint Clairsville
323	114	Urbana City	Urbana
326	113	Madison Local	Middletown
327	111	Highland Local	Sparta
327	111	Mariemont City	Cincinnati
327	111	Westfall Local	Williamsport
330	110	Northwest Local	Mc Dermott
331	109	Amanda-Clearcreek Local	Amanda
331	109	Wheelersburg Local	Wheelersburg
333	108	Girard City SD	Girard
334	106	Southeast Local	Apple Creek
335	103	Fostoria City	Fostoria
336	102	Wickliffe City	Wickliffe
337	101	Zane Trace Local	Chillicothe
338	99	Reading Community City	Reading
339	98	Portsmouth City	Portsmouth
339	98	Wellston City	Wellston
341	94	Alternative Education Academy	Toledo
341	94	South Point Local	South Point
341	94	Washington-Nile Local	West Portsmouth
344	85	Ohio Virtual Academy	Maumee
345	77	Gallipolis City	Gallipolis
346	70	East Holmes Local	Berlin
347	25	Ohio Connections Academy Inc	Cleveland

High School Drop-out Rate

Rank	Percent	District Name	City
1	41.1	Treca Digital Academy	Marion
2	36.5	Electronic Classroom of Tomorrow	Columbus
3	34.7	Alternative Education Academy	Toledo
4	12.8	Cleveland Municipal	Cleveland
5	12.1	Ohio Connections Academy Inc	Cleveland
6	10.7	Lima City	Lima
7	10.2	Painesville City Local	Painesville
8	8.6	Fostoria City	Fostoria
9	8.4	East Cleveland City SD	East Cleveland
10	8.3	Marion City	Marion
11	7.7	Springfield City	Springfield
11	7.7	Youngstown City Schools	Youngstown
13	7.6	Sandusky City	Sandusky
14	7.0	Canton City	Canton
14	7.0	Newark City	Newark
16	6.5	South Point Local	South Point
17	6.4	Alliance City	Alliance
18	6.3	Akron City	Akron
19	6.1	Dayton City	Dayton
20	6.0	Mansfield City	Mansfield
20	6.0	Ohio Virtual Academy	Maumee
22	5.3	Cincinnati City	Cincinnati
23	5.2	Ashtabula Area City	Ashtabula
23	5.2	Urbana City	Urbana
25	4.8	Chillicothe City	Chillicothe
26	4.6	Trotwood-Madison City	Trotwood
27	4.5	Bedford City	Bedford
28	4.4	Xenia Community City	Xenia
29	4.3	Niles City	Niles
30	4.2	Euclid City	Euclid
30	4.2	Lorain City	Lorain
30	4.2	Toledo City	Toledo
30	4.2	Wooster City	Wooster
34	4.1	Greenville City	Greenville
34	4.1	Madison Local	Mansfield
34	4.1	Marietta City	Marietta
37	4.0	Cambridge City	Cambridge
38	3.8	Hamilton Local	Columbus
39	3.7	Circleville City	Circleville
39	3.7	Fremont City	Fremont
39	3.7	Garfield Hgts City Schools	Garfield Hgts
39	3.7	Middletown City	Middletown
39	3.7	Norwood City	Norwood
39	3.7	South-Western City	Grove City
45	3.6	Groveport Madison Local	Groveport
45	3.6	Hillsboro City	Hillsboro
45	3.6	River Valley Local	Caledonia
45	3.6	Warren City	Warren
49	3.5	Southwest Local	Harrison
49	3.5	Washington Local	Toledo
51	3.4	Galion City	Galion
51	3.4	Ravenna City	Ravenna
53	3.3	Gallia County Local	Gallipolis
53	3.3	Mount Vernon City	Mount Vernon
53	3.3	Rossford Exempted Village	Rossford
56	3.2	Gallipolis City	Gallipolis
56	3.2	Rolling Hills Local	Cambridge
56	3.2	Whitehall City	Whitehall
59	3.1	New Lexington City	New Lexington
59	3.1	Winton Woods City	Cincinnati
61	3.0	Cleveland Hgts-University Hgts City	University Hgts
62	2.9	Franklin City	Franklin
63	2.8	Clearview Local	Lorain
63	2.8	Massillon City	Massillon
63	2.8	Northwest Local	Cincinnati
63	2.8	Tecumseh Local	New Carlisle
63	2.8	Tiffin City	Tiffin
68	2.7	Buckeye Local	Ashtabula
68	2.7	Springfield Local	Akron
70	2.6	Celina City	Celina
70	2.6	Eaton Community City	Eaton
70	2.6	Elyria City Schools	Elyria
70	2.6	Harrison Hills City	Cadiz
70	2.6	Huber Heights City	Huber Heights
70	2.6	Mad River Local	Dayton
70	2.6	Southeast Local	Ravenna
70	2.6	Union-Scioto Local	Chillicothe
78	2.5	Bucyrus City	Bucyrus
78	2.5	East Muskingum Local	New Concord
78	2.5	Meigs Local	Pomeroy
78	2.5	New Philadel. City	New Philadel.
78	2.5	New Richmond Exempted Village	New Richmond
78	2.5	Shaker Heights City	Shaker Heights
84	2.4	Clermont Northeastern Local	Batavia
84	2.4	Elida Local	Elida
84	2.4	Lakewood City	Lakewood
84	2.4	Norwalk City	Norwalk
84	2.4	Warren Local	Vincent
89	2.3	Delaware City	Delaware
89	2.3	Logan Elm Local	Circleville
89	2.3	Maple Heights City	Maple Heights
89	2.3	Miamisburg City	Miamisburg
89	2.3	Midview Local	Grafton
89	2.3	Mt Healthy City	Cincinnati
89	2.3	Parma City	Parma
89	2.3	Ross Local	Hamilton
89	2.3	Southwest Licking Local	Pataskala
89	2.3	Switzerland of Ohio Local	Woodsfield
89	2.3	Teays Valley Local	Ashville
89	2.3	Vinton County Local	Mc Arthur
89	2.3	Waverly City	Waverly
102	2.2	Columbus City SD	Columbus
102	2.2	Greenon Local	Enon
102	2.2	Indian Creek Local	Wintersville
102	2.2	Kenton City	Kenton
102	2.2	Mentor Exempted Village	Mentor
102	2.2	Struthers City	Struthers
102	2.2	Three Rivers Local	Cleves
109	2.1	Barberton City	Barberton
109	2.1	Berea City	Berea
109	2.1	Buckeye Local	Dillonvale
109	2.1	Hubbard Exempted Village	Hubbard
109	2.1	Northern Local	Thornville
109	2.1	Springfield Local	Holland
109	2.1	Western Brown Local	Mount Orab
109	2.1	Westerville City	Westerville
109	2.1	Willard City	Willard
118	2.0	Batavia Local	Batavia
118	2.0	Carrollton Exempted Village	Carrollton
118	2.0	Conneaut Area City	Conneaut
118	2.0	Edison Local	Hammondsville
118	2.0	Lancaster City	Lancaster
118	2.0	Piqua City	Piqua
118	2.0	Reynoldsburg City	Reynoldsburg
118	2.0	Salem City	Salem
118	2.0	Sylvania City	Sylvania
118	2.0	West Holmes Local	Millersburg
128	1.9	Clear Fork Valley Local	Bellville
128	1.9	Triway Local	Wooster
130	1.8	Amanda-Clearcreek Local	Amanda
130	1.8	Blanchester Local	Blanchester
130	1.8	Jackson City	Jackson
130	1.8	Madison Local	Madison
130	1.8	Tallmadge City	Tallmadge
130	1.8	West Carrollton City	West Carrollton
130	1.8	Wickliffe City	Wickliffe
137	1.7	Findlay City	Findlay
137	1.7	Indian Lake Local	Lewistown
137	1.7	Jefferson Area Local	Jefferson
137	1.7	North Fork Local	Utica
137	1.7	Zane Trace Local	Chillicothe
142	1.6	Beaver Local	Lisbon
142	1.6	Bellevue City	Bellevue
142	1.6	Claymont City	Dennison
142	1.6	Cloverleaf Local	Lodi
142	1.6	Graham Local	Saint Paris
142	1.6	Lakota Local	Liberty Twp
142	1.6	Madison Local	Middletown
142	1.6	Morgan Local	Mc Connelsville
142	1.6	Upper Sandusky Exempted Village	Upper Sandusky
151	1.5	Defiance City	Defiance
151	1.5	Field Local	Mogadore
151	1.5	Port Clinton City	Port Clinton
151	1.5	River View Local	Warsaw
151	1.5	Van Wert City	Van Wert
151	1.5	Warrensville Hgts City	Warrensville Hgts

Note: This section only includes districts with 1,500 or more students; All categories are ranked from high to low

151	1.5	Washington-Nile Local	West Portsmouth
158	1.4	Amherst Exempted Village	Amherst
158	1.4	Ashland City	Ashland
158	1.4	Clark-Shawnee Local	Springfield
158	1.4	Kent City	Kent
158	1.4	Milford Exempted Village	Milford
158	1.4	Portsmouth City	Portsmouth
158	1.4	Tri-Valley Local	Dresden
158	1.4	West Clermont Local	Cincinnati
158	1.4	Wilmington City	Wilmington
167	1.3	Bath Local	Lima
167	1.3	Carlisle Local	Carlisle
167	1.3	Eastwood Local	Pemberville
167	1.3	Fairland Local	Proctorville
167	1.3	Fairless Local	Navarre
167	1.3	Licking Valley Local	Newark
167	1.3	Marlington Local	Alliance
167	1.3	Marysville Exempted Village	Marysville
167	1.3	North Olmsted City	North Olmsted
167	1.3	Pickerington Local	Pickerington
167	1.3	Shawnee Local	Lima
167	1.3	Tipp City Exempted Village	Tipp City
179	1.2	Buckeye Valley Local	Delaware
179	1.2	Dover City	Dover
179	1.2	Gahanna-Jefferson City	Gahanna
179	1.2	Northwest Local	Canal Fulton
179	1.2	Perkins Local	Sandusky
179	1.2	Twinsburg City	Twinsburg
179	1.2	West Branch Local	Beloit
186	1.1	Canton Local	Canton
186	1.1	Hilliard City	Hilliard
186	1.1	Indian Valley Local Schools	Gnadenhutten
186	1.1	Kings Local	Kings Mills
186	1.1	Lexington Local	Lexington
186	1.1	Nordonia Hills City	Northfield
186	1.1	North College Hill City	Cincinnati
186	1.1	North Royalton City	North Royalton
186	1.1	Northeastern Local	Springfield
186	1.1	Otsego Local	Tontogany
186	1.1	Plain Local	Canton
186	1.1	Reading Community City	Reading
186	1.1	Saint Clairsville-Richland City	Saint Clairsville
186	1.1	Springboro Community City	Springboro
186	1.1	Troy City	Troy
186	1.1	Washington CH City	Washington CH
186	1.1	Westfall Local	Williamsport
186	1.1	Worthington City	Worthington
204	1.0	Adams County/ohio Valley Local	West Union
204	1.0	Buckeye Local	Medina
204	1.0	Clinton-Massie Local	Clarksville
204	1.0	Edgewood City	Trenton
204	1.0	Fairfield City	Fairfield
204	1.0	Geneva Area City	Geneva
204	1.0	Licking Heights Local	Pataskala
204	1.0	Maumee City	Maumee
204	1.0	Napoleon Area City	Napoleon
204	1.0	Paulding Exempted Village	Paulding
204	1.0	Princeton City	Cincinnati
204	1.0	Riverside Local	Painesville
204	1.0	Vermilion Local	Vermilion
217	0.9	Bellefontaine City	Bellefontaine
217	0.9	Boardman Local	Youngstown
217	0.9	Brunswick City	Brunswick
217	0.9	Canal Wnchstr Local	Canal Wnchstr
217	0.9	Clyde-Green Springs Ex. Village	Clyde
217	0.9	Crestwood Local	Mantua
217	0.9	Edison Local (Formerly Berlin-Milan)	Milan
217	0.9	Fairborn City	Fairborn
217	0.9	Fairfield Union Local	Lancaster
217	0.9	Hamilton City	Hamilton
217	0.9	Logan-Hocking Local	Logan
217	0.9	Minerva Local	Minerva
217	0.9	Northmont City	Englewood
217	0.9	Shelby City	Shelby
217	0.9	Willoughby-Eastlake City	Willoughby
232	0.8	Big Walnut Local	Galena
232	0.8	Fairview Park City	Fairview Park
232	0.8	Forest Hills Local	Cincinnati
232	0.8	Greenfield Exempted Village	Greenfield
232	0.8	Medina City SD	Medina
232	0.8	Northwestern Local	Springfield
232	0.8	Perry Local	Massillon
232	0.8	Sheffield-Sheffield Lake City	Sheffield Vllg
232	0.8	South Euclid-Lyndhurst City	Lyndhurst
232	0.8	Streetsboro City	Streetsboro
232	0.8	Westlake City	Westlake
232	0.8	Woodridge Local	Peninsula
244	0.7	Coshocton City	Coshocton
244	0.7	Franklin Local	Duncan Falls
244	0.7	Indian Hill Exempted Village	Cincinnati
244	0.7	Lake Local	Millbury
244	0.7	Louisville City	Louisville
244	0.7	Northridge Local	Dayton
244	0.7	Olmsted Falls City	Olmsted Falls
244	0.7	Sidney City	Sidney
244	0.7	Strongsville City	Strongsville
244	0.7	Sycamore Community City	Cincinnati
244	0.7	Zanesville City	Zanesville
255	0.6	Athens City	The Plains
255	0.6	Beachwood City	Beachwood
255	0.6	Bethel-Tate Local	Bethel
255	0.6	Brecksville-Broadview Hghts City	Brecksville
255	0.6	Bryan City	Bryan
255	0.6	Centerville City	Centerville
255	0.6	Coventry Local	Akron
255	0.6	Green Local	Uniontown
255	0.6	Lake Local	Uniontown
255	0.6	Little Miami Local	Maineville
255	0.6	Loveland City	Loveland
255	0.6	Mayfield City	Mayfield Hgts
255	0.6	Maysville Local	Zanesville
255	0.6	Monroe Local SD	Monroe
255	0.6	Oak Hills Local	Cincinnati
255	0.6	Perry Local	Perry
255	0.6	Valley View Local	Germantown
255	0.6	Wapakoneta City	Wapakoneta
273	0.5	Aurora City	Aurora
273	0.5	Beavercreek City	Beavercreek
273	0.5	Bowling Green City SD	Bowling Green
273	0.5	Chardon Local	Chardon
273	0.5	Cuyahoga Falls City	Cuyahoga Falls
273	0.5	Goshen Local	Goshen
273	0.5	Kettering City	Kettering
273	0.5	Miami Trace Local	Washington CH
273	0.5	Upper Arlington City	Upper Arlington
273	0.5	Wadsworth City	Wadsworth
273	0.5	West Geauga Local	Chesterland
284	0.4	Austintown Local	Youngstown
284	0.4	Copley-Fairlawn City	Copley
284	0.4	Dublin City	Dublin
284	0.4	Lebanon City	Lebanon
284	0.4	N Ridgeville City	N Ridgeville
284	0.4	Olentangy Local	Lewis Center
284	0.4	Solon City	Solon
284	0.4	Stow-Munroe Falls City SD	Stow
292	0.3	Hudson City	Hudson
292	0.3	North Canton City	North Canton
294	0.2	Mason City SD	Mason
n/a	n/a	Benton Carroll Salem Local	Oak Harbor
n/a	n/a	Bexley City	Bexley
n/a	n/a	Canfield Local	Canfield
n/a	n/a	East Liverpool City	East Liverpool
n/a	n/a	Howland Local	Warren
n/a	n/a	Oregon City	Oregon
n/a	n/a	Perrysburg Exempted Village	Perrysburg
n/a	n/a	Wellston City	Wellston
n/a	n/a	Wheelersburg Local	Wheelersburg
n/a	n/a	Alexander Local	Albany
n/a	n/a	Anthony Wayne Local	Whitehouse
n/a	n/a	Avon Lake City	Avon Lake
n/a	n/a	Avon Local	Avon
n/a	n/a	Bay Village City	Bay Village
n/a	n/a	Bellbrook-Sugarcreek Local SD	Bellbrook
n/a	n/a	Benjamin Logan Local	Bellefontaine
n/a	n/a	Bloom-Carroll Local	Carroll
n/a	n/a	Chagrin Falls Exempted Village	Chagrin Falls
n/a	n/a	East Holmes Local	Berlin
n/a	n/a	Firelands Local	South Amherst
n/a	n/a	Girard City SD	Girard
n/a	n/a	Granville Exempted Village	Granville
n/a	n/a	Heath City	Heath
n/a	n/a	Highland Local	Medina
n/a	n/a	Highland Local	Sparta
n/a	n/a	Jackson Local	Massillon
n/a	n/a	Johnstown-Monroe Local	Johnstown
n/a	n/a	Jonathan Alder Local	Plain City
n/a	n/a	Kenston Local	Chagrin Falls
n/a	n/a	Keystone Local	Lagrange
n/a	n/a	Lakeview Local	Cortland
n/a	n/a	Lakewood Local	Hebron
n/a	n/a	London City	London
n/a	n/a	Mariemont City	Cincinnati
n/a	n/a	Minford Local	Minford
n/a	n/a	New Albany-Plain Local	New Albany
n/a	n/a	Northwest Local	Mc Dermott
n/a	n/a	Norton City	Norton
n/a	n/a	Oakwood City	Dayton
n/a	n/a	Ontario Local	Mansfield
n/a	n/a	Orange City	Cleveland
n/a	n/a	Orrville City	Orrville
n/a	n/a	Ottawa-Glandorf Local	Ottawa
n/a	n/a	Poland Local	Poland
n/a	n/a	Revere Local	Bath
n/a	n/a	Rocky River City	Rocky River
n/a	n/a	Saint Marys City	Saint Marys
n/a	n/a	Southeast Local	Apple Creek
n/a	n/a	Steubenville City	Steubenville
n/a	n/a	Talawanda City	Oxford
n/a	n/a	Vandalia-Butler City	Vandalia
n/a	n/a	Wauseon Exempted Village	Wauseon
n/a	n/a	Wyoming City	Wyoming

Average Freshman Graduation Rate

Rank	Percent	District Name	City
1	100.0	Anthony Wayne Local	Whitehouse
1	100.0	Beachwood City	Beachwood
1	100.0	Bloom-Carroll Local	Carroll
1	100.0	Celina City	Celina
1	100.0	Centerville City	Centerville
1	100.0	Electronic Classroom of Tomorrow	Columbus
1	100.0	Highland Local	Medina
1	100.0	Maumee City	Maumee
1	100.0	New Philadel. City	New Philadel.
1	100.0	North Canton City	North Canton
1	100.0	Olentangy Local	Lewis Center
1	100.0	Ottawa-Glandorf Local	Ottawa
1	100.0	Rocky River City	Rocky River
1	100.0	Talawanda City	Oxford
15	99.6	Bellbrook-Sugarcreek Local SD	Bellbrook
15	99.6	Mason City SD	Mason
17	99.3	Kent City	Kent
18	99.1	Beavercreek City	Beavercreek
18	99.1	Big Walnut Local	Galena
20	98.8	Wauseon Exempted Village	Wauseon
21	98.7	Poland Local	Poland
22	98.3	Minford Local	Minford
22	98.3	New Albany-Plain Local	New Albany
24	98.1	Lake Local	Uniontown
25	97.8	Upper Arlington City	Upper Arlington
26	97.7	Canfield Local	Canfield
26	97.7	Wyoming City	Wyoming
28	97.6	Sycamore Community City	Cincinnati
29	97.5	Oak Hills Local	Cincinnati
30	97.4	Avon Local	Avon
31	97.1	Aurora City	Aurora
32	96.9	Avon Lake City	Avon Lake
33	96.8	Jackson Local	Massillon
34	96.6	Perrysburg Exempted Village	Perrysburg
34	96.6	Solon City	Solon
34	96.6	Twinsburg City	Twinsburg
37	96.3	Amherst Exempted Village	Amherst
37	96.3	Springboro Community City	Springboro
37	96.3	Valley View Local	Germantown
40	96.2	Brecksville-Broadview Hghts City	Brecksville
40	96.2	Ross Local	Hamilton
40	96.2	Tri-Valley Local	Dresden
43	96.1	Blanchester Local	Blanchester
43	96.1	Van Wert City	Van Wert
43	96.1	Willoughby-Eastlake City	Willoughby
46	96.0	Dublin City	Dublin
46	96.0	Mentor Exempted Village	Mentor
48	95.9	Marysville Exempted Village	Marysville
49	95.8	Nordonia Hills City	Northfield
50	95.7	Benton Carroll Salem Local	Oak Harbor
50	95.7	Saint Marys City	Saint Marys
52	95.6	Napoleon Area City	Napoleon
52	95.6	Pickerington Local	Pickerington
54	95.5	Chagrin Falls Exempted Village	Chagrin Falls
54	95.5	Otsego Local	Tontogany
56	95.4	Oakwood City	Dayton

Note: This section only includes districts with 1,500 or more students; All categories are ranked from high to low

Rank	Value	District	City
57	95.3	Edgewood City	Trenton
58	95.2	Louisville City	Louisville
59	95.1	Lakota Local	Liberty Twp
60	95.0	North Olmsted City	North Olmsted
61	94.8	North Royalton City	North Royalton
62	94.6	Streetsboro City	Streetsboro
63	94.5	Southwest Licking Local	Pataskala
64	94.4	Olmsted Falls City	Olmsted Falls
65	94.3	Northeastern Local	Springfield
66	94.2	Saint Clairsville-Richland City	Saint Clairsville
67	94.0	Copley-Fairlawn City	Copley
68	93.9	Fairless Local	Navarre
69	93.8	Indian Hill Exempted Village	Cincinnati
69	93.8	Jonathan Alder Local	Plain City
69	93.8	Minerva Local	Minerva
72	93.7	Marlington Local	Alliance
73	93.6	Lake Local	Millbury
73	93.6	Riverside Local	Painesville
75	93.4	Bay Village City	Bay Village
75	93.4	Hudson City	Hudson
77	93.3	Bryan City	Bryan
78	93.1	Wapakoneta City	Wapakoneta
79	93.0	Woodridge Local	Peninsula
80	92.9	Greenon Local	Enon
80	92.9	South Euclid-Lyndhurst City	Lyndhurst
82	92.7	Northwest Local	Canal Fulton
83	92.6	Bowling Green City SD	Bowling Green
83	92.6	Gahanna-Jefferson City	Gahanna
83	92.6	Lakewood Local	Hebron
86	92.5	Bellefontaine City	Bellefontaine
86	92.5	Fairfield City	Fairfield
86	92.5	Loveland City	Loveland
86	92.5	Perry Local	Perry
86	92.5	Revere Local	Bath
91	92.4	Chardon Local	Chardon
92	92.3	Forest Hills Local	Cincinnati
93	92.2	Medina City SD	Medina
93	92.2	Wadsworth City	Wadsworth
93	92.2	West Geauga Local	Chesterland
96	92.1	Bexley City	Bexley
97	92.0	Brunswick City	Brunswick
97	92.0	Clearview Local	Lorain
99	91.7	Strongsville City	Strongsville
100	91.5	Logan Elm Local	Circleville
100	91.5	Sheffield-Sheffield Lake City	Sheffield Vllg
100	91.5	Troy City	Troy
103	91.4	Green Local	Uniontown
103	91.4	Little Miami Local	Maineville
105	91.3	Berea City	Berea
105	91.3	Stow-Munroe Falls City SD	Stow
107	91.0	Granville Exempted Village	Granville
108	90.9	Adams County/ohio Valley Local	West Union
108	90.9	Field Local	Mogadore
110	90.8	North College Hill City	Cincinnati
111	90.6	Northwestern Local	Springfield
111	90.6	Worthington City	Worthington
113	90.5	Meigs Local	Pomeroy
113	90.5	Milford Exempted Village	Milford
115	90.4	Fairland Local	Proctorville
115	90.4	Steubenville City	Steubenville
117	90.2	Westlake City	Westlake
117	90.2	Zane Trace Local	Chillicothe
119	90.0	Boardman Local	Youngstown
119	90.0	Defiance City	Defiance
119	90.0	Eastwood Local	Pemberville
119	90.0	North Fork Local	Utica
123	89.9	Orrville City	Orrville
124	89.8	West Branch Local	Beloit
125	89.7	Ontario Local	Mansfield
125	89.7	Port Clinton City	Port Clinton
125	89.7	Rossford Exempted Village	Rossford
125	89.7	Vandalia-Butler City	Vandalia
129	89.6	Chillicothe City	Chillicothe
130	89.4	Lexington Local	Lexington
130	89.4	Madison Local	Madison
130	89.4	Tipp City Exempted Village	Tipp City
133	89.3	Heath City	Heath
134	89.2	Orange City	Cleveland
134	89.2	Shawnee Local	Lima
134	89.2	Upper Sandusky Exempted Village	Upper Sandusky
137	89.1	Carlisle Local	Carlisle
137	89.1	Mount Vernon City	Mount Vernon
137	89.1	Shelby City	Shelby
140	89.0	Fairview Park City	Fairview Park

Rank	Value	District	City
140	89.0	Union-Scioto Local	Chillicothe
140	89.0	Vermilion Local	Vermilion
143	88.9	East Muskingum Local	New Concord
143	88.9	Kenston Local	Chagrin Falls
145	88.6	Austintown Local	Youngstown
145	88.6	Buckeye Valley Local	Delaware
145	88.6	Sylvania City	Sylvania
148	88.5	Geneva Area City	Geneva
149	88.4	Hillsboro City	Hillsboro
150	88.1	Benjamin Logan Local	Bellefontaine
151	88.0	Ashland City	Ashland
151	88.0	Dover City	Dover
151	88.0	Mayfield City	Mayfield Hgts
154	87.9	New Richmond Exempted Village	New Richmond
155	87.8	Firelands Local	South Amherst
155	87.8	Licking Heights Local	Pataskala
155	87.8	Monroe Local SD	Monroe
158	87.7	Hubbard Exempted Village	Hubbard
158	87.7	Lebanon City	Lebanon
160	87.6	Harrison Hills City	Cadiz
161	87.4	Miamisburg City	Miamisburg
162	87.2	Crestwood Local	Mantua
162	87.2	Wheelersburg Local	Wheelersburg
164	87.1	Oregon City	Oregon
164	87.1	Teays Valley Local	Ashville
166	86.9	Elida Local	Elida
166	86.9	Howland Local	Warren
168	86.8	Bellevue City	Bellevue
169	86.7	Alexander Local	Albany
169	86.7	Buckeye Local	Dillonvale
169	86.7	Graham Local	Saint Paris
169	86.7	Portsmouth City	Portsmouth
169	86.7	West Clermont Local	Cincinnati
174	86.6	Westerville City	Westerville
175	86.5	Tiffin City	Tiffin
176	86.4	Hilliard City	Hilliard
177	86.3	Carrollton Exempted Village	Carrollton
178	86.2	Buckeye Local	Medina
179	86.1	Johnstown-Monroe Local	Johnstown
179	86.1	Northridge Local	Dayton
181	85.9	Canal Wnchstr Local	Canal Wnchstr
182	85.8	Edison Local (Formerly Berlin-Milan)	Milan
183	85.7	Fremont City	Fremont
183	85.7	Perry Local	Massillon
185	85.6	Fairfield Union Local	Lancaster
185	85.6	Logan-Hocking Local	Logan
185	85.6	Marietta City	Marietta
188	85.4	Piqua City	Piqua
189	85.2	Indian Creek Local	Wintersville
189	85.2	Switzerland of Ohio Local	Woodsfield
191	85.1	Northern Local	Thornville
192	85.0	Canton Local	Canton
193	84.9	Kings Local	Kings Mills
194	84.8	Triway Local	Wooster
195	84.7	Clark-Shawnee Local	Springfield
195	84.7	Kettering City	Kettering
195	84.7	Lancaster City	Lancaster
195	84.7	Mariemont City	Cincinnati
195	84.7	Perkins Local	Sandusky
200	84.5	Franklin Local	Duncan Falls
201	84.4	Clear Fork Valley Local	Bellville
201	84.4	Princeton City	Cincinnati
201	84.4	River View Local	Warsaw
204	84.0	Clinton-Massie Local	Clarksville
204	84.0	Paulding Exempted Village	Paulding
206	83.9	Delaware City	Delaware
206	83.9	Licking Valley Local	Newark
208	83.8	Plain Local	Canton
209	83.7	Cloverleaf Local	Lodi
209	83.7	Franklin City	Franklin
209	83.7	Southwest Local	Harrison
209	83.7	Warren Local	Vincent
213	83.6	Springfield Local	Holland
213	83.6	Struthers City	Struthers
213	83.6	Wickliffe City	Wickliffe
213	83.6	Wooster City	Wooster
217	83.4	Morgan Local	Mc Connelsville
218	83.3	Sidney City	Sidney
219	83.2	Clyde-Green Springs Ex. Village	Clyde
220	83.0	River Valley Local	Caledonia
221	82.9	Greenville City	Greenville
222	82.8	Batavia Local	Batavia
222	82.8	Southeast Local	Apple Creek
224	82.6	Bethel-Tate Local	Bethel

Rank	Value	District	City
224	82.6	Indian Valley Local Schools	Gnadenhutten
224	82.6	Western Brown Local	Mount Orab
227	82.5	Canton City	Canton
227	82.5	Norton City	Norton
229	82.4	Buckeye Local	Ashtabula
229	82.4	Eaton Community City	Eaton
231	82.1	Athens City	The Plains
232	81.9	Lakeview Local	Cortland
233	81.7	New Lexington City	New Lexington
234	81.6	Coventry Local	Akron
235	81.4	Maysville Local	Zanesville
236	81.3	Southeast Local	Ravenna
237	81.2	Findlay City	Findlay
238	81.1	Parma City	Parma
239	80.9	Northmont City	Englewood
239	80.9	Northwest Local	Mc Dermott
241	80.7	Madison Local	Middletown
241	80.7	Washington Local	Toledo
243	80.3	Midview Local	Grafton
243	80.3	Tallmadge City	Tallmadge
245	80.2	Beaver Local	Lisbon
245	80.2	Kenton City	Kenton
245	80.2	Keystone Local	Lagrange
248	80.1	Coshocton City	Coshocton
249	79.9	Gallia County Local	Gallipolis
249	79.9	Jackson City	Jackson
251	79.7	Edison Local	Hammondsville
252	79.6	Huber Heights City	Huber Heights
252	79.6	Ravenna City	Ravenna
252	79.6	Three Rivers Local	Cleves
255	79.5	Jefferson Area Local	Jefferson
256	79.4	London City	London
256	79.4	Winton Woods City	Cincinnati
258	79.3	Waverly City	Waverly
258	79.3	Wilmington City	Wilmington
260	79.0	Amanda-Clearcreek Local	Amanda
260	79.0	Bath Local	Lima
262	78.8	N Ridgeville City	N Ridgeville
263	78.7	Highland Local	Sparta
263	78.7	Westfall Local	Williamsport
265	78.5	Cuyahoga Falls City	Cuyahoga Falls
265	78.5	Norwalk City	Norwalk
265	78.5	West Holmes Local	Millersburg
268	78.2	Lakewood City	Lakewood
269	78.0	Indian Lake Local	Lewistown
270	77.8	Shaker Heights City	Shaker Heights
271	77.6	Xenia Community City	Xenia
272	77.4	Sandusky City	Sandusky
273	77.3	Reading Community City	Reading
274	77.2	Clermont Northeastern Local	Batavia
275	76.8	Northwest Local	Cincinnati
276	76.7	Vinton County Local	Mc Arthur
277	76.6	Circleville City	Circleville
277	76.6	Conneaut Area City	Conneaut
279	76.3	Salem City	Salem
280	75.6	Rolling Hills Local	Cambridge
281	75.4	Wellston City	Wellston
282	75.3	Alliance City	Alliance
283	75.0	Madison Local	Mansfield
284	74.8	Goshen Local	Goshen
285	74.7	Bucyrus City	Bucyrus
286	74.6	South Point Local	South Point
287	74.5	Girard City SD	Girard
288	74.0	Washington-Nile Local	West Portsmouth
289	73.6	Springfield Local	Akron
290	73.4	Garfield Hgts City Schools	Garfield Hgts
291	73.2	Reynoldsburg City	Reynoldsburg
292	73.1	West Carrollton City	West Carrollton
293	72.9	Miami Trace Local	Washington CH
294	72.5	Willard City	Willard
295	72.2	Niles City	Niles
296	72.1	Ashtabula Area City	Ashtabula
297	71.4	Claymont City	Dennison
297	71.4	East Liverpool City	East Liverpool
299	71.3	Urbana City	Urbana
300	71.2	Massillon City	Massillon
300	71.2	Tecumseh Local	New Carlisle
302	71.0	Elyria City Schools	Elyria
303	70.4	South-Western City	Grove City
304	69.9	Euclid City	Euclid
305	69.7	Barberton City	Barberton
306	69.1	Greenfield Exempted Village	Greenfield
307	68.9	Hamilton Local	Columbus
308	68.0	East Holmes Local	Berlin

Note: This section only includes districts with 1,500 or more students; All categories are ranked from high to low

Rank	Percent	District Name	City
309	67.7	Newark City	Newark
309	67.7	Washington CH City	Washington CH
311	67.3	Cambridge City	Cambridge
312	67.2	Hamilton City	Hamilton
313	67.0	Groveport Madison Local	Groveport
314	65.6	Fairborn City	Fairborn
315	65.3	Mt Healthy City	Cincinnati
316	65.1	Maple Heights City	Maple Heights
317	65.0	Akron City	Akron
318	64.9	Bedford City	Bedford
319	64.0	Mad River Local	Dayton
320	63.7	Marion City	Marion
321	63.5	Whitehall City	Whitehall
322	63.4	Galion City	Galion
322	63.4	Warrensville Hgts City	Warrensville Hgts
324	63.0	Treca Digital Academy	Marion
325	62.1	Cleveland Hgts-University Hgts City	University Hgts
326	61.9	Warren City	Warren
327	61.7	Trotwood-Madison City	Trotwood
328	61.4	Norwood City	Norwood
329	61.0	Lorain City	Lorain
330	60.0	Middletown City	Middletown
331	58.2	Ohio Virtual Academy	Maumee
332	56.8	Painesville City Local	Painesville
333	56.6	Fostoria City	Fostoria
333	56.6	Lima City	Lima
335	55.0	Columbus City SD	Columbus
336	53.1	Zanesville City	Zanesville
337	52.7	Cincinnati City	Cincinnati
338	51.8	Springfield City	Springfield
339	48.9	Toledo City	Toledo
340	46.1	East Cleveland City SD	East Cleveland
341	45.9	Dayton City	Dayton
342	44.2	Mansfield City	Mansfield
343	42.8	Gallipolis City	Gallipolis
344	42.3	Cleveland Municipal	Cleveland
345	40.0	Youngstown City Schools	Youngstown
346	36.8	Ohio Connections Academy Inc	Cleveland
347	30.7	Alternative Education Academy	Toledo

Note: This section only includes districts with 1,500 or more students; All categories are ranked from high to low

The Nation's Report Card Mathematics 2013 State Snapshot Report

Ohio
Grade 4
Public Schools

Overall Results

- In 2013, the average score of fourth-grade students in Ohio was 246. This was higher than the average score of 241 for public school students in the nation.
- The average score for students in Ohio in 2013 (246) was not significantly different from their average score in 2011 (244) and was higher than their average score in 1992 (219).
- The score gap between higher performing students in Ohio (those at the 75th percentile) and lower performing students (those at the 25th percentile) was 38 points in 2013. This performance gap was not significantly different from that in 1992 (42 points).
- The percentage of students in Ohio who performed at or above the NAEP *Proficient* level was 48 percent in 2013. This percentage was not significantly different from that in 2011 (45 percent) and was greater than that in 1992 (16 percent).
- The percentage of students in Ohio who performed at or above the NAEP *Basic* level was 86 percent in 2013. This percentage was not significantly different from that in 2011 (86 percent) and was greater than that in 1992 (57 percent).

Achievement-Level Percentages and Average Score Results

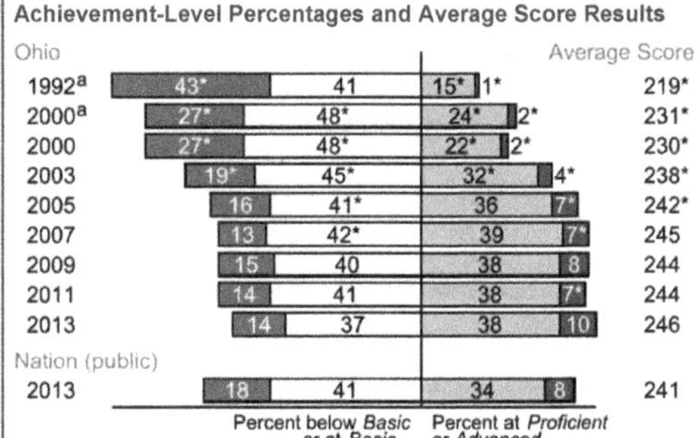

* Significantly different ($p < .05$) from state's results in 2013. Significance tests were performed using unrounded numbers.
a Accommodations not permitted. For information about NAEP accommodations, see http://nces.ed.gov/nationsreportcard/about/inclusion.aspx.

NOTE: Detail may not sum to totals because of rounding.

Compare the Average Score in 2013 to Other States/Jurisdictions

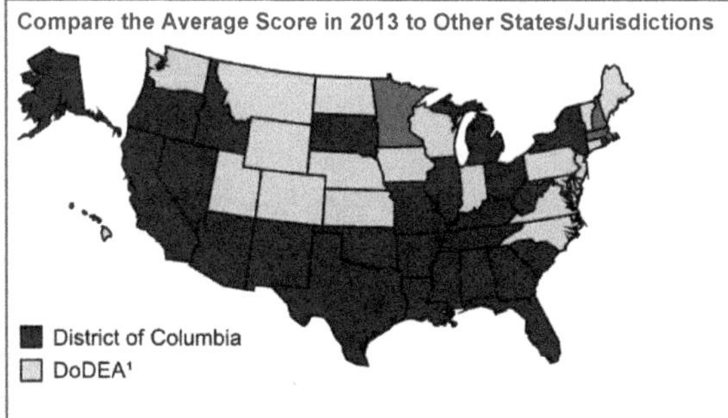

[1] Department of Defense Education Activity (overseas and domestic schools).

In 2013, the average score in Ohio (246) was

- lower than those in 3 states/jurisdictions
- higher than those in 26 states/jurisdictions
- not significantly different from those in 22 states/jurisdictions

Average Scores for State/Jurisdiction and Nation (public)

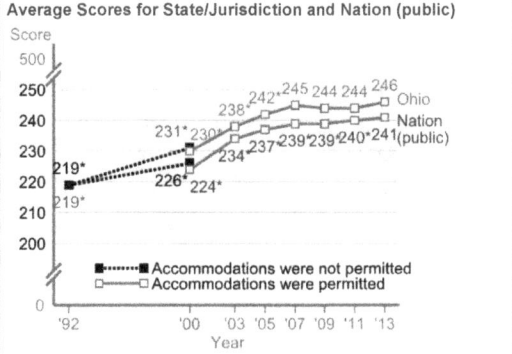

Score: 500, 250, 240, 230, 220, 210, 200, 0
Ohio: 219*, 231*, 230*, 238*, 242*, 245, 244, 244, 246
Nation (public): 219*, 226*, 224*, 234*, 237*, 239*, 239*, 240*, 241
Accommodations were not permitted
Accommodations were permitted
Year: '92, '00, '03, '05, '07, '09, '11, '13

* Significantly different ($p < .05$) from 2013. Significance tests were performed using unrounded numbers.

NOTE: For information about NAEP accommodations, see http://nces.ed.gov/nationsreportcard/about/inclusion.aspx.

Results for Student Groups in 2013

Reporting Groups	Percent of students	Avg. score	Percentages at or above *Basic*	Percentages at or above *Proficient*	Percent at *Advanced*
Race/Ethnicity					
White	71	252	91	56	12
Black	17	222	62	16	1
Hispanic	4	237	81	36	3
Asian	2	261	94	67	26
American Indian/Alaska Native	#	‡	‡	‡	‡
Native Hawaiian/Pacific Islander	#	‡	‡	‡	‡
Two or more races	5	241	84	42	6
Gender					
Male	51	246	85	49	11
Female	49	245	86	47	9
National School Lunch Program					
Eligible	46	232	75	28	2
Not eligible	54	257	94	65	16

\# Rounds to zero. ‡ Reporting standards not met.

NOTE: Detail may not sum to totals because of rounding, and because the "Information not available" category for the National School Lunch Program, which provides free/reduced-price lunches, is not displayed. Black includes African American and Hispanic includes Latino. Race categories exclude Hispanic origin.

Score Gaps for Student Groups

- In 2013, Black students had an average score that was 30 points lower than White students. This performance gap was not significantly different from that in 1992 (28 points).
- In 2013, Hispanic students had an average score that was 15 points lower than White students. Data are not reported for Hispanic students in 1992, because reporting standards were not met.
- In 2013, male students in Ohio had an average score that was not significantly different from female students.
- In 2013, students who were eligible for free/reduced-price school lunch, an indicator of low family income, had an average score that was 25 points lower than students who were not eligible for free/reduced-price school lunch. This performance gap was not significantly different from that in 2000 (22 points).

ies National Center for Education Statistics, Institute of Education Sciences

NOTE: Statistical comparisons are calculated on the basis of unrounded scale scores or percentages.
SOURCE: U.S. Department of Education, Institute of Education Sciences, National Center for Education Statistics, National Assessment of Educational Progress (NAEP), various years, 1992–2013 Mathematics Assessments.

Overall Results

- In 2013, the average score of eighth-grade students in Ohio was 290. This was higher than the average score of 284 for public school students in the nation.
- The average score for students in Ohio in 2013 (290) was not significantly different from their average score in 2011 (289) and was higher than their average score in 1990 (264).
- The score gap between higher performing students in Ohio (those at the 75th percentile) and lower performing students (those at the 25th percentile) was 48 points in 2013. This performance gap was not significantly different from that in 1990 (45 points).
- The percentage of students in Ohio who performed at or above the NAEP *Proficient* level was 40 percent in 2013. This percentage was not significantly different from that in 2011 (39 percent) and was greater than that in 1990 (15 percent).
- The percentage of students in Ohio who performed at or above the NAEP *Basic* level was 79 percent in 2013. This percentage was not significantly different from that in 2011 (79 percent) and was greater than that in 1990 (53 percent).

Achievement-Level Percentages and Average Score Results

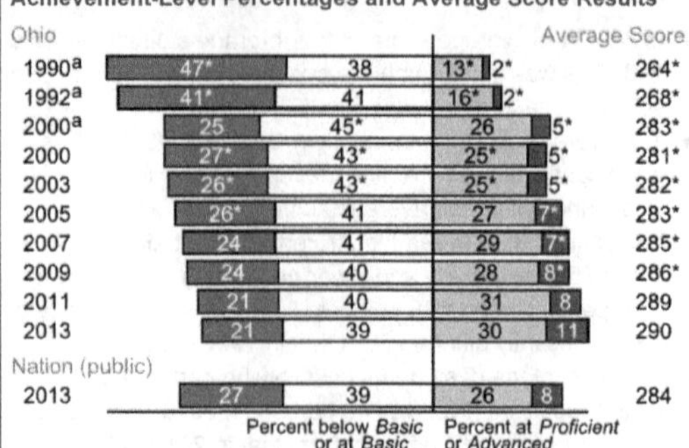

* Significantly different ($p < .05$) from state's results in 2013. Significance tests were performed using unrounded numbers.

[a] Accommodations not permitted. For information about NAEP accommodations, see http://nces.ed.gov/nationsreportcard/about/inclusion.aspx.

NOTE: Detail may not sum to totals because of rounding.

Compare the Average Score in 2013 to Other States/Jurisdictions

[1] Department of Defense Education Activity (overseas and domestic schools).

In 2013, the average score in Ohio (290) was

- lower than those in 5 states/jurisdictions
- higher than those in 31 states/jurisdictions
- not significantly different from those in 15 states/jurisdictions

Average Scores for State/Jurisdiction and Nation (public)

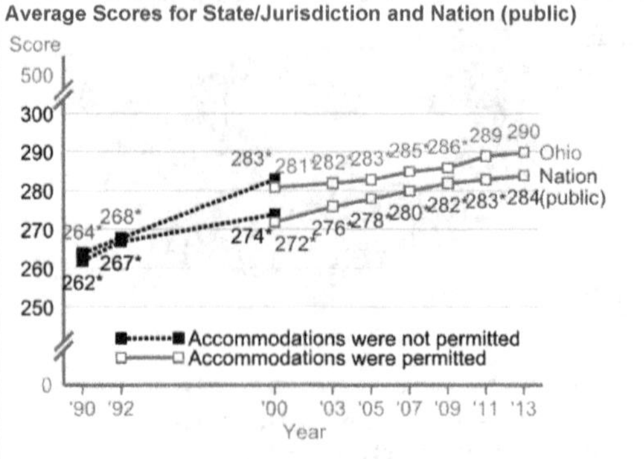

* Significantly different ($p < .05$) from 2013. Significance tests were performed using unrounded numbers.

NOTE: For information about NAEP accommodations, see http://nces.ed.gov/nationsreportcard/about/inclusion.aspx.

Results for Student Groups in 2013

Reporting Groups	Percent of students	Avg. score	Percentages at or above *Basic*	Percentages at or above *Proficient*	Percent at *Advanced*
Race/Ethnicity					
White	76	294	84	45	12
Black	15	267	56	16	1
Hispanic	3	277	66	27	6
Asian	2	312	89	65	33
American Indian/Alaska Native	#	‡	‡	‡	‡
Native Hawaiian/Pacific Islander	#	‡	‡	‡	‡
Two or more races	4	284	77	34	9
Gender					
Male	51	290	79	42	11
Female	49	289	79	39	10
National School Lunch Program					
Eligible	42	274	65	21	3
Not eligible	58	301	88	54	16

\# Rounds to zero. ‡ Reporting standards not met.

NOTE: Detail may not sum to totals because of rounding, and because the "Information not available" category for the National School Lunch Program, which provides free/reduced-price lunches, is not displayed. Black includes African American and Hispanic includes Latino. Race categories exclude Hispanic origin.

Score Gaps for Student Groups

- In 2013, Black students had an average score that was 27 points lower than White students. This performance gap was narrower than that in 1990 (35 points).
- In 2013, Hispanic students had an average score that was 17 points lower than White students. Data are not reported for Hispanic students in 1990, because reporting standards were not met.
- In 2013, male students in Ohio had an average score that was not significantly different from female students.
- In 2013, students who were eligible for free/reduced-price school lunch, an indicator of low family income, had an average score that was 27 points lower than students who were not eligible for free/reduced-price school lunch. This performance gap was not significantly different from that in 2000 (30 points).

NOTE: Statistical comparisons are calculated on the basis of unrounded scale scores or percentages.
SOURCE: U.S. Department of Education, Institute of Education Sciences, National Center for Education Statistics, National Assessment of Educational Progress (NAEP), various years, 1990–2013 Mathematics Assessments.

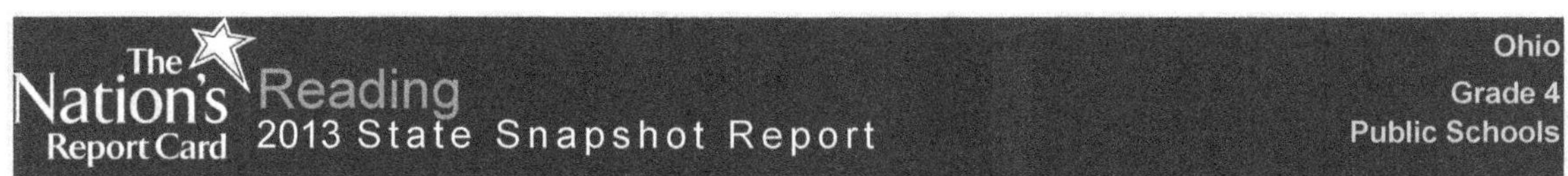

The Nation's Report Card
Reading
2013 State Snapshot Report
Ohio
Grade 4
Public Schools

Overall Results

- In 2013, the average score of fourth-grade students in Ohio was 224. This was higher than the average score of 221 for public school students in the nation.
- The average score for students in Ohio in 2013 (224) was not significantly different from their average score in 2011 (224) and was higher than their average score in 1992 (217).
- The score gap between higher performing students in Ohio (those at the 75th percentile) and lower performing students (those at the 25th percentile) was 46 points in 2013. This performance gap was not significantly different from that in 1992 (43 points).
- The percentage of students in Ohio who performed at or above the NAEP *Proficient* level was 37 percent in 2013. This percentage was not significantly different from that in 2011 (34 percent) and was greater than that in 1992 (27 percent).
- The percentage of students in Ohio who performed at or above the NAEP *Basic* level was 71 percent in 2013. This percentage was not significantly different from that in 2011 (71 percent) and was greater than that in 1992 (63 percent).

Achievement-Level Percentages and Average Score Results

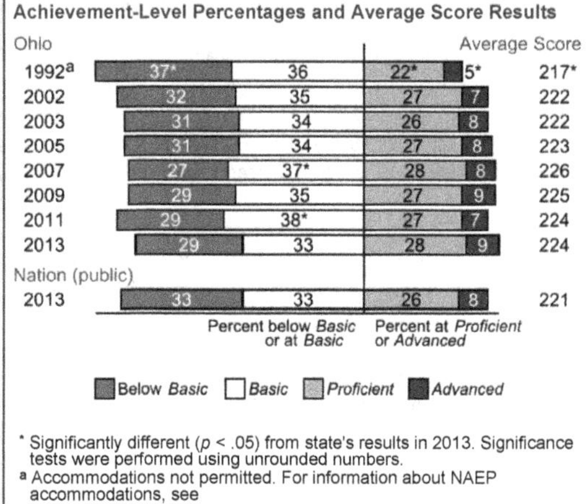

* Significantly different ($p < .05$) from state's results in 2013. Significance tests were performed using unrounded numbers.
a Accommodations not permitted. For information about NAEP accommodations, see http://nces.ed.gov/nationsreportcard/about/inclusion.aspx.

NOTE: Detail may not sum to totals because of rounding.

Compare the Average Score in 2013 to Other States/Jurisdictions

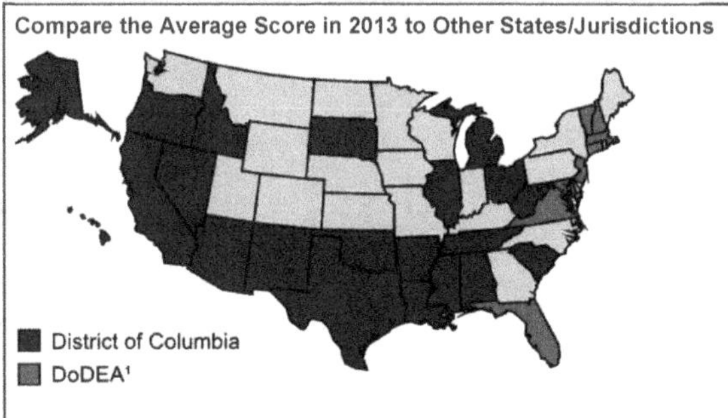

' Department of Defense Education Activity (overseas and domestic schools).

In 2013, the average score in Ohio (224) was

- lower than those in 9 states/jurisdictions
- higher than those in 21 states/jurisdictions
- not significantly different from those in 21 states/jurisdictions

Average Scores for State/Jurisdiction and Nation (public)

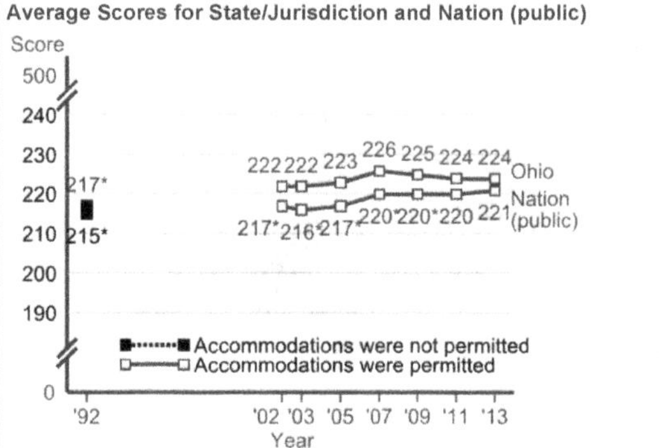

* Significantly different ($p < .05$) from 2013. Significance tests were performed using unrounded numbers.

NOTE: For information about NAEP accommodations, see http://nces.ed.gov/nationsreportcard/about/inclusion.aspx.

Results for Student Groups in 2013

Reporting Groups	Percent of students	Avg. score	Percentages at or above *Basic*	Percentages at or above *Proficient*	Percent at *Advanced*
Race/Ethnicity					
White	71	231	79	44	11
Black	17	195	39	11	1
Hispanic	4	214	57	25	5
Asian	2	244	90	67	19
American Indian/Alaska Native	#	‡	‡	‡	‡
Native Hawaiian/Pacific Islander	#	‡	‡	‡	‡
Two or more races	6	219	69	29	6
Gender					
Male	51	221	68	35	8
Female	49	227	74	40	10
National School Lunch Program					
Eligible	46	208	55	20	3
Not eligible	54	237	84	52	14

\# Rounds to zero. ‡ Reporting standards not met.

NOTE: Detail may not sum to totals because of rounding, and because the "Information not available" category for the National School Lunch Program, which provides free/reduced-price lunches, is not displayed. Black includes African American and Hispanic includes Latino. Race categories exclude Hispanic origin.

Score Gaps for Student Groups

- In 2013, Black students had an average score that was 36 points lower than White students. This performance gap was wider than that in 1992 (23 points).
- In 2013, Hispanic students had an average score that was 17 points lower than White students. Data are not reported for Hispanic students in 1992, because reporting standards were not met.
- In 2013, female students in Ohio had an average score that was higher than male students by 6 points.
- In 2013, students who were eligible for free/reduced-price school lunch, an indicator of low family income, had an average score that was 29 points lower than students who were not eligible for free/reduced-price school lunch. This performance gap was not significantly different from that in 2002 (24 points).

ies NATIONAL CENTER FOR EDUCATION STATISTICS Institute of Education Sciences

NOTE: Statistical comparisons are calculated on the basis of unrounded scale scores or percentages.
SOURCE: U.S. Department of Education, Institute of Education Sciences, National Center for Education Statistics, National Assessment of Educational Progress (NAEP), various years, 1992–2013 Reading Assessments.

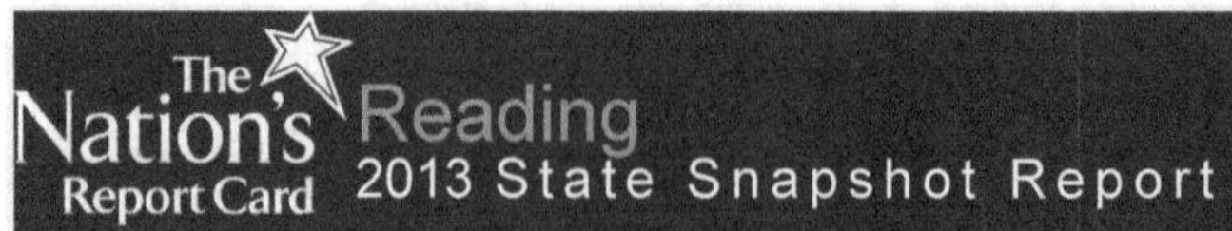

Ohio
Grade 8
Public Schools

Overall Results

- In 2013, the average score of eighth-grade students in Ohio was 269. This was higher than the average score of 266 for public school students in the nation.
- The average score for students in Ohio in 2013 (269) was not significantly different from their average score in 2011 (268) and in 2002 (268).
- The score gap between higher performing students in Ohio (those at the 75th percentile) and lower performing students (those at the 25th percentile) was 46 points in 2013. This performance gap was wider than that in 2002 (39 points).
- The percentage of students in Ohio who performed at or above the NAEP *Proficient* level was 39 percent in 2013. This percentage was not significantly different from that in 2011 (37 percent) and in 2002 (35 percent).
- The percentage of students in Ohio who performed at or above the NAEP *Basic* level was 79 percent in 2013. This percentage was not significantly different from that in 2011 (79 percent) and in 2002 (82 percent).

Achievement-Level Percentages and Average Score Results

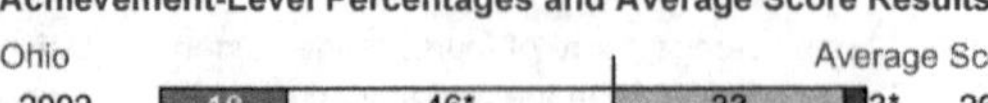

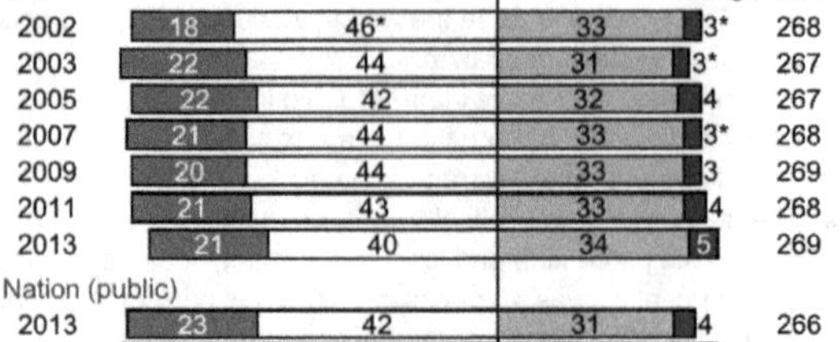

* Significantly different ($p < .05$) from state's results in 2013. Significance tests were performed using unrounded numbers.

NOTE: Detail may not sum to totals because of rounding.

Compare the Average Score in 2013 to Other States/Jurisdictions

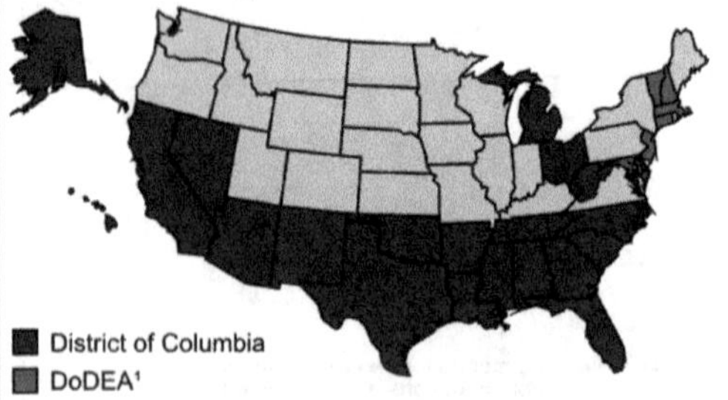

[1] Department of Defense Education Activity (overseas and domestic schools).

In 2013, the average score in Ohio (269) was
- lower than those in 7 states/jurisdictions
- higher than those in 21 states/jurisdictions
- not significantly different from those in 23 states/jurisdictions

Average Scores for State/Jurisdiction and Nation (public)

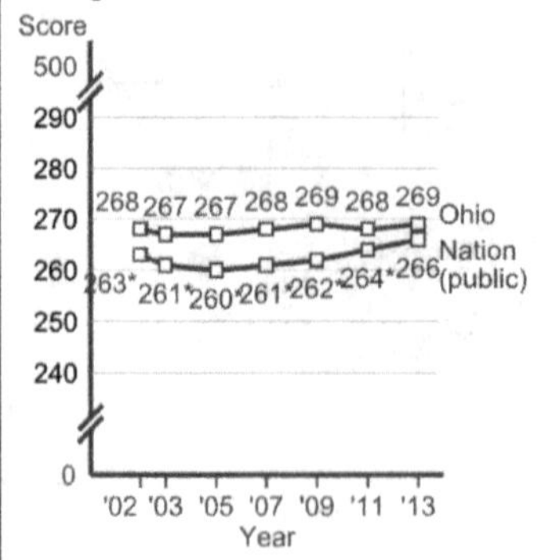

* Significantly different ($p < .05$) from 2013. Significance tests were performed using unrounded numbers.

Results for Student Groups in 2013

Reporting Groups	Percent of students	Avg. score	Percentages at or above *Basic*	Percentages at or above *Proficient*	Percent at *Advanced*
Race/Ethnicity					
White	76	273	82	43	6
Black	15	247	58	16	1
Hispanic	3	266	75	34	3
Asian	2	289	91	61	14
American Indian/Alaska Native	#	‡	‡	‡	‡
Native Hawaiian/Pacific Islander	#	‡	‡	‡	‡
Two or more races	4	268	81	35	2
Gender					
Male	51	264	75	34	3
Female	49	274	83	44	6
National School Lunch Program					
Eligible	41	254	66	22	1
Not eligible	59	280	88	50	8

\# Rounds to zero. ‡ Reporting standards not met.

NOTE: Detail may not sum to totals because of rounding, and because the "Information not available" category for the National School Lunch Program, which provides free/reduced-price lunches, is not displayed. Black includes African American and Hispanic includes Latino. Race categories exclude Hispanic origin.

Score Gaps for Student Groups

- In 2013, Black students had an average score that was 26 points lower than White students. This performance gap was not significantly different from that in 2002 (27 points).
- In 2013, Hispanic students had an average score that was 7 points not significantly different from White students. Data are not reported for Hispanic students in 2002, because reporting standards were not met.
- In 2013, female students in Ohio had an average score that was higher than male students by 10 points.
- In 2013, students who were eligible for free/reduced-price school lunch, an indicator of low family income, had an average score that was 25 points lower than students who were not eligible for free/reduced-price school lunch. This performance gap was not significantly different from that in 2002 (16 points).

ies NATIONAL CENTER FOR EDUCATION STATISTICS Institute of Education Sciences

NOTE: Statistical comparisons are calculated on the basis of unrounded scale scores or percentages.
SOURCE: U.S. Department of Education, Institute of Education Sciences, National Center for Education Statistics, National Assessment of Educational Progress (NAEP), various years, 2002–2013 Reading Assessments.

The Nation's Report Card
Science 2009
State Snapshot Report

Ohio
Grade 4
Public Schools

2009 Science Assessment Content

Guided by a new framework, the NAEP science assessment was updated in 2009 to keep the content current with key developments in science, curriculum standards, assessments, and research. The 2009 framework organizes science content into three broad content areas.

Physical science includes concepts related to properties and changes of matter, forms of energy, energy transfer and conservation, position and motion of objects, and forces affecting motion.

Life science includes concepts related to organization and development, matter and energy transformations, interdependence, heredity and reproduction, and evolution and diversity.

Earth and space sciences includes concepts related to objects in the universe, the history of the Earth, properties of Earth materials, tectonics, energy in Earth systems, climate and weather, and biogeochemical cycles.

The 2009 science assessment was composed of 143 questions at grade 4, 162 at grade 8, and 179 at grade 12. Students responded to only a portion of the questions, which included both multiple-choice questions and questions that required a written response.

Compare the Average Score in 2009 to Other States/Jurisdictions

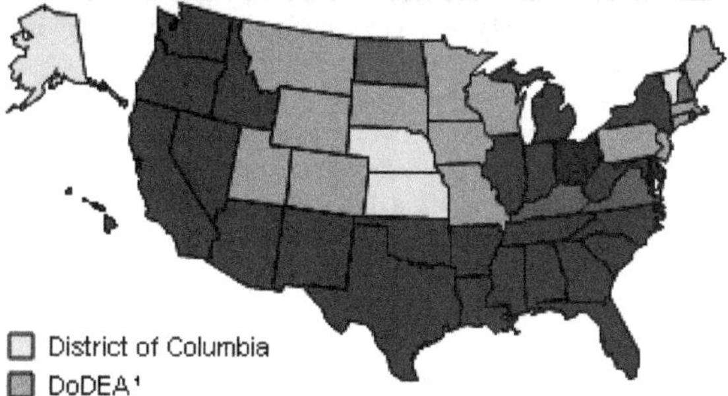

[1] Department of Defense Education Activity (overseas and domestic schools).

In 2009, the average score in **Ohio** was

- lower than those in 4 states/jurisdictions
- higher than those in 27 states/jurisdictions
- not significantly different from those in 15 states/jurisdictions
- 5 states/jurisdictions did not participate

Overall Results

- In 2009, the average score of fourth-grade students in Ohio was 157. This was higher than the average score of 149 for public school students in the nation.
- The percentage of students in Ohio who performed at or above the NAEP *Proficient* level was 41 percent in 2009. This percentage was greater than the nation (32 percent).
- The percentage of students in Ohio who performed at or above the NAEP *Basic* level was 79 percent in 2009. This percentage was greater than the nation (71 percent).

Achievement-Level Percentages and Average Score Results

	Below *Basic*	*Basic*	*Proficient*	*Advanced*	Average Score
Ohio 2009	21	38	40	1	157
Nation (public) 2009	29*	39	32*	1	149*

Percent below *Basic* and at *Basic* — Percent at *Proficient* and *Advanced*

* Significantly different ($p < .05$) from Ohio. Significance tests were performed using unrounded numbers.

NOTE: Detail may not sum to totals because of rounding.

Results for Student Groups in 2009

Reporting Groups	Percent of students	Avg. score	Percentages at or above *Basic*	Percentages at or above *Proficient*	Percent at *Advanced*
Gender					
Male	50	159	81	45	1
Female	50	155	78	38	1
Race/Ethnicity					
White	72	165	89	50	1
Black	19	129	47	10	#
Hispanic	3	140	58	26	1
Asian/Pacific Islander	2	‡	‡	‡	‡
American Indian/Alaska Native	#	‡	‡	‡	‡
National School Lunch Program					
Eligible	40	139	62	20	#
Not eligible	60	169	91	56	2

\# Rounds to zero. ‡ Reporting standards not met.

NOTE: Detail may not sum to totals because of rounding, and because the "Information not available" category for the National School Lunch Program, which provides free/reduced-price lunches, and the "Unclassified" category for race/ethnicity are not displayed.

Score Gaps for Student Groups

- In 2009, male students in Ohio had an average score that was higher than female students.
- In 2009, Black students had an average score that was 37 points lower than White students. This performance gap was not significantly different from the nation (35 points).
- In 2009, Hispanic students had an average score that was 25 points lower than White students. This performance gap was not significantly different from the nation (32 points).
- In 2009, students who were eligible for free/reduced-price school lunch, an indicator of low family income, had an average score that was 30 points lower than students who were not eligible for free/reduced-price school lunch. This performance gap was not significantly different from the nation (29 points).

NOTE: Statistical comparisons are calculated on the basis of unrounded scale scores or percentages.
SOURCE: U.S. Department of Education, Institute of Education Sciences, National Center for Education Statistics, National Assessment of Educational Progress (NAEP), 2009 Science Assessment.

The Nation's Science
Report Card 2011 State Snapshot Report

Ohio
Grade 8
Public Schools

Overall Results

- In 2011, the average score of eighth-grade students in Ohio was 158. This was higher than the average score of 151 for public school students in the nation.
- The average score for students in Ohio in 2011 (158) was not significantly different from their average score in 2009 (158).
- In 2011, the score gap between students in Ohio at the 75th percentile and students at the 25th percentile was 42 points. This performance gap was not significantly different from that of 2009 (40 points).
- The percentage of students in Ohio who performed at or above the NAEP *Proficient* level was 38 percent in 2011. This percentage was not significantly different from that in 2009 (37 percent).
- The percentage of students in Ohio who performed at or above the NAEP *Basic* level was 73 percent in 2011. This percentage was not significantly different from that in 2009 (73 percent).

Achievement-Level Percentages and Average Score Results

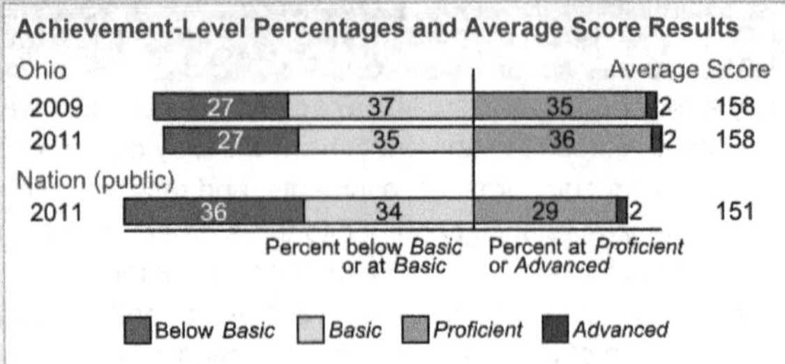

Below *Basic* / *Basic* / *Proficient* / *Advanced*

NOTE: Detail may not sum to totals because of rounding.

Compare the Average Score in 2011 to Other States/Jurisdictions

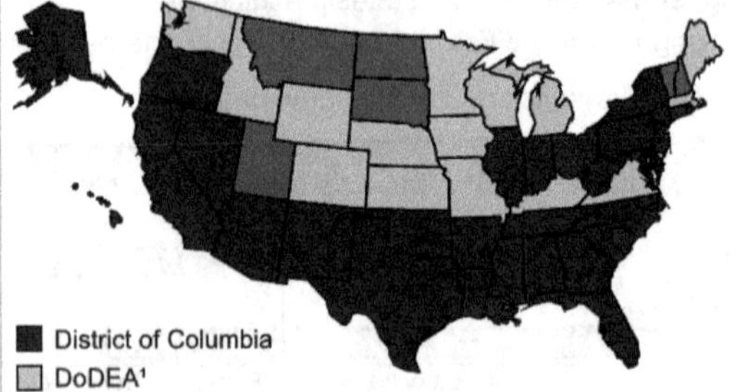

District of Columbia
DoDEA[1]

[1] Department of Defense Education Activity (overseas and domestic schools).

In 2011, the average score in Ohio (158) was

- lower than those in 6 states/jurisdictions
- higher than those in 29 states/jurisdictions
- not significantly different from those in 16 states/jurisdictions

Average Scores for State/Jurisdiction and Nation (public)

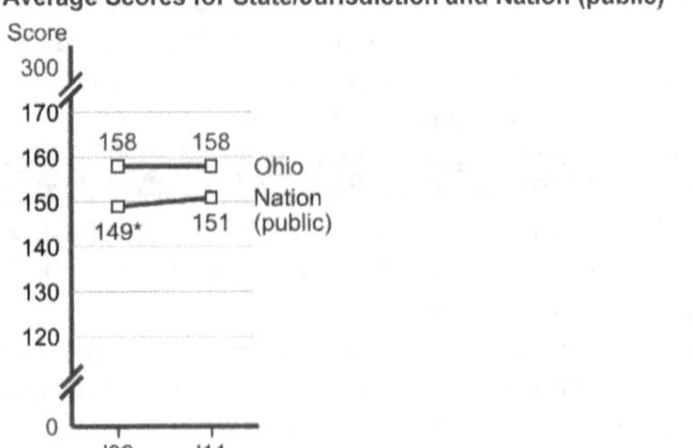

* Significantly different ($p < .05$) from 2011. Significance tests were performed using unrounded numbers.

Results for Student Groups in 2011

Reporting Groups	Percent of students	Avg. score	Percentages at or above *Basic*	Percentages at or above *Proficient*	Percent at *Advanced*
Race/Ethnicity					
White	75	165	81	45	3
Black	17	132	41	8	#
Hispanic	3	151	65	31	2
Asian	1	‡	‡	‡	‡
American Indian/Alaska Native	#	‡	‡	‡	‡
Native Hawaiian/Pacific Islander	#	‡	‡	‡	‡
Two or more races	4	150	64	24	#
Gender					
Male	51	161	75	43	3
Female	49	155	70	33	1
National School Lunch Program					
Eligible	43	144	56	19	1
Not eligible	57	169	86	52	3

Rounds to zero. ‡ Reporting standards not met.

NOTE: Detail may not sum to totals because of rounding, and because the "Information not available" category for the National School Lunch Program, which provides free/reduced-price lunches, is not displayed. Black includes African American and Hispanic includes Latino. Race categories exclude Hispanic origin.

Score Gaps for Student Groups

- In 2011, Black students had an average score that was 33 points lower than White students. This performance gap was not significantly different from that in 2009 (38 points).
- In 2011, Hispanic students had an average score that was 14 points lower than White students. This performance gap was not significantly different from that in 2009 (24 points).
- In 2011, male students in Ohio had an average score that was higher than female students by 6 points.
- In 2011, students who were eligible for free/reduced-price school lunch, an indicator of low family income, had an average score that was 25 points lower than students who were not eligible for free/reduced-price school lunch. This performance gap was not significantly different from that in 2009 (24 points).

NOTE: Statistical comparisons are calculated on the basis of unrounded scale scores or percentages.
SOURCE: U.S. Department of Education, Institute of Education Sciences, National Center for Education Statistics, National Assessment of Educational Progress (NAEP), 2009 and 2011 Science Assessments.

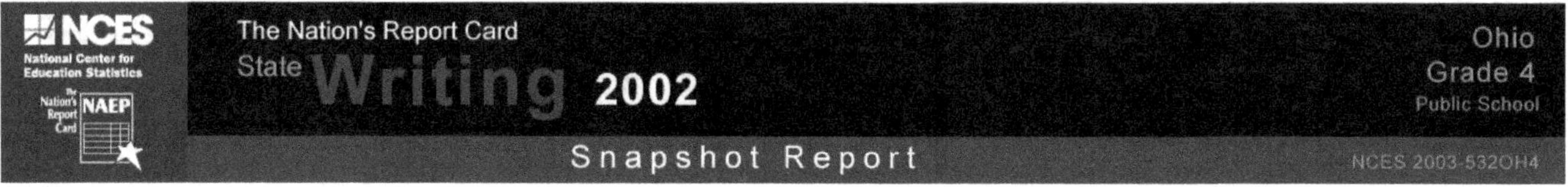

The writing assessment of the National Assessment of Educational Progress (NAEP) measures narrative, informative, and persuasive writing–three purposes identified in the NAEP framework. The NAEP writing scale ranges from 0 to 300.

Overall Writing Results for Ohio

- The average scale score for fourth-grade students in Ohio was 157.
- Ohio's average score (157) was higher[1] than that of the nation's public schools (153).
- Students' average scale scores in Ohio were higher than those in 26 jurisdictions[2], not significantly different from those in 17 jurisdictions, and lower than those in 4 jurisdictions.
- The percentage of students who performed at or above the NAEP *Proficient* level was 28 percent. The percentage of students who performed at or above the *Basic* level was 90 percent.

Student Percentage at Each Achievement Level

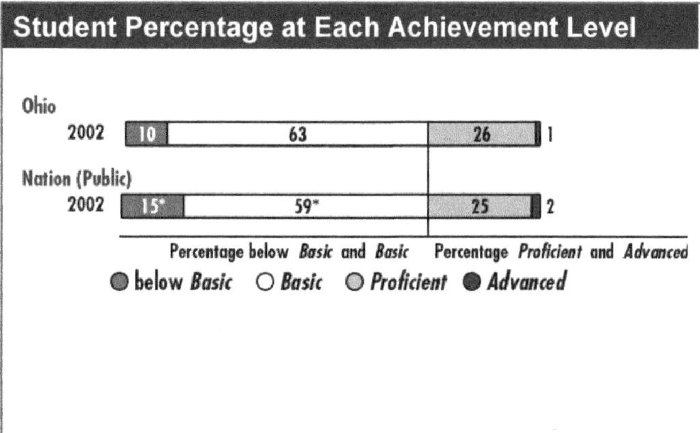

Performance of NAEP Reporting Groups in Ohio

Reporting groups	Percentage of students	Average Score	Below *Basic*	*Basic*	*Proficient*	*Advanced*
			Percentage of students at			
Male	50	150 ↑	13 ↓	67 ↑	19	1
Female	50	164	6 ↓	59	33	2
White	76	162	7 ↓	61 ↑	31	2
Black	20	140	20	68	11	#
Hispanic	2	---	---	---	---	---
Asian/Pacific Islander	1	---	---	---	---	---
American Indian/Alaska Native	#	---	---	---	---	---
Free/reduced-priced school lunch						
Eligible	32	143	18 ↓	69 ↑	14	#
Not eligible	61	164	5 ↓	60	33	2
Information not available	7	158	8	64	26	2

Average Score Gaps Between Selected Groups

- Female students in Ohio had an average score that was higher than that of male students (14 points). This performance gap was not significantly different from that of the Nation (18 points).
- White students had an average score that was higher than that of Black students (22 points). This performance gap was not significantly different from that of the Nation (20 points).
- The sample size was not sufficient to permit a reliable estimate for Hispanic students in Ohio.
- Students who were not eligible for free/reduced-price school lunch had an average score that was higher than that of students who were eligible (21 points). This performance gap was not significantly different from that of the Nation (22 points).

Writing Scale Scores at Selected Percentiles

Scale Score Distribution

	25th Percentile	50th Percentile	75th Percentile
Ohio	*135* ↑	*157* ↑	*179*
Nation (Public)	*128*	*153*	*178*

An examination of scores at different percentiles on the 0-300 NAEP writing scale at each grade indicates how well students at lower, middle, and higher levels of the distribution performed. For example, the data above shows that 75 percent of students in public schools nationally scored below *178,* while 75 percent of students in Ohio scored below *179.*

Percentage rounds to zero. --- Reporting standards not met; sample size insufficient to permit a reliable estimate.

* Significantly different from Ohio. ↑ Significantly higher than, ↓ lower than appropriate subgroup in the nation (public).

[1] Comparisons (higher/lower/not different) are based on statistical tests. The .05 level was used for testing statistical significance.

[2] "Jurisdictions" includes participating states and other jurisdictions (such as Guam or the District of Columbia).

NOTE: Detail may not sum to totals because of rounding. Score gaps are calculated based on differences between unrounded average scale scores.

Visit http://nces.ed.gov/nationsreportcard/states/ for additional results and detailed information.

SOURCE: U.S. Department of Education, Institute of Education Sciences, National Center for Education Statistics, National Assessment of Educational Progress (NAEP), 2002 Writing Assessment.

The National Assessment of Educational Progress (NAEP) assesses writing for three purposes identified in the NAEP framework: narrative, informative, and persuasive. The NAEP writing scale ranges from 0 to 300.

Overall Writing Results for Ohio

- In 2007, the average scale score for eighth-grade students in Ohio was 156. This was not significantly different from their average score in 2002 (160).[1]
- Ohio's average score (156) in 2007 was not significantly different from that of the nation's public schools (154).
- Of the 45 states and one other jurisdiction that participated in the 2007 eighth-grade assessment, students' average scale score in Ohio was higher than those in 15 jurisdictions, not significantly different from those in 22 jurisdictions, and lower than those in 8 jurisdictions.[2]
- The percentage of students in Ohio who performed at or above the NAEP *Proficient* level was 32 percent in 2007. This percentage was smaller than that in 2002 (38 percent).
- The percentage of students in Ohio who performed at or above the NAEP *Basic* level was 90 percent in 2007. This percentage was not significantly different from that in 2002 (89 percent).

Percentages at NAEP Achievement Levels and Average Score

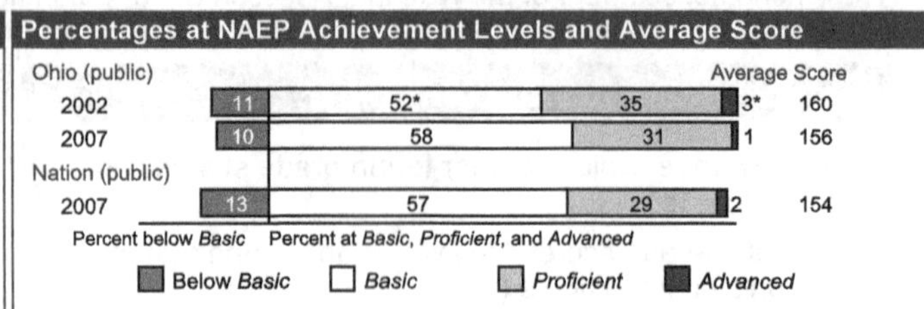

NOTE: The NAEP grade 8 writing achievement levels correspond to the following scale points: Below *Basic*, 113 or lower; *Basic*, 114–172; *Proficient*, 173–223; *Advanced*, 224 or above.

Performance of NAEP Reporting Groups in Ohio: 2007

Reporting groups	Percent of students	Average score	Percent below *Basic*	Percent of students at or above *Basic*	Percent of students at or above *Proficient*	Percent *Advanced*
Male	52	147	15	85	21	#
Female	48	166	5	95	43	2↓
White	76	160	8	92	36	1↓
Black	19	138	20	80	13	#
Hispanic	2	141	26	74	22	#
Asian/Pacific Islander	1	‡	‡	‡	‡	‡
American Indian/Alaska Native	#	‡	‡	‡	‡	‡
Eligible for National School Lunch Program	32	140	19	81	15	#
Not eligible for National School Lunch Program	66	163	6	94	39	1↓

Average Score Gaps Between Selected Groups

- In 2007, male students in Ohio had an average score that was lower than that of female students by 19 points. This performance gap was not significantly different from that of 2002 (20 points).
- In 2007, Black students had an average score that was lower than that of White students by 22 points. This performance gap was not significantly different from that of 2002 (33 points).
- In 2007, Hispanic students had an average score that was lower than that of White students by 20 points. Data are not reported for Hispanic students in 2002, because reporting standards were not met. Therefore, the performance gap results are not reported.
- In 2007, students who were eligible for free/reduced-price school lunch, an indicator of poverty, had an average score that was lower than that of students who were not eligible for free/reduced-price school lunch by 23 points. This performance gap was the same as that of 2002 (23 points).
- In 2007, the score gap between students at the 75th percentile and students at the 25th percentile was 44 points. This performance gap was not significantly different from that of 2002 (47 points).

Writing Scores at Selected Percentiles in Ohio

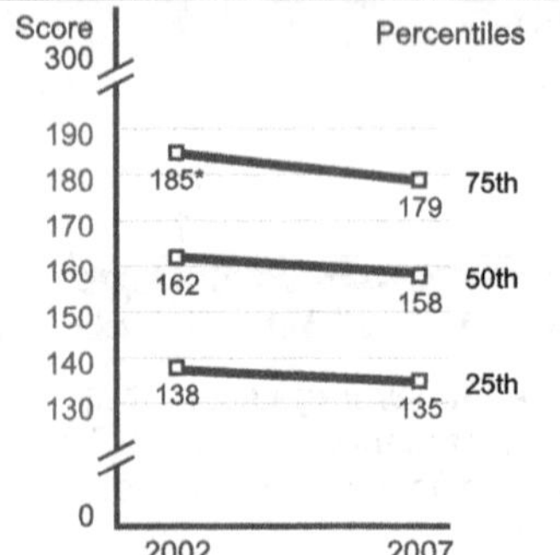

NOTE: Scores at selected percentiles on the NAEP writing scale indicate how well students at lower, middle, and higher levels performed.

\# Rounds to zero.
‡ Reporting standards not met.
* Significantly different from 2007.
↑ Significantly higher than 2002. ↓ Significantly lower than 2002.

[1] Comparisons (higher/lower/narrower/wider/not different) are based on statistical tests. The .05 level with appropriate adjustments for multiple comparisons was used for testing statistical significance. Statistical comparisons are calculated on the basis of unrounded scale scores or percentages. Comparisons across jurisdictions and comparisons with the nation or within a jurisdiction across years may be affected by differences in exclusion rates for students with disabilities (SD) and English language learners (ELL). The exclusion rates for SD and ELL in Ohio were 4 percent and "percentage rounds to zero" in 2007, respectively. For more information on NAEP significance testing, see http://nces.ed.gov/nationsreportcard/writing/interpret-results.asp#statistical.

[2] "Jurisdiction" refers to states, the District of Columbia, and the Department of Defense Education Activity schools.

NOTE: Detail may not sum to totals because of rounding and because the "Information not available" category for the National School Lunch Program, which provides free and reduced-price lunches, and the "Unclassified" category for race/ethnicity are not displayed. Visit http://nces.ed.gov/nationsreportcard/states/ for additional results and detailed information.

SOURCE: U.S. Department of Education, Institute of Education Sciences, National Center for Education Statistics, National Assessment of Educational Progress (NAEP), 2002 and 2007 Writing Assessments.

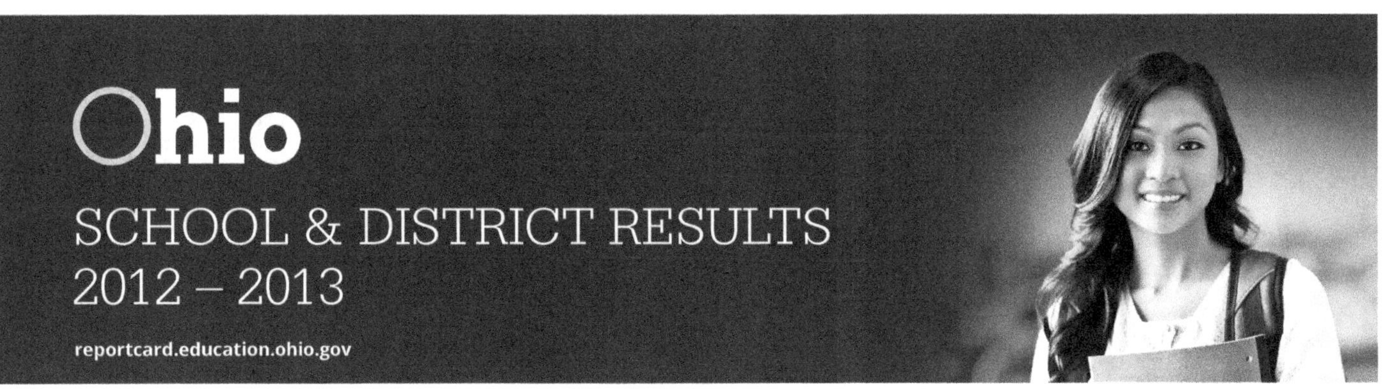

Ohio
SCHOOL & DISTRICT RESULTS
2012 – 2013
reportcard.education.ohio.gov

Dr. Richard A. Ross
Superintendent of Public Instruction

SUPERINTENDENT'S MESSAGE

The 2012–2013 Ohio School Report Cards are the beginning of a new era of greater accountability and higher expectations for Ohio's schools. Moving to a system of A–F letter grades on a broader range of measures will make it clearer for educators, parents and taxpayers to see how their schools are performing.

This new reporting system also sets higher standards for what we consider to be a successful school and district. For too long, too many of our students have left school without a diploma or the skills they need to succeed. This new report card provides data to parents, communities and educators about the strengths of each school and the areas where they need improvement. This is the first step for real discussions and real change.

This year, we are assessing traditional and community schools on up to nine areas. By August 2015, we will assess school performance on 17 items in six categories. Overall grades for each school and district will also be issued in 2015. The measures focus on areas we know are essential to student success, and they pay close attention to the academic achievement of different student demographic and economic groups that were not specifically measured before.

Ohio is also introducing the nation's first-ever A–F report card for career technical programs. These programs are an essential component of Ohio's education system, and we need to count on them to help build our state's economic future.

All the grades for 2012–2013 paint a sharper picture of school performance. The good news is that Ohio is taking bold steps to tackle our state's education challenges. The new Third Grade Reading Guarantee is focusing the efforts of all schools on making sure that our boys and girls get the literacy skills they must have to be successful in every subject, in every grade. And the new Straight A Fund will provide $250 million to Ohio educators with the courage and vision to implement creative solutions to various teaching and learning challenges.

If you are a parent, your school report card will give you the best reading of how well your child is being served every day. When you look at your school and district report cards, take a minute to celebrate their successes and examine the areas where they need improvement. If you have a concern, ask your school principal or district superintendent to explain the story behind it. We all must work together to make sure that every boy and girl, in every school, in every district in Ohio receives the education they need to enjoy a promising future.

To see a specific report card and information on how grades are assigned, please go to reportcard.education.ohio.gov.

School & District Performance

For 2012–2013, schools and districts receive letter grades on up to nine measures of academic performance. Below are the total number of grades earned by districts and schools in each category for 2012–2013.

	DISTRICT RESULTS					SCHOOL RESULTS				
	A	B	C	D	F	A	B	C	D	F
Indicators Met	320	114	82	47	46	1551	310	251	295	863
Performance Index	28	435	128	19	0	217	1780	726	518	48
4-Year Graduation Rate	294	157	92	40	26	327	169	102	59	130
5-Year Graduation Rate	216	237	98	35	24	239	267	119	54	106
Value-Added: Overall	281	52	84	52	141	1023	240	476	208	611
Value-Added: Gifted Students	62	77	270	98	52	164	266	788	272	170
Value-Added: Lowest 20% in Achievement	87	97	296	76	39	298	426	1153	304	174
Value-Added: Students With Disabilities	97	105	255	59	79	312	394	954	280	247
Annual Measurable Objectives	28	183	112	97	190	601	524	340	310	1470
	Total Districts: 610					Total Schools: 3460				

Career-Technical Planning Districts

For the first time, Ohio's 91 career-technical planning districts are receiving A–F letter grades. The 2012–2013 Ohio career-tech report cards are based upon data for students from the graduating class of 2011 in each of Ohio's 91 career-technical districts.

The graduation rates measure the proportion of career-tech students who graduated within four and five years of beginning ninth grade. Students must be concentrating in career-technical studies by the end of their fourth year of high school to be included in these graduation rates. The Post-Program Placement grade is based upon the proportion of students who were enrolled in postsecondary education, advanced training, military service or employed within six months of leaving secondary education.

	A	B	C	D	F
4-Year Graduation Rate	66	17	7	1	0
5-Year Graduation Rate	54	27	7	3	0
Placement	31	22	17	14	7

Ohio's Students 2012–2013

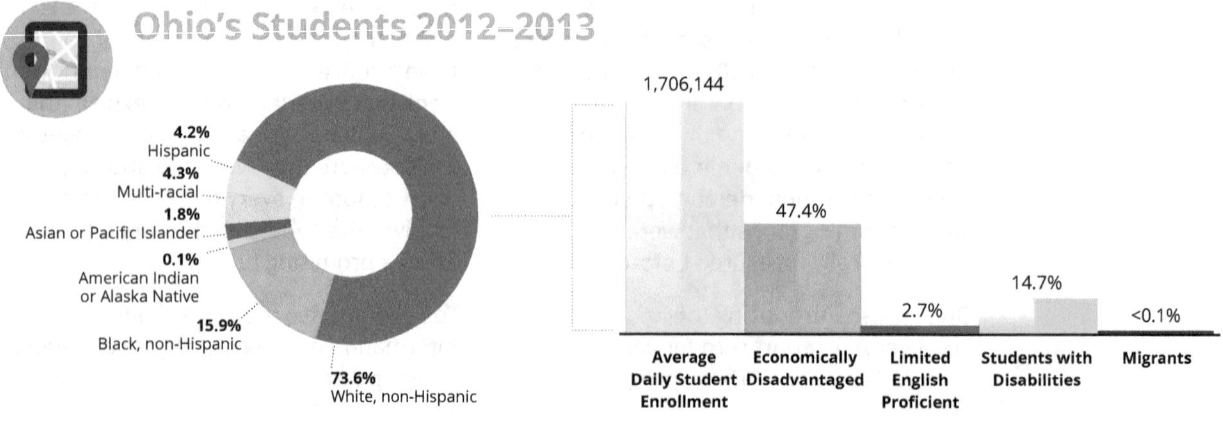

2012-2013 State Report Card Addendum

This addendum to the 2012-2013 Report Card displays updated data based on findings by the Auditor of State. The scores and designations on this addendum are final Report Card ratings.

District and School Performance

For 2012–2013, schools and districts receive letter grades on up to nine measures of academic performance. Below are the total number of grades earned by districts and schools in each category for 2012–2013.

District Performance

Measure	A	B	C	D	F
Indicators Met	320	114	82	47	46
Performance Index	28	435	128	19	0
4 -Year Graduation Rate	294	157	92	40	26
5-Year Graduation Rate	216	237	98	35	24
Value Added:Overall	281	52	84	52	141
Value Added:Gifted Students	62	77	270	98	52
Value Added:Lowest 20% in Achievement	87	97	296	76	39
Value Added:Students with Disabilities	97	105	255	59	79
Annual Measurable Objectives	28	183	112	97	190

School Performance

Measure	A	B	C	D	F
Indicators Met	1551	311	250	296	862
Performance Index	217	1780	727	517	48
4 -Year Graduation Rate	327	169	102	59	130
5-Year Graduation Rate	239	267	119	54	106
Value Added:Overall	1021	242	474	208	613
Value Added:Gifted Students	164	266	788	272	170
Value Added:Lowest 20% in Achievement	298	426	1153	304	174
Value Added:Students with Disabilities	312	394	955	279	247
Annual Measurable Objectives	601	524	341	309	1470

Ancestry and Ethnicity

Ohio State Profile

Population: 11,536,504

Ancestry	Population	%
Afghan (334)	403	<0.01
African, Sub-Saharan (86,101)	98,709	0.86
African (56,965)	66,657	0.58
Cape Verdean (145)	396	<0.01
Ethiopian (4,654)	5,039	0.04
Ghanaian (2,800)	2,919	0.03
Kenyan (805)	948	0.01
Liberian (846)	939	0.01
Nigerian (4,600)	5,051	0.04
Senegalese (438)	537	<0.01
Sierra Leonean (530)	558	<0.01
Somalian (9,821)	10,078	0.09
South African (814)	1,304	0.01
Sudanese (348)	385	<0.01
Ugandan (139)	139	<0.01
Zimbabwean (381)	381	<0.01
Other Sub-Saharan African (2,815)	3,378	0.03
Albanian (3,200)	4,061	0.04
Alsatian (213)	705	0.01
American (911,201)	911,201	7.91
Arab (41,613)	65,834	0.57
Arab (7,980)	10,035	0.09
Egyptian (3,921)	4,801	0.04
Iraqi (1,205)	1,346	0.01
Jordanian (2,350)	2,833	0.02
Lebanese (14,495)	30,056	0.26
Moroccan (1,055)	1,497	0.01
Palestinian (4,116)	4,705	0.04
Syrian (2,939)	6,042	0.05
Other Arab (3,552)	4,519	0.04
Armenian (1,768)	4,333	0.04
Assyrian/Chaldean/Syriac (288)	389	<0.01
Australian (662)	2,134	0.02
Austrian (6,767)	28,071	0.24
Basque (8)	63	<0.01
Belgian (2,787)	10,037	0.09
Brazilian (1,749)	2,500	0.02
British (19,024)	42,018	0.36
Bulgarian (1,401)	2,864	0.02
Cajun (205)	558	<0.01
Canadian (6,805)	15,625	0.14
Carpatho Rusyn (539)	959	0.01
Celtic (1,001)	1,824	0.02
Croatian (15,181)	41,430	0.36
Cypriot (116)	141	<0.01
Czech (19,585)	73,775	0.64
Czechoslovakian (8,047)	18,742	0.16
Danish (4,624)	18,632	0.16
Dutch (34,625)	207,492	1.80
Eastern European (9,338)	10,672	0.09
English (362,859)	1,112,280	9.66
Estonian (461)	663	0.01
European (87,969)	98,058	0.85
Finnish (5,944)	19,872	0.17
French, ex. Basque (46,200)	284,589	2.47
French Canadian (11,090)	32,522	0.28
German (1,247,503)	3,220,180	27.97
German Russian (164)	481	<0.01
Greek (27,899)	58,649	0.51
Guyanese (907)	1,203	0.01
Hungarian (69,178)	210,625	1.83
Icelander (252)	808	0.01
Iranian (3,084)	4,038	0.04
Irish (413,997)	1,666,746	14.48
Israeli (907)	1,650	0.01
Italian (282,256)	748,397	6.50
Latvian (1,324)	2,580	0.02
Lithuanian (8,194)	24,321	0.21
Luxemburger (165)	665	0.01
Macedonian (2,762)	4,613	0.04
Maltese (204)	516	<0.01
New Zealander (154)	387	<0.01
Northern European (3,525)	3,939	0.03
Norwegian (12,651)	42,773	0.37
Pennsylvania German (24,371)	32,246	0.28
Polish (156,163)	462,815	4.02
Portuguese (3,847)	9,658	0.08
Romanian (13,078)	29,751	0.26
Russian (29,493)	80,848	0.70
Scandinavian (3,490)	8,810	0.08
Scotch-Irish (70,567)	190,369	1.65
Scottish (65,322)	229,371	1.99
Serbian (8,080)	17,530	0.15
Slavic (2,824)	8,235	0.07
Slovak (51,528)	144,300	1.25
Slovene (19,901)	55,482	0.48
Soviet Union (23)	36	<0.01
Swedish (17,992)	78,498	0.68
Swiss (19,738)	78,114	0.68
Turkish (2,941)	4,399	0.04
Ukrainian (22,564)	46,993	0.41
Welsh (28,763)	135,998	1.18
West Indian, ex. Hispanic (11,019)	17,473	0.15
Bahamian (276)	396	<0.01
Barbadian (223)	480	<0.01
Belizean (133)	214	<0.01
Bermudan (59)	128	<0.01
British West Indian (323)	457	<0.01
Dutch West Indian (156)	676	0.01
Haitian (2,297)	2,912	0.03
Jamaican (5,799)	8,744	0.08
Trinidadian/Tobagonian (541)	938	0.01
U.S. Virgin Islander (35)	56	<0.01
West Indian (1,168)	2,428	0.02
Other West Indian (9)	44	<0.01
Yugoslavian (6,948)	12,485	0.11

Hispanic Origin	Population	%
Hispanic or Latino (of any race)	354,674	3.07
Central American, ex. Mexican	22,756	0.20
Costa Rican	1,093	0.01
Guatemalan	8,680	0.08
Honduran	3,699	0.03
Nicaraguan	1,383	0.01
Panamanian	2,055	0.02
Salvadoran	5,627	0.05
Other Central American	219	<0.01
Cuban	7,523	0.07
Dominican Republic	6,453	0.06
Mexican	172,029	1.49
Puerto Rican	94,965	0.82
South American	17,571	0.15
Argentinean	1,921	0.02
Bolivian	649	0.01
Chilean	1,065	0.01
Colombian	5,247	0.05
Ecuadorian	2,090	0.02
Paraguayan	205	<0.01
Peruvian	3,741	0.03
Uruguayan	291	<0.01
Venezuelan	2,190	0.02
Other South American	172	<0.01
Other Hispanic or Latino	33,377	0.29

Race*	Population	%
African-American/Black (1,407,681)	1,541,771	13.36
Not Hispanic (1,389,115)	1,511,035	13.10
Hispanic (18,566)	30,736	0.27
American Indian/Alaska Native (25,292)	90,124	0.78
Not Hispanic (20,906)	79,872	0.69
Hispanic (4,386)	10,252	0.09
Alaska Athabascan *(Ala. Nat.)* (47)	100	<0.01
Aleut *(Alaska Native)* (43)	88	<0.01
Apache (362)	1,325	0.01
Arapaho (21)	95	<0.01
Blackfeet (642)	4,916	0.04
Canadian/French Am. Ind. (143)	338	<0.01
Central American Ind. (372)	458	<0.01
Cherokee (5,386)	26,584	0.23
Cheyenne (57)	236	<0.01
Chickasaw (111)	289	<0.01
Chippewa (807)	1,599	0.01
Choctaw (339)	1,194	0.01
Colville (5)	11	<0.01
Comanche (84)	237	<0.01
Cree (64)	194	<0.01
Creek (169)	579	0.01
Crow (38)	204	<0.01
Delaware (252)	608	0.01
Hopi (35)	105	<0.01
Houma (9)	22	<0.01
Inupiat *(Alaska Native)* (56)	115	<0.01
Iroquois (570)	1,807	0.02
Kiowa (33)	70	<0.01
Lumbee (235)	406	<0.01
Menominee (48)	66	<0.01
Mexican American Ind. (862)	1,472	0.01
Navajo (310)	809	0.01
Osage (47)	125	<0.01
Ottawa (91)	229	<0.01
Paiute (21)	39	<0.01
Pima (15)	27	<0.01
Potawatomi (125)	276	<0.01
Pueblo (75)	163	<0.01
Puget Sound Salish (24)	32	<0.01
Seminole (87)	460	<0.01
Shoshone (28)	99	<0.01
Sioux (613)	2,069	0.02
South American Ind. (287)	650	0.01
Spanish American Ind. (81)	124	<0.01
Tlingit-Haida *(Alaska Native)* (48)	77	<0.01
Tohono O'Odham (22)	41	<0.01
Tsimshian *(Alaska Native)* (12)	28	<0.01
Ute (5)	32	<0.01
Yakama (9)	19	<0.01
Yaqui (29)	73	<0.01
Yuman (13)	31	<0.01
Yup'ik *(Alaska Native)* (27)	47	<0.01
Asian (192,233)	238,292	2.07
Not Hispanic (190,765)	234,053	2.03
Hispanic (1,468)	4,239	0.04
Bangladeshi (928)	1,052	0.01
Bhutanese (703)	865	0.01
Burmese (1,258)	1,356	0.01
Cambodian (3,744)	4,570	0.04
Chinese, ex. Taiwanese (41,006)	47,861	0.41
Filipino (16,899)	27,661	0.24
Hmong (539)	589	0.01
Indian (64,187)	71,211	0.62
Indonesian (862)	1,354	0.01
Japanese (10,162)	16,995	0.15
Korean (15,281)	21,207	0.18
Laotian (3,355)	4,183	0.04
Malaysian (335)	528	<0.01
Nepalese (819)	992	0.01
Pakistani (4,644)	5,330	0.05
Sri Lankan (882)	1,029	0.01
Taiwanese (2,672)	3,172	0.03
Thai (2,535)	4,024	0.03
Vietnamese (13,121)	15,639	0.14
Hawaii Native/Pacific Islander (4,066)	10,525	0.09
Not Hispanic (3,400)	8,702	0.08
Hispanic (666)	1,823	0.02
Fijian (46)	90	<0.01
Guamanian/Chamorro (1,145)	1,977	0.02
Marshallese (99)	124	<0.01
Native Hawaiian (928)	3,037	0.03
Samoan (702)	1,278	0.01
Tongan (30)	81	<0.01
White (9,539,437)	9,751,547	84.53
Not Hispanic (9,359,263)	9,543,218	82.72
Hispanic (180,174)	208,329	1.81

*Notes: † The Census 2010 population figure is used to calculate the percentages in the Hispanic Origin and Race categories. Ancestry percentages are based on the 2006-2010 American Community Survey population (not shown); ‡ Numbers in parentheses indicate the number of people reporting a single ancestry; * Numbers in parentheses indicate the number of persons reporting this race alone, not in combination with any other race; Please refer to the User Guide for more information.*

County Profiles

Allen County

Population: 106,331

Ancestry	Population	%
Afghan (0)	0	<0.01
African, Sub-Saharan (1,284)	1,341	1.26
African (1,030)	1,087	1.02
Cape Verdean (0)	0	<0.01
Ethiopian (0)	0	<0.01
Ghanaian (193)	193	0.18
Kenyan (0)	0	<0.01
Liberian (0)	0	<0.01
Nigerian (17)	17	0.02
Senegalese (0)	0	<0.01
Sierra Leonean (0)	0	<0.01
Somalian (34)	34	0.03
South African (0)	0	<0.01
Sudanese (10)	10	0.01
Ugandan (0)	0	<0.01
Zimbabwean (0)	0	<0.01
Other Sub-Saharan African (0)	0	<0.01
Albanian (0)	0	<0.01
Alsatian (15)	15	0.01
American (10,384)	10,384	9.74
Arab (187)	315	0.30
Arab (38)	93	0.09
Egyptian (9)	9	0.01
Iraqi (11)	11	0.01
Jordanian (0)	0	<0.01
Lebanese (102)	158	0.15
Moroccan (0)	0	<0.01
Palestinian (14)	14	0.01
Syrian (13)	30	0.03
Other Arab (0)	0	<0.01
Armenian (0)	0	<0.01
Assyrian/Chaldean/Syriac (0)	0	<0.01
Australian (0)	24	0.02
Austrian (46)	167	0.16
Basque (0)	0	<0.01
Belgian (39)	71	0.07
Brazilian (0)	0	<0.01
British (68)	320	0.30
Bulgarian (7)	7	0.01
Cajun (0)	0	<0.01
Canadian (60)	105	0.10
Carpatho Rusyn (0)	0	<0.01
Celtic (8)	8	0.01
Croatian (8)	28	0.03
Cypriot (0)	0	<0.01
Czech (133)	337	0.32
Czechoslovakian (68)	111	0.10
Danish (10)	39	0.04
Dutch (381)	2,356	2.21
Eastern European (8)	8	0.01
English (2,554)	7,586	7.12
Estonian (0)	0	<0.01
European (738)	750	0.70
Finnish (44)	119	0.11
French, ex. Basque (423)	2,710	2.54
French Canadian (61)	231	0.22
German (17,813)	37,029	34.74
German Russian (0)	0	<0.01
Greek (169)	297	0.28
Guyanese (0)	0	<0.01
Hungarian (188)	436	0.41
Icelander (0)	10	0.01
Iranian (0)	0	<0.01
Irish (3,143)	13,434	12.60
Israeli (0)	0	<0.01
Italian (1,426)	4,111	3.86
Latvian (0)	0	<0.01
Lithuanian (47)	110	0.10
Luxemburger (0)	13	0.01
Macedonian (4)	4	<0.01
Maltese (0)	0	<0.01
New Zealander (0)	0	<0.01
Northern European (69)	69	0.06
Norwegian (21)	207	0.19
Pennsylvania German (56)	77	0.07
Polish (464)	1,589	1.49
Portuguese (10)	47	0.04
Romanian (0)	14	0.01
Russian (82)	343	0.32
Scandinavian (13)	121	0.11
Scotch-Irish (572)	1,491	1.40
Scottish (443)	1,650	1.55
Serbian (0)	34	0.03
Slavic (15)	45	0.04
Slovak (31)	187	0.18
Slovene (10)	10	0.01
Soviet Union (0)	0	<0.01
Swedish (128)	534	0.50
Swiss (570)	1,717	1.61
Turkish (0)	0	<0.01
Ukrainian (54)	70	0.07
Welsh (617)	1,982	1.86
West Indian, ex. Hispanic (130)	240	0.23
Bahamian (14)	14	0.01
Barbadian (0)	0	<0.01
Belizean (0)	0	<0.01
Bermudan (0)	0	<0.01
British West Indian (0)	0	<0.01
Dutch West Indian (0)	0	<0.01
Haitian (14)	56	0.05
Jamaican (91)	159	0.15
Trinidadian/Tobagonian (11)	11	0.01
U.S. Virgin Islander (0)	0	<0.01
West Indian (0)	0	<0.01
Other West Indian (0)	0	<0.01
Yugoslavian (0)	24	0.02

Hispanic Origin	Population	%
Hispanic or Latino (of any race)	2,513	2.36
Central American, ex. Mexican	74	0.07
Costa Rican	17	0.02
Guatemalan	13	0.01
Honduran	7	0.01
Nicaraguan	7	0.01
Panamanian	8	0.01
Salvadoran	22	0.02
Other Central American	0	<0.01
Cuban	54	0.05
Dominican Republic	4	<0.01
Mexican	1,614	1.52
Puerto Rican	202	0.19
South American	55	0.05
Argentinean	3	<0.01
Bolivian	9	0.01
Chilean	9	0.01
Colombian	14	0.01
Ecuadorian	9	0.01
Paraguayan	0	<0.01
Peruvian	5	<0.01
Uruguayan	0	<0.01
Venezuelan	6	0.01
Other South American	0	<0.01
Other Hispanic or Latino	510	0.48

Race*	Population	%
African-American/Black (12,639)	14,616	13.75
Not Hispanic (12,508)	14,331	13.48
Hispanic (131)	285	0.27
American Indian/Alaska Native (207)	790	0.74
Not Hispanic (162)	672	0.63
Hispanic (45)	118	0.11
Alaska Athabascan *(Ala. Nat.)* (0)	0	<0.01
Aleut *(Alaska Native)* (0)	0	<0.01
Apache (6)	15	0.01
Arapaho (0)	0	<0.01
Blackfeet (1)	31	0.03
Canadian/French Am. Ind. (1)	8	0.01
Central American Ind. (0)	0	<0.01
Cherokee (32)	227	0.21
Cheyenne (1)	3	<0.01
Chickasaw (1)	2	<0.01
Chippewa (9)	28	0.03
Choctaw (2)	7	0.01
Colville (0)	0	<0.01
Comanche (0)	0	<0.01
Cree (0)	0	<0.01
Creek (0)	6	0.01
Crow (0)	0	<0.01
Delaware (3)	4	<0.01
Hopi (0)	0	<0.01
Houma (0)	0	<0.01
Inupiat *(Alaska Native)* (0)	1	<0.01
Iroquois (5)	13	0.01
Kiowa (0)	0	<0.01
Lumbee (0)	0	<0.01
Menominee (4)	5	<0.01
Mexican American Ind. (6)	16	0.02
Navajo (0)	3	<0.01
Osage (2)	4	<0.01
Ottawa (0)	0	<0.01
Paiute (0)	0	<0.01
Pima (0)	0	<0.01
Potawatomi (0)	1	<0.01
Pueblo (0)	0	<0.01
Puget Sound Salish (0)	0	<0.01
Seminole (0)	3	<0.01
Shoshone (0)	0	<0.01
Sioux (4)	19	0.02
South American Ind. (5)	5	<0.01
Spanish American Ind. (0)	0	<0.01
Tlingit-Haida *(Alaska Native)* (0)	0	<0.01
Tohono O'Odham (0)	0	<0.01
Tsimshian *(Alaska Native)* (0)	0	<0.01
Ute (0)	0	<0.01
Yakama (0)	0	<0.01
Yaqui (0)	0	<0.01
Yuman (0)	0	<0.01
Yup'ik *(Alaska Native)* (0)	0	<0.01
Asian (740)	1,043	0.98
Not Hispanic (725)	1,004	0.94
Hispanic (15)	39	0.04
Bangladeshi (1)	1	<0.01
Bhutanese (0)	0	<0.01
Burmese (0)	0	<0.01
Cambodian (5)	5	<0.01
Chinese, ex. Taiwanese (83)	134	0.13
Filipino (124)	187	0.18
Hmong (3)	4	<0.01
Indian (224)	258	0.24
Indonesian (1)	2	<0.01
Japanese (37)	69	0.06
Korean (74)	124	0.12
Laotian (37)	50	0.05
Malaysian (0)	0	<0.01
Nepalese (4)	4	<0.01
Pakistani (9)	12	0.01
Sri Lankan (0)	0	<0.01
Taiwanese (11)	16	0.02
Thai (8)	22	0.02
Vietnamese (61)	87	0.08
Hawaii Native/Pacific Islander (15)	71	0.07
Not Hispanic (13)	64	0.06
Hispanic (2)	7	0.01
Fijian (0)	0	<0.01
Guamanian/Chamorro (4)	12	0.01
Marshallese (0)	0	<0.01
Native Hawaiian (5)	22	0.02
Samoan (5)	7	0.01
Tongan (0)	0	<0.01
White (89,089)	91,659	86.20
Not Hispanic (87,708)	89,974	84.62
Hispanic (1,381)	1,685	1.58

*Notes: † The Census 2010 population figure is used to calculate the percentages in the Hispanic Origin and Race categories. Ancestry percentages are based on the 2006-2010 American Community Survey population (not shown); ‡ Numbers in parentheses indicate the number of people reporting a single ancestry; * Numbers in parentheses indicate the number of persons reporting this race alone, not in combination with any other race; Please refer to the User Guide for more information.*

Ashtabula County

Population: 101,497

Ancestry	Population	%
Afghan (0)	0	<0.01
African, Sub-Saharan (119)	195	0.19
African (119)	186	0.18
Cape Verdean (0)	0	<0.01
Ethiopian (0)	9	0.01
Ghanaian (0)	0	<0.01
Kenyan (0)	0	<0.01
Liberian (0)	0	<0.01
Nigerian (0)	0	<0.01
Senegalese (0)	0	<0.01
Sierra Leonean (0)	0	<0.01
Somalian (0)	0	<0.01
South African (0)	0	<0.01
Sudanese (0)	0	<0.01
Ugandan (0)	0	<0.01
Zimbabwean (0)	0	<0.01
Other Sub-Saharan African (0)	0	<0.01
Albanian (0)	11	0.01
Alsatian (0)	0	<0.01
American (10,204)	10,204	10.02
Arab (150)	268	0.26
Arab (0)	0	<0.01
Egyptian (0)	0	<0.01
Iraqi (0)	0	<0.01
Jordanian (0)	0	<0.01
Lebanese (126)	221	0.22
Moroccan (0)	0	<0.01
Palestinian (0)	0	<0.01
Syrian (24)	47	0.05
Other Arab (0)	0	<0.01
Armenian (0)	0	<0.01
Assyrian/Chaldean/Syriac (0)	0	<0.01
Australian (4)	10	0.01
Austrian (145)	359	0.35
Basque (0)	0	<0.01
Belgian (48)	100	0.10
Brazilian (0)	21	0.02
British (98)	163	0.16
Bulgarian (0)	0	<0.01
Cajun (0)	0	<0.01
Canadian (6)	36	0.04
Carpatho Rusyn (0)	0	<0.01
Celtic (0)	14	0.01
Croatian (142)	409	0.40
Cypriot (0)	0	<0.01
Czech (171)	765	0.75
Czechoslovakian (155)	297	0.29
Danish (36)	186	0.18
Dutch (135)	1,900	1.87
Eastern European (0)	10	0.01
English (3,641)	12,816	12.58
Estonian (0)	0	<0.01
European (936)	1,037	1.02
Finnish (995)	3,193	3.13
French, ex. Basque (366)	2,039	2.00
French Canadian (76)	350	0.34
German (7,153)	25,350	24.89
German Russian (0)	0	<0.01
Greek (103)	320	0.31
Guyanese (0)	0	<0.01
Hungarian (1,198)	4,254	4.18
Icelander (0)	0	<0.01
Iranian (21)	21	0.02
Irish (3,195)	16,053	15.76
Israeli (0)	9	0.01
Italian (5,075)	11,334	11.13
Latvian (11)	46	0.05
Lithuanian (88)	270	0.27
Luxemburger (0)	0	<0.01
Macedonian (0)	8	0.01
Maltese (0)	0	<0.01
New Zealander (0)	0	<0.01
Northern European (0)	0	<0.01
Norwegian (101)	425	0.42
Pennsylvania German (701)	836	0.82
Polish (2,107)	5,897	5.79
Portuguese (154)	348	0.34
Romanian (51)	339	0.33
Russian (231)	832	0.82
Scandinavian (91)	91	0.09
Scotch-Irish (476)	2,033	2.00
Scottish (301)	2,062	2.02
Serbian (27)	109	0.11
Slavic (51)	164	0.16
Slovak (612)	1,747	1.71
Slovene (678)	1,392	1.37
Soviet Union (0)	0	<0.01
Swedish (530)	2,018	1.98
Swiss (201)	487	0.48
Turkish (0)	0	<0.01
Ukrainian (55)	145	0.14
Welsh (200)	1,102	1.08
West Indian, ex. Hispanic (40)	40	0.04
Bahamian (0)	0	<0.01
Barbadian (0)	0	<0.01
Belizean (0)	0	<0.01
Bermudan (0)	0	<0.01
British West Indian (0)	0	<0.01
Dutch West Indian (0)	0	<0.01
Haitian (0)	0	<0.01
Jamaican (40)	40	0.04
Trinidadian/Tobagonian (0)	0	<0.01
U.S. Virgin Islander (0)	0	<0.01
West Indian (0)	0	<0.01
Other West Indian (0)	0	<0.01
Yugoslavian (32)	106	0.10

Hispanic Origin	Population	%
Hispanic or Latino (of any race)	3,441	3.39
Central American, ex. Mexican	132	0.13
Costa Rican	1	<0.01
Guatemalan	16	0.02
Honduran	96	0.09
Nicaraguan	1	<0.01
Panamanian	10	0.01
Salvadoran	7	0.01
Other Central American	1	<0.01
Cuban	31	0.03
Dominican Republic	11	0.01
Mexican	948	0.93
Puerto Rican	2,065	2.03
South American	46	0.05
Argentinean	1	<0.01
Bolivian	3	<0.01
Chilean	1	<0.01
Colombian	22	0.02
Ecuadorian	3	<0.01
Paraguayan	1	<0.01
Peruvian	9	0.01
Uruguayan	0	<0.01
Venezuelan	1	<0.01
Other South American	5	<0.01
Other Hispanic or Latino	208	0.20

Race*	Population	%
African-American/Black (3,586)	4,820	4.75
Not Hispanic (3,467)	4,620	4.55
Hispanic (119)	200	0.20
American Indian/Alaska Native (241)	870	0.86
Not Hispanic (208)	779	0.77
Hispanic (33)	91	0.09
Alaska Athabascan *(Ala. Nat.)* (0)	0	<0.01
Aleut *(Alaska Native)* (0)	0	<0.01
Apache (1)	12	0.01
Arapaho (0)	0	<0.01
Blackfeet (4)	50	0.05
Canadian/French Am. Ind. (2)	7	0.01
Central American Ind. (0)	0	<0.01
Cherokee (67)	274	0.27
Cheyenne (1)	2	<0.01
Chickasaw (0)	6	0.01
Chippewa (14)	28	0.03
Choctaw (6)	9	0.01
Colville (0)	0	<0.01
Comanche (0)	1	<0.01
Cree (1)	1	<0.01
Creek (0)	4	<0.01
Crow (0)	5	<0.01
Delaware (4)	15	0.01
Hopi (1)	2	<0.01
Houma (0)	0	<0.01
Inupiat *(Alaska Native)* (1)	1	<0.01
Iroquois (9)	14	0.01
Kiowa (0)	0	<0.01
Lumbee (0)	0	<0.01
Menominee (0)	0	<0.01
Mexican American Ind. (6)	7	0.01
Navajo (2)	7	0.01
Osage (1)	1	<0.01
Ottawa (0)	0	<0.01
Paiute (0)	2	<0.01
Pima (0)	0	<0.01
Potawatomi (0)	1	<0.01
Pueblo (0)	0	<0.01
Puget Sound Salish (0)	0	<0.01
Seminole (1)	3	<0.01
Shoshone (0)	0	<0.01
Sioux (3)	12	0.01
South American Ind. (1)	1	<0.01
Spanish American Ind. (1)	1	<0.01
Tlingit-Haida *(Alaska Native)* (0)	0	<0.01
Tohono O'Odham (0)	3	<0.01
Tsimshian *(Alaska Native)* (0)	0	<0.01
Ute (0)	1	<0.01
Yakama (0)	0	<0.01
Yaqui (0)	1	<0.01
Yuman (0)	0	<0.01
Yup'ik *(Alaska Native)* (0)	0	<0.01
Asian (375)	588	0.58
Not Hispanic (372)	572	0.56
Hispanic (3)	16	0.02
Bangladeshi (3)	3	<0.01
Bhutanese (0)	0	<0.01
Burmese (0)	0	<0.01
Cambodian (1)	3	<0.01
Chinese, ex. Taiwanese (59)	90	0.09
Filipino (62)	127	0.13
Hmong (0)	0	<0.01
Indian (69)	97	0.10
Indonesian (0)	2	<0.01
Japanese (33)	68	0.07
Korean (61)	95	0.09
Laotian (2)	3	<0.01
Malaysian (0)	0	<0.01
Nepalese (0)	0	<0.01
Pakistani (2)	2	<0.01
Sri Lankan (9)	9	0.01
Taiwanese (3)	4	<0.01
Thai (9)	11	0.01
Vietnamese (37)	48	0.05
Hawaii Native/Pacific Islander (22)	76	0.07
Not Hispanic (17)	61	0.06
Hispanic (5)	15	0.01
Fijian (0)	0	<0.01
Guamanian/Chamorro (8)	19	0.02
Marshallese (0)	0	<0.01
Native Hawaiian (10)	29	0.03
Samoan (1)	4	<0.01
Tongan (0)	0	<0.01
White (94,041)	96,058	94.64
Not Hispanic (92,126)	93,866	92.48
Hispanic (1,915)	2,192	2.16

*Notes: † The Census 2010 population figure is used to calculate the percentages in the Hispanic Origin and Race categories. Ancestry percentages are based on the 2006-2010 American Community Survey population (not shown); ‡ Numbers in parentheses indicate the number of people reporting a single ancestry; * Numbers in parentheses indicate the number of persons reporting this race alone, not in combination with any other race; Please refer to the User Guide for more information.*

Butler County

Population: 368,130

Ancestry	Population	%
Afghan (0)	0	<0.01
African, Sub-Saharan (2,444)	2,728	0.75
African (1,625)	1,909	0.53
Cape Verdean (0)	0	<0.01
Ethiopian (47)	47	0.01
Ghanaian (376)	376	0.10
Kenyan (0)	0	<0.01
Liberian (0)	0	<0.01
Nigerian (250)	250	0.07
Senegalese (0)	0	<0.01
Sierra Leonean (0)	0	<0.01
Somalian (0)	0	<0.01
South African (0)	0	<0.01
Sudanese (0)	0	<0.01
Ugandan (8)	8	<0.01
Zimbabwean (19)	19	0.01
Other Sub-Saharan African (119)	119	0.03
Albanian (0)	12	<0.01
Alsatian (0)	0	<0.01
American (53,925)	53,925	14.84
Arab (1,006)	1,229	0.34
Arab (248)	260	0.07
Egyptian (75)	75	0.02
Iraqi (8)	8	<0.01
Jordanian (80)	97	0.03
Lebanese (295)	396	0.11
Moroccan (165)	235	0.06
Palestinian (17)	17	<0.01
Syrian (76)	76	0.02
Other Arab (42)	65	0.02
Armenian (43)	52	0.01
Assyrian/Chaldean/Syriac (0)	0	<0.01
Australian (0)	27	0.01
Austrian (191)	767	0.21
Basque (0)	0	<0.01
Belgian (32)	252	0.07
Brazilian (82)	146	0.04
British (731)	1,647	0.45
Bulgarian (32)	68	0.02
Cajun (12)	12	<0.01
Canadian (110)	295	0.08
Carpatho Rusyn (17)	17	<0.01
Celtic (13)	40	0.01
Croatian (40)	164	0.05
Cypriot (0)	0	<0.01
Czech (352)	1,431	0.39
Czechoslovakian (143)	319	0.09
Danish (309)	603	0.17
Dutch (959)	5,753	1.58
Eastern European (74)	115	0.03
English (12,989)	35,175	9.68
Estonian (79)	79	0.02
European (3,647)	4,103	1.13
Finnish (171)	582	0.16
French, ex. Basque (1,876)	8,367	2.30
French Canadian (320)	628	0.17
German (43,445)	98,300	27.05
German Russian (0)	0	<0.01
Greek (498)	1,102	0.30
Guyanese (0)	0	<0.01
Hungarian (616)	1,949	0.54
Icelander (14)	24	0.01
Iranian (14)	63	0.02
Irish (11,925)	49,474	13.61
Israeli (13)	24	0.01
Italian (6,157)	16,823	4.63
Latvian (35)	46	0.01
Lithuanian (213)	383	0.11
Luxemburger (0)	0	<0.01
Macedonian (16)	16	<0.01
Maltese (0)	0	<0.01
New Zealander (0)	8	<0.01
Northern European (102)	102	0.03
Norwegian (604)	1,864	0.51
Pennsylvania German (55)	69	0.02
Polish (1,561)	6,159	1.69
Portuguese (47)	214	0.06
Romanian (48)	269	0.07
Russian (718)	2,015	0.55
Scandinavian (152)	360	0.10
Scotch-Irish (2,105)	5,738	1.58
Scottish (2,061)	6,619	1.82
Serbian (22)	89	0.02
Slavic (25)	79	0.02
Slovak (280)	834	0.23
Slovene (48)	141	0.04
Soviet Union (0)	0	<0.01
Swedish (576)	2,229	0.61
Swiss (340)	1,054	0.29
Turkish (77)	155	0.04
Ukrainian (204)	577	0.16
Welsh (786)	2,921	0.80
West Indian, ex. Hispanic (165)	255	0.07
Bahamian (0)	0	<0.01
Barbadian (0)	0	<0.01
Belizean (0)	0	<0.01
Bermudan (0)	0	<0.01
British West Indian (0)	0	<0.01
Dutch West Indian (43)	70	0.02
Haitian (0)	0	<0.01
Jamaican (43)	76	0.02
Trinidadian/Tobagonian (59)	89	0.02
U.S. Virgin Islander (0)	0	<0.01
West Indian (20)	20	0.01
Other West Indian (0)	0	<0.01
Yugoslavian (117)	244	0.07

Hispanic Origin	Population	%
Hispanic or Latino (of any race)	14,670	3.99
Central American, ex. Mexican	1,493	0.41
Costa Rican	43	0.01
Guatemalan	824	0.22
Honduran	251	0.07
Nicaraguan	61	0.02
Panamanian	103	0.03
Salvadoran	206	0.06
Other Central American	5	<0.01
Cuban	382	0.10
Dominican Republic	880	0.24
Mexican	8,246	2.24
Puerto Rican	1,366	0.37
South American	990	0.27
Argentinean	63	0.02
Bolivian	17	<0.01
Chilean	38	0.01
Colombian	260	0.07
Ecuadorian	112	0.03
Paraguayan	13	<0.01
Peruvian	355	0.10
Uruguayan	16	<0.01
Venezuelan	105	0.03
Other South American	11	<0.01
Other Hispanic or Latino	1,313	0.36

Race*	Population	%
African-American/Black (26,972)	31,121	8.45
Not Hispanic (26,463)	30,315	8.23
Hispanic (509)	806	0.22
American Indian/Alaska Native (770)	2,496	0.68
Not Hispanic (606)	2,203	0.60
Hispanic (164)	293	0.08
Alaska Athabascan *(Ala. Nat.)* (1)	1	<0.01
Aleut *(Alaska Native)* (1)	4	<0.01
Apache (9)	20	0.01
Arapaho (0)	1	<0.01
Blackfeet (9)	86	0.02
Canadian/French Am. Ind. (16)	17	<0.01
Central American Ind. (12)	12	<0.01
Cherokee (185)	805	0.22
Cheyenne (2)	4	<0.01
Chickasaw (0)	1	<0.01
Chippewa (22)	39	0.01
Choctaw (13)	36	0.01
Colville (0)	0	<0.01
Comanche (6)	9	<0.01
Cree (3)	5	<0.01
Creek (4)	17	<0.01
Crow (1)	4	<0.01
Delaware (4)	6	<0.01
Hopi (0)	0	<0.01
Houma (0)	1	<0.01
Inupiat *(Alaska Native)* (2)	2	<0.01
Iroquois (19)	49	0.01
Kiowa (0)	3	<0.01
Lumbee (6)	6	<0.01
Menominee (0)	0	<0.01
Mexican American Ind. (54)	69	0.02
Navajo (12)	29	0.01
Osage (2)	4	<0.01
Ottawa (0)	0	<0.01
Paiute (0)	0	<0.01
Pima (0)	0	<0.01
Potawatomi (1)	4	<0.01
Pueblo (2)	3	<0.01
Puget Sound Salish (1)	1	<0.01
Seminole (6)	15	<0.01
Shoshone (0)	3	<0.01
Sioux (23)	65	0.02
South American Ind. (10)	18	<0.01
Spanish American Ind. (5)	13	<0.01
Tlingit-Haida *(Alaska Native)* (3)	3	<0.01
Tohono O'Odham (0)	0	<0.01
Tsimshian *(Alaska Native)* (0)	0	<0.01
Ute (0)	0	<0.01
Yakama (0)	5	<0.01
Yaqui (2)	3	<0.01
Yuman (0)	0	<0.01
Yup'ik *(Alaska Native)* (0)	0	<0.01
Asian (8,811)	10,555	2.87
Not Hispanic (8,759)	10,414	2.83
Hispanic (52)	141	0.04
Bangladeshi (28)	34	0.01
Bhutanese (0)	0	<0.01
Burmese (8)	12	<0.01
Cambodian (249)	289	0.08
Chinese, ex. Taiwanese (1,781)	2,042	0.55
Filipino (715)	1,137	0.31
Hmong (5)	5	<0.01
Indian (2,966)	3,272	0.89
Indonesian (23)	42	0.01
Japanese (272)	533	0.14
Korean (520)	740	0.20
Laotian (39)	44	0.01
Malaysian (13)	21	0.01
Nepalese (31)	34	0.01
Pakistani (228)	270	0.07
Sri Lankan (64)	73	0.02
Taiwanese (86)	128	0.03
Thai (113)	169	0.05
Vietnamese (1,351)	1,469	0.40
Hawaii Native/Pacific Islander (288)	503	0.14
Not Hispanic (239)	426	0.12
Hispanic (49)	77	0.02
Fijian (2)	4	<0.01
Guamanian/Chamorro (79)	113	0.03
Marshallese (7)	15	<0.01
Native Hawaiian (46)	101	0.03
Samoan (10)	33	0.01
Tongan (6)	7	<0.01
White (316,667)	323,820	87.96
Not Hispanic (310,183)	316,333	85.93
Hispanic (6,484)	7,487	2.03

*Notes: † The Census 2010 population figure is used to calculate the percentages in the Hispanic Origin and Race categories. Ancestry percentages are based on the 2006-2010 American Community Survey population (not shown); ‡ Numbers in parentheses indicate the number of people reporting a single ancestry; * Numbers in parentheses indicate the number of persons reporting this race alone, not in combination with any other race; Please refer to the User Guide for more information.*

Clark County

Population: 138,333

Ancestry	Population	%
Afghan (0)	0	<0.01
African, Sub-Saharan (670)	776	0.56
African (639)	738	0.53
Cape Verdean (6)	13	0.01
Ethiopian (0)	0	<0.01
Ghanaian (0)	0	<0.01
Kenyan (0)	0	<0.01
Liberian (0)	0	<0.01
Nigerian (25)	25	0.02
Senegalese (0)	0	<0.01
Sierra Leonean (0)	0	<0.01
Somalian (0)	0	<0.01
South African (0)	0	<0.01
Sudanese (0)	0	<0.01
Ugandan (0)	0	<0.01
Zimbabwean (0)	0	<0.01
Other Sub-Saharan African (0)	0	<0.01
Albanian (0)	0	<0.01
Alsatian (5)	5	<0.01
American (19,231)	19,231	13.80
Arab (62)	112	0.08
Arab (0)	0	<0.01
Egyptian (0)	0	<0.01
Iraqi (0)	0	<0.01
Jordanian (27)	35	0.03
Lebanese (0)	29	0.02
Moroccan (0)	0	<0.01
Palestinian (0)	0	<0.01
Syrian (0)	5	<0.01
Other Arab (35)	43	0.03
Armenian (6)	18	0.01
Assyrian/Chaldean/Syriac (0)	0	<0.01
Australian (9)	40	0.03
Austrian (3)	81	0.06
Basque (0)	0	<0.01
Belgian (26)	144	0.10
Brazilian (8)	8	0.01
British (227)	436	0.31
Bulgarian (9)	39	0.03
Cajun (0)	0	<0.01
Canadian (104)	194	0.14
Carpatho Rusyn (0)	0	<0.01
Celtic (12)	12	0.01
Croatian (24)	77	0.06
Cypriot (0)	0	<0.01
Czech (22)	246	0.18
Czechoslovakian (59)	106	0.08
Danish (20)	139	0.10
Dutch (622)	3,291	2.36
Eastern European (0)	0	<0.01
English (5,879)	14,578	10.46
Estonian (0)	0	<0.01
European (1,180)	1,255	0.90
Finnish (126)	163	0.12
French, ex. Basque (678)	2,901	2.08
French Canadian (75)	353	0.25
German (14,560)	35,228	25.28
German Russian (0)	0	<0.01
Greek (199)	537	0.39
Guyanese (0)	0	<0.01
Hungarian (228)	701	0.50
Icelander (8)	8	0.01
Iranian (28)	57	0.04
Irish (6,572)	20,947	15.03
Israeli (0)	0	<0.01
Italian (1,835)	4,266	3.06
Latvian (8)	8	0.01
Lithuanian (64)	150	0.11
Luxemburger (0)	0	<0.01
Macedonian (111)	266	0.19
Maltese (0)	0	<0.01
New Zealander (0)	0	<0.01
Northern European (38)	38	0.03
Norwegian (170)	572	0.41
Pennsylvania German (175)	175	0.13
Polish (638)	1,899	1.36
Portuguese (113)	155	0.11
Romanian (85)	179	0.13
Russian (107)	312	0.22
Scandinavian (76)	94	0.07
Scotch-Irish (1,119)	2,810	2.02
Scottish (1,099)	3,182	2.28
Serbian (0)	0	<0.01
Slavic (0)	53	0.04
Slovak (57)	393	0.28
Slovene (18)	54	0.04
Soviet Union (0)	0	<0.01
Swedish (335)	1,275	0.91
Swiss (110)	354	0.25
Turkish (0)	0	<0.01
Ukrainian (22)	119	0.09
Welsh (426)	1,414	1.01
West Indian, ex. Hispanic (49)	112	0.08
Bahamian (0)	0	<0.01
Barbadian (0)	0	<0.01
Belizean (0)	0	<0.01
Bermudan (0)	0	<0.01
British West Indian (0)	0	<0.01
Dutch West Indian (9)	44	0.03
Haitian (6)	6	<0.01
Jamaican (34)	62	0.04
Trinidadian/Tobagonian (0)	0	<0.01
U.S. Virgin Islander (0)	0	<0.01
West Indian (0)	0	<0.01
Other West Indian (0)	0	<0.01
Yugoslavian (24)	35	0.03

Hispanic Origin	Population	%
Hispanic or Latino (of any race)	3,805	2.75
Central American, ex. Mexican	142	0.10
Costa Rican	3	<0.01
Guatemalan	39	0.03
Honduran	30	0.02
Nicaraguan	19	0.01
Panamanian	23	0.02
Salvadoran	28	0.02
Other Central American	0	<0.01
Cuban	51	0.04
Dominican Republic	22	0.02
Mexican	2,961	2.14
Puerto Rican	204	0.15
South American	31	0.02
Argentinean	0	<0.01
Bolivian	1	<0.01
Chilean	3	<0.01
Colombian	14	0.01
Ecuadorian	3	<0.01
Paraguayan	2	<0.01
Peruvian	4	<0.01
Uruguayan	0	<0.01
Venezuelan	4	<0.01
Other South American	0	<0.01
Other Hispanic or Latino	394	0.28

Race*	Population	%
African-American/Black (12,128)	14,415	10.42
Not Hispanic (11,999)	14,145	10.23
Hispanic (129)	270	0.20
American Indian/Alaska Native (351)	1,287	0.93
Not Hispanic (302)	1,159	0.84
Hispanic (49)	128	0.09
Alaska Athabascan *(Ala. Nat.)* (0)	3	<0.01
Aleut *(Alaska Native)* (1)	1	<0.01
Apache (6)	16	0.01
Arapaho (0)	0	<0.01
Blackfeet (12)	62	0.04
Canadian/French Am. Ind. (0)	4	<0.01
Central American Ind. (0)	1	<0.01
Cherokee (70)	401	0.29
Cheyenne (3)	7	0.01
Chickasaw (1)	2	<0.01
Chippewa (8)	11	0.01
Choctaw (11)	17	0.01
Colville (0)	0	<0.01
Comanche (5)	7	0.01
Cree (1)	2	<0.01
Creek (4)	10	0.01
Crow (1)	2	<0.01
Delaware (2)	12	0.01
Hopi (0)	5	<0.01
Houma (0)	0	<0.01
Inupiat *(Alaska Native)* (1)	4	<0.01
Iroquois (7)	24	0.02
Kiowa (0)	0	<0.01
Lumbee (2)	2	<0.01
Menominee (0)	0	<0.01
Mexican American Ind. (7)	17	0.01
Navajo (0)	3	<0.01
Osage (0)	6	<0.01
Ottawa (1)	1	<0.01
Paiute (0)	0	<0.01
Pima (0)	0	<0.01
Potawatomi (1)	4	<0.01
Pueblo (0)	0	<0.01
Puget Sound Salish (0)	0	<0.01
Seminole (0)	7	0.01
Shoshone (0)	0	<0.01
Sioux (9)	28	0.02
South American Ind. (0)	0	<0.01
Spanish American Ind. (2)	2	<0.01
Tlingit-Haida *(Alaska Native)* (0)	0	<0.01
Tohono O'Odham (3)	3	<0.01
Tsimshian *(Alaska Native)* (0)	0	<0.01
Ute (0)	0	<0.01
Yakama (0)	0	<0.01
Yaqui (1)	1	<0.01
Yuman (0)	0	<0.01
Yup'ik *(Alaska Native)* (0)	0	<0.01
Asian (858)	1,294	0.94
Not Hispanic (849)	1,243	0.90
Hispanic (9)	51	0.04
Bangladeshi (0)	0	<0.01
Bhutanese (0)	0	<0.01
Burmese (0)	0	<0.01
Cambodian (3)	6	<0.01
Chinese, ex. Taiwanese (154)	207	0.15
Filipino (131)	220	0.16
Hmong (0)	0	<0.01
Indian (244)	293	0.21
Indonesian (3)	8	0.01
Japanese (67)	137	0.10
Korean (87)	156	0.11
Laotian (19)	26	0.02
Malaysian (1)	1	<0.01
Nepalese (0)	0	<0.01
Pakistani (46)	51	0.04
Sri Lankan (3)	4	<0.01
Taiwanese (2)	11	0.01
Thai (28)	60	0.04
Vietnamese (33)	63	0.05
Hawaii Native/Pacific Islander (51)	152	0.11
Not Hispanic (47)	123	0.09
Hispanic (4)	29	0.02
Fijian (19)	24	0.02
Guamanian/Chamorro (4)	12	0.01
Marshallese (2)	2	<0.01
Native Hawaiian (6)	29	0.02
Samoan (8)	16	0.01
Tongan (0)	2	<0.01
White (119,440)	122,670	88.68
Not Hispanic (117,976)	120,876	87.38
Hispanic (1,464)	1,794	1.30

*Notes: † The Census 2010 population figure is used to calculate the percentages in the Hispanic Origin and Race categories. Ancestry percentages are based on the 2006-2010 American Community Survey population (not shown); ‡ Numbers in parentheses indicate the number of people reporting a single ancestry; * Numbers in parentheses indicate the number of persons reporting this race alone, not in combination with any other race; Please refer to the User Guide for more information.*

Clermont County

Population: 197,363

Ancestry	Population	%
Afghan (0)	0	<0.01
African, Sub-Saharan (206)	244	0.12
African (192)	230	0.12
Cape Verdean (0)	0	<0.01
Ethiopian (0)	0	<0.01
Ghanaian (14)	14	0.01
Kenyan (0)	0	<0.01
Liberian (0)	0	<0.01
Nigerian (0)	0	<0.01
Senegalese (0)	0	<0.01
Sierra Leonean (0)	0	<0.01
Somalian (0)	0	<0.01
South African (0)	0	<0.01
Sudanese (0)	0	<0.01
Ugandan (0)	0	<0.01
Zimbabwean (0)	0	<0.01
Other Sub-Saharan African (0)	0	<0.01
Albanian (0)	0	<0.01
Alsatian (0)	4	<0.01
American (23,411)	23,411	11.99
Arab (277)	623	0.32
Arab (44)	54	0.03
Egyptian (7)	14	0.01
Iraqi (0)	0	<0.01
Jordanian (14)	14	0.01
Lebanese (113)	423	0.22
Moroccan (0)	0	<0.01
Palestinian (0)	19	0.01
Syrian (0)	0	<0.01
Other Arab (99)	99	0.05
Armenian (0)	16	0.01
Assyrian/Chaldean/Syriac (0)	0	<0.01
Australian (54)	54	0.03
Austrian (101)	505	0.26
Basque (0)	0	<0.01
Belgian (20)	149	0.08
Brazilian (26)	26	0.01
British (548)	971	0.50
Bulgarian (42)	42	0.02
Cajun (0)	0	<0.01
Canadian (107)	327	0.17
Carpatho Rusyn (0)	0	<0.01
Celtic (28)	75	0.04
Croatian (77)	174	0.09
Cypriot (0)	0	<0.01
Czech (68)	427	0.22
Czechoslovakian (22)	134	0.07
Danish (119)	421	0.22
Dutch (589)	3,615	1.85
Eastern European (57)	69	0.04
English (7,598)	21,648	11.08
Estonian (0)	0	<0.01
European (1,949)	2,158	1.10
Finnish (23)	215	0.11
French, ex. Basque (871)	5,377	2.75
French Canadian (230)	522	0.27
German (26,679)	66,435	34.01
German Russian (0)	0	<0.01
Greek (306)	772	0.40
Guyanese (0)	0	<0.01
Hungarian (314)	1,216	0.62
Icelander (0)	31	0.02
Iranian (31)	31	0.02
Irish (7,947)	35,329	18.09
Israeli (11)	11	0.01
Italian (2,963)	8,369	4.28
Latvian (0)	0	<0.01
Lithuanian (84)	287	0.15
Luxemburger (0)	0	<0.01
Macedonian (0)	15	0.01
Maltese (0)	0	<0.01
New Zealander (0)	0	<0.01
Northern European (67)	67	0.03
Norwegian (468)	1,002	0.51
Pennsylvania German (73)	106	0.05
Polish (1,205)	3,481	1.78
Portuguese (15)	137	0.07
Romanian (231)	301	0.15
Russian (325)	710	0.36
Scandinavian (64)	226	0.12
Scotch-Irish (1,192)	3,090	1.58
Scottish (1,598)	4,770	2.44
Serbian (62)	112	0.06
Slavic (0)	188	0.10
Slovak (74)	262	0.13
Slovene (12)	52	0.03
Soviet Union (0)	0	<0.01
Swedish (214)	1,409	0.72
Swiss (118)	560	0.29
Turkish (33)	39	0.02
Ukrainian (300)	500	0.26
Welsh (299)	1,461	0.75
West Indian, ex. Hispanic (50)	194	0.10
Bahamian (0)	0	<0.01
Barbadian (0)	0	<0.01
Belizean (0)	0	<0.01
Bermudan (0)	0	<0.01
British West Indian (0)	23	0.01
Dutch West Indian (0)	0	<0.01
Haitian (38)	79	0.04
Jamaican (0)	23	0.01
Trinidadian/Tobagonian (0)	0	<0.01
U.S. Virgin Islander (0)	0	<0.01
West Indian (12)	69	0.04
Other West Indian (0)	0	<0.01
Yugoslavian (59)	74	0.04

Hispanic Origin	Population	%
Hispanic or Latino (of any race)	2,896	1.47
Central American, ex. Mexican	260	0.13
Costa Rican	45	0.02
Guatemalan	69	0.03
Honduran	41	0.02
Nicaraguan	9	<0.01
Panamanian	40	0.02
Salvadoran	52	0.03
Other Central American	4	<0.01
Cuban	109	0.06
Dominican Republic	36	0.02
Mexican	1,504	0.76
Puerto Rican	407	0.21
South American	244	0.12
Argentinean	17	0.01
Bolivian	13	0.01
Chilean	16	0.01
Colombian	71	0.04
Ecuadorian	24	0.01
Paraguayan	4	<0.01
Peruvian	52	0.03
Uruguayan	3	<0.01
Venezuelan	41	0.02
Other South American	3	<0.01
Other Hispanic or Latino	336	0.17

Race*	Population	%
African-American/Black (2,284)	3,297	1.67
Not Hispanic (2,234)	3,202	1.62
Hispanic (50)	95	0.05
American Indian/Alaska Native (403)	1,343	0.68
Not Hispanic (349)	1,236	0.63
Hispanic (54)	107	0.05
Alaska Athabascan *(Ala. Nat.)* (0)	0	<0.01
Aleut *(Alaska Native)* (0)	3	<0.01
Apache (6)	26	0.01
Arapaho (0)	1	<0.01
Blackfeet (10)	78	0.04
Canadian/French Am. Ind. (0)	2	<0.01
Central American Ind. (2)	2	<0.01
Cherokee (127)	519	0.26
Cheyenne (0)	1	<0.01
Chickasaw (0)	0	<0.01
Chippewa (11)	21	0.01
Choctaw (4)	12	0.01
Colville (0)	0	<0.01
Comanche (0)	2	<0.01
Cree (0)	1	<0.01
Creek (5)	8	<0.01
Crow (5)	8	<0.01
Delaware (1)	4	<0.01
Hopi (1)	1	<0.01
Houma (0)	0	<0.01
Inupiat *(Alaska Native)* (0)	0	<0.01
Iroquois (2)	9	<0.01
Kiowa (0)	0	<0.01
Lumbee (2)	2	<0.01
Menominee (2)	2	<0.01
Mexican American Ind. (11)	15	0.01
Navajo (1)	2	<0.01
Osage (8)	8	<0.01
Ottawa (3)	5	<0.01
Paiute (0)	0	<0.01
Pima (0)	1	<0.01
Potawatomi (7)	7	<0.01
Pueblo (0)	0	<0.01
Puget Sound Salish (0)	1	<0.01
Seminole (1)	8	<0.01
Shoshone (0)	0	<0.01
Sioux (8)	26	0.01
South American Ind. (4)	5	<0.01
Spanish American Ind. (0)	0	<0.01
Tlingit-Haida *(Alaska Native)* (1)	1	<0.01
Tohono O'Odham (0)	0	<0.01
Tsimshian *(Alaska Native)* (0)	3	<0.01
Ute (0)	0	<0.01
Yakama (0)	0	<0.01
Yaqui (0)	0	<0.01
Yuman (0)	0	<0.01
Yup'ik *(Alaska Native)* (0)	0	<0.01
Asian (1,920)	2,544	1.29
Not Hispanic (1,900)	2,509	1.27
Hispanic (20)	35	0.02
Bangladeshi (12)	13	0.01
Bhutanese (0)	0	<0.01
Burmese (0)	0	<0.01
Cambodian (23)	39	0.02
Chinese, ex. Taiwanese (369)	441	0.22
Filipino (205)	388	0.20
Hmong (0)	0	<0.01
Indian (692)	797	0.40
Indonesian (14)	20	0.01
Japanese (84)	176	0.09
Korean (107)	178	0.09
Laotian (1)	3	<0.01
Malaysian (1)	1	<0.01
Nepalese (0)	0	<0.01
Pakistani (25)	31	0.02
Sri Lankan (11)	12	0.01
Taiwanese (17)	20	0.01
Thai (57)	70	0.04
Vietnamese (226)	263	0.13
Hawaii Native/Pacific Islander (61)	138	0.07
Not Hispanic (58)	123	0.06
Hispanic (3)	15	0.01
Fijian (0)	1	<0.01
Guamanian/Chamorro (3)	8	<0.01
Marshallese (2)	2	<0.01
Native Hawaiian (22)	45	0.02
Samoan (14)	32	0.02
Tongan (1)	1	<0.01
White (189,250)	191,819	97.19
Not Hispanic (187,331)	189,662	96.10
Hispanic (1,919)	2,157	1.09

*Notes: † The Census 2010 population figure is used to calculate the percentages in the Hispanic Origin and Race categories. Ancestry percentages are based on the 2006-2010 American Community Survey population (not shown); ‡ Numbers in parentheses indicate the number of people reporting a single ancestry; * Numbers in parentheses indicate the number of persons reporting this race alone, not in combination with any other race; Please refer to the User Guide for more information.*

Columbiana County

Population: 107,841

Ancestry	Population	%
Afghan (0)	0	<0.01
African, Sub-Saharan (120)	134	0.12
African (103)	117	0.11
Cape Verdean (8)	8	0.01
Ethiopian (0)	0	<0.01
Ghanaian (0)	0	<0.01
Kenyan (0)	0	<0.01
Liberian (0)	0	<0.01
Nigerian (9)	9	0.01
Senegalese (0)	0	<0.01
Sierra Leonean (0)	0	<0.01
Somalian (0)	0	<0.01
South African (0)	0	<0.01
Sudanese (0)	0	<0.01
Ugandan (0)	0	<0.01
Zimbabwean (0)	0	<0.01
Other Sub-Saharan African (0)	0	<0.01
Albanian (13)	13	0.01
Alsatian (0)	0	<0.01
American (8,280)	8,280	7.62
Arab (31)	166	0.15
Arab (8)	8	0.01
Egyptian (0)	0	<0.01
Iraqi (0)	0	<0.01
Jordanian (0)	0	<0.01
Lebanese (5)	127	0.12
Moroccan (18)	18	0.02
Palestinian (0)	0	<0.01
Syrian (0)	13	0.01
Other Arab (0)	0	<0.01
Armenian (0)	0	<0.01
Assyrian/Chaldean/Syriac (0)	0	<0.01
Australian (0)	0	<0.01
Austrian (83)	245	0.23
Basque (0)	0	<0.01
Belgian (80)	150	0.14
Brazilian (21)	57	0.05
British (171)	308	0.28
Bulgarian (0)	0	<0.01
Cajun (0)	0	<0.01
Canadian (76)	136	0.13
Carpatho Rusyn (0)	12	0.01
Celtic (57)	79	0.07
Croatian (116)	357	0.33
Cypriot (0)	0	<0.01
Czech (120)	464	0.43
Czechoslovakian (107)	216	0.20
Danish (42)	121	0.11
Dutch (320)	2,422	2.23
Eastern European (9)	9	0.01
English (5,017)	15,893	14.63
Estonian (0)	0	<0.01
European (529)	541	0.50
Finnish (19)	19	0.02
French, ex. Basque (366)	2,166	1.99
French Canadian (80)	340	0.31
German (10,044)	31,734	29.22
German Russian (0)	0	<0.01
Greek (106)	222	0.20
Guyanese (10)	10	0.01
Hungarian (374)	1,020	0.94
Icelander (0)	0	<0.01
Iranian (0)	0	<0.01
Irish (4,371)	19,269	17.74
Israeli (0)	0	<0.01
Italian (4,242)	9,830	9.05
Latvian (11)	11	0.01
Lithuanian (87)	147	0.14
Luxemburger (0)	0	<0.01
Macedonian (0)	0	<0.01
Maltese (0)	0	<0.01
New Zealander (0)	0	<0.01
Northern European (0)	0	<0.01
Norwegian (118)	490	0.45
Pennsylvania German (226)	481	0.44
Polish (846)	3,535	3.25
Portuguese (14)	20	0.02
Romanian (103)	434	0.40
Russian (91)	418	0.38
Scandinavian (0)	18	0.02
Scotch-Irish (1,485)	3,602	3.32
Scottish (816)	3,106	2.86
Serbian (111)	329	0.30
Slavic (52)	162	0.15
Slovak (572)	1,437	1.32
Slovene (65)	92	0.08
Soviet Union (0)	0	<0.01
Swedish (180)	783	0.72
Swiss (505)	1,442	1.33
Turkish (0)	0	<0.01
Ukrainian (144)	429	0.39
Welsh (485)	1,979	1.82
West Indian, ex. Hispanic (30)	65	0.06
Bahamian (14)	14	0.01
Barbadian (0)	0	<0.01
Belizean (0)	0	<0.01
Bermudan (0)	0	<0.01
British West Indian (0)	0	<0.01
Dutch West Indian (0)	0	<0.01
Haitian (0)	0	<0.01
Jamaican (16)	33	0.03
Trinidadian/Tobagonian (0)	18	0.02
U.S. Virgin Islander (0)	0	<0.01
West Indian (0)	0	<0.01
Other West Indian (0)	0	<0.01
Yugoslavian (95)	226	0.21

Hispanic Origin	Population	%
Hispanic or Latino (of any race)	1,348	1.25
Central American, ex. Mexican	189	0.18
Costa Rican	1	<0.01
Guatemalan	155	0.14
Honduran	6	0.01
Nicaraguan	1	<0.01
Panamanian	15	0.01
Salvadoran	9	0.01
Other Central American	2	<0.01
Cuban	30	0.03
Dominican Republic	40	0.04
Mexican	616	0.57
Puerto Rican	269	0.25
South American	54	0.05
Argentinean	2	<0.01
Bolivian	2	<0.01
Chilean	4	<0.01
Colombian	26	0.02
Ecuadorian	6	0.01
Paraguayan	0	<0.01
Peruvian	12	0.01
Uruguayan	0	<0.01
Venezuelan	2	<0.01
Other South American	0	<0.01
Other Hispanic or Latino	150	0.14

Race*	Population	%
African-American/Black (2,405)	3,123	2.90
Not Hispanic (2,323)	3,014	2.79
Hispanic (82)	109	0.10
American Indian/Alaska Native (202)	710	0.66
Not Hispanic (164)	644	0.60
Hispanic (38)	66	0.06
Alaska Athabascan *(Ala. Nat.)* (1)	1	<0.01
Aleut *(Alaska Native)* (0)	1	<0.01
Apache (5)	14	0.01
Arapaho (0)	0	<0.01
Blackfeet (7)	47	0.04
Canadian/French Am. Ind. (6)	6	0.01
Central American Ind. (0)	1	<0.01
Cherokee (34)	227	0.21
Cheyenne (1)	2	<0.01
Chickasaw (1)	5	<0.01
Chippewa (10)	18	0.02
Choctaw (4)	10	0.01
Colville (0)	0	<0.01
Comanche (2)	2	<0.01
Cree (2)	8	0.01
Creek (0)	1	<0.01
Crow (0)	3	<0.01
Delaware (10)	16	0.01
Hopi (0)	0	<0.01
Houma (0)	0	<0.01
Inupiat *(Alaska Native)* (1)	1	<0.01
Iroquois (4)	10	0.01
Kiowa (0)	0	<0.01
Lumbee (4)	6	0.01
Menominee (0)	0	<0.01
Mexican American Ind. (7)	14	0.01
Navajo (0)	4	<0.01
Osage (0)	0	<0.01
Ottawa (2)	5	<0.01
Paiute (0)	1	<0.01
Pima (0)	0	<0.01
Potawatomi (0)	0	<0.01
Pueblo (0)	0	<0.01
Puget Sound Salish (0)	0	<0.01
Seminole (0)	4	<0.01
Shoshone (0)	0	<0.01
Sioux (9)	21	0.02
South American Ind. (6)	12	0.01
Spanish American Ind. (0)	0	<0.01
Tlingit-Haida *(Alaska Native)* (0)	0	<0.01
Tohono O'Odham (0)	0	<0.01
Tsimshian *(Alaska Native)* (0)	0	<0.01
Ute (0)	0	<0.01
Yakama (0)	1	<0.01
Yaqui (3)	3	<0.01
Yuman (0)	0	<0.01
Yup'ik *(Alaska Native)* (0)	0	<0.01
Asian (322)	500	0.46
Not Hispanic (319)	489	0.45
Hispanic (3)	11	0.01
Bangladeshi (0)	0	<0.01
Bhutanese (0)	0	<0.01
Burmese (0)	0	<0.01
Cambodian (0)	1	<0.01
Chinese, ex. Taiwanese (85)	102	0.09
Filipino (80)	139	0.13
Hmong (3)	3	<0.01
Indian (50)	66	0.06
Indonesian (0)	1	<0.01
Japanese (15)	44	0.04
Korean (21)	52	0.05
Laotian (3)	3	<0.01
Malaysian (0)	0	<0.01
Nepalese (0)	0	<0.01
Pakistani (22)	25	0.02
Sri Lankan (0)	0	<0.01
Taiwanese (0)	1	<0.01
Thai (3)	5	<0.01
Vietnamese (20)	27	0.03
Hawaii Native/Pacific Islander (27)	65	0.06
Not Hispanic (20)	57	0.05
Hispanic (7)	8	0.01
Fijian (0)	0	<0.01
Guamanian/Chamorro (11)	18	0.02
Marshallese (0)	0	<0.01
Native Hawaiian (15)	31	0.03
Samoan (0)	3	<0.01
Tongan (0)	0	<0.01
White (102,959)	104,291	96.71
Not Hispanic (102,326)	103,554	96.02
Hispanic (633)	737	0.68

*Notes: † The Census 2010 population figure is used to calculate the percentages in the Hispanic Origin and Race categories. Ancestry percentages are based on the 2006-2010 American Community Survey population (not shown); ‡ Numbers in parentheses indicate the number of people reporting a single ancestry; * Numbers in parentheses indicate the number of persons reporting this race alone, not in combination with any other race; Please refer to the User Guide for more information.*

Cuyahoga County

Population: 1,280,122

Ancestry	Population	%
Afghan (0)	0	<0.01
African, Sub-Saharan (9,385)	11,464	0.89
African (6,600)	8,154	0.63
Cape Verdean (19)	58	<0.01
Ethiopian (21)	31	<0.01
Ghanaian (229)	244	0.02
Kenyan (89)	120	0.01
Liberian (248)	253	0.02
Nigerian (1,014)	1,093	0.08
Senegalese (17)	39	<0.01
Sierra Leonean (36)	36	<0.01
Somalian (212)	246	0.02
South African (179)	326	0.03
Sudanese (117)	117	0.01
Ugandan (29)	29	<0.01
Zimbabwean (0)	0	<0.01
Other Sub-Saharan African (575)	718	0.06
Albanian (1,946)	2,139	0.17
Alsatian (0)	15	<0.01
American (35,629)	35,629	2.75
Arab (12,072)	17,189	1.33
Arab (2,129)	2,644	0.20
Egyptian (1,223)	1,360	0.11
Iraqi (238)	238	0.02
Jordanian (433)	495	0.04
Lebanese (4,616)	8,193	0.63
Moroccan (202)	260	0.02
Palestinian (1,654)	1,741	0.13
Syrian (965)	1,513	0.12
Other Arab (612)	745	0.06
Armenian (458)	958	0.07
Assyrian/Chaldean/Syriac (15)	20	<0.01
Australian (70)	199	0.02
Austrian (942)	5,359	0.41
Basque (0)	12	<0.01
Belgian (149)	762	0.06
Brazilian (178)	240	0.02
British (1,174)	3,030	0.23
Bulgarian (373)	640	0.05
Cajun (37)	46	<0.01
Canadian (458)	1,902	0.15
Carpatho Rusyn (214)	256	0.02
Celtic (79)	125	0.01
Croatian (3,695)	9,707	0.75
Cypriot (12)	12	<0.01
Czech (6,762)	22,584	1.75
Czechoslovakian (1,730)	3,395	0.26
Danish (563)	2,158	0.17
Dutch (1,191)	10,463	0.81
Eastern European (3,823)	4,024	0.31
English (18,135)	80,962	6.26
Estonian (97)	150	0.01
European (6,840)	7,776	0.60
Finnish (491)	2,144	0.17
French, ex. Basque (1,631)	18,173	1.40
French Canadian (892)	2,785	0.22
German (54,613)	225,136	17.40
German Russian (72)	125	0.01
Greek (4,765)	9,414	0.73
Guyanese (337)	403	0.03
Hungarian (14,725)	44,605	3.45
Icelander (51)	95	0.01
Iranian (554)	816	0.06
Irish (42,280)	168,679	13.04
Israeli (331)	648	0.05
Italian (47,317)	118,489	9.16
Latvian (486)	897	0.07
Lithuanian (2,405)	6,678	0.52
Luxemburger (6)	18	<0.01
Macedonian (155)	304	0.02
Maltese (30)	30	<0.01
New Zealander (41)	87	0.01
Northern European (304)	341	0.03
Norwegian (823)	3,363	0.26
Pennsylvania German (189)	547	0.04
Polish (41,516)	111,245	8.60
Portuguese (369)	1,075	0.08
Romanian (4,309)	7,213	0.56
Russian (9,338)	21,861	1.69
Scandinavian (294)	776	0.06
Scotch-Irish (4,893)	15,009	1.16
Scottish (3,655)	16,982	1.31
Serbian (3,085)	5,164	0.40
Slavic (426)	1,177	0.09
Slovak (15,574)	43,131	3.33
Slovene (6,974)	19,262	1.49
Soviet Union (0)	0	<0.01
Swedish (1,524)	7,938	0.61
Swiss (453)	3,615	0.28
Turkish (707)	942	0.07
Ukrainian (10,616)	17,407	1.35
Welsh (1,137)	8,613	0.67
West Indian, ex. Hispanic (3,010)	4,624	0.36
Bahamian (11)	26	<0.01
Barbadian (44)	128	0.01
Belizean (30)	46	<0.01
Bermudan (32)	90	0.01
British West Indian (55)	65	0.01
Dutch West Indian (0)	0	<0.01
Haitian (103)	195	0.02
Jamaican (2,303)	3,087	0.24
Trinidadian/Tobagonian (78)	185	0.01
U.S. Virgin Islander (12)	12	<0.01
West Indian (342)	790	0.06
Other West Indian (0)	0	<0.01
Yugoslavian (978)	1,617	0.12

Hispanic Origin	Population	%
Hispanic or Latino (of any race)	61,270	4.79
Central American, ex. Mexican	3,371	0.26
Costa Rican	108	0.01
Guatemalan	1,187	0.09
Honduran	455	0.04
Nicaraguan	195	0.02
Panamanian	278	0.02
Salvadoran	1,119	0.09
Other Central American	29	<0.01
Cuban	1,153	0.09
Dominican Republic	1,643	0.13
Mexican	8,797	0.69
Puerto Rican	39,068	3.05
South American	3,175	0.25
Argentinean	380	0.03
Bolivian	28	<0.01
Chilean	196	0.02
Colombian	920	0.07
Ecuadorian	280	0.02
Paraguayan	49	<0.01
Peruvian	872	0.07
Uruguayan	105	0.01
Venezuelan	302	0.02
Other South American	43	<0.01
Other Hispanic or Latino	4,063	0.32

Race*	Population	%
African-American/Black (380,198)	396,157	30.95
Not Hispanic (374,968)	388,386	30.34
Hispanic (5,230)	7,771	0.61
American Indian/Alaska Native (2,578)	8,991	0.70
Not Hispanic (2,018)	7,571	0.59
Hispanic (560)	1,420	0.11
Alaska Athabascan *(Ala. Nat.)* (5)	11	<0.01
Aleut *(Alaska Native)* (1)	1	<0.01
Apache (30)	106	0.01
Arapaho (1)	9	<0.01
Blackfeet (75)	560	0.04
Canadian/French Am. Ind. (12)	27	<0.01
Central American Ind. (35)	46	<0.01
Cherokee (297)	2,013	0.16
Cheyenne (12)	23	<0.01
Chickasaw (21)	53	<0.01
Chippewa (87)	146	0.01
Choctaw (49)	178	0.01
Colville (1)	3	<0.01
Comanche (2)	12	<0.01
Cree (2)	8	<0.01
Creek (12)	65	0.01
Crow (4)	14	<0.01
Delaware (8)	28	<0.01
Hopi (0)	5	<0.01
Houma (0)	0	<0.01
Inupiat *(Alaska Native)* (10)	15	<0.01
Iroquois (62)	195	0.02
Kiowa (8)	14	<0.01
Lumbee (18)	38	<0.01
Menominee (2)	4	<0.01
Mexican American Ind. (84)	126	0.01
Navajo (44)	100	0.01
Osage (2)	5	<0.01
Ottawa (8)	17	<0.01
Paiute (0)	0	<0.01
Pima (0)	1	<0.01
Potawatomi (6)	16	<0.01
Pueblo (21)	32	<0.01
Puget Sound Salish (1)	1	<0.01
Seminole (20)	87	0.01
Shoshone (5)	10	<0.01
Sioux (66)	223	0.02
South American Ind. (66)	167	0.01
Spanish American Ind. (11)	13	<0.01
Tlingit-Haida *(Alaska Native)* (13)	21	<0.01
Tohono O'Odham (7)	7	<0.01
Tsimshian *(Alaska Native)* (1)	4	<0.01
Ute (0)	0	<0.01
Yakama (0)	0	<0.01
Yaqui (0)	5	<0.01
Yuman (1)	2	<0.01
Yup'ik *(Alaska Native)* (1)	4	<0.01
Asian (32,883)	39,136	3.06
Not Hispanic (32,615)	38,506	3.01
Hispanic (268)	630	0.05
Bangladeshi (99)	127	0.01
Bhutanese (175)	246	0.02
Burmese (241)	257	0.02
Cambodian (560)	652	0.05
Chinese, ex. Taiwanese (8,541)	9,633	0.75
Filipino (3,308)	4,758	0.37
Hmong (3)	8	<0.01
Indian (11,778)	12,960	1.01
Indonesian (85)	136	0.01
Japanese (947)	1,671	0.13
Korean (2,181)	2,765	0.22
Laotian (169)	221	0.02
Malaysian (27)	47	<0.01
Nepalese (171)	226	0.02
Pakistani (659)	743	0.06
Sri Lankan (92)	127	0.01
Taiwanese (432)	494	0.04
Thai (343)	457	0.04
Vietnamese (2,023)	2,355	0.18
Hawaii Native/Pacific Islander (285)	1,203	0.09
Not Hispanic (217)	896	0.07
Hispanic (68)	307	0.02
Fijian (2)	3	<0.01
Guamanian/Chamorro (87)	155	0.01
Marshallese (2)	2	<0.01
Native Hawaiian (80)	306	0.02
Samoan (14)	58	<0.01
Tongan (10)	19	<0.01
White (814,103)	835,527	65.27
Not Hispanic (785,977)	803,437	62.76
Hispanic (28,126)	32,090	2.51

*Notes: † The Census 2010 population figure is used to calculate the percentages in the Hispanic Origin and Race categories. Ancestry percentages are based on the 2006-2010 American Community Survey population (not shown); ‡ Numbers in parentheses indicate the number of people reporting a single ancestry; * Numbers in parentheses indicate the number of persons reporting this race alone, not in combination with any other race; Please refer to the User Guide for more information.*

Delaware County

Population: 174,214

Ancestry	Population	%
Afghan (9)	44	0.03
African, Sub-Saharan (838)	934	0.56
African (369)	414	0.25
Cape Verdean (0)	0	<0.01
Ethiopian (145)	145	0.09
Ghanaian (18)	31	0.02
Kenyan (0)	0	<0.01
Liberian (0)	0	<0.01
Nigerian (293)	293	0.18
Senegalese (0)	0	<0.01
Sierra Leonean (0)	0	<0.01
Somalian (13)	51	0.03
South African (0)	0	<0.01
Sudanese (0)	0	<0.01
Ugandan (0)	0	<0.01
Zimbabwean (0)	0	<0.01
Other Sub-Saharan African (0)	0	<0.01
Albanian (6)	6	<0.01
Alsatian (0)	9	0.01
American (9,422)	9,422	5.67
Arab (490)	905	0.54
Arab (72)	121	0.07
Egyptian (0)	0	<0.01
Iraqi (39)	58	0.03
Jordanian (24)	82	0.05
Lebanese (260)	465	0.28
Moroccan (0)	0	<0.01
Palestinian (7)	11	0.01
Syrian (15)	71	0.04
Other Arab (73)	97	0.06
Armenian (87)	144	0.09
Assyrian/Chaldean/Syriac (50)	50	0.03
Australian (0)	43	0.03
Austrian (75)	349	0.21
Basque (0)	0	<0.01
Belgian (58)	205	0.12
Brazilian (77)	116	0.07
British (469)	1,224	0.74
Bulgarian (0)	47	0.03
Cajun (0)	0	<0.01
Canadian (269)	461	0.28
Carpatho Rusyn (28)	28	0.02
Celtic (0)	39	0.02
Croatian (145)	514	0.31
Cypriot (37)	37	0.02
Czech (282)	978	0.59
Czechoslovakian (72)	205	0.12
Danish (59)	314	0.19
Dutch (573)	3,085	1.86
Eastern European (154)	197	0.12
English (7,225)	23,193	13.96
Estonian (9)	35	0.02
European (2,102)	2,445	1.47
Finnish (146)	292	0.18
French, ex. Basque (815)	4,571	2.75
French Canadian (292)	547	0.33
German (20,334)	56,848	34.22
German Russian (0)	0	<0.01
Greek (432)	1,038	0.62
Guyanese (0)	0	<0.01
Hungarian (755)	2,137	1.29
Icelander (0)	24	0.01
Iranian (185)	234	0.14
Irish (5,844)	27,048	16.28
Israeli (0)	0	<0.01
Italian (4,570)	13,511	8.13
Latvian (0)	63	0.04
Lithuanian (46)	353	0.21
Luxemburger (6)	6	<0.01
Macedonian (105)	150	0.09
Maltese (0)	0	<0.01
New Zealander (29)	29	0.02
Northern European (66)	66	0.04
Norwegian (341)	1,188	0.72
Pennsylvania German (33)	113	0.07
Polish (1,920)	6,886	4.15
Portuguese (28)	131	0.08
Romanian (121)	451	0.27
Russian (413)	1,131	0.68
Scandinavian (198)	282	0.17
Scotch-Irish (1,350)	3,495	2.10
Scottish (1,605)	5,292	3.19
Serbian (51)	178	0.11
Slavic (60)	158	0.10
Slovak (359)	1,042	0.63
Slovene (104)	335	0.20
Soviet Union (0)	0	<0.01
Swedish (415)	1,715	1.03
Swiss (126)	722	0.43
Turkish (25)	98	0.06
Ukrainian (125)	375	0.23
Welsh (892)	3,864	2.33
West Indian, ex. Hispanic (149)	192	0.12
Bahamian (0)	0	<0.01
Barbadian (0)	0	<0.01
Belizean (0)	0	<0.01
Bermudan (0)	0	<0.01
British West Indian (9)	9	0.01
Dutch West Indian (0)	12	0.01
Haitian (54)	75	0.05
Jamaican (70)	75	0.05
Trinidadian/Tobagonian (16)	21	0.01
U.S. Virgin Islander (0)	0	<0.01
West Indian (0)	0	<0.01
Other West Indian (0)	0	<0.01
Yugoslavian (83)	185	0.11

Hispanic Origin	Population	%
Hispanic or Latino (of any race)	3,669	2.11
Central American, ex. Mexican	326	0.19
Costa Rican	24	0.01
Guatemalan	100	0.06
Honduran	37	0.02
Nicaraguan	36	0.02
Panamanian	36	0.02
Salvadoran	92	0.05
Other Central American	1	<0.01
Cuban	128	0.07
Dominican Republic	61	0.04
Mexican	1,800	1.03
Puerto Rican	481	0.28
South American	489	0.28
Argentinean	28	0.02
Bolivian	20	0.01
Chilean	16	0.01
Colombian	195	0.11
Ecuadorian	49	0.03
Paraguayan	7	<0.01
Peruvian	72	0.04
Uruguayan	4	<0.01
Venezuelan	95	0.05
Other South American	3	<0.01
Other Hispanic or Latino	384	0.22

Race*	Population	%
African-American/Black (5,837)	7,133	4.09
Not Hispanic (5,756)	6,974	4.00
Hispanic (81)	159	0.09
American Indian/Alaska Native (252)	1,001	0.57
Not Hispanic (216)	890	0.51
Hispanic (36)	111	0.06
Alaska Athabascan *(Ala. Nat.)* (2)	2	<0.01
Aleut *(Alaska Native)* (0)	0	<0.01
Apache (5)	17	0.01
Arapaho (0)	0	<0.01
Blackfeet (4)	34	0.02
Canadian/French Am. Ind. (1)	5	<0.01
Central American Ind. (6)	6	<0.01
Cherokee (56)	292	0.17
Cheyenne (0)	1	<0.01
Chickasaw (2)	2	<0.01
Chippewa (8)	16	0.01
Choctaw (1)	5	<0.01
Colville (0)	0	<0.01
Comanche (0)	0	<0.01
Cree (0)	2	<0.01
Creek (1)	10	0.01
Crow (0)	0	<0.01
Delaware (1)	6	<0.01
Hopi (0)	0	<0.01
Houma (0)	0	<0.01
Inupiat *(Alaska Native)* (1)	1	<0.01
Iroquois (1)	31	0.02
Kiowa (1)	1	<0.01
Lumbee (5)	20	0.01
Menominee (0)	0	<0.01
Mexican American Ind. (12)	19	0.01
Navajo (8)	15	0.01
Osage (0)	0	<0.01
Ottawa (0)	2	<0.01
Paiute (0)	1	<0.01
Pima (0)	0	<0.01
Potawatomi (2)	2	<0.01
Pueblo (0)	1	<0.01
Puget Sound Salish (0)	0	<0.01
Seminole (0)	4	<0.01
Shoshone (0)	0	<0.01
Sioux (6)	29	0.02
South American Ind. (1)	6	<0.01
Spanish American Ind. (3)	4	<0.01
Tlingit-Haida *(Alaska Native)* (0)	0	<0.01
Tohono O'Odham (0)	0	<0.01
Tsimshian *(Alaska Native)* (0)	0	<0.01
Ute (0)	0	<0.01
Yakama (0)	0	<0.01
Yaqui (0)	3	<0.01
Yuman (1)	1	<0.01
Yup'ik *(Alaska Native)* (0)	0	<0.01
Asian (7,436)	8,690	4.99
Not Hispanic (7,393)	8,599	4.94
Hispanic (43)	91	0.05
Bangladeshi (50)	51	0.03
Bhutanese (0)	0	<0.01
Burmese (3)	11	0.01
Cambodian (67)	88	0.05
Chinese, ex. Taiwanese (1,548)	1,818	1.04
Filipino (357)	544	0.31
Hmong (0)	1	<0.01
Indian (3,401)	3,648	2.09
Indonesian (43)	62	0.04
Japanese (272)	455	0.26
Korean (605)	779	0.45
Laotian (59)	83	0.05
Malaysian (10)	27	0.02
Nepalese (7)	7	<0.01
Pakistani (137)	149	0.09
Sri Lankan (30)	39	0.02
Taiwanese (74)	105	0.06
Thai (45)	83	0.05
Vietnamese (514)	620	0.36
Hawaii Native/Pacific Islander (51)	152	0.09
Not Hispanic (47)	126	0.07
Hispanic (4)	26	0.01
Fijian (0)	0	<0.01
Guamanian/Chamorro (12)	33	0.02
Marshallese (0)	1	<0.01
Native Hawaiian (21)	59	0.03
Samoan (3)	9	0.01
Tongan (0)	1	<0.01
White (156,328)	159,242	91.41
Not Hispanic (153,969)	156,608	89.89
Hispanic (2,359)	2,634	1.51

*Notes: † The Census 2010 population figure is used to calculate the percentages in the Hispanic Origin and Race categories. Ancestry percentages are based on the 2006-2010 American Community Survey population (not shown); ‡ Numbers in parentheses indicate the number of people reporting a single ancestry; * Numbers in parentheses indicate the number of persons reporting this race alone, not in combination with any other race; Please refer to the User Guide for more information.*

Fairfield County

Population: 146,156

Ancestry	Population	%
Afghan (0)	0	<0.01
African, Sub-Saharan (537)	666	0.46
African (332)	435	0.30
Cape Verdean (0)	0	<0.01
Ethiopian (63)	63	0.04
Ghanaian (0)	8	0.01
Kenyan (0)	0	<0.01
Liberian (7)	15	0.01
Nigerian (0)	0	<0.01
Senegalese (0)	0	<0.01
Sierra Leonean (0)	0	<0.01
Somalian (9)	9	0.01
South African (0)	10	0.01
Sudanese (0)	0	<0.01
Ugandan (0)	0	<0.01
Zimbabwean (0)	0	<0.01
Other Sub-Saharan African (126)	126	0.09
Albanian (16)	35	0.02
Alsatian (0)	0	<0.01
American (12,393)	12,393	8.61
Arab (424)	749	0.52
Arab (50)	79	0.05
Egyptian (82)	82	0.06
Iraqi (0)	0	<0.01
Jordanian (167)	167	0.12
Lebanese (31)	243	0.17
Moroccan (5)	67	0.05
Palestinian (0)	0	<0.01
Syrian (89)	111	0.08
Other Arab (0)	0	<0.01
Armenian (0)	0	<0.01
Assyrian/Chaldean/Syriac (0)	12	0.01
Australian (0)	0	<0.01
Austrian (98)	250	0.17
Basque (0)	0	<0.01
Belgian (66)	147	0.10
Brazilian (52)	118	0.08
British (338)	706	0.49
Bulgarian (0)	0	<0.01
Cajun (14)	36	0.03
Canadian (96)	160	0.11
Carpatho Rusyn (0)	0	<0.01
Celtic (0)	0	<0.01
Croatian (79)	308	0.21
Cypriot (0)	0	<0.01
Czech (125)	459	0.32
Czechoslovakian (46)	153	0.11
Danish (51)	186	0.13
Dutch (641)	3,641	2.53
Eastern European (44)	49	0.03
English (5,465)	16,787	11.66
Estonian (0)	0	<0.01
European (1,394)	1,427	0.99
Finnish (9)	50	0.03
French, ex. Basque (687)	3,594	2.50
French Canadian (133)	328	0.23
German (17,469)	44,962	31.23
German Russian (0)	0	<0.01
Greek (221)	468	0.33
Guyanese (0)	36	0.03
Hungarian (761)	1,436	1.00
Icelander (0)	0	<0.01
Iranian (12)	24	0.02
Irish (6,142)	23,293	16.18
Israeli (0)	0	<0.01
Italian (2,857)	7,503	5.21
Latvian (0)	0	<0.01
Lithuanian (42)	118	0.08
Luxemburger (0)	4	<0.01
Macedonian (169)	262	0.18
Maltese (0)	0	<0.01
New Zealander (14)	14	0.01
Northern European (119)	135	0.09
Norwegian (253)	683	0.47
Pennsylvania German (62)	102	0.07
Polish (672)	2,996	2.08
Portuguese (0)	43	0.03
Romanian (27)	308	0.21
Russian (276)	655	0.46
Scandinavian (58)	105	0.07
Scotch-Irish (1,296)	2,544	1.77
Scottish (927)	3,376	2.35
Serbian (4)	55	0.04
Slavic (11)	69	0.05
Slovak (128)	432	0.30
Slovene (0)	58	0.04
Soviet Union (0)	0	<0.01
Swedish (412)	1,055	0.73
Swiss (157)	675	0.47
Turkish (0)	0	<0.01
Ukrainian (76)	255	0.18
Welsh (414)	2,475	1.72
West Indian, ex. Hispanic (363)	393	0.27
Bahamian (100)	100	0.07
Barbadian (0)	0	<0.01
Belizean (0)	0	<0.01
Bermudan (0)	0	<0.01
British West Indian (0)	0	<0.01
Dutch West Indian (0)	6	<0.01
Haitian (238)	238	0.17
Jamaican (25)	25	0.02
Trinidadian/Tobagonian (0)	0	<0.01
U.S. Virgin Islander (0)	0	<0.01
West Indian (0)	24	0.02
Other West Indian (0)	0	<0.01
Yugoslavian (44)	176	0.12

Hispanic Origin	Population	%
Hispanic or Latino (of any race)	2,510	1.72
Central American, ex. Mexican	208	0.14
Costa Rican	21	0.01
Guatemalan	63	0.04
Honduran	40	0.03
Nicaraguan	4	<0.01
Panamanian	45	0.03
Salvadoran	29	0.02
Other Central American	6	<0.01
Cuban	97	0.07
Dominican Republic	101	0.07
Mexican	1,184	0.81
Puerto Rican	411	0.28
South American	167	0.11
Argentinean	14	0.01
Bolivian	6	<0.01
Chilean	7	<0.01
Colombian	54	0.04
Ecuadorian	20	0.01
Paraguayan	0	<0.01
Peruvian	34	0.02
Uruguayan	6	<0.01
Venezuelan	20	0.01
Other South American	6	<0.01
Other Hispanic or Latino	342	0.23

Race*	Population	%
African-American/Black (8,702)	10,097	6.91
Not Hispanic (8,609)	9,927	6.79
Hispanic (93)	170	0.12
American Indian/Alaska Native (309)	1,253	0.86
Not Hispanic (278)	1,153	0.79
Hispanic (31)	100	0.07
Alaska Athabascan *(Ala. Nat.)* (4)	8	0.01
Aleut *(Alaska Native)* (1)	3	<0.01
Apache (9)	35	0.02
Arapaho (0)	0	<0.01
Blackfeet (6)	63	0.04
Canadian/French Am. Ind. (0)	6	<0.01
Central American Ind. (4)	4	<0.01
Cherokee (55)	361	0.25
Cheyenne (0)	3	<0.01
Chickasaw (0)	0	<0.01
Chippewa (10)	18	0.01
Choctaw (3)	10	0.01
Colville (0)	0	<0.01
Comanche (0)	3	<0.01
Cree (1)	1	<0.01
Creek (2)	19	0.01
Crow (0)	2	<0.01
Delaware (0)	6	<0.01
Hopi (0)	1	<0.01
Houma (0)	0	<0.01
Inupiat *(Alaska Native)* (0)	0	<0.01
Iroquois (7)	28	0.02
Kiowa (0)	0	<0.01
Lumbee (2)	6	<0.01
Menominee (0)	0	<0.01
Mexican American Ind. (9)	16	0.01
Navajo (1)	12	0.01
Osage (0)	0	<0.01
Ottawa (0)	0	<0.01
Paiute (1)	4	<0.01
Pima (0)	0	<0.01
Potawatomi (4)	9	0.01
Pueblo (0)	0	<0.01
Puget Sound Salish (0)	0	<0.01
Seminole (1)	6	<0.01
Shoshone (0)	0	<0.01
Sioux (8)	35	0.02
South American Ind. (1)	1	<0.01
Spanish American Ind. (0)	0	<0.01
Tlingit-Haida *(Alaska Native)* (0)	0	<0.01
Tohono O'Odham (0)	0	<0.01
Tsimshian *(Alaska Native)* (0)	0	<0.01
Ute (0)	0	<0.01
Yakama (0)	0	<0.01
Yaqui (0)	0	<0.01
Yuman (0)	0	<0.01
Yup'ik *(Alaska Native)* (3)	3	<0.01
Asian (1,645)	2,311	1.58
Not Hispanic (1,626)	2,260	1.55
Hispanic (19)	51	0.03
Bangladeshi (2)	4	<0.01
Bhutanese (0)	0	<0.01
Burmese (8)	8	0.01
Cambodian (34)	42	0.03
Chinese, ex. Taiwanese (318)	414	0.28
Filipino (165)	323	0.22
Hmong (4)	6	<0.01
Indian (391)	473	0.32
Indonesian (11)	19	0.01
Japanese (96)	197	0.13
Korean (87)	185	0.13
Laotian (87)	107	0.07
Malaysian (5)	9	0.01
Nepalese (1)	4	<0.01
Pakistani (153)	167	0.11
Sri Lankan (12)	18	0.01
Taiwanese (7)	11	0.01
Thai (28)	71	0.05
Vietnamese (141)	172	0.12
Hawaii Native/Pacific Islander (45)	137	0.09
Not Hispanic (39)	123	0.08
Hispanic (6)	14	0.01
Fijian (1)	2	<0.01
Guamanian/Chamorro (4)	20	0.01
Marshallese (0)	0	<0.01
Native Hawaiian (20)	67	0.05
Samoan (6)	8	0.01
Tongan (0)	0	<0.01
White (131,830)	134,451	91.99
Not Hispanic (130,377)	132,756	90.83
Hispanic (1,453)	1,695	1.16

*Notes: † The Census 2010 population figure is used to calculate the percentages in the Hispanic Origin and Race categories. Ancestry percentages are based on the 2006-2010 American Community Survey population (not shown); ‡ Numbers in parentheses indicate the number of people reporting a single ancestry; * Numbers in parentheses indicate the number of persons reporting this race alone, not in combination with any other race; Please refer to the User Guide for more information.*

Franklin County

Population: 1,163,414

Ancestry	Population	%
Afghan (87)	109	0.01
African, Sub-Saharan (28,783)	30,900	2.71
African (11,345)	12,661	1.11
Cape Verdean (28)	28	<0.01
Ethiopian (2,910)	3,037	0.27
Ghanaian (1,550)	1,575	0.14
Kenyan (490)	574	0.05
Liberian (379)	446	0.04
Nigerian (930)	1,120	0.10
Senegalese (104)	104	0.01
Sierra Leonean (471)	499	0.04
Somalian (9,515)	9,670	0.85
South African (124)	142	0.01
Sudanese (103)	140	0.01
Ugandan (88)	88	0.01
Zimbabwean (125)	125	0.01
Other Sub-Saharan African (621)	691	0.06
Albanian (425)	479	0.04
Alsatian (0)	67	0.01
American (57,318)	57,318	5.02
Arab (5,994)	8,707	0.76
Arab (1,280)	1,476	0.13
Egyptian (1,197)	1,478	0.13
Iraqi (279)	334	0.03
Jordanian (492)	507	0.04
Lebanese (807)	2,288	0.20
Moroccan (396)	513	0.04
Palestinian (785)	914	0.08
Syrian (238)	565	0.05
Other Arab (520)	632	0.06
Armenian (183)	328	0.03
Assyrian/Chaldean/Syriac (148)	148	0.01
Australian (60)	357	0.03
Austrian (645)	2,554	0.22
Basque (0)	0	<0.01
Belgian (447)	1,043	0.09
Brazilian (469)	601	0.05
British (2,691)	6,035	0.53
Bulgarian (110)	261	0.02
Cajun (0)	56	<0.01
Canadian (839)	2,087	0.18
Carpatho Rusyn (12)	45	<0.01
Celtic (97)	178	0.02
Croatian (521)	1,761	0.15
Cypriot (0)	14	<0.01
Czech (1,425)	5,115	0.45
Czechoslovakian (459)	1,339	0.12
Danish (479)	1,925	0.17
Dutch (3,171)	17,752	1.56
Eastern European (1,201)	1,436	0.13
English (32,516)	104,384	9.15
Estonian (39)	53	<0.01
European (11,463)	12,844	1.13
Finnish (495)	1,723	0.15
French, ex. Basque (4,674)	23,955	2.10
French Canadian (1,234)	3,189	0.28
German (99,605)	276,500	24.23
German Russian (33)	62	0.01
Greek (2,545)	6,069	0.53
Guyanese (101)	135	0.01
Hungarian (2,928)	10,887	0.95
Icelander (15)	51	<0.01
Iranian (769)	911	0.08
Irish (47,953)	164,857	14.45
Israeli (125)	220	0.02
Italian (23,468)	63,246	5.54
Latvian (206)	359	0.03
Lithuanian (466)	1,729	0.15
Luxemburger (28)	49	<0.01
Macedonian (568)	702	0.06
Maltese (0)	29	<0.01
New Zealander (62)	62	0.01
Northern European (504)	549	0.05
Norwegian (1,682)	5,861	0.51
Pennsylvania German (370)	716	0.06
Polish (8,491)	29,037	2.54
Portuguese (960)	1,993	0.17
Romanian (759)	1,923	0.17
Russian (4,085)	9,141	0.80
Scandinavian (703)	1,618	0.14
Scotch-Irish (7,654)	20,404	1.79
Scottish (7,727)	24,642	2.16
Serbian (228)	741	0.06
Slavic (275)	783	0.07
Slovak (1,643)	5,279	0.46
Slovene (771)	2,005	0.18
Soviet Union (0)	0	<0.01
Swedish (1,856)	8,493	0.74
Swiss (903)	5,061	0.44
Turkish (685)	881	0.08
Ukrainian (1,565)	3,428	0.30
Welsh (4,053)	18,461	1.62
West Indian, ex. Hispanic (3,018)	4,506	0.39
Bahamian (82)	156	0.01
Barbadian (106)	179	0.02
Belizean (28)	42	<0.01
Bermudan (0)	11	<0.01
British West Indian (157)	173	0.02
Dutch West Indian (0)	84	0.01
Haitian (1,306)	1,547	0.14
Jamaican (833)	1,602	0.14
Trinidadian/Tobagonian (213)	292	0.03
U.S. Virgin Islander (15)	27	<0.01
West Indian (278)	393	0.03
Other West Indian (0)	0	<0.01
Yugoslavian (779)	1,106	0.10

Hispanic Origin	Population	%
Hispanic or Latino (of any race)	55,718	4.79
Central American, ex. Mexican	5,203	0.45
Costa Rican	204	0.02
Guatemalan	845	0.07
Honduran	993	0.09
Nicaraguan	227	0.02
Panamanian	372	0.03
Salvadoran	2,503	0.22
Other Central American	59	0.01
Cuban	1,285	0.11
Dominican Republic	1,879	0.16
Mexican	31,905	2.74
Puerto Rican	6,443	0.55
South American	3,830	0.33
Argentinean	498	0.04
Bolivian	159	0.01
Chilean	183	0.02
Colombian	1,073	0.09
Ecuadorian	597	0.05
Paraguayan	19	<0.01
Peruvian	736	0.06
Uruguayan	56	<0.01
Venezuelan	483	0.04
Other South American	26	<0.01
Other Hispanic or Latino	5,173	0.44

Race*	Population	%
African-American/Black (247,225)	268,432	23.07
Not Hispanic (244,200)	263,683	22.66
Hispanic (3,025)	4,749	0.41
American Indian/Alaska Native (2,852)	11,292	0.97
Not Hispanic (2,280)	9,913	0.85
Hispanic (572)	1,379	0.12
Alaska Athabascan *(Ala. Nat.)* (10)	15	<0.01
Aleut *(Alaska Native)* (6)	15	<0.01
Apache (32)	137	0.01
Arapaho (3)	11	<0.01
Blackfeet (57)	670	0.06
Canadian/French Am. Ind. (4)	27	<0.01
Central American Ind. (11)	19	<0.01
Cherokee (471)	2,950	0.25
Cheyenne (6)	22	<0.01
Chickasaw (11)	29	<0.01
Chippewa (60)	158	0.01
Choctaw (36)	129	0.01
Colville (0)	1	<0.01
Comanche (5)	31	<0.01
Cree (9)	26	<0.01
Creek (14)	70	0.01
Crow (2)	15	<0.01
Delaware (19)	76	0.01
Hopi (3)	11	<0.01
Houma (4)	7	<0.01
Inupiat *(Alaska Native)* (3)	5	<0.01
Iroquois (74)	193	0.02
Kiowa (0)	1	<0.01
Lumbee (58)	90	0.01
Menominee (3)	3	<0.01
Mexican American Ind. (145)	263	0.02
Navajo (37)	89	0.01
Osage (6)	14	<0.01
Ottawa (9)	19	<0.01
Paiute (4)	4	<0.01
Pima (0)	4	<0.01
Potawatomi (10)	31	<0.01
Pueblo (12)	22	<0.01
Puget Sound Salish (0)	1	<0.01
Seminole (4)	60	0.01
Shoshone (3)	10	<0.01
Sioux (56)	235	0.02
South American Ind. (27)	68	0.01
Spanish American Ind. (16)	20	<0.01
Tlingit-Haida *(Alaska Native)* (11)	14	<0.01
Tohono O'Odham (2)	5	<0.01
Tsimshian *(Alaska Native)* (3)	5	<0.01
Ute (2)	6	<0.01
Yakama (0)	0	<0.01
Yaqui (1)	3	<0.01
Yuman (0)	3	<0.01
Yup'ik *(Alaska Native)* (3)	5	<0.01
Asian (44,996)	53,189	4.57
Not Hispanic (44,723)	52,482	4.51
Hispanic (273)	707	0.06
Bangladeshi (436)	476	0.04
Bhutanese (71)	97	0.01
Burmese (219)	233	0.02
Cambodian (1,814)	2,153	0.19
Chinese, ex. Taiwanese (8,824)	10,162	0.87
Filipino (2,353)	3,974	0.34
Hmong (46)	52	<0.01
Indian (14,789)	16,029	1.38
Indonesian (329)	441	0.04
Japanese (2,870)	4,124	0.35
Korean (3,763)	4,788	0.41
Laotian (1,454)	1,771	0.15
Malaysian (101)	140	0.01
Nepalese (202)	230	0.02
Pakistani (1,140)	1,332	0.11
Sri Lankan (248)	273	0.02
Taiwanese (805)	928	0.08
Thai (546)	830	0.07
Vietnamese (2,383)	2,914	0.25
Hawaii Native/Pacific Islander (746)	1,756	0.15
Not Hispanic (676)	1,535	0.13
Hispanic (70)	221	0.02
Fijian (5)	10	<0.01
Guamanian/Chamorro (105)	215	0.02
Marshallese (2)	3	<0.01
Native Hawaiian (113)	419	0.04
Samoan (424)	550	0.05
Tongan (0)	2	<0.01
White (805,617)	835,249	71.79
Not Hispanic (783,048)	809,006	69.54
Hispanic (22,569)	26,243	2.26

*Notes: † The Census 2010 population figure is used to calculate the percentages in the Hispanic Origin and Race categories. Ancestry percentages are based on the 2006-2010 American Community Survey population (not shown); ‡ Numbers in parentheses indicate the number of people reporting a single ancestry; * Numbers in parentheses indicate the number of persons reporting this race alone, not in combination with any other race; Please refer to the User Guide for more information.*

Greene County

Population: 161,573

Ancestry	Population	%
Afghan (0)	0	<0.01
African, Sub-Saharan (487)	550	0.34
African (325)	372	0.23
Cape Verdean (12)	28	0.02
Ethiopian (0)	0	<0.01
Ghanaian (0)	0	<0.01
Kenyan (12)	12	0.01
Liberian (0)	0	<0.01
Nigerian (111)	111	0.07
Senegalese (0)	0	<0.01
Sierra Leonean (0)	0	<0.01
Somalian (0)	0	<0.01
South African (13)	13	0.01
Sudanese (0)	0	<0.01
Ugandan (0)	0	<0.01
Zimbabwean (0)	0	<0.01
Other Sub-Saharan African (14)	14	0.01
Albanian (0)	0	<0.01
Alsatian (0)	0	<0.01
American (25,183)	25,183	15.75
Arab (342)	613	0.38
Arab (17)	79	0.05
Egyptian (24)	34	0.02
Iraqi (0)	0	<0.01
Jordanian (0)	0	<0.01
Lebanese (127)	207	0.13
Moroccan (0)	0	<0.01
Palestinian (9)	9	0.01
Syrian (0)	32	0.02
Other Arab (165)	252	0.16
Armenian (11)	45	0.03
Assyrian/Chaldean/Syriac (0)	0	<0.01
Australian (39)	57	0.04
Austrian (28)	285	0.18
Basque (0)	0	<0.01
Belgian (13)	84	0.05
Brazilian (19)	19	0.01
British (597)	1,427	0.89
Bulgarian (0)	0	<0.01
Cajun (15)	32	0.02
Canadian (117)	251	0.16
Carpatho Rusyn (0)	0	<0.01
Celtic (16)	25	0.02
Croatian (72)	112	0.07
Cypriot (0)	0	<0.01
Czech (161)	742	0.46
Czechoslovakian (45)	185	0.12
Danish (107)	333	0.21
Dutch (646)	3,086	1.93
Eastern European (128)	142	0.09
English (6,488)	17,505	10.94
Estonian (0)	12	0.01
European (1,652)	1,853	1.16
Finnish (46)	101	0.06
French, ex. Basque (844)	4,562	2.85
French Canadian (192)	494	0.31
German (16,801)	42,247	26.41
German Russian (0)	0	<0.01
Greek (269)	492	0.31
Guyanese (0)	0	<0.01
Hungarian (558)	1,680	1.05
Icelander (0)	0	<0.01
Iranian (7)	37	0.02
Irish (5,856)	20,815	13.01
Israeli (10)	50	0.03
Italian (1,941)	5,598	3.50
Latvian (15)	52	0.03
Lithuanian (59)	257	0.16
Luxemburger (0)	0	<0.01
Macedonian (0)	20	0.01
Maltese (11)	11	0.01
New Zealander (0)	0	<0.01
Northern European (119)	133	0.08
Norwegian (312)	1,046	0.65
Pennsylvania German (95)	107	0.07
Polish (1,075)	3,427	2.14
Portuguese (160)	287	0.18
Romanian (132)	260	0.16
Russian (120)	597	0.37
Scandinavian (83)	352	0.22
Scotch-Irish (1,205)	3,287	2.06
Scottish (1,592)	4,603	2.88
Serbian (0)	0	<0.01
Slavic (0)	68	0.04
Slovak (177)	465	0.29
Slovene (9)	119	0.07
Soviet Union (0)	0	<0.01
Swedish (398)	1,438	0.90
Swiss (141)	594	0.37
Turkish (43)	43	0.03
Ukrainian (73)	327	0.20
Welsh (422)	1,975	1.23
West Indian, ex. Hispanic (0)	7	<0.01
Bahamian (0)	0	<0.01
Barbadian (0)	0	<0.01
Belizean (0)	0	<0.01
Bermudan (0)	0	<0.01
British West Indian (0)	0	<0.01
Dutch West Indian (0)	0	<0.01
Haitian (0)	0	<0.01
Jamaican (0)	7	<0.01
Trinidadian/Tobagonian (0)	0	<0.01
U.S. Virgin Islander (0)	0	<0.01
West Indian (0)	0	<0.01
Other West Indian (0)	0	<0.01
Yugoslavian (76)	148	0.09

Hispanic Origin	Population	%
Hispanic or Latino (of any race)	3,439	2.13
Central American, ex. Mexican	254	0.16
Costa Rican	21	0.01
Guatemalan	86	0.05
Honduran	35	0.02
Nicaraguan	26	0.02
Panamanian	60	0.04
Salvadoran	16	0.01
Other Central American	10	0.01
Cuban	137	0.08
Dominican Republic	41	0.03
Mexican	1,577	0.98
Puerto Rican	660	0.41
South American	304	0.19
Argentinean	40	0.02
Bolivian	24	0.01
Chilean	20	0.01
Colombian	115	0.07
Ecuadorian	27	0.02
Paraguayan	2	<0.01
Peruvian	50	0.03
Uruguayan	2	<0.01
Venezuelan	19	0.01
Other South American	5	<0.01
Other Hispanic or Latino	466	0.29

Race*	Population	%
African-American/Black (11,681)	13,716	8.49
Not Hispanic (11,506)	13,419	8.31
Hispanic (175)	297	0.18
American Indian/Alaska Native (428)	1,567	0.97
Not Hispanic (367)	1,416	0.88
Hispanic (61)	151	0.09
Alaska Athabascan *(Ala. Nat.)* (0)	0	<0.01
Aleut *(Alaska Native)* (1)	1	<0.01
Apache (9)	15	0.01
Arapaho (0)	4	<0.01
Blackfeet (9)	49	0.03
Canadian/French Am. Ind. (3)	9	0.01
Central American Ind. (3)	3	<0.01
Cherokee (89)	463	0.29
Cheyenne (0)	0	<0.01
Chickasaw (5)	6	<0.01
Chippewa (24)	47	0.03
Choctaw (9)	33	0.02
Colville (0)	0	<0.01
Comanche (0)	4	<0.01
Cree (0)	2	<0.01
Creek (5)	19	0.01
Crow (1)	2	<0.01
Delaware (1)	6	<0.01
Hopi (1)	3	<0.01
Houma (0)	0	<0.01
Inupiat *(Alaska Native)* (0)	0	<0.01
Iroquois (4)	29	0.02
Kiowa (5)	7	<0.01
Lumbee (0)	1	<0.01
Menominee (0)	0	<0.01
Mexican American Ind. (25)	29	0.02
Navajo (4)	5	<0.01
Osage (2)	5	<0.01
Ottawa (0)	0	<0.01
Paiute (1)	4	<0.01
Pima (0)	0	<0.01
Potawatomi (3)	6	<0.01
Pueblo (1)	6	<0.01
Puget Sound Salish (0)	0	<0.01
Seminole (3)	21	0.01
Shoshone (1)	3	<0.01
Sioux (12)	35	0.02
South American Ind. (2)	4	<0.01
Spanish American Ind. (0)	0	<0.01
Tlingit-Haida *(Alaska Native)* (1)	1	<0.01
Tohono O'Odham (0)	0	<0.01
Tsimshian *(Alaska Native)* (1)	1	<0.01
Ute (0)	1	<0.01
Yakama (1)	1	<0.01
Yaqui (1)	1	<0.01
Yuman (0)	0	<0.01
Yup'ik *(Alaska Native)* (1)	1	<0.01
Asian (4,703)	5,967	3.69
Not Hispanic (4,663)	5,876	3.64
Hispanic (40)	91	0.06
Bangladeshi (15)	15	0.01
Bhutanese (0)	0	<0.01
Burmese (5)	5	<0.01
Cambodian (37)	54	0.03
Chinese, ex. Taiwanese (829)	970	0.60
Filipino (476)	788	0.49
Hmong (1)	1	<0.01
Indian (1,646)	1,807	1.12
Indonesian (8)	13	0.01
Japanese (243)	494	0.31
Korean (603)	798	0.49
Laotian (13)	15	0.01
Malaysian (6)	11	0.01
Nepalese (7)	14	0.01
Pakistani (152)	160	0.10
Sri Lankan (28)	35	0.02
Taiwanese (65)	72	0.04
Thai (72)	130	0.08
Vietnamese (328)	394	0.24
Hawaii Native/Pacific Islander (89)	245	0.15
Not Hispanic (81)	221	0.14
Hispanic (8)	24	0.01
Fijian (2)	6	<0.01
Guamanian/Chamorro (25)	52	0.03
Marshallese (0)	0	<0.01
Native Hawaiian (36)	95	0.06
Samoan (9)	21	0.01
Tongan (0)	0	<0.01
White (139,670)	143,414	88.76
Not Hispanic (137,440)	140,906	87.21
Hispanic (2,230)	2,508	1.55

*Notes: † The Census 2010 population figure is used to calculate the percentages in the Hispanic Origin and Race categories. Ancestry percentages are based on the 2006-2010 American Community Survey population (not shown); ‡ Numbers in parentheses indicate the number of people reporting a single ancestry; * Numbers in parentheses indicate the number of persons reporting this race alone, not in combination with any other race; Please refer to the User Guide for more information.*

Hamilton County

Population: 802,374

Ancestry	Population	%
Afghan (0)	0	<0.01
African, Sub-Saharan (20,067)	21,746	2.71
African (16,797)	18,085	2.25
Cape Verdean (0)	0	<0.01
Ethiopian (774)	902	0.11
Ghanaian (150)	150	0.02
Kenyan (50)	50	0.01
Liberian (73)	73	0.01
Nigerian (786)	786	0.10
Senegalese (289)	358	0.04
Sierra Leonean (0)	0	<0.01
Somalian (0)	0	<0.01
South African (56)	92	0.01
Sudanese (63)	63	0.01
Ugandan (0)	0	<0.01
Zimbabwean (225)	225	0.03
Other Sub-Saharan African (804)	962	0.12
Albanian (0)	0	<0.01
Alsatian (83)	209	0.03
American (52,671)	52,671	6.57
Arab (2,021)	3,515	0.44
Arab (483)	613	0.08
Egyptian (123)	149	0.02
Iraqi (29)	29	<0.01
Jordanian (225)	240	0.03
Lebanese (799)	1,736	0.22
Moroccan (65)	65	0.01
Palestinian (204)	219	0.03
Syrian (11)	292	0.04
Other Arab (82)	172	0.02
Armenian (107)	320	0.04
Assyrian/Chaldean/Syriac (0)	9	<0.01
Australian (154)	193	0.02
Austrian (355)	1,909	0.24
Basque (0)	17	<0.01
Belgian (115)	482	0.06
Brazilian (203)	253	0.03
British (1,795)	3,407	0.42
Bulgarian (81)	81	0.01
Cajun (0)	41	0.01
Canadian (581)	1,055	0.13
Carpatho Rusyn (0)	0	<0.01
Celtic (14)	77	0.01
Croatian (118)	416	0.05
Cypriot (0)	0	<0.01
Czech (591)	2,237	0.28
Czechoslovakian (154)	538	0.07
Danish (259)	1,281	0.16
Dutch (1,696)	10,817	1.35
Eastern European (584)	711	0.09
English (19,015)	61,903	7.72
Estonian (77)	104	0.01
European (7,230)	7,844	0.98
Finnish (123)	491	0.06
French, ex. Basque (2,367)	18,863	2.35
French Canadian (473)	1,508	0.19
German (110,301)	248,340	30.96
German Russian (10)	87	0.01
Greek (2,072)	3,954	0.49
Guyanese (107)	128	0.02
Hungarian (1,340)	4,734	0.59
Icelander (0)	35	<0.01
Iranian (202)	254	0.03
Irish (25,494)	117,831	14.69
Israeli (226)	320	0.04
Italian (12,262)	36,726	4.58
Latvian (80)	151	0.02
Lithuanian (355)	927	0.12
Luxemburger (26)	159	0.02
Macedonian (217)	304	0.04
Maltese (0)	38	<0.01
New Zealander (0)	0	<0.01
Northern European (265)	315	0.04
Norwegian (833)	2,814	0.35
Pennsylvania German (111)	202	0.03
Polish (3,259)	11,895	1.48
Portuguese (156)	451	0.06
Romanian (324)	1,259	0.16
Russian (2,457)	6,004	0.75
Scandinavian (321)	647	0.08
Scotch-Irish (3,677)	10,796	1.35
Scottish (3,616)	13,159	1.64
Serbian (112)	270	0.03
Slavic (136)	329	0.04
Slovak (453)	1,659	0.21
Slovene (139)	513	0.06
Soviet Union (15)	15	<0.01
Swedish (924)	3,936	0.49
Swiss (602)	2,633	0.33
Turkish (130)	155	0.02
Ukrainian (475)	1,053	0.13
Welsh (1,148)	5,952	0.74
West Indian, ex. Hispanic (701)	1,149	0.14
Bahamian (33)	40	<0.01
Barbadian (11)	41	0.01
Belizean (0)	0	<0.01
Bermudan (0)	0	<0.01
British West Indian (16)	36	<0.01
Dutch West Indian (0)	0	<0.01
Haitian (57)	61	0.01
Jamaican (477)	657	0.08
Trinidadian/Tobagonian (29)	127	0.02
U.S. Virgin Islander (0)	0	<0.01
West Indian (69)	168	0.02
Other West Indian (9)	19	<0.01
Yugoslavian (378)	598	0.07

Hispanic Origin	Population	%
Hispanic or Latino (of any race)	20,607	2.57
Central American, ex. Mexican	3,802	0.47
Costa Rican	99	0.01
Guatemalan	2,381	0.30
Honduran	509	0.06
Nicaraguan	178	0.02
Panamanian	198	0.02
Salvadoran	392	0.05
Other Central American	45	0.01
Cuban	682	0.08
Dominican Republic	324	0.04
Mexican	9,583	1.19
Puerto Rican	2,111	0.26
South American	1,785	0.22
Argentinean	206	0.03
Bolivian	48	0.01
Chilean	103	0.01
Colombian	505	0.06
Ecuadorian	142	0.02
Paraguayan	12	<0.01
Peruvian	454	0.06
Uruguayan	12	<0.01
Venezuelan	285	0.04
Other South American	18	<0.01
Other Hispanic or Latino	2,320	0.29

Race*	Population	%
African-American/Black (205,952)	216,782	27.02
Not Hispanic (204,748)	214,889	26.78
Hispanic (1,204)	1,893	0.24
American Indian/Alaska Native (1,617)	5,806	0.72
Not Hispanic (1,219)	5,029	0.63
Hispanic (398)	777	0.10
Alaska Athabascan *(Ala. Nat.)* (1)	11	<0.01
Aleut *(Alaska Native)* (7)	13	<0.01
Apache (27)	88	0.01
Arapaho (1)	8	<0.01
Blackfeet (28)	294	0.04
Canadian/French Am. Ind. (10)	18	<0.01
Central American Ind. (121)	142	0.02
Cherokee (253)	1,605	0.20
Cheyenne (0)	12	<0.01
Chickasaw (8)	18	<0.01
Chippewa (32)	72	0.01
Choctaw (21)	71	0.01
Colville (0)	3	<0.01
Comanche (8)	18	<0.01
Cree (1)	15	<0.01
Creek (19)	40	<0.01
Crow (0)	6	<0.01
Delaware (6)	11	<0.01
Hopi (2)	2	<0.01
Houma (0)	0	<0.01
Inupiat *(Alaska Native)* (1)	3	<0.01
Iroquois (16)	48	0.01
Kiowa (1)	2	<0.01
Lumbee (9)	10	<0.01
Menominee (2)	2	<0.01
Mexican American Ind. (90)	142	0.02
Navajo (32)	81	0.01
Osage (9)	15	<0.01
Ottawa (3)	10	<0.01
Paiute (1)	1	<0.01
Pima (2)	2	<0.01
Potawatomi (13)	26	<0.01
Pueblo (3)	5	<0.01
Puget Sound Salish (0)	0	<0.01
Seminole (4)	34	<0.01
Shoshone (0)	2	<0.01
Sioux (33)	125	0.02
South American Ind. (10)	39	<0.01
Spanish American Ind. (9)	10	<0.01
Tlingit-Haida *(Alaska Native)* (3)	6	<0.01
Tohono O'Odham (1)	7	<0.01
Tsimshian *(Alaska Native)* (0)	1	<0.01
Ute (0)	2	<0.01
Yakama (0)	1	<0.01
Yaqui (1)	4	<0.01
Yuman (2)	2	<0.01
Yup'ik *(Alaska Native)* (0)	0	<0.01
Asian (16,182)	20,016	2.49
Not Hispanic (16,080)	19,665	2.45
Hispanic (102)	351	0.04
Bangladeshi (43)	53	0.01
Bhutanese (120)	133	0.02
Burmese (87)	89	0.01
Cambodian (525)	644	0.08
Chinese, ex. Taiwanese (3,277)	3,987	0.50
Filipino (1,385)	2,314	0.29
Hmong (0)	3	<0.01
Indian (5,612)	6,253	0.78
Indonesian (33)	83	0.01
Japanese (841)	1,353	0.17
Korean (1,344)	1,745	0.22
Laotian (48)	67	0.01
Malaysian (13)	20	<0.01
Nepalese (118)	137	0.02
Pakistani (319)	372	0.05
Sri Lankan (127)	142	0.02
Taiwanese (322)	368	0.05
Thai (214)	305	0.04
Vietnamese (1,142)	1,323	0.16
Hawaii Native/Pacific Islander (603)	1,075	0.13
Not Hispanic (474)	868	0.11
Hispanic (129)	207	0.03
Fijian (3)	6	<0.01
Guamanian/Chamorro (231)	292	0.04
Marshallese (9)	10	<0.01
Native Hawaiian (87)	234	0.03
Samoan (35)	83	0.01
Tongan (2)	3	<0.01
White (552,330)	567,032	70.67
Not Hispanic (542,273)	555,532	69.24
Hispanic (10,057)	11,500	1.43

*Notes: † The Census 2010 population figure is used to calculate the percentages in the Hispanic Origin and Race categories. Ancestry percentages are based on the 2006-2010 American Community Survey population (not shown); ‡ Numbers in parentheses indicate the number of people reporting a single ancestry; * Numbers in parentheses indicate the number of persons reporting this race alone, not in combination with any other race; Please refer to the User Guide for more information.*

Lake County

Population: 230,041

Ancestry	Population	%
Afghan (8)	8	<0.01
African, Sub-Saharan (56)	118	0.05
African (24)	74	0.03
Cape Verdean (0)	0	<0.01
Ethiopian (0)	0	<0.01
Ghanaian (0)	0	<0.01
Kenyan (0)	12	0.01
Liberian (0)	0	<0.01
Nigerian (0)	0	<0.01
Senegalese (0)	0	<0.01
Sierra Leonean (0)	0	<0.01
Somalian (15)	15	0.01
South African (17)	17	0.01
Sudanese (0)	0	<0.01
Ugandan (0)	0	<0.01
Zimbabwean (0)	0	<0.01
Other Sub-Saharan African (0)	0	<0.01
Albanian (141)	215	0.09
Alsatian (9)	53	0.02
American (9,031)	9,031	3.94
Arab (313)	711	0.31
Arab (24)	47	0.02
Egyptian (0)	0	<0.01
Iraqi (0)	0	<0.01
Jordanian (10)	10	<0.01
Lebanese (232)	593	0.26
Moroccan (0)	0	<0.01
Palestinian (0)	0	<0.01
Syrian (22)	36	0.02
Other Arab (25)	25	0.01
Armenian (51)	76	0.03
Assyrian/Chaldean/Syriac (0)	0	<0.01
Australian (0)	35	0.02
Austrian (228)	903	0.39
Basque (0)	0	<0.01
Belgian (21)	87	0.04
Brazilian (0)	24	0.01
British (344)	659	0.29
Bulgarian (25)	25	0.01
Cajun (0)	0	<0.01
Canadian (158)	394	0.17
Carpatho Rusyn (11)	11	<0.01
Celtic (15)	15	0.01
Croatian (3,374)	6,869	2.99
Cypriot (0)	0	<0.01
Czech (686)	2,952	1.29
Czechoslovakian (309)	648	0.28
Danish (115)	547	0.24
Dutch (376)	3,156	1.38
Eastern European (245)	270	0.12
English (6,191)	26,409	11.51
Estonian (17)	17	0.01
European (1,444)	1,645	0.72
Finnish (920)	2,815	1.23
French, ex. Basque (560)	5,340	2.33
French Canadian (368)	1,386	0.60
German (15,119)	60,669	26.44
German Russian (0)	0	<0.01
Greek (541)	1,103	0.48
Guyanese (0)	9	<0.01
Hungarian (4,431)	12,343	5.38
Icelander (4)	4	<0.01
Iranian (28)	28	0.01
Irish (9,514)	43,284	18.87
Israeli (0)	0	<0.01
Italian (13,636)	37,567	16.37
Latvian (29)	46	0.02
Lithuanian (970)	2,468	1.08
Luxemburger (22)	44	0.02
Macedonian (6)	10	<0.01
Maltese (0)	0	<0.01
New Zealander (8)	8	<0.01
Northern European (42)	51	0.02
Norwegian (293)	1,050	0.46
Pennsylvania German (138)	288	0.13
Polish (5,388)	17,548	7.65
Portuguese (53)	257	0.11
Romanian (295)	805	0.35
Russian (830)	2,724	1.19
Scandinavian (85)	139	0.06
Scotch-Irish (1,694)	4,962	2.16
Scottish (1,215)	5,929	2.58
Serbian (173)	491	0.21
Slavic (256)	636	0.28
Slovak (2,193)	6,095	2.66
Slovene (5,406)	14,255	6.21
Soviet Union (0)	0	<0.01
Swedish (461)	2,475	1.08
Swiss (71)	534	0.23
Turkish (15)	53	0.02
Ukrainian (505)	1,413	0.62
Welsh (435)	2,661	1.16
West Indian, ex. Hispanic (0)	7	<0.01
Bahamian (0)	0	<0.01
Barbadian (0)	0	<0.01
Belizean (0)	7	<0.01
Bermudan (0)	0	<0.01
British West Indian (0)	0	<0.01
Dutch West Indian (0)	0	<0.01
Haitian (0)	0	<0.01
Jamaican (0)	0	<0.01
Trinidadian/Tobagonian (0)	0	<0.01
U.S. Virgin Islander (0)	0	<0.01
West Indian (0)	0	<0.01
Other West Indian (0)	0	<0.01
Yugoslavian (756)	893	0.39

Hispanic Origin	Population	%
Hispanic or Latino (of any race)	7,825	3.40
Central American, ex. Mexican	186	0.08
Costa Rican	17	0.01
Guatemalan	55	0.02
Honduran	38	0.02
Nicaraguan	10	<0.01
Panamanian	19	0.01
Salvadoran	47	0.02
Other Central American	0	<0.01
Cuban	115	0.05
Dominican Republic	31	0.01
Mexican	5,378	2.34
Puerto Rican	1,289	0.56
South American	309	0.13
Argentinean	51	0.02
Bolivian	2	<0.01
Chilean	39	0.02
Colombian	86	0.04
Ecuadorian	9	<0.01
Paraguayan	4	<0.01
Peruvian	66	0.03
Uruguayan	7	<0.01
Venezuelan	41	0.02
Other South American	4	<0.01
Other Hispanic or Latino	517	0.22

Race*	Population	%
African-American/Black (7,306)	9,106	3.96
Not Hispanic (7,156)	8,813	3.83
Hispanic (150)	293	0.13
American Indian/Alaska Native (273)	1,141	0.50
Not Hispanic (234)	1,032	0.45
Hispanic (39)	109	0.05
Alaska Athabascan *(Ala. Nat.)* (0)	0	<0.01
Aleut *(Alaska Native)* (1)	1	<0.01
Apache (4)	27	0.01
Arapaho (0)	0	<0.01
Blackfeet (7)	65	0.03
Canadian/French Am. Ind. (3)	5	<0.01
Central American Ind. (2)	3	<0.01
Cherokee (56)	329	0.14
Cheyenne (0)	1	<0.01
Chickasaw (2)	7	<0.01
Chippewa (5)	23	0.01
Choctaw (3)	13	0.01
Colville (0)	0	<0.01
Comanche (0)	1	<0.01
Cree (1)	1	<0.01
Creek (3)	9	<0.01
Crow (0)	3	<0.01
Delaware (2)	5	<0.01
Hopi (0)	1	<0.01
Houma (0)	0	<0.01
Inupiat *(Alaska Native)* (5)	10	<0.01
Iroquois (10)	35	0.02
Kiowa (0)	1	<0.01
Lumbee (3)	3	<0.01
Menominee (0)	0	<0.01
Mexican American Ind. (8)	26	0.01
Navajo (8)	22	0.01
Osage (2)	4	<0.01
Ottawa (5)	5	<0.01
Paiute (0)	0	<0.01
Pima (0)	0	<0.01
Potawatomi (2)	5	<0.01
Pueblo (3)	6	<0.01
Puget Sound Salish (0)	1	<0.01
Seminole (1)	5	<0.01
Shoshone (0)	3	<0.01
Sioux (4)	15	0.01
South American Ind. (5)	6	<0.01
Spanish American Ind. (0)	0	<0.01
Tlingit-Haida *(Alaska Native)* (0)	0	<0.01
Tohono O'Odham (6)	7	<0.01
Tsimshian *(Alaska Native)* (0)	0	<0.01
Ute (0)	0	<0.01
Yakama (0)	0	<0.01
Yaqui (0)	0	<0.01
Yuman (0)	0	<0.01
Yup'ik *(Alaska Native)* (0)	0	<0.01
Asian (2,611)	3,388	1.47
Not Hispanic (2,586)	3,317	1.44
Hispanic (25)	71	0.03
Bangladeshi (2)	2	<0.01
Bhutanese (0)	0	<0.01
Burmese (8)	13	0.01
Cambodian (5)	11	<0.01
Chinese, ex. Taiwanese (503)	620	0.27
Filipino (289)	478	0.21
Hmong (5)	5	<0.01
Indian (998)	1,124	0.49
Indonesian (6)	8	<0.01
Japanese (157)	299	0.13
Korean (245)	344	0.15
Laotian (54)	61	0.03
Malaysian (4)	7	<0.01
Nepalese (7)	9	<0.01
Pakistani (41)	42	0.02
Sri Lankan (3)	3	<0.01
Taiwanese (10)	13	0.01
Thai (28)	49	0.02
Vietnamese (156)	187	0.08
Hawaii Native/Pacific Islander (35)	156	0.07
Not Hispanic (31)	128	0.06
Hispanic (4)	28	0.01
Fijian (2)	3	<0.01
Guamanian/Chamorro (9)	26	0.01
Marshallese (1)	1	<0.01
Native Hawaiian (5)	55	0.02
Samoan (3)	17	0.01
Tongan (0)	1	<0.01
White (212,713)	215,963	93.88
Not Hispanic (208,994)	211,827	92.08
Hispanic (3,719)	4,136	1.80

*Notes: † The Census 2010 population figure is used to calculate the percentages in the Hispanic Origin and Race categories. Ancestry percentages are based on the 2006-2010 American Community Survey population (not shown); ‡ Numbers in parentheses indicate the number of people reporting a single ancestry; * Numbers in parentheses indicate the number of persons reporting this race alone, not in combination with any other race; Please refer to the User Guide for more information.*

Licking County

Population: 166,492

Ancestry	Population	%
Afghan (0)	0	<0.01
African, Sub-Saharan (317)	356	0.22
African (220)	256	0.16
Cape Verdean (0)	0	<0.01
Ethiopian (39)	42	0.03
Ghanaian (0)	0	<0.01
Kenyan (0)	0	<0.01
Liberian (58)	58	0.04
Nigerian (0)	0	<0.01
Senegalese (0)	0	<0.01
Sierra Leonean (0)	0	<0.01
Somalian (0)	0	<0.01
South African (0)	0	<0.01
Sudanese (0)	0	<0.01
Ugandan (0)	0	<0.01
Zimbabwean (0)	0	<0.01
Other Sub-Saharan African (0)	0	<0.01
Albanian (0)	0	<0.01
Alsatian (0)	0	<0.01
American (17,654)	17,654	10.78
Arab (170)	239	0.15
Arab (70)	70	0.04
Egyptian (20)	20	0.01
Iraqi (0)	0	<0.01
Jordanian (0)	0	<0.01
Lebanese (15)	49	0.03
Moroccan (0)	0	<0.01
Palestinian (0)	0	<0.01
Syrian (0)	35	0.02
Other Arab (65)	65	0.04
Armenian (24)	66	0.04
Assyrian/Chaldean/Syriac (0)	0	<0.01
Australian (8)	101	0.06
Austrian (92)	296	0.18
Basque (0)	0	<0.01
Belgian (32)	165	0.10
Brazilian (0)	0	<0.01
British (287)	711	0.43
Bulgarian (0)	21	0.01
Cajun (0)	0	<0.01
Canadian (95)	198	0.12
Carpatho Rusyn (9)	9	0.01
Celtic (19)	19	0.01
Croatian (8)	81	0.05
Cypriot (0)	0	<0.01
Czech (98)	485	0.30
Czechoslovakian (36)	153	0.09
Danish (31)	187	0.11
Dutch (616)	3,931	2.40
Eastern European (78)	78	0.05
English (9,053)	21,334	13.03
Estonian (0)	0	<0.01
European (2,067)	2,271	1.39
Finnish (0)	125	0.08
French, ex. Basque (747)	3,832	2.34
French Canadian (180)	376	0.23
German (17,842)	48,283	29.49
German Russian (0)	0	<0.01
Greek (185)	440	0.27
Guyanese (0)	0	<0.01
Hungarian (548)	1,246	0.76
Icelander (13)	26	0.02
Iranian (41)	57	0.03
Irish (7,125)	26,219	16.02
Israeli (10)	23	0.01
Italian (3,245)	8,958	5.47
Latvian (0)	0	<0.01
Lithuanian (23)	96	0.06
Luxemburger (12)	12	0.01
Macedonian (135)	214	0.13
Maltese (0)	0	<0.01
New Zealander (0)	15	0.01
Northern European (51)	51	0.03
Norwegian (144)	696	0.43
Pennsylvania German (221)	315	0.19
Polish (1,157)	3,439	2.10
Portuguese (139)	219	0.13
Romanian (52)	155	0.09
Russian (265)	886	0.54
Scandinavian (70)	145	0.09
Scotch-Irish (1,300)	3,286	2.01
Scottish (1,441)	4,018	2.45
Serbian (54)	144	0.09
Slavic (24)	151	0.09
Slovak (71)	502	0.31
Slovene (37)	265	0.16
Soviet Union (8)	8	<0.01
Swedish (232)	1,373	0.84
Swiss (83)	700	0.43
Turkish (17)	32	0.02
Ukrainian (156)	334	0.20
Welsh (794)	3,351	2.05
West Indian, ex. Hispanic (157)	279	0.17
Bahamian (0)	0	<0.01
Barbadian (0)	0	<0.01
Belizean (0)	0	<0.01
Bermudan (0)	0	<0.01
British West Indian (0)	31	0.02
Dutch West Indian (0)	40	0.02
Haitian (110)	123	0.08
Jamaican (47)	77	0.05
Trinidadian/Tobagonian (0)	0	<0.01
U.S. Virgin Islander (0)	0	<0.01
West Indian (0)	0	<0.01
Other West Indian (0)	8	<0.01
Yugoslavian (12)	60	0.04

Hispanic Origin	Population	%
Hispanic or Latino (of any race)	2,312	1.39
Central American, ex. Mexican	144	0.09
Costa Rican	12	0.01
Guatemalan	32	0.02
Honduran	18	0.01
Nicaraguan	7	<0.01
Panamanian	19	0.01
Salvadoran	56	0.03
Other Central American	0	<0.01
Cuban	72	0.04
Dominican Republic	43	0.03
Mexican	1,197	0.72
Puerto Rican	400	0.24
South American	174	0.10
Argentinean	14	0.01
Bolivian	7	<0.01
Chilean	18	0.01
Colombian	71	0.04
Ecuadorian	11	0.01
Paraguayan	4	<0.01
Peruvian	26	0.02
Uruguayan	0	<0.01
Venezuelan	23	0.01
Other South American	0	<0.01
Other Hispanic or Latino	282	0.17

Race*	Population	%
African-American/Black (5,701)	7,309	4.39
Not Hispanic (5,643)	7,167	4.30
Hispanic (58)	142	0.09
American Indian/Alaska Native (462)	1,454	0.87
Not Hispanic (436)	1,380	0.83
Hispanic (26)	74	0.04
Alaska Athabascan *(Ala. Nat.)* (0)	0	<0.01
Aleut *(Alaska Native)* (0)	0	<0.01
Apache (11)	21	0.01
Arapaho (0)	0	<0.01
Blackfeet (9)	94	0.06
Canadian/French Am. Ind. (6)	12	0.01
Central American Ind. (0)	0	<0.01
Cherokee (114)	462	0.28
Cheyenne (1)	2	<0.01
Chickasaw (2)	3	<0.01
Chippewa (19)	33	0.02
Choctaw (8)	18	0.01
Colville (0)	0	<0.01
Comanche (4)	5	<0.01
Cree (1)	8	<0.01
Creek (5)	10	0.01
Crow (0)	2	<0.01
Delaware (10)	18	0.01
Hopi (0)	0	<0.01
Houma (0)	0	<0.01
Inupiat *(Alaska Native)* (0)	3	<0.01
Iroquois (12)	22	0.01
Kiowa (0)	1	<0.01
Lumbee (6)	10	0.01
Menominee (0)	0	<0.01
Mexican American Ind. (3)	7	<0.01
Navajo (6)	9	0.01
Osage (0)	1	<0.01
Ottawa (3)	3	<0.01
Paiute (0)	0	<0.01
Pima (0)	0	<0.01
Potawatomi (2)	2	<0.01
Pueblo (1)	1	<0.01
Puget Sound Salish (0)	0	<0.01
Seminole (1)	9	0.01
Shoshone (0)	4	<0.01
Sioux (21)	49	0.03
South American Ind. (0)	2	<0.01
Spanish American Ind. (0)	0	<0.01
Tlingit-Haida *(Alaska Native)* (0)	0	<0.01
Tohono O'Odham (0)	0	<0.01
Tsimshian *(Alaska Native)* (0)	0	<0.01
Ute (0)	1	<0.01
Yakama (0)	0	<0.01
Yaqui (0)	0	<0.01
Yuman (0)	0	<0.01
Yup'ik *(Alaska Native)* (0)	1	<0.01
Asian (1,237)	1,787	1.07
Not Hispanic (1,224)	1,741	1.05
Hispanic (13)	46	0.03
Bangladeshi (2)	2	<0.01
Bhutanese (0)	0	<0.01
Burmese (0)	0	<0.01
Cambodian (26)	46	0.03
Chinese, ex. Taiwanese (291)	378	0.23
Filipino (159)	284	0.17
Hmong (0)	0	<0.01
Indian (219)	305	0.18
Indonesian (7)	17	0.01
Japanese (76)	166	0.10
Korean (148)	219	0.13
Laotian (66)	85	0.05
Malaysian (2)	4	<0.01
Nepalese (3)	5	<0.01
Pakistani (21)	26	0.02
Sri Lankan (5)	6	<0.01
Taiwanese (18)	23	0.01
Thai (36)	81	0.05
Vietnamese (80)	123	0.07
Hawaii Native/Pacific Islander (36)	124	0.07
Not Hispanic (33)	105	0.06
Hispanic (3)	19	0.01
Fijian (0)	0	<0.01
Guamanian/Chamorro (11)	24	0.01
Marshallese (0)	0	<0.01
Native Hawaiian (10)	38	0.02
Samoan (1)	4	<0.01
Tongan (4)	8	<0.01
White (155,190)	158,164	95.00
Not Hispanic (153,811)	156,500	94.00
Hispanic (1,379)	1,664	1.00

*Notes: † The Census 2010 population figure is used to calculate the percentages in the Hispanic Origin and Race categories. Ancestry percentages are based on the 2006-2010 American Community Survey population (not shown); ‡ Numbers in parentheses indicate the number of people reporting a single ancestry; * Numbers in parentheses indicate the number of persons reporting this race alone, not in combination with any other race; Please refer to the User Guide for more information.*

Lorain County

Population: 301,356

Ancestry	Population	%
Afghan (0)	0	<0.01
African, Sub-Saharan (518)	843	0.28
African (418)	705	0.24
Cape Verdean (0)	0	<0.01
Ethiopian (10)	14	<0.01
Ghanaian (0)	11	<0.01
Kenyan (35)	35	0.01
Liberian (0)	0	<0.01
Nigerian (0)	11	<0.01
Senegalese (0)	0	<0.01
Sierra Leonean (0)	0	<0.01
Somalian (0)	0	<0.01
South African (0)	12	<0.01
Sudanese (55)	55	0.02
Ugandan (0)	0	<0.01
Zimbabwean (0)	0	<0.01
Other Sub-Saharan African (0)	0	<0.01
Albanian (3)	12	<0.01
Alsatian (0)	13	<0.01
American (18,528)	18,528	6.18
Arab (683)	1,464	0.49
Arab (309)	322	0.11
Egyptian (23)	23	0.01
Iraqi (0)	0	<0.01
Jordanian (30)	30	0.01
Lebanese (161)	762	0.25
Moroccan (41)	46	0.02
Palestinian (59)	82	0.03
Syrian (60)	185	0.06
Other Arab (0)	14	<0.01
Armenian (37)	103	0.03
Assyrian/Chaldean/Syriac (0)	0	<0.01
Australian (12)	26	0.01
Austrian (240)	1,125	0.38
Basque (0)	0	<0.01
Belgian (0)	76	0.03
Brazilian (0)	28	0.01
British (626)	1,177	0.39
Bulgarian (80)	145	0.05
Cajun (20)	32	0.01
Canadian (195)	487	0.16
Carpatho Rusyn (36)	50	0.02
Celtic (20)	60	0.02
Croatian (637)	1,774	0.59
Cypriot (0)	0	<0.01
Czech (522)	2,564	0.86
Czechoslovakian (321)	1,118	0.37
Danish (206)	734	0.24
Dutch (707)	4,971	1.66
Eastern European (300)	342	0.11
English (7,830)	32,511	10.85
Estonian (5)	17	0.01
European (1,534)	1,671	0.56
Finnish (159)	486	0.16
French, ex. Basque (748)	5,830	1.95
French Canadian (377)	1,229	0.41
German (22,162)	79,530	26.54
German Russian (18)	21	0.01
Greek (966)	2,176	0.73
Guyanese (0)	0	<0.01
Hungarian (5,551)	15,474	5.16
Icelander (0)	0	<0.01
Iranian (57)	57	0.02
Irish (12,155)	50,160	16.74
Israeli (16)	37	0.01
Italian (7,768)	24,705	8.25
Latvian (9)	96	0.03
Lithuanian (191)	836	0.28
Luxemburger (0)	0	<0.01
Macedonian (174)	280	0.09
Maltese (0)	0	<0.01
New Zealander (0)	0	<0.01
Northern European (61)	89	0.03
Norwegian (327)	1,503	0.50
Pennsylvania German (194)	386	0.13
Polish (8,652)	25,192	8.41
Portuguese (25)	247	0.08
Romanian (497)	1,042	0.35
Russian (717)	2,669	0.89
Scandinavian (53)	107	0.04
Scotch-Irish (1,508)	5,015	1.67
Scottish (1,629)	6,620	2.21
Serbian (373)	881	0.29
Slavic (71)	240	0.08
Slovak (3,466)	10,981	3.67
Slovene (614)	2,540	0.85
Soviet Union (0)	0	<0.01
Swedish (460)	2,004	0.67
Swiss (123)	1,198	0.40
Turkish (40)	62	0.02
Ukrainian (885)	2,512	0.84
Welsh (462)	3,341	1.12
West Indian, ex. Hispanic (118)	218	0.07
Bahamian (0)	0	<0.01
Barbadian (0)	0	<0.01
Belizean (0)	0	<0.01
Bermudan (0)	0	<0.01
British West Indian (9)	9	<0.01
Dutch West Indian (0)	0	<0.01
Haitian (43)	43	0.01
Jamaican (53)	116	0.04
Trinidadian/Tobagonian (0)	0	<0.01
U.S. Virgin Islander (0)	0	<0.01
West Indian (13)	50	0.02
Other West Indian (0)	0	<0.01
Yugoslavian (91)	259	0.09

Hispanic Origin	Population	%
Hispanic or Latino (of any race)	25,290	8.39
Central American, ex. Mexican	343	0.11
Costa Rican	27	0.01
Guatemalan	100	0.03
Honduran	53	0.02
Nicaraguan	43	0.01
Panamanian	62	0.02
Salvadoran	57	0.02
Other Central American	1	<0.01
Cuban	236	0.08
Dominican Republic	169	0.06
Mexican	5,490	1.82
Puerto Rican	17,580	5.83
South American	399	0.13
Argentinean	46	0.02
Bolivian	11	<0.01
Chilean	57	0.02
Colombian	111	0.04
Ecuadorian	41	0.01
Paraguayan	5	<0.01
Peruvian	74	0.02
Uruguayan	4	<0.01
Venezuelan	43	0.01
Other South American	7	<0.01
Other Hispanic or Latino	1,073	0.36

Race*	Population	%
African-American/Black (25,799)	30,995	10.29
Not Hispanic (24,289)	28,443	9.44
Hispanic (1,510)	2,552	0.85
American Indian/Alaska Native (883)	3,062	1.02
Not Hispanic (635)	2,468	0.82
Hispanic (248)	594	0.20
Alaska Athabascan *(Ala. Nat.)* (0)	0	<0.01
Aleut *(Alaska Native)* (2)	2	<0.01
Apache (9)	34	0.01
Arapaho (3)	3	<0.01
Blackfeet (21)	183	0.06
Canadian/French Am. Ind. (6)	12	<0.01
Central American Ind. (7)	12	<0.01
Cherokee (159)	861	0.29
Cheyenne (0)	6	<0.01
Chickasaw (8)	19	0.01
Chippewa (26)	48	0.02
Choctaw (16)	47	0.02
Colville (0)	0	<0.01
Comanche (0)	1	<0.01
Cree (2)	3	<0.01
Creek (1)	15	<0.01
Crow (2)	10	<0.01
Delaware (5)	10	<0.01
Hopi (6)	9	<0.01
Houma (0)	1	<0.01
Inupiat *(Alaska Native)* (0)	2	<0.01
Iroquois (24)	90	0.03
Kiowa (1)	3	<0.01
Lumbee (11)	22	0.01
Menominee (0)	0	<0.01
Mexican American Ind. (25)	41	0.01
Navajo (9)	41	0.01
Osage (0)	5	<0.01
Ottawa (3)	4	<0.01
Paiute (3)	4	<0.01
Pima (0)	0	<0.01
Potawatomi (6)	8	<0.01
Pueblo (11)	22	0.01
Puget Sound Salish (0)	1	<0.01
Seminole (7)	13	<0.01
Shoshone (3)	3	<0.01
Sioux (23)	79	0.03
South American Ind. (37)	96	0.03
Spanish American Ind. (1)	1	<0.01
Tlingit-Haida *(Alaska Native)* (4)	6	<0.01
Tohono O'Odham (0)	1	<0.01
Tsimshian *(Alaska Native)* (0)	0	<0.01
Ute (0)	0	<0.01
Yakama (0)	0	<0.01
Yaqui (0)	1	<0.01
Yuman (0)	0	<0.01
Yup'ik *(Alaska Native)* (0)	1	<0.01
Asian (2,811)	3,976	1.32
Not Hispanic (2,758)	3,782	1.25
Hispanic (53)	194	0.06
Bangladeshi (5)	5	<0.01
Bhutanese (0)	0	<0.01
Burmese (1)	8	<0.01
Cambodian (35)	42	0.01
Chinese, ex. Taiwanese (532)	722	0.24
Filipino (540)	878	0.29
Hmong (6)	6	<0.01
Indian (751)	893	0.30
Indonesian (18)	30	0.01
Japanese (154)	337	0.11
Korean (305)	482	0.16
Laotian (0)	5	<0.01
Malaysian (4)	4	<0.01
Nepalese (3)	3	<0.01
Pakistani (72)	78	0.03
Sri Lankan (9)	15	<0.01
Taiwanese (29)	41	0.01
Thai (32)	56	0.02
Vietnamese (217)	267	0.09
Hawaii Native/Pacific Islander (49)	267	0.09
Not Hispanic (35)	148	0.05
Hispanic (14)	119	0.04
Fijian (0)	0	<0.01
Guamanian/Chamorro (12)	31	0.01
Marshallese (1)	1	<0.01
Native Hawaiian (9)	64	0.02
Samoan (11)	23	0.01
Tongan (0)	3	<0.01
White (255,410)	263,438	87.42
Not Hispanic (241,543)	247,632	82.17
Hispanic (13,867)	15,806	5.24

*Notes: † The Census 2010 population figure is used to calculate the percentages in the Hispanic Origin and Race categories. Ancestry percentages are based on the 2006-2010 American Community Survey population (not shown); ‡ Numbers in parentheses indicate the number of people reporting a single ancestry; * Numbers in parentheses indicate the number of persons reporting this race alone, not in combination with any other race; Please refer to the User Guide for more information.*

Lucas County

Population: 441,815

Ancestry	Population	%
Afghan (187)	187	0.04
African, Sub-Saharan (3,067)	3,959	0.89
African (2,136)	2,868	0.65
Cape Verdean (0)	46	0.01
Ethiopian (229)	229	0.05
Ghanaian (69)	69	0.02
Kenyan (19)	19	<0.01
Liberian (0)	0	<0.01
Nigerian (536)	650	0.15
Senegalese (15)	15	<0.01
Sierra Leonean (0)	0	<0.01
Somalian (0)	0	<0.01
South African (27)	27	0.01
Sudanese (0)	0	<0.01
Ugandan (0)	0	<0.01
Zimbabwean (0)	0	<0.01
Other Sub-Saharan African (36)	36	0.01
Albanian (0)	28	0.01
Alsatian (0)	6	<0.01
American (17,015)	17,015	3.83
Arab (4,410)	5,952	1.34
Arab (930)	990	0.22
Egyptian (180)	210	0.05
Iraqi (15)	28	0.01
Jordanian (249)	293	0.07
Lebanese (2,016)	3,005	0.68
Moroccan (0)	0	<0.01
Palestinian (254)	310	0.07
Syrian (342)	648	0.15
Other Arab (424)	468	0.11
Armenian (86)	357	0.08
Assyrian/Chaldean/Syriac (27)	27	0.01
Australian (9)	9	<0.01
Austrian (229)	1,015	0.23
Basque (0)	0	<0.01
Belgian (184)	746	0.17
Brazilian (7)	7	<0.01
British (521)	1,427	0.32
Bulgarian (140)	372	0.08
Cajun (0)	0	<0.01
Canadian (424)	1,003	0.23
Carpatho Rusyn (6)	15	<0.01
Celtic (57)	73	0.02
Croatian (29)	310	0.07
Cypriot (0)	11	<0.01
Czech (341)	1,689	0.38
Czechoslovakian (229)	697	0.16
Danish (151)	893	0.20
Dutch (910)	6,731	1.52
Eastern European (142)	192	0.04
English (8,967)	35,376	7.97
Estonian (30)	30	0.01
European (2,910)	3,204	0.72
Finnish (175)	566	0.13
French, ex. Basque (2,735)	23,487	5.29
French Canadian (1,034)	3,609	0.81
German (48,514)	132,503	29.84
German Russian (0)	0	<0.01
Greek (862)	1,898	0.43
Guyanese (60)	60	0.01
Hungarian (3,663)	11,178	2.52
Icelander (13)	44	0.01
Iranian (123)	160	0.04
Irish (12,847)	58,662	13.21
Israeli (28)	35	0.01
Italian (5,132)	17,011	3.83
Latvian (80)	118	0.03
Lithuanian (158)	603	0.14
Luxemburger (12)	58	0.01
Macedonian (20)	30	0.01
Maltese (23)	49	0.01
New Zealander (0)	0	<0.01
Northern European (120)	120	0.03
Norwegian (360)	1,759	0.40
Pennsylvania German (179)	372	0.08
Polish (18,012)	42,924	9.67
Portuguese (58)	182	0.04
Romanian (166)	752	0.17
Russian (673)	2,219	0.50
Scandinavian (12)	113	0.03
Scotch-Irish (1,494)	4,371	0.98
Scottish (1,722)	7,222	1.63
Serbian (151)	238	0.05
Slavic (27)	110	0.02
Slovak (494)	1,650	0.37
Slovene (109)	322	0.07
Soviet Union (0)	0	<0.01
Swedish (496)	2,805	0.63
Swiss (321)	2,347	0.53
Turkish (193)	373	0.08
Ukrainian (328)	990	0.22
Welsh (531)	2,337	0.53
West Indian, ex. Hispanic (868)	1,151	0.26
Bahamian (0)	0	<0.01
Barbadian (0)	0	<0.01
Belizean (19)	19	<0.01
Bermudan (0)	0	<0.01
British West Indian (22)	22	<0.01
Dutch West Indian (9)	18	<0.01
Haitian (64)	97	0.02
Jamaican (714)	926	0.21
Trinidadian/Tobagonian (11)	11	<0.01
U.S. Virgin Islander (0)	9	<0.01
West Indian (29)	49	0.01
Other West Indian (0)	0	<0.01
Yugoslavian (99)	183	0.04

Hispanic Origin	Population	%
Hispanic or Latino (of any race)	26,974	6.11
Central American, ex. Mexican	396	0.09
Costa Rican	20	<0.01
Guatemalan	114	0.03
Honduran	36	0.01
Nicaraguan	113	0.03
Panamanian	70	0.02
Salvadoran	38	0.01
Other Central American	5	<0.01
Cuban	388	0.09
Dominican Republic	90	0.02
Mexican	22,028	4.99
Puerto Rican	1,482	0.34
South American	460	0.10
Argentinean	55	0.01
Bolivian	11	<0.01
Chilean	40	0.01
Colombian	90	0.02
Ecuadorian	38	0.01
Paraguayan	24	0.01
Peruvian	89	0.02
Uruguayan	5	<0.01
Venezuelan	95	0.02
Other South American	13	<0.01
Other Hispanic or Latino	2,130	0.48

Race*	Population	%
African-American/Black (83,926)	92,260	20.88
Not Hispanic (82,541)	89,631	20.29
Hispanic (1,385)	2,629	0.60
American Indian/Alaska Native (1,349)	4,246	0.96
Not Hispanic (955)	3,390	0.77
Hispanic (394)	856	0.19
Alaska Athabascan *(Ala. Nat.)* (1)	2	<0.01
Aleut *(Alaska Native)* (1)	3	<0.01
Apache (23)	80	0.02
Arapaho (0)	7	<0.01
Blackfeet (38)	187	0.04
Canadian/French Am. Ind. (8)	30	0.01
Central American Ind. (0)	0	<0.01
Cherokee (201)	968	0.22
Cheyenne (1)	8	<0.01
Chickasaw (5)	9	<0.01
Chippewa (104)	200	0.05
Choctaw (19)	69	0.02
Colville (0)	0	<0.01
Comanche (1)	3	<0.01
Cree (5)	15	<0.01
Creek (2)	26	0.01
Crow (1)	10	<0.01
Delaware (9)	11	<0.01
Hopi (4)	5	<0.01
Houma (0)	0	<0.01
Inupiat *(Alaska Native)* (2)	7	<0.01
Iroquois (20)	55	0.01
Kiowa (0)	1	<0.01
Lumbee (6)	16	<0.01
Menominee (9)	11	<0.01
Mexican American Ind. (49)	133	0.03
Navajo (15)	36	0.01
Osage (0)	3	<0.01
Ottawa (11)	54	0.01
Paiute (0)	0	<0.01
Pima (0)	0	<0.01
Potawatomi (15)	36	0.01
Pueblo (7)	16	<0.01
Puget Sound Salish (0)	0	<0.01
Seminole (5)	20	<0.01
Shoshone (1)	7	<0.01
Sioux (23)	57	0.01
South American Ind. (20)	33	0.01
Spanish American Ind. (4)	8	<0.01
Tlingit-Haida *(Alaska Native)* (1)	2	<0.01
Tohono O'Odham (0)	0	<0.01
Tsimshian *(Alaska Native)* (0)	0	<0.01
Ute (0)	1	<0.01
Yakama (0)	0	<0.01
Yaqui (5)	6	<0.01
Yuman (0)	0	<0.01
Yup'ik *(Alaska Native)* (0)	0	<0.01
Asian (6,764)	8,801	1.99
Not Hispanic (6,676)	8,493	1.92
Hispanic (88)	308	0.07
Bangladeshi (23)	26	0.01
Bhutanese (0)	0	<0.01
Burmese (14)	20	<0.01
Cambodian (14)	25	0.01
Chinese, ex. Taiwanese (1,883)	2,174	0.49
Filipino (613)	999	0.23
Hmong (5)	7	<0.01
Indian (2,028)	2,289	0.52
Indonesian (19)	40	0.01
Japanese (194)	464	0.11
Korean (534)	803	0.18
Laotian (110)	162	0.04
Malaysian (23)	42	0.01
Nepalese (37)	45	0.01
Pakistani (306)	354	0.08
Sri Lankan (23)	27	0.01
Taiwanese (62)	84	0.02
Thai (121)	197	0.04
Vietnamese (428)	533	0.12
Hawaii Native/Pacific Islander (113)	382	0.09
Not Hispanic (91)	308	0.07
Hispanic (22)	74	0.02
Fijian (2)	2	<0.01
Guamanian/Chamorro (26)	48	0.01
Marshallese (0)	0	<0.01
Native Hawaiian (29)	119	0.03
Samoan (23)	54	0.01
Tongan (1)	2	<0.01
White (326,868)	339,206	76.78
Not Hispanic (313,596)	322,945	73.10
Hispanic (13,272)	16,261	3.68

*Notes: † The Census 2010 population figure is used to calculate the percentages in the Hispanic Origin and Race categories. Ancestry percentages are based on the 2006-2010 American Community Survey population (not shown); ‡ Numbers in parentheses indicate the number of people reporting a single ancestry; * Numbers in parentheses indicate the number of persons reporting this race alone, not in combination with any other race; Please refer to the User Guide for more information.*

Mahoning County

Population: 238,823

Ancestry	Population	%
Afghan (0)	0	<0.01
African, Sub-Saharan (3,001)	3,338	1.38
African (2,932)	3,188	1.32
Cape Verdean (0)	0	<0.01
Ethiopian (14)	65	0.03
Ghanaian (0)	0	<0.01
Kenyan (0)	0	<0.01
Liberian (0)	0	<0.01
Nigerian (0)	0	<0.01
Senegalese (0)	0	<0.01
Sierra Leonean (0)	0	<0.01
Somalian (0)	0	<0.01
South African (0)	30	0.01
Sudanese (0)	0	<0.01
Ugandan (0)	0	<0.01
Zimbabwean (0)	0	<0.01
Other Sub-Saharan African (55)	55	0.02
Albanian (23)	73	0.03
Alsatian (0)	0	<0.01
American (10,247)	10,247	4.24
Arab (1,473)	2,445	1.01
Arab (556)	696	0.29
Egyptian (146)	196	0.08
Iraqi (0)	0	<0.01
Jordanian (135)	135	0.06
Lebanese (464)	1,098	0.45
Moroccan (0)	0	<0.01
Palestinian (80)	97	0.04
Syrian (14)	141	0.06
Other Arab (78)	82	0.03
Armenian (8)	78	0.03
Assyrian/Chaldean/Syriac (0)	0	<0.01
Australian (0)	79	0.03
Austrian (63)	359	0.15
Basque (0)	0	<0.01
Belgian (0)	122	0.05
Brazilian (0)	0	<0.01
British (317)	544	0.22
Bulgarian (59)	119	0.05
Cajun (0)	0	<0.01
Canadian (45)	145	0.06
Carpatho Rusyn (78)	118	0.05
Celtic (52)	65	0.03
Croatian (1,430)	4,200	1.74
Cypriot (21)	21	0.01
Czech (225)	1,304	0.54
Czechoslovakian (229)	378	0.16
Danish (0)	267	0.11
Dutch (536)	3,379	1.40
Eastern European (71)	96	0.04
English (4,980)	21,540	8.90
Estonian (16)	16	0.01
European (1,104)	1,190	0.49
Finnish (70)	389	0.16
French, ex. Basque (450)	3,826	1.58
French Canadian (186)	570	0.24
German (13,004)	51,681	21.36
German Russian (0)	1	<0.01
Greek (2,071)	4,074	1.68
Guyanese (0)	0	<0.01
Hungarian (2,227)	7,298	3.02
Icelander (0)	0	<0.01
Iranian (10)	29	0.01
Irish (7,655)	40,063	16.56
Israeli (0)	0	<0.01
Italian (19,058)	44,626	18.45
Latvian (0)	0	<0.01
Lithuanian (109)	462	0.19
Luxemburger (0)	7	<0.01
Macedonian (39)	80	0.03
Maltese (0)	152	0.06
New Zealander (0)	0	<0.01
Northern European (121)	143	0.06
Norwegian (126)	475	0.20
Pennsylvania German (382)	859	0.36
Polish (3,620)	11,693	4.83
Portuguese (10)	100	0.04
Romanian (815)	1,741	0.72
Russian (524)	1,838	0.76
Scandinavian (24)	90	0.04
Scotch-Irish (1,401)	3,735	1.54
Scottish (640)	3,641	1.51
Serbian (259)	702	0.29
Slavic (108)	274	0.11
Slovak (6,975)	17,550	7.26
Slovene (150)	418	0.17
Soviet Union (0)	0	<0.01
Swedish (769)	2,630	1.09
Swiss (273)	1,061	0.44
Turkish (12)	12	<0.01
Ukrainian (1,439)	3,465	1.43
Welsh (578)	5,295	2.19
West Indian, ex. Hispanic (115)	238	0.10
Bahamian (0)	0	<0.01
Barbadian (0)	8	<0.01
Belizean (0)	0	<0.01
Bermudan (0)	0	<0.01
British West Indian (0)	0	<0.01
Dutch West Indian (0)	0	<0.01
Haitian (9)	43	0.02
Jamaican (106)	154	0.06
Trinidadian/Tobagonian (0)	0	<0.01
U.S. Virgin Islander (0)	0	<0.01
West Indian (0)	33	0.01
Other West Indian (0)	0	<0.01
Yugoslavian (103)	197	0.08

Hispanic Origin	Population	%
Hispanic or Latino (of any race)	11,136	4.66
Central American, ex. Mexican	265	0.11
Costa Rican	11	<0.01
Guatemalan	72	0.03
Honduran	78	0.03
Nicaraguan	9	<0.01
Panamanian	29	0.01
Salvadoran	65	0.03
Other Central American	1	<0.01
Cuban	172	0.07
Dominican Republic	321	0.13
Mexican	2,326	0.97
Puerto Rican	6,904	2.89
South American	294	0.12
Argentinean	24	0.01
Bolivian	4	<0.01
Chilean	16	0.01
Colombian	130	0.05
Ecuadorian	24	0.01
Paraguayan	5	<0.01
Peruvian	59	0.02
Uruguayan	6	<0.01
Venezuelan	23	0.01
Other South American	3	<0.01
Other Hispanic or Latino	854	0.36

Race*	Population	%
African-American/Black (37,433)	40,500	16.96
Not Hispanic (36,400)	38,901	16.29
Hispanic (1,033)	1,599	0.67
American Indian/Alaska Native (491)	1,808	0.76
Not Hispanic (392)	1,498	0.63
Hispanic (99)	310	0.13
Alaska Athabascan *(Ala. Nat.)* (1)	5	<0.01
Aleut *(Alaska Native)* (2)	2	<0.01
Apache (2)	29	0.01
Arapaho (0)	4	<0.01
Blackfeet (12)	116	0.05
Canadian/French Am. Ind. (1)	1	<0.01
Central American Ind. (1)	2	<0.01
Cherokee (110)	502	0.21
Cheyenne (0)	1	<0.01
Chickasaw (1)	1	<0.01
Chippewa (8)	20	0.01
Choctaw (3)	19	0.01
Colville (0)	0	<0.01
Comanche (3)	7	<0.01
Cree (0)	1	<0.01
Creek (1)	4	<0.01
Crow (0)	3	<0.01
Delaware (6)	9	<0.01
Hopi (3)	3	<0.01
Houma (0)	0	<0.01
Inupiat *(Alaska Native)* (1)	2	<0.01
Iroquois (11)	45	0.02
Kiowa (0)	0	<0.01
Lumbee (2)	2	<0.01
Menominee (0)	1	<0.01
Mexican American Ind. (16)	38	0.02
Navajo (3)	12	0.01
Osage (0)	0	<0.01
Ottawa (0)	0	<0.01
Paiute (0)	0	<0.01
Pima (0)	1	<0.01
Potawatomi (2)	4	<0.01
Pueblo (0)	0	<0.01
Puget Sound Salish (0)	0	<0.01
Seminole (2)	10	<0.01
Shoshone (1)	1	<0.01
Sioux (9)	35	0.01
South American Ind. (15)	32	0.01
Spanish American Ind. (3)	3	<0.01
Tlingit-Haida *(Alaska Native)* (1)	5	<0.01
Tohono O'Odham (0)	2	<0.01
Tsimshian *(Alaska Native)* (0)	0	<0.01
Ute (1)	1	<0.01
Yakama (0)	0	<0.01
Yaqui (2)	2	<0.01
Yuman (0)	0	<0.01
Yup'ik *(Alaska Native)* (0)	0	<0.01
Asian (1,682)	2,364	0.99
Not Hispanic (1,647)	2,264	0.95
Hispanic (35)	100	0.04
Bangladeshi (11)	14	0.01
Bhutanese (0)	0	<0.01
Burmese (0)	0	<0.01
Cambodian (11)	16	0.01
Chinese, ex. Taiwanese (278)	367	0.15
Filipino (172)	311	0.13
Hmong (5)	11	<0.01
Indian (564)	653	0.27
Indonesian (6)	8	<0.01
Japanese (69)	152	0.06
Korean (153)	255	0.11
Laotian (7)	12	0.01
Malaysian (5)	5	<0.01
Nepalese (14)	15	0.01
Pakistani (98)	113	0.05
Sri Lankan (3)	4	<0.01
Taiwanese (6)	7	<0.01
Thai (34)	59	0.02
Vietnamese (154)	197	0.08
Hawaii Native/Pacific Islander (51)	180	0.08
Not Hispanic (36)	128	0.05
Hispanic (15)	52	0.02
Fijian (0)	0	<0.01
Guamanian/Chamorro (13)	24	0.01
Marshallese (0)	0	<0.01
Native Hawaiian (14)	50	0.02
Samoan (7)	15	0.01
Tongan (0)	1	<0.01
White (190,848)	195,006	81.65
Not Hispanic (185,230)	188,538	78.94
Hispanic (5,618)	6,468	2.71

*Notes: † The Census 2010 population figure is used to calculate the percentages in the Hispanic Origin and Race categories. Ancestry percentages are based on the 2006-2010 American Community Survey population (not shown); ‡ Numbers in parentheses indicate the number of people reporting a single ancestry; * Numbers in parentheses indicate the number of persons reporting this race alone, not in combination with any other race; Please refer to the User Guide for more information.*

Medina County

Population: 172,332

Ancestry	Population	%
Afghan (0)	0	<0.01
African, Sub-Saharan (151)	198	0.12
African (130)	155	0.09
Cape Verdean (8)	16	0.01
Ethiopian (0)	0	<0.01
Ghanaian (0)	0	<0.01
Kenyan (0)	0	<0.01
Liberian (0)	0	<0.01
Nigerian (0)	0	<0.01
Senegalese (13)	13	0.01
Sierra Leonean (0)	0	<0.01
Somalian (0)	14	0.01
South African (0)	0	<0.01
Sudanese (0)	0	<0.01
Ugandan (0)	0	<0.01
Zimbabwean (0)	0	<0.01
Other Sub-Saharan African (0)	0	<0.01
Albanian (0)	14	0.01
Alsatian (0)	0	<0.01
American (12,543)	12,543	7.37
Arab (504)	1,097	0.64
Arab (29)	62	0.04
Egyptian (10)	31	0.02
Iraqi (0)	0	<0.01
Jordanian (82)	82	0.05
Lebanese (208)	647	0.38
Moroccan (0)	0	<0.01
Palestinian (152)	188	0.11
Syrian (23)	87	0.05
Other Arab (0)	0	<0.01
Armenian (61)	213	0.13
Assyrian/Chaldean/Syriac (0)	0	<0.01
Australian (0)	0	<0.01
Austrian (164)	647	0.38
Basque (0)	0	<0.01
Belgian (0)	90	0.05
Brazilian (0)	0	<0.01
British (277)	537	0.32
Bulgarian (36)	72	0.04
Cajun (0)	0	<0.01
Canadian (176)	221	0.13
Carpatho Rusyn (0)	38	0.02
Celtic (19)	28	0.02
Croatian (306)	1,083	0.64
Cypriot (0)	0	<0.01
Czech (645)	3,358	1.97
Czechoslovakian (156)	576	0.34
Danish (106)	599	0.35
Dutch (500)	2,909	1.71
Eastern European (34)	71	0.04
English (5,191)	19,753	11.61
Estonian (11)	11	0.01
European (1,146)	1,250	0.73
Finnish (74)	373	0.22
French, ex. Basque (832)	5,622	3.30
French Canadian (131)	702	0.41
German (16,103)	55,560	32.66
German Russian (0)	15	0.01
Greek (484)	1,330	0.78
Guyanese (10)	25	0.01
Hungarian (2,690)	7,887	4.64
Icelander (0)	0	<0.01
Iranian (94)	144	0.08
Irish (6,101)	31,210	18.34
Israeli (11)	11	0.01
Italian (5,370)	18,275	10.74
Latvian (64)	78	0.05
Lithuanian (135)	438	0.26
Luxemburger (0)	0	<0.01
Macedonian (296)	328	0.19
Maltese (9)	37	0.02
New Zealander (0)	0	<0.01
Northern European (47)	65	0.04
Norwegian (161)	886	0.52
Pennsylvania German (301)	465	0.27
Polish (5,177)	17,719	10.41
Portuguese (405)	609	0.36
Romanian (513)	870	0.51
Russian (391)	2,091	1.23
Scandinavian (78)	171	0.10
Scotch-Irish (1,017)	2,972	1.75
Scottish (1,122)	4,219	2.48
Serbian (369)	915	0.54
Slavic (125)	304	0.18
Slovak (2,484)	7,074	4.16
Slovene (321)	1,377	0.81
Soviet Union (0)	0	<0.01
Swedish (322)	1,366	0.80
Swiss (331)	1,698	1.00
Turkish (63)	238	0.14
Ukrainian (837)	2,197	1.29
Welsh (392)	1,943	1.14
West Indian, ex. Hispanic (0)	43	0.03
Bahamian (0)	0	<0.01
Barbadian (0)	0	<0.01
Belizean (0)	0	<0.01
Bermudan (0)	0	<0.01
British West Indian (0)	0	<0.01
Dutch West Indian (0)	10	0.01
Haitian (0)	0	<0.01
Jamaican (0)	33	0.02
Trinidadian/Tobagonian (0)	0	<0.01
U.S. Virgin Islander (0)	0	<0.01
West Indian (0)	0	<0.01
Other West Indian (0)	0	<0.01
Yugoslavian (141)	418	0.25

Hispanic Origin	Population	%
Hispanic or Latino (of any race)	2,747	1.59
Central American, ex. Mexican	193	0.11
Costa Rican	10	0.01
Guatemalan	86	0.05
Honduran	19	0.01
Nicaraguan	15	0.01
Panamanian	28	0.02
Salvadoran	34	0.02
Other Central American	1	<0.01
Cuban	67	0.04
Dominican Republic	25	0.01
Mexican	950	0.55
Puerto Rican	1,016	0.59
South American	193	0.11
Argentinean	37	0.02
Bolivian	1	<0.01
Chilean	13	0.01
Colombian	57	0.03
Ecuadorian	17	0.01
Paraguayan	3	<0.01
Peruvian	39	0.02
Uruguayan	1	<0.01
Venezuelan	25	0.01
Other South American	0	<0.01
Other Hispanic or Latino	303	0.18

Race*	Population	%
African-American/Black (2,027)	2,834	1.64
Not Hispanic (1,982)	2,714	1.57
Hispanic (45)	120	0.07
American Indian/Alaska Native (247)	944	0.55
Not Hispanic (216)	865	0.50
Hispanic (31)	79	0.05
Alaska Athabascan *(Ala. Nat.)* (0)	1	<0.01
Aleut *(Alaska Native)* (0)	0	<0.01
Apache (10)	18	0.01
Arapaho (0)	1	<0.01
Blackfeet (9)	86	0.05
Canadian/French Am. Ind. (2)	5	<0.01
Central American Ind. (1)	4	<0.01
Cherokee (64)	334	0.19
Cheyenne (0)	3	<0.01
Chickasaw (0)	5	<0.01
Chippewa (13)	23	0.01
Choctaw (1)	12	0.01
Colville (0)	0	<0.01
Comanche (4)	8	<0.01
Cree (0)	1	<0.01
Creek (0)	4	<0.01
Crow (0)	4	<0.01
Delaware (0)	4	<0.01
Hopi (0)	1	<0.01
Houma (0)	0	<0.01
Inupiat *(Alaska Native)* (0)	3	<0.01
Iroquois (2)	19	0.01
Kiowa (0)	0	<0.01
Lumbee (8)	13	0.01
Menominee (0)	0	<0.01
Mexican American Ind. (5)	8	<0.01
Navajo (2)	6	<0.01
Osage (0)	0	<0.01
Ottawa (1)	1	<0.01
Paiute (0)	0	<0.01
Pima (0)	0	<0.01
Potawatomi (1)	6	<0.01
Pueblo (0)	2	<0.01
Puget Sound Salish (0)	0	<0.01
Seminole (0)	1	<0.01
Shoshone (0)	0	<0.01
Sioux (11)	30	0.02
South American Ind. (2)	4	<0.01
Spanish American Ind. (0)	0	<0.01
Tlingit-Haida *(Alaska Native)* (0)	0	<0.01
Tohono O'Odham (0)	0	<0.01
Tsimshian *(Alaska Native)* (0)	0	<0.01
Ute (0)	1	<0.01
Yakama (0)	0	<0.01
Yaqui (0)	0	<0.01
Yuman (2)	4	<0.01
Yup'ik *(Alaska Native)* (0)	0	<0.01
Asian (1,660)	2,154	1.25
Not Hispanic (1,638)	2,108	1.22
Hispanic (22)	46	0.03
Bangladeshi (0)	0	<0.01
Bhutanese (0)	0	<0.01
Burmese (0)	0	<0.01
Cambodian (8)	13	0.01
Chinese, ex. Taiwanese (269)	311	0.18
Filipino (233)	373	0.22
Hmong (12)	12	0.01
Indian (532)	629	0.36
Indonesian (12)	14	0.01
Japanese (74)	163	0.09
Korean (193)	265	0.15
Laotian (38)	44	0.03
Malaysian (1)	1	<0.01
Nepalese (0)	0	<0.01
Pakistani (18)	27	0.02
Sri Lankan (0)	1	<0.01
Taiwanese (23)	26	0.02
Thai (10)	15	0.01
Vietnamese (149)	167	0.10
Hawaii Native/Pacific Islander (18)	60	0.03
Not Hispanic (17)	52	0.03
Hispanic (1)	8	<0.01
Fijian (0)	0	<0.01
Guamanian/Chamorro (2)	5	<0.01
Marshallese (1)	1	<0.01
Native Hawaiian (4)	21	0.01
Samoan (3)	4	<0.01
Tongan (0)	0	<0.01
White (165,642)	167,628	97.27
Not Hispanic (163,794)	165,548	96.06
Hispanic (1,848)	2,080	1.21

*Notes: † The Census 2010 population figure is used to calculate the percentages in the Hispanic Origin and Race categories. Ancestry percentages are based on the 2006-2010 American Community Survey population (not shown); ‡ Numbers in parentheses indicate the number of people reporting a single ancestry; * Numbers in parentheses indicate the number of persons reporting this race alone, not in combination with any other race; Please refer to the User Guide for more information.*

Miami County

Population: 102,506

Ancestry	Population	%
Afghan (0)	0	<0.01
African, Sub-Saharan (113)	145	0.14
African (113)	145	0.14
Cape Verdean (0)	0	<0.01
Ethiopian (0)	0	<0.01
Ghanaian (0)	0	<0.01
Kenyan (0)	0	<0.01
Liberian (0)	0	<0.01
Nigerian (0)	0	<0.01
Senegalese (0)	0	<0.01
Sierra Leonean (0)	0	<0.01
Somalian (0)	0	<0.01
South African (0)	0	<0.01
Sudanese (0)	0	<0.01
Ugandan (0)	0	<0.01
Zimbabwean (0)	0	<0.01
Other Sub-Saharan African (0)	0	<0.01
Albanian (24)	30	0.03
Alsatian (0)	7	0.01
American (9,988)	9,988	9.76
Arab (42)	137	0.13
Arab (19)	19	0.02
Egyptian (0)	0	<0.01
Iraqi (0)	0	<0.01
Jordanian (0)	0	<0.01
Lebanese (9)	104	0.10
Moroccan (0)	0	<0.01
Palestinian (0)	0	<0.01
Syrian (14)	14	0.01
Other Arab (0)	0	<0.01
Armenian (0)	0	<0.01
Assyrian/Chaldean/Syriac (0)	0	<0.01
Australian (11)	25	0.02
Austrian (73)	160	0.16
Basque (0)	0	<0.01
Belgian (0)	44	0.04
Brazilian (0)	0	<0.01
British (195)	443	0.43
Bulgarian (0)	0	<0.01
Cajun (0)	0	<0.01
Canadian (95)	137	0.13
Carpatho Rusyn (0)	0	<0.01
Celtic (0)	7	0.01
Croatian (26)	78	0.08
Cypriot (0)	0	<0.01
Czech (90)	274	0.27
Czechoslovakian (98)	151	0.15
Danish (51)	155	0.15
Dutch (445)	2,246	2.20
Eastern European (65)	65	0.06
English (4,240)	10,409	10.17
Estonian (0)	0	<0.01
European (1,110)	1,207	1.18
Finnish (23)	31	0.03
French, ex. Basque (823)	3,488	3.41
French Canadian (97)	209	0.20
German (17,407)	35,267	34.47
German Russian (0)	0	<0.01
Greek (89)	198	0.19
Guyanese (0)	0	<0.01
Hungarian (187)	603	0.59
Icelander (0)	9	0.01
Iranian (0)	0	<0.01
Irish (4,138)	13,801	13.49
Israeli (0)	0	<0.01
Italian (910)	2,915	2.85
Latvian (13)	13	0.01
Lithuanian (0)	83	0.08
Luxemburger (0)	12	0.01
Macedonian (0)	8	0.01
Maltese (10)	10	0.01
New Zealander (0)	0	<0.01
Northern European (49)	80	0.08
Norwegian (83)	348	0.34
Pennsylvania German (134)	189	0.18
Polish (671)	1,928	1.88
Portuguese (34)	86	0.08
Romanian (66)	98	0.10
Russian (72)	169	0.17
Scandinavian (31)	31	0.03
Scotch-Irish (646)	1,966	1.92
Scottish (1,088)	2,588	2.53
Serbian (0)	0	<0.01
Slavic (18)	54	0.05
Slovak (31)	115	0.11
Slovene (0)	47	0.05
Soviet Union (0)	0	<0.01
Swedish (37)	601	0.59
Swiss (62)	510	0.50
Turkish (0)	0	<0.01
Ukrainian (64)	96	0.09
Welsh (300)	1,252	1.22
West Indian, ex. Hispanic (0)	10	0.01
Bahamian (0)	10	0.01
Barbadian (0)	0	<0.01
Belizean (0)	0	<0.01
Bermudan (0)	0	<0.01
British West Indian (0)	0	<0.01
Dutch West Indian (0)	0	<0.01
Haitian (0)	0	<0.01
Jamaican (0)	0	<0.01
Trinidadian/Tobagonian (0)	0	<0.01
U.S. Virgin Islander (0)	0	<0.01
West Indian (0)	0	<0.01
Other West Indian (0)	0	<0.01
Yugoslavian (32)	104	0.10

Hispanic Origin	Population	%
Hispanic or Latino (of any race)	1,341	1.31
Central American, ex. Mexican	57	0.06
Costa Rican	1	<0.01
Guatemalan	42	0.04
Honduran	8	0.01
Nicaraguan	2	<0.01
Panamanian	3	<0.01
Salvadoran	1	<0.01
Other Central American	0	<0.01
Cuban	33	0.03
Dominican Republic	9	0.01
Mexican	855	0.83
Puerto Rican	130	0.13
South American	56	0.05
Argentinean	1	<0.01
Bolivian	2	<0.01
Chilean	5	<0.01
Colombian	23	0.02
Ecuadorian	7	0.01
Paraguayan	0	<0.01
Peruvian	10	0.01
Uruguayan	0	<0.01
Venezuelan	7	0.01
Other South American	1	<0.01
Other Hispanic or Latino	201	0.20

Race*	Population	%
African-American/Black (2,084)	3,137	3.06
Not Hispanic (2,063)	3,087	3.01
Hispanic (21)	50	0.05
American Indian/Alaska Native (189)	665	0.65
Not Hispanic (173)	635	0.62
Hispanic (16)	30	0.03
Alaska Athabascan *(Ala. Nat.)* (0)	1	<0.01
Aleut *(Alaska Native)* (0)	0	<0.01
Apache (0)	2	<0.01
Arapaho (1)	1	<0.01
Blackfeet (7)	36	0.04
Canadian/French Am. Ind. (1)	7	0.01
Central American Ind. (3)	3	<0.01
Cherokee (58)	227	0.22
Cheyenne (0)	2	<0.01
Chickasaw (0)	0	<0.01
Chippewa (4)	7	0.01
Choctaw (4)	6	0.01
Colville (0)	0	<0.01
Comanche (0)	0	<0.01
Cree (0)	0	<0.01
Creek (1)	2	<0.01
Crow (0)	0	<0.01
Delaware (2)	5	<0.01
Hopi (1)	1	<0.01
Houma (0)	0	<0.01
Inupiat *(Alaska Native)* (0)	0	<0.01
Iroquois (7)	14	0.01
Kiowa (0)	0	<0.01
Lumbee (0)	5	<0.01
Menominee (0)	1	<0.01
Mexican American Ind. (3)	5	<0.01
Navajo (0)	2	<0.01
Osage (0)	0	<0.01
Ottawa (0)	0	<0.01
Paiute (0)	0	<0.01
Pima (0)	0	<0.01
Potawatomi (0)	1	<0.01
Pueblo (0)	1	<0.01
Puget Sound Salish (0)	0	<0.01
Seminole (1)	2	<0.01
Shoshone (0)	0	<0.01
Sioux (5)	16	0.02
South American Ind. (0)	0	<0.01
Spanish American Ind. (1)	1	<0.01
Tlingit-Haida *(Alaska Native)* (0)	0	<0.01
Tohono O'Odham (0)	0	<0.01
Tsimshian *(Alaska Native)* (0)	0	<0.01
Ute (0)	0	<0.01
Yakama (0)	0	<0.01
Yaqui (0)	1	<0.01
Yuman (0)	0	<0.01
Yup'ik *(Alaska Native)* (0)	0	<0.01
Asian (1,218)	1,494	1.46
Not Hispanic (1,213)	1,479	1.44
Hispanic (5)	15	0.01
Bangladeshi (7)	7	0.01
Bhutanese (0)	0	<0.01
Burmese (0)	0	<0.01
Cambodian (3)	3	<0.01
Chinese, ex. Taiwanese (167)	186	0.18
Filipino (147)	237	0.23
Hmong (0)	0	<0.01
Indian (334)	355	0.35
Indonesian (7)	13	0.01
Japanese (324)	390	0.38
Korean (74)	108	0.11
Laotian (3)	3	<0.01
Malaysian (1)	3	<0.01
Nepalese (3)	3	<0.01
Pakistani (3)	5	<0.01
Sri Lankan (7)	8	0.01
Taiwanese (13)	13	0.01
Thai (16)	26	0.03
Vietnamese (64)	80	0.08
Hawaii Native/Pacific Islander (15)	42	0.04
Not Hispanic (13)	34	0.03
Hispanic (2)	8	0.01
Fijian (0)	0	<0.01
Guamanian/Chamorro (3)	6	0.01
Marshallese (0)	0	<0.01
Native Hawaiian (5)	18	0.02
Samoan (1)	3	<0.01
Tongan (0)	0	<0.01
White (96,722)	98,447	96.04
Not Hispanic (95,908)	97,527	95.14
Hispanic (814)	920	0.90

*Notes: † The Census 2010 population figure is used to calculate the percentages in the Hispanic Origin and Race categories. Ancestry percentages are based on the 2006-2010 American Community Survey population (not shown); ‡ Numbers in parentheses indicate the number of people reporting a single ancestry; * Numbers in parentheses indicate the number of persons reporting this race alone, not in combination with any other race; Please refer to the User Guide for more information.*

Montgomery County

Population: 535,153

Ancestry	Population	%
Afghan (12)	12	<0.01
African, Sub-Saharan (3,349)	4,246	0.79
African (2,457)	3,166	0.59
Cape Verdean (18)	94	0.02
Ethiopian (87)	103	0.02
Ghanaian (59)	70	0.01
Kenyan (10)	10	<0.01
Liberian (0)	0	<0.01
Nigerian (420)	465	0.09
Senegalese (0)	0	<0.01
Sierra Leonean (0)	0	<0.01
Somalian (0)	0	<0.01
South African (45)	76	0.01
Sudanese (0)	0	<0.01
Ugandan (0)	0	<0.01
Zimbabwean (0)	0	<0.01
Other Sub-Saharan African (253)	262	0.05
Albanian (144)	144	0.03
Alsatian (13)	26	<0.01
American (52,457)	52,457	9.74
Arab (1,900)	2,858	0.53
Arab (387)	398	0.07
Egyptian (165)	251	0.05
Iraqi (401)	401	0.07
Jordanian (150)	279	0.05
Lebanese (342)	922	0.17
Moroccan (66)	94	0.02
Palestinian (219)	239	0.04
Syrian (72)	135	0.03
Other Arab (98)	139	0.03
Armenian (51)	65	0.01
Assyrian/Chaldean/Syriac (25)	44	0.01
Australian (9)	120	0.02
Austrian (231)	853	0.16
Basque (0)	0	<0.01
Belgian (54)	385	0.07
Brazilian (82)	93	0.02
British (1,012)	2,510	0.47
Bulgarian (86)	216	0.04
Cajun (31)	76	0.01
Canadian (207)	547	0.10
Carpatho Rusyn (0)	0	<0.01
Celtic (6)	16	<0.01
Croatian (253)	497	0.09
Cypriot (0)	0	<0.01
Czech (309)	1,310	0.24
Czechoslovakian (231)	625	0.12
Danish (166)	910	0.17
Dutch (1,834)	9,203	1.71
Eastern European (361)	471	0.09
English (17,233)	47,269	8.78
Estonian (0)	39	0.01
European (5,187)	5,893	1.09
Finnish (167)	456	0.08
French, ex. Basque (2,036)	12,340	2.29
French Canadian (620)	1,589	0.30
German (55,815)	134,170	24.92
German Russian (0)	0	<0.01
Greek (1,061)	2,164	0.40
Guyanese (123)	157	0.03
Hungarian (1,753)	4,146	0.77
Icelander (9)	61	0.01
Iranian (121)	166	0.03
Irish (17,193)	68,965	12.81
Israeli (45)	45	0.01
Italian (6,606)	18,464	3.43
Latvian (29)	142	0.03
Lithuanian (278)	1,098	0.20
Luxemburger (0)	13	<0.01
Macedonian (9)	218	0.04
Maltese (0)	0	<0.01
New Zealander (0)	11	<0.01
Northern European (140)	152	0.03
Norwegian (790)	2,193	0.41
Pennsylvania German (269)	486	0.09
Polish (3,463)	10,812	2.01
Portuguese (37)	299	0.06
Romanian (275)	683	0.13
Russian (980)	2,173	0.40
Scandinavian (223)	647	0.12
Scotch-Irish (3,718)	8,851	1.64
Scottish (3,709)	10,342	1.92
Serbian (20)	175	0.03
Slavic (43)	125	0.02
Slovak (432)	1,181	0.22
Slovene (81)	308	0.06
Soviet Union (0)	0	<0.01
Swedish (1,036)	3,796	0.70
Swiss (437)	1,953	0.36
Turkish (208)	276	0.05
Ukrainian (263)	585	0.11
Welsh (1,083)	4,789	0.89
West Indian, ex. Hispanic (517)	977	0.18
Bahamian (0)	0	<0.01
Barbadian (23)	23	<0.01
Belizean (27)	27	0.01
Bermudan (18)	18	<0.01
British West Indian (16)	16	<0.01
Dutch West Indian (37)	107	0.02
Haitian (81)	105	0.02
Jamaican (173)	310	0.06
Trinidadian/Tobagonian (62)	62	0.01
U.S. Virgin Islander (0)	0	<0.01
West Indian (80)	309	0.06
Other West Indian (0)	0	<0.01
Yugoslavian (201)	340	0.06

Hispanic Origin	Population	%
Hispanic or Latino (of any race)	12,177	2.28
Central American, ex. Mexican	839	0.16
Costa Rican	164	0.03
Guatemalan	188	0.04
Honduran	142	0.03
Nicaraguan	39	0.01
Panamanian	159	0.03
Salvadoran	140	0.03
Other Central American	7	<0.01
Cuban	447	0.08
Dominican Republic	183	0.03
Mexican	6,544	1.22
Puerto Rican	1,854	0.35
South American	931	0.17
Argentinean	59	0.01
Bolivian	61	0.01
Chilean	49	0.01
Colombian	215	0.04
Ecuadorian	342	0.06
Paraguayan	7	<0.01
Peruvian	133	0.02
Uruguayan	11	<0.01
Venezuelan	50	0.01
Other South American	4	<0.01
Other Hispanic or Latino	1,379	0.26

Race*	Population	%
African-American/Black (111,870)	119,559	22.34
Not Hispanic (111,105)	118,252	22.10
Hispanic (765)	1,307	0.24
American Indian/Alaska Native (1,242)	4,628	0.86
Not Hispanic (1,096)	4,245	0.79
Hispanic (146)	383	0.07
Alaska Athabascan *(Ala. Nat.)* (1)	2	<0.01
Aleut *(Alaska Native)* (5)	9	<0.01
Apache (21)	52	0.01
Arapaho (3)	11	<0.01
Blackfeet (43)	242	0.05
Canadian/French Am. Ind. (5)	12	<0.01
Central American Ind. (2)	7	<0.01
Cherokee (288)	1,458	0.27
Cheyenne (0)	9	<0.01
Chickasaw (6)	9	<0.01
Chippewa (28)	79	0.01
Choctaw (20)	47	0.01
Colville (0)	0	<0.01
Comanche (7)	10	<0.01
Cree (2)	5	<0.01
Creek (15)	43	0.01
Crow (1)	13	<0.01
Delaware (2)	5	<0.01
Hopi (2)	3	<0.01
Houma (0)	0	<0.01
Inupiat *(Alaska Native)* (3)	5	<0.01
Iroquois (19)	61	0.01
Kiowa (0)	0	<0.01
Lumbee (6)	8	<0.01
Menominee (1)	7	<0.01
Mexican American Ind. (22)	45	0.01
Navajo (20)	45	0.01
Osage (1)	2	<0.01
Ottawa (9)	16	<0.01
Paiute (0)	0	<0.01
Pima (5)	6	<0.01
Potawatomi (6)	7	<0.01
Pueblo (1)	9	<0.01
Puget Sound Salish (2)	4	<0.01
Seminole (5)	28	0.01
Shoshone (3)	6	<0.01
Sioux (35)	114	0.02
South American Ind. (12)	30	0.01
Spanish American Ind. (3)	6	<0.01
Tlingit-Haida *(Alaska Native)* (1)	2	<0.01
Tohono O'Odham (0)	0	<0.01
Tsimshian *(Alaska Native)* (3)	3	<0.01
Ute (1)	5	<0.01
Yakama (0)	0	<0.01
Yaqui (0)	0	<0.01
Yuman (1)	1	<0.01
Yup'ik *(Alaska Native)* (5)	5	<0.01
Asian (9,273)	12,254	2.29
Not Hispanic (9,195)	11,992	2.24
Hispanic (78)	262	0.05
Bangladeshi (30)	38	0.01
Bhutanese (0)	0	<0.01
Burmese (17)	21	<0.01
Cambodian (88)	114	0.02
Chinese, ex. Taiwanese (1,404)	1,716	0.32
Filipino (1,187)	1,996	0.37
Hmong (2)	2	<0.01
Indian (3,182)	3,507	0.66
Indonesian (40)	89	0.02
Japanese (487)	972	0.18
Korean (699)	1,152	0.22
Laotian (45)	69	0.01
Malaysian (21)	23	<0.01
Nepalese (15)	16	<0.01
Pakistani (241)	278	0.05
Sri Lankan (36)	41	0.01
Taiwanese (126)	152	0.03
Thai (148)	247	0.05
Vietnamese (1,178)	1,330	0.25
Hawaii Native/Pacific Islander (177)	548	0.10
Not Hispanic (163)	496	0.09
Hispanic (14)	52	0.01
Fijian (0)	5	<0.01
Guamanian/Chamorro (62)	133	0.02
Marshallese (1)	5	<0.01
Native Hawaiian (64)	195	0.04
Samoan (23)	58	0.01
Tongan (0)	3	<0.01
White (395,272)	406,488	75.96
Not Hispanic (388,917)	399,143	74.58
Hispanic (6,355)	7,345	1.37

*Notes: † The Census 2010 population figure is used to calculate the percentages in the Hispanic Origin and Race categories. Ancestry percentages are based on the 2006-2010 American Community Survey population (not shown); ‡ Numbers in parentheses indicate the number of people reporting a single ancestry; * Numbers in parentheses indicate the number of persons reporting this race alone, not in combination with any other race; Please refer to the User Guide for more information.*

Portage County

Population: 161,419

Ancestry	Population	%
Afghan (0)	0	<0.01
African, Sub-Saharan (177)	363	0.23
African (8)	61	0.04
Cape Verdean (0)	0	<0.01
Ethiopian (0)	0	<0.01
Ghanaian (57)	93	0.06
Kenyan (0)	0	<0.01
Liberian (0)	0	<0.01
Nigerian (76)	76	0.05
Senegalese (0)	0	<0.01
Sierra Leonean (23)	23	0.01
Somalian (0)	0	<0.01
South African (13)	19	0.01
Sudanese (0)	0	<0.01
Ugandan (0)	0	<0.01
Zimbabwean (0)	0	<0.01
Other Sub-Saharan African (0)	91	0.06
Albanian (1)	1	<0.01
Alsatian (0)	0	<0.01
American (9,158)	9,158	5.73
Arab (511)	1,086	0.68
Arab (37)	174	0.11
Egyptian (59)	85	0.05
Iraqi (0)	0	<0.01
Jordanian (94)	94	0.06
Lebanese (147)	251	0.16
Moroccan (0)	63	0.04
Palestinian (18)	146	0.09
Syrian (63)	111	0.07
Other Arab (93)	162	0.10
Armenian (17)	27	0.02
Assyrian/Chaldean/Syriac (0)	0	<0.01
Australian (0)	6	<0.01
Austrian (123)	514	0.32
Basque (0)	0	<0.01
Belgian (59)	262	0.16
Brazilian (29)	29	0.02
British (300)	806	0.50
Bulgarian (0)	14	0.01
Cajun (0)	11	0.01
Canadian (36)	236	0.15
Carpatho Rusyn (16)	65	0.04
Celtic (12)	26	0.02
Croatian (196)	744	0.47
Cypriot (0)	0	<0.01
Czech (555)	2,099	1.31
Czechoslovakian (203)	502	0.31
Danish (121)	387	0.24
Dutch (569)	3,617	2.26
Eastern European (96)	128	0.08
English (4,544)	18,433	11.52
Estonian (0)	0	<0.01
European (1,073)	1,227	0.77
Finnish (66)	258	0.16
French, ex. Basque (584)	4,050	2.53
French Canadian (147)	485	0.30
German (14,445)	49,152	30.73
German Russian (0)	0	<0.01
Greek (317)	830	0.52
Guyanese (16)	16	0.01
Hungarian (1,620)	6,159	3.85
Icelander (0)	10	0.01
Iranian (10)	55	0.03
Irish (6,142)	27,355	17.10
Israeli (0)	0	<0.01
Italian (6,334)	17,622	11.02
Latvian (30)	52	0.03
Lithuanian (134)	512	0.32
Luxemburger (0)	13	0.01
Macedonian (0)	15	0.01
Maltese (0)	0	<0.01
New Zealander (0)	0	<0.01
Northern European (18)	18	0.01
Norwegian (148)	723	0.45
Pennsylvania German (352)	485	0.30
Polish (3,519)	10,497	6.56
Portuguese (15)	46	0.03
Romanian (267)	645	0.40
Russian (406)	1,485	0.93
Scandinavian (23)	90	0.06
Scotch-Irish (1,176)	3,355	2.10
Scottish (919)	4,128	2.58
Serbian (18)	222	0.14
Slavic (133)	224	0.14
Slovak (1,063)	3,826	2.39
Slovene (523)	1,139	0.71
Soviet Union (0)	0	<0.01
Swedish (572)	1,768	1.11
Swiss (164)	1,081	0.68
Turkish (33)	65	0.04
Ukrainian (319)	813	0.51
Welsh (652)	3,117	1.95
West Indian, ex. Hispanic (91)	120	0.08
Bahamian (0)	0	<0.01
Barbadian (0)	0	<0.01
Belizean (0)	0	<0.01
Bermudan (0)	0	<0.01
British West Indian (0)	0	<0.01
Dutch West Indian (0)	0	<0.01
Haitian (0)	0	<0.01
Jamaican (91)	120	0.08
Trinidadian/Tobagonian (0)	0	<0.01
U.S. Virgin Islander (0)	0	<0.01
West Indian (0)	0	<0.01
Other West Indian (0)	0	<0.01
Yugoslavian (90)	326	0.20

Hispanic Origin	Population	%
Hispanic or Latino (of any race)	2,073	1.28
Central American, ex. Mexican	152	0.09
Costa Rican	20	0.01
Guatemalan	40	0.02
Honduran	32	0.02
Nicaraguan	11	0.01
Panamanian	17	0.01
Salvadoran	31	0.02
Other Central American	1	<0.01
Cuban	96	0.06
Dominican Republic	16	0.01
Mexican	875	0.54
Puerto Rican	496	0.31
South American	144	0.09
Argentinean	19	0.01
Bolivian	3	<0.01
Chilean	12	0.01
Colombian	59	0.04
Ecuadorian	11	0.01
Paraguayan	0	<0.01
Peruvian	22	0.01
Uruguayan	3	<0.01
Venezuelan	15	0.01
Other South American	0	<0.01
Other Hispanic or Latino	294	0.18

Race*	Population	%
African-American/Black (6,687)	8,080	5.01
Not Hispanic (6,611)	7,910	4.90
Hispanic (76)	170	0.11
American Indian/Alaska Native (296)	1,136	0.70
Not Hispanic (274)	1,063	0.66
Hispanic (22)	73	0.05
Alaska Athabascan *(Ala. Nat.)* (4)	4	<0.01
Aleut *(Alaska Native)* (0)	0	<0.01
Apache (4)	14	0.01
Arapaho (0)	2	<0.01
Blackfeet (17)	70	0.04
Canadian/French Am. Ind. (2)	2	<0.01
Central American Ind. (0)	0	<0.01
Cherokee (73)	352	0.22
Cheyenne (0)	7	<0.01
Chickasaw (0)	2	<0.01
Chippewa (21)	38	0.02
Choctaw (4)	17	0.01
Colville (0)	0	<0.01
Comanche (0)	2	<0.01
Cree (2)	6	<0.01
Creek (0)	7	<0.01
Crow (0)	3	<0.01
Delaware (0)	5	<0.01
Hopi (0)	0	<0.01
Houma (0)	1	<0.01
Inupiat *(Alaska Native)* (2)	2	<0.01
Iroquois (6)	30	0.02
Kiowa (0)	0	<0.01
Lumbee (4)	6	<0.01
Menominee (1)	1	<0.01
Mexican American Ind. (3)	6	<0.01
Navajo (3)	11	0.01
Osage (0)	2	<0.01
Ottawa (0)	0	<0.01
Paiute (0)	0	<0.01
Pima (1)	1	<0.01
Potawatomi (1)	4	<0.01
Pueblo (0)	0	<0.01
Puget Sound Salish (0)	0	<0.01
Seminole (2)	5	<0.01
Shoshone (0)	2	<0.01
Sioux (15)	32	0.02
South American Ind. (3)	5	<0.01
Spanish American Ind. (0)	0	<0.01
Tlingit-Haida *(Alaska Native)* (0)	0	<0.01
Tohono O'Odham (0)	0	<0.01
Tsimshian *(Alaska Native)* (0)	0	<0.01
Ute (0)	0	<0.01
Yakama (0)	0	<0.01
Yaqui (1)	1	<0.01
Yuman (3)	3	<0.01
Yup'ik *(Alaska Native)* (1)	1	<0.01
Asian (2,305)	2,884	1.79
Not Hispanic (2,283)	2,844	1.76
Hispanic (22)	40	0.02
Bangladeshi (6)	7	<0.01
Bhutanese (16)	16	0.01
Burmese (5)	6	<0.01
Cambodian (4)	8	<0.01
Chinese, ex. Taiwanese (746)	816	0.51
Filipino (180)	307	0.19
Hmong (8)	8	<0.01
Indian (676)	765	0.47
Indonesian (11)	13	0.01
Japanese (84)	182	0.11
Korean (174)	236	0.15
Laotian (11)	21	0.01
Malaysian (14)	16	0.01
Nepalese (55)	55	0.03
Pakistani (37)	41	0.03
Sri Lankan (21)	24	0.01
Taiwanese (51)	59	0.04
Thai (24)	32	0.02
Vietnamese (109)	135	0.08
Hawaii Native/Pacific Islander (40)	136	0.08
Not Hispanic (33)	121	0.07
Hispanic (7)	15	0.01
Fijian (1)	3	<0.01
Guamanian/Chamorro (12)	38	0.02
Marshallese (0)	0	<0.01
Native Hawaiian (5)	36	0.02
Samoan (5)	11	0.01
Tongan (0)	0	<0.01
White (148,936)	151,473	93.84
Not Hispanic (147,527)	149,826	92.82
Hispanic (1,409)	1,647	1.02

*Notes: † The Census 2010 population figure is used to calculate the percentages in the Hispanic Origin and Race categories. Ancestry percentages are based on the 2006-2010 American Community Survey population (not shown); ‡ Numbers in parentheses indicate the number of people reporting a single ancestry; * Numbers in parentheses indicate the number of persons reporting this race alone, not in combination with any other race; Please refer to the User Guide for more information.*

Richland County

Population: 124,475

Ancestry	Population	%
Afghan (0)	0	<0.01
African, Sub-Saharan (751)	950	0.75
African (732)	914	0.73
Cape Verdean (0)	0	<0.01
Ethiopian (0)	0	<0.01
Ghanaian (19)	19	0.02
Kenyan (0)	0	<0.01
Liberian (0)	0	<0.01
Nigerian (0)	0	<0.01
Senegalese (0)	8	0.01
Sierra Leonean (0)	0	<0.01
Somalian (0)	0	<0.01
South African (0)	0	<0.01
Sudanese (0)	0	<0.01
Ugandan (0)	0	<0.01
Zimbabwean (0)	0	<0.01
Other Sub-Saharan African (0)	9	0.01
Albanian (29)	29	0.02
Alsatian (0)	0	<0.01
American (10,022)	10,022	7.96
Arab (212)	217	0.17
Arab (177)	177	0.14
Egyptian (0)	0	<0.01
Iraqi (4)	4	<0.01
Jordanian (18)	18	0.01
Lebanese (0)	0	<0.01
Moroccan (0)	0	<0.01
Palestinian (13)	18	0.01
Syrian (0)	0	<0.01
Other Arab (0)	0	<0.01
Armenian (11)	43	0.03
Assyrian/Chaldean/Syriac (0)	0	<0.01
Australian (20)	80	0.06
Austrian (121)	597	0.47
Basque (0)	0	<0.01
Belgian (12)	80	0.06
Brazilian (23)	64	0.05
British (154)	416	0.33
Bulgarian (6)	15	0.01
Cajun (0)	0	<0.01
Canadian (51)	79	0.06
Carpatho Rusyn (0)	43	0.03
Celtic (13)	13	0.01
Croatian (51)	169	0.13
Cypriot (3)	3	<0.01
Czech (171)	348	0.28
Czechoslovakian (106)	410	0.33
Danish (62)	224	0.18
Dutch (402)	2,808	2.23
Eastern European (18)	18	0.01
English (7,367)	15,829	12.56
Estonian (0)	0	<0.01
European (614)	634	0.50
Finnish (42)	97	0.08
French, ex. Basque (601)	2,831	2.25
French Canadian (157)	274	0.22
German (17,415)	38,612	30.65
German Russian (0)	0	<0.01
Greek (215)	419	0.33
Guyanese (0)	0	<0.01
Hungarian (415)	1,475	1.17
Icelander (0)	0	<0.01
Iranian (0)	0	<0.01
Irish (4,037)	16,794	13.33
Israeli (0)	0	<0.01
Italian (1,609)	4,341	3.45
Latvian (8)	30	0.02
Lithuanian (96)	235	0.19
Luxemburger (0)	4	<0.01
Macedonian (71)	103	0.08
Maltese (26)	26	0.02
New Zealander (0)	0	<0.01
Northern European (0)	0	<0.01
Norwegian (241)	521	0.41
Pennsylvania German (470)	794	0.63
Polish (1,004)	2,803	2.22
Portuguese (12)	12	0.01
Romanian (53)	175	0.14
Russian (55)	215	0.17
Scandinavian (0)	69	0.05
Scotch-Irish (756)	2,632	2.09
Scottish (668)	2,475	1.96
Serbian (32)	140	0.11
Slavic (22)	51	0.04
Slovak (82)	235	0.19
Slovene (12)	29	0.02
Soviet Union (0)	0	<0.01
Swedish (171)	698	0.55
Swiss (606)	1,639	1.30
Turkish (0)	9	0.01
Ukrainian (15)	110	0.09
Welsh (218)	1,327	1.05
West Indian, ex. Hispanic (146)	226	0.18
Bahamian (0)	0	<0.01
Barbadian (0)	40	0.03
Belizean (0)	0	<0.01
Bermudan (0)	0	<0.01
British West Indian (0)	0	<0.01
Dutch West Indian (0)	0	<0.01
Haitian (9)	9	0.01
Jamaican (129)	169	0.13
Trinidadian/Tobagonian (0)	0	<0.01
U.S. Virgin Islander (0)	0	<0.01
West Indian (8)	8	0.01
Other West Indian (0)	0	<0.01
Yugoslavian (319)	777	0.62

Hispanic Origin	Population	%
Hispanic or Latino (of any race)	1,732	1.39
Central American, ex. Mexican	67	0.05
Costa Rican	2	<0.01
Guatemalan	21	0.02
Honduran	4	<0.01
Nicaraguan	8	0.01
Panamanian	20	0.02
Salvadoran	7	0.01
Other Central American	5	<0.01
Cuban	46	0.04
Dominican Republic	18	0.01
Mexican	978	0.79
Puerto Rican	282	0.23
South American	93	0.07
Argentinean	21	0.02
Bolivian	0	<0.01
Chilean	2	<0.01
Colombian	35	0.03
Ecuadorian	7	0.01
Paraguayan	0	<0.01
Peruvian	22	0.02
Uruguayan	0	<0.01
Venezuelan	6	<0.01
Other South American	0	<0.01
Other Hispanic or Latino	248	0.20

Race*	Population	%
African-American/Black (11,709)	13,120	10.54
Not Hispanic (11,612)	12,948	10.40
Hispanic (97)	172	0.14
American Indian/Alaska Native (240)	956	0.77
Not Hispanic (218)	899	0.72
Hispanic (22)	57	0.05
Alaska Athabascan *(Ala. Nat.)* (0)	0	<0.01
Aleut *(Alaska Native)* (0)	1	<0.01
Apache (1)	19	0.02
Arapaho (0)	2	<0.01
Blackfeet (12)	42	0.03
Canadian/French Am. Ind. (1)	6	<0.01
Central American Ind. (0)	0	<0.01
Cherokee (53)	321	0.26
Cheyenne (0)	6	<0.01
Chickasaw (0)	2	<0.01
Chippewa (8)	11	0.01
Choctaw (1)	21	0.02
Colville (0)	0	<0.01
Comanche (0)	2	<0.01
Cree (0)	0	<0.01
Creek (0)	12	0.01
Crow (0)	2	<0.01
Delaware (0)	1	<0.01
Hopi (2)	4	<0.01
Houma (0)	0	<0.01
Inupiat *(Alaska Native)* (0)	0	<0.01
Iroquois (11)	24	0.02
Kiowa (0)	0	<0.01
Lumbee (1)	1	<0.01
Menominee (5)	5	<0.01
Mexican American Ind. (8)	8	0.01
Navajo (2)	4	<0.01
Osage (0)	0	<0.01
Ottawa (0)	2	<0.01
Paiute (0)	0	<0.01
Pima (0)	0	<0.01
Potawatomi (0)	0	<0.01
Pueblo (1)	1	<0.01
Puget Sound Salish (1)	1	<0.01
Seminole (0)	1	<0.01
Shoshone (0)	1	<0.01
Sioux (4)	22	0.02
South American Ind. (0)	0	<0.01
Spanish American Ind. (0)	0	<0.01
Tlingit-Haida *(Alaska Native)* (0)	0	<0.01
Tohono O'Odham (1)	1	<0.01
Tsimshian *(Alaska Native)* (0)	0	<0.01
Ute (0)	0	<0.01
Yakama (2)	4	<0.01
Yaqui (0)	0	<0.01
Yuman (0)	0	<0.01
Yup'ik *(Alaska Native)* (1)	1	<0.01
Asian (808)	1,097	0.88
Not Hispanic (800)	1,078	0.87
Hispanic (8)	19	0.02
Bangladeshi (0)	0	<0.01
Bhutanese (0)	0	<0.01
Burmese (3)	3	<0.01
Cambodian (2)	3	<0.01
Chinese, ex. Taiwanese (106)	141	0.11
Filipino (102)	171	0.14
Hmong (0)	0	<0.01
Indian (264)	300	0.24
Indonesian (2)	2	<0.01
Japanese (63)	109	0.09
Korean (103)	166	0.13
Laotian (5)	5	<0.01
Malaysian (0)	0	<0.01
Nepalese (2)	2	<0.01
Pakistani (13)	17	0.01
Sri Lankan (2)	3	<0.01
Taiwanese (15)	23	0.02
Thai (7)	13	0.01
Vietnamese (75)	85	0.07
Hawaii Native/Pacific Islander (37)	112	0.09
Not Hispanic (32)	101	0.08
Hispanic (5)	11	0.01
Fijian (0)	0	<0.01
Guamanian/Chamorro (15)	35	0.03
Marshallese (0)	0	<0.01
Native Hawaiian (9)	26	0.02
Samoan (6)	22	0.02
Tongan (0)	0	<0.01
White (108,870)	111,108	89.26
Not Hispanic (107,726)	109,824	88.23
Hispanic (1,144)	1,284	1.03

*Notes: † The Census 2010 population figure is used to calculate the percentages in the Hispanic Origin and Race categories. Ancestry percentages are based on the 2006-2010 American Community Survey population (not shown); ‡ Numbers in parentheses indicate the number of people reporting a single ancestry; * Numbers in parentheses indicate the number of persons reporting this race alone, not in combination with any other race; Please refer to the User Guide for more information.*

Stark County

Population: 375,586

Ancestry	Population	%
Afghan (0)	0	<0.01
African, Sub-Saharan (3,722)	4,085	1.09
African (3,501)	3,854	1.02
Cape Verdean (46)	56	0.01
Ethiopian (57)	57	0.02
Ghanaian (0)	0	<0.01
Kenyan (0)	0	<0.01
Liberian (38)	38	0.01
Nigerian (0)	0	<0.01
Senegalese (0)	0	<0.01
Sierra Leonean (0)	0	<0.01
Somalian (0)	0	<0.01
South African (61)	61	0.02
Sudanese (0)	0	<0.01
Ugandan (0)	0	<0.01
Zimbabwean (0)	0	<0.01
Other Sub-Saharan African (19)	19	0.01
Albanian (102)	247	0.07
Alsatian (0)	8	<0.01
American (28,916)	28,916	7.68
Arab (1,165)	2,453	0.65
Arab (280)	408	0.11
Egyptian (9)	50	0.01
Iraqi (15)	15	<0.01
Jordanian (0)	70	0.02
Lebanese (552)	1,314	0.35
Moroccan (0)	0	<0.01
Palestinian (0)	0	<0.01
Syrian (300)	530	0.14
Other Arab (9)	66	0.02
Armenian (9)	127	0.03
Assyrian/Chaldean/Syriac (0)	0	<0.01
Australian (30)	53	0.01
Austrian (417)	1,239	0.33
Basque (0)	0	<0.01
Belgian (16)	379	0.10
Brazilian (154)	154	0.04
British (597)	1,141	0.30
Bulgarian (11)	66	0.02
Cajun (15)	15	<0.01
Canadian (342)	558	0.15
Carpatho Rusyn (0)	13	<0.01
Celtic (32)	83	0.02
Croatian (371)	1,701	0.45
Cypriot (43)	43	0.01
Czech (452)	1,822	0.48
Czechoslovakian (254)	504	0.13
Danish (124)	784	0.21
Dutch (1,226)	9,341	2.48
Eastern European (192)	237	0.06
English (10,395)	38,102	10.12
Estonian (0)	0	<0.01
European (2,258)	2,452	0.65
Finnish (124)	349	0.09
French, ex. Basque (2,120)	14,425	3.83
French Canadian (295)	904	0.24
German (42,182)	126,329	33.57
German Russian (0)	0	<0.01
Greek (2,068)	3,895	1.03
Guyanese (0)	0	<0.01
Hungarian (2,389)	7,189	1.91
Icelander (0)	0	<0.01
Iranian (85)	85	0.02
Irish (13,451)	58,384	15.51
Israeli (0)	0	<0.01
Italian (15,557)	37,971	10.09
Latvian (14)	28	0.01
Lithuanian (201)	695	0.18
Luxemburger (13)	23	0.01
Macedonian (276)	401	0.11
Maltese (0)	0	<0.01
New Zealander (0)	0	<0.01
Northern European (80)	102	0.03
Norwegian (258)	1,065	0.28
Pennsylvania German (779)	1,397	0.37
Polish (3,271)	11,279	3.00
Portuguese (262)	573	0.15
Romanian (1,292)	3,717	0.99
Russian (599)	2,217	0.59
Scandinavian (39)	139	0.04
Scotch-Irish (2,713)	7,885	2.10
Scottish (1,947)	7,932	2.11
Serbian (420)	849	0.23
Slavic (75)	267	0.07
Slovak (1,626)	4,539	1.21
Slovene (229)	585	0.16
Soviet Union (0)	13	<0.01
Swedish (587)	3,093	0.82
Swiss (1,532)	6,978	1.85
Turkish (25)	45	0.01
Ukrainian (687)	1,515	0.40
Welsh (1,219)	6,556	1.74
West Indian, ex. Hispanic (35)	139	0.04
Bahamian (16)	16	<0.01
Barbadian (0)	0	<0.01
Belizean (0)	0	<0.01
Bermudan (0)	0	<0.01
British West Indian (0)	10	<0.01
Dutch West Indian (0)	0	<0.01
Haitian (0)	16	<0.01
Jamaican (19)	67	0.02
Trinidadian/Tobagonian (0)	0	<0.01
U.S. Virgin Islander (0)	0	<0.01
West Indian (0)	30	0.01
Other West Indian (0)	0	<0.01
Yugoslavian (229)	460	0.12

Hispanic Origin	Population	%
Hispanic or Latino (of any race)	5,965	1.59
Central American, ex. Mexican	730	0.19
Costa Rican	18	<0.01
Guatemalan	306	0.08
Honduran	212	0.06
Nicaraguan	40	0.01
Panamanian	57	0.02
Salvadoran	83	0.02
Other Central American	14	<0.01
Cuban	165	0.04
Dominican Republic	64	0.02
Mexican	2,413	0.64
Puerto Rican	924	0.25
South American	279	0.07
Argentinean	56	0.01
Bolivian	14	<0.01
Chilean	11	<0.01
Colombian	99	0.03
Ecuadorian	26	0.01
Paraguayan	4	<0.01
Peruvian	42	0.01
Uruguayan	3	<0.01
Venezuelan	24	0.01
Other South American	0	<0.01
Other Hispanic or Latino	1,390	0.37

Race*	Population	%
African-American/Black (28,537)	34,010	9.06
Not Hispanic (28,272)	33,503	8.92
Hispanic (265)	507	0.13
American Indian/Alaska Native (961)	3,253	0.87
Not Hispanic (808)	2,950	0.79
Hispanic (153)	303	0.08
Alaska Athabascan *(Ala. Nat.)* (0)	1	<0.01
Aleut *(Alaska Native)* (0)	0	<0.01
Apache (9)	44	0.01
Arapaho (0)	0	<0.01
Blackfeet (17)	208	0.06
Canadian/French Am. Ind. (2)	9	<0.01
Central American Ind. (73)	73	0.02
Cherokee (218)	934	0.25
Cheyenne (2)	14	<0.01
Chickasaw (7)	16	<0.01
Chippewa (13)	39	0.01
Choctaw (7)	43	0.01
Colville (0)	0	<0.01
Comanche (1)	13	<0.01
Cree (1)	6	<0.01
Creek (11)	18	<0.01
Crow (1)	13	<0.01
Delaware (84)	147	0.04
Hopi (1)	5	<0.01
Houma (2)	2	<0.01
Inupiat *(Alaska Native)* (6)	8	<0.01
Iroquois (30)	104	0.03
Kiowa (2)	8	<0.01
Lumbee (19)	23	0.01
Menominee (3)	4	<0.01
Mexican American Ind. (33)	43	0.01
Navajo (8)	31	0.01
Osage (0)	4	<0.01
Ottawa (4)	15	<0.01
Paiute (0)	0	<0.01
Pima (1)	2	<0.01
Potawatomi (6)	17	<0.01
Pueblo (2)	4	<0.01
Puget Sound Salish (0)	0	<0.01
Seminole (2)	20	0.01
Shoshone (0)	0	<0.01
Sioux (15)	62	0.02
South American Ind. (4)	11	<0.01
Spanish American Ind. (2)	4	<0.01
Tlingit-Haida *(Alaska Native)* (1)	1	<0.01
Tohono O'Odham (0)	0	<0.01
Tsimshian *(Alaska Native)* (0)	0	<0.01
Ute (0)	0	<0.01
Yakama (0)	0	<0.01
Yaqui (1)	1	<0.01
Yuman (1)	9	<0.01
Yup'ik *(Alaska Native)* (0)	0	<0.01
Asian (2,764)	3,754	1.00
Not Hispanic (2,736)	3,683	0.98
Hispanic (28)	71	0.02
Bangladeshi (8)	8	<0.01
Bhutanese (0)	0	<0.01
Burmese (2)	3	<0.01
Cambodian (1)	5	<0.01
Chinese, ex. Taiwanese (617)	727	0.19
Filipino (364)	671	0.18
Hmong (10)	10	<0.01
Indian (855)	969	0.26
Indonesian (5)	7	<0.01
Japanese (139)	294	0.08
Korean (272)	412	0.11
Laotian (28)	35	0.01
Malaysian (5)	11	<0.01
Nepalese (2)	2	<0.01
Pakistani (96)	106	0.03
Sri Lankan (13)	13	<0.01
Taiwanese (17)	22	0.01
Thai (37)	83	0.02
Vietnamese (194)	245	0.07
Hawaii Native/Pacific Islander (85)	244	0.06
Not Hispanic (63)	197	0.05
Hispanic (22)	47	0.01
Fijian (0)	1	<0.01
Guamanian/Chamorro (32)	58	0.02
Marshallese (0)	0	<0.01
Native Hawaiian (21)	86	0.02
Samoan (3)	14	<0.01
Tongan (0)	2	<0.01
White (333,191)	340,942	90.78
Not Hispanic (329,497)	336,694	89.64
Hispanic (3,694)	4,248	1.13

*Notes: † The Census 2010 population figure is used to calculate the percentages in the Hispanic Origin and Race categories. Ancestry percentages are based on the 2006-2010 American Community Survey population (not shown); ‡ Numbers in parentheses indicate the number of people reporting a single ancestry; * Numbers in parentheses indicate the number of persons reporting this race alone, not in combination with any other race; Please refer to the User Guide for more information.*

Summit County

Population: 541,781

Ancestry	Population	%
Afghan (13)	13	<0.01
African, Sub-Saharan (2,025)	2,791	0.51
African (1,804)	2,372	0.44
Cape Verdean (0)	33	0.01
Ethiopian (14)	42	0.01
Ghanaian (0)	0	<0.01
Kenyan (30)	46	0.01
Liberian (29)	29	0.01
Nigerian (12)	24	<0.01
Senegalese (0)	0	<0.01
Sierra Leonean (0)	0	<0.01
Somalian (23)	23	<0.01
South African (58)	103	0.02
Sudanese (0)	0	<0.01
Ugandan (0)	0	<0.01
Zimbabwean (12)	12	<0.01
Other Sub-Saharan African (43)	107	0.02
Albanian (272)	390	0.07
Alsatian (17)	74	0.01
American (24,520)	24,520	4.51
Arab (2,893)	4,596	0.85
Arab (318)	447	0.08
Egyptian (199)	244	0.04
Iraqi (58)	65	0.01
Jordanian (11)	57	0.01
Lebanese (1,229)	2,545	0.47
Moroccan (0)	13	<0.01
Palestinian (447)	447	0.08
Syrian (147)	285	0.05
Other Arab (484)	493	0.09
Armenian (181)	517	0.10
Assyrian/Chaldean/Syriac (0)	0	<0.01
Australian (0)	103	0.02
Austrian (349)	1,705	0.31
Basque (0)	0	<0.01
Belgian (173)	320	0.06
Brazilian (16)	68	0.01
British (838)	1,803	0.33
Bulgarian (54)	107	0.02
Cajun (9)	61	0.01
Canadian (509)	987	0.18
Carpatho Rusyn (56)	111	0.02
Celtic (6)	24	<0.01
Croatian (1,360)	3,314	0.61
Cypriot (0)	0	<0.01
Czech (1,502)	5,935	1.09
Czechoslovakian (809)	1,368	0.25
Danish (212)	1,047	0.19
Dutch (1,318)	9,167	1.69
Eastern European (564)	677	0.12
English (15,823)	57,459	10.58
Estonian (22)	29	0.01
European (4,981)	5,585	1.03
Finnish (318)	956	0.18
French, ex. Basque (1,649)	12,241	2.25
French Canadian (524)	1,401	0.26
German (38,453)	135,453	24.94
German Russian (0)	78	0.01
Greek (1,777)	3,595	0.66
Guyanese (0)	0	<0.01
Hungarian (5,700)	19,645	3.62
Icelander (29)	51	0.01
Iranian (176)	201	0.04
Irish (19,719)	83,267	15.33
Israeli (19)	50	0.01
Italian (21,644)	55,039	10.13
Latvian (68)	115	0.02
Lithuanian (626)	1,553	0.29
Luxemburger (21)	31	0.01
Macedonian (90)	288	0.05
Maltese (0)	0	<0.01
New Zealander (0)	32	0.01
Northern European (413)	500	0.09
Norwegian (606)	1,840	0.34
Pennsylvania German (661)	1,257	0.23
Polish (8,553)	27,447	5.05
Portuguese (295)	546	0.10
Romanian (1,106)	2,246	0.41
Russian (1,746)	4,648	0.86
Scandinavian (93)	310	0.06
Scotch-Irish (3,976)	10,172	1.87
Scottish (2,691)	11,673	2.15
Serbian (1,641)	3,098	0.57
Slavic (260)	653	0.12
Slovak (3,751)	10,163	1.87
Slovene (1,358)	3,802	0.70
Soviet Union (0)	0	<0.01
Swedish (916)	4,472	0.82
Swiss (682)	3,119	0.57
Turkish (205)	314	0.06
Ukrainian (920)	2,431	0.45
Welsh (1,358)	7,018	1.29
West Indian, ex. Hispanic (267)	469	0.09
Bahamian (0)	0	<0.01
Barbadian (5)	5	<0.01
Belizean (0)	0	<0.01
Bermudan (9)	9	<0.01
British West Indian (39)	39	0.01
Dutch West Indian (0)	0	<0.01
Haitian (9)	36	0.01
Jamaican (133)	287	0.05
Trinidadian/Tobagonian (0)	9	<0.01
U.S. Virgin Islander (0)	0	<0.01
West Indian (72)	84	0.02
Other West Indian (0)	0	<0.01
Yugoslavian (1,235)	1,878	0.35

Hispanic Origin	Population	%
Hispanic or Latino (of any race)	8,660	1.60
Central American, ex. Mexican	658	0.12
Costa Rican	42	0.01
Guatemalan	205	0.04
Honduran	141	0.03
Nicaraguan	59	0.01
Panamanian	76	0.01
Salvadoran	130	0.02
Other Central American	5	<0.01
Cuban	306	0.06
Dominican Republic	87	0.02
Mexican	3,704	0.68
Puerto Rican	2,006	0.37
South American	755	0.14
Argentinean	88	0.02
Bolivian	27	<0.01
Chilean	69	0.01
Colombian	259	0.05
Ecuadorian	75	0.01
Paraguayan	10	<0.01
Peruvian	125	0.02
Uruguayan	14	<0.01
Venezuelan	82	0.02
Other South American	6	<0.01
Other Hispanic or Latino	1,144	0.21

Race*	Population	%
African-American/Black (78,120)	85,046	15.70
Not Hispanic (77,373)	83,851	15.48
Hispanic (747)	1,195	0.22
American Indian/Alaska Native (1,015)	4,185	0.77
Not Hispanic (901)	3,836	0.71
Hispanic (114)	349	0.06
Alaska Athabascan *(Ala. Nat.)* (5)	8	<0.01
Aleut *(Alaska Native)* (1)	1	<0.01
Apache (8)	46	0.01
Arapaho (0)	4	<0.01
Blackfeet (27)	228	0.04
Canadian/French Am. Ind. (18)	27	<0.01
Central American Ind. (3)	3	<0.01
Cherokee (216)	1,218	0.22
Cheyenne (5)	17	<0.01
Chickasaw (5)	19	<0.01
Chippewa (36)	59	0.01
Choctaw (20)	89	0.02
Colville (3)	3	<0.01
Comanche (2)	7	<0.01
Cree (6)	13	<0.01
Creek (6)	24	<0.01
Crow (1)	13	<0.01
Delaware (11)	26	<0.01
Hopi (0)	0	<0.01
Houma (0)	0	<0.01
Inupiat *(Alaska Native)* (2)	6	<0.01
Iroquois (28)	121	0.02
Kiowa (0)	1	<0.01
Lumbee (8)	11	<0.01
Menominee (0)	0	<0.01
Mexican American Ind. (22)	43	0.01
Navajo (11)	38	0.01
Osage (1)	4	<0.01
Ottawa (5)	9	<0.01
Paiute (1)	1	<0.01
Pima (4)	5	<0.01
Potawatomi (4)	5	<0.01
Pueblo (2)	3	<0.01
Puget Sound Salish (0)	0	<0.01
Seminole (4)	29	0.01
Shoshone (4)	14	<0.01
Sioux (33)	112	0.02
South American Ind. (5)	13	<0.01
Spanish American Ind. (2)	6	<0.01
Tlingit-Haida *(Alaska Native)* (0)	2	<0.01
Tohono O'Odham (0)	0	<0.01
Tsimshian *(Alaska Native)* (1)	2	<0.01
Ute (0)	1	<0.01
Yakama (0)	0	<0.01
Yaqui (2)	13	<0.01
Yuman (0)	0	<0.01
Yup'ik *(Alaska Native)* (3)	3	<0.01
Asian (11,885)	14,311	2.64
Not Hispanic (11,841)	14,170	2.62
Hispanic (44)	141	0.03
Bangladeshi (70)	82	0.02
Bhutanese (320)	372	0.07
Burmese (597)	615	0.11
Cambodian (77)	107	0.02
Chinese, ex. Taiwanese (2,126)	2,473	0.46
Filipino (797)	1,316	0.24
Hmong (410)	426	0.08
Indian (3,727)	4,154	0.77
Indonesian (47)	79	0.01
Japanese (416)	728	0.13
Korean (874)	1,154	0.21
Laotian (413)	481	0.09
Malaysian (16)	27	<0.01
Nepalese (72)	106	0.02
Pakistani (161)	175	0.03
Sri Lankan (48)	49	0.01
Taiwanese (171)	195	0.04
Thai (161)	249	0.05
Vietnamese (828)	936	0.17
Hawaii Native/Pacific Islander (133)	373	0.07
Not Hispanic (118)	328	0.06
Hispanic (15)	45	0.01
Fijian (0)	0	<0.01
Guamanian/Chamorro (23)	58	0.01
Marshallese (2)	2	<0.01
Native Hawaiian (59)	150	0.03
Samoan (9)	28	0.01
Tongan (1)	1	<0.01
White (436,487)	446,769	82.46
Not Hispanic (431,624)	441,092	81.42
Hispanic (4,863)	5,677	1.05

*Notes: † The Census 2010 population figure is used to calculate the percentages in the Hispanic Origin and Race categories. Ancestry percentages are based on the 2006-2010 American Community Survey population (not shown); ‡ Numbers in parentheses indicate the number of people reporting a single ancestry; * Numbers in parentheses indicate the number of persons reporting this race alone, not in combination with any other race; Please refer to the User Guide for more information.*

Trumbull County

Population: 210,312

Ancestry	Population	%
Afghan (0)	0	<0.01
African, Sub-Saharan (327)	475	0.22
African (205)	353	0.17
Cape Verdean (0)	0	<0.01
Ethiopian (122)	122	0.06
Ghanaian (0)	0	<0.01
Kenyan (0)	0	<0.01
Liberian (0)	0	<0.01
Nigerian (0)	0	<0.01
Senegalese (0)	0	<0.01
Sierra Leonean (0)	0	<0.01
Somalian (0)	0	<0.01
South African (0)	0	<0.01
Sudanese (0)	0	<0.01
Ugandan (0)	0	<0.01
Zimbabwean (0)	0	<0.01
Other Sub-Saharan African (0)	0	<0.01
Albanian (14)	39	0.02
Alsatian (0)	0	<0.01
American (35,115)	35,115	16.50
Arab (538)	1,014	0.48
Arab (57)	143	0.07
Egyptian (49)	49	0.02
Iraqi (0)	0	<0.01
Jordanian (11)	11	0.01
Lebanese (265)	618	0.29
Moroccan (17)	17	0.01
Palestinian (118)	118	0.06
Syrian (21)	58	0.03
Other Arab (0)	0	<0.01
Armenian (0)	8	<0.01
Assyrian/Chaldean/Syriac (0)	0	<0.01
Australian (12)	12	0.01
Austrian (104)	295	0.14
Basque (0)	0	<0.01
Belgian (38)	189	0.09
Brazilian (72)	72	0.03
British (89)	400	0.19
Bulgarian (0)	10	<0.01
Cajun (13)	13	0.01
Canadian (113)	229	0.11
Carpatho Rusyn (54)	69	0.03
Celtic (39)	88	0.04
Croatian (890)	2,594	1.22
Cypriot (0)	0	<0.01
Czech (210)	1,093	0.51
Czechoslovakian (154)	429	0.20
Danish (23)	181	0.09
Dutch (518)	4,149	1.95
Eastern European (80)	89	0.04
English (6,026)	22,460	10.56
Estonian (0)	0	<0.01
European (643)	728	0.34
Finnish (337)	1,139	0.54
French, ex. Basque (441)	3,486	1.64
French Canadian (94)	494	0.23
German (11,879)	46,006	21.62
German Russian (0)	0	<0.01
Greek (1,318)	2,767	1.30
Guyanese (0)	0	<0.01
Hungarian (2,269)	6,552	3.08
Icelander (0)	0	<0.01
Iranian (74)	74	0.03
Irish (6,169)	30,396	14.29
Israeli (0)	0	<0.01
Italian (13,208)	29,089	13.67
Latvian (12)	12	0.01
Lithuanian (237)	586	0.28
Luxemburger (0)	17	0.01
Macedonian (11)	121	0.06
Maltese (0)	0	<0.01
New Zealander (0)	0	<0.01
Northern European (37)	37	0.02
Norwegian (7)	178	0.08
Pennsylvania German (1,510)	2,069	0.97
Polish (2,756)	9,735	4.58
Portuguese (0)	46	0.02
Romanian (670)	1,351	0.63
Russian (481)	1,626	0.76
Scandinavian (27)	132	0.06
Scotch-Irish (1,006)	3,638	1.71
Scottish (951)	4,070	1.91
Serbian (259)	689	0.32
Slavic (65)	145	0.07
Slovak (2,964)	8,417	3.96
Slovene (339)	883	0.41
Soviet Union (0)	0	<0.01
Swedish (410)	1,475	0.69
Swiss (219)	907	0.43
Turkish (0)	0	<0.01
Ukrainian (765)	1,747	0.82
Welsh (838)	5,069	2.38
West Indian, ex. Hispanic (106)	166	0.08
Bahamian (0)	0	<0.01
Barbadian (0)	8	<0.01
Belizean (0)	0	<0.01
Bermudan (0)	0	<0.01
British West Indian (0)	0	<0.01
Dutch West Indian (0)	0	<0.01
Haitian (12)	12	0.01
Jamaican (37)	75	0.04
Trinidadian/Tobagonian (0)	6	<0.01
U.S. Virgin Islander (0)	0	<0.01
West Indian (57)	65	0.03
Other West Indian (0)	0	<0.01
Yugoslavian (101)	207	0.10

Hispanic Origin	Population	%
Hispanic or Latino (of any race)	2,801	1.33
Central American, ex. Mexican	98	0.05
Costa Rican	0	<0.01
Guatemalan	43	0.02
Honduran	13	0.01
Nicaraguan	8	<0.01
Panamanian	15	0.01
Salvadoran	19	0.01
Other Central American	0	<0.01
Cuban	89	0.04
Dominican Republic	40	0.02
Mexican	1,027	0.49
Puerto Rican	1,023	0.49
South American	112	0.05
Argentinean	10	<0.01
Bolivian	0	<0.01
Chilean	12	0.01
Colombian	40	0.02
Ecuadorian	9	<0.01
Paraguayan	0	<0.01
Peruvian	28	0.01
Uruguayan	0	<0.01
Venezuelan	13	0.01
Other South American	0	<0.01
Other Hispanic or Latino	412	0.20

Race*	Population	%
African-American/Black (17,417)	19,704	9.37
Not Hispanic (17,200)	19,327	9.19
Hispanic (217)	377	0.18
American Indian/Alaska Native (360)	1,456	0.69
Not Hispanic (326)	1,348	0.64
Hispanic (34)	108	0.05
Alaska Athabascan *(Ala. Nat.)* (2)	4	<0.01
Aleut *(Alaska Native)* (0)	0	<0.01
Apache (5)	22	0.01
Arapaho (0)	2	<0.01
Blackfeet (14)	88	0.04
Canadian/French Am. Ind. (0)	1	<0.01
Central American Ind. (1)	2	<0.01
Cherokee (90)	493	0.23
Cheyenne (1)	7	<0.01
Chickasaw (1)	2	<0.01
Chippewa (3)	15	0.01
Choctaw (2)	21	0.01
Colville (0)	0	<0.01
Comanche (1)	9	<0.01
Cree (6)	10	<0.01
Creek (4)	10	<0.01
Crow (2)	2	<0.01
Delaware (3)	5	<0.01
Hopi (4)	8	<0.01
Houma (0)	0	<0.01
Inupiat *(Alaska Native)* (0)	2	<0.01
Iroquois (7)	55	0.03
Kiowa (0)	0	<0.01
Lumbee (1)	1	<0.01
Menominee (0)	0	<0.01
Mexican American Ind. (5)	9	<0.01
Navajo (5)	18	0.01
Osage (1)	1	<0.01
Ottawa (2)	2	<0.01
Paiute (0)	5	<0.01
Pima (0)	0	<0.01
Potawatomi (1)	2	<0.01
Pueblo (0)	0	<0.01
Puget Sound Salish (0)	0	<0.01
Seminole (1)	2	<0.01
Shoshone (1)	1	<0.01
Sioux (10)	36	0.02
South American Ind. (0)	1	<0.01
Spanish American Ind. (0)	0	<0.01
Tlingit-Haida *(Alaska Native)* (0)	2	<0.01
Tohono O'Odham (0)	0	<0.01
Tsimshian *(Alaska Native)* (0)	0	<0.01
Ute (0)	0	<0.01
Yakama (0)	0	<0.01
Yaqui (0)	0	<0.01
Yuman (0)	0	<0.01
Yup'ik *(Alaska Native)* (0)	0	<0.01
Asian (984)	1,469	0.70
Not Hispanic (979)	1,424	0.68
Hispanic (5)	45	0.02
Bangladeshi (3)	3	<0.01
Bhutanese (1)	1	<0.01
Burmese (1)	1	<0.01
Cambodian (3)	3	<0.01
Chinese, ex. Taiwanese (196)	255	0.12
Filipino (130)	236	0.11
Hmong (0)	0	<0.01
Indian (311)	379	0.18
Indonesian (8)	10	<0.01
Japanese (51)	145	0.07
Korean (103)	178	0.08
Laotian (1)	7	<0.01
Malaysian (7)	8	<0.01
Nepalese (3)	5	<0.01
Pakistani (8)	20	0.01
Sri Lankan (5)	5	<0.01
Taiwanese (4)	7	<0.01
Thai (24)	47	0.02
Vietnamese (64)	86	0.04
Hawaii Native/Pacific Islander (41)	118	0.06
Not Hispanic (36)	93	0.04
Hispanic (5)	25	0.01
Fijian (0)	0	<0.01
Guamanian/Chamorro (15)	18	0.01
Marshallese (0)	1	<0.01
Native Hawaiian (9)	39	0.02
Samoan (8)	18	0.01
Tongan (0)	3	<0.01
White (187,113)	190,582	90.62
Not Hispanic (185,388)	188,576	89.66
Hispanic (1,725)	2,006	0.95

*Notes: † The Census 2010 population figure is used to calculate the percentages in the Hispanic Origin and Race categories. Ancestry percentages are based on the 2006-2010 American Community Survey population (not shown); ‡ Numbers in parentheses indicate the number of people reporting a single ancestry; * Numbers in parentheses indicate the number of persons reporting this race alone, not in combination with any other race; Please refer to the User Guide for more information.*

Warren County

Population: 212,693

Ancestry	Population	%
Afghan (0)	12	0.01
African, Sub-Saharan (366)	610	0.29
African (209)	453	0.22
Cape Verdean (0)	0	<0.01
Ethiopian (91)	91	0.04
Ghanaian (0)	0	<0.01
Kenyan (0)	0	<0.01
Liberian (6)	6	<0.01
Nigerian (30)	30	0.01
Senegalese (0)	0	<0.01
Sierra Leonean (0)	0	<0.01
Somalian (0)	0	<0.01
South African (0)	0	<0.01
Sudanese (0)	0	<0.01
Ugandan (0)	0	<0.01
Zimbabwean (0)	0	<0.01
Other Sub-Saharan African (30)	30	0.01
Albanian (10)	20	0.01
Alsatian (0)	8	<0.01
American (24,038)	24,038	11.57
Arab (350)	826	0.40
Arab (57)	118	0.06
Egyptian (105)	113	0.05
Iraqi (0)	0	<0.01
Jordanian (18)	26	0.01
Lebanese (80)	335	0.16
Moroccan (11)	20	0.01
Palestinian (15)	15	0.01
Syrian (24)	64	0.03
Other Arab (40)	135	0.06
Armenian (0)	79	0.04
Assyrian/Chaldean/Syriac (0)	21	0.01
Australian (19)	19	0.01
Austrian (149)	413	0.20
Basque (0)	0	<0.01
Belgian (52)	203	0.10
Brazilian (49)	94	0.05
British (621)	1,206	0.58
Bulgarian (0)	25	0.01
Cajun (0)	0	<0.01
Canadian (150)	331	0.16
Carpatho Rusyn (0)	0	<0.01
Celtic (42)	42	0.02
Croatian (51)	184	0.09
Cypriot (0)	0	<0.01
Czech (100)	673	0.32
Czechoslovakian (16)	138	0.07
Danish (81)	461	0.22
Dutch (739)	3,919	1.89
Eastern European (205)	218	0.10
English (10,025)	24,983	12.02
Estonian (9)	9	<0.01
European (2,731)	3,094	1.49
Finnish (138)	417	0.20
French, ex. Basque (730)	4,785	2.30
French Canadian (102)	422	0.20
German (22,765)	59,637	28.70
German Russian (0)	0	<0.01
Greek (437)	1,118	0.54
Guyanese (0)	0	<0.01
Hungarian (370)	1,377	0.66
Icelander (11)	33	0.02
Iranian (119)	119	0.06
Irish (7,210)	29,249	14.08
Israeli (31)	62	0.03
Italian (3,105)	10,403	5.01
Latvian (12)	31	0.01
Lithuanian (147)	307	0.15
Luxemburger (6)	6	<0.01
Macedonian (14)	14	0.01
Maltese (31)	31	0.01
New Zealander (0)	0	<0.01
Northern European (32)	49	0.02
Norwegian (275)	1,113	0.54
Pennsylvania German (74)	100	0.05
Polish (1,497)	5,547	2.67
Portuguese (12)	125	0.06
Romanian (78)	155	0.07
Russian (891)	1,525	0.73
Scandinavian (92)	198	0.10
Scotch-Irish (1,554)	3,368	1.62
Scottish (1,351)	5,065	2.44
Serbian (25)	165	0.08
Slavic (15)	80	0.04
Slovak (139)	468	0.23
Slovene (29)	198	0.10
Soviet Union (0)	0	<0.01
Swedish (351)	1,671	0.80
Swiss (47)	666	0.32
Turkish (74)	112	0.05
Ukrainian (190)	582	0.28
Welsh (401)	1,691	0.81
West Indian, ex. Hispanic (162)	193	0.09
Bahamian (0)	0	<0.01
Barbadian (22)	36	0.02
Belizean (0)	0	<0.01
Bermudan (0)	0	<0.01
British West Indian (0)	0	<0.01
Dutch West Indian (0)	0	<0.01
Haitian (0)	17	0.01
Jamaican (11)	11	0.01
Trinidadian/Tobagonian (0)	0	<0.01
U.S. Virgin Islander (0)	0	<0.01
West Indian (129)	129	0.06
Other West Indian (0)	0	<0.01
Yugoslavian (154)	220	0.11

Hispanic Origin	Population	%
Hispanic or Latino (of any race)	4,784	2.25
Central American, ex. Mexican	387	0.18
Costa Rican	42	0.02
Guatemalan	152	0.07
Honduran	50	0.02
Nicaraguan	42	0.02
Panamanian	33	0.02
Salvadoran	67	0.03
Other Central American	1	<0.01
Cuban	210	0.10
Dominican Republic	50	0.02
Mexican	2,449	1.15
Puerto Rican	651	0.31
South American	663	0.31
Argentinean	35	0.02
Bolivian	27	0.01
Chilean	21	0.01
Colombian	207	0.10
Ecuadorian	59	0.03
Paraguayan	0	<0.01
Peruvian	95	0.04
Uruguayan	10	<0.01
Venezuelan	206	0.10
Other South American	3	<0.01
Other Hispanic or Latino	374	0.18

Race*	Population	%
African-American/Black (6,940)	8,004	3.76
Not Hispanic (6,838)	7,827	3.68
Hispanic (102)	177	0.08
American Indian/Alaska Native (341)	1,151	0.54
Not Hispanic (289)	1,026	0.48
Hispanic (52)	125	0.06
Alaska Athabascan *(Ala. Nat.)* (0)	1	<0.01
Aleut *(Alaska Native)* (1)	3	<0.01
Apache (6)	22	0.01
Arapaho (0)	0	<0.01
Blackfeet (3)	48	0.02
Canadian/French Am. Ind. (4)	4	<0.01
Central American Ind. (1)	3	<0.01
Cherokee (78)	386	0.18
Cheyenne (0)	9	<0.01
Chickasaw (3)	3	<0.01
Chippewa (22)	25	0.01
Choctaw (8)	25	0.01
Colville (0)	0	<0.01
Comanche (3)	4	<0.01
Cree (0)	0	<0.01
Creek (5)	13	0.01
Crow (0)	4	<0.01
Delaware (0)	0	<0.01
Hopi (0)	2	<0.01
Houma (0)	0	<0.01
Inupiat *(Alaska Native)* (0)	1	<0.01
Iroquois (21)	32	0.02
Kiowa (0)	0	<0.01
Lumbee (0)	2	<0.01
Menominee (0)	0	<0.01
Mexican American Ind. (19)	21	0.01
Navajo (10)	27	0.01
Osage (1)	1	<0.01
Ottawa (0)	0	<0.01
Paiute (0)	0	<0.01
Pima (1)	1	<0.01
Potawatomi (0)	3	<0.01
Pueblo (1)	2	<0.01
Puget Sound Salish (0)	0	<0.01
Seminole (0)	5	<0.01
Shoshone (0)	2	<0.01
Sioux (5)	13	0.01
South American Ind. (2)	7	<0.01
Spanish American Ind. (5)	8	<0.01
Tlingit-Haida *(Alaska Native)* (3)	3	<0.01
Tohono O'Odham (0)	0	<0.01
Tsimshian *(Alaska Native)* (1)	6	<0.01
Ute (1)	4	<0.01
Yakama (0)	0	<0.01
Yaqui (0)	0	<0.01
Yuman (0)	0	<0.01
Yup'ik *(Alaska Native)* (0)	0	<0.01
Asian (8,284)	9,550	4.49
Not Hispanic (8,261)	9,483	4.46
Hispanic (23)	67	0.03
Bangladeshi (22)	22	0.01
Bhutanese (0)	0	<0.01
Burmese (8)	18	0.01
Cambodian (31)	42	0.02
Chinese, ex. Taiwanese (1,734)	1,964	0.92
Filipino (375)	642	0.30
Hmong (0)	0	<0.01
Indian (4,142)	4,373	2.06
Indonesian (8)	23	0.01
Japanese (405)	578	0.27
Korean (445)	632	0.30
Laotian (19)	36	0.02
Malaysian (6)	28	0.01
Nepalese (9)	12	0.01
Pakistani (333)	359	0.17
Sri Lankan (29)	35	0.02
Taiwanese (103)	125	0.06
Thai (42)	71	0.03
Vietnamese (357)	406	0.19
Hawaii Native/Pacific Islander (99)	220	0.10
Not Hispanic (93)	206	0.10
Hispanic (6)	14	0.01
Fijian (0)	0	<0.01
Guamanian/Chamorro (17)	38	0.02
Marshallese (5)	5	<0.01
Native Hawaiian (23)	64	0.03
Samoan (1)	4	<0.01
Tongan (0)	0	<0.01
White (192,431)	195,373	91.86
Not Hispanic (189,305)	191,943	90.24
Hispanic (3,126)	3,430	1.61

*Notes: † The Census 2010 population figure is used to calculate the percentages in the Hispanic Origin and Race categories. Ancestry percentages are based on the 2006-2010 American Community Survey population (not shown); ‡ Numbers in parentheses indicate the number of people reporting a single ancestry; * Numbers in parentheses indicate the number of persons reporting this race alone, not in combination with any other race; Please refer to the User Guide for more information.*

Wayne County

Population: 114,520

Ancestry	Population	%
Afghan (0)	0	<0.01
African, Sub-Saharan (140)	242	0.21
African (124)	208	0.18
Cape Verdean (0)	0	<0.01
Ethiopian (0)	0	<0.01
Ghanaian (16)	16	0.01
Kenyan (0)	0	<0.01
Liberian (0)	0	<0.01
Nigerian (0)	0	<0.01
Senegalese (0)	0	<0.01
Sierra Leonean (0)	0	<0.01
Somalian (0)	0	<0.01
South African (0)	18	0.02
Sudanese (0)	0	<0.01
Ugandan (0)	0	<0.01
Zimbabwean (0)	0	<0.01
Other Sub-Saharan African (0)	0	<0.01
Albanian (0)	0	<0.01
Alsatian (0)	0	<0.01
American (15,164)	15,164	13.25
Arab (100)	177	0.15
Arab (0)	0	<0.01
Egyptian (10)	10	0.01
Iraqi (0)	0	<0.01
Jordanian (0)	0	<0.01
Lebanese (58)	135	0.12
Moroccan (11)	11	0.01
Palestinian (0)	0	<0.01
Syrian (0)	0	<0.01
Other Arab (21)	21	0.02
Armenian (0)	69	0.06
Assyrian/Chaldean/Syriac (0)	0	<0.01
Australian (0)	0	<0.01
Austrian (128)	458	0.40
Basque (0)	0	<0.01
Belgian (0)	37	0.03
Brazilian (0)	8	0.01
British (57)	170	0.15
Bulgarian (25)	66	0.06
Cajun (7)	7	0.01
Canadian (48)	138	0.12
Carpatho Rusyn (0)	0	<0.01
Celtic (9)	19	0.02
Croatian (115)	223	0.19
Cypriot (0)	0	<0.01
Czech (62)	539	0.47
Czechoslovakian (109)	190	0.17
Danish (3)	58	0.05
Dutch (484)	2,735	2.39
Eastern European (18)	18	0.02
English (3,643)	10,250	8.96
Estonian (0)	0	<0.01
European (1,342)	1,471	1.29
Finnish (53)	196	0.17
French, ex. Basque (507)	3,668	3.21
French Canadian (165)	260	0.23
German (15,883)	39,012	34.09
German Russian (0)	0	<0.01
Greek (181)	373	0.33
Guyanese (0)	0	<0.01
Hungarian (591)	1,848	1.61
Icelander (0)	0	<0.01
Iranian (0)	19	0.02
Irish (3,476)	14,717	12.86
Israeli (0)	0	<0.01
Italian (2,066)	5,444	4.76
Latvian (0)	0	<0.01
Lithuanian (9)	146	0.13
Luxemburger (0)	0	<0.01
Macedonian (0)	2	<0.01
Maltese (0)	9	0.01
New Zealander (0)	0	<0.01
Northern European (30)	30	0.03
Norwegian (29)	267	0.23
Pennsylvania German (3,063)	3,330	2.91
Polish (802)	2,823	2.47
Portuguese (0)	104	0.09
Romanian (54)	124	0.11
Russian (126)	572	0.50
Scandinavian (9)	30	0.03
Scotch-Irish (664)	2,007	1.75
Scottish (730)	2,498	2.18
Serbian (0)	42	0.04
Slavic (0)	47	0.04
Slovak (258)	822	0.72
Slovene (60)	161	0.14
Soviet Union (0)	0	<0.01
Swedish (329)	1,134	0.99
Swiss (2,904)	7,223	6.31
Turkish (15)	23	0.02
Ukrainian (83)	181	0.16
Welsh (325)	1,043	0.91
West Indian, ex. Hispanic (83)	97	0.08
Bahamian (0)	0	<0.01
Barbadian (0)	0	<0.01
Belizean (0)	0	<0.01
Bermudan (0)	0	<0.01
British West Indian (0)	0	<0.01
Dutch West Indian (0)	10	0.01
Haitian (45)	45	0.04
Jamaican (38)	42	0.04
Trinidadian/Tobagonian (0)	0	<0.01
U.S. Virgin Islander (0)	0	<0.01
West Indian (0)	0	<0.01
Other West Indian (0)	0	<0.01
Yugoslavian (97)	163	0.14

Hispanic Origin	Population	%
Hispanic or Latino (of any race)	1,800	1.57
Central American, ex. Mexican	174	0.15
Costa Rican	16	0.01
Guatemalan	52	0.05
Honduran	40	0.03
Nicaraguan	4	<0.01
Panamanian	5	<0.01
Salvadoran	53	0.05
Other Central American	4	<0.01
Cuban	71	0.06
Dominican Republic	20	0.02
Mexican	927	0.81
Puerto Rican	235	0.21
South American	125	0.11
Argentinean	9	0.01
Bolivian	13	0.01
Chilean	13	0.01
Colombian	37	0.03
Ecuadorian	24	0.02
Paraguayan	2	<0.01
Peruvian	15	0.01
Uruguayan	3	<0.01
Venezuelan	9	0.01
Other South American	0	<0.01
Other Hispanic or Latino	248	0.22

Race*	Population	%
African-American/Black (1,712)	2,490	2.17
Not Hispanic (1,689)	2,429	2.12
Hispanic (23)	61	0.05
American Indian/Alaska Native (183)	693	0.61
Not Hispanic (152)	629	0.55
Hispanic (31)	64	0.06
Alaska Athabascan *(Ala. Nat.)* (1)	1	<0.01
Aleut *(Alaska Native)* (0)	0	<0.01
Apache (2)	9	0.01
Arapaho (0)	0	<0.01
Blackfeet (2)	38	0.03
Canadian/French Am. Ind. (1)	2	<0.01
Central American Ind. (2)	5	<0.01
Cherokee (58)	248	0.22
Cheyenne (0)	1	<0.01
Chickasaw (0)	0	<0.01
Chippewa (6)	18	0.02
Choctaw (4)	17	0.01
Colville (0)	0	<0.01
Comanche (1)	1	<0.01
Cree (2)	3	<0.01
Creek (5)	5	<0.01
Crow (1)	1	<0.01
Delaware (0)	8	0.01
Hopi (0)	4	<0.01
Houma (1)	3	<0.01
Inupiat *(Alaska Native)* (1)	2	<0.01
Iroquois (4)	18	0.02
Kiowa (0)	0	<0.01
Lumbee (0)	0	<0.01
Menominee (4)	4	<0.01
Mexican American Ind. (4)	10	0.01
Navajo (1)	7	0.01
Osage (1)	1	<0.01
Ottawa (0)	0	<0.01
Paiute (0)	0	<0.01
Pima (0)	0	<0.01
Potawatomi (2)	2	<0.01
Pueblo (0)	0	<0.01
Puget Sound Salish (0)	0	<0.01
Seminole (0)	0	<0.01
Shoshone (0)	0	<0.01
Sioux (10)	19	0.02
South American Ind. (2)	2	<0.01
Spanish American Ind. (1)	3	<0.01
Tlingit-Haida *(Alaska Native)* (2)	4	<0.01
Tohono O'Odham (0)	0	<0.01
Tsimshian *(Alaska Native)* (0)	0	<0.01
Ute (0)	0	<0.01
Yakama (0)	0	<0.01
Yaqui (0)	0	<0.01
Yuman (0)	0	<0.01
Yup'ik *(Alaska Native)* (0)	0	<0.01
Asian (874)	1,148	1.00
Not Hispanic (864)	1,122	0.98
Hispanic (10)	26	0.02
Bangladeshi (0)	1	<0.01
Bhutanese (0)	0	<0.01
Burmese (0)	0	<0.01
Cambodian (2)	2	<0.01
Chinese, ex. Taiwanese (184)	220	0.19
Filipino (84)	161	0.14
Hmong (0)	0	<0.01
Indian (226)	264	0.23
Indonesian (5)	7	0.01
Japanese (28)	74	0.06
Korean (103)	125	0.11
Laotian (128)	155	0.14
Malaysian (0)	1	<0.01
Nepalese (5)	5	<0.01
Pakistani (14)	15	0.01
Sri Lankan (0)	1	<0.01
Taiwanese (2)	3	<0.01
Thai (17)	22	0.02
Vietnamese (50)	70	0.06
Hawaii Native/Pacific Islander (26)	80	0.07
Not Hispanic (22)	73	0.06
Hispanic (4)	7	0.01
Fijian (0)	0	<0.01
Guamanian/Chamorro (10)	25	0.02
Marshallese (0)	0	<0.01
Native Hawaiian (4)	28	0.02
Samoan (4)	8	0.01
Tongan (0)	0	<0.01
White (109,543)	111,077	96.99
Not Hispanic (108,450)	109,832	95.91
Hispanic (1,093)	1,245	1.09

*Notes: † The Census 2010 population figure is used to calculate the percentages in the Hispanic Origin and Race categories. Ancestry percentages are based on the 2006-2010 American Community Survey population (not shown); ‡ Numbers in parentheses indicate the number of people reporting a single ancestry; * Numbers in parentheses indicate the number of persons reporting this race alone, not in combination with any other race; Please refer to the User Guide for more information.*

Wood County

Population: 125,488

Ancestry	Population	%
Afghan (0)	0	<0.01
African, Sub-Saharan (212)	317	0.25
African (154)	227	0.18
Cape Verdean (0)	16	0.01
Ethiopian (0)	0	<0.01
Ghanaian (21)	21	0.02
Kenyan (0)	0	<0.01
Liberian (0)	0	<0.01
Nigerian (20)	20	0.02
Senegalese (0)	0	<0.01
Sierra Leonean (0)	0	<0.01
Somalian (0)	0	<0.01
South African (17)	17	0.01
Sudanese (0)	0	<0.01
Ugandan (0)	0	<0.01
Zimbabwean (0)	0	<0.01
Other Sub-Saharan African (0)	16	0.01
Albanian (0)	0	<0.01
Alsatian (0)	0	<0.01
American (6,552)	6,552	5.23
Arab (370)	602	0.48
Arab (26)	48	0.04
Egyptian (12)	12	0.01
Iraqi (0)	0	<0.01
Jordanian (0)	0	<0.01
Lebanese (159)	327	0.26
Moroccan (24)	24	0.02
Palestinian (0)	0	<0.01
Syrian (75)	114	0.09
Other Arab (74)	77	0.06
Armenian (51)	70	0.06
Assyrian/Chaldean/Syriac (0)	0	<0.01
Australian (14)	32	0.03
Austrian (102)	305	0.24
Basque (0)	18	0.01
Belgian (101)	261	0.21
Brazilian (0)	0	<0.01
British (147)	469	0.37
Bulgarian (45)	65	0.05
Cajun (0)	0	<0.01
Canadian (35)	183	0.15
Carpatho Rusyn (0)	0	<0.01
Celtic (3)	3	<0.01
Croatian (36)	277	0.22
Cypriot (0)	0	<0.01
Czech (262)	1,037	0.83
Czechoslovakian (76)	347	0.28
Danish (92)	379	0.30
Dutch (487)	2,672	2.13
Eastern European (51)	85	0.07
English (3,102)	13,032	10.40
Estonian (0)	0	<0.01
European (1,039)	1,086	0.87
Finnish (91)	181	0.14
French, ex. Basque (744)	4,979	3.97
French Canadian (140)	863	0.69
German (22,082)	51,154	40.83
German Russian (0)	0	<0.01
Greek (178)	554	0.44
Guyanese (0)	0	<0.01
Hungarian (1,147)	3,343	2.67
Icelander (31)	70	0.06
Iranian (68)	68	0.05
Irish (3,606)	17,993	14.36
Israeli (14)	14	0.01
Italian (1,865)	5,664	4.52
Latvian (0)	0	<0.01
Lithuanian (70)	248	0.20
Luxemburger (0)	0	<0.01
Macedonian (17)	38	0.03
Maltese (12)	39	0.03
New Zealander (0)	0	<0.01
Northern European (2)	5	<0.01
Norwegian (266)	710	0.57
Pennsylvania German (105)	208	0.17
Polish (3,125)	8,421	6.72
Portuguese (0)	14	0.01
Romanian (30)	240	0.19
Russian (130)	511	0.41
Scandinavian (35)	93	0.07
Scotch-Irish (523)	1,850	1.48
Scottish (846)	3,070	2.45
Serbian (15)	53	0.04
Slavic (12)	62	0.05
Slovak (537)	1,052	0.84
Slovene (2)	105	0.08
Soviet Union (0)	0	<0.01
Swedish (178)	824	0.66
Swiss (220)	976	0.78
Turkish (207)	207	0.17
Ukrainian (94)	277	0.22
Welsh (180)	1,348	1.08
West Indian, ex. Hispanic (11)	37	0.03
Bahamian (0)	14	0.01
Barbadian (0)	0	<0.01
Belizean (0)	0	<0.01
Bermudan (0)	0	<0.01
British West Indian (0)	0	<0.01
Dutch West Indian (0)	12	0.01
Haitian (0)	0	<0.01
Jamaican (0)	0	<0.01
Trinidadian/Tobagonian (0)	0	<0.01
U.S. Virgin Islander (0)	0	<0.01
West Indian (11)	11	0.01
Other West Indian (0)	0	<0.01
Yugoslavian (0)	29	0.02

Hispanic Origin	Population	%
Hispanic or Latino (of any race)	5,663	4.51
Central American, ex. Mexican	91	0.07
Costa Rican	5	<0.01
Guatemalan	43	0.03
Honduran	8	0.01
Nicaraguan	9	0.01
Panamanian	13	0.01
Salvadoran	13	0.01
Other Central American	0	<0.01
Cuban	74	0.06
Dominican Republic	14	0.01
Mexican	4,502	3.59
Puerto Rican	291	0.23
South American	172	0.14
Argentinean	28	0.02
Bolivian	16	0.01
Chilean	5	<0.01
Colombian	53	0.04
Ecuadorian	11	0.01
Paraguayan	9	0.01
Peruvian	23	0.02
Uruguayan	1	<0.01
Venezuelan	26	0.02
Other South American	0	<0.01
Other Hispanic or Latino	519	0.41

Race*	Population	%
African-American/Black (3,022)	3,799	3.03
Not Hispanic (2,906)	3,582	2.85
Hispanic (116)	217	0.17
American Indian/Alaska Native (286)	919	0.73
Not Hispanic (232)	766	0.61
Hispanic (54)	153	0.12
Alaska Athabascan *(Ala. Nat.)* (0)	0	<0.01
Aleut *(Alaska Native)* (2)	2	<0.01
Apache (9)	21	0.02
Arapaho (1)	2	<0.01
Blackfeet (6)	44	0.04
Canadian/French Am. Ind. (0)	1	<0.01
Central American Ind. (0)	0	<0.01
Cherokee (81)	283	0.23
Cheyenne (1)	2	<0.01
Chickasaw (0)	1	<0.01
Chippewa (12)	28	0.02
Choctaw (1)	7	0.01
Colville (0)	0	<0.01
Comanche (2)	5	<0.01
Cree (0)	2	<0.01
Creek (0)	2	<0.01
Crow (0)	4	<0.01
Delaware (3)	4	<0.01
Hopi (0)	1	<0.01
Houma (1)	3	<0.01
Inupiat *(Alaska Native)* (3)	3	<0.01
Iroquois (12)	28	0.02
Kiowa (0)	0	<0.01
Lumbee (2)	2	<0.01
Menominee (1)	1	<0.01
Mexican American Ind. (11)	20	0.02
Navajo (6)	8	0.01
Osage (1)	1	<0.01
Ottawa (2)	2	<0.01
Paiute (0)	0	<0.01
Pima (0)	0	<0.01
Potawatomi (3)	6	<0.01
Pueblo (0)	0	<0.01
Puget Sound Salish (0)	0	<0.01
Seminole (0)	1	<0.01
Shoshone (1)	3	<0.01
Sioux (11)	27	0.02
South American Ind. (1)	2	<0.01
Spanish American Ind. (0)	0	<0.01
Tlingit-Haida *(Alaska Native)* (0)	0	<0.01
Tohono O'Odham (0)	0	<0.01
Tsimshian *(Alaska Native)* (0)	0	<0.01
Ute (0)	0	<0.01
Yakama (0)	0	<0.01
Yaqui (1)	1	<0.01
Yuman (0)	0	<0.01
Yup'ik *(Alaska Native)* (0)	0	<0.01
Asian (1,943)	2,472	1.97
Not Hispanic (1,924)	2,418	1.93
Hispanic (19)	54	0.04
Bangladeshi (14)	19	0.02
Bhutanese (0)	0	<0.01
Burmese (0)	1	<0.01
Cambodian (6)	9	0.01
Chinese, ex. Taiwanese (546)	619	0.49
Filipino (181)	293	0.23
Hmong (0)	1	<0.01
Indian (503)	581	0.46
Indonesian (12)	17	0.01
Japanese (88)	136	0.11
Korean (201)	276	0.22
Laotian (41)	62	0.05
Malaysian (5)	5	<0.01
Nepalese (10)	10	0.01
Pakistani (91)	110	0.09
Sri Lankan (13)	15	0.01
Taiwanese (12)	16	0.01
Thai (51)	80	0.06
Vietnamese (69)	86	0.07
Hawaii Native/Pacific Islander (37)	82	0.07
Not Hispanic (30)	66	0.05
Hispanic (7)	16	0.01
Fijian (0)	1	<0.01
Guamanian/Chamorro (6)	10	0.01
Marshallese (0)	1	<0.01
Native Hawaiian (12)	23	0.02
Samoan (4)	10	0.01
Tongan (0)	0	<0.01
White (116,422)	118,442	94.39
Not Hispanic (113,021)	114,519	91.26
Hispanic (3,401)	3,923	3.13

*Notes: † The Census 2010 population figure is used to calculate the percentages in the Hispanic Origin and Race categories. Ancestry percentages are based on the 2006-2010 American Community Survey population (not shown); ‡ Numbers in parentheses indicate the number of people reporting a single ancestry; * Numbers in parentheses indicate the number of persons reporting this race alone, not in combination with any other race; Please refer to the User Guide for more information.*

Place Profiles

Akron

Place Type: City
County: Summit
Population: 199,110

Ancestry	Population	%
Afghan (0)	0	<0.01
African, Sub-Saharan (1,717)	2,290	1.13
African (1,579)	2,027	1.00
Cape Verdean (0)	33	0.02
Ethiopian (14)	42	0.02
Ghanaian (0)	0	<0.01
Kenyan (0)	0	<0.01
Liberian (29)	29	0.01
Nigerian (0)	0	<0.01
Senegalese (0)	0	<0.01
Sierra Leonean (0)	0	<0.01
Somalian (23)	23	0.01
South African (17)	17	0.01
Sudanese (0)	0	<0.01
Ugandan (0)	0	<0.01
Zimbabwean (12)	12	0.01
Other Sub-Saharan African (43)	107	0.05
Albanian (214)	304	0.15
Alsatian (0)	26	0.01
American (8,242)	8,242	4.06
Arab (714)	1,396	0.69
Arab (30)	159	0.08
Egyptian (124)	137	0.07
Iraqi (0)	7	<0.01
Jordanian (0)	0	<0.01
Lebanese (407)	914	0.45
Moroccan (0)	0	<0.01
Palestinian (10)	10	<0.01
Syrian (0)	26	0.01
Other Arab (143)	143	0.07
Armenian (26)	82	0.04
Assyrian/Chaldean/Syriac (0)	0	<0.01
Australian (0)	21	0.01
Austrian (108)	450	0.22
Basque (0)	0	<0.01
Belgian (58)	109	0.05
Brazilian (0)	27	0.01
British (201)	508	0.25
Bulgarian (11)	32	0.02
Cajun (0)	27	0.01
Canadian (102)	196	0.10
Carpatho Rusyn (7)	25	0.01
Celtic (0)	0	<0.01
Croatian (225)	584	0.29
Cypriot (0)	0	<0.01
Czech (236)	919	0.45
Czechoslovakian (176)	233	0.11
Danish (76)	260	0.13
Dutch (352)	2,805	1.38
Eastern European (115)	138	0.07
English (4,635)	15,829	7.80
Estonian (0)	0	<0.01
European (1,068)	1,390	0.69
Finnish (12)	84	0.04
French, ex. Basque (524)	3,698	1.82
French Canadian (143)	320	0.16
German (11,486)	39,722	19.59
German Russian (0)	78	0.04
Greek (609)	1,127	0.56
Guyanese (0)	0	<0.01
Hungarian (1,222)	4,508	2.22
Icelander (19)	19	0.01
Iranian (36)	36	0.02
Irish (6,958)	26,458	13.05
Israeli (11)	11	0.01
Italian (5,897)	15,000	7.40
Latvian (27)	27	0.01
Lithuanian (87)	239	0.12
Luxemburger (0)	0	<0.01
Macedonian (43)	56	0.03
Maltese (0)	0	<0.01
New Zealander (0)	0	<0.01
Northern European (103)	103	0.05
Norwegian (220)	541	0.27
Pennsylvania German (177)	444	0.22
Polish (1,639)	4,998	2.46
Portuguese (210)	293	0.14
Romanian (344)	564	0.28
Russian (294)	893	0.44
Scandinavian (49)	130	0.06
Scotch-Irish (1,292)	3,342	1.65
Scottish (734)	2,974	1.47
Serbian (522)	945	0.47
Slavic (25)	106	0.05
Slovak (960)	2,164	1.07
Slovene (180)	588	0.29
Soviet Union (0)	0	<0.01
Swedish (292)	1,161	0.57
Swiss (161)	690	0.34
Turkish (27)	61	0.03
Ukrainian (304)	693	0.34
Welsh (376)	2,022	1.00
West Indian, ex. Hispanic (142)	240	0.12
Bahamian (0)	0	<0.01
Barbadian (5)	5	<0.01
Belizean (0)	0	<0.01
Bermudan (0)	0	<0.01
British West Indian (39)	39	0.02
Dutch West Indian (0)	0	<0.01
Haitian (9)	36	0.02
Jamaican (30)	89	0.04
Trinidadian/Tobagonian (0)	0	<0.01
U.S. Virgin Islander (0)	0	<0.01
West Indian (59)	71	0.04
Other West Indian (0)	0	<0.01
Yugoslavian (858)	1,145	0.56

Hispanic Origin	Population	%
Hispanic or Latino (of any race)	4,255	2.14
Central American, ex. Mexican	341	0.17
Costa Rican	10	0.01
Guatemalan	80	0.04
Honduran	93	0.05
Nicaraguan	38	0.02
Panamanian	47	0.02
Salvadoran	69	0.03
Other Central American	4	<0.01
Cuban	148	0.07
Dominican Republic	50	0.03
Mexican	1,784	0.90
Puerto Rican	1,091	0.55
South American	251	0.13
Argentinean	23	0.01
Bolivian	6	<0.01
Chilean	18	0.01
Colombian	101	0.05
Ecuadorian	39	0.02
Paraguayan	0	<0.01
Peruvian	24	0.01
Uruguayan	6	<0.01
Venezuelan	31	0.02
Other South American	3	<0.01
Other Hispanic or Latino	590	0.30

Race*	Population	%
African-American/Black (62,648)	67,240	33.77
Not Hispanic (62,095)	66,385	33.34
Hispanic (553)	855	0.43
American Indian/Alaska Native (486)	2,083	1.05
Not Hispanic (425)	1,899	0.95
Hispanic (61)	184	0.09
Alaska Athabascan *(Ala. Nat.)* (0)	0	<0.01
Aleut *(Alaska Native)* (1)	1	<0.01
Apache (3)	16	0.01
Arapaho (0)	3	<0.01
Blackfeet (11)	115	0.06
Canadian/French Am. Ind. (12)	18	0.01
Central American Ind. (0)	0	<0.01
Cherokee (91)	534	0.27
Cheyenne (4)	14	0.01
Chickasaw (3)	9	<0.01
Chippewa (13)	20	0.01
Choctaw (10)	42	0.02
Colville (0)	0	<0.01
Comanche (2)	5	<0.01
Cree (4)	8	<0.01
Creek (5)	16	0.01
Crow (0)	6	<0.01
Delaware (5)	17	0.01
Hopi (0)	0	<0.01
Houma (0)	0	<0.01
Inupiat *(Alaska Native)* (2)	4	<0.01
Iroquois (6)	41	0.02
Kiowa (0)	0	<0.01
Lumbee (2)	5	<0.01
Menominee (0)	0	<0.01
Mexican American Ind. (1)	14	0.01
Navajo (3)	15	0.01
Osage (0)	3	<0.01
Ottawa (3)	4	<0.01
Paiute (0)	0	<0.01
Pima (4)	5	<0.01
Potawatomi (2)	2	<0.01
Pueblo (0)	1	<0.01
Puget Sound Salish (0)	0	<0.01
Seminole (1)	17	0.01
Shoshone (4)	10	0.01
Sioux (14)	55	0.03
South American Ind. (4)	7	<0.01
Spanish American Ind. (2)	4	<0.01
Tlingit-Haida *(Alaska Native)* (0)	1	<0.01
Tohono O'Odham (0)	0	<0.01
Tsimshian *(Alaska Native)* (0)	0	<0.01
Ute (0)	1	<0.01
Yakama (0)	0	<0.01
Yaqui (1)	9	<0.01
Yuman (0)	0	<0.01
Yup'ik *(Alaska Native)* (0)	0	<0.01
Asian (4,218)	5,081	2.55
Not Hispanic (4,201)	5,008	2.52
Hispanic (17)	73	0.04
Bangladeshi (15)	15	0.01
Bhutanese (267)	318	0.16
Burmese (585)	603	0.30
Cambodian (55)	69	0.03
Chinese, ex. Taiwanese (486)	607	0.30
Filipino (174)	317	0.16
Hmong (351)	362	0.18
Indian (713)	874	0.44
Indonesian (12)	20	0.01
Japanese (68)	207	0.10
Korean (174)	252	0.13
Laotian (346)	388	0.19
Malaysian (6)	9	<0.01
Nepalese (54)	85	0.04
Pakistani (19)	22	0.01
Sri Lankan (17)	18	0.01
Taiwanese (50)	54	0.03
Thai (77)	116	0.06
Vietnamese (427)	474	0.24
Hawaii Native/Pacific Islander (52)	189	0.09
Not Hispanic (49)	164	0.08
Hispanic (3)	25	0.01
Fijian (0)	0	<0.01
Guamanian/Chamorro (12)	27	0.01
Marshallese (0)	0	<0.01
Native Hawaiian (20)	84	0.04
Samoan (5)	14	0.01
Tongan (1)	1	<0.01
White (123,879)	129,298	64.94
Not Hispanic (121,946)	126,928	63.75
Hispanic (1,933)	2,370	1.19

*Notes: † The Census 2010 population figure is used to calculate the percentages in the Hispanic Origin and Race categories. Ancestry percentages are based on the 2006-2010 American Community Survey population (not shown); ‡ Numbers in parentheses indicate the number of people reporting a single ancestry; * Numbers in parentheses indicate the number of persons reporting this race alone, not in combination with any other race; Please refer to the User Guide for more information.*

Canton

Place Type: City
County: Stark
Population: 73,007

Ancestry	Population	%
Afghan (0)	0	<0.01
African, Sub-Saharan (2,636)	2,852	3.83
African (2,507)	2,713	3.64
Cape Verdean (46)	56	0.08
Ethiopian (0)	0	<0.01
Ghanaian (0)	0	<0.01
Kenyan (0)	0	<0.01
Liberian (38)	38	0.05
Nigerian (0)	0	<0.01
Senegalese (0)	0	<0.01
Sierra Leonean (0)	0	<0.01
Somalian (0)	0	<0.01
South African (45)	45	0.06
Sudanese (0)	0	<0.01
Ugandan (0)	0	<0.01
Zimbabwean (0)	0	<0.01
Other Sub-Saharan African (0)	0	<0.01
Albanian (14)	30	0.04
Alsatian (0)	0	<0.01
American (5,025)	5,025	6.75
Arab (443)	577	0.78
Arab (13)	23	0.03
Egyptian (0)	5	0.01
Iraqi (15)	15	0.02
Jordanian (0)	0	<0.01
Lebanese (278)	358	0.48
Moroccan (0)	0	<0.01
Palestinian (0)	0	<0.01
Syrian (137)	164	0.22
Other Arab (0)	12	0.02
Armenian (9)	35	0.05
Assyrian/Chaldean/Syriac (0)	0	<0.01
Australian (0)	0	<0.01
Austrian (99)	143	0.19
Basque (0)	0	<0.01
Belgian (6)	152	0.20
Brazilian (0)	0	<0.01
British (75)	146	0.20
Bulgarian (11)	11	0.01
Cajun (0)	0	<0.01
Canadian (17)	41	0.06
Carpatho Rusyn (0)	13	0.02
Celtic (0)	39	0.05
Croatian (66)	279	0.37
Cypriot (0)	0	<0.01
Czech (192)	342	0.46
Czechoslovakian (30)	51	0.07
Danish (25)	176	0.24
Dutch (88)	1,441	1.94
Eastern European (0)	0	<0.01
English (1,447)	5,256	7.06
Estonian (0)	0	<0.01
European (341)	358	0.48
Finnish (0)	27	0.04
French, ex. Basque (135)	1,697	2.28
French Canadian (37)	122	0.16
German (5,392)	18,990	25.51
German Russian (0)	0	<0.01
Greek (747)	1,154	1.55
Guyanese (0)	0	<0.01
Hungarian (330)	917	1.23
Icelander (0)	0	<0.01
Iranian (0)	0	<0.01
Irish (2,411)	9,815	13.18
Israeli (0)	0	<0.01
Italian (2,380)	5,958	8.00
Latvian (0)	0	<0.01
Lithuanian (29)	99	0.13
Luxemburger (0)	0	<0.01
Macedonian (0)	0	<0.01
Maltese (0)	0	<0.01
New Zealander (0)	0	<0.01
Northern European (80)	80	0.11
Norwegian (51)	143	0.19
Pennsylvania German (125)	212	0.28
Polish (447)	1,434	1.93
Portuguese (253)	367	0.49
Romanian (171)	682	0.92
Russian (185)	603	0.81
Scandinavian (0)	0	<0.01
Scotch-Irish (392)	1,161	1.56
Scottish (250)	1,294	1.74
Serbian (10)	67	0.09
Slavic (25)	87	0.12
Slovak (197)	577	0.78
Slovene (5)	28	0.04
Soviet Union (0)	0	<0.01
Swedish (57)	420	0.56
Swiss (41)	577	0.78
Turkish (0)	9	0.01
Ukrainian (128)	214	0.29
Welsh (91)	631	0.85
West Indian, ex. Hispanic (22)	32	0.04
Bahamian (16)	16	0.02
Barbadian (0)	0	<0.01
Belizean (0)	0	<0.01
Bermudan (0)	0	<0.01
British West Indian (0)	10	0.01
Dutch West Indian (0)	0	<0.01
Haitian (0)	0	<0.01
Jamaican (6)	6	0.01
Trinidadian/Tobagonian (0)	0	<0.01
U.S. Virgin Islander (0)	0	<0.01
West Indian (0)	0	<0.01
Other West Indian (0)	0	<0.01
Yugoslavian (36)	48	0.06

Hispanic Origin	Population	%
Hispanic or Latino (of any race)	1,899	2.60
Central American, ex. Mexican	348	0.48
Costa Rican	2	<0.01
Guatemalan	138	0.19
Honduran	139	0.19
Nicaraguan	5	0.01
Panamanian	8	0.01
Salvadoran	42	0.06
Other Central American	14	0.02
Cuban	49	0.07
Dominican Republic	27	0.04
Mexican	666	0.91
Puerto Rican	356	0.49
South American	66	0.09
Argentinean	14	0.02
Bolivian	3	<0.01
Chilean	0	<0.01
Colombian	25	0.03
Ecuadorian	6	0.01
Paraguayan	0	<0.01
Peruvian	13	0.02
Uruguayan	1	<0.01
Venezuelan	4	0.01
Other South American	0	<0.01
Other Hispanic or Latino	387	0.53

Race*	Population	%
African-American/Black (17,666)	20,377	27.91
Not Hispanic (17,501)	20,069	27.49
Hispanic (165)	308	0.42
American Indian/Alaska Native (349)	1,243	1.70
Not Hispanic (274)	1,102	1.51
Hispanic (75)	141	0.19
Alaska Athabascan *(Ala. Nat.)* (0)	0	<0.01
Aleut *(Alaska Native)* (0)	0	<0.01
Apache (3)	20	0.03
Arapaho (0)	0	<0.01
Blackfeet (4)	100	0.14
Canadian/French Am. Ind. (2)	5	0.01
Central American Ind. (45)	45	0.06
Cherokee (64)	327	0.45
Cheyenne (2)	5	0.01
Chickasaw (0)	2	<0.01
Chippewa (5)	5	0.01
Choctaw (1)	6	0.01
Colville (0)	0	<0.01
Comanche (1)	5	0.01
Cree (0)	0	<0.01
Creek (4)	5	0.01
Crow (0)	3	<0.01
Delaware (30)	57	0.08
Hopi (1)	4	0.01
Houma (1)	1	<0.01
Inupiat *(Alaska Native)* (1)	2	<0.01
Iroquois (4)	31	0.04
Kiowa (0)	0	<0.01
Lumbee (4)	5	0.01
Menominee (0)	0	<0.01
Mexican American Ind. (19)	24	0.03
Navajo (3)	16	0.02
Osage (0)	0	<0.01
Ottawa (0)	1	<0.01
Paiute (0)	0	<0.01
Pima (0)	0	<0.01
Potawatomi (3)	3	<0.01
Pueblo (1)	1	<0.01
Puget Sound Salish (0)	0	<0.01
Seminole (2)	13	0.02
Shoshone (0)	0	<0.01
Sioux (0)	8	0.01
South American Ind. (0)	4	0.01
Spanish American Ind. (1)	1	<0.01
Tlingit-Haida *(Alaska Native)* (0)	0	<0.01
Tohono O'Odham (0)	0	<0.01
Tsimshian *(Alaska Native)* (0)	0	<0.01
Ute (0)	0	<0.01
Yakama (0)	0	<0.01
Yaqui (0)	0	<0.01
Yuman (1)	5	0.01
Yup'ik *(Alaska Native)* (0)	0	<0.01
Asian (253)	461	0.63
Not Hispanic (243)	442	0.61
Hispanic (10)	19	0.03
Bangladeshi (1)	1	<0.01
Bhutanese (0)	0	<0.01
Burmese (0)	1	<0.01
Cambodian (0)	0	<0.01
Chinese, ex. Taiwanese (55)	78	0.11
Filipino (53)	112	0.15
Hmong (1)	1	<0.01
Indian (43)	58	0.08
Indonesian (0)	0	<0.01
Japanese (22)	60	0.08
Korean (38)	80	0.11
Laotian (2)	2	<0.01
Malaysian (0)	0	<0.01
Nepalese (0)	0	<0.01
Pakistani (1)	1	<0.01
Sri Lankan (1)	1	<0.01
Taiwanese (0)	0	<0.01
Thai (5)	17	0.02
Vietnamese (22)	28	0.04
Hawaii Native/Pacific Islander (35)	93	0.13
Not Hispanic (21)	65	0.09
Hispanic (14)	28	0.04
Fijian (0)	0	<0.01
Guamanian/Chamorro (17)	28	0.04
Marshallese (0)	0	<0.01
Native Hawaiian (8)	32	0.04
Samoan (2)	9	0.01
Tongan (0)	0	<0.01
White (50,458)	53,661	73.50
Not Hispanic (49,591)	52,555	71.99
Hispanic (867)	1,106	1.51

*Notes: † The Census 2010 population figure is used to calculate the percentages in the Hispanic Origin and Race categories. Ancestry percentages are based on the 2006-2010 American Community Survey population (not shown); ‡ Numbers in parentheses indicate the number of people reporting a single ancestry; * Numbers in parentheses indicate the number of persons reporting this race alone, not in combination with any other race; Please refer to the User Guide for more information.*

Cincinnati

Place Type: City
County: Hamilton
Population: 296,943

Ancestry	Population	%
Afghan (0)	0	<0.01
African, Sub-Saharan (16,040)	17,006	5.67
African (14,780)	15,631	5.21
Cape Verdean (0)	0	<0.01
Ethiopian (432)	458	0.15
Ghanaian (23)	23	0.01
Kenyan (12)	12	<0.01
Liberian (26)	26	0.01
Nigerian (158)	158	0.05
Senegalese (144)	195	0.06
Sierra Leonean (0)	0	<0.01
Somalian (0)	0	<0.01
South African (13)	13	<0.01
Sudanese (63)	63	0.02
Ugandan (0)	0	<0.01
Zimbabwean (53)	53	0.02
Other Sub-Saharan African (336)	374	0.12
Albanian (0)	0	<0.01
Alsatian (9)	67	0.02
American (18,156)	18,156	6.05
Arab (941)	1,405	0.47
Arab (142)	199	0.07
Egyptian (107)	133	0.04
Iraqi (14)	14	<0.01
Jordanian (112)	127	0.04
Lebanese (408)	704	0.23
Moroccan (65)	65	0.02
Palestinian (40)	55	0.02
Syrian (0)	38	0.01
Other Arab (53)	70	0.02
Armenian (30)	82	0.03
Assyrian/Chaldean/Syriac (0)	9	<0.01
Australian (45)	50	0.02
Austrian (82)	502	0.17
Basque (0)	0	<0.01
Belgian (48)	185	0.06
Brazilian (16)	23	0.01
British (770)	1,314	0.44
Bulgarian (13)	13	<0.01
Cajun (0)	41	0.01
Canadian (144)	275	0.09
Carpatho Rusyn (0)	0	<0.01
Celtic (0)	29	0.01
Croatian (60)	146	0.05
Cypriot (0)	0	<0.01
Czech (240)	704	0.23
Czechoslovakian (64)	180	0.06
Danish (99)	439	0.15
Dutch (627)	2,867	0.96
Eastern European (147)	172	0.06
English (4,893)	16,011	5.33
Estonian (69)	86	0.03
European (2,291)	2,521	0.84
Finnish (7)	175	0.06
French, ex. Basque (685)	5,247	1.75
French Canadian (127)	503	0.17
German (23,192)	59,441	19.80
German Russian (0)	34	0.01
Greek (499)	840	0.28
Guyanese (77)	77	0.03
Hungarian (350)	1,319	0.44
Icelander (0)	0	<0.01
Iranian (47)	69	0.02
Irish (8,007)	32,799	10.93
Israeli (75)	118	0.04
Italian (3,201)	9,502	3.17
Latvian (36)	67	0.02
Lithuanian (86)	212	0.07
Luxemburger (0)	0	<0.01
Macedonian (13)	46	0.02
Maltese (0)	18	0.01
New Zealander (0)	0	<0.01
Northern European (69)	69	0.02
Norwegian (302)	1,024	0.34
Pennsylvania German (46)	63	0.02
Polish (972)	3,782	1.26
Portuguese (10)	142	0.05
Romanian (46)	356	0.12
Russian (598)	1,528	0.51
Scandinavian (168)	293	0.10
Scotch-Irish (988)	3,249	1.08
Scottish (987)	3,828	1.28
Serbian (10)	10	<0.01
Slavic (9)	63	0.02
Slovak (229)	659	0.22
Slovene (19)	90	0.03
Soviet Union (15)	15	<0.01
Swedish (193)	1,245	0.41
Swiss (128)	796	0.27
Turkish (75)	75	0.02
Ukrainian (128)	313	0.10
Welsh (405)	2,038	0.68
West Indian, ex. Hispanic (270)	478	0.16
Bahamian (33)	33	0.01
Barbadian (0)	0	<0.01
Belizean (0)	0	<0.01
Bermudan (0)	0	<0.01
British West Indian (0)	20	0.01
Dutch West Indian (0)	0	<0.01
Haitian (41)	41	0.01
Jamaican (153)	292	0.10
Trinidadian/Tobagonian (29)	29	0.01
U.S. Virgin Islander (0)	0	<0.01
West Indian (14)	53	0.02
Other West Indian (0)	10	<0.01
Yugoslavian (128)	158	0.05

Hispanic Origin	Population	%
Hispanic or Latino (of any race)	8,308	2.80
Central American, ex. Mexican	1,860	0.63
Costa Rican	39	0.01
Guatemalan	1,257	0.42
Honduran	230	0.08
Nicaraguan	90	0.03
Panamanian	78	0.03
Salvadoran	132	0.04
Other Central American	34	0.01
Cuban	320	0.11
Dominican Republic	119	0.04
Mexican	3,244	1.09
Puerto Rican	973	0.33
South American	668	0.22
Argentinean	83	0.03
Bolivian	14	<0.01
Chilean	50	0.02
Colombian	215	0.07
Ecuadorian	45	0.02
Paraguayan	6	<0.01
Peruvian	138	0.05
Uruguayan	1	<0.01
Venezuelan	107	0.04
Other South American	0	<0.01
Other Hispanic or Latino	1,124	0.38

Race*	Population	%
African-American/Black (133,039)	138,296	46.57
Not Hispanic (132,307)	137,223	46.21
Hispanic (732)	1,073	0.36
American Indian/Alaska Native (759)	2,658	0.90
Not Hispanic (549)	2,276	0.77
Hispanic (210)	382	0.13
Alaska Athabascan *(Ala. Nat.)* (1)	3	<0.01
Aleut *(Alaska Native)* (4)	8	<0.01
Apache (10)	44	0.01
Arapaho (0)	4	<0.01
Blackfeet (16)	160	0.05
Canadian/French Am. Ind. (3)	6	<0.01
Central American Ind. (95)	98	0.03
Cherokee (85)	652	0.22
Cheyenne (0)	0	<0.01
Chickasaw (5)	11	<0.01
Chippewa (13)	29	0.01
Choctaw (6)	26	0.01
Colville (0)	0	<0.01
Comanche (5)	7	<0.01
Cree (0)	6	<0.01
Creek (6)	23	0.01
Crow (0)	5	<0.01
Delaware (2)	5	<0.01
Hopi (0)	0	<0.01
Houma (0)	0	<0.01
Inupiat *(Alaska Native)* (1)	1	<0.01
Iroquois (6)	18	0.01
Kiowa (0)	0	<0.01
Lumbee (4)	4	<0.01
Menominee (1)	1	<0.01
Mexican American Ind. (25)	38	0.01
Navajo (11)	31	0.01
Osage (2)	3	<0.01
Ottawa (0)	1	<0.01
Paiute (0)	0	<0.01
Pima (0)	0	<0.01
Potawatomi (1)	10	<0.01
Pueblo (3)	4	<0.01
Puget Sound Salish (0)	0	<0.01
Seminole (3)	20	0.01
Shoshone (0)	2	<0.01
Sioux (12)	56	0.02
South American Ind. (2)	18	0.01
Spanish American Ind. (6)	6	<0.01
Tlingit-Haida *(Alaska Native)* (0)	0	<0.01
Tohono O'Odham (1)	7	<0.01
Tsimshian *(Alaska Native)* (0)	1	<0.01
Ute (0)	0	<0.01
Yakama (0)	1	<0.01
Yaqui (0)	2	<0.01
Yuman (2)	2	<0.01
Yup'ik *(Alaska Native)* (0)	0	<0.01
Asian (5,481)	6,875	2.32
Not Hispanic (5,434)	6,728	2.27
Hispanic (47)	147	0.05
Bangladeshi (25)	25	0.01
Bhutanese (74)	74	0.02
Burmese (12)	13	<0.01
Cambodian (169)	212	0.07
Chinese, ex. Taiwanese (1,267)	1,558	0.52
Filipino (411)	718	0.24
Hmong (0)	3	<0.01
Indian (1,805)	2,036	0.69
Indonesian (10)	31	0.01
Japanese (222)	399	0.13
Korean (514)	674	0.23
Laotian (9)	14	<0.01
Malaysian (4)	5	<0.01
Nepalese (59)	77	0.03
Pakistani (98)	125	0.04
Sri Lankan (75)	82	0.03
Taiwanese (112)	122	0.04
Thai (108)	143	0.05
Vietnamese (303)	359	0.12
Hawaii Native/Pacific Islander (251)	465	0.16
Not Hispanic (168)	344	0.12
Hispanic (83)	121	0.04
Fijian (1)	1	<0.01
Guamanian/Chamorro (171)	202	0.07
Marshallese (1)	2	<0.01
Native Hawaiian (15)	70	0.02
Samoan (21)	51	0.02
Tongan (0)	0	<0.01
White (146,435)	152,515	51.36
Not Hispanic (142,831)	148,354	49.96
Hispanic (3,604)	4,161	1.40

*Notes: † The Census 2010 population figure is used to calculate the percentages in the Hispanic Origin and Race categories. Ancestry percentages are based on the 2006-2010 American Community Survey population (not shown); ‡ Numbers in parentheses indicate the number of people reporting a single ancestry; * Numbers in parentheses indicate the number of persons reporting this race alone, not in combination with any other race; Please refer to the User Guide for more information.*

Cleveland

Place Type: City
County: Cuyahoga
Population: 396,815

Ancestry	Population	%
Afghan (0)	0	<0.01
African, Sub-Saharan (4,355)	5,454	1.33
African (3,344)	4,279	1.05
Cape Verdean (19)	58	0.01
Ethiopian (21)	21	0.01
Ghanaian (79)	79	0.02
Kenyan (0)	10	<0.01
Liberian (128)	128	0.03
Nigerian (352)	352	0.09
Senegalese (17)	17	<0.01
Sierra Leonean (0)	0	<0.01
Somalian (41)	41	0.01
South African (19)	68	0.02
Sudanese (86)	86	0.02
Ugandan (0)	0	<0.01
Zimbabwean (0)	0	<0.01
Other Sub-Saharan African (249)	315	0.08
Albanian (130)	139	0.03
Alsatian (0)	0	<0.01
American (9,836)	9,836	2.40
Arab (2,382)	3,346	0.82
Arab (466)	663	0.16
Egyptian (318)	326	0.08
Iraqi (85)	85	0.02
Jordanian (115)	115	0.03
Lebanese (551)	1,147	0.28
Moroccan (37)	75	0.02
Palestinian (553)	553	0.14
Syrian (77)	155	0.04
Other Arab (180)	227	0.06
Armenian (61)	91	0.02
Assyrian/Chaldean/Syriac (5)	5	<0.01
Australian (24)	39	0.01
Austrian (85)	589	0.14
Basque (0)	0	<0.01
Belgian (0)	96	0.02
Brazilian (80)	80	0.02
British (102)	474	0.12
Bulgarian (29)	54	0.01
Cajun (29)	29	0.01
Canadian (124)	343	0.08
Carpatho Rusyn (0)	0	<0.01
Celtic (8)	18	<0.01
Croatian (509)	1,547	0.38
Cypriot (0)	0	<0.01
Czech (881)	2,835	0.69
Czechoslovakian (319)	553	0.14
Danish (54)	230	0.06
Dutch (180)	2,881	0.70
Eastern European (140)	140	0.03
English (4,019)	13,765	3.36
Estonian (0)	0	<0.01
European (887)	1,116	0.27
Finnish (79)	376	0.09
French, ex. Basque (428)	4,063	0.99
French Canadian (146)	425	0.10
German (9,110)	40,200	9.82
German Russian (18)	18	<0.01
Greek (536)	1,435	0.35
Guyanese (304)	370	0.09
Hungarian (2,360)	6,822	1.67
Icelander (11)	25	0.01
Iranian (26)	26	0.01
Irish (9,753)	37,296	9.11
Israeli (10)	10	<0.01
Italian (7,160)	19,033	4.65
Latvian (62)	99	0.02
Lithuanian (435)	1,180	0.29
Luxemburger (0)	0	<0.01
Macedonian (0)	10	<0.01
Maltese (0)	0	<0.01
New Zealander (0)	0	<0.01
Northern European (48)	48	0.01
Norwegian (77)	435	0.11
Pennsylvania German (89)	157	0.04
Polish (6,968)	18,227	4.45
Portuguese (73)	277	0.07
Romanian (904)	1,296	0.32
Russian (692)	2,395	0.59
Scandinavian (29)	127	0.03
Scotch-Irish (927)	2,928	0.72
Scottish (682)	3,093	0.76
Serbian (241)	529	0.13
Slavic (72)	232	0.06
Slovak (2,328)	7,074	1.73
Slovene (1,381)	3,214	0.79
Soviet Union (0)	0	<0.01
Swedish (186)	1,163	0.28
Swiss (55)	405	0.10
Turkish (45)	53	0.01
Ukrainian (858)	2,072	0.51
Welsh (131)	1,575	0.38
West Indian, ex. Hispanic (1,118)	1,835	0.45
Bahamian (0)	0	<0.01
Barbadian (0)	0	<0.01
Belizean (0)	16	<0.01
Bermudan (11)	11	<0.01
British West Indian (21)	31	0.01
Dutch West Indian (0)	0	<0.01
Haitian (22)	31	0.01
Jamaican (904)	1,281	0.31
Trinidadian/Tobagonian (45)	94	0.02
U.S. Virgin Islander (7)	7	<0.01
West Indian (108)	364	0.09
Other West Indian (0)	0	<0.01
Yugoslavian (168)	287	0.07

Hispanic Origin	Population	%
Hispanic or Latino (of any race)	39,534	9.96
Central American, ex. Mexican	2,085	0.53
Costa Rican	45	0.01
Guatemalan	786	0.20
Honduran	324	0.08
Nicaraguan	82	0.02
Panamanian	89	0.02
Salvadoran	738	0.19
Other Central American	21	0.01
Cuban	463	0.12
Dominican Republic	1,140	0.29
Mexican	3,593	0.91
Puerto Rican	29,286	7.38
South American	959	0.24
Argentinean	70	0.02
Bolivian	3	<0.01
Chilean	62	0.02
Colombian	320	0.08
Ecuadorian	113	0.03
Paraguayan	8	<0.01
Peruvian	276	0.07
Uruguayan	28	0.01
Venezuelan	54	0.01
Other South American	25	0.01
Other Hispanic or Latino	2,008	0.51

Race*	Population	%
African-American/Black (211,672)	219,027	55.20
Not Hispanic (208,208)	213,920	53.91
Hispanic (3,464)	5,107	1.29
American Indian/Alaska Native (1,340)	4,008	1.01
Not Hispanic (997)	3,202	0.81
Hispanic (343)	806	0.20
Alaska Athabascan *(Ala. Nat.)* (0)	2	<0.01
Aleut *(Alaska Native)* (0)	0	<0.01
Apache (10)	43	0.01
Arapaho (0)	7	<0.01
Blackfeet (39)	240	0.06
Canadian/French Am. Ind. (2)	7	<0.01
Central American Ind. (24)	32	0.01
Cherokee (140)	865	0.22
Cheyenne (5)	7	<0.01
Chickasaw (14)	34	0.01
Chippewa (38)	54	0.01
Choctaw (29)	83	0.02
Colville (1)	3	<0.01
Comanche (1)	3	<0.01
Cree (1)	3	<0.01
Creek (7)	23	0.01
Crow (3)	10	<0.01
Delaware (3)	10	<0.01
Hopi (0)	4	<0.01
Houma (0)	0	<0.01
Inupiat *(Alaska Native)* (3)	6	<0.01
Iroquois (27)	62	0.02
Kiowa (6)	11	<0.01
Lumbee (6)	9	<0.01
Menominee (0)	0	<0.01
Mexican American Ind. (44)	60	0.02
Navajo (16)	31	0.01
Osage (0)	0	<0.01
Ottawa (6)	7	<0.01
Paiute (0)	0	<0.01
Pima (0)	1	<0.01
Potawatomi (1)	4	<0.01
Pueblo (13)	13	<0.01
Puget Sound Salish (0)	0	<0.01
Seminole (9)	30	0.01
Shoshone (3)	4	<0.01
Sioux (34)	91	0.02
South American Ind. (39)	105	0.03
Spanish American Ind. (2)	3	<0.01
Tlingit-Haida *(Alaska Native)* (2)	2	<0.01
Tohono O'Odham (7)	7	<0.01
Tsimshian *(Alaska Native)* (0)	0	<0.01
Ute (0)	0	<0.01
Yakama (0)	0	<0.01
Yaqui (0)	0	<0.01
Yuman (0)	0	<0.01
Yup'ik *(Alaska Native)* (1)	3	<0.01
Asian (7,327)	8,705	2.19
Not Hispanic (7,213)	8,422	2.12
Hispanic (114)	283	0.07
Bangladeshi (8)	11	<0.01
Bhutanese (70)	94	0.02
Burmese (63)	69	0.02
Cambodian (275)	328	0.08
Chinese, ex. Taiwanese (2,620)	2,916	0.73
Filipino (643)	937	0.24
Hmong (2)	7	<0.01
Indian (1,412)	1,649	0.42
Indonesian (18)	25	0.01
Japanese (158)	349	0.09
Korean (418)	533	0.13
Laotian (87)	108	0.03
Malaysian (6)	12	<0.01
Nepalese (79)	108	0.03
Pakistani (55)	61	0.02
Sri Lankan (14)	18	<0.01
Taiwanese (94)	102	0.03
Thai (89)	121	0.03
Vietnamese (882)	990	0.25
Hawaii Native/Pacific Islander (120)	582	0.15
Not Hispanic (70)	347	0.09
Hispanic (50)	235	0.06
Fijian (0)	0	<0.01
Guamanian/Chamorro (47)	73	0.02
Marshallese (0)	0	<0.01
Native Hawaiian (25)	127	0.03
Samoan (7)	24	0.01
Tongan (4)	6	<0.01
White (147,929)	156,136	39.35
Not Hispanic (132,710)	138,590	34.93
Hispanic (15,219)	17,546	4.42

*Notes: † The Census 2010 population figure is used to calculate the percentages in the Hispanic Origin and Race categories. Ancestry percentages are based on the 2006-2010 American Community Survey population (not shown); ‡ Numbers in parentheses indicate the number of people reporting a single ancestry; * Numbers in parentheses indicate the number of persons reporting this race alone, not in combination with any other race; Please refer to the User Guide for more information.*

Columbus

Place Type: City
County: Franklin
Population: 787,033

Ancestry	Population	%
Afghan (67)	89	0.01
African, Sub-Saharan (25,127)	26,987	3.50
African (9,844)	10,986	1.43
Cape Verdean (28)	28	<0.01
Ethiopian (2,080)	2,207	0.29
Ghanaian (1,270)	1,303	0.17
Kenyan (433)	517	0.07
Liberian (376)	384	0.05
Nigerian (703)	861	0.11
Senegalese (104)	104	0.01
Sierra Leonean (433)	461	0.06
Somalian (8,938)	9,093	1.18
South African (97)	115	0.01
Sudanese (53)	90	0.01
Ugandan (0)	0	<0.01
Zimbabwean (125)	125	0.02
Other Sub-Saharan African (643)	713	0.09
Albanian (261)	292	0.04
Alsatian (0)	29	<0.01
American (31,925)	31,925	4.14
Arab (4,438)	6,451	0.84
Arab (974)	1,109	0.14
Egyptian (669)	911	0.12
Iraqi (279)	334	0.04
Jordanian (602)	617	0.08
Lebanese (518)	1,656	0.21
Moroccan (222)	308	0.04
Palestinian (576)	604	0.08
Syrian (163)	415	0.05
Other Arab (435)	497	0.06
Armenian (111)	163	0.02
Assyrian/Chaldean/Syriac (97)	97	0.01
Australian (43)	154	0.02
Austrian (325)	1,440	0.19
Basque (0)	0	<0.01
Belgian (320)	699	0.09
Brazilian (263)	284	0.04
British (1,471)	3,242	0.42
Bulgarian (55)	130	0.02
Cajun (0)	56	0.01
Canadian (509)	1,023	0.13
Carpatho Rusyn (12)	35	<0.01
Celtic (17)	95	0.01
Croatian (428)	1,158	0.15
Cypriot (0)	14	<0.01
Czech (836)	2,996	0.39
Czechoslovakian (251)	819	0.11
Danish (332)	1,200	0.16
Dutch (1,747)	10,822	1.40
Eastern European (701)	867	0.11
English (18,279)	58,155	7.55
Estonian (20)	20	<0.01
European (6,242)	7,099	0.92
Finnish (224)	858	0.11
French, ex. Basque (3,125)	14,605	1.90
French Canadian (763)	1,886	0.24
German (59,347)	163,383	21.21
German Russian (33)	33	<0.01
Greek (1,110)	2,987	0.39
Guyanese (101)	135	0.02
Hungarian (1,716)	6,569	0.85
Icelander (15)	51	0.01
Iranian (408)	466	0.06
Irish (30,407)	99,000	12.85
Israeli (63)	138	0.02
Italian (14,391)	38,883	5.05
Latvian (150)	214	0.03
Lithuanian (193)	1,022	0.13
Luxemburger (14)	23	<0.01
Macedonian (235)	307	0.04
Maltese (0)	29	<0.01
New Zealander (48)	48	0.01
Northern European (188)	220	0.03
Norwegian (1,070)	3,594	0.47
Pennsylvania German (141)	359	0.05
Polish (5,407)	17,936	2.33
Portuguese (819)	1,667	0.22
Romanian (458)	1,256	0.16
Russian (2,348)	5,392	0.70
Scandinavian (453)	1,042	0.14
Scotch-Irish (4,412)	12,017	1.56
Scottish (4,099)	13,797	1.79
Serbian (189)	511	0.07
Slavic (192)	458	0.06
Slovak (1,091)	3,380	0.44
Slovene (592)	1,380	0.18
Soviet Union (0)	0	<0.01
Swedish (985)	4,492	0.58
Swiss (563)	2,745	0.36
Turkish (530)	601	0.08
Ukrainian (989)	1,935	0.25
Welsh (2,202)	10,220	1.33
West Indian, ex. Hispanic (2,879)	3,944	0.51
Bahamian (82)	93	0.01
Barbadian (88)	132	0.02
Belizean (28)	42	0.01
Bermudan (0)	11	<0.01
British West Indian (149)	165	0.02
Dutch West Indian (0)	54	0.01
Haitian (1,450)	1,655	0.21
Jamaican (757)	1,305	0.17
Trinidadian/Tobagonian (68)	103	0.01
U.S. Virgin Islander (15)	27	<0.01
West Indian (242)	357	0.05
Other West Indian (0)	0	<0.01
Yugoslavian (660)	883	0.11

Hispanic Origin	Population	%
Hispanic or Latino (of any race)	44,359	5.64
Central American, ex. Mexican	4,017	0.51
Costa Rican	129	0.02
Guatemalan	645	0.08
Honduran	784	0.10
Nicaraguan	157	0.02
Panamanian	294	0.04
Salvadoran	1,954	0.25
Other Central American	54	0.01
Cuban	922	0.12
Dominican Republic	1,553	0.20
Mexican	25,973	3.30
Puerto Rican	5,034	0.64
South American	2,730	0.35
Argentinean	273	0.03
Bolivian	81	0.01
Chilean	112	0.01
Colombian	797	0.10
Ecuadorian	491	0.06
Paraguayan	9	<0.01
Peruvian	543	0.07
Uruguayan	47	0.01
Venezuelan	355	0.05
Other South American	22	<0.01
Other Hispanic or Latino	4,130	0.52

Race*	Population	%
African-American/Black (220,241)	237,077	30.12
Not Hispanic (217,694)	233,108	29.62
Hispanic (2,547)	3,969	0.50
American Indian/Alaska Native (2,105)	8,353	1.06
Not Hispanic (1,643)	7,286	0.93
Hispanic (462)	1,067	0.14
Alaska Athabascan *(Ala. Nat.)* (8)	11	<0.01
Aleut *(Alaska Native)* (4)	9	<0.01
Apache (21)	109	0.01
Arapaho (0)	3	<0.01
Blackfeet (49)	539	0.07
Canadian/French Am. Ind. (3)	21	<0.01
Central American Ind. (11)	18	<0.01
Cherokee (333)	2,100	0.27
Cheyenne (3)	15	<0.01
Chickasaw (11)	23	<0.01
Chippewa (44)	112	0.01
Choctaw (17)	72	0.01
Colville (0)	1	<0.01
Comanche (3)	17	<0.01
Cree (6)	17	<0.01
Creek (8)	47	0.01
Crow (0)	12	<0.01
Delaware (5)	40	0.01
Hopi (3)	9	<0.01
Houma (0)	0	<0.01
Inupiat *(Alaska Native)* (2)	3	<0.01
Iroquois (50)	126	0.02
Kiowa (0)	1	<0.01
Lumbee (37)	56	0.01
Menominee (3)	3	<0.01
Mexican American Ind. (114)	203	0.03
Navajo (24)	68	0.01
Osage (5)	7	<0.01
Ottawa (6)	13	<0.01
Paiute (1)	1	<0.01
Pima (0)	3	<0.01
Potawatomi (5)	13	<0.01
Pueblo (9)	16	<0.01
Puget Sound Salish (0)	1	<0.01
Seminole (3)	42	0.01
Shoshone (3)	5	<0.01
Sioux (41)	182	0.02
South American Ind. (24)	51	0.01
Spanish American Ind. (14)	18	<0.01
Tlingit-Haida *(Alaska Native)* (9)	10	<0.01
Tohono O'Odham (2)	5	<0.01
Tsimshian *(Alaska Native)* (1)	1	<0.01
Ute (1)	4	<0.01
Yakama (0)	0	<0.01
Yaqui (0)	1	<0.01
Yuman (0)	2	<0.01
Yup'ik *(Alaska Native)* (0)	2	<0.01
Asian (31,965)	37,743	4.80
Not Hispanic (31,734)	37,170	4.72
Hispanic (231)	573	0.07
Bangladeshi (334)	366	0.05
Bhutanese (71)	96	0.01
Burmese (198)	204	0.03
Cambodian (1,521)	1,794	0.23
Chinese, ex. Taiwanese (5,887)	6,780	0.86
Filipino (1,713)	2,827	0.36
Hmong (45)	51	0.01
Indian (10,495)	11,364	1.44
Indonesian (245)	326	0.04
Japanese (1,474)	2,331	0.30
Korean (2,612)	3,330	0.42
Laotian (1,161)	1,412	0.18
Malaysian (92)	121	0.02
Nepalese (163)	190	0.02
Pakistani (787)	927	0.12
Sri Lankan (188)	202	0.03
Taiwanese (535)	626	0.08
Thai (375)	594	0.08
Vietnamese (1,922)	2,319	0.29
Hawaii Native/Pacific Islander (512)	1,346	0.17
Not Hispanic (462)	1,149	0.15
Hispanic (50)	197	0.03
Fijian (4)	7	<0.01
Guamanian/Chamorro (77)	181	0.02
Marshallese (0)	0	<0.01
Native Hawaiian (78)	336	0.04
Samoan (298)	399	0.05
Tongan (0)	2	<0.01
White (483,677)	505,454	64.22
Not Hispanic (466,615)	485,567	61.70
Hispanic (17,062)	19,887	2.53

*Notes: † The Census 2010 population figure is used to calculate the percentages in the Hispanic Origin and Race categories. Ancestry percentages are based on the 2006-2010 American Community Survey population (not shown); ‡ Numbers in parentheses indicate the number of people reporting a single ancestry; * Numbers in parentheses indicate the number of persons reporting this race alone, not in combination with any other race; Please refer to the User Guide for more information.*

Dayton

Place Type: City
County: Montgomery
Population: 141,527

Ancestry	Population	%
Afghan (0)	0	<0.01
African, Sub-Saharan (2,085)	2,395	1.64
African (1,718)	1,956	1.34
Cape Verdean (0)	0	<0.01
Ethiopian (78)	94	0.06
Ghanaian (0)	0	<0.01
Kenyan (10)	10	0.01
Liberian (0)	0	<0.01
Nigerian (104)	138	0.09
Senegalese (0)	0	<0.01
Sierra Leonean (0)	0	<0.01
Somalian (0)	0	<0.01
South African (9)	22	0.02
Sudanese (0)	0	<0.01
Ugandan (0)	0	<0.01
Zimbabwean (0)	0	<0.01
Other Sub-Saharan African (166)	175	0.12
Albanian (0)	0	<0.01
Alsatian (13)	13	0.01
American (16,035)	16,035	11.01
Arab (256)	474	0.33
Arab (39)	39	0.03
Egyptian (28)	46	0.03
Iraqi (123)	123	0.08
Jordanian (0)	39	0.03
Lebanese (51)	184	0.13
Moroccan (0)	28	0.02
Palestinian (15)	15	0.01
Syrian (0)	0	<0.01
Other Arab (0)	0	<0.01
Armenian (0)	0	<0.01
Assyrian/Chaldean/Syriac (0)	0	<0.01
Australian (9)	22	0.02
Austrian (11)	93	0.06
Basque (0)	0	<0.01
Belgian (35)	105	0.07
Brazilian (0)	0	<0.01
British (397)	727	0.50
Bulgarian (62)	125	0.09
Cajun (0)	0	<0.01
Canadian (19)	116	0.08
Carpatho Rusyn (0)	0	<0.01
Celtic (0)	0	<0.01
Croatian (37)	81	0.06
Cypriot (0)	0	<0.01
Czech (69)	231	0.16
Czechoslovakian (27)	179	0.12
Danish (13)	94	0.06
Dutch (260)	1,660	1.14
Eastern European (0)	54	0.04
English (2,681)	7,108	4.88
Estonian (0)	0	<0.01
European (968)	1,113	0.76
Finnish (53)	144	0.10
French, ex. Basque (165)	2,130	1.46
French Canadian (137)	280	0.19
German (8,595)	23,171	15.91
German Russian (0)	0	<0.01
Greek (227)	451	0.31
Guyanese (0)	0	<0.01
Hungarian (312)	792	0.54
Icelander (0)	0	<0.01
Iranian (0)	0	<0.01
Irish (3,119)	14,086	9.67
Israeli (29)	29	0.02
Italian (1,474)	4,059	2.79
Latvian (9)	9	0.01
Lithuanian (47)	244	0.17
Luxemburger (0)	0	<0.01
Macedonian (0)	14	0.01
Maltese (0)	0	<0.01
New Zealander (0)	0	<0.01
Northern European (0)	0	<0.01
Norwegian (78)	346	0.24
Pennsylvania German (21)	80	0.05
Polish (614)	2,017	1.39
Portuguese (0)	45	0.03
Romanian (11)	177	0.12
Russian (121)	358	0.25
Scandinavian (42)	93	0.06
Scotch-Irish (817)	1,768	1.21
Scottish (514)	1,758	1.21
Serbian (7)	30	0.02
Slavic (10)	31	0.02
Slovak (16)	154	0.11
Slovene (14)	132	0.09
Soviet Union (0)	0	<0.01
Swedish (371)	927	0.64
Swiss (84)	346	0.24
Turkish (158)	203	0.14
Ukrainian (79)	150	0.10
Welsh (162)	856	0.59
West Indian, ex. Hispanic (175)	267	0.18
Bahamian (0)	0	<0.01
Barbadian (0)	0	<0.01
Belizean (0)	0	<0.01
Bermudan (0)	0	<0.01
British West Indian (0)	0	<0.01
Dutch West Indian (0)	0	<0.01
Haitian (32)	32	0.02
Jamaican (81)	173	0.12
Trinidadian/Tobagonian (62)	62	0.04
U.S. Virgin Islander (0)	0	<0.01
West Indian (0)	0	<0.01
Other West Indian (0)	0	<0.01
Yugoslavian (28)	28	0.02

Hispanic Origin	Population	%
Hispanic or Latino (of any race)	4,180	2.95
Central American, ex. Mexican	269	0.19
Costa Rican	87	0.06
Guatemalan	51	0.04
Honduran	59	0.04
Nicaraguan	14	0.01
Panamanian	37	0.03
Salvadoran	20	0.01
Other Central American	1	<0.01
Cuban	147	0.10
Dominican Republic	58	0.04
Mexican	2,541	1.80
Puerto Rican	515	0.36
South American	217	0.15
Argentinean	11	0.01
Bolivian	11	0.01
Chilean	8	0.01
Colombian	34	0.02
Ecuadorian	115	0.08
Paraguayan	1	<0.01
Peruvian	25	0.02
Uruguayan	7	<0.01
Venezuelan	5	<0.01
Other South American	0	<0.01
Other Hispanic or Latino	433	0.31

Race*	Population	%
African-American/Black (60,705)	63,535	44.89
Not Hispanic (60,342)	62,972	44.49
Hispanic (363)	563	0.40
American Indian/Alaska Native (417)	1,579	1.12
Not Hispanic (373)	1,460	1.03
Hispanic (44)	119	0.08
Alaska Athabascan *(Ala. Nat.)* (0)	0	<0.01
Aleut *(Alaska Native)* (4)	4	<0.01
Apache (5)	18	0.01
Arapaho (3)	10	0.01
Blackfeet (19)	100	0.07
Canadian/French Am. Ind. (0)	1	<0.01
Central American Ind. (1)	1	<0.01
Cherokee (90)	435	0.31
Cheyenne (0)	4	<0.01
Chickasaw (0)	1	<0.01
Chippewa (9)	23	0.02
Choctaw (1)	9	0.01
Colville (0)	0	<0.01
Comanche (1)	2	<0.01
Cree (0)	0	<0.01
Creek (6)	17	0.01
Crow (0)	0	<0.01
Delaware (0)	1	<0.01
Hopi (0)	1	<0.01
Houma (0)	0	<0.01
Inupiat *(Alaska Native)* (0)	0	<0.01
Iroquois (4)	19	0.01
Kiowa (0)	0	<0.01
Lumbee (1)	2	<0.01
Menominee (1)	6	<0.01
Mexican American Ind. (7)	12	0.01
Navajo (3)	13	0.01
Osage (0)	1	<0.01
Ottawa (2)	6	<0.01
Paiute (0)	0	<0.01
Pima (1)	2	<0.01
Potawatomi (2)	3	<0.01
Pueblo (0)	5	<0.01
Puget Sound Salish (0)	2	<0.01
Seminole (2)	10	0.01
Shoshone (1)	1	<0.01
Sioux (10)	31	0.02
South American Ind. (1)	5	<0.01
Spanish American Ind. (2)	2	<0.01
Tlingit-Haida *(Alaska Native)* (0)	0	<0.01
Tohono O'Odham (0)	0	<0.01
Tsimshian *(Alaska Native)* (0)	0	<0.01
Ute (0)	4	<0.01
Yakama (0)	0	<0.01
Yaqui (0)	0	<0.01
Yuman (0)	0	<0.01
Yup'ik *(Alaska Native)* (0)	0	<0.01
Asian (1,206)	1,864	1.32
Not Hispanic (1,195)	1,813	1.28
Hispanic (11)	51	0.04
Bangladeshi (3)	8	0.01
Bhutanese (0)	0	<0.01
Burmese (2)	2	<0.01
Cambodian (43)	59	0.04
Chinese, ex. Taiwanese (252)	324	0.23
Filipino (196)	334	0.24
Hmong (0)	0	<0.01
Indian (220)	281	0.20
Indonesian (5)	16	0.01
Japanese (51)	147	0.10
Korean (96)	184	0.13
Laotian (0)	1	<0.01
Malaysian (9)	9	0.01
Nepalese (4)	4	<0.01
Pakistani (24)	30	0.02
Sri Lankan (8)	9	0.01
Taiwanese (10)	12	0.01
Thai (30)	54	0.04
Vietnamese (188)	220	0.16
Hawaii Native/Pacific Islander (52)	166	0.12
Not Hispanic (47)	148	0.10
Hispanic (5)	18	0.01
Fijian (0)	0	<0.01
Guamanian/Chamorro (7)	31	0.02
Marshallese (0)	4	<0.01
Native Hawaiian (17)	57	0.04
Samoan (15)	34	0.02
Tongan (0)	2	<0.01
White (73,193)	76,680	54.18
Not Hispanic (71,458)	74,600	52.71
Hispanic (1,735)	2,080	1.47

*Notes: † The Census 2010 population figure is used to calculate the percentages in the Hispanic Origin and Race categories. Ancestry percentages are based on the 2006-2010 American Community Survey population (not shown); ‡ Numbers in parentheses indicate the number of people reporting a single ancestry; * Numbers in parentheses indicate the number of persons reporting this race alone, not in combination with any other race; Please refer to the User Guide for more information.*

Elyria

Place Type: City
County: Lorain
Population: 54,533

Ancestry	Population	%
Afghan (0)	0	<0.01
African, Sub-Saharan (102)	138	0.25
African (29)	65	0.12
Cape Verdean (0)	0	<0.01
Ethiopian (0)	0	<0.01
Ghanaian (0)	0	<0.01
Kenyan (18)	18	0.03
Liberian (0)	0	<0.01
Nigerian (0)	0	<0.01
Senegalese (0)	0	<0.01
Sierra Leonean (0)	0	<0.01
Somalian (0)	0	<0.01
South African (0)	0	<0.01
Sudanese (55)	55	0.10
Ugandan (0)	0	<0.01
Zimbabwean (0)	0	<0.01
Other Sub-Saharan African (0)	0	<0.01
Albanian (0)	0	<0.01
Alsatian (0)	0	<0.01
American (5,042)	5,042	9.17
Arab (31)	112	0.20
Arab (1)	1	<0.01
Egyptian (0)	0	<0.01
Iraqi (0)	0	<0.01
Jordanian (30)	30	0.05
Lebanese (0)	72	0.13
Moroccan (0)	0	<0.01
Palestinian (0)	0	<0.01
Syrian (0)	9	0.02
Other Arab (0)	0	<0.01
Armenian (0)	10	0.02
Assyrian/Chaldean/Syriac (0)	0	<0.01
Australian (0)	0	<0.01
Austrian (30)	154	0.28
Basque (0)	0	<0.01
Belgian (0)	21	0.04
Brazilian (0)	0	<0.01
British (72)	137	0.25
Bulgarian (0)	0	<0.01
Cajun (0)	0	<0.01
Canadian (11)	100	0.18
Carpatho Rusyn (0)	0	<0.01
Celtic (0)	0	<0.01
Croatian (33)	123	0.22
Cypriot (0)	0	<0.01
Czech (85)	556	1.01
Czechoslovakian (26)	312	0.57
Danish (39)	183	0.33
Dutch (123)	1,082	1.97
Eastern European (31)	31	0.06
English (1,799)	6,659	12.11
Estonian (0)	0	<0.01
European (78)	88	0.16
Finnish (6)	36	0.07
French, ex. Basque (74)	896	1.63
French Canadian (78)	376	0.68
German (3,671)	13,579	24.69
German Russian (0)	0	<0.01
Greek (203)	317	0.58
Guyanese (0)	0	<0.01
Hungarian (968)	2,358	4.29
Icelander (0)	0	<0.01
Iranian (0)	0	<0.01
Irish (1,823)	8,207	14.92
Israeli (0)	0	<0.01
Italian (1,155)	3,507	6.38
Latvian (0)	0	<0.01
Lithuanian (64)	132	0.24
Luxemburger (0)	0	<0.01
Macedonian (74)	95	0.17
Maltese (0)	0	<0.01
New Zealander (0)	0	<0.01
Northern European (0)	28	0.05
Norwegian (52)	234	0.43
Pennsylvania German (68)	68	0.12
Polish (1,483)	4,359	7.93
Portuguese (8)	58	0.11
Romanian (89)	165	0.30
Russian (131)	599	1.09
Scandinavian (20)	20	0.04
Scotch-Irish (311)	730	1.33
Scottish (316)	1,571	2.86
Serbian (8)	57	0.10
Slavic (0)	43	0.08
Slovak (531)	1,549	2.82
Slovene (57)	165	0.30
Soviet Union (0)	0	<0.01
Swedish (196)	509	0.93
Swiss (32)	318	0.58
Turkish (0)	0	<0.01
Ukrainian (6)	229	0.42
Welsh (149)	612	1.11
West Indian, ex. Hispanic (10)	22	0.04
Bahamian (0)	0	<0.01
Barbadian (0)	0	<0.01
Belizean (0)	0	<0.01
Bermudan (0)	0	<0.01
British West Indian (0)	0	<0.01
Dutch West Indian (0)	0	<0.01
Haitian (0)	0	<0.01
Jamaican (10)	22	0.04
Trinidadian/Tobagonian (0)	0	<0.01
U.S. Virgin Islander (0)	0	<0.01
West Indian (0)	0	<0.01
Other West Indian (0)	0	<0.01
Yugoslavian (11)	41	0.07

Hispanic Origin	Population	%
Hispanic or Latino (of any race)	2,649	4.86
Central American, ex. Mexican	34	0.06
Costa Rican	3	0.01
Guatemalan	16	0.03
Honduran	3	0.01
Nicaraguan	1	<0.01
Panamanian	3	0.01
Salvadoran	7	0.01
Other Central American	1	<0.01
Cuban	28	0.05
Dominican Republic	18	0.03
Mexican	578	1.06
Puerto Rican	1,719	3.15
South American	50	0.09
Argentinean	2	<0.01
Bolivian	1	<0.01
Chilean	3	0.01
Colombian	16	0.03
Ecuadorian	8	0.01
Paraguayan	0	<0.01
Peruvian	13	0.02
Uruguayan	0	<0.01
Venezuelan	5	0.01
Other South American	2	<0.01
Other Hispanic or Latino	222	0.41

Race*	Population	%
African-American/Black (8,441)	10,098	18.52
Not Hispanic (8,161)	9,622	17.64
Hispanic (280)	476	0.87
American Indian/Alaska Native (162)	631	1.16
Not Hispanic (131)	531	0.97
Hispanic (31)	100	0.18
Alaska Athabascan *(Ala. Nat.)* (0)	0	<0.01
Aleut *(Alaska Native)* (1)	1	<0.01
Apache (0)	6	0.01
Arapaho (1)	1	<0.01
Blackfeet (7)	44	0.08
Canadian/French Am. Ind. (0)	0	<0.01
Central American Ind. (0)	0	<0.01
Cherokee (32)	197	0.36
Cheyenne (0)	4	0.01
Chickasaw (0)	3	0.01
Chippewa (7)	11	0.02
Choctaw (0)	3	0.01
Colville (0)	0	<0.01
Comanche (0)	0	<0.01
Cree (0)	0	<0.01
Creek (0)	0	<0.01
Crow (0)	0	<0.01
Delaware (0)	1	<0.01
Hopi (0)	0	<0.01
Houma (0)	0	<0.01
Inupiat *(Alaska Native)* (0)	1	<0.01
Iroquois (7)	17	0.03
Kiowa (0)	0	<0.01
Lumbee (5)	8	0.01
Menominee (0)	0	<0.01
Mexican American Ind. (3)	4	0.01
Navajo (0)	6	0.01
Osage (0)	1	<0.01
Ottawa (0)	0	<0.01
Paiute (0)	1	<0.01
Pima (0)	0	<0.01
Potawatomi (1)	2	<0.01
Pueblo (1)	1	<0.01
Puget Sound Salish (0)	1	<0.01
Seminole (3)	4	0.01
Shoshone (0)	0	<0.01
Sioux (4)	11	0.02
South American Ind. (3)	3	0.01
Spanish American Ind. (0)	0	<0.01
Tlingit-Haida *(Alaska Native)* (0)	0	<0.01
Tohono O'Odham (0)	0	<0.01
Tsimshian *(Alaska Native)* (0)	0	<0.01
Ute (0)	0	<0.01
Yakama (0)	0	<0.01
Yaqui (0)	0	<0.01
Yuman (0)	0	<0.01
Yup'ik *(Alaska Native)* (0)	0	<0.01
Asian (435)	628	1.15
Not Hispanic (421)	590	1.08
Hispanic (14)	38	0.07
Bangladeshi (0)	0	<0.01
Bhutanese (0)	0	<0.01
Burmese (0)	0	<0.01
Cambodian (0)	1	<0.01
Chinese, ex. Taiwanese (60)	78	0.14
Filipino (185)	273	0.50
Hmong (0)	0	<0.01
Indian (70)	88	0.16
Indonesian (1)	2	<0.01
Japanese (16)	33	0.06
Korean (39)	76	0.14
Laotian (0)	0	<0.01
Malaysian (2)	2	<0.01
Nepalese (0)	0	<0.01
Pakistani (6)	7	0.01
Sri Lankan (2)	8	0.01
Taiwanese (3)	3	0.01
Thai (6)	13	0.02
Vietnamese (25)	31	0.06
Hawaii Native/Pacific Islander (4)	65	0.12
Not Hispanic (3)	45	0.08
Hispanic (1)	20	0.04
Fijian (0)	0	<0.01
Guamanian/Chamorro (2)	13	0.02
Marshallese (0)	0	<0.01
Native Hawaiian (1)	16	0.03
Samoan (1)	5	0.01
Tongan (0)	0	<0.01
White (42,601)	44,643	81.86
Not Hispanic (41,226)	42,979	78.81
Hispanic (1,375)	1,664	3.05

*Notes: † The Census 2010 population figure is used to calculate the percentages in the Hispanic Origin and Race categories. Ancestry percentages are based on the 2006-2010 American Community Survey population (not shown); ‡ Numbers in parentheses indicate the number of people reporting a single ancestry; * Numbers in parentheses indicate the number of persons reporting this race alone, not in combination with any other race; Please refer to the User Guide for more information.*

Hamilton

Place Type: City
County: Butler
Population: 62,477

Ancestry	Population	%
Afghan (0)	0	<0.01
African, Sub-Saharan (289)	348	0.56
African (289)	348	0.56
Cape Verdean (0)	0	<0.01
Ethiopian (0)	0	<0.01
Ghanaian (0)	0	<0.01
Kenyan (0)	0	<0.01
Liberian (0)	0	<0.01
Nigerian (0)	0	<0.01
Senegalese (0)	0	<0.01
Sierra Leonean (0)	0	<0.01
Somalian (0)	0	<0.01
South African (0)	0	<0.01
Sudanese (0)	0	<0.01
Ugandan (0)	0	<0.01
Zimbabwean (0)	0	<0.01
Other Sub-Saharan African (0)	0	<0.01
Albanian (0)	0	<0.01
Alsatian (0)	0	<0.01
American (15,067)	15,067	24.12
Arab (81)	81	0.13
Arab (0)	0	<0.01
Egyptian (0)	0	<0.01
Iraqi (8)	8	0.01
Jordanian (58)	58	0.09
Lebanese (0)	0	<0.01
Moroccan (0)	0	<0.01
Palestinian (0)	0	<0.01
Syrian (0)	0	<0.01
Other Arab (15)	15	0.02
Armenian (0)	0	<0.01
Assyrian/Chaldean/Syriac (0)	0	<0.01
Australian (0)	10	0.02
Austrian (49)	93	0.15
Basque (0)	0	<0.01
Belgian (0)	16	0.03
Brazilian (0)	0	<0.01
British (139)	270	0.43
Bulgarian (0)	0	<0.01
Cajun (0)	0	<0.01
Canadian (0)	0	<0.01
Carpatho Rusyn (0)	0	<0.01
Celtic (0)	0	<0.01
Croatian (0)	0	<0.01
Cypriot (0)	0	<0.01
Czech (10)	114	0.18
Czechoslovakian (0)	36	0.06
Danish (48)	48	0.08
Dutch (179)	873	1.40
Eastern European (24)	24	0.04
English (1,890)	4,631	7.41
Estonian (0)	0	<0.01
European (327)	357	0.57
Finnish (0)	49	0.08
French, ex. Basque (188)	844	1.35
French Canadian (9)	19	0.03
German (6,035)	13,275	21.25
German Russian (0)	0	<0.01
Greek (26)	71	0.11
Guyanese (0)	0	<0.01
Hungarian (64)	193	0.31
Icelander (0)	0	<0.01
Iranian (0)	0	<0.01
Irish (1,930)	6,846	10.96
Israeli (0)	0	<0.01
Italian (1,003)	2,251	3.60
Latvian (0)	0	<0.01
Lithuanian (16)	16	0.03
Luxemburger (0)	0	<0.01
Macedonian (0)	0	<0.01
Maltese (0)	0	<0.01
New Zealander (0)	8	0.01
Northern European (28)	28	0.04
Norwegian (139)	199	0.32
Pennsylvania German (24)	24	0.04
Polish (70)	477	0.76
Portuguese (0)	18	0.03
Romanian (0)	34	0.05
Russian (45)	206	0.33
Scandinavian (0)	0	<0.01
Scotch-Irish (276)	655	1.05
Scottish (239)	801	1.28
Serbian (0)	0	<0.01
Slavic (8)	8	0.01
Slovak (33)	59	0.09
Slovene (0)	0	<0.01
Soviet Union (0)	0	<0.01
Swedish (28)	142	0.23
Swiss (160)	202	0.32
Turkish (0)	0	<0.01
Ukrainian (47)	47	0.08
Welsh (52)	242	0.39
West Indian, ex. Hispanic (29)	29	0.05
Bahamian (0)	0	<0.01
Barbadian (0)	0	<0.01
Belizean (0)	0	<0.01
Bermudan (0)	0	<0.01
British West Indian (0)	0	<0.01
Dutch West Indian (0)	0	<0.01
Haitian (0)	0	<0.01
Jamaican (17)	17	0.03
Trinidadian/Tobagonian (12)	12	0.02
U.S. Virgin Islander (0)	0	<0.01
West Indian (0)	0	<0.01
Other West Indian (0)	0	<0.01
Yugoslavian (0)	15	0.02

Hispanic Origin	Population	%
Hispanic or Latino (of any race)	3,981	6.37
Central American, ex. Mexican	166	0.27
Costa Rican	3	<0.01
Guatemalan	41	0.07
Honduran	64	0.10
Nicaraguan	2	<0.01
Panamanian	3	<0.01
Salvadoran	50	0.08
Other Central American	3	<0.01
Cuban	48	0.08
Dominican Republic	300	0.48
Mexican	2,897	4.64
Puerto Rican	209	0.33
South American	60	0.10
Argentinean	4	0.01
Bolivian	2	<0.01
Chilean	3	<0.01
Colombian	18	0.03
Ecuadorian	5	0.01
Paraguayan	4	0.01
Peruvian	20	0.03
Uruguayan	0	<0.01
Venezuelan	3	<0.01
Other South American	1	<0.01
Other Hispanic or Latino	301	0.48

Race*	Population	%
African-American/Black (5,336)	6,394	10.23
Not Hispanic (5,232)	6,226	9.97
Hispanic (104)	168	0.27
American Indian/Alaska Native (150)	518	0.83
Not Hispanic (113)	451	0.72
Hispanic (37)	67	0.11
Alaska Athabascan *(Ala. Nat.)* (0)	0	<0.01
Aleut *(Alaska Native)* (1)	4	0.01
Apache (1)	6	0.01
Arapaho (0)	1	<0.01
Blackfeet (1)	16	0.03
Canadian/French Am. Ind. (0)	0	<0.01
Central American Ind. (1)	1	<0.01
Cherokee (33)	172	0.28
Cheyenne (1)	2	<0.01
Chickasaw (0)	1	<0.01
Chippewa (0)	4	0.01
Choctaw (6)	6	0.01
Colville (0)	0	<0.01
Comanche (1)	2	<0.01
Cree (2)	2	<0.01
Creek (0)	6	0.01
Crow (0)	0	<0.01
Delaware (0)	0	<0.01
Hopi (0)	0	<0.01
Houma (0)	0	<0.01
Inupiat *(Alaska Native)* (0)	0	<0.01
Iroquois (2)	11	0.02
Kiowa (0)	2	<0.01
Lumbee (0)	0	<0.01
Menominee (0)	0	<0.01
Mexican American Ind. (10)	11	0.02
Navajo (2)	4	0.01
Osage (0)	0	<0.01
Ottawa (0)	0	<0.01
Paiute (0)	0	<0.01
Pima (0)	0	<0.01
Potawatomi (0)	0	<0.01
Pueblo (0)	0	<0.01
Puget Sound Salish (0)	0	<0.01
Seminole (2)	3	<0.01
Shoshone (0)	0	<0.01
Sioux (3)	14	0.02
South American Ind. (1)	5	0.01
Spanish American Ind. (3)	3	<0.01
Tlingit-Haida *(Alaska Native)* (0)	0	<0.01
Tohono O'Odham (0)	0	<0.01
Tsimshian *(Alaska Native)* (0)	0	<0.01
Ute (0)	0	<0.01
Yakama (0)	5	0.01
Yaqui (0)	1	<0.01
Yuman (0)	0	<0.01
Yup'ik *(Alaska Native)* (0)	0	<0.01
Asian (384)	576	0.92
Not Hispanic (379)	552	0.88
Hispanic (5)	24	0.04
Bangladeshi (0)	0	<0.01
Bhutanese (0)	0	<0.01
Burmese (0)	0	<0.01
Cambodian (9)	12	0.02
Chinese, ex. Taiwanese (48)	65	0.10
Filipino (118)	164	0.26
Hmong (0)	0	<0.01
Indian (50)	73	0.12
Indonesian (7)	11	0.02
Japanese (23)	52	0.08
Korean (20)	56	0.09
Laotian (0)	0	<0.01
Malaysian (0)	0	<0.01
Nepalese (3)	3	<0.01
Pakistani (2)	9	0.01
Sri Lankan (0)	1	<0.01
Taiwanese (1)	1	<0.01
Thai (5)	19	0.03
Vietnamese (83)	98	0.16
Hawaii Native/Pacific Islander (46)	104	0.17
Not Hispanic (40)	82	0.13
Hispanic (6)	22	0.04
Fijian (0)	0	<0.01
Guamanian/Chamorro (18)	30	0.05
Marshallese (0)	5	0.01
Native Hawaiian (8)	22	0.04
Samoan (2)	9	0.01
Tongan (6)	7	0.01
White (52,487)	54,183	86.72
Not Hispanic (51,198)	52,579	84.16
Hispanic (1,289)	1,604	2.57

*Notes: † The Census 2010 population figure is used to calculate the percentages in the Hispanic Origin and Race categories. Ancestry percentages are based on the 2006-2010 American Community Survey population (not shown); ‡ Numbers in parentheses indicate the number of people reporting a single ancestry; * Numbers in parentheses indicate the number of persons reporting this race alone, not in combination with any other race; Please refer to the User Guide for more information.*

Kettering

Place Type: City
County: Montgomery
Population: 56,163

Ancestry	Population	%
Afghan (0)	0	<0.01
African, Sub-Saharan (11)	42	0.07
African (0)	31	0.06
Cape Verdean (0)	0	<0.01
Ethiopian (0)	0	<0.01
Ghanaian (0)	0	<0.01
Kenyan (0)	0	<0.01
Liberian (0)	0	<0.01
Nigerian (0)	0	<0.01
Senegalese (0)	0	<0.01
Sierra Leonean (0)	0	<0.01
Somalian (0)	0	<0.01
South African (0)	0	<0.01
Sudanese (0)	0	<0.01
Ugandan (0)	0	<0.01
Zimbabwean (0)	0	<0.01
Other Sub-Saharan African (11)	11	0.02
Albanian (15)	15	0.03
Alsatian (0)	13	0.02
American (4,961)	4,961	8.83
Arab (345)	458	0.82
Arab (0)	11	0.02
Egyptian (10)	10	0.02
Iraqi (0)	0	<0.01
Jordanian (78)	78	0.14
Lebanese (184)	251	0.45
Moroccan (0)	0	<0.01
Palestinian (0)	0	<0.01
Syrian (56)	81	0.14
Other Arab (17)	27	0.05
Armenian (0)	0	<0.01
Assyrian/Chaldean/Syriac (0)	0	<0.01
Australian (0)	4	0.01
Austrian (36)	160	0.28
Basque (0)	0	<0.01
Belgian (19)	63	0.11
Brazilian (59)	59	0.11
British (119)	352	0.63
Bulgarian (0)	0	<0.01
Cajun (31)	66	0.12
Canadian (28)	58	0.10
Carpatho Rusyn (0)	0	<0.01
Celtic (0)	0	<0.01
Croatian (13)	58	0.10
Cypriot (0)	0	<0.01
Czech (53)	220	0.39
Czechoslovakian (36)	136	0.24
Danish (20)	174	0.31
Dutch (254)	1,420	2.53
Eastern European (95)	104	0.19
English (2,059)	6,441	11.46
Estonian (0)	39	0.07
European (633)	692	1.23
Finnish (23)	84	0.15
French, ex. Basque (480)	2,149	3.83
French Canadian (69)	237	0.42
German (8,550)	20,845	37.10
German Russian (0)	0	<0.01
Greek (100)	224	0.40
Guyanese (0)	0	<0.01
Hungarian (298)	714	1.27
Icelander (0)	0	<0.01
Iranian (9)	9	0.02
Irish (2,170)	9,275	16.51
Israeli (0)	0	<0.01
Italian (1,188)	2,845	5.06
Latvian (0)	0	<0.01
Lithuanian (46)	202	0.36
Luxemburger (0)	0	<0.01
Macedonian (0)	0	<0.01
Maltese (0)	0	<0.01
New Zealander (0)	0	<0.01
Northern European (18)	18	0.03
Norwegian (112)	264	0.47
Pennsylvania German (81)	118	0.21
Polish (395)	1,457	2.59
Portuguese (8)	22	0.04
Romanian (55)	70	0.12
Russian (91)	238	0.42
Scandinavian (42)	120	0.21
Scotch-Irish (467)	1,103	1.96
Scottish (452)	1,568	2.79
Serbian (0)	12	0.02
Slavic (0)	15	0.03
Slovak (51)	208	0.37
Slovene (11)	41	0.07
Soviet Union (0)	0	<0.01
Swedish (77)	648	1.15
Swiss (63)	263	0.47
Turkish (0)	0	<0.01
Ukrainian (55)	157	0.28
Welsh (170)	757	1.35
West Indian, ex. Hispanic (8)	74	0.13
Bahamian (0)	0	<0.01
Barbadian (0)	0	<0.01
Belizean (0)	0	<0.01
Bermudan (0)	0	<0.01
British West Indian (0)	0	<0.01
Dutch West Indian (0)	0	<0.01
Haitian (0)	9	0.02
Jamaican (8)	8	0.01
Trinidadian/Tobagonian (0)	0	<0.01
U.S. Virgin Islander (0)	0	<0.01
West Indian (0)	57	0.10
Other West Indian (0)	0	<0.01
Yugoslavian (60)	81	0.14

Hispanic Origin	Population	%
Hispanic or Latino (of any race)	1,178	2.10
Central American, ex. Mexican	116	0.21
Costa Rican	29	0.05
Guatemalan	28	0.05
Honduran	11	0.02
Nicaraguan	5	0.01
Panamanian	28	0.05
Salvadoran	15	0.03
Other Central American	0	<0.01
Cuban	84	0.15
Dominican Republic	7	0.01
Mexican	542	0.97
Puerto Rican	151	0.27
South American	125	0.22
Argentinean	7	0.01
Bolivian	13	0.02
Chilean	5	0.01
Colombian	44	0.08
Ecuadorian	18	0.03
Paraguayan	3	0.01
Peruvian	15	0.03
Uruguayan	3	0.01
Venezuelan	15	0.03
Other South American	2	<0.01
Other Hispanic or Latino	153	0.27

Race*	Population	%
African-American/Black (1,840)	2,386	4.25
Not Hispanic (1,806)	2,323	4.14
Hispanic (34)	63	0.11
American Indian/Alaska Native (106)	414	0.74
Not Hispanic (98)	382	0.68
Hispanic (8)	32	0.06
Alaska Athabascan *(Ala. Nat.)* (0)	0	<0.01
Aleut *(Alaska Native)* (0)	1	<0.01
Apache (1)	5	0.01
Arapaho (0)	0	<0.01
Blackfeet (4)	15	0.03
Canadian/French Am. Ind. (2)	2	<0.01
Central American Ind. (0)	0	<0.01
Cherokee (18)	134	0.24
Cheyenne (0)	0	<0.01
Chickasaw (0)	0	<0.01
Chippewa (4)	8	0.01
Choctaw (3)	5	0.01
Colville (0)	0	<0.01
Comanche (1)	1	<0.01
Cree (0)	0	<0.01
Creek (4)	8	0.01
Crow (0)	1	<0.01
Delaware (0)	0	<0.01
Hopi (0)	0	<0.01
Houma (0)	0	<0.01
Inupiat *(Alaska Native)* (1)	1	<0.01
Iroquois (1)	2	<0.01
Kiowa (0)	0	<0.01
Lumbee (1)	1	<0.01
Menominee (0)	0	<0.01
Mexican American Ind. (0)	1	<0.01
Navajo (3)	6	0.01
Osage (0)	0	<0.01
Ottawa (1)	1	<0.01
Paiute (0)	0	<0.01
Pima (0)	0	<0.01
Potawatomi (0)	0	<0.01
Pueblo (0)	0	<0.01
Puget Sound Salish (0)	0	<0.01
Seminole (0)	1	<0.01
Shoshone (0)	0	<0.01
Sioux (4)	14	0.02
South American Ind. (0)	6	0.01
Spanish American Ind. (0)	3	0.01
Tlingit-Haida *(Alaska Native)* (0)	0	<0.01
Tohono O'Odham (0)	0	<0.01
Tsimshian *(Alaska Native)* (0)	0	<0.01
Ute (1)	1	<0.01
Yakama (0)	0	<0.01
Yaqui (0)	0	<0.01
Yuman (1)	1	<0.01
Yup'ik *(Alaska Native)* (0)	0	<0.01
Asian (752)	1,101	1.96
Not Hispanic (745)	1,080	1.92
Hispanic (7)	21	0.04
Bangladeshi (1)	3	0.01
Bhutanese (0)	0	<0.01
Burmese (7)	7	0.01
Cambodian (20)	23	0.04
Chinese, ex. Taiwanese (161)	197	0.35
Filipino (120)	213	0.38
Hmong (0)	0	<0.01
Indian (148)	182	0.32
Indonesian (2)	13	0.02
Japanese (55)	119	0.21
Korean (58)	124	0.22
Laotian (7)	7	0.01
Malaysian (3)	3	0.01
Nepalese (0)	0	<0.01
Pakistani (14)	21	0.04
Sri Lankan (2)	2	<0.01
Taiwanese (13)	15	0.03
Thai (13)	26	0.05
Vietnamese (96)	116	0.21
Hawaii Native/Pacific Islander (12)	46	0.08
Not Hispanic (12)	45	0.08
Hispanic (0)	1	<0.01
Fijian (0)	0	<0.01
Guamanian/Chamorro (2)	6	0.01
Marshallese (0)	0	<0.01
Native Hawaiian (5)	15	0.03
Samoan (2)	4	0.01
Tongan (0)	0	<0.01
White (51,982)	53,090	94.53
Not Hispanic (51,191)	52,203	92.95
Hispanic (791)	887	1.58

*Notes: † The Census 2010 population figure is used to calculate the percentages in the Hispanic Origin and Race categories. Ancestry percentages are based on the 2006-2010 American Community Survey population (not shown); ‡ Numbers in parentheses indicate the number of people reporting a single ancestry; * Numbers in parentheses indicate the number of persons reporting this race alone, not in combination with any other race; Please refer to the User Guide for more information.*

Lakewood

Place Type: City
County: Cuyahoga
Population: 52,131

Ancestry	Population	%
Afghan (0)	0	<0.01
African, Sub-Saharan (363)	406	0.77
African (159)	169	0.32
Cape Verdean (0)	0	<0.01
Ethiopian (0)	0	<0.01
Ghanaian (67)	67	0.13
Kenyan (13)	13	0.02
Liberian (0)	0	<0.01
Nigerian (19)	52	0.10
Senegalese (0)	0	<0.01
Sierra Leonean (0)	0	<0.01
Somalian (0)	0	<0.01
South African (0)	0	<0.01
Sudanese (23)	23	0.04
Ugandan (9)	9	0.02
Zimbabwean (0)	0	<0.01
Other Sub-Saharan African (73)	73	0.14
Albanian (741)	766	1.45
Alsatian (0)	0	<0.01
American (1,234)	1,234	2.34
Arab (997)	1,450	2.75
Arab (151)	218	0.41
Egyptian (172)	172	0.33
Iraqi (0)	0	<0.01
Jordanian (0)	0	<0.01
Lebanese (360)	706	1.34
Moroccan (0)	0	<0.01
Palestinian (105)	116	0.22
Syrian (207)	213	0.40
Other Arab (2)	25	0.05
Armenian (13)	29	0.06
Assyrian/Chaldean/Syriac (0)	0	<0.01
Australian (0)	10	0.02
Austrian (22)	233	0.44
Basque (0)	0	<0.01
Belgian (24)	53	0.10
Brazilian (0)	21	0.04
British (64)	313	0.59
Bulgarian (23)	23	0.04
Cajun (0)	0	<0.01
Canadian (0)	16	0.03
Carpatho Rusyn (12)	25	0.05
Celtic (0)	0	<0.01
Croatian (108)	563	1.07
Cypriot (12)	12	0.02
Czech (240)	758	1.44
Czechoslovakian (38)	126	0.24
Danish (61)	219	0.42
Dutch (59)	553	1.05
Eastern European (107)	129	0.24
English (1,284)	5,509	10.46
Estonian (9)	9	0.02
European (373)	385	0.73
Finnish (77)	386	0.73
French, ex. Basque (16)	1,255	2.38
French Canadian (55)	227	0.43
German (2,948)	14,246	27.05
German Russian (0)	0	<0.01
Greek (343)	607	1.15
Guyanese (0)	0	<0.01
Hungarian (632)	2,499	4.74
Icelander (0)	0	<0.01
Iranian (0)	118	0.22
Irish (3,451)	12,740	24.19
Israeli (14)	14	0.03
Italian (2,167)	6,124	11.63
Latvian (44)	60	0.11
Lithuanian (140)	291	0.55
Luxemburger (0)	0	<0.01
Macedonian (11)	11	0.02
Maltese (30)	30	0.06
New Zealander (0)	0	<0.01
Northern European (9)	9	0.02
Norwegian (64)	366	0.69
Pennsylvania German (12)	12	0.02
Polish (907)	4,284	8.13
Portuguese (8)	31	0.06
Romanian (147)	293	0.56
Russian (209)	673	1.28
Scandinavian (11)	66	0.13
Scotch-Irish (447)	1,371	2.60
Scottish (236)	1,113	2.11
Serbian (85)	183	0.35
Slavic (27)	47	0.09
Slovak (795)	2,432	4.62
Slovene (199)	761	1.44
Soviet Union (0)	0	<0.01
Swedish (94)	528	1.00
Swiss (29)	154	0.29
Turkish (222)	222	0.42
Ukrainian (235)	528	1.00
Welsh (121)	657	1.25
West Indian, ex. Hispanic (90)	193	0.37
Bahamian (0)	0	<0.01
Barbadian (0)	0	<0.01
Belizean (0)	0	<0.01
Bermudan (0)	0	<0.01
British West Indian (0)	0	<0.01
Dutch West Indian (0)	0	<0.01
Haitian (13)	27	0.05
Jamaican (69)	158	0.30
Trinidadian/Tobagonian (0)	0	<0.01
U.S. Virgin Islander (0)	0	<0.01
West Indian (8)	8	0.02
Other West Indian (0)	0	<0.01
Yugoslavian (87)	109	0.21

Hispanic Origin	Population	%
Hispanic or Latino (of any race)	2,147	4.12
Central American, ex. Mexican	98	0.19
Costa Rican	5	0.01
Guatemalan	21	0.04
Honduran	16	0.03
Nicaraguan	17	0.03
Panamanian	13	0.02
Salvadoran	26	0.05
Other Central American	0	<0.01
Cuban	80	0.15
Dominican Republic	82	0.16
Mexican	442	0.85
Puerto Rican	1,077	2.07
South American	179	0.34
Argentinean	32	0.06
Bolivian	1	<0.01
Chilean	11	0.02
Colombian	37	0.07
Ecuadorian	5	0.01
Paraguayan	1	<0.01
Peruvian	31	0.06
Uruguayan	7	0.01
Venezuelan	52	0.10
Other South American	2	<0.01
Other Hispanic or Latino	189	0.36

Race*	Population	%
African-American/Black (3,340)	4,052	7.77
Not Hispanic (3,238)	3,858	7.40
Hispanic (102)	194	0.37
American Indian/Alaska Native (149)	503	0.96
Not Hispanic (127)	428	0.82
Hispanic (22)	75	0.14
Alaska Athabascan *(Ala. Nat.)* (2)	2	<0.01
Aleut *(Alaska Native)* (1)	1	<0.01
Apache (1)	4	0.01
Arapaho (0)	0	<0.01
Blackfeet (7)	27	0.05
Canadian/French Am. Ind. (0)	1	<0.01
Central American Ind. (3)	3	0.01
Cherokee (26)	132	0.25
Cheyenne (0)	2	<0.01
Chickasaw (2)	6	0.01
Chippewa (9)	11	0.02
Choctaw (1)	9	0.02
Colville (0)	0	<0.01
Comanche (1)	1	<0.01
Cree (1)	1	<0.01
Creek (0)	7	0.01
Crow (0)	0	<0.01
Delaware (2)	4	0.01
Hopi (0)	0	<0.01
Houma (0)	0	<0.01
Inupiat *(Alaska Native)* (0)	0	<0.01
Iroquois (1)	10	0.02
Kiowa (0)	0	<0.01
Lumbee (0)	0	<0.01
Menominee (0)	0	<0.01
Mexican American Ind. (4)	9	0.02
Navajo (5)	13	0.02
Osage (0)	0	<0.01
Ottawa (0)	0	<0.01
Paiute (0)	0	<0.01
Pima (0)	0	<0.01
Potawatomi (1)	1	<0.01
Pueblo (1)	1	<0.01
Puget Sound Salish (0)	0	<0.01
Seminole (1)	7	0.01
Shoshone (0)	0	<0.01
Sioux (15)	35	0.07
South American Ind. (0)	2	<0.01
Spanish American Ind. (5)	5	0.01
Tlingit-Haida *(Alaska Native)* (1)	2	<0.01
Tohono O'Odham (0)	0	<0.01
Tsimshian *(Alaska Native)* (1)	2	<0.01
Ute (0)	0	<0.01
Yakama (0)	0	<0.01
Yaqui (0)	0	<0.01
Yuman (0)	1	<0.01
Yup'ik *(Alaska Native)* (0)	0	<0.01
Asian (988)	1,344	2.58
Not Hispanic (977)	1,323	2.54
Hispanic (11)	21	0.04
Bangladeshi (5)	8	0.02
Bhutanese (29)	49	0.09
Burmese (146)	146	0.28
Cambodian (6)	7	0.01
Chinese, ex. Taiwanese (150)	189	0.36
Filipino (73)	137	0.26
Hmong (0)	0	<0.01
Indian (217)	277	0.53
Indonesian (13)	21	0.04
Japanese (49)	95	0.18
Korean (68)	96	0.18
Laotian (3)	6	0.01
Malaysian (0)	0	<0.01
Nepalese (16)	29	0.06
Pakistani (68)	75	0.14
Sri Lankan (1)	1	<0.01
Taiwanese (8)	8	0.02
Thai (34)	47	0.09
Vietnamese (49)	62	0.12
Hawaii Native/Pacific Islander (9)	41	0.08
Not Hispanic (9)	37	0.07
Hispanic (0)	4	0.01
Fijian (0)	0	<0.01
Guamanian/Chamorro (3)	5	0.01
Marshallese (0)	0	<0.01
Native Hawaiian (4)	8	0.02
Samoan (0)	0	<0.01
Tongan (0)	0	<0.01
White (45,598)	46,836	89.84
Not Hispanic (44,341)	45,393	87.07
Hispanic (1,257)	1,443	2.77

*Notes: † The Census 2010 population figure is used to calculate the percentages in the Hispanic Origin and Race categories. Ancestry percentages are based on the 2006-2010 American Community Survey population (not shown); ‡ Numbers in parentheses indicate the number of people reporting a single ancestry; * Numbers in parentheses indicate the number of persons reporting this race alone, not in combination with any other race; Please refer to the User Guide for more information.*

Lorain

Place Type: City
County: Lorain
Population: 64,097

Ancestry	Population	%
Afghan (0)	0	<0.01
African, Sub-Saharan (258)	473	0.73
African (258)	451	0.69
Cape Verdean (0)	0	<0.01
Ethiopian (0)	0	<0.01
Ghanaian (0)	11	0.02
Kenyan (0)	0	<0.01
Liberian (0)	0	<0.01
Nigerian (0)	11	0.02
Senegalese (0)	0	<0.01
Sierra Leonean (0)	0	<0.01
Somalian (0)	0	<0.01
South African (0)	0	<0.01
Sudanese (0)	0	<0.01
Ugandan (0)	0	<0.01
Zimbabwean (0)	0	<0.01
Other Sub-Saharan African (0)	0	<0.01
Albanian (0)	0	<0.01
Alsatian (0)	0	<0.01
American (2,165)	2,165	3.32
Arab (222)	383	0.59
Arab (211)	211	0.32
Egyptian (0)	0	<0.01
Iraqi (0)	0	<0.01
Jordanian (0)	0	<0.01
Lebanese (0)	153	0.23
Moroccan (0)	0	<0.01
Palestinian (0)	0	<0.01
Syrian (11)	19	0.03
Other Arab (0)	0	<0.01
Armenian (0)	0	<0.01
Assyrian/Chaldean/Syriac (0)	0	<0.01
Australian (0)	0	<0.01
Austrian (24)	110	0.17
Basque (0)	0	<0.01
Belgian (0)	31	0.05
Brazilian (0)	0	<0.01
British (85)	93	0.14
Bulgarian (15)	15	0.02
Cajun (0)	0	<0.01
Canadian (8)	26	0.04
Carpatho Rusyn (26)	26	0.04
Celtic (0)	0	<0.01
Croatian (319)	569	0.87
Cypriot (0)	0	<0.01
Czech (32)	104	0.16
Czechoslovakian (64)	186	0.29
Danish (18)	53	0.08
Dutch (46)	824	1.26
Eastern European (156)	156	0.24
English (581)	3,807	5.84
Estonian (0)	0	<0.01
European (77)	87	0.13
Finnish (11)	23	0.04
French, ex. Basque (190)	1,057	1.62
French Canadian (4)	42	0.06
German (2,443)	9,408	14.42
German Russian (18)	18	0.03
Greek (160)	365	0.56
Guyanese (0)	0	<0.01
Hungarian (1,136)	3,113	4.77
Icelander (0)	0	<0.01
Iranian (0)	0	<0.01
Irish (1,573)	7,298	11.19
Israeli (0)	0	<0.01
Italian (1,682)	4,912	7.53
Latvian (0)	23	0.04
Lithuanian (25)	66	0.10
Luxemburger (0)	0	<0.01
Macedonian (62)	97	0.15
Maltese (0)	0	<0.01
New Zealander (0)	0	<0.01
Northern European (0)	0	<0.01
Norwegian (25)	71	0.11
Pennsylvania German (25)	25	0.04
Polish (1,803)	4,052	6.21
Portuguese (0)	0	<0.01
Romanian (44)	135	0.21
Russian (81)	399	0.61
Scandinavian (0)	33	0.05
Scotch-Irish (232)	1,107	1.70
Scottish (77)	613	0.94
Serbian (95)	206	0.32
Slavic (7)	15	0.02
Slovak (769)	1,882	2.89
Slovene (175)	546	0.84
Soviet Union (0)	0	<0.01
Swedish (27)	125	0.19
Swiss (11)	115	0.18
Turkish (0)	0	<0.01
Ukrainian (284)	521	0.80
Welsh (50)	314	0.48
West Indian, ex. Hispanic (78)	122	0.19
Bahamian (0)	0	<0.01
Barbadian (0)	0	<0.01
Belizean (0)	0	<0.01
Bermudan (0)	0	<0.01
British West Indian (0)	0	<0.01
Dutch West Indian (0)	0	<0.01
Haitian (43)	43	0.07
Jamaican (22)	29	0.04
Trinidadian/Tobagonian (0)	0	<0.01
U.S. Virgin Islander (0)	0	<0.01
West Indian (13)	50	0.08
Other West Indian (0)	0	<0.01
Yugoslavian (0)	23	0.04

Hispanic Origin	Population	%
Hispanic or Latino (of any race)	16,177	25.24
Central American, ex. Mexican	118	0.18
Costa Rican	4	0.01
Guatemalan	32	0.05
Honduran	17	0.03
Nicaraguan	8	0.01
Panamanian	28	0.04
Salvadoran	29	0.05
Other Central American	0	<0.01
Cuban	79	0.12
Dominican Republic	115	0.18
Mexican	2,934	4.58
Puerto Rican	12,413	19.37
South American	60	0.09
Argentinean	9	0.01
Bolivian	4	0.01
Chilean	3	<0.01
Colombian	12	0.02
Ecuadorian	12	0.02
Paraguayan	0	<0.01
Peruvian	10	0.02
Uruguayan	0	<0.01
Venezuelan	10	0.02
Other South American	0	<0.01
Other Hispanic or Latino	458	0.71

Race*	Population	%
African-American/Black (11,262)	13,512	21.08
Not Hispanic (10,245)	11,803	18.41
Hispanic (1,017)	1,709	2.67
American Indian/Alaska Native (324)	966	1.51
Not Hispanic (177)	651	1.02
Hispanic (147)	315	0.49
Alaska Athabascan *(Ala. Nat.)* (0)	0	<0.01
Aleut *(Alaska Native)* (0)	0	<0.01
Apache (2)	13	0.02
Arapaho (2)	2	<0.01
Blackfeet (8)	54	0.08
Canadian/French Am. Ind. (1)	1	<0.01
Central American Ind. (6)	9	0.01
Cherokee (41)	227	0.35
Cheyenne (0)	1	<0.01
Chickasaw (4)	5	0.01
Chippewa (6)	11	0.02
Choctaw (1)	6	0.01
Colville (0)	0	<0.01
Comanche (0)	1	<0.01
Cree (1)	1	<0.01
Creek (0)	4	0.01
Crow (0)	0	<0.01
Delaware (0)	2	<0.01
Hopi (0)	1	<0.01
Houma (0)	0	<0.01
Inupiat *(Alaska Native)* (0)	0	<0.01
Iroquois (3)	14	0.02
Kiowa (1)	2	<0.01
Lumbee (0)	2	<0.01
Menominee (0)	0	<0.01
Mexican American Ind. (10)	16	0.02
Navajo (2)	7	0.01
Osage (0)	0	<0.01
Ottawa (2)	2	<0.01
Paiute (0)	0	<0.01
Pima (0)	0	<0.01
Potawatomi (3)	3	<0.01
Pueblo (7)	14	0.02
Puget Sound Salish (0)	0	<0.01
Seminole (0)	1	<0.01
Shoshone (0)	0	<0.01
Sioux (8)	26	0.04
South American Ind. (31)	79	0.12
Spanish American Ind. (1)	1	<0.01
Tlingit-Haida *(Alaska Native)* (0)	0	<0.01
Tohono O'Odham (0)	0	<0.01
Tsimshian *(Alaska Native)* (0)	0	<0.01
Ute (0)	0	<0.01
Yakama (0)	0	<0.01
Yaqui (0)	1	<0.01
Yuman (0)	0	<0.01
Yup'ik *(Alaska Native)* (0)	0	<0.01
Asian (228)	428	0.67
Not Hispanic (206)	342	0.53
Hispanic (22)	86	0.13
Bangladeshi (0)	0	<0.01
Bhutanese (0)	0	<0.01
Burmese (0)	0	<0.01
Cambodian (0)	3	<0.01
Chinese, ex. Taiwanese (36)	70	0.11
Filipino (70)	131	0.20
Hmong (6)	6	0.01
Indian (38)	59	0.09
Indonesian (4)	5	0.01
Japanese (11)	29	0.05
Korean (25)	53	0.08
Laotian (0)	0	<0.01
Malaysian (0)	0	<0.01
Nepalese (1)	1	<0.01
Pakistani (5)	7	0.01
Sri Lankan (0)	0	<0.01
Taiwanese (0)	0	<0.01
Thai (11)	13	0.02
Vietnamese (13)	22	0.03
Hawaii Native/Pacific Islander (9)	88	0.14
Not Hispanic (4)	27	0.04
Hispanic (5)	61	0.10
Fijian (0)	0	<0.01
Guamanian/Chamorro (4)	6	0.01
Marshallese (0)	0	<0.01
Native Hawaiian (1)	15	0.02
Samoan (1)	4	0.01
Tongan (0)	0	<0.01
White (43,505)	46,446	72.46
Not Hispanic (35,269)	37,080	57.85
Hispanic (8,236)	9,366	14.61

*Notes: † The Census 2010 population figure is used to calculate the percentages in the Hispanic Origin and Race categories. Ancestry percentages are based on the 2006-2010 American Community Survey population (not shown); ‡ Numbers in parentheses indicate the number of people reporting a single ancestry; * Numbers in parentheses indicate the number of persons reporting this race alone, not in combination with any other race; Please refer to the User Guide for more information.*

Parma

Place Type: City
County: Cuyahoga
Population: 81,601

Ancestry	Population	%
Afghan (0)	0	<0.01
African, Sub-Saharan (341)	341	0.42
African (122)	122	0.15
Cape Verdean (0)	0	<0.01
Ethiopian (0)	0	<0.01
Ghanaian (0)	0	<0.01
Kenyan (31)	31	0.04
Liberian (0)	0	<0.01
Nigerian (180)	180	0.22
Senegalese (0)	0	<0.01
Sierra Leonean (0)	0	<0.01
Somalian (0)	0	<0.01
South African (0)	0	<0.01
Sudanese (0)	0	<0.01
Ugandan (8)	8	0.01
Zimbabwean (0)	0	<0.01
Other Sub-Saharan African (0)	0	<0.01
Albanian (26)	41	0.05
Alsatian (0)	0	<0.01
American (3,084)	3,084	3.77
Arab (743)	1,340	1.64
Arab (55)	184	0.22
Egyptian (0)	0	<0.01
Iraqi (153)	153	0.19
Jordanian (0)	0	<0.01
Lebanese (356)	813	0.99
Moroccan (83)	83	0.10
Palestinian (34)	34	0.04
Syrian (62)	62	0.08
Other Arab (0)	11	0.01
Armenian (35)	80	0.10
Assyrian/Chaldean/Syriac (0)	0	<0.01
Australian (0)	44	0.05
Austrian (64)	283	0.35
Basque (0)	0	<0.01
Belgian (0)	163	0.20
Brazilian (0)	0	<0.01
British (66)	189	0.23
Bulgarian (52)	73	0.09
Cajun (0)	0	<0.01
Canadian (43)	85	0.10
Carpatho Rusyn (95)	116	0.14
Celtic (0)	0	<0.01
Croatian (256)	1,112	1.36
Cypriot (0)	0	<0.01
Czech (648)	2,231	2.72
Czechoslovakian (215)	299	0.37
Danish (0)	32	0.04
Dutch (49)	589	0.72
Eastern European (91)	102	0.12
English (959)	5,050	6.17
Estonian (0)	0	<0.01
European (367)	420	0.51
Finnish (20)	42	0.05
French, ex. Basque (83)	1,339	1.64
French Canadian (46)	178	0.22
German (5,153)	21,335	26.05
German Russian (0)	0	<0.01
Greek (712)	1,087	1.33
Guyanese (0)	0	<0.01
Hungarian (1,279)	4,239	5.18
Icelander (0)	0	<0.01
Iranian (24)	24	0.03
Irish (2,406)	11,502	14.04
Israeli (0)	0	<0.01
Italian (3,782)	11,434	13.96
Latvian (24)	24	0.03
Lithuanian (183)	613	0.75
Luxemburger (0)	0	<0.01
Macedonian (10)	10	0.01
Maltese (0)	0	<0.01
New Zealander (0)	0	<0.01
Northern European (0)	0	<0.01
Norwegian (43)	152	0.19
Pennsylvania German (12)	25	0.03
Polish (5,990)	14,703	17.95
Portuguese (50)	97	0.12
Romanian (460)	761	0.93
Russian (437)	1,152	1.41
Scandinavian (0)	0	<0.01
Scotch-Irish (230)	831	1.01
Scottish (146)	883	1.08
Serbian (1,540)	1,778	2.17
Slavic (56)	145	0.18
Slovak (2,503)	6,760	8.25
Slovene (501)	1,677	2.05
Soviet Union (0)	0	<0.01
Swedish (58)	382	0.47
Swiss (36)	206	0.25
Turkish (0)	0	<0.01
Ukrainian (3,660)	4,857	5.93
Welsh (76)	411	0.50
West Indian, ex. Hispanic (139)	160	0.20
Bahamian (0)	0	<0.01
Barbadian (44)	44	0.05
Belizean (0)	0	<0.01
Bermudan (0)	0	<0.01
British West Indian (0)	0	<0.01
Dutch West Indian (0)	0	<0.01
Haitian (0)	21	0.03
Jamaican (0)	0	<0.01
Trinidadian/Tobagonian (0)	0	<0.01
U.S. Virgin Islander (5)	5	0.01
West Indian (90)	90	0.11
Other West Indian (0)	0	<0.01
Yugoslavian (264)	332	0.41

Hispanic Origin	Population	%
Hispanic or Latino (of any race)	2,915	3.57
Central American, ex. Mexican	117	0.14
Costa Rican	6	0.01
Guatemalan	34	0.04
Honduran	19	0.02
Nicaraguan	13	0.02
Panamanian	8	0.01
Salvadoran	37	0.05
Other Central American	0	<0.01
Cuban	58	0.07
Dominican Republic	64	0.08
Mexican	566	0.69
Puerto Rican	1,665	2.04
South American	252	0.31
Argentinean	19	0.02
Bolivian	0	<0.01
Chilean	4	<0.01
Colombian	45	0.06
Ecuadorian	44	0.05
Paraguayan	1	<0.01
Peruvian	129	0.16
Uruguayan	0	<0.01
Venezuelan	7	0.01
Other South American	3	<0.01
Other Hispanic or Latino	193	0.24

Race*	Population	%
African-American/Black (1,887)	2,340	2.87
Not Hispanic (1,797)	2,211	2.71
Hispanic (90)	129	0.16
American Indian/Alaska Native (151)	435	0.53
Not Hispanic (121)	368	0.45
Hispanic (30)	67	0.08
Alaska Athabascan *(Ala. Nat.)* (1)	3	<0.01
Aleut *(Alaska Native)* (0)	0	<0.01
Apache (6)	13	0.02
Arapaho (0)	0	<0.01
Blackfeet (5)	27	0.03
Canadian/French Am. Ind. (0)	0	<0.01
Central American Ind. (3)	3	<0.01
Cherokee (18)	115	0.14
Cheyenne (2)	5	0.01
Chickasaw (0)	1	<0.01
Chippewa (1)	6	0.01
Choctaw (8)	15	0.02
Colville (0)	0	<0.01
Comanche (0)	3	<0.01
Cree (0)	0	<0.01
Creek (0)	0	<0.01
Crow (0)	1	<0.01
Delaware (0)	0	<0.01
Hopi (0)	0	<0.01
Houma (0)	0	<0.01
Inupiat *(Alaska Native)* (1)	2	<0.01
Iroquois (3)	13	0.02
Kiowa (0)	0	<0.01
Lumbee (1)	3	<0.01
Menominee (0)	0	<0.01
Mexican American Ind. (3)	5	0.01
Navajo (7)	13	0.02
Osage (0)	1	<0.01
Ottawa (0)	0	<0.01
Paiute (0)	0	<0.01
Pima (0)	0	<0.01
Potawatomi (0)	3	<0.01
Pueblo (1)	2	<0.01
Puget Sound Salish (0)	0	<0.01
Seminole (0)	0	<0.01
Shoshone (0)	0	<0.01
Sioux (0)	9	0.01
South American Ind. (8)	10	0.01
Spanish American Ind. (1)	1	<0.01
Tlingit-Haida *(Alaska Native)* (5)	6	0.01
Tohono O'Odham (0)	0	<0.01
Tsimshian *(Alaska Native)* (0)	2	<0.01
Ute (0)	0	<0.01
Yakama (0)	0	<0.01
Yaqui (0)	0	<0.01
Yuman (0)	0	<0.01
Yup'ik *(Alaska Native)* (0)	0	<0.01
Asian (1,511)	1,920	2.35
Not Hispanic (1,497)	1,891	2.32
Hispanic (14)	29	0.04
Bangladeshi (0)	1	<0.01
Bhutanese (0)	0	<0.01
Burmese (0)	0	<0.01
Cambodian (52)	54	0.07
Chinese, ex. Taiwanese (174)	218	0.27
Filipino (392)	515	0.63
Hmong (0)	0	<0.01
Indian (543)	630	0.77
Indonesian (1)	4	<0.01
Japanese (48)	86	0.11
Korean (60)	86	0.11
Laotian (16)	18	0.02
Malaysian (0)	0	<0.01
Nepalese (5)	5	0.01
Pakistani (20)	21	0.03
Sri Lankan (5)	8	0.01
Taiwanese (2)	4	<0.01
Thai (12)	16	0.02
Vietnamese (149)	176	0.22
Hawaii Native/Pacific Islander (13)	79	0.10
Not Hispanic (11)	71	0.09
Hispanic (2)	8	0.01
Fijian (0)	0	<0.01
Guamanian/Chamorro (4)	8	0.01
Marshallese (0)	0	<0.01
Native Hawaiian (6)	16	0.02
Samoan (1)	9	0.01
Tongan (0)	0	<0.01
White (75,921)	77,034	94.40
Not Hispanic (74,186)	75,053	91.98
Hispanic (1,735)	1,981	2.43

*Notes: † The Census 2010 population figure is used to calculate the percentages in the Hispanic Origin and Race categories. Ancestry percentages are based on the 2006-2010 American Community Survey population (not shown); ‡ Numbers in parentheses indicate the number of people reporting a single ancestry; * Numbers in parentheses indicate the number of persons reporting this race alone, not in combination with any other race; Please refer to the User Guide for more information.*

Springfield

Place Type: City
County: Clark
Population: 60,608

Ancestry	Population	%
Afghan (0)	0	<0.01
African, Sub-Saharan (658)	729	1.19
African (627)	691	1.12
Cape Verdean (6)	13	0.02
Ethiopian (0)	0	<0.01
Ghanaian (0)	0	<0.01
Kenyan (0)	0	<0.01
Liberian (0)	0	<0.01
Nigerian (25)	25	0.04
Senegalese (0)	0	<0.01
Sierra Leonean (0)	0	<0.01
Somalian (0)	0	<0.01
South African (0)	0	<0.01
Sudanese (0)	0	<0.01
Ugandan (0)	0	<0.01
Zimbabwean (0)	0	<0.01
Other Sub-Saharan African (0)	0	<0.01
Albanian (0)	0	<0.01
Alsatian (0)	0	<0.01
American (8,078)	8,078	13.14
Arab (35)	35	0.06
Arab (0)	0	<0.01
Egyptian (0)	0	<0.01
Iraqi (0)	0	<0.01
Jordanian (0)	0	<0.01
Lebanese (0)	0	<0.01
Moroccan (0)	0	<0.01
Palestinian (0)	0	<0.01
Syrian (0)	0	<0.01
Other Arab (35)	35	0.06
Armenian (0)	12	0.02
Assyrian/Chaldean/Syriac (0)	0	<0.01
Australian (0)	0	<0.01
Austrian (0)	11	0.02
Basque (0)	0	<0.01
Belgian (12)	12	0.02
Brazilian (0)	0	<0.01
British (25)	83	0.13
Bulgarian (0)	22	0.04
Cajun (0)	0	<0.01
Canadian (22)	61	0.10
Carpatho Rusyn (0)	0	<0.01
Celtic (12)	12	0.02
Croatian (0)	0	<0.01
Cypriot (0)	0	<0.01
Czech (16)	153	0.25
Czechoslovakian (15)	15	0.02
Danish (0)	35	0.06
Dutch (186)	1,199	1.95
Eastern European (0)	0	<0.01
English (1,994)	4,701	7.64
Estonian (0)	0	<0.01
European (473)	473	0.77
Finnish (78)	106	0.17
French, ex. Basque (201)	1,220	1.98
French Canadian (19)	177	0.29
German (5,064)	13,145	21.37
German Russian (0)	0	<0.01
Greek (123)	244	0.40
Guyanese (0)	0	<0.01
Hungarian (85)	267	0.43
Icelander (0)	0	<0.01
Iranian (28)	28	0.05
Irish (2,254)	7,564	12.30
Israeli (0)	0	<0.01
Italian (754)	1,570	2.55
Latvian (8)	8	0.01
Lithuanian (26)	84	0.14
Luxemburger (0)	0	<0.01
Macedonian (55)	145	0.24
Maltese (0)	0	<0.01
New Zealander (0)	0	<0.01
Northern European (11)	11	0.02
Norwegian (25)	151	0.25
Pennsylvania German (9)	9	0.01
Polish (134)	661	1.07
Portuguese (87)	116	0.19
Romanian (38)	60	0.10
Russian (81)	192	0.31
Scandinavian (59)	67	0.11
Scotch-Irish (557)	1,143	1.86
Scottish (545)	1,400	2.28
Serbian (0)	0	<0.01
Slavic (0)	14	0.02
Slovak (20)	139	0.23
Slovene (0)	0	<0.01
Soviet Union (0)	0	<0.01
Swedish (212)	498	0.81
Swiss (12)	63	0.10
Turkish (0)	0	<0.01
Ukrainian (0)	41	0.07
Welsh (182)	505	0.82
West Indian, ex. Hispanic (40)	103	0.17
Bahamian (0)	0	<0.01
Barbadian (0)	0	<0.01
Belizean (0)	0	<0.01
Bermudan (0)	0	<0.01
British West Indian (0)	0	<0.01
Dutch West Indian (0)	35	0.06
Haitian (6)	6	0.01
Jamaican (34)	62	0.10
Trinidadian/Tobagonian (0)	0	<0.01
U.S. Virgin Islander (0)	0	<0.01
West Indian (0)	0	<0.01
Other West Indian (0)	0	<0.01
Yugoslavian (0)	11	0.02

Hispanic Origin	Population	%
Hispanic or Latino (of any race)	1,824	3.01
Central American, ex. Mexican	77	0.13
Costa Rican	3	<0.01
Guatemalan	26	0.04
Honduran	10	0.02
Nicaraguan	13	0.02
Panamanian	11	0.02
Salvadoran	14	0.02
Other Central American	0	<0.01
Cuban	40	0.07
Dominican Republic	13	0.02
Mexican	1,342	2.21
Puerto Rican	115	0.19
South American	19	0.03
Argentinean	0	<0.01
Bolivian	0	<0.01
Chilean	0	<0.01
Colombian	12	0.02
Ecuadorian	2	<0.01
Paraguayan	1	<0.01
Peruvian	2	<0.01
Uruguayan	0	<0.01
Venezuelan	2	<0.01
Other South American	0	<0.01
Other Hispanic or Latino	218	0.36

Race*	Population	%
African-American/Black (10,981)	12,807	21.13
Not Hispanic (10,876)	12,597	20.78
Hispanic (105)	210	0.35
American Indian/Alaska Native (201)	748	1.23
Not Hispanic (167)	660	1.09
Hispanic (34)	88	0.15
Alaska Athabascan *(Ala. Nat.)* (0)	0	<0.01
Aleut *(Alaska Native)* (0)	0	<0.01
Apache (4)	9	0.01
Arapaho (0)	0	<0.01
Blackfeet (5)	47	0.08
Canadian/French Am. Ind. (0)	3	<0.01
Central American Ind. (0)	1	<0.01
Cherokee (46)	230	0.38
Cheyenne (2)	4	0.01
Chickasaw (0)	0	<0.01
Chippewa (1)	2	<0.01
Choctaw (7)	9	0.01
Colville (0)	0	<0.01
Comanche (4)	6	0.01
Cree (1)	2	<0.01
Creek (4)	7	0.01
Crow (1)	2	<0.01
Delaware (0)	6	0.01
Hopi (0)	5	0.01
Houma (0)	0	<0.01
Inupiat *(Alaska Native)* (0)	0	<0.01
Iroquois (2)	6	0.01
Kiowa (0)	0	<0.01
Lumbee (1)	1	<0.01
Menominee (0)	0	<0.01
Mexican American Ind. (1)	8	0.01
Navajo (0)	2	<0.01
Osage (0)	6	0.01
Ottawa (1)	1	<0.01
Paiute (0)	0	<0.01
Pima (0)	0	<0.01
Potawatomi (1)	4	0.01
Pueblo (0)	0	<0.01
Puget Sound Salish (0)	0	<0.01
Seminole (0)	7	0.01
Shoshone (0)	0	<0.01
Sioux (3)	12	0.02
South American Ind. (0)	0	<0.01
Spanish American Ind. (2)	2	<0.01
Tlingit-Haida *(Alaska Native)* (0)	0	<0.01
Tohono O'Odham (3)	3	<0.01
Tsimshian *(Alaska Native)* (0)	0	<0.01
Ute (0)	0	<0.01
Yakama (0)	0	<0.01
Yaqui (1)	1	<0.01
Yuman (0)	0	<0.01
Yup'ik *(Alaska Native)* (0)	0	<0.01
Asian (455)	667	1.10
Not Hispanic (446)	634	1.05
Hispanic (9)	33	0.05
Bangladeshi (0)	0	<0.01
Bhutanese (0)	0	<0.01
Burmese (0)	0	<0.01
Cambodian (3)	6	0.01
Chinese, ex. Taiwanese (76)	97	0.16
Filipino (64)	102	0.17
Hmong (0)	0	<0.01
Indian (163)	196	0.32
Indonesian (1)	6	0.01
Japanese (36)	68	0.11
Korean (18)	48	0.08
Laotian (16)	22	0.04
Malaysian (0)	0	<0.01
Nepalese (0)	0	<0.01
Pakistani (35)	38	0.06
Sri Lankan (2)	2	<0.01
Taiwanese (1)	2	<0.01
Thai (5)	16	0.03
Vietnamese (17)	38	0.06
Hawaii Native/Pacific Islander (25)	96	0.16
Not Hispanic (21)	73	0.12
Hispanic (4)	23	0.04
Fijian (7)	11	0.02
Guamanian/Chamorro (4)	12	0.02
Marshallese (1)	1	<0.01
Native Hawaiian (4)	16	0.03
Samoan (6)	10	0.02
Tongan (0)	2	<0.01
White (45,607)	47,786	78.84
Not Hispanic (44,946)	46,921	77.42
Hispanic (661)	865	1.43

*Notes: † The Census 2010 population figure is used to calculate the percentages in the Hispanic Origin and Race categories. Ancestry percentages are based on the 2006-2010 American Community Survey population (not shown); ‡ Numbers in parentheses indicate the number of people reporting a single ancestry; * Numbers in parentheses indicate the number of persons reporting this race alone, not in combination with any other race; Please refer to the User Guide for more information.*

Toledo

Place Type: City
County: Lucas
Population: 287,208

Ancestry	Population	%
Afghan (0)	0	<0.01
African, Sub-Saharan (2,462)	3,260	1.12
African (1,781)	2,419	0.83
Cape Verdean (0)	46	0.02
Ethiopian (0)	0	<0.01
Ghanaian (69)	69	0.02
Kenyan (19)	19	0.01
Liberian (0)	0	<0.01
Nigerian (528)	642	0.22
Senegalese (15)	15	0.01
Sierra Leonean (0)	0	<0.01
Somalian (0)	0	<0.01
South African (27)	27	0.01
Sudanese (0)	0	<0.01
Ugandan (0)	0	<0.01
Zimbabwean (0)	0	<0.01
Other Sub-Saharan African (23)	23	0.01
Albanian (0)	0	<0.01
Alsatian (0)	6	<0.01
American (10,051)	10,051	3.44
Arab (2,777)	3,428	1.17
Arab (592)	614	0.21
Egyptian (9)	28	0.01
Iraqi (15)	28	0.01
Jordanian (201)	201	0.07
Lebanese (1,284)	1,656	0.57
Moroccan (0)	0	<0.01
Palestinian (183)	216	0.07
Syrian (209)	381	0.13
Other Arab (284)	304	0.10
Armenian (48)	234	0.08
Assyrian/Chaldean/Syriac (27)	27	0.01
Australian (9)	9	<0.01
Austrian (103)	628	0.22
Basque (0)	0	<0.01
Belgian (34)	215	0.07
Brazilian (0)	0	<0.01
British (325)	785	0.27
Bulgarian (66)	217	0.07
Cajun (0)	0	<0.01
Canadian (235)	521	0.18
Carpatho Rusyn (6)	15	0.01
Celtic (57)	73	0.03
Croatian (0)	125	0.04
Cypriot (0)	11	<0.01
Czech (143)	833	0.29
Czechoslovakian (116)	304	0.10
Danish (101)	499	0.17
Dutch (454)	3,569	1.22
Eastern European (63)	63	0.02
English (5,068)	18,826	6.45
Estonian (19)	19	0.01
European (1,540)	1,626	0.56
Finnish (95)	295	0.10
French, ex. Basque (1,553)	13,787	4.72
French Canadian (664)	2,025	0.69
German (27,798)	76,635	26.26
German Russian (0)	0	<0.01
Greek (510)	910	0.31
Guyanese (60)	60	0.02
Hungarian (2,245)	6,352	2.18
Icelander (13)	44	0.02
Iranian (73)	73	0.03
Irish (8,029)	34,827	11.93
Israeli (28)	35	0.01
Italian (3,020)	9,356	3.21
Latvian (21)	21	0.01
Lithuanian (38)	264	0.09
Luxemburger (0)	0	<0.01
Macedonian (8)	18	0.01
Maltese (9)	17	0.01
New Zealander (0)	0	<0.01
Northern European (13)	13	<0.01
Norwegian (197)	1,161	0.40
Pennsylvania German (65)	245	0.08
Polish (10,864)	25,480	8.73
Portuguese (48)	154	0.05
Romanian (114)	436	0.15
Russian (227)	959	0.33
Scandinavian (12)	101	0.03
Scotch-Irish (695)	2,388	0.82
Scottish (805)	3,645	1.25
Serbian (35)	69	0.02
Slavic (0)	58	0.02
Slovak (237)	945	0.32
Slovene (70)	149	0.05
Soviet Union (0)	0	<0.01
Swedish (278)	1,344	0.46
Swiss (165)	1,134	0.39
Turkish (120)	120	0.04
Ukrainian (159)	499	0.17
Welsh (246)	1,296	0.44
West Indian, ex. Hispanic (812)	1,077	0.37
Bahamian (0)	0	<0.01
Barbadian (0)	0	<0.01
Belizean (19)	19	0.01
Bermudan (0)	0	<0.01
British West Indian (22)	22	0.01
Dutch West Indian (0)	0	<0.01
Haitian (64)	97	0.03
Jamaican (667)	879	0.30
Trinidadian/Tobagonian (11)	11	<0.01
U.S. Virgin Islander (0)	0	<0.01
West Indian (29)	49	0.02
Other West Indian (0)	0	<0.01
Yugoslavian (75)	115	0.04

Hispanic Origin	Population	%
Hispanic or Latino (of any race)	21,231	7.39
Central American, ex. Mexican	240	0.08
Costa Rican	15	0.01
Guatemalan	61	0.02
Honduran	26	0.01
Nicaraguan	72	0.03
Panamanian	33	0.01
Salvadoran	33	0.01
Other Central American	0	<0.01
Cuban	299	0.10
Dominican Republic	69	0.02
Mexican	17,576	6.12
Puerto Rican	1,143	0.40
South American	219	0.08
Argentinean	24	0.01
Bolivian	4	<0.01
Chilean	18	0.01
Colombian	49	0.02
Ecuadorian	27	0.01
Paraguayan	6	<0.01
Peruvian	51	0.02
Uruguayan	0	<0.01
Venezuelan	32	0.01
Other South American	8	<0.01
Other Hispanic or Latino	1,685	0.59

Race*	Population	%
African-American/Black (78,073)	85,254	29.68
Not Hispanic (76,820)	82,886	28.86
Hispanic (1,253)	2,368	0.82
American Indian/Alaska Native (1,065)	3,359	1.17
Not Hispanic (755)	2,675	0.93
Hispanic (310)	684	0.24
Alaska Athabascan *(Ala. Nat.)* (1)	2	<0.01
Aleut *(Alaska Native)* (1)	2	<0.01
Apache (21)	66	0.02
Arapaho (0)	6	<0.01
Blackfeet (25)	158	0.06
Canadian/French Am. Ind. (7)	23	0.01
Central American Ind. (0)	0	<0.01
Cherokee (163)	784	0.27
Cheyenne (0)	6	<0.01
Chickasaw (3)	7	<0.01
Chippewa (77)	139	0.05
Choctaw (13)	59	0.02
Colville (0)	0	<0.01
Comanche (1)	3	<0.01
Cree (1)	6	<0.01
Creek (2)	23	0.01
Crow (0)	5	<0.01
Delaware (9)	11	<0.01
Hopi (3)	4	<0.01
Houma (0)	0	<0.01
Inupiat *(Alaska Native)* (2)	3	<0.01
Iroquois (15)	39	0.01
Kiowa (0)	1	<0.01
Lumbee (5)	14	<0.01
Menominee (9)	11	<0.01
Mexican American Ind. (38)	96	0.03
Navajo (13)	30	0.01
Osage (0)	3	<0.01
Ottawa (10)	41	0.01
Paiute (0)	0	<0.01
Pima (0)	0	<0.01
Potawatomi (13)	33	0.01
Pueblo (6)	15	0.01
Puget Sound Salish (0)	0	<0.01
Seminole (1)	9	<0.01
Shoshone (0)	3	<0.01
Sioux (14)	39	0.01
South American Ind. (14)	17	0.01
Spanish American Ind. (2)	6	<0.01
Tlingit-Haida *(Alaska Native)* (1)	2	<0.01
Tohono O'Odham (0)	0	<0.01
Tsimshian *(Alaska Native)* (0)	0	<0.01
Ute (0)	0	<0.01
Yakama (0)	0	<0.01
Yaqui (3)	4	<0.01
Yuman (0)	0	<0.01
Yup'ik *(Alaska Native)* (0)	0	<0.01
Asian (3,264)	4,559	1.59
Not Hispanic (3,204)	4,312	1.50
Hispanic (60)	247	0.09
Bangladeshi (2)	5	<0.01
Bhutanese (0)	0	<0.01
Burmese (5)	5	<0.01
Cambodian (2)	7	<0.01
Chinese, ex. Taiwanese (1,015)	1,177	0.41
Filipino (355)	610	0.21
Hmong (4)	4	<0.01
Indian (836)	995	0.35
Indonesian (14)	28	0.01
Japanese (84)	272	0.09
Korean (216)	382	0.13
Laotian (91)	129	0.04
Malaysian (11)	22	0.01
Nepalese (32)	36	0.01
Pakistani (81)	97	0.03
Sri Lankan (16)	18	0.01
Taiwanese (26)	30	0.01
Thai (72)	116	0.04
Vietnamese (236)	286	0.10
Hawaii Native/Pacific Islander (77)	275	0.10
Not Hispanic (64)	220	0.08
Hispanic (13)	55	0.02
Fijian (2)	2	<0.01
Guamanian/Chamorro (13)	28	0.01
Marshallese (0)	0	<0.01
Native Hawaiian (23)	86	0.03
Samoan (17)	34	0.01
Tongan (1)	2	<0.01
White (186,188)	195,953	68.23
Not Hispanic (176,468)	183,797	63.99
Hispanic (9,720)	12,156	4.23

*Notes: † The Census 2010 population figure is used to calculate the percentages in the Hispanic Origin and Race categories. Ancestry percentages are based on the 2006-2010 American Community Survey population (not shown); ‡ Numbers in parentheses indicate the number of people reporting a single ancestry; * Numbers in parentheses indicate the number of persons reporting this race alone, not in combination with any other race; Please refer to the User Guide for more information.*

Youngstown

Place Type: City
County: Mahoning
Population: 66,982

Ancestry	Population	%
Afghan (0)	0	<0.01
African, Sub-Saharan (2,618)	2,765	3.97
African (2,559)	2,655	3.82
Cape Verdean (0)	0	<0.01
Ethiopian (14)	65	0.09
Ghanaian (0)	0	<0.01
Kenyan (0)	0	<0.01
Liberian (0)	0	<0.01
Nigerian (0)	0	<0.01
Senegalese (0)	0	<0.01
Sierra Leonean (0)	0	<0.01
Somalian (0)	0	<0.01
South African (0)	0	<0.01
Sudanese (0)	0	<0.01
Ugandan (0)	0	<0.01
Zimbabwean (0)	0	<0.01
Other Sub-Saharan African (45)	45	0.06
Albanian (10)	22	0.03
Alsatian (0)	0	<0.01
American (2,278)	2,278	3.27
Arab (104)	274	0.39
Arab (84)	110	0.16
Egyptian (0)	0	<0.01
Iraqi (0)	0	<0.01
Jordanian (0)	0	<0.01
Lebanese (20)	139	0.20
Moroccan (0)	0	<0.01
Palestinian (0)	0	<0.01
Syrian (0)	25	0.04
Other Arab (0)	0	<0.01
Armenian (0)	11	0.02
Assyrian/Chaldean/Syriac (0)	0	<0.01
Australian (0)	18	0.03
Austrian (0)	0	<0.01
Basque (0)	0	<0.01
Belgian (0)	0	<0.01
Brazilian (0)	0	<0.01
British (82)	115	0.17
Bulgarian (10)	33	0.05
Cajun (0)	0	<0.01
Canadian (11)	46	0.07
Carpatho Rusyn (0)	20	0.03
Celtic (0)	0	<0.01
Croatian (314)	688	0.99
Cypriot (0)	0	<0.01
Czech (28)	160	0.23
Czechoslovakian (24)	32	0.05
Danish (0)	141	0.20
Dutch (72)	662	0.95
Eastern European (11)	11	0.02
English (656)	3,017	4.34
Estonian (0)	0	<0.01
European (103)	119	0.17
Finnish (0)	29	0.04
French, ex. Basque (130)	542	0.78
French Canadian (58)	106	0.15
German (1,840)	7,654	11.00
German Russian (0)	1	<0.01
Greek (110)	312	0.45
Guyanese (0)	0	<0.01
Hungarian (389)	1,409	2.02
Icelander (0)	0	<0.01
Iranian (0)	0	<0.01
Irish (1,479)	6,661	9.57
Israeli (0)	0	<0.01
Italian (3,495)	7,337	10.54
Latvian (0)	0	<0.01
Lithuanian (33)	79	0.11
Luxemburger (0)	0	<0.01
Macedonian (0)	0	<0.01
Maltese (0)	0	<0.01
New Zealander (0)	0	<0.01
Northern European (7)	7	0.01
Norwegian (7)	22	0.03
Pennsylvania German (19)	113	0.16
Polish (807)	2,036	2.93
Portuguese (10)	25	0.04
Romanian (146)	267	0.38
Russian (152)	351	0.50
Scandinavian (0)	0	<0.01
Scotch-Irish (218)	730	1.05
Scottish (79)	466	0.67
Serbian (16)	43	0.06
Slavic (9)	16	0.02
Slovak (1,477)	3,113	4.47
Slovene (20)	44	0.06
Soviet Union (0)	0	<0.01
Swedish (128)	228	0.33
Swiss (12)	96	0.14
Turkish (12)	12	0.02
Ukrainian (218)	533	0.77
Welsh (70)	877	1.26
West Indian, ex. Hispanic (86)	152	0.22
Bahamian (0)	0	<0.01
Barbadian (0)	8	0.01
Belizean (0)	0	<0.01
Bermudan (0)	0	<0.01
British West Indian (0)	0	<0.01
Dutch West Indian (0)	0	<0.01
Haitian (9)	19	0.03
Jamaican (77)	125	0.18
Trinidadian/Tobagonian (0)	0	<0.01
U.S. Virgin Islander (0)	0	<0.01
West Indian (0)	0	<0.01
Other West Indian (0)	0	<0.01
Yugoslavian (7)	34	0.05

Hispanic Origin	Population	%
Hispanic or Latino (of any race)	6,207	9.27
Central American, ex. Mexican	152	0.23
Costa Rican	5	0.01
Guatemalan	26	0.04
Honduran	46	0.07
Nicaraguan	7	0.01
Panamanian	19	0.03
Salvadoran	49	0.07
Other Central American	0	<0.01
Cuban	98	0.15
Dominican Republic	239	0.36
Mexican	1,270	1.90
Puerto Rican	3,836	5.73
South American	155	0.23
Argentinean	9	0.01
Bolivian	2	<0.01
Chilean	3	<0.01
Colombian	104	0.16
Ecuadorian	7	0.01
Paraguayan	0	<0.01
Peruvian	18	0.03
Uruguayan	1	<0.01
Venezuelan	9	0.01
Other South American	2	<0.01
Other Hispanic or Latino	457	0.68

Race*	Population	%
African-American/Black (30,257)	32,093	47.91
Not Hispanic (29,448)	30,939	46.19
Hispanic (809)	1,154	1.72
American Indian/Alaska Native (237)	870	1.30
Not Hispanic (183)	715	1.07
Hispanic (54)	155	0.23
Alaska Athabascan *(Ala. Nat.)* (0)	3	<0.01
Aleut *(Alaska Native)* (0)	0	<0.01
Apache (1)	19	0.03
Arapaho (0)	4	0.01
Blackfeet (9)	60	0.09
Canadian/French Am. Ind. (0)	0	<0.01
Central American Ind. (0)	0	<0.01
Cherokee (55)	234	0.35
Cheyenne (0)	0	<0.01
Chickasaw (1)	1	<0.01
Chippewa (0)	7	0.01
Choctaw (3)	14	0.02
Colville (0)	0	<0.01
Comanche (2)	6	0.01
Cree (0)	0	<0.01
Creek (0)	1	<0.01
Crow (0)	2	<0.01
Delaware (0)	1	<0.01
Hopi (2)	2	<0.01
Houma (0)	0	<0.01
Inupiat *(Alaska Native)* (1)	2	<0.01
Iroquois (6)	11	0.02
Kiowa (0)	0	<0.01
Lumbee (2)	2	<0.01
Menominee (0)	1	<0.01
Mexican American Ind. (8)	19	0.03
Navajo (2)	3	<0.01
Osage (0)	0	<0.01
Ottawa (0)	0	<0.01
Paiute (0)	0	<0.01
Pima (0)	0	<0.01
Potawatomi (0)	0	<0.01
Pueblo (0)	0	<0.01
Puget Sound Salish (0)	0	<0.01
Seminole (2)	6	0.01
Shoshone (1)	1	<0.01
Sioux (2)	11	0.02
South American Ind. (8)	15	0.02
Spanish American Ind. (3)	3	<0.01
Tlingit-Haida *(Alaska Native)* (0)	1	<0.01
Tohono O'Odham (0)	0	<0.01
Tsimshian *(Alaska Native)* (0)	0	<0.01
Ute (1)	1	<0.01
Yakama (0)	0	<0.01
Yaqui (2)	2	<0.01
Yuman (0)	0	<0.01
Yup'ik *(Alaska Native)* (0)	0	<0.01
Asian (297)	499	0.74
Not Hispanic (283)	449	0.67
Hispanic (14)	50	0.07
Bangladeshi (0)	1	<0.01
Bhutanese (0)	0	<0.01
Burmese (0)	0	<0.01
Cambodian (7)	9	0.01
Chinese, ex. Taiwanese (31)	43	0.06
Filipino (34)	74	0.11
Hmong (3)	3	<0.01
Indian (100)	128	0.19
Indonesian (1)	1	<0.01
Japanese (8)	27	0.04
Korean (19)	59	0.09
Laotian (7)	10	0.01
Malaysian (0)	0	<0.01
Nepalese (6)	7	0.01
Pakistani (11)	12	0.02
Sri Lankan (0)	1	<0.01
Taiwanese (3)	3	<0.01
Thai (1)	3	<0.01
Vietnamese (50)	67	0.10
Hawaii Native/Pacific Islander (17)	87	0.13
Not Hispanic (7)	54	0.08
Hispanic (10)	33	0.05
Fijian (0)	0	<0.01
Guamanian/Chamorro (3)	10	0.01
Marshallese (0)	0	<0.01
Native Hawaiian (5)	25	0.04
Samoan (2)	6	0.01
Tongan (0)	0	<0.01
White (31,508)	33,448	49.94
Not Hispanic (28,918)	30,411	45.40
Hispanic (2,590)	3,037	4.53

*Notes: † The Census 2010 population figure is used to calculate the percentages in the Hispanic Origin and Race categories. Ancestry percentages are based on the 2006-2010 American Community Survey population (not shown); ‡ Numbers in parentheses indicate the number of people reporting a single ancestry; * Numbers in parentheses indicate the number of persons reporting this race alone, not in combination with any other race; Please refer to the User Guide for more information.*

Ancestry Group Rankings

Afghan

Top 10 Places Sorted by Population

Based on all places, regardless of total population

Place	Population	%
Columbus (city) Franklin County	89	0.01
Dublin (city) Franklin County	38	0.10
Tallmadge (city) Summit County	13	0.07
Lebanon (city) Warren County	12	0.06
Wickliffe (city) Lake County	8	0.06
Aberdeen (village) Brown County	0	0.00
Ada (village) Hardin County	0	0.00
Adamsville (village) Muskingum County	0	0.00
Addyston (village) Hamilton County	0	0.00
Adelphi (village) Ross County	0	0.00

Top 10 Places Sorted by Percent of Total Population

Based on all places, regardless of total population

Place	Population	%
Dublin (city) Franklin County	38	0.10
Tallmadge (city) Summit County	13	0.07
Lebanon (city) Warren County	12	0.06
Wickliffe (city) Lake County	8	0.06
Columbus (city) Franklin County	89	0.01
Aberdeen (village) Brown County	0	0.00
Ada (village) Hardin County	0	0.00
Adamsville (village) Muskingum County	0	0.00
Addyston (village) Hamilton County	0	0.00
Adelphi (village) Ross County	0	0.00

Top 10 Places Sorted by Percent of Total Population

Based on places with total population of 50,000 or more

Place	Population	%
Columbus (city) Franklin County	89	0.01
Akron (city) Summit County	0	0.00
Canton (city) Stark County	0	0.00
Cincinnati (city) Hamilton County	0	0.00
Cleveland (city) Cuyahoga County	0	0.00
Dayton (city) Montgomery County	0	0.00
Elyria (city) Lorain County	0	0.00
Hamilton (city) Butler County	0	0.00
Kettering (city) Montgomery County	0	0.00
Lakewood (city) Cuyahoga County	0	0.00

African, Sub-Saharan

Top 10 Places Sorted by Population

Based on all places, regardless of total population

Place	Population	%
Columbus (city) Franklin County	26,987	3.50
Cincinnati (city) Hamilton County	17,006	5.67
Cleveland (city) Cuyahoga County	5,454	1.33
Toledo (city) Lucas County	3,260	1.12
Canton (city) Stark County	2,852	3.83
Youngstown (city) Mahoning County	2,765	3.97
Dayton (city) Montgomery County	2,395	1.64
Akron (city) Summit County	2,290	1.13
Fairfield (city) Butler County	1,080	2.53
Lima (city) Allen County	1,042	2.68

Top 10 Places Sorted by Percent of Total Population

Based on all places, regardless of total population

Place	Population	%
Urbancrest (village) Franklin County	284	27.76
Lockland (village) Hamilton County	451	13.02
Skyline Acres (cdp) Hamilton County	152	7.81
Chesterhill (village) Morgan County	16	6.40
Cincinnati (city) Hamilton County	17,006	5.67
Whitehall (city) Franklin County	932	5.13
Mount Healthy (city) Hamilton County	276	4.53
Kenwood (cdp) Hamilton County	326	4.51
Huber Ridge (cdp) Franklin County	196	4.39
Youngstown (city) Mahoning County	2,765	3.97

Top 10 Places Sorted by Percent of Total Population

Based on places with total population of 50,000 or more

Place	Population	%
Cincinnati (city) Hamilton County	17,006	5.67
Youngstown (city) Mahoning County	2,765	3.97
Canton (city) Stark County	2,852	3.83
Columbus (city) Franklin County	26,987	3.50
Dayton (city) Montgomery County	2,395	1.64
Cleveland (city) Cuyahoga County	5,454	1.33
Springfield (city) Clark County	729	1.19
Akron (city) Summit County	2,290	1.13
Toledo (city) Lucas County	3,260	1.12
Lakewood (city) Cuyahoga County	406	0.77

African, Sub-Saharan: African

Top 10 Places Sorted by Population

Based on all places, regardless of total population

Place	Population	%
Cincinnati (city) Hamilton County	15,631	5.21
Columbus (city) Franklin County	10,986	1.43
Cleveland (city) Cuyahoga County	4,279	1.05
Canton (city) Stark County	2,713	3.64
Youngstown (city) Mahoning County	2,655	3.82
Toledo (city) Lucas County	2,419	0.83
Akron (city) Summit County	2,027	1.00
Dayton (city) Montgomery County	1,956	1.34
Lima (city) Allen County	995	2.56
Mansfield (city) Richland County	827	1.69

Top 10 Places Sorted by Percent of Total Population

Based on all places, regardless of total population

Place	Population	%
Skyline Acres (cdp) Hamilton County	152	7.81
Chesterhill (village) Morgan County	16	6.40
Cincinnati (city) Hamilton County	15,631	5.21
Urbancrest (village) Franklin County	45	4.40
Youngstown (city) Mahoning County	2,655	3.82
Canton (city) Stark County	2,713	3.64
Maplewood Park (cdp) Trumbull County	10	3.44
Addyston (village) Hamilton County	24	3.38
New Weston (village) Darke County	6	3.28
Mount Healthy (city) Hamilton County	193	3.17

Top 10 Places Sorted by Percent of Total Population

Based on places with total population of 50,000 or more

Place	Population	%
Cincinnati (city) Hamilton County	15,631	5.21
Youngstown (city) Mahoning County	2,655	3.82
Canton (city) Stark County	2,713	3.64
Columbus (city) Franklin County	10,986	1.43
Dayton (city) Montgomery County	1,956	1.34
Springfield (city) Clark County	691	1.12
Cleveland (city) Cuyahoga County	4,279	1.05
Akron (city) Summit County	2,027	1.00
Toledo (city) Lucas County	2,419	0.83
Lorain (city) Lorain County	451	0.69

African, Sub-Saharan: Cape Verdean

Top 10 Places Sorted by Population

Based on all places, regardless of total population

Place	Population	%
Englewood (city) Montgomery County	94	0.71
Cleveland (city) Cuyahoga County	58	0.01
Canton (city) Stark County	56	0.08
Toledo (city) Lucas County	46	0.02
Akron (city) Summit County	33	0.02
Fairborn (city) Greene County	28	0.09
Columbus (city) Franklin County	28	<0.01
Springfield (city) Clark County	13	0.02
Aberdeen (village) Brown County	0	0.00
Ada (village) Hardin County	0	0.00

Top 10 Places Sorted by Percent of Total Population

Based on all places, regardless of total population

Place	Population	%
Englewood (city) Montgomery County	94	0.71
Fairborn (city) Greene County	28	0.09
Canton (city) Stark County	56	0.08
Toledo (city) Lucas County	46	0.02
Akron (city) Summit County	33	0.02
Springfield (city) Clark County	13	0.02
Cleveland (city) Cuyahoga County	58	0.01
Columbus (city) Franklin County	28	<0.01
Aberdeen (village) Brown County	0	0.00
Ada (village) Hardin County	0	0.00

Top 10 Places Sorted by Percent of Total Population

Based on places with total population of 50,000 or more

Place	Population	%
Canton (city) Stark County	56	0.08
Toledo (city) Lucas County	46	0.02
Akron (city) Summit County	33	0.02
Springfield (city) Clark County	13	0.02
Cleveland (city) Cuyahoga County	58	0.01
Columbus (city) Franklin County	28	<0.01
Cincinnati (city) Hamilton County	0	0.00
Dayton (city) Montgomery County	0	0.00
Elyria (city) Lorain County	0	0.00
Hamilton (city) Butler County	0	0.00

African, Sub-Saharan: Ethiopian

Top 10 Places Sorted by Population

Based on all places, regardless of total population

Place	Population	%
Columbus (city) Franklin County	2,207	0.29
Whitehall (city) Franklin County	565	3.11
Cincinnati (city) Hamilton County	458	0.15
Reynoldsburg (city) Franklin County	297	0.85
Pleasant Run Farm (cdp) Hamilton County	141	3.19
Forestville (cdp) Hamilton County	96	0.88
Forest Park (city) Hamilton County	96	0.51
Dayton (city) Montgomery County	94	0.06
Kenwood (cdp) Hamilton County	87	1.20
Westerville (city) Franklin County	68	0.19

Top 10 Places Sorted by Percent of Total Population

Based on all places, regardless of total population

Place	Population	%
Pleasant Run Farm (cdp) Hamilton County	141	3.19
Whitehall (city) Franklin County	565	3.11
Urbancrest (village) Franklin County	16	1.56
Kenwood (cdp) Hamilton County	87	1.20
Forestville (cdp) Hamilton County	96	0.88
Reynoldsburg (city) Franklin County	297	0.85
Forest Park (city) Hamilton County	96	0.51
Hartford (village) Licking County	3	0.51
Columbus (city) Franklin County	2,207	0.29
Westerville (city) Franklin County	68	0.19

Top 10 Places Sorted by Percent of Total Population

Based on places with total population of 50,000 or more

Place	Population	%
Columbus (city) Franklin County	2,207	0.29
Cincinnati (city) Hamilton County	458	0.15
Youngstown (city) Mahoning County	65	0.09
Dayton (city) Montgomery County	94	0.06
Akron (city) Summit County	42	0.02
Cleveland (city) Cuyahoga County	21	0.01
Canton (city) Stark County	0	0.00
Elyria (city) Lorain County	0	0.00
Hamilton (city) Butler County	0	0.00
Kettering (city) Montgomery County	0	0.00

African, Sub-Saharan: Ghanaian

Top 10 Places Sorted by Population

Based on all places, regardless of total population

Place	Population	%
Columbus (city) Franklin County	1,303	0.17
Fairfield (city) Butler County	368	0.86
Westerville (city) Franklin County	262	0.73
Cleveland (city) Cuyahoga County	79	0.02
Toledo (city) Lucas County	69	0.02
Lakewood (city) Cuyahoga County	67	0.13
Mount Healthy (city) Hamilton County	42	0.69
Forest Park (city) Hamilton County	39	0.21
South Euclid (city) Cuyahoga County	39	0.17
Solon (city) Cuyahoga County	34	0.15

Top 10 Places Sorted by Percent of Total Population

Based on all places, regardless of total population

Place	Population	%
Fairfield (city) Butler County	368	0.86
Westerville (city) Franklin County	262	0.73
Mount Healthy (city) Hamilton County	42	0.69
Mulberry (cdp) Clermont County	14	0.43
North College Hill (city) Hamilton County	33	0.35
Oakwood (village) Cuyahoga County	10	0.27
Forest Park (city) Hamilton County	39	0.21
Northgate (cdp) Hamilton County	13	0.20
Ada (village) Hardin County	12	0.20
Columbus (city) Franklin County	1,303	0.17

Top 10 Places Sorted by Percent of Total Population

Based on places with total population of 50,000 or more

Place	Population	%
Columbus (city) Franklin County	1,303	0.17
Lakewood (city) Cuyahoga County	67	0.13
Cleveland (city) Cuyahoga County	79	0.02
Toledo (city) Lucas County	69	0.02
Lorain (city) Lorain County	11	0.02
Cincinnati (city) Hamilton County	23	0.01
Akron (city) Summit County	0	0.00
Canton (city) Stark County	0	0.00
Dayton (city) Montgomery County	0	0.00
Elyria (city) Lorain County	0	0.00

African, Sub-Saharan: Kenyan

Top 10 Places Sorted by Population

Based on all places, regardless of total population

Place	Population	%
Columbus (city) Franklin County	517	0.07
Reynoldsburg (city) Franklin County	57	0.16
Garfield Heights (city) Cuyahoga County	51	0.18
Green (city) Summit County	46	0.18
Pleasant Run (cdp) Hamilton County	38	0.80
Parma (city) Cuyahoga County	31	0.04
Toledo (city) Lucas County	19	0.01
Elyria (city) Lorain County	18	0.03
Oberlin (city) Lorain County	17	0.20
Lakewood (city) Cuyahoga County	13	0.02

Top 10 Places Sorted by Percent of Total Population

Based on all places, regardless of total population

Place	Population	%
Pleasant Run (cdp) Hamilton County	38	0.80
North Randall (village) Cuyahoga County	3	0.35
Oberlin (city) Lorain County	17	0.20
Garfield Heights (city) Cuyahoga County	51	0.18
Green (city) Summit County	46	0.18
Reynoldsburg (city) Franklin County	57	0.16
Beachwood (city) Cuyahoga County	12	0.10
Columbus (city) Franklin County	517	0.07
Wilmington (city) Clinton County	9	0.07
Painesville (city) Lake County	12	0.06

Top 10 Places Sorted by Percent of Total Population

Based on places with total population of 50,000 or more

Place	Population	%
Columbus (city) Franklin County	517	0.07
Parma (city) Cuyahoga County	31	0.04
Elyria (city) Lorain County	18	0.03
Lakewood (city) Cuyahoga County	13	0.02
Toledo (city) Lucas County	19	0.01
Dayton (city) Montgomery County	10	0.01
Cincinnati (city) Hamilton County	12	<0.01
Cleveland (city) Cuyahoga County	10	<0.01
Akron (city) Summit County	0	0.00
Canton (city) Stark County	0	0.00

African, Sub-Saharan: Liberian

Top 10 Places Sorted by Population

Based on all places, regardless of total population

Place	Population	%
Columbus (city) Franklin County	384	0.05
Cleveland (city) Cuyahoga County	128	0.03
Richmond Heights (city) Cuyahoga County	65	0.61
Pataskala (city) Licking County	58	0.41
Huber Ridge (cdp) Franklin County	56	1.25
Lockland (village) Hamilton County	47	1.36
Canton (city) Stark County	38	0.05
Akron (city) Summit County	29	0.01
Cleveland Heights (city) Cuyahoga County	28	0.06
Cincinnati (city) Hamilton County	26	0.01

Top 10 Places Sorted by Percent of Total Population

Based on all places, regardless of total population

Place	Population	%
Lockland (village) Hamilton County	47	1.36
Huber Ridge (cdp) Franklin County	56	1.25
Richmond Heights (city) Cuyahoga County	65	0.61
Pataskala (city) Licking County	58	0.41
University Heights (city) Cuyahoga County	25	0.18
Landen (cdp) Warren County	6	0.09
Cleveland Heights (city) Cuyahoga County	28	0.06
Columbus (city) Franklin County	384	0.05
Canton (city) Stark County	38	0.05
Zanesville (city) Muskingum County	13	0.05

Top 10 Places Sorted by Percent of Total Population

Based on places with total population of 50,000 or more

Place	Population	%
Columbus (city) Franklin County	384	0.05
Canton (city) Stark County	38	0.05
Cleveland (city) Cuyahoga County	128	0.03
Akron (city) Summit County	29	0.01
Cincinnati (city) Hamilton County	26	0.01
Dayton (city) Montgomery County	0	0.00
Elyria (city) Lorain County	0	0.00
Hamilton (city) Butler County	0	0.00
Kettering (city) Montgomery County	0	0.00
Lakewood (city) Cuyahoga County	0	0.00

African, Sub-Saharan: Nigerian

Top 10 Places Sorted by Population

Based on all places, regardless of total population

Place	Population	%
Columbus (city) Franklin County	861	0.11
Toledo (city) Lucas County	642	0.22
Cleveland (city) Cuyahoga County	352	0.09
Kenwood (cdp) Hamilton County	239	3.31
Lockland (village) Hamilton County	204	5.89
Parma (city) Cuyahoga County	180	0.22
Solon (city) Cuyahoga County	168	0.73
Cincinnati (city) Hamilton County	158	0.05
Trotwood (city) Montgomery County	153	0.61
Dayton (city) Montgomery County	138	0.09

Top 10 Places Sorted by Percent of Total Population

Based on all places, regardless of total population

Place	Population	%
Lockland (village) Hamilton County	204	5.89
Kenwood (cdp) Hamilton County	239	3.31
Canal Winchester (village) Franklin County	77	1.14
Twinsburg Heights (cdp) Summit County	12	1.07
North Randall (village) Cuyahoga County	9	1.04
Newtown (village) Hamilton County	24	0.92
Solon (city) Cuyahoga County	168	0.73
Trotwood (city) Montgomery County	153	0.61
Bergholz (village) Jefferson County	4	0.60
Blacklick Estates (cdp) Franklin County	44	0.51

Top 10 Places Sorted by Percent of Total Population

Based on places with total population of 50,000 or more

Place	Population	%
Toledo (city) Lucas County	642	0.22
Parma (city) Cuyahoga County	180	0.22
Columbus (city) Franklin County	861	0.11
Lakewood (city) Cuyahoga County	52	0.10
Cleveland (city) Cuyahoga County	352	0.09
Dayton (city) Montgomery County	138	0.09
Cincinnati (city) Hamilton County	158	0.05
Springfield (city) Clark County	25	0.04
Lorain (city) Lorain County	11	0.02
Akron (city) Summit County	0	0.00

African, Sub-Saharan: Senegalese

Top 10 Places Sorted by Population

Based on all places, regardless of total population

Place	Population	%
Cincinnati (city) Hamilton County	195	0.06
Finneytown (cdp) Hamilton County	131	1.01
Columbus (city) Franklin County	104	0.01
Bedford Heights (city) Cuyahoga County	22	0.20
Cleveland (city) Cuyahoga County	17	<0.01
Toledo (city) Lucas County	15	0.01
Northbrook (cdp) Hamilton County	14	0.14
Medina (city) Medina County	13	0.05
Mansfield (city) Richland County	8	0.02
Aberdeen (village) Brown County	0	0.00

Top 10 Places Sorted by Percent of Total Population

Based on all places, regardless of total population

Place	Population	%
Finneytown (cdp) Hamilton County	131	1.01
Bedford Heights (city) Cuyahoga County	22	0.20
Northbrook (cdp) Hamilton County	14	0.14
Cincinnati (city) Hamilton County	195	0.06
Medina (city) Medina County	13	0.05
Mansfield (city) Richland County	8	0.02
Columbus (city) Franklin County	104	0.01
Toledo (city) Lucas County	15	0.01
Cleveland (city) Cuyahoga County	17	<0.01
Aberdeen (village) Brown County	0	0.00

Top 10 Places Sorted by Percent of Total Population

Based on places with total population of 50,000 or more

Place	Population	%
Cincinnati (city) Hamilton County	195	0.06
Columbus (city) Franklin County	104	0.01
Toledo (city) Lucas County	15	0.01
Cleveland (city) Cuyahoga County	17	<0.01
Akron (city) Summit County	0	0.00
Canton (city) Stark County	0	0.00
Dayton (city) Montgomery County	0	0.00
Elyria (city) Lorain County	0	0.00
Hamilton (city) Butler County	0	0.00
Kettering (city) Montgomery County	0	0.00

African, Sub-Saharan: Sierra Leonean

Top 10 Places Sorted by Population

Based on all places, regardless of total population

Place	Population	%
Columbus (city) Franklin County	461	0.06
Lake Darby (cdp) Franklin County	38	0.82
Olmsted Falls (city) Cuyahoga County	36	0.41
Streetsboro (city) Portage County	23	0.15
Aberdeen (village) Brown County	0	0.00
Ada (village) Hardin County	0	0.00
Adamsville (village) Muskingum County	0	0.00
Addyston (village) Hamilton County	0	0.00
Adelphi (village) Ross County	0	0.00
Adena (village) Jefferson County	0	0.00

Top 10 Places Sorted by Percent of Total Population

Based on all places, regardless of total population

Place	Population	%
Lake Darby (cdp) Franklin County	38	0.82
Olmsted Falls (city) Cuyahoga County	36	0.41
Streetsboro (city) Portage County	23	0.15

Place	Population	%
Columbus (city) Franklin County	461	0.06
Aberdeen (village) Brown County	0	0.00
Ada (village) Hardin County	0	0.00
Adamsville (village) Muskingum County	0	0.00
Addyston (village) Hamilton County	0	0.00
Adelphi (village) Ross County	0	0.00
Adena (village) Jefferson County	0	0.00

Top 10 Places Sorted by Percent of Total Population
Based on places with total population of 50,000 or more

Place	Population	%
Columbus (city) Franklin County	461	0.06
Akron (city) Summit County	0	0.00
Canton (city) Stark County	0	0.00
Cincinnati (city) Hamilton County	0	0.00
Cleveland (city) Cuyahoga County	0	0.00
Dayton (city) Montgomery County	0	0.00
Elyria (city) Lorain County	0	0.00
Hamilton (city) Butler County	0	0.00
Kettering (city) Montgomery County	0	0.00
Lakewood (city) Cuyahoga County	0	0.00

African, Sub-Saharan: Somalian

Top 10 Places Sorted by Population
Based on all places, regardless of total population

Place	Population	%
Columbus (city) Franklin County	9,093	1.18
Urbancrest (village) Franklin County	223	21.80
Hilliard (city) Franklin County	130	0.47
Warrensville Heights (city) Cuyahoga County	119	0.87
Dublin (city) Franklin County	77	0.20
Westlake (city) Cuyahoga County	76	0.23
Huber Ridge (cdp) Franklin County	57	1.28
Cleveland (city) Cuyahoga County	41	0.01
Whitehall (city) Franklin County	37	0.20
Lima (city) Allen County	34	0.09

Top 10 Places Sorted by Percent of Total Population
Based on all places, regardless of total population

Place	Population	%
Urbancrest (village) Franklin County	223	21.80
Huber Ridge (cdp) Franklin County	57	1.28
Columbus (city) Franklin County	9,093	1.18
Warrensville Heights (city) Cuyahoga County	119	0.87
Hilliard (city) Franklin County	130	0.47
Westlake (city) Cuyahoga County	76	0.23
Dublin (city) Franklin County	77	0.20
Whitehall (city) Franklin County	37	0.20
Lima (city) Allen County	34	0.09
Grove City (city) Franklin County	28	0.08

Top 10 Places Sorted by Percent of Total Population
Based on places with total population of 50,000 or more

Place	Population	%
Columbus (city) Franklin County	9,093	1.18
Cleveland (city) Cuyahoga County	41	0.01
Akron (city) Summit County	23	0.01
Canton (city) Stark County	0	0.00
Cincinnati (city) Hamilton County	0	0.00
Dayton (city) Montgomery County	0	0.00
Elyria (city) Lorain County	0	0.00
Hamilton (city) Butler County	0	0.00
Kettering (city) Montgomery County	0	0.00
Lakewood (city) Cuyahoga County	0	0.00

African, Sub-Saharan: South African

Top 10 Places Sorted by Population
Based on all places, regardless of total population

Place	Population	%
Columbus (city) Franklin County	115	0.01
Beachwood (city) Cuyahoga County	79	0.66
Greenville (city) Darke County	75	0.57
Cleveland (city) Cuyahoga County	68	0.02
Findlay (city) Hancock County	51	0.12
Montrose-Ghent (cdp) Summit County	46	0.90
Canton (city) Stark County	45	0.06
Monfort Heights (cdp) Hamilton County	36	0.31
Shaker Heights (city) Cuyahoga County	35	0.12
Cleveland Heights (city) Cuyahoga County	35	0.07

Top 10 Places Sorted by Percent of Total Population
Based on all places, regardless of total population

Place	Population	%
Montrose-Ghent (cdp) Summit County	46	0.90
Orange (village) Cuyahoga County	28	0.85
Lockland (village) Hamilton County	25	0.72
Northfield (village) Summit County	26	0.70
Beachwood (city) Cuyahoga County	79	0.66
Greenville (city) Darke County	75	0.57
Brimfield (cdp) Portage County	13	0.39
Monfort Heights (cdp) Hamilton County	36	0.31
New Concord (village) Muskingum County	4	0.16
West Carrollton (city) Montgomery County	18	0.14

Top 10 Places Sorted by Percent of Total Population
Based on places with total population of 50,000 or more

Place	Population	%
Canton (city) Stark County	45	0.06
Cleveland (city) Cuyahoga County	68	0.02
Dayton (city) Montgomery County	22	0.02
Columbus (city) Franklin County	115	0.01
Toledo (city) Lucas County	27	0.01
Akron (city) Summit County	17	0.01
Cincinnati (city) Hamilton County	13	<0.01
Elyria (city) Lorain County	0	0.00
Hamilton (city) Butler County	0	0.00
Kettering (city) Montgomery County	0	0.00

African, Sub-Saharan: Sudanese

Top 10 Places Sorted by Population
Based on all places, regardless of total population

Place	Population	%
Columbus (city) Franklin County	90	0.01
Cleveland (city) Cuyahoga County	86	0.02
Cincinnati (city) Hamilton County	63	0.02
Elyria (city) Lorain County	55	0.10
Whitehall (city) Franklin County	50	0.28
Lakewood (city) Cuyahoga County	23	0.04
Bluffton (village) Allen County	10	0.24
Mayfield Heights (city) Cuyahoga County	8	0.04
Aberdeen (village) Brown County	0	0.00
Ada (village) Hardin County	0	0.00

Top 10 Places Sorted by Percent of Total Population
Based on all places, regardless of total population

Place	Population	%
Whitehall (city) Franklin County	50	0.28
Bluffton (village) Allen County	10	0.24
Elyria (city) Lorain County	55	0.10
Lakewood (city) Cuyahoga County	23	0.04
Mayfield Heights (city) Cuyahoga County	8	0.04
Cleveland (city) Cuyahoga County	86	0.02
Cincinnati (city) Hamilton County	63	0.02
Columbus (city) Franklin County	90	0.01
Aberdeen (village) Brown County	0	0.00
Ada (village) Hardin County	0	0.00

Top 10 Places Sorted by Percent of Total Population
Based on places with total population of 50,000 or more

Place	Population	%
Elyria (city) Lorain County	55	0.10
Lakewood (city) Cuyahoga County	23	0.04
Cleveland (city) Cuyahoga County	86	0.02
Cincinnati (city) Hamilton County	63	0.02
Columbus (city) Franklin County	90	0.01
Akron (city) Summit County	0	0.00
Canton (city) Stark County	0	0.00
Dayton (city) Montgomery County	0	0.00
Hamilton (city) Butler County	0	0.00
Kettering (city) Montgomery County	0	0.00

African, Sub-Saharan: Ugandan

Top 10 Places Sorted by Population
Based on all places, regardless of total population

Place	Population	%
Cleveland Heights (city) Cuyahoga County	12	0.03
Lakewood (city) Cuyahoga County	9	0.02
Oxford (city) Butler County	8	0.04
Parma (city) Cuyahoga County	8	0.01
Athens (city) Athens County	6	0.03
Aberdeen (village) Brown County	0	0.00
Ada (village) Hardin County	0	0.00
Adamsville (village) Muskingum County	0	0.00
Addyston (village) Hamilton County	0	0.00
Adelphi (village) Ross County	0	0.00

Top 10 Places Sorted by Percent of Total Population
Based on all places, regardless of total population

Place	Population	%
Oxford (city) Butler County	8	0.04
Cleveland Heights (city) Cuyahoga County	12	0.03
Athens (city) Athens County	6	0.03
Lakewood (city) Cuyahoga County	9	0.02
Parma (city) Cuyahoga County	8	0.01
Aberdeen (village) Brown County	0	0.00
Ada (village) Hardin County	0	0.00
Adamsville (village) Muskingum County	0	0.00
Addyston (village) Hamilton County	0	0.00
Adelphi (village) Ross County	0	0.00

Top 10 Places Sorted by Percent of Total Population
Based on places with total population of 50,000 or more

Place	Population	%
Lakewood (city) Cuyahoga County	9	0.02
Parma (city) Cuyahoga County	8	0.01
Akron (city) Summit County	0	0.00
Canton (city) Stark County	0	0.00
Cincinnati (city) Hamilton County	0	0.00
Cleveland (city) Cuyahoga County	0	0.00
Columbus (city) Franklin County	0	0.00
Dayton (city) Montgomery County	0	0.00
Elyria (city) Lorain County	0	0.00
Hamilton (city) Butler County	0	0.00

African, Sub-Saharan: Zimbabwean

Top 10 Places Sorted by Population
Based on all places, regardless of total population

Place	Population	%
Blue Ash (city) Hamilton County	172	1.43
Columbus (city) Franklin County	125	0.02
Cincinnati (city) Hamilton County	53	0.02
Akron (city) Summit County	12	0.01
Aberdeen (village) Brown County	0	0.00
Ada (village) Hardin County	0	0.00
Adamsville (village) Muskingum County	0	0.00
Addyston (village) Hamilton County	0	0.00
Adelphi (village) Ross County	0	0.00
Adena (village) Jefferson County	0	0.00

Top 10 Places Sorted by Percent of Total Population
Based on all places, regardless of total population

Place	Population	%
Blue Ash (city) Hamilton County	172	1.43
Columbus (city) Franklin County	125	0.02
Cincinnati (city) Hamilton County	53	0.02
Akron (city) Summit County	12	0.01
Aberdeen (village) Brown County	0	0.00
Ada (village) Hardin County	0	0.00
Adamsville (village) Muskingum County	0	0.00
Addyston (village) Hamilton County	0	0.00
Adelphi (village) Ross County	0	0.00
Adena (village) Jefferson County	0	0.00

Top 10 Places Sorted by Percent of Total Population
Based on places with total population of 50,000 or more

Place	Population	%
Columbus (city) Franklin County	125	0.02
Cincinnati (city) Hamilton County	53	0.02
Akron (city) Summit County	12	0.01
Canton (city) Stark County	0	0.00
Cleveland (city) Cuyahoga County	0	0.00
Dayton (city) Montgomery County	0	0.00
Elyria (city) Lorain County	0	0.00
Hamilton (city) Butler County	0	0.00
Kettering (city) Montgomery County	0	0.00
Lakewood (city) Cuyahoga County	0	0.00

African, Sub-Saharan: Other

Top 10 Places Sorted by Population

Based on all places, regardless of total population

Place	Population	%
Columbus (city) Franklin County	713	0.09
Cincinnati (city) Hamilton County	374	0.12
Forest Park (city) Hamilton County	366	1.96
Cleveland (city) Cuyahoga County	315	0.08
Dayton (city) Montgomery County	175	0.12
Akron (city) Summit County	107	0.05
Euclid (city) Cuyahoga County	105	0.21
Lockland (village) Hamilton County	93	2.69
Parma Heights (city) Cuyahoga County	91	0.44
Streetsboro (city) Portage County	82	0.53

Top 10 Places Sorted by Percent of Total Population

Based on all places, regardless of total population

Place	Population	%
Lockland (village) Hamilton County	93	2.69
Forest Park (city) Hamilton County	366	1.96
Turpin Hills (cdp) Hamilton County	45	0.91
North Randall (village) Cuyahoga County	7	0.81
Hiram (village) Portage County	9	0.73
Baltic (village) Tuscarawas County	3	0.58
Streetsboro (city) Portage County	82	0.53
Parma Heights (city) Cuyahoga County	91	0.44
Beach City (village) Stark County	4	0.36
Sidney (city) Shelby County	64	0.30

Top 10 Places Sorted by Percent of Total Population

Based on places with total population of 50,000 or more

Place	Population	%
Lakewood (city) Cuyahoga County	73	0.14
Cincinnati (city) Hamilton County	374	0.12
Dayton (city) Montgomery County	175	0.12
Columbus (city) Franklin County	713	0.09
Cleveland (city) Cuyahoga County	315	0.08
Youngstown (city) Mahoning County	45	0.06
Akron (city) Summit County	107	0.05
Kettering (city) Montgomery County	11	0.02
Toledo (city) Lucas County	23	0.01
Canton (city) Stark County	0	0.00

Albanian

Top 10 Places Sorted by Population

Based on all places, regardless of total population

Place	Population	%
Lakewood (city) Cuyahoga County	766	1.45
Rocky River (city) Cuyahoga County	328	1.62
Akron (city) Summit County	304	0.15
Columbus (city) Franklin County	292	0.04
Fairview Park (city) Cuyahoga County	223	1.32
North Olmsted (city) Cuyahoga County	176	0.54
Parma Heights (city) Cuyahoga County	164	0.79
Cleveland (city) Cuyahoga County	139	0.03
Willowick (city) Lake County	132	0.93
West Carrollton (city) Montgomery County	129	0.97

Top 10 Places Sorted by Percent of Total Population

Based on all places, regardless of total population

Place	Population	%
Peninsula (village) Summit County	16	2.79
Lake Mohawk (cdp) Carroll County	48	2.76
McKinley Heights (cdp) Trumbull County	25	2.29
Rocky River (city) Cuyahoga County	328	1.62
Lakewood (city) Cuyahoga County	766	1.45
Fairview Park (city) Cuyahoga County	223	1.32
West Carrollton (city) Montgomery County	129	0.97
Willowick (city) Lake County	132	0.93
Montrose-Ghent (cdp) Summit County	42	0.82
Parma Heights (city) Cuyahoga County	164	0.79

Top 10 Places Sorted by Percent of Total Population

Based on places with total population of 50,000 or more

Place	Population	%
Lakewood (city) Cuyahoga County	766	1.45
Akron (city) Summit County	304	0.15
Parma (city) Cuyahoga County	41	0.05
Columbus (city) Franklin County	292	0.04
Canton (city) Stark County	30	0.04
Cleveland (city) Cuyahoga County	139	0.03
Youngstown (city) Mahoning County	22	0.03
Kettering (city) Montgomery County	15	0.03
Cincinnati (city) Hamilton County	0	0.00
Dayton (city) Montgomery County	0	0.00

Alsatian

Top 10 Places Sorted by Population

Based on all places, regardless of total population

Place	Population	%
Ashland (city) Ashland County	69	0.33
Cincinnati (city) Hamilton County	67	0.02
Dent (cdp) Hamilton County	30	0.31
Grove City (city) Franklin County	30	0.09
Columbus (city) Franklin County	29	<0.01
Akron (city) Summit County	26	0.01
Salem Heights (cdp) Hamilton County	25	0.63
Archbold (village) Fulton County	24	0.57
Athens (city) Athens County	21	0.09
White Oak (cdp) Hamilton County	20	0.11

Top 10 Places Sorted by Percent of Total Population

Based on all places, regardless of total population

Place	Population	%
Lake Waynoka (cdp) Brown County	11	1.21
Silver Lake (village) Summit County	17	0.66
Salem Heights (cdp) Hamilton County	25	0.63
Archbold (village) Fulton County	24	0.57
Moreland Hills (village) Cuyahoga County	15	0.45
Sherwood (cdp) Hamilton County	14	0.40
Fredericktown (village) Knox County	10	0.40
Ashland (city) Ashland County	69	0.33
Dent (cdp) Hamilton County	30	0.31
Gibsonburg (village) Sandusky County	6	0.23

Top 10 Places Sorted by Percent of Total Population

Based on places with total population of 50,000 or more

Place	Population	%
Cincinnati (city) Hamilton County	67	0.02
Kettering (city) Montgomery County	13	0.02
Akron (city) Summit County	26	0.01
Dayton (city) Montgomery County	13	0.01
Columbus (city) Franklin County	29	<0.01
Toledo (city) Lucas County	6	<0.01
Canton (city) Stark County	0	0.00
Cleveland (city) Cuyahoga County	0	0.00
Elyria (city) Lorain County	0	0.00
Hamilton (city) Butler County	0	0.00

American

Top 10 Places Sorted by Population

Based on all places, regardless of total population

Place	Population	%
Columbus (city) Franklin County	31,925	4.14
Cincinnati (city) Hamilton County	18,156	6.05
Dayton (city) Montgomery County	16,035	11.01
Hamilton (city) Butler County	15,067	24.12
Toledo (city) Lucas County	10,051	3.44
Cleveland (city) Cuyahoga County	9,836	2.40
Akron (city) Summit County	8,242	4.06
Springfield (city) Clark County	8,078	13.14
Warren (city) Trumbull County	7,537	17.66
Fairborn (city) Greene County	6,052	18.82

Top 10 Places Sorted by Percent of Total Population

Based on all places, regardless of total population

Place	Population	%
Flat Rock (cdp) Seneca County	86	61.87
Kanauga (cdp) Gallia County	75	59.52
Octa (village) Fayette County	28	58.33
Kansas (cdp) Seneca County	166	56.27
Somerville (village) Butler County	147	55.89
Olde West Chester (cdp) Butler County	95	46.57
Cynthiana (cdp) Pike County	26	46.43
Congress (village) Wayne County	78	45.61
Hanging Rock (village) Lawrence County	74	42.77
Darbyville (village) Pickaway County	89	42.38

Top 10 Places Sorted by Percent of Total Population

Based on places with total population of 50,000 or more

Place	Population	%
Hamilton (city) Butler County	15,067	24.12
Springfield (city) Clark County	8,078	13.14
Dayton (city) Montgomery County	16,035	11.01
Elyria (city) Lorain County	5,042	9.17
Kettering (city) Montgomery County	4,961	8.83
Canton (city) Stark County	5,025	6.75
Cincinnati (city) Hamilton County	18,156	6.05
Columbus (city) Franklin County	31,925	4.14
Akron (city) Summit County	8,242	4.06
Parma (city) Cuyahoga County	3,084	3.77

Arab: Total

Top 10 Places Sorted by Population

Based on all places, regardless of total population

Place	Population	%
Columbus (city) Franklin County	6,451	0.84
Toledo (city) Lucas County	3,428	1.17
Cleveland (city) Cuyahoga County	3,346	0.82
Lakewood (city) Cuyahoga County	1,450	2.75
Cincinnati (city) Hamilton County	1,405	0.47
Akron (city) Summit County	1,396	0.69
Parma (city) Cuyahoga County	1,340	1.64
North Olmsted (city) Cuyahoga County	1,223	3.73
Westlake (city) Cuyahoga County	1,183	3.66
Strongsville (city) Cuyahoga County	988	2.23

Top 10 Places Sorted by Percent of Total Population

Based on all places, regardless of total population

Place	Population	%
Damascus (cdp) Mahoning County	23	9.27
Port William (village) Clinton County	17	6.67
Lake Tomahawk (cdp) Columbiana County	21	4.59
Bloomingburg (village) Fayette County	44	4.51
Rosemount (cdp) Scioto County	90	4.09
Olmsted Falls (city) Cuyahoga County	343	3.92
Middleburg Heights (city) Cuyahoga County	596	3.77
North Olmsted (city) Cuyahoga County	1,223	3.73
Linndale (village) Cuyahoga County	5	3.68
Westlake (city) Cuyahoga County	1,183	3.66

Top 10 Places Sorted by Percent of Total Population

Based on places with total population of 50,000 or more

Place	Population	%
Lakewood (city) Cuyahoga County	1,450	2.75
Parma (city) Cuyahoga County	1,340	1.64
Toledo (city) Lucas County	3,428	1.17
Columbus (city) Franklin County	6,451	0.84
Cleveland (city) Cuyahoga County	3,346	0.82
Kettering (city) Montgomery County	458	0.82
Canton (city) Stark County	577	0.78
Akron (city) Summit County	1,396	0.69
Lorain (city) Lorain County	383	0.59
Cincinnati (city) Hamilton County	1,405	0.47

Arab: Arab

Top 10 Places Sorted by Population

Based on all places, regardless of total population

Place	Population	%
Columbus (city) Franklin County	1,109	0.14
Cleveland (city) Cuyahoga County	663	0.16
Toledo (city) Lucas County	614	0.21
North Olmsted (city) Cuyahoga County	447	1.36
Westlake (city) Cuyahoga County	344	1.06
Lakewood (city) Cuyahoga County	218	0.41
Lorain (city) Lorain County	211	0.32
Cincinnati (city) Hamilton County	199	0.07
Boardman (cdp) Mahoning County	198	0.56
Parma (city) Cuyahoga County	184	0.22

Top 10 Places Sorted by Percent of Total Population

Based on all places, regardless of total population

Place	Population	%
Lexington (village) Richland County	168	3.25
Moreland Hills (village) Cuyahoga County	52	1.57
Linndale (village) Cuyahoga County	2	1.47

Place	Population	%
Lincoln Heights (village) Hamilton County	49	1.44
North Olmsted (city) Cuyahoga County	447	1.36
Craig Beach (village) Mahoning County	12	1.07
Westlake (city) Cuyahoga County	344	1.06
Mogadore (village) Summit County	43	1.06
Williamsburg (village) Clermont County	25	1.04
Gates Mills (village) Cuyahoga County	18	0.83

Top 10 Places Sorted by Percent of Total Population

Based on places with total population of 50,000 or more

Place	Population	%
Lakewood (city) Cuyahoga County	218	0.41
Lorain (city) Lorain County	211	0.32
Parma (city) Cuyahoga County	184	0.22
Toledo (city) Lucas County	614	0.21
Cleveland (city) Cuyahoga County	663	0.16
Youngstown (city) Mahoning County	110	0.16
Columbus (city) Franklin County	1,109	0.14
Akron (city) Summit County	159	0.08
Cincinnati (city) Hamilton County	199	0.07
Dayton (city) Montgomery County	39	0.03

Arab: Egyptian

Top 10 Places Sorted by Population

Based on all places, regardless of total population

Place	Population	%
Columbus (city) Franklin County	911	0.12
Cleveland (city) Cuyahoga County	326	0.08
Strongsville (city) Cuyahoga County	179	0.40
Lakewood (city) Cuyahoga County	172	0.33
Dublin (city) Franklin County	164	0.42
Akron (city) Summit County	137	0.07
Cincinnati (city) Hamilton County	133	0.04
Sylvania (city) Lucas County	114	0.60
Westlake (city) Cuyahoga County	111	0.34
Parma Heights (city) Cuyahoga County	110	0.53

Top 10 Places Sorted by Percent of Total Population

Based on all places, regardless of total population

Place	Population	%
Orange (village) Cuyahoga County	56	1.70
Maineville (village) Warren County	8	0.97
New Albany (village) Franklin County	62	0.87
Sylvania (city) Lucas County	114	0.60
Parma Heights (city) Cuyahoga County	110	0.53
Independence (city) Cuyahoga County	36	0.51
Delta (village) Fulton County	15	0.50
Dublin (city) Franklin County	164	0.42
Elida (village) Allen County	9	0.42
Strongsville (city) Cuyahoga County	179	0.40

Top 10 Places Sorted by Percent of Total Population

Based on places with total population of 50,000 or more

Place	Population	%
Lakewood (city) Cuyahoga County	172	0.33
Columbus (city) Franklin County	911	0.12
Cleveland (city) Cuyahoga County	326	0.08
Akron (city) Summit County	137	0.07
Cincinnati (city) Hamilton County	133	0.04
Dayton (city) Montgomery County	46	0.03
Kettering (city) Montgomery County	10	0.02
Toledo (city) Lucas County	28	0.01
Canton (city) Stark County	5	0.01
Elyria (city) Lorain County	0	0.00

Arab: Iraqi

Top 10 Places Sorted by Population

Based on all places, regardless of total population

Place	Population	%
Columbus (city) Franklin County	334	0.04
Centerville (city) Montgomery County	264	1.11
Parma (city) Cuyahoga County	153	0.19
Dayton (city) Montgomery County	123	0.08
Cleveland (city) Cuyahoga County	85	0.02
Delaware (city) Delaware County	58	0.17
Stow (city) Summit County	44	0.13
Toledo (city) Lucas County	28	0.01
Canton (city) Stark County	15	0.02
Miamisburg (city) Montgomery County	14	0.07

Top 10 Places Sorted by Percent of Total Population

Based on all places, regardless of total population

Place	Population	%
Centerville (city) Montgomery County	264	1.11
Bluffton (village) Allen County	11	0.27
Parma (city) Cuyahoga County	153	0.19
Delaware (city) Delaware County	58	0.17
Stow (city) Summit County	44	0.13
Dayton (city) Montgomery County	123	0.08
Miamisburg (city) Montgomery County	14	0.07
Barberton (city) Summit County	14	0.05
Columbus (city) Franklin County	334	0.04
Cleveland (city) Cuyahoga County	85	0.02

Top 10 Places Sorted by Percent of Total Population

Based on places with total population of 50,000 or more

Place	Population	%
Parma (city) Cuyahoga County	153	0.19
Dayton (city) Montgomery County	123	0.08
Columbus (city) Franklin County	334	0.04
Cleveland (city) Cuyahoga County	85	0.02
Canton (city) Stark County	15	0.02
Toledo (city) Lucas County	28	0.01
Hamilton (city) Butler County	8	0.01
Cincinnati (city) Hamilton County	14	<0.01
Akron (city) Summit County	7	<0.01
Elyria (city) Lorain County	0	0.00

Arab: Jordanian

Top 10 Places Sorted by Population

Based on all places, regardless of total population

Place	Population	%
Columbus (city) Franklin County	617	0.08
Toledo (city) Lucas County	201	0.07
Cincinnati (city) Hamilton County	127	0.04
Cleveland (city) Cuyahoga County	115	0.03
Fairview Park (city) Cuyahoga County	107	0.63
Miamisburg (city) Montgomery County	105	0.53
New Burlington (cdp) Hamilton County	99	1.87
Ravenna (city) Portage County	94	0.80
Bellefontaine (city) Logan County	83	0.63
Kettering (city) Montgomery County	78	0.14

Top 10 Places Sorted by Percent of Total Population

Based on all places, regardless of total population

Place	Population	%
New Burlington (cdp) Hamilton County	99	1.87
Ravenna (city) Portage County	94	0.80
Park Layne (cdp) Clark County	35	0.78
Fairview Park (city) Cuyahoga County	107	0.63
Bellefontaine (city) Logan County	83	0.63
Olmsted Falls (city) Cuyahoga County	48	0.55
Miamisburg (city) Montgomery County	105	0.53
Shawnee Hills (village) Delaware County	4	0.51
Rocky River (city) Cuyahoga County	62	0.31
Glendale (village) Hamilton County	7	0.30

Top 10 Places Sorted by Percent of Total Population

Based on places with total population of 50,000 or more

Place	Population	%
Kettering (city) Montgomery County	78	0.14
Hamilton (city) Butler County	58	0.09
Columbus (city) Franklin County	617	0.08
Toledo (city) Lucas County	201	0.07
Elyria (city) Lorain County	30	0.05
Cincinnati (city) Hamilton County	127	0.04
Cleveland (city) Cuyahoga County	115	0.03
Dayton (city) Montgomery County	39	0.03
Akron (city) Summit County	0	0.00
Canton (city) Stark County	0	0.00

Arab: Lebanese

Top 10 Places Sorted by Population

Based on all places, regardless of total population

Place	Population	%
Toledo (city) Lucas County	1,656	0.57
Columbus (city) Franklin County	1,656	0.21
Cleveland (city) Cuyahoga County	1,147	0.28
Akron (city) Summit County	914	0.45
Parma (city) Cuyahoga County	813	0.99
Lakewood (city) Cuyahoga County	706	1.34
Cincinnati (city) Hamilton County	704	0.23
Middleburg Heights (city) Cuyahoga County	479	3.03
Westlake (city) Cuyahoga County	431	1.33
Strongsville (city) Cuyahoga County	410	0.92

Top 10 Places Sorted by Percent of Total Population

Based on all places, regardless of total population

Place	Population	%
Damascus (cdp) Mahoning County	23	9.27
Port William (village) Clinton County	17	6.67
Lake Tomahawk (cdp) Columbiana County	21	4.59
Bloomingburg (village) Fayette County	44	4.51
Five Points (cdp) Warren County	65	3.37
Mulberry (cdp) Clermont County	109	3.35
Middleburg Heights (city) Cuyahoga County	479	3.03
Marble Cliff (village) Franklin County	17	2.91
Savannah (village) Ashland County	7	2.29
Mount Repose (cdp) Clermont County	94	2.21

Top 10 Places Sorted by Percent of Total Population

Based on places with total population of 50,000 or more

Place	Population	%
Lakewood (city) Cuyahoga County	706	1.34
Parma (city) Cuyahoga County	813	0.99
Toledo (city) Lucas County	1,656	0.57
Canton (city) Stark County	358	0.48
Akron (city) Summit County	914	0.45
Kettering (city) Montgomery County	251	0.45
Cleveland (city) Cuyahoga County	1,147	0.28
Cincinnati (city) Hamilton County	704	0.23
Lorain (city) Lorain County	153	0.23
Columbus (city) Franklin County	1,656	0.21

Arab: Moroccan

Top 10 Places Sorted by Population

Based on all places, regardless of total population

Place	Population	%
Columbus (city) Franklin County	308	0.04
Parma (city) Cuyahoga County	83	0.10
Cleveland Heights (city) Cuyahoga County	82	0.18
Cleveland (city) Cuyahoga County	75	0.02
Cincinnati (city) Hamilton County	65	0.02
Aurora (city) Portage County	63	0.41
Englewood (city) Montgomery County	39	0.30
Dublin (city) Franklin County	39	0.10
Bexley (city) Franklin County	38	0.29
Dayton (city) Montgomery County	28	0.02

Top 10 Places Sorted by Percent of Total Population

Based on all places, regardless of total population

Place	Population	%
South Amherst (village) Lorain County	10	0.54
New Holland (village) Pickaway County	3	0.44
Aurora (city) Portage County	63	0.41
Englewood (city) Montgomery County	39	0.30
Bexley (city) Franklin County	38	0.29
South Lebanon (village) Warren County	11	0.29
Amherst (city) Lorain County	27	0.22
Cleveland Heights (city) Cuyahoga County	82	0.18
Grafton (village) Lorain County	9	0.14
Orrville (city) Wayne County	11	0.13

Top 10 Places Sorted by Percent of Total Population

Based on places with total population of 50,000 or more

Place	Population	%
Parma (city) Cuyahoga County	83	0.10
Columbus (city) Franklin County	308	0.04
Cleveland (city) Cuyahoga County	75	0.02
Cincinnati (city) Hamilton County	65	0.02
Dayton (city) Montgomery County	28	0.02
Akron (city) Summit County	0	0.00
Canton (city) Stark County	0	0.00
Elyria (city) Lorain County	0	0.00
Hamilton (city) Butler County	0	0.00
Kettering (city) Montgomery County	0	0.00

Arab: Palestinian

Top 10 Places Sorted by Population
Based on all places, regardless of total population

Place	Population	%
Columbus (city) Franklin County	604	0.08
Cleveland (city) Cuyahoga County	553	0.14
North Olmsted (city) Cuyahoga County	331	1.01
Toledo (city) Lucas County	216	0.07
Macedonia (city) Summit County	213	1.96
Strongsville (city) Cuyahoga County	211	0.48
Tallmadge (city) Summit County	199	1.15
Westlake (city) Cuyahoga County	145	0.45
Lakewood (city) Cuyahoga County	116	0.22
Miamisburg (city) Montgomery County	104	0.52

Top 10 Places Sorted by Percent of Total Population
Based on all places, regardless of total population

Place	Population	%
Lowellville (village) Mahoning County	33	2.86
Salem Heights (cdp) Hamilton County	90	2.26
Macedonia (city) Summit County	213	1.96
Huber Ridge (cdp) Franklin County	83	1.86
Tallmadge (city) Summit County	199	1.15
North Olmsted (city) Cuyahoga County	331	1.01
New Albany (village) Franklin County	59	0.83
Fairview Park (city) Cuyahoga County	94	0.56
Miamisburg (city) Montgomery County	104	0.52
Pepper Pike (city) Cuyahoga County	31	0.52

Top 10 Places Sorted by Percent of Total Population
Based on places with total population of 50,000 or more

Place	Population	%
Lakewood (city) Cuyahoga County	116	0.22
Cleveland (city) Cuyahoga County	553	0.14
Columbus (city) Franklin County	604	0.08
Toledo (city) Lucas County	216	0.07
Parma (city) Cuyahoga County	34	0.04
Cincinnati (city) Hamilton County	55	0.02
Dayton (city) Montgomery County	15	0.01
Akron (city) Summit County	10	<0.01
Canton (city) Stark County	0	0.00
Elyria (city) Lorain County	0	0.00

Arab: Syrian

Top 10 Places Sorted by Population
Based on all places, regardless of total population

Place	Population	%
Columbus (city) Franklin County	415	0.05
Toledo (city) Lucas County	381	0.13
Lakewood (city) Cuyahoga County	213	0.40
Olmsted Falls (city) Cuyahoga County	210	2.40
Canton (city) Stark County	164	0.22
Cleveland (city) Cuyahoga County	155	0.04
Westlake (city) Cuyahoga County	126	0.39
Fairview Park (city) Cuyahoga County	123	0.73
Parma Heights (city) Cuyahoga County	93	0.45
Rocky River (city) Cuyahoga County	89	0.44

Top 10 Places Sorted by Percent of Total Population
Based on all places, regardless of total population

Place	Population	%
Rosemount (cdp) Scioto County	77	3.50
Olmsted Falls (city) Cuyahoga County	210	2.40
Walbridge (village) Wood County	71	2.30
Waterville (village) Lucas County	64	1.18
Clay Center (village) Ottawa County	3	1.06
Waite Hill (village) Lake County	5	1.03
Middlefield (village) Geauga County	26	0.99
Chagrin Falls (village) Cuyahoga County	37	0.91
Caldwell (village) Noble County	12	0.86
Dent (cdp) Hamilton County	82	0.84

Top 10 Places Sorted by Percent of Total Population
Based on places with total population of 50,000 or more

Place	Population	%
Lakewood (city) Cuyahoga County	213	0.40
Canton (city) Stark County	164	0.22
Kettering (city) Montgomery County	81	0.14
Toledo (city) Lucas County	381	0.13
Parma (city) Cuyahoga County	62	0.08
Columbus (city) Franklin County	415	0.05
Cleveland (city) Cuyahoga County	155	0.04
Youngstown (city) Mahoning County	25	0.04
Lorain (city) Lorain County	19	0.03
Elyria (city) Lorain County	9	0.02

Arab: Other

Top 10 Places Sorted by Population
Based on all places, regardless of total population

Place	Population	%
Columbus (city) Franklin County	497	0.06
Toledo (city) Lucas County	304	0.10
Cleveland (city) Cuyahoga County	227	0.06
Cleveland Heights (city) Cuyahoga County	200	0.43
Cuyahoga Falls (city) Summit County	149	0.30
Athens (city) Athens County	148	0.63
Akron (city) Summit County	143	0.07
Findlay (city) Hancock County	137	0.33
Bellbrook (city) Greene County	131	1.87
Beavercreek (city) Greene County	121	0.27

Top 10 Places Sorted by Percent of Total Population
Based on all places, regardless of total population

Place	Population	%
Haskins (village) Wood County	29	2.53
Bellbrook (city) Greene County	131	1.87
Greentown (cdp) Stark County	45	1.40
Frankfort (village) Ross County	12	1.09
Waynesville (village) Warren County	29	1.01
Cherry Grove (cdp) Hamilton County	38	0.84
Higginsport (village) Brown County	2	0.80
Athens (city) Athens County	148	0.63
Mariemont (village) Hamilton County	21	0.62
Streetsboro (city) Portage County	93	0.60

Top 10 Places Sorted by Percent of Total Population
Based on places with total population of 50,000 or more

Place	Population	%
Toledo (city) Lucas County	304	0.10
Akron (city) Summit County	143	0.07
Columbus (city) Franklin County	497	0.06
Cleveland (city) Cuyahoga County	227	0.06
Springfield (city) Clark County	35	0.06
Kettering (city) Montgomery County	27	0.05
Lakewood (city) Cuyahoga County	25	0.05
Cincinnati (city) Hamilton County	70	0.02
Hamilton (city) Butler County	15	0.02
Canton (city) Stark County	12	0.02

Armenian

Top 10 Places Sorted by Population
Based on all places, regardless of total population

Place	Population	%
Toledo (city) Lucas County	234	0.08
Columbus (city) Franklin County	163	0.02
Portsmouth (city) Scioto County	126	0.62
Pepper Pike (city) Cuyahoga County	112	1.88
Cleveland (city) Cuyahoga County	91	0.02
Golf Manor (village) Hamilton County	86	2.36
Akron (city) Summit County	82	0.04
Cincinnati (city) Hamilton County	82	0.03
Parma (city) Cuyahoga County	80	0.10
Northfield (village) Summit County	73	1.97

Top 10 Places Sorted by Percent of Total Population
Based on all places, regardless of total population

Place	Population	%
Malinta (village) Henry County	10	3.36
Bradner (village) Wood County	33	2.67
Golf Manor (village) Hamilton County	86	2.36
Northfield (village) Summit County	73	1.97
Pepper Pike (city) Cuyahoga County	112	1.88
Sebring (village) Mahoning County	59	1.31
Hunting Valley (village) Cuyahoga County	7	1.09
Frankfort (village) Ross County	11	1.00
Chagrin Falls (village) Cuyahoga County	37	0.91
Granville (village) Licking County	42	0.75

Top 10 Places Sorted by Percent of Total Population
Based on places with total population of 50,000 or more

Place	Population	%
Parma (city) Cuyahoga County	80	0.10
Toledo (city) Lucas County	234	0.08
Lakewood (city) Cuyahoga County	29	0.06
Canton (city) Stark County	35	0.05
Akron (city) Summit County	82	0.04
Cincinnati (city) Hamilton County	82	0.03
Columbus (city) Franklin County	163	0.02
Cleveland (city) Cuyahoga County	91	0.02
Springfield (city) Clark County	12	0.02
Youngstown (city) Mahoning County	11	0.02

Assyrian/Chaldean/Syriac

Top 10 Places Sorted by Population
Based on all places, regardless of total population

Place	Population	%
Columbus (city) Franklin County	97	0.01
Upper Arlington (city) Franklin County	51	0.15
Toledo (city) Lucas County	27	0.01
Circleville (city) Pickaway County	13	0.10
Pickerington (city) Fairfield County	12	0.07
Highland Heights (city) Cuyahoga County	10	0.12
Englewood (city) Montgomery County	10	0.08
Defiance (city) Defiance County	10	0.06
Dublin (city) Franklin County	10	0.03
Cincinnati (city) Hamilton County	9	<0.01

Top 10 Places Sorted by Percent of Total Population
Based on all places, regardless of total population

Place	Population	%
Upper Arlington (city) Franklin County	51	0.15
Highland Heights (city) Cuyahoga County	10	0.12
Circleville (city) Pickaway County	13	0.10
Englewood (city) Montgomery County	10	0.08
Pickerington (city) Fairfield County	12	0.07
Defiance (city) Defiance County	10	0.06
Dublin (city) Franklin County	10	0.03
Columbus (city) Franklin County	97	0.01
Toledo (city) Lucas County	27	0.01
Euclid (city) Cuyahoga County	5	0.01

Top 10 Places Sorted by Percent of Total Population
Based on places with total population of 50,000 or more

Place	Population	%
Columbus (city) Franklin County	97	0.01
Toledo (city) Lucas County	27	0.01
Cincinnati (city) Hamilton County	9	<0.01
Cleveland (city) Cuyahoga County	5	<0.01
Akron (city) Summit County	0	0.00
Canton (city) Stark County	0	0.00
Dayton (city) Montgomery County	0	0.00
Elyria (city) Lorain County	0	0.00
Hamilton (city) Butler County	0	0.00
Kettering (city) Montgomery County	0	0.00

Australian

Top 10 Places Sorted by Population
Based on all places, regardless of total population

Place	Population	%
Whitehall (city) Franklin County	156	0.86
Columbus (city) Franklin County	154	0.02
Marion (city) Marion County	59	0.16
Cincinnati (city) Hamilton County	50	0.02
Parma (city) Cuyahoga County	44	0.05
Struthers (city) Mahoning County	42	0.39
Lexington (village) Richland County	41	0.79
Kenwood (cdp) Hamilton County	40	0.55
Mansfield (city) Richland County	39	0.08
Cleveland (city) Cuyahoga County	39	0.01

Top 10 Places Sorted by Percent of Total Population
Based on all places, regardless of total population

Place	Population	%
Lafayette (village) Allen County	13	4.55
Brice (village) Franklin County	3	2.70
Dellroy (village) Carroll County	3	1.01

Whitehall (city) Franklin County	156	0.86
Lexington (village) Richland County	41	0.79
Four Bridges (cdp) Butler County	17	0.73
Orwell (village) Ashtabula County	10	0.68
Fayetteville (village) Brown County	2	0.68
Sherwood (cdp) Hamilton County	23	0.66
Newtown (village) Hamilton County	16	0.61

Top 10 Places Sorted by Percent of Total Population

Based on places with total population of 50,000 or more

Place	Population	%
Parma (city) Cuyahoga County	44	0.05
Youngstown (city) Mahoning County	18	0.03
Columbus (city) Franklin County	154	0.02
Cincinnati (city) Hamilton County	50	0.02
Dayton (city) Montgomery County	22	0.02
Hamilton (city) Butler County	10	0.02
Lakewood (city) Cuyahoga County	10	0.02
Cleveland (city) Cuyahoga County	39	0.01
Akron (city) Summit County	21	0.01
Kettering (city) Montgomery County	4	0.01

Austrian

Top 10 Places Sorted by Population

Based on all places, regardless of total population

Place	Population	%
Columbus (city) Franklin County	1,440	0.19
Toledo (city) Lucas County	628	0.22
Cleveland (city) Cuyahoga County	589	0.14
Cincinnati (city) Hamilton County	502	0.17
Akron (city) Summit County	450	0.22
Solon (city) Cuyahoga County	300	1.31
Parma (city) Cuyahoga County	283	0.35
Hilliard (city) Franklin County	255	0.93
Cleveland Heights (city) Cuyahoga County	255	0.54
Mansfield (city) Richland County	253	0.52

Top 10 Places Sorted by Percent of Total Population

Based on all places, regardless of total population

Place	Population	%
Lafferty (cdp) Belmont County	33	15.07
Port Washington (village) Tuscarawas County	33	6.21
Belle Valley (village) Noble County	19	5.31
Gilboa (village) Putnam County	7	5.00
Rock Creek (village) Ashtabula County	31	4.34
Wetherington (cdp) Butler County	60	4.18
Stone Creek (village) Tuscarawas County	7	3.78
Lake Tomahawk (cdp) Columbiana County	16	3.49
Waite Hill (village) Lake County	15	3.10
Malinta (village) Henry County	9	3.02

Top 10 Places Sorted by Percent of Total Population

Based on places with total population of 50,000 or more

Place	Population	%
Lakewood (city) Cuyahoga County	233	0.44
Parma (city) Cuyahoga County	283	0.35
Kettering (city) Montgomery County	160	0.28
Elyria (city) Lorain County	154	0.28
Toledo (city) Lucas County	628	0.22
Akron (city) Summit County	450	0.22
Columbus (city) Franklin County	1,440	0.19
Canton (city) Stark County	143	0.19
Cincinnati (city) Hamilton County	502	0.17
Lorain (city) Lorain County	110	0.17

Basque

Top 10 Places Sorted by Population

Based on all places, regardless of total population

Place	Population	%
Bowling Green (city) Wood County	18	0.06
Dent (cdp) Hamilton County	17	0.17
Chagrin Falls (village) Cuyahoga County	12	0.29
Aberdeen (village) Brown County	0	0.00
Ada (village) Hardin County	0	0.00
Adamsville (village) Muskingum County	0	0.00
Addyston (village) Hamilton County	0	0.00
Adelphi (village) Ross County	0	0.00
Adena (village) Jefferson County	0	0.00
Akron (city) Summit County	0	0.00

Top 10 Places Sorted by Percent of Total Population

Based on all places, regardless of total population

Place	Population	%
Chagrin Falls (village) Cuyahoga County	12	0.29
Dent (cdp) Hamilton County	17	0.17
Bowling Green (city) Wood County	18	0.06
Aberdeen (village) Brown County	0	0.00
Ada (village) Hardin County	0	0.00
Adamsville (village) Muskingum County	0	0.00
Addyston (village) Hamilton County	0	0.00
Adelphi (village) Ross County	0	0.00
Adena (village) Jefferson County	0	0.00
Akron (city) Summit County	0	0.00

Top 10 Places Sorted by Percent of Total Population

Based on places with total population of 50,000 or more

Place	Population	%
Akron (city) Summit County	0	0.00
Canton (city) Stark County	0	0.00
Cincinnati (city) Hamilton County	0	0.00
Cleveland (city) Cuyahoga County	0	0.00
Columbus (city) Franklin County	0	0.00
Dayton (city) Montgomery County	0	0.00
Elyria (city) Lorain County	0	0.00
Hamilton (city) Butler County	0	0.00
Kettering (city) Montgomery County	0	0.00
Lakewood (city) Cuyahoga County	0	0.00

Belgian

Top 10 Places Sorted by Population

Based on all places, regardless of total population

Place	Population	%
Columbus (city) Franklin County	699	0.09
Toledo (city) Lucas County	215	0.07
Cincinnati (city) Hamilton County	185	0.06
Parma (city) Cuyahoga County	163	0.20
Canton (city) Stark County	152	0.20
Plain City (village) Madison County	145	3.81
Findlay (city) Hancock County	116	0.28
Akron (city) Summit County	109	0.05
Bowling Green (city) Wood County	107	0.35
Dayton (city) Montgomery County	105	0.07

Top 10 Places Sorted by Percent of Total Population

Based on all places, regardless of total population

Place	Population	%
Plumwood (cdp) Madison County	43	24.02
Martinsburg (village) Knox County	10	5.43
Plain City (village) Madison County	145	3.81
Berkey (village) Lucas County	8	3.03
Highland Holiday (cdp) Highland County	11	2.78
Kings Mills (cdp) Warren County	32	2.56
Helena (village) Sandusky County	6	2.39
Bethel (village) Clermont County	58	2.13
Mount Gilead (village) Morrow County	80	2.11
Mutual (village) Champaign County	3	2.07

Top 10 Places Sorted by Percent of Total Population

Based on places with total population of 50,000 or more

Place	Population	%
Parma (city) Cuyahoga County	163	0.20
Canton (city) Stark County	152	0.20
Kettering (city) Montgomery County	63	0.11
Lakewood (city) Cuyahoga County	53	0.10
Columbus (city) Franklin County	699	0.09
Toledo (city) Lucas County	215	0.07
Dayton (city) Montgomery County	105	0.07
Cincinnati (city) Hamilton County	185	0.06
Akron (city) Summit County	109	0.05
Lorain (city) Lorain County	31	0.05

Brazilian

Top 10 Places Sorted by Population

Based on all places, regardless of total population

Place	Population	%
Columbus (city) Franklin County	284	0.04
Dublin (city) Franklin County	155	0.39
Forest Park (city) Hamilton County	135	0.72
Fairfield (city) Butler County	131	0.31
Pickerington (city) Fairfield County	118	0.69
Cleveland (city) Cuyahoga County	80	0.02
Upper Arlington (city) Franklin County	72	0.21
Athens (city) Athens County	68	0.29
Kettering (city) Montgomery County	59	0.11
Arcanum (village) Darke County	53	2.21

Top 10 Places Sorted by Percent of Total Population

Based on all places, regardless of total population

Place	Population	%
Fairview (village) Guernsey County	4	6.56
Arcanum (village) Darke County	53	2.21
West Mansfield (village) Logan County	13	1.88
East Palestine (city) Columbiana County	53	1.11
Fayetteville (village) Brown County	3	1.03
Hanoverton (village) Columbiana County	4	0.97
Forest Park (city) Hamilton County	135	0.72
Pickerington (city) Fairfield County	118	0.69
Canal Fulton (city) Stark County	28	0.52
Fairlawn (city) Summit County	32	0.43

Top 10 Places Sorted by Percent of Total Population

Based on places with total population of 50,000 or more

Place	Population	%
Kettering (city) Montgomery County	59	0.11
Columbus (city) Franklin County	284	0.04
Lakewood (city) Cuyahoga County	21	0.04
Cleveland (city) Cuyahoga County	80	0.02
Akron (city) Summit County	27	0.01
Cincinnati (city) Hamilton County	23	0.01
Canton (city) Stark County	0	0.00
Dayton (city) Montgomery County	0	0.00
Elyria (city) Lorain County	0	0.00
Hamilton (city) Butler County	0	0.00

British

Top 10 Places Sorted by Population

Based on all places, regardless of total population

Place	Population	%
Columbus (city) Franklin County	3,242	0.42
Cincinnati (city) Hamilton County	1,314	0.44
Toledo (city) Lucas County	785	0.27
Dayton (city) Montgomery County	727	0.50
Westerville (city) Franklin County	538	1.50
Akron (city) Summit County	508	0.25
Cleveland (city) Cuyahoga County	474	0.12
Upper Arlington (city) Franklin County	394	1.17
Kettering (city) Montgomery County	352	0.63
Grove City (city) Franklin County	324	0.95

Top 10 Places Sorted by Percent of Total Population

Based on all places, regardless of total population

Place	Population	%
Oceola (cdp) Crawford County	100	45.66
Canal Lewisville (cdp) Coshocton County	23	6.65
Pleasant Plain (village) Warren County	9	6.16
Sherwood (village) Defiance County	31	5.61
Concorde Hills (cdp) Hamilton County	26	5.30
Lafayette (village) Allen County	13	4.55
Old Washington (village) Guernsey County	12	3.99
North Perry (village) Lake County	37	3.85
Bellbrook (city) Greene County	254	3.63
New Straitsville (village) Perry County	17	3.47

Top 10 Places Sorted by Percent of Total Population

Based on places with total population of 50,000 or more

Place	Population	%
Kettering (city) Montgomery County	352	0.63
Lakewood (city) Cuyahoga County	313	0.59
Dayton (city) Montgomery County	727	0.50
Cincinnati (city) Hamilton County	1,314	0.44
Hamilton (city) Butler County	270	0.43
Columbus (city) Franklin County	3,242	0.42
Toledo (city) Lucas County	785	0.27
Akron (city) Summit County	508	0.25
Elyria (city) Lorain County	137	0.25
Parma (city) Cuyahoga County	189	0.23

Bulgarian

Top 10 Places Sorted by Population

Based on all places, regardless of total population

Place	Population	%
Toledo (city) Lucas County	217	0.07
Columbus (city) Franklin County	130	0.02
Dayton (city) Montgomery County	125	0.09
Parma Heights (city) Cuyahoga County	112	0.54
Fairview Park (city) Cuyahoga County	107	0.63
Avon (city) Lorain County	84	0.43
Oregon (city) Lucas County	77	0.38
Parma (city) Cuyahoga County	73	0.09
Upper Arlington (city) Franklin County	67	0.20
Cleveland (city) Cuyahoga County	54	0.01

Top 10 Places Sorted by Percent of Total Population

Based on all places, regardless of total population

Place	Population	%
Woodmere (village) Cuyahoga County	36	3.91
Monroeville (village) Huron County	27	2.02
Gambier (village) Knox County	33	1.50
Belle Valley (village) Noble County	5	1.40
Lyons (village) Fulton County	4	0.78
Northwood (city) Wood County	35	0.66
Oak Harbor (village) Ottawa County	18	0.65
Newtown (village) Hamilton County	17	0.65
Fairview Park (city) Cuyahoga County	107	0.63
Windham (village) Portage County	14	0.61

Top 10 Places Sorted by Percent of Total Population

Based on places with total population of 50,000 or more

Place	Population	%
Dayton (city) Montgomery County	125	0.09
Parma (city) Cuyahoga County	73	0.09
Toledo (city) Lucas County	217	0.07
Youngstown (city) Mahoning County	33	0.05
Lakewood (city) Cuyahoga County	23	0.04
Springfield (city) Clark County	22	0.04
Columbus (city) Franklin County	130	0.02
Akron (city) Summit County	32	0.02
Lorain (city) Lorain County	15	0.02
Cleveland (city) Cuyahoga County	54	0.01

Cajun

Top 10 Places Sorted by Population

Based on all places, regardless of total population

Place	Population	%
Kettering (city) Montgomery County	66	0.12
Columbus (city) Franklin County	56	0.01
Cincinnati (city) Hamilton County	41	0.01
Beavercreek (city) Greene County	29	0.07
Cleveland (city) Cuyahoga County	29	0.01
Akron (city) Summit County	27	0.01
Montrose-Ghent (cdp) Summit County	19	0.37
Green (city) Summit County	15	0.06
Lithopolis (village) Fairfield County	14	2.22
North Ridgeville (city) Lorain County	13	0.05

Top 10 Places Sorted by Percent of Total Population

Based on all places, regardless of total population

Place	Population	%
Lithopolis (village) Fairfield County	14	2.22
Smithville (village) Wayne County	7	0.55
Montrose-Ghent (cdp) Summit County	19	0.37
Kettering (city) Montgomery County	66	0.12
Highland Heights (city) Cuyahoga County	8	0.10
Beavercreek (city) Greene County	29	0.07
Cedarville (village) Greene County	3	0.07
Green (city) Summit County	15	0.06
North Ridgeville (city) Lorain County	13	0.05
Kent (city) Portage County	11	0.04

Top 10 Places Sorted by Percent of Total Population

Based on places with total population of 50,000 or more

Place	Population	%
Kettering (city) Montgomery County	66	0.12
Columbus (city) Franklin County	56	0.01
Cincinnati (city) Hamilton County	41	0.01
Cleveland (city) Cuyahoga County	29	0.01
Akron (city) Summit County	27	0.01
Canton (city) Stark County	0	0.00
Dayton (city) Montgomery County	0	0.00
Elyria (city) Lorain County	0	0.00
Hamilton (city) Butler County	0	0.00
Lakewood (city) Cuyahoga County	0	0.00

Canadian

Top 10 Places Sorted by Population

Based on all places, regardless of total population

Place	Population	%
Columbus (city) Franklin County	1,023	0.13
Toledo (city) Lucas County	521	0.18
Cleveland (city) Cuyahoga County	343	0.08
Cincinnati (city) Hamilton County	275	0.09
Cleveland Heights (city) Cuyahoga County	210	0.45
Hudson (city) Summit County	201	0.90
Akron (city) Summit County	196	0.10
Westerville (city) Franklin County	187	0.52
Hilliard (city) Franklin County	170	0.62
Gahanna (city) Franklin County	157	0.48

Top 10 Places Sorted by Percent of Total Population

Based on all places, regardless of total population

Place	Population	%
Negley (cdp) Columbiana County	40	16.74
Huntsville (village) Logan County	44	11.08
Yankee Lake (village) Trumbull County	4	5.80
Clarksville (village) Clinton County	26	4.26
Kings Mills (cdp) Warren County	48	3.84
Day Heights (cdp) Clermont County	73	2.69
Amberley (village) Hamilton County	95	2.68
Shawnee (cdp) Hamilton County	18	2.49
Green Meadows (cdp) Clark County	58	2.45
St. Paris (village) Champaign County	48	2.42

Top 10 Places Sorted by Percent of Total Population

Based on places with total population of 50,000 or more

Place	Population	%
Toledo (city) Lucas County	521	0.18
Elyria (city) Lorain County	100	0.18
Columbus (city) Franklin County	1,023	0.13
Akron (city) Summit County	196	0.10
Parma (city) Cuyahoga County	85	0.10
Springfield (city) Clark County	61	0.10
Kettering (city) Montgomery County	58	0.10
Cincinnati (city) Hamilton County	275	0.09
Cleveland (city) Cuyahoga County	343	0.08
Dayton (city) Montgomery County	116	0.08

Carpatho Rusyn

Top 10 Places Sorted by Population

Based on all places, regardless of total population

Place	Population	%
Parma (city) Cuyahoga County	116	0.14
Aurora (city) Portage County	65	0.43
Tallmadge (city) Summit County	51	0.29
Mansfield (city) Richland County	43	0.09
Canfield (city) Mahoning County	41	0.55
Columbus (city) Franklin County	35	<0.01
Fairview Park (city) Cuyahoga County	30	0.18
Westerville (city) Franklin County	28	0.08
Lorain (city) Lorain County	26	0.04
Lakewood (city) Cuyahoga County	25	0.05

Top 10 Places Sorted by Percent of Total Population

Based on all places, regardless of total population

Place	Population	%
Canfield (city) Mahoning County	41	0.55
Aurora (city) Portage County	65	0.43
Pleasant City (village) Guernsey County	2	0.43
Tallmadge (city) Summit County	51	0.29
Campbell (city) Mahoning County	17	0.20
Wellington (village) Lorain County	10	0.20
Brooklyn Heights (village) Cuyahoga County	3	0.20
Fairview Park (city) Cuyahoga County	30	0.18
Shadyside (village) Belmont County	7	0.18
Oberlin (city) Lorain County	14	0.17

Top 10 Places Sorted by Percent of Total Population

Based on places with total population of 50,000 or more

Place	Population	%
Parma (city) Cuyahoga County	116	0.14
Lakewood (city) Cuyahoga County	25	0.05
Lorain (city) Lorain County	26	0.04
Youngstown (city) Mahoning County	20	0.03
Canton (city) Stark County	13	0.02
Akron (city) Summit County	25	0.01
Toledo (city) Lucas County	15	0.01
Columbus (city) Franklin County	35	<0.01
Cincinnati (city) Hamilton County	0	0.00
Cleveland (city) Cuyahoga County	0	0.00

Celtic

Top 10 Places Sorted by Population

Based on all places, regardless of total population

Place	Population	%
Columbus (city) Franklin County	95	0.01
Toledo (city) Lucas County	73	0.03
Toronto (city) Jefferson County	70	1.40
Niles (city) Trumbull County	64	0.33
Mount Repose (cdp) Clermont County	60	1.41
Struthers (city) Mahoning County	51	0.47
Gahanna (city) Franklin County	51	0.16
Rocky River (city) Cuyahoga County	42	0.21
Canton (city) Stark County	39	0.05
North Ridgeville (city) Lorain County	31	0.11

Top 10 Places Sorted by Percent of Total Population

Based on all places, regardless of total population

Place	Population	%
Mount Repose (cdp) Clermont County	60	1.41
Toronto (city) Jefferson County	70	1.40
Sugar Bush Knolls (village) Portage County	2	1.32
Laura (village) Miami County	7	1.20
Granville South (cdp) Licking County	19	1.19
Beloit (village) Mahoning County	14	1.13
Riverlea (village) Franklin County	5	1.04
Walton Hills (village) Cuyahoga County	22	0.97
Richfield (village) Summit County	18	0.50
Milford Center (village) Union County	3	0.50

Top 10 Places Sorted by Percent of Total Population

Based on places with total population of 50,000 or more

Place	Population	%
Canton (city) Stark County	39	0.05
Toledo (city) Lucas County	73	0.03
Springfield (city) Clark County	12	0.02
Columbus (city) Franklin County	95	0.01
Cincinnati (city) Hamilton County	29	0.01
Cleveland (city) Cuyahoga County	18	<0.01
Akron (city) Summit County	0	0.00
Dayton (city) Montgomery County	0	0.00
Elyria (city) Lorain County	0	0.00
Hamilton (city) Butler County	0	0.00

Croatian

Top 10 Places Sorted by Population

Based on all places, regardless of total population

Place	Population	%
Mentor (city) Lake County	1,797	3.77
Cleveland (city) Cuyahoga County	1,547	0.38
Columbus (city) Franklin County	1,158	0.15
Parma (city) Cuyahoga County	1,112	1.36
Euclid (city) Cuyahoga County	1,084	2.20
Willoughby (city) Lake County	769	3.46
Boardman (cdp) Mahoning County	733	2.07
Willowick (city) Lake County	705	4.96
Eastlake (city) Lake County	689	3.65
Youngstown (city) Mahoning County	688	0.99

Top 10 Places Sorted by Percent of Total Population

Based on all places, regardless of total population

Place	Population	%
Yankee Lake (village) Trumbull County	10	14.49
Radnor (cdp) Delaware County	16	11.35
McKinley Heights (cdp) Trumbull County	75	6.88

Place	Population	%
Willoughby Hills (city) Lake County	505	5.38
Lakeline (village) Lake County	8	5.30
Waite Hill (village) Lake County	25	5.17
Willowick (city) Lake County	705	4.96
Austinburg (cdp) Ashtabula County	40	4.96
Wickliffe (city) Lake County	580	4.51
Newburgh Heights (village) Cuyahoga County	91	4.32

Top 10 Places Sorted by Percent of Total Population
Based on places with total population of 50,000 or more

Place	Population	%
Parma (city) Cuyahoga County	1,112	1.36
Lakewood (city) Cuyahoga County	563	1.07
Youngstown (city) Mahoning County	688	0.99
Lorain (city) Lorain County	569	0.87
Cleveland (city) Cuyahoga County	1,547	0.38
Canton (city) Stark County	279	0.37
Akron (city) Summit County	584	0.29
Elyria (city) Lorain County	123	0.22
Columbus (city) Franklin County	1,158	0.15
Kettering (city) Montgomery County	58	0.10

Cypriot

Top 10 Places Sorted by Population
Based on all places, regardless of total population

Place	Population	%
North Canton (city) Stark County	15	0.09
Columbus (city) Franklin County	14	<0.01
Lakewood (city) Cuyahoga County	12	0.02
Boardman (cdp) Mahoning County	11	0.03
Toledo (city) Lucas County	11	<0.01
Plymouth (village) Richland County	3	0.15
Aberdeen (village) Brown County	0	0.00
Ada (village) Hardin County	0	0.00
Adamsville (village) Muskingum County	0	0.00
Addyston (village) Hamilton County	0	0.00

Top 10 Places Sorted by Percent of Total Population
Based on all places, regardless of total population

Place	Population	%
Plymouth (village) Richland County	3	0.15
North Canton (city) Stark County	15	0.09
Boardman (cdp) Mahoning County	11	0.03
Lakewood (city) Cuyahoga County	12	0.02
Columbus (city) Franklin County	14	<0.01
Toledo (city) Lucas County	11	<0.01
Aberdeen (village) Brown County	0	0.00
Ada (village) Hardin County	0	0.00
Adamsville (village) Muskingum County	0	0.00
Addyston (village) Hamilton County	0	0.00

Top 10 Places Sorted by Percent of Total Population
Based on places with total population of 50,000 or more

Place	Population	%
Lakewood (city) Cuyahoga County	12	0.02
Columbus (city) Franklin County	14	<0.01
Toledo (city) Lucas County	11	<0.01
Akron (city) Summit County	0	0.00
Canton (city) Stark County	0	0.00
Cincinnati (city) Hamilton County	0	0.00
Cleveland (city) Cuyahoga County	0	0.00
Dayton (city) Montgomery County	0	0.00
Elyria (city) Lorain County	0	0.00
Hamilton (city) Butler County	0	0.00

Czech

Top 10 Places Sorted by Population
Based on all places, regardless of total population

Place	Population	%
Columbus (city) Franklin County	2,996	0.39
Cleveland (city) Cuyahoga County	2,835	0.69
Parma (city) Cuyahoga County	2,231	2.72
North Royalton (city) Cuyahoga County	1,263	4.21
Strongsville (city) Cuyahoga County	1,236	2.79
North Olmsted (city) Cuyahoga County	982	2.99
Garfield Heights (city) Cuyahoga County	945	3.25
Akron (city) Summit County	919	0.45
Toledo (city) Lucas County	833	0.29
Brunswick (city) Medina County	824	2.39

Top 10 Places Sorted by Percent of Total Population
Based on all places, regardless of total population

Place	Population	%
Tippecanoe (cdp) Harrison County	47	60.26
Blakeslee (village) Williams County	7	10.61
Put-in-Bay (village) Ottawa County	13	9.35
Independence (city) Cuyahoga County	531	7.50
Lansing (cdp) Belmont County	27	7.32
Neffs (cdp) Belmont County	72	7.29
Brooklyn Heights (village) Cuyahoga County	98	6.56
West Rushville (village) Fairfield County	7	6.48
Bourneville (cdp) Ross County	11	6.47
Seven Hills (city) Cuyahoga County	756	6.41

Top 10 Places Sorted by Percent of Total Population
Based on places with total population of 50,000 or more

Place	Population	%
Parma (city) Cuyahoga County	2,231	2.72
Lakewood (city) Cuyahoga County	758	1.44
Elyria (city) Lorain County	556	1.01
Cleveland (city) Cuyahoga County	2,835	0.69
Canton (city) Stark County	342	0.46
Akron (city) Summit County	919	0.45
Columbus (city) Franklin County	2,996	0.39
Kettering (city) Montgomery County	220	0.39
Toledo (city) Lucas County	833	0.29
Springfield (city) Clark County	153	0.25

Czechoslovakian

Top 10 Places Sorted by Population
Based on all places, regardless of total population

Place	Population	%
Columbus (city) Franklin County	819	0.11
Cleveland (city) Cuyahoga County	553	0.14
Elyria (city) Lorain County	312	0.57
Toledo (city) Lucas County	304	0.10
Parma (city) Cuyahoga County	299	0.37
Mansfield (city) Richland County	260	0.53
Akron (city) Summit County	233	0.11
Cuyahoga Falls (city) Summit County	222	0.45
Strongsville (city) Cuyahoga County	217	0.49
Westlake (city) Cuyahoga County	204	0.63

Top 10 Places Sorted by Percent of Total Population
Based on all places, regardless of total population

Place	Population	%
Buffalo (cdp) Guernsey County	18	4.68
Kidron (cdp) Wayne County	33	3.17
Leavittsburg (cdp) Trumbull County	50	2.57
Bloomingburg (village) Fayette County	24	2.46
Hannibal (cdp) Monroe County	12	2.45
Jefferson (village) Ashtabula County	73	2.26
Burgoon (village) Sandusky County	4	2.13
Whites Landing (cdp) Erie County	7	1.84
Montpelier (village) Williams County	71	1.71
Adena (village) Jefferson County	14	1.66

Top 10 Places Sorted by Percent of Total Population
Based on places with total population of 50,000 or more

Place	Population	%
Elyria (city) Lorain County	312	0.57
Parma (city) Cuyahoga County	299	0.37
Lorain (city) Lorain County	186	0.29
Kettering (city) Montgomery County	136	0.24
Lakewood (city) Cuyahoga County	126	0.24
Cleveland (city) Cuyahoga County	553	0.14
Dayton (city) Montgomery County	179	0.12
Columbus (city) Franklin County	819	0.11
Akron (city) Summit County	233	0.11
Toledo (city) Lucas County	304	0.10

Danish

Top 10 Places Sorted by Population
Based on all places, regardless of total population

Place	Population	%
Columbus (city) Franklin County	1,200	0.16
Toledo (city) Lucas County	499	0.17
Cincinnati (city) Hamilton County	439	0.15
Cleveland Heights (city) Cuyahoga County	271	0.58
Akron (city) Summit County	260	0.13
Cleveland (city) Cuyahoga County	230	0.06
Lakewood (city) Cuyahoga County	219	0.42
Elyria (city) Lorain County	183	0.33
Canton (city) Stark County	176	0.24
Kettering (city) Montgomery County	174	0.31

Top 10 Places Sorted by Percent of Total Population
Based on all places, regardless of total population

Place	Population	%
Tarlton (village) Pickaway County	20	6.21
Reno (cdp) Washington County	41	4.47
Lewistown (cdp) Logan County	14	3.89
Swanton (village) Fulton County	133	3.49
Sardis (cdp) Monroe County	10	3.02
Concorde Hills (cdp) Hamilton County	12	2.44
Butler (village) Richland County	25	2.43
Caledonia (village) Marion County	12	1.87
Chesterland (cdp) Geauga County	44	1.82
Gratis (village) Preble County	18	1.80

Top 10 Places Sorted by Percent of Total Population
Based on places with total population of 50,000 or more

Place	Population	%
Lakewood (city) Cuyahoga County	219	0.42
Elyria (city) Lorain County	183	0.33
Kettering (city) Montgomery County	174	0.31
Canton (city) Stark County	176	0.24
Youngstown (city) Mahoning County	141	0.20
Toledo (city) Lucas County	499	0.17
Columbus (city) Franklin County	1,200	0.16
Cincinnati (city) Hamilton County	439	0.15
Akron (city) Summit County	260	0.13
Lorain (city) Lorain County	53	0.08

Dutch

Top 10 Places Sorted by Population
Based on all places, regardless of total population

Place	Population	%
Columbus (city) Franklin County	10,822	1.40
Toledo (city) Lucas County	3,569	1.22
Cleveland (city) Cuyahoga County	2,881	0.70
Cincinnati (city) Hamilton County	2,867	0.96
Akron (city) Summit County	2,805	1.38
Dayton (city) Montgomery County	1,660	1.14
Canton (city) Stark County	1,441	1.94
Kettering (city) Montgomery County	1,420	2.53
Lancaster (city) Fairfield County	1,384	3.58
Springfield (city) Clark County	1,199	1.95

Top 10 Places Sorted by Percent of Total Population
Based on all places, regardless of total population

Place	Population	%
Celeryville (cdp) Huron County	59	44.36
Pulaski (cdp) Williams County	26	39.39
Fairview (village) Guernsey County	16	26.23
Elgin (village) Van Wert County	6	26.09
Beulah Beach (cdp) Erie County	9	25.71
East Liberty (cdp) Logan County	81	25.23
Otway (village) Scioto County	26	21.49
Crystal Lakes (cdp) Clark County	229	18.79
Neville (village) Clermont County	20	18.69
Derby (cdp) Pickaway County	76	17.92

Top 10 Places Sorted by Percent of Total Population
Based on places with total population of 50,000 or more

Place	Population	%
Kettering (city) Montgomery County	1,420	2.53
Elyria (city) Lorain County	1,082	1.97
Springfield (city) Clark County	1,199	1.95
Canton (city) Stark County	1,441	1.94
Columbus (city) Franklin County	10,822	1.40
Hamilton (city) Butler County	873	1.40
Akron (city) Summit County	2,805	1.38
Lorain (city) Lorain County	824	1.26
Toledo (city) Lucas County	3,569	1.22
Dayton (city) Montgomery County	1,660	1.14

Eastern European

Top 10 Places Sorted by Population
Based on all places, regardless of total population

Place	Population	%
Columbus (city) Franklin County	867	0.11
Beachwood (city) Cuyahoga County	546	4.58
Shaker Heights (city) Cuyahoga County	545	1.92
Cleveland Heights (city) Cuyahoga County	475	1.02
University Heights (city) Cuyahoga County	457	3.37
Solon (city) Cuyahoga County	420	1.83
Pepper Pike (city) Cuyahoga County	227	3.81
Cincinnati (city) Hamilton County	172	0.06
Lorain (city) Lorain County	156	0.24
Bexley (city) Franklin County	151	1.16

Top 10 Places Sorted by Percent of Total Population
Based on all places, regardless of total population

Place	Population	%
Beachwood (city) Cuyahoga County	546	4.58
Aquilla (village) Geauga County	14	3.83
Pepper Pike (city) Cuyahoga County	227	3.81
University Heights (city) Cuyahoga County	457	3.37
Orange (village) Cuyahoga County	105	3.20
Bentleyville (village) Cuyahoga County	31	2.93
Nellie (village) Coshocton County	3	2.59
Moreland Hills (village) Cuyahoga County	75	2.27
Shaker Heights (city) Cuyahoga County	545	1.92
Hunting Valley (village) Cuyahoga County	12	1.87

Top 10 Places Sorted by Percent of Total Population
Based on places with total population of 50,000 or more

Place	Population	%
Lorain (city) Lorain County	156	0.24
Lakewood (city) Cuyahoga County	129	0.24
Kettering (city) Montgomery County	104	0.19
Parma (city) Cuyahoga County	102	0.12
Columbus (city) Franklin County	867	0.11
Akron (city) Summit County	138	0.07
Cincinnati (city) Hamilton County	172	0.06
Elyria (city) Lorain County	31	0.06
Dayton (city) Montgomery County	54	0.04
Hamilton (city) Butler County	24	0.04

English

Top 10 Places Sorted by Population
Based on all places, regardless of total population

Place	Population	%
Columbus (city) Franklin County	58,155	7.55
Toledo (city) Lucas County	18,826	6.45
Cincinnati (city) Hamilton County	16,011	5.33
Akron (city) Summit County	15,829	7.80
Cleveland (city) Cuyahoga County	13,765	3.36
Dayton (city) Montgomery County	7,108	4.88
Elyria (city) Lorain County	6,659	12.11
Cuyahoga Falls (city) Summit County	6,483	13.04
Kettering (city) Montgomery County	6,441	11.46
Mentor (city) Lake County	6,049	12.70

Top 10 Places Sorted by Percent of Total Population
Based on all places, regardless of total population

Place	Population	%
Cynthiana (cdp) Pike County	30	53.57
Dundee (cdp) Tuscarawas County	174	43.28
Rocky Fork Point (cdp) Highland County	237	43.25
Tuppers Plains (cdp) Meigs County	112	42.42
Brice (village) Franklin County	47	42.34
East Fultonham (cdp) Muskingum County	63	40.13
Howard (cdp) Knox County	136	38.53
Gann (village) Knox County	42	37.84
Old Fort (cdp) Seneca County	39	35.45
Lakeside (cdp) Ottawa County	224	34.09

Top 10 Places Sorted by Percent of Total Population
Based on places with total population of 50,000 or more

Place	Population	%
Elyria (city) Lorain County	6,659	12.11
Kettering (city) Montgomery County	6,441	11.46
Lakewood (city) Cuyahoga County	5,509	10.46
Akron (city) Summit County	15,829	7.80
Springfield (city) Clark County	4,701	7.64
Columbus (city) Franklin County	58,155	7.55
Hamilton (city) Butler County	4,631	7.41
Canton (city) Stark County	5,256	7.06
Toledo (city) Lucas County	18,826	6.45
Parma (city) Cuyahoga County	5,050	6.17

Estonian

Top 10 Places Sorted by Population
Based on all places, regardless of total population

Place	Population	%
Cincinnati (city) Hamilton County	86	0.03
Kettering (city) Montgomery County	39	0.07
North Royalton (city) Cuyahoga County	35	0.12
University Heights (city) Cuyahoga County	30	0.22
Broadview Heights (city) Cuyahoga County	27	0.14
Oxford (city) Butler County	27	0.13
Columbus (city) Franklin County	20	<0.01
Toledo (city) Lucas County	19	0.01
Norwalk (city) Huron County	17	0.10
Mentor (city) Lake County	17	0.04

Top 10 Places Sorted by Percent of Total Population
Based on all places, regardless of total population

Place	Population	%
Marble Cliff (village) Franklin County	3	0.51
Ballville (cdp) Sandusky County	11	0.35
University Heights (city) Cuyahoga County	30	0.22
Richfield (village) Summit County	7	0.19
Archbold (village) Fulton County	7	0.17
Broadview Heights (city) Cuyahoga County	27	0.14
Oxford (city) Butler County	27	0.13
North Royalton (city) Cuyahoga County	35	0.12
Norwalk (city) Huron County	17	0.10
Mount Vernon (city) Knox County	15	0.09

Top 10 Places Sorted by Percent of Total Population
Based on places with total population of 50,000 or more

Place	Population	%
Kettering (city) Montgomery County	39	0.07
Cincinnati (city) Hamilton County	86	0.03
Lakewood (city) Cuyahoga County	9	0.02
Toledo (city) Lucas County	19	0.01
Columbus (city) Franklin County	20	<0.01
Akron (city) Summit County	0	0.00
Canton (city) Stark County	0	0.00
Cleveland (city) Cuyahoga County	0	0.00
Dayton (city) Montgomery County	0	0.00
Elyria (city) Lorain County	0	0.00

European

Top 10 Places Sorted by Population
Based on all places, regardless of total population

Place	Population	%
Columbus (city) Franklin County	7,099	0.92
Cincinnati (city) Hamilton County	2,521	0.84
Toledo (city) Lucas County	1,626	0.56
Akron (city) Summit County	1,390	0.69
Cleveland (city) Cuyahoga County	1,116	0.27
Dayton (city) Montgomery County	1,113	0.76
Newark (city) Licking County	901	1.89
Findlay (city) Hancock County	845	2.05
Dublin (city) Franklin County	836	2.13
Westerville (city) Franklin County	733	2.04

Top 10 Places Sorted by Percent of Total Population
Based on all places, regardless of total population

Place	Population	%
Homeworth (cdp) Columbiana County	163	17.70
Camp Dennison (cdp) Hamilton County	61	13.01
Ithaca (village) Darke County	10	12.82
Richmond Dale (cdp) Ross County	26	12.62
Rawson (village) Hancock County	46	9.64
Fort Seneca (cdp) Seneca County	40	9.55
Wilson (village) Monroe County	10	8.70
Granville South (cdp) Licking County	132	8.26
Pancoastburg (cdp) Fayette County	8	8.08
Plainville (cdp) Hamilton County	15	6.73

Top 10 Places Sorted by Percent of Total Population
Based on places with total population of 50,000 or more

Place	Population	%
Kettering (city) Montgomery County	692	1.23
Columbus (city) Franklin County	7,099	0.92
Cincinnati (city) Hamilton County	2,521	0.84
Springfield (city) Clark County	473	0.77
Dayton (city) Montgomery County	1,113	0.76
Lakewood (city) Cuyahoga County	385	0.73
Akron (city) Summit County	1,390	0.69
Hamilton (city) Butler County	357	0.57
Toledo (city) Lucas County	1,626	0.56
Parma (city) Cuyahoga County	420	0.51

Finnish

Top 10 Places Sorted by Population
Based on all places, regardless of total population

Place	Population	%
Ashtabula (city) Ashtabula County	914	4.69
Columbus (city) Franklin County	858	0.11
Conneaut (city) Ashtabula County	688	5.38
Lakewood (city) Cuyahoga County	386	0.73
Cleveland (city) Cuyahoga County	376	0.09
Fairport Harbor (village) Lake County	356	11.40
Toledo (city) Lucas County	295	0.10
Painesville (city) Lake County	290	1.51
Mentor (city) Lake County	280	0.59
North Madison (cdp) Lake County	226	2.51

Top 10 Places Sorted by Percent of Total Population
Based on all places, regardless of total population

Place	Population	%
Austinburg (cdp) Ashtabula County	97	12.02
Fairport Harbor (village) Lake County	356	11.40
North Kingsville (village) Ashtabula County	179	6.22
Conneaut (city) Ashtabula County	688	5.38
Ashtabula (city) Ashtabula County	914	4.69
Madison (village) Lake County	137	4.37
Jefferson (village) Ashtabula County	133	4.11
Peninsula (village) Summit County	21	3.66
Put-in-Bay (village) Ottawa County	5	3.60
North Madison (cdp) Lake County	226	2.51

Top 10 Places Sorted by Percent of Total Population
Based on places with total population of 50,000 or more

Place	Population	%
Lakewood (city) Cuyahoga County	386	0.73
Springfield (city) Clark County	106	0.17
Kettering (city) Montgomery County	84	0.15
Columbus (city) Franklin County	858	0.11
Toledo (city) Lucas County	295	0.10
Dayton (city) Montgomery County	144	0.10
Cleveland (city) Cuyahoga County	376	0.09
Hamilton (city) Butler County	49	0.08
Elyria (city) Lorain County	36	0.07
Cincinnati (city) Hamilton County	175	0.06

French, except Basque

Top 10 Places Sorted by Population
Based on all places, regardless of total population

Place	Population	%
Columbus (city) Franklin County	14,605	1.90
Toledo (city) Lucas County	13,787	4.72
Cincinnati (city) Hamilton County	5,247	1.75
Cleveland (city) Cuyahoga County	4,063	0.99
Akron (city) Summit County	3,698	1.82
Kettering (city) Montgomery County	2,149	3.83
Dayton (city) Montgomery County	2,130	1.46
Beavercreek (city) Greene County	1,789	4.06
Canton (city) Stark County	1,697	2.28
Oregon (city) Lucas County	1,492	7.42

Top 10 Places Sorted by Percent of Total Population
Based on all places, regardless of total population

Place	Population	%
Maplewood Park (cdp) Trumbull County	112	38.49
Russia (village) Shelby County	243	38.15
Versailles (village) Darke County	895	33.76

Place	Population	%
North Star (village) Darke County	71	33.02
Remington (cdp) Hamilton County	71	29.71
Mifflin (village) Ashland County	28	23.93
Haviland (village) Paulding County	23	18.70
New Hampshire (cdp) Auglaize County	21	15.56
Osgood (village) Darke County	42	15.50
Stony Ridge (cdp) Wood County	55	14.86

Top 10 Places Sorted by Percent of Total Population
Based on places with total population of 50,000 or more

Place	Population	%
Toledo (city) Lucas County	13,787	4.72
Kettering (city) Montgomery County	2,149	3.83
Lakewood (city) Cuyahoga County	1,255	2.38
Canton (city) Stark County	1,697	2.28
Springfield (city) Clark County	1,220	1.98
Columbus (city) Franklin County	14,605	1.90
Akron (city) Summit County	3,698	1.82
Cincinnati (city) Hamilton County	5,247	1.75
Parma (city) Cuyahoga County	1,339	1.64
Elyria (city) Lorain County	896	1.63

French Canadian

Top 10 Places Sorted by Population
Based on all places, regardless of total population

Place	Population	%
Toledo (city) Lucas County	2,025	0.69
Columbus (city) Franklin County	1,886	0.24
Cincinnati (city) Hamilton County	503	0.17
Cleveland (city) Cuyahoga County	425	0.10
Oregon (city) Lucas County	417	2.07
Elyria (city) Lorain County	376	0.68
Mentor (city) Lake County	326	0.68
Akron (city) Summit County	320	0.16
Dayton (city) Montgomery County	280	0.19
Sylvania (city) Lucas County	266	1.40

Top 10 Places Sorted by Percent of Total Population
Based on all places, regardless of total population

Place	Population	%
East Fultonham (cdp) Muskingum County	25	15.92
Trinway (cdp) Muskingum County	40	9.39
Montezuma (village) Mercer County	13	8.39
Caledonia (village) Marion County	37	5.76
Millbury (village) Wood County	77	5.64
Alger (village) Hardin County	45	5.55
Berkey (village) Lucas County	13	4.92
Jerusalem (village) Monroe County	6	4.80
Burgoon (village) Sandusky County	9	4.79
Buckland (village) Auglaize County	9	3.85

Top 10 Places Sorted by Percent of Total Population
Based on places with total population of 50,000 or more

Place	Population	%
Toledo (city) Lucas County	2,025	0.69
Elyria (city) Lorain County	376	0.68
Lakewood (city) Cuyahoga County	227	0.43
Kettering (city) Montgomery County	237	0.42
Springfield (city) Clark County	177	0.29
Columbus (city) Franklin County	1,886	0.24
Parma (city) Cuyahoga County	178	0.22
Dayton (city) Montgomery County	280	0.19
Cincinnati (city) Hamilton County	503	0.17
Akron (city) Summit County	320	0.16

German

Top 10 Places Sorted by Population
Based on all places, regardless of total population

Place	Population	%
Columbus (city) Franklin County	163,383	21.21
Toledo (city) Lucas County	76,635	26.26
Cincinnati (city) Hamilton County	59,441	19.80
Cleveland (city) Cuyahoga County	40,200	9.82
Akron (city) Summit County	39,722	19.59
Dayton (city) Montgomery County	23,171	15.91
Parma (city) Cuyahoga County	21,335	26.05
Kettering (city) Montgomery County	20,845	37.10
Canton (city) Stark County	18,990	25.51
Findlay (city) Hancock County	16,605	40.31

Top 10 Places Sorted by Percent of Total Population
Based on all places, regardless of total population

Place	Population	%
Miamiville (cdp) Clermont County	226	100.00
Miltonsburg (village) Monroe County	7	100.00
Walnut Creek (cdp) Holmes County	373	96.38
Holiday City (village) Williams County	45	91.84
Glandorf (village) Putnam County	869	86.99
Miller City (village) Putnam County	87	84.47
Fort Jennings (village) Putnam County	440	83.81
St Johns (cdp) Auglaize County	60	83.33
Newport (cdp) Shelby County	238	82.64
Kalida (village) Putnam County	836	82.20

Top 10 Places Sorted by Percent of Total Population
Based on places with total population of 50,000 or more

Place	Population	%
Kettering (city) Montgomery County	20,845	37.10
Lakewood (city) Cuyahoga County	14,246	27.05
Toledo (city) Lucas County	76,635	26.26
Parma (city) Cuyahoga County	21,335	26.05
Canton (city) Stark County	18,990	25.51
Elyria (city) Lorain County	13,579	24.69
Springfield (city) Clark County	13,145	21.37
Hamilton (city) Butler County	13,275	21.25
Columbus (city) Franklin County	163,383	21.21
Cincinnati (city) Hamilton County	59,441	19.80

German Russian

Top 10 Places Sorted by Population
Based on all places, regardless of total population

Place	Population	%
Akron (city) Summit County	78	0.04
Maple Heights (city) Cuyahoga County	68	0.29
Cincinnati (city) Hamilton County	34	0.01
Columbus (city) Franklin County	33	<0.01
Grove City (city) Franklin County	29	0.09
Garfield Heights (city) Cuyahoga County	28	0.10
Washington Court House (city) Fayette County	23	0.16
Ashland (city) Ashland County	22	0.11
Lorain (city) Lorain County	18	0.03
Cleveland (city) Cuyahoga County	18	<0.01

Top 10 Places Sorted by Percent of Total Population
Based on all places, regardless of total population

Place	Population	%
North Randall (village) Cuyahoga County	11	1.27
Ridgeway (village) Hardin County	4	0.85
Valley Hi (village) Logan County	2	0.81
West Liberty (village) Logan County	7	0.38
Maple Heights (city) Cuyahoga County	68	0.29
Silverton (city) Hamilton County	14	0.29
Washington Court House (city) Fayette County	23	0.16
South Amherst (village) Lorain County	3	0.16
Ashland (city) Ashland County	22	0.11
Garfield Heights (city) Cuyahoga County	28	0.10

Top 10 Places Sorted by Percent of Total Population
Based on places with total population of 50,000 or more

Place	Population	%
Akron (city) Summit County	78	0.04
Lorain (city) Lorain County	18	0.03
Cincinnati (city) Hamilton County	34	0.01
Columbus (city) Franklin County	33	<0.01
Cleveland (city) Cuyahoga County	18	<0.01
Youngstown (city) Mahoning County	1	<0.01
Canton (city) Stark County	0	0.00
Dayton (city) Montgomery County	0	0.00
Elyria (city) Lorain County	0	0.00
Hamilton (city) Butler County	0	0.00

Greek

Top 10 Places Sorted by Population
Based on all places, regardless of total population

Place	Population	%
Columbus (city) Franklin County	2,987	0.39
Cleveland (city) Cuyahoga County	1,435	0.35
Campbell (city) Mahoning County	1,393	16.50
Canton (city) Stark County	1,154	1.55
Akron (city) Summit County	1,127	0.56
Parma (city) Cuyahoga County	1,087	1.33
Toledo (city) Lucas County	910	0.31
Warren (city) Trumbull County	876	2.05
Cincinnati (city) Hamilton County	840	0.28
Boardman (cdp) Mahoning County	783	2.21

Top 10 Places Sorted by Percent of Total Population
Based on all places, regardless of total population

Place	Population	%
Campbell (city) Mahoning County	1,393	16.50
Lake Mohawk (cdp) Carroll County	187	10.77
Lake Buckhorn (cdp) Holmes County	32	9.30
Mount Orab (village) Brown County	334	8.47
Yorkville (village) Jefferson County	86	6.71
Miami Heights (cdp) Hamilton County	241	5.27
Rayland (village) Jefferson County	18	4.64
Arcadia (village) Hancock County	26	4.46
Linndale (village) Cuyahoga County	6	4.41
Aquilla (village) Geauga County	16	4.37

Top 10 Places Sorted by Percent of Total Population
Based on places with total population of 50,000 or more

Place	Population	%
Canton (city) Stark County	1,154	1.55
Parma (city) Cuyahoga County	1,087	1.33
Lakewood (city) Cuyahoga County	607	1.15
Elyria (city) Lorain County	317	0.58
Akron (city) Summit County	1,127	0.56
Lorain (city) Lorain County	365	0.56
Youngstown (city) Mahoning County	312	0.45
Springfield (city) Clark County	244	0.40
Kettering (city) Montgomery County	224	0.40
Columbus (city) Franklin County	2,987	0.39

Guyanese

Top 10 Places Sorted by Population
Based on all places, regardless of total population

Place	Population	%
Cleveland (city) Cuyahoga County	370	0.09
Columbus (city) Franklin County	135	0.02
Centerville (city) Montgomery County	123	0.52
Mount Vernon (city) Knox County	120	0.71
Ballville (cdp) Sandusky County	88	2.77
Cincinnati (city) Hamilton County	77	0.03
Toledo (city) Lucas County	60	0.02
Middleburg Heights (city) Cuyahoga County	33	0.21
White Oak (cdp) Hamilton County	22	0.12
Springdale (city) Hamilton County	21	0.19

Top 10 Places Sorted by Percent of Total Population
Based on all places, regardless of total population

Place	Population	%
Ballville (cdp) Sandusky County	88	2.77
Mount Vernon (city) Knox County	120	0.71
Centerville (city) Montgomery County	123	0.52
Sixteen Mile Stand (cdp) Hamilton County	8	0.27
Middleburg Heights (city) Cuyahoga County	33	0.21
Springdale (city) Hamilton County	21	0.19
White Oak (cdp) Hamilton County	22	0.12
Cleveland (city) Cuyahoga County	370	0.09
Kent (city) Portage County	16	0.06
Eastlake (city) Lake County	9	0.05

Top 10 Places Sorted by Percent of Total Population
Based on places with total population of 50,000 or more

Place	Population	%
Cleveland (city) Cuyahoga County	370	0.09
Cincinnati (city) Hamilton County	77	0.03
Columbus (city) Franklin County	135	0.02
Toledo (city) Lucas County	60	0.02
Akron (city) Summit County	0	0.00
Canton (city) Stark County	0	0.00
Dayton (city) Montgomery County	0	0.00
Elyria (city) Lorain County	0	0.00
Hamilton (city) Butler County	0	0.00
Kettering (city) Montgomery County	0	0.00

Hungarian

Top 10 Places Sorted by Population
Based on all places, regardless of total population

Place	Population	%
Cleveland (city) Cuyahoga County	6,822	1.67
Columbus (city) Franklin County	6,569	0.85
Toledo (city) Lucas County	6,352	2.18
Akron (city) Summit County	4,508	2.22
Parma (city) Cuyahoga County	4,239	5.18
Lorain (city) Lorain County	3,113	4.77
Mentor (city) Lake County	2,998	6.29
Lakewood (city) Cuyahoga County	2,499	4.74
Elyria (city) Lorain County	2,358	4.29
Brunswick (city) Medina County	1,802	5.24

Top 10 Places Sorted by Percent of Total Population
Based on all places, regardless of total population

Place	Population	%
East Fultonham (cdp) Muskingum County	47	29.94
Williston (cdp) Ottawa County	75	20.27
Crystal Rock (cdp) Erie County	14	19.72
Pigeon Creek (cdp) Summit County	135	18.96
Fairport Harbor (village) Lake County	487	15.59
Bolivar (village) Tuscarawas County	144	11.94
Clifton (village) Greene County	27	11.64
Yankee Lake (village) Trumbull County	8	11.59
Moreland Hills (village) Cuyahoga County	373	11.27
Rayland (village) Jefferson County	42	10.82

Top 10 Places Sorted by Percent of Total Population
Based on places with total population of 50,000 or more

Place	Population	%
Parma (city) Cuyahoga County	4,239	5.18
Lorain (city) Lorain County	3,113	4.77
Lakewood (city) Cuyahoga County	2,499	4.74
Elyria (city) Lorain County	2,358	4.29
Akron (city) Summit County	4,508	2.22
Toledo (city) Lucas County	6,352	2.18
Youngstown (city) Mahoning County	1,409	2.02
Cleveland (city) Cuyahoga County	6,822	1.67
Kettering (city) Montgomery County	714	1.27
Canton (city) Stark County	917	1.23

Icelander

Top 10 Places Sorted by Population
Based on all places, regardless of total population

Place	Population	%
Gambier (village) Knox County	75	3.41
Columbus (city) Franklin County	51	0.01
Toledo (city) Lucas County	44	0.02
Miamisburg (city) Montgomery County	43	0.22
Northwood (city) Wood County	37	0.69
Monfort Heights (cdp) Hamilton County	35	0.30
Westlake (city) Cuyahoga County	33	0.10
Stow (city) Summit County	32	0.09
Strongsville (city) Cuyahoga County	29	0.07
Cleveland (city) Cuyahoga County	25	0.01

Top 10 Places Sorted by Percent of Total Population
Based on all places, regardless of total population

Place	Population	%
Gambier (village) Knox County	75	3.41
Waite Hill (village) Lake County	4	0.83
Northwood (city) Wood County	37	0.69
Beechwood Trails (cdp) Licking County	13	0.40
Monfort Heights (cdp) Hamilton County	35	0.30
Granville (village) Licking County	13	0.23
Miamisburg (city) Montgomery County	43	0.22
Fostoria (city) Seneca County	24	0.18
West Carrollton (city) Montgomery County	18	0.14
Delphos (city) Allen County	10	0.14

Top 10 Places Sorted by Percent of Total Population
Based on places with total population of 50,000 or more

Place	Population	%
Toledo (city) Lucas County	44	0.02
Columbus (city) Franklin County	51	0.01
Cleveland (city) Cuyahoga County	25	0.01
Akron (city) Summit County	19	0.01
Canton (city) Stark County	0	0.00
Cincinnati (city) Hamilton County	0	0.00
Dayton (city) Montgomery County	0	0.00
Elyria (city) Lorain County	0	0.00
Hamilton (city) Butler County	0	0.00
Kettering (city) Montgomery County	0	0.00

Iranian

Top 10 Places Sorted by Population
Based on all places, regardless of total population

Place	Population	%
Columbus (city) Franklin County	466	0.06
Upper Arlington (city) Franklin County	161	0.48
Lakewood (city) Cuyahoga County	118	0.22
Dublin (city) Franklin County	98	0.25
Shaker Heights (city) Cuyahoga County	96	0.34
Springboro (city) Warren County	86	0.50
Strongsville (city) Cuyahoga County	85	0.19
Oakwood (city) Montgomery County	77	0.84
Toledo (city) Lucas County	73	0.03
Cincinnati (city) Hamilton County	69	0.02

Top 10 Places Sorted by Percent of Total Population
Based on all places, regardless of total population

Place	Population	%
Remington (cdp) Hamilton County	8	3.35
Moreland Hills (village) Cuyahoga County	43	1.30
Mayfield (village) Cuyahoga County	42	1.23
Montrose-Ghent (cdp) Summit County	52	1.01
Hunting Valley (village) Cuyahoga County	6	0.93
Oakwood (city) Montgomery County	77	0.84
Brooklyn Heights (village) Cuyahoga County	12	0.80
Ottawa Hills (village) Lucas County	33	0.73
Mariemont (village) Hamilton County	24	0.71
New Albany (village) Franklin County	46	0.65

Top 10 Places Sorted by Percent of Total Population
Based on places with total population of 50,000 or more

Place	Population	%
Lakewood (city) Cuyahoga County	118	0.22
Columbus (city) Franklin County	466	0.06
Springfield (city) Clark County	28	0.05
Toledo (city) Lucas County	73	0.03
Parma (city) Cuyahoga County	24	0.03
Cincinnati (city) Hamilton County	69	0.02
Akron (city) Summit County	36	0.02
Kettering (city) Montgomery County	9	0.02
Cleveland (city) Cuyahoga County	26	0.01
Canton (city) Stark County	0	0.00

Irish

Top 10 Places Sorted by Population
Based on all places, regardless of total population

Place	Population	%
Columbus (city) Franklin County	99,000	12.85
Cleveland (city) Cuyahoga County	37,296	9.11
Toledo (city) Lucas County	34,827	11.93
Cincinnati (city) Hamilton County	32,799	10.93
Akron (city) Summit County	26,458	13.05
Dayton (city) Montgomery County	14,086	9.67
Lakewood (city) Cuyahoga County	12,740	24.19
Parma (city) Cuyahoga County	11,502	14.04
Canton (city) Stark County	9,815	13.18
Cuyahoga Falls (city) Summit County	9,658	19.43

Top 10 Places Sorted by Percent of Total Population
Based on all places, regardless of total population

Place	Population	%
Miltonsburg (village) Monroe County	7	100.00
Kilbourne (cdp) Delaware County	136	74.73
Miamiville (cdp) Clermont County	166	73.45
Pulaski (cdp) Williams County	44	66.67
Wightmans Grove (cdp) Sandusky County	20	60.61
Vaughnsville (cdp) Putnam County	82	59.85
Stockdale (cdp) Pike County	91	52.60
Buford (cdp) Highland County	146	52.33
Glencoe (cdp) Belmont County	45	52.33
East Fultonham (cdp) Muskingum County	80	50.96

Top 10 Places Sorted by Percent of Total Population
Based on places with total population of 50,000 or more

Place	Population	%
Lakewood (city) Cuyahoga County	12,740	24.19
Kettering (city) Montgomery County	9,275	16.51
Elyria (city) Lorain County	8,207	14.92
Parma (city) Cuyahoga County	11,502	14.04
Canton (city) Stark County	9,815	13.18
Akron (city) Summit County	26,458	13.05
Columbus (city) Franklin County	99,000	12.85
Springfield (city) Clark County	7,564	12.30
Toledo (city) Lucas County	34,827	11.93
Lorain (city) Lorain County	7,298	11.19

Israeli

Top 10 Places Sorted by Population
Based on all places, regardless of total population

Place	Population	%
Columbus (city) Franklin County	138	0.02
Lyndhurst (city) Cuyahoga County	136	0.96
Solon (city) Cuyahoga County	124	0.54
Cincinnati (city) Hamilton County	118	0.04
North Olmsted (city) Cuyahoga County	80	0.24
South Euclid (city) Cuyahoga County	69	0.31
Blue Ash (city) Hamilton County	50	0.41
Beavercreek (city) Greene County	50	0.11
Cleveland Heights (city) Cuyahoga County	49	0.10
Kenwood (cdp) Hamilton County	47	0.65

Top 10 Places Sorted by Percent of Total Population
Based on all places, regardless of total population

Place	Population	%
Lyndhurst (city) Cuyahoga County	136	0.96
Kenwood (cdp) Hamilton County	47	0.65
Solon (city) Cuyahoga County	124	0.54
Oberlin (city) Lorain County	37	0.45
Reminderville (village) Summit County	14	0.43
Blue Ash (city) Hamilton County	50	0.41
South Euclid (city) Cuyahoga County	69	0.31
Silver Lake (village) Summit County	8	0.31
University Heights (city) Cuyahoga County	38	0.28
Westfield Center (village) Medina County	3	0.28

Top 10 Places Sorted by Percent of Total Population
Based on places with total population of 50,000 or more

Place	Population	%
Cincinnati (city) Hamilton County	118	0.04
Lakewood (city) Cuyahoga County	14	0.03
Columbus (city) Franklin County	138	0.02
Dayton (city) Montgomery County	29	0.02
Toledo (city) Lucas County	35	0.01
Akron (city) Summit County	11	0.01
Cleveland (city) Cuyahoga County	10	<0.01
Canton (city) Stark County	0	0.00
Elyria (city) Lorain County	0	0.00
Hamilton (city) Butler County	0	0.00

Italian

Top 10 Places Sorted by Population
Based on all places, regardless of total population

Place	Population	%
Columbus (city) Franklin County	38,883	5.05
Cleveland (city) Cuyahoga County	19,033	4.65
Akron (city) Summit County	15,000	7.40
Parma (city) Cuyahoga County	11,434	13.96
Cincinnati (city) Hamilton County	9,502	3.17
Toledo (city) Lucas County	9,356	3.21
Boardman (cdp) Mahoning County	8,683	24.53
Mentor (city) Lake County	8,526	17.90
Youngstown (city) Mahoning County	7,337	10.54
Cuyahoga Falls (city) Summit County	6,168	12.41

Top 10 Places Sorted by Percent of Total Population
Based on all places, regardless of total population

Place	Population	%
Kilbourne (cdp) Delaware County	123	67.58
Wightmans Grove (cdp) Sandusky County	20	60.61
Lafferty (cdp) Belmont County	102	46.58

Place	Population	%
Lowellville (village) Mahoning County	506	43.81
McKinley Heights (cdp) Trumbull County	410	37.61
Poland (village) Mahoning County	825	31.72
New Middletown (village) Mahoning County	565	30.59
Summitville (village) Columbiana County	49	30.43
Brookfield Center (cdp) Trumbull County	427	29.01
Lockbourne (village) Franklin County	112	28.72

Top 10 Places Sorted by Percent of Total Population

Based on places with total population of 50,000 or more

Place	Population	%
Parma (city) Cuyahoga County	11,434	13.96
Lakewood (city) Cuyahoga County	6,124	11.63
Youngstown (city) Mahoning County	7,337	10.54
Canton (city) Stark County	5,958	8.00
Lorain (city) Lorain County	4,912	7.53
Akron (city) Summit County	15,000	7.40
Elyria (city) Lorain County	3,507	6.38
Kettering (city) Montgomery County	2,845	5.06
Columbus (city) Franklin County	38,883	5.05
Cleveland (city) Cuyahoga County	19,033	4.65

Latvian

Top 10 Places Sorted by Population

Based on all places, regardless of total population

Place	Population	%
Columbus (city) Franklin County	214	0.03
Cleveland (city) Cuyahoga County	99	0.02
Middleburg Heights (city) Cuyahoga County	94	0.60
Cincinnati (city) Hamilton County	67	0.02
Shaker Heights (city) Cuyahoga County	63	0.22
Lakewood (city) Cuyahoga County	60	0.11
Waterville (village) Lucas County	59	1.09
Brook Park (city) Cuyahoga County	55	0.28
Hilliard (city) Franklin County	51	0.19
Gahanna (city) Franklin County	48	0.15

Top 10 Places Sorted by Percent of Total Population

Based on all places, regardless of total population

Place	Population	%
Waterville (village) Lucas County	59	1.09
Bentleyville (village) Cuyahoga County	10	0.95
Jamestown (village) Greene County	15	0.80
Moreland Hills (village) Cuyahoga County	22	0.66
Gambier (village) Knox County	14	0.64
Middleburg Heights (city) Cuyahoga County	94	0.60
Ney (village) Defiance County	2	0.60
Bailey Lakes (village) Ashland County	2	0.53
Pepper Pike (city) Cuyahoga County	29	0.49
Hunting Valley (village) Cuyahoga County	3	0.47

Top 10 Places Sorted by Percent of Total Population

Based on places with total population of 50,000 or more

Place	Population	%
Lakewood (city) Cuyahoga County	60	0.11
Lorain (city) Lorain County	23	0.04
Columbus (city) Franklin County	214	0.03
Parma (city) Cuyahoga County	24	0.03
Cleveland (city) Cuyahoga County	99	0.02
Cincinnati (city) Hamilton County	67	0.02
Akron (city) Summit County	27	0.01
Toledo (city) Lucas County	21	0.01
Dayton (city) Montgomery County	9	0.01
Springfield (city) Clark County	8	0.01

Lithuanian

Top 10 Places Sorted by Population

Based on all places, regardless of total population

Place	Population	%
Cleveland (city) Cuyahoga County	1,180	0.29
Columbus (city) Franklin County	1,022	0.13
Parma (city) Cuyahoga County	613	0.75
Euclid (city) Cuyahoga County	568	1.15
Mentor (city) Lake County	497	1.04
Willoughby (city) Lake County	338	1.52
Willowick (city) Lake County	316	2.22
Beachwood (city) Cuyahoga County	299	2.51
Lakewood (city) Cuyahoga County	291	0.55
Eastlake (city) Lake County	286	1.51

Top 10 Places Sorted by Percent of Total Population

Based on all places, regardless of total population

Place	Population	%
Deersville (village) Harrison County	6	5.26
Kettlersville (village) Shelby County	9	4.39
Mount Eaton (village) Wayne County	10	4.15
Timberlake (village) Lake County	22	3.49
Kirtland Hills (village) Lake County	25	3.27
Lockington (village) Shelby County	5	2.98
Cortland (city) Trumbull County	191	2.72
Beachwood (city) Cuyahoga County	299	2.51
South Russell (village) Geauga County	96	2.48
Orange (village) Cuyahoga County	80	2.43

Top 10 Places Sorted by Percent of Total Population

Based on places with total population of 50,000 or more

Place	Population	%
Parma (city) Cuyahoga County	613	0.75
Lakewood (city) Cuyahoga County	291	0.55
Kettering (city) Montgomery County	202	0.36
Cleveland (city) Cuyahoga County	1,180	0.29
Elyria (city) Lorain County	132	0.24
Dayton (city) Montgomery County	244	0.17
Springfield (city) Clark County	84	0.14
Columbus (city) Franklin County	1,022	0.13
Canton (city) Stark County	99	0.13
Akron (city) Summit County	239	0.12

Luxemburger

Top 10 Places Sorted by Population

Based on all places, regardless of total population

Place	Population	%
Tiffin (city) Seneca County	56	0.31
Steubenville (city) Jefferson County	54	0.29
Mentor (city) Lake County	44	0.09
Dry Run (cdp) Hamilton County	29	0.44
Columbus (city) Franklin County	23	<0.01
Greenhills (village) Hamilton County	19	0.52
McKinley Heights (cdp) Trumbull County	17	1.56
Taylor Creek (cdp) Hamilton County	17	0.48
Green (city) Summit County	14	0.06
Aurora (city) Portage County	13	0.09

Top 10 Places Sorted by Percent of Total Population

Based on all places, regardless of total population

Place	Population	%
McKinley Heights (cdp) Trumbull County	17	1.56
Sugar Grove (village) Fairfield County	4	0.82
Greenhills (village) Hamilton County	19	0.52
Taylor Creek (cdp) Hamilton County	17	0.48
Dry Run (cdp) Hamilton County	29	0.44
Terrace Park (village) Hamilton County	9	0.40
Butler (village) Richland County	4	0.39
Tiffin (city) Seneca County	56	0.31
Carey (village) Wyandot County	12	0.31
Steubenville (city) Jefferson County	54	0.29

Top 10 Places Sorted by Percent of Total Population

Based on places with total population of 50,000 or more

Place	Population	%
Columbus (city) Franklin County	23	<0.01
Akron (city) Summit County	0	0.00
Canton (city) Stark County	0	0.00
Cincinnati (city) Hamilton County	0	0.00
Cleveland (city) Cuyahoga County	0	0.00
Dayton (city) Montgomery County	0	0.00
Elyria (city) Lorain County	0	0.00
Hamilton (city) Butler County	0	0.00
Kettering (city) Montgomery County	0	0.00
Lakewood (city) Cuyahoga County	0	0.00

Macedonian

Top 10 Places Sorted by Population

Based on all places, regardless of total population

Place	Population	%
Columbus (city) Franklin County	307	0.04
Brunswick (city) Medina County	222	0.65
Springfield (city) Clark County	145	0.24
White Oak (cdp) Hamilton County	123	0.65
Johnstown (village) Licking County	122	2.47
Pickerington (city) Fairfield County	116	0.68
Gahanna (city) Franklin County	103	0.32
Lorain (city) Lorain County	97	0.15
Elyria (city) Lorain County	95	0.17
Norwalk (city) Huron County	76	0.45

Top 10 Places Sorted by Percent of Total Population

Based on all places, regardless of total population

Place	Population	%
West Manchester (village) Preble County	17	3.82
Johnstown (village) Licking County	122	2.47
Lake Mohawk (cdp) Carroll County	24	1.38
Churchill (cdp) Trumbull County	22	0.83
Pickerington (city) Fairfield County	116	0.68
Brunswick (city) Medina County	222	0.65
White Oak (cdp) Hamilton County	123	0.65
Mack (cdp) Hamilton County	72	0.63
New Albany (village) Franklin County	44	0.62
Poland (village) Mahoning County	16	0.62

Top 10 Places Sorted by Percent of Total Population

Based on places with total population of 50,000 or more

Place	Population	%
Springfield (city) Clark County	145	0.24
Elyria (city) Lorain County	95	0.17
Lorain (city) Lorain County	97	0.15
Columbus (city) Franklin County	307	0.04
Akron (city) Summit County	56	0.03
Cincinnati (city) Hamilton County	46	0.02
Lakewood (city) Cuyahoga County	11	0.02
Toledo (city) Lucas County	18	0.01
Dayton (city) Montgomery County	14	0.01
Parma (city) Cuyahoga County	10	0.01

Maltese

Top 10 Places Sorted by Population

Based on all places, regardless of total population

Place	Population	%
Boardman (cdp) Mahoning County	152	0.43
Perrysburg (city) Wood County	39	0.19
Lakewood (city) Cuyahoga County	30	0.06
Columbus (city) Franklin County	29	<0.01
Mansfield (city) Richland County	26	0.05
Evendale (village) Hamilton County	20	0.71
Ballville (cdp) Sandusky County	19	0.60
Cincinnati (city) Hamilton County	18	0.01
Toledo (city) Lucas County	17	0.01
Norwalk (city) Huron County	11	0.06

Top 10 Places Sorted by Percent of Total Population

Based on all places, regardless of total population

Place	Population	%
Evendale (village) Hamilton County	20	0.71
Ballville (cdp) Sandusky County	19	0.60
Boardman (cdp) Mahoning County	152	0.43
Doylestown (village) Wayne County	9	0.30
Perrysburg (city) Wood County	39	0.19
Union City (village) Darke County	3	0.18
Lakewood (city) Cuyahoga County	30	0.06
Norwalk (city) Huron County	11	0.06
Mansfield (city) Richland County	26	0.05
Sylvania (city) Lucas County	7	0.04

Top 10 Places Sorted by Percent of Total Population

Based on places with total population of 50,000 or more

Place	Population	%
Lakewood (city) Cuyahoga County	30	0.06
Cincinnati (city) Hamilton County	18	0.01
Toledo (city) Lucas County	17	0.01
Columbus (city) Franklin County	29	<0.01
Akron (city) Summit County	0	0.00
Canton (city) Stark County	0	0.00
Cleveland (city) Cuyahoga County	0	0.00
Dayton (city) Montgomery County	0	0.00
Elyria (city) Lorain County	0	0.00
Hamilton (city) Butler County	0	0.00

New Zealander

Top 10 Places Sorted by Population

Based on all places, regardless of total population

Place	Population	%
Ballville (cdp) Sandusky County	62	1.95
Chagrin Falls (village) Cuyahoga County	55	1.35
Columbus (city) Franklin County	48	0.01
Cuyahoga Falls (city) Summit County	32	0.06
Delaware (city) Delaware County	29	0.09
University Heights (city) Cuyahoga County	22	0.16
Granville (village) Licking County	15	0.27
Gahanna (city) Franklin County	14	0.04
Oakwood (city) Montgomery County	11	0.12
Cleveland Heights (city) Cuyahoga County	10	0.02

Top 10 Places Sorted by Percent of Total Population

Based on all places, regardless of total population

Place	Population	%
Ballville (cdp) Sandusky County	62	1.95
Chagrin Falls (village) Cuyahoga County	55	1.35
Granville (village) Licking County	15	0.27
University Heights (city) Cuyahoga County	22	0.16
Oakwood (city) Montgomery County	11	0.12
Delaware (city) Delaware County	29	0.09
Willoughby Hills (city) Lake County	8	0.09
Cuyahoga Falls (city) Summit County	32	0.06
Gahanna (city) Franklin County	14	0.04
Cleveland Heights (city) Cuyahoga County	10	0.02

Top 10 Places Sorted by Percent of Total Population

Based on places with total population of 50,000 or more

Place	Population	%
Columbus (city) Franklin County	48	0.01
Hamilton (city) Butler County	8	0.01
Akron (city) Summit County	0	0.00
Canton (city) Stark County	0	0.00
Cincinnati (city) Hamilton County	0	0.00
Cleveland (city) Cuyahoga County	0	0.00
Dayton (city) Montgomery County	0	0.00
Elyria (city) Lorain County	0	0.00
Kettering (city) Montgomery County	0	0.00
Lakewood (city) Cuyahoga County	0	0.00

Northern European

Top 10 Places Sorted by Population

Based on all places, regardless of total population

Place	Population	%
Columbus (city) Franklin County	220	0.03
Boardman (cdp) Mahoning County	109	0.31
Akron (city) Summit County	103	0.05
Grove City (city) Franklin County	80	0.24
Canton (city) Stark County	80	0.11
Beavercreek (city) Greene County	79	0.18
Dublin (city) Franklin County	77	0.20
Cuyahoga Falls (city) Summit County	73	0.15
Cincinnati (city) Hamilton County	69	0.02
Shaker Heights (city) Cuyahoga County	55	0.19

Top 10 Places Sorted by Percent of Total Population

Based on all places, regardless of total population

Place	Population	%
Duncan Falls (cdp) Muskingum County	22	2.57
Silver Lake (village) Summit County	39	1.52
Sixteen Mile Stand (cdp) Hamilton County	35	1.19
Glendale (village) Hamilton County	24	1.04
Chagrin Falls (village) Cuyahoga County	36	0.88
Newcomerstown (village) Tuscarawas County	34	0.88
Richfield (village) Summit County	30	0.83
Kenwood (cdp) Hamilton County	50	0.69
Millersport (village) Fairfield County	6	0.63
Cherry Grove (cdp) Hamilton County	26	0.57

Top 10 Places Sorted by Percent of Total Population

Based on places with total population of 50,000 or more

Place	Population	%
Canton (city) Stark County	80	0.11
Akron (city) Summit County	103	0.05
Elyria (city) Lorain County	28	0.05
Hamilton (city) Butler County	28	0.04
Columbus (city) Franklin County	220	0.03
Kettering (city) Montgomery County	18	0.03
Cincinnati (city) Hamilton County	69	0.02
Springfield (city) Clark County	11	0.02
Lakewood (city) Cuyahoga County	9	0.02
Cleveland (city) Cuyahoga County	48	0.01

Norwegian

Top 10 Places Sorted by Population

Based on all places, regardless of total population

Place	Population	%
Columbus (city) Franklin County	3,594	0.47
Toledo (city) Lucas County	1,161	0.40
Cincinnati (city) Hamilton County	1,024	0.34
Akron (city) Summit County	541	0.27
Cleveland (city) Cuyahoga County	435	0.11
Upper Arlington (city) Franklin County	392	1.17
Lakewood (city) Cuyahoga County	366	0.69
Beavercreek (city) Greene County	349	0.79
Dayton (city) Montgomery County	346	0.24
Mason (city) Warren County	338	1.13

Top 10 Places Sorted by Percent of Total Population

Based on all places, regardless of total population

Place	Population	%
Mount Blanchard (village) Hancock County	34	6.18
Wright-Patterson AFB (cdp) Greene County	180	5.71
Tuppers Plains (cdp) Meigs County	13	4.92
Casstown (village) Miami County	12	4.40
New Straitsville (village) Perry County	20	4.08
Lewistown (cdp) Logan County	14	3.89
Luckey (village) Wood County	39	3.87
Mount Gilead (village) Morrow County	139	3.67
Johnstown (village) Licking County	170	3.45
Clifton (village) Greene County	7	3.02

Top 10 Places Sorted by Percent of Total Population

Based on places with total population of 50,000 or more

Place	Population	%
Lakewood (city) Cuyahoga County	366	0.69
Columbus (city) Franklin County	3,594	0.47
Kettering (city) Montgomery County	264	0.47
Elyria (city) Lorain County	234	0.43
Toledo (city) Lucas County	1,161	0.40
Cincinnati (city) Hamilton County	1,024	0.34
Hamilton (city) Butler County	199	0.32
Akron (city) Summit County	541	0.27
Springfield (city) Clark County	151	0.25
Dayton (city) Montgomery County	346	0.24

Pennsylvania German

Top 10 Places Sorted by Population

Based on all places, regardless of total population

Place	Population	%
Akron (city) Summit County	444	0.22
Columbus (city) Franklin County	359	0.05
Ashland (city) Ashland County	283	1.37
Boardman (cdp) Mahoning County	275	0.78
Toledo (city) Lucas County	245	0.08
Canton (city) Stark County	212	0.28
Newark (city) Licking County	202	0.42
Cleveland (city) Cuyahoga County	157	0.04
Kent (city) Portage County	156	0.54
Ontario (city) Richland County	153	2.51

Top 10 Places Sorted by Percent of Total Population

Based on all places, regardless of total population

Place	Population	%
Whites Landing (cdp) Erie County	136	35.70
Jacksonburg (village) Butler County	4	6.25
West Millgrove (village) Wood County	8	5.71
North Robinson (village) Crawford County	10	5.21
Hartville (village) Stark County	138	4.82
Holmesville (village) Holmes County	19	4.68
Green Camp (village) Marion County	13	4.42
New Haven (cdp) Huron County	11	4.12
Walnut Creek (cdp) Holmes County	14	3.62
Shiloh (village) Richland County	17	3.49

Top 10 Places Sorted by Percent of Total Population

Based on places with total population of 50,000 or more

Place	Population	%
Canton (city) Stark County	212	0.28
Akron (city) Summit County	444	0.22
Kettering (city) Montgomery County	118	0.21
Youngstown (city) Mahoning County	113	0.16
Elyria (city) Lorain County	68	0.12
Toledo (city) Lucas County	245	0.08
Columbus (city) Franklin County	359	0.05
Dayton (city) Montgomery County	80	0.05
Cleveland (city) Cuyahoga County	157	0.04
Lorain (city) Lorain County	25	0.04

Polish

Top 10 Places Sorted by Population

Based on all places, regardless of total population

Place	Population	%
Toledo (city) Lucas County	25,480	8.73
Cleveland (city) Cuyahoga County	18,227	4.45
Columbus (city) Franklin County	17,936	2.33
Parma (city) Cuyahoga County	14,703	17.95
Garfield Heights (city) Cuyahoga County	6,009	20.68
Strongsville (city) Cuyahoga County	5,938	13.39
North Royalton (city) Cuyahoga County	5,749	19.19
Brunswick (city) Medina County	5,132	14.92
Akron (city) Summit County	4,998	2.46
Elyria (city) Lorain County	4,359	7.93

Top 10 Places Sorted by Percent of Total Population

Based on all places, regardless of total population

Place	Population	%
Plumwood (cdp) Madison County	73	40.78
Cuyahoga Heights (village) Cuyahoga County	216	39.49
Independence (city) Cuyahoga County	2,591	36.60
Newburgh Heights (village) Cuyahoga County	706	33.49
Hockingport (cdp) Athens County	26	31.33
Valley View (village) Cuyahoga County	531	27.29
Brooklyn Heights (village) Cuyahoga County	357	23.90
Neapolis (cdp) Lucas County	112	23.88
Lansing (cdp) Belmont County	88	23.85
Rocky Ridge (village) Ottawa County	96	22.97

Top 10 Places Sorted by Percent of Total Population

Based on places with total population of 50,000 or more

Place	Population	%
Parma (city) Cuyahoga County	14,703	17.95
Toledo (city) Lucas County	25,480	8.73
Lakewood (city) Cuyahoga County	4,284	8.13
Elyria (city) Lorain County	4,359	7.93
Lorain (city) Lorain County	4,052	6.21
Cleveland (city) Cuyahoga County	18,227	4.45
Youngstown (city) Mahoning County	2,036	2.93
Kettering (city) Montgomery County	1,457	2.59
Akron (city) Summit County	4,998	2.46
Columbus (city) Franklin County	17,936	2.33

Portuguese

Top 10 Places Sorted by Population

Based on all places, regardless of total population

Place	Population	%
Columbus (city) Franklin County	1,667	0.22
Canton (city) Stark County	367	0.49
Akron (city) Summit County	293	0.14
Cleveland (city) Cuyahoga County	277	0.07
Medina (city) Medina County	214	0.80
Newark (city) Licking County	186	0.39
Mentor (city) Lake County	184	0.39
Wadsworth (city) Medina County	170	0.80
Toledo (city) Lucas County	154	0.05
Cincinnati (city) Hamilton County	142	0.05

Top 10 Places Sorted by Percent of Total Population

Based on all places, regardless of total population

Place	Population	%
Bolivar (village) Tuscarawas County	85	7.05
Wilson (village) Monroe County	4	3.48
St. Paris (village) Champaign County	60	3.02

Place	Population	%
Summerfield (village) Noble County	7	2.33
Union City (village) Darke County	37	2.22
Fort Recovery (village) Mercer County	24	2.13
Kipton (village) Lorain County	6	1.90
Leesburg (village) Highland County	28	1.87
East Liberty (cdp) Logan County	6	1.87
Mendon (village) Mercer County	10	1.78

Top 10 Places Sorted by Percent of Total Population
Based on places with total population of 50,000 or more

Place	Population	%
Canton (city) Stark County	367	0.49
Columbus (city) Franklin County	1,667	0.22
Springfield (city) Clark County	116	0.19
Akron (city) Summit County	293	0.14
Parma (city) Cuyahoga County	97	0.12
Elyria (city) Lorain County	58	0.11
Cleveland (city) Cuyahoga County	277	0.07
Lakewood (city) Cuyahoga County	31	0.06
Toledo (city) Lucas County	154	0.05
Cincinnati (city) Hamilton County	142	0.05

Romanian

Top 10 Places Sorted by Population
Based on all places, regardless of total population

Place	Population	%
Cleveland (city) Cuyahoga County	1,296	0.32
Columbus (city) Franklin County	1,256	0.16
Parma (city) Cuyahoga County	761	0.93
Canton (city) Stark County	682	0.92
Akron (city) Summit County	564	0.28
Parma Heights (city) Cuyahoga County	549	2.64
Strongsville (city) Cuyahoga County	468	1.06
Toledo (city) Lucas County	436	0.15
North Olmsted (city) Cuyahoga County	398	1.21
Warren (city) Trumbull County	372	0.87

Top 10 Places Sorted by Percent of Total Population
Based on all places, regardless of total population

Place	Population	%
Remington (cdp) Hamilton County	16	6.69
Vienna Center (cdp) Trumbull County	44	6.14
Celeryville (cdp) Huron County	7	5.26
North Robinson (village) Crawford County	8	4.17
Pepper Pike (city) Cuyahoga County	243	4.08
Fairlawn (city) Summit County	254	3.40
Newburgh Heights (village) Cuyahoga County	66	3.13
Parma Heights (city) Cuyahoga County	549	2.64
Brimfield (cdp) Portage County	85	2.56
Sixteen Mile Stand (cdp) Hamilton County	70	2.39

Top 10 Places Sorted by Percent of Total Population
Based on places with total population of 50,000 or more

Place	Population	%
Parma (city) Cuyahoga County	761	0.93
Canton (city) Stark County	682	0.92
Lakewood (city) Cuyahoga County	293	0.56
Youngstown (city) Mahoning County	267	0.38
Cleveland (city) Cuyahoga County	1,296	0.32
Elyria (city) Lorain County	165	0.30
Akron (city) Summit County	564	0.28
Lorain (city) Lorain County	135	0.21
Columbus (city) Franklin County	1,256	0.16
Toledo (city) Lucas County	436	0.15

Russian

Top 10 Places Sorted by Population
Based on all places, regardless of total population

Place	Population	%
Columbus (city) Franklin County	5,392	0.70
Cleveland (city) Cuyahoga County	2,395	0.59
Beachwood (city) Cuyahoga County	1,926	16.14
Cincinnati (city) Hamilton County	1,528	0.51
Solon (city) Cuyahoga County	1,498	6.52
Cleveland Heights (city) Cuyahoga County	1,231	2.63
Bexley (city) Franklin County	1,210	9.29
Mayfield Heights (city) Cuyahoga County	1,185	6.20
Parma (city) Cuyahoga County	1,152	1.41
Shaker Heights (city) Cuyahoga County	1,019	3.58

Top 10 Places Sorted by Percent of Total Population
Based on all places, regardless of total population

Place	Population	%
East Liberty (cdp) Logan County	81	25.23
Beachwood (city) Cuyahoga County	1,926	16.14
Loveland Park (cdp) Warren County	146	12.09
Pepper Pike (city) Cuyahoga County	675	11.34
New Pittsburg (cdp) Wayne County	28	10.53
Amberley (village) Hamilton County	367	10.36
Bexley (city) Franklin County	1,210	9.29
Sixteen Mile Stand (cdp) Hamilton County	265	9.04
Moreland Hills (village) Cuyahoga County	275	8.31
Woodmere (village) Cuyahoga County	74	8.03

Top 10 Places Sorted by Percent of Total Population
Based on places with total population of 50,000 or more

Place	Population	%
Parma (city) Cuyahoga County	1,152	1.41
Lakewood (city) Cuyahoga County	673	1.28
Elyria (city) Lorain County	599	1.09
Canton (city) Stark County	603	0.81
Columbus (city) Franklin County	5,392	0.70
Lorain (city) Lorain County	399	0.61
Cleveland (city) Cuyahoga County	2,395	0.59
Cincinnati (city) Hamilton County	1,528	0.51
Youngstown (city) Mahoning County	351	0.50
Akron (city) Summit County	893	0.44

Scandinavian

Top 10 Places Sorted by Population
Based on all places, regardless of total population

Place	Population	%
Columbus (city) Franklin County	1,042	0.14
Cincinnati (city) Hamilton County	293	0.10
Beavercreek (city) Greene County	156	0.35
Akron (city) Summit County	130	0.06
Huber Heights (city) Montgomery County	128	0.34
Cleveland (city) Cuyahoga County	127	0.03
Wright-Patterson AFB (cdp) Greene County	121	3.84
Dublin (city) Franklin County	121	0.31
Kettering (city) Montgomery County	120	0.21
Newark (city) Licking County	102	0.21

Top 10 Places Sorted by Percent of Total Population
Based on all places, regardless of total population

Place	Population	%
Wilkesville (village) Vinton County	4	3.92
Wright-Patterson AFB (cdp) Greene County	121	3.84
Shiloh (village) Richland County	13	2.67
Warsaw (village) Coshocton County	22	2.43
Venedocia (village) Van Wert County	2	1.77
Caledonia (village) Marion County	11	1.71
Williamsburg (village) Clermont County	40	1.66
Geneva-on-the-Lake (village) Ashtabula County	22	1.58
Tuscarawas (village) Tuscarawas County	14	1.40
Fairfax (village) Hamilton County	22	1.25

Top 10 Places Sorted by Percent of Total Population
Based on places with total population of 50,000 or more

Place	Population	%
Kettering (city) Montgomery County	120	0.21
Columbus (city) Franklin County	1,042	0.14
Lakewood (city) Cuyahoga County	66	0.13
Springfield (city) Clark County	67	0.11
Cincinnati (city) Hamilton County	293	0.10
Akron (city) Summit County	130	0.06
Dayton (city) Montgomery County	93	0.06
Lorain (city) Lorain County	33	0.05
Elyria (city) Lorain County	20	0.04
Cleveland (city) Cuyahoga County	127	0.03

Scotch-Irish

Top 10 Places Sorted by Population
Based on all places, regardless of total population

Place	Population	%
Columbus (city) Franklin County	12,017	1.56
Akron (city) Summit County	3,342	1.65
Cincinnati (city) Hamilton County	3,249	1.08
Cleveland (city) Cuyahoga County	2,928	0.72
Toledo (city) Lucas County	2,388	0.82
Dayton (city) Montgomery County	1,768	1.21
Lakewood (city) Cuyahoga County	1,371	2.60
Cuyahoga Falls (city) Summit County	1,222	2.46
Newark (city) Licking County	1,163	2.44
Canton (city) Stark County	1,161	1.56

Top 10 Places Sorted by Percent of Total Population
Based on all places, regardless of total population

Place	Population	%
Hessville (cdp) Sandusky County	17	21.52
Kunkle (cdp) Williams County	29	20.42
Newport (cdp) Shelby County	53	18.40
Stewart (cdp) Athens County	12	17.65
Elgin (village) Van Wert County	4	17.39
Tuppers Plains (cdp) Meigs County	41	15.53
Lansing (cdp) Belmont County	57	15.45
Pottery Addition (cdp) Jefferson County	25	13.02
Salesville (village) Guernsey County	24	12.90
Sulphur Springs (cdp) Crawford County	32	11.43

Top 10 Places Sorted by Percent of Total Population
Based on places with total population of 50,000 or more

Place	Population	%
Lakewood (city) Cuyahoga County	1,371	2.60
Kettering (city) Montgomery County	1,103	1.96
Springfield (city) Clark County	1,143	1.86
Lorain (city) Lorain County	1,107	1.70
Akron (city) Summit County	3,342	1.65
Columbus (city) Franklin County	12,017	1.56
Canton (city) Stark County	1,161	1.56
Elyria (city) Lorain County	730	1.33
Dayton (city) Montgomery County	1,768	1.21
Cincinnati (city) Hamilton County	3,249	1.08

Scottish

Top 10 Places Sorted by Population
Based on all places, regardless of total population

Place	Population	%
Columbus (city) Franklin County	13,797	1.79
Cincinnati (city) Hamilton County	3,828	1.28
Toledo (city) Lucas County	3,645	1.25
Cleveland (city) Cuyahoga County	3,093	0.76
Akron (city) Summit County	2,974	1.47
Dayton (city) Montgomery County	1,758	1.21
Elyria (city) Lorain County	1,571	2.86
Kettering (city) Montgomery County	1,568	2.79
Mentor (city) Lake County	1,464	3.07
Westerville (city) Franklin County	1,430	3.98

Top 10 Places Sorted by Percent of Total Population
Based on all places, regardless of total population

Place	Population	%
Vickery (cdp) Sandusky County	43	47.25
Gann (village) Knox County	31	27.93
Plainville (cdp) Hamilton County	54	24.22
Raymond (cdp) Union County	52	19.77
Howard (cdp) Knox County	68	19.26
Minford (cdp) Scioto County	96	18.60
Sandyville (cdp) Tuscarawas County	48	15.43
Rosewood (cdp) Champaign County	39	14.66
Glenford (village) Perry County	33	12.99
Polk (village) Ashland County	38	12.71

Top 10 Places Sorted by Percent of Total Population
Based on places with total population of 50,000 or more

Place	Population	%
Elyria (city) Lorain County	1,571	2.86
Kettering (city) Montgomery County	1,568	2.79
Springfield (city) Clark County	1,400	2.28
Lakewood (city) Cuyahoga County	1,113	2.11
Columbus (city) Franklin County	13,797	1.79
Canton (city) Stark County	1,294	1.74
Akron (city) Summit County	2,974	1.47
Cincinnati (city) Hamilton County	3,828	1.28
Hamilton (city) Butler County	801	1.28
Toledo (city) Lucas County	3,645	1.25

Serbian

Top 10 Places Sorted by Population

Based on all places, regardless of total population

Place	Population	%
Parma (city) Cuyahoga County	1,778	2.17
Akron (city) Summit County	945	0.47
Cleveland (city) Cuyahoga County	529	0.13
Columbus (city) Franklin County	511	0.07
North Royalton (city) Cuyahoga County	433	1.45
Brunswick (city) Medina County	399	1.16
Barberton (city) Summit County	358	1.33
Cuyahoga Falls (city) Summit County	264	0.53
Parma Heights (city) Cuyahoga County	234	1.13
Broadview Heights (city) Cuyahoga County	230	1.23

Top 10 Places Sorted by Percent of Total Population

Based on all places, regardless of total population

Place	Population	%
Plainville (cdp) Hamilton County	18	8.07
Silver Lake (village) Summit County	70	2.73
Franklin Furnace (cdp) Scioto County	37	2.21
Parma (city) Cuyahoga County	1,778	2.17
Mingo Junction (village) Jefferson County	74	2.14
Orange (village) Cuyahoga County	67	2.04
Orangeville (village) Trumbull County	3	1.96
Lindsey (village) Sandusky County	9	1.91
Kipton (village) Lorain County	6	1.90
Antwerp (village) Paulding County	31	1.84

Top 10 Places Sorted by Percent of Total Population

Based on places with total population of 50,000 or more

Place	Population	%
Parma (city) Cuyahoga County	1,778	2.17
Akron (city) Summit County	945	0.47
Lakewood (city) Cuyahoga County	183	0.35
Lorain (city) Lorain County	206	0.32
Cleveland (city) Cuyahoga County	529	0.13
Elyria (city) Lorain County	57	0.10
Canton (city) Stark County	67	0.09
Columbus (city) Franklin County	511	0.07
Youngstown (city) Mahoning County	43	0.06
Toledo (city) Lucas County	69	0.02

Slavic

Top 10 Places Sorted by Population

Based on all places, regardless of total population

Place	Population	%
Columbus (city) Franklin County	458	0.06
Cleveland (city) Cuyahoga County	232	0.06
Parma (city) Cuyahoga County	145	0.18
Cuyahoga Falls (city) Summit County	132	0.27
Brunswick (city) Medina County	117	0.34
Mentor (city) Lake County	112	0.24
Zanesville (city) Muskingum County	108	0.42
Akron (city) Summit County	106	0.05
Willoughby (city) Lake County	94	0.42
Eastlake (city) Lake County	91	0.48

Top 10 Places Sorted by Percent of Total Population

Based on all places, regardless of total population

Place	Population	%
Lafferty (cdp) Belmont County	35	15.98
Cinnamon Lake (cdp) Ashland County	74	8.15
Washingtonville (village) Columbiana County	62	6.87
Marshallville (village) Wayne County	21	2.62
Alexandria (village) Licking County	4	1.67
Mingo Junction (village) Jefferson County	50	1.44
Oak Harbor (village) Ottawa County	35	1.26
Richfield (village) Summit County	44	1.22
Peninsula (village) Summit County	7	1.22
Blue Jay (cdp) Hamilton County	14	1.17

Top 10 Places Sorted by Percent of Total Population

Based on places with total population of 50,000 or more

Place	Population	%
Parma (city) Cuyahoga County	145	0.18
Canton (city) Stark County	87	0.12
Lakewood (city) Cuyahoga County	47	0.09
Elyria (city) Lorain County	43	0.08
Columbus (city) Franklin County	458	0.06
Cleveland (city) Cuyahoga County	232	0.06
Akron (city) Summit County	106	0.05
Kettering (city) Montgomery County	15	0.03
Cincinnati (city) Hamilton County	63	0.02
Toledo (city) Lucas County	58	0.02

Slovak

Top 10 Places Sorted by Population

Based on all places, regardless of total population

Place	Population	%
Cleveland (city) Cuyahoga County	7,074	1.73
Parma (city) Cuyahoga County	6,760	8.25
Columbus (city) Franklin County	3,380	0.44
Youngstown (city) Mahoning County	3,113	4.47
Strongsville (city) Cuyahoga County	2,962	6.68
Boardman (cdp) Mahoning County	2,764	7.81
Lakewood (city) Cuyahoga County	2,432	4.62
Austintown (cdp) Mahoning County	2,267	7.50
Akron (city) Summit County	2,164	1.07
North Olmsted (city) Cuyahoga County	2,024	6.17

Top 10 Places Sorted by Percent of Total Population

Based on all places, regardless of total population

Place	Population	%
Yankee Lake (village) Trumbull County	18	26.09
Brookfield Center (cdp) Trumbull County	244	16.58
New Middletown (village) Mahoning County	293	15.86
Put-in-Bay (village) Ottawa County	20	14.39
Struthers (city) Mahoning County	1,441	13.23
Lowellville (village) Mahoning County	148	12.81
Stratton (village) Jefferson County	35	12.59
Mingo Junction (village) Jefferson County	385	11.12
Marblehead (village) Ottawa County	86	10.71
Campbell (city) Mahoning County	892	10.56

Top 10 Places Sorted by Percent of Total Population

Based on places with total population of 50,000 or more

Place	Population	%
Parma (city) Cuyahoga County	6,760	8.25
Lakewood (city) Cuyahoga County	2,432	4.62
Youngstown (city) Mahoning County	3,113	4.47
Lorain (city) Lorain County	1,882	2.89
Elyria (city) Lorain County	1,549	2.82
Cleveland (city) Cuyahoga County	7,074	1.73
Akron (city) Summit County	2,164	1.07
Canton (city) Stark County	577	0.78
Columbus (city) Franklin County	3,380	0.44
Kettering (city) Montgomery County	208	0.37

Slovene

Top 10 Places Sorted by Population

Based on all places, regardless of total population

Place	Population	%
Cleveland (city) Cuyahoga County	3,214	0.79
Mentor (city) Lake County	3,037	6.38
Euclid (city) Cuyahoga County	2,895	5.87
Willoughby (city) Lake County	1,861	8.37
Parma (city) Cuyahoga County	1,677	2.05
Eastlake (city) Lake County	1,595	8.45
Columbus (city) Franklin County	1,380	0.18
Willowick (city) Lake County	1,273	8.96
Wickliffe (city) Lake County	1,137	8.85
Lakewood (city) Cuyahoga County	761	1.44

Top 10 Places Sorted by Percent of Total Population

Based on all places, regardless of total population

Place	Population	%
Lakeline (village) Lake County	22	14.57
Grand River (village) Lake County	48	13.68
Kirtland Hills (village) Lake County	94	12.30
Willowick (city) Lake County	1,273	8.96
Mayfield (village) Cuyahoga County	305	8.90
Wickliffe (city) Lake County	1,137	8.85
Kirtland (city) Lake County	581	8.50
Eastlake (city) Lake County	1,595	8.45
Willoughby (city) Lake County	1,861	8.37
Mentor-on-the-Lake (city) Lake County	601	7.92

Top 10 Places Sorted by Percent of Total Population

Based on places with total population of 50,000 or more

Place	Population	%
Parma (city) Cuyahoga County	1,677	2.05
Lakewood (city) Cuyahoga County	761	1.44
Lorain (city) Lorain County	546	0.84
Cleveland (city) Cuyahoga County	3,214	0.79
Elyria (city) Lorain County	165	0.30
Akron (city) Summit County	588	0.29
Columbus (city) Franklin County	1,380	0.18
Dayton (city) Montgomery County	132	0.09
Kettering (city) Montgomery County	41	0.07
Youngstown (city) Mahoning County	44	0.06

Soviet Union

Top 10 Places Sorted by Population

Based on all places, regardless of total population

Place	Population	%
Cincinnati (city) Hamilton County	15	<0.01
Perry Heights (cdp) Stark County	13	0.15
Aberdeen (village) Brown County	0	0.00
Ada (village) Hardin County	0	0.00
Adamsville (village) Muskingum County	0	0.00
Addyston (village) Hamilton County	0	0.00
Adelphi (village) Ross County	0	0.00
Adena (village) Jefferson County	0	0.00
Akron (city) Summit County	0	0.00
Albany (village) Athens County	0	0.00

Top 10 Places Sorted by Percent of Total Population

Based on all places, regardless of total population

Place	Population	%
Perry Heights (cdp) Stark County	13	0.15
Cincinnati (city) Hamilton County	15	<0.01
Aberdeen (village) Brown County	0	0.00
Ada (village) Hardin County	0	0.00
Adamsville (village) Muskingum County	0	0.00
Addyston (village) Hamilton County	0	0.00
Adelphi (village) Ross County	0	0.00
Adena (village) Jefferson County	0	0.00
Akron (city) Summit County	0	0.00
Albany (village) Athens County	0	0.00

Top 10 Places Sorted by Percent of Total Population

Based on places with total population of 50,000 or more

Place	Population	%
Cincinnati (city) Hamilton County	15	<0.01
Akron (city) Summit County	0	0.00
Canton (city) Stark County	0	0.00
Cleveland (city) Cuyahoga County	0	0.00
Columbus (city) Franklin County	0	0.00
Dayton (city) Montgomery County	0	0.00
Elyria (city) Lorain County	0	0.00
Hamilton (city) Butler County	0	0.00
Kettering (city) Montgomery County	0	0.00
Lakewood (city) Cuyahoga County	0	0.00

Swedish

Top 10 Places Sorted by Population

Based on all places, regardless of total population

Place	Population	%
Columbus (city) Franklin County	4,492	0.58
Toledo (city) Lucas County	1,344	0.46
Cincinnati (city) Hamilton County	1,245	0.41
Cleveland (city) Cuyahoga County	1,163	0.28
Akron (city) Summit County	1,161	0.57
Dublin (city) Franklin County	978	2.49
Dayton (city) Montgomery County	927	0.64
Kettering (city) Montgomery County	648	1.15
Cuyahoga Falls (city) Summit County	642	1.29
Austintown (cdp) Mahoning County	579	1.91

Top 10 Places Sorted by Percent of Total Population

Based on all places, regardless of total population

Place	Population	%
Pleasant Grove (cdp) Muskingum County	271	14.23
Congress (village) Wayne County	21	12.28
Darbydale (cdp) Franklin County	57	9.98

Please refer to the Explanation of Data in the front of the book for more detailed information.

Place	Population	%
New Bavaria (village) Henry County	5	7.25
Ridgeville Corners (cdp) Henry County	21	6.75
Plainville (cdp) Hamilton County	14	6.28
Hartford (village) Licking County	36	6.09
Brimfield (cdp) Portage County	175	5.27
Gratiot (village) Licking County	15	5.23
La Croft (cdp) Columbiana County	60	5.17

Top 10 Places Sorted by Percent of Total Population
Based on places with total population of 50,000 or more

Place	Population	%
Kettering (city) Montgomery County	648	1.15
Lakewood (city) Cuyahoga County	528	1.00
Elyria (city) Lorain County	509	0.93
Springfield (city) Clark County	498	0.81
Dayton (city) Montgomery County	927	0.64
Columbus (city) Franklin County	4,492	0.58
Akron (city) Summit County	1,161	0.57
Canton (city) Stark County	420	0.56
Parma (city) Cuyahoga County	382	0.47
Toledo (city) Lucas County	1,344	0.46

Swiss

Top 10 Places Sorted by Population
Based on all places, regardless of total population

Place	Population	%
Columbus (city) Franklin County	2,745	0.36
Toledo (city) Lucas County	1,134	0.39
Cincinnati (city) Hamilton County	796	0.27
Wooster (city) Wayne County	722	2.77
Akron (city) Summit County	690	0.34
Orrville (city) Wayne County	622	7.37
New Philadelphia (city) Tuscarawas County	620	3.59
Canton (city) Stark County	577	0.78
Dover (city) Tuscarawas County	541	4.23
Alliance (city) Stark County	540	2.40

Top 10 Places Sorted by Percent of Total Population
Based on all places, regardless of total population

Place	Population	%
Berlin (cdp) Holmes County	390	41.40
Mount Eaton (village) Wayne County	70	29.05
Sterling (cdp) Wayne County	96	28.24
Kidron (cdp) Wayne County	253	24.33
Antioch (village) Monroe County	50	23.04
Wilmot (village) Stark County	51	21.98
Walnut Creek (cdp) Holmes County	82	21.19
Sugarcreek (village) Tuscarawas County	448	20.06
Pandora (village) Putnam County	205	17.95
Gilboa (village) Putnam County	24	17.14

Top 10 Places Sorted by Percent of Total Population
Based on places with total population of 50,000 or more

Place	Population	%
Canton (city) Stark County	577	0.78
Elyria (city) Lorain County	318	0.58
Kettering (city) Montgomery County	263	0.47
Toledo (city) Lucas County	1,134	0.39
Columbus (city) Franklin County	2,745	0.36
Akron (city) Summit County	690	0.34
Hamilton (city) Butler County	202	0.32
Lakewood (city) Cuyahoga County	154	0.29
Cincinnati (city) Hamilton County	796	0.27
Parma (city) Cuyahoga County	206	0.25

Turkish

Top 10 Places Sorted by Population
Based on all places, regardless of total population

Place	Population	%
Columbus (city) Franklin County	601	0.08
Lakewood (city) Cuyahoga County	222	0.42
Dayton (city) Montgomery County	203	0.14
Medina (city) Medina County	199	0.75
Perrysburg (city) Wood County	176	0.87
Stow (city) Summit County	152	0.44
Toledo (city) Lucas County	120	0.04
Solon (city) Cuyahoga County	112	0.49
Westlake (city) Cuyahoga County	83	0.26
Richmond Heights (city) Cuyahoga County	75	0.71

Top 10 Places Sorted by Percent of Total Population
Based on all places, regardless of total population

Place	Population	%
Van Buren (village) Hancock County	7	2.12
Newtonsville (village) Clermont County	6	1.99
West Union (village) Adams County	28	1.00
Perrysburg (city) Wood County	176	0.87
Medina (city) Medina County	199	0.75
Richmond Heights (city) Cuyahoga County	75	0.71
Bailey Lakes (village) Ashland County	2	0.53
Beachwood (city) Cuyahoga County	60	0.50
Solon (city) Cuyahoga County	112	0.49
Stow (city) Summit County	152	0.44

Top 10 Places Sorted by Percent of Total Population
Based on places with total population of 50,000 or more

Place	Population	%
Lakewood (city) Cuyahoga County	222	0.42
Dayton (city) Montgomery County	203	0.14
Columbus (city) Franklin County	601	0.08
Toledo (city) Lucas County	120	0.04
Akron (city) Summit County	61	0.03
Cincinnati (city) Hamilton County	75	0.02
Youngstown (city) Mahoning County	12	0.02
Cleveland (city) Cuyahoga County	53	0.01
Canton (city) Stark County	9	0.01
Elyria (city) Lorain County	0	0.00

Ukrainian

Top 10 Places Sorted by Population
Based on all places, regardless of total population

Place	Population	%
Parma (city) Cuyahoga County	4,857	5.93
Cleveland (city) Cuyahoga County	2,072	0.51
Columbus (city) Franklin County	1,935	0.25
North Royalton (city) Cuyahoga County	1,113	3.71
Parma Heights (city) Cuyahoga County	883	4.25
Strongsville (city) Cuyahoga County	741	1.67
Akron (city) Summit County	693	0.34
Austintown (cdp) Mahoning County	666	2.20
Boardman (cdp) Mahoning County	653	1.84
Mayfield Heights (city) Cuyahoga County	649	3.40

Top 10 Places Sorted by Percent of Total Population
Based on all places, regardless of total population

Place	Population	%
Negley (cdp) Columbiana County	48	20.08
Collins (cdp) Huron County	41	7.84
Parma (city) Cuyahoga County	4,857	5.93
Independence (city) Cuyahoga County	390	5.51
Kipton (village) Lorain County	17	5.38
Parma Heights (city) Cuyahoga County	883	4.25
Marne (cdp) Licking County	23	3.99
North Royalton (city) Cuyahoga County	1,113	3.71
Highland Hills (village) Cuyahoga County	56	3.67
Loveland Park (cdp) Warren County	44	3.64

Top 10 Places Sorted by Percent of Total Population
Based on places with total population of 50,000 or more

Place	Population	%
Parma (city) Cuyahoga County	4,857	5.93
Lakewood (city) Cuyahoga County	528	1.00
Lorain (city) Lorain County	521	0.80
Youngstown (city) Mahoning County	533	0.77
Cleveland (city) Cuyahoga County	2,072	0.51
Elyria (city) Lorain County	229	0.42
Akron (city) Summit County	693	0.34
Canton (city) Stark County	214	0.29
Kettering (city) Montgomery County	157	0.28
Columbus (city) Franklin County	1,935	0.25

Welsh

Top 10 Places Sorted by Population
Based on all places, regardless of total population

Place	Population	%
Columbus (city) Franklin County	10,220	1.33
Cincinnati (city) Hamilton County	2,038	0.68
Akron (city) Summit County	2,022	1.00
Cleveland (city) Cuyahoga County	1,575	0.38
Toledo (city) Lucas County	1,296	0.44
Boardman (cdp) Mahoning County	1,078	3.04
Delaware (city) Delaware County	998	2.96
Upper Arlington (city) Franklin County	983	2.92
Gahanna (city) Franklin County	927	2.84
Niles (city) Trumbull County	898	4.61

Top 10 Places Sorted by Percent of Total Population
Based on all places, regardless of total population

Place	Population	%
Glencoe (cdp) Belmont County	37	43.02
Vaughnsville (cdp) Putnam County	32	23.36
Venedocia (village) Van Wert County	16	14.16
Sandyville (cdp) Tuscarawas County	38	12.22
Bannock (cdp) Belmont County	25	12.02
Radnor (cdp) Delaware County	15	10.64
Oak Hill (village) Jackson County	182	10.30
Cardington (village) Morrow County	221	10.18
Yankee Lake (village) Trumbull County	7	10.14
Senecaville (village) Guernsey County	32	9.82

Top 10 Places Sorted by Percent of Total Population
Based on places with total population of 50,000 or more

Place	Population	%
Kettering (city) Montgomery County	757	1.35
Columbus (city) Franklin County	10,220	1.33
Youngstown (city) Mahoning County	877	1.26
Lakewood (city) Cuyahoga County	657	1.25
Elyria (city) Lorain County	612	1.11
Akron (city) Summit County	2,022	1.00
Canton (city) Stark County	631	0.85
Springfield (city) Clark County	505	0.82
Cincinnati (city) Hamilton County	2,038	0.68
Dayton (city) Montgomery County	856	0.59

West Indian, excluding Hispanic

Top 10 Places Sorted by Population
Based on all places, regardless of total population

Place	Population	%
Columbus (city) Franklin County	3,944	0.51
Cleveland (city) Cuyahoga County	1,835	0.45
Toledo (city) Lucas County	1,077	0.37
Cincinnati (city) Hamilton County	478	0.16
Cleveland Heights (city) Cuyahoga County	351	0.75
Reynoldsburg (city) Franklin County	270	0.77
Dayton (city) Montgomery County	267	0.18
Strongsville (city) Cuyahoga County	250	0.56
Bedford Heights (city) Cuyahoga County	249	2.31
Akron (city) Summit County	240	0.12

Top 10 Places Sorted by Percent of Total Population
Based on all places, regardless of total population

Place	Population	%
Oceola (cdp) Crawford County	22	10.05
Mount Healthy Heights (cdp) Hamilton County	214	6.15
Woodmere (village) Cuyahoga County	50	5.43
Moreland Hills (village) Cuyahoga County	94	2.84
Sciotodale (cdp) Scioto County	19	2.55
North Randall (village) Cuyahoga County	21	2.42
Bedford Heights (city) Cuyahoga County	249	2.31
Holland (village) Lucas County	39	2.01
Nelsonville (city) Athens County	79	1.51
Aquilla (village) Geauga County	5	1.37

Top 10 Places Sorted by Percent of Total Population
Based on places with total population of 50,000 or more

Place	Population	%
Columbus (city) Franklin County	3,944	0.51
Cleveland (city) Cuyahoga County	1,835	0.45
Toledo (city) Lucas County	1,077	0.37
Lakewood (city) Cuyahoga County	193	0.37
Youngstown (city) Mahoning County	152	0.22
Parma (city) Cuyahoga County	160	0.20
Lorain (city) Lorain County	122	0.19
Dayton (city) Montgomery County	267	0.18
Springfield (city) Clark County	103	0.17
Cincinnati (city) Hamilton County	478	0.16

West Indian: Bahamian, excluding Hispanic

Top 10 Places Sorted by Population
Based on all places, regardless of total population

Place	Population	%
Pickerington (city) Fairfield County	100	0.59
Columbus (city) Franklin County	93	0.01
Worthington (city) Franklin County	63	0.46
Cincinnati (city) Hamilton County	33	0.01
Canton (city) Stark County	16	0.02
Euclid (city) Cuyahoga County	15	0.03
Fort Shawnee (village) Allen County	14	0.37
Bowling Green (city) Wood County	14	0.05
Warrensville Heights (city) Cuyahoga County	11	0.08
Troy (city) Miami County	10	0.04

Top 10 Places Sorted by Percent of Total Population
Based on all places, regardless of total population

Place	Population	%
Pickerington (city) Fairfield County	100	0.59
Worthington (city) Franklin County	63	0.46
Fort Shawnee (village) Allen County	14	0.37
Warrensville Heights (city) Cuyahoga County	11	0.08
Bowling Green (city) Wood County	14	0.05
Troy (city) Miami County	10	0.04
Euclid (city) Cuyahoga County	15	0.03
Tiffin (city) Seneca County	6	0.03
Canton (city) Stark County	16	0.02
Columbus (city) Franklin County	93	0.01

Top 10 Places Sorted by Percent of Total Population
Based on places with total population of 50,000 or more

Place	Population	%
Canton (city) Stark County	16	0.02
Columbus (city) Franklin County	93	0.01
Cincinnati (city) Hamilton County	33	0.01
Akron (city) Summit County	0	0.00
Cleveland (city) Cuyahoga County	0	0.00
Dayton (city) Montgomery County	0	0.00
Elyria (city) Lorain County	0	0.00
Hamilton (city) Butler County	0	0.00
Kettering (city) Montgomery County	0	0.00
Lakewood (city) Cuyahoga County	0	0.00

West Indian: Barbadian, excluding Hispanic

Top 10 Places Sorted by Population
Based on all places, regardless of total population

Place	Population	%
Columbus (city) Franklin County	132	0.02
North Olmsted (city) Cuyahoga County	74	0.23
Reynoldsburg (city) Franklin County	47	0.13
Parma (city) Cuyahoga County	44	0.05
Wyoming (city) Hamilton County	41	0.49
Mansfield (city) Richland County	40	0.08
Middletown (city) Butler County	36	0.07
West Carrollton (city) Montgomery County	10	0.08
Euclid (city) Cuyahoga County	10	0.02
Defiance (city) Defiance County	8	0.05

Top 10 Places Sorted by Percent of Total Population
Based on all places, regardless of total population

Place	Population	%
Wyoming (city) Hamilton County	41	0.49
North Olmsted (city) Cuyahoga County	74	0.23
Reynoldsburg (city) Franklin County	47	0.13
Mansfield (city) Richland County	40	0.08
West Carrollton (city) Montgomery County	10	0.08
Middletown (city) Butler County	36	0.07
Parma (city) Cuyahoga County	44	0.05
Defiance (city) Defiance County	8	0.05
Columbus (city) Franklin County	132	0.02
Euclid (city) Cuyahoga County	10	0.02

Top 10 Places Sorted by Percent of Total Population
Based on places with total population of 50,000 or more

Place	Population	%
Parma (city) Cuyahoga County	44	0.05
Columbus (city) Franklin County	132	0.02
Youngstown (city) Mahoning County	8	0.01
Akron (city) Summit County	5	<0.01
Canton (city) Stark County	0	0.00
Cincinnati (city) Hamilton County	0	0.00
Cleveland (city) Cuyahoga County	0	0.00
Dayton (city) Montgomery County	0	0.00
Elyria (city) Lorain County	0	0.00
Hamilton (city) Butler County	0	0.00

West Indian: Belizean, excluding Hispanic

Top 10 Places Sorted by Population
Based on all places, regardless of total population

Place	Population	%
Columbus (city) Franklin County	42	0.01
Marysville (city) Union County	20	0.09
Toledo (city) Lucas County	19	0.01
Cleveland (city) Cuyahoga County	16	<0.01
Bay Village (city) Cuyahoga County	12	0.08
Euclid (city) Cuyahoga County	10	0.02
Bedford Heights (city) Cuyahoga County	8	0.07
North Madison (cdp) Lake County	7	0.08
Aberdeen (village) Brown County	0	0.00
Ada (village) Hardin County	0	0.00

Top 10 Places Sorted by Percent of Total Population
Based on all places, regardless of total population

Place	Population	%
Marysville (city) Union County	20	0.09
Bay Village (city) Cuyahoga County	12	0.08
North Madison (cdp) Lake County	7	0.08
Bedford Heights (city) Cuyahoga County	8	0.07
Euclid (city) Cuyahoga County	10	0.02
Columbus (city) Franklin County	42	0.01
Toledo (city) Lucas County	19	0.01
Cleveland (city) Cuyahoga County	16	<0.01
Aberdeen (village) Brown County	0	0.00
Ada (village) Hardin County	0	0.00

Top 10 Places Sorted by Percent of Total Population
Based on places with total population of 50,000 or more

Place	Population	%
Columbus (city) Franklin County	42	0.01
Toledo (city) Lucas County	19	0.01
Cleveland (city) Cuyahoga County	16	<0.01
Akron (city) Summit County	0	0.00
Canton (city) Stark County	0	0.00
Cincinnati (city) Hamilton County	0	0.00
Dayton (city) Montgomery County	0	0.00
Elyria (city) Lorain County	0	0.00
Hamilton (city) Butler County	0	0.00
Kettering (city) Montgomery County	0	0.00

West Indian: Bermudan, excluding Hispanic

Top 10 Places Sorted by Population
Based on all places, regardless of total population

Place	Population	%
North Royalton (city) Cuyahoga County	45	0.15
Clayton (city) Montgomery County	18	0.14
Berea (city) Cuyahoga County	13	0.07
Cleveland Heights (city) Cuyahoga County	11	0.02
Cleveland (city) Cuyahoga County	11	<0.01
Columbus (city) Franklin County	11	<0.01
Shaker Heights (city) Cuyahoga County	10	0.04
Macedonia (city) Summit County	9	0.08
Aberdeen (village) Brown County	0	0.00
Ada (village) Hardin County	0	0.00

Top 10 Places Sorted by Percent of Total Population
Based on all places, regardless of total population

Place	Population	%
North Royalton (city) Cuyahoga County	45	0.15
Clayton (city) Montgomery County	18	0.14
Macedonia (city) Summit County	9	0.08
Berea (city) Cuyahoga County	13	0.07
Shaker Heights (city) Cuyahoga County	10	0.04
Cleveland Heights (city) Cuyahoga County	11	0.02
Cleveland (city) Cuyahoga County	11	<0.01
Columbus (city) Franklin County	11	<0.01
Aberdeen (village) Brown County	0	0.00
Ada (village) Hardin County	0	0.00

Top 10 Places Sorted by Percent of Total Population
Based on places with total population of 50,000 or more

Place	Population	%
Cleveland (city) Cuyahoga County	11	<0.01
Columbus (city) Franklin County	11	<0.01
Akron (city) Summit County	0	0.00
Canton (city) Stark County	0	0.00
Cincinnati (city) Hamilton County	0	0.00
Dayton (city) Montgomery County	0	0.00
Elyria (city) Lorain County	0	0.00
Hamilton (city) Butler County	0	0.00
Kettering (city) Montgomery County	0	0.00
Lakewood (city) Cuyahoga County	0	0.00

West Indian: British West Indian, excluding Hispanic

Top 10 Places Sorted by Population
Based on all places, regardless of total population

Place	Population	%
Columbus (city) Franklin County	165	0.02
Akron (city) Summit County	39	0.02
Bedford Heights (city) Cuyahoga County	34	0.31
Heath (city) Licking County	31	0.31
Cleveland (city) Cuyahoga County	31	0.01
Toledo (city) Lucas County	22	0.01
Cincinnati (city) Hamilton County	20	0.01
Dent (cdp) Hamilton County	16	0.16
Rosemount (cdp) Scioto County	15	0.68
Canton (city) Stark County	10	0.01

Top 10 Places Sorted by Percent of Total Population
Based on all places, regardless of total population

Place	Population	%
Rosemount (cdp) Scioto County	15	0.68
Bedford Heights (city) Cuyahoga County	34	0.31
Heath (city) Licking County	31	0.31
Dent (cdp) Hamilton County	16	0.16
Grafton (village) Lorain County	9	0.14
Delaware (city) Delaware County	9	0.03
Hilliard (city) Franklin County	8	0.03
Columbus (city) Franklin County	165	0.02
Akron (city) Summit County	39	0.02
Cleveland (city) Cuyahoga County	31	0.01

Top 10 Places Sorted by Percent of Total Population
Based on places with total population of 50,000 or more

Place	Population	%
Columbus (city) Franklin County	165	0.02
Akron (city) Summit County	39	0.02
Cleveland (city) Cuyahoga County	31	0.01
Toledo (city) Lucas County	22	0.01
Cincinnati (city) Hamilton County	20	0.01
Canton (city) Stark County	10	0.01
Dayton (city) Montgomery County	0	0.00
Elyria (city) Lorain County	0	0.00
Hamilton (city) Butler County	0	0.00
Kettering (city) Montgomery County	0	0.00

West Indian: Dutch West Indian, excluding Hispanic

Top 10 Places Sorted by Population
Based on all places, regardless of total population

Place	Population	%
Columbus (city) Franklin County	54	0.01
Huber Heights (city) Montgomery County	43	0.11
Springfield (city) Clark County	35	0.06
Nelsonville (city) Athens County	26	0.50
Riverside (city) Montgomery County	26	0.10
Hilliard (city) Franklin County	21	0.08
Maumee (city) Lucas County	18	0.12
Choctaw Lake (cdp) Madison County	17	1.09
Upper Sandusky (city) Wyandot County	13	0.20
Washington Court House (city) Fayette County	13	0.09

Top 10 Places Sorted by Percent of Total Population

Based on all places, regardless of total population

Place	Population	%
Choctaw Lake (cdp) Madison County	17	1.09
Bainbridge (village) Ross County	7	0.82
Nelsonville (city) Athens County	26	0.50
Buchtel (village) Athens County	3	0.50
Mount Sterling (village) Madison County	8	0.44
Bremen (village) Fairfield County	6	0.42
Cadiz (village) Harrison County	9	0.27
Northwood (city) Wood County	12	0.23
Upper Sandusky (city) Wyandot County	13	0.20
St. Paris (village) Champaign County	3	0.15

Top 10 Places Sorted by Percent of Total Population

Based on places with total population of 50,000 or more

Place	Population	%
Springfield (city) Clark County	35	0.06
Columbus (city) Franklin County	54	0.01
Akron (city) Summit County	0	0.00
Canton (city) Stark County	0	0.00
Cincinnati (city) Hamilton County	0	0.00
Cleveland (city) Cuyahoga County	0	0.00
Dayton (city) Montgomery County	0	0.00
Elyria (city) Lorain County	0	0.00
Hamilton (city) Butler County	0	0.00
Kettering (city) Montgomery County	0	0.00

West Indian: Haitian, excluding Hispanic

Top 10 Places Sorted by Population

Based on all places, regardless of total population

Place	Population	%
Columbus (city) Franklin County	1,655	0.21
Reynoldsburg (city) Franklin County	145	0.41
Toledo (city) Lucas County	97	0.03
Lima (city) Allen County	52	0.13
Euclid (city) Cuyahoga County	49	0.10
Lorain (city) Lorain County	43	0.07
Cincinnati (city) Hamilton County	41	0.01
Akron (city) Summit County	36	0.02
Dayton (city) Montgomery County	32	0.02
Chillicothe (city) Ross County	31	0.14

Top 10 Places Sorted by Percent of Total Population

Based on all places, regardless of total population

Place	Population	%
Dunkirk (village) Hardin County	11	1.20
Richville (cdp) Stark County	16	0.47
Reynoldsburg (city) Franklin County	145	0.41
McDonald (village) Trumbull County	12	0.36
North Randall (village) Cuyahoga County	3	0.35
Granville (village) Licking County	13	0.23
Dillonvale (cdp) Hamilton County	8	0.23
Castalia (village) Erie County	2	0.23
Columbus (city) Franklin County	1,655	0.21
Fruit Hill (cdp) Hamilton County	8	0.20

Top 10 Places Sorted by Percent of Total Population

Based on places with total population of 50,000 or more

Place	Population	%
Columbus (city) Franklin County	1,655	0.21
Lorain (city) Lorain County	43	0.07
Lakewood (city) Cuyahoga County	27	0.05
Toledo (city) Lucas County	97	0.03
Parma (city) Cuyahoga County	21	0.03
Youngstown (city) Mahoning County	19	0.03
Akron (city) Summit County	36	0.02
Dayton (city) Montgomery County	32	0.02
Kettering (city) Montgomery County	9	0.02
Cincinnati (city) Hamilton County	41	0.01

West Indian: Jamaican, excluding Hispanic

Top 10 Places Sorted by Population

Based on all places, regardless of total population

Place	Population	%
Columbus (city) Franklin County	1,305	0.17
Cleveland (city) Cuyahoga County	1,281	0.31
Toledo (city) Lucas County	879	0.30
Cleveland Heights (city) Cuyahoga County	315	0.67
Cincinnati (city) Hamilton County	292	0.10
Strongsville (city) Cuyahoga County	236	0.53
Mount Healthy Heights (cdp) Hamilton County	214	6.15
Maple Heights (city) Cuyahoga County	182	0.77
Dayton (city) Montgomery County	173	0.12
Mansfield (city) Richland County	169	0.35

Top 10 Places Sorted by Percent of Total Population

Based on all places, regardless of total population

Place	Population	%
Mount Healthy Heights (cdp) Hamilton County	214	6.15
Woodmere (village) Cuyahoga County	40	4.34
Moreland Hills (village) Cuyahoga County	94	2.84
Sciotodale (cdp) Scioto County	19	2.55
Holland (village) Lucas County	39	2.01
North Randall (village) Cuyahoga County	15	1.73
Bedford Heights (city) Cuyahoga County	155	1.44
Aquilla (village) Geauga County	5	1.37
Midvale (village) Tuscarawas County	6	1.14
Nelsonville (city) Athens County	53	1.01

Top 10 Places Sorted by Percent of Total Population

Based on places with total population of 50,000 or more

Place	Population	%
Cleveland (city) Cuyahoga County	1,281	0.31
Toledo (city) Lucas County	879	0.30
Lakewood (city) Cuyahoga County	158	0.30
Youngstown (city) Mahoning County	125	0.18
Columbus (city) Franklin County	1,305	0.17
Dayton (city) Montgomery County	173	0.12
Cincinnati (city) Hamilton County	292	0.10
Springfield (city) Clark County	62	0.10
Akron (city) Summit County	89	0.04
Lorain (city) Lorain County	29	0.04

West Indian: Trinidadian and Tobagonian, excluding Hispanic

Top 10 Places Sorted by Population

Based on all places, regardless of total population

Place	Population	%
Columbus (city) Franklin County	103	0.01
Springdale (city) Hamilton County	98	0.89
Cleveland (city) Cuyahoga County	94	0.02
Dayton (city) Montgomery County	62	0.04
Warrensville Heights (city) Cuyahoga County	33	0.24
Ballville (cdp) Sandusky County	31	0.98
Reynoldsburg (city) Franklin County	29	0.08
Cincinnati (city) Hamilton County	29	0.01
Blacklick Estates (cdp) Franklin County	25	0.29
Chillicothe (city) Ross County	23	0.10

Top 10 Places Sorted by Percent of Total Population

Based on all places, regardless of total population

Place	Population	%
Oceola (cdp) Crawford County	22	10.05
Ballville (cdp) Sandusky County	31	0.98
Springdale (city) Hamilton County	98	0.89
Highland Hills (village) Cuyahoga County	7	0.46
Blacklick Estates (cdp) Franklin County	25	0.29
Warrensville Heights (city) Cuyahoga County	33	0.24
Chillicothe (city) Ross County	23	0.10
Reynoldsburg (city) Franklin County	29	0.08
Berea (city) Cuyahoga County	16	0.08
Shaker Heights (city) Cuyahoga County	21	0.07

Top 10 Places Sorted by Percent of Total Population

Based on places with total population of 50,000 or more

Place	Population	%
Dayton (city) Montgomery County	62	0.04
Cleveland (city) Cuyahoga County	94	0.02
Hamilton (city) Butler County	12	0.02
Columbus (city) Franklin County	103	0.01
Cincinnati (city) Hamilton County	29	0.01
Toledo (city) Lucas County	11	<0.01
Akron (city) Summit County	0	0.00
Canton (city) Stark County	0	0.00
Elyria (city) Lorain County	0	0.00
Kettering (city) Montgomery County	0	0.00

West Indian: U.S. Virgin Islander, excluding Hispanic

Top 10 Places Sorted by Population

Based on all places, regardless of total population

Place	Population	%
Columbus (city) Franklin County	27	<0.01
Findlay (city) Hancock County	8	0.02
Cleveland (city) Cuyahoga County	7	<0.01
Parma (city) Cuyahoga County	5	0.01
Aberdeen (village) Brown County	0	0.00
Ada (village) Hardin County	0	0.00
Adamsville (village) Muskingum County	0	0.00
Addyston (village) Hamilton County	0	0.00
Adelphi (village) Ross County	0	0.00
Adena (village) Jefferson County	0	0.00

Top 10 Places Sorted by Percent of Total Population

Based on all places, regardless of total population

Place	Population	%
Findlay (city) Hancock County	8	0.02
Parma (city) Cuyahoga County	5	0.01
Columbus (city) Franklin County	27	<0.01
Cleveland (city) Cuyahoga County	7	<0.01
Aberdeen (village) Brown County	0	0.00
Ada (village) Hardin County	0	0.00
Adamsville (village) Muskingum County	0	0.00
Addyston (village) Hamilton County	0	0.00
Adelphi (village) Ross County	0	0.00
Adena (village) Jefferson County	0	0.00

Top 10 Places Sorted by Percent of Total Population

Based on places with total population of 50,000 or more

Place	Population	%
Parma (city) Cuyahoga County	5	0.01
Columbus (city) Franklin County	27	<0.01
Cleveland (city) Cuyahoga County	7	<0.01
Akron (city) Summit County	0	0.00
Canton (city) Stark County	0	0.00
Cincinnati (city) Hamilton County	0	0.00
Dayton (city) Montgomery County	0	0.00
Elyria (city) Lorain County	0	0.00
Hamilton (city) Butler County	0	0.00
Kettering (city) Montgomery County	0	0.00

West Indian: West Indian, excluding Hispanic

Top 10 Places Sorted by Population

Based on all places, regardless of total population

Place	Population	%
Cleveland (city) Cuyahoga County	364	0.09
Columbus (city) Franklin County	357	0.05
Franklin (city) Warren County	129	1.08
Trotwood (city) Montgomery County	121	0.49
Euclid (city) Cuyahoga County	108	0.22
Parma (city) Cuyahoga County	90	0.11
Sandusky (city) Erie County	72	0.28
Akron (city) Summit County	71	0.04
Warren (city) Trumbull County	65	0.15
Kettering (city) Montgomery County	57	0.10

Top 10 Places Sorted by Percent of Total Population

Based on all places, regardless of total population

Place	Population	%
Woodmere (village) Cuyahoga County	10	1.09
Franklin (city) Warren County	129	1.08
Richwood (village) Union County	16	0.72
Columbiana (city) Columbiana County	33	0.52
Trotwood (city) Montgomery County	121	0.49
Bedford Heights (city) Cuyahoga County	52	0.48
Milford (city) Clermont County	28	0.42
North Randall (village) Cuyahoga County	3	0.35
Vandalia (city) Montgomery County	51	0.34
Greenwich (village) Huron County	4	0.30

Top 10 Places Sorted by Percent of Total Population

Based on places with total population of 50,000 or more

Place	Population	%
Parma (city) Cuyahoga County	90	0.11

Place	Population	%
Kettering (city) Montgomery County	57	0.10
Cleveland (city) Cuyahoga County	364	0.09
Lorain (city) Lorain County	50	0.08
Columbus (city) Franklin County	357	0.05
Akron (city) Summit County	71	0.04
Cincinnati (city) Hamilton County	53	0.02
Toledo (city) Lucas County	49	0.02
Lakewood (city) Cuyahoga County	8	0.02
Canton (city) Stark County	0	0.00

West Indian: Other, excluding Hispanic

Top 10 Places Sorted by Population

Based on all places, regardless of total population

Place	Population	%
Ashland (city) Ashland County	17	0.08
Cincinnati (city) Hamilton County	10	<0.01
Montgomery (city) Hamilton County	9	0.09
Newark (city) Licking County	8	0.02
Aberdeen (village) Brown County	0	0.00
Ada (village) Hardin County	0	0.00
Adamsville (village) Muskingum County	0	0.00
Addyston (village) Hamilton County	0	0.00
Adelphi (village) Ross County	0	0.00
Adena (village) Jefferson County	0	0.00

Top 10 Places Sorted by Percent of Total Population

Based on all places, regardless of total population

Place	Population	%
Montgomery (city) Hamilton County	9	0.09
Ashland (city) Ashland County	17	0.08
Newark (city) Licking County	8	0.02
Cincinnati (city) Hamilton County	10	<0.01
Aberdeen (village) Brown County	0	0.00
Ada (village) Hardin County	0	0.00
Adamsville (village) Muskingum County	0	0.00
Addyston (village) Hamilton County	0	0.00
Adelphi (village) Ross County	0	0.00
Adena (village) Jefferson County	0	0.00

Top 10 Places Sorted by Percent of Total Population

Based on places with total population of 50,000 or more

Place	Population	%
Cincinnati (city) Hamilton County	10	<0.01
Akron (city) Summit County	0	0.00
Canton (city) Stark County	0	0.00
Cleveland (city) Cuyahoga County	0	0.00
Columbus (city) Franklin County	0	0.00
Dayton (city) Montgomery County	0	0.00
Elyria (city) Lorain County	0	0.00
Hamilton (city) Butler County	0	0.00
Kettering (city) Montgomery County	0	0.00
Lakewood (city) Cuyahoga County	0	0.00

Yugoslavian

Top 10 Places Sorted by Population

Based on all places, regardless of total population

Place	Population	%
Akron (city) Summit County	1,145	0.56
Columbus (city) Franklin County	883	0.11
Parma (city) Cuyahoga County	332	0.41
Mansfield (city) Richland County	307	0.63
Cleveland (city) Cuyahoga County	287	0.07
Medina (city) Medina County	278	1.04
Eastlake (city) Lake County	265	1.40
Mentor (city) Lake County	241	0.51
Barberton (city) Summit County	178	0.66
Cincinnati (city) Hamilton County	158	0.05

Top 10 Places Sorted by Percent of Total Population

Based on all places, regardless of total population

Place	Population	%
Frankfort (village) Ross County	53	4.83
North Lawrence (cdp) Stark County	8	4.47
Hayesville (village) Ashland County	8	2.27
Four Bridges (cdp) Butler County	43	1.84
Mount Pleasant (village) Jefferson County	8	1.66
North Randall (village) Cuyahoga County	14	1.61
Thurston (village) Fairfield County	9	1.57
Mount Sterling (village) Madison County	26	1.43
Eastlake (city) Lake County	265	1.40
Dalton (village) Wayne County	27	1.40

Top 10 Places Sorted by Percent of Total Population

Based on places with total population of 50,000 or more

Place	Population	%
Akron (city) Summit County	1,145	0.56
Parma (city) Cuyahoga County	332	0.41
Lakewood (city) Cuyahoga County	109	0.21
Kettering (city) Montgomery County	81	0.14
Columbus (city) Franklin County	883	0.11
Cleveland (city) Cuyahoga County	287	0.07
Elyria (city) Lorain County	41	0.07
Canton (city) Stark County	48	0.06
Cincinnati (city) Hamilton County	158	0.05
Youngstown (city) Mahoning County	34	0.05

Hispanic Origin Rankings

Hispanic or Latino (of any race)

Top 10 Places Sorted by Population
Based on all places, regardless of total population

Place	Population	%
Columbus (city) Franklin County	44,359	5.64
Cleveland (city) Cuyahoga County	39,534	9.96
Toledo (city) Lucas County	21,231	7.39
Lorain (city) Lorain County	16,177	25.24
Cincinnati (city) Hamilton County	8,308	2.80
Youngstown (city) Mahoning County	6,207	9.27
Painesville (city) Lake County	4,298	21.97
Akron (city) Summit County	4,255	2.14
Dayton (city) Montgomery County	4,180	2.95
Hamilton (city) Butler County	3,981	6.37

Top 10 Places Sorted by Percent of Total Population
Based on all places, regardless of total population

Place	Population	%
Leipsic (village) Putnam County	656	31.34
Tedrow (cdp) Fulton County	53	30.64
West Leipsic (village) Putnam County	61	29.61
Belmore (village) Putnam County	42	29.37
Brecon (cdp) Hamilton County	69	28.28
Hessville (cdp) Sandusky County	55	25.70
Lorain (city) Lorain County	16,177	25.24
Milton Center (village) Wood County	33	22.92
Painesville (city) Lake County	4,298	21.97
Hamler (village) Henry County	124	21.53

Top 10 Places Sorted by Percent of Total Population
Based on places with total population of 50,000 or more

Place	Population	%
Lorain (city) Lorain County	16,177	25.24
Cleveland (city) Cuyahoga County	39,534	9.96
Youngstown (city) Mahoning County	6,207	9.27
Toledo (city) Lucas County	21,231	7.39
Hamilton (city) Butler County	3,981	6.37
Columbus (city) Franklin County	44,359	5.64
Elyria (city) Lorain County	2,649	4.86
Lakewood (city) Cuyahoga County	2,147	4.12
Parma (city) Cuyahoga County	2,915	3.57
Springfield (city) Clark County	1,824	3.01

Central American, excluding Mexican

Top 10 Places Sorted by Population
Based on all places, regardless of total population

Place	Population	%
Columbus (city) Franklin County	4,017	0.51
Cleveland (city) Cuyahoga County	2,085	0.53
Cincinnati (city) Hamilton County	1,860	0.63
Springdale (city) Hamilton County	613	5.46
New Philadelphia (city) Tuscarawas County	365	2.11
Canton (city) Stark County	348	0.48
Akron (city) Summit County	341	0.17
Whitehall (city) Franklin County	338	1.87
Fairfield (city) Butler County	299	0.70
Dover (city) Tuscarawas County	280	2.18

Top 10 Places Sorted by Percent of Total Population
Based on all places, regardless of total population

Place	Population	%
Springdale (city) Hamilton County	613	5.46
Parral (village) Tuscarawas County	5	2.29
Dover (city) Tuscarawas County	280	2.18
New Philadelphia (city) Tuscarawas County	365	2.11
North Robinson (village) Crawford County	4	1.95
Whitehall (city) Franklin County	338	1.87
Sugar Bush Knolls (village) Portage County	3	1.69
Brecon (cdp) Hamilton County	4	1.64
Sandyville (cdp) Tuscarawas County	6	1.63
Wilson (village) Monroe County	2	1.60

Top 10 Places Sorted by Percent of Total Population
Based on places with total population of 50,000 or more

Place	Population	%
Cincinnati (city) Hamilton County	1,860	0.63
Cleveland (city) Cuyahoga County	2,085	0.53
Columbus (city) Franklin County	4,017	0.51
Canton (city) Stark County	348	0.48
Hamilton (city) Butler County	166	0.27
Youngstown (city) Mahoning County	152	0.23
Kettering (city) Montgomery County	116	0.21
Dayton (city) Montgomery County	269	0.19
Lakewood (city) Cuyahoga County	98	0.19
Lorain (city) Lorain County	118	0.18

Central American: Costa Rican

Top 10 Places Sorted by Population
Based on all places, regardless of total population

Place	Population	%
Columbus (city) Franklin County	129	0.02
Dayton (city) Montgomery County	87	0.06
Cleveland (city) Cuyahoga County	45	0.01
Cincinnati (city) Hamilton County	39	0.01
Kettering (city) Montgomery County	29	0.05
Toledo (city) Lucas County	15	0.01
Hudson (city) Summit County	14	0.06
Whitehall (city) Franklin County	13	0.07
North Ridgeville (city) Lorain County	11	0.04
Fairborn (city) Greene County	11	0.03

Top 10 Places Sorted by Percent of Total Population
Based on all places, regardless of total population

Place	Population	%
Waldo (village) Marion County	2	0.59
Coldstream (cdp) Hamilton County	3	0.26
Fredericksburg (village) Wayne County	1	0.24
Loveland Park (cdp) Warren County	3	0.20
Pettisville (cdp) Fulton County	1	0.20
Marble Cliff (village) Franklin County	1	0.17
Kidron (cdp) Wayne County	1	0.11
Canal Winchester (village) Franklin County	7	0.10
Apple Valley (cdp) Knox County	5	0.10
Turpin Hills (cdp) Hamilton County	5	0.10

Top 10 Places Sorted by Percent of Total Population
Based on places with total population of 50,000 or more

Place	Population	%
Dayton (city) Montgomery County	87	0.06
Kettering (city) Montgomery County	29	0.05
Columbus (city) Franklin County	129	0.02
Cleveland (city) Cuyahoga County	45	0.01
Cincinnati (city) Hamilton County	39	0.01
Toledo (city) Lucas County	15	0.01
Akron (city) Summit County	10	0.01
Parma (city) Cuyahoga County	6	0.01
Lakewood (city) Cuyahoga County	5	0.01
Youngstown (city) Mahoning County	5	0.01

Central American: Guatemalan

Top 10 Places Sorted by Population
Based on all places, regardless of total population

Place	Population	%
Cincinnati (city) Hamilton County	1,257	0.42
Cleveland (city) Cuyahoga County	786	0.20
Columbus (city) Franklin County	645	0.08
Springdale (city) Hamilton County	562	5.01
New Philadelphia (city) Tuscarawas County	353	2.04
Dover (city) Tuscarawas County	273	2.13
Forest Park (city) Hamilton County	148	0.79
Canton (city) Stark County	138	0.19
Salem (city) Columbiana County	133	1.08
Fairfield (city) Butler County	133	0.31

Top 10 Places Sorted by Percent of Total Population
Based on all places, regardless of total population

Place	Population	%
Springdale (city) Hamilton County	562	5.01
Parral (village) Tuscarawas County	5	2.29
Dover (city) Tuscarawas County	273	2.13
New Philadelphia (city) Tuscarawas County	353	2.04
Brecon (cdp) Hamilton County	4	1.64
Sandyville (cdp) Tuscarawas County	6	1.63
Plumwood (cdp) Madison County	4	1.25
Leipsic (village) Putnam County	25	1.19
Salem (city) Columbiana County	133	1.08
South Vienna (village) Clark County	4	1.04

Top 10 Places Sorted by Percent of Total Population
Based on places with total population of 50,000 or more

Place	Population	%
Cincinnati (city) Hamilton County	1,257	0.42
Cleveland (city) Cuyahoga County	786	0.20
Canton (city) Stark County	138	0.19
Columbus (city) Franklin County	645	0.08
Hamilton (city) Butler County	41	0.07
Lorain (city) Lorain County	32	0.05
Kettering (city) Montgomery County	28	0.05
Akron (city) Summit County	80	0.04
Dayton (city) Montgomery County	51	0.04
Parma (city) Cuyahoga County	34	0.04

Central American: Honduran

Top 10 Places Sorted by Population
Based on all places, regardless of total population

Place	Population	%
Columbus (city) Franklin County	784	0.10
Cleveland (city) Cuyahoga County	324	0.08
Cincinnati (city) Hamilton County	230	0.08
Canton (city) Stark County	139	0.19
Akron (city) Summit County	93	0.05
Norwood (city) Hamilton County	81	0.42
Fairfield (city) Butler County	79	0.19
Hamilton (city) Butler County	64	0.10
Dayton (city) Montgomery County	59	0.04
Youngstown (city) Mahoning County	46	0.07

Top 10 Places Sorted by Percent of Total Population
Based on all places, regardless of total population

Place	Population	%
Midway (village) Madison County	5	1.55
Valleyview (village) Franklin County	9	1.45
Hooven (cdp) Hamilton County	3	0.56
Fredericksburg (village) Wayne County	2	0.47
Norwood (city) Hamilton County	81	0.42
Riverlea (village) Franklin County	2	0.37
Lincoln Village (cdp) Franklin County	32	0.35
Geneva-on-the-Lake (village) Ashtabula County	4	0.31
Robertsville (cdp) Stark County	1	0.30
Crystal Lakes (cdp) Clark County	4	0.27

Top 10 Places Sorted by Percent of Total Population
Based on places with total population of 50,000 or more

Place	Population	%
Canton (city) Stark County	139	0.19
Columbus (city) Franklin County	784	0.10
Hamilton (city) Butler County	64	0.10
Cleveland (city) Cuyahoga County	324	0.08
Cincinnati (city) Hamilton County	230	0.08
Youngstown (city) Mahoning County	46	0.07
Akron (city) Summit County	93	0.05
Dayton (city) Montgomery County	59	0.04
Lorain (city) Lorain County	17	0.03
Lakewood (city) Cuyahoga County	16	0.03

Central American: Nicaraguan

Top 10 Places Sorted by Population
Based on all places, regardless of total population

Place	Population	%
Columbus (city) Franklin County	157	0.02
Cincinnati (city) Hamilton County	90	0.03
Cleveland (city) Cuyahoga County	82	0.02
Toledo (city) Lucas County	72	0.03
Akron (city) Summit County	38	0.02
Norwood (city) Hamilton County	25	0.13
Reynoldsburg (city) Franklin County	22	0.06
North Ridgeville (city) Lorain County	18	0.06
Middletown (city) Butler County	18	0.04
Beavercreek (city) Greene County	17	0.04

Top 10 Places Sorted by Percent of Total Population
Based on all places, regardless of total population

Place	Population	%
Kipton (village) Lorain County	1	0.41
Flushing (village) Belmont County	3	0.34
New Marshfield (cdp) Athens County	1	0.31
Spring Valley (village) Greene County	1	0.21
Willard (city) Huron County	11	0.18
Rossmoyne (cdp) Hamilton County	4	0.18
Napoleon (city) Henry County	14	0.16
Greentown (cdp) Stark County	6	0.16
Etna (cdp) Licking County	2	0.16
Ostrander (village) Delaware County	1	0.16

Top 10 Places Sorted by Percent of Total Population
Based on places with total population of 50,000 or more

Place	Population	%
Cincinnati (city) Hamilton County	90	0.03
Toledo (city) Lucas County	72	0.03
Lakewood (city) Cuyahoga County	17	0.03
Columbus (city) Franklin County	157	0.02
Cleveland (city) Cuyahoga County	82	0.02
Akron (city) Summit County	38	0.02
Parma (city) Cuyahoga County	13	0.02
Springfield (city) Clark County	13	0.02
Dayton (city) Montgomery County	14	0.01
Lorain (city) Lorain County	8	0.01

Central American: Panamanian

Top 10 Places Sorted by Population
Based on all places, regardless of total population

Place	Population	%
Columbus (city) Franklin County	294	0.04
Cleveland (city) Cuyahoga County	89	0.02
Cincinnati (city) Hamilton County	78	0.03
Middletown (city) Butler County	47	0.10
Akron (city) Summit County	47	0.02
Dayton (city) Montgomery County	37	0.03
Toledo (city) Lucas County	33	0.01
Beavercreek (city) Greene County	30	0.07
Kettering (city) Montgomery County	28	0.05
Lorain (city) Lorain County	28	0.04

Top 10 Places Sorted by Percent of Total Population
Based on all places, regardless of total population

Place	Population	%
North Robinson (village) Crawford County	4	1.95
Wilson (village) Monroe County	2	1.60
Hanging Rock (village) Lawrence County	3	1.36
Barnhill (village) Tuscarawas County	5	1.26
Hills and Dales (village) Stark County	1	0.45
Mount Blanchard (village) Hancock County	2	0.41
Atwater (cdp) Portage County	3	0.40
Jeromesville (village) Ashland County	2	0.36
Woodmere (village) Cuyahoga County	3	0.34
Seaman (village) Adams County	3	0.32

Top 10 Places Sorted by Percent of Total Population
Based on places with total population of 50,000 or more

Place	Population	%
Kettering (city) Montgomery County	28	0.05
Columbus (city) Franklin County	294	0.04
Lorain (city) Lorain County	28	0.04
Cincinnati (city) Hamilton County	78	0.03
Dayton (city) Montgomery County	37	0.03
Youngstown (city) Mahoning County	19	0.03
Cleveland (city) Cuyahoga County	89	0.02
Akron (city) Summit County	47	0.02
Lakewood (city) Cuyahoga County	13	0.02
Springfield (city) Clark County	11	0.02

Central American: Salvadoran

Top 10 Places Sorted by Population
Based on all places, regardless of total population

Place	Population	%
Columbus (city) Franklin County	1,954	0.25
Cleveland (city) Cuyahoga County	738	0.19
Whitehall (city) Franklin County	236	1.31
Cincinnati (city) Hamilton County	132	0.04
Forest Park (city) Hamilton County	93	0.50
Grove City (city) Franklin County	77	0.22
Akron (city) Summit County	69	0.03
Fairfield (city) Butler County	62	0.15
Cleveland Heights (city) Cuyahoga County	61	0.13
Lincoln Village (cdp) Franklin County	54	0.60

Top 10 Places Sorted by Percent of Total Population
Based on all places, regardless of total population

Place	Population	%
Sugar Bush Knolls (village) Portage County	3	1.69
Chatfield (village) Crawford County	3	1.59
Whitehall (city) Franklin County	236	1.31
Hooven (cdp) Hamilton County	5	0.94
Willard (city) Huron County	50	0.80
New Haven (cdp) Huron County	3	0.75
Minerva Park (village) Franklin County	8	0.63
Lincoln Village (cdp) Franklin County	54	0.60
Linndale (village) Cuyahoga County	1	0.56
Forest Park (city) Hamilton County	93	0.50

Top 10 Places Sorted by Percent of Total Population
Based on places with total population of 50,000 or more

Place	Population	%
Columbus (city) Franklin County	1,954	0.25
Cleveland (city) Cuyahoga County	738	0.19
Hamilton (city) Butler County	50	0.08
Youngstown (city) Mahoning County	49	0.07
Canton (city) Stark County	42	0.06
Parma (city) Cuyahoga County	37	0.05
Lorain (city) Lorain County	29	0.05
Lakewood (city) Cuyahoga County	26	0.05
Cincinnati (city) Hamilton County	132	0.04
Akron (city) Summit County	69	0.03

Central American: Other Central American

Top 10 Places Sorted by Population
Based on all places, regardless of total population

Place	Population	%
Columbus (city) Franklin County	54	0.01
Cincinnati (city) Hamilton County	34	0.01
Cleveland (city) Cuyahoga County	21	0.01
Canton (city) Stark County	14	0.02
Beavercreek (city) Greene County	6	0.01
Cheviot (city) Hamilton County	5	0.06
Dublin (city) Franklin County	5	0.01
Mansfield (city) Richland County	5	0.01
Bellefontaine (city) Logan County	4	0.03
Middleburg Heights (city) Cuyahoga County	4	0.03

Top 10 Places Sorted by Percent of Total Population
Based on all places, regardless of total population

Place	Population	%
Cheviot (city) Hamilton County	5	0.06
Oakwood (village) Cuyahoga County	2	0.05
Ottawa Hills (village) Lucas County	2	0.04
Bellefontaine (city) Logan County	4	0.03
Middleburg Heights (city) Cuyahoga County	4	0.03
North Kingsville (village) Ashtabula County	1	0.03
Canton (city) Stark County	14	0.02
Forest Park (city) Hamilton County	4	0.02
Wooster (city) Wayne County	4	0.02
Springdale (city) Hamilton County	2	0.02

Top 10 Places Sorted by Percent of Total Population
Based on places with total population of 50,000 or more

Place	Population	%
Canton (city) Stark County	14	0.02
Columbus (city) Franklin County	54	0.01
Cincinnati (city) Hamilton County	34	0.01
Cleveland (city) Cuyahoga County	21	0.01
Akron (city) Summit County	4	<0.01
Hamilton (city) Butler County	3	<0.01
Dayton (city) Montgomery County	1	<0.01
Elyria (city) Lorain County	1	<0.01
Kettering (city) Montgomery County	0	0.00
Lakewood (city) Cuyahoga County	0	0.00

Cuban

Top 10 Places Sorted by Population
Based on all places, regardless of total population

Place	Population	%
Columbus (city) Franklin County	922	0.12
Cleveland (city) Cuyahoga County	463	0.12
Cincinnati (city) Hamilton County	320	0.11
Toledo (city) Lucas County	299	0.10
Akron (city) Summit County	148	0.07
Dayton (city) Montgomery County	147	0.10
Youngstown (city) Mahoning County	98	0.15
Kettering (city) Montgomery County	84	0.15
Lakewood (city) Cuyahoga County	80	0.15
Lorain (city) Lorain County	79	0.12

Top 10 Places Sorted by Percent of Total Population
Based on all places, regardless of total population

Place	Population	%
Amesville (village) Athens County	4	2.60
Olde West Chester (cdp) Butler County	4	1.67
Millfield (cdp) Athens County	5	1.47
Orangeville (village) Trumbull County	2	1.02
Vanlue (village) Hancock County	3	0.84
Clay Center (village) Ottawa County	2	0.72
Woodmere (village) Cuyahoga County	6	0.68
Amsterdam (village) Jefferson County	3	0.59
Sixteen Mile Stand (cdp) Hamilton County	15	0.51
Marne (cdp) Licking County	4	0.51

Top 10 Places Sorted by Percent of Total Population
Based on places with total population of 50,000 or more

Place	Population	%
Youngstown (city) Mahoning County	98	0.15
Kettering (city) Montgomery County	84	0.15
Lakewood (city) Cuyahoga County	80	0.15
Columbus (city) Franklin County	922	0.12
Cleveland (city) Cuyahoga County	463	0.12
Lorain (city) Lorain County	79	0.12
Cincinnati (city) Hamilton County	320	0.11
Toledo (city) Lucas County	299	0.10
Dayton (city) Montgomery County	147	0.10
Hamilton (city) Butler County	48	0.08

Dominican Republic

Top 10 Places Sorted by Population
Based on all places, regardless of total population

Place	Population	%
Columbus (city) Franklin County	1,553	0.20
Cleveland (city) Cuyahoga County	1,140	0.29
Hamilton (city) Butler County	300	0.48
Youngstown (city) Mahoning County	239	0.36
Fairfield (city) Butler County	233	0.55
Middletown (city) Butler County	182	0.37
Cincinnati (city) Hamilton County	119	0.04
Lorain (city) Lorain County	115	0.18
Reynoldsburg (city) Franklin County	109	0.30
Lakewood (city) Cuyahoga County	82	0.16

Top 10 Places Sorted by Percent of Total Population
Based on all places, regardless of total population

Place	Population	%
Fairfield (city) Butler County	233	0.55
Hamilton (city) Butler County	300	0.48
Lincoln Village (cdp) Franklin County	38	0.42

Middletown (city) Butler County	182	0.37
Youngstown (city) Mahoning County	239	0.36
New Burlington (cdp) Hamilton County	18	0.36
Phillipsburg (village) Montgomery County	2	0.36
Willard (city) Huron County	22	0.35
Meyers Lake (village) Stark County	2	0.35
Lake Lorelei (cdp) Brown County	4	0.34

Top 10 Places Sorted by Percent of Total Population
Based on places with total population of 50,000 or more

Place	Population	%
Hamilton (city) Butler County	300	0.48
Youngstown (city) Mahoning County	239	0.36
Cleveland (city) Cuyahoga County	1,140	0.29
Columbus (city) Franklin County	1,553	0.20
Lorain (city) Lorain County	115	0.18
Lakewood (city) Cuyahoga County	82	0.16
Parma (city) Cuyahoga County	64	0.08
Cincinnati (city) Hamilton County	119	0.04
Dayton (city) Montgomery County	58	0.04
Canton (city) Stark County	27	0.04

Mexican

Top 10 Places Sorted by Population
Based on all places, regardless of total population

Place	Population	%
Columbus (city) Franklin County	25,973	3.30
Toledo (city) Lucas County	17,576	6.12
Painesville (city) Lake County	3,614	18.47
Cleveland (city) Cuyahoga County	3,593	0.91
Cincinnati (city) Hamilton County	3,244	1.09
Lorain (city) Lorain County	2,934	4.58
Hamilton (city) Butler County	2,897	4.64
Dayton (city) Montgomery County	2,541	1.80
Fremont (city) Sandusky County	2,331	13.93
Findlay (city) Hancock County	1,926	4.67

Top 10 Places Sorted by Percent of Total Population
Based on all places, regardless of total population

Place	Population	%
Tedrow (cdp) Fulton County	53	30.64
West Leipsic (village) Putnam County	61	29.61
Belmore (village) Putnam County	42	29.37
Leipsic (village) Putnam County	547	26.13
Brecon (cdp) Hamilton County	63	25.82
Hessville (cdp) Sandusky County	54	25.23
Milton Center (village) Wood County	32	22.22
Hamler (village) Henry County	118	20.49
Painesville (city) Lake County	3,614	18.47
Holgate (village) Henry County	179	16.14

Top 10 Places Sorted by Percent of Total Population
Based on places with total population of 50,000 or more

Place	Population	%
Toledo (city) Lucas County	17,576	6.12
Hamilton (city) Butler County	2,897	4.64
Lorain (city) Lorain County	2,934	4.58
Columbus (city) Franklin County	25,973	3.30
Springfield (city) Clark County	1,342	2.21
Youngstown (city) Mahoning County	1,270	1.90
Dayton (city) Montgomery County	2,541	1.80
Cincinnati (city) Hamilton County	3,244	1.09
Elyria (city) Lorain County	578	1.06
Kettering (city) Montgomery County	542	0.97

Puerto Rican

Top 10 Places Sorted by Population
Based on all places, regardless of total population

Place	Population	%
Cleveland (city) Cuyahoga County	29,286	7.38
Lorain (city) Lorain County	12,413	19.37
Columbus (city) Franklin County	5,034	0.64
Youngstown (city) Mahoning County	3,836	5.73
Elyria (city) Lorain County	1,719	3.15
Parma (city) Cuyahoga County	1,665	2.04
Ashtabula (city) Ashtabula County	1,156	6.04
Toledo (city) Lucas County	1,143	0.40
Akron (city) Summit County	1,091	0.55
Campbell (city) Mahoning County	1,090	13.24

Top 10 Places Sorted by Percent of Total Population
Based on all places, regardless of total population

Place	Population	%
Lorain (city) Lorain County	12,413	19.37
Linndale (village) Cuyahoga County	29	16.20
Campbell (city) Mahoning County	1,090	13.24
Brooklyn (city) Cuyahoga County	896	8.02
Cleveland (city) Cuyahoga County	29,286	7.38
Ashtabula (city) Ashtabula County	1,156	6.04
Youngstown (city) Mahoning County	3,836	5.73
Summitville (village) Columbiana County	6	4.44
Geneva (city) Ashtabula County	246	3.96
Beulah Beach (cdp) Erie County	2	3.77

Top 10 Places Sorted by Percent of Total Population
Based on places with total population of 50,000 or more

Place	Population	%
Lorain (city) Lorain County	12,413	19.37
Cleveland (city) Cuyahoga County	29,286	7.38
Youngstown (city) Mahoning County	3,836	5.73
Elyria (city) Lorain County	1,719	3.15
Lakewood (city) Cuyahoga County	1,077	2.07
Parma (city) Cuyahoga County	1,665	2.04
Columbus (city) Franklin County	5,034	0.64
Akron (city) Summit County	1,091	0.55
Canton (city) Stark County	356	0.49
Toledo (city) Lucas County	1,143	0.40

South American

Top 10 Places Sorted by Population
Based on all places, regardless of total population

Place	Population	%
Columbus (city) Franklin County	2,730	0.35
Cleveland (city) Cuyahoga County	959	0.24
Cincinnati (city) Hamilton County	668	0.22
Parma (city) Cuyahoga County	252	0.31
Akron (city) Summit County	251	0.13
Fairfield (city) Butler County	250	0.59
Toledo (city) Lucas County	219	0.08
Dayton (city) Montgomery County	217	0.15
Lakewood (city) Cuyahoga County	179	0.34
Mason (city) Warren County	172	0.56

Top 10 Places Sorted by Percent of Total Population
Based on all places, regardless of total population

Place	Population	%
Cloverdale (village) Putnam County	4	2.38
Concorde Hills (cdp) Hamilton County	14	2.11
Pettisville (cdp) Fulton County	10	2.01
Hills and Dales (village) Stark County	3	1.36
Sixteen Mile Stand (cdp) Hamilton County	28	0.96
Moraine (city) Montgomery County	52	0.82
Kenwood (cdp) Hamilton County	53	0.76
Gambier (village) Knox County	18	0.75
West Rushville (village) Fairfield County	1	0.75
Proctorville (village) Lawrence County	4	0.70

Top 10 Places Sorted by Percent of Total Population
Based on places with total population of 50,000 or more

Place	Population	%
Columbus (city) Franklin County	2,730	0.35
Lakewood (city) Cuyahoga County	179	0.34
Parma (city) Cuyahoga County	252	0.31
Cleveland (city) Cuyahoga County	959	0.24
Youngstown (city) Mahoning County	155	0.23
Cincinnati (city) Hamilton County	668	0.22
Kettering (city) Montgomery County	125	0.22
Dayton (city) Montgomery County	217	0.15
Akron (city) Summit County	251	0.13
Hamilton (city) Butler County	60	0.10

South American: Argentinean

Top 10 Places Sorted by Population
Based on all places, regardless of total population

Place	Population	%
Columbus (city) Franklin County	273	0.03
Whitehall (city) Franklin County	100	0.55
Cincinnati (city) Hamilton County	83	0.03
Cleveland (city) Cuyahoga County	70	0.02
Upper Arlington (city) Franklin County	35	0.10
Shaker Heights (city) Cuyahoga County	32	0.11
Lakewood (city) Cuyahoga County	32	0.06
Beavercreek (city) Greene County	24	0.05
Toledo (city) Lucas County	24	0.01
Akron (city) Summit County	23	0.01

Top 10 Places Sorted by Percent of Total Population
Based on all places, regardless of total population

Place	Population	%
Whitehall (city) Franklin County	100	0.55
Spencer (village) Medina County	4	0.53
Port William (village) Clinton County	1	0.39
Gambier (village) Knox County	6	0.25
Stony Ridge (cdp) Wood County	1	0.24
Dry Ridge (cdp) Hamilton County	5	0.18
Rossmoyne (cdp) Hamilton County	4	0.18
Amberley (village) Hamilton County	6	0.17
Morrow (village) Warren County	2	0.17
Fairport Harbor (village) Lake County	5	0.16

Top 10 Places Sorted by Percent of Total Population
Based on places with total population of 50,000 or more

Place	Population	%
Lakewood (city) Cuyahoga County	32	0.06
Columbus (city) Franklin County	273	0.03
Cincinnati (city) Hamilton County	83	0.03
Cleveland (city) Cuyahoga County	70	0.02
Parma (city) Cuyahoga County	19	0.02
Canton (city) Stark County	14	0.02
Toledo (city) Lucas County	24	0.01
Akron (city) Summit County	23	0.01
Dayton (city) Montgomery County	11	0.01
Lorain (city) Lorain County	9	0.01

South American: Bolivian

Top 10 Places Sorted by Population
Based on all places, regardless of total population

Place	Population	%
Columbus (city) Franklin County	81	0.01
Wauseon (city) Fulton County	36	0.49
Dublin (city) Franklin County	14	0.03
Cincinnati (city) Hamilton County	14	<0.01
Beavercreek (city) Greene County	13	0.03
Kettering (city) Montgomery County	13	0.02
Burlington (cdp) Lawrence County	11	0.41
Upper Arlington (city) Franklin County	11	0.03
Dayton (city) Montgomery County	11	0.01
Westerville (city) Franklin County	10	0.03

Top 10 Places Sorted by Percent of Total Population
Based on all places, regardless of total population

Place	Population	%
Pettisville (cdp) Fulton County	9	1.81
Wauseon (city) Fulton County	36	0.49
Burlington (cdp) Lawrence County	11	0.41
Fletcher (village) Miami County	1	0.21
Smithville (village) Wayne County	2	0.16
Elmwood Place (village) Hamilton County	3	0.14
Napoleon (city) Henry County	7	0.08
Grandview Heights (city) Franklin County	5	0.08
Amberley (village) Hamilton County	3	0.08
West Carrollton (city) Montgomery County	9	0.07

Top 10 Places Sorted by Percent of Total Population
Based on places with total population of 50,000 or more

Place	Population	%
Kettering (city) Montgomery County	13	0.02
Columbus (city) Franklin County	81	0.01
Dayton (city) Montgomery County	11	0.01
Lorain (city) Lorain County	4	0.01
Cincinnati (city) Hamilton County	14	<0.01
Akron (city) Summit County	6	<0.01
Toledo (city) Lucas County	4	<0.01
Canton (city) Stark County	3	<0.01
Cleveland (city) Cuyahoga County	3	<0.01
Hamilton (city) Butler County	2	<0.01

South American: Chilean

Top 10 Places Sorted by Population
Based on all places, regardless of total population

Place	Population	%
Columbus (city) Franklin County	112	0.01
Cleveland (city) Cuyahoga County	62	0.02
Cincinnati (city) Hamilton County	50	0.02
North Ridgeville (city) Lorain County	24	0.08
Huber Heights (city) Montgomery County	22	0.06
Akron (city) Summit County	18	0.01
Toledo (city) Lucas County	18	0.01
Athens (city) Athens County	16	0.07
Hudson (city) Summit County	16	0.07
Cleveland Heights (city) Cuyahoga County	16	0.03

Top 10 Places Sorted by Percent of Total Population
Based on all places, regardless of total population

Place	Population	%
Cloverdale (village) Putnam County	4	2.38
Hunting Valley (village) Cuyahoga County	2	0.28
Sixteen Mile Stand (cdp) Hamilton County	8	0.27
Ottawa Hills (village) Lucas County	8	0.18
Timberlake (village) Lake County	1	0.15
Wellston (city) Jackson County	7	0.12
Covedale (cdp) Hamilton County	6	0.09
Green Meadows (cdp) Clark County	2	0.09
West Hill (cdp) Trumbull County	2	0.09
North Ridgeville (city) Lorain County	24	0.08

Top 10 Places Sorted by Percent of Total Population
Based on places with total population of 50,000 or more

Place	Population	%
Cleveland (city) Cuyahoga County	62	0.02
Cincinnati (city) Hamilton County	50	0.02
Lakewood (city) Cuyahoga County	11	0.02
Columbus (city) Franklin County	112	0.01
Akron (city) Summit County	18	0.01
Toledo (city) Lucas County	18	0.01
Dayton (city) Montgomery County	8	0.01
Kettering (city) Montgomery County	5	0.01
Elyria (city) Lorain County	3	0.01
Parma (city) Cuyahoga County	4	<0.01

South American: Colombian

Top 10 Places Sorted by Population
Based on all places, regardless of total population

Place	Population	%
Columbus (city) Franklin County	797	0.10
Cleveland (city) Cuyahoga County	320	0.08
Cincinnati (city) Hamilton County	215	0.07
Youngstown (city) Mahoning County	104	0.16
Akron (city) Summit County	101	0.05
Beavercreek (city) Greene County	53	0.12
Westlake (city) Cuyahoga County	51	0.16
Toledo (city) Lucas County	49	0.02
Dublin (city) Franklin County	47	0.11
Fairfield (city) Butler County	47	0.11

Top 10 Places Sorted by Percent of Total Population
Based on all places, regardless of total population

Place	Population	%
Hills and Dales (village) Stark County	3	1.36
Zoar (village) Tuscarawas County	1	0.59
Celeryville (cdp) Huron County	1	0.48
Milan (village) Erie County	5	0.37
Marble Cliff (village) Franklin County	2	0.35
Thurston (village) Fairfield County	2	0.33
Sixteen Mile Stand (cdp) Hamilton County	9	0.31
Wetherington (cdp) Butler County	4	0.31
Kenwood (cdp) Hamilton County	20	0.29
Beckett Ridge (cdp) Butler County	26	0.28

Top 10 Places Sorted by Percent of Total Population
Based on places with total population of 50,000 or more

Place	Population	%
Youngstown (city) Mahoning County	104	0.16
Columbus (city) Franklin County	797	0.10
Cleveland (city) Cuyahoga County	320	0.08
Kettering (city) Montgomery County	44	0.08
Cincinnati (city) Hamilton County	215	0.07
Lakewood (city) Cuyahoga County	37	0.07
Parma (city) Cuyahoga County	45	0.06
Akron (city) Summit County	101	0.05
Canton (city) Stark County	25	0.03
Hamilton (city) Butler County	18	0.03

South American: Ecuadorian

Top 10 Places Sorted by Population
Based on all places, regardless of total population

Place	Population	%
Columbus (city) Franklin County	491	0.06
Dayton (city) Montgomery County	115	0.08
Cleveland (city) Cuyahoga County	113	0.03
Moraine (city) Montgomery County	48	0.76
Cincinnati (city) Hamilton County	45	0.02
Parma (city) Cuyahoga County	44	0.05
Akron (city) Summit County	39	0.02
Huber Heights (city) Montgomery County	27	0.07
Toledo (city) Lucas County	27	0.01
Fairfield (city) Butler County	25	0.06

Top 10 Places Sorted by Percent of Total Population
Based on all places, regardless of total population

Place	Population	%
Moraine (city) Montgomery County	48	0.76
West Rushville (village) Fairfield County	1	0.75
Killbuck (village) Holmes County	4	0.49
Newtown (village) Hamilton County	7	0.26
South Amherst (village) Lorain County	4	0.24
New Concord (village) Muskingum County	5	0.20
Canal Winchester (village) Franklin County	13	0.18
Craig Beach (village) Mahoning County	2	0.17
Marble Cliff (village) Franklin County	1	0.17
Orange (village) Cuyahoga County	5	0.15

Top 10 Places Sorted by Percent of Total Population
Based on places with total population of 50,000 or more

Place	Population	%
Dayton (city) Montgomery County	115	0.08
Columbus (city) Franklin County	491	0.06
Parma (city) Cuyahoga County	44	0.05
Cleveland (city) Cuyahoga County	113	0.03
Kettering (city) Montgomery County	18	0.03
Cincinnati (city) Hamilton County	45	0.02
Akron (city) Summit County	39	0.02
Lorain (city) Lorain County	12	0.02
Toledo (city) Lucas County	27	0.01
Elyria (city) Lorain County	8	0.01

South American: Paraguayan

Top 10 Places Sorted by Population
Based on all places, regardless of total population

Place	Population	%
Columbus (city) Franklin County	9	<0.01
Fairview Park (city) Cuyahoga County	8	0.05
Cleveland (city) Cuyahoga County	8	<0.01
Strongsville (city) Cuyahoga County	7	0.02
Perrysburg (city) Wood County	6	0.03
Sylvania (city) Lucas County	6	0.03
Cincinnati (city) Hamilton County	6	<0.01
Toledo (city) Lucas County	6	<0.01
Athens (city) Athens County	5	0.02
North Royalton (city) Cuyahoga County	5	0.02

Top 10 Places Sorted by Percent of Total Population
Based on all places, regardless of total population

Place	Population	%
Phillipsburg (village) Montgomery County	1	0.18
Malta (village) Morgan County	1	0.15
Coldstream (cdp) Hamilton County	1	0.09
Fairview Park (city) Cuyahoga County	8	0.05
Edgerton (village) Williams County	1	0.05
Glendale (village) Hamilton County	1	0.05
Fairlawn (city) Summit County	3	0.04
Highland Heights (city) Cuyahoga County	3	0.04
Kirtland (city) Lake County	3	0.04
Oberlin (city) Lorain County	3	0.04

Top 10 Places Sorted by Percent of Total Population
Based on places with total population of 50,000 or more

Place	Population	%
Hamilton (city) Butler County	4	0.01
Kettering (city) Montgomery County	3	0.01
Columbus (city) Franklin County	9	<0.01
Cleveland (city) Cuyahoga County	8	<0.01
Cincinnati (city) Hamilton County	6	<0.01
Toledo (city) Lucas County	6	<0.01
Dayton (city) Montgomery County	1	<0.01
Lakewood (city) Cuyahoga County	1	<0.01
Parma (city) Cuyahoga County	1	<0.01
Springfield (city) Clark County	1	<0.01

South American: Peruvian

Top 10 Places Sorted by Population
Based on all places, regardless of total population

Place	Population	%
Columbus (city) Franklin County	543	0.07
Cleveland (city) Cuyahoga County	276	0.07
Fairfield (city) Butler County	145	0.34
Cincinnati (city) Hamilton County	138	0.05
Parma (city) Cuyahoga County	129	0.16
Toledo (city) Lucas County	51	0.02
Mentor (city) Lake County	33	0.07
Shaker Heights (city) Cuyahoga County	31	0.11
Lakewood (city) Cuyahoga County	31	0.06
Strongsville (city) Cuyahoga County	30	0.07

Top 10 Places Sorted by Percent of Total Population
Based on all places, regardless of total population

Place	Population	%
Proctorville (village) Lawrence County	4	0.70
Austinburg (cdp) Ashtabula County	3	0.58
Fairfield (city) Butler County	145	0.34
Hebron (village) Licking County	7	0.30
Pleasant Run (cdp) Hamilton County	14	0.28
Pleasant Run Farm (cdp) Hamilton County	12	0.26
Campbell (city) Mahoning County	20	0.24
Landen (cdp) Warren County	16	0.24
Bedford Heights (city) Cuyahoga County	25	0.23
Salem Heights (cdp) Hamilton County	9	0.23

Top 10 Places Sorted by Percent of Total Population
Based on places with total population of 50,000 or more

Place	Population	%
Parma (city) Cuyahoga County	129	0.16
Columbus (city) Franklin County	543	0.07
Cleveland (city) Cuyahoga County	276	0.07
Lakewood (city) Cuyahoga County	31	0.06
Cincinnati (city) Hamilton County	138	0.05
Hamilton (city) Butler County	20	0.03
Youngstown (city) Mahoning County	18	0.03
Kettering (city) Montgomery County	15	0.03
Toledo (city) Lucas County	51	0.02
Dayton (city) Montgomery County	25	0.02

South American: Uruguayan

Top 10 Places Sorted by Population
Based on all places, regardless of total population

Place	Population	%
Columbus (city) Franklin County	47	0.01
Cleveland (city) Cuyahoga County	28	0.01
Mayfield Heights (city) Cuyahoga County	15	0.08
Shaker Heights (city) Cuyahoga County	12	0.04
Richmond Heights (city) Cuyahoga County	10	0.09
Lakewood (city) Cuyahoga County	7	0.01
Dayton (city) Montgomery County	7	<0.01
Oxford (city) Butler County	6	0.03
Euclid (city) Cuyahoga County	6	0.01
Akron (city) Summit County	6	<0.01

Top 10 Places Sorted by Percent of Total Population
Based on all places, regardless of total population

Place	Population	%
Terrace Park (village) Hamilton County	3	0.13
Richmond Heights (city) Cuyahoga County	10	0.09
Mayfield Heights (city) Cuyahoga County	15	0.08

Place	Population	%
Highland Heights (city) Cuyahoga County	4	0.05
Windham (village) Portage County	1	0.05
Shaker Heights (city) Cuyahoga County	12	0.04
Gambier (village) Knox County	1	0.04
Oxford (city) Butler County	6	0.03
Groesbeck (cdp) Hamilton County	2	0.03
New Albany (village) Franklin County	2	0.03

Top 10 Places Sorted by Percent of Total Population

Based on places with total population of 50,000 or more

Place	Population	%
Columbus (city) Franklin County	47	0.01
Cleveland (city) Cuyahoga County	28	0.01
Lakewood (city) Cuyahoga County	7	0.01
Kettering (city) Montgomery County	3	0.01
Dayton (city) Montgomery County	7	<0.01
Akron (city) Summit County	6	<0.01
Canton (city) Stark County	1	<0.01
Cincinnati (city) Hamilton County	1	<0.01
Youngstown (city) Mahoning County	1	<0.01
Elyria (city) Lorain County	0	0.00

South American: Venezuelan

Top 10 Places Sorted by Population

Based on all places, regardless of total population

Place	Population	%
Columbus (city) Franklin County	355	0.05
Cincinnati (city) Hamilton County	107	0.04
Mason (city) Warren County	78	0.25
Cleveland (city) Cuyahoga County	54	0.01
Lakewood (city) Cuyahoga County	52	0.10
Dublin (city) Franklin County	37	0.09
Toledo (city) Lucas County	32	0.01
Akron (city) Summit County	31	0.02
Beachwood (city) Cuyahoga County	22	0.18
Upper Arlington (city) Franklin County	21	0.06

Top 10 Places Sorted by Percent of Total Population

Based on all places, regardless of total population

Place	Population	%
Concorde Hills (cdp) Hamilton County	13	1.96
Miamiville (cdp) Clermont County	1	0.41
The Village of Indian Hill (city) Hamilton County	20	0.35
East Liberty (cdp) Logan County	1	0.27
Mason (city) Warren County	78	0.25
Kenwood (cdp) Hamilton County	16	0.23
Sixteen Mile Stand (cdp) Hamilton County	6	0.20
Pettisville (cdp) Fulton County	1	0.20
Beachwood (city) Cuyahoga County	22	0.18
Nelsonville (city) Athens County	9	0.17

Top 10 Places Sorted by Percent of Total Population

Based on places with total population of 50,000 or more

Place	Population	%
Lakewood (city) Cuyahoga County	52	0.10
Columbus (city) Franklin County	355	0.05
Cincinnati (city) Hamilton County	107	0.04
Kettering (city) Montgomery County	15	0.03
Akron (city) Summit County	31	0.02
Lorain (city) Lorain County	10	0.02
Cleveland (city) Cuyahoga County	54	0.01
Toledo (city) Lucas County	32	0.01
Youngstown (city) Mahoning County	9	0.01
Parma (city) Cuyahoga County	7	0.01

South American: Other South American

Top 10 Places Sorted by Population

Based on all places, regardless of total population

Place	Population	%
Cleveland (city) Cuyahoga County	25	0.01
Columbus (city) Franklin County	22	<0.01
Cincinnati (city) Hamilton County	9	<0.01
Toledo (city) Lucas County	8	<0.01
Ashtabula (city) Ashtabula County	4	0.02
Mentor-on-the-Lake (city) Lake County	3	0.04
Cambridge (city) Guernsey County	3	0.03
Sheffield Lake (city) Lorain County	3	0.03
Lyndhurst (city) Cuyahoga County	3	0.02
Pickerington (city) Fairfield County	3	0.02

Top 10 Places Sorted by Percent of Total Population

Based on all places, regardless of total population

Place	Population	%
East Liberty (cdp) Logan County	1	0.27
Jamestown (village) Greene County	2	0.10
Lincoln Heights (village) Hamilton County	2	0.06
Mentor-on-the-Lake (city) Lake County	3	0.04
Wilberforce (cdp) Greene County	1	0.04
Cambridge (city) Guernsey County	3	0.03
Sheffield Lake (city) Lorain County	3	0.03
Deer Park (city) Hamilton County	2	0.03
Ashtabula (city) Ashtabula County	4	0.02
Lyndhurst (city) Cuyahoga County	3	0.02

Top 10 Places Sorted by Percent of Total Population

Based on places with total population of 50,000 or more

Place	Population	%
Cleveland (city) Cuyahoga County	25	0.01
Columbus (city) Franklin County	22	<0.01
Cincinnati (city) Hamilton County	9	<0.01
Toledo (city) Lucas County	8	<0.01
Akron (city) Summit County	3	<0.01
Parma (city) Cuyahoga County	3	<0.01
Elyria (city) Lorain County	2	<0.01
Kettering (city) Montgomery County	2	<0.01
Lakewood (city) Cuyahoga County	2	<0.01
Youngstown (city) Mahoning County	2	<0.01

Other Hispanic or Latino

Top 10 Places Sorted by Population

Based on all places, regardless of total population

Place	Population	%
Columbus (city) Franklin County	4,130	0.52
Cleveland (city) Cuyahoga County	2,008	0.51
Toledo (city) Lucas County	1,685	0.59
Cincinnati (city) Hamilton County	1,124	0.38
Akron (city) Summit County	590	0.30
Lorain (city) Lorain County	458	0.71
Youngstown (city) Mahoning County	457	0.68
Dayton (city) Montgomery County	433	0.31
Canton (city) Stark County	387	0.53
Lima (city) Allen County	380	0.98

Top 10 Places Sorted by Percent of Total Population

Based on all places, regardless of total population

Place	Population	%
Portage (village) Wood County	17	3.88
Leipsic (village) Putnam County	81	3.87
Ithaca (village) Darke County	5	3.68
Tontogany (village) Wood County	12	3.27
South Vienna (village) Clark County	11	2.86
Gilboa (village) Putnam County	5	2.72
St Johns (cdp) Auglaize County	5	2.70
Holgate (village) Henry County	26	2.34
Buckland (village) Auglaize County	5	2.15
Old Fort (cdp) Seneca County	4	2.15

Top 10 Places Sorted by Percent of Total Population

Based on places with total population of 50,000 or more

Place	Population	%
Lorain (city) Lorain County	458	0.71
Youngstown (city) Mahoning County	457	0.68
Toledo (city) Lucas County	1,685	0.59
Canton (city) Stark County	387	0.53
Columbus (city) Franklin County	4,130	0.52
Cleveland (city) Cuyahoga County	2,008	0.51
Hamilton (city) Butler County	301	0.48
Elyria (city) Lorain County	222	0.41
Cincinnati (city) Hamilton County	1,124	0.38
Springfield (city) Clark County	218	0.36

Racial Group Rankings

African-American/Black

Top 10 Places Sorted by Population

Based on all places, regardless of total population

Place	Population	%
Columbus (city) Franklin County	237,077	30.12
Cleveland (city) Cuyahoga County	219,027	55.20
Cincinnati (city) Hamilton County	138,296	46.57
Toledo (city) Lucas County	85,254	29.68
Akron (city) Summit County	67,240	33.77
Dayton (city) Montgomery County	63,535	44.89
Youngstown (city) Mahoning County	32,093	47.91
Euclid (city) Cuyahoga County	26,672	54.52
Cleveland Heights (city) Cuyahoga County	20,487	44.42
Canton (city) Stark County	20,377	27.91

Top 10 Places Sorted by Percent of Total Population

Based on all places, regardless of total population

Place	Population	%
Lincoln Heights (village) Hamilton County	3,203	97.47
Warrensville Heights (city) Cuyahoga County	12,909	95.33
East Cleveland (city) Cuyahoga County	16,901	94.72
Twinsburg Heights (cdp) Summit County	810	87.57
North Randall (village) Cuyahoga County	898	87.44
Wilberforce (cdp) Greene County	1,950	85.87
Skyline Acres (cdp) Hamilton County	1,435	83.58
Bedford Heights (city) Cuyahoga County	8,458	78.67
Highland Hills (village) Cuyahoga County	858	75.93
Golf Manor (village) Hamilton County	2,698	74.72

Top 10 Places Sorted by Percent of Total Population

Based on places with total population of 50,000 or more

Place	Population	%
Cleveland (city) Cuyahoga County	219,027	55.20
Youngstown (city) Mahoning County	32,093	47.91
Cincinnati (city) Hamilton County	138,296	46.57
Dayton (city) Montgomery County	63,535	44.89
Akron (city) Summit County	67,240	33.77
Columbus (city) Franklin County	237,077	30.12
Toledo (city) Lucas County	85,254	29.68
Canton (city) Stark County	20,377	27.91
Springfield (city) Clark County	12,807	21.13
Lorain (city) Lorain County	13,512	21.08

African-American/Black: Not Hispanic

Top 10 Places Sorted by Population

Based on all places, regardless of total population

Place	Population	%
Columbus (city) Franklin County	233,108	29.62
Cleveland (city) Cuyahoga County	213,920	53.91
Cincinnati (city) Hamilton County	137,223	46.21
Toledo (city) Lucas County	82,886	28.86
Akron (city) Summit County	66,385	33.34
Dayton (city) Montgomery County	62,972	44.49
Youngstown (city) Mahoning County	30,939	46.19
Euclid (city) Cuyahoga County	26,370	53.90
Cleveland Heights (city) Cuyahoga County	20,266	43.94
Canton (city) Stark County	20,069	27.49

Top 10 Places Sorted by Percent of Total Population

Based on all places, regardless of total population

Place	Population	%
Lincoln Heights (village) Hamilton County	3,193	97.17
Warrensville Heights (city) Cuyahoga County	12,764	94.25
East Cleveland (city) Cuyahoga County	16,770	93.99
North Randall (village) Cuyahoga County	897	87.34
Twinsburg Heights (cdp) Summit County	800	86.49
Wilberforce (cdp) Greene County	1,917	84.41
Skyline Acres (cdp) Hamilton County	1,433	83.46
Bedford Heights (city) Cuyahoga County	8,383	77.97
Highland Hills (village) Cuyahoga County	851	75.31
Golf Manor (village) Hamilton County	2,677	74.13

Top 10 Places Sorted by Percent of Total Population

Based on places with total population of 50,000 or more

Place	Population	%
Cleveland (city) Cuyahoga County	213,920	53.91
Cincinnati (city) Hamilton County	137,223	46.21
Youngstown (city) Mahoning County	30,939	46.19
Dayton (city) Montgomery County	62,972	44.49
Akron (city) Summit County	66,385	33.34
Columbus (city) Franklin County	233,108	29.62
Toledo (city) Lucas County	82,886	28.86
Canton (city) Stark County	20,069	27.49
Springfield (city) Clark County	12,597	20.78
Lorain (city) Lorain County	11,803	18.41

African-American/Black: Hispanic

Top 10 Places Sorted by Population

Based on all places, regardless of total population

Place	Population	%
Cleveland (city) Cuyahoga County	5,107	1.29
Columbus (city) Franklin County	3,969	0.50
Toledo (city) Lucas County	2,368	0.82
Lorain (city) Lorain County	1,709	2.67
Youngstown (city) Mahoning County	1,154	1.72
Cincinnati (city) Hamilton County	1,073	0.36
Akron (city) Summit County	855	0.43
Dayton (city) Montgomery County	563	0.40
Elyria (city) Lorain County	476	0.87
Canton (city) Stark County	308	0.42

Top 10 Places Sorted by Percent of Total Population

Based on all places, regardless of total population

Place	Population	%
Lorain (city) Lorain County	1,709	2.67
Campbell (city) Mahoning County	154	1.87
Youngstown (city) Mahoning County	1,154	1.72
Summitville (village) Columbiana County	2	1.48
Wilberforce (cdp) Greene County	33	1.45
Woodmere (village) Cuyahoga County	12	1.36
Oakwood (village) Paulding County	8	1.32
Drexel (cdp) Montgomery County	27	1.30
Cleveland (city) Cuyahoga County	5,107	1.29
Fairview (village) Guernsey County	1	1.20

Top 10 Places Sorted by Percent of Total Population

Based on places with total population of 50,000 or more

Place	Population	%
Lorain (city) Lorain County	1,709	2.67
Youngstown (city) Mahoning County	1,154	1.72
Cleveland (city) Cuyahoga County	5,107	1.29
Elyria (city) Lorain County	476	0.87
Toledo (city) Lucas County	2,368	0.82
Columbus (city) Franklin County	3,969	0.50
Akron (city) Summit County	855	0.43
Canton (city) Stark County	308	0.42
Dayton (city) Montgomery County	563	0.40
Lakewood (city) Cuyahoga County	194	0.37

American Indian/Alaska Native

Top 10 Places Sorted by Population

Based on all places, regardless of total population

Place	Population	%
Columbus (city) Franklin County	8,353	1.06
Cleveland (city) Cuyahoga County	4,008	1.01
Toledo (city) Lucas County	3,359	1.17
Cincinnati (city) Hamilton County	2,658	0.90
Akron (city) Summit County	2,083	1.05
Dayton (city) Montgomery County	1,579	1.12
Canton (city) Stark County	1,243	1.70
Lorain (city) Lorain County	966	1.51
Youngstown (city) Mahoning County	870	1.30
Springfield (city) Clark County	748	1.23

Top 10 Places Sorted by Percent of Total Population

Based on all places, regardless of total population

Place	Population	%
Rendville (village) Perry County	4	11.11
Graysville (village) Monroe County	8	10.53
Chesterhill (village) Morgan County	21	7.27
Otway (village) Scioto County	5	5.75
Latty (village) Paulding County	10	5.18
Jacksonburg (village) Butler County	3	4.76
Rome (village) Adams County	4	4.26
Yorkshire (village) Darke County	4	4.17
Whites Landing (cdp) Erie County	15	4.00
Clifton (village) Greene County	6	3.95

Top 10 Places Sorted by Percent of Total Population

Based on places with total population of 50,000 or more

Place	Population	%
Canton (city) Stark County	1,243	1.70
Lorain (city) Lorain County	966	1.51
Youngstown (city) Mahoning County	870	1.30
Springfield (city) Clark County	748	1.23
Toledo (city) Lucas County	3,359	1.17
Elyria (city) Lorain County	631	1.16
Dayton (city) Montgomery County	1,579	1.12
Columbus (city) Franklin County	8,353	1.06
Akron (city) Summit County	2,083	1.05
Cleveland (city) Cuyahoga County	4,008	1.01

American Indian/Alaska Native: Not Hispanic

Top 10 Places Sorted by Population

Based on all places, regardless of total population

Place	Population	%
Columbus (city) Franklin County	7,286	0.93
Cleveland (city) Cuyahoga County	3,202	0.81
Toledo (city) Lucas County	2,675	0.93
Cincinnati (city) Hamilton County	2,276	0.77
Akron (city) Summit County	1,899	0.95
Dayton (city) Montgomery County	1,460	1.03
Canton (city) Stark County	1,102	1.51
Youngstown (city) Mahoning County	715	1.07
Springfield (city) Clark County	660	1.09
Lorain (city) Lorain County	651	1.02

Top 10 Places Sorted by Percent of Total Population

Based on all places, regardless of total population

Place	Population	%
Rendville (village) Perry County	4	11.11
Graysville (village) Monroe County	8	10.53
Chesterhill (village) Morgan County	21	7.27
Otway (village) Scioto County	5	5.75
Jacksonburg (village) Butler County	3	4.76
Rome (village) Adams County	4	4.26
Yorkshire (village) Darke County	4	4.17
Whites Landing (cdp) Erie County	15	4.00
Clifton (village) Greene County	6	3.95
Potsdam (village) Miami County	11	3.82

Top 10 Places Sorted by Percent of Total Population

Based on places with total population of 50,000 or more

Place	Population	%
Canton (city) Stark County	1,102	1.51
Springfield (city) Clark County	660	1.09
Youngstown (city) Mahoning County	715	1.07
Dayton (city) Montgomery County	1,460	1.03
Lorain (city) Lorain County	651	1.02
Elyria (city) Lorain County	531	0.97
Akron (city) Summit County	1,899	0.95
Columbus (city) Franklin County	7,286	0.93
Toledo (city) Lucas County	2,675	0.93
Lakewood (city) Cuyahoga County	428	0.82

Please refer to the Explanation of Data in the front of the book for more detailed information.

American Indian/Alaska Native: Hispanic

Top 10 Places Sorted by Population
Based on all places, regardless of total population

Place	Population	%
Columbus (city) Franklin County	1,067	0.14
Cleveland (city) Cuyahoga County	806	0.20
Toledo (city) Lucas County	684	0.24
Cincinnati (city) Hamilton County	382	0.13
Lorain (city) Lorain County	315	0.49
Akron (city) Summit County	184	0.09
Youngstown (city) Mahoning County	155	0.23
Canton (city) Stark County	141	0.19
Dayton (city) Montgomery County	119	0.08
Elyria (city) Lorain County	100	0.18

Top 10 Places Sorted by Percent of Total Population
Based on all places, regardless of total population

Place	Population	%
Latty (village) Paulding County	6	3.11
New Bloomington (village) Marion County	11	2.14
Hooven (cdp) Hamilton County	9	1.69
Valley Hi (village) Logan County	3	1.42
Milton Center (village) Wood County	2	1.39
Highland (village) Highland County	3	1.18
Oakwood (village) Paulding County	6	0.99
Wayne (village) Wood County	8	0.90
Jeromesville (village) Ashland County	5	0.89
Rudolph (cdp) Wood County	4	0.87

Top 10 Places Sorted by Percent of Total Population
Based on places with total population of 50,000 or more

Place	Population	%
Lorain (city) Lorain County	315	0.49
Toledo (city) Lucas County	684	0.24
Youngstown (city) Mahoning County	155	0.23
Cleveland (city) Cuyahoga County	806	0.20
Canton (city) Stark County	141	0.19
Elyria (city) Lorain County	100	0.18
Springfield (city) Clark County	88	0.15
Columbus (city) Franklin County	1,067	0.14
Lakewood (city) Cuyahoga County	75	0.14
Cincinnati (city) Hamilton County	382	0.13

Alaska Native: Alaska Athabascan

Top 10 Places Sorted by Population
Based on all places, regardless of total population

Place	Population	%
Columbus (city) Franklin County	11	<0.01
Pleasant Run Farm (cdp) Hamilton County	5	0.11
Hudson (city) Summit County	4	0.02
Minerva (village) Stark County	3	0.08
Jackson (city) Jackson County	3	0.05
Groesbeck (cdp) Hamilton County	3	0.04
Northridge (cdp) Clark County	3	0.04
Circleville (city) Pickaway County	3	0.02
Tallmadge (city) Summit County	3	0.02
Shaker Heights (city) Cuyahoga County	3	0.01

Top 10 Places Sorted by Percent of Total Population
Based on all places, regardless of total population

Place	Population	%
Pleasant Run Farm (cdp) Hamilton County	5	0.11
Minerva (village) Stark County	3	0.08
North Lewisburg (village) Champaign County	1	0.07
Jackson (city) Jackson County	3	0.05
Leipsic (village) Putnam County	1	0.05
Groesbeck (cdp) Hamilton County	3	0.04
Northridge (cdp) Clark County	3	0.04
Richfield (village) Summit County	1	0.03
Hudson (city) Summit County	4	0.02
Circleville (city) Pickaway County	3	0.02

Top 10 Places Sorted by Percent of Total Population
Based on places with total population of 50,000 or more

Place	Population	%
Columbus (city) Franklin County	11	<0.01
Cincinnati (city) Hamilton County	3	<0.01
Parma (city) Cuyahoga County	3	<0.01
Youngstown (city) Mahoning County	3	<0.01
Cleveland (city) Cuyahoga County	2	<0.01
Lakewood (city) Cuyahoga County	2	<0.01
Toledo (city) Lucas County	2	<0.01
Akron (city) Summit County	0	0.00
Canton (city) Stark County	0	0.00
Dayton (city) Montgomery County	0	0.00

Alaska Native: Aleut

Top 10 Places Sorted by Population
Based on all places, regardless of total population

Place	Population	%
Columbus (city) Franklin County	9	<0.01
Cincinnati (city) Hamilton County	8	<0.01
Milford Center (village) Union County	4	0.51
Hamilton (city) Butler County	4	0.01
Dayton (city) Montgomery County	4	<0.01
Minerva (village) Stark County	3	0.08
Wilmington (city) Clinton County	3	0.02
Lockland (village) Hamilton County	2	0.06
Milford (city) Clermont County	2	0.03
Boardman (cdp) Mahoning County	2	0.01

Top 10 Places Sorted by Percent of Total Population
Based on all places, regardless of total population

Place	Population	%
Milford Center (village) Union County	4	0.51
West Manchester (village) Preble County	1	0.21
Minerva (village) Stark County	3	0.08
Fayette (village) Fulton County	1	0.08
Grandview (cdp) Hamilton County	1	0.07
Lockland (village) Hamilton County	2	0.06
Franklin Furnace (cdp) Scioto County	1	0.06
South Bloomfield (village) Pickaway County	1	0.06
Milford (city) Clermont County	2	0.03
Wellsville (village) Columbiana County	1	0.03

Top 10 Places Sorted by Percent of Total Population
Based on places with total population of 50,000 or more

Place	Population	%
Hamilton (city) Butler County	4	0.01
Columbus (city) Franklin County	9	<0.01
Cincinnati (city) Hamilton County	8	<0.01
Dayton (city) Montgomery County	4	<0.01
Toledo (city) Lucas County	2	<0.01
Akron (city) Summit County	1	<0.01
Elyria (city) Lorain County	1	<0.01
Kettering (city) Montgomery County	1	<0.01
Lakewood (city) Cuyahoga County	1	<0.01
Canton (city) Stark County	0	0.00

American Indian: Apache

Top 10 Places Sorted by Population
Based on all places, regardless of total population

Place	Population	%
Columbus (city) Franklin County	109	0.01
Toledo (city) Lucas County	66	0.02
Cincinnati (city) Hamilton County	44	0.01
Cleveland (city) Cuyahoga County	43	0.01
Canton (city) Stark County	20	0.03
Sandusky (city) Erie County	19	0.07
Lancaster (city) Fairfield County	19	0.05
Youngstown (city) Mahoning County	19	0.03
Dayton (city) Montgomery County	18	0.01
Akron (city) Summit County	16	0.01

Top 10 Places Sorted by Percent of Total Population
Based on all places, regardless of total population

Place	Population	%
Whites Landing (cdp) Erie County	5	1.33
Dunkirk (village) Hardin County	8	0.91
College Corner (village) Preble County	3	0.74
Milton Center (village) Wood County	1	0.69
Gilboa (village) Putnam County	1	0.54
Camp Dennison (cdp) Hamilton County	2	0.53
Wren (village) Van Wert County	1	0.52
La Rue (village) Marion County	3	0.40
Glenmont (village) Holmes County	1	0.37
Russells Point (village) Logan County	5	0.36

Top 10 Places Sorted by Percent of Total Population
Based on places with total population of 50,000 or more

Place	Population	%
Canton (city) Stark County	20	0.03
Youngstown (city) Mahoning County	19	0.03
Toledo (city) Lucas County	66	0.02
Lorain (city) Lorain County	13	0.02
Parma (city) Cuyahoga County	13	0.02
Columbus (city) Franklin County	109	0.01
Cincinnati (city) Hamilton County	44	0.01
Cleveland (city) Cuyahoga County	43	0.01
Dayton (city) Montgomery County	18	0.01
Akron (city) Summit County	16	0.01

American Indian: Arapaho

Top 10 Places Sorted by Population
Based on all places, regardless of total population

Place	Population	%
Dayton (city) Montgomery County	10	0.01
Cleveland (city) Cuyahoga County	7	<0.01
Toledo (city) Lucas County	6	<0.01
Youngstown (city) Mahoning County	4	0.01
Cincinnati (city) Hamilton County	4	<0.01
Uhrichsville (city) Tuscarawas County	3	0.06
Montgomery (city) Hamilton County	3	0.03
Upper Arlington (city) Franklin County	3	0.01
Zanesville (city) Muskingum County	3	0.01
Akron (city) Summit County	3	<0.01

Top 10 Places Sorted by Percent of Total Population
Based on all places, regardless of total population

Place	Population	%
Otway (village) Scioto County	1	1.15
Uhrichsville (city) Tuscarawas County	3	0.06
Manchester (village) Adams County	1	0.05
Montgomery (city) Hamilton County	3	0.03
Mulberry (cdp) Clermont County	1	0.03
North Baltimore (village) Wood County	1	0.03
Reminderville (village) Summit County	1	0.03
London (city) Madison County	2	0.02
Dayton (city) Montgomery County	10	0.01
Youngstown (city) Mahoning County	4	0.01

Top 10 Places Sorted by Percent of Total Population
Based on places with total population of 50,000 or more

Place	Population	%
Dayton (city) Montgomery County	10	0.01
Youngstown (city) Mahoning County	4	0.01
Cleveland (city) Cuyahoga County	7	<0.01
Toledo (city) Lucas County	6	<0.01
Cincinnati (city) Hamilton County	4	<0.01
Akron (city) Summit County	3	<0.01
Columbus (city) Franklin County	3	<0.01
Lorain (city) Lorain County	2	<0.01
Elyria (city) Lorain County	1	<0.01
Hamilton (city) Butler County	1	<0.01

American Indian: Blackfeet

Top 10 Places Sorted by Population
Based on all places, regardless of total population

Place	Population	%
Columbus (city) Franklin County	539	0.07
Cleveland (city) Cuyahoga County	240	0.06
Cincinnati (city) Hamilton County	160	0.05
Toledo (city) Lucas County	158	0.06
Akron (city) Summit County	115	0.06
Canton (city) Stark County	100	0.14
Dayton (city) Montgomery County	100	0.07
Youngstown (city) Mahoning County	60	0.09
Lorain (city) Lorain County	54	0.08
Springfield (city) Clark County	47	0.08

Top 10 Places Sorted by Percent of Total Population
Based on all places, regardless of total population

Place	Population	%
Hollansburg (village) Darke County	3	1.32
Millfield (cdp) Athens County	4	1.17
Harveysburg (village) Warren County	6	1.10

Place	Population	%
Camp Dennison (cdp) Hamilton County	4	1.07
Trinway (cdp) Muskingum County	3	0.82
Stewart (cdp) Athens County	2	0.81
Magnetic Springs (village) Union County	2	0.75
Pleasant City (village) Guernsey County	3	0.67
Cloverdale (village) Putnam County	1	0.60
Maple Ridge (cdp) Mahoning County	4	0.53

Top 10 Places Sorted by Percent of Total Population
Based on places with total population of 50,000 or more

Place	Population	%
Canton (city) Stark County	100	0.14
Youngstown (city) Mahoning County	60	0.09
Lorain (city) Lorain County	54	0.08
Springfield (city) Clark County	47	0.08
Elyria (city) Lorain County	44	0.08
Columbus (city) Franklin County	539	0.07
Dayton (city) Montgomery County	100	0.07
Cleveland (city) Cuyahoga County	240	0.06
Toledo (city) Lucas County	158	0.06
Akron (city) Summit County	115	0.06

American Indian: Canadian/French American Indian

Top 10 Places Sorted by Population
Based on all places, regardless of total population

Place	Population	%
Toledo (city) Lucas County	23	0.01
Columbus (city) Franklin County	21	<0.01
Akron (city) Summit County	18	0.01
Cleveland (city) Cuyahoga County	7	<0.01
Salem (city) Columbiana County	6	0.05
Cincinnati (city) Hamilton County	6	<0.01
Amherst (city) Lorain County	5	0.04
Canton (city) Stark County	5	0.01
Euclid (city) Cuyahoga County	5	0.01
Findlay (city) Hancock County	5	0.01

Top 10 Places Sorted by Percent of Total Population
Based on all places, regardless of total population

Place	Population	%
Rushville (village) Fairfield County	4	1.32
McGuffey (village) Hardin County	2	0.40
Sherwood (cdp) Hamilton County	4	0.11
Shawnee Hills (cdp) Greene County	2	0.09
Fairport Harbor (village) Lake County	2	0.06
Salem (city) Columbiana County	6	0.05
Northfield (village) Summit County	2	0.05
LaGrange (village) Lorain County	1	0.05
Leipsic (village) Putnam County	1	0.05
Amherst (city) Lorain County	5	0.04

Top 10 Places Sorted by Percent of Total Population
Based on places with total population of 50,000 or more

Place	Population	%
Toledo (city) Lucas County	23	0.01
Akron (city) Summit County	18	0.01
Canton (city) Stark County	5	0.01
Columbus (city) Franklin County	21	<0.01
Cleveland (city) Cuyahoga County	7	<0.01
Cincinnati (city) Hamilton County	6	<0.01
Springfield (city) Clark County	3	<0.01
Kettering (city) Montgomery County	2	<0.01
Dayton (city) Montgomery County	1	<0.01
Lakewood (city) Cuyahoga County	1	<0.01

American Indian: Central American Indian

Top 10 Places Sorted by Population
Based on all places, regardless of total population

Place	Population	%
Cincinnati (city) Hamilton County	98	0.03
Canton (city) Stark County	45	0.06
New Philadelphia (city) Tuscarawas County	35	0.20
Dover (city) Tuscarawas County	33	0.26
Cleveland (city) Cuyahoga County	32	0.01
Massillon (city) Stark County	27	0.08
Columbus (city) Franklin County	18	<0.01
Springdale (city) Hamilton County	14	0.12
Northbrook (cdp) Hamilton County	10	0.09
Lorain (city) Lorain County	9	0.01

Top 10 Places Sorted by Percent of Total Population
Based on all places, regardless of total population

Place	Population	%
Dover (city) Tuscarawas County	33	0.26
New Philadelphia (city) Tuscarawas County	35	0.20
Cleves (village) Hamilton County	5	0.15
Crestline (city) Crawford County	6	0.13
Springdale (city) Hamilton County	14	0.12
Northbrook (cdp) Hamilton County	10	0.09
Massillon (city) Stark County	27	0.08
Canton (city) Stark County	45	0.06
Norwood (city) Hamilton County	8	0.04
Sharonville (city) Hamilton County	6	0.04

Top 10 Places Sorted by Percent of Total Population
Based on places with total population of 50,000 or more

Place	Population	%
Canton (city) Stark County	45	0.06
Cincinnati (city) Hamilton County	98	0.03
Cleveland (city) Cuyahoga County	32	0.01
Lorain (city) Lorain County	9	0.01
Lakewood (city) Cuyahoga County	3	0.01
Columbus (city) Franklin County	18	<0.01
Parma (city) Cuyahoga County	3	<0.01
Dayton (city) Montgomery County	1	<0.01
Hamilton (city) Butler County	1	<0.01
Springfield (city) Clark County	1	<0.01

American Indian: Cherokee

Top 10 Places Sorted by Population
Based on all places, regardless of total population

Place	Population	%
Columbus (city) Franklin County	2,100	0.27
Cleveland (city) Cuyahoga County	865	0.22
Toledo (city) Lucas County	784	0.27
Cincinnati (city) Hamilton County	652	0.22
Akron (city) Summit County	534	0.27
Dayton (city) Montgomery County	435	0.31
Canton (city) Stark County	327	0.45
Youngstown (city) Mahoning County	234	0.35
Springfield (city) Clark County	230	0.38
Lorain (city) Lorain County	227	0.35

Top 10 Places Sorted by Percent of Total Population
Based on all places, regardless of total population

Place	Population	%
Jacksonburg (village) Butler County	3	4.76
Rendville (village) Perry County	1	2.78
Graysville (village) Monroe County	2	2.63
West Millgrove (village) Wood County	4	2.30
Summitville (village) Columbiana County	3	2.22
Rome (village) Adams County	2	2.13
Richmond Dale (cdp) Ross County	8	2.12
Beaver (village) Pike County	9	2.00
North Robinson (village) Crawford County	4	1.95
Malinta (village) Henry County	5	1.89

Top 10 Places Sorted by Percent of Total Population
Based on places with total population of 50,000 or more

Place	Population	%
Canton (city) Stark County	327	0.45
Springfield (city) Clark County	230	0.38
Elyria (city) Lorain County	197	0.36
Youngstown (city) Mahoning County	234	0.35
Lorain (city) Lorain County	227	0.35
Dayton (city) Montgomery County	435	0.31
Hamilton (city) Butler County	172	0.28
Columbus (city) Franklin County	2,100	0.27
Toledo (city) Lucas County	784	0.27
Akron (city) Summit County	534	0.27

American Indian: Cheyenne

Top 10 Places Sorted by Population
Based on all places, regardless of total population

Place	Population	%
Columbus (city) Franklin County	15	<0.01
Akron (city) Summit County	14	0.01
Franklin (city) Warren County	7	0.06
Cleveland (city) Cuyahoga County	7	<0.01
Zanesville (city) Muskingum County	6	0.02
Warren (city) Trumbull County	6	0.01
Toledo (city) Lucas County	6	<0.01
Tuppers Plains (cdp) Meigs County	5	1.08
Canton (city) Stark County	5	0.01
Parma (city) Cuyahoga County	5	0.01

Top 10 Places Sorted by Percent of Total Population
Based on all places, regardless of total population

Place	Population	%
Tuppers Plains (cdp) Meigs County	5	1.08
South Vienna (village) Clark County	2	0.52
Rocky Ridge (village) Ottawa County	1	0.24
Coolville (village) Athens County	1	0.20
Brookside (village) Belmont County	1	0.16
Smithfield (village) Jefferson County	1	0.12
Franklin (city) Warren County	7	0.06
Logan (city) Hocking County	4	0.06
Holland (village) Lucas County	1	0.06
Pleasant Grove (cdp) Muskingum County	1	0.06

Top 10 Places Sorted by Percent of Total Population
Based on places with total population of 50,000 or more

Place	Population	%
Akron (city) Summit County	14	0.01
Canton (city) Stark County	5	0.01
Parma (city) Cuyahoga County	5	0.01
Elyria (city) Lorain County	4	0.01
Springfield (city) Clark County	4	0.01
Columbus (city) Franklin County	15	<0.01
Cleveland (city) Cuyahoga County	7	<0.01
Toledo (city) Lucas County	6	<0.01
Dayton (city) Montgomery County	4	<0.01
Hamilton (city) Butler County	2	<0.01

American Indian: Chickasaw

Top 10 Places Sorted by Population
Based on all places, regardless of total population

Place	Population	%
Cleveland (city) Cuyahoga County	34	0.01
Columbus (city) Franklin County	23	<0.01
Cincinnati (city) Hamilton County	11	<0.01
Akron (city) Summit County	9	<0.01
Napoleon (city) Henry County	8	0.09
Toledo (city) Lucas County	7	<0.01
Lakewood (city) Cuyahoga County	6	0.01
Nevada (village) Wyandot County	5	0.66
Fairborn (city) Greene County	5	0.02
Lorain (city) Lorain County	5	0.01

Top 10 Places Sorted by Percent of Total Population
Based on all places, regardless of total population

Place	Population	%
Nevada (village) Wyandot County	5	0.66
Latty (village) Paulding County	1	0.52
Holiday Lakes (cdp) Huron County	1	0.13
Napoleon (city) Henry County	8	0.09
Crestline (city) Crawford County	4	0.09
Tuscarawas (village) Tuscarawas County	1	0.09
Crystal Lakes (cdp) Clark County	1	0.07
McArthur (village) Vinton County	1	0.06
Elmwood Place (village) Hamilton County	1	0.05
Oberlin (city) Lorain County	3	0.04

Top 10 Places Sorted by Percent of Total Population
Based on places with total population of 50,000 or more

Place	Population	%
Cleveland (city) Cuyahoga County	34	0.01
Lakewood (city) Cuyahoga County	6	0.01
Lorain (city) Lorain County	5	0.01
Elyria (city) Lorain County	3	0.01
Columbus (city) Franklin County	23	<0.01
Cincinnati (city) Hamilton County	11	<0.01
Akron (city) Summit County	9	<0.01
Toledo (city) Lucas County	7	<0.01
Canton (city) Stark County	2	<0.01
Dayton (city) Montgomery County	1	<0.01

American Indian: Chippewa

Top 10 Places Sorted by Population
Based on all places, regardless of total population

Place	Population	%
Toledo (city) Lucas County	139	0.05
Columbus (city) Franklin County	112	0.01
Cleveland (city) Cuyahoga County	54	0.01
Cincinnati (city) Hamilton County	29	0.01
Dayton (city) Montgomery County	23	0.02
Akron (city) Summit County	20	0.01
Lima (city) Allen County	12	0.03
Cuyahoga Falls (city) Summit County	12	0.02
Oregon (city) Lucas County	11	0.05
Elyria (city) Lorain County	11	0.02

Top 10 Places Sorted by Percent of Total Population
Based on all places, regardless of total population

Place	Population	%
Port William (village) Clinton County	3	1.18
Castine (village) Darke County	1	0.77
Cherry Fork (village) Adams County	1	0.65
Plumwood (cdp) Madison County	2	0.63
Lake Tomahawk (cdp) Columbiana County	2	0.41
Orwell (village) Ashtabula County	4	0.24
Skyline Acres (cdp) Hamilton County	4	0.23
Portage (village) Wood County	1	0.23
Mount Pleasant (village) Jefferson County	1	0.21
Spring Valley (village) Greene County	1	0.21

Top 10 Places Sorted by Percent of Total Population
Based on places with total population of 50,000 or more

Place	Population	%
Toledo (city) Lucas County	139	0.05
Dayton (city) Montgomery County	23	0.02
Elyria (city) Lorain County	11	0.02
Lakewood (city) Cuyahoga County	11	0.02
Lorain (city) Lorain County	11	0.02
Columbus (city) Franklin County	112	0.01
Cleveland (city) Cuyahoga County	54	0.01
Cincinnati (city) Hamilton County	29	0.01
Akron (city) Summit County	20	0.01
Kettering (city) Montgomery County	8	0.01

American Indian: Choctaw

Top 10 Places Sorted by Population
Based on all places, regardless of total population

Place	Population	%
Cleveland (city) Cuyahoga County	83	0.02
Columbus (city) Franklin County	72	0.01
Toledo (city) Lucas County	59	0.02
Akron (city) Summit County	42	0.02
Cincinnati (city) Hamilton County	26	0.01
Parma (city) Cuyahoga County	15	0.02
Youngstown (city) Mahoning County	14	0.02
Gahanna (city) Franklin County	13	0.04
Warren (city) Trumbull County	13	0.03
Shaker Heights (city) Cuyahoga County	11	0.04

Top 10 Places Sorted by Percent of Total Population
Based on all places, regardless of total population

Place	Population	%
South Amherst (village) Lorain County	9	0.53
Brady Lake (village) Portage County	2	0.43
Christiansburg (village) Champaign County	2	0.38
Commercial Point (village) Pickaway County	5	0.32
Gibsonburg (village) Sandusky County	7	0.27
Bloomville (village) Seneca County	2	0.21
North Randall (village) Cuyahoga County	2	0.19
Cairo (village) Allen County	1	0.19
Dry Ridge (cdp) Hamilton County	5	0.18
Harveysburg (village) Warren County	1	0.18

Top 10 Places Sorted by Percent of Total Population
Based on places with total population of 50,000 or more

Place	Population	%
Cleveland (city) Cuyahoga County	83	0.02
Toledo (city) Lucas County	59	0.02
Akron (city) Summit County	42	0.02
Parma (city) Cuyahoga County	15	0.02
Youngstown (city) Mahoning County	14	0.02
Lakewood (city) Cuyahoga County	9	0.02
Columbus (city) Franklin County	72	0.01
Cincinnati (city) Hamilton County	26	0.01
Dayton (city) Montgomery County	9	0.01
Springfield (city) Clark County	9	0.01

American Indian: Colville

Top 10 Places Sorted by Population
Based on all places, regardless of total population

Place	Population	%
Dent (cdp) Hamilton County	3	0.03
Cleveland (city) Cuyahoga County	3	<0.01
Hudson (city) Summit County	2	0.01
Silver Lake (village) Summit County	1	0.04
Jackson (city) Jackson County	1	0.02
Columbus (city) Franklin County	1	<0.01
Aberdeen (village) Brown County	0	0.00
Ada (village) Hardin County	0	0.00
Adamsville (village) Muskingum County	0	0.00
Addyston (village) Hamilton County	0	0.00

Top 10 Places Sorted by Percent of Total Population
Based on all places, regardless of total population

Place	Population	%
Silver Lake (village) Summit County	1	0.04
Dent (cdp) Hamilton County	3	0.03
Jackson (city) Jackson County	1	0.02
Hudson (city) Summit County	2	0.01
Cleveland (city) Cuyahoga County	3	<0.01
Columbus (city) Franklin County	1	<0.01
Aberdeen (village) Brown County	0	0.00
Ada (village) Hardin County	0	0.00
Adamsville (village) Muskingum County	0	0.00
Addyston (village) Hamilton County	0	0.00

Top 10 Places Sorted by Percent of Total Population
Based on places with total population of 50,000 or more

Place	Population	%
Cleveland (city) Cuyahoga County	3	<0.01
Columbus (city) Franklin County	1	<0.01
Akron (city) Summit County	0	0.00
Canton (city) Stark County	0	0.00
Cincinnati (city) Hamilton County	0	0.00
Dayton (city) Montgomery County	0	0.00
Elyria (city) Lorain County	0	0.00
Hamilton (city) Butler County	0	0.00
Kettering (city) Montgomery County	0	0.00
Lakewood (city) Cuyahoga County	0	0.00

American Indian: Comanche

Top 10 Places Sorted by Population
Based on all places, regardless of total population

Place	Population	%
Columbus (city) Franklin County	17	<0.01
Wadsworth (city) Medina County	8	0.04
Grove City (city) Franklin County	8	0.02
Cincinnati (city) Hamilton County	7	<0.01
Steubenville (city) Jefferson County	6	0.03
Springfield (city) Clark County	6	0.01
Warren (city) Trumbull County	6	0.01
Youngstown (city) Mahoning County	6	0.01
Canton (city) Stark County	5	0.01
Akron (city) Summit County	5	<0.01

Top 10 Places Sorted by Percent of Total Population
Based on all places, regardless of total population

Place	Population	%
Seaman (village) Adams County	1	0.11
Bethesda (village) Belmont County	1	0.08
Mariemont (village) Hamilton County	2	0.06
Lewisburg (village) Preble County	1	0.05
Newburgh Heights (village) Cuyahoga County	1	0.05
Wadsworth (city) Medina County	8	0.04
Celina (city) Mercer County	4	0.04
Heath (city) Licking County	4	0.04
Wellston (city) Jackson County	2	0.04
Gambier (village) Knox County	1	0.04

Top 10 Places Sorted by Percent of Total Population
Based on places with total population of 50,000 or more

Place	Population	%
Springfield (city) Clark County	6	0.01
Youngstown (city) Mahoning County	6	0.01
Canton (city) Stark County	5	0.01
Columbus (city) Franklin County	17	<0.01
Cincinnati (city) Hamilton County	7	<0.01
Akron (city) Summit County	5	<0.01
Cleveland (city) Cuyahoga County	3	<0.01
Parma (city) Cuyahoga County	3	<0.01
Toledo (city) Lucas County	3	<0.01
Dayton (city) Montgomery County	2	<0.01

American Indian: Cree

Top 10 Places Sorted by Population
Based on all places, regardless of total population

Place	Population	%
Columbus (city) Franklin County	17	<0.01
Akron (city) Summit County	8	<0.01
Zanesville (city) Muskingum County	6	0.02
Cincinnati (city) Hamilton County	6	<0.01
Toledo (city) Lucas County	6	<0.01
Newtown (village) Hamilton County	5	0.19
Warren (city) Trumbull County	5	0.01
McDermott (cdp) Scioto County	4	0.92
Bainbridge (cdp) Geauga County	3	0.09
Greenhills (village) Hamilton County	3	0.08

Top 10 Places Sorted by Percent of Total Population
Based on all places, regardless of total population

Place	Population	%
McDermott (cdp) Scioto County	4	0.92
Newtown (village) Hamilton County	5	0.19
Clarksville (village) Clinton County	1	0.18
Bainbridge (cdp) Geauga County	3	0.09
Greenhills (village) Hamilton County	3	0.08
Smithville (village) Wayne County	1	0.08
Hiram (village) Portage County	1	0.07
Peebles (village) Adams County	1	0.06
Union City (village) Darke County	1	0.06
Glenmoor (cdp) Columbiana County	1	0.05

Top 10 Places Sorted by Percent of Total Population
Based on places with total population of 50,000 or more

Place	Population	%
Columbus (city) Franklin County	17	<0.01
Akron (city) Summit County	8	<0.01
Cincinnati (city) Hamilton County	6	<0.01
Toledo (city) Lucas County	6	<0.01
Cleveland (city) Cuyahoga County	3	<0.01
Hamilton (city) Butler County	2	<0.01
Springfield (city) Clark County	2	<0.01
Lakewood (city) Cuyahoga County	1	<0.01
Lorain (city) Lorain County	1	<0.01
Canton (city) Stark County	0	0.00

American Indian: Creek

Top 10 Places Sorted by Population
Based on all places, regardless of total population

Place	Population	%
Columbus (city) Franklin County	47	0.01
Cincinnati (city) Hamilton County	23	0.01
Cleveland (city) Cuyahoga County	23	0.01
Toledo (city) Lucas County	23	0.01
Dayton (city) Montgomery County	17	0.01
Akron (city) Summit County	16	0.01
Lancaster (city) Fairfield County	12	0.03
Kettering (city) Montgomery County	8	0.01
Dennison (village) Tuscarawas County	7	0.26
Sheffield Lake (city) Lorain County	7	0.08

Top 10 Places Sorted by Percent of Total Population
Based on all places, regardless of total population

Place	Population	%
Lake Lorelei (cdp) Brown County	4	0.34
Thurston (village) Fairfield County	2	0.33
Pomeroy (village) Meigs County	5	0.27

Whites Landing (cdp) Erie County	1	0.27
Dennison (village) Tuscarawas County	7	0.26
Rocky Ridge (village) Ottawa County	1	0.24
Lake Waynoka (cdp) Brown County	2	0.17
Fredericktown (village) Knox County	4	0.16
Kinsman Center (cdp) Trumbull County	1	0.16
Buckeye Lake (village) Licking County	3	0.11

Top 10 Places Sorted by Percent of Total Population

Based on places with total population of 50,000 or more

Place	Population	%
Columbus (city) Franklin County	47	0.01
Cincinnati (city) Hamilton County	23	0.01
Cleveland (city) Cuyahoga County	23	0.01
Toledo (city) Lucas County	23	0.01
Dayton (city) Montgomery County	17	0.01
Akron (city) Summit County	16	0.01
Kettering (city) Montgomery County	8	0.01
Lakewood (city) Cuyahoga County	7	0.01
Springfield (city) Clark County	7	0.01
Hamilton (city) Butler County	6	0.01

American Indian: Crow

Top 10 Places Sorted by Population

Based on all places, regardless of total population

Place	Population	%
Columbus (city) Franklin County	12	<0.01
Cleveland (city) Cuyahoga County	10	<0.01
Alliance (city) Stark County	7	0.03
Akron (city) Summit County	6	<0.01
Centerville (city) Montgomery County	5	0.02
Cincinnati (city) Hamilton County	5	<0.01
Toledo (city) Lucas County	5	<0.01
Loveland (city) Hamilton County	4	0.03
Latty (village) Paulding County	3	1.55
Oakwood (city) Montgomery County	3	0.03

Top 10 Places Sorted by Percent of Total Population

Based on all places, regardless of total population

Place	Population	%
Latty (village) Paulding County	3	1.55
Collins (cdp) Huron County	1	0.16
Shawnee (village) Perry County	1	0.15
Woodsfield (village) Monroe County	2	0.08
Jackson Center (village) Shelby County	1	0.07
Gallipolis (village) Gallia County	2	0.05
Glenmoor (cdp) Columbiana County	1	0.05
Lucasville (cdp) Scioto County	1	0.04
Alliance (city) Stark County	7	0.03
Loveland (city) Hamilton County	4	0.03

Top 10 Places Sorted by Percent of Total Population

Based on places with total population of 50,000 or more

Place	Population	%
Columbus (city) Franklin County	12	<0.01
Cleveland (city) Cuyahoga County	10	<0.01
Akron (city) Summit County	6	<0.01
Cincinnati (city) Hamilton County	5	<0.01
Toledo (city) Lucas County	5	<0.01
Canton (city) Stark County	3	<0.01
Springfield (city) Clark County	2	<0.01
Youngstown (city) Mahoning County	2	<0.01
Kettering (city) Montgomery County	1	<0.01
Parma (city) Cuyahoga County	1	<0.01

American Indian: Delaware

Top 10 Places Sorted by Population

Based on all places, regardless of total population

Place	Population	%
Canton (city) Stark County	57	0.08
Columbus (city) Franklin County	40	0.01
Akron (city) Summit County	17	0.01
Zanesville (city) Muskingum County	12	0.05
Toledo (city) Lucas County	11	<0.01
Cleveland (city) Cuyahoga County	10	<0.01
New Philadelphia (city) Tuscarawas County	8	0.05
Massillon (city) Stark County	7	0.02
Newark (city) Licking County	7	0.01
Ashtabula (city) Ashtabula County	6	0.03

Top 10 Places Sorted by Percent of Total Population

Based on all places, regardless of total population

Place	Population	%
Bailey Lakes (village) Ashland County	4	1.08
Robertsville (cdp) Stark County	3	0.91
Dexter City (village) Noble County	1	0.78
Kimbolton (cdp) Guernsey County	1	0.69
Sherrodsville (village) Carroll County	2	0.66
Belle Valley (village) Noble County	1	0.45
Eaton Estates (cdp) Lorain County	5	0.41
Urbancrest (village) Franklin County	3	0.31
New Concord (village) Muskingum County	4	0.16
Rocky Fork Point (cdp) Highland County	1	0.16

Top 10 Places Sorted by Percent of Total Population

Based on places with total population of 50,000 or more

Place	Population	%
Canton (city) Stark County	57	0.08
Columbus (city) Franklin County	40	0.01
Akron (city) Summit County	17	0.01
Springfield (city) Clark County	6	0.01
Lakewood (city) Cuyahoga County	4	0.01
Toledo (city) Lucas County	11	<0.01
Cleveland (city) Cuyahoga County	10	<0.01
Cincinnati (city) Hamilton County	5	<0.01
Lorain (city) Lorain County	2	<0.01
Dayton (city) Montgomery County	1	<0.01

American Indian: Hopi

Top 10 Places Sorted by Population

Based on all places, regardless of total population

Place	Population	%
Columbus (city) Franklin County	9	<0.01
LaGrange (village) Lorain County	6	0.29
Latty (village) Paulding County	5	2.59
Jackson (city) Jackson County	5	0.08
Springfield (city) Clark County	5	0.01
Canton (city) Stark County	4	0.01
Cleveland (city) Cuyahoga County	4	<0.01
Toledo (city) Lucas County	4	<0.01
Columbus Grove (village) Putnam County	3	0.14
McDonald (village) Trumbull County	3	0.09

Top 10 Places Sorted by Percent of Total Population

Based on all places, regardless of total population

Place	Population	%
Latty (village) Paulding County	5	2.59
LaGrange (village) Lorain County	6	0.29
Columbus Grove (village) Putnam County	3	0.14
West Salem (village) Wayne County	2	0.14
McDonald (village) Trumbull County	3	0.09
Jackson (city) Jackson County	5	0.08
Eaton Estates (cdp) Lorain County	1	0.08
Yellow Springs (village) Greene County	2	0.06
Leavittsburg (cdp) Trumbull County	1	0.05
Leipsic (village) Putnam County	1	0.05

Top 10 Places Sorted by Percent of Total Population

Based on places with total population of 50,000 or more

Place	Population	%
Springfield (city) Clark County	5	0.01
Canton (city) Stark County	4	0.01
Columbus (city) Franklin County	9	<0.01
Cleveland (city) Cuyahoga County	4	<0.01
Toledo (city) Lucas County	4	<0.01
Youngstown (city) Mahoning County	2	<0.01
Dayton (city) Montgomery County	1	<0.01
Lorain (city) Lorain County	1	<0.01
Akron (city) Summit County	0	0.00
Cincinnati (city) Hamilton County	0	0.00

American Indian: Houma

Top 10 Places Sorted by Population

Based on all places, regardless of total population

Place	Population	%
Groveport (village) Franklin County	4	0.07
Vermilion (city) Lorain County	3	0.03
Reynoldsburg (city) Franklin County	3	0.01
Wooster (city) Wayne County	3	0.01
Bowling Green (city) Wood County	2	0.01
Risingsun (village) Wood County	1	0.17
Oberlin (city) Lorain County	1	0.01
Canton (city) Stark County	1	<0.01
Middletown (city) Butler County	1	<0.01
Aberdeen (village) Brown County	0	0.00

Top 10 Places Sorted by Percent of Total Population

Based on all places, regardless of total population

Place	Population	%
Risingsun (village) Wood County	1	0.17
Groveport (village) Franklin County	4	0.07
Vermilion (city) Lorain County	3	0.03
Reynoldsburg (city) Franklin County	3	0.01
Wooster (city) Wayne County	3	0.01
Bowling Green (city) Wood County	2	0.01
Oberlin (city) Lorain County	1	0.01
Canton (city) Stark County	1	<0.01
Middletown (city) Butler County	1	<0.01
Aberdeen (village) Brown County	0	0.00

Top 10 Places Sorted by Percent of Total Population

Based on places with total population of 50,000 or more

Place	Population	%
Canton (city) Stark County	1	<0.01
Akron (city) Summit County	0	0.00
Cincinnati (city) Hamilton County	0	0.00
Cleveland (city) Cuyahoga County	0	0.00
Columbus (city) Franklin County	0	0.00
Dayton (city) Montgomery County	0	0.00
Elyria (city) Lorain County	0	0.00
Hamilton (city) Butler County	0	0.00
Kettering (city) Montgomery County	0	0.00
Lakewood (city) Cuyahoga County	0	0.00

Alaska Native: Inupiat (Eskimo)

Top 10 Places Sorted by Population

Based on all places, regardless of total population

Place	Population	%
Willowick (city) Lake County	7	0.05
Fremont (city) Sandusky County	6	0.04
Cleveland (city) Cuyahoga County	6	<0.01
New Carlisle (city) Clark County	4	0.07
Sylvania (city) Lucas County	4	0.02
Akron (city) Summit County	4	<0.01
North Canton (city) Stark County	3	0.02
Perrysburg (city) Wood County	3	0.01
Columbus (city) Franklin County	3	<0.01
Toledo (city) Lucas County	3	<0.01

Top 10 Places Sorted by Percent of Total Population

Based on all places, regardless of total population

Place	Population	%
East Fultonham (cdp) Muskingum County	1	0.30
Williamsdale (cdp) Butler County	1	0.17
Monroeville (village) Huron County	2	0.14
New Carlisle (city) Clark County	4	0.07
Lodi (village) Medina County	2	0.07
Willowick (city) Lake County	7	0.05
Brewster (village) Stark County	1	0.05
Fremont (city) Sandusky County	6	0.04
Beechwood Trails (cdp) Licking County	1	0.03
Sylvania (city) Lucas County	4	0.02

Top 10 Places Sorted by Percent of Total Population

Based on places with total population of 50,000 or more

Place	Population	%
Cleveland (city) Cuyahoga County	6	<0.01
Akron (city) Summit County	4	<0.01
Columbus (city) Franklin County	3	<0.01
Toledo (city) Lucas County	3	<0.01
Canton (city) Stark County	2	<0.01
Parma (city) Cuyahoga County	2	<0.01
Youngstown (city) Mahoning County	2	<0.01
Cincinnati (city) Hamilton County	1	<0.01
Elyria (city) Lorain County	1	<0.01
Kettering (city) Montgomery County	1	<0.01

American Indian: Iroquois

Top 10 Places Sorted by Population

Based on all places, regardless of total population

Place	Population	%
Columbus (city) Franklin County	126	0.02
Cleveland (city) Cuyahoga County	62	0.02
Akron (city) Summit County	41	0.02
Toledo (city) Lucas County	39	0.01
Canton (city) Stark County	31	0.04
Dayton (city) Montgomery County	19	0.01
Cincinnati (city) Hamilton County	18	0.01
Elyria (city) Lorain County	17	0.03
Cleveland Heights (city) Cuyahoga County	15	0.03
Lorain (city) Lorain County	14	0.02

Top 10 Places Sorted by Percent of Total Population

Based on all places, regardless of total population

Place	Population	%
Stafford (village) Monroe County	1	1.23
Cygnet (village) Wood County	4	0.67
Matamoras (village) Washington County	4	0.45
Flat Rock (cdp) Seneca County	1	0.43
Miamiville (cdp) Clermont County	1	0.41
Marshallville (village) Wayne County	3	0.40
Maple Ridge (cdp) Mahoning County	3	0.39
Beverly (village) Washington County	5	0.38
Hamler (village) Henry County	2	0.35
Potsdam (village) Miami County	1	0.35

Top 10 Places Sorted by Percent of Total Population

Based on places with total population of 50,000 or more

Place	Population	%
Canton (city) Stark County	31	0.04
Elyria (city) Lorain County	17	0.03
Columbus (city) Franklin County	126	0.02
Cleveland (city) Cuyahoga County	62	0.02
Akron (city) Summit County	41	0.02
Lorain (city) Lorain County	14	0.02
Parma (city) Cuyahoga County	13	0.02
Hamilton (city) Butler County	11	0.02
Youngstown (city) Mahoning County	11	0.02
Lakewood (city) Cuyahoga County	10	0.02

American Indian: Kiowa

Top 10 Places Sorted by Population

Based on all places, regardless of total population

Place	Population	%
Cleveland (city) Cuyahoga County	11	<0.01
Yellow Springs (village) Greene County	5	0.14
Jackson (city) Jackson County	4	0.06
St. Marys (city) Auglaize County	4	0.05
Minerva (village) Stark County	3	0.08
Ironton (city) Lawrence County	3	0.03
Marysville (city) Union County	2	0.01
Xenia (city) Greene County	2	0.01
Hamilton (city) Butler County	2	<0.01
Lorain (city) Lorain County	2	<0.01

Top 10 Places Sorted by Percent of Total Population

Based on all places, regardless of total population

Place	Population	%
Yellow Springs (village) Greene County	5	0.14
Minerva (village) Stark County	3	0.08
Jackson (city) Jackson County	4	0.06
Anna (village) Shelby County	1	0.06
St. Marys (city) Auglaize County	4	0.05
Rossmoyne (cdp) Hamilton County	1	0.04
Ironton (city) Lawrence County	3	0.03
Sixteen Mile Stand (cdp) Hamilton County	1	0.03
Marysville (city) Union County	2	0.01
Xenia (city) Greene County	2	0.01

Top 10 Places Sorted by Percent of Total Population

Based on places with total population of 50,000 or more

Place	Population	%
Cleveland (city) Cuyahoga County	11	<0.01
Hamilton (city) Butler County	2	<0.01
Lorain (city) Lorain County	2	<0.01
Columbus (city) Franklin County	1	<0.01
Toledo (city) Lucas County	1	<0.01
Akron (city) Summit County	0	0.00
Canton (city) Stark County	0	0.00
Cincinnati (city) Hamilton County	0	0.00
Dayton (city) Montgomery County	0	0.00
Elyria (city) Lorain County	0	0.00

American Indian: Lumbee

Top 10 Places Sorted by Population

Based on all places, regardless of total population

Place	Population	%
Columbus (city) Franklin County	56	0.01
Toledo (city) Lucas County	14	<0.01
Strongsville (city) Cuyahoga County	12	0.03
Cleveland (city) Cuyahoga County	9	<0.01
Delaware (city) Delaware County	8	0.02
Elyria (city) Lorain County	8	0.01
London (city) Madison County	6	0.06
Middleport (village) Meigs County	5	0.20
Blanchester (village) Clinton County	5	0.12
Alliance (city) Stark County	5	0.02

Top 10 Places Sorted by Percent of Total Population

Based on all places, regardless of total population

Place	Population	%
Marseilles (village) Wyandot County	1	0.89
Gratis (village) Preble County	3	0.34
Middleport (village) Meigs County	5	0.20
Hamersville (village) Brown County	1	0.18
Jeffersonville (village) Fayette County	2	0.17
Proctorville (village) Lawrence County	1	0.17
Piketon (village) Pike County	3	0.14
Blanchester (village) Clinton County	5	0.12
Rio Grande (village) Gallia County	1	0.12
Greentown (cdp) Stark County	3	0.08

Top 10 Places Sorted by Percent of Total Population

Based on places with total population of 50,000 or more

Place	Population	%
Columbus (city) Franklin County	56	0.01
Elyria (city) Lorain County	8	0.01
Canton (city) Stark County	5	0.01
Toledo (city) Lucas County	14	<0.01
Cleveland (city) Cuyahoga County	9	<0.01
Akron (city) Summit County	5	<0.01
Cincinnati (city) Hamilton County	4	<0.01
Parma (city) Cuyahoga County	3	<0.01
Dayton (city) Montgomery County	2	<0.01
Lorain (city) Lorain County	2	<0.01

American Indian: Menominee

Top 10 Places Sorted by Population

Based on all places, regardless of total population

Place	Population	%
Toledo (city) Lucas County	11	<0.01
Dayton (city) Montgomery County	6	<0.01
Lima (city) Allen County	4	0.01
New Knoxville (village) Auglaize County	3	0.34
Columbus (city) Franklin County	3	<0.01
Martins Ferry (city) Belmont County	2	0.03
Euclid (city) Cuyahoga County	2	<0.01
Franklin Furnace (cdp) Scioto County	1	0.06
Northwood (city) Wood County	1	0.02
Bedford Heights (city) Cuyahoga County	1	0.01

Top 10 Places Sorted by Percent of Total Population

Based on all places, regardless of total population

Place	Population	%
New Knoxville (village) Auglaize County	3	0.34
Franklin Furnace (cdp) Scioto County	1	0.06
Martins Ferry (city) Belmont County	2	0.03
Northwood (city) Wood County	1	0.02
Lima (city) Allen County	4	0.01
Bedford Heights (city) Cuyahoga County	1	0.01
Greenville (city) Darke County	1	0.01
Marietta (city) Washington County	1	0.01
Monfort Heights (cdp) Hamilton County	1	0.01
Ravenna (city) Portage County	1	0.01

Top 10 Places Sorted by Percent of Total Population

Based on places with total population of 50,000 or more

Place	Population	%
Toledo (city) Lucas County	11	<0.01
Dayton (city) Montgomery County	6	<0.01
Columbus (city) Franklin County	3	<0.01
Cincinnati (city) Hamilton County	1	<0.01
Youngstown (city) Mahoning County	1	<0.01
Akron (city) Summit County	0	0.00
Canton (city) Stark County	0	0.00
Cleveland (city) Cuyahoga County	0	0.00
Elyria (city) Lorain County	0	0.00
Hamilton (city) Butler County	0	0.00

American Indian: Mexican American Indian

Top 10 Places Sorted by Population

Based on all places, regardless of total population

Place	Population	%
Columbus (city) Franklin County	203	0.03
Toledo (city) Lucas County	96	0.03
Cleveland (city) Cuyahoga County	60	0.02
Cincinnati (city) Hamilton County	38	0.01
Northbrook (cdp) Hamilton County	30	0.28
Canton (city) Stark County	24	0.03
New Philadelphia (city) Tuscarawas County	21	0.12
Youngstown (city) Mahoning County	19	0.03
Lorain (city) Lorain County	16	0.02
Akron (city) Summit County	14	0.01

Top 10 Places Sorted by Percent of Total Population

Based on all places, regardless of total population

Place	Population	%
Highland (village) Highland County	3	1.18
Beaverdam (village) Allen County	3	0.79
Hooven (cdp) Hamilton County	4	0.75
Castalia (village) Erie County	5	0.59
Hessville (cdp) Sandusky County	1	0.47
Alvordton (cdp) Williams County	1	0.46
Addyston (village) Hamilton County	4	0.43
Malinta (village) Henry County	1	0.38
Berlin (cdp) Holmes County	3	0.33
New Marshfield (cdp) Athens County	1	0.31

Top 10 Places Sorted by Percent of Total Population

Based on places with total population of 50,000 or more

Place	Population	%
Columbus (city) Franklin County	203	0.03
Toledo (city) Lucas County	96	0.03
Canton (city) Stark County	24	0.03
Youngstown (city) Mahoning County	19	0.03
Cleveland (city) Cuyahoga County	60	0.02
Lorain (city) Lorain County	16	0.02
Hamilton (city) Butler County	11	0.02
Lakewood (city) Cuyahoga County	9	0.02
Cincinnati (city) Hamilton County	38	0.01
Akron (city) Summit County	14	0.01

American Indian: Navajo

Top 10 Places Sorted by Population

Based on all places, regardless of total population

Place	Population	%
Columbus (city) Franklin County	68	0.01
Cincinnati (city) Hamilton County	31	0.01
Cleveland (city) Cuyahoga County	31	0.01
Toledo (city) Lucas County	30	0.01
Canton (city) Stark County	16	0.02
Akron (city) Summit County	15	0.01
Lakewood (city) Cuyahoga County	13	0.02
Parma (city) Cuyahoga County	13	0.02
Dayton (city) Montgomery County	13	0.01
Miamisburg (city) Montgomery County	11	0.05

Top 10 Places Sorted by Percent of Total Population

Based on all places, regardless of total population

Place	Population	%
Higginsport (village) Brown County	2	0.80
Quincy (village) Logan County	2	0.28

South Solon (village) Madison County	1	0.28
Weston (village) Wood County	4	0.25
Buffalo (cdp) Guernsey County	1	0.25
South Amherst (village) Lorain County	3	0.18
Highland Holiday (cdp) Highland County	1	0.18
The Plains (cdp) Athens County	5	0.16
Waynesville (village) Warren County	4	0.14
New Straitsville (village) Perry County	1	0.14

Top 10 Places Sorted by Percent of Total Population

Based on places with total population of 50,000 or more

Place	Population	%
Canton (city) Stark County	16	0.02
Lakewood (city) Cuyahoga County	13	0.02
Parma (city) Cuyahoga County	13	0.02
Columbus (city) Franklin County	68	0.01
Cincinnati (city) Hamilton County	31	0.01
Cleveland (city) Cuyahoga County	31	0.01
Toledo (city) Lucas County	30	0.01
Akron (city) Summit County	15	0.01
Dayton (city) Montgomery County	13	0.01
Lorain (city) Lorain County	7	0.01

American Indian: Osage

Top 10 Places Sorted by Population

Based on all places, regardless of total population

Place	Population	%
Columbus (city) Franklin County	7	<0.01
Springfield (city) Clark County	6	0.01
Zanesville (city) Muskingum County	5	0.02
Coldstream (cdp) Hamilton County	3	0.26
Minerva Park (village) Franklin County	3	0.24
Byesville (village) Guernsey County	3	0.12
Cleves (village) Hamilton County	3	0.09
Avon Lake (city) Lorain County	3	0.01
Beavercreek (city) Greene County	3	0.01
Lima (city) Allen County	3	0.01

Top 10 Places Sorted by Percent of Total Population

Based on all places, regardless of total population

Place	Population	%
New Haven (cdp) Hamilton County	2	0.34
Coldstream (cdp) Hamilton County	3	0.26
Minerva Park (village) Franklin County	3	0.24
Pioneer (village) Williams County	2	0.14
Byesville (village) Guernsey County	3	0.12
Cleves (village) Hamilton County	3	0.09
Williamsburg (village) Clermont County	1	0.04
Withamsville (cdp) Clermont County	2	0.03
Fort Shawnee (village) Allen County	1	0.03
Mount Healthy Heights (cdp) Hamilton County	1	0.03

Top 10 Places Sorted by Percent of Total Population

Based on places with total population of 50,000 or more

Place	Population	%
Springfield (city) Clark County	6	0.01
Columbus (city) Franklin County	7	<0.01
Akron (city) Summit County	3	<0.01
Cincinnati (city) Hamilton County	3	<0.01
Toledo (city) Lucas County	3	<0.01
Dayton (city) Montgomery County	1	<0.01
Elyria (city) Lorain County	1	<0.01
Parma (city) Cuyahoga County	1	<0.01
Canton (city) Stark County	0	0.00
Cleveland (city) Cuyahoga County	0	0.00

American Indian: Ottawa

Top 10 Places Sorted by Population

Based on all places, regardless of total population

Place	Population	%
Toledo (city) Lucas County	41	0.01
Columbus (city) Franklin County	13	<0.01
Sandusky (city) Erie County	9	0.03
Cleveland (city) Cuyahoga County	7	<0.01
Dayton (city) Montgomery County	6	<0.01
Germantown (village) Montgomery County	5	0.09
Pomeroy (village) Meigs County	4	0.22
Bedford Heights (city) Cuyahoga County	4	0.04
Cuyahoga Falls (city) Summit County	4	0.01
Akron (city) Summit County	4	<0.01

Top 10 Places Sorted by Percent of Total Population

Based on all places, regardless of total population

Place	Population	%
Crystal Rock (cdp) Erie County	1	0.57
Hooven (cdp) Hamilton County	3	0.56
Athalia (village) Lawrence County	1	0.27
Pomeroy (village) Meigs County	4	0.22
Bay View (village) Erie County	1	0.16
Ashley (village) Delaware County	2	0.15
Genoa (village) Ottawa County	3	0.13
Germantown (village) Montgomery County	5	0.09
Caldwell (village) Noble County	1	0.06
Plain City (village) Madison County	2	0.05

Top 10 Places Sorted by Percent of Total Population

Based on places with total population of 50,000 or more

Place	Population	%
Toledo (city) Lucas County	41	0.01
Columbus (city) Franklin County	13	<0.01
Cleveland (city) Cuyahoga County	7	<0.01
Dayton (city) Montgomery County	6	<0.01
Akron (city) Summit County	4	<0.01
Lorain (city) Lorain County	2	<0.01
Canton (city) Stark County	1	<0.01
Cincinnati (city) Hamilton County	1	<0.01
Kettering (city) Montgomery County	1	<0.01
Springfield (city) Clark County	1	<0.01

American Indian: Paiute

Top 10 Places Sorted by Population

Based on all places, regardless of total population

Place	Population	%
Warren (city) Trumbull County	5	0.01
Pickerington (city) Fairfield County	3	0.02
Beavercreek (city) Greene County	3	0.01
Wheelersburg (cdp) Scioto County	2	0.03
Amherst (city) Lorain County	2	0.02
Reynoldsburg (city) Franklin County	2	0.01
Roseville (village) Perry County	1	0.05
Munroe Falls (city) Summit County	1	0.02
Pleasant Run (cdp) Hamilton County	1	0.02
East Liverpool (city) Columbiana County	1	0.01

Top 10 Places Sorted by Percent of Total Population

Based on all places, regardless of total population

Place	Population	%
Roseville (village) Perry County	1	0.05
Wheelersburg (cdp) Scioto County	2	0.03
Pickerington (city) Fairfield County	3	0.02
Amherst (city) Lorain County	2	0.02
Munroe Falls (city) Summit County	1	0.02
Pleasant Run (cdp) Hamilton County	1	0.02
Warren (city) Trumbull County	5	0.01
Beavercreek (city) Greene County	3	0.01
Reynoldsburg (city) Franklin County	2	0.01
East Liverpool (city) Columbiana County	1	0.01

Top 10 Places Sorted by Percent of Total Population

Based on places with total population of 50,000 or more

Place	Population	%
Columbus (city) Franklin County	1	<0.01
Elyria (city) Lorain County	1	<0.01
Akron (city) Summit County	0	0.00
Canton (city) Stark County	0	0.00
Cincinnati (city) Hamilton County	0	0.00
Cleveland (city) Cuyahoga County	0	0.00
Dayton (city) Montgomery County	0	0.00
Hamilton (city) Butler County	0	0.00
Kettering (city) Montgomery County	0	0.00
Lakewood (city) Cuyahoga County	0	0.00

American Indian: Pima

Top 10 Places Sorted by Population

Based on all places, regardless of total population

Place	Population	%
Akron (city) Summit County	5	<0.01
Columbus (city) Franklin County	3	<0.01
Dayton (city) Montgomery County	2	<0.01
Lockland (village) Hamilton County	1	0.03
Aurora (city) Portage County	1	0.01
North Canton (city) Stark County	1	0.01
Sharonville (city) Hamilton County	1	0.01
Wilmington (city) Clinton County	1	0.01
Alliance (city) Stark County	1	<0.01
Boardman (cdp) Mahoning County	1	<0.01

Top 10 Places Sorted by Percent of Total Population

Based on all places, regardless of total population

Place	Population	%
Lockland (village) Hamilton County	1	0.03
Aurora (city) Portage County	1	0.01
North Canton (city) Stark County	1	0.01
Sharonville (city) Hamilton County	1	0.01
Wilmington (city) Clinton County	1	0.01
Akron (city) Summit County	5	<0.01
Columbus (city) Franklin County	3	<0.01
Dayton (city) Montgomery County	2	<0.01
Alliance (city) Stark County	1	<0.01
Boardman (cdp) Mahoning County	1	<0.01

Top 10 Places Sorted by Percent of Total Population

Based on places with total population of 50,000 or more

Place	Population	%
Akron (city) Summit County	5	<0.01
Columbus (city) Franklin County	3	<0.01
Dayton (city) Montgomery County	2	<0.01
Cleveland (city) Cuyahoga County	1	<0.01
Canton (city) Stark County	0	0.00
Cincinnati (city) Hamilton County	0	0.00
Elyria (city) Lorain County	0	0.00
Hamilton (city) Butler County	0	0.00
Kettering (city) Montgomery County	0	0.00
Lakewood (city) Cuyahoga County	0	0.00

American Indian: Potawatomi

Top 10 Places Sorted by Population

Based on all places, regardless of total population

Place	Population	%
Toledo (city) Lucas County	33	0.01
Columbus (city) Franklin County	13	<0.01
Cincinnati (city) Hamilton County	10	<0.01
Sandusky (city) Erie County	6	0.02
Hilliard (city) Franklin County	5	0.02
Xenia (city) Greene County	5	0.02
Upper Arlington (city) Franklin County	5	0.01
Amesville (village) Athens County	4	2.60
Brunswick (city) Medina County	4	0.01
Springfield (city) Clark County	4	0.01

Top 10 Places Sorted by Percent of Total Population

Based on all places, regardless of total population

Place	Population	%
Amesville (village) Athens County	4	2.60
Bremen (village) Fairfield County	3	0.21
Williston (cdp) Ottawa County	1	0.21
Reminderville (village) Summit County	3	0.09
Chesterland (cdp) Geauga County	2	0.08
Obetz (village) Franklin County	3	0.07
Lodi (village) Medina County	2	0.07
Wellston (city) Jackson County	3	0.05
Miami Heights (cdp) Hamilton County	2	0.04
Van Wert (city) Van Wert County	3	0.03

Top 10 Places Sorted by Percent of Total Population

Based on places with total population of 50,000 or more

Place	Population	%
Toledo (city) Lucas County	33	0.01
Springfield (city) Clark County	4	0.01
Columbus (city) Franklin County	13	<0.01
Cincinnati (city) Hamilton County	10	<0.01
Cleveland (city) Cuyahoga County	4	<0.01
Canton (city) Stark County	3	<0.01
Dayton (city) Montgomery County	3	<0.01
Lorain (city) Lorain County	3	<0.01
Parma (city) Cuyahoga County	3	<0.01
Akron (city) Summit County	2	<0.01

American Indian: Pueblo

Top 10 Places Sorted by Population
Based on all places, regardless of total population

Place	Population	%
Columbus (city) Franklin County	16	<0.01
Toledo (city) Lucas County	15	0.01
Lorain (city) Lorain County	14	0.02
Cleveland (city) Cuyahoga County	13	<0.01
North Madison (cdp) Lake County	5	0.06
Fairborn (city) Greene County	5	0.02
Rocky River (city) Cuyahoga County	5	0.02
Dayton (city) Montgomery County	5	<0.01
Middlefield (village) Geauga County	4	0.15
Cincinnati (city) Hamilton County	4	<0.01

Top 10 Places Sorted by Percent of Total Population
Based on all places, regardless of total population

Place	Population	%
Middlefield (village) Geauga County	4	0.15
Russells Point (village) Logan County	2	0.14
La Rue (village) Marion County	1	0.13
North Madison (cdp) Lake County	5	0.06
Sugarcreek (village) Tuscarawas County	1	0.05
New Lexington (village) Perry County	2	0.04
Gambier (village) Knox County	1	0.04
Grandview Heights (city) Franklin County	2	0.03
Ballville (cdp) Sandusky County	1	0.03
Yellow Springs (village) Greene County	1	0.03

Top 10 Places Sorted by Percent of Total Population
Based on places with total population of 50,000 or more

Place	Population	%
Lorain (city) Lorain County	14	0.02
Toledo (city) Lucas County	15	0.01
Columbus (city) Franklin County	16	<0.01
Cleveland (city) Cuyahoga County	13	<0.01
Dayton (city) Montgomery County	5	<0.01
Cincinnati (city) Hamilton County	4	<0.01
Parma (city) Cuyahoga County	2	<0.01
Akron (city) Summit County	1	<0.01
Canton (city) Stark County	1	<0.01
Elyria (city) Lorain County	1	<0.01

American Indian: Puget Sound Salish

Top 10 Places Sorted by Population
Based on all places, regardless of total population

Place	Population	%
Belmont (village) Belmont County	6	1.32
Findlay (city) Hancock County	4	0.01
Dayton (city) Montgomery County	2	<0.01
Batavia (village) Clermont County	1	0.07
Minster (village) Auglaize County	1	0.04
Napoleon (city) Henry County	1	0.01
Willoughby Hills (city) Lake County	1	0.01
Centerville (city) Montgomery County	1	<0.01
Cleveland Heights (city) Cuyahoga County	1	<0.01
Columbus (city) Franklin County	1	<0.01

Top 10 Places Sorted by Percent of Total Population
Based on all places, regardless of total population

Place	Population	%
Belmont (village) Belmont County	6	1.32
Batavia (village) Clermont County	1	0.07
Minster (village) Auglaize County	1	0.04
Findlay (city) Hancock County	4	0.01
Napoleon (city) Henry County	1	0.01
Willoughby Hills (city) Lake County	1	0.01
Dayton (city) Montgomery County	2	<0.01
Centerville (city) Montgomery County	1	<0.01
Cleveland Heights (city) Cuyahoga County	1	<0.01
Columbus (city) Franklin County	1	<0.01

Top 10 Places Sorted by Percent of Total Population
Based on places with total population of 50,000 or more

Place	Population	%
Dayton (city) Montgomery County	2	<0.01
Columbus (city) Franklin County	1	<0.01
Elyria (city) Lorain County	1	<0.01
Akron (city) Summit County	0	0.00
Canton (city) Stark County	0	0.00
Cincinnati (city) Hamilton County	0	0.00
Cleveland (city) Cuyahoga County	0	0.00
Hamilton (city) Butler County	0	0.00
Kettering (city) Montgomery County	0	0.00
Lakewood (city) Cuyahoga County	0	0.00

American Indian: Seminole

Top 10 Places Sorted by Population
Based on all places, regardless of total population

Place	Population	%
Columbus (city) Franklin County	42	0.01
Cleveland (city) Cuyahoga County	30	0.01
Cincinnati (city) Hamilton County	20	0.01
Akron (city) Summit County	17	0.01
Euclid (city) Cuyahoga County	13	0.03
Canton (city) Stark County	13	0.02
Cleveland Heights (city) Cuyahoga County	10	0.02
Dayton (city) Montgomery County	10	0.01
Toledo (city) Lucas County	9	<0.01
Wilberforce (cdp) Greene County	7	0.31

Top 10 Places Sorted by Percent of Total Population
Based on all places, regardless of total population

Place	Population	%
Antioch (village) Monroe County	1	1.16
Twinsburg Heights (cdp) Summit County	3	0.32
Wilberforce (cdp) Greene County	7	0.31
Athalia (village) Lawrence County	1	0.27
Pleasant Hills (cdp) Hamilton County	1	0.17
Smithfield (village) Jefferson County	1	0.12
Bridgeport (village) Belmont County	2	0.11
Sheffield Lake (city) Lorain County	7	0.08
Moraine (city) Montgomery County	5	0.08
New Vienna (village) Clinton County	1	0.08

Top 10 Places Sorted by Percent of Total Population
Based on places with total population of 50,000 or more

Place	Population	%
Canton (city) Stark County	13	0.02
Columbus (city) Franklin County	42	0.01
Cleveland (city) Cuyahoga County	30	0.01
Cincinnati (city) Hamilton County	20	0.01
Akron (city) Summit County	17	0.01
Dayton (city) Montgomery County	10	0.01
Lakewood (city) Cuyahoga County	7	0.01
Springfield (city) Clark County	7	0.01
Youngstown (city) Mahoning County	6	0.01
Elyria (city) Lorain County	4	0.01

American Indian: Shoshone

Top 10 Places Sorted by Population
Based on all places, regardless of total population

Place	Population	%
Akron (city) Summit County	10	0.01
Columbus (city) Franklin County	5	<0.01
Castalia (village) Erie County	4	0.47
Pataskala (city) Licking County	4	0.03
Garfield Heights (city) Cuyahoga County	4	0.01
Westerville (city) Franklin County	4	0.01
Cleveland (city) Cuyahoga County	4	<0.01
Avon (city) Lorain County	3	0.01
Toledo (city) Lucas County	3	<0.01
Reminderville (village) Summit County	2	0.06

Top 10 Places Sorted by Percent of Total Population
Based on all places, regardless of total population

Place	Population	%
Castalia (village) Erie County	4	0.47
Seaman (village) Adams County	1	0.11
Reminderville (village) Summit County	2	0.06
Yellow Springs (village) Greene County	2	0.06
Bolindale (cdp) Trumbull County	1	0.05
Pataskala (city) Licking County	4	0.03
Bellaire (village) Belmont County	1	0.02
Jackson (city) Jackson County	1	0.02
Nelsonville (city) Athens County	1	0.02
Upper Sandusky (city) Wyandot County	1	0.02

Top 10 Places Sorted by Percent of Total Population
Based on places with total population of 50,000 or more

Place	Population	%
Akron (city) Summit County	10	0.01
Columbus (city) Franklin County	5	<0.01
Cleveland (city) Cuyahoga County	4	<0.01
Toledo (city) Lucas County	3	<0.01
Cincinnati (city) Hamilton County	2	<0.01
Dayton (city) Montgomery County	1	<0.01
Youngstown (city) Mahoning County	1	<0.01
Canton (city) Stark County	0	0.00
Elyria (city) Lorain County	0	0.00
Hamilton (city) Butler County	0	0.00

American Indian: Sioux

Top 10 Places Sorted by Population
Based on all places, regardless of total population

Place	Population	%
Columbus (city) Franklin County	182	0.02
Cleveland (city) Cuyahoga County	91	0.02
Cincinnati (city) Hamilton County	56	0.02
Akron (city) Summit County	55	0.03
Toledo (city) Lucas County	39	0.01
Lakewood (city) Cuyahoga County	35	0.07
Dayton (city) Montgomery County	31	0.02
Lorain (city) Lorain County	26	0.04
Reynoldsburg (city) Franklin County	21	0.06
Beavercreek (city) Greene County	14	0.03

Top 10 Places Sorted by Percent of Total Population
Based on all places, regardless of total population

Place	Population	%
Clifton (village) Greene County	4	2.63
Potsdam (village) Miami County	4	1.39
Otway (village) Scioto County	1	1.15
Orient (village) Pickaway County	3	1.11
College Corner (village) Preble County	2	0.49
Jewett (village) Harrison County	3	0.43
Carbon Hill (cdp) Hocking County	1	0.43
Florida (village) Henry County	1	0.43
Christiansburg (village) Champaign County	2	0.38
Dundee (cdp) Tuscarawas County	1	0.34

Top 10 Places Sorted by Percent of Total Population
Based on places with total population of 50,000 or more

Place	Population	%
Lakewood (city) Cuyahoga County	35	0.07
Lorain (city) Lorain County	26	0.04
Akron (city) Summit County	55	0.03
Columbus (city) Franklin County	182	0.02
Cleveland (city) Cuyahoga County	91	0.02
Cincinnati (city) Hamilton County	56	0.02
Dayton (city) Montgomery County	31	0.02
Hamilton (city) Butler County	14	0.02
Kettering (city) Montgomery County	14	0.02
Springfield (city) Clark County	12	0.02

American Indian: South American Indian

Top 10 Places Sorted by Population
Based on all places, regardless of total population

Place	Population	%
Cleveland (city) Cuyahoga County	105	0.03
Lorain (city) Lorain County	79	0.12
Columbus (city) Franklin County	51	0.01
Cincinnati (city) Hamilton County	18	0.01
Toledo (city) Lucas County	17	0.01
Youngstown (city) Mahoning County	15	0.02
Parma (city) Cuyahoga County	10	0.01
Boardman (cdp) Mahoning County	9	0.03
Strongsville (city) Cuyahoga County	7	0.02
Upper Arlington (city) Franklin County	7	0.02

Top 10 Places Sorted by Percent of Total Population
Based on all places, regardless of total population

Place	Population	%
Jeromesville (village) Ashland County	5	0.89
Brooklyn Heights (village) Cuyahoga County	5	0.32
Rayland (village) Jefferson County	1	0.24

Place	Population	%
Pettisville (cdp) Fulton County	1	0.20
Malta (village) Morgan County	1	0.15
Lorain (city) Lorain County	79	0.12
Salem Heights (cdp) Hamilton County	4	0.10
The Village of Indian Hill (city) Hamilton County	5	0.09
Rockford (village) Mercer County	1	0.09
Devola (cdp) Washington County	2	0.08

Top 10 Places Sorted by Percent of Total Population

Based on places with total population of 50,000 or more

Place	Population	%
Lorain (city) Lorain County	79	0.12
Cleveland (city) Cuyahoga County	105	0.03
Youngstown (city) Mahoning County	15	0.02
Columbus (city) Franklin County	51	0.01
Cincinnati (city) Hamilton County	18	0.01
Toledo (city) Lucas County	17	0.01
Parma (city) Cuyahoga County	10	0.01
Kettering (city) Montgomery County	6	0.01
Hamilton (city) Butler County	5	0.01
Canton (city) Stark County	4	0.01

American Indian: Spanish American Indian

Top 10 Places Sorted by Population

Based on all places, regardless of total population

Place	Population	%
Columbus (city) Franklin County	18	<0.01
Cincinnati (city) Hamilton County	6	<0.01
Toledo (city) Lucas County	6	<0.01
Ottawa (village) Putnam County	5	0.11
Lakewood (city) Cuyahoga County	5	0.01
Bryan (city) Williams County	4	0.05
Defiance (city) Defiance County	4	0.02
Akron (city) Summit County	4	<0.01
Fairfield (city) Butler County	3	0.01
Kettering (city) Montgomery County	3	0.01

Top 10 Places Sorted by Percent of Total Population

Based on all places, regardless of total population

Place	Population	%
Port William (village) Clinton County	1	0.39
Wayne Lakes (village) Darke County	1	0.14
Ottawa (village) Putnam County	5	0.11
Hartville (village) Stark County	2	0.07
Bryan (city) Williams County	4	0.05
Defiance (city) Defiance County	4	0.02
Jackson (city) Jackson County	1	0.02
Pleasant Run (cdp) Hamilton County	1	0.02
Lakewood (city) Cuyahoga County	5	0.01
Fairfield (city) Butler County	3	0.01

Top 10 Places Sorted by Percent of Total Population

Based on places with total population of 50,000 or more

Place	Population	%
Lakewood (city) Cuyahoga County	5	0.01
Kettering (city) Montgomery County	3	0.01
Columbus (city) Franklin County	18	<0.01
Cincinnati (city) Hamilton County	6	<0.01
Toledo (city) Lucas County	6	<0.01
Akron (city) Summit County	4	<0.01
Cleveland (city) Cuyahoga County	3	<0.01
Hamilton (city) Butler County	3	<0.01
Youngstown (city) Mahoning County	3	<0.01
Dayton (city) Montgomery County	2	<0.01

Alaska Native: Tlingit-Haida

Top 10 Places Sorted by Population

Based on all places, regardless of total population

Place	Population	%
Columbus (city) Franklin County	10	<0.01
North Olmsted (city) Cuyahoga County	6	0.02
Parma (city) Cuyahoga County	6	0.01
LaGrange (village) Lorain County	3	0.14
Rittman (city) Wayne County	3	0.05
Berea (city) Cuyahoga County	3	0.02
Gahanna (city) Franklin County	2	0.01
Niles (city) Trumbull County	2	0.01
Cleveland (city) Cuyahoga County	2	<0.01
Lakewood (city) Cuyahoga County	2	<0.01

Top 10 Places Sorted by Percent of Total Population

Based on all places, regardless of total population

Place	Population	%
LaGrange (village) Lorain County	3	0.14
Rittman (city) Wayne County	3	0.05
North Olmsted (city) Cuyahoga County	6	0.02
Berea (city) Cuyahoga County	3	0.02
Ada (village) Hardin County	1	0.02
Nelsonville (city) Athens County	1	0.02
Parma (city) Cuyahoga County	6	0.01
Gahanna (city) Franklin County	2	0.01
Niles (city) Trumbull County	2	0.01
Blue Ash (city) Hamilton County	1	0.01

Top 10 Places Sorted by Percent of Total Population

Based on places with total population of 50,000 or more

Place	Population	%
Parma (city) Cuyahoga County	6	0.01
Columbus (city) Franklin County	10	<0.01
Cleveland (city) Cuyahoga County	2	<0.01
Lakewood (city) Cuyahoga County	2	<0.01
Toledo (city) Lucas County	2	<0.01
Akron (city) Summit County	1	<0.01
Youngstown (city) Mahoning County	1	<0.01
Canton (city) Stark County	0	0.00
Cincinnati (city) Hamilton County	0	0.00
Dayton (city) Montgomery County	0	0.00

American Indian: Tohono O'Odham

Top 10 Places Sorted by Population

Based on all places, regardless of total population

Place	Population	%
Cincinnati (city) Hamilton County	7	<0.01
Cleveland (city) Cuyahoga County	7	<0.01
Columbus (city) Franklin County	5	<0.01
Mentor-on-the-Lake (city) Lake County	3	0.04
Conneaut (city) Ashtabula County	3	0.02
Eastlake (city) Lake County	3	0.02
Springfield (city) Clark County	3	<0.01
Campbell (city) Mahoning County	2	0.02
Ashville (village) Pickaway County	1	0.02
Oberlin (city) Lorain County	1	0.01

Top 10 Places Sorted by Percent of Total Population

Based on all places, regardless of total population

Place	Population	%
Mentor-on-the-Lake (city) Lake County	3	0.04
Conneaut (city) Ashtabula County	3	0.02
Eastlake (city) Lake County	3	0.02
Campbell (city) Mahoning County	2	0.02
Ashville (village) Pickaway County	1	0.02
Oberlin (city) Lorain County	1	0.01
Tiffin (city) Seneca County	1	0.01
Wilmington (city) Clinton County	1	0.01
Cincinnati (city) Hamilton County	7	<0.01
Cleveland (city) Cuyahoga County	7	<0.01

Top 10 Places Sorted by Percent of Total Population

Based on places with total population of 50,000 or more

Place	Population	%
Cincinnati (city) Hamilton County	7	<0.01
Cleveland (city) Cuyahoga County	7	<0.01
Columbus (city) Franklin County	5	<0.01
Springfield (city) Clark County	3	<0.01
Akron (city) Summit County	0	0.00
Canton (city) Stark County	0	0.00
Dayton (city) Montgomery County	0	0.00
Elyria (city) Lorain County	0	0.00
Hamilton (city) Butler County	0	0.00
Kettering (city) Montgomery County	0	0.00

Alaska Native: Tsimshian

Top 10 Places Sorted by Population

Based on all places, regardless of total population

Place	Population	%
Brookville (city) Montgomery County	2	0.03
Gahanna (city) Franklin County	2	0.01
Green (city) Summit County	2	0.01
Lakewood (city) Cuyahoga County	2	<0.01
Parma (city) Cuyahoga County	2	<0.01
West Manchester (village) Preble County	1	0.21
Moraine (city) Montgomery County	1	0.02
Bellbrook (city) Greene County	1	0.01
Cincinnati (city) Hamilton County	1	<0.01
Columbus (city) Franklin County	1	<0.01

Top 10 Places Sorted by Percent of Total Population

Based on all places, regardless of total population

Place	Population	%
West Manchester (village) Preble County	1	0.21
Brookville (city) Montgomery County	2	0.03
Moraine (city) Montgomery County	1	0.02
Gahanna (city) Franklin County	2	0.01
Green (city) Summit County	2	0.01
Bellbrook (city) Greene County	1	0.01
Lakewood (city) Cuyahoga County	2	<0.01
Parma (city) Cuyahoga County	2	<0.01
Cincinnati (city) Hamilton County	1	<0.01
Columbus (city) Franklin County	1	<0.01

Top 10 Places Sorted by Percent of Total Population

Based on places with total population of 50,000 or more

Place	Population	%
Lakewood (city) Cuyahoga County	2	<0.01
Parma (city) Cuyahoga County	2	<0.01
Cincinnati (city) Hamilton County	1	<0.01
Columbus (city) Franklin County	1	<0.01
Akron (city) Summit County	0	0.00
Canton (city) Stark County	0	0.00
Cleveland (city) Cuyahoga County	0	0.00
Dayton (city) Montgomery County	0	0.00
Elyria (city) Lorain County	0	0.00
Hamilton (city) Butler County	0	0.00

American Indian: Ute

Top 10 Places Sorted by Population

Based on all places, regardless of total population

Place	Population	%
Franklin (city) Warren County	4	0.03
Columbus (city) Franklin County	4	<0.01
Dayton (city) Montgomery County	4	<0.01
St. Marys (city) Auglaize County	2	0.02
White Oak (cdp) Hamilton County	2	0.01
Edgewood (cdp) Ashtabula County	1	0.02
Delphos (city) Allen County	1	0.01
Akron (city) Summit County	1	<0.01
Brunswick (city) Medina County	1	<0.01
Kettering (city) Montgomery County	1	<0.01

Top 10 Places Sorted by Percent of Total Population

Based on all places, regardless of total population

Place	Population	%
Franklin (city) Warren County	4	0.03
St. Marys (city) Auglaize County	2	0.02
Edgewood (cdp) Ashtabula County	1	0.02
White Oak (cdp) Hamilton County	2	0.01
Delphos (city) Allen County	1	0.01
Columbus (city) Franklin County	4	<0.01
Dayton (city) Montgomery County	4	<0.01
Akron (city) Summit County	1	<0.01
Brunswick (city) Medina County	1	<0.01
Kettering (city) Montgomery County	1	<0.01

Top 10 Places Sorted by Percent of Total Population

Based on places with total population of 50,000 or more

Place	Population	%
Columbus (city) Franklin County	4	<0.01
Dayton (city) Montgomery County	4	<0.01
Akron (city) Summit County	1	<0.01
Kettering (city) Montgomery County	1	<0.01
Youngstown (city) Mahoning County	1	<0.01
Canton (city) Stark County	0	0.00
Cincinnati (city) Hamilton County	0	0.00
Cleveland (city) Cuyahoga County	0	0.00
Elyria (city) Lorain County	0	0.00
Hamilton (city) Butler County	0	0.00

American Indian: Yakama

Top 10 Places Sorted by Population

Based on all places, regardless of total population

Place	Population	%
Hamilton (city) Butler County	5	0.01
Mansfield (city) Richland County	4	0.01
Fremont (city) Sandusky County	2	0.01
Port Clinton (city) Ottawa County	1	0.02
Wheelersburg (cdp) Scioto County	1	0.02
Cincinnati (city) Hamilton County	1	<0.01
Aberdeen (village) Brown County	0	0.00
Ada (village) Hardin County	0	0.00
Adamsville (village) Muskingum County	0	0.00
Addyston (village) Hamilton County	0	0.00

Top 10 Places Sorted by Percent of Total Population

Based on all places, regardless of total population

Place	Population	%
Port Clinton (city) Ottawa County	1	0.02
Wheelersburg (cdp) Scioto County	1	0.02
Hamilton (city) Butler County	5	0.01
Mansfield (city) Richland County	4	0.01
Fremont (city) Sandusky County	2	0.01
Cincinnati (city) Hamilton County	1	<0.01
Aberdeen (village) Brown County	0	0.00
Ada (village) Hardin County	0	0.00
Adamsville (village) Muskingum County	0	0.00
Addyston (village) Hamilton County	0	0.00

Top 10 Places Sorted by Percent of Total Population

Based on places with total population of 50,000 or more

Place	Population	%
Hamilton (city) Butler County	5	0.01
Cincinnati (city) Hamilton County	1	<0.01
Akron (city) Summit County	0	0.00
Canton (city) Stark County	0	0.00
Cleveland (city) Cuyahoga County	0	0.00
Columbus (city) Franklin County	0	0.00
Dayton (city) Montgomery County	0	0.00
Elyria (city) Lorain County	0	0.00
Kettering (city) Montgomery County	0	0.00
Lakewood (city) Cuyahoga County	0	0.00

American Indian: Yaqui

Top 10 Places Sorted by Population

Based on all places, regardless of total population

Place	Population	%
Akron (city) Summit County	9	<0.01
Marietta (city) Washington County	4	0.03
Toledo (city) Lucas County	4	<0.01
Glenmoor (cdp) Columbiana County	3	0.15
Archbold (village) Fulton County	3	0.07
Barberton (city) Summit County	3	0.01
Strongsville (city) Cuyahoga County	3	0.01
Steubenville (city) Jefferson County	2	0.01
Cincinnati (city) Hamilton County	2	<0.01
Youngstown (city) Mahoning County	2	<0.01

Top 10 Places Sorted by Percent of Total Population

Based on all places, regardless of total population

Place	Population	%
Glenmoor (cdp) Columbiana County	3	0.15
Bloomville (village) Seneca County	1	0.10
Archbold (village) Fulton County	3	0.07
Orwell (village) Ashtabula County	1	0.06
Marietta (city) Washington County	4	0.03
Groveport (village) Franklin County	1	0.02
Miami Heights (cdp) Hamilton County	1	0.02
Port Clinton (city) Ottawa County	1	0.02
Barberton (city) Summit County	3	0.01
Strongsville (city) Cuyahoga County	3	0.01

Top 10 Places Sorted by Percent of Total Population

Based on places with total population of 50,000 or more

Place	Population	%
Akron (city) Summit County	9	<0.01
Toledo (city) Lucas County	4	<0.01
Cincinnati (city) Hamilton County	2	<0.01
Youngstown (city) Mahoning County	2	<0.01
Columbus (city) Franklin County	1	<0.01
Hamilton (city) Butler County	1	<0.01
Lorain (city) Lorain County	1	<0.01
Springfield (city) Clark County	1	<0.01
Canton (city) Stark County	0	0.00
Cleveland (city) Cuyahoga County	0	0.00

American Indian: Yuman

Top 10 Places Sorted by Population

Based on all places, regardless of total population

Place	Population	%
Canton (city) Stark County	5	0.01
Wadsworth (city) Medina County	4	0.02
Mogadore (village) Summit County	3	0.08
Cincinnati (city) Hamilton County	2	<0.01
Columbus (city) Franklin County	2	<0.01
McArthur (village) Vinton County	1	0.06
Bedford Heights (city) Cuyahoga County	1	0.01
Bexley (city) Franklin County	1	0.01
Kettering (city) Montgomery County	1	<0.01
Lakewood (city) Cuyahoga County	1	<0.01

Top 10 Places Sorted by Percent of Total Population

Based on all places, regardless of total population

Place	Population	%
Mogadore (village) Summit County	3	0.08
McArthur (village) Vinton County	1	0.06
Wadsworth (city) Medina County	4	0.02
Canton (city) Stark County	5	0.01
Bedford Heights (city) Cuyahoga County	1	0.01
Bexley (city) Franklin County	1	0.01
Cincinnati (city) Hamilton County	2	<0.01
Columbus (city) Franklin County	2	<0.01
Kettering (city) Montgomery County	1	<0.01
Lakewood (city) Cuyahoga County	1	<0.01

Top 10 Places Sorted by Percent of Total Population

Based on places with total population of 50,000 or more

Place	Population	%
Canton (city) Stark County	5	0.01
Cincinnati (city) Hamilton County	2	<0.01
Columbus (city) Franklin County	2	<0.01
Kettering (city) Montgomery County	1	<0.01
Lakewood (city) Cuyahoga County	1	<0.01
Akron (city) Summit County	0	0.00
Cleveland (city) Cuyahoga County	0	0.00
Dayton (city) Montgomery County	0	0.00
Elyria (city) Lorain County	0	0.00
Hamilton (city) Butler County	0	0.00

Alaska Native: Yup'ik

Top 10 Places Sorted by Population

Based on all places, regardless of total population

Place	Population	%
Huber Heights (city) Montgomery County	5	0.01
Green (city) Summit County	3	0.01
Sandusky (city) Erie County	3	0.01
Cleveland (city) Cuyahoga County	3	<0.01
Columbus (city) Franklin County	2	<0.01
Hebron (village) Licking County	1	0.04
Amherst (city) Lorain County	1	0.01
Berea (city) Cuyahoga County	1	0.01
Defiance (city) Defiance County	1	0.01
Marietta (city) Washington County	1	0.01

Top 10 Places Sorted by Percent of Total Population

Based on all places, regardless of total population

Place	Population	%
Hebron (village) Licking County	1	0.04
Huber Heights (city) Montgomery County	5	0.01
Green (city) Summit County	3	0.01
Sandusky (city) Erie County	3	0.01
Amherst (city) Lorain County	1	0.01
Berea (city) Cuyahoga County	1	0.01
Defiance (city) Defiance County	1	0.01
Marietta (city) Washington County	1	0.01
Cleveland (city) Cuyahoga County	3	<0.01
Columbus (city) Franklin County	2	<0.01

Top 10 Places Sorted by Percent of Total Population

Based on places with total population of 50,000 or more

Place	Population	%
Cleveland (city) Cuyahoga County	3	<0.01
Columbus (city) Franklin County	2	<0.01
Akron (city) Summit County	0	0.00
Canton (city) Stark County	0	0.00
Cincinnati (city) Hamilton County	0	0.00
Dayton (city) Montgomery County	0	0.00
Elyria (city) Lorain County	0	0.00
Hamilton (city) Butler County	0	0.00
Kettering (city) Montgomery County	0	0.00
Lakewood (city) Cuyahoga County	0	0.00

Asian

Top 10 Places Sorted by Population

Based on all places, regardless of total population

Place	Population	%
Columbus (city) Franklin County	37,743	4.80
Cleveland (city) Cuyahoga County	8,705	2.19
Dublin (city) Franklin County	6,891	16.50
Cincinnati (city) Hamilton County	6,875	2.32
Akron (city) Summit County	5,081	2.55
Toledo (city) Lucas County	4,559	1.59
Beavercreek (city) Greene County	3,170	7.01
Mason (city) Warren County	3,049	9.93
Solon (city) Cuyahoga County	2,491	10.67
Cleveland Heights (city) Cuyahoga County	2,267	4.92

Top 10 Places Sorted by Percent of Total Population

Based on all places, regardless of total population

Place	Population	%
Dublin (city) Franklin County	6,891	16.50
Sixteen Mile Stand (cdp) Hamilton County	435	14.86
Remington (cdp) Hamilton County	41	12.50
Blue Ash (city) Hamilton County	1,406	11.61
Glenwillow (village) Cuyahoga County	102	11.05
Solon (city) Cuyahoga County	2,491	10.67
Mason (city) Warren County	3,049	9.93
Powell (city) Delaware County	955	8.30
Beachwood (city) Cuyahoga County	939	7.86
New Albany (village) Franklin County	601	7.78

Top 10 Places Sorted by Percent of Total Population

Based on places with total population of 50,000 or more

Place	Population	%
Columbus (city) Franklin County	37,743	4.80
Lakewood (city) Cuyahoga County	1,344	2.58
Akron (city) Summit County	5,081	2.55
Parma (city) Cuyahoga County	1,920	2.35
Cincinnati (city) Hamilton County	6,875	2.32
Cleveland (city) Cuyahoga County	8,705	2.19
Kettering (city) Montgomery County	1,101	1.96
Toledo (city) Lucas County	4,559	1.59
Dayton (city) Montgomery County	1,864	1.32
Elyria (city) Lorain County	628	1.15

Asian: Not Hispanic

Top 10 Places Sorted by Population

Based on all places, regardless of total population

Place	Population	%
Columbus (city) Franklin County	37,170	4.72
Cleveland (city) Cuyahoga County	8,422	2.12
Dublin (city) Franklin County	6,866	16.45
Cincinnati (city) Hamilton County	6,728	2.27
Akron (city) Summit County	5,008	2.52
Toledo (city) Lucas County	4,312	1.50
Beavercreek (city) Greene County	3,130	6.93
Mason (city) Warren County	3,035	9.88
Solon (city) Cuyahoga County	2,482	10.63
Cleveland Heights (city) Cuyahoga County	2,236	4.85

Top 10 Places Sorted by Percent of Total Population

Based on all places, regardless of total population

Place	Population	%
Dublin (city) Franklin County	6,866	16.45
Sixteen Mile Stand (cdp) Hamilton County	433	14.79
Remington (cdp) Hamilton County	41	12.50

Blue Ash (city) Hamilton County	1,393	11.50
Glenwillow (village) Cuyahoga County	102	11.05
Solon (city) Cuyahoga County	2,482	10.63
Mason (city) Warren County	3,035	9.88
Powell (city) Delaware County	951	8.27
Beachwood (city) Cuyahoga County	937	7.84
New Albany (village) Franklin County	595	7.70

Top 10 Places Sorted by Percent of Total Population

Based on places with total population of 50,000 or more

Place	Population	%
Columbus (city) Franklin County	37,170	4.72
Lakewood (city) Cuyahoga County	1,323	2.54
Akron (city) Summit County	5,008	2.52
Parma (city) Cuyahoga County	1,891	2.32
Cincinnati (city) Hamilton County	6,728	2.27
Cleveland (city) Cuyahoga County	8,422	2.12
Kettering (city) Montgomery County	1,080	1.92
Toledo (city) Lucas County	4,312	1.50
Dayton (city) Montgomery County	1,813	1.28
Elyria (city) Lorain County	590	1.08

Asian: Hispanic

Top 10 Places Sorted by Population

Based on all places, regardless of total population

Place	Population	%
Columbus (city) Franklin County	573	0.07
Cleveland (city) Cuyahoga County	283	0.07
Toledo (city) Lucas County	247	0.09
Cincinnati (city) Hamilton County	147	0.05
Lorain (city) Lorain County	86	0.13
Akron (city) Summit County	73	0.04
Dayton (city) Montgomery County	51	0.04
Youngstown (city) Mahoning County	50	0.07
Beavercreek (city) Greene County	40	0.09
Elyria (city) Lorain County	38	0.07

Top 10 Places Sorted by Percent of Total Population

Based on all places, regardless of total population

Place	Population	%
Burgoon (village) Sandusky County	1	0.58
Congress (village) Wayne County	1	0.54
Woodmere (village) Cuyahoga County	4	0.45
Spencer (village) Medina County	3	0.40
Pettisville (cdp) Fulton County	2	0.40
North Fairfield (village) Huron County	2	0.36
Collins (cdp) Huron County	2	0.32
Rockford (village) Mercer County	3	0.27
Cumberland (village) Guernsey County	1	0.27
Whites Landing (cdp) Erie County	1	0.27

Top 10 Places Sorted by Percent of Total Population

Based on places with total population of 50,000 or more

Place	Population	%
Lorain (city) Lorain County	86	0.13
Toledo (city) Lucas County	247	0.09
Columbus (city) Franklin County	573	0.07
Cleveland (city) Cuyahoga County	283	0.07
Youngstown (city) Mahoning County	50	0.07
Elyria (city) Lorain County	38	0.07
Cincinnati (city) Hamilton County	147	0.05
Springfield (city) Clark County	33	0.05
Akron (city) Summit County	73	0.04
Dayton (city) Montgomery County	51	0.04

Asian: Bangladeshi

Top 10 Places Sorted by Population

Based on all places, regardless of total population

Place	Population	%
Columbus (city) Franklin County	366	0.05
Dublin (city) Franklin County	53	0.13
Hilliard (city) Franklin County	28	0.10
Cincinnati (city) Hamilton County	25	0.01
Akron (city) Summit County	15	0.01
Kenwood (cdp) Hamilton County	12	0.17
Twinsburg (city) Summit County	12	0.06
Fairborn (city) Greene County	12	0.04
Strongsville (city) Cuyahoga County	12	0.03
Parma Heights (city) Cuyahoga County	11	0.05

Top 10 Places Sorted by Percent of Total Population

Based on all places, regardless of total population

Place	Population	%
Peninsula (village) Summit County	3	0.53
Concorde Hills (cdp) Hamilton County	3	0.45
Pigeon Creek (cdp) Summit County	3	0.34
Woodmere (village) Cuyahoga County	2	0.23
Northfield (village) Summit County	8	0.22
Obetz (village) Franklin County	9	0.20
Kenwood (cdp) Hamilton County	12	0.17
Dublin (city) Franklin County	53	0.13
Hilliard (city) Franklin County	28	0.10
Lake Darby (cdp) Franklin County	4	0.09

Top 10 Places Sorted by Percent of Total Population

Based on places with total population of 50,000 or more

Place	Population	%
Columbus (city) Franklin County	366	0.05
Lakewood (city) Cuyahoga County	8	0.02
Cincinnati (city) Hamilton County	25	0.01
Akron (city) Summit County	15	0.01
Dayton (city) Montgomery County	8	0.01
Kettering (city) Montgomery County	3	0.01
Cleveland (city) Cuyahoga County	11	<0.01
Toledo (city) Lucas County	5	<0.01
Canton (city) Stark County	1	<0.01
Parma (city) Cuyahoga County	1	<0.01

Asian: Bhutanese

Top 10 Places Sorted by Population

Based on all places, regardless of total population

Place	Population	%
Akron (city) Summit County	318	0.16
Columbus (city) Franklin County	96	0.01
Cleveland (city) Cuyahoga County	94	0.02
Cincinnati (city) Hamilton County	74	0.02
South Euclid (city) Cuyahoga County	55	0.25
Cuyahoga Falls (city) Summit County	54	0.11
Lakewood (city) Cuyahoga County	49	0.09
Cleveland Heights (city) Cuyahoga County	48	0.10
Finneytown (cdp) Hamilton County	25	0.20
White Oak (cdp) Hamilton County	16	0.08

Top 10 Places Sorted by Percent of Total Population

Based on all places, regardless of total population

Place	Population	%
South Euclid (city) Cuyahoga County	55	0.25
Finneytown (cdp) Hamilton County	25	0.20
Akron (city) Summit County	318	0.16
Cuyahoga Falls (city) Summit County	54	0.11
Cleveland Heights (city) Cuyahoga County	48	0.10
Lakewood (city) Cuyahoga County	49	0.09
White Oak (cdp) Hamilton County	16	0.08
Hiram (village) Portage County	1	0.07
Kent (city) Portage County	15	0.05
Monfort Heights (cdp) Hamilton County	6	0.05

Top 10 Places Sorted by Percent of Total Population

Based on places with total population of 50,000 or more

Place	Population	%
Akron (city) Summit County	318	0.16
Lakewood (city) Cuyahoga County	49	0.09
Cleveland (city) Cuyahoga County	94	0.02
Cincinnati (city) Hamilton County	74	0.02
Columbus (city) Franklin County	96	0.01
Canton (city) Stark County	0	0.00
Dayton (city) Montgomery County	0	0.00
Elyria (city) Lorain County	0	0.00
Hamilton (city) Butler County	0	0.00
Kettering (city) Montgomery County	0	0.00

Asian: Burmese

Top 10 Places Sorted by Population

Based on all places, regardless of total population

Place	Population	%
Akron (city) Summit County	603	0.30
Columbus (city) Franklin County	204	0.03
Lakewood (city) Cuyahoga County	146	0.28
Cleveland (city) Cuyahoga County	69	0.02
Blue Ash (city) Hamilton County	26	0.21
Montgomery (city) Hamilton County	17	0.17
Cincinnati (city) Hamilton County	13	<0.01
Strongsville (city) Cuyahoga County	12	0.03
Dover (city) Tuscarawas County	10	0.08
Madeira (city) Hamilton County	9	0.10

Top 10 Places Sorted by Percent of Total Population

Based on all places, regardless of total population

Place	Population	%
Akron (city) Summit County	603	0.30
Lakewood (city) Cuyahoga County	146	0.28
Blue Ash (city) Hamilton County	26	0.21
Montgomery (city) Hamilton County	17	0.17
Hiram (village) Portage County	2	0.14
Madeira (city) Hamilton County	9	0.10
Deer Park (city) Hamilton County	5	0.09
Dover (city) Tuscarawas County	10	0.08
Lincoln Village (cdp) Franklin County	7	0.08
Pleasant Run (cdp) Hamilton County	4	0.08

Top 10 Places Sorted by Percent of Total Population

Based on places with total population of 50,000 or more

Place	Population	%
Akron (city) Summit County	603	0.30
Lakewood (city) Cuyahoga County	146	0.28
Columbus (city) Franklin County	204	0.03
Cleveland (city) Cuyahoga County	69	0.02
Kettering (city) Montgomery County	7	0.01
Cincinnati (city) Hamilton County	13	<0.01
Toledo (city) Lucas County	5	<0.01
Dayton (city) Montgomery County	2	<0.01
Canton (city) Stark County	1	<0.01
Elyria (city) Lorain County	0	0.00

Asian: Cambodian

Top 10 Places Sorted by Population

Based on all places, regardless of total population

Place	Population	%
Columbus (city) Franklin County	1,794	0.23
Cleveland (city) Cuyahoga County	328	0.08
Cincinnati (city) Hamilton County	212	0.07
Fairfield (city) Butler County	133	0.31
Grove City (city) Franklin County	87	0.24
Akron (city) Summit County	69	0.03
Dayton (city) Montgomery County	59	0.04
Strongsville (city) Cuyahoga County	56	0.13
Pleasant Run (cdp) Hamilton County	54	1.09
Parma (city) Cuyahoga County	54	0.07

Top 10 Places Sorted by Percent of Total Population

Based on all places, regardless of total population

Place	Population	%
Urbancrest (village) Franklin County	23	2.40
Pleasant Run (cdp) Hamilton County	54	1.09
West Elkton (village) Preble County	2	1.02
Rossmoyne (cdp) Hamilton County	17	0.76
Obetz (village) Franklin County	27	0.60
Pleasant Hills (cdp) Hamilton County	3	0.50
Mount Victory (village) Hardin County	3	0.48
Madeira (city) Hamilton County	40	0.46
Kenwood (cdp) Hamilton County	32	0.46
Northgate (cdp) Hamilton County	33	0.45

Top 10 Places Sorted by Percent of Total Population

Based on places with total population of 50,000 or more

Place	Population	%
Columbus (city) Franklin County	1,794	0.23
Cleveland (city) Cuyahoga County	328	0.08
Cincinnati (city) Hamilton County	212	0.07
Parma (city) Cuyahoga County	54	0.07
Dayton (city) Montgomery County	59	0.04
Kettering (city) Montgomery County	23	0.04
Akron (city) Summit County	69	0.03
Hamilton (city) Butler County	12	0.02
Youngstown (city) Mahoning County	9	0.01
Lakewood (city) Cuyahoga County	7	0.01

Asian: Chinese, except Taiwanese

Top 10 Places Sorted by Population

Based on all places, regardless of total population

Place	Population	%
Columbus (city) Franklin County	6,780	0.86
Cleveland (city) Cuyahoga County	2,916	0.73
Cincinnati (city) Hamilton County	1,558	0.52
Dublin (city) Franklin County	1,343	3.22
Toledo (city) Lucas County	1,177	0.41
Solon (city) Cuyahoga County	965	4.13
Athens (city) Athens County	900	3.78
Upper Arlington (city) Franklin County	758	2.24
Oxford (city) Butler County	716	3.35
Mason (city) Warren County	667	2.17

Top 10 Places Sorted by Percent of Total Population

Based on all places, regardless of total population

Place	Population	%
Glenwillow (village) Cuyahoga County	49	5.31
Remington (cdp) Hamilton County	15	4.57
Solon (city) Cuyahoga County	965	4.13
Athens (city) Athens County	900	3.78
Oxford (city) Butler County	716	3.35
Harbor View (village) Lucas County	4	3.25
Dublin (city) Franklin County	1,343	3.22
Beachwood (city) Cuyahoga County	303	2.53
Bairdstown (village) Wood County	3	2.31
Upper Arlington (city) Franklin County	758	2.24

Top 10 Places Sorted by Percent of Total Population

Based on places with total population of 50,000 or more

Place	Population	%
Columbus (city) Franklin County	6,780	0.86
Cleveland (city) Cuyahoga County	2,916	0.73
Cincinnati (city) Hamilton County	1,558	0.52
Toledo (city) Lucas County	1,177	0.41
Lakewood (city) Cuyahoga County	189	0.36
Kettering (city) Montgomery County	197	0.35
Akron (city) Summit County	607	0.30
Parma (city) Cuyahoga County	218	0.27
Dayton (city) Montgomery County	324	0.23
Springfield (city) Clark County	97	0.16

Asian: Filipino

Top 10 Places Sorted by Population

Based on all places, regardless of total population

Place	Population	%
Columbus (city) Franklin County	2,827	0.36
Cleveland (city) Cuyahoga County	937	0.24
Cincinnati (city) Hamilton County	718	0.24
Toledo (city) Lucas County	610	0.21
Parma (city) Cuyahoga County	515	0.63
Huber Heights (city) Montgomery County	382	1.00
Beavercreek (city) Greene County	347	0.77
Dayton (city) Montgomery County	334	0.24
Akron (city) Summit County	317	0.16
Elyria (city) Lorain County	273	0.50

Top 10 Places Sorted by Percent of Total Population

Based on all places, regardless of total population

Place	Population	%
Bairdstown (village) Wood County	5	3.85
Melmore (cdp) Seneca County	4	2.61
Wright-Patterson AFB (cdp) Greene County	43	2.36
Hills and Dales (village) Stark County	5	2.26
Beulah Beach (cdp) Erie County	1	1.89
Milledgeville (village) Fayette County	2	1.79
Vaughnsville (cdp) Putnam County	4	1.53
Lockington (village) Shelby County	2	1.42
Deersville (village) Harrison County	1	1.27
Pleasantville (village) Fairfield County	11	1.15

Top 10 Places Sorted by Percent of Total Population

Based on places with total population of 50,000 or more

Place	Population	%
Parma (city) Cuyahoga County	515	0.63
Elyria (city) Lorain County	273	0.50
Kettering (city) Montgomery County	213	0.38
Columbus (city) Franklin County	2,827	0.36
Hamilton (city) Butler County	164	0.26
Lakewood (city) Cuyahoga County	137	0.26
Cleveland (city) Cuyahoga County	937	0.24
Cincinnati (city) Hamilton County	718	0.24
Dayton (city) Montgomery County	334	0.24
Toledo (city) Lucas County	610	0.21

Asian: Hmong

Top 10 Places Sorted by Population

Based on all places, regardless of total population

Place	Population	%
Akron (city) Summit County	362	0.18
Columbus (city) Franklin County	51	0.01
Green (city) Summit County	31	0.12
New Franklin (city) Summit County	12	0.08
Medina (city) Medina County	7	0.03
Cleveland (city) Cuyahoga County	7	<0.01
Lorain (city) Lorain County	6	0.01
Tallmadge (city) Summit County	5	0.03
Athens (city) Athens County	5	0.02
Upper Arlington (city) Franklin County	4	0.01

Top 10 Places Sorted by Percent of Total Population

Based on all places, regardless of total population

Place	Population	%
Holloway (village) Belmont County	1	0.30
Akron (city) Summit County	362	0.18
Green (city) Summit County	31	0.12
New Franklin (city) Summit County	12	0.08
Silver Lake (village) Summit County	2	0.08
Hiram (village) Portage County	1	0.07
Fairport Harbor (village) Lake County	2	0.06
West Union (village) Adams County	2	0.06
Weston (village) Wood County	1	0.06
Medina (city) Medina County	7	0.03

Top 10 Places Sorted by Percent of Total Population

Based on places with total population of 50,000 or more

Place	Population	%
Akron (city) Summit County	362	0.18
Columbus (city) Franklin County	51	0.01
Lorain (city) Lorain County	6	0.01
Cleveland (city) Cuyahoga County	7	<0.01
Toledo (city) Lucas County	4	<0.01
Cincinnati (city) Hamilton County	3	<0.01
Youngstown (city) Mahoning County	3	<0.01
Canton (city) Stark County	1	<0.01
Dayton (city) Montgomery County	0	0.00
Elyria (city) Lorain County	0	0.00

Asian: Indian

Top 10 Places Sorted by Population

Based on all places, regardless of total population

Place	Population	%
Columbus (city) Franklin County	11,364	1.44
Dublin (city) Franklin County	2,986	7.15
Cincinnati (city) Hamilton County	2,036	0.69
Cleveland (city) Cuyahoga County	1,649	0.42
Mason (city) Warren County	1,384	4.51
Beavercreek (city) Greene County	1,127	2.49
Solon (city) Cuyahoga County	1,107	4.74
Toledo (city) Lucas County	995	0.35
Strongsville (city) Cuyahoga County	971	2.17
Akron (city) Summit County	874	0.44

Top 10 Places Sorted by Percent of Total Population

Based on all places, regardless of total population

Place	Population	%
Dublin (city) Franklin County	2,986	7.15
Blue Ash (city) Hamilton County	807	6.66
Sixteen Mile Stand (cdp) Hamilton County	185	6.32
Glenwillow (village) Cuyahoga County	50	5.42
Northfield (village) Summit County	179	4.87
Solon (city) Cuyahoga County	1,107	4.74
Powell (city) Delaware County	530	4.61
Mason (city) Warren County	1,384	4.51
Wetherington (cdp) Butler County	58	4.45
Mayfield Heights (city) Cuyahoga County	836	4.36

Top 10 Places Sorted by Percent of Total Population

Based on places with total population of 50,000 or more

Place	Population	%
Columbus (city) Franklin County	11,364	1.44
Parma (city) Cuyahoga County	630	0.77
Cincinnati (city) Hamilton County	2,036	0.69
Lakewood (city) Cuyahoga County	277	0.53
Akron (city) Summit County	874	0.44
Cleveland (city) Cuyahoga County	1,649	0.42
Toledo (city) Lucas County	995	0.35
Springfield (city) Clark County	196	0.32
Kettering (city) Montgomery County	182	0.32
Dayton (city) Montgomery County	281	0.20

Asian: Indonesian

Top 10 Places Sorted by Population

Based on all places, regardless of total population

Place	Population	%
Columbus (city) Franklin County	326	0.04
Athens (city) Athens County	41	0.17
Hilliard (city) Franklin County	38	0.13
Cincinnati (city) Hamilton County	31	0.01
Dublin (city) Franklin County	30	0.07
Toledo (city) Lucas County	28	0.01
Cleveland (city) Cuyahoga County	25	0.01
Upper Arlington (city) Franklin County	23	0.07
Lakewood (city) Cuyahoga County	21	0.04
Akron (city) Summit County	20	0.01

Top 10 Places Sorted by Percent of Total Population

Based on all places, regardless of total population

Place	Population	%
Amesville (village) Athens County	7	4.55
Glenwillow (village) Cuyahoga County	3	0.33
Lake Lorelei (cdp) Brown County	3	0.26
Clarktown (cdp) Scioto County	2	0.21
Highpoint (cdp) Hamilton County	3	0.20
Rushsylvania (village) Logan County	1	0.19
Athens (city) Athens County	41	0.17
McConnelsville (village) Morgan County	3	0.17
Hilliard (city) Franklin County	38	0.13
Atwater (cdp) Portage County	1	0.13

Top 10 Places Sorted by Percent of Total Population

Based on places with total population of 50,000 or more

Place	Population	%
Columbus (city) Franklin County	326	0.04
Lakewood (city) Cuyahoga County	21	0.04
Kettering (city) Montgomery County	13	0.02
Hamilton (city) Butler County	11	0.02
Cincinnati (city) Hamilton County	31	0.01
Toledo (city) Lucas County	28	0.01
Cleveland (city) Cuyahoga County	25	0.01
Akron (city) Summit County	20	0.01
Dayton (city) Montgomery County	16	0.01
Springfield (city) Clark County	6	0.01

Asian: Japanese

Top 10 Places Sorted by Population

Based on all places, regardless of total population

Place	Population	%
Columbus (city) Franklin County	2,331	0.30
Dublin (city) Franklin County	1,154	2.76
Cincinnati (city) Hamilton County	399	0.13
Cleveland (city) Cuyahoga County	349	0.09
Findlay (city) Hancock County	274	0.67
Toledo (city) Lucas County	272	0.09
Troy (city) Miami County	251	1.00
Beavercreek (city) Greene County	214	0.47
Akron (city) Summit County	207	0.10
Sidney (city) Shelby County	178	0.84

Top 10 Places Sorted by Percent of Total Population

Based on all places, regardless of total population

Place	Population	%
Batesville (village) Noble County	2	2.82
Dublin (city) Franklin County	1,154	2.76
Deersville (village) Harrison County	2	2.53

Place	Population	%
Sugar Bush Knolls (village) Portage County	4	2.26
Sixteen Mile Stand (cdp) Hamilton County	65	2.22
Hollansburg (village) Darke County	3	1.32
Melmore (cdp) Seneca County	2	1.31
Buckland (village) Auglaize County	3	1.29
Carbon Hill (cdp) Hocking County	3	1.29
Woodmere (village) Cuyahoga County	11	1.24

Top 10 Places Sorted by Percent of Total Population

Based on places with total population of 50,000 or more

Place	Population	%
Columbus (city) Franklin County	2,331	0.30
Kettering (city) Montgomery County	119	0.21
Lakewood (city) Cuyahoga County	95	0.18
Cincinnati (city) Hamilton County	399	0.13
Parma (city) Cuyahoga County	86	0.11
Springfield (city) Clark County	68	0.11
Akron (city) Summit County	207	0.10
Dayton (city) Montgomery County	147	0.10
Cleveland (city) Cuyahoga County	349	0.09
Toledo (city) Lucas County	272	0.09

Asian: Korean

Top 10 Places Sorted by Population

Based on all places, regardless of total population

Place	Population	%
Columbus (city) Franklin County	3,330	0.42
Cincinnati (city) Hamilton County	674	0.23
Dublin (city) Franklin County	611	1.46
Cleveland (city) Cuyahoga County	533	0.13
Beavercreek (city) Greene County	410	0.91
Toledo (city) Lucas County	382	0.13
Akron (city) Summit County	252	0.13
Upper Arlington (city) Franklin County	214	0.63
Mason (city) Warren County	192	0.63
Cleveland Heights (city) Cuyahoga County	186	0.40

Top 10 Places Sorted by Percent of Total Population

Based on all places, regardless of total population

Place	Population	%
Remington (cdp) Hamilton County	7	2.13
Sixteen Mile Stand (cdp) Hamilton County	53	1.81
Brice (village) Franklin County	2	1.75
Dublin (city) Franklin County	611	1.46
Lafayette (village) Allen County	6	1.35
Plumwood (cdp) Madison County	4	1.25
Sugar Bush Knolls (village) Portage County	2	1.13
Oberlin (city) Lorain County	85	1.03
West Elkton (village) Preble County	2	1.02
Beachwood (city) Cuyahoga County	110	0.92

Top 10 Places Sorted by Percent of Total Population

Based on places with total population of 50,000 or more

Place	Population	%
Columbus (city) Franklin County	3,330	0.42
Cincinnati (city) Hamilton County	674	0.23
Kettering (city) Montgomery County	124	0.22
Lakewood (city) Cuyahoga County	96	0.18
Elyria (city) Lorain County	76	0.14
Cleveland (city) Cuyahoga County	533	0.13
Toledo (city) Lucas County	382	0.13
Akron (city) Summit County	252	0.13
Dayton (city) Montgomery County	184	0.13
Parma (city) Cuyahoga County	86	0.11

Asian: Laotian

Top 10 Places Sorted by Population

Based on all places, regardless of total population

Place	Population	%
Columbus (city) Franklin County	1,412	0.18
Akron (city) Summit County	388	0.19
Findlay (city) Hancock County	133	0.32
Toledo (city) Lucas County	129	0.04
Cleveland (city) Cuyahoga County	108	0.03
Orrville (city) Wayne County	76	0.91
Reynoldsburg (city) Franklin County	70	0.20
Whitehall (city) Franklin County	56	0.31
Groveport (village) Franklin County	49	0.91
Blacklick Estates (cdp) Franklin County	47	0.54

Top 10 Places Sorted by Percent of Total Population

Based on all places, regardless of total population

Place	Population	%
Unionville Center (village) Union County	6	2.58
Maplewood Park (cdp) Trumbull County	3	1.07
Carey (village) Wyandot County	35	0.95
Orrville (city) Wayne County	76	0.91
Groveport (village) Franklin County	49	0.91
Montpelier (village) Williams County	37	0.91
Pettisville (cdp) Fulton County	4	0.80
Luckey (village) Wood County	8	0.79
New Haven (cdp) Huron County	3	0.75
Etna (cdp) Licking County	9	0.74

Top 10 Places Sorted by Percent of Total Population

Based on places with total population of 50,000 or more

Place	Population	%
Akron (city) Summit County	388	0.19
Columbus (city) Franklin County	1,412	0.18
Toledo (city) Lucas County	129	0.04
Springfield (city) Clark County	22	0.04
Cleveland (city) Cuyahoga County	108	0.03
Parma (city) Cuyahoga County	18	0.02
Youngstown (city) Mahoning County	10	0.01
Kettering (city) Montgomery County	7	0.01
Lakewood (city) Cuyahoga County	6	0.01
Cincinnati (city) Hamilton County	14	<0.01

Asian: Malaysian

Top 10 Places Sorted by Population

Based on all places, regardless of total population

Place	Population	%
Columbus (city) Franklin County	121	0.02
Toledo (city) Lucas County	22	0.01
Mason (city) Warren County	17	0.06
Athens (city) Athens County	12	0.05
Cleveland (city) Cuyahoga County	12	<0.01
Kent (city) Portage County	10	0.03
Dayton (city) Montgomery County	9	0.01
Akron (city) Summit County	9	<0.01
Beavercreek (city) Greene County	8	0.02
Oxford (city) Butler County	7	0.03

Top 10 Places Sorted by Percent of Total Population

Based on all places, regardless of total population

Place	Population	%
Northfield (village) Summit County	6	0.16
Bremen (village) Fairfield County	2	0.14
Chauncey (village) Athens County	1	0.10
Sunbury (village) Delaware County	4	0.09
Ada (village) Hardin County	4	0.07
Mason (city) Warren County	17	0.06
Athens (city) Athens County	12	0.05
Worthington (city) Franklin County	6	0.04
Montgomery (city) Hamilton County	4	0.04
Fairlawn (city) Summit County	3	0.04

Top 10 Places Sorted by Percent of Total Population

Based on places with total population of 50,000 or more

Place	Population	%
Columbus (city) Franklin County	121	0.02
Toledo (city) Lucas County	22	0.01
Dayton (city) Montgomery County	9	0.01
Kettering (city) Montgomery County	3	0.01
Cleveland (city) Cuyahoga County	12	<0.01
Akron (city) Summit County	9	<0.01
Cincinnati (city) Hamilton County	5	<0.01
Elyria (city) Lorain County	2	<0.01
Canton (city) Stark County	0	0.00
Hamilton (city) Butler County	0	0.00

Asian: Nepalese

Top 10 Places Sorted by Population

Based on all places, regardless of total population

Place	Population	%
Columbus (city) Franklin County	190	0.02
Cleveland (city) Cuyahoga County	108	0.03
Akron (city) Summit County	85	0.04
Cincinnati (city) Hamilton County	77	0.03
Kent (city) Portage County	39	0.13
Toledo (city) Lucas County	36	0.01
Cleveland Heights (city) Cuyahoga County	34	0.07
Lakewood (city) Cuyahoga County	29	0.06
Upper Arlington (city) Franklin County	23	0.07
South Euclid (city) Cuyahoga County	22	0.10

Top 10 Places Sorted by Percent of Total Population

Based on all places, regardless of total population

Place	Population	%
Derby (cdp) Pickaway County	4	0.98
Hiram (village) Portage County	13	0.92
Harrisburg (village) Franklin County	1	0.31
Kent (city) Portage County	39	0.13
South Euclid (city) Cuyahoga County	22	0.10
Oxford (city) Butler County	21	0.10
Sixteen Mile Stand (cdp) Hamilton County	3	0.10
Ottawa Hills (village) Lucas County	4	0.09
Montgomery (city) Hamilton County	8	0.08
Cleveland Heights (city) Cuyahoga County	34	0.07

Top 10 Places Sorted by Percent of Total Population

Based on places with total population of 50,000 or more

Place	Population	%
Lakewood (city) Cuyahoga County	29	0.06
Akron (city) Summit County	85	0.04
Cleveland (city) Cuyahoga County	108	0.03
Cincinnati (city) Hamilton County	77	0.03
Columbus (city) Franklin County	190	0.02
Toledo (city) Lucas County	36	0.01
Youngstown (city) Mahoning County	7	0.01
Parma (city) Cuyahoga County	5	0.01
Dayton (city) Montgomery County	4	<0.01
Hamilton (city) Butler County	3	<0.01

Asian: Pakistani

Top 10 Places Sorted by Population

Based on all places, regardless of total population

Place	Population	%
Columbus (city) Franklin County	927	0.12
Mason (city) Warren County	190	0.62
Hilliard (city) Franklin County	177	0.62
Cincinnati (city) Hamilton County	125	0.04
Beavercreek (city) Greene County	113	0.25
Dublin (city) Franklin County	105	0.25
Westlake (city) Cuyahoga County	98	0.30
Toledo (city) Lucas County	97	0.03
Pickerington (city) Fairfield County	89	0.49
Lakewood (city) Cuyahoga County	75	0.14

Top 10 Places Sorted by Percent of Total Population

Based on all places, regardless of total population

Place	Population	%
Mineral City (village) Tuscarawas County	7	0.96
Brady Lake (village) Portage County	4	0.86
Orange (village) Cuyahoga County	25	0.75
Mason (city) Warren County	190	0.62
Hilliard (city) Franklin County	177	0.62
Sixteen Mile Stand (cdp) Hamilton County	17	0.58
Etna (cdp) Licking County	7	0.58
Millbury (village) Wood County	6	0.50
Pickerington (city) Fairfield County	89	0.49
Bentleyville (village) Cuyahoga County	4	0.46

Top 10 Places Sorted by Percent of Total Population

Based on places with total population of 50,000 or more

Place	Population	%
Lakewood (city) Cuyahoga County	75	0.14
Columbus (city) Franklin County	927	0.12
Springfield (city) Clark County	38	0.06
Cincinnati (city) Hamilton County	125	0.04
Kettering (city) Montgomery County	21	0.04
Toledo (city) Lucas County	97	0.03
Parma (city) Cuyahoga County	21	0.03
Cleveland (city) Cuyahoga County	61	0.02
Dayton (city) Montgomery County	30	0.02
Youngstown (city) Mahoning County	12	0.02

Asian: Sri Lankan

Top 10 Places Sorted by Population

Based on all places, regardless of total population

Place	Population	%
Columbus (city) Franklin County	202	0.03
Cincinnati (city) Hamilton County	82	0.03
Dublin (city) Franklin County	35	0.08
Hilliard (city) Franklin County	21	0.07
Akron (city) Summit County	18	0.01
Toledo (city) Lucas County	18	0.01
Cleveland (city) Cuyahoga County	18	<0.01
Cleveland Heights (city) Cuyahoga County	17	0.04
Beavercreek (city) Greene County	16	0.04
Mason (city) Warren County	15	0.05

Top 10 Places Sorted by Percent of Total Population

Based on all places, regardless of total population

Place	Population	%
Fairfax (village) Hamilton County	9	0.53
Four Bridges (cdp) Butler County	11	0.38
Gates Mills (village) Cuyahoga County	4	0.18
Union City (village) Darke County	3	0.18
Kenwood (cdp) Hamilton County	9	0.13
Fairlawn (city) Summit County	9	0.12
Greentown (cdp) Stark County	4	0.11
Sixteen Mile Stand (cdp) Hamilton County	3	0.10
Dublin (city) Franklin County	35	0.08
Dry Run (cdp) Hamilton County	6	0.08

Top 10 Places Sorted by Percent of Total Population

Based on places with total population of 50,000 or more

Place	Population	%
Columbus (city) Franklin County	202	0.03
Cincinnati (city) Hamilton County	82	0.03
Akron (city) Summit County	18	0.01
Toledo (city) Lucas County	18	0.01
Dayton (city) Montgomery County	9	0.01
Elyria (city) Lorain County	8	0.01
Parma (city) Cuyahoga County	8	0.01
Cleveland (city) Cuyahoga County	18	<0.01
Kettering (city) Montgomery County	2	<0.01
Springfield (city) Clark County	2	<0.01

Asian: Taiwanese

Top 10 Places Sorted by Population

Based on all places, regardless of total population

Place	Population	%
Columbus (city) Franklin County	626	0.08
Cincinnati (city) Hamilton County	122	0.04
Dublin (city) Franklin County	121	0.29
Upper Arlington (city) Franklin County	109	0.32
Cleveland (city) Cuyahoga County	102	0.03
Cleveland Heights (city) Cuyahoga County	83	0.18
Mason (city) Warren County	56	0.18
Akron (city) Summit County	54	0.03
Solon (city) Cuyahoga County	52	0.22
Beavercreek (city) Greene County	52	0.12

Top 10 Places Sorted by Percent of Total Population

Based on all places, regardless of total population

Place	Population	%
Evendale (village) Hamilton County	18	0.65
Sixteen Mile Stand (cdp) Hamilton County	17	0.58
Pigeon Creek (cdp) Summit County	3	0.34
Upper Arlington (city) Franklin County	109	0.32
The Village of Indian Hill (city) Hamilton County	18	0.31
Dublin (city) Franklin County	121	0.29
Blue Ash (city) Hamilton County	31	0.26
Oberlin (city) Lorain County	21	0.25
Solon (city) Cuyahoga County	52	0.22
Wyoming (city) Hamilton County	18	0.21

Top 10 Places Sorted by Percent of Total Population

Based on places with total population of 50,000 or more

Place	Population	%
Columbus (city) Franklin County	626	0.08
Cincinnati (city) Hamilton County	122	0.04
Cleveland (city) Cuyahoga County	102	0.03
Akron (city) Summit County	54	0.03
Kettering (city) Montgomery County	15	0.03
Lakewood (city) Cuyahoga County	8	0.02
Toledo (city) Lucas County	30	0.01
Dayton (city) Montgomery County	12	0.01
Elyria (city) Lorain County	3	0.01
Parma (city) Cuyahoga County	4	<0.01

Asian: Thai

Top 10 Places Sorted by Population

Based on all places, regardless of total population

Place	Population	%
Columbus (city) Franklin County	594	0.08
Cincinnati (city) Hamilton County	143	0.05
Cleveland (city) Cuyahoga County	121	0.03
Akron (city) Summit County	116	0.06
Toledo (city) Lucas County	116	0.04
Cleveland Heights (city) Cuyahoga County	68	0.15
Fairborn (city) Greene County	63	0.19
Dayton (city) Montgomery County	54	0.04
Huber Heights (city) Montgomery County	49	0.13
Lakewood (city) Cuyahoga County	47	0.09

Top 10 Places Sorted by Percent of Total Population

Based on all places, regardless of total population

Place	Population	%
Kimbolton (cdp) Guernsey County	2	1.39
Etna (cdp) Licking County	6	0.49
Crown City (village) Gallia County	2	0.48
Hebron (village) Licking County	11	0.47
Albany (village) Athens County	3	0.36
Green Meadows (cdp) Clark County	8	0.34
New Vienna (village) Clinton County	4	0.33
Donnelsville (village) Clark County	1	0.33
Minerva Park (village) Franklin County	4	0.31
Urbancrest (village) Franklin County	3	0.31

Top 10 Places Sorted by Percent of Total Population

Based on places with total population of 50,000 or more

Place	Population	%
Lakewood (city) Cuyahoga County	47	0.09
Columbus (city) Franklin County	594	0.08
Akron (city) Summit County	116	0.06
Cincinnati (city) Hamilton County	143	0.05
Kettering (city) Montgomery County	26	0.05
Toledo (city) Lucas County	116	0.04
Dayton (city) Montgomery County	54	0.04
Cleveland (city) Cuyahoga County	121	0.03
Hamilton (city) Butler County	19	0.03
Springfield (city) Clark County	16	0.03

Asian: Vietnamese

Top 10 Places Sorted by Population

Based on all places, regardless of total population

Place	Population	%
Columbus (city) Franklin County	2,319	0.29
Cleveland (city) Cuyahoga County	990	0.25
Akron (city) Summit County	474	0.24
Cincinnati (city) Hamilton County	359	0.12
Huber Heights (city) Montgomery County	294	0.77
Toledo (city) Lucas County	286	0.10
Fairfield (city) Butler County	224	0.53
Dayton (city) Montgomery County	220	0.16
Brooklyn (city) Cuyahoga County	193	1.73
Beavercreek (city) Greene County	188	0.42

Top 10 Places Sorted by Percent of Total Population

Based on all places, regardless of total population

Place	Population	%
Brooklyn (city) Cuyahoga County	193	1.73
West Leipsic (village) Putnam County	3	1.46
Sheffield (village) Lorain County	50	1.26
Galena (village) Delaware County	7	1.07
Beckett Ridge (cdp) Butler County	92	1.00
Waldo (village) Marion County	3	0.89
Springdale (city) Hamilton County	92	0.82
Four Bridges (cdp) Butler County	23	0.79
Huber Heights (city) Montgomery County	294	0.77
Bettsville (village) Seneca County	5	0.76

Top 10 Places Sorted by Percent of Total Population

Based on places with total population of 50,000 or more

Place	Population	%
Columbus (city) Franklin County	2,319	0.29
Cleveland (city) Cuyahoga County	990	0.25
Akron (city) Summit County	474	0.24
Parma (city) Cuyahoga County	176	0.22
Kettering (city) Montgomery County	116	0.21
Dayton (city) Montgomery County	220	0.16
Hamilton (city) Butler County	98	0.16
Cincinnati (city) Hamilton County	359	0.12
Lakewood (city) Cuyahoga County	62	0.12
Toledo (city) Lucas County	286	0.10

Hawaii Native/Pacific Islander

Top 10 Places Sorted by Population

Based on all places, regardless of total population

Place	Population	%
Columbus (city) Franklin County	1,346	0.17
Cleveland (city) Cuyahoga County	582	0.15
Cincinnati (city) Hamilton County	465	0.16
Toledo (city) Lucas County	275	0.10
Akron (city) Summit County	189	0.09
Dayton (city) Montgomery County	166	0.12
Hamilton (city) Butler County	104	0.17
Dover (city) Tuscarawas County	100	0.78
Urbancrest (village) Franklin County	97	10.10
Springfield (city) Clark County	96	0.16

Top 10 Places Sorted by Percent of Total Population

Based on all places, regardless of total population

Place	Population	%
Urbancrest (village) Franklin County	97	10.10
Brecon (cdp) Hamilton County	5	2.05
Linndale (village) Cuyahoga County	3	1.68
Haydenville (cdp) Hocking County	6	1.57
Highpoint (cdp) Hamilton County	18	1.20
Kettlersville (village) Shelby County	2	1.12
Zanesfield (village) Logan County	2	1.02
Valleyview (village) Franklin County	6	0.97
Elmwood Place (village) Hamilton County	21	0.96
Plumwood (cdp) Madison County	3	0.94

Top 10 Places Sorted by Percent of Total Population

Based on places with total population of 50,000 or more

Place	Population	%
Columbus (city) Franklin County	1,346	0.17
Hamilton (city) Butler County	104	0.17
Cincinnati (city) Hamilton County	465	0.16
Springfield (city) Clark County	96	0.16
Cleveland (city) Cuyahoga County	582	0.15
Lorain (city) Lorain County	88	0.14
Canton (city) Stark County	93	0.13
Youngstown (city) Mahoning County	87	0.13
Dayton (city) Montgomery County	166	0.12
Elyria (city) Lorain County	65	0.12

Hawaii Native/Pacific Islander: Not Hispanic

Top 10 Places Sorted by Population

Based on all places, regardless of total population

Place	Population	%
Columbus (city) Franklin County	1,149	0.15
Cleveland (city) Cuyahoga County	347	0.09
Cincinnati (city) Hamilton County	344	0.12
Toledo (city) Lucas County	220	0.08
Akron (city) Summit County	164	0.08
Dayton (city) Montgomery County	148	0.10
Urbancrest (village) Franklin County	97	10.10
Hamilton (city) Butler County	82	0.13
Huber Heights (city) Montgomery County	74	0.19
Springfield (city) Clark County	73	0.12

Top 10 Places Sorted by Percent of Total Population

Based on all places, regardless of total population

Place	Population	%
Urbancrest (village) Franklin County	97	10.10
Brecon (cdp) Hamilton County	5	2.05

Place	Population	%
Linndale (village) Cuyahoga County	3	1.68
Highpoint (cdp) Hamilton County	18	1.20
Kettlersville (village) Shelby County	2	1.12
Zanesfield (village) Logan County	2	1.02
Valleyview (village) Franklin County	6	0.97
Elmwood Place (village) Hamilton County	21	0.96
Plumwood (cdp) Madison County	3	0.94
Polk (village) Ashland County	3	0.89

Top 10 Places Sorted by Percent of Total Population

Based on places with total population of 50,000 or more

Place	Population	%
Columbus (city) Franklin County	1,149	0.15
Hamilton (city) Butler County	82	0.13
Cincinnati (city) Hamilton County	344	0.12
Springfield (city) Clark County	73	0.12
Dayton (city) Montgomery County	148	0.10
Cleveland (city) Cuyahoga County	347	0.09
Parma (city) Cuyahoga County	71	0.09
Canton (city) Stark County	65	0.09
Toledo (city) Lucas County	220	0.08
Akron (city) Summit County	164	0.08

Hawaii Native/Pacific Islander: Hispanic

Top 10 Places Sorted by Population

Based on all places, regardless of total population

Place	Population	%
Cleveland (city) Cuyahoga County	235	0.06
Columbus (city) Franklin County	197	0.03
Cincinnati (city) Hamilton County	121	0.04
Lorain (city) Lorain County	61	0.10
Dover (city) Tuscarawas County	59	0.46
Toledo (city) Lucas County	55	0.02
New Philadelphia (city) Tuscarawas County	50	0.29
Youngstown (city) Mahoning County	33	0.05
Canton (city) Stark County	28	0.04
Akron (city) Summit County	25	0.01

Top 10 Places Sorted by Percent of Total Population

Based on all places, regardless of total population

Place	Population	%
Haydenville (cdp) Hocking County	6	1.57
Celeryville (cdp) Huron County	1	0.48
Dover (city) Tuscarawas County	59	0.46
New Philadelphia (city) Tuscarawas County	50	0.29
Spencer (village) Medina County	2	0.27
Strasburg (village) Tuscarawas County	6	0.23
Lake Tomahawk (cdp) Columbiana County	1	0.21
Hebron (village) Licking County	4	0.17
Calcutta (cdp) Columbiana County	6	0.16
Valley View (village) Cuyahoga County	3	0.15

Top 10 Places Sorted by Percent of Total Population

Based on places with total population of 50,000 or more

Place	Population	%
Lorain (city) Lorain County	61	0.10
Cleveland (city) Cuyahoga County	235	0.06
Youngstown (city) Mahoning County	33	0.05
Cincinnati (city) Hamilton County	121	0.04
Canton (city) Stark County	28	0.04
Springfield (city) Clark County	23	0.04
Hamilton (city) Butler County	22	0.04
Elyria (city) Lorain County	20	0.04
Columbus (city) Franklin County	197	0.03
Toledo (city) Lucas County	55	0.02

Hawaii Native/Pacific Islander: Fijian

Top 10 Places Sorted by Population

Based on all places, regardless of total population

Place	Population	%
Springfield (city) Clark County	11	0.02
Columbus (city) Franklin County	7	<0.01
Fremont (city) Sandusky County	6	0.04
Huber Heights (city) Montgomery County	5	0.01
Elmwood Place (village) Hamilton County	3	0.14
Middletown (city) Butler County	3	0.01
Chillicothe (city) Ross County	2	0.01
Gahanna (city) Franklin County	2	0.01
Painesville (city) Lake County	2	0.01
Toledo (city) Lucas County	2	<0.01

Top 10 Places Sorted by Percent of Total Population

Based on all places, regardless of total population

Place	Population	%
Elmwood Place (village) Hamilton County	3	0.14
Adena (village) Jefferson County	1	0.13
Bethesda (village) Belmont County	1	0.08
Fremont (city) Sandusky County	6	0.04
Fruit Hill (cdp) Hamilton County	1	0.03
Springfield (city) Clark County	11	0.02
St. Bernard (city) Hamilton County	1	0.02
Huber Heights (city) Montgomery County	5	0.01
Middletown (city) Butler County	3	0.01
Chillicothe (city) Ross County	2	0.01

Top 10 Places Sorted by Percent of Total Population

Based on places with total population of 50,000 or more

Place	Population	%
Springfield (city) Clark County	11	0.02
Columbus (city) Franklin County	7	<0.01
Toledo (city) Lucas County	2	<0.01
Cincinnati (city) Hamilton County	1	<0.01
Akron (city) Summit County	0	0.00
Canton (city) Stark County	0	0.00
Cleveland (city) Cuyahoga County	0	0.00
Dayton (city) Montgomery County	0	0.00
Elyria (city) Lorain County	0	0.00
Hamilton (city) Butler County	0	0.00

Hawaii Native/Pacific Islander: Guamanian or Chamorro

Top 10 Places Sorted by Population

Based on all places, regardless of total population

Place	Population	%
Cincinnati (city) Hamilton County	202	0.07
Columbus (city) Franklin County	181	0.02
Dover (city) Tuscarawas County	89	0.69
Cleveland (city) Cuyahoga County	73	0.02
New Philadelphia (city) Tuscarawas County	65	0.38
Huber Heights (city) Montgomery County	33	0.09
Dayton (city) Montgomery County	31	0.02
Hamilton (city) Butler County	30	0.05
Sidney (city) Shelby County	29	0.14
Canton (city) Stark County	28	0.04

Top 10 Places Sorted by Percent of Total Population

Based on all places, regardless of total population

Place	Population	%
Brice (village) Franklin County	1	0.88
Dover (city) Tuscarawas County	89	0.69
Strasburg (village) Tuscarawas County	15	0.58
Sulphur Springs (cdp) Crawford County	1	0.52
Bourneville (cdp) Ross County	1	0.50
New Philadelphia (city) Tuscarawas County	65	0.38
Grand Rapids (village) Wood County	3	0.31
Elmwood Place (village) Hamilton County	6	0.27
Whites Landing (cdp) Erie County	1	0.27
Willshire (village) Van Wert County	1	0.25

Top 10 Places Sorted by Percent of Total Population

Based on places with total population of 50,000 or more

Place	Population	%
Cincinnati (city) Hamilton County	202	0.07
Hamilton (city) Butler County	30	0.05
Canton (city) Stark County	28	0.04
Columbus (city) Franklin County	181	0.02
Cleveland (city) Cuyahoga County	73	0.02
Dayton (city) Montgomery County	31	0.02
Elyria (city) Lorain County	13	0.02
Springfield (city) Clark County	12	0.02
Toledo (city) Lucas County	28	0.01
Akron (city) Summit County	27	0.01

Hawaii Native/Pacific Islander: Marshallese

Top 10 Places Sorted by Population

Based on all places, regardless of total population

Place	Population	%
Celina (city) Mercer County	24	0.23
Coldwater (village) Mercer County	9	0.20
St. Marys (city) Auglaize County	6	0.07
Mount Healthy (city) Hamilton County	5	0.08
Hamilton (city) Butler County	5	0.01
Dayton (city) Montgomery County	4	<0.01
Zanesfield (village) Logan County	2	1.02
De Graff (village) Logan County	2	0.16
Wyoming (city) Hamilton County	2	0.02
Athens (city) Athens County	2	0.01

Top 10 Places Sorted by Percent of Total Population

Based on all places, regardless of total population

Place	Population	%
Zanesfield (village) Logan County	2	1.02
Celina (city) Mercer County	24	0.23
Coldwater (village) Mercer County	9	0.20
De Graff (village) Logan County	2	0.16
Mount Healthy (city) Hamilton County	5	0.08
St. Marys (city) Auglaize County	6	0.07
West Liberty (village) Logan County	1	0.06
Waynesville (village) Warren County	1	0.04
Greenhills (village) Hamilton County	1	0.03
Wyoming (city) Hamilton County	2	0.02

Top 10 Places Sorted by Percent of Total Population

Based on places with total population of 50,000 or more

Place	Population	%
Hamilton (city) Butler County	5	0.01
Dayton (city) Montgomery County	4	<0.01
Cincinnati (city) Hamilton County	2	<0.01
Springfield (city) Clark County	1	<0.01
Akron (city) Summit County	0	0.00
Canton (city) Stark County	0	0.00
Cleveland (city) Cuyahoga County	0	0.00
Columbus (city) Franklin County	0	0.00
Elyria (city) Lorain County	0	0.00
Kettering (city) Montgomery County	0	0.00

Hawaii Native/Pacific Islander: Native Hawaiian

Top 10 Places Sorted by Population

Based on all places, regardless of total population

Place	Population	%
Columbus (city) Franklin County	336	0.04
Cleveland (city) Cuyahoga County	127	0.03
Toledo (city) Lucas County	86	0.03
Akron (city) Summit County	84	0.04
Cincinnati (city) Hamilton County	70	0.02
Dayton (city) Montgomery County	57	0.04
Canton (city) Stark County	32	0.04
Fairborn (city) Greene County	30	0.09
Beavercreek (city) Greene County	29	0.06
Strongsville (city) Cuyahoga County	26	0.06

Top 10 Places Sorted by Percent of Total Population

Based on all places, regardless of total population

Place	Population	%
Linndale (village) Cuyahoga County	3	1.68
Plumwood (cdp) Madison County	3	0.94
Clarington (village) Monroe County	3	0.78
Cairo (village) Allen County	4	0.76
Elmwood Place (village) Hamilton County	12	0.55
Haviland (village) Paulding County	1	0.47
Portage (village) Wood County	2	0.46
Hollansburg (village) Darke County	1	0.44
Amanda (village) Fairfield County	3	0.41
Alexandria (village) Licking County	2	0.39

Top 10 Places Sorted by Percent of Total Population

Based on places with total population of 50,000 or more

Place	Population	%
Columbus (city) Franklin County	336	0.04

Place	Population	%
Akron (city) Summit County	84	0.04
Dayton (city) Montgomery County	57	0.04
Canton (city) Stark County	32	0.04
Youngstown (city) Mahoning County	25	0.04
Hamilton (city) Butler County	22	0.04
Cleveland (city) Cuyahoga County	127	0.03
Toledo (city) Lucas County	86	0.03
Elyria (city) Lorain County	16	0.03
Springfield (city) Clark County	16	0.03

Hawaii Native/Pacific Islander: Samoan

Top 10 Places Sorted by Population

Based on all places, regardless of total population

Place	Population	%
Columbus (city) Franklin County	399	0.05
Urbancrest (village) Franklin County	93	9.69
Cincinnati (city) Hamilton County	51	0.02
Dayton (city) Montgomery County	34	0.02
Toledo (city) Lucas County	34	0.01
Cleveland (city) Cuyahoga County	24	0.01
Mansfield (city) Richland County	14	0.03
Akron (city) Summit County	14	0.01
Springfield (city) Clark County	10	0.02
Blacklick Estates (cdp) Franklin County	9	0.10

Top 10 Places Sorted by Percent of Total Population

Based on all places, regardless of total population

Place	Population	%
Urbancrest (village) Franklin County	93	9.69
Valleyview (village) Franklin County	6	0.97
Hilltop (cdp) Trumbull County	3	0.56
New Riegel (village) Seneca County	1	0.40
Rosewood (cdp) Champaign County	1	0.39
Bethel (village) Clermont County	8	0.30
Mendon (village) Mercer County	2	0.30
Blacklick Estates (cdp) Franklin County	9	0.10
New Albany (village) Franklin County	8	0.10
Spencerville (village) Allen County	2	0.09

Top 10 Places Sorted by Percent of Total Population

Based on places with total population of 50,000 or more

Place	Population	%
Columbus (city) Franklin County	399	0.05
Cincinnati (city) Hamilton County	51	0.02
Dayton (city) Montgomery County	34	0.02
Springfield (city) Clark County	10	0.02
Toledo (city) Lucas County	34	0.01
Cleveland (city) Cuyahoga County	24	0.01
Akron (city) Summit County	14	0.01
Canton (city) Stark County	9	0.01
Hamilton (city) Butler County	9	0.01
Parma (city) Cuyahoga County	9	0.01

Hawaii Native/Pacific Islander: Tongan

Top 10 Places Sorted by Population

Based on all places, regardless of total population

Place	Population	%
Newark (city) Licking County	8	0.02
Hamilton (city) Butler County	7	0.01
Fremont (city) Sandusky County	6	0.04
Cleveland (city) Cuyahoga County	6	<0.01
Brook Park (city) Cuyahoga County	4	0.02
Middleburg Heights (city) Cuyahoga County	3	0.02
Avon (city) Lorain County	3	0.01
Cleveland Heights (city) Cuyahoga County	3	0.01
St. Bernard (city) Hamilton County	2	0.05
Wilmington (city) Clinton County	2	0.02

Top 10 Places Sorted by Percent of Total Population

Based on all places, regardless of total population

Place	Population	%
St. Bernard (city) Hamilton County	2	0.05
Fremont (city) Sandusky County	6	0.04
New Richmond (village) Clermont County	1	0.04
Fairport Harbor (village) Lake County	1	0.03
Newark (city) Licking County	8	0.02
Brook Park (city) Cuyahoga County	4	0.02
Middleburg Heights (city) Cuyahoga County	3	0.02
Wilmington (city) Clinton County	2	0.02
Chagrin Falls (village) Cuyahoga County	1	0.02
Hamilton (city) Butler County	7	0.01

Top 10 Places Sorted by Percent of Total Population

Based on places with total population of 50,000 or more

Place	Population	%
Hamilton (city) Butler County	7	0.01
Cleveland (city) Cuyahoga County	6	<0.01
Columbus (city) Franklin County	2	<0.01
Dayton (city) Montgomery County	2	<0.01
Springfield (city) Clark County	2	<0.01
Toledo (city) Lucas County	2	<0.01
Akron (city) Summit County	1	<0.01
Canton (city) Stark County	0	0.00
Cincinnati (city) Hamilton County	0	0.00
Elyria (city) Lorain County	0	0.00

White

Top 10 Places Sorted by Population

Based on all places, regardless of total population

Place	Population	%
Columbus (city) Franklin County	505,454	64.22
Toledo (city) Lucas County	195,953	68.23
Cleveland (city) Cuyahoga County	156,136	39.35
Cincinnati (city) Hamilton County	152,515	51.36
Akron (city) Summit County	129,298	64.94
Parma (city) Cuyahoga County	77,034	94.40
Dayton (city) Montgomery County	76,680	54.18
Hamilton (city) Butler County	54,183	86.72
Canton (city) Stark County	53,661	73.50
Kettering (city) Montgomery County	53,090	94.53

Top 10 Places Sorted by Percent of Total Population

Based on all places, regardless of total population

Place	Population	%
Scio (village) Harrison County	763	100.00
Russia (village) Shelby County	640	100.00
Stoutsville (village) Fairfield County	560	100.00
Verona (village) Preble County	494	100.00
McDermott (cdp) Scioto County	434	100.00
Harrod (village) Allen County	417	100.00
Beallsville (village) Monroe County	409	100.00
Hanoverton (village) Columbiana County	408	100.00
Bascom (cdp) Seneca County	390	100.00
Green Camp (village) Marion County	374	100.00

Top 10 Places Sorted by Percent of Total Population

Based on places with total population of 50,000 or more

Place	Population	%
Kettering (city) Montgomery County	53,090	94.53
Parma (city) Cuyahoga County	77,034	94.40
Lakewood (city) Cuyahoga County	46,836	89.84
Hamilton (city) Butler County	54,183	86.72
Elyria (city) Lorain County	44,643	81.86
Springfield (city) Clark County	47,786	78.84
Canton (city) Stark County	53,661	73.50
Lorain (city) Lorain County	46,446	72.46
Toledo (city) Lucas County	195,953	68.23
Akron (city) Summit County	129,298	64.94

White: Not Hispanic

Top 10 Places Sorted by Population

Based on all places, regardless of total population

Place	Population	%
Columbus (city) Franklin County	485,567	61.70
Toledo (city) Lucas County	183,797	63.99
Cincinnati (city) Hamilton County	148,354	49.96
Cleveland (city) Cuyahoga County	138,590	34.93
Akron (city) Summit County	126,928	63.75
Parma (city) Cuyahoga County	75,053	91.98
Dayton (city) Montgomery County	74,600	52.71
Hamilton (city) Butler County	52,579	84.16
Canton (city) Stark County	52,555	71.99
Kettering (city) Montgomery County	52,203	92.95

Top 10 Places Sorted by Percent of Total Population

Based on all places, regardless of total population

Place	Population	%
Verona (village) Preble County	494	100.00
Beallsville (village) Monroe County	409	100.00
Hanoverton (village) Columbiana County	408	100.00
Port Jefferson (village) Shelby County	371	100.00
Freeport (village) Harrison County	369	100.00
Winesburg (cdp) Holmes County	352	100.00
Conesville (village) Coshocton County	347	100.00
Somerville (village) Butler County	281	100.00
Casstown (village) Miami County	267	100.00
North Star (village) Darke County	236	100.00

Top 10 Places Sorted by Percent of Total Population

Based on places with total population of 50,000 or more

Place	Population	%
Kettering (city) Montgomery County	52,203	92.95
Parma (city) Cuyahoga County	75,053	91.98
Lakewood (city) Cuyahoga County	45,393	87.07
Hamilton (city) Butler County	52,579	84.16
Elyria (city) Lorain County	42,979	78.81
Springfield (city) Clark County	46,921	77.42
Canton (city) Stark County	52,555	71.99
Toledo (city) Lucas County	183,797	63.99
Akron (city) Summit County	126,928	63.75
Columbus (city) Franklin County	485,567	61.70

White: Hispanic

Top 10 Places Sorted by Population

Based on all places, regardless of total population

Place	Population	%
Columbus (city) Franklin County	19,887	2.53
Cleveland (city) Cuyahoga County	17,546	4.42
Toledo (city) Lucas County	12,156	4.23
Lorain (city) Lorain County	9,366	14.61
Cincinnati (city) Hamilton County	4,161	1.40
Youngstown (city) Mahoning County	3,037	4.53
Akron (city) Summit County	2,370	1.19
Dayton (city) Montgomery County	2,080	1.47
Parma (city) Cuyahoga County	1,981	2.43
Fremont (city) Sandusky County	1,724	10.30

Top 10 Places Sorted by Percent of Total Population

Based on all places, regardless of total population

Place	Population	%
Tedrow (cdp) Fulton County	41	23.70
Brecon (cdp) Hamilton County	50	20.49
Hessville (cdp) Sandusky County	41	19.16
Milton Center (village) Wood County	24	16.67
West Leipsic (village) Putnam County	33	16.02
Hamler (village) Henry County	87	15.10
Lorain (city) Lorain County	9,366	14.61
Leipsic (village) Putnam County	270	12.90
Willard (city) Huron County	803	12.88
Linndale (village) Cuyahoga County	22	12.29

Top 10 Places Sorted by Percent of Total Population

Based on places with total population of 50,000 or more

Place	Population	%
Lorain (city) Lorain County	9,366	14.61
Youngstown (city) Mahoning County	3,037	4.53
Cleveland (city) Cuyahoga County	17,546	4.42
Toledo (city) Lucas County	12,156	4.23
Elyria (city) Lorain County	1,664	3.05
Lakewood (city) Cuyahoga County	1,443	2.77
Hamilton (city) Butler County	1,604	2.57
Columbus (city) Franklin County	19,887	2.53
Parma (city) Cuyahoga County	1,981	2.43
Kettering (city) Montgomery County	887	1.58

Climate

Ohio Physical Features and Climate Narrative

PHYSICAL FEATURES AND GENERAL CLIMATE. The climate of Ohio is remarkably varied. Less than one-half of its area is occupied by typical plains, while most of eastern and much of southern Ohio is hilly. Topography ranges in elevation from 430 feet above sea level at the junction of the Great Miami and Ohio Rivers up to 1,550 feet on a summit near Bellefontaine. In addition to this high point there are innumerable other hills which rise above 1,400 feet (mean sea level). These are located mainly along the dividing line between the Ohio River and Lake Erie drainage basins. Large areas in the State have elevations above 1,000 feet. An extensive area in northwestern Ohio is occupied by a flat lake plain — once the bottom of glacial Lake Maumee which was much larger than the present Lake Erie. The greater part of eastern Ohio is within the Allegheny Plateau, an unglaciated area consisting of picturesque hills, many of which rise above 1,300 feet and comprise many winding rivers and streams.

The Ohio River, which forms the southern and southeastern boundaries of Ohio, and its tributaries drain the greater portion of the State. A number of streams drain northward into Lake Erie. Although this area comprises nearly a third of the State, the divide between the two drainages is only 20 to 40 miles from the lake shore for a distance of more than 100 miles until it dips south of the arrowhead-shaped Maumee Basin. The largest streams in this region are the Maumee, Sandusky, and Cuyahoga Rivers. Principal tributaries flowing southward into the Ohio River include the Muskingum in the east, the Scioto in the central section, and the Great Miami in the west. A small portion in the west-central region drains westward into the Wabash River basin of Indiana.

Located west of the Appalachian Mountains, Ohio has a climate essentially continental in nature, characterized by moderate extremes of heat and cold, and wetness and dryness. Summers are moderately warm and humid, with occasional days when temperatures exceed 100°F.; winters are reasonably cold, with an average of about two days of subzero weather; and autumns are predominately cool, dry, and invigorating. Spring is the wettest season and vegetation is lush and profuse.

PRECIPITATION. Annual precipitation is slightly in excess of the national average and is well distributed, though with peaks in early spring and summer. In spite of the relatively small range in latitude and the compact shape of Ohio, rainfall varies considerably in amount and seasonal distribution. This is accounted for not only by the presence of Lake Erie on the north, but also by its topography and proximity to rain producing storm paths. Annual precipitation averages about 38 inches, being most generous in spring (about four inches in April) and least in the fall (about 2.5 inches in October). Greatest amounts are measured in the southwest where Wilmington has an average of 44.36 inches; the lake shore is driest, with Gilbralter Island having a normal of only 29.06 inches.

The southern half of the State is visited more frequently by productive rainstorms which, together with the general roughness of terrain, accounts for the larger total precipitation. The lifting of moist air masses over the hills tends to increase the yield of rainfall, especially in winter and spring. There is a marked tendency during the cold season for northeastern counties to receive snowfall amounts substantially in excess of those measured elsewhere. Northerly winds have a long fetch across Lake Huron and the widest part of Lake Erie, thus picking up moisture and heat from the lakes. This moisture is then forced to condense as the air is lifted abruptly over the divide a short distance from the lake. Average snowfall ranges from 60 inches in parts of Lake and adjoining counties down to 16 inches or less along the Ohio River.

TEMPERATURE. The normal annual temperature for the State ranges from 49.6°F. at Hiram in Portage County up to 56.9°F. at Portsmouth on the Ohio River. Variations over the State are due mainly to differences in latitude and topography, but the immediate lake shore area experiences a moderating effect due to its proximity to a large body of water. Widest temperature ranges are found generally among the eastern hills. In an average year, 90°F. heat may be expected about 20 times in summer with 100°F. or more once or twice. Readings of zero or lower are generally to be expected on two to four days each winter, and these are just as likely to occur in the south as the north. However, one winter out of six or eight will pass without experiencing zero readings anywhere in the State.

OTHER CLIMATIC ELEMENTS. The growing season, as defined by the period 32°F. or higher, ranges widely because of latitude and proximity to Lake Erie. The longest is about 200 days on the lake shore and the shortest is in the northeastern valleys within the Ohio River drainage. Dates of the average last freezing temperature in spring range from April 15 to May 18 and the mean first freeze date in fall varies from September 30 to November 6, the latter being on the western lake shore.

Damaging windstorms are mostly associated with heavy thunderstorms or line squalls. Three or four tornadoes may be expected to strike in Ohio each year. Most tornadoes, however, are of limited effect having paths that are short and narrow.

Most floods in Ohio are caused by unusual precipitation. The storms causing floods may bring rainfall of unusual intensity or of unusual duration and extent. Some floods may be caused by a series of ordinary storms which follow one another in rapid succession. Others may result from rain falling at relatively high temperatures on snow-covered areas. At times, though infrequent, flood conditions are caused or aggravated by ice gorges, especially in the tributary streams. Severe thunderstorms frequently cause local flash flooding. General flooding occurs most frequently during January to March and rarely occurs during August to October.

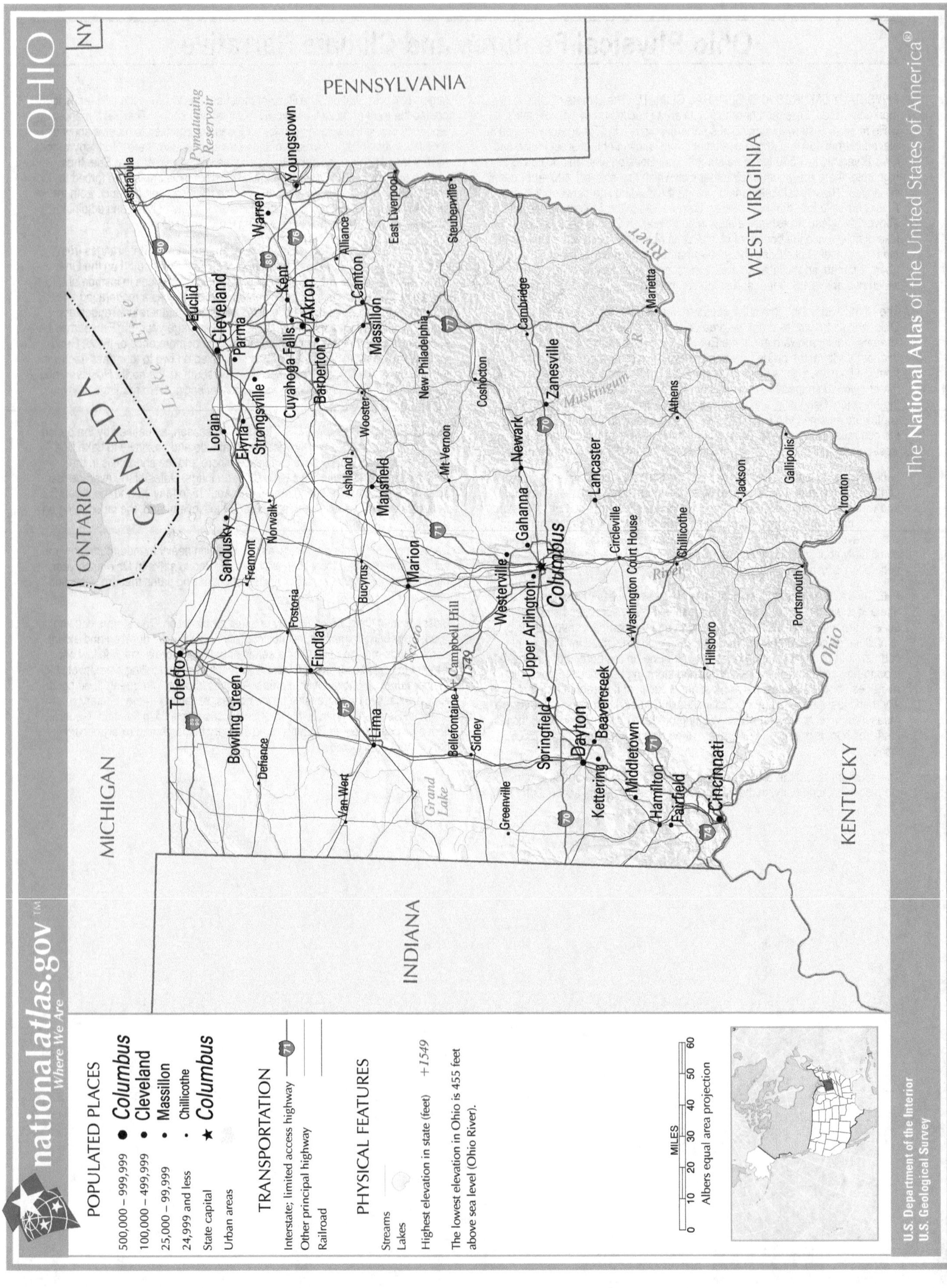

nationalatlas.gov™
Where We Are

OHIO

POPULATED PLACES

500,000 – 999,999	● Columbus
100,000 – 499,999	• Cleveland
25,000 – 99,999	• Massillon
24,999 and less	· Chillicothe
State capital	★ Columbus
Urban areas	

TRANSPORTATION

Interstate; limited access highway
Other principal highway
Railroad

PHYSICAL FEATURES

Streams
Lakes
Highest elevation in state (feet) +1549

The lowest elevation in Ohio is 455 feet above sea level (Ohio River).

MILES
0 10 20 30 40 50 60
Albers equal area projection

U.S. Department of the Interior
U.S. Geological Survey

The National Atlas of the United States of America®

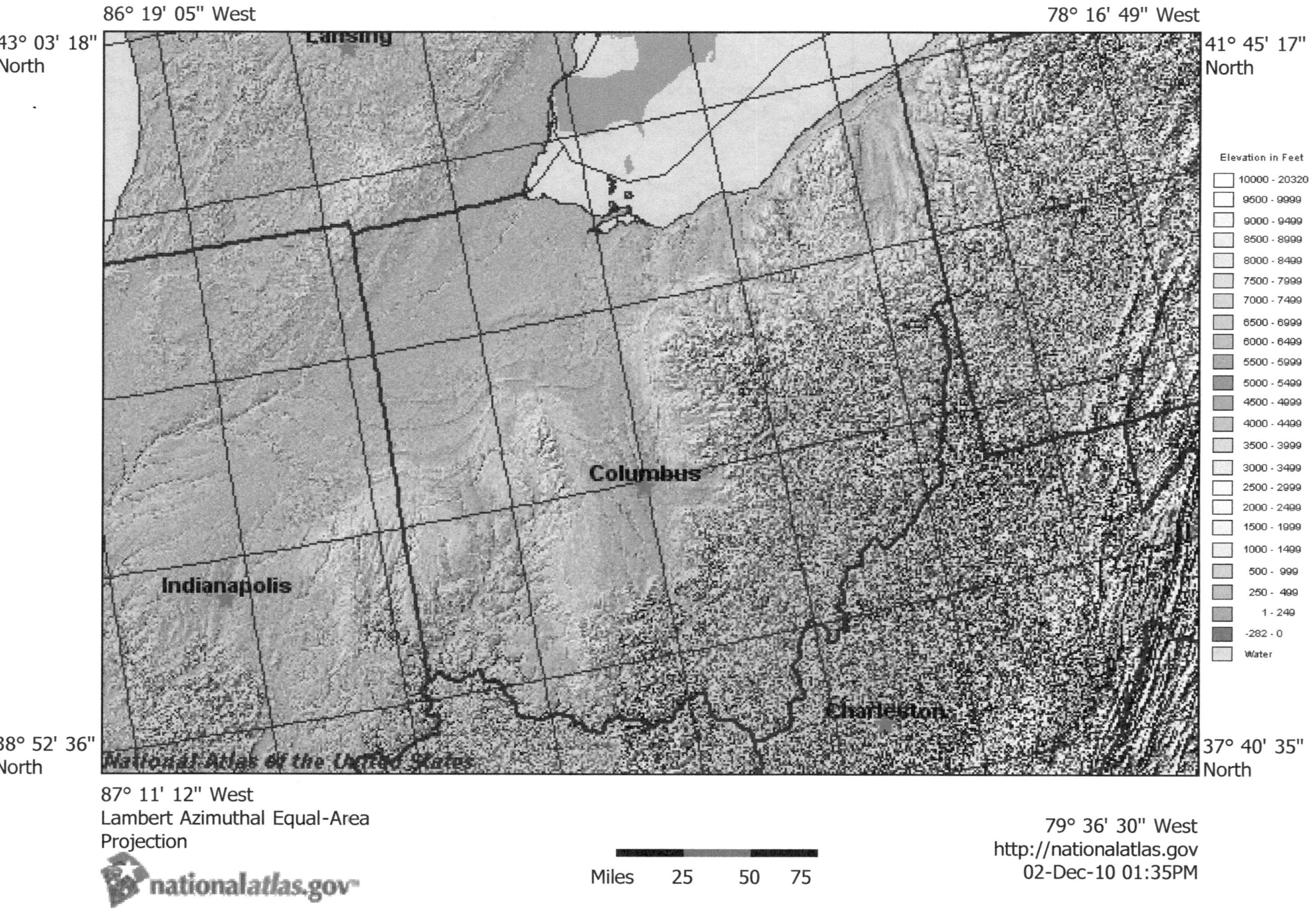
86° 19' 05" West
78° 16' 49" West
43° 03' 18" North
41° 45' 17" North
Lansing
Columbus
Indianapolis
Charleston
National Atlas of the United States
Elevation in Feet
10000 - 20320
9500 - 9999
9000 - 9499
8500 - 8999
8000 - 8499
7500 - 7999
7000 - 7499
6500 - 6999
6000 - 6499
5500 - 5999
5000 - 5499
4500 - 4999
4000 - 4499
3500 - 3999
3000 - 3499
2500 - 2999
2000 - 2499
1500 - 1999
1000 - 1499
500 - 999
250 - 499
1 - 249
-282 - 0
Water
38° 52' 36" North
37° 40' 35" North
87° 11' 12" West
Lambert Azimuthal Equal-Area Projection
nationalatlas.gov
Miles 25 50 75
79° 36' 30" West
http://nationalatlas.gov
02-Dec-10 01:35PM

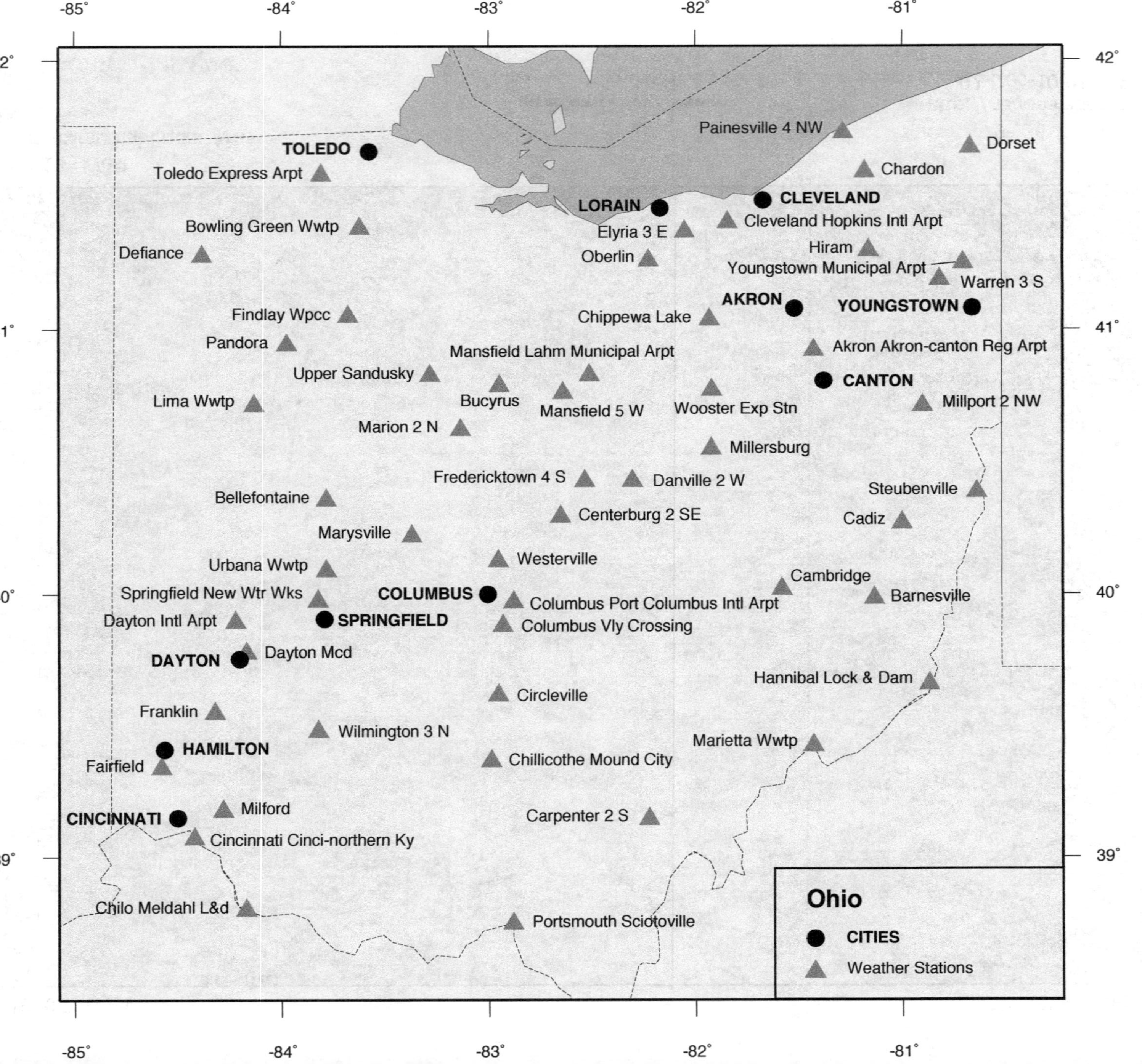
-85°
-84°
-83°
-82°
-81°
42°
41°
40°
39°
TOLEDO
Toledo Express Arpt
Painesville 4 NW
Dorset
Chardon
LORAIN
CLEVELAND
Bowling Green Wwtp
Elyria 3 E
Cleveland Hopkins Intl Arpt
Defiance
Oberlin
Hiram
Youngstown Municipal Arpt
Warren 3 S
AKRON
YOUNGSTOWN
Findlay Wpcc
Chippewa Lake
Pandora
Akron Akron-canton Reg Arpt
Mansfield Lahm Municipal Arpt
Upper Sandusky
CANTON
Lima Wwtp
Bucyrus
Mansfield 5 W
Wooster Exp Stn
Millport 2 NW
Marion 2 N
Millersburg
Fredericktown 4 S
Danville 2 W
Steubenville
Bellefontaine
Centerburg 2 SE
Cadiz
Marysville
Westerville
Urbana Wwtp
Cambridge
Springfield New Wtr Wks
COLUMBUS
Columbus Port Columbus Intl Arpt
Barnesville
Dayton Intl Arpt
SPRINGFIELD
Columbus Vly Crossing
Dayton Mcd
DAYTON
Hannibal Lock & Dam
Circleville
Franklin
Wilmington 3 N
Marietta Wwtp
HAMILTON
Chillicothe Mound City
Fairfield
Milford
CINCINNATI
Carpenter 2 S
Cincinnati Cinci-northern Ky
Chilo Meldahl L&d
Portsmouth Sciotoville
Ohio
CITIES
Weather Stations

Ohio Weather Stations by County

County	Station Name
Allen	Lima WWTP
Ashtabula	Dorset
Belmont	Barnesville
Boone	Cincinnati-Northern Kentucky
Butler	Fairfield
Champaign	Urbana WWTP
Clark	Springfield New Water Works
Clermont	Chilo Meldahl L&D Milford
Clinton	Wilmington 3 N
Columbiana	Millport 2 NW
Crawford	Bucyrus
Cuyahoga	Cleveland Hopkins Intl Arpt
Defiance	Defiance
Franklin	Columbus Valley Crossing Columbus-Port Columbus Intl Westerville
Geauga	Chardon
Guernsey	Cambridge
Hancock	Findlay Wpcc
Harrison	Cadiz
Holmes	Millersburg
Jefferson	Steubenville
Knox	Centerburg 2 SE Danville 2 W Fredericktown 4 S
Lake	Painesville 4 NW
Logan	Bellefontaine
Lorain	Elyria 3 E Oberlin
Lucas	Toledo Express Arpt
Marion	Marion 2 N
Medina	Chippewa Lake
Meigs	Carpenter 2 S
Monroe	Hannibal Lock & Dam

County	Station Name
Montgomery	Dayton Intl Arpt Dayton Mcd
Pickaway	Circleville
Portage	Hiram
Putnam	Pandora
Richland	Mansfield 5 W Mansfield Lahm Municipal Arpt
Ross	Chillicothe Mound City
Scioto	Portsmouth Sciotoville
Summit	Akron Akron-Canton Reg Arpt
Trumbull	Warren 3 S Youngstown Municipal Arpt
Union	Marysville
Warren	Franklin
Washington	Marietta Wwtp
Wayne	Wooster Exp Stn
Wood	Bowling Green WWTP
Wyandot	Upper Sandusky

See User Guide for station inclusion criteria.

Ohio Weather Stations by City

City	Station Name	Miles
Akron	Akron Akron-Canton Reg Arpt	11.9
	Chippewa Lake	21.7
	Hiram	24.6
Beavercreek	Dayton Mcd	6.9
	Dayton Intl Arpt	14.4
	Franklin	18.2
	Springfield New Water Works	21.1
	Wilmington 3 N	21.4
Boardman	Warren 3 S	13.9
	Youngstown Municipal Arpt	14.9
Brunswick	Chippewa Lake	14.8
	Cleveland Hopkins Intl Arpt	10.6
	Elyria 3 E	15.0
	Oberlin	20.5
Canton	Akron Akron-Canton Reg Arpt	7.9
Cincinnati	Cincinnati-Northern Kentucky	10.6
	Fairfield	14.8
	Milford	12.5
Cleveland	Cleveland Hopkins Intl Arpt	11.1
	Elyria 3 E	21.0
Cleveland Heights	Chardon	20.2
	Cleveland Hopkins Intl Arpt	16.8
	Painesville 4 NW	21.3
Columbus	Columbus Valley Crossing	7.6
	Columbus-Port Columbus Intl	6.0
	Westerville	9.5
Cuyahoga Falls	Akron Akron-Canton Reg Arpt	16.0
	Chippewa Lake	24.0
	Hiram	20.7
Dayton	Dayton Mcd	0.6
	Dayton Intl Arpt	9.6
	Franklin	16.1
	Springfield New Water Works	24.5
Delaware	Centerburg 2 SE	22.6
	Columbus-Port Columbus Intl	24.2
	Marion 2 N	22.1
	Marysville	15.9
	Westerville	13.3
Dublin	Columbus Valley Crossing	18.6
	Columbus-Port Columbus Intl	16.4
	Marysville	14.4
	Westerville	10.1
Elyria	Chippewa Lake	23.9
	Cleveland Hopkins Intl Arpt	13.1
	Elyria 3 E	2.7
	Oberlin	9.5
Euclid	Chardon	17.4
	Cleveland Hopkins Intl Arpt	21.8
	Painesville 4 NW	15.6

City	Station Name	Miles
Fairborn	Dayton Mcd	8.9
	Dayton Intl Arpt	12.3
	Franklin	23.5
	Springfield New Water Works	15.7
	Urbana WWTP	24.1
	Wilmington 3 N	24.6
Fairfield	Cincinnati-Northern Kentucky	20.2
	Fairfield	2.7
	Franklin	19.6
	Milford	17.1
Findlay	Bowling Green WWTP	23.4
	Findlay Wpcc	1.4
	Pandora	18.2
	Upper Sandusky	23.7
Gahanna	Centerburg 2 SE	22.1
	Columbus Valley Crossing	9.5
	Columbus-Port Columbus Intl	3.2
	Westerville	8.3
Grove City	Circleville	19.1
	Columbus Valley Crossing	7.8
	Columbus-Port Columbus Intl	12.6
	Westerville	19.0
Hamilton	Brookville, IN	24.0
	Cincinnati-Northern Kentucky	24.6
	Fairfield	3.4
	Franklin	17.0
	Milford	21.2
Huber Heights	Dayton Mcd	6.8
	Dayton Intl Arpt	5.7
	Franklin	23.4
	Springfield New Water Works	18.1
	Urbana WWTP	24.8
Kettering	Dayton Mcd	5.3
	Dayton Intl Arpt	14.7
	Franklin	13.5
	Wilmington 3 N	22.9
Lakewood	Cleveland Hopkins Intl Arpt	6.4
	Elyria 3 E	14.8
Lancaster	Circleville	19.9
	Columbus Valley Crossing	21.5
	Columbus-Port Columbus Intl	23.5
Lima	Lima WWTP	2.1
	Pandora	16.2
Lorain	Cleveland Hopkins Intl Arpt	16.9
	Elyria 3 E	7.6
	Oberlin	12.7
Mansfield	Bucyrus	23.5
	Danville 2 W	25.0
	Fredericktown 4 S	23.1
	Mansfield Lahm Municipal Arpt	4.5
	Mansfield 5 W	4.9

See User Guide for station inclusion criteria.

City	Station Name	Miles
Marion	Bucyrus	17.8
	Marion 2 N	2.0
	Upper Sandusky	18.8
Mason	Fairfield	14.4
	Franklin	13.5
	Milford	12.0
Massillon	Akron Akron-Canton Reg Arpt	9.5
	Wooster Exp Stn	20.6
Mentor	Chardon	10.9
	Painesville 4 NW	4.8
Middletown	Dayton Mcd	20.5
	Fairfield	15.6
	Franklin	4.2
	Milford	22.9
Newark	Centerburg 2 SE	20.3
North Olmsted	Cleveland Hopkins Intl Arpt	3.6
	Elyria 3 E	7.5
	Oberlin	18.9
Parma	Cleveland Hopkins Intl Arpt	6.5
	Elyria 3 E	16.8
Reynoldsburg	Centerburg 2 SE	24.9
	Circleville	24.9
	Columbus Valley Crossing	8.1
	Columbus-Port Columbus Intl	4.6
	Westerville	14.3
Springfield	Dayton Mcd	23.2
	Dayton Intl Arpt	22.2
	Springfield New Water Works	2.8
	Urbana WWTP	11.9
Stow	Akron Akron-Canton Reg Arpt	17.9
	Hiram	16.8
Strongsville	Chippewa Lake	18.9
	Cleveland Hopkins Intl Arpt	6.2
	Elyria 3 E	12.5
	Oberlin	20.3
Toledo	Bowling Green WWTP	19.5
	Toledo Express Arpt	12.5
Upper Arlington	Columbus Valley Crossing	11.1
	Columbus-Port Columbus Intl	10.2
	Marysville	21.4
	Westerville	9.9
Warren	Hiram	17.8
	Warren 3 S	2.7
	Youngstown Municipal Arpt	7.8
Westerville	Centerburg 2 SE	18.8
	Columbus Valley Crossing	15.3
	Columbus-Port Columbus Intl	9.7
	Marysville	25.0
	Westerville	1.9

City	Station Name	Miles
Westlake	Cleveland Hopkins Intl Arpt	5.3
	Elyria 3 E	8.0
	Oberlin	19.8
Youngstown	Warren 3 S	11.3
	Youngstown Municipal Arpt	11.0
	Mercer, PA	23.6

Note: Miles is the distance between the geographic center of the city and the weather station.

Ohio Weather Stations by Elevation

Feet	Station Name
1,350	Mansfield 5 W
1,294	Mansfield Lahm Municipal Arpt
1,259	Cadiz
1,240	Barnesville
1,229	Hiram
1,208	Akron Akron-Canton Reg Arpt
1,205	Centerburg 2 SE
1,185	Bellefontaine
1,180	Chippewa Lake
1,180	Youngstown Municipal Arpt
1,149	Millport 2 NW
1,129	Chardon
1,049	Fredericktown 4 S
1,029	Wilmington 3 N
1,020	Wooster Exp Stn
1,000	Dayton Intl Arpt
1,000	Marysville
1,000	Urbana WWTP
992	Steubenville
979	Dorset
970	Danville 2 W
964	Marion 2 N
955	Bucyrus
930	Springfield New Water Works
899	Warren 3 S
869	Cincinnati-Northern Kentucky
854	Upper Sandusky
850	Lima WWTP
821	Carpenter 2 S
818	Millersburg
815	Oberlin
810	Columbus-Port Columbus Intl
810	Westerville
799	Cambridge
770	Cleveland Hopkins Intl Arpt
770	Pandora
768	Findlay Wpcc
745	Dayton Mcd
734	Columbus Valley Crossing
729	Elyria 3 E
700	Defiance
674	Bowling Green WWTP
672	Circleville
669	Franklin
668	Toledo Express Arpt
649	Chillicothe Mound City
620	Hannibal Lock & Dam
600	Painesville 4 NW
580	Marietta Wwtp
575	Fairfield
540	Portsmouth Sciotoville
520	Milford
500	Chilo Meldahl L&D

See User Guide for station inclusion criteria.

Akron-Canton Regional Airport

The station at the Akron-Canton Airport is located about midway between Akron and Canton, a few miles south of the crest separating the Lake Erie and Muskingum River drainage areas. Precipitation at the station and southward drains through the Muskingum River into the Ohio, while northward of the crest the Cuyahoga and other streams flow into Lake Erie. The terrain is rolling with highest elevations near 1,300 feet above sea level and many small lakes provide water for local industry as well as recreational facilities for the densely populated region. The area is mainly industrial, agricultural operations having diminished rapidly in recent years.

Lake Erie has considerable influence on the area weather, tempering cold air masses during the late fall and winter, as well as contributing to the formation of brief, but heavy snow squalls until the lake freezes over.

The arrival of spring is late in this area, allowing growing of normally frost-susceptible fruits. Summers are moderately warm, but quite humid, while the months of September, October, and sometimes November are usually pleasant although with considerable morning fog. The average last occurrence of freezing temperatures in spring is the end of April, and the first occurrence in fall is late October. In past years, growing seasons for most vegetation has varied from 120 to 211 days. Temperatures and occurences of frost vary widely over the area because of the hilly terrain. Due to the influence of Lake Erie, snowfall is usually much heavier north of the station.

Akron-Canton Regional Airport *Summit County* Elevation: 1,208 ft. Latitude: 40° 55' N Longitude: 81° 26' W

	JAN	FEB	MAR	APR	MAY	JUN	JUL	AUG	SEP	OCT	NOV	DEC	YEAR
Mean Maximum Temp. (°F)	33.7	37.1	46.9	59.8	69.8	78.3	82.4	80.7	73.4	61.3	49.5	37.7	59.2
Mean Temp. (°F)	26.5	29.2	37.7	49.3	59.2	68.0	72.2	70.8	63.5	51.9	41.8	30.9	50.1
Mean Minimum Temp. (°F)	19.3	21.3	28.4	38.7	48.6	57.6	61.9	60.8	53.4	42.4	34.0	24.1	40.9
Extreme Maximum Temp. (°F)	68	72	81	88	93	100	101	97	93	86	76	76	101
Extreme Minimum Temp. (°F)	-25	-8	-3	15	27	33	43	41	33	22	8	-16	-25
Days Maximum Temp. ≥ 90°F	0	0	0	0	0	2	3	2	0	0	0	0	7
Days Maximum Temp. ≤ 32°F	14	10	4	0	0	0	0	0	0	0	1	10	39
Days Minimum Temp. ≤ 32°F	27	24	21	8	0	0	0	0	0	4	14	25	123
Days Minimum Temp. ≤ 0°F	2	1	0	0	0	0	0	0	0	0	0	1	4
Heating Degree Days (base 65°F)	1,186	1,005	841	472	214	47	5	12	110	407	690	1,050	6,039
Cooling Degree Days (base 65°F)	0	0	1	7	41	142	234	199	70	7	0	0	701
Mean Precipitation (in.)	2.60	2.26	3.03	3.58	4.32	3.76	4.12	3.67	3.38	2.83	3.19	2.84	39.58
Maximum Precipitation (in.)*	8.7	5.2	8.8	6.5	9.6	8.4	11.4	8.2	9.0	8.4	9.4	6.7	65.7
Minimum Precipitation (in.)*	0.7	0.3	1.0	0.9	1.0	0.4	0.7	0.5	0.2	0.4	0.6	0.3	23.8
Extreme Maximum Daily Precip. (in.)	2.04	1.66	1.48	1.99	2.29	2.31	3.98	3.67	3.70	2.07	2.31	1.71	3.98
Days With ≥ 0.1" Precipitation	7	6	8	8	9	8	7	6	6	6	8	8	87
Days With ≥ 0.5" Precipitation	1	1	2	2	3	3	3	2	2	2	2	1	24
Days With ≥ 1.0" Precipitation	0	0	0	1	1	1	1	1	1	0	0	0	6
Mean Snowfall (in.)	12.2	9.6	8.4	2.8	0.1	trace	0.0	trace	trace	0.5	2.9	9.9	46.4
Maximum Snowfall (in.)*	38	20	21	21	3	0	0	0	0	7	22	29	72
Maximum 24-hr. Snowfall (in.)*	9	10	8	20	3	0	0	0	0	4	7	16	20
Maximum Snow Depth (in.)	14	17	17	13	trace	trace	0	trace	trace	2	4	11	17
Days With ≥ 1.0" Snow Depth	15	12	6	1	0	0	0	0	0	0	1	10	45
Thunderstorm Days*	< 1	< 1	2	4	6	7	8	6	3	1	1	< 1	38
Foggy Days*	13	12	13	13	14	15	17	19	17	15	13	14	175
Predominant Sky Cover*	OVR	OVR	OVR	OVR	OVR	OVR	OVR	OVR	OVR	OVR	OVR	OVR	OVR
Mean Relative Humidity 7am (%)*	80	80	79	77	77	80	84	87	88	84	80	81	82
Mean Relative Humidity 4pm (%)*	69	65	59	53	52	54	54	55	56	56	64	70	59
Mean Dewpoint (°F)*	19	20	27	36	47	56	61	60	53	42	32	24	40
Prevailing Wind Direction*	SW	WSW	W	SW	SW	SW	SW	SW	S	S	S	WSW	SW
Prevailing Wind Speed (mph)*	13	12	13	12	10	9	8	8	8	9	12	13	10
Maximum Wind Gust (mph)*	76	58	64	60	56	63	68	62	52	51	58	61	76

Note: (*) Period of record is 1948-1995

The period of record for National Weather Service station data is 1980 – 2009 except where noted. See User Guide for detailed explanation of data.

Cincinnati Covington Airport

Greater Cincinnati Airport is located on a gently rolling plateau about 12 miles southwest of downtown Cincinnati and two miles south of the Ohio River at its nearest point. The river valley is rather narrow and steep-sided varying from one to three miles in width and the river bed is 500 feet below the level of the airport.

The climate is continental with a rather wide range of temperatures from winter to summer. A precipitation maximum occurs during winter and spring with a late summer and fall minimum. On the average, the maximum snowfall occurs during January, although the heaviest 24-hour amounts have been recorded during late November and February.

The heaviest precipitation, as well as the precipitation of the longest duration, is normally associated with low pressure disturbances moving in a general southwest to northeast direction through the Ohio valley and south of the Cincinnati area.

Summers are warm and rather humid. The temperature will reach 100 degrees or more in one year out of three. However, the temperature will reach 90 degrees or higher on about 19 days each year. Winters are moderately cold with frequent periods of extensive cloudiness.

The freeze free period lasts on the average 187 days from mid-April to the latter part of October.

Cincinnati Covington Airport *Boone County* Elevation: 869 ft. Latitude: 39° 03' N Longitude: 84° 40' W

	JAN	FEB	MAR	APR	MAY	JUN	JUL	AUG	SEP	OCT	NOV	DEC	YEAR
Mean Maximum Temp. (°F)	38.9	42.9	52.9	64.4	73.7	82.0	85.6	84.8	78.0	65.9	53.8	41.9	63.7
Mean Temp. (°F)	30.8	34.2	43.1	53.7	63.2	71.7	75.6	74.6	67.3	55.4	44.8	34.1	54.0
Mean Minimum Temp. (°F)	22.6	25.4	33.2	42.9	52.6	61.4	65.5	64.3	56.6	44.9	35.7	26.3	44.3
Extreme Maximum Temp. (°F)	70	75	84	87	91	102	103	101	97	91	81	75	103
Extreme Minimum Temp. (°F)	-24	-11	-11	15	30	41	47	43	31	20	10	-20	-24
Days Maximum Temp. ≥ 90°F	0	0	0	0	0	4	7	7	2	0	0	0	20
Days Maximum Temp. ≤ 32°F	9	6	1	0	0	0	0	0	0	0	0	7	23
Days Minimum Temp. ≤ 32°F	25	21	16	4	0	0	0	0	0	3	12	22	103
Days Minimum Temp. ≤ 0°F	2	1	0	0	0	0	0	0	0	0	0	1	4
Heating Degree Days (base 65°F)	1,055	866	674	350	125	15	0	2	60	312	602	951	5,012
Cooling Degree Days (base 65°F)	0	0	3	17	75	223	336	306	136	22	1	0	1,119
Mean Precipitation (in.)	3.01	2.77	3.99	3.89	4.90	3.94	3.86	3.51	2.67	3.36	3.28	3.35	42.53
Maximum Precipitation (in.)*	9.4	6.7	12.2	7.2	9.5	7.4	8.4	7.7	8.6	8.6	7.5	7.9	57.6
Minimum Precipitation (in.)*	0.6	0.3	1.1	1.0	1.1	0.9	1.2	0.3	0.2	0.3	0.4	0.5	28.0
Extreme Maximum Daily Precip. (in.)	3.23	2.84	3.25	2.41	2.96	3.04	3.11	3.52	2.55	4.30	1.87	2.47	4.30
Days With ≥ 0.1" Precipitation	6	6	8	8	9	7	7	6	5	6	7	7	82
Days With ≥ 0.5" Precipitation	2	1	2	3	3	3	3	2	2	2	2	2	27
Days With ≥ 1.0" Precipitation	1	1	1	1	1	1	1	1	1	1	1	1	12
Mean Snowfall (in.)	6.6	6.1	3.3	0.5	trace	trace	trace	trace	0.0	0.4	0.4	4.3	21.6
Maximum Snowfall (in.)*	32	20	13	4	trace	0	0	0	0	6	12	13	54
Maximum 24-hr. Snowfall (in.)*	8	9	10	3	trace	0	0	0	0	6	9	8	10
Maximum Snow Depth (in.)	14	14	11	5	trace	trace	trace	trace	0	4	1	9	14
Days With ≥ 1.0" Snow Depth	8	6	2	0	0	0	0	0	0	0	0	4	20
Thunderstorm Days*	1	1	3	4	6	7	8	6	3	1	1	< 1	41
Foggy Days*	13	12	12	9	12	13	16	19	16	14	12	14	162
Predominant Sky Cover*	OVR	OVR	OVR	OVR	OVR	OVR	OVR	OVR	OVR	OVR	OVR	OVR	OVR
Mean Relative Humidity 7am (%)*	80	79	77	76	80	82	85	88	87	83	79	80	81
Mean Relative Humidity 4pm (%)*	65	60	55	50	52	53	54	53	52	51	59	65	56
Mean Dewpoint (°F)*	22	24	31	40	51	60	64	63	56	44	34	26	43
Prevailing Wind Direction*	SSW	SSW	SSW	SSW	SSW	SSW	SW	SSW	SSW	SSW	SSW	SSW	SSW
Prevailing Wind Speed (mph)*	12	12	13	12	9	9	8	7	8	9	12	12	10
Maximum Wind Gust (mph)*	71	55	64	71	59	67	83	62	54	59	56	61	83

Note: (*) Period of record is 1948-1995

The period of record for National Weather Service station data is 1980 – 2009 except where noted. See User Guide for detailed explanation of data.

Cleveland Hopkins Int'l Airport

Cleveland is on the south shore of Lake Erie in northeast Ohio. The metropolitan area has a lake frontage of 3l miles. The surrounding terrain is generally level except for an abrupt ridge on the eastern edge of the city which rises some 500 feet above the shore terrain. The Cuyahoga River, which flows through a rather deep but narrow north-south valley, bisects the city.

Local climate is continental in character but with strong modifying influences by Lake Erie. West to northerly winds blowing off Lake Erie tend to lower daily high temperatures in summer and raise temperatures in winter. Temperatures at Hopkins Airport which is 5 miles south of the lakeshore average from two to four degrees higher than the lakeshore in summer, while overnight low temperatures average from two to four degrees lower than the lakefront during all seasons.

In this area, summers are moderately warm and humid with occasional days when temperatures exceed 90 degrees. Winters are relatively cold and cloudy with an average of five days with sub-zero temperatures. Weather changes occur every few days from the passing of cold fronts.

The daily range in temperature is usually greatest in late summer and least in winter. Annual extremes in temperature normally occur soon after late June and December. Maximum temperatures below freezing occur most often in December, January, and February. Temperatures of 100 degrees or higher are rare. On the average, freezing temperatures in fall are first recorded in October while the last freezing temperature in spring normally occurs in April.

As is characteristic of continental climates, precipitation varies widely from year to year. However, it is normally abundant and well distributed throughout the year with spring being the wettest season. Showers and thunderstorms account for most of the rainfall during the growing season. Thunderstorms are most frequent from April through August. Snowfall may fluctuate widely. Mean annual snowfall increases from west to east in Cuyahoga County ranging from about 45 inches in the west to more than 90 inches in the extreme east.

Damaging winds of 50 mph or greater are usually associated with thunderstorms. Tornadoes, one of the most destructive of all atmospheric storms, occasionally occur in Cuyahoga County.

Cleveland Hopkins Int'l Airport *Cuyahoga County* Elevation: 770 ft. Latitude: 41° 24' N Longitude: 81° 51' W

	JAN	FEB	MAR	APR	MAY	JUN	JUL	AUG	SEP	OCT	NOV	DEC	YEAR
Mean Maximum Temp. (°F)	34.2	37.1	46.0	58.5	69.1	78.2	82.3	80.5	73.7	61.9	50.4	38.2	59.2
Mean Temp. (°F)	27.3	29.6	37.4	48.8	59.0	68.3	72.7	71.3	64.3	53.0	43.1	31.8	50.5
Mean Minimum Temp. (°F)	20.3	22.1	28.7	39.0	48.8	58.4	63.1	62.0	54.8	44.0	35.7	25.3	41.9
Extreme Maximum Temp. (°F)	68	74	82	88	91	104	100	99	93	88	79	77	104
Extreme Minimum Temp. (°F)	-20	-10	-5	11	27	37	45	38	34	19	13	-15	-20
Days Maximum Temp. ≥ 90°F	0	0	0	0	0	2	4	3	0	0	0	0	9
Days Maximum Temp. ≤ 32°F	14	11	4	0	0	0	0	0	0	0	1	9	39
Days Minimum Temp. ≤ 32°F	27	24	21	7	0	0	0	0	0	2	12	24	117
Days Minimum Temp. ≤ 0°F	2	1	0	0	0	0	0	0	0	0	0	1	4
Heating Degree Days (base 65°F)	1,161	994	850	489	223	47	5	10	97	377	652	1,023	5,928
Cooling Degree Days (base 65°F)	0	0	2	9	43	153	250	211	82	11	1	0	762
Mean Precipitation (in.)	2.70	2.28	2.99	3.51	3.62	3.37	3.49	3.53	3.81	3.07	3.51	3.12	39.00
Maximum Precipitation (in.)*	7.0	4.7	6.1	6.6	9.1	9.1	9.1	9.0	7.3	9.5	8.8	8.6	53.8
Minimum Precipitation (in.)*	0.4	0.5	0.8	1.2	1.0	0.6	1.2	0.5	0.7	0.6	0.8	0.7	18.8
Extreme Maximum Daily Precip. (in.)	2.53	1.73	1.87	2.10	2.02	2.57	2.11	3.55	4.59	2.26	2.33	2.39	4.59
Days With ≥ 0.1" Precipitation	7	6	8	8	8	7	7	6	7	7	8	8	87
Days With ≥ 0.5" Precipitation	1	1	2	2	2	2	2	2	3	2	2	2	23
Days With ≥ 1.0" Precipitation	0	0	0	1	1	1	1	1	1	0	1	0	7
Mean Snowfall (in.)	18.4	14.5	12.6	3.3	trace	trace	trace	trace	trace	0.2	4.5	14.1	67.6
Maximum Snowfall (in.)*	43	39	26	13	2	0	0	0	0	8	22	30	97
Maximum 24-hr. Snowfall (in.)*	10	14	11	9	2	0	0	0	0	7	13	12	14
Maximum Snow Depth (in.)	17	22	15	14	trace	trace	trace	trace	trace	trace	9	14	22
Days With ≥ 1.0" Snow Depth	17	13	7	1	0	0	0	0	0	0	2	11	51
Thunderstorm Days*	< 1	< 1	2	3	5	6	6	5	3	2	1	< 1	33
Foggy Days*	13	12	13	12	13	11	12	14	12	11	12	13	148
Predominant Sky Cover*	OVR	OVR	OVR	OVR	OVR	OVR	OVR	OVR	OVR	OVR	OVR	OVR	OVR
Mean Relative Humidity 7am (%)*	79	79	79	76	77	79	81	85	84	81	78	78	80
Mean Relative Humidity 4pm (%)*	70	67	62	56	54	55	55	58	58	58	65	70	61
Mean Dewpoint (°F)*	19	21	27	37	47	57	61	61	54	43	33	24	40
Prevailing Wind Direction*	SW	SW	SW	S	N	SSW	SW	SW	S	SSW	SW	SW	SW
Prevailing Wind Speed (mph)*	13	13	14	13	9	10	9	8	9	10	13	13	12
Maximum Wind Gust (mph)*	82	64	63	78	55	77	67	51	58	54	59	71	82

Note: (*) Period of record is 1948-1995

Columbus-Port Columbus Int'l

Columbus is located in the center of the state and in the drainage area of the Ohio River. The airport is located at the eastern boundary of the city approximately seven miles from the center of the business district.

Four nearly parallel streams run through or adjacent to the city. The Scioto River is the principal stream and flows from the northwest into the center of the city and then flows straight south toward the Ohio River. The Olentangy River runs almost due south and empties into the Scioto just west of the business district. Alum Creek empties into the Big Walnut southeast of the city and the Big Walnut Creek empties into the Scioto a few miles downstream.

The narrow valleys associated with the streams flowing through the city supply the only variation in the micro-climate of the area. The city proper shows the typical metropolitan effect with shrubs and flowers blossoming earlier than in the immediate surroundings and in retarding light frost on clear quiet nights. Many small areas to the southeast and to the north and northeast show marked effects of air drainage as evidenced by the frequent formation of shallow ground fog at daybreak during the summer and fall months and the higher frequency of frost in the spring and fall.

The average occurrence of the last freezing temperature in the spring within the city proper is mid-April, and the first freeze in the fall is very late October, but in the immediate surroundings there is much variation. For example, at Valley Crossing located at the southeastern outskirts of the city, the average occurrence of the last 32 degree temperature in the spring is very early May, while the first 32 degree temperature in the fall is mid-October.

The records show a high frequency of calm or very low wind speeds during the late evening and early morning hours, from June through September. The rolling landscape is conducive to calm winds from the Weather Service location at the airport these are toward the northwest with the wind direction indicated as southeast, at speeds generally 4 mph or less.

Columbus is located in the area of changeable weather. Air masses from central and northwest Canada frequently invade this region. Air from the Gulf of Mexico often reaches central Ohio during the summer and to a much lesser extent in the fall and winter. There are also occasional weather changes brought about by cool outbreaks from the Hudson Bay region of Canada, especially during the spring months. At infrequent intervals the general circulation will bring showers or snow to Columbus from the Atlantic.

Columbus-Port Columbus Int'l *Franklin County* Elevation: 810 ft. Latitude: 39° 59' N Longitude: 82° 53' W

	JAN	FEB	MAR	APR	MAY	JUN	JUL	AUG	SEP	OCT	NOV	DEC	YEAR
Mean Maximum Temp. (°F)	36.7	40.6	50.9	63.2	72.9	81.4	84.8	83.7	77.0	64.9	52.4	40.4	62.4
Mean Temp. (°F)	29.3	32.4	41.3	52.4	62.1	71.0	74.9	73.6	66.5	54.5	43.9	33.3	52.9
Mean Minimum Temp. (°F)	21.9	24.2	31.7	41.6	51.3	60.5	64.8	63.5	55.9	44.1	35.4	26.2	43.4
Extreme Maximum Temp. (°F)	70	75	83	88	93	101	100	101	97	91	80	76	101
Extreme Minimum Temp. (°F)	-22	-10	-6	14	30	39	44	40	33	21	12	-17	-22
Days Maximum Temp. ≥ 90°F	0	0	0	0	0	4	6	5	1	0	0	0	16
Days Maximum Temp. ≤ 32°F	11	8	2	0	0	0	0	0	0	0	1	8	30
Days Minimum Temp. ≤ 32°F	26	22	18	5	0	0	0	0	0	3	12	22	108
Days Minimum Temp. ≤ 0°F	2	1	0	0	0	0	0	0	0	0	0	1	4
Heating Degree Days (base 65°F)	1,100	915	730	383	149	21	1	4	68	334	626	976	5,307
Cooling Degree Days (base 65°F)	0	0	2	12	66	207	313	278	118	16	1	0	1,013
Mean Precipitation (in.)	2.70	2.21	3.05	3.37	4.19	4.00	4.74	3.46	2.85	2.64	3.12	2.99	39.32
Maximum Precipitation (in.)*	8.3	5.1	9.6	6.4	9.1	9.8	12.4	8.6	6.8	5.2	10.7	7.0	53.2
Minimum Precipitation (in.)*	0.6	0.3	1.0	0.7	0.9	0.7	1.0	0.6	0.5	0.1	0.6	0.5	24.5
Extreme Maximum Daily Precip. (in.)	2.41	1.72	1.95	2.23	2.67	2.89	5.13	3.17	2.36	2.31	2.38	2.56	5.13
Days With ≥ 0.1" Precipitation	6	6	7	7	9	7	7	6	5	5	7	7	79
Days With ≥ 0.5" Precipitation	1	1	2	2	3	3	3	2	2	2	2	2	25
Days With ≥ 1.0" Precipitation	0	0	0	0	1	1	1	1	1	1	1	0	7
Mean Snowfall (in.)	9.3	6.3	4.4	1.1	trace	trace	trace	trace	trace	0.2	1.2	5.4	27.9
Maximum Snowfall (in.)*	34	16	14	13	1	0	0	0	trace	5	15	17	48
Maximum 24-hr. Snowfall (in.)*	7	9	9	12	1	0	0	0	trace	4	8	8	12
Maximum Snow Depth (in.)	13	13	18	10	trace	trace	trace	trace	trace	trace	5	7	18
Days With ≥ 1.0" Snow Depth	11	7	3	0	0	0	0	0	0	0	0	5	26
Thunderstorm Days*	< 1	1	2	4	6	8	8	6	3	1	1	< 1	40
Foggy Days*	13	11	12	10	13	14	16	19	15	14	12	14	163
Predominant Sky Cover*	OVR	OVR	OVR	OVR	OVR	OVR	OVR	SCT	OVR	OVR	OVR	OVR	OVR
Mean Relative Humidity 7am (%)*	78	78	76	76	79	81	84	87	87	83	80	80	81
Mean Relative Humidity 4pm (%)*	67	62	55	51	52	53	54	53	53	52	61	67	57
Mean Dewpoint (°F)*	20	22	29	38	49	59	63	62	55	43	34	25	42
Prevailing Wind Direction*	S	S	WNW	S	S	S	S	S	S	S	S	S	S
Prevailing Wind Speed (mph)*	9	9	12	9	8	8	7	7	8	8	9	9	9
Maximum Wind Gust (mph)*	69	58	62	78	76	68	67	66	62	53	53	61	78

Note: (*) Period of record is 1948-1995

Dayton Int'l Airport

Dayton is located near the center of the Miami River Valley, which is a nearly flat plain, 50 to 200 feet below the general elevation of the adjacent rolling country. Three Miami River tributaries, the Mad River, the Stillwater River, and Wolf Creek converge, fanwise, from the north to join the master stream within the city limits of Dayton. Heavy rains in March 1913 caused the worst flood disaster in the history of the Miami Valley. During the flood more than 400 people lost their lives and property damage amounted to $100 million. After the 1913 flood, dams were built on the streams north of Dayton, forming retarding basins. No floods have occurred at Dayton since the construction of these dams.

The elevation of the city of Dayton is about 750 feet. Terrain north of the city slopes gradually upward to about 1,100 feet at Indian Lake. Ten miles southeast of Indian Lake, near Bellefontaine, is the highest point in the state, with an elevation of about 1,550 feet. South of the city, the terrain slopes gradually downward to about 450 feet where the Miami River empties into the Ohio River.

Precipitation, which is rather evenly distributed throughout the year, and moderate temperatures help to make the Miami Valley a rich agricultural region. High relative humidities during much of the year cause some discomfort to people with allergies. Temperatures of zero or below will be experienced in about four years out of five, while 100 degrees or higher will be recorded in about one year out of five. Extreme temperatures are usually of short duration. The downward slope of about 700 feet in the 163 miles of the Miami River may have some moderating influence on the winter temperatures in the Miami Valley.

Based on the 1951-1980 period, the average last occurrence in the spring of freezing temperatures is mid-April, and the average first occurrence in the autumn is late October.

Cold, polar air, flowing across the Great Lakes, causes much cloudiness during the winter, and is accompanied by frequent snow flurries. These add little to the total snowfall.

Dayton Int'l Airport *Montgomery County* Elevation: 1,000 ft. Latitude: 39° 54' N Longitude: 84° 13' W

	JAN	FEB	MAR	APR	MAY	JUN	JUL	AUG	SEP	OCT	NOV	DEC	YEAR
Mean Maximum Temp. (°F)	35.3	39.4	49.8	62.1	71.9	80.7	84.4	83.1	76.4	64.0	51.4	38.9	61.4
Mean Temp. (°F)	27.8	31.2	40.4	51.6	61.6	70.7	74.4	73.0	65.6	53.9	43.0	31.7	52.1
Mean Minimum Temp. (°F)	20.3	23.0	31.0	41.1	51.2	60.6	64.4	62.8	54.9	43.8	34.6	24.5	42.7
Extreme Maximum Temp. (°F)	66	73	82	88	92	102	102	102	95	89	77	72	102
Extreme Minimum Temp. (°F)	-25	-12	-7	17	31	40	46	41	33	23	11	-20	-25
Days Maximum Temp. ≥ 90°F	0	0	0	0	0	3	6	5	1	0	0	0	15
Days Maximum Temp. ≤ 32°F	13	9	3	0	0	0	0	0	0	0	1	9	35
Days Minimum Temp. ≤ 32°F	27	23	18	6	0	0	0	0	0	3	14	24	115
Days Minimum Temp. ≤ 0°F	2	1	0	0	0	0	0	0	0	0	0	1	4
Heating Degree Days (base 65°F)	1,146	950	758	407	162	21	2	5	80	352	654	1,026	5,563
Cooling Degree Days (base 65°F)	0	0	2	12	62	197	300	259	106	14	0	0	952
Mean Precipitation (in.)	2.76	2.28	3.41	4.12	4.64	4.28	4.06	3.08	3.11	2.98	3.29	3.12	41.13
Maximum Precipitation (in.)*	9.9	5.8	7.6	6.8	9.0	10.9	8.5	8.0	5.7	6.3	8.1	10.0	59.8
Minimum Precipitation (in.)*	0.3	0.2	1.1	0.6	1.5	0.3	0.5	0.3	0.3	0.2	0.5	0.4	24.2
Extreme Maximum Daily Precip. (in.)	2.58	1.68	1.86	2.53	3.17	3.76	2.82	3.38	3.81	3.54	2.05	2.85	3.81
Days With ≥ 0.1" Precipitation	6	5	8	9	9	7	7	5	5	5	7	7	80
Days With ≥ 0.5" Precipitation	1	1	2	3	3	3	3	2	2	2	2	2	26
Days With ≥ 1.0" Precipitation	0	0	1	1	1	1	1	1	1	1	1	1	10
Mean Snowfall (in.)	8.0	6.3	4.1	0.6	trace	0.0	trace	trace	trace	0.4	0.8	5.1	25.3
Maximum Snowfall (in.)*	40	18	14	5	trace	0	0	0	0	6	13	16	53
Maximum 24-hr. Snowfall (in.)*	12	7	11	5	trace	0	0	0	0	5	8	6	12
Maximum Snow Depth (in.)	16	10	13	6	trace	0	trace	trace	trace	4	5	16	16
Days With ≥ 1.0" Snow Depth	10	8	3	0	0	0	0	0	0	0	0	6	27
Thunderstorm Days*	< 1	1	2	4	6	7	8	6	3	2	1	< 1	40
Foggy Days*	15	12	14	12	13	13	15	18	15	14	14	15	170
Predominant Sky Cover*	OVR	OVR	OVR	OVR	OVR	OVR	OVR	OVR	OVR	OVR	OVR	OVR	OVR
Mean Relative Humidity 7am (%)*	80	79	79	77	78	80	83	86	87	83	81	81	81
Mean Relative Humidity 4pm (%)*	68	64	59	53	52	52	53	53	52	52	63	69	57
Mean Dewpoint (°F)*	20	22	30	39	49	58	63	62	54	43	33	25	42
Prevailing Wind Direction*	W	WNW	WNW	SSW	SSW	SSW	SW	SW	SSW	SSW	SSW	SSW	SSW
Prevailing Wind Speed (mph)*	13	13	13	13	12	10	9	9	9	10	13	13	12
Maximum Wind Gust (mph)*	69	52	67	63	60	60	71	61	48	46	54	62	71

Note: (*) Period of record is 1948-1995

Mansfield Lahm Municipal Airport

Mansfield is in the north central highlands at the geographical and climatological junction of central Ohio, northwest Ohio, and northeast Ohio. The station is on a plateau 3 miles north of the city of Mansfield and surrounded by rolling open farmland. The general elevation ranges from around 1,300 to 1,400 feet above sea level with the 1,000-foot contour east to west some 15 miles to the north. The climate is continental, with the modifying effects of Lake Erie most pronounced in winter. Lake Erie is just 38 miles due north.

The lake influence, plus the elevation, produce cloudy skies and considerable snow shower activity from late November into April with any wind flow from northwest through northeast. Because of this, any windshift with a cold frontal passage in winter does not bring the clearing skies, indeed, more snow is often measured from the flurry activity behind the front than from the pre-frontal conditions. A frozen Lake Erie will allow clearing skies, but an open lake dictates overcast and snow flurries. Usually the lake is open enough to set off the flurries and cloudy conditions. The major snow producer will be an intense storm moving out of the southwest with the Gulf of Mexico moisture available. Snow cover is almost constant from December through March due to almost daily snow flurries, but the depth of cover is rarely more than 8 inches. Daytime winter temperatures are not above the freezing mark too often.

Spring is a short period of rapid transition from hard winter to summer conditions. April usually brings abundant shower activity and the crops and vegetation get a quick start.

Summer is a pleasant season with low humidities and no extremely high temperatures. Rarely does the temperature climb above the 90 degree point. Thunderstorms average about once every three days during the season from June through September. Highest winds are associated with the heavier thunderstorms, and while hail does not occur often, it is of major concern to the applegrowers in the area. Flooding problems are confined to the flash-flood type on the small streams in the area.

The growing season is normally about 153 days. Autumn usually produces many clear warm days and cool invigorating nights. Ground fog is at a maximum incidence during the autumn. Little rainfall occurs to interfere with harvest time and county fair time.

Mansfield Lahm Municipal Airport *Richland County* Elevation: 1,294 ft. Latitude: 40° 49' N Longitude: 82° 31' W

	JAN	FEB	MAR	APR	MAY	JUN	JUL	AUG	SEP	OCT	NOV	DEC	YEAR
Mean Maximum Temp. (°F)	33.2	36.3	46.2	59.2	69.4	78.0	81.7	80.0	73.4	61.5	49.3	37.0	58.8
Mean Temp. (°F)	26.1	28.6	37.3	48.9	58.9	67.8	71.8	70.3	63.3	52.0	41.6	30.3	49.7
Mean Minimum Temp. (°F)	18.9	20.9	28.3	38.6	48.4	57.6	61.8	60.6	53.2	42.4	33.8	23.5	40.7
Extreme Maximum Temp. (°F)	65	71	82	86	90	101	100	97	92	87	76	73	101
Extreme Minimum Temp. (°F)	-22	-11	-6	8	27	37	43	42	33	20	10	-17	-22
Days Maximum Temp. ≥ 90°F	0	0	0	0	0	1	2	2	0	0	0	0	5
Days Maximum Temp. ≤ 32°F	15	11	5	0	0	0	0	0	0	0	2	11	44
Days Minimum Temp. ≤ 32°F	28	24	21	9	0	0	0	0	0	4	15	25	126
Days Minimum Temp. ≤ 0°F	3	1	0	0	0	0	0	0	0	0	0	1	5
Heating Degree Days (base 65°F)	1,200	1,022	854	485	223	51	7	15	114	405	696	1,069	6,141
Cooling Degree Days (base 65°F)	0	0	1	8	42	142	224	187	70	9	0	0	683
Mean Precipitation (in.)	2.85	2.31	3.48	4.19	4.54	4.66	4.46	4.43	3.33	2.94	3.72	3.33	44.24
Maximum Precipitation (in.)*	11.5	5.4	7.0	7.0	8.8	10.0	13.2	8.6	7.8	6.4	12.8	11.2	67.2
Minimum Precipitation (in.)*	0.4	0.3	1.2	0.8	1.1	0.6	0.9	0.6	0.7	0.4	0.7	0.7	21.8
Extreme Maximum Daily Precip. (in.)	1.97	1.63	2.04	2.66	2.62	2.93	3.39	4.34	2.22	3.33	3.11	2.62	4.34
Days With ≥ 0.1" Precipitation	7	6	8	9	10	8	7	7	6	6	7	8	89
Days With ≥ 0.5" Precipitation	2	1	2	3	3	4	3	3	2	2	2	2	29
Days With ≥ 1.0" Precipitation	1	0	1	1	1	1	1	1	1	1	1	1	11
Mean Snowfall (in.)	13.1	10.3	8.0	2.7	trace	trace	0.0	0.0	0.0	0.6	2.5	10.5	47.7
Maximum Snowfall (in.)*	42	18	17	13	1	0	0	0	0	10	12	23	59
Maximum 24-hr. Snowfall (in.)*	10	9	8	12	1	0	0	0	0	8	5	12	12
Maximum Snow Depth (in.)	20	13	15	10	0	trace	0	0	0	2	4	15	20
Days With ≥ 1.0" Snow Depth	15	14	6	1	0	0	0	0	0	0	2	11	49
Thunderstorm Days*	< 1	< 1	2	3	5	6	7	6	3	1	1	< 1	34
Foggy Days*	13	12	14	13	14	13	14	17	15	13	13	15	166
Predominant Sky Cover*	OVR	OVR	OVR	OVR	OVR	OVR	SCT	SCT	OVR	OVR	OVR	OVR	OVR
Mean Relative Humidity 7am (%)*	82	81	81	78	78	81	83	87	87	83	82	83	82
Mean Relative Humidity 4pm (%)*	72	69	64	56	55	56	56	57	58	56	67	74	62
Mean Dewpoint (°F)*	20	21	28	37	47	58	62	61	54	42	33	24	40
Prevailing Wind Direction*	WSW	WSW	WSW	WSW	SSW	SSW	SW	SSW	S	S	SW	WSW	WSW
Prevailing Wind Speed (mph)*	15	14	15	14	13	12	10	10	9	10	14	14	13
Maximum Wind Gust (mph)*	62	59	62	68	60	68	81	69	61	53	69	69	81

Note: (*) Period of record is 1948-1995

Toledo Express Airport

Toledo is located on the western end of Lake Erie at the mouth of the Maumee River. Except for a bank up from the river about 30 feet, the terrain is generally level with only a slight slope toward the river and Lake Erie. The city has quite a diversified industrial section and excellent harbor facilities, making it a large transportation center for rail, water, and motor freight. Generally rich agricultural land is found in the surrounding area, especially up the Maumee Valley toward the Indiana state line.

Rainfall is usually sufficient for general agriculture. The terrain is level and drainage rather poor, therefore, a little less than the normal precipitation during the growing season is better than excessive amounts. Snowfall is generally light in this area, distributed throughout the winter from November to March with frequent thaws.

The nearness of Lake Erie and the other Great Lakes has a moderating effect on the temperature, and extremes are seldom recorded. On average, only fifteen days a year experience temperatures of 90 degrees or higher, and only eight days when it drops to zero or lower. The growing season averages 160 days, but has ranged from over 220 to less than 125 days.

Humidity is rather high throughout the year in this area, and there is an excessive amount of cloudiness. In the winter months the sun shines during only about 30 percent of the daylight hours. December and January, the cloudiest months, sometimes have as little as 16 percent of the possible hours of sunshine.

Severe windstorms, causing more than minor damage, occur infrequently. There are on the average twenty-three days per year having a sustained wind velocity of 32 mph or more.

Flooding in the Toledo area is produced by several factors. Heavy rains of one inch or more will cause a sudden rise in creeks and drainage ditches to the point of overflow. The western shores of Lake Erie are subject to flooding when the lake level is high and prolonged periods of east to northeast winds prevail.

Toledo Express Airport *Lucas County* Elevation: 668 ft. Latitude: 41° 35' N Longitude: 83° 48' W

	JAN	FEB	MAR	APR	MAY	JUN	JUL	AUG	SEP	OCT	NOV	DEC	YEAR
Mean Maximum Temp. (°F)	32.5	35.7	46.3	59.6	70.8	80.4	84.3	82.0	75.2	62.4	49.3	36.4	59.6
Mean Temp. (°F)	25.2	27.9	37.1	49.0	59.5	69.1	73.2	71.3	63.9	51.9	41.1	29.6	49.9
Mean Minimum Temp. (°F)	18.0	20.1	27.8	38.3	48.1	57.7	62.1	60.6	52.5	41.3	32.9	22.8	40.2
Extreme Maximum Temp. (°F)	66	71	81	88	94	104	104	99	96	89	80	70	104
Extreme Minimum Temp. (°F)	-20	-14	-6	8	25	37	40	34	30	16	9	-19	-20
Days Maximum Temp. ≥ 90°F	0	0	0	0	1	4	6	4	1	0	0	0	16
Days Maximum Temp. ≤ 32°F	16	11	4	0	0	0	0	0	0	0	1	11	43
Days Minimum Temp. ≤ 32°F	28	25	22	8	1	0	0	0	0	5	15	26	130
Days Minimum Temp. ≤ 0°F	3	2	0	0	0	0	0	0	0	0	0	1	6
Heating Degree Days (base 65°F)	1,226	1,041	859	482	209	37	3	12	108	409	710	1,090	6,186
Cooling Degree Days (base 65°F)	0	0	1	9	45	166	264	215	80	9	0	0	789
Mean Precipitation (in.)	2.05	2.03	2.52	3.13	3.48	3.54	3.21	3.26	2.78	2.62	2.78	2.71	34.11
Maximum Precipitation (in.)*	4.6	5.4	5.7	6.1	5.1	8.5	6.8	8.5	8.1	5.5	6.9	6.8	40.8
Minimum Precipitation (in.)*	0.3	0.3	0.6	0.9	1.0	0.3	0.3	0.4	0.6	0.3	0.5	0.5	22.0
Extreme Maximum Daily Precip. (in.)	1.30	2.59	2.60	2.81	1.85	3.12	3.15	2.21	2.70	2.88	2.71	2.51	3.15
Days With ≥ 0.1" Precipitation	5	5	7	7	7	6	6	6	5	5	6	7	72
Days With ≥ 0.5" Precipitation	1	1	1	2	2	2	2	2	2	2	2	2	21
Days With ≥ 1.0" Precipitation	0	0	0	0	1	1	1	1	1	1	1	0	7
Mean Snowfall (in.)	***11.3***	***8.6***	***5.9***	***1.4***	na	na	na	na	na	na	***1.9***	***7.4***	na
Maximum Snowfall (in.)*	31	17	18	12	1	0	0	0	trace	2	18	24	72
Maximum 24-hr. Snowfall (in.)*	10	8	9	7	1	0	0	0	trace	2	7	14	14
Maximum Snow Depth (in.)	***12***	***16***	***8***	***7***	***1***	na	na	na	na	na	***3***	***7***	na
Days With ≥ 1.0" Snow Depth	***15***	***13***	***6***	***1***	***0***	na	na	***0***	na	na	***1***	***10***	na
Thunderstorm Days*	< 1	1	2	4	5	7	7	6	4	1	1	< 1	38
Foggy Days*	13	11	14	12	12	11	14	18	15	13	14	15	162
Predominant Sky Cover*	OVR	OVR	OVR	OVR	OVR	OVR	SCT	SCT	OVR	OVR	OVR	OVR	OVR
Mean Relative Humidity 7am (%)*	80	80	81	80	80	82	86	91	91	86	83	83	84
Mean Relative Humidity 4pm (%)*	68	65	59	53	51	52	53	56	54	55	65	72	58
Mean Dewpoint (°F)*	17	19	27	36	47	57	62	61	54	42	32	23	40
Prevailing Wind Direction*	WSW	WSW	ENE	WSW	WSW	SW	SW	SW	SW	SW	WSW	WSW	WSW
Prevailing Wind Speed (mph)*	13	13	12	13	12	9	8	8	9	10	13	13	12
Maximum Wind Gust (mph)*	62	52	64	63	58	59	66	75	54	49	55	56	75

Note: (*) Period of record is 1955-1995

Youngstown Municipal Airport

The Youngstown Municipal Airport is located in northeastern Ohio approximately eight miles north of the city of Youngstown in Trumbull County. Airport elevation is 1,178 feet, about 200 feet higher than most communities in the Mahoning and Shenango River Valleys. There are numerous natural and man-made lakes in the region, including Lake Erie, 45 miles to the north. Drainage from the area flows southward through the Mahoning and Shenango Rivers which join to form the Beaver River at New Castle, Pennsylvania. The Beaver empties into the Ohio River at Rochester, Pennsylvania.

This entire area experiences frequent outbreaks of cold Canadian air masses which may be modified by passage over Lake Erie. This effect produces widespread cloudiness especially during the cool months of the year. The winter months are characterized by persistent cloudiness and intermittent snow flurries. The daily temperature range during most winter days is quite small. During most winters, the bulk of the snow falls as flurries of 2 inches or less per occurrence, although several snowstorms per year will produce amounts in the four to 10 inch range.

Destructive storms seldom occur, and tornadoes are not common. During recent years flood control projects have all but eliminated the threat of serious river flooding. Flash flooding of small streams and creeks rarely affects residential areas. Certain communities have well known areas of urban flooding during periods of prolonged heavy thunderstorms.

The climate of the Youngstown district has had an important role in the growth and development of this industrial area. Temperatures seldom reach extreme values especially during the summer months. However, high humidity during most days of the year tends to accentuate the temperature. Rainfall, reasonably well distributed throughout the year, provides a more than adequate supply of water for agriculture, industrial, and residential use.

Based on the 1951-1980 period, the average first occurrence of 32 degrees Fahrenheit in the fall is October 14 and the average last occurrence in the spring is May 6.

Youngstown Municipal Airport *Trumbull County* Elevation: 1,180 ft. Latitude: 41° 15' N Longitude: 80° 40' W

	JAN	FEB	MAR	APR	MAY	JUN	JUL	AUG	SEP	OCT	NOV	DEC	YEAR
Mean Maximum Temp. (°F)	33.2	36.6	46.1	59.3	69.5	77.9	81.9	80.5	73.0	61.0	49.3	37.3	58.8
Mean Temp. (°F)	26.1	28.6	36.7	48.6	58.0	66.6	70.8	69.4	62.2	51.2	41.6	30.6	49.2
Mean Minimum Temp. (°F)	19.0	20.5	27.4	37.7	46.5	55.1	59.6	58.3	51.4	41.3	33.9	23.9	39.6
Extreme Maximum Temp. (°F)	68	73	82	88	90	99	100	97	92	87	78	76	100
Extreme Minimum Temp. (°F)	-22	-8	-10	14	25	34	40	32	29	20	12	-12	-22
Days Maximum Temp. ≥ 90°F	0	0	0	0	0	1	3	2	0	0	0	0	6
Days Maximum Temp. ≤ 32°F	15	11	5	0	0	0	0	0	0	0	2	11	44
Days Minimum Temp. ≤ 32°F	27	24	22	10	1	0	0	0	0	4	15	26	129
Days Minimum Temp. ≤ 0°F	2	1	0	0	0	0	0	0	0	0	0	1	4
Heating Degree Days (base 65°F)	1,199	1,023	871	495	243	65	11	22	133	427	696	1,058	6,243
Cooling Degree Days (base 65°F)	0	0	1	8	34	118	197	166	57	7	0	0	588
Mean Precipitation (in.)	2.51	2.09	3.02	3.36	3.70	3.86	4.41	3.41	3.82	2.74	3.09	2.91	38.92
Maximum Precipitation (in.)*	7.6	5.3	6.2	6.4	6.2	10.7	9.7	7.9	6.1	8.6	9.1	6.5	48.6
Minimum Precipitation (in.)*	0.7	0.5	1.1	1.0	0.8	0.7	1.6	0.5	0.3	0.4	0.9	0.9	23.8
Extreme Maximum Daily Precip. (in.)	1.34	1.63	1.41	1.53	1.95	3.57	4.65	3.47	4.09	2.05	2.73	1.55	4.65
Days With ≥ 0.1" Precipitation	7	6	8	8	9	8	7	6	7	6	7	8	87
Days With ≥ 0.5" Precipitation	1	1	2	2	2	2	3	2	3	2	2	1	23
Days With ≥ 1.0" Precipitation	0	0	0	1	1	1	1	1	1	0	0	0	6
Mean Snowfall (in.)	15.9	11.9	10.8	3.0	trace	trace	trace	trace	trace	0.8	4.0	13.3	59.7
Maximum Snowfall (in.)*	36	23	31	12	5	0	0	0	trace	8	31	30	91
Maximum 24-hr. Snowfall (in.)*	17	9	15	12	5	0	0	0	trace	5	17	12	17
Maximum Snow Depth (in.)	18	14	11	10	trace	trace	trace	trace	trace	1	6	13	18
Days With ≥ 1.0" Snow Depth	17	14	7	1	0	0	0	0	0	0	2	13	54
Thunderstorm Days*	< 1	< 1	2	3	4	7	7	5	3	1	1	< 1	33
Foggy Days*	13	12	14	13	15	16	17	20	17	15	13	14	179
Predominant Sky Cover*	OVR	OVR	OVR	OVR	OVR	OVR	OVR	OVR	OVR	OVR	OVR	OVR	OVR
Mean Relative Humidity 7am (%)*	81	80	80	77	79	82	85	88	89	85	81	82	82
Mean Relative Humidity 4pm (%)*	70	66	60	54	52	54	55	55	57	57	66	72	60
Mean Dewpoint (°F)*	18	19	26	36	46	56	60	60	53	42	32	23	39
Prevailing Wind Direction*	WSW	WSW	W	SW	SW	SW	SW	SW	SW	SW	SW	WSW	SW
Prevailing Wind Speed (mph)*	14	13	13	13	12	9	9	8	9	10	12	14	12
Maximum Wind Gust (mph)*	67	54	78	75	70	58	66	58	62	51	53	62	78

Note: (*) Period of record is 1948-1995

Barnesville *Belmont County* Elevation: 1,240 ft. Latitude: 39° 59' N Longitude: 81° 09' W

	JAN	FEB	MAR	APR	MAY	JUN	JUL	AUG	SEP	OCT	NOV	DEC	YEAR
Mean Maximum Temp. (°F)	35.5	38.8	48.6	61.1	70.2	78.7	82.5	81.3	74.3	62.8	50.9	39.4	60.4
Mean Temp. (°F)	27.6	30.1	38.5	49.8	59.4	68.1	72.3	70.6	63.4	52.2	42.0	31.9	50.5
Mean Minimum Temp. (°F)	19.7	21.2	28.4	38.5	48.4	57.4	62.1	59.9	52.4	41.4	33.1	24.3	40.6
Extreme Maximum Temp. (°F)	71	76	82	87	90	96	100	97	93	85	76	75	100
Extreme Minimum Temp. (°F)	-23	-10	-5	15	26	33	45	38	30	18	na	-17	na
Days Maximum Temp. ≥ 90°F	0	0	0	0	0	1	2	3	1	0	0	0	7
Days Maximum Temp. ≤ 32°F	13	9	3	0	0	0	0	0	0	0	2	8	35
Days Minimum Temp. ≤ 32°F	27	24	21	9	1	0	0	0	0	5	15	24	126
Days Minimum Temp. ≤ 0°F	2	1	0	0	0	0	0	0	0	0	0	1	4
Heating Degree Days (base 65°F)	1,151	980	815	458	207	44	6	14	115	399	684	1,019	5,892
Cooling Degree Days (base 65°F)	0	0	2	9	40	144	239	196	72	8	0	0	710
Mean Precipitation (in.)	2.97	2.62	3.54	3.91	4.50	4.63	4.39	3.74	3.23	3.09	4.01	2.97	43.60
Extreme Maximum Daily Precip. (in.)	2.03	2.17	1.69	1.74	2.32	2.28	3.67	5.12	2.42	1.56	2.91	1.56	5.12
Days With ≥ 0.1" Precipitation	7	6	8	9	9	8	7	6	6	6	8	7	87
Days With ≥ 0.5" Precipitation	2	2	2	3	3	3	3	2	2	2	3	2	29
Days With ≥ 1.0" Precipitation	0	0	1	1	1	1	1	1	1	1	1	0	9
Mean Snowfall (in.)	10.1	7.7	4.9	1.2	trace	0.0	0.0	trace	0.0	0.1	1.8	5.8	31.6
Maximum Snow Depth (in.)	16	20	17	12	trace	0	0	trace	0	2	4	8	20
Days With ≥ 1.0" Snow Depth	12	9	4	0	0	0	0	0	0	0	2	7	34

Bellefontaine *Logan County* Elevation: 1,185 ft. Latitude: 40° 21' N Longitude: 83° 46' W

	JAN	FEB	MAR	APR	MAY	JUN	JUL	AUG	SEP	OCT	NOV	DEC	YEAR
Mean Maximum Temp. (°F)	33.4	37.5	47.6	60.6	71.1	79.5	82.9	81.8	75.9	63.4	50.4	37.6	60.2
Mean Temp. (°F)	25.7	28.9	38.1	49.8	60.4	69.3	72.8	71.6	64.8	52.8	41.8	30.1	50.5
Mean Minimum Temp. (°F)	17.9	20.2	28.5	38.9	49.6	59.0	62.6	61.4	53.8	42.2	33.0	22.6	40.8
Extreme Maximum Temp. (°F)	66	72	82	87	90	101	99	101	95	89	77	71	101
Extreme Minimum Temp. (°F)	-27	-13	-12	9	28	37	45	39	30	17	8	-22	-27
Days Maximum Temp. ≥ 90°F	0	0	0	0	0	2	4	3	1	0	0	0	10
Days Maximum Temp. ≤ 32°F	14	10	4	0	0	0	0	0	0	0	2	10	40
Days Minimum Temp. ≤ 32°F	28	24	21	8	1	0	0	0	0	5	16	26	129
Days Minimum Temp. ≤ 0°F	3	2	0	0	0	0	0	0	0	0	0	2	7
Heating Degree Days (base 65°F)	1,212	1,014	828	457	188	34	4	10	92	384	691	1,074	5,988
Cooling Degree Days (base 65°F)	0	0	1	8	50	169	253	222	94	13	0	0	810
Mean Precipitation (in.)	2.64	2.13	2.93	3.58	4.13	4.44	4.19	3.57	2.81	2.62	3.17	3.03	39.24
Extreme Maximum Daily Precip. (in.)	3.29	2.30	1.85	2.37	2.47	3.30	4.45	3.02	2.40	2.47	1.78	2.96	4.45
Days With ≥ 0.1" Precipitation	6	5	7	8	9	8	7	6	5	6	7	7	81
Days With ≥ 0.5" Precipitation	1	1	2	3	3	3	3	2	2	1	2	2	25
Days With ≥ 1.0" Precipitation	0	0	0	1	1	1	1	1	1	1	1	1	9
Mean Snowfall (in.)	na	3.2	1.2	0.2	0.0	0.0	0.0	0.0	0.0	0.2	0.4	2.5	na
Maximum Snow Depth (in.)	19	14	10	1	0	0	0	0	0	1	4	11	19
Days With ≥ 1.0" Snow Depth	7	4	1	0	0	0	0	0	0	0	0	3	15

Bowling Green WWTP *Wood County* Elevation: 674 ft. Latitude: 41° 23' N Longitude: 83° 37' W

	JAN	FEB	MAR	APR	MAY	JUN	JUL	AUG	SEP	OCT	NOV	DEC	YEAR
Mean Maximum Temp. (°F)	32.2	35.7	46.0	59.4	70.7	80.7	84.1	82.1	75.9	63.0	49.6	36.5	59.7
Mean Temp. (°F)	24.9	27.9	36.6	48.5	59.4	69.7	73.1	71.0	64.1	52.2	41.1	29.6	49.8
Mean Minimum Temp. (°F)	17.6	20.0	27.2	37.5	48.1	58.6	62.0	59.9	52.2	41.4	32.6	22.6	40.0
Extreme Maximum Temp. (°F)	66	72	80	88	92	104	101	98	95	90	78	70	104
Extreme Minimum Temp. (°F)	-20	-13	-5	8	28	39	45	38	30	21	11	-19	-20
Days Maximum Temp. ≥ 90°F	0	0	0	0	1	4	6	4	1	0	0	0	16
Days Maximum Temp. ≤ 32°F	16	11	4	0	0	0	0	0	0	0	1	11	43
Days Minimum Temp. ≤ 32°F	28	25	22	9	0	0	0	0	0	4	16	26	130
Days Minimum Temp. ≤ 0°F	4	2	0	0	0	0	0	0	0	0	0	1	7
Heating Degree Days (base 65°F)	1,238	1,044	873	496	211	32	3	13	103	402	710	1,090	6,215
Cooling Degree Days (base 65°F)	0	0	1	8	46	180	261	206	83	11	0	0	796
Mean Precipitation (in.)	1.91	1.84	2.17	3.14	3.76	3.37	3.66	3.64	2.61	2.82	2.57	2.43	33.92
Extreme Maximum Daily Precip. (in.)	1.47	2.00	1.68	1.90	2.66	4.25	4.08	3.31	2.49	3.37	2.12	2.11	4.25
Days With ≥ 0.1" Precipitation	5	4	6	7	8	7	7	6	5	6	6	6	73
Days With ≥ 0.5" Precipitation	1	1	1	2	2	2	3	2	2	2	2	1	21
Days With ≥ 1.0" Precipitation	0	0	0	1	1	1	1	1	1	1	0	0	7
Mean Snowfall (in.)	7.1	5.4	3.2	0.6	trace	0.0	0.0	0.0	0.0	0.0	0.6	4.7	21.6
Maximum Snow Depth (in.)	14	18	10	7	1	0	0	0	0	0	3	11	18
Days With ≥ 1.0" Snow Depth	14	11	5	0	0	0	0	0	0	0	1	7	38

Bucyrus *Crawford County* Elevation: 955 ft. Latitude: 40° 49' N Longitude: 82° 58' W

	JAN	FEB	MAR	APR	MAY	JUN	JUL	AUG	SEP	OCT	NOV	DEC	YEAR
Mean Maximum Temp. (°F)	32.6	35.7	45.6	59.6	70.2	79.5	83.1	81.4	74.8	61.9	49.2	36.6	59.2
Mean Temp. (°F)	25.2	27.6	36.3	48.5	58.8	68.4	72.3	70.5	63.4	51.4	40.8	29.7	49.4
Mean Minimum Temp. (°F)	17.8	19.5	26.9	37.4	47.4	57.3	61.4	59.6	52.0	40.8	32.4	22.7	39.6
Extreme Maximum Temp. (°F)	64	71	81	88	91	102	100	99	95	87	77	72	102
Extreme Minimum Temp. (°F)	-26	-18	-11	10	27	37	43	39	30	20	12	-18	-26
Days Maximum Temp. ≥ 90°F	0	0	0	0	0	3	4	3	1	0	0	0	11
Days Maximum Temp. ≤ 32°F	16	11	5	0	0	0	0	0	0	0	2	11	45
Days Minimum Temp. ≤ 32°F	27	25	23	10	0	0	0	0	0	5	16	26	132
Days Minimum Temp. ≤ 0°F	3	2	0	0	0	0	0	0	0	0	0	1	6
Heating Degree Days (base 65°F)	1,227	1,052	884	495	225	45	7	16	114	423	721	1,088	6,297
Cooling Degree Days (base 65°F)	0	0	1	7	40	154	240	195	74	9	0	0	720
Mean Precipitation (in.)	2.48	2.02	2.66	3.42	4.26	4.21	4.44	3.84	3.19	2.62	3.07	2.86	39.07
Extreme Maximum Daily Precip. (in.)	2.20	1.45	1.50	1.80	2.18	3.27	3.42	8.68	3.58	2.51	1.57	1.95	8.68
Days With ≥ 0.1" Precipitation	6	5	7	8	9	8	8	6	6	6	7	7	83
Days With ≥ 0.5" Precipitation	1	1	2	2	3	3	3	3	2	1	2	2	25
Days With ≥ 1.0" Precipitation	1	0	0	0	1	1	1	1	1	0	1	0	7
Mean Snowfall (in.)	7.4	4.6	3.4	0.9	0.1	0.0	0.0	0.0	0.0	0.1	0.9	5.1	22.5
Maximum Snow Depth (in.)	14	13	10	8	2	0	0	0	0	1	3	17	17
Days With ≥ 1.0" Snow Depth	12	7	3	0	0	0	0	0	0	0	1	6	29

The period of record for all cooperative weather station data is 1980 – 2009. See User Guide for detailed explanation of data.

Cadiz *Harrison County* Elevation: 1,259 ft. Latitude: 40° 16' N Longitude: 81° 00' W

	JAN	FEB	MAR	APR	MAY	JUN	JUL	AUG	SEP	OCT	NOV	DEC	YEAR
Mean Maximum Temp. (°F)	35.2	38.9	48.5	61.1	70.3	78.5	82.2	81.3	74.7	63.1	50.6	39.0	60.3
Mean Temp. (°F)	27.2	30.3	38.9	50.3	60.0	68.5	72.6	71.1	64.3	52.8	42.0	31.6	50.8
Mean Minimum Temp. (°F)	19.5	21.5	29.1	39.6	49.5	58.3	62.8	61.1	53.9	42.5	33.5	24.1	41.3
Extreme Maximum Temp. (°F)	69	76	81	89	89	95	101	97	94	87	79	75	101
Extreme Minimum Temp. (°F)	-24	-10	-6	14	26	35	47	40	35	22	10	-17	-24
Days Maximum Temp. ≥ 90°F	0	0	0	0	0	1	3	3	1	0	0	0	8
Days Maximum Temp. ≤ 32°F	14	9	4	0	0	0	0	0	0	0	1	9	37
Days Minimum Temp. ≤ 32°F	26	22	18	7	1	0	0	0	0	4	14	24	116
Days Minimum Temp. ≤ 0°F	2	1	0	0	0	0	0	0	0	0	0	1	4
Heating Degree Days (base 65°F)	1,168	978	805	446	196	38	4	11	99	381	683	1,031	5,840
Cooling Degree Days (base 65°F)	0	0	1	12	46	148	246	208	85	11	1	0	758
Mean Precipitation (in.)	3.02	2.37	3.17	3.48	4.39	4.27	4.31	3.80	3.43	2.75	3.37	2.90	41.26
Extreme Maximum Daily Precip. (in.)	2.07	1.75	1.64	2.00	2.32	5.00	3.28	2.70	5.09	1.93	2.90	2.05	5.09
Days With ≥ 0.1" Precipitation	7	6	8	9	9	8	8	6	6	6	7	7	87
Days With ≥ 0.5" Precipitation	2	1	2	2	3	3	3	3	2	2	2	2	27
Days With ≥ 1.0" Precipitation	0	0	0	1	1	1	1	1	1	1	0	0	7
Mean Snowfall (in.)	8.8	6.1	4.9	1.2	0.0	0.0	0.0	0.0	0.0	0.1	1.5	5.6	28.2
Maximum Snow Depth (in.)	***10***	***15***	***12***	2	0	0	0	0	0	***trace***	***3***	na	na
Days With ≥ 1.0" Snow Depth	***9***	6	3	0	0	0	0	0	0	0	1	***6***	***25***

Cambridge *Guernsey County* Elevation: 799 ft. Latitude: 40° 01' N Longitude: 81° 35' W

	JAN	FEB	MAR	APR	MAY	JUN	JUL	AUG	SEP	OCT	NOV	DEC	YEAR
Mean Maximum Temp. (°F)	38.0	42.6	52.9	65.7	74.2	82.0	85.2	84.2	77.6	66.0	53.8	41.6	63.6
Mean Temp. (°F)	30.0	33.3	42.0	53.3	62.0	70.2	74.1	73.0	66.0	54.4	44.1	33.7	53.0
Mean Minimum Temp. (°F)	21.8	23.9	31.0	40.8	49.7	58.4	63.0	61.7	54.4	42.7	34.5	25.7	42.3
Extreme Maximum Temp. (°F)	72	76	83	90	92	98	102	99	96	90	80	77	102
Extreme Minimum Temp. (°F)	-32	-12	-3	17	29	38	42	37	32	19	9	-17	-32
Days Maximum Temp. ≥ 90°F	0	0	0	0	0	3	6	5	1	0	0	0	15
Days Maximum Temp. ≤ 32°F	9	6	1	0	0	0	0	0	0	0	1	6	23
Days Minimum Temp. ≤ 32°F	25	22	18	6	1	0	0	0	0	5	13	23	113
Days Minimum Temp. ≤ 0°F	2	1	0	0	0	0	0	0	0	0	0	1	4
Heating Degree Days (base 65°F)	1,080	891	709	359	144	21	2	5	71	335	619	964	5,200
Cooling Degree Days (base 65°F)	0	0	2	14	57	185	292	259	107	13	0	0	929
Mean Precipitation (in.)	2.95	2.19	3.09	3.52	4.18	3.92	4.25	3.62	3.32	2.78	3.26	2.79	39.87
Extreme Maximum Daily Precip. (in.)	2.17	1.83	2.08	2.29	2.01	4.97	2.74	5.45	5.33	2.37	2.32	1.65	5.45
Days With ≥ 0.1" Precipitation	6	6	8	7	9	8	8	6	5	6	7	7	83
Days With ≥ 0.5" Precipitation	2	1	2	2	3	3	3	2	2	2	2	2	26
Days With ≥ 1.0" Precipitation	1	0	0	1	1	1	1	1	1	1	1	0	9
Mean Snowfall (in.)	6.3	4.5	2.8	0.7	trace	0.0	0.0	0.0	0.0	trace	0.7	3.2	18.2
Maximum Snow Depth (in.)	9	19	9	10	trace	0	0	0	0	trace	5	6	19
Days With ≥ 1.0" Snow Depth	11	7	2	0	0	0	0	0	0	0	0	5	25

Carpenter 2 S *Meigs County* Elevation: 821 ft. Latitude: 39° 09' N Longitude: 82° 13' W

	JAN	FEB	MAR	APR	MAY	JUN	JUL	AUG	SEP	OCT	NOV	DEC	YEAR
Mean Maximum Temp. (°F)	***39.0***	42.8	53.2	64.9	73.3	***81.2***	***84.7***	***84.0***	77.2	66.3	***54.6***	***42.9***	***63.7***
Mean Temp. (°F)	***30.2***	33.0	41.9	52.6	61.2	***69.5***	***73.3***	***72.1***	64.7	53.4	***43.9***	***33.9***	***52.5***
Mean Minimum Temp. (°F)	***21.3***	23.1	30.5	40.2	49.1	***57.7***	***61.9***	***60.2***	52.1	40.6	***33.2***	***24.9***	***41.2***
Extreme Maximum Temp. (°F)	***75***	***77***	***83***	***89***	***90***	***99***	***101***	***101***	***97***	***87***	***80***	***78***	***101***
Extreme Minimum Temp. (°F)	***-25***	***-11***	***-5***	***15***	***27***	***37***	***44***	***35***	***29***	***17***	***8***	***-4***	***-25***
Days Maximum Temp. ≥ 90°F	***0***	0	0	0	0	2	5	5	1	0	***0***	***0***	***13***
Days Maximum Temp. ≤ 32°F	***9***	6	1	0	0	0	0	0	0	0	***0***	***7***	***23***
Days Minimum Temp. ≤ 32°F	***26***	23	18	7	1	0	0	0	0	7	***15***	***23***	***120***
Days Minimum Temp. ≤ 0°F	***2***	1	0	0	0	0	0	0	0	0	***0***	***1***	***4***
Heating Degree Days (base 65°F)	***1,073***	899	714	381	163	***25***	***3***	***7***	93	364	***627***	***958***	***5,307***
Cooling Degree Days (base 65°F)	***0***	0	3	15	53	***167***	***267***	***234***	90	12	***2***	***0***	***843***
Mean Precipitation (in.)	***2.90***	***2.82***	3.67	3.55	4.39	3.76	4.47	3.32	3.22	2.90	***3.22***	***2.82***	***41.04***
Extreme Maximum Daily Precip. (in.)	***1.81***	***3.60***	***4.87***	***1.80***	***2.96***	***2.23***	***2.76***	***3.22***	***4.34***	***2.20***	***2.00***	na	na
Days With ≥ 0.1" Precipitation	***7***	***6***	7	8	8	***7***	8	6	6	6	***7***	***6***	***82***
Days With ≥ 0.5" Precipitation	***2***	***2***	3	2	3	***3***	3	2	2	2	***2***	***2***	***28***
Days With ≥ 1.0" Precipitation	***0***	***1***	1	1	1	1	1	1	1	1	***1***	***0***	***10***
Mean Snowfall (in.)	***6.9***	***4.4***	***2.7***	0.9	trace	0.0	0.0	0.0	0.0	trace	***0.6***	***3.1***	***18.6***
Maximum Snow Depth (in.)	na	na	na	na	na	na	na	na	na	na	na	na	na
Days With ≥ 1.0" Snow Depth	na	na	***1***	0	0	0	0	0	0	***0***	***0***	na	na

Centerburg 2 SE *Knox County* Elevation: 1,205 ft. Latitude: 40° 18' N Longitude: 82° 39' W

	JAN	FEB	MAR	APR	MAY	JUN	JUL	AUG	SEP	OCT	NOV	DEC	YEAR
Mean Maximum Temp. (°F)	33.7	37.3	47.6	60.9	70.6	79.2	82.6	81.4	74.7	62.6	50.3	37.3	59.8
Mean Temp. (°F)	25.8	28.4	37.8	49.9	59.6	68.6	72.2	70.8	63.5	51.6	41.3	29.7	49.9
Mean Minimum Temp. (°F)	17.4	19.6	28.0	38.6	48.6	57.9	61.6	60.0	52.2	40.6	32.3	22.3	39.9
Extreme Maximum Temp. (°F)	67	73	82	87	89	99	99	97	94	88	78	70	99
Extreme Minimum Temp. (°F)	-29	-16	-6	11	27	37	44	38	32	21	7	-23	-29
Days Maximum Temp. ≥ 90°F	0	0	0	0	0	2	3	3	1	0	0	0	9
Days Maximum Temp. ≤ 32°F	14	10	4	0	0	0	0	0	0	0	2	10	40
Days Minimum Temp. ≤ 32°F	28	25	21	8	1	0	0	0	0	6	16	26	131
Days Minimum Temp. ≤ 0°F	4	2	0	0	0	0	0	0	0	0	0	1	7
Heating Degree Days (base 65°F)	1,210	1,027	836	456	203	39	5	13	108	417	704	1,088	6,106
Cooling Degree Days (base 65°F)	0	0	1	9	42	152	234	201	70	8	0	0	717
Mean Precipitation (in.)	2.85	2.40	3.05	3.76	4.51	4.56	4.43	3.74	3.15	2.90	3.45	3.14	41.94
Extreme Maximum Daily Precip. (in.)	2.82	2.75	2.25	2.11	2.75	3.46	2.95	3.34	2.76	2.81	1.70	2.31	3.46
Days With ≥ 0.1" Precipitation	6	6	7	8	8	8	7	6	5	6	7	7	81
Days With ≥ 0.5" Precipitation	2	2	2	2	3	3	3	3	2	2	3	2	29
Days With ≥ 1.0" Precipitation	0	0	0	1	1	1	1	1	1	1	1	1	9
Mean Snowfall (in.)	4.6	2.1	2.1	0.2	trace	0.0	0.0	0.0	0.0	0.1	0.8	2.5	12.4
Maximum Snow Depth (in.)	23	9	10	7	1	0	0	0	0	1	4	10	23
Days With ≥ 1.0" Snow Depth	9	7	3	1	0	0	0	0	0	0	1	5	26

The period of record for all cooperative weather station data is 1980 – 2009. See User Guide for detailed explanation of data.

Chardon *Geauga County* Elevation: 1,129 ft. Latitude: 41° 35' N Longitude: 81° 11' W

	JAN	FEB	MAR	APR	MAY	JUN	JUL	AUG	SEP	OCT	NOV	DEC	YEAR
Mean Maximum Temp. (°F)	32.3	35.1	43.7	57.1	67.7	76.7	80.4	79.0	72.1	60.2	48.5	36.6	57.5
Mean Temp. (°F)	24.4	25.9	33.9	46.1	56.2	65.3	69.4	68.0	61.0	50.0	40.5	29.5	47.5
Mean Minimum Temp. (°F)	16.3	16.7	24.2	35.0	44.6	53.9	58.3	56.9	49.8	39.7	32.4	22.4	37.5
Extreme Maximum Temp. (°F)	67	73	82	88	90	100	98	96	92	85	79	73	100
Extreme Minimum Temp. (°F)	-23	-17	-17	5	23	33	40	33	29	17	4	-21	-23
Days Maximum Temp. ≥ 90°F	0	0	0	0	0	1	2	2	0	0	0	0	5
Days Maximum Temp. ≤ 32°F	16	13	7	0	0	0	0	0	0	0	2	11	49
Days Minimum Temp. ≤ 32°F	28	26	25	13	2	0	0	0	0	6	16	26	142
Days Minimum Temp. ≤ 0°F	4	3	1	0	0	0	0	0	0	0	0	1	9
Heating Degree Days (base 65°F)	1,253	1,099	956	565	290	86	24	36	160	463	729	1,093	6,754
Cooling Degree Days (base 65°F)	0	0	1	4	23	102	166	136	46	4	0	0	482
Mean Precipitation (in.)	3.59	2.79	3.27	4.03	4.42	4.46	4.38	4.24	4.30	4.06	4.30	4.40	48.24
Extreme Maximum Daily Precip. (in.)	1.78	2.33	2.25	2.30	3.13	3.66	5.50	3.75	2.65	2.00	2.89	2.14	5.50
Days With ≥ 0.1" Precipitation	10	8	9	10	9	8	8	7	8	9	10	12	108
Days With ≥ 0.5" Precipitation	2	1	2	3	3	3	3	3	3	3	3	3	32
Days With ≥ 1.0" Precipitation	0	0	0	1	1	1	1	1	1	1	1	1	9
Mean Snowfall (in.)	28.6	19.2	14.4	4.5	trace	0.0	0.0	0.0	0.0	0.9	9.5	25.7	102.8
Maximum Snow Depth (in.)	23	22	20	14	trace	0	0	0	0	7	47	23	47
Days With ≥ 1.0" Snow Depth	23	20	12	2	0	0	0	0	0	1	5	17	80

Chillicothe Mound City *Ross County* Elevation: 649 ft. Latitude: 39° 22' N Longitude: 83° 00' W

	JAN	FEB	MAR	APR	MAY	JUN	JUL	AUG	SEP	OCT	NOV	DEC	YEAR
Mean Maximum Temp. (°F)	***38.0***	***43.0***	***52.3***	***64.6***	***73.5***	82.5	***85.7***	***85.0***	***78.4***	***67.0***	***54.3***	***42.4***	***63.9***
Mean Temp. (°F)	***29.1***	***33.3***	***41.3***	***52.4***	***61.7***	***70.9***	***74.6***	***73.2***	***65.8***	***54.2***	***44.0***	***33.8***	***52.8***
Mean Minimum Temp. (°F)	***20.1***	***23.4***	***30.2***	***40.1***	***49.8***	***59.2***	***63.4***	***61.4***	***53.0***	***41.4***	***33.6***	***25.0***	***41.7***
Extreme Maximum Temp. (°F)	73	77	88	90	93	103	103	105	100	92	82	80	105
Extreme Minimum Temp. (°F)	-29	-14	-10	16	29	36	41	39	32	17	11	-21	-29
Days Maximum Temp. ≥ 90°F	0	0	0	0	0	4	7	6	2	0	0	0	19
Days Maximum Temp. ≤ 32°F	9	5	1	0	0	0	0	0	0	0	0	6	21
Days Minimum Temp. ≤ 32°F	25	22	18	6	0	0	0	0	0	5	14	22	112
Days Minimum Temp. ≤ 0°F	2	1	0	0	0	0	0	0	0	0	0	1	4
Heating Degree Days (base 65°F)	***1,107***	***891***	***729***	***387***	***157***	***21***	***1***	***6***	***83***	***341***	***625***	***960***	***5,308***
Cooling Degree Days (base 65°F)	***0***	***0***	***3***	***14***	***61***	***205***	***306***	***268***	***112***	***15***	***1***	***0***	***985***
Mean Precipitation (in.)	2.62	2.46	3.49	3.55	4.64	3.26	4.04	3.05	2.67	2.58	2.93	2.82	38.11
Extreme Maximum Daily Precip. (in.)	***1.95***	***2.21***	***1.96***	***3.05***	3.01	4.10	***2.45***	***3.98***	3.06	2.88	***2.04***	***1.72***	***4.10***
Days With ≥ 0.1" Precipitation	5	5	7	7	8	6	7	5	4	5	6	5	70
Days With ≥ 0.5" Precipitation	2	2	2	2	3	2	3	2	2	2	2	2	26
Days With ≥ 1.0" Precipitation	0	1	1	1	1	1	1	1	1	1	0	0	9
Mean Snowfall (in.)	5.2	4.0	2.4	0.4	trace	0.0	0.0	0.0	0.0	0.1	0.4	2.3	14.8
Maximum Snow Depth (in.)	11	10	9	11	trace	0	0	0	0	1	4	8	11
Days With ≥ 1.0" Snow Depth	8	5	2	0	0	0	0	0	0	0	0	3	18

Chilo Meldahl L&D *Clermont County* Elevation: 500 ft. Latitude: 38° 48' N Longitude: 84° 10' W

	JAN	FEB	MAR	APR	MAY	JUN	JUL	AUG	SEP	OCT	NOV	DEC	YEAR
Mean Maximum Temp. (°F)	39.9	43.8	53.8	65.5	73.7	82.3	86.0	85.6	79.5	67.9	55.6	43.7	64.8
Mean Temp. (°F)	31.2	34.2	42.8	53.5	62.4	71.2	75.4	74.8	68.0	56.4	45.6	35.2	54.2
Mean Minimum Temp. (°F)	22.6	24.4	31.7	41.5	51.0	60.1	64.8	63.9	56.3	44.8	35.7	26.6	43.6
Extreme Maximum Temp. (°F)	71	73	83	89	91	98	101	107	98	92	82	73	107
Extreme Minimum Temp. (°F)	-22	-6	-4	22	29	42	48	44	35	23	13	-15	-22
Days Maximum Temp. ≥ 90°F	0	0	0	0	0	3	8	7	2	0	0	0	20
Days Maximum Temp. ≤ 32°F	8	5	1	0	0	0	0	0	0	0	0	5	19
Days Minimum Temp. ≤ 32°F	26	22	18	4	0	0	0	0	0	2	12	23	107
Days Minimum Temp. ≤ 0°F	1	1	0	0	0	0	0	0	0	0	0	1	3
Heating Degree Days (base 65°F)	1,039	865	683	349	134	17	0	2	47	281	575	917	4,909
Cooling Degree Days (base 65°F)	0	0	1	12	59	209	332	313	143	21	0	0	1,090
Mean Precipitation (in.)	2.88	2.82	4.30	3.42	4.64	3.61	3.92	3.21	2.82	3.08	2.90	2.98	40.58
Extreme Maximum Daily Precip. (in.)	2.88	2.00	7.20	2.08	3.80	2.80	3.82	4.45	4.11	5.00	2.46	2.85	7.20
Days With ≥ 0.1" Precipitation	6	6	7	7	8	6	6	5	4	5	6	6	72
Days With ≥ 0.5" Precipitation	2	2	3	2	3	2	3	2	2	2	2	2	27
Days With ≥ 1.0" Precipitation	1	1	1	1	1	1	1	1	1	1	1	1	12
Mean Snowfall (in.)	***0.6***	na	***0.7***	0.0	0.0	0.0	0.0	0.0	0.0	0.0	trace	***1.3***	na
Maximum Snow Depth (in.)	***16***	***5***	***11***	0	0	0	0	***0***	0	***0***	*trace*	***3***	***16***
Days With ≥ 1.0" Snow Depth	***2***	***2***	***0***	0	0	0	0	0	0	0	0	***0***	***4***

Chippewa Lake *Medina County* Elevation: 1,180 ft. Latitude: 41° 03' N Longitude: 81° 56' W

	JAN	FEB	MAR	APR	MAY	JUN	JUL	AUG	SEP	OCT	NOV	DEC	YEAR
Mean Maximum Temp. (°F)	33.3	36.7	46.1	59.4	69.6	78.8	82.5	81.1	74.2	62.2	49.7	37.2	59.2
Mean Temp. (°F)	25.7	28.0	36.4	48.3	58.2	67.6	71.5	70.2	63.1	51.7	41.2	29.9	49.3
Mean Minimum Temp. (°F)	18.0	19.2	26.7	37.2	46.7	56.4	60.4	59.2	52.0	41.1	32.6	22.6	39.3
Extreme Maximum Temp. (°F)	68	74	83	88	90	102	102	99	92	88	78	75	102
Extreme Minimum Temp. (°F)	-26	-17	-14	8	25	34	39	34	31	16	8	-18	-26
Days Maximum Temp. ≥ 90°F	0	0	0	0	0	2	4	2	0	0	0	0	8
Days Maximum Temp. ≤ 32°F	15	11	5	0	0	0	0	0	0	0	2	11	44
Days Minimum Temp. ≤ 32°F	28	25	22	10	1	0	0	0	0	5	16	26	133
Days Minimum Temp. ≤ 0°F	3	2	0	0	0	0	0	0	0	0	0	1	6
Heating Degree Days (base 65°F)	1,213	1,039	880	500	236	51	8	16	118	413	708	1,081	6,263
Cooling Degree Days (base 65°F)	0	0	1	6	33	138	216	185	68	7	0	0	654
Mean Precipitation (in.)	2.54	2.12	2.94	3.46	3.98	3.89	4.21	3.66	3.44	2.79	3.29	3.00	39.32
Extreme Maximum Daily Precip. (in.)	1.93	1.83	1.44	1.63	2.72	2.25	3.91	4.30	3.40	2.29	2.16	2.45	4.30
Days With ≥ 0.1" Precipitation	7	6	8	9	9	7	7	6	6	7	8	7	87
Days With ≥ 0.5" Precipitation	1	1	2	2	2	3	3	3	2	2	2	2	25
Days With ≥ 1.0" Precipitation	0	0	0	1	1	1	1	1	1	0	0	0	6
Mean Snowfall (in.)	9.4	7.1	6.7	1.9	trace	0.0	0.0	0.0	0.0	0.1	2.6	8.1	35.9
Maximum Snow Depth (in.)	16	15	15	6	trace	0	0	0	0	1	7	24	24
Days With ≥ 1.0" Snow Depth	14	12	6	1	0	0	0	0	0	0	2	10	45

The period of record for all cooperative weather station data is 1980 – 2009. See User Guide for detailed explanation of data.

Circleville *Pickaway County* Elevation: 672 ft. Latitude: 39° 37' N Longitude: 82° 57' W

	JAN	FEB	MAR	APR	MAY	JUN	JUL	AUG	SEP	OCT	NOV	DEC	YEAR
Mean Maximum Temp. (°F)	37.6	40.9	51.3	63.9	73.2	81.8	85.0	84.1	78.0	66.2	53.6	41.1	63.1
Mean Temp. (°F)	29.8	32.2	41.0	52.2	61.9	70.8	74.2	72.9	66.1	54.6	44.0	33.4	52.8
Mean Minimum Temp. (°F)	21.9	23.5	30.6	40.5	50.5	59.9	63.5	61.7	54.2	42.9	34.4	25.6	42.4
Extreme Maximum Temp. (°F)	70	76	83	90	92	100	100	101	97	91	81	79	101
Extreme Minimum Temp. (°F)	-22	-14	-4	17	31	42	42	40	33	21	12	-19	-22
Days Maximum Temp. ≥ 90°F	0	0	0	0	0	4	7	6	1	0	0	0	18
Days Maximum Temp. ≤ 32°F	10	7	2	0	0	0	0	0	0	0	1	7	27
Days Minimum Temp. ≤ 32°F	25	22	19	6	0	0	0	0	0	4	14	23	113
Days Minimum Temp. ≤ 0°F	2	1	0	0	0	0	0	0	0	0	0	1	4
Heating Degree Days (base 65°F)	1,085	920	739	388	152	20	1	5	70	333	623	974	5,310
Cooling Degree Days (base 65°F)	0	0	2	13	61	201	295	259	112	18	1	0	962
Mean Precipitation (in.)	2.60	2.16	2.97	3.52	4.80	3.65	3.96	3.41	2.92	2.96	3.02	2.83	38.80
Extreme Maximum Daily Precip. (in.)	2.43	1.77	2.07	2.00	3.35	4.12	2.75	2.58	2.70	2.62	1.70	2.73	4.12
Days With ≥ 0.1" Precipitation	6	5	7	8	9	7	7	6	5	6	6	6	78
Days With ≥ 0.5" Precipitation	2	1	2	2	4	2	3	3	2	2	2	2	27
Days With ≥ 1.0" Precipitation	0	0	1	1	1	1	1	1	1	1	1	0	9
Mean Snowfall (in.)	5.5	3.9	1.7	0.4	0.0	0.0	0.0	0.0	0.0	0.0	0.3	2.1	13.9
Maximum Snow Depth (in.)	15	9	7	10	0	0	0	0	0	0	3	***7***	***15***
Days With ≥ 1.0" Snow Depth	7	6	2	0	0	0	0	0	0	0	0	4	19

Columbus Valley Crossing *Franklin County* Elevation: 734 ft. Latitude: 39° 54' N Longitude: 82° 56' W

	JAN	FEB	MAR	APR	MAY	JUN	JUL	AUG	SEP	OCT	NOV	DEC	YEAR
Mean Maximum Temp. (°F)	37.1	41.1	51.5	64.2	73.5	81.9	84.9	83.6	77.8	66.1	53.6	40.6	63.0
Mean Temp. (°F)	29.2	32.3	41.3	52.5	62.1	70.8	74.4	72.8	66.0	54.4	43.9	32.9	52.7
Mean Minimum Temp. (°F)	21.3	23.5	31.0	40.7	50.6	59.8	63.8	61.9	54.1	42.6	34.2	25.2	42.4
Extreme Maximum Temp. (°F)	70	75	83	90	92	100	100	100	96	91	79	76	100
Extreme Minimum Temp. (°F)	-28	-13	-2	17	29	39	45	38	28	20	10	-21	-28
Days Maximum Temp. ≥ 90°F	0	0	0	0	0	3	6	4	1	0	0	0	14
Days Maximum Temp. ≤ 32°F	10	6	2	0	0	0	0	0	0	0	1	7	26
Days Minimum Temp. ≤ 32°F	26	22	18	6	0	0	0	0	0	4	14	24	114
Days Minimum Temp. ≤ 0°F	2	1	0	0	0	0	0	0	0	0	0	1	4
Heating Degree Days (base 65°F)	1,103	917	728	379	144	19	1	4	72	337	627	987	5,318
Cooling Degree Days (base 65°F)	0	0	1	10	61	200	297	251	108	14	1	0	943
Mean Precipitation (in.)	2.93	2.13	3.30	3.74	4.46	4.00	4.45	3.30	3.00	2.85	3.22	3.01	40.39
Extreme Maximum Daily Precip. (in.)	2.34	1.43	2.07	2.76	2.16	3.46	3.77	3.72	2.76	2.36	1.74	2.16	3.77
Days With ≥ 0.1" Precipitation	6	5	7	7	8	6	7	5	5	5	7	6	74
Days With ≥ 0.5" Precipitation	2	1	2	3	3	3	3	2	2	2	2	2	27
Days With ≥ 1.0" Precipitation	1	0	0	1	1	1	1	1	1	1	1	0	9
Mean Snowfall (in.)	5.7	4.0	1.6	0.5	trace	0.0	0.0	0.0	0.0	trace	0.4	2.7	14.9
Maximum Snow Depth (in.)	13	***10***	10	5	trace	0	0	0	0	trace	trace	***6***	***13***
Days With ≥ 1.0" Snow Depth	6	3	1	0	0	0	0	0	0	0	0	3	13

Danville 2 W *Knox County* Elevation: 970 ft. Latitude: 40° 26' N Longitude: 82° 18' W

	JAN	FEB	MAR	APR	MAY	JUN	JUL	AUG	SEP	OCT	NOV	DEC	YEAR
Mean Maximum Temp. (°F)	34.8	38.7	48.9	61.4	71.0	79.8	83.4	82.5	75.7	63.8	51.4	39.0	60.9
Mean Temp. (°F)	25.9	28.7	37.5	48.3	58.0	67.2	71.0	69.7	62.3	50.5	40.8	30.3	49.2
Mean Minimum Temp. (°F)	16.9	18.5	26.2	35.2	44.9	54.6	58.6	56.9	48.9	37.2	30.1	21.5	37.5
Extreme Maximum Temp. (°F)	69	74	83	89	94	102	102	98	96	88	78	74	102
Extreme Minimum Temp. (°F)	-35	-22	-18	9	23	35	35	32	27	15	7	-22	-35
Days Maximum Temp. ≥ 90°F	0	0	0	0	0	2	4	3	1	0	0	0	10
Days Maximum Temp. ≤ 32°F	13	9	3	0	0	0	0	0	0	0	1	9	35
Days Minimum Temp. ≤ 32°F	28	25	23	13	3	0	0	0	1	12	19	26	150
Days Minimum Temp. ≤ 0°F	4	2	0	0	0	0	0	0	0	0	0	2	8
Heating Degree Days (base 65°F)	1,207	1,021	845	496	239	52	10	19	131	448	720	1,070	6,258
Cooling Degree Days (base 65°F)	0	0	0	3	30	125	204	171	58	6	0	0	597
Mean Precipitation (in.)	2.83	2.39	3.20	3.55	4.72	4.58	4.57	3.67	3.14	2.79	3.21	3.22	41.87
Extreme Maximum Daily Precip. (in.)	2.65	2.30	1.45	2.72	2.31	3.20	3.96	5.12	2.30	2.87	2.07	2.30	5.12
Days With ≥ 0.1" Precipitation	6	6	8	8	9	8	8	6	6	6	7	7	85
Days With ≥ 0.5" Precipitation	2	1	2	2	3	3	3	3	2	2	2	2	27
Days With ≥ 1.0" Precipitation	0	0	1	1	1	1	1	1	1	0	1	1	9
Mean Snowfall (in.)	12.2	8.5	6.2	1.8	trace	0.0	0.0	0.0	0.0	trace	2.2	8.2	39.1
Maximum Snow Depth (in.)	22	15	15	5	1	0	0	0	0	1	4	9	22
Days With ≥ 1.0" Snow Depth	15	11	5	1	0	0	0	0	0	0	2	9	43

Dayton Mcd *Montgomery County* Elevation: 745 ft. Latitude: 39° 46' N Longitude: 84° 11' W

	JAN	FEB	MAR	APR	MAY	JUN	JUL	AUG	SEP	OCT	NOV	DEC	YEAR
Mean Maximum Temp. (°F)	36.4	40.9	50.6	63.7	74.3	83.5	87.5	86.2	79.1	66.1	53.0	40.5	63.5
Mean Temp. (°F)	29.3	32.8	41.2	53.3	63.8	73.3	77.3	75.8	68.1	55.7	44.6	33.5	54.0
Mean Minimum Temp. (°F)	22.2	24.6	31.8	42.8	53.3	62.9	67.0	65.2	57.1	45.2	36.1	26.5	44.5
Extreme Maximum Temp. (°F)	69	77	84	90	95	103	104	103	99	92	81	75	104
Extreme Minimum Temp. (°F)	-21	-8	2	19	33	42	51	45	35	26	13	-16	-21
Days Maximum Temp. ≥ 90°F	0	0	0	0	2	8	12	10	3	0	0	0	35
Days Maximum Temp. ≤ 32°F	12	7	2	0	0	0	0	0	0	0	1	8	30
Days Minimum Temp. ≤ 32°F	25	22	17	3	0	0	0	0	0	2	12	22	103
Days Minimum Temp. ≤ 0°F	1	1	0	0	0	0	0	0	0	0	0	1	3
Heating Degree Days (base 65°F)	1,101	906	733	365	122	15	0	2	54	308	606	970	5,182
Cooling Degree Days (base 65°F)	0	0	3	20	92	269	387	342	154	26	1	0	1,294
Mean Precipitation (in.)	2.86	2.31	3.28	4.01	4.94	4.07	4.39	3.01	2.65	2.92	3.21	3.01	40.66
Extreme Maximum Daily Precip. (in.)	2.50	2.28	2.41	2.85	3.90	4.10	2.77	3.15	4.36	2.98	2.20	2.06	4.36
Days With ≥ 0.1" Precipitation	6	5	7	8	9	7	7	5	4	5	6	7	76
Days With ≥ 0.5" Precipitation	2	1	2	3	3	3	3	2	2	2	2	2	27
Days With ≥ 1.0" Precipitation	1	0	0	1	1	1	1	1	1	1	1	1	10
Mean Snowfall (in.)	4.8	2.7	1.6	0.1	0.0	0.0	0.0	0.0	0.0	trace	0.3	2.9	12.4
Maximum Snow Depth (in.)	12	10	7	2	0	0	0	0	0	1	6	7	12
Days With ≥ 1.0" Snow Depth	8	5	2	0	0	0	0	0	0	0	0	4	19

The period of record for all cooperative weather station data is 1980 – 2009. See User Guide for detailed explanation of data.

Defiance *Defiance County* Elevation: 700 ft. Latitude: 41° 17' N Longitude: 84° 23' W

	JAN	FEB	MAR	APR	MAY	JUN	JUL	AUG	SEP	OCT	NOV	DEC	YEAR
Mean Maximum Temp. (°F)	32.3	35.5	46.0	59.7	70.9	80.7	84.4	82.5	75.9	62.7	49.3	36.3	59.7
Mean Temp. (°F)	24.7	27.3	36.5	48.7	59.5	69.5	73.4	71.7	64.4	52.2	40.9	29.3	49.8
Mean Minimum Temp. (°F)	17.0	19.0	27.0	37.6	48.1	58.4	62.3	60.8	52.9	41.5	32.4	22.3	40.0
Extreme Maximum Temp. (°F)	65	73	80	89	93	104	101	99	95	90	78	70	104
Extreme Minimum Temp. (°F)	-22	-19	-5	4	28	39	46	43	32	18	11	-19	-22
Days Maximum Temp. ≥ 90°F	0	0	0	0	1	4	7	4	1	0	0	0	17
Days Maximum Temp. ≤ 32°F	15	12	4	0	0	0	0	0	0	0	1	11	43
Days Minimum Temp. ≤ 32°F	28	25	23	8	0	0	0	0	0	4	16	26	130
Days Minimum Temp. ≤ 0°F	4	3	0	0	0	0	0	0	0	0	0	2	9
Heating Degree Days (base 65°F)	1,243	1,060	877	491	208	35	3	10	99	402	716	1,100	6,244
Cooling Degree Days (base 65°F)	0	0	1	9	46	178	269	223	88	11	0	0	825
Mean Precipitation (in.)	2.01	2.09	2.47	3.36	3.87	3.59	4.10	3.17	3.30	2.98	2.97	2.73	36.64
Extreme Maximum Daily Precip. (in.)	1.93	2.19	1.90	1.87	1.95	2.65	3.37	3.02	2.58	3.89	3.13	2.14	3.89
Days With ≥ 0.1" Precipitation	5	5	6	7	8	7	7	6	6	6	7	7	77
Days With ≥ 0.5" Precipitation	1	1	2	2	3	2	3	2	2	2	2	2	24
Days With ≥ 1.0" Precipitation	0	0	0	1	1	1	1	1	1	1	1	0	8
Mean Snowfall (in.)	6.7	5.6	2.4	0.5	trace	0.0	0.0	0.0	0.0	0.1	0.9	4.5	20.7
Maximum Snow Depth (in.)	12	17	8	4	trace	0	0	0	0	trace	4	10	17
Days With ≥ 1.0" Snow Depth	14	11	4	0	0	0	0	0	0	0	1	8	38

Dorset *Ashtabula County* Elevation: 979 ft. Latitude: 41° 41' N Longitude: 80° 40' W

	JAN	FEB	MAR	APR	MAY	JUN	JUL	AUG	SEP	OCT	NOV	DEC	YEAR
Mean Maximum Temp. (°F)	32.6	35.5	44.6	57.9	68.5	77.3	81.3	79.9	73.5	61.4	49.2	37.0	58.2
Mean Temp. (°F)	24.5	26.2	34.7	46.5	56.5	65.5	69.5	68.2	61.7	50.6	40.9	29.7	47.9
Mean Minimum Temp. (°F)	16.2	16.9	24.7	35.1	44.4	53.6	57.7	56.6	49.9	39.8	32.5	22.3	37.5
Extreme Maximum Temp. (°F)	68	74	83	88	90	99	100	98	95	86	83	74	100
Extreme Minimum Temp. (°F)	-28	-21	-20	-4	22	30	39	30	26	17	4	-22	-28
Days Maximum Temp. ≥ 90°F	0	0	0	0	0	1	3	2	1	0	0	0	7
Days Maximum Temp. ≤ 32°F	16	12	6	0	0	0	0	0	0	0	1	10	45
Days Minimum Temp. ≤ 32°F	28	26	24	13	3	0	0	0	1	6	16	26	143
Days Minimum Temp. ≤ 0°F	4	3	1	0	0	0	0	0	0	0	0	1	9
Heating Degree Days (base 65°F)	1,250	1,091	933	552	284	83	25	34	149	443	716	1,088	6,648
Cooling Degree Days (base 65°F)	0	0	0	5	26	104	172	141	57	5	0	0	510
Mean Precipitation (in.)	2.63	2.15	2.88	3.59	3.94	4.51	4.80	3.82	4.40	3.96	3.72	3.18	43.58
Extreme Maximum Daily Precip. (in.)	1.65	1.85	2.04	1.63	2.50	3.22	3.60	2.80	2.98	2.23	4.29	2.00	4.29
Days With ≥ 0.1" Precipitation	7	6	7	9	8	8	8	7	8	9	9	8	94
Days With ≥ 0.5" Precipitation	1	1	2	2	3	4	3	3	3	3	2	2	29
Days With ≥ 1.0" Precipitation	0	0	0	1	1	1	1	1	1	1	0	0	7
Mean Snowfall (in.)	21.2	13.5	11.6	3.5	trace	0.0	0.0	0.0	0.0	0.5	8.3	20.4	79.0
Maximum Snow Depth (in.)	20	18	20	16	trace	0	0	0	0	4	15	18	20
Days With ≥ 1.0" Snow Depth	21	17	10	2	0	0	0	0	0	0	4	15	69

Elyria 3 E *Lorain County* Elevation: 729 ft. Latitude: 41° 23' N Longitude: 82° 03' W

	JAN	FEB	MAR	APR	MAY	JUN	JUL	AUG	SEP	OCT	NOV	DEC	YEAR
Mean Maximum Temp. (°F)	35.4	38.9	48.3	61.5	71.9	80.9	84.6	82.7	76.1	64.3	52.0	39.3	61.3
Mean Temp. (°F)	28.1	30.6	38.7	50.3	60.5	69.7	73.9	72.3	65.5	54.3	43.8	32.4	51.7
Mean Minimum Temp. (°F)	20.7	22.2	29.1	39.2	49.0	58.6	63.1	61.9	54.9	44.3	35.6	25.5	42.0
Extreme Maximum Temp. (°F)	68	76	84	89	93	104	102	100	94	90	80	76	104
Extreme Minimum Temp. (°F)	-22	-14	-10	11	28	38	44	40	32	18	14	-14	-22
Days Maximum Temp. ≥ 90°F	0	0	0	0	1	4	7	5	1	0	0	0	18
Days Maximum Temp. ≤ 32°F	12	8	3	0	0	0	0	0	0	0	0	8	31
Days Minimum Temp. ≤ 32°F	26	24	21	8	1	0	0	0	0	2	12	24	118
Days Minimum Temp. ≤ 0°F	2	1	0	0	0	0	0	0	0	0	0	1	4
Heating Degree Days (base 65°F)	1,137	967	809	445	186	31	2	7	77	338	629	1,003	5,631
Cooling Degree Days (base 65°F)	0	0	2	12	53	180	284	240	100	14	0	0	885
Mean Precipitation (in.)	2.56	2.25	2.82	3.40	3.72	3.75	3.79	3.82	3.69	3.10	3.27	3.20	39.37
Extreme Maximum Daily Precip. (in.)	1.66	1.92	1.79	2.06	2.45	3.28	2.80	3.25	5.75	3.10	1.80	2.30	5.75
Days With ≥ 0.1" Precipitation	7	7	7	8	9	7	7	7	7	7	8	8	89
Days With ≥ 0.5" Precipitation	1	1	2	2	2	2	3	3	3	2	2	2	25
Days With ≥ 1.0" Precipitation	0	0	0	0	1	1	1	1	1	1	1	0	7
Mean Snowfall (in.)	11.6	9.0	7.2	2.2	trace	trace	0.0	0.0	0.0	trace	2.4	8.6	41.0
Maximum Snow Depth (in.)	13	15	14	6	trace	trace	0	0	0	trace	3	13	15
Days With ≥ 1.0" Snow Depth	15	12	5	1	0	0	0	0	0	0	1	9	43

Fairfield *Butler County* Elevation: 575 ft. Latitude: 39° 21' N Longitude: 84° 35' W

	JAN	FEB	MAR	APR	MAY	JUN	JUL	AUG	SEP	OCT	NOV	DEC	YEAR
Mean Maximum Temp. (°F)	39.7	43.3	53.6	65.8	75.4	84.2	87.8	87.3	80.4	67.7	54.6	42.4	65.2
Mean Temp. (°F)	31.1	33.8	42.5	53.4	63.4	72.6	76.4	75.3	67.8	55.2	44.3	34.0	54.1
Mean Minimum Temp. (°F)	22.4	24.2	31.4	40.9	51.4	60.9	65.0	63.3	55.2	42.7	34.0	25.5	43.1
Extreme Maximum Temp. (°F)	69	76	85	90	93	103	103	104	101	93	82	74	104
Extreme Minimum Temp. (°F)	-23	-10	4	19	30	40	48	41	33	22	11	-19	-23
Days Maximum Temp. ≥ 90°F	0	0	0	0	1	8	12	11	3	0	0	0	35
Days Maximum Temp. ≤ 32°F	8	5	1	0	0	0	0	0	0	0	0	6	20
Days Minimum Temp. ≤ 32°F	25	22	18	5	0	0	0	0	0	4	14	23	111
Days Minimum Temp. ≤ 0°F	1	1	0	0	0	0	0	0	0	0	0	1	3
Heating Degree Days (base 65°F)	1,045	875	693	356	123	14	0	2	51	317	615	955	5,046
Cooling Degree Days (base 65°F)	0	0	3	15	81	248	360	329	142	20	1	0	1,199
Mean Precipitation (in.)	3.24	2.85	3.84	4.49	5.02	4.06	4.19	3.18	3.09	3.22	2.96	3.66	43.80
Extreme Maximum Daily Precip. (in.)	2.55	2.36	3.82	3.66	4.67	2.60	4.15	3.55	3.98	3.55	2.30	2.73	4.67
Days With ≥ 0.1" Precipitation	6	6	7	9	9	7	7	5	5	5	6	7	79
Days With ≥ 0.5" Precipitation	2	2	3	3	3	3	3	2	2	2	2	3	30
Days With ≥ 1.0" Precipitation	1	0	1	1	1	1	1	1	1	1	1	1	11
Mean Snowfall (in.)	3.1	2.1	0.8	0.0	0.0	0.0	0.0	0.0	0.0	0.2	0.1	1.5	7.8
Maximum Snow Depth (in.)	na	na	na	na	na	na	na	na	na	na	na	na	na
Days With ≥ 1.0" Snow Depth	na	na	0	0	0	0	0	0	0	0	0	na	na

The period of record for all cooperative weather station data is 1980 – 2009. See User Guide for detailed explanation of data.

Findlay Wpcc *Hancock County* Elevation: 768 ft. Latitude: 41° 03' N Longitude: 83° 40' W

	JAN	FEB	MAR	APR	MAY	JUN	JUL	AUG	SEP	OCT	NOV	DEC	YEAR
Mean Maximum Temp. (°F)	33.1	36.5	47.2	60.3	71.3	80.3	83.8	81.9	75.6	62.9	49.7	36.9	60.0
Mean Temp. (°F)	26.3	29.2	38.3	50.1	60.9	70.3	74.0	72.3	65.2	53.2	41.9	30.4	51.0
Mean Minimum Temp. (°F)	19.4	21.7	29.3	39.8	50.4	60.2	64.2	62.7	54.9	43.5	34.1	24.0	42.0
Extreme Maximum Temp. (°F)	66	73	81	86	93	104	101	99	95	90	78	70	104
Extreme Minimum Temp. (°F)	-20	-11	-11	8	29	40	47	42	33	21	9	-18	-20
Days Maximum Temp. ≥ 90°F	0	0	0	0	1	4	5	3	1	0	0	0	14
Days Maximum Temp. ≤ 32°F	15	11	4	0	0	0	0	0	0	0	1	11	42
Days Minimum Temp. ≤ 32°F	27	24	20	6	0	0	0	0	0	3	14	25	119
Days Minimum Temp. ≤ 0°F	2	1	0	0	0	0	0	0	0	0	0	1	4
Heating Degree Days (base 65°F)	1,193	1,007	823	451	178	28	2	7	86	371	685	1,064	5,895
Cooling Degree Days (base 65°F)	0	0	1	10	57	192	288	241	100	13	0	0	902
Mean Precipitation (in.)	2.32	2.08	2.63	3.43	4.06	4.17	3.99	3.77	2.72	2.65	2.85	2.77	37.44
Extreme Maximum Daily Precip. (in.)	2.30	2.04	2.70	1.94	3.80	4.47	2.76	5.62	2.95	2.40	1.54	1.33	5.62
Days With ≥ 0.1" Precipitation	6	5	7	8	8	8	7	6	5	6	6	7	79
Days With ≥ 0.5" Precipitation	1	1	2	2	2	3	3	2	2	2	2	2	24
Days With ≥ 1.0" Precipitation	0	0	0	1	1	1	1	1	1	0	1	0	7
Mean Snowfall (in.)	8.4	5.5	4.4	1.1	0.1	0.0	0.0	0.0	0.0	0.2	1.3	5.9	26.9
Maximum Snow Depth (in.)	14	14	12	4	trace	0	0	0	0	trace	7	12	14
Days With ≥ 1.0" Snow Depth	14	10	3	0	0	0	0	0	0	0	1	8	36

Franklin *Warren County* Elevation: 669 ft. Latitude: 39° 33' N Longitude: 84° 19' W

	JAN	FEB	MAR	APR	MAY	JUN	JUL	AUG	SEP	OCT	NOV	DEC	YEAR
Mean Maximum Temp. (°F)	37.4	41.4	51.5	63.4	73.3	81.8	85.4	84.7	78.1	65.6	53.3	41.0	63.1
Mean Temp. (°F)	28.8	31.9	40.8	51.5	61.5	70.4	74.1	72.9	65.4	53.0	43.3	32.6	52.2
Mean Minimum Temp. (°F)	20.2	22.4	30.0	39.5	49.7	58.9	62.8	61.1	52.6	40.4	33.1	24.2	41.2
Extreme Maximum Temp. (°F)	68	75	86	88	96	100	104	100	96	87	79	74	104
Extreme Minimum Temp. (°F)	-24	-12	-7	18	30	38	42	39	32	19	10	-21	-24
Days Maximum Temp. ≥ 90°F	0	0	0	0	0	4	7	6	2	0	0	0	19
Days Maximum Temp. ≤ 32°F	10	7	2	0	0	0	0	0	0	0	1	7	27
Days Minimum Temp. ≤ 32°F	26	23	19	7	0	0	0	0	0	6	15	24	120
Days Minimum Temp. ≤ 0°F	2	1	0	0	0	0	0	0	0	0	0	1	4
Heating Degree Days (base 65°F)	1,114	927	744	408	158	25	2	6	83	375	646	996	5,484
Cooling Degree Days (base 65°F)	0	0	2	9	57	193	291	258	101	10	0	0	921
Mean Precipitation (in.)	2.49	2.37	3.25	3.70	4.74	3.77	4.06	2.89	2.51	3.05	3.21	3.07	39.11
Extreme Maximum Daily Precip. (in.)	2.49	2.27	3.00	2.79	3.61	2.89	3.66	3.10	3.76	2.83	2.08	2.68	3.76
Days With ≥ 0.1" Precipitation	5	5	7	8	9	7	7	4	4	5	6	6	73
Days With ≥ 0.5" Precipitation	1	1	2	2	3	2	3	2	2	2	2	2	24
Days With ≥ 1.0" Precipitation	0	0	1	1	1	1	1	1	1	1	1	1	10
Mean Snowfall (in.)	***0.9***	***1.4***	***0.4***	trace	0.0	0.0	0.0	0.0	0.0	0.0	0.2	na	na
Maximum Snow Depth (in.)	***4***	na	***6***	3	0	0	0	***0***	0	***0***	***5***	na	na
Days With ≥ 1.0" Snow Depth	***3***	***3***	1	0	0	0	0	0	0	0	0	***1***	***8***

Fredericktown 4 S *Knox County* Elevation: 1,049 ft. Latitude: 40° 25' N Longitude: 82° 32' W

	JAN	FEB	MAR	APR	MAY	JUN	JUL	AUG	SEP	OCT	NOV	DEC	YEAR
Mean Maximum Temp. (°F)	33.2	37.2	46.9	60.1	70.0	78.9	82.3	80.9	74.8	62.7	50.5	38.5	59.7
Mean Temp. (°F)	24.2	27.6	36.3	47.9	57.9	67.0	70.6	68.6	61.7	50.1	40.4	30.3	48.5
Mean Minimum Temp. (°F)	15.2	18.0	25.7	35.7	45.7	55.2	58.8	56.2	48.7	37.4	30.2	22.0	37.4
Extreme Maximum Temp. (°F)	67	72	82	88	91	100	98	98	94	***86***	78	75	***100***
Extreme Minimum Temp. (°F)	-30	-26	-21	12	24	36	38	32	29	***17***	4	-20	***-30***
Days Maximum Temp. ≥ 90°F	0	0	0	0	0	2	3	2	1	0	0	0	8
Days Maximum Temp. ≤ 32°F	15	10	4	0	0	0	0	0	0	0	1	9	39
Days Minimum Temp. ≤ 32°F	28	26	24	12	2	0	0	0	1	10	19	25	147
Days Minimum Temp. ≤ 0°F	5	2	1	0	0	0	0	0	0	0	0	1	9
Heating Degree Days (base 65°F)	1,259	1,051	884	511	244	55	13	28	142	460	732	1,070	6,449
Cooling Degree Days (base 65°F)	0	0	0	5	30	122	192	145	50	4	0	0	548
Mean Precipitation (in.)	2.43	1.87	3.00	3.43	4.32	4.12	4.33	3.35	3.12	2.65	3.02	2.68	38.32
Extreme Maximum Daily Precip. (in.)	2.40	2.10	2.01	3.00	2.70	2.43	2.48	2.30	2.71	2.25	***1.60***	***1.80***	***3.00***
Days With ≥ 0.1" Precipitation	4	4	6	7	8	7	7	5	5	6	6	5	70
Days With ≥ 0.5" Precipitation	1	1	2	3	3	2	3	2	2	2	2	2	25
Days With ≥ 1.0" Precipitation	1	0	0	1	1	1	1	1	1	1	1	1	10
Mean Snowfall (in.)	8.7	5.5	3.5	0.6	trace	0.0	0.0	0.0	0.0	0.0	1.1	5.4	24.8
Maximum Snow Depth (in.)	na	na	na	***trace***	***0***	na	na	***0***	na	na	na	na	na
Days With ≥ 1.0" Snow Depth	na	na	0	0	0	0	0	0	0	0	0	***0***	na

Hannibal Lock & Dam *Monroe County* Elevation: 620 ft. Latitude: 39° 40' N Longitude: 80° 52' W

	JAN	FEB	MAR	APR	MAY	JUN	JUL	AUG	SEP	OCT	NOV	DEC	YEAR
Mean Maximum Temp. (°F)	38.5	42.0	51.1	63.6	72.3	80.5	83.7	83.1	76.6	65.3	53.9	42.1	62.7
Mean Temp. (°F)	29.9	32.5	40.1	51.0	60.2	68.8	73.1	72.6	65.6	54.0	43.8	33.8	52.1
Mean Minimum Temp. (°F)	21.2	22.9	29.0	38.5	48.0	57.0	62.3	61.9	54.6	42.7	33.6	25.6	41.4
Extreme Maximum Temp. (°F)	72	75	83	89	91	96	99	100	95	90	80	74	100
Extreme Minimum Temp. (°F)	-24	-10	-8	18	30	38	44	42	34	22	13	-14	-24
Days Maximum Temp. ≥ 90°F	0	0	0	0	0	2	4	4	1	0	0	0	11
Days Maximum Temp. ≤ 32°F	9	6	2	0	0	0	0	0	0	0	0	6	23
Days Minimum Temp. ≤ 32°F	26	23	21	8	1	0	0	0	0	3	15	23	120
Days Minimum Temp. ≤ 0°F	2	1	0	0	0	0	0	0	0	0	0	0	3
Heating Degree Days (base 65°F)	1,082	914	765	418	178	28	2	5	69	344	631	959	5,395
Cooling Degree Days (base 65°F)	0	0	0	6	37	149	258	246	94	10	0	0	800
Mean Precipitation (in.)	3.06	2.81	3.66	3.41	4.34	3.99	4.41	3.47	3.16	2.57	3.36	3.10	41.34
Extreme Maximum Daily Precip. (in.)	2.84	2.45	3.45	2.43	1.92	2.98	2.49	3.23	4.28	1.93	3.47	3.40	4.28
Days With ≥ 0.1" Precipitation	7	7	7	8	9	7	8	6	5	6	7	7	84
Days With ≥ 0.5" Precipitation	2	2	3	2	3	3	3	2	2	2	2	2	28
Days With ≥ 1.0" Precipitation	1	0	1	0	1	1	1	1	1	0	1	0	8
Mean Snowfall (in.)	na	na	1.9	trace	0.0	0.0	0.0	0.0	0.0	0.0	trace	0.5	na
Maximum Snow Depth (in.)	***15***	***23***	***4***	0	0	0	0	0	0	0	1	6	***23***
Days With ≥ 1.0" Snow Depth	***5***	2	0	0	0	0	0	0	0	0	0	3	***10***

The period of record for all cooperative weather station data is 1980 – 2009. See User Guide for detailed explanation of data.

Hiram *Portage County* Elevation: 1,229 ft. Latitude: 41° 18' N Longitude: 81° 09' W

	JAN	FEB	MAR	APR	MAY	JUN	JUL	AUG	SEP	OCT	NOV	DEC	YEAR
Mean Maximum Temp. (°F)	32.1	35.7	45.0	58.2	68.3	76.9	81.0	79.7	72.5	60.4	48.9	36.3	57.9
Mean Temp. (°F)	24.7	27.3	35.7	47.8	57.8	66.6	70.8	69.6	62.4	51.0	40.8	29.3	48.6
Mean Minimum Temp. (°F)	17.2	18.8	26.3	37.4	47.1	56.2	60.6	59.6	52.3	41.4	32.6	22.2	39.3
Extreme Maximum Temp. (°F)	69	72	81	87	90	100	99	95	91	85	77	73	100
Extreme Minimum Temp. (°F)	-25	-14	-6	12	27	37	41	38	32	22	4	-15	-25
Days Maximum Temp. ≥ 90°F	0	0	0	0	0	1	2	2	0	0	0	0	5
Days Maximum Temp. ≤ 32°F	16	12	5	0	0	0	0	0	0	0	1	12	46
Days Minimum Temp. ≤ 32°F	28	25	23	9	1	0	0	0	0	4	17	27	134
Days Minimum Temp. ≤ 0°F	3	2	0	0	0	0	0	0	0	0	0	1	6
Heating Degree Days (base 65°F)	1,243	1,060	902	515	248	63	11	19	127	434	720	1,100	6,442
Cooling Degree Days (base 65°F)	0	0	1	7	30	116	199	169	55	5	0	0	582
Mean Precipitation (in.)	3.03	2.42	3.32	3.77	4.06	4.00	4.05	3.72	3.82	3.44	3.59	3.45	42.67
Extreme Maximum Daily Precip. (in.)	1.71	1.64	2.93	1.76	2.19	3.22	4.05	3.42	3.30	2.13	2.41	1.98	4.05
Days With ≥ 0.1" Precipitation	8	7	8	9	9	9	7	6	7	8	8	9	95
Days With ≥ 0.5" Precipitation	2	1	2	2	3	2	3	2	3	2	2	2	26
Days With ≥ 1.0" Precipitation	0	0	0	1	1	1	1	1	1	1	0	0	7
Mean Snowfall (in.)	18.2	12.7	10.4	1.9	trace	0.0	0.0	0.0	0.0	0.4	5.3	14.3	63.2
Maximum Snow Depth (in.)	22	15	18	9	trace	0	0	0	0	2	16	16	22
Days With ≥ 1.0" Snow Depth	20	17	9	1	0	0	0	0	0	0	3	14	64

Lima WWTP *Allen County* Elevation: 850 ft. Latitude: 40° 43' N Longitude: 84° 08' W

	JAN	FEB	MAR	APR	MAY	JUN	JUL	AUG	SEP	OCT	NOV	DEC	YEAR
Mean Maximum Temp. (°F)	34.1	37.7	48.0	61.1	71.7	80.5	84.0	82.4	76.5	64.1	50.8	37.8	60.7
Mean Temp. (°F)	26.9	29.7	38.9	50.6	61.1	70.4	74.0	72.6	65.9	54.0	42.8	31.0	51.5
Mean Minimum Temp. (°F)	19.7	21.7	29.7	40.1	50.5	60.3	64.0	62.7	55.3	43.9	34.7	24.1	42.2
Extreme Maximum Temp. (°F)	66	72	81	89	93	97	100	99	95	90	77	70	100
Extreme Minimum Temp. (°F)	-21	-12	-3	8	30	39	46	42	31	19	9	-17	-21
Days Maximum Temp. ≥ 90°F	0	0	0	0	1	3	5	4	1	0	0	0	14
Days Maximum Temp. ≤ 32°F	14	10	3	0	0	0	0	0	0	0	1	10	38
Days Minimum Temp. ≤ 32°F	27	23	20	7	0	0	0	0	0	3	14	25	119
Days Minimum Temp. ≤ 0°F	3	1	0	0	0	0	0	0	0	0	0	1	5
Heating Degree Days (base 65°F)	1,174	989	804	437	174	26	2	7	75	349	657	1,047	5,741
Cooling Degree Days (base 65°F)	0	0	1	12	61	195	289	250	109	16	0	0	933
Mean Precipitation (in.)	2.44	2.18	2.71	3.44	4.16	3.87	4.34	3.50	3.15	2.72	3.26	2.78	38.55
Extreme Maximum Daily Precip. (in.)	2.08	1.98	1.95	2.15	2.50	4.38	2.97	5.08	2.78	3.03	2.10	2.96	5.08
Days With ≥ 0.1" Precipitation	6	5	6	8	9	7	8	6	6	6	7	6	80
Days With ≥ 0.5" Precipitation	1	2	1	2	3	3	3	2	2	2	2	2	25
Days With ≥ 1.0" Precipitation	0	0	0	1	1	1	1	1	1	0	0	0	6
Mean Snowfall (in.)	na	na	na	trace	0.0	0.0	0.0	0.0	0.0	0.0	***0.1***	na	na
Maximum Snow Depth (in.)	na	na	na	***1***	***0***	***0***	***0***	***0***	***0***	na	na	na	na
Days With ≥ 1.0" Snow Depth	na	na	na	0	0	0	0	0	0	0	***0***	na	na

Mansfield 5 W *Richland County* Elevation: 1,350 ft. Latitude: 40° 46' N Longitude: 82° 37' W

	JAN	FEB	MAR	APR	MAY	JUN	JUL	AUG	SEP	OCT	NOV	DEC	YEAR
Mean Maximum Temp. (°F)	32.5	36.2	46.1	59.3	69.7	78.3	81.6	80.2	73.6	61.0	48.8	36.6	58.7
Mean Temp. (°F)	24.5	27.7	36.4	48.4	58.5	67.2	70.9	69.5	62.7	50.8	40.4	29.2	48.8
Mean Minimum Temp. (°F)	16.5	19.2	26.6	37.3	47.2	56.0	60.1	58.8	51.8	40.5	32.0	21.7	39.0
Extreme Maximum Temp. (°F)	66	72	81	87	91	100	99	97	94	84	76	69	100
Extreme Minimum Temp. (°F)	-25	-15	-8	5	24	33	40	37	28	18	9	-19	-25
Days Maximum Temp. ≥ 90°F	0	0	0	0	0	2	2	2	0	0	0	0	6
Days Maximum Temp. ≤ 32°F	16	12	5	0	0	0	0	0	0	0	2	12	47
Days Minimum Temp. ≤ 32°F	28	25	22	11	1	0	0	0	0	7	16	26	136
Days Minimum Temp. ≤ 0°F	4	2	0	0	0	0	0	0	0	0	0	1	7
Heating Degree Days (base 65°F)	1,249	1,047	882	500	231	57	11	20	127	442	731	1,104	6,401
Cooling Degree Days (base 65°F)	0	0	1	8	36	128	200	169	66	7	0	0	615
Mean Precipitation (in.)	2.23	1.81	2.77	3.64	4.55	4.40	4.02	3.80	3.23	2.83	3.08	2.88	39.24
Extreme Maximum Daily Precip. (in.)	2.47	1.87	***2.04***	***1.80***	2.13	4.08	2.55	5.19	2.22	2.02	1.91	2.00	***5.19***
Days With ≥ 0.1" Precipitation	5	5	6	8	10	7	7	7	6	6	7	6	80
Days With ≥ 0.5" Precipitation	1	1	2	2	3	3	3	2	2	2	2	2	25
Days With ≥ 1.0" Precipitation	0	0	0	1	1	1	1	1	1	1	1	0	8
Mean Snowfall (in.)	na	na	na	0.4	0.0	0.0	0.0	0.0	0.0	trace	***0.4***	na	na
Maximum Snow Depth (in.)	na	na	na	***4***	***0***	***0***	***0***	***0***	***0***	na	na	na	na
Days With ≥ 1.0" Snow Depth	na	na	***1***	0	0	0	0	0	0	0	***0***	na	na

Marietta Wwtp *Washington County* Elevation: 580 ft. Latitude: 39° 25' N Longitude: 81° 26' W

	JAN	FEB	MAR	APR	MAY	JUN	JUL	AUG	SEP	OCT	NOV	DEC	YEAR
Mean Maximum Temp. (°F)	39.9	43.7	53.3	65.5	74.0	82.0	85.4	84.7	78.1	66.5	54.9	43.4	64.3
Mean Temp. (°F)	31.4	34.1	42.4	53.3	62.2	70.8	74.7	73.7	66.6	54.8	44.7	35.0	53.6
Mean Minimum Temp. (°F)	22.8	24.6	31.3	41.0	50.3	59.6	64.0	62.6	55.0	43.1	34.4	26.5	42.9
Extreme Maximum Temp. (°F)	74	77	85	91	93	99	102	100	97	91	81	78	102
Extreme Minimum Temp. (°F)	-23	-7	0	19	31	40	44	38	33	23	12	-11	-23
Days Maximum Temp. ≥ 90°F	0	0	0	0	1	4	7	6	1	0	0	0	19
Days Maximum Temp. ≤ 32°F	8	5	1	0	0	0	0	0	0	0	0	6	20
Days Minimum Temp. ≤ 32°F	25	22	18	5	0	0	0	0	0	4	14	22	110
Days Minimum Temp. ≤ 0°F	1	1	0	0	0	0	0	0	0	0	0	0	2
Heating Degree Days (base 65°F)	1,036	866	697	357	141	17	1	3	61	322	603	924	5,028
Cooling Degree Days (base 65°F)	0	0	1	12	59	199	309	278	114	14	1	0	987
Mean Precipitation (in.)	3.12	2.76	3.83	3.41	4.26	4.57	4.54	3.70	3.24	2.91	3.21	3.26	42.81
Extreme Maximum Daily Precip. (in.)	1.60	2.83	3.15	2.12	2.60	4.00	2.70	4.78	4.27	1.93	2.01	2.25	4.78
Days With ≥ 0.1" Precipitation	7	6	8	8	9	8	8	7	6	6	7	7	87
Days With ≥ 0.5" Precipitation	2	2	3	2	3	3	3	3	2	2	2	2	29
Days With ≥ 1.0" Precipitation	0	0	1	1	1	1	1	1	1	1	0	0	8
Mean Snowfall (in.)	7.0	4.6	3.0	0.6	0.0	0.0	0.0	0.0	0.0	trace	0.6	3.0	18.8
Maximum Snow Depth (in.)	19	16	20	10	0	0	0	0	0	trace	2	5	20
Days With ≥ 1.0" Snow Depth	7	4	1	0	0	0	0	0	0	0	0	3	15

The period of record for all cooperative weather station data is 1980 – 2009. See User Guide for detailed explanation of data.

Marion 2 N *Marion County* Elevation: 964 ft. Latitude: 40° 37' N Longitude: 83° 08' W

	JAN	FEB	MAR	APR	MAY	JUN	JUL	AUG	SEP	OCT	NOV	DEC	YEAR
Mean Maximum Temp. (°F)	33.2	37.0	46.9	60.4	70.5	80.0	83.4	82.0	75.6	63.3	50.4	37.5	60.0
Mean Temp. (°F)	25.5	28.5	37.3	49.2	59.6	69.3	72.9	71.1	64.0	52.2	41.5	30.1	50.1
Mean Minimum Temp. (°F)	17.7	20.0	27.6	38.0	48.6	58.6	62.3	60.2	52.3	41.1	32.6	22.7	40.1
Extreme Maximum Temp. (°F)	67	73	81	87	91	103	100	99	97	89	79	73	103
Extreme Minimum Temp. (°F)	-23	-20	-5	8	29	39	43	35	24	17	11	-19	-23
Days Maximum Temp. ≥ 90°F	0	0	0	0	0	3	5	4	1	0	0	0	13
Days Maximum Temp. ≤ 32°F	15	10	4	0	0	0	0	0	0	0	1	10	40
Days Minimum Temp. ≤ 32°F	28	25	22	9	0	0	0	0	0	5	16	25	130
Days Minimum Temp. ≤ 0°F	3	2	0	0	0	0	0	0	0	0	0	1	6
Heating Degree Days (base 65°F)	1,219	1,024	853	475	211	37	5	15	106	402	698	1,075	6,120
Cooling Degree Days (base 65°F)	0	0	2	8	49	174	256	212	82	12	0	0	795
Mean Precipitation (in.)	2.45	1.85	2.32	3.56	4.45	4.35	4.31	3.78	3.21	2.90	3.01	2.84	39.03
Extreme Maximum Daily Precip. (in.)	2.00	1.35	1.37	1.80	2.68	3.82	5.33	3.11	2.91	2.25	1.57	1.84	5.33
Days With ≥ 0.1" Precipitation	5	5	6	9	9	7	7	6	6	6	7	6	79
Days With ≥ 0.5" Precipitation	1	1	1	2	3	3	3	3	2	2	2	2	25
Days With ≥ 1.0" Precipitation	1	0	0	1	1	1	1	1	1	1	1	0	9
Mean Snowfall (in.)	7.6	5.2	3.5	0.6	0.0	0.0	0.0	0.0	0.0	trace	0.8	5.3	23.0
Maximum Snow Depth (in.)	15	15	13	2	0	0	0	0	0	trace	3	15	15
Days With ≥ 1.0" Snow Depth	11	9	2	0	0	0	0	0	0	0	0	5	27

Marysville *Union County* Elevation: 1,000 ft. Latitude: 40° 14' N Longitude: 83° 22' W

	JAN	FEB	MAR	APR	MAY	JUN	JUL	AUG	SEP	OCT	NOV	DEC	YEAR
Mean Maximum Temp. (°F)	34.5	38.6	49.2	62.0	72.3	80.8	84.3	82.9	76.3	63.9	50.8	38.3	61.2
Mean Temp. (°F)	27.2	30.4	39.5	51.2	61.4	70.2	74.0	72.4	65.2	53.4	42.4	31.2	51.5
Mean Minimum Temp. (°F)	19.8	22.3	29.8	40.2	50.4	59.5	63.6	61.9	54.0	42.8	34.0	24.1	41.9
Extreme Maximum Temp. (°F)	66	73	82	88	92	101	100	99	96	91	79	74	101
Extreme Minimum Temp. (°F)	-23	-18	-11	12	29	38	44	41	32	18	12	-20	-23
Days Maximum Temp. ≥ 90°F	0	0	0	0	0	3	6	4	1	0	0	0	14
Days Maximum Temp. ≤ 32°F	13	9	3	0	0	0	0	0	0	0	1	9	35
Days Minimum Temp. ≤ 32°F	26	24	20	6	0	0	0	0	0	3	14	24	117
Days Minimum Temp. ≤ 0°F	2	1	0	0	0	0	0	0	0	0	0	1	4
Heating Degree Days (base 65°F)	1,165	971	785	419	165	25	2	7	85	364	671	1,040	5,699
Cooling Degree Days (base 65°F)	0	0	1	11	59	187	287	244	97	11	0	0	897
Mean Precipitation (in.)	2.35	2.00	2.73	3.30	4.43	4.28	4.26	3.25	2.91	2.61	2.99	2.77	37.88
Extreme Maximum Daily Precip. (in.)	2.60	1.18	1.50	2.75	2.37	4.82	3.50	3.28	2.56	2.48	1.66	1.88	4.82
Days With ≥ 0.1" Precipitation	6	5	6	8	9	7	7	6	5	6	6	6	77
Days With ≥ 0.5" Precipitation	1	1	2	2	3	3	3	2	2	2	2	2	25
Days With ≥ 1.0" Precipitation	0	0	0	0	1	1	1	1	1	1	1	0	7
Mean Snowfall (in.)	6.2	4.6	3.8	0.4	0.0	0.0	0.0	0.0	0.0	0.1	0.9	4.5	20.5
Maximum Snow Depth (in.)	16	12	15	4	0	0	0	0	0	3	5	17	17
Days With ≥ 1.0" Snow Depth	12	8	4	0	0	0	0	0	0	0	1	6	31

Milford *Clermont County* Elevation: 520 ft. Latitude: 39° 11' N Longitude: 84° 17' W

	JAN	FEB	MAR	APR	MAY	JUN	JUL	AUG	SEP	OCT	NOV	DEC	YEAR
Mean Maximum Temp. (°F)	38.4	43.1	52.9	64.8	75.1	82.8	87.2	85.9	78.9	67.7	54.8	42.5	64.5
Mean Temp. (°F)	29.3	33.1	41.5	52.2	62.7	71.0	75.4	73.9	66.1	54.5	43.9	33.6	53.1
Mean Minimum Temp. (°F)	20.1	23.1	30.0	39.7	50.1	59.1	63.5	61.9	53.2	41.1	32.7	24.7	41.6
Extreme Maximum Temp. (°F)	72	76	84	89	93	96	104	101	98	87	81	75	104
Extreme Minimum Temp. (°F)	-23	-13	-10	19	31	36	45	41	26	20	12	-22	-23
Days Maximum Temp. ≥ 90°F	0	0	0	0	1	5	11	9	2	0	0	0	28
Days Maximum Temp. ≤ 32°F	9	6	1	0	0	0	0	0	0	0	0	6	22
Days Minimum Temp. ≤ 32°F	26	23	19	7	0	0	0	0	0	5	16	23	119
Days Minimum Temp. ≤ 0°F	2	1	0	0	0	0	0	0	0	0	0	1	4
Heating Degree Days (base 65°F)	1,101	896	724	390	136	19	1	3	75	334	626	966	5,271
Cooling Degree Days (base 65°F)	0	0	2	12	70	206	329	286	115	14	0	0	1,034
Mean Precipitation (in.)	3.06	2.62	3.73	4.14	5.55	4.35	4.27	4.10	3.01	2.96	3.60	3.33	44.72
Extreme Maximum Daily Precip. (in.)	3.10	2.38	2.03	2.50	3.55	2.86	4.45	4.63	3.34	2.53	2.45	2.41	4.63
Days With ≥ 0.1" Precipitation	6	6	7	9	9	8	7	6	5	6	7	6	82
Days With ≥ 0.5" Precipitation	2	2	3	3	4	3	3	3	2	2	3	2	32
Days With ≥ 1.0" Precipitation	1	0	1	1	1	1	1	1	1	1	1	1	11
Mean Snowfall (in.)	na	4.5	1.3	0.3	trace	0.0	0.0	trace	0.0	0.2	0.1	2.6	na
Maximum Snow Depth (in.)	na	na	na	trace	trace	na	0	na	na	na	na	na	na
Days With ≥ 1.0" Snow Depth	na	5	1	0	0	0	0	0	0	0	0	3	na

Millersburg *Holmes County* Elevation: 818 ft. Latitude: 40° 33' N Longitude: 81° 55' W

	JAN	FEB	MAR	APR	MAY	JUN	JUL	AUG	SEP	OCT	NOV	DEC	YEAR
Mean Maximum Temp. (°F)	36.2	38.9	49.1	61.7	71.1	80.4	83.8	82.6	75.9	63.9	51.6	39.3	61.2
Mean Temp. (°F)	27.3	29.1	37.9	48.9	58.3	68.1	71.8	70.4	63.0	51.0	41.2	30.8	49.8
Mean Minimum Temp. (°F)	18.4	19.3	26.7	36.1	45.5	55.7	59.7	58.2	50.1	38.1	30.8	22.2	38.4
Extreme Maximum Temp. (°F)	70	75	82	87	90	95	97	98	95	88	80	76	98
Extreme Minimum Temp. (°F)	-35	-13	-7	14	20	36	43	35	29	19	10	-24	-35
Days Maximum Temp. ≥ 90°F	0	0	0	0	0	3	5	4	1	0	0	0	13
Days Maximum Temp. ≤ 32°F	12	9	3	0	0	0	0	0	0	0	1	8	33
Days Minimum Temp. ≤ 32°F	27	25	23	12	2	0	0	0	0	9	18	26	142
Days Minimum Temp. ≤ 0°F	3	2	0	0	0	0	0	0	0	0	0	1	6
Heating Degree Days (base 65°F)	1,162	1,007	833	480	229	43	6	14	116	434	707	1,055	6,086
Cooling Degree Days (base 65°F)	0	0	0	5	29	142	223	188	61	6	0	0	654
Mean Precipitation (in.)	2.85	1.83	2.89	3.48	4.57	4.81	4.33	3.52	3.14	2.87	2.83	2.67	39.79
Extreme Maximum Daily Precip. (in.)	2.95	1.58	1.63	1.83	1.78	3.42	3.28	3.85	2.86	2.54	1.87	2.38	3.85
Days With ≥ 0.1" Precipitation	6	5	6	7	9	8	8	6	6	6	6	6	79
Days With ≥ 0.5" Precipitation	2	1	2	2	3	3	3	2	2	2	2	2	26
Days With ≥ 1.0" Precipitation	0	0	0	1	1	1	1	1	1	1	0	0	7
Mean Snowfall (in.)	6.3	3.8	2.5	0.3	trace	0.0	0.0	0.0	0.0	trace	0.7	3.9	17.5
Maximum Snow Depth (in.)	11	10	13	6	trace	0	0	0	0	1	4	7	13
Days With ≥ 1.0" Snow Depth	10	8	2	0	0	0	0	0	0	0	1	5	26

The period of record for all cooperative weather station data is 1980 – 2009. See User Guide for detailed explanation of data.

Millport 2 NW *Columbiana County* Elevation: 1,149 ft. Latitude: 40° 43' N Longitude: 80° 54' W

	JAN	FEB	MAR	APR	MAY	JUN	JUL	AUG	SEP	OCT	NOV	DEC	YEAR
Mean Maximum Temp. (°F)	35.7	39.9	49.6	62.1	71.5	79.9	83.6	82.4	75.6	63.9	51.2	39.1	61.2
Mean Temp. (°F)	26.9	29.9	38.2	49.4	58.6	67.3	71.2	69.8	62.8	51.5	41.3	30.7	49.8
Mean Minimum Temp. (°F)	18.1	19.9	26.7	36.7	45.7	54.7	58.9	57.0	49.9	39.1	31.3	22.2	38.4
Extreme Maximum Temp. (°F)	69	77	82	90	91	98	103	99	94	87	79	74	103
Extreme Minimum Temp. (°F)	-34	-19	-17	10	20	33	38	27	26	14	3	-20	-34
Days Maximum Temp. ≥ 90°F	0	0	0	0	0	2	5	4	1	0	0	0	12
Days Maximum Temp. ≤ 32°F	12	8	3	0	0	0	0	0	0	0	1	9	33
Days Minimum Temp. ≤ 32°F	27	25	22	11	3	0	0	0	1	9	17	26	141
Days Minimum Temp. ≤ 0°F	3	2	1	0	0	0	0	0	0	0	0	1	7
Heating Degree Days (base 65°F)	1,175	985	825	467	221	49	8	19	122	419	704	1,057	6,051
Cooling Degree Days (base 65°F)	0	0	0	6	30	125	209	174	61	7	0	0	612
Mean Precipitation (in.)	2.53	2.15	2.83	3.25	3.97	3.78	4.01	3.29	3.28	2.60	3.13	2.81	37.63
Extreme Maximum Daily Precip. (in.)	1.93	1.70	1.61	1.85	3.71	3.70	2.74	3.20	4.80	3.30	2.86	1.93	4.80
Days With ≥ 0.1" Precipitation	7	6	7	8	8	7	7	6	6	6	8	8	84
Days With ≥ 0.5" Precipitation	1	1	2	2	3	3	3	2	2	1	2	2	24
Days With ≥ 1.0" Precipitation	0	0	0	1	1	1	1	1	1	0	0	0	6
Mean Snowfall (in.)	8.0	6.6	5.1	1.5	trace	0.0	0.0	0.0	0.0	trace	1.6	5.9	28.7
Maximum Snow Depth (in.)	***12***	***15***	***6***	10	trace	0	0	0	0	***1***	***5***	***7***	***15***
Days With ≥ 1.0" Snow Depth	***4***	***6***	***1***	0	0	0	0	0	0	0	***1***	***3***	***15***

Oberlin *Lorain County* Elevation: 815 ft. Latitude: 41° 16' N Longitude: 82° 13' W

	JAN	FEB	MAR	APR	MAY	JUN	JUL	AUG	SEP	OCT	NOV	DEC	YEAR
Mean Maximum Temp. (°F)	33.6	36.8	45.9	59.3	70.0	79.2	83.2	81.4	75.0	62.7	50.0	37.6	59.6
Mean Temp. (°F)	25.7	28.2	36.6	48.4	58.8	68.2	72.3	70.4	63.4	51.9	41.6	30.2	49.6
Mean Minimum Temp. (°F)	17.8	19.5	27.3	37.5	47.5	57.1	61.5	59.4	51.7	41.0	33.2	22.8	39.7
Extreme Maximum Temp. (°F)	67	76	82	87	91	104	100	100	94	89	77	75	104
Extreme Minimum Temp. (°F)	-23	-18	-15	11	27	35	41	32	25	16	7	-18	-23
Days Maximum Temp. ≥ 90°F	0	0	0	0	0	3	5	3	1	0	0	0	12
Days Maximum Temp. ≤ 32°F	15	11	5	0	0	0	0	0	0	0	1	10	42
Days Minimum Temp. ≤ 32°F	28	25	22	10	1	0	0	0	0	5	15	25	131
Days Minimum Temp. ≤ 0°F	3	2	0	0	0	0	0	0	0	0	0	1	6
Heating Degree Days (base 65°F)	1,210	1,034	874	500	228	52	8	16	116	408	695	1,071	6,212
Cooling Degree Days (base 65°F)	0	0	1	8	42	153	241	192	74	9	0	0	720
Mean Precipitation (in.)	2.54	2.14	2.74	3.38	3.89	3.69	3.86	3.36	3.31	2.87	3.13	2.84	37.75
Extreme Maximum Daily Precip. (in.)	2.35	2.35	2.06	1.75	2.35	2.72	2.83	2.92	2.64	2.88	1.80	2.00	2.92
Days With ≥ 0.1" Precipitation	6	6	7	8	9	8	7	6	6	7	7	7	84
Days With ≥ 0.5" Precipitation	1	1	2	2	2	2	3	2	2	2	2	2	23
Days With ≥ 1.0" Precipitation	0	0	0	0	1	1	1	1	1	0	1	0	6
Mean Snowfall (in.)	13.3	10.0	8.6	2.2	trace	0.0	0.0	0.0	0.0	trace	2.1	9.6	45.8
Maximum Snow Depth (in.)	17	17	16	7	trace	0	0	0	0	trace	5	15	17
Days With ≥ 1.0" Snow Depth	18	14	7	1	0	0	0	0	0	0	2	11	53

Painesville 4 NW *Lake County* Elevation: 600 ft. Latitude: 41° 45' N Longitude: 81° 18' W

	JAN	FEB	MAR	APR	MAY	JUN	JUL	AUG	SEP	OCT	NOV	DEC	YEAR
Mean Maximum Temp. (°F)	35.2	37.2	45.3	56.8	67.3	76.6	80.9	79.8	74.2	63.0	51.5	39.7	58.9
Mean Temp. (°F)	28.7	30.0	37.2	48.2	58.5	68.1	72.9	71.9	65.8	55.0	44.7	33.6	51.2
Mean Minimum Temp. (°F)	22.2	22.8	29.0	39.5	49.8	59.6	64.8	64.0	57.3	47.0	37.9	27.5	43.4
Extreme Maximum Temp. (°F)	70	76	82	91	92	98	96	93	94	88	77	75	98
Extreme Minimum Temp. (°F)	-19	-4	0	17	30	40	47	39	33	24	16	-11	-19
Days Maximum Temp. ≥ 90°F	0	0	0	0	0	1	2	1	0	0	0	0	4
Days Maximum Temp. ≤ 32°F	13	10	4	0	0	0	0	0	0	0	0	7	34
Days Minimum Temp. ≤ 32°F	26	24	20	6	0	0	0	0	0	1	8	21	106
Days Minimum Temp. ≤ 0°F	1	0	0	0	0	0	0	0	0	0	0	0	1
Heating Degree Days (base 65°F)	1,119	983	857	505	229	42	2	4	67	317	604	966	5,695
Cooling Degree Days (base 65°F)	0	0	1	7	36	143	253	226	97	14	0	0	777
Mean Precipitation (in.)	2.40	1.98	2.80	3.31	3.31	3.66	3.80	3.39	4.03	3.47	3.50	2.98	38.63
Extreme Maximum Daily Precip. (in.)	2.25	2.10	1.97	3.64	2.02	3.10	4.57	2.41	2.51	2.97	2.37	2.70	4.57
Days With ≥ 0.1" Precipitation	7	5	7	8	7	7	7	6	7	8	8	8	85
Days With ≥ 0.5" Precipitation	1	1	2	2	2	2	3	2	3	2	2	1	23
Days With ≥ 1.0" Precipitation	0	0	0	0	1	1	1	1	1	0	1	0	6
Mean Snowfall (in.)	11.5	8.1	6.5	1.2	trace	0.0	0.0	0.0	0.0	trace	2.2	9.7	39.2
Maximum Snow Depth (in.)	24	25	25	7	trace	0	0	0	0	trace	16	15	25
Days With ≥ 1.0" Snow Depth	17	11	5	0	0	0	0	0	0	0	1	9	43

Pandora *Putnam County* Elevation: 770 ft. Latitude: 40° 57' N Longitude: 83° 58' W

	JAN	FEB	MAR	APR	MAY	JUN	JUL	AUG	SEP	OCT	NOV	DEC	YEAR
Mean Maximum Temp. (°F)	32.9	36.6	47.5	60.5	71.5	80.4	83.9	82.0	75.7	62.7	49.7	36.7	60.0
Mean Temp. (°F)	25.7	28.8	38.0	49.7	60.5	69.7	73.2	71.3	64.2	52.5	41.6	29.9	50.4
Mean Minimum Temp. (°F)	18.4	20.9	28.5	38.7	49.5	59.0	62.5	60.5	52.8	42.2	33.4	23.1	40.8
Extreme Maximum Temp. (°F)	67	73	82	89	94	103	101	100	96	90	78	71	103
Extreme Minimum Temp. (°F)	-21	-13	-13	6	26	38	44	40	29	19	8	-19	-21
Days Maximum Temp. ≥ 90°F	0	0	0	0	1	4	6	3	1	0	0	0	15
Days Maximum Temp. ≤ 32°F	15	11	4	0	0	0	0	0	0	0	1	11	42
Days Minimum Temp. ≤ 32°F	28	24	21	8	0	0	0	0	0	4	15	26	126
Days Minimum Temp. ≤ 0°F	4	2	0	0	0	0	0	0	0	0	0	1	7
Heating Degree Days (base 65°F)	1,212	1,018	831	464	189	31	3	12	100	393	696	1,080	6,029
Cooling Degree Days (base 65°F)	0	0	1	10	56	180	265	212	85	12	0	0	821
Mean Precipitation (in.)	2.26	2.01	2.65	3.47	3.94	4.10	3.95	3.43	2.98	2.67	3.07	2.66	37.19
Extreme Maximum Daily Precip. (in.)	1.83	1.76	3.01	1.73	3.41	3.69	2.58	6.19	2.54	2.80	1.91	1.31	6.19
Days With ≥ 0.1" Precipitation	6	5	7	8	8	7	7	6	6	6	7	6	79
Days With ≥ 0.5" Precipitation	1	1	1	2	3	3	3	3	2	2	2	2	25
Days With ≥ 1.0" Precipitation	0	0	0	0	1	1	1	1	1	0	1	0	6
Mean Snowfall (in.)	9.4	6.9	4.4	1.2	trace	0.0	0.0	0.0	trace	0.1	1.9	6.6	30.5
Maximum Snow Depth (in.)	13	16	10	7	trace	0	0	0	trace	trace	5	11	16
Days With ≥ 1.0" Snow Depth	14	11	4	0	0	0	0	0	0	0	1	9	39

The period of record for all cooperative weather station data is 1980 – 2009. See User Guide for detailed explanation of data.

Portsmouth Sciotoville *Scioto County* Elevation: 540 ft. Latitude: 38° 45' N Longitude: 82° 53' W

	JAN	FEB	MAR	APR	MAY	JUN	JUL	AUG	SEP	OCT	NOV	DEC	YEAR
Mean Maximum Temp. (°F)	40.6	44.9	54.9	66.5	75.3	83.2	86.6	86.0	79.8	68.4	56.3	44.4	65.6
Mean Temp. (°F)	31.7	35.0	43.8	54.2	63.4	71.7	75.3	73.9	67.0	55.4	45.3	35.4	54.3
Mean Minimum Temp. (°F)	22.7	25.0	32.7	42.1	51.5	60.1	63.9	61.9	54.0	42.5	34.2	26.3	43.1
Extreme Maximum Temp. (°F)	74	76	84	99	93	101	104	104	100	92	82	75	104
Extreme Minimum Temp. (°F)	-29	-8	0	12	28	38	40	35	31	22	10	-18	-29
Days Maximum Temp. ≥ 90°F	0	0	0	0	1	5	10	8	3	0	0	0	27
Days Maximum Temp. ≤ 32°F	7	4	1	0	0	0	0	0	0	0	0	4	16
Days Minimum Temp. ≤ 32°F	25	22	16	5	0	0	0	0	0	4	14	22	108
Days Minimum Temp. ≤ 0°F	1	1	0	0	0	0	0	0	0	0	0	1	3
Heating Degree Days (base 65°F)	1,025	842	652	333	119	14	1	5	61	306	585	912	4,855
Cooling Degree Days (base 65°F)	0	0	2	16	77	221	328	288	126	17	1	0	1,076
Mean Precipitation (in.)	3.06	2.77	3.76	3.61	4.71	3.42	4.39	3.78	2.57	2.62	3.05	3.19	40.93
Extreme Maximum Daily Precip. (in.)	2.52	2.42	3.74	3.95	2.18	2.50	3.69	5.20	2.82	2.17	1.86	2.50	5.20
Days With ≥ 0.1" Precipitation	7	6	8	8	9	7	8	6	5	5	6	7	82
Days With ≥ 0.5" Precipitation	2	2	3	2	3	2	3	2	2	2	2	2	27
Days With ≥ 1.0" Precipitation	1	1	1	1	1	1	1	1	1	0	1	0	10
Mean Snowfall (in.)	3.4	2.1	1.2	0.2	trace	0.0	0.0	0.0	0.0	0.0	0.1	1.0	8.0
Maximum Snow Depth (in.)	21	7	8	5	trace	0	0	0	0	0	1	5	21
Days With ≥ 1.0" Snow Depth	4	2	1	0	0	0	0	0	0	0	0	1	8

Springfield New Water Works *Clark County* Elevation: 930 ft. Latitude: 39° 58' N Longitude: 83° 49' W

	JAN	FEB	MAR	APR	MAY	JUN	JUL	AUG	SEP	OCT	NOV	DEC	YEAR
Mean Maximum Temp. (°F)	35.3	38.9	48.8	61.4	71.6	80.4	83.5	82.8	76.6	64.2	51.5	39.2	61.2
Mean Temp. (°F)	27.0	29.8	38.7	49.9	60.2	69.5	72.8	71.4	64.3	52.5	42.0	31.3	50.8
Mean Minimum Temp. (°F)	18.6	20.5	28.5	38.4	48.7	58.6	62.0	59.9	51.9	40.7	32.4	23.2	40.3
Extreme Maximum Temp. (°F)	68	74	81	87	91	98	98	100	95	89	79	72	100
Extreme Minimum Temp. (°F)	-26	-18	-13	14	29	37	46	39	29	16	10	-26	-26
Days Maximum Temp. ≥ 90°F	0	0	0	0	0	3	4	4	1	0	0	0	12
Days Maximum Temp. ≤ 32°F	12	9	3	0	0	0	0	0	0	0	1	9	34
Days Minimum Temp. ≤ 32°F	27	24	21	8	1	0	0	0	0	6	16	25	128
Days Minimum Temp. ≤ 0°F	3	2	0	0	0	0	0	0	0	0	0	1	6
Heating Degree Days (base 65°F)	1,172	991	810	453	191	33	4	10	100	393	683	1,040	5,880
Cooling Degree Days (base 65°F)	0	0	1	8	49	175	253	215	86	11	0	0	798
Mean Precipitation (in.)	2.40	1.79	2.43	3.41	4.68	4.38	4.60	3.34	3.08	2.82	2.94	2.70	38.57
Extreme Maximum Daily Precip. (in.)	2.51	2.26	1.73	2.80	3.09	3.60	3.78	3.60	3.14	2.65	2.55	2.68	3.78
Days With ≥ 0.1" Precipitation	5	5	6	7	9	8	7	5	5	5	6	6	74
Days With ≥ 0.5" Precipitation	1	1	2	2	4	3	3	2	2	2	2	2	26
Days With ≥ 1.0" Precipitation	0	0	0	1	1	1	1	1	1	1	1	1	9
Mean Snowfall (in.)	na	***2.7***	na	trace	0.0	0.0	0.0	0.0	0.0	trace	trace	***1.4***	na
Maximum Snow Depth (in.)	na	na	na	***trace***	***0***	***0***	***0***	***0***	***0***	***trace***	***trace***	na	na
Days With ≥ 1.0" Snow Depth	na	na	***0***	0	0	0	0	0	0	0	0	na	na

Steubenville *Jefferson County* Elevation: 992 ft. Latitude: 40° 23' N Longitude: 80° 38' W

	JAN	FEB	MAR	APR	MAY	JUN	JUL	AUG	SEP	OCT	NOV	DEC	YEAR
Mean Maximum Temp. (°F)	37.5	41.1	50.3	62.9	71.8	79.9	83.0	82.3	75.6	63.6	52.4	40.7	61.8
Mean Temp. (°F)	29.7	32.3	40.2	51.6	60.7	69.4	73.3	72.4	65.5	53.5	43.7	33.1	52.1
Mean Minimum Temp. (°F)	21.8	23.5	30.2	40.2	49.7	58.9	63.5	62.5	55.4	43.3	34.9	25.4	42.4
Extreme Maximum Temp. (°F)	72	77	83	89	91	97	102	96	93	85	80	77	102
Extreme Minimum Temp. (°F)	-22	-8	-1	16	29	39	46	42	34	22	12	-14	-22
Days Maximum Temp. ≥ 90°F	0	0	0	0	0	2	4	3	1	0	0	0	10
Days Maximum Temp. ≤ 32°F	11	7	2	0	0	0	0	0	0	0	1	8	29
Days Minimum Temp. ≤ 32°F	25	22	19	6	1	0	0	0	0	2	13	24	112
Days Minimum Temp. ≤ 0°F	1	1	0	0	0	0	0	0	0	0	0	0	2
Heating Degree Days (base 65°F)	1,088	917	763	406	174	29	2	6	75	360	634	984	5,438
Cooling Degree Days (base 65°F)	0	0	2	11	49	167	267	244	97	9	1	0	847
Mean Precipitation (in.)	3.00	2.31	3.27	3.41	4.35	4.21	4.38	3.96	3.37	2.81	3.47	2.98	41.52
Extreme Maximum Daily Precip. (in.)	1.75	1.32	1.48	1.56	2.25	3.14	3.42	2.72	5.36	2.37	2.90	1.80	5.36
Days With ≥ 0.1" Precipitation	7	6	8	8	9	8	8	7	6	6	8	7	88
Days With ≥ 0.5" Precipitation	2	1	2	2	3	3	3	3	2	2	2	2	27
Days With ≥ 1.0" Precipitation	1	0	0	0	1	1	1	1	1	0	1	0	7
Mean Snowfall (in.)	na	na	***0.4***	trace	0.0	0.0	0.0	0.0	0.0	0.2	0.2	na	na
Maximum Snow Depth (in.)	na	na	na	na	na	na	na	na	na	na	na	na	na
Days With ≥ 1.0" Snow Depth	na	na	***0***	0	0	0	0	0	0	0	0	na	na

Upper Sandusky *Wyandot County* Elevation: 854 ft. Latitude: 40° 50' N Longitude: 83° 17' W

	JAN	FEB	MAR	APR	MAY	JUN	JUL	AUG	SEP	OCT	NOV	DEC	YEAR
Mean Maximum Temp. (°F)	33.0	37.0	47.1	60.6	70.8	80.2	84.0	82.6	76.6	63.7	50.4	37.1	60.3
Mean Temp. (°F)	25.5	28.7	37.6	49.4	59.6	69.4	73.2	71.6	64.8	52.6	41.6	30.0	50.3
Mean Minimum Temp. (°F)	18.0	20.4	28.0	38.1	48.4	58.6	62.4	60.5	52.8	41.4	32.7	22.8	40.4
Extreme Maximum Temp. (°F)	67	73	82	87	91	104	102	99	97	89	79	72	104
Extreme Minimum Temp. (°F)	-23	-16	-8	9	27	38	43	40	29	18	9	-20	-23
Days Maximum Temp. ≥ 90°F	0	0	0	0	0	4	5	4	1	0	0	0	14
Days Maximum Temp. ≤ 32°F	14	10	4	0	0	0	0	0	0	0	1	10	39
Days Minimum Temp. ≤ 32°F	26	25	21	9	1	0	0	0	0	5	16	25	128
Days Minimum Temp. ≤ 0°F	3	1	0	0	0	0	0	0	0	0	0	1	5
Heating Degree Days (base 65°F)	1,217	1,022	844	472	208	36	4	11	94	393	696	1,078	6,075
Cooling Degree Days (base 65°F)	0	0	1	9	47	176	266	224	94	13	0	0	830
Mean Precipitation (in.)	1.98	1.89	2.50	3.51	4.52	3.92	4.46	3.49	3.13	2.36	3.20	2.56	37.52
Extreme Maximum Daily Precip. (in.)	1.78	1.60	2.05	1.74	2.27	3.21	2.50	9.35	3.74	2.46	2.00	2.05	9.35
Days With ≥ 0.1" Precipitation	5	5	6	8	9	7	7	6	5	6	7	6	77
Days With ≥ 0.5" Precipitation	1	1	1	2	3	3	3	2	2	1	2	1	22
Days With ≥ 1.0" Precipitation	0	0	0	1	1	1	2	1	1	0	1	0	8
Mean Snowfall (in.)	6.4	3.8	2.2	1.1	trace	0.0	0.0	0.0	0.0	trace	0.8	5.1	19.4
Maximum Snow Depth (in.)	12	11	13	9	0	0	0	0	0	trace	4	***19***	***19***
Days With ≥ 1.0" Snow Depth	9	6	2	0	0	0	0	0	0	0	1	4	22

The period of record for all cooperative weather station data is 1980 – 2009. See User Guide for detailed explanation of data.

Urbana WWTP *Champaign County* Elevation: 1,000 ft. Latitude: 40° 06' N Longitude: 83° 47' W

	JAN	FEB	MAR	APR	MAY	JUN	JUL	AUG	SEP	OCT	NOV	DEC	YEAR
Mean Maximum Temp. (°F)	34.5	38.6	47.9	60.8	71.0	80.4	84.1	82.9	76.2	63.5	50.9	38.2	60.7
Mean Temp. (°F)	26.7	30.1	38.3	50.0	60.2	69.5	73.1	71.5	64.3	52.4	42.0	30.8	50.7
Mean Minimum Temp. (°F)	19.0	21.6	28.7	39.1	49.3	58.6	62.0	60.0	52.4	41.2	33.1	23.3	40.7
Extreme Maximum Temp. (°F)	66	71	80	86	91	99	100	101	96	87	76	72	101
Extreme Minimum Temp. (°F)	-26	-18	-6	14	29	36	42	39	28	18	11	-22	-26
Days Maximum Temp. ≥ 90°F	0	0	0	0	0	3	6	4	1	0	0	0	14
Days Maximum Temp. ≤ 32°F	13	9	3	0	0	0	0	0	0	0	1	9	35
Days Minimum Temp. ≤ 32°F	27	24	20	7	0	0	0	0	0	6	15	25	124
Days Minimum Temp. ≤ 0°F	3	1	0	0	0	0	0	0	0	0	0	1	5
Heating Degree Days (base 65°F)	1,179	980	820	452	190	34	4	10	98	394	682	1,054	5,897
Cooling Degree Days (base 65°F)	0	0	0	7	47	175	261	218	84	9	0	0	801
Mean Precipitation (in.)	2.64	2.06	2.81	3.76	4.78	4.50	5.49	3.42	3.08	2.94	3.19	3.04	41.71
Extreme Maximum Daily Precip. (in.)	2.61	1.60	1.82	2.70	2.47	3.50	3.97	3.72	3.60	3.05	1.80	2.30	3.97
Days With ≥ 0.1" Precipitation	6	6	7	8	9	8	7	6	5	6	7	6	81
Days With ≥ 0.5" Precipitation	1	1	2	3	3	3	4	2	2	2	2	2	27
Days With ≥ 1.0" Precipitation	1	0	0	1	1	1	2	1	1	1	1	1	11
Mean Snowfall (in.)	na	na	na	0.1	0.0	0.0	0.0	0.0	0.0	0.0	trace	na	na
Maximum Snow Depth (in.)	na	na	na	*trace*	*0*	*0*	*0*	na	*0*	na	na	na	na
Days With ≥ 1.0" Snow Depth	na	na	na	0	0	0	0	0	0	0	0	na	na

Warren 3 S *Trumbull County* Elevation: 899 ft. Latitude: 41° 12' N Longitude: 80° 49' W

	JAN	FEB	MAR	APR	MAY	JUN	JUL	AUG	SEP	OCT	NOV	DEC	YEAR
Mean Maximum Temp. (°F)	34.7	37.9	47.4	60.6	70.7	79.3	83.1	81.7	74.5	62.6	50.7	38.7	60.2
Mean Temp. (°F)	26.1	28.1	36.4	48.0	57.6	66.6	70.7	69.4	62.1	50.8	41.1	30.5	48.9
Mean Minimum Temp. (°F)	17.3	18.3	25.3	35.3	44.4	53.9	58.2	57.0	49.7	38.9	31.4	22.3	37.7
Extreme Maximum Temp. (°F)	69	75	82	90	91	99	101	99	93	87	79	76	101
Extreme Minimum Temp. (°F)	-26	-13	-11	10	23	32	40	30	28	16	7	-17	-26
Days Maximum Temp. ≥ 90°F	0	0	0	0	0	2	4	3	0	0	0	0	9
Days Maximum Temp. ≤ 32°F	13	10	4	0	0	0	0	0	0	0	1	9	37
Days Minimum Temp. ≤ 32°F	28	25	24	13	3	0	0	0	1	8	18	26	146
Days Minimum Temp. ≤ 0°F	4	2	0	0	0	0	0	0	0	0	0	1	7
Heating Degree Days (base 65°F)	1,200	1,037	881	509	250	61	12	22	136	438	711	1,062	6,319
Cooling Degree Days (base 65°F)	0	0	0	5	28	116	195	164	55	4	0	0	567
Mean Precipitation (in.)	2.60	1.82	3.06	3.51	3.97	3.96	4.80	3.46	3.79	2.92	3.10	2.79	39.78
Extreme Maximum Daily Precip. (in.)	1.81	1.40	1.84	1.80	1.80	2.26	4.41	2.96	3.87	1.74	2.60	1.56	4.41
Days With ≥ 0.1" Precipitation	7	6	8	9	9	8	7	7	7	7	7	7	89
Days With ≥ 0.5" Precipitation	1	1	2	2	3	3	3	2	2	2	2	1	24
Days With ≥ 1.0" Precipitation	0	0	0	1	1	1	1	1	1	0	0	0	6
Mean Snowfall (in.)	11.5	6.9	5.2	0.4	0.0	0.0	0.0	0.0	0.0	trace	0.8	7.0	31.8
Maximum Snow Depth (in.)	16	14	15	6	0	0	0	0	0	trace	3	13	16
Days With ≥ 1.0" Snow Depth	13	9	4	0	0	0	0	0	0	0	1	8	35

Westerville *Franklin County* Elevation: 810 ft. Latitude: 40° 08' N Longitude: 82° 57' W

	JAN	FEB	MAR	APR	MAY	JUN	JUL	AUG	SEP	OCT	NOV	DEC	YEAR
Mean Maximum Temp. (°F)	36.9	41.5	52.1	65.0	74.2	82.4	85.4	84.4	78.2	66.4	53.4	40.7	63.4
Mean Temp. (°F)	28.9	32.3	41.4	52.8	62.2	70.8	74.3	73.2	66.3	54.7	44.2	33.1	52.9
Mean Minimum Temp. (°F)	20.9	23.1	30.7	40.5	50.2	59.2	63.2	61.9	54.3	43.0	34.9	25.5	42.3
Extreme Maximum Temp. (°F)	68	74	82	88	92	100	101	101	97	89	79	76	101
Extreme Minimum Temp. (°F)	-27	-20	-5	14	28	36	41	36	31	18	12	-25	-27
Days Maximum Temp. ≥ 90°F	0	0	0	0	0	4	7	6	2	0	0	0	19
Days Maximum Temp. ≤ 32°F	11	7	2	0	0	0	0	0	0	0	1	7	28
Days Minimum Temp. ≤ 32°F	25	23	18	7	1	0	0	0	0	4	13	23	114
Days Minimum Temp. ≤ 0°F	2	1	0	0	0	0	0	0	0	0	0	1	4
Heating Degree Days (base 65°F)	1,114	918	726	371	146	21	1	5	70	327	619	982	5,300
Cooling Degree Days (base 65°F)	0	0	2	13	67	202	298	265	115	16	0	0	978
Mean Precipitation (in.)	2.66	2.22	2.94	3.49	4.35	4.46	4.27	3.21	2.81	2.78	3.13	2.94	39.26
Extreme Maximum Daily Precip. (in.)	1.95	1.96	1.55	3.84	1.78	3.32	3.19	2.79	2.17	3.06	1.64	1.77	3.84
Days With ≥ 0.1" Precipitation	6	6	7	8	9	8	7	6	5	6	7	7	82
Days With ≥ 0.5" Precipitation	2	1	2	2	3	3	3	2	2	2	2	2	26
Days With ≥ 1.0" Precipitation	1	0	0	0	1	1	1	1	1	0	1	1	8
Mean Snowfall (in.)	6.9	4.6	2.5	0.5	trace	0.0	0.0	0.0	0.0	trace	0.3	3.7	18.5
Maximum Snow Depth (in.)	12	13	11	3	trace	0	0	0	0	trace	1	7	13
Days With ≥ 1.0" Snow Depth	10	6	2	0	0	0	0	0	0	0	0	5	23

Wilmington 3 N *Clinton County* Elevation: 1,029 ft. Latitude: 39° 29' N Longitude: 83° 49' W

	JAN	FEB	MAR	APR	MAY	JUN	JUL	AUG	SEP	OCT	NOV	DEC	YEAR
Mean Maximum Temp. (°F)	35.8	39.5	49.5	61.9	71.6	80.2	83.7	82.8	76.9	65.0	52.3	39.4	61.6
Mean Temp. (°F)	27.9	30.8	39.6	50.8	60.8	69.7	73.1	71.5	64.7	53.4	43.0	31.8	51.4
Mean Minimum Temp. (°F)	19.9	22.1	29.5	39.7	50.0	59.2	62.5	60.1	52.5	41.8	33.5	24.1	41.2
Extreme Maximum Temp. (°F)	69	73	81	87	90	99	99	99	95	91	78	73	99
Extreme Minimum Temp. (°F)	-25	-20	-10	17	29	39	40	37	32	17	11	-24	-25
Days Maximum Temp. ≥ 90°F	0	0	0	0	0	2	4	4	1	0	0	0	11
Days Maximum Temp. ≤ 32°F	12	9	3	0	0	0	0	0	0	0	1	9	34
Days Minimum Temp. ≤ 32°F	27	23	20	6	0	0	0	0	0	5	15	24	120
Days Minimum Temp. ≤ 0°F	3	2	0	0	0	0	0	0	0	0	0	1	6
Heating Degree Days (base 65°F)	1,144	960	783	429	173	29	3	10	90	366	655	1,022	5,664
Cooling Degree Days (base 65°F)	0	0	1	10	50	177	261	218	90	14	1	0	822
Mean Precipitation (in.)	2.81	2.35	3.50	3.92	5.22	3.79	4.19	3.02	2.82	3.10	3.13	2.95	40.80
Extreme Maximum Daily Precip. (in.)	3.42	2.23	1.67	2.85	2.14	2.53	3.03	3.39	2.43	2.83	1.70	2.40	3.42
Days With ≥ 0.1" Precipitation	6	5	7	9	9	8	8	5	5	6	7	7	82
Days With ≥ 0.5" Precipitation	2	1	2	3	4	2	3	2	2	2	2	2	27
Days With ≥ 1.0" Precipitation	1	0	1	1	1	1	1	1	1	1	1	0	10
Mean Snowfall (in.)	6.9	5.8	3.3	0.4	trace	0.0	0.0	0.0	0.0	0.2	0.9	3.5	21.0
Maximum Snow Depth (in.)	16	14	18	5	trace	0	0	0	0	2	5	7	18
Days With ≥ 1.0" Snow Depth	10	8	3	0	0	0	0	0	0	0	0	5	26

The period of record for all cooperative weather station data is 1980 – 2009. See User Guide for detailed explanation of data.

Wooster Exp Stn *Wayne County* Elevation: 1,020 ft. Latitude: 40° 47' N Longitude: 81° 55' W

	JAN	FEB	MAR	APR	MAY	JUN	JUL	AUG	SEP	OCT	NOV	DEC	YEAR
Mean Maximum Temp. (°F)	33.4	36.8	46.7	59.6	69.5	78.2	81.8	80.3	73.3	61.3	49.5	37.4	59.0
Mean Temp. (°F)	26.2	28.8	37.5	49.0	58.7	67.5	71.3	69.8	62.4	51.0	41.2	30.5	49.5
Mean Minimum Temp. (°F)	19.0	20.7	28.2	38.3	47.8	56.8	60.8	59.2	51.6	40.7	32.8	23.5	39.9
Extreme Maximum Temp. (°F)	69	71	80	86	90	100	101	96	94	88	76	74	101
Extreme Minimum Temp. (°F)	-24	-13	-6	14	26	37	41	36	30	17	9	-17	-24
Days Maximum Temp. ≥ 90°F	0	0	0	0	0	1	2	2	0	0	0	0	5
Days Maximum Temp. ≤ 32°F	15	11	4	0	0	0	0	0	0	0	1	11	42
Days Minimum Temp. ≤ 32°F	27	24	21	9	1	0	0	0	0	6	16	26	130
Days Minimum Temp. ≤ 0°F	3	1	0	0	0	0	0	0	0	0	0	1	5
Heating Degree Days (base 65°F)	1,195	1,019	847	480	223	51	8	18	128	432	707	1,064	6,172
Cooling Degree Days (base 65°F)	0	0	1	6	34	133	210	172	57	6	0	0	619
Mean Precipitation (in.)	2.29	1.95	2.83	3.66	4.43	4.34	4.24	4.10	3.36	3.03	3.06	2.70	39.99
Extreme Maximum Daily Precip. (in.)	2.59	1.39	1.63	1.96	2.37	2.47	2.95	3.60	3.25	2.37	2.09	2.08	3.60
Days With ≥ 0.1" Precipitation	6	5	7	8	9	8	7	6	6	6	7	6	81
Days With ≥ 0.5" Precipitation	1	1	2	3	3	3	3	3	2	2	2	2	27
Days With ≥ 1.0" Precipitation	0	0	0	1	1	1	1	1	1	1	0	0	7
Mean Snowfall (in.)	8.4	6.4	5.6	1.1	trace	0.0	0.0	trace	0.0	0.1	1.5	6.2	29.3
Maximum Snow Depth (in.)	13	17	13	8	0	0	0	trace	0	2	4	8	17
Days With ≥ 1.0" Snow Depth	15	12	6	1	0	0	0	0	0	0	1	10	45

The period of record for all cooperative weather station data is 1980 – 2009. See User Guide for detailed explanation of data.

Ohio Weather Station Rankings

Annual Extreme Maximum Temperature

Highest			Lowest		
Rank	**Station Name**	**°F**	**Rank**	**Station Name**	**°F**
1	Chilo Meldahl L&D	107	1	Millersburg	***98***
2	Chillicothe Mound City	105	1	Painesville 4 NW	98
3	Bowling Green WWTP	104	3	Centerburg 2 SE	99
3	Cleveland Hopkins Intl Arpt	104	3	Wilmington 3 N	99
3	Dayton Mcd	104	5	Barnesville	***100***
3	Defiance	104	5	Chardon	100
3	Elyria 3 E	104	5	Columbus Valley Crossing	100
3	Fairfield	***104***	5	Dorset	100
3	Findlay Wpcc	104	5	Fredericktown 4 S	***100***
3	Franklin	104	5	Hannibal Lock & Dam	100
3	Milford	***104***	5	Hiram	100
3	Oberlin	104	5	Lima WWTP	100
3	Portsmouth Sciotoville	104	5	Mansfield 5 W	100
3	Toledo Express Arpt	104	5	Springfield New Water Works	100
3	Upper Sandusky	104	5	Youngstown Municipal Arpt	100
16	Cincinnati-Northern Kentucky	103	16	Akron Akron-Canton Reg Arpt	101
16	Marion 2 N	103	16	Bellefontaine	101
16	Millport 2 NW	103	16	Cadiz	101
16	Pandora	103	16	Carpenter 2 S	***101***
20	Bucyrus	102	16	Circleville	101
20	Cambridge	102	16	Columbus-Port Columbus Intl	101
20	Chippewa Lake	102	16	Mansfield Lahm Municipal Arpt	101
20	Danville 2 W	102	16	Marysville	101
20	Dayton Intl Arpt	102	16	Urbana WWTP	101
20	Marietta Wwtp	102	16	Warren 3 S	101

Annual Mean Maximum Temperature

Highest			Lowest		
Rank	**Station Name**	**°F**	**Rank**	**Station Name**	**°F**
1	Portsmouth Sciotoville	65.6	1	Chardon	57.5
2	Fairfield	***65.2***	2	Hiram	57.9
3	Chilo Meldahl L&D	64.8	3	Dorset	58.2
4	Milford	***64.5***	4	Mansfield 5 W	58.7
5	Marietta Wwtp	64.3	5	Mansfield Lahm Municipal Arpt	58.8
6	Chillicothe Mound City	***63.9***	5	Youngstown Municipal Arpt	58.8
7	Carpenter 2 S	***63.7***	7	Painesville 4 NW	59.0
7	Cincinnati-Northern Kentucky	63.7	7	Wooster Exp Stn	59.0
9	Cambridge	63.6	9	Akron Akron-Canton Reg Arpt	59.2
10	Dayton Mcd	63.5	9	Bucyrus	59.2
11	Westerville	63.4	9	Chippewa Lake	59.2
12	Circleville	63.1	9	Cleveland Hopkins Intl Arpt	59.2
12	Franklin	63.1	13	Oberlin	59.6
14	Columbus Valley Crossing	63.0	13	Toledo Express Arpt	59.6
15	Hannibal Lock & Dam	62.7	15	Bowling Green WWTP	59.7
16	Columbus-Port Columbus Intl	62.4	15	Defiance	59.7
17	Steubenville	61.8	15	Fredericktown 4 S	59.7
18	Wilmington 3 N	61.6	18	Centerburg 2 SE	59.8
19	Dayton Intl Arpt	61.4	19	Findlay Wpcc	60.0
20	Elyria 3 E	61.3	19	Marion 2 N	60.0
21	Marysville	61.2	19	Pandora	60.0
21	Millersburg	***61.2***	22	Bellefontaine	60.2
21	Millport 2 NW	61.2	22	Warren 3 S	60.2
21	Springfield New Water Works	61.2	24	Cadiz	60.3
25	Danville 2 W	60.9	24	Upper Sandusky	60.3

Rankings include 25 highest/lowest stations. If state has less than 25 stations, all stations are included. The period of record is 1980–2009. See User Guide for detailed explanation of data.

Annual Mean Temperature

Highest Rank	Station Name	°F	Lowest Rank	Station Name	°F
1	Portsmouth Sciotoville	54.4	1	Chardon	47.5
2	Chilo Meldahl L&D	54.2	2	Dorset	47.9
2	Fairfield	***54.2***	3	Fredericktown 4 S	48.5
4	Cincinnati-Northern Kentucky	54.0	4	Hiram	48.6
4	Dayton Mcd	54.0	5	Mansfield 5 W	48.8
6	Marietta Wwtp	53.6	6	Warren 3 S	48.9
7	Milford	***53.1***	7	Danville 2 W	49.2
8	Cambridge	53.0	7	Youngstown Municipal Arpt	49.2
9	Columbus-Port Columbus Intl	52.9	9	Chippewa Lake	49.3
9	Westerville	52.9	10	Bucyrus	49.4
11	Chillicothe Mound City	***52.8***	11	Wooster Exp Stn	49.5
11	Circleville	52.8	12	Oberlin	49.6
13	Columbus Valley Crossing	52.7	13	Mansfield Lahm Municipal Arpt	49.7
14	Carpenter 2 S	***52.5***	14	Bowling Green WWTP	49.8
15	Franklin	52.2	14	Defiance	49.8
16	Dayton Intl Arpt	52.1	14	Millersburg	***49.8***
16	Hannibal Lock & Dam	52.1	14	Millport 2 NW	49.8
16	Steubenville	52.1	18	Centerburg 2 SE	49.9
19	Elyria 3 E	51.7	18	Toledo Express Arpt	49.9
20	Lima WWTP	51.5	20	Akron Akron-Canton Reg Arpt	50.1
20	Marysville	51.5	20	Marion 2 N	50.1
22	Wilmington 3 N	51.4	22	Upper Sandusky	50.3
23	Painesville 4 NW	51.2	23	Pandora	50.4
24	Findlay Wpcc	51.0	24	Barnesville	***50.5***
25	Cadiz	50.8	24	Bellefontaine	50.5

Annual Mean Minimum Temperature

Highest Rank	Station Name	°F	Lowest Rank	Station Name	°F
1	Dayton Mcd	44.6	1	Fredericktown 4 S	37.4
2	Cincinnati-Northern Kentucky	44.3	2	Chardon	37.5
3	Chilo Meldahl L&D	43.6	2	Danville 2 W	37.5
4	Columbus-Port Columbus Intl	43.4	2	Dorset	37.5
4	Painesville 4 NW	43.4	5	Warren 3 S	37.7
6	Fairfield	***43.1***	6	Millersburg	***38.4***
6	Portsmouth Sciotoville	43.1	6	Millport 2 NW	38.4
8	Marietta Wwtp	42.9	8	Mansfield 5 W	39.0
9	Dayton Intl Arpt	42.7	9	Chippewa Lake	39.3
10	Circleville	42.4	9	Hiram	39.3
10	Columbus Valley Crossing	42.4	11	Bucyrus	39.6
10	Steubenville	42.4	11	Youngstown Municipal Arpt	39.6
13	Cambridge	42.3	13	Oberlin	39.7
13	Westerville	42.3	14	Centerburg 2 SE	39.9
15	Lima WWTP	42.2	15	Bowling Green WWTP	40.0
16	Elyria 3 E	42.0	15	Defiance	40.0
16	Findlay Wpcc	42.0	15	Wooster Exp Stn	40.0
18	Cleveland Hopkins Intl Arpt	41.9	18	Marion 2 N	40.1
18	Marysville	41.9	19	Toledo Express Arpt	40.2
20	Chillicothe Mound City	***41.7***	20	Springfield New Water Works	40.3
21	Milford	***41.6***	21	Upper Sandusky	40.4
22	Hannibal Lock & Dam	41.4	22	Barnesville	***40.6***
23	Cadiz	41.3	23	Mansfield Lahm Municipal Arpt	40.7
23	Franklin	41.3	23	Urbana WWTP	40.7
23	Wilmington 3 N	41.3	25	Bellefontaine	40.8

Rankings include 25 highest/lowest stations. If state has less than 25 stations, all stations are included. The period of record is 1980–2009. See User Guide for detailed explanation of data.

Annual Extreme Minimum Temperature

Highest			Lowest		
Rank	Station Name	°F	Rank	Station Name	°F
1	Painesville 4 NW	-19	1	Danville 2 W	-35
2	Bowling Green WWTP	-20	1	Millersburg	***-35***
2	Cleveland Hopkins Intl Arpt	-20	3	Millport 2 NW	-34
2	Findlay Wpcc	-20	4	Cambridge	-32
2	Toledo Express Arpt	-20	5	Fredericktown 4 S	***-30***
6	Dayton Mcd	-21	6	Centerburg 2 SE	-29
6	Lima WWTP	-21	6	Chillicothe Mound City	-29
6	Pandora	-21	6	Portsmouth Sciotoville	-29
9	Chilo Meldahl L&D	-22	9	Columbus Valley Crossing	-28
9	Circleville	-22	9	Dorset	-28
9	Columbus-Port Columbus Intl	-22	11	Bellefontaine	-27
9	Defiance	-22	11	Westerville	-27
9	Elyria 3 E	-22	13	Bucyrus	-26
9	Mansfield Lahm Municipal Arpt	-22	13	Chippewa Lake	-26
9	Steubenville	-22	13	Springfield New Water Works	-26
9	Youngstown Municipal Arpt	-22	13	Urbana WWTP	-26
17	Chardon	-23	13	Warren 3 S	-26
17	Fairfield	***-23***	18	Akron Akron-Canton Reg Arpt	-25
17	Marietta Wwtp	-23	18	Carpenter 2 S	***-25***
17	Marion 2 N	-23	18	Dayton Intl Arpt	-25
17	Marysville	-23	18	Hiram	-25
17	Milford	***-23***	18	Mansfield 5 W	-25
17	Oberlin	-23	18	Wilmington 3 N	-25
17	Upper Sandusky	-23	24	Cadiz	-24
25	Cadiz	-24	24	Cincinnati-Northern Kentucky	-24

July Mean Maximum Temperature

Highest			Lowest		
Rank	Station Name	°F	Rank	Station Name	°F
1	Fairfield	***87.8***	1	Chardon	80.4
2	Dayton Mcd	87.5	2	Painesville 4 NW	80.9
3	Milford	***87.2***	3	Hiram	81.0
4	Portsmouth Sciotoville	86.6	4	Dorset	81.3
5	Chilo Meldahl L&D	86.0	5	Mansfield 5 W	81.6
6	Chillicothe Mound City	***85.7***	6	Mansfield Lahm Municipal Arpt	81.7
7	Cincinnati-Northern Kentucky	85.6	7	Wooster Exp Stn	81.8
8	Franklin	85.4	8	Youngstown Municipal Arpt	81.9
8	Marietta Wwtp	85.4	9	Cadiz	82.2
8	Westerville	85.4	10	Cleveland Hopkins Intl Arpt	82.3
11	Cambridge	85.2	10	Fredericktown 4 S	82.3
12	Circleville	85.0	12	Akron Akron-Canton Reg Arpt	82.4
13	Columbus Valley Crossing	84.9	13	Barnesville	***82.5***
14	Columbus-Port Columbus Intl	84.8	13	Chippewa Lake	82.5
15	Carpenter 2 S	***84.7***	15	Centerburg 2 SE	82.6
16	Elyria 3 E	84.6	16	Bellefontaine	82.9
17	Dayton Intl Arpt	84.4	17	Steubenville	83.0
17	Defiance	84.4	18	Bucyrus	83.1
19	Marysville	84.3	18	Warren 3 S	83.1
19	Toledo Express Arpt	84.3	20	Oberlin	83.2
21	Bowling Green WWTP	84.1	21	Danville 2 W	83.4
21	Urbana WWTP	84.1	21	Marion 2 N	83.4
23	Lima WWTP	84.0	23	Springfield New Water Works	83.5
23	Upper Sandusky	84.0	24	Millport 2 NW	83.6
25	Pandora	83.9	25	Hannibal Lock & Dam	83.7

Rankings include 25 highest/lowest stations. If state has less than 25 stations, all stations are included. The period of record is 1980–2009. See User Guide for detailed explanation of data.

January Mean Minimum Temperature

Highest			Lowest		
Rank	Station Name	°F	Rank	Station Name	°F
1	Marietta Wwtp	22.8	1	Fredericktown 4 S	15.2
2	Portsmouth Sciotoville	22.7	2	Dorset	16.2
3	Chilo Meldahl L&D	22.6	3	Chardon	16.3
3	Cincinnati-Northern Kentucky	22.6	4	Mansfield 5 W	16.5
5	Fairfield	***22.4***	5	Danville 2 W	16.9
6	Dayton Mcd	22.2	6	Defiance	17.0
6	Painesville 4 NW	22.2	7	Hiram	17.2
8	Circleville	21.9	8	Warren 3 S	17.3
8	Columbus-Port Columbus Intl	21.9	9	Centerburg 2 SE	17.4
10	Cambridge	21.8	10	Bowling Green WWTP	17.6
10	Steubenville	21.8	11	Marion 2 N	17.7
12	Carpenter 2 S	***21.3***	12	Bucyrus	17.8
12	Columbus Valley Crossing	21.3	12	Oberlin	17.8
14	Hannibal Lock & Dam	21.2	14	Bellefontaine	17.9
15	Westerville	20.9	15	Chippewa Lake	18.0
16	Elyria 3 E	20.7	15	Toledo Express Arpt	18.0
17	Cleveland Hopkins Intl Arpt	20.3	15	Upper Sandusky	18.0
17	Dayton Intl Arpt	20.3	18	Millport 2 NW	18.1
19	Franklin	20.2	19	Millersburg	***18.4***
20	Chillicothe Mound City	***20.1***	19	Pandora	18.4
20	Milford	***20.1***	21	Springfield New Water Works	18.6
22	Wilmington 3 N	19.9	22	Mansfield Lahm Municipal Arpt	18.9
23	Lima WWTP	19.8	23	Urbana WWTP	19.0
23	Marysville	19.8	23	Wooster Exp Stn	19.0
25	Barnesville	***19.7***	23	Youngstown Municipal Arpt	19.0

Number of Days Annually Maximum Temperature ≥ 90°F

Highest			Lowest		
Rank	Station Name	Days	Rank	Station Name	Days
1	Dayton Mcd	35	1	Painesville 4 NW	4
1	Fairfield	***35***	2	Chardon	5
3	Milford	***28***	2	Hiram	5
4	Portsmouth Sciotoville	27	2	Mansfield Lahm Municipal Arpt	5
5	Chilo Meldahl L&D	20	2	Wooster Exp Stn	5
5	Cincinnati-Northern Kentucky	20	6	Mansfield 5 W	6
7	Chillicothe Mound City	19	6	Youngstown Municipal Arpt	6
7	Franklin	19	8	Akron Akron-Canton Reg Arpt	7
7	Marietta Wwtp	19	8	Barnesville	***7***
7	Westerville	19	8	Dorset	7
11	Circleville	18	11	Cadiz	8
11	Elyria 3 E	18	11	Chippewa Lake	8
13	Defiance	17	11	Fredericktown 4 S	8
14	Bowling Green WWTP	16	14	Centerburg 2 SE	9
14	Columbus-Port Columbus Intl	16	14	Cleveland Hopkins Intl Arpt	9
14	Toledo Express Arpt	16	14	Warren 3 S	9
17	Cambridge	15	17	Bellefontaine	10
17	Dayton Intl Arpt	15	17	Danville 2 W	10
17	Pandora	15	17	Steubenville	10
20	Columbus Valley Crossing	14	20	Bucyrus	11
20	Findlay Wpcc	14	20	Hannibal Lock & Dam	11
20	Lima WWTP	14	20	Wilmington 3 N	11
20	Marysville	14	23	Millport 2 NW	12
20	Upper Sandusky	14	23	Oberlin	12
20	Urbana WWTP	14	23	Springfield New Water Works	12

Rankings include 25 highest/lowest stations. If state has less than 25 stations, all stations are included. The period of record is 1980–2009. See User Guide for detailed explanation of data.

Number of Days Annually Maximum Temperature ≤ 32°F

Highest			Lowest		
Rank	Station Name	Days	Rank	Station Name	Days
1	Chardon	49	1	Portsmouth Sciotoville	16
2	Mansfield 5 W	47	2	Chilo Meldahl L&D	19
3	Hiram	46	3	Fairfield	***20***
4	Bucyrus	45	3	Marietta Wwtp	20
4	Dorset	45	5	Chillicothe Mound City	21
6	Chippewa Lake	44	6	Milford	***22***
6	Mansfield Lahm Municipal Arpt	44	7	Cambridge	23
6	Youngstown Municipal Arpt	44	7	Carpenter 2 S	***23***
9	Bowling Green WWTP	43	7	Cincinnati-Northern Kentucky	23
9	Defiance	43	7	Hannibal Lock & Dam	23
9	Toledo Express Arpt	43	11	Columbus Valley Crossing	26
12	Findlay Wpcc	42	12	Circleville	27
12	Oberlin	42	12	Franklin	27
12	Pandora	42	14	Westerville	28
12	Wooster Exp Stn	42	15	Steubenville	29
16	Bellefontaine	40	16	Columbus-Port Columbus Intl	30
16	Centerburg 2 SE	40	16	Dayton Mcd	30
16	Marion 2 N	40	18	Elyria 3 E	31
19	Akron Akron-Canton Reg Arpt	39	19	Millersburg	***33***
19	Cleveland Hopkins Intl Arpt	39	19	Millport 2 NW	33
19	Fredericktown 4 S	39	21	Painesville 4 NW	34
19	Upper Sandusky	39	21	Springfield New Water Works	34
23	Lima WWTP	38	21	Wilmington 3 N	34
24	Cadiz	37	24	Barnesville	***35***
24	Warren 3 S	37	24	Danville 2 W	35

Number of Days Annually Minimum Temperature ≤ 32°F

Highest			Lowest		
Rank	Station Name	Days	Rank	Station Name	Days
1	Danville 2 W	150	1	Cincinnati-Northern Kentucky	103
2	Fredericktown 4 S	147	1	Dayton Mcd	103
3	Warren 3 S	146	3	Painesville 4 NW	106
4	Dorset	143	4	Chilo Meldahl L&D	107
5	Chardon	142	5	Columbus-Port Columbus Intl	108
5	Millersburg	***142***	5	Portsmouth Sciotoville	108
7	Millport 2 NW	141	7	Marietta Wwtp	110
8	Mansfield 5 W	136	8	Fairfield	***111***
9	Hiram	134	9	Chillicothe Mound City	112
10	Chippewa Lake	133	9	Steubenville	112
11	Bucyrus	132	11	Cambridge	113
12	Centerburg 2 SE	131	11	Circleville	113
12	Oberlin	131	13	Columbus Valley Crossing	114
14	Bowling Green WWTP	130	13	Westerville	114
14	Defiance	130	15	Dayton Intl Arpt	115
14	Marion 2 N	130	16	Cadiz	116
14	Toledo Express Arpt	130	17	Cleveland Hopkins Intl Arpt	117
14	Wooster Exp Stn	130	17	Marysville	117
19	Bellefontaine	129	19	Elyria 3 E	118
19	Youngstown Municipal Arpt	129	20	Findlay Wpcc	119
21	Springfield New Water Works	128	20	Lima WWTP	119
21	Upper Sandusky	128	20	Milford	***119***
23	Barnesville	***126***	23	Carpenter 2 S	***120***
23	Mansfield Lahm Municipal Arpt	126	23	Franklin	120
23	Pandora	126	23	Hannibal Lock & Dam	120

Rankings include 25 highest/lowest stations. If state has less than 25 stations, all stations are included. The period of record is 1980–2009. See User Guide for detailed explanation of data.

Number of Days Annually Minimum Temperature ≤ 0°F

Highest			Lowest		
Rank	Station Name	Days	Rank	Station Name	Days
1	Chardon	9	1	Painesville 4 NW	1
1	Defiance	9	2	Marietta Wwtp	2
1	Dorset	9	2	Steubenville	2
1	Fredericktown 4 S	9	4	Chilo Meldahl L&D	3
5	Danville 2 W	8	4	Dayton Mcd	3
6	Bellefontaine	7	4	Fairfield	***3***
6	Bowling Green WWTP	7	4	Hannibal Lock & Dam	3
6	Centerburg 2 SE	7	4	Portsmouth Sciotoville	3
6	Mansfield 5 W	7	9	Akron Akron-Canton Reg Arpt	4
6	Millport 2 NW	7	9	Barnesville	***4***
6	Pandora	7	9	Cadiz	4
6	Warren 3 S	7	9	Cambridge	4
13	Bucyrus	6	9	Carpenter 2 S	***4***
13	Chippewa Lake	6	9	Chillicothe Mound City	4
13	Hiram	6	9	Cincinnati-Northern Kentucky	4
13	Marion 2 N	6	9	Circleville	4
13	Millersburg	***6***	9	Cleveland Hopkins Intl Arpt	4
13	Oberlin	6	9	Columbus-Port Columbus Intl	4
13	Springfield New Water Works	6	9	Columbus Valley Crossing	4
13	Toledo Express Arpt	6	9	Dayton Intl Arpt	4
13	Wilmington 3 N	6	9	Elyria 3 E	4
22	Lima WWTP	5	9	Findlay Wpcc	4
22	Mansfield Lahm Municipal Arpt	5	9	Franklin	4
22	Upper Sandusky	5	9	Marysville	4
22	Urbana WWTP	5	9	Milford	***4***

Number of Annual Heating Degree Days

Highest			Lowest		
Rank	Station Name	Num.	Rank	Station Name	Num.
1	Chardon	6,754	1	Portsmouth Sciotoville	4,855
2	Dorset	6,648	2	Chilo Meldahl L&D	4,909
3	Fredericktown 4 S	6,449	3	Cincinnati-Northern Kentucky	5,012
4	Hiram	6,442	4	Marietta Wwtp	5,028
5	Mansfield 5 W	6,401	5	Fairfield	***5,046***
6	Warren 3 S	6,319	6	Dayton Mcd	5,182
7	Bucyrus	6,297	7	Cambridge	5,200
8	Chippewa Lake	6,263	8	Milford	***5,271***
9	Danville 2 W	6,258	9	Westerville	5,300
10	Defiance	6,244	10	Carpenter 2 S	***5,307***
11	Youngstown Municipal Arpt	6,243	10	Columbus-Port Columbus Intl	5,307
12	Bowling Green WWTP	6,215	12	Chillicothe Mound City	***5,308***
13	Oberlin	6,212	13	Circleville	5,310
14	Toledo Express Arpt	6,186	14	Columbus Valley Crossing	5,318
15	Wooster Exp Stn	6,172	15	Hannibal Lock & Dam	5,395
16	Mansfield Lahm Municipal Arpt	6,141	16	Steubenville	5,438
17	Marion 2 N	6,120	17	Franklin	5,484
18	Centerburg 2 SE	6,106	18	Dayton Intl Arpt	5,563
19	Millersburg	***6,086***	19	Elyria 3 E	5,631
20	Upper Sandusky	6,075	20	Wilmington 3 N	5,664
21	Millport 2 NW	6,051	21	Painesville 4 NW	5,695
22	Akron Akron-Canton Reg Arpt	6,039	22	Marysville	5,699
23	Pandora	6,029	23	Lima WWTP	5,741
24	Bellefontaine	5,988	24	Cadiz	5,840
25	Cleveland Hopkins Intl Arpt	5,928	25	Springfield New Water Works	5,880

Rankings include 25 highest/lowest stations. If state has less than 25 stations, all stations are included. The period of record is 1980–2009. See User Guide for detailed explanation of data.

Number of Annual Cooling Degree Days

Highest			Lowest		
Rank	Station Name	Num.	Rank	Station Name	Num.
1	Dayton Mcd	1,294	1	Chardon	482
2	Fairfield	***1,199***	2	Dorset	510
3	Cincinnati-Northern Kentucky	1,119	3	Fredericktown 4 S	548
4	Chilo Meldahl L&D	1,090	4	Warren 3 S	567
5	Portsmouth Sciotoville	1,076	5	Hiram	582
6	Milford	***1,034***	6	Youngstown Municipal Arpt	588
7	Columbus-Port Columbus Intl	1,013	7	Danville 2 W	597
8	Marietta Wwtp	987	8	Millport 2 NW	612
9	Chillicothe Mound City	***985***	9	Mansfield 5 W	615
10	Westerville	978	10	Wooster Exp Stn	619
11	Circleville	962	11	Chippewa Lake	654
12	Dayton Intl Arpt	952	11	Millersburg	***654***
13	Columbus Valley Crossing	943	13	Mansfield Lahm Municipal Arpt	683
14	Lima WWTP	933	14	Akron Akron-Canton Reg Arpt	701
15	Cambridge	929	15	Barnesville	***710***
16	Franklin	921	16	Centerburg 2 SE	717
17	Findlay Wpcc	902	17	Bucyrus	720
18	Marysville	897	17	Oberlin	720
19	Elyria 3 E	885	19	Cadiz	758
20	Steubenville	847	20	Cleveland Hopkins Intl Arpt	762
21	Carpenter 2 S	***843***	21	Painesville 4 NW	777
22	Upper Sandusky	830	22	Toledo Express Arpt	789
23	Defiance	825	23	Marion 2 N	795
24	Wilmington 3 N	822	24	Bowling Green WWTP	796
25	Pandora	821	25	Springfield New Water Works	798

Annual Precipitation

Highest			Lowest		
Rank	Station Name	Inches	Rank	Station Name	Inches
1	Chardon	48.24	1	Bowling Green WWTP	33.92
2	Milford	***44.72***	2	Toledo Express Arpt	34.11
3	Mansfield Lahm Municipal Arpt	44.24	3	Defiance	36.64
4	Fairfield	***43.80***	4	Pandora	37.19
5	Barnesville	***43.60***	5	Findlay Wpcc	37.44
6	Dorset	43.58	6	Upper Sandusky	37.52
7	Marietta Wwtp	42.81	7	Millport 2 NW	37.63
8	Hiram	42.67	8	Oberlin	37.75
9	Cincinnati-Northern Kentucky	42.53	9	Marysville	37.88
10	Centerburg 2 SE	41.94	10	Chillicothe Mound City	38.11
11	Danville 2 W	41.87	11	Fredericktown 4 S	38.32
12	Urbana WWTP	41.71	12	Lima WWTP	38.55
13	Steubenville	41.52	13	Springfield New Water Works	38.57
14	Hannibal Lock & Dam	41.34	14	Painesville 4 NW	38.63
15	Cadiz	41.26	15	Circleville	38.80
16	Dayton Intl Arpt	41.13	16	Youngstown Municipal Arpt	38.92
17	Carpenter 2 S	***41.04***	17	Cleveland Hopkins Intl Arpt	39.00
18	Portsmouth Sciotoville	40.93	18	Marion 2 N	39.03
19	Wilmington 3 N	40.80	19	Bucyrus	39.07
20	Dayton Mcd	40.66	20	Franklin	39.11
21	Chilo Meldahl L&D	40.58	21	Bellefontaine	39.24
22	Columbus Valley Crossing	40.39	21	Mansfield 5 W	39.24
23	Wooster Exp Stn	39.99	23	Westerville	39.26
24	Cambridge	39.87	24	Chippewa Lake	39.32
25	Millersburg	***39.79***	24	Columbus-Port Columbus Intl	39.32

Rankings include 25 highest/lowest stations. If state has less than 25 stations, all stations are included. The period of record is 1980–2009. See User Guide for detailed explanation of data.

Annual Extreme Maximum Daily Precipitation

Highest			Lowest		
Rank	Station Name	Inches	Rank	Station Name	Inches
1	Upper Sandusky	9.35	1	Oberlin	2.92
2	Bucyrus	8.68	2	Fredericktown 4 S	***3.00***
3	Chilo Meldahl L&D	7.20	3	Toledo Express Arpt	3.15
4	Pandora	6.19	4	Wilmington 3 N	3.42
5	Elyria 3 E	5.75	5	Centerburg 2 SE	3.46
6	Findlay Wpcc	5.62	6	Wooster Exp Stn	3.60
7	Chardon	5.50	7	Franklin	3.76
8	Cambridge	5.45	8	Columbus Valley Crossing	3.77
9	Steubenville	5.36	9	Springfield New Water Works	3.78
10	Marion 2 N	5.33	10	Dayton Intl Arpt	3.81
11	Portsmouth Sciotoville	5.20	11	Westerville	3.84
12	Mansfield 5 W	***5.19***	12	Millersburg	***3.85***
13	Columbus-Port Columbus Intl	5.13	13	Defiance	3.89
14	Barnesville	***5.12***	14	Urbana WWTP	3.97
14	Danville 2 W	5.12	15	Akron Akron-Canton Reg Arpt	3.98
16	Cadiz	5.09	16	Hiram	4.05
17	Lima WWTP	5.08	17	Chillicothe Mound City	***4.10***
18	Marysville	4.82	18	Circleville	4.12
19	Millport 2 NW	4.80	19	Bowling Green WWTP	4.25
20	Marietta Wwtp	4.78	20	Hannibal Lock & Dam	4.28
21	Fairfield	***4.67***	21	Dorset	4.29
22	Youngstown Municipal Arpt	4.65	22	Chippewa Lake	4.30
23	Milford	***4.63***	22	Cincinnati-Northern Kentucky	4.30
24	Cleveland Hopkins Intl Arpt	4.59	24	Mansfield Lahm Municipal Arpt	4.34
25	Painesville 4 NW	4.57	25	Dayton Mcd	4.36

Number of Days Annually With ≥ 0.1 Inches of Precipitation

Highest			Lowest		
Rank	Station Name	Days	Rank	Station Name	Days
1	Chardon	108	1	Chillicothe Mound City	70
2	Hiram	95	1	Fredericktown 4 S	70
3	Dorset	94	3	Chilo Meldahl L&D	72
4	Elyria 3 E	89	3	Toledo Express Arpt	72
4	Mansfield Lahm Municipal Arpt	89	5	Bowling Green WWTP	73
4	Warren 3 S	89	5	Franklin	73
7	Steubenville	88	7	Columbus Valley Crossing	74
8	Akron Akron-Canton Reg Arpt	87	7	Springfield New Water Works	74
8	Barnesville	***87***	9	Dayton Mcd	76
8	Cadiz	87	10	Defiance	77
8	Chippewa Lake	87	10	Marysville	77
8	Cleveland Hopkins Intl Arpt	87	10	Upper Sandusky	77
8	Marietta Wwtp	87	13	Circleville	78
8	Youngstown Municipal Arpt	87	14	Columbus-Port Columbus Intl	79
15	Danville 2 W	85	14	Fairfield	***79***
15	Painesville 4 NW	85	14	Findlay Wpcc	79
17	Hannibal Lock & Dam	84	14	Marion 2 N	79
17	Millport 2 NW	84	14	Millersburg	***79***
17	Oberlin	84	14	Pandora	79
20	Bucyrus	83	20	Dayton Intl Arpt	80
20	Cambridge	83	20	Lima WWTP	80
22	Carpenter 2 S	***82***	20	Mansfield 5 W	80
22	Cincinnati-Northern Kentucky	82	23	Bellefontaine	81
22	Milford	***82***	23	Centerburg 2 SE	81
22	Portsmouth Sciotoville	82	23	Urbana WWTP	81

Rankings include 25 highest/lowest stations. If state has less than 25 stations, all stations are included. The period of record is 1980–2009. See User Guide for detailed explanation of data.

Number of Days Annually With ≥ 0.5 Inches of Precipitation

Highest			Lowest		
Rank	Station Name	Days	Rank	Station Name	Days
1	Chardon	32	1	Bowling Green WWTP	21
1	Milford	***32***	1	Toledo Express Arpt	21
3	Fairfield	***30***	3	Upper Sandusky	22
4	Barnesville	***29***	4	Cleveland Hopkins Intl Arpt	23
4	Centerburg 2 SE	29	4	Oberlin	23
4	Dorset	29	4	Painesville 4 NW	23
4	Mansfield Lahm Municipal Arpt	29	4	Youngstown Municipal Arpt	23
4	Marietta Wwtp	29	8	Akron Akron-Canton Reg Arpt	24
9	Carpenter 2 S	***28***	8	Defiance	24
9	Hannibal Lock & Dam	28	8	Findlay Wpcc	24
11	Cadiz	27	8	Franklin	24
11	Chilo Meldahl L&D	27	8	Millport 2 NW	24
11	Cincinnati-Northern Kentucky	27	8	Warren 3 S	24
11	Circleville	27	14	Bellefontaine	25
11	Columbus Valley Crossing	27	14	Bucyrus	25
11	Danville 2 W	27	14	Chippewa Lake	25
11	Dayton Mcd	27	14	Columbus-Port Columbus Intl	25
11	Portsmouth Sciotoville	27	14	Elyria 3 E	25
11	Steubenville	27	14	Fredericktown 4 S	25
11	Urbana WWTP	27	14	Lima WWTP	25
11	Wilmington 3 N	27	14	Mansfield 5 W	25
11	Wooster Exp Stn	27	14	Marion 2 N	25
23	Cambridge	26	14	Marysville	25
23	Chillicothe Mound City	26	14	Pandora	25
23	Dayton Intl Arpt	26	25	Cambridge	26

Number of Days Annually With ≥ 1.0 Inches of Precipitation

Highest			Lowest		
Rank	Station Name	Days	Rank	Station Name	Days
1	Chilo Meldahl L&D	12	1	Akron Akron-Canton Reg Arpt	6
1	Cincinnati-Northern Kentucky	12	1	Chippewa Lake	6
3	Fairfield	***11***	1	Lima WWTP	6
3	Mansfield Lahm Municipal Arpt	11	1	Millport 2 NW	6
3	Milford	***11***	1	Oberlin	6
3	Urbana WWTP	11	1	Painesville 4 NW	6
7	Carpenter 2 S	***10***	1	Pandora	6
7	Dayton Intl Arpt	10	1	Warren 3 S	6
7	Dayton Mcd	10	1	Youngstown Municipal Arpt	6
7	Franklin	10	10	Bowling Green WWTP	7
7	Fredericktown 4 S	10	10	Bucyrus	7
7	Portsmouth Sciotoville	10	10	Cadiz	7
7	Wilmington 3 N	10	10	Cleveland Hopkins Intl Arpt	7
14	Barnesville	***9***	10	Columbus-Port Columbus Intl	7
14	Bellefontaine	9	10	Dorset	7
14	Cambridge	9	10	Elyria 3 E	7
14	Centerburg 2 SE	9	10	Findlay Wpcc	7
14	Chardon	9	10	Hiram	7
14	Chillicothe Mound City	9	10	Marysville	7
14	Circleville	9	10	Millersburg	***7***
14	Columbus Valley Crossing	9	10	Steubenville	7
14	Danville 2 W	9	10	Toledo Express Arpt	7
14	Marion 2 N	9	10	Wooster Exp Stn	7
14	Springfield New Water Works	9	24	Defiance	8
25	Defiance	8	24	Hannibal Lock & Dam	8

Rankings include 25 highest/lowest stations. If state has less than 25 stations, all stations are included. The period of record is 1980–2009. See User Guide for detailed explanation of data.

Annual Snowfall

Highest Rank	Station Name	Inches	Lowest Rank	Station Name	Inches
1	Chardon	102.8	1	Fairfield	***7.8***
2	Dorset	79.0	2	Portsmouth Sciotoville	8.0
3	Cleveland Hopkins Intl Arpt	67.6	3	Centerburg 2 SE	12.4
4	Hiram	63.2	3	Dayton Mcd	12.4
5	Youngstown Municipal Arpt	59.7	5	Circleville	13.9
6	Mansfield Lahm Municipal Arpt	47.7	6	Chillicothe Mound City	14.8
7	Akron Akron-Canton Reg Arpt	46.4	7	Columbus Valley Crossing	14.9
8	Oberlin	45.8	8	Millersburg	***17.5***
9	Elyria 3 E	41.0	9	Cambridge	18.2
10	Painesville 4 NW	39.2	10	Westerville	18.5
11	Danville 2 W	39.1	11	Carpenter 2 S	***18.6***
12	Chippewa Lake	35.9	12	Marietta Wwtp	18.8
13	Warren 3 S	31.8	13	Upper Sandusky	19.4
14	Barnesville	***31.6***	14	Marysville	20.5
15	Pandora	30.5	15	Defiance	20.7
16	Wooster Exp Stn	29.3	16	Wilmington 3 N	21.0
17	Millport 2 NW	28.7	17	Bowling Green WWTP	21.6
18	Cadiz	28.2	17	Cincinnati-Northern Kentucky	21.6
19	Columbus-Port Columbus Intl	27.9	19	Bucyrus	22.5
20	Findlay Wpcc	26.9	20	Marion 2 N	23.0
21	Dayton Intl Arpt	25.3	21	Fredericktown 4 S	24.8
22	Fredericktown 4 S	24.8	22	Dayton Intl Arpt	25.3
23	Marion 2 N	23.0	23	Findlay Wpcc	26.9
24	Bucyrus	22.5	24	Columbus-Port Columbus Intl	27.9
25	Bowling Green WWTP	21.6	25	Cadiz	28.2

Annual Maximum Snow Depth

Highest Rank	Station Name	Inches	Lowest Rank	Station Name	Inches
1	Chardon	47	1	Chillicothe Mound City	11
2	Painesville 4 NW	25	2	Dayton Mcd	12
3	Chippewa Lake	24	3	Columbus Valley Crossing	***13***
4	Centerburg 2 SE	23	3	Millersburg	***13***
4	Hannibal Lock & Dam	***23***	3	Westerville	13
6	Cleveland Hopkins Intl Arpt	22	6	Cincinnati-Northern Kentucky	14
6	Danville 2 W	22	6	Findlay Wpcc	14
6	Hiram	22	8	Circleville	***15***
9	Portsmouth Sciotoville	21	8	Elyria 3 E	15
10	Barnesville	***20***	8	Marion 2 N	***15***
10	Dorset	20	8	Millport 2 NW	***15***
10	Mansfield Lahm Municipal Arpt	20	12	Chilo Meldahl L&D	***16***
10	Marietta Wwtp	20	12	Dayton Intl Arpt	16
14	Bellefontaine	***19***	12	Pandora	16
14	Cambridge	19	12	Warren 3 S	16
14	Upper Sandusky	***19***	16	Akron Akron-Canton Reg Arpt	17
17	Bowling Green WWTP	18	16	Bucyrus	17
17	Columbus-Port Columbus Intl	18	16	Defiance	17
17	Wilmington 3 N	18	16	Marysville	17
17	Youngstown Municipal Arpt	18	16	Oberlin	17
21	Akron Akron-Canton Reg Arpt	17	16	Wooster Exp Stn	17
21	Bucyrus	17	22	Bowling Green WWTP	18
21	Defiance	17	22	Columbus-Port Columbus Intl	18
21	Marysville	17	22	Wilmington 3 N	18
21	Oberlin	17	22	Youngstown Municipal Arpt	18

Rankings include 25 highest/lowest stations. If state has less than 25 stations, all stations are included. The period of record is 1980–2009. See User Guide for detailed explanation of data.

Number of Days Annually With ≥ 1.0 Inch Snow Depth

Highest			Lowest		
Rank	Station Name	Days	Rank	Station Name	Days
1	Chardon	80	1	Chilo Meldahl L&D	***4***
2	Dorset	69	2	Franklin	***8***
3	Hiram	64	2	Portsmouth Sciotoville	8
4	Youngstown Municipal Arpt	54	4	Hannibal Lock & Dam	***10***
5	Oberlin	53	5	Columbus Valley Crossing	13
6	Cleveland Hopkins Intl Arpt	51	6	Bellefontaine	***15***
7	Mansfield Lahm Municipal Arpt	49	6	Marietta Wwtp	15
8	Akron Akron-Canton Reg Arpt	45	6	Millport 2 NW	***15***
8	Chippewa Lake	45	9	Chillicothe Mound City	18
8	Wooster Exp Stn	45	10	Circleville	19
11	Danville 2 W	43	10	Dayton Mcd	19
11	Elyria 3 E	43	12	Cincinnati-Northern Kentucky	20
11	Painesville 4 NW	43	13	Upper Sandusky	22
14	Pandora	39	14	Westerville	23
15	Bowling Green WWTP	38	15	Cadiz	***25***
15	Defiance	38	15	Cambridge	25
17	Findlay Wpcc	36	17	Centerburg 2 SE	26
18	Warren 3 S	35	17	Columbus-Port Columbus Intl	26
19	Barnesville	***34***	17	Millersburg	***26***
20	Marysville	31	17	Wilmington 3 N	26
21	Bucyrus	29	21	Dayton Intl Arpt	27
22	Dayton Intl Arpt	27	21	Marion 2 N	***27***
22	Marion 2 N	***27***	23	Bucyrus	29
24	Centerburg 2 SE	26	24	Marysville	31
24	Columbus-Port Columbus Intl	26	25	Barnesville	***34***

Rankings include 25 highest/lowest stations. If state has less than 25 stations, all stations are included. The period of record is 1980–2009. See User Guide for detailed explanation of data.

Significant Storm Events in Ohio: 2000 – 2009

Location or County	Date	Type	Mag.	Deaths	Injuries	Property Damage ($mil.)	Crop Damage ($mil.)
Preble County	02/07/00	Fog	na	1	14	0.2	0.0
Greene	09/20/00	Tornado	F4	1	100	15.0	0.0
Montgomery	04/09/01	Hail	1.75 in.	0	0	70.0	0.0
Western and Southern Ohio	03/09/02	High Wind	84 mph	1	12	0.9	0.0
Stark	04/28/02	Tornado	F2	0	2	45.5	0.0
Van Wert	11/10/02	Tornado	F4	2	17	30.0	0.0
Franklin	04/20/03	Hail	1.75 in.	0	0	80.0	0.0
Delaware	04/20/03	Hail	1.50 in.	0	0	65.0	0.0
Summit	07/21/03	Flash Flood	na	3	0	100.0	0.0
Stark	07/27/03	Flash Flood	na	0	0	52.0	0.0
Northern Ohio	12/22/04	Winter Storm	na	0	0	54.9	0.0
Northern Ohio	01/05/05	Ice Storm	na	0	0	124.9	0.0
Lake	07/28/06	Flash Flood	na	1	0	320.0	0.0
Licking	10/04/06	Hail	1.75 in.	0	1	100.0	0.0
Franklin	10/04/06	Hail	2.00 in.	0	0	100.0	0.0
Franklin	10/11/06	Tornado	F2	0	0	50.0	0.0
Summit	06/08/07	Hail	4.25 in.	0	0	105.0	0.0
Hancock	08/21/07	Flash Flood	na	0	0	100.0	5.0
Richland	08/21/07	Flash Flood	na	0	0	70.0	5.0
Crawford	08/21/07	Flash Flood	na	0	0	62.0	3.0
Knox, Stark, and Trumbull Counties	03/07/08	Winter Storm	na	0	0	750.0	0.0
Franklin and Logan Counties	09/14/08	High Wind	75 mph	0	0	128.7	0.0
Hamilton County	09/14/08	High Wind	61 mph	1	0	96.6	0.0
Montgomery County	09/14/08	High Wind	69 mph	0	0	63.7	0.0

Note: Deaths, injuries, and damages are date and location specific.

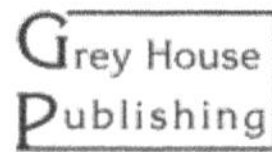

2015 Title List

Visit www.GreyHouse.com for Product Information, Table of Contents, and Sample Pages.

eneral Reference

n African Biographical Dictionary
merica's College Museums
merican Environmental Leaders: From Colonial Times to the Present
ncyclopedia of African-American Writing
ncyclopedia of Constitutional Amendments
ncyclopedia of Gun Control & Gun Rights
n Encyclopedia of Human Rights in the United States
ncyclopedia of Invasions & Conquests
ncyclopedia of Prisoners of War & Internment
ncyclopedia of Religion & Law in America
ncyclopedia of Rural America
ncyclopedia of the Continental Congress
ncyclopedia of the United States Cabinet, 1789-2010
ncyclopedia of War Journalism
ncyclopedia of Warrior Peoples & Fighting Groups
he Environmental Debate: A Documentary History
he Evolution Wars: A Guide to the Debates
rom Suffrage to the Senate: America's Political Women
lobal Terror & Political Risk Assessment
edia & Communications 1900-2020
ations of the World
olitical Corruption in America
rivacy Rights in the Digital Era
he Religious Right: A Reference Handbook
peakers of the House of Representatives, 1789-2009
his is Who We Were: 1880-1900
his is Who We Were: A Companion to the 1940 Census
his is Who We Were: In the 1910s
his is Who We Were: In the 1920s
his is Who We Were: In the 1940s
his is Who We Were: In the 1950s
his is Who We Were: In the 1960s
his is Who We Were: In the 1970s
.S. Land & Natural Resource Policy
he Value of a Dollar 1600-1865: Colonial Era to the Civil War
he Value of a Dollar: 1860-2014
Vorking Americans 1770-1869 Vol. IX: Revolutionary War to the Civil War
Vorking Americans 1880-1999 Vol. I: The Working Class
Vorking Americans 1880-1999 Vol. II: The Middle Class
Vorking Americans 1880-1999 Vol. III: The Upper Class
Vorking Americans 1880-1999 Vol. IV: Their Children
Vorking Americans 1880-2015 Vol. V: Americans At War
Vorking Americans 1880-2005 Vol. VI: Women at Work
Vorking Americans 1880-2006 Vol. VII: Social Movements
Vorking Americans 1880-2007 Vol. VIII: Immigrants
Vorking Americans 1880-2009 Vol. X: Sports & Recreation
Vorking Americans 1880-2010 Vol. XI: Inventors & Entrepreneurs
Vorking Americans 1880-2011 Vol. XII: Our History through Music
Vorking Americans 1880-2012 Vol. XIII: Education & Educators
Vorld Cultural Leaders of the 20th & 21st Centuries

ducation Information

harter School Movement
omparative Guide to American Elementary & Secondary Schools
omplete Learning Disabilities Directory
ducators Resource Directory
pecial Education: A Reference Book for Policy and Curriculum
Development

ealth Information

omparative Guide to American Hospitals
omplete Directory for Pediatric Disorders
omplete Directory for People with Chronic Illness
omplete Directory for People with Disabilities
omplete Mental Health Directory
iabetes in America: Analysis of an Epidemic
irectory of Drug & Alcohol Residential Rehab Facilities
irectory of Health Care Group Purchasing Organizations
irectory of Hospital Personnel
MO/PPO Directory
ledical Device Register
lder Americans Information Directory

Business Information

Complete Television, Radio & Cable Industry Directory
Directory of Business Information Resources
Directory of Mail Order Catalogs
Directory of Venture Capital & Private Equity Firms
Environmental Resource Handbook
Food & Beverage Market Place
Grey House Homeland Security Directory
Grey House Performing Arts Directory
Grey House Safety & Security Directory
Grey House Transportation Security Directory
Hudson's Washington News Media Contacts Directory
New York State Directory
Rauch Market Research Guides
Sports Market Place Directory

Statistics & Demographics

American Tally
America's Top-Rated Cities
America's Top-Rated Smaller Cities
America's Top-Rated Small Towns & Cities
Ancestry & Ethnicity in America
The Asian Databook
Comparative Guide to American Suburbs
The Hispanic Databook
Profiles of America
"Profiles of" Series - State Handbooks
Weather America

Financial Ratings Series

TheStreet Ratings' Guide to Bond & Money Market Mutual Funds
TheStreet Ratings' Guide to Common Stocks
TheStreet Ratings' Guide to Exchange-Traded Funds
TheStreet Ratings' Guide to Stock Mutual Funds
TheStreet Ratings' Ultimate Guided Tour of Stock Investing
Weiss Ratings' Consumer Guides
Weiss Ratings' Guide to Banks
Weiss Ratings' Guide to Credit Unions
Weiss Ratings' Guide to Health Insurers
Weiss Ratings' Guide to Life & Annuity Insurers
Weiss Ratings' Guide to Property & Casualty Insurers

Bowker's Books In Print® Titles

American Book Publishing Record® Annual
American Book Publishing Record® Monthly
Books In Print®
Books In Print® Supplement
Books Out Loud™
Bowker's Complete Video Directory™
Children's Books In Print®
El-Hi Textbooks & Serials In Print®
Forthcoming Books®
Large Print Books & Serials™
Law Books & Serials In Print™
Medical & Health Care Books In Print™
Publishers, Distributors & Wholesalers of the US™
Subject Guide to Books In Print®
Subject Guide to Children's Books In Print®

Canadian General Reference

Associations Canada
Canadian Almanac & Directory
Canadian Environmental Resource Guide
Canadian Parliamentary Guide
Canadian Venture Capital & Private Equity Firms
Financial Services Canada
Governments Canada
Health Guide Canada
The History of Canada
Libraries Canada
Major Canadian Cities

2015 Title List

Visit www.SalemPress.com for Product Information, Table of Contents, and Sample Pages.

Science, Careers & Mathematics

Ancient Creatures: Unearthed
Applied Science
Applied Science: Engineering & Mathematics
Applied Science: Science & Medicine
Applied Science: Technology
Biomes and Ecosystems
Careers in Business
Careers in Chemistry
Careers in Communications & Media
Careers in Environment & Conservation
Careers in Healthcare
Careers in Hospitality & Tourism
Careers in Human Services
Careers in Law, Criminal Justice & Emergency Services
Careers in Physics
Careers in Technology Services & Repair
Computer Technology Innovators
Contemporary Biographies in Business
Contemporary Biographies in Chemistry
Contemporary Biographies in Communications & Media
Contemporary Biographies in Environment & Conservation
Contemporary Biographies in Healthcare
Contemporary Biographies in Hospitality & Tourism
Contemporary Biographies in Law & Criminal Justice
Contemporary Biographies in Physics
Earth Science
Earth Science: Earth Materials & Resources
Earth Science: Earth's Surface and History
Earth Science: Physics & Chemistry of the Earth
Earth Science: Weather, Water & Atmosphere
Encyclopedia of Energy
Encyclopedia of Environmental Issues
Encyclopedia of Environmental Issues: Atmosphere and Air Pollution
Encyclopedia of Environmental Issues: Ecology and Ecosystems
Encyclopedia of Environmental Issues: Energy and Energy Use
Encyclopedia of Environmental Issues: Policy and Activism
Encyclopedia of Environmental Issues: Preservation/Wilderness Issues
Encyclopedia of Environmental Issues: Water and Water Pollution
Encyclopedia of Global Resources
Encyclopedia of Global Warming
Encyclopedia of Mathematics & Society
Encyclopedia of Mathematics & Society: Engineering, Tech, Medicine
Encyclopedia of Mathematics & Society: Great Mathematicians
Encyclopedia of Mathematics & Society: Math & Social Sciences
Encyclopedia of Mathematics & Society: Math Development/Concepts
Encyclopedia of Mathematics & Society: Math in Culture & Society
Encyclopedia of Mathematics & Society: Space, Science, Environment
Encyclopedia of the Ancient World
Forensic Science
Geography Basics
Internet Innovators
Inventions and Inventors
Magill's Encyclopedia of Science: Animal Life
Magill's Encyclopedia of Science: Plant life
Notable Natural Disasters
Principles of Chemistry
Science and Scientists
Solar System
Solar System: Great Astronomers
Solar System: Study of the Universe
Solar System: The Inner Planets
Solar System: The Moon and Other Small Bodies
Solar System: The Outer Planets
Solar System: The Sun and Other Stars
World Geography

Literature

American Ethnic Writers
Classics of Science Fiction & Fantasy Literature
Critical Insights: Authors
Critical Insights: New Literary Collection Bundles
Critical Insights: Themes
Critical Insights: Works
Critical Survey of Drama
Critical Survey of Graphic Novels: Heroes & Super Heroes
Critical Survey of Graphic Novels: History, Theme & Technique
Critical Survey of Graphic Novels: Independents/Underground Classics
Critical Survey of Graphic Novels: Manga
Critical Survey of Long Fiction
Critical Survey of Mystery & Detective Fiction
Critical Survey of Mythology and Folklore: Heroes and Heroines
Critical Survey of Mythology and Folklore: Love, Sexuality & Desire
Critical Survey of Mythology and Folklore: World Mythology
Critical Survey of Poetry
Critical Survey of Poetry: American Poets
Critical Survey of Poetry: British, Irish & Commonwealth Poets
Critical Survey of Poetry: Cumulative Index
Critical Survey of Poetry: European Poets
Critical Survey of Poetry: Topical Essays
Critical Survey of Poetry: World Poets
Critical Survey of Shakespeare's Sonnets
Critical Survey of Short Fiction
Critical Survey of Short Fiction: American Writers
Critical Survey of Short Fiction: British, Irish, Commonwealth Writers
Critical Survey of Short Fiction: Cumulative Index
Critical Survey of Short Fiction: European Writers
Critical Survey of Short Fiction: Topical Essays
Critical Survey of Short Fiction: World Writers
Cyclopedia of Literary Characters
Holocaust Literature
Introduction to Literary Context: American Poetry of the 20th Century
Introduction to Literary Context: American Post-Modernist Novels
Introduction to Literary Context: American Short Fiction
Introduction to Literary Context: English Literature
Introduction to Literary Context: Plays
Introduction to Literary Context: World Literature
Magill's Literary Annual 2015
Magill's Survey of American Literature
Magill's Survey of World Literature
Masterplots
Masterplots II: African American Literature
Masterplots II: American Fiction Series
Masterplots II: British & Commonwealth Fiction Series
Masterplots II: Christian Literature
Masterplots II: Drama Series
Masterplots II: Juvenile & Young Adult Literature, Supplement
Masterplots II: Nonfiction Series
Masterplots II: Poetry Series
Masterplots II: Short Story Series
Masterplots II: Women's Literature Series
Notable African American Writers
Notable American Novelists
Notable Playwrights
Notable Poets
Recommended Reading: 500 Classics Reviewed
Short Story Writers

2015 Title List

Visit www.SalemPress.com for Product Information, Table of Contents, and Sample Pages.

istory and Social Science

ne 2000s in America
) States
rican American History
griculture in History
merican First Ladies
merican Heroes
merican Indian Culture
merican Indian History
merican Indian Tribes
merican Presidents
merican Villains
merica's Historic Sites
ncient Greece
he Bill of Rights
he Civil Rights Movement
he Cold War
ountries, Peoples & Cultures
ountries, Peoples & Cultures: Central & South America
ountries, Peoples & Cultures: Central, South & Southeast Asia
ountries, Peoples & Cultures: East & South Africa
ountries, Peoples & Cultures: East Asia & the Pacific
ountries, Peoples & Cultures: Eastern Europe
ountries, Peoples & Cultures: Middle East & North Africa
ountries, Peoples & Cultures: North America & the Caribbean
ountries, Peoples & Cultures: West & Central Africa
ountries, Peoples & Cultures: Western Europe
efining Documents: American Revolution (1754-1805)
efining Documents: Civil War (1860-1865)
efining Documents: Emergence of Modern America (1868-1918)
efining Documents: Exploration & Colonial America (1492-1755)
efining Documents: Manifest Destiny (1803-1860)
efining Documents: Post-War 1940s (1945-1949)
efining Documents: Reconstruction (1865-1880)
efining Documents: The 1920s
efining Documents: The 1930s
efining Documents: The American West (1836-1900)
efining Documents: The Ancient World (2700 B.C.E.-50 C.E.)
efining Documents: The Middle Ages (524-1431)
efining Documents: World War I
efining Documents: World War II (1939-1946)
he Eighties in America
ncyclopedia of American Immigration
ncyclopedia of Flight
ncyclopedia of the Ancient World
he Fifties in America
he Forties in America
reat Athletes
reat Athletes: Baseball
reat Athletes: Basketball
reat Athletes: Boxing & Soccer
reat Athletes: Cumulative Index
reat Athletes: Football
reat Athletes: Golf & Tennis
reat Athletes: Olympics
reat Athletes: Racing & Individual Sports
reat Events from History: 17th Century
reat Events from History: 18th Century
reat Events from History: 19th Century
reat Events from History: 20th Century (1901-1940)
reat Events from History: 20th Century (1941-1970)
reat Events from History: 20th Century (1971-2000)
reat Events from History: Ancient World
reat Events from History: Cumulative Indexes
reat Events from History: Gay, Lesbian, Bisexual, Transgender Events
reat Events from History: Middle Ages
reat Events from History: Modern Scandals
reat Events from History: Renaissance & Early Modern Era
Great Lives from History: 17th Century
Great Lives from History: 18th Century
Great Lives from History: 19th Century
Great Lives from History: 20th Century
Great Lives from History: African Americans
Great Lives from History: Ancient World
Great Lives from History: Asian & Pacific Islander Americans
Great Lives from History: Cumulative Indexes
Great Lives from History: Incredibly Wealthy
Great Lives from History: Inventors & Inventions
Great Lives from History: Jewish Americans
Great Lives from History: Latinos
Great Lives from History: Middle Ages
Great Lives from History: Notorious Lives
Great Lives from History: Renaissance & Early Modern Era
Great Lives from History: Scientists & Science
Historical Encyclopedia of American Business
Immigration in U.S. History
Magill's Guide to Military History
Milestone Documents in African American History
Milestone Documents in American History
Milestone Documents in World History
Milestone Documents of American Leaders
Milestone Documents of World Religions
Musicians & Composers 20th Century
The Nineties in America
The Seventies in America
The Sixties in America
Survey of American Industry and Careers
The Thirties in America
The Twenties in America
United States at War
U.S.A. in Space
U.S. Court Cases
U.S. Government Leaders
U.S. Laws, Acts, and Treaties
U.S. Legal System
U.S. Supreme Court
Weapons and Warfare
World Conflicts: Asia and the Middle East

Health

Addictions & Substance Abuse
Adolescent Health
Cancer
Complementary & Alternative Medicine
Genetics & Inherited Conditions
Health Issues
Infectious Diseases & Conditions
Magill's Medical Guide
Psychology & Behavioral Health
Psychology Basics

2015 Title List

Visit www.HWWilsonInPrint.com for Product Information, Table of Contents and Sample Pages

Current Biography
Current Biography Cumulative Index 1946-2013
Current Biography Monthly Magazine
Current Biography Yearbook: 2003
Current Biography Yearbook: 2004
Current Biography Yearbook: 2005
Current Biography Yearbook: 2006
Current Biography Yearbook: 2007
Current Biography Yearbook: 2008
Current Biography Yearbook: 2009
Current Biography Yearbook: 2010
Current Biography Yearbook: 2011
Current Biography Yearbook: 2012
Current Biography Yearbook: 2013
Current Biography Yearbook: 2014
Current Biography Yearbook: 2015

Core Collections
Children's Core Collection
Fiction Core Collection
Middle & Junior High School Core
Public Library Core Collection: Nonfiction
Senior High Core Collection

The Reference Shelf
Aging in America
American Military Presence Overseas
The Arab Spring
The Brain
The Business of Food
Conspiracy Theories
The Digital Age
Dinosaurs
Embracing New Paradigms in Education
Faith & Science
Families: Traditional and New Structures
The Future of U.S. Economic Relations: Mexico, Cuba, and Venezuela
Global Climate Change
Graphic Novels and Comic Books
Immigration in the U.S.
Internet Safety
Marijuana Reform
The News and its Future
The Paranormal
Politics of the Ocean
Reality Television
Representative American Speeches: 2008-2009
Representative American Speeches: 2009-2010
Representative American Speeches: 2010-2011
Representative American Speeches: 2011-2012
Representative American Speeches: 2012-2013
Representative American Speeches: 2013-2014
Representative American Speeches: 2014-2015
Revisiting Gender
Robotics
Russia
Social Networking
Social Services for the Poor
Space Exploration & Development
Sports in America
The Supreme Court
The Transformation of American Cities
U.S. Infrastructure
U.S. National Debate Topic: Surveillance
U.S. National Debate Topic: The Ocean
U.S. National Debate Topic: Transportation Infrastructure
Whistleblowers

Readers' Guide
Abridged Readers' Guide to Periodical Literature
Readers' Guide to Periodical Literature

Indexes
Index to Legal Periodicals & Books
Short Story Index
Book Review Digest

Sears List
Sears List of Subject Headings
Sears: Lista de Encabezamientos de Materia

Facts About Series
Facts About American Immigration
Facts About China
Facts About the 20th Century
Facts About the Presidents
Facts About the World's Languages

Nobel Prize Winners
Nobel Prize Winners: 1901-1986
Nobel Prize Winners: 1987-1991
Nobel Prize Winners: 1992-1996
Nobel Prize Winners: 1997-2001

World Authors
World Authors: 1995-2000
World Authors: 2000-2005

Famous First Facts
Famous First Facts
Famous First Facts About American Politics
Famous First Facts About Sports
Famous First Facts About the Environment
Famous First Facts: International Edition

American Book of Days
The American Book of Days
The International Book of Days

Junior Authors & Illustrators
Tenth Book of Junior Authors & Illustrations

Monographs
The Barnhart Dictionary of Etymology
Celebrate the World
Guide to the Ancient World
Indexing from A to Z
The Poetry Break
Radical Change: Books for Youth in a Digital Age

Wilson Chronology
Wilson Chronology of Asia and the Pacific
Wilson Chronology of Human Rights
Wilson Chronology of Ideas
Wilson Chronology of the Arts
Wilson Chronology of the World's Religions
Wilson Chronology of Women's Achievements